International Financial Reporting Standards®

as issued at 1 January 2010

This edition published in two parts

PART B

International Financial Reporting Standards®

as issued at 1 January 2010

This edition published in two parts

PART B

The consolidated text of documents accompanying International Financial Reporting Standards (IFRSs®) including International Accounting Standards (IASs®) and Interpretations, as published at 1 January 2010, together with the IASB Framework, IASC Foundation procedural documents and the Glossary of Terms.

For the unaccompanied IFRSs, see Part A of this edition

International Accounting Standards Board®
30 Cannon Street
London EC4M 6XH
United Kingdom

Telephone: +44 (0)20 7246 6410
Fax: +44 (0)20 7246 6411
Email: iasb@iasb.org

Publications Telephone: +44 (0)20 7332 2730
Publications Fax: +44 (0)20 7332 2749
Publications Email: publications@iasb.org
Web: www.iasb.org

IFRSs together with their accompanying documents are issued by the International Accounting Standards Board (IASB), 30 Cannon Street, London EC4M 6XH, United Kingdom. Tel: +44 (0)20 7246 6410 Fax: +44 (0)20 7246 6411 Email: iasb@iasb.org Web: www.iasb.org

ISBN for this part: 978-1-907026-62-1
ISBN for complete publication (two parts): 978-1-907026-60-7

International
Accounting Standards
Board®

Contents

Documents accompanying:

International Financial Reporting Standards (IFRSs)

International Accounting Standards (IASs)

IASB documents published to accompany

International Financial Reporting Standard 1

First-time Adoption of International Financial Reporting Standards

This version includes amendments resulting from IFRSs issued up to 31 December 2009.

The text of the unaccompanied IFRS 1 is contained in Part A of this edition. Its effective date is 1 July 2009. The effective date of the latest amendments is 1 January 2013. This part presents the following accompanying documents:

Approval by the Board of IFRS 1 issued in November 2008

International Financial Reporting Standard 1 *First-time Adoption of International Financial Reporting Standards* (as revised in 2008) was approved for issue by the thirteen members of the International Accounting Standards Board.[*]

Sir David Tweedie	Chairman
Thomas E Jones	Vice-Chairman
Mary E Barth	
Stephen Cooper	
Philippe Danjou	
Jan Engström	
Robert P Garnett	
Gilbert Gélard	
James J Leisenring	
Warren J McGregor	
John T Smith	
Tatsumi Yamada	
Wei-Guo Zhang	

---

[*] Professor Barth and Mr Danjou dissented from *Cost of an Investment in a Subsidiary, Jointly Controlled Entity or Associate* (Amendments to IFRS 1 and IAS 27) issued in May 2008. Their dissenting opinions are set out after the Basis for Conclusions on IAS 27.

Approval by the Board of *Additional Exemptions for First-time Adopters* (Amendments to IFRS 1) issued in July 2009

Additional Exemptions for First-time Adopters (Amendments to IFRS 1) was approved for issue by the fourteen members of the International Accounting Standards Board.

Sir David Tweedie   Chairman

Thomas E Jones   Vice-Chairman

Mary E Barth

Stephen Cooper

Philippe Danjou

Jan Engström

Robert P Garnett

Gilbert Gélard

Prabhakar Kalavacherla

James J Leisenring

Warren J McGregor

John T Smith

Tatsumi Yamada

Wei-Guo Zhang

CONTENTS

Basis for Conclusions on
IFRS 1 *First-time Adoption of International Financial Reporting Standards*

This Basis for Conclusions accompanies, but is not part of, IFRS 1.

In this Basis for Conclusions the terminology has not been amended to reflect the changes made by IAS 1 Presentation of Financial Statements (as revised in 2007).

This Basis for Conclusions has not been revised to reflect the restructuring of IFRS 1 in November 2008, but cross-references have been updated.

Introduction

BC1   This Basis for Conclusions summarises the International Accounting Standards Board's considerations in reaching the conclusions in IFRS 1 *First-time Adoption of International Financial Reporting Standards*. Individual Board members gave greater weight to some factors than to others.

BC2   SIC-8 *First-time Application of IASs as the Primary Basis of Accounting*, issued in 1998, dealt with matters that arose when an entity first adopted IASs. In 2001, the Board began a project to review SIC-8. In July 2002, the Board published ED 1 *First-time Application of International Financial Reporting Standards*, with a comment deadline of 31 October 2002. The Board received 83 comment letters on ED 1. IFRS 1 was issued by the Board in June 2003.

BC2A   IFRS 1 replaced SIC-8. The Board developed the IFRS to address concerns that:

(a)   some aspects of SIC-8's requirement for full retrospective application caused costs that exceeded the likely benefits for users of financial statements. Moreover, although SIC-8 did not require retrospective application when this would be impracticable, it did not explain whether a first-time adopter should interpret impracticability as a high hurdle or a low hurdle and it did not specify any particular treatment in cases of impracticability.

(b)   SIC-8 could require a first-time adopter to apply two different versions of a standard if a new version were introduced during the periods covered by its first financial statements prepared under IASs and the new version prohibited retrospective application.

(c)   SIC-8 did not state clearly whether a first-time adopter should use hindsight in applying recognition and measurement decisions retrospectively.

(d)   there was some doubt about how SIC-8 interacted with specific transitional provisions in individual standards.

BC2B   Like SIC-8, IFRS 1 requires retrospective application in most areas. Unlike SIC-8, it:

(a)   includes targeted exemptions to avoid costs that would be likely to exceed the benefits to users of financial statements, and a small number of other exceptions for practical reasons.

(b)   clarifies that an entity applies the latest version of IFRSs.

    (c)   clarifies how a first-time adopter's estimates in accordance with IFRSs relate to the estimates it made for the same date in accordance with previous GAAP.

    (d)   specifies that the transitional provisions in other IFRSs do not apply to a first-time adopter.

    (e)   requires enhanced disclosure about the transition to IFRSs.

BC3   The project took on added significance because of the requirement for listed European Union companies to adopt IFRSs in their consolidated financial statements from 2005. Several other countries announced that they would permit or require entities to adopt IFRSs in the next few years. Nevertheless, the Board's aim in developing the IFRS was to find solutions that would be appropriate for any entity, in any part of the world, regardless of whether adoption occurs in 2005 or at a different time.

Restructuring of the IFRS

BC3A   Since it was issued in 2003, IFRS 1 has been amended many times to accommodate first-time adoption requirements resulting from new or amended IFRSs. Because of the way IFRS 1 was structured, those amendments made the IFRS more complex and less clear. As more amendments become necessary, this problem will become worse.

BC3B   As part of its improvements project in 2007, therefore, the Board proposed to change the structure of IFRS 1 without amending its substance. Respondents to the exposure draft published in October 2007 supported the restructuring. The revised structure of the IFRS issued in November 2008 is easier for the reader to understand and is better designed to accommodate future changes. The focus of the restructuring was to move to appendices all specific exemptions and exceptions from the requirements of IFRSs. Exemptions are categorised into business combinations, exemptions and short-term exemptions. Exemptions are applicable to all first-time adopters regardless of their date of transition to IFRSs. Short-term exemptions are those exemptions applicable to users for a short time. Once those exemptions have become out of date, they will be deleted.

Scope

BC4   The IFRS applies to an entity that presents its first IFRS financial statements (a first-time adopter). Some suggested that an entity should not be regarded as a first-time adopter if its previous financial statements contained an explicit statement of compliance with IFRSs, except for specified (and explicit) departures. They argued that an explicit statement of compliance establishes that an entity regards IFRSs as its basis of accounting, even if the entity does not comply with every requirement of every IFRS. Some regarded this argument as especially strong if an entity previously complied with all recognition and measurement requirements of IFRSs, but did not give some required disclosures—for example, segmental disclosures that IAS 14 *Segment Reporting** requires or the explicit statement of compliance with IFRSs that IAS 1 *Presentation of Financial Statements* requires.

BC5 To implement that approach, it would be necessary to establish how many departures are needed—and how serious they must be—before an entity would conclude that it has not adopted IFRSs. In the Board's view, this would lead to complexity and uncertainty. Also, an entity should not be regarded as having adopted IFRSs if it does not give all disclosures required by IFRSs, because that approach would diminish the importance of disclosures and undermine efforts to promote full compliance with IFRSs. Therefore, the IFRS contains a simple test that gives an unambiguous answer: an entity has adopted IFRSs if, and only if, its financial statements contain an explicit and unreserved statement of compliance with IFRSs (paragraph 3 of the IFRS).

BC6 If an entity's financial statements in previous years contained that statement, any material disclosed or undisclosed departures from IFRSs are errors. The entity applies IAS 8 *Accounting Policies, Changes in Accounting Estimates and Errors* in correcting them.

Basic concepts

Useful information for users

BC7 In developing recognition and measurement requirements for an entity's opening IFRS balance sheet, the Board referred to the objective of financial statements, as set out in the *Framework for the Preparation and Presentation of Financial Statements*. The *Framework* states that the objective of financial statements is to provide information about the financial position, performance and changes in financial position of an entity that is useful to a wide range of users in making economic decisions.

BC8 The *Framework* identifies four qualitative characteristics that make information in financial statements useful to users. In summary, the information should be:

(a) readily understandable by users.

(b) relevant to the decision-making needs of users.

(c) reliable, in other words financial statements should:

    (i) represent faithfully the transactions and other events they either purport to represent or could reasonably be expected to represent;

    (ii) represent transactions and other events in accordance with their substance and economic reality and not merely their legal form;

    (iii) be neutral, that is to say, free from bias;

    (iv) contend with the uncertainties that inevitably surround many events and circumstances by the exercise of prudence; and

    (v) be complete within the bounds of materiality and cost.

---

* In 2006 IAS 14 was replaced by IFRS 8 *Operating Segments*.

(d)   comparable with information provided by the entity in its financial statements through time and with information provided in the financial statements of other entities.

Comparability

BC9   The previous paragraph notes the need for comparability. Ideally, a regime for first-time adoption of IFRSs would achieve comparability:

(a)   within an entity over time;

(b)   between different first-time adopters; and

(c)   between first-time adopters and entities that already apply IFRSs.

BC10   SIC-8 gave priority to ensuring comparability between a first-time adopter and entities that already applied IASs. It was based on the principle that a first-time adopter should comply with the same standards as an entity that already applied IASs. However, the Board decided that it is more important to achieve comparability over time within a first-time adopter's first IFRS financial statements and between different entities adopting IFRSs for the first time at a given date; achieving comparability between first-time adopters and entities that already apply IFRSs is a secondary objective.

Current version of IFRSs

BC11   Paragraphs 7–9 of the IFRS require a first-time adopter to apply the current version of IFRSs, without considering superseded or amended versions. This:

(a)   enhances comparability, because the information in a first-time adopter's first IFRS financial statements is prepared on a consistent basis over time;

(b)   gives users comparative information prepared using later versions of IFRSs that the Board regards as superior to superseded versions; and

(c)   avoids unnecessary costs.

BC12   In general, the transitional provisions in other IFRSs do not apply to a first-time adopter (paragraph 9 of the IFRS). Some of these transitional provisions require or permit an entity already reporting in accordance with IFRSs to apply a new requirement prospectively. These provisions generally reflect a conclusion that one or both of the following factors are present in a particular case:

(a)   Retrospective application may be difficult or involve costs exceeding the likely benefits. The IFRS permits prospective application in specific cases where this could occur (paragraphs BC30–BC73).

(b)   There is a danger of abuse if retrospective application would require judgements by management about past conditions after the outcome of a particular transaction is already known. The IFRS prohibits retrospective application in some areas where this could occur (paragraphs BC74–BC84).

BC13   Some have suggested three further reasons for permitting or requiring prospective application in some cases:

(a)   to alleviate unforeseen consequences of a new IFRS if another party uses financial statements to monitor compliance with a contract or agreement. However, in the Board's view, it is up to the parties to an agreement to determine whether to insulate the agreement from the effects of a future IFRS and, if not, how they might renegotiate it so that it reflects changes in the underlying financial condition rather than changes in reporting (paragraph 21 of the *Preface to International Financial Reporting Standards*).

(b)   to give a first-time adopter the same accounting options as an entity that already applies IFRSs. However, permitting prospective application by a first-time adopter would conflict with the Board's primary objective of comparability within an entity's first IFRS financial statements (paragraph BC10). Therefore, the Board did not adopt a general policy of giving first-time adopters the same accounting options of prospective application that existing IFRSs give to entities that already apply IFRSs. Paragraphs BC20–BC23 discuss one specific case, namely derecognition of financial assets and financial liabilities.

(c)   to avoid difficult distinctions between changes in estimates and changes in the basis for making estimates. However, a first-time adopter need not make this distinction in preparing its opening IFRS balance sheet, so the IFRS does not include exemptions on these grounds. If an entity becomes aware of errors made under previous GAAP, the IFRS requires it to disclose the correction of the errors (paragraph 26 of the IFRS).

BC14   The Board will consider case by case when it issues a new IFRS whether a first-time adopter should apply that IFRS retrospectively or prospectively. The Board expects that retrospective application will be appropriate in most cases, given its primary objective of comparability over time within a first-time adopter's first IFRS financial statements. However, if the Board concludes in a particular case that prospective application by a first-time adopter is justified, it will amend the IFRS on first-time adoption of IFRSs. As a result, IFRS 1 will contain all material on first-time adoption of IFRSs and other IFRSs will not refer to first-time adopters (except, when needed, in the Basis for Conclusions and consequential amendments).

BC15   Under the proposals in ED 1, a first-time adopter could have elected to apply IFRSs as if it had always applied IFRSs. This alternative approach was intended mainly to help an entity that did not wish to use any of the exemptions proposed in ED 1 because it had already been accumulating information in accordance with IFRSs without presenting IFRS financial statements. To enable an entity using this approach to use the information it had already accumulated, ED 1 would have required it to consider superseded versions of IFRSs if more recent versions required prospective application. However, as explained in paragraphs BC28 and BC29, the Board abandoned ED 1's all-or-nothing approach to exemptions. Because this eliminated the reason for the alternative approach, the Board deleted it in finalising the IFRS.

Opening IFRS balance sheet

BC16   An entity's opening IFRS balance sheet is the starting point for its accounting in accordance with IFRSs. The following paragraphs explain how the Board used the *Framework* in developing recognition and measurement requirements for the opening IFRS balance sheet.

Recognition

BC17   The Board considered a suggestion that the IFRS should not require a first-time adopter to investigate transactions that occurred before the beginning of a 'look back' period of, say, three to five years before the date of transition to IFRSs. Some argued that this would be a practical way for a first-time adopter to give a high level of transparency and comparability, without incurring the cost of investigating very old transactions. They noted two particular precedents for transitional provisions that have permitted an entity to omit some assets and liabilities from its balance sheet:

(a)   A previous version of IAS 39 *Financial Instruments: Recognition and Measurement* prohibited restatement of securitisation, transfer or other derecognition transactions entered into before the beginning of the financial year in which it was initially applied.

(b)   Some national accounting standards and IAS 17 *Accounting for Leases* (superseded in 1997 by IAS 17 *Leases*) permitted prospective application of a requirement for lessees to capitalise finance leases. Under this approach, a lessee would not be required to recognise finance lease obligations and the related leased assets for leases that began before a specified date.

BC18   However, limiting the look back period could lead to the omission of material assets or liabilities from an entity's opening IFRS balance sheet. Material omissions would undermine the understandability, relevance, reliability and comparability of an entity's first IFRS financial statements. Therefore, the Board concluded that an entity's opening IFRS balance sheet should:

(a)   include all assets and liabilities whose recognition is required by IFRSs, except:

(i)   some financial assets or financial liabilities derecognised in accordance with previous GAAP before the date of transition to IFRSs (paragraphs BC20–BC23); and

(ii)   goodwill and other assets acquired, and liabilities assumed, in a past business combination that were not recognised in the acquirer's consolidated balance sheet in accordance with previous GAAP and also would not qualify for recognition in accordance with IFRSs in the balance sheet of the acquiree (paragraphs BC31–BC40).

(b)   not report items as assets or liabilities if they do not qualify for recognition in accordance with IFRSs.

BC19   Some financial instruments may be classified as equity in accordance with previous GAAP but as financial liabilities in accordance with IAS 32 *Financial Instruments: Presentation*. Some respondents to ED 1 requested an extended transitional period to enable the issuer of such instruments to renegotiate contracts that refer to debt-equity ratios. However, although a new IFRS may have unforeseen consequences if another party uses financial statements to monitor compliance with a contract or agreement, that possibility does not, in the Board's view, justify prospective application (paragraph BC13(a)).

Derecognition in accordance with previous GAAP

BC20   An entity may have derecognised financial assets or financial liabilities in accordance with its previous GAAP that do not qualify for derecognition in accordance with IAS 39. ED 1 proposed that a first-time adopter should recognise those assets and liabilities in its opening IFRS balance sheet. Some respondents to ED 1 requested the Board to permit or require a first-time adopter not to restate past derecognition transactions, on the following grounds:

   (a)   Restating past derecognition transactions would be costly, especially if restatement involves determining the fair value of retained servicing assets and liabilities and other components retained in a complex securitisation. Furthermore, it may be difficult to obtain information on financial assets held by transferees that are not under the transferor's control.

   (b)   Restatement undermines the legal certainty expected by parties who entered into transactions on the basis of the accounting rules in effect at the time.

   (c)   IAS 39 did not, before the improvements proposed in June 2002, require (or even permit) entities to restate past derecognition transactions. Without a similar exemption, first-time adopters would be unfairly disadvantaged.

   (d)   Retrospective application would not result in consistent measurement, as entities would need to recreate information about past transactions with the benefit of hindsight.

BC21   The Board had considered these arguments in developing ED 1. The Board's reasons for the proposal in ED 1 were as follows:

   (a)   The omission of material assets or liabilities would undermine the understandability, relevance, reliability and comparability of an entity's financial statements. Many of the transactions under discussion are large and will have effects for many years.

   (b)   Such an exemption would be inconsistent with the June 2002 exposure draft of improvements to IAS 39.

   (c)   The Board's primary objective is to achieve comparability over time within an entity's first IFRS financial statements. Prospective application by a first-time adopter would conflict with that primary objective, even if prospective application were available to entities already applying IFRSs.

(d)   Although a new IFRS may have unforeseen consequences if another party uses financial statements to monitor compliance with a contract or agreement, that possibility does not justify prospective application (paragraph BC13(a)).

BC22   Nevertheless, in finalising the IFRS, the Board concluded that it would be premature to require a treatment different from the current version of IAS 39 before completing the proposed improvements to IAS 39. Accordingly, the IFRS originally required the same treatment as the then current version of IAS 39 for derecognition transactions before the effective date of the then current version of IAS 39, namely that any financial assets or financial liabilities derecognised in accordance with previous GAAP before financial years beginning on 1 January 2001 remain derecognised. The Board agreed that when it completed the improvements to IAS 39, it might amend or delete this exemption.

BC22A   The Board reconsidered this issue in completing the revision of IAS 39 in 2003. The Board decided to retain the transition requirements as set out in IFRS 1, for the reasons given in paragraph BC20. However, the Board amended the date from which prospective application was required to transactions that occur on or after 1 January 2004 in order to overcome the practical difficulties of restating transactions that had been derecognised before that date.

BC22B   The Board also noted that financial statements that include financial assets and financial liabilities that would otherwise be omitted under the provisions of the IFRS would be more complete and therefore more useful to users of financial statements. The Board therefore decided to permit retrospective application of the derecognition requirements. It also decided that retrospective application should be limited to cases when the information needed to apply the IFRS to past transactions was obtained at the time of initially accounting for those transactions. This limitation prevents the unacceptable use of hindsight.

BC23   The Board removed from IAS 39 the following consequential amendments to IAS 39 made when IFRS 1 was issued, because, for first-time adopters, these clarifications are clear in paragraphs IG26–IG31 and IG53 of the guidance on implementing IFRS 1. These were:

(a)   the clarification that an entity is required to apply IAS 39 to all derivatives or other interests retained after a derecognition transaction, even if the transaction occurred before the effective date of IAS 39; and

(b)   the confirmation that there are no exemptions for special purpose entities that existed before the date of transition to IFRSs.

Measurement

BC24   The Board considered whether it should require a first-time adopter to measure all assets and liabilities at fair value in the opening IFRS balance sheet. Some argued that this would result in more relevant information than an aggregation of costs incurred at different dates, or of costs and fair values. However, the Board concluded that a requirement to measure all assets and liabilities at fair value at the date of transition to IFRSs would be unreasonable, given that an entity may use an IFRS-compliant cost-based measurement before and after that date for some items.

BC25   The Board decided as a general principle that a first-time adopter should measure all assets and liabilities recognised in its opening IFRS balance sheet on the basis required by the relevant IFRSs. This is needed for an entity's first IFRS financial statements to present understandable, relevant, reliable and comparable information.

Benefits and costs

BC26   The *Framework* acknowledges that the need for a balance between the benefits of information and the cost of providing it may constrain the provision of relevant and reliable information. The Board considered these cost-benefit constraints and developed targeted exemptions from the general principle described in paragraph BC25. SIC-8 did not include specific exemptions of this kind, although it provided general exemptions from:

(a)   retrospective adjustments to the opening balance of retained earnings 'when the amount of the adjustment relating to prior periods cannot be reasonably determined'.

(b)   provision of comparative information when it is 'impracticable' to provide such information.

BC27   The Board expects that most first-time adopters will begin planning on a timely basis for the transition to IFRSs. Accordingly, in balancing benefits and costs, the Board took as its benchmark an entity that plans the transition well in advance and can collect most information needed for its opening IFRS balance sheet at, or very soon after, the date of transition to IFRSs.

BC28   ED 1 proposed that a first-time adopter should use either all the exemptions in ED 1 or none. However, some respondents disagreed with this all-or-nothing approach for the following reasons:

(a)   Many of the exemptions are not interdependent, so there is no conceptual reason to condition use of one exemption on use of other exemptions.

(b)   Although it is necessary to permit some exemptions on pragmatic grounds, entities should be encouraged to use as few exemptions as possible.

(c)   Some of the exemptions proposed in ED 1 were implicit options because they relied on the entity's own judgement of undue cost or effort and some others were explicit options. Only a few exemptions were really mandatory.

(d)   Unlike the other exceptions to retrospective application, the requirement to apply hedge accounting prospectively was not intended as a pragmatic concession on cost-benefit grounds. Retrospective application in an area that relies on designation by management would not be acceptable, even if an entity applied all other aspects of IFRSs retrospectively.

BC29   The Board found these comments persuasive. In finalising the IFRS, the Board grouped the exceptions to retrospective application into two categories:

(a)   Some exceptions consist of optional exemptions (paragraphs BC30–BC63E).

(b)   The other exceptions prohibit full retrospective application of IFRSs to some aspects of derecognition (paragraphs BC20–BC23), hedge accounting (paragraphs BC75–BC80), and estimates (paragraph BC84).

Exemptions from other IFRSs

BC30   An entity may elect to use one or more of the following exemptions:

(a)   business combinations (paragraphs BC31–BC40);

(b)   deemed cost (paragraphs BC41–BC47E);

(c)   employee benefits (paragraphs BC48–BC52);

(d)   cumulative translation differences (paragraphs BC53–BC55);

(e)   compound financial instruments (paragraphs BC56–BC58);

(f)   investments in subsidiaries, jointly controlled entities and associates (paragraphs BC58A–BC58M);

(g)   assets and liabilities of subsidiaries, associates and joint ventures (paragraphs BC59–BC63);

(h)   designation of previously recognised financial instruments (paragraph BC63A);

(i)   share-based payment transactions (paragraph BC63B);

(j)   changes in existing decommissioning, restoration and similar liabilities included in the cost of property, plant and equipment (paragraphs BC63C and BC63CA);

(k)   leases (paragraphs BC63D–BC63DB); and

(l)   borrowing costs (paragraph BC63E).

Business combinations

BC31   The following paragraphs discuss various aspects of accounting for business combinations that an entity recognised in accordance with previous GAAP before the date of transition to IFRSs:

(a)   whether retrospective restatement of past business combinations should be prohibited, permitted or required (paragraphs BC32–BC34).

(b)   whether an entity should recognise assets acquired and liabilities assumed in a past business combination if it did not recognise them in accordance with previous GAAP (paragraph BC35).

(c)   whether an entity should restate amounts assigned to the assets and liabilities of the combining entities if previous GAAP brought forward unchanged their pre-combination carrying amounts (paragraph BC36).

(d)   whether an entity should restate goodwill for adjustments made in its opening IFRS balance sheet to the carrying amounts of assets acquired and liabilities assumed in past business combinations (paragraphs BC37–BC40).

BC32   Retrospective application of IFRS 3 *Business Combinations* could require an entity to recreate data that it did not capture at the date of a past business combination and make subjective estimates about conditions that existed at that date. These factors could reduce the relevance and reliability of the entity's first IFRS financial statements. Therefore, ED 1 would have prohibited restatement of past business combinations (unless an entity used the proposed alternative approach, discussed in paragraph BC15, of applying IFRSs as if it had always applied IFRSs). Some respondents agreed, arguing that restatement of past business combinations would involve subjective, and potentially selective, use of hindsight that would diminish the relevance and reliability of financial statements.

BC33 Other respondents disagreed. They argued that:

(a) effects of business combination accounting can last for many years. Previous GAAP may differ significantly from IFRSs, and in some countries there are no accounting requirements at all for business combinations. Previous GAAP balances might not result in decision-useful information in these countries.

(b) restatement is preferable and may not involve as much cost or effort for more recent business combinations.

BC34 In the light of these comments, the Board concluded that restatement of past business combinations is conceptually preferable, although for cost-benefit reasons this should be permitted but not required. The Board decided to place some limits on this election and noted that information is more likely to be available for more recent business combinations. Therefore, if a first-time adopter restates any business combination, the IFRS requires it to restate all later business combinations (paragraph C1 of the IFRS).

BC35 If an entity did not recognise a particular asset or liability in accordance with previous GAAP at the date of the business combination, ED 1 proposed that its deemed cost in accordance with IFRSs would be zero. As a result, the entity's opening IFRS balance sheet would not have included that asset or liability if IFRSs permit or require a cost-based measurement. Some respondents to ED 1 argued that this would be an unjustifiable departure from the principle that the opening IFRS balance sheet should include all assets and liabilities. The Board agreed with that conclusion. Therefore, paragraph C4(f) of the IFRS requires that the acquirer should recognise those assets and liabilities and measure them on the basis that IFRSs would require in the separate balance sheet of the acquiree.

BC36 In accordance with previous GAAP, an entity might have brought forward unchanged the pre-combination carrying amounts of the combining entities' assets and liabilities. Some argued that it would be inconsistent to use these carrying amounts as deemed cost in accordance with IFRSs, given that the IFRS does not permit the use of similar carrying amounts as deemed cost for assets and liabilities that were not acquired in a business combination. However, the Board identified no specific form of past business combination, and no specific form of accounting for past business combinations, for which it would not be acceptable to bring forward cost-based measurements made in accordance with previous GAAP.

BC37 Although the IFRS treats amounts assigned in accordance with previous GAAP to goodwill and other assets acquired and liabilities assumed in a past business combination as their deemed cost in accordance with IFRSs at the date of the business combination, an entity needs to adjust their carrying amounts in its opening IFRS balance sheet, as follows.

(a)   Assets and liabilities measured in accordance with IFRSs at fair value or other forms of current value: remeasure to fair value or that other current value.

(b)   Assets (other than goodwill) and liabilities for which IFRSs apply a cost-based measurement: adjust the accumulated depreciation or amortisation since the date of the business combination if it does not comply with IFRSs. Depreciation is based on deemed cost, which is the carrying amount in accordance with previous GAAP immediately following the business combination.

(c)   Assets (other than goodwill) and liabilities not recognised in accordance with previous GAAP: measure on the basis that IFRSs would require in the separate balance sheet of the acquiree.

(d)   Items that do not qualify for recognition as assets and liabilities in accordance with IFRSs: eliminate from the opening IFRS balance sheet.

BC38   The Board considered whether a first-time adopter should recognise the resulting adjustments by restating goodwill. Because intangible assets and goodwill are closely related, the Board decided that a first-time adopter should restate goodwill when it:

(a)   eliminates an item that was recognised in accordance with previous GAAP as an intangible asset but does not qualify for separate recognition in accordance with IFRSs; or

(b)   recognises an intangible asset that was subsumed within goodwill in accordance with previous GAAP.

However, to avoid costs that would exceed the likely benefits to users, the IFRS prohibits restatement of goodwill for most other adjustments reflected in the opening IFRS balance sheet, unless a first-time adopter elects to apply IFRS 3 retrospectively (paragraph C4(g) of the IFRS).

BC39   To minimise the possibility of double-counting an item that was included in goodwill in accordance with previous GAAP, and is included in accordance with IFRSs either within the measurement of another asset or as a deduction from a liability, the IFRS requires an entity to test goodwill recognised in its opening IFRS balance sheet for impairment (paragraph C4(g)(ii) of the IFRS). This does not prevent the implicit recognition of internally generated goodwill that arose after the date of the business combination. However, the Board concluded that an attempt to exclude such internally generated goodwill would be costly and lead to arbitrary results.

BC40   Some respondents to ED 1 suggested that a formal impairment test should be required only if there is a possibility of double-counting—ie when additional, previously unrecognised, assets relating to a past business combination are recognised in the opening IFRS balance sheet (or an indicator of impairment is present). However, the Board decided that a first-time adopter should carry out a formal impairment test of all goodwill recognised in its opening IFRS balance sheet, as previous GAAP might not have required a test of comparable rigour.

Deemed cost

BC41   Some measurements in accordance with IFRSs are based on an accumulation of past costs or other transaction data. If an entity has not previously collected the necessary information, collecting or estimating it retrospectively may be costly. To avoid excessive cost, ED 1 proposed that an entity could use the fair value of an item of property, plant and equipment at the date of transition to IFRSs as its deemed cost at that date if determining a cost-based measurement in accordance with IFRSs would involve undue cost or effort.

BC42   In finalising the IFRS, the Board noted that reconstructed cost data might be less relevant to users, and less reliable, than current fair value data. Furthermore, the Board concluded that balancing costs and benefits was a task for the Board when it sets accounting requirements rather than for entities when they apply those requirements. Therefore, the IFRS permits an entity to use fair value as deemed cost in some cases without any need to demonstrate undue cost or effort.

BC43   Some expressed concerns that the use of fair value would lead to lack of comparability. However, cost is generally equivalent to fair value at the date of acquisition. Therefore, the use of fair value as the deemed cost of an asset means that an entity will report the same cost data as if it had acquired an asset with the same remaining service potential at the date of transition to IFRSs. If there is any lack of comparability, it arises from the aggregation of costs incurred at different dates, rather than from the targeted use of fair value as deemed cost for some assets. The Board regarded this approach as justified to solve the unique problem of introducing IFRSs in a cost-effective way without damaging transparency.

BC44   The IFRS restricts the use of fair value as deemed cost to those assets for which reconstructing costs is likely to be of limited benefit to users and particularly onerous: property, plant and equipment, investment property (if an entity elects to use the cost method in IAS 40 *Investment Property*) and intangible assets that meet restrictive criteria (paragraphs D5 and D7 of the IFRS).

BC45   Under the revaluation model in IAS 16 *Property, Plant and Equipment*, if an entity revalues an asset, it must revalue all assets in that class. This restriction prevents selective revaluation of only those assets whose revaluation would lead to a particular result. Some suggested a similar restriction on the use of fair value as deemed cost. However, IAS 36 *Impairment of Assets* requires an impairment test if there is any indication that an asset is impaired. Thus, if an entity uses fair value as deemed cost for assets whose fair value is above cost, it cannot ignore indications that the recoverable amount of other assets may have fallen below their carrying amount. Therefore, the IFRS does not restrict the use of fair value as deemed cost to entire classes of asset.

BC46   Some revaluations in accordance with previous GAAP might be more relevant to users than original cost. If so, it would not be reasonable to require time-consuming and expensive reconstruction of a cost that complies with IFRSs. In consequence, the IFRS permits an entity to use amounts determined using previous GAAP as deemed cost for IFRSs in the following cases:

(a)   if an entity revalued one of the assets described in paragraph BC44 using its previous GAAP and the revaluation met specified criteria (paragraphs D6 and D7 of the IFRS).

(b) if an entity established a deemed cost in accordance with previous GAAP for some or all assets and liabilities by measuring them at their fair value at one particular date because of an event such as a privatisation or initial public offering (paragraph D8 of the IFRS).

BC47 Paragraph D6 of the IFRS refers to revaluations that are broadly comparable to fair value or reflect an index applied to a cost that is broadly comparable to cost determined in accordance with IFRSs. It may not always be clear whether a previous revaluation was intended as a measure of fair value or differs materially from fair value. The flexibility in this area permits a cost-effective solution for the unique problem of transition to IFRSs. It allows a first-time adopter to establish a deemed cost using a measurement that is already available and is a reasonable starting point for a cost-based measurement.

BC47A Under their previous GAAP many oil and gas entities accounted for exploration and development costs for properties in development or production in cost centres that include all properties in a large geographical area. (In some jurisdictions, this is referred to as full cost accounting.) Those entities will in most cases have to determine the carrying amounts for oil and gas assets at the date of transition to IFRSs. Information about oil and gas assets recorded in an accounting system using this method of accounting will almost always be at a larger unit of account than the unit of account that is acceptable under IFRSs. Amortisation at the IFRS unit of account level would also have to be calculated (on a unit of production basis) for each year, using a reserves base that has changed over time because of changes in factors such as geological understanding and prices for oil and gas. In many cases, particularly for older assets, this information may not be available. The Board was advised that even if such information is available the effort and associated cost to determine the opening balances at the date of transition would usually be very high.

BC47B IFRS 1 permits an entity to measure an item of property, plant and equipment at its fair value at the date of transition to IFRSs and to use that fair value as the item's deemed cost at that date. Determining the fair value of oil and gas assets is a complex process that begins with the difficult task of estimating the volume of reserves and resources. When the fair value amounts must be audited, determining significant inputs to the estimates generally requires the use of qualified external experts. For entities with many oil and gas assets, the use of this fair value as deemed cost alternative would not meet the Board's stated intention of avoiding excessive cost (see paragraph BC41).

BC47C The Board decided that for oil and gas assets in the development or production phases, it would permit entities that used the method of accounting described in paragraph BC47A under their previous GAAP to determine the deemed cost at the date of transition to IFRSs using an allocation of the amount determined for a cost centre under the entity's previous GAAP on the basis of the reserves associated with the oil and gas assets in that cost centre.

BC47D The deemed cost of oil and gas assets determined in this way may include amounts that would not have been capitalised in accordance with IFRSs, such as some overhead costs, costs that were incurred before the entity obtained legal rights to explore a specific area (and cannot be capitalised in accordance with IAS 38 Intangible Assets) and, most significantly, unsuccessful exploration costs.

This is a consequence of having included these costs in the single carrying amount under the method of accounting described in paragraph BC47A. To avoid the use of deemed costs resulting in an oil and gas asset being measured at more than its recoverable amount, the Board decided that oil and gas assets should be tested for impairment at the date of transition to IFRSs.

BC47E   Not all oil and gas entities used the method of accounting described in paragraph BC47A under their previous GAAP. Some used a method of accounting that requires a unit of account that is generally consistent with IFRSs and does not cause similar transition issues. Therefore, the Board decided that the exemption would apply only to entities that used the method of accounting described in paragraph BC47A under their previous GAAP.

Employee benefits

BC48   If an entity elects to use the 'corridor' approach in IAS 19 *Employee Benefits*, full retrospective application of IAS 19 would require the entity to determine actuarial gains or losses for each year since the inception of the plan in order to determine the net cumulative unrecognised gains or losses at the date of transition to IFRSs. The Board concluded that this would not benefit users and would be costly. Therefore, the IFRS permits a first-time adopter to recognise all actuarial gains or losses up to the date of transition to IFRSs, even if its accounting policy in accordance with IAS 19 involves leaving some later actuarial gains and losses unrecognised (paragraph D10 of the IFRS).

BC49   The revision of IAS 19 in 1998 increased the reported employee benefit liabilities of some entities. IAS 19 permitted entities to amortise that increase over up to five years. Some suggested a similar transitional treatment for first-time adopters. However, the Board has no general policy of exempting transactions occurring before a specific date from the requirements of new IFRSs (paragraph 21 of the *Preface to International Financial Reporting Standards*). Therefore, the Board did not include a similar transitional provision for first-time adopters.

BC50   An entity's first IFRS financial statements may reflect measurements of pension liabilities at three dates: the reporting date, the end of the comparative year and the date of transition to IFRSs. Some suggested that obtaining three separate actuarial valuations for a single set of financial statements would be costly. Therefore, they proposed that the Board should permit an entity to use a single actuarial valuation, based, for example, on assumptions valid at the reporting date, with service costs and interest costs based on those assumptions for each of the periods presented.

BC51   However, the Board concluded that a general exemption from the principle of measurement at each date would conflict with the objective of providing understandable, relevant, reliable and comparable information for users. If an entity obtains a full actuarial valuation at one or two of these dates and rolls that (those) valuation(s) forward or back to the other date(s), any such roll forward or roll back needs to reflect material transactions and other material events (including changes in market prices and interest rates) between those dates (IAS 19 paragraph 57).

BC52　Some suggested that the Board should exempt a first-time adopter from the requirement to identify and amortise the unvested portion of past service cost at the date of transition to IFRSs. However, this requirement is less onerous than the retrospective application of the corridor for actuarial gains and losses because it does not require the recreation of data since the inception of the plan. The Board concluded that no exemption was justified for past service cost.

Cumulative translation differences

BC53　IAS 21 *The Effects of Changes in Foreign Exchange Rates* requires an entity to classify some cumulative translation differences (CTDs) relating to a net investment in a foreign operation as a separate component of equity. The entity transfers the CTDs to the income statement on subsequent disposal of the foreign operation. The proposals in ED 1 would have permitted a first-time adopter to use the CTDs in accordance with previous GAAP as the deemed CTDs in accordance with IFRSs if reconstructing CTDs would have involved undue cost or effort.

BC54　Some respondents to ED 1 argued that it would be more transparent and comparable to exempt an entity from the requirement to identify CTDs at the date of transition to IFRSs, for the following reasons:

(a)　An entity might know the aggregate CTDs, but might not know the amount for each subsidiary. If so, it could not transfer that amount to the income statement on disposal of that subsidiary. This would defeat the objective of identifying CTDs as a separate component of equity.

(b)　The amount of CTDs in accordance with previous GAAP might be inappropriate as it might be affected by adjustments made on transition to IFRSs to assets and liabilities of foreign entities.

BC55　The Board found these arguments persuasive. Therefore, a first-time adopter need not identify the CTDs at the date of transition to IFRSs (paragraphs D12 and D13 of the IFRS). The first-time adopter need not show that identifying the CTDs would involve undue cost or effort.

Compound financial instruments

BC56　IAS 32 requires an entity to split a compound financial instrument at inception into separate liability and equity components. Even if the liability component is no longer outstanding, retrospective application of IAS 32 would involve separating two portions of equity. The first portion is in retained earnings and represents the cumulative interest accreted on the liability component. The other portion represents the original equity component of the instrument.

BC57　Some respondents to ED 1 argued that separating these two portions would be costly if the liability component of the compound instrument is no longer outstanding at the date of transition to IFRSs. The Board agreed with those comments. Therefore, if the liability component is no longer outstanding at the date of transition to IFRSs, a first-time adopter need not separate the cumulative interest on the liability component from the equity component (paragraph D18 of the IFRS).

BC58   Some respondents requested an exemption for compound instruments even if still outstanding at the date of transition to IFRSs. One possible approach would be to use the fair value of the components at the date of transition to IFRSs as deemed cost. However, as the IFRS does not include any exemptions for financial liabilities, the Board concluded that it would be inconsistent to create such an exemption for the liability component of a compound instrument.

Investments in subsidiaries, jointly controlled entities and associates

BC58A   IAS 27 *Consolidated and Separate Financial Statements* requires an entity, in its separate financial statements, to account for investments in subsidiaries, jointly controlled entities and associates either at cost or in accordance with IAS 39.* For those investments that are measured at cost, the previous version of IAS 27 (before *Cost of an Investment* in a *Subsidiary, Jointly Controlled Entity or Associate* was issued in May 2008) required an entity to recognise income from the investment only to the extent the entity received distributions from post-acquisition retained earnings (the 'cost method'). Distributions received in excess of such profits were regarded as a recovery of investment and were recognised as a reduction in the cost of the investment.

BC58B   For some jurisdictions, these aspects of IAS 27 led to practical difficulties on transition to IFRSs. In order to apply IAS 27 retrospectively, it would be necessary:

     (a)   to measure the fair value of the consideration given at the date of acquisition; and

     (b)   to determine whether any dividends received from a subsidiary after its acquisition were paid out of pre-acquisition retained earnings, which would reduce the carrying amount of the investment in the subsidiary in the parent's separate financial statements.

BC58C   If a parent held an investment in a subsidiary for many years, such an exercise might be difficult, or even impossible, and perhaps costly. For example, in some jurisdictions, entities accounted for some previous acquisitions that were share-for-share exchanges using so-called 'merger relief' or 'group reconstruction relief'. In this situation, the carrying amount of the investment in the parent's separate financial statements was based on the nominal value of the shares given rather than the value of the purchase consideration. This might make it difficult or impossible to measure the fair value of the shares given.

BC58D   The Board published *Cost of an Investment in a Subsidiary*, an exposure draft of proposed amendments to IFRS 1, in January 2007. In response to the issues outlined in paragraphs BC58A–BC58C, the Board proposed two exemptions from applying the requirements of IAS 27 retrospectively upon first-time adoption of IFRSs:

     (a)   an alternative approach for determining the cost of an investment in a subsidiary in the separate financial statements of a parent; and

     (b)   simplification of the process for determining the pre-acquisition retained earnings of that subsidiary.

---

*   In November 2009 the IASB amended some of the requirements of IAS 39 and relocated them to IFRS 9 *Financial Instruments*.

           © IASCF

BC58E In developing that exposure draft, the Board considered three ways of determining a deemed cost of an investment in a subsidiary at the parent's date of transition to IFRSs in its separate financial statements. These were:

(a) the previous GAAP cost of the investment (previous GAAP deemed cost).

(b) the parent's interest in the subsidiary's assets less liabilities, using the carrying amounts that IFRSs would require in the subsidiary's statement of financial position (net asset deemed cost).

(c) the fair value of the investment (fair value deemed cost).

BC58F The Board decided that the net asset deemed cost option would provide relevant information to users about the subsidiary's financial position at the date of transition to IFRSs and would be relatively easy to determine. The fair value deemed cost option would provide relevant information at the date of transition to IFRSs, but might be more costly and difficult to determine.

BC58G In some situations, the cost of an investment in a subsidiary determined using the previous GAAP carrying amount might bear little resemblance to cost determined in accordance with IAS 27. Therefore, the Board rejected the use of a deemed cost based on the previous GAAP carrying amount. The Board proposed to allow entities a choice between the net asset deemed cost and the fair value deemed cost.

BC58H Respondents to the exposure draft stated that the previous GAAP carrying amount is a more appropriate deemed cost. They argued that:

(a) a net asset deemed cost would not include goodwill or other intangible assets that might be present in a carrying amount determined in accordance with previous GAAP. When this is the case, the net asset deemed cost option would understate the assets of the entities for which it is used. The resulting reduction in the carrying amount of the investment could reduce the distributable profits of the parent.

(b) it was difficult to see why, in the light of the exemption in IFRS 1 from applying IFRS 3 retrospectively, the Board did not propose to permit the cost of the investment in a subsidiary in accordance with previous GAAP to be used as a deemed cost. When an entity had chosen not to apply IFRS 3 retrospectively to a past business combination, it would be logical not to require it to restate the cost of the related investment in the separate financial statements of the parent.

BC58I In the light of respondents' comments, the Board observed that, in many instances, neither the previous GAAP carrying amount nor the net asset deemed cost represents 'cost'—both numbers could be viewed as being equally arbitrary.

BC58J In order to reduce the cost of adopting IFRSs in the parent entity's separate financial statements without significantly reducing the benefits of those statements, the Board decided to allow entities a choice between the previous GAAP carrying amount and the fair value as deemed cost.

BC58K The Board also agreed with respondents that similar issues arise for investments in associates and jointly controlled entities. As a result, paragraph D15 of the IFRS applies to such investments.

BC58L   The Board published its revised proposals in *Cost of an Investment in a Subsidiary, Jointly Controlled Entity or Associate*, an exposure draft of proposed amendments to IFRS 1 and IAS 27, in December 2007. Respondents generally supported the proposed amendments to IFRS 1. The Board included the amendments in *Cost of an Investment in a Subsidiary, Jointly Controlled Entity or Associate* issued in May 2008.

BC58M   In developing the December 2007 exposure draft, the Board decided to address the simplification of the process for determining the pre-acquisition retained earnings of a subsidiary more generally through an amendment to IAS 27 (see paragraph 38A of IAS 27 and paragraphs BC66D–BC66J of the Basis for Conclusions on IAS 27).

Assets and liabilities of subsidiaries, associates and joint ventures

BC59   A subsidiary may have reported to its parent in the previous period using IFRSs without presenting a full set of financial statements in accordance with IFRSs. If the subsidiary subsequently begins to present financial statements that contain an explicit and unreserved statement of compliance with IFRSs, it becomes a first-time adopter at that time. This might compel the subsidiary to keep two parallel sets of accounting records based on different dates of transition to IFRSs, because some measurements in accordance with the IFRS depend on the date of transition to IFRSs.

BC60   In developing ED 1, the Board concluded that a requirement to keep two parallel sets of records would be burdensome and not be beneficial to users. Therefore, ED 1 proposed that a subsidiary would not be treated as a first-time adopter for recognition and measurement purposes if the subsidiary was consolidated in IFRS financial statements for the previous period and all owners of the minority interests consented.*

BC61   Some respondents to ED 1 opposed the exemption, on the following grounds:

(a)   The exemption would not eliminate all differences between the group reporting package and the subsidiary's own financial statements. The reporting package does not constitute a full set of financial statements, the parent may have made adjustments to the reported numbers (for example, if pension cost adjustments were made centrally), and the group materiality threshold may be higher than for the subsidiary.

(b)   The Board's objective of comparability between different entities adopting IFRSs for the first time at the same date (paragraph BC10) should apply equally to any entity, including subsidiaries, particularly if the subsidiary's debt or equity securities are publicly traded.

BC62   However, the Board retained the exemption because it will ease some practical problems. Although the exemption does not eliminate all differences between the subsidiary's financial statements and a group reporting package, it does reduce them. Furthermore, the exemption does not diminish the relevance and reliability of the subsidiary's financial statements because it permits a

---

*   In January 2008 the IASB issued an amended IAS 27 *Consolidated and Separate Financial Statements*, which amended 'minority interests' to 'non-controlling interests'.

measurement that is already acceptable in accordance with IFRSs in the consolidated financial statements of the parent. Therefore, the Board also eliminated the proposal in ED 1 that the exemption should be conditional on the consent of minorities.

BC63   In finalising the IFRS, the Board simplified the description of the exemption for a subsidiary that adopts IFRSs after its parent. In accordance with the IFRS, the subsidiary may measure its assets and liabilities at the carrying amounts that would be included in the parent's consolidated financial statements, based on the parent's date of transition to IFRSs, if no adjustments were made for consolidation procedures and for the effects of the business combination in which the parent acquired the subsidiary. Alternatively, it may elect to measure them at the carrying amounts required by the rest of the IFRS, based on the subsidiary's date of transition to IFRSs. The Board also extended the exemption to an associate or joint venture that becomes a first-time adopter later than an entity that has significant influence or joint control over it (paragraph D16 of the IFRS). However, if a parent adopts IFRSs later than a subsidiary, the parent cannot, in its consolidated financial statements, elect to change IFRS measurements that the subsidiary has already used in its financial statements, except to adjust for consolidation procedures and for the effects of the business combination in which the parent acquired the subsidiary (paragraph D17 of the IFRS).

Designation of previously recognised financial instruments

BC63A   IAS 39* permits an entity to designate, on initial recognition only, a financial instrument as (a) available for sale (for a financial asset) or (b) a financial asset or financial liability at fair value through profit or loss (provided the asset or liability qualifies for such designation in accordance with paragraph 9(b)(i), 9(b)(ii) or 11A of IAS 39). Despite this requirement, an entity that had already applied IFRSs before the effective date of IAS 39 (as revised in March 2004) may (a) designate a previously recognised financial asset as available for sale on initial application of IAS 39 (as revised in March 2004), or (b) designate a previously recognised financial instrument as at fair value through profit or loss in the circumstances specified in paragraph 105B of IAS 39. The Board decided that the same considerations apply to first-time adopters as to entities that already apply IFRSs. Accordingly, a first-time adopter of IFRSs may similarly designate a previously recognised financial instrument in accordance with paragraph D19 of the IFRS. Such an entity shall disclose the fair value of the financial assets or financial liabilities designated into each category at the date of designation and their classification and carrying amount in the previous financial statements.

Share-based payment transactions

BC63B   IFRS 2 *Share-based Payment* contains various transitional provisions. For example, for equity-settled share-based payment arrangements, IFRS 2 requires an entity to apply IFRS 2 to shares, share options or other equity instruments that were granted after 7 November 2002 and had not vested at the effective date of IFRS 2.

---

*   In November 2009 the IASB amended the requirements of IAS 39 relating to classification and measurement of assets within the scope of IAS 39 and relocated them to IFRS 9 *Financial Instruments*. IFRS 9 applies to all assets within the scope of IAS 39. This paragraph refers to matters relevant when IFRS 1 was issued.

IFRS 2 is effective for annual periods beginning on or after 1 January 2005. There are also transitional arrangements for liabilities arising from cash-settled share-based payment transactions, and for modifications of the terms or conditions of a grant of equity instruments to which IFRS 2 has not been applied, if the modification occurs after the effective date of IFRS 2. The Board decided that, in general, first-time adopters should be treated in the same way as entities that already apply IFRSs. For example, a first-time adopter should not be required to apply IFRS 2 to equity instruments that were granted on or before 7 November 2002. Similarly, a first-time adopter should not be required to apply IFRS 2 to equity instruments that were granted after 7 November 2002 if those equity instruments vested before 1 January 2005. In addition, the Board decided that a first-time adopter should not be required to apply IFRS 2 to equity instruments that were granted after 7 November 2002 if those equity instruments vested before the date of transition to IFRSs. Similarly, the Board decided that a first-time adopter should not be required to apply IFRS 2 to liabilities arising from cash-settled share-based payment transactions if those liabilities were settled before the date of transition to IFRSs.

Changes in existing decommissioning, restoration and similar liabilities included in the cost of property, plant and equipment

BC63C   IFRIC 1 *Changes in Existing Decommissioning, Restoration and Similar Liabilities* requires specified changes in decommissioning, restoration and similar liabilities to be added to, or deducted from, the cost of the assets to which they relate, and the adjusted depreciable amount to be depreciated prospectively over the remaining useful life of those assets. Retrospective application of this requirement at the date of transition would require an entity to construct a historical record of all such adjustments that would have been made in the past. In many cases this will not be practicable. The Board agreed that, as an alternative to complying with this requirement, an entity should be permitted to include in the depreciated cost of the asset, at the date of transition to IFRSs, an amount calculated by discounting the liability at that date back to, and depreciating it from, when the liability was first incurred.

BC63CA   Paragraph D21 of the IFRS exempts from the requirements of IFRIC 1 *Changes in Existing Decommissioning, Restoration and Similar Liabilities* changes in decommissioning costs incurred before the date of transition to IFRSs. Use of this exemption would require detailed calculations that would not be practicable for entities that used the method of accounting described in paragraph BC47A under their previous GAAP. The Board noted that adjustments to liabilities as a result of initial adoption of IFRSs arise from events and transactions before the date of transition to IFRSs and are generally recognised in retained earnings. Therefore, the Board decided that, for entities that used the method of accounting described in paragraph BC47A, any adjustment for a difference between decommissioning, restoration and similar liabilities measured in accordance with IAS 37 and the liability determined under the entity's previous GAAP should be accounted for in the same manner.

Leases

BC63D IFRIC 4 *Determining whether an Arrangement contains a Lease* contains transitional provisions because the IFRIC acknowledged the practical difficulties raised by full retrospective application of the Interpretation, in particular the difficulty of going back potentially many years and making a meaningful assessment of whether the arrangement satisfied the criteria at that time. The Board decided to treat first-time adopters in the same way as entities that already apply IFRSs.

BC63DA IFRIC 4 permits an entity to apply its requirements to arrangements existing at the start of the earliest period for which comparative information is presented on the basis of facts and circumstances existing at the start of that period. Before adopting IFRSs, a jurisdiction might adopt a national standard having the same effect as the requirements of IFRIC 4, including the same transitional provisions. An entity in that jurisdiction might then apply requirements having the same effect as the requirements of IFRIC 4 to some or all arrangements (even if the wording of those requirements is not identical). However, the entity might apply the requirements at a date different from the date in the transitional provisions of IFRIC 4. IFRS 1 would require such an entity to reassess that accounting retrospectively on first-time adoption. This might result in additional costs, with no obvious benefits. Accordingly, the Board decided that if a first-time adopter made the same determination under previous GAAP as that required by IFRIC 4 but at a date other than that required by IFRIC 4, the first-time adopter need not reassess that determination when it adopts IFRSs.

BC63DB The Board considered a more general modification to IFRS 1. It considered whether to modify IFRS 1 so that entities need not reassess, at the date of transition to IFRSs, prior accounting if that prior accounting permitted the same prospective application as IFRSs with the only difference from IFRSs being the effective date from when that accounting was applied. In this regard, the Board noted that any such proposal must apply to assessments resulting in the *same* determination, rather than *similar* determinations, because it would be too difficult to determine and enforce what constitutes a sufficient degree of similarity. The Board noted that many of the circumstances in which this situation might arise have been dealt with in IFRS 1 or other IFRSs. Accordingly, the Board decided to focus on IFRIC 4 only.

Borrowing costs

BC63E IAS 23 *Borrowing Costs* (as revised in 2007) contains transitional provisions because the Board acknowledged that if an entity has been following the accounting policy of immediately recognising borrowing costs as an expense and has not previously gathered the necessary information for capitalisation of borrowing costs, getting the information retrospectively may be costly. First-time adopters of IFRSs face problems similar to those facing entities that already apply IFRSs. Moreover, although first-time adopters have the option of using fair value as the deemed cost of an asset at the date of transition to IFRSs, this option is not applicable to all qualifying assets, such as inventories. Furthermore, the Board concluded that the existence of the deemed cost option is not sufficient to justify a more stringent requirement for the application of IAS 23 for first-time adopters than for entities that already apply IFRSs. A more stringent requirement for the adoption of the capitalisation treatment could be justified when IFRS 1 was originally issued because capitalisation was then an option. The requirements for the application of mandatory capitalisation, on the other hand, should be the same for entities that already apply IFRSs and for first-time adopters. Therefore, the Board decided to amend IFRS 1, allowing first-time adopters transitional provisions equivalent to those available to entities that already apply IFRSs in paragraphs 27 and 28 of IAS 23, as revised in 2007.

Other possible exemptions rejected

BC64   The Board considered and rejected suggestions for other exemptions. Each such exemption would have moved the IFRS away from a principle-based approach, diminished transparency for users, decreased comparability over time within an entity's first IFRS financial statements and created additional complexity. In the Board's view, any cost savings generated would not have outweighed these disadvantages. Paragraphs BC65–BC73 discuss some of the specific suggestions the Board considered for embedded derivatives, hyperinflation, intangible assets and transaction costs on financial instruments.

Embedded derivatives

BC65   IAS 39[*] requires an entity to account separately for some embedded derivatives at fair value. Some respondents to ED 1 argued that retrospective application of this requirement would be costly. Some suggested either an exemption from retrospective application of this requirement, or a requirement or option to use the fair value of the host instrument at the date of transition to IFRSs as its deemed cost at that date.

BC66   The Board noted that US GAAP provides an option in this area. Under the transitional provisions of SFAS 133 *Accounting for Derivative Instruments and Hedging Activities*, an entity need not account separately for some pre-existing embedded derivatives. Nevertheless, the Board concluded that the failure to measure embedded derivatives at fair value would diminish the relevance and reliability of an entity's first IFRS financial statements. The Board also observed that IAS 39[*] addresses an inability to measure an embedded derivative and the host contract separately. In such cases, IAS 39 requires an entity to measure the entire combined contract at fair value.

Hyperinflation

BC67   Some argued that the cost of restating financial statements for the effects of hyperinflation in periods before the date of transition to IFRSs would exceed the benefits, particularly if the currency is no longer hyperinflationary. However, the Board concluded that such restatement should be required, because hyperinflation can make unadjusted financial statements meaningless or misleading.

---

[*]   IFRS 9 *Financial Instruments*, issued in November 2009, amended the requirements in IAS 39 to identify and separately account for derivatives embedded in a financial host within the scope of IFRS 9. The requirements in IAS 39 continue to apply for derivatives embedded in non-financial hosts and financial hosts outside the scope of IFRS 9. This Basis for Conclusions has not been updated for changes in requirements since IFRIC 9 *Reassessment of Embedded Derivatives* was issued in March 2006.

Intangible assets

BC68 For the following reasons, some proposed that a first-time adopter's opening IFRS balance sheet should exclude intangible assets that it did not recognise in accordance with previous GAAP:

(a) Using hindsight to assess retrospectively when the recognition criteria for intangible assets were met could be subjective, open up possibilities for manipulation and involve costs that might exceed the benefits to users.

(b) The benefits expected from intangible assets are often not related directly to the costs incurred. Therefore, capitalising the costs incurred is of limited benefit to users, particularly if the costs were incurred in the distant past.

(c) Such an exclusion would be consistent with the transitional provisions in IAS 38 *Intangible Assets*. These encourage (but do not require) the recognition of intangible assets acquired in a previous business combination that was an acquisition and prohibit the recognition of all other previously unrecognised intangible assets.

BC69 In many cases, internally generated intangible assets do not qualify for recognition in accordance with IAS 38 at the date of transition to IFRSs because an entity did not, in accordance with previous GAAP, accumulate cost information or did not carry out contemporaneous assessments of future economic benefits. In these cases, there is no need for a specific requirement to exclude those assets. Furthermore, when these assets do not qualify for recognition, first-time adopters will not generally, in the Board's view, need to perform extensive work to reach this conclusion.

BC70 In other cases, an entity may have accumulated and retained sufficient information about costs and future economic benefits to determine which intangible assets (whether internally generated or acquired in a business combination or separately) qualify in accordance with IAS 38 for recognition in its opening IFRS balance sheet. If that information is available, no exclusion is justified.

BC71 Some argued that fair value should be used as deemed cost for intangible assets in the opening IFRS balance sheet (by analogy with a business combination). ED 1 would not have permitted this. However, in finalising the IFRS, the Board concluded that this approach should be available for those intangible assets for which IFRSs already permit fair value measurements. Therefore, in accordance with the IFRS, a first-time adopter may elect to use fair value or some previous GAAP revaluations of intangible assets as deemed cost for IFRSs, but only if the intangible assets meet:

(a) the recognition criteria in IAS 38 (including reliable measurement of original cost); and

(b) the criteria in IAS 38 for revaluation (including the existence of an active market) (paragraph D7 of the IFRS).

Transaction costs: financial instruments

BC72   To determine the amortised cost of a financial asset or financial liability using the effective interest method, it is necessary to determine the transaction costs incurred when the asset or liability was originated. Some respondents to ED 1 argued that determining these transaction costs could involve undue cost or effort for financial assets or financial liabilities originated long before the date of transition to IFRSs. They suggested that the Board should permit a first-time adopter:

(a)   to use the fair value of the financial asset or financial liability at the date of transition to IFRSs as its deemed cost at that date; or

(b)   to determine amortised cost without considering transaction costs.

BC73   In the Board's view, the unamortised portion of transaction costs at the date of transition to IFRSs is unlikely to be material for most financial assets and financial liabilities. Even when the unamortised portion is material, reasonable estimates should be possible. Therefore, the Board created no exemption in this area.

Retrospective designation

BC74   The Board considered practical implementation difficulties that could arise from the retrospective application of aspects of IAS 39:*

(a)   hedge accounting (paragraphs BC75–BC80);

(b)   the treatment of cumulative fair value changes on available-for-sale financial assets at the date of transition to IFRSs (paragraphs BC81–BC83); and

(c)   'day 1' gain or loss recognition (paragraph BC83A).

Hedge accounting

BC75   Before beginning their preparations for adopting IAS 39 (or a local standard based on IAS 39), it is unlikely that most entities would have adopted IAS 39's criteria for (a) documenting hedges at their inception and (b) testing the hedges for effectiveness, even if they intended to continue the same hedging strategies after adopting IAS 39. Furthermore, retrospective designation of hedges (or retrospective reversal of their designation) could lead to selective designation of some hedges to report a particular result.

BC76   To overcome these problems, the transitional requirements in IAS 39 require an entity already applying IFRSs to apply the hedging requirements prospectively when it adopts IAS 39. As the same problems arise for a first-time adopter, the IFRS requires prospective application by a first-time adopter.

---

*   In November 2009 the IASB amended the requirements of IAS 39 relating to classification and measurement of assets within the scope of IAS 39 and relocated them to IFRS 9 *Financial Instruments*. IFRS 9 applies to all assets within the scope of IAS 39. Paragraphs BC74(b) and (c) and BC81–BC83A discuss matters relevant when IFRS 1 was issued.

BC77   ED 1 included a redrafted version of the transitional provisions in IAS 39 and related *Questions and Answers* (Q&As) developed by the IAS 39 Implementation Guidance Committee. The Board confirmed in the Basis for Conclusions published with ED 1 that it did not intend the redrafting to create substantive changes. However, in the light of responses to ED 1, the Board decided in finalising IFRS 1 that the redrafting would not make it easier for first-time adopters and others to understand and apply the transitional provisions and Q&As. However, the project to improve IAS 32 and IAS 39 resulted in certain amendments to the transition requirements. In addition, this project incorporated selected other Q&As (ie not on transition) into IAS 39. The Board therefore took this opportunity to consolidate all the guidance for first-time adopters in one place, by incorporating the Q&As on transition into IFRS 1.

BC78   Some respondents to ED 1 asked the Board to clarify what would happen if hedge accounting in accordance with previous GAAP involved hedging relationships of a type that does not qualify for hedge accounting in accordance with IAS 39. The problem can be seen most clearly for a hedge of a net position (macro hedge). If a first-time adopter were to use hedge accounting in its opening IFRS balance sheet for a hedge of a net position, this would involve either:

   (a)   recognising deferred debits and credits that are not assets and liabilities (for a fair value hedge); or

   (b)   deferring gains or losses in equity when there is, at best, a weak link to an underlying item that defines when they should be transferred to the income statement (for a cash flow hedge).

BC79   As either of these treatments would diminish the relevance and reliability of an entity's first IFRS financial statements, the Board decided that an entity should not apply hedge accounting in its opening IFRS balance sheet to a hedge of a net position that does not qualify as a hedged item in accordance with IAS 39. However, the Board concluded that it would be reasonable (and consistent with IAS 39 paragraph 133[*]) to permit a first-time adopter to designate an individual item as a hedged item within the net position, provided that it does so no later than the date of transition to IFRSs, to prevent selective designation. For similar reasons, the Board prohibited hedge accounting in the opening IFRS balance sheet for any hedging relationship of a type that does not qualify for hedge accounting in accordance with IAS 39 (see paragraph B5 of the IFRS).

BC80   Some respondents to ED 1 suggested that an entity adopting IFRSs for the first time in 2005 could not meet IAS 39's documentation and effectiveness criteria by the date of transition to IFRSs (1 January 2004 for many entities). Some requested an exemption from these criteria until the beginning of the latest period covered by the first IFRS financial statements (1 January 2005 for many entities). However, for the following reasons, the Board did not create an exemption in this area:

   (a)   The Board's primary objective is comparability within a first-time adopter's first IFRS financial statements and between different first-time adopters switching to IFRSs at the same time (paragraph BC10).

---

[*]   In IAS 39, as revised in 2003, paragraph 133 was replaced by paragraphs 84 and AG101.

(b)   The continuation of previous GAAP hedge accounting practices could permit the non-recognition of derivatives or the recognition of deferred debits and credits that are not assets and liabilities.

(c)   The Board's benchmark for cost-benefit assessments was an entity that has planned the transition to IFRSs and is able to collect the necessary information at, or very soon after, the date of transition to IFRSs (paragraph BC27). Entities should not be 'rewarded' by concessions if they failed to plan for transition, nor should that failure be allowed to undermine the integrity of their opening IFRS balance sheet. Entities switching to IFRSs in 2005 need to have their hedge accounting systems in place by the beginning of 2004. In the Board's view, that is a challenging but achievable timetable. Entities preparing to switch to IFRSs in 2004 should have been aware of the implications of IAS 39 already and the exposure draft of improvements to IAS 39, published in June 2002, proposed very few changes in this area, so delayed transition is not justified for these entities either.

Available-for-sale financial assets[*]

BC81   Retrospective application of IAS 39 to available-for-sale financial assets requires a first-time adopter to recognise the cumulative fair value changes in a separate component of equity in the opening IFRS balance sheet, and transfer those fair value changes to the income statement on subsequent disposal or impairment of the asset. This could allow, for example, selective classification of assets with cumulative gains as available for sale (with subsequent transfers to the income statement on disposal) and assets with cumulative losses as held for trading (with no transfers on disposal).

BC82   IAS 39 confirmed the proposal in the exposure draft of June 2002 to give an entity that already applies IFRSs an option to designate any financial asset as at fair value through profit or loss when it first applies the proposed improvements. Although this requirement could increase the risk of selective classification by first-time adopters of the kind discussed in the previous paragraph, the Board noted that an entity could achieve a similar result by selective disposal of some assets before the date of transition to IFRSs. Therefore, the Board concluded that it should treat first-time adopters in the same way as entities that already apply IFRSs by requiring retrospective application.

BC83   Some respondents to ED 1 commented that the cost of determining the amount to be included in a separate component of equity would exceed the benefits. However, the Board noted that these costs would be minimal if a first-time adopter carried the available-for-sale financial assets in accordance with previous GAAP at cost or the lower of cost and market value. These costs might be more significant if it carried them at fair value, but in that case it might well classify the assets as held for trading. Therefore, the Board made no changes to ED 1's proposal that a first-time adopter should apply IAS 39 retrospectively to available-for-sale financial assets.

---

[*]   IFRS 9 *Financial Instruments*, issued in November 2009, eliminated the category of available-for-sale financial assets. Paragraphs BC81–BC83A discuss matters relevant when IFRS 1 was issued.

BC83A IFRS 1 originally required retrospective application of the 'day 1' gain or loss recognition requirements in IAS 39 paragraph AG76. After the revised IAS 39 was issued, constituents raised concerns that retrospective application would diverge from the requirements of US GAAP, would be difficult and expensive to implement, and might require subjective assumptions about what was observable and what was not. In response to these concerns, the Board decided to permit entities to apply the requirements in the last sentence of IAS 39 paragraph AG76 and in paragraph AG76A, in any one of the following ways:

(a) retrospectively;

(b) prospectively to transactions entered into after 25 October 2002; or

(c) prospectively to transactions entered into after 1 January 2004.

Estimates

BC84 An entity will have made estimates in accordance with previous GAAP at the date of transition to IFRSs. Events between that date and the reporting date for the entity's first IFRS financial statements might suggest a need to change those estimates. Some of those events might qualify as adjusting events in accordance with IAS 10 *Events after the Balance Sheet Date.*[*] However, if the entity made those estimates on a basis consistent with IFRSs, the Board concluded that it would be more helpful to users—and more consistent with IAS 8—to recognise the revision of those estimates as income or expense in the period when the entity made the revision, rather than in preparing the opening IFRS balance sheet (paragraphs 14–17 of the IFRS).

Presentation and disclosure

Comparative information

BC85 IAS 1 requires an entity to disclose comparative information (in accordance with IFRSs) for the previous period. Some suggested that a first-time adopter should disclose comparative information for more than one previous period. For entities that already apply IFRSs, users normally have access to financial statements prepared on a comparable basis for several years. However, this is not the case for a first-time adopter.

BC86 Nevertheless, the Board did not require a first-time adopter to present more comparative information than IAS 1 requires, because such a requirement would impose costs out of proportion to the benefits to users, and increase the risk that preparers might need to make arbitrary assumptions in applying hindsight.

---

[*] In September 2007 the IASB amended the title of IAS 10 *Events after the Balance Sheet Date* to *Events after the Reporting Period* as a consequence of the revision of IAS 1 *Presentation of Financial Statements* in 2007.

BC87　ED 1 proposed that if the first IFRS financial statements include more than one year of comparative information, the additional comparative information should comply with IFRSs. Some respondents to ED 1 noted that some regulators require entities to prepare more than two years of comparatives. They argued the following:

(a)　A requirement to restate two years of comparatives would impose excessive costs and lead to arbitrary restatements that might be biased by hindsight.

(b)　Consider an entity adopting IFRSs in 2005 and required by its regulator to give two years of comparatives. Its date of transition to IFRSs would be 1 January 2003—several months before the publication of the IFRS and of the standards resulting from the improvements project. This could contradict the Board's assertion in paragraph BC27 above that most preparers could gather most information they need for their opening IFRS balance sheet at, or soon after, the date of transition to IFRSs.

BC88　In response to these comments, the Board deleted this proposal. Instead, if a first-time adopter elects to give more than one year of comparative information, the additional comparative information need not comply with IFRSs, but the IFRS requires the entity:

(a)　to label previous GAAP information prominently as not being prepared in accordance with IFRSs.

(b)　to disclose the nature of the main adjustments that would make it comply with IFRSs (paragraph 22 of the IFRS).

BC89　Some respondents to ED 1 suggested that it would be onerous to prepare comparative information in accordance with IAS 32 and IAS 39[*] about financial instruments. They suggested that an entity should be able to apply IAS 39 prospectively from the beginning of the year of its first IFRS financial statements (eg 1 January 2005 for many first-time adopters). They noted that US companies were not required to restate comparatives on the introduction of SFAS 133 *Accounting for Derivative Instruments and Hedging Activities*. However, given the Board's emphasis on comparability within the first IFRS financial statements (paragraph BC10) and the assumption of timely planning (paragraph BC27), the Board introduced no general exemption in this area.

BC89A　Nevertheless, the Board noted that the revised IAS 32 and IAS 39[*] were not issued until December 2003. Additionally, the Board's decision to re-expose its proposals for portfolio hedges of interest rate risk had the effect that some of the requirements will not be finalised until early 2004. The Board was sympathetic to concerns that entities that will be required to comply with IFRSs for the first time in 2005 could not make a timely transition to IFRSs because IAS 39 will not be issued in final form until after the start of 2004. Therefore, the Board decided to exempt entities adopting IFRSs for the first time before 1 January 2006 from producing comparative information that complies with IAS 32 and IAS 39, as revised in 2003, in their first IFRS financial statements.

---

[*]　In November 2009 the IASB amended the requirements of IAS 39 relating to classification and measurement of assets within the scope of IAS 39 and relocated them to IFRS 9 *Financial Instruments*. IFRS 9 applies to all assets within the scope of IAS 39. This paragraph refers to matters relevant when IFRS 1 was issued.

Historical summaries

BC90   Some entities choose, or are required, to present in their financial statements historical summaries of selected data covering periods before the first period for which they present full comparative information. Some argued that an entity should present this information in accordance with IFRSs, to ensure comparability over time. However, the Board concluded that such a requirement would cause costs out of proportion to the benefit to users. The IFRS requires disclosure of the nature of the main adjustments needed to make historical summaries included in financial statements or interim financial reports comply with IFRSs (paragraph 22 of the IFRS). Historical summaries published outside financial statements or interim financial reports are beyond the scope of the IFRS.

Explanation of transition to IFRSs

BC91   The IFRS requires disclosures about the effect of the transition from previous GAAP to IFRSs. The Board concluded that such disclosures are essential, in the first (annual) IFRS financial statements as well as in interim financial reports (if any), because they help users understand the effect and implications of the transition to IFRSs and how they need to change their analytical models to make the best use of information presented using IFRSs. The required disclosures relate to both:

(a)   the most recent information published in accordance with previous GAAP, so that users have the most up-to-date information; and

(b)   the date of transition to IFRSs. This is an important focus of attention for users, preparers and auditors because the opening IFRS balance sheet is the starting point for accounting in accordance with IFRSs.

BC92   Paragraph 24(a) and (b) of the IFRS requires reconciliations of equity and total comprehensive income. The Board concluded that users would also find it helpful to have information about the other adjustments that affect the opening IFRS balance sheet but do not appear in these reconciliations. Because a reconciliation could be voluminous, the IFRS requires disclosure of narrative information about these adjustments, as well as about adjustments to the cash flow statement (paragraph 25 of the IFRS).

BC92A   The Board decided to require a first-time adopter to include in its first IFRS financial statements a reconciliation of total comprehensive income (or, if an entity did not report such a total, profit or loss) in accordance with previous GAAP to total comprehensive income in accordance with IFRSs for the latest period reported in accordance with previous GAAP.

BC92B   The Board observed that the amendments to IAS 1 in 2007 regarding the presentation of income and expense might result in users having to change their analytical models to include both income and expense that are recognised in profit or loss and those recognised outside profit or loss. Accordingly, the Board concluded that it would be helpful to those users to provide information on the effect and implication of the transition to IFRSs on all items of income and expense, not only those recognised in profit or loss.

BC92C   The Board acknowledged that GAAP in other jurisdictions might not have a notion of total comprehensive income. Accordingly, it decided that an entity should reconcile to total comprehensive income in accordance with IFRSs from the previous GAAP equivalent of total comprehensive income. The previous GAAP equivalent might be profit or loss.

BC93   Paragraph 26 of the IFRS states that the reconciliations should distinguish changes in accounting policies from the correction of errors. Some respondents to ED 1 argued that complying with this requirement could be difficult or costly. However, the Board concluded that both components are important and their disclosure should be required because:

    (a)   information about changes in accounting policies helps explain the transition to IFRSs.

    (b)   information about errors helps users assess the reliability of financial information. Furthermore, a failure to disclose the effect of material errors would obscure the 'results of the stewardship of management, or the accountability of management for the resources entrusted to it' (*Framework*, paragraph 14).

BC94   For impairment losses (and reversals) recognised in preparing the opening IFRS balance sheet, paragraph 24(c) of the IFRS requires the disclosures that IAS 36 would require if those impairment losses (and reversals) were recognised during the period beginning with the date of transition to IFRSs. The rationale for this requirement is that there is inevitably subjectivity about impairment losses. This disclosure provides transparency about impairment losses recognised on transition to IFRSs. These losses might otherwise receive less attention than impairment losses recognised in earlier or later periods.

BC95   Paragraph 30 of the IFRS requires disclosures about the use of fair value as deemed cost. Although the adjustment arising from the use of this exemption appears in the reconciliations discussed above, this more specific disclosure highlights it. Furthermore, this exemption differs from the other exemptions that might apply for property, plant and equipment (previous GAAP revaluation or event-driven fair value measurement). The latter two exemptions do not lead to a restatement on transition to IFRSs because they apply only if the measurement was already used in previous GAAP financial statements.

Interim financial reports

BC96   IAS 34 *Interim Financial Reporting* states that the interim financial report is 'intended to provide an update on the latest complete set of annual financial statements' (paragraph 6). Thus, IAS 34 requires less disclosure in interim financial statements than IFRSs require in annual financial statements. However, an entity's interim financial report in accordance with IAS 34 is less helpful to users if the entity's latest annual financial statements were prepared using previous GAAP than if they were prepared in accordance with IFRSs. Therefore, the Board concluded that a first-time adopter's first interim financial report in accordance with IAS 34 should include sufficient information to enable users to understand how the transition to IFRSs affected previously reported annual, as well as interim, figures (paragraphs 32 and 33 of the IFRS).

Appendix
Amendments to Basis for Conclusions
on other IFRSs

This appendix contains amendments to the Basis for Conclusions on other IFRSs that are necessary to ensure consistency with IFRS 1 (as revised in 2008).

* * * * *

The amendments contained in this appendix when the revised IFRS 1 was issued in 2008 have been incorporated into the text of the Basis for Conclusions on IFRS 6 and IASs 27 and 39 as issued at 27 November 2008.

CONTENTS

© IASCF

LIST OF EXAMPLES

Guidance on implementing
IFRS 1 *First-time Adoption*
of International Financial Reporting Standards

This guidance accompanies, but is not part of, IFRS 1.

Introduction

IG1   This implementation guidance:

     (a)   explains how the requirements of the IFRS interact with the requirements of some other IFRSs (paragraphs IG2–IG62, IG64 and IG65). This explanation addresses those IFRSs that are most likely to involve questions that are specific to first-time adopters.

     (b)   includes an illustrative example to show how a first-time adopter might disclose how the transition to IFRSs affected its reported financial position, financial performance and cash flows, as required by paragraphs 24(a) and (b), 25 and 26 of the IFRS (paragraph IG63).

IAS 10 *Events after the Reporting Period*

IG2   Except as described in paragraph IG3, an entity applies IAS 10 in determining whether:

     (a)   its opening IFRS statement of financial position reflects an event that occurred after the date of transition to IFRSs; and

     (b)   comparative amounts in its first IFRS financial statements reflect an event that occurred after the end of that comparative period.

IG3   Paragraphs 14–17 of the IFRS require some modifications to the principles in IAS 10 when a first-time adopter determines whether changes in estimates are adjusting or non-adjusting events at the date of transition to IFRSs (or, when applicable, the end of the comparative period). Cases 1 and 2 below illustrate those modifications. In case 3 below, paragraphs 14–17 of the IFRS do not require modifications to the principles in IAS 10.

     (a)   Case 1—Previous GAAP required estimates of similar items for the date of transition to IFRSs, using an accounting policy that is consistent with IFRSs. In this case, the estimates in accordance with IFRSs need to be consistent with estimates made for that date in accordance with previous GAAP, unless there is objective evidence that those estimates were in error (see IAS 8 *Accounting Policies, Changes in Accounting Estimates and Errors*). The entity reports later revisions to those estimates as events of the period in which it makes the revisions, rather than as adjusting events resulting from the receipt of further evidence about conditions that existed at the date of transition to IFRSs.

     (b)   Case 2—Previous GAAP required estimates of similar items for the date of transition to IFRSs, but the entity made those estimates using accounting policies that are not consistent with its accounting policies in accordance with IFRSs. In this case, the estimates in accordance with IFRSs need to be consistent with the estimates required in accordance with previous GAAP for that date (unless there is objective evidence that those estimates were in error), after adjusting for the difference in accounting policies. The opening IFRS statement of financial position reflects those adjustments for the difference in accounting policies. As in case 1, the entity reports later revisions to those estimates as events of the period in which it makes the revisions.

For example, previous GAAP may have required an entity to recognise and measure provisions on a basis consistent with IAS 37 *Provisions, Contingent Liabilities and Contingent Assets*, except that the previous GAAP measurement was on an undiscounted basis. In this example, the entity uses the estimates in accordance with previous GAAP as inputs in making the discounted measurement required by IAS 37.

(c)   Case 3—Previous GAAP did not require estimates of similar items for the date of transition to IFRSs. Estimates in accordance with IFRSs for that date reflect conditions existing at that date. In particular, estimates of market prices, interest rates or foreign exchange rates at the date of transition to IFRSs reflect market conditions at that date. This is consistent with the distinction in IAS 10 between adjusting events after the reporting period and non-adjusting events after the reporting period.

IG Example 1   Estimates

Background

Entity A's first IFRS financial statements are for a period that ends on 31 December 20X5 and include comparative information for one year. In its previous GAAP financial statements for 31 December 20X3 and 20X4, entity A:

(a)   made estimates of accrued expenses and provisions at those dates;

(b)   accounted on a cash basis for a defined benefit pension plan; and

(c)   did not recognise a provision for a court case arising from events that occurred in September 20X4. When the court case was concluded on 30 June 20X5, entity A was required to pay CU1,000[*] and paid this on 10 July 20X5.

In preparing its first IFRS financial statements, entity A concludes that its estimates in accordance with previous GAAP of accrued expenses and provisions at 31 December 20X3 and 20X4 were made on a basis consistent with its accounting policies in accordance with IFRSs. Although some of the accruals and provisions turned out to be overestimates and others to be underestimates, entity A concludes that its estimates were reasonable and that, therefore, no error had occurred. As a result, accounting for those overestimates and underestimates involves the routine adjustment of estimates in accordance with IAS 8.

continued...

---

[*]   In this guidance monetary amounts are denominated in 'currency units (CU)'.

...continued

IG Example 1 Estimates

Application of requirements

In preparing its opening IFRS statement of financial position at 1 January 20X4 and in its comparative statement of financial position at 31 December 20X4, entity A:

(a) does not adjust the previous estimates for accrued expenses and provisions; and

(b) makes estimates (in the form of actuarial assumptions) necessary to account for the pension plan in accordance with IAS 19 *Employee Benefits*. Entity A's actuarial assumptions at 1 January 20X4 and 31 December 20X4 do not reflect conditions that arose after those dates. For example, entity A's:

    (i) discount rates at 1 January 20X4 and 31 December 20X4 for the pension plan and for provisions reflect market conditions at those dates; and

    (ii) actuarial assumptions at 1 January 20X4 and 31 December 20X4 about future employee turnover rates do not reflect conditions that arose after those dates—such as a significant increase in estimated employee turnover rates as a result of a curtailment of the pension plan in 20X5.

The treatment of the court case at 31 December 20X4 depends on the reason why entity A did not recognise a provision in accordance with previous GAAP at that date.

Assumption 1 – Previous GAAP was consistent with IAS 37 *Provisions, Contingent Liabilities and Contingent Assets*. Entity A concluded that the recognition criteria were not met. In this case, entity A's assumptions in accordance with IFRSs are consistent with its assumptions in accordance with previous GAAP. Therefore, entity A does not recognise a provision at 31 December 20X4.

Assumption 2 – Previous GAAP was not consistent with IAS 37. Therefore, entity A develops estimates in accordance with IAS 37. Under IAS 37, an entity determines whether an obligation exists at the end of the reporting period by taking account of all available evidence, including any additional evidence provided by events after the reporting period. Similarly, in accordance with IAS 10 *Events after the Reporting Period*, the resolution of a court case after the reporting period is an adjusting event after the reporting period if it confirms that the entity had a present obligation at that date. In this instance, the resolution of the court case confirms that entity A had a liability in September 20X4 (when the events occurred that gave rise to the court case). Therefore, entity A recognises a provision at 31 December 20X4. Entity A measures that provision by discounting the CU1,000 paid on 10 July 20X5 to its present value, using a discount rate that complies with IAS 37 and reflects market conditions at 31 December 20X4.

IG4 Paragraphs 14–17 of the IFRS do not override requirements in other IFRSs that base classifications or measurements on circumstances existing at a particular date. Examples include:

(a) the distinction between finance leases and operating leases (see IAS 17 *Leases*);

(b) the restrictions in IAS 38 *Intangible Assets* that prohibit capitalisation of expenditure on an internally generated intangible asset if the asset did not qualify for recognition when the expenditure was incurred; and

(c) the distinction between financial liabilities and equity instruments (see IAS 32 *Financial Instruments: Presentation*).

IAS 12 *Income Taxes*

IG5 An entity applies IAS 12 to temporary differences between the carrying amount of the assets and liabilities in its opening IFRS statement of financial position and their tax bases.

IG6 In accordance with IAS 12, the measurement of current and deferred tax reflects tax rates and tax laws that have been enacted or substantively enacted by the end of the reporting period. An entity accounts for the effect of changes in tax rates and tax laws when those changes are enacted or substantively enacted.

IAS 16 *Property, Plant and Equipment*

IG7 If an entity's depreciation methods and rates in accordance with previous GAAP are acceptable in accordance with IFRSs, it accounts for any change in estimated useful life or depreciation pattern prospectively from when it makes that change in estimate (paragraphs 14 and 15 of the IFRS and paragraph 61 of IAS 16). However, in some cases, an entity's depreciation methods and rates in accordance with previous GAAP may differ from those that would be acceptable in accordance with IFRSs (for example, if they were adopted solely for tax purposes and do not reflect a reasonable estimate of the asset's useful life). If those differences have a material effect on the financial statements, the entity adjusts accumulated depreciation in its opening IFRS statement of financial position retrospectively so that it complies with IFRSs.

IG8 An entity may elect to use one of the following amounts as the deemed cost of an item of property, plant and equipment:

(a) fair value at the date of transition to IFRSs (paragraph D5 of the IFRS), in which case the entity gives the disclosures required by paragraph 30 of the IFRS;

(b) a revaluation in accordance with previous GAAP that meets the criteria in paragraph D6 of the IFRS;

(c) fair value at the date of an event such as a privatisation or initial public offering (paragraph D8 of the IFRS); or

(d) an allocation of an amount determined under previous GAAP that meets the criteria in paragraph D8A of the IFRS.

IG9 Subsequent depreciation is based on that deemed cost and starts from the date for which the entity established the deemed cost.

IG10 If an entity chooses as its accounting policy the revaluation model in IAS 16 for some or all classes of property, plant and equipment, it presents the cumulative revaluation surplus as a separate component of equity. The revaluation surplus at the date of transition to IFRSs is based on a comparison of the carrying amount of the asset at that date with its cost or deemed cost. If the deemed cost is the fair value at the date of transition to IFRSs, the entity gives the disclosures required by paragraph 30 of the IFRS.

IG11 If revaluations in accordance with previous GAAP did not satisfy the criteria in paragraph D6 or D8 of the IFRS, an entity measures the revalued assets in its opening statement of financial position on one of the following bases:

(a) cost (or deemed cost) less any accumulated depreciation and any accumulated impairment losses under the cost model in IAS 16;

(b) deemed cost, being the fair value at the date of transition to IFRSs (paragraph D5 of the IFRS); or

(c) revalued amount, if the entity adopts the revaluation model in IAS 16 as its accounting policy in accordance with IFRSs for all items of property, plant and equipment in the same class.

IG12 IAS 16 requires each part of an item of property, plant and equipment with a cost that is significant in relation to the total cost of the item to be depreciated separately. However, IAS 16 does not prescribe the unit of measure for recognition of an asset, ie what constitutes an item of property, plant and equipment. Thus, judgement is required in applying the recognition criteria to an entity's specific circumstances (see IAS 16 paragraphs 9 and 43).

IG13 In some cases, the construction or commissioning of an asset results in an obligation for an entity to dismantle or remove the asset and restore the site on which the asset stands. An entity applies IAS 37 *Provisions, Contingent Liabilities and Contingent Assets* in recognising and measuring any resulting provision. The entity applies IAS 16 in determining the resulting amount included in the cost of the asset, before depreciation and impairment losses. Items such as depreciation and, when applicable, impairment losses cause differences between the carrying amount of the liability and the amount included in the carrying amount of the asset. An entity accounts for changes in such liabilities in accordance with IFRIC 1 *Changes in Existing Decommissioning, Restoration and Similar Liabilities*. However, paragraph D21 of IFRS 1 provides an exemption for changes that occurred before the date of transition to IFRSs, and prescribes an alternative treatment where the exemption is used. An example of the first-time adoption of IFRIC 1, which illustrates the use of this exemption, is given at paragraphs IG201–IG203.

IAS 17 *Leases*

IG14   At the date of transition to IFRSs, a lessee or lessor classifies leases as operating leases or finance leases on the basis of circumstances existing at the inception of the lease (IAS 17 paragraph 13). In some cases, the lessee and the lessor may agree to change the provisions of the lease, other than by renewing the lease, in a manner that would have resulted in a different classification in accordance with IAS 17 had the changed terms been in effect at the inception of the lease. If so, the revised agreement is considered as a new agreement over its term. However, changes in estimates (for example, changes in estimates of the economic life or of the residual value of the leased property) or changes in circumstances (for example, default by the lessee) do not give rise to a new classification of a lease.

IG15   When IAS 17 was revised in 1997, the net cash investment method for recognising finance income of lessors was eliminated. IAS 17 permits finance lessors to eliminate this method prospectively. However, the transitional provisions in IAS 17 do not apply to an entity's opening IFRS statement of financial position (paragraph 9 of the IFRS). Therefore, a finance lessor measures finance lease receivables in its opening IFRS statement of financial position as if the net cash investment method had never been permitted.

IG16   SIC-15 *Operating Leases—Incentives* applies to lease terms beginning on or after 1 January 1999. However, a first-time adopter applies SIC-15 to all leases, whether they started before or after that date.

IAS 18 *Revenue*

IG17   If an entity has received amounts that do not yet qualify for recognition as revenue in accordance with IAS 18 (for example, the proceeds of a sale that does not qualify for revenue recognition), the entity recognises the amounts received as a liability in its opening IFRS statement of financial position and measures that liability at the amount received.

IAS 19 *Employee Benefits*

IG18   At the date of transition to IFRSs, an entity applies IAS 19 in measuring net employee benefit assets or liabilities under defined benefit plans, but it may elect to recognise all cumulative actuarial gains or losses from the inception of the plan until the date of transition to IFRSs even if its accounting policy in accordance with IAS 19 will involve leaving some later actuarial gains and losses unrecognised (paragraph D10 of the IFRS). The transitional provisions in IAS 19 do not apply to an entity's opening IFRS statement of financial position (paragraph 9 of the IFRS).

IG19 An entity's actuarial assumptions at the date of transition to IFRSs are consistent with actuarial assumptions made for the same date in accordance with previous GAAP (after adjustments to reflect any difference in accounting policies), unless there is objective evidence that those assumptions were in error (paragraph 14 of the IFRS). The impact of any later revisions to those assumptions is an actuarial gain or loss of the period in which the entity makes the revisions.

IG20 An entity may need to make actuarial assumptions at the date of transition to IFRSs that were not necessary in accordance with its previous GAAP. Such actuarial assumptions do not reflect conditions that arose after the date of transition to IFRSs. In particular, discount rates and the fair value of plan assets at the date of transition to IFRSs reflect market conditions at that date. Similarly, the entity's actuarial assumptions at the date of transition to IFRSs about future employee turnover rates do not reflect a significant increase in estimated employee turnover rates as a result of a curtailment of the pension plan that occurred after the date of transition to IFRSs (paragraph 16 of the IFRS).

IG21 In many cases, an entity's first IFRS financial statements will reflect measurements of employee benefit obligations at three dates: the end of the first IFRS reporting period, the date of the comparative statement of financial position and the date of transition to IFRSs. IAS 19 encourages an entity to involve a qualified actuary in the measurement of all material post-employment benefit obligations. To minimise costs, an entity may request a qualified actuary to carry out a detailed actuarial valuation at one or two of these dates and roll the valuation(s) forward or back to the other date(s). Any such roll forward or roll back reflects any material transactions and other material events (including changes in market prices and interest rates) between those dates (IAS 19 paragraph 57).

IAS 21 *The Effects of Changes in Foreign Exchange Rates*

IG21A An entity may, in accordance with previous GAAP, have treated goodwill arising on the acquisition of a foreign operation and any fair value adjustments to the carrying amounts of assets and liabilities arising on the acquisition of that foreign operation as assets and liabilities of the entity rather than as assets and liabilities of the foreign operation. If so, the entity is permitted to apply prospectively the requirements of paragraph 47 of IAS 21 to all acquisitions occurring after the date of transition to IFRSs.

IFRS 3 *Business Combinations*

IG22   The following examples illustrate the effect of Appendix C of the IFRS, assuming that a first-time adopter uses the exemption.

IG Example 2   Business combination

Background

Entity B's first IFRS financial statements are for a period that ends on 31 December 20X5 and include comparative information for 20X4 only. On 1 July 20X1, entity B acquired 100 per cent of subsidiary C. In accordance with its previous GAAP, entity B:

(a)   classified the business combination as an acquisition by entity B.

(b)   measured the assets acquired and liabilities assumed at the following amounts in accordance with previous GAAP at 31 December 20X3 (date of transition to IFRSs):

    (i)   identifiable assets less liabilities for which IFRSs require cost-based measurement at a date after the business combination: CU200 (with a tax base of CU150 and an applicable tax rate of 30 per cent).

    (ii)   pension liability (for which the present value of the defined benefit obligation measured in accordance with IAS 19 *Employee Benefits* is CU130 and the fair value of plan assets is CU100): nil (because entity B used a pay-as-you-go cash method of accounting for pensions in accordance with its previous GAAP). The tax base of the pension liability is also nil.

    (iii)   goodwill: CU180.

(c)   did not, at the acquisition date, recognise deferred tax arising from temporary differences associated with the identifiable assets acquired and liabilities assumed.

continued...

...continued
IG Example 2   Business combination

Application of requirements

In its opening (consolidated) IFRS statement of financial position, entity B:

(a)   classifies the business combination as an acquisition by entity B even if the business combination would have qualified in accordance with IFRS 3 as a reverse acquisition by subsidiary C (paragraph C4(a) of the IFRS).

(b)   does not adjust the accumulated amortisation of goodwill. Entity B tests the goodwill for impairment in accordance with IAS 36 *Impairment of Assets* and recognises any resulting impairment loss, based on conditions that existed at the date of transition to IFRSs. If no impairment exists, the carrying amount of the goodwill remains at CU180 (paragraph C4(g) of the IFRS).

(c)   for those net identifiable assets acquired for which IFRSs require cost-based measurement at a date after the business combination, treats their carrying amount in accordance with previous GAAP immediately after the business combination as their deemed cost at that date (paragraph C4(e) of the IFRS).

(d)   does not restate the accumulated depreciation and amortisation of the net identifiable assets in (c), unless the depreciation methods and rates in accordance with previous GAAP result in amounts that differ materially from those required in accordance with IFRSs (for example, if they were adopted solely for tax purposes and do not reflect a reasonable estimate of the asset's useful life in accordance with IFRSs). If no such restatement is made, the carrying amount of those assets in the opening IFRS statement of financial position equals their carrying amount in accordance with previous GAAP at the date of transition to IFRSs (CU200) (paragraph IG7).

(e)   if there is any indication that identifiable assets are impaired, tests those assets for impairment, based on conditions that existed at the date of transition to IFRSs (see IAS 36).

(f)   recognises the pension liability, and measures it, at the present value of the defined benefit obligation (CU130) less the fair value of the plan assets (CU100), giving a carrying amount of CU30, with a corresponding debit of CU30 to retained earnings (paragraph C4(d) of the IFRS). However, if subsidiary C had already adopted IFRSs in an earlier period, entity B would measure the pension liability at the same amount as in subsidiary C's financial statements (paragraph D17 of the IFRS and IG Example 9).

continued...

...continued
IG Example 2   Business combination

(g)   recognises a net deferred tax liability of CU6 (CU20 at 30 per cent) arising
       from:

   (i)   the taxable temporary difference of CU50 (CU200 less CU150)
          associated with the identifiable assets acquired and non-pension
          liabilities assumed, less

   (ii)   the deductible temporary difference of CU30 (CU30 less nil)
          associated with the pension liability.

   The entity recognises the resulting increase in the deferred tax liability
   as a deduction from retained earnings (paragraph C4(k) of the IFRS). If a
   taxable temporary difference arises from the initial recognition of the
   goodwill, entity B does not recognise the resulting deferred tax liability
   (paragraph 15(a) of IAS 12 *Income Taxes*).

IG Example 3   Business combination—restructuring provision

Background

Entity D's first IFRS financial statements are for a period that ends on
31 December 20X5 and include comparative information for 20X4 only.
On 1 July 20X3, entity D acquired 100 per cent of subsidiary E. In accordance
with its previous GAAP, entity D recognised an (undiscounted) restructuring
provision of CU100 that would not have qualified as an identifiable liability in
accordance with IFRS 3. The recognition of this restructuring provision
increased goodwill by CU100. At 31 December 20X3 (date of transition to IFRSs),
entity D:

(a)   had paid restructuring costs of CU60; and

(b)   estimated that it would pay further costs of CU40 in 20X4, and that the
       effects of discounting were immaterial. At 31 December 20X3, those
       further costs did not qualify for recognition as a provision in accordance
       with IAS 37 *Provisions, Contingent Liabilities and Contingent Assets*.

Application of requirements

In its opening IFRS statement of financial position, entity D:

(a)   does not recognise a restructuring provision (paragraph C4(c) of the IFRS).

(b)   does not adjust the amount assigned to goodwill. However, entity D tests
       the goodwill for impairment in accordance with IAS 36 *Impairment of
       Assets*, and recognises any resulting impairment loss (paragraph C4(g) of
       the IFRS).

(c)   as a result of (a) and (b), reports retained earnings in its opening IFRS
       statement of financial position that are higher by CU40 (before income
       taxes, and before recognising any impairment loss) than in the statement
       of financial position at the same date in accordance with previous GAAP.

IG Example 4 Business combination—intangible assets

Background

Entity F's first IFRS financial statements are for a period that ends on 31 December 20X5 and include comparative information for 20X4 only. On 1 July 20X1 entity F acquired 75 per cent of subsidiary G. In accordance with its previous GAAP, entity F assigned an initial carrying amount of CU200 to intangible assets that would not have qualified for recognition in accordance with IAS 38 *Intangible Assets*. The tax base of the intangible assets was nil, giving rise to a deferred tax liability (at 30 per cent) of CU60.

On 31 December 20X3 (the date of transition to IFRSs) the carrying amount of the intangible assets in accordance with previous GAAP was CU160, and the carrying amount of the related deferred tax liability was CU48 (30 per cent of CU160).

Application of requirements

Because the intangible assets do not qualify for recognition as separate assets in accordance with IAS 38, entity F transfers them to goodwill, together with the related deferred tax liability (CU48) and non-controlling interests (paragraph C4(g)(i) of the IFRS). The related non-controlling interests amount to CU28 (25 per cent of [CU160 – CU48 = CU112]). Thus, the increase in goodwill is CU84—intangible assets (CU160) less deferred tax liability (CU48) less non-controlling interests (CU28).

Entity F tests the goodwill for impairment in accordance with IAS 36 *Impairment of Assets* and recognises any resulting impairment loss, based on conditions that existed at the date of transition to IFRSs (paragraph C4(g)(ii) of the IFRS).

IG Example 5 Business combination—goodwill deducted from equity and treatment of related intangible assets

Background

Entity H acquired a subsidiary before the date of transition to IFRSs. In accordance with its previous GAAP, entity H:

(a) recognised goodwill as an immediate deduction from equity;

(b) recognised an intangible asset of the subsidiary that does not qualify for recognition as an asset in accordance with IAS 38 *Intangible Assets*; and

(c) did not recognise an intangible asset of the subsidiary that would qualify in accordance with IAS 38 for recognition as an asset in the financial statements of the subsidiary. The subsidiary held the asset at the date of its acquisition by entity H.

continued...

...continued
IG Example 5 Business combination—goodwill deducted from equity and treatment of related intangible assets

Application of requirements

In its opening IFRS statement of financial position, entity H:

(a)   does not recognise the goodwill, as it did not recognise the goodwill as an asset in accordance with previous GAAP (paragraph C4(g)–(i) of the IFRS).

(b)   does not recognise the intangible asset that does not qualify for recognition as an asset in accordance with IAS 38. Because entity H deducted goodwill from equity in accordance with its previous GAAP, the elimination of this intangible asset reduces retained earnings (paragraph C4(c)(ii) of the IFRS).

(c)   recognises the intangible asset that qualifies in accordance with IAS 38 for recognition as an asset in the financial statements of the subsidiary, even though the amount assigned to it in accordance with previous GAAP in entity H's consolidated financial statements was nil (paragraph C4(f) of the IFRS). The recognition criteria in IAS 38 include the availability of a reliable measurement of cost (paragraphs IG45–IG48) and entity H measures the asset at cost less accumulated depreciation and less any impairment losses identified in accordance with IAS 36 *Impairment of Assets*. Because entity H deducted goodwill from equity in accordance with its previous GAAP, the recognition of this intangible asset increases retained earnings (paragraph C4(c)(ii) of the IFRS). However, if this intangible asset had been subsumed in goodwill recognised as an asset in accordance with previous GAAP, entity H would have decreased the carrying amount of that goodwill accordingly (and, if applicable, adjusted deferred tax and non-controlling interests) (paragraph C4(g)(i) of the IFRS).

IG Example 6   Business combination—subsidiary not consolidated in accordance with previous GAAP

Background

Parent J's date of transition to IFRSs is 1 January 20X4. In accordance with its previous GAAP, parent J did not consolidate its 75 per cent subsidiary K, acquired in a business combination on 15 July 20X1. On 1 January 20X4:

(a)   the cost of parent J's investment in subsidiary K is CU180.

(b)   in accordance with IFRSs, subsidiary K would measure its assets at CU500 and its liabilities (including deferred tax in accordance with IAS 12 *Income Taxes*) at CU300. On this basis, subsidiary K's net assets are CU200 in accordance with IFRSs.

Application of requirements

Parent J consolidates subsidiary K. The consolidated statement of financial position at 1 January 20X4 includes:

(a)   subsidiary K's assets at CU500 and liabilities at CU300;

(b)   non-controlling interests of CU50 (25 per cent of [CU500 – CU300]); and

(c)   goodwill of CU30 (cost of CU180 less 75 per cent of [CU500 – CU300]) (paragraph C4(j) of the IFRS). Parent J tests the goodwill for impairment in accordance with IAS 36 *Impairment of Assets* and recognises any resulting impairment loss, based on conditions that existed at the date of transition to IFRSs (paragraph C4(g)(ii) of the IFRS).

IG Example 7   Business combination—finance lease not capitalised in accordance with previous GAAP

Background

Parent L's date of transition to IFRSs is 1 January 20X4. Parent L acquired subsidiary M on 15 January 20X1 and did not capitalise subsidiary M's finance leases. If subsidiary M prepared financial statements in accordance with IFRSs, it would recognise finance lease obligations of 300 and leased assets of 250 at 1 January 20X4.

Application of requirements

In its consolidated opening IFRS statement of financial position, parent L recognises finance lease obligations of CU300 and leased assets of CU250, and charges CU50 to retained earnings (paragraph C4(f)).

IAS 23 *Borrowing Costs*

IG23 On first adopting IFRSs, an entity begins capitalising borrowing costs (IAS 23 as revised in 2007). In accordance with paragraph D23 of the IFRS, an entity:

(a) capitalises borrowing costs relating to qualifying assets for which the commencement date for capitalisation is on or after 1 January 2009 or the date of transition to IFRSs (whichever is later);

(b) may elect to designate any date before 1 January 2009 or the date of transition to IFRSs (whichever is later) and to capitalise borrowing costs relating to all qualifying assets for which the commencement date for capitalisation is on or after that date.

However, if the entity established a deemed cost for an asset, the entity does not capitalise borrowing costs incurred before the date of the measurement that established the deemed cost.

IG24 IAS 23 requires disclosure of interest capitalised during the period. Neither IAS 23 nor the IFRS requires disclosure of the cumulative amount capitalised.

IG25 [Deleted]

IAS 27 *Consolidated and Separate Financial Statements*

IG26 A first-time adopter consolidates all subsidiaries (as defined in IAS 27), unless IAS 27 requires otherwise.

IG27 If a first-time adopter did not consolidate a subsidiary in accordance with previous GAAP, then:

(a) in its consolidated financial statements, the first-time adopter measures the subsidiary's assets and liabilities at the same carrying amounts as in the IFRS financial statements of the subsidiary, after adjusting for consolidation procedures and for the effects of the business combination in which it acquired the subsidiary (paragraph D17 of the IFRS). If the subsidiary has not adopted IFRSs in its financial statements, the carrying amounts described in the previous sentence are those that IFRSs would require in those financial statements (paragraph C4(j) of the IFRS).

(b) if the parent acquired the subsidiary in a business combination before the date of transition to IFRS, the parent recognises goodwill, as explained in IG Example 6.

(c) if the parent did not acquire the subsidiary in a business combination because it created the subsidiary, the parent does not recognise goodwill.

IG28 When a first-time adopter adjusts the carrying amounts of assets and liabilities of its subsidiaries in preparing its opening IFRS statement of financial position, this may affect non-controlling interests and deferred tax.

IG29   IG Examples 8 and 9 illustrate paragraphs D16 and D17 of the IFRS, which address cases where a parent and its subsidiary become first-time adopters at different dates.

IG Example 8   Parent adopts IFRSs before subsidiary

Background

Parent N presents its (consolidated) first IFRS financial statements in 20X5. Its foreign subsidiary O, wholly owned by parent N since formation, prepares information in accordance with IFRSs for internal consolidation purposes from that date, but subsidiary O does not present its first IFRS financial statements until 20X7.

Application of requirements

If subsidiary O applies paragraph D16(a) of the IFRS, the carrying amounts of its assets and liabilities are the same in both its opening IFRS statement of financial position at 1 January 20X6 and parent N's consolidated statement of financial position (except for adjustments for consolidation procedures) and are based on parent N's date of transition to IFRSs.

Alternatively, subsidiary O may, in accordance with paragraph D16(b) of the IFRS, measure all its assets or liabilities based on its own date of transition to IFRSs (1 January 20X6). However, the fact that subsidiary O becomes a first-time adopter in 20X7 does not change the carrying amounts of its assets and liabilities in parent N's consolidated financial statements.

IG Example 9   Subsidiary adopts IFRSs before parent

Background

Parent P presents its (consolidated) first IFRS financial statements in 20X7. Its foreign subsidiary Q, wholly owned by parent P since formation, presented its first IFRS financial statements in 20X5. Until 20X7, subsidiary Q prepared information for internal consolidation purposes in accordance with parent P's previous GAAP.

Application of requirements

The carrying amounts of subsidiary Q's assets and liabilities at 1 January 20X6 are the same in both parent P's (consolidated) opening IFRS statement of financial position and subsidiary Q's financial statements (except for adjustments for consolidation procedures) and are based on subsidiary Q's date of transition to IFRSs. The fact that parent P becomes a first-time adopter in 20X7 does not change those carrying amounts (paragraph D17 of the IFRS).

IG30   Paragraphs D16 and D17 of the IFRS do not override the following requirements:

(a)   to apply Appendix C of the IFRS to assets acquired, and liabilities assumed, in a business combination that occurred before the acquirer's date of transition to IFRSs. However, the acquirer applies paragraph D17 to new assets acquired, and liabilities assumed, by the acquiree after that business combination and still held at the acquirer's date of transition to IFRSs.

(b)   to apply the rest of the IFRS in measuring all assets and liabilities for which paragraphs D16 and D17 are not relevant.

(c)   to give all disclosures required by the IFRS as of the first-time adopter's own date of transition to IFRSs.

IG31   Paragraph D16 of the IFRS applies if a subsidiary becomes a first-time adopter later than its parent, for example if the subsidiary previously prepared a reporting package in accordance with IFRSs for consolidation purposes but did not present a full set of financial statements in accordance with IFRSs. This may be relevant not only when a subsidiary's reporting package complies fully with the recognition and measurement requirements of IFRSs, but also when it is adjusted centrally for matters such as review of events after the reporting period and central allocation of pension costs. For the disclosure required by paragraph 26 of the IFRS, adjustments made centrally to an unpublished reporting package are not corrections of errors. However, paragraph D16 does not permit a subsidiary to ignore misstatements that are immaterial to the consolidated financial statements of its parent but material to its own financial statements.

IAS 29 *Financial Reporting in Hyperinflationary Economies*

IG32   An entity complies with IAS 21 *The Effects of Changes in Foreign Exchange Rates* in determining its functional currency and presentation currency. When the entity prepares its opening IFRS statement of financial position, it applies IAS 29 to any periods during which the economy of the functional currency or presentation currency was hyperinflationary.

IG33   An entity may elect to use the fair value of an item of property, plant and equipment at the date of transition to IFRSs as its deemed cost at that date (paragraph D5 of the IFRS), in which case it gives the disclosures required by paragraph 30 of the IFRS.

IG34   If an entity elects to use the exemptions in paragraphs D5–D8 of the IFRS, it applies IAS 29 to periods after the date for which the revalued amount or fair value was determined.

IAS 32 *Financial Instruments: Presentation*

IG35   In its opening IFRS statement of financial position, an entity applies the criteria in IAS 32 to classify financial instruments issued (or components of compound instruments issued) as either financial liabilities or equity instruments in accordance with the substance of the contractual arrangement when the instrument first satisfied the recognition criteria in IAS 32 (paragraphs 15 and 30), without considering events after that date (other than changes to the terms of the instruments).

IG36   For compound instruments outstanding at the date of transition to IFRSs, an entity determines the initial carrying amounts of the components on the basis of circumstances existing when the instrument was issued (IAS 32 paragraph 30). An entity determines those carrying amounts using the version of IAS 32 effective at the end of its first IFRS reporting period. If the liability component is no longer outstanding at the date of transition to IFRSs, a first-time adopter need not separate the initial equity component of the instrument from the cumulative interest accreted on the liability component (paragraph D18 of the IFRS).

IAS 34 *Interim Financial Reporting*

IG37   IAS 34 applies if an entity is required, or elects, to present an interim financial report in accordance with IFRSs. Accordingly, neither IAS 34 nor the IFRS requires an entity:

(a)   to present interim financial reports that comply with IAS 34; or

(b)   to prepare new versions of interim financial reports presented in accordance with previous GAAP. However, if an entity does prepare an interim financial report in accordance with IAS 34 for part of the period covered by its first IFRS financial statements, the entity restates the comparative information presented in that report so that it complies with IFRSs.

IG38   An entity applies the IFRS in each interim financial report that it presents in accordance with IAS 34 for part of the period covered by its first IFRS financial statements. In particular, paragraph 32 of the IFRS requires an entity to disclose various reconciliations (see IG Example 10).

IG Example 10   Interim financial reporting

Background

Entity R's first IFRS financial statements are for a period that ends on 31 December 20X5, and its first interim financial report in accordance with IAS 34 is for the quarter ended 31 March 20X5. Entity R prepared previous GAAP annual financial statements for the year ended 31 December 20X4, and prepared quarterly reports throughout 20X4 .

Application of requirements

In each quarterly interim financial report for 20X5, entity R includes reconciliations of:

(a)   its equity in accordance with previous GAAP at the end of the comparable quarter of 20X4 to its equity in accordance with IFRSs at that date; and

(b)   its total comprehensive income (or, if it did not report such a total, profit or loss) in accordance with previous GAAP for the comparable quarter of 20X4 (current and year to date) to its total comprehensive income in accordance with IFRSs.

continued...

> **...continued**
> **IG Example 10 Interim financial reporting**
>
> In addition to the reconciliations required by (a) and (b) and the disclosures required by IAS 34, entity R's interim financial report for the first quarter of 20X5 includes reconciliations of (or a cross-reference to another published document that includes these reconciliations):
>
> (a) its equity in accordance with previous GAAP at 1 January 20X4 and 31 December 20X4 to its equity in accordance with IFRSs at those dates; and
>
> (b) its total comprehensive income (or, if it did not report such a total, profit or loss) for 20X4 in accordance with previous GAAP to its total comprehensive income for 20X4 in accordance with IFRSs.
>
> Each of the above reconciliations gives sufficient detail to enable users to understand the material adjustments to the statement of financial position and statement of comprehensive income. Entity R also explains the material adjustments to the statement of cash flows.
>
> If entity R becomes aware of errors made in accordance with previous GAAP, the reconciliations distinguish the correction of those errors from changes in accounting policies.
>
> If entity R did not, in its most recent annual financial statements in accordance with previous GAAP, disclose information material to an understanding of the current interim period, its interim financial reports for 20X5 disclose that information or include a cross-reference to another published document that includes it (paragraph 33 of the IFRS).

IAS 36 *Impairment of Assets* and IAS 37 *Provisions, Contingent Liabilities and Contingent Assets*

IG39   An entity applies IAS 36 in:

  (a)   determining whether any impairment loss exists at the date of transition to IFRSs; and

  (b)   measuring any impairment loss that exists at that date, and reversing any impairment loss that no longer exists at that date. An entity's first IFRS financial statements include the disclosures that IAS 36 would have required if the entity had recognised those impairment losses or reversals in the period beginning with the date of transition to IFRSs (paragraph 24(c) of the IFRS).

IG40   The estimates used to determine whether an entity recognises an impairment loss or provision (and to measure any such impairment loss or provision) at the date of transition to IFRSs are consistent with estimates made for the same date in accordance with previous GAAP (after adjustments to reflect any difference in accounting policies), unless there is objective evidence that those estimates were in error (paragraphs 14 and 15 of the IFRS). The entity reports the impact of any later revisions to those estimates as an event of the period in which it makes the revisions.

IG41 In assessing whether it needs to recognise an impairment loss or provision (and in measuring any such impairment loss or provision) at the date of transition to IFRSs, an entity may need to make estimates for that date that were not necessary in accordance with its previous GAAP. Such estimates and assumptions do not reflect conditions that arose after the date of transition to IFRSs (paragraph 16 of the IFRS).

IG42 The transitional provisions in IAS 36 and IAS 37 do not apply to an entity's opening IFRS statement of financial position (paragraph 9 of the IFRS).

IG43 IAS 36 requires the reversal of impairment losses in some cases. If an entity's opening IFRS statement of financial position reflects impairment losses, the entity recognises any later reversal of those impairment losses in profit or loss (except when IAS 36 requires the entity to treat that reversal as a revaluation). This applies to both impairment losses recognised in accordance with previous GAAP and additional impairment losses recognised on transition to IFRSs.

IAS 38 *Intangible Assets*

IG44 An entity's opening IFRS statement of financial position:

(a) excludes all intangible assets and other intangible items that do not meet the criteria for recognition in accordance with IAS 38 at the date of transition to IFRSs; and

(b) includes all intangible assets that meet the recognition criteria in IAS 38 at that date, except for intangible assets acquired in a business combination that were not recognised in the acquirer's consolidated statement of financial position in accordance with previous GAAP and also would not qualify for recognition in accordance with IAS 38 in the separate statement of financial position of the acquiree (see paragraph C4(f) of the IFRS).

IG45 The criteria in IAS 38 require an entity to recognise an intangible asset if, and only if:

(a) it is probable that the future economic benefits that are attributable to the asset will flow to the entity; and

(b) the cost of the asset can be measured reliably.

IAS 38 supplements these two criteria with further, more specific, criteria for internally generated intangible assets.

IG46 In accordance with paragraphs 65 and 71 of IAS 38, an entity capitalises the costs of creating internally generated intangible assets prospectively from the date when the recognition criteria are met. IAS 38 does not permit an entity to use hindsight to conclude retrospectively that these recognition criteria are met.

Therefore, even if an entity concludes retrospectively that a future inflow of economic benefits from an internally generated intangible asset is probable and the entity is able to reconstruct the costs reliably, IAS 38 prohibits it from capitalising the costs incurred before the date when the entity both:

(a) concludes, based on an assessment made and documented at the date of that conclusion, that it is probable that future economic benefits from the asset will flow to the entity; and

(b) has a reliable system for accumulating the costs of internally generated intangible assets when, or shortly after, they are incurred.

IG47 If an internally generated intangible asset qualifies for recognition at the date of transition to IFRSs, an entity recognises the asset in its opening IFRS statement of financial position even if it had recognised the related expenditure as an expense in accordance with previous GAAP. If the asset does not qualify for recognition in accordance with IAS 38 until a later date, its cost is the sum of the expenditure incurred from that later date.

IG48 The criteria discussed in paragraph IG45 also apply to an intangible asset acquired separately. In many cases, contemporaneous documentation prepared to support the decision to acquire the asset will contain an assessment of the future economic benefits. Furthermore, as explained in paragraph 26 of IAS 38, the cost of a separately acquired intangible asset can usually be measured reliably.

IG49 For an intangible asset acquired in a business combination before the date of transition to IFRSs, its carrying amount in accordance with previous GAAP immediately after the business combination is its deemed cost in accordance with IFRSs at that date (paragraph C4(e) of the IFRS). If that carrying amount was zero, the acquirer does not recognise the intangible asset in its consolidated opening IFRS statement of financial position, unless it would qualify in accordance with IAS 38, applying the criteria discussed in paragraphs IG45–IG48, for recognition at the date of transition to IFRSs in the statement of financial position of the acquiree (paragraph C4(f) of the IFRS). If those recognition criteria are met, the acquirer measures the asset on the basis that IAS 38 would require in the statement of financial position of the acquiree. The resulting adjustment affects goodwill (paragraph C4(g)(i) of the IFRS).

IG50 A first-time adopter may elect to use the fair value of an intangible asset at the date of an event such as a privatisation or initial public offering as its deemed cost at the date of that event (paragraph D8 of the IFRS), provided that the intangible asset qualifies for recognition in accordance with IAS 38 (paragraph 10 of the IFRS). In addition, if, and only if, an intangible asset meets both the recognition criteria in IAS 38 (including reliable measurement of original cost) and the criteria in IAS 38 for revaluation (including the existence of an active market), a first-time adopter may elect to use one of the following amounts as its deemed cost (paragraph D7 of the IFRS):

(a) fair value at the date of transition to IFRSs (paragraph D5 of the IFRS), in which case the entity gives the disclosures required by paragraph 30 of the IFRS; or

(b) a revaluation in accordance with previous GAAP that meets the criteria in paragraph D6 of the IFRS.

IG51   If an entity's amortisation methods and rates in accordance with previous GAAP would be acceptable in accordance with IFRSs, the entity does not restate the accumulated amortisation in its opening IFRS statement of financial position. Instead, the entity accounts for any change in estimated useful life or amortisation pattern prospectively from the period when it makes that change in estimate (paragraph 14 of the IFRS and paragraph 104 of IAS 38). However, in some cases, an entity's amortisation methods and rates in accordance with previous GAAP may differ from those that would be acceptable in accordance with IFRSs (for example, if they were adopted solely for tax purposes and do not reflect a reasonable estimate of the asset's useful life). If those differences have a material effect on the financial statements, the entity adjusts the accumulated amortisation in its opening IFRS statement of financial position retrospectively so that it complies with IFRSs (paragraph 14 of the IFRS).

IAS 39 *Financial Instruments: Recognition and Measurement* and IFRS 9 *Financial Instruments*

IG52   An entity recognises and measures all financial assets and financial liabilities in its opening IFRS statement of financial position in accordance with IFRS 9 and IAS 39 respectively, except as specified in paragraphs B2–B6 of the IFRS, which address derecognition and hedge accounting.

Recognition

IG53   An entity recognises all financial assets and financial liabilities (including all derivatives) that qualify for recognition in accordance with IAS 39 and IFRS 9 and have not yet qualified for derecognition in accordance with IAS 39, except non-derivative financial assets and non-derivative financial liabilities derecognised in accordance with previous GAAP before 1 January 2004, to which the entity does not choose to apply paragraph B3 (see paragraphs B2 and B3 of the IFRS). For example, an entity that does not apply paragraph B3 does not recognise assets transferred in a securitisation, transfer or other derecognition transaction that occurred before 1 January 2004 if those transactions qualified for derecognition in accordance with previous GAAP. However, if the entity uses the same securitisation arrangement or other derecognition arrangement for further transfers after 1 January 2004, those further transfers qualify for derecognition only if they meet the derecognition criteria of IAS 39.

IG54   An entity does not recognise financial assets and financial liabilities that do not qualify for recognition in accordance with IAS 39 or IFRS 9, or have already qualified for derecognition in accordance with IAS 39.

Embedded derivatives

IG55   When IAS 39 requires an entity to separate an embedded derivative from a host contract outside the scope of IFRS 9, the initial carrying amounts of the components at the date when the instrument first satisfies the recognition criteria in IAS 39 reflect circumstances at that date (IAS 39 paragraph 11). If the entity cannot determine the initial carrying amounts of the embedded derivative and host contract reliably, it designates the entire combined contract as at fair value through profit or loss (IAS 39 paragraph 12).

Measurement

IG56   In preparing its opening IFRS statement of financial position, an entity applies the criteria in IAS 39 and IFRS 9 to identify on the basis of the facts and circumstances that exist at the date of transition to IFRSs those financial assets and financial liabilities that are measured at fair value and those that are measured at amortised cost. The resulting classifications are applied retrospectively.

IG57   For those financial assets and financial liabilities measured at amortised cost in the opening IFRS statement of financial position, an entity determines their cost on the basis of circumstances existing when the assets and liabilities first satisfied the recognition criteria in IAS 39 or IFRS 9. However, if the entity acquired those financial assets and financial liabilities in a past business combination, their carrying amount in accordance with previous GAAP immediately following the business combination is their deemed cost in accordance with IFRSs at that date (paragraph C4(e) of the IFRS).

IG58   An entity's estimates of impairments of financial assets measured at amortised cost at the date of transition to IFRSs are consistent with estimates made for the same date in accordance with previous GAAP (after adjustments to reflect any difference in accounting policies), unless there is objective evidence that those assumptions were in error (paragraph 14 of the IFRS). The entity treats the impact of any later revisions to those estimates as impairment losses (or, if the criteria in IAS 39 are met, reversals of impairment losses) of the period in which it makes the revisions.

Transition adjustments

IG58A   An entity shall treat an adjustment to the carrying amount of a financial asset or financial liability as a transition adjustment to be recognised in the opening balance of retained earnings at the date of transition to IFRSs only to the extent that it results from adopting IAS 39 and IFRS 9. Because all derivatives, other than those that are financial guarantee contracts or are designated and effective hedging instruments, are measured at fair value through profit or loss, the differences between the previous carrying amount (which may have been zero) and the fair value of the derivatives are recognised as an adjustment of the balance of retained earnings at the beginning of the financial year in which IAS 39 and IFRS 9 are is initially applied (other than for a derivative that is a financial guarantee contract or a designated and effective hedging instrument).

IG58B   IAS 8 (as revised in 2003) applies to adjustments resulting from changes in estimates. If an entity is unable to determine whether a particular portion of the adjustment is a transition adjustment or a change in estimate, it treats that portion as a change in accounting estimate in accordance with IAS 8, with appropriate disclosures (IAS 8 paragraphs 32–40).

IG59   An entity may, in accordance with its previous GAAP, have measured investments at fair value and recognised the revaluation gain outside profit or loss. If an investment is classified as at fair value through profit or loss, the pre-IFRS 9 revaluation gain that had been recognised outside profit or loss is reclassified into retained earnings on initial application of IFRS 9. If, on initial application of IFRS 9, an investment is classified as at fair value through other comprehensive income, then the pre-IFRS 9 revaluation gain is recognised in a separate component of equity. Subsequently, the entity recognises gains and losses on the financial asset in other comprehensive income (except dividends, which are recognised in profit or loss) and accumulates the cumulative gains and losses in that separate component of equity. On subsequent derecognition, the entity may transfer that separate component of equity within equity.

Hedge accounting

IG60   Paragraphs B4–B6 of the IFRS deal with hedge accounting. The designation and documentation of a hedge relationship must be completed on or before the date of transition to IFRSs if the hedge relationship is to qualify for hedge accounting from that date. Hedge accounting can be applied prospectively only from the date that the hedge relationship is fully designated and documented.

IG60A   An entity may, in accordance with its previous GAAP, have deferred or not recognised gains and losses on a fair value hedge of a hedged item that is not measured at fair value. For such a fair value hedge, an entity adjusts the carrying amount of the hedged item at the date of transition to IFRSs. The adjustment is the lower of:

(a)   that portion of the cumulative change in the fair value of the hedged item that reflects the designated hedged risk and was not recognised in accordance with previous GAAP; and

(b)   that portion of the cumulative change in the fair value of the hedging instrument that reflects the designated hedged risk and, in accordance with previous GAAP, was either (i) not recognised or (ii) deferred in the statement of financial position as an asset or liability.

IG60B   An entity may, in accordance with its previous GAAP, have deferred gains and losses on a cash flow hedge of a forecast transaction. If, at the date of transition to IFRSs, the hedged forecast transaction is not highly probable, but is expected to occur, the entire deferred gain or loss is recognised in equity. Any net cumulative gain or loss that has been reclassified to equity on initial application of IAS 39 remains in equity until (a) the forecast transaction subsequently results in the recognition of a non-financial asset or non-financial liability, (b) the forecast transaction affects profit or loss or (c) subsequently circumstances change and the forecast transaction is no longer expected to occur, in which case any related net cumulative gain or loss is reclassified from equity to profit or loss. If the hedging instrument is still held, but the hedge does not qualify as a cash flow hedge in accordance with IAS 39, hedge accounting is no longer appropriate starting from the date of transition to IFRSs.

IAS 40 *Investment Property*

IG61   An entity that adopts the fair value model in IAS 40 measures its investment property at fair value at the date of transition to IFRSs. The transitional requirements of IAS 40 do not apply (paragraph 9 of the IFRS).

IG62   An entity that adopts the cost model in IAS 40 applies paragraphs IG7–IG13 on property, plant and equipment.

Explanation of transition to IFRSs

IG63   Paragraphs 24(a) and (b), 25 and 26 of the IFRS require a first-time adopter to disclose reconciliations that give sufficient detail to enable users to understand the material adjustments to the statement of financial position, statement of comprehensive income and, if applicable, statement of cash flows. Paragraph 24(a) and (b) requires specific reconciliations of equity and total comprehensive income. IG Example 11 shows one way of satisfying these requirements.

IG Example 11   Reconciliation of equity and total comprehensive income

Background

An entity first adopted IFRSs in 20X5, with a date of transition to IFRSs of 1 January 20X4. Its last financial statements in accordance with previous GAAP were for the year ended 31 December 20X4.

Application of requirements

The entity's first IFRS financial statements include the reconciliations and related notes shown below.

Among other things, this example includes a reconciliation of equity at the date of transition to IFRSs (1 January 20X4). The IFRS also requires a reconciliation at the end of the last period presented in accordance with previous GAAP (not included in this example).

In practice, it may be helpful to include cross-references to accounting policies and supporting analyses that give further explanation of the adjustments shown in the reconciliations below.

If a first-time adopter becomes aware of errors made in accordance with previous GAAP, the reconciliations distinguish the correction of those errors from changes in accounting policies (paragraph 26 of the IFRS). This example does not illustrate disclosure of a correction of an error.

continued...

...continued

IG Example 11   Reconciliation of equity and total comprehensive income

Reconciliation of equity at 1 January 20X4 (date of transition to IFRSs)

Note		Previous GAAP CU	Effect of transition to IFRSs CU	IFRSs CU
1	Property, plant and equipment	8,299	100	8,399
2	Goodwill	1,220	150	1,370
2	Intangible assets	208	(150)	58
3	Financial assets	3,471	420	3,891
	Total non-current assets	13,198	520	13,718
	Trade and other receivables	3,710	0	3,710
4	Inventories	2,962	400	3,362
5	Other receivables	333	431	764
	Cash and cash equivalents	748	0	748
	Total current assets	7,753	831	8,584
	Total assets	20,951	1,351	22,302
	Interest-bearing loans	9,396	0	9,396
	Trade and other payables	4,124	0	4,124
6	Employee benefits	0	66	66
7	Restructuring provision	250	(250)	0
	Current tax liability	42	0	42
8	Deferred tax liability	579	460	1,039
	Total liabilities	14,391	276	14,667
	Total assets less total liabilities	6,560	1,075	7,635
	Issued capital	1,500	0	1,500
5	Hedging reserve	0	302	302
9	Retained earnings	5,060	773	5,833
	Total equity	6,560	1,075	7,635

continued...

...continued
IG Example 11 Reconciliation of equity and total comprehensive income

Notes to the reconciliation of equity at 1 January 20X4:

1   Depreciation was influenced by tax requirements in accordance with previous GAAP, but in accordance with IFRSs reflects the useful life of the assets. The cumulative adjustment increased the carrying amount of property, plant and equipment by 100.

2   Intangible assets in accordance with previous GAAP included CU150 for items that are transferred to goodwill because they do not qualify for recognition as intangible assets in accordance with IFRSs.

3   Financial assets are all classified as at fair value through profit or loss in accordance with IFRSs and are carried at their fair value of CU3,891. They were carried at cost of CU3,471 in accordance with previous GAAP. The resulting gains of CU294 (CU420, less related deferred tax of CU126) are included in retained earnings.

4   Inventories include fixed and variable production overhead of CU400 in accordance with IFRSs, but this overhead was excluded in accordance with previous GAAP.

5   Unrealised gains of CU431 on unmatured forward foreign exchange contracts are recognised in accordance with IFRSs, but were not recognised in accordance with previous GAAP. The resulting gains of CU302 (CU431, less related deferred tax of CU129) are included in the hedging reserve because the contracts hedge forecast sales.

6   A pension liability of CU66 is recognised in accordance with IFRSs, but was not recognised in accordance with previous GAAP, which used a cash basis.

7   A restructuring provision of CU250 relating to head office activities was recognised in accordance with previous GAAP, but does not qualify for recognition as a liability in accordance with IFRSs.

8   The above changes increased the deferred tax liability as follows:

	CU
Hedging reserve (note 5)	129
Retained earnings	331
Increase in deferred tax liability	460

Because the tax base at 1 January 20X4 of the items reclassified from intangible assets to goodwill (note 2) equalled their carrying amount at that date, the reclassification did not affect deferred tax liabilities.

continued...

...continued
IG Example 11 Reconciliation of equity and total comprehensive income

9   The adjustments to retained earnings are as follows:

	CU
Depreciation (note 1)	100
Financial assets (note 3)	420
Production overhead (note 4)	400
Pension liability (note 6)	(66)
Restructuring provision (note 7)	250
Tax effect of the above	(331)
Total adjustment to retained earnings	773

Reconciliation of total comprehensive income for 20X4

Note		Previous GAAP CU	Effect of transition to IFRSs CU	IFRSs CU
	Revenue	20,910	0	20,910
1,2,3	Cost of sales	(15,283)	(97)	(15,380)
	Gross profit	5,627	(97)	5,530
6	Other income	0	180	180
1	Distribution costs	(1,907)	(30)	(1,937)
1,4	Administrative expenses	(2,842)	(300)	(3,142)
	Finance income	1,446	0	1,446
	Finance costs	(1,902)	0	(1,902)
	Profit before tax	422	(247)	175
5	Tax expense	(158)	74	(84)
	Profit (loss) for the year	264	(173)	91
7	Cash flow hedges	0	(40)	(40)
8	Tax relating to other comprehensive income	0	(29)	(29)
	Other comprehensive income	0	(69)	(69)
	Total comprehensive income	264	(242)	22

continued...

...continued

IG Example 11   Reconciliation of equity and total comprehensive income

Notes to the reconciliation of total comprehensive income for 20X4:

1. A pension liability is recognised in accordance with IFRSs, but was not recognised in accordance with previous GAAP. The pension liability increased by CU130 during 20X4, which caused increases in cost of sales (CU50), distribution costs (CU30) and administrative expenses (CU50).

2. Cost of sales is higher by CU47 in accordance with IFRSs because inventories include fixed and variable production overhead in accordance with IFRSs but not in accordance with previous GAAP.

3. Depreciation was influenced by tax requirements in accordance with previous GAAP, but reflects the useful life of the assets in accordance with IFRSs. The effect on the profit for 20X4 was not material.

4. A restructuring provision of CU250 was recognised in accordance with previous GAAP at 1 January 20X4, but did not qualify for recognition in accordance with IFRSs until the year ended 31 December 20X4. This increases administrative expenses for 20X4 in accordance with IFRSs.

5. Adjustments 1–4 above lead to a reduction of CU128 in deferred tax expense.

6. Financial assets at fair value through profit or loss increased in value by CU180 during 20X4. They were carried at cost in accordance with previous GAAP. Fair value changes have been included in 'Other income'.

7. The fair value of forward foreign exchange contracts that are effective hedges of forecast transactions decreased by CU40 during 20X4.

8. Adjustments 6 and 7 above lead to an increase of CU29 in deferred tax expense.

Explanation of material adjustments to the statement of cash flows for 20X4:

Income taxes of CU133 paid during 20X4 are classified as operating cash flows in accordance with IFRSs, but were included in a separate category of tax cash flows in accordance with previous GAAP. There are no other material differences between the statement of cash flows presented in accordance with IFRSs and the statement of cash flows presented in accordance with previous GAAP.

IFRS 2 *Share-based Payment*

IG64   A first-time adopter is encouraged, but not required, to apply IFRS 2 *Share-based Payment* to equity instruments that were granted after 7 November 2002 that vested before the later of (a) the date of transition to IFRSs and (b) 1 January 2005.

IG65   For example, if an entity's date of transition to IFRSs is 1 January 2004, the entity applies IFRS 2 to shares, share options or other equity instruments that were granted after 7 November 2002 and had not yet vested at 1 January 2005. Conversely, if an entity's date of transition to IFRSs is 1 January 2010, the entity applies IFRS 2 to shares, share options or other equity instruments that were granted after 7 November 2002 and had not yet vested at 1 January 2010.

[Paragraphs IG66–IG200 reserved for possible guidance on future standards]

IFRIC Interpretations

IFRIC 1 *Changes in Existing Decommissioning, Restoration and Similar Liabilities*

IG201   IAS 16 requires the cost of an item of property, plant and equipment to include the initial estimate of the costs of dismantling and removing the asset and restoring the site on which it is located. IAS 37 requires the liability, both initially and subsequently, to be measured at the amount required to settle the present obligation at the end of the reporting period, reflecting a current market-based discount rate.

IG202   IFRIC 1 requires that, subject to specified conditions, changes in an existing decommissioning, restoration or similar liability are added to or deducted from the cost of the related asset. The resulting depreciable amount of the asset is depreciated over its useful life, and the periodic unwinding of the discount on the liability is recognised in profit or loss as it occurs.

IG203   Paragraph D21 of IFRS 1 provides a transitional exemption. Instead of retrospectively accounting for changes in this way, entities can include in the depreciated cost of the asset an amount calculated by discounting the liability at the date of transition to IFRSs back to, and depreciating it from, when the liability was first incurred. IG Example 201 illustrates the effect of applying this exemption, assuming that the entity accounts for its property, plant and equipment using the cost model.

IG Example 201   Changes in existing decommissioning, restoration and similar liabilities

Background

An entity's first IFRS financial statements are for a period that ends on 31 December 20X5 and include comparative information for 20X4 only. Its date of transition to IFRSs is therefore 1 January 20X4.

The entity acquired an energy plant on 1 January 20X1, with a life of 40 years.

As at the date of transition to IFRSs, the entity estimates the decommissioning cost in 37 years' time to be 470, and estimates that the appropriate risk-adjusted discount rate for the liability is 5 per cent. It judges that the appropriate discount rate has not changed since 1 January 20X1.

Application of requirements

The decommissioning liability recognised at the transition date is CU77 (CU470 discounted for 37 years at 5 per cent).

Discounting this liability back for a further three years to 1 January 20X1 gives an estimated liability at acquisition, to be included in the cost of the asset, of CU67. Accumulated depreciation on the asset is $CU67 \times 3/40 = CU5$.

The amounts recognised in the opening IFRS statement of financial position on the date of transition to IFRSs (1 January 20X4) are, in summary:

	CU
Decommissioning cost included in cost of plant	67
Accumulated depreciation	(5)
Decommissioning liability	(77)
Net assets/retained earnings	(15)

IFRIC 4 *Determining whether an Arrangement contains a Lease*

IG204   IFRIC 4 specifies criteria for determining, at the inception of an arrangement, whether the arrangement contains a lease. It also specifies when an arrangement should be reassessed subsequently.

IG205   Paragraph D9 of the IFRS provides a transitional exemption. Instead of determining retrospectively whether an arrangement contains a lease at the inception of the arrangement and subsequently reassessing that arrangement as required in the periods before transition to IFRSs, entities may determine whether arrangements in existence on the date of transition to IFRSs contain leases by applying paragraphs 6–9 of IFRIC 4 to those arrangements on the basis of facts and circumstances existing on that date.

IG Example 202   Determining whether an arrangement contains a lease
Background
An entity's first IFRS financial statements are for a period that ends on 31 December 20Y7 and include comparative information for 20Y6 only. Its date of transition to IFRSs is therefore 1 January 20Y6.
On 1 January 20X5 the entity entered into a take-or-pay arrangement to supply gas. On 1 January 20Y0, there was a change in the contractual terms of the arrangement.
Application of requirements
On 1 January 20Y6 the entity may determine whether the arrangement contains a lease by applying the criteria in paragraphs 6–9 of IFRIC 4 on the basis of facts and circumstances existing on that date. Alternatively, the entity applies those criteria on the basis of facts and circumstances existing on 1 January 20X5 and reassesses the arrangement on 1 January 20Y0. If the arrangement is determined to contain a lease, the entity follows the guidance in paragraphs IG14–IG16.

IG206   Paragraph D9A of IFRS 1 provides a transitional exemption in addition to that discussed in paragraph IG205. The exemption in paragraph D9A applies only to arrangements that were assessed in the same manner as required by IFRIC 4. If arrangements exist at the date of transition to IFRSs that an entity did not assess under previous GAAP in the same manner as required by IFRIC 4 to determine whether they contain a lease, the entity may apply the transition exemption discussed in paragraph IG205.

Table of Concordance

This table shows how the contents of the superseded version of IFRS 1 and the revised version of IFRS 1 correspond.

Superseded IFRS 1 paragraph	Revised IFRS 1 paragraph	Superseded IFRS 1 paragraph	Revised IFRS 1 paragraph	Superseded IFRS 1 paragraph	Revised IFRS 1 paragraph
1	1	25A	D19	38	23
2	2	25B	D2	39	24
3	3	25C	D3	40	25
4	4	25D	D4	41	26
5	5	25E	D21	42	27
6	6	25F	D9	43	28
7	7	25G	D20	43A	29
8	8	25H	D22	44	30
9	9	25I	D23	44A	31
10	10	26	B1	45	32
11	11	27	B2	46	33
12	12	27A	B3	47	34
13	D1	28	B4	47A	None
14	19	29	B5	47B	None
15	None	30	B6	47C	None
16	D5	31	14	47D	None
17	D6	32	15	47E	None
18	D7	33	16	47F	None
19	D8	34	17	47G	35
20	D10	34A	None	47H	None
20A	D11	34B	None	47I	36
21	D12	34C	B7	47J	37
22	D13	35	20	47K	38
23	D18	36	21	47L	39
23A	D14	36A	None	Appendix A	Appendix A
23B	D15	36B	None	Appendix B	Appendix C
24	D16	36C	None	None	13, 18, 40
25	D17	37	22		

IASB documents published to accompany

International Financial Reporting Standard 2

Share-based Payment

This version includes amendments resulting from IFRSs issued up to 31 December 2009.

The text of the unaccompanied IFRS 2 is contained in Part A of this edition. Its effective date, when issued, was 1 January 2005. The effective date of the most recent amendments is 1 January 2013. This part presents the following accompanying documents:

Approval by the Board of IFRS 2 issued in February 2004

International Financial Reporting Standard 2 *Share-based Payment* was approved for issue by the fourteen members of the International Accounting Standards Board.

Sir David Tweedie	Chairman
Thomas E Jones	Vice-Chairman
Mary E Barth	
Hans-Georg Bruns	
Anthony T Cope	
Robert P Garnett	
Gilbert Gélard	
James J Leisenring	
Warren J McGregor	
Patricia L O'Malley	
Harry K Schmid	
John T Smith	
Geoffrey Whittington	
Tatsumi Yamada	

Approval by the Board of *Vesting Conditions and Cancellations* (Amendments to IFRS 2) issued in January 2008

Vesting Conditions and Cancellations (Amendments to IFRS 2) was approved for issue by the thirteen members of the International Accounting Standards Board.

Sir David Tweedie	Chairman
Thomas E Jones	Vice-Chairman
Mary E Barth	
Stephen Cooper	
Philippe Danjou	
Jan Engström	
Robert P Garnett	
Gilbert Gélard	
James J Leisenring	
Warren J McGregor	
John T Smith	
Tatsumi Yamada	
Wei-Guo Zhang	

Approval by the Board of *Group Cash-settled Share-based Payment Transactions* (Amendments to IFRS 2) issued in June 2009

Group Cash-settled Share-based Payment Transactions (Amendments to IFRS 2) was approved for issue by thirteen of the fourteen members of the International Accounting Standards Board. Mr Kalavacherla abstained in view of his recent appointment to the Board.

Sir David Tweedie   Chairman

Thomas E Jones   Vice-Chairman

Mary E Barth

Stephen Cooper

Philippe Danjou

Jan Engström

Robert P Garnett

Gilbert Gélard

Prabhakar Kalavacherla

James J Leisenring

Warren J McGregor

John T Smith

Tatsumi Yamada

Wei-Guo Zhang

CONTENTS

© IASCF

Basis for Conclusions on
IFRS 2 *Share-based Payment*

This Basis for Conclusions accompanies, but is not part of, IFRS 2.

Introduction

BC1   This Basis for Conclusions summarises the International Accounting Standards Board's considerations in reaching the conclusions in IFRS 2 *Share-based Payment*. Individual Board members gave greater weight to some factors than to others.

BC2   Entities often issue* shares or share options to pay employees or other parties. Share plans and share option plans are a common feature of employee remuneration, not only for directors and senior executives, but also for many other employees. Some entities issue shares or share options to pay suppliers, such as suppliers of professional services.

BC3   Until the issue of IFRS 2, there has been no International Financial Reporting Standard (IFRS) covering the recognition and measurement of these transactions. Concerns have been raised about this gap in international standards. For example, the International Organization of Securities Commissions (IOSCO), in its 2000 report on international standards, stated that IASC (the IASB's predecessor body) should consider the accounting treatment of share-based payment.

BC4   Few countries have standards on the topic. This is a concern in many countries, because the use of share-based payment has increased in recent years and continues to spread. Various standard-setting bodies have been working on this issue. At the time the IASB added a project on share-based payment to its agenda in July 2001, some standard-setters had recently published proposals. For example, the German Accounting Standards Committee published a draft accounting standard *Accounting for Share Option Plans and Similar Compensation Arrangements* in June 2001. The UK Accounting Standards Board led the development of the Discussion Paper *Accounting for Share-based Payment*, published in July 2000 by IASC, the ASB and other bodies represented in the G4+1.† The Danish Institute of State Authorised Public Accountants issued a Discussion Paper *The Accounting Treatment of Share-based Payment* in April 2000. More recently, in December 2002, the Accounting Standards Board of Japan published a Summary Issues Paper on share-based payment. In March 2003, the US Financial Accounting Standards Board (FASB) added to its agenda a project to review US accounting requirements on share-based payment. Also, the Canadian

---

*   The word 'issue' is used in a broad sense. For example, a transfer of shares held in treasury (own shares held) to another party is regarded as an 'issue' of equity instruments. Some argue that if options or shares are granted with vesting conditions, they are not 'issued' until those vesting conditions have been satisfied. However, even if this argument is accepted, it does not change the Board's conclusions on the requirements of the IFRS, and therefore the word 'issue' is used broadly, to include situations in which equity instruments are conditionally transferred to the counterparty, subject to the satisfaction of specified vesting conditions.

†   The G4+1 comprised members of the national accounting standard-setting bodies of Australia, Canada, New Zealand, the UK and the US, and IASC.

Accounting Standards Board (AcSB) recently completed its project on share-based payment. The AcSB standard requires recognition of all share-based payment transactions, including transactions in which share options are granted to employees (discussed further in paragraphs BC281 and BC282).

BC5 Users of financial statements and other commentators are calling for improvements in the accounting treatment of share-based payment. For example, the proposal in the IASC/G4+1 Discussion Paper and ED 2 *Share-based Payment*, that share-based payment transactions should be recognised in the financial statements, resulting in an expense when the goods or services are consumed, received strong support from investors and other users of financial statements. Recent economic events have emphasised the importance of high quality financial statements that provide neutral, transparent and comparable information to help users make economic decisions. In particular, the omission of expenses arising from share-based payment transactions with employees has been highlighted by investors, other users of financial statements and other commentators as causing economic distortions and corporate governance concerns.

BC6 As noted above, the Board began a project to develop an IFRS on share-based payment in July 2001. In September 2001, the Board invited additional comment on the IASC/G4+1 Discussion Paper, with a comment deadline of 15 December 2001. The Board received over 270 letters. During the development of ED 2, the Board was also assisted by an Advisory Group, consisting of individuals from various countries and with a range of backgrounds, including persons from the investment, corporate, audit, academic, compensation consultancy, valuation and regulatory communities. The Board received further assistance from other experts at a panel discussion held in New York in July 2002. In November 2002, the Board published an Exposure Draft, ED 2 *Share-based Payment*, with a comment deadline of 7 March 2003. The Board received over 240 letters. The Board also worked with the FASB after that body added to its agenda a project to review US accounting requirements on share-based payment. This included participating in meetings of the FASB's Option Valuation Group and meeting the FASB to discuss convergence issues.

BC6A In 2007 the Board added to its agenda a project to clarify the scope and accounting for group cash-settled share-based payment transactions in the separate or individual financial statements of the entity receiving the goods or services when that entity has no obligation to settle the share-based payment. In December 2007 the Board published *Group Cash-settled Share-based Payment Transactions* (proposed amendments to IFRS 2). The resulting amendments issued in June 2009 also incorporate the requirements of two Interpretations—IFRIC 8 *Scope of IFRS 2* and IFRIC 11 *IFRS 2—Group and Treasury Share Transactions*. As a consequence, the Board withdrew both Interpretations.

Scope

BC7 Much of the controversy and complexity surrounding the accounting for share-based payment relates to employee share options. However, the scope of IFRS 2 is broader than that. It applies to transactions in which shares or other equity instruments are granted to employees. It also applies to transactions with parties other than employees, in which goods or services are received as consideration for the issue of shares, share options or other equity instruments. The term 'goods' includes inventories, consumables, property, plant and equipment, intangible assets and other non-financial assets. Lastly, the IFRS applies to payments in cash (or other assets) that are 'share-based' because the amount of the payment is based on the price of the entity's shares or other equity instruments, eg cash share appreciation rights.

Broad-based employee share plans, including employee share purchase plans

BC8   Some employee share plans are described as 'broad-based' or 'all-employee' plans, in which all (or virtually all) employees have the opportunity to participate, whereas other plans are more selective, covering individual or specific groups of employees (eg senior executives). Employee share purchase plans are often broad-based plans. Typically, employee share purchase plans provide employees with an opportunity to buy a specific number of shares at a discounted price, ie at an amount that is less than the fair value of the shares. The employee's entitlement to discounted shares is usually conditional upon specific conditions being satisfied, such as remaining in the service of the entity for a specified period.

BC9   The issues that arise with respect to employee share purchase plans are:

(a)   are these plans somehow so different from other employee share plans that a different accounting treatment is appropriate?

(b)   even if the answer to the above question is 'no', are there circumstances, such as when the discount is very small, when it is appropriate to exempt employee share purchase plans from an accounting standard on share-based payment?

BC10   Some respondents to ED 2 argued that broad-based employee share plans should be exempt from an accounting standard on share-based payment. The reason usually given was that these plans are different from other types of employee share plans and, in particular, are not a part of remuneration for employee services. Some argued that requiring the recognition of an expense in respect of these types of plans was perceived to be contrary to government policy to encourage employee share ownership. In contrast, other respondents saw no difference between employee share purchase plans and other employee share plans, and argued that the same accounting requirements should therefore apply. However, some suggested that there should be an exemption if the discount is small.

BC11   The Board concluded that, in principle, there is no reason to treat broad-based employee share plans, including broad-based employee share purchase plans, differently from other employee share plans (the issue of 'small' discounts is considered later). The Board noted that the fact that these schemes are available only to employees is in itself sufficient to conclude that the benefits provided represent employee remuneration. Moreover, the term 'remuneration' is not limited to remuneration provided as part of an individual employee's contract:

it encompasses all benefits provided to employees. Similarly, the term services encompasses all benefits provided by the employees in return, including increased productivity, commitment or other enhancements in employee work performance as a result of the incentives provided by the share plan.

BC12　Moreover, distinguishing regular employee services from the additional benefits received from broad-based employee share plans would not change the conclusion that it is necessary to account for such plans. No matter what label is placed on the benefits provided by employees—or the benefits provided by the entity—the transaction should be recognised in the financial statements.

BC13　Furthermore, that governments in some countries have a policy of encouraging employee share ownership is not a valid reason for according these types of plans a different accounting treatment, because it is not the role of financial reporting to give favourable accounting treatment to particular transactions to encourage entities to enter into them. For example, governments might wish to encourage entities to provide pensions to their employees, to lessen the future burden on the state, but that does not mean that pension costs should be excluded from the financial statements. To do so would impair the quality of financial reporting. The purpose of financial reporting is to provide information to users of financial statements, to assist them in making economic decisions. The omission of expenses from the financial statements does not change the fact that those expenses have been incurred. The omission of expenses causes reported profits to be overstated and hence the financial statements are not neutral, are less transparent and comparable, and are potentially misleading to users.

BC14　There remains the question whether there should be an exemption for some plans, when the discount is small. For example, FASB Statement of Financial Accounting Standards No.123 *Accounting for Stock-Based Compensation* contains an exemption for employee share purchase plans that meet specified criteria, of which one is that the discount is small.

BC15　On the one hand, it seems reasonable to exempt an employee share purchase plan if it has substantially no option features and the discount is small. In such situations, the rights given to the employees under the plan probably do not have a significant value, from the entity's perspective.

BC16　On the other hand, even if one accepts that an exemption is appropriate, specifying its scope is problematic, eg deciding what constitutes a small discount. Some argue that a 5 per cent discount from the market price (as specified in SFAS 123) is too high, noting that a block of shares can be sold on the market at a price close to the current share price. Furthermore, it could be argued that it is unnecessary to exempt these plans from the standard. If the rights given to the employees do not have a significant value, this suggests that the amounts involved are immaterial. Because it is not necessary to include immaterial information in the financial statements, there is no need for a specific exclusion in an accounting standard.

BC17　For the reasons given in the preceding paragraph, the Board concluded that broad-based employee share plans, including broad-based employee share purchase plans, should not be exempted from the IFRS.

BC18 However, the Board noted that there might be instances when an entity engages in a transaction with an employee in his/her capacity as a holder of equity instruments, rather than in his/her capacity as an employee. For example, an entity might grant all holders of a particular class of its equity instruments the right to acquire additional equity instruments of the entity at a price that is less than the fair value of those equity instruments. If an employee receives such a right because he/she is a holder of that particular class of equity instruments, the Board concluded that the granting or exercise of that right should not be subject to the requirements of the IFRS, because the employee has received that right in his/her capacity as a shareholder, rather than as an employee.

Transactions in which an entity cannot identify some or all of the goods or services received (paragraph 2)[*]

BC18A The Board incorporated into IFRS 2 the consensus of IFRIC 8 in *Group Cash-settled Share-based Payment Transactions* issued in June 2009. This section summarises the IFRIC's considerations in reaching that consensus, as approved by the Board.

BC18B IFRS 2 applies to share-based payment transactions in which the entity receives or acquires goods or services. However, in some situations it might be difficult to demonstrate that the entity has received goods or services. This raises the question of whether IFRS 2 applies to such transactions. In addition, if the entity has made a share-based payment and the identifiable consideration received (if any) appears to be less than the fair value of the share-based payment, does this situation indicate that goods or services have been received, even though those goods or services are not specifically identified, and therefore that IFRS 2 applies?

BC18C When the Board developed IFRS 2, it concluded that the directors of an entity would expect to receive some goods or services in return for equity instruments issued (paragraph BC37). This implies that it is not necessary to identify the specific goods or services received in return for the equity instruments granted to conclude that goods or services have been (or will be) received. Furthermore, paragraph 8 of the IFRS establishes that it is not necessary for the goods or services received to qualify for recognition as an asset in order for the share-based payment to be within the scope of IFRS 2. In this case, the IFRS requires the cost of the goods or services received or receivable to be recognised as expenses.

BC18D Accordingly, the Board concluded that the scope of IFRS 2 includes transactions in which the entity cannot identify some or all of the specific goods or services received. If the value of the identifiable consideration received appears to be less than the fair value of the equity instruments granted or liability incurred, typically,[†] this circumstance indicates that other consideration (ie unidentifiable goods or services) has been (or will be) received.

---

[*] Paragraphs BC18A–BC18D are added as a consequence of *Group Cash-settled Share-based Payment Transactions* (Amendments to IFRS 2) issued in June 2009.

[†] In some cases, the reason for the transfer would explain why no goods or services have been or will be received. For example, a principal shareholder, as part of estate planning, transfers some of his shares to a family member. In the absence of factors that indicate that the family member has provided, or is expected to provide, any goods or services to the entity in return for the shares, such a transaction would be outside the scope of IFRS 2.

Transfers of equity instruments to employees (paragraphs 3 and 3A)[*]

BC19   In some situations, an entity might not issue shares or share options to employees (or other parties) direct. Instead, a shareholder (or shareholders) might transfer equity instruments to the employees (or other parties).

BC20   Under this arrangement, the entity has received services (or goods) that were paid for by its shareholders. The arrangement could be viewed as being, in substance, two transactions—one transaction in which the entity has reacquired equity instruments for nil consideration, and a second transaction in which the entity has received services (or goods) as consideration for equity instruments issued to the employees (or other parties).

BC21   The second transaction is a share-based payment transaction. Therefore, the Board concluded that the entity should account for transfers of equity instruments by shareholders to employees or other parties in the same way as other share-based payment transactions. The Board reached the same conclusion with respect to transfers of equity instruments of the entity's parent, or of another entity within the same group as the entity, to the entity's employees or other suppliers.

BC22   However, such a transfer is not a share-based payment transaction if the transfer of equity instruments to an employee or other party is clearly for a purpose other than payment for goods or services supplied to the entity. This would be the case, for example, if the transfer is to settle a shareholder's personal obligation to an employee that is unrelated to employment by the entity, or if the shareholder and employee are related and the transfer is a personal gift because of that relationship.

BC22A   In December 2007 the Board published an exposure draft *Group Cash-settled Share-based Payment Transactions* proposing amendments to IFRS 2 and IFRIC 11 to clarify the accounting for such transactions in the separate or individual financial statements of the entity receiving goods or services. The Board proposed to include specified types of such transactions within the scope of IFRS 2 (not IAS 19 *Employee Benefits*), regardless of whether the group share-based payment transaction is cash-settled or equity-settled.

BC22B   Nearly all of the respondents to the exposure draft agreed that the group cash-settled transactions between a parent and a subsidiary described in the exposure draft should be within the scope of IFRS 2. Respondents generally believed that including these transactions is consistent with IFRS 2's main principle that the entity should recognise the goods or services that it receives in a share-based transaction. However, respondents also expressed concerns that the proposed scope:

(a)   adopted a case-by-case approach and was inconsistent with the definitions of share-based payment transactions in IFRS 2.

(b)   was unclear and increased the inconsistency in the scope requirements among the applicable IFRSs, including IFRIC 11.

---

[*]   Paragraphs BC22A–BC22G are added as a consequence of *Group Cash-settled Share-based Payment Transactions* (Amendments to IFRS 2) issued in June 2009.

BC22C   Many respondents expressed concerns that similar transactions would continue to be treated differently. Because no amendments to the definitions of share-based payment transactions were proposed, some transactions might not be included within the scope of IFRS 2 because they did not meet those definitions. The Board agreed with respondents that the proposals did not achieve the objective of including all share-based payment transactions within the scope of IFRS 2 as intended.

BC22D   When finalising the amendments issued in June 2009, the Board reaffirmed the view it had intended to convey in the proposed amendments, namely that the entity receiving the goods or services should account for group share-based payment transactions in accordance with IFRS 2. Consequently, IFRS 2 applies even when the entity receiving the goods or services has no obligation to settle the transaction and regardless of whether the payments to the suppliers are equity-settled or cash-settled. To avoid the need for further guidance on the scope of IFRS 2 for group transactions, the Board decided to amend some of the defined terms and to supersede paragraph 3 by a new paragraph 3A to state clearly the principles applicable to those transactions.

BC22E   During its redeliberations of the proposed amendments, the Board agreed with respondents' comments that, as proposed, the scope of IFRS 2 remained unclear and inconsistent between the standard and related Interpretations. For example, the terms 'shareholder' and 'parent' have different meanings: a shareholder is not necessarily a parent, and a parent does not have to be a shareholder. The Board noted that share-based payment transactions among group entities are often directed by the parent, indicating a level of control. Therefore, the Board clarified the boundaries of a 'group' by adopting the same definition as in paragraph 4 of IAS 27 *Consolidated and Separate Financial Statements*, which includes only a parent and its subsidiaries.

BC22F   Some respondents to the exposure draft questioned whether the proposals should apply to joint ventures. Before the Board's amendments, the guidance in paragraph 3 (now superseded by paragraph 3A) stated that when a shareholder transferred equity instruments of the entity (or another group entity), the transaction would be within the scope of IFRS 2 for the entity receiving the goods or services. However, that guidance did not specify the accounting by a shareholder transferor. The Board noted that the defined terms in Appendix A, as amended, would clearly state that any entity (including a joint venture) that receives goods or services in a share-based payment transaction should account for the transaction in accordance with the IFRS, regardless of whether that entity also settles the transaction.

BC22G   Furthermore, the Board noted that the exposure draft and related discussions focused on clarifying guidance for transactions involving group entities in the separate or individual financial statements of the entity receiving the goods or services. Addressing transactions involving related parties outside a group structure in their separate or individual financial statements would significantly expand the scope of the project and change the scope of IFRS 2. Therefore, the Board decided not to address transactions between entities not in the same group that are similar to share-based payment transactions but outside the definitions as amended. This carries forward the existing guidance of IFRS 2 for entities not in the same group and the Board does not intend to change that guidance.

Transactions within the scope of IFRS 3 *Business Combinations*

BC23   An entity might acquire goods (or other non-financial assets) as part of the net assets acquired in a business combination for which the consideration paid included shares or other equity instruments issued by the entity. Because IFRS 3 applies to the acquisition of assets and issue of shares in connection with a business combination, that is the more specific standard that should be applied to that transaction.

BC24   Therefore, equity instruments issued in a business combination in exchange for control of the acquiree are not within the scope of IFRS 2. However, equity instruments granted to employees of the acquiree in their capacity as employees, eg in return for continued service, are within the scope of IFRS 2. Also, the cancellation, replacement, or other modifications to share-based payment arrangements because of a business combination or other equity restructuring should be accounted for in accordance with IFRS 2.

BC24A   IFRS 3 (as revised in 2008) changed the definition of a business combination. The previous definition of a business combination was 'the bringing together of separate entities or businesses into one reporting entity'. The revised definition of a business combination is 'a transaction or other event in which an acquirer obtains control of one or more businesses'.

BC24B   The Board was advised that the changes to that definition caused the accounting for the contribution of a business in exchange for shares issued on formation of a joint venture by the venturers to be within the scope of IFRS 2. The Board noted that common control transactions may also be within the scope of IFRS 2 depending on which level of the group reporting entity is assessing the combination.

BC24C   The Board noted that during the development of revised IFRS 3 it did not discuss whether it intended IFRS 2 to apply to these types of transactions. The Board also noted that the reason for excluding common control transactions and the accounting by a joint venture upon its formation from the scope of revised IFRS 3 was to give the Board more time to consider the relevant accounting issues. When the Board revised IFRS 3, it did not intend to change existing practice by bringing such transactions within the scope of IFRS 2, which does not specifically address them.

BC24D   Accordingly, in *Improvements to IFRSs* issued in April 2009, the Board amended paragraph 5 of IFRS 2 to confirm that the contribution of a business on the formation of a joint venture and common control transactions are not within the scope of IFRS 2.

Transactions within the scope of IAS 32 *Financial Instruments: Presentation* and IAS 39 *Financial Instruments: Recognition and Measurement**

BC25 The IFRS includes consequential amendments to IAS 32 and IAS 39 (both as revised in 2003)† to exclude from their scope transactions within the scope of IFRS 2.

BC26 For example, suppose the entity enters into a contract to purchase cloth for use in its clothing manufacturing business, whereby it is required to pay cash to the counterparty in an amount equal to the value of 1,000 of the entity's shares at the date of delivery of the cloth. The entity will acquire goods and pay cash at an amount based on its share price. This meets the definition of a share-based payment transaction. Moreover, because the contract is to purchase cloth, which is a non-financial item, and the contract was entered into for the purpose of taking delivery of the cloth for use in the entity's manufacturing business, the contract is not within the scope of IAS 32 and IAS 39.

BC27 The scope of IAS 32 and IAS 39 includes contracts to buy non-financial items that can be settled net in cash or another financial instrument, or by exchanging financial instruments, with the exception of contracts that were entered into and continue to be held for the purpose of the receipt or delivery of a non-financial item in accordance with the entity's expected purchase, sale or usage requirements. A contract that can be settled net in cash or another financial instrument or by exchanging financial instruments includes (a) when the terms of the contract permit either party to settle it net in cash or another financial instrument or by exchanging financial instruments; (b) when the ability to settle net in cash or another financial instrument, or by exchanging financial instruments, is not explicit in the terms of the contract, but the entity has a practice of settling similar contracts net in cash or another financial instrument, or by exchanging financial instruments (whether with the counterparty, by entering into offsetting contracts, or by selling the contract before its exercise or lapse); (c) when, for similar contracts, the entity has a practice of taking delivery of the underlying and selling it within a short period after delivery for the purpose of generating a profit from short-term fluctuations in price or dealer's margin; and (d) when the non-financial item that is the subject of the contract is readily convertible to cash (IAS 32, paragraphs 8–10 and IAS 39, paragraphs 5–7).

BC28 The Board concluded that the contracts discussed in paragraph BC27 should remain within the scope of IAS 32 and IAS 39 and they are therefore excluded from the scope of IFRS 2.

Recognition of equity-settled share-based payment transactions

BC29 When it developed ED 2, the Board first considered conceptual arguments relating to the recognition of an expense arising from equity-settled share-based payment transactions, including arguments advanced by respondents to the Discussion Paper and other commentators. Some respondents who disagreed

---

* In November 2009 the IASB amended some of the requirements of IAS 39 and relocated them to IFRS 9 *Financial Instruments*. IFRS 9 applies to all assets within the scope of IAS 39.

† The title of IAS 32 was amended in 2005.

with the recognition of an expense arising from particular share-based payment transactions (ie those involving employee share options) did so for practical, rather than conceptual, reasons. The Board considered those practical issues later (see paragraphs BC294–BC310).

BC30   The Board focused its discussions on employee share options, because that is where most of the complexity and controversy lies, but the question of whether expense recognition is appropriate is broader than that—it covers all transactions involving the issue of shares, share options or other equity instruments to employees or suppliers of goods and services. For example, the Board noted that arguments made by respondents and other commentators against expense recognition are directed solely at employee share options. However, if conceptual arguments made against recognition of an expense in relation to employee share options are valid (eg that there is no cost to the entity), those arguments ought to apply equally to transactions involving other equity instruments (eg shares) and to equity instruments issued to other parties (eg suppliers of professional services).

BC31   The rationale for recognising all types of share-based payment transactions— irrespective of whether the equity instrument is a share or a share option, and irrespective of whether the equity instrument is granted to an employee or to some other party—is that the entity has engaged in a transaction that is in essence the same as any other issue of equity instruments. In other words, the entity has received resources (goods or services) as consideration for the issue of shares, share options or other equity instruments. It should therefore account for the inflow of resources (goods or services) and the increase in equity. Subsequently, either at the time of receipt of the goods or services or at some later date, the entity should also account for the expense arising from the consumption of those resources.

BC32   Many respondents to ED 2 agreed with this conclusion. Of those who disagreed, some disagreed in principle, some disagreed for practical reasons, and some disagreed for both reasons. The arguments against expense recognition in principle were considered by the Board when it developed ED 2, as were the arguments against expense recognition for practical reasons, as explained below and in paragraphs BC294–BC310.

BC33   Arguments commonly made against expense recognition include:

(a)   the transaction is between the shareholders and the employees, not the entity and the employees.

(b)   the employees do not provide services for the options.

(c)   there is no cost to the entity, because no cash or other assets are given up; the shareholders bear the cost, in the form of dilution of their ownership interests, not the entity.

(d)   the recognition of an expense is inconsistent with the definition of an expense in the conceptual frameworks used by accounting standard-setters, including the IASB's *Framework for the Preparation and Presentation of Financial Statements*.

(e) the cost borne by the shareholders is recognised in the dilution of earnings per share (EPS); if the transaction is recognised in the entity's accounts, the resulting charge to the income statement would mean that EPS is 'hit twice'.

(f) requiring the recognition of a charge would have adverse economic consequences, because it would discourage entities from introducing or continuing employee share plans.

'The entity is not a party to the transaction'

BC34 Some argue that the effect of employee share plans is that the existing shareholders transfer some of their ownership interests to the employees and that the entity is not a party to this transaction.

BC35 The Board did not accept this argument. Entities, not shareholders, set up employee share plans and entities, not shareholders, issue share options to their employees. Even if that were not the case, eg if shareholders transferred shares or share options direct to the employees, this would not mean that the entity is not a party to the transaction. The equity instruments are issued in return for services rendered by the employees and the entity, not the shareholders, receives those services. Therefore, the Board concluded that the entity should account for the services received in return for the equity instruments issued. The Board noted that this is no different from other situations in which equity instruments are issued. For example, if an entity issues warrants for cash, the entity recognises the cash received in return for the warrants issued. Although the effect of an issue, and subsequent exercise, of warrants might be described as a transfer of ownership interests from the existing shareholders to the warrant holders, the entity nevertheless is a party to the transaction because it receives resources (cash) for the issue of warrants and further resources (cash) for the issue of shares upon exercise of the warrants. Similarly, with employee share options, the entity receives resources (employee services) for the issue of the options and further resources (cash) for the issue of shares on the exercise of options.

'The employees do not provide services'

BC36 Some who argue that the entity is not a party to the transaction counter the points made above with the argument that employees do not provide services for the options, because the employees are paid in cash (or other assets) for their services.

BC37 Again, the Board was not convinced by this argument. If it were true that employees do not provide services for their share options, this would mean that entities are issuing valuable share options and getting nothing in return. Employees do not pay cash for the share options they receive. Hence, if they do not provide services for the options, the employees are providing nothing in return. If this were true, by issuing such options the entity's directors would be in breach of their fiduciary duties to their shareholders.

BC38 Typically, shares or share options granted to employees form one part of their remuneration package. For example, an employee might have a remuneration package consisting of a basic cash salary, company car, pension, healthcare benefits, and other benefits including shares and share options. It is usually not possible to identify the services received in respect of individual components of that remuneration package, eg the services received in respect of healthcare benefits. But that does not mean that the employee does not provide services for those healthcare benefits. Rather, the employee provides services for the entire remuneration package.

BC39 In summary, shares, share options or other equity instruments are granted to employees because they are employees. The equity instruments granted form a part of their total remuneration package, regardless of whether that represents a large part or a small part.

'There is no cost to the entity, therefore there is no expense'

BC40 Some argue that because share-based payments do not require the entity to sacrifice any cash or other assets, there is no cost to the entity, and therefore no expense should be recognised.

BC41 The Board regards this argument as unsound, because it overlooks that:

(a) every time an entity receives resources as consideration for the issue of equity instruments, there is no outflow of cash or other assets, and on every other occasion the resources received as consideration for the issue of equity instruments are recognised in the financial statements; and

(b) the expense arises from the consumption of those resources, not from an outflow of assets.

BC42 In other words, irrespective of whether one accepts that there is a cost to the entity, an accounting entry is required to recognise the resources received as consideration for the issue of equity instruments, just as it is on other occasions when equity instruments are issued. For example, when shares are issued for cash, an entry is required to recognise the cash received. If a non-monetary asset, such as plant and machinery, is received for those shares instead of cash, an entry is required to recognise the asset received. If the entity acquires another business or entity by issuing shares in a business combination, the entity recognises the net assets acquired.

BC43 The recognition of an expense arising out of such a transaction represents the consumption of resources received, ie the 'using up' of the resources received for the shares or share options. In the case of the plant and machinery mentioned above, the asset would be depreciated over its expected life, resulting in the recognition of an expense each year. Eventually, the entire amount recognised for the resources received when the shares were issued would be recognised as an expense (including any residual value, which would form part of the measurement of the gain or loss on disposal of the asset). Similarly, if another business or entity is acquired by an issue of shares, an expense is recognised when the assets acquired are consumed. For example, inventories acquired will be recognised as an expense when sold, even though no cash or other assets were disbursed to acquire those inventories.

BC44   The only difference in the case of employee services (or other services) received as consideration for the issue of shares or share options is that usually the resources received are consumed immediately upon receipt. This means that an expense for the consumption of resources is recognised immediately, rather than over a period of time. The Board concluded that the timing of consumption does not change the principle; the financial statements should recognise the receipt and consumption of resources, even when consumption occurs at the same time as, or soon after, receipt. This point is discussed further in paragraphs BC45–BC53.

'Expense recognition is inconsistent with the definition of an expense'

BC45   Some have questioned whether recognition of an expense arising from particular share-based payment transactions is consistent with accounting standard-setters' conceptual frameworks, in particular, the *Framework*, which states:

> Expenses are decreases in economic benefits during the accounting period in the form of outflows or *depletions of assets* or incurrences of liabilities that result in decreases in equity, other than those relating to distributions to equity participants. (paragraph 70, emphasis added)

BC46   Some argue that if services are received in a share-based payment transaction, there is no transaction or event that meets the definition of an expense. They contend that there is no outflow of assets and that no liability is incurred. Furthermore, because services usually do not meet the criteria for recognition as an asset, it is argued that the consumption of those services does not represent a depletion of assets.

BC47   The *Framework* defines an asset and explains that the term 'asset' is not limited to resources that can be recognised as assets in the balance sheet (*Framework*, paragraphs 49 and 50). Although services to be received in the future might not meet the definition of an asset, *services are assets when received. These assets are usually consumed immediately. This is explained in FASB Statement of Financial Accounting Concepts No. 6 *Elements of Financial Statements*:

> Services provided by other entities, including personal services, cannot be stored and are received and used simultaneously. They can be assets of an entity only momentarily—as the entity receives and uses them—although their use may create or add value to other assets of the entity ... (paragraph 31)

BC48   This applies to all types of services, eg employee services, legal services and telephone services. It also applies irrespective of the form of payment. For example, if an entity purchases services for cash, the accounting entry is:

Dr   Services received

    Cr   Cash paid

BC49   Sometimes, those services are consumed in the creation of a recognisable asset, such as inventories, in which case the debit for services received is capitalised as part of a recognised asset. But often the services do not create or form part of a recognisable asset, in which case the debit for services received is charged

---

*   For example, the entity might not have control over future services.

immediately to the income statement as an expense. The debit entry above (and the resulting expense) does not represent the cash outflow—that is what the credit entry was for. Nor does it represent some sort of balancing item, to make the accounts balance. The debit entry above represents the resources received, and the resulting expense represents the consumption of those resources.

BC50 The same analysis applies if the services are acquired with payment made in shares or share options. The resulting expense represents the consumption of services, ie a depletion of assets.

BC51 To illustrate this point, suppose that an entity has two buildings, both with gas heating, and the entity issues shares to the gas supplier instead of paying cash. Suppose that, for one building, the gas is supplied through a pipeline, and so is consumed immediately upon receipt. Suppose that, for the other building, the gas is supplied in bottles, and is consumed over a period of time. In both cases, the entity has received assets as consideration for the issue of equity instruments, and should therefore recognise the assets received, and a corresponding contribution to equity. If the assets are consumed immediately (the gas received through the pipeline), an expense is recognised immediately; if the assets are consumed later (the gas received in bottles), an expense is recognised later when the assets are consumed.

BC52 Therefore, the Board concluded that the recognition of an expense arising from share-based payment transactions is consistent with the definition of an expense in the *Framework*.

BC53 The FASB considered the same issue and reached the same conclusion in SFAS 123:

> Some respondents pointed out that the definition of expenses in FASB Concepts Statement No. 6, *Elements of Financial Statements*, says that expenses result from outflows or using up of assets or incurring of liabilities (or both). They asserted that because the issuance of stock options does not result in the incurrence of a liability, no expense should be recognised. The Board agrees that employee stock options are not a liability—like stock purchase warrants, employee stock options are equity instruments of the issuer. However, equity instruments, including employee stock options, are valuable financial instruments and thus are issued for valuable consideration, which...for employee stock options is employee services. Using in the entity's operations the benefits embodied in the asset received results in an expense ... (Concepts Statement 6, paragraph 81, footnote 43, notes that, in concept most expenses decrease assets. However, if receipt of an asset, such as services, and its use occur virtually simultaneously, the asset often is not recorded.) [paragraph 88]

'Earnings per share is "hit twice"'

BC54 Some argue that any cost arising from share-based payment transactions is already recognised in the dilution of earnings per share (EPS). If an expense were recognised in the income statement, EPS would be 'hit twice'.

BC55 However, the Board noted that this result is appropriate. For example, if the entity paid the employees in cash for their services and the cash was then returned to the entity, as consideration for the issue of share options, the effect on EPS would be the same as issuing those options direct to the employees.

BC56   The dual effect on EPS simply reflects the two economic events that have occurred: the entity has issued shares or share options, thereby increasing the number of shares included in the EPS calculation—although, in the case of options, only to the extent that the options are regarded as dilutive—and it has also consumed the resources it received for those options, thereby decreasing earnings. This is illustrated by the plant and machinery example mentioned in paragraphs BC42 and BC43. Issuing shares affects the number of shares in the EPS calculation, and the consumption (depreciation) of the asset affects earnings.

BC57   In summary, the Board concluded that the dual effect on diluted EPS is not double-counting the effects of a share or share option grant—the same effect is not counted twice. Rather, two different effects are each counted once.

'Adverse economic consequences'

BC58   Some argue that to require recognition (or greater recognition) of employee share-based payment would have adverse economic consequences, in that it might discourage entities from introducing or continuing employee share plans.

BC59   Others argue that if the introduction of accounting changes did lead to a reduction in the use of employee share plans, it might be because the requirement for entities to account properly for employee share plans had revealed the economic consequences of such plans. They argue that this would correct the present economic distortion, whereby entities obtain and consume resources by issuing valuable shares or share options without accounting for those transactions.

BC60   In any event, the Board noted that the role of accounting is to report transactions and events in a neutral manner, not to give 'favourable' treatment to particular transactions to encourage entities to engage in those transactions. To do so would impair the quality of financial reporting. The omission of expenses from the financial statements does not change the fact that those expenses have been incurred. Hence, if expenses are omitted from the income statement, reported profits are overstated. The financial statements are not neutral, are less transparent and are potentially misleading to users. Comparability is impaired, given that expenses arising from employee share-based payment transactions vary from entity to entity, from sector to sector, and from year to year. More fundamentally, accountability is impaired, because the entities are not accounting for transactions they have entered into and the consequences of those transactions.

Measurement of equity-settled share-based payment transactions

BC61   To recognise equity-settled share-based payment transactions, it is necessary to decide how the transactions should be measured. The Board began by considering how to measure share-based payment transactions in principle. Later, it considered practical issues arising from the application of its preferred measurement approach. In terms of accounting principles, there are two basic questions:

     (a)   which measurement basis should be applied?

     (b)   when should that measurement basis be applied?

BC62   To answer these questions, the Board considered the accounting principles applying to equity transactions. The *Framework* states:

> Equity is the residual interest in the assets of the enterprise after deducting all of its liabilities ... The amount at which equity is shown in the balance sheet is dependent upon the measurement of assets and liabilities. Normally, the aggregate amount of equity only by coincidence corresponds with the aggregate market value of the shares of the enterprise ... (paragraphs 49 and 67)

BC63   The accounting equation that corresponds to this definition of equity is:

> assets minus liabilities equals equity

BC64   Equity is a residual interest, dependent on the measurement of assets and liabilities. Therefore, accounting focuses on recording changes in the left side of the equation (assets minus liabilities, or net assets), rather than the right side. Changes in equity arise from changes in net assets. For example, if an entity issues shares for cash, it recognises the cash received and a corresponding increase in equity. Subsequent changes in the market price of the shares do not affect the entity's net assets and therefore those changes in value are not recognised.

BC65   Hence, the Board concluded that, when accounting for an equity-settled share-based payment transaction, the primary accounting objective is to account for the goods or services received as consideration for the issue of equity instruments. Therefore, equity-settled share-based payment transactions should be accounted for in the same way as other issues of equity instruments, by recognising the consideration received (the change in net assets), and a corresponding increase in equity.

BC66   Given this objective, the Board concluded that, in principle, the goods or services received should be measured at their fair value at the date when the entity obtains those goods or as the services are received. In other words, because a change in net assets occurs when the entity obtains the goods or as the services are received, the fair value of those goods or services at that date provides an appropriate measure of the change in net assets.

BC67   However, for share-based payment transactions with employees, it is usually difficult to measure directly the fair value of the services received. As noted earlier, typically shares or share options are granted to employees as one component of their remuneration package. It is usually not possible to identify the services rendered in respect of individual components of that package. It might also not be possible to measure independently the fair value of the total package, without measuring directly the fair value of the equity instruments granted. Furthermore, options or shares are sometimes granted as part of a bonus arrangement, rather than as a part of basic remuneration, eg as an incentive to the employees to remain in the entity's employ, or to reward them for their efforts in improving the entity's performance. By granting share options, in addition to other remuneration, the entity is paying additional remuneration to obtain additional benefits. Estimating the fair value of those additional benefits is likely to be difficult.

BC68 Given these practical difficulties in measuring directly the fair value of the employee services received, the Board concluded that it is necessary to measure the other side of the transaction, ie the fair value of the equity instruments granted, as a surrogate measure of the fair value of the services received. In this context, the Board considered the same basic questions, as mentioned above:

    (a) which measurement basis should be applied?

    (b) when should that measurement basis be applied?

Measurement basis

BC69 The Board discussed the following measurement bases, to decide which should be applied in principle:

    (a) historical cost

    (b) intrinsic value

    (c) minimum value

    (d) fair value.

Historical cost

BC70 In jurisdictions where legislation permits, entities commonly repurchase their own shares, either directly or through a vehicle such as a trust, which are used to fulfil promised grants of shares to employees or the exercise of employee share options. A possible basis for measuring a grant of options or shares would be the historical cost (purchase price) of its own shares that an entity holds (own shares held), even if they were acquired before the award was made.

BC71 For share options, this would entail comparing the historical cost of own shares held with the exercise price of options granted to employees. Any shortfall would be recognised as an expense. Also, presumably, if the exercise price exceeded the historical cost of own shares held, the excess would be recognised as a gain.

BC72 At first sight, if one simply focuses on the cash flows involved, the historical cost basis appears reasonable: there is a cash outflow to acquire the shares, followed by a cash inflow when those shares are transferred to the employees (the exercise price), with any shortfall representing a cost to the entity. If the cash flows related to anything other than the entity's own shares, this approach would be appropriate. For example, suppose ABC Ltd bought shares in another entity, XYZ Ltd, for a total cost of CU500,000,[*] and later sold the shares to employees for a total of CU400,000. The entity would recognise an expense for the CU100,000 shortfall.

---

[*] All monetary amounts in this Basis for Conclusions are denominated in 'currency units (CU)'.

BC73   But when this analysis is applied to the entity's own shares, the logic breaks down. The entity's own shares are not an asset of the entity.* Rather, the shares are an interest in the entity's assets. Hence, the distribution of cash to buy back shares is a return of capital to shareholders, and should therefore be recognised as a decrease in equity. Similarly, when the shares are subsequently reissued or transferred, the inflow of cash is an increase in shareholders' capital, and should therefore be recognised as an increase in equity. It follows that no revenue or expense should be recognised. Just as the issue of shares does not represent revenue to the entity, the repurchase of those shares does not represent an expense.

BC74   Therefore, the Board concluded that historical cost is not an appropriate basis upon which to measure equity-settled share-based payment transactions.

Intrinsic value

BC75   An equity instrument could be measured at its intrinsic value. The intrinsic value of a share option at any point in time is the difference between the market price of the underlying shares and the exercise price of the option.

BC76   Often, employee share options have zero intrinsic value at the date of grant— commonly the exercise price is at the market value of the shares at grant date. Therefore, in many cases, valuing share options at their intrinsic value at grant date is equivalent to attributing no value to the options.

BC77   However, the intrinsic value of an option does not fully reflect its value. Options sell in the market for more than their intrinsic value. This is because the holder of an option need not exercise it immediately and benefits from any increase in the value of the underlying shares. In other words, although the ultimate benefit realised by the option holder is the option's intrinsic value at the date of exercise, the option holder is able to realise that future intrinsic value because of having held the option. Thus, the option holder benefits from the right to participate in future gains from increases in the share price. In addition, the option holder benefits from the right to defer payment of the exercise price until the end of the option term. These benefits are commonly referred to as the option's 'time value'.

BC78   For many options, time value represents a substantial part of their value. As noted earlier, many employee share options have zero intrinsic value at grant date, and hence the option's value consists entirely of time value. In such cases, ignoring time value by applying the intrinsic value method at grant date understates the value of the option by 100 per cent.

---

*   The Discussion Paper discusses this point: Accounting practice in some jurisdictions may present own shares acquired as an asset, but they lack the essential feature of an asset—the ability to provide future economic benefits. The future economic benefits usually provided by an interest in shares are the right to receive dividends and the right to gain from an increase in value of the shares. When a company has an interest in its own shares, it will receive dividends on those shares only if it elects to pay them, and such dividends do not represent a gain to the company, as there is no change in net assets: the flow of funds is simply circular. Whilst it is true that a company that holds its own shares in treasury may sell them and receive a higher amount if their value has increased, a company is generally able to issue shares to third parties at (or near) the current market price. Although there may be legal, regulatory or administrative reasons why it is easier to sell shares that are held as treasury shares than it would be to issue new shares, such considerations do not seem to amount to a fundamental contrast between the two cases. (Footnote to paragraph 4.7)

BC79   The Board concluded that, in general, the intrinsic value measurement basis is not appropriate for measuring share-based payment transactions, because omitting the option's time value ignores a potentially substantial part of an option's total value. Measuring share-based payment transactions at such an understated value would fail to represent those transactions faithfully in the financial statements.

Minimum value

BC80   A share option could be measured at its minimum value. Minimum value is based on the premise that someone who wants to buy a call option on a share would be willing to pay at least (and the option writer would demand at least) the value of the right to defer payment of the exercise price until the end of the option's term. Therefore, minimum value can be calculated using a present value technique. For a dividend-paying share, the calculation is:

(a)   the current price of the share, minus

(b)   the present value of expected dividends on that share during the option term (if the option holder does not receive dividends), minus

(c)   the present value of the exercise price.

BC81   Minimum value can also be calculated using an option pricing model with an expected volatility of effectively zero (not exactly zero, because some option pricing models use volatility as a divisor, and zero cannot be a divisor).

BC82   The minimum value measurement basis captures part of the time value of options, being the value of the right to defer payment of the exercise price until the end of the option's term. It does not capture the effects of volatility. Option holders benefit from volatility because they have the right to participate in gains from increases in the share price during the option term without having to bear the full risk of loss from decreases in the share price. By ignoring volatility, the minimum value method produces a value that is lower, and often much lower, than values produced by methods designed to estimate the fair value of an option.

BC83   The Board concluded that minimum value is not an appropriate measurement basis, because ignoring the effects of volatility ignores a potentially large part of an option's value. As with intrinsic value, measuring share-based payment transactions at the option's minimum value would fail to represent those transactions faithfully in the financial statements.

Fair value

BC84   Fair value is already used in other areas of accounting, including other transactions in which non-cash resources are acquired through the issue of equity instruments. For example, consideration transferred in a business combination is measured at fair value, including the fair value of any equity instruments issued by the entity.

BC85   Fair value, which is the amount at which an equity instrument granted could be exchanged between knowledgeable, willing parties in an arm's length transaction, captures both intrinsic value and time value and therefore provides a measure of the share option's total value (unlike intrinsic value or minimum value). It is the value that reflects the bargain between the entity and its employees, whereby the entity has agreed to grant share options to employees for their services to the entity. Hence, measuring share-based payment transactions at fair value ensures that those transactions are represented faithfully in the financial statements, and consistently with other transactions in which the entity receives resources as consideration for the issue of equity instruments.

BC86   Therefore, the Board concluded that shares, share options or other equity instruments granted should be measured at their fair value.

BC87   Of the respondents to ED 2 who addressed this issue, many agreed with the proposal to measure the equity instruments granted at their fair value. Some respondents who disagreed with the proposal, or who agreed with reservations, expressed concerns about measurement reliability, particularly in the case of smaller or unlisted entities. The issues of measurement reliability and unlisted entities are discussed in paragraphs BC294–BC310 and BC137–BC144, respectively.

Measurement date

BC88   The Board first considered at which date the fair value of equity instruments should be determined for the purpose of measuring share-based payment transactions with employees (and others providing similar services).* The possible measurement dates discussed were grant date, service date, vesting date and exercise date. Much of this discussion was in the context of share options rather than shares or other equity instruments, because only options have an exercise date.

BC89   In the context of an employee share option, grant date is when the entity and the employee enter into an agreement, whereby the employee is granted rights to the share option, provided that specified conditions are met, such as the employee's remaining in the entity's employ for a specified period. Service date is the date when the employee renders the services necessary to become entitled to the share option.† Vesting date is the date when the employee has satisfied all the conditions necessary to become entitled to the share option. For example, if the employee is required to remain in the entity's employ for three years, vesting date is at the end of that three-year period. Exercise date is when the share option is exercised.

---

*   When the Board developed the proposals in ED 2, it focused on the measurement of equity-settled transactions with employees and with parties other than employees. ED 2 did not propose a definition of the term 'employees'. When the Board reconsidered the proposals in ED 2 in the light of comments received, it discussed whether the term might be interpreted too narrowly. This could result in a different accounting treatment of services received from individuals who are regarded as employees (eg for legal or tax purposes) and substantially similar services received from other individuals. The Board therefore concluded that the requirements of the IFRS for transactions with employees should also apply to transactions with other parties providing similar services. This includes services received from (1) individuals who work for the entity under its direction in the same way as individuals who are regarded as employees for legal or tax purposes and (2) individuals who are not employees but who render personal services to the entity similar to those rendered by employees. All references to employees therefore include other parties providing similar services.

†   Service date measurement theoretically requires the entity to measure the fair value of the share option at each date when services are received. For pragmatic reasons, an approximation would probably be used, such as the fair value of the share option at the end of each accounting period, or the value of the share option measured at regular intervals during each accounting period.

BC90   To help determine the appropriate measurement date, the Board applied the accounting concepts in the *Framework* to each side of the transaction. For transactions with employees, the Board concluded that grant date is the appropriate measurement date, as explained in paragraphs BC91–BC105. The Board also considered some other issues, as explained in paragraphs BC106–BC118. For transactions with parties other than employees, the Board concluded that delivery date is the appropriate measurement date (ie the date the goods or services are received, referred to as service date in the context of transactions with employees), as explained in paragraphs BC119–BC128.

The debit side of the transaction

BC91   Focusing on the debit side of the transaction means focusing on measuring the fair value of the resources received. This measurement objective is consistent with the primary objective of accounting for the goods or services received as consideration for the issue of equity instruments (see paragraphs BC64–BC66). The Board therefore concluded that, in principle, the goods or services received should be measured at their fair value at the date when the entity obtains those goods or as the services are received.

BC92   However, if the fair value of the services received is not readily determinable, then a surrogate measure must be used, such as the fair value of the share options or shares granted. This is the case for employee services.

BC93   If the fair value of the equity instruments granted is used as a surrogate measure of the fair value of the services received, both vesting date and exercise date measurement are inappropriate because the fair value of the services received during a particular accounting period is not affected by subsequent changes in the fair value of the equity instrument. For example, suppose that services are received during years 1–3 as the consideration for share options that are exercised at the end of year 5. For services received in year 1, subsequent changes in the value of the share option in years 2–5 are unrelated to, and have no effect on, the fair value of those services when received.

BC94   Service date measurement measures the fair value of the equity instrument at the same time as the services are received. This means that changes in the fair value of the equity instrument during the vesting period affect the amount attributed to the services received. Some argue that this is appropriate, because, in their view, there is a correlation between changes in the fair value of the equity instrument and the fair value of the services received. For example, they argue that if the fair value of a share option falls, so does its incentive effects, which causes employees to reduce the level of services provided for that option, or demand extra remuneration. Some argue that when the fair value of a share option falls because of a general decline in share prices, remuneration levels also fall, and therefore service date measurement reflects this decline in remuneration levels.

BC95   The Board concluded, however, that there is unlikely to be a high correlation between changes in the fair value of an equity instrument and the fair value of the services received. For example, if the fair value of a share option doubles, it is unlikely that the employees work twice as hard, or accept a reduction in the rest of their remuneration package. Similarly, even if a general rise in share prices is accompanied by a rise in remuneration levels, it is unlikely that there is a high correlation between the two. Furthermore, it is likely that any link between share prices and remuneration levels is not universally applicable to all industry sectors.

BC96 The Board concluded that, at grant date, it is reasonable to presume that the fair value of both sides of the contract are substantially the same, ie the fair value of the services expected to be received is substantially the same as the fair value of the equity instruments granted. This conclusion, together with the Board's conclusion that there is unlikely to be a high correlation between the fair value of the services received and the fair value of the equity instruments granted at later measurement dates, led the Board to conclude that grant date is the most appropriate measurement date for the purposes of providing a surrogate measure of the fair value of the services received.

The credit side of the transaction

BC97 Although focusing on the debit side of the transaction is consistent with the primary accounting objective, some approach the measurement date question from the perspective of the credit side of the transaction, ie the issue of an equity instrument. The Board therefore considered the matter from this perspective too.

Exercise date

BC98 Under exercise date measurement, the entity recognises the resources received (eg employee services) for the issue of share options, and also recognises changes in the fair value of the option until it is exercised or lapses. Thus, if the option is exercised, the transaction amount is ultimately 'trued up' to equal the gain made by the option holder on exercise of the option. However, if the option lapses at the end of the exercise period, any amounts previously recognised are effectively reversed, hence the transaction amount is ultimately trued up to equal zero. The Board rejected exercise date measurement because it requires share options to be treated as liabilities, which is inconsistent with the definition of liabilities in the *Framework*. Exercise date measurement requires share options to be treated as liabilities because it requires the remeasurement of share options after initial recognition, which is inappropriate if the share options are equity instruments. A share option does not meet the definition of a liability, because it does not contain an obligation to transfer cash or other assets.

Vesting date, service date and grant date

BC99 The Board noted that the IASC/G4+1 Discussion Paper supported vesting date measurement, and rejected grant date and service date measurement, because it concluded that the share option is not issued until vesting date. It noted that the employees must perform their side of the arrangement by providing the necessary services and meeting any other performance criteria before the entity is obliged to perform its side of the arrangement. The provision of services by the employees is not merely a condition of the arrangement, it is the consideration they use to 'pay' for the share option. Therefore, the Discussion Paper concluded, in economic terms the share option is not issued until vesting date. Because the entity performs its side of the arrangement on vesting date, that is the appropriate measurement date.

BC100 The Discussion Paper also proposed recognising an accrual in equity during the vesting period to ensure that the services are recognised when they are received. It proposed that this accrual should be revised on vesting date to equal the fair value of the share option at that date. This means that amounts credited to equity during the vesting period will be subsequently remeasured to reflect changes in the value of that equity interest before vesting date. That is inconsistent with the *Framework* because equity interests are not subsequently remeasured, ie any changes in their value are not recognised. The Discussion Paper justified this remeasurement by arguing that because the share option is not issued until vesting date, the option is not being remeasured. The credit to equity during the vesting period is merely an interim measure that is used to recognise the partially completed transaction.

BC101 However, the Board noted that even if one accepts that the share option is not issued until vesting date, this does not mean that there is no equity interest until then. If an equity interest exists before vesting date, that interest should not be remeasured. Moreover, the conversion of one type of equity interest into another should not, in itself, cause a change in total equity, because no change in net assets has occurred.

BC102 Some supporters of vesting date suggest that the accrual during the performance period meets the definition of a liability. However, the basis for this conclusion is unclear. The entity is not required to transfer cash or other assets to the employees. Its only commitment is to issue equity instruments.

BC103 The Board concluded that vesting date measurement is inconsistent with the *Framework*, because it requires the remeasurement of equity.

BC104 Service date measurement does not require remeasurement of equity interests after initial recognition. However, as explained earlier, the Board concluded that incorporating changes in the fair value of the share option into the transaction amount is unlikely to produce an amount that fairly reflects the fair value of the services received, which is the primary objective.

BC105 The Board therefore concluded that, no matter which side of the transaction one focuses upon (ie the receipt of resources or the issue of an equity instrument), grant date is the appropriate measurement date under the *Framework*, because it does not require remeasurement of equity interests and it provides a reasonable surrogate measure of the fair value of the services received from employees.

Other issues

IAS 32 Financial Instruments: Disclosure and Presentation[*]

BC106 As discussed above, under the definitions of liabilities and equity in the *Framework*, both shares and share options are equity instruments, because neither instrument requires the entity to transfer cash or other assets. Similarly, all contracts or arrangements that will be settled by the entity issuing shares or share options are classified as equity. However, this differs from the distinction between liabilities and equity applied in IAS 32. Although IAS 32 also considers, in its debt/equity distinction, whether an instrument contains an obligation to

---

[*] In August 2005 IAS 32 was amended as IAS 32 *Financial Instruments: Presentation*.

transfer cash or other assets, this is supplemented by a second criterion, which considers whether the number of shares to be issued (and cash to be received) on settlement is fixed or variable. IAS 32 classifies a contract that will or may be settled in the entity's own equity instruments as a liability if the contract is a non-derivative for which the entity is or may be obliged to deliver a variable number of the entity's own equity instruments; or a derivative that will or may be settled other than by the exchange of a fixed amount of cash or another financial asset for a fixed number of the entity's own equity instruments.

BC107 In some cases, the number of share options to which employees are entitled varies. For example, the number of share options to which the employees will be entitled on vesting date might vary depending on whether, and to the extent that, a particular performance target is exceeded. Another example is share appreciation rights settled in shares. In this situation, a variable number of shares will be issued, equal in value to the appreciation of the entity's share price over a period of time.

BC108 Therefore, if the requirements of IAS 32 were applied to equity-settled share-based payment transactions, in some situations an obligation to issue equity instruments would be classified as a liability. In such cases, final measurement of the transaction would be at a measurement date later than grant date.

BC109 The Board concluded that different considerations applied in developing IFRS 2. For example, drawing a distinction between fixed and variable option plans and requiring a later measurement date for variable option plans has undesirable consequences, as discussed in paragraphs BC272–BC275.

BC110 The Board concluded that the requirements in IAS 32, whereby some obligations to issue equity instruments are classified as liabilities, should not be applied in the IFRS on share-based payment. The Board recognises that this creates a difference between IFRS 2 and IAS 32. Before deciding whether and how that difference should be eliminated, the Board concluded that it is necessary to address this issue in a broader context, as part of a fundamental review of the definitions of liabilities and equity in the *Framework*, particularly because this is not the only debt/equity classification issue that has arisen in the share-based payment project, as explained below.

Suggestions to change the definitions of liabilities and equity

BC111 In concluding that, for transactions with employees, grant date is the appropriate measurement date under the *Framework*, the Board noted that some respondents to ED 2 and the Discussion Paper support other measurement dates because they believe that the definitions of liabilities and equity in the *Framework* should be revised.

BC112 For example, some supporters of vesting date argue that receipt of employee services between grant date and vesting date creates an obligation for the entity to pay for those services, and that the method of settlement should not matter. In other words, it should not matter whether that obligation is settled in cash or in equity instruments—both ought to be treated as liabilities. Therefore, the definition of a liability should be modified so that all types of obligations, however settled, are included in liabilities. But it is not clear that this approach would necessarily result in vesting date measurement. A share option contains an obligation to issue shares. Hence, if all types of obligations are classified as liabilities, then a share option would be a liability, which would result in exercise date measurement.

BC113 Some support exercise date measurement on the grounds that it produces the same accounting result as 'economically similar' cash-settled share-based payments. For example, it is argued that share appreciation rights (SARs) settled in cash are substantially similar to SARs settled in shares, because in both cases the employee receives consideration to the same value. Also, if the SARs are settled in shares and the shares are immediately sold, the employee ends up in exactly the same position as under a cash-settled SAR, ie with cash equal to the appreciation in the entity's share price over the specified period. Similarly, some argue that share options and cash-settled SARs are economically similar. This is particularly true when the employee realises the gain on the exercise of share options by selling the shares immediately after exercise, as commonly occurs. Either way, the employee ends up with an amount of cash that is based on the appreciation of the share price over a period of time. If cash-settled transactions and equity-settled transactions are economically similar, the accounting treatment should be the same.

BC114 However, it is not clear that changing the distinction between liabilities and equity to be consistent with exercise date measurement is the only way to achieve the same accounting treatment. For example, the distinction could be changed so that cash-settled employee share plans are measured at grant date, with the subsequent cash payment debited directly to equity, as a distribution to equity participants.

BC115 Others who support exercise date measurement do not regard share option holders as part of the ownership group, and therefore believe that options should not be classified as equity. Option holders, some argue, are only potential owners of the entity. But it is not clear whether this view is held generally, ie applied to all types of options. For example, some who support exercise date measurement for employee share options do not necessarily advocate the same approach for share options or warrants issued for cash in the market. However, any revision to the definitions of liabilities and equity in the *Framework* would affect the classification of all options and warrants issued by the entity.

BC116 Given that there is more than one suggestion to change the definitions of liabilities and equity, and these suggestions have not been fully explored, it is not clear exactly what changes to the definitions are being proposed.

BC117 Moreover, the Board concluded that these suggestions should not be considered in isolation, because changing the distinction between liabilities and equity affects all sorts of financial interests, not just those relating to employee share plans. All of the implications of any suggested changes should be explored in a broader project to review the definitions of liabilities and equity in the *Framework*. If such a review resulted in changes to the definitions, the Board would then consider whether the IFRS on share-based payment should be revised.

BC118   Therefore, after considering the issues discussed above, the Board confirmed its conclusion that grant date is the appropriate date at which to measure the fair value of the equity instruments granted for the purposes of providing a surrogate measure of the fair value of services received from employees.

Share-based payment transactions with parties other than employees

BC119   In many share-based payment transactions with parties other than employees, it should be possible to measure reliably the fair value of the goods or services received. The Board therefore concluded that the IFRS should require an entity to presume that the fair value of the goods or services received can be measured reliably.* However, in rare cases in which the presumption is rebutted, it is necessary to measure the transaction at the fair value of the equity instruments granted.

BC120   Some measurement issues that arise in respect of share-based payment transactions with employees also arise in transactions with other parties. For example, there might be performance (ie vesting) conditions that must be met before the other party is entitled to the shares or share options. Therefore, any conclusions reached on how to treat vesting conditions in the context of share-based payment transactions with employees also apply to transactions with other parties.

BC121   Similarly, performance by the other party might take place over a period of time, rather than on one specific date, which again raises the question of the appropriate measurement date.

BC122   SFAS 123 does not specify a measurement date for share-based payment transactions with parties other than employees, on the grounds that this is usually a minor issue in such transactions. However, the date at which to estimate the fair value of equity instruments issued to parties other than employees is specified in the US interpretation EITF 96-18 *Accounting for Equity Instruments That Are Issued to Other Than Employees for Acquiring, or in Conjunction with Selling, Goods or Services*:

> [The measurement date is] the earlier of the following:
>
> (a)   The date at which a commitment for performance by the counterparty to earn the equity instruments is reached (a "performance commitment"), or
>
> (b)   The date at which the counterparty's performance is complete.
> (extract from Issue 1, footnotes excluded)

---

*   ED 2 proposed that equity-settled share-based payment transactions should be measured at the fair value of the goods or services received, or by reference to the fair value of the equity instruments granted, whichever fair value is more readily determinable. For transactions with parties other than employees, ED 2 proposed that there should be a rebuttable presumption that the fair value of the goods or services received is the more readily determinable fair value. The Board reconsidered these proposed requirements when finalising the IFRS. It concluded that it would be more consistent with the primary accounting objective (explained in paragraphs BC64–BC66) to require equity-settled share-based payment transactions to be measured at the fair value of the goods or services received, unless that fair value cannot be estimated reliably (eg in transactions with employees). For transactions with parties other than employees, the Board concluded that, in many cases, it should be possible to measure reliably the fair value of the goods or services received, as noted above. Hence, the Board concluded that the IFRS should require an entity to presume that the fair value of the goods or services received can be measured reliably.

BC123   The second of these two dates corresponds to vesting date, because vesting date is when the other party has satisfied all the conditions necessary to become unconditionally entitled to the share options or shares. The first of the two dates does not necessarily correspond to grant date. For example, under an employee share plan, the employees are (usually) not committed to providing the necessary services, because they are usually able to leave at any time. Indeed, EITF 96-18 makes it clear that the fact that the equity instrument will be forfeited if the counterparty fails to perform is not sufficient evidence of a performance commitment (Issue 1, footnote 3). Therefore, in the context of share-based payment transactions with parties other than employees, if the other party is not committed to perform, there would be no performance commitment date, in which case the measurement date would be vesting date.

BC124   Accordingly, under SFAS 123 and EITF 96-18, the measurement date for share-based payment transactions with employees is grant date, but for transactions with other parties the measurement date could be vesting date, or some other date between grant date and vesting date.

BC125   In developing the proposals in ED 2, the Board concluded that for transactions with parties other than employees that are measured by reference to the fair value of the equity instruments granted, the equity instruments should be measured at grant date, the same as for transactions with employees.

BC126   However, the Board reconsidered this conclusion during its redeliberations of the proposals in ED 2. The Board considered whether the delivery (service) date fair value of the equity instruments granted provided a better surrogate measure of the fair value of the goods or services received from parties other than employees than the grant date fair value of those instruments. For example, some argue that if the counterparty is not firmly committed to delivering the goods or services, the counterparty would consider whether the fair value of the equity instruments at the delivery date is sufficient payment for the goods or services when deciding whether to deliver the goods or services. This suggests that there is a high correlation between the fair value of the equity instruments at the date the goods or services are received and the fair value of those goods or services. The Board noted that it had considered and rejected a similar argument in the context of transactions with employees (see paragraphs BC94 and BC95). However, the Board found the argument more compelling in the case of transactions with parties other than employees, particularly for transactions in which the counterparty delivers the goods or services on a single date (or over a short period of time) that is substantially later than grant date, compared with transactions with employees in which the services are received over a continuous period that typically begins on grant date.

BC127   The Board was also concerned that permitting entities to measure transactions with parties other than employees on the basis of the fair value of the equity instruments at grant date would provide opportunities for entities to structure transactions to achieve a particular accounting result, causing the carrying amount of the goods or services received, and the resulting expense for the consumption of those goods or services, to be understated.

BC128   The Board therefore concluded that for transactions with parties other than employees in which the entity cannot measure reliably the fair value of the goods or services received at the date of receipt, the fair value of those goods or services should be measured indirectly, based on the fair value of the equity instruments granted, measured at the date the goods or services are received.

Transactions in which the entity cannot identify specifically some or all of the goods or services received (paragraph 13A)[*]

BC128A   The Board incorporated into IFRS 2 the consensus of IFRIC 8 in *Group Cash-settled Share-based Payment Transactions* issued in June 2009. This section summarises the IFRIC's considerations in reaching that consensus, as approved by the Board.

BC128B   IFRS 2 presumes that the consideration received for share-based payments is consistent with the fair value of those share-based payments. For example, if the entity cannot estimate reliably the fair value of the goods or services received, paragraph 10 of the IFRS requires the entity to measure the fair value of the goods or services received by reference to the fair value of the share-based payment made to acquire those goods or services.

BC128C   The Board noted that it is neither necessary nor appropriate to measure the fair value of goods or services as well as the fair value of the share-based payment for every transaction in which the entity receives goods or non-employee services. However, when the value of the identifiable consideration received appears to be less than the fair value of the share-based payment, measurement of both the goods or the services received and the share-based payment may be necessary in order to measure the value of the unidentifiable goods or services received.

BC128D   Paragraph 13 of the IFRS stipulates a rebuttable presumption that the value of identifiable goods or services received can be reliably measured. The Board noted that goods or services that are unidentifiable cannot be reliably measured and that this rebuttable presumption is relevant only for identifiable goods or services.

BC128E   The Board noted that when the goods or services received are identifiable, the measurement principles in the IFRS should be applied. When the goods or services received are unidentifiable, the Board concluded that the grant date is the most appropriate date for the purposes of providing a surrogate measure of the value of the unidentifiable goods or services received (or to be received).

BC128F   The Board noted that some transactions include identifiable and unidentifiable goods or services. In this case, it would be necessary to measure at the grant date the fair value of the unidentifiable goods or services received and to measure the value of the identifiable goods or services in accordance with the IFRS.

BC128G   For cash-settled transactions in which unidentifiable goods or services are received, it is necessary to remeasure the liability at each subsequent reporting date in order to be consistent with the IFRS.

---

[*]   Paragraphs BC128A–BC128H are added as a consequence of amendments to IFRS 2 *Group Cash-settled Share-based Payment Transactions* issued in June 2009.

           © IASCF

BC128H The Board noted that the IFRS's requirements in respect of the recognition of the expense arising from share-based payments would apply to identifiable and unidentifiable goods or services. Therefore, the Board decided not to issue additional guidance on this point.

Fair value of employee share options

BC129 The Board spent much time discussing how to measure the fair value of employee share options, including how to take into account common features of employee share options, such as vesting conditions and non-transferability. These discussions focused on measuring fair value at grant date, not only because the Board regarded grant date as the appropriate measurement date for transactions with employees, but also because more measurement issues arise at grant date than at later measurement dates. In reaching its conclusions in ED 2, the Board received assistance from the project's Advisory Group and from a panel of experts. During its redeliberations of the proposals in ED 2, the Board considered comments by respondents and advice received from valuation experts on the FASB's Option Valuation Group.

BC130 Market prices provide the best evidence of the fair value of share options. However, share options with terms and conditions similar to employee share options are seldom traded in the markets. The Board therefore concluded that, if market prices are not available, it will be necessary to apply an option pricing model to estimate the fair value of share options.

BC131 The Board decided that it is not necessary or appropriate to prescribe the precise formula or model to be used for option valuation. There is no particular option pricing model that is regarded as theoretically superior to the others, and there is the risk that any model specified might be superseded by improved methodologies in the future. Entities should select whichever model is most appropriate in the circumstances. For example, many employee share options have long lives, are usually exercisable during the period between vesting date and the end of the option's life, and are often exercised early. These factors should be considered when estimating the grant date fair value of share options. For many entities, this might preclude the use of the Black-Scholes-Merton formula, which does not take into account the possibility of exercise before the end of the share option's life and may not adequately reflect the effects of expected early exercise. This is discussed further below (paragraphs BC160–BC162).

BC132 All option pricing models take into account the following option features:

- the exercise price of the option

- the current market price of the share

- the expected volatility of the share price

- the dividends expected to be paid on the shares

- the rate of interest available in the market

- the term of the option.

BC133 The first two items define the intrinsic value of a share option; the remaining four are relevant to the share option's time value. Expected volatility, dividends and interest rate are all based on expectations over the option term. Therefore, the option term is an important part of calculating time value, because it affects the other inputs.

BC134 One aspect of time value is the value of the right to participate in future gains, if any. The valuation does not attempt to predict what the future gain will be, only the amount that a buyer would pay at the valuation date to obtain the right to participate in any future gains. In other words, option pricing models estimate the value of the share option at the measurement date, not the value of the underlying share at some future date.

BC135 The Board noted that some argue that any estimate of the fair value of a share option is inherently uncertain, because it is not known what the ultimate outcome will be, eg whether the share option will expire worthless or whether the employee (or other party) will make a large gain on exercise. However, the valuation objective is to measure the fair value of the rights granted, not to predict the outcome of having granted those rights. Hence, irrespective of whether the option expires worthless or the employee makes a large gain on exercise, that outcome does not mean that the grant date estimate of the fair value of the option was unreliable or wrong.

BC136 A similar analysis applies to the argument that share options do not have any value until they are in the money, ie the share price is greater than the exercise price. This argument refers to the share option's intrinsic value only. Share options also have a time value, which is why they are traded in the markets at prices greater than their intrinsic value. The option holder has a valuable right to participate in any future increases in the share price. So even share options that are at the money have a value when granted. The subsequent outcome of that option grant, even if it expires worthless, does not change the fact that the share option had a value at grant date.

Application of option pricing models to unlisted and newly listed entities

BC137 As explained above, two of the inputs to an option pricing model are the entity's share price and the expected volatility of its share price. For an unlisted entity, there is no published share price information. The entity would therefore need to estimate the fair value of its shares (eg based on the share price of similar entities that are listed, or on a net assets or earnings basis). It would also need to estimate the expected volatility of that value.

BC138 The Board considered whether unlisted entities should be permitted to use the minimum value method instead of a fair value measurement method. The minimum value method is explained earlier, in paragraphs BC80–BC83. Because it excludes the effects of expected volatility, the minimum value method produces a value that is lower, often much lower, than that produced by methods designed to estimate the fair value of an option. Therefore, the Board discussed how an unlisted entity could estimate expected volatility.

BC139   An unlisted entity that regularly issues share options or shares to employees (or other parties) might have an internal market for its shares. The volatility of the internal market share prices provides a basis for estimating expected volatility. Alternatively, an entity could use the historical or implied volatility of similar entities that are listed, and for which share price or option price information is available, as the basis for an estimate of expected volatility. This would be appropriate if the entity has estimated the value of its shares by reference to the share prices of these similar listed entities. If the entity has instead used another methodology to value its shares, the entity could derive an estimate of expected volatility consistent with that methodology. For example, the entity might value its shares on the basis of net asset values or earnings, in which case it could use the expected volatility of those net asset values or earnings as a basis for estimating expected share price volatility.

BC140   The Board acknowledged that these approaches for estimating the expected volatility of an unlisted entity's shares are somewhat subjective. However, the Board thought it likely that, in practice, the application of these approaches would result in underestimates of expected volatility, rather than overestimates, because entities were likely to exercise caution in making such estimates, to ensure that the resulting option values are not overstated. Therefore, estimating expected volatility is likely to produce a more reliable measure of the fair value of share options granted by unlisted entities than an alternative valuation method, such as the minimum value method.

BC141   Newly listed entities would not need to estimate their share price. However, like unlisted entities, newly listed entities could have difficulties in estimating expected volatility when valuing share options, because they might not have sufficient historical share price information upon which to base an estimate of expected volatility.

BC142   SFAS 123 requires such entities to consider the historical volatility of similar entities during a comparable period in their lives:

> For example, an entity that has been publicly traded for only one year that grants options with an average expected life of five years might consider the pattern and level of historical volatility of more mature entities in the same industry for the first six years the stock of those entities were publicly traded. (paragraph 285b)

BC143   The Board concluded that, in general, unlisted and newly listed entities should not be exempt from a requirement to apply fair value measurement and that the IFRS should include implementation guidance on estimating expected volatility for the purposes of applying an option pricing model to share options granted by unlisted and newly listed entities.

BC144   However, the Board acknowledged that there might be some instances in which an entity—such as (but not limited to) an unlisted or newly listed entity—cannot estimate reliably the grant date fair value of share options granted. In this situation, the Board concluded that the entity should measure the share option at its intrinsic value, initially at the date the entity obtains the goods or the counterparty renders service and subsequently at each reporting date until the final settlement of the share-based payment arrangement, with the effects of the remeasurement recognised in profit or loss. For a grant of share options, the share-based payment arrangement is finally settled when the options are exercised, forfeited (eg upon cessation of employment) or lapse (eg at the end of the option's life). For a grant of shares, the share-based payment arrangement is finally settled when the shares vest or are forfeited.

Application of option pricing models to employee share options

BC145 Option pricing models are widely used in, and accepted by, the financial markets. However, there are differences between employee share options and traded share options. The Board considered the valuation implications of these differences, with assistance from its Advisory Group and other experts, including experts in the FASB's Option Valuation Group, and comments made by respondents to ED 2. Employee share options usually differ from traded options in the following ways, which are discussed further below:

(a) there is a vesting period, during which time the share options are not exercisable;

(b) the options are non-transferable;

(c) there are conditions attached to vesting which, if not satisfied, cause the options to be forfeited; and

(d) the option term is significantly longer.

Inability to exercise during the vesting period

BC146 Typically, employee share options have a vesting period, during which the options cannot be exercised. For example, a share option might be granted with a ten-year life and a vesting period of three years, so the option is not exercisable for the first three years and can then be exercised at any time during the remaining seven years. Employee share options cannot be exercised during the vesting period because the employees must first 'pay' for the options, by providing the necessary services. Furthermore, there might be other specified periods during which an employee share option cannot be exercised (eg during a closed period).

BC147 In the finance literature, employee share options are sometimes called Bermudian options, being partly European and partly American. An American share option can be exercised at any time during the option's life, whereas a European share option can be exercised only at the end of the option's life. An American share option is more valuable than a European share option, although the difference in value is not usually significant.

BC148 Therefore, other things being equal, an employee share option would have a higher value than a European share option and a lower value than an American share option, but the difference between the three values is unlikely to be significant.

BC149 If the entity uses the Black-Scholes-Merton formula, or another option pricing model that values European share options, there is no need to adjust the model for the inability to exercise an option in the vesting period (or any other period), because the model already assumes that the option cannot be exercised during that period.

BC150   If the entity uses an option pricing model that values American share options, such as the binomial model, the inability to exercise an option during the vesting period can be taken into account in applying such a model.

BC151   Although the inability to exercise the share option during the vesting period does not, in itself, have a significant effect on the value of the option, there is still the question whether this restriction has an effect when combined with non-transferability. This is discussed in the following section.

BC152   The Board therefore concluded that:

(a)   if the entity uses an option pricing model that values European share options, such as the Black-Scholes-Merton formula, no adjustment is required for the inability to exercise the options during the vesting period, because the model already assumes that they cannot be exercised during that period.

(b)   if the entity uses an option pricing model that values American share options, such as a binomial model, the application of the model should take account of the inability to exercise the options during the vesting period.

Non-transferability

BC153   From the option holder's perspective, the inability to transfer a share option limits the opportunities available when the option has some time yet to run and the holder wishes either to terminate the exposure to future price changes or to liquidate the position. For example, the holder might believe that over the remaining term of the share option the share price is more likely to decrease than to increase. Also, employee share option plans typically require employees to exercise vested options within a fixed period of time after the employee leaves the entity, or to forfeit the options.

BC154   In the case of a conventional share option, the holder would sell the option rather than exercise it and then sell the shares. Selling the share option enables the holder to receive the option's fair value, including both its intrinsic value and remaining time value, whereas exercising the option enables the holder to receive intrinsic value only.

BC155   However, the option holder is not able to sell a non-transferable share option. Usually, the only possibility open to the option holder is to exercise it, which entails forgoing the remaining time value. (This is not always true. The use of other derivatives, in effect, to sell or gain protection from future changes in the value of the option is discussed later.)

BC156   At first sight, the inability to transfer a share option could seem irrelevant from the entity's perspective, because the entity must issue shares at the exercise price upon exercise of the option, no matter who holds it. In other words, from the entity's perspective, its commitments under the contract are unaffected by whether the shares are issued to the original option holder or to someone else. Therefore, in valuing the entity's side of the contract, from the entity's perspective, non-transferability seems irrelevant.

BC157　However, the lack of transferability often results in early exercise of the share option, because that is the only way for the employees to liquidate their position. Therefore, by imposing the restriction on transferability, the entity has caused the option holder to exercise the option early, thereby resulting in the loss of time value. For example, one aspect of time value is the value of the right to defer payment of the exercise price until the end of the option term. If the option is exercised early because of non-transferability, the entity receives the exercise price much earlier than it would otherwise have done.

BC158　Non-transferability is not the only reason why employees might exercise share options early. Other reasons include risk aversion, lack of wealth diversification, and termination of employment (typically, employees must exercise vested options soon after termination of employment; otherwise the options are forfeited).

BC159　Recent accounting standards and proposed standards (including ED 2) address the issue of early exercise by requiring the expected life of a non-transferable share option to be used in valuing it, rather than the contractual option term. Expected life can be estimated either for the entire share option plan or for subgroups of employees participating in the plan. The estimate takes into account factors such as the length of the vesting period, the average length of time similar options have remained outstanding in the past and the expected volatility of the underlying shares.

BC160　However, comments from respondents to ED 2 and advice received from valuation experts during the Board's redeliberations led the Board to conclude that using a single expected life as an input into an option pricing model (eg the Black-Scholes-Merton formula) was not the best solution for reflecting in the share option valuation the effects of early exercise. For example, such an approach does not take into account the correlation between the share price and early exercise. It would also mean that the share option valuation does not take into account the possibility that the option might be exercised at a date that is later than the end of its expected life. Therefore, in many instances, a more flexible model, such as a binomial model, that uses the share option's contractual life as an input and takes into account the possibility of early exercise on a range of different dates in the option's life, allowing for factors such as the correlation between the share price and early exercise and expected employee turnover, is likely to produce a more accurate estimate of the option's fair value.

BC161　Binomial lattice and similar option pricing models also have the advantage of permitting the inputs to the model to vary over the share option's life. For example, instead of using a single expected volatility, a binomial lattice or similar option pricing model can allow for the possibility that volatility might change over the share option's life. This would be particularly appropriate when valuing share options granted by entities experiencing higher than usual volatility, because volatility tends to revert to its mean over time.

BC162　For these reasons, the Board considered whether it should require the use of a more flexible model, rather than the more commonly used Black-Scholes-Merton formula. However, the Board concluded that it was not necessary to prohibit the use of the Black-Scholes-Merton formula, because there might be instances in which the formula produces a sufficiently reliable estimate of the fair value of the share options granted. For example, if the entity has not granted many share options, the effects of applying a more flexible model might not have a material impact on the entity's financial statements. Also, for share options with relatively short contractual lives, or share options that must be exercised within a short period of time after vesting date, the issues discussed in paragraph BC160 may not be relevant, and hence the Black-Scholes-Merton formula may produce a value that is substantially the same as that produced by a more flexible option pricing model. Therefore, rather than prohibit the use of the Black-Scholes-Merton formula, the Board concluded that the IFRS should include guidance on selecting the most appropriate model to apply. This includes the requirement that the entity should consider factors that knowledgeable, willing market participants would consider in selecting the option pricing model to apply.

BC163 Although non-transferability often results in the early exercise of employee share options, some employees can mitigate the effects of non-transferability, because they are able, in effect, to sell the options or protect themselves from future changes in the value of the options by selling or buying other derivatives. For example, the employee might be able, in effect, to sell an employee share option by entering into an arrangement with an investment bank whereby the employee sells a similar call option to the bank, ie an option with the same exercise price and term. A zero-cost collar is one means of obtaining protection from changes in the value of an employee share option, by selling a call option and buying a put option.

BC164 However, it appears that such arrangements are not always available. For example, the amounts involved have to be sufficiently large to make it worthwhile for the investment bank, which would probably exclude many employees (unless a collective arrangement was made). Also, it appears that investment banks are unlikely to enter into such an arrangement unless the entity is a top listed company, with shares traded in a deep and active market, to enable the investment bank to hedge its own position.

BC165 It would not be feasible to stipulate in an accounting standard that an adjustment to take account of non-transferability is necessary only if the employees cannot mitigate the effects of non-transferability through the use of other derivatives. However, using expected life as an input into an option pricing model, or modelling early exercise in a binomial or similar model, copes with both situations. If employees were able to mitigate the effects of non-transferability by using derivatives, this would often result in the employee share options being exercised later than they would otherwise have been. By taking this factor into account, the estimated fair value of the share option would be higher, which makes sense, given that non-transferability is not a constraint in this case. If the employees cannot mitigate the effects of non-transferability through the use of derivatives, they are likely to exercise the share options much earlier than is optimal. In this case, allowing for the effects of early exercise would significantly reduce the estimated value of the share option.

BC166 This still leaves the question whether there is a need for further adjustment for the combined effect of being unable to exercise or transfer the share option during the vesting period. In other words, the inability to exercise a share option does not, in itself, appear to have a significant effect on its value. But if the share option cannot be transferred and cannot be exercised, and assuming that other derivatives are not available, the holder is unable to extract value from the share option or protect its value during the vesting period.

BC167 However, it should be noted why these restrictions are in place: the employee has not yet 'paid' for the share option by providing the required services (and fulfilling any other performance conditions). The employee cannot exercise or transfer a share option to which he/she is not yet entitled. The share option will either vest or fail to vest, depending on whether the vesting conditions are satisfied. The possibility of forfeiture resulting from failure to fulfil the vesting conditions is taken into account through the application of the modified grant date method (discussed in paragraphs BC170–BC184).

BC168 Moreover, for accounting purposes, the objective is to estimate the fair value of the share option, not the value from the employee's perspective. The fair value of any item depends on the expected amounts, timing, and uncertainty of the future cash flows relating to the item. The share option grant gives the employee the right to subscribe to the entity's shares at the exercise price, provided that the vesting conditions are satisfied and the exercise price is paid during the specified period. The effect of the vesting conditions is considered below. The effect of the share option being non-exercisable during the vesting period has already been considered above, as has the effect of non-transferability. There does not seem to be any additional effect on the expected amounts, timing or uncertainty of the future cash flows arising from the combination of non-exercisability and non-transferability during the vesting period.

BC169 After considering all of the above points, the Board concluded that the effects of early exercise, because of non-transferability and other factors, should be taken into account when estimating the fair value of the share option, either by modelling early exercise in a binomial or similar model, or using expected life rather than contracted life as an input into an option pricing model, such as the Black-Scholes-Merton formula.

Vesting conditions

BC170 Employee share options usually have vesting conditions. The most common condition is that the employee must remain in the entity's employ for a specified period, say three years. If the employee leaves during that period, the options are forfeited. There might also be other performance conditions, eg that the entity achieves a specified growth in share price or earnings.

BC171 Vesting conditions ensure that the employees provide the services required to 'pay' for their share options. For example, the usual reason for imposing service conditions is to retain staff; the usual reason for imposing other performance conditions is to provide an incentive for the employees to work towards specified performance targets.

BC171A In 2005 the Board decided to take on a project to clarify the definition of vesting conditions and the accounting treatment of cancellations. In particular, the Board noted that it is important to distinguish between non-vesting conditions, which need to be satisfied for the counterparty to become entitled to the equity instrument, and vesting conditions such as performance conditions. In February 2006 the Board published an exposure draft *Vesting Conditions and Cancellations*, which proposed to restrict vesting conditions to service conditions and performance conditions. Those are the only conditions that determine whether *the entity receives the services* that entitle the counterparty to the share-based payment, and therefore whether the share-based payment vests. In particular, a share-based payment may vest even if some non-vesting conditions have not been met. The feature that distinguishes a performance condition from a non-vesting condition is that the former has an explicit or implicit service requirement and the latter does not.

BC171B In general, respondents to the exposure draft agreed with the Board's proposals but asked for clarification of whether particular restrictive conditions, such as 'non-compete provisions', are vesting conditions. The Board noted that a share-based payment vests when the counterparty's entitlement to it is no longer conditional on future service or performance conditions. Therefore, conditions such as non-compete provisions and transfer restrictions, which apply after the counterparty has become entitled to the share-based payment, are not vesting conditions. The Board revised the definition of 'vest' accordingly.

BC172 Some argue that the existence of vesting conditions does not necessarily imply that the value of employee share options is significantly less than the value of traded share options. The employees have to satisfy the vesting conditions to fulfil their side of the arrangement. In other words, the employees' performance of their side of the arrangement is what they do to pay for their share options. Employees do not pay for the options with cash, as do the holders of traded share options; they pay with their services. Having to pay for the share options does not make them less valuable. On the contrary, it proves that the share options are valuable.

BC173 Others argue that the possibility of forfeiture without compensation for part-performance suggests that the share options are less valuable. The employees might partly perform their side of the arrangement, eg by working for part of the period, then have to leave for some reason, and forfeit the share options without compensation for that part performance. If there are other performance conditions, such as achieving a specified growth in the share price or earnings, the employees might work for the entire vesting period, but fail to meet the vesting conditions and therefore forfeit the share options.

BC174 Similarly, some argue that the entity would take into account the possibility of forfeiture when entering into the agreement at grant date. In other words, in deciding how many share options to grant in total, the entity would allow for expected forfeitures. Hence, if the objective is to estimate at grant date the fair value of the entity's commitments under the share option agreement, that valuation should take into account that the entity's commitment to fulfil its side of the option agreement is conditional upon the vesting conditions being satisfied.

BC175   In developing the proposals in ED 2, the Board concluded that the valuation of rights to share options or shares granted to employees (or other parties) should take into account all types of vesting conditions, including both service conditions and performance conditions. In other words, the grant date valuation should be reduced to allow for the possibility of forfeiture due to failure to satisfy the vesting conditions.

BC176   Such a reduction might be achieved by adapting an option pricing model to incorporate vesting conditions. Alternatively, a more simplistic approach might be applied. One such approach is to estimate the possibility of forfeiture at grant date, and reduce the value produced by an option pricing model accordingly. For example, if the valuation calculated using an option pricing model was CU15, and the entity estimated that 20 per cent of the share options would be forfeited because of failure to satisfy the vesting conditions, allowing for the possibility of forfeiture would reduce the grant date value of each option granted from CU15 to CU12.

BC177   The Board decided against proposing detailed guidance on how the grant date value should be adjusted to allow for the possibility of forfeiture. This is consistent with the Board's objective of setting principles-based standards. The measurement objective is to estimate fair value. That objective might not be achieved if detailed, prescriptive rules were specified, which would probably become outdated by future developments in valuation methodologies.

BC178   However, respondents to ED 2 raised a variety of concerns about the inclusion of vesting conditions in the grant date valuation. Some respondents were concerned about the practicality and subjectivity of including non-market performance conditions in the share option valuation. Some were also concerned about the practicality of including service conditions in the grant date valuation, particularly in conjunction with the units of service method proposed in ED 2 (discussed further in paragraphs BC203–BC217).

BC179   Some respondents suggested the alternative approach applied in SFAS 123, referred to as the modified grant date method. Under this method, service conditions and non-market performance conditions are excluded from the grant date valuation (ie the possibility of forfeiture is not taken into account when estimating the grant date fair value of the share options or other equity instruments, thereby producing a higher grant date fair value), but are instead taken into account by requiring the transaction amount to be based on the number of equity instruments that eventually vest. Under this method, on a cumulative basis, no amount is recognised for goods or services received if the equity instruments granted do not vest because of failure to satisfy a vesting condition (other than a market condition), eg the counterparty fails to complete a specified service period, or a performance condition (other than a market condition) is not satisfied.

BC180   After considering respondents' comments and obtaining further advice from valuation experts, the Board decided to adopt the modified grant date method applied in SFAS 123. However, the Board decided that it should not permit the choice available in SFAS 123 to account for the effects of expected or actual forfeitures of share options or other equity instruments because of failure to satisfy a service condition. For a grant of equity instruments with a service condition, SFAS 123 permits an entity to choose at grant date to recognise the services received based on an estimate of the number of share options or other equity instruments expected to vest, and to revise that estimate, if necessary, if subsequent information indicates that actual forfeitures are likely to differ from previous estimates. Alternatively, an entity may begin recognising the services received as if all the equity instruments granted that are subject to a service requirement are expected to vest. The effects of forfeitures are then recognised when those forfeitures occur, by reversing any amounts previously recognised for services received as consideration for equity instruments that are forfeited.

BC181　The Board decided that the latter method should not be permitted. Given that the transaction amount is ultimately based on the number of equity instruments that vest, it is appropriate to estimate the number of expected forfeitures when recognising the services received during the vesting period. Furthermore, by ignoring expected forfeitures until those forfeitures occur, the effects of reversing any amounts previously recognised might result in a distortion of remuneration expense recognised during the vesting period. For example, an entity that experiences a high level of forfeitures might recognise a large amount of remuneration expense in one period, which is then reversed in a later period.

BC182　Therefore, the Board decided that the IFRS should require an entity to estimate the number of equity instruments expected to vest and to revise that estimate, if necessary, if subsequent information indicates that actual forfeitures are likely to differ from previous estimates.

BC183　Under SFAS 123, market conditions (eg a condition involving a target share price, or specified amount of intrinsic value on which vesting or exercisability is conditioned) are included in the grant date valuation, without subsequent reversal. That is to say, when estimating the fair value of the equity instruments at grant date, the entity takes into account the possibility that the market condition may not be satisfied. Having allowed for that possibility in the grant date valuation of the equity instruments, no adjustment is made to the number of equity instruments included in the calculation of the transaction amount, irrespective of the outcome of the market condition. In other words, the entity recognises the goods or services received from a counterparty that satisfies all other vesting conditions (eg services received from an employee who remains in service for the specified service period), irrespective of whether that market condition is satisfied. The treatment of market conditions therefore contrasts with the treatment of other types of vesting conditions. As explained in paragraph BC179, under the modified grant date method, vesting conditions are not taken into account when estimating the fair value of the equity instruments at grant date, but are instead taken into account by requiring the transaction amount to be based on the number of equity instruments that eventually vest.

BC184　The Board considered whether it should apply the same approach to market conditions as is applied in SFAS 123. It might be argued that it is not appropriate to distinguish between market conditions and other types of performance conditions, because to do so could create opportunities for arbitrage, or cause an economic distortion by encouraging entities to favour one type of performance condition over another. However, the Board noted that it is not clear what the result would be. On the one hand, some entities might prefer the 'truing up' aspect of the modified grant date method, because it permits a reversal of remuneration expense if the condition is not met. On the other hand, if the performance condition is met, and it has not been incorporated into the grant date valuation (as is the case when the modified grant date method is used), the expense will be higher than it would otherwise have been (ie if the performance condition had been incorporated into the grant date valuation). Furthermore, some entities might prefer to avoid the potential volatility caused by the truing up mechanism. Therefore, it is not clear whether having a different treatment for market and non-market performance conditions will necessarily cause entities to favour market conditions over non-market performance conditions, or vice versa. Furthermore, the practical difficulties that led the Board to conclude that non-market performance conditions should be dealt with via the modified grant date method rather than being included in the grant date valuation do not apply to market conditions, because market conditions can be incorporated into option pricing models. Moreover, it is difficult to distinguish between market conditions, such as a target share price, and the market condition that is inherent in the option itself, ie that the option will be exercised only if the share price on the date of exercise exceeds the exercise price. For these reasons, the Board concluded that the IFRS should apply the same approach as is applied in SFAS 123.

Option term

BC185 Employee share options often have a long contractual life, eg ten years. Traded options typically have short lives, often only a few months. Estimating the inputs required by an option pricing model, such as expected volatility, over long periods can be difficult, giving rise to the possibility of significant estimation error. This is not usually a problem with traded share options, given their much shorter lives.

BC186 However, some share options traded over the counter have long lives, such as ten or fifteen years. Option pricing models are used to value them. Therefore, contrary to the argument sometimes advanced, option pricing models can be (and are being) applied to long-lived share options.

BC187 Moreover, the potential for estimation error is mitigated by using a binomial or similar model that allows for changes in model inputs over the share option's life, such as expected volatility, and interest and dividend rates, that could occur and the probability of those changes occurring during the term of the share option. The potential for estimation error is further mitigated by taking into account the possibility of early exercise, either by using expected life rather than contracted life as an input into an option pricing model or by modelling exercise behaviour in a binomial or similar model, because this reduces the expected term of the share option. Because employees often exercise their share options relatively early in the share option's life, the expected term is usually much shorter than contracted life.

Other features of employee share options

BC188 Whilst the features discussed above are common to most employee share options, some might include other features. For example, some share options have a reload feature. This entitles the employee to automatic grants of additional share options whenever he/she exercises previously granted share options and pays the exercise price in the entity's shares rather than in cash. Typically, the employee is granted a new share option, called a reload option, for each share surrendered when exercising the previous share option. The exercise price of the reload option is usually set at the market price of the shares on the date the reload option is granted.

BC189 When SFAS 123 was developed, the FASB concluded that, ideally, the value of the reload feature should be included in the valuation of the original share option at grant date. However, at that time the FASB believed that it was not possible to do so. Accordingly, SFAS 123 does not require the reload feature to be included in the grant date valuation of the original share option. Instead, reload options granted upon exercise of the original share options are accounted for as a new share option grant.

BC190 However, recent academic research indicates that it is possible to value the reload feature at grant date, eg Saly, Jagannathan and Huddart (1999).[*] However, if significant uncertainties exist, such as the number and timing of expected grants of reload options, it might not be practicable to include the reload feature in the grant date valuation.

BC191 When it developed ED 2, the Board concluded that the reload feature should be taken into account, where practicable, when measuring the fair value of the share options granted. However, if the reload feature was not taken into account, then when the reload option is granted, it should be accounted for as a new share option grant.

BC192 Many respondents to ED 2 agreed with the proposals in ED 2. However, some disagreed. For example, some disagreed with there being a choice of treatments. Some respondents supported always treating reload options granted as new grants whereas others supported always including the reload feature in the grant date valuation. Some expressed concerns about the practicality of including the reload feature in the grant date valuation. After reconsidering this issue, the Board concluded that the reload feature should not be included in the grant date valuation and therefore all reload options granted should be accounted for as new share option grants.

BC193 There may be other features of employee (and other) share options that the Board has not yet considered. But even if the Board were to consider every conceivable feature of employee (and other) share options that exist at present, new features might be developed in the future.

BC194 The Board therefore concluded that the IFRS should focus on setting out clear principles to be applied to share-based payment transactions, and provide guidance on the more common features of employee share options, but should not prescribe extensive application guidance, which would be likely to become outdated.

BC195 Nevertheless, the Board considered whether there are share options with such unusual or complex features that it is too difficult to make a reliable estimate of their fair value and, if so, what the accounting treatment should be.

---

[*] P J Saly, R Jagannathan and S J Huddart. 1999. Valuing the Reload Features of Executive Stock Options. *Accounting Horizons* 13 (3): 219–240.

BC196 SFAS 123 states that 'it should be possible to reasonably estimate the fair value of most stock options and other equity instruments at the date they are granted' (paragraph 21). However, it states that, 'in unusual circumstances, the terms of the stock option or other equity instrument may make it virtually impossible to reasonably estimate the instrument's fair value at the date it is granted'. The standard requires that, in such situations, measurement should be delayed until it is possible to estimate reasonably the instrument's fair value. It notes that this is likely to be the date at which the number of shares to which the employee is entitled and the exercise price are determinable. This could be vesting date. The standard requires that estimates of compensation expense for earlier periods (ie until it is possible to estimate fair value) should be based on current intrinsic value.

BC197 The Board thought it unlikely that entities could not reasonably determine the fair value of share options at grant date, particularly after excluding vesting conditions* and reload features from the grant date valuation. The share options form part of the employee's remuneration package, and it seems reasonable to presume that an entity's management would consider the value of the share options to satisfy itself that the employee's remuneration package is fair and reasonable.

BC198 When it developed ED 2, the Board concluded that there should be no exceptions to the requirement to apply a fair value measurement basis, and therefore it was not necessary to include in the proposed IFRS specific accounting requirements for share options that are difficult to value.

BC199 However, after considering respondents' comments, particularly with regard to unlisted entities, the Board reconsidered this issue. The Board concluded that, in rare cases only, in which the entity could not estimate reliably the grant date fair value of the equity instruments granted, the entity should measure the equity instruments at intrinsic value, initially at grant date and subsequently at each reporting date until the final settlement of the share-based payment arrangement, with the effects of the remeasurement recognised in profit or loss. For a grant of share options, the share-based payment arrangement is finally settled when the share options are exercised, are forfeited (eg upon cessation of employment) or lapse (eg at the end of the option's life). For a grant of shares, the share-based payment arrangement is finally settled when the shares vest or are forfeited. This requirement would apply to all entities, including listed and unlisted entities.

Recognition and measurement of services received in an equity-settled share-based payment transaction

During the vesting period

BC200 In an equity-settled share-based payment transaction, the accounting objective is to recognise the goods or services received as consideration for the entity's equity instruments, measured at the fair value of those goods or services when received. For transactions in which the entity receives employee services, it is often difficult

---

* ie vesting conditions other than market conditions.

to measure directly the fair value of the services received. In this case, the Board concluded that the fair value of the equity instruments granted should be used as a surrogate measure of the fair value of the services received. This raises the question how to use that surrogate measure to derive an amount to attribute to the services received. Another related question is how the entity should determine when the services are received.

BC201 Starting with the latter question, some argue that shares or share options are often granted to employees for past services rather than future services, or mostly for past services, irrespective of whether the employees are required to continue working for the entity for a specified future period before their rights to those shares or share options vest. Conversely, some argue that shares or share options granted provide a future incentive to the employees and those incentive effects continue after vesting date, which implies that the entity receives services from employees during a period that extends beyond vesting date. For share options in particular, some argue that employees render services beyond vesting date, because employees are able to benefit from an option's time value between vesting date and exercise date only if they continue to work for the entity (since usually a departing employee must exercise the share options within a short period, otherwise they are forfeited).

BC202 However, the Board concluded that if the employees are required to complete a specified service period to become entitled to the shares or share options, this requirement provides the best evidence of when the employees render services in return for the shares or share options. Consequently, the Board concluded that the entity should presume that the services are received during the vesting period. If the shares or share options vest immediately, it should be presumed that the entity has already received the services, in the absence of evidence to the contrary. An example of when immediately vested shares or share options are not for past services is when the employee concerned has only recently begun working for the entity, and the shares or share options are granted as a signing bonus. But in this situation, it might nevertheless be necessary to recognise an expense immediately, if the future employee services do not meet the definition of an asset.

BC203 Returning to the first question in paragraph BC200, when the Board developed ED 2 it developed an approach whereby the fair value of the shares or share options granted, measured at grant date and allowing for all vesting conditions, is divided by the number of units of service expected to be received to determine the deemed fair value of each unit of service subsequently received.

BC204 For example, suppose that the fair value of share options granted, before taking into account the possibility of forfeiture, is CU750,000. Suppose that the entity estimates the possibility of forfeiture because of failure of the employees to complete the required three-year period of service is 20 per cent (based on a weighted average probability), and hence it estimates the fair value of the options granted at CU600,000 (CU750,000 × 80%). The entity expects to receive 1,350 units of service over the three-year vesting period.

BC205   Under the units of service method proposed in ED 2, the deemed fair value per unit of service subsequently received is CU444.44 (CU600,000/1,350). If everything turns out as expected, the amount recognised for services received is CU600,000 (CU444.44 × 1,350).

BC206   This approach is based on the presumption that there is a fairly bargained contract at grant date. Thus the entity has granted share options valued at CU600,000 and expects to receive services valued at CU600,000 in return. It does not expect all share options granted to vest because it does not expect all employees to complete three years' service. Expectations of forfeiture because of employee departures are taken into account when estimating the fair value of the share options granted, and when determining the fair value of the services to be received in return.

BC207   Under the units of service method, the amount recognised for services received during the vesting period might exceed CU600,000, if the entity receives more services than expected. This is because the objective is to account for the services subsequently received, not the fair value of the share options granted. In other words, the objective is not to estimate the fair value of the share options granted and then spread that amount over the vesting period. Rather, the objective is to account for the services subsequently received, because it is the receipt of those services that causes a change in net assets and hence a change in equity. Because of the practical difficulty of valuing those services directly, the fair value of the share options granted is used as a surrogate measure to determine the fair value of each unit of service subsequently received, and therefore the transaction amount is dependent upon the number of units of service actually received. If more are received than expected, the transaction amount will be greater than CU600,000. If fewer services are received, the transaction amount will be less than CU600,000.

BC208   Hence, a grant date measurement method is used as a practical expedient to achieve the accounting objective, which is to account for the services actually received in the vesting period. The Board noted that many who support grant date measurement do so for reasons that focus on the entity's commitments under the contract, not the services received. They take the view that the entity has conveyed to its employees valuable equity instruments at grant date and that the accounting objective should be to account for the equity instruments conveyed. Similarly, supporters of vesting date measurement argue that the entity does not convey valuable equity instruments to the employees until vesting date, and that the accounting objective should be to account for the equity instruments conveyed at vesting date. Supporters of exercise date measurement argue that, ultimately, the valuable equity instruments conveyed by the entity to the employees are the shares issued on exercise date and the objective should be to account for the value given up by the entity by issuing equity instruments at less than their fair value.

BC209   Hence all of these arguments for various measurement dates are focused entirely on what the entity (or its shareholders) has given up under the share-based payment arrangement, and accounting for that sacrifice. Therefore, if 'grant date measurement' were applied as a matter of principle, the primary objective would be to account for the value of the rights granted. Depending on whether the services have already been received and whether a prepayment for services to be received in the future meets the definition of an asset, the other side of the transaction would either be recognised as an expense at grant date, or capitalised as a prepayment and amortised over some period of time, such as over the vesting period or over the expected life of the share option. Under this view of grant date measurement, there would be no subsequent adjustment for actual outcomes. No matter how many share options vest or how many share options are exercised, that does not change the value of the rights given to the employees at grant date.

BC210 Therefore, the reason why some support grant date measurement differs from the reason why the Board concluded that the fair value of the equity instruments granted should be measured at grant date. This means that some will have different views about the consequences of applying grant date measurement. Because the units of service method is based on using the fair value of the equity instruments granted, measured at grant date, as a surrogate measure of the fair value of the services received, the total transaction amount is dependent upon the number of units of service received.

BC211 Some respondents to ED 2 disagreed with the units of service method in principle, because they did not accept that the fair value of the services received should be the accounting focus. Rather, the respondents focused on accounting for the 'cost' of the equity instruments issued (ie the credit side of the transaction rather than the debit side), and took the view that if the share options or shares are forfeited, no cost was incurred, and thus any amounts recognised previously should be reversed, as would happen with a cash-settled transaction.

BC212 Some respondents also disagreed with the treatment of performance conditions under the units of service method, because if the employee completes the required service period but the equity instruments do not vest because of the performance condition not being satisfied, there is no reversal of amounts recognised during the vesting period. Some argue that this result is unreasonable because, if the performance condition is not satisfied, then the employee did not perform as required, hence it is inappropriate to recognise an expense for services received or consumed, because the entity did not receive the specified services.

BC213 The Board considered and rejected the above arguments made against the units of service method in principle. For example, the Board noted that the objective of accounting for the services received, rather than the cost of the equity instruments issued, is consistent with the accounting treatment of other issues of equity instruments, and with the IASB *Framework*. With regard to performance conditions, the Board noted that the strength of the argument in paragraph BC212 depends on the extent to which the employee has control or influence over the achievement of the performance target. One cannot necessarily conclude that the non-attainment of the performance target is a good indication that the employee has failed to perform his/her side of the arrangement (ie failed to provide services).

BC214 Therefore, the Board was not persuaded by those respondents who disagreed with the units of service method in principle. However, the Board also noted that some respondents raised practical concerns about the method. Some respondents regarded the units of service method as too complex and burdensome to apply in practice. For example, if an entity granted share options to a group of employees but did not grant the same number of share options to each employee (eg the number might vary according to their salary or position in the entity), it would be necessary to calculate a different deemed fair value per unit of service for each individual employee (or for each subgroup of employees, if there are groups of employees who each received the same number of options). Then the entity would have to track each employee, to calculate the amount to recognise for each employee. Furthermore, in some circumstances, an employee share or share option scheme might not require the employee to forfeit the shares or share options if the employee leaves during the vesting period in specified circumstances. Under the terms of some schemes, employees can retain their share options or shares if they are classified as a 'good leaver', eg a departure resulting from circumstances not within the employee's control, such as compulsory retirement, ill health or redundancy. Therefore, in estimating the possibility of forfeiture, it is not simply a matter of estimating the possibility of employee departure during the vesting period. It is also necessary to estimate whether those departures will be 'good leavers' or 'bad leavers'. And because the share options or shares will vest upon departure of 'good leavers', the expected number of units to be received and the expected length of the vesting period will be shorter for this group of employees. These factors would need to be incorporated into the application of the units of service method.

BC215 Some respondents also raised practical concerns about applying the units of service method to grants with performance conditions. These concerns include the difficulty of incorporating non-market and complex performance conditions into the grant date valuation, the additional subjectivity that this introduces, and that it was unclear how to apply the method when the length of the vesting period is not fixed, because it depends on when a performance condition is satisfied.

BC216 The Board considered the practical concerns raised by respondents, and obtained further advice from valuation experts concerning the difficulties highlighted by respondents of including non-market performance conditions in the grant date valuation. Because of these practical considerations, the Board concluded that the units of service method should not be retained in the IFRS. Instead, the Board decided to adopt the modified grant date method applied in SFAS 123. Under this method, service conditions and non-market performance conditions are excluded from the grant date valuation (ie the possibility of forfeiture is not taken into account when estimating the grant date fair value of the share options or other equity instruments, thereby producing a higher grant date fair value), but are instead taken into account by requiring that the transaction amount be based on the number of equity instruments that eventually vest.[*] Under this method, on a cumulative basis, no amount is recognised for goods or services received if the equity instruments granted do not vest because of failure to satisfy a vesting condition (other than a market condition), eg the counterparty fails to complete a specified service period, or a performance condition (other than a market condition) is not satisfied.

---

[*] The treatment of market conditions is discussed in paragraphs BC183 and BC184. As noted in paragraph BC184, the practical difficulties that led the Board to conclude that non-market conditions should be dealt with via the modified grant date method rather than being included in the grant date valuation do not apply to market conditions, because market conditions can be incorporated into option pricing models.

BC217 However, as discussed earlier (paragraphs BC180–BC182), the Board decided that it should not permit the choice available in SFAS 123 to account for the effects of expected or actual forfeitures of share options or other equity instruments because of failure to satisfy a service condition. The Board decided that the IFRS should require an entity to estimate the number of equity instruments expected to vest and to revise that estimate, if necessary, if subsequent information indicates that actual forfeitures are likely to differ from previous estimates.

Share options that are forfeited or lapse after the end of the vesting period

BC218 Some share options might not be exercised. For example, a share option holder is unlikely to exercise a share option if the share price is below the exercise price throughout the exercise period. Once the last date for exercise is passed, the share option will lapse.

BC219 The lapse of a share option at the end of the exercise period does not change the fact that the original transaction occurred, ie goods or services were received as consideration for the issue of an equity instrument (the share option). The lapsing of the share option does not represent a gain to the entity, because there is no change to the entity's net assets. In other words, although some might see such an event as being a benefit to the remaining shareholders, it has no effect on the entity's financial position. In effect, one type of equity interest (the share option holders' interest) becomes part of another type of equity interest (the shareholders' interest). The Board therefore concluded that the only accounting entry that might be required is a movement within equity, to reflect that the share options are no longer outstanding (ie as a transfer from one type of equity interest to another).

BC220 This is consistent with the treatment of other equity instruments, such as warrants issued for cash. When warrants subsequently lapse unexercised, this is not treated as a gain; instead the amount previously recognised when the warrants were issued remains within equity.*

BC221 The same analysis applies to equity instruments that are forfeited after the end of the vesting period. For example, an employee with vested share options typically must exercise those options within a short period after cessation of employment, otherwise the options are forfeited. If the share options are not in the money, the employee is unlikely to exercise the options and hence they will be forfeited. For the same reasons as are given in paragraph BC219, no adjustment is made to the amounts previously recognised for services received as consideration for the share options. The only accounting entry that might be required is a movement within equity, to reflect that the share options are no longer outstanding.

---

* However, an alternative approach is followed in some jurisdictions (eg Japan and the UK), where the entity recognises a gain when warrants lapse. But under the *Framework*, recognising a gain on the lapse of warrants would be appropriate only if warrants were liabilities, which they are not.

Modifications to the terms and conditions of share-based payment arrangements

BC222 An entity might modify the terms of or conditions under which the equity instruments were granted. For example, the entity might reduce the exercise price of share options granted to employees (ie reprice the options), which increases the fair value of those options. During the development of ED 2, the Board focused mainly on the repricing of share options.

BC223 The Board noted that the IASC/G4+1 Discussion Paper argued that if the entity reprices its share options it has, in effect, replaced the original share option with a more valuable share option. The entity presumably believes that it will receive an equivalent amount of benefit from doing so, because otherwise the directors would not be acting in the best interests of the entity or its shareholders. This suggests that the entity expects to receive additional or enhanced employee services equivalent in value to the incremental value of the repriced share options. The Discussion Paper therefore proposed that the incremental value given (ie the difference between the value of the original share option and the value of the repriced share option, as at the date of repricing) should be recognised as additional remuneration expense. Although the Discussion Paper discussed repricing in the context of vesting date measurement, SFAS 123, which applies a grant date measurement basis for employee share-based payment, contains reasoning similar to that in the Discussion Paper.

BC224 This reasoning seems appropriate if grant date measurement is applied on the grounds that the entity made a payment to the employees on grant date by granting them valuable rights to equity instruments of the entity. If the entity is prepared to replace that payment with a more valuable payment, it must believe it will receive an equivalent amount of benefit from doing so.

BC225 The same conclusion is drawn if grant date measurement is applied on the grounds that some type of equity interest is created at grant date, and thereafter changes in the value of that equity interest accrue to the option holders as equity participants, not as employees. Repricing is inconsistent with the view that share option holders bear changes in value as equity participants. Hence it follows that the incremental value has been granted to the share option holders in their capacity as employees (rather than equity participants), as part of their remuneration for services to the entity. Therefore additional remuneration expense arises in respect of the incremental value given.

BC226 It could be argued that if (a) grant date measurement is used as a surrogate measure of the fair value of the services received and (b) the repricing occurs between grant date and vesting date and (c) the repricing merely restores the share option's original value at grant date, then the entity may not receive additional services. Rather, the repricing might simply be a means of ensuring that the entity receives the services it originally expected to receive when the share options were granted. Under this view, it is not appropriate to recognise additional remuneration expense to the extent that the repricing restores the share option's original value at grant date.

BC227　Some argue that the effect of a repricing is to create a new deal between the entity and its employees, and therefore the entity should estimate the fair value of the repriced share options at the date of repricing to calculate a new measure of the fair value of the services received subsequent to repricing. Under this view, the entity would cease using the grant date fair value of the share options when measuring services received after the repricing date, but without reversal of amounts recognised previously. The entity would then measure the services received between the date of repricing and the end of the vesting period by reference to the fair value of the modified share options, measured at the date of repricing. If the repricing occurs after the end of the vesting period, the same process applies. That is to say, there is no adjustment to previously recognised amounts, and the entity recognises—either immediately or over the vesting period, depending on whether the employees are required to complete an additional period of service to become entitled to the repriced share options—an amount equal to the fair value of the modified share options, measured at the date of repricing.

BC228　In the context of measuring the fair value of the equity instruments as a surrogate measure of the fair value of the services received, after considering the above points, the Board concluded when it developed ED 2 that the incremental value granted on repricing should be taken into account when measuring the services received, because:

(a)　there is an underlying presumption that the fair value of the equity instruments, at grant date, provides a surrogate measure of the fair value of the services received. That fair value is based on the share option's original terms and conditions. Therefore, if those terms or conditions are modified, the modification should be taken into account when measuring the services received.

(b)　a share option that will be repriced if the share price falls is more valuable than one that will not be repriced. Therefore, by presuming at grant date that the share option will not be repriced, the entity underestimated the fair value of that option. The Board concluded that, because it is impractical to include the possibility of repricing in the estimate of fair value at grant date, the incremental value granted on repricing should be taken into account as and when the repricing occurs.

BC229　Many of the respondents to ED 2 who addressed the issue of repricing agreed with the proposed requirements. After considering respondents' comments, the Board decided to retain the approach to repricing as proposed in ED 2, ie recognise the incremental value granted on repricing, in addition to continuing to recognise amounts based on the fair value of the original grant.

BC230　The Board also discussed situations in which repricing might be effected by cancelling share options and issuing replacement share options. For example, suppose an entity grants at-the-money share options with an estimated fair value of CU20 each. Suppose the share price falls, so that the share options become significantly out of the money, and are now worth CU2 each. Suppose the entity is considering repricing, so that the share options are again at the money, which would result in them being worth, say, CU10 each. (Note that the share options are still worth less than at grant date, because the share price is now lower. Other things being equal, an at-the-money option on a low priced share is worth less than an at-the-money option on a high priced share.)

BC231 Under ED 2's proposed treatment of repricing, the incremental value given on repricing (CU10 – CU2 = CU8 increment in fair value per share option) would be accounted for when measuring the services rendered, resulting in the recognition of additional expense, ie additional to any amounts recognised in the future in respect of the original share option grant (valued at CU20). If the entity instead cancelled the existing share options and then issued what were, in effect, replacement share options, but treated the replacement share options as a new share option grant, this could reduce the expense recognised. Although the new grant would be valued at CU10 rather than incremental value of CU8, the entity would not recognise any further expense in respect of the original share option grant, valued at CU20. Although some regard such a result as appropriate (and consistent with their views on repricing, as explained in paragraph BC227), it is inconsistent with the Board's treatment of repricing.

BC232 By this means, the entity could, in effect, reduce its remuneration expense if the share price falls, without having to increase the expense if the share price rises (because no repricing would be necessary in this case). In other words, the entity could structure a repricing so as to achieve a form of service date measurement if the share price falls and grant date measurement if the share price rises, ie an asymmetrical treatment of share price changes.

BC233 When it developed ED 2, the Board concluded that if an entity cancels a share or share option grant during the vesting period (other than cancellations because of employees' failing to satisfy the vesting conditions), it should nevertheless continue to account for services received, as if that share or share option grant had not been cancelled. In the Board's view, it is very unlikely that a share or share option grant would be cancelled without some compensation to the counterparty, either in the form of cash or replacement share options. Moreover, the Board saw no difference between a repricing of share options and a cancellation of share options followed by the granting of replacement share options at a lower exercise price, and therefore concluded that the accounting treatment should be the same. If cash is paid on the cancellation of the share or share option grant, the Board concluded that the payment should be accounted for as the repurchase of an equity interest, ie as a deduction from equity.

BC234 The Board noted that its proposed treatment means that an entity would continue to recognise services received during the remainder of the original vesting period, even though the entity might have paid cash compensation to the counterparty upon cancellation of the share or share option grant. The Board discussed an alternative approach applied in SFAS 123: if an entity settles unvested shares or share options in cash, those shares or share options are treated as having immediately vested. The entity is required to recognise immediately an expense for the amount of compensation expense that would otherwise have been recognised during the remainder of the original vesting period. Although the Board would have preferred to adopt this approach, it would have been difficult to apply in the context of the proposed accounting method in ED 2, given that there is not a specific amount of unrecognised compensation expense—the amount recognised in the future would have depended on the number of units of service received in the future.

BC235 Many respondents who commented on the treatment of cancellations disagreed with the proposals in ED 2. They commented that it was inappropriate to continue recognising an expense after a grant has been cancelled. Some suggested other approaches, including the approach applied in SFAS 123. After considering these comments, and given that the Board had decided to replace the units of service method with the modified grant date method in SFAS 123, the Board concluded that it should adopt the same approach as applied in SFAS 123 to cancellations and settlements. Under SFAS 123, a settlement (including a cancellation) is regarded as resulting in the immediate vesting of the equity instruments. The amount of remuneration expense measured at grant date but not yet recognised is recognised immediately at the date of settlement or cancellation.

BC236 In addition to the above issues, during its redeliberation of the proposals in ED 2 the Board also considered more detailed issues relating to modifications and cancellations. Specifically, the Board considered:

(a) a modification that results in a decrease in fair value (ie the fair value of the modified instrument is less than the fair value of the original instrument, measured at the date of the modification).

(b) a change in the number of equity instruments granted (increase and decrease).

(c) a change in services conditions, thereby changing the length of the vesting period (increase and decrease).

(d) a change in performance conditions, thereby changing the probability of vesting (increase and decrease).

(e) a change in the classification of the grant, from equity to liabilities.

BC237 The Board concluded that having adopted a grant date measurement method, the requirements for modifications and cancellations should ensure that the entity cannot, by modifying or cancelling the grant of shares or share options, avoid recognising remuneration expense based on the grant date fair values. Therefore, the Board concluded that, for arrangements that are classified as equity-settled arrangements (at least initially), the entity must recognise the grant date fair value of the equity instruments over the vesting period, unless the employee fails to vest in those equity instruments under the terms of the original vesting conditions.

BC237A During the deliberations of its proposals in the exposure draft *Vesting Conditions and Cancellations* published in February 2006, the Board considered how failure to meet a non-vesting condition should be treated. The Board concluded that in order to be consistent with the grant date measurement method, failure to meet a non-vesting condition should have no accounting effect when neither the entity nor the counterparty can choose whether that condition is met. The entity should continue to recognise the expense, based on the grant date fair value, over the vesting period unless the employee fails to meet a vesting condition.

BC237B However, the Board concluded that the entity's failure to meet a non-vesting condition is a cancellation if the entity can choose whether that non-vesting condition is met. Furthermore, the Board noted that no non-arbitrary or unambiguous criteria exist to distinguish between a decision by the counterparty not to meet a non-vesting condition and a cancellation by the entity. The Board considered establishing a rebuttable presumption that a counterparty's failure to meet a non-vesting condition is (or is not) a cancellation, unless it can be demonstrated that the entity had no (or had some) influence over the counterparty's decision. The Board did not believe that the information about the entity's decision-making processes that is publicly available would be sufficient to determine whether the presumption has been rebutted. Therefore, the Board concluded that a failure to meet a non-vesting condition should be treated as a cancellation when either the entity or the counterparty can choose whether that non-vesting condition is met.

Share appreciation rights settled in cash

BC238 Some transactions are 'share-based', even though they do not involve the issue of shares, share options or any other form of equity instrument. Share appreciation rights (SARs) settled in cash are transactions in which the amount of cash paid to the employee (or another party) is based upon the increase in the share price over a specified period, usually subject to vesting conditions, such as the employee's remaining with the entity during the specified period. (Note that the following discussion focuses on SARs granted to employees, but also applies to SARs granted to other parties.)

BC239 In terms of accounting concepts, share-based payment transactions involving an outflow of cash (or other assets) are different from transactions in which goods or services are received as consideration for the issue of equity instruments.

BC240 In an equity-settled transaction, only one side of the transaction causes a change in assets, ie an asset (services) is received but no assets are disbursed. The other side of the transaction increases equity; it does not cause a change in assets. Accordingly, not only is it not necessary to remeasure the transaction amount upon settlement, it is not appropriate, because equity interests are not remeasured.

BC241 In contrast, in a cash-settled transaction, both sides of the transaction cause a change in assets, ie an asset (services) is received and an asset (cash) is ultimately disbursed. Therefore, no matter what value is attributed to the first asset (services received), eventually it will be necessary to recognise the change in assets when the second asset (cash) is disbursed. Thus, no matter how the transaction is accounted for between the receipt of services and the settlement in cash, it will be 'trued up' to equal the amount of cash paid out, to account for both changes in assets.

BC242 Because cash-settled SARs involve an outflow of cash (rather than the issue of equity instruments) cash SARs should be accounted for in accordance with the usual accounting for similar liabilities. That sounds straightforward, but there are some questions to consider:

(a) should a liability be recognised before vesting date, ie before the employees have fulfilled the conditions to become unconditionally entitled to the cash payment?

(b) if so, how should that liability be measured?

(c) how should the expense be presented in the income statement?

Is there a liability before vesting date?

BC243 It could be argued that the entity does not have a liability until vesting date, because the entity does not have a present obligation to pay cash to the employees until the employees fulfil the conditions to become unconditionally entitled to the cash; between grant date and vesting date there is only a contingent liability.

BC244 The Board noted that this argument applies to all sorts of employee benefits settled in cash, not just SARs. For example, it could be argued that an entity has no liability for pension payments to employees until the employees have met the specified vesting conditions. This argument was considered by IASC in IAS 19 *Employee Benefits*. The Basis for Conclusions states:

> Paragraph 54 of the new IAS 19 summarises the recognition and measurement of liabilities arising from defined benefit plans ... Paragraph 54 of the new IAS 19 is based on the definition of, and recognition criteria for, a liability in IASC's *Framework* ... The Board believes that an enterprise has an obligation under a defined benefit plan when an employee has rendered service in return for the benefits promised under the plan ... The Board believes that an obligation exists even if a benefit is not vested, in other words if the employee's right to receive the benefit is conditional upon future employment. For example, consider an enterprise that provides a benefit of 100 to employees who remain in service for two years. At the end of the first year, the employee and the enterprise are not in the same position as at the beginning of the first year, because the employee will only need to work for one year, instead of two, before becoming entitled to the benefit. Although there is a possibility that the benefit may not vest, that difference is an obligation and, in the Board's view, should result in the recognition of a liability at the end of the first year. The measurement of that obligation at its present value reflects the enterprise's best estimate of the probability that the benefit may not vest. (IAS 19, Basis for Conclusions, paragraphs BC11–BC14)

BC245 Therefore, the Board concluded that, to be consistent with IAS 19, which covers other cash-settled employee benefits, a liability should be recognised in respect of cash-settled SARs during the vesting period, as services are rendered by the employees. Thus, no matter how the liability is measured, the Board concluded that it should be accrued over the vesting period, to the extent that the employees have performed their side of the arrangement. For example, if the terms of the arrangement require the employees to perform services over a three-year period, the liability would be accrued over that three-year period, consistently with the treatment of other cash-settled employee benefits.

How should the liability be measured?

BC246 A simple approach would be to base the accrual on the entity's share price at the end of each reporting period. If the entity's share price increased over the vesting period, expenses would be larger in later reporting periods compared with earlier reporting periods. This is because each reporting period will include the effects of (a) an increase in the liability in respect of the employee services received during that reporting period and (b) an increase in the liability attributable to the increase in the entity's share price during the reporting period, which increases the amount payable in respect of past employee services received.

BC247 This approach is consistent with SFAS 123 (paragraph 25) and FASB Interpretation No. 28 *Accounting for Stock Appreciation Rights and Other Variable Stock Option or Award Plans.*

BC248 However, this is not a fair value approach. Like share options, the fair value of SARs includes both their intrinsic value (the increase in the share price to date) and their time value (the value of the right to participate in future increases in the share price, if any, that may occur between the valuation date and the settlement date). An option pricing model can be used to estimate the fair value of SARs.

BC249 Ultimately, however, no matter how the liability is measured during the vesting period, the liability—and therefore the expense—will be remeasured, when the SARs are settled, to equal the amount of the cash paid out. The amount of cash paid will be based on the SARs' intrinsic value at the settlement date. Some support measuring the SAR liability at intrinsic value for this reason, and because intrinsic value is easier to measure.

BC250 The Board concluded that measuring SARs at intrinsic value would be inconsistent with the fair value measurement basis applied, in most cases, in the rest of the IFRS. Furthermore, although a fair value measurement basis is more complex to apply, it was likely that many entities would be measuring the fair value of similar instruments regularly, eg new SAR or share option grants, which would provide much of the information required to remeasure the fair value of the SAR at each reporting date. Moreover, because the intrinsic value measurement basis does not include time value, it is not an adequate measure of either the SAR liability or the cost of services consumed.

BC251 The question of how to measure the liability is linked with the question how to present the associated expense in the income statement, as explained below.

How should the associated expense be presented in the income statement?

BC252 SARs are economically similar to share options. Hence some argue that the accounting treatment of SARs should be the same as the treatment of share options, as discussed earlier (paragraph BC113). However, as noted in paragraphs BC240 and BC241, in an equity-settled transaction there is one change in net assets (the goods or services received) whereas in a cash-settled transaction there are two changes in net assets (the goods or services received and the cash or other assets paid out). To differentiate between the effects of each change in net assets in a cash-settled transaction, the expense could be separated into two components:

- an amount based on the fair value of the SARs at grant date, recognised over the vesting period, in a manner similar to accounting for equity-settled share-based payment transactions, and

- changes in estimate between grant date and settlement date, ie all changes required to remeasure the transaction amount to equal the amount paid out on settlement date.

BC253   In developing ED 2, the Board concluded that information about these two components would be helpful to users of financial statements. For example, users of financial statements regard the effects of remeasuring the liability as having little predictive value. Therefore, the Board concluded that there should be separate disclosure, either on the face of the income statement or in the notes, of that portion of the expense recognised during each accounting period that is attributable to changes in the estimated fair value of the liability between grant date and settlement date.

BC254   However, some respondents to ED 2 disagreed with the proposed disclosure, arguing that it was burdensome and inappropriate to require the entity to account for the transaction as a cash-settled transaction and also calculate, for the purposes of the disclosure, what the transaction amount would have been if the arrangement was an equity-settled transaction.

BC255   The Board considered these comments and also noted that its decision to adopt the SFAS 123 modified grant date method will make it more complex for entities to determine the amount to disclose, because it will be necessary to distinguish between the effects of forfeitures and the effects of fair value changes when calculating the amount to disclose. The Board therefore concluded that the disclosure should not be retained as a mandatory requirement, but instead should be given as an example of an additional disclosure that entities should consider providing. For example, entities with a significant amount of cash-settled arrangements that experience significant share price volatility will probably find that the disclosure is helpful to users of their financial statements.

Share-based payment transactions with cash alternatives

BC256   Under some employee share-based payment arrangements the employees can choose to receive cash instead of shares or share options, or instead of exercising share options. There are many possible variations of share-based payment arrangements under which a cash alternative may be paid. For example, the employees may have more than one opportunity to elect to receive the cash alternative, eg the employees may be able to elect to receive cash instead of shares or share options on vesting date, or elect to receive cash instead of exercising the share options. The terms of the arrangement may provide the entity with a choice of settlement, ie whether to pay the cash alternative instead of issuing shares or share options on vesting date or instead of issuing shares upon the exercise of the share options. The amount of the cash alternative may be fixed or variable and, if variable, may be determinable in a manner that is related, or unrelated, to the price of the entity's shares.

BC257   The IFRS contains different accounting methods for cash-settled and equity-settled share-based payment transactions. Hence, if the entity or the employee has the choice of settlement, it is necessary to determine which accounting method should be applied. The Board considered situations when the terms of the arrangement provide (a) the employee with a choice of settlement and (b) the entity with a choice of settlement.

The terms of the arrangement provide the employee with a choice of settlement

BC258   Share-based payment transactions without cash alternatives do not give rise to liabilities under the *Framework*, because the entity is not required to transfer cash or other assets to the other party. However, this is not so if the contract between the entity and the employee gives the employee the contractual right to demand the cash alternative. In this situation, the entity has an obligation to transfer cash to the employee and hence a liability exists. Furthermore, because the employee has the right to demand settlement in equity instead of cash, the employee also has a conditional right to equity instruments. Hence, on grant date the employee was granted rights to a compound financial instrument, ie a financial instrument that includes both debt and equity components.

BC259   It is common for the alternatives to be structured so that the fair value of the cash alternative is always the same as the fair value of the equity alternative, eg where the employee has a choice between share options and SARs. However, if this is not so, then the fair value of the compound financial instrument will usually exceed both the individual fair value of the cash alternative (because of the possibility that the shares or share options may be more valuable than the cash alternative) and that of the shares or options (because of the possibility that the cash alternative may be more valuable than the shares or options).

BC260   Under IAS 32, a financial instrument that is accounted for as a compound instrument is separated into its debt and equity components, by allocating the proceeds received for the issue of a compound instrument to its debt and equity components. This entails determining the fair value of the liability component and then assigning the remainder of the proceeds received to the equity component. This is possible if those proceeds are cash or non-cash consideration whose fair value can be reliably measured. If that is not the case, it will be necessary to estimate the fair value of the compound instrument itself.

BC261   The Board concluded that the compound instrument should be measured by first valuing the liability component (the cash alternative) and then valuing the equity component (the equity instrument)—with that valuation taking into account that the employee must forfeit the cash alternative to receive the equity instrument—and adding the two component values together. This is consistent with the approach adopted in IAS 32, whereby the liability component is measured first and the residual is allocated to equity. If the fair value of each settlement alternative is always the same, then the fair value of the equity component of the compound instrument will be zero and hence the fair value of the compound instrument will be the same as the fair value of the liability component.

BC262　The Board concluded that the entity should separately account for the services rendered in respect of each component of the compound financial instrument, to ensure consistency with the IFRS's requirements for equity-settled and cash-settled share-based payment transactions. Hence, for the debt component, the entity should recognise the services received, and a liability to pay for those services, as the employees render services, in the same manner as other cash-settled share-based payment transactions (eg SARs). For the equity component (if any), the entity should recognise the services received, and an increase in equity, as the employees render services, in the same way as other equity-settled share-based payment transactions.

BC263　The Board concluded that the liability should be remeasured to its fair value as at the date of settlement, before accounting for the settlement of the liability. This ensures that, if the entity settles the liability by issuing equity instruments, the resulting increase in equity is measured at the fair value of the consideration received for the equity instruments issued, being the fair value of the liability settled.

BC264　The Board also concluded that, if the entity pays cash rather than issuing equity instruments on settlement, any contributions to equity previously recognised in respect of the equity component should remain in equity. By electing to receive cash rather than equity instruments, the employee has surrendered his/her rights to receive equity instruments. That event does not cause a change in net assets and hence there is no change in total equity. This is consistent with the Board's conclusions on other lapses of equity instruments (see paragraphs BC218–BC221).

The terms of the arrangement provide the entity with a choice of settlement

BC265　For share-based payment transactions in which the terms of the arrangement provide the entity with a choice of whether to settle in cash or by issuing equity instruments, the entity would need first to determine whether it has an obligation to settle in cash and therefore does not, in effect, have a choice of settlement. Although the contract might specify that the entity can choose whether to settle in cash or by issuing equity instruments, the Board concluded that the entity will have an obligation to settle in cash if the choice of settlement in equity has no commercial substance (eg because the entity is legally prohibited from issuing shares), or if the entity has a past practice or a stated policy of settling in cash, or generally settles in cash whenever the counterparty asks for cash settlement. The entity will also have an obligation to settle in cash if the shares issued (including shares issued upon the exercise of share options) are redeemable, either mandatorily (eg upon cessation of employment) or at the counterparty's option.

BC266　During its redeliberations of the proposals in ED 2, the Board noted that the classification as liabilities or equity of arrangements in which the entity appears to have the choice of settlement differs from the classification under IAS 32, which requires such an arrangement to be classified either wholly as a liability (if the contract is a derivative contract) or as a compound instrument (if the contract is a non-derivative contract). However, consistently with its conclusions on the other differences between IFRS 2 and IAS 32 (see paragraphs BC106–BC110), the Board decided to retain this difference, pending the outcome of its longer-term Concepts project, which includes reviewing the definitions of liabilities and equity.

BC267 Even if the entity is not obliged to settle in cash until it chooses to do so, at the time it makes that election a liability will arise for the amount of the cash payment. This raises the question how to account for the debit side of the entry. It could be argued that any difference between (a) the amount of the cash payment and (b) the total expense recognised for services received and consumed up to the date of settlement (which would be based on the grant date value of the equity settlement alternative) should be recognised as an adjustment to the employee remuneration expense. However, given that the cash payment is to settle an equity interest, the Board concluded that it is consistent with the *Framework* to treat the cash payment as the repurchase of an equity interest, ie as a deduction from equity. In this case, no adjustment to remuneration expense is required on settlement.

BC268 However, the Board concluded that an additional expense should be recognised if the entity chooses the settlement alternative with the higher fair value because, given that the entity has voluntarily paid more than it needed to, presumably it expects to receive (or has already received) additional services from the employees in return for the additional value given.

Share-based payment transactions among group entities (2009 amendments)[*]

BC268A This section summarises the Board's considerations when finalising its proposals contained in the exposure draft *Group Cash-settled Share-based Payment Transactions* published in December 2007. Until the Board amended IFRS 2 in 2009, IFRIC 11 provided guidance on how an entity that received the goods or services from its suppliers should account for some specific group equity-settled share-based payment transactions in its separate or individual financial statements. Therefore, the amendments issued in June 2009 incorporated substantially the same consensus contained in IFRIC 11. The relevant matters the IFRIC considered when reaching the consensus contained in IFRIC 11, as approved by the Board, are also carried forward in this section.

BC268B The exposure draft published in December 2007 addressed two arrangements in which the parent (not the entity itself) has an obligation to make the required cash payments to the suppliers of the entity:

(a)   Arrangement 1 – the supplier of the entity will receive cash payments that are linked to the price of the equity instruments of the entity.

(b)   Arrangement 2 – the supplier of the entity will receive cash payments that are linked to the price of the equity instruments of the parent of the entity.

---

[*]   Paragraphs BC268A–BC268O are added as a consequence of amendments to IFRS 2 *Group Cash-settled Share-based Payment Transactions* issued in June 2009.

BC268C The Board noted that like those group equity-settled share-based payment transactions originally addressed in IFRIC 11, the two arrangements described in paragraph BC268B did not meet the definition of either an equity-settled or a cash-settled share-based payment transaction. The Board considered whether a different conclusion should be reached for such arrangements merely because they are cash-settled rather than equity-settled. Paragraphs BC22A–BC22F explain the Board's considerations in finalising the amendments to clarify the scope of IFRS 2. The section below summarises the Board's considerations in finalising the amendments relating to the measurement of such transactions.

BC268D The Board noted that the arrangements described in paragraph BC268B are

(a) for the purpose of providing benefits to the employees of the subsidiary in return for employee services, and

(b) share-based and cash-settled.

In addition, the Board noted that the guidance in paragraph 3 (now superseded by paragraph 3A) already stated that when a shareholder transferred equity instruments of the entity (or another group entity), the transaction would be within the scope of IFRS 2 for the entity receiving the goods or services.

BC268E For these reasons, in the exposure draft published in December 2007 the Board proposed to amend IFRS 2 and IFRIC 11 to require that, in the separate or individual financial statements of the entity receiving the goods or services, the entity should measure the employee services in accordance with the requirements applicable to cash-settled share-based payment transactions on the basis of the fair value of the corresponding liability incurred by the parent. Specifically, until the liability incurred by the parent is settled, the entity should recognise any changes in the fair value of the liability in profit or loss and changes in the entity's equity as adjustments to contributions from the parent.

BC268F Because group cash-settled share-based payment transactions did not meet the definition of either an equity-settled or a cash-settled share-based payment transaction, some respondents did not object to measuring them as cash-settled on the basis that the accounting reflects the form of the payment received by the entity's suppliers. However, many respondents questioned the basis for the conclusions reached, citing reasons that included:

(a) the lack of a 'push-down' accounting concept in current IFRSs that would require the parent's costs incurred on behalf of the subsidiary to be attributed to the subsidiary,

(b) conflicts with the Framework and with other IFRSs that prohibit remeasurement of equity, and

(c) conflicts with the rationale in the Basis for Conclusions on IFRS 2 related to the remeasurement of cash-settled share-based payment transactions when the entity itself has no obligation to its suppliers.

BC268G The Board agreed with respondents that the entity receiving goods or services has no obligation to distribute assets and that the parent's settlement is an equity contribution to the entity. The Board noted that regardless of how such group transactions are structured or accounted for in the separate or individual financial statements of the group entities, the accounting measurement in the consolidated financial statements of the group will be the same. The Board also noted that the share-based payment expense measured on grant date results in the same fair value for both the entity receiving goods or services and the entity settling the transaction, regardless of whether it is measured as equity-settled or as cash-settled.

BC268H To address the comments received from respondents, the Board reviewed two issues to determine the appropriate subsequent measurement in the separate or individual financial statements of the entity receiving the goods or services. The first issue was whether the entity should recognise in its separate or individual financial statements:

(a) Approach 1 – an expense of the same amount as in the consolidated financial statements, or

(b) Approach 2 – an expense measured by classifying the transaction as equity-settled or cash-settled evaluated from its own perspective, which may not always be the same as the amount recognised by the consolidated group.

BC268I The Board noted that IFRSs have no broad-based guidance to address push-down accounting or the accounting in separate or individual financial statements for the allocation of costs among group entities. When addressing defined benefit plans that share risks between entities under common control, IAS 19 requires an expense to be recognised by the subsidiary on the basis of the cash amount charged by the group plan. When there are no repayment arrangements, in the separate or individual financial statements, the subsidiary should recognise a cost equal to its contribution payable for the period. This is consistent with Approach 2 described in paragraph BC268H.

BC268J The Board therefore decided to adopt Approach 2. However, the approach adopted in IFRS 2 is different from that in IAS 19 in that the entity receiving goods or services in a share-based payment transaction recognises an expense even when it has no obligation to pay cash or other assets. The Board concluded that this approach is consistent with the expense attribution principles underlying IFRS 2.

BC268K The Board noted that Approach 2 is consistent with the rationale that the information provided by general purpose financial reporting should 'reflect the perspective of the entity rather than the perspective of the entity's equity investors ....' because the reporting entity is deemed to have substance of its own, separate from that of its owners. Approach 1 reflects the perspective of the entity's owners (the group) rather than the rights and obligations of the entity itself.

BC268L The Board also noted that the consensus reached in IFRIC 11 reflected Approach 1 described in paragraph BC268H for some scenarios and Approach 2 for others. The Board concluded that this was undesirable and decided that there should be a single approach to measurement that would apply in all situations.

BC268M The second issue the Board considered was identifying the criteria for classifying group share-based payment transactions as equity-settled or cash-settled. How a transaction is classified determines the subsequent measurement in the separate or individual financial statements of both the entity receiving the goods or services and the entity settling the transaction, if different. The Board reviewed the two classification criteria set out in the consensus in IFRIC 11 for group equity-settled transactions:

(a) based on the nature of the award given to the employees—therefore, classified as *equity-settled* if the entity's own equity instruments are given, regardless of which entity grants or settles it; otherwise classified as *cash-settled* even when the entity receiving the goods or services has no obligation.

(b) based on the entity's own rights and obligations—therefore, classified as *cash-settled* if the entity has an obligation to settle, regardless of the nature of the consideration; otherwise classified as *equity-settled*.

BC268N The Board noted that, on its own, either of the two criteria described above would not consistently reflect the entity's perspective when assessing the appropriate classification for transactions described in paragraph BC268B. The Board concluded that the entity should consider both criteria in IFRIC 11, ie *equity-settled* when suppliers are given the entity's own equity instruments or when the entity receiving the goods or services has no obligation to settle and *cash-settled* in all other circumstances. The Board also noted that when the entity receiving goods or services has no obligation to deliver cash or other assets to its suppliers, accounting for the transaction as cash-settled in its separate or individual financial statements is not appropriate. The equity-settled basis is more consistent with the principles and rationales in both IFRS 2 and IFRIC 11. Therefore, the Board decided that the entity receiving the goods or services should classify both of the group cash-settled share-based payment transactions described in paragraph BC268B as *equity-settled* in its separate or individual financial statements.

BC268O This conclusion is the main change to the proposals in the exposure draft. The Board concluded that the broader principles it developed during its redeliberations addressed the three main concerns expressed by respondents described in paragraph BC268F. Those principles apply to all group share-based payment transactions, whether they are cash-settled or equity-settled. The Board's conclusions do not result in any changes to the guidance in IFRIC 11 that addressed similar group equity-settled share-based payment transactions. Other than the change described above, the Board reaffirmed the proposals in the exposure draft. Therefore, the Board concluded that it was not necessary to re-expose the amendments before finalising them.

Transfers of employees between group entities (paragraphs B59–B61)

BC268P When it developed the consensus in IFRIC 11, the IFRIC noted that some share-based payment arrangements involve a parent granting rights to the employees of more than one subsidiary with a vesting condition that requires the employees to work for the group for a particular period. Sometimes, an employee of one subsidiary transfers employment to another subsidiary during the vesting period, without the employee's rights under the original share-based payment arrangements being affected.

BC268Q The IFRIC noted that the terms of the original share-based payment arrangement require the employees to work for the group, rather than for a particular group entity. Thus, the IFRIC concluded that the change of employment should not result in a new grant of equity instruments in the financial statements of the subsidiary to which the employees transferred employment. The subsidiary to which the employee transfers employment should measure the fair value of the services received from the employee by reference to the fair value of the equity instruments at the date those equity instruments were originally granted to the employee by the parent. For the same reason, the IFRIC concluded that the transfer itself should not be treated as an employee's failure to satisfy a vesting condition. Thus, the transfer should not trigger any reversal of the charge previously recognised in respect of the services received from the employee in the separate or individual financial statements of the subsidiary from which the employee transfers employment.

BC268R The IFRIC noted that paragraph 19 of the IFRS requires the cumulative amount recognised for goods or services as consideration for the equity instruments granted to be based on the number of equity instruments that eventually vest. Accordingly, on a cumulative basis, no amount is recognised for goods or services if the equity instruments do not vest because of failure to satisfy a vesting condition other than a market condition as defined in Appendix A. Applying the principles in paragraph 19, the IFRIC concluded that when the employee fails to satisfy a vesting condition other than a market condition, the services from that employee recognised in the financial statements of each group entity during the vesting period should be reversed.

BC268S When finalising the 2009 amendments to IFRS 2 for group share-based payment transactions, the Board concluded that the guidance in IFRIC 11 should apply to all group share-based payment transactions classified as equity-settled in the entity's separate or individual financial statements in accordance with paragraphs 43A–43C.

Overall conclusions on accounting for employee share options

BC269 The Board first considered all major issues relating to the recognition and measurement of share-based payment transactions, and reached conclusions on those issues. It then drew some overall conclusions, particularly on the treatment of employee share options, which is one of the most controversial aspects of the project. In arriving at those conclusions, the Board considered the following issues:

- convergence with US GAAP
- recognition versus disclosure of expenses arising from employee share-based payment transactions
- reliability of measurement of the fair value of employee share options.

Convergence with US GAAP

BC270 Some respondents to the Discussion Paper and ED 2 urged the Board to develop an IFRS that was based on existing requirements under US generally accepted accounting principles (US GAAP).

BC271 More specifically, respondents urged the Board to develop a standard based on SFAS 123. However, given that convergence of accounting standards was commonly given as a reason for this suggestion, the Board considered US GAAP overall, not just one aspect of it. The main pronouncements of US GAAP on share-based payment are Accounting Principles Board Opinion No. 25 *Accounting for Stock Issued to Employees*, and SFAS 123.

APB 25

BC272 APB 25 was issued in 1972. It deals with employee share plans only, and draws a distinction between non-performance-related (fixed) plans and performance-related and other variable plans.

BC273 For fixed plans, an expense is measured at intrinsic value (ie the difference between the share price and the exercise price), if any, at grant date. Typically, this results in no expense being recognised for fixed plans, because most share options granted under fixed plans are granted at the money. For performance-related and other variable plans, an expense is measured at intrinsic value at the measurement date. The measurement date is when both the number of shares or share options that the employee is entitled to receive and the exercise price are fixed. Because this measurement date is likely to be much later than grant date, any expense is subject to uncertainty and, if the share price is increasing, the expense for performance-related plans would be larger than for fixed plans.

BC274 In SFAS 123, the FASB noted that APB 25 is criticised for producing anomalous results and for lacking any underlying conceptual rationale. For example, the requirements of APB 25 typically result in the recognition of an expense for performance-related share options but usually no expense is recognised for fixed share options. This result is anomalous because fixed share options are usually more valuable at grant date than performance-related share options. Moreover, the omission of an expense for fixed share options impairs the quality of financial statements:

> The resulting financial statements are less credible than they could be, and the financial statements of entities that use fixed employee share options extensively are not comparable to those of entities that do not make significant use of fixed options. (SFAS 123, paragraph 56)

BC275　The Discussion Paper, in its discussion of US GAAP, noted that the different accounting treatments for fixed and performance-related plans also had the perverse effect of discouraging entities from setting up performance-related employee share plans.

SFAS 123

BC276　SFAS 123 was issued in 1995. It requires recognition of share-based payment transactions with parties other than employees, based on the fair value of the shares or share options issued or the fair value of the goods or services received, whichever is more reliably measurable. Entities are also encouraged, but not required, to apply the fair value accounting method in SFAS 123 to share-based payment transactions with employees. Generally speaking, SFAS 123 draws no distinction between fixed and performance-related plans.

BC277　If an entity applies the accounting method in APB 25 rather than that in SFAS 123, SFAS 123 requires disclosures of pro forma net income and earnings per share in the annual financial statements, as if the standard had been applied. Recently, a significant number of major US companies have voluntarily adopted the fair value accounting method in SFAS 123 for transactions with employees.

BC278　The FASB regards SFAS 123 as superior to APB 25, and would have preferred recognition based on the fair value of employee options to be mandatory, not optional. SFAS 123 makes it clear that the FASB decided to permit the disclosure-based alternative for political reasons, not because it thought that it was the best accounting solution:

> ... the Board ... continues to believe that disclosure is not an adequate substitute for recognition of assets, liabilities, equity, revenues and expenses in financial statements ... The Board chose a disclosure-based solution for stock-based employee compensation to bring closure to the divisive debate on this issue—not because it believes that solution is the best way to improve financial accounting and reporting.
> (SFAS 123, paragraphs 61 and 62)

BC279　Under US GAAP, the accounting treatment of share-based payment transactions differs, depending on whether the other party to the transaction is an employee or non-employee, and whether the entity chooses to apply SFAS 123 or APB 25 to transactions with employees. Having a choice of accounting methods is generally regarded as undesirable. Indeed, the Board recently devoted much time and effort to developing improvements to existing international standards, one of the objectives of which is to eliminate choices of accounting methods.

BC280　Research in the US demonstrates that choosing one accounting method over the other has a significant impact on the reported earnings of US entities. For example, research by Bear Stearns and Credit Suisse First Boston on the S&P 500 shows that, had the fair value measurement method in SFAS 123 been applied for the purposes of recognising an expense for employee stock-based compensation, the earnings of the S&P 500 companies would have been significantly lower, and that the effect is growing. The effect on reported earnings is substantial in some sectors, where companies make heavy use of share options.

BC281 The Canadian Accounting Standards Board (AcSB) recently completed its project on share-based payment. In accordance with the AcSB's policy of harmonising Canadian standards with those in the US, the AcSB initially proposed a standard that was based on US GAAP, including APB 25. After considering respondents' comments, the AcSB decided to delete the guidance drawn from APB 25. The AcSB reached this decision for various reasons, including that, in its view, the intrinsic value method is flawed. Also, incorporating the requirements of APB 25 into an accounting standard would result in preparers of financial statements incurring substantial costs for which users of financial statements would derive no benefit—entities would spend a great deal of time and effort on understanding the rules and then redesigning option plans, usually by deleting existing performance conditions, to avoid recognising an expense in respect of such plans, thereby producing no improvement in the accounting for share option plans.

BC282 The Canadian standard was initially consistent with SFAS 123. That included permitting a choice between fair value-based accounting for employee stock-based compensation expense in the income statement and disclosure of pro forma amounts in the notes to both interim and annual financial statements. However, the AcSB recently amended its standard to remove the choice between recognition and disclosure, and therefore expense recognition is mandatory for financial periods beginning on or after 1 January 2004.

BC283 Because APB 25 contains serious flaws, the Board concluded that basing an IFRS on it is unlikely to represent much, if any, improvement in financial reporting. Moreover, the perverse effects of APB 25, particularly in discouraging performance-related share option plans, may cause economic distortions. Accounting standards are intended to be neutral, not to give favourable or unfavourable accounting treatments to particular transactions to encourage or discourage entities from entering into those transactions. APB 25 fails to achieve that objective. Performance-related employee share plans are common in Europe (performance conditions are often required by law) and in other parts of the world outside the US, and investors are calling for greater use of performance conditions. Therefore, the Board concluded that introducing an accounting standard based on APB 25 would be inconsistent with its objective of developing high quality accounting standards.

BC284 That leaves SFAS 123. Comments from the FASB, in the SFAS 123 Basis for Conclusions, and from the Canadian AcSB when it developed a standard based on SFAS 123, indicate that both standard-setters regard it as inadequate, because it permits a choice between recognition and disclosure. (This issue is discussed further below.) The FASB added to its agenda in March 2003 a project to review US accounting requirements on share-based payment, including removing the disclosure alternative in SFAS 123, so that expense recognition is mandatory. The Chairman of the FASB commented:

> Recent events have served as a reminder to all of us that clear, credible and comparable financial information is essential to the health and vitality of our capital market system. In the wake of the market meltdown and corporate reporting scandals, the FASB has received numerous requests from individual and institutional investors, financial analysts and many others urging the Board to mandate the expensing of the compensation cost relating to employee stock options ... While a number of major companies have voluntarily opted to reflect these costs as an expense in reporting their earnings, other companies continue to show these costs in the footnotes to their

financial statements. In addition, a move to require an expense treatment would be consistent with the FASB's commitment to work toward convergence between U.S. and international accounting standards. In taking all of these factors into consideration, the Board concluded that it was critical that it now revisit this important subject. (FASB News Release, 12 March 2003)

BC285 During the Board's redeliberations of the proposals in ED 2, the Board worked with the FASB to achieve convergence of international and US standards, to the extent possible, bearing in mind that the FASB was at an earlier stage in its project—the FASB was developing an Exposure Draft to revise SFAS 123 whereas the IASB was finalising its IFRS. The Board concluded that, although convergence is an important objective, it would not be appropriate to delay the issue of the IFRS, because of the pressing need for a standard on share-based payment, as explained in paragraphs BC2–BC5. In any event, at the time the IASB concluded its deliberations, a substantial amount of convergence had been achieved. For example, the FASB agreed with the IASB that all share-based payment transactions should be recognised in the financial statements, measured on a fair value measurement basis, including transactions in which share options are granted to employees. Hence, the FASB agreed that the disclosure alternative in SFAS 123 should be eliminated.

BC286 The IASB and FASB also agreed that, once both boards have issued final standards on share-based payment, the two boards will consider undertaking a convergence project, with the objective of eliminating any remaining areas of divergence between international and US standards on this topic.

Recognition versus disclosure

BC287 A basic accounting concept is that disclosure of financial information is not an adequate substitute for recognition in the financial statements. For example, the *Framework* states:

> Items that meet the recognition criteria should be recognised in the balance sheet or income statement. The failure to recognise such items is not rectified by disclosure of the accounting policies used nor by notes or explanatory material. (paragraph 82)

BC288 A key aspect of the recognition criteria is that the item can be measured with reliability. This issue is discussed further below. Therefore, this discussion focuses on the 'recognition versus disclosure' issue in principle, not on measurement reliability. Once it has been determined that an item meets the criteria for recognition in the financial statements, failing to recognise it is inconsistent with the basic concept that disclosure is not an adequate substitute for recognition.

BC289 Some disagree with this concept, arguing that it makes no difference whether information is recognised in the financial statements or disclosed in the notes. Either way, users of financial statements have the information they require to make economic decisions. Hence, they believe that note disclosure of expenses arising from particular employee share-based payment transactions (ie those involving awards of share options to employees), rather than recognition in the income statement, is acceptable.

BC290 The Board did not accept this argument. The Board noted that if note disclosure is acceptable, because it makes no difference whether the expense is recognised or disclosed, then recognition in the financial statements must also be acceptable for the same reason. If recognition is acceptable, and recognition rather than mere disclosure accords with the accounting principles applied to all other expense items, it is not acceptable to leave one particular expense item out of the income statement.

BC291 The Board also noted that there is significant evidence that there is a difference between recognition and disclosure. First, academic research indicates that whether information is recognised or merely disclosed affects market prices (eg Barth, Clinch and Shibano, 2003).* If information is disclosed only in the notes, users of financial statements have to expend time and effort to become sufficiently expert in accounting to know (a) that there are items that are not recognised in the financial statements, (b) that there is information about those items in the notes, and (c) how to assess the note disclosures. Because gaining that expertise comes at a cost, and not all users of financial statements will become accounting experts, information that is merely disclosed may not be fully reflected in share prices.

BC292 Second, both preparers and users of financial statements appear to agree that there is an important difference between recognition and disclosure. Users of financial statements have strongly expressed the view that all forms of share-based payment, including employee share options, should be recognised in the financial statements, resulting in the recognition of an expense when the goods or services received are consumed, and that note disclosure alone is inadequate. Their views have been expressed by various means, including:

(a) users' responses to the Discussion Paper and ED 2.

(b) the 2001 survey by the Association for Investment Management and Research of analysts and fund managers—83 per cent of survey respondents said the accounting method for all share-based payment transactions should require recognition of an expense in the income statement.

(c) public comments by users of financial statements, such as those reported in the press or made at recent US Senate hearings.

BC293 Preparers of financial statements also see a major difference between recognition and disclosure. For example, some preparers who responded to the Discussion Paper and ED 2 were concerned that unless expense recognition is required in all countries, entities that are required to recognise an expense would be at a competitive disadvantage compared with entities that are permitted a choice between recognition and disclosure. Comments such as these indicate that preparers of financial statements regard expense recognition as having consequences that are different from those of disclosure.

---

* M E Barth, G Clinch and T Shibano. 2003. Market Effects of Recognition and Disclosure. *Journal of Accounting Research* 41(4): 581–609.

Reliability of measurement

BC294 One reason commonly given by those who oppose the recognition of an expense arising from transactions involving grants of share options to employees is that it is not possible to measure those transactions reliably.

BC295 The Board discussed these concerns about reliability, after first putting the issue into context. For example, the Board noted that when estimating the fair value of share options, the objective is to measure that fair value at the measurement date, not the value of the underlying share at some future date. Some regard the fair value estimate as inherently uncertain because it is not known, at the measurement date, what the final outcome will be, ie how much the gain on exercise (if any) will be. However, the valuation does not attempt to estimate the future gain, only the amount that the other party would pay to obtain the right to participate in any future gains. Therefore, even if the share option expires worthless or the employee makes a large gain on exercise, this does not mean that the grant date estimate of the fair value of that option was unreliable or wrong.

BC296 The Board also noted that accounting often involves making estimates, and therefore reporting an estimated fair value is not objectionable merely because that amount represents an estimate rather than a precise measure. Examples of other estimates made in accounting, which may have a material effect on the income statement and the balance sheet, include estimates of the collectability of doubtful debts, estimates of the useful life of fixed assets and the pattern of their consumption, and estimates of employee pension liabilities.

BC297 However, some argue that including in the financial statements an estimate of the fair value of employee share options is different from including other estimates, because there is no subsequent correction of the estimate. Other estimates, such as employee pension costs, will ultimately be revised to equal the amount of the cash paid out. In contrast, because equity is not remeasured, if the estimated fair value of employee share options is recognised, there is no remeasurement of the fair value estimate—unless exercise date measurement is used—so any estimation error is permanently embedded in the financial statements.

BC298 The FASB considered and rejected this argument in developing SFAS 123. For example, for employee pension costs, the total cost is never completely trued up unless the scheme is terminated, the amount attributed to any particular year is never trued up, and it can take decades before the amounts relating to particular employees are trued up. In the meantime, users of financial statements have made economic decisions based on the estimated costs.

BC299 Moreover, the Board noted that if no expense (or an expense based on intrinsic value only, which is typically zero) is recognised in respect of employee share options, that also means that there is an error that is permanently embedded in the financial statements. Reporting zero (or an amount based on intrinsic value, if any) is never trued up.

BC300 The Board also considered the meaning of reliability. Arguments about whether estimates of the fair value of employee share options are sufficiently reliable focus on one aspect of reliability only—whether the estimate is free from material error. The *Framework*, in common with the conceptual frameworks of other accounting standard-setters, makes it clear that another important aspect of reliability is whether the information can be depended upon by users of financial statements to represent faithfully what it purports to represent. Therefore, in assessing whether a particular accounting method produces reliable financial information, it is necessary to consider whether that information is representationally faithful. This is one way in which reliability is linked to another important qualitative characteristic of financial information, relevance.

BC301 For example, in the context of share-based payment, some commentators advocate measuring employee share options at intrinsic value rather than fair value, because intrinsic value is regarded as a much more reliable measure. Whether intrinsic value is a more reliable measure is doubtful—it is certainly less subject to estimation error, but is unlikely to be a representationally faithful measure of remuneration. Nor is intrinsic value a relevant measure, especially when measured at grant date. Many employee share options are issued at the money, so have no intrinsic value at grant date. A share option with no intrinsic value consists entirely of time value. If a share option is measured at intrinsic value at grant date, zero value is attributed to the share option. Therefore, by ignoring time value, the amount attributed to the share option is 100 per cent understated.

BC302 Another qualitative characteristic is comparability. Some argue that, given the uncertainties relating to estimating the fair value of employee share options, it is better for all entities to report zero, because this will make financial statements more comparable. They argue that if, for example, for two entities the 'true' amount of expense relating to employee share options is CU500,000, and estimation uncertainties cause one entity to report CU450,000 and the other to report CU550,000, the two entities' financial statements would be more comparable if both reported zero, rather than these divergent figures.

BC303 However, it is unlikely that any two entities will have the same amount of employee share-based remuneration expense. Research (eg by Bear Stearns and Credit Suisse First Boston) indicates that the expense varies widely from industry to industry, from entity to entity, and from year to year. Reporting zero rather than an estimated amount is likely to make the financial statements much less comparable, not more comparable. For example, if the estimated employee share-based remuneration expense of Company A, Company B and Company C is CU10,000, CU100,000 and CU1,000,000 respectively, reporting zero for all three companies will not make their financial statements comparable.

BC304 In the context of the foregoing discussion of reliability, the Board addressed the question whether transactions involving share options granted to employees can be measured with sufficient reliability for the purpose of recognition in the financial statements. The Board noted that many respondents to the Discussion Paper asserted that this is not possible. They argue that option pricing models cannot be applied to employee share options, because of the differences between employee options and traded options.

BC305 The Board considered these differences, with the assistance of the project's Advisory Group and other experts, and has reached conclusions on how to take account of these differences when estimating the fair value of employee share options, as explained in paragraphs BC145–BC199. In doing so, the Board noted that the objective is to measure the fair value of the share options, ie an estimate of what the price of those equity instruments would have been on grant date in an arm's length transaction between knowledgeable, willing parties. The valuation methodology applied should therefore be consistent with valuation methodologies that market participants would use for pricing similar financial instruments, and should incorporate all factors and assumptions that knowledgeable, willing market participants would consider in setting the price.

BC306 Hence, factors that a knowledgeable, willing market participant would not consider in setting the price of an option are not relevant when estimating the fair value of shares, share options or other equity instruments granted. For example, for share options granted to employees, factors that affect the value of the option from the individual employee's perspective only are not relevant to estimating the price that would be set by a knowledgeable, willing market participant. Many respondents' comments about measurement reliability, and the differences between employee share options and traded options, often focused on the value of the option from the employee's perspective. Therefore, the Board concluded that the IFRS should emphasise that the objective is to estimate the fair value of the share option, not an employee-specific value.

BC307 The Board noted that there is evidence to support a conclusion that it is possible to make a reliable estimate of the fair value of employee share options. First, there is academic research to support this conclusion (eg Carpenter 1998, Maller, Tan and Van De Vyver 2002).[*] Second, users of financial statements regard the estimated fair values as sufficiently reliable for recognition in the financial statements. Evidence of this can be found in a variety of sources, such as the comment letters received from users of financial statements who responded to the Discussion Paper and ED 2. Users' views are important, because the objective of financial statements is to provide high quality, transparent and comparable information to help users make economic decisions. In other words, financial statements are intended to meet the needs of users, rather than preparers or other interest groups. The purpose of setting accounting standards is to ensure that, wherever possible, the information provided in the financial statements meets users' needs. Therefore, if the people who use the financial statements in making economic decisions regard the fair value estimates as sufficiently reliable for recognition in the financial statements, this provides strong evidence of measurement reliability.

BC308 The Board also noted that, although the FASB decided to permit a choice between recognition and disclosure of expenses arising from employee share-based payment transactions, it did so for non-technical reasons, not because it agreed with the view that reliable measurement was not possible:

> The Board continues to believe that use of option-pricing models, as modified in this statement, will produce estimates of the fair value of stock options that are sufficiently reliable to justify recognition in financial statements. Imprecision in those estimates does not justify failure to recognize compensation cost stemming from employee stock options. That belief underlies the Board's encouragement to

---

[*] J N Carpenter. 1998. The exercise and valuation of executive stock options. *Journal of Financial Economics* 48: 127–158.
R A Maller, R Tan and M Van De Vyver. 2002. How Might Companies Value ESOs? *Australian Accounting Review* 12 (1): 11–24.

entities to adopt the fair value based method of recognizing stock-based employee compensation cost in their financial statements.
(SFAS 123, Basis for Conclusions, paragraph 117)

BC309 In summary, if expenses arising from grants of share options to employees are omitted from the financial statements, or recognised using the intrinsic value method (which typically results in zero expense) or the minimum value method, there will be a permanent error embedded in the financial statements. So the question is, which accounting method is more likely to produce the smallest amount of error and the most relevant, comparable information—a fair value estimate, which might result in some understatement or overstatement of the associated expense, or another measurement basis, such as intrinsic value (especially if measured at grant date), that will definitely result in substantial understatement of the associated expense?

BC310 Taking all of the above into consideration, the Board concluded that, in virtually all cases, the estimated fair value of employee share options at grant date can be measured with sufficient reliability for the purposes of recognising employee share-based payment transactions in the financial statements. The Board therefore concluded that, in general, the IFRS on share-based payment should require a fair value measurement method to be applied to all types of share-based payment transactions, including all types of employee share-based payment. Hence, the Board concluded that the IFRS should not allow a choice between a fair value measurement method and an intrinsic value measurement method, and should not permit a choice between recognition and disclosure of expenses arising from employee share-based payment transactions.

Transitional provisions

Share-based payment transactions among group entities

BC310A The Board noted a potential difficulty when an entity retrospectively applies the amendments made by *Group Cash-settled Share-based Payment Transactions* issued in June 2009. An entity might not have accounted for some group share-based payment transactions in accordance with IFRS 2 in its separate or individual financial statements. In a few cases, an entity that settles a group share-based payment transaction may have to apply hindsight to measure the fair value of awards now required to be accounted for as cash-settled. However, the Board noted that such transactions would have been accounted for in accordance with IFRS 2 in the group's consolidated financial statements. For these reasons and those outlined in paragraph BC268G, if the information necessary for retrospective application is not available, the Board decided to require an entity to use amounts previously recognised in the group's consolidated financial statements when applying the new requirements retrospectively in the entity's separate or individual financial statements.

Consequential amendments to other Standards

Tax effects of share-based payment transactions

BC311   Whether expenses arising from share-based payment transactions are deductible, and if so, whether the amount of the tax deduction is the same as the reported expense and whether the tax deduction arises in the same accounting period, varies from country to country.

BC312   If the amount of the tax deduction is the same as the reported expense, but the tax deduction arises in a later accounting period, this will result in a deductible temporary difference under IAS 12 *Income Taxes*. Temporary differences usually arise from differences between the carrying amount of assets and liabilities and the amount attributed to those assets and liabilities for tax purposes. However, IAS 12 also deals with items that have a tax base but are not recognised as assets and liabilities in the balance sheet. It gives an example of research costs that are recognised as an expense in the financial statements in the period in which the costs are incurred, but are deductible for tax purposes in a later accounting period. The Standard states that the difference between the tax base of the research costs, being the amount that will be deductible in a future accounting period, and the carrying amount of nil is a deductible temporary difference that results in a deferred tax asset (IAS 12, paragraph 9).

BC313   Applying this guidance indicates that if an expense arising from a share-based payment transaction is recognised in the financial statements in one accounting period and is tax-deductible in a later accounting period, this should be accounted for as a deductible temporary difference under IAS 12. Under that Standard, a deferred tax asset is recognised for all deductible temporary differences to the extent that it is probable that taxable profit will be available against which the deductible temporary difference can be used (IAS 12, paragraph 24).

BC314   Whilst IAS 12 does not discuss reverse situations, the same logic applies. For example, suppose the entity is able to claim a tax deduction for the total transaction amount at the date of grant but the entity recognises an expense arising from that transaction over the vesting period. Applying the guidance in IAS 12 suggests that this should be accounted for as a taxable temporary difference, and hence a deferred tax liability should be recognised.

BC315   However, the amount of the tax deduction might differ from the amount of the expense recognised in the financial statements. For example, the measurement basis applied for accounting purposes might not be the same as that used for tax purposes, eg intrinsic value might be used for tax purposes and fair value for accounting purposes. Similarly, the measurement date might differ. For example, US entities receive a tax deduction based on intrinsic value at the date of exercise in respect of some share options, whereas for accounting purposes an entity applying SFAS 123 would recognise an expense based on the option's fair value, measured at the date of grant. There could also be other differences in the measurement method applied for accounting and tax purposes, eg differences in the treatment of forfeitures or different valuation methodologies applied.

BC316   SFAS 123 requires that, if the amount of the tax deduction exceeds the total expense recognised in the financial statements, the tax benefit for the excess deduction should be recognised as additional paid-in capital, ie as a direct credit to equity. Conversely, if the tax deduction is less than the total expense recognised for accounting purposes, the write-off of the related deferred tax asset in excess of the benefits of the tax deduction is recognised in the income statement, except to the extent that there is remaining additional paid-in capital from excess tax deductions from previous share-based payment transactions (SFAS 123, paragraph 44).

BC317   At first sight, it may seem questionable to credit or debit directly to equity amounts that relate to differences between the amount of the tax deduction and the total recognised expense. The tax effects of any such differences would ordinarily flow through the income statement. However, some argue that the approach in SFAS 123 is appropriate if the reason for the difference between the amount of the tax deduction and the recognised expense is that a different measurement date is applied.

BC318   For example, suppose grant date measurement is used for accounting purposes and exercise date measurement is used for tax purposes. Under grant date measurement, any changes in the value of the equity instrument after grant date accrue to the employee (or other party) in their capacity as equity participants. Therefore, some argue that any tax effects arising from those valuation changes should be credited to equity (or debited to equity, if the value of the equity instrument declines).

BC319   Similarly, some argue that the tax deduction arises from an equity transaction (the exercise of options), and hence the tax effects should be reported in equity. It can also be argued that this treatment is consistent with the requirement in IAS 12 to account for the tax effects of transactions or events in the same way as the entity accounts for those transactions or events themselves. If the tax deduction relates to both an income statement item and an equity item, the associated tax effects should be allocated between the income statement and equity.

BC320   Others disagree, arguing that the tax deduction relates to employee remuneration expense, ie an income statement item only, and therefore all of the tax effects of the deduction should be recognised in the income statement. The fact that the taxing authority applies a different method in measuring the amount of the tax deduction does not change this conclusion. A further argument is that this treatment is consistent with the *Framework*, because reporting amounts directly in equity would be inappropriate, given that the government is not an owner of the entity.

BC321   The Board noted that, if one accepts that it might be appropriate to debit/credit to equity the tax effect of the difference between the amount of the tax deduction and the total recognised expense where that difference relates to changes in the value of equity interests, there could be other reasons why the amount of the tax deduction differs from the total recognised expense. For example, grant date measurement may be used for both tax and accounting purposes, but the valuation methodology used for tax purposes might produce a higher value than the methodology used for accounting purposes (eg the effects of early exercise might be ignored when valuing an option for tax purposes). The Board saw no reason why, in this situation, the excess tax benefits should be credited to equity.

BC322   In developing ED 2, the Board concluded that the tax effects of share-based payment transactions should be recognised in the income statement by being taken into account in the determination of tax expense. It agreed that this should be explained in the form of a worked example in a consequential amendment to IAS 12.

BC323   During the Board's redeliberation of the proposals in ED 2, the Board reconsidered the points above, and concluded that the tax effects of an equity-settled share-based payment transaction should be allocated between the income statement and equity. The Board then considered how this allocation should be made and related issues, such as the measurement of the deferred tax asset.

BC324   Under IAS 12, the deferred tax asset for a deductible temporary difference is based on the amount the taxation authorities will permit as a deduction in future periods. Therefore, the Board concluded that the measurement of the deferred tax asset should be based on an estimate of the future tax deduction. If changes in the share price affect that future tax deduction, the estimate of the expected future tax deduction should be based on the current share price.

BC325   These conclusions are consistent with the proposals in ED 2 concerning the measurement of the deferred tax asset. However, this approach differs from SFAS 123, which measures the deferred tax asset on the basis of the cumulative recognised expense. The Board rejected the SFAS 123 method of measuring the deferred tax asset because it is inconsistent with IAS 12. As noted above, under IAS 12, the deferred tax asset for a deductible temporary difference is based on the amount the taxation authorities will permit as a deduction in future periods. If a later measurement date is applied for tax purposes, it is very unlikely that the tax deduction will ever equal the cumulative expense, except by coincidence. For example, if share options are granted to employees, and the entity receives a tax deduction measured as the difference between the share price and the exercise price at the date of exercise, it is extremely unlikely that the tax deduction will ever equal the cumulative expense. By basing the measurement of the deferred tax asset on the cumulative expense, the SFAS 123 method is likely to result in the understatement or overstatement of the deferred tax asset. In some situations, such as when share options are significantly out of the money, SFAS 123 requires the entity to continue to recognise a deferred tax asset even when the possibility of the entity recovering that asset is remote. Continuing to recognise a deferred tax asset in this situation is not only inconsistent with IAS 12, it is inconsistent with the definition of an asset in the *Framework*, and the requirements of other IFRSs for the recognition and measurement of assets, including requirements to assess impairment.

BC326   The Board also concluded that:

   (a)   if the tax deduction received (or expected to be received, measured as described in paragraph BC324) is less than or equal to the cumulative expense, the associated tax benefits received (or expected to be received) should be recognised as tax income and included in profit or loss for the period.

(b) if the tax deduction received (or expected to be received, measured as described in paragraph BC324) exceeds the cumulative expense, the excess associated tax benefits received (or expected to be received) should be recognised directly in equity.

BC327 The above allocation method is similar to that applied in SFAS 123, with some exceptions. First, the above allocation method ensures that the total tax benefits recognised in the income statement in respect of a particular share-based payment transaction do not exceed the tax benefits ultimately received. The Board disagreed with the approach in SFAS 123, which sometimes results in the total tax benefits recognised in the income statement exceeding the tax benefits ultimately received because, in some situations, SFAS 123 permits the unrecovered portion of the deferred tax asset to be written off to equity.

BC328 Second, the Board concluded that the above allocation method should be applied irrespective of why the tax deduction received (or expected to be received) differs from the cumulative expense. The SFAS 123 method is based on US tax legislation, under which the excess tax benefits credited to equity (if any) arise from the use of a later measurement date for tax purposes. The Board agreed with respondents who commented that the accounting treatment must be capable of being applied in various tax jurisdictions. The Board was concerned that requiring entities to examine the reasons why there is a difference between the tax deduction and the cumulative expense, and then account for the tax effects accordingly, would be too complex to be applied consistently across a wide range of different tax jurisdictions.

BC329 The Board noted that it might need to reconsider its conclusions on accounting for the tax effects of share-based payment transactions in the future, for example, if the Board reviews IAS 12 more broadly.

Accounting for own shares held

BC330 IAS 32 requires the acquisition of treasury shares to be deducted from equity, and no gain or loss is to be recognised on the sale, issue or cancellation of treasury shares. Consideration received on the subsequent sale or issue of treasury shares is credited to equity.

BC331 This is consistent with the *Framework*. The repurchase of shares and their subsequent reissue or transfer to other parties are transactions with equity participants that should be recognised as changes in equity. In accounting terms, there is no difference between shares that are repurchased and cancelled, and shares that are repurchased and held by the entity. In both cases, the repurchase involves an outflow of resources to shareholders (ie a distribution), thereby reducing shareholders' investment in the entity. Similarly, there is no difference between a new issue of shares and an issue of shares previously repurchased and held in treasury. In both cases, there is an inflow of resources from shareholders, thereby increasing shareholders' investment in the entity. Although accounting practice in some jurisdictions treats own shares held as assets, this is not consistent with the definition of assets in the *Framework* and the conceptual frameworks of other standard-setters, as explained in the Discussion Paper (footnote to paragraph 4.7 of the Discussion Paper, reproduced earlier in the footnote to paragraph BC73).

BC332 Given that treasury shares are treated as an asset in some jurisdictions, it will be necessary to change that accounting treatment when this IFRS is applied, because otherwise an entity would be faced with two expense items—an expense arising from the share-based payment transaction (for the consumption of goods and services received as consideration for the issue of an equity instrument) and another expense arising from the write-down of the 'asset' for treasury shares issued or transferred to employees at an exercise price that is less than their purchase price.

BC333 Hence, the Board concluded that the requirements in the relevant paragraphs of IAS 32 regarding treasury shares should also be applied to treasury shares purchased, sold, issued or cancelled in connection with employee share plans or other share-based payment arrangements.

CONTENTS

Guidance on implementing
IFRS 2 *Share-based Payment*

This guidance accompanies, but is not part of, IFRS 2.

Definition of grant date

IG1   IFRS 2 defines grant date as the date at which the entity and the employee (or other party providing similar services) agree to a share-based payment arrangement, being when the entity and the counterparty have a shared understanding of the terms and conditions of the arrangement. At grant date the entity confers on the counterparty the right to cash, other assets, or equity instruments of the entity, provided the specified vesting conditions, if any, are met.   If that agreement is subject to an approval process (for example, by shareholders), grant date is the date when that approval is obtained.

IG2   As noted above, grant date is when both parties agree to a share-based payment arrangement. The word 'agree' is used in its usual sense, which means that there must be both an offer and acceptance of that offer. Hence, the date at which one party makes an offer to another party is not grant date. The date of grant is when that other party accepts the offer.   In some instances, the counterparty explicitly agrees to the arrangement, eg by signing a contract.   In other instances, agreement might be implicit, eg for many share-based payment arrangements with employees, the employees' agreement is evidenced by their commencing to render services.

IG3   Furthermore, for both parties to have agreed to the share-based payment arrangement, both parties must have a shared understanding of the terms and conditions of the arrangement. Therefore, if some of the terms and conditions of the arrangement are agreed on one date, with the remainder of the terms and conditions agreed on a later date, then grant date is on that later date, when all of the terms and conditions have been agreed. For example, if an entity agrees to issue share options to an employee, but the exercise price of the options will be set by a compensation committee that meets in three months' time, grant date is when the exercise price is set by the compensation committee.

IG4   In some cases, grant date might occur after the employees to whom the equity instruments were granted have begun rendering services. For example, if a grant of equity instruments is subject to shareholder approval, grant date might occur some months after the employees have begun rendering services in respect of that grant. The IFRS requires the entity to recognise the services when received. In this situation, the entity should estimate the grant date fair value of the equity instruments (eg by estimating the fair value of the equity instruments at the end of the reporting period), for the purposes of recognising the services received during the period between service commencement date and grant date. Once the date of grant has been established, the entity should revise the earlier estimate so that the amounts recognised for services received in respect of the grant are ultimately based on the grant date fair value of the equity instruments.

Definition of vesting conditions

IG4A   IFRS 2 defines vesting conditions as the conditions that determine whether the entity receives the services that entitle the counterparty to receive cash, other assets or equity instruments of the entity under a share-based payment arrangement. The following flowchart illustrates the evaluation of whether a condition is a service or performance condition or a non-vesting condition.

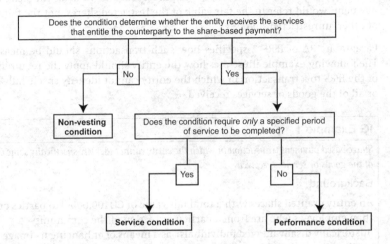

Transactions with parties other than employees

IG5   For transactions with parties other than employees (and others providing similar services) that are measured by reference to the fair value of the equity instruments granted, paragraph 13 of IFRS 2 includes a rebuttable presumption that the fair value of the goods or services received can be estimated reliably. In these situations, paragraph 13 of IFRS 2 requires the entity to measure that fair value at the date the entity obtains the goods or the counterparty renders service.

Transaction in which the entity cannot identify specifically some or all of the goods or services received

IG5A   In some cases, however, it might be difficult to demonstrate that goods or services have been (or will be) received. For example, an entity may grant shares to a charitable organisation for nil consideration. It is usually not possible to identify the specific goods or services received in return for such a transaction. A similar situation might arise in transactions with other parties.

IG5B   Paragraph 11 of IFRS 2 requires transactions in which share-based payments are made to employees to be measured by reference to the fair value of the share-based payments at grant date.[*] Hence, the entity is not required to measure directly the fair value of the employee services received.

---

[*]   In IFRS 2, all references to employees include others providing similar services.

IG5C   It should be noted that the phrase 'the fair value of the share-based payment' refers to the fair value of the particular share-based payment concerned. For example, an entity might be required by government legislation to issue some portion of its shares to nationals of a particular country that may be transferred only to other nationals of that country. Such a transfer restriction may affect the fair value of the shares concerned, and therefore those shares may have a fair value that is less than the fair value of otherwise identical shares that do not carry such restrictions. In this situation, the phrase 'the fair value of the share-based payment' would refer to the fair value of the restricted shares, not the fair value of other, unrestricted shares.

IG5D   Paragraph 13A of IFRS 2 specifies how such transactions should be measured. The following example illustrates how the entity should apply the requirements of the IFRS to a transaction in which the entity cannot identify specifically some or all of the goods or services received.

IG Example 1

Share-based payment transaction in which the entity cannot identify specifically some or all of the goods or services received

Background

An entity granted shares with a total fair value of CU100,000[a] to parties other than employees who are from a particular section of the community (historically disadvantaged individuals), as a means of enhancing its image as a good corporate citizen. The economic benefits derived from enhancing its corporate image could take a variety of forms, such as increasing its customer base, attracting or retaining employees, or improving or maintaining its ability to tender successfully for business contracts.

The entity cannot identify the specific consideration received. For example, no cash was received and no service conditions were imposed. Therefore, the identifiable consideration (nil) is less than the fair value of the equity instruments granted (CU100,000).

Application of requirements

Although the entity cannot identify the specific goods or services received, the circumstances indicate that goods or services have been (or will be) received, and therefore IFRS 2 applies.

In this situation, because the entity cannot identify the specific goods or services received, the rebuttable presumption in paragraph 13 of IFRS 2, that the fair value of the goods or services received can be estimated reliably, does not apply. The entity should instead measure the goods or services received by reference to the fair value of the equity instruments granted.

(a) In this example, and in all other examples in this guidance, monetary amounts are denominated in 'currency units (CU)'.

Measurement date for transactions with parties other than employees

IG6   If the goods or services are received on more than one date, the entity should measure the fair value of the equity instruments granted on each date when goods or services are received. The entity should apply that fair value when measuring the goods or services received on that date.

IG7   However, an approximation could be used in some cases. For example, if an entity received services continuously during a three-month period, and its share price did not change significantly during that period, the entity could use the average share price during the three-month period when estimating the fair value of the equity instruments granted.

Transitional arrangements

IG8   In paragraph 54 of IFRS 2, the entity is encouraged, but not required, to apply the requirements of the IFRS to other grants of equity instruments (ie grants other than those specified in paragraph 53 of the IFRS), if the entity has disclosed publicly the fair value of those equity instruments, measured at the measurement date. For example, such equity instruments include equity instruments for which the entity has disclosed in the notes to its financial statements the information required in the US by SFAS 123 *Accounting for Stock-based Compensation*.

Equity-settled share-based payment transactions

IG9   For equity-settled transactions measured by reference to the fair value of the equity instruments granted, paragraph 19 of IFRS 2 states that vesting conditions, other than market conditions,* are not taken into account when estimating the fair value of the shares or share options at the measurement date (ie grant date, for transactions with employees and others providing similar services). Instead, vesting conditions are taken into account by adjusting the number of equity instruments included in the measurement of the transaction amount so that, ultimately, the amount recognised for goods or services received as consideration for the equity instruments granted is based on the number of equity instruments that eventually vest. Hence, on a cumulative basis, no amount is recognised for goods or services received if the equity instruments granted do not vest because of failure to satisfy a vesting condition, eg the counterparty fails to complete a specified service period, or a performance condition is not satisfied. This accounting method is known as the modified grant date method, because the number of equity instruments included in the determination of the transaction amount is adjusted to reflect the outcome of the vesting conditions, but no adjustment is made to the fair value of those equity instruments. That fair value is estimated at grant date (for transactions with employees and others providing similar services) and not subsequently revised. Hence, neither increases nor decreases in the fair value of the equity instruments after grant date are taken

---

* In the remainder of this paragraph, the discussion of vesting conditions excludes market conditions, which are subject to the requirements of paragraph 21 of IFRS 2.

into account when determining the transaction amount (other than in the context of measuring the incremental fair value transferred if a grant of equity instruments is subsequently modified).

IG10　To apply these requirements, paragraph 20 of IFRS 2 requires the entity to recognise the goods or services received during the vesting period based on the best available estimate of the number of equity instruments expected to vest and to revise that estimate, if necessary, if subsequent information indicates that the number of equity instruments expected to vest differs from previous estimates. On vesting date, the entity revises the estimate to equal the number of equity instruments that ultimately vested (subject to the requirements of paragraph 21 concerning market conditions).

IG11　In the examples below, the share options granted all vest at the same time, at the end of a specified period. In some situations, share options or other equity instruments granted might vest in instalments over the vesting period. For example, suppose an employee is granted 100 share options, which will vest in instalments of 25 share options at the end of each year over the next four years. To apply the requirements of the IFRS, the entity should treat each instalment as a separate share option grant, because each instalment has a different vesting period, and hence the fair value of each instalment will differ (because the length of the vesting period affects, for example, the likely timing of cash flows arising from the exercise of the options).

IG Example 1A

Background

An entity grants 100 share options to each of its 500 employees. Each grant is conditional upon the employee working for the entity over the next three years. The entity estimates that the fair value of each share option is CU15.

On the basis of a weighted average probability, the entity estimates that 20 per cent of employees will leave during the three-year period and therefore forfeit their rights to the share options.

Application of requirements

Scenario 1

If everything turns out exactly as expected, the entity recognises the following amounts during the vesting period, for services received as consideration for the share options.

Year	Calculation	Remuneration expense for period CU	Cumulative remuneration expense CU
1	50,000 options × 80% × CU15 × ⅓ years	200,000	200,000
2	(50,000 options × 80% × CU15 × ⅔ years) – CU200,000	200,000	400,000
3	(50,000 options × 80% × CU15 × ³⁄₃ years) – CU400,000	200,000	600,000

continued...

　　　　　　　　　　© IASCF

...continued
IG Example 1A

Scenario 2

During year 1, 20 employees leave. The entity revises its estimate of total employee departures over the three-year period from 20 per cent (100 employees) to 15 per cent (75 employees). During year 2, a further 22 employees leave. The entity revises its estimate of total employee departures over the three-year period from 15 per cent to 12 per cent (60 employees). During year 3, a further 15 employees leave. Hence, a total of 57 employees forfeited their rights to the share options during the three-year period, and a total of 44,300 share options (443 employees × 100 options per employee) vested at the end of year 3.

Year	Calculation	Remuneration expense for period	Cumulative remuneration expense
		CU	CU
1	50,000 options × 85% × CU15 × ⅓ years	212,500	212,500
2	(50,000 options × 88% × CU15 × ⅔ years) – CU212,500	227,500	440,000
3	(44,300 options × CU15) – CU440,000	224,500	664,500

IG12   In Example 1A, the share options were granted conditionally upon the employees' completing a specified service period. In some cases, a share option or share grant might also be conditional upon the achievement of a specified performance target. Examples 2, 3 and 4 illustrate the application of the IFRS to share option or share grants with performance conditions (other than market conditions, which are discussed in paragraph IG13 and illustrated in Examples 5 and 6). In Example 2, the length of the vesting period varies, depending on when the performance condition is satisfied. Paragraph 15 of the IFRS requires the entity to estimate the length of the expected vesting period, based on the most likely outcome of the performance condition, and to revise that estimate, if necessary, if subsequent information indicates that the length of the vesting period is likely to differ from previous estimates.

IG Example 2

Grant with a performance condition, in which the length of the vesting period varies

Background

At the beginning of year 1, the entity grants 100 shares each to 500 employees, conditional upon the employees' remaining in the entity's employ during the vesting period. The shares will vest at the end of year 1 if the entity's earnings increase by more than 18 per cent; at the end of year 2 if the entity's earnings increase by more than an average of 13 per cent per year over the two-year period; and at the end of year 3 if the entity's earnings increase by more than an average of 10 per cent per year over the three-year period. The shares have a fair value of CU30 per share at the start of year 1, which equals the share price at grant date. No dividends are expected to be paid over the three-year period.

By the end of year 1, the entity's earnings have increased by 14 per cent, and 30 employees have left. The entity expects that earnings will continue to increase at a similar rate in year 2, and therefore expects that the shares will vest at the end of year 2. The entity expects, on the basis of a weighted average probability, that a further 30 employees will leave during year 2, and therefore expects that 440 employees will vest in 100 shares each at the end of year 2.

By the end of year 2, the entity's earnings have increased by only 10 per cent and therefore the shares do not vest at the end of year 2. 28 employees have left during the year. The entity expects that a further 25 employees will leave during year 3, and that the entity's earnings will increase by at least 6 per cent, thereby achieving the average of 10 per cent per year.

By the end of year 3, 23 employees have left and the entity's earnings had increased by 8 per cent, resulting in an average increase of 10.67 per cent per year. Therefore, 419 employees received 100 shares at the end of year 3.

Application of requirements

Year	Calculation	Remuneration expense for period CU	Cumulative remuneration expense CU
1	440 employees × 100 shares × CU30 × ½	660,000	660,000
2	(417 employees × 100 shares × CU30 × ⅔) − CU660,000	174,000	834,000
3	(419 employees × 100 shares × CU30 × ⅓) − CU834,000	423,000	1,257,000

IG Example 3

Grant with a performance condition, in which the number of equity instruments varies

Background

At the beginning of year 1, Entity A grants share options to each of its 100 employees working in the sales department. The share options will vest at the end of year 3, provided that the employees remain in the entity's employ, and provided that the volume of sales of a particular product increases by at least an average of 5 per cent per year. If the volume of sales of the product increases by an average of between 5 per cent and 10 per cent per year, each employee will receive 100 share options. If the volume of sales increases by an average of between 10 per cent and 15 per cent each year, each employee will receive 200 share options. If the volume of sales increases by an average of 15 per cent or more, each employee will receive 300 share options.

On grant date, Entity A estimates that the share options have a fair value of CU20 per option. Entity A also estimates that the volume of sales of the product will increase by an average of between 10 per cent and 15 per cent per year, and therefore expects that, for each employee who remains in service until the end of year 3, 200 share options will vest. The entity also estimates, on the basis of a weighted average probability, that 20 per cent of employees will leave before the end of year 3.

By the end of year 1, seven employees have left and the entity still expects that a total of 20 employees will leave by the end of year 3. Hence, the entity expects that 80 employees will remain in service for the three-year period. Product sales have increased by 12 per cent and the entity expects this rate of increase to continue over the next 2 years.

By the end of year 2, a further five employees have left, bringing the total to 12 to date. The entity now expects only three more employees will leave during year 3, and therefore expects a total of 15 employees will have left during the three-year period, and hence 85 employees are expected to remain. Product sales have increased by 18 per cent, resulting in an average of 15 per cent over the two years to date. The entity now expects that sales will average 15 per cent or more over the three-year period, and hence expects each sales employee to receive 300 share options at the end of year 3.

By the end of year 3, a further two employees have left. Hence, 14 employees have left during the three-year period, and 86 employees remain. The entity's sales have increased by an average of 16 per cent over the three years. Therefore, each of the 86 employees receives 300 share options.

continued...

...continued
IG Example 3

Application of requirements

Year	Calculation	Remuneration expense for period	Cumulative remuneration expense
		CU	CU
1	80 employees × 200 options × CU20 × ⅓	106,667	106,667
2	(85 employees × 300 options × CU20 × ⅔) – CU106,667	233,333	340,000
3	(86 employees × 300 options × CU20 × ¾) – CU340,000	176,000	516,000

IG Example 4

Grant with a performance condition, in which the exercise price varies

Background

At the beginning of year 1, an entity grants to a senior executive 10,000 share options, conditional upon the executive's remaining in the entity's employ until the end of year 3. The exercise price is CU40. However, the exercise price drops to CU30 if the entity's earnings increase by at least an average of 10 per cent per year over the three-year period.

On grant date, the entity estimates that the fair value of the share options, with an exercise price of CU30, is CU16 per option. If the exercise price is CU40, the entity estimates that the share options have a fair value of CU12 per option.

During year 1, the entity's earnings increased by 12 per cent, and the entity expects that earnings will continue to increase at this rate over the next two years. The entity therefore expects that the earnings target will be achieved, and hence the share options will have an exercise price of CU30.

During year 2, the entity's earnings increased by 13 per cent, and the entity continues to expect that the earnings target will be achieved.

During year 3, the entity's earnings increased by only 3 per cent, and therefore the earnings target was not achieved. The executive completes three years' service, and therefore satisfies the service condition. Because the earnings target was not achieved, the 10,000 vested share options have an exercise price of CU40.

continued...

© IASCF

...*continued*
IG Example 4

Application of requirements

Because the exercise price varies depending on the outcome of a performance condition that is not a market condition, the effect of that performance condition (ie the possibility that the exercise price might be CU40 and the possibility that the exercise price might be CU30) is not taken into account when estimating the fair value of the share options at grant date. Instead, the entity estimates the fair value of the share options at grant date under each scenario (ie exercise price of CU40 and exercise price of CU30) and ultimately revises the transaction amount to reflect the outcome of that performance condition, as illustrated below.

Year	Calculation	Remuneration expense for period	Cumulative remuneration expense
		CU	CU
1	10,000 options × CU16 × ⅓	53,333	53,333
2	(10,000 options × CU16 × ⅔) – CU53,333	53,334	106,667
3	(10,000 options × CU12 × ¾) – CU106,667	13,333	120,000

IG13   Paragraph 21 of the IFRS requires market conditions, such as a target share price upon which vesting (or exercisability) is conditional, to be taken into account when estimating the fair value of the equity instruments granted. Therefore, for grants of equity instruments with market conditions, the entity recognises the goods or services received from a counterparty who satisfies all other vesting conditions (eg services received from an employee who remains in service for the specified period of service), irrespective of whether that market condition is satisfied. Example 5 illustrates these requirements.

IG Example 5

Grant with a market condition

Background

At the beginning of year 1, an entity grants to a senior executive 10,000 share options, conditional upon the executive remaining in the entity's employ until the end of year 3. However, the share options cannot be exercised unless the share price has increased from CU50 at the beginning of year 1 to above CU65 at the end of year 3. If the share price is above CU65 at the end of year 3, the share options can be exercised at any time during the next seven years, ie by the end of year 10.

The entity applies a binomial option pricing model, which takes into account the possibility that the share price will exceed CU65 at the end of year 3 (and hence the share options become exercisable) and the possibility that the share price will not exceed CU65 at the end of year 3 (and hence the options will be forfeited). It estimates the fair value of the share options with this market condition to be CU24 per option.

Application of requirements

Because paragraph 21 of the IFRS requires the entity to recognise the services received from a counterparty who satisfies all other vesting conditions (eg services received from an employee who remains in service for the specified service period), irrespective of whether that market condition is satisfied, it makes no difference whether the share price target is achieved. The possibility that the share price target might not be achieved has already been taken into account when estimating the fair value of the share options at grant date. Therefore, if the entity expects the executive to complete the three-year service period, and the executive does so, the entity recognises the following amounts in years 1, 2 and 3:

Year	Calculation	Remuneration expense for period	Cumulative remuneration expense
		CU	CU
1	10,000 options × CU24 × ⅓	80,000	80,000
2	(10,000 options × CU24 × ⅔) – CU80,000	80,000	160,000
3	(10,000 options × CU24) – CU160,000	80,000	240,000

As noted above, these amounts are recognised irrespective of the outcome of the market condition. However, if the executive left during year 2 (or year 3), the amount recognised during year 1 (and year 2) would be reversed in year 2 (or year 3). This is because the service condition, in contrast to the market condition, was not taken into account when estimating the fair value of the share options at grant date. Instead, the service condition is taken into account by adjusting the transaction amount to be based on the number of equity instruments that ultimately vest, in accordance with paragraphs 19 and 20 of the IFRS.

IG14   In Example 5, the outcome of the market condition did not change the length of the vesting period. However, if the length of the vesting period varies depending on when a performance condition is satisfied, paragraph 15 of the IFRS requires the entity to presume that the services to be rendered by the employees as consideration for the equity instruments granted will be received in the future, over the expected vesting period. The entity is required to estimate the length of the expected vesting period at grant date, based on the most likely outcome of the performance condition. If the performance condition is a market condition, the estimate of the length of the expected vesting period must be consistent with the assumptions used in estimating the fair value of the share options granted, and is not subsequently revised. Example 6 illustrates these requirements.

IG Example 6

Grant with a market condition, in which the length of the vesting period varies

Background

At the beginning of year 1, an entity grants 10,000 share options with a ten-year life to each of ten senior executives. The share options will vest and become exercisable immediately if and when the entity's share price increases from CU50 to CU70, provided that the executive remains in service until the share price target is achieved.

The entity applies a binomial option pricing model, which takes into account the possibility that the share price target will be achieved during the ten-year life of the options, and the possibility that the target will not be achieved. The entity estimates that the fair value of the share options at grant date is CU25 per option. From the option pricing model, the entity determines that the mode of the distribution of possible vesting dates is five years. In other words, of all the possible outcomes, the most likely outcome of the market condition is that the share price target will be achieved at the end of year 5. Therefore, the entity estimates that the expected vesting period is five years. The entity also estimates that two executives will have left by the end of year 5, and therefore expects that 80,000 share options (10,000 share options × 8 executives) will vest at the end of year 5.

Throughout years 1–4, the entity continues to estimate that a total of two executives will leave by the end of year 5. However, in total three executives leave, one in each of years 3, 4 and 5. The share price target is achieved at the end of year 6. Another executive leaves during year 6, before the share price target is achieved.

continued...

...continued
IG Example 6

Application of requirements

Paragraph 15 of the IFRS requires the entity to recognise the services received over the expected vesting period, as estimated at grant date, and also requires the entity not to revise that estimate. Therefore, the entity recognises the services received from the executives over years 1–5. Hence, the transaction amount is ultimately based on 70,000 share options (10,000 share options × 7 executives who remain in service at the end of year 5).

Although another executive left during year 6, no adjustment is made, because the executive had already completed the expected vesting period of five years. Therefore, the entity recognises the following amounts in years 1–5:

Year	Calculation	Remuneration expense for period	Cumulative remuneration expense
		CU	CU
1	80,000 options × CU25 × $\frac{1}{5}$	400,000	400,000
2	(80,000 options × CU25 × $\frac{2}{5}$) – CU400,000	400,000	800,000
3	(80,000 options × CU25 × $\frac{3}{5}$) – CU800,000	400,000	1,200,000
4	(80,000 options × CU25 × $\frac{4}{5}$) – CU1,200,000	400,000	1,600,000
5	(70,000 options × CU25) – CU1,600,000	150,000	1,750,000

IG15 Paragraphs 26–29 and B42–B44 of the IFRS set out requirements that apply if a share option is repriced (or the entity otherwise modifies the terms or conditions of a share-based payment arrangement). Examples 7–9 illustrate some of these requirements.

IG Example 7

Grant of share options that are subsequently repriced

Background

At the beginning of year 1, an entity grants 100 share options to each of its 500 employees. Each grant is conditional upon the employee remaining in service over the next three years. The entity estimates that the fair value of each option is CU15. On the basis of a weighted average probability, the entity estimates that 100 employees will leave during the three-year period and therefore forfeit their rights to the share options.

continued...

...continued
IG Example 7

Suppose that 40 employees leave during year 1. Also suppose that by the end of year 1, the entity's share price has dropped, and the entity reprices its share options, and that the repriced share options vest at the end of year 3. The entity estimates that a further 70 employees will leave during years 2 and 3, and hence the total expected employee departures over the three-year vesting period is 110 employees. During year 2, a further 35 employees leave, and the entity estimates that a further 30 employees will leave during year 3, to bring the total expected employee departures over the three-year vesting period to 105 employees. During year 3, a total of 28 employees leave, and hence a total of 103 employees ceased employment during the vesting period. For the remaining 397 employees, the share options vested at the end of year 3.

The entity estimates that, at the date of repricing, the fair value of each of the original share options granted (ie before taking into account the repricing) is CU5 and that the fair value of each repriced share option is CU8.

Application of requirements

Paragraph 27 of the IFRS requires the entity to recognise the effects of modifications that increase the total fair value of the share-based payment arrangement or are otherwise beneficial to the employee. If the modification increases the fair value of the equity instruments granted (eg by reducing the exercise price), measured immediately before and after the modification, paragraph B43(a) of Appendix B requires the entity to include the incremental fair value granted (ie the difference between the fair value of the modified equity instrument and that of the original equity instrument, both estimated as at the date of the modification) in the measurement of the amount recognised for services received as consideration for the equity instruments granted. If the modification occurs during the vesting period, the incremental fair value granted is included in the measurement of the amount recognised for services received over the period from the modification date until the date when the modified equity instruments vest, in addition to the amount based on the grant date fair value of the original equity instruments, which is recognised over the remainder of the original vesting period.

The incremental value is CU3 per share option (CU8 - CU5). This amount is recognised over the remaining two years of the vesting period, along with remuneration expense based on the original option value of CU15.

The amounts recognised in years 1–3 are as follows:

Year	Calculation	Remuneration expense for period CU	Cumulative remuneration expense CU
1	(500 – 110) employees × 100 options × CU15 × ⅓	195,000	195,000
2	(500 – 105) employees × 100 options × (CU15 × ⅔ + CU3 × ½) – CU195,000	259,250	454,250
3	(500 – 103) employees × 100 options × (CU15 + CU3) – CU454,250	260,350	714,600

IG Example 8

Grant of share options with a vesting condition that is subsequently modified

Background

At the beginning of year 1, the entity grants 1,000 share options to each member of its sales team, conditional upon the employee's remaining in the entity's employ for three years, and the team selling more than 50,000 units of a particular product over the three-year period. The fair value of the share options is CU15 per option at the date of grant.

During year 2, the entity increases the sales target to 100,000 units. By the end of year 3, the entity has sold 55,000 units, and the share options are forfeited. Twelve members of the sales team have remained in service for the three-year period.

Application of requirements

Paragraph 20 of the IFRS requires, for a performance condition that is not a market condition, the entity to recognise the services received during the vesting period based on the best available estimate of the number of equity instruments expected to vest and to revise that estimate, if necessary, if subsequent information indicates that the number of equity instruments expected to vest differs from previous estimates. On vesting date, the entity revises the estimate to equal the number of equity instruments that ultimately vested. However, paragraph 27 of the IFRS requires, irrespective of any modifications to the terms and conditions on which the equity instruments were granted, or a cancellation or settlement of that grant of equity instruments, the entity to recognise, as a minimum, the services received, measured at the grant date fair value of the equity instruments granted, unless those equity instruments do not vest because of failure to satisfy a vesting condition (other than a market condition) that was specified at grant date. Furthermore, paragraph B44(c) of Appendix B specifies that, if the entity modifies the vesting conditions in a manner that is not beneficial to the employee, the entity does not take the modified vesting conditions into account when applying the requirements of paragraphs 19–21 of the IFRS.

Therefore, because the modification to the performance condition made it less likely that the share options will vest, which was not beneficial to the employee, the entity takes no account of the modified performance condition when recognising the services received. Instead, it continues to recognise the services received over the three-year period based on the original vesting conditions. Hence, the entity ultimately recognises cumulative remuneration expense of CU180,000 over the three-year period (12 employees × 1,000 options × CU15).

The same result would have occurred if, instead of modifying the performance target, the entity had increased the number of years of service required for the share options to vest from three years to ten years. Because such a modification would make it less likely that the options will vest, which would not be beneficial to the employees, the entity would take no account of the modified service condition when recognising the services received. Instead, it would recognise the services received from the twelve employees who remained in service over the original three-year vesting period.

IG Example 9

Grant of shares, with a cash alternative subsequently added

Background

At the beginning of year 1, the entity grants 10,000 shares with a fair value of CU33 per share to a senior executive, conditional upon the completion of three years' service. By the end of year 2, the share price has dropped to CU25 per share. At that date, the entity adds a cash alternative to the grant, whereby the executive can choose whether to receive 10,000 shares or cash equal to the value of 10,000 shares on vesting date. The share price is CU22 on vesting date.

Application of requirements

Paragraph 27 of the IFRS requires, irrespective of any modifications to the terms and conditions on which the equity instruments were granted, or a cancellation or settlement of that grant of equity instruments, the entity to recognise, as a minimum, the services received measured at the grant date fair value of the equity instruments granted, unless those equity instruments do not vest because of failure to satisfy a vesting condition (other than a market condition) that was specified at grant date. Therefore, the entity recognises the services received over the three-year period, based on the grant date fair value of the shares.

Furthermore, the addition of the cash alternative at the end of year 2 creates an obligation to settle in cash. In accordance with the requirements for cash-settled share-based payment transactions (paragraphs 30–33 of the IFRS), the entity recognises the liability to settle in cash at the modification date, based on the fair value of the shares at the modification date and the extent to which the specified services have been received. Furthermore, the entity remeasures the fair value of the liability at the end of each reporting period and at the date of settlement, with any changes in fair value recognised in profit or loss for the period. Therefore, the entity recognises the following amounts:

continued...

...continued
IG Example 9

Year	Calculation	Expense CU	Equity CU	Liability CU
1	Remuneration expense for year: 10,000 shares × CU33 × ⅓	110,000	110,000	
2	Remuneration expense for year: (10,000 shares × CU33 × ⅔) − CU110,000	110,000	110,000	
	Reclassify equity to liabilities: 10,000 shares × CU25 × ⅔		(166,667)	166,667
3	Remuneration expense for year: (10,000 shares × CU33 × ³⁄₃) − CU220,000	110,000	26,667[a]	83,333[a]
	Adjust liability to closing fair value: (CU166,667 + CU83,333) − (CU22 × 10,000 shares)	(30,000)		(30,000)
	Total	300,000	80,000	220,000

(a) Allocated between liabilities and equity, to bring in the final third of the liability based on the fair value of the shares as at the date of the modification.

IG15A If a share-based payment has a non-vesting condition that the counterparty can choose not to meet and the counterparty does not meet that non-vesting condition during the vesting period, paragraph 28A of the IFRS requires that event to be treated as a cancellation. Example 9A illustrates the accounting for this type of event.

IG Example 9A

Share-based payment with vesting and non-vesting conditions when the counterparty can choose whether the non-vesting condition is met

Background

An entity grants an employee the opportunity to participate in a plan in which the employee obtains share options if he agrees to save 25 per cent of his monthly salary of CU400 for a three-year period. The monthly payments are made by deduction from the employee's salary. The employee may use the accumulated savings to exercise his options at the end of three years, or take a refund of his contributions at any point during the three-year period. The estimated annual expense for the share-based payment arrangement is CU120.

After 18 months, the employee stops paying contributions to the plan and takes a refund of contributions paid to date of CU1,800.

continued...

...continued
IG Example 9A

Application of requirements

There are three components to this plan: paid salary, salary deduction paid to the savings plan and share-based payment. The entity recognises an expense in respect of each component and a corresponding increase in liability or equity as appropriate. The requirement to pay contributions to the plan is a non-vesting condition, which the employee chooses not to meet in the second year. Therefore, in accordance with paragraphs 28(b) and 28A of the IFRS, the repayment of contributions is treated as an extinguishment of the liability and the cessation of contributions in year 2 is treated as a cancellation.

YEAR 1	Expense	Cash	Liability	Equity
	CU	CU	CU	CU
Paid salary	3,600	(3,600)		
	(75% × 400 × 12)			
Salary deduction paid to the savings plan	1,200 (25% × 400 × 12)		(1,200)	
Share-based payment	120			(120)
Total	4,920	(3,600)	(1,200)	(120)

YEAR 2	Expense	Cash	Liability	Equity
	CU	CU	CU	CU
Paid salary	4,200 (75% × 400 × 6 + 100% × 400 × 6)	(4,200)		
Salary deduction paid to the savings plan	600 (25% × 400 × 6)		(600)	
Refund of contributions to the employee		(1,800)	1,800	
Share-based payment (acceleration of remaining expense)	240 (120 × 3 – 120)			(240)
Total	5,040	(6,000)	1,200	(240)

IG16   Paragraph 24 of the IFRS requires that, in rare cases only, in which the IFRS requires the entity to measure an equity-settled share-based payment transaction by reference to the fair value of the equity instruments granted, but the entity is unable to estimate reliably that fair value at the specified measurement date (eg grant date, for transactions with employees), the entity shall instead measure the transaction using an intrinsic value measurement method. Paragraph 24 also contains requirements on how to apply this method. The following example illustrates these requirements.

IG Example 10

Grant of share options that is accounted for by applying the intrinsic value method

Background

At the beginning of year 1, an entity grants 1,000 share options to 50 employees. The share options will vest at the end of year 3, provided the employees remain in service until then. The share options have a life of 10 years. The exercise price is CU60 and the entity's share price is also CU60 at the date of grant.

At the date of grant, the entity concludes that it cannot estimate reliably the fair value of the share options granted.

At the end of year 1, three employees have ceased employment and the entity estimates that a further seven employees will leave during years 2 and 3. Hence, the entity estimates that 80 per cent of the share options will vest.

Two employees leave during year 2, and the entity revises its estimate of the number of share options that it expects will vest to 86 per cent.

Two employees leave during year 3. Hence, 43,000 share options vested at the end of year 3.

The entity's share price during years 1–10, and the number of share options exercised during years 4–10, are set out below. Share options that were exercised during a particular year were all exercised at the end of that year.

continued...

...continued
IG Example 10

Year	Share price at year-end	Number of share options exercised at year-end
1	63	0
2	65	0
3	75	0
4	88	6,000
5	100	8,000
6	90	5,000
7	96	9,000
8	105	8,000
9	108	5,000
10	115	2,000

Application of requirements

In accordance with paragraph 24 of the IFRS, the entity recognises the following amounts in years 1–10.

Year	Calculation	Expense for period CU	Cumulative expense CU
1	50,000 options × 80% × (CU63 – CU60) × ⅓ years	40,000	40,000
2	50,000 options × 86% × (CU65 – CU60) × ⅔ years – CU40,000	103,333	143,333
3	43,000 options × (CU75 – CU60) – CU143,333	501,667	645,000
4	37,000 outstanding options × (CU88 – CU75) + 6,000 exercised options × (CU88 – CU75)	559,000	1,204,000
5	29,000 outstanding options × (CU100 – CU88) + 8,000 exercised options × (CU100 – CU88)	444,000	1,648,000
6	24,000 outstanding options × (CU90 – CU100) + 5,000 exercised options × (CU90 – CU100)	(290,000)	1,358,000
7	15,000 outstanding options × (CU96 – CU90) + 9,000 exercised options × (CU96 – CU90)	144,000	1,502,000
8	7,000 outstanding options × (CU105 – CU96) + 8,000 exercised options × (CU105 – CU96)	135,000	1,637,000
9	2,000 outstanding options × (CU108 – CU105) + 5,000 exercised options × (CU108 – CU105)	21,000	1,658,000
10	2,000 exercised options × (CU115 – CU108)	14,000	1,672,000

IG17 There are many different types of employee share and share option plans. The following example illustrates the application of IFRS 2 to one particular type of plan—an employee share purchase plan. Typically, an employee share purchase plan provides employees with the opportunity to purchase the entity's shares at a discounted price. The terms and conditions under which employee share purchase plans operate differ from country to country. That is to say, not only are there many different types of employee share and share options plans, there are also many different types of employee share purchase plans. Therefore, the following example illustrates the application of IFRS 2 to one specific employee share purchase plan.

IG Example 11

Employee share purchase plan

Background

An entity offers all its 1,000 employees the opportunity to participate in an employee share purchase plan. The employees have two weeks to decide whether to accept the offer. Under the terms of the plan, the employees are entitled to purchase a maximum of 100 shares each. The purchase price will be 20 per cent less than the market price of the entity's shares at the date the offer is accepted, and the purchase price must be paid immediately upon acceptance of the offer. All shares purchased must be held in trust for the employees, and cannot be sold for five years. The employee is not permitted to withdraw from the plan during that period. For example, if the employee ceases employment during the five-year period, the shares must nevertheless remain in the plan until the end of the five-year period. Any dividends paid during the five-year period will be held in trust for the employees until the end of the five-year period.

In total, 800 employees accept the offer and each employee purchases, on average, 80 shares, ie the employees purchase a total of 64,000 shares. The weighted-average market price of the shares at the purchase date is CU30 per share, and the weighted-average purchase price is CU24 per share.

Application of requirements

For transactions with employees, IFRS 2 requires the transaction amount to be measured by reference to the fair value of the equity instruments granted (IFRS 2, paragraph 11). To apply this requirement, it is necessary first to determine the type of equity instrument granted to the employees. Although the plan is described as an employee share purchase plan (ESPP), some ESPPs include option features and are therefore, in effect, share option plans. For example, an ESPP might include a 'look-back feature', whereby the employee is able to purchase shares at a discount, and choose whether the discount is applied to the entity's share price at the date of grant or its share price at the date of purchase. Or an ESPP might specify the purchase price, and then allow the employees a significant period of time to decide whether to participate in the plan. Another example of an option feature is an ESPP that permits the participating employees to cancel their participation before or at the end of a specified period and obtain a refund of amounts previously paid into the plan.

continued...

...continued
IG Example 11

However, in this example, the plan includes no option features. The discount is applied to the share price at the purchase date, and the employees are not permitted to withdraw from the plan.

Another factor to consider is the effect of post-vesting transfer restrictions, if any. Paragraph B3 of IFRS 2 states that, if shares are subject to restrictions on transfer after vesting date, that factor should be taken into account when estimating the fair value of those shares, but only to the extent that the post-vesting restrictions affect the price that a knowledgeable, willing market participant would pay for that share. For example, if the shares are actively traded in a deep and liquid market, post-vesting transfer restrictions may have little, if any, effect on the price that a knowledgeable, willing market participant would pay for those shares.

In this example, the shares are vested when purchased, but cannot be sold for five years after the date of purchase. Therefore, the entity should consider the valuation effect of the five-year post-vesting transfer restriction. This entails using a valuation technique to estimate what the price of the restricted share would have been on the purchase date in an arm's length transaction between knowledgeable, willing parties. Suppose that, in this example, the entity estimates that the fair value of each restricted share is CU28. In this case, the fair value of the equity instruments granted is CU4 per share (being the fair value of the restricted share of CU28 less the purchase price of CU24). Because 64,000 shares were purchased, the total fair value of the equity instruments granted is CU256,000.

In this example, there is no vesting period. Therefore, in accordance with paragraph 14 of IFRS 2, the entity should recognise an expense of CU256,000 immediately.

However, in some cases, the expense relating to an ESPP might not be material. IAS 8 *Accounting Policies, Changes in Accounting Policies and Errors* states that the accounting policies in IFRSs need not be applied when the effect of applying them is immaterial (IAS 8, paragraph 8). IAS 8 also states that an omission or misstatement of an item is material if it could, individually or collectively, influence the economic decisions that users make on the basis of the financial statements. Materiality depends on the size and nature of the omission or misstatement judged in the surrounding circumstances. The size or nature of the item, or a combination of both, could be the determining factor (IAS 8, paragraph 5). Therefore, in this example, the entity should consider whether the expense of CU256,000 is material.

Cash-settled share-based payment transactions

IG18   Paragraphs 30–33 of the IFRS set out requirements for transactions in which an entity acquires goods or services by incurring liabilities to the supplier of those goods or services in amounts based on the price of the entity's shares or other equity instruments. The entity is required to recognise initially the goods or services acquired, and a liability to pay for those goods or services, when the entity obtains the goods or as the services are rendered, measured at the fair value of the liability. Thereafter, until the liability is settled, the entity is required to recognise changes in the fair value of the liability.

IG19 For example, an entity might grant share appreciation rights to employees as part of their remuneration package, whereby the employees will become entitled to a future cash payment (rather than an equity instrument), based on the increase in the entity's share price from a specified level over a specified period of time. If the share appreciation rights do not vest until the employees have completed a specified period of service, the entity recognises the services received, and a liability to pay for them, as the employees render service during that period. The liability is measured, initially and at the end of each reporting period until settled, at the fair value of the share appreciation rights, by applying an option pricing model, and the extent to which the employees have rendered service to date. Changes in fair value are recognised in profit or loss. Therefore, if the amount recognised for the services received was included in the carrying amount of an asset recognised in the entity's statement of financial position (eg inventory), the carrying amount of that asset is not adjusted for the effects of the liability remeasurement. Example 12 illustrates these requirements.

IG Example 12

Background

An entity grants 100 cash share appreciation rights (SARs) to each of its 500 employees, on condition that the employees remain in its employ for the next three years.

During year 1, 35 employees leave. The entity estimates that a further 60 will leave during years 2 and 3. During year 2, 40 employees leave and the entity estimates that a further 25 will leave during year 3. During year 3, 22 employees leave. At the end of year 3, 150 employees exercise their SARs, another 140 employees exercise their SARs at the end of year 4 and the remaining 113 employees exercise their SARs at the end of year 5.

The entity estimates the fair value of the SARs at the end of each year in which a liability exists as shown below. At the end of year 3, all SARs held by the remaining employees vest. The intrinsic values of the SARs at the date of exercise (which equal the cash paid out) at the end of years 3, 4 and 5 are also shown below.

Year	Fair value	Intrinsic value
1	CU14.40	
2	CU15.50	
3	CU18.20	CU15.00
4	CU21.40	CU20.00
5		CU25.00

continued...

...continued
IG Example 12

Application of requirements

Year	Calculation	Expense CU	Liability CU
1	(500 – 95) employees × 100 SARs × CU14.40 × ⅓	194,400	194,400
2	(500 – 100) employees × 100 SARs × CU15.50 × ⅔ – CU194,400	218,933	413,333
3	(500 – 97 – 150) employees × 100 SARs × CU18.20 – CU413,333	47,127	460,460
	+ 150 employees × 100 SARs × CU15.00	225,000	
	Total	272,127	
4	(253 – 140) employees × 100 SARs × CU21.40 – CU460,460	(218,640)	241,820
	+ 140 employees × 100 SARs × CU20.00	280,000	
	Total	61,360	
5	CU0 – CU241,820	(241,820)	0
	+ 113 employees × 100 SARs × CU25.00	282,500	
	Total	40,680	
	Total	787,500	

Share-based payment arrangements with cash alternatives

IG20   Some employee share-based payment arrangements permit the employee to choose whether to receive cash or equity instruments. In this situation, a compound financial instrument has been granted, ie a financial instrument with debt and equity components. Paragraph 37 of the IFRS requires the entity to estimate the fair value of the compound financial instrument at grant date, by first measuring the fair value of the debt component, and then measuring the fair value of the equity component—taking into account that the employee must forfeit the right to receive cash to receive the equity instrument.

IG21   Typically, share-based payment arrangements with cash alternatives are structured so that the fair value of one settlement alternative is the same as the other. For example, the employee might have the choice of receiving share options or cash share appreciation rights. In such cases, the fair value of the equity component will be zero, and hence the fair value of the compound financial instrument will be the same as the fair value of the debt component.

However, if the fair values of the settlement alternatives differ, usually the fair value of the equity component will be greater than zero, in which case the fair value of the compound financial instrument will be greater than the fair value of the debt component.

IG22   Paragraph 38 of the IFRS requires the entity to account separately for the services received in respect of each component of the compound financial instrument. For the debt component, the entity recognises the services received, and a liability to pay for those services, as the counterparty renders service, in accordance with the requirements applying to cash-settled share-based payment transactions. For the equity component (if any), the entity recognises the services received, and an increase in equity, as the counterparty renders service, in accordance with the requirements applying to equity-settled share-based payment transactions. Example 13 illustrates these requirements.

IG Example 13

Background

An entity grants to an employee the right to choose either 1,000 phantom shares, ie a right to a cash payment equal to the value of 1,000 shares, or 1,200 shares. The grant is conditional upon the completion of three years' service. If the employee chooses the share alternative, the shares must be held for three years after vesting date.

At grant date, the entity's share price is CU50 per share. At the end of years 1, 2 and 3, the share price is CU52, CU55 and CU60 respectively. The entity does not expect to pay dividends in the next three years. After taking into account the effects of the post-vesting transfer restrictions, the entity estimates that the grant date fair value of the share alternative is CU48 per share.

At the end of year 3, the employee chooses:

Scenario 1: The cash alternative

Scenario 2: The equity alternative

continued...

...continued
IG Example 13

Application of requirements

The fair value of the equity alternative is CU57,600 (1,200 shares × CU48). The fair value of the cash alternative is CU50,000 (1,000 phantom shares × CU50). Therefore, the fair value of the equity component of the compound instrument is CU7,600 (CU57,600 − CU50,000).

The entity recognises the following amounts:

Year		Expense CU	Equity CU	Liability CU
1	Liability component: (1,000 × CU52 × ⅓)	17,333		17,333
	Equity component: (CU7,600 × ⅓)	2,533	2,533	
2	Liability component: (1,000 × CU55 × ⅔) − CU17,333	19,333		19,333
	Equity component: (CU7,600 × ⅓)	2,533	2,533	
3	Liability component: (1,000 × CU60) − CU36,666	23,334		23,334
	Equity component: (CU7,600 × ⅓)	2,534	2,534	
End Year 3	Scenario 1: cash of CU60,000 paid			(60,000)
	Scenario 1 totals	67,600	7,600	0
	Scenario 2: 1,200 shares issued		60,000	(60,000)
	Scenario 2 totals	67,600	67,600	0

Share-based payment transactions among group entities

IG22A   Paragraphs 43A and 43B of IFRS 2 specify the accounting requirements for share-based payment transactions among group entities in the separate or individual financial statements of the entity receiving the goods or services. Example 14 illustrates the journal entries in the separate or individual financial statements for a group transaction in which a parent grants rights to its equity instruments to the employees of its subsidiary.

IG Example 14

Share-based payment transactions in which a parent grants rights to its equity instruments to the employees of its subsidiary

Background

A parent grants 200 share options to each of 100 employees of its subsidiary, conditional upon the completion of two years' service with the subsidiary. The fair value of the share options on grant date is CU30 each. At grant date, the subsidiary estimates that 80 per cent of the employees will complete the two-year service period. This estimate does not change during the vesting period. At the end of the vesting period, 81 employees complete the required two years of service. The parent does not require the subsidiary to pay for the shares needed to settle the grant of share options.

Application of requirements

As required by paragraph B53 of the IFRS, over the two-year vesting period, the subsidiary measures the services received from the employees in accordance with the requirements applicable to equity-settled share-based payment transactions. Thus, the subsidiary measures the services received from the employees on the basis of the fair value of the share options at grant date. An increase in equity is recognised as a contribution from the parent in the separate or individual financial statements of the subsidiary.

The journal entries recorded by the subsidiary for each of the two years are as follows:

Year 1

Dr Remuneration expense		
(200 × 100 × CU30 × 0.8/2)	CU240,000	
Cr Equity (Contribution from the parent)		CU240,000

Year 2

Dr Remuneration expense		
(200 × 100 × CU30 × 0.81 − 240,000)	CU246,000	
Cr Equity (Contribution from the parent)		CU246,000

Illustrative disclosures

IG23 The following example illustrates the disclosure requirements in paragraphs 44–52 of the IFRS.*

Extract from the Notes to the Financial Statements of Company Z for the year ended 31 December 20X5.

Share-based Payment

During the period ended 31 December 20X5, the Company had four share-based payment arrangements, which are described below.

Type of arrangement	Senior management share option plan	General employee share option plan	Executive share plan	Senior management share appreciation cash plan
Date of grant	1 January 20X4	1 January 20X5	1 January 20X5	1 July 20X5
Number granted	50,000	75,000	50,000	25,000
Contractual life	10 years	10 years	N/A	10 years
Vesting conditions	1.5 years' service and achievement of a share price target, which was achieved.	Three years' service.	Three years' service and achievement of a target growth in earnings per share.	Three years' service and achievement of a target increase in market share.

The estimated fair value of each share option granted in the general employee share option plan is CU23.60. This was calculated by applying a binomial option pricing model. The model inputs were the share price at grant date of CU50, exercise price of CU50, expected volatility of 30 per cent, no expected dividends, contractual life of ten years, and a risk-free interest rate of 5 per cent. To allow for the effects of early exercise, it was assumed that the employees would exercise the options after vesting date when the share price was twice the exercise price. Historical volatility was 40 per cent, which includes the early years of the Company's life; the Company expects the volatility of its share price to reduce as it matures.

The estimated fair value of each share granted in the executive share plan is CU50.00, which is equal to the share price at the date of grant.

---

* Note that the illustrative example is not intended to be a template or model and is therefore not exhaustive. For example, it does not illustrate the disclosure requirements in paragraphs 47(c), 48 and 49 of the IFRS.

Further details of the two share option plans are as follows:

	20X4		20X5	
	Number of options	Weighted average exercise price	Number of options	Weighted average exercise price
Outstanding at start of year	0	–	45,000	CU40
Granted	50,000	CU40	75,000	CU50
Forfeited	(5,000)	CU40	(8,000)	CU46
Exercised	0	–	(4,000)	CU40
Outstanding at end of year	45,000	CU40	108,000	CU46
Exercisable at end of year	0	CU40	38,000	CU40

The weighted average share price at the date of exercise for share options exercised during the period was CU52. The options outstanding at 31 December 20X5 had an exercise price of CU40 or CU50, and a weighted average remaining contractual life of 8.64 years.

	20X4	20X5
	CU	CU
Expense arising from share-based payment transactions	495,000	1,105,867
Expense arising from share and share option plans	495,000	1,007,000
Closing balance of liability for cash share appreciation plan	–	98,867
Expense arising from increase in fair value of liability for cash share appreciation plan	–	9,200

Summary of conditions for a counterparty to receive an equity instrument granted and of accounting treatments

IG24 The table below categorises, with examples, the various conditions that determine whether a counterparty receives an equity instrument granted and the accounting treatment of share-based payments with those conditions.

Summary of conditions that determine whether a counterparty receives an equity instrument granted						
	VESTING CONDITIONS			**NON-VESTING CONDITIONS**		
	Service conditions	Performance conditions		Neither the entity nor the counterparty can choose whether the condition is met	Counterparty can choose whether to meet the condition	Entity can choose whether to meet the condition
		Performance conditions that are market conditions	Other performance conditions			
Example conditions	Requirement to remain in service for three years	Target based on the market price of the entity's equity instruments	Target based on a successful initial public offering with a specified service requirement	Target based on a commodity index	Paying contributions towards the exercise price of a share-based payment	Continuation of the plan by the entity
Include in grant-date fair value?	No	Yes	No	Yes	Yes	Yes[(a)]
Accounting treatment if the condition is not met after the grant date and during the vesting period	Forfeiture. The entity revises the expense to reflect the best available estimate of the number of equity instruments expected to vest. (paragraph 19)	No change to accounting. The entity continues to recognise the expense over the remainder of the vesting period. (paragraph 21)	Forfeiture. The entity revises the expense to reflect the best available estimate of the number of equity instruments expected to vest. (paragraph 19)	No change to accounting. The entity continues to recognise the expense over the remainder of the vesting period. (paragraph 21A)	Cancellation. The entity recognises immediately the amount of the expense that would otherwise have been recognised over the remainder of the vesting period. (paragraph 28A)	Cancellation. The entity recognises immediately the amount of the expense that would otherwise have been recognised over the remainder of the vesting period. (paragraph 28A)

(a) In the calculation of the fair value of the share-based payment, the probability of continuation of the plan by the entity is assumed to be 100 per cent.

Table of Concordance

This table shows how the contents of IFRIC 8 and IFRIC 11 correspond with IFRS 2 (as amended in 2009).

IFRIC 8 paragraph	IFRS 2 (amended) paragraph	IFRIC 11 paragraph	IFRS 2 (amended) paragraph
1	2	1	B48
2, 3	IG5A, IG5B	2, 3	B51, B52
4	None	4–6	B46
5	IG5C	7	B49
6	2	8	B53
7, 8	2	9	B59
9	2	10	B61
9–12	13A	11	B55
13, 14	64	12, 13	64
IE1–IE4	IG Example 1	IE1–IE4	IG Example 14
BC1–BC5	BC18A–BC18D	BC1, BC2	None
BC6–BC12	BC128B–BC128H	BC3–BC18	None
BC13	None	BC19	BC268P
		BC20	None
		BC21, BC22	BC268Q, BC268R

IASB documents published to accompany

International Financial Reporting Standard 3

Business Combinations

This version includes amendments resulting from IFRSs issued up to 31 December 2009.

The text of the unaccompanied IFRS 3 is contained in Part A of this edition. Its effective date is 1 July 2009. The effective date of the amendments is 1 January 2013. This part presents the following accompanying documents:

Approval by the Board of IFRS 3 issued in January 2008

International Financial Reporting Standard 3 *Business Combinations* (as revised in 2008) was approved for issue by eleven of the fourteen members of the International Accounting Standards Board. Professor Barth and Messrs Garnett and Smith dissented. Their dissenting opinions are set out after the Basis for Conclusions.

Sir David Tweedie	Chairman
Thomas E Jones	Vice-Chairman
Mary E Barth	
Hans-Georg Bruns	
Anthony T Cope	
Philippe Danjou	
Jan Engström	
Robert P Garnett	
Gilbert Gélard	
James J Leisenring	
Warren J McGregor	
Patricia L O'Malley	
John T Smith	
Tatsumi Yamada	

CONTENTS

Basis for Conclusions on
IFRS 3 *Business Combinations*

This Basis for Conclusions and its appendix accompany, but are not part of, IFRS 3.

Background information

In 2001 the International Accounting Standards Board began a project to review IAS 22 *Business Combinations* (revised in 1998) as part of its initial agenda, with the objective of improving the quality of, and seeking international convergence on, the accounting for business combinations. The Board decided to address the accounting for business combinations in two phases.

As part of the first phase, the Board published in December 2002 ED 3 *Business Combinations*, together with an exposure draft of proposed related amendments to IAS 36 *Impairment of Assets* and IAS 38 *Intangible Assets*, with a comment deadline of 4 April 2003. The Board received 136 comment letters.

The Board concluded the first phase in March 2004 by issuing simultaneously IFRS 3 *Business Combinations* and revised versions of IAS 36 and IAS 38. The Board's primary conclusion in the first phase was that virtually all business combinations are acquisitions. Accordingly, the Board decided to require the use of one method of accounting for business combinations—the acquisition method.

The US Financial Accounting Standards Board (FASB) also conducted a project on business combinations in multiple phases. The FASB concluded its first phase in June 2001 by issuing FASB Statements No. 141 *Business Combinations* (SFAS 141) and No. 142 *Goodwill and Other Intangible Assets*. The scope of that first phase was similar to IFRS 3 and the FASB reached similar conclusions on the major issues.

The two boards began deliberating the second phase of their projects at about the same time. They decided that a significant improvement could be made to financial reporting if they had similar standards for accounting for business combinations. They therefore agreed to conduct the second phase of the project as a joint effort with the objective of reaching the same conclusions.

The second phase of the project addressed the guidance for applying the acquisition method. In June 2005 the boards published an exposure draft of revisions to IFRS 3 and SFAS 141, together with exposure drafts of related amendments to IAS 27 *Consolidated and Separate Financial Statements* and Accounting Research Bulletin No. 51 *Consolidated Financial Statements*, with a comment deadline of 28 October 2005. The boards received more than 280 comment letters.

The boards concluded the second phase of the project by issuing their revised standards, IFRS 3 *Business Combinations* (as revised in 2008) and FASB Statement No. 141 (revised 2007) *Business Combinations* and the related amendments to IAS 27 and FASB Statement No. 160 *Noncontrolling Interests in Consolidated Financial Statements*.

Introduction

BC1　This Basis for Conclusions summarises the considerations of the International Accounting Standards Board (IASB) and the US Financial Accounting Standards Board (FASB) in reaching the conclusions in their revised standards, IFRS 3 *Business Combinations* (as revised in 2008) and FASB Statement No. 141 (revised 2007) *Business Combinations* (SFAS 141(R)). It includes the reasons why each board accepted particular approaches and rejected others. Individual board members gave greater weight to some factors than to others.

BC2　The revised IFRS 3 and SFAS 141(R) carry forward without reconsideration the primary conclusions each board reached in IFRS 3 (issued in 2004) and FASB Statement No. 141 (SFAS 141, issued in 2001), both of which were titled *Business Combinations*. The conclusions carried forward include, among others, the requirement to apply the *purchase method* (which the revised standards refer to as the *acquisition method*) to account for all business combinations and the identifiability criteria for recognising an intangible asset separately from goodwill. This Basis for Conclusions includes the reasons for those conclusions, as well as the reasons for the conclusions the boards reached in their joint deliberations that led to the revised standards. Because the provisions of the revised standards on applying the acquisition method represent a more extensive change to SFAS 141 than to the previous version of IFRS 3, this Basis for Conclusions includes more discussion of the FASB's conclusions than of the IASB's in the second phase of their respective business combinations projects.

BC3　In discussing the boards' consideration of comments on exposure drafts, this Basis for Conclusions refers to the exposure draft that preceded the previous version of IFRS 3 as *ED 3* and to the one that preceded SFAS 141 as the *1999 Exposure Draft*; it refers to the joint exposure draft that preceded the revised standards as the *2005 Exposure Draft*. Other exposure drafts published by each board in developing IFRS 3 or SFAS 141 are explained in the context of the issues they addressed. As used in this Basis for Conclusions, *the revised IFRS 3, SFAS 141(R)* and *the revised standards* refer to the revised versions of IFRS 3 and SFAS 141; references to *IFRS 3* and *SFAS 141* are to the original versions of those standards.

BC4　The IASB and the FASB concurrently deliberated the issues in the second phase of the project and reached the same conclusions on most of them. The table of differences between the revised IFRS 3 and SFAS 141(R) (presented after the illustrative examples) describes the substantive differences that remain; the most significant difference is the measurement of a non-controlling interest in an acquiree (see paragraphs BC205–BC221). In addition, the application of some provisions of the revised standards on which the boards reached the same conclusions may differ because of differences in:

(a)　other accounting standards of the boards to which the revised standards refer. For example, recognition and measurement requirements for a few particular assets acquired (eg a deferred tax asset) and liabilities assumed (eg an employee benefit obligation) refer to existing IFRSs or US generally accepted accounting principles (GAAP) rather than fair value measures.

(b)   disclosure practices of the boards. For example, the FASB requires particular supplementary information or particular disclosures by public entities only. The IASB has no similar requirements for supplementary information and does not distinguish between listed and unlisted entities.

(c)   particular transition provisions for changes to past accounting practices of US and non-US companies that previously differed.

Definition of a business combination

BC5   The FASB's 1999 Exposure Draft proposed that a *business combination* should be defined as occurring when one entity acquires net assets that constitute a business or acquires equity interests in one or more other entities and thereby obtains control over that entity or entities. Many respondents who commented on the proposed definition said that it would exclude certain transactions covered by APB Opinion No. 16 *Business Combinations* (APB Opinion 16), in particular, transactions in which none of the former shareholder groups of the combining entities obtained control over the combined entity (such as roll-ups, put-togethers and so-called mergers of equals). During its redeliberations of the 1999 Exposure Draft, the FASB concluded that those transactions should be included in the definition of a business combination and in the scope of SFAS 141. Therefore, paragraph 10 of SFAS 141 indicated that it also applied to business combinations in which none of the owners of the combining entities as a group retain or receive a majority of the voting rights of the combined entity. However, the FASB acknowledged at that time that some of those business combinations might not be acquisitions and said that it intended to consider in another project whether business combinations that are not acquisitions should be accounted for using the fresh start method rather than the purchase method.

BC6   IFRS 3 defined a business combination as 'the bringing together of separate entities or businesses into one reporting entity.' In developing IFRS 3, the IASB considered adopting the definition of a business combination in SFAS 141. It did not do so because that definition excluded some forms of combinations encompassed in IAS 22 *Business Combinations* (which IFRS 3 replaced), such as those described in paragraph BC5 in which none of the former shareholder groups of the combining entities obtained control over the combined entity. Accordingly, IFRS 3 essentially retained the definition of a business combination from IAS 22.

BC7   The definition of a business combination was an item of divergence between IFRS 3 and SFAS 141. In addition, the definition in SFAS 141 excluded combinations in which control is obtained by means other than acquiring net assets or equity interests. An objective of the second phase of the FASB's project leading to SFAS 141(R) was to reconsider whether the accounting for a change in control resulting in the acquisition of a business should differ because of the way in which control is obtained.

BC8   The FASB considered several alternatives for improving the definition of a business combination, including adopting the definition of a business combination in IFRS 3. That definition would encompass all transactions or other events that are within the scope of the revised standards. The FASB concluded, however, that the definition of a business combination in IFRS 3 was too broad for its purposes because it would allow for the inclusion in a business combination of one or more businesses that the acquirer does not control.

BC9   Because the FASB considers all changes of control in which an entity acquires a business to be economically similar transactions or events, it decided to expand the definition of a business combination to include all transactions or other events in which an entity obtains control of a business. Application of the expanded definition will improve the consistency of accounting guidance and the relevance, completeness and comparability of the resulting information about the assets, liabilities and activities of an acquired business.

BC10   The IASB also reconsidered the definition of a business combination. The result was that the IASB and the FASB adopted the same definition. The IASB observed that the IFRS 3 definition could be read to include circumstances in which there may be no triggering economic event or transaction and thus no change in an economic entity, per se. For example, under the IFRS 3 definition, an individual's decision to prepare combined financial statements for all or some of the entities that he or she controls could qualify as a business combination. The IASB concluded that a business combination should be described in terms of an economic event rather than in terms of consolidation accounting and that the definition in the revised standards satisfies that condition.

BC11   The IASB also observed that, although the IFRS 3 definition of a business combination was sufficiently broad to include them, formations of joint ventures were excluded from the scope of IFRS 3. Because joint ventures are also excluded from the scope of the revised standards, the revised definition of a business combination is intended to include all of the types of transactions and other events initially included in the scope of IFRS 3.

BC12   Some respondents to the 2005 Exposure Draft who consider particular combinations of businesses to be 'true mergers' said that the definition of a business combination as a transaction or other event in which an acquirer obtains control of one or more businesses seemed to exclude true mergers. The boards concluded that the most straightforward way of indicating that the scope of the revised standards, and the definition of a business combination, is intended to include true mergers, if any occur, is simply to state that fact.

BC13   Some respondents to the 2005 Exposure Draft also said that it was not clear that the definition of a business combination, and thus the scope of the revised standards, includes reverse acquisitions and perhaps other combinations of businesses. The boards observed that in a reverse acquisition, one entity—the one whose equity interests are acquired—obtains economic (although not legal) control over the other and is therefore the acquirer, as indicated in paragraph B15 of the revised IFRS 3. Therefore, the boards concluded that it is unnecessary to state explicitly that reverse acquisitions are included in the definition of a business combination and thus within the scope of the revised standards.

Change in terminology

BC14   As defined in the revised standards, a business combination could occur in the absence of a purchase transaction. Accordingly, the boards decided to replace the term *purchase method*, which was previously used to describe the method of accounting for business combinations that the revised standards require, with the term *acquisition method*. To avoid confusion, this Basis for Conclusions uses that term throughout, including when it refers to IFRS 3 and SFAS 141 (and earlier exposure drafts or other documents), which used the term *purchase method*.

Definition of a business

BC15   The definition of a business combination in the revised standards provides that a transaction or other event is a business combination only if the assets acquired and liabilities assumed constitute a business (an acquiree), and Appendix A defines a *business*.

BC16   SFAS 141 did not include a definition of a business. Instead, it referred to EITF Issue No. 98-3 *Determining Whether a Nonmonetary Transaction Involves Receipt of Productive Assets or of a Business* for guidance on whether a group of net assets constitutes a business. Some constituents said that particular aspects of the definition and the related guidance in EITF Issue 98-3 were both unnecessarily restrictive and open to misinterpretation. They suggested that the FASB should reconsider that definition and guidance as part of this phase of the project, and it agreed to do so. In addition to considering how its definition and guidance might be improved, the FASB, in conjunction with the IASB, decided that the boards should strive to develop a joint definition of a business.

BC17   Before issuing IFRS 3, the IASB did not have a definition of a business or guidance similar to that in EITF Issue 98-3. Consistently with the suggestions of respondents to ED 3, the IASB decided to provide a definition of a business in IFRS 3. In developing that definition, the IASB also considered the guidance in EITF Issue 98-3. However, the definition in IFRS 3 benefited from deliberations in this project to that date, and it differed from EITF Issue 98-3 in some aspects. For example, the definition in IFRS 3 did not include either of the following factors, both of which were in EITF Issue 98-3:

(a)   a requirement that a business be self-sustaining; or

(b)   a presumption that a transferred set of activities and assets in the development stage that has not commenced planned principal operations cannot be a business.

BC18   In the second phase of their business combinations projects, both boards considered the suitability of their existing definitions of a business in an attempt to develop an improved, common definition. To address the perceived deficiencies and misinterpretations, the boards modified their respective definitions of a business and clarified the related guidance. The more significant modifications, and the reasons for them, are:

(a)   to continue to exclude self-sustaining as the definition in IFRS 3 did, and instead, provide that the integrated set of activities and assets must be **capable** of being conducted and managed for the purpose of providing a return in the form of dividends, lower costs or other economic benefits directly to investors or other owners, members or participants. Focusing on the capability to achieve the purposes of the business helps avoid the unduly restrictive interpretations that existed in accordance with the former guidance.

(b) to clarify the meanings of the terms *inputs, processes* and *outputs* that were used in both EITF Issue 98-3 and IFRS 3. Clarifying the meanings of those terms, together with other modifications, helps eliminate the need for extensive detailed guidance and the misinterpretations that sometimes stem from such guidance.

(c) to clarify that inputs and processes applied to those inputs are essential and that although the resulting outputs are normally present, they need not be present. Therefore, an integrated set of assets and activities could qualify as a business if the integrated set is capable of being conducted and managed to produce the resulting outputs. Together with item (a), clarifying that outputs need not be present for an integrated set to be a business helps avoid the unduly restrictive interpretations of the guidance in EITF Issue 98-3.

(d) to clarify that a business need not include all of the inputs or processes that the seller used in operating that business if a market participant is capable of continuing to produce outputs, for example, by integrating the business with its own inputs and processes. This clarification also helps avoid the need for extensive detailed guidance and assessments about whether a missing input or process is minor.

(e) to continue to exclude a presumption that an integrated set in the development stage is not a business merely because it has not yet begun its planned principal operations, as IFRS 3 did. Eliminating that presumption is consistent with focusing on assessing the capability to achieve the purposes of the business (item (a)) and helps avoid the unduly restrictive interpretations that existed with the former guidance.

BC19 The boards also considered whether to include in the revised standards a presumption similar to the one in EITF Issue 98-3 that an asset group is a business if goodwill is present. Some members of the FASB's resource group suggested that that presumption results in circular logic that is not especially useful guidance in practice. Although the boards had some sympathy with those views, they noted that such a presumption could be useful in avoiding interpretations of the definition of a business that would hinder the stated intention of applying the revised standards' guidance to economically similar transactions. The presumption might also simplify the assessment of whether a particular set of activities and assets meets the definition of a business. Therefore, the revised standards' application guidance retains that presumption.

BC20 The boards considered whether to expand the scope of the revised standards to all acquisitions of groups of assets. They noted that doing so would avoid the need to distinguish between those groups that are businesses and those that are not. However, both boards noted that broadening the scope of the revised standards beyond acquisitions of businesses would require further research and deliberation of additional issues and delay the implementation of the revised standards' improvements to practice. The boards therefore did not extend the scope of the revised standards to acquisitions of all asset groups. Paragraph 2(b) of the revised IFRS 3 describes the typical accounting for an asset acquisition.

BC21   SFAS 141(R) amends FASB Interpretation No. 46 (revised December 2003) *Consolidation of Variable Interest Entities* (FASB Interpretation 46(R)) to clarify that the initial consolidation of a variable interest entity that is a business is a business combination. Therefore, the assets, liabilities and non-controlling interests of the variable interest entity should be measured in accordance with the requirements of SFAS 141(R). Previously, FASB Interpretation 46(R) required assets, liabilities and non-controlling interests of variable interest entities that are businesses to be measured at fair value. The FASB concluded that variable interest entities that are businesses should be afforded the same exceptions to fair value measurement and recognition that are provided for assets and liabilities of acquired businesses. The FASB also decided that upon the initial consolidation of a variable interest entity that is not a business, the assets (other than goodwill), liabilities and non-controlling interests should be recognised and measured in accordance with the requirements of SFAS 141(R), rather than at fair value as previously required by FASB Interpretation 46(R). The FASB reached that decision for the same reasons described above, ie if SFAS 141(R) allows an exception to fair value measurement for a particular asset or liability, it would be inconsistent to require the same type of asset or liability to be measured at fair value. Except for that provision, the FASB did not reconsider the requirements in FASB Interpretation 46(R) for the initial consolidation of a variable interest entity that is not a business.

Method of accounting for business combinations

BC22   Both IAS 22 and APB Opinion 16 permitted use of either the acquisition method or the pooling of interests (pooling) method of accounting for a business combination, although the two methods were not intended as alternatives for the same set of facts and circumstances. ED 3 and the 1999 Exposure Draft proposed, and IFRS 3 and SFAS 141 required, use of the acquisition method to account for all business combinations. The boards did not redeliberate that conclusion during the project that led to the revised standards.

BC23   In developing IFRS 3 and SFAS 141, the IASB and the FASB considered three possible methods of accounting for business combinations—the pooling method, the acquisition method and the fresh start method. In assessing those methods, both boards were mindful of the disadvantages of having more than one method of accounting for business combinations, as evidenced by the experience with IAS 22 and APB Opinion 16. The boards concluded that having more than one method could be justified only if the alternative method (or methods) could be demonstrated to produce information that is more decision-useful and if unambiguous and non-arbitrary boundaries could be established that unequivocally distinguish when one method is to be applied instead of another. The boards also concluded that most business combinations are acquisitions and, for the reasons discussed in paragraphs BC24–BC28, that the acquisition method is the appropriate method for those business combinations. Respondents to ED 3 and the 1999 Exposure Draft generally agreed. Therefore, neither the pooling method nor the fresh start method could be appropriately used for all business combinations.

Reasons for adopting the acquisition method

BC24 Both boards concluded that the acquisition method is the appropriate method of accounting for all business combinations in which one entity obtains control of one or more other businesses because that method is consistent with how the accounting model generally accounts for transactions in which assets are acquired and liabilities are assumed or incurred. Therefore, it produces information that is comparable with other accounting information.

BC25 The acquisition method views a combination from the perspective of the acquirer—the entity that obtains control of the other combining businesses. The acquirer purchases or otherwise obtains control over net assets and recognises in its financial statements the assets acquired and liabilities assumed, including those not previously recognised by the acquiree. Consequently, users of financial statements are better able to assess the initial investments made and the subsequent performance of those investments and compare them with the performance of other entities. In addition, by initially recognising almost all of the assets acquired and liabilities assumed at their fair values, the acquisition method includes in the financial statements more information about the market's expectation of the value of the future cash flows associated with those assets and liabilities, which enhances the relevance of that information.

BC26 Most of the respondents to ED 3 supported the proposal to eliminate the pooling method and to require all business combinations to be accounted for by applying the acquisition method, pending the IASB's future consideration of whether the fresh start method might be applied to some combinations. Respondents to the 1999 Exposure Draft generally agreed that most business combinations are acquisitions, and many said that all combinations involving only two entities are acquisitions. Respondents also agreed that the acquisition method is the appropriate method of accounting for business combinations in which one of the combining entities obtains control over the other combining entities. However, some qualified their support for the acquisition method as contingent upon the FASB's decisions about some aspects of applying that method, particularly the accounting for goodwill.

BC27 The boards concluded that most business combinations, both two-party transactions and those involving three or more entities (multi-party combinations), are acquisitions. The boards acknowledged that some multi-party combinations (in particular, those that are commonly referred to as roll-up or put-together transactions) might not be acquisitions; however, they noted that the acquisition method has generally been used to account for them. The boards decided not to change that practice at this time. Consequently, the revised standards require the acquisition method to be used to account for all business combinations, including those that some might not consider acquisitions.

BC28 Both boards considered assertions that exceptions to the acquisition method should be provided for circumstances in which identifying the acquirer is difficult. Respondents taking that view generally said that the pooling method would provide better information in those circumstances. Although acknowledging that identifying the acquirer sometimes may be difficult, the boards concluded that it would be practicable to identify an acquirer in all business combinations. Moreover, in some jurisdictions an acquirer must be identified for tax purposes, regardless of how difficult it may be to do so. Both boards also concluded that in no circumstances does the pooling method provide better information than the acquisition method.

Reasons for rejecting the pooling method

Mergers and acquisitions are economically similar

BC29 Some observers, including some respondents to the ED 3 and to the 1999 Exposure Draft, argued that business combinations in which the predominant form of consideration is equity interests, generally referred to as *mergers*, are different from acquisitions and should be accounted for differently. They said that the pooling method is appropriate for a merger because ownership interests are continued (either completely or substantially), no new capital is invested and no assets are distributed, post-combination ownership interests are proportional to those before the combination, and the intention is to unite commercial strategies. Those respondents said that a merger should be accounted for in terms of the carrying amounts of the assets and liabilities of the combining entities because, unlike acquisitions in which only the acquirer survives the combination, all of the combining entities effectively survive a merger.

BC30 Most respondents who favoured retaining the pooling method also supported limiting its application. Many of those respondents suggested limiting use of the pooling method to 'true mergers' or 'mergers of equals', which they described as combinations of entities of approximately equal size or those in which it is difficult to identify an acquirer.

BC31 The boards also considered the assertion that the pooling method properly portrays true mergers as a transaction between the owners of the combining entities rather than between the combining entities. The boards rejected that assertion, noting that business combinations are initiated by, and take place because of, a transaction between the combining entities themselves. The entities—not their owners—engage in the negotiations necessary to carry out the combination, although the owners must eventually participate in and approve the transaction.

BC32 Many respondents agreed with the boards that although ownership interests are continued in a combination effected by an exchange of equity instruments, those interests **change** as a result of the combination. The former owners of each entity no longer have an exclusive interest in the net assets of the pre-combination entities. Rather, after the business combination, the owners of the combining entities have a residual interest in the net assets of the combined entity. The information provided by the pooling method fails to reflect that and is therefore not a faithful representation.

BC33 Both boards observed that all business combinations entail some bringing together of commercial strategies. Accordingly, the intention to unite commercial strategies is not unique to mergers and does not support applying a different accounting method to some combinations from that applied to others.

BC34　Some respondents said that, economically, mergers are virtually identical to acquisitions, making them in-substance acquisitions. Some noted that shares could have been issued for cash and that cash then used to effect the combination, with the result being economically the same as if shares had been used to effect the combination.

BC35　Both boards concluded that 'true mergers' or 'mergers of equals' in which none of the combining entities obtains control of the others are so rare as to be virtually non-existent, and many respondents agreed. Other respondents stated that even if a true merger or merger of equals did occur, it would be so rare that a separate accounting treatment is not warranted. The boards also observed that respondents and other constituents were unable to suggest an unambiguous and non-arbitrary boundary for distinguishing true mergers or mergers of equals from other business combinations and concluded that developing such an operational boundary would not be feasible. Moreover, even if those mergers could feasibly be distinguished from other combinations, both boards noted that it does not follow that mergers should be accounted for on a carry-over basis. If they were to be accounted for using a method other than the acquisition method, the fresh start method would be better than the pooling method.

Information provided is not decision-useful

BC36　Some proponents of the pooling method argued that it provides decision-useful information for the business combinations for which they favour its use. They said that the information is a more faithful representation than the information that the acquisition method would provide for those combinations. However, other respondents said that the information provided by the acquisition method is more revealing than that provided by the pooling method. Respondents also noted that the pooling method does not hold management accountable for the investment made and the subsequent performance of that investment. In contrast, the accountability that results from applying the acquisition method forces management to examine business combination deals carefully to see that they make economic sense.

BC37　Both boards observed that an important part of decision-useful information is information about cash-generating abilities and cash flows generated. The IASB's *Framework for the Preparation and Presentation of Financial Statements* says that 'The economic decisions that are taken by users of financial statements require an evaluation of the ability of an entity to generate cash and cash equivalents and of the timing and certainty of their generation' (paragraph 15). FASB Concepts Statement No. 1 *Objectives of Financial Reporting by Business Enterprises* indicates that '... financial reporting should provide information to help investors, creditors, and others assess the amounts, timing, and uncertainty of prospective net cash inflows to the related enterprise' (paragraph 37; footnote reference omitted). Neither the cash-generating abilities of the combined entity nor its future cash flows generally are affected by the method used to account for the combination. However, fair values reflect the expected cash flows associated with acquired assets and assumed liabilities. Because the pooling method records the net assets acquired at their carrying amounts rather than at their fair values, the information that the pooling method provides about the cash-generating abilities of those net assets is less useful than that provided by the acquisition method.

BC38   Both boards also concluded that the information provided by the pooling method is less relevant because it has less predictive value and feedback value than the information that is provided by other methods. It is also less complete because it does not reflect assets acquired or liabilities assumed that were not included in the pre-combination financial statements of the combining entities. The pooling method also provides a less faithful representation of the combined entity's performance in periods after the combination. For example, by recording assets and liabilities at the carrying amounts of predecessor entities, post-combination revenues may be overstated (and expenses understated) as the result of embedded gains that were generated by predecessor entities but not recognised by them.

BC39   The *Framework* and FASB Concepts Statement No. 2 *Qualitative Characteristics of Accounting Information* describe comparability as an important characteristic of decision-useful information. Use of different accounting methods for the same set of facts and circumstances makes the resulting information less comparable and thus less useful for making economic decisions. As discussed in paragraphs BC29–BC35, the boards concluded that all business combinations are economically similar. Accordingly, use of the same method to account for all combinations enhances the comparability of the resulting financial reporting information. Both boards observed that the acquisition method, but not the pooling method, could reasonably be applied to all business combinations in which one party to the combination obtains control over the combined entity.

BC40   Opponents of the pooling method generally said that eliminating that method would enhance the comparability of financial statements of entities that grow by means of acquisitions. Both boards agreed.

Inconsistent with historical cost accounting model

BC41   Both boards observed that the pooling method is an exception to the general concept that exchange transactions are accounted for in terms of the fair values of the items exchanged. Because the pooling method records the combination in terms of the pre-combination carrying amounts of the parties to the transaction, it fails to record and thus to hold management accountable for the investment made in the combination.

BC42   Some respondents to the FASB's 1999 Exposure Draft who advocated use of the pooling method asserted that it is consistent with the historical cost model and that eliminating the pooling method would be a step towards adopting a fair value model. They argued that before eliminating the pooling method, the FASB should resolve the broad issue of whether to adopt a fair value model in place of the historical cost model. The FASB disagreed, noting that, regardless of the merits of a fair value model, the pooling method is an aberration that is inconsistent with the historical cost model.

BC43   Although the historical cost model is frequently described as being 'transaction based', the fair value model also records all transactions. In both models, transactions are recognised on the basis of the fair values exchanged at the transaction date. In contrast, the pooling method does not result in recognising in the records of the combined entity the values exchanged; instead, only the carrying amounts of the predecessor entities are recognised. Failure to record those values can adversely affect the relevance and reliability of the combined entity's financial statements for years—and even decades—to come. For those reasons, both boards concluded that the pooling method is inconsistent with the historical cost model. Requiring use of the acquisition method is not a step towards adopting a fair value accounting model. Rather, it eliminates an exception to the historical cost model and requires accounting for assets acquired and liabilities assumed in a business combination consistently with other acquisitions of assets and incurrences of liabilities.

Disclosure not an adequate response

BC44 In urging that the pooling method should be retained, a few respondents to the 1999 Exposure Draft said that any perceived problems with having two methods of accounting could be addressed by enhanced disclosures in the notes to the financial statements. However, they generally did not specify what those disclosures should be and how they would help overcome the comparability problems that inevitably result from having two methods.

BC45 The FASB considered whether enhanced disclosures might compensate for the deficiencies of the pooling method but doubted the usefulness of almost any disclosures short of disclosing what the results would have been had the acquisition method been used to account for the business combination. Providing disclosures that would enable users of financial statements to determine what the results would have been had the transaction been accounted for by the acquisition method would be a costly solution that begs the question of why the acquisition method was not used to account for the transaction in the first place. Thus, the FASB rejected enhanced disclosures as a viable alternative.

Not cost-beneficial

BC46 Some of the boards' constituents cited cost-benefit considerations as a reason for retaining the pooling method. They argued that the pooling method is a quicker and less expensive way to account for a business combination because it does not require an entity to hire valuation experts to value assets for accounting purposes.

BC47 Other constituents favoured eliminating the pooling method for cost-benefit reasons. Some argued that the pooling method causes preparers of financial statements, auditors, regulators and others to spend unproductive time dealing with the detailed criteria required by IAS 22 or APB Opinion 16 in attempts to qualify some business combinations for the pooling method. Others noted that using the acquisition method of accounting for all business combinations would eliminate the enormous amount of interpretative guidance necessary to accommodate the pooling method. They also said that the benefits derived from making the acquisition method the only method of accounting for business combinations would significantly outweigh any issues that might arise from accounting for the very rare true merger or merger of equals by the acquisition method.

BC48 Both boards concluded that requiring a single method of accounting is preferable because having more than one method would lead to higher costs associated with applying, auditing, enforcing and analysing the information produced by the different methods. The IASB's conclusions on benefits and costs are more fully discussed in paragraphs BC435–BC439.

Perceived economic consequences not a valid reason for retention

BC49   Some of the respondents to ED 3 and the 1999 Exposure Draft who favoured retaining the pooling method cited public policy considerations or other perceived economic consequences of eliminating it. Some argued that eliminating the pooling method would require some investors to adjust to different measures of performance, potentially affecting market valuations adversely in some industries during the transition period. Others argued that it would impede desirable consolidation in some industries, reduce the amount of capital flowing into those industries, slow the development of new technology and adversely affect entrepreneurial culture. Some argued that eliminating the pooling method would reduce the options available to some regulatory agencies and possibly require regulated entities to maintain a second set of accounting records.

BC50   Other respondents did not share those views. Some said that because business combinations are (or should be) driven by economic rather than accounting considerations, economically sound deals would be completed regardless of the method used to account for them. Others noted that the financial community values business combinations in terms of their fair values rather than book values; therefore, those transactions should initially be recognised in the financial statements at fair value.

BC51   Both boards have long held that accounting standards should be neutral; they should not be slanted to favour one set of economic interests over another. Neutrality is the absence of bias intended to attain a predetermined result or to induce a particular behaviour. Neutrality is an essential aspect of decision-useful financial information because biased financial reporting information cannot faithfully represent economic phenomena. The consequences of a new financial reporting standard may indeed be negative for some interests in either the short term or the long term. But the dissemination of unreliable and potentially misleading information is, in the long run, harmful for all interests.

BC52   Both boards rejected the view that the pooling method should be retained because eliminating it could have adverse consequences for some economic interests. Accounting requirements for business combinations should seek neither to encourage nor to discourage business combinations. Instead, those standards should produce unbiased information about those combinations that is useful to investors, creditors and others in making economic decisions about the combined entity.

Acquisition method flaws remedied

BC53   Some respondents to ED 3 or to the 1999 Exposure Draft supported retaining the pooling method because of perceived problems associated with the acquisition method. Most of those comments focused on the effects of goodwill amortisation.

BC54   Both boards concluded that the pooling method is so fundamentally flawed that it does not warrant retention, regardless of perceived problems with the acquisition method. The boards also observed that the most frequently cited concern is remedied by the requirement of IAS 36 *Impairment of Assets* and FASB Statement No. 142 *Goodwill and Other Intangible Assets* (SFAS 142) to test goodwill for impairment and recognise a loss if it is impaired rather than to amortise goodwill.

The fresh start method

BC55 In the fresh start method, none of the combining entities is viewed as having survived the combination as an independent reporting entity. Rather, the combination is viewed as the transfer of the net assets of the combining entities to a new entity that assumes control over them. The history of that new entity, by definition, begins with the combination.

BC56 In the first part of their respective business combinations projects, both the IASB and the FASB acknowledged that a case could be made for using the fresh start method to account for the relatively rare business combination that does not clearly qualify as an acquisition. Such a combination might be defined either as one in which an acquirer cannot be identified or as one in which the acquirer is substantially modified by the transaction. However, the boards observed that those transactions have been accounted for by the acquisition method and they decided not to change that practice.

BC57 Neither the IASB nor the FASB has on its agenda a project to consider the fresh start method. However, both boards have expressed interest in considering whether joint venture formations and some formations of new entities in multi-party business combinations should be accounted for by the fresh start method. Depending on the relative priorities of that topic and other topics competing for their agendas when time becomes available, the boards might undertake a joint project to consider those issues at some future date.

Scope

BC58 The revised standards exclude from their scope some transactions that were also excluded from the scope of both IFRS 3 and SFAS 141. However, the revised standards include within their scope combinations involving only mutual entities and combinations achieved by contract alone, which were excluded from the scope of IFRS 3 and SFAS 141. Paragraphs BC59–BC79 discuss the boards' reasons for those conclusions.

Joint ventures and combinations of entities under common control

BC59 Formations of joint ventures and combinations of entities under common control are excluded from the scope of the revised standards. Those transactions were also excluded from the scope of both IFRS 3 and SFAS 141, and the boards continue to believe that issues related to such combinations are appropriately excluded from the scope of this project. The boards are aware of nothing that has happened since IFRS 3 and SFAS 141 were issued to suggest that the revised standards should be delayed to address the accounting for those events.

BC60 In developing IFRS 3, the IASB considered whether it should amend the definition of joint control in IAS 31 *Interests in Joint Ventures* because it was concerned that its decision to eliminate the pooling method would create incentives for business combinations to be structured to meet the definition of a joint venture. After considering comments on the definition proposed in ED 3, the IASB revised the definition of joint control in IAS 31 to clarify that:

(a) unanimous consent on **all** financial and operating decisions is not necessary for an arrangement to satisfy the definition of a joint venture—unanimous consent on only strategic decisions is sufficient.

(b) in the absence of a contractual agreement requiring unanimous consent to strategic financial and operating decisions, a transaction in which the owners of multiple businesses agree to combine their businesses into a new entity (sometimes referred to as a roll-up transaction) should be accounted for by the acquisition method. Majority consent on such decisions is not sufficient.

BC61   In developing SFAS 141, the FASB noted that constituents consider the guidance in paragraph 3(d) of APB Opinion No. 18 *The Equity Method of Accounting for Investments in Common Stock* in assessing whether an entity is a joint venture, and it decided not to change that practice in its project on business combinations.

Not-for-profit organisations

BC62   The FASB also decided to exclude from the scope of SFAS 141(R) business combinations of not-for-profit organisations and acquisitions of for-profit businesses by not-for-profit organisations. Some aspects of combinations of not-for-profit organisations are different from combinations of business entities. For example, it cannot be presumed that combinations of organisations that serve a public interest are necessarily exchange transactions in which willing parties exchange equal values. For that reason, the FASB is addressing the accounting for combinations of not-for-profit organisations in a separate project. It published an exposure draft in October 2006 that addresses accounting for combinations of not-for-profit organisations.

BC63   IFRSs generally do not have scope limitations for not-for-profit activities in the private or public sector. Although IFRSs are developed for profit-oriented entities, a not-for-profit entity might be required, or choose, to apply IFRSs. A scope exclusion for combinations of not-for-profit organisations is not necessary.

Combinations of mutual entities

BC64   During its deliberations leading to SFAS 141, the FASB concluded that combinations involving only mutual entities should also be accounted for using the acquisition method but decided not to mandate its use until the FASB had considered implementation questions raised about the application of that method. Similarly, IFRS 3 did not require use of the acquisition method for combinations of mutual entities, although the IASB had also concluded that the acquisition method was appropriate for those combinations. Instead, as part of the first phase of its business combinations project, the IASB published an exposure draft of proposed amendments to IFRS 3—*Combinations by Contract Alone or Involving Mutual Entities*, which proposed an interim approach for accounting for those combinations until the IASB had considered related implementation issues in the second phase of its project. In the light of respondents' comments, the IASB decided not to proceed with the proposals in the exposure draft, primarily for reasons of timing and impending consideration of those issues in the second phase of this project.

BC65　After SFAS 141 was issued, the FASB began a joint project with the Canadian Accounting Standards Board (AcSB). The objective of that project was to develop guidance for combinations of two or more mutual entities. In October 2001 the FASB and the AcSB held a round-table discussion with representatives of mutual banks, credit unions, co-operatives and other mutual entities. In January 2004 the FASB met representatives of organisations of co-operative and other mutual entities to discuss its tentative conclusions and specific concerns raised by constituents. In addition, the FASB conducted field visits to three mutual entities in 2004.

BC66　A few participants in those meetings indicated a preference for the fresh start method as an alternative to the acquisition method for particular mergers, especially for those in which it is difficult to identify the acquirer. On both occasions, however, those participants acknowledged the costs and practical difficulties that a fresh start alternative would impose, especially on entities with recurring combinations. After considering those views, the FASB concluded that any potential advantages of using the fresh start method for some combinations of mutual entities would be outweighed by the disadvantages of having two methods of accounting.

BC67　During the deliberations leading to the 2005 Exposure Draft, some representatives of mutual entities reiterated concerns expressed during the development of SFAS 141 about requiring all combinations of mutual entities to be accounted for using the acquisition method. Many of those constituents reiterated public policy concerns similar to those discussed in paragraphs BC49–BC52. For example, some said that eliminating the pooling method could impede desirable combinations and reduce the amount of capital flowing into their industries. They suggested, for example, that the requirement to identify an acquirer could impede mergers of neighbouring mutual entities when both the fact and appearance of a merger of equals are of paramount importance to their directors, members and communities. The boards did not find those arguments persuasive for the same reasons discussed in paragraphs BC49–BC52.

BC68　Although mutual entities have particular characteristics that distinguish them from other business entities, the boards noted that the two types of entities also have many common characteristics. The boards also observed that the economic motivations for combinations of mutual entities, such as to provide their constituents with a broader range of, or access to, services and cost savings through economies of scale, are similar to those for combinations of other business entities. For example:

(a)　although mutual entities generally do not have shareholders in the traditional sense of investor-owners, they are in effect 'owned' by their members and are in business to serve their members or other stakeholders. Like other businesses, mutual entities strive to provide their members with a financial return or benefits. A mutual entity generally does that by focusing on providing its members with its products and services at lower prices. For example, the benefit provided by a credit union may be a lower interest rate on a borrowing than might be obtainable through an investor-owned financial institution. In a wholesale buying co-operative, the benefit might be lower net costs, after reflecting patronage dividends.

(b) members' interests in a mutual entity are generally not transferable like other ownership interests. However, they usually include a right to share in the net assets of the mutual entity in the event of its liquidation or conversion to another form of entity.

(c) a higher percentage of combinations of mutual entities than of combinations of other business entities occur without an exchange of cash or other readily measurable consideration, but such combinations are not unique to mutual entities. Business combinations of other entities, particularly private entities, also take place without an exchange of cash or other readily measurable consideration.

BC69 Thus, the boards concluded that the attributes of mutual entities are not sufficiently different from those of other entities to justify different accounting for business combinations. The boards also concluded that the benefits of requiring combinations of mutual entities to be accounted for by the acquisition method would justify the related costs. Therefore, combinations of mutual entities were included within the scope of the 2005 Exposure Draft.

BC70 Many of the respondents to the 2005 Exposure Draft who commented on combinations of mutual entities objected to including them in the scope of the revised standards and thus requiring them to be accounted for by the acquisition method. Respondents objected to the use of the acquisition method for conceptual, practical and cost-benefit reasons. For example, some said that a combination involving only mutual entities is a 'true pooling of interests' and that the acquisition method would not reflect the economics of the transactions. Some also said that it would often be difficult to identify an acquirer. Some also noted the absence of readily measurable consideration transferred in many combinations of mutual entities, which would make it necessary to use other valuation techniques to develop the fair values needed to apply the acquisition method. For those reasons, respondents also said that using the acquisition method for combinations of mutual entities would not be cost-beneficial. Respondents proposed other methods of accounting for mutual entities, including the pooling method, the fresh start method and a net asset method that was the same as the modified version of the acquisition method proposed by the IASB in its exposure draft mentioned in paragraph BC64.

BC71 In considering those comments, the boards noted that respondents' reasons for their objections to the acquisition method were generally the same as the factors discussed in paragraphs BC67 and BC68. For the same reasons discussed in those paragraphs, the boards affirmed their conclusion that the attributes of mutual entities are not sufficiently different from those of investor-owned entities to justify a different method of accounting for combinations of mutual entities. The boards also noted that, regardless of the intentions of the combining entities, the general result of a combination involving only mutual entities is that one entity obtains control of the other entity (or entities). Thus, combinations involving only mutual entities are included in the scope of the revised standards.

BC72 Some representatives of mutual entities suggested that the revised standards should permit an acquisition of a mutual entity to be reported as an increase in the retained earnings of the acquirer (combined entity) as had been the practice in accordance with the pooling method of accounting. The boards observed that in a combination of two investor-owned entities in which the acquirer issues its equity shares as consideration for all of the acquiree's equity shares, the fair value of the acquiree's equity is recognised as an addition to the acquirer's equity—generally as an increase to the acquirer's ordinary shares and capital. Thus, the equity (net assets) of the combined entity is increased from the acquisition of the acquiree (and the fair value of its net assets), but retained earnings of the acquirer are unaffected. The boards concluded that business combinations of two investor-owned entities are economically similar to those of two mutual entities in which the acquirer issues member interests for all the member interests of the acquiree. Thus, the boards concluded that those similar transactions should be similarly reported. Therefore, the revised standards clarify that if the only consideration exchanged is the member interests of the acquiree for the member interests of the acquirer (or the member interests of the newly combined entity), the amount of the acquiree's net assets is recognised as a direct addition to capital or equity, not retained earnings (paragraph B47 of the revised IFRS 3).

BC73   During the boards' redeliberations of the 2005 Exposure Draft, some representatives of mutual entities also proposed that the entire amount of the acquiree's net assets recognised in accordance with the revised standards should be considered a gain on a bargain purchase. They contended that the exchange of member interests in at least some forms of mutual entities does not constitute consideration because the interests the acquirer transfers have no economic value. The boards disagreed, noting that one mutual entity—the acquiree—would presumably not be willing to transfer its net assets to the control of another—the acquirer—in exchange for nothing of value.

BC74   The FASB also considered more specific concerns of representatives of credit unions about adverse economic consequences for those entities. Those representatives argued that requiring the application of the acquisition method would impede consolidation within that industry and might misrepresent the financial soundness and regulatory capital of two credit unions that combine their operations. They noted that in the United States, applicable federal law defines net worth for credit unions as the 'retained earnings balance of the credit union, as determined under generally accepted accounting principles.' Because the regulatory definition of net worth is narrower than equity under US GAAP, they expressed concern that the exclusion of the equity of an acquired credit union from retained earnings of the combined entity could make a financially sound combined entity appear to be financially unsound. Thus, they suggested that credit unions should be permitted to continue to report the equity of an acquired mutual entity as an addition to retained earnings of the combined entity. The FASB was not persuaded by those arguments; it believes that Statement 141(R) will not affect the ability of credit unions to restructure and combine with other credit unions.

BC75   Additionally, constituents told the FASB that the number of combinations of credit unions in which the regulatory net worth calculation could be significantly affected is relatively small in any given year. The FASB also noted that the regulatory filings of credit unions and other entities and the needs of their regulators are separate matters beyond the purpose of financial statements. The FASB's Concepts Statement 2 states that a necessary and important characteristic of accounting information is neutrality. In the context of business combinations, neutrality means that accounting standards should neither encourage nor discourage business combinations but rather provide information about those combinations that is fair and even-handed. The FASB observed that its public policy goal is to issue accounting standards that result in neutral and representationally faithful financial information. Eliminating use of the pooling method for all entities and requiring all entities, including mutual entities, to report the resulting increase directly in equity other than retained earnings is consistent with that public policy goal.

BC76   Some respondents to the 2005 Exposure Draft said that co-operatives do not fit within the definition of a mutual entity and that co-operatives are sufficiently different from other entities to justify a different method of accounting for combinations involving only co-operatives. To support their view, they cited factors such as differences in legal characteristics and different purposes of co-operatives in addition to providing economic benefits to members.

BC77   The boards considered the differences between, for example, a co-operative that provides electricity to its members in a rural area and other types of mutual entities, such as a mutual insurance company. The boards acknowledged particular differences between the two types of entities, for example, the co-operative issues member shares and the mutual insurance company does not. In addition, the objective of the co-operative may include providing more social and cultural benefits to its community in addition to the economic benefits provided to its members than does another type of mutual entity. However, the boards concluded that co-operatives generally provide direct and indirect economic benefits such as dividends and lower costs of services, including credit, or other products directly to its members. The boards concluded that differences in the amount of social and cultural benefits an entity seeks to provide do not justify a conclusion that co-operatives are sufficiently different from other mutual entities that they do not fit within the definition of a mutual entity in the revised standards. Thus, co-operatives are included in the definition of a mutual entity in the revised standards.

Combinations achieved by contract alone

BC78   Both boards also concluded that business combinations achieved by contract alone should be included in the scope of the revised standards. Those combinations were not included in the scope of either IFRS 3 or SFAS 141, although the boards understand that practice in the United States generally was to account for them in accordance with SFAS 141. For example, in EITF Issue No. 97-2 *Application of FASB Statement No. 94 and APB Opinion No. 16 to Physician Practice Management Entities and Certain Other Entities with Contractual Management Arrangements*, the Task Force reached a consensus that a transaction in which a physician practice management entity executes a management agreement with the physician practice should be accounted for as a business combination. Technically, that transaction would not meet the definition of a business combination in APB Opinion 16 or SFAS 141 because the physician practice management entity does not acquire either equity interests in, or the net assets of, the physician practice.

BC79   The boards understand that difficulties may arise in applying the acquisition method to combinations achieved by contract alone. In particular, such business combinations normally do not involve the payment of readily measurable consideration and in rare circumstances it might be difficult to identify the acquirer. However, as for combinations of mutual entities and for the reasons discussed above, the boards concluded that the acquisition method can and should be applied in accounting for such business combinations. In reaching that conclusion, the boards also concluded that in a business combination achieved by contract alone:

(a)   difficulties in identifying the acquirer are not a sufficient reason to justify a different accounting treatment, and no further guidance is necessary for identifying the acquirer for combinations by contract alone.

(b)   in the United States, these transactions are already being accounted for by the acquisition method and insurmountable issues have not been encountered.

(c)   determining the fair value of the identifiable assets acquired and liabilities assumed and calculating the related goodwill should be consistent with decisions reached in the second phase of the project.

Applying the acquisition method

BC80   The 2005 Exposure Draft identified four steps in applying the acquisition method, and it discussed the requirements for applying the acquisition method in terms of those steps:

(a)   identifying the acquirer;

(b)   determining the acquisition date;

(c)   measuring the fair value of the acquiree; and

(d)   measuring and recognising the assets acquired and the liabilities assumed.

BC80A   In contrast, the revised standards indicate (paragraph 5 of the revised IFRS 3) that applying the acquisition method requires:

(a)   identifying the acquirer;

(b)   determining the acquisition date;

(c)   recognising and measuring the identifiable assets acquired, liabilities assumed and any non-controlling interest in the acquiree; and

(d)   recognising and measuring goodwill or a gain from a bargain purchase.

BC81   The main changes to the list of steps in applying the acquisition method are to eliminate measuring the fair value of the acquiree as a whole and to add recognising and measuring goodwill as a separate step. The primary reason for those changes is the boards' decision to focus on measuring the components of the business combination, including any non-controlling interest in the acquiree, rather than measuring the fair value of the acquiree as a whole. The boards observed that neither the requirements of the 2005 Exposure Draft nor those of the revised standards for applying the acquisition method result in a fair value measure of either the acquiree as a whole or the acquirer's interest in the acquiree. For example, the revised standards do not provide for recognising a loss if the acquirer overpays for the acquiree, ie if the acquisition-date fair value of the consideration transferred exceeds the acquisition-date fair value of the acquirer's interest in the acquiree. The IASB's decision to allow an acquirer to choose to measure any non-controlling interest in the acquiree at fair value or on the basis of its proportionate interest in the acquiree's identifiable net assets adds another potential difference between the results of applying the requirements of the revised IFRS 3 and measuring the acquisition-date fair value of the acquiree as a whole. (See paragraphs BC209–BC221 for discussion of the reasons why the IASB provided that choice.) Paragraphs BC330 and BC331 discuss the reasons why the revised standards also eliminate the related presumption in the 2005 Exposure Draft that the consideration transferred in exchange for the acquiree measures the fair value of the acquirer's interest in the acquiree.

Identifying the acquirer

BC82   The boards' decision that all business combinations within the scope of the revised standards should be accounted for by the acquisition method means that the acquirer must be identified in every business combination.

BC83   The IASB and the FASB separately developed the guidance on identifying the acquirer that appeared in IFRS 3 and SFAS 141, respectively. Paragraphs BC84–BC92 discuss the FASB's development of the guidance in SFAS 141 and paragraphs BC93–BC101 discuss the IASB's development of the guidance in IFRS 3. Paragraphs BC102–BC105 discuss the boards' joint consideration of how to identify the acquirer in a business combination in the second phase of their projects on business combinations.

Developing the guidance in SFAS 141

BC84   SFAS 141's guidance on identifying the acquirer focused on the types of business combinations included in its scope, which excluded transactions in which one entity obtains control over one or more other entities by means other than transferring assets, incurring liabilities or issuing equity securities. Thus, SFAS 141 did not include the general guidance that the entity that obtains control is the acquirer, although that was the effect of the guidance for the combinations within its scope.

BC85   In developing its 1999 Exposure Draft, the FASB affirmed the guidance in APB Opinion 16 that in a business combination effected primarily through the distribution of cash or other assets or by incurring liabilities, the acquirer is generally the entity that distributes cash or other assets or assumes or incurs liabilities. The FASB considered a variety of suggestions on factors that should be considered in identifying the acquirer in a business combination effected through an exchange of equity interests. The guidance proposed in the 1999 Exposure Draft reflected the FASB's conclusion that all pertinent facts and circumstances should be considered when identifying the acquirer, particularly the relative voting rights in the combined entity after the combination. That proposed guidance said that the existence of unusual or special voting arrangements and options, warrants or convertible securities should be considered in determining which shareholder group retained or received the larger portion of the voting rights in the combined entity. In addition, factors related to the composition of the board of directors and senior management of the combined entity should be considered and should be weighted equally with the factors related to voting rights.

BC86   Respondents to the 1999 Exposure Draft who commented on the proposed criteria for identifying the acquirer generally agreed that they were appropriate. Some respondents said that the proposed guidance was an improvement over APB Opinion 16 because it provided additional factors to consider in determining which shareholder group retained or received the larger share of the voting rights in the combined entity. However, many respondents suggested improvements to the proposed criteria, and some suggested that the FASB should consider other criteria.

BC87   Several respondents suggested that the FASB should retain the presumptive approach in APB Opinion 16 for identifying the acquirer in transactions effected through an exchange of equity interests. That approach presumes that, in the absence of evidence to the contrary, the acquirer is the combining entity whose owners as a group retain or receive the larger share of the voting rights in the combined entity. Other respondents suggested that the factors to be considered in identifying the acquirer should be provided in the form of a hierarchy. Some of those respondents also suggested that the FASB should provide additional guidance explaining how factors relating to voting rights (unusual special voting arrangements and options, warrants or convertible securities) would affect the determination of the acquirer.

BC88   In considering those suggestions, the FASB observed, as it did in developing the 1999 Exposure Draft, that because each business combination is unique, the facts and circumstances relevant to identifying the acquirer in one combination may be less relevant in another. Therefore, SFAS 141 did not retain the presumptive approach in APB Opinion 16 nor did it provide hierarchical guidance because to do so would have implied that some factors are always more important than others in identifying the acquirer. However, as suggested by respondents, the FASB modified the proposed guidance to explain how some of the factors influence the identification of the acquirer.

BC89   The 1999 Exposure Draft did not propose requiring consideration of the payment of a premium over the market value of the equity securities acquired as evidence of the identity of the acquirer. Some respondents to the 1999 Exposure Draft said that the payment of a premium is a strong indicator of the identity of the acquirer. Upon reconsideration, the FASB decided to include in SFAS 141 the payment of a premium as a criterion to be considered in identifying the acquirer.

BC90   In developing SFAS 141, the FASB observed that identifying the acquirer might be difficult in some multi-party business combinations, particularly those that might not be acquisitions but are required to be accounted for as such. The FASB noted that in those circumstances it might be helpful to consider additional factors such as which of the entities initiated the combination and whether the reported amounts of assets, revenues and earnings of one of the combining entities significantly exceed those of the others. Respondents to the 1999 Exposure Draft generally agreed, and SFAS 141 included that guidance.

BC91   In addition, as suggested by respondents, the FASB decided that SFAS 141 should explicitly state that in some business combinations, such as reverse acquisitions, the entity that issues the equity interests may not be the acquirer. In a reverse acquisition, one entity (Entity A) obtains ownership of the equity instruments of another entity (Entity B), but Entity A issues enough of its own voting equity instruments as consideration in the exchange transaction for control of the combined entity to pass to the owners of Entity B.

BC92   If a new entity is formed to issue equity instruments to effect a business combination, SFAS 141 required that one of the combining entities that existed before the combination must be identified as the acquirer for essentially the same reasons as those discussed in paragraphs BC98–BC101 in the context of IFRS 3's similar requirement.

Developing the guidance in IFRS 3

BC93   As proposed in ED 3, IFRS 3 carried forward from IAS 22 the principle that in a business combination accounted for using the acquisition method the acquirer is the combining entity that obtains control of the other combining entities or businesses. The IASB observed that using the control concept as the basis for identifying the acquirer is consistent with using the control concept in IAS 27 *Consolidated and Separate Financial Statements* to define the boundaries of the reporting entity and to provide the basis for establishing the existence of a parent-subsidiary relationship. IFRS 3 also carried forward the guidance in IAS 22 that control is the power to govern the financial and operating policies of the other entity so as to obtain benefits from its activities. IFRS 3 also provided the same guidance as IAS 22 for identifying the acquirer if one of the combining entities might have obtained control even if it does not acquire more than one-half of the voting rights of another combining entity.

Identifying an acquirer in a business combination effected through an exchange of equity interests

BC94   In developing ED 3 and IFRS 3, the IASB decided not to carry forward the guidance in IAS 22 on identifying which of the combining entities is the acquirer in a reverse acquisition. IAS 22 required the entity whose owners control the combined entity to be treated as the acquirer. That approach presumed that in a business combination effected through an exchange of equity interests, the entity whose owners control the combined entity is always the entity with the power to govern the financial and operating policies of the other entity so as to obtain benefits from its activities. The IASB observed that because the presumption is not always accurate, carrying it forward would in effect override the control concept for identifying the acquirer.

BC95   The IASB observed that the control concept focuses on the relationship between two entities, in particular, whether one entity has the power to govern the financial and operating policies of another so as to obtain benefits from its activities. Therefore, determining which of the combining entities has, as a consequence of the combination, the power to govern the financial and operating policies of the other so as to obtain benefits from its activities is fundamental to identifying the acquirer, regardless of the form of the consideration.

BC96   The IASB also observed that in some reverse acquisitions, the acquirer may be the entity whose equity interests have been acquired and the acquiree is the issuing entity. For example, a private entity might arrange to have itself 'acquired' by a smaller public entity through an exchange of equity interests as a means of obtaining a stock exchange listing. As part of the agreement, the directors of the public entity resign and are replaced by directors appointed by the private entity and its former owners. The IASB observed that in such circumstances, the private entity, which is the legal subsidiary, has the power to govern the financial and operating policies of the combined entity so as to obtain benefits from its activities. Treating the legal subsidiary as the acquirer in such circumstances is thus consistent with applying the control concept for identifying the acquirer. Treating the legal parent as the acquirer in such circumstances would place the form of the transaction over its substance, thereby providing less useful information than would be provided using the control concept to identify the acquirer.

BC97   Therefore, the IASB proposed in ED 3 that the acquirer in a business combination effected through an issue of equity interests should be identified by considering all pertinent facts and circumstances to determine which of the combining entities has the power to govern the financial and operating policies of the other so as to obtain benefits from its activities. Pertinent facts and circumstances include, but are not limited to, the relative ownership interests of the owners of the combining entities. Respondents to ED 3 generally supported that requirement, which was consistent with the requirement of SFAS 141.

Identifying an acquirer if a new entity is formed to effect a business combination

BC98   If a new entity is formed to issue equity instruments to effect a business combination, ED 3 proposed and IFRS 3 required one of the combining entities that existed before the combination to be identified as the acquirer on the basis of the evidence available. In considering that requirement, the IASB identified two approaches to applying the acquisition method that had been applied in various jurisdictions. The first approach viewed business combinations from the perspective of one of the combining entities that existed before the combination. Under that approach, the acquirer must be one of the combining entities that existed before the combination and therefore cannot be a new entity formed to issue equity instruments to effect a combination. The second approach viewed business combinations from the perspective of the entity providing the consideration, which could be a newly formed entity. Under that approach, the acquirer must be the entity providing the consideration. Some jurisdictions interpreted IAS 22 as requiring the first approach; other jurisdictions interpreted IAS 22 as requiring the second approach.

BC99   If a new entity is formed to issue equity instruments to effect a business combination involving two or more other entities, viewing the combination from the perspective of the entity providing the consideration would result in the newly formed entity applying the acquisition method to each of the other combining entities. The IASB noted that the result would be the same as applying the fresh start method to account for the business combination, which would potentially provide users of the financial statements with more relevant information than requiring one of the pre-existing entities to be treated as the acquirer.

BC100   The IASB also considered whether treating a new entity formed to issue equity instruments to effect a business combination as the acquirer would place the form of the transaction over its substance, because the new entity may have no economic substance. The formation of such entities is often related to legal, tax or other business considerations that do not affect the identification of the acquirer. For example, a combination of two entities that is structured so that one entity directs the formation of a new entity to issue equity instruments to the owners of both of the combining entities is, in substance, no different from a transaction in which one of the combining entities directly acquires the other. Therefore, the transaction should be accounted for in the same way as a transaction in which one of the combining entities directly acquires the other. To do otherwise would impair both the comparability and the reliability of the information.

BC101   The IASB concluded that the users of an entity's financial statements are provided with more useful information about a business combination when that information faithfully represents the transaction it purports to represent. Therefore, IFRS 3 required the acquirer to be one of the combining entities that existed before the combination.

Convergence and clarification of SFAS 141's and IFRS 3's guidance for identifying the acquirer

BC102   The deliberations of the FASB and the IASB described in paragraphs BC84–BC101 resulted in similar but not identical guidance for identifying the acquirer in SFAS 141 and IFRS 3. But the guidance was worded differently, and the boards were concerned that differences in identifying the acquirer could arise. Therefore, as part of the effort to develop a common standard on accounting for business combinations, the boards decided to develop common guidance for identifying the acquirer that could be applied internationally. For example, the FASB adopted the IASB's definition of an acquirer as the entity that obtains control of the other combining entities, and both boards decided to include in the revised standards an explicit reference to their other standards that provide guidance for identifying the acquirer. That guidance, although previously implicit, was not in SFAS 141. The intention of the boards is to conform and clarify their guidance but not to change the substance of the provisions for identifying an acquirer previously provided in SFAS 141 and IFRS 3.

BC103   Some respondents to the 2005 Exposure Draft noted that the existing IASB and FASB definitions of control in their respective consolidations standards are somewhat different and, in rare instances, may lead to identifications of different acquirers. The boards agreed with that observation, but they affirmed their conclusion in developing the 2005 Exposure Draft that developing a common definition of control is outside the scope of the business combinations project.

Identifying the acquirer in business combinations involving only mutual entities

BC104   The boards considered whether differences between mutual entities and investor-owned entities or differences between combinations of mutual entities and combinations of investor-owned entities result in a need for different or additional guidance for identifying the acquirer in combinations of mutual entities. The boards did not note any such differences. As a result, the boards concluded that an acquirer must be identified for all business combinations, including those involving only mutual entities.

BC105   The boards also concluded that the indicators for identifying the acquirer in a business combination are applicable to mutual entities and that no additional indicators are needed to identify the acquirer in those combinations. Both boards acknowledged that difficulties may arise in identifying the acquirer in combinations of two virtually equal mutual entities but observed that those difficulties also arise in combinations of two virtually equal investor-owned entities. The boards concluded that those difficulties, which are not unique to mutual entities, could be resolved in practice.

Determining the acquisition date

BC106   IFRS 3 and SFAS 141 carried forward without reconsideration the provisions of IAS 22 and APB Opinion 16, respectively, on determining the acquisition date. With one exception that applies only to SFAS 141 (see paragraphs BC108–BC110), that guidance resulted in the same acquisition date as the guidance in the revised standards.

BC107   In both IFRS 3 and SFAS 141, the guidance on the acquisition date, which IFRS 3 also referred to as the *exchange date*, was incorporated within the guidance on determining the cost of the acquisition rather than being stated separately. The revised standards clarify the acquisition-date guidance to make explicit that the acquisition date is the date that the acquirer obtains control of the acquiree. Paragraphs BC338–BC342 discuss the related issue of the measurement date for equity securities transferred as consideration in a business combination and the changes the revised standards make to the previous requirements on that issue.

BC108   The FASB also eliminated the 'convenience' exception that SFAS 141 carried forward from APB Opinion 16 and the reporting alternative permitted by Accounting Research Bulletin No. 51 *Consolidated Financial Statements* (ARB 51). SFAS 141, paragraph 48, permitted an acquirer to designate an effective date other than the date that assets or equity interests are transferred or liabilities are assumed or incurred (the acquisition date) if it also reduced the cost of the acquiree and net income as required by that paragraph to compensate for recognising income before consideration was transferred. Paragraph 11 of ARB 51 permitted an acquirer to include a subsidiary that was purchased during the year in the consolidation as though it had been acquired at the beginning of the year and to deduct the pre-acquisition earnings at the bottom of the consolidated income statement.

BC109   The FASB concluded that to represent faithfully an acquirer's financial position and results of operations, the acquirer should account for all business combinations at the acquisition date. In other words, its financial position should reflect the assets acquired and liabilities assumed at the acquisition date—not before or after they are obtained or assumed. Moreover, the acquirer's financial statements for the period should include only the cash inflows and outflows, revenues and expenses and other effects of the acquiree's operations after the acquisition date.

BC110   Very few respondents to the 2005 Exposure Draft commented on the proposed guidance on determining the acquisition date. Those who did so generally raised practicability issues related to eliminating the ability to designate an effective date other than the acquisition date. The boards concluded that the financial statement effects of eliminating that exception were rarely likely to be material. For example, for convenience an entity might wish to designate an acquisition date of the end (or the beginning) of a month, the date on which it closes its books, rather than the actual acquisition date during the month. Unless events between the 'convenience' date and the actual acquisition date result in material changes in the amounts recognised, that entity's practice would comply with the requirements of the revised standards. Therefore, the boards decided to retain the guidance in the 2005 Exposure Draft about determining the acquisition date.

Recognising and measuring the identifiable assets acquired, the liabilities assumed and any non-controlling interest in the acquiree

Recognition

BC111   The revised standards' recognition principle is stated in paragraph 10 of the revised IFRS 3. Paragraphs BC112–BC130 discuss the recognition conditions the acquirer is to use in applying the recognition principle. The revised standards also provide guidance for recognising particular assets and liabilities, which is discussed in paragraphs BC131–BC184. The revised standards' guidance on classifying and designating assets acquired and liabilities assumed is discussed in paragraphs BC185–BC188, and the limited exceptions to the recognition principle provided in the revised standards are discussed in paragraphs BC263–BC303.

Conditions for recognition

BC112   The boards decided that to achieve a reasonably high degree of consistency in practice and to resolve existing inconsistencies, the revised standards should provide guidance on applying the recognition principle. That guidance emphasises two fundamental conditions. To measure and recognise an item as part of applying the acquisition method, the item acquired or assumed must be:

(a)   an asset or liability at the acquisition date; and

(b)   part of the business acquired (the acquiree) rather than the result of a separate transaction.

An asset or a liability at the acquisition date

BC113   In determining whether an item should be recognised at the acquisition date as part of the business combination, the boards decided that the appropriate first step is to apply the definitions of assets and liabilities in the IASB's *Framework* or FASB Concepts Statement No. 6 *Elements of Financial Statements*, respectively.

BC114   The boards observed that in accordance with both IFRS 3 and SFAS 141, and their predecessors and the related interpretative guidance, particular items were recognised **as if** they were assets acquired or liabilities assumed at the acquisition date even though they did not meet the definition of an asset or a liability. That practice was related to the previous emphasis on measuring the cost of (or investment in) the acquiree rather than the acquisition-date fair values of the assets acquired and liabilities assumed. For example, as discussed in paragraphs BC365–BC370, some expenses for services received in connection with a business combination were capitalised as part of the cost of the acquiree (and recognised as part of goodwill) **as if** they were an asset at the acquisition date. In addition, some future costs that an acquirer expected to incur often were viewed as a cost of the acquiree and recognised **as if** they were a liability at the acquisition date— expected restructuring costs were an example. The boards concluded that the representational faithfulness, consistency and understandability of financial reporting would be improved by eliminating such practices.

Part of the business combination

BC115   The second condition for recognising an asset acquired or a liability assumed or incurred in a business combination is that the asset or liability must be part of the business combination transaction rather than an asset or a liability resulting from a separate transaction. Making that distinction requires an acquirer to identify the components of a transaction in which it obtains control over an acquiree. The objective of the condition and the guidance on identifying the components of a business combination is to ensure that each component is accounted for in accordance with its economic substance.

BC116   The boards decided to provide application guidance to help address concerns about the difficulty of determining whether a part of the consideration transferred is for the acquiree or is for another purpose. The boards observed that parties directly involved in the negotiations of an impending business combination may take on the characteristics of related parties. Therefore, they may be willing to enter into other agreements or include as part of the business combination agreement some arrangements that are designed primarily for the benefit of the acquirer or the combined entity, for example, to achieve more favourable financial reporting outcomes after the business combination. Because of those concerns the boards decided to develop a principle for determining whether a particular transaction or arrangement entered into by the parties to the combination is part of what the acquirer and acquiree exchange in the business combination or is a separate transaction.

BC117   The boards concluded that a transaction that is designed primarily for the economic benefit of the acquirer or the combined entity (rather than the acquiree or its former owners before the business combination) is not part of the exchange for the acquiree. Those transactions should be accounted for separately from the business combination. The boards acknowledge that judgement may be required to determine whether part of the consideration paid or the assets acquired and liabilities assumed stems from a separate transaction. Accordingly, the 2005 Exposure Draft included both a general principle and implementation guidance for applying that principle, including several examples.

BC118　Respondents' comments on the proposed guidance on identifying the components of a business combination transaction were mixed. For example, some respondents said that the general principle was clear and provided adequate guidance; others said that the proposed principle was not clear. Several respondents said that the focus on determining whether a transaction benefits the acquiree or the acquirer was not clear because a transaction or event that benefits the acquiree would also benefit the combined entity because the acquiree is part of the combined entity.

BC119　The boards agreed with respondents that the proposed principle for distinguishing between components of a business combination needed improvement. Accordingly, they revised the principle to focus on whether a transaction is entered into by or on behalf of the acquirer or **primarily** for the benefit of the acquirer or the combined entity, rather than **primarily** for the benefit of the acquiree or its former owners **before the combination** (paragraph 52 of the revised IFRS 3).

BC120　The boards also concluded that the focus of the principle should be on identifying whether a business combination includes separate transactions that should be accounted for separately in accordance with their economic substance rather than solely on assessing whether a transaction is part of the exchange for the acquiree (paragraph 51 of the revised IFRS 3). Focusing solely on whether assets or liabilities are part of the exchange for the acquiree might not result in all transactions being accounted for in accordance with their economic substance. For example, if an acquirer asks the acquiree to pay some or all of the acquisition-related costs on its behalf and the acquiree has paid those costs before the acquisition date, at the acquisition date the acquiree will show no liability for those costs. Therefore, some might think that the principle as stated in the 2005 Exposure Draft does not apply to the transactions giving rise to the acquisition-related costs. The boards concluded that focusing instead on whether a transaction is separate from the business combination will more clearly convey the intention of the principle and thus will provide users with more relevant information about the financial effects of transactions and events entered into by the acquirer. The acquirer's financial statements will reflect the financial effects of all transactions for which the acquirer is responsible in accordance with their economic substance.

BC121　To help in applying the principle, paragraph 52 of the revised IFRS 3 includes three examples of transactions that are separate from the transaction in which an acquirer obtains control over an acquiree, and Appendix B provides additional application guidance.

BC122　The first example in paragraph 52 is directed at ensuring that a transaction that in effect settles a pre-existing relationship between the acquirer and the acquiree is excluded from the accounting for the business combination. Assume, for example, that a potential acquiree has an asset (receivable) for an unresolved claim against the potential acquirer. The acquirer and the acquiree's owners agree to settle that claim as part of an agreement to sell the acquiree to the acquirer. The boards concluded that if the acquirer makes a lump sum payment to the seller-owner, part of that payment is to settle the claim and is not part of the consideration transferred to acquire the business. Thus, the portion of the payment that relates to the claim settlement should be excluded from the accounting for the business combination and accounted for separately. In effect, the acquiree relinquished its claim (receivable) against the acquirer by transferring it (as a dividend) to the acquiree's owner. Thus, at the acquisition date the acquiree has no receivable (asset) to be acquired as part of the combination, and the acquirer would account for its settlement payment separately. The FASB observed that the conclusion that a transaction that settles a pre-existing relationship is not part of applying the acquisition method is consistent with the conclusion in EITF Issue No. 04-1 *Accounting for Preexisting Relationships between the Parties to a Business Combination*, which is incorporated into SFAS 141(R) and therefore superseded.

BC123 The second and third examples are also directed at ensuring that payments that are not part of the consideration transferred for the acquiree are excluded from the business combination accounting. The boards concluded that the payments for such transactions or arrangements should be accounted for separately in accordance with the applicable requirements for those transactions. Paragraph BC370 also discusses potential abuses related to the third example— payments to reimburse the acquiree or its former owners for paying the acquirer's costs incurred in connection with the business combination.

BC124 To provide additional help in identifying the components of a business combination, paragraph B50 of the revised IFRS 3 includes three factors to be considered in assessing a business combination transaction: (a) the reason for the transaction, (b) who initiated the transaction and (c) the timing of the transaction. Although those factors are neither mutually exclusive nor individually conclusive, the boards decided that the factors could help in considering whether a transaction or event is arranged primarily for the economic benefit of the acquirer or the combined entity or primarily for the benefit of the acquiree and its former owners before the business combination.

IFRS 3's criterion on reliability of measurement

BC125 IFRS 3 included another recognition criterion for assets acquired or liabilities assumed in a business combination. That criterion required an asset or liability to be recognised separately from goodwill only if it could be reliably measured. In its deliberations leading to the revised IFRS 3, the IASB decided to eliminate reliability of measurement as an overall criterion, which it observed is unnecessary because reliability of measurement is a part of the overall recognition criteria in the *Framework*.

IFRS 3's criterion on probability of an inflow or outflow of benefits

BC126 IFRS 3 provided that an acquirer should recognise the acquiree's identifiable assets (other than intangible assets) and liabilities (other than contingent liabilities) only if it is probable that the asset or liability will result in an inflow or outflow of economic benefits. The revised IFRS 3 does not contain that probability recognition criterion and thus it requires the acquirer to recognise identifiable assets acquired and liabilities assumed regardless of the degree of probability of an inflow or outflow of economic benefits.

BC127 The recognition criteria in the *Framework* include the concept of probability to refer to the degree of uncertainty that the future economic benefits associated with an asset or liability will flow to or from the entity.

BC128 During the development of the revised IFRS 3, the IASB reconsidered items described in IAS 37 *Provisions, Contingent Liabilities and Contingent Assets* as contingent assets and contingent liabilities. Analysing the rights or obligations in such items to determine which are conditional and which are unconditional clarifies the question of whether the entity has an asset or a liability at the acquisition date.* As a result, the IASB concluded that many items previously described as contingent assets or contingent liabilities meet the definition of an asset or a liability in the *Framework* because they contain unconditional rights or obligations as well as conditional rights or obligations. Once the unconditional right in an asset (the unconditional obligation in a liability) is identified, the question to be addressed becomes what is the inflow (outflow) of economic benefits relating to that unconditional right (unconditional obligation).

BC129 The IASB noted that the *Framework* articulates the probability recognition criterion in terms of a flow of economic benefits rather than just direct cash flows. If an entity has an unconditional obligation, it is certain that an outflow of economic benefits from the entity is required, even if there is uncertainty about the timing and the amount of the outflow of benefits associated with a related conditional obligation. Hence, the IASB concluded that the liability (the unconditional obligation) satisfies the *Framework*'s probability recognition criterion. That conclusion applies equally to unconditional rights. Thus, if an entity has an unconditional right, it is certain that it has the right to an inflow of economic benefits, and the probability recognition criterion is satisfied.

BC130 Therefore, the IASB decided that inclusion of the probability criterion in the revised IFRS 3 is unnecessary because an unconditional right or obligation will always satisfy the criterion. In addition, the IASB made consequential amendments to paragraphs 25 and 33 of IAS 38 *Intangible Assets* to clarify the reason for its conclusion that the probability recognition criterion is always considered to be satisfied for intangible assets that are acquired separately or in a business combination. Specifically, the amendment indicates that an entity expects there to be an inflow of economic benefits embodied in an intangible asset acquired separately or in a business combination, even if there is uncertainty about the timing and the amount of the inflow.

Recognising particular identifiable assets acquired and liabilities assumed

BC131 To help ensure the consistent application of the requirements of the revised standards, the boards decided to provide specific recognition guidance for particular types of identifiable assets acquired and liabilities assumed in a business combination. That guidance and the reasons for it are discussed in the following paragraphs.

---

* Paragraphs BC11–BC17 and BC22–BC26 of the Basis for Conclusions on the draft amendments to IAS 37, published for comment in June 2005, discuss this issue in more detail.

Liabilities associated with restructuring or exit activities of the acquiree

BC132 The revised standards explain that an acquirer recognises liabilities for restructuring or exit activities acquired in a business combination only if they meet the definition of a liability at the acquisition date (paragraph 11 of the revised IFRS 3). Costs associated with restructuring or exiting an acquiree's activities that are not liabilities at that date are recognised as post-combination activities or transactions of the combined entity when the costs are incurred. In considering acquired restructuring or exit activities the FASB and the IASB began at different points because the requirements of SFAS 141 and IFRS 3 on the issue differed.

BC133 In applying SFAS 141, acquirers looked to EITF Issue No. 95-3 *Recognition of Liabilities in Connection with a Purchase Business Combination* for guidance on recognising liabilities associated with restructuring or exit activities of an acquirer. EITF Issue 95-3 provided that the costs of an acquirer's plan (a) to exit an activity of an acquired company, (b) to involuntarily terminate the employment of employees of an acquired company or (c) to relocate employees of an acquired company should be recognised as liabilities assumed in a purchase business combination if specified conditions were met. Those conditions did not require the existence of a present obligation to another party. In developing the 2005 Exposure Draft, the FASB concluded, as it did in FASB Statement No. 146 *Accounting for Costs Associated with Exit or Disposal Activities* (SFAS 146), that only present obligations to others are liabilities under the definition in the FASB's Concepts Statement 6. An exit or disposal plan, by itself, does not create a present obligation to others for costs an entity expects to incur under the plan. Thus, an entity's commitment to an exit or disposal plan, by itself, is not a sufficient condition for recognition of a liability. Consistently with that conclusion, SFAS 141(R) nullifies the guidance in EITF Issue 95-3, which was not consistent with SFAS 146.

BC134 Before the IASB issued IFRS 3, IAS 22, like EITF Issue 95-3, required the acquirer to recognise as part of allocating the cost of a combination a provision for terminating or reducing the activities of the acquiree (*a restructuring provision*) that was not a liability of the acquiree at the acquisition date, provided that the acquirer had satisfied specified criteria. The criteria in IAS 22 were similar to those in EITF Issue 95-3. In developing ED 3 and IFRS 3, the IASB considered the view that a restructuring provision that was not a liability of the acquiree at the acquisition date should nonetheless be recognised by the acquirer as part of allocating the cost of the combination if the specified conditions were met. Those supporting this view, including some respondents to ED 3, argued that:

(a) the estimated cost of terminating or reducing the activities of the acquiree would have influenced the price paid by the acquirer for the acquiree and therefore should be taken into account in measuring goodwill.

(b) the acquirer is committed to the costs of terminating or reducing the activities of the acquiree because of the business combination. In other words, the combination is the past event that gives rise to a present obligation to terminate or reduce the activities of the acquiree.

BC135   In developing IFRS 3, the IASB rejected those arguments, noting that the price paid by the acquirer would also be influenced by future losses and other 'unavoidable' costs that relate to the future conduct of the business, such as costs of investing in new systems. IFRS 3 did not provide for recognising those costs as liabilities because they do not represent liabilities of the acquiree at the acquisition date, although the expected future outflows may affect the value of existing recognised assets. The IASB concluded that it would be inconsistent to recognise 'unavoidable' restructuring costs that arise in a business combination but to prohibit recognition of a liability for other 'unavoidable' costs to be incurred as a result of the combination.

BC136   The IASB's general criteria for identifying and recognising restructuring provisions are set out in IAS 37. IAS 37 states that a constructive obligation to restructure (and therefore a liability) arises only when the entity has developed a detailed formal plan for the restructuring and either raised a valid expectation in those affected that it will carry out the restructuring by publicly announcing details of the plan or begun implementing the plan. IAS 37 requires such a liability to be recognised when it becomes probable that an outflow of resources embodying economic benefits will be required to settle the obligation and the amount of the obligation can be reliably estimated.

BC137   IFRS 3 reflected the IASB's conclusion that if the criteria in paragraph 31 of IAS 22 for the recognition of a restructuring provision were carried forward, similar items would be accounted for differently. The timing of the recognition of restructuring provisions would differ, depending on whether a plan to restructure arises in connection with, or in the absence of, a business combination. The IASB decided that such a difference would impair the usefulness of the information provided to users about an entity's plans to restructure because both comparability and reliability would be diminished. Accordingly, IFRS 3 contained the same requirements as the revised IFRS 3 for recognising liabilities associated with restructuring or exit activities.

BC138   Few of the comments on the 2005 Exposure Draft from respondents who apply IFRSs in preparing their financial statements addressed its proposal on accounting for costs to restructure or exit activities of an acquiree (restructuring costs). Those who did so generally agreed with its proposal to carry forward the requirement of IFRS 3 for recognising liabilities associated with restructuring or exit activities of an acquiree. But the provisions of the 2005 Exposure Draft on that issue represented a change to GAAP in the United States, and the FASB received several responses objecting to the proposed change. It also received some responses that agreed with them, generally for the same reasons that the boards proposed the provisions in the 2005 Exposure Draft.

BC139   Respondents who disagreed with the proposed accounting for liabilities associated with restructuring or exit activities of an acquiree generally cited one or more of the following reasons in support of their view:

(a)   Acquirers factor restructuring costs into the amount they are willing to pay for the acquiree. Therefore, those costs should be included in accounting for the business combination.

(b)   It is not clear why the boards decided that restructuring costs should not be recognised as liabilities assumed in the business combination when those costs are more likely to be incurred than some of the liabilities related to contingencies that the boards proposed to recognise as liabilities assumed in a combination.

(c)   Capitalising restructuring costs as part of a business combination would be consistent with the accounting for other asset acquisitions in which the amount capitalised is equal to the amount paid to acquire and place the asset in service.

BC140   The boards were not persuaded by those views. They observed that the view described in paragraph BC139(a) is essentially the same as the view of some respondents to ED 3 discussed in paragraph BC134(a). In addition, the boards noted that the acquirer does not pay the acquiree or its owners for the anticipated costs to restructure or exit activities and the acquirer's plans to do so do not give rise to an obligation and associated liability at the acquisition date. The acquirer ordinarily incurs a liability associated with such costs after it gains control of the acquiree's business.

BC141   The boards also disagreed with the view that the accounting for costs to restructure or exit some of an acquiree's activities is inconsistent with the requirements of the revised standards on contingencies. On the contrary, the two requirements are consistent with each other because both require recognition of a liability only if an obligation that meets the definition of a liability exists at the acquisition date.

BC142   The boards also observed that the requirements of the revised standards on restructuring costs are consistent with current practice in accounting for many similar costs expected to be incurred in conjunction with other acquisitions of assets. For example, one airline might acquire an aircraft from another airline. The acquirer was likely to consider the costs of changing the logo on the aircraft and making any other intended changes to its configuration in deciding what it was willing to pay for the aircraft. Other airlines bidding for the aircraft might also have plans to change the aircraft if they were the successful bidders. The nature and extent of the changes each airline expected to make and the costs each would incur were likely to differ.

BC143   In accordance with both US GAAP and IFRSs, the airline would recognise none of those expected, post-acquisition costs at the date the aircraft is acquired. Instead, those costs are accounted for after control of the aircraft is obtained. If the costs add to the value of the aircraft and meet the related requirements of US GAAP or IFRSs, they will be recognised as assets (probably as an addition to the carrying amount of the aircraft). Otherwise, those additional costs are likely to be charged to expense when incurred.

Operating leases

BC144   In accordance with both FASB Statement No. 13 *Accounting for Leases* (SFAS 13) and IAS 17 *Leases*, an acquiree that is the lessee in an operating lease does not recognise separately the rights and obligations embodied in operating leases. The boards considered whether to require, for example, the separate recognition of an asset acquired for an acquiree's rights to use property for the specified period and related renewal options or other rights and a liability assumed for an acquiree's obligations to make required lease payments for an operating lease acquired in a business combination. However, at the time they considered how to account for operating leases in a business combination, they were considering adding to their agendas a joint project on accounting for leases. That project was added in 2006. Accordingly, the boards concluded that the revised standards should be consistent with the existing accounting requirements on accounting for leases. Therefore, the revised standards provide that the acquirer recognises no assets or liabilities related to an operating lease in which the acquiree is the lessee other than those referred to in paragraphs B29 and B30 of the revised IFRS 3, which are discussed in the following paragraphs.

BC145   The 2005 Exposure Draft proposed that the amount by which the terms of an operating lease are favourable or unfavourable in relation to market terms should be recognised as a separate intangible asset, regardless of whether the acquiree is the lessee or the lessor. For the FASB, that proposal would have carried forward the related guidance in SFAS 141 for leases in which the acquiree is the lessee. Some respondents suggested that, instead, the measure of the fair value of an asset subject to an operating lease in which the acquiree is the lessor should take into account the favourable or unfavourable aspect of the lease terms.

BC146   The boards considered this issue in the context of their respective guidance in other standards on how to determine the fair value of an asset. As noted above, the proposal in the 2005 Exposure Draft was generally consistent with US GAAP for business combinations. However, FASB Statement No. 157 *Fair Value Measurements* (SFAS 157) does not provide guidance on the *unit of valuation*—the level at which an asset or liability is aggregated or disaggregated to determine what is being measured. The IASB also does not have general guidance on determining the unit of valuation. However, IAS 40 *Investment Property* provides that the fair value of investment property takes into account rental income from current leases, and the IASB understands that practice in measuring the fair value of investment property is to take into account the contractual terms of the leases and other contracts in place relating to the asset.

BC147   The FASB concluded that SFAS 141 should retain the guidance in the 2005 Exposure Draft that the favourable or unfavourable aspect of an operating lease in which the acquiree is the lessor should be separately recognised as an intangible asset or liability. It concluded that separately reporting that amount rather than embedding an aspect of a lease contract in the fair value of the leased asset would provide more complete information to users of the post-combination financial statements. In addition, the FASB noted that reporting the favourable or unfavourable aspect of the lease contract separately would facilitate appropriate amortisation of that amount over the term of the lease rather than over the remaining life of the leased asset. Unlike IAS 16 *Property, Plant and Equipment*, US GAAP does not require an item of property, plant or equipment to be separated into components, with the components depreciated or amortised over different useful lives.

BC148   The IASB decided to require the acquirer in a business combination to follow the guidance in IAS 40 for assets subject to operating leases in which the acquiree is the lessor. The IASB observed that, for lessors who choose the cost option in IAS 40, both IAS 16 and IAS 38 require use of a depreciation or amortisation method that reflects the pattern in which the entity expects to consume the asset's future economic benefits. In addition, IAS 16 requires each part of an item of property, plant and equipment that has a cost that is significant in relation to the total cost of the item to be depreciated separately. Thus, an entity would be required to adjust the depreciation or amortisation method for the leased asset to reflect the timing of cash flows attributable to the underlying leases. Therefore, although the presentation of operating leases and the underlying leased assets in the statement of financial position will differ depending on whether an entity applies IFRSs or US GAAP, the IASB observed that the identifiable net assets and the depreciation or amortisation recognised in the post-combination financial statements will be the same.

Research and development assets

BC149 The revised standards require an acquirer to recognise all tangible and intangible research and development assets acquired in a business combination, as was proposed in the 2005 Exposure Draft. Previously, FASB Interpretation No. 4 *Applicability of FASB Statement No. 2 to Business Combinations Accounted for by the Purchase Method* (FASB Interpretation 4) required an acquirer to measure and immediately recognise as expense tangible and intangible assets to be used in research and development that had no alternative future use. A research and development asset was recognised as such only if it had an alternative future use. In contrast, IFRS 3 did not require a research and development asset to have an alternative future use for it to be recognised. The revised standards therefore do not change the provisions of IFRS 3 on that issue. Accordingly, most of the discussion in paragraphs BC150–BC156 pertains to the FASB's consideration of this issue.

BC150 The FASB concluded that the requirement to write off assets to be used in research and development activities immediately if they have no alternative future use resulted in information that was not representationally faithful. In addition, eliminating that requirement furthers the goal of international convergence of accounting standards. Therefore, SFAS 141(R) supersedes FASB Interpretation 4 and requires research and development assets acquired in a business combination to be recognised regardless of whether they have an alternative future use.

BC151 Relatively few respondents to the 2005 Exposure Draft commented on the proposed accounting for research and development assets. Those who did so generally disagreed with those proposals (they also generally applied US GAAP rather than IFRSs), citing either or both of the following concerns as support for their view:

(a) In-process research and development may not meet the definition of an asset in the FASB's Concepts Statement 6 because its low likelihood of success does not represent **probable** future economic benefits.

(b) The fair value of in-process research and development may not be measurable with sufficient reliability for recognition in financial statements.

The boards rejected both of those views for the reasons explained in the following paragraphs.

BC152 The boards agreed with respondents that the likelihood that an individual research and development project will result in a profitable product is often low. However, the boards also noted that the use of the word *probable* in the FASB's Concepts Statement 6 refers only to something that is not certain. The definition does not use that term as a recognition criterion that specifies the degree of probability of the inflow or outflow of future economic benefits that must be present for an item to qualify for recognition. Therefore, the boards concluded that in-process research and development acquired in a business combination will generally satisfy the definition of an asset because the observable exchange at the acquisition date provides evidence that the parties to the exchange expect future economic benefits to result from that research and development. Uncertainty about the outcome of an individual project is reflected in measuring its fair value.

BC153 The boards also agreed that determining the fair value of in-process research and development requires the use of estimates and judgement, and the resulting amount will generally not be as reliable as the fair values of other assets for which quoted prices in active markets are available. However, the boards observed that use of estimates and judgement, by itself, does not mean that information is unreliable; reliability does not require precision or certainty. For example, paragraph 86 of the IASB's *Framework* says that 'In many cases, cost or value must be estimated; the use of reasonable estimates is an essential part of the preparation of financial statements and does not undermine their reliability.' The boards also noted that the requirement to measure the fair value of in-process research and development assets acquired in a business combination is not new—not even in US GAAP. In accordance with FASB Interpretation 4, that amount was measured but immediately written off. Moreover, respondents to the 2005 Exposure Draft that apply IFRSs generally did not mention any problems with complying with the provisions of IFRS 3 on research and development assets, which are the same as those in the revised standards.

BC154 In developing the 2005 Exposure Draft, the FASB also considered whether it could make further improvements by extending the recognition provisions of SFAS 141(R) for research and development assets to purchases of in-process research and development assets outside a business combination. At that time, the FASB decided not to do so because the additional time needed to deliberate the related issues would have unduly delayed the revised standards.

BC155 Some respondents to the 2005 Exposure Draft objected to the resulting inconsistent US GAAP requirements for research and development assets acquired in a business combination and those acquired in another type of transaction. The FASB agreed with respondents that inconsistent accounting for research and development assets depending on how they are acquired is undesirable. Therefore, the FASB expects to reconsider the accounting for research and development assets acquired by means other than in a business combination separately from its project on business combinations.

BC156 The FASB also decided to provide guidance on the impairment testing of in-process research and development projects that are temporarily idled or abandoned. It did that by means of an amendment to SFAS 142.

Distinguishing identifiable intangible assets from goodwill

BC157 Early in their respective projects on accounting for business combinations, the IASB and the FASB both observed that intangible assets make up an increasing proportion of the assets of many (if not most) entities. The boards also observed that intangible assets acquired in a business combination were often included in the amount recognised as goodwill.

BC158 Both the IASB and the FASB decided that they needed to provide explicit criteria for determining whether an acquired intangible asset should be recognised separately from goodwill. The FASB provided such criteria in SFAS 141 and the IASB provided similar, although not identical, criteria in IAS 38.* One reason for providing such criteria was the boards' conclusion that the decision-usefulness of financial statements would be enhanced if intangible assets acquired in a business combination were distinguished from goodwill. For example, the FASB's Concepts Statement No. 5 *Recognition and Measurement in Financial Statements of Business Enterprises* says that classification in financial statements facilitates analysis by grouping items with essentially similar characteristics and separating items with essentially different characteristics. Analysis aimed at objectives such as predicting amounts, timing and uncertainty of future cash flows requires financial information segregated into reasonably homogeneous groups.

BC159 In developing its 1999 Exposure Draft, the FASB considered various characteristics that might distinguish other intangible assets from goodwill. Because the FASB concluded that identifiability is the characteristic that conceptually distinguishes other intangible assets from goodwill, the 1999 Exposure Draft proposed that intangible assets that are identifiable and reliably measurable should be recognised as assets separately from goodwill. Most respondents to the 1999 Exposure Draft agreed that many intangible assets are identifiable and that various intangible assets are reliably measurable. However, respondents' views on the proposed recognition criteria varied. Many of those respondents suggested alternative recognition criteria and many urged the FASB to clarify the term *reliably measurable*.

BC160 The FASB considered those suggestions and decided to modify the proposed recognition criteria to provide a clearer distinction between intangible assets that should be recognised separately from goodwill and those that should be subsumed into goodwill. The FASB then published a revised exposure draft *Business Combinations and Intangible Assets—Accounting for Goodwill* (2001 Exposure Draft) which proposed that an intangible asset should be recognised separately from goodwill if either:

(a) control over the future economic benefits of the asset results from contractual or other legal rights (the contractual-legal criterion); or

(b) the intangible asset is capable of being separated or divided and sold, transferred, licensed, rented or exchanged (either separately or as part of a group of assets) (the separability criterion).

---

* More detailed information about the IASB's reasoning in developing the criteria in IAS 38 is available in its Basis for Conclusions.

The FASB concluded that sufficient information should exist to measure reliably the fair value of an asset that satisfies either of those criteria. Thus, the change in the recognition criteria eliminated the need explicitly to include *reliably measurable* as a recognition criterion or to clarify the meaning of that term.

BC161 IAS 38 (as issued by the IASB's predecessor body in 1998) clarified that the definition of an intangible asset required an intangible asset to be identifiable to distinguish it from goodwill. However, it did not define the term *identifiable*. Instead, IAS 38 stated that an intangible asset could be distinguished from goodwill if the asset was separable, though separability was not a necessary condition for identifiability.

BC162 In developing IFRS 3, the IASB affirmed the conclusion in IAS 38 that identifiability is the characteristic that conceptually distinguishes other intangible assets from goodwill. In addition, the IASB concluded that to provide a definitive basis for identifying and recognising intangible assets separately from goodwill, the concept of identifiability needed to be articulated more clearly. As a result of that consideration, which is discussed in paragraphs BC163–BC165, the IASB developed more definitive criteria for distinguishing between identifiable intangible assets and goodwill and included those criteria in both IFRS 3 and IAS 38 (as revised in 2004).

Reasons for the contractual-legal criterion

BC163 In developing IFRS 3 and SFAS 141, the IASB and the FASB observed that many intangible assets arise from rights conveyed legally by contract, statute or similar means. For example, franchises are granted to car dealers, fast food outlets and professional sports teams. Trademarks and service marks may be registered with the government. Contracts are often negotiated with customers or suppliers. Technological innovations are often protected by patents. In contrast, goodwill arises from the collection of assembled assets that make up an acquiree or the value created by assembling a collection of assets through a business combination, such as the synergies that are expected to result from combining two or more businesses. Therefore, both boards concluded that the fact that an intangible asset arises from contractual or other legal rights is an important characteristic that distinguishes many intangible assets from goodwill and an acquired intangible asset with that characteristic should be recognised separately from goodwill.

Reasons for the separability criterion

BC164 As already noted (paragraph BC161), the original version of IAS 38 included separability as a characteristic that helps to distinguish intangible assets from goodwill. In developing IFRS 3, the IASB affirmed that conclusion for the reasons discussed in the following paragraphs.

BC165 In developing IFRS 3 and SFAS 141, the IASB and the FASB observed that some intangible assets that do not arise from rights conveyed by contract or other legal means are nonetheless capable of being separated from the acquiree and exchanged for something else of value. Others, like goodwill, cannot be separated from an entity and sold or otherwise transferred. Both boards thus concluded that separability is another important characteristic that distinguishes many intangible assets from goodwill. An acquired intangible asset with that characteristic should be recognised separately from goodwill.

BC166   The FASB's 2001 Exposure Draft proposed that an intangible asset that was not separable individually would meet the separability criterion if it could be sold, transferred, licensed, rented or exchanged along with a group of related assets or liabilities. Some respondents suggested that the FASB should eliminate that requirement, arguing that unless the asset is separable individually it should be included in the amount recognised as goodwill. Others asked the FASB to clarify the meaning of the term *group of related assets*, noting that even goodwill can be separated from the acquiree if the asset group sold constitutes a business.

BC167   The FASB noted that some intangible assets are so closely related to another asset or liability that they are usually sold as a 'package' (eg deposit liabilities and the related depositor relationship intangible asset). If those intangible assets were subsumed into goodwill, gains might be inappropriately recognised if the intangible asset was later sold along with the related asset or obligation. However, the FASB agreed that the proposed requirement to recognise an intangible asset separately from goodwill if it could be sold or transferred as part of an asset group was a broader criterion than it had intended. For those reasons, SFAS 141 provided, as do the revised standards, that an intangible asset that is not separable individually meets the separability criterion if it can be separated from the entity and sold, transferred, licensed, rented or exchanged in combination with a related contract, other identifiable asset or other liability.

BC168   Some respondents to the 2001 Exposure Draft suggested limiting the separability criterion to intangible assets that are separable **and** are traded in observable exchange transactions. Although the FASB agreed that exchange transactions provide evidence of an asset's separability, it concluded that those transactions were not necessarily the only evidence of separability and it did not adopt that suggestion.

BC169   Other respondents suggested that the separability criterion should be modified to require recognition of an intangible asset separately from goodwill only if management of the entity **intends** to sell, lease or otherwise exchange the asset. The FASB rejected that suggestion because it concluded that the asset's **capability** of being separated from the entity and exchanged for something else of value is the pertinent characteristic of an intangible asset that distinguishes it from goodwill. In contrast, management's intentions are not a characteristic of an asset.

The FASB's reasons for rejecting other recognition criteria suggested for SFAS 141

BC170   Some respondents suggested that the FASB should eliminate the requirement to recognise intangible assets separately from goodwill. Others suggested that all intangible assets with characteristics similar to goodwill should be included in the amount recorded as goodwill. The FASB rejected those suggestions because they would diminish rather than improve the decision-usefulness of reported financial information.

BC171   Some respondents doubted their ability to measure reliably the fair values of many intangible assets. They suggested that the only intangible assets that should be recognised separately from goodwill are those that have direct cash flows and those that are bought and sold in observable exchange transactions. The FASB rejected that suggestion. Although the fair value measures of some identifiable intangible assets might lack the precision of the measures for other assets, the FASB concluded that the information that will be provided by recognising intangible assets at their estimated fair values is a more faithful representation than that which would be provided if those intangible assets were subsumed into goodwill. Moreover, including finite-lived intangible assets in goodwill that is not being amortised would further diminish the representational faithfulness of financial statements.

Convergence of criteria in SFAS 141 and IFRS 3

BC172   The criteria in IFRS 3 for determining if an intangible asset is identifiable and thus should be recognised separately from goodwill included the same contractual or legal and separability conditions as SFAS 141. However, IFRS 3 also included a requirement that the fair value of an identifiable intangible asset should be reliably measurable to be recognised separately. In developing the 2005 Exposure Draft, the boards considered how best to achieve convergence of their respective recognition criteria for intangible assets.

BC173   In developing IFRS 3, the IASB noted that the fair value of identifiable intangible assets acquired in a business combination is normally measurable with sufficient reliability to be recognised separately from goodwill. The effects of uncertainty because of a range of possible outcomes with different probabilities are reflected in measuring the asset's fair value; the existence of such a range does not demonstrate an inability to measure fair value reliably. IAS 38 (before amendment by the revised IFRS 3) included a rebuttable presumption that the fair value of an intangible asset with a finite useful life acquired in a business combination can be measured reliably. The IASB had concluded that it might not always be possible to measure reliably the fair value of an asset that has an underlying contractual or legal basis. However, IAS 38 provided that the only circumstances in which it might not be possible to measure reliably the fair value of an intangible asset that arises from legal or other contractual rights acquired in a business combination were if it either:

(a)   is not separable; or

(b)   is separable, but there is no history or evidence of exchange transactions for the same or similar assets, and otherwise estimating fair value would depend on immeasurable variables.

BC174   In developing the 2005 Exposure Draft, the IASB concluded that separate recognition of intangible assets, on the basis of an estimate of fair value, rather than subsuming them in goodwill, provides better information to the users of financial statements even if a significant degree of judgement is required to estimate fair value. For that reason, the IASB decided to propose consequential amendments to IAS 38 to remove the reliability of measurement criterion for intangible assets acquired in a business combination. In redeliberating the proposals in the 2005 Exposure Draft, the IASB affirmed those amendments to IAS 38.

Illustrative list of intangible assets

BC175   The illustrative examples that accompanied IFRS 3 included a list of examples of identifiable intangible assets that might be acquired in a business combination. A similar list accompanies the revised IFRS 3 (see the illustrative examples). The list reflects various changes to similar lists in the exposure drafts that the boards published earlier in their respective projects on business combinations. The boards observed that the list is not exhaustive, and a particular type of intangible asset that was included on an earlier list might not be mentioned in the illustrative examples. That does not necessarily mean that the intangible asset does not qualify as identifiable in accordance with the criteria in the revised standards. An acquirer must consider the nature of each acquired intangible asset in determining whether those criteria are met.

Assembled workforce

BC176   In developing SFAS 141, the FASB did not consider whether an assembled workforce met either the contractual-legal or the separability criterion for recognition as an identifiable intangible asset. Instead, SFAS 141 precluded separate recognition of an assembled workforce because of the FASB's conclusion that techniques to measure the value of an assembled workforce with sufficient reliability were not currently available. IFRS 3 and IAS 38, on the other hand, did not explicitly preclude separate recognition of an assembled workforce. However, paragraph 15 of IAS 38 noted that an entity would not usually have sufficient control over the expected future economic benefits arising from an assembled workforce for it to meet the definition of a separate intangible asset.

BC177   In developing the 2005 Exposure Draft, the boards concluded that an acquirer should not recognise an assembled workforce as a separate intangible asset because it meets neither the contractual-legal nor the separability criterion. The views of respondents who commented on recognition of an assembled workforce were mixed. Some agreed with its proposed recognition prohibition. Others suggested that the boards should reconsider that prohibition; they generally said that an assembled workforce is already valued in many situations for the purpose of calculating a 'contributory asset charge' in determining the fair value of some intangible assets. (In using an 'excess earnings' income valuation technique, a contributory asset charge is required to isolate the cash flows generated by the intangible asset being valued from the contribution to those cash flows made by other assets, including other intangible assets. Contributory asset charges are hypothetical 'rental' charges for the use of those other contributing assets.) Those respondents opposed a prohibition on recognising an assembled workforce as a separate intangible asset; they favoured permitting acquirers to assess whether an assembled workforce is separable in each situation and to recognise those that are separable.

BC178   In reconsidering the proposal in the 2005 Exposure Draft, the boards concluded that the prohibition of recognising an assembled workforce should be retained. Because an assembled workforce is a collection of employees rather than an individual employee, it does not arise from contractual or legal rights. Although individual employees might have employment contracts with the employer, the collection of employees, as a whole, does not have such a contract. In addition, an assembled workforce is not separable, either as individual employees or together with a related contract, identifiable asset or liability. An assembled workforce cannot be sold, transferred, licensed, rented or otherwise exchanged without causing disruption to the acquirer's business. In contrast, an entity could continue to operate after transferring an identifiable asset. Therefore, an assembled workforce is not an identifiable intangible asset to be recognised separately from goodwill.

BC179 The boards observed that neither IAS 38 nor SFAS 141 defined an assembled workforce, and that inconsistencies have resulted in practice. In addition, some who objected to the recognition prohibition in the 2005 Exposure Draft apparently consider that an assembled workforce represents the intellectual capital of the skilled workforce—the (often specialised) knowledge and experience that employees of an acquiree bring to their jobs. However, the boards view an assembled workforce as an existing collection of employees that permits an acquirer to continue to operate an acquired business from the acquisition date and they decided to include that definition in the revised standards (paragraph B37 of the revised IFRS 3).

BC180 The boards observed that the value of intellectual capital is, in effect, recognised because it is part of the fair value of the entity's other intangible assets, such as proprietary technologies and processes and customer contracts and relationships. In that situation, a process or methodology can be documented and followed to the extent that the business would not be materially affected if a particular employee left the entity. In most jurisdictions, the employer usually 'owns' the intellectual capital of an employee. Most employment contracts stipulate that the employer retains the rights to and ownership of any intellectual property created by the employee. For example, a software program created by a particular employee (or group of employees) would be documented and generally would be the property of the entity. The particular programmer who created the program could be replaced by another software programmer with equivalent expertise without significantly affecting the ability of the entity to continue to operate. But the intellectual property created in the form of a software program is part of the fair value of that program and is an identifiable intangible asset if it is separable from the entity. In other words, the prohibition of recognising an assembled workforce as an intangible asset does not apply to intellectual property; it applies only to the value of having a workforce in place on the acquisition date so that the acquirer can continue the acquiree's operations without having to hire and train a workforce.

Reacquired rights

BC181 As part of a business combination, an acquirer may reacquire a right that it had previously granted to the acquiree to use the acquirer's recognised or unrecognised intangible assets. Examples of such rights include a right to use the acquirer's trade name under a franchise agreement or a right to use the acquirer's technology under a technology licensing agreement. The 2005 Exposure Draft proposed, and the revised standards require, an acquirer to recognise such a reacquired right as an identifiable intangible asset (paragraph B35 of the revised IFRS 3). The fair value of a reacquired right is to be amortised over the remaining term of the contract that gave rise to the right. For entities applying US GAAP, that guidance is not new; it is the same as the related guidance in EITF Issue 04-1. (Paragraphs BC308–BC310 discuss the measurement of reacquired rights.)

BC182 A few respondents to the 2005 Exposure Draft disagreed with recognising a reacquired right as an identifiable intangible asset because they considered that doing so was the same as recognising an internally generated intangible asset. Some suggested recognising a reacquired right as the settlement of a pre-existing relationship; others said that a reacquired right should be recognised as part of goodwill.

BC183　The boards rejected the alternative of treating a reacquired right as the termination of a pre-existing relationship because reacquisition of, for example, a franchise right does not terminate the right. After a business combination, the right to operate a franchised outlet in a particular region continues to exist. The difference is that the acquirer, rather than the acquiree by itself, now controls the franchise right.

BC184　The boards also rejected recognising a reacquired right as part of goodwill. Supporters of that alternative consider that such a right differs from other identifiable intangible assets recognised in a business combination because, from the perspective of the combined entity, a franchising relationship with an outside party no longer exists. As already noted, however, the reacquired right and the related cash flows continue to exist. The boards concluded that recognising that right separately from goodwill provides users of the financial statements of the combined entity with more decision-useful information than subsuming the right into goodwill. The boards also observed that a reacquired right meets the contractual-legal and the separability criteria and therefore qualifies as an identifiable intangible asset.

Classifying and designating assets acquired and liabilities assumed

BC185　In some situations, IFRSs and US GAAP provide for different accounting depending on how a particular asset or liability is classified or designated. For example, in accordance with both IAS 39 *Financial Instruments: Recognition and Measurement*[*] and FASB Statement No. 115 *Accounting for Certain Investments in Debt and Equity Securities*, the accounting for particular financial instruments differs depending on how the instrument is classified, for example, as at fair value through profit or loss, available for sale or held to maturity. Another example is the accounting for a derivative instrument in accordance with either IAS 39 or FASB Statement No. 133 *Accounting for Derivative Instruments and Hedging Activities* (SFAS 133), which depends on whether the derivative is designated as a hedge, and if so, the type of hedge designated.

BC186　The 2005 Exposure Draft proposed that the classification of an acquired lease would not change from the acquiree's classification at lease inception unless the terms of the lease were modified as a result of the business combination in a way that would require a different classification in accordance with IAS 17 or SFAS 13. But that exposure draft did not address classification or designation issues pertaining to other types of contracts. Some respondents and others asked the boards to provide additional guidance on when the acquirer in a business combination should reconsider and perhaps change the classification or designation of a contract for the purpose of applying other accounting requirements.

BC187　The boards decided that providing a general principle for classifying or designating contracts acquired in a business combination would facilitate consistent implementation of the revised standards. They observed that application of the acquisition method results in the initial recognition in the

---

[*]　In November 2009 the IASB amended the requirements of IAS 39 relating to classification and measurement of assets within the scope of IAS 39 and relocated them to IFRS 9 *Financial Instruments*. IFRS 9 applies to all assets within the scope of IAS 39. This paragraph discusses matters relevant when IFRS 3 was issued.

acquirer's financial statements of the assets acquired and liabilities assumed in a business combination. Therefore, in concept, the acquirer should classify and designate all items acquired in a business combination at the acquisition date in the context of the contractual terms, economic conditions and other pertinent factors at that date. That concept underlies the classification and designation principle (paragraph 15 of the revised IFRS 3).

BC188　In the two situations described in paragraph 17 of the revised IFRS 3, classification of a lease contract as an operating lease or a finance lease and classification of a contract as an insurance or reinsurance contract or a deposit contract, other IFRSs and US GAAP require an entity to classify a contract only at its inception, on the basis of contractual terms and other factors at that date. Because those requirements apply to specific types of contracts regardless of the identity of the parties to the contract, the boards concluded that such requirements should also apply in accounting for a business combination. Thus, the revised standards provide an exception to the principle for classifying and designating assets acquired and liabilities assumed in a business combination for the two types of contracts identified in paragraph 17.

Recognition, classification and measurement guidance for insurance and reinsurance contracts

BC189　SFAS 141(R) provides guidance specific to insurance and reinsurance contracts acquired or assumed in a business combination, primarily by means of amendments to other insurance-related standards. Paragraphs BC190–BC195 discuss that guidance. Paragraph BC196 discusses the IASB's guidance on recognition and measurement of insurance contracts in a business combination, which is provided in IFRS 4 *Insurance Contracts*.

BC190　The FASB decided that insurance and reinsurance contracts acquired in a business combination should be accounted for on a fresh start (new contract) basis. Accordingly, all assets and liabilities arising from the rights and obligations of insurance and reinsurance contracts acquired in a business combination are recognised at the acquisition date, measured at their acquisition-date fair values. That recognition and measurement might include a reinsurance recoverable, a liability to pay future contract claims and claims expenses on the unexpired portion of the acquired contracts and a liability to pay incurred contract claims and claims expenses. However, those assets acquired and liabilities assumed would not include the acquiree's insurance and reinsurance contract accounts such as deferred acquisition costs and unearned premiums that do not represent future cash flows. The FASB considers that model the most consistent with the acquisition method and with the accounting for other types of contracts acquired in a business combination.

BC191　The FASB also decided to require the acquirer to carry forward the acquiree's classification of a contract as an insurance or reinsurance contract (rather than a deposit) on the basis of the terms of the acquired contract and any related contracts or agreements at the inception of the contract. If the terms of those contracts or agreements have been modified in a manner that would change the classification, the acquirer determines the classification of the contract on the basis of its terms and other pertinent factors as of the modification date, which may be the acquisition date. Consideration of related contracts and arrangements is important in assessing whether a contract qualifies as insurance or reinsurance because they can significantly affect the amount of risk transferred.

BC192 SFAS 141(R) also requires the fair value of the insurance and reinsurance contracts acquired in a business combination to be separated into (a) insurance and reinsurance US GAAP accounting balances using the acquirer's accounting policies and (b) an intangible asset (or, at times that are expected to be rare, another liability). That guidance permits the acquirer to report the acquired business subsequently on the same basis as its written business (with the exception of the amortisation of the intangible asset). Other contracts providing for third-party contingent commissions would be accounted for in the same way as other contingencies, and contracts that provide guarantees of the adequacy of claims liabilities would be accounted for as indemnifications.

BC193 The FASB concluded that the intangible asset should be amortised on a basis consistent with the measurement of the liability. For example, for most short-duration contracts such as property and liability insurance contracts, US GAAP claims liabilities are not discounted, so amortising the intangible asset like a discount using an interest method could be an appropriate method. For particular long-duration contracts such as most traditional life insurance contracts, using a basis consistent with the measurement of the liability would be similar to the guidance provided in paragraph 31 of FASB Statement No. 60 *Accounting and Reporting by Insurance Enterprises* (SFAS 60).

BC194 The FASB considered several implementation issues identified by respondents to the 2005 Exposure Draft but decided that specifying the fresh start model for acquired insurance and reinsurance contracts and providing limited guidance on subsequent accounting, including requiring the intangible asset to be amortised on a basis consistent with the liability, should be sufficient to resolve most practice issues. That level of guidance is also consistent with the limited guidance provided by IFRS 4.

BC195 The FASB decided to provide the guidance on recognition and measurement, including subsequent measurement, of insurance and reinsurance contracts acquired in a business combination by means of an amendment to SFAS 60. That parallels the location of the IASB's business combination guidance for insurance contracts in IFRS 4 and will make it easier to address any changes in that guidance that might result if the FASB and the IASB eventually undertake a joint project to reconsider comprehensively the accounting for insurance contracts.

BC196 Paragraphs 31–33 of IFRS 4 deal with limited aspects of insurance contracts acquired in a business combination. That guidance was developed in phase I of the IASB's project on insurance contracts. The IASB decided not to amend those paragraphs in phase II of the business combinations project, so as not to pre-empt phase II of the IASB's project on insurance contracts. In May 2007 the IASB published its initial thoughts for phase II of that project in a discussion paper *Preliminary Views on Insurance Contracts*.

Measurement

BC197 Paragraph 18 of the revised IFRS 3 establishes the principle that the identifiable assets acquired and liabilities assumed should be measured at their acquisition-date fair values. The reasons for that principle and its application to contingencies and non-controlling interests are discussed in paragraphs BC198–BC245, and the definition of fair value is discussed in paragraphs BC246–BC251. The revised standards provide guidance on determining the acquisition-date fair value of particular types of assets acquired, which is discussed in paragraphs BC252–BC262. The exceptions to the measurement principle are discussed in paragraphs BC279–BC311.

Why establish fair value as the measurement principle?

Identifiable assets acquired and liabilities assumed

BC198 In developing the measurement principle in the revised standards, the boards concluded that fair value is the most relevant attribute for assets acquired and liabilities assumed in a business combination. Measurement at fair value also provides information that is more comparable and understandable than measurement at cost or on the basis of allocating the total cost of an acquisition. Both IFRS 3 and SFAS 141 required allocation of that cost on the basis of the fair value of the assets acquired and the liabilities assumed. However, other guidance in those standards required measurements that were other than fair value. Moveover, SFAS 141's requirements for measuring identifiable assets acquired and liabilities assumed in an acquisition achieved in stages (a step acquisition) and in acquisitions of less than all of the equity interests in the acquiree resulted in another difference between fair value measurement of identifiable assets and liabilities and the process of accumulating and allocating costs. Those requirements were the same as the benchmark treatment in IAS 22, which IFRS 3 replaced. The following paragraphs discuss both the IASB's reasons for that change to IAS 22 and the FASB's reasons for the change to SFAS 141's requirements for step acquisitions, as well as providing additional discussion of the reasons for the fair value measurement principle in the revised standards.

BC199 In developing IFRS 3 and SFAS 141(R), respectively, the boards examined the inconsistencies that resulted from applying the benchmark treatment in IAS 22 and the provisions of SFAS 141, and the related implementation guidance, to acquisitions of businesses. For a step acquisition, that process involved accumulating the costs or carrying amounts of earlier purchases of interests in an entity, which may have occurred years or decades ago. Those amounts were added to the current costs to purchase incremental interests in the acquiree on the acquisition date. The accumulated amounts of those purchases were then allocated to the assets acquired and liabilities assumed. Allocating the accumulated amounts generally resulted in recognising the identifiable assets and liabilities of the acquiree at a mixture of current exchange prices and carry-forward book values for each earlier purchase rather than at their acquisition-date fair values. Users of financial statements have long criticised those practices as resulting in information that lacks consistency, understandability and usefulness. For example, in response to the September 1991 FASB Discussion Memorandum *Consolidation Policy and Procedures*, an organisation representing lending officers said:

> [We believe] that the assets and liabilities of the subsidiary [acquiree] reported in the consolidation should reflect the full values established by the exchange transaction in which they were purchased. . . . [We believe] the current practice of reporting individual assets and liabilities at a mixture of some current exchange prices and some carry-forward book values is **dangerously misleading.** [emphasis added]

BC200 The boards concluded that no useful purpose is served by reporting the assets or liabilities of a newly acquired business using a mixture of their fair values at the date acquired and the acquirer's historical costs or carrying amounts. Amounts that relate to transactions and events occurring before the business is included in the acquirer's financial statements are not relevant to users of those financial statements.

BC201 The boards also observed the criticisms of the information resulting from application of the cost accumulation and allocation process to acquisitions of businesses that resulted in ownership of less than all of the equity interests in the acquiree. In those circumstances, application of the cost accumulation and allocation process also resulted in identifiable assets and liabilities being assigned amounts that were generally not their acquisition-date fair values. For example, in its 1993 Position Paper *Financial Reporting in the 1990s and Beyond* the Association for Investment Management and Research (AIMR)* said:

> An even more difficult situation arises when Firm B acquires less than total ownership of Firm A. Under current practice, only the proportionate share of Firm A's assets and liabilities owned by Firm B are re-valued, but all of Firm A's assets and liabilities—partially re-valued, partially not—are consolidated with those of Firm B, none of whose assets and liabilities have been re-valued. What a mélange! **The result is a combination of historic and current values that only a mystic could sort out with precision.** [page 28, emphasis added]

BC202 In contrast, if all of the interests in the business were acquired in a single purchase, the process of assigning that current purchase price generally resulted in the assets and liabilities being measured and recognised at their acquisition-date fair values. Thus, the reported amounts of assets and liabilities differed depending on whether an acquirer purchased all of the equity interests in an acquiree in one transaction or in multiple transactions.

BC203 The boards concluded that measuring assets acquired or liabilities assumed at amounts other than their fair values at the acquisition date does not faithfully represent their economic values or the acquirer's economic circumstances resulting from the business combination. As discussed in paragraph BC37, an important purpose of financial statements is to provide users with relevant and reliable information about the performance of the entity and the resources under its control. That applies regardless of the extent of the ownership interest a parent holds in a particular subsidiary. The boards concluded that measurement at fair value enables users to make a better assessment of the cash-generating abilities of the identifiable net assets acquired in the business combination and the accountability of management for the resources entrusted to it. Thus, the fair value measurement principle in the revised standards will improve the completeness, reliability and relevance of the information reported in an acquirer's financial statements. The boards also concluded that application of

---

* Subsequently, the AIMR changed its name to the CFA Institute. References to the organisation in this Basis for Conclusions use its name at the date it published a particular paper.

that measurement principle should not impose undue incremental costs on entities because it was also necessary to measure the fair values of assets acquired and liabilities assumed under the provisions of IFRS 3 and SFAS 141, even though those fair values were not always the amounts at which assets and liabilities were recognised.

BC204 Thus, the revised standards reflect the decisions of the IASB and the FASB to develop a standard (and related application guidance) for measuring assets acquired and liabilities assumed in a business combination that:

(a) is consistent with the general principle of initially measuring assets acquired and liabilities assumed at their fair values, thereby improving the relevance and comparability of the resulting information about the assets acquired and liabilities assumed;

(b) eliminates inconsistencies and other deficiencies of the purchase price allocation process, including those in acquisitions of businesses that occur in stages and those in which the acquirer obtains a business without purchasing all, or perhaps any, of the acquiree's equity interests on the acquisition date; and

(c) can be applied in practice with a reasonably high degree of consistency and without imposing undue costs.

Non-controlling interests

BC205 The 2005 Exposure Draft proposed that a non-controlling interest in an acquiree should be determined as the sum of the non-controlling interest's proportional interest in the identifiable assets acquired and liabilities assumed plus the non-controlling interest's share of goodwill. Thus, because goodwill is measured as a residual, the amount recognised for a non-controlling interest in an acquiree would also have been a residual. Also, an important issue in deciding how to measure a non-controlling interest was whether its share of goodwill should be recognised (often referred to as the 'full goodwill versus partial goodwill issue'). In developing the 2005 Exposure Draft, the boards concluded that it should be recognised (in other words, they selected the 'full goodwill' alternative).

BC206 In redeliberating the 2005 Exposure Draft, the boards observed that they had specified the mechanics of determining the reported amount of a non-controlling interest but had not identified its measurement attribute. The result of those mechanics would have been that the non-controlling interest was effectively measured as the 'final residual' in a business combination. That is to say, the reported amount of the non-controlling interest depended on the amount of goodwill attributed to it, and goodwill is measured as a residual. Thus, in a sense, a non-controlling interest would have been the residual after allocating the residual, or the residual of a residual.

BC207 The boards concluded that, in principle, it is undesirable to have two residual amounts in accounting for a business combination. They also observed that goodwill cannot be measured as other than as a residual; measuring the fair value of goodwill directly would not be possible. In contrast, an acquirer can measure the fair value of a non-controlling interest, for example, on the basis of market prices for the shares held by non-controlling shareholders or by applying another valuation technique. The non-controlling interest in the acquiree is a component of a business combination in which less than 100 per cent of the equity interests are acquired, and the boards concluded that, in concept, the non-controlling interest, like other components of the combination, should be measured at fair value. The boards concluded that the decision-usefulness of information about a non-controlling interest would be improved if the revised standards specified a measurement attribute for a non-controlling interest rather than merely mechanics for determining that amount. They also concluded that, in principle, the measurement attribute should be fair value. The boards also understand from consultation with some constituents who use financial statements for making (or making recommendations about) investment decisions that information about the acquisition-date fair value of a non-controlling interest would be helpful in estimating the value of shares of the parent company, not only at the acquisition date but also at future dates.

BC208 The boards also observed that a non-controlling interest is a component of equity in the acquirer's consolidated financial statements and that measuring a non-controlling interest at its acquisition-date fair value is consistent with the way in which other components of equity are measured. For example, outstanding shares of the parent company, including shares issued to former owners of an acquiree to effect a business combination, were measured in the financial statements at their fair value (market price) on the date they were issued. Accordingly, the fair value measurement principle in SFAS 141(R) applies to a non-controlling interest in an acquiree, and the revised IFRS 3 permits an acquirer to measure a non-controlling interest in an acquiree at its acquisition-date fair value.

IFRS 3's choice of measurement basis for a non-controlling interest

BC209 The IASB concluded that, in principle, an acquirer should measure all components of a business combination, including any non-controlling interest in an acquiree, at their acquisition-date fair values. However, the revised IFRS 3 permits an acquirer to choose whether to measure any non-controlling interest in an acquiree at its fair value or as the non-controlling interests' proportionate share of the acquiree's identifiable net assets.

BC210 Introducing a choice of measurement basis for non-controlling interests was not the IASB's first preference. In general, the IASB believes that alternative accounting methods reduce the comparability of financial statements. However, the IASB was not able to agree on a single measurement basis for non-controlling interests because neither of the alternatives considered (fair value and proportionate share of the acquiree's identifiable net assets) was supported by enough board members to enable a revised business combinations standard to be issued. The IASB decided to permit a choice of measurement basis for non-controlling interests because it concluded that the benefits of the other improvements to, and the convergence of, the accounting for business combinations developed in this project outweigh the disadvantages of allowing this particular option.

BC211 The following sections (a) provide additional information about the measurement alternatives considered by the IASB, (b) summarise the main effects of permitting a choice in measurement basis and (c) discuss the effect on convergence.

Measurement alternatives

BC212   Although the IASB supports the principle of measuring all components of a business combination at fair value, support for that principle was not unanimous. Some IASB members did not support that principle because it would require measuring non-controlling interests at fair value. For that reason, those IASB members supported making an exception to the measurement principle for the non-controlling interest in an acquiree.

BC213   Some other IASB members supported an exception for the non-controlling interest for different reasons. Some advocated an exception on the basis that they did not have sufficient evidence to assess the marginal benefits of reporting the acquisition-date fair value of non-controlling interests. Those members concluded that, generally, the fair value of the non-controlling interest could be measured reliably, but they noted that it would be more costly to do so than measuring it at its proportionate share of the acquiree's identifiable net assets. Those members observed that many respondents had indicated that they saw little information of value in the reported non-controlling interest, no matter how it is measured.

BC214   Those IASB members who did not support making an exception concluded that the marginal benefits of reporting the acquisition-date fair value of non-controlling interests exceed the marginal costs of measuring it.

BC215   The IASB considered making it a requirement to measure non-controlling interests at fair value unless doing so would impose undue cost or effort on the acquirer. However, feedback from constituents and staff research indicated that it was unlikely that the term *undue cost or effort* would be applied consistently. Therefore, such a requirement would be unlikely to increase appreciably the consistency with which different entities measured non-controlling interests.

BC216   The IASB reluctantly concluded that the only way the revised IFRS 3 would receive sufficient votes to be issued was if it permitted an acquirer to measure a non-controlling interest either at fair value or at its proportionate share of the acquiree's identifiable net assets, on a transaction-by-transaction basis.

Effects of the optional measurement of non-controlling interests

BC217   The IASB noted that there are likely to be three main differences in outcome that occur when the non-controlling interest is measured as its proportionate share of the acquiree's identifiable net assets, rather than at fair value. First, the amounts recognised in a business combination for non-controlling interests and goodwill are likely to be lower (and these should be the only two items affected on initial recognition). Second, if a cash-generating unit is subsequently impaired, any resulting impairment of goodwill recognised through income is likely to be lower than it would have been if the non-controlling interest had been measured at fair value (although it does not affect the impairment loss attributable to the controlling interest).

BC218   The third difference arises if the acquirer subsequently purchases some (or all) of the shares held by the non-controlling shareholders. If the non-controlling interests are acquired, presumably at fair value, the equity of the group is reduced by the non-controlling interests' share of any unrecognised changes in the fair value of the net assets of the business, including goodwill. If the non-controlling interest is measured initially as a proportionate share of the acquiree's identifiable net assets, rather than at fair value, that reduction in the reported equity attributable to the acquirer is likely to be larger. This matter was considered further in the IASB's deliberations on the proposed amendments to IAS 27.

Convergence

BC219   Both boards decided that, although they would have preferred to have a common measurement attribute for non-controlling interests, they had considered and removed as many differences between IFRS 3 and SFAS 141 as was practicable.

BC220   The boards were unable to achieve convergence of their respective requirements in several areas because of existing differences between IFRSs and US GAAP requirements outside a business combination. The boards observed that the accounting for impairments in IFRSs is different from that in US GAAP. This means that even if the boards converged on the initial measurement of non-controlling interests, and therefore goodwill, the subsequent accounting for goodwill would not have converged. Although this is not a good reason for allowing divergence in the initial measurement of non-controlling interests, it was a mitigating factor.

BC221   Because most business combinations do not involve a non-controlling interest, the boards also observed that the revised standards will align most of the accounting for most business combinations regardless of the different accounting for non-controlling interests in the revised standards.

Measuring assets and liabilities arising from contingencies, including subsequent measurement

BC222   FASB Statement No. 5 *Accounting for Contingencies* (SFAS 5) defines a *contingency* as an existing condition, situation or set of circumstances involving uncertainty as to possible gain or loss to an entity that will ultimately be resolved when one or more future events occur or fail to occur. SFAS 141(R) refers to the assets and liabilities to which contingencies relate as *assets and liabilities arising from contingencies*. For ease of discussion, this Basis for Conclusions also uses that term to refer broadly to the issues related to contingencies, including the issues that the IASB considered in developing its requirements on recognising and measuring contingent liabilities in a business combination (paragraphs BC242–BC245 and BC272–BC278).

BC223   The revised standards require the assets and liabilities arising from contingencies that are recognised as of the acquisition date to be measured at their acquisition-date fair values. That requirement is generally consistent with the measurement requirements of IFRS 3, but it represents a change in the way entities generally applied SFAS 141. In addition, the IASB's measurement guidance on contingent liabilities carries forward the related guidance in IFRS 3, pending completion of the project to revise IAS 37 (paragraphs BC272–BC276). Accordingly, the FASB's and the IASB's conclusions on measuring assets and liabilities arising from contingencies are discussed separately.

The FASB's conclusions on measuring assets and liabilities arising from contingencies

BC224　The amount of an asset or a liability arising from a contingency recognised in accordance with SFAS 141 was seldom the acquisition-date fair value. Rather, it was often the settlement amount or a best estimate of the expected settlement amount on the basis of circumstances existing at a date after the acquisition date.

BC225　In developing the 2005 Exposure Draft, the FASB considered whether to require a strict SFAS 5 approach for the initial measurement and recognition of all contingencies in a business combination. That would mean that contingencies that did not meet the SFAS 5 'probability' criterion would be measured at zero (or at a minimum amount that qualifies as probable) rather than at fair value. Some constituents said that applying SFAS 5 in accounting for a business combination might be a practical way to reduce the costs and measurement difficulties involved in obtaining the information and legal counsel needed to measure the fair value of numerous contingencies that the acquiree had not recognised in accordance with SFAS 5.

BC226　The FASB observed that paragraph 17(a) of SFAS 5 states that 'Contingencies that might result in gains usually are not reflected in the accounts since to do so might be to recognize revenue prior to its realization.' Thus, to apply SFAS 5 in accounting for a business combination in the same way it is applied in other situations was likely to result in non-recognition of gain contingencies, including those for which all of the needed information is available at the acquisition date. The FASB concluded that that would be a step backwards; SFAS 141 already required the recognition of gain contingencies at the acquisition date and for which fair value is determinable (paragraphs 39 and 40(a) of SFAS 141). Also, in accordance with SFAS 5's requirements, contingent losses that arise outside a business combination are not recognised unless there is a high likelihood of a future outflow of resources. In addition, because goodwill is calculated as a residual, omitting an asset for an identifiable contingent gain would also result in overstating goodwill. Similarly, omitting a liability for a contingent loss would result in understating goodwill. Thus, the FASB rejected the SFAS 5 approach in accounting for a business combination.

BC227　The FASB also considered but rejected retaining existing practice based on FASB Statement No. 38 *Accounting for Preacquisition Contingencies of Purchased Enterprises* (SFAS 38), which SFAS 141 carried forward without reconsideration. For the reasons described in the preceding paragraph, the FASB concluded that continuing to permit the delayed recognition of most assets and liabilities arising from contingencies that occurred in applying SFAS 141 and the related guidance would fail to bring about needed improvements in the accounting for business combinations. The FASB decided that requiring an acquirer to measure at fair value and recognise any assets and liabilities arising from contingencies that meet the conceptual elements definition would help bring about those needed improvements, in particular, improvements in the completeness of reported financial information.

BC228　Some respondents to the 2005 Exposure Draft were concerned about the ability to measure reliably the fair value of assets and liabilities arising from contingencies at the acquisition date. The FASB concluded that measuring the fair value of an asset or a liability arising from a contractual contingency with sufficient reliability as of the acquisition date should not be more difficult than measuring the fair value of many other assets and liabilities that the revised standards require to be measured at fair value as of that date. The terms of the contract, together with information developed during the acquisition process, for example, to determine the price to be paid, should provide the needed information. Sufficient information is also likely to be available to measure the acquisition-date fair value of assets and liabilities arising from non-contractual contingencies that satisfy the more-likely-than-not criterion (see paragraphs BC270 and BC271). The FASB acknowledges that non-contractual assets and liabilities that do not meet that criterion at the acquisition date are most likely to raise difficult measurement issues and concerns about the reliability of those measures. To address those reliability concerns, the FASB decided that an acquirer should not measure and recognise such assets and liabilities. Rather, assets and liabilities arising from non-contractual contingencies that do not satisfy the more-likely-than-not criterion at the acquisition date are accounted for in accordance with other US GAAP, including SFAS 5.

BC229 The FASB also observed that respondents who are concerned about the reliability with which the fair values of assets and liabilities arising from contingencies can be measured may be interpreting *reliable measurement* differently from the FASB. To determine a reliable measure of the fair value of a contingency, the acquirer need not be able to determine, predict or otherwise know the ultimate settlement amount of that contingency at the acquisition date (or within the measurement period) with certainty or precision.

BC230 In 2006 the FASB and the IASB published for comment the first discussion paper in their joint project to improve their respective conceptual frameworks. Paragraph QC21 of that paper—*Preliminary Views on an improved Conceptual Framework for Financial Reporting: The Objective of Financial Reporting and Qualitative Characteristics of Decision-useful Financial Reporting Information*—discusses the relationship between faithful representation, the quality of decision-useful financial reporting information that pertains to the reliability of information, and precision. It says that accuracy of estimates is desirable and some minimum level of accuracy is necessary for an estimate to be a faithful representation of an economic phenomenon. However, faithful representation implies neither absolute precision in the estimate nor certainty about the outcome.

BC231 The FASB concluded that the fair values of assets and liabilities arising from contingencies meeting the recognition criteria of SFAS 141(R) are measurable with sufficient reliability as of the acquisition date for recognition in accounting for a business combination if the estimates are based on the appropriate inputs and each input reflects the best available information about that factor. The FASB acknowledges that the fair value measured at the acquisition date will not be the amount for which the asset or liability is ultimately settled, but it provides information about the current value of an asset or a liability by incorporating uncertainty into the measure.

Subsequent measurement of assets and liabilities arising from contingencies

BC232 The FASB observed that applying SFAS 5 in the post-combination period to a recognised liability or asset arising from a contingency that did not meet the SFAS 5 probability threshold at the acquisition date would result in derecognising that liability or asset and reporting a gain or loss in income of the post-combination period. That result would not faithfully represent the economic events occurring in that period. The FASB noted that similar concerns about the potential for misleading reporting consequences do not exist for many financial instruments arising from contingencies, such as options, forward contracts and other derivatives. Such assets and liabilities generally would continue to be measured at fair value in accordance with other applicable US GAAP, which also provides guidance on how to report subsequent changes in the fair values of financial instruments in earnings or comprehensive income. Thus, the FASB decided that it must address the subsequent measurement of assets and liabilities arising from contingencies recognised in a business combination. However, it limited the scope of that effort to assets and liabilities that would be subsequently subject to SFAS 5.

BC233 The FASB considered five alternatives for subsequent measurement of assets and liabilities arising from contingencies that would be subject to SFAS 5 if not acquired or assumed in a business combination:

Alternative 1— Subsequently measuring at fair value

Alternative 2—Subsequently reporting amounts initially recognised in a business combination at their acquisition-date fair values until the acquirer obtains new information about the possible outcome of the contingency. When new information is obtained the acquirer evaluates that new information and measures a liability at the **higher** of its acquisition-date fair value or the amount that would be recognised if applying SFAS 5 and an asset at the **lower** of its acquisition-date fair value or the best estimate of its future settlement amount

Alternative 3—'Freezing' amounts initially recognised in a business combination

Alternative 4—Applying an interest allocation method (similar to the model in FASB Statement No. 143 *Accounting for Asset Retirement Obligations* (SFAS 143))

Alternative 5—Applying a deferred revenue method, but only to those items that relate to revenue-generating activities.

BC234 Paragraphs BC224–BC231 discuss the reasons for the FASB's decision to require fair value measurement for initial recognition of assets and liabilities arising from contingencies. For many of those same reasons, the FASB considered requiring Alternative 1—subsequent measurement at fair value. For a variety of reasons, the FASB ultimately rejected that alternative. Adopting this alternative would mean that for some entities (maybe many entities) assets and liabilities arising from contingencies acquired in a business combination would be reported at fair value, while other similar assets and liabilities would be reported at SFAS 5 amounts—different measurement of similar assets and liabilities would make financial reports more difficult to understand. The FASB noted that a project on business combinations would not be the appropriate place to address broadly perceived deficiencies in SFAS 5. Moreover, at the same time as SFAS 141(R) was finalised, the FASB was considering adding a project to its technical agenda to reconsider comprehensively the accounting for contingencies in SFAS 5. (The FASB added a project to reconsider the accounting for contingencies to its agenda in September 2007.) The FASB concluded that requiring assets and liabilities arising from contingencies to be subsequently measured at fair value was premature and might prejudice the outcome of its deliberations in that project.

BC235 The FASB decided, as a practical alternative, to require Alternative 2. In accordance with that approach, the acquirer continues to report an asset or liability arising from a contingency recognised as of the acquisition date at its acquisition-date fair value in the absence of new information about the possible outcome of the contingency. When such new information is obtained, the acquirer evaluates that information and measures the asset or liability as follows:

(a) a liability is measured at the **higher** of:

(i) its acquisition-date fair value; and

(ii) the amount that would be recognised if applying SFAS 5.

(b) an asset is measured at the **lower** of:

(i) its acquisition-date fair value; or

(ii) the best estimate of its future settlement amount.

BC236 The FASB concluded that this alternative was a practical bridge between improved reporting at the acquisition date and subsequent accounting under the existing requirements of SFAS 5. It would not prejudice the outcome of deliberations that the FASB will have in a project to reconsider SFAS 5. It also addressed the concerns of some constituents that requiring contingencies to be subsequently measured at fair value would result in contingencies acquired or assumed in a business combination being measured differently from contingencies that arise outside of a business combination.

BC237 The FASB observed that this alternative provides slightly different guidance for liabilities from its guidance for assets. Unlike liabilities, it could not require assets to be measured at the lower of their acquisition-date fair values or *the amounts that would be recognised if applying* SFAS 5. Because SFAS 5 does not allow recognition of gain contingencies, the amount that would be recognised by applying SFAS 5 to an asset would be zero. Thus, the FASB decided that an asset arising from a contingency should be measured at the lower of its acquisition-date fair value or *the best estimate of its future settlement amount.* The FASB believes that that measure is similar to the measure required by SFAS 5 for liabilities (loss contingencies). The FASB also observed that the approach for assets allows for the recognition of impairments to the asset; it requires an asset to be decreased to the current estimate of the amount the acquirer expects to collect.

BC238 The FASB rejected Alternative 3—freezing the amounts initially recognised. The FASB observed that this alternative results in less relevant information than Alternative 2. Because the FASB views Alternative 2 as a practical and operational solution, it saw no compelling reason to adopt a less optimal alternative. The FASB also rejected Alternative 4—the interest allocation method. In accordance with that method, the contingency would be remeasured using a convention similar to SFAS 143 whereby interest rates are held constant for initial cash flow assumptions. The FASB noted that the reasons for selecting the interest allocation method in SFAS 143 for long-term asset retirement obligations, including concerns about income statement volatility, are not compelling for contingencies such as warranties and pending litigation that generally have shorter lives.

BC239　In accordance with Alternative 5—the deferred revenue method—the acquisition-date fair value of a deferred revenue liability (performance obligation) would be amortised after the acquisition date, like the approach for separately priced extended warranties and product maintenance contracts acquired outside a business combination. Accruals would be added to the contingency for subsequent direct costs. The FASB acknowledged that the costs to apply that measurement approach would be lower than other measurement approaches. However, the FASB concluded that the potential reduction in costs does not justify (a) creating inconsistencies in the subsequent accounting for particular classes of contingencies acquired or assumed in a business combination and (b) the diminished relevance of the resulting information. Thus, the FASB also rejected Alternative 5. Some respondents to the 2005 Exposure Draft supported recognition of subsequent changes in the amounts recognised for assets and liabilities arising from contingencies either as adjustments to goodwill or in comprehensive income rather than in earnings. Some who favoured reporting such changes as adjustments to goodwill did so at least in part because of the difficulties they see in distinguishing between changes that result from changes in circumstances after the acquisition date and changes that pertain more to obtaining better information about circumstances that existed at that date. They noted that the latter are measurement period adjustments, many of which result in adjustments to goodwill.

BC240　The FASB understands that distinguishing between measurement period adjustments and other changes in the amounts of assets and liabilities arising from contingencies will sometimes be difficult. It observed, however, that similar difficulties exist for other assets acquired and liabilities assumed in a business combination; changes in the amounts of those assets and liabilities after the acquisition date are included in earnings. The FASB saw no compelling reason to treat items arising from contingencies differently.

BC241　Those who favoured reporting subsequent changes in the amounts recognised for assets and liabilities arising from contingencies in other comprehensive income rather than in earnings generally analogised to the present accounting for available-for-sale securities. They said that items arising from contingencies were not 'realised' until the contingency is resolved. The FASB rejected that alternative because it saw no compelling reason to add to the category of items that are initially recognised as other comprehensive income and later 'recycled' to earnings. The FASB considers reporting subsequent changes in the amounts of items arising from contingencies in earnings not only conceptually superior to reporting those changes only in comprehensive income but also consistent with the way in which other changes in amounts of items acquired or assumed in a business combination are recognised.

The IASB's conclusions on initial and subsequent measurement of contingent liabilities

BC242　As noted in paragraph BC223, the IASB's measurement guidance on contingencies carries forward the related guidance in IFRS 3 (except for clarifying that an acquirer cannot recognise a contingency that is not a liability), pending completion of the project to revise IAS 37. Accordingly, contingent liabilities recognised in a business combination are initially measured at their acquisition-date fair values.

BC243 In developing IFRS 3, the IASB observed that not specifying the subsequent accounting for contingent liabilities recognised in a business combination might result in inappropriately derecognising some or all of those contingent liabilities immediately after the combination.

BC244 In ED 3 the IASB proposed that a contingent liability recognised in a business combination should be excluded from the scope of IAS 37 and subsequently measured at fair value with changes in fair value recognised in profit or loss until the liability is settled or the uncertain future event described in the definition of a contingent liability is resolved. In considering respondents' comments on this issue, the IASB noted that subsequently measuring such contingent liabilities at fair value would be inconsistent with the conclusions it reached on the accounting for financial guarantees and commitments to provide loans at below-market interest rates when it revised IAS 39.*

BC245 The IASB decided to revise the proposal in ED 3 for consistency with IAS 39. Therefore, the revised IFRS 3 requires contingent liabilities recognised in a business combination to be measured after their initial recognition at the higher of:

(a) the amount that would be recognised in accordance with IAS 37; or

(b) the amount initially recognised less, when appropriate, cumulative amortisation recognised in accordance with IAS 18 *Revenue*.

Definition of fair value

BC246 The revised IFRS 3 and SFAS 141(R) each use the same definition of fair value that the IASB and the FASB respectively use in their other standards. Specifically, IAS 39 and other IFRSs define fair value as 'the amount for which an asset could be exchanged, or a liability settled, between knowledgeable, willing parties in an arm's length transaction' and the revised IFRS 3 uses that definition. SFAS 157, on the other hand, defines fair value as 'the price that would be received to sell an asset or paid to transfer a liability in an orderly transaction between market participants at the measurement date' and that definition is used in SFAS 141(R).

BC247 The IASB considered also using the definition of fair value from SFAS 157 but decided that to do so would prejudge the outcome of its project on fair value measurements. Similarly, the FASB considered using the definition of fair value from IFRS 3 but decided that to do so would be inappropriate in the light of SFAS 157, which it intends for use in all situations in which a new standard requires measurement at fair value.

BC248 The boards acknowledge that the differing definitions of fair value might result in measuring the fair values of assets acquired and liabilities assumed in a business combination differently depending on whether the combination is accounted for in accordance with the revised IFRS 3 or SFAS 141(R). However, the

---

* In November 2009 the IASB relocated to IFRS 9 *Financial Instruments* the requirements on the accounting for financial guarantees and commitments to provide loans at below-market interest rates.

boards consulted valuation experts on the likely effects of the differing definitions of fair value. As a result of that consultation, the boards understand that such differences are unlikely to occur often. The boards also observed that the definitions use different words to articulate essentially the same concepts in two general areas—the non-performance risk and credit standing of financial liabilities and the market-based measurement objective.

BC249   SFAS 157 defines non-performance risk as the risk that an obligation will not be fulfilled and indicates that it affects the fair value of a liability. Non-performance risk includes but may not be limited to the reporting entity's own credit risk. In comparison, IFRSs do not use the term *non-performance risk* in discussing the fair value of a liability. However, IAS 39 requires the fair value of a financial liability to reflect its credit risk. Although the words are different, the boards believe that the underlying concepts are essentially the same.

BC250   The definition of fair value from SFAS 157 indicates that it is a price in an orderly transaction between market participants. In comparison, IFRSs indicate that fair value reflects an arm's length transaction between knowledgeable, willing parties. Paragraphs 42–44 of IAS 40 discuss what a *transaction between knowledgeable, willing parties* means:

> ... In this context, 'knowledgeable' means that both the willing buyer and the willing seller are reasonably informed about the nature and characteristics of the investment property, its actual and potential uses, and market conditions at the end of the reporting period ...

> ... The willing seller is motivated to sell the investment property at market terms for the best price obtainable. The factual circumstances of the actual investment property owner are not a part of this consideration because the willing seller is a hypothetical owner (eg a willing seller would not take into account the particular tax circumstances of the investment property owner).

> The definition of fair value refers to an arm's length transaction. An arm's length transaction is one between parties that do not have a particular or special relationship that makes prices of transactions uncharacteristic of market conditions. The transaction is presumed to be between unrelated parties, each acting independently.

Thus, although the two definitions use different words, the concept is the same—fair value is a market-based measure in a transaction between unrelated parties.

BC251   However, differences in the results of applying the different definitions of fair value may occur in particular areas. For example, SFAS 157 defines fair value as an exit price between market participants and IFRSs define fair value as an exchange price in an arm's length transaction. Most valuation experts the boards consulted said that, because transaction costs are not a component of fair value in either definition, an exit price for an asset or liability acquired or assumed in a business combination would differ from an exchange price (entry or exit) only (a) if the asset is acquired for its defensive value or (b) if a liability is measured on the basis of settling it with the creditor rather than transferring it to a third party. However, the boards understand that ways of measuring assets on the basis of their defensive value in accordance with paragraph A12 of SFAS 157 are developing, and it is too early to tell the significance of any differences that might result. It is also not clear that entities will use different methods of measuring the fair value of liabilities assumed in a business combination.

Measuring the acquisition-date fair values of particular assets acquired

Assets with uncertain cash flows (valuation allowances)

BC252　Both IFRS 3 and SFAS 141 required receivables to be measured at the present values of amounts to be received determined at appropriate current interest rates, less allowances for uncollectibility and collection costs, if necessary. The boards considered whether an exception to the fair value measurement principle is necessary for assets such as trade receivables and other short-term and long-term receivables acquired in a business combination. Several of the boards' constituents suggested that an exception should be permitted for practical and other reasons, including concerns about comparing credit losses on loans acquired in a business combination with those on originated loans. In developing the 2005 Exposure Draft, however, the boards saw no compelling reason for such an exception. The boards observed that using an acquiree's carrying basis and including collection costs is inconsistent with the revised standards' fair value measurement requirement and the underlying notion that the acquirer's initial measurement, recognition and classification of the assets acquired and liabilities assumed begins on the acquisition date. Because uncertainty about collections and future cash flows is included in the fair value measure of a receivable, the 2005 Exposure Draft proposed that the acquirer should not recognise a separate valuation allowance for acquired assets measured at fair value.

BC253　In developing the 2005 Exposure Draft, the FASB acknowledged that including uncertainties about future cash flows in a fair value measure, with no separate allowance for uncollectible amounts, differed from the current practice for SEC registrants. That practice was established in SEC Staff Accounting Bulletin Topic 2.A.5 *Adjustments to Allowances for Loan Losses in Connection with Business Combinations* which states that generally the acquirer's estimation of the uncollectible portion of the acquiree's loans should not change from the acquiree's estimation before the acquisition. However, the FASB also observed that fair value measurement is consistent with guidance in AICPA Statement of Position 03-3 *Accounting for Certain Loans or Debt Securities Acquired in a Transfer* (AICPA SOP 03-3), which prohibits 'carrying over' or creating valuation allowances in the initial accounting of all loans acquired in transfers that are within its scope, including business combinations accounted for as an acquisition.

BC254　In developing the 2005 Exposure Draft, the boards also acknowledged that the fair value measurement approach has implications for the capital requirements for financial institutions, particularly banks. The boards noted, however, that regulatory reporting requirements are a separate matter that is beyond the scope of general purpose financial reporting.

BC255　Some respondents to the 2005 Exposure Draft who commented on this issue agreed with the proposal, but many who commented on it disagreed with not recognising a separate valuation allowance for receivables and similar assets. Some of those respondents favoured retaining the guidance in IFRS 3 and SFAS 141. They said that the costs of measuring the fair value of trade receivables, loans, receivables under financing leases and the like would be high; they did not think the related benefits would justify those costs. Some also said that software systems currently available for loans and other receivables do not provide for separate accounting for acquired and originated loans; they have to account manually for loans to which AICPA SOP 03-3 applies, incurring significant costs to do so.

BC256   As they did in developing the 2005 Exposure Draft, the boards acknowledged that the requirement to measure receivables and similar assets at fair value with no separate valuation allowance may lead to additional costs for some entities. However, the boards observed that entities that apply IAS 39[*] are required to measure financial assets acquired outside a business combination, as well as those originated, at fair value on initial recognition. The boards do not think financial or other assets should be measured differently because of the nature of the transaction in which they are acquired. Because the boards saw no compelling reason to provide an exception to the measurement principle for receivables or other assets with credit risk, they affirmed their conclusion that the benefits of measuring receivables and similar assets at fair value justify the related costs.

BC257   Some respondents to the 2005 Exposure Draft said that separate recognition of valuation allowances for loans and similar assets was important to users in evaluating the credit assumptions built into loan valuations. They suggested that the fair value of receivables should be split into three components: (a) the gross contractual amounts, (b) a separate discount or premium for changes in interest rates and (c) a valuation allowance for the credit risk, which would be based on the contractual cash flows expected to be uncollectible. In evaluating that alternative presentation, the boards noted that the valuation allowance presented would differ from the valuation allowance for receivables under IAS 39 and SFAS 5, each of which is determined on the basis of incurred, rather than expected, losses. Thus, how to determine the valuation allowance on an ongoing basis would be problematic. For example, if requirements for other receivables were applied, an immediate gain would be recognised for the difference between incurred losses and expected losses. In contrast, if the valuation allowance for receivables acquired by transfer, including in a business combination, rather than by origination was determined subsequently on an expected loss basis, the result would be a new accounting model for those receivables. The boards concluded that this project is not the place to consider the broader issues of how best to determine the valuation allowances for receivables, regardless of the manner in which the receivables are acquired.

Disclosure of information about receivables acquired

BC258   Some constituents asked the boards to consider requiring additional disclosures about receivables measured at fair value to help in assessing considerations of credit quality included in the fair value measures, including expectations about receivables that will be uncollectible. Those constituents were concerned that without additional disclosure, it would be impossible to determine the contractual cash flows and the amount of the contractual cash flows not expected to be collected if receivables were recognised at fair value. In response to those

---

[*]   In November 2009 the IASB amended the requirements of IAS 39 relating to classification and measurement of assets within the scope of IAS 39 and relocated them to IFRS 9 *Financial Instruments*. IFRS 9 applies to all assets within the scope of IAS 39. This paragraph discusses matters relevant when IFRS 3 was issued.

comments, the boards decided to require disclosure of the fair value of receivables acquired, the gross contractual amounts receivable and the best estimate at the acquisition date of the contractual cash flows not expected to be collected. The disclosures are required for each major class of receivable.

BC259 In January 2007 the FASB added a project to its technical agenda to improve disclosures relating to the allowance for credit losses associated with financing receivables. As part of that project, the FASB is considering potential new disclosures and enhanced current disclosures about the credit quality of an entity's portfolio, the entity's credit risk exposures, its accounting policies on valuation allowances and possibly other areas.

BC260 The boards observed that the work involved in developing a complete set of credit quality disclosures to be made for receivables acquired in a business combination would be similar to that required in the FASB's disclosure project related to valuation allowances. Combining those efforts would be a more efficient use of resources. Accordingly, the FASB decided to include disclosures that should be made in a business combination in the scope of its project on disclosures related to valuation allowances and credit quality, and the IASB will monitor that project. In the interim, the disclosures required by the revised standards (paragraph B64(h) of the revised IFRS 3) will provide at least some, although perhaps not all, of the information users need to evaluate the credit quality of receivables acquired.

Assets that the acquirer intends not to use or to use in a way that is different from the way other market participants would use them

BC261 While the revised standards were being developed, the FASB received enquiries about inconsistencies in practice in accordance with SFAS 141 related to measuring particular intangible assets that an acquirer intends not to use or intends to use in a way different from the way other market participants would use them. For example, if the acquirer did not intend to use a brand name acquired in a business combination, some entities assigned no value to the asset and other entities measured it at the amount at which market participants could be expected to exchange the asset, ie at its fair value.

BC262 To avoid such inconsistencies in practice, the boards decided to clarify the measurement of assets that an acquirer intends not to use (paragraph B43 of the revised IFRS 3). The intention of both IFRS 3 and SFAS 141 was that assets, both tangible and intangible, should be measured at their fair values regardless of how or whether the acquirer intends to use them. The FASB observed that measuring such assets in accordance with their highest and best use is consistent with SFAS 157. Paragraph A12 of SFAS 157 illustrates determining the fair value of an in-process research and development project acquired in a business combination that the acquirer does not intend to complete. The IASB understands from its consultation with preparers, valuation experts and auditors that IFRS 3 was applied in the way the revised standards require.

Exceptions to the recognition or measurement principle

BC263 As indicated in paragraphs 14 and 20 of the revised IFRS 3, the revised standards include limited exceptions to its recognition and measurement principles. Paragraphs BC265–BC311 discuss the types of identifiable assets and liabilities for which exceptions are provided and the reasons for those exceptions.

BC264   It is important to note that not every item that falls into a particular type of asset or liability is an exception to either the recognition or the measurement principle (or both). For example, contingent liabilities are identified as an exception to the recognition principle because the revised IFRS 3 includes a recognition condition for them in addition to the recognition conditions in paragraphs 11 and 12. Although applying that additional condition will result in not recognising some contingent liabilities, those that meet the additional condition will be recognised in accordance with the recognition principle. Another example is employee benefits, which are identified as a type of asset or liability for which exceptions to both the recognition and the measurement principles are provided. As discussed further in paragraphs BC296–BC300, the acquirer is required to recognise and measure liabilities and any related assets resulting from the acquiree's employee benefit arrangements in accordance with IAS 19 *Employee Benefits* rather than by applying the recognition and measurement principles in the revised IFRS 3. Applying the requirements of IAS 19 will result in recognising many, if not most, types of employee benefit liabilities in the same way as would result from applying the recognition principle (see paragraph BC297). However, others, for example withdrawal liabilities from multi-employer plans for entities applying US GAAP, are not necessarily consistent with the recognition principle. In addition, applying the requirements of IAS 19 generally will result in measuring liabilities for employee benefits (and any related assets) on a basis other than their acquisition-date fair values. However, applying the requirements of SFAS 146 to one-off termination benefits results in measuring liabilities for those benefits at their acquisition-date fair values.

Exception to the recognition principle

Assets and liabilities arising from contingencies

BC265   Both the FASB's conclusions on recognising assets and liabilities arising from contingencies and the IASB's conclusions on recognising contingent liabilities resulted in exceptions to the recognition principle in the revised standards because both will result in some items being unrecognised at the acquisition date. However, the details of the exceptions differ. The reasons for those exceptions and the differences between them are discussed in paragraphs BC266–BC278.

The FASB's conclusions on assets and liabilities arising from contingencies

BC266   SFAS 141 carried forward without reconsideration the requirements of SFAS 38, which required an acquirer to include in the purchase price allocation the fair value of an acquiree's contingencies if their fair value could be determined during the allocation period. For those contingencies whose fair value could not be determined during the allocation period, SFAS 141 required the acquirer to recognise the contingency in earnings when the occurrence of the contingency became probable and its amount could be reasonably estimated.

BC267   Members of its resource group and others told the FASB that in practice acquirers often did not recognise an acquiree's assets and liabilities arising from contingencies at the acquisition date. Instead, contingencies were recognised after the acquisition date at an amount determined at that later date either because their amount could not be 'reasonably estimated' or because the contingency was determined not to meet the SFAS 5 'probability' criterion for recognition.

BC268   The 2005 Exposure Draft proposed that an acquirer should recognise all assets and liabilities arising from an acquiree's contingencies if they meet the definition of an asset or a liability in the FASB's Concepts Statement 6 regardless of whether a contingency meets the recognition criteria in SFAS 5. The FASB, like the IASB, concluded that to represent faithfully the economic circumstances at the acquisition date, in principle, all identifiable assets acquired and liabilities assumed should be recognised separately from goodwill, including assets and liabilities arising from contingencies at the acquisition date.

BC269   Respondents to the 2005 Exposure Draft that apply US GAAP expressed concern about how to deal with uncertainty about whether and when a contingency gives rise to an asset or a liability that meets the definition in the FASB's Concepts Statement 6, referred to as *element uncertainty*. An example cited by some respondents involved an acquiree's negotiations with another party at the acquisition date for reimbursement of costs incurred on the other party's behalf. How should the acquirer determine whether that contingency gave rise to an asset that should be recognised as part of the accounting for the business combination? Respondents suggested several means of dealing with element uncertainty, which generally involved introducing a threshold either for all contingencies or for the non-contractual contingencies an acquirer is required to recognise at the acquisition date. Other respondents suggested requiring recognition of only those assets and liabilities arising from contingencies whose fair values can be reliably determined, which would be similar to the requirements of SFAS 141.

BC270   The FASB understands the potential difficulty of resolving element uncertainty, especially for assets or liabilities arising from non-contractual contingencies. It considered whether to deal with element uncertainty by requiring assets and liabilities arising from contingencies to be recognised only if their fair values are reliably measurable. The FASB concluded that applying the guidance in SFAS 157 on measuring fair value should result in an estimate of the fair value of assets and liabilities arising from contingencies that is sufficiently reliable for recognition. The FASB also observed that adding a measurement condition is an indirect way of dealing with uncertainty involving recognition; it would be better to deal with such uncertainty more directly.

BC271   The FASB concluded that most cases of significant uncertainty about whether a potential asset or liability arising from a contingency meets the pertinent definition (element uncertainty) are likely to involve non-contractual contingencies. To help preparers and their auditors deal with element uncertainty, the FASB decided to add a requirement for the acquirer to assess whether it is **more likely than not** that the contingency gives rise to an asset or a liability as defined in the FASB's Concepts Statement 6. For an asset arising from a contingency, applying that criterion focuses on whether it is more likely than not that the acquirer has obtained control of a future economic benefit as a result of a past transaction or other event. For a liability, the more-likely-than-not criterion focuses on whether the acquirer has a present obligation to sacrifice future economic benefits as a result of a past transaction or other event. If that criterion is met at the acquisition date, the acquirer recognises the asset or liability, measured at its acquisition-date fair value, as part of the accounting for the business combination. If that criterion is not met at the acquisition date, the acquirer accounts for the non-contractual contingency in accordance with other

US GAAP, including SFAS 5, as appropriate. The FASB concluded that adding the more-likely-than-not criterion would permit acquirers to focus their efforts on the more readily identifiable contingencies of acquirees, thereby avoiding spending disproportionate amounts of time searching for contingencies that, even if identified, would have less significant effects.

The IASB's conclusions on contingent liabilities

BC272   In developing the 2005 Exposure Draft, the IASB concluded that an asset or a liability should be recognised separately from goodwill if it satisfies the definitions in the *Framework*. In some cases, the amount of the future economic benefits embodied in the asset or required to settle the liability is contingent (or conditional) on the occurrence or non-occurrence of one or more uncertain future events. That uncertainty is reflected in measurement. The FASB reached a consistent conclusion.

BC273   At the same time as it published the 2005 Exposure Draft, the IASB also published for comment a separate exposure draft containing similar proposals on the accounting for contingent assets and contingent liabilities within the scope of IAS 37. At that time, the IASB expected that the effective date of the revised IAS 37 would be the same as the effective date of the revised IFRS 3. However, the IASB now expects to issue a revised IAS 37 at a later date. Accordingly, except for clarifying that an acquirer should not recognise a so-called contingent liability that is not an obligation at the acquisition date, the IASB decided to carry forward the related requirements in the original IFRS 3. The IASB expects to reconsider and, if necessary, amend the requirements in the revised IFRS 3 when it issues the revised IAS 37.

BC274   The IASB concluded that an acquirer should recognise a contingent liability assumed in a business combination only if it satisfies the definition of a liability in the *Framework*. This is consistent with the overall objective of the second phase of the project on business combinations in which an acquirer recognises the assets acquired and liabilities assumed at the date control is obtained.

BC275   However, the IASB observed that the definition of a contingent liability in IAS 37 includes both (a) 'possible obligations' and (b) present obligations for which either it is not probable that an outflow of resources embodying economic benefits will be required to settle the obligation or the amount of the obligation cannot be measured reliably. The IASB concluded that a contingent liability assumed in a business combination should be recognised only if it is a present obligation. Therefore, unlike the previous version of IFRS 3, the revised IFRS 3 does not permit the recognition of 'possible obligations'.

BC276   Like its decision on the recognition of contingent liabilities assumed in a business combination, the IASB concluded that an acquirer should recognise a contingent asset acquired in a business combination only if it satisfies the definition of an asset in the *Framework*. However, the IASB observed that the definition of a contingent asset in IAS 37 includes only 'possible assets'. A contingent asset arises when it is uncertain whether an entity has an asset at the end of the reporting period, but it is expected that some future event will confirm whether the entity has an asset. Accordingly, the IASB concluded that contingent assets should not be recognised, even if it is virtually certain that they will become unconditional or non-contingent. If an entity determines that an asset exists at the acquisition date (ie that it has an unconditional right at the acquisition date), that asset is not a contingent asset and should be accounted for in accordance with the appropriate IFRS.

Convergence

BC277 The result of the FASB's and the IASB's conclusions on recognising assets and liabilities arising from contingencies is that the criteria for determining which items to recognise at the acquisition date differ, at least for the short term. That lack of convergence is inevitable at this time, given the status of the IASB's redeliberations on its revision of IAS 37 and the fact that the FASB had no project on its agenda to reconsider the requirements of SFAS 5 while the boards were developing the revised standards. (The FASB added a project to reconsider the accounting for contingencies to its agenda in September 2007.) To attempt to converge on guidance for recognising assets and liabilities arising from contingencies in a business combination now would run the risk of establishing requirements for a business combination that would be inconsistent with the eventual requirements for assets and liabilities arising from contingencies acquired or incurred by means other than a business combination.

BC278 However, the boards observed that the assets or liabilities arising from contingencies that are recognised in accordance with the FASB's recognition guidance and the contingent liabilities recognised in accordance with the IASB's recognition guidance will be measured consistently. In other words, the initial measurement requirements for assets and liabilities arising from contingencies recognised at the acquisition date have converged. However, the boards acknowledge that the subsequent measurement requirements differ because SFAS 5's measurement guidance differs from that in IAS 37. The reasons for the boards' conclusion on measuring those assets and liabilities are discussed in paragraphs BC224–BC245.

Exceptions to both the recognition and measurement principles

Income taxes

BC279 The 2005 Exposure Draft proposed, and the revised standards require, that a deferred tax asset or liability should be recognised and measured in accordance with either IAS 12 *Income Taxes* or FASB Statement No. 109 *Accounting for Income Taxes* (SFAS 109) respectively. IAS 12 and SFAS 109 establish requirements for recognising and measuring deferred tax assets and liabilities—requirements that are not necessarily consistent with the recognition and measurement principles in the revised standards.

BC280 The boards considered identifying deferred tax assets and liabilities as an exception to only the measurement principle because most, if not all, of the requirements of IAS 12 and SFAS 109 are arguably consistent with the revised standards' recognition principle. The recognition principle requires the acquirer to recognise at the acquisition date the assets acquired and liabilities assumed that meet the conceptual definition of an asset or a liability at that date. However, the boards concluded that exempting deferred tax assets and liabilities from both the recognition and the measurement principles would more clearly indicate that the acquirer should apply the recognition and measurement provisions of IAS 12 and SFAS 109 and their related interpretations or amendments.

BC281   Deferred tax assets or liabilities generally are measured at undiscounted amounts in accordance with IAS 12 and SFAS 109. The boards decided not to require deferred tax assets or liabilities acquired in a business combination to be measured at fair value because they observed that:

(a)   if those assets and liabilities were measured at their acquisition-date fair values, their subsequent measurement in accordance with IAS 12 or SFAS 109 would result in reported post-combination gains or losses in the period immediately following the acquisition even though the underlying economic circumstances did not change. That would not faithfully represent the results of the post-combination period and would be inconsistent with the notion that a business combination that is a fair value exchange should not give rise to the recognition of immediate post-combination gains or losses.

(b)   to measure those assets and liabilities at their acquisition-date fair values and overcome the reporting problem noted in (a) would require a comprehensive consideration of whether and how to modify the requirements of IAS 12 and SFAS 109 for the subsequent measurement of deferred tax assets or liabilities acquired in a business combination. Because of the complexities of IAS 12 and SFAS 109 and the added complexities that would be involved in tracking deferred tax assets acquired and liabilities assumed in a business combination, the boards concluded that the benefits of applying the revised standards' fair value measurement principle would not warrant the costs or complexities that would cause.

Respondents to the 2005 Exposure Draft generally supported that exception to the fair value measurement requirements.

BC282   To align IAS 12 and SFAS 109 more closely and to make the accounting more consistent with the principles in the revised standards, the boards decided to address four specific issues pertaining to the acquirer's income tax accounting in connection with a business combination:

(a)   accounting for a change in the acquirer's recognised deferred tax asset that results from a business combination;

(b)   accounting for a change after the acquisition date in the deferred tax benefits for the acquiree's deductible temporary differences or operating loss or tax credit carryforwards acquired in a business combination;

(c)   accounting for tax benefits arising from tax-deductible goodwill in excess of goodwill for financial reporting; and

(d)   accounting for changes after the acquisition date in the uncertainties pertaining to acquired tax positions.

BC283   The boards addressed the first issue because the existing requirements of IAS 12 and SFAS 109 differed, with IAS 12 accounting for a change in recognised deferred tax assets separately from the business combination and SFAS 109 including a change in the acquirer's valuation allowance for its deferred tax asset in the business combination accounting. The FASB decided to converge with the IAS 12 requirement on the first issue, which the IASB decided to retain. Thus, the acquirer would recognise the change in its recognised deferred tax assets as income or expense (or a change in equity), as required by IAS 12, in the period of the business combination.

BC284 Because the boards considered the first issue primarily in an attempt to achieve convergence, they limited their consideration to the requirements of IAS 12 and SFAS 109. The FASB acknowledged that both alternatives are defensible on conceptual grounds. However, it concluded that on balance the benefits of converging with the IAS 12 method outweigh the costs related to a change in the accounting in accordance with SFAS 109. SFAS 141(R) therefore amends SFAS 109 accordingly.

BC285 Most of the respondents to the 2005 Exposure Draft supported its proposal on accounting for changes to the acquirer's own deferred taxes in conjunction with a business combination. But some disagreed; they said that an acquirer factors its expected tax synergies into the price it is willing to pay for the acquiree, and therefore those tax synergies constitute goodwill. Those respondents were concerned about the potential for double-counting the synergies once in the consideration and a second time by separately recognising the changes in the acquirer's income taxes.

BC286 The boards acknowledged that in some situations a portion of the tax synergies might be factored into the price paid in the business combination. However, they concluded that it would be difficult, if not impossible, to identify that portion. In addition, an acquirer would not pay more for an acquiree because of tax synergies unless another bidder would also pay more; an acquirer would not knowingly pay more than necessary for the acquiree. Therefore, in some situations none (or only a very small portion) of the tax synergies are likely to be factored into the price paid. The boards also observed that the revised standards (paragraph 51 of the revised IFRS 3) require only the portion of the consideration transferred for the acquiree and the assets acquired and liabilities assumed in the exchange for the acquiree to be included in applying the acquisition method. Excluding effects on the acquirer's ability to utilise its deferred tax asset is consistent with that requirement. Therefore, the boards decided to retain the treatment of changes in an acquirer's tax assets and liabilities proposed in the 2005 Exposure Draft.

BC287 The revised standards also amend IAS 12 and SFAS 109 to require disclosure of the amount of the deferred tax benefit (or expense) recognised in income in the period of the acquisition for the reduction (or increase) of the acquirer's valuation allowance for its deferred tax asset that results from a business combination. The boards decided that disclosure of that amount is necessary to enable users of the acquirer's financial statements to evaluate the nature and financial effect of a business combination.

BC288 The second issue listed in paragraph BC282 relates to changes after the acquisition date in the amounts recognised for deferred tax benefits acquired in a business combination. IAS 12 and SFAS 109 both required subsequent recognition of acquired tax benefits to reduce goodwill. However, IAS 12 and SFAS 109 differed in that:

(a) IAS 12 did not permit the reduction of other non-current intangible assets, which SFAS 109 required; and

(b) IAS 12 required the recognition of offsetting income and expense in the acquirer's profit or loss when subsequent changes are recognised.

BC289 In developing the 2005 Exposure Draft, the FASB concluded that the fair value of other long-lived assets acquired in a business combination should no longer be reduced for changes in a valuation allowance after the acquisition date. That decision is consistent with the boards' decision not to adjust other acquired assets or assumed liabilities, with a corresponding adjustment to goodwill, for the effects of other events occurring after the acquisition date.

BC290 Few respondents to the 2005 Exposure Draft addressed this issue, and the views of those who commented differed. Some favoured providing for reduction of goodwill indefinitely because they view the measurement exception for deferred tax assets as resulting in a measure that is drastically different from fair value. Those who supported not permitting the indefinite reduction of goodwill said that, conceptually, changes in estimates pertaining to deferred taxes recognised in a business combination should be treated the same as other revisions to the amounts recorded at acquisition. The boards agreed with those respondents that a measurement exception should not result in potentially indefinite adjustments to goodwill. The revised standards provide other limited exceptions to the recognition and measurement principles, for example, for employee benefits—none of which result in indefinite adjustments to goodwill for subsequent changes.

BC291 The 2005 Exposure Draft proposed a rebuttable presumption that the subsequent recognition of acquired tax benefits within one year of the acquisition date should be accounted for by reducing goodwill. The rebuttable presumption could have been overcome if the subsequent recognition of the tax benefits resulted from a discrete event or circumstance occurring after the acquisition date. Recognition of acquired tax benefits after the one-year period would be accounted for in profit or loss (or, if IAS 12 or SFAS 109 so requires, outside profit or loss). Respondents suggested particular modifications to that proposal, including removing the rebuttable presumption about subsequent recognition of acquired tax benefits within one year of the acquisition date and treating increases and decreases in deferred tax assets consistently. (IAS 12 and SFAS 109 provided guidance on accounting for decreases.) The boards agreed with those suggestions and revised the requirements of the revised standards accordingly.

BC292 As described in paragraph BC282(c), the boards considered whether a deferred tax asset should be recognised in a business combination for any excess amount of tax-deductible goodwill over the goodwill for financial reporting purposes (excess tax goodwill). From a conceptual standpoint, the excess tax goodwill meets the definition of a temporary difference. Not recognising the tax benefit of that temporary difference at the date of the business combination would be inappropriate and inconsistent with IAS 12 and SFAS 109; it would also be inconsistent with the recognition principle in the revised standards. Thus, the revised IFRS 3 clarifies IAS 12 and SFAS 141(R) amends SFAS 109 accordingly.

BC293 On the issue in paragraph BC282(d), respondents to the 2005 Exposure Draft suggested that the revised standards should address how to account for subsequent adjustments to amounts recognised for acquired income tax uncertainties. Respondents supported accounting for subsequent adjustments to amounts recognised for tax uncertainties using the same approach as the accounting for subsequent adjustments to acquired deferred tax benefits.

BC294 The FASB agreed with respondents' suggestion that an acquirer should recognise changes to acquired income tax uncertainties after the acquisition in the same way as changes in acquired deferred tax benefits. Therefore, SFAS 141(R) amends FASB Interpretation No. 48 *Accounting for Uncertainty in Income Taxes* (FASB Interpretation 48) to require a change to an acquired income tax uncertainty within the measurement period that results from new information about facts and circumstances that existed at the acquisition date to be recognised through a corresponding adjustment to goodwill. If that reduces goodwill to zero, an acquirer would recognise any additional increases of the recognised income tax uncertainty as a reduction of income tax expense. All other changes in the acquired income tax uncertainties would be accounted for in accordance with FASB Interpretation 48.

BC295 The IASB also considered whether to address the accounting for changes in acquired income tax uncertainties in a business combination. IAS 12 is silent on income tax uncertainties. The IASB is considering tax uncertainties as part of the convergence income tax project. Therefore, the IASB decided not to modify IAS 12 as part of this project to address specifically the accounting for changes in acquired income tax uncertainties in a business combination.

Employee benefits

BC296 The revised standards provide exceptions to both the recognition and measurement principles for liabilities and any related assets resulting from the employee benefit arrangements of an acquiree. The acquirer is required to recognise and measure those assets and liabilities in accordance with IAS 19 or applicable US GAAP.

BC297 As with deferred tax assets and liabilities, the boards considered identifying employee benefits as an exception only to the measurement principle. The boards concluded that essentially the same considerations discussed in paragraph BC280 for deferred tax assets and liabilities also apply to employee benefits. In addition, the FASB observed that FASB Statements No. 43 *Accounting for Compensated Absences* and 112 *Employers' Accounting for Postemployment Benefits* require recognition of a liability for compensated absences or post-employment benefits, respectively, only if payment is probable. Arguably, a liability for those benefits exists, at least in some circumstances, regardless of whether payment is probable. Accordingly, to make it clear that the acquirer should apply the recognition and measurement requirements of IAS 19 or applicable US GAAP without separately considering the extent to which those requirements are consistent with the principles in the revised standards, the boards exempted employee benefit obligations from both the recognition and the measurement principles.

BC298 The FASB decided to amend FASB Statements No. 87 *Employers' Accounting for Pensions* (SFAS 87) and 106 *Employers' Accounting for Postretirement Benefits Other Than Pensions* (SFAS 106) to require the acquirer to exclude from the liability it recognises for a single-employer pension or other post-retirement benefit plan the effects of expected plan amendments, terminations or curtailments that it has no obligation to make at the acquisition date. However, those amendments also require the acquirer to include in the liability it recognises at the acquisition date the expected withdrawal liability for a multi-employer plan if it is probable at that date that the acquirer will withdraw from the plan. For a pension or other post-retirement benefit plan, the latter requirement brings into the authoritative literature a provision that previously appeared only in the Basis for Conclusions on SFASs 87 and 106. The FASB acknowledges that the provisions for single-employer and multi-employer plans are not necessarily consistent, and it considered amending SFASs 87 and 106 to require recognition of withdrawal liabilities not yet incurred in post-combination financial statements of the periods in which withdrawals occur. However, it observed that the liability recognised upon withdrawal from a multi-employer plan represents the previously unrecognised portion of the accumulated benefits obligation, which is recognised as it arises for a single-employer plan. In addition, the FASB observed that some might consider the employer's contractual obligation upon withdrawal from a multi-employer plan an unconditional obligation to 'stand ready' to pay if withdrawal occurs and therefore a present obligation. Therefore, the FASB decided not to require the same accounting for expected withdrawals from a multi-employer plan as it requires for expected terminations or curtailments of a single-employer plan.

BC299 The effect of the revised standards' measurement exception for liabilities and any related assets resulting from the acquiree's employee benefit plans is more significant than the related recognition exception. The boards concluded that it was not feasible to require all employee benefit obligations assumed in a business combination to be measured at their acquisition-date fair values. To do so would effectively require the boards to reconsider comprehensively the relevant standards for those employee benefits as a part of their business combinations projects. Given the complexities in accounting for employee benefit obligations in accordance with existing requirements, the boards decided that the only practicable alternative is to require those obligations, and any related assets, to be measured in accordance with their applicable standards.

BC300 The 2005 Exposure Draft proposed exempting only employee benefits subject to SFASs 87 and 106 from its fair value measurement requirement. Some respondents observed that existing measurement requirements for other types of employee benefits are not consistent with fair value and said that those benefits should also be exempted. The FASB agreed and modified the measurement exception for employee benefits accordingly.

Indemnification assets

BC301 A few constituents asked about the potential inconsistency if an asset for an indemnification is measured at fair value at the acquisition date and the related liability is measured using a different measurement attribute. Members of the FASB's resource group raised the issue primarily in the context of FASB Interpretation 48, which requires an entity to measure a tax position that meets the more-likely-than-not recognition threshold at the largest amount of tax benefit that is more than 50 per cent likely to be realised upon ultimate settlement with a taxing authority.

BC302　The boards understand that a business combination sometimes includes an indemnification agreement under which the former owners of the acquiree are required to reimburse the acquirer for any payments the acquirer eventually makes upon settlement of a particular liability. If the indemnification pertains to uncertainty about a position taken in the acquiree's tax returns for prior years or to another item for which the revised standards provide a recognition or measurement exception, not providing a related exception for the indemnification asset would result in recognition or measurement anomalies. For example, for an indemnification pertaining to a deferred tax liability, the acquirer would recognise at the acquisition date a liability to the taxing authority for the deferred taxes and an asset for the indemnification due from the former owners of the acquiree. In the absence of an exception, the asset would be measured at fair value, and the liability would be measured in accordance with the pertinent income tax accounting requirements, such as FASB Interpretation 48 for an entity that applies US GAAP, because income taxes are an exception to the fair value measurement principle. Those two amounts would differ. The boards agreed with constituents that an asset representing an indemnification related to a specific liability should be recognised and measured on the same basis as that liability.

BC303　The boards also provided an exception to the recognition principle for indemnification assets. The reasons for that exception are much the same as the reasons why the boards exempted deferred tax assets and liabilities and employee benefits from that principle. Providing an exception to the recognition principle for indemnification assets clarifies that the acquirer does not apply that principle in determining whether or when to recognise such an asset. Rather, the acquirer recognises the asset when it recognises the related liability. Therefore, the revised standards provide an exception to the recognition and measurement principles for indemnification assets.

Exceptions to the measurement principle

BC304　In addition to the exceptions to both the recognition and measurement principles discussed above, the revised standards provide exceptions to the measurement principle for particular types of assets acquired or liabilities assumed in a business combination. Those exceptions are discussed in paragraphs BC305–BC311.

Temporary exception for assets held for sale

BC305　The 2005 Exposure Draft proposed that non-current assets qualifying as held for sale at the acquisition date under IFRS 5 *Non-current Assets Held for Sale and Discontinued Operations* or FASB Statement No. 144 *Accounting for the Impairment or Disposal of Long-Lived Assets* (SFAS 144) should be measured as those standards require—at fair value less costs to sell. The purpose of that proposed exception was to avoid the need to recognise a loss for the selling costs immediately after a business combination (referred to as a *Day 2 loss* because in theory it would be recognised on the day after the acquisition date). That Day 2 loss would result if the assets were initially measured at fair value but the acquirer then applied either IFRS 5 or SFAS 144, requiring measurement at fair value less costs to sell, for subsequent accounting. Because that loss would stem entirely from different measurement requirements for assets held for sale acquired in a business combination and for assets already held that are classified as held for sale, the reported loss would not faithfully represent the activities of the acquirer.

BC306　After considering responses to the 2005 Exposure Draft, the boards decided that the exception to the measurement principle for assets held for sale should be eliminated. The definitions of fair value in the revised standards, and their application in other areas focuses on market data. Costs that a buyer (acquirer) incurs to purchase or expects to incur to sell an asset are excluded from the amount at which an asset is measured. The boards concluded that disposal costs should also be excluded from the measurement of assets held for sale.

BC307　However, avoiding the Day 2 loss described in paragraph BC305 will require the boards to amend IFRS 5 and SFAS 144 to require assets classified as held for sale to be measured at fair value rather than at fair value less costs to sell. The boards decided to do that, but their respective due process procedures require those amendments to be made in separate projects to give constituents the opportunity to comment on the proposed changes. Although the boards intend the amendments of IFRS 5 and SFAS 144 to be effective at the same time as the revised standards, they decided as an interim step to include a measurement exception until completion of the amendments.

Reacquired rights

BC308　The revised standards (paragraph 29 of the revised IFRS 3) require the fair value of a reacquired right recognised as an intangible asset to be measured on the basis of the remaining contractual term of the contract that gave rise to the right, without taking into account potential renewals of that contract. In developing the 2005 Exposure Draft, the boards observed that a reacquired right is no longer a contract with a third party. An acquirer who controls a reacquired right could assume indefinite renewals of its contractual term, effectively making the reacquired right an intangible asset with an indefinite life. (The boards understood that some entities had been classifying reacquired rights in that way.) The boards concluded that a right reacquired from an acquiree has in substance a finite life; a renewal of the contractual term after the business combination is not part of what was acquired in the business combination. Accordingly, the 2005 Exposure Draft proposed, and the revised standards require, limiting the period over which the intangible asset is amortised (its useful life) to the remaining contractual term of the contract from which the reacquired right stems.

BC309　The 2005 Exposure Draft did not include guidance on determining the fair value of a reacquired right. Some constituents indicated that determining that value is a problem in practice, and the boards agreed that the revised standards should include guidance on that point. To be consistent with the requirement for determining the useful life of a reacquired right, the boards concluded that the fair value of the right should be based on the remaining term of the contract giving rise to the right. The boards acknowledge that market participants would generally reflect expected renewals of the term of a contractual right in the fair value of a right traded in the market. The boards decided, however, that determining the fair value of a reacquired right in that manner would be inconsistent with amortising its value over the remaining contractual term. The boards also observed that a contractual right transferred to a third party (traded in the market) is not a **reacquired** right. Accordingly, the boards decided that departing from the assumptions that market participants would use in measuring the fair value of a reacquired right is appropriate.

BC310   A few constituents asked for guidance on accounting for the sale of a reacquired right after the business combination. The boards concluded that the sale of a reacquired right is in substance the sale of an intangible asset, and the revised standards require the sale of a reacquired right to be accounted for in the same way as sales of other assets (paragraph 55 of the revised IFRS 3). Thus, the carrying amount of the right is to be included in determining the gain or loss on the sale.

Share-based payment awards

BC311   FASB Statement No. 123 (revised 2004) *Share-Based Payment* (SFAS 123(R)) requires measurement of share-based payment awards using what it describes as the *fair-value-based method*. IFRS 2 *Share-based Payment* requires essentially the same measurement method, which the revised IFRS 3 refers to as the *market-based measure*. For reasons identified in those standards, application of the measurement methods they require generally does not result in the amount at which market participants would exchange an award at a particular date—its fair value at that date. Therefore, the revised standards provide an exception to the measurement principle for share-based payment awards. The reasons for that exception are essentially the same as the reasons already discussed for other exceptions to its recognition and measurement principles that the revised standards provide. For example, as with both deferred tax assets and liabilities and assets and liabilities related to employee benefit arrangements, initial measurement of share-based payment awards at their acquisition-date fair values would cause difficulties with the subsequent accounting for those awards in accordance with IFRS 2 or SFAS 123(R).

Recognising and measuring goodwill or a gain from a bargain purchase

BC312   Consistently with IFRS 3 and SFAS 141, the revised standards require the acquirer to recognise goodwill as an asset and to measure it as a residual.

Goodwill qualifies as an asset

BC313   The FASB's 1999 and 2001 Exposure Drafts listed six components of the amount that in practice, under authoritative guidance in effect at that time, had been recognised as goodwill. The IASB's ED 3 included a similar, but not identical, discussion. The components and their descriptions, taken from the FASB's exposure drafts, were:

Component 1—The excess of the fair values over the book values of the acquiree's net assets at the date of acquisition.

Component 2—The fair values of other net assets that the acquiree had not previously recognised. They may not have been recognised because they failed to meet the recognition criteria (perhaps because of measurement difficulties), because of a requirement that prohibited their recognition, or because the acquiree concluded that the costs of recognising them separately were not justified by the benefits.

Component 3—The fair value of the *going concern* element of the acquiree's existing business. The going concern element represents the ability of the established business to earn a higher rate of return on an assembled collection of net assets than would be expected if those net assets had to be acquired separately. That value stems from the synergies of the net assets of the business, as well as from other benefits (such as factors related to market imperfections, including the ability to earn monopoly profits and barriers to market entry—either legal or because of transaction costs—by potential competitors).

Component 4—The fair value of the expected synergies and other benefits from combining the acquirer's and acquiree's net assets and businesses. Those synergies and other benefits are unique to each combination, and different combinations would produce different synergies and, hence, different values.

Component 5—Overvaluation of the consideration paid by the acquirer stemming from errors in valuing the consideration tendered. Although the purchase price in an all-cash transaction would not be subject to measurement error, the same may not necessarily be said of a transaction involving the acquirer's equity interests. For example, the number of ordinary shares being traded daily may be small relative to the number of shares issued in the combination. If so, imputing the current market price to all of the shares issued to effect the combination may produce a higher value than those shares would command if they were sold for cash and the cash then used to effect the combination.

Component 6—Overpayment or underpayment by the acquirer. Overpayment might occur, for example, if the price is driven up in the course of bidding for the acquiree; underpayment may occur in a distress sale (sometimes termed a fire sale).

BC314　The boards observed that the first two components, both of which relate to the acquiree, are conceptually not part of goodwill. The first component is not itself an asset; instead, it reflects gains that the acquiree had not recognised on its net assets. As such, that component is part of those assets rather than part of goodwill. The second component is also not part of goodwill conceptually; it primarily reflects intangible assets that might be recognised as individual assets.

BC315　The fifth and sixth components, both of which relate to the acquirer, are also not conceptually part of goodwill. The fifth component is not an asset in and of itself or even part of an asset but, rather, is a measurement error. The sixth component is also not an asset; conceptually it represents a loss (in the case of overpayment) or a gain (in the case of underpayment) to the acquirer. Thus, neither of those components is conceptually part of goodwill.

BC316　The boards also observed that the third and fourth components are part of goodwill. The third component relates to the acquiree and reflects the excess assembled value of the acquiree's net assets. It represents the pre-existing goodwill that was either internally generated by the acquiree or acquired by it in prior business combinations. The fourth component relates to the acquiree and the acquirer jointly and reflects the excess assembled value that is created by the combination—the synergies that are expected from combining those businesses. The boards described the third and fourth components collectively as 'core goodwill'.

BC317　The revised standards try to avoid subsuming the first, second and fifth components of goodwill into the amount initially recognised as goodwill. Specifically, an acquirer is required to make every effort:

(a)　to measure the consideration accurately (eliminating or reducing component 5);

(b)　to recognise the identifiable net assets acquired at their fair values rather than their carrying amounts (eliminating or reducing component 1); and

(c)　to recognise all acquired intangible assets meeting the criteria in the revised standards (paragraph B31 of the revised IFRS 3) so that they are not subsumed into the amount initially recognised as goodwill (reducing component 2).

BC318　In developing IFRS 3 and SFAS 141, the IASB and the FASB both considered whether 'core goodwill' (the third and fourth components) qualifies as an asset under the definition in their respective conceptual frameworks. (That consideration was based on the existing conceptual frameworks. In 2004, the IASB and the FASB began work on a joint project to develop an improved conceptual framework that, among other things, would eliminate both substantive and wording differences between their existing frameworks. Although the asset definition is likely to change as a result of that project, the boards observed that nothing in their deliberations to date indicates that any such changes are likely to call into question whether goodwill continues to qualify as an asset.)

Asset definition in the FASB's Concepts Statement 6

BC319　Paragraph 172 of the FASB's Concepts Statement 6 says that an item that has future economic benefits has the capacity to serve the entity by being exchanged for something else of value to the entity, by being used to produce something of value to the entity or by being used to settle its liabilities.

BC320　The FASB noted that goodwill cannot be exchanged for something else of value to the entity and it cannot be used to settle the entity's liabilities. Goodwill also lacks the capacity singly to produce future net cash inflows, although it can—in combination with other assets—produce cash flows. Thus, the future benefit associated with goodwill is generally more nebulous and may be less certain than the benefit associated with most other assets. Nevertheless, goodwill generally provides future economic benefit. The FASB's Concepts Statement 6 observes that 'Anything that is commonly bought and sold has future economic benefit, including the individual items that a buyer obtains and is willing to pay for in a "basket purchase" of several items or in a business combination' (paragraph 173).

BC321　For the future economic benefit embodied in goodwill to qualify as an asset, the acquirer must control that benefit. The FASB observed that the acquirer's control is demonstrated by means of its ability to direct the policies and management of the acquiree. The FASB also observed that the past transaction or event necessary for goodwill to qualify as the acquirer's asset is the transaction in which it obtained the controlling interest in the acquiree.

Asset definition in the IASB's Framework

BC322 Paragraph 53 of the IASB's *Framework* explains that 'The future economic benefit embodied in an asset is the potential to contribute, directly or indirectly, to the flow of cash and cash equivalents to the entity.'

BC323 The IASB concluded that core goodwill represents resources from which future economic benefits are expected to flow to the entity. In considering whether core goodwill represents a resource **controlled** by the entity, the IASB considered the assertion that core goodwill arises, at least in part, through factors such as a well-trained workforce, loyal customers and so on, and that these factors cannot be regarded as controlled by the entity because the workforce could leave and the customers could go elsewhere. However, the IASB, like the FASB, concluded that control of core goodwill is provided by means of the acquirer's power to direct the policies and management of the acquiree. Therefore, both the IASB and the FASB concluded that core goodwill meets the conceptual definition of an asset.

Relevance of information about goodwill

BC324 In developing SFAS 141, the FASB also considered the relevance of information about goodwill. Although the IASB's Basis for Conclusions on IFRS 3 did not explicitly discuss the relevance of information about goodwill, the FASB's analysis of that issue was available to the IASB members as they developed IFRS 3, and they saw no reason not to accept that analysis.

BC325 More specifically, in developing SFAS 141, the FASB considered the views of users as reported by the AICPA Special Committee[*] and as expressed by the Financial Accounting Policy Committee (FAPC) of the Association for Investment Management and Research (AIMR) in its 1993 position paper *Financial Reporting in the 1990s and Beyond*. The FASB observed that users have mixed views about whether goodwill should be recognised as an asset. Some are troubled by the lack of comparability between internally generated goodwill and acquired goodwill that results under present standards, but others do not appear to be particularly bothered by it. However, users appear to be reluctant to give up information about goodwill acquired in a business combination. In the view of the AICPA Special Committee, users want to retain the option of being able to use that information. Similarly, the FAPC said that goodwill should be recognised in financial statements.

BC326 The FASB also considered the growing use of 'economic value added' (EVA)[†] and similar measures, which are increasingly being employed as means of assessing performance. The FASB observed that such measures commonly incorporate goodwill, and in business combinations accounted for by the pooling method, an adjustment was commonly made to incorporate a measure of the goodwill that was not recognised under that method. As a result, the aggregate amount of goodwill is included in the base that is subject to a capital charge that is part of the EVA measure and management is held accountable for the total investment in the acquiree.

---

[*] AICPA Special Committee on Financial Reporting, *Improving Business Reporting—A Customer Focus* (New York: AICPA, 1994).

[†] EVA was developed by the consulting firm of Stern Stewart & Company (and is a registered trademark of Stern Stewart) as a financial performance measure that improves management's ability to make decisions that enhance shareholder value.

BC327 The FASB also considered evidence about the relevance of goodwill provided by a number of research studies that empirically examined the relationship between goodwill and the market value of business entities. Those studies generally found a positive relationship between the reported goodwill of entities and their market values, thereby indicating that investors in the markets behave as if they view goodwill as an asset.

Measuring goodwill as a residual

BC328 The revised standards require the acquirer to measure goodwill as the excess of one amount (described in paragraph 32(a) of the revised IFRS 3) over another (described in paragraph 32(b) of the revised IFRS 3). Therefore, goodwill is measured as a residual, which is consistent with IFRS 3 and SFAS 141, in which the IASB and the FASB, respectively, concluded that direct measurement of goodwill is not possible. The boards did not reconsider measuring goodwill as a residual in the second phase of the business combinations project. However, the boards simplified the measurement of goodwill acquired in a business combination achieved in stages (a step acquisition). In accordance with IFRS 3 and SFAS 141, an entity that acquired another entity in a step acquisition measured goodwill by reference to the cost of each step and the related fair value of the underlying identifiable net assets acquired. This process was costly because it required the acquirer in a step acquisition to determine the amounts allocated to the identifiable net assets acquired at the date of each acquisition, even if those steps occurred years or decades earlier. In contrast, the revised standards require goodwill to be measured once—at the acquisition date. Thus, the revised standards reduce the complexity and costs of accounting for step acquisitions.

BC329 Both boards decided that all assets acquired and liabilities assumed, including those of an acquiree (subsidiary) that is not wholly-owned, as well as, in principle, any non-controlling interest in the acquiree, should be measured at their acquisition-date fair values (or in limited situations, their amounts determined in accordance with other US GAAP or IFRSs). Thus, SFAS 141(R) eliminates the past practice of not recognising the portion of goodwill related to the non-controlling interests in subsidiaries that are not wholly-owned. However, as discussed in paragraphs BC209–BC211, the IASB concluded that the revised IFRS 3 should permit entities to measure any non-controlling interest in an acquiree as its proportionate share of the acquiree's identifiable net assets. If an entity chooses that alternative, only the goodwill related to the acquirer is recognised.

---

* Refer to, for example, Eli Amir, Trevor S Harris and Elizabeth K Venuti, 'A Comparison of the Value-Relevance of U.S. versus Non-U.S. GAAP Accounting Measures Using Form 20-F Reconciliations', *Journal of Accounting Research*, Supplement (1993): 230–264; Mary Barth and Greg Clinch, 'International Accounting Differences and Their Relation to Share Prices: Evidence from U.K., Australian and Canadian Firms', *Contemporary Accounting Research* (spring 1996): 135–170; Keith W Chauvin and Mark Hirschey, 'Goodwill, Profitability, and the Market Value of the Firm', *Journal of Accounting and Public Policy* (summer 1994): 159–180; Ross Jennings, John Robinson, Robert B Thompson and Linda Duvall, 'The Relation between Accounting Goodwill Numbers and Equity Values', *Journal of Business Finance and Accounting* (June 1996): 513–533; and Mark G McCarthy and Douglas K Schneider, 'Market Perception of Goodwill: Some Empirical Evidence', *Accounting and Business Research* (winter 1995): 69–81.

Using the acquisition-date fair value of consideration to measure goodwill

BC330   As discussed in paragraph BC81, the revised standards do not focus on measuring the acquisition-date fair value of either the acquiree as a whole or the acquirer's interest in the acquiree as the 2005 Exposure Draft did. Consistently with that change, the boards also eliminated the presumption in the 2005 Exposure Draft that, in the absence of evidence to the contrary, the acquisition-date fair value of the consideration transferred is the best evidence of the fair value of the acquirer's interest in the acquiree at that date. Therefore, the revised standards describe the measurement of goodwill in terms of the recognised amount of the consideration transferred—generally its acquisition-date fair value (paragraph 32 of the revised IFRS 3)—and specify how to measure goodwill if the fair value of the acquiree is more reliably measurable than the fair value of the consideration transferred or if no consideration is transferred (paragraph 33 of the revised IFRS 3).

BC331   Because business combinations are generally exchange transactions in which knowledgeable, unrelated willing parties exchange equal values, the boards continue to believe that the acquisition-date fair value of the consideration transferred provides the best evidence of the acquisition-date fair value of the acquirer's interest in the acquiree in many, if not most, situations. However, that is not the case if the acquirer either makes a bargain purchase or pays more than the acquiree is worth at the acquisition date—if the acquirer underpays or overpays. The revised standards provide for recognising a gain in the event of a bargain purchase, but they do not provide for recognising a loss in the event of an overpayment (paragraph BC382). Therefore, the boards concluded that focusing directly on the fair value of the consideration transferred rather than on the fair value of the acquirer's interest in the acquiree, with a presumption that the two amounts are usually equal, would be a more straightforward way of describing how to measure goodwill. (The same conclusion applies to measuring the gain on a bargain purchase, which is discussed in paragraphs BC371–BC381.) That change in focus will also avoid unproductive disputes in practice about whether the consideration transferred or another valuation technique provides the best evidence for measuring the acquirer's interest in the acquiree in a particular situation.

Using the acquirer's interest in the acquiree to measure goodwill

BC332   The boards acknowledge that in the absence of measurable consideration, the acquirer is likely to incur costs to measure the acquisition-date fair value of its interest in the acquiree and incremental costs to have that measure independently verified. The boards observed that in many of those circumstances companies already incur such costs as part of their due diligence procedures. For example, an acquisition of a privately held entity by another privately held entity is often accomplished by an exchange of equity shares that do not have observable market prices. To determine the exchange ratio, those entities generally engage advisers and valuation experts to assist them in valuing the acquiree as well as the equity transferred by the acquirer in exchange for the acquiree. Similarly, a combination of two mutual entities is often accomplished by an exchange of member interests of the acquirer for all of the member interests of the acquiree. In many, but not necessarily all, of those cases the directors and managers of the entities also assess the relative fair values of the combining entities to ensure that the exchange of member interests is equitable to the members of both entities.

BC333   The boards concluded that the benefits in terms of improved financial information resulting from the revised standards outweigh the incremental measurement costs that the revised standards may require. Those improvements include the increased relevance and understandability of information resulting from applying the revised standards' measurement principle and guidance on recognising and measuring goodwill, which are consistent with reflecting the change in economic circumstances that occurs at that date.

BC334   The 2005 Exposure Draft included illustrative guidance for applying the fair value measurement requirement if no consideration is transferred or the consideration transferred is not the best evidence of the acquisition-date fair value of the acquiree. That illustrative guidance drew on related guidance in the FASB's exposure draft that preceded SFAS 157. Because SFAS 157 provides guidance on using valuation techniques such as the market approach and the income approach for measuring fair value, the FASB decided that it is unnecessary for SFAS 141(R) to provide the same guidance.

BC335   The IASB decided not to include in the revised IFRS 3 guidance on using valuation techniques to measure the acquisition-date fair value of the acquirer's interest in the acquiree. The IASB has on its agenda a project to develop guidance on measuring fair value. While deliberations on that project are in progress, the IASB considers it inappropriate to include fair value measurement guidance in IFRSs.

BC336   The FASB, on the other hand, completed its project on fair value measurement when it issued SFAS 157. SFAS 141(R), together with SFAS 157, provides broadly applicable measurement guidance that is relevant and useful in measuring the acquirer's interest in the acquiree. However, both boards were concerned that without some discussion of special considerations for measuring the fair value of mutual entities, some acquirers might neglect to consider relevant assumptions that market participants would make about future member benefits when using a valuation technique. For example, the acquirer of a co-operative entity should consider the value of the member discounts in its determination of the fair value of its interest in the acquiree. Therefore, the boards decided to include a discussion of special considerations in measuring the fair value of mutual entities (paragraphs B47–B49 of the revised IFRS 3).

Measuring consideration and determining whether particular items are part of the consideration transferred for the acquiree

BC337   Paragraphs BC338–BC360 discuss the boards' conclusions on measuring specific items of consideration that are often transferred by acquirers. Paragraphs BC361–BC370 then discuss whether particular replacement awards of share-based remuneration and acquisition-related costs incurred by acquirers are part of the consideration transferred for the acquiree.

Measurement date for equity securities transferred

BC338   The guidance in IFRS 3 and SFAS 141 on the measurement date for equity securities transferred as consideration in a business combination differed, and SFAS 141's guidance on that issue was contradictory. Paragraph 22 of SFAS 141, which was carried forward from APB Opinion 16, said that the market price for a reasonable period before and after the date that the terms of the acquisition are agreed to and announced should be considered in determining the fair value of the securities issued. That effectively established the agreement date as the measurement date for equity securities issued as consideration. However, paragraph 49 of SFAS 141, which was also carried forward from APB Opinion 16, said that the cost of an acquiree should be determined as of the acquisition date. IFRS 3, on the other hand, required measuring the consideration transferred in a business combination at its fair value on the exchange date, which was the acquisition date for a combination in which control is achieved in a single transaction. (IFRS 3, like SFAS 141, included special guidance on determining the cost of a business combination in which control is achieved in stages.) In their deliberations leading to the 2005 Exposure Draft, the boards decided that the fair value of equity securities issued as consideration in a business combination should be measured at the acquisition date.

BC339   In reaching their conclusions on this issue, the boards considered the reasons for the consensus reached in EITF Issue No. 99-12 *Determination of the Measurement Date for the Market Price of Acquirer Securities Issued in a Purchase Business Combination.* That consensus states that the value of the acquirer's marketable equity securities issued to effect a business combination should be determined on the basis of the market price of the securities over a reasonable period before and after the terms of the acquisition are agreed to and announced. The arguments for that consensus are based on the view that the announcement of a transaction, and the related agreements, normally bind the parties to the transaction so that the acquirer is obliged at that point to issue the equity securities at the closing date. If the parties are bound to the transaction at the agreement (announcement) date, the value of the underlying securities on that date best reflects the value of the bargained exchange. The boards did not find those arguments compelling. The boards observed that to make the announcement of a recommended transaction binding generally requires shareholders' authorisation or another binding event, which also gives rise to the change in control of the acquiree.

BC340   Additionally, the boards noted that measuring the fair value of equity securities issued on the agreement date (or on the basis of the market price of the securities for a short period before and after that date) did not result in a consistent measure of the consideration transferred. The fair values of all other forms of consideration transferred are measured at the acquisition date. The boards decided that all forms of consideration transferred should be valued on the same date, which should also be the same date as when the assets acquired and liabilities assumed are measured. The boards also observed that negotiations between an acquirer and an acquiree typically provide for share adjustments in the event of material events and circumstances between the agreement date and acquisition date. In addition, ongoing negotiations after announcement of agreements, which are not unusual, provide evidence that agreements are generally not binding at the date they are announced. Lastly, the boards also observed that the parties typically provide for cancellation options if the number of shares to be issued at the acquisition date would not reflect an exchange of approximately equal fair values at that date.

BC341 Respondents to the 2005 Exposure Draft expressed mixed views on the measurement date for equity securities. Some supported the proposal to measure equity securities at their fair value on the acquisition date, generally for the same reasons given in that exposure draft. Others, however, favoured use of the agreement date. They generally cited one or more of the following as support for their view:

(a) An acquirer and a target entity both consider the fair value of a target entity on the agreement date in negotiating the amount of consideration to be paid. Measuring equity securities issued as consideration at fair value on the agreement date reflects the values taken into account in negotiations.

(b) Changes in the fair value of the acquirer's equity securities between the agreement date and the acquisition date may be caused by factors unrelated to the business combination.

(c) Changes in the fair value of the acquirer's equity securities between the agreement date and the acquisition date may result in inappropriate recognition of either a bargain purchase or artificially inflated goodwill if the fair value of those securities is measured at the acquisition date.

BC342 In considering those comments, the boards observed, as they did in the 2005 Exposure Draft, that valid conceptual arguments can be made for both the agreement date and the acquisition date. However, they also observed that the parties to a business combination are likely to take into account expected changes between the agreement date and the acquisition date in the fair value of the acquirer and the market price of the acquirer's securities issued as consideration. The argument against acquisition date measurement of equity securities noted in paragraph BC341(a) is mitigated if acquirers and targets generally consider their best estimates at the agreement date of the fair values of the amounts to be exchanged on the acquisition dates. The boards also noted that measuring the equity securities on the acquisition date avoids the complexities of dealing with situations in which the number of shares or other consideration transferred can change between the agreement date and the acquisition date. The boards therefore concluded that equity instruments issued as consideration in a business combination should be measured at their fair values on the acquisition date.

Contingent consideration, including subsequent measurement

BC343 In accordance with the guidance in SFAS 141, which was carried forward from APB Opinion 16 without reconsideration, an acquirer's obligations to make payments conditional on the outcome of future events (often called *contingent consideration*) were not usually recognised at the acquisition date. Rather, acquirers usually recognised those obligations when the contingency was resolved and consideration was issued or became issuable. In general, issuing additional securities or distributing additional cash or other assets upon resolving contingencies on the basis of reaching particular earnings levels resulted in delayed recognition of an additional element of cost of an acquiree.

In contrast, issuing additional securities or distributing additional assets upon resolving contingencies on the basis of security prices did not change the recognised cost of an acquiree.

BC344 The IASB carried forward in IFRS 3 the requirements for contingent consideration from IAS 22 without reconsideration. In accordance with IFRS 3, an acquirer recognised consideration that is contingent on future events at the acquisition date only if it is probable and can be measured reliably. If the required level of probability or reliability for recognition was reached only after the acquisition date, the additional consideration was treated as an adjustment to the accounting for the business combination and to goodwill at that later date.

BC345 Therefore, in accordance with both SFAS 141 and IFRS 3, unlike other forms of consideration, an obligation for contingent consideration was not always measured at its acquisition-date fair value and its remeasurement either sometimes (SFAS 141) or always (IFRS 3) resulted in an adjustment to the business combination accounting.

BC346 In developing the 2005 Exposure Draft, both boards concluded that the delayed recognition of contingent consideration in their previous standards on business combinations was unacceptable because it ignored that the acquirer's agreement to make contingent payments is the obligating event in a business combination transaction. Although the amount of the future payments the acquirer will make is conditional on future events, the obligation to make them if the specified future events occur is unconditional. The same is true for a right to the return of previously transferred consideration if specified conditions are met. Failure to recognise that obligation or right at the acquisition date would not faithfully represent the economic consideration exchanged at that date. Thus, both boards concluded that obligations and rights associated with contingent consideration arrangements should be measured and recognised at their acquisition-date fair values.

BC347 The boards considered arguments that it might be difficult to measure the fair value of contingent consideration at the acquisition date. The boards acknowledged that measuring the fair value of some contingent payments may be difficult, but they concluded that to delay recognition of, or otherwise ignore, assets or liabilities that are difficult to measure would cause financial reporting to be incomplete and thus diminish its usefulness in making economic decisions.

BC348 Moreover, a contingent consideration arrangement is inherently part of the economic considerations in the negotiations between the buyer and seller. Such arrangements are commonly used by buyers and sellers to reach an agreement by sharing particular specified economic risks related to uncertainties about future outcomes. Differences in the views of the buyer and seller about those uncertainties are often reconciled by their agreeing to share the risks in such ways that favourable future outcomes generally result in additional payments to the seller and unfavourable outcomes result in no or lower payments. The boards observed that information used in those negotiations will often be helpful in estimating the fair value of the contingent obligation assumed by the acquirer.

BC349 The boards noted that most contingent consideration obligations are financial instruments, and many are derivative instruments. Reporting entities that use such instruments extensively, auditors and valuation professionals are familiar with the use of valuation techniques for estimating the fair values of financial instruments. The boards concluded that acquirers should be able to use valuation techniques to develop estimates of the fair values of contingent consideration obligations that are sufficiently reliable for recognition. The boards also observed that an effective estimate of zero for the acquisition-date fair value of contingent consideration, which was often the result under IFRS 3 and SFAS 141, was unreliable.

BC350   Some respondents to the 2005 Exposure Draft were especially concerned about the reliability with which the fair value of performance-based contingent consideration can be measured. The IASB and the FASB considered those concerns in the context of related requirements in their standards on share-based payments (IFRS 2 and SFAS 123(R), respectively), neither of which requires performance conditions that are not market conditions to be included in the market-based measure of an award of share-based payment at the grant date. For example, remuneration cost is recognised for a share option with vesting requirements that depend on achievement of an earnings target based on the number of equity instruments expected to vest and any such cost recognised during the vesting period is reversed if the target is not achieved. Both IFRS 2 and SFAS 123(R) cite constituents' concerns about the measurability at the grant date of the expected outcomes associated with performance conditions as part of the reason for that treatment.

BC351   The boards concluded that the requirements for awards of share-based payment subject to performance conditions should not determine the requirements for contingent (or conditional) consideration in a business combination. In addition, the boards concluded that the negotiations between buyer and seller inherent in a contingent consideration arrangement in a business combination provide better evidence of its fair value than is likely to be available for most share-based payment arrangements with performance conditions.

BC352   The boards also noted that some contingent consideration arrangements oblige the acquirer to deliver its equity securities if specified future events occur. The boards concluded that the classification of such instruments as either equity or a liability should be based on existing IFRSs or US GAAP, as indicated in paragraph 40 of the revised IFRS 3.

Subsequent measurement of contingent consideration

BC353   For reasons similar to those discussed in the context of contingent liabilities (paragraphs BC232 and BC243), the boards concluded that the revised standards must address subsequent accounting for contingent consideration. For consistency with the accounting for other obligations that require an entity to deliver its equity shares, the boards concluded that obligations for contingent payments that are classified as equity should not be remeasured after the acquisition date.

BC354   The boards observed that many obligations for contingent consideration that qualify for classification as liabilities meet the definition of derivative instruments in IAS 39 or SFAS 133. To improve transparency in reporting particular instruments, the boards concluded that all contracts that would otherwise be within the scope of those standards (if not issued in a business combination) should be subject to their requirements if issued in a business combination. Therefore, the boards decided to eliminate their respective provisions (paragraph 2(f) of IAS 39 and paragraph 11(c) of SFAS 133) that excluded contingent consideration in a business combination from the scope of those standards. Accordingly, liabilities for payments of contingent consideration that are subject to the requirements of IAS 39 or SFAS 133 would subsequently be measured at fair value at the end of each reporting period, with changes in fair value recognised in accordance with whichever of those standards an entity applies in its financial statements.

BC355 In considering the subsequent accounting for contingent payments that are liabilities but are not derivatives, the boards concluded that, in concept, all liabilities for contingent payments should be accounted for similarly. Therefore, liabilities for contingent payments that are not derivative instruments should also be remeasured at fair value after the acquisition date. The boards concluded that applying those provisions would faithfully represent the fair value of the liability for the contingent payment of consideration that remains a liability until settled.

BC356 The boards also considered whether subsequent changes in the fair values of liabilities for contingent consideration should be reflected as adjustments to the consideration transferred in the business combination (usually in goodwill). Some respondents to the 2005 Exposure Draft favoured that alternative because they thought that changes in the fair value of contingent consideration effectively resolve differing views of the acquirer and the former owners of the acquiree about the acquisition-date fair value of the acquiree. The boards acknowledged that a conclusive determination at the acquisition date of the fair value of a liability for contingent consideration might not be practicable in the limited circumstances in which particular information is not available at that date. As discussed in more detail in paragraphs BC390–BC400, the boards decided that the revised standards should provide for provisional measurement of the fair value of assets acquired or liabilities assumed or incurred, including liabilities for contingent payments, in those circumstances.

BC357 Except for adjustments during the measurement period to provisional estimates of fair values at the acquisition date, the boards concluded that subsequent changes in the fair value of a liability for contingent consideration do not affect the acquisition-date fair value of the consideration transferred. Rather, those subsequent changes in value are generally directly related to post-combination events and changes in circumstances related to the combined entity. Thus, subsequent changes in value for post-combination events and circumstances should not affect the measurement of the consideration transferred or goodwill on the acquisition date. (The boards acknowledge that some changes in fair value might result from events and circumstances related in part to a pre-combination period. But that part of the change is usually indistinguishable from the part related to the post-combination period and the boards concluded that the benefits in those limited circumstances that might result from making such fine distinctions would not justify the costs that such a requirement would impose.)

BC358 The boards also considered arguments that the results of the requirements of the revised standards for recognition of changes in the fair value of contingent consideration after the acquisition date are counter-intuitive because they will result in:

(a)   recognising gains if the specified milestone or event requiring the contingent payment is not met. For example, the acquirer would recognise a gain on the reversal of the liability if an earnings target in an earn-out arrangement is not achieved.

(b)   recognising losses if the combined entity is successful and the amount paid exceeds the estimated fair value of the liability at the acquisition date.

BC359   The boards accept the consequence that recognising the fair value of a liability for payment of contingent consideration is likely to result subsequently in a gain if smaller or no payments are required or result in a loss if greater payments are required. That is a consequence of entering into contingent consideration arrangements related to future changes in the value of a specified asset or liability or earnings of the acquiree after the acquisition date. For example, if a contingent consideration arrangement relates to the level of future earnings of the combined entity, higher earnings in the specified periods may be partially offset by increases in the liability to make contingent payments based on earnings because the acquirer has agreed to share those increases with former owners of the acquiree.

BC360   The boards also observed that liabilities for contingent payments may be related to contingencies surrounding an outcome for a particular asset or another liability. In those cases, the effect on income of the period of a change in the fair value of the liability for the contingent payment may be offset by a change in the value of the asset or other liability. For example, after an acquisition the combined entity might reach a favourable settlement of pending litigation of the acquiree for which it had a contingent consideration arrangement. If the combined entity is thus required to make a contingent payment to the seller of the acquiree that exceeds the initially estimated fair value of the liability for contingent consideration, the effect of the increase in that liability may be offset in part by the reduction in the liability to the litigation claimant. Similarly, if the acquirer is not required to make a contingent payment to the seller because an acquired research and development project failed to result in a viable product, the gain from the elimination of the liability may be offset, in whole or in part, by an impairment charge to the asset acquired.

Replacement awards

BC361   An acquirer sometimes issues replacement awards to benefit the employees of the acquiree for past services, for future services or for both. Accordingly, the 2005 Exposure Draft included guidance for determining the extent to which replacement awards are for past services (and thus part of the consideration transferred in the business combination) or future services (and thus not part of the consideration transferred). In developing that guidance, the boards' objective was, as far as possible, to be consistent with the guidance in their respective standards on share-based payments.

BC362   Few respondents to the 2005 Exposure Draft commented on this issue, and those who did so generally agreed with the proposals, at least as they related to entities that apply IFRS 2 in accounting for share-based payment awards granted otherwise than in a business combination. However, in redeliberating the 2005 Exposure Draft, the FASB observed that some of its proposals on share-based payment awards were not consistent with SFAS 123(R), which was published after the related deliberations in the second phase of its business combinations project. For example, the 2005 Exposure Draft proposed that the excess, if any, of the fair value of replacement awards over the fair value of the replaced acquiree awards should be immediately recognised as remuneration cost in the post-combination financial statements even if employees were required to render future service to earn the rights to the replacement awards. SFAS 123(R), on the other hand, requires recognition of additional remuneration cost arising in a modification of the terms of an award (which is the same as the replacement of one award with another) over the requisite service period. The FASB concluded that, in general, the requirements of SFAS 141(R) on accounting for replacements of share-based payment awards should be consistent with the requirements for other share-based payment awards in SFAS 123(R). To achieve that goal the FASB modified the guidance in SFAS 141(R) on accounting for any excess of the fair value of replacement awards over the fair value of the replaced awards.

BC363 In addition, the FASB's constituents raised questions about other aspects of the guidance on accounting for the replacement of share-based payment awards. Those questions generally related to interpretative guidance that SFAS 123(R) superseded or nullified without providing comparable guidance—specifically, FASB Interpretation No. 44 *Accounting for Certain Transactions involving Stock Compensation* and EITF Issue No. 00-23 *Issues Related to the Accounting for Stock Compensation under APB Opinion No. 25 and FASB Interpretation No. 44*. Paragraphs B56–B62 of the revised IFRS 3 provide guidance to help in resolving those implementation questions. In developing that guidance, the FASB sought to apply the same principles to the replacement of share-based payment awards in a business combination that are applied to share-based payment awards in other situations. The IASB agreed with that goal, and it decided that the guidance on accounting for replacement awards of share-based payment is consistent with the guidance in IFRS 2 on accounting for modification of share-based payment awards.

BC364 The boards concluded that the guidance in the revised standards is consistent with the objective that the consideration transferred for an acquired business includes those payments that are for the business and excludes those payments that are for other purposes. Remuneration for future services to be rendered to the acquirer by former owners or other employees of the acquiree is not, in substance, consideration for the business acquired.

Acquisition-related costs

BC365 The boards considered whether acquisition-related costs are part of the consideration transferred in exchange for the acquiree. Those costs include an acquirer's costs incurred in connection with a business combination (a) for the services of lawyers, investment bankers, accountants and other third parties and (b) for issuing debt or equity instruments used to effect the business combination (issue costs). Generally, acquisition-related costs are charged to expense as incurred, but the costs to issue debt or equity securities are an exception. Currently, the accounting for issue costs is mixed and conflicting practices have developed in the absence of clear accounting guidance. The FASB is addressing issue costs in its project on liabilities and equity and has tentatively decided that those costs should be recognised as expenses as incurred. Some FASB members would have preferred to require issue costs to effect a business combination to be recognised as expenses, but they did not think that the business combinations project was the place to make that decision. Therefore, the FASB decided to allow mixed practices for accounting for issue costs to continue until the project on liabilities and equity resolves the issue broadly.

BC366 The boards concluded that acquisition-related costs are not part of the fair value exchange between the buyer and seller for the business. Rather, they are separate transactions in which the buyer pays for the fair value of services received. The boards also observed that those costs, whether for services performed by external parties or internal staff of the acquirer, do not generally represent assets of the acquirer at the acquisition date because the benefits obtained are consumed as the services are received.

BC367 Thus, the 2005 Exposure Draft proposed, and the revised standards require, the acquirer to exclude acquisition-related costs from the measurement of the fair value of both the consideration transferred and the assets acquired or liabilities assumed as part of the business combination. Those costs are to be accounted for separately from the business combination, and generally recognised as expenses when incurred. The revised standards therefore resolve inconsistencies in accounting for acquisition-related costs in accordance with the cost-accumulation approach in IFRS 3 and SFAS 141, which provided that the cost of an acquiree included *direct* costs incurred for an acquisition of a business but excluded *indirect* costs. Direct costs included out-of-pocket or incremental costs, for example, finder's fees and fees paid to outside consultants for accounting, legal or valuation services for a successful acquisition, but direct costs incurred in unsuccessful negotiations were recognised as expenses as incurred. Indirect costs included recurring internal costs, such as maintaining an acquisition department. Although those costs also could be directly related to a successful acquisition, they were recognised as expenses as incurred.

BC368 Some respondents to the 2005 Exposure Draft said that acquisition-related costs, including costs of due diligence, are unavoidable costs of the investment in a business. They suggested that, because the acquirer intends to recover its due diligence cost through the post-acquisition operations of the business, that transaction cost should be capitalised as part of the total investment in the business. Some also argued that the buyer specifically considers those costs in determining the amount that it is willing to pay for the acquiree. The boards rejected those arguments. They found no persuasive evidence indicating that the seller of a particular business is willing to accept less than fair value as consideration for its business merely because a particular buyer may incur more (or less) acquisition-related costs than other potential buyers for that business. Furthermore, the boards concluded that the intentions of a particular buyer, including its plans to recover such costs, are a separate matter that is distinct from the fair value measurement objective in the revised standards.

BC369 The boards acknowledge that the cost-accumulation models in IFRS 3 and SFAS 141 included some acquisition-related costs as part of the carrying amount of the assets acquired. The boards also acknowledge that all asset acquisitions are similar transactions that, in concept, should be accounted for similarly, regardless of whether assets are acquired separately or as part of a group of assets that may meet the definition of a business. However, as noted in paragraph BC20, the boards decided not to extend the scope of the revised standards to all acquisitions of groups of assets. Therefore, the boards accept that, at this time, accounting for most acquisition-related costs separately from the business combination, generally as an expense as incurred for services received in connection with a combination, differs from some standards or accepted practices that require or permit particular acquisition-related costs to be included in the cost of an asset acquisition. The boards concluded, however, that the revised standards improve financial reporting by eliminating inconsistencies in accounting for acquisition-related costs in connection with a business combination and by applying the fair value measurement principle to all business combinations. The boards also observed that in practice under IFRS 3 and SFAS 141, most acquisition-related costs were subsumed in goodwill, which was also not consistent with accounting for asset acquisitions.

BC370 The boards also considered concerns about the potential for abuse. Some constituents, including some respondents to the 2005 Exposure Draft, said that if acquirers could no longer capitalise acquisition-related costs as part of the cost of the business acquired, they might modify transactions to avoid recognising those costs as expenses. For example, some said that a buyer might ask a seller to make payments to the buyer's vendors on its behalf. To facilitate the negotiations and sale of the business, the seller might agree to make those payments if the total amount to be paid to it upon closing of the business combination is sufficient to reimburse the seller for payments it made on the buyer's behalf. If the disguised reimbursements were treated as part of the consideration transferred for the business, the acquirer might not recognise those expenses. Rather, the measure of the fair value of the business and the amount of goodwill recognised for that business might be overstated. To mitigate such concerns, the revised standards require any payments to an acquiree (or its former owners) in connection with a business combination that are payments for goods or services that are not part of the acquired business to be assigned to those goods or services and accounted for as a separate transaction. The revised standards specifically require an acquirer to determine whether any portion of the amounts transferred by the acquirer are separate from the consideration exchanged for the acquiree and the assets acquired and liabilities assumed in the business combination. The revised standards (see paragraphs 51–53 and B50 of the revised IFRS 3) provide guidance for making that determination.

Bargain purchases

BC371 Paragraphs 34–36 of the revised IFRS 3 set out the accounting requirements for a bargain purchase. The boards consider bargain purchases anomalous transactions—business entities and their owners generally do not knowingly and willingly sell assets or businesses at prices below their fair values. However, bargain purchases have occurred and are likely to continue to occur. Circumstances in which they occur include a forced liquidation or distress sale (eg after the death of a founder or key manager) in which owners need to sell a business quickly, which may result in a price that is less than fair value.

BC372 The boards observed that an economic gain is inherent in a bargain purchase. At the acquisition date, the acquirer is better off by the amount by which the fair value of what is acquired exceeds the fair value of the consideration transferred (paid) for it. The boards concluded that, in concept, the acquirer should recognise that gain at the acquisition date. However, the boards acknowledged that although the reasons for a forced liquidation or distress sale are often apparent, sometimes clear evidence might not exist, for example, if a seller uses a closed (private) process for the sale and to maintain its negotiating position is unwilling to reveal the main reason for the sale. The appearance of a bargain purchase without evidence of the underlying reasons would raise concerns in practice about the existence of measurement errors.

BC373   Constituents, including some respondents to the 2005 Exposure Draft, expressed concerns about recognising gains upon the acquisition of a business, particularly if it is difficult to determine whether a particular acquisition is in fact a bargain purchase. They also suggested that an initial determination of an excess of the acquisition-date fair value (or other recognised amounts) of the identifiable net assets acquired over the fair value of the consideration paid by the acquirer plus the recognised amount of any non-controlling interest in the acquiree might arise from other factors, including:

    (a)   errors in measuring the fair values of (i) the consideration paid for the business, (ii) the assets acquired or (iii) the liabilities assumed; and

    (b)   using measures in accordance with IFRSs or US GAAP that are not fair values.

Distinguishing a bargain purchase from measurement errors

BC374   The boards acknowledged concerns raised by constituents that a requirement to recognise gains on a bargain purchase might provide an opportunity for inappropriate gain recognition from intentional errors resulting from the acquirer's:

    (a)   understating or failing to identify the value of items of consideration that it transferred;

    (b)   overstating values attributed to particular assets acquired; or

    (c)   understating or failing to identify and recognise particular liabilities assumed.

BC375   The boards think that problems surrounding intentional measurement errors by acquirers are generally best addressed by means other than setting standards specifically intended to avoid abuse. Strong internal control systems and the use of independent valuation experts and external auditors are among the means by which both intentional and unintentional measurement errors are minimised. Standards specifically designed to avoid abuse would inevitably lack neutrality. (See paragraph BC51 for a discussion of the need for neutrality in accounting and accounting standards.) However, the boards share constituents' concerns about the potential for inappropriate gain recognition resulting from measurement bias or undetected measurement errors. Thus, the boards decided (see paragraph 36 of the revised IFRS 3) to require the acquirer to reassess whether it has correctly identified all of the assets acquired and all of the liabilities assumed before recognising a gain on a bargain purchase. The acquirer must then review the procedures used to measure the amounts the revised standards require to be recognised at the acquisition date for all of the following:

    (a)   the identifiable assets acquired and liabilities assumed;

    (b)   the non-controlling interest in the acquiree, if any;

(c)   for a business combination achieved in stages, the acquirer's previously held equity interest in the acquiree; and

(d)   the consideration transferred.

The objective of that review is to ensure that appropriate consideration has been given to all available information in identifying the items to be measured and recognised and in determining their fair values. The boards believe that the required review will mitigate, if not eliminate, undetected errors that might have existed in the initial measurements.

BC376   The boards acknowledged, however, that the required review might be insufficient to eliminate concerns about unintentional measurement bias. They decided to address that concern by limiting the extent of gain that can be recognised. Thus, the revised standards provide that a gain on a bargain purchase is measured as the excess of:

(a)   the net of the acquisition-date amounts of the identifiable assets acquired and liabilities assumed; over

(b)   the acquisition-date fair value of the consideration transferred plus the recognised amount of any non-controlling interest in the acquiree and, if the transaction is an acquisition achieved in stages, the acquisition-date fair value of the acquirer's previously held equity interest in the acquiree.

That means that a gain on a bargain purchase and goodwill cannot both be recognised for the same business combination. The 2005 Exposure Draft defined a bargain purchase as a transaction in which the fair value of the acquirer's interest in the acquiree exceeds the consideration transferred for it, but it would have required that any resulting goodwill should be written off before a gain was recognised. The result of the revised standards' requirement is the same, but there will be no goodwill to write off if the gain is measured with reference to the identifiable net assets acquired rather than the fair value of the acquirer's interest in the acquiree. In addition, the revised standards require (paragraph B64(n) of the revised IFRS 3) the acquirer to disclose information about a gain recognised on a bargain purchase.

BC377   The main purpose of the limitation on gain recognition is to mitigate the potential for inappropriate gain recognition through measurement errors, particularly those that might result from unintended measurement bias. The main purpose of the disclosure requirement is to provide information that enables users of an acquirer's financial statements to evaluate the nature and financial effect of business combinations that occur during the period. The boards acknowledged, however, that the limitation and disclosure requirements may also help to mitigate constituents' concerns about potential abuse, although that is not their primary objective.

BC378   Moreover, the boards believe that concerns about abuse resulting from the opportunity for gain recognition may be overstated. Financial analysts and other users have often told the boards that they give little weight to one-off or unusual gains, such as those resulting from a bargain purchase transaction. In addition, the boards noted that managers of entities generally have no incentive to overstate assets acquired or understate liabilities assumed in a business combination because that would generally result in higher post-combination expenses—when the assets are used or become impaired or liabilities are remeasured or settled.

Distinguishing a bargain purchase from a 'negative goodwill result'

BC379　The boards acknowledged that a so-called negative goodwill result remains a possibility (although in most situations, a remote possibility) because the revised standards continue to require particular assets acquired and liabilities assumed to be measured at amounts other than their acquisition-date fair values. The boards observed, however, that the revised standards address most deficiencies in past requirements on accounting for business combinations that previously led to negative goodwill results—ie a result that had the appearance but not the economic substance of a bargain purchase. For example, often no liability was recognised for some contingent payment arrangements (eg earn-outs) at the acquisition date, which could result in the appearance of a bargain purchase by understating the consideration paid. The revised standards, in contrast, require the measurement and recognition of substantially all liabilities at their fair values on the acquisition date.

BC380　The boards also considered concerns raised by some constituents that a buyer's expectations of future losses and its need to incur future costs to make a business viable might give rise to a negative goodwill result. In other words, a buyer would be willing to pay a seller only an amount that is, according to that view, less than the fair value of the acquiree (or its identifiable net assets) because to make a fair return on the business the buyer would need to make further investments in that business to bring its condition to fair value. The boards disagreed with that view for the reasons noted in paragraphs BC134–BC143 in the context of liabilities associated with restructuring or exit activities of the acquiree, as well as those that follow.

BC381　Fair values are measured by reference to unrelated buyers and sellers that are knowledgeable and have a common understanding about factors relevant to the business and the transaction and are also willing and able to transact business in the same market(s) and have the legal and financial ability to do so. The boards are aware of no compelling reason to believe that, in the absence of duress, a seller would willingly and knowingly sell a business for an amount less than its fair value. Thus, the boards concluded that careful application of the revised standards' fair value measurement requirements will mitigate concerns that negative goodwill might result and be misinterpreted as a bargain purchase transaction.

Overpayments

BC382　The boards considered whether the revised standards should include special provisions to account for a business combination in which a buyer overpays for its interest in the acquiree. The boards acknowledged that overpayments are possible and, in concept, an overpayment should lead to the acquirer's recognition of an expense (or loss) in the period of the acquisition. However, the boards believe that in practice any overpayment is unlikely to be detectable or known at the acquisition date. In other words, the boards are not aware of instances in which a buyer knowingly overpays or is compelled to overpay a seller to acquire a business. Even if an acquirer thinks it might have overpaid in some sense, the amount of overpayment would be difficult, if not impossible, to quantify. Thus, the boards concluded that in practice it is not possible to identify and reliably measure an overpayment at the acquisition date. Accounting for overpayments is best addressed through subsequent impairment testing when evidence of a potential overpayment first arises.

Additional guidance for particular types of business combinations

BC383   To help entities apply the acquisition method as required by the revised standards, the boards decided to provide additional guidance for business combinations achieved in stages and those achieved without the transfer of consideration. Paragraphs BC384–BC389 discuss the guidance provided on business combinations achieved in stages. The guidance on combinations achieved without the transfer of consideration merely responds to a question about how to report the acquiree's net assets in the equity section of the acquirer's post-combination statement of financial position, and this Basis for Conclusions does not discuss that guidance further.

Business combinations achieved in stages

BC384   In a business combination achieved in stages, the acquirer remeasures its previously held equity interest at its acquisition-date fair value and recognises the related gain or loss in profit or loss (paragraph 42 of the revised IFRS 3). The boards concluded that a change from holding a non-controlling investment in an entity to obtaining control of that entity is a significant change in the nature of and economic circumstances surrounding that investment. That change warrants a change in the classification and measurement of that investment. Once it obtains control, the acquirer is no longer the owner of a non-controlling investment asset in the acquiree. As in present practice, the acquirer ceases its accounting for an investment asset and begins reporting in its financial statements the underlying assets, liabilities and results of operations of the acquiree. In effect, the acquirer exchanges its status as an owner of an investment asset in an entity for a controlling financial interest in all of the underlying assets and liabilities of that entity (acquiree) and the right to direct how the acquiree and its management use those assets in its operations.

BC385   In August 2003 the FASB held a round-table meeting with members of its resource group on business combinations and other constituents to discuss, among other things, the decision to require an acquirer to remeasure any previously held equity investment in an acquiree at its acquisition-date fair value and to recognise in earnings any gain or loss. The users of financial statements indicated they did not have significant concerns with that change to present practice, as long as the amount of the gain or loss is clearly disclosed in the financial statements or in the notes. Paragraph B64(p) of the revised IFRS 3 requires that disclosure.

BC386   The boards rejected the view expressed by some constituents that the carrying amount of any pre-acquisition investment should be retained in the initial accounting for the cost of the business acquired. The boards concluded that cost-accumulation practices led to many of the inconsistencies and deficiencies in financial reporting as required by SFAS 141 and, to a lesser extent, by IFRS 3 (see paragraphs BC198–BC202).

BC387 Some constituents also expressed concern about what they described as allowing an opportunity for gain recognition on a purchase transaction. The boards noted that the required remeasurement could also result in loss recognition. Moreover, the boards rejected the characterisation that the result is to recognise a gain or loss on a purchase. Rather, under today's mixed attribute accounting model, economic gains and losses are recognised as they occur for some, but not all, financial instruments. If an equity interest in an entity is not required to be measured at its fair value, the recognition of a gain or loss at the acquisition date is merely a consequence of the delayed recognition of the economic gain or loss that is present in that financial instrument. If the investment asset had been measured at fair value at the end of each reporting period, the gain or loss would have been recognised as it occurred and measurement of the asset at its acquisition-date fair value would result in no further gain or loss.

BC388 Some respondents who agreed that an acquirer should remeasure its previously held equity interest at fair value would recognise any resulting gain or loss in other comprehensive income rather than in profit or loss. Those respondents said that the accounting for previously held equity interests is similar to the accounting for available-for-sale securities. Changes in the value of available-for-sale securities are recognised in other comprehensive income. They view each step in a step acquisition as a transaction in which the acquirer only obtains more shares in the acquiree. Because the shares that the acquirer previously held have not been exchanged or sold, they think that the recognition of profit or loss is not appropriate.

BC389 The boards understand that the required treatment of a previously held equity investment in a step acquisition is different from the initial recognition of gains or losses on available-for-sale securities. However, the boards noted that changes in the value of available-for-sale securities are recognised in profit or loss when the securities are derecognised. In a business combination achieved in stages, the acquirer derecognises its investment asset in an entity in its consolidated financial statements when it achieves control. Thus, the boards concluded that it is appropriate to recognise any resulting gain or loss in profit or loss at the acquisition date.

Measurement period

BC390 The revised standards provide an acquirer with a reasonable period after the acquisition date, a *measurement period*, during which to obtain the information necessary to identify and measure the items specified in paragraph 46 of the revised IFRS 3 as of the acquisition date in accordance with the requirements of the revised standards. If sufficient information is not available at the acquisition date to measure those amounts, the acquirer determines and recognises provisional amounts until the necessary information becomes available.

BC391 The boards concluded that providing for retrospective adjustments during the measurement period should help to resolve concerns about the quality and availability of information at the acquisition date for measuring the fair values of particular items at that date. Constituents especially indicated such concerns about contingent liabilities and contingent consideration arrangements, which also affect the amount of goodwill or the gain recognised on a bargain purchase.

BC392　The boards decided to place constraints on the period for which it is deemed reasonable to be seeking information necessary to complete the accounting for a business combination. The measurement period ends as soon as the acquirer receives the necessary information about facts and circumstances that existed as of the acquisition date or learns that the information is not obtainable. However, in no circumstances may the measurement period exceed one year from the acquisition date. The boards concluded that allowing a measurement period longer than one year would not be especially helpful; obtaining reliable information about circumstances and conditions that existed more than a year ago is likely to become more difficult as time passes. Of course, the outcome of some contingencies and similar matters may not be known within a year. But the objective of the measurement period is to provide time to obtain the information necessary to measure the fair value of the item as of the acquisition date. Determining the ultimate settlement amount of a contingency or other item is not necessary. Uncertainties about the timing and amount of future cash flows are part of the measure of the fair value of an asset or liability.

BC393　The boards also concluded that acquirers should provide users of their financial statements with relevant information about the status of items that have been measured only provisionally. Thus, paragraph B67(a) of the revised IFRS 3 specifies particular disclosures about those items.

BC394　Both IFRS 3 and SFAS 141 included a period during which an acquirer might measure particular amounts provisionally if the necessary information was not available at the acquisition date. Neither of those provisions was identical to the measurement period guidance in the revised standards, although IFRS 3's was quite similar. However, the measurement period provisions in the revised standards differ in important ways from the allocation period guidance of SFAS 141 and its cost-allocation method. The revised standards emphasise the principle that assets acquired, liabilities assumed and any non-controlling interest in the acquiree should be measured at their acquisition-date fair values. SFAS 141's allocation period and its post-combination adjustments delayed the recognition of assets and liabilities, and those assets and liabilities were not measured at their acquisition-date fair values when they were recognised. Therefore, the FASB decided to replace the SFAS 141 term *allocation period* and its guidance with the measurement period guidance in the revised standards.

BC395　The FASB also decided that to improve the quality of comparative information reported in financial statements and to converge with the requirements of IFRS 3, SFAS 141(R) should require an acquirer:

(a)　to recognise adjustments made during the measurement period to the provisional values of the assets acquired and liabilities assumed as if the accounting for the business combination had been completed at the acquisition date.

(b)　to adjust comparative information in previously issued financial statements, including any change in depreciation, amortisation or other income effect recognised as a result of completing the initial accounting.

BC396   SFAS 141 was silent about whether adjustments during its allocation period were to be reported retrospectively, but the FASB noted that in practice the effects of those adjustments were typically reported in the post-combination period, not retrospectively. The FASB acknowledged concerns that retrospective adjustments and adjusting previously issued comparative information are more costly. The FASB observed, however, that applying measurement period adjustments retrospectively would result in at least two significant benefits: (a) improvements in comparative period information and (b) avoidance of divergent accounting between US entities and others and the reduction of reconciling items and their attendant costs. The FASB concluded, as had the IASB in developing IFRS 3, that those overall benefits outweigh the potential costs of retrospective application.

BC397   Some respondents to the 2005 Exposure Draft (generally those who apply US GAAP rather than IFRSs) disagreed with retrospective application of measurement period adjustments. They regarded measurement period adjustments as similar to changes in estimates, which are accounted for prospectively. They noted that FASB Statement No. 154 *Accounting Changes and Error Corrections* (SFAS 154) and IAS 8 *Accounting Policies, Changes in Accounting Estimates and Errors* both require retrospective adjustment only for changes in accounting policy or restatement for errors.

BC398   In considering those responses, the boards observed that measurement period adjustments in a business combination differ from the changes in estimates dealt with by SFAS 154 and IAS 8. Measurement period adjustments result from information about assets, liabilities and non-controlling interests **as of** the acquisition date that becomes available only after that date. In contrast, adjustments for changes in estimates generally result from changes in facts and circumstances that affect an estimate, for example, a change in technology that affects the useful life of an asset.

BC399   The boards concluded that adjustments during the measurement period following a business combination are more analogous to adjusting events after the end of the reporting period (IAS 10 *Events after the Reporting Period*) than to changes in estimates. The effects of events that occur after the end of an accounting period but before the financial statements for the period are authorised for issue and provide evidence of a condition that existed at the date of the financial statements are reflected in financial statements as of that date. Similarly, the effects of information that first becomes available during the measurement period and provides evidence of conditions or circumstances that existed at the acquisition date should be reflected in the accounting as of that date.

BC400   To recognise measurement period adjustments only prospectively would be inconsistent with the recognition and measurement principles in the revised standards. Thus, although the boards understand the practical and other difficulties with retrospective adjustments, on balance, they concluded that requiring such adjustments in this situation is appropriate.

Disclosures

BC401   Because a business combination often results in a significant change to an entity's operations, the nature and extent of the information disclosed about the transaction bear on users' abilities to assess the effects of such changes on post-combination profit or loss and cash flows. Accordingly, as part of their respective projects that led to IFRS 3 and SFAS 141, the IASB and the FASB both considered the usefulness of the disclosure requirements required by IAS 22 and APB Opinion 16, respectively, for the acquisition method. IFRS 3 and SFAS 141 carried forward disclosures from the earlier requirements for business combinations that remained relevant, eliminated those that did not and modified those that were affected by changes in the recognition or measurement requirements. In the second phase of their projects on business combinations, the boards undertook essentially the same sort of reconsideration of the disclosure requirements in IFRS 3 and SFAS 141, and they also considered particular disclosures requested by respondents to the 2005 Exposure Draft.

BC402   The remainder of this section first reviews the changes that SFAS 141 and IFRS 3 made to the disclosure requirements of APB Opinion 16 and IAS 22 respectively (paragraphs BC403–BC418). Paragraphs BC419–BC428 then discuss the changes the revised standards make to the disclosure requirements of SFAS 141 and IFRS 3.

Disclosure requirements of SFAS 141

Disclosure of information about the purchase price allocation and pro forma sales and earnings

BC403   The 1999 Exposure Draft would have required tabular disclosure of the fair values allocated to each of the major classes of assets and liabilities presented in the statement of financial position and the acquiree's related carrying amounts immediately before its acquisition. That exposure draft also proposed eliminating the pro forma sales and earnings disclosures required by APB Opinion 16.

BC404   Approximately half of the respondents who commented on the proposed requirement to disclose information about the purchase price allocation agreed that the information would be useful in assessing post-acquisition earnings and cash flows of the acquirer. However, some respondents questioned the usefulness of the proposed disclosure of information about the acquiree's carrying amounts of assets acquired and liabilities assumed, particularly if the financial statements of the acquiree were not audited or were prepared on a basis other than US GAAP. After considering those views, the FASB affirmed its conclusion that information about the allocation of the purchase price to major classes of assets and liabilities in the statement of financial position would be useful in assessing the amount and timing of future cash flows. However, it agreed that information about the related carrying amounts might be of limited usefulness. Thus, SFAS 141 required disclosure of information about the allocation of the purchase price to each major class of asset and liability in the acquiree's statement of financial position but not their previous carrying amounts.

BC405   After considering respondents' views, the FASB included in SFAS 141 the pro forma disclosure requirements from APB Opinion 16. However, the FASB also continued the exemption of non-public entities from the pro forma disclosure requirements. Preparers and auditors of financial statements of non-public entities urged the FASB to continue that exemption, which was initially provided by FASB Statement No. 79 *Elimination of Certain Disclosures for Business Combinations by Nonpublic Enterprises*.

Disclosures related to goodwill

BC406 The FASB's 2001 Exposure Draft (see paragraph BC160 for a discussion of that exposure draft) would have required the acquirer to disclose (a) the reasons for the acquisition, including a description of the factors that led to a purchase price that resulted in goodwill and (b) the amount of goodwill assigned to each reportable segment. The requirement to disclose goodwill by reportable segment was limited to entities that are within the scope of FASB Statement No. 131 *Disclosures about Segments of an Enterprise and Related Information*. That exposure draft also proposed requiring disclosure of the amount of goodwill expected to be deductible for tax purposes if the goodwill initially recognised in a material business combination was significant in relation to the total cost of the acquiree. After considering the comments of respondents, the FASB affirmed its conclusion that the information would be useful in estimating the amount and timing of future impairment losses, and SFAS 141 required that disclosure.

Disclosure of information about intangible assets other than goodwill

BC407 If the amount assigned to intangible assets was significant in relation to the total cost of an acquiree, SFAS 141 required disclosure of the following information to help users of financial statements assess the amount and timing of future cash flows:

(a) the total amount assigned to intangible assets subject to amortisation and the total amount assigned to those that are not subject to amortisation;

(b) the amount assigned to each major intangible asset class;

(c) for intangible assets subject to amortisation, the weighted average amortisation period in total and for each major intangible asset class; and

(d) the amount of any significant residual value assumed, both in total and for each major class of intangible asset.

Other disclosure requirements

BC408 The 1999 Exposure Draft proposed, and SFAS 141 required, disclosure of specified information for a series of immaterial business combinations that are material in the aggregate completed in a reporting period:

(a) the number of entities acquired and a brief description of them;

(b) the aggregate cost of the acquired entities, the number of equity interests issued or issuable and the value assigned to them;

(c) the aggregate amount of any contingent payments, options or commitments and the accounting treatment that will be followed should any such contingency occur (if potentially significant in relation to the aggregate cost of the acquired entities); and

(d) the information about goodwill required for a material acquisition if the aggregate amount assigned to goodwill or to other intangible assets acquired was significant in relation to the aggregate cost of the acquired entities.

BC409 In addition, the 1999 Exposure Draft proposed, and SFAS 141 required, that the information required to be disclosed for a completed business combination would also be disclosed for a material business combination completed after the balance sheet date but before the financial statements are authorised for issue (unless disclosure of such information was not practicable). That requirement was consistent with auditing standards on subsequent events.

Disclosures in interim financial information

BC410 Several analysts and other users recommended that the FASB should require disclosure of supplemental pro forma revenues and earnings in interim financial information because that information would be more useful if it was available earlier. SFAS 141 amended APB Opinion No. 28 *Interim Financial Reporting* to require disclosure of that information.

Disclosure requirements of IFRS 3

BC411 IFRS 3 identified three objectives that its disclosure requirements were intended to meet, specifically, to provide the users of an acquirer's financial statements with information that enables them to evaluate:

(a) the nature and financial effect of business combinations that were effected during the reporting period or after the balance sheet date but before the financial statements were authorised for issue.

(b) the financial effects of gains, losses, error corrections and other adjustments recognised in the current period that relate to business combinations that were effected in the current period or in previous periods.

(c) changes in the carrying amount of goodwill during the period.

BC412 The IASB began its discussion of the disclosure requirements necessary to meet the objectives by assessing the disclosure requirements in SIC-28 *Business Combinations—"Date of Exchange" and Fair Value of Equity Instruments* and IAS 22. The IASB concluded that information disclosed in accordance with SIC-28 about equity instruments issued as part of the cost of a business combination helped to meet the first of the three objectives outlined above. Therefore, IFRS 3 carried forward the disclosure requirements in SIC-28.

BC413 The IASB also concluded that information previously disclosed in accordance with IAS 22 about business combinations classified as acquisitions and goodwill helped to meet the objectives in paragraph BC411. Therefore, IFRS 3 carried forward the related disclosure requirements in IAS 22, amended as necessary to reflect changes IFRS 3 made to the provisions of IAS 22. For example, IAS 22 required disclosure of the amount of any adjustment during the period to goodwill or 'negative goodwill' resulting from subsequent identification or changes in value of the acquiree's identifiable assets and liabilities. IFRS 3 required an acquirer, with specified exceptions, to adjust the initial accounting for a combination after that accounting was complete only to correct an error. Thus, IFRS 3 revised the IAS 22 disclosure requirement to require disclosure of information about error corrections required to be disclosed by IAS 8.

BC414 The IASB then assessed whether any additional disclosure requirements should be included in IFRS 3 to ensure that the three disclosure objectives were met and considered the disclosure requirements in the corresponding standards of its partner standard-setters. As a result, and after considering respondents' comments on ED 3, the IASB identified, and IFRS 3 required, the following additional disclosures to help meet the first of the three disclosure objectives in paragraph BC411:

    (a)   For each business combination effected during the period:

        (i)   the amounts recognised at the acquisition date for each class of the acquiree's assets, liabilities and contingent liabilities and, if practicable, the carrying amounts of each of those classes, determined in accordance with IFRSs, immediately before the combination. If such disclosure was impracticable, an entity disclosed that fact, together with an explanation of why disclosure was impracticable.

        (ii)   a description of the factors that contributed to the recognition of goodwill—including a description of each intangible asset that was not recognised separately from goodwill and an explanation of why the intangible asset's fair value could not be measured reliably. If the acquirer's interest in the acquiree's identifiable net assets exceeded the cost, the acquirer was required to describe the nature of that excess.

        (iii)   the amount of the acquiree's profit or loss since the acquisition date included in the acquirer's profit or loss for the period, unless disclosure was impracticable. If such disclosure was impracticable, the acquirer disclosed that fact, together with an explanation of why disclosure was impracticable.

    (b)   The information required to be disclosed for each business combination that was effected during the period in aggregate for business combinations that are individually immaterial.

    (c)   The revenue and profit or loss of the combined entity for the period as though the acquisition date for all business combinations that were effected during the period had been the beginning of that period, unless such disclosure was impracticable.

BC415 To aid in meeting the second disclosure objective in paragraph BC411, IFRS 3 also required disclosure of the amount and an explanation of any gain or loss recognised in the current period that both:

    (a)   related to the identifiable assets acquired or liabilities or contingent liabilities assumed in a business combination that was effected in the current or a previous period; and

    (b)   was of such size, nature or incidence that disclosure was relevant to an understanding of the combined entity's financial performance.

BC416　To help achieve the third disclosure objective in paragraph BC411, the IASB concluded that the previous requirement to disclose a reconciliation of the carrying amount of goodwill at the beginning and end of the period should be amended to require separate disclosure of net exchange rate differences arising during the period in accordance with IAS 21 *The Effects of Changes in Foreign Exchange Rates*.

BC417　The IASB observed that there might be situations in which the information disclosed under the specific requirements would not completely satisfy IFRS 3's three disclosure objectives. In that situation, IFRS 3 required disclosure of any additional information necessary to meet those objectives.

BC418　IFRS 3 also required the acquirer to disclose the number of equity instruments issued or issuable as part of the cost of a business combination, the fair value of those instruments and the basis for determining that fair value. Although IAS 22 did not explicitly require disclosure of that information, the IASB concluded that the acquirer should have provided it as part of disclosing the cost of acquisition and a description of the purchase consideration paid or contingently payable in accordance with paragraph 87(b) of IAS 22. The IASB decided that to avoid inconsistent application, IFRS 3 should explicitly require disclosure of that information.

Disclosure requirements of the revised standards

BC419　The boards decided that the revised standards should include overall objectives for the disclosure of information that would be useful to investors, creditors and others in evaluating the financial effects of a business combination. The objectives, which are stated in paragraphs 59 and 61 of the revised IFRS 3, are, in substance, the same as those in IFRS 3 and the 2005 Exposure Draft. Respondents to the 2005 Exposure Draft who discussed the proposed disclosures generally agreed with the disclosure objectives. In reconsidering that exposure draft, however, the boards noted that the third objective in IFRS 3, to provide information that enables users of an entity's financial statements to evaluate changes in the carrying amount of goodwill during the period, is effectively included in the objective in paragraph 61. Thus, the boards combined those two objectives.

BC420　In addition, both boards concluded, as the IASB did in developing IFRS 3, that it is not necessary (or possible) to identify all of the specific information that may be necessary to meet those objectives for all business combinations. Rather, the revised standards specify particular disclosures that are generally required to meet those objectives and require acquirers to disclose any additional information about the circumstances surrounding a particular business combination that they consider necessary to meet those objectives (paragraph 63 of the revised IFRS 3).

BC421　Changes to the disclosure requirements of IFRS 3 and SFAS 141 include the elimination of disclosures of amounts or information that was based on applying the cost allocation (purchase price) method for assigning amounts to assets and liabilities that is replaced by the revised standards' fair value measurement principle. Some of those disclosures are modified to retain the information but conform the amounts to be disclosed with the fair value measurement principle.

BC422   The boards added some disclosure requirements to those in IFRS 3, SFAS 141 or both and modified or eliminated others. Those changes are described below, together with an indication of how the changes relate to each board's previous requirements and references to related discussions in other parts of this Basis for Conclusions where pertinent.

(a)   In response to requests from some commentators on the 2005 Exposure Draft, the boards added to both IFRS 3 and SFAS 141 disclosure of information about receivables acquired. (paragraphs BC258–BC260)

(b)   The boards modified both IFRS 3's and SFAS 141's disclosures about contingent consideration in a business combination to make them consistent with the revised standards' requirements for contingent consideration. Paragraph B64(g) of the revised IFRS 3 describes the specific disclosures now required.

(c)   The FASB added to SFAS 141 disclosure of the revenue and earnings of the acquiree, if practicable, for a minimum of the period from the acquisition date to the end of the current year. The disclosure is required only from public business entities for the current year, the current interim period and cumulative interim periods from the acquisition date to the end of the current year. IFRS 3 already required disclosure of the amount of the acquiree's profit or loss included in the acquirer's profit or loss for the period, unless that was impracticable; the IASB added revenues to that disclosure. (paragraphs BC423–BC428)

(d)   The FASB modified SFAS 141's disclosure of supplemental pro forma information about results of operations for the comparable prior period presented to focus on revenue and earnings of the combined entity for the comparable prior reporting period as though the acquisition date for all business combinations during the current year had been the beginning of the comparable prior annual reporting period. The disclosure is required only from public entities and only if practicable. The IASB decided not to add that disclosure. (paragraph BC428)

(e)   The FASB replaced SFAS 141's disclosure of the period for which the results of operations of the acquiree are included in the income statement of the combined entity with disclosure of the acquisition date—a disclosure that IFRS 3 already required. SFAS 141(R) no longer permits the alternative practice of reporting revenues and expenses of the acquiree as if the acquisition occurred as of the beginning of the year (or a designated date) with a reduction to eliminate the acquiree's pre-acquisition period earnings. (paragraphs BC108–BC110)

(f)   The boards revised both IFRS 3's and SFAS 141's disclosures about contingencies, at the acquisition date and subsequently, to make them consistent with the requirement of the revised standards on assets and liabilities arising from contingencies. The IASB's and the FASB's disclosures on contingencies differ because the recognition requirements to which they relate differ. (paragraphs BC265–BC278)

(g)   The FASB added to SFAS 141 disclosure of the amount of acquisition-related costs, which IFRS 3 already required, and the boards added to both IFRS 3 and SFAS 141 disclosure of the amount of acquisition-related costs recognised as expense and the statement of comprehensive income line item in which that expense is reported.

(h) The FASB eliminated SFAS 141's requirement to disclose the amount of in-process research and development acquired that had been measured and immediately written off to expense in accordance with FASB Interpretation 4. SFAS 141(R) no longer permits that practice. (paragraphs BC149–BC155)

(i) The boards added to both IFRS 3 and SFAS 141 disclosure of the acquisition-date fair value or other recognised amount of the non-controlling interest in the acquiree and the valuation techniques and key model inputs used for determining that value. An entity that prepares its financial statements in accordance with IFRSs also discloses the measurement basis selected for the non-controlling interest.

(j) For a business combination achieved in stages, the boards added to both IFRS 3 and SFAS 141 disclosure of the fair value of the acquirer's previously held equity interest in the acquiree, the amount of gain or loss recognised in accordance with paragraph 42 of the revised IFRS 3 and the line item in the statement of comprehensive income in which that gain or loss is recognised.

(k) The FASB replaced SFAS 141's disclosure of extraordinary gains recognised for 'negative goodwill' with disclosure of the amount of any gain recognised in the period for a bargain purchase, the line item in the statement of comprehensive income in which it is recognised and a description of the reasons why the transaction resulted in a gain (paragraphs BC371–BC381). IFRS 3 already required disclosure of that amount (although it was not called a gain on a bargain purchase).

(l) The boards added to both IFRS 3 and SFAS 141 the disclosures described in paragraph B64(l) of the revised IFRS 3 about transactions that are separate from the acquisition of assets and assumption of liabilities in the exchange for the acquiree. The 2005 Exposure Draft proposed requiring disclosures about only pre-existing relationships between the acquirer and acquiree. The boards broadened the disclosure to all separate transactions in response to comments on the exposure draft.

(m) The boards revised the disclosures in IFRS 3 and SFAS 141 about aspects of the purchase price allocation not yet completed to make them consistent with the requirements of the revised standards about the measurement period. The specific disclosures required are in paragraph B67(a) of the revised IFRS 3.

(n) The IASB eliminated IFRS 3's required disclosure of the acquiree's carrying amounts in accordance with IFRSs for each class of its assets and liabilities immediately before the combination. The IASB concluded that providing that disclosure could often involve significant costs because the acquiree might not be applying IFRSs and that those costs might exceed the benefits of the information to users.

Disclosure of information about post-combination revenue and profit or loss of the acquiree

BC423   Paragraph B64(q) of the revised IFRS 3 requires an entity to disclose, for each business combination (and for individually immaterial business combinations that are material collectively), the amounts of revenue and profit or loss of the acquiree since the acquisition date included in the consolidated statement of comprehensive income for the period. At its August 2003 round-table discussion with users of financial statements, the FASB discussed the potential usefulness of information about increases or decreases in post-combination revenues and earnings from acquired businesses versus revenues and earnings from the operations already owned by the acquirer (organic growth). The FASB also asked whether that information would be preferable to the pro forma supplemental disclosure of revenue and results of operations of the combined entity for the current period as though the acquisition date for all business combinations during the year had been as of the beginning of the annual reporting period. SFAS 141 carried that disclosure forward from APB Opinion 16 and IFRS 3 required a similar disclosure.

BC424   The FASB also questioned whether those disclosures are directed at similar objectives and, if so, whether one may be preferable. The FASB observed that making post-combination distinctions might be too costly or impossible if the operations of the acquiree are integrated with those of the acquirer. Although users acknowledged that point, they indicated that information about actual post-combination revenues and earnings is preferable to the pro forma disclosures and should be required whenever possible. Some also said that distinguishing acquired revenues from organic revenues is most important and suggested that acquirers should be required to provide that information for a twelve-month period following an acquisition rather than only to the end of the annual period.

BC425   The boards agreed with users that the information about post-combination revenues and profit or loss of the acquiree is useful. However, for practical reasons, the boards concluded that the revised standards should provide an exception to that requirement if distinguishing the post-combination earnings of the acquiree from earnings of the combined entity is impracticable. The boards also decided that in those circumstances the acquirer should disclose that fact and the reasons why it is impracticable to provide the post-combination information. The period for that disclosure is limited to the end of the current annual period because the boards concluded that the information needed to provide the disclosure during that period will generally be available. A short period is often required to integrate an acquiree's operations fully with those of the acquirer. The boards also observed that the usefulness of the separate information diminishes as the operations of the acquiree are integrated with the combined entity.

BC426   The FASB proposed in its version of the 2005 Exposure Draft that the post-combination disclosures should focus on *results of operations* rather than on revenues and earnings. *Results of operations* was defined as revenue, income before extraordinary items and the cumulative effect of accounting changes, earnings and earnings per share. In considering the responses to the exposure draft and opportunities for further convergence, the FASB decided to revise its disclosures to focus on revenues and earnings, which is consistent with the related requirements of the IASB. The boards observed that the term *results of operations* is not used or defined in IFRSs; it would thus have been more difficult for the IASB to converge with the disclosures initially proposed by the FASB.

BC427 The FASB considered expanding the disclosure of post-combination revenues and earnings of an acquiree to all entities because the information would be valuable to any investor, not merely investors in public business entities. To do so would also converge with the requirements of the IASB. However, the FASB was concerned about imposing the additional costs on non-public entities because it believes that the benefits to users of those entities would not be sufficient to warrant imposing those costs. The FASB also observed that the IASB has not completed its separate deliberations on its small and medium-sized entities project and thus does not have an established practice of differential disclosure for circumstances in which it is clear that the benefits would be sufficient for some entities but not so clear for all entities. Because of those cost-benefit concerns, the FASB decided not to extend this disclosure requirement to all entities.

BC428 If comparative financial statements are presented, the FASB decided to require disclosure of supplemental pro forma information about the revenue and earnings of the combined entity for the comparable prior reporting period as though the acquisition date for all business combinations during the current year had been the beginning of the comparable prior annual reporting period. The disclosure is required only for public entities and only if practicable. The IASB considered also requiring that disclosure, but it observed that the needed information would be particularly difficult and costly to obtain in the international environment. An entity that prepares its financial statements in accordance with IFRSs might in a given year acquire other entities that had previously applied the domestic reporting requirements of several different countries. Because the IASB did not consider it feasible to require the disclosure in the international environment, the revised IFRS 3 requires only disclosure of revenues and profit or loss for the current reporting period determined as though the acquisition date for all combinations during the period had been as of the beginning of the annual reporting period.

Effective date and transition

BC429 SFAS 141(R) is effective for business combinations for which the acquisition date is on or after the beginning of the first annual reporting period beginning on or after 15 December 2008, ie for 2009 financial statements. The IASB decided to provide a slightly later effective date. The revised IFRS 3 is effective for business combinations for which the acquisition date is on or after the beginning of the first annual reporting period beginning on or after 1 July 2009. The IASB made a commitment to its constituents that there would be a transition period of approximately 18 months between the publication date and the effective date of the revised IFRS 3 as part of its commitment to have a period of stability following the initial transition to IFRSs. The FASB decided to make SFAS 141(R) effective as soon as practicable, ie for 2009 financial statements. The FASB believes that that effective date provides sufficient time for entities and their auditors to analyse, interpret and prepare for implementation of the provisions of SFAS 141(R).

BC430   The boards also concluded that the effective date of the revised standards should be the same as that of the amendments to their respective consolidation standards (FASB Statement No. 160 *Noncontrolling Interests in Consolidated Financial Statements* and the IASB's amendments to IAS 27). Particular provisions in those amendments, which address the subsequent accounting for an acquiree in consolidated financial statements, are related to provisions in the revised standards that address the initial accounting for an acquiree at the acquisition date. The boards concluded that linking the timing of the changes in accounting required by those amendments to those required by the revised standards would minimise disruptions to practice, which benefits both preparers and users of financial statements.

BC431   SFAS 141(R) prohibits early application and the revised IFRS 3 permits early application. The FASB's Investors Technical Advisory Committee and other users of financial statements told the FASB that providing alternatives for when entities adopt a new standard impairs comparability. The IASB observed, however, that the changes to IFRS 3 are less extensive than the changes to SFAS 141. In addition, the IASB observed that IAS 27 is silent on the accounting for changes in controlling ownership interests in a subsidiary and it wanted entities to be able to adopt the guidance in the amended IAS 27 as soon as it is published. Accordingly, the IASB retained the proposal in the 2005 Exposure Draft to permit entities to adopt the revised IFRS 3 early if they so choose.

BC432   The IASB and the FASB also concluded that the revised standards should be applied prospectively. As with most other requirements that relate to particular types of transactions, applying the revised standards retrospectively would not be feasible.

Effective date and transition for combinations of mutual entities or by contract alone

BC433   IFRS 3 excluded from its scope combinations of mutual entities and those achieved by contract alone. In developing IFRS 3, the IASB decided that these combinations should be excluded from its scope until the IASB published interpretative guidance for the application of the acquisition method to those transactions. The revised IFRS 3 provides that guidance. The effective date for combinations of mutual entities and those achieved by contract alone is the same as the effective date for all other entities applying the revised IFRS 3.

BC434   For the reasons outlined in paragraph BC180 of IFRS 3 the IASB concluded that the transitional provisions for combinations involving mutual entities only or those achieved by contract alone should be prospective. Given that these combinations were not within the scope of IFRS 3, they may have been accounted for differently from what IFRS 3 required. The transitional provisions in IFRS 3 took into consideration that entities may have used a range of alternatives in accounting for combinations in the past. The IASB concluded that the transitional provisions for these combinations should incorporate the transitional provisions in IFRS 3 for other business combinations. In addition, the IASB concluded that the transitional provisions should provide that an entity should continue to classify prior combinations in accordance with its previous accounting for such combinations. This is consistent with the prospective approach. Those provisions are contained in paragraphs B68 and B69 of the revised IFRS 3.

Benefits and costs

BC435 The objective of financial statements is to provide information about the financial position, performance and changes in financial position of an entity that is useful to a wide range of users in making economic decisions. However, the benefits derived from information should exceed the cost of providing it. The evaluation of benefits and costs is substantially a judgemental process. Furthermore, the costs do not necessarily fall on those who enjoy the benefits. For these reasons, it is difficult to apply a cost-benefit test in any particular case. In making its judgement, the IASB considers:

(a) the costs incurred by preparers of financial statements;

(b) the costs incurred by users of financial statements when information is not available;

(c) the comparative advantage that preparers have in developing information, when compared with the costs that users would incur to develop surrogate information; and

(d) the benefit of better economic decision-making as a result of improved financial reporting.

In the second phase of the business combinations project the IASB also considered the costs and benefits of the revised IFRS 3 relative to IFRS 3.

BC436 The IASB concluded that the revised IFRS 3 benefits both preparers and users of financial statements by converging to common high quality, understandable and enforceable accounting standards for business combinations in IFRSs and US GAAP. This improves the comparability of financial information around the world and it also simplifies and reduces the costs of accounting for entities that issue financial statements in accordance with both IFRSs and US GAAP.

BC437 The revised IFRS 3 builds on the core principles established by IFRS 3. However, the IASB sought to improve the understandability, relevance, reliability and comparability of information provided to users of financial statements as follows:

(a) **Scope**

The revised IFRS 3 has a broader scope than IFRS 3. Those entities that will now be required to apply the acquisition method might incur additional costs to obtain valuations and account for intangible assets and goodwill after the acquisition date. However, the IASB observes that much of the information required to account for a business combination by applying the acquisition method is already prepared by those entities that are currently applying the pooling of interests method. There might be additional costs associated with presenting this information within the financial statements, such as audit costs, but much of the information will already be available to management. The IASB concluded therefore that the benefits of improved comparability and faithful representation outweigh the costs that those entities will incur.

(b) **Non-controlling interest**

Paragraph 19 of the revised IFRS 3 provides preparers of financial statements with a choice for each business combination to measure

© IASCF

initially a non-controlling interest either at fair value or as the non-controlling interest's proportionate share of the acquiree's identifiable net assets. Paragraphs BC209–BC221 discuss the benefits and costs associated with granting a choice on how non-controlling interests should be measured.

(c)   **Contingent consideration**

Paragraph 58 of the revised IFRS 3 requires contingent consideration that is classified as a liability and is within the scope of IAS 39[*] to be remeasured to fair value (or for those within the scope of IAS 37 or another IFRS, to be accounted for in accordance with that IFRS) and that contingent consideration classified as equity is not remeasured. The IASB understands that remeasuring the fair value of contingent consideration after the acquisition date results in additional costs to preparers. Preparers will need to measure the fair value of these arrangements or will need to obtain external valuations at the end of each reporting period. However, users have stated that the information they receive under IFRS 3 is too late to be useful. The IASB concluded therefore that the benefits of relevance and representational faithfulness and the increased information that would be provided to users outweigh the costs.

(d)   **Acquisition-related costs**

Paragraph 53 of the revised IFRS 3 requires the costs the acquirer incurs in connection with a business combination to be accounted for separately from the business combination. The IASB concluded that this treatment would improve the understandability of the information provided to users of financial statements. The IASB observed that the new requirement does not create significant additional costs for preparers of financial statements because paragraph 67(d) of IFRS 3 already required disclosure of acquisition-related costs.

(e)   **Business combinations achieved in stages**

The revised IFRS 3 establishes the acquisition date as the single measurement date for all assets acquired, liabilities assumed and any non-controlling interest in the acquiree. In a business combination achieved in stages, the acquirer also remeasures its previously held equity interest in the acquiree at its acquisition-date fair value and recognises the resulting gain or loss, if any, in profit or loss. In contrast, IFRS 3 required that for a business combination achieved in stages each exchange transaction should be treated separately by the acquirer, using the cost of the transaction and fair value information at the date of each exchange transaction, to determine the amount of any goodwill associated with that transaction. Therefore, the previous treatment required a comparison of the cost of the individual investments with the acquirer's interest in the fair values of the acquiree's identifiable assets and liabilities at each step. The IASB concluded that the revised treatment of business combinations

---

[*]   In November 2009 the IASB amended the requirements of IAS 39 relating to classification and measurement of assets within the scope of IAS 39 and relocated them to IFRS 9 *Financial Instruments*. IFRS 9 applies to all assets within the scope of IAS 39. This paragraph discusses matters relevant when IFRS 3 was issued.

achieved in stages would improve understandability and relevance of the information provided as well as reduce the cost of accounting for such transactions.

BC438   The IASB concluded that the guidance in the revised IFRS 3 is not unduly complex. Indeed, it eliminates guidance that many have found to be complex, costly and arbitrary and that has been the source of considerable uncertainties and costs in the marketplace. Moreover, the revised IFRS 3 does not introduce a new method of accounting but rather expands the use of the acquisition-method of accounting that is familiar, has been widely used and for which there is a substantial base of experience. However, the IASB also sought to reduce the costs of applying the revised IFRS 3 by:

(a)   requiring particular assets and liabilities (eg those related to deferred taxes and employee benefits) to continue to be measured in accordance with existing accounting standards rather than at fair value;

(b)   carrying over the basic requirements of IFRS 3 on contingent liabilities assumed in a business combination into the revised IFRS 3 until the IASB has comprehensively reconsidered the accounting for contingencies in its liabilities project; and

(c)   requiring the revised IFRS 3 to be applied prospectively rather than retrospectively.

BC439   The IASB acknowledges that those steps may result in some sacrifice to the benefits of improved information in financial statements in accordance with the revised IFRS 3. However, the IASB concluded that the complexities and related costs that would result from applying the fair value measurement requirement to all assets and liabilities, at this time, and requiring retrospective application are not justified.

Appendix
Amendments to the Basis for Conclusions on other IFRSs

This appendix contains amendments to the Basis for Conclusions on other IFRSs that are necessary in order to ensure consistency with IFRS 3 (as revised in 2008) and the related amendments to other IFRSs. Amended paragraphs are shown with new text underlined and deleted text struck through.

* * * * *

The amendments contained in this appendix when the revised IFRS 3 was issued in 2008 have been incorporated into the text of the Basis for Conclusions on IFRSs 2, 4 and 5 and on IASs 36 and 38 as issued at 10 January 2008.

Dissenting opinions

Dissent of Mary E Barth, Robert P Garnett and John T Smith

DO1   Professor Barth and Messrs Garnett and Smith dissent from the publication of IFRS 3 *Business Combinations* (as revised in 2008), for the reasons set out below.

Measurement of non-controlling interest

DO2   Professor Barth and Mr Smith disagree with the Board's decision to make an exception to the IFRS's measurement principle and permit acquirers a free choice, acquisition by acquisition, to measure any non-controlling interest in an acquiree as the non-controlling interest's proportionate share of the acquiree's identifiable net assets, rather than at fair value (paragraph 19 of the IFRS).

DO3   Professor Barth and Mr Smith agree with the measurement principle as explained in paragraph BC207 that the acquirer should recognise the identifiable assets acquired, the liabilities assumed and any non-controlling interest in the acquiree at their acquisition-date fair values. Paragraph BC209 indicates that the Board also supports this principle, but decided to make an exception. Professor Barth and Mr Smith support the Board's general view that exceptions should be avoided because they undermine principle-based standards, but understand that they are necessary in well-justified circumstances. Professor Barth and Mr Smith do not believe that an exception to this principle, with a free choice in applying it, is justified in this situation.

DO4   First, Professor Barth and Mr Smith are among those Board members mentioned in paragraph BC213 who believe that non-controlling interests can be measured reliably. Second, Professor Barth and Mr Smith believe that the benefits of consistently measuring all assets acquired and liabilities assumed outweigh the costs involved in conducting the measurement. To address concerns about costs exceeding benefits in particular acquisitions, they would have supported an exception to the principle based on undue cost or effort. Such an exception would not have been a free choice, but would have required assessment of the facts and circumstances associated with the acquisition. Professor Barth and Mr Smith disagree with the Board's decision to permit a free choice, rather than to adopt such an exception. They also disagree with the Board's decision not to require fair value measurement even for acquisitions of listed acquirees, for which the cost would be nil. Third, a consequence of failure to measure non-controlling interests at fair value is that acquired goodwill is not measured at fair value. In addition to being an exception to the IFRS's measurement principle, this has several undesirable effects beyond the initial accounting for goodwill. The Board acknowledges these in paragraphs BC217 and BC218. In particular, if goodwill is impaired the impairment loss is understated, and if the acquirer subsequently purchases more of the non-controlling interests equity is reduced more than it would be had goodwill been measured initially at fair value. Fourth, based on staff research, the choice will benefit only a minority of acquirers because most acquisitions are for 100 per cent of the acquiree. As noted above, any benefit is reduced if such acquirers subsequently impair goodwill or acquire more of the non-controlling interest because of the resulting anomalous accounting results.

DO5   Professor Barth and Mr Smith agree with the Board that permitting entities a choice between alternative accounting methods impairs comparability, as noted in paragraph BC210. They disagree with the Board's decision not to support a single method, particularly a method consistent with the IFRS's measurement principle. However, Professor Barth and Mr Smith disagree with the Board that the benefits of other changes to the IFRS outweigh the disadvantages of permitting entities that acquire less than 100 per cent of an acquiree a free choice as to how to account for the acquisition. Although Professor Barth and Mr Smith agree with the other changes to IFRS 3, they believe that these changes are not as important as having a consistent measurement principle.

DO6   In addition to improving the accounting for business combinations, a primary goal of the business combinations project was to achieve convergence between IFRS 3 and FASB Statement No. 141 (revised 2007) *Business Combinations* (SFAS 141(R)). Professor Barth and Mr Smith strongly support that goal. The Board's decision to make the exception to the measurement principle for non-controlling interests creates a divergence from SFAS 141(R). Both the FASB and the IASB made compromises to achieve a converged result in other aspects of the IFRS, and the FASB made a number of changes to its standard that conform to IFRS 3 (as issued in 2004). Professor Barth and Mr Smith believe that the Board's compromise on this particular issue diminishes the importance of convergence, establishes a precedent for allowing a choice when the two boards cannot reach agreement and may suggest that full convergence in the long term cannot be achieved. This is particularly concerning for this decision given that the Board supports the principle underlying the FASB's answer, there are comparability costs inherent in a free choice of accounting methods and there are likely to be few benefits arising from the exception.

DO7   Mr Garnett dissents from the issue of the IFRS because it both establishes a measurement principle for non-controlling interests with which he disagrees, and permits an exception to that principle. Whilst the exception permits the accounting that he considers appropriate, the use of alternative accounting methods reduces the comparability of financial statements.

DO8   Mr Garnett observes that the application of the measurement principle that an acquirer should measure the components of a business combination, including non-controlling interests, at their acquisition-date fair values results in the recognition of not only the purchased goodwill attributable to the acquirer as a result of the acquisition transaction, but also the goodwill attributable to the non-controlling interest in the acquiree. This is often referred to as the 'full goodwill' method.

DO9   Mr Garnett considers that goodwill is unlike other assets since it cannot be identified separately, or measured directly. Purchased goodwill is a residual resulting from a calculation that absorbs the effects of recognition and measurement exceptions made in the IFRS (such as the accounting for employee benefit plans and deferred taxes) and any differences between an entry price used in valuing the business as a whole and the valuation of the individual assets and liabilities acquired.

DO10 Mr Garnett notes that the 'parent-only' approach to goodwill in the previous version of IFRS 3 (as issued in 2004) avoids this difficulty by measuring goodwill as the difference between the fair value of the consideration paid by the parent for the acquiree and its share of the fair value of the identifiable net assets of the acquiree. Thus, purchased goodwill is the amount implicit in the acquisition transaction and excludes any goodwill attributable to non-controlling interests. This method gives rise to more reliable measurement because it is based on the purchase consideration, which can usually be reliably measured, and it reflects faithfully the acquisition transaction to which the non-controlling interests were not a party.

A business combination achieved in stages

DO11 Mr Garnett disagrees with the requirement in a business combination achieved in stages to recognise the effect of remeasuring any previously-held equity interest in the acquiree to fair value through profit or loss (paragraph 42 of the IFRS), because that investment was not part of the exchange. Mr Garnett agrees that gaining control is a significant economic event that warrants a change from investment accounting to consolidation. However, the previous investment has not been sold. Under current IFRSs, gains and losses on cost method, available-for-sale and equity method investments are recognised in profit or loss only when the investment is sold (other than impairment). Mr Garnett would have recognised the effect of those remeasurements as a separate component of other comprehensive income instead of profit or loss.

CONTENTS

IFRS 3 *Business Combinations*
Illustrative examples

These examples accompany, but are not part of, IFRS 3.

Reverse acquisitions

Illustrating the consequences of recognising a reverse acquisition by applying paragraphs B19–B27 of IFRS 3.

IE1   This example illustrates the accounting for a reverse acquisition in which Entity B, the legal subsidiary, acquires Entity A, the entity issuing equity instruments and therefore the legal parent, in a reverse acquisition on 30 September 20X6. This example ignores the accounting for any income tax effects.

IE2   The statements of financial position of Entity A and Entity B immediately before the business combination are:

	Entity A (legal parent, accounting acquiree)	Entity B (legal subsidiary, accounting acquirer)
	CU*	CU
Current assets	500	700
Non-current assets	1,300	3,000
Total assets	1,800	3,700
Current liabilities	300	600
Non-current liabilities	400	1,100
Total liabilities	700	1,700
Shareholders' equity		
Retained earnings	800	1,400
Issued equity		
100 ordinary shares	300	
60 ordinary shares		600
Total shareholders' equity	1,100	2,000
Total liabilities and shareholders' equity	1,800	3,700

IE3   This example also uses the following information:

(a)   On 30 September 20X6 Entity A issues 2.5 shares in exchange for each ordinary share of Entity B. All of Entity B's shareholders exchange their shares in Entity B. Therefore, Entity A issues 150 ordinary shares in exchange for all 60 ordinary shares of Entity B.

---

*   In these examples monetary amounts are denominated in 'currency units (CU)'.

© IASCF

(b) The fair value of each ordinary share of Entity B at 30 September 20X6 is CU40. The quoted market price of Entity A's ordinary shares at that date is CU16.

(c) The fair values of Entity A's identifiable assets and liabilities at 30 September 20X6 are the same as their carrying amounts, except that the fair value of Entity A's non-current assets at 30 September 20X6 is CU1,500.

Calculating the fair value of the consideration transferred

IE4   As a result of Entity A (legal parent, accounting acquiree) issuing 150 ordinary shares, Entity B's shareholders own 60 per cent of the issued shares of the combined entity (ie 150 of 250 issued shares). The remaining 40 per cent are owned by Entity A's shareholders. If the business combination had taken the form of Entity B issuing additional ordinary shares to Entity A's shareholders in exchange for their ordinary shares in Entity A, Entity B would have had to issue 40 shares for the ratio of ownership interest in the combined entity to be the same. Entity B's shareholders would then own 60 of the 100 issued shares of Entity B—60 per cent of the combined entity. As a result, the fair value of the consideration effectively transferred by Entity B and the group's interest in Entity A is CU1,600 (40 shares with a fair value per share of CU40).

IE5   The fair value of the consideration effectively transferred should be based on the most reliable measure. In this example, the quoted market price of Entity A's shares provides a more reliable basis for measuring the consideration effectively transferred than the estimated fair value of the shares in Entity B, and the consideration is measured using the market price of Entity A's shares—100 shares with a fair value per share of CU16.

Measuring goodwill

IE6   Goodwill is measured as the excess of the fair value of the consideration effectively transferred (the group's interest in Entity A) over the net amount of Entity A's recognised identifiable assets and liabilities, as follows:

	CU	CU
Consideration effectively transferred		1,600
Net recognised values of Entity A's identifiable assets and liabilities		
Current assets	500	
Non-current assets	1,500	
Current liabilities	(300)	
Non-current liabilities	(400)	(1,300)
Goodwill		300

Consolidated statement of financial position at 30 September 20X6

IE7   The consolidated statement of financial position immediately after the business combination is:

	CU
Current assets [CU700 + CU500]	1,200
Non-current assets [CU3,000 + CU1,500]	4,500
Goodwill	300
Total assets	6,000
Current liabilities [CU600 + CU300]	900
Non-current liabilities [CU1,100 + CU400]	1,500
Total liabilities	2,400
Shareholders' equity	
Retained earnings	1,400
Issued equity	
250 ordinary shares [CU600 + CU1,600]	2,200
Total shareholders' equity	3,600
Total liabilities and shareholders' equity	6,000

IE8   The amount recognised as issued equity interests in the consolidated financial statements (CU2,200) is determined by adding the issued equity of the legal subsidiary immediately before the business combination (CU600) and the fair value of the consideration effectively transferred (CU1,600). However, the equity structure appearing in the consolidated financial statements (ie the number and type of equity interests issued) must reflect the equity structure of the legal parent, including the equity interests issued by the legal parent to effect the combination.

Earnings per share

IE9 Assume that Entity B's earnings for the annual period ended 31 December 20X5 were CU600 and that the consolidated earnings for the annual period ended 31 December 20X6 were CU800. Assume also that there was no change in the number of ordinary shares issued by Entity B during the annual period ended 31 December 20X5 and during the period from 1 January 20X6 to the date of the reverse acquisition on 30 September 20X6. Earnings per share for the annual period ended 31 December 20X6 is calculated as follows:

Number of shares deemed to be outstanding for the period from 1 January 20X6 to the acquisition date (ie the number of ordinary shares issued by Entity A (legal parent, accounting acquiree) in the reverse acquisition)	150
Number of shares outstanding from the acquisition date to 31 December 20X6	250
Weighted average number of ordinary shares outstanding [(150 × 9/12) + (250 × 3/12)]	175
Earnings per share [800/175]	CU4.57

IE10 Restated earnings per share for the annual period ended 31 December 20X5 is CU4.00 (calculated as the earnings of Entity B of 600 divided by the number of ordinary shares Entity A issued in the reverse acquisition (150)).

Non-controlling interest

IE11 Assume the same facts as above, except that only 56 of Entity B's 60 ordinary shares are exchanged. Because Entity A issues 2.5 shares in exchange for each ordinary share of Entity B, Entity A issues only 140 (rather than 150) shares. As a result, Entity B's shareholders own 58.3 per cent of the issued shares of the combined entity (140 of 240 issued shares). The fair value of the consideration transferred for Entity A, the accounting acquiree, is calculated by assuming that the combination had been effected by Entity B issuing additional ordinary shares to the shareholders of Entity A in exchange for their ordinary shares in Entity A. That is because Entity A is the accounting acquirer, and paragraph B20 of IFRS 3 requires the acquirer to measure the consideration exchanged for the accounting acquiree.

IE12 In calculating the number of shares that Entity B would have had to issue, the non-controlling interest is excluded from the calculation. The majority shareholders own 56 shares of Entity B. For that to represent a 58.3 per cent equity interest, Entity B would have had to issue an additional 40 shares. The majority shareholders would then own 56 of the 96 issued shares of Entity B and, therefore, 58.3 per cent of the combined entity. As a result, the fair value of the consideration transferred for Entity A, the accounting acquiree, is CU1,600 (ie 40 shares, each with a fair value of CU40). That is the same amount as when all 60 of Entity B's shareholders tender all 60 of its ordinary shares for exchange. The recognised amount of the group's interest in Entity A, the accounting acquiree, does not change if some of Entity B's shareholders do not participate in the exchange.

IE13   The non-controlling interest is represented by the four shares of the total 60 shares of Entity B that are not exchanged for shares of Entity A. Therefore, the non-controlling interest is 6.7 per cent. The non-controlling interest reflects the proportionate interest of the non-controlling shareholders in the pre-combination carrying amounts of the net assets of Entity B, the legal subsidiary. Therefore, the consolidated statement of financial position is adjusted to show a non-controlling interest of 6.7 per cent of the pre-combination carrying amounts of Entity B's net assets (ie CU134 or 6.7 per cent of CU2,000).

IE14   The consolidated statement of financial position at 30 September 20X6, reflecting the non-controlling interest, is as follows:

	CU
Current assets [CU700 + CU500]	1,200
Non-current assets [CU3,000 + CU1,500]	4,500
Goodwill	300
Total assets	6,000
Current liabilities [CU600 + CU300]	900
Non-current liabilities [CU1,100 + CU400]	1,500
Total liabilities	2,400
Shareholders' equity	
Retained earnings [CU1,400 x 93.3 per cent]	1,306
Issued equity	
240 ordinary shares [CU560 + CU1,600]	2,160
Non-controlling interest	134
Total shareholders' equity	3,600
Total liabilities and shareholders' equity	6,000

IE15   The non-controlling interest of CU134 has two components. The first component is the reclassification of the non-controlling interest's share of the accounting acquirer's retained earnings immediately before the acquisition (CU1,400 × 6.7 per cent or CU93.80). The second component represents the reclassification of the non-controlling interest's share of the accounting acquirer's issued equity (CU600 × 6.7 per cent or CU40.20).

Identifiable intangible assets

Illustrating the consequences of applying paragraphs 10–14 and B31–B40 of IFRS 3.

IE16   The following are examples of identifiable intangible assets acquired in a business combination. Some of the examples may have characteristics of assets other than intangible assets. The acquirer should account for those assets in accordance with their substance. The examples are not intended to be all-inclusive.

IE17   Intangible assets identified as having a contractual basis are those that arise from contractual or other legal rights. Those designated as having a non-contractual basis do not arise from contractual or other legal rights but are separable. Intangible assets identified as having a contractual basis might also be separable but separability is not a necessary condition for an asset to meet the contractual-legal criterion.

Marketing-related intangible assets

IE18   Marketing-related intangible assets are used primarily in the marketing or promotion of products or services. Examples of marketing-related intangible assets are:

Class	Basis
Trademarks, trade names, service marks, collective marks and certification marks	Contractual
Trade dress (unique colour, shape or package design)	Contractual
Newspaper mastheads	Contractual
Internet domain names	Contractual
Non-competition agreements	Contractual

Trademarks, trade names, service marks, collective marks and certification marks

IE19   Trademarks are words, names, symbols or other devices used in trade to indicate the source of a product and to distinguish it from the products of others. A service mark identifies and distinguishes the source of a service rather than a product. Collective marks identify the goods or services of members of a group. Certification marks certify the geographical origin or other characteristics of a good or service.

IE20   Trademarks, trade names, service marks, collective marks and certification marks may be protected legally through registration with governmental agencies, continuous use in commerce or by other means. If it is protected legally through registration or other means, a trademark or other mark acquired in a business combination is an intangible asset that meets the contractual-legal criterion. Otherwise, a trademark or other mark acquired in a business combination can be recognised separately from goodwill if the separability criterion is met, which normally it would be.

IE21   The terms *brand* and *brand name*, often used as synonyms for trademarks and other marks, are general marketing terms that typically refer to a group of complementary assets such as a trademark (or service mark) and its related trade name, formulas, recipes and technological expertise. IFRS 3 does not preclude an entity from recognising, as a single asset separately from goodwill, a group of complementary intangible assets commonly referred to as a brand if the assets that make up that group have similar useful lives.

Internet domain names

IE22   An Internet domain name is a unique alphanumeric name that is used to identify a particular numeric Internet address. Registration of a domain name creates an association between that name and a designated computer on the Internet for the period of the registration. Those registrations are renewable. A registered domain name acquired in a business combination meets the contractual-legal criterion.

Customer-related intangible assets

IE23   Examples of customer-related intangible assets are:

Class	Basis
Customer lists	Non-contractual
Order or production backlog	Contractual
Customer contracts and related customer relationships	Contractual
Non-contractual customer relationships	Non-contractual

Customer lists

IE24   A customer list consists of information about customers, such as their names and contact information. A customer list also may be in the form of a database that includes other information about the customers, such as their order histories and demographic information. A customer list does not usually arise from contractual or other legal rights. However, customer lists are often leased or exchanged. Therefore, a customer list acquired in a business combination normally meets the separability criterion.

Order or production backlog

IE25   An order or production backlog arises from contracts such as purchase or sales orders. An order or production backlog acquired in a business combination meets the contractual-legal criterion even if the purchase or sales orders can be cancelled.

Customer contracts and the related customer relationships

IE26   If an entity establishes relationships with its customers through contracts, those customer relationships arise from contractual rights. Therefore, customer contracts and the related customer relationships acquired in a business combination meet the contractual-legal criterion, even if confidentiality or other contractual terms prohibit the sale or transfer of a contract separately from the acquiree.

IE27   A customer contract and the related customer relationship may represent two distinct intangible assets. Both the useful lives and the pattern in which the economic benefits of the two assets are consumed may differ.

IE28   A customer relationship exists between an entity and its customer if (a) the entity has information about the customer and has regular contact with the customer and (b) the customer has the ability to make direct contact with the entity. Customer relationships meet the contractual-legal criterion if an entity has a practice of establishing contracts with its customers, regardless of whether a contract exists at the acquisition date. Customer relationships may also arise through means other than contracts, such as through regular contact by sales or service representatives.

IE29   As noted in paragraph IE25, an order or a production backlog arises from contracts such as purchase or sales orders and is therefore considered a contractual right. Consequently, if an entity has relationships with its customers through these types of contracts, the customer relationships also arise from contractual rights and therefore meet the contractual-legal criterion.

Examples

IE30   The following examples illustrate the recognition of customer contract and customer relationship intangible assets acquired in a business combination.

(a)   Acquirer Company (AC) acquires Target Company (TC) in a business combination on 31 December 20X5. TC has a five-year agreement to supply goods to Customer. Both TC and AC believe that Customer will renew the agreement at the end of the current contract. The agreement is not separable.

The agreement, whether cancellable or not, meets the contractual-legal criterion. Additionally, because TC establishes its relationship with Customer through a contract, not only the agreement itself but also TC's customer relationship with Customer meet the contractual-legal criterion.

(b)   AC acquires TC in a business combination on 31 December 20X5. TC manufactures goods in two distinct lines of business: sporting goods and electronics. Customer purchases both sporting goods and electronics from TC. TC has a contract with Customer to be its exclusive provider of sporting goods but has no contract for the supply of electronics to Customer. Both TC and AC believe that only one overall customer relationship exists between TC and Customer.

The contract to be Customer's exclusive supplier of sporting goods, whether cancellable or not, meets the contractual-legal criterion. Additionally, because TC establishes its relationship with Customer through a contract, the customer relationship with Customer meets the contractual-legal criterion. Because TC has only one customer relationship with Customer, the fair value of that relationship incorporates assumptions about TC's relationship with Customer related to both sporting goods and electronics. However, if AC determines that the customer relationships with Customer for sporting goods and for electronics are separate from each other, AC would assess whether the customer relationship for electronics meets the separability criterion for identification as an intangible asset.

(c)   AC acquires TC in a business combination on 31 December 20X5. TC does business with its customers solely through purchase and sales orders. At 31 December 20X5, TC has a backlog of customer purchase orders from

60 per cent of its customers, all of whom are recurring customers. The other 40 per cent of TC's customers are also recurring customers. However, as of 31 December 20X5, TC has no open purchase orders or other contracts with those customers.

Regardless of whether they are cancellable or not, the purchase orders from 60 per cent of TC's customers meet the contractual-legal criterion. Additionally, because TC has established its relationship with 60 per cent of its customers through contracts, not only the purchase orders but also TC's customer relationships meet the contractual-legal criterion. Because TC has a practice of establishing contracts with the remaining 40 per cent of its customers, its relationship with those customers also arises through contractual rights and therefore meets the contractual-legal criterion even though TC does not have contracts with those customers at 31 December 20X5.

(d) AC acquires TC, an insurer, in a business combination on 31 December 20X5. TC has a portfolio of one-year motor insurance contracts that are cancellable by policyholders.

Because TC establishes its relationships with policyholders through insurance contracts, the customer relationship with policyholders meets the contractual-legal criterion. IAS 36 *Impairment of Assets* and IAS 38 *Intangible Assets* apply to the customer relationship intangible asset.

Non-contractual customer relationships

IE31   A customer relationship acquired in a business combination that does not arise from a contract may nevertheless be identifiable because the relationship is separable. Exchange transactions for the same asset or a similar asset that indicate that other entities have sold or otherwise transferred a particular type of non-contractual customer relationship would provide evidence that the relationship is separable.

Artistic-related intangible assets

IE32   Examples of artistic-related intangible assets are:

Class	Basis
Plays, operas and ballets	Contractual
Books, magazines, newspapers and other literary works	Contractual
Musical works such as compositions, song lyrics and advertising jingles	Contractual
Pictures and photographs	Contractual
Video and audiovisual material, including motion pictures or films, music videos and television programmes	Contractual

IE33   Artistic-related assets acquired in a business combination are identifiable if they arise from contractual or legal rights such as those provided by copyright. The holder can transfer a copyright, either in whole through an assignment or in part through a licensing agreement. An acquirer is not precluded from recognising a copyright intangible asset and any related assignments or licence agreements as a single asset, provided they have similar useful lives.

Contract-based intangible assets

IE34   Contract-based intangible assets represent the value of rights that arise from contractual arrangements. Customer contracts are one type of contract-based intangible asset. If the terms of a contract give rise to a liability (for example, if the terms of an operating lease or customer contract are unfavourable relative to market terms), the acquirer recognises it as a liability assumed in the business combination. Examples of contract-based intangible assets are:

Class	Basis
Licensing, royalty and standstill agreements	Contractual
Advertising, construction, management, service or supply contracts	Contractual
Lease agreements (whether the acquiree is the lessee or the lessor)	Contractual
Construction permits	Contractual
Franchise agreements	Contractual
Operating and broadcast rights	Contractual
Servicing contracts, such as mortgage servicing contracts	Contractual
Employment contracts	Contractual
Use rights, such as drilling, water, air, timber cutting and route authorities	Contractual

Servicing contracts, such as mortgage servicing contracts

IE35   Contracts to service financial assets are one type of contract-based intangible asset. Although servicing is inherent in all financial assets, it becomes a distinct asset (or liability) by one of the following:

(a)   when contractually separated from the underlying financial asset by sale or securitisation of the assets with servicing retained;

(b)   through the separate purchase and assumption of the servicing.

IE36   If mortgage loans, credit card receivables or other financial assets are acquired in a business combination with servicing retained, the inherent servicing rights are not a separate intangible asset because the fair value of those servicing rights is included in the measurement of the fair value of the acquired financial asset.

Employment contracts

IE37   Employment contracts that are beneficial contracts from the perspective of the employer because the pricing of those contracts is favourable relative to market terms are one type of contract-based intangible asset.

Use rights

IE38   Use rights include rights for drilling, water, air, timber cutting and route authorities. Some use rights are contract-based intangible assets to be accounted for separately from goodwill. Other use rights may have characteristics of tangible assets rather than of intangible assets. An acquirer should account for use rights on the basis of their nature.

Technology-based intangible assets

IE39   Examples of technology-based intangible assets are:

Class	Basis
Patented technology	Contractual
Computer software and mask works	Contractual
Unpatented technology	Non-contractual
Databases, including title plants	Non-contractual
Trade secrets, such as secret formulas, processes and recipes	Contractual

Computer software and mask works

IE40   Computer software and program formats acquired in a business combination that are protected legally, such as by patent or copyright, meet the contractual-legal criterion for identification as intangible assets.

IE41   Mask works are software permanently stored on a read-only memory chip as a series of stencils or integrated circuitry. Mask works may have legal protection. Mask works with legal protection that are acquired in a business combination meet the contractual-legal criterion for identification as intangible assets.

Databases, including title plants

IE42   Databases are collections of information, often stored in electronic form (such as on computer disks or files). A database that includes original works of authorship may be entitled to copyright protection. A database acquired in a business combination and protected by copyright meets the contractual-legal criterion. However, a database typically includes information created as a consequence of an entity's normal operations, such as customer lists, or specialised information, such as scientific data or credit information. Databases that are not protected by copyright can be, and often are, exchanged, licensed or leased to others in their entirety or in part. Therefore, even if the future economic benefits from a database do not arise from legal rights, a database acquired in a business combination meets the separability criterion.

IE43   Title plants constitute a historical record of all matters affecting title to parcels of land in a particular geographical area. Title plant assets are bought and sold, either in whole or in part, in exchange transactions or are licensed. Therefore, title plant assets acquired in a business combination meet the separability criterion.

Trade secrets, such as secret formulas, processes and recipes

IE44   A trade secret is 'information, including a formula, pattern, recipe, compilation, program, device, method, technique, or process that (a) derives independent economic value, actual or potential, from not being generally known and (b) is the subject of efforts that are reasonable under the circumstances to maintain its secrecy.[*] If the future economic benefits from a trade secret acquired in a business combination are legally protected, that asset meets the contractual-legal criterion. Otherwise, trade secrets acquired in a business combination are identifiable only if the separability criterion is met, which is likely to be the case.

Gain on a bargain purchase

Illustrating the consequences of recognising and measuring a gain from a bargain purchase by applying paragraphs 32–36 of IFRS 3.

IE45   The following example illustrates the accounting for a business combination in which a gain on a bargain purchase is recognised.

IE46   On 1 January 20X5 AC acquires 80 per cent of the equity interests of TC, a private entity, in exchange for cash of CU150. Because the former owners of TC needed to dispose of their investments in TC by a specified date, they did not have sufficient time to market TC to multiple potential buyers. The management of AC initially measures the separately recognisable identifiable assets acquired and the liabilities assumed as of the acquisition date in accordance with the requirements of IFRS 3. The identifiable assets are measured at CU250 and the liabilities assumed are measured at CU50. AC engages an independent consultant, who determines that the fair value of the 20 per cent non-controlling interest in TC is CU42.

IE47   The amount of TC's identifiable net assets (CU200, calculated as CU250 – CU50) exceeds the fair value of the consideration transferred plus the fair value of the non-controlling interest in TC. Therefore, AC reviews the procedures it used to identify and measure the assets acquired and liabilities assumed and to measure

---

[*]   Melvin Simensky and Lanning Bryer, *The New Role of Intellectual Property in Commercial Transactions* (New York: John Wiley & Sons, 1998), page 293.

the fair value of both the non-controlling interest in TC and the consideration transferred. After that review, AC decides that the procedures and resulting measures were appropriate. AC measures the gain on its purchase of the 80 per cent interest as follows:

	CU
Amount of the identifiable net assets acquired (CU250 – CU50)	200

	CU	CU
Less: Fair value of the consideration transferred for AC's 80 per cent interest in TC; plus	150	
Fair value of non-controlling interest in TC	42	
		192
Gain on bargain purchase of 80 per cent interest		8

IE48   AC would record its acquisition of TC in its consolidated financial statements as follows:

	CU	CU
Dr Identifiable assets acquired	250	
Cr Cash		150
Cr Liabilities assumed		50
Cr Gain on the bargain purchase		8
Cr Equity—non-controlling interest in TC		42

IE49   If the acquirer chose to measure the non-controlling interest in TC on the basis of its proportionate interest in the identifiable net assets of the acquiree, the recognised amount of the non-controlling interest would be CU40 (CU200 x 0.20). The gain on the bargain purchase then would be CU10 (CU200 – (CU150 + CU40)).

Measurement period

Illustrating the consequences of applying paragraphs 45–50 of IFRS 3.

IE50   If the initial accounting for a business combination is not complete at the end of the financial reporting period in which the combination occurs, paragraph 45 of IFRS 3 requires the acquirer to recognise in its financial statements provisional amounts for the items for which the accounting is incomplete. During the measurement period, the acquirer recognises adjustments to the provisional amounts needed to reflect new information obtained about facts and circumstances that existed as of the acquisition date and, if known, would have affected the measurement of the amounts recognised as of that date. Paragraph 49 of IFRS 3 requires the acquirer to recognise such adjustments as if the accounting for the business combination had been completed at the acquisition date. Measurement period adjustments are not included in profit or loss.

IE51   Suppose that AC acquires TC on 30 September 20X7. AC seeks an independent valuation for an item of property, plant and equipment acquired in the combination, and the valuation was not complete by the time AC authorised for issue its financial statements for the year ended 31 December 20X7. In its 20X7 annual financial statements, AC recognised a provisional fair value for the asset of CU30,000. At the acquisition date, the item of property, plant and equipment had a remaining useful life of five years. Five months after the acquisition date, AC received the independent valuation, which estimated the asset's acquisition-date fair value as CU40,000.

IE52   In its financial statements for the year ended 31 December 20X8, AC retrospectively adjusts the 20X7 prior year information as follows:

(a)   The carrying amount of property, plant and equipment as of 31 December 20X7 is increased by CU9,500. That adjustment is measured as the fair value adjustment at the acquisition date of CU10,000 less the additional depreciation that would have been recognised if the asset's fair value at the acquisition date had been recognised from that date (CU500 for three months' depreciation).

(b)   The carrying amount of goodwill as of 31 December 20X7 is decreased by CU10,000.

(c)   Depreciation expense for 20X7 is increased by CU500.

IE53   In accordance with paragraph B67 of IFRS 3, AC discloses:

(a)   in its 20X7 financial statements, that the initial accounting for the business combination has not been completed because the valuation of property, plant and equipment has not yet been received.

(b)   in its 20X8 financial statements, the amounts and explanations of the adjustments to the provisional values recognised during the current reporting period. Therefore, AC discloses that the 20X7 comparative information is adjusted retrospectively to increase the fair value of the item of property, plant and equipment at the acquisition date by CU9,500, offset by a decrease to goodwill of CU10,000 and an increase in depreciation expense of CU500.

Determining what is part of the business combination transaction

Settlement of a pre-existing relationship

Illustrating the consequences of applying paragraphs 51, 52 and B50–B53 of IFRS 3.

IE54   AC purchases electronic components from TC under a five-year supply contract at fixed rates. Currently, the fixed rates are higher than the rates at which AC could purchase similar electronic components from another supplier. The supply contract allows AC to terminate the contract before the end of the initial five-year term but only by paying a CU6 million penalty. With three years remaining under the supply contract, AC pays CU50 million to acquire TC, which is the fair value of TC based on what other market participants would be willing to pay.

IE55   Included in the total fair value of TC is CU8 million related to the fair value of the supply contract with AC. The CU8 million represents a CU3 million component that is 'at market' because the pricing is comparable to pricing for current market transactions for the same or similar items (selling effort, customer relationships and so on) and a CU5 million component for pricing that is unfavourable to AC because it exceeds the price of current market transactions for similar items. TC has no other identifiable assets or liabilities related to the supply contract, and AC has not recognised any assets or liabilities related to the supply contract before the business combination.

IE56   In this example, AC calculates a loss of CU5 million (the lesser of the CU6 million stated settlement amount and the amount by which the contract is unfavourable to the acquirer) separately from the business combination. The CU3 million 'at-market' component of the contract is part of goodwill.

IE57   Whether AC had recognised previously an amount in its financial statements related to a pre-existing relationship will affect the amount recognised as a gain or loss for the effective settlement of the relationship. Suppose that IFRSs had required AC to recognise a CU6 million liability for the supply contract before the business combination. In that situation, AC recognises a CU1 million settlement gain on the contract in profit or loss at the acquisition date (the CU5 million measured loss on the contract less the CU6 million loss previously recognised). In other words, AC has in effect settled a recognised liability of CU6 million for CU5 million, resulting in a gain of CU1 million.

Contingent payments to employees

Illustrating the consequences of applying paragraphs 51, 52, B50, B54 and B55 of IFRS 3.

IE58   TC appointed a candidate as its new CEO under a ten-year contract. The contract required TC to pay the candidate CU5 million if TC is acquired before the contract expires. AC acquires TC eight years later. The CEO was still employed at the acquisition date and will receive the additional payment under the existing contract.

IE59   In this example, TC entered into the employment agreement before the negotiations of the combination began, and the purpose of the agreement was to obtain the services of CEO. Thus, there is no evidence that the agreement was arranged primarily to provide benefits to AC or the combined entity. Therefore, the liability to pay CU5 million is included in the application of the acquisition method.

IE60   In other circumstances, TC might enter into a similar agreement with CEO at the suggestion of AC during the negotiations for the business combination. If so, the primary purpose of the agreement might be to provide severance pay to CEO, and the agreement may primarily benefit AC or the combined entity rather than TC or its former owners. In that situation, AC accounts for the liability to pay CEO in its post-combination financial statements separately from application of the acquisition method.

Replacement awards

Illustrating the consequences of applying paragraphs 51, 52 and B56–B62 of IFRS 3.

IE61　The following examples illustrate replacement awards that the acquirer was obliged to issue in the following circumstances:

		Acquiree awards	
		Has the vesting period been completed before the business combination?	
		Completed	Not completed
Replacement awards Are employees required to provide additional service after the acquisition date?	Not required	Example 1	Example 4
	Required	Example 2	Example 3

IE62　The examples assume that all awards are classified as equity.

Example 1

Acquiree awards	Vesting period **completed** before the business combination
Replacement awards	Additional employee services **are not** required after the acquisition date

IE63　AC issues replacement awards of CU110 (market-based measure) at the acquisition date for TC awards of CU100 (market-based measure) at the acquisition date. No post-combination services are required for the replacement awards and TC's employees had rendered all of the required service for the acquiree awards as of the acquisition date.

IE64　The amount attributable to pre-combination service is the market-based measure of TC's awards (CU100) at the acquisition date; that amount is included in the consideration transferred in the business combination. The amount attributable to post-combination service is CU10, which is the difference between the total value of the replacement awards (CU110) and the portion attributable to pre-combination service (CU100). Because no post-combination service is required for the replacement awards, AC immediately recognises CU10 as remuneration cost in its post-combination financial statements.

Example 2

Acquiree awards	Vesting period **completed** before the business combination
Replacement awards	Additional employee services **are** required after the acquisition date

IE65   AC exchanges replacement awards that require one year of post-combination service for share-based payment awards of TC, for which employees had completed the vesting period before the business combination. The market-based measure of both awards is CU100 at the acquisition date. When originally granted, TC's awards had a vesting period of four years. As of the acquisition date, the TC employees holding unexercised awards had rendered a total of seven years of service since the grant date.

IE66   Even though TC employees had already rendered all of the service, AC attributes a portion of the replacement award to post-combination remuneration cost in accordance with paragraph B59 of IFRS 3, because the replacement awards require one year of post-combination service. The total vesting period is five years—the vesting period for the original acquiree award completed before the acquisition date (four years) plus the vesting period for the replacement award (one year).

IE67   The portion attributable to pre-combination services equals the market-based measure of the acquiree award (CU100) multiplied by the ratio of the pre-combination vesting period (four years) to the total vesting period (five years). Thus, CU80 (CU100 x 4/5 years) is attributed to the pre-combination vesting period and therefore included in the consideration transferred in the business combination. The remaining CU20 is attributed to the post-combination vesting period and is therefore recognised as remuneration cost in AC's post-combination financial statements in accordance with IFRS 2.

Example 3

Acquiree awards	Vesting period **not completed** before the business combination
Replacement awards	Additional employee services **are** required after the acquisition date

IE68   AC exchanges replacement awards that require one year of post-combination service for share-based payment awards of TC, for which employees had not yet rendered all of the service as of the acquisition date. The market-based measure of both awards is CU100 at the acquisition date. When originally granted, the awards of TC had a vesting period of four years. As of the acquisition date, the TC employees had rendered two years' service, and they would have been required to render two additional years of service after the acquisition date for their awards to vest. Accordingly, only a portion of the TC awards is attributable to pre-combination service.

IE69   The replacement awards require only one year of post-combination service. Because employees have already rendered two years of service, the total vesting period is three years. The portion attributable to pre-combination services equals the market-based measure of the acquiree award (CU100) multiplied by the ratio of the pre-combination vesting period (two years) to the **greater of** the total vesting period (three years) or the original vesting period of TC's award (four years). Thus, CU50 (CU100 x 2/4 years) is attributable to pre-combination service and therefore included in the consideration transferred for the acquiree. The remaining CU50 is attributable to post-combination service and therefore recognised as remuneration cost in AC's post-combination financial statements.

Example 4

Acquiree awards	Vesting period **not completed** before the business combination
Replacement awards	Additional employee services **are not** required after the acquisition date

IE70   Assume the same facts as in Example 3 above, except that AC exchanges replacement awards that require no post-combination service for share-based payment awards of TC for which employees had not yet rendered all of the service as of the acquisition date. The terms of the replaced TC awards did not eliminate any remaining vesting period upon a change in control. (If the TC awards had included a provision that eliminated any remaining vesting period upon a change in control, the guidance in Example 1 would apply.) The market-based measure of both awards is CU100. Because employees have already rendered two years of service and the replacement awards do not require any post-combination service, the total vesting period is two years.

IE71   The portion of the market-based measure of the replacement awards attributable to pre-combination services equals the market-based measure of the acquiree award (CU100) multiplied by the ratio of the pre-combination vesting period (two years) to the **greater of** the total vesting period (two years) or the original vesting period of TC's award (four years). Thus, CU50 (CU100 × 2/4 years) is attributable to pre-combination service and therefore included in the consideration transferred for the acquiree. The remaining CU50 is attributable to post-combination service. Because no post-combination service is required to vest in the replacement award, AC recognises the entire CU50 immediately as remuneration cost in the post-combination financial statements.

Disclosure requirements

Illustrating the consequences of applying the disclosure requirements in paragraphs 59–63 and B64–B67 of IFRS 3.

IE72   The following example illustrates some of the disclosure requirements of IFRS 3; it is not based on an actual transaction. The example assumes that AC is a listed entity and that TC is an unlisted entity. The illustration presents the disclosures in a tabular format that refers to the specific disclosure requirements illustrated. An actual footnote might present many of the disclosures illustrated in a simple narrative format.

Footnote X: Acquisitions

Paragraph reference		
B64(a–d)	On 30 June 20X0 AC acquired 15 per cent of the outstanding ordinary shares of TC. On 30 June 20X2 AC acquired 60 per cent of the outstanding ordinary shares of TC and obtained control of TC. TC is a provider of data networking products and services in Canada and Mexico. As a result of the acquisition, AC is expected to be the leading provider of data networking products and services in those markets. It also expects to reduce costs through economies of scale.	
B64(e)	The goodwill of CU2,500 arising from the acquisition consists largely of the synergies and economies of scale expected from combining the operations of AC and TC.	
B64(k)	None of the goodwill recognised is expected to be deductible for income tax purposes. The following table summarises the consideration paid for TC and the amounts of the assets acquired and liabilities assumed recognised at the acquisition date, as well as the fair value at the acquisition date of the non-controlling interest in TC.	

At 30 June 20X2

	Consideration	CU
B64(f)(i)	Cash	5,000
B64(f)(iv)	Equity instruments (100,000 ordinary shares of AC)	4,000
B64(f)(iii); B64(g)(i)	Contingent consideration arrangement	1,000
B64(f)	**Total consideration transferred**	10,000
B64(p)(i)	**Fair value of AC's equity interest in TC held before the business combination**	2,000
		12,000
B64(m)	**Acquisition-related costs** (included in selling, general and administrative expenses in AC's statement of comprehensive income for the year ended 31 December 20X2)	1,250
B64(i)	**Recognised amounts of identifiable assets acquired and liabilities assumed**	
	Financial assets	3,500
	Inventory	1,000
	Property, plant and equipment	10,000
	Identifiable intangible assets	3,300
	Financial liabilities	(4,000)
	Contingent liability	(1,000)
	Total identifiable net assets	12,800
B64(o)(i)	**Non-controlling interest in TC**	(3,300)
	Goodwill	2,500
		12,000

B64(f)(iv)	The fair value of the 100,000 ordinary shares issued as part of the consideration paid for TC (CU4,000) was determined on the basis of the closing market price of AC's ordinary shares on the acquisition date.
B64(f)(iii)	The contingent consideration arrangement requires AC to pay the former owners of TC 5 per cent of the revenues of XC, an unconsolidated equity
B64(g)	investment owned by TC, in excess of CU7,500 for 20X3, up to a maximum
B67(b)	amount of CU2,500 (undiscounted).

The potential undiscounted amount of all future payments that AC could be required to make under the contingent consideration arrangement is between CU0 and CU2,500.

The fair value of the contingent consideration arrangement of CU1,000 was estimated by applying the income approach. The fair value estimates are based on an assumed discount rate range of 20–25 per cent and assumed probability-adjusted revenues in XC of CU10,000–20,000.

As of 31 December 20X2, neither the amount recognised for the contingent consideration arrangement, nor the range of outcomes or the assumptions used to develop the estimates had changed.

B64(h)	The fair value of the financial assets acquired includes receivables under finance leases of data networking equipment with a fair value of CU2,375. The gross amount due under the contracts is CU3,100, of which CU450 is expected to be uncollectible.
B67(a)	The fair value of the acquired identifiable intangible assets of CU3,300 is provisional pending receipt of the final valuations for those assets.
B64(j)	A contingent liability of CU1,000 has been recognised for expected warranty claims on products sold by TC during the last three years. We expect that the
B67(c)	majority of this expenditure will be incurred in 20X3 and that all will be
IAS 37.84, 85	incurred by the end of 20X4. The potential undiscounted amount of all future payments that AC could be required to make under the warranty arrangements is estimated to be between CU500 and CU1,500. As of 31 December 20X2, there has been no change since 30 June 20X2 in the amount recognised for the liability or any change in the range of outcomes or assumptions used to develop the estimates.
B64(o)	The fair value of the non-controlling interest in TC, an unlisted company, was estimated by applying a market approach and an income approach. The fair value estimates are based on:

(a)   an assumed discount rate range of 20–25 per cent;

(b)   an assumed terminal value based on a range of terminal EBITDA multiples between 3 and 5 times (or, if appropriate, based on long-term sustainable growth rates ranging from 3 to 6 per cent);

(c)   assumed financial multiples of companies deemed to be similar to TC; and

(d)   assumed adjustments because of the lack of control or lack of marketability that market participants would consider when estimating the fair value of the non-controlling interest in TC.

B64(p)(ii)   AC recognised a gain of CU500 as a result of measuring at fair value its 15 per cent equity interest in TC held before the business combination. The gain is included in other income in AC's statement of comprehensive income for the year ending 31 December 20X2.

B64(q)(i)   The revenue included in the consolidated statement of comprehensive income since 30 June 20X2 contributed by TC was CU4,090. TC also contributed profit of CU1,710 over the same period.

B64(q)(ii)   Had TC been consolidated from 1 January 20X2 the consolidated statement of comprehensive income would have included revenue of CU27,670 and profit of CU12,870.

Appendix
Amendments to guidance on other IFRSs

The following amendments to guidance on other IFRSs are necessary in order to ensure consistency with IFRS 3 (as revised in 2008) and the related amendments to other IFRSs. In the amended paragraphs, new text is underlined and deleted text is struck through.

* * * * *

The amendments contained in this appendix when IFRS 3 was issued in 2008 have been incorporated into the text of the Guidance on Implementing IFRS 5, Appendices A and B of IAS 12 and the Illustrative Examples of IAS 36, as issued at 10 January 2008.

Comparison of IFRS 3 (as revised in 2008) and SFAS 141(R)

1   IFRS 3 *Business Combinations* (as revised in 2008) and FASB Statement No. 141 (revised 2007) *Business Combinations* (SFAS 141(R)) are the result of the IASB's and the FASB's projects to improve the accounting for and reporting of business combinations. The first phase of those projects led to IFRS 3 (issued in 2004) and FASB Statement No. 141 (issued in 2001). In 2002, the IASB and the FASB agreed to reconsider jointly their guidance for applying the purchase method (now called the acquisition method) of accounting for business combinations. The objective of the joint effort was to develop a common and comprehensive standard for the accounting for business combinations that could be used for both domestic and international financial reporting. Although the boards reached the same conclusions on most of the issues addressed in the project, they reached different conclusions on a few matters.

2   On those matters on which the boards reached different conclusions, each board includes its own requirements in its version of the standard. The following table identifies and compares those paragraphs in which the IASB and the FASB have different requirements. The table does not identify non-substantive differences. For example, the table does not identify differences in terminology that do not change the meaning of the guidance, such as the IASB using the term *profit or loss* and the FASB using the term *earnings*.

3   Most of the differences identified in the table arise because of the boards' decision to provide guidance for accounting for business combinations that is consistent with other IFRSs or FASB standards. Many of those differences are being considered in current projects or are candidates for future convergence projects, which is why the boards allowed those differences to continue at this time.

Guidance	IFRS 3 (as revised in 2008)	SFAS 141(R)
Scope exception for not-for-profit organisations	IFRSs generally do not have scope limitations for not-for-profit activities in the private or public sector. Therefore, this scope exception is not necessary for the revised IFRS 3.	SFAS 141(R) does not apply to combinations of not-for-profit organisations or the acquisition of a for-profit business by a not-for-profit organisation. The FASB is developing guidance for the accounting for mergers and acquisitions by not-for-profit organisations in a separate project. [paragraph 2(d)]
Identifying the acquirer	The guidance on control in IAS 27 *Consolidated and Separate Financial Statements* is used to identify the acquirer. The revised IFRS 3 does not have guidance for primary beneficiaries because it does not have consolidation guidance equivalent to FASB Interpretation No. 46 (revised December 2003) *Consolidation of Variable Interest Entities* (FASB Interpretation 46(R)). [Appendix A and paragraph 7]	The guidance on *controlling financial interest* in ARB No. 51 *Consolidated Financial Statements* (ARB 51), as amended, is used to identify the acquirer, unless the acquirer is the primary beneficiary of a variable interest entity. The primary beneficiary of a variable interest entity is always the acquirer and the determination of which party is the primary beneficiary is made in accordance with FASB Interpretation 46(R), not based on the guidance in ARB 51 or paragraphs A11–A15 of SFAS 141(R). [paragraphs 3(b) and 9]
Definition of control	*Control* is defined as the power to govern the financial and operating policies of an entity so as to obtain benefits from its activities. [Appendix A]	*Control* has the meaning of *controlling financial interest* in paragraph 2 of ARB 51, as amended, and interpreted by FASB Interpretation 46(R). [paragraph 3(g)]

Guidance	IFRS 3 (as revised in 2008)	SFAS 141(R)
Definition of fair value	*Fair value* is defined as the amount for which an asset could be exchanged, or a liability settled, between knowledgeable, willing parties in an arm's length transaction. The IASB has a separate project in which it is considering the definition of fair value and related measurement guidance. [Appendix A]	*Fair value* is defined in paragraph 5 of FASB Statement No. 157 *Fair Value Measurements* as the price that would be received to sell an asset or paid to transfer a liability in an orderly transaction between market participants at the measurement date. [paragraph 3(i)]
Operating leases	The revised IFRS 3 requires the acquirer to take into account the terms of a lease in measuring the acquisition-date fair value of an asset that is subject to an operating lease in which the acquiree is the lessor. This is consistent with the guidance in IAS 40 *Investment Property*. Accordingly, the revised IFRS 3 does not require the acquirer of an operating lease in which the acquiree is the lessor to recognise a separate asset or liability if the terms of an operating lease are favourable or unfavourable compared with market terms as is required for leases in which the acquiree is the lessee. [paragraphs B29 and B42]	Regardless of whether the acquiree is the lessee or the lessor, SFAS 141(R) requires the acquirer to recognise an intangible asset if the terms of an operating lease are favourable relative to market terms or a liability if the terms are unfavourable relative to market terms. Accordingly, an acquirer measures the acquisition-date fair value of an asset that is subject to an operating lease in which the acquiree is the lessor separately from the lease contract. [paragraphs A17 and A58]
Non-controlling interest in an acquiree	**Initial recognition** The revised IFRS 3 permits an acquirer to measure the non-controlling interest in an acquiree either at fair value or as its proportionate share of the acquiree's identifiable net assets. [paragraph 19]	**Initial recognition** SFAS 141(R) requires the non-controlling interest in an acquiree to be measured at fair value. [paragraph 20]

Guidance	IFRS 3 (as revised in 2008)	SFAS 141(R)
Non-controlling interest in an acquiree	**Disclosures** Because an acquirer is permitted to choose between two measurement bases for the non-controlling interest in an acquiree, the revised IFRS 3 requires an acquirer to disclose the measurement basis used. If the non-controlling interest is measured at fair value, the acquirer must disclose the valuation techniques and key model inputs used. [paragraph B64(o)]	**Disclosures** SFAS 141(R) requires an acquirer to disclose the valuation technique(s) and significant inputs used to measure fair value. [paragraph 68(p)]
Assets and liabilities arising from contingencies	**Initial recognition** The revised IFRS 3 requires the acquirer to recognise a contingent liability assumed in a business combination if it is a present obligation that arises from past events and its fair value can be measured reliably. [paragraphs 22 and 23]	**Initial recognition** SFAS 141(R) requires the acquirer to recognise as of the acquisition date the assets acquired and liabilities assumed that arise from *contractual contingencies*, measured at their acquisition-date fair values. For all other contingencies (referred to as *non-contractual contingencies*), the acquirer recognises an asset or liability as of the acquisition date if it is **more likely than not** that the contingency gives rise to an asset or a liability as defined in FASB Concepts Statement No. 6 *Elements of Financial Statements*. Non-contractual contingencies that do not meet the recognition threshold as of the acquisition date are accounted for in accordance with other GAAP, including FASB Statement No. 5 *Accounting for Contingencies* (SFAS 5) as appropriate. [paragraphs 23–25]

Guidance	IFRS 3 (as revised in 2008)	SFAS 141(R)

Assets and liabilities arising from contingencies	**Subsequent measurement**
	
	The revised IFRS 3 carries forward the existing requirements that a contingent liability recognised in a business combination must be measured subsequently at the higher of the amount that would be recognised in accordance with IAS 37 *Provisions, Contingent Liabilities and Contingent Assets* or the amount initially recognised less, if appropriate, cumulative amortisation recognised in accordance with IAS 18 *Revenue*. [paragraph 56]
		Subsequent measurement
		
		SFAS 141(R) requires an acquirer to continue to report an asset or liability arising from a contractual or non-contractual contingency that is recognised as of the acquisition date that would be in the scope of SFAS 5 if not acquired or assumed in a business combination at its acquisition-date fair value until the acquirer obtains new information about the possible outcome of the contingency. The acquirer evaluates that new information and measures the asset or liability as follows:
		
		(a) a liability is measured at the *higher* of:
		
		   (i) its acquisition-date fair value; or
		
		   (ii) the amount that would be recognised if applying SFAS 5.
		
		(b) an asset is measured at the *lower* of:
		
		   (i) its acquisition-date fair value; or
		
		   (ii) the best estimate of its future settlement amount.
		[paragraphs 62 and 63]

Guidance	IFRS 3 (as revised in 2008)	SFAS 141(R)
Assets and liabilities arising from contingencies	**Disclosures** SFAS 141(R)'s disclosures related to assets and liabilities arising from contingencies are slightly different from those required by the revised IFRS 3 because the IASB's disclosures are based on the requirements in IAS 37. [the revised IFRS 3, paragraphs B64(j) and B67(c); SFAS 141(R), paragraphs 68(j) and 72(c)] **Application guidance** SFAS 141(R) provides application guidance for applying the more-likely-than-not criterion for recognising non-contractual contingencies. The revised IFRS 3 does not have equivalent guidance. [SFAS 141(R), paragraphs A62–A65]	
Assets and liabilities for which the acquirer applies other IFRSs or US GAAP rather than the recognition and measurement principles	The revised IFRS 3 and SFAS 141(R) provide exceptions to the recognition and measurement principles for particular assets and liabilities that the acquirer accounts for in accordance with other IFRSs or US GAAP. For example, income taxes and employee benefit arrangements are accounted for in accordance with existing IFRSs or US GAAP. Differences in the existing guidance might result in differences in the amounts recognised in a business combination. For example, differences between the recognition and measurement guidance in IAS 12 *Income Taxes* and FASB Statement No. 109 *Accounting for Income Taxes* (SFAS 109) might result in differences in the amounts recognised in a business combination related to income taxes. [the revised IFRS 3, paragraphs 24–26; SFAS 141(R), paragraphs 26–28]	
Replacement share-based payment awards	The revised IFRS 3 requires an acquirer to account for share-based payment awards that it exchanges for awards held by employees of the acquiree in accordance with IFRS 2 *Share-based Payment* and SFAS 141(R) requires the acquirer to account for those awards in accordance with FASB Statement No. 123 (revised 2004) *Share-Based Payment* (SFAS 123(R)). Differences between IFRS 2 and SFAS 123(R) might cause differences in the accounting for share-based payment awards entered into as part of the business combination. In addition, the implementation guidance differs because of the different requirements in IFRS 2 and SFAS 123(R). [the revised IFRS 3, paragraphs 30 and B56–B62; SFAS 141(R), paragraphs 32, 43–46 and A91–A106]	

Guidance	IFRS 3 (as revised in 2008)	SFAS 141(R)
Contingent consideration	**Initial classification** The revised IFRS 3 and SFAS 141(R) require an acquirer to classify contingent consideration as an asset, a liability or equity on the basis of other IFRSs or US GAAP, respectively. Differences between the related IFRSs and US GAAP might cause differences in the initial classification and, therefore, might cause differences in the subsequent accounting. [the revised IFRS 3, paragraph 40; SFAS 141(R), paragraph 42]	
	Subsequent measurement Contingent consideration classified as an asset or liability that: (a) is a financial instrument and is within the scope of IAS 39 *Financial Instruments: Recognition and Measurement* is measured at fair value, with any resulting gain or loss recognised either in profit or loss or in other comprehensive income in accordance with that IFRS. (b) is not within the scope of IAS 39 is accounted for in accordance with IAS 37 or other IFRSs as appropriate. [paragraph 58]	**Subsequent measurement** Contingent consideration classified as an asset or liability is measured subsequently at fair value. The changes in fair value are recognised in earnings unless the contingent consideration is a hedging instrument for which FASB Statement No. 133 *Accounting for Derivative Instruments and Hedging Activities* requires the subsequent changes to be recognised in other comprehensive income. [paragraph 65]
Subsequent measurement and accounting for assets, liabilities or equity instruments	In general, after a business combination an acquirer measures and accounts for assets acquired, liabilities assumed or incurred and equity instruments issued in accordance with other applicable IFRSs or US GAAP, depending on their nature. Differences in the other applicable guidance might cause differences in the subsequent measurement and accounting for those assets, liabilities and equity instruments. [the revised IFRS 3, paragraphs 54 and B63; SFAS 141(R), paragraphs 60 and 66]	

Guidance	IFRS 3 (as revised in 2008)	SFAS 141(R)
Goodwill by reportable segment	The disclosure of goodwill by reportable segment is not required by the revised IFRS 3. Paragraph 134 of IAS 36 *Impairment of Assets* requires an entity to disclose the aggregate carrying amount of goodwill allocated to each cash-generating unit (group of units) for which the carrying amount of goodwill allocated to that unit (group of units) is significant in comparison with the entity's total carrying amount of goodwill. This information is not required to be disclosed for each material business combination that occurs during the period or in the aggregate for individually immaterial business combinations that are material collectively and occur during the period.	SFAS 141(R) requires the acquirer to disclose **for each business combination that occurs during the period or in the aggregate for individually immaterial business combinations that are material collectively and that occur during the period,** the amount of goodwill by reportable segment, if the combined entity is required to disclose segment information in accordance with FASB Statement No. 131 *Disclosures about Segments of an Enterprise and Related Information* (SFAS 131) unless such disclosure is impracticable. Like IAS 36, paragraph 45 of FASB Statement No. 142 *Goodwill and Other Intangible Assets* (SFAS 142) requires disclosure of this information in the aggregate by each reportable segment, not for each material business combination that occurs during the period or in the aggregate for individually immaterial business combinations that are material collectively and occur during the period. [paragraph 68(l)]

Guidance	IFRS 3 (as revised in 2008)	SFAS 141(R)
Pro forma disclosures	The disclosures required by this paragraph apply to all acquirers. The revised IFRS 3 does not require the disclosure of *revenue and profit or loss* of the combined entity for the comparable prior period even if comparative financial statements are presented. [paragraph B64(q)]	The disclosures required by this paragraph apply only to acquirers that are *public business enterprises*, as described in paragraph 9 of SFAS 131. If comparative financial statements are presented, SFAS 141(R) requires disclosure of *revenue and earnings* of the combined entity for the comparable prior reporting period as though the acquisition date for all business combinations that occurred during the current year had occurred as of the beginning of the comparable prior annual reporting period (*supplemental pro forma* information). [paragraph 68(r)]
Goodwill reconciliation	The revised IFRS 3 requires an acquirer to provide a goodwill reconciliation and provides a detailed list of items that should be shown separately. [paragraph B67(d)]	SFAS 141(R) requires an acquirer to provide a goodwill reconciliation in accordance with the requirements of SFAS 142. SFAS 141(R) amends the requirement in SFAS 142 to align the level of detail in the reconciliation with that required by the IASB. As a result, there is no substantive difference between the FASB's and the IASB's requirements; however, the guidance is contained in different standards. [paragraph 72(d)]

Guidance	IFRS 3 (as revised in 2008)	SFAS 141(R)
Disclosures of the financial effects of adjustments to the amounts recognised in a business combination	The revised IFRS 3 requires the acquirer to disclose the amount and an explanation of any gain or loss recognised in the current period that (a) relates to the identifiable assets acquired or liabilities assumed in a business combination that was effected in the current or previous reporting period and (b) is of such a size, nature or incidence that disclosure is relevant to understanding the combined entity's financial statements. [paragraph B67(e)]	SFAS 141(R) does not require this disclosure.
Effective date	The revised IFRS 3 is required to be applied prospectively to business combinations for which the acquisition date is on or after the beginning of the first annual reporting period beginning on or after 1 July 2009. Early application is permitted. [paragraph 64]	SFAS 141(R) is required to be applied prospectively to business combinations for which the acquisition date is on or after the beginning of the first annual reporting period beginning on or after 15 December 2008. Early application is prohibited. [paragraph 74]
Income taxes	The revised IFRS 3 and SFAS 141(R) require the subsequent recognition of acquired deferred tax benefits in accordance with IAS 12 or SFAS 109, respectively. Differences between IAS 12 and SFAS 109 might cause differences in the subsequent recognition. Also, in accordance with US GAAP, the acquirer is required to recognise changes in the acquired income tax positions in accordance with FASB Interpretation No. 48 *Accounting for Uncertainty in Income Taxes*, as amended by SFAS 141(R). [the revised IFRS 3, paragraph 67; SFAS 141(R), paragraph 77]	

The revised IFRS 3 and SFAS 141(R) have also been structured to be consistent with the style of other IFRSs and FASB standards. As a result, the paragraph numbers of the revised standards are not the same, even though the wording in the paragraphs is consistent (except for the differences identified above). This table shows how the paragraph numbers of the revised standards correspond.

IFRS 3 (revised 2008) paragraph	SFAS 141(R) paragraph	IFRS 3 (revised 2008) paragraph	SFAS 141(R) paragraph	IFRS 3 (revised 2008) paragraph	SFAS 141(R) paragraph
1	1	28	30	55	61
2	2	29	31	56	62, 63
3	4, 5	30	32	57	64
4	6	31	33	58	65
5	7	32	34	59	67
6	8	33	35	60	68
7	9	34	36	61	71
8	10	35	37	62	72
9	11	36	38	63	73
10	12	37	39	64	74
11	13	38	40	65	75
12	14	39	41	66	76
13	15	40	42	67	77
14	16	41	47	68	None
15	17	42	48	Appendix A	3
16	18	43	49	B1–B4	D8–D14
17	19	44	50	B5	A2
18	20	45	51	B6	A3
19	20	46	52	B7	A4
20	21	47	53	B8	A5
21	22	48	54	B9	A6
22	23	49	55	B10	A7
23	24, 25	50	56	B11	A8
24	26	51	57	B12	A9
25	27	52	58	B13	A10
26	28	53	59	B14	A11
27	29	54	60	B15	A12

IFRS 3 (revised 2008) paragraph	SFAS 141(R) paragraph	IFRS 3 (revised 2008) paragraph	SFAS 141(R) paragraph	IFRS 3 (revised 2008) paragraph	SFAS 141(R) paragraph
B16	A13	B47	A67	IE10	A125
B17	A14	B48	A68	IE11	A126
B18	A15	B49	A69	IE12	A126
B19	A108	B50	A77	IE13	A127
B20	A109	B51	A78	IE14	A128
B21	A110	B52	A79, A80	IE15	A129
B22	A111	B53	A81	IE16	A29
B23	A112	B54	A86	IE17	A30
B24	A113	B55	A87	IE18	A31
B25	A114	B56	43, 44	IE19	A32
B26	A115	B57	45, A92	IE20	A33
B27	A116	B58	A93	IE21	A34
B28	A16	B59	46, A94	IE22	A35
B29	A17	B60	A95	IE23	A36
B30	A18	B61	A96	IE24	A37
B31	A19	B62	A97–A99	IE25	A38
B32	A20	B63	66	IE26	A39
B33	A21	B64	68	IE27	A40
B34	A22	B65	69	IE28	A41
B35	A23	B66	70	IE29	A41
B36	A24	B67	72	IE30	A43
B37	A25	B68, B69	A130–A134	IE31	A42
B38	A26	IE1	A117	IE32	A44
B39	A27	IE2	A118	IE33	A45
B40	A28	IE3	A119	IE34	A46
B41	A57	IE4	A120	IE35	A47
B42	A58	IE5	A120	IE36	A48
B43	A59	IE6	A121	IE37	A49
B44	A60	IE7	A122	IE38	A50
B45	A61	IE8	A123	IE39	A51
B46	A66	IE9	A124	IE40	A52

IFRS 3 (revised 2008) paragraph	SFAS 141(R) paragraph	IFRS 3 (revised 2008) paragraph	SFAS 141(R) paragraph	IFRS 3 (revised 2008) paragraph	SFAS 141(R) paragraph
IE41	A53	IE52	A75	IE63	A101
IE42	A54	IE53	A76	IE64	A102
IE43	A55	IE54	A82	IE65	A103
IE44	A56	IE55	A83	IE66	A103
IE45	A70	IE56	A84	IE67	A103
IE46	A71	IE57	A85	IE68	A104
IE47	A71	IE58	A88	IE69	A105
IE48	A72	IE59	A89	IE70	A106
IE49	None	IE60	A90	IE71	A106
IE50	A73	IE61	A100	IE72	A107
IE51	A74	IE62	A100		

Table of Concordance

This table shows how the contents of the superseded version of IFRS 3 and the revised version of IFRS 3 correspond. Paragraphs are treated as corresponding if they broadly address the same matter even though the guidance may differ.

Superseded IFRS 3 paragraph	Revised IFRS 3 paragraph	Superseded IFRS 3 paragraph	Revised IFRS 3 paragraph	Superseded IFRS 3 paragraph	Revised IFRS 3 paragraph
1	1	25	8, 41, 42	65	IAS 12.68
2	2	26	None	66	59
3	2	27	None	67	60, B64
4	2, 3	28	11	68	B65
5	B5, B6	29–31	53	69	B67(a)
6	B6	32–35	39, 40, 58	70	B64(q)
7	B6	36	10, 18, 31	71	B66
8	43	37	10	72	61
9	None	38	IAS 27.26	73	62, B67
10	B1	39	8, 9	74–76	B67(d)
11	B2	40	19	77	63
12	B3	41	11	78–85	64–67, B68, B69
13	B4	42	None	86, 87	68
14	4	43	11	Appendix A	Appendix A, B7, B12
15	None	44	13	B1–B3	B19
16	5	45, 46	B31–B34	B4–B6	B20
17	6, 7	47–50	22, 23, 56, B64(j), B67(c)	B7–B9	B21, B22
18	None	51	32	B10, B11	B23, B24
19	7	52	Appendix A	B12–B15	B25–B27
20	B13–B16	53	35	B16	None
21	B15	54, 55	B63(a)	B17	None
22	B18	56, 57	34–36	None	12, 14–17, 20, 21, 24–30, 33, 44, 51, 52, 54, 55, 57
23	B17	58–60	41, 42	None	B8–B11, B28–B30, B35–B62
24	37, 38	61–64	45–50		

The main revisions made in 2008 were:

- The scope was broadened to cover business combinations involving only mutual entities and business combinations achieved by contract alone.

- The definitions of a *business* and a *business combination* were amended and additional guidance was added for identifying when a group of assets constitutes a business.

- For each business combination, the acquirer must measure any non-controlling interest in the acquiree either at fair value or as the non-controlling interest's proportionate share of the acquiree's net identifiable assets. Previously, only the latter was permitted.

- The requirements for how the acquirer makes any classifications, designations or assessments for the identifiable assets acquired and liabilities assumed in a business combination were clarified.

- The period during which changes to deferred tax benefits acquired in a business combination can be adjusted against goodwill has been limited to the measurement period (through a consequential amendment to IAS 12 *Income Taxes*).

- An acquirer is no longer permitted to recognise contingencies acquired in a business combination that do not meet the definition of a liability.

- Costs the acquirer incurs in connection with the business combination must be accounted for separately from the business combination, which usually means that they are recognised as expenses (rather than included in goodwill).

- Consideration transferred by the acquirer, including contingent consideration, must be measured and recognised at fair value at the acquisition date. Subsequent changes in the fair value of contingent consideration classified as liabilities are recognised in accordance with IAS 39, IAS 37 or other IFRSs, as appropriate (rather than by adjusting goodwill). The disclosures required to be made in relation to contingent consideration were enhanced.

- Application guidance was added in relation to when the acquirer is obliged to replace the acquiree's share-based payment awards; measuring indemnification assets; rights sold previously that are reacquired in a business combination; operating leases; and valuation allowances related to financial assets such as receivables and loans.

- For business combinations achieved in stages, having the acquisition date as the single measurement date was extended to include the measurement of goodwill. An acquirer must remeasure any equity interest it holds in the acquiree immediately before achieving control at its acquisition-date fair value and recognise the resulting gain or loss, if any, in profit or loss.

IASB documents published to accompany

International Financial Reporting Standard 4

Insurance Contracts

This version includes amendments resulting from IFRSs issued up to 31 December 2009.

The text of the unaccompanied IFRS 4 is contained in Part A of this edition. Its effective date, when issued, was 1 January 2005. The effective date of the most recent amendments is 1 January 2013. This part presents the following accompanying documents:

Approval by the Board of IFRS 4 issued in March 2004

International Financial Reporting Standard 4 *Insurance Contracts* was approved for issue by eight of the fourteen members of the International Accounting Standards Board. Professor Barth and Messrs Garnett, Gélard, Leisenring, Smith and Yamada dissented. Their dissenting opinions are set out after the Basis for Conclusions on IFRS 4.

Sir David Tweedie   Chairman

Thomas E Jones   Vice-Chairman

Mary E Barth

Hans-Georg Bruns

Anthony T Cope

Robert P Garnett

Gilbert Gélard

James J Leisenring

Warren J McGregor

Patricia L O'Malley

Harry K Schmid

John T Smith

Geoffrey Whittington

Tatsumi Yamada

Approval by the Board of *Financial Guarantee Contracts* (Amendments to IAS 39 and IFRS 4) issued in August 2005

Financial Guarantee Contracts (Amendments to IAS 39 *Financial Instruments: Recognition and Measurement* and to IFRS 4 *Insurance Contracts*) was approved for issue by the fourteen members of the International Accounting Standards Board.

Sir David Tweedie   Chairman

Thomas E Jones   Vice-Chairman

Mary E Barth

Hans-Georg Bruns

Anthony T Cope

Jan Engström

Robert P Garnett

Gilbert Gélard

James J Leisenring

Warren J McGregor

Patricia L O'Malley

John T Smith

Geoffrey Whittington

Tatsumi Yamada

CONTENTS

Basis for Conclusions on
IFRS 4 *Insurance Contracts*

This Basis for Conclusions accompanies, but is not part of, IFRS 4.

Introduction

BC1 This Basis for Conclusions summarises the International Accounting Standards Board's considerations in reaching the conclusions in IFRS 4 *Insurance Contracts*. Individual Board members gave greater weight to some factors than to others.

Background

BC2 The Board decided to develop an International Financial Reporting Standard (IFRS) on insurance contracts because:

(a) there was no IFRS on insurance contracts, and insurance contracts were excluded from the scope of existing IFRSs that would otherwise have been relevant (eg IFRSs on provisions, financial instruments and intangible assets).

(b) accounting practices for insurance contracts were diverse, and also often differed from practices in other sectors.

BC3 The Board's predecessor organisation, the International Accounting Standards Committee (IASC), set up a Steering Committee in 1997 to carry out the initial work on this project. In December 1999, the Steering Committee published an *Issues Paper*, which attracted 138 comment letters. The Steering Committee reviewed the comment letters and concluded its work by developing a report to the Board in the form of a *Draft Statement of Principles* (DSOP). The Board started discussing the DSOP in November 2001. The Board did not approve the DSOP or invite formal comments on it, but made it available to the public on the IASB's Website.

BC4 Few insurers report using IFRSs at present, although many more are expected to do so from 2005. Because it was not feasible to complete this project for implementation in 2005, the Board split the project into two phases so that insurers could implement some aspects in 2005. The Board published its proposals for phase I in July 2003 as ED 5 *Insurance Contracts*. The deadline for comments was 31 October 2003 and the Board received 135 responses. After reviewing the responses, the Board issued IFRS 4 in March 2004.

BC5 The Board's objectives for phase I were:

(a) to make limited improvements to accounting practices for insurance contracts, without requiring major changes that may need to be reversed in phase II.

(b) to require disclosure that (i) identifies and explains the amounts in an insurer's financial statements arising from insurance contracts and (ii) helps users of those financial statements understand the amount, timing and uncertainty of future cash flows from insurance contracts.

Tentative conclusions for phase II

BC6   The Board sees phase I as a stepping stone to phase II and is committed to completing phase II without delay once it has investigated all relevant conceptual and practical questions and completed its due process. In January 2003, the Board reached the following tentative conclusions for phase II:

    (a)   The approach should be an asset-and-liability approach that would require an entity to identify and measure directly the contractual rights and obligations arising from insurance contracts, rather than create deferrals of inflows and outflows.

    (b)   Assets and liabilities arising from insurance contracts should be measured at their fair value, with the following two caveats:

        (i)   Recognising the lack of market transactions, an entity may use entity-specific assumptions and information when market-based information is not available without undue cost and effort.

        (ii)   In the absence of market evidence to the contrary, the estimated fair value of an insurance liability shall not be less, but may be more, than the entity would charge to accept new contracts with identical contractual terms and remaining maturity from new policyholders. It follows that an insurer would not recognise a net gain at inception of an insurance contract, unless such market evidence is available.

    (c)   As implied by the definition of fair value:

        (i)   an undiscounted measure is inconsistent with fair value.

        (ii)   expectations about the performance of assets should not be incorporated into the measurement of an insurance contract, directly or indirectly (unless the amounts payable to a policyholder depend on the performance of specific assets).

        (iii)   the measurement of fair value should include an adjustment for the premium that marketplace participants would demand for risks and mark-up in addition to the expected cash flows.

        (iv)   fair value measurement of an insurance contract should reflect the credit characteristics of that contract, including the effect of policyholder protections and insurance provided by governmental bodies or other guarantors.

    (d)   The measurement of contractual rights and obligations associated with the closed book of insurance contracts should include future premiums specified in the contracts (and claims, benefits, expenses, and other additional cash flows resulting from those premiums) if, and only if:

        (i)   policyholders hold non-cancellable continuation or renewal rights that significantly constrain the insurer's ability to reprice the contract to rates that would apply for new policyholders whose characteristics are similar to those of the existing policyholders; and

        (ii)   those rights will lapse if the policyholders stop paying premiums.

    (e)   Acquisition costs should be recognised as an expense when incurred.

    (f)   The Board will consider two more questions later in phase II:

        (i)   Should the measurement model unbundle the individual elements of an insurance contract and measure them individually?

        (ii)   How should an insurer measure its liability to holders of participating contracts?

BC7   In two areas, those tentative conclusions differ from the IASC Steering Committee's recommendations in the DSOP:

    (a)   the use of a fair value measurement objective rather than entity-specific value. However, that change is not as significant as it might seem because entity-specific value as described in the DSOP is indistinguishable in most respects from estimates of fair value determined using measurement guidance that the Board has tentatively adopted in phase II of its project on business combinations.[*]

    (b)   the criteria used to determine whether measurement should reflect future premiums and related cash flows (paragraph BC6(d)).

BC8   Since January 2003, constraints on Board and staff resources have prevented the Board from continuing work to determine whether its tentative conclusions for phase II can be developed into a standard that is consistent with the IASB *Framework* and workable in practice. The Board intends to return to phase II of the project in the second quarter of 2004. It plans to focus at that time on both conceptual and practical issues, as in any project. Only after completing its deliberations will the Board proceed with an Exposure Draft of a proposed IFRS. The Board's deliberations in all projects include a consideration of alternatives and whether those alternatives represent conceptually superior approaches to financial reporting issues. Consequently, the Board will examine existing practices throughout the world to ascertain whether any could be deemed to be a superior answer suitable for international adoption.

BC9   As discussed in paragraph BC84, ED 5 proposed a 'sunset clause', which the Board deleted in finalising the IFRS. Although respondents generally opposed the sunset clause, many applauded the Board's signal of its commitment to complete phase II without delay.

Scope

BC10   Some argued that the IFRS should deal with all aspects of financial reporting by insurers, to ensure that the financial reporting for insurers is internally consistent. They noted that regulatory requirements, and some national accounting requirements, often cover all aspects of an insurer's business. However, for the following reasons, the IFRS deals with insurance contracts of all entities and does not address other aspects of accounting by insurers:

---

[*]   The Board completed the second phase of its project on business combinations in 2008 by issuing a revised IFRS 3 *Business Combinations* and an amended version of IAS 27 *Consolidated and Separate Financial Statements*.

(a) It would be difficult, and perhaps impossible, to create a robust definition of an insurer that could be applied consistently from country to country. Among other things, an increasing number of entities have major activities in both insurance and other areas.

(b) It would be undesirable for an insurer to account for a transaction in one way and for a non-insurer to account in a different way for the same transaction.

(c) The project should not reopen issues addressed by other IFRSs, unless specific features of insurance contracts justify a different treatment. Paragraphs BC166–BC180 discuss the treatment of assets backing insurance contracts.

Definition of insurance contract

BC11 The definition of an insurance contract determines which contracts are within the scope of IFRS 4 rather than other IFRSs. Some argued that phase I should use existing national definitions of insurance contracts, on the following grounds:

(a) Before phase II gives guidance on applying IAS 39 *Financial Instruments: Recognition and Measurement*[*] to difficult areas such as discretionary participation features and cancellation and renewal rights, it would be premature to require insurers to apply IAS 39 to contracts that contain these features and rights.

(b) The definition adopted for phase I may need to be amended again for phase II. This could compel insurers to make extensive changes twice in a short time.

BC12 However, in the Board's view, it is unsatisfactory to base the definition used in IFRSs on local definitions that may vary from country to country and may not be most relevant for deciding which IFRS ought to apply to a particular type of contract.

BC13 Some expressed concerns that the adoption of a particular definition by the IASB could lead ultimately to inappropriate changes in definitions used for other purposes, such as insurance law, insurance supervision or tax. The Board emphasises that any definition used in IFRSs is solely for financial reporting and is not intended to change or pre-empt definitions used for other purposes.

BC14 Various Standards issued by IASC used definitions or descriptions of insurance contracts to exclude insurance contracts from their scope. The scope of IAS 37 *Provisions, Contingent Liabilities and Contingent Assets* and of IAS 38 *Intangible Assets* excluded provisions, contingent liabilities, contingent assets and intangible assets that arise in insurance enterprises from contracts with policyholders. IASC used this wording when its insurance project had just started, to avoid prejudging whether the project would address insurance contracts or a broader class of contracts. Similarly, the scope of IAS 18 *Revenue* excluded revenue arising from insurance contracts of insurance enterprises.

---

[*] In November 2009 the IASB amended some of the requirements of IAS 39 and relocated them to IFRS 9 *Financial Instruments*. IFRS 9 applies to all assets within the scope of IAS 39. This paragraph discusses matters relevant when IFRS 4 was issued.

BC15   The following definition of insurance contracts was used to exclude insurance contracts from the scope of an earlier version of IAS 32 *Financial Instruments: Disclosure and Presentation* and IAS 39.

> An insurance contract is a contract that exposes the insurer to identified risks of loss from events or circumstances occurring or discovered within a specified period, including death (in the case of an annuity, the survival of the annuitant), sickness, disability, property damage, injury to others and business interruption.

BC16   This definition was supplemented by a statement that IAS 32 and IAS 39 did, nevertheless, apply when a financial instrument 'takes the form of an insurance contract but principally involves the transfer of financial risks.'

BC17   For the following reasons, the Board discarded the previous definition in IAS 32 and IAS 39:

(a)   The definition gave a list of examples, but did not define the characteristics of the risks that it was intended to include.

(b)   A clearer definition reduces the uncertainty about the meaning of the phrase 'principally involves the transfer of financial risks'. This will help insurers adopting IFRSs for the first-time ('first-time adopters') in 2005 and minimises the likelihood of further changes in classification for phase II. Furthermore, the previous test could have led to many contracts being classified as financial instruments even though they transfer significant insurance risk.

BC18   In developing a new definition, the Board also considered US GAAP. The main FASB statements for insurers deal with financial reporting by insurance entities and do not define insurance contracts explicitly. However, paragraph 1 of SFAS 113 *Accounting and Reporting for Reinsurance of Short-Duration and Long-Duration Contracts* states:

> Insurance provides indemnification against loss or liability from specified events and circumstances that may occur or be discovered during a specified period. In exchange for a payment from the policyholder (a premium), an insurance enterprise agrees to pay the policyholder if specified events occur or are discovered.

BC19   Paragraph 6 of SFAS 113 applies to any transaction, regardless of its form, that indemnifies an insurer against loss or liability relating to insurance risk. The glossary appended to SFAS 113 defines insurance risk as:

> The risk arising from uncertainties about both (a) the ultimate amount of net cash flows from premiums, commissions, claims, and claim settlement expenses paid under a contract (often referred to as underwriting risk) and (b) the timing of the receipt and payment of those cash flows (often referred to as timing risk). Actual or imputed investment returns are not an element of insurance risk. Insurance risk is fortuitous—the possibility of adverse events occurring is outside the control of the insured.

BC20   Having reviewed these definitions from US GAAP, the Board developed a new definition of insurance contract for the IFRS and expects to use the same definition for phase II. The following aspects of the definition are discussed below:

(a)   insurance risk (paragraphs BC21–BC24);

(b)   insurable interest (paragraphs BC25–BC29);

           © IASCF

(c) quantity of insurance risk (paragraphs BC30–BC37);

(d) expiry of insurance-contingent rights and obligations (paragraphs BC38 and BC39);

(e) unbundling (paragraphs BC40–BC54); and

(f) weather derivatives (paragraphs BC55–BC60).

Insurance risk

BC21 The definition of an insurance contract in the IFRS focuses on the feature that causes accounting problems unique to insurance contracts, namely insurance risk. The definition of insurance risk excludes financial risk, defined using a list of risks that also appears in IAS 39's definition of a derivative.

BC22 Some contracts have the legal form of insurance contracts but do not transfer significant insurance risk to the issuer. Some argue that all such contracts should be treated as insurance contracts, for the following reasons:

(a) These contracts are traditionally described as insurance contracts and are generally subject to regulation by insurance supervisors.

(b) Phase I will not achieve great comparability between insurers because it will permit a diverse range of treatments for insurance contracts. It would be preferable to ensure consistency at least within a single insurer.

(c) Accounting for some contracts under IAS 39[*] and others under local GAAP is unhelpful to users. Moreover, some argued that IAS 39 contains insufficient, and possibly inappropriate, guidance for investment contracts.[†]

(d) The guidance proposed in ED 5 on significant insurance risk was too vague, would be applied inconsistently and relied on actuarial resources in short supply in many countries.

BC23 However, as explained in the *Framework*, financial statements should reflect economic substance and not merely legal form. Furthermore, accounting arbitrage could occur if the addition of an insignificant amount of insurance risk made a significant difference to the accounting. Therefore, the Board decided that contracts described in the previous paragraph should not be treated as insurance contracts for financial reporting.

BC24 Some respondents suggested that an insurance contract is any contract under which the policyholder exchanges a fixed amount (ie the premium) for an amount payable if an insured event occurs. However, not all insurance contracts have explicit premiums (eg insurance cover bundled with some credit card contracts). Adding a reference to premiums would have introduced no more clarity and might have required more supporting guidance and explanations.

---

[*] In November 2009 the IASB amended some of the requirements of IAS 39 and relocated them to IFRS 9 *Financial Instruments*. IFRS 9 applies to all assets within the scope of IAS 39. This paragraph discusses matters relevant when IFRS 4 was issued.

[†] 'Investment contract' is an informal term referring to a contract issued by an insurer that does not expose the insurer to significant insurance risk and is therefore within the scope of IAS 39.

Insurable interest

BC25   In some countries, the legal definition of insurance requires that the policyholder or other beneficiary should have an insurable interest in the insured event. For the following reasons, the definition proposed in 1999 by the former IASC Steering Committee in the Issues Paper did not refer to insurable interest:

   (a)   Insurable interest is defined in different ways in different countries. Also, it is difficult to find a simple definition of insurable interest that is adequate for such different types of insurance as insurance against fire, term life insurance and annuities.

   (b)   Contracts that require payment if a specified uncertain future event occurs cause similar types of economic exposure, whether or not the other party has an insurable interest.

BC26   Because the definition proposed in the Issues Paper did not include a notion of insurable interest, it would have encompassed gambling. Several commentators on the Issues Paper stressed the important social, moral, legal and regulatory differences between insurance and gambling. They noted that policyholders buy insurance to reduce risk, whereas gamblers take on risk (unless they use a gambling contract as a hedge). In the light of these comments, the definition of an insurance contract in the IFRS incorporates the notion of insurable interest. Specifically, it refers to the fact that the insurer accepts risk from the policyholder by agreeing to compensate the policyholder if an uncertain event adversely affects the policyholder. The notion of insurable interest also appears in the definition of financial risk, which refers to a non-financial variable not specific to a party to the contract.

BC27   This reference to an adverse effect is open to the objections set out in paragraph BC25. However, without this reference, the definition of an insurance contract might have captured any prepaid contract to provide services whose cost is uncertain (see paragraphs BC74–BC76 for further discussion). This would have extended the meaning of the term 'insurance contract' too far beyond its traditional meaning.

BC28   Some respondents to ED 5 were opposed to including the notion of insurable interest, on the following grounds:

   (a)   In life insurance, there is no direct link between the adverse event and the financial loss to the policyholder. Moreover, it is not clear that survival adversely affects an annuitant. Any contract that is contingent on human life should meet the definition of insurance contract.

   (b)   This notion excludes some contracts that are, in substance, used as insurance, such as weather derivatives (see paragraphs BC55–BC60 for further discussion). The test should be whether there is a reasonable expectation of some indemnification to policyholders. A tradable contract could be brought within the scope of IAS 39.[*]

---

[*]   In November 2009 the IASB amended some of the requirements of IAS 39 and relocated them to IFRS 9 *Financial Instruments*. IFRS 9 applies to all assets within the scope of IAS 39. This paragraph discusses matters relevant when IFRS 4 was issued.

(c) It would be preferable to eliminate the notion of insurable interest and replace it with the notion that insurance is a business that involves assembling risks into a pool that is managed together.

BC29 The Board decided to retain the notion of insurable interest because it gives a principle-based distinction, particularly between insurance contracts and other contracts that happen to be used for hedging. Furthermore, it is preferable to base a distinction on the type of contract, rather than the way an entity manages a contract or group of contracts. Moreover, the Board decided that it was unnecessary to refine this notion for a life insurance contract or life-contingent annuity, because such contracts typically provide for a predetermined amount to quantify the adverse effect (see paragraph B13 of the IFRS).

Quantity of insurance risk

BC30 Paragraphs B22–B28 of Appendix B of the IFRS discuss how much insurance risk must be present before a contract qualifies as an insurance contract. In developing this material, the Board noted the conditions in US GAAP for a contract to be treated as an insurance contract. SFAS 113 requires two conditions for a contract to be eligible for reinsurance accounting, rather than deposit accounting:

(a) the contract transfers significant insurance risk from the cedant to the reinsurer (which does not occur if the probability of a significant variation in either the amount or timing of payments by the reinsurer is remote); and

(b) either:

(i) there is a reasonable possibility that the reinsurer will suffer a significant loss (based on the present value of all cash flows between the ceding and assuming enterprises under reasonably possible outcomes); or

(ii) the reinsurer has assumed substantially all of the insurance risk relating to the reinsured portions of the underlying insurance contracts (and the cedant has retained only insignificant insurance risk on the reinsured portions).

BC31 Under paragraph 8 of SFAS 97 *Accounting and Reporting by Insurance Enterprises for Certain Long-Duration Contracts and for Realized Gains and Losses from the Sale of Investments*, an annuity contract is considered an insurance contract unless (a) the probability that life contingent payments will be made is remote[*] or (b) the present value of the expected life-contingent payments relative to the present value of all expected payments under the contract is insignificant.

---

[*] Paragraph 8 of SFAS 97 notes that the term remote is defined in paragraph 3 of SFAS 5 *Accounting for Contingencies* as 'the chance of the future event or events occurring is slight.'

BC32　The Board noted that some practitioners use the following guideline in applying US GAAP: a reasonable possibility of a significant loss is a 10 per cent probability of a 10 per cent loss. In this light, the Board considered whether it should define the amount of insurance risk in quantitative terms in relation to, for example:

(a)　the probability that payments under the contract will exceed the expected (ie probability-weighted average) level of payments; or

(b)　a measure of the range of outcomes, such as the range between the highest and lowest level of payments or the standard deviation of payments.

BC33　Quantitative guidance creates an arbitrary dividing line that results in different accounting treatments for similar transactions that fall marginally on different sides of the line. It also creates opportunities for accounting arbitrage by encouraging transactions that fall marginally on one side or the other of the line. For these reasons, the IFRS does not include quantitative guidance.

BC34　The Board also considered whether it should define the significance of insurance risk by referring to materiality, which the *Framework* describes as follows. 'Information is material if its omission or misstatement could influence the economic decisions of users taken on the basis of the financial statements.' However, a single contract, or even a single book of similar contracts, could rarely generate a loss that is material in relation to the financial statements as a whole. Therefore, the IFRS defines the significance of insurance risk in relation to the individual contract (paragraph B25). The Board had two reasons for this:

(a)　Although insurers manage contracts on a portfolio basis, and often measure them on that basis, the contractual rights and obligations arise from individual contracts.

(b)　An assessment contract by contract is likely to increase the proportion of contracts that qualify as insurance contracts. If a relatively homogeneous book of contracts is known to consist of contracts that all transfer insurance risk, the Board did not intend to require insurers to examine each contract within that book to identify a few non-derivative contracts that transfer insignificant insurance risk (paragraph B25 of the IFRS). The Board intended to make it easier, not harder, for a contract to meet the definition.

BC35　The Board also rejected the notion of defining the significance of insurance risk by expressing the expected (ie probability-weighted) average of the present values of the adverse outcomes as a proportion of the expected present value of all outcomes, or as a proportion of the premium. This notion had some intuitive appeal because it would consider both amount and probability. However, it would have meant that a contract could start as an investment contract (ie a financial liability) and become an insurance contract as time passes or probabilities are reassessed. In the Board's view, requiring continuous monitoring over the life of the contract would be too onerous. Instead, the Board adopted an approach that requires this decision to be made once only, at the inception of a contract. The guidance in paragraphs B22–B28 of the IFRS focuses on whether insured events could cause an insurer to pay additional amounts, judged contract by contract.

　　　　　　　　　　　　© IASCF

BC36 Some respondents objected to ED 5's proposal that insurance risk would be significant if a single plausible event could cause a loss that is more than trivial. They suggested that such a broad notion of significant insurance risk might permit abuse. Instead, they suggested referring to a reasonable possibility of a significant loss. However, the Board rejected this suggestion because it would have required insurers to monitor the level of insurance risk continually, which could have given rise to frequent reclassifications. It might also have been too difficult to apply this notion to remote catastrophic scenarios; indeed, some respondents asked the Board to clarify whether the assessment should include such scenarios. In finalising the IFRS, the Board clarified the terminology by (a) replacing the notion of a plausible scenario with an explanation of the need to ignore scenarios that have no commercial substance and (b) replacing the term 'trivial' with the term 'insignificant'.

BC37 Some respondents asked the Board to clarify the basis of comparison for the significance test, because of uncertainty about the meaning of the phrase 'net cash flows arising from the contract' in ED 5. Some suggested that this would require a comparison with the profit that the issuer expects from the contract. However, the Board had not intended this reading, which would have led to the absurd conclusion that any contract with a profitability of close to zero might qualify as an insurance contract. In finalising the IFRS, the Board confirmed in paragraphs B22–B28 that:

(a) the comparison is between the amounts payable if an insured event occurs and the amounts payable if no insured event occurs. Implementation Guidance in IG Example 1.3 addresses a contract in which the death benefit in a unit-linked contract is 101 per cent of the unit value.

(b) surrender charges that might be waived on death are not relevant in assessing how much insurance risk a contract transfers because their waiver does not compensate the policyholder for a pre-existing risk. Implementation Guidance in IG Examples 1.23 and 1.24 is relevant.

Expiry of insurance-contingent rights and obligations

BC38 Some respondents suggested that a contract should no longer be treated as an insurance contract after all insurance-contingent rights and obligations have expired. However, this suggestion could have required insurers to set up new systems to identify these contracts. Therefore, paragraph B30 states that an insurance contract remains an insurance contract until all rights and obligations expire. IG Example 2.19 in the Implementation Guidance addresses dual-trigger contracts.

BC39 Some respondents suggested that a contract should not be regarded as an insurance contract if the insurance-contingent rights and obligations expire after a very short time. The IFRS includes material that may be relevant: paragraph B23 explains the need to ignore scenarios that lack commercial substance and paragraph B24(b) notes that there is no significant transfer of pre-existing risk in some contracts that waive surrender penalties on death.

Unbundling

BC40   The definition of an insurance contact distinguishes insurance contracts within the scope of the IFRS from investments and deposits within the scope of IAS 39.* However, many insurance contracts contain a significant deposit component (ie a component that would, if it were a separate instrument, be within the scope of IAS 39).* Indeed, virtually all insurance contracts have an implicit or explicit deposit component, because the policyholder is generally required to pay premiums before the period of risk; therefore, the time value of money is likely to be one factor that insurers consider in pricing contracts.

BC41   To reduce the need for guidance on the definition of an insurance contract, some argue that an insurer should 'unbundle' the deposit component from the insurance component. Unbundling has the following consequences:

(a)   The insurance component is measured as an insurance contract.

(b)   The deposit component is measured under IAS 39* at either amortised cost or fair value. This might not be consistent with the basis used for insurance contracts.

(c)   Premium receipts for the deposit component are recognised not as revenue, but rather as changes in the deposit liability. Premium receipts for the insurance element are typically recognised as revenue.

(d)   A portion of the transaction costs incurred at inception is allocated to the deposit component if this allocation has a material effect.

BC42   Supporters of unbundling deposit components argue that:

(a)   an entity should account in the same way for the deposit component of an insurance contract as for an otherwise identical financial instrument that does not transfer significant insurance risk.

(b)   the tendency in some countries for banks to own insurers (and vice versa) and the similarity of products offered by the insurance and fund management sectors suggest that insurers, banks and fund managers should account for the deposit component in a similar manner.

(c)   many groups sell products ranging from pure investments to pure insurance, with all variations in between. Unbundling would avoid sharp discontinuities in the accounting between a product that transfers just enough insurance risk to be an insurance contract, and another product that falls marginally on the other side of the line.

(d)   financial statements should make a clear distinction between premium revenue derived from products that transfer significant insurance risk and premium receipts that are, in substance, investment or deposit receipts.

---

*   In November 2009 the IASB amended some of the requirements of IAS 39 and relocated them to IFRS 9 *Financial Instruments*. IFRS 9 applies to all assets within the scope of IAS 39. This paragraph discusses matters relevant when IFRS 4 was issued.

© IASCF

BC43 The Issues Paper published in 1999 proposed that the deposit component should be unbundled if it is either disclosed explicitly to the policyholder or clearly identifiable from the terms of the contract. However, commentators on the Issues Paper generally opposed unbundling, giving the following reasons:

(a) The components are closely interrelated and the value of the bundled product is not necessarily equal to the sum of the individual values of the components.

(b) Unbundling would require significant and costly systems changes.

(c) Contracts of this kind are a single product, regulated as insurance business by insurance supervisors and should be treated in a similar way for financial reporting.

(d) Some users of financial statements would prefer that either all products are unbundled or no products are unbundled, because they regard information about gross premium inflows as important. A consistent use of a single measurement basis might be more useful as an aid to economic decisions than mixing one measurement basis for the deposit component with another measurement basis for the insurance component.

BC44 In the light of these arguments, the DSOP proposed that an insurer or policyholder should not unbundle these components. However, that was against the background of an assumption that the treatments of the two components would be reasonably similar. This may not be the case in phase I, because phase I permits a wide range of accounting treatments for insurance components. Nevertheless, the Board did not wish to require costly changes in phase I that might be reversed in phase II. Therefore, the Board decided to require unbundling only when it is easiest to perform and the effect is likely to be greatest (paragraphs 10–12 of the IFRS and IG Example 3 in the Implementation Guidance).

BC45 The Board acknowledges that there is no clear conceptual line between the cases when unbundling is required and the cases when unbundling is not required. At one extreme, the Board regards unbundling as appropriate for large customised contracts, such as some financial reinsurance contracts, if a failure to unbundle them could lead to the complete omission from the balance sheet of material contractual rights and obligations. This may be especially important if a contract was deliberately structured to achieve a specific accounting result. Furthermore, the practical problems cited in paragraph BC43 are much less significant for these contracts.

BC46 At the other extreme, unbundling the surrender values in a large portfolio of traditional life insurance contracts would require significant systems changes beyond the intended scope of phase I. Furthermore, failing to unbundle these contracts would affect the measurement of these liabilities, but not lead to their complete omission from the insurer's balance sheet. In addition, a desire to achieve a particular accounting result is much less likely to influence the precise structure of these transactions.

BC47   The option for the policyholder to surrender a traditional life insurance contract at an amount that differs significantly from its carrying amount is an embedded derivative and IAS 39* would require the insurer to separate it and measure it at fair value. That treatment would have the same disadvantages, described in the previous paragraph, as unbundling the surrender value. Therefore, paragraph 8 of the IFRS exempts an insurer from applying this requirement to some surrender options embedded in insurance contracts. However, the Board saw no conceptual or practical reason to create such an exemption for surrender options in non-insurance financial instruments issued by insurers or by others.

BC48   Some respondents opposed unbundling in phase I on the following grounds, in addition to the reasons given in paragraph BC43:

(a)   Insurance contracts are, in general, designed, priced and managed as packages of benefits. Furthermore, the insurer cannot unilaterally terminate the agreement or sell parts of it. In consequence, any unbundling required solely for accounting would be artificial. Insurance contracts should not be unbundled unless the structure of the contract is clearly artificial.

(b)   Unbundling may require extensive systems changes that would increase the administrative burden for 2005 and not be needed for phase II.

(c)   There would be no need to require unbundling if the Board strengthened the liability adequacy test, defined significant insurance risk more narrowly and confirmed that contracts combined artificially are separate contracts.

(d)   The unbundling conditions in ED 5 were vague and did not explain the underlying principle.

(e)   Because ED 5 did not propose recognition criteria, insurers would use local GAAP to judge whether assets and liabilities were omitted. This would defeat the stated reason for unbundling.

(f)   If a contract is unbundled, the premium for the deposit component is recognised not as premium revenue but as a balance sheet movement (ie as a deposit receipt). Requiring this would be premature before the Board completes its project on reporting comprehensive income.

BC49   Some suggested other criteria for unbundling:

(a)   All contracts should be unbundled, or unbundling should always be permitted at least. Unbundling is required in Australia and New Zealand.

(b)   All non-insurance components (for example, service components) should be unbundled, not only deposit components.

---

*   IFRS 9 *Financial Instruments*, issued in November 2009, amended the requirements in IAS 39 to identify and separately account for derivatives embedded in a financial host within the scope of IFRS 9. The requirements in IAS 39 continue to apply for derivatives embedded in non-financial hosts and financial hosts outside the scope of IFRS 9. This Basis for Conclusions has not been updated for changes in requirements since IFRIC 9 *Reassessment of Embedded Derivatives* was issued in March 2006.

(c) Unbundling should be required only when the components are completely separable, or when there is an account in the name of the policyholder.

(d) Unbundling could affect the presentation of revenue more than it affects liability recognition. Therefore, unbundling should also be required if it would have a significant effect on reported revenue and is easy to perform.

BC50 Some respondents argued that the test for unbundling should be two-sided (ie the cash flows of the insurance component and the investment component do not interact) rather than the one-sided test proposed in ED 5 (ie the cash flows from the insurance component do not affect the cash flows from the deposit component). Here is an example where this might make a difference: in some life insurance contracts, the death benefit is the difference between (a) a fixed amount and (b) the value of a deposit component (for example, a unit-linked investment). The deposit component can be measured independently, but the death benefit depends on the unit value so the insurance component cannot be measured independently.

BC51 The Board decided that phase I should not require insurers to set up systems to unbundle the products described in the previous paragraph. However, the Board decided to rely on the condition that provides an exemption from unbundling if all the rights and obligations under the deposit component are recognised. If this condition is not met, unbundling is appropriate.

BC52 Some argued that it is irrelevant whether the insurance component affects the deposit component. They suggested that a deposit component exists if the policyholder will receive a minimum fixed amount of future cash flows in the form of either a return of premium (if no insured event occurs) or an insurance recovery (if an insured event occurs). However, the Board noted that this focus on a single cash flow would not result in unbundling if a financial instrument and an insurance contract are combined artificially into a single contract and the cash flows from one component offset cash flows from the other component. The Board regarded that result as inappropriate and open to abuse.

BC53 In summary, the Board retained the approach broadly as in ED 5. This requires unbundling if that is needed to ensure the recognition of rights and obligations arising from the deposit component and those rights and obligations can be measured separately. If only the second of these conditions is met, the IFRS permits unbundling, but does not require it.

BC54 Some respondents suggested that if a contract has been artificially separated through the use of side letters, the separate components of the contract should be considered together. The Board did not address this because it is a wider issue for the Board's possible future work on linkage (ie accounting for separate transactions that are connected in some way). The footnote to paragraph B25 refers to simultaneous contracts with the same counterparty.

Weather derivatives

BC55 The scope of IAS 39* previously excluded contracts that require a payment based on climatic, geological, or other physical variables (if based on climatic variables, sometimes described as weather derivatives). It is convenient to divide these contracts into two categories:

(a) contracts that require a payment only if a particular level of the underlying climatic, geological, or other physical variables adversely affects the contract holder. These are insurance contracts as defined in the IFRS.

(b) contracts that require a payment based on a specified level of the underlying variable regardless of whether there is an adverse effect on the contract holder. These are derivatives and the IFRS removes a previous scope exclusion to bring them within the scope of IAS 39.*

BC56 The previous scope exclusion was created mainly because the holder might use such a derivative in a way that resembles the use of an insurance contract. However, the definition of an insurance contract in the IFRS now provides a principled basis for deciding which of these contracts are treated as insurance contracts and which are treated as derivatives. Therefore, the Board removed the scope exclusion from IAS 39 (see paragraph C3 of Appendix C of the IFRS). Such contracts are within the scope of the IFRS if payment is contingent on changes in a physical variable that is specific to a party to the contract, and within the scope of IAS 39 in all other cases.

BC57 Some respondents suggested that a weather derivative should be treated as:

(a) an insurance contract if it is expected to be highly effective in mitigating an existing risk exposure.

(b) a derivative financial instrument otherwise.

BC58 Some argued that some weather derivatives are, in substance, insurance contracts. For example, under some contracts, the policyholder can claim a fixed sum based on rainfall levels at the nearest weather station. The contract was purchased to provide insurance against low rainfall but was structured like this because of difficulties in measuring actual loss suffered and because of the moral hazard of having a rainfall gauge on the policyholder's property. It can reasonably be expected that the rainfall at the nearest weather station will affect the holder, but the physical variable specified in the contract (ie rainfall) is not specific to a party to the contract. Similarly, some insurers use weather derivatives as a hedge against insurance contracts they issue and view them as similar to reinsurance.

BC59 Some suggested that weather derivatives should be excluded from the scope of the IFRS because they are tradable instruments that behave like other derivatives and have an observable market value, rather than because there is no contractual link between the holder and the event that triggers payment.

---

* In November 2009 the IASB amended some of the requirements of IAS 39 and relocated them to IFRS 9 *Financial Instruments*. IFRS 9 applies to all assets within the scope of IAS 39. This paragraph discusses matters relevant when IFRS 4 was issued.

BC60 The IFRS distinguishes an insurance contract (in which an adverse effect on the policyholder is a contractual precondition for payment) from other instruments, such as derivatives and weather derivatives (in which an adverse effect is not a contractual precondition for payment, although the counterparty may, in fact, use the instrument to hedge an existing exposure). In the Board's view, this is an important and useful distinction. It is much easier to base a classification on the terms of the contract than on an assessment of the counterparty's motive (ie hedging or trading). Consequently, the Board made no change to ED 5's proposals for the treatment of weather derivatives.

Scope exclusions

BC61 The scope of the IFRS excludes various items that may meet the definition of insurance contracts, but are, or will be, covered by existing or proposed future IFRSs (paragraph 4). The following paragraphs discuss:

(a) financial guarantees and insurance against credit risk (paragraphs BC62–BC68);

(b) product warranties (paragraphs BC69–BC72);

(c) accounting by policyholders (paragraph BC73); and

(d) prepaid service contracts (paragraphs BC74–BC76).

Financial guarantees and insurance against credit risk

BC62 The Basis for Conclusions on IAS 39 explains the reasons for the Board's conclusions on financial guarantee contracts.

BC63–
BC68 [Deleted]

Product warranties

BC69 A product warranty clearly meets the definition of an insurance contract if an entity issues it on behalf of another party (such as a manufacturer, dealer or retailer). The scope of the IFRS includes such warranties.

BC70 A product warranty issued directly by a manufacturer, dealer or retailer also meets the definition of an insurance contract. Although some might think of this as 'self-insurance', the risk retained arises from existing contractual obligations towards the customer. Some may reason that the definition of insurance contracts should exclude such direct warranties because they do not involve a transfer of risk from buyer to seller, but rather a crystallisation of an existing responsibility. However, in the Board's view, excluding these warranties from the definition of insurance contracts would complicate the definition for only marginal benefit.

BC71 Although such direct warranties create economic exposures similar to warranties issued on behalf of the manufacturer, dealer or retailer by another party (ie the insurer), the scope of the IFRS excludes them because they are closely related to the underlying sale of goods and because IAS 37 addresses product warranties. IAS 18 deals with the revenue received for such warranties.

BC72   In a separate project, the Board is exploring an asset and liability approach to revenue recognition. If this approach is implemented, the accounting model for these direct product warranties may change.

Accounting by policyholders

BC73   The IFRS does not address accounting and disclosure by policyholders for direct insurance contracts because the Board does not regard this as a high priority for phase I. The Board intends to address accounting by policyholders in phase II (see IASB *Update* February 2002 for the Board's discussion of accounting by policyholders). IFRSs address some aspects of accounting by policyholders for insurance contracts:

(a)   IAS 37 addresses accounting for reimbursements from insurers for expenditure required to settle a provision.

(b)   IAS 16 addresses some aspects of compensation from third parties for property, plant and equipment that was impaired, lost or given up.

(c)   Because policyholder accounting is outside the scope of the IFRS, the hierarchy of criteria in paragraphs 10–12 of IAS 8 *Accounting Policies, Changes in Accounting Estimates and Errors* applies to policyholder accounting (see paragraphs BC77–BC86).

(d)   A policyholder's rights and obligations under insurance contracts are outside the scope of IAS 32 and IAS 39.[*]

Prepaid service contracts

BC74   Some respondents noted that the definition proposed in ED 5 captured some prepaid contracts to provide services whose cost is uncertain. Because these contracts are not normally regarded as insurance contracts, these respondents suggested that the Board should change the definition or exclude these contracts from the scope of the IFRS. Respondents cited two specific examples.

(a)   Fixed fee service contracts if the level of service depends on an uncertain event, for example maintenance contracts if the service provider agrees to repair specified equipment after a malfunction. The fixed service fee is based on the expected number of malfunctions, although it is uncertain that the machines will actually break down. The malfunction of the equipment adversely affects its owner and the contract compensates the owner (in kind, rather than cash).

(b)   Some car breakdown assistance if (i) each breakdown has little incremental cost because employed patrols provide most of the assistance, (ii) the motorist pays for all parts and repairs, (iii) the service provider's only responsibility is to take the car to a specified destination (eg the nearest garage, home or the original destination), (iv) the need to provide assistance (and the related cost) is known within hours and (v) the number of call-outs is limited.

---

[*]   In November 2009 the IASB amended some of the requirements of IAS 39 and relocated them to IFRS 9 *Financial Instruments*. IFRS 9 applies to all assets within the scope of IAS 39. This paragraph discusses matters relevant when IFRS 4 was issued.

BC75　The Board saw no conceptual reason to change either the definition of insurance contracts or the scope of the IFRS in the light of the two examples cited by respondents. Paragraphs B6 and B7 of the IFRS note that complying with the IFRS in phase I is unlikely to be particularly burdensome in these two examples, for materiality reasons. The Board may need to review this conclusion in phase II.

BC76　Some respondents argued that the proposals in ED 5 were directed primarily at entities that are generally regarded as insurers. They suggested that the Board should not impose these proposals on entities that have a relatively small amount of a given transaction type. The Board concluded that these comments were primarily about materiality. IAS 1 *Presentation of Financial Statements* and IAS 8 address materiality and the Board decided that no further guidance or specific exemption was needed in this case.

Temporary exemption from some other IFRSs

BC77　Paragraphs 10–12 of IAS 8 specify a hierarchy of criteria that an entity should use in developing an accounting policy if no IFRS applies specifically to an item. Without changes made in the IFRS, an insurer adopting IFRSs in 2005 would have needed to assess whether its accounting policies for insurance contracts comply with these requirements. In the absence of guidance, there might have been uncertainty about what would be acceptable. Establishing what would be acceptable could have been costly and some insurers might have made major changes in 2005 followed by further significant changes in phase II.

BC78　To avoid unnecessary disruption for both users and preparers in phase I that would not have eased the transition to phase II, the Board decided to limit the need for insurers to change their existing accounting policies for insurance contracts. The Board did this by the following measures:

(a)　creating a temporary exemption from the hierarchy in IAS 8 that specifies the criteria an entity uses in developing an accounting policy if no IFRS applies specifically to an item. The exemption applies to insurers, but not to policyholders.

(b)　limiting the impact of that exemption from the hierarchy by five specific requirements (relating to catastrophe provisions, liability adequacy, derecognition, offsetting and impairment of reinsurance assets, see paragraphs BC87–BC114).

(c)　permitting some existing practices to continue but prohibiting their introduction (paragraphs BC123–BC146).

BC79　Some respondents opposed the exemption from the hierarchy on the grounds that it would permit too much diversity and allow fundamental departures from the *Framework* that could prevent an insurer's financial statements from presenting information that is understandable, relevant, reliable and comparable. The Board did not grant the exemption from the hierarchy in IAS 8 lightly, but took this unusual step to minimise disruption in 2005 for both users (eg lack of continuity of trend data) and preparers (eg systems changes).

BC80   ED 6 *Exploration for and Evaluation of Mineral Resources* proposes a temporary exemption from paragraphs 11 and 12 of IAS 8 (ie sources of guidance), but not from paragraph 10 (ie relevance and reliability). That proposed exemption is narrower than in IFRS 4 because ED 6 leaves a relatively narrow range of issues unaddressed. In contrast, because IFRS 4 leaves many significant aspects of accounting for insurance contracts until phase II, a requirement to apply paragraph 10 of IAS 8 to insurance contracts would have had much more pervasive effects and insurers would have needed to address matters such as completeness, substance over form and neutrality.

BC81   Some suggested that the Board should specifically require an insurer to follow its national accounting requirements (national GAAP) in accounting for insurance contracts during phase I, to prevent selection of accounting policies that do not form a comprehensive basis of accounting to achieve a predetermined result ('cherry-picking'). However, defining national GAAP would have posed problems. Further definitional problems could have arisen because some insurers do not apply the national GAAP of their own country. For example, some non-US insurers with a US listing apply US GAAP. Moreover, it is unusual and, arguably, beyond the Board's mandate to impose requirements set by another body.

BC82   In addition, an insurer might wish to improve its accounting policies to reflect other accounting developments with no counterpart in national GAAP. For example, an insurer adopting IFRSs for the first time might wish to amend its accounting policies for insurance contracts for greater consistency with accounting policies that it uses for contracts within the scope of IAS 39.[*] Similarly, an insurer might wish to improve its accounting for embedded options and guarantees by addressing both their time value and their intrinsic value, even if no similar improvements are made to its national GAAP.

BC83   Therefore, the Board decided that an insurer could continue to follow the accounting policies that it was using when it first applied the phase I requirements, with some exceptions noted below. An insurer could also improve those accounting policies if specified criteria are met (see paragraphs 21–30 of the IFRS).

BC84   The criteria in paragraphs 10–12 of IAS 8 include relevance and reliability. Granting an exemption from those criteria, even temporarily, is a highly unusual step. The Board was prepared to contemplate that step only as part of an orderly and relatively fast transition to phase II. Because the exemption is so exceptional, ED 5 proposed that it would apply only for accounting periods beginning before 1 January 2007. Some described this time limit as a 'sunset clause'.

BC85   Many respondents opposed the sunset clause. They argued the following:

(a)   If the exemption expired in 2007 before phase II is in force, there would be considerable confusion, disruption and cost for both users and preparers. It would not be appropriate to penalise users and preparers if the Board does not complete phase II on time.

---

[*]   In November 2009 the IASB amended some of the requirements of IAS 39 and relocated them to IFRS 9 *Financial Instruments*. IFRS 9 applies to all assets within the scope of IAS 39. This paragraph discusses matters relevant when IFRS 4 was issued.

(b)   The sunset clause might be perceived as putting pressure on the Board to complete phase II without adequate consultation, investigation and testing.

The Board accepted the validity of these objections to the sunset clause and deleted it.

BC86   The Board decided to maintain some requirements that follow from the criteria in IAS 8. The Board acknowledges that it is difficult to make piecemeal changes to recognition and measurement practices in phase I because many aspects of accounting for insurance contracts are interrelated with aspects that will not be completed until phase II. However, abandoning these particular requirements would detract from the relevance and reliability of an insurer's financial statements to an unacceptable degree. Moreover, these requirements are not interrelated to a great extent with other aspects of recognition and measurement and the Board does not expect phase II to reverse these requirements. The following points are discussed below:

(a)   catastrophe and equalisation provisions (paragraphs BC87–BC93)

(b)   liability adequacy (paragraphs BC94–BC104)

(c)   derecognition (paragraph BC105)

(d)   offsetting (paragraph BC106)

(e)   impairment of reinsurance assets (paragraphs BC107–BC114).

Catastrophe and equalisation provisions

BC87   Some insurance contracts expose the insurer to infrequent but severe catastrophic losses caused by events such as damage to nuclear installations or satellites or earthquake damage. Some jurisdictions permit or require catastrophe provisions for contracts of this type. The catastrophe provisions are generally built up gradually over the years out of the premiums received, usually following a prescribed formula, until a specified limit is reached. They are intended to be used on the occurrence of a future catastrophic loss that is covered by current or future contracts of this type. Some countries also permit or require equalisation provisions to cover random fluctuations of claim expenses around the expected value of claims for some types of insurance contract (eg hail, credit, guarantee and fidelity insurance) using a formula based on experience over a number of years.

BC88   Those who favour recognising catastrophe or equalisation provisions as liabilities base their view on one or more of the following arguments:

(a)   Such provisions represent a deferral of unearned premiums that are designed to provide for events that are not expected, on average, to occur in any single contract period but are expected to occur over an entire cycle of several contract periods. Although contracts cover only one period in form, in substance contracts are commonly renewed, leading to pooling of risks over time rather than within a single period. Indeed, some jurisdictions make it difficult for an insurer to stop offering insurance against some forms of risk, such as hurricanes.

(b)   In some jurisdictions, an insurer is required to segregate part of the premium (the catastrophe premium). The catastrophe premium is not available for distribution to shareholders (except on liquidation) and, if the insurer transfers the contract to another insurer, it must also transfer the catastrophe premium.

(c)   In years when no catastrophe occurs (or when claims are abnormally low), such provisions portray an insurer's long-term profitability faithfully because they match the insurer's costs and revenue over the long term. Also, they show a pattern of profit similar to one obtained through reinsurance, but with less cost and administrative burden.

(d)   Such provisions enhance solvency protection by restricting the amounts distributed to shareholders and by restricting a weak company's ability to expand or enter new markets.

(e)   Such provisions encourage insurers to accept risks that they might otherwise decline. Some countries reinforce this encouragement with tax deductions.

BC89   For the following reasons, the IFRS prohibits the recognition as a liability of provisions for possible future claims under contracts that are not in existence at the reporting date (such as catastrophe and equalisation provisions):

(a)   Such provisions are not liabilities as defined in the *Framework*, because the insurer has no present obligation for losses that will occur after the end of the current contract period. As the *Framework* states, the matching concept does not allow the recognition of items in the balance sheet that do not meet the definition of assets or liabilities. Recognising deferred credits as if they were liabilities would diminish the relevance and reliability of an insurer's financial statements.

(b)   Even if the insurance law requires an insurer to segregate catastrophe premiums so that they are not available for distribution to shareholders in any circumstances, earnings on those segregated premiums will ultimately be available to shareholders. Therefore, those segregated amounts are appropriately classified as equity, not as a liability.

(c)   Recognising such provisions obscures users' ability to examine the impact of past catastrophes and does not contribute to their analysis of an insurer's exposure to future catastrophes. Given adequate disclosure, knowledgeable users understand that some types of insurance expose an insurer to infrequent but severe losses. Moreover, the analogy with reinsurance contracts is irrelevant, because reinsurance actually changes the insurer's risk profile.

(d)   The objective of general purpose financial statements is not to enhance solvency but to provide information that is useful to a wide range of users for economic decisions. Moreover, the recognition of provisions does not, by itself, enhance solvency. However, if the objective of financial statements were to enhance solvency and such provisions were an appropriate means of enhancing solvency, it would follow that the insurer should recognise the entire provision immediately, rather than accumulating it over time. Furthermore, if catastrophes (or unusual experience) in one period are independent of those in other periods, the insurer should not reduce the liability when a catastrophe (or unusually bad experience) occurs. Also, if diversification over time were a valid basis for accounting, above-average losses in early years should be recognised as assets, yet proponents of catastrophe and equalisation provisions do not advocate this.

(e)   Recognising catastrophe or equalisation provisions is not the only way to limit distributions to shareholders. Other measures, such as solvency margin requirements and risk-based capital requirements, could play an important role. Another possibility is for an insurer to segregate a portion of its equity for retention to meet possible losses in future years.

(f)   The objective of general purpose financial statements is not to encourage or discourage particular transactions or activities, but to report neutral information about transactions and activities. Therefore, accounting requirements should not try to encourage insurers to accept or decline particular types of risks.

(g)   If an insurer expects to continue writing catastrophe cover, presumably it believes that the future business will be profitable. It would not be representationally faithful to recognise a liability for future contracts that are expected to be profitable.

(h)   There is no objective way to measure catastrophe and equalisation provisions, unless an arbitrary formula is used.

BC90   Some suggested that it is not appropriate to eliminate catastrophe and equalisation provisions in phase I as a piecemeal amendment to existing approaches. However, the Board concluded that it could prohibit these provisions without undermining other components of existing approaches. There is no credible basis for arguing that catastrophe or equalisation 'provisions' are recognisable liabilities under IFRSs and there is no realistic prospect that the Board will permit them in phase II. Indeed, as noted above, paragraphs 10–12 of IAS 8 require an entity to consider various criteria in developing an accounting policy for an item if no IFRS applies specifically to that item. In the Board's view, if the IFRS had not suspended that requirement, it would clearly have prohibited the recognition of such items as a liability. Accordingly, the IFRS preserves this prohibition (see paragraph 14(a) of the IFRS).

BC91   Some respondents presented additional arguments for permitting the recognition of catastrophe and equalisation provisions as a liability:

(a)   Some insurers measure insurance contracts without margins for risk, but instead recognise catastrophe or equalisation provisions. If catastrophe provisions are eliminated in phase I, this change might be partly reversed in phase II if insurers are then required to include margins for risk.

(b)   Some insurers regard these provisions as relating partly to existing contracts and partly to future contracts. Splitting these components may be difficult and involve systems changes that might not be needed in phase II.

BC92   For the following reasons, these arguments did not persuade the Board:

    (a)   Present imperfections in the measurement of recognisable liabilities do not justify the recognition of other items that do not meet the definition of a liability.

    (b)   Additions to these provisions are often based on a percentage of premium revenue. If the risk period has already expired, that premium does not relate to an existing contractual obligation. If the risk period has not yet fully expired, the related portion of the premium relates to an existing contractual obligation, but most existing models defer all the related premium as unearned premium, so recognising an additional provision would be double-counting (unless the contract were known to be underpriced).

BC93   Accordingly, the Board retained the proposal in ED 5 to eliminate these provisions. However, although the IFRS prohibits their recognition as a liability, it does not prohibit the segregation of a component of equity. Changes in a component of equity are not recognised in profit or loss. IAS 1 requires a statement of changes in equity.

Liability adequacy

BC94   Many existing accounting models have tests to confirm that insurance liabilities are not understated, and that related amounts recognised as assets, such as deferred acquisition costs, are not overstated. The precise form of the test depends on the underlying measurement approach. However, there is no guarantee that these tests exist everywhere and the credibility of IFRSs could suffer if an insurer claims to comply with IFRSs but fails to recognise material and reasonably foreseeable losses arising from existing contractual obligations. To avoid this, the IFRS requires a liability adequacy test* (see paragraphs 15–19).

BC95   The Board's intention was not to introduce piecemeal elements of a parallel measurement model, but to create a mechanism that reduces the possibility that material losses remain unrecognised during phase I. With this in mind, paragraph 16 of the IFRS defines minimum requirements that an insurer's existing test must meet. If the insurer does not apply a test that meets those requirements, it must apply a test specified by the Board. To specify a test on a basis that already exists in IFRSs and minimise the need for exceptions to existing principles, the Board decided to draw on IAS 37.

BC96   The liability adequacy test also applies to deferred acquisition costs and to intangible assets representing the contractual rights acquired in a business combination or portfolio transfer. As a result, when the Board revised IAS 36 *Impairment of Assets* in 2004, it excluded deferred acquisition costs and those intangible assets from the scope of IAS 36.

BC97   The Board considered whether it should retain the impairment model in IAS 36 for deferred acquisition costs, and perhaps also the related insurance liabilities. However, the IAS 36 model cannot be applied to deferred acquisition costs alone, without also considering the cash flows relating to the recognised liability.

---

*   ED 5 described this as a 'loss recognition test'.

Indeed, some insurers capitalise acquisition costs implicitly through deductions in the measurement of the liability. Moreover, it would be confusing and difficult to apply this model to liabilities without some re-engineering. In the Board's view, it is simpler to use a model that is designed for liabilities, namely the IAS 37 model. In practice, a re-engineered IAS 36 model and IAS 37 might not lead to very different results.

BC98 Some respondents suggested that the Board should specify that the cash flows considered in a liability adequacy test should include the effect of embedded options and guarantees, such as guaranteed annuity rates. They expressed concerns that many national practices have not required insurers to recognise these exposures, which can be very large.

BC99 Although the Board's objective was not to develop a detailed liability adequacy test, it observed that the size of exposures to embedded guarantees and options and the failings of many national practices in this area warranted specific requirements, even in phase I. Accordingly, the Board decided that the minimum requirements for an existing liability adequacy test should include considering cash flows resulting from embedded options and guarantees. The Board did not specify how those cash flows should be considered but noted that an insurer would consider this matter in developing disclosures of its accounting policies. If an existing liability adequacy test does not meet the minimum requirements, a comparison is made with the measurement that IAS 37 would require. IAS 37 refers to the amount that an entity would rationally pay to settle the obligation or transfer it to a third party. Implicitly, this amount would consider the possible effect of embedded options and guarantees.

BC100 ED 5 did not specify the level of aggregation for the liability adequacy test and some respondents asked the Board to clarify this. Paragraph 18 of the IFRS confirms that the aggregation requirements of the existing liability adequacy test apply if the test meets the minimum requirements specified in paragraph 16 of the IFRS. If that test does not meet those minimum requirements, there is no conceptual justification for offsetting a loss on one contract against an otherwise unrecognisable gain on another contract. However, the Board concluded that a contract-by-contract assessment would impose costs that exceed the likely benefits to users. Therefore, paragraph 18 states that the comparison is made at the level of a portfolio of contracts that are subject to broadly similar risks and managed together as a portfolio. More precise definition would be difficult and is not needed, given the Board's restricted objective of ensuring at least a minimum level of testing for the limited life of phase I.

BC101 It is beyond the scope of phase I to create a detailed accounting regime for insurance contracts. Therefore, the IFRS does not specify:

(a) what criteria determine when existing contracts end and future contracts start.

(b) whether or how the cash flows are discounted to reflect the time value of money or adjusted for risk and uncertainty.

(c) whether the liability adequacy test considers both the time value and the intrinsic value of embedded options and guarantees.

(d)   whether additional losses recognised because of the liability adequacy test are recognised by reducing the carrying amount of deferred acquisition costs or by increasing the carrying amount of the related insurance liabilities.

BC102   Some respondents asked the Board to clarify that no formal liability adequacy test is needed if an entity can demonstrate that its method of measuring insurance liabilities means that they are not understated. Paragraph 15 of the IFRS requires an insurer to 'assess whether its recognised insurance liabilities are adequate, using current estimates of future cash flows'. The fundamental point is that future cash flows must be considered in some way, and not merely be assumed to support the existing carrying amount. The IFRS does not specify the precise means of ensuring this, as long as the minimum requirements in paragraph 16 are met.

BC103   Some respondents read the liability adequacy test proposed in ED 5 as requiring fair value measurement as a minimum. That was not the Board's intention. An insurer needs to refer to IAS 37 only if the minimum requirements in paragraph 16 are not met.

BC104   Some respondents noted that many existing liability adequacy tests require measurements that do not include a risk margin. However, IAS 37 requires such a margin. To achieve consistency, these respondents suggested that a liability adequacy test under IAS 37 should also exclude these margins. The Board did not adopt this suggestion. The idea behind using IAS 37 for phase I was to take an existing measurement basis 'off the shelf' rather than create a new model.

Derecognition

BC105   The Board identified no reasons why derecognition requirements for insurance liabilities and insurance assets should differ from those for financial liabilities and financial assets. Therefore, the derecognition requirements for insurance liabilities are the same as for financial liabilities (see paragraph 14(c) of the IFRS). However, because derecognition of financial assets is a controversial topic, the IFRS does not address derecognition of insurance assets.

Offsetting

BC106   A cedant (ie the insurer that is the policyholder under a reinsurance contract) does not normally have a right to offset amounts due from a reinsurer against amounts due to the underlying policyholder. Normal offsetting criteria prohibit offsetting when no such right exists. When these criteria are not met, a gross presentation gives a clearer picture of the cedant's rights and obligations, and related income and expense (see paragraph 14(d) of the IFRS).

Reinsurance assets

Impairment of reinsurance assets

BC107   ED 5 proposed that a cedant should apply IAS 36 *Impairment of Assets* to its reinsurance assets. Respondents opposed this proposal for the following reasons:

(a)   This would compel many cedants to change their accounting model for reinsurance contracts in a way that is inconsistent with the accounting for the underlying direct insurance liability.

(b)   IAS 36 would require the cedant to address matters that are beyond the scope of phase I for the underlying direct insurance liability, such as the cash flows to be discounted, the discount rate and the approach to risk. Some saw IAS 36 as an indirect way of imposing something similar to a fair value model. There would also have been systems implications.

(c)   Reinsurance assets are essentially a form of financial asset and should be subject, for impairment testing, to IAS 39 rather than IAS 36.

BC108   The Board concluded that an impairment test for phase I (a) should focus on credit risk (arising from the risk of default by the reinsurer and also from disputes over coverage) and (b) should not address matters arising from the measurement of the underlying direct insurance liability. The Board decided that the most appropriate way to achieve this was an incurred loss model based on that in IAS 39 (see paragraph 20 of the IFRS).

Gains and losses on buying reinsurance

BC109   The IFRS defines a reinsurance contract as an insurance contract issued by one insurer (the reinsurer) to compensate another insurer (the cedant) for losses on one or more contracts issued by the cedant. One consequence is that the level of insurance risk required to meet the definition of an insurance contract is the same for a reinsurance contract as for a direct insurance contract.

BC110   National accounting requirements often define reinsurance contracts more strictly than direct insurance contracts to avoid distortion through contracts that have the legal form of reinsurance but do not transfer significant insurance risk (sometimes known as financial reinsurance). One source of such distortions is the failure to discount many non-life insurance claims liabilities. If the insurer buys reinsurance, the premium paid to the reinsurer reflects the present value of the liability and is, therefore, less than the previous carrying amount of the liability. Reporting a gain on buying the reinsurance is not representationally faithful if no economic gain occurred at that time. The accounting gain arises largely because of the failure to use discounting for the underlying liability. Similar problems arise if the underlying insurance liability is measured with excessive prudence.

BC111   The Board decided that it would not use the definition of a reinsurance contract to address these problems because the Board found no conceptual reason to define a reinsurance contract more or less strictly than a direct insurance contract. Instead, ED 5 addressed these problems through the following proposals:

(a)   prohibiting derecognition if the liability is not extinguished (paragraphs 14(c) of the IFRS and BC105) and prohibiting the offsetting of reinsurance assets against the related direct insurance liabilities (paragraphs 14(d) of the IFRS and BC106).

(b)   requiring unbundling in some cases (paragraphs 10–12 of the IFRS, IG Example 3 in the Implementation Guidance and paragraphs BC40–BC54).

(c) limiting the recognition of gains when an insurer buys reinsurance.

BC112 Respondents to ED 5 generally opposed the proposal described in paragraph BC111(c), on the following grounds:

(a) These piecemeal amendments to existing accounting models were beyond the scope of phase I and would require new systems that might not be needed in phase II.

(b) The proposals would have been difficult to apply to more complex reinsurance contracts, including excess of loss contracts and contracts that reinsure different layers of a portfolio of underlying direct insurance contracts.

(c) The proposals would have created inconsistencies with the measurement of the underlying direct insurance contracts.

(d) The artificial gain recognised at inception of some reinsurance contracts mitigates an artificial loss that arose earlier from excessive prudence or lack of discounting. If the net exposure has been reduced by reinsurance, there is no reason to continue to overstate the original liability.

(e) Any deferral of profit on buying reinsurance should be recognised as a liability, not as a reduction in the carrying amount of the reinsurance asset. This would permit assets and liabilities relating to the same underlying insurance contracts to be measured on a consistent basis and would also be consistent with other accounting bases such as US GAAP.

(f) Any restrictions in phase I should be targeted more precisely at financial reinsurance transactions (ie transactions that do not meet the definition of an insurance contract or that have significant financial components) or contracts that provide retroactive cover (ie ones that cover events that have already occurred).

(g) The liability adequacy test and unbundling proposals would have provided sufficient safeguards against the recognition of excessive profits.

BC113 The Board considered limiting the proposed requirements to cases where significant distortions in reported profit were most likely to occur, for example retroactive contracts. However, developing such a distinction would have been time-consuming and difficult, and there would have been no guarantee of success. The Board also considered drawing on requirements in US GAAP but decided not to include detailed requirements of this kind as a temporary and only partly effective solution. The proposals in ED 5 were an attempt to develop a simpler temporary solution. The responses indicated that the proposed solution contained too many imperfections to achieve its purpose.

BC114 The Board decided to delete the proposal in ED 5 and replace it with a specific disclosure requirement for gains and losses that arose on buying reinsurance (see paragraph 37(b) of the IFRS).

Other existing practices

BC115 The IFRS does not address:

(a) acquisition costs (paragraphs BC116–BC119);

(b) salvage and subrogation (paragraphs BC120 and BC121); and

(c) policy loans (paragraph BC122).

Acquisition costs

BC116 Acquisition costs are the costs that an insurer incurs to sell, underwrite and initiate a new insurance contract. The IFRS neither prohibits nor requires the deferral of acquisition costs, nor does it prescribe what acquisition costs are deferrable, the period and method of their amortisation or whether an insurer should present deferred acquisition costs as an asset or as a reduction in insurance liabilities. The treatment of deferred acquisition costs is an integral part of existing models and cannot be amended easily without a more fundamental review of those models in phase II.

BC117 The treatment of acquisition costs for insurance contracts in phase I may differ from the treatment of transaction costs incurred for investment contracts (ie financial liabilities). IAS 39 requires specified transaction costs to be presented as a deduction in determining the initial carrying amount of a financial liability. The Board did not wish to create exceptions to the definition of the transaction costs to which this treatment applies. Those costs may be defined more broadly or more narrowly than the acquisition costs that an insurer is required or permitted to defer using its existing accounting policies.

BC118 Some entities incur significant costs in originating long-term savings contracts. Some respondents argued that most, if not all, of these costs relate to the right to charge future investment management fees rather than to the financial liability that is created when the first instalment is received. They asked the Board to clarify whether the cost of originating those rights could be recognised as a separate asset rather than as a deduction in determining the initial carrying amount of the financial liability. They noted that this treatment would:

(a) simplify the application of the effective interest method for a financial liability carried at amortised cost.

(b) prevent the recognition of a misleading loss at inception for a financial liability that contains a demand feature and is carried at fair value. IAS 39 states that the fair value of such a liability is not less than the amount payable on demand (discounted, if applicable, from the first date when that amount could be required to be paid).

BC119 In response to these comments, the Board decided that incremental costs directly attributable to securing an investment management contract should be recognised as an asset if they meet specified criteria, and that incremental costs should be defined in the same way as in IAS 39. The Board clarified these points by adding guidance to the appendix of IAS 18 *Revenue*.

Salvage and subrogation

BC120   Some insurance contracts permit the insurer to sell (usually damaged) property acquired in settling the claim (ie salvage). The insurer may also have the right to pursue third parties for payment of some or all costs (ie subrogation). The Board will consider salvage and subrogation in phase II.

BC121   In the following two related areas, the IFRS does not amend IAS 37:

(a)   Gains on the expected disposal of assets are not taken into account in measuring a provision, even if the expected disposal is closely linked to the event giving rise to the provision. Instead, an entity recognises gains on expected disposals of assets at the time specified by the IFRS dealing with the assets concerned (paragraphs 51 and 52 of IAS 37).

(b)   Paragraphs 53–58 of IAS 37 address reimbursements for some or all of the expenditure required to settle a provision.

The Board is working on a project to amend various aspects of IAS 37.

Policy loans

BC122   Some insurance contracts permit the policyholder to obtain a loan from the insurer. The DSOP proposed that an insurer should treat these loans as a prepayment of the insurance liability, rather than as the creation of a separate financial asset. Because the Board does not regard this issue as a priority, phase I does not address it.

Changes in accounting policies

Relevance and reliability

BC123   IAS 8 prohibits a change in accounting policies that is not required by an IFRS, unless the change will result in the provision of reliable and more relevant information. Although the Board wished to avoid imposing unnecessary changes in phase I, it saw no need to exempt insurers from the requirement to justify changes in accounting policies. Therefore, paragraph 22 of the IFRS permits an insurer to change its accounting policies for insurance contracts if, and only if, the change makes the financial statements more relevant and no less reliable or more reliable and no less relevant, judged by the criteria in IAS 8.[*] As the Board's conclusions for phase II develop (see paragraphs BC6–BC8), they will give insurers further context for judgements about whether a change in accounting policies will make their financial statements more relevant and reliable.

---

[*]   Unlike IAS 8, paragraph 22 of the IFRS permits changes in accounting policies that make the financial statements more reliable and no less relevant. This permits improvements that make financial statements more reliable even if they do not achieve full reliability. In IAS 8 and the *Framework*, reliability is not synonymous with verifiability but includes characteristics such as neutrality and substance over form.

BC124   The IFRS contains further specific requirements supporting paragraph 22:

(a)   paragraph 24 permits an insurer to change its accounting policies for some insurance liabilities that it designates, without satisfying the normal requirement in IAS 8 that an accounting policy should be applied to all similar items (paragraphs BC174–BC177).

(b)   paragraph 25 permits the following practices to continue but prohibits their introduction:

(i)   measuring insurance liabilities on an undiscounted basis (paragraphs BC126 and BC127).

(ii)   measuring contractual rights to future investment management fees at an amount that exceeds their fair value as implied by a comparison with current fees charged by other market participants for similar services (paragraphs BC128–BC130).

(iii)   using non-uniform accounting policies for the insurance contracts of subsidiaries (paragraphs BC131 and BC132).

(c)   paragraph 26 prohibits the introduction of additional prudence if an insurer already measures insurance liabilities with sufficient prudence (paragraph BC133).

(d)   paragraphs 27–29 create a rebuttable presumption against the introduction of future investment margins in the measurement of insurance contracts (paragraphs BC134–BC144).

(e)   paragraph 30 addresses 'shadow accounting' (paragraphs BC181–BC184).

(f)   paragraph 45 permits an insurer to redesignate financial assets as 'at fair value through profit or loss' when it changes its accounting policies for insurance liabilities (paragraphs BC145 and BC146).

BC125   Some respondents suggested that phase I should not permit changes in accounting policies, to prevent lack of comparability (especially within a country) and management discretion to make arbitrary changes. However, the Board decided to permit changes in accounting policies for insurance contracts if they make the financial statements more relevant and no less reliable, or more reliable and no less relevant.

Discounting

BC126   In present practice, most general insurance claims liabilities are not discounted. In the Board's view, discounting of insurance liabilities results in financial statements that are more relevant and reliable. However, because the Board will not address discount rates and the basis for risk adjustments until phase II, the Board concluded that it could not require discounting in phase I. Nevertheless, the IFRS prohibits a change from an accounting policy that involves discounting to one that does not involve discounting (paragraph 25(a)).

BC127   Some respondents to ED 5 opposed discounting for contracts in which almost all the cash flows are expected to arise within one year, on materiality and cost-benefit grounds. The Board decided to create no specific exemption for these liabilities, because the normal materiality criteria in IAS 8 apply.

Investment management fees

BC128   Under some insurance contracts, the insurer is entitled to receive a periodic investment management fee. Some suggest that the insurer should, in determining the fair value of its contractual rights and obligations, discount the estimated future cash flows at a discount rate that reflects the risks associated with the cash flows. Some insurers use this approach in determining embedded values.

BC129   However, in the Board's view, this approach can lead to results that are not consistent with a fair value measurement. If the insurer's contractual asset management fee is in line with the fee charged by other insurers and asset managers for comparable asset management services, the fair value of the insurer's contractual right to that fee would be approximately equal to what it would cost insurers and asset managers to acquire similar contractual rights.* Therefore, paragraph 25(b) of the IFRS confirms that an insurer cannot introduce an accounting policy that measures those contractual rights at more than their fair value as implied by fees charged by others for comparable services; however, if an insurer's existing accounting policies involve such measurements, it may continue to use them in phase I.

BC130   The Board's agenda includes a project on revenue recognition.

Uniform accounting policies on consolidation

BC131   IAS 27 *Consolidated and Separate Financial Statements* requires entities to use uniform accounting policies. However, under current national requirements, some insurers consolidate subsidiaries without conforming the measurement of insurance liabilities using the subsidiaries' own local GAAP to the accounting policies used by the rest of the group.

BC132   The use of non-uniform accounting policies reduces the relevance and reliability of financial statements. However, prohibiting this would force some insurers to change their accounting policies for the insurance liabilities of some subsidiaries in phase I. This could have required systems changes that might no longer be needed in phase II. Therefore, the Board decided that an insurer already using non-uniform accounting policies for insurance contracts could continue to do so in phase I. However, if an insurer already uses uniform accounting policies for insurance contracts, it could not switch to a policy of using non-uniform accounting policies (paragraph 25(c) of the IFRS).

Excessive prudence

BC133   Insurers sometimes measure insurance liabilities on what is intended to be a highly prudent basis that lacks the neutrality required by the *Framework*. However, phase I does not define how much prudence is appropriate and cannot, therefore, eliminate excessive prudence. Consequently, the IFRS does not attempt to prohibit existing measurements of insurance liabilities that lack neutrality because of excessive prudence. Nevertheless, it prohibits the introduction of

---

*   This approach is consistent with the discussion of servicing rights and obligations in IAS 39.

additional prudence if an insurer already measures insurance liabilities with sufficient prudence (see paragraph 26 of the IFRS). The liability adequacy test in paragraphs 15–19 addresses the converse problem of understated insurance liabilities.

Future investment margins

BC134　In the Board's view, the cash flows from an asset are irrelevant for the measurement of a liability (unless those cash flows affect (a) the cash flows arising from the liability or (b) the credit characteristics of the liability). Many existing measurement practices for insurance liabilities conflict with this principle because they use a discount rate based on the estimated return from the assets that are deemed to back the insurance liabilities. However, the Board concluded that it could not eliminate these practices until phase II gives guidance on discount rates and the basis for risk adjustments.

BC135　ED 5 stated that an accounting policy change makes financial statements less relevant and reliable if it introduces a practice of including future investment margins. On the following grounds, some respondents opposed this proposal, which would have prohibited the introduction of any measurements that reflect future investment margins:

(a)　The proposal prejudges a phase II issue. Most actuaries and insurers believe that a fair value measure (ie one calibrated to transactions involving insurance contracts) must include some consideration of asset performance because product pricing, reinsurance and market transactions are observed to reflect this feature.

(b)　A current market rate results in more relevant and reliable information than an out-of-date discount rate prescribed by a regulator, even if the current market rate reflects expected asset returns.

(c)　Asset-based discount rates are a feature of most existing national systems, including some modern systems that use current estimates of future cash flows and current (albeit asset-based) discount rates. The prohibition proposed in ED 5 would have prevented an insurer from replacing its existing accounting policies for insurance contracts with another comprehensive basis of accounting for insurance contracts that is, in aggregate, more relevant and reliable despite the disadvantage of using an asset-based discount rate.

(d)　Because US GAAP uses an asset-based discount rate for some insurance liabilities, the prohibition would have prevented insurers from adopting US GAAP for their insurance liabilities in phase I. This would have been unfair because some insurers that have already adopted IFRSs apply US GAAP to their insurance contracts and could continue to do so in phase I.

BC136　In the light of these comments, the Board replaced the prohibition proposed in ED 5 with a rebuttable presumption, which could be overcome if the other components of a change in accounting policies increase the relevance and reliability of an insurer's financial statements sufficiently to outweigh the disadvantage of introducing the practice in question (see paragraph 28 of the IFRS for an example).

BC137   The IFRS identifies two practices that include future investment margins in the measurement of insurance liabilities: (a) using a discount rate that reflects the estimated return on the insurer's assets,[*] (b) projecting the returns on those assets at an estimated rate of return, discounting those projected returns at a different rate and including the result in the measurement of the liability. Some suggested that (b) should be eliminated in phase I because they regarded it as less acceptable than (a). However, the Board noted that although (b) appears more obviously incorrect than (a), these two practices have the same effect and are logically equivalent.

Future investment margins and embedded value

BC138   In addition to considering asset-based discount rates in general, the Board also considered a specific measurement technique that, at least in present practice, typically reflects future investment margins, namely embedded value. Embedded value is an indirect method of measuring an insurance liability. Indirect methods measure the liability by discounting all cash flows arising from both the book of insurance contracts and the assets supporting the book, to arrive at a net measurement for the contracts and supporting assets. The measurement of the assets is then deducted to arrive at a measurement of the book of contracts.[†] In contrast, direct methods measure the liability by discounting future cash flows arising from the book of insurance contracts only. If the same assumptions are made in both methods, direct and indirect methods can produce the same results.[§]

BC139   Life insurers in an increasing number of countries disclose embedded value information. Most disclose this information outside the financial statements or as supplementary information (usually unaudited), but a few use it as a measurement in their balance sheets.[ø]

BC140   Some respondents felt that embedded value methodology is far more relevant and reliable than most local accounting methods, and insurers should be permitted to adopt it. They noted that embedded values are often an important consideration in determining prices for acquisitions of insurers and of blocks of insurance contracts. Furthermore, embedded value and similar indirect methods are often used in accounting for the insurance liabilities assumed in these acquisitions.

---

[*]   Some approaches attempt to find a portfolio of assets ('replicating portfolio') with characteristics that replicate the characteristics of the liability very closely. If such a portfolio can be found, it may be appropriate to use the expected return on the replicating portfolio as the discount rate for the liability, with suitable adjustments for differences in their characteristics. However, replicating portfolio approaches should not be regarded as using an asset-based discount rate because they attempt to measure the characteristics of the liability. They are not based on the characteristics of the actual assets held, which may or may not match those of the liability.

[†]   If embedded values are recognised in the statement of financial position, they are typically presented as two components: an insurance liability and a separate intangible asset. This is similar to the expanded presentation that the IFRS permits in a business combination or portfolio transfer.

[§]   Luke N Girard, *Market Value of Insurance Liabilities: Reconciling the Actuarial Appraisal and Option Pricing Methods*, North American Actuarial Journal, Volume 4, Number 1

[ø]   IAS 1 *Presentation of Financial Statements* (as revised in 2007) replaced the term 'balance sheet' with 'statement of financial position'.

BC141　For the following reasons, some suggested that phase I should prohibit embedded value measurements in the balance sheet.

(a)　Embedded value approaches are largely unregulated at present and there is diversity in their application. For example, some view the methods used to reflect risk as fairly crude, diverse and not always fully consistent with capital market prices.

(b)　Embedded value methods today typically involve two practices whose introduction ED 5 regarded as unacceptable:

(i)　reflecting future investment margins in the measurement of the 'embedded value' asset associated with insurance liabilities (see paragraphs BC134–BC144).

(ii)　measuring contractual rights to future investment management fees at an amount that exceeds their fair value as implied by a comparison with current fees charged by other market participants for similar services (see paragraphs BC128–BC130).

(c)　In current practice, embedded values are generally determined on a single best estimate basis that does not reflect the full range of possible outcomes. This does not generally adequately address embedded guarantees and options, such as embedded interest rate guarantees. Until recently, embedded values would have ignored these items if they were out of the money. Indeed, in some cases, they might have been ignored even if they were in the money, because of assumptions about future investment performance. More attention is now being devoted to these options and guarantees and embedded value methods may begin to address them more rigorously, but that development is not yet complete.

BC142　However, for the following reasons, the IFRS permits continued use of embedded value measurements:

(a)　One objective of phase I is to avoid disturbing existing practice for insurance contracts, unless a change creates a significant improvement and leads in a direction consistent with the likely direction of phase II. Prohibiting the continued use of embedded values would not meet that criterion.

(b)　Embedded value methods are based on estimates of future cash flows, not an accumulation of past transactions. The advantages of this may, in some cases, outweigh the disadvantage of including future investment margins. Therefore, eliminating embedded value methods may not result in more relevant and reliable financial statements in every case.

(c)　Given that the Board did not prohibit asset-based discount rates for other measurements of insurance liabilities in phase I, there is no compelling reason in phase I to prohibit embedded value measurements that contain future investment margins.

(d)　Although embedded value measurements today typically include future investment margins, some practitioners have suggested improving embedded value methods by adjusting the asset cash flows fully for risk to make them consistent with market prices.

BC143 It follows from the Board's conclusions on relevance and reliability (paragraphs BC123–BC125), investment management fees (paragraphs BC128–BC130) and future investment margins (paragraphs BC134–BC137) that an insurer can introduce embedded value measurements in its balance sheet only if all the following conditions are met:

(a) the new accounting policy will result in more relevant and reliable financial statements (paragraph 22 of the IFRS). This is not an automatic decision and will depend on a comparison of the insurer's existing accounting with the way in which it intends to apply embedded value.

(b) this increase in relevance and reliability is sufficient to overcome the rebuttable presumption against including future investment margins (paragraph 29 of the IFRS).

(c) the embedded values include contractual rights to future investment management fees at an amount that does not exceed their fair value as implied by a comparison with current fees charged by other market participants for similar services (paragraph 25(b) of the IFRS and paragraphs BC128–BC130).

BC144 In some measurement approaches, the discount rate is used to determine the present value of a future profit margin, which is then attributed to different periods using a formula. However, in other approaches (such as most applications of embedded value), the discount rate determines the measurement of the liability directly. The Board concluded that it is highly unlikely that an insurer could overcome the rebuttable presumption in the latter case (see paragraph 29 of the IFRS).

Redesignation of financial assets

BC145 When an insurer changes its accounting policies for insurance liabilities, it is permitted, but not required, to reclassify some or all financial assets as 'at fair value through profit or loss'. This permits an insurer to avoid artificial mismatches when it improves its accounting policies for insurance liabilities. The Board also decided:

(a) not to restrict redesignation to assets backing the insurance contracts for which the accounting policies were changed. The Board did not wish to create unnecessary barriers for those insurers that wish to move to a more consistent measurement basis that reflects fair values.

(b) not to introduce an option to reclassify financial assets as 'available for sale'.* Such reclassification would have caused changes in carrying amount to be recognised directly in equity for assets, but in profit or loss for insurance liabilities. An insurer can avoid this inconsistency by classifying the financial assets as 'at fair value through profit or loss'.

BC146 IAS 39 permits redesignation of assets in specified circumstances when an entity adopts the revised IAS 39. IFRS 1 *First-time Adoption of International Financial Reporting Standards* contains corresponding provisions for first-time adopters.

---

* IFRS 9 *Financial Instruments*, issued in November 2009, eliminated the category of available-for-sale financial assets.

Acquisition of insurance contracts in business combinations and portfolio transfers

BC147 When an entity acquires another entity in a business combination, IFRS 3 *Business Combinations* requires the acquirer to measure at fair value the identifiable assets and liabilities acquired. Similar requirements exist under many national accounting frameworks. Nevertheless, in practice, insurers have often used an expanded presentation that splits the fair value of acquired insurance contracts into two components:

(a) a liability measured in accordance with the insurer's accounting policies for insurance contracts that it issues; and

(b) an intangible asset, representing the difference between (i) the fair value of the contractual insurance rights acquired and insurance obligations assumed and (ii) the amount described in (a). Life insurers often describe this intangible asset by names such as the present value of in force business (PVIF), present value of future profits (PVFP or PVP) or value of business acquired (VOBA). Similar principles apply in non-life insurance, for example if claims liabilities are not discounted.

BC148 For the following reasons, the Board decided to permit these existing practices during phase I (paragraph 31 of the IFRS):

(a) One objective of phase I is to avoid prejudging most phase II issues and to avoid requiring systems changes for phase I that might need to be reversed for phase II. In the meantime, disclosure about the nature of, and changes in, the related intangible asset provides transparency for users.

(b) The IFRS gives no guidance on how to determine the fair value of the insurance liabilities, because that would be premature in phase I. Thus, fair values identified during phase I might need to be changed in phase II.

(c) It may be difficult to integrate a fair value measurement at the date of a business combination into subsequent insurance contract accounting without requiring systems changes that could become obsolete in phase II.

BC149 The intangible asset described above is generally amortised over the estimated life of the contracts. Some insurers use an interest method of amortisation, which appears appropriate for an asset that essentially comprises the present value of a set of contractual cash flows. However, it is doubtful whether IAS 38 *Intangible Assets* would have permitted its use. Therefore, the Board decided that this asset should remain outside the scope of IAS 38 and its subsequent measurement should be consistent with the measurement of the related insurance liability (paragraph 31(b) of the IFRS). Because this asset would be covered by the liability adequacy test in paragraphs 15–19, the Board also excluded it from the scope of IAS 36 *Impairment of Assets*.

BC150 IAS 36 and IAS 38 still apply to customer lists and customer relationships reflecting the expectation of contracts that are not part of the contractual insurance rights and contractual insurance obligations that existed at the date of a business combination. An illustrative example published with IFRS 3 deals with customer relationships acquired together with a portfolio of one-year motor insurance contracts.

BC151 Measurements of the intangible asset described in paragraph BC147(b) sometimes include future investment margins. Those margins are subject to the same requirements as future investment margins included in the measurement of the related insurance liability (see paragraphs BC134–BC144).

BC152 In some cases, an insurer's accounting policies under previous GAAP (ie those used before it adopted IFRSs) involved measuring the intangible asset described in paragraph BC147(b) on a basis derived from the carrying amounts of other assets and liabilities. In such cases, if an entity changes the measurements of its assets and liabilities on adopting IFRSs for the first time, shadow accounting may become relevant (see paragraphs BC181–BC184 for a discussion of shadow accounting).

BC153 Some respondents requested an exemption from fair value measurement for insurance liabilities assumed in a business combination. They argued that there is still too much uncertainty about how fair value should be defined and determined. However, insurers have apparently been able to cope with the existing requirements in IFRSs and in national standards. The Board saw no compelling reason for a new exemption.

Discretionary participation features

BC154 Some insurance contracts contain a discretionary participation feature as well as a guaranteed element. The insurer has discretion over the amount and/or timing of distributions to policyholders, although that discretion may be subject to some contractual constraints (including related legal and regulatory constraints) and competitive constraints. Distributions are typically made to policyholders whose contracts are still in force when the distribution is made. Thus, in many cases, a change in the timing of a distribution means that a different generation of policyholders will benefit.

BC155 Although the issuer has contractual discretion over distributions, it is usually likely that current or future policyholders will ultimately receive some part of the accumulated surplus available, at the reporting date, for distribution to holders of contracts with discretionary participation features (ie distributable surplus). The main accounting question is whether that part of the distributable surplus is a liability or a component of equity. The Board will explore that question in phase II.

BC156 Features of this kind are found not only in insurance contracts but also in some investment contracts (ie financial liabilities). Requiring a particular accounting treatment in phase I for investment contracts with these features would create the risk that the Board might decide on a different treatment in phase II. Furthermore, in some cases, holders of insurance contracts and investment contracts have a contractual right to share in discretionary payments out of the same pool of assets. If the Board required a particular treatment for the discretionary participation features of the investment contracts in phase I, it might prejudge the treatment of these features in insurance contracts that are linked to the same pool of assets.

BC157 For these reasons, the Board decided not to address most aspects of the accounting treatment of such features in phase I, in either insurance contracts or investment contracts. However, paragraphs 34 and 35 of the IFRS confirm that it is unacceptable to classify a discretionary participation feature as an intermediate category that is neither liability nor equity, because this would be inconsistent with the *Framework*. If a balance sheet item does not meet the *Framework*'s definition of, and recognition criteria for, assets or liabilities, that item is included in equity.

BC158 Furthermore, ED 5 proposed a requirement for the issuer of an investment contract containing such a feature to recognise a liability measured at no less than the amount that would result from applying IAS 39 to the guaranteed element of the contract. Because issuers need not determine the IAS 39 measurement of the guaranteed element if the total recognised liability is clearly higher, ED 5 noted the Board's expectation that issuers would not need extensive new systems to comply with this requirement.

BC159 Some respondents objected that determining the result of applying IAS 39 to the guaranteed element would either have virtually no effect (in which case the requirement would be unnecessary) or require extensive new systems (causing costs exceeding the likely benefit to users). In finalising the IFRS, the Board adopted a more flexible approach that limits the need for systems to apply IAS 39 to the guaranteed element alone, while still requiring some rigour to avoid the understatement of the financial liability. Specifically, paragraph 35 permits two approaches for a discretionary participation feature in a financial liability:

(a) The issuer may classify the entire discretionary participation feature as a liability, but need not separate it from the guaranteed element (and so need not determine the result of applying IAS 39 to the guaranteed element). An issuer choosing this approach is required to apply the liability adequacy test in paragraphs 15–19 of the IFRS to the contract.

(b) The issuer may classify part or all of the feature as a separate component of equity. If so, the liability recognised cannot be less than the result of applying IAS 39 to the guaranteed element. The issuer need not determine that measurement if the total liability recognised is clearly higher.

BC160 There may be timing differences between retained earnings under IFRSs and distributable surplus (ie the accumulated amount that is contractually eligible for distribution to holders of discretionary participation features). For example, distributable surplus may exclude unrealised investment gains that are recognised under IFRSs. The resulting timing differences are analogous, in some respects, to temporary differences between the carrying amounts of assets and liabilities and their tax bases. The IFRS does not address the classification of these timing differences because the Board will not determine until phase II whether the distributable surplus is all equity, all liability or part equity and part liability.

BC161   The factor that makes it difficult to determine the appropriate accounting for these features is constrained discretion, in other words, the combination of discretion and constraints on that discretion. If participation features lack discretion, they are embedded derivatives and within the scope of IAS 39[*].

BC162   The definition of a discretionary participation feature does not capture an unconstrained contractual discretion to set a 'crediting rate' that is used to credit interest or other returns to policyholders (as found in the contracts described in some countries as 'universal life' contracts). Some view these features as similar to discretionary participation features because crediting rates are constrained by market forces and the insurer's resources. The Board will revisit the treatment of these features in phase II.

BC163   Some respondents asked the Board to clarify the treatment of premiums received for financial instruments containing discretionary participation features. Conceptually the premium for the guaranteed element is not revenue, but the treatment of the premium for the discretionary participation feature could depend on matters that will not be resolved until phase II. Furthermore, requiring the premium to be split could involve system changes that might become redundant in phase II. To avoid unnecessary disruption in phase I, the Board decided that entities could continue presenting premiums as revenue, with a corresponding expense representing the change in the liability.

BC164   Conceptually, if part or all of a discretionary participation feature is classified as a component of equity, the related portion of the premium should not be included in profit or loss. However, the Board concluded that requiring each incoming premium to be split would require systems changes beyond the scope of phase I. Therefore, the Board decided that an issuer could recognise the entire premium as revenue without separating the portion that relates to the equity component. However, the Board confirmed that the portion of profit or loss attributable to the equity component is presented as an allocation of profit or loss (in a manner similar to the presentation of minority interests[†]), not as expense or income.

BC165   Some suggested that investment contracts containing a discretionary participation feature should be excluded from the fair value disclosure required by IAS 32.[§] They noted both conceptual and practical problems in determining the fair value of an instrument of this kind. However, instead of creating a new exclusion from the required disclosure of fair value, the Board added new paragraph 91A to IAS 32. This extends existing requirements in IAS 32 governing those unquoted equity instruments whose fair value cannot be determined reliably.

---

[*] IFRS 9 *Financial Instruments*, issued in November 2009, amended the requirements in IAS 39 to identify and separately account for derivatives embedded in a financial host within the scope of IFRS 9. The requirements in IAS 39 continue to apply for derivatives embedded in non-financial hosts and financial hosts outside the scope of IFRS 9. This Basis for Conclusions has not been updated for changes in requirements since IFRIC 9 *Reassessment of Embedded Derivatives* was issued in March 2006.

[†] In January 2008 the IASB issued an amended IAS 27 *Consolidated and Separate Financial Statements*, which amended 'minority interests' to 'non-controlling interests'.

[§] In August 2005, the IASB relocated all disclosures relating to financial instruments to IFRS 7 *Financial Instruments: Disclosures*.

Issues related to IAS 39[*]

Assets held to back insurance contracts

BC166 The IFRS does not address financial or non-financial assets held by insurers to back insurance contracts. IAS 39 identifies four categories of financial asset, with three different accounting treatments. In developing IAS 39, the Board's predecessor (IASC) acknowledged that most countries had a mixed measurement model, measuring some financial assets at amortised cost and others at fair value. IASC decided to retain, but regulate and structure, the different approaches as follows:

(a) financial assets classified as 'at fair value through profit or loss' (including all financial assets held for trading) are measured at fair value, with all changes in their fair value recognised in profit or loss. Furthermore, all derivatives are deemed to be held for trading, and hence measured at fair value, because this is the only method that provides sufficient transparency in the financial statements.

(b) available-for-sale assets (ie those that do not fall into any of the other categories) are measured at fair value, with changes in their fair value recognised in equity until the asset is derecognised or becomes impaired. Measurement at fair value is appropriate given that available-for-sale assets may be sold in response to, for example, changes in market prices or a liquidity shortage.

(c) assets with a fixed maturity may be measured at amortised cost if the entity intends to hold them to maturity and shows that it has the ability to do so. This treatment is based on the view of some that changes in market prices are irrelevant if an asset is held to maturity because those changes will reverse before maturity (unless the asset becomes impaired).

(d) loans and receivables are measured at amortised cost. IASC was persuaded that there are difficulties in estimating the fair value of such loans, and that further progress was needed in valuation techniques before fair value should be required.

BC167 Some expressed concerns that accounting mismatches would arise in phase I if financial assets (particularly interest-bearing investments) held to back insurance contracts are measured at fair value under IAS 39 whilst insurance liabilities are measured on a different basis. If the insurer classifies the assets as 'available for sale', this difference in measurement basis would not affect profit or loss but it could lead to some volatility in equity. Some do not regard that volatility as a faithful representation of changes in the insurer's financial position.

---

[*] In November 2009 the IASB amended the requirements of IAS 39 relating to classification and measurement of assets within the scope of IAS 39 and relocated them to IFRS 9 *Financial Instruments*. IFRS 9 applies to all assets within the scope of IAS 39. Paragraphs BC166–BC194 discuss matters relevant when IFRS 4 was issued.

In developing ED 5, after discussing various suggestions for reducing that volatility,* the Board decided:

(a)   not to relax the criteria in IAS 39 for classifying financial assets as 'held to maturity'. Relaxing those criteria would undermine the fundamental assertion that an entity has both the intent and ability to hold the assets until maturity. The Board noted that an insurer may be able to classify some of its fixed maturity financial assets as held to maturity if it intends not to sell them before maturity and, in addition to meeting the other conditions set out in IAS 39, concludes that an unexpected increase in lapses or claims would not compel it to sell those assets (except in the 'disaster scenario' discussed in IAS 39 paragraph AG21).

(b)   not to create a new category of assets carried at amortised cost: assets held to back insurance liabilities. The creation of such a category would lead to a need for arbitrary distinctions and complex attribution procedures that would not make an insurer's financial statements more relevant and reliable, and could require insurers to develop costly systems. The Board reviewed a precedent that exists in Japan for such a category, but was not persuaded that the procedures adopted there can overcome these difficulties. Moreover, if an insurer may sell assets in response to, for example, changes in market prices or a liquidity shortage, the only appropriate measurement is fair value.

(c)   not to create a new category of 'available-for-settlement' liabilities, analogous to available-for-sale assets, measured at fair value, with changes in fair value recognised in equity. The creation of such a category would make it necessary to find some basis for distinguishing between that category and the existing category of non-trading financial liabilities, or to permit a free choice of accounting treatments. The Board has identified no basis for such a distinction, nor for deciding which of these two categories would be the new residual category. Furthermore, creating such a category could require insurers to develop new systems with no certainty that those systems would be needed in phase II.

BC168   In developing ED 5, the Board concluded that the reasons given above outweigh the effects of any accounting mismatch on an insurer's reported equity. Therefore, the Board decided not to exempt insurers from these existing requirements, even temporarily.

BC169   Insurers may be particularly sensitive to equity reported in general purpose financial statements in some countries where this amount is used in assessing compliance with regulatory capital requirements. However, although insurance supervisors are important users of general purpose financial statements, those financial statements are not directed at specific needs of insurance supervisors that other users do not share. Furthermore, supervisors generally have the power

---

*   The Board discussed this subject at its meeting in November 2002. It was also one of the major topics raised by insurance participants at two half-day sessions during the financial instruments round tables in March 2003. Before finalising ED 5, the Board discussed the subject again in April 2003.

to obtain additional information that meets their specific needs. In the Board's view, creating new exemptions from IAS 39 in this area would not have been the best way to meet the common needs of users (including insurance supervisors) of an insurer's general purpose financial statements.

BC170 Some argued that banks enjoy an 'advantage' that is not available to insurers. Under IAS 39, a bank may measure its core banking-book assets and liabilities (loans and receivables and non-trading financial liabilities) at amortised cost, whereas an insurer would have no such option for many of the assets held to back its core insurance activities. However, as noted in paragraph BC166(d), IASC permitted amortised cost measurement for loans and receivables because it had concerns about difficulties in establishing their fair value. This factor does not apply to many assets held by insurers to back insurance liabilities.

BC171 Many of the respondents to ED 5 urged the Board to explore ways of reducing the accounting mismatch described above. The Board discussed this subject at length at all three meetings at which it discussed the responses to ED 5 before finalising the IFRS. In addition, the Board discussed it with the Standards Advisory Council. It was also raised at a meeting of the Board's Insurance Advisory Committee in September 2003, which six Board members attended together with the project staff. Individual Board members and staff also had many discussions with interested parties, including users, insurers, actuaries, auditors and regulators.

BC172 It is important to distinguish two different types of mismatch:

(a) *accounting mismatch* arises if changes in economic conditions affect assets and liabilities to the same extent, but the carrying amounts of those assets and liabilities do not respond equally to those economic changes. Specifically, accounting mismatch occurs if an entity uses different measurement bases for assets and liabilities.

(b) *economic mismatch* arises if the values of, or cash flows from, assets and liabilities respond differently to changes in economic conditions. It is worth noting that economic mismatch is not necessarily eliminated by an asset-liability management programme that involves investing in assets to provide the optimal risk-return trade-off for the package of assets and liabilities.

BC173 Ideally, a measurement model would report all the economic mismatch that exists and would not report any accounting mismatch. The Board considered various alternatives, observing that all had advantages and disadvantages. Some alternatives would have amended IAS 39 to extend the use of cost or amortised cost measurements. However, the Board noted the following:

(a) Fair value is a more relevant measurement than amortised cost for financial assets that an entity might sell in response to changing market and other conditions.

(b) In its response to ED 5, the Association for Investment Management and Research (AIMR) strongly urged the Board not to extend the use of amortised cost in IAS 39. The AIMR is a non-profit professional association of more than 67,200 financial analysts, portfolio managers, and other investment professionals in 116 countries.

(c) An accounting model that measured both assets and liabilities at amounts based on current interest rates would provide information about the degree of economic mismatch. A model that measured both at historical values, or ignored the time value of money in measuring some insurance liabilities, would not. Financial analysts often observe that information about economic mismatch is very important to them.

(d) Some suggested that insurers wish to follow a strategy that involves holding fixed maturity investments to maturity, with some flexibility to sell investments if insurance claims or lapses are unusually high. They recommended relaxing restrictions in IAS 39 so that insurers using such a strategy could use the held-to-maturity category more easily. However, in discussions with individual Board members and staff, insurers generally indicated that they also wished to keep the flexibility to make sales in the light of changing demographic and economic conditions so that they can seek the best trade-off between risk and return. That is a valid and understandable business objective, but it is difficult to argue that cost could be more relevant than fair value in such cases. Although IAS 32[*] requires disclosure of the fair value of financial assets carried at amortised cost, disclosure does not rectify inappropriate measurement.

(e) Some noted that they wished to keep the flexibility to sell corporate bonds before a major downgrade occurs. They viewed the guidance in IAS 39 as restricting their ability to do this. Moreover, because a 'tainting' requirement in IAS 39 prohibits the use of the held-to-maturity category after most sales from this category, insurers are reluctant to use this classification for corporate bonds. The application guidance in IAS 39 gives examples of cases when sales of held-to-maturity investments do not 'taint' all other such investments. For example, paragraph AG22(a) of IAS 39 refers to a sale following a significant deterioration in the issuer's creditworthiness. The Board noted that some appeared to read that guidance as limited to changes in a credit rating by an external credit rating agency, although the guidance also refers to internal ratings that meet particular criteria.

(f) The Japanese precedent mentioned in paragraph BC167(b) creates some discipline by placing restrictions on the use of amortised cost, but for systems or other reasons not all insurers in Japan adopt this approach. Furthermore, this approach permits a cost approach if the durations (ie average maturities) of insurance liabilities match those of the related assets within a specified band of 80–125 per cent. If any economic mismatch arises within that band, this approach does not recognise it. In addition, gains and losses on selling assets held at amortised cost are generally recognised immediately in profit or loss (except that some gains are deferred and amortised if sales are not compatible with the duration matching strategy).

(g) Some Board members and staff met representatives of major European insurers to explore the possibility of (i) extending the use of amortised cost

---

[*] In August 2005, the IASB relocated all disclosures relating to financial instruments to IFRS 7 *Financial Instruments: Disclosures.*

if specified, relatively strict, criteria are met and (ii) combining that with a simplified attempt to identify 'ineffectiveness' resulting from the fact that the assets and liabilities would not respond identically to changes in interest rates. This approach would have avoided some of the practical and conceptual problems inherent in the Japanese approach discussed above. However, this untried approach had been developed at short notice and not all details had been worked through. Moreover, many insurers may not be able or willing to invest in systems that could need amendment in phase II.

(h) That a mixed measurement model can create an accounting mismatch is undeniable. Furthermore, it costs time and money for insurers to explain the effects even to sophisticated users. Insurers are very concerned that less sophisticated users may misinterpret the resulting information. If a simple, transparent and conceptually acceptable way could have been found to eliminate the accounting mismatch at an acceptable cost without also obscuring the economic mismatch, that change might have been beneficial. However, the Board could find no such way in the short term. The Board also noted that any change could have required major systems changes and that there appeared to be no consensus among insurers on a single method.

(i) Extending the use of amortised cost would have created an inconsistency with US GAAP. The accounting mismatch described in paragraphs BC167 and BC172 has existed for some years in US GAAP, which requires insurers to account for their financial assets in broadly the same way as under IAS 39. Furthermore, the US Financial Accounting Standards Board decided in January 2004 not to add to its agenda a project to reconsider US GAAP for investments held by life insurance companies.

BC174 In the light of these considerations, the Board concluded that changing the measurement requirements in IAS 39 for financial assets, even temporarily, would diminish the relevance and reliability of an insurer's financial statements. The Board observed that the accounting mismatch arose more from imperfections in existing measurement models for insurance liabilities than from deficiencies in the measurement of the assets. It would have been a retrograde step to try to mitigate the accounting mismatch by adopting a less relevant measurement of the assets—a measurement that would also have obscured some of the economic mismatch.

BC175 The Board considered whether it could mitigate the accounting mismatch by permitting improvements to the measurement of insurance liabilities. The Board noted that introducing a current market-based discount rate for insurance liabilities rather than a historical discount rate would improve the relevance and reliability of an insurer's financial statements. Therefore, such a change would have been permitted by the proposals in ED 5 and is also permitted by the IFRS. However, IAS 8 requires consistent accounting policies for similar transactions. For systems and other reasons, some insurers may not wish, or be able, in phase I to introduce a current market-based discount rate for all insurance liabilities.

BC176 The Board concluded that the increase in relevance and reliability from introducing a current discount rate could outweigh the disadvantages of permitting accounting policies that are not applied consistently to all similar liabilities. Accordingly, the Board decided to permit, but not require, an insurer to change its accounting policies so that it remeasures designated insurance liabilities for changes in interest rates. This election permits a change in accounting policies that is applied to some liabilities, but not to all similar liabilities as IAS 8 would otherwise require. The Board noted that insurers might sometimes be able to develop simplified models that give a reasonable estimate of the effect of interest rate changes.

BC177 The Board also noted the following:

(a) No single proposal would have eliminated the accounting mismatch for a broad cross-section of insurers without also obscuring the economic mismatch.

(b) No single proposal would have been acceptable to a broad cross-section of insurers.

(c) No single proposal could have been implemented by a broad cross-section of insurers without major systems changes. In other words, no solution was available that built on common industry approaches and systems. Furthermore, the systems needed to implement successfully the approach discussed with some European insurers (see paragraph BC173(g)) would also allow the approach permitted by paragraph 24 of the IFRS (adjusting designated liabilities for changes in interest rates). Indeed, paragraph 24 imposes fewer restrictions than the approach discussed with European insurers because it does not require the assets to match the liability cash flows closely, since any mismatch in cash flows is reflected in profit or loss.

(d) Adjusting the discount rate for designated liabilities will not eliminate all the accounting mismatch described above and some, perhaps many, insurers will choose not to make that adjustment. The reasons for this are as follows:

(i) As noted above, many insurers may not have systems to adjust liabilities for changes in interest rates and may not wish to develop such systems, even for designated liabilities as opposed to all liabilities.

(ii) Changes in discount rates would not affect the measurement of insurance liabilities that are carried at an accumulated account value.

(iii) Changes in discount rates would not affect the measurement of financial liabilities with a demand feature, because IAS 39 states that their fair value is not less than the amount payable on demand (discounted, if applicable, from the first date when that amount could be required to be paid). Although this last point is not strictly relevant for insurance contracts, many life insurers issue investment contracts for which it is relevant.

BC178 In summary, the Board decided not to amend existing measurement requirements in IAS 39 for financial assets because such amendments would have reduced the relevance and reliability of financial statements to an unacceptable extent. Although such amendments could have eliminated some of the accounting mismatch, they would also have obscured any economic mismatch that exists. The following points summarise amendments made to ED 5 that might mitigate the accounting mismatch in some cases, as well as relevant observations made by the Board:

(a) The Board decided to permit, but not require, an insurer to change its accounting policies so that it remeasures designated insurance liabilities for changes in interest rates (see paragraph BC176).

(b) The Board clarified the applicability of the practice sometimes known as 'shadow accounting' (paragraphs BC181–BC184).

(c) The Board amended IAS 40 *Investment Property* to permit two separate elections when an entity selects the fair value model or the cost model for investment property. One election is for investment property backing contracts (which could be either insurance contracts or financial instruments) that pay a return linked directly to the fair value of, or returns from, specified assets including that investment property. The other election is for all other investment property (see paragraph C12 of the IFRS).*

(d) The Board observed that some entities appeared to have misread the application guidance in IAS 39 on sales of held-to-maturity investments following a significant deterioration in the issuer's creditworthiness. Specifically, as noted in paragraph BC173(e), some appeared to have read it as limited to changes in a credit rating by an external credit rating agency, although the guidance also refers to internal ratings that meet particular criteria.

(e) The Board observed that IAS 1 and IAS 32 do not preclude a presentation identifying a separate component of equity to report a portion of the change (and cumulative change) in the carrying amount of fixed-maturity available-for-sale financial assets. An insurer could use such a presentation to highlight the effect on equity of changes in interest rates that (i) changed the carrying amount of assets but (ii) did not change the carrying amount of liabilities that respond economically to those changing interest rates.

BC179 IAS 40 permits an entity to use a fair value model for investment property, but IAS 16 does not permit this model for owner-occupied property. An entity may measure its owner-occupied property at fair value using the revaluation model in IAS 16, but changes in its fair value must be recognised in revaluation surplus rather than in profit or loss. Some insurers regard their owner-occupied property as an investment and prefer to use a fair value model for it. However, the Board decided not to make piecemeal changes to IAS 16 and IAS 40 at this stage.

BC180 The Board noted that shadow accounting (paragraphs BC181–BC184) may be relevant if there is a contractual link between payments to policyholders and the carrying amount of, or returns from, owner-occupied property. If an insurer elects to use shadow accounting, changes in the measurement of the liability resulting from revaluations of the property are recognised directly in equity, through the statement of changes in equity.

---

* The amendments contained in paragraph C12 are now incorporated as paragraphs 32A–32C of IAS 40.

Shadow accounting

BC181 In some accounting models, realised gains or losses on an insurer's assets have a direct effect on the measurement of some or all of its insurance liabilities.[*]

BC182 When many of those models were constructed, unrealised gains and most unrealised losses were not recognised in financial statements. Some of those models were extended later to require some financial assets to be measured at fair value, with changes in fair value recognised directly in equity (ie the same treatment as for available-for-sale financial assets under IAS 39). When this happened, a practice sometimes known as 'shadow accounting' was developed with the following two features:

    (a)   A recognised but unrealised gain or loss on an asset affects the measurement of the insurance liability in the same way that a realised gain or loss does.

    (b)   If unrealised gains or losses on an asset are recognised directly in equity, the resulting change in the carrying amount of the insurance liability is also recognised in equity.

BC183 Some respondents asked the Board to clarify whether the proposals in ED 5 permitted shadow accounting. The Board concluded the following:

    (a)   In principle, gains and losses on an asset should not influence the measurement of an insurance liability (unless the gains or losses on the asset alter the amounts payable to policyholders). Nevertheless, this is a feature of some existing measurement models for insurance liabilities and the Board decided that it was not feasible to eliminate this practice in phase I (see paragraph BC134 for further discussion in the context of future investment margins).

    (b)   Shadow accounting permits all recognised gains and losses on assets to affect the measurement of insurance liabilities in the same way, regardless of whether (i) the gains and losses are realised or unrealised and (ii) unrealised gains and losses are recognised in profit or loss or directly in equity. This is a logical application of a feature of some existing models.

    (c)   Because the Board does not expect that feature of existing models to survive in phase II, insurers should not be required to develop systems to apply shadow accounting.

    (d)   If an unrealised gain or loss on an asset triggers a shadow accounting adjustment to a liability, that adjustment should be recognised in the same way as the unrealised gain or loss.

    (e)   In some cases and to some extent, shadow accounting might mitigate volatility caused by differences between the measurement basis for assets and the measurement basis for insurance liabilities. However, that is a by-product of shadow accounting and not its primary purpose.

---

[*] Throughout this section, references to insurance liabilities are also relevant for (a) related deferred acquisition costs and (b) intangible assets relating to insurance contracts acquired in a business combination or portfolio transfer.

BC184 Paragraph 30 of the IFRS permits, but does not require, shadow accounting. The Implementation Guidance includes an illustrative example to show how shadow accounting might become relevant in an environment where the accounting for assets changes so that unrealised gains are recognised (IG Example 4). Because the Board does not expect the feature underlying the use of shadow accounting to survive in phase II, the Board decided not to give further guidance.

Investment contracts

BC185 Many insurers issue investment contracts (ie financial instruments that do not transfer enough insurance risk to qualify as insurance contracts). Under IAS 39, the issuer measures investment contracts at either amortised cost or, with appropriate designation at inception, at fair value. Some aspects of the measurements under IAS 39 differ from the measurements that are often used at present under national accounting requirements for these contracts:

(a) The definition and treatment of transaction costs under IAS 39 may differ from the definition and treatment of acquisition costs in some national requirements.

(b) The condition in IAS 39 for treating a modification of a financial liability (or the exchange of the new liability for an old liability) as an extinguishment of the original liability may differ from equivalent national requirements.

(c) Future cash flows from assets do not affect the amortised cost or fair value of investment contract liabilities (unless the cash flows from the liabilities are contractually linked to the cash flows from the assets).

(d) The amortised cost of a financial liability is not adjusted when market interest rates change, even if the return on available assets is below the effective interest rate on the liability (unless the change in rates causes the liability cash flows to change).

(e) The fair value of a financial liability with a demand feature is not less than the amount payable on demand.

(f) The fair value of a financial instrument reflects its credit characteristics.

(g) Premiums received for an investment contract are not recognised as revenue under IAS 39, but as balance sheet movements, in the same way as a deposit received.

BC186 Some argued that the Board should not require insurers to change their accounting for investment contracts in phase I because the scope of phase I is intended to be limited and because the current treatment of such contracts is often very similar to the treatment of insurance contracts. However, the Board saw no reason to delay the application of IAS 39 to contracts that do not transfer significant insurance risk. The Board noted that some of these contracts have features, such as long maturities, recurring premiums and high initial transaction costs, that are less common in other financial instruments. Nevertheless, applying a single set of accounting requirements to all financial instruments will make an insurer's financial statements more relevant and reliable.

BC187 Some contracts within the scope of IAS 39 grant cancellation or renewal rights to the holder. The cancellation or renewal rights are embedded derivatives and IAS 39 requires the issuer to measure them separately at fair value if they are not closely related to their host contract (unless the issuer elects to measure the entire contract at fair value).

Embedded derivatives

BC188 Some suggested that the Board should exempt insurers from the requirement to separate embedded derivatives contained in a host insurance contract and measure them at fair value under IAS 39. They argued that:

(a) separating these derivatives would require extensive and costly systems changes that might not be needed for phase II.

(b) some of these derivatives are intertwined with the host insurance contract in a way that would make separate measurement arbitrary and perhaps misleading, because the fair value of the whole contract might differ from the sum of the fair values of its components.

BC189 Some suggested that the inclusion of embedded options and guarantees in the cash flows used for a liability adequacy test could permit the Board to exempt some embedded derivatives from fair value measurement under IAS 39. Most proponents of this exemption implied that including only the intrinsic value of these items (ie without their time value) would suffice. However, because excluding the time value of these items could make an entity's financial statements much less relevant and reliable, the Board did not create such an exemption.

BC190 In the Board's view, fair value is the only relevant measurement basis for derivatives, because it is the only method that provides sufficient transparency in the financial statements. The cost of most derivatives is nil or immaterial. Hence if derivatives were measured at cost, they would not be included in the balance sheet and their success (or otherwise) in reducing risk, or their role in increasing risk, would not be visible. In addition, the value of derivatives often changes disproportionately in response to market movements (put another way, they are highly leveraged or carry a high level of risk). Fair value is the only measurement basis that can capture this leveraged nature of derivatives—information that is essential to communicate to users the nature of the rights and obligations inherent in derivatives.

BC191 IAS 39 requires entities to account separately for derivatives embedded in non-derivative contracts. This is necessary:

(a) to ensure that contractual rights and obligations that create similar risk exposures are treated in the same way whether or not they are embedded in a non-derivative contract.

(b)   to counter the possibility that entities might seek to avoid the requirement to measure derivatives at fair value by embedding a derivative in a non-derivative contract.

BC192   The requirement to separate embedded derivatives already applied to a host contract of any kind before the IFRS was issued. Exempting insurance contracts from that existing requirement would have been a retrograde step. Furthermore, much of the effort needed to measure embedded derivatives at fair value arises from the need to identify the derivatives and from other steps that will still be needed if the Board requires fair value measurement for phase II. In the Board's view, the incremental effort needed to identify the embedded derivatives separately in phase I is relatively small and is justified by the increased transparency that fair value measurement brings. IG Example 2 in the Implementation Guidance gives guidance on the treatment of various forms of embedded derivative.

BC193   Some embedded derivatives meet the definition of an insurance contract. It would be contradictory to require a fair value measurement in phase I of an insurance contract that is embedded in a larger contract when such measurement is not required for a stand-alone insurance contract. Therefore, the IFRS confirms that this is not required (paragraph 8). For the same reason, the Board concluded that an embedded derivative is closely related to the host insurance contract if the embedded derivative and host insurance contract are so interdependent that an entity cannot measure the embedded derivative separately (see new paragraph AG33(h) of IAS 39). Without this conclusion, paragraph 12 of IAS 39 would have required the insurer to measure the entire contract at fair value. An alternative approach would have been to retain that requirement, but require measurement at cost if an insurance contract cannot be measured reliably at fair value in its entirety, building on a similar treatment in IAS 39 for unquoted equity instruments. However, the Board did not intend to require fair value measurement for insurance contracts in phase I. Therefore, the Board decided not to require this even when it is possible to measure reliably the fair value of an insurance contract containing an embedded derivative.

BC194   The Board acknowledges that insurers need not, during phase I, recognise some potentially large exposures to items such as guaranteed annuity options and guaranteed minimum death benefits. These items create risks that many regard as predominantly financial, but if the payout is contingent on an event that creates significant insurance risk, these embedded derivatives meet the definition of an insurance contract. The IFRS requires specific disclosures about these items (paragraph 39(e)). In addition, the liability adequacy test requires an entity to consider them (see paragraphs BC94–BC104).

Elimination of internal items

BC195   Some respondents suggested that financial instruments issued by one entity to a life insurer in the same group should not be eliminated from the group's consolidated financial statements if the life insurer's assets are earmarked as security for policyholders' savings.

BC196   The Board noted that these financial instruments are not assets and liabilities from the group's perspective. The Board saw no justification for departing from the general principle that all intragroup transactions are eliminated, even if they are between components of an entity that have different stakeholders, for example policyholder funds and shareholder funds. However, although the transactions are eliminated, they may affect future cash flows. Hence, they may be relevant in measuring liabilities.

BC197   Some respondents argued that non-elimination would be consistent with the fact that financial instruments issued can (unless they are non-transferable) be plan assets in defined benefit plans under IAS 19 *Employee Benefits*. However, the Board did not view IAS 19 as a precedent in this area. IAS 19 requires a presentation net of plan assets because investment in plan assets reduces the obligation (IAS 19 Basis for Conclusions paragraph BC66). This presentation does not result in the recognition of new assets and liabilities.

Income taxes

BC198   Some respondents argued that discounting should be required, or at least permitted, for deferred tax relating to insurance contracts. The Board noted that discounting of a temporary difference is not relevant if an item's tax base and carrying amount are both determined on a present value basis.

Disclosure

BC199   The disclosure requirements are designed as a pair of high level principles, supplemented by some specified disclosures to meet those objectives. Implementation Guidance, published in a separate booklet,* discusses how an insurer might satisfy the requirements.

BC200   Although they agreed that insurers should be allowed flexibility in determining the levels of aggregation and amount of disclosure, some respondents suggested that the Board should introduce more specific and standardised disclosure requirements. Others suggested that the draft Implementation Guidance published with ED 5 was at too high a level to ensure consistency and comparability and that its non-mandatory nature might diminish its usefulness. Some were concerned that different levels of aggregation by different insurers could reduce comparability.

BC201   Nevertheless, the Board retained ED 5's approach. The Board viewed this as superior to requiring a long list of detailed and descriptive disclosures, because concentrating on the underlying principles:

    (a)   makes it easier for insurers to understand the rationale for the requirements, which promotes compliance.

    (b)   avoids 'hard-wiring' into the IFRS disclosures that may become obsolete, and encourages experimentation that will lead to improvements as techniques develop.

---

*   but included in this volume.

(c)   avoids requiring specific disclosures that may not be needed to meet the underlying objectives in the circumstances of every insurer and could lead to information overload that obscures important information in a mass of detail.

(d)   gives insurers flexibility to decide on an appropriate level of aggregation that enables users to see the overall picture but without combining information that has different characteristics.

BC202   Some respondents expressed the following general concerns about the proposed disclosure requirements in ED 5:

(a)   The proposed volume of disclosure was excessive and some of it would duplicate extensive material included in some countries in prudential returns.

(b)   Some of the proposed disclosures would be difficult and costly to prepare and audit, make it difficult to prepare timely financial statements and provide users with little value.

(c)   The proposals in ED 5 would require excessive disclosure of sensitive pricing information and other confidential proprietary information.

(d)   Some of the disclosures exceeded those required in other industries, which singled out insurers unfairly. Some felt that the level of disclosure would be particularly burdensome for small insurers, whereas others referred to the difficulty of aggregating information in a meaningful way for large international groups.

BC203   The two principles and most of the supporting requirements are applications of existing requirements in IFRSs, or relatively straightforward analogies with existing IFRS requirements (particularly IFRS 7 *Financial Instruments: Disclosures*).

BC203A   IFRS 7 was issued in August 2005 and replaced the disclosure requirements in IAS 32, including those on which the disclosures originally in IFRS 4 were based. Accordingly, the Board amended the disclosure requirements in IFRS 4 to be consistent with IFRS 7, when possible. The Board noted that:

(a)   insurers will have both insurance contracts and financial instruments. In particular, some of the investment products issued by insurers are financial instruments, not insurance contracts as defined in IFRS 4. It is more useful for users and easier for preparers if the risk disclosures for insurance contracts and financial instruments are the same.

(b)   making the disclosure requirements of IFRS 4 consistent with IFRS 7 makes the disclosures easier to prepare. In particular, IFRS 7 removes the 'terms and conditions' disclosure previously in paragraph 39(b) of IFRS 4. Some commentators on ED 5 (the Exposure Draft that preceded IFRS 4) objected to this disclosure requirement, believing it to be onerous and not to provide the most useful information.

(c)   the disclosures in IFRS 7 are designed to be implemented as a package, and if implemented piecemeal would result in less useful information for users. For example, the risk disclosures replace the 'terms and conditions' disclosure previously in paragraph 60(a) of IAS 32 and paragraph 39(b) of

IFRS 4. Merely updating the reference in paragraph 39(d) from IAS 32 to IFRS 7 would have resulted in some, but not all, of the risk disclosures being applicable to insurance contracts and the 'terms and conditions' disclosure being retained.

(d) as discussed in paragraph BC207, significant changes to the risk disclosures in paragraphs 38–39A are not expected as a result of phase II of the project on insurance contracts (although consequential changes may be needed to the accounting-related disclosures in paragraphs 36 and 37).

BC203B Some respondents, particularly preparers, did not agree that IFRS 4 should be amended as part of IFRS 7. In particular, some respondents argued that sensitivity analysis of market risk would be problematic for insurance contracts; they disagreed that such an analysis would be relatively easy to understand or calculate while issues relating to the measurement of fair value for insurance contracts remain unresolved. Those respondents suggested that disclosure requirements on sensitivity analysis should be considered during phase II of the project on insurance contracts, rather than in finalising IFRS 7. The Board noted that this requirement should not be unduly onerous for insurers, nor require them to provide quantitative information, because the sensitivity analysis applies only to changes in market risk variables that have an effect on profit or loss and equity in the period being reported. In addition, the Board noted that a sensitivity analysis is intended to replace the terms and conditions disclosures, which entities found onerous. The Board did not want to *require* insurers to comply with the older terms and conditions disclosures while allowing other entities to use the less onerous sensitivity analysis. However, the Board also noted that providing the sensitivity analysis would mean systems changes for some entities. Because the purpose of IFRS 4 was to minimise such changes pending the outcome of phase II, the Board did not want to require extensive systems changes for insurance contracts as a result of IFRS 7.

BC203C To address the concerns of those who do not want to make systems changes and those who want to substitute the new sensitivity analysis for the terms and conditions disclosures, the Board decided to permit a choice of sensitivity analysis disclosures for insurance risk only. Paragraph 39A of IFRS 4 has been added so that entities will be able to choose between providing:

(a) the terms and conditions disclosures, together with the qualitative sensitivity analysis currently permitted by IFRS 4; or

(b) the quantitative sensitivity analysis required by IFRS 7 (and permitted, but not required, by IFRS 4).

The Board permitted entities to choose to disclose a combination of qualitative and quantitative sensitivity analysis for insurance risk because it believes that entities should not be prevented from providing more useful information for some insurance risks, even if they do not have the ability to provide this information for all insurance risks. The Board noted that this option was a temporary solution to the problems cited in paragraph BC203B and would be eliminated in phase II.

BC204　Many respondents asked the Board to clarify the status of the Implementation Guidance. In particular, some felt that the Implementation Guidance appeared to impose detailed and voluminous requirements that contradicted the Board's stated intention in paragraph BC201. In response to requests from respondents, the Board added paragraph IG12 to clarify the status of the implementation guidance on disclosure.

BC205　Some suggested that some of the disclosures, particularly those that are qualitative rather than quantitative or convey management's assertions about possible future developments, should be located outside the financial statements in a financial review by management. However, in the Board's view, the disclosure requirements are all essential and should be part of the financial statements.

BC206　Some argued that the disclosure requirements could be particularly onerous and less relevant for a subsidiary, especially if the parent guarantees the liabilities or the parent reinsures all the liabilities. However, the Board decided that no exemptions from the disclosure principles were justified. Nevertheless, the high level and flexible approach adopted by the Board enables a subsidiary to disclose the required information in a way that suits its circumstances.

BC207　Some respondents expressed concerns that the disclosure proposals in ED 5 might require extensive systems changes in phase I that might not be needed in phase II. The Board expects that both disclosure principles will remain largely unchanged for phase II, although the guidance to support them may need refinement because different information will be available and because insurers will have experience of developing systems to meet the disclosure principles in phase I.

Materiality

BC208　Some respondents expressed concerns that the IFRS (reinforced by the Implementation Guidance) might require disclosure of excessively detailed information that might not be beneficial to users. In response to these concerns, the Board included in the Implementation Guidance a discussion of materiality taken from IAS 1.

BC209　Some respondents suggested that some of the qualitative disclosures should not be subject to the normal materiality threshold, which might, in their view, lead to excessive disclosure. They proposed using different terminology, such as 'significant', to reinforce that message. However, the Board noted that not requiring disclosure of material information would be inconsistent with the definition of materiality. Thus, the Board concluded that the disclosure should, in general, rely solely on the normal definition of materiality.

BC210　In one place, the IFRS refers to a different notion. Paragraph 37(c) refers to 'the assumptions that have the greatest effect on the measurement of' assets, liabilities, income and expense arising from insurance contracts'. Because many assumptions could be relevant, the Board decided to narrow the scope of the disclosure somewhat.

Explanation of recognised amounts

Assumptions

BC211 The first disclosure principle in the IFRS requires disclosure of amounts in an insurer's balance sheet* and income statement† that arise from insurance contracts (paragraph 36 of the IFRS). In support of this principle, paragraph 37(c) and (d) requires disclosure about assumptions and changes in assumptions. The disclosure of assumptions both assists users in testing reported information for sensitivity to changes in those assumptions and enhances their confidence in the transparency and comparability of the information.

BC212 Some expressed concerns that information about assumptions and changes in assumptions might be costly to prepare and of limited usefulness. There are many possible assumptions that could be disclosed: excessive aggregation would result in meaningless information, whereas excessive disaggregation could be costly, lead to information overload, and reveal commercially sensitive information. In response to these concerns, the disclosure about the assumptions focuses on the process used to derive them.

BC213 Some respondents argued that it is difficult to disclose meaningful information about changes in interdependent assumptions. As a result, an analysis by sources of change often depends on the order in which the analysis is performed. To acknowledge this difficulty, the IFRS does not specify a rigid format or contents for this analysis. This allows insurers to analyse the changes in a way that meets the objective of the disclosure and is appropriate for the risks they face and the systems that they have, or can enhance at a reasonable cost.

Changes in insurance liabilities

BC214 Paragraph 37(e) of the IFRS requires a reconciliation of changes in insurance liabilities, reinsurance assets and, if any, deferred acquisition costs. IAS 37 requires broadly comparable disclosure of changes in provisions, but the scope of IAS 37 excludes insurance contracts. Disclosure about changes in deferred acquisition costs is important because some existing methods use adjustments to deferred acquisition costs as a means of recognising some effects of remeasuring the future cash flows from an insurance contract (for example, to reflect the result of a liability adequacy test).

Nature and extent of risks arising from insurance contracts

BC215 The second disclosure principle in the IFRS requires disclosure of information that enables users to understand the nature and extent of risks arising from insurance contracts (paragraph 38 of the IFRS). The Implementation Guidance supporting this principle builds largely on existing requirements in IFRSs, particularly the disclosures for financial instruments in IFRS 7.

---

*   IAS 1 *Presentation of Financial Statements* (as revised in 2007) replaced the term 'balance sheet' with 'statement of financial position'.

†   IAS 1 (revised 2007) requires an entity to present all income and expense items in one statement of comprehensive income or in two statements (a separate income statement and a statement of comprehensive income).

BC216 Some respondents read the draft Implementation Guidance accompanying ED 5 as implying that the IFRS would require disclosures of estimated cash flows. That was not the Board's intention because insurers cannot be expected to have systems to prepare detailed estimates of cash flows in phase I (beyond what is needed for the liability adequacy test). The Board revised the Implementation Guidance to emphasise that the second disclosure principle requires disclosure **about** cash flows (ie disclosure that helps users understand their amount, timing and uncertainty), not disclosure of cash flows.[*]

Insurance risk

BC217 For insurance risk (paragraph 39(c)), the disclosures are intended to be consistent with the spirit of the disclosures required by IAS 32.[†] The usefulness of particular disclosures about insurance risk depends on the circumstances of a particular insurer. Therefore, the requirements are written in general terms to allow practice in this area to evolve.

Sensitivity analysis

BC218 Paragraph 39(c)(i) requires disclosure of a sensitivity analysis. The Board decided not to include specific requirements that may not be appropriate in every case and could impede the development of more useful forms of disclosure or become obsolete.

BC219 IAS 32[†] requires disclosure of a sensitivity analysis only for assumptions that are not supported by observable market prices or rates. However, because the IFRS does not require a specific method of accounting for embedded options and guarantees, including some that are partly dependent on observable market prices or rates, paragraph 39(c)(i) requires a sensitivity analysis for all variables that have a material effect, including variables that are observable market prices or rates.

Claims development

BC220 Paragraph 39(c)(iii) requires disclosure about claims development. The US Securities and Exchange Commission requires property and casualty insurers to provide a table showing the development of provisions for unpaid claims and claim adjustment expenses for the previous ten years, if the provisions exceed 50 per cent of equity. The Board noted that the period of ten years is arbitrary and decided instead to set the period covered by this disclosure by reference to the length of the claims settlement cycle. Therefore, the IFRS requires that the disclosure should go back to the period when the earliest material claim arose for which there is still uncertainty about the amount and timing of the claims payments, but need not go back more than ten years (subject to transitional exemptions in paragraph 44 of the IFRS). Furthermore, the proposal applies to all insurers, not only to property and casualty insurers. However, because an insurer need not disclose this information for claims for

---

[*] IFRS 7 replaced the required disclosures about cash flows with required disclosures about the nature and extent of risks.

[†] In August 2005, the IASB relocated all disclosures relating to financial instruments to IFRS 7 *Financial Instruments: Disclosures*.

which uncertainty about the amount and timing of claims payments is typically resolved within one year, it is unlikely that many life insurers would need to give this disclosure.

BC221 In the US, disclosure of claims development is generally presented in management's discussion and analysis, rather than in the financial statements. However, this disclosure is important because it gives users insights into the uncertainty surrounding estimates about future claims, and also indicates whether a particular insurer has tended to overestimate or underestimate ultimate payments. Therefore, the IFRS requires it in the financial statements.

Probable maximum loss

BC222 Some suggested that an insurer—particularly a general insurer—should disclose the probable maximum loss (PML) that it would expect if a reasonably extreme event occurred. For example, an insurer might disclose the loss that it would suffer from a severe earthquake of the kind that would be expected to recur every one hundred years, on average. However, given the lack of a widely agreed definition of PML, the Board concluded that it is not feasible to require disclosure of PML or similar measures.

Exposures to interest rate risk or market risk

BC223 As discussed in paragraphs BC193 and BC194, the Board confirmed that an insurer need not account at fair value for embedded derivatives that meet the definition of an insurance contract, but also create material exposures to interest rate risk or market risk. For many insurers, these exposures can be large. Therefore, paragraph 39(e) of the IFRS specifically requires disclosures about these exposures.

Fair value of insurance liabilities and insurance assets

BC224 ED 5 proposed that an insurer should disclose the fair value of its insurance liabilities and insurance assets. This proposal was intended (a) to give useful information to users of an insurer's financial statements and (b) to encourage insurers to begin work on systems that use updated information, to minimise the transition period for phase II.

BC225 Some respondents supported the proposed disclosure of fair value, arguing that it is important information for users. Some felt that this would be particularly important given the range of measurement practices in phase I. However, many respondents (including some who supported a fair value disclosure requirement in principle) suggested that the Board should delete this requirement or suspend it until phase II is completed. They offered the following arguments:

(a) Requiring such disclosure would be premature before the Board resolves significant issues about fair value measurement and gives adequate guidance on how to determine fair value. The lack of guidance would lead to lack of comparability for users, place unreasonable demands on preparers and pose problems of auditability. Furthermore, disclosure cannot rectify that lack of comparability because it is difficult to describe the features of different models clearly and concisely.

(b) Disclosure by 2006 (as proposed in ED 5) would be impracticable because insurers would not have time to create and test the necessary systems.

(c) Expecting insurers to begin work on an unknown objective would be costly and waste time. Furthermore, in the absence of agreed methods for developing fair value, the systems developed for phase I disclosures of fair value might need changes for phase II.

(d) The proposal asked for a mandate for the IASB to interpret its own requirement before explaining what it means.

BC226 The Board did not view the proposed requirement to disclose fair value as conditional on the measurement model for phase II. In the Board's view, disclosure of the fair value of insurance liabilities and insurance assets would provide relevant and reliable information for users even if phase II does not result in a fair value model. However, the Board agreed with respondents that requiring disclosure of fair value would not be appropriate at this stage.

Summary of changes from ED 5

BC227 The following is a summary of the main changes from ED 5 to the IFRS. The Board:

(a) clarified aspects of the definition of an insurance contract (paragraphs BC36 and BC37).

(b) clarified the requirement to unbundle deposit components in some (limited) circumstances (paragraphs BC40–BC54).

(c) deleted the 'sunset clause' proposed in ED 5 (paragraphs BC84 and BC85).

(d) clarified the need to consider embedded options and guarantees in a liability adequacy test (paragraph BC99) and clarified the level of aggregation for the liability adequacy test (paragraph BC100).

(e) replaced the impairment test for reinsurance assets. Instead of referring to IAS 36 (which contained no scope exclusion for reinsurance assets before the Board issued IFRS 4), the test will refer to IAS 39 (paragraphs BC107 and BC108).

(f) deleted the proposed ban on recognising a gain at inception of a reinsurance contract, and replaced this with a disclosure requirement (paragraphs BC109–BC114).

(g) clarified the treatment of acquisition costs for contracts that involve the provision of investment management services (paragraphs BC118 and BC119).

(h) changed the prohibition on introducing asset-based discount rates into a rebuttable presumption (paragraphs BC134–BC144).

(i) clarified aspects of the treatment of discretionary participation features (paragraphs BC154–BC165) and created an explicit new exemption from the requirement to separate, and measure at fair value, some options to surrender a contract with a discretionary participation feature (paragraph 9 of the IFRS).

(j)   introduced an option for an insurer to change its accounting policies so that it remeasures designated insurance liabilities in each period for changes in interest rates. This election permits a change in accounting policies that is applied to some liabilities, but not to all similar liabilities as IAS 8 would otherwise require (paragraphs BC174–BC177).

(k)   amended IAS 40 to permit two separate elections for investment property when an entity selects the fair value model or the cost model. One election is for investment property backing contracts that pay a return linked directly to the fair value of, or returns from, that investment property. The other election is for all other investment property (paragraph BC178).

(l)   clarified the applicability of shadow accounting (paragraphs BC181–BC184).

(m)   clarified that an embedded derivative is closely related to the host insurance contract if they are so interdependent that an entity cannot measure the embedded derivative separately (ie without considering the host contract) (paragraph BC193).

(n)   clarified that the Implementation Guidance does not impose new disclosure requirements (paragraph BC204).

(o)   deleted the proposed requirement to disclose the fair value of insurance contracts from 2006 (paragraphs BC224–BC226).

(p)   provided an exemption from applying most disclosure requirements for insurance contracts to comparatives that relate to 2004 (paragraphs 42–44 of the IFRS).

(q)   confirmed that unit-denominated payments can be measured at current unit values, for both insurance contracts and investment contracts, avoiding the apparent need to separate an 'embedded derivative' (paragraph AG33(g) of IAS 39, inserted by the IFRS).

Dissenting opinions

DO1   Professor Barth and Messrs Garnett, Gélard, Leisenring, Smith and Yamada dissent from the issue of IFRS 4.

Dissent of Mary E Barth, Robert P Garnett, Gilbert Gélard, James J Leisenring and John T Smith

DO2   Messrs Garnett and Gélard dissent for the reasons given in paragraphs DO3 and DO4 and Mr Garnett also dissents for the reasons given in paragraphs DO5 and DO6. Professor Barth and Messrs Leisenring and Smith dissent for the reasons given in paragraphs DO3–DO8 and Mr Smith also dissents for the reasons given in paragraphs DO9–DO13.

Temporary exemption from paragraphs 10–12 of IAS 8

DO3   Professor Barth and Messrs Garnett, Gélard, Leisenring and Smith dissent because IFRS 4 exempts an entity from applying paragraphs 10–12 of IAS 8 *Accounting Policies, Changes in Accounting Estimates and Errors* when accounting for insurance and reinsurance contracts. They believe that all entities should be required to apply these paragraphs. These Board members believe that the requirements in IAS 8 have particular relevance and applicability when an IFRS lacks specificities, as does IFRS 4, which allows the continuation of a variety of measurement bases for insurance and reinsurance contracts. Because of the failure to consider the IASB *Framework*, continuation of such practices may result in the inappropriate recognition of, or inappropriate failure to recognise, assets, liabilities, equity, income and expense. In these Board members' view, if an entity cannot meet the basic requirements of paragraphs 10–12 of IAS 8, it should not be allowed to describe its financial statements as being in accordance with International Financial Reporting Standards.

DO4   These Board members' concerns are heightened by the delay in completing phase II of the Board's project on accounting for insurance contracts. Although phase II is on the Board's active agenda, it is unlikely that the Board will be able to develop an IFRS on insurance contracts in the near term. Accordingly, it is likely that the exemption from IAS 8 will be in place for some time.

Future investment margins and shadow accounting

DO5   Professor Barth and Messrs Garnett, Leisenring and Smith dissent for the further reason that they would not permit entities to change their accounting policies for insurance and reinsurance contracts to policies that include using future investment margins in the measurement of insurance liabilities. They agree with the view expressed in paragraph BC134 that cash flows from an asset are irrelevant for the measurement of a liability (unless those cash flows affect the cash flows arising from the liability or the credit characteristics of the liability). Therefore, they believe that changing to an accounting policy for insurance contracts that uses future investment margins to measure liabilities arising from insurance contracts reduces the relevance and reliability of an insurer's financial statements. They do not believe that other aspects of an accounting model for insurance contracts can outweigh this reduction.

DO6 These four Board members also would not permit entities to change their accounting policies for insurance and reinsurance contracts to policies that include using what is called shadow accounting. They do not believe that the changes in the carrying amount of insurance liabilities (including related deferred acquisition costs and intangible assets) under shadow accounting should be recognised directly in equity. That these changes in the measurement of the liability are calculated on the basis of changes in the measurement of assets is irrelevant. These Board members believe that these changes in insurance liabilities result in expenses that under the IASB *Framework* should be recognised in profit or loss.

Financial instruments with a discretionary participation feature*

DO7 Professor Barth and Messrs Leisenring and Smith would not permit entities to account for a financial instrument with a discretionary participation feature on a basis that differs from that required by IAS 32 *Financial Instruments: Disclosure and Presentation* and IAS 39 *Financial Instruments: Recognition and Measurement*. Those Standards require entities to separate the components of a compound financial instrument, recognise the liability component initially at fair value, and attribute any residual to the equity component. These three Board members believe that the difficulty in determining whether a discretionary participation feature is a liability or equity does not preclude applying the measurement requirements in IAS 39 to the liability and equity components once the entity makes that determination. These three Board members believe that an entity would misstate interest expense if the financial liability component is not initially measured at its fair value.

DO8 These three Board members would require entities to ensure in all cases that the liability recognised for financial instruments with a discretionary participation feature is no less than the amount that would result from applying IAS 39 to the guaranteed element. Paragraph 35 of IFRS 4 requires this if an entity classifies none or some of the feature as a liability, but not if it classifies all of the feature as a liability.

Financial instruments*

DO9 Mr Smith also dissents from IFRS 4 because he believes it defines insurance contracts too broadly and makes unnecessary exceptions to the scope of IAS 32 and IAS 39. In his view, this permits the structuring of contractual provisions to avoid the requirements of those Standards, diminishing their effectiveness and adding considerable complexity in interpreting and applying them and IFRS 4. He believes that many of the exceptions, based on the desire to avoid systems changes, are unnecessary because they generally are unrelated to the second

---

* In November 2009 the IASB amended the requirements of IAS 39 relating to classification and measurement of assets within the scope of IAS 39 and relocated them to IFRS 9 *Financial Instruments*. IFRS 9 applies to all assets within the scope of IAS 39.

phase of the project on insurance contracts, and they create a disincentive to enhance systems before the second phase of that project is completed. Mr Smith believes that IAS 32 and IAS 39 already contain the appropriate solutions when measurements cannot be made reliably and those solutions make systems limitations transparent.

DO10 Paragraph 10 of IFRS 4 requires an insurer to unbundle a deposit component of an insurance contract if the insurer can measure the deposit component separately and the insurer's accounting policies do not otherwise require it to recognise all rights and obligations arising from the deposit component. Mr Smith notes that the deposit component consists entirely of financial liabilities or financial assets. Therefore, he believes that the deposit component of all insurance contracts should be unbundled. Mr Smith notes that IAS 32 already requires the liability component of a compound financial instrument to be separated at its fair value with any residual accounted for as equity. He believes this approach could be applied by analogy when an insurance contract contains a financial liability and would represent a superior solution.

DO11 IFRS 4 amends IAS 39 by stating that an embedded derivative and the host insurance contract are closely related if they are so interdependent that the entity cannot measure the embedded derivative separately. This creates an exemption from the requirement in IAS 39 to account for such embedded derivatives at fair value. Mr Smith disagrees with that change. In particular, if a contract permits a policyholder to obtain a derivative-based cash settlement in lieu of maintaining insurance, Mr Smith believes that the derivative-based cash settlement alternative is a financial liability and should be measured at fair value.

DO12 For the contracts discussed in the previous paragraph, Mr Smith believes that IAS 39 already provides a superior solution that will not promote structuring to take advantage of an exception to IAS 39. It requires the entire contract to be measured at fair value when an embedded derivative cannot be reliably separated from the host contract. However, Mr Smith would amend IAS 39 to require measurement at cost if a contract cannot be measured reliably at fair value in its entirety and contains a significant insurance component as well as an embedded derivative. This amendment would be consistent with similar requirements in IAS 39 for unquoted equity instruments. To make systems limitations more transparent, Mr Smith would add the disclosure required by IAS 32, including the fact that fair value cannot be measured reliably, a description of the insurance contracts in question, their carrying amounts, an explanation of why fair value cannot be measured reliably and, if possible, the range of estimates within which fair value is likely to fall.

DO13 Mr Smith would exclude from the definition of an insurance contract those contracts that are regarded as transferring significant insurance risk at inception only because they include a pricing option permitting the holder to purchase insurance at a specified price at a later date. He would also exclude from the definition those contracts in which the insurance component has expired. He believes that any remaining obligation is a financial instrument that should be accounted for under IAS 39.

Dissent of Tatsumi Yamada

DO14   Mr Yamada dissents from the issue of IFRS 4 because he believes that it does not resolve appropriately the mismatch in measurement base between financial assets of insurers and their insurance liabilities. Specifically:

(a)   he disagrees with the inclusion of an option to introduce a current discount rate for designated insurance liabilities.

(b)   he believes that the Board should have provided a practicable means to reduce the effect of the accounting mismatch using methods based partly on some existing practices that involve broader, but constrained, use of amortised cost.

Option to introduce a current discount rate

DO15   Mr Yamada disagrees with paragraph 24 of the IFRS, which creates an option to introduce a current market-based discount rate for designated insurance liabilities. He has sympathy for the view expressed in paragraph BC175 that introducing a current market-based discount rate for insurance liabilities rather than a historical discount rate would improve the relevance and reliability of an insurer's financial statements. However, as explained in paragraph BC126, 'the Board will not address discount rates and the basis for risk adjustments until phase II.' Therefore, Mr Yamada believes that it is not appropriate to deal with measurement of insurance liabilities in phase I of this project.

DO16   In addition, Mr Yamada believes that there should be a stringent test to assess whether changes in the carrying amount of the designated insurance liabilities mitigate the changes in carrying amount of financial assets. Without such a test, management will have a free choice to decide the extent to which it introduces remeasurement of insurance liabilities. Therefore, he does not agree with the Board's conclusion in paragraph BC176 that 'the increase in relevance and reliability from introducing a current discount rate could outweigh the disadvantages of permitting accounting policies that are not applied consistently to all similar liabilities'.

DO17   Furthermore, the option introduced by paragraph 24 is not an effective way to reduce the accounting mismatch, in Mr Yamada's view. He agrees with the Board's analysis that 'many insurers may not have systems to adjust liabilities for changes in interest rates and may not wish to develop such systems, even for designated liabilities as opposed to all liabilities', as explained in paragraph BC177(d)(i).

Assets held to back insurance liabilities[*]

DO18   As stated in paragraph BC171, many of the respondents to ED 5 urged the Board to explore ways of reducing the accounting mismatch. Mr Yamada notes that IFRS 4 provides some limited solutions for the accounting mismatch by clarifying that shadow accounting can be used and amending IAS 40 to permit two separate

---

[*]   In November 2009 the IASB amended the requirements of IAS 39 relating to classification and measurement of assets within the scope of IAS 39 and relocated them to IFRS 9 *Financial Instruments*. IFRS 9 applies to all assets within the scope of IAS 39.

elections when an entity selects the fair value model or the cost model for investment property. IFRS 4 also provides an option to introduce a current market-based discount rate for designated insurance liabilities but, for reasons given in paragraphs DO15–DO17, Mr Yamada does not support that option.

DO19   Mr Yamada believes that it would have been appropriate to provide a more broadly applicable way of mitigating the effect of the accounting mismatch. Because phase I is only a stepping stone to phase II, Mr Yamada is of the view that the only practicable solution in the short term is one based on the existing practices of insurers. He believes that if remeasurement of insurance liabilities by a current market-based discount rate is allowed as means of resolving the mismatch, a new category of assets carried at amortised cost such as the Japanese 'debt securities earmarked for policy reserve' (DSR) should also have been allowed in phase I.

DO20   Although Mr Yamada acknowledges that the DSR approach would not lead to more relevant and reliable measurements, he notes that insurers have several years' experience of using this approach, which was created in 2000 when Japan introduced an accounting standard for financial instruments that is similar to IASs 32 and 39. He believes that no perfect solution is available in phase I and together with the disclosure of fair value information required by IAS 32, the DSR approach would provide a reasonable solution for phase I. Therefore he does not agree with the Board's conclusion in paragraph BC178 that amending the existing measurement requirements in IAS 39 for financial assets 'would have reduced the relevance and reliability of financial statements to an unacceptable extent'. Indeed, Mr Yamada believes the exemption in IFRS 4 from paragraphs 10–12 of IAS 8 could impair the relevance and reliability of financial statements more than introducing the DSR approach would have done.

CONTENTS

          © IASCF

Guidance on implementing
IFRS 4 *Insurance Contracts*

This guidance accompanies, but is not part of, IFRS 4.

Introduction

IG1   This implementation guidance:

(a)   illustrates which contracts and embedded derivatives are within the scope of the IFRS (see paragraphs IG2–IG4).

(b)   includes an example of an insurance contract containing a deposit component that needs to be unbundled (paragraph IG5).

(c)   illustrates shadow accounting (paragraphs IG6–IG10).

(d)   discusses how an insurer might satisfy the disclosure requirements in the IFRS (paragraphs IG11–IG71).

Definition of insurance contract

IG2   IG Example 1 illustrates the application of the definition of an insurance contract. The example does not illustrate all possible circumstances.

IG Example 1: Application of the definition of an insurance contract

Contract type	Treatment in phase I
1.1 Insurance contract (see definition in Appendix A of the IFRS and guidance in Appendix B).	Within the scope of the IFRS, unless covered by scope exclusions in paragraph 4 of the IFRS. Some embedded derivatives and deposit components must be separated (see IG Examples 2 and 3 and paragraphs 7–12 of the IFRS).
1.2 Death benefit that could exceed amounts payable on surrender or maturity.	Insurance contract (unless contingent amount is insignificant in all scenarios that have commercial substance). Insurer could suffer a significant loss on an individual contract if the policyholder dies early. See IG Examples 1.23–27 for further discussion of surrender penalties.
1.3 A unit-linked contract that pays benefits linked to the fair value of a pool of assets. The benefit is 100 per cent of the unit value on surrender or maturity and 101 per cent of the unit value on death.	This contract contains a deposit component (100 per cent of unit value) and an insurance component (additional death benefit of 1 per cent). Paragraph 10 of the IFRS permits unbundling (but requires it only if the insurance component is material and the issuer would not otherwise recognise all obligations and rights arising under the deposit component). If the insurance component is not unbundled, the whole contract is an investment contract because the insurance component is insignificant in relation to the whole contract.

continued...

...continued

IG Example 1: Application of the definition of an insurance contract

Contract type	Treatment in phase I
1.4 Life-contingent annuity.	Insurance contract (unless contingent amount is insignificant in all scenarios that have commercial substance). Insurer could suffer a significant loss on an individual contract if the annuitant survives longer than expected.
1.5 Pure endowment. The insured person receives a payment on survival to a specified date, but beneficiaries receive nothing if the insured person dies before then.	Insurance contract (unless the transfer of insurance risk is insignificant). If a relatively homogeneous book of pure endowments is known to consist of contracts that all transfer insurance risk, the insurer may classify the entire book as insurance contracts without examining each contract to identify a few non-derivative pure endowments that transfer insignificant insurance risk (see paragraph B25).
1.6 Deferred annuity: policyholder will receive, or can elect to receive, a life-contingent annuity at rates guaranteed at inception.	Insurance contract (unless the transfer of insurance risk is insignificant). The contract transfers mortality risk to the insurer at inception, because the insurer might have to pay significant additional benefits for an individual contract if the annuitant elects to take the life-contingent annuity and survives longer than expected (unless the contingent amount is insignificant in all scenarios that have commercial substance).
1.7 Deferred annuity: policyholder will receive, or can elect to receive, a life-contingent annuity at rates prevailing when the annuity begins.	Not an insurance contract at inception, if the insurer can reprice the mortality risk without constraints. Within the scope of IAS 39 *Financial Instruments: Recognition and Measurement* unless the contract contains a discretionary participation feature. Will become an insurance contract when the annuity rate is fixed (unless the contingent amount is insignificant in all scenarios that have commercial substance).
1.8 Investment contract[(a)] that does not contain a discretionary participation feature.	Within the scope of IAS 39.
1.9 Investment contract containing a discretionary participation feature.	Paragraph 35 of the IFRS sets out requirements for these contracts, which are excluded from the scope of IAS 39.
1.10 Investment contract in which payments are contractually linked (with no discretion) to returns on a specified pool of assets held by the issuer.	Within the scope of IAS 39. Payments denominated in unit values representing the fair value of the specified assets are measured at current unit value (see paragraph AG33(g) of Appendix A of IAS 39).

continued...

...continued

IG Example 1: Application of the definition of an insurance contract

Contract type	Treatment in phase I
1.11 Contract that requires the issuer to make specified payments to reimburse the holder for a loss it incurs because a specified debtor fails to make payment when due under the original or modified terms of a debt instrument. The contract may have various legal forms (eg insurance contract, guarantee or letter of credit).	Insurance contract, but within the scope of IAS 39, not IFRS 4. However, if the issuer has previously asserted explicitly that it regards such contracts as insurance contracts and has used accounting applicable to insurance contracts, the issuer may elect to apply either IAS 39 and IAS 32[b] or IFRS 4 to such financial guarantee contracts. The legal form of the contract does not affect its recognition and measurement. Accounting by the holder of such a contract is excluded from the scope of IAS 39 and IFRS 4 (unless the contract is a reinsurance contract). Therefore, paragraphs 10–12 of IAS 8 *Accounting Policies, Changes in Accounting Estimates and Errors* apply. Those paragraphs specify criteria to use in developing an accounting policy if no IFRS applies specifically to an item.
1.12 A credit-related guarantee that does not, as a precondition for payment, require that the holder is exposed to, and has incurred a loss on, the failure of the debtor to make payments on the guaranteed asset when due. An example of such a guarantee is one that requires payments in response to changes in a specified credit rating or credit index.	Not an insurance contract. A derivative within the scope of IAS 39.
1.13 Guarantee fund established by contract. The contract requires all participants to pay contributions to the fund so that it can meet obligations incurred by participants (and, perhaps, others). Participants would typically be from a single industry, eg insurance, banking or travel.	The contract that establishes the guarantee fund is an insurance contract (see IG Example 1.11).
1.14 Guarantee fund established by law.	The commitment of participants to contribute to the fund is not established by a contract, so there is no insurance contract. Within the scope of IAS 37 *Provisions, Contingent Liabilities and Contingent Assets*.

continued...

...*continued*	
IG Example 1: Application of the definition of an insurance contract	
Contract type	*Treatment in phase I*
1.15 Residual value insurance or residual value guarantee. Guarantee by one party of the fair value at a future date of a non-financial asset held by a beneficiary of the insurance or guarantee.	Insurance contract within the scope of the IFRS (unless changes in the condition of the asset have an insignificant effect). The risk of changes in the fair value of the non-financial asset is not a financial risk because the fair value reflects not only changes in market prices for such assets (a financial variable) but also the condition of the specific asset held (a non-financial variable). However, if the contract compensates the beneficiary only for changes in market prices and not for changes in the condition of the beneficiary's asset, the contract is a derivative and within the scope of IAS 39. Residual value guarantees given by a lessee under a finance lease are within the scope of IAS 17 *Leases*.
1.16 Product warranties issued directly by a manufacturer, dealer or retailer.	Insurance contracts, but excluded from the scope of the IFRS (see IAS 18 *Revenue* and IAS 37).
1.17 Product warranties issued by a third party.	Insurance contracts, no scope exclusion. Same treatment as other insurance contracts.
1.18 Group insurance contract that gives the insurer an enforceable and non-cancellable contractual right to recover all claims paid out of future premiums, with appropriate compensation for the time value of money.	Insurance risk is insignificant. Therefore, the contract is a financial asset within the scope of IFRS 9. Servicing fees are within the scope of IAS 18 (recognise as services are provided, subject to various conditions).
1.19 Catastrophe bond: bond in which principal, interest payments or both are reduced if a specified triggering event occurs and the triggering event does not include a condition that the issuer of the bond suffered a loss.	Financial instrument with embedded derivative. Both the holder and the issuer measure the embedded derivative at fair value.
	continued...

...continued
IG Example 1: Application of the definition of an insurance contract

Contract type	Treatment in phase I
1.20 Catastrophe bond: bond in which principal, interest payments or both are reduced significantly if a specified triggering event occurs and the triggering event includes a condition that the issuer of the bond suffered a loss.	The contract is an insurance contract, and contains an insurance component (with the issuer as policyholder and the holder as the insurer) and a deposit component. (a) If specified conditions are met, paragraph 10 of the IFRS requires the holder to unbundle the deposit component and apply IAS 39 to it. (b) The issuer accounts for the insurance component as reinsurance if it uses the bond for that purpose. If the issuer does not use the insurance component as reinsurance, it is not within the scope of the IFRS, which does not address accounting by policyholders for direct insurance contracts. (c) Under paragraph 13 of the IFRS, the holder could continue its existing accounting for the insurance component, unless that involves the practices prohibited by paragraph 14.
1.21 An insurance contract issued by an insurer to a defined benefit pension plan covering the employees of the insurer, or of another entity consolidated within the same financial statements as the insurer.	The contract will generally be eliminated from the financial statements, which will include: (a) the full amount of the pension obligation under IAS 19 *Employee Benefits*, with no deduction for the plan's rights under the contract. (b) no liability to policyholders under the contract. (c) the assets backing the contract.
1.22 An insurance contract issued to employees as a result of a defined contribution pension plan. The contractual benefits for employee service in the current and prior periods are not contingent on future service. The insurer also issues similar contracts on the same terms to third parties.	Insurance contract within the scope of the IFRS. If the employer pays part or all of the employee's premiums, the payment by the employer is an employee benefit within the scope of IAS 19. See also IAS 19, paragraphs 39–42 and 104–104D. Furthermore, a 'qualifying insurance policy' as defined in IAS 19 need not meet the definition of an insurance contract in this IFRS.

continued...

...continued	
IG Example 1: Application of the definition of an insurance contract	
Contract type	**Treatment in phase I**
1.23 Loan contract containing a prepayment fee that is waived if prepayment results from the borrower's death.	Not an insurance contract. Before entering into the contract, the borrower faced no risk corresponding to the prepayment fee. Hence, although the loan contract exposes the lender to mortality risk, it does not transfer a pre-existing risk from the borrower. Thus, the risk associated with the possible waiver on death of the prepayment fee is not insurance risk (paragraphs B12 and B24(b) of Appendix B of the IFRS).
1.24 Loan contract that waives repayment of the entire loan balance if the borrower dies.	This contract contains a deposit component (the loan) and an insurance component (waiver of the loan balance on death, equivalent to a cash death benefit). If specified conditions are met, paragraph 10 of the IFRS requires or permits unbundling. If the insurance component is not unbundled, the contract is an insurance contract if the insurance component is significant in relation to the whole contract.
1.25 A contract permits the issuer to deduct a market value adjustment (MVA) from surrender values or death benefits to reflect current market prices for the underlying assets. The contract does not permit an MVA for maturity benefits.	The policyholder obtains an additional survival benefit because no MVA is applied at maturity. That benefit is a pure endowment (see IG Example 1.5). If the risk transferred by that benefit is significant, the contract is an insurance contract.
1.26 A contract permits the issuer to deduct an MVA from surrender values or maturity payments to reflect current market prices for the underlying assets. The contract does not permit an MVA for death benefits.	The policyholder obtains an additional death benefit because no MVA is applied on death. If the risk transferred by that benefit is significant, the contract is an insurance contract.
1.27 A contract permits the issuer to deduct an MVA from surrender payments to reflect current market prices for the underlying assets. The contract does not permit an MVA for death and maturity benefits. The amount payable on death or maturity is the amount originally invested plus interest.	The policyholder obtains an additional benefit because no MVA is applied on death or maturity. However, that benefit does not transfer insurance risk from the policyholder because it is certain that the policyholder will live or die and the amount payable on death or maturity is adjusted for the time value of money (see paragraph B27 of the IFRS). The contract is an investment contract. This contract combines the two features discussed in IG Examples 1.25 and 1.26. When considered separately, those two features transfer insurance risk. However, when combined, they do not transfer insurance risk. Therefore, it is not appropriate to separate this contract into two 'insurance' components.
	continued...

　　　　　　　　© IASCF

...continued	
IG Example 1: Application of the definition of an insurance contract	
Contract type	*Treatment in phase I*
	If the amount payable on death were not adjusted in full for the time value of money, or were adjusted in some other way, the contract might transfer insurance risk. If that insurance risk is significant, the contract is an insurance contract.
1.28 A contract meets the definition of an insurance contract. It was issued by one entity in a group (for example a captive insurer) to another entity in the same group.	If the entities present individual or separate financial statements, they treat the contract as an insurance contract in those individual or separate financial statements (see IAS 27 *Consolidated and Separate Financial Statements*).
	The transaction is eliminated from the group's consolidated financial statements.
	If the intragroup contract is reinsured with a third party that is not part of the group, the reinsurance contract is treated as a direct insurance contract in the consolidated financial statements because the intragroup contract is eliminated on consolidation.
1.29 An agreement that entity A will compensate entity B for losses on one or more contracts issued by entity B that do not transfer significant insurance risk.	The contract is an insurance contract if it transfers significant insurance risk from entity B to entity A, even if some or all of the individual contracts do not transfer significant insurance risk to entity B.
	The contract is a reinsurance contract if any of the contracts issued by entity B are insurance contracts. Otherwise, the contract is a direct insurance contract.
(a) The term 'investment contract' is an informal term used for ease of discussion. It refers to a financial instrument that does not meet the definition of an insurance contract.	
(b) When an entity applies IFRS 7 *Financial Instruments: Disclosures*, the reference to IAS 32 is replaced by a reference to IFRS 7.	

Embedded derivatives

IG3   IAS 39 requires an entity to separate embedded derivatives that meet specified conditions from the host instrument that contains them, measure the embedded derivatives at fair value and recognise changes in their fair value in profit or loss. However, an insurer need not separate an embedded derivative that itself meets the definition of an insurance contract (paragraph 7 of the IFRS). Nevertheless, separation and fair value measurement of such an embedded derivative are not prohibited if the insurer's existing accounting policies require such separation, or if an insurer changes its accounting policies and that change meets the criteria in paragraph 22 of the IFRS.

IG4   IG Example 2 illustrates the treatment of embedded derivatives contained in insurance contracts and investment contracts. The term 'investment contract' is an informal term used for ease of discussion. It refers to a financial instrument that does not meet the definition of an insurance contract. The example does not illustrate all possible circumstances. Throughout the example, the phrase 'fair value measurement is required' indicates that the issuer of the contract is required:

(a) to measure the embedded derivative at fair value and include changes in its fair value in profit or loss.

(b) to separate the embedded derivative from the host contract, unless it measures the entire contract at fair value and includes changes in that fair value in profit or loss.

IG Example 2: Embedded derivatives

	Type of embedded derivative	Treatment if embedded in a host insurance contract	Treatment if embedded in a host investment contract
2.1	Death benefit linked to equity prices or equity index, payable only on death or annuitisation and not on surrender or maturity.	The equity-index feature is an insurance contract (unless the life-contingent payments are insignificant), because the policyholder benefits from it only when the insured event occurs. Fair value measurement is not required (but not prohibited).	Not applicable. The entire contract is an insurance contract (unless the life-contingent payments are insignificant).
2.2	Death benefit that is the greater of: (a) unit value of an investment fund (equal to the amount payable on surrender or maturity); and (b) guaranteed minimum.	Excess of guaranteed minimum over unit value is a death benefit (similar to the payout on a dual trigger contract, see IG Example 2.19). This meets the definition of an insurance contract (unless the life-contingent payments are insignificant) and fair value measurement is not required (but not prohibited).	Not applicable. The entire contract is an insurance contract (unless the life-contingent payments are insignificant).
2.3	Option to take a life-contingent annuity at guaranteed rate (combined guarantee of interest rates and mortality charges).	The embedded option is an insurance contract (unless the life-contingent payments are insignificant). Fair value measurement is not required (but not prohibited).	Not applicable. The entire contract is an insurance contract (unless the life-contingent payments are insignificant).

continued...

...continued
IG Example 2: Embedded derivatives

Type of embedded derivative		Treatment if embedded in a host insurance contract	Treatment if embedded in a host investment contract
2.4	Embedded guarantee of minimum interest rates in determining surrender or maturity values that is at or out of the money on issue, and not leveraged.	The embedded guarantee is not an insurance contract (unless significant payments are life-contingent[(a)]). However, it is closely related to the host contract (paragraph AG33(b) of Appendix A of IAS 39). Fair value measurement is not required (but not prohibited). If significant payments are life-contingent, the contract is an insurance contract and contains a deposit component (the guaranteed minimum). However, an insurer is not required to unbundle the contract if it recognises all obligations arising from the deposit component (paragraph 10 of the IFRS). If cancelling the deposit component requires the policyholder to cancel the insurance component, the two cancellation options may be interdependent; if the option to cancel the deposit component cannot be measured separately (ie without considering the other option), both options are regarded as part of the insurance component (paragraph AG33(h) of IAS 39).	Fair value measurement is not permitted (paragraph AG33(b) of IAS 39).
2.5	Embedded guarantee of minimum interest rates in determining surrender or maturity values: in the money on issue, or leveraged.	The embedded guarantee is not an insurance contract (unless the embedded guarantee is life-contingent to a significant extent). Fair value measurement is required (paragraph AG33(b) of IAS 39).	Fair value measurement is required (paragraph AG33(b) of IAS 39).

continued...

...continued

IG Example 2: Embedded derivatives

Type of embedded derivative	Treatment if embedded in a host insurance contract	Treatment if embedded in a host investment contract
2.6 Embedded guarantee of minimum annuity payments if the annuity payments are contractually linked to investment returns or asset prices:		
(a) guarantee relates only to payments that are life-contingent.	The embedded guarantee is an insurance contract (unless the life-contingent payments are insignificant). Fair value measurement is not required (but not prohibited).	Not applicable. The entire contract is an insurance contract (unless the life-contingent payments are insignificant).
(b) guarantee relates only to payments that are not life-contingent.	The embedded derivative is not an insurance contract. Fair value measurement is required (unless the guarantee is regarded as closely related to the host contract because the guarantee is an unleveraged interest floor that is at or out of the money at inception, see paragraph AG33(b) of IAS 39).	Fair value measurement is required (unless the guarantee is regarded as closely related to the host contract because the guarantee is an unleveraged interest floor that is at or out of the money at inception, see paragraph AG33(b) of IAS 39).

continued...

...continued

IG Example 2: Embedded derivatives

Type of embedded derivative	Treatment if embedded in a host insurance contract	Treatment if embedded in a host investment contract
(c) policyholder can elect to receive life-contingent payments or payments that are not life-contingent, and the guarantee relates to both. When the policyholder makes its election, the issuer cannot adjust the pricing of the life-contingent payments to reflect the risk that the insurer assumes at that time (see paragraph B29 of the IFRS for discussion of contracts with separate accumulation and payout phases).	The embedded option to benefit from a guarantee of life-contingent payments is an insurance contract (unless the life-contingent payments are insignificant). Fair value measurement is not required (but not prohibited). The embedded option to receive payments that are not life-contingent ('the second option') is not an insurance contract. However, because the second option and the life-contingent option are alternatives, their fair values are interdependent. If they are so interdependent that the issuer cannot measure the second option separately (ie without considering the life-contingent option), the second option is closely related to the insurance contract. In that case, fair value measurement is not required (but not prohibited).	Not applicable. The entire contract is an insurance contract (unless the life-contingent payments are insignificant).
2.7 Embedded guarantee of minimum equity returns on surrender or maturity.	The embedded guarantee is not an insurance contract (unless the embedded guarantee is life-contingent to a significant extent) and is not closely related to the host insurance contract. Fair value measurement is required.	Fair value measurement is required.
2.8 Equity-linked return available on surrender or maturity.	The embedded derivative is not an insurance contract (unless the equity-linked return is life-contingent to a significant extent) and is not closely related to the host insurance contract. Fair value measurement is required.	Fair value measurement is required.

continued...

...continued
IG Example 2: Embedded derivatives

Type of embedded derivative		Treatment if embedded in a host insurance contract	Treatment if embedded in a host investment contract
2.9	Embedded guarantee of minimum equity returns that is available only if the policyholder elects to take a life-contingent annuity.	The embedded guarantee is an insurance contract (unless the life-contingent payments are insignificant), because the policyholder can benefit from the guarantee only by taking the annuity option (whether annuity rates are set at inception or at the date of annuitisation). Fair value measurement is not required (but not prohibited).	Not applicable. The entire contract is an insurance contract (unless the life-contingent payments are insignificant).
2.10	Embedded guarantee of minimum equity returns available to the policyholder as either (a) a cash payment, (b) a period-certain annuity or (c) a life-contingent annuity, at annuity rates prevailing at the **date of annuitisation**.	If the guaranteed payments are not contingent to a significant extent on survival, the option to take the life-contingent annuity does not transfer insurance risk until the policyholder opts to take the annuity. Therefore, the embedded guarantee is not an insurance contract and is not closely related to the host insurance contract. Fair value measurement is required. If the guaranteed payments are contingent to a significant extent on survival, the guarantee is an insurance contract (similar to a pure endowment). Fair value measurement is not required (but not prohibited).	Fair value measurement is required.

continued...

...continued

IG Example 2: Embedded derivatives

Type of embedded derivative		Treatment if embedded in a host insurance contract	Treatment if embedded in a host investment contract
2.11	Embedded guarantee of minimum equity returns available to the policyholder as either (a) a cash payment (b) a period-certain annuity or (c) a life-contingent annuity, at annuity rates set at **inception**.	The whole contract is an insurance contract from inception (unless the life-contingent payments are insignificant). The option to take the life-contingent annuity is an embedded insurance contract, so fair value measurement is not required (but not prohibited). The option to take the cash payment or the period-certain annuity ('the second option') is not an insurance contract (unless the option is contingent to a significant extent on survival), so it must be separated. However, because the second option and the life-contingent option are alternatives, their fair values are interdependent. If they are so interdependent that the issuer cannot measure the second option separately (ie without considering the life-contingent option), the second option is closely related to the host insurance contract. In that case, fair value measurement is not required (but not prohibited).	Not applicable.
2.12	Policyholder option to surrender a contract for a cash surrender value specified in a schedule (ie not indexed and not accumulating interest).	Fair value measurement is not required (but not prohibited: paragraph 8 of the IFRS). The surrender value may be viewed as a deposit component, but the IFRS does not require an insurer to unbundle a contract if it recognises all its obligations arising under the deposit component (paragraph 10).	The surrender option is closely related to the host contract if the surrender value is approximately equal to the amortised cost at each exercise date (paragraph AG30(g) of IAS 39). Otherwise, the surrender option is measured at fair value.

continued...

...continued
IG Example 2: Embedded derivatives

Type of embedded derivative	Treatment if embedded in a host insurance contract	Treatment if embedded in a host investment contract
2.13 Policyholder option to surrender a contract for account value based on a principal amount and a fixed or variable interest rate (or based on the fair value of a pool of interest-bearing securities), possibly after deducting a surrender charge.	Same as for a cash surrender value (IG Example 2.12).	Same as for a cash surrender value (IG Example 2.12).
2.14 Policyholder option to surrender a contract for a surrender value based on an equity or commodity price or index.	The option is not closely related to the host contract (unless the option is life-contingent to a significant extent). Fair value measurement is required (paragraphs 8 of the IFRS and AG30(d) and (e) of IAS 39).	Fair value measurement is required (paragraph AG30(d) and (e) of IAS 39).
2.15 Policyholder option to surrender a contract for account value equal to the fair value of a pool of equity investments, possibly after deducting a surrender charge.	If the insurer measures that portion of its obligation at account value, no further adjustment is needed for the option (unless the surrender value differs significantly from account value) (see paragraph AG33(g) of IAS 39). Otherwise, fair value measurement is required.	If the insurer regards the account value as the amortised cost or fair value of that portion of its obligation, no further adjustment is needed for the option (unless the surrender value differs significantly from account value). Otherwise, fair value measurement is required.
2.16 Contractual feature that provides a return contractually linked (with no discretion) to the return on specified assets.	The embedded derivative is not an insurance contract and is not closely related to the contract (paragraph AG30(h) of IAS 39). Fair value measurement is required.	Fair value measurement is required.

continued...

...continued

IG Example 2: Embedded derivatives

Type of embedded derivative	Treatment if embedded in a host insurance contract	Treatment if embedded in a host investment contract
2.17 Persistency bonus paid at maturity in cash (or as a period-certain annuity).	The embedded derivative (option to receive the persistency bonus) is not an insurance contract (unless the persistency bonus is life-contingent to a significant extent). Insurance risk does not include lapse or persistency risk (paragraph B15 of the IFRS). Fair value measurement is required.	An option or automatic provision to extend the remaining term to maturity of a debt instrument is not closely related to the host debt instrument unless there is a concurrent adjustment to the approximate current market rate of interest at the time of the extension (paragraph AG30(c) of IAS 39). If the option or provision is not closely related to the host instrument, fair value measurement is required.
2.18 Persistency bonus paid at maturity as an enhanced life-contingent annuity.	The embedded derivative is an insurance contract (unless the life-contingent payments are insignificant). Fair value measurement is not required (but not prohibited).	Not applicable. The entire contract is an insurance contract (unless the life-contingent payments are insignificant).
2.19 Dual trigger contract, eg contract requiring a payment that is contingent on a breakdown in power supply that adversely affects the holder (first trigger) and a specified level of electricity prices (second trigger). The contingent payment is made only if both triggering events occur.	The embedded derivative is an insurance contract (unless the first trigger lacks commercial substance). A contract that qualifies as an insurance contract, whether at inception or later, remains an insurance contract until all rights and obligations are extinguished or expire (paragraph B30 of the IFRS). Therefore, although the remaining exposure is similar to a financial derivative after the insured event has occurred, the embedded derivative is still an insurance contract and fair value measurement is not required (but not prohibited).	Not applicable. The entire contract is an insurance contract (unless the first trigger lacks commercial substance).

continued...

...continued

IG Example 2: Embedded derivatives

Type of embedded derivative	Treatment if embedded in a host insurance contract	Treatment if embedded in a host investment contract
2.20 Non-guaranteed participating dividend contained in a life insurance contract. The amount is contractually at the discretion of the insurer but is contractually based on the insurer's actual experience on the related block of insurance contracts.	The contract contains a discretionary participation feature, rather than an embedded derivative (paragraph 34 of the IFRS).	Not applicable. The entire contract is an insurance contract (unless the life-contingent payments are insignificant).

(a) Payments are life-contingent if they are contingent on death or contingent on survival.

Unbundling a deposit component

IG5   Paragraph 10 of the IFRS requires an insurer to unbundle some insurance contracts that contain a deposit component. IG Example 3 illustrates this requirement. Although arrangements of this kind are more common in reinsurance, the same principle applies in direct insurance. However, unbundling is not required if the insurer recognises all obligations or rights arising from the deposit component.

IG Example 3: Unbundling a deposit component of a reinsurance contract

Background

A reinsurance contract has the following features:

(a)   The cedant pays premiums of CU10[(a)] every year for five years.

(b)   An experience account is established, equal to 90 per cent of cumulative premiums (including the additional premiums discussed in (c) below) less 90 per cent of cumulative claims.

(c)   If the balance in the experience account is negative (ie cumulative claims exceed cumulative premiums), the cedant pays an additional premium equal to the experience account balance divided by the number of years left to run on the contract.

(d)   At the end of the contract, if the experience account balance is positive (ie cumulative premiums exceed cumulative claims), it is refunded to the cedant; if the balance is negative, the cedant pays the balance to the reinsurer as an additional premium.

(e)   Neither party can cancel the contract before maturity.

(f)   The maximum loss that the reinsurer is required to pay in any period is CU200.

This contract is an insurance contract because it transfers significant insurance risk to the reinsurer. For example, in case 2 discussed below, the reinsurer is required to pay additional benefits with a present value, in year 1, of CU35, which is clearly significant in relation to the contract.

continued...

...continued
IG Example 3: Unbundling a deposit component of a reinsurance contract

---

The following discussion addresses the accounting by the reinsurer. Similar principles apply to the accounting by the cedant.

Application of requirements: case 1—no claims

If there are no claims, the cedant will receive CU45 in year 5 (90 per cent of the cumulative premiums of CU50). In substance, the cedant has made a loan, which the reinsurer will repay in one instalment of CU45 in year 5.

If the reinsurer's accounting policies require it to recognise its contractual liability to repay the loan to the cedant, unbundling is permitted but not required. However, if the reinsurer's accounting policies would not require it to recognise the liability to repay the loan, the reinsurer is required to unbundle the contract (paragraph 10 of the IFRS).

If the reinsurer is required, or elects, to unbundle the contract, it does so as follows. Each payment by the cedant has two components: a loan advance (deposit component) and a payment for insurance cover (insurance component). Applying IAS 39 to the deposit component, the reinsurer is required to measure it initially at fair value. Fair value could be determined by discounting the future cash flows from the deposit component. Assume that an appropriate discount rate is 10 per cent and that the insurance cover is equal in each year, so that the payment for insurance cover is the same in every year. Each payment of CU10 by the cedant is then made up of a loan advance of CU6.7 and an insurance premium of CU3.3.

The reinsurer accounts for the insurance component in the same way that it accounts for a separate insurance contract with an annual premium of CU3.3.

The movements in the loan are shown below.

Year	Opening balance CU	Interest at 10 per cent CU	Advance (repayment) CU	Closing balance CU
0	0.00	0.00	6.70	6.70
1	6.70	0.67	6.70	14.07
2	14.07	1.41	6.70	22.18
3	22.18	2.21	6.70	31.09
4	31.09	3.11	6.70	40.90
5	40.90	4.10	(45.00)	0.00
Total		11.50	(11.50)	

continued...

...continued

IG Example 3: Unbundling a deposit component of a reinsurance contract

Application of requirements: case 2—claim of CU150 in year 1

Consider now what happens if the reinsurer pays a claim of CU150 in year 1. The changes in the experience account, and resulting additional premiums, are as follows.

Year	Premium	Additional premium	Total premium	Cumulative premium	Claims	Cumulative claims	Cumulative premiums less claims	Experience account
	CU	CU	CU	CU	CU	CU	CU	CU
0	10	0	10	10	0	0	10	9
1	10	0	10	20	(150)	(150)	(130)	(117)
2	10	39	49	69	0	(150)	(81)	(73)
3	10	36	46	115	0	(150)	(35)	(31)
4	10	31	41	156	0	(150)	6	6
		106	156		(150)			

Incremental cash flows because of the claim in year 1

The claim in year 1 leads to the following incremental cash flows, compared with case 1:

Year	Additional Premium	Claims	Refund in case 2	Refund in case 1	Net incremental cash flow	Present value at 10 per cent
	CU	CU	CU	CU	CU	CU
0	0	0			0	0
1	0	(150)			(150)	(150)
2	39	0			39	35
3	36	0			36	30
4	31	0			31	23
5	0	0	(6)	(45)	39	27
Total	106	(150)	(6)	(45)	(5)	(35)

continued...

...continued

IG Example 3: Unbundling a deposit component of a reinsurance contract

The incremental cash flows have a present value, in year 1, of CU35 (assuming a discount rate of 10 per cent is appropriate). Applying paragraphs 10–12 of the IFRS, the cedant unbundles the contract and applies IAS 39 to this deposit component (unless the cedant already recognises its contractual obligation to repay the deposit component to the reinsurer). If this were not done, the cedant might recognise the CU150 received in year 1 as income, and the incremental payments in years 2–5 as expenses. However, in substance, the reinsurer has paid a claim of CU35 and made a loan of CU115 (CU150 less CU35) that will be repaid in instalments.

The following table shows the changes in the loan balance. The table assumes that the original loan shown in case 1 and the new loan in case 2 met the criteria for offsetting in IAS 32. Amounts shown in the table are rounded.

Loan to (from) the reinsurer

Year	Opening balance	Interest at 10 per cent	Payments per original schedule	Additional payments in case 2	Closing balance
	CU	CU	CU	CU	CU
0	–	–	6	–	6
1	6	1	7	(115)	(101)
2	(101)	(10)	7	39	(65)
3	(65)	(7)	7	36	(29)
4	(29)	(3)	6	31	5
5	5	1	(45)	39	0
Total		(18)	(12)	30	

(a) In this Implementation Guidance monetary amounts are denominated in 'currency units (CU)'.

Shadow accounting

IG6 Paragraph 30 of the IFRS permits, but does not require, a practice sometimes described as 'shadow accounting'. IG Example 4 illustrates shadow accounting.

IG7 Shadow accounting is not the same as fair value hedge accounting under IAS 39 and will not usually have the same effect. Under IAS 39, a non-derivative financial asset or non-derivative financial liability may be designated as a hedging instrument only for a hedge of foreign currency risk.

IG8   Shadow accounting is not applicable for liabilities arising from investment contracts (ie contracts within the scope of IAS 39) because the underlying measurement of those liabilities (including the treatment of related transaction costs) does not depend on asset values or asset returns. However, shadow accounting may be applicable for a discretionary participation feature within an investment contract if the measurement of that feature depends on asset values or asset returns.

IG9   Shadow accounting is not applicable if the measurement of an insurance liability is not driven directly by realised gains and losses on assets held. For example, assume that financial assets are measured at fair value and insurance liabilities are measured using a discount rate that reflects current market rates but does not depend directly on the actual assets held. The measurements of the assets and the liability both reflect changes in interest rates, but the measurement of the liability does not depend directly on the carrying amount of the assets held. Therefore, shadow accounting is not applicable and changes in the carrying amount of the liability are recognised in profit or loss because IAS 1 *Presentation of Financial Statements* requires all items of income or expense to be recognised in profit or loss unless an IFRS requires otherwise.

IG10   Shadow accounting may be relevant if there is a contractual link between payments to policyholders and the carrying amount of, or returns from, owner-occupied property. If an entity uses the revaluation model in IAS 16 *Property, Plant and Equipment*, it recognises changes in the carrying amount of the owner-occupied property in revaluation surplus. If it also elects to use shadow accounting, the changes in the measurement of the insurance liability resulting from revaluations of the property are also recognised in revaluation surplus.

IG Example 4: Shadow accounting

Background

Under some national requirements for some insurance contracts, deferred acquisition costs (DAC) are amortised over the life of the contract as a constant proportion of estimated gross profits (EGP). EGP includes investment returns, including realised (but not unrealised) gains and losses. Interest is applied to both DAC and EGP, to preserve present value relationships. For simplicity, this example ignores interest and ignores re-estimation of EGP.

At the inception of a contract, insurer A has DAC of CU20 relating to that contract and the present value, at inception, of EGP is CU100. In other words, DAC is 20 per cent of EGP at inception. Thus, for each CU1 of realised gross profits, insurer A amortises DAC by CU0.20. For example, if insurer A sells assets and recognises a gain of CU10, insurer A amortises DAC by CU2 (20 per cent of CU10).

continued...

...*continued*
IG Example 4: Shadow accounting

Before adopting IFRSs for the first time in 20X5, insurer A measured financial assets on a cost basis. (Therefore, EGP under those national requirements considers only realised gains and losses.) However, under IFRSs, it classifies its financial assets as measured at fair value through profit or loss.

In 20X5 insurer A recognises unrealised gains of CU10 on the assets backing the contract and in 20X6 it sells the assets for an amount equal to their fair value at the end of 20X5.

Application of paragraph 30 of the IFRS

Paragraph 30 of the IFRS permits, but does not require, insurer A to adopt shadow accounting. If insurer A adopts shadow accounting, it amortises DAC in 20X5 by an additional CU2 (20 per cent of CU10) as a result of the change in the fair value of the assets. Insurer A recognises the additional amortisation of CU2 in profit or loss.

When insurer A sells the assets in 20X6, it makes no further adjustment to DAC.

In summary, shadow accounting treats an unrealised gain in the same way as a realised gain. If insurer A does not adopt shadow accounting, unrealised gains on assets do not affect the amortisation of DAC.

Disclosure

Purpose of this guidance

IG11   The guidance in paragraphs IG12–IG71 suggests possible ways to apply the disclosure requirements in paragraphs 36–39A of the IFRS. As explained in paragraphs 36 and 38 of the IFRS, the objective of the disclosures is:

  (a)   to identify and explain the amounts in an insurer's financial statements arising from insurance contracts; and

  (b)   to enable users of those financial statements to evaluate the nature and extent of risks arising from insurance contracts.

IG12   An insurer decides in the light of its circumstances how much detail it gives to satisfy those requirements, how much emphasis it places on different aspects of the requirements and how it aggregates information to display the overall picture without combining information that has materially different characteristics. It is necessary to strike a balance so that important information is not obscured either by the inclusion of a large amount of insignificant detail or by the aggregation of items that have materially different characteristics. For example:

  (a)   a large international insurance group that operates in a wide range of regulatory jurisdictions typically provides disclosures that differ in format, content and detail from those provided by a specialised niche insurer operating in one jurisdiction.

(b)   many insurance contracts have similar characteristics. When no single contract is individually material, a summary by classes of contracts is appropriate.

(c)   information about an individual contract may be material when it is, for example, a significant contributor to an insurer's risk profile.

To satisfy the requirements, an insurer would not typically need to disclose all the information suggested in the guidance. This guidance does not create additional requirements.

IG13   IAS 1 *Presentation of Financial Statements* requires an entity to 'provide additional disclosures when compliance with the specific requirements in IFRSs is insufficient to enable users to understand the impact of particular transactions, other events and conditions on the entity's financial position and financial performance.'

IG14   For convenience, this Implementation Guidance discusses each disclosure requirement in the IFRS separately. In practice, disclosures would normally be presented as an integrated package and individual disclosures may satisfy more than one requirement. For example, information about the assumptions that have the greatest effect on the measurement of amounts arising from insurance contracts may help to convey information about insurance risk and market risk.

Materiality

IG15   IAS 1 notes that a specific disclosure requirement in an IFRS need not be satisfied if the information is not material. IAS 1 defines materiality as follows:

> Omissions or misstatements of items are material if they could, individually or collectively, influence the economic decisions that users make on the basis of the financial statements. Materiality depends on the size and nature of the omission or misstatement judged in the surrounding circumstances. The size or nature of the item, or a combination of both, could be the determining factor.

IG16   IAS 1 also explains the following:

> Assessing whether an omission or misstatement could influence economic decisions of users, and so be material, requires consideration of the characteristics of those users. The *Framework for the Preparation and Presentation of Financial Statements* states in paragraph 25 that 'users are assumed to have a reasonable knowledge of business and economic activities and accounting and a willingness to study the information with reasonable diligence.' Therefore, the assessment needs to take into account how users with such attributes could reasonably be expected to be influenced in making economic decisions.

Explanation of recognised amounts (paragraphs 36 and 37 of the IFRS)

Accounting policies

IG17   IAS 1 requires disclosure of accounting policies and paragraph 37(a) of the IFRS highlights this requirement. In developing disclosures about accounting policies for insurance contracts, an insurer might conclude that it needs to address the treatment of, for example, some or all of the following, if applicable:

(a)   premiums (including the treatment of unearned premiums, renewals and lapses, premiums collected by agents and brokers but not yet passed on and premium taxes or other levies on premiums).

(b)   fees or other charges made to policyholders.

(c)   acquisition costs (including a description of their nature).

(d)   claims incurred (both reported and not reported), claims handling costs (including a description of their nature) and liability adequacy tests (including a description of the cash flows included in the test, whether and how the cash flows are discounted and the treatment of embedded options and guarantees in those tests, see paragraphs 15–19 of the IFRS). An insurer might disclose whether insurance liabilities are discounted and, if they are discounted, explain the methodology used.

(e)   the objective of methods used to adjust insurance liabilities for risk and uncertainty (for example, in terms of a level of assurance or level of sufficiency), the nature of those models, and the source of information used in the models.

(f)   embedded options and guarantees (including a description of whether (i) the measurement of insurance liabilities reflects the intrinsic value and time value of these items and (ii) their measurement is consistent with observed current market prices).

(g)   discretionary participation features (including a clear statement of how the insurer applies paragraphs 34 and 35 of the IFRS in classifying that feature as a liability or as a component of equity) and other features that permit policyholders to share in investment performance.

(h)   salvage, subrogation or other recoveries from third parties.

(i)   reinsurance held.

(j)   underwriting pools, coinsurance and guarantee fund arrangements.

(k)   insurance contracts acquired in business combinations and portfolio transfers, and the treatment of related intangible assets.

(l)   as required by IAS 1, the judgements, apart from those involving estimations, management has made in the process of applying the accounting policies that have the most significant effect on the amounts recognised in the financial statements. The classification of discretionary participation features is an example of an accounting policy that might have a significant effect.

IG18   If the financial statements disclose supplementary information, for example embedded value information, that is not prepared on the basis used for other measurements in the financial statements, it is appropriate to explain the basis. Disclosures about embedded value methodology might include information similar to that described in paragraph IG17, as well as disclosure of whether, and how, embedded values are affected by estimated returns from assets and by locked-in capital and how those effects are estimated.

Assets, liabilities, income and expense

IG19 Paragraph 37(b) of the IFRS requires an insurer to disclose the assets, liabilities, income and expenses that arise from insurance contracts. If an insurer presents its statement of cash flows using the direct method, paragraph 37(b) requires it also to disclose the cash flows that arise from insurance contracts. The IFRS does not require disclosure of specific cash flows. The following paragraphs discuss how an insurer might satisfy those general requirements.

IG20 IAS 1 requires minimum disclosures in the statement of financial position. An insurer might conclude that, to satisfy those requirements, it needs to present separately in its statement of financial position the following amounts arising from insurance contracts:

(a) liabilities under insurance contracts and reinsurance contracts issued.

(b) assets under insurance contracts and reinsurance contracts issued.

(c) assets under reinsurance ceded. Under paragraph 14(d)(i) of the IFRS, these assets are not offset against the related insurance liabilities.

IG21 Neither IAS 1 nor the IFRS prescribes the descriptions and ordering of the line items presented in the statement of financial position. An insurer could amend the descriptions and ordering to suit the nature of its transactions.

IG22 IAS 1 requires disclosure, either in the statement of financial position or in the notes, of subclassifications of the line items presented, classified in a manner appropriate to the entity's operations. Appropriate subclassifications of insurance liabilities will depend on the circumstances, but might include items such as:

(a) unearned premiums.

(b) claims reported by policyholders.

(c) claims incurred but not reported (IBNR).

(d) provisions arising from liability adequacy tests.

(e) provisions for future non-participating benefits.

(f) liabilities or components of equity relating to discretionary participation features (see paragraphs 34 and 35 of the IFRS). If an insurer classifies these features as a component of equity, disclosure is needed to comply with IAS 1, which requires an entity to disclose 'a description of the nature and purpose of each reserve within equity.'

(g) receivables and payables related to insurance contracts (amounts currently due to and from agents, brokers and policyholders related to insurance contracts).

(h) non-insurance assets acquired by exercising rights to recoveries.

IG23 Similar subclassifications may also be appropriate for reinsurance assets, depending on their materiality and other relevant circumstances. For assets under insurance contracts and reinsurance contracts issued, an insurer might conclude that it needs to distinguish:

(a)   deferred acquisition costs; and

(b)   intangible assets relating to insurance contracts acquired in business combinations or portfolio transfers.

IG23A   Paragraph 14 of IFRS 7 *Financial Instruments: Disclosures* requires an entity to disclose the carrying amount of financial assets pledged as collateral for liabilities, the carrying amount of financial assets pledged as collateral for contingent liabilities, and any terms and conditions relating to assets pledged as collateral. In complying with this requirement, an insurer might also conclude that it needs to disclose segregation requirements that are intended to protect policyholders by restricting the use of some of the insurer's assets.

IG24   IAS 1 lists minimum line items that an entity should present in its statement of comprehensive income. It also requires the presentation of additional line items when this is necessary to present fairly the entity's financial performance. An insurer might conclude that, to satisfy these requirements, it needs to present the following amounts in its statement of comprehensive income:

(a)   revenue from insurance contracts issued (without any reduction for reinsurance held).

(b)   income from contracts with reinsurers.

(c)   expense for policyholder claims and benefits (without any reduction for reinsurance held).

(d)   expenses arising from reinsurance held.

IG25   IAS 18 requires an entity to disclose the amount of each significant category of revenue recognised during the period, and specifically requires disclosure of revenue arising from the rendering of services. Although revenue from insurance contracts is outside the scope of IAS 18, similar disclosures may be appropriate for insurance contracts. The IFRS does not prescribe a particular method for recognising revenue and various models exist:

(a)   Under some models, an insurer recognises premiums earned during the period as revenue and recognises claims arising during the period (including estimates of claims incurred but not reported) as an expense.

(b)   Under some other models, an insurer recognises premiums received as revenue and at the same time recognises an expense representing the resulting increase in the insurance liability.

(c)   Under yet other models, an insurer recognises premiums received as deposit receipts. Its revenue includes charges for items such as mortality, and its expenses include the policyholder claims and benefits related to those charges.

IG26   IAS 1 requires additional disclosure of various items of income and expense. An insurer might conclude that, to satisfy these requirements, it needs to disclose the following additional items, either in its statement of comprehensive income or in the notes:

(a)   acquisition costs (distinguishing those recognised as an expense immediately from the amortisation of deferred acquisition costs).

(b)   the effect of changes in estimates and assumptions.

(c)   losses recognised as a result of applying liability adequacy tests.

(d)   for insurance liabilities measured on a discounted basis:

    (i)   accretion of interest to reflect the passage of time; and

    (ii)   the effect of changes in discount rates.

(e)   distributions or allocations to holders of contracts that contain discretionary participation features. The portion of profit or loss that relates to any equity component of those contracts is an allocation of profit or loss, not expense or income (paragraph 34(c) of the IFRS).

IG27   Some insurers present a detailed analysis of the sources of their earnings from insurance activities either in the statement of comprehensive income or in the notes. Such an analysis may provide useful information about both the income and expense of the current period and the risk exposures faced during the period.

IG28   The items described in paragraph IG26 are not offset against income or expense arising from reinsurance held (paragraph 14(d)(ii) of the IFRS).

IG29   Paragraph 37(b) also requires specific disclosure about gains or losses recognised on buying reinsurance. This disclosure informs users about gains or losses that may, using some measurement models, arise from imperfect measurements of the underlying direct insurance liability. Furthermore, some measurement models require a cedant to defer some of those gains and losses and amortise them over the period of the related risk exposures, or some other period. Paragraph 37(b) also requires a cedant to disclose information about such deferred gains and losses.

IG30   If an insurer does not adopt uniform accounting policies for the insurance liabilities of its subsidiaries, it might conclude that it needs to disaggregate the disclosures about amounts reported in its financial statements to give meaningful information about amounts determined using different accounting policies.

Significant assumptions and other sources of estimation uncertainty

IG31   Paragraph 37(c) of the IFRS requires an insurer to describe the process used to determine the assumptions that have the greatest effect on the measurement of assets, liabilities, income and expense arising from insurance contracts and, when practicable, give quantified disclosure of those assumptions. For some disclosures, such as discount rates or assumptions about future trends or general inflation, it may be relatively easy to disclose the assumptions used (aggregated at a reasonable but not excessive level, when necessary). For other assumptions, such as mortality tables, it may not be practicable to disclose quantified assumptions because there are too many, in which case it is more important to describe the process used to generate the assumptions.

IG32   The description of the process used to determine assumptions might include a summary of the most significant of the following:

(a)   the objective of the assumptions. For example, an insurer might disclose whether the assumptions are intended to be neutral estimates of the most likely or expected outcome ('best estimates') or to provide a given level of assurance or level of sufficiency. If they are intended to provide a quantitative or qualitative level of assurance, an insurer might disclose that level.

(b)   the source of data used as inputs for the assumptions that have the greatest effect. For example, an insurer might disclose whether the inputs are internal, external or a mixture of the two. For data derived from detailed studies that are not carried out annually, an insurer might disclose the criteria used to determine when the studies are updated and the date of the latest update.

(c)   the extent to which the assumptions are consistent with observable market prices or other published information.

(d)   a description of how past experience, current conditions and other relevant benchmarks are taken into account in developing estimates and assumptions. If a relationship would normally be expected between experience and future results, an insurer might explain the reasons for using assumptions that differ from past experience and indicate the extent of the difference.

(e)   a description of how the insurer developed assumptions about future trends, such as changes in mortality, healthcare costs or litigation awards.

(f)   an explanation of how the insurer identifies correlations between different assumptions.

(g)   the insurer's policy in making allocations or distributions for contracts with discretionary participation features, the related assumptions that are reflected in the financial statements, the nature and extent of any significant uncertainty about the relative interests of policyholders and shareholders in the unallocated surplus associated with those contracts, and the effect on the financial statements of any changes during the period in that policy or those assumptions.

(h)   the nature and extent of uncertainties affecting specific assumptions. In addition, to comply with paragraphs 125–131 of IAS 1, an insurer may need to disclose that it is reasonably possible, based on existing knowledge, that outcomes within the next financial year that are different from assumptions could require a material adjustment to the carrying amount of insurance liabilities and insurance assets. Paragraph 129 of IAS 1 gives further guidance on this disclosure.

IG33   The IFRS does not prescribe specific assumptions that would be disclosed, because different assumptions will be more significant for different types of contract.

Changes in assumptions

IG34   Paragraph 37(d) of the IFRS requires an insurer to disclose the effect of changes in assumptions used to measure insurance assets and insurance liabilities. This is consistent with IAS 8, which requires disclosure of the nature and amount of a change in an accounting estimate that has an effect in the current period or is expected to have an effect in future periods.

IG35   Assumptions are often interdependent. When this is the case, analysis of changes by assumption may depend on the order in which the analysis is performed and may be arbitrary to some extent. Therefore, the IFRS does not specify a rigid format or content for this analysis. This allows insurers to analyse the changes in a way that meets the objective of the disclosure and is appropriate for their particular circumstances. If practicable, an insurer might disclose separately the impact of changes in different assumptions, particularly if changes in some assumptions have an adverse effect and others have a beneficial effect. An insurer might also describe the impact of interdependencies between assumptions and the resulting limitations of any analysis of the effect of changes in assumption.

IG36   An insurer might disclose the effects of changes in assumptions both before and after reinsurance held, especially if the insurer expects a significant change in the nature or extent of its reinsurance programme or if an analysis before reinsurance is relevant for an analysis of the credit risk arising from reinsurance held.

Changes in insurance liabilities and related items

IG37   Paragraph 37(e) of the IFRS requires an insurer to disclose reconciliations of changes in insurance liabilities. It also requires disclosure of changes in reinsurance assets. An insurer need not disaggregate those changes into broad classes, but might do that if different forms of analysis are more relevant for different types of liability. The changes might include:

(a)   the carrying amount at the beginning and end of the period.

(b)   additional insurance liabilities arising during the period.

(c)   cash paid.

(d)   income and expense included in profit or loss.

(e)   liabilities acquired from, or transferred to, other insurers.

(f)   net exchange differences arising on the translation of the financial statements into a different presentation currency, and on the translation of a foreign operation into the presentation currency of the reporting entity.

IG38   An insurer discloses the changes in insurance liabilities and reinsurance assets in all prior periods for which it reports full comparative information.

IG39   Paragraph 37(e) of the IFRS also requires an insurer to disclose changes in deferred acquisition costs, if applicable. The reconciliation might disclose:

(a)   the carrying amount at the beginning and end of the period.

(b)   the amounts incurred during the period.

(c)   the amortisation for the period.

(d)   impairment losses recognised during the period.

(e)   other changes categorised by cause and type.

IG40   An insurer may have recognised intangible assets related to insurance contracts acquired in a business combination or portfolio transfer. IAS 38 *Intangible Assets* contains disclosure requirements for intangible assets, including a requirement to give a reconciliation of changes in intangible assets. The IFRS does not require additional disclosures about these assets.

Nature and extent of risks arising from insurance contracts (paragraphs 38–39A of the IFRS)

IG41   The disclosures about the nature and extent of risks arising from insurance contracts are based on two foundations:

(a)   There should be a balance between quantitative and qualitative disclosures, enabling users to understand the nature of risk exposures and their potential impact.

(b)   Disclosures should be consistent with how management perceives its activities and risks, and the objectives, policies and processes that management uses to manage those risks. This approach is likely:

(i)   to generate information that has more predictive value than information based on assumptions and methods that management does not use, for instance, in considering the insurer's ability to react to adverse situations.

(ii)   to be more effective in adapting to the continuing change in risk measurement and management techniques and developments in the external environment over time.

IG42   In developing disclosures to satisfy paragraphs 38–39A of the IFRS, an insurer decides in the light of its circumstances how it would aggregate information to display the overall picture without combining information that has materially different characteristics, so that the information is useful. An insurer might group insurance contracts into broad classes appropriate for the nature of the information to be disclosed, taking into account matters such as the risks covered, the characteristics of the contracts and the measurement basis applied. The broad classes may correspond to classes established for legal or regulatory purposes, but the IFRS does not require this.

IG43   Under IFRS 8 *Operating Segments*, the identification of reportable segments reflects the way in which management allocates resources and assesses performance. An insurer might adopt a similar approach to identify broad classes of insurance contracts for disclosure purposes, although it might be appropriate to disaggregate disclosures down to the next level.   For example, if an insurer identifies life insurance as a reportable segment for IFRS 8, it might be appropriate to report separate information about, say, life insurance, annuities in the accumulation phase and annuities in the payout phase.

IG44   [Deleted]

IG45   In identifying broad classes for separate disclosure, an insurer might consider how best to indicate the level of uncertainty associated with the risks underwritten, to inform users whether outcomes are likely to be within a wider or a narrower range. For example, an insurer might disclose information about exposures where there are significant amounts of provisions for claims incurred but not reported (IBNR) or where outcomes and risks are unusually difficult to assess (eg asbestos).

IG46   It may be useful to disclose sufficient information about the broad classes identified to permit a reconciliation to relevant line items in the statement of financial position.

IG47   Information about the nature and extent of risks arising from insurance contracts is more useful if it highlights any relationship between classes of insurance contracts (and between insurance contracts and other items, such as financial instruments) that can affect those risks. If the effect of any relationship would not be apparent from disclosures required by the IFRS, further disclosure might be useful.

Risk management objectives and policies for mitigating risks arising from insurance contracts

IG48   Paragraph 39(a) of the IFRS requires an insurer to disclose its objectives, policies and processes for managing risks arising from insurance contracts and the methods used to manage those risks. Such discussion provides an additional perspective that complements information about contracts outstanding at a particular time. Such disclosure might include information about:

(a)   the structure and organisation of the insurer's risk management function(s), including a discussion of independence and accountability.

(b)   the scope and nature of the insurer's risk reporting or measurement systems, such as internal risk measurement models, sensitivity analyses, scenario analysis, and stress testing, and how the insurer integrates them into its operating activities. Useful disclosure might include a summary description of the approach used, associated assumptions and parameters (including confidence intervals, computation frequencies and historical observation periods) and strengths and limitations of the approach.

(c)   the insurer's processes for accepting, measuring, monitoring and controlling insurance risks and the underwriting strategy to ensure that there are appropriate risk classification and premium levels.

(d)   the extent to which insurance risks are assessed and managed on an entity-wide basis.

(e)   the methods the insurer employs to limit or transfer insurance risk exposures and avoid undue concentrations of risk, such as retention limits, inclusion of options in contracts, and reinsurance.

(f)   asset and liability management (ALM) techniques.

(g)   the insurer's processes for managing, monitoring and controlling commitments received (or given) to accept (or contribute) additional debt or equity capital when specified events occur.

These disclosures might be provided both for individual types of risks insured and overall, and might include a combination of narrative descriptions and specific quantified data, as appropriate to the nature of the insurance contracts and their relative significance to the insurer.

IG49   [Deleted]

IG50   [Deleted]

Insurance risk

IG51   Paragraph 39(c) of the IFRS requires disclosures about insurance risk. Disclosures to satisfy this requirement might build on the following foundations:

(a)   Information about insurance risk might be consistent with (though less detailed than) the information provided internally to the entity's key management personnel (as defined in IAS 24 *Related Party Disclosures*), so that users can assess the insurer's financial position, performance and cash flows 'through the eyes of management'.

(b)   Information about risk exposures might report exposures both gross and net of reinsurance (or other risk mitigating elements, such as catastrophe bonds issued or policyholder participation features), especially if the insurer expects a significant change in the nature or extent of its reinsurance programme or if an analysis before reinsurance is relevant for an analysis of the credit risk arising from reinsurance held.

(c)   In reporting quantitative information about insurance risk, an insurer might disclose the methods used, the strengths and limitations of those methods, the assumptions made, and the effect of reinsurance, policyholder participation and other mitigating elements.

(d)   Insurers might classify risk along more than one dimension. For example, life insurers might classify contracts by both the level of mortality risk and the level of investment risk. It may sometimes be convenient to display this information in a matrix format.

(e)   If an insurer's risk exposures at the end of the reporting period are unrepresentative of its exposures during the period, it might be useful to disclose that fact.

(f)   The following disclosures required by paragraph 39 of the IFRS might also be relevant:

(i)   the sensitivity of profit or loss and equity to changes in variables that have a material effect on them.

(ii)   concentrations of insurance risk.

(iii)   the development of prior year insurance liabilities.

IG51A   Disclosures about insurance risk might include:

(a)   information about the nature of the risk covered, with a brief summary description of the class (such as annuities, pensions, other life insurance, motor, property and liability).

(b)   information about the general nature of participation features whereby policyholders share in the performance (and related risks) of individual contracts or pools of contracts or entities, including the general nature of any formula for the participation and the extent of any discretion held by the insurer.

(c)   information about the terms of any obligation or contingent obligation for the insurer to contribute to government or other guarantee funds (see also IAS 37 *Provisions, Contingent Liabilities and Contingent Assets*).

Sensitivity to insurance risk

IG52   Paragraph 39(c)(i) of the IFRS requires disclosure about sensitivity to insurance risk. To permit meaningful aggregation, the sensitivity disclosures focus on summary indicators, namely profit or loss and equity. Although sensitivity tests can provide useful information, such tests have limitations. An insurer might disclose the strengths and limitations of sensitivity analyses performed.

IG52A   Paragraph 39A permits two alternative approaches for this disclosure: quantitative disclosure of effects on profit or loss and equity (paragraph 39A(a)) or qualitative disclosure and disclosure about terms and conditions (paragraph 39A(b)). An insurer may provide quantitative disclosures for some insurance risks (in accordance with paragraph 39A(a)), and provide qualitative information about sensitivity and information about terms and conditions (in accordance with paragraph 39A(b)) for other insurance risks.

IG53   Informative disclosure avoids giving a misleading sensitivity analysis if there are significant non-linearities in sensitivities to variables that have a material effect. For example, if a change of 1 per cent in a variable has a negligible effect, but a change of 1.1 per cent has a material effect, it might be misleading to disclose the effect of a 1 per cent change without further explanation.

IG53A   If an insurer chooses to disclose a quantitative sensitivity analysis in accordance with paragraph 39A(a), and that sensitivity analysis does not reflect significant correlations between key variables, the insurer might explain the effect of those correlations.

IG54   [Deleted]

IG54A   If an insurer chooses to disclose qualitative information about sensitivity in accordance with paragraph 39A(b), it is required to disclose information about those terms and conditions of insurance contracts that have a material effect on the amount, timing and uncertainty of cash flows. To achieve this, an insurer might disclose the qualitative information suggested by paragraphs IG51–IG58 on insurance risk and paragraphs IG62–IG65G on credit risk, liquidity risk and market risk. As stated in paragraph IG12, an insurer decides in the light of its circumstances how it aggregates information to display the overall picture without combining information with different characteristics. An insurer might conclude that qualitative information needs to be more disaggregated if it is not supplemented with quantitative information.

Concentrations of insurance risk

IG55   Paragraph 39(c)(ii) of the IFRS refers to the need to disclose concentrations of insurance risk. Such concentration could arise from, for example:

(a)   a single insurance contract, or a small number of related contracts, for instance, when an insurance contract covers low-frequency, high-severity risks such as earthquakes.

(b)   single incidents that expose an insurer to risk under several different types of insurance contract. For example, a major terrorist incident could create exposure under life insurance contracts, property insurance contracts, business interruption and civil liability.

(c)   exposure to unexpected changes in trends, for example, unexpected changes in human mortality or in policyholder behaviour.

(d)   exposure to possible major changes in financial market conditions that could cause options held by policyholders to come into the money. For example, when interest rates decline significantly, interest rate and annuity guarantees may result in significant losses.

(e)   significant litigation or legislative risks that could cause a large single loss, or have a pervasive effect on many contracts.

(f)   correlations and interdependencies between different risks.

(g)   significant non-linearities, such as stop-loss or excess of loss features, especially if a key variable is close to a level that triggers a material change in future cash flows.

(h)   geographical and sectoral concentrations.

IG56   Disclosure of concentrations of insurance risk might include a description of the shared characteristic that identifies each concentration and an indication of the possible exposure, both before and after reinsurance held, associated with all insurance liabilities sharing that characteristic.

IG57   Disclosure about an insurer's historical performance on low-frequency, high-severity risks might be one way to help users to assess cash flow uncertainty associated with those risks. Consider an insurance contract that covers an earthquake that is expected to happen every 50 years, on average. If the insured event occurs during the current contract period, the insurer will report a large loss. If the insured event does not occur during the current period, the insurer will report a profit. Without adequate disclosure of the source of historical profits, it could be misleading for the insurer to report 49 years of reasonable profits, followed by one large loss; users may misinterpret the insurer's long-term ability to generate cash flows over the complete cycle of 50 years. Therefore, it might be useful to describe the extent of the exposure to risks of this kind and the estimated frequency of losses. If circumstances have not changed significantly, disclosure of the insurer's experience with this exposure may be one way to convey information about estimated frequencies.

IG58   For regulatory or other reasons, some entities produce special purpose financial reports that show catastrophe or equalisation reserves as liabilities. However, in financial statements prepared using IFRSs, those reserves are not liabilities but are a component of equity. Therefore they are subject to the disclosure requirements in IAS 1 for equity. IAS 1 requires an entity to disclose:

(a)   a description of the nature and purpose of each reserve within equity;

(b)   information that enables users to understand the entity's objectives, policies and processes for managing capital; and

(c)   the nature of any externally imposed capital requirements, how those requirements are incorporated into the management of capital and whether during the period it complied with any externally imposed capital requirements to which it is subject.

Claims development

IG59   Paragraph 39(c)(iii) of the IFRS requires disclosure of claims development information (subject to transitional relief in paragraph 44). Informative disclosure might reconcile this information to amounts reported in the statement of financial position. An insurer might disclose unusual claims expenses or developments separately, allowing users to identify the underlying trends in performance.

IG60   As explained in paragraph 39(c)(iii) of the IFRS, disclosures about claims development are not required for claims for which uncertainty about the amount and timing of claims payments is typically resolved within one year. Therefore, these disclosures are not normally required for most life insurance contracts. Furthermore, claims development disclosure is not normally needed for annuity contracts because each periodic payment arises, in effect, from a separate claim about which there is no uncertainty.

IG61   IG Example 5 shows one possible format for presenting claims development information. Other possible formats might, for example, present information by accident year rather than underwriting year. Although the example illustrates a format that might be useful if insurance liabilities are discounted, the IFRS does not require discounting (paragraph 25(a) of the IFRS).

IG Example 5: Disclosure of claims development

This example illustrates a possible format for a claims development table for a general insurer. The top half of the table shows how the insurer's estimates of total claims for each underwriting year develop over time. For example, at the end of 20X1, the insurer estimated that it would pay claims of CU680 for insured events relating to insurance contracts underwritten in 20X1. By the end of 20X2, the insurer had revised the estimate of cumulative claims (both those paid and those still to be paid) to CU673.

The lower half of the table reconciles the cumulative claims to the amount appearing in the statement of financial position. First, the cumulative payments are deducted to give the cumulative unpaid claims for each year on an undiscounted basis. Second, if the claims liabilities are discounted, the effect of discounting is deducted to give the carrying amount in the statement of financial position.

Underwriting year	20X1	20X2	20X3	20X4	20X5	Total
	CU	CU	CU	CU	CU	CU
Estimate of cumulative claims:						
At end of underwriting year	680	790	823	920	968	
One year later	673	785	840	903		
Two years later	692	776	845			
Three years later	697	771				
Four years later	702					
Estimate of cumulative claims	702	771	845	903	968	
Cumulative payments	(702)	(689)	(570)	(350)	(217)	
	–	82	275	553	751	1,661
Effect of discounting	–	(14)	(68)	(175)	(285)	(542)
Present value recognised in the statement of financial position	–	68	207	378	466	1,119

Credit risk, liquidity risk and market risk

IG62   Paragraph 39(d) of the IFRS requires an insurer to disclose information about credit risk, liquidity risk and market risk that paragraphs 31–42 of IFRS 7 would require if insurance contracts were within its scope. Such disclosure includes:

(a)   summary quantitative data about the insurer's exposure to those risks based on information provided internally to its key management personnel (as defined in IAS 24); and

(b)   to the extent not already covered by the disclosures discussed above, the information described in paragraphs 36–42 of IFRS 7.

The disclosures about credit risk, liquidity risk and market risk may be either provided in the financial statements or incorporated by cross-reference to some other statement, such as a management commentary or risk report, that is available to users of the financial statements on the same terms as the financial statements and at the same time.

IG63   [Deleted]

IG64   Informative disclosure about credit risk, liquidity risk and market risk might include:

(a)   information about the extent to which features such as policyholder participation features mitigate or compound those risks.

(b)   a summary of significant guarantees, and of the levels at which guarantees of market prices or interest rates are likely to alter the insurer's cash flows.

(c)   the basis for determining investment returns credited to policyholders, such as whether the returns are fixed, based contractually on the return of specified assets or partly or wholly subject to the insurer's discretion.

Credit risk

IG64A   Paragraphs 36–38 of IFRS 7 require disclosure about credit risk. Credit risk is defined as 'the risk that one party to a financial instrument will fail to discharge an obligation and cause the other party to incur a financial loss'. Thus, for an insurance contract, credit risk includes the risk that an insurer incurs a financial loss because a reinsurer defaults on its obligations under the reinsurance contract. Furthermore, disputes with the reinsurer could lead to an impairment of the cedant's reinsurance asset. The risk of such disputes may have an effect similar to credit risk. Thus, similar disclosure might be relevant. Balances due from agents or brokers may also be subject to credit risk.

IG64B   A financial guarantee contract reimburses a loss incurred by the holder because a specified debtor fails to make payment when due. The holder is exposed to credit risk, and IFRS 7 requires the holder to provide disclosures about that credit risk. However, from the perspective of the issuer, the risk assumed by the issuer is insurance risk rather than credit risk.

IG65   [Deleted]

IG65A The issuer of a financial guarantee contract provides disclosures complying with IFRS 7 if it applies IAS 39 in recognising and measuring the contract. If the issuer elects, when permitted by paragraph 4(d) of IFRS 4, to apply IFRS 4 in recognising and measuring the contract, it provides disclosures complying with IFRS 4. The main implications are as follows:

(a) IFRS 4 requires disclosure about actual claims compared with previous estimates (claims development), but does not require disclosure of the fair value of the contract.

(b) IFRS 7 requires disclosure of the fair value of the contract, but does not require disclosure of claims development.

Liquidity risk

IG65B Paragraph 39(a) and (b) of IFRS 7 requires disclosure of a maturity analysis for financial liabilities that shows the remaining contractual maturities. For insurance contracts, the contractual maturity refers to the estimated date when contractually required cash flows will occur. This depends on factors such as when the insured event occurs and the possibility of lapse. However, IFRS 4 permits various existing accounting practices for insurance contracts to continue. As a result, an insurer may not need to make detailed estimates of cash flows to determine the amounts it recognises in the statement of financial position. To avoid requiring detailed cash flow estimates that are not required for measurement purposes, paragraph 39(d)(i) of IFRS 4 states that an insurer need not provide the maturity analyses required by paragraph 39(a) and (b) of IFRS 7 (ie that show the remaining contractual maturities of insurance contracts) if it discloses an analysis, by estimated timing, of the amounts recognised in the statement of financial position.

IG65C An insurer might also disclose a summary narrative description of how the maturity analysis (or analysis by estimated timing) flows could change if policyholders exercised lapse or surrender options in different ways. If an insurer considers that lapse behaviour is likely to be sensitive to interest rates, the insurer might disclose that fact and state whether the disclosures about market risk reflect that interdependence.

Market risk

IG65D Paragraph 40(a) of IFRS 7 requires a sensitivity analysis for each type of market risk at the end of the reporting period, showing the effect of reasonably possible changes in the relevant risk variable on profit or loss or equity. If no reasonably possible change in the relevant risk variable would affect profit or loss or equity, an entity discloses that fact to comply with paragraph 40(a) of IFRS 7. A reasonably possible change in the relevant risk variable might not affect profit or loss in the following examples:

(a) if a non-life insurance liability is not discounted, changes in market interest rates would not affect profit or loss.

(b) some insurers may use valuation factors that blend together the effect of various market and non-market assumptions that do not change unless the insurer assesses that its recognised insurance liability is not adequate. In some cases a reasonably possible change in the relevant risk variable would not affect the adequacy of the recognised insurance liability.

IG65E   In some accounting models, a regulator specifies discount rates or other assumptions about market risk variables that the insurer uses in measuring its insurance liabilities and the regulator does not amend those assumptions to reflect current market conditions at all times. In such cases, the insurer might comply with paragraph 40(a) of IFRS 7 by disclosing:

(a)   the effect on profit or loss or equity of a reasonably possible change in the assumption set by the regulator.

(b)   the fact that the assumption set by the regulator would not necessarily change at the same time, by the same amount, or in the same direction, as changes in market prices, or market rates, would imply.

IG65F   An insurer might be able to take action to reduce the effect of changes in market conditions. For example, an insurer may have discretion to change surrender values or maturity benefits, or to vary the amount or timing of policyholder benefits arising from discretionary participation features. Paragraph 40(a) of IFRS 7 does not require entities to consider the potential effect of future management actions that may offset the effect of the disclosed changes in the relevant risk variable. However, paragraph 40(b) of IFRS 7 requires an entity to disclose the methods and assumptions used to prepare the sensitivity analysis. To comply with this requirement, an insurer might conclude that it needs to disclose the extent of available management actions and their effect on the sensitivity analysis.

IG65G   Some insurers manage sensitivity to market conditions using a method that differs from the method described by paragraph 40(a) of IFRS 7. For example, some insurers use an analysis of the sensitivity of embedded value to changes in market risk. Paragraph 39(d)(ii) of IFRS 4 permits an insurer to use that sensitivity analysis to meet the requirement in paragraph 40(a) of IFRS 7. IFRS 4 and IFRS 7 require an insurer to provide sensitivity analyses for all classes of financial instruments and insurance contracts, but an insurer might use different approaches for different classes. IFRS 4 and IFRS 7 specify the following approaches:

(a)   the sensitivity analysis described in paragraph 40(a) of IFRS 7 for financial instruments or insurance contracts;

(b)   the method described in paragraph 41 of IFRS 7 for financial instruments or insurance contracts; or

(c)   the method permitted by paragraph 39(d)(ii) of IFRS 4 for insurance contracts.

Exposures to market risk under embedded derivatives

IG66   Paragraph 39(e) of the IFRS requires an insurer to disclose information about exposures to market risk under embedded derivatives contained in a host insurance contract if the insurer is not required to, and does not, measure the embedded derivative at fair value (for example, guaranteed annuity options and guaranteed minimum death benefits).

IG67   An example of a contract containing a guaranteed annuity option is one in which the policyholder pays a fixed monthly premium for thirty years. At maturity, the policyholder can elect to take either (a) a lump sum equal to the accumulated investment value or (b) a lifetime annuity at a rate guaranteed at inception (ie when the contract started). For policyholders electing to receive the annuity, the insurer could suffer a significant loss if interest rates decline substantially or if the policyholder lives much longer than the average. The insurer is exposed to both market risk and significant insurance risk (mortality risk) and a transfer of insurance risk occurs at inception, because the insurer fixed the price for mortality risk at that date. Therefore, the contract is an insurance contract from inception. Moreover, the embedded guaranteed annuity option itself meets the definition of an insurance contract, and so separation is not required.

IG68   An example of a contract containing minimum guaranteed death benefits is one in which the policyholder pays a monthly premium for 30 years. Most of the premiums are invested in a mutual fund. The rest is used to buy life cover and to cover expenses. On maturity or surrender, the insurer pays the value of the mutual fund units at that date. On death before final maturity, the insurer pays the greater of (a) the current unit value and (b) a fixed amount. This contract could be viewed as a hybrid contract comprising (a) a mutual fund investment and (b) an embedded life insurance contract that pays a death benefit equal to the fixed amount less the current unit value (but zero if the current unit value is more than the fixed amount).

IG69   Both these embedded derivatives meet the definition of an insurance contract if the insurance risk is significant. However, in both cases market risk may be much more significant than the mortality risk. If interest rates or equity markets fall substantially, these guarantees would be well in the money. Given the long-term nature of the guarantees and the size of the exposures, an insurer might face extremely large losses. Therefore, an insurer might place particular emphasis on disclosures about such exposures.

IG70   Useful disclosures about such exposures might include:

(a)   the sensitivity analysis discussed above.

(b)   information about the levels where these exposures start to have a material effect on the insurer's cash flows (paragraph IG64(b)).

(c)   the fair value of the embedded derivative, although neither the IFRS nor IFRS 7 requires disclosure of that fair value.

Key performance indicators

IG71   Some insurers present disclosures about what they regard as key performance indicators, such as lapse and renewal rates, total sum insured, average cost per claim, average number of claims per contract, new business volumes, claims ratio, expense ratio and combined ratio. The IFRS does not require such disclosures. However, such disclosures might be a useful way for an insurer to explain its financial performance during the period and to give an insight into the risks arising from insurance contracts.

IASB documents published to accompany

International Financial Reporting Standard 5

Non-current Assets Held for Sale and Discontinued Operations

This version includes amendments resulting from IFRSs issued up to 31 December 2009.

The text of the unaccompanied IFRS 5 is contained in Part A of this edition. Its effective date, when issued, was 1 January 2005. The effective date of the most recent amendment is 1 January 2013. This part presents the following accompanying documents:

Approval by the Board of IFRS 5 issued in March 2004

International Financial Reporting Standard 5 *Non-current Assets Held for Sale and Discontinued Operations* was approved for issue by twelve of the fourteen members of the International Accounting Standards Board. Messrs Cope and Schmid dissented. Their dissenting opinions are set out after the Basis for Conclusions on IFRS 5.

Sir David Tweedie	Chairman
Thomas E Jones	Vice-Chairman
Mary E Barth	
Hans-Georg Bruns	
Anthony T Cope	
Robert P Garnett	
Gilbert Gélard	
James J Leisenring	
Warren J McGregor	
Patricia L O'Malley	
Harry K Schmid	
John T Smith	
Geoffrey Whittington	
Tatsumi Yamada	

CONTENTS

Basis for Conclusions on
IFRS 5 *Non-current Assets Held for Sale*
and Discontinued Operations

This Basis for Conclusions accompanies, but is not part of, IFRS 5.

Introduction

BC1 This Basis for Conclusions summarises the International Accounting Standards Board's considerations in reaching the conclusions in IFRS 5 *Non-current Assets Held for Sale and Discontinued Operations*. Individual Board members gave greater weight to some factors than to others.

BC2 In September 2002 the Board agreed to add a short-term convergence project to its active agenda. The objective of the project is to reduce differences between IFRSs and US GAAP that are capable of resolution in a relatively short time and can be addressed outside major projects. The project is a joint project with the US Financial Accounting Standards Board (FASB).

BC3 As part of the project, the two boards agreed to review each other's deliberations on each of the selected possible convergence topics, and choose the highest quality solution as the basis for convergence. For topics recently considered by either board, there is an expectation that whichever board has more recently deliberated that topic will have the higher quality solution.

BC4 As part of the review of topics recently considered by the FASB, the Board discussed the requirements of SFAS 144 *Accounting for the Impairment or Disposal of Long-Lived Assets*, as they relate to assets held for sale and discontinued operations. The Board did not consider the requirements of SFAS 144 relating to the impairment of assets held for use. Impairment of such assets is an issue that is being addressed in the IASB research project on measurement being led by the Canadian Accounting Standards Board.

BC5 Until the issue of IFRS 5, the requirements of SFAS 144 on assets held for sale and discontinued operations differed from IFRSs in the following ways:

(a) if specified criteria are met, SFAS 144 requires non-current assets that are to be disposed of to be classified as held for sale. Such assets are remeasured at the lower of carrying amount and fair value less costs to sell and are not depreciated or amortised. IFRSs did not require non-current assets that are to be disposed of to be classified separately or measured differently from other non-current assets.

(b) the definition of discontinued operations in SFAS 144 was different from the definition of discontinuing operations in IAS 35 *Discontinuing Operations* and the presentation of such operations required by the two standards was also different.

BC6 As discussed in more detail below, the Board concluded that introducing a classification of assets that are held for sale would substantially improve the information available to users of financial statements about assets to be sold.

BC7   The Board published its proposals in an Exposure Draft, ED 4 *Disposal of Non-current Assets and Presentation of Discontinued Operations*, in July 2003 with a comment deadline of 24 October 2003. The Board received over 80 comment letters on the Exposure Draft.

Scope of the IFRS

BC8   In ED 4, the Board proposed that the IFRS should apply to all non-current assets except:

(a)   goodwill,

(b)   financial instruments within the scope of IAS 39 *Financial Instruments: Recognition and Measurement,*[*]

(c)   financial assets under leases, and

(d)   deferred tax assets and assets arising from employee benefits.

BC9   In reconsidering the scope, the Board noted that the use of the term 'non-current' caused the following problems:

(a)   assets that are acquired with the intention of resale were clearly intended to be within the scope of ED 4, but would also be within the definition of current assets and so might be thought to be excluded. The same was true for assets that had been classified as non-current but were now expected to be realised within twelve months.

(b)   it was not clear how the scope would apply to assets presented in accordance with a liquidity presentation.

BC10   The Board noted that it had not intended that assets classified as non-current in accordance with IAS 1 *Presentation of Financial Statements* would be reclassified as current assets simply because of management's intention to sell or because they reached their final twelve months of expected use by the entity. The Board decided to clarify in IFRS 5 that assets classified as non-current are not reclassified as current assets until they meet the criteria to be classified as held for sale in accordance with the IFRS. Further, assets of a class that an entity would normally regard as non-current and are acquired exclusively with a view to resale are not classified as current unless they meet the criteria to be classified as held for sale in accordance with the IFRS.

BC11   In relation to assets presented in accordance with a liquidity presentation, the Board decided that non-current should be taken to mean assets that include amounts expected to be recovered more than twelve months after the balance sheet date.

BC12   These clarifications ensure that all assets of the type normally regarded by the entity as non-current will be within the scope of the IFRS.

---

[*]   In November 2009 the IASB amended some of the requirements of IAS 39 and relocated them to IFRS 9 *Financial Instruments*. IFRS 9 applies to all assets within the scope of IAS 39.

BC13　　The Board also reconsidered the exclusions from the scope proposed in ED 4. The Board noted that the classification and presentation requirements of the IFRS are applicable to all non-current assets and concluded that any exclusions should relate only to the measurement requirements. In relation to the measurement requirements, the Board decided that non-current assets should be excluded only if (i) they are already carried at fair value with changes in fair value recognised in profit or loss or (ii) there would be difficulties in determining their fair value less costs to sell. The Board therefore concluded that only the following non-current assets should be excluded from the measurement requirements of the IFRS:

Assets already carried at fair value with changes in fair value recognised in profit or loss:

(a)　　financial assets within the scope of IAS 39.[*]

(b)　　non-current assets that have been accounted for using the fair value model in IAS 40 *Investment Property*.

(c)　　non-current assets that have been measured at fair value less estimated point-of-sale costs in accordance with IAS 41 *Agriculture*.[†]

Assets for which there might be difficulties in determining their fair value:

(a)　　deferred tax assets.

(b)　　assets arising from employee benefits.

(c)　　assets arising from insurance contracts.

BC14　　The Board acknowledged that the scope of the IFRS would differ from that of SFAS 144 but noted that SFAS 144 covers the impairment of non-current assets held for use as well as those held for sale. Furthermore, other requirements in US GAAP affect the scope of SFAS 144. The Board therefore concluded that convergence with the scope of SFAS 144 would not be possible.

BC14A　　The Board identified a need to clarify the disclosure requirements for non-current assets (or disposal groups) classified as held for sale or discontinued operations in accordance with IFRS 5. Some believed that IFRS 5 and other IFRSs that specifically refer to non-current assets (or disposal groups) classified as held for sale or discontinued operations set out all the disclosures required in respect of those assets or operations. Others believed that all disclosures required by IFRSs whose scope does not specifically exclude non-current assets (or disposal groups) classified as held for sale or discontinued operations apply to such assets (or disposal groups).[§]

---

[*]　　In November 2009 the IASB amended some of the requirements of IAS 39 and relocated them to IFRS 9 *Financial Instruments*. IFRS 9 applies to all assets within the scope of IAS 39.

[†]　　In *Improvements to IFRSs* issued in May 2008 the Board amended IAS 41: the term 'estimated point-of-sale costs' was replaced by 'costs to sell'.

[§]　　Paragraphs BC14A–BC14E were added as a consequence of amendments to IFRS 5 by *Improvements to IFRSs* issued in April 2009.

　　　　　　　　　　　　　　　　　© IASCF

BC14B   The Board noted that paragraph 30 of IFRS 5 requires an entity to 'present and disclose information that enables users of the financial statements to evaluate the financial effects of discontinued operations and disposals of non-current assets (or disposal groups).' Paragraph BC17 below states that 'the Board concluded that providing information about assets and groups of assets and liabilities to be disposed of is of benefit to users of financial statements. Such information should assist users in assessing the timing, amount and uncertainty of future cash flows.'

BC14C   The Board noted that some IFRSs other than IFRS 5 require specific disclosures for non-current assets (or disposal groups) classified as held for sale or discontinued operations. For instance, paragraph 68 of IAS 33 *Earnings per Share* requires an entity to disclose the amount per share for discontinued operations. The Board also noted that the requirements of IAS 1 on fair presentation and materiality also apply to such assets (or disposal groups).

BC14D   The Board also noted that when a disposal group includes assets and liabilities that are not within the scope of the measurement requirements of IFRS 5, disclosures about measurement of those assets and liabilities are normally provided in the other notes to the financial statements and do not need to be repeated, unless they better enable users of the financial statements to evaluate the financial effects of discontinued operations and disposals of non-current assets (or disposal groups).

BC14E   Consequently, in *Improvements to IFRSs* issued in April 2009, the Board clarified that IFRS 5 and other IFRSs that specifically refer to non-current assets (or disposal groups) classified as held for sale or discontinued operations set out all the disclosures required in respect of those assets or operations. Additional disclosures about non-current assets (or disposal groups) classified as held for sale may be necessary to comply with the general requirements of IAS 1, in particular paragraphs 15 and 125 of that Standard.

Classification of non-current assets to be disposed of as held for sale

BC15   Under SFAS 144, long-lived assets are classified as either (i) held and used or (ii) held for sale. Before the issue of this IFRS, no distinction was made in IFRSs between non-current assets held and used and non-current assets held for sale, except in relation to financial instruments.

BC16   The Board considered whether a separate classification for non-current assets held for sale would create unnecessary complexity in IFRSs and introduce an element of management intent into the accounting. Some commentators suggested that the categorisation 'assets held for sale' is unnecessary, and that if the focus were changed to 'assets *retired* from active use' much of the complexity could be eliminated, because the latter classification would be based on actuality rather than what they perceive as management intent. They assert that it is the potential abuse of the classification that necessitates many of the detailed requirements in SFAS 144. Others suggested that, if existing IFRSs were amended to specify that assets retired from active use are measured at fair value less costs to sell and to require additional disclosure, some convergence with SFAS 144 could be achieved without creating a new IFRS.

BC17   However, the Board concluded that providing information about assets and groups of assets and liabilities to be disposed of is of benefit to users of financial statements. Such information should assist users in assessing the timing, amount and uncertainty of future cash flows. The Board understands that this was also the assessment underpinning SFAS 144. Therefore the Board concluded that introducing the notion of assets and disposal groups held for sale makes IFRSs more complete.

BC18   Furthermore, although the held for sale classification begins from an intention to sell the asset, the other criteria for this classification are tightly drawn and are significantly more objective than simply specifying an intention or commitment to sell. Some might argue that the criteria are too specific. However, the Board believes that the criteria should be specific to achieve comparability of classification between entities. The Board does not believe that a classification 'retired from active use' would necessarily require fewer criteria to support it. For example, it would be necessary to establish a distinction between assets retired from active use and those that are held as back-up spares or are temporarily idle.

BC19   Lastly, if the classification and measurement of assets held for sale in IFRSs are the same as in US GAAP, convergence will have been achieved in an area of importance to users of financial statements.

BC20   Most respondents to ED 4 agreed that a separate classification for non-current assets that are no longer held to be used is desirable. However, the proposals in ED 4 were criticised for the following reasons:

(a)   the criteria were too restrictive and rules-based.

(b)   a commitment to sell needs to be demonstrated, consistently with the requirements of IAS 37 *Provisions, Contingent Liabilities and Contingent Assets* relating to restructuring provisions.

(c)   the classification should be for assets retired from active use.

(d)   assets to be abandoned should be treated in the same way as assets to be sold.

BC21   The Board noted that a more flexible definition would be open to abuse. Further, changing the criteria for classification could cause divergence from US GAAP. The Board has, however, reordered the criteria to highlight the principles.

BC22   The Board also noted that the requirements of IAS 37 establish when a liability is incurred, whereas the requirements of the IFRS relate to the measurement and presentation of assets that are already recognised.

BC23   Finally, the Board reconfirmed the principle behind the classification proposals in ED 4, which is that the carrying amount of the assets will be recovered principally through sale. Applying this principle to assets retired from active use, the Board decided that assets retired from active use that do not meet the criteria for classification as assets held for sale should not be presented separately because the carrying amount of the asset may not be recovered principally through sale. Conversely, the Board decided that assets that meet the criteria to be classified as held for sale and are being used should not be precluded from being separately classified. This is because, if a non-current asset is available for immediate sale, the remaining use of the asset is incidental to its recovery through sale and the carrying amount of the asset will be recovered principally through sale.

BC24 Applying the same principle to assets to be abandoned, the Board noted that their carrying value will never be recovered principally through sale.

Plan to sell the controlling interest in a subsidiary[*]

BC24A In 2007 the Board considered situations in which an entity is committed to a plan to sell the controlling interest in a subsidiary and, after the sale, retains a non-controlling interest in its former subsidiary, taking the form of an investment in an associate, an investment in a joint venture or a financial asset. The Board considered how the classification as held for sale applies to the subsidiary in the consolidated financial statements of the entity.

BC24B The Board noted that paragraph 6 states that 'An entity shall classify a non-current asset (or disposal group) as held for sale if its carrying amount will be recovered principally through a sale transaction rather than through continuing use.' The Board also noted that IAS 27 *Consolidated and Separate Financial Statements* (as amended in January 2008) defines control and requires a parent to consolidate a subsidiary until control is lost. At the date control is lost, all the subsidiary's assets and liabilities are derecognised and any investment retained in the former subsidiary is recognised. Loss of control is a significant economic event that changes the nature of an investment. The parent-subsidiary relationship ceases to exist and an investor-investee relationship begins that differs significantly from the former parent-subsidiary relationship. Therefore, the new investor-investee relationship is recognised and measured initially at the date when control is lost.

BC24C The Board concluded that, under the sale plan described above, the controlling interest in the subsidiary is, in substance, exchanged for a non-controlling interest. Therefore, in the Board's view, being committed to a plan involving loss of control of a subsidiary should trigger classification as held for sale. The Board also noted that this conclusion is consistent with IAS 27.

BC24D The Board noted that the subsidiary's assets and liabilities meet the definition of a disposal group in accordance with paragraph 4. Therefore, the Board concluded that all the subsidiary's assets and liabilities should be classified as held for sale, not only the portion of the interest to be disposed of, regardless of whether the entity will retain a non-controlling interest.

BC24E The Board considered the comments received on the proposal set out in its exposure draft of October 2007. In response to comments from some respondents, the Board clarified in the amendment that the criteria for classification as held for sale need to be met.

---

[*] This section and paragraphs BC77A and BC79A were added as a consequence of amendments to IFRS 5 by *Improvements to IFRSs* issued in May 2008.

Assets to be exchanged for other non-current assets

BC25 Under SFAS 144, long-lived assets that are to be exchanged for similar productive assets cannot be classified as held for sale. They are regarded as disposed of only when exchanged. The Basis for Conclusions on SFAS 144 explains that this is because the exchange of such assets is accounted for at amounts based on the carrying amount of the assets, not at fair value, and that using the carrying amount is more consistent with the accounting for a long-lived asset to be held and used than for a long-lived asset to be sold.

BC26 Under IAS 16 *Property, Plant and Equipment*, as revised in 2003, an exchange of assets is normally measured at fair value. The SFAS 144 reasoning for the classification of such assets as held for sale does not, therefore, apply. Consistently with IAS 16, the IFRS treats an exchange of assets as a disposal and acquisition of assets unless the exchange has no commercial substance.

BC27 The FASB has published an exposure draft proposing to converge with the requirements in IAS 16 for an exchange of assets to be measured at fair value. The exposure draft also proposes a consequential amendment to SFAS 144 that would make exchanges of assets that have commercial substance eligible for classification as held for sale.

Measurement of non-current assets held for sale

BC28 SFAS 144 requires a long-lived asset or a disposal group classified as held for sale to be measured at the lower of its carrying amount and fair value less costs to sell. A long-lived asset classified as held for sale (or included within a disposal group) is not depreciated, but interest and other expenses attributable to the liabilities of a disposal group are recognised.

BC29 As explained in the Basis for Conclusions on SFAS 144, the remaining use in operations of an asset that is to be sold is incidental to the recovery of the carrying amount through sale. The accounting for such an asset should therefore be a process of valuation rather than allocation.

BC30 The FASB further observed that once the asset is remeasured, to depreciate the asset would reduce its carrying amount below its fair value less costs to sell. It also noted that should there be a decline in the value of the asset after initial classification as held for sale and before eventual sale, the loss would be recognised in the period of decline because the fair value less costs to sell is evaluated each period.

BC31 The counter-argument is that, although classified as held for sale, the asset is still being used in operations, and hence cessation of depreciation is inconsistent with the basic principle that the cost of an asset should be allocated over the period during which benefits are obtained from its use. Furthermore, although the decline in the value of the asset through its use would be reflected in the recognised change in fair value, it might also be masked by an increase arising from changes in the market prices of the asset.

BC32   However, the Board noted that IAS 16 requires an entity to keep the expected useful life and residual values of property, plant and equipment up to date, and IAS 36 *Impairment of Assets* requires an immediate write-down to the higher of value in use and fair value less costs to sell. An entity should, therefore, often achieve a measurement effect for individual assets that are about to be sold under other IFRSs similar to that required by this IFRS as follows. Under other IFRSs, if the fair value less costs to sell is higher than carrying amount there will be no impairment and no depreciation (because the residual value will have been updated). If fair value less costs to sell is lower than carrying amount, there will be an impairment loss that reduces the carrying amount to fair value less costs to sell and then no depreciation (because the residual value will have been updated), unless value in use is higher than fair value less costs to sell. If value in use is higher than fair value less costs to sell, there would be small differences between the treatment that would arise under other IFRSs and the treatment under IFRS 5. Under other IFRSs there would be an impairment loss to the extent that the carrying amount exceeds value in use rather than to the extent that the carrying amount exceeds fair value less costs to sell. Under other IFRSs, there would also then be depreciation of the excess of value in use (the new carrying amount of the asset) over fair value less costs to sell (its residual value). However, for assets classified as held for sale, value in use will differ from fair value less costs to sell only to the extent of the net cash flows expected to arise before the sale. If the period to sale is short, this amount will usually be relatively small. The difference in impairment loss recognised and subsequent depreciation under other IFRSs compared with the impairment loss and no subsequent depreciation under IFRS 5 would, therefore, also be small.

BC33   The Board concluded that the measurement requirements of IFRS 5 for individual assets would often not involve a significant change from the requirements of other IFRSs. Furthermore, the Board agreed with the FASB that the cash flows arising from the asset's remaining use were incidental to the recovery of the asset through sale and, hence, concluded that individual assets classified as held for sale should be measured at the lower of carrying amount and fair value less costs to sell and should not be depreciated.

BC34   For disposal groups, there could be greater differences between the requirements in other IFRSs and the requirements of IFRS 5. For example, the fair value less costs to sell of a disposal group may reflect internally generated goodwill to the extent that it is higher than the carrying value of the net assets in the disposal group. The residual value of the non-current assets in the disposal group may, nonetheless, be such that, if they were accounted for in accordance with IAS 16, those assets would be depreciated.

BC35   In such a situation, some might view the requirements in IFRS 5 as allowing internally generated goodwill to stop the depreciation of non-current assets. However, the Board does not agree with that view. Rather, the Board believes that the internally generated goodwill provides a buffer against the recognition of an impairment loss on the disposal group. The same effect arises from the impairment requirements in IAS 36. The non-depreciation of the non-current assets in the disposal group is, as with individual assets, a consequence of the basic principle underlying the separate classification, that the carrying amount of the asset will be recovered principally through sale, not continuing use, and that amounts recovered through continuing use will be incidental.

BC36   In addition, it is important to emphasise that IFRS 5 permits only an asset (or disposal group) that is to be *sold* to be classified as held for sale. Assets to be abandoned are classified as held and used until disposed of, and thus are depreciated. The Board agrees with the FASB's observation that a distinction can be drawn between an asset that is to be sold and an asset that is to be abandoned, because the former will be recovered principally through sale and the latter through its continuing use. Therefore, it is logical that depreciation should cease in the former but not the latter case.

BC37   When an asset or a disposal group held for sale is part of a foreign operation with a functional currency that is different from the presentation currency of the group, an exchange difference will have been recognised in equity* arising from the translation of the asset or disposal group into the presentation currency of the group. IAS 21 *The Effects of Changes in Foreign Exchange Rates* requires the exchange difference to be 'recycled' from equity to profit or loss on disposal of the operation. The question arises whether classification as held for sale should trigger the recycling of any exchange differences. Under US GAAP (EITF 01-5 *Application of FASB Statement No. 52 to an Investment Being Evaluated for Impairment That Will Be Disposed Of)* the accumulated foreign currency translation adjustments previously recognised in other comprehensive income that are expected to be recycled in income at the time of sale are included in the carrying amount of the asset (or disposal group) being tested for impairment.

BC38   In its project on reporting comprehensive income, the Board may reconsider the issue of recycling. Therefore, it did not wish to make any interim changes to the requirements in IAS 21. Hence, the IFRS does not permit any exchange differences to be recycled on the classification of an asset or a disposal group as held for sale. The recycling will take place when the asset or disposal group is sold.

The allocation of an impairment loss to a disposal group

BC39   Under SFAS 144 and the proposals in ED 4, assets within the disposal group that are not within the scope of the IFRS are adjusted in accordance with other standards before measuring the fair value less costs to sell of the disposal group. Any loss or gain recognised on adjusting the carrying amount of the disposal group is allocated to the carrying amount of the long-lived assets of the group.

BC40   This is different from the requirements of IAS 36 for the allocation of an impairment loss arising on a cash-generating unit. IAS 36 requires an impairment loss on a cash-generating unit to be allocated first to reduce the carrying amount of goodwill and then to reduce pro rata the carrying amounts of the other assets in the unit.

BC41   The Board considered whether the allocation of an impairment loss for a disposal group should be consistent with the requirements of IAS 36 or with the requirements of SFAS 144. The Board concluded that it would be simplest to require the same allocation as is required by IAS 36 for cash-generating units. Although this is different from SFAS 144, the disposal group as a whole will be measured at the same amount.

---

*   As a consequence of the revision of IAS 1 *Presentation of Financial Statements* (as revised in 2007) such a difference is recognised in other comprehensive income.

Newly acquired assets

BC42   SFAS 144 requires, and ED 4 proposed, newly acquired assets that meet the criteria to be classified as held for sale to be measured at fair value less costs to sell on initial recognition. So, in those instances, other than in a business combination, in which an entity acquires a non-current asset that meets the criteria to be classified as held for sale, a loss is recognised in profit or loss if the cost of the asset exceeds its fair value less costs to sell. In the more common cases in which an entity acquires, as part of a business combination, a non-current asset (or disposal group) that meets the criteria to be classified as held for sale, the difference between fair value and fair value less costs to sell is recognised in goodwill.

BC43   Some respondents to ED 4 noted that measuring newly acquired assets not part of a business combination at fair value less costs to sell was inconsistent with the general proposal that assets classified as held for sale should be measured at *the lower of carrying amount* and fair value less costs to sell. The Board agreed and amended the requirement so that it is clear that the newly acquired assets (or disposal groups) are measured on initial recognition at the lower of what their carrying amount would be were they not classified as held for sale (ie cost) and fair value less costs to sell.

BC44   In relation to business combinations, the Board noted that conceptually the assets should be recognised initially at fair value and then immediately classified as held for sale, with the result that the costs to sell are recognised in profit or loss, not goodwill. In theory, if the entity had factored the costs to sell into the purchase price, the reduced price would lead to the creation of negative goodwill, the immediate recognition of which in profit or loss would offset the loss arising from the costs to sell. Of course, in practice, the reduced price will usually result in lower net positive goodwill rather than negative goodwill to be recognised in profit or loss. For that reason, and for the sake of convergence, the Board concluded that in a business combination non-current assets that meet the criteria to be classified as held for sale on acquisition should be measured at fair value less costs to sell on initial recognition.

BC45   The Board and the FASB are considering which items should form part of the business combination transaction more generally in their joint project on the application of the purchase method. This consideration includes whether the assets and liabilities recognised in the transaction should be based on the acquirer's or the acquiree's perspective. The outcome of those deliberations may affect the decision discussed in paragraph BC44.[*]

Recognition of subsequent increases in fair value less costs to sell

BC46   The Board considered whether a subsequent increase in fair value less costs to sell should be recognised to the extent that it reversed previous impairments.

---

[*]   In their joint project on the application of the acquisition method, the Board and the FASB clarified that the classification of assets acquired in a business combination as held for sale should be based on the acquirer's perspective. Therefore, the acquirer would have to satisfy the criteria in paragraphs 6–11 of IFRS 5 at the acquisition date in order to classify assets acquired as held for sale on initial recognition.

SFAS 144 requires the recognition of a subsequent increase in fair value less costs to sell, but not in excess of the cumulative loss previously recognised for a write-down to fair value less costs to sell. The Board decided that, under IFRSs, a gain should be recognised to the extent that it reverses any impairment of the asset, either in accordance with the IFRS or previously in accordance with IAS 36. Recognising a gain for the reversal of an impairment that occurred before the classification of the asset as held for sale is consistent with the requirement in IAS 36 to recognise reversals of impairment.

Recognition of impairment losses and subsequent gains for assets that, before classification as held for sale, were measured at revalued amounts in accordance with another IFRS

BC47   ED 4 proposed that impairment losses and subsequent gains for assets that, before classification as held for sale, were measured at revalued amounts in accordance with another IFRS should be treated as revaluation decreases and increases according to the standard under which the assets had previously been revalued, consistently with the requirements of IAS 36, except to the extent that the losses and gains are caused by the initial recognition of, or changes in, costs to sell. ED 4 also proposed that costs to sell should always be recognised in profit or loss.

BC48   Many respondents disagreed with these proposals, because of their complexity and because of the resulting inconsistent treatment of assets classified as held for sale. The Board considered the issues raised and decided that assets that were already carried at fair value with changes in fair value recognised in profit or loss should not be subject to the measurement requirements of the IFRS. The Board believes that, for such assets, continued measurement at fair value gives better information than measurement at the lower of carrying amount and fair value less costs to sell. The Board did not, however, believe that such treatment was appropriate for assets that had been revalued in accordance with IAS 16 and IAS 38, because those standards require depreciation to continue and the revaluation change would not necessarily be recognised in profit or loss. The Board concluded that assets that had been revalued in accordance with IAS 16 and IAS 38 should be treated in the same way as any assets that, before classification as held for sale, had not been revalued. Such an approach results in a consistent treatment for assets that are within the scope of the measurement requirements of the IFRS and, hence, a simpler standard.

Measurement of assets reclassified as held for use

BC49   Under SFAS 144, when an entity changes its plan to sell the asset and reclassifies a long-lived asset from held for sale to held and used, the asset is measured at the lower of (a) the carrying amount before the asset (or disposal group) was classified as held for sale, adjusted for any depreciation (or amortisation) that would have been recognised had the asset (or disposal group) been continuously classified as held and used and (b) its fair value at the date of the decision not to sell.

BC50 The underlying principle is to restore the carrying value of the asset to what it would have been had it never been classified as held for sale, taking into account any impairments that may have occurred. In fact, SFAS 144 requires that, for held and used assets, an impairment is recognised only if the carrying amount of the asset exceeds the sum of the undiscounted cash flows expected to result from its use and eventual disposal. Thus, the carrying amount of the asset if it had never been classified as held for sale might exceed its fair value. As a result, SFAS 144 does not necessarily lead to the asset reverting to its original carrying amount. However, the Basis for Conclusions on SFAS 144 notes that the FASB concluded it would be inappropriate to write up the carrying amount of the asset to an amount greater than its fair value solely on the basis of an undiscounted cash flow test. Hence, it arrived at the requirement for measurement at the lower of (a) the asset's carrying amount had it not been classified as held for sale and (b) fair value at the date of the decision not to sell the asset.

BC51 IAS 36 has a different measurement basis for impaired assets, ie recoverable amount. The Board concluded that to be consistent with the principle of SFAS 144 and also to be consistent with the requirements of IAS 36, an asset that ceases to be classified as held for sale should be measured at the lower of (a) the carrying amount that would have been recognised had the asset not been classified as held for sale and (b) its recoverable amount at the date of reclassification. Whilst this is not full convergence, the difference arises from differences in the US GAAP and IFRS impairment models.

Removal of exemption from consolidation for subsidiaries acquired and held exclusively with a view to resale

BC52 SFAS 144 removed the exemption from consolidation in US GAAP for subsidiaries held on a temporary basis on the grounds that all assets held for sale should be treated in the same way, ie as required by SFAS 144 rather than having some assets consolidated and some not.

BC53 The Board agreed that all subsidiaries should be consolidated and that all assets (and disposal groups) that meet the criteria to be classified as held for sale should be treated in the same way. The exemption from consolidation in IAS 27 *Consolidated and Separate Financial Statements* for subsidiaries acquired and held exclusively with a view to resale prevents those assets and disposal groups within such subsidiaries that meet the criteria to be classified as held for sale from being treated consistently with other assets and disposal groups. ED 4 therefore proposed that the exemption in IAS 27 should be removed.

BC54 Some respondents disagreed with this proposal, on the grounds that the information provided by consolidation of such subsidiaries would be less useful than that provided by the current requirement to measure the investment in such subsidiaries at fair value. The Board noted that the impact of the proposals in ED 4 would be limited to the following:

(a) the measurement of a subsidiary that currently is within the scope of the exemptions would change from fair value as required by IAS 39 to the lower of cost and fair value less costs to sell.

(b) any change in fair value of the investment in the subsidiary would, in accordance with the current requirements in IAS 27, be presented as a single amount in profit or loss as a held-for-trading financial asset in accordance with IAS 39.* As discussed in paragraph BC72, the subsidiary would be a discontinued operation and, in accordance with the IFRS's requirements (see paragraphs BC73–BC76), any recognised change in the value of the disposal group that comprises the subsidiary would be presented as a single amount in profit or loss.

(c) the presentation in the balance sheet would change from a single amount for the investment in the subsidiary to two amounts—one for the assets and one for the liabilities of the disposal group that is the subsidiary.†

BC55 The Board reaffirmed its conclusion set out in paragraph BC53. However, it noted that the limited impact of the proposals apply only to the amounts required to be presented on the face of the balance sheet and the income statement. Providing the required analyses of those amounts in the notes could potentially involve the entity having to obtain significantly more information. The Board therefore decided not to require the disclosure of the analyses of the amounts presented on the face of the balance sheet and income statement for newly acquired subsidiaries and to clarify in an example the computational short cuts that could be used to arrive at the amounts to be presented on the face of the balance sheet and income statement.

Presentation of non-current assets held for sale

BC56 SFAS 144 requires an entity to present:

(a) a long-lived asset classified as held for sale separately in the balance sheet; and

(b) the assets and liabilities of a disposal group classified as held for sale separately in the asset and liability sections of the balance sheet. The major classes of those assets and liabilities are separately disclosed either on the face of the balance sheet or in the notes.

BC57 In the Basis for Conclusions on SFAS 144 the FASB noted that information about the nature of both assets and liabilities of a disposal group is useful to users. Separately presenting those items in the balance sheet provides information that is relevant. Separate presentation also distinguishes those assets that are not being depreciated from those that are being depreciated. The Board agreed with the FASB's views.

BC58 Respondents to ED 4 noted that the separate presentation within equity of amounts relating to assets and disposal groups classified as held for sale (such as, for example, unrealised gains and losses on available-for-sale assets§ and foreign

---

* IFRS 9 *Financial Instruments*, issued in November 2009, eliminated the category of held-for-trading financial assets. Paragraph BC54 discusses matters relevant when IFRS 5 was issued.

† Greater disaggregation of the disposal group in the statement of financial position is permitted but not required.

§ IFRS 9 *Financial Instruments*, issued in November 2009, eliminated the category of held-for-trading financial assets. Paragraph BC58 discusses matters relevant when IFRS 5 was issued.

currency translation adjustments) would also provide useful information. The Board agreed and has added such a requirement to the IFRS.

Timing of classification as, and definition of, discontinued operations

BC59   With the introduction of SFAS 144, the FASB broadened the scope of a discontinued operation from a 'segment of a business' to a 'component of an entity'. A component is widely drawn, the criterion being that it comprises 'operations and cash flows that can be clearly distinguished, operationally and for financial reporting purposes, from the rest of the entity'. SFAS 144 states that a component may be a segment, a reporting unit, a subsidiary or an asset group.

BC60   However, at the same time, the FASB specified more restrictive criteria for determining *when* the component is classified as discontinued and hence when its results are presented as discontinued. SFAS 144 requires a component to be classified as discontinued only if it has been disposed of or if it meets the criteria for classification as an asset 'held for sale'.

BC61   The definition of a discontinuing operation in IAS 35 as a 'major line of business' or 'geographical area of operations' is closer to the former, and narrower, US GAAP definition. The trigger in IAS 35 for classifying the operation as discontinuing is the earlier of (a) the entity entering into a binding sale agreement and (b) the board of directors approving and announcing a formal disposal plan. Although IAS 35 refers to IAS 37 for further guidance on what constitutes a plan, the criteria are less restrictive than those in SFAS 144.

BC62   Paragraph 12 of the *Framework* states that the objective of financial statements is to provide information about the financial position, performance and changes in financial position of an entity that is useful to a wide range of users in making economic decisions. Paragraph 15 of the *Framework* goes on to state that the economic decisions that are taken by users of financial statements require an evaluation of the ability of an entity to generate cash and cash equivalents. Separately highlighting the results of discontinued operations provides users with information that is relevant in assessing the ongoing ability of the entity to generate cash flows.

BC63   In terms of the timing of classifying an operation as discontinued, the Board considered whether more useful information is provided by making the classification conditional upon a firm decision to discontinue an operation (the current IAS 35 approach) or conditional upon the classification of an operation as held for sale.

BC64   The Board decided that, to be consistent with the presentation of assets held for disposal and in the interests of convergence, an operation should be classified as discontinued when it is disposed of or classified as held for sale.

BC65   IAS 35 also adopts a different approach from US GAAP when criteria for classification as discontinued are met after the period-end but before the financial statements are issued. SFAS 144 requires some disclosure; however, the component is *not* presented as a discontinued operation. IAS 35 requires the component to be classified as discontinuing.

BC66   The Board believes that, consistently with IAS 10 *Events after the Balance Sheet Date,*[*] a component should not be classified as discontinued in the financial statements unless it meets the criteria to be so classified at the balance sheet date.

BC67   In terms of the definition of a discontinued operation, ED 4 proposed adopting the SFAS 144 definition of a discontinued operation. The Board argued that under existing IAS 35 there may be disposal transactions that, although likely to have an impact on the ongoing operations of the entity, do not meet the criteria for classification as a discontinuing activity. For example, an entity might dispose of a significant portion, but not all, of its cash-generating units operating in a particular geographical area. Under IAS 35, that might not meet the definition of a discontinuing operation. Under SFAS 144, if the relevant criteria were met, it would.

BC68   However, a substantial majority of respondents to ED 4 disagreed with this proposal. They preferred instead to retain the IAS 35 criterion that a discontinued operation should be a major line of business or geographical area of operations.

BC69   The Board reconsidered the issue in the light of the comments received and concluded that the size of unit that could be classified as discontinued in accordance with SFAS 144 was too small, with the result that the information provided by separately presenting discontinued operations may not be as useful as it could be.

BC70   The Board also noted that the FASB Emerging Issues Task Force (EITF) is considering practical problems that have arisen in implementing the criteria for discontinued operations in SFAS 144. Specifically, the EITF is considering (a) the cash flows of the component that should be considered in the determination of whether cash flows have been or will be eliminated from the ongoing operations of the entity and (b) the types of continuing involvement that constitute significant continuing involvement in the operations of the disposal component. As a result of these practical problems, the Board further concluded that it was not appropriate to change the definition of a discontinued operation in a way that was likely to cause the same problems in practice as have arisen under SFAS 144.

BC71   The Board therefore decided that it would retain the requirement in IAS 35 that a discontinued operation should be a major line of business or geographical area of operations, noting that this will include operations that would have been excluded from the US definition before SFAS 144, which was based on a reporting segment. However, the Board regards this as an interim measure and intends to work with the FASB to arrive at a converged definition within a relatively short time.

BC72   Lastly, the Board considered whether newly acquired subsidiaries that meet the criteria to be classified as held for sale should always be classified as discontinued. The Board concluded that they should be so classified because they are being disposed of for one of the following reasons:

(a)   the subsidiary is in a different line of business from the entity, so disposing of it is similar to disposing of a major line of business.

---

[*]   In September 2007 the title of IAS 10 was amended from *Events after the Balance Sheet Date* to *Events after the Reporting Period* as a consequence of the revision of IAS 1 *Presentation of Financial Statements* in 2007.

(b)   the subsidiary is required to be disposed of by regulators because the entity would otherwise have too much of a particular type of operation in a particular geographical area. In such a case the subsidiary must be a significant operation.

Presentation of discontinued operations

BC73   SFAS 144 requires the results of a discontinued operation to be presented as a separate component in the income statement (net of income tax) for all periods presented.

BC74   IAS 35 did not require the results of a discontinuing operation to be presented as a net amount on the face of the income statement. Instead, specified items are disclosed either in the notes or on the face of the income statement.

BC75   In ED 4, the Board noted that it was considering the presentation of discontinued operations in the income statement in its project on reporting comprehensive income and that it did not wish to prejudge the outcome of that project by changing the requirements of IAS 35 in respect of the components to be disclosed. Given that the project on reporting comprehensive income will not be completed as soon as previously expected, the Board decided to proceed with its decisions on the presentation of discontinued operations in this IFRS.

BC76   The Board believes that discontinued operations should be shown in a section of the income statement separately from continuing operations because of the different cash flows expected to arise from the two types of operations. The Board concluded that it is sufficient to show a single net figure for discontinued operations on the face of the income statement because of the limited future cash flows expected to arise from the operations. The IFRS therefore permits an analysis of the single net amount to be presented either in the notes or in the income statement.*

BC77   A substantial majority of the respondents to ED 4 supported such a presentation.

BC77A The Board considered the comments received on the draft amendments in the 2007 exposure draft of proposed *Improvements to International Financial Reporting Standards.* Some respondents asked the Board to clarify the effects of the proposed amendment on the income statement when the disposal group meets the definition of a discontinued operation. The Board concluded that when a subsidiary is a disposal group that meets the definition of a discontinued operation in accordance with paragraph 32, an entity that is committed to a sale plan involving loss of control of the subsidiary should disclose the information required by paragraphs 33–36. The Board agreed with respondents that presentation should not differ simply because of the form of the disposal group.

---

*   IAS 1 *Presentation of Financial Statements* (as revised in 2007) requires an entity to present all income and expense items in one statement of comprehensive income or in two statements (a separate income statement and a statement of comprehensive income).

Transitional arrangements

BC78   Some respondents to ED 4 noted that there could be difficulties in obtaining the information necessary to apply the IFRS retrospectively. The Board agreed that hindsight might be involved in determining at what date assets or disposal groups met the criteria to be classified as held for sale and their fair value at that date. Problems might also arise in separating the results of operations that would have been classified as discontinued operations in prior periods and that had been derecognised in full before the effective date of the IFRS.

BC79   The Board therefore decided to require application of the IFRS prospectively and allow retrospective application only when the necessary information had been obtained in the prior periods in question.

BC79A   The Board concluded that the effective date of the amendments in paragraphs 8A and 36A for presentation purposes should be 1 July 2009 to be consistent with the effective date of the amendments to IAS 27 (as amended in January 2008) for measurement purposes. Because paragraph 45(c) of IAS 27 provides an exception to retrospective application of the amendments relating to the loss of control of a subsidiary for measurement purposes, the Board required an entity to consider the applicable transitional provisions in IAS 27 when implementing the amendments in paragraphs 8A and 36A.

Terminology

BC80   Two issues of terminology arose in developing the IFRS:

    (a)   the use of the term 'probable' and

    (b)   the use of the term 'fair value less costs to sell'.

BC81   In SFAS 144, the term *probable* is described as referring to a future sale that is 'likely to occur'. For the purposes of IFRSs, probable is defined as 'more likely than not'. To converge on the same meaning as SFAS 144 and to avoid using the term 'probable' with different meanings in IFRSs, this IFRS uses the phrase 'highly probable'. The Board regards 'highly probable' as implying a significantly higher probability than 'more likely than not' and as implying the same probability as the FASB's phrase 'likely to occur'. This is consistent with the Board's use of 'highly probable' in IAS 39.

BC82   The measurement basis 'fair value less costs to sell' used in SFAS 144 is the same as the measurement 'net selling price' used in IAS 36 (as issued in 1998). SFAS 144 defines fair value of an asset as 'the amount at which that asset could be bought or sold in a current transaction between willing parties, that is, other than in a forced or liquidation sale', and costs to sell as 'the incremental direct costs to transact a sale, that is, the costs that result directly from and are essential to a sale transaction and that would not have been incurred by the entity had the decision to sell not been made.' IAS 36 defines net selling price as the amount obtainable from the sale of an asset in an arm's length transaction between knowledgeable, willing parties, less the costs of disposal. Costs of disposal are incremental costs directly attributable to the disposal of an asset, excluding finance costs and income tax expenses.

BC83   The Board considered using the phrase 'net selling price' to be consistent with IAS 36. However, it noted that 'fair value' is used in many IFRSs. The Board concluded that it would be preferable to use the same phrase as SFAS 144 so that it is clear that convergence on this point had been achieved and to amend IAS 36 so that the terminology in IAS 36 is consistent with other IFRSs. Therefore, a consequential amendment made by IFRS 5 replaces 'net selling price' with 'fair value less costs to sell' throughout IAS 36.

Summary of changes from ED 4

BC84   The major changes from the proposals in ED 4 are:

(a)   clarification that assets classified as non-current are not reclassified as current until they meet the criteria to be classified as held for sale (paragraph BC10).

(b)   goodwill and financial assets under leases are included in the scope of the measurement provisions of the IFRS (paragraphs BC8–BC14).

(c)   non-current assets carried at fair value with changes recognised in profit or loss are excluded from the measurement provisions of the IFRS (paragraphs BC8–BC14).

(d)   assets that are revalued in accordance with IAS 16 or IAS 38 are, when classified as held for sale, treated consistently with assets that had not previously been revalued (paragraphs BC47 and BC48).

(e)   the allocation of an impairment loss on a disposal group is consistent with the order of allocation of impairment losses in IAS 36 (paragraphs BC39–BC41).

(f)   the criterion in IAS 35 that a discontinued operation should be a major line of business or area of geographical operations has been added (paragraphs BC67–BC71).

(g)   discontinued operations can be presented on the face of the income statement as a single amount (paragraphs BC73–BC77).

Comparison with relevant aspects of SFAS 144

BC85   The following table sets out the extent of convergence with SFAS 144:

Requirement	Extent of convergence with SFAS 144
Scope	Some differences in scope arising from other differences between IFRSs and US GAAP.
Criteria for classification as held for sale	Fully converged.
Treatment of assets to be exchanged	Fully converged if FASB proposals on exchanges of non-monetary assets are finalised.
Treatment of assets to be abandoned	Fully converged.
Measurement on initial classification	Converged, other than cumulative exchange differences recognised directly in equity[a] that are included in the carrying amount of the asset (or disposal group) under US GAAP but are not under IFRS 5.
Subsequent measurement	Converged on the principles, but some differences arising from different requirements on reversals of previous impairments.
Changes to a plan to sell	Converged on reclassification and on measurement, except for differences arising from different requirements on reversals of previous impairments.
Presentation of assets classified as held for sale	Fully converged.
Definition of a discontinued operation	Not converged but the Board intends to work with the FASB to arrive at a converged definition within a relatively short time.
Timing of classification of an operation as discontinued	Fully converged.
Presentation of a discontinued operation	Converged except that SFAS 144 requires the presentation of pre- and post-tax profits on the face of the income statement and IFRS 5 requires the presentation of post-tax profit only (although disaggregation is permitted).

(a)   As a consequence of the revision of IAS 1 *Presentation of Financial Statements* (as revised in 2007) such differences are recognised in other comprehensive income.

Dissenting opinions

Dissent of Anthony T Cope and Harry K Schmid

DO1 Messrs Cope and Schmid dissent from the issue of IFRS 5.

Dissent of Anthony T Cope

DO2 Mr Cope dissents because, in his view, the IFRS fails to meet fully the needs of users in this important area.

DO3 In deciding to undertake this project, the Board had two objectives—to improve users' ability to assess the amount, timing and uncertainty of future cash flows, and to converge with US GAAP. The ability to identify assets (or asset groups) whose value will be recovered principally through sale rather than through operations has significant implications for future cash flows. Similarly, separate presentation of discontinued operations enables users to distinguish those parts of a business that will not contribute to future cash flows.

DO4 The importance of identifying and disaggregating these components was emphasised in the 1994 report of the Special Committee on Financial Reporting of the American Institute of Certified Public Accountants (the AICPA Jenkins Committee). The Jenkins Committee report, arguably the most extensive and authoritative survey of user needs ever undertaken, recommended that:

> [The definition of discontinued operations] should be broadened to include all significant discontinued operations whose assets and results of operations and activities can be distinguished physically and operationally and for business reporting purposes.

The sections of SFAS 144 dealing with discontinued operations were the direct response of the FASB to this recommendation.

DO5 Indeed, the Board appeared to agree in its initial deliberations. In ED 4, the Board stated:

> [The Board] further concluded that the definition of discontinued operations in SFAS 144 leads to more useful information being presented and disclosed for a wider range of operations than did the existing definition in IAS 35. That information is important to users in their assessment of the amount, timing and uncertainty of future cash flows.

Mr Cope continues to agree with that statement.

DO6 However, the Board ultimately has decided to retain the definition in IAS 35, thus failing to gain convergence on an important point in a project designed to achieve such convergence, and failing to respond to the stated needs of users.

DO7 The reason given for the Board's action is that implementation problems with SFAS 144 have emerged in the US. (Most of these problems seem to be with the guidance concerning the definition in SFAS 144, rather than the definition itself.) In paragraph BC71, the Board describes its action as an interim measure, and plans to work with the FASB to arrive promptly at a converged solution. In Mr Cope's view, it would have been much preferable to have converged first, and then dealt with any implementation problems jointly with the FASB.

Dissent of Harry K Schmid

DO8 The main reasons for Mr Schmid's dissent are:

(a) depreciation/amortisation of non-current assets that are still in active use should not cease only because of a management decision to sell the assets that has not yet been fully carried out; and

(b) measurement of assets should not be based on a management decision that has not yet been fully carried out, requiring a very rule-based Standard.

DO9 Mr Schmid believes that not depreciating/amortising assets classified as held for sale but still in active use is conceptually wrong and is especially problematic for discontinued operations because such operations represent a separate major line of business or geographical area of operations. Mr Schmid does not accept that measurement at the lower of carrying amount and fair value less costs to sell acts as a proxy for depreciation because, in most such cases, the fair value less costs to sell will be higher than the carrying amount as the fair value of such disposal groups will often reflect internally generated goodwill. Therefore, non-current assets in such disposal groups will simply remain at their carrying amounts even though they are still actively used, up to one year or even longer. In addition, the net profit shown separately in the income statement for discontinued operations will not be meaningful because depreciation/amortisation charges are not deducted for the continued use of the assets and this profit cannot be compared with the information restated in comparative periods where depreciation had been charged.

DO10 The proposed classification 'held for sale' and resulting measurement of non-current assets (or disposal groups) so classified is based on a management decision that has not yet been fully carried out and demands detailed (anti-abuse) rules to define the classification and to fix the time boundaries during which these assets can remain within the classification. The final result is, in Mr Schmid's view, an excessively detailed and rule-based Standard.

DO11 Mr Schmid believes that a more simple and straightforward solution would have been possible by creating a special category of non-current assets retired from active use. The concept 'retired from active use' would have been simple to apply and management intentions would be removed from the Standard. The classification would equally apply to any form of disposal (sale, abandonment, exchange, spin-off etc); no detailed (anti-abuse) rules and no illustrations would be necessary and the Standard would be simple and based on a clear and unambiguous principle. Mr Schmid, on this point, does not agree with the conclusions in paragraph BC18 that a classification 'retired from active use' would not require fewer criteria to support it than the category 'assets held for sale'.

DO12 Mr Schmid agrees with paragraph BC17 of the Basis for Conclusions, but in order to provide information of intended sales of non-current assets, especially discontinued operations, disclosure could have been required to take effect as soon as such assets are likely to be sold, even if they are still in active use.

DO13 Mr Schmid is fully in favour of seeking, whenever possible, convergence with US GAAP, but only if the converged solution is of high quality. He is of the opinion that this is not the case for this Standard for the reasons given.

CONTENTS

GUIDANCE ON IMPLEMENTING
IFRS 5 *NON-CURRENT ASSETS HELD FOR SALE*
AND DISCONTINUED OPERATIONS

Guidance on implementing
IFRS 5 *Non-current Assets Held for Sale and Discontinued Operations*

This guidance accompanies, but is not part of, IFRS 5.

Availability for immediate sale (paragraph 7)

To qualify for classification as held for sale, a non-current asset (or disposal group) must be available for immediate sale in its present condition subject only to terms that are usual and customary for sales of such assets (or disposal groups) (paragraph 7). A non-current asset (or disposal group) is available for immediate sale if an entity currently has the intention and ability to transfer the asset (or disposal group) to a buyer in its present condition. Examples 1–3 illustrate situations in which the criterion in paragraph 7 would or would not be met.

Example 1

An entity is committed to a plan to sell its headquarters building and has initiated actions to locate a buyer.

(a) The entity intends to transfer the building to a buyer after it vacates the building. The time necessary to vacate the building is usual and customary for sales of such assets. The criterion in paragraph 7 would be met at the plan commitment date.

(b) The entity will continue to use the building until construction of a new headquarters building is completed. The entity does not intend to transfer the existing building to a buyer until after construction of the new building is completed (and it vacates the existing building). The delay in the timing of the transfer of the existing building imposed by the entity (seller) demonstrates that the building is not available for immediate sale. The criterion in paragraph 7 would not be met until construction of the new building is completed, even if a firm purchase commitment for the future transfer of the existing building is obtained earlier.

Example 2

An entity is committed to a plan to sell a manufacturing facility and has initiated actions to locate a buyer. At the plan commitment date, there is a backlog of uncompleted customer orders.

(a) The entity intends to sell the manufacturing facility with its operations. Any uncompleted customer orders at the sale date will be transferred to the buyer. The transfer of uncompleted customer orders at the sale date will not affect the timing of the transfer of the facility. The criterion in paragraph 7 would be met at the plan commitment date.

(b) The entity intends to sell the manufacturing facility, but without its operations. The entity does not intend to transfer the facility to a buyer until after it ceases all operations of the facility and eliminates the backlog of uncompleted customer orders. The delay in the timing of the transfer of the facility imposed by the entity (seller) demonstrates that the facility is not available for immediate sale.

The criterion in paragraph 7 would not be met until the operations of the facility cease, even if a firm purchase commitment for the future transfer of the facility were obtained earlier.

Example 3

An entity acquires through foreclosure a property comprising land and buildings that it intends to sell.

(a) The entity does not intend to transfer the property to a buyer until after it completes renovations to increase the property's sales value. The delay in the timing of the transfer of the property imposed by the entity (seller) demonstrates that the property is not available for immediate sale. The criterion in paragraph 7 would not be met until the renovations are completed.

(b) After the renovations are completed and the property is classified as held for sale but before a firm purchase commitment is obtained, the entity becomes aware of environmental damage requiring remediation. The entity still intends to sell the property. However, the entity does not have the ability to transfer the property to a buyer until after the remediation is completed. The delay in the timing of the transfer of the property imposed by others before a firm purchase commitment is obtained demonstrates that the property is not available for immediate sale. The criterion in paragraph 7 would not continue to be met. The property would be reclassified as held and used in accordance with paragraph 26.

Completion of sale expected within one year (paragraph 8)

Example 4

To qualify for classification as held for sale, the sale of a non-current asset (or disposal group) must be highly probable (paragraph 7), and transfer of the asset (or disposal group) must be expected to qualify for recognition as a completed sale within one year (paragraph 8). That criterion would not be met if, for example:

(a) an entity that is a commercial leasing and finance company is holding for sale or lease equipment that has recently ceased to be leased and the ultimate form of a future transaction (sale or lease) has not yet been determined.

(b) an entity is committed to a plan to 'sell' a property that is in use, and the transfer of the property will be accounted for as a sale and finance leaseback.

Exceptions to the criterion in paragraph 8

An exception to the one-year requirement in paragraph 8 applies in limited situations in which the period required to complete the sale of a non-current asset (or disposal group) will be (or has been) extended by events or circumstances beyond an entity's control and specified conditions are met (paragraphs 9 and B1). Examples 5–7 illustrate those situations.

Example 5

An entity in the power generating industry is committed to a plan to sell a disposal group that represents a significant portion of its regulated operations. The sale requires regulatory approval, which could extend the period required to complete the sale beyond one year. Actions necessary to obtain that approval cannot be initiated until after a buyer is known and a firm purchase commitment is obtained. However, a firm purchase commitment is highly probable within one year. In that situation, the conditions in paragraph B1(a) for an exception to the one-year requirement in paragraph 8 would be met.

Example 6

An entity is committed to a plan to sell a manufacturing facility in its present condition and classifies the facility as held for sale at that date. After a firm purchase commitment is obtained, the buyer's inspection of the property identifies environmental damage not previously known to exist. The entity is required by the buyer to make good the damage, which will extend the period required to complete the sale beyond one year. However, the entity has initiated actions to make good the damage, and satisfactory rectification of the damage is highly probable. In that situation, the conditions in paragraph B1(b) for an exception to the one-year requirement in paragraph 8 would be met.

Example 7

An entity is committed to a plan to sell a non-current asset and classifies the asset as held for sale at that date.

(a) During the initial one-year period, the market conditions that existed at the date the asset was classified initially as held for sale deteriorate and, as a result, the asset is not sold by the end of that period. During that period, the entity actively solicited but did not receive any reasonable offers to purchase the asset and, in response, reduced the price. The asset continues to be actively marketed at a price that is reasonable given the change in market conditions, and the criteria in paragraphs 7 and 8 are therefore met. In that situation, the conditions in paragraph B1(c) for an exception to the one-year requirement in paragraph 8 would be met. At the end of the initial one-year period, the asset would continue to be classified as held for sale.

(b) During the following one-year period, market conditions deteriorate further, and the asset is not sold by the end of that period. The entity believes that the market conditions will improve and has not further reduced the price of the asset. The asset continues to be held for sale, but at a price in excess of its current fair value. In that situation, the absence of a price reduction demonstrates that the asset is not available for immediate sale as required by paragraph 7. In addition, paragraph 8 also requires an asset to be marketed at a price that is reasonable in relation to its current fair value. Therefore, the conditions in paragraph B1(c) for an exception to the one-year requirement in paragraph 8 would not be met. The asset would be reclassified as held and used in accordance with paragraph 26.

Determining whether an asset has been abandoned

Paragraphs 13 and 14 of the IFRS specify requirements for when assets are to be treated as abandoned. Example 8 illustrates when an asset has not been abandoned.

Example 8

An entity ceases to use a manufacturing plant because demand for its product has declined. However, the plant is maintained in workable condition and it is expected that it will be brought back into use if demand picks up. The plant is not regarded as abandoned.

Presenting a discontinued operation that has been abandoned

Paragraph 13 of the IFRS prohibits assets that will be abandoned from being classified as held for sale. However, if the assets to be abandoned are a major line of business or geographical area of operations, they are reported in discontinued operations at the date at which they are abandoned. Example 9 illustrates this.

Example 9

In October 20X5 an entity decides to abandon all of its cotton mills, which constitute a major line of business. All work stops at the cotton mills during the year ended 31 December 20X6. In the financial statements for the year ended 31 December 20X5, results and cash flows of the cotton mills are treated as continuing operations. In the financial statements for the year ended 31 December 20X6, the results and cash flows of the cotton mills are treated as discontinued operations and the entity makes the disclosures required by paragraphs 33 and 34 of the IFRS.

Allocation of an impairment loss on a disposal group

Paragraph 23 of the IFRS requires an impairment loss (or any subsequent gain) recognised for a disposal group to reduce (or increase) the carrying amount of the non-current assets in the group that are within the scope of the measurement requirements of the IFRS, in the order of allocation set out in paragraphs 104 and 122 of IAS 36 (as revised in 2004). Example 10 illustrates the allocation of an impairment loss on a disposal group.

Example 10

An entity plans to dispose of a group of its assets (as an asset sale). The assets form a disposal group, and are measured as follows:

	Carrying amount at the end of the reporting period before classification as held for sale	Carrying amount as remeasured immediately before classification as held for sale
	CU(a)	CU
Goodwill	1,500	1,500
Property, plant and equipment (carried at revalued amounts)	4,600	4,000
Property, plant and equipment (carried at cost)	5,700	5,700
Inventory	2,400	2,200
AFS financial assets	1,800	1,500
Total	**16,000**	**14,900**

(a) In this guidance, monetary amounts are denominated in 'currency units (CU)'.

The entity recognises the loss of CU1,100 (CU16,000 – CU14,900) immediately before classifying the disposal group as held for sale.

The entity estimates that fair value less costs to sell of the disposal group amounts to CU13,000. Because an entity measures a disposal group classified as held for sale at the lower of its carrying amount and fair value less costs to sell, the entity recognises an impairment loss of CU1,900 (CU14,900 – CU13,000) when the group is initially classified as held for sale.

The impairment loss is allocated to non-current assets to which the measurement requirements of the IFRS are applicable. Therefore, no impairment loss is allocated to inventory and AFS financial assets. The loss is allocated to the other assets in the order of allocation set out in paragraphs 104 and 122 of IAS 36 (as revised in 2004).

The allocation can be illustrated as follows:

	Carrying amount as remeasured immediately before classification as held for sale	Allocated impairment loss	Carrying amount after allocation of impairment loss
	CU	CU	CU
Goodwill	1,500	(1,500)	0
Property, plant and equipment (carried at revalued amounts)	4,000	(165)	3,835
Property, plant and equipment (carried at cost)	5,700	(235)	5,465
Inventory	2,200	–	2,200
AFS financial assets	1,500	–	1,500
Total	**14,900**	**(1,900)**	**13,000**

First, the impairment loss reduces any amount of goodwill. Then, the residual loss is allocated to other assets pro rata based on the carrying amounts of those assets.

Presenting discontinued operations in the statement of comprehensive income

Paragraph 33 of the IFRS requires an entity to disclose a single amount in the statement of comprehensive income for discontinued operations with an analysis in the notes or in a section of the statement of comprehensive income separate from continuing operations. Example 11 illustrates how these requirements might be met.

Example 11

XYZ GROUP – STATEMENT OF COMPREHENSIVE INCOME FOR THE YEAR ENDED 31 DECEMBER 20X2
(illustrating the classification of expenses by function)

(in thousands of currency units)	20X2	20X1
Continuing operations		
Revenue	X	X
Cost of sales	(X)	(X)
Gross profit	X	X
Other income	X	X
Distribution costs	(X)	(X)
Administrative expenses	(X)	(X)
Other expenses	(X)	(X)
Finance costs	(X)	(X)
Share of profit of associates	X	X
Profit before tax	X	X
Income tax expense	(X)	(X)
Profit for the period from continuing operations	X	X
Discontinued operations		
Profit for the period from discontinued operations[a]	X	X
Profit for the period	X	X
Attributable to:		
Owners of the parent		
Profit for the period from continuing operations	X	X
Profit for the period from discontinued operations	X	X
Profit for the period attributable to owners of the parent	X	X
Non-controlling interests		
Profit for the period from continuing operations	X	X
Profit for the period from discontinued operations	X	X
Profit for the period attributable to non-controlling interests	X	X
	X	X

(a) The required analysis would be given in the notes.

Presenting non-current assets or disposal groups classified as held for sale

Paragraph 38 of the IFRS requires an entity to present a non-current asset classified as held for sale and the assets of a disposal group classified as held for sale separately from other assets in the statement of financial position. The liabilities of a disposal group classified as held for sale are also presented separately from other liabilities in the statement of financial position. Those assets and liabilities are not offset and presented as a single amount. Example 12 illustrates these requirements.

Example 12

At the end of 20X5, an entity decides to dispose of part of its assets (and directly associated liabilities). The disposal, which meets the criteria in paragraphs 7 and 8 to be classified as held for sale, takes the form of two disposal groups, as follows:

	Carrying amount after classification as held for sale	
	Disposal group I: CU	Disposal group II: CU
Property, plant and equipment	4,900	1,700
AFS financial asset	1,400[(a)]	–
Liabilities	(2,400)	(900)
Net carrying amount of disposal group	**3,900**	**800**

(a) An amount of CU400 relating to these assets has been recognised in other comprehensive income and accumulated in equity.

The presentation in the entity's statement of financial position of the disposal groups classified as held for sale can be shown as follows:

	20X5	20X4
ASSETS		
Non-current assets		
AAA	X	X
BBB	X	X
CCC	X	X
	X	X
Current assets		
DDD	X	X
EEE	X	X
	X	X
Non-current assets classified as held for sale	8,000	–
	X	X
Total assets	X	X

continued...

...continued

	20X5	20X4
EQUITY AND LIABILITIES		
Equity attributable to owners of the parent		
FFF	X	X
GGG	X	X
Amounts recognised in other comprehensive income and accumulated in equity relating to non-current assets held for sale	400	–
	X	X
Non-controlling interests	X	X
Total equity	X	X
Non-current liabilities		
HHH	X	X
III	X	X
JJJ	X	X
	X	X
Current liabilities		
KKK	X	X
LLL	X	X
MMM	X	X
Liabilities directly associated with non-current assets classified as held for sale	3,300	–
	X	X
Total liabilities	X	X
Total equity and liabilities	X	X

The presentation requirements for assets (or disposal groups) classified as held for sale at the end of the reporting period do not apply retrospectively. The comparative statements of financial position for any previous periods are therefore not re-presented.

Measuring and presenting subsidiaries acquired with a view to resale and classified as held for sale

A subsidiary acquired with a view to sale is not exempt from consolidation in accordance with IAS 27 *Consolidated and Separate Financial Statements*. However, if it meets the criteria in paragraph 11, it is presented as a disposal group classified as held for sale. Example 13 illustrates these requirements.

Example 13

Entity A acquires an entity H, which is a holding company with two subsidiaries, S1 and S2. S2 is acquired exclusively with a view to sale and meets the criteria to be classified as held for sale. In accordance with paragraph 32(c), S2 is also a discontinued operation.

The estimated fair value less costs to sell of S2 is CU135. A accounts for S2 as follows:

- initially, A measures the identifiable liabilities of S2 at fair value, say at CU40

- initially, A measures the acquired assets as the fair value less costs to sell of S2 (CU135) plus the fair value of the identifiable liabilities (CU40), ie at CU175

- at the end of the reporting period, A remeasures the disposal group at the lower of its cost and fair value less costs to sell, say at CU130. The liabilities are remeasured in accordance with applicable IFRSs, say at CU35. The total assets are measured at CU130 + CU35, ie at CU165

- at the end of the reporting period, A presents the assets and liabilities separately from other assets and liabilities in its consolidated financial statements as illustrated in Example 12 *Presenting non-current assets or disposal groups classified as held for sale*, and

- in the statement of comprehensive income, A presents the total of the post-tax profit or loss of S2 and the post-tax gain or loss recognised on the subsequent remeasurement of S2, which equals the remeasurement of the disposal group from CU135 to CU130.

Further analysis of the assets and liabilities or of the change in value of the disposal group is not required.

IASB documents published to accompany

International Financial Reporting Standard 6

Exploration for and Evaluation of Mineral Resources

This version includes amendments resulting from IFRSs issued up to 31 December 2009.

The text of the unaccompanied IFRS 6 is contained in Part A of this edition. Its effective date is 1 January 2006. The effective date of the most recent amendment is 1 January 2010. This part presents the following accompanying documents:

Approval by the Board of IFRS 6 issued in December 2004

International Financial Reporting Standard 6 *Exploration for and Evaluation of Mineral Resources* was approved for issue by ten of the fourteen members of the International Accounting Standards Board. Messrs Garnett, Leisenring, McGregor and Smith dissented. Their dissenting opinions are set out after the Basis for Conclusions.

Sir David Tweedie	Chairman
Thomas E Jones	Vice-Chairman
Mary E Barth	
Hans-Georg Bruns	
Anthony T Cope	
Jan Engström	
Robert P Garnett	
Gilbert Gélard	
James J Leisenring	
Warren J McGregor	
Patricia L O'Malley	
John T Smith	
Geoffrey Whittington	
Tatsumi Yamada	

Approval by the Board of Amendments to IFRS 1 and IFRS 6 issued in June 2005

These Amendments to International Financial Reporting Standard 1 *First-time Adoption of International Financial Reporting Standards* and International Financial Reporting Standard 6 *Exploration for and Evaluation of Mineral Resources* were approved for issue by the fourteen members of the International Accounting Standards Board.

Sir David Tweedie	Chairman
Thomas E Jones	Vice-Chairman
Mary E Barth	
Hans-Georg Bruns	
Anthony T Cope	
Jan Engström	
Robert P Garnett	
Gilbert Gélard	
James J Leisenring	
Warren J McGregor	
Patricia L O'Malley	
John T Smith	
Geoffrey Whittington	
Tatsumi Yamada	

CONTENTS

Basis for Conclusions on
IFRS 6 *Exploration for and Evaluation of Mineral Resources*

This Basis for Conclusions accompanies, but is not part of, IFRS 6.

Introduction

BC1   This Basis for Conclusions summarises the International Accounting Standards Board's considerations in reaching the conclusions in IFRS 6 *Exploration for and Evaluation of Mineral Resources*. Individual Board members gave greater weight to some factors than to others.

Reasons for issuing the IFRS

BC2   Paragraphs 10–12 of IAS 8 *Accounting Policies, Changes in Accounting Estimates and Errors* specify a hierarchy of criteria that an entity should use in developing an accounting policy if no IFRS applies specifically to an item. Without the exemption in IFRS 6, an entity adopting IFRSs in 2005 would have needed to assess whether its accounting policies for the exploration for and evaluation of mineral resources complied with those requirements. In the absence of guidance, there might have been uncertainty about what would be acceptable. Establishing what would be acceptable could have been costly and some entities might have made major changes in 2005 followed by further significant changes once the Board completes its comprehensive review of accounting for extractive activities.

BC3   To avoid unnecessary disruption for both users and preparers at this time, the Board proposed to limit the need for entities to change their existing accounting policies for exploration and evaluation assets. The Board did this by:

(a)   creating a temporary exemption from parts of the hierarchy in IAS 8 that specify the criteria an entity uses in developing an accounting policy if no IFRS applies specifically.

(b)   limiting the impact of that exemption from the hierarchy by identifying expenditures to be included in and excluded from exploration and evaluation assets and requiring all exploration and evaluation assets to be assessed for impairment.

BC4   The Board published its proposals in January 2004. ED 6 *Exploration for and Evaluation of Mineral Resources* had a comment deadline of 16 April 2004. The Board received 55 comment letters.

BC5   In April 2004 the Board approved a research project to be undertaken by staff from the national standard-setters in Australia, Canada, Norway and South Africa that will address accounting for extractive activities generally. The research project team is assisted by an advisory panel, which includes members from industry (oil and gas and mining sectors), accounting firms, users and securities regulators from around the world.

Scope

BC6   In the Board's view, even though no IFRS has addressed extractive activities directly, all IFRSs (including International Accounting Standards and Interpretations) are applicable to entities engaged in the exploration for and evaluation of mineral resources that make an unreserved statement of compliance with IFRSs in accordance with IAS 1 *Presentation of Financial Statements*. Consequently, each IFRS must be applied by all such entities.

BC7   Some respondents to ED 6 encouraged the Board to develop standards for other stages in the process of exploring for and evaluating mineral resources, including pre-exploration activities (ie activities preceding the exploration for and evaluation of mineral resources) and development activities (ie activities after the technical feasibility and commercial viability of extracting a mineral resource are demonstrable). The Board decided not to do this for two reasons. First, it did not want to prejudge the comprehensive review of the accounting for such activities. Second, the Board concluded that an appropriate accounting policy for pre-exploration activities could be developed from an application of existing IFRSs, from the *Framework's* definitions of assets and expenses, and by applying the general principles of asset recognition in IAS 16 *Property, Plant and Equipment* and IAS 38 *Intangible Assets*.

BC8   The Board also decided not to expand the scope of IFRS 6 beyond that proposed in ED 6 because to do so would require additional due process, possibly including another exposure draft. In view of the many entities engaged in extractive activities that would be required to apply IFRSs from 1 January 2005, the Board decided that it should not delay issuing guidance by expanding the scope of the IFRS beyond the exploration for and evaluation of mineral resources.

Definition of exploration and evaluation assets

BC9   Most respondents to ED 6 agreed with the Board's proposed definition of exploration and evaluation assets, but asked for changes or clarifications to make the Board's intentions clearer:

(a)   some respondents asked the Board to distinguish between exploration and pre-exploration expenditures.

(b)   others asked the Board to define exploration and evaluation activities separately, reflecting the different risk profiles of such activities or the requirements of other jurisdictions.

(c)   other respondents asked for further guidance on what constitute mineral resources, principally examples of what constitutes a mineral reserve.

Expenditures incurred before the exploration for and evaluation of mineral resources

BC10 Respondents seemed to be concerned that the Board was extending the scope of the proposals to include expenditures incurred before the acquisition of legal rights to explore in a specific area in the definition of exploration and evaluation expenditure. Some were concerned that such an extension would open the way for the recognition of such expenditures as assets; others preferred this result. In drafting IFRS 6, the Board could not identify any reason why the *Framework* was not applicable to such expenditures.

BC11 The Board decided not to define pre-acquisition or pre-exploration expenditures. However, the IFRS clarifies that expenditures before the entity has obtained legal rights to explore in a specific area are not exploration and evaluation expenditures and are therefore outside the scope of the IFRS.

BC12 The Board noted that an appropriate application of IFRSs might require pre-acquisition expenditures related to the acquisition of an intangible asset (eg expenditures directly attributable to the acquisition of an exploration licence) to be recognised as part of the intangible asset in accordance with IAS 38. Paragraph 27(a) of IAS 38 states that the cost of a separately acquired intangible asset comprises its purchase price, including import duties and non-refundable purchase taxes, and some directly attributable costs.

BC13 Similarly, the Board understands that expenditures incurred before the exploration for and evaluation of mineral resources cannot usually be associated with any specific mineral property and thus are likely to be recognised as an expense as incurred. However, such expenditures need to be distinguished from expenditures on infrastructure—for example access roads—necessary for the exploration work to proceed. Such expenditures should be recognised as property, plant and equipment in accordance with paragraph 3 of IAS 16.

Separate definitions of 'exploration' and 'evaluation'

BC14 Some respondents asked the Board to provide separate definitions of exploration and evaluation. The Board considered using the definitions provided in the Issues Paper *Extractive Industries* published by its predecessor, the Board of the International Accounting Standards Committee, in November 2000, because those definitions would be acceptable to many respondents, particularly because they are based on definitions that have been used for a number of years in both the mining and the oil and gas sectors.

BC15 The Board concluded that distinguishing between evaluation and exploration would not improve the IFRS. Exploration and evaluation are accounted for in the same way.

Mineral resources

BC16 Some respondents asked the Board to define mineral resources more precisely. The Board concluded that, for the purposes of the IFRS, elaboration was unnecessary. The items listed in the definition of exploration for and evaluation of mineral resources were sufficient to convey the Board's intentions.

Recognition of exploration and evaluation assets

Temporary exemption from IAS 8 paragraphs 11 and 12

BC17 A variety of accounting practices are followed by entities engaged in the exploration for and evaluation of mineral resources. These practices range from deferring on the balance sheet nearly all exploration and evaluation expenditure to recognising all such expenditure in profit or loss as incurred. The IFRS permits these various accounting practices to continue. Given this diversity, some respondents to ED 6 opposed any exemption from paragraphs 11 and 12 of IAS 8. These respondents were concerned that entities could give the appearance of compliance with IFRSs while being inconsistent with the stated objectives of the IASB, ie to provide users of financial statements with financial information that was of high quality, transparent and comparable. The Board did not grant the exemption from parts of IAS 8 lightly, but took this step to minimise disruption, especially in 2006 (or 2005, for those entities that adopt the IFRS early), both for users (eg lack of continuity of trend data) and for preparers (eg systems changes).

BC18 IFRS 4 *Insurance Contracts* provides a temporary exemption from paragraphs 10–12 of IAS 8. That exemption is broader than in IFRS 6 because IFRS 4 leaves many significant aspects of accounting for insurance contracts until phase II of the Board's project on that topic. A requirement to apply paragraph 10 of IAS 8 to insurance contracts would have had much more pervasive effects and insurers would have needed to address matters such as completeness, substance over form and neutrality. In contrast, IFRS 6 leaves a relatively narrow range of issues unaddressed and the Board did not think that an exemption from paragraph 10 of IAS 8 was necessary.

BC19 ED 6 made it clear that the Board intended to suspend only paragraphs 11 and 12 of IAS 8, implying that paragraph 10 should be followed when an entity was determining its accounting policies for exploration and evaluation assets. However, it was apparent from some comments received that the Board's intention had not been understood clearly. Consequently, the IFRS contains a specific statement that complying with paragraph 10 of IAS 8 is mandatory.

BC20 Respondents who objected to the Board's proposal in ED 6 to permit some accounting practices to continue found it difficult to draw a meaningful distinction between the exploration for and evaluation of mineral resources and scientific research. Both activities can be costly and have significant risks of failure. These respondents would support bringing the exploration for and evaluation of mineral resources within the scope of IAS 16 and IAS 38. The Board is similarly concerned that existing accounting practices might result in the inappropriate recognition of exploration and evaluation assets. However, it is also concerned that accounting for exploration and evaluation expenditures in accordance with IAS 38 might result in the overstatement of expenses. In the absence of internationally accepted standards for such expenditures, the Board concluded that it could not make an informed judgement in advance of the comprehensive review of accounting for extractive activities.

BC21   Some suggested that the Board should require an entity to follow its national accounting requirements (ie national GAAP) in accounting for the exploration for and evaluation of mineral resources until the Board completes its comprehensive review of accounting for extractive activities, to prevent the selection of accounting policies that do not form a comprehensive basis of accounting. Consistently with its conclusions in IFRS 4, the Board concluded that defining national GAAP would have posed problems. Further definitional problems could have arisen because some entities do not apply the national GAAP of their own country. For example, some non-US entities with extractive activities in the oil and gas sector apply US GAAP. Moreover, it is unusual and, arguably, beyond the Board's mandate to impose requirements set by another body.

BC22   Therefore, the Board decided that an entity could continue to follow the accounting policies that it was using when it first applied the IFRS's requirements, provided they satisfy the requirements of paragraph 10 of IAS 8 and with some exceptions noted below. An entity could also improve those accounting policies if specified criteria are met (see paragraphs 13 and 14 of the IFRS).

BC23   The Board acknowledges that it is difficult to make piecemeal changes to recognition and measurement practices at this time because many aspects of accounting for extractive activities are interrelated with aspects that will not be considered until the Board completes its comprehensive review of accounting for extractive activities. However, not imposing the requirements in the IFRS would detract from the relevance and reliability of an entity's financial statements to an unacceptable degree.

BC23A   In 2008, as part of its annual improvements project, the Board considered the guidance on the treatment in IAS 7 *Statement of Cash Flows* of some types of expenditures incurred with the objective of generating future cash flows when those expenditures are not recognised as assets in accordance with IFRSs. Some entities classify such expenditures as cash flows from operating activities and others classify them as investing activities. Examples of such expenditures are those for exploration and evaluation activities, which can be recognised according to IFRS 6 as either an asset or an expense.[*]

BC23B   The Board noted that the exemption in IFRS 6 applies only to recognition and measurement of exploration and evaluation assets, not to the classification of related expenditures in the statement of cash flows. Consequently, the Board amended paragraph 16 of IAS 7 to state that only an expenditure that results in a recognised asset can be classified as a cash flow from investing activities.

Elements of cost of exploration and evaluation assets

BC24   ED 6 paragraph 7 listed examples of expenditures related to the exploration for and evaluation of mineral resources that might be included in the cost of an exploration and evaluation asset. ED 6 paragraph 8 listed expenditures that could not be recognised as an exploration and evaluation asset. Respondents expressed a desire for greater clarity with respect to these paragraphs and more examples of types of expenditures that would be included or excluded.

---

[*]   Paragraphs BC23A and BC23B were added as a consequence of an amendment to IAS 7 included in *Improvements to IFRSs* issued in April 2009.

BC25   In the light of the responses, the Board decided to redraft the guidance to state that the list is not exhaustive and that the items noted are examples of expenditures that might, but need not always, satisfy the definition of exploration and evaluation expenditure. In addition, the Board noted that IFRSs require that expenditures should be treated consistently for comparable activities and between reporting periods. Any change in what is deemed to be an expenditure qualifying for recognition as an exploration and evaluation asset should be treated as a change in an accounting policy accounted for in accordance with IAS 8. Pending the comprehensive review of accounting for extractive activities, the Board does not think that it is feasible to define what expenditures should be included or excluded.

BC26   ED 6 paragraph 8 proposed to prohibit expenditure related to the development of a mineral resource from being recognised as an exploration and evaluation asset. Respondents expressed difficulty identifying expenditures on 'development'. The Board did not define 'development of a mineral resource' because this is beyond the scope of the IFRS.

BC27   However, the Board noted that development of a mineral resource once the technical feasibility and commercial viability of extracting the mineral resource had been determined was an example of the development phase of an internal project. Paragraph 57 of IAS 38 provides guidance that should be followed in developing an accounting policy for this activity.

BC28   ED 6 proposed that administration and other general overhead costs should be excluded from the initial measurement of exploration and evaluation assets. Several respondents suggested that general and administrative and overhead costs *directly attributable* to the exploration and evaluation activities should qualify for inclusion in the carrying amount of the asset. These respondents saw this treatment as consistent with the treatment of such costs with respect to inventory (paragraph 11 of IAS 2 *Inventories*) and intangible assets (paragraph 67(a) of IAS 38). However, the Board noted that such a treatment would seem to be inconsistent with paragraph 19(d) of IAS 16. The IFRS was not regarded as the appropriate Standard in which to resolve this inconsistency, and the Board decided to delete the reference in the IFRS to administrative and other general overheads. The treatment of such expenditures would be an accounting policy choice; the chosen policy should be consistent with one of the treatments available under IFRSs.

Measurement after recognition

BC29   The IFRS permits an entity recognising exploration and evaluation assets to measure such assets, after recognition, using either the cost model or the revaluation model in IAS 16 and IAS 38. The model chosen should be consistent with how the entity classifies the exploration and evaluation assets. Those revaluation models permit the revaluation of assets when specified requirements are met (see paragraphs 31–42 of IAS 16 and paragraphs 72–84 of IAS 38). The revaluation model in IAS 38 can be used only if the asset's fair value can be determined by reference to an active market; the revaluation model in IAS 16 refers only to 'market-based evidence'. The Board was troubled by this inconsistency and was concerned that entities might choose accounting policies to achieve a more advantageous measurement of exploration and evaluation assets.

BC30　A few respondents were also concerned with the option proposed in ED 6. Some did not agree that exploration and evaluation assets should be revalued, preferring an arbitrary prohibition of remeasurement. Others were concerned about the reliability of the measure. The Board concluded that no substantive reasons had been presented for reaching a conclusion different from that in ED 6. Although the revaluation of an exploration asset in accordance with IAS 16 or IAS 38 might not be widespread, it was not appropriate to prohibit remeasurement of specific types of IAS 16 or IAS 38 assets on a selective basis.

BC31　Exploration and evaluation assets may arise as a result of a business combination. The Board noted that IFRS 3 *Business Combinations* applies to all entities asserting compliance with IFRSs and that any exploration and evaluation assets acquired in a business combination should be accounted for in accordance with IFRS 3.

Presentation of exploration and evaluation assets

BC32　ED 6 noted that the Board had not yet considered whether exploration and evaluation assets are tangible or intangible. Several respondents suggested that the Board should give some direction on this issue.

BC33　Some exploration and evaluation assets are treated as intangible assets (eg drilling rights), whereas others are clearly tangible (eg vehicles and drilling rigs). A tangible asset may be used in the development of an intangible one. For example, a portable drilling rig may be used to drill test wells or take core samples, clearly part of the exploration activity. To the extent that the tangible asset is consumed in developing an intangible asset, the amount reflecting that consumption is part of the cost of the intangible asset. However, using the drilling rig to develop an intangible asset does not change a tangible asset into an intangible asset.

BC34　Pending completion of the comprehensive review of accounting practices for extractive activities, the Board did not wish to decide whether and which exploration and evaluation assets should be classified as tangible or intangible. However, the Board concluded that an entity should classify the elements of exploration and evaluation assets as tangible or intangible according to their nature and apply this classification consistently. This classification is the foundation for other accounting policy choices as described in paragraphs BC29–BC31 and for the disclosures required by the IFRS.

Impairment of exploration and evaluation assets

BC35　When it developed ED 6, the Board decided that an entity recognising exploration and evaluation assets should test those assets for impairment, and that the impairment test to be applied should be that in IAS 36 *Impairment of Assets*. Respondents accepted the general proposition that exploration and evaluation assets should be tested for impairment. However, the Board's proposals for a special 'cash-generating unit for exploration and evaluation assets' (the special CGU) were not thought appropriate or useful.

Assessment of impairment

BC36 In some cases, and particularly in exploration-only entities, exploration and evaluation assets do not generate cash flows and there is insufficient information about the mineral resources in a specific area for an entity to make reasonable estimates of exploration and evaluation assets' recoverable amount. This is because the exploration for and evaluation of the mineral resources has not reached a stage at which information sufficient to estimate future cash flows is available to the entity. Without such information, it is not possible to estimate either fair value less costs to sell or value in use, the two measures of recoverable amount in IAS 36. Respondents noted that this would lead to an immediate write-off of exploration assets in many cases.

BC37 The Board was persuaded by respondents' arguments that recognising impairment losses on this basis was potentially inconsistent with permitting existing methods of accounting for exploration and evaluation assets to continue. Therefore, pending completion of the comprehensive review of accounting for extractive activities, the Board decided to change the approach to recognition of impairment; the assessment of impairment should be triggered by changes in facts and circumstances. However, it also confirmed that, once an entity had determined that an exploration and evaluation asset was impaired, IAS 36 should be used to measure, present and disclose that impairment in the financial statements, subject to special requirements with respect to the level at which impairment is assessed.

BC38 Paragraph 12 of ED 6 proposed that an entity that had recognised exploration and evaluation assets should assess those assets for impairment annually and recognise any resulting impairment loss in accordance with IAS 36. Paragraph 13 proposed a set of indicators of impairment that an entity would consider in addition to those in IAS 36. Respondents stated that these indicators would not achieve the Board's intended result, especially in circumstances in which the information necessary for an assessment of mineral reserves was not available.

BC39 The Board replaced the proposals in paragraphs 12 and 13 of ED 6 with an exception to the recognition requirements in IAS 36. The Board decided that, until the entity had sufficient data to determine technical feasibility and commercial viability, exploration and evaluation assets need not be assessed for impairment. However, when such information becomes available, or other facts and circumstances suggest that the asset might be impaired, the exploration and evaluation assets must be assessed for impairment. The IFRS suggests possible indicators of impairment.

The level at which impairment is assessed

BC40 When it developed ED 6, the Board decided that there was a need for consistency between the level at which costs were accumulated and the level at which impairment was assessed. Without this consistency, there was a danger that expenditures that would form part of the cost of an exploration and evaluation asset under one of the common methods of accounting for the exploration for and evaluation of mineral resources would need to be recognised in profit or loss in accordance with IAS 36. Consequently, ED 6 proposed that an entity recognising exploration and evaluation assets should make a one-time election to test those assets either at the level of the IAS 36 cash-generating unit (CGU) or at the level of a special CGU. ED 6 explained that any assets other than exploration and evaluation assets included within the special CGU should continue to be subject to separate impairment testing in accordance with IAS 36, and that impairment test should be performed before the special CGU was tested for impairment.

BC41 Respondents disagreed with the Board's proposal. In particular, and for various reasons, they did not accept that the special CGU would provide the relief it was intended to provide, because:

(a) small, start-up or exploration-only entities might not have adequate cash flows to support exploration and evaluation assets that were not cash-generating.

(b) entities applying the successful efforts method of accounting typically conduct impairment tests property by property. However, because of the way in which the special CGU was defined in ED 6 such entities would be forced to carry out impairment tests at the CGU level.

(c) the special CGU permitted management extensive discretion.

In addition, there was concern that, because the exploration and evaluation assets could be aggregated with other assets in the special CGU, there would be confusion about the appropriate measurement model to apply (fair value less costs to sell or value in use). As a result, many respondents to ED 6 did not think that the Board had achieved its intention in this respect, and said that they preferred to apply IAS 36 without the special CGU.

BC42 Although the Board disagreed with some of the arguments put forward by respondents, it acknowledged that the special CGU seemed to be more confusing than helpful. This suggested that it was not needed. Paragraph BC20 of the Basis for Conclusions on ED 6 noted the Board's reluctance to introduce a special CGU. Removing the special CGU would eliminate much of the complexity in the proposed IFRS and the confusion among constituents. It would also mean that entities with extractive activities would assess their assets for impairment at the same level as other entities—providing a higher level of comparability than might otherwise be the case.

BC43 Board members noted that paragraph 22 of IAS 36 requires impairment to be assessed at the individual asset level 'unless the asset does not generate cash inflows that are largely independent of those from other assets or groups of assets'. In addition, paragraph 70 of IAS 36 requires that 'if an active market exists for the output produced by an asset or group of assets, that asset or group of assets shall be identified as a cash-generating unit'. In some cases in which exploration and evaluation assets are recognised, eg in the petroleum sector, each well is potentially capable of producing cash inflows that are observable and capable of reliable measurement because there is an active market for crude oil.

The Board was concerned that removing the special CGU would cause entities recognising exploration and evaluation assets to test for impairment at a very low level.

BC44 The issue was highlighted in the July 2004 issue of *IASB Update*, in the project summary and in the *Effect of Redeliberations* documents available on the IASB's Website. These documents were also sent to the Board's research project team and others with a request to encourage their constituents to respond to the issues raised. The Board received 16 comment letters.

BC45 The majority of respondents continued to support the elimination of the special CGU. They also supported the notion that entities should test impairment at the level of the cost centre and suggested that the Board should consider defining an 'asset' as it applied to exploration and evaluation assets. The respondents argued that such an approach would reflect more accurately the way in which the industry manages its operations. The Board was persuaded by these arguments and decided that it should permit entities some flexibility in allocating exploration and evaluation assets to cash-generating units or groups of units, subject to an upper limit on the size of the units or groups of units.

BC46 The Board decided that its approach to the impairment of goodwill in the 2004 revisions to IAS 36 paragraphs 80–82 offered the best model available within IFRSs to accomplish its objective. It noted that entities might be able to monitor exploration and evaluation assets for internal management purposes at the level of an oilfield or a contiguous ore body. The Board did not intend to require impairment to be assessed at such a low level. Consequently, the IFRS permits CGUs to be aggregated. However, the Board decided to require the level at which impairment was assessed to be no larger than a segment, based on either the entity's primary or the entity's secondary segment reporting format in accordance with IAS 14 *Segment Reporting*. The Board concluded, consistently with the approach to goodwill in IAS 36, that this approach was necessary to ensure that entities managed on a matrix basis could test exploration and evaluation assets for impairment at the level of reporting that reflects the way they manage their operations. This requirement is no less rigorous than ED 6's requirement that the special CGU should 'be no larger than a segment'.[*]

BC47 Consequently, the Board decided to remove the proposed special CGU. In doing so, it noted that eliminating this requirement would have the following benefits:

(a) once an impairment was identified, the measurement, presentation and disclosure of impairment would be more consistent across entities recognising exploration and evaluation assets.

(b) it would remove the confusion about what practices entities recognising exploration and evaluation assets for the first time should follow.

(c) it would remove the risk noted in some comment letters that the special CGU could become the 'industry norm', limiting the Board's options when the comprehensive review of accounting for extractive activities is completed.

---

[*] In 2006 IAS 14 was replaced by IFRS 8 *Operating Segments*, which does not require the identification of primary and secondary segments. See paragraph BC150A of the Basis for Conclusions on IAS 36 *Impairment of Assets*.

Reversal of impairment losses

BC48   The reversal of impairment losses when specified requirements (ie those set out in paragraphs 109–123 of IAS 36) are met is required of all entities for all assets (excluding goodwill and equity investments classified as available for sale). Respondents to ED 6 who commented on this issue and who disagreed with the ability to reverse impairment losses advanced no new arguments why the Board should prohibit reversal of impairment losses in the case of exploration and evaluation assets. Consequently, the Board reaffirmed its conclusion that it would not be appropriate to propose an exemption from the requirement to reverse impairment losses for exploration and evaluation assets.

Changes in accounting policies

BC49   IAS 8 prohibits a change in accounting policies that is not required by an IFRS, unless the change will result in the provision of reliable and more relevant information. Although the Board wished to avoid imposing unnecessary changes in this IFRS, it did not believe it should exempt entities from the requirement to justify changes in accounting policies. Consistently with its conclusions in IFRS 4, the Board decided to permit changes in accounting policies for exploration and evaluation assets if they make the financial statements more relevant and no less reliable, or more reliable and no less relevant judged by the criteria in IAS 8.

Disclosures

BC50   The disclosure requirements in the IFRS are based on a principle that an entity should disclose information that identifies and explains the amounts recognised in its financial statements that arise from the exploration for and evaluation of mineral resources, supplemented by specified disclosures to meet that objective.

BC51   Although respondents agreed that entities should be allowed flexibility in determining the levels of aggregation and amount of disclosure, they suggested that the Board should introduce more specific and standardised disclosure requirements. Some respondents were concerned that the variety of accounting for the exploration for and evaluation of mineral resources could reduce comparability.

BC52   The Board concluded that the ED 6 approach was superior to requiring a long list of detailed and prescriptive disclosures because concentrating on the underlying principle:

(a)   makes it easier for entities to understand the rationale for the requirements, which promotes compliance.

(b)   avoids requiring specific disclosures that may not be needed to meet the underlying objectives in the circumstances of every entity and could lead to information overload that obscures important information in a mass of detail.

(c)   gives entities flexibility to decide on an appropriate level of aggregation that enables users to see the overall picture, but without combining information that has different characteristics.

(d)   permits reporting exploration and evaluation expenditure by segment on either an annual basis or an accumulated basis.

BC53   Some respondents suggested that the Board should require disclosures similar to those in paragraphs 73 and 74 of IAS 16 or in paragraphs 118–125 of IAS 38. Both IAS 16 and IAS 38 contain scope exclusions for exploration and evaluation assets. Therefore, entities recognising these assets could claim that the requirements were not applicable. The Board decided that, although the scope of those standards excludes exploration and evaluation assets, their required disclosures would provide information relevant to an understanding of the financial statements and useful to users. Consequently, the Board concluded that the IFRS should confirm that the disclosures of IASs 16 and 38 are required consistently with how the entity classifies its exploration and evaluation assets (ie tangible (IAS 16) or intangible (IAS 38)).

BC54   In addition, some respondents suggested that the Board should require disclosure of non-financial information, including:

(a)   commercial reserve quantities;

(b)   rights to explore for, develop and produce wasting resources;

(c)   disclosures about stages after exploration and evaluation; and

(d)   the number of years since exploration started, and an estimation of the time remaining until a decision could be made about the technical feasibility and commercial viability of extracting the mineral resource.

Commercial reserves

BC55   The Board acknowledged that information about commercial reserve quantities is, perhaps, the most important disclosure for an entity with extractive activities. However, it noted that commercial reserves are usually determined after the exploration and evaluation stage has ended and it concluded that such disclosure was beyond the stated scope of the IFRS.

Stages after exploration and evaluation

BC56   As with commercial reserves, the Board concluded that, although information about stages after exploration and evaluation would be useful to users of financial statements, such disclosure is beyond the scope of the IFRS.

Project timing

BC57   The Board also concluded that disclosure of the number of years since exploration started and the estimated time remaining until a decision could be made about development would apply only to large scale exploration activities. It noted that if the project is significant, paragraph 112(c) of IAS 1 already requires its disclosure, ie as additional information that is necessary for an understanding of the financial statements.

                    © IASCF

Effective date

BC58   ED 6 proposed that the IFRS should be effective for annual periods beginning on or after 1 January 2005. The Board decided to change the effective date to 1 January 2006 to allow entities more time to make the transition to the IFRS. It also decided to permit an entity that wishes or is required to adopt IFRSs before 1 January 2006 to adopt IFRS 6 early.

Transition

BC59   The Board did not propose any special transition in ED 6. Consequently, paragraphs 14–27 of IAS 8 would apply to any changes in accounting that are necessary as a result of the IFRS.

BC60   Some respondents expressed concern about the application of the proposals to prior periods—especially those related to impairment and the inclusion or exclusion of some expenditures from exploration and evaluation assets. In particular, respondents requested that if the Board were to require restatement, it should give transitional guidance on how to identify elements previously recognised as exploration and evaluation assets now outside the definition.

BC61   IAS 8 would require entities recognising exploration and evaluation assets to determine whether there were any facts and circumstances indicating impairment in prior periods. The Board concluded that retrospective application was not likely to involve the use of hindsight because the facts and circumstances identified in the IFRS are generally objective indicators and whether they existed at a particular date should be a question of fact. However, the Board noted that it provided transitional relief in IFRS 4 for applying the liability adequacy test to comparative periods on the basis of impracticability, principally because the liability adequacy test involves the use of current estimates of future cash flows from an entity's insurance contracts. The Board does not expect that IFRS 6's approach to impairment will involve current estimates of future cash flows and other variables to the same extent. However, it is aware that the variety of approaches to assessing recoverability means that current estimates of future cash flows and other variables are likely to be in use by some entities.

BC62   Therefore, consistently with IFRS 4, the Board concluded that if it is impracticable to apply the impairment test to comparative information that relates to annual periods beginning before 1 January 2006, an entity should disclose that fact.

BC63   Some respondents were concerned that entities would have difficulty in compiling the information necessary for 2004 comparative figures, and suggested that entities should be exempted from restating comparatives on transition, given that the IFRS would be introduced close to 1 January 2005, and could result in substantial changes.

BC64   The Board considered a similar issue when it developed ED 7 *Financial Instruments: Disclosures*, in which it concluded that entities that apply the requirements proposed in ED 7 only when they become mandatory should be required to provide comparative disclosures because such entities will have enough time to prepare the information.

BC65   In ED 7, the Board decided to propose that an entity that both (a) adopts IFRSs for the first time before 1 January 2006 and (b) applies the IFRS before that date should be exempt from the requirement to produce comparative information in the first year of application. The Board compared the concerns raised by constituents in response to ED 6 and the issues it considered in developing ED 7 and decided that its conclusions in ED 7 were also appropriate for the IFRS.

BC65A   [Deleted]*

Summary of changes from ED 6

BC66   The following is a summary of the main changes from ED 6 to the IFRS. The Board:

(a)   deleted the specific prohibition against including administration and other general overhead costs in the initial measurement of an exploration and evaluation asset (paragraph BC28).

(b)   introduced a requirement for the entity to classify exploration and evaluation assets as either tangible or intangible according to the nature of the asset acquired and to apply this classification consistently (paragraphs BC32–BC34).

(c)   amended the impairment principle so that an impairment is recognised on the basis of an assessment of facts and circumstances and measured, presented and disclosed in accordance with IAS 36, subject to the modification of the level at which the impairment is assessed (paragraphs BC36–BC39).

(d)   deleted the indicators of impairment proposed in ED 6 and replaced them with examples of facts and circumstances that would suggest that an exploration and evaluation asset was impaired (paragraphs BC36–BC39).

(e)   deleted the special cash-generating unit for exploration and evaluation assets and instead required that the entity determine an accounting policy for allocating exploration and evaluation assets to a cash-generating unit or units for the purpose of the impairment test (paragraphs BC40–BC47).

(f)   amended the effective date of the IFRS so that the IFRS is effective for annual periods beginning on or after 1 January 2006 (paragraph BC58).

(g)   provided transitional relief for entities adopting IFRSs for the first time and adopting the IFRS before 1 January 2006 (paragraphs BC59–BC65).

---

*   Paragraph BC65A was deleted as a result of revisions to IFRS 1 *First-time Adoption of International Financial Reporting Standards* in November 2008 as it was no longer applicable.

Dissenting opinions

Dissent of Robert P Garnett, James J Leisenring, Warren J McGregor and John T Smith

DO1   Messrs Garnett, Leisenring, McGregor and Smith dissent from the issue of IFRS 6.

DO2   These four Board members dissent because they would not permit entities the alternative of continuing their existing accounting treatment for exploration and evaluation assets. In particular, they believe that all entities should be required to apply paragraphs 11 and 12 of IAS 8 *Accounting Policies, Changes in Accounting Estimates and Errors* when developing an accounting policy for exploration and evaluation assets. These Board members believe that the requirements in IAS 8 have particular relevance and applicability when an IFRS lacks specificities, as is the case for entities recognising exploration and evaluation assets. This is especially true because the IFRS allows the continuation of a variety of measurement bases for these items and, because of the failure to consider the *Framework*, may result in the inappropriate recognition of assets. In the view of these Board members, if an entity cannot meet those requirements, it should not be allowed to describe its financial statements as being in accordance with International Financial Reporting Standards.

DO3   Messrs Garnett and McGregor also disagree with the modifications to the requirements of IAS 36 for the purpose of assessing exploration and evaluation assets for impairment contained in paragraphs 18–22 of the IFRS. They think that the requirements of IAS 36 should be applied in their entirety to exploration and evaluation assets. Failure to do so could result in exploration and evaluation assets continuing to be carried forward when such assets are not known to be recoverable. This could result in the exclusion of relevant information from the financial statements because of the failure to recognise impairment losses on a timely basis and the inclusion of unreliable information because of the inclusion of assets that do not faithfully represent the transactions and other events that they purport to represent.

DO4   The four Board members' concerns are heightened by the absence as yet from the Board's main agenda of a project on accounting for exploration for and evaluation of mineral resources generally. Although a research project has begun, it is unlikely that the Board will be able to develop financial reporting standards in the medium term. Accordingly, it is likely that the concession referred to in paragraph DO2 and, in Messrs Garnett and McGregor's cases, in paragraph DO3, will remain in place for some time.

IASB documents published to accompany

International Financial Reporting Standard 7

Financial Instruments: Disclosures

This version includes amendments resulting from IFRSs issued up to 31 December 2009.

The text of the unaccompanied IFRS 7 is contained in Part A of this edition. Its effective date when issued was 1 January 2007. The effective date of the most recent amendments is 1 January 2013. This part presents the following accompanying documents:

Approval by the Board of IFRS 7 issued in August 2005

International Financial Reporting Standard 7 *Financial Instruments: Disclosures* was approved for issue by the fourteen members of the International Accounting Standards Board.

Sir David Tweedie	Chairman
Thomas E Jones	Vice-Chairman
Mary E Barth	
Hans-Georg Bruns	
Anthony T Cope	
Jan Engström	
Robert P Garnett	
Gilbert Gélard	
James J Leisenring	
Warren J McGregor	
Patricia L O'Malley	
John T Smith	
Geoffrey Whittington	
Tatsumi Yamada	

Approval by the Board of *Reclassification of Financial Assets* (Amendments to IAS 39 and IFRS 7) issued in October 2008

Reclassification of Financial Assets (Amendments to IAS 39 *Financial Instruments: Recognition and Measurement* and IFRS 7 *Financial Instruments: Disclosures*) was approved for issue by eleven of the thirteen members of the International Accounting Standards Board. Messrs Leisenring and Smith dissented. Their dissenting opinions are set out after the Basis for Conclusions on IAS 39.

Sir David Tweedie   Chairman

Thomas E Jones   Vice-Chairman

Mary E Barth

Stephen Cooper

Philippe Danjou

Jan Engström

Robert P Garnett

Gilbert Gélard

James J Leisenring

Warren J McGregor

John T Smith

Tatsumi Yamada

Wei-Guo Zhang

Approval by the Board of *Reclassification of Financial Assets—Effective Date and Transition* (Amendments to IAS 39 and IFRS 7) issued in November 2008

Reclassification of Financial Assets—Effective Date and Transition (Amendments to IAS 39 *Financial Instruments: Recognition and Measurement* and IFRS 7 *Financial Instruments: Disclosures*) was approved for issue by the thirteen members of the International Accounting Standards Board.

Sir David Tweedie	Chairman
Thomas E Jones	Vice-Chairman
Mary E Barth	
Stephen Cooper	
Philippe Danjou	
Jan Engström	
Robert P Garnett	
Gilbert Gélard	
James J Leisenring	
Warren J McGregor	
John T Smith	
Tatsumi Yamada	
Wei-Guo Zhang	

Approval by the Board of *Improving Disclosures about Financial Instruments* (Amendments to IFRS 7) issued in March 2009

Improving Disclosures about Financial Instruments (Amendments to IFRS 7) was approved for issue by the fourteen members of the International Accounting Standards Board.

Sir David Tweedie	Chairman
Thomas E Jones	Vice-Chairman
Mary E Barth	
Stephen Cooper	
Philippe Danjou	
Jan Engström	
Robert P Garnett	
Gilbert Gélard	
Prabhakar Kalavacherla	
James J Leisenring	
Warren J McGregor	
John T Smith	
Tatsumi Yamada	
Wei-Guo Zhang	

CONTENTS

Basis for Conclusions on
IFRS 7 *Financial Instruments: Disclosures*

This Basis for Conclusions accompanies, but is not part of, IFRS 7.

In this Basis for Conclusions the terminology has not been amended to reflect the changes made by IAS 1 Presentation of Financial Statements *(as revised in 2007).*

In November 2009 the requirements of IAS 39 relating to classification and measurement of assets within the scope of IAS 39 were relocated to IFRS 9 Financial Instruments. *The text of this Basis for Conclusions has been marked up to reflect those changes: new text is underlined and deleted text is struck through.*

Introduction

BC1   This Basis for Conclusions summarises the International Accounting Standards Board's considerations in reaching the conclusions in IFRS 7 *Financial Instruments: Disclosures.* Individual Board members gave greater weight to some factors than to others.

BC2   During the late 1990s, the need for a comprehensive review of IAS 30 *Disclosures in the Financial Statements of Banks and Similar Financial Institutions* became apparent. The Board's predecessor, the International Accounting Standards Committee (IASC), issued a number of Standards that addressed, more comprehensively, some of the topics previously addressed only for banks in IAS 30. Also, fundamental changes were taking place in the financial services industry and in the way in which financial institutions manage their activities and risk exposures. This made it increasingly difficult for users of banks' financial statements to assess and compare their financial position and performance, their associated risk exposures, and their processes for measuring and managing those risks.

BC3   In 1999 IASC added a project to its agenda to revise IAS 30 and in 2000 it appointed a steering committee.

BC4   In 2001 the Board added this project to its agenda. To assist and advise it, the Board retained the IAS 30 steering committee, renamed the Financial Activities Advisory Committee (FAAC), as an expert advisory group. FAAC members had experience and expertise in banks, finance companies and insurance companies and included auditors, financial analysts, preparers and regulators. The FAAC's role was:

(a)   to provide input from the perspective of preparers and auditors of financial statements of entities that have significant exposures to financial instruments; and

(b)   to assist the Board in developing a standard and implementation guidance for risk disclosures arising from financial instruments and for other related disclosures.

BC5   The Board published its proposals in July 2004 as ED 7 *Financial Instruments: Disclosures*. The deadline for comments was 27 October 2004. The Board received 105 comment letters. After reviewing the responses, the Board issued IFRS 7 in August 2005.

BC5A   In October 2008 the Board published an exposure draft *Improving Disclosures about Financial Instruments* (proposed amendments to IFRS 7). The aim of the proposed amendments was to enhance disclosures about fair value and liquidity risk. The Board received 89 comment letters. After reviewing the responses, the Board issued amendments to IFRS 7 in March 2009. The Board decided to require application of the amendments for periods beginning on or after 1 January 2009. The Board noted that, although the effective date of IFRSs and amendments to IFRSs is usually 6–18 months after issue, the urgent need for enhanced disclosures about financial instruments demanded earlier application.

Scope (paragraphs 3–5)

The entities to which the IFRS applies

BC6   Although IFRS 7 arose from a project to revise IAS 30 (a Standard that applied only to banks and similar financial institutions), it applies to all entities that have financial instruments. The Board observed that the reduction in regulatory barriers in many countries and increasing competition between banks, non-bank financial services firms, and financial conglomerates have resulted in many entities providing financial services that were traditionally provided only by entities regulated and supervised as banks. The Board concluded that this development would make it inappropriate to limit this project to banks and similar financial institutions.

BC7   The Board considered whether entities that undertake specified activities commonly undertaken by banks and other financial institutions, namely deposit-taking, lending and securities activities, face unique risks that would require a standard specific to them. However, the Board decided that the scope of this project should include disclosures about risks arising from financial instruments in all entities for the following reasons:

    (a)   disclosures about risks associated with financial instruments are useful to users of the financial statements of all entities.

    (b)   the Board found it could not satisfactorily define deposit-taking, lending, and securities activities. In particular, it could not satisfactorily differentiate an entity with securities activities from an entity holding a portfolio of financial assets for investment and liquidity management purposes.

    (c)   responses to the Exposure Draft of Improvements to IAS 32 *Financial Instruments: Disclosure and Presentation*, published in June 2002, indicated that IAS 32's risk disclosure requirements, applicable to all entities, could be improved.

    (d)   the exclusion of some financial instruments would increase the danger that risk disclosures could be incomplete and possibly misleading.

For example, a debt instrument issued by an entity could significantly affect its exposures to liquidity risk, interest rate risk and currency risk even if that instrument is not held as part of deposit-taking, lending and securities activities.

(e)   users of financial statements need to be able to compare similar activities, transactions and events of different entities on a consistent basis. Hence, the disclosure principles that apply to regulated entities should not differ from those that apply to non-regulated, but otherwise similar, entities.

BC8   The Board decided that the scope of the IFRS should be the same as that of IAS 32 with one exception. The Board concluded that the IFRS should not apply to derivatives based on interests in subsidiaries, associates or joint ventures if the derivatives meet the definition of an equity instrument in IAS 32. This is because equity instruments are not remeasured and hence:

(a)   they do not expose the issuer to balance sheet and income statement risk; and

(b)   the disclosures about the significance of financial instruments for financial position and performance are not relevant to equity instruments.

Although these instruments are excluded from the scope of IFRS 7, they are within the scope of IAS 32 for the purpose of determining whether they meet the definition of equity instruments.

Exemptions considered by the Board

Insurers

BC9   The Board considered whether the IFRS should apply to entities that both have financial instruments and issue insurance contracts. The Board did not exempt these entities because financial instruments expose all entities to risks regardless of what other assets and liabilities they have. Accordingly, an entity that both issues insurance contracts and has financial instruments applies IFRS 4 *Insurance Contracts* to its insurance contracts and IFRS 7 to its financial assets and financial liabilities. However, many of the disclosure requirements in IFRS 4 were applications of, or relatively straightforward analogies with, existing requirements in IAS 32. Therefore, the Board also updated the disclosures required by IFRS 4 to make them consistent with IFRS 7, with modifications that reflect the interim nature of IFRS 4.

Small and medium-sized entities

BC10   The Board considered whether it should exempt small and medium-sized entities from the scope of the IFRS. The Board noted that the extent of disclosures required by the IFRS will depend on the extent to which the entity uses financial instruments and the extent to which it has assumed associated risks. The IFRS requires entities with few financial instruments and few risks to give few disclosures. Also, many of the requirements in the IFRS are based on information provided internally to the entity's key management personnel. This helps to avoid unduly onerous requirements that would not be appropriate for smaller entities. Accordingly, the Board decided not to exempt such entities from the scope of IFRS 7. However, it will keep this decision under review in its project on financial reporting for small and medium-sized entities.

Subsidiaries

BC11   Some respondents to ED 7 stated that there is little public interest in the financial statements of some entities, such as a wholly-owned subsidiary whose parent issues publicly available financial statements. These respondents stated that such subsidiaries should be exempt from some of the requirements of IFRS 7 in their individual financial statements. However, deciding whether such an entity should prepare general purpose financial statements is a matter for the entity and local legislators and regulators. If such an entity prepares financial statements in accordance with IFRSs, users of those statements should receive information of the same quality as users of any general purpose financial statements prepared in accordance with IFRSs. The Board confirmed its view that no exemptions from the general requirements of any Standard should be given for the financial statements of subsidiaries.

Disclosures about the significance of financial instruments for financial position and performance (paragraphs 7–30, B4 and B5)

BC12   The Board relocated disclosures from IAS 32 to IFRS 7, so that all disclosure requirements for financial instruments are in one Standard. Many of the disclosure requirements about the significance of financial instruments for an entity's financial position and performance were previously in IAS 32. For these disclosures, the relevant paragraphs from the Basis for Conclusions on IAS 32 have been incorporated into this Basis for Conclusions. This Basis for Conclusions does not discuss requirements that the Board did not reconsider either in revising IAS 32 in 2003 or in developing IFRS 7.

The principle (paragraph 7)

BC13   The Board decided that the disclosure requirements of IFRS 7 should result from the explicit disclosure principle in paragraph 7. The Board also decided to specify disclosures to satisfy this principle. In the Board's view, entities could not satisfy the principle in paragraph 7 unless they disclose the information required by paragraphs 8–30.

Balance sheet disclosures (paragraphs 8–19 and B4)

Categories of financial assets and financial liabilities (paragraph 8)

BC14   Paragraph 8 requires entities to disclose financial assets by the measurement categories in IFRS 9 *Financial Instruments* and financial liabilities by the measurement categories in IAS 39 *Financial Instruments: Recognition and Measurement*. The Board concluded that disclosures for each measurement category would assist users in understanding the extent to which accounting policies affect the amounts at which financial assets and financial liabilities are recognised.

BC15 The Board also concluded that separate disclosure of the carrying amounts of financial assets and financial liabilities that are ~~classified as held for trading and those~~ designated upon initial recognition as financial assets and financial liabilities at fair value through profit or loss and those mandatorily measured at fair value is useful because such designation is at the discretion of the entity.

Financial assets or financial liabilities at fair value through profit or loss (paragraphs 9–11, B4 and B5)

BC16 IAS 39 permits entities to designate a non-derivative financial liability as at fair value through profit or loss, if specified conditions are met. If entities do so, they are required to provide the disclosures in paragraphs 10 and 11. The Board's reasons for these disclosures are set out in the Basis for Conclusions on IAS 39, paragraphs BC87–BC92.

BC17 The requirements in paragraphs 9, 11 and B5(a) are related to the Amendments to IAS 39 Financial Instruments: Recognition and Measurement—*The Fair Value Option*, issued in June 2005. The reasons for those requirements are discussed in the Basis for Conclusions on those Amendments.

BC18 Paragraph 10(a) requires disclosure of the change in fair value of a financial liability designated as at fair value through profit or loss that is attributable to changes in the liability's credit risk. The Board previously considered this disclosure in its deliberations on the fair value measurement of financial liabilities in IAS 39.

BC19 Although quantifying such changes might be difficult in practice, the Board concluded that disclosure of such information would be useful to users of financial statements and would help alleviate concerns that users may misinterpret the profit or loss effects of changes in credit risk, especially in the absence of disclosures. Therefore, in finalising the revisions to IAS 32 in 2003, it decided to require disclosure of the change in fair value of the financial liability that is not attributable to changes in a benchmark interest rate. The Board believed that this is often a reasonable proxy for the change in fair value that is attributable to changes in the liability's credit risk, in particular when such changes are large, and would provide users with information with which to understand the profit or loss effect of such a change in credit risk.

BC20 However, some respondents to ED 7 stated that they did not agree that the IAS 32 disclosure provided a reasonable proxy, except for straightforward debt instruments. In particular, there could be other factors involved in the change in an instrument's fair value unrelated to the benchmark interest rate, such as the effect of an embedded derivative. Respondents also cited difficulties for unit-linked insurance contracts, for which the amount of the liability reflects the performance of a defined pool of assets. The Board noted that the proxy that was developed in IAS 32 assumed that it is not practicable for entities to determine directly the change in fair value arising from changes in credit risk. However, the Board acknowledged and shared these concerns.

BC21 As a result, the Board amended this requirement to focus directly on the objective of providing information about the effects of changes in credit risk:

(a) by permitting entities to provide a more faithful representation of the amount of change in fair value that is attributable to changes in credit risk if they could do so. However, such entities are also required to disclose the methods used and provide their justification for concluding that those methods give a more faithful representation than the proxy in paragraph 10(a)(i).

(b) by amending the proxy disclosure to be the amount of change in fair value that is not attributable to changes in market conditions that give rise to market risk. For example, some entities may be able to identify part of the change in the fair value of the liability as attributable to a change in an index. In these cases, the proxy disclosure would exclude the amount of change attributable to a change in an index. Similarly, excluding the amount attributable to a change in an internal or external investment fund makes the proxy more suitable for unit-linked insurance contracts.

BC22 The Board decided that when an entity has designated a financial liability as at fair value through profit or loss, it should disclose the difference between the carrying amount and the amount the entity would contractually be required to pay at maturity to the holders of the liability (see paragraph 10(b)). The fair value may differ significantly from the settlement amount, in particular for financial liabilities with a long duration when an entity has experienced a significant deterioration in creditworthiness since their issue. The Board concluded that knowledge of this difference would be useful to users of financial statements. Also, the settlement amount is important to some financial statement users, particularly creditors.

Reclassification (paragraphs ~~12 and 12A~~ 12B–12D)

BC23 IAS 32 required disclosure of the reason for reclassification of financial assets at cost or amortised cost rather than at fair value. The Board extended this requirement to include disclosure of the reason for reclassifications and of the amount reclassified into and out of each category. As noted in paragraph BC14, the Board regards such information as useful because the categorisation of financial instruments has a significant effect on their measurement.

BC23A In October and November 2008 the Board amended IAS 39 to permit reclassification of particular financial assets in some circumstances. The Board decided to require additional disclosures about the situations in which any such reclassification is made, and the effects on the financial statements. The Board regards such information as useful because the reclassification of a financial asset can have a significant effect on the financial statements.

BC23B <u>In November 2009 the Board revised the requirements relating to reclassification of financial assets in IFRS 9 *Financial Instruments*. Accordingly, the Board revised the disclosure requirements relating to reclassification of financial assets.</u>

Derecognition (paragraph 13)

BC24   An entity may have transferred financial assets in such a way that part or all of them do not qualify for derecognition (see paragraphs 15–37 of IAS 39). If the entity either continues to recognise all of the assets or continues to recognise the assets to the extent of its continuing involvement, paragraph 13 requires disclosure of the nature of the financial assets, the extent of the entity's continuing involvement, and any associated liabilities. Such disclosure helps users of the financial statements evaluate the significance of the risks retained.

Collateral (paragraphs 14 and 15)

BC25   Paragraph 15 requires disclosures about collateral that the entity holds if it is permitted to sell or repledge the collateral in the absence of default by the owner. Some respondents to ED 7 argued for an exemption from this disclosure if it is impracticable to obtain the fair value of the collateral held. However, the Board concluded that it is reasonable to expect an entity to know the fair value of collateral that it holds and can sell even if there is no default.

Allowance account for credit losses (paragraph 16)

BC26   When a separate account is used to record impairment losses (such as an allowance account or similar account used to record a collective impairment of assets), paragraph 16 requires a reconciliation of that account to be disclosed. The Board was informed that analysts and other users find this information useful in assessing the adequacy of the allowance for impairment losses for such entities and when comparing one entity with another. However, the Board decided not to specify the components of the reconciliation. This allows entities flexibility in determining the most appropriate format for their needs.

BC27   Respondents to ED 7 asked the Board to require entities to provide equivalent information if they do not use an allowance account. The Board decided not to add this disclosure in finalising the IFRS. It concluded that, for virtually all entities, IAS 39's requirement to consider impairment on a group basis would necessitate the use of an allowance or similar account. The accounting policy disclosures required by paragraph B5(d) also include information about the use of direct adjustments to carrying amounts of financial assets.

Compound financial instruments with multiple embedded derivatives (paragraph 17)

BC28   IAS 32 requires the separation of the liability and equity components of a compound financial instrument. The Board notes that this is more complicated for compound financial instruments with multiple embedded derivative features whose values are interdependent (for example, a convertible debt instrument that gives the issuer a right to call the instrument back from the holder, or the holder a right to put the instrument back to the issuer) than for those without such features. If the embedded equity and non-equity derivative features are interdependent, the sum of the separately determined values of the liability and equity components will not equal the value of the compound financial instrument as a whole.

BC29　For example, the values of an embedded call option feature and an equity conversion option feature in a callable convertible debt instrument depend in part on each other if the holder's equity conversion option is extinguished when the entity exercises the call option or vice versa. The following diagram illustrates the joint value arising from the interaction between a call option and an equity conversion option in a callable convertible bond. Circle L represents the value of the liability component, ie the value of the straight debt and the embedded call option on the straight debt, and Circle E represents the value of the equity component, ie the equity conversion option on the straight debt.

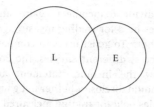

The total area of the two circles represents the value of the callable convertible bond. The difference between the value of the callable convertible bond as a whole and the sum of the separately determined values for the liability and equity components is the joint value attributable to the interdependence between the call option feature and the equity conversion feature. It is represented by the intersection between the two circles.

BC30　Under the approach in IAS 32, the joint value attributable to the interdependence between multiple embedded derivative features is included in the liability component. A numerical example is set out as Illustrative Example 10 accompanying IAS 32.

BC31　Even though this approach is consistent with the definition of equity as a residual interest, the Board recognises that the allocation of the joint value to either the liability component or the equity component is arbitrary because it is, by its nature, joint. Therefore, the Board concluded that it is important to disclose the existence of issued compound financial instruments with multiple embedded derivative features that have interdependent values. Such disclosure highlights the effect of multiple embedded derivative features on the amounts recognised as liabilities and equity.

Defaults and breaches (paragraphs 18 and 19)

BC32　Paragraphs 18 and 19 require disclosures about defaults and breaches of loans payable and other loan agreements. The Board concluded that such disclosures provide relevant information about the entity's creditworthiness and its prospects of obtaining future loans.

Income statement and equity (paragraph 20)

Items of income, expenses, gains or losses (paragraph 20(a))

BC33   Paragraph 20(a) requires disclosure of income statement gains and losses by the measurement categories in IAS 39 and measurement classifications in IFRS 9 (which complement the balance sheet disclosure requirement described in paragraph BC14). The Board concluded that the disclosure is needed for users to understand the financial performance of an entity's financial instruments, given the different measurement bases in IAS 39 and IFRS 9.

BC34   Some entities include interest and dividend income in gains and losses on financial assets and financial liabilities held for trading measured at fair value through profit or loss and others do not. To assist users in comparing income arising from financial instruments across different entities, the Board decided that an entity should disclose how the income statement amounts are determined. For example, an entity should disclose whether net gains and losses on financial assets or financial liabilities held for trading measured at fair value through profit or loss include interest and dividend income (see Appendix B, paragraph B5(e)).

Fee income and expense (paragraph 20(c))

BC35   Paragraph 20(c) requires disclosure of fee income and expense (other than amounts included in determining the effective interest rate) arising from financial assets or financial liabilities and from trust and other fiduciary activities that result in the entity holding or placing assets on behalf of individuals, trusts, retirement benefit plans, and other institutions. This information indicates the level of such activities and helps users to estimate possible future income of the entity.

Other disclosures—fair value (paragraphs 25–30)

BC36   Many entities use fair value information internally in determining their overall financial position and in making decisions about individual financial instruments. It is also relevant to many decisions made by users of financial statements because, in many circumstances, it reflects the judgement of the financial markets about the present value of expected future cash flows relating to an instrument. Fair value information permits comparisons of financial instruments having substantially the same economic characteristics, regardless of why they are held and when and by whom they were issued or acquired. Fair values provide a neutral basis for assessing management's stewardship by indicating the effects of its decisions to buy, sell or hold financial assets and to incur, maintain or discharge financial liabilities. The Board decided that when an entity does not measure a financial asset or financial liability in its balance sheet at fair value, it should provide fair value information through supplementary disclosures to assist users to compare entities on a consistent basis.

BC37   Disclosure of fair value is not required for investments in unquoted equity instruments and derivatives linked to such equity instruments if their fair value cannot be measured reliably. Similarly, IFRS 4 does not specify the accounting required for contracts containing a discretionary participation feature pending phase II of the Board's project on insurance contracts. Accordingly, disclosure of fair value is not required for contracts containing a discretionary participation feature, if the fair value of that feature cannot be measured reliably. For all other financial assets and financial liabilities, it is reasonable to expect that fair value can be determined with sufficient reliability within constraints of timeliness and cost. Therefore, the Board concluded that there should be no other exception from the requirement to disclose fair value information for financial assets or financial liabilities.

BC38   To provide users of financial statements with a sense of the potential variability of fair value estimates, the Board decided that information about the use of valuation techniques should be disclosed, in particular the sensitivities of fair value estimates to the main valuation assumptions. In forming this conclusion, the Board considered the view that disclosure of sensitivities could be difficult, particularly when there are many assumptions to which the disclosure would apply and these assumptions are interdependent. However, the Board noted that a detailed quantitative disclosure of sensitivity to all assumptions is not required (only those that could result in a significantly different estimate of fair value are required) and that the disclosure does not require the entity to reflect interdependencies between assumptions when making the disclosure. Additionally, the Board considered whether this disclosure might imply that a fair value established by a valuation technique is less reliable than one established by other means. However, the Board noted that fair values estimated by valuation techniques are more subjective than those established from an observable market price, and concluded that users need information to help them assess the extent of this subjectivity.

BC39   Paragraph 28 requires disclosure about the difference that arises if the transaction price differs from the fair value of a financial instrument that is determined in accordance with paragraph AG76 of IAS 39. Those disclosures relate to matters addressed in the December 2004 amendment to IAS 39 *Transition and Initial Recognition of Financial Assets and Financial Liabilities*. That amendment does not specify how entities should account for those initial differences in subsequent periods. The disclosures required by paragraph 28 inform users about the amount of gain or loss that will be recognised in profit or loss in future periods. The Board noted that the information required to provide these disclosures would be readily available to the entities affected.

BC39A   Statement of Financial Accounting Standards No. 157 *Fair Value Measurements* (SFAS 157) issued by the US Financial Accounting Standards Board requires disclosures that are based on a three-level fair value hierarchy for the inputs used in valuation techniques to measure fair value. The Board was asked by some users of financial statements to include similar disclosure requirements in IFRS 7 to provide more information about the relative reliability of the inputs to fair value measurements. The Board concluded that such a hierarchy would improve comparability between entities about the effects of fair value measurements as well as increase the convergence of IFRSs and US generally accepted accounting principles (GAAP). Therefore, the Board decided to require disclosures for financial instruments on the basis of a fair value hierarchy.

BC39B   Because its own fair value measurement project was not yet completed, the Board decided not to propose a fair value hierarchy for measurement, but only for disclosures. The fair value hierarchy for disclosures is the same as that in SFAS 157 but uses IFRS language pending completion of the fair value measurement project. Although the implicit fair value hierarchy for measurement in IAS 39 is different from the fair value hierarchy in SFAS 157, the Board recognised the importance of using a three-level hierarchy for disclosures that is the same as that in SFAS 157.

BC39C   The Board noted the following three-level measurement hierarchy implicit in IAS 39:

(a)   financial instruments quoted in an active market;

(b)   financial instruments whose fair value is evidenced by comparison with other observable current market transactions in the same instrument (ie without modification or repackaging) or based on a valuation technique whose variables include only data from observable markets; and

(c)   financial instruments whose fair value is determined in whole or in part using a valuation technique based on assumptions that are not supported by prices from observable current market transactions in the same instrument (ie without modification or repackaging) and not based on available observable market data.

BC39D   For example, the Board acknowledged that some financial instruments that for measurement purposes are considered to have an active market in accordance with paragraphs AG71–AG73 of IAS 39 might be in Level 2 for disclosure purposes. Also, the application of paragraph AG76A of IAS 39 might result in no gain or loss being recognised on the initial recognition of a financial instrument that is in Level 2 for disclosure purposes.

BC39E   The introduction of the fair value disclosure hierarchy does not affect any measurement or recognition requirements of other standards. In particular, the Board noted that the recognition of gains or losses at inception of a financial instrument (as required by paragraph AG76 of IAS 39) would not change as a result of the fair value disclosure hierarchy.

BC39F   The Board decided to require additional disclosures for instruments with fair value measurements that are in Level 3 of the fair value hierarchy. These disclosures inform users of financial statements about the effects of those fair value measurements that use the most subjective inputs.

BC39G   After reviewing comments received on the exposure draft, the Board decided not to require disclosure by level of the fair value hierarchy for financial instruments that are not measured at fair value in the statement of financial position. The Board noted that paragraphs 25 and 27 of IFRS 7, which require the disclosure of the fair value of each class of assets and liabilities in a way that permits it to be compared with its carrying amount, and the methods and assumptions applied in determining fair values, were retained.

Disclosures about the nature and extent of risks arising from financial instruments (paragraphs 31–42 and B6–B28)

BC40   The Board was informed that users of financial statements value information about the risks arising from financial instruments, such as credit risk, liquidity risk and market risk, to which entities are exposed, and the techniques used to identify, measure, monitor and control those risks. Therefore, the Board decided to require disclosure of this information. The Board also decided to balance two objectives:

    (a)   consistent requirements should apply to all entities so that users receive comparable information about the risks to which entities are exposed.

    (b)   the disclosures provided should depend on the extent of an entity's use of financial instruments and the extent to which it assumes associated risks. Entities with many financial instruments and related risks should provide more disclosure to communicate those risks to users of financial statements. Conversely, entities with few financial instruments and related risks may provide less extensive disclosure.

BC41   The Board decided to balance these two objectives by developing an IFRS that sets out principles and minimum requirements applicable to all entities, supported by guidance on implementing the IFRS. The requirements in paragraphs 33–42 combine qualitative disclosures of the entity's exposure to risks arising from financial instruments, and the way in which management views and manages these risks, with quantitative disclosures about material risks arising from financial instruments. The extent of disclosure depends on the extent of the entity's exposure to risks arising from financial instruments. The guidance on implementing the IFRS illustrates how an entity might apply the IFRS. This guidance is consistent with the disclosure requirements for banks developed by the Basel Committee (known as Pillar 3), so that banks can prepare, and users receive, a single co-ordinated set of disclosures about financial risk.

BC42   The Board noted that because entities view and manage risk in different ways, disclosures based on how an entity manages risk are unlikely to be comparable between entities. In addition, for an entity that undertakes limited management of risks arising from financial instruments, such disclosures would convey little or no information about the risks the entity has assumed. To overcome these limitations, the Board decided to specify disclosures about risk exposures applicable to all entities. These disclosures provide a common benchmark for financial statement users when comparing risk exposures across different entities and are expected to be relatively easy for entities to prepare. Entities with more developed risk management systems would provide more detailed information.

Location of disclosures of risks arising from financial instruments (paragraph B6)

BC43   Many respondents to ED 7 argued that disclosures about risks in paragraphs 31–42 should not be part of the financial statements for the following reasons:

    (a)   the information would be difficult and costly to audit.

(b)   the information is different from information generally included in financial statements because it is subjective, forward-looking and based on management's judgement. Thus, the information does not meet the criteria of comparability, faithful representation and completeness.

(c)   inclusion of such information in a management commentary section outside the financial statements would be consistent with practice in other jurisdictions, including the US. Having this information in the financial statements would put IFRS preparers at a disadvantage relative to their US peers.

BC44   Respondents raised concerns that the disclosure of sensitivity analysis in particular should not be part of the financial statements. Respondents stated that sensitivity analysis cannot be prepared with the degree of reliability expected of information in the financial statements, and that the subjectivity in the sensitivity analysis and the hypothetical alternative values could undermine the credibility of the fair values recognised in the financial statements.

BC45   The Board considered whether the disclosures should be part of the information provided by management outside the financial statements. The Board noted that respondents generally regarded the disclosures proposed in ED 7 as useful, even if they did not agree that they should be located in the financial statements. The Board's view is that financial statements would be incomplete and potentially misleading without disclosures about risks arising from financial instruments. Hence, it concluded that such disclosures should be part of the financial statements. The Board rejected the argument that increased transparency puts an entity at a disadvantage; greater certainty on the part of investors can provide a significant advantage by lowering the entity's cost of capital.

BC46   The Board also noted that some entities might prefer to present the information required by the IFRS together with material such as a management commentary or risk report that is not part of the financial statements. Some entities might be required by regulatory authorities to provide in a separate report information similar to that required by the IFRS. Accordingly, the Board decided these disclosures should be given in the financial statements or incorporated by cross-reference from the financial statements to some other statement that is available to users of the financial statements on the same terms as the financial statements and at the same time.

Quantitative disclosures (paragraphs 34–42 and B7–B28)

Information based on how the entity manages risk (paragraphs 34 and B7)

BC47   The Board concluded that disclosures about an entity's exposure to risks arising from financial instruments should be required, and should be based on how the entity views and manages its risks, ie using the information provided to key management personnel (for example, its board of directors or chief executive officer). This approach:

(a)   provides a useful insight into how the entity views and manages risk;

(b) results in information that has more predictive value than information based on assumptions and methods that management does not use, for instance, in considering the entity's ability to react to adverse situations;

(c) is more effective in adapting to changes in risk measurement and management techniques and developments in the external environment;

(d) has practical advantages for preparers of financial statements, because it allows them to use the data they use in managing risk; and

(e) is consistent with the approach used in IAS 14 *Segment Reporting.*[*]

Information on averages

BC48 The Board considered whether it should require quantitative information about average risk exposures during the period. It noted that information about averages is more informative if the risk exposure at the reporting date is not typical of the exposure during the period. However, information about averages is also more onerous to prepare. On balance, the Board decided to require disclosure of the exposures at the reporting date in all cases and to require additional information only if the information provided at the reporting date is unrepresentative of the entity's exposure to risk during the period.

Credit risk (paragraphs 36–38, B9 and B10)

Maximum exposure to credit risk (paragraphs 36(a), B9 and B10)

BC49 Paragraph 36(a) requires disclosure of an entity's maximum exposure to credit risk at the reporting date. Some respondents to ED 7 stated that these disclosures would not provide useful information when there are no identified problems in a loan portfolio, and it is not likely that collateral would be called on. However, the Board disagreed because it believes that such information:

(a) provides users of financial statements with a consistent measure of an entity's exposure to credit risk; and

(b) takes into account the possibility that the maximum exposure to loss may differ from the amount recognised in the balance sheet.

BC50 Some respondents to ED 7 questioned whether the maximum exposure to credit risk for a derivative contract is its carrying amount because fair value does not always reflect potential future exposure to credit risk (see paragraph B10(b)). However, the Board noted that paragraph 36(a) requires disclosure of the amount that best represents the maximum exposure to credit risk *at the reporting date*, which is the carrying amount.

---

[*] In 2006 IAS 14 was replaced by IFRS 8 *Operating Segments.*

Collateral held as security and other credit enhancements (paragraphs 36(b) and 37(c))

BC51   ED 7 proposed that, unless impracticable, the entity should disclose the fair value of collateral held as security and other credit enhancements, to provide information about the loss the entity might incur in the event of default. However, many respondents to ED 7 disagreed with this proposal on cost/benefit grounds. Respondents indicated that fair value information might not be available for:

(a)   small entities and entities other than banks, which may find it onerous to acquire information about collateral;

(b)   banks that collect precise information on the value of collateral only on origination, for loans whose payments are made on time and in full (for example a mortgage portfolio secured by properties, for which valuations are not kept up to date on an asset-by-asset basis);

(c)   particular types of collateral, such as a floating charge on all the assets of an entity; and

(d)   insurers that hold collateral for which fair value information is not readily available.

BC52   The Board also noted respondents' concerns that an aggregate disclosure of the fair value of collateral held would be misleading when some loans in a portfolio are over-collateralised, and other loans have insufficient collateral. In these circumstances, netting the fair value of the two types of collateral would under-report the amount of credit risk. The Board agreed with respondents that the information useful to users is not the total amount of credit exposure less the total amount of collateral, but rather is the amount of credit exposure that is left after available collateral is taken into account.

BC53   Therefore, the Board decided not to require disclosure of the fair value of collateral held, but to require disclosure of only a description of collateral held as security and other credit enhancements. The Board noted that such disclosure does not require an entity to establish fair values for all its collateral (in particular when the entity has determined that the fair value of some collateral exceeds the carrying amount of the loan) and, thus, would be less onerous for entities to provide than fair values.

Credit quality of financial assets that are neither past due nor impaired (paragraph 36(c))

BC54   The Board noted that information about credit quality gives a greater insight into the credit risk of assets and helps users assess whether such assets are more or less likely to become impaired in the future. Because this information will vary between entities, the Board decided not to specify a particular method for giving this information, but rather to allow each entity to devise a method that is appropriate to its circumstances.

           © IASCF

Financial assets that are either past due or impaired (paragraph 37)

BC55 The Board decided to require separate disclosure of financial assets that are past due or impaired to provide users with information about financial assets with the greatest credit risk (paragraph 37). This includes:

(a) an analysis of the age of financial assets, including trade receivables, that are past due at the reporting date, but not impaired (paragraph 37(a)). This information provides users with information about those financial assets that are more likely to become impaired and helps users to estimate the level of future impairment losses.

(b) an analysis of financial assets that are individually determined to be impaired at the reporting date, including the factors the entity considered in determining that the financial assets are impaired (paragraph 37(b)). The Board concluded that an analysis of impaired financial assets by factors other than age (eg nature of the counterparty, or geographical analysis of impaired assets) would be useful because it helps users to understand why the impairment occurred.

Collateral and other credit enhancements obtained (paragraph 38)

BC56 Paragraph 38 requires the entity to disclose the nature and carrying amount of assets obtained by taking possession of collateral held as security or calling on other credit enhancements and its policy for disposing of such assets. The Board concluded that this information is useful because it provides information about the frequency of such activities and the entity's ability to obtain and realise the value of the collateral. ED 7 had proposed that the entity should disclose the fair value of the assets obtained less the cost of selling them, rather than the carrying amount. The Board noted that this amount might be more relevant in the case of collateral obtained that is expected to be sold. However, it also noted that such an amount would be included in the impairment calculation that is reflected in the amount recognised in the balance sheet and the purpose of the disclosure is to indicate the amount recognised in the balance sheet for such assets.

Liquidity risk (paragraphs 34(a), 39, B10A and B11A–B11F)

BC57 The Board decided to require disclosure of a maturity analysis for financial liabilities showing the remaining earliest contractual maturities (paragraph 39(a) and paragraphs B11–B16 of Appendix B).[*] Liquidity risk, ie the risk that the entity will encounter difficulty in meeting commitments associated with financial liabilities, arises because of the possibility (which may often be remote) that the entity could be required to pay its liabilities earlier than expected. The Board decided to require disclosure based on the earliest contractual maturity date because this disclosure shows a worst case scenario.

BC58 Some respondents expressed concerns that such a contractual maturity analysis does not reveal the expected maturity of liabilities, which, for some entities— eg banks with many demand deposits—may be very different. They suggested that a contractual maturity analysis alone does not provide information about the

---

[*] Amendments to IFRS 7 issued in March 2009 amended paragraph 39 and paragraphs B11–B16. The paragraph references in paragraph BC57 have not been amended as a result of these amendments.

conditions expected in normal circumstances or how the entity manages deviations from expected maturity. Therefore, the Board decided to require a description of how the entity manages the liquidity risk portrayed by the contractual maturity analysis.

BC58A   In March 2009 the Board amended the disclosure requirements on the nature and extent of liquidity risk by:

(a)   amending the definition of liquidity risk to clarify that paragraph 39 applies only to financial liabilities that will result in the outflow of cash or another financial asset.   This clarifies that the disclosure requirements would not apply to financial liabilities that will be settled in the entity's own equity instruments and to liabilities within the scope of IFRS 7 that are settled with non-financial assets.

(b)   emphasising that an entity must provide summary quantitative data about its exposure to liquidity risk based on information provided internally to key management personnel of the entity as required by paragraph 34(a). This reinforces the principles of IFRS 7.

(c)   amending the requirement in paragraph 39 to disclose a contractual maturity analysis.

BC58B   The requirements in paragraph 39(a) and (b) relate to minimum benchmark disclosures as set out in paragraph 34(b) and are expected to be relatively easy to apply.   However, the Board noted that the requirement to provide disclosures based on the remaining contractual maturities was difficult to apply for some derivative financial liabilities and did not always result in information that reflects how many entities manage liquidity risk for such instruments. Hence, for some circumstances the Board eliminated the previous requirement to disclose contractual maturity information for derivative financial liabilities.   However, the Board retained minimum contractual maturity disclosures for non-derivative financial liabilities (including issued financial guarantee contracts within the scope of the IFRS) and for some derivative financial liabilities.

BC58C   The Board noted that for non-derivative financial liabilities (including issued financial guarantee contracts within the scope of the IFRS) and some derivative financial liabilities, contractual maturities are essential for an understanding of the timing of cash flows associated with the liabilities.   Therefore, this information is useful to users of financial statements.   The Board concluded that disclosures based on the remaining contractual maturities of these financial liabilities should continue to be required.

BC58D   The Board also emphasised the existing requirement to disclose a maturity analysis for financial assets held for managing liquidity risk, if that information is required to enable users of its financial statements to evaluate the nature and extent of liquidity risk.   The Board also emphasised that an entity must explain the relationship between qualitative and quantitative disclosures about liquidity risk so that users of financial statements can evaluate the nature and extent of liquidity risk.

Market risk (paragraphs 40–42 and B17–B28)

BC59 The Board decided to require disclosure of a sensitivity analysis for each type of market risk (paragraph 40) because:

(a) users have consistently emphasised the fundamental importance of sensitivity analysis;

(b) a sensitivity analysis can be disclosed for all types of market risk and by all entities, and is relatively easy to understand and calculate; and

(c) it is suitable for all entities—including non-financial entities—that have financial instruments. It is supported by disclosures of how the entity manages the risk. Thus, it is a simpler and more suitable disclosure than other approaches, including the disclosures of terms and conditions and the gap analysis of interest rate risk previously required by IAS 32.

The Board noted that information provided by a simple sensitivity analysis would not be comparable across entities. This is because the methodologies used to prepare the sensitivity analysis and the resulting disclosures would vary according to the nature of the entity and the complexity of its risk management systems.

BC60 The Board acknowledged that a simple sensitivity analysis that shows a change in only one variable has limitations. For example, the analysis may not reveal non-linearities in sensitivities or the effects of interdependencies between variables. The Board decided to meet the first concern by requiring additional disclosure when the sensitivity analysis is unrepresentative of a risk inherent in a financial instrument (paragraph 42). The Board noted that it could meet the second concern by requiring a more complex sensitivity analysis that takes into account the interdependencies between risks. Although more informative, such an analysis is also more complex and costly to prepare. Accordingly, the Board decided not to require such an analysis, but to permit its disclosure as an alternative to the minimum requirement when it is used by management to manage risk.

BC61 Respondents to ED 7 noted that a value-at-risk amount would not show the effect on profit or loss or equity. However, entities that manage on the basis of value at risk would not want to prepare a separate sensitivity analysis solely for the purpose of this disclosure. The Board's objective was to require disclosures about sensitivity, not to mandate a particular form of sensitivity disclosure. Therefore, the Board decided not to require disclosure of the effects on profit or loss and equity if an alternative disclosure of sensitivity is made.

BC62 Respondents to ED 7 requested the Board to provide more guidance and clarification about the sensitivity analysis, in particular:

(a) what is a reasonably possible change in the relevant risk variable?

(b) what is the appropriate level of aggregation in the disclosures?

(c) what methodology should be used in preparing the sensitivity analysis?

BC63 The Board concluded that it would not be possible to provide comprehensive guidance on the methodology to be used in preparing the sensitivity analysis. The Board noted that more comparable information would be obtained if it imposed specific requirements about the inputs, process and methodology of the analysis, for example disclosure of the effects of a parallel shift of the yield curve by 100 basis points. However, the Board decided against such a specific requirement because a reasonably possible change in a relevant risk variable (such as interest rates) in one economic environment may not be reasonably possible in another (such as an economy with higher inflation). Moreover, the effect of a reasonably possible change will vary depending on the entity's risk exposures. As a result, entities are required to judge what those reasonably possible changes are.

BC64 However, the Board decided that it would provide high level application guidance about how the entity should assess what is a reasonably possible change and on the appropriate level of aggregation in the disclosures. In response to comments received on ED 7, the Board also decided to clarify that:

(a) an entity should not aggregate information about material exposures to risk from significantly different economic environments. However, if it has exposure to only one type of market risk in only one economic environment, it might not show disaggregated information.

(b) the sensitivity analysis does not require entities to determine what the profit or loss for the period would have been had the relevant risk variable been different. The sensitivity analysis shows the effect on current period profit or loss and equity if a reasonably possible change in the relevant risk variable had been applied to the risk exposures in existence at the balance sheet date.

(c) a reasonably possible change is judged relative to the economic environments in which the entity operates, and does not include remote or 'worst case' scenarios or 'stress tests'.

(d) entities are required to disclose only the effects of the changes at the limits of the reasonably possible range of the relevant risk variable, rather than all reasonably possible changes.

(e) the time frame for which entities should make an assessment about what is reasonably possible is the period until the entity next presents these disclosures, usually its next annual reporting period.

The Board also decided to add a simple example of what a sensitivity analysis might look like.

Operational risk

BC65 The Board discussed whether it should require disclosure of information about operational risk. However, the Board noted that the definition and measurement of operational risk are in their infancy and are not necessarily related to financial instruments. It also decided that such disclosures would be more appropriately located outside the financial statements. Therefore, the Board decided to defer this issue to its research project on management commentary.

Effective date and transition (paragraphs 43 and 44)

BC66 The Board is committed to maintaining a 'stable platform' of substantially unchanged Standards for annual periods beginning on or before 1 January 2005, when many entities will adopt IFRSs for the first time. In addition, some preparers will need time to make the system changes necessary to comply with the IFRS. Therefore, the Board decided that the effective date of IFRS 7 should be annual periods beginning on or after 1 January 2007, with earlier application encouraged.

BC67 The Board noted that entities that apply IFRS 7 only when it becomes mandatory will have sufficient time to prepare comparative information. This conclusion does not apply to entities that apply IFRS 7 early. In particular, the time would be extremely short for those entities that would like to apply IFRS 7 when they first adopt IFRSs in 2005, to avoid changing from local GAAP to IAS 32 and IAS 30 when they adopt IFRSs and then changing again to IFRS 7 only one or two years later. Therefore, the Board gave an exemption from providing comparative disclosure in the first year of application of IFRS 7 to any entity that both (a) is a first-time adopter of IFRSs and (b) applies IFRS 7 before 1 January 2006. The Board noted that such an exemption for first-time adopters exists in IAS 32 and IFRS 4 and that the reasons for providing the exemption apply equally to IFRS 7.

BC68 The Board also considered whether it should provide an exemption from presenting all or some of the comparative information to encourage early adoption of IFRS 7 by entities that already apply IFRSs.

BC69 The Board noted that IFRS 7 contains two types of disclosures: accounting disclosures (in paragraphs 7–30) that are based on requirements previously in IAS 32 and new risk disclosures (in paragraphs 31–42). The Board concluded that existing users of IFRSs already will have complied with the requirements of IAS 32 and will not encounter difficulty in providing comparative information for the accounting disclosures.

BC70 The Board noted that most of the risk disclosures, in particular those about market risk, are based on information collected at the end of the reporting period. The Board concluded that although IFRS 7 was published in August 2005, it will still be possible for entities to collect the information that they require to comply with IFRS 7 for accounting periods beginning in 2005. However, it would not always be possible to collect the information needed to provide comparative information about accounting periods that began in 2004. As a result, the Board decided that entities that apply IFRS 7 for accounting periods beginning in 2005 (ie before 1 January 2006) need not present comparative information about the risk disclosures.

BC71 The Board also noted that comparative disclosures about risk are less relevant because these disclosures are intended to have predictive value. As a result information about risk loses relevance more quickly than other types of disclosure, and any disclosures required by previous GAAP are unlikely to be comparable with those required by IFRS 7. Accordingly, the Board decided that an entity that is not a first-time adopter and applies IFRS 7 for annual periods beginning before 1 January 2006 need not present comparative disclosures about the nature and extent of risks arising from financial instruments. In reaching this conclusion, the Board noted that the advantages of encouraging more entities to apply IFRS 7 early outweighed the disadvantage of the reduced information provided.

BC72 The Board considered and rejected arguments that it should extend the exemption:

(a) from providing comparative information to first-time adopters that applied IFRS 7 before 1 January 2007 (rather than only those that applied IFRS 7 before 1 January 2006). The Board concluded that an entity that intends to adopt IFRSs for the first time on or after 1 January 2006 will have sufficient time to collect information for its accounting period beginning on or after 1 January 2005 and, thus, should not have difficulty in providing the comparative disclosures for accounting periods beginning on or after 1 January 2006.

(b) from providing comparative disclosures about the significance of financial instruments to all entities adopting the IFRS for annual periods beginning before 1 January 2006 (rather than only to first-time adopters). The Board concluded that only first-time adopters warranted special relief so that they would be able to adopt IFRS 7 early without first having to adopt IAS 32 and IAS 30 for only one period. Entities that are not first-time adopters already apply IAS 32 and IAS 30 and have no particular need to adopt IFRS 7 before 1 January 2007.

(c) from providing comparative disclosures about risk to periods beginning before 1 January 2007 (rather than 2006). The Board noted that entities adopting IFRS 7 after 1 January 2006 would have a full calendar year to prepare after the publication of the IFRS.

Summary of main changes from the Exposure Draft

BC73 The main changes to the proposals in ED 7 are:

(a) ED 7 proposed disclosure of the amount of change in the fair value of a financial liability designated as at fair value through profit or loss that is not attributable to changes in a benchmark interest rate as a proxy for the amount of change in fair value attributable to changes in the instrument's credit risk. The IFRS permits entities to determine the amount of change in fair value attributable to changes in the instrument's credit risk using an alternative method if the entity believes that its alternative method gives more faithful representation. The proxy disclosure has been amended to be the amount of change in fair value that is not attributable to changes in market conditions that give rise to market risk. As a result, entities may exclude factors other than a change in a benchmark interest rate when calculating the proxy.

(b) a requirement has been added for disclosures about the difference between the transaction price at initial recognition (used as fair value in accordance with paragraph AG76 of IAS 39) and the results of a valuation technique that will be used for subsequent measurement.

(c)   no disclosure is required of the fair value of collateral pledged as security and other credit enhancements as was proposed in ED 7.

(d)   the sensitivity analysis requirements have been clarified.

(e)   the exemption from presenting comparatives has been widened.

(f)   the capital disclosures are a stand-alone amendment to IAS 1, rather than part of the IFRS. No disclosure is required of whether the entity has complied with capital targets set by management and of the consequences of any non-compliance with those targets.

(g)   the amendments to IFRS 4 related to IFRS 7 have been modified to reduce systems changes for insurers.

Appendix
Amendments to Basis for Conclusions on other IFRSs

This appendix contains amendments to the Basis for Conclusions on other IFRSs that are necessary in order to ensure consistency with IFRS 7. In the amended paragraphs, new text is underlined and deleted text is struck through.

* * * * *

The amendments contained in this appendix when IFRS 7 was issued in 2005 have been incorporated into the text of the Basis of Conclusions on IFRS 4 and on IASs 32, 39 and 41 as issued at 18 August 2005.

CONTENTS

Guidance on implementing
IFRS 7 *Financial Instruments: Disclosures*

This guidance accompanies, but is not part of, IFRS 7.

Introduction

IG1   This guidance suggests possible ways to apply some of the disclosure requirements in IFRS 7. The guidance does not create additional requirements.

IG2   For convenience, each disclosure requirement in the IFRS is discussed separately. In practice, disclosures would normally be presented as an integrated package and individual disclosures might satisfy more than one requirement. For example, information about concentrations of risk might also convey information about exposure to credit or other risk.

Materiality

IG3   IAS 1 *Presentation of Financial Statements* notes that a specific disclosure requirement in an IFRS need not be satisfied if the information is not material. IAS 1 defines materiality as follows:

> Omissions or misstatements of items are material if they could, individually or collectively, influence the economic decisions that users make on the basis of the financial statements. Materiality depends on the size and nature of the omission or misstatement judged in the surrounding circumstances. The size or nature of the item, or a combination of both, could be the determining factor.

IG4   IAS 1 also explains that definition as follows:

> Assessing whether an omission or misstatement could influence economic decisions of users, and so be material, requires consideration of the characteristics of those users. The *Framework for the Preparation and Presentation of Financial Statements* states in paragraph 25 that 'users are assumed to have a reasonable knowledge of business and economic activities and accounting and a willingness to study the information with reasonable diligence.' Therefore, the assessment needs to take into account how users with such attributes could reasonably be expected to be influenced in making economic decisions.

Classes of financial instruments and level of disclosure (paragraphs 6 and B1–B3)

IG5   Paragraph B3 states that 'an entity decides in the light of its circumstances how much detail it provides to satisfy the requirements of this IFRS, how much emphasis it places on different aspects of the requirements and how it aggregates information to display the overall picture without combining information with different characteristics.' To satisfy the requirements, an entity may not need to disclose all the information suggested in this guidance.

IG6   Paragraph 17(c) of IAS 1 requires an entity to 'provide additional disclosures when compliance with the specific requirements in IFRSs is insufficient to enable users to understand the impact of particular transactions, other events and conditions on the entity's financial position and financial performance.'

© IASCF

Significance of financial instruments for financial position and performance (paragraphs 7–30, B4 and B5)

Financial liabilities at fair value through profit or loss (paragraphs 10(a)(i) and B4)

IG7   The following example illustrates the calculation that an entity might perform in accordance with paragraph B4 of Appendix B of the IFRS.

IG8   On 1 January 20X1, an entity issues a 10-year bond with a par value of CU150,000* and an annual fixed coupon rate of 8 per cent, which is consistent with market rates for bonds with similar characteristics.

IG9   The entity uses LIBOR as its observable (benchmark) interest rate. At the date of inception of the bond, LIBOR is 5 per cent. At the end of the first year:

(a)   LIBOR has decreased to 4.75 per cent.

(b)   the fair value for the bond is CU153,811, consistent with an interest rate of 7.6 per cent.[†]

IG10   The entity assumes a flat yield curve, all changes in interest rates result from a parallel shift in the yield curve, and the changes in LIBOR are the only relevant changes in market conditions.

IG11   The entity estimates the amount of change in the fair value of the bond that is not attributable to changes in market conditions that give rise to market risk as follows:

[paragraph B4(a)]	
First, the entity computes the liability's internal rate of return at the start of the period using the observed market price of the liability and the liability's contractual cash flows at the start of the period. It deducts from this rate of return the observed (benchmark) interest rate at the start of the period, to arrive at an instrument-specific component of the internal rate of return.	At the start of the period of a 10-year bond with a coupon of 8 per cent, the bond's internal rate of return is 8 per cent. Because the observed (benchmark) interest rate (LIBOR) is 5 per cent, the instrument-specific component of the internal rate of return is 3 per cent.

continued...

---

*   In this guidance monetary amounts are denominated in 'currency units (CU)'.

†   This reflects a shift in LIBOR from 5 per cent to 4.75 per cent and a movement of 0.15 per cent which, in the absence of other relevant changes in market conditions, is assumed to reflect changes in credit risk of the instrument.

...continued	
[paragraph B4(b)]	
Next, the entity calculates the present value of the cash flows associated with the liability using the liability's contractual cash flows at the end of the period and a discount rate equal to the sum of (i) the observed (benchmark) interest rate at the end of the period and (ii) the instrument-specific component of the internal rate of return as determined in accordance with paragraph B4(a).	The contractual cash flows of the instrument at the end of the period are: • interest: CU12,000[a] per year for each of years 2–10. • principal: CU150,000 in year 10. The discount rate to be used to calculate the present value of the bond is thus 7.75 per cent, which is 4.75 per cent end of period LIBOR rate, plus the 3 per cent instrument-specific component. This gives a present value of CU152,367.[b]
[paragraph B4(c)]	
The difference between the observed market price of the liability at the end of the period and the amount determined in accordance with paragraph B4(b) is the change in fair value that is not attributable to changes in the observed (benchmark) interest rate. This is the amount to be disclosed.	The market price of the liability at the end of the period is CU153,811.[c] Thus, the entity discloses CU1,444, which is CU153,811 − CU152,367, as the increase in fair value of the bond that is not attributable to changes in market conditions that give rise to market risk.
(a) CU150,000 × 8% = CU12,000 (b) $PV = [CU12,000 \times (1 - (1 + 0.0775)^{-9})/0.0775] + CU150,000 \times (1 + 0.0775)^{-9}$ (c) market price $= [CU12,000 \times (1 - (1 + 0.076)^{-9})/0.076] + CU150,000 \times (1 + 0.076)^{-9}$	

Defaults and breaches (paragraphs 18 and 19)

IG12   Paragraphs 18 and 19 require disclosures when there are any defaults or breaches of loans payable. Any defaults or breaches may affect the classification of the liability as current or non-current in accordance with IAS 1.

Total interest expense (paragraph 20(b))*

IG13   Total interest expense disclosed in accordance with paragraph 20(b) is a component of finance costs, which paragraph 82(b) of IAS 1 requires to be presented separately in the statement of comprehensive income. The line item for finance costs may also include amounts associated with non-financial liabilities.

Fair value (paragraphs 27–28)

IG13A   IFRS 7 requires disclosures about the level in the fair value hierarchy in which fair value measurements are categorised for assets and liabilities measured in the statement of financial position. A tabular format is required unless another format is more appropriate. An entity might disclose the following for assets to comply with paragraph 27B(a). (Disclosure of comparative information is also required, but is not included in the following example.)

Assets measured at fair value				
		Fair value measurement at end of the reporting period using:		
		Level 1	Level 2	Level 3
Description	31 Dec 20X2	CU million	CU million	CU million
Financial assets at fair value through profit or loss				
Trading securities	100	40	55	5
Trading derivatives	39	17	20	2
Financial assets at fair value through comprehensive income				
Equity investments	75	30	40	5
Total	214	87	115	12

(Note: For liabilities, a similar table might be presented.)

---

*   In *Improvements to IFRSs* issued in May 2008, the Board amended paragraph IG13 and removed 'total interest income' as a component of finance costs. This amendment removed an inconsistency with paragraph 32 of IAS 1 *Presentation of Financial Statements*, which precludes the offsetting of income and expenses (except when required or permitted by an IFRS).

IG13B   IFRS 7 requires a reconciliation from beginning to ending balances for those assets and liabilities that are measured in the statement of financial position at fair value based on a valuation technique for which any significant input is not based on observable market data (Level 3). A tabular format is required unless another format is more appropriate. An entity might disclose the following for assets to comply with paragraph 27B(c). (Disclosure of comparative information is also required, but is not included in the following example.)

Assets measured at fair value based on Level 3

	Fair value measurement at the end of the reporting period			
	Financial assets at fair value			Total
	Trading securities	Trading derivatives	Equity investments	
	CU million	CU million	CU million	CU million
Opening balance	6	5	3	14
Total gains or losses				
in profit or loss	(2)	(2)	–	(4)
in other comprehensive income	–	–	1	1
Purchases	1	2	1	4
Issues	–	–	–	–
Settlements	–	(1)	–	(1)
Transfers out of Level 3	–	(2)	–	(2)
Closing balance	5	2	5	12
Total gains or losses for the period included in profit or loss for assets held at the end of the reporting period	(1)	(1)	–	(2)

Gains or losses included in profit or loss for the period (above) are presented in trading income and in other income as follows:

	Trading income
Total gains or losses included in profit or loss for the period	(4)
Total gains or losses for the period included in profit or loss for assets held at the end of the reporting period	(2)

(Note: For liabilities, a similar table might be presented.)

IG14   The fair value at initial recognition of financial instruments that are not traded in active markets is determined in accordance with paragraph AG76 of IAS 39. However, when, after initial recognition, an entity will use a valuation technique that incorporates data not obtained from observable markets, there may be a difference between the transaction price at initial recognition and the amount determined at initial recognition using that valuation technique. In these circumstances, the difference will be recognised in profit or loss in subsequent periods in accordance with IAS 39 (for financial liabilities) or IFRS 9 (for financial assets) and the entity's accounting policy. Such recognition reflects changes in factors (including time) that market participants would consider in setting a price (see paragraph AG76A of IAS 39). Paragraph 28 requires disclosures in these circumstances. An entity might disclose the following to comply with paragraph 28:

Background

On 1 January 20X1 an entity purchases for CU15 million financial assets that are not traded in an active market. The entity has only one class of such financial assets.

The transaction price of CU15 million is the fair value at initial recognition.

After initial recognition, the entity will apply a valuation technique to establish the financial assets' fair value. This valuation technique includes variables other than data from observable markets.

At initial recognition, the same valuation technique would have resulted in an amount of CU14 million, which differs from fair value by CU1 million.

The entity has existing differences of CU5 million at 1 January 20X1.

Application of requirements

The entity's 20X2 disclosure would include the following:

Accounting policies

The entity uses the following valuation technique to determine the fair value of financial instruments that are not traded in an active market: [description of technique, not included in this example]. Differences may arise between the fair value at initial recognition (which, in accordance with IFRS 9, is generally the transaction price) and the amount determined at initial recognition using the valuation technique. Any such differences are [description of the entity's accounting policy].

In the notes to the financial statements

As discussed in note X, the entity uses [name of valuation technique] to measure the fair value of the following financial instruments that are not traded in an active market. However, in accordance with IFRS 9, the fair value of an instrument at inception is generally the transaction price. If the transaction price differs from the amount determined at inception using the valuation technique, that difference is [description of the entity's accounting policy].

continued...

...continued The differences yet to be recognised in profit or loss are as follows:	31 Dec X2 CU million	31 Dec X1 CU million
Balance at beginning of year	5.3	5.0
New transactions	–	1.0
Amounts recognised in profit or loss during the year	(0.7)	(0.8)
Other increases	–	0.2
Other decreases	(0.1)	(0.1)
Balance at end of year	4.5	5.3

Nature and extent of risks arising from financial instruments (paragraphs 31–42 and B6–B28)

Qualitative disclosures (paragraph 33)

IG15   The type of qualitative information an entity might disclose to meet the requirements in paragraph 33 includes, but is not limited to, a narrative description of:

(a)   the entity's exposures to risk and how they arose. Information about risk exposures might describe exposures both gross and net of risk transfer and other risk-mitigating transactions.

(b)   the entity's policies and processes for accepting, measuring, monitoring and controlling risk, which might include:

(i)   the structure and organisation of the entity's risk management function(s), including a discussion of independence and accountability;

(ii)   the scope and nature of the entity's risk reporting or measurement systems;

(iii)   the entity's policies for hedging or mitigating risk, including its policies and procedures for taking collateral; and

(iv)   the entity's processes for monitoring the continuing effectiveness of such hedges or mitigating devices.

(c)   the entity's policies and procedures for avoiding excessive concentrations of risk.

IG16   Information about the nature and extent of risks arising from financial instruments is more useful if it highlights any relationship between financial instruments that can affect the amount, timing or uncertainty of an entity's future cash flows. The extent to which a risk exposure is altered by such relationships might be apparent to users from the disclosures required by this Standard, but in some cases further disclosures might be useful.

IG17   In accordance with paragraph 33(c), entities disclose any change in the qualitative information from the previous period and explain the reasons for the change. Such changes may result from changes in exposure to risk or from changes in the way those exposures are managed.

Quantitative disclosures (paragraphs 34–42 and B7–B28)

IG18   Paragraph 34 requires disclosure of quantitative data about concentrations of risk. For example, concentrations of credit risk may arise from:

(a)   industry sectors. Thus, if an entity's counterparties are concentrated in one or more industry sectors (such as retail or wholesale), it would disclose separately exposure to risks arising from each concentration of counterparties.

(b)   credit rating or other measure of credit quality. Thus, if an entity's counterparties are concentrated in one or more credit qualities (such as secured loans or unsecured loans) or in one or more credit ratings (such as investment grade or speculative grade), it would disclose separately exposure to risks arising from each concentration of counterparties.

(c)   geographical distribution. Thus, if an entity's counterparties are concentrated in one or more geographical markets (such as Asia or Europe), it would disclose separately exposure to risks arising from each concentration of counterparties.

(d)   a limited number of individual counterparties or groups of closely related counterparties.

Similar principles apply to identifying concentrations of other risks, including liquidity risk and market risk. For example, concentrations of liquidity risk may arise from the repayment terms of financial liabilities, sources of borrowing facilities or reliance on a particular market in which to realise liquid assets. Concentrations of foreign exchange risk may arise if an entity has a significant net open position in a single foreign currency, or aggregate net open positions in several currencies that tend to move together.

IG19   In accordance with paragraph B8, disclosure of concentrations of risk includes a description of the shared characteristic that identifies each concentration. For example, the shared characteristic may refer to geographical distribution of counterparties by groups of countries, individual countries or regions within countries.

IG20   When quantitative information at the end of the reporting period is unrepresentative of the entity's exposure to risk during the period, paragraph 35 requires further disclosure. To meet this requirement, an entity might disclose the highest, lowest and average amount of risk to which it was exposed during the period. For example, if an entity typically has a large exposure to a particular currency, but at year-end unwinds the position, the entity might disclose a graph that shows the exposure at various times during the period, or disclose the highest, lowest and average exposures.

Credit risk (paragraphs 36–38, B9 and B10)

IG21 Paragraph 36 requires an entity to disclose information about its exposure to credit risk by class of financial instrument. Financial instruments in the same class share economic characteristics with respect to the risk being disclosed (in this case, credit risk). For example, an entity might determine that residential mortgages, unsecured consumer loans, and commercial loans each have different economic characteristics.

Collateral and other credit enhancements pledged (paragraph 36(b))

IG22 Paragraph 36(b) requires an entity to describe collateral available as security for assets it holds and other credit enhancements obtained. An entity might meet this requirement by disclosing:

(a) the policies and processes for valuing and managing collateral and other credit enhancements obtained;

(b) a description of the main types of collateral and other credit enhancements (examples of the latter being guarantees, credit derivatives, and netting agreements that do not qualify for offset in accordance with IAS 32);

(c) the main types of counterparties to collateral and other credit enhancements and their creditworthiness; and

(d) information about risk concentrations within the collateral or other credit enhancements.

Credit quality (paragraph 36(c))

IG23 Paragraph 36(c) requires an entity to disclose information about the credit quality of financial assets with credit risk that are neither past due nor impaired. In doing so, an entity might disclose the following information:

(a) an analysis of credit exposures using an external or internal credit grading system;

(b) the nature of the counterparty;

(c) historical information about counterparty default rates; and

(d) any other information used to assess credit quality.

IG24 When the entity considers external ratings when managing and monitoring credit quality, the entity might disclose information about:

(a) the amounts of credit exposures for each external credit grade;

(b) the rating agencies used;

(c) the amount of an entity's rated and unrated credit exposures; and

(d) the relationship between internal and external ratings.

IG25   When the entity considers internal credit ratings when managing and monitoring credit quality, the entity might disclose information about:

(a)   the internal credit ratings process;

(b)   the amounts of credit exposures for each internal credit grade; and

(c)   the relationship between internal and external ratings.

Financial assets that are either past due or impaired (paragraph 37)

IG26   A financial asset is past due when the counterparty has failed to make a payment when contractually due. As an example, an entity enters into a lending agreement that requires interest to be paid every month. On the first day of the next month, if interest has not been paid, the loan is past due. Past due does not mean that a counterparty will never pay, but it can trigger various actions such as renegotiation, enforcement of covenants, or legal proceedings.

IG27   When the terms and conditions of financial assets that have been classified as past due are renegotiated, the terms and conditions of the new contractual arrangement apply in determining whether the financial asset remains past due.

IG28   Paragraph 37(a) requires an analysis by class of the age of financial assets that are past due but not impaired. An entity uses its judgement to determine an appropriate number of time bands. For example, an entity might determine that the following time bands are appropriate:

(a)   not more than three months;

(b)   more than three months and not more than six months;

(c)   more than six months and not more than one year; and

(d)   more than one year.

IG29   Paragraph 37(b) requires an analysis of impaired financial assets by class. This analysis might include:

(a)   the carrying amount, before deducting any impairment loss;

(b)   the amount of any related impairment loss; and

(c)   the nature and fair value of collateral available and other credit enhancements obtained.

IG30–   [Deleted]
IG31

Market risk (paragraphs 40–42 and B17–B28)

IG32   Paragraph 40(a) requires a sensitivity analysis for each type of market risk to which the entity is exposed. There are three types of market risk: interest rate risk, currency risk and other price risk. Other price risk may include risks such as equity price risk, commodity price risk, prepayment risk (ie the risk that one party to a financial asset will incur a financial loss because the other party repays earlier or later than expected), and residual value risk (eg a lessor of motor cars that writes residual value guarantees is exposed to residual value risk). Risk variables that are relevant to disclosing market risk include, but are not limited to:

(a) the yield curve of market interest rates. It may be necessary to consider both parallel and non-parallel shifts in the yield curve.

(b) foreign exchange rates.

(c) prices of equity instruments.

(d) market prices of commodities.

IG33 Paragraph 40(a) requires the sensitivity analysis to show the effect on profit or loss and equity of reasonably possible changes in the relevant risk variable. For example, relevant risk variables might include:

(a) prevailing market interest rates, for interest-sensitive financial instruments such as a variable-rate loan; or

(b) currency rates and interest rates, for foreign currency financial instruments such as foreign currency bonds.

IG34 For interest rate risk, the sensitivity analysis might show separately the effect of a change in market interest rates on:

(a) interest income and expense;

(b) other line items of profit or loss (such as trading gains and losses); and

(c) when applicable, equity.

An entity might disclose a sensitivity analysis for interest rate risk for each currency in which the entity has material exposures to interest rate risk.

IG35 Because the factors affecting market risk vary depending on the specific circumstances of each entity, the appropriate range to be considered in providing a sensitivity analysis of market risk varies for each entity and for each type of market risk.

IG36 The following example illustrates the application of the disclosure requirement in paragraph 40(a):

Interest rate risk

At 31 December 20X2, if interest rates at that date had been 10 basis points lower with all other variables held constant, post-tax profit for the year would have been CU1.7 million (20X1—CU2.4 million) higher, arising mainly as a result of lower interest expense on variable borrowings. If interest rates had been 10 basis points higher, with all other variables held constant, post-tax profit would have been CU1.5 million (20X1—CU2.1 million) lower, arising mainly as a result of higher interest expense on variable borrowings. Profit is more sensitive to interest rate decreases than increases because of borrowings with capped interest rates. The sensitivity is lower in 20X2 than in 20X1 because of a reduction in outstanding borrowings that has occurred as the entity's debt has matured (see note X).[a]

Foreign currency exchange rate risk

At 31 December 20X2, if the CU had weakened 10 per cent against the US dollar with all other variables held constant, post-tax profit for the year would have been CU2.8 million (20X1—CU6.4 million) lower, and other comprehensive income would have been CU1.2 million (20X1—CU1.1 million) higher. Conversely, if the CU had strengthened 10 per cent against the US dollar with all other variables held constant, post-tax profit would have been CU2.8 million (20X1—CU6.4 million) higher, and other comprehensive income would have been CU1.2 million (20X1—CU1.1 million) lower. The lower foreign currency exchange rate sensitivity in profit in 20X2 compared with 20X1 is attributable to a reduction in foreign currency denominated debt. Equity is more sensitive in 20X2 than in 20X1 because of the increased use of hedges of foreign currency purchases, offset by the reduction in foreign currency debt.

(a) Paragraph 39(a) requires disclosure of a maturity analysis of liabilities.

Other market risk disclosures (paragraph 42)

IG37 Paragraph 42 requires the disclosure of additional information when the sensitivity analysis disclosed is unrepresentative of a risk inherent in a financial instrument. For example, this can occur when:

(a) a financial instrument contains terms and conditions whose effects are not apparent from the sensitivity analysis, eg options that remain out of (or in) the money for the chosen change in the risk variable;

(b) financial assets are illiquid, eg when there is a low volume of transactions in similar assets and an entity finds it difficult to find a counterparty; or

(c) an entity has a large holding of a financial asset that, if sold in its entirety, would be sold at a discount or premium to the quoted market price for a smaller holding.

IG38 In the situation in paragraph IG37(a), additional disclosure might include:

(a) the terms and conditions of the financial instrument (eg the options);

(b)   the effect on profit or loss if the term or condition were met (ie if the options were exercised); and

(c)   a description of how the risk is hedged.

For example, an entity may acquire a zero-cost interest rate collar that includes an out-of-the-money leveraged written option (eg the entity pays ten times the amount of the difference between a specified interest rate floor and the current market interest rate). The entity may regard the collar as an inexpensive economic hedge against a reasonably possible increase in interest rates. However, an unexpectedly large decrease in interest rates might trigger payments under the written option that, because of the leverage, might be significantly larger than the benefit of lower interest rates. Neither the fair value of the collar nor a sensitivity analysis based on reasonably possible changes in market variables would indicate this exposure. In this case, the entity might provide the additional information described above.

IG39   In the situation described in paragraph IG37(b), additional disclosure might include the reasons for the lack of liquidity and how the entity hedges the risk.

IG40   In the situation described in paragraph IG37(c), additional disclosure might include:

(a)   the nature of the security (eg entity name);

(b)   the extent of holding (eg 15 per cent of the issued shares);

(c)   the effect on profit or loss; and

(d)   how the entity hedges the risk.

Transition (paragraph 44)

IG41   The following table summarises the effect of the exemption from presenting comparative accounting and risk disclosures for accounting periods beginning before 1 January 2006, before 1 January 2007, and on or after 1 January 2007. In this table:

(a)   a **first-time adopter** is an entity preparing its first IFRS financial statements (see IFRS 1 *First-time Adoption of International Financial Reporting Standards*).

(b)   an **existing IFRS user** is an entity preparing its second or subsequent IFRS financial statements.

	Accounting disclosures (paragraphs 7–30)	Risk disclosures (paragraphs 31–42)
Accounting periods beginning before 1 January 2006		
First-time adopter not applying IFRS 7 early	*Applies IAS 32 but exempt from providing IAS 32 comparative information*	*Applies IAS 32 but exempt from providing IAS 32 comparative information*
First-time adopter applying IFRS 7 early	**Exempt from presenting IFRS 7 comparative information**	**Exempt from presenting IFRS 7 comparative information**
Existing IFRS user not applying IFRS 7 early	Applies IAS 32. Provides full IAS 32 comparative information	Applies IAS 32. Provides full IAS 32 comparative information
Existing IFRS user applying IFRS 7 early	Provides full IFRS 7 comparative information	**Exempt from presenting IFRS 7 comparative information**[(a)]
Accounting periods beginning on or after 1 January 2006 and before 1 January 2007		
First-time adopter not applying IFRS 7 early	Applies IAS 32. Provides full IAS 32 comparative information	Applies IAS 32. Provides full IAS 32 comparative information
First-time adopter applying IFRS 7 early	Provides full IFRS 7 comparative information	Provides full IFRS 7 comparative information
Existing IFRS user not applying IFRS 7 early	Applies IAS 32. Provides full IAS 32 comparative information	Applies IAS 32. Provides full IAS 32 comparative information
Existing IFRS user applying IFRS 7 early	Provides full IFRS 7 comparative information	Provides full IFRS 7 comparative information
Accounting periods beginning on or after 1 January 2007 (mandatory application of IFRS 7)		
First-time adopter	Provides full IFRS 7 comparative information	Provides full IFRS 7 comparative information
Existing IFRS user	Provides full IFRS 7 comparative information	Provides full IFRS 7 comparative information
(a) See paragraph 44 of IFRS 7		

Appendix
Amendments to guidance on other IFRSs

This appendix contains amendments to guidance on IFRSs other than IFRS 4 that are necessary in order to ensure consistency with IFRS 7. Amendments to the Guidance on Implementing IFRS 4 will be published at a later date. In the amended paragraphs, new text is underlined and deleted text is struck through.

* * * * *

The amendments contained in this appendix when IFRS 7 was issued in 2005 have been incorporated into the text of the Guidance on Implementing IAS 39 as issued at 18 August 2005. The revised Guidance on Implementing IFRS 4 was published in December 2005.

IASB documents published to accompany

International Financial Reporting Standard 8

Operating Segments

This version includes amendments resulting from IFRSs issued up to 31 December 2009.

The text of the unaccompanied IFRS 8 is contained in Part A of this edition. Its effective date when issued was 1 January 2009. The effective date of the most recent amendment is 1 January 2011. This part presents the following accompanying documents:

Approval by the Board of IFRS 8 issued in November 2006

International Financial Reporting Standard 8 *Operating Segments* was approved for issue by eleven of the thirteen members of the International Accounting Standards Board. Messrs Gélard and Leisenring dissented. Their dissenting opinions are set out after the Basis for Conclusions.

Sir David Tweedie	Chairman
Thomas E Jones	Vice-Chairman
Mary E Barth	
Hans-Georg Bruns	
Anthony T Cope	
Jan Engström	
Robert P Garnett	
Gilbert Gélard	
James J Leisenring	
Warren J McGregor	
Patricia L O'Malley	
John T Smith	
Tatsumi Yamada	

CONTENTS

Basis for Conclusions on
IFRS 8 *Operating Segments*

This Basis for Conclusions and its appendices accompany, but are not part of, IFRS 8.

Introduction

BC1 This Basis for Conclusions summarises the International Accounting Standards Board's considerations in reaching the conclusions in IFRS 8 *Operating Segments*. Individual Board members gave greater weight to some factors than to others.

BC2 In September 2002 the Board decided to add a short-term convergence project to its active agenda. The project is being conducted jointly with the United States standard-setter, the Financial Accounting Standards Board (FASB). The objective of the project is to reduce differences between IFRSs and US generally accepted accounting principles (US GAAP) that are capable of resolution in a relatively short time and can be addressed outside major projects.

BC3 As part of the project, the Board identified differences between IAS 14 *Segment Reporting* and the US standard SFAS 131 *Disclosures about Segments of an Enterprise and Related Information*, reviewed academic research findings on segment reporting, in particular relating to the implementation of SFAS 131, and had meetings with users of financial statements.

Differences between IAS 14 and SFAS 131

BC4 The requirements of SFAS 131 are based on the way that management regards an entity, focusing on information about the components of the business that management uses to make decisions about operating matters. In contrast, IAS 14 requires the disaggregation of the entity's financial statements into segments based on related products and services, and on geographical areas.

BC5 The requirements of SFAS 14 *Financial Reporting for Segments of a Business Enterprise*, the predecessor to SFAS 131, were similar to those of IAS 14. In particular, both standards required the accounting policies underlying the disaggregated information to be the same as those underlying the entity information, since segment information was regarded as a disaggregation of the entity information. The approach to segment disclosures in SFAS 14 was criticised for not providing information about segments based on the structure of an entity's internal organisation that could enhance a user's ability to predict actions or reactions of management that could significantly affect the entity's future cash flow prospects.

Academic research findings

BC6 Most of the academic research findings on segment reporting indicated that application of SFAS 131 resulted in more useful information than its predecessor, SFAS 14. According to the research, the management approach of SFAS 131:

(a) increased the number of reported segments and provided more information;

(b)   enabled users to see an entity through the eyes of management;

(c)   enabled an entity to provide timely segment information for external interim reporting with relatively low incremental cost;

(d)   enhanced consistency with the management discussion and analysis or other annual report disclosures; and

(e)   provided various measures of segment performance.

Meetings with users

BC7   The Board discussed segment reporting at several meetings with users of financial statements. Most of the users supported the management approach of SFAS 131 for the reasons mentioned in the previous paragraph. In particular, they supported an approach that would enable more segment information to be provided in interim financial reports.

BC8   Consequently the Board decided to adopt the US approach and published its proposals as an exposure draft in ED 8 *Operating Segments* in January 2006. The deadline for comments was 19 May 2006. The Board received 182 comment letters. After reviewing the responses, the Board issued IFRS 8 in November 2006.

Adoption of management approach

BC9   In the Basis for Conclusions on ED 8, the Board noted that the primary benefits of adopting the management approach in SFAS 131 are that:

(a)   entities will report segments that correspond to internal management reports;

(b)   entities will report segment information that will be more consistent with other parts of their annual reports;

(c)   some entities will report more segments; and

(d)   entities will report more segment information in interim financial reports.

In addition, the Board noted that the proposed IFRS would reduce the cost of providing disaggregated information for many entities because it uses segment information that is generated for management's use.

BC10   Most respondents to the Exposure Draft supported the adoption of the management approach. They considered the management approach appropriate, and superior to the approach of IAS 14. These respondents observed that the management approach for segment reporting allows users to review an entity's operations from the same perspective as management. They noted that although the IAS 14 approach would enhance comparability by requiring entities to report segment information that is consistent with IFRSs, the disclosures will not necessarily correspond to segment information that is reported to management and is used for making decisions.

BC11   Other respondents disagreed with the management approach. They argued that convergence should instead be achieved by changing SFAS 131 to IAS 14. In their view the latter approach is superior because it provides comparability of information across entities by defining measures of segment revenue, segment expense, segment result, segment assets and segment liabilities.

BC12   Yet other respondents agreed with the management approach for the identification of segment assets, but disagreed with the management approach for the measurement of the various segment disclosures. In particular, they doubted whether the publication of internally reported amounts would generate significant benefit for investors if those amounts differ from IFRS amounts.

BC13   The Board noted that if IFRS amounts could be prepared reliably and on a timely basis for segments identified using the management approach, that approach would provide the most useful information. However, the Board observed that IFRS amounts for segments cannot always be prepared on a sufficiently timely basis for interim reporting.

BC14   The Board also noted the requirements in the IFRS for an explanation of the measurements of segment profit or loss and segment assets and for reconciliations of the segment amounts to the amounts recognised in the entity's financial statements. The Board was satisfied that users would be able to understand and judge appropriately the basis on which the segment amounts were determined.

BC15   The Board concluded that the advantages of the management approach, in particular the ability of entities to prepare segment information on a sufficiently timely basis for inclusion in interim financial reports, outweighed any disadvantages arising from the potential for segments to be reported in accordance with non-IFRS accounting policies.

BC16   Given the Board's support for the principles of the management approach required by SFAS 131 and the objectives of the short-term convergence project, the Board decided that the simplest and most complete way to achieve convergence would be to use the text of SFAS 131 for the IFRS.

BC17   The FASB's thinking behind the management approach of SFAS 131 is presented in its Background Information and Basis for Conclusions. Because the Board has adopted that approach, the FASB's Background Information and Basis for Conclusions are reproduced in Appendix A to this Basis for Conclusions. The few differences from SFAS 131 that the Board has included in the IFRS are noted in paragraph BC60 below.

Scope of the standard

BC18   In ED 8, the Board proposed extending the scope of the IFRS to all entities that have public accountability rather than just entities whose securities are publicly traded. The Board noted that it was premature to adopt the proposed definition of public accountability that is being considered in a separate Board project on small and medium-sized entities (SMEs). However, the Board decided that the scope of the standard should be extended to include entities that hold assets in a fiduciary capacity for a broad group of outsiders. The Board concluded that the SMEs project is the most appropriate context in which to decide whether to extend the scope of the requirements on segment reporting to other entities.

BC19   Some respondents to ED 8 commented that the scope of the IFRS should not be extended until the Board has reached a conclusion on the definitions of 'fiduciary capacity' and 'public accountability' in the SMEs project. They argued that the terms needed clarification and definition.

BC20   The Board accepted these concerns and decided that the IFRS should not apply to entities that hold assets in a fiduciary capacity. However, the Board decided that publicly accountable entities should be within the scope of the IFRS, and that a future amendment of the scope of the IFRS should be proposed to include publicly accountable entities once the definition has been properly developed in the SMEs project. The proposed amendment will therefore be exposed at the same time as the exposure draft of the proposed IFRS for SMEs.

BC21   A number of respondents to ED 8 suggested that the scope exemption of paragraph 6 of IAS 14 should be included in the IFRS. This paragraph provided an exemption from segment reporting in the separate financial statements of the parent when a financial report contains both consolidated financial statements and the parent's separate financial statements. The Board agreed that on practical grounds such an exemption was appropriate.

BC22   In ED 8 the Board proposed that if an entity not required to apply the IFRS chooses to disclose segment information in financial statements that comply with IFRSs, that entity would be required to comply with the requirements of the IFRS. Respondents commented that this was unnecessarily restrictive. For example, they observed that requiring full compliance with the IFRS would prevent an entity outside its scope from voluntarily disclosing sales information for segments without also disclosing segment profit or loss. The Board concluded that an entity should be able to provide segment information on a voluntary basis without triggering the need to comply fully with the IFRS, so long as the disclosure is not referred to as segment information.

BC23   A respondent to ED 8 asked for clarification on whether the scope of the proposed IFRS included the consolidated financial statements of a group whose parent has no listed financial instruments, but includes a listed minority interest[*] or a subsidiary with listed debt. The Board decided that such consolidated financial statements should not be included in the scope and that the scope should be clarified accordingly. The Board also noted that the same clarification should be made to the scope of IAS 33 *Earnings per Share*.

---

[*]   In January 2008 the IASB issued an amended IAS 27 *Consolidated and Separate Financial Statements*, which amended 'minority interest' to 'non-controlling interests'.

Aspects of the management approach

Specific measurement requirements for some items

BC24 In ED 8, the Board invited comments on whether the proposed IFRS should depart from the management approach in SFAS 131 by setting measurement requirements for specified items. Some respondents to ED 8 supported an approach that would define the measurement of the key terms such as segment revenues, segment expenses, segment results, segment assets and segment liabilities in order to enhance comparability between reporting entities. Other respondents disagreed with any departure from SFAS 131 on the grounds that defined measurements for specified items would eliminate the major benefits of the management approach.

BC25 The IFRS requires the entity to explain the measurements of segment profit or loss and segment assets and liabilities and to provide reconciliations of the total segment amounts to the amounts recognised in the entity's financial statements. The Board believes that such reconciliations will enable users to understand and judge the basis on which the segment amounts were determined. The Board also noted that to define the measurement of such amounts would be a departure from the requirements of SFAS 131 that would involve additional time and cost for entities and would be inconsistent with the management perspective on segment information.

BC26 Therefore, the Board decided not to require defined measures of segment revenues, segment expenses, segment result, segment assets and segment liabilities.

Matrix form of organisations

BC27 In ED 8 the Board proposed that when more than one set of segments could be identified, for example when entities use a matrix form of organisation, the components based on products and services should be the basis for the operating segments. Some respondents noted that matrix organisational structures are commonly used for large complex organisations and that mandating the use of components based on products and services was inconsistent with the management approach. The Board agreed with this view. Accordingly, the IFRS requires the identification of operating segments to be made by reference to the core principle of the IFRS.

Quantitative thresholds

BC28 In ED 8 the Board proposed quantitative thresholds for identifying reportable segments. Some respondents argued that such requirements represent adoption of a rule-based, rather than a principle-based, approach. In addition, some respondents commented that the inclusion of a 10 per cent threshold could create a precedent for determining materiality in other areas.

BC29   The Board considered an approach whereby any material operating segment would be required to be disclosed separately. However, the Board was concerned that there might be uncertainty about the meaning of materiality in relation to disclosure. Furthermore, such a requirement would be a significant change from the wording of SFAS 131. Thus, the Board was concerned that the change would be from an easily understandable and familiar set of words that converges with SFAS 131 to a potentially confusing principle. Accordingly, the Board decided to retain the quantitative thresholds.

Interaction of aggregation criteria and quantitative thresholds

BC30   One respondent commented that the ranking of the aggregation criteria for operating segments and the quantitative thresholds for determining reportable segments was unclear in ED 8. However, the flow chart in paragraph IG7 of the implementation guidance indicates that the aggregation criteria take precedence over the quantitative thresholds. The Board also noted that the wording in SFAS 131 was clear because the paragraph on aggregation refers to aggregation into a 'single operating segment'. The quantitative thresholds then determine which operating segments are reportable segments. The term 'operating' has been inserted in paragraph 12 of the IFRS.

Inclusion of US guidance

BC31   The Board discussed the extent to which the IFRS should address the practical problems that have arisen from applying SFAS 131 in the US. The Board considered the FASB Q&A 131 Segment Information: Guidance on Applying Statement 131 and Emerging Issues Task Force (EITF) 04-10 Determining Whether to Aggregate Operating Segments that do not Meet the Quantitative Threshold.

BC32   EITF 04-10 addresses the issue of whether to aggregate operating segments that do not meet the quantitative thresholds. It requires quantitative thresholds to be aggregated only if aggregation is consistent with the objective and core principles of SFAS 131, the segments have similar economic characteristics, and the segments share a majority of the aggregation criteria listed in paragraph 17(a)–(e) of SFAS 131. The Board agreed with the approach adopted in EITF 04-10 and concluded that the same requirement should be included in the IFRS.

BC33   FASB Q&A 131—Segment Information: Guidance on Applying Statement 131 is an implementation guide that provides the views of the FASB staff on certain questions on SFAS 131. Because it was not issued by the FASB itself, the Board decided not to include this material in the IFRS.

Information about segment assets

BC34   Several respondents noted that, whilst a measure of segment profit or loss can be expected in every entity's internal reporting, a measure of segment assets is not always available, particularly in service industries or other industries with low utilisation of physical assets. Respondents suggested that in such circumstances a measure of segment assets should be disclosed only if those amounts were regularly provided to the chief operating decision maker.

BC35   ~~The Board noted that requiring disclosure of a measure of segment assets only when such a measure is reviewed by the chief operating decision maker would create divergence from SFAS 131. The Board also supported a minimum disclosure of segment profit or loss and segment assets. The Board therefore concluded that measures of segment profit or loss and total segment assets should be disclosed for all segments regardless of whether those measures are reviewed by the chief operating decision maker.~~ *

BC35A   After IFRS 8 was issued, the Board was informed that the reasons originally set out in paragraph BC35 contradict long-standing interpretations published in the US for the application of SFAS 131 and create an unintended difference from practice in the US under SFAS 131. After reconsideration and discussion of the interaction between the disclosure and measurement requirements in the IFRS (paragraphs 23 and 25), the Board concluded that those reasons no longer reflected its thinking. Therefore, the Board amended paragraph 23 by *Improvements to IFRSs* issued in April 2009 to clarify that a measure of segment assets should be disclosed only if that amount is regularly provided to the chief operating decision maker.

Information about segment liabilities

BC36   ED 8 did not propose disclosure of segment liabilities because there is no such requirement in SFAS 131. The reasons for this are set out in paragraph 96 of the Basis for Conclusions on SFAS 131, included as Appendix A to this Basis for Conclusions.

BC37   Some respondents proposed adding a requirement for each entity to disclose information about segment liabilities, if such information is regularly provided to the chief operating decision maker. They argued that information about segment liabilities would be helpful to users. Other respondents favoured information about net segment assets rather than gross segment assets.

BC38   The Board noted that if segment liabilities are considered in assessing the performance of, and allocating resources to, the segments of an entity, such disclosure would be consistent with the management approach. The Board also noted support for this disclosure from some commentators, particularly users of financial statements. Accordingly the Board decided to require disclosure of a measure of segment liabilities if those amounts are regularly provided to the chief operating decision maker notwithstanding that such a requirement would create divergence from SFAS 131.

Level of reconciliations

BC39   ED 8 proposed that an entity should provide reconciliations of total reportable segment amounts for specified items to amounts the entity recognised in accordance with IFRSs. It did not propose such reconciliations for individual reportable segments.

---

*   Paragraph BC35 was deleted and paragraph BC35A added as a consequence of *Improvements to IFRSs* issued in April 2009.

© IASCF

BC40   Several respondents expressed concern about the level of detail provided by the proposed reconciliations. They argued that if the IFRS allows segment information to be measured on the basis of management information, it should require reconciliations for individual reportable segments between the segment amounts and the equivalent amounts measured in accordance with an entity's IFRS accounting policies. They added that reconciling only total reportable segment amounts to amounts presented in the financial statements does not provide useful information.

BC41   Other respondents supported the proposed reconciliations on the grounds that more detailed reconciliations would not be more understandable to users and might be confusing. They believed that the additional costs to reporting entities were not justified.

BC42   The Board noted that a requirement to provide reconciliations at the individual reportable segment level would effectively lead to two complete segment reports—one according to internal measures and the other according to IFRSs. The Board concluded that the cost of providing two sets of segment information would outweigh the benefits.

Lack of a competitive harm exemption

BC43   The Board discussed whether entities should be exempt from aspects of the IFRS if disclosure could cause competitive damage or erosion of shareholder value. The Board considered an alternative approach whereby entities could be required to provide reasons for non-disclosure on a 'comply or explain' basis.

BC44   The Board concluded that a 'competitive harm' exemption would be inappropriate because it would provide a means for broad non-compliance with the IFRS. The Board noted that entities would be unlikely to suffer competitive harm from the required disclosures since most competitors have sources of detailed information about an entity other than its financial statements.

BC45   Respondents also commented that the requirements of the IFRS would place small listed companies at a disadvantage to non-listed companies, which are outside the scope of the IFRS. The Board noted that the relative advantage/disadvantage of an entity being publicly listed is not a matter for the Board to consider.

Adoption of the term 'impracticable'

BC46   Some respondents to ED 8 expressed concern that entities were to be allowed not to give entity-wide disclosures about products and services and geographical areas if '... the necessary information is not available and the cost to develop it would be excessive.' They argued that the test to be applied for non-disclosure should be that of impracticability as defined in IAS 1 *Presentation of Financial Statements*.

BC47   The Board noted that the wording in ED 8 ensures convergence with SFAS 131. Using the term 'impracticable' as defined in IAS 1 would change the requirement and create divergence from SFAS 131. Therefore, the Board decided to retain the wording of ED 8.

Entity-wide disclosures

Geographical information

BC48   The IFRS requires an entity to disclose geographical information about non-current assets, excluding specified items. The Board considered comments made by some respondents who advocated country-by-country disclosure, others who requested specific items of geographical information to be disclosed, and some who expressed reservations with the proposed requirement relating to disclosure of country of domicile.

BC49   A coalition of over 300 organisations from more than 50 countries known as the Publish What You Pay campaign requested that the scope of the IFRS should be extended to require additional disclosure on a country-by-country basis. The objective of such additional disclosure would be to promote greater transparency in the management of amounts paid by the oil, gas and mining industries to governments in developing or transitional countries that are resource-rich. The view of these campaigners was that publication of specific payments made by those companies to governments is in the interest of all users of financial statements.

BC50   Because the IFRS is being developed in a short-term convergence project to converge with SFAS 131, the Board decided that issues raised by the Publish What You Pay campaign relating to country-by-country disclosures should not be addressed in the IFRS. The Board was of the view that such issues merit further discussion with bodies that are currently engaged in similar issues, for example the United Nations, International Public Sector Accounting Standards Board, International Monetary Fund, World Bank, regional development banks and Financial Stability Forum.

Exemption from entity-wide disclosures

BC51   Several respondents suggested different geographical disclosures from those proposed in ED 8. For example, some preferred disclosures by geographical areas rather than by individual country. Others favoured geographical disclosure of profit or loss as well as non-current assets. Several respondents expressed the view that disclosure of total assets would be more relevant than non-current assets. Some took the view that disclosures should be made of both current and non-current assets. Other respondents recommended that financial assets should be disclosed as well as non-current assets. Some respondents expressed the view that disclosure of non-current assets should not be required if those amounts are not reviewed by the chief operating decision maker.

BC52   In developing ED 8, the Board decided to adopt the requirements in SFAS 131. Paragraphs 104–107 of the Basis for Conclusions on SFAS 131 provide the rationale for the geographical disclosures required.

BC53   None of the suggested alternative disclosures was broadly supported by the user responses. The Board noted that entities that wish to give additional information are free to do so. The Board therefore concluded that the disclosure requirement taken from SFAS 131 should not be changed.

Country of domicile

BC54 Some respondents asserted that disclosures relating to the country of domicile were inappropriate for many entities. They expressed the view that such information would be relevant when a large proportion of an entity's business is carried out in its country of domicile. They noted, however, that in many circumstances the country of domicile represents a small proportion of the entity's business and in these cases the information required would not be relevant. In addition, they argued that SFAS 131 had been designed for entities in the US, for whom the 'country of domicile' is in itself a significant geographical area. These respondents suggested that disclosures should instead be required about the country of principal activities.

BC55 The IFRS requires disclosures for any country that is individually material. The Board noted that identifying the country of principal activities may be difficult and subjective. Accordingly, the Board decided not to require entities to identify the country of principal activities.

Subtotal for tangible non-current assets

BC56 Paragraphs 14 and 15 of the Basis for Conclusions on ED 8 highlighted a potential difference from SFAS 131. SFAS 131 requires disclosure of 'long-lived assets' excluding intangible assets, whereas ED 8 proposed disclosure of 'non-current assets' including intangible assets. The Board reconsidered whether, in the interest of convergence, the IFRS should require disclosure of the subtotal of tangible non-current assets.

BC57 The Board concluded that a separate disclosure of a subtotal of tangible non-current assets was unnecessary on the grounds that the incremental benefit does not justify such disclosure. However, the Board noted that entities that wish to provide that information are free to do so.

Information about major customers

BC58 ED 8 proposed that, in respect of the disclosures about major customers, a group of entities known to be under common control should be treated as a single customer. Some respondents noted that this could be difficult when entities are state-controlled. The Board noted that it was considering proposals to amend IAS 24 *Related Party Disclosures* with regard to state-controlled entities, and a consequential amendment to the IFRS on reporting segments might result from those proposals. In the meantime, the Board decided to require in the IFRS that a government (whether national, state, provincial, territorial, local or foreign) and entities known to the reporting entity to be controlled by that government should be treated as a single customer. This makes the requirements relating to government-controlled entities the same as those relating to privately controlled entities.

Interim financial information

BC59 The Board decided that the changes to IAS 34 *Interim Financial Reporting* proposed in ED 8 should be amended to clarify that interim disclosure of information on segment profit or loss items is required only if the specified amounts are included in the measure of segment profit or loss reviewed by the chief operating decision maker. The Board reached this conclusion because it noted that such disclosure is consistent with the management approach.

Differences from SFAS 131

BC60 In developing the IFRS, the Board included the following differences from SFAS 131:

(a) The FASB *Guidance on Applying Statement 131* indicates that the FASB staff believe that 'long-lived assets', as that phrase is used in paragraph 38 of SFAS 131, implies hard assets that cannot be readily removed, which would appear to exclude intangibles. Non-current assets in the IFRS include intangibles (see paragraphs BC56 and BC57).

(b) SFAS 131 does not require disclosure of a measure of segment liabilities. The IFRS requires disclosure of segment liabilities if such a measure is regularly provided to the chief operating decision maker (see paragraphs BC36–BC38).

(c) SFAS 131 requires an entity with a matrix form of organisation to determine operating segments based on products and services. The IFRS requires such an entity to determine operating segments by reference to the core principle of the IFRS (see paragraph BC27).

Transitional provisions

BC61 Under its transitional provisions, SFAS 131 was not required to be applied to interim financial statements in the initial year of its application. However, in the second year of application, comparative information relating to interim periods in the initial year of application was required. The Basis for Conclusions on SFAS 131 explained that the reason for these transitional requirements was that some of the information that is required to be reported for interim periods is based on information reported in the most recent annual financial statements. Interim segment information would not be as meaningful without a full set of annual segment information to use as a comparison and to provide an understanding of the basis on which it is provided.

BC62 The Board did not agree with the transitional provision for interim financial statements in SFAS 131. The Board noted that the IFRS is not effective until 2009, giving entities adequate time to prepare. Furthermore, the Board was aware that some entities adopting IFRSs for the first time may wish to present comparative information in accordance with the IFRS rather than IAS 14.

CONTENTS

Background information and basis for conclusions of the US Financial Accounting Standards Board on SFAS 131

Introduction

41.   This appendix summarizes considerations that were deemed significant by Board members in reaching the conclusions in this Statement. It includes reasons for accepting certain approaches and rejecting others. Individual Board members gave greater weight to some factors than to others.

Background Information

42.   FASB Statement No. 14, *Financial Reporting for Segments of a Business Enterprise*, was issued in 1976. That Statement required that business enterprises report segment information on two bases: by industry and by geographic area. It also required disclosure of information about export sales and major customers.

43.   The Board concluded at the time it issued Statement 14 that information about components of an enterprise, the products and services that it offers, its foreign operations, and its major customers is useful for understanding and making decisions about the enterprise as a whole. Financial statement users observe that the evaluation of the prospects for future cash flows is the central element of investment and lending decisions. The evaluation of prospects requires assessment of the uncertainty that surrounds both the timing and the amount of the expected cash flows to the enterprise, which in turn affect potential cash flows to the investor or creditor. Users also observe that uncertainty results in part from factors related to the products and services an enterprise offers and the geographic areas in which it operates.

44.   In its 1993 position paper, *Financial Reporting in the 1990s and Beyond*, the Association for Investment Management and Research (AIMR) said:

> [Segment data] is vital, essential, fundamental, indispensable, and integral to the investment analysis process. Analysts need to know and understand how the various components of a multifaceted enterprise behave economically. One weak member of the group is analogous to a section of blight on a piece of fruit; it has the potential to spread rot over the entirety. Even in the absence of weakness, different segments will generate dissimilar streams of cash flows to which are attached disparate risks and which bring about unique values. Thus, without disaggregation, there is no sensible way to predict the overall amounts, timing, or risks of a complete enterprise's future cash flows. There is little dispute over the analytic usefulness of disaggregated financial data. [pages 59 and 60]

45.   Over the years, financial analysts consistently requested that financial statement data be disaggregated to a much greater degree than it is in current practice. Many analysts said that they found Statement 14 helpful but inadequate. In its 1993 position paper, the AIMR emphasized that:

> There is no disagreement among AIMR members that segment information is totally vital to their work. There also is general agreement among them that the current segment reporting standard, Financial Accounting Standard No. 14, is inadequate. Recent work by a subcommittee of the [Financial Accounting Policy Committee] has confirmed that a substantial majority of analysts seek and, when it is available, use quarterly segment data. [page 5]

46. The Canadian Institute of Chartered Accountants (CICA) published a Research Study, *Financial Reporting for Segments*, in August 1992. An FASB Research Report, *Reporting Disaggregated Information*, was published in February 1993. In March 1993, the FASB and the Accounting Standards Board (AcSB) of the CICA agreed to pursue their projects jointly.

47. In May 1993, the FASB and the AcSB jointly issued an Invitation to Comment, *Reporting Disaggregated Information by Business Enterprises*. That Invitation to Comment identified certain issues related to disclosure of information about segments, solicited comments on those issues, and asked readers to identify additional issues. The boards received 129 comment letters from U.S. and Canadian respondents.

48. In late 1993, the FASB and the AcSB formed the Disaggregated Disclosures Advisory Group to advise and otherwise support the two boards in their efforts to improve disaggregated disclosures. The members of the group included financial statement issuers, auditors, financial analysts, and academics from both the United States and Canada. In January 1994, the FASB and the AcSB began discussing changes to Statement 14 and *CICA Handbook* Section 1700, "Segmented Information." The two boards met with and otherwise actively solicited the views of analysts and preparers of financial statements about possible improvements to the current segment reporting requirements. FASB and AcSB members and staff also discussed disaggregated disclosures at meetings of several groups of analysts, including the AIMR's Financial Accounting Policy Committee.

49. In 1991, the AICPA formed the Special Committee on Financial Reporting (the Special Committee) to make recommendations to improve the relevance and usefulness of business reporting. The Special Committee, which comprised financial statement auditors and preparers, established focus groups of credit analysts and equity analysts to assist in formulating its recommendations. The Special Committee issued its report, *Improving Business Reporting—A Customer Focus*, in 1994. That report listed improvements in disclosures of business segment information as its first recommendation and included the following commentary:

> ... for users analyzing a company involved in diverse businesses, financial information about business segments often is as important as information about the company as a whole. Users suggest that standard setters assign the highest priority to improving segment reporting because of its importance to their work and the perceived problems with current reporting of segment information. [page 68]

50. The report of the Special Committee listed the following as among the most important improvements needed:

(a) Disclosure of segment information in interim financial reports

(b) Greater number of segments for some enterprises

(c) More information about segments

(d) Segmentation that corresponds to internal management reports

(e) Consistency of segment information with other parts of an annual report.

Similar recommendations had been made in each of the last 20 years in evaluations of corporate reporting conducted by the AIMR.

51.   The two boards reached tentative conclusions about an approach to segment reporting that was substantially different from the approach in Statement 14 and Section 1700. Key characteristics of the new approach were that (a) information would be provided about segments of the enterprise that corresponded to the structure of the enterprise's internal organization, that is, about the divisions, departments, subsidiaries, or other internal units that the chief operating decision maker uses to make operating decisions and to assess an enterprise's performance, (b) specific amounts would be allocated to segments only if they were allocated in reports used by the chief operating decision maker for evaluation of segment performance, and (c) accounting policies used to produce the disaggregated information would be the same as those used in the reports used by the chief operating decision maker in allocating resources and assessing segment performance.

52.   In February 1995, the staffs of the FASB and the CICA distributed a paper, "Tentative Conclusions on Financial Reporting for Segments" (Tentative Conclusions), to selected securities analysts, the FASB Task Force on Consolidations and Related Matters, the Disaggregated Disclosures Advisory Group, the FASB's Emerging Issues Task Force, the Financial Accounting Standards Advisory Council, the AcSB's list of Associates,* and members of representative organizations that regularly work with the boards. The paper also was announced in FASB and CICA publications and was sent to anyone who requested a copy. Board and staff members discussed the Tentative Conclusions with various analyst and preparer groups. Approximately 80 comment letters were received from U.S. and Canadian respondents.

53.   In January 1996, the FASB and the AcSB issued virtually identical Exposure Drafts, *Reporting Disaggregated Information about a Business Enterprise.* The FASB received 221 comment letters and the AcSB received 73 comment letters in response to the Exposure Drafts. A field test of the proposals was conducted in March 1996. A public meeting was held in Toronto in October 1996 to discuss results and concerns with field test participants. Other interested parties attended a public meeting in Norwalk in October 1996 to discuss their concerns about the proposals in the Exposure Drafts. The FASB decided that it could reach an informed decision on the project without holding a public hearing.

54.   The FASB and the AcSB exchanged information during the course of redeliberating the proposals in their respective Exposure Drafts. AcSB members and CICA staff attended FASB meetings, and FASB members and staff attended AcSB meetings in late 1996 and in 1997 to discuss the issues raised by respondents. Both boards reached agreement on all of the substantive issues to achieve virtually identical standards for segment reporting in the United States and Canada. Members of the Segment Disclosures Advisory Group (formerly the Disaggregated Disclosures Advisory Group) discussed a draft of the standards section in March 1997.

---

* Associates are individuals and organizations with a particular interest in financial reporting issues that have volunteered to provide an outside reaction to AcSB positions at an early stage in the AcSB's deliberations.

55.   The International Accounting Standards Committee (IASC) issued an Exposure Draft of a proposed International Accounting Standard that would replace International Accounting Standard IAS 14, *Reporting Financial Information by Segment*, in December 1995. Although many of its provisions are similar to those of the FASB and AcSB Exposure Drafts, the IASC's proposal is based on different objectives and is different from those Exposure Drafts. A member of the IASC Segments Steering Committee participated in FASB meetings during the redeliberations of the Exposure Draft, and members of the FASB participated in meetings of the IASC Segments Steering Committee. Many of the respondents to the Exposure Drafts encouraged the FASB and the AcSB to work closely with the IASC to achieve similar standards for segment reporting. The IASC expects to issue a standard on segment reporting later in 1997. Although there likely will be differences between the IASC's requirements for segment reporting and those of this Statement, the boards expect that it will be possible to prepare one set of segment information that complies with both the IASC requirements and those of this Statement.

56.   This Statement addresses the following key issues:

(a)   What is the appropriate basis for defining segments?

(b)   What accounting principles and allocations should be used?

(c)   What specific items of information should be reported?

(d)   Should segment information be reported in condensed financial statements for interim periods?

Defining Operating Segments of an Enterprise

57.   The Board concluded that the *industry approach* to segment disclosures in Statement 14 was not providing the information required by financial statement users and that disclosure of disaggregated information should be based on operating segments. This Statement defines an operating segment as a component of an enterprise (a) that engages in business activities from which it may earn revenues and incur expenses, (b) whose operating results are regularly reviewed by the enterprise's chief operating decision maker to make decisions about resources to be allocated to the segment and to assess its performance, and (c) for which discrete financial information is available.

58.   The AIMR's 1993 position paper and the report of the AICPA Special Committee criticized Statement 14's industry segment approach to reporting segment information. The AIMR's position paper included the following:

> FAS 14 requires disclosure of line-of-business information classified by "industry segment." Its definition of segment is necessarily imprecise, recognizing that there are numerous practical problems in applying that definition to different business entities operating under disparate circumstances. That weakness in FAS 14 has been exploited by many enterprises to suit their own financial reporting purposes. As a result, we have seen one of the ten largest firms in the country report all of its operations as being in a single, very broadly defined industry segment. [page 60]

The report of the Special Committee said that "[financial statement users] believe that many companies define industry segments too broadly for business reporting and thus report on too few industry segments" (page 69).

59. The report of the AICPA Special Committee also said that "… the primary means to improving industry segment reporting should be to align business reporting with internal reporting" (page 69), and the AIMR's 1993 position paper recommended that:

> … priority should be given to the production and dissemination of financial data that reflects and reports sensibly the operations of specific enterprises. If we could obtain reports showing the details of how an individual business firm is organized and managed, we would assume more responsibility for making meaningful comparisons of those data to the unlike data of other firms that conduct their business differently. [pages 60 and 61]

Almost all of the users and many other constituents who responded to the Exposure Draft or who met with Board and staff members agreed that defining segments based on the structure of an enterprise's internal organization would result in improved information. They said that not only would enterprises be likely to report more detailed information but knowledge of the structure of an enterprise's internal organization is valuable in itself because it highlights the risks and opportunities that management believes are important.

60. Segments based on the structure of an enterprise's internal organization have at least three other significant advantages. First, an ability to see an enterprise "through the eyes of management" enhances a user's ability to predict actions or reactions of management that can significantly affect the enterprise's prospects for future cash flows. Second, because information about those segments is generated for management's use, the incremental cost of providing information for external reporting should be relatively low. Third, practice has demonstrated that the term *industry* is subjective. Segments based on an existing internal structure should be less subjective.

61. The AIMR and other users have commented that segment information is more useful if it is consistent with explanatory information provided elsewhere in the annual report. They note that the business review section and the chairman's letter in an annual report frequently discuss the enterprise's operations on a basis different from that of the segment information in the notes to the financial statements and the management's discussion and analysis section, which is required by SEC rules to correspond to the segment information provided to comply with Statement 14. That appears to occur if the enterprise is not managed in a way that corresponds to the way it defines segments under the requirements of Statement 14. Segmentation based on the structure of an enterprise's internal organization should facilitate consistent discussion of segment financial results throughout an enterprise's annual report.

62. Some respondents to the Exposure Draft opposed the Board's approach for several reasons. Segments based on the structure of an enterprise's internal organization may not be comparable between enterprises that engage in similar activities and may not be comparable from year to year for an individual enterprise. In addition, an enterprise may not be organized based on products and services or geographic areas, and thus the enterprise's segments may not be susceptible to analysis using macroeconomic models. Finally, some asserted that because enterprises are organized strategically, the information that would be reported may be competitively harmful to the reporting enterprise.

63. The Board acknowledges that comparability of accounting information is important. The summary of principal conclusions in FASB Concepts Statement No. 2, *Qualitative Characteristics of Accounting Information*, says: "Comparability between enterprises and consistency in the application of methods over time increases the informational value of comparisons of relative economic opportunities or performance. The significance of information, especially quantitative information, depends to a great extent on the user's ability to relate it to some benchmark." However, Concepts Statement 2 also notes a danger:

> Improving comparability may destroy or weaken relevance or reliability if, to secure comparability between two measures, one of them has to be obtained by a method yielding less relevant or less reliable information. Historically, extreme examples of this have been provided in some European countries in which the use of standardized charts of accounts has been made mandatory in the interest of interfirm comparability but at the expense of relevance and often reliability as well. That kind of uniformity may even adversely affect comparability of information if it conceals real differences between enterprises. [paragraph 116]

64. The Board was concerned that segments defined using the approach in Statement 14 may appear to be more comparable between enterprises than they actually are. Statement 14 included the following:

> Information prepared in conformity with [Statement 14] may be of limited usefulness for comparing an industry segment of one enterprise with a similar industry segment of another enterprise (i.e., for interenterprise comparison). Interenterprise comparison of industry segments would require a fairly detailed prescription of the basis or bases of disaggregation to be followed by all enterprises, as well as specification of the basis of accounting for intersegment transfers and methods of allocating costs common to two or more segments. [paragraph 76]

65. Statement 14 explained why the Board chose not to develop a detailed prescription of the bases of disaggregation:

> ... differences among enterprises in the nature of their operations and in the extent to which components of the enterprise share common facilities, equipment, materials and supplies, or labor force make unworkable the prescription of highly detailed rules and procedures that must be followed by all enterprises. Moreover, ... differences in the accounting systems of business enterprises are a practical constraint on the degree of specificity with which standards of financial accounting and reporting for disaggregated information can be established. [paragraph 74]

Those same considerations persuaded the Board not to adopt more specific requirements in this Statement. Both relevance and comparability will not be achievable in all cases, and relevance should be the overriding concern.

66. The AICPA Special Committee, some respondents to the Exposure Draft, and other constituents recommended that the Board require that an enterprise use an alternative method of segmentation for external reporting if its internal organization is not based on differences in products and services or geography. Some specifically recommended adoption of the proposal in the IASC Exposure Draft that was commonly referred to as a "safety net." The IASC Exposure Draft approach to identifying primary and secondary operating segments calls for review of management's organization of segments, but both primary and secondary segments are required to be defined either on the basis of related

products and services or on the basis of geography. That is, regardless of management's organization, segments must be grouped either by related products and services or by geographic areas, and one set must be presented as primary segments and the other as secondary segments.

67. The Board recognizes that an enterprise may not be divided into components with similar products and services or geographic areas for internal purposes and that some users of financial statements have expressed a desire for information organized on those bases. However, instead of an alternative method of segmentation, which would call for multiple sets of segment information in many circumstances, the Board chose to require disclosure of additional information about products and services and about geographic areas of operations for the enterprise as a whole if the basic segment disclosures do not provide it.

68. One reason for not prescribing segmentation along bases of only related products and services or geography is that it is difficult to define clearly the circumstances in which an alternative method that differs from the management approach would be applied consistently. An enterprise with a relatively narrow product line may not consider two products to be similar, while an enterprise with a broad product line may consider those same two products to be similar. For example, a highly diversified enterprise may consider all consumer products to be similar if it has other businesses such as financial services and road construction. However, an enterprise that sells only consumer products might consider razor blades to be different from toasters.

69. A second reason for rejecting that approach is that an alternative method of segmentation would increase the cost to some enterprises to prepare the information. A management approach to defining segments allows enterprises to present the information that they use internally and facilitates consistent descriptions of the components of an enterprise from one part of the annual report to another. An enterprise could be organized by its products and services, geography, a mixture of both products and services and geography, or other bases, such as customer type, and the segment information required by this Statement would be consistent with that method of organization. Furthermore, the enterprise-wide disclosures about products and services will provide information about the total revenues from related products and services, and the enterprise-wide disclosures about geography will provide information about the revenues and assets of an enterprise both inside and outside its home country. If material, individual foreign country information also is required.

70. The Board recognizes that some enterprises organize their segments on more than one basis. Other enterprises may produce reports in which their activities are presented in a variety of ways. In those situations, reportable segments are to be determined based on a review of other factors to identify the enterprise's operating segments, including the nature of the activities of each component, the existence of managers responsible for them, and the information provided to the board of directors. In many enterprises, only one set of data is provided to the board of directors. That set of data generally is indicative of how management views the enterprise's activities.

Reportable Segments

71.   The Board included a notion of reportable segments, a subset of operating segments, in this Statement by defining aggregation criteria and quantitative thresholds for determining which operating segments should be reported separately in the financial statements.

72.   A so-called pure management approach to segment reporting might require that an enterprise report all of the information that is reviewed by the chief operating decision maker to make decisions about resource allocations and to assess the performance of the enterprise. However, that level of detail may not be useful to readers of external financial statements, and it also may be cumbersome for an enterprise to present. Therefore, this Statement uses a modified management approach that includes both aggregation criteria and quantitative thresholds for determining reportable operating segments. However, an enterprise need not aggregate similar segments, and it may present segments that fall below the quantitative thresholds.

Aggregation of Similar Operating Segments

73.   The Board believes that separate reporting of segment information will not add significantly to an investor's understanding of an enterprise if its operating segments have characteristics so similar that they can be expected to have essentially the same future prospects. The Board concluded that although information about each segment may be available, in those circumstances the benefit would be insufficient to justify its disclosure. For example, a retail chain may have 10 stores that individually meet the definition of an operating segment, but each store may be essentially the same as the others.

74.   Most respondents commented on the aggregation criteria in the Exposure Draft. Many said that the criteria were unreasonably strict, to the extent that nearly identical segments might not qualify for aggregation. Some respondents linked their concerns about competitive harm and too many segments directly to the aggregation criteria, indicating that a relaxation of the criteria would significantly reduce those concerns. To better convey its intent, the Board revised the wording of the aggregation criteria and the introduction to them. However, the Board rejected recommendations that the criteria be indicators rather than tests and that the guidance require only the expectation of similar long-term performance of segments to justify aggregation because those changes might result in a level of aggregation that would cause a loss of potentially valuable information. For the same reason, the Board also rejected suggestions that segments need be similar in only a majority of the characteristics in paragraph 17 to justify aggregation. The Board recognizes that determining when two segments are sufficiently similar to justify aggregating them is difficult and subjective. However, the Board notes that one of the reasons that the information provided under Statement 14 did not satisfy financial statement users' needs is that segments with different characteristics in important areas were at times aggregated.

Quantitative Thresholds

75. In developing the Exposure Draft, the Board had concluded that quantitative criteria might interfere with the determination of operating segments and, if anything, might unnecessarily reduce the number of segments disclosed. Respondents to the Exposure Draft and others urged the Board to include quantitative criteria for determining which segments to report because they said that some enterprises would be required to report too many segments unless specific quantitative guidelines allowed them to omit small segments. Some respondents said that the Exposure Draft would have required disclosure of as many as 25 operating segments, which was not a result anticipated by the Board in its deliberations preceding the Exposure Draft. Others said that enterprises would report information that was too highly aggregated unless quantitative guidelines prevented it. The Board decided that the addition of quantitative thresholds would be a practical way to address respondents' concerns about competitive harm and proliferation of segments without fundamentally changing the management approach to segment definition.

76. Similar to the requirements in Statement 14, the Board decided to require that any operating segment that constitutes 10 percent or more of reported revenues, assets, or profit or loss be reported separately and that reportable segments account for at least 75 percent of an enterprise's external revenues. The Board decided to retain that guidance for the quantitative thresholds because it can be objectively applied and because preparers and users of financial statements already understand it.

77. Inclusion of quantitative thresholds similar to those in Statement 14 necessitates guidance on how to report operating segments that do not meet the thresholds. The Board concluded that enterprises should be permitted to aggregate information about operating segments that do not meet the thresholds with information about other operating segments that do not meet the thresholds if a majority of the aggregation criteria in paragraph 17 are met. That is a more liberal aggregation provision than that for individually material operating segments, but it prohibits aggregation of segments that are dissimilar.

78. Paragraph 125 of Concepts Statement 2 states that "... magnitude by itself, without regard to the nature of the item and the circumstances in which the judgment has to be made, will not generally be a sufficient basis for a materiality judgment." That guidance applies to segment information. An understanding of the material segments of an enterprise is important for understanding the enterprise as a whole, and individual items of segment information are important for understanding the segments. Thus, an item of segment information that, if omitted, would change a user's decision about that segment so significantly that it would change the user's decision about the enterprise as a whole is material even though an item of a similar magnitude might not be considered material if it were omitted from the consolidated financial statements. Therefore, enterprises are encouraged to report information about segments that do not meet the quantitative thresholds if management believes that it is material. Those who are familiar with the particular circumstances of each enterprise must decide what constitutes *material*.

Vertically Integrated Enterprises

79. The Board concluded that the definition of an operating segment should include components of an enterprise that sell primarily or exclusively to other operating segments of the enterprise if the enterprise is managed that way. Information about the components engaged in each stage of production is particularly important for understanding vertically integrated enterprises in certain businesses, for example, oil and gas enterprises. Different activities within the enterprise may have significantly different prospects for future cash flows, and users of financial statements have asserted that they need to know results of each operation.

80. Some respondents to the Exposure Draft opposed the requirement to report vertically integrated segments separately. They said that the segment results may not be comparable between enterprises and that transfer prices are not sufficiently reliable for external reporting purposes. The Board considered an approach that would have required separate reporting of vertically integrated segments only if transfer prices were based on quoted market prices and if there was no basis for combining the selling segment and the buying segment. However, that would have been a significant departure from the management approach to defining segments. The Board also was concerned that the criteria would be unworkable. Therefore, the Board decided to retain the Exposure Draft's provisions for vertically integrated segments.

Accounting Principles and Allocations

81. The Board decided that the information to be reported about each segment should be measured on the same basis as the information used by the chief operating decision maker for purposes of allocating resources to segments and assessing segments' performance. That is a management approach to measuring segment information as proposed in the Exposure Draft. The Board does not think that a separate measure of segment profit or loss or assets should have to be developed solely for the purpose of disclosing segment information. For example, an enterprise that accounts for inventory using a specialized valuation method for internal purposes should not be required to restate inventory amounts for each segment, and an enterprise that accounts for pension expense only on a consolidated basis should not be required to allocate pension expense to each operating segment.

82. The report of the AICPA Special Committee said that the Board "should allow companies to report a statistic on the same basis it is reported for internal purposes, if the statistic is reported internally. The usefulness of information prepared only for [external] reporting is questionable. Users want to understand management's perspective on the company and the implications of key statistics." It also said that "key statistics to be reported [should] be limited to statistics a company has available..." (page 72).

83. Respondents to the Exposure Draft had mixed reactions to its measurement guidance. Very few suggested that the Board require allocations solely for external reporting purposes. Most agreed that allocations are inherently arbitrary and may not be meaningful if they are not used for management purposes. No respondents suggested that intersegment transfers should be

reported on any basis other than that used internally. However, some respondents recommended that information about each segment be provided based on the accounting principles used in the enterprise's general-purpose financial statements. Some observed that unadjusted information from internal sources would not necessarily comply with generally accepted accounting principles and, for that reason, might be difficult for users to understand. Other respondents argued that comparability between enterprises would be improved if the segment information were provided on the basis of generally accepted accounting principles. Finally, a few questioned the verifiability of the information.

84. The Board decided not to require that segment information be provided in accordance with the same generally accepted accounting principles used to prepare the consolidated financial statements for several reasons. Preparing segment information in accordance with the generally accepted accounting principles used at the consolidated level would be difficult because some generally accepted accounting principles are not intended to apply at a segment level. Examples include allocation of the cost of an acquisition to individual assets and liabilities of a subsidiary using the purchase method of accounting, accounting for the cost of enterprise-wide employee benefit plans, accounting for income taxes in an enterprise that files a consolidated income tax return, and accounting for inventory on a last-in, first-out basis if the pools include items in more than one segment. In addition, there are no generally accepted accounting principles for allocating joint costs, jointly used assets, or jointly incurred liabilities to segments or for pricing intersegment transfers. As a consequence, it generally is not feasible to present segment profitability in accordance with generally accepted accounting principles.

85. The Board recognizes that segment information is subject to certain limitations and that some of that information may not be susceptible to the same degree of verifiability as some other financial information. However, verifiability is not the only important qualitative characteristic of accounting information. Verifiability is a component of reliability, which is one of two characteristics that contribute to the usefulness of accounting information. The other is relevance, which is equally important. Concepts Statement 2 states:

> Although financial information must be both relevant and reliable to be useful, information may possess both characteristics to varying degrees. It may be possible to trade relevance for reliability or vice versa, though not to the point of dispensing with one of them altogether. ... trade-offs between characteristics may be necessary or beneficial.

> In a particular situation, the importance attached to relevance in relation to the importance of other decision specific qualities of accounting information (for example, reliability) will be different for different information users, and their willingness to trade one quality for another will also differ. [paragraphs 42 and 45]

86. It is apparent that users are willing to trade a degree of reliability in segment information for more relevant information. The AIMR's 1993 position paper states:

> Analysts need financial statements structured so as to be consistent with how the business is organized and managed. That means that two different companies in the

same industry may have to report segment data differently because they are structured differently themselves. [page 20]

But, as previously noted, the position paper says that, under those circumstances, analysts "would assume more responsibility for making meaningful comparisons of those data to the unlike data of other firms that conduct their business differently" (page 61).

87. The Board believes that the information required by this Statement meets the objective of reliability of which both representational faithfulness and verifiability are components. An auditor can determine whether the information reported in the notes to the financial statements came from the required source by reviewing management reports or minutes from meetings of the board of directors. The information is not required to be provided on a specified basis, but the enterprise is required to explain the basis on which it is provided and to reconcile the segment information to consolidated enterprise totals. Adequate explanation and an appropriate reconciliation will enable a user to understand the information and its limitations in the context of the enterprise's financial statements. The auditor can test both the explanation of segment amounts and the reconciliations to consolidated totals. Furthermore, because management uses that information in its decision-making processes, that information is likely to be highly reliable. The information provided to comply with Statement 14 was more difficult to verify in many situations and was less reliable. Because it was prepared solely for external reporting purposes, it required allocations that may have been arbitrary, and it was based on accounting principles that may have been difficult to apply at the segment level.

88. Paragraph 29 requires amounts allocated to a segment to be allocated on a reasonable basis. However, the Board believes that the potential increased reliability that might have been achieved by requiring allocation of consolidated amounts is illusory because expenses incurred at the consolidated level could be allocated to segments in a variety of ways that could be considered "reasonable." For example, an enterprise could use either the number of employees in each segment or the segment's total salary expense in relation to the consolidated amounts as a basis for allocating pension expense to segments. Those two approaches to allocation could result in significantly different measures of segment profit or loss. However, both the number of employees and the total salary expense might be reasonable bases on which to allocate total pension expense. In contrast, it would not seem reasonable for an enterprise to allocate pension expense to a segment that had no employees eligible for the pension plan. Because of the potential for misleading information that may result from such allocations, the Board decided that it is appropriate for this Statement to require that amounts allocated to a segment be allocated on a reasonable basis.

89. The Board also considered explicitly requiring that revenues and expenses directly incurred by or directly attributable to an operating segment be reported by that segment. However, it decided that, in some cases, whether an item of revenue or expense is attributable to an operating segment is a matter of judgment. Further, such an explicit requirement would be an additional

modification of the management approach to measurement. While the Board decided not to include an explicit requirement, it believes that many items of revenue or expense clearly relate to a particular segment and that it would be unlikely that the information used by management would omit those items.

90.   To assist users of financial statements in understanding segment disclosures, this Statement requires that enterprises provide sufficient explanation of the basis on which the information was prepared. That disclosure must include any differences in the basis of measurement between the consolidated amounts and the segment amounts. It also must indicate whether allocations of items were made symmetrically. An enterprise may allocate an expense to a segment without allocating the related asset; however, disclosure of that fact is required. Enterprises also are required to reconcile to the consolidated totals in the enterprise's financial statements the totals of reportable segment assets, segment revenues, segment profit or loss, and any other significant segment information that is disclosed.

91.   In addition, the advantages of reporting unadjusted management information are significant. That practice is consistent with defining segments based on the structure of the enterprise's internal organization. It imposes little incremental cost on the enterprise and requires little incremental time to prepare. Thus, the enterprise can more easily report segment information in condensed financial statements for interim periods and can report more information about each segment in annual financial statements. Information used by management also highlights for a user of financial statements the risks and opportunities that management considers important.

Information to Be Disclosed about Segments

92.   The items of information about each reportable operating segment that must be disclosed as described in paragraphs 25–31 represent a balance between the needs of users of financial statements who may want a complete set of financial statements for each segment and the costs to preparers who may prefer not to disclose any segment information. Statement 14 required disclosure of internal and external revenues; profit or loss; depreciation, depletion, and amortization expense; and unusual items as defined in APB Opinion No. 30, *Reporting the Results of Operations—Reporting the Effects of Disposal of a Segment of a Business, and Extraordinary, Unusual and Infrequently Occurring Events and Transactions*, for each segment. Statement 14 also required disclosure of total assets, equity in the net income of investees accounted for by the equity method, the amount of investment in equity method investees, and total expenditures for additions to long-lived assets. Some respondents to the Exposure Draft objected to disclosing any information that was not required by Statement 14, while others recommended disclosure of additional items that are not required by this Statement. This Statement calls for the following additional disclosures only if the items are included in the measure of segment profit or loss that is reviewed by the chief operating decision maker: significant noncash items, interest revenue, interest expense, and income tax expense.

93.   Some respondents to the Exposure Draft expressed concern that the proposals would increase the sheer volume of information compared to what was required to be reported under Statement 14. The Board considers that concern to be overstated for several reasons. Although this Statement requires disclosure of more information about an individual operating segment than Statement 14 required for an industry segment, this Statement requires disclosure of information about only one type of segment–reportable operating segments– while Statement 14 required information about two types of segments–industry segments and geographic segments. Moreover, Statement 14 required that many enterprises create information solely for external reporting, while almost all of the segment information that this Statement requires is already available in management reports. The Board recognizes, however, that some enterprises may find it necessary to create the enterprise-wide information about products and services, geographic areas, and major customers required by paragraphs 36–39.

94.   The Board decided to require disclosure of significant noncash items included in the measure of segment profit or loss and information about total expenditures for additions to long-lived segment assets (other than financial instruments, long-term customer relationships of a financial institution, mortgage and other servicing rights, deferred policy acquisition costs, and deferred tax assets) if that information is reported internally because it improves financial statement users' abilities to estimate cash-generating potential and cash requirements of operating segments. As an alternative, the Board considered requiring disclosure of operating cash flow for each operating segment. However, many respondents said that disclosing operating cash flow in accordance with FASB Statement No. 95, *Statement of Cash Flows*, would require that they gather and process information solely for external reporting purposes. They said that management often evaluates cash generated or required by segments in ways other than by calculating operating cash flow in accordance with Statement 95. For that reason, the Board decided not to require disclosure of cash flow by segment.

95.   Disclosure of interest revenue and interest expense included in reported segment profit or loss is intended to provide information about the financing activities of a segment. The Exposure Draft proposed that an enterprise disclose gross interest revenue and gross interest expense for all segments in which reported profit or loss includes those items. Some respondents said that financial services segments generally are managed based on net interest revenue, or the "spread," and that management looks only to that data in its decision-making process. Therefore those segments should be required to disclose only the net amount and not both gross interest revenue and expense. Those respondents noted that requiring disclosure of both gross amounts would be analogous to requiring nonfinancial services segments to disclose both sales and cost of sales. The Board decided that segments that derive a majority of revenue from interest should be permitted to disclose net interest revenue instead of gross interest revenue and gross interest expense if management finds that amount to be more relevant in managing the segment. Information about interest is most important if a single segment comprises a mix of financial and nonfinancial operations. If a segment is primarily a financial operation, interest revenue probably constitutes most of

segment revenues and interest expense will constitute most of the difference between reported segment revenues and reported segment profit or loss. If the segment has no financial operations or only immaterial financial operations, no information about interest is required.

96.   The Board decided not to require the disclosure of segment liabilities. The Exposure Draft proposed that an enterprise disclose segment liabilities because the Board believed that liabilities are an important disclosure for understanding the financing activities of a segment. The Board also noted that the requirement in FASB Statement No. 94, *Consolidation of All Majority-Owned Subsidiaries*, to disclose assets, liabilities, and profit or loss about previously unconsolidated subsidiaries was continued from APB Opinion No. 18, *The Equity Method of Accounting for Investments in Common Stock*, pending completion of the project on disaggregated disclosures. However, in commenting on the disclosures that should be required by this Statement, many respondents said that liabilities are incurred centrally and that enterprises often do not allocate those amounts to segments. The Board concluded that the value of information about segment liabilities in assessing the performance of the segments of an enterprise was limited.

97.   The Board decided not to require disclosure of research and development expense included in the measure of segment profit or loss. The Exposure Draft would have required that disclosure to provide financial statement users with information about the operating segments in which an enterprise is focusing its product development efforts. Disclosure of research and development expense was requested by a number of financial statement users and was specifically requested in both the report of the AICPA's Special Committee and the AIMR's 1993 position paper. However, respondents said that disclosing research and development expense by segment may result in competitive harm by providing competitors with early insight into the strategic plans of an enterprise. Other respondents observed that research and development is only one of a number of items that indicate where an enterprise is focusing its efforts and that it is much more significant in some enterprises than in others. For example, costs of employee training and advertising were cited as items that often are more important to some enterprises than research and development, calling into question the relevance of disclosing only research and development expense. Additionally, many respondents said that research and development expense often is incurred centrally and not allocated to segments. The Board therefore decided not to require the disclosure of research and development expense by segment.

Interim Period Information

98.   This Statement requires disclosure of limited segment information in condensed financial statements that are included in quarterly reports to shareholders, as was proposed in the Exposure Draft. Statement 14 did not apply to those condensed financial statements because of the expense and the time required for producing segment information under Statement 14. A few respondents to the Exposure Draft said that reporting segment information in interim financial statements would be unnecessarily burdensome. However, users contended that, to be

timely, segment information is needed more often than annually and that the difficulties of preparing it on an interim basis could be overcome by an approach like the one in this Statement. Managers of many enterprises agree and have voluntarily provided segment information for interim periods.

99. The Board decided that the condensed financial statements in interim reports issued to shareholders should include disclosure of segment revenues from external customers, intersegment revenues, a measure of segment profit or loss, material changes in segment assets, differences in the basis of segmentation or the way segment profit or loss was measured in the previous annual period, and a reconciliation to the enterprise's total profit or loss. That decision is a compromise between the needs of users who want the same segment information for interim periods as that required in annual financial statements and the costs to preparers who must report the information. Users will have some key information on a timely basis. Enterprises should not incur significant incremental costs to provide the information because it is based on information that is used internally and therefore already available.

Restatement of Previously Reported Information

100. The Board decided to require restatement of previously reported segment information following a change in the composition of an enterprise's segments unless it is impracticable to do so. Changes in the composition of segments interrupt trends, and trend analysis is important to users of financial statements. Some financial statement issuers have said that their policy is to restate one or more prior years for internal trend analysis. Many reorganizations result in discrete profit centers' being reassigned from one segment to another and lead to relatively simple restatements. However, if an enterprise undergoes a fundamental reorganization, restatement may be very difficult and expensive. The Board concluded that in those situations restatement may be impracticable and, therefore, should not be required. However, if an enterprise does not restate its segment information, the enterprise is required to provide current-period segment information on both the old and new bases of segmentation in the year in which the change occurs unless it is impracticable to do so.

Enterprise-Wide Disclosures

101. Paragraphs 36–39 require disclosure of information about an enterprise's products and services, geographic areas, and major customers, regardless of the enterprise's organization. The required disclosures need be provided only if they are not included as part of the disclosures about segments. The Exposure Draft proposed requiring additional disclosures about products and services and geographic areas *by segment*. Many respondents said that that proposal would have resulted in disclosure of excessive amounts of information. Some enterprises providing a variety of products and services throughout many countries, for example, would have been required to present a large quantity of information that would have been time-consuming to prepare and of questionable benefit to most financial statement users. The Board decided that additional disclosures provided on an enterprise-wide basis rather than on a segment basis would be appropriate and not unduly burdensome. The Board also

agreed that those enterprise-wide disclosures are appropriate for all enterprises including those that have a single operating segment if the enterprise offers a range of products and services, derives revenues from customers in more than one country, or both.

102. Based on reviews of published information about public enterprises, discussions with constituents, and a field test of the Exposure Draft, the Board believes that most enterprises are organized by products and services or by geography and will report one or both of those types of information in their reportable operating segment disclosures. However, some enterprises will be required by paragraphs 36–39 to report additional information because the enterprise-wide disclosures are required for all enterprises, even those that have a single reportable segment.

Information about Products and Services

103. This Statement requires that enterprises report revenues from external customers for each product and service or each group of similar products and services for the enterprise as a whole. Analysts said that an analysis of trends in revenues from products and services is important in assessing both past performance and prospects for future growth. Those trends can be compared to benchmarks such as industry statistics or information reported by competitors. Information about the assets that are used to produce specific products and deliver specific services also might be useful. However, in many enterprises, assets are not dedicated to specific products and services and reporting assets by products and services would require arbitrary allocations.

Information about Geographic Areas

104. This Statement requires disclosure of information about both revenues and assets by geographic area. Analysts said that information about revenues from customers in different geographic areas assists them in understanding concentrations of risks due to negative changes in economic conditions and prospects for growth due to positive economic changes. They said that information about assets located in different areas assists them in understanding concentrations of risks (for example, political risks such as expropriation).

105. Statement 14 requires disclosure of geographic information by geographic region, whereas this Statement requires disclosure of individually material countries as well as information for the enterprise's country of domicile and all foreign countries in the aggregate. This Statement's approach has two significant benefits. First, it will reduce the burden on preparers of financial statements because most enterprises are likely to have material operations in only a few countries or perhaps only in their country of domicile. Second, and more important, it will provide information that is more useful in assessing the impact of concentrations of risk. Information disclosed by country is more useful because it is easier to interpret. Countries in contiguous areas often experience different rates of growth and other differences in economic conditions. Under the requirements of Statement 14, enterprises often reported information about broad geographic areas that included groupings such as Europe, Africa, and the Middle East. Analysts and others have questioned the usefulness of that type of broad disclosure.

106.   Respondents to the Exposure Draft questioned how revenues should be allocated to individual countries. For example, guidance was requested for situations in which products are shipped to one location but the customer resides in another location. The Board decided to provide flexibility concerning the basis on which enterprises attribute revenues to individual countries rather than requiring that revenues be attributed to countries according to the location of customers. The Board also decided to require that enterprises disclose the basis they have adopted for attributing revenues to countries to permit financial statement users to understand the geographic information provided.

107.   As a result of its decision to require geographic information on an enterprise-wide basis, the Board decided not to require disclosure of capital expenditures on certain long-lived assets by geographic area. Such information on an enterprise-wide basis is not necessarily helpful in forecasting future cash flows of operating segments.

Information about Major Customers

108.   The Board decided to retain the requirement in Statement 14, as amended by FASB Statement No. 30, *Disclosure of Information about Major Customers*, to report information about major customers because major customers of an enterprise represent a significant concentration of risk. The 10 percent threshold is arbitrary; however, it has been accepted practice since Statement 14 was issued, and few have suggested changing it.

Competitive Harm

109.   A number of respondents to the Exposure Draft noted the potential for competitive harm as a result of disclosing segment information in accordance with this Statement. The Board considered adopting special provisions to reduce the potential for competitive harm from certain segment information but decided against it. In the Invitation to Comment, the Tentative Conclusions, and the Exposure Draft, the Board asked constituents for specific illustrations of competitive harm that has resulted from disclosing segment information. Some respondents said that public enterprises may be at a disadvantage to nonpublic enterprises or foreign competitors that do not have to disclose segment information. Other respondents suggested that information about narrowly defined segments may put an enterprise at a disadvantage in price negotiations with customers or in competitive bid situations.

110.   Some respondents said that if a competitive disadvantage exists, it is a consequence of an obligation that enterprises have accepted to gain greater access to capital markets, which gives them certain advantages over nonpublic enterprises and many foreign enterprises. Other respondents said that enterprises are not likely to suffer competitive harm because most competitors have other sources of more detailed information about an enterprise than that disclosed in the financial statements. In addition, the information that is required to be disclosed about an operating segment is no more detailed or specific than the information typically provided by a smaller enterprise with a single operation.

111.   The Board was sympathetic to specific concerns raised by certain constituents; however, it decided that a competitive-harm exemption was inappropriate because it would provide a means for broad noncompliance with this Statement. Some form of relief for single-product or single-service segments was explored; however, there are many enterprises that produce a single product or a single service that are required to issue general-purpose financial statements. Those statements would include the same information that would be reported by single-product or single-service segments of an enterprise. The Board concluded that it was not necessary to provide an exemption for single-product or single-service segments because enterprises that produce a single product or service that are required to issue general-purpose financial statements have that same exposure to competitive harm. The Board noted that concerns about competitive harm were addressed to the extent feasible by four changes made during redeliberations: (a) modifying the aggregation criteria, (b) adding quantitative materiality thresholds for identifying reportable segments, (c) eliminating the requirements to disclose research and development expense and liabilities by segment, and (d) changing the second-level disclosure requirements about products and services and geography from a segment basis to an enterprise-wide basis.

Cost-Benefit Considerations

112.   One of the precepts of the Board's mission is to promulgate standards only if the expected benefits of the resulting information exceed the perceived costs. The Board strives to determine that a proposed standard will fill a significant need and that the costs incurred to satisfy that need, as compared with other alternatives, are justified in relation to the overall benefits of the resulting information. The Board concluded that the benefits that will result from this Statement will exceed the related costs.

113.   The Board believes that the primary benefits of this Statement are that enterprises will report segment information in interim financial reports, some enterprises will report a greater number of segments, most enterprises will report more items of information about each segment, enterprises will report segments that correspond to internal management reports, and enterprises will report segment information that will be more consistent with other parts of their annual reports.

114.   This Statement will reduce the cost of providing disaggregated information for many enterprises. Statement 14 required that enterprises define segments by both industry and by geographical area, ways that often did not match the way that information was used internally. Even if the reported segments aligned with the internal organization, the information required was often created solely for external reporting because Statement 14 required certain allocations of costs, prohibited other cost allocations, and required allocations of assets to segments. This Statement requires that information about operating segments be provided on the same basis that it is used internally. The Board believes that most of the enterprise-wide disclosures in this Statement about products and services, geography, and major customers typically are provided in current financial statements or can be prepared with minimal incremental cost.

Applicability to Nonpublic Enterprises and Not-for-Profit Organizations

115.   The Board decided to continue to exempt nonpublic enterprises from the requirement to report segment information. Few users of nonpublic enterprises' financial statements have requested that the Board require that those enterprises provide segment information.

116.   At the time the Board began considering improvements to disclosures about segment information, FASB Statement No. 117, *Financial Statements of Not-for-Profit Organizations*, had not been issued and there were no effective standards for consolidated financial statements of not-for-profit organizations. Most not-for-profit organizations provided financial information for each of their funds, which is a form of disaggregated information. The situation in Canada was similar. Thus, when the two boards agreed to pursue a joint project, they decided to limit the scope to public business enterprises.

117.   The Board provided a limited form of disaggregated information in paragraph 26 of Statement 117, which requires disclosure of expense by functional classification. However, the Board acknowledges that the application of that Statement may increase the need for disaggregated information about not-for-profit organizations. A final Statement expected to result from the FASB Exposure Draft, *Consolidated Financial Statements: Policy and Procedures*, also may increase that need by requiring aggregation of information about more entities in the financial statements of not-for-profit organizations.

118.   The general approach of providing information based on the structure of an enterprise's internal organization may be appropriate for not-for-profit organizations. However, the Board decided not to add not-for-profit organizations to the scope of this Statement. Users of financial statements of not-for-profit organizations have not urged the Board to include those organizations, perhaps because they have not yet seen the effects of Statement 117 and the Exposure Draft on consolidations. Furthermore, the term *not-for-profit organizations* applies to a wide variety of entities, some of which are similar to business enterprises and some of which are very different. There are likely to be unique characteristics of some of those entities or special user needs that require special provisions, which the Board has not studied. In addition, the AcSB has recently adopted standards for reporting by not-for-profit organizations that are different from Statement 117. In the interest of completing this joint project in a timely manner, the Board decided not to undertake the research and deliberations that would be necessary to adapt the requirements of this Statement to not-for-profit organizations at this time. Few respondents to the Exposure Draft disagreed with the Board's position.

Effective Date and Transition

119.   The Board concluded that this Statement should be effective for financial statements issued for fiscal years beginning after December 15, 1997. In developing the Exposure Draft, the Board had decided on an effective date of December 15, 1996. The Board believed that that time frame was reasonable because almost all of the information that this Statement requires is generated by

systems already in place within an enterprise and a final Statement was expected to be issued before the end of 1996. However, respondents said that some enterprises may need more time to comply with the requirements of this Statement than would have been provided under the Exposure Draft.

120. The Board also decided not to require that segment information be reported in financial statements for interim periods in the initial year of application. Some of the information that is required to be reported for interim periods is based on information that would have been reported in the most recent annual financial statements. Without a full set of segment information to use as a comparison and to provide an understanding of the basis on which it is provided, interim information would not be as meaningful.

Appendix B

Amendments to Basis for Conclusions on other IFRSs

This appendix contains amendments to the Basis for Conclusions on other IFRSs that are necessary in order to note the replacement of IAS 14 by IFRS 8.

*****

The amendments contained in this appendix when IFRS 8 was issued in 2006 have been incorporated into the text of the Basis for Conclusions on IFRSs 1, 6 and 7 and IASs 27 and 36 as issued at 30 November 2006.

Dissenting opinions

Dissent of Gilbert Gélard and James J Leisenring

DO1   Messrs Gélard and Leisenring dissent from the issue of the IFRS because it does not require a defined measure of segment profit or loss to be disclosed and does not require the measure of profit or loss reported to be consistent with the attribution of assets to reportable segments.

DO2   By not defining segment profit or loss, the IFRS allows the reporting of any measure of segment profit or loss as long as that measure is reviewed by the chief operating decision maker. Items of revenue and expense directly attributable to a segment need not be included in the reported profit or loss of that segment, and allocation of items not directly attributable to any given segment is not required. Messrs Gélard and Leisenring believe that the IFRS should require amounts directly incurred by or directly attributable to a segment to be included in that segment's profit or loss, and measurement of a segment's profit or loss to be consistent with the attribution of assets to the segment.

DO3   Messrs Gélard and Leisenring support the disclosure of information to enable users of financial statements to evaluate the activities of an entity and the economic environment in which it operates. However, they believe that the IFRS will not meet this objective, even with the required disclosures and reconciliation to the entity's annual financial statements, because it does not define segment profit or loss and does not require consistent attribution of assets and profit or loss to segments.

DO4   Messrs Gélard and Leisenring support the management approach for defining reportable segments and support requiring disclosure of selected segment information in interim financial reports. They believe, however, that the definitions of segment revenue, expense, result, assets and liabilities in paragraph 16 of IAS 14 *Segment Reporting* should be retained in the IFRS and applied to segments identified by the management approach. They believe that proper external reporting of segment information should not permit the use of non-GAAP measures because they might mislead users.

DO5   Messrs Gélard and Leisenring also believe that the changes from IAS 14 are not justified by the need for convergence with US GAAP. IAS 14 is a disclosure standard and therefore does not affect the reconciliation of IFRS amounts to US GAAP, though additional disclosure from what is required now by IAS 14 might be needed to comply with US GAAP.

Dissent of Stephen Cooper from the amendment issued in April 2009

DO1   Mr Cooper dissents from the amendment to IFRS 8 *Operating Segments* made by *Improvements to IFRSs* issued in April 2009.

DO2   In his view the changes are unnecessary considering that the provisions in the *Framework* regarding materiality already enable a reporting entity not to disclose segment assets when those assets are small relative to segment profit and not relevant to the understanding of the business. Mr Cooper believes that allowing a reporting entity not to disclose segment assets merely because this is not reported to the chief operating decision maker weakens IFRS 8, and may result in segment assets not being disclosed even when they are important to understanding the performance and financial position of that business.

CONTENTS

Guidance on implementing
IFRS 8 *Operating Segments*

This guidance accompanies, but is not part of, IFRS 8.

Introduction

IG1   This implementation guidance provides examples that illustrate the disclosures required by IFRS 8 and a diagram to assist in identifying reportable segments. The formats in the illustrations are not requirements. The Board encourages a format that provides the information in the most understandable manner in the specific circumstances. The following illustrations are for a single hypothetical entity referred to as Diversified Company.

Descriptive information about an entity's reportable segments

IG2   The following illustrates the disclosure of descriptive information about an entity's reportable segments (the paragraph references are to the relevant requirements in the IFRS).

Description of the types of products and services from which each reportable segment derives its revenues (paragraph 22(b))

Diversified Company has five reportable segments: car parts, motor vessels, software, electronics and finance. The car parts segment produces replacement parts for sale to car parts retailers. The motor vessels segment produces small motor vessels to serve the offshore oil industry and similar businesses. The software segment produces application software for sale to computer manufacturers and retailers. The electronics segment produces integrated circuits and related products for sale to computer manufacturers. The finance segment is responsible for portions of the company's financial operations including financing customer purchases of products from other segments and property lending operations.

Measurement of operating segment profit or loss, assets and liabilities (paragraph 27)

The accounting policies of the operating segments are the same as those described in the summary of significant accounting policies except that pension expense for each operating segment is recognised and measured on the basis of cash payments to the pension plan. Diversified Company evaluates performance on the basis of profit or loss from operations before tax expense not including non-recurring gains and losses and foreign exchange gains and losses.

Diversified Company accounts for intersegment sales and transfers as if the sales or transfers were to third parties, ie at current market prices.

Factors that management used to identify the entity's reportable segments (paragraph 22(a))

> Diversified Company's reportable segments are strategic business units that offer different products and services. They are managed separately because each business requires different technology and marketing strategies. Most of the businesses were acquired as individual units, and the management at the time of the acquisition was retained.

Information about reportable segment profit or loss, assets and liabilities

IG3 The following table illustrates a suggested format for disclosing information about reportable segment profit or loss, assets and liabilities (paragraphs 23 and 24). The same type of information is required for each year for which a statement of comprehensive income is presented. Diversified Company does not allocate tax expense (tax income) or non-recurring gains and losses to reportable segments. In addition, not all reportable segments have material non-cash items other than depreciation and amortisation in profit or loss. The amounts in this illustration, denominated as 'currency units (CU)', are assumed to be the amounts in reports used by the chief operating decision maker.

	Car parts	Motor vessels	Software	Electronics	Finance	All other	Totals
	CU	CU	CU	CU	CU	CU	CU
Revenues from external customers	3,000	5,000	9,500	12,000	5,000	1,000[(a)]	35,500
Intersegment revenues	–	–	3,000	1,500	–	–	4,500
Interest revenue	450	800	1,000	1,500	–	–	3,750
Interest expense	350	600	700	1,100	–	–	2,750
Net interest revenue[(b)]	–	–	–	–	1,000	–	1,000
Depreciation and amortisation	200	100	50	1,500	1,100	–	2,950
Reportable segment profit	200	70	900	2,300	500	100	4,070
Other material non-cash items:							
Impairment of assets	–	200	–	–	–	–	200
Reportable segment assets	2,000	5,000	3,000	12,000	57,000	2,000	81,000
Expenditures for reportable segment non-current assets	300	700	500	800	600	–	2,900
Reportable segment liabilities	1,050	3,000	1,800	8,000	30,000	–	43,850

(a) Revenues from segments below the quantitative thresholds are attributable to four operating segments of Diversified Company. Those segments include a small property business, an electronics equipment rental business, a software consulting practice and a warehouse leasing operation. None of those segments has ever met any of the quantitative thresholds for determining reportable segments.

(b) The finance segment derives a majority of its revenue from interest. Management primarily relies on net interest revenue, not the gross revenue and expense amounts, in managing that segment. Therefore, as permitted by paragraph 23, only the net amount is disclosed.

Reconciliations of reportable segment revenues, profit or loss, assets and liabilities

IG4   The following illustrate reconciliations of reportable segment revenues, profit or loss, assets and liabilities to the entity's corresponding amounts (paragraph 28(a)–(d)). Reconciliations also are required to be shown for every other material item of information disclosed (paragraph 28(e)). The entity's financial statements are assumed not to include discontinued operations. As discussed in paragraph IG2, the entity recognises and measures pension expense of its reportable segments on the basis of cash payments to the pension plan, and it does not allocate certain items to its reportable segments.

Revenues	CU
Total revenues for reportable segments	39,000
Other revenues	1,000
Elimination of intersegment revenues	(4,500)
Entity's revenues	35,500

Profit or loss	CU
Total profit or loss for reportable segments	3,970
Other profit or loss	100
Elimination of intersegment profits	(500)
Unallocated amounts:	
Litigation settlement received	500
Other corporate expenses	(750)
Adjustment to pension expense in consolidation	(250)
Income before income tax expense	3,070

Assets	CU
Total assets for reportable segments	79,000
Other assets	2,000
Elimination of receivable from corporate headquarters	(1,000)
Other unallocated amounts	1,500
Entity's assets	81,500

Liabilities	CU
Total liabilities for reportable segments	43,850
Unallocated defined benefit pension liabilities	25,000
Entity's liabilities	68,850

Other material items	Reportable segment totals CU	Adjustments CU	Entity totals CU
Interest revenue	3,750	75	3,825
Interest expense	2,750	(50)	2,700
Net interest revenue (finance segment only)	1,000	–	1,000
Expenditures for assets	2,900	1,000	3,900
Depreciation and amortisation	2,950	–	2,950
Impairment of assets	200	–	200

The reconciling item to adjust expenditures for assets is the amount incurred for the corporate headquarters building, which is not included in segment information. None of the other adjustments are material.

Geographical information

IG5 The following illustrates the geographical information required by paragraph 33. (Because Diversified Company's reportable segments are based on differences in products and services, no additional disclosures of revenue information about products and services are required (paragraph 32).)

Geographical information	Revenues[a] CU	Non-current assets CU
United States	19,000	11,000
Canada	4,200	–
China	3,400	6,500
Japan	2,900	3,500
Other countries	6,000	3,000
Total	35,500	24,000

(a) Revenues are attributed to countries on the basis of the customer's location.

Information about major customers

IG6 The following illustrates the information about major customers required by paragraph 34. Neither the identity of the customer nor the amount of revenues for each operating segment is required.

Revenues from one customer of Diversified Company's software and electronics segments represent approximately CU5,000 of the Company's total revenues.

Diagram to assist in identifying reportable segments

IG7   The following diagram illustrates how to apply the main provisions for identifying reportable segments as defined in the IFRS. The diagram is a visual supplement to the IFRS. It should not be interpreted as altering or adding to any requirements of the IFRS nor should it be regarded as a substitute for the requirements.

Diagram for identifying reportable segments

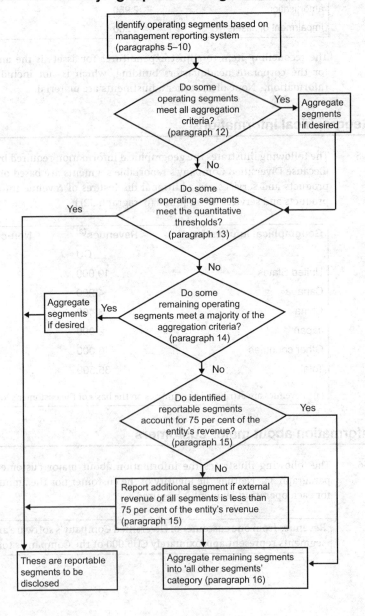

© IASCF

Appendix
Amendments to other implementation guidance

This appendix contains amendments to guidance on other IFRSs that are necessary in order to ensure consistency with IFRS 8. In the amended paragraphs, new text is underlined and deleted text is struck through.

* * * * *

The amendments contained in this appendix when IFRS 8 was issued in 2006 have been incorporated into the text of the Guidance on Implementing IFRS 4 and the illustrative examples accompanying IAS 36, both as issued at 30 November 2006.

IASB documents published to accompany

International Financial Reporting Standard 9

Financial Instruments

The text of the unaccompanied IFRS 9 is contained in Part A of this edition. Its effective date is 1 January 2013. This part presents the following accompanying documents:

Approval by the Board of IFRS 9 issued in November 2009

International Financial Reporting Standard 9 *Financial Instruments* was approved for issue by thirteen of the fifteen members of the International Accounting Standards Board. Mr Leisenring and Ms McConnell dissented from the issue of the IFRS. Their dissenting opinions are set out after the Basis for Conclusions.

Sir David Tweedie   Chairman

Stephen Cooper

Philippe Danjou

Jan Engström

Patrick Finnegan

Robert P Garnett

Gilbert Gélard

Amaro Luiz de Oliveira Gomes

Prabhakar Kalavacherla

James J Leisenring

Patricia McConnell

Warren J McGregor

John T Smith

Tatsumi Yamada

Wei-Guo Zhang

Contents

Basis for Conclusions on
IFRS 9 *Financial Instruments*

This Basis for Conclusions accompanies, but is not part of, IFRS 9.

Introduction

BC1   This Basis for Conclusions summarises the International Accounting Standards Board's considerations in developing IFRS 9 *Financial Instruments*. Individual Board members gave greater weight to some factors than to others.

BC2   The Board has long acknowledged the need to improve the requirements for financial reporting of financial instruments to make it easier for users of financial statements to understand financial reporting information. To meet the heightened urgency of that need in the light of the financial crisis, the Board proposes to replace IAS 39 *Financial Instruments: Recognition and Measurement* by the end of 2010. To make progress as quickly as possible the Board has divided the project into several phases. In adopting this approach, the Board acknowledged the difficulties that might be created by differences in timing between this project and others, in particular phase II of the project on insurance contracts. (Paragraphs BC91(b), BC93 and BC113–BC117 discuss issues relating to insurance contracts.)

BC3   IFRS 9 is a new standard dealing with the accounting for financial instruments. In developing IFRS 9, the Board considered the responses to its exposure draft *Financial Instruments: Classification and Measurement*, published in July 2009. As a result, in November 2009 the Board finalised the first part of IFRS 9, dealing with classification and measurement of financial assets. In the Board's view, requirements on classification and measurement are the foundation for any financial reporting standard, and requirements on associated matters (for example, on impairment and hedge accounting) have to reflect those requirements. In addition, the Board noted that many of the application issues that have arisen in the financial crisis are related to the classification and measurement of financial assets in accordance with IAS 39.

BC4   The Board sees this first phase of the project to replace IAS 39 as a stepping stone to future improvements in the financial reporting of financial instruments and is committed to completing its project on financial instruments expeditiously. The Board is also committed to the convergence of IFRSs and US GAAP requirements for financial instruments. There are many detailed differences between them, making it impossible to achieve convergence on the basis of existing requirements. The Board will consider publishing for comment any proposals that the US Financial Accounting Standards Board (FASB) may publish, to the extent that they are different from IFRSs or proposed IFRSs.

Scope

BC5   The Board has not yet considered the scope of IFRS 9. The scope of IAS 39 and its interaction with other IFRSs have resulted in some application and interpretation issues. However, the Board believes that it should address the issue of scope comprehensively rather than only in the context of classification and measurement. The scope of IAS 39 has not been raised as a matter of concern during the financial crisis and, hence, the Board believes that the scope of IFRS 9 should be based on that of IAS 39 until it considers the scope more generally in a later phase of the project to replace IAS 39.

BC6 The exposure draft contained proposals for all items within the scope of IAS 39. However, some respondents to the exposure draft said that the Board should restrict its proposals on classification and measurement to financial assets and retain the existing requirements for financial liabilities (including the requirements for embedded derivatives and the fair value option) until the Board has more fully considered and debated the issues relating to financial liabilities. Those respondents pointed out that the Board accelerated its project on financial instruments because of the global financial crisis, which placed more emphasis on issues in the accounting for financial assets than for financial liabilities. They suggested that the Board should consider issues that arise from its projects on own credit risk and other related projects more fully before finalising the requirements for classification and measurement of financial liabilities.

BC7 The Board noted those concerns and decided that IFRS 9 should at this stage apply only to assets within the scope of IAS 39. Thus, financial liabilities, including derivative liabilities, remain within the scope of IAS 39. Accordingly, this Basis for Conclusions discusses the responses to the exposure draft as they apply to the classification and measurement of financial assets. Taking this course will enable the Board to obtain further feedback on the accounting for financial liabilities, including how best to address accounting for changes in own credit risk.

Classification

BC8 In IFRS 9 the Board aimed to improve the ability of users to understand the financial reporting of financial assets by:

(a) reducing the number of classification categories and providing a clearer rationale for measuring financial assets in a particular way that replaces the numerous categories in IAS 39, each of which has specific rules dictating how an asset can or must be classified;

(b) applying a single impairment method to all financial assets not measured at fair value, which replaces the many different impairment methods that are associated with the numerous classification categories in IAS 39; and

(c) aligning the measurement attribute of financial assets to the way the entity manages its financial assets ('business model') and their contractual cash flow characteristics, thus providing relevant and useful information to users for their assessment of the amounts, timing and uncertainty of the entity's future cash flows.

BC9 The Board believes that IFRS 9 both improves the ability of users to understand and use the financial reporting of financial assets and eliminates much of the complexity in IAS 39. The Board disagrees with the assertion made by a dissenting Board member that IFRS 9 does not meet the objective of reducing the number of classification categories for financial assets and eliminating the specific rules associated with those categories. Unlike IAS 39, IFRS 9 provides a clear rationale for measuring a financial asset at either amortised cost or fair value, and hence improves the ability of users to understand the financial reporting of financial assets. IFRS 9 aligns the measurement attribute of financial assets to the way the entity manages its financial assets ('business model') and their contractual cash flow characteristics. In so doing, IFRS 9 significantly reduces complexity by eliminating the numerous rules associated with each classification category in IAS 39. Consistently with all other financial assets, hybrid contracts with financial asset hosts are classified and measured in their entirety, thereby eliminating the complex and rule-based requirements in IAS 39 for embedded derivatives. Furthermore, IFRS 9 requires a single impairment method, which replaces the different impairment methods associated with the many classification categories in IAS 39. The Board believes that these changes will improve the ability of users to understand the financial reporting of financial assets and to better assess the amounts, timing and uncertainty of future cash flows.

Measurement categories

BC10   Some users of financial statements support a single measurement method—fair value—for all financial assets. They view fair value as more relevant than other measurements in helping them to assess the effect of current economic events on an entity. They assert that having one measurement attribute for all financial assets promotes consistency in valuation, presentation and disclosure and improves the usefulness of financial statements.

BC11   However, many users and others, including many preparers and auditors of financial statements and regulators, do not support the recognition in the statement of comprehensive income of changes in fair value for financial assets that are not held for trading or are not managed on a fair value basis. Some users say that they often value an entity on the basis of its business model and that in some circumstances cost-based information provides relevant information that can be used to predict likely actual cash flows.

BC12   Some, including some of those who generally support the broad application of fair value for financial assets, raise concerns about the use of fair value when fair value cannot be determined within a narrow range. Those views were consistent with the general concerns raised during the financial crisis. Many also believe that other issues, including financial statement presentation, need to be addressed before a comprehensive fair value measurement requirement would be feasible.

BC13   In response to those views, the Board decided that measuring all financial assets at fair value is not the most appropriate approach to improving the financial reporting for financial instruments. Accordingly, the exposure draft proposed that entities should classify financial assets into two primary measurement categories: amortised cost and fair value (the 'mixed attribute approach'). The Board noted that both of those measurement methods can provide useful information to users of financial statements for particular types of financial assets in particular circumstances.

BC14   Almost all respondents to the exposure draft supported the mixed attribute approach, stating that amortised cost provides relevant and useful information about particular financial assets in particular circumstances because it provides information about the entity's likely actual cash flows. Some respondents said that fair value does not provide such information because it assumes that the financial asset is sold or transferred on the measurement date.

BC15 Accordingly, IFRS 9 requires some financial assets to be measured at amortised cost if particular conditions are met.

Fair value information in the statements of financial position and financial performance

BC16 Some respondents to the exposure draft proposed that fair value information should be presented in the statement of financial position for financial assets measured at amortised cost. Some of those supporting such presentation said that the information provided would be more reliable and timely if it were required to be presented in the statement of financial position rather than in the notes.

BC17 The Board also considered whether the total gains and losses for the period related to fair value measurements in Level 3 of the fair value measurement hierarchy (paragraph 27A of IFRS 7 *Financial Instruments: Disclosures* describes the levels in the fair value hierarchy) should be presented separately in the statement of comprehensive income. Those supporting such presentation said that its prominence would draw attention to how much of the total fair value gain or loss for the period was attributable to fair value measurements that are subject to more measurement uncertainty.

BC18 The Board decided that it would reconsider both issues at a future date. The Board noted that the Level 3 gains or losses for the period are required to be disclosed in the notes to the financial statements in accordance with IFRS 7. The Board also noted that neither proposal had been exposed for public comment and further consultation was required. The Board decided that these two issues should form part of convergence discussions with the FASB.

Approach to classification

BC19 The exposure draft proposed that an entity should classify its financial assets into two primary measurement categories on the basis of the financial assets' characteristics and the entity's business model for managing them. Thus, a financial asset would be measured at amortised cost if two conditions were met:

(a) the financial asset has only basic loan features; and

(b) the financial asset is managed on a contractual yield basis.

A financial asset that did not meet both conditions would be measured at fair value.

BC20 Most respondents supported classification based on the contractual terms of the financial asset and how an entity manages groups of financial assets. Although they agreed with the principles proposed in the exposure draft, some did not agree with the way the approach was described and said that more application guidance was needed, in particular to address the following issues:

(a) the order in which the two conditions are considered;

(b) how the 'managed on a contractual yield basis' condition should be applied; and

(c) how the 'basic loan features' condition should be applied.

BC21 Most respondents agreed that the two conditions for determining how financial assets are measured were necessary. However, many questioned the order in which the two conditions should be considered. The Board agreed with those comment letters that stated that it would be more efficient for an entity to consider the business model condition first. Therefore, the Board clarified that entities would consider the business model first. However, the Board noted that the contractual cash flow characteristics of any financial asset within a business model that has the objective of collecting contractual cash flows must also be assessed to ensure that amortised cost provides relevant information to users.

The entity's business model

BC22 The Board concluded that an entity's business model affects the predictive quality of contractual cash flows—ie whether the likely actual cash flows will result primarily from the collection of contractual cash flows. Accordingly, the exposure draft proposed that a financial asset should be measured at amortised cost only if it is 'managed on a contractual yield basis'. This condition was intended to ensure that the measurement of a financial asset provides information that is useful to users of financial statements in predicting likely actual cash flows.

BC23 Almost all respondents to the exposure draft agreed that classification and measurement should reflect how an entity manages its financial assets. However, most expressed concern that the term 'managed on a contractual yield basis' would not adequately describe that principle and that more guidance was needed.

BC24 In August 2009 the FASB posted on its website a description of its tentative approach to classification and measurement of financial instruments. That approach also considers the entity's business model. Under that approach, financial instruments would be measured at fair value through profit or loss unless:

> ... an entity's business strategy is to hold debt instruments with principal amounts for collection or payment(s) of contractual cash flows rather than to sell or settle the financial instruments with a third party ...

The FASB also provided explanatory text:

> ... an entity's business strategy for a financial instrument would be evaluated based on how the entity manages its financial instruments rather than based on the entity's intent for an individual financial instrument. The entity also would demonstrate that it holds a high proportion of similar instruments for long periods of time relative to their contractual terms.

BC25 The Board had intended 'managed on a contractual yield basis' to describe a similar condition. However, it decided not to use the FASB's proposed guidance because the additional guidance included would still necessitate significant judgement. In addition, the Board noted that the FASB's proposed approach might be viewed as very similar to the notion of 'held to maturity' in IAS 39, which could result in 'bright line' guidance on how to apply it. Most respondents believed the Board should avoid such bright lines and that an entity should be required to exercise judgement.

BC26   Therefore, in response to the concerns noted in paragraph BC23, the Board clarified the condition by requiring an entity to measure a financial asset at amortised cost only if the objective of the entity's business model is to hold the financial asset to collect the contractual cash flows. The Board also clarified in the application guidance that:

(a)   it is expected that an entity may sell some financial assets that it holds with an objective of collecting the contractual cash flows. Very few business models entail holding all instruments until maturity. However, frequent buying and selling of financial assets is not consistent with a business model of holding financial assets to collect contractual cash flows.

(b)   an entity needs to use judgement to determine at what level this condition should be applied. That determination is made on the basis of how an entity manages its business. It is not made at the level of an individual financial asset.

BC27   The Board noted that an entity's business model does not relate to a choice (ie it is not a voluntary designation) but rather it is a matter of fact that can be observed by the way an entity is managed and information is provided to its management.

BC28   For example, if an investment bank uses a trading business model, it could not easily become a savings bank that uses an 'originate and hold' business model. Therefore, a business model is very different from 'management intentions' which can relate to a single instrument. The Board concluded that sales or transfers of financial instruments before maturity would not be inconsistent with a business model with an objective of collecting contractual cash flows, as long as such transactions were consistent with that business model, rather than with a business model that has the objective of realising changes in fair values.

Contractual cash flow characteristics

BC29   The exposure draft proposed that only financial instruments with basic loan features could be measured at amortised cost. It specified that a financial instrument has basic loan features if its contractual terms give rise on specified dates to cash flows that are solely payments of principal and interest on the principal amount outstanding. For the purposes of this condition, interest is consideration for the time value of money and the credit risk associated with the principal amount outstanding during a particular period of time, which may include a premium for liquidity risk.

BC30   The objective of the effective interest method for financial instruments measured at amortised cost is to allocate interest revenue or expense to the relevant period. Cash flows that are interest always have a close relation to the amount advanced to the debtor (the 'funded' amount) because interest is consideration for the time value of money and the credit risk associated with the issuer of the instrument and with the instrument itself. The Board noted that the effective interest method is not an appropriate method to allocate cash flows that are not principal or interest on the principal amount outstanding. The Board concluded that if a financial asset contains contractual cash flows that are not principal or interest on the principal amount outstanding then a valuation overlay to contractual cash flows (fair value) is required to ensure that the reported financial information provides useful information.

BC31 Most respondents to the exposure draft agreed with the principle that classification should reflect the contractual terms of the financial asset. However, many objected to the label 'basic loan features' and requested more guidance to apply the principle to particular financial assets. Respondents were also concerned that the exposure draft did not discuss 'immaterial' or 'insignificant' features that they believed ought not to affect classification.

BC32 The Board decided to clarify how contractual cash flow characteristics should affect classification and improve the examples that illustrate how the condition should be applied. It decided not to add application guidance clarifying that the notion of materiality applies to this condition, because that notion applies to every item in the financial statements. However, it did add application guidance that a contractual cash flow characteristic does not affect the classification of a financial asset if it is 'not genuine'.

Application of the two classification conditions to particular financial assets

Investments in contractually linked instruments (tranches)

BC33 A structured investment vehicle may issue different tranches to create a 'waterfall' structure that prioritises the payments by the issuer to the holders of the different tranches. In typical waterfall structures, multiple contractually linked instruments effect concentrations of credit risk in which payments to holders are prioritised. Such structures specify the order in which any losses that the issuer incurs are allocated to the tranches. The exposure draft concluded that tranches providing credit protection (albeit on a contingent basis) to other tranches are leveraged because they expose themselves to higher credit risk by writing credit protection to other tranches. Hence their cash flows do not represent solely payments of principal and interest on the principal amount outstanding. Thus, only the most senior tranche could have basic loan features and might qualify for measurement at amortised cost, because only the most senior tranche would receive credit protection in all situations.

BC34 The exposure draft proposed that the classification principle should be based on whether a tranche could provide credit protection to any other tranches in *any* possible scenario. In the Board's view, a contract that contains credit concentration features that create ongoing subordination (not only in a liquidation scenario) would include contractual cash flows that represent a premium for providing credit protection to other tranches. Only the most senior tranche does not receive such a premium.

BC35 In proposing this approach, the Board concluded that subordination in itself should not preclude amortised cost measurement. The ranking of an entity's instruments is a common form of subordination that affects almost all lending transactions. Commercial law (including bankruptcy law) typically sets out a basic ranking for creditors. This is required because not all creditors' claims are contractual (eg claims regarding damages for unlawful behaviour and for tax liabilities or social insurance contributions). Although it is often difficult to determine exactly the degree of leverage resulting from this subordination, the Board believes that it is reasonable to assume that commercial law does not intend to create leveraged credit exposure for general creditors such as trade creditors. Thus, the Board believes that the credit risk associated with general creditors does not preclude the contractual cash flows representing the payments of principal and interest on the principal amount outstanding. Consequently, the credit risk associated with any secured or senior liabilities ranking above general creditors should also not preclude the contractual cash flows from representing payments of principal and interest on the principal amount outstanding.

BC36 Almost all respondents disagreed with the approach in the exposure draft for investments in contractually linked instruments for the following reasons:

(a) It focused on form and legal structure rather than the economic characteristics of the financial instruments.

(b) It would create structuring opportunities because of the focus on the existence of a waterfall structure, without consideration of the characteristics of the underlying instruments.

(c) It would be an exception to the overall classification model, driven by anti-abuse considerations.

BC37 In particular, respondents argued that the proposals in the exposure draft would conclude that some tranches provide credit protection and therefore were ineligible for measurement at amortised cost, even though that tranche might have a lower credit risk than the underlying pool of instruments that would themselves be eligible for measurement at amortised cost.

BC38 The Board did not agree that the proposals in the exposure draft were an exception to the overall classification model. In the Board's view, those proposals were consistent with many respondents' view that any financial instrument that creates contractual subordination should be subject to the proposed classification criteria and no specific guidance should be required to apply the classification approach to these instruments. However, it noted that, for contractually linked instruments that effect concentrations of credit risk, many respondents did not agree that the contractual cash flow characteristics determined by the terms and conditions of the financial asset in isolation best reflected the economic characteristics of that financial asset.

BC39 Respondents proposed other approaches in which an investor 'looks through' to the underlying pool of instruments of a waterfall structure and measures the instruments at fair value if looking through is not possible. They made the following points:

(a) *Practicability:* The securitisation transactions intended to be addressed were generally over-the-counter transactions in which the parties involved had sufficient information about the assets to perform an analysis of the underlying pool of instruments.

(b) *Complexity:* Complex accounting judgement was appropriate to reflect the complex economic characteristics of the instrument. In particular, in order to obtain an understanding of the effects of the contractual terms and conditions, an investor would have to understand the underlying pool of instruments. Also, requiring fair value measurement if it were not practicable to look through to the underlying pool of instruments would allow an entity to avoid such complexity.

(c) *Mechanics:* Amortised cost measurement should be available only if all of the instruments in the underlying pool of instruments had contractual cash flows that represented payments of principal and interest on the principal amount outstanding. Some also suggested that instruments that change the cash flow variability of the underlying pool of instruments in a way that is consistent with representing solely payments of principal and interest on the principal amount outstanding, or aligned currency/interest rates with the issued notes, should not preclude amortised cost measurement.

(d) *Relative exposure to credit risk:* Many favoured use of a probability-weighted approach to assess whether an instrument has a lower or higher exposure to credit risk than the average credit risk of the underlying pool of instruments.

BC40 The Board was persuaded that classification based solely on the contractual features of the financial asset being assessed for classification would not capture the economic characteristics of the instruments when a concentrated credit risk arises through contractual linkage. Therefore, the Board decided that, unless it is impracticable, an entity should 'look through' to assess the underlying cash flow characteristics of the financial assets and to assess the exposure to credit risk of those financial assets relative to the underlying pool of instruments.

BC41 The Board concluded that the nature of contractually linked instruments that effect concentrations of credit risk justifies this approach because the variability of cash flows from the underlying pool of instruments is a reference point, and tranching only reallocates credit risk. Thus, if the contractual cash flows of the assets in the underlying pool represent payments of principal and interest on the principal amount outstanding, any tranche that is exposed to the same or lower credit risk (as evidenced by the cash flow variability of the tranche relative to the overall cash flow variability of the underlying instrument pool) would also be deemed to represent payments of principal and interest on the principal amount outstanding. The Board also took the view that such an approach would address many of the concerns raised in the comment letters with regard to structuring opportunities and the focus on the contractual form of the financial asset, rather than its underlying economic characteristics. The Board also noted that in order to understand and make the judgement about whether particular types of financial assets have the required cash flow characteristics, an entity would have to understand the characteristics of the underlying issuer to ensure that the instrument's cash flows are solely payments of principal and interest on the principal amount outstanding.

BC42 To apply this approach, the Board decided that an entity should:

(a) determine whether the contractual terms of the issued instrument (the financial asset being classified) give rise to cash flows that are solely payments of principal and interest on the principal amount outstanding. The Board concluded that the issued instrument must have contractual cash flows that are solely payments of principal and interest on the principal amount outstanding.

(b) look through to the underlying pool of instruments until it can identify the instruments that are creating (rather than simply passing through) the cash flows.

(c) determine whether one or more of the instruments in the underlying pool has contractual cash flows that are solely payments of principal and interest on the principal amount outstanding. The Board concluded the underlying pool must contain one or more instruments that have contractual cash flows that are solely payments of principal and interest on the principal amount outstanding.

(d) assess whether any other instruments in the underlying pool only:

  (i) reduce the cash flow variability of the underlying pool of instruments in a way that is consistent with representing solely payments of principal and interest on the principal amount outstanding, or

  (ii) align the cash flows of the issued financial assets with the underlying pool of financial instruments.

  The Board concluded that the existence of such instruments does not preclude the cash flows from representing solely payments of principal and interest on the principal amount outstanding. The Board determined that the existence of other instruments in the pool would, however, preclude the cash flows representing solely payments of principal and interest on the principal amount outstanding. For example, an underlying pool that contains government bonds and an instrument that swaps government credit risk for (riskier) corporate credit risk would not have cash flows that represent solely principal and interest on the principal amount outstanding.

(e) measure at fair value any issued instrument in which any of the financial instruments in the underlying pool:

  (i) have cash flows that do not represent solely payments of principal and interest on the principal amount outstanding; or

  (ii) could change so that cash flows may not represent solely payments of principal and interest on the principal amount outstanding at any point in the future.

(f) measure at fair value any issued instrument whose exposure to credit risk in the underlying pool of financial instruments is greater than the exposure to credit risk of the underlying pool of financial instruments. The Board decided that if the range of expected losses on the issued instrument is greater than the weighted average range of expected losses on the underlying pool of financial instruments, then the issued instrument should be measured at fair value.

BC43 The Board also decided that if it were not practicable to look through to the underlying pool of financial instruments, entities should measure the issued instrument at fair value.

Financial assets acquired at a discount that reflects incurred credit losses

BC44 The exposure draft proposed that if a financial asset is acquired at a discount that reflects incurred credit losses, it cannot be measured at amortised cost because:

(a) the entity does not hold such financial assets to collect the cash flows arising from those assets' contractual terms; and

(b) an investor acquiring a financial asset at such a discount believes that the actual losses will be less than the losses that are reflected in the purchase price. Thus, that asset creates exposure to significant variability in actual cash flows and such variability is not interest.

BC45 Almost all respondents disagreed with the Board's conclusion that these assets cannot be held to collect the contractual cash flows. They regarded that conclusion as an exception to a classification approach based on the entity's business model for managing the financial assets. In particular, they noted that entities could acquire and subsequently manage such assets as part of an otherwise performing asset portfolio for which the objective of the entity's business model is to hold the assets to collect contractual cash flows.

BC46 Respondents also noted that an entity's expectations about actual future cash flows are not the same as the contractual cash flows of the financial asset. Those expectations are irrelevant to an assessment of the financial asset's contractual cash flow characteristics.

BC47 The Board agreed that the general classification approach in IFRS 9 should apply to financial assets acquired at a discount that reflects incurred credit losses. Thus, when such assets meet the conditions in paragraph 4.2, they are measured at amortised cost.

Alternative approaches to classification

BC48 In its deliberations leading to the exposure draft, the Board discussed alternative approaches to classification and measurement. In particular, it considered an approach in which financial assets that have basic loan features, are managed on a contractual yield basis and meet the definition of loans and receivables in IAS 39 would be measured at amortised cost. All other financial assets would be measured at fair value. The fair value changes for each period for those financial assets with basic loan features that are managed on a contractual yield basis would be disaggregated and presented as follows:

(a) changes in recognised value determined on an amortised cost basis (including impairments determined using the incurred loss impairment requirements in IAS 39) would be presented in profit or loss; and

(b) any difference between the amortised cost measure in (a) and the fair value change for the period would be presented in other comprehensive income.

BC49 The Board also considered variants in which all financial assets and financial liabilities would be measured at fair value. One variant would be to present both the amounts in paragraph BC48(a) and (b) in profit or loss, but separately. Another variant would be to measure all financial instruments (including financial assets that meet the two conditions specified in the exposure draft and meet the definition of loans and receivables in IAS 39) at fair value in the statement of financial position. All financial instruments (including financial liabilities) with basic loan features that are managed on a contractual yield basis would be disaggregated and presented as described in paragraph BC48(a) and (b).

BC50 Respondents noted that the alternative approach described in paragraph BC48 and both variants described in paragraph BC49 would result in more financial assets and financial liabilities being measured at fair value. Respondents also noted that the alternative approach would apply only to financial assets. Lastly, almost all respondents noted that splitting gains and losses between profit or loss and other comprehensive income would increase complexity and reduce understandability. The Board concluded that those approaches would not result in more useful information than the approach in IFRS 9 and did not consider them further.

BC51 The Board also considered and rejected the following approaches to classification:

(a) *Classification based on the definition of held for trading:* A few respondents suggested that all financial assets and financial liabilities that are not 'held for trading' should be eligible for measurement at amortised cost. However, in the Board's view, the notion of 'held for trading' is too narrow and cannot appropriately reflect all situations in which amortised cost does not provide useful information.

(b) *Three-category approach:* Some respondents suggested retaining a three-category approach, ie including a third category similar to the available-for-sale category in IAS 39. However, in the Board's view, such an approach would neither significantly improve nor reduce the complexity of the reporting for financial instruments.

(c) *Classification based only on the business model:* A small number of respondents thought the contractual terms of the instrument condition was unnecessary and that classification should depend solely on the entity's business model for managing financial instruments. However, in the Board's view, determining classification solely on the basis of how an entity manages its financial instruments would result in misleading information that is not useful to a user in understanding the risks associated with complex or risky instruments. The Board concluded, as had almost all respondents, that the contractual cash flow characteristics condition is required to ensure that amortised cost is used only when it provides information that is useful in predicting the entity's future cash flows.

(d) *Amortised cost as the default option:* The Board considered developing conditions that specified when a financial asset must be measured at fair value, with the requirement that all other financial instruments would be measured at amortised cost. The Board rejected that approach because it believes that new conditions would have to be developed in the future to address innovative financial products. In addition, the Board noted that such an approach would not be practical because an entity can apply amortised cost only to some types of financial instruments.

(e)   *Originated loan approach:* In developing an approach to distinguish between financial assets measured at fair value and amortised cost the Board considered a model in which only loans originated by the entity would qualify for amortised cost measurement. The Board acknowledged that for originated instruments the entity potentially has better information about the future contractual cash flows and credit risk than for purchased loans. However, the Board decided not to pursue that approach, mainly because some entities manage originated and purchased loans in the same portfolio. Distinguishing between originated and purchased loans, which would be done mainly for accounting purposes, would involve systems changes. In addition, the Board noted that 'originated loans' might easily be created by placing purchased loans into an investment vehicle. The Board also noted that the definition of loans and receivables in IAS 39 had created application problems in practice.

Tainting

BC52   The Board considered whether it should prohibit an entity from classifying a financial asset as measured at amortised cost if the entity had previously sold or reclassified financial assets rather than holding them to collect the contractual cash flows. A restriction of this kind is often called 'tainting'. However, the Board believes that classification based on the entity's business model for managing financial assets and the contractual cash flow characteristics of those financial assets provides a clear rationale for measurement. A tainting provision would increase the complexity of application, be unduly prohibitive in the context of that approach and could give rise to classification inconsistent with the classification approach. However, the Board amended IAS 1 *Presentation of Financial Statements* to require an entity to present separately in the statement of comprehensive income all gains and losses arising from the derecognition of financial assets measured at amortised cost. The Board also amended IFRS 7 to require an entity to disclose an analysis of those gains and losses, including the reasons for derecognising those financial assets. Those requirements enable users of financial statements to understand the effects of derecognising before maturity instruments measured at amortised cost and also provides transparency in situations where an entity has measured financial assets at amortised cost on the basis of having an objective of managing those assets in order to collect the contractual cash flows but regularly sells them.

Embedded derivatives

BC53   An embedded derivative is a derivative component of a hybrid (combined) contract that also includes a non-derivative host, with the effect that some of the cash flows of the combined contract vary like the cash flows of a stand-alone derivative contract. IAS 39 requires an entity to assess all contracts to determine whether they contain one or more embedded derivatives that are required to be separated from the host and accounted for as stand-alone derivatives.

BC54   Many respondents to the discussion paper *Reducing Complexity in Reporting Financial Instruments* commented that the requirements and guidance in IAS 39 are complex, rule-based and internally inconsistent. Respondents, and others, also noted the many application problems that arise from requirements to assess all non-derivative contracts for embedded derivatives and, if required, to account for and measure those embedded derivatives separately as stand-alone derivatives.

BC55   The Board discussed three approaches for accounting for embedded derivatives:

(a)   to maintain the requirements in IAS 39;

(b)   to use 'closely related' (used in IAS 39 to determine whether an embedded derivative is required to be separated from the host) to determine the classification for the contract in its entirety; and

(c)   to use the same classification approach for all financial assets (including hybrid contracts).

BC56   The Board rejected the first two approaches. The Board noted that both would rely on the assessment of whether an embedded derivative is 'closely related' to the host. The 'closely related' assessment in IAS 39 is based on a list of examples that are inconsistent and unclear. That assessment is also a significant source of complexity. Both approaches would result in hybrid contracts being classified using conditions different from those that would be applied to all non-hybrid financial instruments. Consequently, some hybrid contracts whose contractual cash flows do not solely represent payments of principal and interest on the principal amount outstanding might be measured at amortised cost. Similarly, some hybrid contracts whose contractual cash flows do meet the conditions for measurement at amortised cost might be measured at fair value. The Board also believes that neither approach would make it easier for users of financial statements to understand the information that financial statements present about financial instruments.

BC57   Therefore, the exposure draft proposed that entities should use the same classification approach for all financial instruments, including hybrid contracts with hosts within the scope of the proposed IFRS ('financial hosts'). The Board concluded that a single classification approach for all financial instruments and hybrid contracts with financial hosts was the only approach that responded adequately to the criticisms described above. The Board noted that using a single classification approach improves comparability by ensuring consistency in classification, and hence makes it easier for users to understand the information that financial statements present about financial instruments.

BC58   In the responses to the exposure draft, some respondents, mainly preparers, stated their preference for keeping or modifying the bifurcation model that was in IAS 39. They noted that:

(a)   eliminating the requirement to account for embedded derivatives as stand-alone derivatives would lead to increased volatility in profit or loss and result in accounting that did not reflect the underlying economics and risk management or business model considerations in a transaction. For example, the components of some hybrid financial instruments may be managed separately.

(b) structuring opportunities would be created, for example if an entity entered into two transactions that have the same economic effect as entering into a single hybrid contract.

BC59 However, the Board confirmed the proposals in the exposure draft for the following reasons:

(a) The elimination of the embedded derivatives guidance for hybrid contracts with financial hosts reduces the complexity in financial reporting of financial assets by eliminating another classification approach and improves the reporting for financial instruments. Many constituents agreed with this conclusion.

(b) In the Board's view, the underlying rationale for separate accounting for embedded derivatives is not to reflect risk management activities, but to avoid entities circumventing the recognition and measurement requirements for derivatives. Accordingly it is an exception to the definition of the unit of account (the contract) motivated by a wish to avoid abuse. It would reduce complexity to eliminate an anti-abuse exception.

(c) The Board noted the concerns about structuring opportunities referred to in paragraph BC58(b). However, two contracts represent two units of account. Reconsideration of the unit of account forms part of a far broader issue for financial reporting that is outside the scope of the Board's considerations in IFRS 9. In addition, embedded derivative features often do not have contractual cash flows that represent payments of principal and interest on the principal amount outstanding and thus the entire hybrid contract would not be eligible to be measured at amortised cost. However, the Board noted that this would provide more relevant information because the embedded derivative feature affects the cash flows ultimately arising from the hybrid contract. Thus, applying the classification approach to the hybrid contract in its entirety would depict more faithfully the amount, timing and uncertainty of future cash flows.

(d) In the Board's view, accounting for the hybrid contract as one unit of account is consistent with the project's objective—to improve the usefulness for users in their assessment of the timing, amount and uncertainty of future cash flows of financial instruments and to reduce the complexity in reporting financial instruments.

Because the Board decided that the scope of IFRS 9 at this stage should be assets within the scope of IAS 39, this decision applies only to hybrid contracts with financial asset hosts.

BC60 The Board decided not to consider at this time changes to the requirements in IAS 39 for embedded derivatives in hybrid contracts with non-financial hosts. The Board acknowledged that those requirements are also complex and have resulted in some application problems, including the question of whether particular types of non-financial contracts are within the scope of IAS 39. The Board accepted the importance of ensuring that any proposals for hybrid contracts with non-financial hosts should also address which non-financial contracts should be within the scope of IFRS 9. The Board also noted the importance for many non-financial entities of hedge accounting for non-financial items, and the relationship to both scope and embedded derivative requirements. Therefore, the Board concluded that the requirements for hybrid contracts with non-financial hosts should be addressed in a later phase of the project to replace IAS 39.

Option to designate a financial asset at fair value

BC61   IAS 39 allows entities an option to designate on initial recognition any financial asset or financial liability as measured at fair value through profit or loss if one (or more) of the following three conditions is met:

(a)   Doing so eliminates or significantly reduces a measurement or recognition inconsistency (sometimes referred to as an 'accounting mismatch') that would otherwise arise from measuring assets or liabilities on different bases or recognising the gains and losses on them on different bases.

(b)   A group of financial assets, financial liabilities or both is managed and its performance is evaluated on a fair value basis, in accordance with a documented risk management or investment strategy, and information about the group is provided internally on that basis to the entity's key management personnel.

(c)   The financial asset or financial liability contains one or more embedded derivatives (and particular other conditions described in paragraph 11A of IAS 39 are met) and the entity elects to account for the hybrid (combined) contract in its entirety.

BC62   However, in contrast to IAS 39, IFRS 9 requires:

(a)   any financial asset that is not managed within a business model that has the objective of collecting contractual cash flows to be measured at fair value; and

(b)   hybrid contracts with financial asset hosts to be classified in their entirety, hence eliminating the requirement to identify and account for embedded derivatives separately.

Accordingly, the Board concluded that the conditions described in paragraph BC61(b) and (c) are unnecessary for financial assets.

BC63   The Board retained the eligibility condition described in paragraph BC61(a) because it mitigates some anomalies that result from the different measurement attributes used for financial instruments. In particular, it eliminates the need for fair value hedge accounting of fair value exposures when there are natural offsets. It also avoids problems arising from a mixed measurement model when some financial assets are measured at amortised cost and related financial liabilities are measured at fair value. A separate phase of the project is considering hedge accounting, and the fair value option will be better considered in that context. The Board also noted that particular industry sectors believe it is important to be able to mitigate such anomalies until other IASB projects are completed (eg insurance contracts). The Board decided to defer consideration of changes to the eligibility condition set out in paragraph BC61(a) as part of the future exposure draft on hedge accounting.

BC64   Almost all the respondents to the exposure draft supported the proposal to retain the fair value option if such designation eliminates or significantly reduces an accounting mismatch. Although some respondents would prefer an unrestricted fair value option, they acknowledged that an unrestricted fair value option has been opposed by many in the past and it is not appropriate to pursue it now.

Reclassification between fair value and amortised cost categories

BC65   The exposure draft proposed to prohibit reclassification of financial assets between the amortised cost and fair value categories. The Board's rationale for that proposal was as follows:

(a)   Requiring (or permitting) reclassifications would not make it easier for users of financial statements to understand the information that financial statements provide about financial instruments.

(b)   Requiring (or permitting) reclassifications would increase complexity because detailed guidance would be required to specify when reclassifications would be required (or permitted) and the subsequent accounting for reclassified financial instruments.

(c)   Reclassification should not be necessary because classification is based on the entity's business model and that business model is not expected to change.

BC66   In their responses, some users questioned the usefulness of reclassified information, noting concerns about the consistency and rigour with which any requirements would be applied. Some were also concerned that opportunistic reclassifications would be possible.

BC67   However, almost all respondents (including most users) argued that prohibiting reclassification is inconsistent with a classification approach based on how an entity manages its financial assets. They noted that in an approach based on an entity's business model for managing financial assets, reclassifications would provide useful, relevant and comparable information to users because it would ensure that financial statements faithfully represent how those financial assets are managed at the reporting date. In particular, most users stated that, conceptually, reclassifications should not be prohibited when the classification no longer reflects how the instruments would be classified if the items were newly acquired. If reclassification were prohibited, the reported information would not reflect the amounts, timing and uncertainty of future cash flows.

BC68   The Board was persuaded by these arguments and decided that reclassification should not be prohibited. The Board noted that prohibiting reclassification decreases comparability for like instruments managed in the same way.

BC69   Some respondents contended that reclassifications should be permitted, rather than required, but did not explain their justification. However, the Board noted that permitting reclassification would decrease comparability, both between different entities and for instruments held by a single entity, and would enable an entity to manage its profit or loss by selecting the timing of when future gains or losses are recognised. Therefore, the Board decided that reclassification should be required when the entity's business model for managing those financial assets changes.

BC70   The Board noted that, as highlighted by many respondents, such changes in business model would be very infrequent, significant and demonstrable and determined by the entity's senior management as a result of external or internal change.

BC71   The Board considered arguments that reclassification should also be permitted or required when contractual cash flow characteristics of a financial asset vary (or may vary) over that asset's life based on its original contractual terms. However, the Board noted that, unlike a change in business model, the contractual terms of a financial asset are known at initial recognition. An entity classifies the financial asset at initial recognition on the basis of the contractual terms over the life of the instrument. Therefore the Board decided that reclassification on the basis of a financial asset's contractual cash flows should not be permitted.

BC72   The Board considered how reclassifications should be accounted for. Almost all respondents said that reclassifications should be accounted for prospectively and should be accompanied by robust disclosures. The Board reasoned that if classification and reclassification are based on the business model within which they are managed, classification should always reflect the business model within which the financial asset was managed at the reporting date. To apply the reclassification retrospectively would not reflect how the financial assets were managed at the prior reporting dates.

BC73   The Board also considered the date at which reclassifications could take effect. Some respondents stated that reclassifications should be reflected in the entity's financial statements as soon as the entity's business model for the relevant instruments changes. To do otherwise would be contradictory to the objective of reclassification—ie to reflect how the instruments are managed. However, the Board decided that reclassifications should take effect from the beginning of the following reporting period. In the Board's view, entities should be prevented from choosing a reclassification date to achieve an accounting result. The Board also noted that a change in an entity's business model is a significant and demonstrable event; therefore, an entity will most likely disclose such an event in its financial statements in the reporting period in which the change in business model takes place.

BC74   The Board also considered and rejected the following approaches:

(a)   *Disclosure approach:* Quantitative and qualitative disclosure (instead of reclassification) could be used to address when the classification no longer reflects how the financial assets would be classified if they were newly acquired. However, in the Board's view, disclosure is not an adequate substitute for recognition.

(b)   *One-way reclassification:* Reclassification would be required only to fair value measurement, ie reclassification to amortised cost measurement would be prohibited. Proponents of this approach indicated that such an approach might minimise abuse of the reclassification requirements and result in more instruments being measured at fair value. However, in the Board's view, there is no conceptual reason to require reclassification in one direction but not the other.

Measurement

Exception in IAS 39 from fair value measurement for some unquoted equity instruments (and some derivatives linked to those instruments)

BC75 The Board believes that measurement at amortised cost is not applicable to equity investments because such financial assets have no contractual cash flows and hence there are no contractual cash flows to amortise. IAS 39 contains an exception from fair value measurement for investments in equity instruments (and some derivatives linked to those investments) that do not have a quoted price in an active market and whose fair value cannot be reliably measured. Those equity investments are required to be measured at cost less impairment, if any. Impairment losses are measured as the difference between the carrying amount of the financial asset and the present value of estimated future cash flows discounted at the current market rate of return for a similar financial asset.

BC76 The exposure draft proposed that all investments in equity instruments (and derivatives linked to those investments) should be measured at fair value for the following reasons:

(a) For investments in equity instruments and derivatives, fair value provides the most relevant information. Cost provides little, if any, information with predictive value about the timing, amount and uncertainty of the future cash flows arising from the instrument. In many cases, fair value will differ significantly from historical cost (this is particularly true for derivatives measured at cost under the exception).

(b) To ensure that a financial asset accounted for under the cost exception is not carried above its recoverable amount, IAS 39 requires an entity to monitor instruments measured at cost for any impairment. Calculating any impairment loss is similar to determining fair value (ie the estimated future cash flows are discounted using the current market rate of return for a similar financial asset and compared with the carrying amount).

(c) Removing the exception would reduce complexity because the classification model for financial assets would not have a third measurement attribute and would not require an additional impairment methodology. Although there might be an increase in the complexity of determining fair values on a recurring basis that complexity would be offset (at least partially) by the fact that all equity instruments and derivatives have one common measurement attribute; thus the impairment requirements would be eliminated.

BC77 Many respondents agreed that cost does not provide useful information about future cash flows arising from equity instruments and that conceptually such equity instruments should be measured using a current measurement attribute such as fair value. Some of those respondents generally agreed with the removal of the exception, but suggested that disclosures would have to include information about the uncertainties surrounding measurement.

BC78   However, many respondents (mainly preparers from non-financial entities and some auditors) disagreed with the proposal to eliminate the current cost exception on the grounds of the reliability and usefulness of fair value measurement and the cost and difficulty involved in determining fair value on a recurring basis. They generally preferred to keep a cost exception, similar to that in IAS 39. Some noted that the proposals would not reduce complexity, because they would increase complexity in measurement. Furthermore, a few believed that cost could provide useful information if the financial asset is held for the long term.

BC79   The Board considered those arguments as follows:

(a)   *Reliability and usefulness of fair value measurement*

Respondents noted that IAS 39 included a cost exception because of the lack of reliability of fair value measurement for particular equity instruments and contended that this rationale is still valid. They believe that, given the lack of available reliable information, any fair value measurement would require significant management judgement or might be impossible. They also believe that comparability would be impaired by the requirement to measure such equity instruments at fair value. However, those respondents had considered the question of reliability of fair value for the instruments concerned in isolation. In the Board's view, the usefulness of information must be assessed against all four of the qualitative characteristics in the *Framework*: reliability, understandability, relevance and comparability. Thus, cost is a reliable (and objective) amount, but has little, if any, relevance. In the Board's view measuring all equity instruments at fair value, including those that are currently measured using the cost exception in IAS 39, meets the criteria in the *Framework* for information to be reliable if appropriate measurement techniques and inputs are employed. The Board noted that its project on fair value measurement will provide guidance on how to meet that objective.

(b)   *Cost and difficulty involved in determining fair value on a recurring basis*

Many respondents, particularly in emerging economies, said that they faced difficulty in obtaining information that might be relied on to use in valuation. Others said that they would inevitably rely heavily on external experts at significant cost. Many questioned whether the requirement to determine fair value on a recurring basis would involve significant costs and efforts that are not offset by the incremental benefit to usefulness from fair value. The Board considered the costs of requiring such equity investments to be measured at fair value from the perspectives of valuation methodology and expertise, as well as the ability to obtain the information required for a fair value measurement. The Board noted that valuation methods for equity investments are well-developed and are often far less complex than those required for other financial instruments that are required to be measured at fair value, including many complex derivative products. Although some expressed concern that smaller entities applying IFRSs might not have internal systems or expertise to determine easily the fair value of equity investments held, the Board noted that basic shareholder rights generally enable an entity to obtain the necessary information to perform a valuation. The Board acknowledged that there are circumstances in which the cost of determining fair value could outweigh the benefits from fair value measurement. In particular, the Board noted that, in some jurisdictions, entities hold high numbers of unquoted equity instruments that are currently accounted for under the cost exception and the value of a single investment is considered low. However, the Board concluded that if the volume of the investments individually or aggregated is material the incremental benefit of fair value generally outweighs the additional cost because of the impact of the investments on the financial performance and position of the entity.

BC80   The Board noted that there are some circumstances in which cost might be representative of fair value and decided to provide additional application guidance on those circumstances to alleviate some of the concerns expressed. However, the Board also noted that those circumstances would never apply to equity investments held by particular entities such as financial institutions and investment funds.

BC81   The Board considered whether a simplified approach to measurement should be provided for equity instruments when fair value measurement was impracticable. The Board also discussed possible simplified measurement approaches, including management's best estimate of the price it would accept to sell or buy the instrument, or changes in the share of net assets. However, the Board concluded that a simplified measurement approach would add complexity to the classification approach and reduce the usefulness of information to users of financial statements. Those disadvantages would not be offset by the benefit of reduced cost to preparers of financial statements.

Gains and losses

Investments in equity instruments

BC82   IFRS 9 permits an entity to make an irrevocable election to present in other comprehensive income changes in the value of any investment in equity instruments that is not held for trading. The term 'equity instrument' is defined in IAS 32 *Financial Instruments: Presentation*. The Board noted that in particular circumstances a puttable instrument (or an instrument that imposes on the entity an obligation to deliver to another party a pro rata share of the net assets of the entity only on liquidation) is classified as equity. However, the Board noted that such instruments do not meet the definition of an equity instrument.

BC83   In the Board's view, fair value provides the most useful information about investments in equity instruments to users of financial statements. However, the Board noted arguments that presenting fair value gains and losses in profit or loss for some equity investments may not be indicative of the performance of the entity, particularly if the entity holds those equity instruments for non-contractual benefits, rather than primarily for increases in the value of the investment. An example could be a requirement to hold such an investment if an entity sells its products in a particular country.

BC84   The Board also noted that, in their valuation of an entity, users of financial statements often differentiate between fair value changes arising from equity investments held for purposes other than generating investment returns and equity investments held for trading. Thus, the Board believes that separate presentation in other comprehensive income of gains and losses for some investments could provide useful information to users of financial statements because it would allow them to identify easily, and value accordingly, the associated fair value changes.

BC85 Almost all respondents to the exposure draft supported recognition of fair value gains and losses in other comprehensive income for particular equity investments. They agreed that an entity should make an irrevocable election to identify those equity instruments. However, some users did not support these proposals in the exposure draft.

BC86 The concerns expressed in the comment letters were as follows:

(a) *Dividends:* The exposure draft proposed that dividends on equity instruments measured at fair value with changes recognised in other comprehensive income would also be recognised in other comprehensive income. Nearly all respondents objected to that proposal. They argued that dividends are a form of income that should be presented in profit or loss in accordance with IAS 18 *Revenue* and noted that those equity investments are sometimes funded with debt instruments whose interest expense is recognised in profit or loss. As a result, presenting dividends in other comprehensive income would create a 'mismatch'. Some listed investment funds stated that without recognising dividend income in profit or loss their financial statements would become meaningless to their investors. The Board agreed with those arguments. The Board noted that structuring opportunities may remain because dividends could represent a return of investment, rather than a return on investment. Therefore, the Board decided that dividends that clearly represent a recovery of part of the cost of the investment are not recognised in profit or loss. However, in the Board's view, those structuring opportunities would be limited because an entity with the ability to control or significantly influence the dividend policy of the investment would not account for those investments in accordance with IFRS 9. Furthermore, the Board decided to require disclosures that would allow a user to compare easily the dividends recognised in profit or loss and the other fair value changes.

(b) *Recycling:* Many respondents, including many users, did not support the proposal to prohibit subsequent transfer ('recycling') of fair value changes to profit or loss (on derecognition of the investments in an equity instrument). Those respondents supported an approach that maintains a distinction between realised and unrealised gains and losses and said that an entity's performance should include all realised gains and losses. However, the Board concluded that a gain or loss on those investments should be recognised once only; therefore, recognising a gain or loss in other comprehensive income and subsequently transferring it to profit or loss is inappropriate. In addition, the Board noted that recycling of gains and losses to profit or loss would create something similar to the available-for-sale category in IAS 39 and would create the requirement to assess the equity instrument for impairment, which had created application problems. That would not significantly improve or reduce the complexity of the financial reporting for financial assets. Accordingly, the Board decided to prohibit recycling of gains and losses into profit or loss when an equity instrument is derecognised.

(c) *Scope of exception:* Some respondents asked the Board to identify a principle that defined the equity instruments to which the exception should apply. However, they did not specify what that principle should be. The Board previously considered developing a principle to identify other equity investments whose fair value changes should be presented in profit or loss (or other comprehensive income), including a distinction based on whether the equity instruments represented a 'strategic investment'. However, the Board decided that it would be difficult, and perhaps impossible, to develop a clear and robust principle that would identify investments that are different enough to justify a different presentation requirement. The Board considered whether a list of indicators could be used to support the principle, but decided that such a list would inevitably be rule-based and could not be comprehensive enough to address all possible situations and factors. Moreover, the Board noted that such an approach would create complexity in application without necessarily increasing the usefulness of information to users of financial statements.

(d) *Irrevocability of the exception:* A small number of respondents believed that an entity should be able to reclassify equity instruments into and out of the fair value through other comprehensive income category if an entity starts or ceases to hold the investments for trading purposes. However, the Board decided that the option must be irrevocable to provide discipline to its application. The Board also noted that the option to designate a financial asset as measured at fair value is also irrevocable.

BC87 An entity may transfer the cumulative gain or loss within equity. In the light of jurisdiction-specific restrictions on components of equity, the Board decided not to provide specific requirements related to that transfer.

BC88 IFRS 9 amends IFRS 7 to require additional disclosures about investments in equity instruments that are measured at fair value through other comprehensive income. The Board believes those disclosures will provide useful information to users of financial statements about instruments presented in that manner and the effect of that presentation.

BC89 The Board noted that permitting an option for entities to present some gains and losses in other comprehensive income is an exception to the overall classification and measurement approach and adds complexity. However, the Board believes that the requirement that the election is irrevocable, together with the additional disclosures required, addresses many of those concerns.

Effective date

BC90 The Board recognises that many countries require time for translation and for introducing the mandatory requirements into law. In addition, entities require time to implement new standards. The Board usually sets an effective date of between six and eighteen months after issuing an IFRS. However, the Board has adopted a phased approach to publishing IFRS 9, so this is not possible.

BC91   In the response to the exposure draft, respondents urged that:

(a)   it would be helpful to preparers if the Board were to permit all phases of the project to replace IAS 39 to be adopted at the same time.

(b)   it would be helpful to entities that issue insurance contracts if the effective date of IFRS 9 were aligned to the forthcoming IFRS on accounting for insurance contracts. Most of an insurer's assets are financial assets and most of its liabilities are insurance liabilities or financial liabilities. Thus, if an insurer applies IFRS 9 before it applies any new IFRS on insurance, it might face two rounds of major change in a short period. This would be disruptive for both users and preparers.

(c)   because a number of countries will adopt IFRSs in the next few years, it would be helpful to entities in those countries if the Board did not require them to make two changes in a short period of time.

BC92   With these factors in mind, the Board decided it should require entities to apply the requirements of IFRS 9 for annual periods beginning on or after 1 January 2013. The Board intends that this date will allow entities to adopt at the same time the guidance from all phases of the project to replace IAS 39.

BC93   The Board will consider delaying the effective date of IFRS 9 if the impairment phase of the project to replace IAS 39 makes such a delay necessary, or if the new IFRS on insurance contracts has a mandatory effective date later than 2013, to avoid an insurer having to face two rounds of changes in a short period.

BC94   The Board decided to permit earlier application of IFRS 9 to allow an entity to apply the new requirements on classification and measurement of financial assets. This enables entities to use IFRS 9 in their 2009 annual financial statements and meets one of the objectives of the phased approach, ie to have improved classification and measurement requirements for financial assets in place for 2009 year-ends.

BC95   The effect of transition will be significant for some entities. As a result, there will be less comparability between entities that apply IFRS 9 and those that do not. Accordingly, IFRS 9 includes additional disclosures about the transition to IFRS 9.

Transition

BC96   IAS 8 *Accounting Policies, Changes in Accounting Estimates and Errors* states that retrospective application results in the most useful information to users because the information presented for all periods is comparable. Therefore, the exposure draft proposed retrospective application subject to some transition relief in particular circumstances. The Board considered the difficulties and associated costs of full retrospective application of the proposals in the exposure draft.

BC97   Most respondents agreed, in principle, with requiring retrospective application, but many questioned the practicability of the approach. In particular, many noted that the extensive exceptions to retrospective application that would be required to make such transition practicable significantly reduced (and possibly eliminated) any benefit that users might obtain from requiring comparative information to be restated.

BC98   The Board considered whether to require prospective application, but noted that such an approach does not provide comparable information for users of financial statements. In addition, the Board noted that any transition approach (such as prospective application) that requires resetting the effective interest rate for financial assets measured at amortised cost reduces the usefulness of information about interest income.

BC99   The Board decided to require retrospective application but provide transition relief to address particular difficulties that might arise from retrospective application. The Board also noted that IAS 8 sets out transition requirements that apply if retrospective application is impracticable and prohibits the use of hindsight when applying a new accounting policy to a prior period.

Transition relief

Impracticability exceptions

BC100   The Board acknowledged that it may be impracticable for an entity to apply the effective interest method or impairment requirements in IAS 39 retrospectively in some situations. The process would be cumbersome, in particular for an entity with a large number of financial assets that were previously measured at fair value but are measured at amortised cost in accordance with the approach in IFRS 9. Several loss events and reversals might have occurred between the date when the asset was initially recognised and the date of initial application of the IFRS. IFRS 9 requires that if applying the impairment requirements is impracticable or requires the use of hindsight, an entity should use previously determined fair value information to determine whether a financial asset was impaired in comparative periods. IFRS 9 also requires that the fair value at the date of initial application of the new requirements should be treated as the new amortised cost carrying amount of that financial asset in that case. The Board rejected proposals that entities should be permitted, but not required, to treat the fair value at the date of initial application as amortised cost because it would impair comparability and require significant guidance about when such an option should be permitted.

BC101   The Board noted that an entity would not have determined the fair value of an investment in an unquoted equity instrument (or a derivative on such an investment) that was previously accounted for in accordance with paragraphs 46(c) and 66 of IAS 39. Moreover, an entity will not have the necessary information to determine fair value retrospectively without using hindsight. Accordingly, IFRS 9 requires such instruments to be measured at fair value at the date of initial application.

Hybrid contracts

BC102   An entity may not have previously determined the fair value of a hybrid contract in its entirety. Moreover, an entity will not have the necessary information to determine fair value retrospectively without using hindsight. However, an entity would have been required to measure both the embedded derivative and host separately at fair value to apply the disclosure requirements in IFRS 7. Therefore, in comparative periods, IFRS 9 requires the sum of the fair value of the embedded derivative and the host to be used as an approximation of the fair value of the entire hybrid contract.

           © IASCF

BC103   The proposals in the exposure draft would have resulted in fair value measurement for many hybrid contracts for which the embedded derivative was accounted for separately in accordance with IAS 39. Some respondents asked for such treatment under IAS 39 to be 'grandfathered'. The Board noted that many such requests had been related to the proposed treatment of hybrid contracts with financial liability hosts, which are not included in the IFRS. Therefore the Board decided not to permit an option to grandfather hybrid contracts with financial hosts that were bifurcated in accordance with IAS 39 as an accounting policy choice because it would impair comparability, and because some such contracts may still have a significant remaining maturity.

Assessment of the objective of the entity's business model for managing financial assets

BC104   IFRS 9 requires an entity to assess whether the objective of an entity's business model is to manage financial assets to collect the contractual cash flows on the basis of circumstances at the date of initial application. The Board believes it would be difficult, and perhaps impossible, to assess that condition on the basis of circumstances when the instrument first satisfied the recognition criterion in IAS 39.

Assessment of qualifying criteria for fair value option

BC105   The Board decided that the assessment of whether a financial asset or financial liability meets the eligibility criterion for designation under the fair value option should be based on the circumstances at the date of initial application. IFRS 9 changes the classification of some financial assets, including eliminating two of the three eligibility criteria in IAS 39 for the fair value option for financial assets. Therefore, the Board believes that an entity should reconsider at transition its original assessment of whether to designate a financial asset or financial liability as at fair value through profit or loss.

Comparative information

BC106   As noted above, many respondents were concerned that the inevitable exceptions to full retrospective application would result in restated information that is incomplete. They proposed an approach similar to that used on first-time adoption of IFRSs and when entities adopted IAS 39 in 2005, in which the requirement to provide comparative information was waived. Some respondents believe that such an approach would address the concerns that, although IAS 1 requires only one year of comparative information, the legal and regulatory frameworks in many jurisdictions require further comparative periods to be presented. In those situations, the restatement of comparatives would be virtually impossible for an entity wishing to adopt IFRS 9 early.

BC107   In the Board's view, waiving the requirement to restate comparatives strikes a balance between the conceptually preferable method of full retrospective application (as stated in IAS 8) and the practicability of adopting the new classification model within a short time frame. Accordingly, the Board decided that it would permit, but not require, restatement of comparative periods by entities that implement IFRS 9 for reporting periods beginning before 1 January 2012. However, those considerations would be less applicable for entities that adopted outside a short time frame. Therefore, restated comparative information is required if an entity adopts IFRS 9 for reporting periods beginning after 1 January 2012.

Date of initial application

BC108   The exposure draft stated that the date of initial application would be the date when an entity first applies the requirements in the IFRS. Many respondents questioned whether the date of initial application could be an arbitrary date between the date of issue of the IFRS (or even earlier) and the mandatory effective date, resulting in a loss of comparability over a long period of time. The Board agreed that a free choice would impair comparability, but noted it intended that entities should be able to apply the IFRS in 2009 or 2010 financial statements. Accordingly, the IFRS requires the date of initial application to be the beginning of a reporting period, but provides relief from this requirement for entities applying the IFRS for reporting periods beginning on or before 1 January 2011.

Hedge accounting

BC109   The Board decided not to carry forward the specific transition provisions on hedge accounting proposed in the exposure draft because they are not necessary.

Transitional disclosures

BC110   The exposure draft proposed disclosures for entities that apply the new IFRS 9 early. However, many noted that such disclosures would be useful for all entities applying IFRS 9 for the first time, and not only early adopters. The Board noted that the information necessary to make those disclosures would be readily available to the entity to make the necessary journal entries on transition and to account for the financial assets in the future. Accordingly, IFRS 9 requires all entities to supply additional disclosures on transition.

BC111   The Board rejected a proposal in the comment letters that entities should apply disclosures similar to those based on IFRS 1 *First-time Adoption of International Financial Reporting Standards* explaining the transition to the new IFRS. The Board noted that the disclosures in IFRS 1 relate to first-time adoption and not to changes in accounting policies. Disclosures about changes in an accounting policy are required by IAS 8.

Transition for future phases

BC112   The Board does not intend to require entities that apply IFRS 9 early also to apply early any future requirements arising from the project to improve IAS 39. However, to reduce the number of versions of IFRSs that can be applied, the Board intends that any future additions to IFRS 9 can be applied only if the entity also applies requirements published before them.

Transitional insurance issues

BC113 The Board noted that insurers may face particular problems if they apply IFRS 9 before they apply the phase II standard on insurance contracts ('the new IFRS 4'). To avoid accounting mismatches in profit or loss, many insurers classify many of their financial assets as available for sale. If those insurers apply IFRS 9 before the new IFRS 4, they might decide to classify many of their financial assets at amortised cost (assuming they meet the relevant conditions in IFRS 9). When those insurers later apply the new IFRS 4, they may wish to reclassify those assets from amortised cost to fair value through profit or loss, but that may not generally be possible in accordance with IFRS 9. Thus, those insurers might have either to classify those assets at fair value through profit or loss during the intervening period or to continue to classify them at amortised cost when they apply the new IFRS 4. Either choice might lead to an accounting mismatch.

BC114 The Board considered whether it could reduce such mismatches by maintaining the available-for-sale category for insurers until they can apply the new IFRS 4. However, if the Board did so, it would have to create detailed and arbitrary descriptions of the entities and instruments to which that approach would apply. The Board concluded that permitting the continuation of that category would not provide more useful information for users.

BC115 The Board will consider in developing the new IFRS 4 whether to provide an option for insurers to reclassify some or all financial assets when they first apply the new IFRS 4. This would be similar to the option in paragraph 45 of IFRS 4 *Insurance Contracts* and paragraph D4 of IFRS 1. The Board included such an option in IFRS 4 for reasons that may be equally valid for phase II.

Shadow accounting for participating contracts

BC116 Some insurers expressed concerns that an accounting mismatch will arise if the assets backing participating insurance liabilities include equity investments and the insurer elects to present gains and losses on those investments in other comprehensive income. That accounting mismatch would arise because paragraph 30 of IFRS 4 does not give explicit authority to apply 'shadow accounting' in such cases.

BC117 The Board acknowledges that this accounting mismatch is undesirable. However, for the following reasons, the Board did not amend paragraph 30 of IFRS 4:

(a) This accounting mismatch will arise only if an insurer elects to present gains and losses on equity investments in other comprehensive income.

(b) As described in paragraph BC84, in creating the option to present gains and losses on equity investments in other comprehensive income, the Board's intention was to provide a presentation alternative for some equity investments in which presenting fair value gains and losses in profit or loss may not be indicative of the performance of the entity, particularly if the entity holds those equity instruments for non-contractual benefits, rather than primarily to generate increases in the value of the investment. The Board did not intend to provide an alternative for investments in any other circumstances, including if an entity intends to hold an equity investment over a long time frame. In the Board's view, if an insurer holds investments with the primary objective of realising a profit from increases in their value, for the benefit of either the insurer itself or its policyholders, the most transparent place to present those value changes is in profit or loss.

Summary of main changes from the exposure draft

BC118 The main changes from the exposure draft are:

(a) At this stage, IFRS 9 deals with the classification and measurement of financial assets only, rather than financial assets and financial liabilities as proposed in the exposure draft.

(b) IFRS 9 requires entities to classify financial assets on the basis of the objective of the entity's business model for managing the financial assets and the characteristics of the contractual cash flows. It points out that the entity's business model should be considered first, and that the contractual cash flow characteristics should be considered only for financial assets that are eligible to be measured at amortised cost because of the business model. It states that both classification conditions are essential to ensure that amortised cost provides useful information.

(c) Additional application guidance has been added on how to apply the conditions necessary for amortised cost measurement.

(d) IFRS 9 requires a 'look through' approach for investments in contractually linked instruments that effect concentrations of credit risk. The exposure draft had proposed that only the most senior tranche could have cash flows that represented payments of principal and interest on the principal amount outstanding.

(e) IFRS 9 requires (unless the fair value option is elected) financial assets purchased in the secondary market to be recognised at amortised cost if the instruments are managed within a business model that has an objective of collecting contractual cash flows and the financial asset has only contractual cash flows representing principal and interest on the principal amount outstanding even if such assets are acquired at a discount that reflects incurred credit losses.

(f) IFRS 9 requires that when an entity elects to present gains and losses on equity instruments measured at fair value in other comprehensive income, dividends are to be recognised in profit or loss. The exposure draft had proposed that those dividends would be recognised in other comprehensive income.

(g) IFRS 9 requires reclassifications between amortised cost and fair value classifications when the entity's business model changes. The exposure draft had proposed prohibiting reclassification.

(h) For entities that adopt IFRS 9 for reporting periods before 1 January 2012 IFRS 9 provides transition relief from restating comparative information.

(i) IFRS 9 requires additional disclosures for all entities when they first apply the IFRS.

Cost-benefit considerations

BC119 The objective of financial statements is to provide information about the financial position, performance and changes in financial position of an entity that is useful to a wide range of users in making economic decisions. To attain this objective, the Board endeavours to ensure that an IFRS will meet a significant need and that the overall benefits of the resulting information justify the costs of providing it. Although the costs to implement a new IFRS might not be borne evenly, users of financial statements benefit from improvements in financial reporting, thereby facilitating the functioning of markets for capital and credit and the efficient allocation of resources in the economy.

BC120 The evaluation of costs and benefits is necessarily subjective. In making its judgement, the Board considered the following:

(a) the costs incurred by preparers of financial statements;

(b) the costs incurred by users of financial statements when information is not available;

(c) the comparative advantage that preparers have in developing information, compared with the costs that users would incur to develop surrogate information;

(d) the benefit of better economic decision-making as result of improved financial reporting; and

(e) the costs of transition for users, preparers and others.

BC121 The objective of IFRS 9 is to present information that is useful to users for their assessment of the amounts, timing and uncertainty of future cash flows of financial assets. However, the Board also considered the cost of implementing IFRS 9 and applying it on a continuous basis. During the development of IFRS 9 the Board conducted an extensive outreach programme to consult users, preparers, auditors, regulators and others. Those activities helped the Board evaluate the relative costs and benefits of IFRS 9.

BC122 IFRS 9 should improve the ability of users to understand the financial reporting for financial assets by:

(a) reducing the number of classification categories. All financial assets will be subsequently measured at either amortised cost or fair value. Hybrid contracts with financial asset hosts will be classified and measured in their entirety thereby eliminating the complex and rule-based requirements in IAS 39.

(b) having a single impairment methodology that is applied to all financial assets that are not measured at fair value. Many constituents criticised the multitude of impairment methodologies in IAS 39.

(c) providing a clear rationale for why financial assets are measured in a particular way, which aligns the measurement attribute to the way that an entity manages its financial assets and their contractual cash flow characteristics.

BC123   There are costs involved in the adoption and ongoing application of IFRS 9. Those costs will depend on an entity's volume and complexity of financial instruments as well the industry and jurisdiction in which the entity operates. However, those costs should be minimised because IFRS 9 is less complex and rule-based than the equivalent requirements in IAS 39. Consequently, the Board believes that the benefits of IFRS 9 outweigh the costs.

Appendix
Amendments to the Basis for Conclusions on other IFRSs

This appendix contains amendments to the Basis for Conclusions on other IFRSs that are necessary in order to ensure consistency with IFRS 9 and the related amendments to other IFRSs. Amended paragraphs are shown with new text underlined and deleted text struck through.

* * * * *

The amendments contained in this appendix when IFRS 9 was issued in 2009 have been incorporated into the Basis for Conclusions on the relevant IFRSs published in this volume.

Dissenting opinions

Dissenting opinion of James J Leisenring

DO1 Mr Leisenring supports efforts to reduce the complexity of accounting for financial instruments. In that regard, he supports requiring all financial instruments to be measured at fair value, with that measurement being recognised in profit or loss. He finds no compelling reason related to improving financial reporting to reject that approach. It is an approach that maximises comparability and minimises complexity.

DO2 It maximises comparability because all financial instruments would be measured at one attribute within an entity and across entities. No measurement or presentation would change to reflect either arbitrary distinctions or management behaviour or intentions. IFRS 9 emphasises management intentions and behaviour, which substantially undermines comparability.

DO3 Complexity of accounting would be drastically reduced if all financial instruments were measured at fair value. The approach favoured by Mr Leisenring provides at least the following simplifications:

(a) no impairment model is necessary.

(b) criteria for when a given instrument must or can be measured with a given attribute are unnecessary.

(c) there is no need to bifurcate embedded derivatives or to identify financial derivatives.

(d) it eliminates the need for fair value hedge accounting for financial instruments.

(e) it eliminates the disparity in the measurement of derivatives within and outside the scope of IAS 39.

(f) it minimises the incentives for structuring transactions to achieve a particular accounting outcome.

(g) no fair value option would be needed to eliminate accounting mismatches.

(h) it provides a superior foundation for developing a comprehensive standard for the derecognition of financial instruments that is not present in a mixed attribute model.

DO4 Mr Leisenring accepts that measuring more instruments at fair value increases measurement complexity, but this increase is minimal compared with the reductions in complexity that would be otherwise achieved. There is no disagreement that derivatives must be measured at fair value. Those instruments raise the most difficult measurement issues, as cash instruments have many fewer problems. Indeed, some suggestions for an impairment model would measure at fair value the credit loss component of cash instruments. If that were to be the conclusion on impairment (an expected loss approach), it would minimise the incremental fair value measurement complexity of recording at fair value instruments now at amortised cost.

DO5 Mr Leisenring recognises that measuring all instruments at fair value through profit or loss raises presentation issues about disaggregation of fair value changes. However, he does not believe that these issues are insurmountable.

DO6 Investors have often told both the IASB and the FASB that fair value of financial instruments recognised in profit or loss provides the most useful information for their purposes. There is a worldwide demand for an improved and common solution to the accounting for financial instruments. Investors are disappointed that the Board will not take this opportunity to make, with other standard-setters, truly substantive changes rather than these minimal changes that perpetuate all the legitimate concerns that have been expressed about the mixed attribute model.

DO7 IFRS 9 does to some extent reduce complexity but that reduction is minimal. Certain measurement classifications are eliminated but others have been added. Mr Leisenring does not think that, on balance, this is an improvement over IAS 39.

DO8 Fundamental to IFRS 9 is the distinction between financial instruments measured at amortised cost and those at fair value. Mr Leisenring is concerned that neither of the two conditions necessary for that determination is operational. Paragraph BC56 criticises IAS 39 because the embedded derivative requirement of that standard is based on a list of examples. However, the basic classification model of IFRS 9 is based on lists of examples in paragraphs B4.4, B4.13 and B4.14. The examples are helpful but are far from exhaustive of the issues that will be problematic in applying the two criteria for classification at amortised cost.

DO9 Mr Leisenring also thinks that the two criteria are inconsistently applied. When the objective of the entity's business model is to hold the assets to collect the contracted cash flows of an instrument there is no requirement that the entity must actually do so. The cash flow characteristics of the instrument are also ignored when the guidance is applied to investments in contractually linked instruments (tranches). In those circumstances the contractual cash flows of the instrument are ignored and one is required to look through to the composition of assets and liabilities of the issuing entity. This 'look through' requirement is also potentially complex and in Mr Leisenring's opinion is likely to be not very operational. Mr Leisenring also objects to eliminating the requirement to bifurcate derivatives embedded in cash instruments. This objection is primarily because of concern that the two criteria to qualify for amortised cost will not be operational. The pressure on those two conditions will be enormous because there will be an incentive to embed derivatives in a cash instrument in anticipation that the instrument might qualify for amortised cost. Derivatives should be at fair value whether embedded or standing alone and a bifurcation requirement would achieve that accounting. If Mr Leisenring were confident that the criteria for amortised cost could be applied as intended he would not be as concerned because instruments with embedded derivatives would be at fair value in their entirety.

DO10 Mr Leisenring is concerned that, in the current crisis, instruments that have provided some of the most significant losses when measured at fair value would be eligible for amortised cost. That conclusion is not responsive to the present environment. The approach also allows actively traded debt instruments, including treasury securities, to be at amortised cost. These results are unacceptable and reduce the usefulness of reported information for investors.

DO11   The Board is required by its *Framework* to be neutral in its decision-making and to strive to produce neutral information to maximise the usefulness of financial information. IFRS 9 fails in that regard because it produces information based on free choice, management intention and management behaviour. Reporting that will result from this approach will not produce neutral information and diminishes the usefulness of financial reporting.

DO12   The Board is insistent in paragraph BC27 that accounting based on a business model is not free choice but never explains why selection of a business model is not a management choice. The existence of a trading account, a fair value option and the objective of a business model are all free choices.

DO13   The classification of selected equity instruments at fair value with the result of the remeasurement reported outside profit or loss is also a free choice. The Board concludes that reporting fair value changes in profit or loss may not reflect the operating performance of an entity. Mr Leisenring could accept accounting for changes in fair value of some instruments outside profit or loss in other comprehensive income. That accounting, however, should not be a free choice and why that presentation is superior in defined circumstances should be developed. In addition, when these securities are sold any realised gains and losses are not 'recycled' to profit or loss. That conclusion is inconsistent with the Board's conclusion that dividends received on these instruments should be reported in profit or loss. Such dividends would represent a return on investment or a form of 'recycling' of changes in the value of the instruments.

DO14   Mr Leisenring believes that a business model is rarely relevant in writing accounting standards. Identical transactions, rights and obligations should be accounted for in the same way if comparability of financial information is to be achieved. The result of applying IFRS 9 ignores any concern for comparability of financial information.

DO15   The credit crisis has provided confirmation that a drastic change in accounting for financial instruments is desirable. However, many have said that while they agree that the approach suggested by Mr Leisenring would be superior, and a significant improvement, the world is not ready to embrace such change. It is unclear to Mr Leisenring what factors need to be present for the optimal solution to be acceptable. He has concluded that it is hard to envisage circumstances that would make the case any more compelling for fundamental change and improvement than the present circumstances. Therefore, IFRS 9 will inevitably preserve a mixed attribute model and the resulting complexity for a significant period of time.

DO16   An objective of replacing IAS 39 was to provide a basis for convergence with accounting standards issued by the FASB. Mr Leisenring is concerned that IFRS 9 does not provide such a basis. As a consequence, allowing early adoption of the IFRS is undesirable. For convergence to be achieved significant changes in the IFRS are inevitable. Early adoption of the IFRS will therefore necessitate another costly accounting change when convergence is achieved. Permitting early adoption of this IFRS is also undesirable as it permits a lack of comparability in accounting for many years due to the deferred required effective date.

DO17   Mr Leisenring would accept that if, for reasons other than the desire to provide useful information to investors, his approach is politically unattainable, an alternative could be developed that would be operational. That approach would require all financial assets and financial liabilities to be recorded at fair value through profit or loss except originated loans retained by the originator, trade receivables and accounts payable. If certain derivatives were embedded in an instrument to be accounted for at amortised cost the derivative would be either bifurcated and accounted for at fair value or the entire instrument would be measured at fair value. Either approach would be acceptable.

Dissenting opinion of Patricia McConnell

DO18   Ms McConnell believes that fair value is the most relevant and useful measurement attribute for financial assets. However, she acknowledges that many investors prefer not to measure all financial assets at fair value. Those investors believe that both amortised cost and fair value can provide useful information for particular kinds of financial assets in particular circumstances. Therefore, in order to meet the objective of developing high quality, global accounting standards that serve the interests of all investors, Ms McConnell believes that no single measurement attribute should have primacy over another. Thus any new IFRS setting classification and measurement principles for financial assets should require disclosure of sufficient information in the primary financial statements to permit determination of profit or loss and financial position using both amortised cost and fair value. For example, when a measurement attribute other than fair value is used for financial assets, information about fair value should be displayed prominently in the statement of financial position. The Board did not adopt such disclosure in IFRS 9, as discussed in paragraphs BC16–BC18 of the Board's Basis for Conclusions.

DO19   As stated in paragraph BC8, an objective of the Board in developing IFRS 9 was to reduce the number of classification categories for financial instruments. However, Ms McConnell believes that IFRS 9 has not accomplished that objective. IFRS 9 would permit or require the following categories: (1) amortised cost, (2) a fair value option through profit or loss for financial assets that qualify for amortised cost but for which amortised cost would create an accounting mismatch, (3) fair value through profit or loss for debt instruments that fail to qualify for amortised cost, (4) fair value though profit or loss for trading securities, (5) fair value through profit or loss for equity securities not held for trading and (6) fair value through other comprehensive income for equity investments not held for trading. Ms McConnell does not view those six categories as a significant improvement over the six categories in IAS 39; like the categories in IAS 39, they will hinder investors' understanding of an already complex area of financial reporting.

DO20   IFRS 9 sets out two criteria for measuring financial assets at amortised cost: (1) the way the entity manages its financial assets ('business model') and (2) the contractual cash flow characteristics of its financial assets. On the surface, this appears to be an improvement over IAS 39's criterion that was based on management's intention to trade, hold available for sale, hold to maturity, or hold for the foreseeable future. However, Ms McConnell finds it difficult to see how IFRS 9's criterion based on the objective of the entity's business model differs significantly from management's intention. In her opinion selection of a business model is a management choice, as is the decision to have a trading account, use the fair value option for debt instruments or the fair value option for equity instruments with gains and losses reported in other comprehensive income. In paragraphs BC27 and BC28 the Board argues that selection of a measurement method based on an entity's business model is not a free choice. Ms McConnell does not find the arguments persuasive.

DO21 IFRS 9 permits an entity to make an irrevocable election to present in other comprehensive income changes in the value of any investment in equity instruments that is not held for trading. Ms McConnell could accept accounting for changes in fair value of some instruments outside profit or loss in other comprehensive income. However, that treatment should not be a free choice; criteria for that presentation should be developed. In addition, the Board decided that when those securities are sold any realised gains and losses are not 'reclassified' to profit or loss. That conclusion is inconsistent with the Board's decision to report dividends received on these investments in profit or loss. Such dividends represent a return on investment or a form of 'reclassifying' changes in the value of the instruments.

DO22 In addition, Ms McConnell believes the 'look through' guidance for contractually linked investments (tranches) is an exception to one of the criteria necessary for applying amortised cost, namely the contractual cash flow characteristics of the instrument. In those circumstances the contractual cash flows of the instrument are ignored. Instead an entity is required to 'look through' to the underlying pool of instruments and access their cash flow characteristics and credit risk relative to a direct investment in the underlying instruments. Ms McConnell believes that this provision adds complexity to the IFRS and reduces the usefulness of the reporting for financial assets. Moreover, since an entity is required to 'look through' only upon initial recognition of the financial asset, subsequent changes in the relative exposure to credit risk over the life of a structured investment vehicle would be ignored. Consequently, Ms McConnell believes it is possible that highly volatile investments, such as those owning sub-prime residential mortgage loans, would be reported at amortised cost.

Amendments to guidance on other IFRSs

The following amendments to guidance on IFRSs are necessary in order to ensure consistency with IFRS 9 Financial Instruments *and the related amendments to other IFRSs. In the amended paragraphs, new text is underlined and deleted text is struck through.*

* * * * *

The amendments accompanying IFRS 9 when it was issued in 2009 have been incorporated into the guidance on the relevant IFRSs published in this edition.

IASB documents published to accompany

International Accounting Standard 1

Presentation of Financial Statements

This version includes amendments resulting from IFRSs issued up to 31 December 2009.

The text of the unaccompanied IAS 1 is contained in Part A of this edition. Its effective date when issued was 1 January 2009. The effective date of the most recent amendment is 1 January 2013. This part presents the following accompanying documents:

Approval by the Board of IAS 1 issued in September 2007

International Accounting Standard 1 *Presentation of Financial Statements* (as revised in 2007) was approved for issue by ten of the fourteen members of the International Accounting Standards Board.   Professor Barth and Messrs Cope, Garnett and Leisenring dissented. Their dissenting opinions are set out after the Basis for Conclusions.

Sir David Tweedie   Chairman

Thomas E Jones   Vice-Chairman

Mary E Barth

Hans-Georg Bruns

Anthony T Cope

Philippe Danjou

Jan Engström

Robert P Garnett

Gilbert Gélard

James J Leisenring

Warren J McGregor

Patricia L O'Malley

John T Smith

Tatsumi Yamada

Approval by the Board of *Puttable Financial Instruments and Obligations Arising on Liquidation* (Amendments to IAS 32 and IAS 1) issued in February 2008

Puttable Financial Instruments and Obligations Arising on Liquidation (Amendments to IAS 32 *Financial Instruments: Presentation* and IAS 1 *Presentation of Financial Statements*) was approved for issue by eleven of the thirteen members of the International Accounting Standards Board. Professor Barth and Mr Garnett dissented. Their dissenting opinions are set out after the Basis for Conclusions on IAS 32.

Sir David Tweedie	Chairman
Thomas E Jones	Vice-Chairman
Mary E Barth	
Stephen Cooper	
Philippe Danjou	
Jan Engström	
Robert P Garnett	
Gilbert Gélard	
James J Leisenring	
Warren J McGregor	
John T Smith	
Tatsumi Yamada	
Wei-Guo Zhang	

CONTENTS

© IASCF

Basis for Conclusions on
IAS 1 *Presentation of Financial Statements*

The International Accounting Standards Board revised IAS 1 Presentation of Financial Statements *in 2007 as part of its project on financial statement presentation. It was not the Board's intention to reconsider as part of that project all the requirements in IAS 1.*

For convenience, the Board has incorporated into this Basis for Conclusions relevant material from the Basis for Conclusions on the revision of IAS 1 in 2003 and its amendment in 2005. Paragraphs have been renumbered and reorganised as necessary to reflect the new structure of the Standard.

This Basis for Conclusions accompanies, but is not part of, IAS 1.

Introduction

BC1   The International Accounting Standards Committee (IASC) issued the first version of IAS 1 *Disclosure of Accounting Policies* in 1975. It was reformatted in 1994 and superseded in 1997 by IAS 1 *Presentation of Financial Statements.*[*] In 2003 the International Accounting Standards Board revised IAS 1 as part of the Improvements project and in 2005 the Board amended it as a consequence of issuing IFRS 7 *Financial Instruments: Disclosures.* In 2007 the Board revised IAS 1 again as part of its project on financial statement presentation. This Basis for Conclusions summarises the Board's considerations in reaching its conclusions on revising IAS 1 in 2003, on amending it in 2005 and revising it in 2007. It includes reasons for accepting some approaches and rejecting others. Individual Board members gave greater weight to some factors than to others.

The Improvements project—revision of IAS 1 (2003)

BC2   In July 2001 the Board announced that, as part of its initial agenda of technical projects, it would undertake a project to improve a number of standards, including IAS 1. The project was undertaken in the light of queries and criticisms raised in relation to the standards by securities regulators, professional accountants and other interested parties. The objectives of the Improvements project were to reduce or eliminate alternatives, redundancies and conflicts within standards, to deal with some convergence issues and to make other improvements. The Board's intention was not to reconsider the fundamental approach to the presentation of financial statements established by IAS 1 in 1997.

BC3   In May 2002 the Board published an exposure draft of proposed *Improvements to International Accounting Standards*, which contained proposals to revise IAS 1. The Board received more than 160 comment letters. After considering the responses the Board issued in 2003 a revised version of IAS 1. In its revision the Board's main objectives were:

(a)   to provide a framework within which an entity assesses how to present fairly the effects of transactions and other events, and assesses whether the result of complying with a requirement in an IFRS would be so misleading that it would not give a fair presentation;

---

[*]   IASC did not publish a Basis for Conclusions.

© IASCF

(b)   to base the criteria for classifying liabilities as current or non-current solely on the conditions existing at the balance sheet date;

(c)   to prohibit the presentation of items of income and expense as 'extraordinary items';

(d)   to specify disclosures about the judgements that management has made in the process of applying the entity's accounting policies, apart from those involving estimations, and that have the most significant effect on the amounts recognised in the financial statements; and

(e)   to specify disclosures about sources of estimation uncertainty at the balance sheet date that have a significant risk of causing a material adjustment to the carrying amounts of assets and liabilities within the next financial year.

BC4   The following sections summarise the Board's considerations in reaching its conclusions as part of its Improvements project in 2003:

(a)   departures from IFRSs (paragraphs BC23–BC30)

(b)   criterion for exemption from requirements (paragraphs BC34–BC36)

(c)   effect of events after the reporting period on the classification of liabilities (paragraphs BC39–BC48)

(d)   results of operating activities (paragraphs BC55 and BC56)

(e)   minority interest (paragraph BC59)[*]

(f)   extraordinary items (paragraphs BC60–BC64)

(g)   disclosure of the judgements management has made in the process of applying the entity's accounting policies (paragraphs BC77 and BC78)

(h)   disclosure of major sources of estimation uncertainty (paragraphs BC79–BC84).

Amendment to IAS 1—*Capital Disclosures* (2005)

BC5   In August 2005 the Board issued an Amendment to IAS 1—*Capital Disclosures*. The amendment added to IAS 1 requirements for disclosure of:

(a)   the entity's objectives, policies and processes for managing capital.

(b)   quantitative data about what the entity regards as capital.

(c)   whether the entity has complied with any capital requirements; and if it has not complied, the consequences of such non-compliance.

BC6   The following sections summarise the Board's considerations in reaching its conclusions as part of its amendment to IAS 1 in 2005:

(a)   disclosures about capital (paragraphs BC85–BC89)

(b)   objectives, policies and processes for managing capital (paragraphs BC90 and BC91)

---

[*]   In January 2008 the IASB issued an amended IAS 27 *Consolidated and Separate Financial Statements*, which amended 'minority interest' to 'non-controlling interests'.

(c)   externally imposed capital requirements (paragraphs BC92–BC97)

(d)   internal capital targets (paragraphs BC98–BC100).

Amendments to IAS 32 and IAS 1—*Puttable Financial Instruments and Obligations Arising on Liquidation* (2008)

BC6A   In July 2006 the Board published an exposure draft of proposed amendments to IAS 32 and IAS 1 relating to the classification of puttable instruments and instruments with obligations arising only on liquidation. The Board subsequently confirmed the proposals and in February 2008 issued an amendment that now forms part of IAS 1.

Financial statement presentation—Joint project

BC7   In September 2001 the Board added to its agenda the performance reporting project (in March 2006 renamed the 'financial statement presentation project'). The objective of the project was to enhance the usefulness of information presented in the income statement. The Board developed a possible new model for reporting income and expenses and conducted preliminary testing. Similarly, in the United States, the Financial Accounting Standards Board (FASB) added a project on performance reporting to its agenda in October 2001, developed its model and conducted preliminary testing. Constituents raised concerns about both models and about the fact that they were different.

BC8   In April 2004 the Board and the FASB decided to work on financial statement presentation as a joint project. They agreed that the project should address presentation and display not only in the income statement, but also in the other statements that, together with the income statement, would constitute a complete set of financial statements—the balance sheet, the statement of changes in equity, and the cash flow statement. The Board decided to approach the project in two phases. Phase A would address the statements that constitute a complete set of financial statements and the periods for which they are required to be presented. Phase B would be undertaken jointly with the FASB and would address more fundamental issues relating to presentation and display of information in the financial statements, including:

(a)   consistent principles for aggregating information in each financial statement.

(b)   the totals and subtotals that should be reported in each financial statement.

(c)   whether components of other comprehensive income should be reclassified to profit or loss and, if so, the characteristics of the transactions and events that should be reclassified and when reclassification should be made.

(d)   whether the direct or the indirect method of presenting operating cash flows provides more useful information.

BC9   In March 2006, as a result of its work in phase A, the Board published an exposure draft of proposed amendments to IAS 1—*A Revised Presentation*. The Board received more than 130 comment letters. The exposure draft proposed amendments that affected the presentation of owner changes in equity and the presentation of comprehensive income, but did not propose to change the recognition, measurement or disclosure of specific transactions and other events required by other IFRSs. It also proposed to bring IAS 1 largely into line with the US standard—SFAS 130 *Reporting Comprehensive Income*. After considering the responses to the exposure draft the Board issued a revised version of IAS 1. The FASB decided to consider phases A and B issues together, and therefore did not publish an exposure draft on phase A.

BC10   The following sections summarise the Board's considerations in reaching its conclusions as part of its revision in 2007:

   (a) general purpose financial statements (paragraphs BC11–BC13)

   (b) titles of financial statements (paragraphs BC14–BC21)

   (c) equal prominence (paragraph BC22)

   (d) a statement of financial position as at the beginning of the earliest comparative period (paragraphs BC31 and BC32)

   (e) IAS 34 *Interim Financial Reporting* (paragraph BC33)

   (f) reporting owner and non-owner changes in equity (paragraphs BC37 and BC38)

   (g) reporting comprehensive income (paragraphs BC49–BC54)

   (h) subtotal for profit or loss (paragraphs BC57 and BC58)

   (i) other comprehensive income-related tax effects (paragraphs BC65–BC68)

   (j) reclassification adjustments (paragraphs BC69–BC73)

   (k) effects of retrospective application or retrospective restatement (paragraph BC74)

   (l) presentation of dividends (paragraph BC75)

   (m) IAS 7 *Cash Flow Statements* (paragraph BC76)

   (n) presentation of measures per share (paragraphs BC101–BC104)

   (o) effective date and transition (paragraph BC105)

   (p) differences from SFAS 130 (paragraph BC106).

Definitions

General purpose financial statements (paragraph 7)

BC11   The exposure draft of 2006 proposed a change to the explanatory paragraph of what 'general purpose financial statements' include, in order to produce a more generic definition of a set of financial statements. Paragraph 7 of the exposure draft stated:

> General purpose financial statements include those that are presented separately or within other *public* documents such as a *regulatory filing* or report to shareholders. [emphasis added]

BC12   Respondents expressed concern about the proposed change. They argued that it could be understood as defining as general purpose financial statements any financial statement or set of financial statements filed with a regulator and could capture documents other than annual reports and prospectuses. They saw this change as expanding the scope of IAS 1 to documents that previously would not have contained all of the disclosures required by IAS 1. Respondents pointed out that the change would particularly affect some entities (such as small private companies and subsidiaries of public companies with no external users of financial reports) that are required by law to place their financial statements on a public file.

BC13   The Board acknowledged that in some countries the law requires entities, whether public or private, to report to regulatory authorities and include information in those reports that could be beyond the scope of IAS 1. Because the Board did not intend to extend the definition of general purpose financial statements, it decided to eliminate the explanatory paragraph of what 'general purpose financial statements' include, while retaining the definition of 'general purpose financial statements'.

Financial statements

Complete set of financial statements

Titles of financial statements (paragraph 10)

BC14   The exposure draft of 2006 proposed changes to the titles of some of the financial statements—from 'balance sheet' to 'statement of financial position', from 'income statement' to 'statement of profit or loss' and from 'cash flow statement' to 'statement of cash flows'. In addition, the exposure draft proposed a 'statement of recognised income and expense' and that all owner changes in equity should be included in a 'statement of changes in equity'. The Board did not propose to make any of these changes of nomenclature mandatory.

BC15   Many respondents opposed the proposed changes, pointing out that the existing titles had a long tradition and were well understood. However, the Board reaffirmed its view that the proposed new titles better reflect the function of each financial statement, and pointed out that an entity could choose to use other titles in its financial report.

BC16   The Board reaffirmed its conclusion that the title 'statement of financial position' not only better reflects the function of the statement but is consistent with the *Framework for the Preparation and Presentation of Financial Statements*, which contains several references to 'financial position'. Paragraph 12 of the *Framework* states that the objective of financial statements is to provide information about the financial position, performance and changes in financial position of an entity; paragraph 19 of the *Framework* states that information about financial position is primarily provided in a balance sheet. In the Board's view, the title 'balance sheet' simply reflects that double entry bookkeeping requires debits to equal credits. It does not identify the content or purpose of the statement. The Board also noted that 'financial position' is a well-known and accepted term, as it has been used in auditors' opinions internationally for more than 20 years to describe what the 'balance sheet' presents. The Board decided that aligning the statement's title with its content and the opinion rendered by the auditor would help the users of financial statements.

BC17   As to the other statements, respondents suggested that renaming the balance sheet the 'statement of financial position' implied that the 'cash flow statement' and the 'statement of recognised income and expense' do not also reflect an entity's financial position. The Board observed that although the latter statements reflect changes in an entity's financial position, neither can be called a 'statement of changes in financial position', as this would not depict their true function and objective (ie to present cash flows and performance, respectively). The Board acknowledged that the titles 'income statement' and 'statement of profit or loss' are similar in meaning and could be used interchangeably, and decided to retain the title 'income statement' as this is more commonly used.

BC18   The title of the proposed new statement, the 'statement of recognised income and expense', reflects a broader content than the former 'income statement'. The statement encompasses both income and expenses recognised in profit or loss and income and expenses recognised outside profit or loss.

BC19   Many respondents opposed the title 'statement of recognised income and expense', objecting particularly to the use of the term 'recognised'. The Board acknowledged that the term 'recognised' could also be used to describe the content of other primary statements as 'recognition', explained in paragraph 82 of the *Framework*, is 'the process of incorporating in the balance sheet or income statement an item that meets the definition of an element and satisfies the criteria for recognition set out in paragraph 83.' Many respondents suggested the term 'statement of comprehensive income' instead.

BC20   In response to respondents' concerns and to converge with SFAS 130, the Board decided to rename the new statement a 'statement of comprehensive income'. The term 'comprehensive income' is not defined in the *Framework* but is used in IAS 1 to describe the change in equity of an entity during a period from transactions, events and circumstances other than those resulting from transactions with owners in their capacity as owners. Although the term 'comprehensive income' is used to describe the aggregate of all components of comprehensive income, including profit or loss, the term 'other comprehensive income' refers to income and expenses that under IFRSs are included in comprehensive income but excluded from profit or loss.

BC21   In finalising its revision, the Board confirmed that the titles of financial statements used in this Standard would not be mandatory. The titles will be used in future IFRSs but are not required to be used by entities in their financial statements. Some respondents to the exposure draft expressed concern that non-mandatory titles will result in confusion. However, the Board believes that making use of the titles non-mandatory will allow time for entities to implement changes gradually as the new titles become more familiar.

Equal prominence (paragraphs 11 and 12)

BC22   The Board noted that the financial performance of an entity is not assessed by reference to a single financial statement or a single measure within a financial statement. The Board believes that the financial performance of an entity can be assessed only after all aspects of the financial statements are taken into account and understood in their entirety. Accordingly, the Board decided that in order to help users of the financial statements to understand the financial performance of an entity comprehensively, all financial statements within the complete set of financial statements should be presented with equal prominence.

Departures from IFRSs (paragraphs 19–24)

BC23   IAS 1 (as issued in 1997) permitted an entity to depart from a requirement in a Standard 'in the extremely rare circumstances when management concludes that compliance with a requirement in a Standard would be misleading, and therefore that departure from a requirement is necessary to achieve a fair presentation' (paragraph 17, now paragraph 19). When such a departure occurred, paragraph 18 (now paragraph 20) required extensive disclosure of the facts and circumstances surrounding the departure and the treatment adopted.

BC24   The Board decided to clarify in paragraph 15 of the Standard that for financial statements to present fairly the financial position, financial performance and cash flows of an entity, they must represent faithfully the effects of transactions and other events in accordance with the definitions and recognition criteria for assets, liabilities, income and expenses set out in the *Framework*.

BC25   The Board decided to limit the occasions on which an entity should depart from a requirement in an IFRS to the extremely rare circumstances in which management concludes that compliance with the requirement would be so misleading that it would conflict with the objective of financial statements set out in the *Framework*. Guidance on this criterion states that an item of information would conflict with the objective of financial statements when it does not represent faithfully the transactions, other events or conditions that it either purports to represent or could reasonably be expected to represent and, consequently, it would be likely to influence economic decisions made by users of financial statements.

BC26   These amendments provide a framework within which an entity assesses how to present fairly the effects of transactions, other events and conditions, and whether the result of complying with a requirement in an IFRS would be so misleading that it would not give a fair presentation.

BC27   The Board considered whether IAS 1 should be silent on departures from IFRSs. The Board decided against making that change, because it would remove the Board's capability to specify the criteria under which departures from IFRSs should occur.

BC28   Departing from a requirement in an IFRS when considered necessary to achieve a fair presentation would conflict with the regulatory framework in some jurisdictions. The revised IAS 1 takes into account the existence of different regulatory requirements. It requires that when an entity's circumstances satisfy the criterion described in paragraph BC25 for departure from a requirement in an IFRS, the entity should proceed as follows:

   (a)   When the relevant regulatory framework requires—or otherwise does not prohibit—a departure from the requirement, the entity should make that departure and the disclosures set out in paragraph 20.

   (b)   When the relevant regulatory framework prohibits departure from the requirement, the entity should, to the maximum extent possible, reduce the perceived misleading aspects of compliance by making the disclosures set out in paragraph 23.

   This amendment enables entities to comply with the requirements of IAS 1 when the relevant regulatory framework prohibits departures from accounting standards, while retaining the principle that entities should, to the maximum extent possible, ensure that financial statements provide a fair presentation.

BC29   After considering the comments received on the exposure draft of 2002, the Board added to IAS 1 a requirement in paragraph 21 to disclose the effect of a departure from a requirement of an IFRS in a prior period on the current period's financial statements. Without this disclosure, users of the entity's financial statements could be unaware of the continuing effects of prior period departures.

BC30   In view of the strict criteria for departure from a requirement in an IFRS, IAS 1 includes a rebuttable presumption that if other entities in similar circumstances comply with the requirement, the entity's compliance with the requirement would not be so misleading that it would conflict with the objective of financial statements set out in the *Framework*.

Comparative information

A statement of financial position as at the beginning of the earliest comparative period (paragraph 39)

BC31   The exposure draft of 2006 proposed that a statement of financial position as at the beginning of the earliest comparative period should be presented as part of a complete set of financial statements. This statement would provide a basis for investors and creditors to evaluate information about the entity's performance during the period. However, many respondents expressed concern that the requirement would unnecessarily increase disclosures in financial statements, or would be impracticable, excessive and costly.

BC32   By adding a statement of financial position as at the beginning of the earliest comparative period, the exposure draft proposed that an entity should present three statements of financial position and two of each of the other statements. Considering that financial statements from prior years are readily available for financial analysis, the Board decided to require only two statements of financial position, except when the financial statements have been affected by retrospective application or retrospective restatement, as defined in IAS 8 *Accounting Policies, Changes in Accounting Estimates and Errors*, or when a reclassification has been made. In those circumstances three statements of financial position are required.

IAS 34 *Interim Financial Reporting*

BC33   The Board decided not to reflect in paragraph 8 of IAS 34 (ie the minimum components of an interim financial report) its decision to require the inclusion of a statement of financial position as at the beginning of the earliest comparative period in a complete set of financial statements. IAS 34 has a year-to-date approach to interim reporting and does not replicate the requirements of IAS 1 in terms of comparative information.

Criterion for exemption from requirements (paragraphs 41–44)

BC34   IAS 1 as issued in 1997 specified that when the presentation or classification of items in the financial statements is amended, comparative amounts should be reclassified unless it is impracticable to do so. Applying a requirement is impracticable when the entity cannot apply it after making every reasonable effort to do so.

BC35   The exposure draft of 2002 proposed a different criterion for exemption from particular requirements. For the reclassification of comparative amounts, and its proposed new requirement to disclose key assumptions and other sources of estimation uncertainty at the end of the reporting period (discussed in paragraphs BC79–BC84), the exposure draft proposed that the criterion for exemption should be that applying the requirements would require undue cost or effort.

BC36   In the light of respondents' comments on the exposure draft, the Board decided that an exemption based on management's assessment of undue cost or effort was too subjective to be applied consistently by different entities. Moreover, balancing costs and benefits was a task for the Board when it sets accounting requirements rather than for entities when they apply them. Therefore, the Board retained the 'impracticability' criterion for exemption. This affects the exemptions now set out in paragraphs 41–43 and 131 of IAS 1. Impracticability is the only basis on which IFRSs allow specific exemptions from applying particular requirements when the effect of applying them is material.[*]

---

[*]   In 2006 the IASB issued IFRS 8 *Operating Segments*. As explained in paragraphs BC46 and BC47 of the Basis for Conclusions on IFRS 8, that IFRS includes an exemption from some requirements if the necessary information is not available and the cost to develop it would be excessive.

                              © IASCF

Reporting owner and non-owner changes in equity

BC37   The exposure draft of 2006 proposed to separate changes in equity of an entity during a period arising from transactions with owners in their capacity as owners (ie all owner changes in equity) from other changes in equity (ie non-owner changes in equity). All owner changes in equity would be presented in the statement of changes in equity, separately from non-owner changes in equity.

BC38   Most respondents welcomed this proposal and saw this change as an improvement of financial reporting, by increasing the transparency of those items recognised in equity that are not reported as part of profit or loss. However, some respondents pointed out that the terms 'owner' and 'non-owner' were not defined in the exposure draft, the *Framework* or elsewhere in IFRSs, although they are extensively used in national accounting standards. They also noted that the terms 'owner' and 'equity holder' were used interchangeably in the exposure draft. The Board decided to adopt the term 'owner' and use it throughout IAS 1 to converge with SFAS 130, which uses the term in the definition of 'comprehensive income'.

Statement of financial position

Current assets and current liabilities (paragraphs 68 and 71)

BC38A   As part of its improvements project in 2007, the Board identified inconsistent guidance regarding the current/non-current classification of derivatives. Some might read the guidance included in paragraph 71 as implying that financial liabilities classified as held for trading in accordance with IAS 39 *Financial Instruments: Recognition and Measurement*[*] are always required to be presented as current.

BC38B   The Board expects the criteria set out in paragraph 69 to be used to assess whether a financial liability should be presented as current or non-current. The 'held for trading' category in paragraph 9 of IAS 39[*] is for measurement purposes and includes financial assets and liabilities that may not be held primarily for trading purposes.

BC38C   The Board reaffirmed that if a financial liability is held primarily for trading purposes it should be presented as current regardless of its maturity date. However, a financial liability that is not held for trading purposes, such as a derivative that is not a financial guarantee contract or a designated hedging instrument, should be presented as current or non-current on the basis of its settlement date. For example, derivatives that have a maturity of more than twelve months and are expected to be held for more than twelve months after the reporting period should be presented as non-current assets or liabilities.

---

[*]   In November 2009 the IASB amended the requirements of IAS 39 relating to classification and measurement of assets within the scope of IAS 39 and relocated them to IFRS 9 *Financial Instruments*. IFRS 9 applies to all assets within the scope of IAS 39. Paragraphs BC38A–BC38D discuss matters relevant when IAS 1 was issued.

BC38D   Therefore, the Board decided to remove the identified inconsistency by amending the examples of current liabilities in paragraph 71. The Board also amended paragraph 68 in respect of current assets to remove a similar inconsistency.

Classification of the liability component of a convertible instrument (paragraph 69)

BC38E   As part of its improvements project in 2007, the Board considered the classification of the liability component of a convertible instrument as current or non-current. Paragraph 69(d) of IAS 1 states that when an entity does not have an unconditional right to defer settlement of a liability for at least twelve months after the reporting period, the liability should be classified as current. According to the *Framework*, conversion of a liability into equity is a form of settlement.

BC38F   The application of these requirements means that if the conversion option can be exercised by the holder at any time, the liability component would be classified as current. This classification would be required even if the entity would not be required to settle unconverted instruments with cash or other assets for more than twelve months after the reporting period.

BC38G   IAS 1 and the *Framework* state that information about the liquidity and solvency positions of an entity is useful to users. The terms 'liquidity' and 'solvency' are associated with the availability of cash to an entity. Issuing equity does not result in an outflow of cash or other assets of the entity.

BC38H   The Board concluded that classifying the liability on the basis of the requirements to transfer cash or other assets rather than on settlement better reflects the liquidity and solvency position of an entity, and therefore it decided to amend IAS 1 accordingly.

BC38I   The Board discussed the comments received in response to its exposure draft of proposed *Improvements to IFRSs* published in 2007 and noted that some respondents were concerned that the proposal in the exposure draft would apply to all liabilities, not just those that are components of convertible instruments as originally contemplated in the exposure draft. Consequently, in *Improvements to IFRSs* issued in April 2009, the Board amended the proposed wording to clarify that the amendment applies only to the classification of a liability that can, at the option of the counterparty, be settled by the issue of the entity's equity instruments.

Effect of events after the reporting period on the classification of liabilities (paragraphs 69–76)

BC39   Paragraph 63 of IAS 1 (as issued in 1997) included the following:

> An enterprise should continue to classify its long-term interest-bearing liabilities as non-current, even when they are due to be settled within twelve months of the balance sheet date if:
>
> (a)   the original term was for a period of more than twelve months;
>
> (b)   the enterprise intends to refinance the obligation on a long-term basis; and
>
> (c)   that intention is supported by an agreement to refinance, or to reschedule payments, which is completed before the financial statements are authorised for issue.

BC40   Paragraph 65 stated:

> Some borrowing agreements incorporate undertakings by the borrower (covenants) which have the effect that the liability becomes payable on demand if certain conditions related to the borrower's financial position are breached. In these circumstances, the liability is classified as non-current only when:
>
> (a) the lender has agreed, prior to the authorisation of the financial statements for issue, not to demand payment as a consequence of the breach; and
>
> (b) it is not probable that further breaches will occur within twelve months of the balance sheet date.

BC41   The Board considered these requirements and concluded that refinancing, or the receipt of a waiver of the lender's right to demand payment, that occurs after the reporting period should not be taken into account in the classification of a liability.

BC42   Therefore, the exposure draft of 2002 proposed:

(a) to amend paragraph 63 to specify that a long-term financial liability due to be settled within twelve months of the balance sheet date should not be classified as a non-current liability because an agreement to refinance, or to reschedule payments, on a long-term basis is completed after the balance sheet date and before the financial statements are authorised for issue. This amendment would not affect the classification of a liability as non-current when the entity has, under the terms of an existing loan facility, the discretion to refinance or roll over its obligations for at least twelve months after the balance sheet date.

(b) to amend paragraph 65 to specify that a long-term financial liability that is payable on demand because the entity breached a condition of its loan agreement should be classified as current at the balance sheet date even if the lender has agreed after the balance sheet date, and before the financial statements are authorised for issue, not to demand payment as a consequence of the breach. However, if the lender has agreed by the balance sheet date to provide a period of grace within which the entity can rectify the breach and during which the lender cannot demand immediate repayment, the liability is classified as non-current if it is due for settlement, without that breach of the loan agreement, at least twelve months after the balance sheet date and:

(i) the entity rectifies the breach within the period of grace; or

(ii) when the financial statements are authorised for issue, the period of grace is incomplete and it is probable that the breach will be rectified.

BC43   Some respondents disagreed with these proposals. They advocated classifying a liability as current or non-current according to whether it is expected to use current assets of the entity, rather than strictly on the basis of its date of maturity and whether it is callable at the end of the reporting period. In their view, this would provide more relevant information about the liability's future effect on the timing of the entity's resource flows.

BC44   However, the Board decided that the following arguments for changing paragraphs 63 and 65 were more persuasive:

(a)   refinancing a liability after the balance sheet date does not affect the entity's liquidity and solvency *at the balance sheet date*, the reporting of which should reflect contractual arrangements in force on that date. Therefore, it is a non-adjusting event in accordance with IAS 10 *Events after the Balance Sheet Date* and should not affect the presentation of the entity's balance sheet.

(b)   it is illogical to adopt a criterion that 'non-current' classification of short-term obligations expected to be rolled over for at least twelve months after the balance sheet date depends on whether the roll-over is at the discretion of the entity, and then to provide an exception based on refinancing occurring after the balance sheet date.

(c)   in the circumstances set out in paragraph 65, unless the lender has waived its right to demand immediate repayment or granted a period of grace within which the entity may rectify the breach of the loan agreement, the financial condition of the entity at the balance sheet date was that the entity did not hold an absolute right to defer repayment, based on the terms of the loan agreement. The granting of a waiver or a period of grace changes the terms of the loan agreement. Therefore, an entity's receipt from the lender, after the balance sheet date, of a waiver or a period of grace of at least twelve months does not change the nature of the liability to non-current until it occurs.

BC45   IAS 1 now includes the amendments proposed in 2002, with one change. The change relates to the classification of a long-term loan when, at the end of the reporting period, the lender has provided a period of grace within which a breach of the loan agreement can be rectified, and during which period the lender cannot demand immediate repayment of the loan.

BC46   The exposure draft proposed that such a loan should be classified as non-current if it is due for settlement, without the breach, at least twelve months after the balance sheet date and:

(a)   the entity rectifies the breach within the period of grace; or

(b)   when the financial statements are authorised for issue, the period of grace is incomplete and it is probable that the breach will be rectified.

BC47   After considering respondents' comments, the Board decided that the occurrence or probability of a rectification of a breach after the reporting period is irrelevant to the conditions existing at the end of the reporting period. The revised IAS 1 requires that, for the loan to be classified as non-current, the period of grace must end at least twelve months after the reporting period (see paragraph 75). Therefore, the conditions (a) and (b) in paragraph BC46 are redundant.

BC48   The Board considered arguments that if a period of grace to remedy a breach of a long-term loan agreement is provided before the end of the reporting period, the loan should be classified as non-current regardless of the length of the period of grace. These arguments are based on the view that, at the end of the reporting period, the lender does not have an unconditional legal right to demand repayment before the original maturity date (ie if the entity remedies the breach during the period of grace, it is entitled to repay the loan on the original maturity date). However, the Board concluded that an entity should classify a loan as non-current only if it has an unconditional right to defer settlement of the loan for at least twelve months after the reporting period. This criterion focuses on the legal rights of the entity, rather than those of the lender.

Statement of comprehensive income

Reporting comprehensive income (paragraph 81)

BC49   The exposure draft of 2006 proposed that all non-owner changes in equity should be presented in a single statement or in two statements. In a single-statement presentation, all items of income and expense are presented together. In a two-statement presentation, the first statement ('income statement') presents income and expenses recognised in profit or loss and the second statement ('statement of comprehensive income') begins with profit or loss and presents, in addition, items of income and expense that IFRSs require or permit to be recognised outside profit or loss. Such items include, for example, translation differences related to foreign operations and gains or losses on available-for-sale[*] financial assets. The statement of comprehensive income does not include transactions with owners in their capacity as owners. Such transactions are presented in the statement of changes in equity.

BC50   Respondents to the exposure draft had mixed views about whether the Board should permit a choice of displaying non-owner changes in equity in one statement or two statements. Many respondents agreed with the Board's proposal to maintain the two-statement approach and the single-statement approach as alternatives and a few urged the Board to mandate one of them. However, most respondents preferred the two-statement approach because it distinguishes profit or loss and total comprehensive income; they believe that with the two-statement approach, the 'income statement' remains a primary financial statement. Respondents supported the presentation of two separate statements as a transition measure until the Board develops principles to determine the criteria for inclusion of items in profit or loss or in other comprehensive income.

BC51   The exposure draft of 2006 expressed the Board's preference for a single statement of all non-owner changes in equity. The Board provided several reasons for this preference. All items of non-owner changes in equity meet the definitions of income and expenses in the *Framework*. The *Framework* does not define profit or loss, nor does it provide criteria for distinguishing the characteristics of items that should be included in profit or loss from those items that should be excluded from profit or loss. Therefore, the Board decided that it was conceptually correct for an entity to present all non-owner changes in equity (ie all income and expenses recognised in a period) in a single statement because there are no clear principles or common characteristics that can be used to separate income and expenses into two statements.

---

[*] IFRS 9 *Financial Instruments*, issued in November 2009, eliminated the category of available-for-sale financial assets. This paragraph discusses matters relevant when IAS 1 was issued.

BC52   However, in the Board's discussions with interested parties, it was clear that many were strongly opposed to the concept of a single statement. They argued that there would be undue focus on the bottom line of the single statement. In addition, many argued that it was premature for the Board to conclude that presentation of income and expense in a single statement was an improvement in financial reporting without also addressing the other aspects of presentation and display, namely deciding what categories and line items should be presented in a statement of recognised income and expense.

BC53   In the light of these views, although it preferred a single statement, the Board decided that an entity should have the choice of presenting all income and expenses recognised in a period in one statement or in two statements. An entity is prohibited from presenting components of income and expense (ie non-owner changes in equity) in the statement of changes in equity.

BC54   Many respondents disagreed with the Board's preference and thought that a decision at this stage would be premature. In their view the decision about a single-statement or two-statement approach should be subject to further consideration. They urged the Board to address other aspects of presentation and display, namely deciding which categories and line items should be presented in a 'statement of comprehensive income'. The Board reaffirmed its reasons for preferring a single-statement approach and agreed to address other aspects of display and presentation in the next stage of the project.

Results of operating activities

BC55   IAS 1 omits the requirement in the 1997 version to disclose the results of operating activities as a line item in the income statement. 'Operating activities' are not defined in IAS 1, and the Board decided not to require disclosure of an undefined item.

BC56   The Board recognises that an entity may elect to disclose the results of operating activities, or a similar line item, even though this term is not defined. In such cases, the Board notes that the entity should ensure that the amount disclosed is representative of activities that would normally be regarded as 'operating'. In the Board's view, it would be misleading and would impair the comparability of financial statements if items of an operating nature were excluded from the results of operating activities, even if that had been industry practice. For example, it would be inappropriate to exclude items clearly related to operations (such as inventory write-downs and restructuring and relocation expenses) because they occur irregularly or infrequently or are unusual in amount. Similarly, it would be inappropriate to exclude items on the grounds that they do not involve cash flows, such as depreciation and amortisation expenses.

Subtotal for profit or loss (paragraph 82)

BC57   As revised, IAS 1 requires a subtotal for profit or loss in the statement of comprehensive income. If an entity chooses to present comprehensive income by using two statements, it should begin the second statement with profit or loss—the bottom line of the first statement (the 'income statement')—and display the components of other comprehensive income immediately after that. The Board concluded that this is the best way to achieve the objective of equal prominence (see paragraph BC22) for the presentation of income and expenses. An entity that chooses to display comprehensive income in one statement should include profit or loss as a subtotal within that statement.

BC58 The Board acknowledged that the items included in profit or loss do not possess any unique characteristics that allow them to be distinguished from items that are included in other comprehensive income. However, the Board and its predecessor have required some items to be recognised outside profit or loss. The Board will deliberate in the next stage of the project how items of income and expense should be presented in the statement of comprehensive income.

Minority interest (paragraph 83)[*]

BC59 IAS 1 requires the 'profit or loss attributable to minority interest' and 'profit or loss attributable to owners of the parent' each to be presented in the income statement in accordance with paragraph 83. These amounts are to be presented as allocations of profit or loss, not as items of income or expense. A similar requirement has been added for the statement of changes in equity, in paragraph 106(a). These changes are consistent with IAS 27 *Consolidated and Separate Financial Statements*, which requires that in a consolidated balance sheet (now called 'statement of financial position'), minority interest is presented within equity because it does not meet the definition of a liability in the *Framework*.

Extraordinary items (paragraph 87)

BC60 IAS 8 *Net Profit or Loss for the Period, Fundamental Errors and Changes in Accounting Policies* (issued in 1993) required extraordinary items to be disclosed in the income statement separately from the profit or loss from ordinary activities. That standard defined 'extraordinary items' as 'income or expenses that arise from events or transactions that are clearly distinct from the ordinary activities of the enterprise and therefore are not expected to recur frequently or regularly'.

BC61 In 2002, the Board decided to eliminate the concept of extraordinary items from IAS 8 and to prohibit the presentation of items of income and expense as 'extraordinary items' in the income statement and the notes. Therefore, in accordance with IAS 1, no items of income and expense are to be presented as arising from outside the entity's ordinary activities.

BC62 Some respondents to the exposure draft of 2002 argued that extraordinary items should be presented in a separate component of the income statement because they are clearly distinct from all of the other items of income and expense, and because such presentation highlights to users of financial statements the items of income and expense to which the least attention should be given when predicting an entity's future performance.

---

[*] In January 2008 the IASB issued an amended IAS 27 *Consolidated and Separate Financial Statements*, which amended 'minority interest' to 'non-controlling interests'.

BC63   The Board decided that items treated as extraordinary result from the normal business risks faced by an entity and do not warrant presentation in a separate component of the income statement. The nature or function of a transaction or other event, rather than its frequency, should determine its presentation within the income statement. Items currently classified as 'extraordinary' are only a subset of the items of income and expense that may warrant disclosure to assist users in predicting an entity's future performance.

BC64   Eliminating the category of extraordinary items eliminates the need for arbitrary segregation of the effects of related external events—some recurring and others not—on the profit or loss of an entity for a period. For example, arbitrary allocations would have been necessary to estimate the financial effect of an earthquake on an entity's profit or loss if it occurs during a major cyclical downturn in economic activity. In addition, paragraph 97 of IAS 1 requires disclosure of the nature and amount of material items of income and expense.

Other comprehensive income—related tax effects (paragraphs 90 and 91)

BC65   The exposure draft of 2006 proposed to allow components of 'other recognised income and expense' (now 'other comprehensive income') to be presented before tax effects ('gross presentation') or after their related tax effects ('net presentation'). The 'gross presentation' facilitated the traceability of other comprehensive income items to profit or loss, because items of profit or loss are generally displayed before tax. The 'net presentation' facilitated the identification of other comprehensive income items in the equity section of the statement of financial position. A majority of respondents supported allowing both approaches. The Board reaffirmed its conclusion that components of other comprehensive income could be displayed either (a) net of related tax effects or (b) before related tax effects.

BC66   Regardless of whether a pre-tax or post-tax display was used, the exposure draft proposed to require disclosure of the amount of income tax expense or benefit allocated separately to individual components of other comprehensive income, in line with SFAS 130. Many respondents agreed in principle with this disclosure, because they agreed that it helped to improve the clarity and transparency of such information, particularly when components of other comprehensive income are taxed at rates different from those applied to profit or loss.

BC67   However, most respondents expressed concern about having to trace the tax effect for each one of the components of other comprehensive income. Several observed that the tax allocation process is arbitrary (eg it may involve the application of subjectively determined tax rates) and some pointed out that this information is not readily available for some industries (eg the insurance sector), where components of other comprehensive income are multiple and tax allocation involves a high degree of subjectivity. Others commented that they did not understand why tax should be attributed to components of comprehensive income line by line, when this is not a requirement for items in profit or loss.

BC68   The Board decided to maintain the disclosure of income tax expense or benefit allocated to each component of other comprehensive income. Users of financial statements often requested further information on tax amounts relating to components of other comprehensive income, because tax rates often differed from those applied to profit or loss. The Board also observed that an entity should have such tax information available and that a disclosure requirement would therefore not involve additional cost for preparers of financial statements.

Reclassification adjustments (paragraphs 92–96)

BC69   In the exposure draft of 2006, the Board proposed that an entity should separately present reclassification adjustments. These adjustments are the amounts reclassified to profit or loss in the current period that were previously recognised in other comprehensive income. The Board decided that adjustments necessary to avoid double-counting items in total comprehensive income when those items are reclassified to profit or loss in accordance with IFRSs. The Board's view was that separate presentation of reclassification adjustments is essential to inform users of those amounts that are included as income and expenses in different periods—as income or expenses in other comprehensive income in previous periods and as income or expenses in profit or loss in the current period. Without such information, users may find it difficult to assess the effect of reclassifications on profit or loss and to calculate the overall gain or loss associated with available-for-sale* financial assets, cash flow hedges and on translation or disposal of foreign operations.

BC70   Most respondents agreed with the Board's decision and believe that the disclosure of reclassification adjustments is important to understanding how components recognised in profit or loss are related to other items recognised in equity in two different periods. However, some respondents suggested that the Board should use the term 'recycling', rather than 'reclassification' as the former term is more common. The Board concluded that both terms are similar in meaning, but decided to use the term 'reclassification adjustment' to converge with the terminology used in SFAS 130.

BC71   The exposure draft proposed to allow the presentation of reclassification adjustments in the statement of recognised income and expense (now 'statement of comprehensive income') or in the notes. Most respondents supported this approach.

BC72   Some respondents noted some inconsistencies in the definition of 'reclassification adjustments' in the exposure draft (now paragraphs 7 and 93 of IAS 1). Respondents suggested that the Board should expand the definition in paragraph 7 to include gains and losses recognised in current periods in addition to those recognised in earlier periods, to make the definition consistent with paragraph 93. They commented that, without clarification, there could be differences between interim and annual reporting, for reclassifications of items that arise in one interim period and reverse out in a different interim period within the same annual period.

---

*   IFRS 9 *Financial Instruments*, issued in November 2009, eliminated the category of available-for-sale financial assets. This paragraph discusses matters relevant when IAS 1 was issued.

BC73   The Board decided to align the definition of reclassification adjustments with SFAS 130 and include an additional reference to 'current periods' in paragraph 7.

Statement of changes in equity

Effects of retrospective application or retrospective restatement (paragraph 106(b))

BC74   Some respondents to the exposure draft of 2006 asked the Board to clarify whether the effects of retrospective application or retrospective restatement, as defined in IAS 8, should be regarded as non-owner changes in equity. The Board noted that IAS 1 specifies that these effects are included in the statement of changes in equity. However, the Board decided to clarify that the effects of retrospective application or retrospective restatement are not changes in equity in the period, but provide a reconciliation between the previous period's closing balance and the opening balance in the statement of changes in equity.

Presentation of dividends (paragraph 107)

BC75   The Board reaffirmed its conclusion to require the presentation of dividends in the statement of changes in equity or in the notes, because dividends are distributions to owners in their capacity as owners and the statement of changes in equity presents all owner changes in equity. The Board concluded that an entity should not present dividends in the statement of comprehensive income because that statement presents non-owner changes in equity.

Statement of cash flows

IAS 7 *Cash Flow Statements* (paragraph 111)

BC76   The Board considered whether the operating section of an indirect method statement of cash flows should begin with total comprehensive income instead of profit or loss as is required by IAS 7 *Cash Flow Statements*. When components of other comprehensive income are non-cash items, they would become reconciling items in arriving at cash flows from operating activities and would add items to the statement of cash flows without adding information content. The Board concluded that an amendment to IAS 7 is not required; however, as mentioned in paragraph BC14 the Board decided to relabel this financial statement as 'statement of cash flows'.

Notes

Disclosure of the judgements that management has made in the process of applying the entity's accounting policies (paragraphs 122–124)

BC77   The revised IAS 1 requires disclosure of the judgements, apart from those involving estimations, that management has made in the process of applying the entity's accounting policies and that have the most significant effect on the amounts recognised in the financial statements (see paragraph 122). An example of these judgements is how management determines whether financial assets are held-to-maturity investments. The Board decided that disclosure of the most important of these judgements would enable users of financial statements to understand better how the accounting policies are applied and to make comparisons between entities regarding the basis on which managements make these judgements.

BC78 Comments received on the exposure draft of 2002 indicated that the purpose of the proposed disclosure was unclear. Accordingly, the Board amended the disclosure explicitly to exclude judgements involving estimations (which are the subject of the disclosure in paragraph 125) and added another four examples of the types of judgements disclosed (see paragraphs 123 and 124).

Disclosure of major sources of estimation uncertainty (paragraphs 125–133)

BC79 IAS 1 requires disclosure of the assumptions concerning the future, and other major sources of estimation uncertainty at the end of the reporting period, that have a significant risk of causing a material adjustment to the carrying amounts of assets and liabilities within the next financial year. For those assets and liabilities, the proposed disclosures include details of:

(a) their nature; and

(b) their carrying amount as at the end of the reporting period (see paragraph 125).

BC80 Determining the carrying amounts of some assets and liabilities requires estimation of the effects of uncertain future events on those assets and liabilities at the end of the reporting period. For example, in the absence of recently observed market prices used to measure the following assets and liabilities, future-oriented estimates are necessary to measure the recoverable amount of classes of property, plant and equipment, the effect of technological obsolescence of inventories, provisions subject to the future outcome of litigation in progress, and long-term employee benefit liabilities such as pension obligations. These estimates involve assumptions about items such as the risk adjustment to cash flows or discount rates used, future changes in salaries and future changes in prices affecting other costs. No matter how diligently an entity estimates the carrying amounts of assets and liabilities subject to significant estimation uncertainty at the end of the reporting period, the reporting of point estimates in the statement of financial position cannot provide information about the estimation uncertainties involved in measuring those assets and liabilities and the implications of those uncertainties for the period's profit or loss.

BC81 The *Framework* states that 'The economic decisions that are made by users of financial statements require an evaluation of the ability of an entity to generate cash and cash equivalents and of the timing and certainty of their generation.' The Board decided that disclosure of information about assumptions and other major sources of estimation uncertainty at the end of the reporting period enhances the relevance, reliability and understandability of the information reported in financial statements. These assumptions and other sources of estimation uncertainty relate to estimates that require management's most difficult, subjective or complex judgements. Therefore, disclosure in accordance with paragraph 125 of the revised IAS 1 would be made in respect of relatively few assets or liabilities (or classes of them).

BC82 The exposure draft of 2002 proposed the disclosure of some 'sources of measurement uncertainty'. In the light of comments received that the purpose of this disclosure was unclear, the Board decided:

(a) to amend the subject of that disclosure to 'sources of estimation uncertainty at the end of the reporting period'; and

(b) to clarify in the revised Standard that the disclosure does not apply to assets and liabilities measured at fair value based on recently observed market prices (see paragraph 128 of IAS 1).

BC83 When assets and liabilities are measured at fair value on the basis of recently observed market prices, future changes in carrying amounts would not result from using estimates to measure the assets and liabilities at the end of the reporting period. Using observed market prices to measure assets or liabilities obviates the need for estimates at the end of the reporting period. The market prices properly reflect the fair values at the end of the reporting period, even though future market prices could be different. The objective of fair value measurement is to reflect fair value at the measurement date, not to predict a future value.

BC84 IAS 1 does not prescribe the particular form or detail of the disclosures. Circumstances differ from entity to entity, and the nature of estimation uncertainty at the end of the reporting period has many facets. IAS 1 limits the scope of the disclosures to items that have a significant risk of causing a material adjustment to the carrying amounts of assets and liabilities within the next financial year. The longer the future period to which the disclosures relate, the greater the range of items that would qualify for disclosure, and the less specific are the disclosures that could be made about particular assets or liabilities. A period longer than the next financial year might obscure the most relevant information with other disclosures.

Disclosures about capital (paragraphs 134 and 135)

BC85 In July 2004 the Board published an exposure draft—ED 7 *Financial Instruments: Disclosures*. As part of that project, the Board considered whether it should require disclosures about capital.

BC86 The level of an entity's capital and how it manages capital are important factors for users to consider in assessing the risk profile of an entity and its ability to withstand unexpected adverse events. The level of capital might also affect the entity's ability to pay dividends. Consequently, ED 7 proposed disclosures about capital.

BC87 In ED 7 the Board decided that it should not limit the requirements for disclosures about capital to entities that are subject to external capital requirements (eg regulatory capital requirements established by legislation or other regulation). The Board believes that information about capital is useful for all entities, as is evidenced by the fact that some entities set internal capital requirements and norms have been established for some industries. The Board noted that the capital disclosures are not intended to replace disclosures required by regulators. The Board also noted that the financial statements should not be regarded as a substitute for disclosures to regulators (which may not be available to all users) because the function of disclosures made to regulators may differ from the function of those to other users. Therefore, the Board decided that information about capital should be required of all entities because it is useful to users of general purpose financial statements. Accordingly, the Board did not distinguish between the requirements for regulated and non-regulated entities.

BC88 Some respondents to ED 7 questioned the relevance of the capital disclosures in an IFRS dealing with disclosures relating to financial instruments. The Board noted that an entity's capital does not relate solely to financial instruments and, thus, capital disclosures have more general relevance. Accordingly, the Board included these disclosures in IAS 1, rather than IFRS 7 *Financial Instruments: Disclosures*, the IFRS resulting from ED 7.

BC89 The Board also decided that an entity's decision to adopt the amendments to IAS 1 should be independent of the entity's decision to adopt IFRS 7. The Board noted that issuing a separate amendment facilitates separate adoption decisions.

Objectives, policies and processes for managing capital (paragraph 136)

BC90 The Board decided that disclosure about capital should be placed in the context of a discussion of the entity's objectives, policies and processes for managing capital. This is because the Board believes that such a discussion both communicates important information about the entity's capital strategy and provides the context for other disclosures.

BC91 The Board considered whether an entity can have a view of capital that differs from what IFRSs define as equity. The Board noted that, although for the purposes of this disclosure capital would often equate with equity as defined in IFRSs, it might also include or exclude some components. The Board also noted that this disclosure is intended to give entities the opportunity to describe how they view the components of capital they manage, if this is different from what IFRSs define as equity.

Externally imposed capital requirements (paragraph 136)

BC92 The Board considered whether it should require disclosure of any externally imposed capital requirements. Such a capital requirement could be:

(a) an industry-wide requirement with which all entities in the industry must comply; or

(b) an entity-specific requirement imposed on a particular entity by its prudential supervisor or other regulator.

BC93 The Board noted that some industries and countries have industry-wide capital requirements, and others do not. Thus, the Board concluded that it should not require disclosure of industry-wide requirements, or compliance with such requirements, because such disclosure would not lead to comparability between different entities or between similar entities in different countries.

BC94   The Board concluded that disclosure of the existence and level of entity-specific capital requirements is important information for users, because it informs them about the risk assessment of the regulator. Such disclosure improves transparency and market discipline.

BC95   However, the Board noted the following arguments against requiring disclosure of externally imposed entity-specific capital requirements.

(a)   Users of financial statements might rely primarily on the regulator's assessment of solvency risk without making their own risk assessment.

(b)   The focus of a regulator's risk assessment is for those whose interests the regulations are intended to protect (eg depositors or policyholders). This emphasis is different from that of a shareholder. Thus, it could be misleading to suggest that the regulator's risk assessment could, or should, be a substitute for independent analysis by investors.

(c)   The disclosure of entity-specific capital requirements imposed by a regulator might undermine that regulator's ability to impose such requirements. For example, the information could cause depositors to withdraw funds, a prospect that might discourage regulators from imposing requirements. Furthermore, an entity's regulatory dialogue would become public, which might not be appropriate in all circumstances.

(d)   Because different regulators have different tools available, for example formal requirements and moral suasion, a requirement to disclose entity-specific capital requirements could not be framed in a way that would lead to the provision of information that is comparable across entities.

(e)   Disclosure of capital requirements (and hence, regulatory judgements) could hamper clear communication to the entity of the regulator's assessment by creating incentives to use moral suasion and other informal mechanisms.

(f)   Disclosure requirements should not focus on entity-specific capital requirements in isolation, but should focus on how entity-specific capital requirements affect how an entity manages and determines the adequacy of its capital resources.

(g)   A requirement to disclose entity-specific capital requirements imposed by a regulator is not part of Pillar 3 of the Basel II Framework developed by the Basel Committee on Banking Supervision.

BC96   Taking into account all of the above arguments, the Board decided not to require quantitative disclosure of externally imposed capital requirements. Rather, it decided to require disclosures about whether the entity complied with any externally imposed capital requirements during the period and, if not, the consequences of non-compliance. This retains confidentiality between regulators and the entity, but alerts users to breaches of capital requirements and their consequences.

BC97   Some respondents to ED 7 did not agree that breaches of externally imposed capital requirements should be disclosed. They argued that disclosure about breaches of externally imposed capital requirements and the associated regulatory measures subsequently imposed could be disproportionately damaging to entities. The Board was not persuaded by these arguments because it believes that such concerns indicate that information about breaches of externally imposed capital requirements may often be material by its nature. The *Framework* states that 'Information is material if its omission or misstatement could influence the economic decisions of users taken on the basis of the financial statements.' Similarly, the Board decided not to provide an exemption for temporary non-compliance with regulatory requirements during the year. Information that an entity is sufficiently close to its limits to breach them, even on a temporary basis, is useful for users.

Internal capital targets

BC98   The Board proposed in ED 7 that the requirement to disclose information about breaches of capital requirements should apply equally to breaches of internally imposed requirements, because it believed the information is also useful to a user of the financial statements.

BC99   However, this proposal was criticised by respondents to ED 7 for the following reasons:

(a)   The information is subjective and, thus, not comparable between entities. In particular, different entities will set internal targets for different reasons, so a breach of a requirement might signify different things for different entities. In contrast, a breach of an external requirement has similar implications for all entities required to comply with similar requirements.

(b)   Capital targets are not more important than other internally set financial targets, and to require disclosure only of capital targets would provide users with incomplete, and perhaps misleading, information.

(c)   Internal targets are estimates that are subject to change by the entity. It is not appropriate to require the entity's performance against this benchmark to be disclosed.

(d)   An internally set capital target can be manipulated by management. The disclosure requirement could cause management to set the target so that it would always be achieved, providing little useful information to users and potentially reducing the effectiveness of the entity's capital management.

BC100   As a result, the Board decided not to require disclosure of the capital targets set by management, whether the entity has complied with those targets, or the consequences of any non-compliance. However, the Board confirmed its view that when an entity has policies and processes for managing capital, qualitative disclosures about these policies and processes are useful. The Board also concluded that these disclosures, together with disclosure of the components of equity and their changes during the year (required by paragraphs 106–110), would give sufficient information about entities that are not regulated or subject to externally imposed capital requirements.

Puttable financial instruments and obligations arising on liquidation

BC100A The Board decided to require disclosure of information about puttable instruments and instruments that impose on the entity an obligation to deliver to another party a pro rata share of the net assets of the entity only on liquidation that are reclassified in accordance with paragraphs 16E and 16F of IAS 32. This is because the Board concluded that this disclosure allows users of financial statements to understand the effects of any reclassifications.

BC100B The Board also concluded that entities with puttable financial instruments classified as equity should be required to disclose additional information to allow users to assess any effect on the entity's liquidity arising from the ability of the holder to put the instruments to the issuer. Financial instruments classified as equity usually do not include any obligation for the entity to deliver a financial asset to another party. Therefore, the Board concluded that additional disclosures are needed in these circumstances. In particular, the Board concluded that entities should disclose the expected cash outflow on redemption or repurchase of those financial instruments that are classified as equity and information about how that amount was determined. That information allows liquidity risk associated with the put obligation and future cash flows to be evaluated.

Presentation of measures per share

BC101 The exposure draft of 2006 did not propose to change the requirements of IAS 33 *Earnings per Share* on the presentation of basic and diluted earnings per share. A majority of respondents agreed with this decision. In their opinion, earnings per share should be the only measure per share permitted or required in the statement of comprehensive income and changing those requirements was beyond the scope of this stage of the financial statement presentation project.

BC102 However, some respondents would like to see alternative measures per share whenever earnings per share is not viewed as the most relevant measure for financial analysts (ie credit rating agencies that focus on other measures). A few respondents proposed that an entity should also display an amount per share for total comprehensive income, because this was considered a useful measure. The Board did not support including alternative measures per share in the financial statements, until totals and subtotals, and principles for aggregating and disaggregating items, are addressed and discussed as part of the next stage of the financial statement presentation project.

BC103 Some respondents also interpreted the current provisions in IAS 33 as allowing de facto a display of alternative measures in the income statement. In its deliberations, the Board was clear that paragraph 73 of IAS 33 did not leave room for confusion. However, it decided that the wording in paragraph 73 could be improved to clarify that alternative measures should be shown 'only in the notes'. This will be done when IAS 33 is revisited or as part of the annual improvements process.

BC104   One respondent commented that the use of the word 'earnings' was inappropriate in the light of changes proposed in the exposure draft and that the measure should be denominated 'profit or loss per share', instead. The Board considered that this particular change in terminology was beyond the scope of IAS 1.

Transition and effective date

BC105   The Board is committed to maintaining a 'stable platform' of substantially unchanged standards for annual periods beginning between 1 January 2006 and 31 December 2008. In addition, some preparers will need time to make the system changes necessary to comply with the revisions to IAS 1. Therefore, the Board decided that the effective date of IAS 1 should be annual periods beginning on or after 1 January 2009, with earlier application permitted.

Differences from SFAS 130

BC106   In developing IAS 1, the Board identified the following differences from SFAS 130:

(a)   **Reporting and display of comprehensive income** Paragraph 22 of SFAS 130 permits a choice of displaying comprehensive income and its components, in one or two statements of financial performance or in a statement of changes in equity. IAS 1 (as revised in 2007) does not permit display in a statement of changes in equity.

(b)   **Reporting other comprehensive income in the equity section of a statement of financial position** Paragraph 26 of SFAS 130 specifically states that the *total of other comprehensive income* is reported separately from retained earnings and additional paid-in capital in a statement of financial position at the end of the period. A descriptive title such as *accumulated other comprehensive income* is used for that component of equity. An entity discloses accumulated balances for each classification in that separate component of equity in a statement of financial position, in a statement of changes in equity, or in notes to the financial statements. IAS 1 (as revised in 2007) does not specifically require the display of a total of accumulated other comprehensive income in the statement of financial position.

(c)   **Display of the share of other comprehensive income items of associates and joint ventures accounted for using the equity method** Paragraph 82 of IAS 1 (as revised in 2007) requires the display in the statement of comprehensive income of the investor's share of the investee's other comprehensive income. Paragraph 122 of SFAS 130 does not specify how that information should be displayed. An investor is permitted to combine its proportionate share of other comprehensive income amounts with its own other comprehensive income items and display the aggregate of those amounts in an income statement type format or in a statement of changes in equity.

Appendix
Amendments to the Basis for Conclusions on other IFRSs

This appendix contains amendments to the Basis for Conclusions on other IFRSs that are necessary in order to ensure consistency with the revised IAS 1. Amended paragraphs are shown with the new text underlined and deleted text struck through.

* * * * *

The amendments contained in this appendix when this Standard was revised in 2007 have been incorporated into the relevant pronouncements published in this volume.

Dissenting opinions

Dissent of Mary E Barth, Anthony T Cope, Robert P Garnett and James J Leisenring from IAS 1 (as revised in September 2007)

DO1 Professor Barth and Messrs Cope, Garnett and Leisenring voted against the issue of IAS 1 *Presentation of Financial Statements* in 2007. The reasons for their dissent are set out below.

DO2 Those Board members agree with the requirement to report all items of income and expense separately from changes in net assets that arise from transactions with owners in their capacity as owners. Making that distinction clearly is a significant improvement in financial reporting.

DO3 However, they believe that the decision to permit entities to divide the statement of comprehensive income into two separate statements is both conceptually unsound and unwise.

DO4 As noted in paragraph BC51, the *Framework* does not define profit or loss, or net income. It also does not indicate what criteria should be used to distinguish between those items of recognised income and expense that should be included in profit or loss and those items that should not. In some cases, it is even possible for identical transactions to be reported inside or outside profit or loss. Indeed, in that same paragraph, the Board acknowledges these facts, and indicates that it had a preference for reporting all items of income and expense in a single statement, believing that a single statement is the conceptually correct approach. Those Board members believe that some items of income and expense that will potentially bypass the statement of profit and loss can be as significant to the assessment of an entity's performance as items that will be included. Until a conceptual distinction can be developed to determine whether any items should be reported in profit or loss or elsewhere, financial statements will lack neutrality and comparability unless all items are reported in a single statement. In such a statement, profit or loss can be shown as a subtotal, reflecting current conventions.

DO5 In the light of those considerations, it is puzzling that most respondents to the exposure draft that proposed these amendments favoured permitting a two-statement approach, reasoning that it 'distinguishes between profit and loss and total comprehensive income' (paragraph BC50). Distinguishing between those items reported in profit or loss and those reported elsewhere is accomplished by the requirement for relevant subtotals to be included in a statement of comprehensive income. Respondents also stated that a two-statement approach gives primacy to the 'income statement'; that conflicts with the Board's requirement in paragraph 11 of IAS 1 to give equal prominence to all financial statements within a set of financial statements.

DO6 Those Board members also believe that the amendments are flawed by offering entities a choice of presentation methods. The Board has expressed a desire to reduce alternatives in IFRSs. The *Preface to International Financial Reporting Standards*, in paragraph 13, states: 'the IASB intends not to permit choices in accounting treatment ... and will continue to reconsider ... those transactions and events for which IASs permit a choice of accounting treatment, with the objective of reducing the number of those choices.' The *Preface* extends this objective to both accounting and reporting. The same paragraph states: 'The IASB's objective is to require like transactions and events to be accounted for *and reported* in a like way and unlike transactions and events to be accounted for *and reported* differently' (emphasis added). By permitting a choice in this instance, the IASB has abandoned that principle.

DO7   Finally, the four Board members believe that allowing a choice of presentation at this time will ingrain practice, and make achievement of the conceptually correct presentation more difficult as the long-term project on financial statement presentation proceeds.

Guidance on implementing
IAS 1 *Presentation of Financial Statements*

This guidance accompanies, but is not part of, IAS 1.

Illustrative financial statement structure

IG1   IAS 1 sets out the components of financial statements and minimum requirements for disclosure in the statements of financial position, comprehensive income and changes in equity. It also describes further items that may be presented either in the relevant financial statement or in the notes. This guidance provides simple examples of ways in which the requirements of IAS 1 for the presentation of the statements of financial position, comprehensive income and changes in equity might be met. An entity should change the order of presentation, the titles of the statements and the descriptions used for line items when necessary to suit its particular circumstances.

IG2   The guidance is in two sections. Paragraphs IG3–IG6 provide examples of the presentation of financial statements. Paragraphs IG7–IG9 have been deleted. Paragraphs IG10 and IG11 provide examples of capital disclosures.

IG3   The illustrative statement of financial position shows one way in which an entity may present a statement of financial position distinguishing between current and non-current items. Other formats may be equally appropriate, provided the distinction is clear.

IG4   The illustrations use the term 'comprehensive income' to label the total of all components of comprehensive income, including profit or loss. The illustrations use the term 'other comprehensive income' to label income and expenses that are included in comprehensive income but excluded from profit or loss. IAS 1 does not require an entity to use those terms in its financial statements.

IG5   Two statements of comprehensive income are provided, to illustrate the alternative presentations of income and expenses in a single statement or in two statements. The single statement of comprehensive income illustrates the classification of income and expenses within profit or loss by function. The separate statement (in this example, 'the income statement') illustrates the classification of income and expenses within profit by nature.

IG6   The examples are not intended to illustrate all aspects of IFRSs, nor do they constitute a complete set of financial statements, which would also include a statement of cash flows, a summary of significant accounting policies and other explanatory information.

Part I: Illustrative presentation of financial statements

XYZ Group – Statement of financial position as at 31 December 20X7

(in thousands of currency units)

	31 Dec 20X7	31 Dec 20X6
ASSETS		
Non-current assets		
Property, plant and equipment	350,700	360,020
Goodwill	80,800	91,200
Other intangible assets	227,470	227,470
Investments in associates	100,150	110,770
Investments in equity instruments	142,500	156,000
	901,620	945,460
Current assets		
Inventories	135,230	132,500
Trade receivables	91,600	110,800
Other current assets	25,650	12,540
Cash and cash equivalents	312,400	322,900
	564,880	578,740
Total assets	1,466,500	1,524,200

continued...

...continued

XYZ Group – Statement of financial position as at 31 December 20X7
(in thousands of currency units)

	31 Dec 20X7	31 Dec 20X6
EQUITY AND LIABILITIES		
Equity attributable to owners of the parent		
Share capital	650,000	600,000
Retained earnings	243,500	161,700
Other components of equity	10,200	21,200
	903,700	782,900
Non-controlling interests	70,050	48,600
Total equity	973,750	831,500
Non-current liabilities		
Long-term borrowings	120,000	160,000
Deferred tax	28,800	26,040
Long-term provisions	28,850	52,240
Total non-current liabilities	177,650	238,280
Current liabilities		
Trade and other payables	115,100	187,620
Short-term borrowings	150,000	200,000
Current portion of long-term borrowings	10,000	20,000
Current tax payable	35,000	42,000
Short-term provisions	5,000	4,800
Total current liabilities	315,100	454,420
Total liabilities	492,750	692,700
Total equity and liabilities	1,466,500	1,524,200

XYZ Group – Statement of comprehensive income for the year ended 31 December 20X7

(illustrating the presentation of comprehensive income in one statement and the classification of expenses within profit by function)

(in thousands of currency units)

	20X7	20X6
Revenue	390,000	355,000
Cost of sales	(245,000)	(230,000)
Gross profit	145,000	125,000
Other income	20,667	11,300
Distribution costs	(9,000)	(8,700)
Administrative expenses	(20,000)	(21,000)
Other expenses	(2,100)	(1,200)
Finance costs	(8,000)	(7,500)
Share of profit of associates[a]	35,100	30,100
Profit before tax	161,667	128,000
Income tax expense	(40,417)	(32,000)
Profit for the year from continuing operations	121,250	96,000
Loss for the year from discontinued operations	–	(30,500)
PROFIT FOR THE YEAR	121,250	65,500
Other comprehensive income:		
Exchange differences on translating foreign operations[b]	5,334	10,667
Investments in equity instruments	(24,000)	26,667
Cash flow hedges[b]	(667)	(4,000)
Gains on property revaluation	933	3,367
Actuarial gains (losses) on defined benefit pension plans	(667)	1,333
Share of other comprehensive income of associates[c]	400	(700)
Income tax relating to components of other comprehensive income[d]	4,667	(9,334)
Other comprehensive income for the year, net of tax	(14,000)	28,000
TOTAL COMPREHENSIVE INCOME FOR THE YEAR	107,250	93,500

continued...

...continued

XYZ Group – Statement of comprehensive income for the year ended 31 December 20X7

(illustrating the presentation of comprehensive income in one statement and the classification of expenses within profit by function)

(in thousands of currency units)

	20X7	20X6
Profit attributable to:		
Owners of the parent	97,000	52,400
Non-controlling interests	24,250	13,100
	121,250	65,500
Total comprehensive income attributable to:		
Owners of the parent	85,800	74,800
Non-controlling interests	21,450	18,700
	107,250	93,500
Earnings per share (in currency units):		
Basic and diluted	0.46	0.30

Alternatively, components of other comprehensive income could be presented in the statement of comprehensive income net of tax:

Other comprehensive income for the year, after tax:	20X7	20X7
Exchange differences on translating foreign operations	4,000	8,000
Investments in equity instruments	(18,000)	20,000
Cash flow hedges	(500)	(3000)
Gains on property revaluation	600	2,700
Actuarial gains (losses) on defined benefit pension plans	(500)	1,000
Share of other comprehensive income of associates	400	(700)
Other comprehensive income for the year, net of tax[d]	(14,000)	28,000

(a) This means the share of associates' other comprehensive income attributable to owners of the associates, ie it is after tax and non-controlling interests in the associates.

(b) This illustrates the aggregated presentation, with disclosure of the current year gain or loss and reclassification adjustment presented in the notes. Alternatively, a gross presentation can be used.

(c) This means the share of associates' other comprehensive income attributable to owners of the associates, ie it is after tax and non-controlling interests in the associates.

(d) The income tax relating to each component of other comprehensive income is disclosed in the notes.

XYZ Group – Income statement for the year ended 31 December 20X7

(illustrating the presentation of comprehensive income in two statements and classification of expenses within profit by nature)

(in thousands of currency units)

	20X7	20X6
Revenue	390,000	355,000
Other income	20,667	11,300
Changes in inventories of finished goods and work in progress	(115,100)	(107,900)
Work performed by the entity and capitalised	16,000	15,000
Raw material and consumables used	(96,000)	(92,000)
Employee benefits expense	(45,000)	(43,000)
Depreciation and amortisation expense	(19,000)	(17,000)
Impairment of property, plant and equipment	(4,000)	–
Other expenses	(6,000)	(5,500)
Finance costs	(15,000)	(18,000)
Share of profit of associates[(e)]	35,100	30,100
Profit before tax	161,667	128,000
Income tax expense	(40,417)	(32,000)
Profit for the year from continuing operations	121,250	96,000
Loss for the year from discontinued operations	–	(30,500)
PROFIT FOR THE YEAR	121,250	65,500
Profit attributable to:		
Owners of the parent	97,000	52,400
Non-controlling interests	24,250	13,100
	121,250	65,500
Earnings per share (in currency units):		
Basic and diluted	0.46	0.30

(e) This means the share of associates' profit attributable to owners of the associates, ie it is after tax and non-controlling interests in the associates.

XYZ Group – Statement of comprehensive income for the year ended 31 December 20X7

(illustrating the presentation of comprehensive income in two statements)

(in thousands of currency units)

	20X7	20X6
Profit for the year	121,250	65,500
Other comprehensive income:		
Exchange differences on translating foreign operations	5,334	10,667
Investments in equity instruments	(24,000)	26,667
Cash flow hedges	(667)	(4,000)
Gains on property revaluation	933	3,367
Actuarial gains (losses) on defined benefit pension plans	(667)	1,333
Share of other comprehensive income of associates[(f)]	400	(700)
Income tax relating to components of other comprehensive income[(g)]	4,667	(9,334)
Other comprehensive income for the year, net of tax	(14,000)	28,000
TOTAL COMPREHENSIVE INCOME FOR THE YEAR	107,250	93,500
Total comprehensive income attributable to:		
Owners of the parent	85,800	74,800
Non-controlling interests	21,450	18,700
	107,250	93,500

Alternatively, components of other comprehensive income could be presented, net of tax. Refer to the statement of comprehensive income illustrating the presentation of income and expenses in one statement.

(f)   This means the share of associates' other comprehensive income attributable to owners of the associates, ie it is after tax and non-controlling interests in the associates.

(g)   The income tax relating to each component of other comprehensive income is disclosed in the notes.

XYZ Group

Disclosure of components of other comprehensive income[h]

Notes

Year ended 31 December 20X7

(in thousands of currency units)

			20X7		20X6
Other comprehensive income:					
Exchange differences on translating foreign operations[i]			5,334		10,667
Investments in equity instruments			(24,000)		26,667
Cash flow hedges:					
Gains (losses) arising during the year	(4,667)			(4,000)	
Less: Reclassification adjustments for gains (losses) included in profit or loss	3,333			–	
Less: Adjustments for amounts transferred to initial carrying amount of hedged items	667	(667)		–	(4,000)
Gains on property revaluation			933		3,367
Actuarial gains (losses) on defined benefit pension plans			(667)		1,333
Share of other comprehensive income of associates			400		(700)
Other comprehensive income			(18,667)		37,334
Income tax relating to components of other comprehensive income[j]			4,667		(9,334)
Other comprehensive income for the year			(14,000)		28,000

(h) When an entity chooses an aggregated presentation in the statement of comprehensive income, the amounts for reclassification adjustments and current year gain or loss are presented in the notes.

(i) There was no disposal of a foreign operation. Therefore, there is no reclassification adjustment for the years presented.

(j) The income tax relating to each component of other comprehensive income is disclosed in the notes.

XYZ Group

Disclosure of tax effects relating to each component of other comprehensive income

Notes

Year ended 31 December 20X7

(in thousands of currency units)

	20X7			20X6		
	Before-tax amount	Tax (expense) benefit	Net-of-tax amount	Before-tax amount	Tax (expense) benefit	Net-of-tax amount
Exchange differences on translating foreign operations	5,334	(1,334)	4,000	10,667	(2,667)	8,000
Investments in equity instruments	(24,000)	6,000	(18,000)	26,667	(6,667)	20,000
Cash flow hedges	(667)	167	(500)	(4,000)	1,000	(3,000)
Gains on property revaluation	933	(333)	600	3,367	(667)	2,700
Actuarial gains (losses) on defined benefit pension plans	(667)	167	(500)	1,333	(333)	1,000
Share of other comprehensive income of associates	400	–	400	(700)	–	(700)
Other comprehensive income	(18,667)	4,667	(14,000)	37,334	(9,334)	28,000

XYZ Group – Statement of changes in equity for the year ended 31 December 20X7

(in thousands of currency units)

	Share capital	Retained earnings	Translation of foreign operations	Available-for-sale financial assets	Cash flow hedges	Revaluation surplus	Total	Non-controlling interests	Total equity
Balance at 1 January 20X6	600,000	118,100	(4,000)	1,600	2,000	–	717,700	29,800	747,500
Changes in accounting policy	–	400	–	–	–	–	400	100	500
Restated balance	600,000	118,500	(4,000)	1,600	2,000	–	718,100	29,900	748,000
Changes in equity for 20X6									
Dividends	–	(10,000)	–	–	–	–	(10,000)	–	(10,000)
Total comprehensive income for the year(k)	–	53,200	6,400	16,000	(2,400)	1,600	74,800	18,700	93,500
Balance at 31 December 20X6	600,000	161,700	2,400	17,600	(400)	1,600	782,900	48,600	831,500
Changes in equity for 20X7									
Issue of share capital	50,000	–	–	–	–	–	50,000	–	50,000
Dividends	–	(15,000)	–	–	–	–	(15,000)	–	(15,000)
Total comprehensive income for the year(l)	–	96,600	3,200	(14,400)	(400)	800	85,800	21,450	107,250
Transfer to retained earnings	–	200	–	–	–	200	–	–	–
Balance at 31 December 20X7	650,000	243,500	5,600	3,200	(800)	2,200	903,700	70,050	973,750

(k)   The amount included in retained earnings for 20X6 of 53,200 represents profit attributable to owners of the parent of 52,400 plus actuarial gains on defined benefit pension plans of 800 (1,333, less tax 333, less non-controlling interests 200).

The amount included in the translation, investments in equity instruments and cash flow hedge reserves represent other comprehensive income for each component, net of tax and non-controlling interests, eg other comprehensive income related to investments in equity instruments for 20X6 of 16,000 is 26,667, less tax 6,667, less non-controlling interests 4,000.

The amount included in the revaluation surplus of 1,600 represents the share of other comprehensive income of associates of (700) plus gains on property revaluation of 2,300 (3,367, less tax 667, less non-controlling interests 400). Other comprehensive income of associates relates solely to gains or losses on property revaluation.

(l)   The amount included in retained earnings for 20X7 of 96,600 represents profit attributable to owners of the parent of 97,000 plus actuarial losses on defined benefit pension plans of 400 (667, less tax 167, less non-controlling interests 100).

The amount included in the translation, investments in equity instruments and cash flow hedge reserves represent other comprehensive income for each component, net of tax and non-controlling interests, eg other comprehensive income related to the translation of foreign operations for 20X7 of 3,200 is 5,334, less tax 1,334, less non-controlling interests 800.

The amount included in the revaluation surplus of 800 represents the share of other comprehensive income of associates of 400 plus gains on property revaluation of 400 (933, less tax 333, less non-controlling interests 200). Other comprehensive income of associates relates solely to gains or losses on property revaluation.

IG7–IG9 [Deleted]

Part III: Illustrative examples of capital disclosures (paragraphs 134–136)
An entity that is not a regulated financial institution

IG10   The following example illustrates the application of paragraphs 134 and 135 for an entity that is not a financial institution and is not subject to an externally imposed capital requirement. In this example, the entity monitors capital using a debt-to-adjusted capital ratio. Other entities may use different methods to monitor capital. The example is also relatively simple. An entity decides, in the light of its circumstances, how much detail it provides to satisfy the requirements of paragraphs 134 and 135.

Facts

Group A manufactures and sells cars. Group A includes a finance subsidiary that provides finance to customers, primarily in the form of leases. Group A is not subject to any externally imposed capital requirements.

Example disclosure

The Group's objectives when managing capital are:

- to safeguard the entity's ability to continue as a going concern, so that it can continue to provide returns for shareholders and benefits for other stakeholders, and

- to provide an adequate return to shareholders by pricing products and services commensurately with the level of risk.

The Group sets the amount of capital in proportion to risk. The Group manages the capital structure and makes adjustments to it in the light of changes in economic conditions and the risk characteristics of the underlying assets. In order to maintain or adjust the capital structure, the Group may adjust the amount of dividends paid to shareholders, return capital to shareholders, issue new shares, or sell assets to reduce debt.

Consistently with others in the industry, the Group monitors capital on the basis of the debt-to-adjusted capital ratio. This ratio is calculated as net debt ÷ adjusted capital. Net debt is calculated as total debt (as shown in the statement of financial position) less cash and cash equivalents. Adjusted capital comprises all components of equity (ie share capital, share premium, non-controlling interests, retained earnings, and revaluation surplus) other than amounts accumulated in equity relating to cash flow hedges, and includes some forms of subordinated debt.

continued...

...continued

During 20X4, the Group's strategy, which was unchanged from 20X3, was to maintain the debt-to-adjusted capital ratio at the lower end of the range 6:1 to 7:1, in order to secure access to finance at a reasonable cost by maintaining a BB credit rating. The debt-to-adjusted capital ratios at 31 December 20X4 and at 31 December 20X3 were as follows:

	31 Dec 20X4 CU million	31 Dec 20X3 CU million
Total debt	1,000	1,100
Less: cash and cash equivalents	(90)	(150)
Net debt	910	950
Total equity	110	105
Add: subordinated debt instruments	38	38
Less: amounts accumulated in equity relating to cash flow hedges	(10)	(5)
Adjusted capital	138	138
Debt-to-adjusted capital ratio	6.6	6.9

The decrease in the debt-to-adjusted capital ratio during 20X4 resulted primarily from the reduction in net debt that occurred on the sale of subsidiary Z. As a result of this reduction in net debt, improved profitability and lower levels of managed receivables, the dividend payment was increased to CU2.8 million for 20X4 (from CU2.5 million for 20X3).

An entity that has not complied with externally imposed capital requirements

IG11   The following example illustrates the application of paragraph 135(e) when an entity has not complied with externally imposed capital requirements during the period. Other disclosures would be provided to comply with the other requirements of paragraphs 134 and 135.

Facts

Entity A provides financial services to its customers and is subject to capital requirements imposed by Regulator B. During the year ended 31 December 20X7, Entity A did not comply with the capital requirements imposed by Regulator B. In its financial statements for the year ended 31 December 20X7, Entity A provides the following disclosure relating to its non-compliance.

Example disclosure

Entity A filed its quarterly regulatory capital return for 30 September 20X7 on 20 October 20X7. At that date, Entity A's regulatory capital was below the capital requirement imposed by Regulator B by CU1 million. As a result, Entity A was required to submit a plan to the regulator indicating how it would increase its regulatory capital to the amount required. Entity A submitted a plan that entailed selling part of its unquoted equities portfolio with a carrying amount of CU11.5 million in the fourth quarter of 20X7. In the fourth quarter of 20X7, Entity A sold its fixed interest investment portfolio for CU12.6 million and met its regulatory capital requirement.

Appendix
Amendments to guidance on other IFRSs

The following amendments to guidance on other IFRSs are necessary in order to ensure consistency with the revised IAS 1. In the amended paragraphs, new text is underlined and deleted text is struck through.

*****

The amendments contained in this appendix when IAS 1 was revised in 2007 have been incorporated into the guidance on the relevant IFRSs, published in this volume.

Table of Concordance

This table shows how the contents of IAS 1 (revised 2003 and amended in 2005) and IAS 1 (as revised in 2007) correspond. Paragraphs are treated as corresponding if they broadly address the same matter even though the guidance may differ.

Superseded IAS 1 paragraph	IAS 1 (revised 2007) paragraph	Superseded IAS 1 paragraph	IAS 1 (revised 2007) paragraph	Superseded IAS 1 paragraph	IAS 1 (revised 2007) paragraph
1	1, 3	42, 43	47, 48	101	None
2	2	44–48	49–53	102	111
3	4, 7	49, 50	36, 37	103–107	112–116
4	None	51–67	60–76	108–115	117–124
5	5	68	54	116–124	125–133
6	6	68A	54	124A–124C	134–136
7	9	69–73	55–59	125, 126	137, 138
8	10	74–77	77–80	127	139
9, 10	13, 14	None	81	127A	None
11	7	78	88	127B	None
12	7	79	89	128	140
None	8	80	89	IG1	IG1
None	11, 12	81	82	None	IG2
13–22	15–24	82	83	IG2	IG3
23, 24	25, 26	None	84	None	IG4
25, 26	27, 28	83–85	85–87	IG3, IG4	IG5, IG6
27, 28	45, 46	None	90–96	None	IG7
29–31	29–31	86–94	97–105	None	IG8
32–35	32–35	95	107	None	IG9
36	38	None	108	IG5, IG6	IG10, IG11
None	39	96, 97	106, 107		
37–41	40–44	98	109		

IASB documents published to accompany

International Accounting Standard 2

Inventories

This version includes amendments resulting from IFRSs issued up to 31 December 2009.

The text of the unaccompanied IAS 2 is contained in Part A of this edition. Its effective date is 1 January 2005. The effective date of the latest amendment is 1 January 2013. This part presents the following accompanying documents:

Approval by the Board of IAS 2 issued in December 2003

International Accounting Standard 2 *Inventories* (as revised in 2003) was approved for issue by the fourteen members of the International Accounting Standards Board.

Sir David Tweedie	Chairman
Thomas E Jones	Vice-Chairman
Mary E Barth	
Hans-Georg Bruns	
Anthony T Cope	
Robert P Garnett	
Gilbert Gélard	
James J Leisenring	
Warren J McGregor	
Patricia L O'Malley	
Harry K Schmid	
John T Smith	
Geoffrey Whittington	
Tatsumi Yamada	

Basis for Conclusions on
IAS 2 *Inventories*

This Basis for Conclusions accompanies, but is not part of, IAS 2.

Introduction

BC1   This Basis for Conclusions summarises the International Accounting Standards Board's considerations in reaching its conclusions on revising IAS 2 *Inventories* in 2003. Individual Board members gave greater weight to some factors than to others.

BC2   In July 2001 the Board announced that, as part of its initial agenda of technical projects, it would undertake a project to improve a number of Standards, including IAS 2. The project was undertaken in the light of queries and criticisms raised in relation to the Standards by securities regulators, professional accountants and other interested parties. The objectives of the Improvements project were to reduce or eliminate alternatives, redundancies and conflicts within Standards, to deal with some convergence issues and to make other improvements. In May 2002 the Board published its proposals in an Exposure Draft of *Improvements to International Accounting Standards*, with a comment deadline of 16 September 2002. The Board received over 160 comment letters on the Exposure Draft.

BC3   Because the Board's intention was not to reconsider the fundamental approach to the accounting for inventories established by IAS 2, this Basis for Conclusions does not discuss requirements in IAS 2 that the Board has not reconsidered.

Scope

Reference to historical cost system

BC4   Both the objective and the scope of the previous version of IAS 2 referred to 'the accounting treatment for inventories under the historical cost system.' Some had interpreted those words as meaning that the Standard applied only under a historical cost system and permitted entities the choice of applying other measurement bases, for example fair value.

BC5   The Board agreed that those words could be seen as permitting a choice, resulting in inconsistent application of the Standard. Accordingly, it deleted the words 'in the context of the historical cost system in accounting for inventories' to clarify that the Standard applies to all inventories that are not specifically exempted from its scope.

Inventories of broker-traders

BC6   The Exposure Draft proposed excluding from the scope of the Standard inventories of non-producers of agricultural and forest products and mineral ores to the extent that these inventories are measured at net realisable value in accordance with well-established industry practices. However, some respondents disagreed with this scope exemption for the following reasons:

(a) the scope exemption should apply to all types of inventories of broker-traders;

(b) established practice is for broker-traders to follow a mark-to-market approach rather than to value these inventories at net realisable value;

(c) the guidance on net realisable value in IAS 2 is not appropriate for the valuation of inventories of broker-traders.

BC7 The Board found these comments persuasive. Therefore it decided that the Standard should not apply to the measurement of inventories of:

(a) producers of agricultural and forest products, agricultural produce after harvest, and minerals and mineral products, to the extent that they are measured at net realisable value (as in the previous version of IAS 2), or

(b) commodity broker-traders when their inventories are measured at fair value less costs to sell.

BC8 The Board further decided that the measurement of the effect of inventories on profit or loss for the period needed to be consistent with the measurement attribute of inventories for which such exemption is allowed. Accordingly, to qualify under (a) or (b), the Standard requires changes in the recognised amount of inventories to be included in profit or loss for the period. The Board believes this is particularly appropriate in the case of commodity broker-traders because they seek to profit from fluctuations in prices and trade margins.

Cost formulas

BC9 The combination of the previous version of IAS 2 and SIC-1 *Consistency—Different Cost Formulas for Inventories* allowed some choice between first-in, first-out (FIFO) or weighted average cost formulas (benchmark treatment) and the last-in, first-out (LIFO) method (allowed alternative treatment). The Board decided to eliminate the allowed alternative of using the LIFO method.

BC10 The LIFO method treats the newest items of inventory as being sold first, and consequently the items remaining in inventory are recognised as if they were the oldest. This is generally not a reliable representation of actual inventory flows.

BC11 The LIFO method is an attempt to meet a perceived deficiency of the conventional accounting model (the measurement of cost of goods sold expense by reference to outdated prices for the inventories sold, whereas sales revenue is measured at current prices). It does so by imposing an unrealistic cost flow assumption.

BC12 The use of LIFO in financial reporting is often tax-driven, because it results in cost of goods sold expense calculated using the most recent prices being deducted from revenue in the determination of the gross margin. The LIFO method reduces (increases) profits in a manner that tends to reflect the effect that increased (decreased) prices would have on the cost of replacing inventories sold. However, this effect depends on the relationship between the prices of the most recent inventory acquisitions and the replacement cost at the end of the period. Thus, it is not a truly systematic method for determining the effect of changing prices on profits.

BC13　The use of LIFO results in inventories being recognised in the balance sheet at amounts that bear little relationship to recent cost levels of inventories. However, LIFO can distort profit or loss, especially when 'preserved' older 'layers' of inventory are presumed to have been used when inventories are substantially reduced. It is more likely in these circumstances that relatively new inventories will have been used to meet the increased demands on inventory.

BC14　Some respondents argued that the use of LIFO has merit in certain circumstances because it partially adjusts profit or loss for the effects of price changes. The Board concluded that it is not appropriate to allow an approach that results in a measurement of profit or loss for the period that is inconsistent with the measurement of inventories for balance sheet purposes.

BC15　Other respondents argued that in some industries, such as the oil and gas industry, inventory levels are driven by security considerations and often represent a minimum of 90 days of sales. They argue that, in these industries, the use of LIFO better reflects an entity's performance because inventories held as security stocks are closer to long-term assets than to working capital.

BC16　The Board was not convinced by these arguments because these security stocks do not match historical layers under a LIFO computation.

BC17　Other respondents argued that in some cases, for example, when measuring coal dumps, piles of iron or metal scraps (when stock bins are replenished by 'topping up'), the LIFO method reflects the actual physical flow of inventories.

BC18　The Board concluded that valuation of these inventories follows a direct costing approach where actual physical flows are matched with direct costs, which is a method different from LIFO.

BC19　The Board decided to eliminate the LIFO method because of its lack of representational faithfulness of inventory flows. This decision does not rule out specific cost methods that reflect inventory flows that are similar to LIFO.

BC20　The Board recognised that, in some jurisdictions, use of the LIFO method for tax purposes is possible only if that method is also used for accounting purposes. It concluded, however, that tax considerations do not provide an adequate conceptual basis for selecting an appropriate accounting treatment and that it is not acceptable to allow an inferior accounting treatment purely because of tax regulations and advantages in particular jurisdictions. This may be an issue for local taxation authorities.

BC21　IAS 2 continues to allow the use of both the FIFO and the weighted average methods for interchangeable inventories.

Cost of inventories recognised as an expense in the period

BC22   The Exposure Draft proposed deleting paragraphs in the previous version of IAS 2 that required disclosure of the cost of inventories recognised as an expense in the period, because this disclosure is required in IAS 1 *Presentation of Financial Statements*.

BC23   Some respondents observed that IAS 1 does not specifically require disclosure of the cost of inventories recognised as an expense in the period when presenting an analysis of expenses using a classification based on their function. They argued that this information is important to understand the financial statements. Therefore the Board decided to require this disclosure specifically in IAS 2.

IASB documents published to accompany

International Accounting Standard 7

Statement of Cash Flows

This version includes amendments resulting from IFRSs issued up to 31 December 2009.

The text of the unaccompanied IAS 7 is contained in Part A of this edition. Its effective date when issued was 1 January 1994. The effective date of the most recent amendments is 1 January 2010. This part presents the following accompanying documents:

Basis for Conclusions on
IAS 7 *Statement of Cash Flows*

This Basis for Conclusions accompanies, but is not part of, IAS 7.

BC1   This Basis for Conclusions summarises the considerations of the International Accounting Standards Board in reaching its conclusions on amending IAS 7 *Statement of Cash Flows* as part of *Improvements to IFRSs* issued in April 2009. Individual Board members gave greater weight to some factors than to others.

BC2   IAS 7 was developed by the International Accounting Standards Committee in 1992 and was not accompanied by a Basis for Conclusions. This Basis refers to clarification of guidance on classification of cash flows from investing activities.

Classification of expenditures on unrecognised assets

BC3   In 2008 the International Financial Reporting Interpretations Committee (IFRIC) reported to the Board that practice differed for the classification of cash flows for expenditures incurred with the objective of generating future cash flows when those expenditures are not recognised as assets in accordance with IFRSs. Some entities classified such expenditures as cash flows from operating activities and others classified them as investing activities. Examples of such expenditures are those for exploration and evaluation activities, which IFRS 6 *Exploration for and Evaluation of Mineral Resources* permits to be recognised as either an asset or an expense depending on the entity's previous accounting policies for those expenditures. Expenditures on advertising and promotional activities, staff training, and research and development could also raise the same issue.

BC4   The IFRIC decided not to add this issue to its agenda but recommended that the Board should amend IAS 7 to state explicitly that only an expenditure that results in a recognised asset can be classified as a cash flow from investing activity.

BC5   In 2008, as part of its annual improvements project, the Board considered the principles in IAS 7, specifically guidance on the treatment of such expenditures in the statement of cash flows. The Board noted that even though paragraphs 14 and 16 of IAS 7 appear to be clear that only expenditure that results in the recognition of an asset should be classified as cash flows from investing activities, the wording is not definitive in this respect. Some might have misinterpreted the reference in paragraph 11 of IAS 7 for an entity to assess classification by activity that is most appropriate to its business to imply that the assessment is an accounting policy choice.

BC6   Consequently, in *Improvements to IFRSs* issued in April 2009, the Board removed the potential misinterpretation by amending paragraph 16 of IAS 7 to state explicitly that only an expenditure that results in a recognised asset can be classified as a cash flow from investing activities.

BC7　The Board concluded that this amendment better aligns the classification of cash flows from investing activities in the statement of cash flows and the presentation of recognised assets in the statement of financial position, reduces divergence in practice and, therefore, results in financial statements that are easier for users to understand.

BC8　The Board also amended the Basis for Conclusions on IFRS 6 to clarify the Board's view that the exemption in IFRS 6 applies only to recognition and measurement of exploration and evaluation assets, not to the classification of related expenditures in the statement of cash flows, for the same reasons set out in paragraph BC7.

Illustrative examples

These illustrative examples accompany, but are not part of, IAS 7.

A   Statement of cash flows for an entity other than a financial institution

1   The examples show only current period amounts. Corresponding amounts for the preceding period are required to be presented in accordance with IAS 1 *Presentation of Financial Statements.*

2   Information from the statement of comprehensive income and statement of financial position is provided to show how the statements of cash flows under the direct method and indirect method have been derived. Neither the statement of comprehensive income nor the statement of financial position is presented in conformity with the disclosure and presentation requirements of other Standards.

3   The following additional information is also relevant for the preparation of the statements of cash flows:

- all of the shares of a subsidiary were acquired for 590. The fair values of assets acquired and liabilities assumed were as follows:

Inventories	100
Accounts receivable	100
Cash	40
Property, plant and equipment	650
Trade payables	100
Long-term debt	200

- 250 was raised from the issue of share capital and a further 250 was raised from long-term borrowings.

- interest expense was 400, of which 170 was paid during the period. Also, 100 relating to interest expense of the prior period was paid during the period.

- dividends paid were 1,200.

- the liability for tax at the beginning and end of the period was 1,000 and 400 respectively. During the period, a further 200 tax was provided for. Withholding tax on dividends received amounted to 100.

- during the period, the group acquired property, plant and equipment with an aggregate cost of 1,250 of which 900 was acquired by means of finance leases. Cash payments of 350 were made to purchase property, plant and equipment.

- plant with original cost of 80 and accumulated depreciation of 60 was sold for 20.

- accounts receivable as at the end of 20X2 include 100 of interest receivable.

Consolidated statement of comprehensive income for the period ended 20X2[a]

Sales	30,650
Cost of sales	(26,000)
Gross profit	4,650
Depreciation	(450)
Administrative and selling expenses	(910)
Interest expense	(400)
Investment income	500
Foreign exchange loss	(40)
Profit before taxation	3,350
Taxes on income	(300)
Profit	3,050

(a) The entity did not recognise any components of other comprehensive income in the period ended 20X2

Consolidated statement of financial position as at end of 20X2

	20X2		20X1
Assets			
Cash and cash equivalents		230	160
Accounts receivable		1,900	1,200
Inventory		1,000	1,950
Portfolio investments		2,500	2,500
Property, plant and equipment at cost	3,730		1,910
Accumulated depreciation	(1,450)		(1,060)
Property, plant and equipment net		2,280	850
Total assets		7,910	6,660
Liabilities			
Trade payables		250	1,890
Interest payable		230	100
Income taxes payable		400	1,000
Long-term debt		2,300	1,040
Total liabilities		3,180	4,030
Shareholders' equity			
Share capital		1,500	1,250
Retained earnings		3,230	1,380
Total shareholders' equity		4,730	2,630
Total liabilities and shareholders' equity		7,910	6,660

Direct method statement of cash flows (paragraph 18(a))

	20X2
Cash flows from operating activities	
Cash receipts from customers	30,150
Cash paid to suppliers and employees	(27,600)
Cash generated from operations	2,550
Interest paid	(270)
Income taxes paid	(900)
Net cash from operating activities	1,380
Cash flows from investing activities	
Acquisition of subsidiary X, net of cash acquired (Note A)	(550)
Purchase of property, plant and equipment (Note B)	(350)
Proceeds from sale of equipment	20
Interest received	200
Dividends received	200
Net cash used in investing activities	(480)
Cash flows from financing activities	
Proceeds from issue of share capital	250
Proceeds from long-term borrowings	250
Payment of finance lease liabilities	(90)
Dividends paid[(a)]	(1,200)
Net cash used in financing activities	(790)
Net increase in cash and cash equivalents	110
Cash and cash equivalents at beginning of period (Note C)	120
Cash and cash equivalents at end of period (Note C)	230

(a) This could also be shown as an operating cash flow.

Indirect method statement of cash flows (paragraph 18(b))

	20X2	
Cash flows from operating activities		
Profit before taxation	3,350	
Adjustments for:		
Depreciation	450	
Foreign exchange loss	40	
Investment income	(500)	
Interest expense	400	
	3,740	
Increase in trade and other receivables	(500)	
Decrease in inventories	1,050	
Decrease in trade payables	(1,740)	
Cash generated from operations	2,550	
Interest paid	(270)	
Income taxes paid	(900)	
Net cash from operating activities		1,380
Cash flows from investing activities		
Acquisition of subsidiary X net of cash acquired (Note A)	(550)	
Purchase of property, plant and equipment (Note B)	(350)	
Proceeds from sale of equipment	20	
Interest received	200	
Dividends received	200	
Net cash used in investing activities		(480)
Cash flows from financing activities		
Proceeds from issue of share capital	250	
Proceeds from long-term borrowings	250	
Payment of finance lease liabilities	(90)	
Dividends paid[(a)]	(1,200)	
Net cash used in financing activities		(790)
Net increase in cash and cash equivalents		110
Cash and cash equivalents at beginning of period (Note C)		120
Cash and cash equivalents at end of period (Note C)		230

(a) This could also be shown as an operating cash flow.

Notes to the statement of cash flows (direct method and indirect method)

A. Obtaining control of subsidiary

During the period the Group obtained control of subsidiary X. The fair values of assets acquired and liabilities assumed were as follows:

Cash	40
Inventories	100
Accounts receivable	100
Property, plant and equipment	650
Trade payables	(100)
Long-term debt	(200)
Total purchase price paid in cash	590
Less: Cash of subsidiary X acquired	(40)
Cash paid to obtain control net of cash acquired	550

B. Property, plant and equipment

During the period, the Group acquired property, plant and equipment with an aggregate cost of 1,250 of which 900 was acquired by means of finance leases. Cash payments of 350 were made to purchase property, plant and equipment.

C. Cash and cash equivalents

Cash and cash equivalents consist of cash on hand and balances with banks, and investments in money market instruments. Cash and cash equivalents included in the statement of cash flows comprise the following amounts in the statement of financial position:

	20X2	20X1
Cash on hand and balances with banks	40	25
Short-term investments	190	135
Cash and cash equivalents as previously reported	230	160
Effect of exchange rate changes	–	(40)
Cash and cash equivalents as restated	230	120

Cash and cash equivalents at the end of the period include deposits with banks of 100 held by a subsidiary which are not freely remissible to the holding company because of currency exchange restrictions.

The Group has undrawn borrowing facilities of 2,000 of which 700 may be used only for future expansion.

D. Segment information

	Segment A	Segment B	Total
Cash flows from:			
Operating activities	1,520	(140)	1,380
Investing activities	(640)	160	(480)
Financing activities	(570)	(220)	(790)
	310	(200)	110

Alternative presentation (indirect method)

As an alternative, in an indirect method statement of cash flows, operating profit before working capital changes is sometimes presented as follows:

Revenues excluding investment income	30,650
Operating expense excluding depreciation	(26,910)
Operating profit before working capital changes	3,740

B   Statement of cash flows for a financial institution

1   The example shows only current period amounts. Comparative amounts for the preceding period are required to be presented in accordance with IAS 1 *Presentation of Financial Statements.*

2   The example is presented using the direct method.

	20X2
Cash flows from operating activities	
Interest and commission receipts	28,447
Interest payments	(23,463)
Recoveries on loans previously written off	237
Cash payments to employees and suppliers	(997)
	4,224
(Increase) decrease in operating assets:	
Short-term funds	(650)
Deposits held for regulatory or monetary control purposes	234
Funds advanced to customers	(288)
Net increase in credit card receivables	(360)
Other short-term negotiable securities	(120)
Increase (decrease) in operating liabilities:	
Deposits from customers	600
Negotiable certificates of deposit	(200)
Net cash from operating activities before income tax	3,440
Income taxes paid	(100)

Net cash from operating activities 3,340

Cash flows from investing activities	
Disposal of subsidiary Y	50
Dividends received	200
Interest received	300
Proceeds from sales of non-dealing securities	1,200
Purchase of non-dealing securities	(600)
Purchase of property, plant and equipment	(500)

Net cash from investing activities 650

continued...

...continued

Cash flows from financing activities

Issue of loan capital	1,000	
Issue of preference shares by subsidiary undertaking	800	
Repayment of long-term borrowings	(200)	
Net decrease in other borrowings	(1,000)	
Dividends paid	(400)	
Net cash from financing activities		200
Effects of exchange rate changes on cash and cash equivalents		600
Net increase in cash and cash equivalents		4,790
Cash and cash equivalents at beginning of period		4,050
Cash and cash equivalents at end of period		8,840

...continued

Cash flows from financing activities

Issue of share capital	1,000
Issue of preference shares by subsidiary undertaking	300
Repayment of long-term borrowings	(200)
Net decrease in other borrowings	(1,000)
Dividends paid	(400)
Net cash from financing activities	200
Effects of exchange rate changes on cash and cash equivalents	300
Net increase in cash and cash equivalents	4,790
Cash and cash equivalents at beginning of period	4,040
Cash and cash equivalents at end of period	8,840

IASB documents published to accompany

International Accounting Standard 8

Accounting Policies, Changes in Accounting Estimates and Errors

This version includes amendments resulting from IFRSs issued up to 31 December 2009.

The text of the unaccompanied IAS 8 is contained in Part A of this edition. Its effective date when issued was 1 January 2005. The effective date of the most recent amendments is 1 January 2013. This part presents the following accompanying documents:

Approval by the Board of IAS 8 issued in December 2003

International Accounting Standard 8 *Accounting Policies, Changes in Accounting Estimates and Errors* (as revised in 2003) was approved for issue by the fourteen members of the International Accounting Standards Board.

Sir David Tweedie   Chairman

Thomas E Jones   Vice-Chairman

Mary E Barth

Hans-Georg Bruns

Anthony T Cope

Robert P Garnett

Gilbert Gélard

James J Leisenring

Warren J McGregor

Patricia L O'Malley

Harry K Schmid

John T Smith

Geoffrey Whittington

Tatsumi Yamada

Basis for Conclusions on
IAS 8 *Accounting Policies, Changes in Accounting Estimates and Errors*

This Basis for Conclusions accompanies, but is not part of, IAS 8.

Introduction

BC1 This Basis for Conclusions summarises the International Accounting Standards Board's considerations in reaching its conclusions on revising IAS 8 *Net Profit or Loss for the Period, Fundamental Errors and Changes in Accounting Policies* in 2003. Individual Board members gave greater weight to some factors than to others.

BC2 In July 2001 the Board announced that, as part of its initial agenda of technical projects, it would undertake a project to improve a number of Standards, including IAS 8. The project was undertaken in the light of queries and criticisms raised in relation to the Standards by securities regulators, professional accountants and other interested parties. The objectives of the Improvements project were to reduce or eliminate alternatives, redundancies and conflicts within Standards, to deal with some convergence issues and to make other improvements. In May 2002 the Board published its proposals in an Exposure Draft of *Improvements to International Accounting Standards*, with a comment deadline of 16 September 2002. The Board received over 160 comment letters on the Exposure Draft.

BC3 The Standard includes extensive changes to the previous version of IAS 8. The Board's intention was not to reconsider all of the previous Standard's requirements for selecting and applying accounting policies, and accounting for changes in accounting policies, changes in accounting estimates and corrections of errors. Accordingly, this Basis for Conclusions does not discuss requirements in IAS 8 that the Board did not reconsider.

Removing allowed alternative treatments

BC4 The previous version of IAS 8 included allowed alternative treatments of voluntary changes in accounting policies (paragraphs 54–57) and corrections of fundamental errors (paragraphs 38–40). Under those allowed alternatives:

(a) the adjustment resulting from retrospective application of a change in an accounting policy was included in profit or loss for the current period; and

(b) the amount of the correction of a fundamental error was included in profit or loss for the current period.

BC5 In both circumstances, comparative information was presented as it was presented in the financial statements of prior periods.

BC6   The Board identified the removal of optional treatments for changes in accounting policies and corrections of errors as an important improvement to the previous version of IAS 8. The Standard removes the allowed alternative treatments and requires changes in accounting policies and corrections of prior period errors to be accounted for retrospectively.

BC7   The Board concluded that retrospective application made by amending the comparative information presented for prior periods is preferable to the previously allowed alternative treatments because, under the now required method of retrospective application:

(a)   profit or loss for the period of the change does not include the effects of changes in accounting policies or errors relating to prior periods.

(b)   information presented about prior periods is prepared on the same basis as information about the current period, and is therefore comparable. This information possesses a qualitative characteristic identified in the *Framework for the Preparation and Presentation of Financial Statements*, and provides the most useful information for trend analysis of income and expenses.

(c)   prior period errors are not repeated in comparative information presented for prior periods.

BC8   Some respondents to the Exposure Draft argued that the previously allowed alternative treatments are preferable because:

(a)   correcting prior period errors by restating prior period information involves an unjustifiable use of hindsight;

(b)   recognising the effects of changes in accounting policies and corrections of errors in current period profit or loss makes them more prominent to users of financial statements; and

(c)   each amount credited or debited to retained earnings as a result of an entity's activities has been recognised in profit or loss in some period.

BC9   The Board concluded that restating prior period information to correct a prior period error does not involve an unjustifiable use of hindsight because prior period errors are defined in terms of a failure to use, or misuse of, reliable information that was available when the prior period financial statements were authorised for issue and could reasonably be expected to have been obtained and taken into account in the preparation and presentation of those financial statements.

BC10   The Board also concluded that the disclosures about changes in accounting policies and corrections of prior period errors in paragraphs 28, 29 and 49 of the Standard should ensure that their effects are sufficiently prominent to users of financial statements.

BC11   The Board further concluded that it is less important for each amount credited or debited to retained earnings as a result of an entity's activities to be recognised in profit or loss in some period than for the profit or loss for each period presented to represent faithfully the effects of transactions and other events occurring in that period.

Eliminating the distinction between fundamental errors and other material prior period errors

BC12   The Standard eliminates the distinction between fundamental errors and other material prior period errors. As a result, all material prior period errors are accounted for in the same way as a fundamental error was accounted for under the retrospective treatment in the previous version of IAS 8. The Board concluded that the definition of 'fundamental errors' in the previous version was difficult to interpret consistently because the main feature of the definition—that the error causes the financial statements of one or more prior periods no longer to be considered to have been reliable—was also a feature of all material prior period errors.

Applying a Standard or an Interpretation that specifically applies to an item

BC13   The Exposure Draft proposed that when a Standard or an Interpretation applies to an item in the financial statements, the accounting policy (or policies) applied to that item is (are) determined by considering the following in descending order:

(a)   the Standard (including any Appendices that form part of the Standard);

(b)   the Interpretation;

(c)   Appendices to the Standard that do not form a part of the Standard; and

(d)   Implementation Guidance issued in respect of the Standard.

BC14   The Board decided not to set out a hierarchy of requirements for these circumstances. The Standard requires only applicable IFRSs to be applied. In addition, it does not mention Appendices.

BC15   The Board decided not to rank Standards above Interpretations because the definition of International Financial Reporting Standards (IFRSs) includes Interpretations, which are equal in status to Standards. The rubric to each Standard clarifies what material constitutes the requirements of an IFRS and what is Implementation Guidance.[*] The term 'Appendix' is retained only for material that is part of an IFRS.

Pronouncements of other standard-setting bodies

BC16   The Exposure Draft proposed that in the absence of a Standard or an Interpretation specifically applying to an item, management should develop and apply an accounting policy by considering, among other guidance, pronouncements of other standard-setting bodies that use a similar conceptual framework to develop accounting standards. Respondents to the Exposure Draft commented that this could *require* entities to consider the pronouncements of

---

[*]   In 2007 the Board was advised that paragraphs 7 and 9 may appear to conflict, and may be misinterpreted to require mandatory consideration of Implementation Guidance. The Board amended paragraphs 7, 9 and 11 by *Improvements to IFRSs* issued in May 2008 to state that only guidance that is identified as an integral part of IFRSs is mandatory.

various other standard-setting bodies when IASB guidance does not exist. Some commentators argued that, for example, it could require consideration of all components of US GAAP on some topics. After considering these comments, the Board decided that the Standard should indicate that considering such pronouncements is voluntary (see paragraph 12 of the Standard).

BC17 As proposed in the Exposure Draft, the Standard states that pronouncements of other standard-setting bodies are used only if they do not conflict with:

(a) the requirements and guidance in IFRSs dealing with similar and related issues; and

(b) the definitions, recognition criteria and measurement concepts for assets, liabilities, income and expenses in the *Framework*.

BC18 The Standard refers to the most recent pronouncements of other standard-setting bodies because if pronouncements are withdrawn or superseded, the relevant standard-setting body no longer thinks they include the best accounting policies to apply.

BC19 Comments received indicated that it was unclear from the Exposure Draft whether a change in accounting policy following a change in a pronouncement of another standard-setting body should be accounted for under the transitional provisions in that pronouncement. As noted above, the Standard does not mandate using pronouncements of other standard-setting bodies in any circumstances. Accordingly, the Board decided to clarify that such a change in accounting policy is accounted for and disclosed as a voluntary change in accounting policy (see paragraph 21 of the Standard). Thus, an entity is precluded from applying transitional provisions specified by the other standard-setting body if they are inconsistent with the treatment of voluntary changes in accounting policies specified by the Standard.

Materiality

BC20 The Standard states that accounting policies specified by IFRSs need not be applied when the effect of applying them is immaterial. It also states that financial statements do not comply with IFRSs if they contain material errors, and that material prior period errors are to be corrected in the first set of financial statements authorised for issue after their discovery. The Standard includes a definition of material omissions or misstatements, which is based on the description of materiality in IAS 1 *Presentation of Financial Statements* (as issued in 1997) and in the *Framework*.

BC21 The former *Preface to Statements of International Accounting Standards* stated that International Accounting Standards were not intended to apply to immaterial items. There is no equivalent statement in the *Preface to International Financial Reporting Standards*. The Board received comments that the absence of such a statement from the *Preface* could be interpreted as requiring an entity to apply accounting policies (including measurement requirements) specified by IFRSs to immaterial items. However, the Board decided that the application of the concept of materiality should be in Standards rather than in the *Preface*.

BC22   The application of the concept of materiality is set out in two Standards. IAS 1 (as revised in 2007) continues to specify its application to disclosures. IAS 8 specifies the application of materiality in applying accounting policies and correcting errors (including errors in measuring items).

Criterion for exemption from requirements

BC23   The previous version of IAS 8 included an impracticability criterion for exemption from retrospective application of voluntary changes in accounting policies and retrospective restatement for fundamental errors, and from making related disclosures, when the allowed alternative treatment of those items was not applied. The Exposure Draft proposed instead an exemption from retrospective application and retrospective restatement when it gives rise to undue cost or effort.

BC24   In the light of comments received on the Exposure Draft, the Board decided that an exemption based on management's assessment of undue cost or effort is too subjective to be applied consistently by different entities. Moreover, the Board decided that balancing costs and benefits is a task for the Board when it sets accounting requirements rather than for entities when they apply those requirements. Therefore, the Board decided to retain the impracticability criterion for exemption in the previous version of IAS 8. This affects the exemptions in paragraphs 23–25, 39 and 43–45 of the Standard. Impracticability is the only basis on which specific exemptions are provided in IFRSs from applying particular requirements when the effect of applying them is material.*

Definition of 'impracticable'

BC25   The Board decided to clarify the meaning of 'impracticable' in relation to retrospective application of a change in accounting policy and retrospective restatement to correct a prior period error.

BC26   Some commentators suggested that retrospective application of a change in accounting policy and retrospective restatement to correct a prior period error are impracticable for a particular prior period whenever significant estimates are required as of a date in that period. However, the Board decided to specify a narrower definition of impracticable because the fact that significant estimates are frequently required when amending comparative information presented for prior periods does not prevent reliable adjustment or correction of the comparative information. Thus, the Board decided that an inability to distinguish objectively information that both provides evidence of circumstances that existed on the date(s) as at which those amounts are to be recognised, measured or disclosed and would have been available when the financial statements for that prior period were authorised for issue from other information is the factor that prevents reliable adjustment or correction of comparative information for prior periods (see part (c) of the definition of 'impracticable' and paragraphs 51 and 52 of the Standard).

---

*   In 2006 the IASB issued IFRS 8 *Operating Segments*. As explained in paragraphs BC46 and BC47 of the Basis for Conclusions on IFRS 8, that IFRS includes an exemption from some requirements if the necessary information is not available and the cost to develop it would be excessive.

BC27   The Standard specifies that hindsight should not be used when applying a new accounting policy to, or correcting amounts for, a prior period, either in making assumptions about what management's intentions would have been in a prior period or estimating the amounts in a prior period. This is because management's intentions in a prior period cannot be objectively established in a later period, and using information that would have been unavailable when the financial statements for the prior period(s) affected were authorised for issue is inconsistent with the definitions of retrospective application and retrospective restatement.

Applying the impracticability exemption

BC28   The Standard specifies that when it is impracticable to determine the cumulative effect of applying a new accounting policy to all prior periods, or the cumulative effect of an error on all prior periods, the entity changes the comparative information as if the new accounting policy had been applied, or the error had been corrected, prospectively from the earliest date practicable (see paragraphs 25 and 45 of the Standard). This is similar to paragraph 52 of the previous version of IAS 8, but it is no longer restricted to changes in accounting policies. The Board decided to include such provisions in the Standard because it agrees with comments received that it is preferable to require prospective application from the start of the earliest period practicable than to permit a change in accounting policy only when the entity can determine the cumulative effect of the change for all prior periods at the beginning of the current period.

BC29   Consistently with the Exposure Draft's proposals, the Standard provides an impracticability exemption from retrospective application of changes in accounting policies, including retrospective application of changes made in accordance with the transitional provisions in an IFRS. The previous version of IAS 8 specified the impracticability exemption for retrospective application of only *voluntary* changes in accounting policies. Thus, the applicability of the exemption to changes made in accordance with the transitional provisions in an IFRS depended on the text of that IFRS. The Board extended the applicability of the exemption because it decided that the need for the exemption applies equally to all changes in accounting policies applied retrospectively.

Disclosures about impending application of newly issued IFRSs

BC30   The Standard requires an entity to provide disclosures when it has not yet applied a new IFRS that has been issued but is not yet effective. The entity is required to disclose that it has not yet applied the IFRS, and known or reasonably estimable information relevant to assessing the possible impact that initial application of the new IFRS will have on the entity's financial statements in the period of initial application (paragraph 30). The Standard also includes guidance on specific disclosures the entity should consider when applying this requirement (paragraph 31).

                    © IASCF

BC31   Paragraphs 30 and 31 of the Standard differ from the proposals in the Exposure Draft in the following respects:

(a)   they specify that an entity needs to disclose information only if it is known or reasonably estimable. This clarification responds to comments on the Exposure Draft that the proposed disclosures would sometimes be impracticable.

(b)   whereas the Exposure Draft proposed to mandate the disclosures now in paragraph 31, the Standard sets out these disclosures as items an entity should consider disclosing to meet the general requirement in paragraph 30. This amendment focuses the requirement on the objective of the disclosure, and, in response to comments on the Exposure Draft that the proposed disclosures were more onerous than the disclosures in US GAAP, clarifies that the Board's intention was to converge with US requirements, rather than to be more onerous.

Recognising the effects of changes in accounting estimates

BC32   The Exposure Draft proposed to retain without exception the requirement in the previous version of IAS 8 that the effect of a change in accounting estimate is *recognised in profit or loss* in:

(a)   the period of the change, if the change affects that period only; or

(b)   the period of the change and future periods, if the change affects both.

BC33   Some respondents to the Exposure Draft disagreed with requiring the effects of all changes in accounting estimates to be recognised in profit or loss. They argued that this is inappropriate to the extent that a change in an accounting estimate gives rise to changes in assets and liabilities, because the entity's equity does not change as a result. These commentators also argued that it is inappropriate to preclude recognising the effects of changes in accounting estimates directly in equity when that is required or permitted by a Standard or an Interpretation. The Board concurs, and decided to provide an exception to the requirement described in paragraph BC32 for these circumstances.

Guidance on implementing
IAS 8 *Accounting Policies, Changes in Accounting Estimates and Errors*

This guidance accompanies, but is not part of, IAS 8.

Example 1 – Retrospective restatement of errors

1.1 During 20X2, Beta Co discovered that some products that had been sold during 20X1 were incorrectly included in inventory at 31 December 20X1 at CU6,500.[*]

1.2 Beta's accounting records for 20X2 show sales of CU104,000, cost of goods sold of CU86,500 (including CU6,500 for the error in opening inventory), and income taxes of CU5,250.

1.3 In 20X1, Beta reported:

	CU
Sales	73,500
Cost of goods sold	(53,500)
Profit before income taxes	20,000
Income taxes	(6,000)
Profit	14,000

1.4 20X1 opening retained earnings was CU20,000 and closing retained earnings was CU34,000.

1.5 Beta's income tax rate was 30 per cent for 20X2 and 20X1. It had no other income or expenses.

1.6 Beta had CU5,000 of share capital throughout, and no other components of equity except for retained earnings. Its shares are not publicly traded and it does not disclose earnings per share.

Beta Co
Extract from the statement of comprehensive income

	20X2	(restated) 20X1
	CU	CU
Sales	104,000	73,500
Cost of goods sold	(80,000)	(60,000)
Profit before income taxes	24,000	13,500
Income taxes	(7,200)	(4,050)
Profit	16,800	9,450

---

[*] In these examples, monetary amounts are denominated in 'currency units (CU)'.

continued...

...continued

Beta Co
Statement of changes in equity

	Share capital	Retained earnings	Total
	CU	CU	CU
Balance at 31 December 20X0	5,000	20,000	25,000
Profit for the year ended 31 December 20X1 as restated		9,450	9,450
Balance at 31 December 20X1	5,000	29,450	34,450
Profit for the year ended 31 December 20X2		16,800	16,800
Balance at 31 December 20X2	5,000	46,250	51,250

Extracts from the notes

1   Some products that had been sold in 20X1 were incorrectly included in inventory at 31 December 20X1 at CU6,500. The financial statements of 20X1 have been restated to correct this error. The effect of the restatement on those financial statements is summarised below. There is no effect in 20X2.

	Effect on 20X1
	CU
(Increase) in cost of goods sold	(6,500)
Decrease in income tax expense	1,950
(Decrease) in profit	(4,550)
(Decrease) in inventory	(6,500)
Decrease in income tax payable	1,950
(Decrease) in equity	(4,550)

Example 2 – Change in accounting policy with retrospective application

[Deleted]

Example 3 – Prospective application of a change in accounting policy when retrospective application is not practicable

3.1 During 20X2, Delta Co changed its accounting policy for depreciating property, plant and equipment, so as to apply much more fully a components approach, whilst at the same time adopting the revaluation model.

3.2 In years before 20X2, Delta's asset records were not sufficiently detailed to apply a components approach fully. At the end of 20X1, management commissioned an engineering survey, which provided information on the components held and their fair values, useful lives, estimated residual values and depreciable amounts at the beginning of 20X2. However, the survey did not provide a sufficient basis for reliably estimating the cost of those components that had not previously been accounted for separately, and the existing records before the survey did not permit this information to be reconstructed.

3.3 Delta's management considered how to account for each of the two aspects of the accounting change. They determined that it was not practicable to account for the change to a fuller components approach retrospectively, or to account for that change prospectively from any earlier date than the start of 20X2. Also, the change from a cost model to a revaluation model is required to be accounted for prospectively. Therefore, management concluded that it should apply Delta's new policy prospectively from the start of 20X2.

3.4 Additional information:

Delta's tax rate is 30 per cent.

	CU
Property, plant and equipment at the end of 20X1:	
Cost	25,000
Depreciation	(14,000)
Net book value	11,000
Prospective depreciation expense for 20X2 (old basis)	1,500
Some results of the engineering survey:	
Valuation	17,000
Estimated residual value	3,000
Average remaining asset life (years)	7
Depreciation expense on existing property, plant and equipment for 20X2 (new basis)	2,000

continued...

...continued

Extract from the notes

1   From the start of 20X2, Delta changed its accounting policy for depreciating property, plant and equipment, so as to apply much more fully a components approach, whilst at the same time adopting the revaluation model. Management takes the view that this policy provides reliable and more relevant information because it deals more accurately with the components of property, plant and equipment and is based on up-to-date values. The policy has been applied prospectively from the start of 20X2 because it was not practicable to estimate the effects of applying the policy either retrospectively, or prospectively from any earlier date. Accordingly, the adoption of the new policy has no effect on prior years. The effect on the current year is to increase the carrying amount of property, plant and equipment at the start of the year by CU6,000; increase the opening deferred tax provision by CU1,800; create a revaluation surplus at the start of the year of CU4,200; increase depreciation expense by CU500; and reduce tax expense by CU150.

IASB documents published to accompany

International Accounting Standard 10

Events after the Reporting Period

This version includes amendments resulting from IFRSs issued up to 31 December 2009.

The text of the unaccompanied IAS 10 is contained in Part A of this edition. Its effective date when issued was 1 January 2005. The effective date of the most recent amendments is 1 July 2009. This part presents the following accompanying documents:

Approval by the Board of IAS 10 issued in December 2003

International Accounting Standard 10 *Events after the Balance Sheet Date* (as revised in 2003) was approved for issue by the fourteen members of the International Accounting Standards Board.

Sir David Tweedie   Chairman

Thomas E Jones   Vice-Chairman

Mary E Barth

Hans-Georg Bruns

Anthony T Cope

Robert P Garnett

Gilbert Gélard

James J Leisenring

Warren J McGregor

Patricia L O'Malley

Harry K Schmid

John T Smith

Geoffrey Whittington

Tatsumi Yamada

Basis for Conclusions on
IAS 10 *Events after the Reporting Period**

This Basis for Conclusions accompanies, but is not part of, IAS 10.

Introduction

BC1　This Basis for Conclusions summarises the International Accounting Standards Board's considerations in reaching its conclusions on revising IAS 10 *Events After the Balance Sheet Date* in 2003. Individual Board members gave greater weight to some factors than to others.

BC2　In July 2001 the Board announced that, as part of its initial agenda of technical projects, it would undertake a project to improve a number of Standards, including IAS 10. The project was undertaken in the light of queries and criticisms raised in relation to the Standards by securities regulators, professional accountants and other interested parties. The objectives of the Improvements project were to reduce or eliminate alternatives, redundancies and conflicts within Standards, to deal with some convergence issues and to make other improvements. In May 2002 the Board published its proposals in an Exposure Draft of *Improvements to International Accounting Standards*, with a comment deadline of 16 September 2002. The Board received over 160 comment letters on the Exposure Draft.

BC3　Because the Board's intention was not to reconsider the fundamental approach to the accounting for events after the balance sheet date established by IAS 10, this Basis for Conclusions does not discuss requirements in IAS 10 that the Board has not reconsidered.

Limited clarification

BC4　For this limited clarification of IAS 10 the main change made is in paragraphs 12 and 13 (paragraphs 11 and 12 of the previous version of IAS 10). As revised, those paragraphs state that if dividends are declared after the balance sheet date,[†] an entity shall not recognise those dividends as a liability at the balance sheet date. This is because undeclared dividends do not meet the criteria of a present obligation in IAS 37 *Provisions, Contingent Liabilities and Contingent Assets*. The Board discussed whether or not an entity's past practice of paying dividends could be considered a constructive obligation. The Board concluded that such practices do not give rise to a liability to pay dividends.[§]

---

[*]　In September 2007 the IASB amended the title of IAS 10 from *Events after the Balance Sheet Date* to *Events after the Reporting Period* as a consequence of the amendments in IAS 1 *Presentation of Financial Statements* (as revised in 2007).

[†]　IAS 1 *Presentation of Financial Statements* (as revised in 2007) replaced the term 'balance sheet date' with 'end of the reporting period'.

[§]　In 2007 the Board was advised that paragraph 13, taken in isolation, could be read to imply that a liability should be recognised in some circumstances on the basis that a constructive obligation exists, such as when there is an established pattern of paying a dividend. Therefore, the Board amended paragraph 13 by *Improvements to IFRSs* issued in May 2008 to state that no such obligation exists.

IASB document published to accompany

International Accounting Standard 11

Construction Contracts

This version includes amendments resulting from IFRSs issued up to 31 December 2009.

The text of the unaccompanied IAS 11 is contained in Part A of this edition. Its effective date when issued was 1 January 1995. The effective date of the most recent amendment is 1 January 2009. This part presents the following accompanying document:

Illustrative examples

These illustrative examples accompany, but are not part of, IAS 11.

Disclosure of accounting policies

The following are examples of accounting policy disclosures:

Revenue from fixed price construction contracts is recognised on the percentage of completion method, measured by reference to the percentage of labour hours incurred to date to estimated total labour hours for each contract.

Revenue from cost plus contracts is recognised by reference to the recoverable costs incurred during the period plus the fee earned, measured by the proportion that costs incurred to date bear to the estimated total costs of the contract.

The determination of contract revenue and expenses

The following example illustrates one method of determining the stage of completion of a contract and the timing of the recognition of contract revenue and expenses (see paragraphs 22–35 of the Standard).

A construction contractor has a fixed price contract for 9,000 to build a bridge. The initial amount of revenue agreed in the contract is 9,000. The contractor's initial estimate of contract costs is 8,000. It will take 3 years to build the bridge.

By the end of year 1, the contractor's estimate of contract costs has increased to 8,050.

In year 2, the customer approves a variation resulting in an increase in contract revenue of 200 and estimated additional contract costs of 150. At the end of year 2, costs incurred include 100 for standard materials stored at the site to be used in year 3 to complete the project.

The contractor determines the stage of completion of the contract by calculating the proportion that contract costs incurred for work performed to date bear to the latest estimated total contract costs. A summary of the financial data during the construction period is as follows:

	Year 1	Year 2	Year 3
Initial amount of revenue agreed in contract	9,000	9,000	9,000
Variation	–	200	200
Total contract revenue	9,000	9,200	9,200
Contract costs incurred to date	2,093	6,168	8,200
Contract costs to complete	5,957	2,032	–
Total estimated contract costs	8,050	8,200	8,200
Estimated profit	950	1,000	1,000
Stage of completion	26%	74%	100%

The stage of completion for year 2 (74%) is determined by excluding from contract costs incurred for work performed to date the 100 of standard materials stored at the site for use in year 3.

The amounts of revenue, expenses and profit recognised in the statement of comprehensive income in the three years are as follows:

	To date	Recognised in prior years	Recognised in current year
Year 1			
Revenue (9,000 × .26)	2,340	–	2,340
Expenses (8,050 × .26)	2,093	–	2,093
Profit	247	–	247
Year 2			
Revenue (9,200 × .74)	6,808	2,340	4,468
Expenses (8,200 × .74)	6,068	2,093	3,975
Profit	740	247	493
Year 3			
Revenue (9,200 × 1.00)	9,200	6,808	2,392
Expenses	8,200	6,068	2,132
Profit	1,000	740	260

Contract disclosures

A contractor has reached the end of its first year of operations. All its contract costs incurred have been paid for in cash and all its progress billings and advances have been received in cash. Contract costs incurred for contracts B, C and E include the cost of materials that have been purchased for the contract but which have not been used in contract performance to date. For contracts B, C and E, the customers have made advances to the contractor for work not yet performed.

The status of its five contracts in progress at the end of year 1 is as follows:

	A	B	C	D	E	Total
Contract revenue recognised in accordance with paragraph 22	145	520	380	200	55	1,300
Contract expenses recognised in accordance with paragraph 22	110	450	350	250	55	1,215
Expected losses recognised in accordance with paragraph 36	–	–	–	40	30	70
Recognised profits less recognised losses	35	70	30	(90)	(30)	15
Contract costs incurred in the period	110	510	450	250	100	1,420
Contract costs incurred recognised as contract expenses in the period in accordance with paragraph 22	110	450	350	250	55	1,215
Contract costs that relate to future activity recognised as an asset in accordance with paragraph 27	–	60	100	–	45	205
Contract revenue (see above)	145	520	380	200	55	1,300
Progress billings (paragraph 41)	100	520	380	180	55	1,235
Unbilled contract revenue	45	–	–	20	–	65
Advances (paragraph 41)	–	80	20	–	25	125

The amounts to be disclosed in accordance with the Standard are as follows:

Contract revenue recognised as revenue in the period (paragraph 39(a))	1,300
Contract costs incurred and recognised profits (less recognised losses) to date (paragraph 40(a))	1,435
Advances received (paragraph 40(b))	125
Gross amount due from customers for contract work – presented as an asset in accordance with paragraph 42(a)	220
Gross amount due to customers for contract work – presented as a liability in accordance with paragraph 42(b)	(20)

The amounts to be disclosed in accordance with paragraphs 40(a), 42(a) and 42(b) are calculated as follows:

	A	B	C	D	E	Total
Contract						
Contract costs incurred	110	510	450	250	100	1,420
Recognised profits less recognised losses	35	70	30	(90)	(30)	15
	145	580	480	160	70	1,435
Progress billings	100	520	380	180	55	1,235
Due from customers	45	60	100	–	15	220
Due to customers	–	–	–	(20)	–	(20)

The amount disclosed in accordance with paragraph 40(a) is the same as the amount for the current period because the disclosures relate to the first year of operation.

IASB documents published to accompany

International Accounting Standard 12

Income Taxes

This version includes amendments resulting from IFRSs issued up to 31 December 2009.

The text of the unaccompanied IAS 12 is contained in Part A of this edition. Its effective date when issued was 1 January 1998. The effective date of the most recent amendments is 1 January 2013. This part presents the following accompanying documents:

Illustrative examples

These illustrative examples accompany, but are not part of, IAS 12.

Examples of temporary differences

A. Examples of circumstances that give rise to taxable temporary differences

All taxable temporary differences give rise to a deferred tax liability.

Transactions that affect profit or loss

1   Interest revenue is received in arrears and is included in accounting profit on a time apportionment basis but is included in taxable profit on a cash basis.

2   Revenue from the sale of goods is included in accounting profit when goods are delivered but is included in taxable profit when cash is collected. (*note: as explained in B3 below, there is also a* **deductible** *temporary difference associated with any related inventory*).

3   Depreciation of an asset is accelerated for tax purposes.

4   Development costs have been capitalised and will be amortised to the statement of comprehensive income but were deducted in determining taxable profit in the period in which they were incurred.

5   Prepaid expenses have already been deducted on a cash basis in determining the taxable profit of the current or previous periods.

Transactions that affect the statement of financial position

6   Depreciation of an asset is not deductible for tax purposes and no deduction will be available for tax purposes when the asset is sold or scrapped. (*note: paragraph 15(b) of the Standard prohibits recognition of the resulting deferred tax liability unless the asset was acquired in a business combination, see also paragraph 22 of the Standard.*)

7   A borrower records a loan at the proceeds received (which equal the amount due at maturity), less transaction costs. Subsequently, the carrying amount of the loan is increased by amortisation of the transaction costs to accounting profit. The transaction costs were deducted for tax purposes in the period when the loan was first recognised. (*notes: (1) the taxable temporary difference is the amount of transaction costs already deducted in determining the taxable profit of current or prior periods, less the cumulative amount amortised to accounting profit; and (2) as the initial recognition of the loan affects taxable profit, the exception in paragraph 15(b) of the Standard does not apply. Therefore, the borrower recognises the deferred tax liability.*)

8   A loan payable was measured on initial recognition at the amount of the net proceeds, net of transaction costs. The transaction costs are amortised to accounting profit over the life of the loan. Those transaction costs are not deductible in determining the taxable profit of future, current or prior periods. (*notes: (1) the taxable temporary difference is the amount of unamortised transaction costs; and (2) paragraph 15(b) of the Standard prohibits recognition of the resulting deferred tax liability.*)

9   The liability component of a compound financial instrument (for example a convertible bond) is measured at a discount to the amount repayable on maturity (see IAS 32 *Financial Instruments: Presentation*). The discount is not deductible in determining taxable profit (tax loss).

Fair value adjustments and revaluations

10   Financial assets or investment property are carried at fair value which exceeds cost but no equivalent adjustment is made for tax purposes.

11   An entity revalues property, plant and equipment (under the revaluation model treatment in IAS 16 *Property, Plant and Equipment*) but no equivalent adjustment is made for tax purposes. (*note: paragraph 61A of the Standard requires the related deferred tax to be recognised in other comprehensive income.*)

Business combinations and consolidation

12   The carrying amount of an asset is increased to fair value in a business combination and no equivalent adjustment is made for tax purposes. (*Note that on initial recognition, the resulting deferred tax liability increases goodwill or decreases the amount of any bargain purchase gain recognised. See paragraph 66 of the Standard.*)

13   Reductions in the carrying amount of goodwill are not deductible in determining taxable profit and the cost of the goodwill would not be deductible on disposal of the business. (*Note that paragraph 15(a) of the Standard prohibits recognition of the resulting deferred tax liability.*)

14   Unrealised losses resulting from intragroup transactions are eliminated by inclusion in the carrying amount of inventory or property, plant and equipment.

15   Retained earnings of subsidiaries, branches, associates and joint ventures are included in consolidated retained earnings, but income taxes will be payable if the profits are distributed to the reporting parent. (*note: paragraph 39 of the Standard prohibits recognition of the resulting deferred tax liability if the parent, investor or venturer is able to control the timing of the reversal of the temporary difference and it is probable that the temporary difference will not reverse in the foreseeable future.*)

16   Investments in foreign subsidiaries, branches or associates or interests in foreign joint ventures are affected by changes in foreign exchange rates. (*notes: (1) there may be either a taxable temporary difference or a deductible temporary difference; and (2) paragraph 39 of the Standard prohibits recognition of the resulting deferred tax liability if the parent, investor or venturer is able to control the timing of the reversal of the temporary difference and it is probable that the temporary difference will not reverse in the foreseeable future.*)

17   The non-monetary assets and liabilities of an entity are measured in its functional currency but the taxable profit or tax loss is determined in a different currency. (*notes: (1) there may be either a taxable temporary difference or a deductible temporary difference; (2) where there is a taxable temporary difference, the resulting deferred tax liability is recognised (paragraph 41 of the Standard); and (3) the deferred tax is recognised in profit or loss, see paragraph 58 of the Standard.*)

Hyperinflation

18   Non-monetary assets are restated in terms of the measuring unit current at the end of the reporting period (see IAS 29 *Financial Reporting in Hyperinflationary Economies*) and no equivalent adjustment is made for tax purposes. *(notes: (1) the deferred tax is recognised in profit or loss; and (2) if, in addition to the restatement, the non-monetary assets are also revalued, the deferred tax relating to the revaluation is recognised in other comprehensive income and the deferred tax relating to the restatement is recognised in profit or loss.)*

B. Examples of circumstances that give rise to deductible temporary differences

All deductible temporary differences give rise to a deferred tax asset. However, some deferred tax assets may not satisfy the recognition criteria in paragraph 24 of the Standard.

Transactions that affect profit or loss

1   Retirement benefit costs are deducted in determining accounting profit as service is provided by the employee, but are not deducted in determining taxable profit until the entity pays either retirement benefits or contributions to a fund. *(note: similar deductible temporary differences arise where other expenses, such as product warranty costs or interest, are deductible on a cash basis in determining taxable profit.)*

2   Accumulated depreciation of an asset in the financial statements is greater than the cumulative depreciation allowed up to the end of the reporting period for tax purposes.

3   The cost of inventories sold before the end of the reporting period is deducted in determining accounting profit when goods or services are delivered but is deducted in determining taxable profit when cash is collected. *(note: as explained in A2 above, there is also a **taxable** temporary difference associated with the related trade receivable.)*

4   The net realisable value of an item of inventory, or the recoverable amount of an item of property, plant or equipment, is less than the previous carrying amount and an entity therefore reduces the carrying amount of the asset, but that reduction is ignored for tax purposes until the asset is sold.

5   Research costs (or organisation or other start up costs) are recognised as an expense in determining accounting profit but are not permitted as a deduction in determining taxable profit until a later period.

6   Income is deferred in the statement of financial position but has already been included in taxable profit in current or prior periods.

7   A government grant which is included in the statement of financial position as deferred income will not be taxable in future periods. *(note: paragraph 24 of the Standard prohibits the recognition of the resulting deferred tax asset, see also paragraph 33 of the Standard.)*

Fair value adjustments and revaluations

8   Financial assets or investment property are carried at fair value which is less than cost, but no equivalent adjustment is made for tax purposes.

Business combinations and consolidation

9   A liability is recognised at its fair value in a business combination, but none of the related expense is deducted in determining taxable profit until a later period. *(Note that the resulting deferred tax asset decreases goodwill or increases the amount of any bargain purchase gain recognised. See paragraph 66 of the Standard.)*

10   [Deleted]

11   Unrealised profits resulting from intragroup transactions are eliminated from the carrying amount of assets, such as inventory or property, plant or equipment, but no equivalent adjustment is made for tax purposes.

12   Investments in foreign subsidiaries, branches or associates or interests in foreign joint ventures are affected by changes in foreign exchange rates. *(notes: (1) there may be a taxable temporary difference or a deductible temporary difference; and (2) paragraph 44 of the Standard requires recognition of the resulting deferred tax asset to the extent, and only to the extent, that it is probable that: (a) the temporary difference will reverse in the foreseeable future; and (b) taxable profit will be available against which the temporary difference can be utilised).*

13   The non-monetary assets and liabilities of an entity are measured in its functional currency but the taxable profit or tax loss is determined in a different currency. *(notes: (1) there may be either a taxable temporary difference or a deductible temporary difference; (2) where there is a deductible temporary difference, the resulting deferred tax asset is recognised to the extent that it is probable that sufficient taxable profit will be available (paragraph 41 of the Standard); and (3) the deferred tax is recognised in profit or loss, see paragraph 58 of the Standard.)*

C. Examples of circumstances where the carrying amount of an asset or liability is equal to its tax base

1   Accrued expenses have already been deducted in determining an entity's current tax liability for the current or earlier periods.

2   A loan payable is measured at the amount originally received and this amount is the same as the amount repayable on final maturity of the loan.

3   Accrued expenses will never be deductible for tax purposes.

4   Accrued income will never be taxable.

Illustrative computations and presentation

Extracts from statements of financial position and statements of comprehensive income are provided to show the effects on these financial statements of the transactions described below. These extracts do not necessarily conform with all the disclosure and presentation requirements of other Standards.

All the examples below assume that the entities concerned have no transaction other than those described.

Example 1 – Depreciable assets

An entity buys equipment for 10,000 and depreciates it on a straight-line basis over its expected useful life of five years. For tax purposes, the equipment is depreciated at 25% a year on a straight-line basis. Tax losses may be carried back against taxable profit of the previous five years. In year 0, the entity's taxable profit was 5,000. The tax rate is 40%.

The entity will recover the carrying amount of the equipment by using it to manufacture goods for resale. Therefore, the entity's current tax computation is as follows:

	Year				
	1	2	3	4	5
Taxable income	2,000	2,000	2,000	2,000	2,000
Depreciation for tax purposes	2,500	2,500	2,500	2,500	0
Taxable profit (tax loss)	(500)	(500)	(500)	(500)	2,000
Current tax expense (income) at 40%	(200)	(200)	(200)	(200)	800

The entity recognises a current tax asset at the end of years 1 to 4 because it recovers the benefit of the tax loss against the taxable profit of year 0.

The temporary differences associated with the equipment and the resulting deferred tax asset and liability and deferred tax expense and income are as follows:

	Year				
	1	2	3	4	5
Carrying amount	8,000	6,000	4,000	2,000	0
Tax base	7,500	5,000	2,500	0	0
Taxable temporary difference	500	1,000	1,500	2,000	0
Opening deferred tax liability	0	200	400	600	800
Deferred tax expense (income)	200	200	200	200	(800)
Closing deferred tax liability	200	400	600	800	0

The entity recognises the deferred tax liability in years 1 to 4 because the reversal of the taxable temporary difference will create taxable income in subsequent years. The entity's statement of comprehensive income includes the following:

	Year				
	1	2	3	4	5
Income	2,000	2,000	2,000	2,000	2,000
Depreciation	2,000	2,000	2,000	2,000	2,000
Profit before tax	0	0	0	0	0
Current tax expense (income)	(200)	(200)	(200)	(200)	800
Deferred tax expense (income)	200	200	200	200	(800)
Total tax expense (income)	0	0	0	0	0
Profit for the period	0	0	0	0	0

Example 2 – Deferred tax assets and liabilities

The example deals with an entity over the two-year period, X5 and X6. In X5 the enacted income tax rate was 40% of taxable profit. In X6 the enacted income tax rate was 35% of taxable profit.

Charitable donations are recognised as an expense when they are paid and are not deductible for tax purposes.

In X5, the entity was notified by the relevant authorities that they intend to pursue an action against the entity with respect to sulphur emissions. Although as at December X6 the action had not yet come to court the entity recognised a liability of 700 in X5 being its best estimate of the fine arising from the action. Fines are not deductible for tax purposes.

In X2, the entity incurred 1,250 of costs in relation to the development of a new product. These costs were deducted for tax purposes in X2. For accounting purposes, the entity capitalised this expenditure and amortised it on the straight-line basis over five years. At 31/12/X4, the unamortised balance of these product development costs was 500.

In X5, the entity entered into an agreement with its existing employees to provide healthcare benefits to retirees. The entity recognises as an expense the cost of this plan as employees provide service. No payments to retirees were made for such benefits in X5 or X6. Healthcare costs are deductible for tax purposes when payments are made to retirees. The entity has determined that it is probable that taxable profit will be available against which any resulting deferred tax asset can be utilised.

Buildings are depreciated for accounting purposes at 5% a year on a straight-line basis and at 10% a year on a straight-line basis for tax purposes. Motor vehicles are depreciated for accounting purposes at 20% a year on a straight-line basis and at 25% a year on a straight-line basis for tax purposes. A full year's depreciation is charged for accounting purposes in the year that an asset is acquired.

At 1/1/X6, the building was revalued to 65,000 and the entity estimated that the remaining useful life of the building was 20 years from the date of the revaluation. The revaluation did not affect taxable profit in X6 and the taxation authorities did not adjust the tax base of the building to reflect the revaluation. In X6, the entity transferred 1,033 from revaluation surplus to retained earnings. This represents the difference of 1,590 between the actual depreciation on the building (3,250) and equivalent depreciation based on the cost of the building (1,660, which is the book value at 1/1/X6 of 33,200 divided by the remaining useful life of 20 years), less the related deferred tax of 557 (see paragraph 64 of the Standard).

Current tax expense

	X5	X6
Accounting profit	8,775	8,740
Add		
Depreciation for accounting purposes	4,800	8,250
Charitable donations	500	350
Fine for environmental pollution	700	–
Product development costs	250	250
Healthcare benefits	2,000	1,000
	17,025	18,590
Deduct		
Depreciation for tax purposes	(8,100)	(11,850)
Taxable profit	8,925	6,740
Current tax expense at 40%	3,570	
Current tax expense at 35%		2,359

Carrying amounts of property, plant and equipment

Cost	Building	Motor vehicles	Total
Balance at 31/12/X4	50,000	10,000	60,000
Additions X5	6,000	–	6,000
Balance at 31/12/X5	56,000	10,000	66,000
Elimination of accumulated depreciation on revaluation at 1/1/X6	(22,800)	–	(22,800)
Revaluation at 1/1/X6	31,800	–	31,800
Balance at 1/1/X6	65,000	10,000	75,000
Additions X6	–	15,000	15,000
	65,000	25,000	90,000

continued...

...continued

Carrying amounts of property, plant and equipment

Cost	Building	Motor vehicles	Total
Accumulated depreciation	5%	20%	
Balance at 31/12/X4	20,000	4,000	24,000
Depreciation X5	2,800	2,000	4,800
Balance at 31/12/X5	22,800	6,000	28,800
Revaluation at 1/1/X6	(22,800)	–	(22,800)
Balance at 1/1/X6	–	6,000	6,000
Depreciation X6	3,250	5,000	8,250
Balance at 31/12/X6	3,250	11,000	14,250
Carrying amount			
31/12/X4	30,000	6,000	36,000
31/12/X5	33,200	4,000	37,200
31/12/X6	61,750	14,000	75,750

Tax base of property, plant and equipment

Cost	Building	Motor vehicles	Total
Balance at 31/12/X4	50,000	10,000	60,000
Additions X5	6,000	–	6,000
Balance at 31/12/X5	56,000	10,000	66,000
Additions X6	–	15,000	15,000
Balance at 31/12/X6	56,000	25,000	81,000
Accumulated depreciation	10%	25%	
Balance at 31/12/X4	40,000	5,000	45,000
Depreciation X5	5,600	2,500	8,100
Balance at 31/12/X5	45,600	7,500	53,100
Depreciation X6	5,600	6,250	11,850
Balance 31/12/X6	51,200	13,750	64,950
Tax base			
31/12/X4	10,000	5,000	15,000
31/12/X5	10,400	2,500	12,900
31/12/X6	4,800	11,250	16,050

Deferred tax assets, liabilities and expense at 31/12/X4

	Carrying amount	Tax base	Temporary differences
Accounts receivable	500	500	–
Inventory	2,000	2,000	–
Product development costs	500	–	500
Investments	33,000	33,000	–
Property, plant & equipment	36,000	15,000	21,000
TOTAL ASSETS	72,000	50,500	21,500
Current income taxes payable	3,000	3,000	–
Accounts payable	500	500	–
Fines payable	–	–	–
Liability for healthcare benefits	–	–	–
Long-term debt	20,000	20,000	–
Deferred income taxes	8,600	8,600	–
TOTAL LIABILITIES	32,100	32,100	
Share capital	5,000	5,000	–
Revaluation surplus	–		–
Retained earnings	34,900	13,400	
TOTAL LIABILITIES/EQUITY	72,000	50,500	

TEMPORARY DIFFERENCES		21,500
Deferred tax liability	21,500 at 40%	8,600
Deferred tax asset	–	–
Net deferred tax liability		8,600

Deferred tax assets, liabilities and expense at 31/12/X5

	Carrying amount	Tax base	Temporary differences
Accounts receivable	500	500	–
Inventory	2,000	2,000	–
Product development costs	250	–	250
Investments	33,000	33,000	–
Property, plant & equipment	37,200	12,900	24,300
TOTAL ASSETS	72,950	48,400	24,550
Current income taxes payable	3,570	3,570	–
Accounts payable	500	500	–
Fines payable	700	700	–
Liability for healthcare benefits	2,000	–	(2,000)
Long-term debt	12,475	12,475	–
Deferred income taxes	9,020	9,020	
TOTAL LIABILITIES	28,265	26,265	(2,000)
Share capital	5,000	5,000	–
Revaluation surplus	–	–	–
Retained earnings	39,685	17,135	
TOTAL LIABILITIES/EQUITY	72,950	48,400	
TEMPORARY DIFFERENCES			22,550

Deferred tax liability	24,550 at 40%	9,820
Deferred tax asset	2,000 at 40%	(800)
Net deferred tax liability		9,020
Less: Opening deferred tax liability		(8,600)
Deferred tax expense (income) related to the origination and reversal of temporary differences		420

Deferred tax assets, liabilities and expense at 31/12/X6

	Carrying amount	Tax base	Temporary differences
Accounts receivable	500	500	–
Inventory	2,000	2,000	–
Product development costs	–	–	–
Investments	33,000	33,000	–
Property, plant & equipment	75,750	16,050	59,700
TOTAL ASSETS	111,250	51,550	59,700
Current income taxes payable	2,359	2,359	–
Accounts payable	500	500	–
Fines payable	700	700	–
Liability for healthcare benefits	3,000	–	(3,000)
Long-term debt	12,805	12,805	–
Deferred income taxes	19,845	19,845	–
TOTAL LIABILITIES	39,209	36,209	(3,000)
Share capital	5,000	5,000	–
Revaluation surplus	19,637	–	–
Retained earnings	47,404	10,341	
TOTAL LIABILITIES/EQUITY	111,250	51,550	

TEMPORARY DIFFERENCES		56,700
Deferred tax liability	59,700 at 35%	20,895
Deferred tax asset	3,000 at 35%	(1,050)
Net deferred tax liability		19,845
Less: Opening deferred tax liability		(9,020)
Adjustment to opening deferred tax liability resulting from reduction in tax rate	22,550 at 5%	1,127
Deferred tax attributable to revaluation surplus	31,800 at 35%	(11,130)
Deferred tax expense (income) related to the origination and reversal of temporary differences		822

Illustrative disclosure

The amounts to be disclosed in accordance with the Standard are as follows:

Major components of tax expense (income) (paragraph 79)

	X5	X6
Current tax expense	3,570	2,359
Deferred tax expense relating to the origination and reversal of temporary differences:	420	822
Deferred tax expense (income) resulting from reduction in tax rate	–	(1,127)
Tax expense	3,990	2,054

Income tax relating to the components of other comprehensive income (paragraph 81(ab))

Deferred tax relating to revaluation of building	–	(11,130)

In addition, deferred tax of 557 was transferred in X6 from retained earnings to revaluation surplus. This relates to the difference between the actual depreciation on the building and equivalent depreciation based on the cost of the building.

Explanation of the relationship between tax expense and accounting profit (paragraph 81(c))

The Standard permits two alternative methods of explaining the relationship between tax expense (income) and accounting profit. Both of these formats are illustrated below.

(i) a numerical reconciliation between tax expense (income) and the product of accounting profit multiplied by the applicable tax rate(s), disclosing also the basis on which the applicable tax rate(s) is (are) computed

	X5	X6
Accounting profit	8,775	8,740
Tax at the applicable tax rate of 35% (X5: 40%)	3,510	3,059
Tax effect of expenses that are not deductible in determining taxable profit:		
Charitable donations	200	122
Fines for environmental pollution	280	–
Reduction in opening deferred taxes resulting from reduction in tax rate	–	(1,127)
Tax expense	3,990	2,054

The applicable tax rate is the aggregate of the national income tax rate of 30% (X5: 35%) and the local income tax rate of 5%.

(ii) a numerical reconciliation between the average effective tax rate and the applicable tax rate, disclosing also the basis on which the applicable tax rate is computed

	X5	X6
	%	%
Applicable tax rate	40.0	35.0
Tax effect of expenses that are not deductible for tax purposes:		
Charitable donations	2.3	1.4
Fines for environmental pollution	3.2	–
Effect on opening deferred taxes of reduction in tax rate	–	(12.9)
Average effective tax rate (tax expense divided by profit before tax)	45.5	23.5

The applicable tax rate is the aggregate of the national income tax rate of 30% (X5: 35%) and the local income tax rate of 5%.

An explanation of changes in the applicable tax rate(s) compared to the previous accounting period (paragraph 81(d))

In X6, the government enacted a change in the national income tax rate from 35% to 30%.

In respect of each type of temporary difference, and in respect of each type of unused tax losses and unused tax credits:

(i) the amount of the deferred tax assets and liabilities recognised in the statement of financial position for each period presented;

(ii) the amount of the deferred tax income or expense recognised in profit or loss for each period presented, if this is not apparent from the changes in the amounts recognised in the statement of financial position (paragraph 81(g))

	X5	X6
Accelerated depreciation for tax purposes	9,720	10,322
Liabilities for healthcare benefits that are deducted for tax purposes only when paid	(800)	(1,050)
Product development costs deducted from taxable profit in earlier years	100	–
Revaluation, net of related depreciation	–	10,573
Deferred tax liability	9,020	19,845

(note: the amount of the deferred tax income or expense recognised in profit or loss for the current year is apparent from the changes in the amounts recognised in the statement of financial position)

Example 3 – Business combinations

On 1 January X5 entity A acquired 100 per cent of the shares of entity B at a cost of 600. At the acquisition date, the tax base in A's tax jurisdiction of A's investment in B is 600. Reductions in the carrying amount of goodwill are not deductible for tax purposes, and the cost of the goodwill would also not be deductible if B were to dispose of its underlying business. The tax rate in A's tax jurisdiction is 30 per cent and the tax rate in B's tax jurisdiction is 40 per cent.

The fair value of the identifiable assets acquired and liabilities assumed (excluding deferred tax assets and liabilities) by A is set out in the following table, together with their tax bases in B's tax jurisdiction and the resulting temporary differences.

	Amount recognised at acquisition	Tax base	Temporary differences
Property, plant and equipment	270	155	115
Accounts receivable	210	210	–
Inventory	174	124	50
Retirement benefit obligations	(30)	–	(30)
Accounts payable	(120)	(120)	–
Identifiable assets acquired and liabilities assumed, excluding deferred tax	504	369	135

The deferred tax asset arising from the retirement benefit obligations is offset against the deferred tax liabilities arising from the property, plant and equipment and inventory (see paragraph 74 of the Standard).

No deduction is available in B's tax jurisdiction for the cost of the goodwill. Therefore, the tax base of the goodwill in B's jurisdiction is nil. However, in accordance with paragraph 15(a) of the Standard, A recognises no deferred tax liability for the taxable temporary difference associated with the goodwill in B's tax jurisdiction.

The carrying amount, in A's consolidated financial statements, of its investment in B is made up as follows:

Fair value of identifiable assets acquired and liabilities assumed, excluding deferred tax	504
Deferred tax liability (135 at 40%)	(54)
Fair value of identifiable assets acquired and liabilities assumed	450
Goodwill	150
Carrying amount	600

Because, at the acquisition date, the tax base in A's tax jurisdiction, of A's investment in B is 600, no temporary difference is associated in A's tax jurisdiction with the investment.

During X5, B's equity (incorporating the fair value adjustments made as a result of the business combination) changed as follows:

At 1 January X5	450
Retained profit for X5 (net profit of 150, less dividend payable of 80)	70
At 31 December X5	520

A recognises a liability for any withholding tax or other taxes that it will incur on the accrued dividend receivable of 80.

At 31 December X5, the carrying amount of A's underlying investment in B, excluding the accrued dividend receivable, is as follows:

Net assets of B	520
Goodwill	150
Carrying amount	670

The temporary difference associated with A's underlying investment is 70. This amount is equal to the cumulative retained profit since the acquisition date.

If A has determined that it will not sell the investment in the foreseeable future and that B will not distribute its retained profits in the foreseeable future, no deferred tax liability is recognised in relation to A's investment in B (see paragraphs 39 and 40 of the Standard). Note that this exception would apply for an investment in an associate only if there is an agreement requiring that the profits of the associate will not be distributed in the foreseeable future (see paragraph 42 of the Standard). A discloses the amount of the temporary difference for which no deferred tax is recognised, ie 70 (see paragraph 81(f) of the Standard).

If A expects to sell the investment in B, or that B will distribute its retained profits in the foreseeable future, A recognises a deferred tax liability to the extent that the temporary difference is expected to reverse. The tax rate reflects the manner in which A expects to recover the carrying amount of its investment (see paragraph 51 of the Standard). A recognises the deferred tax in other comprehensive income to the extent that the deferred tax results from foreign exchange translation differences that have been recognised in other comprehensive income (paragraph 61A of the Standard). A discloses separately:

(a) the amount of deferred tax that has been recognised in other comprehensive income (paragraph 81(ab) of the Standard); and

(b) the amount of any remaining temporary difference which is not expected to reverse in the foreseeable future and for which, therefore, no deferred tax is recognised (see paragraph 81(f) of the Standard).

Example 4 – Compound financial instruments

An entity receives a non-interest-bearing convertible loan of 1,000 on 31 December X4 repayable at par on 1 January X8. In accordance with IAS 32 *Financial Instruments: Presentation* the entity classifies the instrument's liability component as a liability and the equity component as equity. The entity assigns an initial carrying amount of 751 to the liability component of the convertible loan and 249 to the equity component. Subsequently, the entity recognises imputed discount as interest expense at an annual rate of 10% on the carrying amount of the liability component at the beginning of the year. The tax authorities do not allow the entity to claim any deduction for the imputed discount on the liability component of the convertible loan. The tax rate is 40%.

The temporary differences associated with the liability component and the resulting deferred tax liability and deferred tax expense and income are as follows:

	Year			
	X4	X5	X6	X7
Carrying amount of liability component	751	826	909	1,000
Tax base	1,000	1,000	1,000	1,000
Taxable temporary difference	249	174	91	–
Opening deferred tax liability at 40%	0	100	70	37
Deferred tax charged to equity	100	–	–	–
Deferred tax expense (income)	–	(30)	(33)	(37)
Closing deferred tax liability at 40%	100	70	37	–

As explained in paragraph 23 of the Standard, at 31 December X4, the entity recognises the resulting deferred tax liability by adjusting the initial carrying amount of the equity component of the convertible liability. Therefore, the amounts recognised at that date are as follows:

Liability component	751
Deferred tax liability	100
Equity component (249 less 100)	149
	1,000

Subsequent changes in the deferred tax liability are recognised in profit or loss as tax income (see paragraph 23 of the Standard). Therefore, the entity's profit or loss includes the following:

	Year			
	X4	X5	X6	X7
Interest expense (imputed discount)	–	75	83	91
Deferred tax expense (income)	–	(30)	(33)	(37)
	–	45	50	54

Example 5 – Share-based payment transactions

In accordance with IFRS 2 *Share-based Payment*, an entity has recognised an expense for the consumption of employee services received as consideration for share options granted. A tax deduction will not arise until the options are exercised, and the deduction is based on the options' intrinsic value at exercise date.

As explained in paragraph 68B of the Standard, the difference between the tax base of the employee services received to date (being the amount the taxation authorities will permit as a deduction in future periods in respect of those services), and the carrying amount of nil, is a deductible temporary difference that results in a deferred tax asset. Paragraph 68B requires that, if the amount the taxation authorities will permit as a deduction in future periods is not known at the end of the period, it should be estimated, based on information available at the end of the period. If the amount that the taxation authorities will permit as a deduction in future periods is dependent upon the entity's share price at a future date, the measurement of the deductible temporary difference should be based on the entity's share price at the end of the period. Therefore, in this example, the estimated future tax deduction (and hence the measurement of the deferred tax asset) should be based on the options' intrinsic value at the end of the period.

As explained in paragraph 68C of the Standard, if the tax deduction (or estimated future tax deduction) exceeds the amount of the related cumulative remuneration expense, this indicates that the tax deduction relates not only to remuneration expense but also to an equity item. In this situation, paragraph 68C requires that the excess of the associated current or deferred tax should be recognised directly in equity.

The entity's tax rate is 40 per cent. The options were granted at the start of year 1, vested at the end of year 3 and were exercised at the end of year 5. Details of the expense recognised for employee services received and consumed in each accounting period, the number of options outstanding at each year-end, and the intrinsic value of the options at each year-end, are as follows:

	Employee services expense	Number of options at year-end	Intrinsic value per option
Year 1	188,000	50,000	5
Year 2	185,000	45,000	8
Year 3	190,000	40,000	13
Year 4	0	40,000	17
Year 5	0	40,000	20

The entity recognises a deferred tax asset and deferred tax income in years 1–4 and current tax income in year 5 as follows. In years 4 and 5, some of the deferred and current tax income is recognised directly in equity, because the estimated (and actual) tax deduction exceeds the cumulative remuneration expense.

Year 1

Deferred tax asset and deferred tax income:

$(50,000 \times 5 \times \frac{1}{3}$ [a] $\times 0.40) =$ 33,333

(a) The tax base of the employee services received is based on the intrinsic value of the options, and those options were granted for three years' services. Because only one year's services have been received to date, it is necessary to multiply the option's intrinsic value by one-third to arrive at the tax base of the employee services received in year 1.

The deferred tax income is all recognised in profit or loss, because the estimated future tax deduction of 83,333 (50,000 × 5 × ⅓) is less than the cumulative remuneration expense of 188,000.

Year 2

Deferred tax asset at year-end:

$(45,000 \times 8 \times \frac{2}{3} \times 0.40) =$	96,000
Less deferred tax asset at start of year	(33,333)
Deferred tax income for year	62,667*

* This amount consists of the following:

Deferred tax income for the temporary difference between the tax base of the employee services received during the year and their carrying amount of nil:

$(45,000 \times 8 \times \frac{1}{3} \times 0.40)$	48,000

Tax income resulting from an adjustment to the tax base of employee services received in previous years:

(a)	increase in intrinsic value: $(45,000 \times 3 \times \frac{1}{3} \times 0.40)$	18,000
(b)	decrease in number of options: $(5,000 \times 5 \times \frac{1}{3} \times 0.40)$	(3,333)
	Deferred tax income for year	62,667

The deferred tax income is all recognised in profit or loss, because the estimated future tax deduction of 240,000 (45,000 × 8 × ⅔) is less than the cumulative remuneration expense of 373,000 (188,000 + 185,000).

Year 3

Deferred tax asset at year-end:

$(40,000 \times 13 \times 0.40) =$	208,000
Less deferred tax asset at start of year	(96,000)
Deferred tax income for year	112,000

The deferred tax income is all recognised in profit or loss, because the estimated future tax deduction of 520,000 (40,000 × 13) is less than the cumulative remuneration expense of 563,000 (188,000 + 185,000 + 190,000).

Year 4

Deferred tax asset at year-end:

(40,000 × 17 × 0.40) =	272,000
Less deferred tax asset at start of year	(208,000)
Deferred tax income for year	64,000

The deferred tax income is recognised partly in profit or loss and partly directly in equity as follows:

Estimated future tax deduction (40,000 × 17) =	680,000	
Cumulative remuneration expense	563,000	
Excess tax deduction		117,000
Deferred tax income for year	64,000	
Excess recognised directly in equity (117,000 × 0.40) =	46,800	
Recognised in profit or loss		17,200

Year 5

Deferred tax expense (reversal of deferred tax asset)	272,000
Amount recognised directly in equity (reversal of cumulative deferred tax income recognised directly in equity)	46,800
Amount recognised in profit or loss	225,200
Current tax income based on intrinsic value of options at exercise date (40,000 × 20 × 0.40) =	320,000
Amount recognised in profit or loss (563,000 × 0.40) =	225,200
Amount recognised directly in equity	94,800

Summary

	Statement of comprehensive income				Statement of financial position	
	Employee services expense	Current tax expense (income)	Deferred tax expense (income)	Total tax expense (income)	Equity	Deferred tax asset
Year 1	188,000	0	(33,333)	(33,333)	0	33,333
Year 2	185,000	0	(62,667)	(62,667)	0	96,000
Year 3	190,000	0	(112,000)	(112,000)	0	208,000
Year 4	0	0	(17,200)	(17,200)	(46,800)	272,000
Year 5	0	(225,200)	225,200	0	46,800	0
					(94,800)	
Totals	563,000	(225,200)	0	(225,200)	(94,800)	0

Example 6 – Replacement awards in a business combination

On 1 January 20X1 Entity A acquired 100 per cent of Entity B. Entity A pays cash consideration of CU400 to the former owners of Entity B.

At the acquisition date Entity B had outstanding employee share options with a market-based measure of CU100. The share options were fully vested. As part of the business combination Entity B's outstanding share options are replaced by share options of Entity A (replacement awards) with a market-based measure of CU100 and an intrinsic value of CU80. The replacement awards are fully vested. In accordance with paragraphs B56–B62 of IFRS 3 *Business Combinations* (as revised in 2008), the replacement awards are part of the consideration transferred for Entity B. A tax deduction for the replacement awards will not arise until the options are exercised. The tax deduction will be based on the share options' intrinsic value at that date. Entity A's tax rate is 40 per cent. Entity A recognises a deferred tax asset of CU32 (CU80 intrinsic value × 40%) on the replacement awards at the acquisition date.

Entity A measures the identifiable net assets obtained in the business combination (excluding deferred tax assets and liabilities) at CU450. The tax base of the identifiable net assets obtained is CU300. Entity A recognises a deferred tax liability of CU60 ((CU450 – CU300) × 40%) on the identifiable net assets at the acquisition date.

Goodwill is calculated as follows:

	CU
Cash consideration	400
Market-based measure of replacement awards	100
Total consideration transferred	500
Identifiable net assets, excluding deferred tax assets and liabilities	(450)
Deferred tax asset	32
Deferred tax liability	60
Goodwill	**78**

Reductions in the carrying amount of goodwill are not deductible for tax purposes. In accordance with paragraph 15(a) of the Standard, Entity A recognises no deferred tax liability for the taxable temporary difference associated with the goodwill recognised in the business combination.

The accounting entry for the business combination is as follows:

		CU	CU
Dr	Goodwill	78	
Dr	Identifiable net assets	450	
Dr	Deferred tax asset	32	
	Cr	Cash	400
	Cr	Equity (replacement awards)	100
	Cr	Deferred tax liability	60

On 31 December 20X1 the intrinsic value of the replacement awards is CU120. Entity A recognises a deferred tax asset of CU48 (CU120 × 40%). Entity A recognises deferred tax income of CU16 (CU48 – CU32) from the increase in the intrinsic value of the replacement awards. The accounting entry is as follows:

		CU	CU
Dr	Deferred tax asset	16	
	Cr Deferred tax income		16

If the replacement awards had not been tax-deductible under current tax law, Entity A would not have recognised a deferred tax asset on the acquisition date. Entity A would have accounted for any subsequent events that result in a tax deduction related to the replacement award in the deferred tax income or expense of the period in which the subsequent event occurred.

Paragraphs B56–B62 of IFRS 3 provide guidance on determining which portion of a replacement award is part of the consideration transferred in a business combination and which portion is attributable to future service and thus a post-combination remuneration expense. Deferred tax assets and liabilities on replacement awards that are post-combination expenses are accounted for in accordance with the general principles as illustrated in Example 5.

IASB documents published to accompany

International Accounting Standard 16

Property, Plant and Equipment

This version includes amendments resulting from IFRSs issued up to 31 December 2009.

The text of the unaccompanied IAS 16 is contained in Part A of this edition. Its effective date when issued was 1 January 2005. The effective date of the latest amendments is 1 July 2009. This part presents the following accompanying documents:

Approval by the Board of IAS 16 issued in December 2003

International Accounting Standard 16 *Property, Plant and Equipment* (as revised in 2003) was approved for issue by the fourteen members of the International Accounting Standards Board.

Sir David Tweedie	Chairman
Thomas E Jones	Vice-Chairman
Mary E Barth	
Hans-Georg Bruns	
Anthony T Cope	
Robert P Garnett	
Gilbert Gélard	
James J Leisenring	
Warren J McGregor	
Patricia L O'Malley	
Harry K Schmid	
John T Smith	
Geoffrey Whittington	
Tatsumi Yamada	

CONTENTS

Basis for Conclusions on
IAS 16 *Property, Plant and Equipment*

This Basis for Conclusions accompanies, but is not part of, IAS 16.

Introduction

BC1   This Basis for Conclusions summarises the International Accounting Standards Board's considerations in reaching its conclusions on revising IAS 16 *Property, Plant and Equipment* in 2003. Individual Board members gave greater weight to some factors than to others.

BC2   In July 2001 the Board announced that, as part of its initial agenda of technical projects, it would undertake a project to improve a number of Standards, including IAS 16. The project was undertaken in the light of queries and criticisms raised in relation to the Standards by securities regulators, professional accountants and other interested parties. The objectives of the Improvements project were to reduce or eliminate alternatives, redundancies and conflicts within Standards, to deal with some convergence issues and to make other improvements. In May 2002 the Board published its proposals in an Exposure Draft of *Improvements to International Accounting Standards*, with a comment deadline of 16 September 2002. The Board received over 160 comment letters on the Exposure Draft.

BC3   Because the Board's intention was not to reconsider the fundamental approach to the accounting for property, plant and equipment that was established by IAS 16, this Basis for Conclusions does not discuss requirements in IAS 16 that the Board has not reconsidered.

Scope

BC4   The Board clarified that the requirements of IAS 16 apply to items of property, plant and equipment that an entity uses to develop or maintain (a) biological assets and (b) mineral rights and mineral reserves such as oil, natural gas and similar non-regenerative resources. The Board noted that items of property, plant and equipment that an entity uses for these purposes possess the same characteristics as other items of property, plant and equipment.

Recognition

BC5   In considering potential improvements to the previous version of IAS 16, the Board reviewed its subsequent expenditure recognition principle for two reasons. First, the existing subsequent expenditure recognition principle did not align with the asset recognition principle in the *Framework*. Second, the Board noted difficulties in practice in making the distinction it required between expenditures that maintain, and those that enhance, an item of property, plant and equipment. Some expenditures seem to do both.

BC6   The Board ultimately decided that the separate recognition principle for subsequent expenditure was not needed. As a result, an entity will evaluate all its property, plant and equipment costs under IAS 16's general recognition principle. Also, if the cost of a replacement for part of an item of property, plant and equipment is recognised in the carrying amount of an asset, then an entity will derecognise the carrying amount of what was replaced to avoid carrying both the replacement and the replaced portion as assets. This derecognition occurs whether or not what is replaced is a part of an item that the entity depreciates separately.

BC7   The Board's decision on how to handle the recognition principles was not reached easily. In the Exposure Draft (ED), the Board proposed to include within IAS 16's general recognition principle only the recognition of subsequent expenditures that are replacements of a part of an item of property, plant and equipment. Also in the ED, the Board proposed to modify the subsequent expenditure recognition principle to distinguish more clearly the expenditures to which it would continue to apply.

BC8   Respondents to the ED agreed that it was appropriate for subsequent expenditures that were replacements of a part of an item of property, plant and equipment that an entity depreciated separately to be covered by the general recognition principle. However, the respondents argued, and the Board agreed, that the modified second principle was not clearer because it would result in an entity recognising in the carrying amount of an asset and then depreciating subsequent expenditures that were for the day-to-day servicing of items of property, plant and equipment, those that might commonly be regarded as for 'repairs and maintenance'. That result was not the Board's intention.

BC9   In its redeliberation of the ED, the Board concluded it could not retain the proposed modified subsequent expenditure recognition principle. It also concluded that it could not revert to the subsequent expenditure principle in the previous version of IAS 16 because, if it did, nothing was improved; the *Framework* conflict was not resolved and the practice issues were not addressed.

BC10   The Board concluded that it was best for all subsequent expenditures to be covered by IAS 16's general recognition principle. This solution had the following advantages:

(a)   use of IAS 16's general recognition principle fits the *Framework*.

(b)   use of a single recognition principle is a straightforward approach.

(c)   retaining IAS 16's general recognition principle and combining it with the derecognition principle will result in financial statements that reflect what is occurring, ie both the flow of property, plant and equipment through an entity and the economics of the acquisition and disposal process.

(d)   use of one recognition principle fosters consistency. With two principles, consistency is not achieved unless it is clear when each should apply. Because IAS 16 does not address what constitutes an 'item' of property, plant and equipment, this clarity was not assured because some might characterise a particular cost as the initial cost of a new item of property, plant and equipment and others might regard it as a subsequent cost of an existing item of property, plant and equipment.

BC11   As a consequence of placing all subsequent expenditures under IAS 16's general recognition principle, the Board also included those expenditures under IAS 16's derecognition principle. In the ED, the Board proposed the derecognition of the carrying amount of a part of an item that was depreciated separately and was replaced by a subsequent expenditure that an entity recognised in the carrying amount of the asset under the general recognition principle. With this change, replacements of a part of an item that are not depreciated separately are subject to the same approach.

BC12   The Board noted that some subsequent expenditures on property, plant and equipment, although arguably incurred in the pursuit of future economic benefits, are not sufficiently certain to be recognised in the carrying amount of an asset under the general recognition principle. Thus, the Board decided to state in the Standard that an entity recognises in profit or loss as incurred the costs of the day-to-day servicing of property, plant and equipment.

Measurement at recognition

Asset dismantlement, removal and restoration costs

BC13   The previous version of IAS 16 provided that in initially measuring an item of property, plant and equipment at its cost, an entity would include the cost of dismantling and removing that item and restoring the site on which it is located to the extent it had recognised an obligation for that cost. As part of its deliberations, the Board evaluated whether it could improve this guidance by addressing associated issues that have arisen in practice.

BC14   The Board concluded that the relatively limited scope of the Improvements project warranted addressing only one matter. That matter was whether the cost of an item of property, plant and equipment should include the initial estimate of the cost of dismantlement, removal and restoration that an entity incurs as a consequence of using the item (instead of as a consequence of acquiring it). Therefore, the Board did not address how an entity should account for (a) changes in the amount of the initial estimate of a recognised obligation, (b) the effects of accretion of, or changes in interest rates on, a recognised obligation or (c) the cost of obligations an entity did not face when it acquired the item, such as an obligation triggered by a law change enacted after the asset was acquired.

BC15   The Board observed that whether the obligation is incurred upon acquisition of the item or while it is being used, its underlying nature and its association with the asset are the same. Therefore, the Board decided that the cost of an item should include the costs of dismantlement, removal or restoration, the obligation for which an entity has incurred as a consequence of having used the item during a particular period other than to produce inventories during that period. An entity applies IAS 2 *Inventories* to the costs of these obligations that are incurred as a consequence of having used the item during a particular period to produce inventories during that period. The Board observed that accounting for these costs initially in accordance with IAS 2 acknowledges their nature. Furthermore, doing so achieves the same result as including these costs as an element of the cost of an item of property, plant and equipment, depreciating them over the production period just completed and identifying the depreciation charge as a cost to produce another asset (inventory), in which case the depreciation charge constitutes part of the cost of that other asset.

BC16   The Board noted that because IAS 16's initial measurement provisions are not affected by an entity's subsequent decision to carry an item under the cost model or the revaluation model, the Board's decision applies to assets that an entity carries under either treatment.

Asset exchange transactions

BC17   Paragraph 22 of the previous version of IAS 16 indicated that if (a) an item of property, plant and equipment is acquired in exchange for a similar asset that has a similar use in the same line of business and has a similar fair value or (b) an item of property, plant and equipment is sold in exchange for an equity interest in a similar asset, then no gain or loss is recognised on the transaction. The cost of the new asset is the carrying amount of the asset given up (rather than the fair value of the purchase consideration given for the new asset).

BC18   This requirement in the previous version of IAS 16 was consistent with views that:

(a)   gains should not be recognised on exchanges of assets unless the exchanges represent the culmination of an earning process;

(b)   exchanges of assets of a similar nature and value are not a substantive event warranting the recognition of gains; and

(c)   requiring or permitting the recognition of gains from such exchanges enables entities to 'manufacture' gains by attributing inflated values to the assets exchanged, if the assets do not have observable market prices in active markets.

BC19   The approach described above raised issues about how to identify whether assets exchanged are similar in nature and value. The Board reviewed this topic, and noted views that:

(a)   under the *Framework*, the recognition of income from an exchange of assets does not depend on whether the assets exchanged are dissimilar;

(b)   income is not necessarily earned only at the culmination of an earning process, and in some cases it is arbitrary to determine when an earning process culminates;

(c)   generally, under both measurement bases after recognition that are permitted under IAS 16, gain recognition is not deferred beyond the date at which assets are exchanged; and

(d)   removing 'existing carrying amount' measurement of property, plant and equipment acquired in exchange for similar assets would increase the consistency of measurement of acquisitions of assets.

BC20   The Board decided to require in IAS 16 that all items of property, plant and equipment acquired in exchange for non-monetary assets or a combination of monetary and non-monetary assets should be measured at fair value, except that, if the exchange transaction lacks commercial substance or the fair value of neither of the assets exchanged can be determined reliably, then the cost of the asset acquired in the exchange should be measured at the carrying amount of the asset given up.

BC21   The Board added the 'commercial substance' test in response to a concern raised in the comments it received on the ED. This concern was that, under the Board's proposal, an entity would measure at fair value an asset acquired in a transaction that did not have commercial substance, ie the transaction did not have a discernible effect on an entity's economics. The Board agreed that requiring an evaluation of commercial substance would help to give users of the financial statements assurance that the substance of a transaction in which the acquired asset is measured at fair value (and often, consequentially, a gain on the disposal of the transferred asset is recognised in income) is the same as its legal form.

BC22   The Board concluded that in evaluating whether a transaction has commercial substance, an entity should calculate the present value of the post-tax cash flows that it can reasonably expect to derive from the portion of its operations affected by the transaction. The discount rate should reflect the entity's current assessment of the time value of money and the risks specific to those operations rather than those that marketplace participants would make.

BC23   The Board included the 'reliable measurement' test for using fair value to measure these exchanges to minimise the risk that entities could 'manufacture' gains by attributing inflated values to the assets exchanged. Taking into consideration its project for the convergence of IFRSs and US GAAP, the Board discussed whether to change the manner in which its 'reliable measurement' test is described. The Board observed this was unnecessary because it believes that its guidance and that contained in US GAAP are intended to have the same meaning.

BC24   The Board decided to retain, in IAS 18 *Revenue*, its prohibition on recognising revenue from exchanges or swaps of goods or services of a similar nature and value. The Board has on its agenda a project on revenue recognition and does not propose to make any significant amendments to IAS 18 until that project is completed.

Measurement after recognition

Revaluation model

BC25   The Board is taking part in research activities with national standard-setters on revaluations of property, plant and equipment. This research is intended to promote international convergence of standards. One of the most important issues is identifying the preferred measurement attribute for revaluations. This research could lead to proposals to amend IAS 16.

Depreciation: unit of measure

BC26 The Board's discussions about the potential improvements to the depreciation principle in the previous version of IAS 16 included consideration of the unit of measure an entity uses to depreciate its items of property, plant and equipment. Of particular concern to the Board were situations in which the unit of measure is the 'item as a whole' even though that item may be composed of significant parts with individually varying useful lives or consumption patterns. The Board did not believe that, in these situations, an entity's use of approximation techniques, such as a weighted average useful life for the item as a whole, resulted in depreciation that faithfully represents an entity's varying expectations for the significant parts.

BC27 The Board sought to improve the previous version of IAS 16 by proposing in the ED revisions to existing guidance on separating an item into its parts and then further clarifying in the Standard the need for an entity to depreciate separately any significant parts of an item of property, plant and equipment. By doing so an entity will also separately depreciate the item's remainder.

Depreciation: depreciable amount

BC28 During its discussion of depreciation principles, the Board noted the concern that, under the cost model, the previous version of IAS 16 does not state clearly why an entity deducts an asset's residual value from its cost to determine the asset's depreciable amount. Some argue that the objective is one of precision, ie reducing the amount of depreciation so that it reflects the item's net cost. Others argue that the objective is one of economics, ie stopping depreciation if, because of inflation or otherwise, an entity expects that during its useful life an asset will increase in value by an amount greater than it will diminish.

BC29 The Board decided to improve the previous version of IAS 16 by making clear the objective of deducting a residual value in determining an asset's depreciable amount. In doing so, the Board did not adopt completely either the 'net cost' or the 'economics' objective. Given the concept of depreciation as a cost allocation technique, the Board concluded that an entity's expectation of increases in an asset's value, because of inflation or otherwise, does not override the need to depreciate it. Thus, the Board changed the definition of residual value to the amount an entity could receive for the asset currently (at the financial reporting date) if the asset were already as old and worn as it will be when the entity expects to dispose of it. Thus, an increase in the expected residual value of an asset because of past events will affect the depreciable amount; expectations of future changes in residual value other than the effects of expected wear and tear will not.

Depreciation: depreciation period

BC30 The Board decided that the useful life of an asset should encompass the entire time it is available for use, regardless of whether during that time it is in use or is idle. Idle periods most commonly occur just after an asset is acquired and just before it is disposed of, the latter while the asset is held either for sale or for another form of disposal.

BC31   The Board concluded that, whether idle or not, it is appropriate to depreciate an asset with a limited useful life so that the financial statements reflect the consumption of the asset's service potential that occurs while the asset is held. The Board also discussed but decided not to address the measurement of assets held for sale. The Board concluded that whether to apply a different measurement model to assets held for sale—which may or may not be idle—was a different question and was beyond the scope of the Improvements project.

BC32   In July 2003 the Board published ED 4 *Disposal of Non-current Assets and Presentation of Discontinued Operations*. ED 4 was published as part of the Board's short-term convergence project, the scope of which was broader than that of the Improvements project. In ED 4, the Board proposed that an entity should classify some of its assets as 'assets held for sale' if specified criteria are met. Among other things, the Board proposed that an entity should cease depreciating an asset classified in this manner, irrespective of whether the asset is idle. The basis for this proposal was that the carrying amount of an asset held for sale will be recovered principally through sale rather than future operations, and therefore accounting for the asset should be a process of valuation rather than allocation. The Board will amend IAS 16 accordingly when ED 4 is finalised.

Depreciation: depreciation method

BC33   The Board considered how an entity should account for a change in a depreciation method. The Board concluded that a change in a depreciation method is a change in the technique used to apply the entity's accounting policy to recognise depreciation as an asset's future economic benefits are consumed. Therefore, it is a change in an accounting estimate.

Derecognition

Derecognition date

BC34   The Board decided that an entity should apply the revenue recognition principle in IAS 18 for sales of goods to its gains from the sales of items of property, plant and equipment. The requirements in that principle ensure the representational faithfulness of an entity's recognised revenue. Representational faithfulness is also the appropriate objective for an entity's recognised gains. However, in IAS 16, the revenue recognition principle's criteria drive derecognition of the asset disposed of rather than recognition of the proceeds received. Applying the principle instead to the recognition of the proceeds might lead to the conclusion that an entity will recognise a deferred gain. Deferred gains do not meet the definition of a liability under the *Framework*. Thus, the Board decided that an entity does not derecognise an item of property, plant and equipment until the requirements in IAS 18 to recognise revenue on the sale of goods are met.

Gain classification

BC35   Although the Board concluded that an entity should apply the recognition principle for revenue from sales of goods to its recognition of gains on disposals of items of property, plant and equipment, the Board concluded that the respective approaches to income statement display should differ. The Board concluded that users of financial statements would consider these gains and the proceeds from an entity's sale of goods in the course of its ordinary activities differently in their evaluation of an entity's past results and their projections of future cash flows. This is because revenue from the sale of goods is typically more likely to recur in comparable amounts than are gains from sales of items of property, plant and equipment. Accordingly, the Board concluded that an entity should not classify as revenue gains on disposals of items of property, plant and equipment.

Assets held for rental to others[*]

BC35A   The Board identified that, in some industries, entities are in the business of renting and subsequently selling the same assets.

BC35B   The Board noted that the Standard prohibits classification as revenue of gains arising from derecognition of items of property, plant and equipment. The Board also noted that paragraph BC35 states the reason for this is 'users of financial statements would consider these gains and the proceeds from an entity's sale of goods in the course of its ordinary activities differently in their evaluation of an entity's past results and their projections of future cash flows.'

BC35C   Consistently with that reason, the Board concluded that entities whose ordinary activities include renting and subsequently selling the same assets should recognise revenue from both renting and selling the assets. In the Board's view, the presentation of gross selling revenue, rather than a net gain or loss on the sale of the assets, would better reflect the ordinary activities of such entities.

BC35D   The Board concluded that the disclosure requirements of IAS 16, IAS 2 and IAS 18 would lead an entity to disclose relevant information for users.

BC35E   The Board also concluded that paragraph 14 of IAS 7 *Statement of Cash Flows* should be amended to present within operating activities cash payments to manufacture or acquire such assets and cash receipts from rents and sales of such assets.

BC35F   The Board discussed the comments received in response to its exposure draft of proposed *Improvements to International Financial Reporting Standards* published in 2007 and noted that a few respondents would prefer the issue to be included in one of the Board's major projects such as the revenue recognition project or the financial statement presentation project. However, the Board noted that the proposed amendment would improve financial statement presentation before

---

[*]   Paragraphs BC35A–BC35F were added as a consequence of amendments to IAS 16 by *Improvements to IFRSs* issued in May 2008. At the same time, the Board also amended paragraph 6 by replacing the term 'net selling price' in the definition of 'recoverable amount' with 'fair value less costs to sell' for consistency with the wording used in IFRS 5 *Non-current Assets Held for Sale and Discontinued Operations* and IAS 36 *Impairment of Assets*.

those projects could be completed and decided to add paragraph 68A as previously exposed. A few respondents raised the concern that the term 'held for sale' in the amendment could be confused with the notion of held for sale in accordance with IFRS 5 *Non-current Assets Held for Sale and Discontinued Operations*. Consequently, the Board clarified in the amendment that IFRS 5 should not be applied in those circumstances.

Transitional provisions

BC36   The Board concluded that it would be impracticable for an entity to determine retrospectively whether a previous transaction involving an exchange of non-monetary assets had commercial substance. This is because it would not be possible for management to avoid using hindsight in making the necessary estimates as of earlier dates. Accordingly, the Board decided that in accordance with the provisions of IAS 8 an entity should consider commercial substance only in evaluating the initial measurement of future transactions involving an exchange of non-monetary assets.

Summary of changes from the Exposure Draft

BC37   The main changes from the ED proposals to the revised Standard are as follows:

(a)   The ED contained two recognition principles, one applying to subsequent expenditures on existing items of property, plant and equipment. The Standard contains a single recognition principle that applies to costs incurred initially to acquire an item and costs incurred subsequently to add to, replace part of or service an item. An entity applies the recognition principle to the latter costs at the time it incurs them.

(b)   Under the approach proposed in the ED, an entity measured an item of property, plant and equipment acquired in exchange for a non-monetary asset at fair value irrespective of whether the exchange transaction in which it was acquired had commercial substance. Under the Standard, a lack of commercial substance is cause for an entity to measure the acquired asset at the carrying amount of the asset given up.

(c)   Compared with the Standard, the ED did not as clearly set out the principle that an entity separately depreciates at least the parts of an item of property, plant and equipment that are of significant cost.

(d)   Under the approach proposed in the ED, an entity derecognised the carrying amount of a replaced part of an item of property, plant and equipment if it recognised in the carrying amount of the asset the cost of the replacement under the general recognition principle. In the Standard, an entity also applies this approach to a replacement of a part of an item that is not depreciated separately.

(e)   In finalising the Standard, the Board identified further necessary consequential amendments to IFRS 1, IAS 14, IAS 34, IAS 36, IAS 37, IAS 38, IAS 40, SIC-13, SIC-21, SIC-22 and SIC-32.

IASB documents published to accompany

International Accounting Standard 17

Leases

This version includes amendments resulting from IFRSs issued up to 31 December 2009.

The text of the unaccompanied IAS 17 is contained in Part A of this edition. Its effective date when issued was 1 January 2005. The effective date of the latest amendments is 1 January 2013. This part presents the following accompanying documents:

Approval by the Board of IAS 17 issued in December 2003

International Accounting Standard 17 *Leases* (as revised in 2003) was approved for issue by the fourteen members of the International Accounting Standards Board.

Sir David Tweedie	Chairman
Thomas E Jones	Vice-Chairman
Mary E Barth	
Hans-Georg Bruns	
Anthony T Cope	
Robert P Garnett	
Gilbert Gélard	
James J Leisenring	
Warren J McGregor	
Patricia L O'Malley	
Harry K Schmid	
John T Smith	
Geoffrey Whittington	
Tatsumi Yamada	

Basis for Conclusions on
IAS 17 *Leases*

This Basis for Conclusions accompanies, but is not part of, IAS 17.

Introduction

BC1   This Basis for Conclusions summarises the International Accounting Standards Board's considerations in reaching its conclusions on revising IAS 17 *Leases* in 2003. Individual Board members gave greater weight to some factors than to others.

BC2   In July 2001 the Board announced that, as part of its initial agenda of technical projects, it would undertake a project to improve a number of Standards, including IAS 17. The project was undertaken in the light of queries and criticisms raised in relation to the Standards by securities regulators, professional accountants and other interested parties. The objectives of the Improvements project were to reduce or eliminate alternatives, redundancies and conflicts within existing Standards, to deal with some convergence issues and to make other improvements. In May 2002 the Board published its proposals in an Exposure Draft of *Improvements to International Accounting Standards*, with a comment deadline of 16 September 2002. The Board received over 160 comment letters on the Exposure Draft.

BC3   Because the Board's intention was not to reconsider the fundamental approach to the accounting for leases established by IAS 17, this Basis for Conclusions does not discuss requirements in IAS 17 that the Board has not reconsidered.

Classification of leases—leases of land and buildings (2003 amendment)

BC4   Paragraph 14 of the Standard requires a lease of land with an indefinite economic life to be normally classified as an operating lease, unless title is expected to pass to the lessee by the end of the lease term. The previous version of IAS 17 (as amended in 2000) was not explicit about how to classify a lease of land and buildings.

BC5   This is a matter of concern in countries where property rights are obtained under long-term leases and the substance of those leases differs little from buying a property. Therefore, the Board decided to deal with this matter in its Improvements project in 2001 and not to defer its resolution until the more fundamental project on leases was completed.

BC6   The Board noted that two approaches are applied in practice. The first is to treat such a lease as a single unit and to classify it as an operating lease in its entirety. The second is to split the lease into two elements—a lease of land and a lease of buildings. The Board decided that the first approach does not adequately reflect the assets controlled by the entity or their usage and financing. It is also inconsistent with the classification and the measurement of other leases. Therefore, the Board rejected the first approach of classifying a lease of land and buildings as an operating lease in its entirety.

BC7   The Board agreed on the second approach of splitting the lease into two elements—a lease of land and a lease of buildings. The land element would normally be classified as an operating lease in accordance with paragraph 14 of the revised Standard and the buildings element classified as an operating or finance lease by applying the conditions in paragraphs 7–13. The Board noted that generally accepted accounting principles in Australia, Canada and the United States all explicitly require a lease of land and buildings to be split into two elements.

BC8   The Board also discussed a third approach, namely whether to delete the requirement (in paragraph 14 of the Standard) normally to classify a lease of land as an operating lease when title does not pass at the end of the lease and to require such a lease to be classified as a finance lease when all other conditions for finance lease classification in the Standard are met. The Board noted that such an accounting treatment would conflict with the criteria for lease classification in the Standard, which are based on the extent to which the risks and rewards incidental to ownership of a leased asset lie with the lessor or the lessee. Indeed, land normally has an indefinite economic life and hence there are significant risks and rewards associated with the land at the end of the lease term, which do not pass to the lessee. Therefore, the Board rejected this approach when issuing the amendments to IAS 17 in December 2003.

Land element in long-term leases (2009 amendment)[*]

BC8A   As part of its annual improvements project in 2007, the Board reconsidered the decisions it made in 2003, specifically the perceived inconsistency between the general lease classification guidance in paragraphs 7–13 and the specific lease classification guidance in paragraphs 14 and 15 related to long-term leases of land and buildings. The Board concluded that the guidance in paragraphs 14 and 15 might lead to a conclusion on the classification of land leases that does not reflect the substance of the transaction.

BC8B   For example, consider a 999-year lease of land and buildings. In this situation, significant risks and rewards associated with the land during the lease term would have been transferred to the lessee despite there being no transfer of title.

BC8C   The Board noted that the lessee in leases of this type will typically be in a position economically similar to an entity that purchased the land and buildings. The present value of the residual value of the property in a lease with a term of several decades would be negligible. The Board concluded that the accounting for the land element as a finance lease in such circumstances would be consistent with the economic position of the lessee.

BC8D   The Board noted that this amendment reversed the decision it made in amending IAS 17 in December 2003. The Board also noted that the amendment differed from the International Financial Reporting Interpretations Committee's agenda decision in March 2006 based on the IAS 17 guidance that such long-term leases of land would be classified as an operating lease unless title or significant risks and rewards of ownership passed to the lessee, irrespective of the term of the

---

[*]   Paragraphs BC8A–BC8F were added as a consequence of amendments to IAS 17 made by *Improvements to IFRSs* issued in April 2009.

lease. However, the Board believed that this change improves the accounting for leases by removing a rule and an exception to the general principles applicable to the classification of leases.

BC8E Some respondents to the exposure draft proposing this amendment agreed with the direction of this proposal but suggested that it should be incorporated into the Board's project on leases. The Board acknowledged that the project on leases is expected to produce a standard in 2011. However, the Board decided to issue the amendment now because of the improvement in accounting for leases that would result and the significance of this issue in countries in which property rights are obtained under long-term leases. Therefore, the Board decided to remove this potential inconsistency by deleting the guidance in paragraphs 14 and 15.

BC8F Some respondents raised concerns about the proposed requirement to apply the amendment retrospectively. The land and buildings elements of a long-term finance lease may have different amortisation bases. Accordingly, entities must obtain relative fair values even when both elements are classified as finance leases. The Board noted that this information should already be available because entities would have had to obtain it to adopt the 2003 amendment to IAS 17 that required the split between land and buildings elements for the purposes of lease classification. However, the Board acknowledged that the fair values at the inception of the leases might not be available in some situations. The Board noted that determining the fair value of the land element at the inception of long-term leases in these instances would require the use of hindsight and might not achieve comparability. Accordingly, the Board decided not to require retrospective application when the necessary information is not available. The Board also rejected prospective application of the amendment because the land element in existing long-term leases would be accounted for inconsistently. Therefore, the Board decided to adopt the modified retrospective transition requirement in paragraph 68A of IAS 17.

Allocation of minimum lease payments between land and buildings

BC9 The Exposure Draft proposed that the allocation of the minimum lease payments between land and buildings should be made in proportion to their relative fair values at the inception of the lease. Respondents to the Exposure Draft questioned whether the allocation basis referred to the land and buildings components of the fair value of the property or the fair value of those components to the extent they were the subject of the lease.

BC10 The Board noted that an allocation of the minimum lease payments by reference to the relative fair values of the land and buildings would not reflect the fact that land often has an indefinite economic life, and therefore would be expected to maintain its value beyond the lease term. In contrast, the future economic benefits of a building are likely to be used up, at the least to some extent, over the lease term. Therefore, it would be reasonable to expect that the lease payments relating to the building would be set at a level that enabled the lessor not only to make a return on initial investment, but also to recoup the value of the building used up over the term of the lease. In the case of land, the lessor would not normally need compensation for using up the land.

BC11　Therefore, the Board decided to clarify in the Standard that the allocation of the minimum lease payments is weighted to reflect their role in compensating the lessor, and not by reference to the relative fair values of the land and buildings. In other words, the weighting should reflect the lessee's leasehold interest in the land and the buildings. In the extreme case that a building is fully depreciated over the lease term, the minimum lease payments would need to be weighted to provide a return plus the full depreciation of the building's value at the inception of the lease. The leasehold interest in the land would, assuming a residual value that equals its value at the inception of the lease, have a weighting that reflects only a return on the initial investment.

Impracticability of split between land and buildings

BC12　A question that arises is how to treat leases for which it is not possible to measure the two elements reliably (eg because similar land and buildings are not sold or leased separately). One possibility would be to classify the entire lease as a finance lease. This would prevent a lessee from avoiding finance lease treatment for the buildings by asserting that it cannot separately measure the two elements. However, it may be apparent from the circumstances that classifying the entire lease as a finance lease is not representationally faithful. In view of this, the Board decided that when it is not possible to measure the two elements reliably, the entire lease should be classified as a finance lease unless it is clear that both elements should be classified as an operating lease.

Exception to the requirement to separate the land and buildings elements

BC13　The Board discussed whether to allow or require an exception from the requirement to separate the land and buildings elements in cases in which the present value of the land element at the inception of the lease is small in relation to the value of the entire lease. In such cases the benefits of separating the lease into two elements and accounting for each separately may not outweigh the costs. The Board noted that generally accepted accounting principles in Australia, Canada and the United States allow or require such leases to be classified and accounted for as a single unit, with finance lease treatment being used when the relevant criteria are met. The Board decided to allow land and buildings to be treated as a single unit when the land element is immaterial.

BC14　Some respondents to the Exposure Draft requested guidance on how small the relative value of the land element needs to be in relation to the total value of the lease. The Board decided not to introduce a bright line such as a specific percentage threshold. The Board decided that the normal provisions on materiality should apply.

Transitional provisions

BC15　The Board decided that the requirement to separate the land and buildings elements in a lease of land and buildings should be applied retrospectively. It noted that there will be cases when it will be impracticable to reassess the treatment of these leases retrospectively, because doing so requires estimating what the fair value of the two elements was at the inception of the lease, which may have been many years before. The Board also noted that IAS 8 *Accounting Policies, Changes in Accounting Estimates and Errors* contains guidance on when it is impracticable to apply retrospectively a change in accounting policy and therefore decided not to provide specific transitional provisions for the implementation of this revision to IAS 17.

Inception of the lease and commencement of the lease term

BC16   The previous version of IAS 17 did not define the commencement of the lease term. It implicitly assumed that commencement (when the lease begins) and inception (when the agreement is entered into) are simultaneous. Some respondents questioned what should happen if there is a time lag between the two dates, particularly if the amounts change—for example, because the asset is under construction and the final cost is not known at inception. The Standard now specifies that recognition takes place at commencement, based on values measured at inception. However, if the lease is adjusted for changes in the lessor's costs between the inception of the lease and the commencement of the lease term, the effect of any such changes is deemed to have taken place at inception. These revisions are consistent with generally accepted accounting principles in Australia, Canada and the United States, and are consistent with the present accounting treatment of most ordinary purchases and sales.

BC17   In agreeing on this treatment, the Board noted that measurement at commencement would have been more satisfactory in principle. However, this cannot be done properly within the framework of IAS 17 because the Standard generally requires a finance lease receivable or payable to be recognised at an amount based on the fair value of the asset, which is inappropriate at any date after inception.

Leases in the financial statements of lessors other than manufacturers and dealers

BC18   Lessors may incur direct costs in negotiating a lease, such as commissions, brokers' fees and legal fees. The previous version of IAS 17 contained a choice on how to account for such costs—they might be either charged as an expense as incurred or allocated over the lease term. The choice of treatment applied to operating and finance leases. In the case of a finance lease, paragraph 33 of the previous version of IAS 17 stated that allocation over the lease term might be achieved by recognising the cost as an expense and, in the same period, recognising an equal amount of unearned finance income.

BC19   The Board decided that this treatment was not in accordance with the *Framework for the Preparation and Presentation of Financial Statements*. Its effect was to recognise some future finance income as income and an asset at the commencement of the lease term. However, at that date, the *Framework*'s definitions of income and assets are not met. Therefore, the Board decided that if direct costs incurred by lessors are to be allocated over the lease term, this should be achieved by including them in the carrying amount of the lease asset.

BC20   The Board noted that standard-setters in Australia, Canada, France, Japan, the United Kingdom and the United States either permit or require initial direct costs to be allocated over the lease term. The Board also noted that other Standards permit or require the recognition of a range of similar costs in the carrying amount of assets, generally subject to those costs being directly attributable to the acquisition of the asset in question. Hence, for reasons of convergence and comparability with other Standards, the Board decided to require initial direct costs to be included in the carrying amount of the lease asset.

BC21   For consistency with other Standards, in particular IAS 39 *Financial Instruments: Recognition and Measurement*,* the Board decided that recognition in the carrying amount of assets should be restricted to costs that are incremental and directly attributable to negotiating and arranging a lease.

---

*   In November 2009 the IASB amended some of the requirements of IAS 39 and relocated them to IFRS 9 *Financial Instruments*.

Dissenting opinion

Dissent of James J Leisenring from the amendment issued in April 2009

DO1   Mr Leisenring dissents from the amendment to IAS 17 *Leases* made by *Improvements to IFRSs* issued in April 2009.

DO2   Mr Leisenring believes that the amendment inappropriately permits an accounting that does not reflect the economic position of the lessee. In his view, land normally has an indefinite economic life, unlike other properties with finite useful lives. Therefore, it is not the lessee's land at the end of the lease even if the lease term is 999 years. He does not believe that a lessee is in a position economically similar to the purchaser of the land. Any appreciation in the land value does not accrue to the lessee at the termination of the lease. Furthermore, it is unclear how long the lease term must be for the Board to conclude that a lessee and a purchaser are in the same economic position.

DO3   This amendment also reverses the decision the Board made in amending IAS 17 in December 2003 and creates a divergence from US generally accepted accounting principles. Mr Leisenring agrees with some respondents that it is best to incorporate this amendment into the Board's broader project on lease accounting.

Guidance on implementing
IAS 17 *Leases*

This guidance accompanies, but is not part of, IAS 17.

Illustrative examples of sale and leaseback transactions that result in operating leases

A sale and leaseback transaction that results in an operating lease may give rise to profit or a loss, the determination and treatment of which depends on the leased asset's carrying amount, fair value and selling price. The table below shows the requirements of the Standard in various circumstances.

Sale price at fair value (paragraph 61)	Carrying amount equal to fair value	Carrying amount less than fair value	Carrying amount above fair value
Profit	no profit	recognise profit immediately	not applicable
Loss	no loss	not applicable	recognise loss immediately

Sale price below fair value (paragraph 61)			
Profit	no profit	recognise profit immediately	no profit (note 1)
Loss **not** compensated for by future lease payments at below market price	recognise loss immediately	recognise loss immediately	(note 1)
Loss compensated for by future lease payments at below market price	defer and amortise loss	defer and amortise loss	(note 1)

Sale price above fair value (paragraph 61)			
Profit	defer and amortise profit	defer and amortise excess profit (note 3)	defer and amortise profit (note 2)
Loss	no loss	no loss	(note 1)

Note 1   These parts of the table represent circumstances dealt with in paragraph 63 of the Standard. Paragraph 63 requires the carrying amount of an asset to be written down to fair value where it is subject to a sale and leaseback.

Note 2   Profit is the difference between fair value and sale price because the carrying amount would have been written down to fair value in accordance with paragraph 63.

Note 3   The excess profit (the excess of sale price over fair value) is deferred and amortised over the period for which the asset is expected to be used. Any excess of fair value over carrying amount is recognised immediately.

IASB document published to accompany

International Accounting Standard 18

Revenue

This version includes amendments resulting from IFRSs issued up to 31 December 2009.

The text of the unaccompanied IAS 18 is contained in Part A of this edition. Its effective date when issued was 1 January 1995. The effective date of the latest amendments is 1 January 2013. This part presents the following accompanying document:

Illustrative examples

These illustrative examples accompany, but are not part of, IAS 18. The examples focus on particular aspects of a transaction and are not a comprehensive discussion of all the relevant factors that might influence the recognition of revenue. The examples generally assume that the amount of revenue can be measured reliably, it is probable that the economic benefits will flow to the entity and the costs incurred or to be incurred can be measured reliably.

Sale of goods

The law in different countries may mean the recognition criteria in this Standard are met at different times. In particular, the law may determine the point in time at which the entity transfers the significant risks and rewards of ownership. Therefore, the examples in this section of the appendix need to be read in the context of the laws relating to the sale of goods in the country in which the transaction takes place.

1   *'Bill and hold' sales, in which delivery is delayed at the buyer's request but the buyer takes title and accepts billing.*

Revenue is recognised when the buyer takes title, provided:

(a)   it is probable that delivery will be made;

(b)   the item is on hand, identified and ready for delivery to the buyer at the time the sale is recognised;

(c)   the buyer specifically acknowledges the deferred delivery instructions; and

(d)   the usual payment terms apply.

Revenue is not recognised when there is simply an intention to acquire or manufacture the goods in time for delivery.

2   *Goods shipped subject to conditions.*

(a)   *installation and inspection.*

Revenue is normally recognised when the buyer accepts delivery, and installation and inspection are complete. However, revenue is recognised immediately upon the buyer's acceptance of delivery when:

(i)   the installation process is simple in nature, for example the installation of a factory tested television receiver which only requires unpacking and connection of power and antennae; or

(ii)   the inspection is performed only for purposes of final determination of contract prices, for example, shipments of iron ore, sugar or soya beans.

(b)   *on approval when the buyer has negotiated a limited right of return.*

If there is uncertainty about the possibility of return, revenue is recognised when the shipment has been formally accepted by the buyer or the goods have been delivered and the time period for rejection has elapsed.

(c) *consignment sales under which the recipient (buyer) undertakes to sell the goods on behalf of the shipper (seller).*

Revenue is recognised by the shipper when the goods are sold by the recipient to a third party.

(d) *cash on delivery sales.*

Revenue is recognised when delivery is made and cash is received by the seller or its agent.

3 *Lay away sales under which the goods are delivered only when the buyer makes the final payment in a series of instalments.*

Revenue from such sales is recognised when the goods are delivered. However, when experience indicates that most such sales are consummated, revenue may be recognised when a significant deposit is received provided the goods are on hand, identified and ready for delivery to the buyer.

4 *Orders when payment (or partial payment) is received in advance of delivery for goods not presently held in inventory, for example, the goods are still to be manufactured or will be delivered directly to the customer from a third party.*

Revenue is recognised when the goods are delivered to the buyer.

5 *Sale and repurchase agreements (other than swap transactions) under which the seller concurrently agrees to repurchase the same goods at a later date, or when the seller has a call option to repurchase, or the buyer has a put option to require the repurchase, by the seller, of the goods.*

For a sale and repurchase agreement on an asset other than a financial asset, the terms of the agreement need to be analysed to ascertain whether, in substance, the seller has transferred the risks and rewards of ownership to the buyer and hence revenue is recognised. When the seller has retained the risks and rewards of ownership, even though legal title has been transferred, the transaction is a financing arrangement and does not give rise to revenue. For a sale and repurchase agreement on a financial asset, IFRS 9 *Financial Instruments* and IAS 39 *Financial Instruments: Recognition and Measurement* apply.

6 *Sales to intermediate parties, such as distributors, dealers or others for resale.*

Revenue from such sales is generally recognised when the risks and rewards of ownership have passed. However, when the buyer is acting, in substance, as an agent, the sale is treated as a consignment sale.

7 *Subscriptions to publications and similar items.*

When the items involved are of similar value in each time period, revenue is recognised on a straight-line basis over the period in which the items are despatched. When the items vary in value from period to period, revenue is recognised on the basis of the sales value of the item despatched in relation to the total estimated sales value of all items covered by the subscription.

8 *Instalment sales, under which the consideration is receivable in instalments.*

Revenue attributable to the sales price, exclusive of interest, is recognised at the date of sale. The sale price is the present value of the consideration, determined by discounting the instalments receivable at the imputed rate of interest. The interest element is recognised as revenue as it is earned, using the effective interest method.

9 *Real estate sales.*

This example has been superseded by IFRIC Interpretation 15 *Agreements for the Construction of Real Estate.*

Rendering of services

10 *Installation fees.*

Installation fees are recognised as revenue by reference to the stage of completion of the installation, unless they are incidental to the sale of a product, in which case they are recognised when the goods are sold.

11 *Servicing fees included in the price of the product.*

When the selling price of a product includes an identifiable amount for subsequent servicing (for example, after sales support and product enhancement on the sale of software), that amount is deferred and recognised as revenue over the period during which the service is performed. The amount deferred is that which will cover the expected costs of the services under the agreement, together with a reasonable profit on those services.

12 *Advertising commissions.*

Media commissions are recognised when the related advertisement or commercial appears before the public. Production commissions are recognised by reference to the stage of completion of the project.

13 *Insurance agency commissions.*

Insurance agency commissions received or receivable which do not require the agent to render further service are recognised as revenue by the agent on the effective commencement or renewal dates of the related policies. However, when it is probable that the agent will be required to render further services during the life of the policy, the commission, or part thereof, is deferred and recognised as revenue over the period during which the policy is in force.

14 *Financial service fees.*

The recognition of revenue for financial service fees depends on the purposes for which the fees are assessed and the basis of accounting for any associated financial instrument. The description of fees for financial services may not be indicative of the nature and substance of the services provided. Therefore, it is necessary to distinguish between fees that are an integral part of the effective interest rate of a financial instrument, fees that are earned as services are provided, and fees that are earned on the execution of a significant act.

(a) *Fees that are an integral part of the effective interest rate of a financial instrument.*

Such fees are generally treated as an adjustment to the effective interest rate. However, when the financial instrument is measured at fair value with the change in fair value recognised in profit or loss, the fees are recognised as revenue when the instrument is initially recognised.

(i) *Origination fees received by the entity relating to the creation or acquisition of a financial asset other than one that under IFRS 9 is measured at fair value through profit or loss.*

Such fees may include compensation for activities such as evaluating the borrower's financial condition, evaluating and recording guarantees, collateral and other security arrangements, negotiating the terms of the instrument, preparing and processing documents and closing the transaction. These fees are an integral part of generating an involvement with the resulting financial instrument and, together with the related transaction costs* (as defined in IAS 39), are deferred and recognised as an adjustment to the effective interest rate.

(ii) *Commitment fees received by the entity to originate a loan when the loan commitment is outside the scope of IAS 39.*

If it is probable that the entity will enter into a specific lending arrangement and the loan commitment is not within the scope of IAS 39, the commitment fee received is regarded as compensation for an ongoing involvement with the acquisition of a financial instrument and, together with the related transaction costs (as defined in IAS 39), is deferred and recognised as an adjustment to the effective interest rate. If the commitment expires without the entity making the loan, the fee is recognised as revenue on expiry. Loan commitments that are within the scope of IAS 39 are accounted for as derivatives and measured at fair value.

(iii) *Origination fees received on issuing financial liabilities measured at amortised cost.*

These fees are an integral part of generating an involvement with a financial liability. When a financial liability is not classified as 'at fair value through profit or loss', the origination fees received are included, with the related transaction costs (as defined in IAS 39) incurred, in the initial carrying amount of the financial liability and recognised as an adjustment to the effective interest rate. An entity distinguishes fees and costs that are an integral part of the effective interest rate for the financial liability from origination fees and transaction costs relating to the right to provide services, such as investment management services.

---

* In *Improvements to IFRSs* issued in May 2008, the Board replaced the term 'direct costs' with 'transaction costs' as defined in paragraph 9 of IAS 39. This amendment removed an inconsistency for costs incurred in originating financial assets and liabilities that should be deferred and recognised as an adjustment to the underlying effective interest rate. 'Direct costs', as previously defined, did not require such costs to be incremental.

(b) *Fees earned as services are provided.*

    (i) *Fees charged for servicing a loan.*

Fees charged by an entity for servicing a loan are recognised as revenue as the services are provided.

    (ii) *Commitment fees to originate a loan when the loan commitment is outside the scope of IAS 39.*

If it is unlikely that a specific lending arrangement will be entered into and the loan commitment is outside the scope of IAS 39, the commitment fee is recognised as revenue on a time proportion basis over the commitment period. Loan commitments that are within the scope of IAS 39 are accounted for as derivatives and measured at fair value.

    (iii) *Investment management fees.*

Fees charged for managing investments are recognised as revenue as the services are provided.

Incremental costs that are directly attributable to securing an investment management contract are recognised as an asset if they can be identified separately and measured reliably and if it is probable that they will be recovered. As in IAS 39, an incremental cost is one that would not have been incurred if the entity had not secured the investment management contract. The asset represents the entity's contractual right to benefit from providing investment management services, and is amortised as the entity recognises the related revenue. If the entity has a portfolio of investment management contracts, it may assess their recoverability on a portfolio basis.

Some financial services contracts involve both the origination of one or more financial instruments and the provision of investment management services. An example is a long-term monthly saving contract linked to the management of a pool of equity securities. The provider of the contract distinguishes the transaction costs relating to the origination of the financial instrument from the costs of securing the right to provide investment management services.

(c) *Fees that are earned on the execution of a significant act.*

The fees are recognised as revenue when the significant act has been completed, as in the examples below.

    (i) *Commission on the allotment of shares to a client.*

The commission is recognised as revenue when the shares have been allotted.

    (ii) *Placement fees for arranging a loan between a borrower and an investor.*

The fee is recognised as revenue when the loan has been arranged.

       (iii)   *Loan syndication fees.*

A syndication fee received by an entity that arranges a loan and retains no part of the loan package for itself (or retains a part at the same effective interest rate for comparable risk as other participants) is compensation for the service of syndication. Such a fee is recognised as revenue when the syndication has been completed.

15   *Admission fees.*

Revenue from artistic performances, banquets and other special events is recognised when the event takes place. When a subscription to a number of events is sold, the fee is allocated to each event on a basis which reflects the extent to which services are performed at each event.

16   *Tuition fees.*

Revenue is recognised over the period of instruction.

17   *Initiation, entrance and membership fees.*

Revenue recognition depends on the nature of the services provided. If the fee permits only membership, and all other services or products are paid for separately, or if there is a separate annual subscription, the fee is recognised as revenue when no significant uncertainty as to its collectibility exists. If the fee entitles the member to services or publications to be provided during the membership period, or to purchase goods or services at prices lower than those charged to non-members, it is recognised on a basis that reflects the timing, nature and value of the benefits provided.

18   *Franchise fees.*

Franchise fees may cover the supply of initial and subsequent services, equipment and other tangible assets, and know-how. Accordingly, franchise fees are recognised as revenue on a basis that reflects the purpose for which the fees were charged. The following methods of franchise fee recognition are appropriate:

      (a)   *Supplies of equipment and other tangible assets.*

The amount, based on the fair value of the assets sold, is recognised as revenue when the items are delivered or title passes.

      (b)   *Supplies of initial and subsequent services.*

Fees for the provision of continuing services, whether part of the initial fee or a separate fee, are recognised as revenue as the services are rendered. When the separate fee does not cover the cost of continuing services together with a reasonable profit, part of the initial fee, sufficient to cover the costs of continuing services and to provide a reasonable profit on those services, is deferred and recognised as revenue as the services are rendered.

The franchise agreement may provide for the franchisor to supply equipment, inventories, or other tangible assets, at a price lower than that charged to others or a price that does not provide a reasonable profit on those sales. In these circumstances, part of the initial fee, sufficient to cover estimated costs in excess of that price and to provide a reasonable profit on those sales, is deferred and recognised over the period the goods are likely to be sold to the franchisee. The balance of an initial fee is recognised as revenue when performance of all the initial services and other obligations required of the franchisor (such as assistance with site selection, staff training, financing and advertising) has been substantially accomplished.

The initial services and other obligations under an area franchise agreement may depend on the number of individual outlets established in the area. In this case, the fees attributable to the initial services are recognised as revenue in proportion to the number of outlets for which the initial services have been substantially completed.

If the initial fee is collectible over an extended period and there is a significant uncertainty that it will be collected in full, the fee is recognised as cash instalments are received.

(c) *Continuing franchise fees.*

Fees charged for the use of continuing rights granted by the agreement, or for other services provided during the period of the agreement, are recognised as revenue as the services are provided or the rights used.

(d) *Agency transactions.*

Transactions may take place between the franchisor and the franchisee which, in substance, involve the franchisor acting as agent for the franchisee. For example, the franchisor may order supplies and arrange for their delivery to the franchisee at no profit. Such transactions do not give rise to revenue.

19 *Fees from the development of customised software.*

Fees from the development of customised software are recognised as revenue by reference to the stage of completion of the development, including completion of services provided for post-delivery service support.

Interest, royalties and dividends

20 *Licence fees and royalties.*

Fees and royalties paid for the use of an entity's assets (such as trademarks, patents, software, music copyright, record masters and motion picture films) are normally recognised in accordance with the substance of the agreement. As a practical matter, this may be on a straight-line basis over the life of the agreement, for example, when a licensee has the right to use certain technology for a specified period of time.

An assignment of rights for a fixed fee or non-refundable guarantee under a non-cancellable contract which permits the licensee to exploit those rights freely and the licensor has no remaining obligations to perform is, in substance, a sale. An example is a licensing agreement for the use of software when the licensor has no obligations subsequent to delivery. Another example is the granting of rights to exhibit a motion picture film in markets where the licensor has no control over the distributor and expects to receive no further revenues from the box office receipts. In such cases, revenue is recognised at the time of sale.

In some cases, whether or not a licence fee or royalty will be received is contingent on the occurrence of a future event. In such cases, revenue is recognised only when it is probable that the fee or royalty will be received, which is normally when the event has occurred.

Recognition and measurement

21   *Determining whether an entity is acting as a principal or as an agent (2009 amendment).*

Paragraph 8 states that 'in an agency relationship, the gross inflows of economic benefits include amounts collected on behalf of the principal and which do not result in increases in equity for the entity. The amounts collected on behalf of the principal are not revenue. Instead, revenue is the amount of commission.' Determining whether an entity is acting as a principal or as an agent requires judgement and consideration of all relevant facts and circumstances.

An entity is acting as a principal when it has exposure to the significant risks and rewards associated with the sale of goods or the rendering of services. Features that indicate that an entity is acting as a principal include:

(a)   the entity has the primary responsibility for providing the goods or services to the customer or for fulfilling the order, for example by being responsible for the acceptability of the products or services ordered or purchased by the customer;

(b)   the entity has inventory risk before or after the customer order, during shipping or on return;

(c)   the entity has latitude in establishing prices, either directly or indirectly, for example by providing additional goods or services; and

(d)   the entity bears the customer's credit risk for the amount receivable from the customer.

An entity is acting as an agent when it does not have exposure to the significant risks and rewards associated with the sale of goods or the rendering of services. One feature indicating that an entity is acting as an agent is that the amount the entity earns is predetermined, being either a fixed fee per transaction or a stated percentage of the amount billed to the customer.

IASB documents published to accompany

International Accounting Standard 19

Employee Benefits

This version includes amendments resulting from IFRSs issued up to 31 December 2009.

The text of the unaccompanied IAS 19 is contained in Part A of this edition. Its effective date when issued was 1 January 1999. The effective date of the most recent amendment is 1 January 2013. This part presents the following accompanying documents:

Approval by the Board of *Employee Benefits: The Asset Ceiling* (Amendment to IAS 19) issued in May 2002

Employee Benefits: The Asset Ceiling (Amendment to IAS 19) was approved for issue by thirteen of the fourteen members of the International Accounting Standards Board. Ms O'Malley dissented. Her dissenting opinion is set out after the Basis for Conclusions.

Sir David Tweedie	Chairman
Thomas E Jones	Vice-Chairman
Mary E Barth	
Hans-Georg Bruns	
Anthony T Cope	
Robert P Garnett	
Gilbert Gélard	
James J Leisenring	
Warren J McGregor	
Patricia L O'Malley	
Harry K Schmid	
John T Smith	
Geoffrey Whittington	
Tatsumi Yamada	

Approval by the Board of *Actuarial Gains and Losses, Group Plans and Disclosures* (Amendment to IAS 19) issued in December 2004

Actuarial Gains and Losses, Group Plans and Disclosures (Amendment to IAS 19) was approved for issue by twelve of the fourteen members of the International Accounting Standards Board. Messrs Leisenring and Yamada dissented. Their dissenting opinions are set out after the Basis for Conclusions.

Sir David Tweedie	Chairman
Thomas E Jones	Vice-Chairman
Mary E Barth	
Hans-Georg Bruns	
Anthony T Cope	
Jan Engström	
Robert P Garnett	
Gilbert Gélard	
James J Leisenring	
Warren J McGregor	
Patricia L O'Malley	
John T Smith	
Geoffrey Whittington	
Tatsumi Yamada	

CONTENTS

© IASCF

Basis for Conclusions on
IAS 19 *Employee Benefits*

The original text has been marked up to reflect the revision of IAS 39 Financial Instruments: Recognition and Measurement *in 2003 and the issue of IFRS 2* Share-based Payment *in 2004 and* Improvements to IFRSs *in May 2008; new text is underlined and deleted text is struck through. The terminology has not been amended to reflect the changes made by IAS 1* Presentation of Financial Statements *(as revised in 2007).*

For greater clarity and for consistency with other IFRSs, paragraph numbers have been prefixed BC.

This Basis for Conclusions gives the Board's reasons for rejecting certain alternative solutions. Individual Board members gave greater weight to some factors than to others. Paragraphs BC9A–BC9D, BC10A–BC10K, BC48A–BC48EE and BC85A–BC85E were added in relation to the amendment to IAS 19 issued in December 2004. Paragraphs BC4A–BC4C, BC62A, BC62B and BC97 were added by Improvements to IFRSs *issued in May 2008.*

Background

BC1   The IASC Board (the 'Board') approved IAS 19 *Accounting for Retirement Benefits in the Financial Statements of Employers*, in 1983. Following a limited review, the Board approved a revised Standard IAS 19 *Retirement Benefit Costs* ('the old IAS 19'), in 1993. The Board began a more comprehensive review of IAS 19 in November 1994. In August 1995, the IASC Staff published an Issues Paper on *Retirement Benefit and Other Employee Benefit Costs*. In October 1996, the Board approved E54 *Employee Benefits*, with a comment deadline of 31 January 1997. The Board received more than 130 comment letters on E54 from over 20 countries. The Board approved IAS 19 *Employee Benefits* ('the new IAS 19') in January 1998.

BC2   The Board believes that the new IAS 19 is a significant improvement over the old IAS 19. Nevertheless, the Board believes that further improvement may be possible in due course. In particular, several Board members believe that it would be preferable to recognise all actuarial gains and losses immediately in a statement of financial performance. However, the Board believes that such a solution is not feasible for actuarial gains and losses until the Board makes further progress on various issues relating to the reporting of financial performance. When the Board makes further progress with those issues, it may decide to revisit the treatment of actuarial gains and losses.

Summary of changes to IAS 19

BC3   The most significant feature of the new IAS 19 is a market-based approach to measurement. The main consequences are that the discount rate is based on market yields at the balance sheet date and any plan assets are measured at fair value. In summary, the main changes from the old IAS 19 are the following:

(a)   there is a revised definition of defined contribution plans and related guidance (see paragraphs BC5 and BC6 below), including more detailed guidance than the old IAS 19 on multi-employer plans and state plans (see paragraphs BC7–BC10 below) and on insured plans;

(b) there is improved guidance on the balance sheet treatment of liabilities and assets arising from defined benefit plans (see paragraphs BC11–BC14 below).

(c) defined benefit obligations should be measured with sufficient regularity that the amounts recognised in the financial statements do not differ materially from the amounts that would be determined at the balance sheet date (see paragraphs BC15 and BC16 below);

(d) projected benefit methods are eliminated and there is a requirement to use the accrued benefit method known as the Projected Unit Credit Method (see paragraphs BC17–BC22 below). The use of an accrued benefit method makes it essential to give detailed guidance on the attribution of benefit to individual periods of service (see paragraphs BC23–BC25 below);

(e) the rate used to discount post-employment benefit obligations and other long-term employee benefit obligations (both funded and unfunded) should be determined by reference to market yields at the balance sheet date on high quality corporate bonds. In countries where there is no deep market in such bonds, the market yields (at the balance sheet date) on government bonds should be used. The currency and term of the corporate bonds or government bonds should be consistent with the currency and estimated term of the post-employment benefit obligations (see paragraphs BC26–BC34 below);

(f) defined benefit obligations should consider all benefit increases that are set out in the terms of the plan (or result from any constructive obligation that goes beyond those terms) at the balance sheet date (see paragraphs BC35–BC37 below);

(g) an entity should recognise, as a minimum, a specified portion of those actuarial gains and losses (arising from both defined benefit obligations and any related plan assets) that fall outside a 'corridor'. An entity is permitted, but not required, to adopt certain systematic methods of faster recognition. Such methods include, among others, immediate recognition of all actuarial gains and losses (see paragraphs BC38–BC48 below);

(h) an entity should recognise past service cost on a straight-line basis over the average period until the benefits become vested. To the extent that the benefits are already vested immediately, an entity should recognise past service cost immediately (see paragraphs BC49–BC62 below);

(i) plan assets should be measured at fair value. Fair value is estimated by discounting expected future cash flows only if no market price is available (see paragraphs BC66–BC75 below);

(j) amounts recognised by the reporting entity as an asset should not exceed the net total of:

(i) any unrecognised actuarial losses and past service cost; and

(ii) the present value of any economic benefits available in the form of refunds from the plan or reductions in contributions to the plan (see paragraphs BC76–BC78 below);

(k)   curtailment and settlement losses should be recognised not when it is probable that the settlement or curtailment will occur, but when the settlement or curtailment occurs (see paragraphs BC79 and BC80 below);

(l)   improvements have been made to the disclosure requirements (see paragraphs BC81–BC85 below);

(m)   the new IAS 19 deals with all employee benefits, whereas IAS 19 deals only with retirement benefits and certain similar post-employment benefits (see paragraphs BC86–BC94 below); and

(n)   the transitional provisions for defined benefit plans are amended (see paragraphs BC95 and BC96 below).

The Board rejected a proposal to require recognition of an 'additional minimum liability' in certain cases (see paragraphs BC63–BC65 below).

Summary of changes to E54

BC4   The new IAS 19 makes the following principal changes to the proposals in E54:

(a)   an entity should attribute benefit to periods of service following the plan's benefit formula, but the straight-line basis should be used if employee service in later years leads to a materially higher level of benefit than in earlier years (see paragraphs BC23–BC25 below);

(b)   actuarial assumptions should include estimates of benefit increases not if there is reliable evidence that they will occur, but only if the increases are set out in the terms of the plan (or result from any constructive obligation that goes beyond those terms) at the balance sheet date (see paragraphs BC35–BC37 below);

(c)   actuarial gains and losses that fall outside the 10% 'corridor' need not be recognised immediately as proposed in E54. The minimum amount that an entity should recognise for each defined benefit plan is the part that fell outside the 'corridor' as at the end of the previous reporting period, divided by the expected average remaining working lives of the employees participating in that plan. The new IAS 19 also permits certain systematic methods of faster recognition. Such methods include, among others, immediate recognition of all actuarial gains and losses (see paragraphs BC38–BC48 below);

(d)   E54 set out two alternative treatments for past service cost and indicated that the Board would eliminate one of these treatments after considering comments on the Exposure Draft. One treatment was immediate recognition of all past service cost. The other treatment was immediate recognition for former employees, with amortisation for current employees over the remaining working lives of the current employees. The new IAS 19 requires that an entity should recognise past service cost on a straight-line basis over the average period until the benefits become vested. To the extent that the benefits are already vested immediately an entity should recognise past service cost immediately (see paragraphs BC49–BC59 below);

(e)   the effect of 'negative plan amendments' should not be recognised immediately (as proposed in E54) but treated in the same way as past service cost (see paragraphs BC60–BC62 below);

(f)   non-transferable securities issued by the reporting entity have been excluded from the definition of plan assets (see paragraphs BC67 and BC68 below);

(g)   plan assets should be measured at fair value rather than market value, as defined in E54 (see paragraphs BC69 and BC70 below);

(h)   plan administration costs (not just investment administration costs, as proposed in E54) are to be deducted in determining the return on plan assets (see paragraph BC75 below);

(i)   the limit on the recognition of plan assets has been changed in two respects from the proposals in E54. The limit does not override the corridor for actuarial losses or the deferred recognition of past service cost. Also, the limit refers to **available** refunds or reductions in future contributions. E54 referred to the **expected** refunds or reductions in future contributions (see paragraphs BC76–BC78 below);

(j)   unlike E54, the new IAS 19 does not specify whether an income statement should present interest cost and the expected return on plan assets in the same line item as current service cost. The new IAS 19 requires an entity to disclose the line items in which they are included;

(k)   improvements have been made to the disclosure requirements (see paragraphs BC81–BC85 below);

(l)   the guidance in certain areas (particularly termination benefits, curtailments and settlements, profit-sharing and bonus plans and various references to constructive obligations) has been conformed to the proposals in E59 *Provisions, Contingent Liabilities and Contingent Assets*. Also, the Board has added explicit guidance on the measurement of termination benefits, requiring discounting for termination benefits not payable within one year (see paragraphs BC91–BC93 below); and

(m)   on initial adoption of the new IAS 19, there is a transitional option to recognise an increase in defined benefit liabilities over not more than five years. The new IAS 19 is operative for financial statements covering periods beginning on or after 1 January 1999, rather than 2001 as proposed in E54 (see paragraphs BC95 and BC96 below).

Definitions

BC4A   The IASB identified a perceived inconsistency in the definitions when a compensated absence that is due to the employee but is not expected to occur for more than twelve months is neither an 'other long-term employee benefit' nor a 'short-term compensated absence' as previously defined in paragraphs 7 and 8(b). The IASB decided to amend those definitions and replace the term 'fall due' to remove this potential gap as part of the *Improvements to IFRSs* issued in May 2008.

BC4B   Noting respondents' comments on the exposure draft of proposed *Improvements to International Financial Reporting Standards* published in 2007, the IASB concluded that the critical factor in distinguishing between long-term and short-term benefits is the timing of the expected settlement. Therefore, the IASB clarified that other long-term benefits are those that are not *due to be settled* within twelve months after the end of the period in which the employees rendered the service.

BC4C   The IASB noted that this distinction between short-term and long-term benefits is consistent with the current/non-current liability distinction in IAS 1 *Presentation of Financial Statements*. However, the fact that for presentation purposes a long-term benefit may be split into current and non-current portions does not change how the entire long-term benefit would be measured.

Defined contribution plans (paragraphs 24–47 of the standard)

BC5   The old IAS 19 defined:

(a)   **defined contribution plans** as retirement benefit plans under which amounts to be paid as retirement benefits are determined by reference to contributions to a fund together with investment earnings thereon; and

(b)   **defined benefit plans** as retirement benefit plans under which amounts to be paid as retirement benefits are determined by reference to a formula usually based on employees' remuneration and/or years of service.

The Board considers these definitions unsatisfactory because they focus on the benefit receivable by the employee, rather than on the cost to the entity. The definitions in paragraph 7 of the new IAS 19 focus on the downside risk that the cost to the entity may increase. The definition of defined contribution plans does not exclude the upside potential that the cost to the entity may be less than expected.

BC6   The new IAS 19 does not change the accounting for defined contribution plans, which is straightforward because there is no need for actuarial assumptions and an entity has no possibility of any actuarial gain or loss. The new IAS 19 gives no guidance equivalent to paragraphs 20 (past service costs in defined contribution plans) and 21 (curtailment of defined contribution plans) of the old IAS 19. The Board believes that these issues are not relevant to defined contribution plans.

Multi-employer plans and state plans (paragraphs 29–38 of the Standard)

BC7   An entity may not always be able to obtain sufficient information from multi-employer plans to use defined benefit accounting. The Board considered three approaches to this problem:

(a)   use defined contribution accounting for some and defined benefit accounting for others;

(b)   use defined contribution accounting for all multi-employer plans, with additional disclosure where the multi-employer plan is a defined benefit plan; or

(c)   use defined benefit accounting for those multi-employer plans that are defined benefit plans. However, where sufficient information is not available to use defined benefit accounting, an entity should disclose that fact and use defined contribution accounting.

BC8   The Board believes that there is no conceptually sound, workable and objective way to draw a distinction so that an entity could use defined contribution accounting for some multi-employer defined benefit plans and defined benefit accounting for others. Also, the Board believes that it is misleading to use defined contribution accounting for multi-employer plans that are defined benefit plans. This is illustrated by the case of French banks that used defined contribution accounting for defined benefit pension plans operated under industry-wide collective agreements on a pay-as-you-go basis. Demographic trends made these plans unsustainable and a major reform in 1993 replaced these by defined contribution arrangements for future service. At this point, the banks were compelled to quantify their obligations. Those obligations had previously existed, but had not been recognised as liabilities.

BC9   The Board concluded that an entity should use defined benefit accounting for those multi-employer plans that are defined benefit plans. However, where sufficient information is not available to use defined benefit accounting, an entity should disclose that fact and use defined contribution accounting. The Board agreed to apply the same principle to state plans. The new IAS 19 notes that most state plans are defined contribution plans.

Multi-employer plans: amendment issued by the IASB in December 2004

BC9A   In April 2004 the International Financial Reporting Interpretations Committee (IFRIC) published a draft Interpretation, D6 *Multi-employer Plans*, which proposed the following guidance on how multi-employer plans should apply defined benefit accounting, if possible:

(a)   the plan should be measured in accordance with IAS 19 using assumptions appropriate for the plan as a whole

(b)   the plan should be allocated to plan participants so that they recognise an asset or liability that reflects the impact of the surplus or deficit on the future contributions from the participant.

BC9B   The concerns raised by respondents to D6 about the availability of the information about the plan as a whole, the difficulties in making an allocation as proposed and the resulting lack of usefulness of the information provided by defined benefit accounting were such that the IFRIC decided not to proceed with the proposals.

BC9C   The International Accounting Standards Board (IASB), when discussing group plans (see paragraphs BC10A–BC10K) noted that, if there were a contractual agreement between a multi-employer plan and its participants on how a surplus would be distributed or deficit funded, the same principle that applied to group plans should apply to multi-employer plans, ie the participants should recognise an asset or liability. In relation to the funding of a deficit, the IASB regarded this principle as consistent with the recognition of a provision in accordance with IAS 37.

BC9D   The IASB therefore decided to clarify in IAS 19 that, if a participant in a defined
        benefit multi-employer plan:

        (a)   accounts for that participation on a defined contribution basis in
               accordance with paragraph 30 of IAS 19 because it had insufficient
               information to apply defined benefit accounting but

        (b)   has a contractual agreement that determined how a surplus would be
               distributed or a deficit funded,

        it recognises the asset or liability arising from that contractual agreement.

BC10   In response to comments on E54, the Board considered a proposal to exempt
        wholly owned subsidiaries (and their parents) participating in group defined
        benefit plans from the recognition and measurement requirements in their
        individual non-consolidated financial statements, on cost-benefit grounds.
        The Board concluded that such an exemption would not be appropriate.

Application of IAS 19 in the separate or individual financial statements of entities in a consolidated group: amendment issued by the IASB in December 2004

BC10A   Some constituents asked the IASB to consider whether entities participating in a
        group defined benefit plan should, in their separate or individual financial
        statements, either have an unqualified exemption from defined benefit
        accounting or be able to treat the plan as a multi-employer plan.

BC10B   In developing the exposure draft, the IASB did not agree that an unqualified
        exemption from defined benefit accounting for group defined benefit plans in
        the separate or individual financial statements of group entities was appropriate.
        In principle, the requirements of International Financial Reporting Standards
        (IFRSs) should apply to separate or individual financial statements in the same
        way as they apply to any other financial statements. Following that principle
        would mean amending IAS 19 to allow group entities that participate in a plan
        that meets the definition of a multi-employer plan, except that the participants
        are under common control, to be treated as participants in a multi-employer plan
        in their separate or individual financial statements.

BC10C   However, in the exposure draft, the IASB concluded that entities within a group
        should always be presumed to be able to obtain the necessary information about
        the plan as a whole. This implies that, in accordance with the requirements for
        multi-employer plans, defined benefit accounting should be applied if there is a
        consistent and reliable basis for allocating the assets and obligations of the plan.

BC10D   In the exposure draft, the IASB acknowledged that entities within a group might
        not be able to identify a consistent and reliable basis for allocating the plan that
        results in the entity recognising an asset or liability that reflects the extent to
        which a surplus or deficit in the plan would affect their future contributions. This
        is because there may be uncertainty in the terms of the plan about how surpluses
        will be used or deficits funded across the consolidated group. However, the IASB
        concluded that entities within a group should always be able to make at least a
        consistent and *reasonable* allocation, for example on the basis of a percentage of
        pensionable pay.

BC10E   The IASB then considered whether, for some group entities, the benefits of defined benefit accounting using a consistent and *reasonable* basis of allocation were worth the costs involved in obtaining the information. The IASB decided that this was not the case for entities that meet criteria similar to those in IAS 27 *Consolidated and Separate Financial Statements* for the exemption from preparing consolidated financial statements.

BC10F   The exposure draft therefore proposed that:

(a)   entities that participate in a plan that would meet the definition of a multi-employer plan except that the participants are under common control, and that meet the criteria set out in paragraph 34 of IAS 19 as proposed to be amended in the exposure draft, should be treated as if they were participants in a multi-employer plan. This means that if there is no consistent and reliable basis for allocating the assets and liabilities of the plan, the entity should use defined contribution accounting and provide additional disclosures.

(b)   all other entities that participate in a plan that would meet the definition of a multi-employer plan except that the participants are under common control should be required to apply defined benefit accounting by making a consistent and reasonable allocation of the assets and liabilities of the plan.

BC10G   Respondents to the exposure draft generally supported the proposal to extend the requirements in IAS 19 on multi-employer plans to group entities. However, many disagreed with the criteria proposed in the exposure draft, for the following reasons:

(a)   the proposed amendments and the interaction with D6 were unclear.

(b)   the provisions for multi-employer accounting should be extended to a listed parent company.

(c)   the provisions for multi-employer accounting should be extended to group entities with listed debt.

(d)   the provisions for multi-employer plan accounting should be extended to all group entities, including partly-owned subsidiaries.

(e)   there should be a blanket exemption from defined benefit accounting for all group entities.

BC10H   The IASB agreed that the proposed requirements for group plans were unnecessarily complex. The IASB also concluded that it would be better to treat group plans separately from multi-employer plans because of the difference in information available to the participants: in a group plan information about the plan as a whole should generally be available. The IASB further noted that, if the parent wishes to comply with IFRSs in its separate financial statements or wishes its subsidiaries to comply with IFRSs in their individual financial statements, then it must obtain and provide the necessary information for the purposes of disclosure, at least.

BC10I   The IASB noted that, if there were a contractual agreement or stated policy on charging the net defined benefit cost to group entities, that agreement or policy would determine the cost for each entity. If there is no such contractual agreement or stated policy, the entity that is the sponsoring employer by default bears the risk relating to the plan. The IASB therefore concluded that a group plan should be allocated to the individual entities within a group in accordance with any contractual agreement or stated policy. If there is no such agreement or policy, the net defined benefit cost is allocated to the sponsoring employer. The other group entities recognise a cost equal to any contribution collected by the sponsoring employer.

BC10J   This approach has the advantages of (a) all group entities recognising the cost they have to bear for the defined benefit promise and (b) being simple to apply.

BC10K   The IASB also noted that participation in a group plan is a related party transaction. As such, disclosures are required to comply with IAS 24 *Related Party Disclosures*. Paragraph 20 of IAS 24 requires an entity to disclose the nature of the related party relationship as well as information about the transactions and outstanding balances necessary for an understanding of the potential effect of the relationship on the financial statements. The IASB noted that information about each of (a) the policy on charging the defined benefit cost, (b) the policy on charging current contributions and (c) the status of the plan as a whole was required to give an understanding of the potential effect of the participation in the group plan on the entity's separate or individual financial statements.

Defined benefit plans

Recognition and measurement: balance sheet (paragraphs 49–60 of the Standard)

BC11   Paragraph 54 of the new IAS 19 summarises the recognition and measurement of liabilities arising from defined benefit plans and paragraphs 55–107 of the new IAS 19 describe various aspects of recognition and measurement in greater detail. Although the old IAS 19 did not deal explicitly with the recognition of retirement benefit obligations as a liability, it is likely that most entities would recognise a liability for retirement benefit obligations at the same time under both Standards. However, the two Standards differ in the measurement of the resulting liability.

BC12   Paragraph 54 of the new IAS 19 is based on the definition of, and recognition criteria for, a liability in IASC's *Framework for the Preparation and Presentation of Financial Statements* (the 'Framework'). The *Framework* defines a liability as *a present obligation of the entity arising from past events, the settlement of which is expected to result in an outflow from the entity of resources embodying economic benefits.* The *Framework* states that an item which meets the definition of a liability should be recognised if:

(a)   it is probable that any future economic benefit associated with the item will flow from the entity; and

(b)   the item has a cost or value that can be measured with reliability.

BC13　The Board believes that:

    (a)　an entity has an obligation under a defined benefit plan when an employee has rendered service in return for the benefits promised under the plan. Paragraphs 67–71 of the new IAS 19 deal with the attribution of benefit to individual periods of service in order to determine whether an obligation exists;

    (b)　an entity should use actuarial assumptions to determine whether the entity will pay those benefits in future reporting periods (see paragraphs 72–91 of the Standard); and

    (c)　actuarial techniques allow an entity to measure the obligation with sufficient reliability to justify recognition of a liability.

BC14　The Board believes that an obligation exists even if a benefit is not vested, in other words if the employee's right to receive the benefit is conditional on future employment. For example, consider an entity that provides a benefit of 100 to employees who remain in service for two years. At the end of the first year, the employee and the entity are not in the same position as at the beginning of the first year, because the employee will only need to work for one year, instead of two, before becoming entitled to the benefit. Although there is a possibility that the benefit may not vest, that difference is an obligation and, in the Board's view, should result in the recognition of a liability at the end of the first year. The measurement of that obligation at its present value reflects the entity's best estimate of the probability that the benefit may not vest.

Measurement date (paragraphs 56 and 57 of the Standard)

BC15　Some national standards permit entities to measure the present value of defined benefit obligations at a date up to three months before the balance sheet date. However, the Board decided that entities should measure the present value of defined benefit obligations, and the fair value of any plan assets, at the balance sheet date. Therefore, if an entity carries out a detailed valuation of the obligation at an earlier date, the results of that valuation should be updated to take account of any significant transactions and other significant changes in circumstances up to the balance sheet date.

BC16　In response to comments on E54, the Board has clarified that full actuarial valuation is not required at the balance sheet date, provided that an entity determines the present value of defined benefit obligations and the fair value of any plan assets with sufficient regularity that the amounts recognised in the financial statements do not differ materially from the amounts that would be determined at the balance sheet date.

Actuarial valuation method (paragraphs 64–66 of the Standard)

BC17　The old IAS 19 permitted both accrued benefit valuation methods (benchmark treatment) and projected benefit valuation methods (allowed alternative treatment). The two groups of methods are based on fundamentally different, and incompatible, views of the objectives of accounting for employee benefits:

(a) **accrued benefit methods** (sometimes known as 'benefit', 'unit credit' or 'single premium' methods) determine the present value of employee benefits attributable to service to date; but

(b) **projected benefit methods** (sometimes described as 'cost', 'level contribution' or 'level premium' methods) project the estimated total obligation at retirement and then calculate a level funding cost, taking into account investment earnings, that will provide the total benefit at retirement.

The differences between the two groups of methods were discussed in more detail in the Issues Paper published in August 1995.

BC18   The two methods may have similar effects on the income statement, but only by chance or if the number and age distribution of participating employees remains relatively stable over time. There can be significant differences in the measurement of liabilities under the two groups of methods. For these reasons, the Board believes that a requirement to use a single group of methods will significantly enhance comparability.

BC19   The Board considered whether it should continue to permit projected benefit methods as an allowed alternative treatment while introducing a new requirement to disclose information equivalent to the use of an accrued benefit method. However, the Board believes that disclosure cannot rectify inappropriate accounting in the balance sheet and income statement. The Board concluded that projected benefit methods are not appropriate, and should be eliminated, because such methods:

(a) focus on future events (future service) as well as past events, whereas accrued benefit methods focus only on past events;

(b) generate a liability which does not represent a measure of any real amount and can be described only as the result of cost allocations; and

(c) do not attempt to measure fair value and cannot, therefore, be used in a business combination, as required by IAS 22 *Business Combinations.*[*] If an entity uses an accrued benefit method in a business combination, it would not be feasible for the entity to use a projected benefit method to account for the same obligation in subsequent periods.

BC20   The old IAS 19 did not specify which forms of accrued benefit valuation method should be permitted under the benchmark treatment. The new IAS 19 requires a single accrued benefit method: the most widely used accrued benefit method, which is known as the Projected Unit Credit Method (sometimes known as the 'accrued benefit method pro-rated on service' or as the 'benefit/years of service method').

---

[*]   IAS 22 was withdrawn in 2004 and replaced by IFRS 3 *Business Combinations*.

BC21 The Board acknowledges that the elimination of projected benefit methods, and of accrued benefit methods other than the Projected Unit Credit Method, has cost implications. However, with modern computing power, it will be only marginally more expensive to run a valuation on two different bases and the advantages of improved comparability will outweigh the additional cost.

BC22 An actuary may sometimes, for example, in the case of a closed fund, recommend a method other than the Projected Unit Credit Method for funding purposes. Nevertheless, the Board agreed to require the use of the Projected Unit Credit Method in all cases because that method is more consistent with the accounting objectives laid down in the new IAS 19.

Attributing benefit to periods of service (paragraphs 67–71 of the Standard)

BC23 As explained in paragraph BC13 above, the Board believes that an entity has an obligation under a defined benefit plan when an employee has rendered service in return for the benefits promised under the plan. The Board considered three alternative methods of accounting for a defined benefit plan which attributes different amounts of benefit to different periods:

(a) apportion the entire benefit on a straight-line basis over the entire period to the date when further service by the employee will lead to no material amount of further benefits under the plan, other than from further salary increases;

(b) apportion benefit under the plan's benefit formula. However, a straight-line basis should be used if the plan's benefit formula attributes a materially higher benefit to later years; or

(c) apportion the benefit that vests at each interim date on a straight-line basis over the period between that date and the previous interim vesting date.

The three methods are illustrated by the following two examples.

Example 1

A plan provides a benefit of 400 if an employee retires after more than ten and less than twenty years of service and a further benefit of 100 (500 in total) if an employee retires after twenty or more years of service.

The amounts attributed to each year are as follows:

	Years 1–10	Years 11–20
Method (a)	25	25
Method (b)	40	10
Method (c)	40	10

> **Example 2**
>
> A plan provides a benefit of 100 if an employee retires after more than ten and less than twenty years of service and a further benefit of 400 (500 in total) if an employee retires after twenty or more years of service.
>
> *The amounts attributed to each year are as follows:*
>
> | | Years 1–10 | Years 11–20 |
> |---|---|---|
> | Method (a) | 25 | 25 |
> | Method (b) | 25 | 25 |
> | Method (c) | 10 | 40 |
>
> *Note: this plan attributes a higher benefit to later years, whereas the plan in Example 1 attributes a higher benefit to earlier years.*

BC24   In approving E54, the Board adopted method (a) on the grounds that this method was the most straightforward and that there were no compelling reasons to attribute different amounts of benefit to different years, as would occur under either of the other methods.

BC25   A significant minority of commentators on E54 favoured following the benefit formula (or alternatively, if the final Standard were to retain straight-line attribution, the recognition of a minimum liability based on the benefit formula). The Board agreed with these comments and decided to require method (b).

Actuarial assumptions: discount rate (paragraphs 78–82 of the Standard)

BC26   One of the most important issues in measuring defined benefit obligations is the selection of the criteria used to determine the discount rate. According to the old IAS 19, the discount rate assumed in determining the actuarial present value of promised retirement benefits reflected the long-term rates, or an approximation thereto, at which such obligations are expected to be settled. The Board rejected the use of such a rate because it is not relevant for an entity that does not contemplate settlement and it is an artificial construct, as there may be no market for settlement of such obligations.

BC27   Some believe that, for funded benefits, the discount rate should be the expected rate of return on the plan assets actually held by a plan, on the grounds that the return on plan assets represents faithfully the expected ultimate cash outflow (ie future contributions). The Board rejected this approach because the fact that a fund has chosen to invest in certain kinds of asset does not affect the nature or amount of the obligation. In particular, assets with a higher expected return carry more risk and an entity should not recognise a smaller liability merely because the plan has chosen to invest in riskier assets with a higher expected return. Therefore, the measurement of the obligation should be independent of the measurement of any plan assets actually held by a plan.

BC28   The most significant decision is whether the discount rate should be a risk-adjusted rate (one that attempts to capture the risks associated with the obligation). Some argue that the most appropriate risk-adjusted rate is given by the expected return on an appropriate portfolio of plan assets that would, over the long term, provide an effective hedge against such an obligation. An appropriate portfolio might include:

   (a)   fixed-interest securities for obligations to former employees to the extent that the obligations are not linked, in form or in substance, to inflation;

   (b)   index-linked securities for index-linked obligations to former employees; and

   (c)   equity securities for benefit obligations towards current employees that are linked to final pay. This is based on the view that the long-term performance of equity securities is correlated with general salary progression in the economy as a whole and hence with the final-pay element of a benefit obligation.

   It is important to note that the portfolio actually held need not necessarily be an appropriate portfolio in this sense. Indeed, in some countries, regulatory constraints may prevent plans from holding an appropriate portfolio. For example, in some countries, plans are required to hold a certain proportion of their assets in the form of fixed-interest securities. Furthermore, if an appropriate portfolio is a valid reference point, it is equally valid for both funded and unfunded plans.

BC29   Those who support using the interest rate on an appropriate portfolio as a risk-adjusted discount rate argue that:

   (a)   portfolio theory suggests that the expected return on an asset (or the interest rate inherent in a liability) is related to the undiversifiable risk associated with that asset (or liability). Undiversifiable risk reflects not the variability of the returns (payments) in **absolute** terms but the **correlation** of the returns (or payments) with the returns on other assets. If cash inflows from a portfolio of assets react to changing economic conditions over the long term in the same way as the cash outflows of a defined benefit obligation, the undiversifiable risk of the obligation (and hence the appropriate discount rate) must be the same as that of the portfolio of assets;

   (b)   an important aspect of the economic reality underlying final salary plans is the correlation between final salary and equity returns that arises because they both reflect the same long-term economic forces. Although the correlation is not perfect, it is sufficiently strong that ignoring it will lead to systematic overstatement of the liability. Also, ignoring this correlation will result in misleading volatility due to short-term fluctuations between the rate used to discount the obligation and the discount rate that is implicit in the fair value of the plan assets. These factors will deter entities from operating defined benefit plans and lead to switches from equities to fixed interest investments. Where defined benefit plans are largely funded by equities, this could have a serious impact on share prices. This switch will also increase the cost of pensions. There will be pressure on companies to remove the apparent (but non-existent) shortfall;

(c)   if an entity settled its obligation by purchasing an annuity, the insurance company would determine the annuity rates by looking to a portfolio of assets that provides cash inflows that substantially offset all the cash flows from the benefit obligation as those cash flows fall due. Therefore, the expected return on an appropriate portfolio measures the obligation at an amount that is close to its market value. In practice, it is not possible to settle a final pay obligation by buying annuities since no insurance company would insure a final pay decision that remained at the discretion of the person insured. However, evidence can be derived from the purchase/sale of businesses that include a final salary pension scheme. In this situation the vendor and purchaser would negotiate a price for the pension obligation by reference to its present value, discounted at the rate of return on an appropriate portfolio;

(d)   although investment risk is present even in a well-diversified portfolio of equity securities, any general decline in securities would, in the long term, be reflected in declining salaries. Since employees accepted that risk by agreeing to a final salary plan, the exclusion of that risk from the measurement of the obligation would introduce a systematic bias into the measurement; and

(e)   time-honoured funding practices in some countries use the expected return on an appropriate portfolio as the discount rate. Although funding considerations are distinct from accounting issues, the long history of this approach calls for careful scrutiny of any other proposed approach.

BC30   Those who oppose a risk-adjusted rate argue that:

(a)   it is incorrect to look at returns on assets in determining the discount rate for liabilities;

(b)   if a sufficiently strong correlation between asset returns and final pay actually existed, a market for final salary obligations would develop, yet this has not happened. Furthermore, where any such apparent correlation does exist, it is not clear whether the correlation results from shared characteristics of the portfolio and the obligations or from changes in the contractual pension promise;

(c)   the return on equity securities does not correlate with other risks associated with defined benefit plans, such as variability in mortality, timing of retirement, disability and adverse selection;

(d)   in order to evaluate a liability with uncertain cash flows, an entity would normally use a discount rate lower than the risk-free rate, yet the expected return on an appropriate portfolio is higher than the risk-free rate;

(e)   the assertion that final salary is strongly correlated with asset returns implies that final salary will tend to decrease if asset prices fall, yet experience shows that salaries tend not to decline;

(f)   the notion that equities are not risky in the long term, and the associated notion of long-term value, are based on the fallacious view that the market always bounces back after a crash. Shareholders do not get credit in the market for any additional long-term value if they sell their shares today.

Even if some correlation exists over long periods, benefits must be paid as they become due. An entity that funds its obligations with equity securities runs the risk that equity prices may be down when benefits must be paid. Also, the hypothesis that the real return on equities is uncorrelated with inflation does not mean that equities offer a risk-free return, even in the long term; and

(g) the expected long-term rate of return on an appropriate portfolio cannot be determined sufficiently objectively in practice to provide an adequate basis for an accounting standard. The practical difficulties include specifying the characteristics of the appropriate portfolio, selecting the time horizon for estimating returns on the portfolio and estimating those returns.

BC31 The Board has not identified clear evidence that the expected return on an appropriate portfolio of assets provides a relevant and reliable indication of the risks associated with a defined benefit obligation, or that such a rate can be determined with reasonable objectivity. Therefore, the Board decided that the discount rate should reflect the time value of money but should not attempt to capture those risks. Furthermore, the discount rate should not reflect the entity's own credit rating, as otherwise an entity with a lower credit rating would recognise a smaller liability. The rate that best achieves these objectives is the yield on high quality corporate bonds. In countries where there is no deep market in such bonds, the yield on government bonds should be used.

BC32 Another issue is whether the discount rate should be the long-term average rate, based on past experience over a number of years, or the current market yield at the balance sheet date for an obligation of the appropriate term. Those who support a long-term average rate argue that:

(a) a long-term approach is consistent with the transaction-based historical cost approach that is either required or permitted in other International Accounting Standards;

(b) point in time estimates pursue a level of precision that is not attainable in practice and lead to volatility in reported profit that may not be a faithful representation of changes in the obligation but may simply reflect an unavoidable inability to predict accurately the future events that are anticipated in making period-to-period measures;

(c) for an obligation based on final salary, neither market annuity prices nor simulation by discounting expected future cash flows can determine an unambiguous annuity price; and

(d) over the long term, a suitable portfolio of plan assets may provide a reasonably effective hedge against an employee benefit obligation that increases in line with salary growth. However, there is much less assurance that, at a given measurement date, market interest rates will match the salary growth built into the obligation.

BC33 The Board decided that the discount rate should be determined by reference to market yields at the balance sheet date as:

(a) there is no rational basis for expecting efficient market prices to drift towards any assumed long-term average, because prices in a market of sufficient liquidity and depth incorporate all publicly available information and are more relevant and reliable than an estimate of long-term trends by any individual market participant;

(b) the cost of benefits attributed to service during the current period should reflect prices of that period;

(c) if expected future benefits are defined in terms of projected future salaries that reflect current estimates of future inflation rates, the discount rate should be based on current market interest rates (in nominal terms), as these also reflect current market expectations of inflation rates; and

(d) if plan assets are measured at a current value (ie fair value), the related obligation should be discounted at a current discount rate in order to avoid introducing irrelevant volatility through a difference in the measurement basis.

BC34 The reference to market yields at the balance sheet date does not mean that short-term discount rates should be used to discount long-term obligations. The new IAS 19 requires that the discount rate should reflect market yields (at the balance sheet date) on bonds with an expected term consistent with the expected term of the obligations.

Actuarial assumptions: salaries, benefits and medical costs (paragraphs 83–91 of the Standard)

BC35 Some argue that estimates of future increases in salaries, benefits and medical costs should not affect the measurement of assets and liabilities until they are granted, on the grounds that:

(a) future increases are future events; and

(b) such estimates are too subjective.

BC36 The Board believes that the assumptions are used not to determine whether an obligation exists, but to measure an existing obligation on a basis which provides the most relevant measure of the estimated outflow of resources. If no increase is assumed, this is an implicit assumption that no change will occur and it would be misleading to assume no change if an entity expects a change. The new IAS 19 maintains the existing requirement that measurement should take account of estimated future salary increases. The Board also believes that increases in future medical costs can be estimated with sufficient reliability to justify incorporation of those estimated increases in the measurement of the obligation.

BC37 E54 proposed that measurement should also assume future benefit increases if there is reliable evidence that those benefit increases will occur. In response to comments, the Board concluded that future benefit increases do not give rise to a present obligation and that there would be no reliable or objective way of deciding which future benefit increases were reliable enough to be incorporated in actuarial assumptions. Therefore, the new IAS 19 requires that future benefit increases should be assumed only if they are set out in the terms of the plan (or result from any constructive obligation that goes beyond the formal terms) at the balance sheet date.

Actuarial gains and losses (paragraphs 92–95 of the Standard)

BC38   The Board considered five methods of accounting for actuarial gains and losses:

(a)   deferred recognition in both the balance sheet and the income statement over the average expected remaining working life of the employees concerned (see paragraph BC39 below);

(b)   immediate recognition both in the balance sheet and outside the income statement in equity (IAS 1 *Presentation of Financial Statements* sets out requirements for the presentation or disclosure of such movements in equity)* (see paragraphs BC40 and BC41 below);

(c)   a 'corridor' approach, with immediate recognition in both the balance sheet and the income statement for amounts falling outside a 'corridor' (see paragraph BC42 below);

(d)   a modified 'corridor' approach with deferred recognition of items within the 'corridor' and immediate recognition for amounts falling outside the 'corridor' (see paragraph BC43 below); and

(e)   deferred recognition for amounts falling outside a 'corridor' (see paragraphs BC44–BC46 below).

BC39   The old IAS 19 required a deferred recognition approach: actuarial gains and losses were recognised as an expense or as income systematically over the expected remaining working lives of those employees. Arguments for this approach are that:

(a)   immediate recognition (even when reduced by a 'corridor') can cause volatile fluctuations in liability and expense and implies a degree of accuracy which can rarely apply in practice. This volatility may not be a faithful representation of changes in the obligation but may simply reflect an unavoidable inability to predict accurately the future events that are anticipated in making period-to-period measures; and

(b)   in the long term, actuarial gains and losses may offset one another. Actuarial assumptions are projected over many years, for example, until the expected date of death of the last pensioner, and are, accordingly, long-term in nature. Departures from the assumptions do not normally denote definite changes in the underlying assets or liability, but are indicators which, if not reversed, may accumulate to denote such changes in the future. They are not a gain or loss of the period but a fine tuning of the cost that emerges over the long term; and

(c)   the immediate recognition of actuarial gains and losses in the income statement would cause unacceptable volatility.

---

*   IAS 1 (as revised in 2007) requires non-owner transactions to be presented separately from owner transactions in a statement of comprehensive income.

© IASCF

BC40 Arguments for an immediate recognition approach are that:

(a) deferred recognition and 'corridor' approaches are complex, artificial and difficult to understand. They add to cost by requiring entities to keep complex records. They also require complex provisions to deal with curtailments, settlements and transitional matters. Also, as such approaches are not used for other uncertain assets and liabilities, it is not clear why they should be used for post-employment benefits;

(b) it requires less disclosure because all actuarial gains and losses are recognised;

(c) it represents faithfully the entity's financial position. An entity will report an asset only when a plan is in surplus and a liability only when a plan has a deficit. Paragraph 95 of the *Framework* notes that the application of the matching concept does not allow the recognition of items in the balance sheet which do not meet the definition of assets or liabilities. Deferred actuarial losses do not represent future benefits and hence do not meet the *Framework*'s definition of an asset, even if offset against a related liability. Similarly, deferred actuarial gains do not meet the *Framework*'s definition of a liability;

(d) the balance sheet treatment is consistent with the proposals in the Financial Instruments Steering Committee's March 1997 Discussion Paper *Accounting for Financial Assets and Liabilities*;

(e) it generates income and expense items that are not arbitrary and that have information content;

(f) it is not reasonable to assume that all actuarial gains or losses will be offset in future years; on the contrary, if the original actuarial assumptions are still valid, future fluctuations will, on average, offset each other and thus will not offset past fluctuations;

(g) deferred recognition attempts to avoid volatility. However, a financial measure should be volatile if it purports to represent faithfully transactions and other events that are themselves volatile. Moreover, concerns about volatility could be addressed adequately by using a second performance statement or a statement of changes in equity;

(h) immediate recognition is consistent with IAS 8 *Accounting Policies, Changes in Accounting Estimates and Errors*. Under IAS 8, the effect of changes in accounting estimates should be included in profit or loss for the period if the change affects the current period only but not future periods. Actuarial gains and losses are not an estimate of future events, but result from events before the balance sheet date that resolve a past estimate (experience adjustments) or from changes in the estimated cost of employee service before the balance sheet date (changes in actuarial assumptions);

(i) any amortisation period (or the width of a 'corridor') is arbitrary. In addition, the amount of benefit remaining at a subsequent date is not objectively determinable and this makes it difficult to carry out an impairment test on any expense that is deferred; and

(j) in some cases, even supporters of amortisation or the 'corridor' may prefer immediate recognition. One possible example is where plan assets are stolen. Another possible example is a major change in the basis of taxing pension plans (such as the abolition of dividend tax credits for UK pension plans in 1997). However, although there might be agreement on extreme cases, it would prove very difficult to develop objective and non-arbitrary criteria for identifying such cases.

BC41 The Board found the immediate recognition approach attractive. However, the Board believes that it is not feasible to use this approach for actuarial gains and losses until the Board resolves substantial issues about performance reporting. These issues include:

(a) whether financial performance includes those items that are recognised directly in equity;

(b) the conceptual basis for determining whether items are recognised in the income statement or directly in equity;

(c) whether net cumulative actuarial losses should be recognised in the income statement, rather than directly in equity; and

(d) whether certain items reported initially in equity should subsequently be reported in the income statement ('recycling').

When the Board makes further progress with those issues, it may decide to revisit the treatment of actuarial gains and losses.

BC42 E54 proposed a 'corridor approach'. Under this approach, an entity does not recognise actuarial gains and losses to the extent that the cumulative unrecognised amounts do not exceed 10% of the present value of the obligation (or, if greater, 10% of the fair value of plan assets). Arguments for such approaches are that they:

(a) acknowledge that estimates of post-employment benefit obligations are best viewed as a range around the best estimate. As long as any new best estimate of the liability stays within that range, it would be difficult to say that the liability has really changed. However, once the new best estimate moves outside that range, it is not reasonable to assume that actuarial gains or losses will be offset in future years. If the original actuarial assumptions are still valid, future fluctuations will, on average, offset each other and thus will not offset past fluctuations;

(b) are easy to understand, do not require entities to keep complex records and do not require complex provisions to deal with settlements, curtailments and transitional matters;

(c) result in the recognition of an actuarial loss only when the liability (net of plan assets) has increased in the current period and an actuarial gain only when the (net) liability has decreased. By contrast, amortisation methods sometimes result in the recognition of an actuarial loss even if the (net) liability is unchanged or has decreased in the current period, or an actuarial gain even if the (net) liability is unchanged or has increased;

(d) represent faithfully transactions and other events that are themselves volatile. Paragraph 34 of the *Framework* notes that it may be relevant to recognise items and to disclose the risk of error surrounding their recognition and measurement despite inherent difficulties either in identifying the transactions and other events to be measured or in devising and applying measurement and presentation techniques that can convey messages that correspond with those transactions and events; and

(e) are consistent with IAS 8 *Accounting Policies, Changes in Accounting Estimates and Errors*. Under IAS 8, the effect of changes in accounting estimates is included in profit or loss for the period if the change affects the current period only but not future periods. Actuarial gains and losses are not an estimate of future events, but arise from events before the balance sheet date that resolve a past estimate (experience adjustments) or from changes in the estimated cost of employee service before the balance sheet date (changes in actuarial assumptions).

BC43 Some commentators on E54 argued that an entity should, over a period, recognise actuarial gains and losses within the 'corridor'. Otherwise, certain gains and losses would be deferred permanently, even though it would be more appropriate to recognise them (for example, to recognise gains and losses that persist for a number of years without reversal or to avoid a cumulative effect on the income statement where the net liability returns ultimately to the original level). However, the Board concluded that such a requirement would add complexity for little benefit.

BC44 The 'corridor' approach was supported by fewer than a quarter of the commentators on E54. In particular, the vast majority of preparers argued that the resulting volatility would not be a realistic portrayal of the long-term nature of post-employment benefit obligations. The Board concluded that there was not sufficient support from its constituents for such a significant change in current practice.

BC45 Approximately one third of the commentators on E54 supported the deferred recognition approach. Approximately another third of the respondents proposed a version of the corridor approach which applies deferred recognition to amounts falling outside the corridor. It results in less volatility than the corridor alone or deferred recognition alone. In the absence of any compelling conceptual reasons for choosing between these two approaches, the Board concluded that the latter approach would be a pragmatic means of avoiding a level of volatility that many of its constituents consider to be unrealistic.

BC46   In approving the final Standard, the Board decided to specify the minimum amount of actuarial gains or losses to be recognised, but permit any systematic method of faster recognition, provided that the same basis is applied to both gains and losses and the basis is applied consistently from period to period. The Board was persuaded by the following arguments:

(a)   both the extent of volatility reduction and the mechanism adopted to effect it are essentially practical issues. From a conceptual point of view, the Board found the immediate recognition approach attractive. Therefore, the Board saw no reason to preclude entities from adopting faster methods of recognising actuarial gains and losses. In particular, the Board did not wish to discourage entities from adopting a consistent policy of recognising all actuarial gains and losses immediately. Similarly, the Board did not wish to discourage national standard-setters from requiring immediate recognition; and

(b)   where mechanisms are in place to reduce volatility, the amount of actuarial gains and losses recognised during the period is largely arbitrary and has little information content. Also, the new IAS 19 requires an entity to disclose both the recognised and unrecognised amounts. Therefore, although there is some loss of comparability in allowing entities to use different mechanisms, the needs of users are not likely to be compromised if faster (and systematic) recognition methods are permitted.

BC47   The Board noted that changes in the fair value of any plan assets are, in effect, the results of changing estimates by market participants and are, therefore, inextricably linked with changes in the present value of the obligation. Consequently, the Board decided that changes in the fair value of plan assets are actuarial gains and losses and should be treated in the same way as the changes in the related obligation.

BC48   The width of a 'corridor' (ie the point at which it becomes necessary to recognise gains and losses) is arbitrary. To enhance comparability, the Board decided that the width of the 'corridor' should be consistent with the current requirement in those countries that have already adopted a 'corridor' approach, notably the USA. The Board noted that a significantly narrower 'corridor' would suffer from the disadvantages of the 'corridor', without being large enough to generate the advantages. On the other hand, a significantly wider 'corridor' would lack credibility.

An additional option for the recognition of actuarial gains and losses: amendment adopted by the IASB in December 2004

BC48A   In 2004 the IASB published an exposure draft proposing an additional option for the recognition of actuarial gains and losses. The proposed option allowed an entity that recognised actuarial gains and losses in full in the period in which they occurred to recognise them outside profit or loss in a statement of recognised income and expense.

BC48B   The argument for immediate recognition of actuarial gains and losses is that they are economic events of the period. Recognising them when they occur provides a faithful representation of those events. It also results in a faithful representation of the plan in the balance sheet. In contrast, when recognition is deferred, the information provided is partial and potentially misleading. Furthermore, any net cumulative deferred actuarial losses can give rise to a debit item in the balance sheet that does not meet the definition of an asset. Similarly, any net cumulative deferred actuarial gains can give rise to a credit item in the balance sheet that does not meet the definition of a liability.

BC48C   The arguments put forward for deferred recognition of actuarial gains and losses are, as noted above:

(a)   immediate recognition can cause volatile fluctuations in the balance sheet and income statement. It implies a degree of accuracy of measurement that rarely applies in practice. As a result, the volatility may not be a faithful representation of changes in the defined benefit asset or liability, but may simply reflect an unavoidable inability to predict accurately the future events that are anticipated in making period-to-period measurements.

(b)   in the long term, actuarial gains and losses may offset one another.

(c)   whether or not the volatility resulting from immediate recognition reflects economic events of the period, it is too great to be acceptable in the financial statements. It could overwhelm the profit or loss and financial position of other business operations.

BC48D   The IASB does not accept arguments (a) and (b) as reasons for deferred recognition. It believes that the defined benefit asset or liability can be measured with sufficient reliability to justify its recognition. Recognition in a transparent manner of the current best estimate of the events of the period and the resulting asset and liability provides better information than non-recognition of an arbitrary amount of that current best estimate. Further, it is not reasonable to assume that existing actuarial gains and losses will be offset in future years. This implies an ability to predict future market prices.

BC48E   The IASB also does not accept argument (c) in relation to the balance sheet. If the post-employment benefit amounts are large and volatile, the post-employment plan must be large and risky compared with other business operations. However, the IASB accepts that requiring actuarial gains and losses to be recognised in full in profit or loss in the period in which they occur is not appropriate at this time because the IASB has yet to develop fully the appropriate presentation of profit or loss and other items of recognised income and expense.

BC48F   The IASB noted that the UK standard FRS 17 *Retirement Benefits* requires recognition of actuarial gains and losses in full as they occur outside profit or loss in a statement of total recognised gains and losses.

BC48G   The IASB does not believe that immediate recognition of actuarial gains and losses outside profit or loss is necessarily ideal. However, it provides more transparent information than deferred recognition. The IASB therefore decided to propose such an option pending further developments on the presentation of profit or loss and other items of recognised income and expense.

BC48H IAS 1 (as revised in 2003) requires income and expense recognised outside profit or loss to be presented in a statement of changes in equity.* The statement of changes in equity must present the total income and expense for the period, being the profit or loss for the period and each item of income and expense for the period that, as required or permitted by other IFRSs, is recognised directly in equity. IAS 1 also permits these items, together with the effect of changes in accounting policies and the correction of errors, to be the only items shown in the statement of changes in equity.

BC48I To emphasise its view that actuarial gains and losses are items of income or expense, the IASB decided that actuarial gains and losses that are recognised outside profit or loss must be presented in the form of a statement of changes in equity that excludes transactions with equity holders acting in their capacity as equity holders. The IASB decided that this statement should be titled 'the statement of recognised income and expense'.

BC48J The responses from the UK to the exposure draft strongly supported the proposed option. The responses from outside the UK were divided. The main concerns expressed were:

(a) the option is not a conceptual improvement compared with immediate recognition of actuarial gains and losses in profit or loss.

(b) the option prejudges issues relating to IAS 1 that should be resolved in the project on reporting comprehensive income.

(c) adding options to Standards is not desirable and obstructs comparability.

(d) the IASB should not tinker with IAS 19 before undertaking a comprehensive review of the Standard.

(e) the option could lead to divergence from US GAAP.

(f) deferred recognition is preferable to immediate recognition.

BC48K The IASB agrees that actuarial gains and losses are items of income and expense. However, it believes that it would be premature to require their immediate recognition in profit or loss before a comprehensive review of both accounting for post-employment benefits and reporting comprehensive income. The requirement that actuarial gains and losses that are recognised outside profit or loss must be recognised in a statement of recognised income and expense does not prejudge any of the discussions the IASB is yet to have on reporting comprehensive income. Rather, the IASB is allowing an accounting treatment currently accepted by a national standard-setter (the UK ASB) to continue, pending the comprehensive review of accounting for post-employment benefits and reporting comprehensive income.

BC48L The IASB also agrees that adding options to Standards is generally undesirable because of the resulting lack of comparability between entities. However, IAS 19 permits an entity to choose *any* systematic method of recognition for actuarial gains and losses that results in faster recognition than the minimum required by

---

* IAS 1 *Presentation of Financial Statements* (as revised in 2007) requires non-owner transactions to be presented separately from owner transactions in a statement of comprehensive income.

the Standard. Furthermore, the amount to be recognised under any deferral method will depend on when that method was first applied, ie when an entity first adopted IAS 19 or started a defined benefit plan. There is, therefore, little or no comparability because of the existing options in IAS 19.

BC48M The IASB further agrees that a fundamental review of accounting for post-employment benefits is needed. However, such a review is likely to take some time to complete. In the meantime, the IASB believes that it would be wrong to prohibit a method of recognising actuarial gains and losses that is accepted by a national standard-setter and provides more transparent information about the costs and risks of running a defined benefit plan.

BC48N The IASB agrees that the new option could lead to divergence from US GAAP. However, although IAS 19 and US GAAP share the same basic approach, they differ in several respects. The IASB has decided not to address these issues now. Furthermore, the option is just that. No entity is obliged to create such divergence.

BC48O Lastly, as discussed above, the IASB does not agree that deferred recognition is better than immediate recognition of actuarial gains and losses. The amounts recognised under a deferral method are opaque and not representationally faithful, and the inclusion of deferral methods creates a complex difficult standard.

BC48P The IASB considered whether actuarial gains and losses that have been recognised outside profit or loss should be recognised in profit or loss in a later period (ie recycled). The IASB noted that there is not a consistent policy on recycling in IFRSs and that recycling in general is an issue to be resolved in its project on reporting comprehensive income. Furthermore, it is difficult to see a rational basis on which actuarial gains and losses could be recycled. The exposure draft therefore proposed prohibiting recycling of actuarial gains and losses that have been recognised in the statement of recognised income and expense.

BC48Q Most respondents supported not recycling actuarial gains and losses. However, many argued in favour of recycling, for the following reasons:

(a) all income and expense should be recognised in profit or loss at some time.

(b) a ban on recycling is a new approach in IFRSs and should not be introduced before a fundamental review of reporting comprehensive income.

(c) to ban recycling could encourage abuse in setting over-optimistic actuarial assumptions.

BC48R The IASB notes that most items under IFRSs that are recognised outside profit or loss are recycled, but not all. Revaluation gains and losses on property, plant and equipment and intangibles are not recycled. The question of recycling therefore remains open in IFRSs. The IASB does not believe that a general decision on the matter should be made in the context of these amendments. The decision in these amendments not to recycle actuarial gains and losses is made because of the pragmatic inability to identify a suitable basis and does not prejudice the wider debate that will take place in the project on reporting comprehensive income.

BC48S   In the meantime, the IASB acknowledges the concern of some respondents that some items of income or expense will not be recognised in profit or loss in any period. The IASB has therefore required disclosure of the cumulative amounts recognised in the statement of recognised income and expense so that users of the financial statements can assess the effect of this policy.

BC48T   The IASB also notes the argument that to ban recycling could lead to abuse in setting over-optimistic assumptions. A lower cost could be recognised in profit or loss with resulting experience losses being recognised in the statement of recognised income and expense. Some of the new disclosures help to counter such concerns, for example, the narrative description of the basis for the expected rate of return and the five-year history of experience gains and losses. The IASB also notes that under a deferred recognition approach, if over-optimistic assumptions are used, a lower cost is recognised immediately in profit or loss and the resulting experience losses are recognised only gradually over the next 10–15 years. The incentive for such abuse is just as great under deferred recognition as it is under immediate recognition outside profit or loss.

BC48U   The IASB also considered whether actuarial gains and losses recognised outside profit or loss should be recognised immediately in a separate component of equity and transferred to retained earnings at a later period. Again the IASB concluded that there is no rational basis for a transfer to retained earnings in later periods. Hence, the exposure draft proposed that actuarial gains and losses that are recognised outside profit or loss should be recognised in retained earnings immediately.

BC48V   A small majority of the respondents supported this proposal. The arguments put forward against immediate recognition in retained earnings were:

    (a)   the IASB should not set requirements on the component of equity in which items should be recognised before a fundamental review of the issue.

    (b)   retained earnings should be the cumulative total of profit or loss less amounts distributed to owners.

    (c)   the volatility of the amounts means that separate presentation would be helpful.

    (d)   the impact on distributions needs to be considered.

    (e)   actuarial gains and losses are temporary in nature and hence should be excluded from retained earnings.

BC48W   In IFRSs, the phrase 'retained earnings' is not defined and the IASB has not discussed what it should mean. In particular, retained earnings is not defined as the cumulative total of profit or loss less amounts distributed to owners. As with recycling, practice varies under IFRSs. Some amounts that are recognised outside profit or loss are required to be presented in a separate component of equity, for example exchange gains and losses on foreign subsidiaries. Other such amounts are not, for example gains and losses on available-for-sale financial assets.[*]

---

[*]   IFRS 9 *Financial Instruments,* issued in November 2009, eliminated the category of available-for-sale financial assets.

BC48X   The IASB does not believe that it is appropriate to introduce a definition of retained earnings in the context of these amendments to IAS 19. The proposal in the exposure draft was based on practical considerations. As with recycling, there is no rational basis for transferring actuarial gains and losses from a separate component in equity into retained earnings at a later date. As discussed above, the IASB has added a requirement to disclose the cumulative amount recognised in the statement of recognised income and expense to provide users with further information.

BC48Y   Consideration of the implications of IFRSs on the ability of an entity to make distributions to equity holders is not within the IASB's remit. In addition, the IASB does not agree that even if actuarial gains and losses were temporary in nature this would justify excluding them from retained earnings.

BC48Z   Finally, the IASB considered whether, if actuarial gains and losses are recognised when they occur, entities should be required to present separately in retained earnings an amount equal to the defined benefit asset or liability. Such a presentation is required by FRS 17. The IASB noted that such a presentation is not required by IFRSs for any other item, however significant its size or volatility, and that entities can provide the information if they wish. The IASB therefore decided not to require such a presentation.

BC48AA IAS 19 limits the amount of a surplus that can be recognised as an asset ('the asset ceiling') to the present value of any economic benefits available to an entity in the form of refunds from the plan or reductions in future contributions to the plan.[*] The IASB considered whether the effect of this limit should be recognised outside profit or loss, if that is the entity's accounting policy for actuarial gains and losses, or treated as an adjustment of the other components of the defined benefit cost and recognised in profit or loss.

BC48BB The IASB decided that the effect of the limit is similar to an actuarial gain or loss because it arises from a remeasurement of the benefits available to an entity from a surplus in the plan. The IASB therefore concluded that, if the entity's accounting policy is to recognise actuarial gains and losses as they occur outside profit or loss, the effect of the limit should also be recognised outside profit or loss in the statement of recognised income and expense.

BC48CC Most respondents supported this proposal. The arguments opposing the proposal were:

   (a)   the adjustment arising from the asset ceiling is not necessarily caused by actuarial gains and losses and should not be treated in the same way.

   (b)   it is not consistent with FRS 17, which allocates the change in the recoverable surplus to various events and hence to different components of the defined benefit cost.

BC48DD The IASB agrees that the adjustment from the asset ceiling is not necessarily caused by actuarial gains and losses. The asset ceiling effectively imposes a different measurement basis for the asset to be recognised (present value of refunds and reductions in future contributions) from that used to derive the actuarial gains and losses and other components of the defined benefit cost

---

[*]   The limit also includes unrecognised actuarial gains and losses and past service costs.

(fair value of plan assets less projected unit credit value of plan liabilities). Changes in the recognised asset arise from changes in the present value of refunds and reductions in future contributions. Such changes can be caused by events of the same type as those that cause actuarial gains and losses, for example changes in interest rates or assumptions about longevity, or by events that do not cause actuarial gains and losses, for example trustees agreeing to a refund in exchange for benefit enhancements or a management decision to curtail the plan.

BC48EE Because the asset ceiling imposes a different measurement basis for the asset to be recognised, the IASB does not believe it is possible to allocate the effect of the asset ceiling to the components of the defined benefit cost other than on an arbitrary basis. The IASB reaffirmed its view that the adjustment arising from the asset ceiling should, therefore, be regarded as a remeasurement and similar to an actuarial gain or loss. This treatment also has the advantages of (a) being simple and (b) giving transparent information because the cost of the defined benefit promise (ie the service costs and interest cost) remains unaffected by the funding of the plan.

Past service cost (paragraphs 96–101 of the Standard)

BC49 E54 included two alternative treatments for past service cost. The first approach was similar to that used in the old IAS 19 (amortisation for current employees and immediate recognition for former employees). The second approach was immediate recognition of all past service cost.

BC50 Those who support the first approach argue that:

(a) an entity introduces or improves employee benefits for current employees in order to generate future economic benefits in the form of reduced employee turnover, improved productivity, reduced demands for increases in cash compensation and improved prospects for attracting additional qualified employees;

(b) although it may not be feasible to improve benefits for current employees without also improving benefits for former employees, it would be impracticable to assess the resulting economic benefits for an entity and the period over which those benefits will flow to the entity; and

(c) immediate recognition is too revolutionary. It would also have undesirable social consequences because it would deter companies from improving benefits.

BC51 Those who support immediate recognition of all past service cost argue that:

(a) amortisation of past service cost is inconsistent with the view of employee benefits as an exchange between an entity and its employees for services rendered: past service cost relates to past events and affects the employer's present obligation arising from employees' past service. Although an entity may improve benefits in the expectation of future benefits, an obligation exists and should be recognised;

(b) deferred recognition of the liability reduces comparability; an entity that retrospectively improves benefits relating to past service will report lower liabilities than an entity that granted identical benefits at an earlier date, yet both have identical benefit obligations. Also, deferred recognition encourages entities to increase pensions instead of salaries;

(c) past service cost does not give an entity control over a resource and thus does not meet the *Framework*'s definition of an asset. Therefore, it is not appropriate to defer recognition of the expense; and

(d) there is not likely to be a close relationship between cost—the only available measure of the effect of the amendment—and any related benefits in the form of increased loyalty.

BC52 Under the old IAS 19, past service cost for current employees was recognised as an expense systematically over the expected remaining working lives of the employees concerned. Similarly, under the first approach set out in E54, past service cost was to be amortised over the average expected remaining working lives of the employees concerned. However, E54 also proposed that the attribution period for current service cost should end when the employee's entitlement to receive all significant benefits due under the plan is no longer conditional on further service. Some commentators on E54 felt that these two provisions were inconsistent.

BC53 In the light of comments received, the Board concluded that past service cost should be amortised over the average period until the amended benefits become vested, because:

(a) once the benefits become vested, there is clearly a liability that should be recognised; and

(b) although non-vested benefits give rise to an obligation, any method of attributing non-vested benefits to individual periods is essentially arbitrary. In determining how that obligation builds up, no single method is demonstrably superior to all others.

BC54 Some argue that a 'corridor' approach should be used for past service cost because the use of a different accounting treatment for past service cost than for actuarial gains and losses may create an opportunity for accounting arbitrage. However, the purpose of the 'corridor' is to deal with the inevitable imprecision in the measurement of defined benefit obligations. Past service cost results from a management decision, rather than inherent measurement uncertainty. Consequently, the Board rejected the 'corridor' approach for past service cost.

BC55 The Board rejected proposals that:

(a) past service cost should (as under the old IAS 19) be recognised over a shorter period where plan amendments provide an entity with economic benefits over that shorter period: for example, when plan amendments were made regularly, the old IAS 19 stated that the additional cost may be recognised as an expense or income systematically over the period to the next expected plan amendment. The Board believes that the actuarial assumptions should allow for such regular plan amendments and that subsequent differences between the assumed increase and the actual increase are actuarial gains or losses, not a past service cost;

(b)   past service cost should be recognised over the remaining life expectancy of the participants if all or most plan participants are inactive. The Board believes that it is not clear that the past service cost will lead to economic benefits to the entity over that period; and

(c)   even if past service cost is generally recognised on a delayed basis, past service cost should not be recognised immediately if the past service cost results from legislative changes (such as a new requirement to equalise retirement ages for men and women) or from decisions by trustees who are not controlled, or influenced, by the entity's management. The Board decided that such a distinction would not be practicable.

BC56   The old IAS 19 did not specify the basis upon which an entity should amortise the unrecognised balance of past service cost. The Board agreed that any amortisation method is arbitrary and decided to require straight-line amortisation, as that is the simplest method to apply and understand. To enhance comparability, the Board decided to require a single method and not to permit alternative methods, such as methods that assign:

(a)   an equal amount of past service cost to each expected year of employee service; or

(b)   past service cost to each period in proportion to estimated total salaries in that period.

Paragraph 99 confirms that the amortisation schedule is not amended for subsequent changes in the average remaining working life, unless there is a curtailment or settlement.

BC57   Unlike the old IAS 19, the new IAS 19 treats past service cost for current employees differently from actuarial gains. This means that some benefit improvements may be funded out of actuarial gains that have not yet been recognised in the financial statements. Some argue that the resulting past service cost should not be recognised because:

(a)   the cost of the improvements does not meet the *Framework*'s definition of an expense, as there is no outflow or depletion of any asset which was previously recognised in the balance sheet; and

(b)   in some cases, benefit improvements may have been granted only because of actuarial gains.

The Board decided to require the same accounting treatment for all past service cost (ie recognise over the average period until the amended benefits become vested) whether or not they are funded out of an actuarial gain that is already recognised in the entity's balance sheet.

BC58   Some commentators on E54 argued that the recognition of actuarial gains should be limited if there is unamortised past service cost. The Board rejected this proposal because it would introduce additional complexity for limited benefit. Other commentators would prohibit the recognition of actuarial gains that are earmarked for future benefit improvements. However, the Board believes that if such earmarking is set out in the formal (or constructive) terms of the plan, the benefit improvements should be included in the actuarial assumptions. In other cases, there is insufficient linkage between the actuarial gains and the benefit improvements to justify an exceptional treatment.

BC59 The old IAS 19 did not specify the balance sheet treatment for past service cost. Some argue that an entity should recognise past service cost immediately both as an addition to the liability and as an asset (prepaid expense) on the grounds that deferred recognition of the liability offsets a liability against an asset (unamortised past service cost) that cannot be used to settle the liability. However, the Board decided that an entity should recognise past service cost for current employees as an addition to the liability gradually over a period, because:

(a) past service cost does not give an entity control over a resource and thus does not meet the *Framework*'s definition of an asset;

(b) separate presentation of a liability and a prepaid expense may confuse users; and

(c) although non-vested benefits give rise to an obligation, any method of attributing non-vested benefits to individual periods is essentially arbitrary. In determining how that obligation builds up, no single method is demonstrably superior to all others.

BC60 The old IAS 19 appeared to treat plan amendments that reduce benefits as negative past service cost (ie amortisation for current employees, immediate recognition for former employees). However, some argue that this results in the recognition of deferred income that conflicts with the *Framework*. They also argue that there is only an arbitrary distinction between amendments that should be treated in this way and curtailments or settlements. Therefore, E54 proposed that:

(a) plan amendments are:

(i) a curtailment if the amendment reduces benefits for future service; and

(ii) a settlement if the amendment reduces benefits for past service; and

(b) any gain or loss on the curtailment or settlement should be recognised immediately when the curtailment or settlement occurs.

BC61 Some commentators on E54 argued that such 'negative plan amendments' should be treated as negative past service cost by being recognised as deferred income and amortised into the income statement over the working lives of the employees concerned. The basis for this view is that 'negative' amendments reduce employee morale in the same way that 'positive' amendments increase morale. Also, a consistent treatment avoids the abuses that might occur if an entity could improve benefits in one period (and recognise the resulting expense over an extended period) and then reduce the benefits (and recognise the resulting income immediately). The Board agreed with this view. Therefore, the new IAS 19 treats both 'positive' and 'negative' plan amendments in the same way.

BC62 The distinction between negative past service cost and curtailments would be important if:

(a) a material amount of negative past service cost were amortised over a long period (this is unlikely, as the new IAS 19 requires that negative past service cost should be amortised until the time when those (reduced) benefits that relate to prior service are vested); or

(b) unrecognised past service cost or actuarial gains exist. For a curtailment these would be recognised immediately, whereas they would not be affected directly by negative past service cost.

~~The Board believes that the distinction between negative past service cost and curtailments is unlikely to have any significant effect in practice and that any attempt to deal with exceptional cases would result in excessive complexity.~~ *

BC62A In 2007 the IFRIC reported that practices differ for the recognition of gains or losses on plan amendments that reduce existing benefits, and that such differences in practices can lead to substantial differences in amounts that entities recognise in profit or loss. The IFRIC asked the IASB to clarify when entities should account for those plan amendments as a curtailment instead of as negative past service costs.

BC62B As part of *Improvements to IFRSs* issued in May 2008, the IASB made the distinction between curtailments and negative past service costs clearer. In particular, the Board clarified how a reduction in the extent to which future salary increases are linked to the benefits payable for past service should be treated. The Board noted that an employee is entitled to future salary increases after the reporting date only as a result of future service. Therefore, if a change to a benefit plan affects the extent to which future salary increases after the reporting date are linked to benefits payable for past service, all of the effect of that change on the present value of the defined benefit obligation should be treated as a curtailment, not a negative past service cost. This is consistent with the treatment of a change related to future service.

Recognition and measurement: an additional minimum liability

BC63 The Board considered whether it should require an entity to recognise an additional minimum liability where:

(a) an entity's immediate obligation if it discontinued a plan at the balance sheet date would be greater than the present value of the liability that would otherwise be recognised in the balance sheet;

(b) vested post-employment benefits are payable at the date when an employee leaves the entity. Consequently, because of the effect of discounting, the present value of the vested benefit would be greater if an employee left immediately after the balance sheet date than if the employee completes the expected period of service; or

(c) the present value of vested benefits exceeds the amount of the liability that would otherwise be recognised in the balance sheet. This could occur where a large proportion of the benefits are fully vested and an entity has not recognised actuarial losses or past service cost.

---

* Text deleted as a consequence of amendments by *Improvements to IFRSs* issued in May 2008.

BC64   One example of a requirement for an entity to recognise an additional minimum liability is in the US Standard SFAS 87 *Employers' Accounting for Pensions*: the minimum liability is based on current salaries and excludes the effect of deferring certain past service cost and actuarial gains and losses. If the minimum liability exceeds the obligation measured on the normal projected salary basis (with deferred recognition of certain income and expense), the excess is recognised as an intangible asset (not exceeding the amount of any unamortised past service cost, with any further excess deducted directly from equity) and as an additional minimum liability.

BC65   The Board believes that such additional measures of the liability are potentially confusing and do not provide relevant information. They would also conflict with the *Framework*'s going concern assumption and with its definition of a liability. The new IAS 19 does not require the recognition of an additional minimum liability. Certain of the circumstances discussed in the preceding two paragraphs may give rise to contingent liabilities requiring disclosure under IAS 10 *Events after the Balance Sheet Date.*[*]

Plan assets (paragraphs 102–107 of the Standard)

BC66   The new IAS 19 requires explicitly that defined benefit obligations should be recognised as a liability after deducting plan assets (if any) out of which the obligations are to be settled directly (see paragraph 54 of the Standard). This is already widespread, and probably universal, practice. The Board believes that plan assets reduce (but do not extinguish) an entity's own obligation and result in a single, net liability. Although the presentation of that net liability as a single amount in the balance sheet differs conceptually from the offsetting of separate assets and liabilities, the Board decided in issuing IAS 19 in 1998 that the definition of plan assets should be consistent with the offsetting criteria in IAS 32 *Financial Instruments: Disclosure and Presentation.*[†] IAS 32 states that a financial asset and a financial liability should be offset and the net amount reported in the balance sheet when an entity:

(a)   has a legally enforceable right to set off the recognised amounts; and

(b)   intends either to settle on a net basis, or to realise the asset and settle the liability simultaneously.

BC67   IAS 19 (revised 1998) defined plan assets as assets (other than non-transferable financial instruments issued by the reporting entity) held by an entity (a fund) that satisfies all of the following conditions:

(a)   the entity is legally separate from the reporting entity;

(b)   the assets of the fund are to be used only to settle the employee benefit obligations, are not available to the entity's own creditors and cannot be returned to the entity (or can be returned to the entity only if the

---

[*]   In September 2007 the IASB amended the title of IAS 10 from *Events after the Balance Sheet Date* to *Events after the Reporting Period* as a consequence of the revision of IAS 1 *Presentation of Financial Statements* in 2007.

[†]   In 2005 the IASB amended IAS 32 as *Financial Instruments: Presentation.*

remaining assets of the fund are sufficient to meet the plan's obligations); and

(c)   to the extent that sufficient assets are in the fund, the entity will have no legal or constructive obligation to pay the related employee benefits directly.

BC67A   In issuing IAS 19 in 1998, the Board considered whether the definition of plan assets should include a fourth condition: that the entity does not control the fund. The Board concluded that control is not relevant in determining whether the assets in a fund reduce an entity's own obligation.

BC68   In response to comments on E54, the Board decided to modify the definition of plan assets to exclude non-transferable financial instruments issued by the reporting entity. If this were not done, an entity could reduce its liabilities, and increase its equity, by issuing non-transferable equity instruments to a defined benefit plan.

Plan assets: revised definition adopted in 2000

BC68A   In 1999, the Board began a limited scope project to consider the accounting for assets held by a fund that satisfies parts (a) and (b) of the definition set out in paragraph BC67 above, but does not satisfy condition (c) because the entity retains a legal or constructive obligation to pay the benefits directly. IAS 19 (revised 1998) did not address assets held by such funds.

BC68B   The Board considered two main approaches to such funds:

(a)   a **net** approach – the entity recognises its entire obligation as a liability after deducting the fair value of the assets held by the fund; and

(b)   a **gross** approach – the entity recognises its entire obligation as a liability and recognises its rights to a refund from the fund as a separate asset.

BC68C   Supporters of a net approach made one or more of the following arguments:

(a)   a gross presentation would be misleading, because:

(i)   where conditions (a) and (b) of the definition in paragraph BC67 above are met, the entity does not control the assets held by the fund; and

(ii)   even if the entity retains a legal obligation to pay the entire amount of the benefits directly, this legal obligation is a matter of form rather than substance;

(b)   a gross presentation would be an unnecessary change from current practice, which generally permits a net presentation. It would introduce excessive complexity into the Standard, for limited benefit to users, given that paragraph 120A(c) already requires disclosure of the gross amounts;

(c)   a gross approach may lead to measurement difficulties because of the interaction with the 10% corridor for the obligation.

(i)   One possibility would be to measure the assets at fair value, with all changes in fair value recognised immediately. This might seem inconsistent with the treatment of plan assets, because changes in the fair value of plan assets are one component of the actuarial gains and losses to which the corridor is applied under IAS 19. In other words, this approach would deny entities the opportunity of offsetting gains and losses on the assets against gains and losses on the liability.

  (ii)   A second possibility would be to defer changes in the fair value of the assets to the extent that there are unrecognised actuarial gains and losses on the obligations. However, the carrying amount of the assets would then have no easily describable meaning. It would probably also require complex and arbitrary rules to match the gains and losses on the assets with gains and losses on the obligation.

  (iii) A third possibility would be to measure the assets at fair value, but to aggregate the changes in fair value with actuarial gains and losses on the liability. In other words, the assets would be treated in the same way as plan assets, except the balance sheet presentation would be gross rather than net. However, this would mean that changes in the fair value of the assets could affect the measurement of the obligation; and

(d)   a net approach might be viewed as analogous to the treatment of joint and several liabilities under paragraph 29 of IAS 37. An entity recognises a provision for the part of the obligation for which an outflow of resources embodying economic benefits is probable. The part of the obligation that is expected to be met by other parties is treated as a contingent liability.

BC68D   Supporters of a gross approach advocated that approach for one or more of the following reasons:

(a)   paragraph BC66 above gives an explanation for presenting defined benefit obligations net of plan assets. The explanation focuses on whether offsetting is appropriate. Part (c) of the 1998 definition focuses on offsetting. This suggests that assets that satisfy parts (a) and (b) of the definition, but fail part (c) of the definition, should be treated in the same way as plan assets for recognition and measurement purposes, but should be shown gross on the face of the balance sheet without offsetting;

(b)   if offsetting is allowed when condition (c) is not met, this would seem to be equivalent to permitting a net presentation for 'in-substance defeasance' and other analogous cases where IAS 32 indicates explicitly that offsetting is inappropriate. The Board has rejected 'in-substance defeasance' for financial instruments (see IAS 39 Application Guidance, paragraph AG59) and there is no obvious reason to permit it in accounting for defined benefit plans. In these cases the entity retains an obligation that should be recognised as a liability and the entity's right to reimbursement from the plan is a source of economic benefits that should be recognised as an asset. Offsetting would be permitted if the conditions in paragraph 3342 of IAS 32 are satisfied;

(c)   the Board decided in IAS 37 to require a gross presentation for reimbursements related to provisions, even though this was not previously general practice. There is no conceptual reason to require a different treatment for employee benefits;

(d)   although some consider that a gross approach requires an entity to recognise assets that it does not control, others believe that this view is incorrect. A gross approach requires the entity to recognise an asset representing its right to receive reimbursement from the fund that holds those assets. It does not require the entity to recognise the underlying assets of the fund;

(e)   in a plan with plan assets that meet the definition adopted in 1998, the employees' first claim is against the fund—they have no claim against the entity if sufficient assets are in the fund. In the view of some, the fact that employees must first claim against the fund is more than just a difference in form—it changes the substance of the obligation; and

(f)   defined benefit plans might be regarded under SIC-12 *Consolidation—Special Purpose Entities* as special purpose entities that the entity controls—and should consolidate. As the offsetting criterion in IAS 19 is consistent with offsetting criteria in other International Accounting Standards, it is relatively unimportant whether the pension plan is consolidated in cases where the obligation and the plan assets qualify for offset. If the assets are presented as a deduction from the related benefit obligations in cases where condition (c) is not met, it could become important to assess whether the entity should consolidate the plan.

BC68E   Some argued that a net approach should be permitted when an entity retains an obligation to pay the entire amount of the benefits directly, but the obligation is considered unlikely to have any substantive effect in practice. The Board concluded that it would not be practicable to establish guidance of this kind that could be applied in a consistent manner.

BC68F   The Board also considered the possibility of adopting a 'linked presentation' that UK Financial Reporting Standard FRS 5 *Reporting the Substance of Transactions*, requires for non-recourse finance. Under FRS 5, the face of the balance sheet presents both the gross amount of the asset and, as a direct deduction, the related non-recourse debt. Supporters of this approach argued that it portrays the close link between related assets and liabilities without compromising general offsetting requirements. Opponents of the linked presentation argued that it creates a form of balance sheet presentation that IASC has not used previously and may cause confusion. The Board decided not to adopt the linked presentation.

BC68G   The Board concluded that a net presentation is justified where there are restrictions (including restrictions that apply on bankruptcy of the reporting entity) on the use of the assets so that the assets can be used only to pay or fund employee benefits. Accordingly, the Board decided to modify the definition of plan assets set out in paragraph BC67 above by:

(a)   emphasising that the creditors of the entity should not have access to the assets held by the fund, even on bankruptcy of the reporting entity; and

(b)   deleting condition (c), so that the existence of a legal or constructive obligation to pay the employee benefits directly does not preclude a net presentation, and modifying condition (b) to explicitly permit the fund to reimburse the entity for paying the long-term employee benefits.

BC68H   When an entity retains a direct obligation to the employees, the Board acknowledges that the net presentation is inconsistent with the derecognition requirements for financial instruments in IAS 39 and with the offsetting requirements in IAS 32. However, in the Board's view, the restrictions on the use of the assets create a sufficiently strong link with the employee benefit obligations that a net presentation is more relevant than a gross presentation, even if the entity retains a direct obligation to the employees.

BC68I   The Board believes that such restrictions are unique to employee benefit plans and does not intend to permit this net presentation for other liabilities if the conditions in IAS 32 and IAS 39 are not met. Accordingly, condition (a) in the new definition refers to the reason for the existence of the fund. The Board believes that an arbitrary restriction of this kind is the only practical way to permit a pragmatic exception to IASC's general offsetting criteria without permitting an unacceptable extension of this exception to other cases.

BC68J   In some plans that exist in some countries, an entity is entitled to receive a reimbursement of employee benefits from a separate fund but the entity has discretion to delay receipt of the reimbursement or to claim less than the full reimbursement. Some argue that this element of discretion weakens the link between the benefits and the reimbursement so much that a net presentation is not justifiable. They believe that the definition of plan assets should exclude assets held by such funds and that a gross approach should be used in such cases. The Board concluded that the link between the benefits and the reimbursement is strong enough in such cases that a net approach is still appropriate.

BC68K   The Board's proposal for extending the definition of plan assets was set out in Exposure Draft E67 *Pension Plan Assets*, published in July 2000. The vast majority of the 39 respondents to E67 supported the proposal.

BC68L   A number of respondents to E67 proposed a further extension of the definition to include certain insurance policies that have similar economic effects to funds whose assets qualify as plan assets under the revised definition proposed in E67. Accordingly, the Board decided to extend the definition of plan assets to include certain insurance policies (now described in IAS 19 as qualifying insurance policies) that satisfy the same conditions as other plan assets. These decisions were implemented in a revised IAS 19, approved by the Board in October 2000.[*]

Plan assets: measurement

BC69   The old IAS 19 stated that plan assets are valued at fair value, but did not define fair value. However, other International Accounting Standards define fair value as 'the amount for which an asset could be exchanged or a liability settled between knowledgeable, willing parties in an arm's length transaction'. This may imply that no deduction is made for the estimated costs necessary to sell the asset (in other words, it is a mid-market value, with no adjustment for transaction costs). However, some argue that a plan will eventually have to dispose of its assets in order to pay benefits. Therefore, the Board concluded in E54 that plan assets should be measured at market value. Market value was defined, as in IAS 25 *Accounting for Investments*,[†] as the amount obtainable from the sale of an asset in an active market.

---

[*]   The definition of a qualifying insurance policy refers to a related party as defined by IAS 24 *Related Party Disclosures*. IAS 24 (as revised in 2009) amended the definition of a related party.

[†]   superseded by IAS 39 *Financial Instruments: Recognition and Measurement* and IAS 40 *Investment Property*.

BC70   Some commentators on E54 felt that the proposal to measure plan assets at market value would not be consistent with IAS 22 *Business Combinations** and with the measurement of financial assets as proposed in the discussion paper *Accounting for Financial Assets and Financial Liabilities* published by IASC's Financial Instruments Steering Committee in March 1997. Therefore, the Board decided that plan assets should be measured at fair value.

BC71   Some argue that concerns about volatility in reported profit should be countered by permitting or requiring entities to measure plan assets at a market-related value that reflects changes in fair value over an arbitrary period, such as five years. The Board believes that the use of market-related values would add excessive and unnecessary complexity and that the combination of the 'corridor' approach to actuarial gains and losses with deferred recognition outside the 'corridor' is sufficient to deal with concerns about volatility.

BC72   The old IAS 19 stated that, when fair values were estimated by discounting future cash flows, the long-term rate of return reflected the average rate of total income (interest, dividends and appreciation in value) expected to be earned on the plan assets during the time period until benefits are paid. It was not clear whether the old IAS 19 allowed a free choice between market values and discounted cash flows, or whether discounted cash flows could be used only when no market value was available. The Board decided that plan assets should be measured by techniques such as discounting expected future cash flows only when no market value is available.

BC73   Some believe that plan assets should be measured on the following basis, which is required by IAS 25 *Accounting for Investments:*†

(a)   long-term investments are carried in the balance sheet at either cost, revalued amounts or, in the case of marketable equity securities, the lower of cost and market value determined on a portfolio basis. The carrying amount of a long-term investment is reduced to recognise a decline other than temporary in the value of the investment; and

(b)   current investments are carried in the balance sheet at either market value or the lower of cost and market value.

The Board rejected this basis because it is not consistent with the basis used for measuring the related obligations.

BC74   The Board decided that there should not be a different basis for measuring investments that have a fixed redemption value and that match the obligations of the plan, or specific parts thereof. IAS 26 *Accounting and Reporting by Retirement Benefit Plans* permits such investments to be measured on an amortised cost basis.

BC75   In response to comments on E54, the Board decided that all plan administration costs (not just investment administration costs, as proposed in E54), should be deducted in determining the return on plan assets. The IASB concluded that if the actuarial assumptions used to measure the defined benefit obligation include an allowance for plan administration costs, the deduction of such costs in calculating the return on plan assets would result in double-counting them.

---

*   IAS 22 was withdrawn in 2004 and replaced by IFRS 3 *Business Combinations*.

†   superseded by IAS 39 *Financial Instruments: Recognition and Measurement* and IAS 40 *Investment Property*.

Therefore, as part of *Improvements to IFRSs* issued in May 2008, the IASB amended the definition of the return on plan assets to require the deduction of plan administration costs only to the extent that such costs have not been reflected in the measurement of the defined benefit obligation.

Reimbursements (paragraphs 104A–104D of the Standard)

BC75A   Paragraph 41 of IAS 19 states that an entity recognises its rights under an insurance policy as an asset if the policy is held by the entity itself. IAS 19 (revised 1998) did not address the measurement of these insurance policies. The entity's rights under the insurance policy might be regarded as a financial asset. However, rights and obligations arising under insurance contracts are excluded from the scope of IAS 39 *Financial Instruments: Recognition and Measurement.** Also, IAS 39 does not apply to 'employers' assets and liabilities rights and obligations under employee benefit plans, to which IAS 19 *Employee Benefits* applies'. Paragraphs 39–42 of IAS 19 discuss insured benefits in distinguishing defined contribution plans and defined benefit plans, but this discussion does not deal with measurement.

BC75B   In reviewing the definition of plan assets (see paragraphs BC68A–BC68L above), the Board decided to review the treatment of insurance policies that an entity holds in order to fund employee benefits. Even under the revised definition adopted in 2000, the entity's rights under an insurance policy that is not a qualifying insurance policy (as defined in the 2000 revision to IAS 19) are not plan assets.

BC75C   In 2000, the Board decided to introduce recognition and measurement requirements for reimbursements under such insurance policies (see paragraphs 104A–104D). The Board based these requirements on the treatment of reimbursements under paragraphs 53–58 of IAS 37 *Provisions, Contingent Liabilities and Contingent Assets*. In particular, the Standard requires an entity to recognise a right to reimbursement of post-employment benefits as a separate asset, rather than as a deduction from the related obligations. In all other respects (for example, the use of the 'corridor') the Standard requires an entity to treat such reimbursement rights in the same way as plan assets. This requirement reflects the close link between the reimbursement right and the related obligation.

BC75D   Paragraph 104 states that where plan assets include insurance policies that exactly match the amount and timing of some or all of the benefits payable under the plan, the plan's rights under those insurance policies are measured at the same amount as the related obligations. Paragraph 104D extends that conclusion to insurance policies that are assets of the entity itself.

BC75E   IAS 37 states that the amount recognised for the reimbursement should not exceed the amount of the provision. Paragraph 104A of the Standard contains no similar restriction, because the asset limit in paragraph 58 already applies to prevent the recognition of an asset that exceeds the available economic benefits.

---

*   In November 2009 the IASB amended some of the requirements of IAS 39 and relocated them to IFRS 9 *Financial Instruments*. IFRS 9 applies to all assets within the scope of IAS 39.

Limit on the recognition of an asset (paragraphs 58–60 of the Standard)

BC76　In certain cases, paragraph 54 of the new IAS 19 would require an entity to recognise an asset. E54 proposed that the amount of the asset recognised should not exceed the aggregate of the present values of:

(a)　any refunds expected from the plan; and

(b)　any expected reduction in future contributions arising from the surplus.

In approving E54, the Board took the view that an entity should not recognise an asset at an amount that exceeds the present value of the future benefits that are expected to flow to the entity from that asset. This view is consistent with the Board's proposal that assets should not be carried at more than their recoverable amount (see E55 *Impairment of Assets*). The old IAS 19 contained no such restriction.

BC77　On reviewing the responses to E54, the Board concluded that the limit on the recognition of an asset should not over-ride the treatments of actuarial losses or past service cost in order not to defeat the purpose of these treatments. Consequently, the limit is likely to come into play only where:

(a)　an entity has chosen the transitional option to recognise the effect of adopting the new IAS 19 over up to five years, but has funded the obligation more quickly; or

(b)　the plan is very mature and has a very large surplus that is more than large enough to eliminate all future contributions and cannot be returned to the entity.

BC78　Some commentators argued that the limit in E54 was not operable because it would require an entity to make extremely subjective forecasts of expected refunds or reductions in contributions. In response to these comments, the Board agreed that the limit should reflect the available refunds or reductions in contributions.

Asset ceiling: amendment issued in May 2002

BC78A　In May 2002 the Board issued an amendment to the limit on the recognition of an asset (the asset ceiling) in paragraph 58 of the Standard. The objective of the amendment was to prevent gains (losses) being recognised solely as a result of the deferred recognition of past service cost and actuarial losses (gains).

BC78B　The asset ceiling is specified in paragraph 58 of IAS 19, which requires a defined benefit asset to be measured at the lower of:

(a)　the amount determined under paragraph 54; and

(b)　the total of:

(i)　any cumulative unrecognised net actuarial losses and past service cost; and

(ii)　the present value of any economic benefits available in the form of refunds from the plan or reductions in future contributions to the plan.

BC78C   The problem arises when an entity defers recognition of actuarial losses or past service cost in determining the amount specified in paragraph 54 but is required to measure the defined benefit asset at the net total specified in paragraph 58(b). Paragraph 58(b)(i) could result in the entity recognising an increased asset because of actuarial losses or past service cost in the period. The increase in the asset would be reported as a gain in income. Examples illustrating the issue are given in part C of the implementation guidance accompanying the Standard.

BC78D   The Board agreed that recognising gains (losses) arising from past service cost and actuarial losses (gains) is not representationally faithful. Further, the Board holds the view that this issue demonstrates that IAS 19 can give rise to serious problems. The Board intends to undertake a comprehensive review of the aspects of IAS 19 that cause concern, including the interaction of the asset ceiling and the options to defer recognition of certain gains and losses. In the meantime, the Board regards as an improvement a limited amendment to prevent their interaction giving rise to unfaithful representations of events.

BC78E   Paragraph 58A, therefore, prevents gains (losses) from being recognised solely as a result of the deferred recognition of past service cost or actuarial losses (gains).

BC78F   Some Board members and respondents to the exposure draft of this amendment suggested that the issue be dealt with by removing paragraph 58(b)(i). Paragraph 58(b)(i) is the component of the asset ceiling that gives rise to the problem: losses that are unrecognised under paragraph 54 are added to the amount that can be recognised as an asset. However, deleting paragraph 58(b)(i) effectively removes the option of deferred recognition of actuarial losses for all entities that have a defined benefit asset. Removing this option would have wide reaching implications for the deferred recognition approach in IAS 19 that can be considered fully only within the context of the comprehensive review noted above.

Curtailments and settlements (paragraphs 109–115 of the Standard)

BC79   Under the old IAS 19, curtailment and settlement **gains** were recognised when the curtailment or settlement **occurred**, but **losses** were recognised when it was **probable** that the curtailment or settlement would occur. The Board concluded that management's intent to curtail or settle a defined benefit plan is not a sufficient basis to recognise a loss. The new IAS 19 requires that curtailment and settlement losses, as well as gains, should be recognised when the curtailment or settlement occurs. The guidance on the recognition of curtailments and settlements has been conformed to the proposals in E59 *Provisions, Contingent Liabilities and Contingent Assets.*

BC80   Under some national standards:

(a)   the gain or loss on a curtailment includes any unamortised past service cost (on the grounds that a curtailment eliminates the previously expected motivational effect of the benefit improvement), but excludes unrecognised actuarial gains or losses (on the grounds that the entity is still exposed to actuarial risk); and

(b)   the gain or loss on a settlement includes any unrecognised actuarial gains or losses (on the grounds that the entity is no longer exposed to actuarial risk), but excludes unamortised past service cost (on the grounds that the previously expected motivational effect of the benefit improvement is still present).

The Board considers that this approach has some conceptual merit, but it leads to considerable complexity. The new IAS 19 requires that the gain or loss on a curtailment or settlement should include the related unrecognised actuarial gains and losses and past service cost. This is consistent with the old IAS 19.

Presentation and disclosure (paragraphs 116–125 of the Standard)

BC81   The Board decided not to specify whether an entity should distinguish current and non-current portions of assets and liabilities arising from post-employment benefits, because such a distinction may sometimes be arbitrary.

BC82   Information about defined benefit plans is particularly important to users of financial statements because other information published by an entity will not allow users to estimate the nature and extent of defined benefit obligations and to assess the risks associated with those obligations. The disclosure requirements are based on the following principles:

(a)   the most important information about employee benefits is information about the uncertainty attaching to measures of employee benefit obligations and costs and about the potential consequences of such uncertainty for future cash flows;

(b)   employee benefit arrangements are often complex, and this makes it particularly important for disclosures to be clear, concise and relevant;

(c)   given the wide range of views on the treatment of actuarial gains and losses and past service cost, the required disclosures should highlight their impact on the income statement and the impact of any unrecognised actuarial gains and losses and unamortised past service cost on the balance sheet; and

(d)   the benefits derived from information should exceed the cost of providing it.

BC83   The Board agreed the following changes to the disclosure requirements proposed in E54:

(a)   the description of a defined benefit plan need only be a general description of the type of plan: for example, flat salary pension plans should be distinguished from final salary plans and from post-employment medical plans. Further detail would not be required;

(b)   an entity should disclose the amounts, if any, included in the fair value of plan assets not only for each category of the reporting entity's own financial instruments, but also for any property occupied by, or other assets used by, the entity;

(c)   an entity should disclose not just the expected return on plan assets, but also the actual return on plan assets;

(d) an entity should disclose a reconciliation of the movements in the net liability (or asset) recognised in its balance sheet; and

(e) an entity should disclose any amount not recognised as an asset because of the new limit in paragraph 58(b) of the Standard.

BC84 Some commentators on E54, especially preparers, felt that the disclosures were excessive. A particular concern expressed by several respondents was aggregation: how should an entity aggregate information about many different plans in a concise, meaningful and cost-effective way? Two disclosures that seemed to cause special concern were the analysis of the overall charge in the income statement and the actuarial assumptions. In particular, a number of commentators felt that the requirement to disclose expected rates of salary increases would cause difficulties with employees. However, the Board concluded that all the disclosures were essential.

BC85 The Board considered whether smaller or non-public entities could be exempted from any of the disclosure requirements. However, the Board concluded that any such exemptions would either prevent disclosure of essential information or do little to reduce the cost of the disclosures.

Disclosures: amendment issued by the IASB in December 2004

BC85A From a review of national standards on accounting for post-employment benefits, the IASB identified the following disclosures that it proposed should be added to IAS 19:

(a) reconciliations showing the changes in plan assets and defined benefit obligations. The IASB believed that these reconciliations give clearer information about the plan. Unlike the reconciliation previously required by IAS 19 that showed the changes in the recognised net liability or asset, the new reconciliations include amounts whose recognition has been deferred. The reconciliation previously required was eliminated.

(b) information about plan assets. The IASB believed that more information is needed about the plan assets because, without such information, users cannot assess the level of risk inherent in the plan. The exposure draft proposed:

(i) disclosure of the percentage that the major classes of assets held by the plan constitute of the total fair value of the plan assets;

(ii) disclosure of the expected rate of return for each class of asset; and

(iii) a narrative description of the basis used to determine the overall expected rate of return on assets.

(c) information about the sensitivity of defined benefit plans to changes in medical cost trend rates. The IASB believed that this is necessary because the effects of changes in a plan's medical cost trend rate are difficult to assess. The way in which healthcare cost assumptions interact with caps, cost-sharing provisions, and other factors in the plan precludes reasonable estimates of the effects of those changes. The IASB also noted that the disclosure of a change of one percentage point would be appropriate for plans operating in low inflation environments but would not provide useful information for plans operating in high inflation environments.

(d) information about trends in the plan. The IASB believed that information about trends is important so that users have a view of the plan over time, not just at the balance sheet date. Without such information, users may misinterpret the future cash flow implications of the plan. The exposure draft proposed disclosure of five-year histories of the plan liabilities, plan assets, the surplus or deficit and experience adjustments.

(e) information about contributions to the plan. The IASB believed that this will provide useful information about the entity's cash flows in the immediate future that cannot be determined from the other disclosures about the plan. It proposed the disclosure of the employer's best estimate, as soon as it can reasonably be determined, of contributions expected to be paid to the plan during the next fiscal year beginning after the balance sheet date.

(f) information about the nature of the plan. The IASB proposed an addition to paragraph 121 of IAS 19 to ensure that the description of the plan is complete and includes all the terms of the plan that are used in the determination of the defined benefit obligation.

BC85B The proposed disclosures were generally supported by respondents to the exposure draft, except for the expected rate of return for each major category of plan assets, sensitivity information about medical cost trend rates and the information about trends in the plan.

BC85C In relation to the expected rate of return for each major category of plan assets, respondents argued that the problems of aggregation for entities with many plans in different geographical areas were such that this information would not be useful. The IASB accepted this argument and decided not to proceed with the proposed disclosure. However, the IASB decided to specify that the narrative description of the basis for the overall expected rate of return should include the effect of the major categories of plan assets.

BC85D Respondents also expressed concerns that the sensitivity information about medical cost trend rates gave undue prominence to that assumption, even though medical costs might not be significant compared with other defined benefit costs. The IASB noted that the sensitivity information need be given only if the medical costs are material and that IAS 1 requires information to be given about all key assumptions and key sources of estimation uncertainty.

BC85E Finally, some respondents argued that requiring five-year histories would give rise to information overload and was unnecessary because the information was available from previous financial statements. The IASB reconfirmed its view that the trend information was useful and noted that it was considerably easier for an entity to take the information from previous financial statements and present it in the current financial statements than it would be for users to find the figures for previous periods. However, the IASB agreed that as a transitional measure entities should be permitted to build up the trend information over time.

Benefits other than post-employment benefits

Compensated absences
(paragraphs 11–16 of the Standard)

BC86   Some argue that an employee's entitlement to future compensated absences does
       not create an obligation if that entitlement is conditional on future events other
       than future service. However, the Board believes that an obligation arises as an
       employee renders service which increases the employee's entitlement
       (conditional or unconditional) to future compensated absences; for example,
       accumulating paid sick leave creates an obligation because any unused
       entitlement increases the employee's entitlement to sick leave in future periods.
       The probability that the employee will be sick in those future periods affects the
       measurement of that obligation, but does not determine whether that obligation
       exists.

BC87   The Board considered three alternative approaches to measuring the obligation
       that results from unused entitlement to accumulating compensated absences:

   (a)   recognise the entire unused entitlement as a liability, on the basis that any
         future payments are made first out of unused entitlement and only
         subsequently out of entitlement that will accumulate in future periods
         (a FIFO approach);

   (b)   recognise a liability to the extent that future payments for the employee
         group as a whole are expected to exceed the future payments that would
         have been expected in the absence of the accumulation feature (a group
         LIFO approach); or

   (c)   recognise a liability to the extent that future payments for individual
         employees are expected to exceed the future payments that would have
         been expected in the absence of the accumulation feature (an individual
         LIFO approach).

These methods are illustrated by the following example.

Example

An entity has 100 employees, who are each entitled to five working days of paid sick leave for each year. Unused sick leave may be carried forward for one year. Such leave is taken first out of the current year's entitlement and then out of any balance brought forward from the previous year (a LIFO basis).

At 31 December 20X1, the average unused entitlement is two days per employee. The entity expects, based on past experience which is expected to continue, that 92 employees will take no more than four days of paid sick leave in 20X2 and that the remaining 8 employees will take an average of six and a half days each.

Method (a):   *The entity recognises a liability equal to the undiscounted amount of 200 days of sick pay (two days each, for 100 employees). It is assumed that the first 200 days of paid sick leave result from the unused entitlement.*

Method (b):   *The entity recognises no liability because paid sick leave for the employee group as a whole is not expected to exceed the entitlement of five days each in 20X2.*

Method (c):   *The entity recognises a liability equal to the undiscounted amount of 12 days of sick pay (one and a half days each, for 8 employees).*

BC88   The Board selected method (c), the individual LIFO approach, because that method measures the obligation at the present value of the additional future payments that are expected to arise solely from the accumulation feature. The new IAS 19 notes that, in many cases, the resulting liability will not be material.

Death-in-service benefits

BC89   E54 gave guidance on cases where death-in-service benefits are not insured externally and are not provided through a post-employment benefit plan. The Board concluded that such cases will be rare. Accordingly, the Board agreed to delete the guidance on death-in-service benefits.

Other long-term employee benefits (paragraphs 126–131 of the Standard)

BC90   The Board decided, for simplicity, not to permit or require a 'corridor' approach for other long-term employee benefits, as such benefits do not present measurement difficulties to the same extent as post-employment benefits. For the same reason, the Board decided to require immediate recognition of all past service cost for such benefits and not to permit any transitional option for such benefits.

Termination benefits (paragraphs 132–143 of the Standard)

BC91 Under some national standards, termination benefits are not recognised until employees have accepted the offer of the termination benefits. However, the Board decided that the communication of an offer to employees (or their representatives) creates an obligation and that obligation should be recognised as a liability if there is a detailed formal plan. The detailed formal plan both makes it probable that there will be an outflow of resources embodying economic benefits and also enables the obligation to be measured reliably.

BC92 Some argue that a distinction should be made between:

(a) termination benefits resulting from an explicit contractual or legal requirement; and

(b) termination benefits resulting from an offer to encourage voluntary redundancy.

The Board believes that such a distinction is irrelevant; an entity offers termination benefits to encourage voluntary redundancy because the entity already has a constructive obligation. The communication of an offer enables an entity to measure the obligation reliably. E54 proposed some limited flexibility to allow that communication to take place shortly after the balance sheet date. However, in response to comments on E54, and for consistency with E59 *Provisions, Contingent Liabilities and Contingent Assets*, the Board decided to remove that flexibility.

BC93 Termination benefits are often closely linked with curtailments and settlements and with restructuring provisions. Therefore, the Board decided that there is a need for recognition and measurement principles to be similar. The guidance on the recognition of termination benefits (and of curtailments and settlements) has been conformed to the proposals in E59 *Provisions, Contingent Liabilities and Contingent Assets*. The Board agreed to add explicit guidance (not given in E54) on the measurement of termination benefits, requiring discounting for termination benefits not payable within one year.

Equity compensation benefits (paragraphs 144–152 of the Standard)

BC94 The Board decided that the new IAS 19 should not:

(a) include recognition and measurement requirements for equity compensation benefits, in view of the lack of international consensus on the recognition and measurement of the resulting obligations and costs; or

(b) require disclosure of the fair value of employee share options, in view of the lack of international consensus on the fair value of many employee share options.*

---

* Paragraphs 144–152 of IAS 19 were deleted by IFRS 2 *Share-based Payment*.

Transition and effective date (paragraphs 153–158 of the Standard)

BC95   The Board recognises that the new IAS 19 will lead to significant changes for some entities. E54 proposed to mitigate this problem by delaying the effective date of the new IAS 19 until 3 years after its approval. In response to comments on E54, the Board introduced a transitional option to amortise an increase in defined benefit liabilities over not more than five years. In consequence, the Board decided that it was not necessary to delay the effective date.

BC96   E54 proposed no specific transitional provisions. Consequently, an entity applying the new IAS 19 for the first time would have been required to compute the effect of the 'corridor' retrospectively. Some commentators felt that this would be impracticable and would not generate useful information. The Board agreed with these comments. Accordingly, the new IAS 19 confirms that, on initial adoption, an entity does not compute the effect of the 'corridor' retrospectively.

BC97   The IASB concluded that the amendments to paragraphs 7, 8(b) and 32B simply clarified the existing requirements and thus should be applied retrospectively. The amendments to the paragraphs concerning the distinction between negative past service costs and curtailments are to be applied prospectively. The IASB concluded that the cost of analysing past plan amendments using the clarified definitions and restating them would exceed the benefits.

Dissenting opinions

Dissent of Patricia L O'Malley from the issue in May 2002 of *Employee Benefits: The Asset Ceiling* (Amendment to IAS 19)

DO1   Ms O'Malley dissents from this amendment of IAS 19. In her view, the perceived problem being addressed is an inevitable result of the interaction of two fundamentally inconsistent notions in IAS 19. The corridor approach allowed by IAS 19 permits the recognition of amounts on the balance sheet that do not meet the *Framework*'s definition of assets. The asset ceiling then imposes a limitation on the recognition of some of those assets based on a recoverability notion. A far preferable limited amendment would be to delete the asset ceiling in paragraph 58. This would resolve the identified problem and at least remove the internal inconsistency in IAS 19.

DO2   It is asserted that the amendment to the standard will result in a more representationally faithful portrayal of economic events. Ms O'Malley believes that it is impossible to improve the representational faithfulness of a standard that permits recording an asset relating to a pension plan that actually has a deficiency, or a liability in respect of a plan that actually has a surplus.

Dissent of James J Leisenring and Tatsumi Yamada from the issue in December 2004 of *Actuarial Gains and Losses, Group Plans and Disclosures* (Amendment to IAS 19)

Mr Leisenring

DO1   Mr Leisenring dissents from the issue of the Amendment to IAS 19 Employee Benefits—*Actuarial Gains and Losses, Group Plans and Disclosures.*

DO2   Mr Leisenring dissents because he disagrees with the deletion of the last sentence in paragraph 34 and the addition of paragraphs 34A and 34B. He believes that group entities that give a defined benefit promise to their employees should account for that defined benefit promise in their separate or individual financial statements. He further believes that separate or individual financial statements that purport to be prepared in accordance with IFRSs should comply with the same requirements as other financial statements that are prepared in accordance with IFRSs. He therefore disagrees with the removal of the requirement for group entities to treat defined benefit plans that share risks between entities under common control as defined benefit plans and the introduction instead of the requirements of paragraph 34A.

DO3   Mr Leisenring notes that group entities are required to give disclosures about the plan as a whole but does not believe that disclosures are an adequate substitute for recognition and measurement in accordance with the requirements of IAS 19.

Mr Yamada

DO4   Mr Yamada dissents from the issue of the Amendment to IAS 19 Employee Benefits—*Actuarial Gains and Losses, Group Plans and Disclosures.*

DO5   Mr Yamada agrees that an option should be added to IAS 19 that allows entities that recognise actuarial gains and losses in full in the period in which they occur to recognise them outside profit or loss in a statement of recognised income and expense, even though under the existing IAS 19 they can be recognised in profit or loss in full in the period in which they occur. He agrees that the option provides more transparent information than the deferred recognition options commonly chosen under IAS 19. However, he also believes that all items of income and expense should be recognised in profit or loss in some period. Until they have been so recognised, they should be included in a component of equity separate from retained earnings. They should be transferred from that separate component of equity into retained earnings when they are recognised in profit or loss. Mr Yamada does not, therefore, agree with the requirements of paragraph 93D.

DO6   Mr Yamada acknowledges the difficulty in finding a rational basis for recognising actuarial gains and losses in profit or loss in periods after their initial recognition in a statement of recognised income and expense when the plan is ongoing. He also acknowledges that, under IFRSs, some gains and losses are recognised directly in a separate component of equity and are not subsequently recognised in profit or loss. However, Mr Yamada does not believe that this justifies expanding this treatment to actuarial gains and losses.

DO7   The cumulative actuarial gains and losses could be recognised in profit or loss when a plan is wound up or transferred outside the entity. The cumulative amount recognised in a separate component of equity would be transferred to retained earnings at the same time. This would be consistent with the treatment of exchange gains and losses on subsidiaries that have a measurement currency different from the presentation currency of the group.

DO8   Therefore, Mr Yamada believes that the requirements of paragraph 93D mean that the option is not an improvement to financial reporting because it allows gains and losses to be excluded permanently from profit or loss and yet be recognised immediately in retained earnings.

Guidance on implementing
IAS 19 *Employee Benefits*

This guidance accompanies, but is not part of, IAS 19.

A Illustrative example

Extracts from statements of comprehensive income and statements of financial position are provided to show the effects of the transactions described below. These extracts do not necessarily conform with all the disclosure and presentation requirements of other Standards.

Background information

The following information is given about a funded defined benefit plan. To keep interest computations simple, all transactions are assumed to occur at the year-end. The present value of the obligation and the fair value of the plan assets were both 1,000 at 1 January 20X1. Net cumulative unrecognised actuarial gains at that date were 140.

	20X1	20X2	20X3
Discount rate at start of year	10.0%	9.0%	8.0%
Expected rate of return on plan assets at start of year	12.0%	11.1%	10.3%
Current service cost	130	140	150
Benefits paid	150	180	190
Contributions paid	90	100	110
Present value of obligation at 31 December	1,141	1,197	1,295
Fair value of plan assets at 31 December	1,092	1,109	1,093
Expected average remaining working lives of employees (years)	10	10	10

In 20X2, the plan was amended to provide additional benefits with effect from 1 January 20X2. The present value as at 1 January 20X2 of additional benefits for employee service before 1 January 20X2 was 50 for vested benefits and 30 for non-vested benefits. As at 1 January 20X2, the entity estimated that the average period until the non-vested benefits would become vested was three years; the past service cost arising from additional non-vested benefits is therefore recognised on a straight-line basis over three years. The past service cost arising from additional vested benefits is recognised immediately (paragraph 96 of the Standard). The entity has adopted a policy of recognising actuarial gains and losses under the minimum requirements of paragraph 93.

Changes in the present value of the obligation and in the fair value of the plan assets

The first step is to summarise the changes in the present value of the obligation and in the fair value of the plan assets and use this to determine the amount of the actuarial gains or losses for the period. These are as follows:

	20X1	20X2	20X3
Present value of obligation, 1 January	1,000	1,141	1,197
Interest cost	100	103	96
Current service cost	130	140	150
Past service cost—non-vested benefits	–	30	–
Past service cost—vested benefits	–	50	–
Benefits paid	(150)	(180)	(190)
Actuarial (gain) loss on obligation (balancing figure)	61	(87)	42
Present value of obligation, 31 December	1,141	1,197	1,295
Fair value of plan assets, 1 January	1,000	1,092	1,109
Expected return on plan assets	120	121	114
Contributions	90	100	110
Benefits paid	(150)	(180)	(190)
Actuarial gain (loss) on plan assets (balancing figure)	32	(24)	(50)
Fair value of plan assets, 31 December	1,092	1,109	1,093

Limits of the 'corridor'

The next step is to determine the limits of the corridor and then compare these with the cumulative unrecognised actuarial gains and losses in order to determine the net actuarial gain or loss to be recognised in the following period. Under paragraph 92 of the Standard, the limits of the 'corridor' are set at the greater of:

(a)   10% of the present value of the obligation before deducting plan assets; and

(b)   10% of the fair value of any plan assets.

These limits, and the recognised and unrecognised actuarial gains and losses, are as follows:

	20X1	20X2	20X3
Net cumulative unrecognised actuarial gains (losses) at 1 January	140	107	170
Limits of 'corridor' at 1 January	100	114	120
Excess [A]	40	–	50
Average expected remaining working lives (years) [B]	10	10	10
Actuarial gain (loss) to be recognised [$^A/_B$]	4	–	5
Unrecognised actuarial gains (losses) at 1 January	140	107	170
Actuarial gain (loss) for year—obligation	(61)	87	(42)
Actuarial gain (loss) for year—plan assets	32	(24)	(50)
Subtotal	111	170	78
Actuarial (gain) loss recognised	(4)	–	(5)
Unrecognised actuarial gains (losses) at 31 December	107	170	73

Amounts recognised in the statement of financial position and profit or loss, and related analyses

The final step is to determine the amounts to be recognised in the statement of financial position and profit or loss, and the related analyses to be disclosed in accordance with paragraph 120A(f), (g) and (m) of the Standard (the analyses required to be disclosed in accordance with paragraph 120A(c) and (e) are given above in the section 'Changes in the present value of the obligation and in the fair value of the plan assets'). These are as follows.

	20X1	20X2	20X3
Present value of the obligation	1,141	1,197	1,295
Fair value of plan assets	(1,092)	(1,109)	(1,093)
	49	88	202
Unrecognised actuarial gains (losses)	107	170	73
Unrecognised past service cost—non-vested benefits	–	(20)	(10)
Liability recognised in statement of financial position	**156**	**238**	**265**
Current service cost	130	140	150
Interest cost	100	103	96
Expected return on plan assets	(120)	(121)	(114)
Net actuarial (gain) loss recognised in year	(4)	–	(5)
Past service cost—non-vested benefits	–	10	10
Past service cost—vested benefits	–	50	–
Expense recognised in profit or loss	**106**	**182**	**137**
Actual return on plan assets			
Expected return on plan assets	120	121	114
Actuarial gain (loss) on plan assets	32	(24)	(50)
Actual return on plan assets	152	97	64

Note: see example illustrating paragraphs 104A–104C for presentation of reimbursements.

B Illustrative disclosures

Extracts from notes show how the required disclosures may be aggregated in the case of a large multinational group that provides a variety of employee benefits. These extracts do not necessarily conform with all the disclosure and presentation requirements of IAS 19 and other Standards. In particular, they do not illustrate the disclosure of:

(a)   accounting policies for employee benefits (see IAS 1 **Presentation of Financial Statements**). Paragraph 120A(a) of the Standard requires this disclosure to include the entity's accounting policy for recognising actuarial gains and losses.

(b)   a general description of the type of plan (paragraph 120A(b)).

(c)   amounts recognised in other comprehensive income (paragraph 120A(h) and (i)).

(d)   a narrative description of the basis used to determine the overall expected rate of return on assets (paragraph 120A(l)).

(e)   employee benefits granted to directors and key management personnel (see IAS 24 **Related Party Disclosures**).

(f)   share-based employee benefits (see IFRS 2 **Share-based Payment**).

Employee benefit obligations

The amounts recognised in the statement of financial position are as follows:

	Defined benefit pension plans		Post-employment medical benefits	
	20X2	20X1	20X2	20X1
Present value of funded obligations	20,300	17,400	–	–
Fair value of plan assets	(18,420)	(17,280)	–	–
	1,880	120	–	–
Present value of unfunded obligations	2,000	1,000	7,337	6,405
Unrecognised actuarial gains (losses)	(1,605)	840	(2,707)	(2,607)
Unrecognised past service cost	(450)	(650)	–	–
Net liability	1,825	1,310	4,630	3,798

Amounts in the statement of financial position:				
liabilities	1,825	1,400	4,630	3,798
assets	–	(90)	–	–
Net liability	1,825	1,310	4,630	3,798

The pension plan assets include ordinary shares issued by [name of reporting entity] with a fair value of 317 (20X1: 281). Plan assets also include property occupied by [name of reporting entity] with a fair value of 200 (20X1: 185).

The amounts recognised in profit or loss are as follows:

	Defined benefit pension plans		Post-employment medical benefits	
	20X2	20X1	20X2	20X1
Current service cost	850	750	479	411
Interest on obligation	950	1,000	803	705
Expected return on plan assets	(900)	(650)		
Net actuarial losses (gains) recognised in year	(70)	(20)	150	140
Past service cost	200	200		
Losses (gains) on curtailments and settlements	175	(390)		
Total, included in 'employee benefits expense'	1,205	890	1,432	1,256
Actual return on plan assets	600	2,250	–	–

Changes in the present value of the defined benefit obligation are as follows:

	Defined benefit pension plans		Post-employment medical benefits	
	20X2	20X1	20X2	20X1
Opening defined benefit obligation	18,400	11,600	6,405	5,439
Service cost	850	750	479	411
Interest cost	950	1,000	803	705
Actuarial losses (gains)	2,350	950	250	400
Losses (gains) on curtailments	(500)	–		
Liabilities extinguished on settlements	–	(350)		
Liabilities assumed in a business combination	–	5,000		
Exchange differences on foreign plans	900	(150)		
Benefits paid	(650)	(400)	(600)	(550)
Closing defined benefit obligation	22,300	18,400	7,337	6,405

Changes in the fair value of plan assets are as follows:

	Defined benefit pension plans	
	20X2	20X1
Opening fair value of plan assets	17,280	9,200
Expected return	900	650
Actuarial gains and (losses)	(300)	1,600
Assets distributed on settlements	(400)	–
Contributions by employer	700	350
Assets acquired in a business combination	–	6,000
Exchange differences on foreign plans	890	(120)
Benefits paid	(650)	(400)
	18,420	17,280

The group expects to contribute 900 to its defined benefit pension plans in 20X3.

The major categories of plan assets as a percentage of total plan assets are as follows:

	20X2	20X1
European equities	30%	35%
North American equities	16%	15%
European bonds	31%	28%
North American bonds	18%	17%
Property	5%	5%

Principal actuarial assumptions at the end of the reporting period (expressed as weighted averages):

	20X2	20X1
Discount rate at 31 December	5.0%	6.5%
Expected return on plan assets at 31 December	5.4%	7.0%
Future salary increases	5%	4%
Future pension increases	3%	2%
Proportion of employees opting for early retirement	30%	30%
Annual increase in healthcare costs	8%	8%
Future changes in maximum state healthcare benefits	3%	2%

Assumed healthcare cost trend rates have a significant effect on the amounts recognised in profit or loss. A one percentage point change in assumed healthcare cost trend rates would have the following effects:

	One percentage point increase	One percentage point decrease
Effect on the aggregate of the service cost and interest cost	190	(150)
Effect on defined benefit obligation	1,000	(900)

Amounts for the current and previous four periods are as follows:

Defined benefit pension plans

	20X2	20X1	20X0	20W9	20W8
Defined benefit obligation	(22,300)	(18,400)	(11,600)	(10,582)	(9,144)
Plan assets	18,420	17,280	9,200	8,502	10,000
Surplus/(deficit)	(3,880)	(1,120)	(2,400)	(2,080)	856
Experience adjustments on plan liabilities	(1,111)	(768)	(69)	543	(642)
Experience adjustments on plan assets	(300)	1,600	(1,078)	(2,890)	2,777

Post-employment medical benefits

	20X2	20X1	20X0	20W9	20W8
Defined benefit obligation	7,337	6,405	5,439	4,923	4,221
Experience adjustments on plan liabilities	(232)	829	490	(174)	(103)

The group also participates in an industry-wide defined benefit plan that provides pensions linked to final salaries and is funded on a pay-as-you-go basis. It is not practicable to determine the present value of the group's obligation or the related current service cost as the plan computes its obligations on a basis that differs materially from the basis used in [name of reporting entity]'s financial statements. [describe basis] On that basis, the plan's financial statements to 30 June 20X0 show an unfunded liability of 27,525. The unfunded liability will result in future payments by participating employers. The plan has approximately 75,000 members, of whom approximately 5,000 are current or former employees of [name of reporting entity] or their dependants. The expense recognised in profit or loss, which is equal to contributions due for the year, and is not included in the above amounts, was 230 (20X1: 215). The group's future contributions may be increased substantially if other entities withdraw from the plan.

C Illustration of the application of paragraph 58A

The issue

Paragraph 58 of the Standard imposes a ceiling on the defined benefit asset that can be recognised.

58 **The amount determined under paragraph 54 may be negative (an asset). An entity shall measure the resulting asset at the lower of:**

(a) **the amount determined under paragraph 54** [ie the surplus/deficit in the plan plus (minus) any unrecognised losses (gains)]; **and**

(b) **the total of:**

(i) **any cumulative unrecognised net actuarial losses and past service cost (see paragraphs 92, 93 and 96); and**

(ii) **the present value of any economic benefits available in the form of refunds from the plan or reductions in future contributions to the plan. The present value of these economic benefits shall be determined using the discount rate specified in paragraph 78.**

Without paragraph 58A (see below), paragraph 58(b)(i) has the following consequence: sometimes deferring the recognition of an actuarial loss (gain) in determining the amount specified by paragraph 54 leads to a gain (loss) being recognised in profit or loss.

The following example illustrates the effect of applying paragraph 58 without paragraph 58A. The example assumes that the entity's accounting policy is not to recognise actuarial gains and losses within the 'corridor' and to amortise actuarial gains and losses outside the 'corridor'. (Whether the 'corridor' is used is not significant. The issue can arise whenever there is deferred recognition under paragraph 54.)

Example 1

	A	B	C	D = A + C	E = B + C	F = lower of D and E	G
Year	Surplus in plan	Economic benefits available (paragraph 58(b)(ii))	Losses unrecognised under paragraph 54	Paragraph 54	Paragraph 58(b)	Asset ceiling, ie recognised asset	Gain recognised in year 2
1	100	0	0	100	0	0	–
2	70	0	30	100	30	30	30

At the end of year 1, there is a surplus of 100 in the plan (column A in the table above), but no economic benefits are available to the entity either from refunds or reductions in future contributions* (column B). There are no unrecognised gains and losses under paragraph 54 (column C). So, if there were no asset ceiling, an asset of 100 would be recognised, being the amount specified by paragraph 54 (column D). The asset ceiling in paragraph 58 restricts the asset to nil (column F).

In year 2 there is an actuarial loss in the plan of 30 that reduces the surplus from 100 to 70 (column A) the recognition of which is deferred under paragraph 54 (column C). So, if there were no asset ceiling, an asset of 100 (column D) would be recognised. The asset ceiling without paragraph 58A would be 30 (column E). An asset of 30 would be recognised (column F), giving rise to a gain in income (column G) even though all that has happened is that a surplus from which the entity cannot benefit has decreased.

A similarly counter-intuitive effect could arise with actuarial gains (to the extent that they reduce cumulative unrecognised actuarial losses).

Paragraph 58A

Paragraph 58A prohibits the recognition of gains (losses) that arise solely from past service cost and actuarial losses (gains).

58   **The application of paragraph 58 shall not result in a gain being recognised solely as a result of an actuarial loss or past service cost in the current period or in a loss being recognised solely as a result of an actuarial gain in the current period. The entity shall therefore recognise immediately under paragraph 54 the following, to the extent that they arise while the defined benefit asset is determined in accordance with paragraph 58(b):**

   (a)   **net actuarial losses of the current period and past service cost of the current period to the extent that they exceed any reduction in the present value of the economic benefits specified in paragraph 58(b)(ii). If there is no change or an increase in the present value of the economic benefits, the entire net actuarial losses of the current period and past service cost of the current period shall be recognised immediately under paragraph 54.**

   (b)   **net actuarial gains of the current period after the deduction of past service cost of the current period to the extent that they exceed any increase in the present value of the economic benefits specified in paragraph 58(b)(ii). If there is no change or a decrease in the present value of the economic benefits, the entire net actuarial gains of the current period after the deduction of past service cost of the current period shall be recognised immediately under paragraph 54.**

---

*   based on the current terms of the plan.

Examples

The following examples illustrate the result of applying paragraph 58A. As above, it is assumed that the entity's accounting policy is not to recognise actuarial gains and losses within the 'corridor' and to amortise actuarial gains and losses outside the 'corridor'. For the sake of simplicity the periodic amortisation of unrecognised gains and losses outside the corridor is ignored in the examples.

Example 1 continued – Adjustment when there are actuarial losses and no change in the economic benefits available

	A	B	C	D = A + C	E = B + C	F = lower of D and E	G
Year	Surplus in plan	Economic benefits available (paragraph 58(b)(ii))	Losses unrecognise d under paragraph 54	Paragraph 54	Paragraph 58(b)	Asset ceiling, ie recognised asset	Gain recognised in year 2
1	100	0	0	100	0	0	–
2	70	0	0	70	0	0	0

The facts are as in example 1 above. Applying paragraph 58A, there is no change in the economic benefits available to the entity* so the entire actuarial loss of 30 is recognised immediately under paragraph 54 (column D). The asset ceiling remains at nil (column F) and no gain is recognised.

In effect, the actuarial loss of 30 is recognised immediately, but is offset by the reduction in the effect of the asset ceiling.

	Statement of financial position asset under paragraph 54 (column D above)	Effect of the asset ceiling	Asset ceiling (column F above)
Year 1	100	(100)	0
Year 2	70	(70)	0
Gain/(loss)	(30)	30	0

In the above example, there is no change in the present value of the economic benefits available to the entity. The application of paragraph 58A becomes more complex when there are changes in present value of the economic benefits available, as illustrated in the following examples.

---

* The term 'economic benefits available to the entity' is used to refer to those economic benefits that qualify for recognition under paragraph 58(b)(ii).

Example 2 – Adjustment when there are actuarial losses and a decrease in the economic benefits available

	A	B	C	D = A + C	E = B + C	F = lower of D and E	G
Year	Surplus in plan	Economic benefits available (paragraph 58(b)(ii))	Losses unrecognise d under paragraph 54	Paragraph 54	Paragraph 58(b)	Asset ceiling, ie recognised asset	Gain recognised in year 2
1	60	30	40	100	70	70	–
2	25	20	50	75	70	70	0

At the end of year 1, there is a surplus of 60 in the plan (column A) and economic benefits available to the entity of 30 (column B). There are unrecognised losses of 40 under paragraph 54* (column C). So, if there were no asset ceiling, an asset of 100 would be recognised (column D). The asset ceiling restricts the asset to 70 (column F).

In year 2, an actuarial loss of 35 in the plan reduces the surplus from 60 to 25 (column A). The economic benefits available to the entity fall by 10 from 30 to 20 (column B). Applying paragraph 58A, the actuarial loss of 35 is analysed as follows:

Actuarial loss equal to the reduction in economic benefits	10
Actuarial loss that exceeds the reduction in economic benefits	25

In accordance with paragraph 58A, 25 of the actuarial loss is recognised immediately under paragraph 54 (column D). The reduction in economic benefits of 10 is included in the cumulative unrecognised losses that increase to 50 (column C). The asset ceiling, therefore, also remains at 70 (column E) and no gain is recognised.

In effect, an actuarial loss of 25 is recognised immediately, but is offset by the reduction in the effect of the asset ceiling.

	Statement of financial position asset under paragraph 54 (column D above)	Effect of the asset ceiling	Asset ceiling (column F above)
Year 1	100	(30)	70
Year 2	75	(5)	70
Gain/(loss)	(25)	25	0

* The application of paragraph 58A allows the recognition of some actuarial gains and losses to be deferred under paragraph 54 and, hence, to be included in the calculation of the asset ceiling. For example, cumulative unrecognised actuarial losses that have built up while the amount specified by paragraph 58(b) is not lower than the amount specified by paragraph 54 will not be recognised immediately at the point that the amount specified by paragraph 58(b) becomes lower. Instead their recognition will continue to be deferred in line with the entity's accounting policy. The cumulative unrecognised losses in this example are losses the recognition of which is deferred even though paragraph 58A applies.

Example 3 – Adjustment when there are actuarial gains and a decrease in the economic benefits available to the entity

	A	B	C	D = A + C	E = B + C	F = lower of D and E	G
Year	Surplus in plan	Economic benefits available (paragraph 58(b)(ii))	Losses unrecognised under paragraph 54	Paragraph 54	Paragraph 58(b)	Asset ceiling, ie recognised asset	Gain recognised in year 2
1	60	30	40	100	70	70	–
2	110	25	40	150	65	65	(5)

At the end of year 1 there is a surplus of 60 in the plan (column A) and economic benefits available to the entity of 30 (column B). There are unrecognised losses of 40 under paragraph 54 that arose before the asset ceiling had any effect (column C). So, if there were no asset ceiling, an asset of 100 would be recognised (column D). The asset ceiling restricts the asset to 70 (column F).

In year 2, an actuarial gain of 50 in the plan increases the surplus from 60 to 110 (column A). The economic benefits available to the entity decrease by 5 (column B). Applying paragraph 58A, there is no increase in economic benefits available to the entity. Therefore, the entire actuarial gain of 50 is recognised immediately under paragraph 54 (column D) and the cumulative unrecognised loss under paragraph 54 remains at 40 (column C). The asset ceiling decreases to 65 because of the reduction in economic benefits. That reduction is not an actuarial loss as defined by IAS 19 and therefore does not qualify for deferred recognition.

In effect, an actuarial gain of 50 is recognised immediately, but is (more than) offset by the increase in the effect of the asset ceiling.

	Statement of financial position asset under paragraph 54 (column D above)	Effect of the asset ceiling	Asset ceiling (column F above)
Year 1	100	(30)	70
Year 2	150	(85)	65
Gain/(loss)	50	(55)	(5)

In both examples 2 and 3 there is a reduction in economic benefits available to the entity. However, in example 2 no loss is recognised whereas in example 3 a loss is recognised. This difference in treatment is consistent with the treatment of changes in the present value of economic benefits before paragraph 58A was introduced. The purpose of paragraph 58A is solely to prevent gains (losses) being recognised because of past service cost or actuarial losses (gains). As far as is possible, all other consequences of deferred recognition and the asset ceiling are left unchanged.

Example 4 – Adjustment in a period in which the asset ceiling ceases to have an effect

	A	B	C	D = A + C	E = B + C	F = lower of D and E	G
Year	Surplus in plan	Economic benefits available (paragraph 58(b)(ii))	Losses unrecognised under paragraph 54	Paragraph 54	Paragraph 58(b)	Asset ceiling, ie recognised asset	Gain recognised in year 2
1	60	25	40	100	65	65	–
2	(50)	0	115	65	115	65	0

At the end of year 1 there is a surplus of 60 in the plan (column A) and economic benefits are available to the entity of 25 (column B). There are unrecognised losses of 40 under paragraph 54 that arose before the asset ceiling had any effect (column C). So, if there were no asset ceiling, an asset of 100 would be recognised (column D). The asset ceiling restricts the asset to 65 (column F).

In year 2, an actuarial loss of 110 in the plan reduces the surplus from 60 to a deficit of 50 (column A). The economic benefits available to the entity decrease from 25 to 0 (column B). To apply paragraph 58A it is necessary to determine how much of the actuarial loss arises while the defined benefit asset is determined in accordance with paragraph 58(b). Once the surplus becomes a deficit, the amount determined by paragraph 54 is lower than the net total under paragraph 58(b). So, the actuarial loss that arises while the defined benefit asset is determined in accordance with paragraph 58(b) is the loss that reduces the surplus to nil, ie 60. The actuarial loss is, therefore, analysed as follows:

Actuarial loss that arises while the defined benefit asset is measured under paragraph 58(b):	
Actuarial loss that equals the reduction in economic benefits	25
Actuarial loss that exceeds the reduction in economic benefits	35
	60
Actuarial loss that arises while the defined benefit asset is measured under paragraph 54	50
Total actuarial loss	110

In accordance with paragraph 58A, 35 of the actuarial loss is recognised immediately under paragraph 54 (column D); 75 (25 + 50) of the actuarial loss is included in the cumulative unrecognised losses which increase to 115 (column C). The amount determined under paragraph 54 becomes 65 (column D) and under paragraph 58(b) becomes 115 (column E). The recognised asset is the lower of the two, ie 65 (column F), and no gain or loss is recognised (column G).

In effect, an actuarial loss of 35 is recognised immediately, but is offset by the reduction in the effect of the asset ceiling.

	Statement of financial position asset under paragraph 54 (column D above)	Effect of the asset ceiling	Asset ceiling (column F above)
Year 1	100	(35)	65
Year 2	65	0	65
Gain/(loss)	(35)	35	0

Notes

1   In applying paragraph 58A in situations when there is an increase in the present value of the economic benefits available to the entity, it is important to remember that the present value of the economic benefits available cannot exceed the surplus in the plan.*

2   In practice, benefit improvements often result in a past service cost and an increase in expected future contributions due to increased current service costs of future years. The increase in expected future contributions may increase the economic benefits available to the entity in the form of anticipated reductions in those future contributions. The prohibition against recognising a gain solely as a result of past service cost in the current period does not prevent the recognition of a gain because of an increase in economic benefits. Similarly, a change in actuarial assumptions that causes an actuarial loss may also increase expected future contributions and, hence, the economic benefits available to the entity in the form of anticipated reductions in future contributions. Again, the prohibition against recognising a gain solely as a result of an actuarial loss in the current period does not prevent the recognition of a gain because of an increase in economic benefits.

---

*   The example following paragraph 60 of IAS 19 is corrected so that the present value of available future refunds and reductions in contributions equals the surplus in the plan of 90 (rather than 100), with a further correction to make the limit 270 (rather than 280).

IASB document published to accompany

International Accounting Standard 20

Accounting for Government Grants and Disclosure of Government Assistance

This version includes amendments resulting from IFRSs issued up to 31 December 2009.

The text of the unaccompanied IAS 20 is contained in Part A of this edition. Its effective date when issued was 1 January 1984. The effective date of the latest amendments is 1 January 2009. This part presents the following accompanying document:

page

BASIS FOR CONCLUSIONS   **B864**

Basis for Conclusions on
IAS 20 *Accounting for Government Grants and Disclosure of Government Assistance*

This Basis for Conclusions accompanies, but is not part of, IAS 20.

BC1   This Basis for Conclusions summarises the International Accounting Standards Board's considerations in amending IAS 20 *Accounting for Government Grants and Disclosure of Government Assistance* as part of *Improvements to IFRSs* issued in May 2008.

BC2   IAS 20 was developed by the International Accounting Standards Committee in 1983 and did not include a Basis for Conclusions. This Basis refers to the insertion of paragraphs 10A and 43 and the deletion of paragraph 37. Those changes require government loans with below-market rates of interest to be recognised and measured in accordance with IAS 39 *Financial Instruments: Recognition and Measurement* and the benefit of the reduced interest to be accounted for using IAS 20.

Accounting for loans from government with a below-market rate of interest

BC3   The Board identified an apparent inconsistency between the guidance in IAS 20 and IAS 39. It related to the accounting for loans with a below-market rate of interest received from a government. IAS 20 stated that no interest should be imputed for such a loan, whereas IAS 39 required all loans to be recognised at fair value, thus requiring interest to be imputed to loans with a below-market rate of interest.

BC4   The Board decided to remove this inconsistency. It believed that the imputation of interest provides more relevant information to a user of the financial statements. Accordingly the Board amended IAS 20 to require that loans received from a government that have a below-market rate of interest should be recognised and measured in accordance with IAS 39. The benefit of the government loan is measured at the inception of the loan as the difference between the cash received and the amount at which the loan is initially recognised in the statement of financial position. This benefit is accounted for in accordance with IAS 20.

BC5   Noting that applying IAS 39 to loans retrospectively may require entities to measure the fair value of loans at a past date, the Board decided that the amendment should be applied prospectively to new loans.

IASB documents published to accompany

International Accounting Standard 21

The Effects of Changes in Foreign Exchange Rates

This version includes amendments resulting from IFRSs issued up to 31 December 2009.

The text of the unaccompanied IAS 21 is contained in Part A of this edition. Its effective date when issued was 1 January 2005. The effective date of the most recent amendments is 1 January 2013. This part presents the following accompanying documents:

Approval by the Board of IAS 21 issued in December 2003

International Accounting Standard 21 *The Effects of Changes in Foreign Exchange Rates* (as revised in 2003) was approved for issue by the fourteen members of the International Accounting Standards Board.

Sir David Tweedie   Chairman

Thomas E Jones   Vice-Chairman

Mary E Barth

Hans-Georg Bruns

Anthony T Cope

Robert P Garnett

Gilbert Gélard

James J Leisenring

Warren J McGregor

Patricia L O'Malley

Harry K Schmid

John T Smith

Geoffrey Whittington

Tatsumi Yamada

Approval by the Board of *Net Investment in a Foreign Operation* (Amendment to IAS 21) issued in December 2005

Net Investment in a Foreign Operation (Amendment to IAS 21) was approved for issue by the fourteen members of the International Accounting Standards Board.

Sir David Tweedie   Chairman

Thomas E Jones   Vice-Chairman

Mary E Barth

Hans-Georg Bruns

Anthony T Cope

Jan Engström

Robert P Garnett

Gilbert Gélard

James J Leisenring

Warren J McGregor

Patricia L O'Malley

John T Smith

Geoffrey Whittington

Tatsumi Yamada

Basis for Conclusions on
IAS 21 *The Effects of Changes in Foreign Exchange Rates*

This Basis for Conclusions accompanies, but is not part of, IAS 21.

Paragraph BC1 was amended and paragraphs BC25A–BC25F were added in relation to the amendment to IAS 21 issued in December 2005.

In this Basis for Conclusions the terminology has not been amended to reflect the changes made by IAS 1 Presentation of Financial Statements (as revised in 2007).

Introduction

BC1   This Basis for Conclusions summarises the International Accounting Standards Board's considerations in reaching its conclusions on revising IAS 21 *The Effects of Changes in Foreign Exchange Rates* in 2003, and on the amendment to IAS 21 *Net Investment in a Foreign Operation* in December 2005. Individual Board members gave greater weight to some factors than to others.

BC2   In July 2001 the Board announced that, as part of its initial agenda of technical projects, it would undertake a project to improve a number of Standards, including IAS 21. The project was undertaken in the light of queries and criticisms raised in relation to the Standards by securities regulators, professional accountants and other interested parties. The objectives of the Improvements project were to reduce or eliminate alternatives, redundancies and conflicts within Standards, to deal with some convergence issues and to make other improvements. In May 2002 the Board published its proposals in an Exposure Draft of *Improvements to International Accounting Standards*, with a comment deadline of 16 September 2002. The Board received over 160 comment letters on the Exposure Draft.

BC3   Because the Board's intention was not to reconsider the fundamental approach to accounting for the effects of changes in foreign exchange rates established by IAS 21, this Basis for Conclusions does not discuss requirements in IAS 21 that the Board has not reconsidered.

Functional currency

BC4   The term 'reporting currency' was previously defined as 'the currency used in presenting the financial statements'. This definition comprises two separate notions (which were identified in SIC-19 *Reporting Currency—Measurement and Presentation of Financial Statements under IAS 21 and IAS 29*):

- the measurement currency (the currency in which the entity measures the items in the financial statements); and

- the presentation currency (the currency in which the entity presents its financial statements).

The Board decided to revise the previous version of IAS 21 to incorporate the SIC-19 approach of separating these two notions. The Board also noted that the term 'functional currency' is more commonly used than 'measurement currency' and decided to adopt the more common term.

BC5 The Board noted a concern that the guidance in SIC-19 on determining a measurement currency could permit entities to choose one of several currencies, or to select an inappropriate currency. In particular, some believed that SIC-19 placed too much emphasis on the currency in which transactions are denominated and too little emphasis on the underlying economy that determines the pricing of those transactions. To meet these concerns, the Board defined functional currency as 'the currency of the primary economic environment in which the entity operates'. The Board also provided guidance on how to determine the functional currency (see paragraphs 9–14 of the Standard). This guidance draws heavily on SIC-19 and equivalent guidance in US and other national standards, but also reflects the Board's decision that some factors merit greater emphasis than others.

BC6 The Board also discussed whether a foreign operation that is integral to the reporting entity (as described in the previous version of IAS 21) could have a functional currency that is different from that of its 'parent'.* The Board decided that the functional currencies will always be the same, because it would be contradictory for an integral foreign operation that 'carries on business as if it were an extension of the reporting enterprise's operations'† to operate in a primary economic environment different from its parent.

BC7 It follows that it is not necessary to translate the results and financial position of an integral foreign operation when incorporating them into the financial statements of the parent—they will already be measured in the parent's functional currency. Furthermore, it is not necessary to distinguish between an integral foreign operation and a foreign entity. When a foreign operation's functional currency is different from that of its parent, it is a foreign entity, and the translation method in paragraphs 38–49 of the Standard applies.

BC8 The Board also decided that the principles in the previous version of IAS 21 for distinguishing an integral foreign operation from a foreign entity are relevant in determining an operation's functional currency. Hence it incorporated these principles into the Standard in that context.

BC9 The Board agreed that the indicators in paragraph 9 are the primary indicators for determining the functional currency and that paragraphs 10 and 11 are secondary. This is because the indicators in paragraphs 10 and 11 are not linked to the primary economic environment in which the entity operates but provide additional supporting evidence to determine an entity's functional currency.

---

* The term 'parent' is used broadly in this context to mean an entity that has a branch, associate or joint venture, as well as one with a subsidiary.

† IAS 21 (revised 1993), paragraph 24

Presentation currency

BC10   A further issue is whether an entity should be permitted to present its financial statements in a currency (or currencies) other than its functional currency. Some believe it should not. They believe that the functional currency, being the currency of the primary economic environment in which the entity operates, most usefully portrays the economic effect of transactions and events on the entity. For a group that comprises operations with a number of functional currencies, they believe that the consolidated financial statements should be presented in the functional currency that management uses when controlling and monitoring the performance and financial position of the group. They also believe that allowing an entity to present its financial statements in more than one currency may confuse, rather than help, users of those financial statements. Supporters of this view believe that any presentation in a currency other than that described above should be regarded as a 'convenience translation' that is outside the scope of IFRSs.

BC11   Others believe that the choice of presentation currency should be limited, for example, to the functional currency of one of the substantive entities within a group. However, such a restriction might be easily overcome—an entity that wished to present its financial statements in a different currency might establish a substantive, but relatively small operation with that functional currency.

BC12   Still others believe that, given the rising trend towards globalisation, entities should be permitted to present their financial statements in any currency. They note that most large groups do not have a single functional currency, but rather comprise operations with a number of functional currencies. For such entities, they believe it is not clear which currency should be the presentation currency, or why one currency is preferable to another. They also point out that management may not use a single currency when controlling and monitoring the performance and financial position of such a group. In addition, they note that in some jurisdictions, entities are required to present their financial statements in the local currency, even when this is not the functional currency.[*] Hence, if IFRSs required the financial statements to be presented in the functional currency, some entities would have to present two sets of financial statements: financial statements that comply with IFRSs presented in the functional currency and financial statements that comply with local regulations presented in a different currency.

BC13   The Board was persuaded by the arguments in the previous paragraph. Accordingly, it decided that entities should be permitted to present their financial statements in any currency (or currencies).

BC14   The Board also clarified that the Standard does not prohibit the entity from providing, as supplementary information, a 'convenience translation'. Such a 'convenience translation' may display financial statements (or selected portions of financial statements) in a currency other than the presentation currency, as a convenience to some users. The 'convenience translation' may be prepared using

---

[*] This includes entities operating in another country and, for example, publishing financial statements to comply with a listing requirement of that country.

a translation method other than that required by the Standard. These types of 'convenience translations' should be clearly identified as supplementary information to distinguish them from information required by IFRSs and translated in accordance with the Standard.

Translation method

BC15   The Board debated which method should be used to translate financial statements from an entity's functional currency into a different presentation currency.

BC16   The Board agreed that the translation method should not have the effect of substituting another currency for the functional currency. Put another way, presenting the financial statements in a different currency should not change the way in which the underlying items are measured. Rather, the translation method should merely express the underlying amounts, as measured in the functional currency, in a different currency.

BC17   Given this, the Board considered two possible translation methods. The first is to translate all amounts (including comparatives) at the most recent closing rate. This method has several advantages: it is simple to apply; it does not generate any new gains and losses; and it does not change ratios such as return on assets. This method is supported by those who believe that the process of merely expressing amounts in a different currency should preserve the relationships among amounts as measured in the functional currency and, as such, should not lead to any new gains or losses.

BC18   The second method considered by the Board is the one that the previous version of IAS 21 required for translating the financial statements of a foreign operation.[*] This method results in the same amounts in the presentation currency regardless of whether the financial statements of a foreign operation are:

(a)   first translated into the functional currency of another group entity (eg the parent) and then into the presentation currency, or

(b)   translated directly into the presentation currency.

BC19   This method avoids the need to decide the currency in which to express the financial statements of a multinational group before they are translated into the presentation currency. As noted above, many large groups do not have a single functional currency, but comprise operations with a number of functional currencies. For such entities it is not clear which functional currency should be chosen in which to express amounts before they are translated into the presentation currency, or why one currency is preferable to another. In addition, this method produces the same amounts in the presentation currency for a stand-alone entity as for an identical subsidiary of a parent whose functional currency is the presentation currency.

---

[*]   This is to translate balance sheet items at the closing rate and income and expense items at actual (or average) rates, except for an entity whose functional currency is that of a hyperinflationary economy.

BC20   The Board decided to require the second method, ie that the financial statements of any entity (whether a stand-alone entity, a parent or an operation within a group) whose functional currency differs from the presentation currency used by the reporting entity are translated using the method set out in paragraphs 38–49 of the Standard.

BC21   With respect to translation of comparative amounts, the Board adopted the approach required by SIC-30 for:

(a)   an entity whose functional currency is not the currency of the hyperinflationary economy (assets and liabilities in the comparative balance sheet are translated at the closing rate at the date of that balance sheet and income and expenses in the comparative income statement are translated at exchange rates at the dates of the transactions); and

(b)   an entity whose functional currency is the currency of a hyperinflationary economy, and for which the comparative amounts are being translated into the currency of a hyperinflationary economy (both balance sheet and income statement items are translated at the closing rate of the most recent balance sheet presented).

BC22   However, the Board decided not to adopt the SIC-30 approach for the translation of comparatives for an entity whose functional currency is the currency of a hyperinflationary economy, and for which the comparative amounts are being translated into a presentation currency of a non-hyperinflationary economy. The Board noted that in such a case, the SIC-30 approach requires restating the comparative amounts from those shown in last year's financial statements for both the effects of inflation and for changes in exchange rates. If exchange rates fully reflect differing price levels between the two economies to which they relate, the SIC-30 approach will result in the same amounts for the comparatives as were reported as current year amounts in the prior year financial statements. Furthermore, the Board noted that in the prior year, the relevant amounts had been already expressed in the non-hyperinflationary presentation currency, and there was no reason to change them. For these reasons the Board decided to require that all comparative amounts are those presented in the prior year financial statements (ie there is no adjustment for either subsequent changes in the price level or subsequent changes in exchange rates).

BC23   The Board decided to incorporate into the Standard most of the disclosure requirements of SIC-30 *Reporting Currency—Translation from Measurement Currency to Presentation Currency* that apply when a different translation method is used or other supplementary information, such as an extract from the full financial statements, is displayed in a currency other than the functional currency (see paragraph 57 of the Standard). These disclosures enable users to distinguish information prepared in accordance with IFRSs from information that may be useful to users but is not the subject of IFRSs, and also tell users how the latter information has been prepared.

Capitalisation of exchange differences

BC24   The previous version of IAS 21 allowed a limited choice of accounting for exchange differences that arise 'from a severe devaluation or depreciation of a currency against which there is no practical means of hedging and that affects liabilities which cannot be settled and which arise directly on the recent acquisition of an asset'.* The benchmark treatment was to recognise such exchange differences in profit or loss. The allowed alternative was to recognise them as an asset.

BC25   The Board noted that the allowed alternative (of recognition as an asset) was not in accordance with the *Framework for the Preparation and Presentation of Financial Statements* because exchange losses do not meet the definition of an asset. Moreover, recognition of exchange losses as an asset is neither allowed nor required by any liaison standard-setter, so its deletion would improve convergence. Finally, in many cases when the conditions for recognition as an asset are met, the asset would be restated in accordance with IAS 29 *Financial Reporting in Hyperinflationary Economies*. Thus, to the extent that an exchange loss reflects hyperinflation, this effect is taken into account by IAS 29. For all of these reasons, the Board removed the allowed alternative treatment and the related SIC Interpretation is superseded.

Net investment in a foreign operation

BC25A   The principle in paragraph 32 is that exchange differences arising on a monetary item that is, in substance, part of the reporting entity's net investment in a foreign operation are initially recognised in a separate component of equity[†] in the consolidated financial statements of the reporting entity. Among the revisions to IAS 21 made in 2003 was the provision of guidance on this principle that required the monetary item to be denominated in the functional currency of either the reporting entity or the foreign operation. The previous version of IAS 21 did not include such guidance.

BC25B   The requirements can be illustrated by the following example. Parent P owns 100 per cent of Subsidiary S. Parent P has a functional currency of UK sterling. Subsidiary S has a functional currency of Mexican pesos. Parent P grants a loan of 100 US dollars to Subsidiary S, for which settlement is neither planned nor likely to occur in the foreseeable future. IAS 21 (as revised in 2003) requires the exchange differences arising on the loan to be recognised in profit or loss in the consolidated financial statements of Parent P, whereas those differences would be recognised initially in equity[†] in the consolidated financial statements of Parent P, if the loan were to be denominated in sterling or Mexican pesos.

BC25C   After the revised IAS 21 was issued in 2003, constituents raised the following concerns:

(a)   It is common practice for a monetary item that forms part of an entity's investment in a foreign operation to be denominated in a currency that is

---

*   IAS 21 (revised 1993), paragraph 21.

†   As a consequence of the revision of IAS 1 *Presentation of Financial Statements* in 2007 such differences are recognised in other comprehensive income.

not the functional currency of either the reporting entity or the foreign operation. An example is a monetary item denominated in a currency that is more readily convertible than the local domestic currency of the foreign operation.

(b) An investment in a foreign operation denominated in a currency that is not the functional currency of the reporting entity or the foreign operation does not expose the group to a greater foreign currency exchange difference than arises when the investment is denominated in the functional currency of the reporting entity or the foreign operation. It simply results in exchange differences arising in the foreign operation's individual financial statements and the reporting entity's separate financial statements.

(c) It is not clear whether the term 'reporting entity' in paragraph 32 should be interpreted as the single entity or the group comprising a parent and all its subsidiaries. As a result, constituents questioned whether the monetary item must be transacted between the foreign operation and the reporting entity, or whether it could be transacted between the foreign operation and any member of the consolidated group, ie the reporting entity or any of its subsidiaries.

BC25D The Board noted that the nature of the monetary item referred to in paragraph 15 is similar to an equity investment in a foreign operation, ie settlement of the monetary item is neither planned nor likely to occur in the foreseeable future. Therefore, the principle in paragraph 32 to recognise exchange differences arising on a monetary item initially in a separate component of equity* effectively results in the monetary item being accounted for in the same way as an equity investment in the foreign operation when consolidated financial statements are prepared. The Board concluded that the accounting treatment in the consolidated financial statements should not be dependent on the currency in which the monetary item is denominated, nor on which entity within the group conducts the transaction with the foreign operation.

BC25E Accordingly, in 2005 the Board decided to amend IAS 21. The amendment requires exchange differences arising on a monetary item that forms part of a reporting entity's net investment in a foreign operation to be recognised initially in a separate component of equity* in the consolidated financial statements. This requirement applies irrespective of the currency of the monetary item and of whether the monetary item results from a transaction with the reporting entity or any of its subsidiaries.

BC25F The Board also proposed amending IAS 21 to clarify that an investment in a foreign operation made by an associate of the reporting entity is not part of the reporting entity's net investment in that foreign operation. Respondents to the exposure draft disagreed with this proposal. Many respondents said that the proposed amendment added a detailed rule that was not required because the principle in paragraph 15 was clear. In redeliberations, the Board agreed with those comments and decided not to proceed with that proposed amendment.

---

* As a consequence of the revision of IAS 1 *Presentation of Financial Statements* in 2007 such differences are recognised in other comprehensive income.

Goodwill and fair value adjustments

BC26   The previous version of IAS 21 allowed a choice of translating goodwill and fair value adjustments to assets and liabilities that arise on the acquisition of a foreign entity at (a) the closing rate or (b) the historical transaction rate.

BC27   The Board agreed that, conceptually, the correct treatment depends on whether goodwill and fair value adjustments are part of:

(a)   the assets and liabilities of the acquired entity (which would imply translating them at the closing rate); or

(b)   the assets and liabilities of the parent (which would imply translating them at the historical rate).

BC28   The Board agreed that fair value adjustments clearly relate to the identifiable assets and liabilities of the acquired entity and should therefore be translated at the closing rate.

BC29   Goodwill is more complex, partly because it is measured as a residual. In addition, the Board noted that difficult issues can arise when the acquired entity comprises businesses that have different functional currencies (eg if the acquired entity is a multinational group). The Board discussed how to assess any resulting goodwill for impairment and, in particular, whether the goodwill would need to be 'pushed down' to the level of each different functional currency or could be accounted for and assessed at a higher level.

BC30   One view is that when the parent acquires a multinational operation comprising businesses with many different functional currencies, any goodwill may be treated as an asset of the parent/acquirer and tested for impairment at a consolidated level. Those who support this view believe that, in economic terms, the goodwill is an asset of the parent because it is part of the acquisition price paid by the parent. Thus, they believe, it would be incorrect to allocate the goodwill to the many acquired businesses and translate it into their various functional currencies. Rather, the goodwill, being treated as an asset of the parent, is not exposed to foreign currency risks, and translation differences associated with it should not be recognised. In addition, they believe that such goodwill should be tested for impairment at a consolidated level. Under this view, allocating or 'pushing down' the goodwill to a lower level, such as each different functional currency within the acquired foreign operation, would not serve any purpose.

BC31   Others take a different view. They believe that the goodwill is part of the parent's net investment in the acquired entity. In their view, goodwill should be treated no differently from other assets of the acquired entity, in particular intangible assets, because a significant part of the goodwill is likely to comprise intangible assets that do not qualify for separate recognition. They also note that goodwill arises only because of the investment in the foreign entity and has no existence apart from that entity. Lastly, they point out that when the acquired entity comprises a number of businesses with different functional currencies, the cash flows that support the continued recognition of goodwill are generated in those different functional currencies.

BC32 The Board was persuaded by the reasons set out in the preceding paragraph and decided that goodwill is treated as an asset of the foreign operation and translated at the closing rate. Consequently, goodwill should be allocated to the level of each functional currency of the acquired foreign operation. This means that the level to which goodwill is allocated for foreign currency translation purposes may be different from the level at which the goodwill is tested for impairment. Entities follow the requirements in IAS 36 *Impairment of Assets* to determine the level at which goodwill is tested for impairment.

Disposal or partial disposal of a foreign operation[*]

BC33 In the second phase of the business combinations project the Board decided that the loss of control, significant influence or joint control of an entity is accounted for as a disposal for the purposes of IAS 21. Accordingly, a former parent accounts for the loss of control over a subsidiary as a disposal of the subsidiary, even if the former subsidiary becomes an associate or jointly controlled entity of the former parent. Similarly an investor accounts for the loss of significant influence over an associate or the loss of joint control over a jointly controlled entity as a disposal. The Board decided that the change in the nature of the investment is a significant economic event.

BC34 The Board also decided in the second phase of the business combinations project that:

 (a) changes in the parent's ownership interest in a subsidiary that do not result in a loss of control are accounted for as equity transactions (ie transactions with owners in their capacity as owners);

 (b) if a parent loses control of a subsidiary, the parent reclassifies from equity to profit or loss (as a reclassification adjustment) the parent's share of the exchange differences recognised in other comprehensive income relating to a foreign operation in that subsidiary; and

 (c) if an investor loses significant influence over an associate or loses joint control over a jointly controlled entity, the investor reclassifies from equity to profit or loss (as a reclassification adjustment) the exchange differences recognised in other comprehensive income relating to a foreign operation in that associate or jointly controlled entity.

 The amendments in paragraphs 48A–49 of the Standard reflect those decisions for the disposal or partial disposal of a foreign operation.

BC35 As part of *Cost of an Investment in a Subsidiary, Jointly Controlled Entity or Associate (Amendments to IFRS 1 First-time Adoption of International Financial Reporting Standards and IAS 27 Consolidated and Separate Financial Statements)*, issued in May 2008, the Board amended IAS 27 to remove the definition of the 'cost method'. The cost method required an entity to recognise distributions as income only if they came from post-acquisition retained earnings. Distributions received in excess of such profits were regarded as a recovery of the investment and were

---

[*] This heading and paragraphs BC33 and BC34 were added as a consequence of amendments to IAS 27 *Consolidated and Separate Financial Statements* made as part of the second phase of the business combinations project in 2008.

recognised as a reduction of its cost. Consequently, the Board amended paragraph 49 to remove the reference to pre-acquisition profits and to clarify that a dividend accounted for in accordance with paragraph 38A of IAS 27 cannot be a disposal or partial disposal of a net investment in IAS 21.

IASB documents published to accompany

International Accounting Standard 23

Borrowing Costs

This version includes amendments resulting from IFRSs issued up to 31 December 2009.

The text of the unaccompanied IAS 23 is contained in Part A of this edition. Its effective date when issued was 1 January 2009. The effective date of the amendments is also 1 January 2009. This part presents the following accompanying documents:

Approval by the Board of IAS 23 issued in March 2007

International Accounting Standard 23 *Borrowing Costs* (as revised in 2007) was approved for issue by eleven of the fourteen members of the International Accounting Standards Board. Messrs Cope, Danjou and Garnett dissented. Their dissenting opinions are set out after the Basis for Conclusions.

Sir David Tweedie	Chairman
Thomas E Jones	Vice-Chairman
Mary E Barth	
Hans-Georg Bruns	
Anthony T Cope	
Philippe Danjou	
Jan Engström	
Robert P Garnett	
Gilbert Gélard	
James J Leisenring	
Warren J McGregor	
Patricia L O'Malley	
John T Smith	
Tatsumi Yamada	

Basis for Conclusions on
IAS 23 *Borrowing Costs*

This Basis for Conclusions accompanies, but is not part of, IAS 23.

Introduction

BC1　This Basis for Conclusions summarises the International Accounting Standards Board's considerations in reaching its conclusions on revising IAS 23 *Borrowing Costs* in 2007. Individual Board members gave greater weight to some factors than to others.

BC2　The revisions to IAS 23 result from the Board's Short-term Convergence project. The project is being conducted jointly with the United States standard-setter, the Financial Accounting Standards Board (FASB). The objective of the project is to reduce differences between IFRSs and US generally accepted accounting principles (GAAP) that are capable of resolution in a relatively short time and can be addressed outside major projects. The revisions to IAS 23 are principally concerned with the elimination of one of the two treatments that exist for borrowing costs directly attributable to the acquisition, construction or production of a qualifying asset. The application of only one method will enhance comparability. For the reasons set out below, the Board decided to eliminate the option of immediate recognition of such borrowing costs as an expense. It believes this will result in an improvement in financial reporting as well as achieving convergence in principle with US GAAP.

BC3　The Board considered whether to seek convergence on the detailed requirements for the capitalisation of borrowing costs directly attributable to the acquisition, construction or production of a qualifying asset. However, the Board noted statements by the US Securities and Exchange Commission (SEC) and the European Commission that the IASB and FASB should focus their short-term convergence effort on eliminating major differences of principle between IFRSs and US GAAP. For their purposes, convergence on the detailed aspects of accounting treatments is not necessary. The Board further noted that both IAS 23 and SFAS 34 *Capitalization of Interest Cost* were developed some years ago. Consequently, neither set of specific provisions may be regarded as being of a clearly higher quality than the other. Therefore, the Board concluded that it should not spend time and resources considering aspects of IAS 23 beyond the choice between capitalisation and immediate recognition as an expense. This Basis for Conclusions does not, therefore, discuss aspects of IAS 23 that the Board did not reconsider. Paragraphs BC19–BC26 analyse the differences between IAS 23 and SFAS 34.

Amendments to the scope

Assets measured at fair value

BC4　The exposure draft of proposed amendments to IAS 23 proposed excluding from the scope of IAS 23 assets measured at fair value. Some respondents objected to the proposal, interpreting the scope exclusion as limiting capitalisation of borrowing costs to qualifying assets measured at cost. The Board confirmed its decision not to require capitalisation of borrowing costs relating to assets that are measured at fair value. The measurement of such assets will not be affected by the amount of borrowing costs incurred during their construction or production period. Therefore, requirements on how to account for borrowing costs are unnecessary, as paragraphs B61 and B62 of the Basis for Conclusions on IAS 41 *Agriculture* explain. But the Board noted that the exclusion of assets measured at fair value from the requirements of IAS 23 does not prohibit an entity from presenting items in profit or loss as if borrowing costs had been capitalised on such assets before measuring them at fair value.

Inventories that are manufactured, or otherwise produced, in large quantities on a repetitive basis

BC5   The US standard, SFAS 34, requires an entity to recognise as an expense interest costs for inventories that are routinely manufactured or otherwise produced in large quantities on a repetitive basis because, in the FASB's view, the informational benefit from capitalising interest costs does not justify the cost. The exposure draft did not make an exception for borrowing costs relating to such inventories. The exposure draft, therefore, proposed to require an entity to capitalise borrowing costs relating to inventories that are manufactured in large quantities on a repetitive basis and take a substantial period of time to get ready for sale. Respondents argued that capitalising those borrowing costs would create a significant administrative burden, would not be informative to users and would create a reconciling item between IFRSs and US GAAP.

BC6   The Board decided to exclude from the scope of IAS 23 inventories that are manufactured, or otherwise produced, in large quantities on a repetitive basis, even if they take a substantial period of time to get ready for sale. The Board acknowledges the difficulty in both allocating borrowing costs to inventories that are manufactured in large quantities on a repetitive basis and monitoring those borrowing costs until the inventory is sold. It concluded that it should not require an entity to capitalise borrowing costs on such inventories because the costs of capitalisation are likely to exceed the potential benefits.

Elimination of the option of immediate recognition as an expense of borrowing costs directly attributable to the acquisition, construction or production of a qualifying asset

BC7   The previous version of IAS 23 permitted two treatments for accounting for borrowing costs that are directly attributable to the acquisition, construction or production of a qualifying asset. They could be capitalised or, alternatively, recognised immediately as an expense. SFAS 34 requires the capitalisation of such borrowing costs.

BC8   The Board proposed in the exposure draft to eliminate the option of immediate recognition as an expense. Many respondents disagreed with the Board's proposal in the exposure draft, arguing that:

(a)   borrowing costs should not be the subject of a short-term convergence project.

(b)   the Board had not explored in sufficient detail the merits of both accounting options.

(c)   the proposal did not result in benefits for users of financial statements because:

  (i)   it addressed only one of the differences between IAS 23 and SFAS 34.

  (ii)   comparability would not be enhanced because the capital structure of an entity could affect the cost of an asset.

  (iii)   credit analysts reverse capitalised borrowing costs when calculating coverage ratios.

(d)   the costs of implementing the capitalisation model in IAS 23 would be burdensome.

(e)   the proposal was not consistent with the Board's approach on other projects (in particular, the second phase of the Business Combinations project).

BC9   The Board concluded that borrowing costs that are directly attributable to the acquisition, construction or production of a qualifying asset are part of the cost of that asset. During the period when an asset is under development, the expenditures for the resources used must be financed. Financing has a cost. The cost of the asset should include all costs necessarily incurred to get the asset ready for its intended use or sale, including the cost incurred in financing the expenditures as a part of the asset's acquisition cost. The Board reasoned that recognising immediately as an expense borrowing costs relating to qualifying assets does not give a faithful representation of the cost of the asset.

BC10   The Board confirmed that the objective of the project is not to achieve full convergence on all aspects of accounting for borrowing costs. Rather, it is to reduce differences between IFRSs and US GAAP that are capable of resolution in a relatively short time. The removal of a choice of accounting treatment and convergence in principle with US GAAP will enhance comparability. The Board acknowledges that capitalising borrowing costs does not achieve comparability between assets that are financed with borrowings and those financed with equity. However, it achieves comparability among all non-equity financed assets, which is an improvement.

BC11   A requirement to recognise immediately as an expense borrowing costs relating to qualifying assets would not enhance comparability. Rather, comparability between assets that are internally developed and those acquired from third parties would be impaired. The purchase price of a completed asset purchased from a third party would include financing costs incurred by the third party during the development phase.

BC12   Respondents to the exposure draft argued that requiring the capitalisation of borrowing costs is not consistent with the Board's proposal in the second phase of the Business Combinations project to require an entity to treat as an expense acquisition costs relating to a business combination. The Board disagrees with those respondents. Acquisition costs as defined in the context of a business combination are different from borrowing costs incurred in constructing or producing a qualifying asset. Borrowing costs are part of the cost necessarily incurred to get the asset ready for its intended use or sale. Acquisition costs relating to a business combination are costs incurred for services performed to help with the acquisition, such as due diligence and professional fees. They are not costs of assets acquired in a business combination.

BC13 The Board concluded that the additional benefits in terms of higher comparability, improvements in financial reporting and achieving convergence in principle with US GAAP exceed any additional costs of implementation. Achieving convergence in principle with US GAAP on this topic is a milestone in the Memorandum of Understanding published by the FASB and IASB in February 2006, which is a step towards removal of the requirement imposed on foreign registrants with the SEC to reconcile their financial statements to US GAAP.

BC14 The Board observes that there is an unavoidable cost of complying with any new financial reporting standard. Accordingly, the Board carefully considers the costs and benefits of any new pronouncement. In this case, the Board has not been told that preparers who elected to capitalise borrowing costs under the previous version of IAS 23 found doing so unnecessarily burdensome. In the Board's judgement, any additional costs of capitalising an item of cost of an asset are offset by the advantage of having all entities account for that item in the same way.

Effective date and transition

BC15 Development of a qualifying asset may take a long time. Additionally, some assets currently in use may have undergone and completed their production or construction process many years ago. If the entity has been following the accounting policy of immediately recognising borrowing costs as an expense, the costs of gathering the information required to capitalise them retrospectively and to adjust the carrying amount of the asset may exceed the potential benefits. Hence, the Board decided to require prospective application, which was supported by respondents to the exposure draft.

BC16 The Board noted that the revisions would result in information that is more comparable between entities. On that basis, if an entity wished to apply the revised Standard from any date before the effective date, users of the entity's financial statements would receive more useful and comparable information than previously.

BC17 Therefore, an entity is permitted to apply the revised Standard from any designated date before the effective date. However, if an entity applies the Standard from such an earlier date, it should apply the Standard to all qualifying assets for which the commencement date for capitalisation is on or after that designated date.

BC18 The Board recognises that the Standard may require an entity that reconciles its IFRS financial statements to US GAAP to maintain two sets of capitalisation information—one set that complies with the requirements of IAS 23 and one that complies with the requirements of SFAS 34. The Board wishes to avoid imposing on such entities the need to maintain two sets of capitalisation information. Therefore, before the effective date, the Board will consider what actions it might take to avoid this outcome.

Differences between IAS 23 and SFAS 34

BC19   The following paragraphs summarise the main differences between IAS 23 and SFAS 34.

Definition of borrowing costs

BC20   IAS 23 uses the term 'borrowing costs' whereas SFAS 34 uses the term 'interest costs'. 'Borrowing costs' reflects the broader definition in IAS 23, which encompasses interest and other costs, such as:

(a)   exchange differences arising from foreign currency borrowings to the extent that they are regarded as an adjustment to interest costs; and

(b)   amortisation of ancillary costs incurred in connection with the arrangement of borrowings.

BC21   EITF Issue No. 99-9 concludes that derivative gains and losses (arising from the effective portion of a derivative instrument that qualifies as a fair value hedge) are part of the capitalised interest cost. IAS 23 does not address such derivative gains and losses.

Definition of a qualifying asset

BC22   The main differences are as follows:

(a)   IAS 23 defines a qualifying asset as one that takes a substantial period of time to get ready for its intended use or sale. The SFAS 34 definition does not include the term *substantial*.

(b)   IAS 23 excludes from its scope qualifying assets that are measured at fair value. SFAS 34 does not address assets measured at fair value.

(c)   SFAS 34 includes as qualifying assets investments in investees accounted for using the equity method, in some circumstances.[†] Such investments are not qualifying assets according to IAS 23.

(d)   SFAS 34 does not permit the capitalisation of interest costs on assets acquired with gifts or grants that are restricted by the donor or grantor in some situations. IAS 23 does not address such assets.

---

*   In 2007 the Board was advised that some of the components of borrowing costs in paragraph 6 are broadly equivalent to the components of interest expense calculated using the effective interest method in accordance with IAS 39 *Financial Instruments: Recognition and Measurement*. Therefore, the Board amended paragraph 6 to refer to the relevant guidance in IAS 39 when describing the components of borrowing costs.

†   While the investee has activities in progress necessary to commence its planned principal operations provided that the investee's activities include the use of funds to acquire qualifying assets for its operations.

Measurement

BC23   When an entity borrows funds specifically for the purpose of obtaining a qualifying asset:

(a)   IAS 23 requires an entity to capitalise the actual borrowing costs incurred on that borrowing. SFAS 34 states that an entity may use the rate of that borrowing.

(b)   IAS 23 requires an entity to deduct any income earned on the temporary investment of actual borrowings from the amount of borrowing costs to be capitalised. SFAS 34 does not generally permit this deduction, unless particular tax-exempt borrowings are involved.

BC24   SFAS 34 requires an entity to use judgement in determining the capitalisation rate to apply to the expenditures on the asset—an entity selects the borrowings that it considers appropriate to meet the objective of capitalising the interest costs incurred that otherwise could have been avoided. When an entity borrows funds generally and uses them to obtain a qualifying asset, IAS 23 permits some flexibility in determining the capitalisation rate, but requires an entity to use all outstanding borrowings other than those made specifically to obtain a qualifying asset.

Disclosure requirements

BC25   IAS 23 requires disclosure of the capitalisation rate used to determine the amount of borrowing costs eligible for capitalisation. SFAS 34 does not require this disclosure.

BC26   SFAS 34 requires disclosure of the total amount of interest cost incurred during the period, including the amount capitalised and the amount recognised as an expense. IAS 23 requires disclosure only of the amount of borrowing costs capitalised during the period. IAS 1 *Presentation of Financial Statements* requires the disclosure of finance costs for the period.

Consequential amendments to IAS 11 *Construction Contracts*

BC27   IAS 11 paragraph 18 states that 'costs that may be attributable to contract activity in general and can be allocated to specific contracts also include borrowing costs when the contractor adopts the allowed alternative treatment in IAS 23 *Borrowing Costs*.' The Board decided to delete the reference to IAS 23 in this paragraph because it is unnecessary. Attributing borrowing costs to contracts is not a matter of capitalisation. Rather, it is a matter of identifying the contract costs. The inclusion of borrowing costs in contract costs affects the presentation of borrowing costs in profit or loss. It does not affect the recognition of borrowing costs as specified in IAS 23.

Appendix
Amendments to Basis for Conclusions on other pronouncements

This appendix contains amendments to the Basis for Conclusions on other pronouncements that are necessary in order to ensure consistency with the revised IAS 23.

* * * * *

The amendments contained in this appendix when IAS 23 was issued in 2007 have been incorporated into the text of the Basis for Conclusions on IFRS 1 and IFRICs 1 and 12.

Dissenting opinions

Dissent of Anthony T Cope, Philippe Danjou and Robert P Garnett

DO1   The Board's decision to require the capitalisation of borrowing costs relating to qualifying assets will cause a significant change in accounting for the many preparers that currently apply the benchmark treatment of recognising borrowing costs as an expense. Messrs Cope, Danjou and Garnett believe that such a change will require the establishment of cumbersome measurement processes and monitoring of capitalised costs over a long period. This is likely to involve considerable accounting work and incremental auditing costs.

DO2   Users of financial statements responding to the exposure draft did not support the change because they saw no informational benefit in a model that capitalises costs, other than the capitalisation of the actual economic cost of capital of the investment. In addition, Messrs Cope, Danjou and Garnett believe that a standard requiring the capitalisation of borrowing costs should discuss more extensively which assets qualify for the purpose of capitalising which borrowing costs.

DO3   As a consequence, Messrs Cope, Danjou and Garnett dissent because, in their view, the costs of this particular change will far outweigh the benefits to users.

DO4   In addition, this requirement to capitalise borrowing costs will achieve only limited convergence with US GAAP—differences will remain that could lead to materially different capitalised amounts. Furthermore, entities that are required to reconcile net income and shareholders' equity to US GAAP already have the option to capitalise borrowing costs and, thus, may recognise amounts that are more comparable to, albeit still potentially materially different from, those recognised in accordance with US GAAP.

DO5   The Memorandum of Understanding published by the FASB and the IASB states that trying to eliminate differences between standards that are both in need of significant improvement is not the best use of resources. Messrs Cope, Danjou and Garnett support the convergence work programme, but only if it results in higher quality standards and improved financial reporting. They are of the opinion that IAS 23 and SFAS 34 are both in need of significant improvement and should not have been addressed as part of short-term convergence.

Amendments to guidance on other pronouncements

The following amendments to guidance on other pronouncements are necessary in order to ensure consistency with the revised IAS 23. In the amended paragraphs, new text is underlined and deleted text is struck through.

* * * * *

The amendments contained in this appendix when IAS 23 was issued in 2007 have been applied in the guidance on implementing IFRS 1 and IAS 8 and the illustrative examples accompanying IFRIC 12.

Table of Concordance

This table shows how the contents of the superseded version of IAS 23 and the revised version of IAS 23 correspond. Paragraphs are treated as corresponding if they broadly address the same matter even though the guidance may differ.

Superseded IAS 23 paragraph	Revised IAS 23 paragraph	Superseded IAS 23 paragraph	Revised IAS 23 paragraph
Objective	1	18	15
1	2	19	16
2	None	20	17
3	3	21	18
4	5	22	19
5	6	23	20
6	7	24	21
7	None	25	22
8	None	26	23
9	None	27	24
10	8	28	25
11	None	29	26
12	9	30	None
13	10	31	None
14	11	None	4
15	12	None	27, 28
16	13	None	29
17	14	None	30

IASB documents published to accompany

International Accounting Standard 24

Related Party Disclosures

The text of the unaccompanied IAS 24 is contained in Part A of this edition. Its effective date is 1 January 2011. This part presents the following accompanying documents:

Approval by the Board of IAS 24 issued in November 2009

International Accounting Standard 24 *Related Party Disclosures* (as revised in 2009) was approved for issue by thirteen of the fifteen members of the International Accounting Standards Board. Mr Garnett dissented. His dissenting opinion is set out after the Basis for Conclusions. Ms McConnell abstained from voting in view of her recent appointment to the Board.

Sir David Tweedie   Chairman

Stephen Cooper

Philippe Danjou

Jan Engström

Patrick Finnegan

Robert P Garnett

Gilbert Gélard

Amaro Luiz de Oliveira Gomes

Prabhakar Kalavacherla

James J Leisenring

Patricia McConnell

Warren J McGregor

John T Smith

Tatsumi Yamada

Wei-Guo Zhang

Basis for Conclusions on
IAS 24 *Related Party Disclosures*

This Basis for Conclusions accompanies, but is not part of, IAS 24.

Introduction

BC1   This Basis for Conclusions summarises the International Accounting Standards Board's considerations in reaching its conclusions on revising IAS 24 *Related Party Disclosures* in 2003 and 2009. Individual Board members gave greater weight to some factors than to others.

BC2   In July 2001 the Board announced that, as part of its initial agenda of technical projects, it would undertake a project to improve a number of standards, including IAS 24. The project was undertaken in the light of queries and criticisms raised in relation to the standards by securities regulators, professional accountants and other interested parties. The objectives of the Improvements project were to reduce or eliminate alternatives, redundancies and conflicts within existing standards, to deal with some convergence issues and to make other improvements. In May 2002 the Board published its proposals in an exposure draft of *Improvements to International Accounting Standards* (the 2002 ED), with a comment deadline of 16 September 2002. The Board received over 160 comment letters on the exposure draft. After reviewing the responses, the Board issued a revised version of IAS 24 in December 2003.

BC3   In February 2007 the Board published an exposure draft *State-controlled Entities and the Definition of a Related Party* (the 2007 ED), proposing:

(a)   an exemption from the disclosure requirements in IAS 24 for transactions between entities that are controlled, jointly controlled or significantly influenced by a state ('state-controlled entities*'); and

(b)   amendments to the definition of a related party.

BC4   The Board received 72 comment letters on the 2007 ED. After considering those comments, in December 2008 the Board published revised proposals in an exposure draft *Relationships with the State* (the 2008 ED). The 2008 ED:

(a)   presented revised proposals for state-controlled entities; and

(b)   proposed one further amendment to the definition of a related party.

BC5   The Board received 75 comment letters on the 2008 ED. After reviewing the responses, the Board issued a revised version of IAS 24 in November 2009.

BC6   Because the Board's intention was not to reconsider the fundamental approach to related party disclosures established by IAS 24, this Basis for Conclusions discusses only the following requirements in IAS 24:

(a)   management compensation (paragraphs BC7–BC10);

(b)   related party disclosures in separate financial statements (paragraphs BC11–BC17);

---

*   In finalising the revised version of IAS 24 in 2009, the Board replaced the term 'state' with 'government'.

(c)   definition of a related party (paragraphs BC18–BC32);

(d)   government-related entities (paragraphs BC33–BC48); and

(e)   other minor changes made in 2009 (paragraph BC49).

Management compensation

BC7   The version of IAS 24 issued by the Board's predecessor in 1984 had no exemption for the disclosure of key management personnel compensation. In developing the 2002 ED, the Board proposed that the disclosure of management compensation, expense allowances and similar items paid in the ordinary course of business should not be required because:

(a)   the approval processes for key management personnel compensation in some jurisdictions remove the rationale for related party disclosures;

(b)   privacy issues arise in some jurisdictions where accountability mechanisms other than disclosure in financial statements exist; and

(c)   requiring these disclosures placed weight on the determination of 'key management personnel' and 'compensation', which was likely to prove contentious. In addition, comparability of these disclosures would be unlikely until measurement requirements are developed for all forms of compensation.

BC8   However, some respondents to the 2002 ED objected to the proposed exemption because they were concerned that information relating to management compensation is relevant to users' information needs and that an exemption based on 'items paid in the ordinary course of business' could lead to abuse. Establishing a disclosure exemption on such a criterion without a definition of the terms could lead to exempting other transactions with management from being disclosed, because they could all be structured as 'compensation paid in the ordinary course of an entity's operations'. Respondents argued that such an exemption could lead to abuse because it could potentially apply to any transactions with management.

BC9   The Board was persuaded by the respondents' views on the 2002 ED and decided that the Standard should require disclosure of key management personnel compensation because:

(a)   the principle underpinning the requirements in IAS 24 is that transactions with related parties should be disclosed, and key management personnel are related parties of an entity.

(b)   key management personnel compensation is relevant to decisions made by users of financial statements when it represents a material amount. The structure and amount of compensation are major drivers in the implementation of the business strategy.

(c)   the benefit of this information to users of financial statements largely outweighs the potential lack of comparability arising from the absence of recognition and measurement requirements for all forms of compensation.

BC10   The Board believes that although some jurisdictions have processes for approving compensation for key management personnel in an attempt to ensure an arm's length result, it is clear that some jurisdictions do not. Furthermore, although approval processes for management compensation may involve other parties such as shareholders or investors, key management personnel may still have a significant input. In addition, the Board noted that disclosing key management personnel compensation would improve transparency and comparability, thereby enabling users of financial statements to make a better assessment of the impact of such compensation on the entity's financial position and profit or loss. The Board also noted that the definition of key management personnel and the guidance on compensation in IAS 19 *Employee Benefits* are sufficient to enable entities to disclose the relevant information.

Related party disclosures in separate financial statements

BC11   The version of IAS 24 issued by the Board's predecessor in 1984 exempted disclosures about related party transactions in:

(a)   parents' financial statements when they are made available or published with the consolidated statements; and

(b)   financial statements of a wholly-owned subsidiary if its parent is incorporated in the same country and provides consolidated financial statements in that country.

BC12   In the 2002 ED the Board proposed to continue exempting separate financial statements of parents and financial statements of wholly-owned subsidiaries from disclosures about any related parties in specified circumstances. It proposed that disclosure of related party transactions and outstanding balances in the separate financial statements of a parent or the financial statements of a wholly-owned subsidiary would not be required, but only if those statements were made available or published with consolidated financial statements for the group.

BC13   The Board proposed to retain this exemption so that entities that are required by law to produce financial statements available for public use in accordance with International Financial Reporting Standards (IFRSs) in addition to the group's consolidated financial statements would not be unduly burdened. The Board noted that in some circumstances, users can find sufficient information for their purposes regarding a subsidiary from either its financial statements or the group's consolidated financial statements. In addition, the users of financial statements of a subsidiary often have, or can obtain access to, more information. The Board also noted that users should be aware that amounts recognised in the financial statements of a wholly-owned subsidiary can be affected significantly by the subsidiary's relationship with its parent.

BC14   However, respondents to the 2002 ED objected to this exemption, on the grounds that disclosure of related party transactions and outstanding balances is essential information for external users, who need to be aware of the level of support provided by related parties. The respondents also argued that financial statements prepared in accordance with IFRSs could be presented on a stand-alone basis. Therefore, financial statements prepared on the basis of this proposed exemption would not achieve a fair presentation without related party disclosures.

BC15 The Board was persuaded by those arguments and decided to require the disclosure of related party transactions and outstanding balances in separate financial statements of a parent, investor or venturer in addition to the disclosure requirements in IAS 27 *Consolidated and Separate Financial Statements*, IAS 28 *Investments in Associates* and IAS 31 *Interests in Joint Ventures*.

BC16 The Board noted that the financial statements of an entity that is part of a consolidated group may include the effects of extensive intragroup transactions. Indeed, potentially all of the revenues and expenses for such an entity may derive from related party transactions. The Board concluded that the disclosures required by IAS 24 are essential to understanding the financial position and financial performance of such an entity and therefore should be required for separate financial statements presented in accordance with IAS 27.

BC17 The Board also believed that disclosure of such transactions is essential because the external users need to be aware of the interrelationships between related parties, including the level of support provided by related parties, to assist external users in their economic decisions.

Definition of a related party

BC18 The definition of a related party in IAS 24 was widely considered to be too complex and difficult to apply in practice. The Board noted that the existing definition of a related party had weaknesses: it was cumbersome and included several cross-references that made it difficult to read (and to translate). Therefore, the 2007 and 2008 EDs proposed revised definitions.

BC19 In revising the definition, the Board adopted the following approach:

(a) When an entity assesses whether two parties are related, it would treat significant influence as equivalent to the relationship that exists between an entity and a member of its key management personnel. However, those relationships are not as close as a relationship of control or joint control.

(b) If two entities are both subject to control (or joint control) by the same entity or person, the two entities are related to each other.

(c) If one entity (or person) controls (or jointly controls) a second entity and the first entity (or person) has significant influence over a third entity, the second and third entities are related to each other.

(d) Conversely, if two entities are both subject to significant influence by the same entity (or person), the two entities are not related to each other.

(e) If the revised definition treats one party as related to a second party, the definition should also treat the second party as related to the first party, by symmetry.

BC20 The new definition was not intended to change the meaning of a related party except in the three respects detailed in paragraphs BC21–BC26. The 2008 ED proposed other amendments to the definition for one additional case that had been inadvertently omitted from the 2007 ED and the elimination of further inconsistencies (paragraphs BC27–BC29). In finalising the amendments in 2009, the Board also removed the term 'significant voting power' from the definition of a related party (paragraphs BC30 and BC31).

An associate of a subsidiary's controlling investor

BC21 First, the Board considered the relationship between an associate and a subsidiary of an investor that has significant influence over the associate. The Board observed that when an associate prepares individual or separate financial statements, its investor is a related party. If the investor has a subsidiary, that subsidiary is also related to the associate, because the subsidiary is part of the group that has significant influence over the associate. Although the definition in the 2003 version of IAS 24 incorporated such relationships, the Board concluded that the revised definition should state this more clearly.

BC22 In contrast, when a subsidiary prepares individual or separate financial statements, an associate of the subsidiary's controlling investor was not a related party as defined in the 2003 version of IAS 24. The subsidiary does not have significant influence over the associate, nor is it significantly influenced by the associate.

BC23 However, the Board decided that, for the same reasons that the parties described in paragraph BC21 are related, the parties described in paragraph BC22 are also related. Thus, the Board amended the definition of a related party to include the relationship discussed in paragraph BC22.

BC24 Furthermore, the Board decided that in the situations described in paragraphs BC21 and BC22, if the investor is a person who has significant influence over one entity and control or joint control over another entity, sufficient influence exists to warrant concluding that the two entities are related.

Two associates of a person

BC25 Secondly, the Board considered the relationship between associates of the investor. IAS 24 does not define associates as related to each other if the investor is an entity. This is because there is insufficient influence through the common investment in two associates. However, the Board noted a discrepancy in that if a person significantly influences one entity and a close member of that person's family significantly influences another entity, those entities were treated as related parties of each other. The Board amended the definition to exclude the entities described in the latter scenario, thereby ensuring a consistent treatment of associates.

Investments of members of key management personnel

BC26   Thirdly, IAS 24 treats some investees of the key management personnel of a reporting entity as related to that entity. However, the definition in the 2003 version of IAS 24 did not include the reciprocal of this—ie for the financial statements of the investee, the other entity managed by the key management personnel was not a related party. To eliminate this inconsistency, the Board amended the definition so that for both sets of financial statements the entities are related parties.

Joint control

BC27   Respondents to the 2007 ED pointed out that one case had been excluded from the restructured definition without being explicitly stated as a change to IAS 24. When a person has joint control over a reporting entity and a close member of that person's family has joint control or significant influence over the other entity, the 2003 version of IAS 24 defined the other entity as related to the reporting entity.

BC28   The Board noted that joint control is generally regarded as influence that is stronger than significant influence. Therefore, the Board concluded that the relationship described in paragraph BC27 should continue to be treated as a related party relationship.

BC29   The definition in the 2003 version of IAS 24 did not include the reciprocal of the case described in paragraph BC27, nor did it deal with cases when a person or a third entity has joint control or significant influence over the two entities. The definition proposed in the 2007 ED would not have rectified these omissions. The Board decided to include these cases in the definition, to treat similar relationships in a consistent manner. In summary, whenever a person or entity has both joint control over a second entity and joint control or significant influence over a third entity, the amendments described in this paragraph and paragraph BC27 treat the second and third entities as related to each other.

Removal of 'significant voting power'

BC30   Respondents to the 2007 and 2008 EDs raised concerns about the term 'significant voting power' in the definition of a related party. They identified anomalies in its use such as when significant voting power created a related party relationship only when that power is held by individuals, not when that power is held by an entity. A further anomaly arose because two entities were classified as related to each other when a third person was a member of the key management personnel of one and had significant voting power in the other; however, they were not treated as related when a third person had significant voting power in both entities.

BC31   In response to these comments, the Board deleted the reference to 'significant voting power' because it was undefined, used inconsistently and created unnecessary complexity. The Board concluded that if the effect of 'significant voting power' was considered to be the same as 'significant influence', its deletion would have no effect because 'significant influence' is in the definition. On the other hand, if the effect of 'significant voting power' was considered to be different from that of 'significant influence', IAS 24 did not explain what that difference was.

Other minor changes to the definition of a related party

BC32 The revisions to IAS 24 in 2009 included the following other minor changes:

(a) The definition of a **related party** is amended:

(i) to replace references to 'individual' with 'person';

(ii) to clarify that an associate includes subsidiaries of an associate and a joint venture includes subsidiaries of the joint venture; and

(iii) to clarify that two entities are not related parties simply because a member of key management personnel of one entity has significant influence over the other entity.

(b) The definition of a **close member of the family** is amended:

(i) to replace references to 'individual' with 'person'; and

(ii) to delete 'may' from the list of examples to state that close members of a person's family include (rather than 'may include') that person's spouse or domestic partner and children.

Government-related entities

Exemption (paragraph 25)

BC33 The version of IAS 24 that preceded its revision in 2003 did not require 'state-controlled' entities to disclose transactions with other such entities. The revised version of IAS 24 issued in 2003 omitted this exemption because at the time the Board concluded that the disclosure requirements would not be a burden for those entities.

BC34 Subsequently concerns were raised that in environments where government control is pervasive, compliance with IAS 24 was problematic. To address those concerns, the 2007 ED proposed an exemption from the disclosure requirements now in paragraph 18 of IAS 24 for government-related entities. In developing that proposal, the Board noted the following:

(a) It can be difficult to identify other government-related entities, particularly in jurisdictions with a large number of such entities. Such entities might not even be aware that an entity with which they have transactions is a related party.

(b) For these transactions, the cost of meeting the requirements in IAS 24 was not always offset by the benefit of increased information for users of financial statements. More specifically:

(i) extensive disclosures were required for transactions that are unaffected by the relationship;

(ii)   if some entities are not aware that their transactions are with other government-related entities, the disclosures provided would be incomplete; and

(iii)   transactions that are affected by the relationship might well be obscured by excessive disclosures about unaffected transactions.

(c)   Some governments establish subsidiaries, joint ventures and associates to compete with each other. In this case, transactions between such entities are likely to be conducted as if they are unrelated parties.

BC35   Respondents to the 2007 ED generally supported an exemption for government-related entities. However, they expressed concerns about the complexity of the specific proposal and asked the Board to clarify various aspects of it. After considering all comments received, the Board proposed a revised exemption for those entities in the 2008 ED.

BC36   Respondents to the 2008 ED generally supported the revised proposal, but some argued that the exemption should not apply to transactions:

(a)   between members of a group that is controlled by a government (paragraph BC37); and

(b)   between government-related entities that are related for a reason in addition to their relationship with the same government (paragraph BC38).

BC37   Some respondents reasoned that the exemption should not apply to transactions between members of a group that is controlled by a government, for example between a government-related entity and its parent or its fellow subsidiaries. Those respondents noted that the relationship within such a group might sometimes be closer and more influential than between government-related entities in an environment where government control is pervasive. However, for the following reasons the Board concluded that the exemption should also apply within such groups:

(a)   Sometimes, requiring disclosure in such cases would negate the purpose of the exemption and could lead to significant differences in the level of disclosure when the substance of the relationships and transactions could be very similar. For example, suppose one government controls all entities directly but another government has similar entities and controls them all through a single holding company. The entities controlled by the first government would all qualify for the exemption but those controlled by the second government would not.

(b)   Requiring disclosure in such cases would place considerable pressure on the definition of the boundary between government and entities controlled by the government. For example, suppose a government controls entities through an intermediate institution. It would be necessary to determine whether that institution is an entity controlled by the government (in which case the exemption would not apply) or part of the government (in which case the exemption would apply). This may be answered easily if the institution is a company incorporated under normal company law that simply happens to have the government as a controlling shareholder. It may be less clear if the institution is, for example, a government agency or department.

BC38   The Board identified only one case when government-related entities might be related to each other for reasons other than their relationships with the same government: a government might control both a post-employment benefit plan and the sponsoring employer. However, the main transactions between such a plan and the sponsoring employer are (a) employer contributions and (b) investments by the plan in the employer or in assets used by the employer. IAS 19 already requires a sponsoring employer to disclose most, if not all, of the information that IAS 24 would require if the exemption did not apply. Thus the Board concluded that no significant loss of disclosure would arise from applying the exemption in these cases.

BC39   Paragraph BC34 explains why the Board provided an exemption from the disclosure requirements in paragraph 18 of IAS 24 for government-related entities. It was beyond the scope of the project to consider whether similar exemptions would be appropriate in other circumstances.

BC40   Some respondents to the 2008 ED noted that many financial institutions had recently become government-related entities when governments took significant and sometimes controlling equity interests in them during the global financial crisis. They queried whether the exemption was appropriate in such cases. In finalising the amendments in 2009, the Board identified no reason to treat such entities differently from other government-related entities. The Board noted that in addition to the disclosure requirements in IAS 24, IAS 20 *Accounting for Government Grants and Disclosure of Government Assistance* requires the reporting entity to disclose information about the receipt of government grants or assistance.

BC41   Respondents to the 2008 ED noted that the proposed definition of 'state' was similar to the definition of 'government' in IAS 20. To avoid confusion and provide consistency, the Board adopted the latter definition when finalising the amendments to IAS 24 in 2009. The Board decided that it need not provide a more comprehensive definition or additional guidance on how to determine what is meant by 'government'. In the Board's view, a more detailed definition could not capture every conceivable government structure across every jurisdiction. In addition, judgement is required by the reporting entity when applying the definition because every jurisdiction has its own way of organising government-related activities.

Disclosure requirements when the exemption applies (paragraph 26)

BC42   The Board considered whether the disclosure requirements in paragraph 26:

(a)   met the objective of IAS 24 (paragraphs BC43–BC46); and

(b)   were operational (paragraphs BC47 and BC48).

BC43   The objective of IAS 24 is to provide 'disclosures necessary to draw attention to the possibility that [the entity's] financial position and profit or loss may have been affected by the existence of related parties and by transactions and outstanding balances, including commitments, with such parties.' To meet that objective, paragraph 26 requires some disclosure when the exemption applies. Those disclosures are intended to put users on notice that related party transactions have occurred and to give an indication of their extent. The Board did not intend to require the reporting entity to identify **every** government-related entity, or to quantify in detail **every** transaction with such entities, because such a requirement would negate the exemption.

BC44 Some respondents to the 2008 ED were concerned that qualitative disclosure of individually significant related party transactions alone would not meet the objective of IAS 24 and that combining individually significant transactions with collectively significant transactions would not provide sufficient transparency. The Board concluded that it should require an entity to disclose:

(a) the nature and amount of each individually significant transaction; and

(b) quantitative or qualitative information about other types of transactions that are collectively, but not individually, significant.

BC45 The Board noted that this requirement should not be too onerous for the reporting entity because:

(a) individually significant transactions should be a small subset, by number, of total related party transactions;

(b) the reporting entity should know what those transactions are; and

(c) reporting such items on an exceptional basis takes into account cost-benefit considerations.

BC46 The Board also noted that more disclosure of individually significant transactions would better meet the objective of IAS 24 because this approach focuses on transactions that, through their nature or size, are of more interest to users and are more likely to be affected by the related party relationship.

BC47 Some respondents raised concerns about whether the reporting entity would be able to identify whether the counterparty to individually significant or collectively significant transactions is a related party because it is controlled, jointly controlled or significantly influenced by the same government. The problem of identifying all such counterparties was one of the primary reasons for the exemption.

BC48 However, as discussed in paragraph BC43, it was not the Board's intention to require the reporting entity to identify every government-related entity, or to quantify every transaction with such entities. Moreover, individually significant transactions are likely to attract more scrutiny by management. The Board concluded that management will know, or will apply more effort in establishing, who the counterparty to an individually significant transaction is and will have, or be able to obtain, background information on the counterparty.

Other minor changes made in 2009

BC49 The revisions to IAS 24 in 2009 included the following other changes:

(a) The list of examples of **related party transactions** is amended to include in paragraph 21(i) commitments to do something if a particular event occurs or does not occur in the future, including executory contracts. The Board concluded that commitments were one type of transaction, but to avoid doubt decided to make explicit reference to them.

(b)   Paragraph 3 relating to the **scope** of IAS 24 is amended to clarify that the Standard applies to individual, as well as separate and consolidated, financial statements because individual financial statements relate to something different from the defined term in IAS 27.

(c)   Paragraph 34 of IFRS 8 *Operating Segments* is amended. The Board recognised that in applying the requirements in IFRS 8 it may not be practicable or meaningful to regard all government-related entities as a single customer, especially for environments in which government control is pervasive.

(d)   A consequential amendment to the Basis for Conclusions on IAS 19 draws attention to the new definition of a related party. The definition of a qualifying insurance policy in IAS 19 refers to this definition.

Appendix
Amendment to the Basis for Conclusions on
IAS 19 *Employee Benefits*

The amendment contained in this appendix when IAS 24 (as revised) was issued in 2009 has been incorporated into the Basis for Conclusions on IAS 19 published in this volume.

Dissenting opinion

Dissent of Robert P Garnett

DO1　Mr Garnett disagrees with the Board's decision to exempt only government-related entities from the requirements of paragraph 18 to disclose information about all transactions with related parties. He also disagrees with the decision not to require all entities to provide information about each individually significant transaction with a related party as set out in paragraph 26(b)(i).

DO2　The Basis for Conclusions sets out clearly the need to remove the unnecessary burden of collecting data for all transactions, entered into and priced on normal business terms, because the counterparty was identified as a related party. It also explains the need to inform investors of individually significant transactions with related parties. Mr Garnett agrees with the explanations in paragraphs BC33–BC48.

DO3　Paragraph 25, however, restricts these changes to entities that are controlled, jointly controlled or significantly influenced by the same government. Mr Garnett sees no reason to make such a distinction, other than to provide limited relief to certain entities.

Illustrative examples

The following examples accompany, but are not part of, IAS 24 Related Party Disclosures. They illustrate:

- *the partial exemption for government-related entities; and*

- *how the definition of a related party would apply in specified circumstances.*

In the examples, references to 'financial statements' relate to the individual, separate or consolidated financial statements.

Partial exemption for government-related entities

Example 1 – Exemption from disclosure (paragraph 25)

IE1   Government G directly or indirectly controls Entities 1 and 2 and Entities A, B, C and D. Person X is a member of the key management personnel of Entity 1.

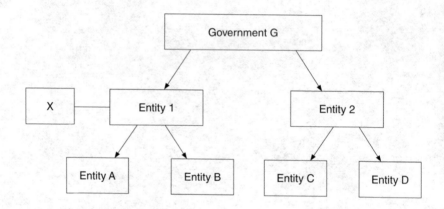

IE2   For Entity A's financial statements, the exemption in paragraph 25 applies to:

(a)   transactions with Government G; and

(b)   transactions with Entities 1 and 2 and Entities B, C and D.

However, that exemption does not apply to transactions with Person X.

Disclosure requirements when exemption applies (paragraph 26)

IE3   In Entity A's financial statements, an example of disclosure to comply with paragraph 26(b)(i) for **individually** significant transactions could be:

Example of disclosure for individually significant transaction carried out on non-market terms

On 15 January 20X1 Entity A, a utility company in which Government G indirectly owns 75 per cent of outstanding shares, sold a 10 hectare piece of land to another government-related utility company for CU5 million.* On 31 December 20X0 a plot of land in a similar location, of a similar size and with similar characteristics, was sold for CU3 million. There had not been any appreciation or depreciation of the land in the intervening period. See note X [of the financial statements] for disclosure of government assistance as required by IAS 20 *Accounting for Government Grants and Disclosure of Government Assistance* and notes Y and Z [of the financial statements] for compliance with other relevant IFRSs.

Example of disclosure for individually significant transaction because of size of transaction

In the year ended December 20X1 Government G provided Entity A, a utility company in which Government G indirectly owns 75 per cent of outstanding shares, with a loan equivalent to 50 per cent of its funding requirement, repayable in quarterly instalments over the next five years. Interest is charged on the loan at a rate of 3 per cent, which is comparable to that charged on Entity A's bank loans.† See notes Y and Z [of the financial statements] for compliance with other relevant IFRSs.

Example of disclosure of collectively significant transactions

In Entity A's financial statements, an example of disclosure to comply with paragraph 26(b)(ii) for **collectively** significant transactions could be:

Government G, indirectly, owns 75 per cent of Entity A's outstanding shares. Entity A's significant transactions with Government G and other entities controlled, jointly controlled or significantly influenced by Government G are [a large portion of its sales of goods and purchases of raw materials] or [about 50 per cent of its sales of goods and about 35 per cent of its purchases of raw materials].

The company also benefits from guarantees by Government G of the company's bank borrowing. See note X [of the financial statements] for disclosure of government assistance as required by IAS 20 *Accounting for Government Grants and Disclosure of Government Assistance* and notes Y and Z [of the financial statements] for compliance with other relevant IFRSs.

---

*   In these examples monetary amounts are denominated in 'currency units (CU)'.

†   If the reporting entity had concluded that this transaction constituted government assistance it would have needed to consider the disclosure requirements in IAS 20.

Definition of a related party

*The references are to subparagraphs of the definition of a **related party** in paragraph 9 of IAS 24.*

Example 2 – Associates and subsidiaries

IE4   Parent entity has a controlling interest in Subsidiaries A, B and C and has significant influence over Associates 1 and 2. Subsidiary C has significant influence over Associate 3.

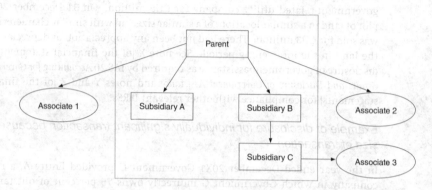

IE5   For Parent's separate financial statements, Subsidiaries A, B and C and Associates 1, 2 and 3 are related parties. *[Paragraph 9(b)(i) and (ii)]*

IE6   For Subsidiary A's financial statements, Parent, Subsidiaries B and C and Associates 1, 2 and 3 are related parties. For Subsidiary B's separate financial statements, Parent, Subsidiaries A and C and Associates 1, 2 and 3 are related parties. For Subsidiary C's financial statements, Parent, Subsidiaries A and B and Associates 1, 2 and 3 are related parties. *[Paragraph 9(b)(i) and (ii)]*

IE7   For the financial statements of Associates 1, 2 and 3, Parent and Subsidiaries A, B and C are related parties. Associates 1, 2 and 3 are not related to each other. *[Paragraph 9(b)(ii)]*

IE8   For Parent's consolidated financial statements, Associates 1, 2 and 3 are related to the Group. *[Paragraph 9(b)(ii)]*

Example 3 – Key management personnel

IE9   A person, X, has a 100 per cent investment in Entity A and is a member of the key management personnel of Entity C. Entity B has a 100 per cent investment in Entity C.

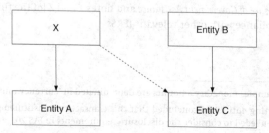

IE10   For Entity C's financial statements, Entity A is related to Entity C because X controls Entity A and is a member of the key management personnel of Entity C. [*Paragraph 9(b)(vi)–(a)(iii)*]

IE11   For Entity C's financial statements, Entity A is also related to Entity C if X is a member of the key management personnel of Entity B and not of Entity C. [*Paragraph 9(b)(vi)–(a)(iii)*]

IE12   Furthermore, the outcome described in paragraphs IE10 and IE11 will be the same if X has joint control over Entity A. [*Paragraph 9(b)(vi)–(a)(iii)*] (If X had only significant influence over Entity A and not control or joint control, then Entities A and C would not be related to each other.)

IE13   For Entity A's financial statements, Entity C is related to Entity A because X controls A and is a member of Entity C's key management personnel. [*Paragraph 9(b)(vii)–(a)(i)*]

IE14   Furthermore, the outcome described in paragraph IE13 will be the same if X has joint control over Entity A. The outcome will also be the same if X is a member of key management personnel of Entity B and not of Entity C. [*Paragraph 9(b)(vii)–(a)(i)*]

IE15   For Entity B's consolidated financial statements, Entity A is a related party of the Group if X is a member of key management personnel of the Group. [*Paragraph 9(b)(vi)–(a)(iii)*]

Example 4 – Person as investor

IE16   A person, X, has an investment in Entity A and Entity B.

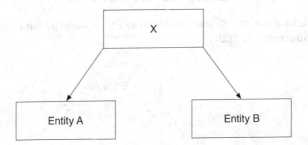

IE17   For Entity A's financial statements, if X controls or jointly controls Entity A, Entity B is related to Entity A when X has control, joint control or significant influence over Entity B. [*Paragraph 9(b)(vi)–(a)(i) and 9(b)(vii)–(a)(i)*]

IE18   For Entity B's financial statements, if X controls or jointly controls Entity A, Entity A is related to Entity B when X has control, joint control or significant influence over Entity B. [*Paragraph 9(b)(vi)–(a)(i) and 9(b)(vi)–(a)(ii)*]

IE19   If X has significant influence over both Entity A and Entity B, Entities A and B are not related to each other.

Example 5 – Close members of the family holding investments

IE20   A person, X, is the domestic partner of Y. X has an investment in Entity A and Y has an investment in Entity B.

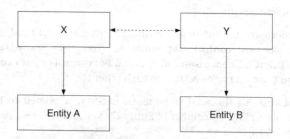

IE21   For Entity A's financial statements, if X controls or jointly controls Entity A, Entity B is related to Entity A when Y has control, joint control or significant influence over Entity B. [*Paragraph 9(b)(vi)–(a)(i) and 9(b)(vii)–(a)(i)*]

IE22   For Entity B's financial statements, if X controls or jointly controls Entity A, Entity A is related to Entity B when Y has control, joint control or significant influence over Entity B. [*Paragraph 9(b)(vi)–(a)(i) and 9(b)(vi)–(a)(ii)*]

IE23   If X has significant influence over Entity A and Y has significant influence over Entity B, Entities A and B are not related to each other.

Example 6 – Entity with joint control

IE24   Entity A has both (i) joint control over Entity B and (ii) joint control or significant influence over Entity C.

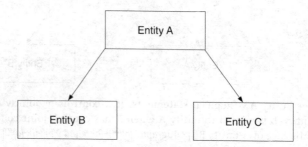

IE25   For Entity B's financial statements, Entity C is related to Entity B. [*Paragraph 9(b)(iii) and (iv)*]

IE26   Similarly, for Entity C's financial statements, Entity B is related to Entity C. [*Paragraph 9(b)(iii) and (iv)*]

Table of Concordance

This table shows how the contents of the superseded version of IAS 24 and the revised version of IAS 24 correspond. Paragraphs are treated as corresponding if they broadly address the same matter even though the guidance may differ.

Superseded IAS 24 paragraph	Revised IAS 24 paragraph	Superseded IAS 24 paragraph	Revised IAS 24 paragraph	Superseded IAS 24 paragraph	Revised IAS 24 paragraph
1	1	11	11	20	21
2	2	None	12	20	22
3	3	12	13	21	23
4	4	13	14	22	24
5	5	14	15	None	25
6	6	15	16	None	26
7	7	16	17	None	27
8	8	17	18	23	28
9	9	18	19	23A	None
10	10	19	20	24	29

IASB documents published to accompany

International Accounting Standard 27

Consolidated and Separate Financial Statements

This version includes amendments resulting from IFRSs issued up to 31 December 2009.

The text of the unaccompanied IAS 27 is contained in Part A of this edition. Its effective date when issued was 1 January 2005. The effective date of the most recent amendments is 1 January 2013. This part presents the following accompanying documents:

Approval by the Board of IAS 27 issued in December 2003

International Accounting Standard 27 *Consolidated and Separate Financial Statements* (as revised in 2003) was approved for issue by thirteen of the fourteen members of the International Accounting Standards Board. Mr Yamada dissented. His dissenting opinion is set out after the Basis for Conclusions.

Sir David Tweedie	Chairman
Thomas E Jones	Vice-Chairman
Mary E Barth	
Hans-Georg Bruns	
Anthony T Cope	
Robert P Garnett	
Gilbert Gélard	
James J Leisenring	
Warren J McGregor	
Patricia L O'Malley	
Harry K Schmid	
John T Smith	
Geoffrey Whittington	
Tatsumi Yamada	

Approval by the Board of amendments to IAS 27 issued in January 2008

The amendments to International Accounting Standard 27 *Consolidated and Separate Financial Statements* in 2008 were approved for issue by nine of the fourteen members of the International Accounting Standards Board. Messrs Danjou, Engström, Garnett, Gélard and Yamada dissented. Their dissenting opinions are set out after the Basis for Conclusions.

Sir David Tweedie	Chairman
Thomas E Jones	Vice-Chairman
Mary E Barth	
Hans-Georg Bruns	
Anthony T Cope	
Philippe Danjou	
Jan Engström	
Robert P Garnett	
Gilbert Gélard	
James J Leisenring	
Warren J McGregor	
Patricia L O'Malley	
John T Smith	
Tatsumi Yamada	

Approval by the Board of *Cost of an Investment in a Subsidiary, Jointly Controlled Entity or Associate* (amendments to IFRS 1 and IAS 27) issued in May 2008

Cost of an Investment in a Subsidiary, Jointly Controlled Entity or Associate (Amendments to IFRS 1 *First-time Adoption of International Financial Reporting Standards* and IAS 27) was approved for issue by eleven of the thirteen members of the International Accounting Standards Board. Professor Barth and Mr Danjou dissented. Their dissenting opinions are set out after the Basis for Conclusions.

Sir David Tweedie	Chairman
Thomas E Jones	Vice-Chairman
Mary E Barth	
Stephen Cooper	
Philippe Danjou	
Jan Engström	
Robert P Garnett	
Gilbert Gélard	
James J Leisenring	
Warren J McGregor	
John T Smith	
Tatsumi Yamada	
Wei-Guo Zhang	

Basis for Conclusions on
IAS 27 *Consolidated and Separate Financial Statements*

This Basis for Conclusions accompanies, but is not part of, IAS 27.

Introduction

BC1   This Basis for Conclusions summarises the International Accounting Standards Board's considerations in reaching its conclusions on revising IAS 27 *Consolidated Financial Statements and Accounting for Investments in Subsidiaries* in 2003 and on amending IAS 27 *Consolidated and Separate Financial Statements* in 2008. Individual Board members gave greater weight to some factors than to others.

BC2   In July 2001 the Board announced that, as part of its initial agenda of technical projects, it would undertake a project to improve a number of standards, including IAS 27 (as revised in 2000). The project was undertaken in the light of queries and criticisms raised in relation to the standards by securities regulators, professional accountants and other interested parties. The objectives of the Improvements project were to reduce or eliminate alternatives, redundancies and conflicts within standards, to deal with some convergence issues and to make other improvements. In May 2002 the Board published its proposals in an exposure draft of *Improvements to International Accounting Standards*, with a comment deadline of 16 September 2002. The Board received over 160 comment letters on the exposure draft. After redeliberating the issues in the light of the comments received, the Board issued a revised IAS 27 in December 2003.

BC3   In July 2001 the Board added a project on business combinations to its agenda. Phase I of the project resulted in the Board issuing in March 2004 IFRS 3 *Business Combinations* and revised versions of IAS 36 *Impairment of Assets* and IAS 38 *Intangible Assets*. The second phase of the project was conducted jointly with the US Financial Accounting Standards Board (FASB), and focused primarily on the application of the acquisition method.

BC4   Part of the second phase of the business combinations project was the reconsideration of business combinations in which an acquirer obtains control of a subsidiary through the acquisition of some, but not all, of the equity interests in that subsidiary. In those business combinations, non-controlling interests in the subsidiary exist at the date of the business combination.

BC5   When the Board revised IAS 27 in 2003, it acknowledged that additional guidance was needed on the recognition and measurement of non-controlling interests and the treatment of transactions with non-controlling interests. The Board was aware of diversity in practice in the absence of guidance in IFRSs, with as many as five methods being used to account for acquisitions of non-controlling interests after control is obtained.

BC6   In June 2005 the Board published an exposure draft of proposed amendments to IAS 27 in conjunction with an exposure draft of proposed amendments to IFRS 3 as part of the second phase of the business combinations project. The Board received 95 comment letters on the exposure draft of amendments to IAS 27.

BC7   After redeliberating the issues in the light of the comments received, in 2008 the Board issued a revised IFRS 3 together with an amended version of IAS 27. Close to the same time, the FASB issued Statement No. 141 (revised 2007) *Business Combinations* and Statement No. 160 *Noncontrolling Interests in Consolidated Financial Statements*, which amended Accounting Research Bulletin No. 51, *Consolidated Financial Statements* (ARB 51). In developing the amendments, the Board did not reconsider all of the requirements in IAS 27, and the FASB did not discuss all of the requirements of ARB 51. The changes primarily relate to accounting for non-controlling interests and the loss of control of subsidiaries. The boards reached the same conclusions on all of the issues considered jointly.

BC8   Because the Board's intention was not to reconsider the fundamental approach to consolidation established in IAS 27, this Basis for Conclusions does not discuss requirements in IAS 27 that the Board has not reconsidered. The Board is considering the other requirements of IAS 27 as part of its project on consolidation.

Presentation of consolidated financial statements (2003 revision)

Exemption from preparing consolidated financial statements

BC9   Paragraph 7 of IAS 27 (as revised in 2000) required consolidated financial statements to be presented. However, paragraph 8 permitted a parent that is a wholly-owned or virtually wholly-owned subsidiary not to prepare consolidated financial statements. The Board considered whether to withdraw or amend this exemption from the general requirement.

BC10   The Board decided to retain an exemption, so that entities in a group that are required by law to produce financial statements available for public use in accordance with International Financial Reporting Standards, in addition to consolidated financial statements, would not be unduly burdened.

BC11   The Board noted that in some circumstances users can find sufficient information for their purposes regarding a subsidiary from either its separate financial statements or consolidated financial statements. In addition, the users of financial statements of a subsidiary often have, or can get access to, more information.

BC12   Having agreed to retain an exemption, the Board decided to modify the circumstances in which an entity would be exempt and considered the following criteria.

Unanimous agreement of the owners of the minority interests[*]

BC13   The 2002 exposure draft proposed to extend the exemption to a parent that is not wholly-owned if the owners of the minority interest, including those not otherwise entitled to vote, unanimously agree.

---

*   IAS 27 (as amended in 2008) changed the term 'minority interest' to 'non-controlling interest'. For further discussion see paragraph BC28.

BC14　Some respondents disagreed with the proposal for unanimous agreement of minority shareholders to be a condition for exemption, in particular because of the practical difficulties in obtaining responses from all of those shareholders. The Board decided that the exemption should be available to a parent that is not wholly-owned when the owners of the minority interests have been informed about, and do not object to, consolidated financial statements not being presented.

Exemption available only to non-public entities

BC15　The Board believes that the information needs of users of financial statements of entities whose debt or equity instruments are traded in a public market are best served when investments in subsidiaries, jointly controlled entities and associates are accounted for in accordance with IAS 27, IAS 28 *Investments in Associates* and IAS 31 *Interests in Joint Ventures*. The Board therefore decided that the exemption from preparing such consolidated financial statements should not be available to such entities or to entities in the process of issuing instruments in a public market.

BC16　The Board decided that a parent that meets the criteria for exemption from the requirement to prepare consolidated financial statements should, in its separate financial statements, account for those subsidiaries in the same way as other parents, venturers with interests in jointly controlled entities or investors in associates account for investments in their separate financial statements. The Board draws a distinction between accounting for such investments as equity investments and accounting for the economic entity that the parent controls. In relation to the former, the Board decided that each category of investment should be accounted for consistently.

BC17　The Board decided that the same approach to accounting for investments in separate financial statements should apply irrespective of the circumstances for which they are prepared. Thus, parents that present consolidated financial statements, and those that do not because they are exempted, should present the same form of separate financial statements.

Scope of consolidated financial statements (2003 revision)

Scope exclusions

BC18　Paragraph 13 of IAS 27 (as revised in 2000) required a subsidiary to be excluded from consolidation when control is intended to be temporary or when the subsidiary operates under severe long-term restrictions.

Temporary control

BC19　The Board considered whether to remove this scope exclusion and thereby converge with other standard-setters that had recently eliminated a similar exclusion. The Board decided to consider this issue as part of a comprehensive standard dealing with asset disposals. It decided to retain an exemption from consolidating a subsidiary when there is evidence that the subsidiary is acquired with the intention to dispose of it within twelve months and that management is actively seeking a buyer. The Board's exposure draft ED 4 *Disposal of Non-current Assets and Presentation of Discontinued Operations* proposed to measure and present assets held for sale in a consistent manner irrespective of whether they are held by an investor or in a subsidiary. Therefore, ED 4 proposed to eliminate the exemption from consolidation when control is intended to be temporary and it contained a draft consequential amendment to IAS 27 to achieve this.[*]

Severe long-term restrictions impairing ability to transfer funds to the parent

BC20   The Board decided to remove the exclusion of a subsidiary from consolidation when there are severe long-term restrictions that impair a subsidiary's ability to transfer funds to the parent. It did so because such circumstances may not preclude control. The Board decided that a parent, when assessing its ability to control a subsidiary, should consider restrictions on the transfer of funds from the subsidiary to the parent. In themselves, such restrictions do not preclude control.

Venture capital organisations, private equity entities and similar organisations

BC21   The 2002 exposure draft of IAS 27 proposed to clarify that a subsidiary should not be excluded from consolidation simply because the entity is a venture capital organisation, mutual fund, unit trust or similar entity. Some respondents from the private equity industry disagreed with this proposed clarification. They argued that private equity entities should not be required to consolidate the investments they control in accordance with the requirements in IAS 27. They argued that they should measure those investments at fair value. Those respondents raised varying arguments—some based on whether control is exercised, some on the length of time that should be provided before consolidation is required, and some on whether consolidation was an appropriate basis for private equity entities or the type of investments they make.

BC22   Some respondents also noted that the Board decided to exclude venture capital organisations and similar entities from the scope of IASs 28 and 31 when investments in associates or jointly controlled entities are measured at fair value in accordance with IAS 39 *Financial Instruments: Recognition and Measurement*.[†] In the view of those respondents, the Board was proposing that similar assets should be accounted for in dissimilar ways.

BC23   The Board did not accept these arguments. The Board noted that those issues are not specific to the private equity industry. It confirmed that a subsidiary should not be excluded from consolidation on the basis of the nature of the controlling entity. Consolidation is based on the parent's ability to control the investee, which captures both the power to control (ie the ability exists but it is not exercised) and actual control (ie the ability is exercised). Consolidation is triggered by control and should not be affected by whether management intends to hold an investment in an entity that it controls for the short term.

---

[*]   In March 2004, the Board issued IFRS 5 *Non-current Assets Held for Sale and Discontinued Operations*. IFRS 5 removed this scope exclusion and eliminated the exemption from consolidation when control is intended to be temporary. For further discussion see the Basis for Conclusions on IFRS 5.

[†]   In November 2009 the Board amended some of the requirements of IAS 39 and relocated them to IFRS 9 *Financial Instruments*.

BC24   The Board noted that the exception from the consolidation principle in IAS 27 (as revised in 2000), when control of a subsidiary is intended to be temporary, might have been misread or interpreted loosely. Some respondents to the exposure draft had interpreted 'near future' as covering a period of up to five years. The Board decided to remove these words and to restrict the exception to subsidiaries acquired and held exclusively for disposal within twelve months, providing that management is actively seeking a buyer.

BC25   The Board did not agree that it should differentiate between types of entity, or types of investment, when applying a control model of consolidation. It also did not agree that management intention should be a determinant of control. Even if it had wished to make such differentiations, the Board did not see how or why it would be meaningful to distinguish private equity investors from other types of entities.

BC26   The Board believes that the diversity of the investment portfolios of entities operating in the private equity sector is not different from the diversification of portfolios held by a conglomerate, which is an industrial group made up of entities that often have diverse and unrelated interests. The Board acknowledged that financial information about an entity's different types of products and services and its operations in different geographical areas—segment information—is relevant to assessing the risks and returns of a diversified or multinational entity and may not be determinable from the aggregated data presented in the consolidated balance sheet.[*] The Board noted that IAS 14 *Segment Reporting* establishes principles for reporting segment information by entities whose equity or debt instruments are publicly traded, or any entity that discloses segment information voluntarily.[†]

BC27   The Board concluded that for investments under the control of private equity entities, users' information needs are best served by financial statements in which those investments are consolidated, thus revealing the extent of the operations of the entities they control. The Board noted that a parent can either present information about the fair value of those investments in the notes to the consolidated financial statements or prepare separate financial statements in addition to its consolidated financial statements, presenting those investments at cost or at fair value. By contrast, the Board decided that information needs of users of financial statements would not be well served if those controlling investments were measured only at fair value. This would leave unreported the assets and liabilities of a controlled entity. It is conceivable that an investment in a large, highly geared subsidiary would have only a small fair value. Reporting that value alone would preclude a user from being able to assess the financial position, results and cash flows of the group.

Non-controlling interests (2003 revision and 2008 amendments)

BC28   The 2008 amendments to IAS 27 changed the term 'minority interest' to 'non-controlling interest'. The change in terminology reflects the fact that the owner of a minority interest in an entity might control that entity and,

---

[*]   IAS 1 *Presentation of Financial Statements* (as revised in 2007) replaced the term 'balance sheet' with 'statement of financial position'.

[†]   In 2006 IAS 14 *Segment Reporting* was replaced by IFRS 8 *Operating Segments*.

conversely, that the owners of a majority interest might not control the entity. 'Non-controlling interest' is a more accurate description than 'minority interest' of the interests of those owners who do not have a controlling interest in an entity.

BC29   Non-controlling interest is defined in IAS 27 as the equity in a subsidiary not attributable, directly or indirectly, to a parent. Paragraph 26 of IAS 27 (as revised in 2000) required minority (non-controlling) interests to be presented in the consolidated balance sheet separately from liabilities and the equity of the shareholders of the parent.

BC30   As part of the 2003 revision of IAS 27, the Board decided to amend this requirement to require minority (non-controlling) interests to be presented in the consolidated balance sheet within equity, separately from the equity of the shareholders of the parent. The Board concluded that a minority (non-controlling) interest is not a liability of a group because it does not meet the definition of a liability in the *Framework for the Preparation and Presentation of Financial Statements*.

BC31   Paragraph 49(b) of the *Framework* states that a liability is a present obligation of the entity arising from past events, the settlement of which is expected to result in an outflow from the entity of resources embodying economic benefits. Paragraph 60 of the *Framework* further indicates that an essential characteristic of a liability is that the entity has a present obligation and that an obligation is a duty or responsibility to act or perform in a particular way. The Board noted that the existence of a minority (non-controlling) interest in the net assets of a subsidiary does not give rise to a present obligation of the group, the settlement of which is expected to result in an outflow of economic benefits from the group.

BC32   Rather, the Board noted that minority (non-controlling) interests represent the residual interest in the net assets of those subsidiaries held by some of the shareholders of the subsidiaries within the group, and therefore meet the *Framework*'s definition of equity. Paragraph 49(c) of the *Framework* states that equity is the residual interest in the assets of the entity after deducting all of its liabilities.

Attribution of losses (2008 amendments)

BC33   IAS 27 (as revised in 2003) stated that when losses attributed to the minority (non-controlling) interests exceed the minority's interests in the subsidiary's equity the excess, and any further losses applicable to the minority, is allocated against the majority interest except to the extent that the minority has a binding obligation and is able to make an additional investment to cover the losses.

BC34   The Board decided that this treatment was inconsistent with its conclusion that non-controlling interests are part of the equity of the group and proposed that an entity should attribute total comprehensive income applicable to non-controlling interests to them, even if this results in the non-controlling interests having a deficit balance.

BC35   If the parent enters into an arrangement that places it under an obligation to the subsidiary or to the non-controlling interests, the Board believes that the entity should account for that arrangement separately and the arrangement should not affect the way the entity attributes comprehensive income to the controlling and non-controlling interests.

BC36   Some respondents to the 2005 exposure draft agreed with the proposal, noting that non-controlling interests share proportionately in the risks and rewards of the investment in the subsidiary and that the proposal is consistent with the classification of non-controlling interests as equity.

BC37   Other respondents disagreed with the proposal, often on the grounds that controlling and non-controlling interests have different characteristics and should not be treated the same way. Those respondents argued that there was no need to change the guidance in IAS 27 (as revised in 2003) (ie that an entity should allocate excess losses to the controlling interest unless the non-controlling interests have a binding obligation and are able to make an additional investment to cover the losses). The reasons offered by those respondents were:

(a)   The non-controlling interests are not compelled to cover the deficit (unless they have otherwise specifically agreed to do so) and it is reasonable to assume that, should the subsidiary require additional capital in order to continue operations, the non-controlling interests would abandon their investments. In contrast, respondents asserted that in practice the controlling interest often has an implicit obligation to maintain the subsidiary as a going concern.

(b)   Often guarantees or other support arrangements by the parent, without any effect on the way losses are attributed to the controlling and non-controlling interests, protect the non-controlling interests from losses of the subsidiary in excess of equity. Respondents believe that allocating those losses to the parent and non-controlling interests and recognising separately a guarantee would not reflect the underlying economics, which are that only the parent absorbs the losses of the subsidiary. In their view, it is misleading for financial statements to imply that the non-controlling interests have an obligation to make additional investments.

(c)   Recognising guarantees separately is contrary to the principle of the non-recognition of transactions between owners.

(d)   Loss allocation should take into account legal, regulatory or contractual constraints, some of which may prevent entities from recognising negative non-controlling interests, especially for regulated businesses (eg banks and insurers).

BC38   The Board considered these arguments but observed that, although it is true that non-controlling interests have no further obligation to contribute assets to the subsidiary, neither does the parent. Non-controlling interests participate proportionally in the risks and rewards of an investment in the subsidiary.

BC39   Some respondents asked the Board to provide guidance on the accounting for guarantees and similar arrangements between the parent and the subsidiary or the non-controlling interests. They also suggested that the Board should require additional disclosures about inter-company guarantees and the extent of deficits, if any, of non-controlling interests.

BC40   The Board considered these requests but observed that this is an issue that is wider than negative non-controlling interests. Similarly, the parent is not necessarily responsible for the liabilities of a subsidiary, and often there are factors that restrict the ability of a parent entity to move assets around in a group, which means that the assets of the group are not necessarily freely available to that entity. The Board decided that it would be more appropriate to address comprehensively disclosures about non-controlling interests.

Changes in ownership interests in subsidiaries (2008 amendments)

BC41   The Board decided that after control of an entity is obtained, changes in a parent's ownership interest that do not result in a loss of control are accounted for as equity transactions (ie transactions with owners in their capacity as owners). This means that no gain or loss from these changes should be recognised in profit or loss. It also means that no change in the carrying amounts of the subsidiary's assets (including goodwill) or liabilities should be recognised as a result of such transactions.

BC42   The Board reached this conclusion because it believes that the approach adopted in these amendments is consistent with its previous decision that non-controlling interests are a separate component of equity (see paragraphs BC29–BC32).

BC43   Some respondents agreed that non-controlling interests are equity but stated that they should be treated as a special class of equity. Other respondents disagreed with the requirement because they believe that recognising transactions with non-controlling interests as equity transactions means that the Board has adopted an entity approach whereas the respondents prefer a proprietary approach. The Board disagreed with this characterisation of the accounting treatment, noting that the accounting proposed is a consequence of classifying non-controlling interests as equity. The Board did not consider comprehensively the entity and proprietary approaches as part of the amendments to IAS 27 in 2008.

BC44   Many respondents to the 2005 exposure draft suggested alternative approaches for the accounting for changes in controlling ownership interests. The most commonly suggested alternative would result in increases in controlling ownership interests giving rise to the recognition of additional goodwill, measured as the excess of the purchase consideration over the carrying amount of the separately identified assets in the subsidiary attributable to the additional interest acquired.

BC45   Some respondents suggested that when an entity reduces its ownership interest in a subsidiary, without losing control, it should recognise a gain or loss attributable to the controlling interest. They would measure that gain or loss as the difference between the consideration received and the proportion of the carrying amount of the subsidiary's assets (including recognised goodwill) attributable to the ownership interest being disposed of. Respondents supporting this alternative believed that it would provide relevant information about the gains and losses attributable to the controlling interest arising on the partial disposal of ownership interests in subsidiaries.

BC46 The Board rejected this alternative. Recognising a change in any of the assets of the business, including goodwill, is inconsistent with the Board's decision in IFRS 3 (as revised in 2008) that obtaining control in a business combination is a significant economic event. That event causes the initial recognition and measurement of all the assets acquired and liabilities assumed in the business combination. Subsequent transactions with owners should not affect the measurement of those assets and liabilities.

BC47 The parent already controls the assets of the business, although it must share the income from those assets with the non-controlling interests. By acquiring the non-controlling interests the parent is obtaining the rights to some, or all, of the income to which the non-controlling interests previously had rights. Generally, the wealth-generating ability of those assets is unaffected by the acquisition of the non-controlling interests. That is to say, the parent is not investing in more or new assets. It is acquiring more rights to the income from the assets it already controls.

BC48 By acquiring some, or all, of the non-controlling interests the parent will be allocated a greater proportion of the profits or losses of the subsidiary in periods after the additional interests are acquired. The adjustment to the controlling interest will be equal to the unrecognised share of the value changes that the parent will be allocated when those value changes are recognised by the subsidiary. Failure to make that adjustment will cause the controlling interest to be overstated.

BC49 The Board noted that accounting for changes in controlling ownership interests as equity transactions, as well as ensuring that the income of the group and the reported controlling interests are faithfully represented, is less complex than the other alternatives considered.

BC50 Some respondents disagreed with the proposal because they were concerned about the effect on reported equity of the subsequent acquisition of non-controlling interests by the parent. Those respondents seemed to be particularly concerned about the effect on the reported leverage of an entity that acquires non-controlling interests and whether this might, for example, cause those entities to have to renegotiate loan agreements.

BC51 The Board observed that all acquisitions of an entity's equity reduce the entity's equity, regardless of whether it is an acquisition of the parent's ordinary or preference shares or non-controlling interests. Hence, the treatment of a subsequent acquisition of non-controlling interests is consistent with the general accounting for the acquisition by an entity of instruments classified as equity.

BC52 The Board understands the importance of providing owners of the parent with information about the total changes in their reported equity. Therefore, the Board decided to require entities to present in a separate schedule the effects of any changes in a parent's ownership interest in a subsidiary that do not result in a loss of control on the equity attributable to owners of the parent.

Loss of control (2008 amendments)

BC53   A parent loses control of a subsidiary when it loses the power to govern the financial and operating policies of an investee so as to obtain benefit from its activities. Loss of control can result from the sale of an ownership interest or by other means, such as when a subsidiary issues new ownership interests to third parties. Loss of control can also occur in the absence of a transaction. It may, for example, occur on the expiry of an agreement that previously allowed an entity to control a subsidiary.

BC54   On loss of control, the parent-subsidiary relationship ceases to exist. The parent no longer controls the subsidiary's individual assets and liabilities. Therefore, the parent derecognises the individual assets, liabilities and equity related to that subsidiary. Equity includes any non-controlling interests as well as amounts previously recognised in other comprehensive income in relation to, for example, available-for-sale financial instruments and foreign currency translation.

BC55   The Board decided that any investment the parent has in the former subsidiary after control is lost should be measured at fair value at the date that control is lost and that any resulting gain or loss should be recognised in profit or loss. Some respondents disagreed with that decision. Those respondents asserted that the principles for revenue and gain recognition in the *Framework* would not be satisfied for the retained interest. The Board disagreed with those respondents. Measuring the investment at fair value reflects the Board's view that the loss of control of a subsidiary is a significant economic event. The parent-subsidiary relationship ceases to exist and an investor-investee relationship begins that differs significantly from the former parent-subsidiary relationship. Therefore, the new investor-investee relationship is recognised and measured initially at the date when control is lost.

BC56   The Board decided that the loss of control of a subsidiary is, from the group's perspective, the loss of control over some of the group's individual assets and liabilities. Accordingly, the general requirements in IFRSs should be applied in accounting for the derecognition from the group's financial statements of the subsidiary's assets and liabilities. If a gain or loss previously recognised in other comprehensive income would be reclassified to profit or loss on the separate disposal of those assets and liabilities, the parent reclassifies the gain or loss from equity to profit or loss on the indirect disposal of those assets and liabilities through loss of control of a subsidiary. For example, if a subsidiary sells one of its available-for-sale financial assets in a separate transaction, a gain or loss previously recognised in other comprehensive income would be reclassified to profit or loss. Similarly, on the loss of control of a subsidiary, the entire gain or loss attributed to the parent on that former subsidiary's available-for-sale financial assets previously recognised in other comprehensive income would be reclassified to profit or loss.

BC57   The Board also discussed the accounting when an entity transfers its shares in a subsidiary to its own shareholders with the result that the entity loses control of the subsidiary (commonly referred to as a spin-off). The International Financial Reporting Interpretations Committee had previously discussed this matter, but decided not to take it on to its agenda while the business combinations project was in progress. The Board observed that the issue is outside the scope of the business combinations project. Therefore, the Board decided not to address the measurement basis of distributions to owners in the amendments to IAS 27.

Multiple arrangements

BC58 The Board considered whether its decision that a gain or loss on the disposal of a subsidiary should be recognised only when that disposal results in a loss of control could give rise to opportunities to structure transactions to achieve a particular accounting outcome. For example, would an entity be motivated to structure a transaction or arrangement as multiple steps to maximise gains or minimise losses if an entity was planning to dispose of its controlling interest in a subsidiary? Consider the following example. Entity P controls 70 per cent of entity S. P intends to sell all of its 70 per cent controlling interest in S. P could initially sell 19 per cent of its ownership interest in S without loss of control and then, soon afterwards, sell the remaining 51 per cent and lose control. Alternatively, P could sell all of its 70 per cent interest in S in one transaction. In the first case, any difference between the amount by which the non-controlling interests are adjusted and the fair value of the consideration received on the sale of the 19 per cent interest would be recognised directly in equity, whereas the gain or loss from the sale of the remaining 51 per cent interest would be recognised in profit or loss. In the second case, a gain or loss on the sale of the whole 70 per cent interest would be recognised in profit or loss.

BC59 The Board noted that the opportunity to conceal losses through structuring would be reduced by the requirements of IAS 36 and IFRS 5 *Non-current Assets Held for Sale and Discontinued Operations*. Paragraph 12 of IAS 36 includes significant changes in how an entity uses or expects to use an asset as one of the indicators that the asset might be impaired.

BC60 Once an asset meets the criteria to be classified as held for sale (or is included in a disposal group that is classified as held for sale), it is excluded from the scope of IAS 36 and is accounted for in accordance with IFRS 5. In accordance with paragraph 20 of IFRS 5 'an entity shall recognise an impairment loss for any initial or subsequent write-down of the asset (or disposal group) to fair value less costs to sell ...'. Therefore, if appropriate, an impairment loss would be recognised for the goodwill and non-current assets of a subsidiary that will be sold or otherwise disposed of before control of the subsidiary is lost. Accordingly, the Board concluded that the principal risk is the minimising of gains, which entities are unlikely to strive to do.

BC61 The Board decided that the possibility of such structuring could be overcome by requiring entities to consider whether multiple arrangements should be accounted for as a single transaction to ensure that the principle of faithful representation is adhered to. The Board believes that all of the terms and conditions of the arrangements and their economic effects should be considered in determining whether multiple arrangements should be accounted for as a single arrangement. Accordingly, the Board included indicators in paragraph 33 to assist in identifying when multiple arrangements that result in the loss of control of a subsidiary should be treated as a single arrangement.

BC62   Some respondents disagreed with the indicators that were provided in the exposure draft. Some respondents stated that the need for guidance on when multiple arrangements should be accounted for as a single arrangement indicates a conceptual weakness in the accounting model developed in the exposure draft. They also stated that such guidance would be unnecessary under other alternatives for accounting for decreases in ownership interests. The Board acknowledges that guidance on multiple arrangements would be unnecessary under some of the other accounting alternatives. However, the Board believes that this does not mean that those models are conceptually superior.

BC63   Some respondents suggested that IAS 27 should include examples rather than indicators for when multiple transactions should be treated as a single transaction or arrangement, but that those examples should not be considered a complete list. The Board considered that suggestion, but decided to affirm the indicators that were in the exposure draft. The Board believed that the indicators could be applied to a variety of situations and are preferable to providing what could be an endless list of examples to try to capture every possible arrangement.

Loss of significant influence or joint control

BC64   The Board observed that the loss of control of a subsidiary, the loss of significant influence over an associate and the loss of joint control over a jointly controlled entity are economically similar events; thus they should be accounted for similarly. The loss of control as well as the loss of significant influence or joint control represents a significant economic event that changes the nature of an investment. Therefore, the Board concluded that the accounting guidance on the loss of control of a subsidiary should be extended to events or transactions in which an investor loses significant influence over an associate or joint control over a jointly controlled entity. Thus, the investor's investment after significant influence or joint control is lost should be recognised and measured initially at fair value and the amount of any resulting gain or loss should be recognised in profit or loss. Therefore, the Board decided to amend IAS 21 *The Effects of Changes in Foreign Exchange Rates*, IAS 28 and IAS 31, accordingly. The FASB considered whether to address that same issue as part of this project. The FASB concluded that the accounting for investments that no longer qualify for equity method accounting was outside the scope of the project.

Measurement of investments in subsidiaries, jointly controlled entities and associates in separate financial statements (2003 revision and 2008 amendments)

BC65   Paragraph 29 of IAS 27 (as revised in 2000) permitted investments in subsidiaries to be measured in any one of three ways in a parent's separate financial statements. These were cost, the equity method, or as available-for-sale financial assets in accordance with IAS 39.* Paragraph 12 of IAS 28 (as revised in 2000) permitted the same choices for investments in associates in separate financial statements, and paragraph 38 of IAS 31 (as revised in 2000) mentioned that IAS 31 did not indicate a preference for any particular treatment for accounting for

---

*   IFRS 9 *Financial Instruments*, issued in November 2009, eliminated the category of available-for-sale financial assets.

interests in jointly controlled entities in a venturer's separate financial statements. The Board decided to require use of cost or IAS 39* for all investments included in separate financial statements.

BC66 Although the equity method would provide users with some profit and loss information similar to that obtained from consolidation, the Board noted that such information is reflected in the investor's economic entity financial statements and does not need to be provided to the users of its separate financial statements. For separate statements, the focus is upon the performance of the assets as investments. The Board concluded that separate financial statements prepared using either the fair value method in accordance with IAS 39* or the cost method would be relevant. Using the fair value method in accordance with IAS 39* would provide a measure of the economic value of the investments. Using the cost method can result in relevant information, depending on the purpose of preparing the separate financial statements. For example, they may be needed only by particular parties to determine the dividend income from subsidiaries.

BC66A As part of its annual improvements project begun in 2007, the Board identified an apparent inconsistency with IFRS 5. The inconsistency relates to the accounting by a parent in its separate financial statements when investments it accounts for in accordance with IAS 39* are classified as held for sale in accordance with IFRS 5. Paragraph 38 requires an entity that prepares separate financial statements to account for such investments that are classified as held for sale (or included in a disposal group that is classified as held for sale) in accordance with IFRS 5. However, financial assets that an entity accounts for in accordance with IAS 39* are excluded from IFRS 5's measurement requirements.

BC66B Paragraph BC13 of the Basis for Conclusions on IFRS 5 explains that the Board decided that non-current assets should be excluded from the measurement scope of IFRS 5 only 'if (i) they are already carried at fair value with changes in fair value recognised in profit or loss or (ii) there would be difficulties in determining their fair value less costs to sell.' The Board acknowledged in the Basis for Conclusions on IFRS 5 that not all financial assets within the scope of IAS 39* are recognised at fair value with changes in fair value recognised in profit or loss, but it did not want to make any further changes to the accounting for financial assets at that time.

BC66C Therefore, the Board amended paragraph 38 by *Improvements to IFRSs* issued in May 2008 to align the accounting in separate financial statements for those investments that are accounted for in accordance with IAS 39* with the measurement exclusion that IFRS 5 provides for other assets that are accounted for in accordance with IAS 39 before classification as held for sale. Thus, an entity should continue to account for such investments in accordance with IAS 39 when they meet the held for sale criteria in IFRS 5.

---

* In November 2009 the Board amended the requirements of IAS 39 relating to classification and measurement of assets within the scope of IAS 39 and relocated them to IFRS 9 *Financial Instruments*.

Dividend received from a subsidiary, jointly controlled entity or associate

BC66D   Before *Cost of an Investment in a Subsidiary, Jointly Controlled Entity or Associate* was issued in May 2008, IAS 27 described a 'cost method'. This required an entity to recognise distributions as income only if they came from post-acquisition retained earnings. Distributions received in excess of such profits were regarded as a recovery of investment and were recognised as a reduction in the cost of the investment. To apply that method retrospectively upon first-time adoption of IFRSs in its separate financial statements, an investor would need to know the subsidiary's pre-acquisition retained earnings in accordance with IFRSs.

BC66E   Restating pre-acquisition retained earnings would be a task tantamount to restating the business combination (for which IFRS 1 *First-time Adoption of International Financial Reporting Standards* provides an exemption in Appendix B).* It might involve subjective use of hindsight, which would diminish the relevance and reliability of the information. In some cases, the restatement would be time-consuming and difficult. In other cases, it would be impossible (because it would involve making judgements about the fair values of the assets and liabilities of a subsidiary at the acquisition date).

BC66F   Therefore, in *Cost of an Investment in a Subsidiary*, an exposure draft of proposed amendments to IFRS 1 (published in January 2007), the Board proposed to give first-time adopters an exemption from restating the retained earnings of the subsidiary at the date of acquisition for the purpose of applying the cost method.

BC66G   In considering the responses to that exposure draft, the Board observed that the principle underpinning the cost method is that a return of an investment should be deducted from the carrying amount of the investment. However, the wording in the previous version of IAS 27 created a problem in some jurisdictions because it made specific reference to retained earnings as the means of making that assessment. The Board determined that the best way to resolve this issue was to delete the definition of the cost method.

BC66H   In removing the definition of the cost method, the Board concluded that an investor should recognise a dividend from a subsidiary, jointly controlled entity or associate as income in its separate financial statements. Consequently, the requirement to separate the retained earnings of an entity into pre-acquisition and post-acquisition components as a method for assessing whether a dividend is a recovery of its associated investment has been removed from IFRSs.

BC66I   To reduce the risk that removing the definition of the cost method would lead to investments in subsidiaries, jointly controlled entities and associates being overstated in the separate financial statements of the investor, the Board proposed that the related investment should be tested for impairment in accordance with IAS 36.

BC66J   The Board published its revised proposals in *Cost of an Investment in a Subsidiary, Jointly Controlled Entity or Associate*, an exposure draft of proposed amendments to IFRS 1 and IAS 27, in December 2007. Respondents generally supported the proposed amendments to IAS 27, except for the proposal to require impairment

---

*   As a result of the revision of IFRS 1 *First-time Adoption of International Financial Reporting Standards* in November 2008, Appendix B became Appendix C.

testing of the related investment when an investor recognises a dividend. In the light of the comments received, the Board revised its proposal and identified specific indicators of impairment. This was done to narrow the circumstances under which impairment testing of the related investment would be required when an investor recognises a dividend (see paragraph 12(h) of IAS 36). The Board included the amendments in *Cost of an Investment in a Subsidiary, Jointly Controlled Entity or Associate* issued in May 2008.

Measurement of cost in the separate financial statements of a new parent

BC66K In 2007 the Board received enquiries about the application of paragraph 38(a) when a parent reorganises the structure of its group by establishing a new entity as its parent. The new parent obtains control of the original parent by issuing equity instruments in exchange for existing equity instruments of the original parent.

BC66L In this type of reorganisation, the assets and liabilities of the new group and the original group are the same immediately before and after the reorganisation. In addition, the owners of the original parent have the same relative and absolute interests in the net assets of the new group immediately after the reorganisation as they had in the net assets of the original group before the reorganisation. Finally, this type of reorganisation involves an existing entity and its shareholders agreeing to create a new parent between them. In contrast, many transactions or events that result in a parent-subsidiary relationship are initiated by a parent over an entity that will be positioned below it in the structure of the group.

BC66M Therefore, the Board decided that in applying paragraph 38(a) *in the limited circumstances in which a parent establishes a new parent in this particular manner*, the new parent should measure the cost of its investment in the original parent at the carrying amount of its share of the equity items shown in the separate financial statements of the original parent at the date of the reorganisation. In December 2007 the Board published an exposure draft proposing to amend IAS 27 to add a paragraph with that requirement.

BC66N In response to comments received from respondents to that exposure draft, the Board modified the drafting of the amendment (paragraphs 38B and 38C of the Standard) to clarify that it applies to the following types of reorganisations when they satisfy the criteria specified in the amendment:

(a) reorganisations in which the new parent does not acquire all of the equity instruments of the original parent. For example, a new parent might issue equity instruments in exchange for ordinary shares of the original parent, but not acquire the preference shares of the original parent. In addition, a new parent might obtain control of the original parent, but not acquire all of the ordinary shares of the original parent.

(b) the establishment of an intermediate parent within a group, as well as the establishment of a new ultimate parent of a group.

(c) reorganisations in which an entity that is not a parent establishes a new entity as its parent.

BC66O   In addition, the Board clarified that the amendment focuses on the measurement of one asset—the new parent's investment in the original parent in the new parent's separate financial statements. The amendment does not apply to the measurement of any other assets or liabilities in the separate financial statements of either the original parent or the new parent or in the consolidated financial statements.

BC66P   The Board included the amendment in *Cost of an Investment in a Subsidiary, Jointly Controlled Entity or Associate* issued in May 2008.

BC66Q   The Board did not consider the accounting for other types of reorganisations or for common control transactions more broadly. Accordingly, paragraphs 38B and 38C apply only when the criteria in those paragraphs are satisfied. Therefore, the Board expects that entities would continue to account for transactions that do not satisfy the criteria in paragraphs 38B and 38C in accordance with their accounting policies for such transactions. The Board plans to consider the definition of common control and the accounting for business combinations under common control in its project on common control transactions.

Disclosure (2008 amendments)

BC67   In considering the 2008 amendments to IAS 27 the Board discussed whether any additional disclosures were necessary. The Board decided that the amount of any gain or loss arising on the loss of control of a subsidiary, including the portion of the gain or loss attributable to recognising any investment retained in the former subsidiary at its fair value at the date when control is lost, and the line item in the statement of comprehensive income in which the gains or losses are recognised should be disclosed. This disclosure will provide information about the effect of the loss of control of a subsidiary on the financial position at the end of, and performance for, the reporting period.

BC68   In its deliberations in the second phase of the business combinations project, the FASB decided to require entities with one or more partially-owned subsidiaries to disclose in the notes to the consolidated financial statements a schedule showing the effects on the controlling interest's equity of changes in a parent's ownership interest in a subsidiary that do not result in a loss of control.

BC69   In the 2005 exposure draft, the Board did not propose to require this disclosure. The Board noted that IFRSs require this information to be provided in the statement of changes in equity or in the notes to the financial statements. This is because IAS 1 *Presentation of Financial Statements* requires an entity to present, within the statement of changes in equity, a reconciliation between the carrying amount of each component of equity at the beginning and end of the period, disclosing separately each change.

BC70   Many respondents to the 2005 exposure draft requested more prominent disclosure of the effects of transactions with non-controlling interests on the equity of the owners of the parent. Therefore, the Board decided to converge with the FASB's disclosure requirement and to require that if a parent has equity transactions with non-controlling interests, it should disclose in a separate schedule the effects of those transactions on the equity of the owners of the parent.

BC71 The Board understands that some users will be interested in information pertaining only to the owners of the parent. The Board expects that the presentation and disclosure requirements of IAS 27, as revised, will meet their information needs.

Transitional provisions (2008 amendments)

BC72 To improve the comparability of financial information across entities, amendments to IFRSs are usually applied retrospectively. Therefore, the Board proposed in its 2005 exposure draft to require retrospective application of the amendments to IAS 27, on the basis that the benefits of retrospective application outweigh the costs. However, in the 2005 exposure draft the Board identified two circumstances in which it concluded that retrospective application would be impracticable:

(a) accounting for increases in a parent's ownership interest in a subsidiary that occurred before the effective date of the amendments. Therefore, the accounting for any previous increase in a parent's ownership interest in a subsidiary before the effective date of the amendments should not be adjusted.

(b) accounting for a parent's investment in a former subsidiary over which control was lost before the effective date of the amendments. Therefore, the carrying amount of any investment in a former subsidiary should not be adjusted to its fair value on the date when control was lost. In addition, an entity should not recalculate any gain or loss on loss of control of a subsidiary if the loss of control occurred before the effective date of the amendments.

BC73 The Board concluded that the implementation difficulties and costs associated with applying the amendments retrospectively in these circumstances outweigh the benefit of improved comparability of financial information. Therefore, the Board decided to require prospective application. In addition, the Board concluded that identifying those provisions for which retrospective application of the amendments would be impracticable, and thus prospective application would be required, would reduce implementation costs and result in greater comparability between entities.

BC74 Some respondents were concerned that the transitional provisions were different for increases and decreases in ownership interests. They argued that accounting for decreases in non-controlling interests retrospectively imposes compliance costs that are not justifiable, mainly because the requirement to account for increases prospectively reduces comparability anyway. The Board accepted those arguments and decided that prospective application would be required for all changes in ownership interests. The revised transitional provisions mean that increases and decreases in ownership interests will be treated symmetrically and that recasting of financial statements is limited to disclosure and presentation. The recognition and measurement of previous transactions will not be changed upon transition.

BC75 In response to practical concerns raised by respondents, the Board also decided to require prospective application of the requirement to allocate losses in excess of the non-controlling interests in the equity of a subsidiary to the non-controlling interests, even if that would result in the non-controlling interests being reported as a deficit.

Appendix
Amendments to the Basis for Conclusions on other IFRSs

This appendix contains amendments to the Basis for Conclusions on other IFRSs that are necessary in order to ensure consistency with the amendments to IAS 27 and the related amendments to other IFRSs.

* * * * *

The amendments contained in this appendix when IAS 27, as amended in 2008, was issued have been incorporated into the Basis for Conclusions on IASs 21, 28 and 31 and on SIC-7 as issued at 10 January 2008.

Dissenting opinions

Dissent of Tatsumi Yamada from IAS 27 (as revised in 2003)

DO1 Mr Yamada dissents from this Standard because he believes that the change in classification of minority interests in the consolidated balance sheet, that is to say, the requirement that it be shown as equity, should not be made as part of the Improvements project. He agrees that minority interests do not meet the definition of a liability under the *Framework for the Preparation and Presentation of Financial Statements*, as stated in paragraph BC31 of the Basis for Conclusions, and that the current requirement, for minority interests to be presented separately from liabilities and the parent shareholders' equity, is not desirable. However, he does not believe that this requirement should be altered at this stage. He believes that before making the change in classification, which will have a wide variety of impacts on current consolidation practices, various issues related to this change need to be considered comprehensively by the Board. These include consideration of the objectives of consolidated financial statements and the accounting procedures that should flow from those objectives. Even though the Board concluded as noted in paragraph BC27, he believes that the decision related to the classification of minority interests should not be made until such a comprehensive consideration of recognition and measurement is completed.*

DO2 Traditionally, there are two views of the objectives of consolidated financial statements; they are implicit in the parent company view and the economic entity view. Mr Yamada believes that the objectives, that is to say, what information should be provided and to whom, should be considered by the Board before it makes its decision on the classification of minority interests in IAS 27. He is of the view that the Board is taking the economic entity view without giving enough consideration to this fundamental issue.

DO3 Step acquisitions are being discussed in the second phase of the Business Combinations project, which is not yet finalised at the time of finalising IAS 27 under the Improvements project. When the ownership interest of the parent increases, the Board has tentatively decided that the difference between the consideration paid by the parent to minority interests and the carrying value of the ownership interests acquired by the parent is recognised as part of equity, which is different from the current practice of recognising a change in the amount of goodwill. If the parent retains control of a subsidiary but its ownership interest decreases, the difference between the consideration received by the parent and the carrying value of the ownership interests transferred is also recognised as part of equity, which is different from the current practice of recognising a gain or a loss. Mr Yamada believes that the results of this discussion

---

* Paragraph BC27 of IAS 27 (as revised in 2003) was deleted as part of the 2008 amendments to IAS 27. That paragraph stated:

> The Board acknowledged that this decision gives rise to questions about the recognition and measurement of minority interests but it concluded that the proposed presentation is consistent with current standards and the *Framework* and would provide better comparability than presentation in the consolidated balance sheet with either liabilities or parent shareholders' equity. It decided that the recognition and measurement questions should be addressed as part of its project on business combinations.

are predetermined by the decision related to the classification of minority interests as equity. The changes in accounting treatments are fundamental and he believes that the decision on which of the two views should govern the consolidated financial statements should be taken only after careful consideration of the ramifications. He believes that the amendment of IAS 27 relating to the classification of minority interests should not be made before completion of the second phase of the Business Combinations project.

Dissent of Philippe Danjou, Jan Engström, Robert P Garnett, Gilbert Gélard and Tatsumi Yamada from the amendments to IAS 27 issued in January 2008 on the accounting for non-controlling interests and the loss of control of a subsidiary

DO1　Messrs Danjou, Engström, Garnett, Gélard and Yamada dissent from the 2008 amendments to IAS 27.

Accounting for changes in ownership interests in a subsidiary

DO2　Messrs Danjou, Engström, Gélard and Yamada do not agree that acquisitions of non-controlling interests in a subsidiary by the parent should be accounted for in full as equity transactions.

DO3　Those Board members observe that the consideration paid for an additional interest in a subsidiary will reflect the additional interest's share in:

(a)　the carrying amount of the subsidiary's net assets at that date;

(b)　additionally acquired goodwill; and

(c)　unrecognised increases in the fair value of the subsidiary's net assets (including goodwill) since the date when control was obtained.

DO4　Paragraphs 30 and 31 of the Standard require such a transaction to be accounted for as an equity transaction, by adjusting the relative interests of the parent and the non-controlling interests. As a consequence, the additionally acquired goodwill and any unrecognised increases in the fair value of the subsidiary's net assets would be deducted from equity. Those Board members disagree that such accounting faithfully represents the economics of such a transaction.

DO5　Those Board members believe that an increase in ownership interests in a subsidiary is likely to provide additional benefits to the parent. Although control has already been obtained, a higher ownership interest might increase synergies accruing to the parent, for example, by meeting legal thresholds provided in company law, which would give the parent an additional level of discretion over the subsidiary. If the additional ownership interest has been acquired in an arm's length exchange transaction in which knowledgeable, willing parties exchange equal values, these additional benefits are reflected in the purchase price of the additional ownership interest. Those Board members believe that the acquisition of non-controlling interests by the parent should give rise to the recognition of goodwill, measured as the excess of the consideration transferred over the carrying amount of the subsidiary's net assets attributable to the additional interest acquired. Those Board members acknowledge that this amount also includes unrecognised increases in the fair value of the subsidiary's net assets since the date when control was obtained. However, on the basis of cost-benefit considerations, they believe that it is a reasonable approximation of the additionally acquired goodwill.

DO6 Messrs Danjou, Gélard and Yamada agree that, in conformity with the *Framework for the Preparation and Presentation of Financial Statements*, non-controlling interests should be presented within the group's equity, because they are not liabilities. However, they believe that until the debates over the objectives of consolidated financial statements (ie what information should be provided and to whom) and the definition of the reporting entity have been settled at the conceptual level, transactions between the parent and non-controlling interests should not be accounted for in the same manner as transactions in which the parent entity acquires its own shares and reduces its equity. In their view, non-controlling interests cannot be considered equivalent to the ordinary ownership interests of the owners of the parent. The owners of the parent and the holders of non-controlling interests in a subsidiary do not share the same risks and rewards in relation to the group's operations and net assets because ownership interests in a subsidiary share only the risks and rewards associated with that subsidiary.

DO7 In addition, Messrs Danjou and Gélard observe that IFRS 3 *Business Combinations* (as revised in 2008) provides an option to measure non-controlling interests in a business combination as their proportionate share of the acquiree's net identifiable assets rather than at their fair value. However, paragraph BC207 of the Basis for Conclusions on IFRS 3 (as revised in 2008) states that accounting for the non-controlling interests at fair value is conceptually superior to this alternative measurement. This view implies that the subsidiary's portion of goodwill attributable to the non-controlling interests at the date when control was obtained is an asset at that date and there is no conceptual reason for it no longer to be an asset at the time of any subsequent acquisitions of non-controlling interests.

DO8 Mr Garnett disagrees with the treatment of changes in controlling interests in subsidiaries after control is established (paragraphs BC41–BC52 of the Basis for Conclusions). He believes that it is important that the consequences of such changes for the owners of the parent entity are reported clearly in the financial statements.

DO9 Mr Garnett believes that the amendments to IAS 27 adopt the economic entity approach that treats all equity interests in the group as being homogeneous. Transactions between controlling and non-controlling interests are regarded as mere transfers within the total equity interest and no gain or loss is recognised on such transactions. Mr Garnett observes that the non-controlling interests represent equity claims that are restricted to particular subsidiaries, whereas the controlling interests are affected by the performance of the entire group. The consolidated financial statements should therefore report performance from the perspective of the controlling interest (a parent entity perspective) in addition to the wider perspective provided by the economic entity approach. This implies the recognition of additional goodwill on purchases, and gains or losses on disposals of the parent entity's interest in a subsidiary.

DO10 If, as Mr Garnett would prefer, the full goodwill method were not used (see paragraphs DO7–DO10 of the dissenting views on IFRS 3), the acquisition of an additional interest in a subsidiary would give rise to the recognition of additional purchased goodwill, measured as the excess of the consideration transferred over the carrying amount of the subsidiary's net assets attributable to the additional interest acquired.

DO11   Mr Garnett does not agree with the requirement in paragraph 31 of the Standard that, in respect of a partial disposal of the parent's ownership interest in a subsidiary that does not result in a loss of control, the carrying amount of the non-controlling interests should be adjusted to reflect the change in the parent's interest in the subsidiary's net assets. On the contrary, he believes that the carrying amount of the non-controlling interests should be adjusted by the fair value of the consideration paid by the non-controlling interests to acquire that additional interest.

DO12   Mr Garnett also believes that it is important to provide the owners of the parent entity with information about the effects of a partial disposal of holdings in subsidiaries, including the difference between the fair value of the consideration received and the proportion of the carrying amount of the subsidiary's assets (including purchased goodwill) attributable to the disposal.

Loss of control

DO13   Mr Garnett disagrees with the requirement in paragraph 34 of the Standard that if a parent loses control of a subsidiary, it measures any retained investment in the former subsidiary at fair value and any difference between the carrying amount of the retained investment and its fair value is recognised in profit or loss, because the retained investment was not part of the exchange. The loss of control of a subsidiary is a significant economic event that warrants deconsolidation. However, the retained investment has not been sold. Under current IFRSs, gains and losses on cost method, available-for-sale and equity method investments are recognised in profit or loss only when the investment is sold (other than impairment). Mr Garnett would have recognised the effect of measuring the retained investment at fair value as a separate component of other comprehensive income instead of profit or loss.

Accounting for losses attributable to non-controlling interests

DO14   Mr Danjou disagrees with paragraph 28 of the Standard according to which losses can be attributed without limitation to the non-controlling interests even if this results in the non-controlling interests having a deficit balance.

DO15   In many circumstances, in the absence of any commitment or binding obligation of the non-controlling interests to make an additional investment to cover the excess losses of the subsidiary, the continuation of the operations of a subsidiary will be funded through the contribution of additional capital by the parent and with the non-controlling interests being diluted. In those circumstances, the deficit balance attributable to the non-controlling interests that would result from the amendment in paragraph 28 does not present faithfully the equity of the consolidating entity.

DO16   Mr Danjou believes that the Standard should therefore not preclude the allocation against the parent equity of losses that exceed the non-controlling interests in a consolidated subsidiary when the facts and circumstances are as outlined in paragraph DO15.

Dissent of Mary E Barth and Philippe Danjou from *Cost of an Investment in a Subsidiary, Jointly Controlled Entity or Associate* (amendments to IFRS 1 and IAS 27) issued in May 2008

DO1   Professor Barth and Mr Danjou voted against the publication of *Cost of an Investment in a Subsidiary, Jointly Controlled Entity or Associate* (Amendments to IFRS 1 *First-time Adoption of International Financial Reporting Standards* and IAS 27 *Consolidated and Separate Financial Statements*). The reasons for their dissent are set out below.

DO2   These Board members disagree with the **requirement** in paragraphs 38B and 38C of IAS 27 that when a reorganisation satisfies the criteria specified in those paragraphs and the resulting new parent accounts for its investment in the original parent at cost in accordance with paragraph 38(a) of IAS 27, the new parent must measure the cost at the carrying amount of its share of the equity items shown in the separate financial statements of the original parent at the date of the reorganisation.

DO3   These Board members acknowledge that a new parent could choose to apply paragraph 38(b) of IAS 27 and account for its investment in the original parent in accordance with IAS 39 *Financial Instruments: Recognition and Measurement.*[*] However, the new parent then would be required to account for the investment in accordance with IAS 39[*] in subsequent periods and to account for all other investments in the same category in accordance with IAS 39.[*]

DO4   These Board members also acknowledge, as outlined in paragraph BC66L of the Basis for Conclusions on IAS 27, that this type of reorganisation is different from other types of reorganisations in that the assets and liabilities of the new group and the original group are the same immediately before and after the reorganisation, as are the interests of the owners of the original parent in the net assets of those groups. Therefore, using the previous carrying amount to measure the cost of the new parent's investment in the original parent might be appropriate on the basis that the separate financial statements of the new parent would reflect its position as part of a pre-existing group.

DO5   However, these Board members believe that it is inappropriate to preclude a new parent from measuring the cost of its investment in the original parent at the fair value of the shares that it issues as part of the reorganisation. Separate financial statements are prepared to reflect the parent as a separate legal entity (ie not considering that the entity might be part of a group). Although such a reorganisation does not change the assets and liabilities of the group and therefore should have no accounting effect at the consolidated level, from the perspective of the new parent as a separate legal entity, its position has changed— it has issued shares and acquired an investment that it did not have previously. Also, in many jurisdictions, commercial law or corporate governance regulations require entities to measure new shares that they issue at the fair value of the consideration received for the shares.

---

[*]   In November 2009 the Board amended the requirements of IAS 39 relating to classification and measurement of assets within the scope of IAS 39 and relocated them to IFRS 9 *Financial Instruments*.

DO6   These Board members believe that the appropriate measurement basis for the new parent's cost of its investment in the original parent depends on the Board's view of separate financial statements. The Board is or will be discussing related issues in the reporting entity phase of its Conceptual Framework project and in its project on common control transactions. Accordingly, these Board members believe that the Board should have permitted a new parent to measure the cost of its investment in the original parent either at the carrying amount of its share of the equity items shown in the separate financial statements of the original parent or at the fair value of the equity instruments that it issues until the Board discusses the related issues in its projects on reporting entity and common control transactions.

Guidance on implementing
IAS 27 *Consolidated and Separate Financial Statements,*
IAS 28 *Investments in Associates* and
IAS 31 *Interests in Joint Ventures*

This guidance accompanies IAS 27, IAS 28 and IAS 31, but is not part of them.

Consideration of potential voting rights

Introduction

IG1 Paragraphs 14, 15 and 19 of IAS 27 *Consolidated and Separate Financial Statements* (as amended in 2008) and paragraphs 8 and 9 of IAS 28 *Investments in Associates* require an entity to consider the existence and effect of all potential voting rights that are currently exercisable or convertible. They also require all facts and circumstances that affect potential voting rights to be examined, except the intention of management and the financial ability to exercise or convert potential voting rights. Because the definition of joint control in paragraph 3 of IAS 31 *Interests in Joint Ventures* depends upon the definition of control, and because that Standard is linked to IAS 28 for application of the equity method, this guidance is also relevant to IAS 31.

Guidance

IG2 Paragraph 4 of IAS 27 defines control as the power to govern the financial and operating policies of an entity so as to obtain benefits from its activities. Paragraph 2 of IAS 28 defines significant influence as the power to participate in the financial and operating policy decisions of the investee but not to control those policies. Paragraph 3 of IAS 31 defines joint control as the contractually agreed sharing of control over an economic activity. In these contexts, power refers to the ability to do or effect something. Consequently, an entity has control, joint control or significant influence when it currently has the ability to exercise that power, regardless of whether control, joint control or significant influence is actively demonstrated or is passive in nature. Potential voting rights held by an entity that are currently exercisable or convertible provide this ability. The ability to exercise power does not exist when potential voting rights lack economic substance (eg the exercise price is set in a manner that precludes exercise or conversion in any feasible scenario). Consequently, potential voting rights are considered when, in substance, they provide the ability to exercise power.

IG3 Control and significant influence also arise in the circumstances described in paragraph 13 of IAS 27 and paragraphs 6 and 7 of IAS 28 respectively, which include consideration of the relative ownership of voting rights. IAS 31 depends on IAS 27 and IAS 28 and references to IAS 27 and IAS 28 from this point onwards should be read as being relevant to IAS 31. Nevertheless it should be borne in mind that joint control involves contractual sharing of control and this contractual aspect is likely to be the critical determinant. Potential voting rights such as share call options and convertible debt are capable of changing an entity's voting power over another entity—if the potential voting rights are exercised or converted, then the relative ownership of the ordinary shares carrying voting rights changes. Consequently, the existence of control (the definition of which permits only one entity to have control of another entity) and significant influence are determined only after assessing all the factors described in paragraph 13 of IAS 27 and paragraphs 6 and 7 of IAS 28 respectively, and considering the existence and effect of potential voting rights. In addition, the entity examines all facts and circumstances that affect potential voting rights except the intention of management and the financial ability to exercise or convert such rights. The intention of management does not affect the existence of power and the financial ability of an entity to exercise or convert potential voting rights is difficult to assess.

IG4 An entity may initially conclude that it controls or significantly influences another entity after considering the potential voting rights that it can currently exercise or convert. However, the entity may not control or significantly influence the other entity when potential voting rights held by other parties are also currently exercisable or convertible. Consequently, an entity considers all potential voting rights held by it and by other parties that are currently exercisable or convertible when determining whether it controls or significantly influences another entity. For example, all share call options are considered, whether held by the entity or another party. Furthermore, the definition of control in paragraph 4 of IAS 27 permits only one entity to have control of another entity. Therefore, when two or more entities each hold significant voting rights, both actual and potential, the factors in paragraph 13 of IAS 27 are reassessed to determine which entity has control.

IG5 The proportion allocated to the parent and non-controlling interests in preparing consolidated financial statements in accordance with IAS 27, and the proportion allocated to an investor that accounts for its investment using the equity method in accordance with IAS 28, are determined solely on the basis of present ownership interests. The proportion allocated is determined taking into account the eventual exercise of potential voting rights and other derivatives that, in substance, give access at present to the economic benefits associated with an ownership interest.

IG6 In some circumstances an entity has, in substance, a present ownership as a result of a transaction that gives it access to the economic benefits associated with an ownership interest. In such circumstances, the proportion allocated is determined taking into account the eventual exercise of those potential voting rights and other derivatives that give the entity access to the economic benefits at present.

IG7 IAS 39 *Financial Instruments: Recognition and Measurement* and IFRS 9 *Financial Instruments* do not apply to interests in subsidiaries, associates and jointly controlled entities that are consolidated, accounted for using the equity method or proportionately consolidated in accordance with IAS 27, IAS 28 and IAS 31 respectively. When instruments containing potential voting rights in substance currently give access to the economic benefits associated with an ownership interest, and the investment is accounted for in one of the above ways, the instruments are not subject to the requirements of IAS 39 and IFRS 9. In all other cases, instruments containing potential voting rights are accounted for in accordance with IAS 39 and IFRS 9.

Illustrative examples

IG8   The five examples below each illustrate one aspect of a potential voting right. In applying IAS 27, IAS 28 or IAS 31, an entity considers all aspects. The existence of control, significant influence and joint control can be determined only after assessing the other factors described in IAS 27, IAS 28 and IAS 31. For the purpose of these examples, however, those other factors are presumed not to affect the determination, even though they may affect it when assessed.

Example 1: Options are out of the money

Entities A and B own 80 per cent and 20 per cent respectively of the ordinary shares that carry voting rights at a general meeting of shareholders of Entity C. Entity A sells one-half of its interest to Entity D and buys call options from Entity D that are exercisable at any time at a premium to the market price when issued, and if exercised would give Entity A its original 80 per cent ownership interest and voting rights.

Though the options are out of the money, they are currently exercisable and give Entity A the power to continue to set the operating and financial policies of Entity C, because Entity A could exercise its options now. The existence of the potential voting rights, as well as the other factors described in paragraph 13 of IAS 27, are considered and it is determined that Entity A controls Entity C.

Example 2: Possibility of exercise or conversion

Entities A, B and C own 40 per cent, 30 per cent and 30 per cent respectively of the ordinary shares that carry voting rights at a general meeting of shareholders of Entity D. Entity A also owns call options that are exercisable at any time at the fair value of the underlying shares and if exercised would give it an additional 20 per cent of the voting rights in Entity D and reduce Entity B's and Entity C's interests to 20 per cent each. If the options are exercised, Entity A will have control over more than one-half of the voting power. The existence of the potential voting rights, as well as the other factors described in paragraph 13 of IAS 27 and paragraphs 6 and 7 of IAS 28, are considered and it is determined that Entity A controls Entity D.

Example 3: Other rights that have the potential to increase an entity's voting power or reduce another entity's voting power

Entities A, B and C own 25 per cent, 35 per cent and 40 per cent respectively of the ordinary shares that carry voting rights at a general meeting of shareholders of Entity D. Entities B and C also have share warrants that are exercisable at any time at a fixed price and provide potential voting rights. Entity A has a call option to purchase these share warrants at any time for a nominal amount. If the call option is exercised, Entity A would have the potential to increase its ownership interest, and thereby its voting rights, in Entity D to 51 per cent (and dilute Entity B's interest to 23 per cent and Entity C's interest to 26 per cent).

Although the share warrants are not owned by Entity A, they are considered in assessing control because they are currently exercisable by Entities B and C. Normally, if an action (eg purchase or exercise of another right) is required before an entity has ownership of a potential voting right, the potential voting right is not regarded as held by the entity. However, the share warrants are, in substance, held by Entity A, because the terms of the call option are designed to ensure Entity A's position. The combination of the call option and share warrants gives Entity A the power to set the operating and financial policies of Entity D, because Entity A could currently exercise the option and share warrants. The other factors described in paragraph 13 of IAS 27 and paragraphs 6 and 7 of IAS 28 are also considered, and it is determined that Entity A, not Entity B or C, controls Entity D.

Example 4: Management intention

Entities A, B and C each own 33 per cent of the ordinary shares that carry voting rights at a general meeting of shareholders of Entity D. Entities A, B and C each have the right to appoint two directors to the board of Entity D. Entity A also owns call options that are exercisable at a fixed price at any time and if exercised would give it all the voting rights in Entity D. The management of Entity A does not intend to exercise the call options, even if Entities B and C do not vote in the same manner as Entity A. The existence of the potential voting rights, as well as the other factors described in paragraph 13 of IAS 27 and paragraphs 6 and 7 of IAS 28, are considered and it is determined that Entity A controls Entity D. The intention of Entity A's management does not influence the assessment.

Example 5: Financial ability

Entities A and B own 55 per cent and 45 per cent respectively of the ordinary shares that carry voting rights at a general meeting of shareholders of Entity C. Entity B also holds debt instruments that are convertible into ordinary shares of Entity C. The debt can be converted at a substantial price, in comparison with Entity B's net assets, at any time and if converted would require Entity B to borrow additional funds to make the payment. If the debt were to be converted, Entity B would hold 70 per cent of the voting rights and Entity A's interest would reduce to 30 per cent.

Although the debt instruments are convertible at a substantial price, they are currently convertible and the conversion feature gives Entity B the power to set the operating and financial policies of Entity C. The existence of the potential voting rights, as well as the other factors described in paragraph 13 of IAS 27, are considered and it is determined that Entity B, not Entity A, controls Entity C. The financial ability of Entity B to pay the conversion price does not influence the assessment.

Appendix
Amendments to guidance on other IFRSs

The following amendments to guidance on other IFRSs are necessary in order to ensure consistency with the amendments to IAS 27 and the related amendments to other IFRSs. In the amended paragraphs, new text is underlined and deleted text is struck through.

* * * * *

The amendments contained in this appendix when IAS 27, as amended in 2008, was issued have been incorporated into the guidance on implementing IFRSs 1 and 5 and IAS 1, and the appendix accompanying IAS 7, as published at 10 January 2008.

Table of Concordance

This table shows how the contents of the superseded version of IAS 27 and the amended version of IAS 27 correspond. Paragraphs are treated as corresponding if they broadly address the same matter even though the guidance may differ.

Superseded IAS 27 paragraph	Amended IAS 27 paragraph	Superseded IAS 27 paragraph	Amended IAS 27 paragraph	Superseded IAS 27 paragraph	Amended IAS 27 paragraph
1	1	17	None	33	27
2	2	18	None	34	28
3	3	19	16	35	28
4	4	20	17	36	29
5	5	21	32	37	38
6	6	22	18	38	39
7	7	23	19	39	40
8	8	24	20	40	41
9	9	25	21	41	42
10	10	26	22	42	43
11	11	27	23	43	44
12	12	28	24	44	46
13	13	29	25	45	None
14	14	30	26	None	30,31, 33–35, 38A–38C, 45–45C
15	15	31	36		
16	None	32	37		

The main amendments made in January 2008 were:

•   The term *minority interest* was replaced by the term *non-controlling interest*, with a new definition.

•   An entity must attribute total comprehensive income to the owners of the parent and to the non-controlling interests even if this results in the non-controlling interests having a deficit balance. The previous version required excess losses to be allocated to the owners of the parent, except to the extent that the non-controlling interests had a binding obligation and were able to make an additional investment to cover the losses.

•   Requirements were added to specify that changes in a parent's ownership interest in a subsidiary that do not result in the loss of control must be accounted for as equity transactions. The previous version did not have requirements for such transactions.

•   Requirements were added to specify how an entity measures any gain or loss arising on the loss of control of a subsidiary. Any such gain or loss is recognised in profit or loss. Any investment retained in the former subsidiary is measured at its fair value at the date when control is lost. The previous version required the carrying amount of an investment retained in the former subsidiary to be regarded as its cost on initial measurement of the financial asset in accordance with IAS 39 *Financial Instruments: Recognition and Measurement.*

The amendments also changed the structure of IAS 27, by moving some paragraphs within the standard. The paragraphs were renumbered for ease of reading.

IASB documents published to accompany

International Accounting Standard 28

Investments in Associates

This version includes amendments resulting from IFRSs issued up to 31 December 2009.

The text of the unaccompanied IAS 28 is contained in Part A of this edition. Its effective date when issued was 1 January 2005. The effective date of the most recent amendments is 1 January 2013. This part presents the following accompanying documents:

Approval by the Board of IAS 28 issued in December 2003

International Accounting Standard 28 *Investments in Associates* (as revised in 2003) was approved for issue by the fourteen members of the International Accounting Standards Board.

Sir David Tweedie	Chairman
Thomas E Jones	Vice-Chairman
Mary E Barth	
Hans-Georg Bruns	
Anthony T Cope	
Robert P Garnett	
Gilbert Gélard	
James J Leisenring	
Warren J McGregor	
Patricia L O'Malley	
Harry K Schmid	
John T Smith	
Geoffrey Whittington	
Tatsumi Yamada	

Basis for Conclusions on
IAS 28 *Investments in Associates*

This Basis for Conclusions accompanies, but is not part of, IAS 28.

Introduction

BC1   This Basis for Conclusions summarises the International Accounting Standards
        Board's considerations in reaching its conclusions on revising IAS 28 *Accounting for
        Investments in Associates* in 2003. Individual Board members gave greater weight to
        some factors than to others.

BC2   In July 2001 the Board announced that, as part of its initial agenda of technical
        projects, it would undertake a project to improve a number of Standards,
        including IAS 28. The project was undertaken in the light of queries and criticisms
        raised in relation to the Standards by securities regulators, professional
        accountants and other interested parties. The objectives of the Improvements
        project were to reduce or eliminate alternatives, redundancies and conflicts
        within Standards, to deal with some convergence issues and to make other
        improvements. In May 2002 the Board published its proposals in an Exposure
        Draft of *Improvements to International Accounting Standards*, with a comment deadline
        of 16 September 2002. The Board received over 160 comment letters on the
        Exposure Draft.

BC3   Because the Board's intention was not to reconsider the fundamental approach to
        the accounting for investments in associates established by IAS 28, this Basis for
        Conclusions does not discuss requirements in IAS 28 that the Board has not
        reconsidered.

Scope exclusion: investments in associates held by venture capital organisations, mutual funds, unit trusts and similar entities

BC4   There are no specific requirements that address accounting for investments by
        venture capital organisations, mutual funds, unit trusts and similar entities.
        As a result, depending on whether an entity has control, joint control or
        significant influence over an investee, one of the following Standards is applied:

        (a)   IAS 27 *Consolidated and Separate Financial Statements*,

        (b)   IAS 28 *Investments in Associates*, or

        (c)   IAS 31 *Interests in Joint Ventures*.

BC5   The Board considered whether another approach is appropriate for these
        investors when they have joint control or significant influence over their
        investees. The Board noted that use of the equity or proportionate consolidation
        methods for investments held by venture capital organisations, mutual funds,
        unit trusts and similar entities often produces information that is not relevant to
        their management and investors and that fair value measurement produces more
        relevant information.

BC6   In addition, the Board noted that there may be frequent changes in the level of ownership in these investments and that financial statements are less useful if there are frequent changes in the method of accounting for an investment.

Measurement at fair value in accordance with IAS 39

BC7   Accordingly, the Board decided that investments held by venture capital organisations, mutual funds, unit trusts and similar entities including investment-linked insurance funds should be excluded from the scope of IAS 28 and IAS 31 when they are measured at fair value in accordance with IAS 39 *Financial Instruments: Recognition and Measurement.*[*] The Board understands that fair value information is often readily available because fair value measurement is a well-established practice in these industries including for investments in entities in the early stages of their development or in non-listed entities.

Treatment of changes in fair value

BC8   The Board decided that if venture capital organisations, mutual funds, unit trusts and similar entities are to be excluded from the scope of IAS 28, it should be only when they recognise changes in the fair value of their investments in associates in profit or loss in the period in which those changes occur. This is to achieve the same treatment as for investments in subsidiaries or associates that are not consolidated or accounted for using the equity method because control or significant influence is intended to be temporary. The Board's approach distinguishes between accounting for the investment and accounting for the economic entity. In relation to the former, the Board decided that there should be consistency in the treatment of all investments, including changes in the fair value of these investments.

BC9   The Board noted that if such investments were classified in accordance with IAS 39,[†] they would not always meet the definition of investments classified as held for trading because venture capital organisations may hold an investment for a period of 3–5 years. In accordance with IAS 39 such an investment is classified as available for sale (unless the entity elects to designate the investment on initial recognition at fair value through profit or loss). Classification as available for sale would not result in recognising changes in fair value in profit or loss. To achieve a similar effect on income to that of applying the equity method, the Board decided to exempt investments held by venture capital organisations, mutual funds, unit trusts and similar entities from this Standard only when they are measured at fair value through profit or loss (either by designation or because they meet the definition in IAS 39 of held for trading).

---

[*]   In November 2009 the Board amended some of the requirements of IAS 39 and relocated them to IFRS 9 *Financial Instruments.* IFRS 9 applies to all assets within the scope of IAS 39.

[†]   In November 2009 the Board amended the requirements of IAS 39 relating to classification and measurement of assets within the scope of IAS 39 and relocated them to IFRS 9 *Financial Instruments.* IFRS 9 eliminated the available-for-sale category and permits entities to make an irrevocable election to present in other comprehensive income subsequent changes in the fair value of an investment in an equity instrument that is not held for trading.

Reference to 'well-established' industry practices

BC10   The Exposure Draft proposed to limit the availability of the scope exclusion to situations in which well-established industry practice existed. Some respondents noted that the development of industry practice to measure such investments at fair value would have been precluded in industries established in countries already applying IFRSs. The Board confirmed that the main purpose of the reference to 'well-established' practice in the Exposure Draft was to emphasise that the exclusion would apply generally to those investments for which fair value is already available.

BC11   Therefore, the Board decided that the availability of the exclusion should be based only on the nature of an entity's activities and to delete the reference to 'well-established' practices. The Board understands that measurement of these investments at fair value is 'well-established' practice in these industries.

Definition of 'venture capital organisations'

BC12   The Board decided not to define further those 'venture capital organisations and similar entities' excluded from the scope of the Standard. Apart from recognising the difficulties of arriving at a universally applicable definition, the Board did not want inadvertently to make it difficult for entities to measure investments at fair value. However, the Board decided to clarify that the reference to 'similar entities' in the scope exclusion includes investment-linked insurance funds.

BC13   The Board decided, however, that if an investee is a subsidiary in accordance with IAS 27, it should be consolidated. The Board concluded that if an investor controls an investee, the investee is part of a group and part of the structure through which the group operates its business and thus consolidation of the investee is appropriate.

Application of the equity method

Temporary significant influence

BC14   The Board considered whether to remove the exemption from applying the equity method when significant influence over an associate is intended to be temporary. The Board decided to consider this issue as part of a comprehensive standard dealing with asset disposals. It decided to retain an exemption from applying the equity method when there is evidence that an associate is acquired with the intention to dispose of it within twelve months and that management is actively seeking a buyer. The Board's Exposure Draft ED 4 *Disposal of Non-current Assets and Presentation of Discontinued Operations* proposes to measure and present assets held for sale in a consistent manner irrespective of whether they are held by an investor in an associate or in a subsidiary.*

---

*   In March 2004, the Board issued IFRS 5 *Non-current Assets Held for Sale and Discontinued Operations*. IFRS 5 removes this scope exclusion and now eliminates the exemption from applying the equity method when significant influence over an associate is intended to be temporary. See IFRS 5 Basis for Conclusions for further discussion.

Severe long-term restrictions impairing ability to transfer funds to the investor

BC15   The Board decided to remove the exemption from applying the equity method for an associate that previously applied when severe long-term restrictions impaired an associate's ability to transfer funds to the investor. It did so because such circumstances may not preclude the investor's significant influence over the associate. The Board decided that an investor should, when assessing its ability to exercise significant influence over an entity, consider restrictions on the transfer of funds from the associate to the investor. In themselves, such restrictions do not preclude the existence of significant influence.

Non-coterminous year-ends

BC16   The Exposure Draft of May 2002 proposed to limit to three months any difference between the reporting dates of the investor and the associate when applying the equity method. Some respondents to that Exposure Draft believed that it could be impracticable for the investor to prepare financial statements as of the same date when the date of the investor's and the associate's financial statements differ by more than three months. The Board noted that a three-month limit operates in several jurisdictions and it was concerned that a longer period, such as six months, would lead to the recognition of stale information. Therefore, it decided to retain the three-month limit.

Recognition of losses

BC17   The previous version of IAS 28 and SIC-20 *Equity Accounting Method—Recognition of Losses* restricted application of the equity method when, in accounting for the investor's share of losses, the carrying amount of the investment is reduced to zero.

BC18   The Board decided that the base to be reduced to zero should be broader than residual equity interests and should also include other non-equity interests that are in substance part of the net investment in the associate, such as long-term receivables. Therefore, the Board decided to withdraw SIC-20.

BC19   The Board also noted that if non-equity investments are not included in the base to be reduced to zero, an investor could restructure its investment to fund the majority in non-equity investments to avoid recognising the losses of the associate under the equity method.

BC20   In widening the base against which losses are to be recognised, the Board also clarified the application of the impairment provisions of IAS 39 to the financial assets that form part of the net investment.

                                               © IASCF

Loss of significant influence over an associate[*]

BC21   In the second phase of the Board's project on business combinations, the Board observed that the loss of control of an entity and the loss of significant influence over an entity are economically similar events; thus they should be accounted for similarly. The loss of significant influence is an economic event that changes the nature of the investment. The Board concluded that the accounting guidance on the loss of control of a subsidiary should be extended to events, transactions or other changes in circumstances in which an investor loses significant influence over an investee.   Thus, when an investor loses significant influence over an associate, the investor measures any retained investment at fair value. Any difference between the carrying amount of the associate when significant influence is lost, the disposal proceeds (if any) and the fair value of any retained interest is recognised in profit or loss.

Scope (2008 amendment)[†]

BC22   The Board identified an apparent inconsistency in the disclosure requirements for entities that are eligible and elect to account for investments in associates at fair value in accordance with IAS 39.[§] These investments are excluded from the scope of IAS 28 and entities are therefore not required to make the disclosures that the Standard would otherwise require. However, IAS 32 *Financial Instruments: Presentation* and IFRS 7 *Financial Instruments: Disclosures* both require entities that account for investments in associates in accordance with IAS 39 to make the disclosures required by IAS 28 in addition to the disclosures they require.

BC23   The Board decided to remove this inconsistency by deleting from IAS 32 and IFRS 7 the general requirement to make the IAS 28 disclosures, and instead identifying the specific disclosures that should be made. The Board concluded that the specific disclosures it identified would be relevant because of the significant interest entities hold in such investments. The Board also decided to delete from IAS 32 and IFRS 7 the requirement to make the disclosures in IAS 27 because it duplicates the requirement in IAS 27.

Impairment losses (2008 amendment)[†]

BC24   The Board identified unclear guidance in IAS 28 regarding the extent to which an impairment reversal should be recognised as an adjustment to the carrying amount of an investment in an associate.

---

[*]   This heading and paragraph BC21 were added as a consequence of amendments to IAS 27 *Consolidated and Separate Financial Statements* made as part of the second phase of the business combinations project in 2008.

[†]   Paragraphs BC22–BC28 were added as a consequence of amendments to IAS 28 by *Improvements to IFRSs* issued in May 2008.

[§]   In November 2009 the Board amended the requirements of IAS 39 relating to classification and measurement of assets within the scope of IAS 39 and relocated them to IFRS 9 *Financial Instruments*. IFRS 9 applies to all assets within the scope of IAS 39.

BC25　The Board noted that applying the equity method involves adjusting the investor's share of the impairment loss recognised by the associate on assets such as goodwill or property, plant and equipment to take account of the acquisition date fair values of those assets. The Board proposed in the exposure draft *Improvements to International Financial Reporting Standards* published in October 2007 that an additional impairment recorded by the investor, after applying the equity method, should not be allocated to any asset, including goodwill, that forms part of the carrying amount of the investment. Therefore, such an impairment charge should be reversed in a subsequent period to the extent that the recoverable amount of the investment increases.

BC26　Some respondents to the exposure draft expressed the view that the proposed amendment was not consistent with IAS 39* (regarding reversal of an impairment loss on an available-for-sale equity instrument), or with IAS 36 *Impairment of Assets*, IAS 27 and the proportionate consolidation method in IAS 31 (regarding the allocation of an impairment loss to goodwill and any reversal of an impairment loss relating to goodwill).

BC27　In its redeliberations, the Board affirmed its previous decisions but, in response to the comments made, decided to clarify the reasons for the amendments to paragraph 33. The Board decided that an investor should not allocate an impairment loss to any asset that forms part of the carrying amount of the investment in the associate because the investment is the only asset that the investor controls and recognises.

BC28　The Board also decided that any reversal of this impairment loss should be recognised as an adjustment to the investment in the associate to the extent that the recoverable amount of the investment increases. This requirement is consistent with IAS 36, which permits the reversal of impairment losses for assets other than goodwill. The Board did not propose aligning the requirements for the reversal of an impairment loss with those in IAS 39 relating to equity instruments because an entity recognises an impairment loss on an investment in an associate in accordance with IAS 36, rather than IAS 39.

---

*　IFRS 9 *Financial Instruments*, issued in November 2009, eliminated the category of available-for-sale financial assets.

　　　　　　　　　　　© IASCF

Dissenting opinion on amendment issued in May 2008

Dissent of Tatsumi Yamada

DO1 Mr Yamada voted against one of the amendments to IAS 28 *Investments in Associates* issued in *Improvements to IFRSs* in May 2008.

DO2 Mr Yamada believes it is inappropriate not to allocate any additional impairment losses to the goodwill and other assets that form part of the carrying amount of the investment in the associate. In his view, because he believes that an investor can identify attributable goodwill when it makes an investment, all impairment losses recognised with respect to the investor's investment in an associate should be allocated to the goodwill and other assets that form part of the carrying amount of the investment.

DO3 Mr Yamada also believes that all impairment losses allocated to goodwill should not be subsequently reversed. In his view the non-allocation of impairment losses to goodwill as required by the amendment and the subsequent reversal of such impairment losses in substance leads to the recognition of internally generated goodwill. He believes that the amendment to IAS 28 is not consistent with paragraphs 124 and 125 of IAS 36 *Impairment of Assets*, which prohibit the reversal of impairment losses related to goodwill.

IASB document published to accompany

International Accounting Standard 29

Financial Reporting in Hyperinflationary Economies

This version includes amendments resulting from IFRSs issued up to 31 December 2009.

The text of the unaccompanied IAS 29 is contained in Part A of this edition. Its effective date when issued was 1 January 1990. The effective date of the latest amendments is 1 January 2009. This part presents the following accompanying document:

page

BASIS FOR CONCLUSIONS   B962

Basis for Conclusions on
IAS 29 *Financial Reporting in Hyperinflationary Economies*

This Basis for Conclusions accompanies, but is not part of, IAS 29.

BC1　This Basis for Conclusions summarises the International Accounting Standards Board's considerations in reaching its conclusions on amending IAS 29 *Financial Reporting in Hyperinflationary Economies* in 2008. Individual Board members gave greater weight to some factors than to others.

BC2　Paragraph 6 of the previous version of the Standard did not reflect the fact that a number of assets and liabilities may or must be measured on the basis of a current value rather than a historical value. Therefore, the Board included examples rather than a definitive list of such items by *Improvements to IFRSs* issued in May 2008.

IASB documents published to accompany

International Accounting Standard 31

Interests in Joint Ventures

This version includes amendments resulting from IFRSs issued up to 31 December 2009.

The text of the unaccompanied IAS 31 is contained in Part A of this edition. Its effective date when issued was 1 January 2005. The effective date of the most recent amendments is 1 January 2013. This part presents the following accompanying documents:

Approval by the Board of IAS 31 issued in December 2003

International Accounting Standard 31 *Interests in Joint Ventures* (as revised in 2003) was approved for issue by the fourteen members of the International Accounting Standards Board.

Sir David Tweedie   Chairman

Thomas E Jones   Vice-Chairman

Mary E Barth

Hans-Georg Bruns

Anthony T Cope

Robert P Garnett

Gilbert Gélard

James J Leisenring

Warren J McGregor

Patricia L O'Malley

Harry K Schmid

John T Smith

Geoffrey Whittington

Tatsumi Yamada

Basis for Conclusions on
IAS 31 *Interests in Joint Ventures*

This Basis for Conclusions accompanies, but is not part of, IAS 31.

Introduction

BC1   This Basis for Conclusions summarises the International Accounting Standards Board's considerations in reaching its conclusions on revising IAS 31 *Financial Reporting of Interests in Joint Ventures* in 2003. Individual Board members gave greater weight to some factors than to others.

BC2   In July 2001 the Board announced that, as part of its initial agenda of technical projects, it would undertake a project to improve a number of Standards, including IAS 27 *Consolidated Financial Statements and Accounting for Investments in Subsidiaries* and IAS 28 *Accounting for Investments in Associates*. The project was undertaken in the light of queries and criticisms raised in relation to the Standards by securities regulators, professional accountants and other interested parties. The objectives of the Improvements project were to reduce or eliminate alternatives, redundancies and conflicts within Standards, to deal with some convergence issues and to make other improvements. Because of the changes that were to be proposed for the revised versions of IAS 27 *Consolidated and Separate Financial Statements* and IAS 28 *Investments in Associates*, the Board also proposed to make some important consequential amendments to IAS 31 *Financial Reporting of Interests in Joint Ventures*.

BC3   Because the Board's intention was not to reconsider the fundamental approach to the accounting for joint ventures established by IAS 31 and to reflect only those changes related to its decisions in the Improvements project, in particular in relation to IAS 27 and IAS 28, this Basis for Conclusions does not discuss requirements in IAS 31 that the Board has not reconsidered. However, because of the scale of the amendments to the Standard, the Board believes it will be helpful to users to issue IAS 31 along with the Standards that were previously identified for revision as part of the Improvements project.

Scope exclusion: investments in joint ventures held by venture capital organisations, mutual funds, unit trusts and similar entities

BC4   There are no specific requirements that address accounting for investments by venture capital organisations, mutual funds, unit trusts and similar entities. As a result, depending on whether an entity has control, joint control or significant influence over an investee, one of the following Standards is applied:

(a)   IAS 27 *Consolidated and Separate Financial Statements*,

(b)   IAS 28 *Investments in Associates*, or

(c)   IAS 31 *Interests in Joint Ventures*.

BC5   The Board considered whether another approach is appropriate for these investors when they do not have control but have joint control or significant influence over their investees. The Board noted that use of proportionate consolidation or the equity method for investments held by venture capital organisations, mutual funds, unit trusts and similar entities often produces information that is not relevant to their management and investors and that fair value measurement produces more relevant information in these circumstances. As noted in the Basis for Conclusions on IAS 27, the Board confirmed that a subsidiary should not be excluded from consolidation on the basis of the nature of the controlling entity. Consolidation is based on the parent's ability to control the investee and should not be affected by whether management intends to hold an investment in an entity that it controls for the short term. The Board concluded that for investments under the control of private equity entities, users' information needs are best served by financial statements in which those investments are consolidated, thus revealing the extent of the operations of the entities they control.

BC6   In addition, the Board noted that there may be frequent changes in the level of ownership in these investments and that financial statements are less useful if there are frequent changes in the method of accounting for an investment.

Measurement at fair value in accordance with IAS 39

BC7   Accordingly, the Board decided that investments held by venture capital organisations, mutual funds, unit trusts and similar entities including investment-linked insurance funds should be excluded from the scope of IAS 31 when they are measured at fair value in accordance with IAS 39 *Financial Instruments: Recognition and Measurement.* The Board understands that fair value information is often readily available because fair value measurement is a well-established practice in these industries including for investments in entities in the early stages of their development or in non-listed entities.

Treatment of changes in fair value

BC8   The Board decided that if venture capital organisations, mutual funds, unit trusts and similar entities are to be excluded from the scope of IAS 31, it should be only when they recognise changes in the fair value of their interests in joint ventures in profit or loss in the period in which those changes occur. This is to achieve the same treatment as for investments in subsidiaries or associates that are not consolidated or accounted for using the equity method because control or significant influence is intended to be temporary. The Board's approach distinguishes between accounting for the investment and accounting for the economic entity. In relation to the former, the Board decided that there should be consistency in the treatment of all investments, including changes in the fair value of these investments.

---

*   In November 2009 the Board amended some of the requirements of IAS 39 and relocated them to IFRS 9 *Financial Instruments*. IFRS 9 applies to all assets within the scope of IAS 39.

© IASCF

BC9   The Board noted that if such investments were classified in accordance with IAS 39,[*] they would not always meet the definition of investments classified as held for trading because venture capital organisations may hold an investment for a period of 3–5 years. In accordance with IAS 39 such an investment is classified as available for sale (unless the entity elects to designate the investment on initial recognition at fair value through profit or loss). Classification as available for sale would not result in recognising changes in fair value in profit or loss. To achieve a similar effect on income to that of applying proportionate consolidation or the equity method, the Board decided to exempt investments held by venture capital organisations, mutual funds, unit trusts and similar entities from this Standard only when they are measured at fair value through profit or loss (either by designation or because they meet the definition in IAS 39 of held for trading).

Reference to 'well-established' industry practices

BC10   The Exposure Draft of IAS 28 proposed to limit the availability of the scope exclusion to situations in which well-established industry practice existed. Some respondents noted that the development of industry practice to measure such investments at fair value would have been precluded in industries established in countries already applying IFRSs. The Board confirmed that the main purpose of the reference to 'well-established' practice in the Exposure Draft was to emphasise that the exclusion would apply generally to those investments for which fair value is already available.

BC11   Therefore, the Board decided that the availability of the exclusion from the scope of IAS 31 should be based only on the nature of an entity's activities and to delete the reference to 'well-established' practices. The Board understands that measurement of these investments at fair value is 'well-established' practice in these industries.

Definition of 'venture capital organisations'

BC12   The Board decided not to define further those 'venture capital organisations and similar entities' excluded from the scope of IAS 31. Apart from recognising the difficulties of arriving at a universally applicable definition, the Board did not want inadvertently to make it difficult for entities to measure investments at fair value. However, the Board decided to clarify that the reference to 'similar entities' in the scope exclusion includes investment-linked insurance funds.

---

[*] In November 2009 the Board amended the requirements of IAS 39 relating to classification and measurement of assets within the scope of IAS 39 and relocated them to IFRS 9 *Financial Instruments*. IFRS 9 eliminated the available-for-sale category and permits entities to make an irrevocable election to present in other comprehensive income subsequent changes in the fair value of an investment in an equity instrument that is not held for trading.

Application of proportionate consolidation or the equity method

Temporary joint control

BC13   The Board considered whether to remove the exemption from applying proportionate consolidation or the equity method when joint control in a joint venture is intended to be temporary. The Board decided to consider this issue as part of a comprehensive standard dealing with asset disposals. It decided to retain an exemption from applying proportionate consolidation or the equity method when there is evidence that an interest in a joint venture is acquired with the intention to dispose of it within twelve months and that management is actively seeking a buyer. The Board's Exposure Draft ED 4 *Disposal of Non-current Assets and Presentation of Discontinued Operations* proposes to measure and present assets held for sale in a consistent manner irrespective of whether they are held by an investor in an associate, a joint venture or a subsidiary.*

Severe long-term restrictions impairing ability to transfer funds to the investor

BC14   The Board decided to remove the exemption from applying proportionate consolidation or the equity method for an interest in a joint venture that previously applied when severe long-term restrictions impaired a venture's ability to transfer funds to the venturer. It did so because such circumstances may not preclude the venturer's joint control over the venture. The Board decided that an investor should, when assessing its ability to exercise joint control over an entity, consider restrictions on the transfer of funds from the entity to the investor. In themselves, such restrictions do not preclude the existence of joint control.

Non-coterminous year-ends

BC15   The Exposure Draft of May 2002 proposed to limit to three months any difference between the reporting dates of the venturer and the venture when applying proportionate consolidation or the equity method. Some respondents to that Exposure Draft believed that it could be impracticable for the venturer to prepare financial statements as of the same date when the date of the venturer's and the venture's financial statements differ by more than three months. The Board noted that a three-month limit operates in several jurisdictions and it was concerned that a longer period, such as six months, would lead to the recognition of stale information. Therefore, it decided to retain the three-month limit.

---

*   In March 2004 the Board issued IFRS 5 *Non-current Assets Held for Sale and Discontinued Operations*. IFRS 5 removes this scope exclusion and now eliminates the exemption from applying proportionate consolidation or the equity method when joint control of a joint venture is intended to be temporary. See IFRS 5 Basis for Conclusions for further discussion.

Loss of joint control over a jointly controlled entity*

BC16   In the second phase of the Board's project on business combinations, the Board observed that the loss of control of an investee and the loss of joint control of an investee are economically similar events; thus they should be accounted for similarly. The loss of joint control represents an economic event that changes the nature of the investment. The Board concluded that the accounting guidance on the loss of control of a subsidiary should be extended to events, transactions or other changes in circumstances in which an investor loses joint control of an investee. Thus, when an investor loses joint control of an investee, the investor measures any retained investment at fair value. Any difference between the carrying amount of the jointly controlled entity when joint control is lost, the disposal proceeds (if any) and the fair value of any retained interest is recognised in profit or loss.

Scope (2008 amendment)†

BC17   The Board identified an apparent inconsistency in the disclosure requirements for entities that are eligible and elect to account for their interests in jointly controlled entities at fair value in accordance with IAS 39.§ Those interests are excluded from the scope of IAS 31 and the entities are therefore not required to make the disclosures that the Standard would otherwise require. However, IAS 32 *Financial Instruments: Presentation* and IFRS 7 *Financial Instruments: Disclosures* both require entities that account for interests in jointly controlled entities in accordance with IAS 39 to make the disclosures required by IAS 31 in addition to the disclosures they require.

BC18   The Board decided to remove this inconsistency by deleting from IAS 32 and IFRS 7 the general requirement to make the IAS 31 disclosures, and instead identifying the specific disclosures that should be made. The Board noted that the specific disclosures identified would be relevant because of the significant interest venturers hold in such investments. The Board also decided to delete from IAS 32 and IFRS 7 the requirement to make the disclosures in IAS 27 because it duplicates the requirement in IAS 27.

---

*   This heading and paragraph BC16 were added as a consequence of amendments to IAS 27 *Consolidated and Separate Financial Statements* made as part of the second phase of the business combinations project in 2008.

†   This section was added as a consequence of an amendment to IAS 31 by *Improvements to IFRSs* issued in May 2008.

§   In November 2009 the IASB amended the requirements of IAS 39 relating to classification and measurement of assets within the scope of IAS 39 and relocated them to IFRS 9 *Financial Instruments*. IFRS 9 applies to all assets within the scope of IAS 39.

IASB documents published to accompany

International Accounting Standard 32

Financial Instruments: Presentation

This version includes amendments resulting from IFRSs issued up to 31 December 2009.

The text of the unaccompanied IAS 32 is contained in Part A of this edition. Its effective date when issued was 1 January 2005. The effective date of the most recent amendments is 1 January 2013. This part presents the following accompanying documents:

Approval by the Board of IAS 32 issued in December 2003

International Accounting Standard 32 *Financial Instruments: Disclosure and Presentation* (as revised in 2003) was approved for issue by thirteen of the fourteen members of the International Accounting Standards Board. Mr Leisenring dissented. His dissenting opinion is set out after the Basis for Conclusions.

Sir David Tweedie	Chairman
Thomas E Jones	Vice-Chairman
Mary E Barth	
Hans-Georg Bruns	
Anthony T Cope	
Robert P Garnett	
Gilbert Gélard	
James J Leisenring	
Warren J McGregor	
Patricia L O'Malley	
Harry K Schmid	
John T Smith	
Geoffrey Whittington	
Tatsumi Yamada	

Approval by the Board of *Puttable Financial Instruments and Obligations Arising on Liquidation* (Amendments to IAS 32 and IAS 1) issued in February 2008

Puttable Financial Instruments and Obligations Arising on Liquidation (Amendments to IAS 32 and IAS 1 *Presentation of Financial Statements*) was approved for issue by eleven of the thirteen members of the International Accounting Standards Board. Professor Barth and Mr Garnett dissented. Their dissenting opinions are set out after the Basis for Conclusions.

Sir David Tweedie	Chairman
Thomas E Jones	Vice-Chairman
Mary E Barth	
Stephen Cooper	
Philippe Danjou	
Jan Engström	
Robert P Garnett	
Gilbert Gélard	
James J Leisenring	
Warren J McGregor	
John T Smith	
Tatsumi Yamada	
Wei-Guo Zhang	

Approval by the Board of *Classification of Rights Issues* (Amendment to IAS 32) issued in October 2009

Classification of Rights Issues (Amendment to IAS 32) was approved for issue by thirteen of the fifteen members of the International Accounting Standards Board. Messrs Leisenring and Smith dissented from the issue of the amendment. Their dissenting opinions are set out after the Basis for Conclusions.

Sir David Tweedie   Chairman

Stephen Cooper

Philippe Danjou

Jan Engström

Patrick Finnegan

Robert P Garnett

Gilbert Gélard

Amaro Luiz de Oliveira Gomes

Prabhakar Kalavacherla

James J Leisenring

Patricia McConnell

Warren J McGregor

John T Smith

Tatsumi Yamada

Wei-Guo Zhang

CONTENTS

Basis for Conclusions on
IAS 32 *Financial Instruments: Presentation*

This Basis for Conclusions accompanies, but is not part of, IAS 32.

BC1   This Basis for Conclusions summarises the International Accounting Standards Board's considerations in reaching its conclusions on revising IAS 32 *Financial Instruments: Disclosure and Presentation** in 2003. Individual Board members gave greater weight to some factors than to others.

BC2   In July 2001 the Board announced that, as part of its initial agenda of technical projects, it would undertake a project to improve a number of Standards, including IAS 32 and IAS 39 *Financial Instruments: Recognition and Measurement*.† The objectives of the Improvements project were to reduce the complexity in the Standards by clarifying and adding guidance, eliminating internal inconsistencies, and incorporating into the Standards elements of Standing Interpretations Committee (SIC) Interpretations and IAS 39 implementation guidance. In June 2002 the Board published its proposals in an Exposure Draft of proposed amendments to IAS 32 *Financial Instruments: Disclosure and Presentation* and IAS 39 *Financial Instruments: Recognition and Measurement*, with a comment deadline of 14 October 2002. The Board received over 170 comment letters on the Exposure Draft.

BC3   Because the Board did not reconsider the fundamental approach to the accounting for financial instruments established by IAS 32 and IAS 39, this Basis for Conclusions does not discuss requirements in IAS 32 that the Board has not reconsidered.

BC3A   In July 2006 the Board published an exposure draft of proposed amendments to IAS 32 relating to the classification of puttable instruments and instruments with obligations arising on liquidation. The Board subsequently confirmed the proposals and in 2008 issued an amendment that now forms part of IAS 32. A summary of the Board's considerations and reasons for its conclusions is in paragraphs BC50–BC74.

Definitions (paragraphs 11–14 and AG3–AG24)

Financial asset, financial liability and equity instrument (paragraphs 11 and AG3–AG14)

BC4   The revised IAS 32 addresses the classification as financial assets, financial liabilities or equity instruments of financial instruments that are indexed to, or settled in, an entity's own equity instruments. As discussed further in paragraphs BC6–BC15, the Board decided to preclude equity classification for such contracts

---

*   In August 2005, the IASB relocated all disclosures relating to financial instruments to IFRS 7. The paragraphs relating to disclosures that were originally published in this Basis for Conclusions were relocated, if still relevant, to the Basis for Conclusions on IFRS 7.

†   In November 2009 the Board amended some of the requirements of IAS 39 and relocated them to IFRS 9 *Financial Instruments*.

when they (a) involve an obligation to deliver cash or another financial asset or to exchange financial assets or financial liabilities under conditions that are potentially unfavourable to the entity, (b) in the case of a non-derivative, are not for the receipt or delivery of a fixed number of shares or (c) in the case of a derivative, are not for the exchange of a fixed number of shares for a fixed amount of cash or another financial asset. The Board also decided to preclude equity classification for contracts that are derivatives on derivatives on an entity's own equity. Consistently with this decision, the Board also decided to amend the definitions of financial asset, financial liability and equity instrument in IAS 32 to make them consistent with the guidance about contracts on an entity's own equity instruments. The Board did not reconsider other aspects of the definitions as part of this project to revise IAS 32, for example the other changes to the definitions proposed by the Joint Working Group in its Draft Standard *Financial Instruments and Similar Items* published by the Board's predecessor body, IASC, in 2000.

Foreign currency denominated pro rata rights issues

BC4A   In 2005 the International Financial Reporting Interpretations Committee (IFRIC) was asked whether the equity conversion option embedded in a convertible bond denominated in a foreign currency met IAS 32's requirements to be classified as an equity instrument. IAS 32 states that a derivative instrument relating to the purchase or issue of an entity's own equity instruments is classified as equity only if it results in the exchange of a fixed number of equity instruments for a fixed amount of cash or other assets. At that time, the IFRIC concluded that if the conversion option was denominated in a currency other than the issuing entity's functional currency, the amount of cash to be received in the functional currency would be variable. Consequently, the instrument was a derivative liability that should be measured at its fair value with changes in fair value included in profit or loss.

BC4B   However, the IFRIC also concluded that this outcome was not consistent with the Board's approach when it introduced the 'fixed for fixed' notion in IAS 32. Therefore, the IFRIC decided to recommend that the Board amend IAS 32 to permit a conversion or stand-alone option to be classified as equity if the exercise price was fixed in any currency. In September 2005 the Board decided not to proceed with the proposed amendment.

BC4C   In 2009 the Board was asked by the IFRIC to consider a similar issue. This issue was whether a right entitling the holder to receive a fixed number of the issuing entity's own equity instruments for a fixed amount of a currency other than the issuing entity's functional currency (foreign currency) should be accounted for as a derivative liability.

BC4D   These rights are commonly described as 'rights issues' and include rights, options and warrants. Laws or regulations in many jurisdictions throughout the world require the use of rights issues when raising capital. The entity issues one or more rights to acquire a fixed number of additional shares pro rata to all existing shareholders of a class of non-derivative equity instruments. The exercise price is normally below the current market price of the shares. Consequently, a shareholder must exercise its rights if it does not wish its proportionate interest in the entity to be diluted. Issues with those characteristics are discussed in IFRS 2 *Share-based Payment* and IAS 33 *Earnings per Share*.

BC4E   The Board was advised that rights with the characteristics discussed above were being issued frequently in the current economic environment. The Board was also advised that many issuing entities fixed the exercise price of the rights in currencies other than their functional currency because the entities were listed in more than one jurisdiction and might be required to do so by law or regulation. Therefore, the accounting conclusions affected a significant number of entities in many jurisdictions. In addition, because these are usually relatively large transactions, they can have a substantial effect on entities' financial statement amounts.

BC4F   The Board agreed with the IFRIC's 2005 conclusion that a contract with an exercise price denominated in a foreign currency would not result in the entity receiving a fixed amount of cash. However, the Board also agreed with the IFRIC that classifying rights as derivative liabilities was not consistent with the substance of the transaction. Rights issues are issued only to existing shareholders on the basis of the number of shares they already own. In this respect they partially resemble dividends paid in shares.

BC4G   The Board decided that a financial instrument that gives the holder the right to acquire a fixed number of the entity's own equity instruments for a fixed amount of any currency is an equity instrument if, and only if, the entity offers the financial instrument pro rata to all of its existing owners of the same class of its own non-derivative equity instruments.

BC4H   In excluding grants of rights with these features from the scope of IFRS 2, the Board explicitly recognised that the holder of the right receives it as a holder of equity instruments, ie as an owner. The Board noted that IAS 1 *Presentation of Financial Statements* requires transactions with owners in their capacity as owners to be recognised in the statement of changes in equity rather than in the statement of comprehensive income.

BC4I   Consistently with its conclusion in IFRS 2, the Board decided that a pro rata issue of rights to all existing shareholders to acquire additional shares is a transaction with an entity's owners in their capacity as owners. Consequently, those transactions should be recognised in equity, not comprehensive income. Because the Board concluded that the rights were equity instruments, it decided to amend the definition of a financial liability to exclude them.

BC4J   Some respondents to the exposure draft expressed concerns that the wording of the amendment was too open-ended and could lead to structuring risks. The Board rejected this argument because of the extremely narrow amendment that requires the entity to treat all of its existing owners of the same class of its own non-derivative equity instruments equally. The Board also noted that a change in the capital structure of an entity to create a new class of non-derivative equity instruments would be transparent because of the presentation and disclosure requirements in IFRSs.

BC4K The Board decided not to extend this conclusion to other instruments that grant the holder the right to purchase the entity's own equity instruments such as the conversion feature in convertible bonds. The Board also noted that long-dated foreign currency rights issues are not primarily transactions with owners in their capacity as owners. The equal treatment of all owners of the same class of equity instruments was also the basis on which, in IFRIC 17 *Distributions of Non-cash Assets to Owners*, the IFRIC distinguished non-reciprocal distributions to owners from exchange transactions. The fact that the rights are distributed pro rata to existing shareholders is critical to the Board's conclusion to provide an exception to the 'fixed for fixed' concept in IAS 32 as this is a narrow targeted transaction with owners in their capacity as owners.

Presentation (paragraphs 15–50 and AG25–AG39)

Liabilities and equity (paragraphs 15–27 and AG25–AG29)

BC5 The revised IAS 32 addresses whether derivative and non-derivative contracts indexed to, or settled in, an entity's own equity instruments are financial assets, financial liabilities or equity instruments. The original IAS 32 dealt with aspects of this issue piecemeal and it was not clear how various transactions (eg net share settled contracts and contracts with settlement options) should be treated under the Standard. The Board concluded that it needed to clarify the accounting treatment for such transactions.

BC6 The approach agreed by the Board can be summarised as follows:

A contract on an entity's own equity is an equity instrument if, and only if:

(a) it contains no contractual obligation to transfer cash or another financial asset, or to exchange financial assets or financial liabilities with another entity under conditions that are potentially unfavourable to the entity; and

(b) if the instrument will or may be settled in the entity's own equity instruments, it is either (i) a non-derivative that includes no contractual obligation for the entity to deliver a variable number of its own equity instruments, or (ii) a derivative that will be settled by the entity exchanging a fixed amount of cash or another financial asset for a fixed number of its own equity instruments.

No contractual obligation to deliver cash or another financial asset (paragraphs 17–20, AG25 and AG26)

Puttable instruments (paragraph 18(b))

BC7 The Board decided that a financial instrument that gives the holder the right to put the instrument back to the entity for cash or another financial asset is a financial liability of the entity. Such financial instruments are commonly issued by mutual funds, unit trusts, co-operative and similar entities, often with the redemption amount being equal to a proportionate share in the net assets of the entity. Although the legal form of such financial instruments often includes a right to the residual interest in the assets of an entity available to holders of such instruments, the inclusion of an option for the holder to put the instrument back to the entity for cash or another financial asset means that the instrument meets the definition of a financial liability. The classification as a financial liability is independent of considerations such as when the right is exercisable, how the amount payable or receivable upon exercise of the right is determined, and whether the puttable instrument has a fixed maturity.

BC7A   The Board reconsidered its conclusions with regards to some puttable instruments and amended IAS 32 in February 2008 (see paragraphs BC50–BC74).

BC8   The Board noted that the classification of a puttable instrument as a financial liability does not preclude the use of descriptors such as 'net assets attributable to unitholders' and 'change in net assets attributable to unitholders' on the face of the financial statements of an entity that has no equity (such as some mutual funds and unit trusts) or whose share capital is a financial liability under IAS 32 (such as some co-operatives). The Board also agreed that it should provide examples of how such entities might present their income statement[*] and balance sheet[†] (see Illustrative Examples 7 and 8).

Implicit obligations (paragraph 20)

BC9   The Board did not debate whether an obligation can be established implicitly rather than explicitly because this is not within the scope of an improvements project. This question will be considered by the Board in its project on revenue, liabilities and equity. Consequently, the Board retained the existing notion that an instrument may establish an obligation indirectly through its terms and conditions (see paragraph 20). However, it decided that the example of a preference share with a contractually accelerating dividend which, within the foreseeable future, is scheduled to yield a dividend so high that the entity will be economically compelled to redeem the instrument, was insufficiently clear. The example was therefore removed and replaced with others that are clearer and deal with situations that have proved problematic in practice.

Settlement in the entity's own equity instruments (paragraphs 21–24 and AG27)

BC10   The approach taken in the revised IAS 32 includes two main conclusions:

(a)   When an entity has an obligation to purchase its own shares for cash (such as under a forward contract to purchase its own shares), there is a financial liability for the amount of cash that the entity has an obligation to pay.

(b)   When an entity uses its own equity instruments 'as currency' in a contract to receive or deliver a variable number of shares whose value equals a fixed amount or an amount based on changes in an underlying variable (eg a commodity price), the contract is not an equity instrument, but is a financial asset or a financial liability. In other words, when a contract is

---

[*]   IAS 1 *Presentation of Financial Statements* (as revised in 2007) requires an entity to present all income and expense items in one statement of comprehensive income or in two statements (a separate income statement and a statement of comprehensive income).

[†]   IAS 1 (revised 2007) replaced the term 'balance sheet' with 'statement of financial position'.

settled in a variable number of the entity's own equity instruments, or by the entity exchanging a fixed number of its own equity instruments for a variable amount of cash or another financial asset, the contract is not an equity instrument but is a financial asset or a financial liability.

When an entity has an obligation to purchase its own shares for cash, there is a financial liability for the amount of cash that the entity has an obligation to pay.

BC11 An entity's obligation to purchase its own shares establishes a maturity date for the shares that are subject to the contract. Therefore, to the extent of the obligation, those shares cease to be equity instruments when the entity assumes the obligation. This treatment under IAS 32 is consistent with the treatment of shares that provide for mandatory redemption by the entity. Without a requirement to recognise a financial liability for the present value of the share redemption amount, entities with identical obligations to deliver cash in exchange for their own equity instruments could report different information in their financial statements depending on whether the redemption clause is embedded in the equity instrument or is a free-standing derivative contract.

BC12 Some respondents to the Exposure Draft suggested that when an entity writes an option that, if exercised, will result in the entity paying cash in return for receiving its own shares, it is incorrect to treat the full amount of the exercise price as a financial liability because the obligation is conditional upon the option being exercised. The Board rejected this argument because the entity has an obligation to pay the full redemption amount and cannot avoid settlement in cash or another financial asset for the full redemption amount unless the counterparty decides not to exercise its redemption right or specified future events or circumstances beyond the control of the entity occur or do not occur. The Board also noted that a change would require a reconsideration of other provisions in IAS 32 that require liability treatment for obligations that are conditional on events or choices that are beyond the entity's control. These include, for example, (a) the treatment of financial instruments with contingent settlement provisions as financial liabilities for the full amount of the conditional obligation, (b) the treatment of preference shares that are redeemable at the option of the holder as financial liabilities for the full amount of the conditional obligation, and (c) the treatment of financial instruments (puttable instruments) that give the holder the right to put the instrument back to the issuer for cash or another financial asset, the amount of which is determined by reference to an index, and which therefore has the potential to increase and decrease, as financial liabilities for the full amount of the conditional obligation.

When an entity uses its own equity instruments as currency in a contract to receive or deliver a variable number of shares, the contract is not an equity instrument, but is a financial asset or a financial liability.

BC13 The Board agreed that it would be inappropriate to account for a contract as an equity instrument when an entity's own equity instruments are used as currency in a contract to receive or deliver a variable number of shares whose value equals a fixed amount or an amount based on changes in an underlying variable (eg a net share-settled derivative contract on gold or an obligation to deliver as many shares as are equal in value to CU10,000). Such a contract represents a right or obligation of a specified amount rather than a specified equity interest. A contract to pay or receive a specified amount (rather than a specified equity interest) is not an equity instrument. For such a contract, the entity does not know, before the transaction is settled, how many of its own shares (or how much cash) it will receive or deliver and the entity may not even know whether it will receive or deliver its own shares.

BC14   In addition, the Board noted that precluding equity treatment for such a contract limits incentives for structuring potentially favourable or unfavourable transactions to obtain equity treatment. For example, the Board believes that an entity should not be able to obtain equity treatment for a transaction simply by including a share settlement clause when the contract is for a specified value, rather than a specified equity interest.

BC15   The Board rejected the argument that a contract that is settled in the entity's own shares must be an equity instrument because no change in assets or liabilities, and thus no gain or loss, arises on settlement of the contract. The Board noted that any gain or loss arises before settlement of the transaction, not when it is settled.

Contingent settlement provisions (paragraphs 25 and AG28)

BC16   The revised Standard incorporates the conclusion previously in SIC-5 *Classification of Financial Instruments—Contingent Settlement Provisions* that a financial instrument for which the manner of settlement depends on the occurrence or non-occurrence of uncertain future events, or on the outcome of uncertain circumstances that are beyond the control of both the issuer and the holder (ie a 'contingent settlement provision'), is a financial liability.

BC17   The amendments do not include the exception previously provided in paragraph 6 of SIC-5 for circumstances in which the possibility of the entity being required to settle in cash or another financial asset is remote at the time the financial instrument is issued. The Board concluded that it is not consistent with the definitions of financial liabilities and equity instruments to classify an obligation to deliver cash or another financial asset as a financial liability only when settlement in cash is probable. There is a contractual obligation to transfer economic benefits as a result of past events because the entity is unable to avoid a settlement in cash or another financial asset unless an event occurs or does not occur in the future.

BC18   However, the Board also concluded that contingent settlement provisions that would apply only in the event of liquidation of an entity should not influence the classification of the instrument because to do so would be inconsistent with a going concern assumption. A contingent settlement provision that provides for payment in cash or another financial asset only on the liquidation of the entity is similar to an equity instrument that has priority in liquidation and therefore should be ignored in classifying the instrument.

BC19   Additionally, the Board decided that if the part of a contingent settlement provision that could require settlement in cash or a variable number of own shares is not genuine, it should be ignored for the purposes of classifying the instrument. The Board also agreed to provide guidance on the meaning of 'genuine' in this context (see paragraph AG28).

Settlement options (paragraphs 26 and 27)

BC20   The revised Standard requires that if one of the parties to a contract has one or more options as to how it is settled (eg net in cash or by exchanging shares for cash), the contract is a financial asset or a financial liability unless all of the settlement alternatives would result in equity classification. The Board concluded that entities should not be able to circumvent the accounting requirements for financial assets and financial liabilities simply by including an option to settle a contract through the exchange of a fixed number of shares for a fixed amount. The Board had proposed in the Exposure Draft that past practice and management intentions should be considered in determining the classification of such instruments. However, respondents to the Exposure Draft noted that such requirements can be difficult to apply because some entities do not have any history of similar transactions and the assessment of whether an established practice exists and of what is management's intention can be subjective. The Board agreed with these comments and accordingly concluded that past practice and management intentions should not be determining factors.

Alternative approaches considered

BC21   In finalising the revisions to IAS 32 the Board considered, but rejected, a number of alternative approaches:

(a)   To classify as an equity instrument any contract that will be settled in the entity's own shares. The Board rejected this approach because it does not deal adequately with transactions in which an entity is using its own shares as currency, eg when an entity has an obligation to pay a fixed or determinable amount that is settled in a variable number of its own shares.

(b)   To classify a contract as an equity instrument only if (i) the contract will be settled in the entity's own shares, and (ii) the changes in the fair value of the contract move in the same direction as the changes in the fair value of the shares from the perspective of the counterparty. Under this approach, contracts that will be settled in the entity's own shares would be financial assets or financial liabilities if, from the perspective of the counterparty, their value moves inversely with the price of the entity's own shares. An example is an entity's obligation to buy back its own shares. The Board rejected this approach because its adoption would represent a fundamental shift in the concept of equity. The Board also noted that it would result in a change to the classification of some transactions, compared with the existing *Framework* and IAS 32, that had not been exposed for comment.

(c)   To classify as an equity instrument a contract that will be settled in the entity's own shares unless its value changes in response to something other than the price of the entity's own shares. The Board rejected this approach to avoid an exception to the principle that non-derivative contracts that are settled in a variable number of an entity's own shares should be treated as financial assets or financial liabilities.

(d) To limit classification as equity instruments to outstanding ordinary shares, and classify as financial assets or financial liabilities all contracts that involve future receipt or delivery of the entity's own shares. The Board rejected this approach because its adoption would represent a fundamental shift in the concept of equity. The Board also noted that it would result in a change to the classification of some transactions compared with the existing IAS 32 that had not been exposed for comment.

Compound financial instruments (paragraphs 28–32 and AG30–AG35)

BC22 The Standard requires the separate presentation in an entity's balance sheet* of liability and equity components of a single financial instrument. It is more a matter of form than a matter of substance that both liabilities and equity interests are created by a single financial instrument rather than two or more separate instruments. The Board believes that an entity's financial position is more faithfully represented by separate presentation of liability and equity components contained in a single instrument.

Allocation of the initial carrying amount to the liability and equity components (paragraphs 31, 32 and AG36–AG38 and Illustrative Examples 9–12)

BC23 The previous version of IAS 32 did not prescribe a particular method for assigning the initial carrying amount of a compound financial instrument to its separated liability and equity components. Rather, it suggested approaches that might be considered, such as:

(a) assigning to the less easily measurable component (often the equity component) the residual amount after deducting from the instrument as a whole the amount separately determined for the component that is more easily determinable (a 'with-and-without' method); and

(b) measuring the liability and equity components separately and, to the extent necessary, adjusting these amounts pro rata so that the sum of the components equals the amount of the instrument as a whole (a 'relative fair value' method).

BC24 This choice was originally justified on the grounds that IAS 32 did not deal with the measurement of financial assets, financial liabilities and equity instruments.

BC25 However, since the issue of IAS 39, IFRSs contain requirements for the measurement of financial assets and financial liabilities. Therefore, the view that IAS 32 should not prescribe a particular method for separating compound financial instruments because of the absence of measurement requirements for

---

* IAS 1 (as revised in 2007) replaced the term 'balance sheet' with 'statement of financial position'.

financial instruments is no longer valid. IAS 39, paragraph 43,* requires a financial liability to be measured on initial recognition at its fair value. Therefore, a relative fair value method could result in an initial measurement of the liability component that is not in compliance with IAS 39.

BC26   After initial recognition, a financial liability that is classified as at fair value through profit or loss is measured at fair value under IAS 39,[†] and other financial liabilities are measured at amortised cost. If the liability component of a compound financial instrument is classified as at fair value through profit or loss, an entity could recognise an immediate gain or loss after initial recognition if it applies a relative fair value method. This is contrary to IAS 32, paragraph 31, which states that no gain or loss arises from recognising the components of the instrument separately.

BC27   Under the *Framework*, and IASs 32 and 39, an equity instrument is defined as any contract that evidences a residual interest in the assets of an entity after deducting all of its liabilities. Paragraph 67 of the *Framework* further states that the amount at which equity is recognised in the balance sheet is dependent on the measurement of assets and liabilities.

BC28   The Board concluded that the alternatives in IAS 32 to measure on initial recognition the liability component of a compound financial instrument as a residual amount after separating the equity component or on the basis of a relative fair value method should be eliminated. Instead the liability component should be measured first (including the value of any embedded non-equity derivative features, such as an embedded call feature), and the residual amount assigned to the equity component.

BC29   The objective of this amendment is to make the requirements about the entity's separation of the liability and equity components of a single compound financial instrument consistent with the requirements about the initial measurement of a financial liability in IAS 39[†] and the definitions in IAS 32 and the *Framework* of an equity instrument as a residual interest.

BC30   This approach removes the need to estimate inputs to, and apply, complex option pricing models to measure the equity component of some compound financial instruments. The Board also noted that the absence of a prescribed approach led to a lack of comparability among entities applying IAS 32 and that it therefore was desirable to specify a single approach.

BC31   The Board noted that a requirement to use the with-and-without method, under which the liability component is determined first, is consistent with the proposals of the Joint Working Group of Standard Setters in its Draft Standard and Basis for Conclusions in *Financial Instruments and Similar Items*, published by IASC in December 2000 (see Draft Standard, paragraphs 74 and 75 and Application Supplement, paragraph 318).

---

*   In November 2009 the requirements of IAS 39, paragraph 43 relating to the initial measurement of financial assets were relocated to paragraph 5.1.1 of IFRS 9 *Financial Instruments*.

†   In November 2009 the requirements on measurement of assets within the scope of IAS 39 were moved from IAS 39 to IFRS 9 *Financial Instruments*.

Treasury shares (paragraphs 33, 34 and AG36)

BC32   The revised Standard incorporates the guidance in SIC-16 *Share Capital—Reacquired Own Equity Instruments (Treasury Shares)*. The acquisition and subsequent resale by an entity of its own equity instruments represents a transfer between those holders of equity instruments who have given up their equity interest and those who continue to hold an equity instrument, rather than a gain or loss to the entity.

Interest, dividends, losses and gains (paragraphs 35–41 and AG37)

Costs of an equity transaction (paragraphs 35 and 37–39)

BC33   The revised Standard incorporates the guidance in SIC-17 *Equity—Costs of an Equity Transaction*. Transaction costs incurred as a necessary part of completing an equity transaction are accounted for as part of the transaction to which they relate. Linking the equity transaction and costs of the transaction reflects in equity the total cost of the transaction.

BC34–   [Deleted]
BC48

Summary of changes from the Exposure Draft

BC49   The main changes from the Exposure Draft's proposals are as follows:

(a)   The Exposure Draft proposed to define a financial liability as a contractual obligation to deliver cash or another financial asset to another entity or to exchange financial instruments with another entity under conditions that are potentially unfavourable. The definition in the Standard has been expanded to include some contracts that will or may be settled in the entity's own equity instruments. The Standard's definition of a financial asset has been similarly expanded.

(b)   The Exposure Draft proposed that a financial instrument that gives the holder the right to put it back to the entity for cash or another financial asset is a financial liability. The Standard retains this conclusion, but provides additional guidance and illustrative examples to assist entities that, as a result of this requirement, either have no equity as defined in IAS 32 or whose share capital is not equity as defined in IAS 32.

(c)   The Standard retains and clarifies the proposal in the Exposure Draft that terms and conditions of a financial instrument may indirectly create an obligation.

(d)   The Exposure Draft proposed to incorporate in IAS 32 the conclusion previously in SIC-5. This is that a financial instrument for which the manner of settlement depends on the occurrence or non-occurrence of uncertain future events or on the outcome of uncertain circumstances that are beyond the control of both the issuer and the holder is a financial liability. The Standard clarifies this conclusion by requiring contingent

© IASCF

settlement provisions that apply only in the event of liquidation of an entity or are not genuine to be ignored.

(e) The Exposure Draft proposed that a derivative contract that contains an option as to how it is settled meets the definition of an equity instrument if the entity had all of the following: (i) an unconditional right and ability to settle the contract gross; (ii) an established practice of such settlement; and (iii) the intention to settle the contract gross. These conditions have not been carried forward into the Standard. Rather, a derivative with settlement options is classified as a financial asset or a financial liability unless all the settlement alternatives would result in equity classification.

(f) The Standard provides explicit guidance on accounting for the repurchase of a convertible instrument.

(g) The Standard provides explicit guidance on accounting for the amendment of the terms of a convertible instrument to induce early conversion.

(h) The Exposure Draft proposed that a financial instrument that is an equity instrument of a subsidiary should be eliminated on consolidation when held by the parent, or presented in the consolidated balance sheet within equity when not held by the parent (as a minority interest* separate from the equity of the parent). The Standard requires all terms and conditions agreed between members of the group and the holders of the instrument to be considered when determining if the group as a whole has an obligation that would give rise to a financial liability. To the extent there is such an obligation, the instrument (or component of the instrument that is subject to the obligation) is a financial liability in consolidated financial statements.

(i) [Deleted]

(j) [Deleted]

(k) In August 2005, the IASB issued IFRS 7 *Financial Instruments: Disclosures*. As a result, disclosures relating to financial instruments, if still relevant, were relocated to IFRS 7.

Amendments for some puttable instruments and some instruments that impose on the entity an obligation to deliver to another party a pro rata share of the net assets of the entity only on liquidation

Amendment for puttable instruments

BC50   As discussed in paragraphs BC7 and BC8, puttable instruments meet the definition of a financial liability and the Board concluded that all such instruments should be classified as liabilities. However, constituents raised the following concerns about classifying such instruments as financial liabilities if they represent the residual claim to the net assets of the entity:

---

*   In January 2008 the IASB issued an amended IAS 27 *Consolidated and Separate Financial Statements*, which amended 'minority interest' to 'non-controlling interests'.

(a)   On an ongoing basis, the liability is recognised at not less than the amount payable on demand. This can result in the entire market capitalisation of the entity being recognised as a liability depending on the basis for which the redemption value of the financial instrument is calculated.

(b)   Changes in the carrying value of the liability are recognised in profit or loss. This results in counter-intuitive accounting (if the redemption value is linked to the performance of the entity) because:

    (i)   when an entity performs well, the present value of the settlement amount of the liabilities increases, and a loss is recognised.

    (ii)   when the entity performs poorly, the present value of the settlement amount of the liability decreases, and a gain is recognised.

(c)   It is possible, again depending on the basis for which the redemption value is calculated, that the entity will report negative net assets because of unrecognised intangible assets and goodwill, and because the measurement of recognised assets and liabilities may not be at fair value.

(d)   The issuing entity's statement of financial position portrays the entity as wholly, or mostly, debt funded.

(e)   Distributions of profits to shareholders are recognised as expenses. Hence, it may appear that profit or loss is a function of the distribution policy, not performance.

Furthermore, constituents contended that additional disclosures and adapting the format of the statement of comprehensive income and statement of financial position did not resolve these concerns.

BC51   The Board agreed with constituents that many puttable instruments, despite meeting the definition of a financial liability, represent a residual interest in the net assets of the entity. The Board also agreed with constituents that additional disclosures and adapting the format of the entity's financial statements did not resolve the problem of the lack of relevance and understandability of that current accounting treatment. Therefore, the Board decided to amend IAS 32 to improve the financial reporting of these instruments.

BC52   The Board considered the following ways to improve the financial reporting of instruments that represent a residual interest in the net assets of the entity:

(a)   to continue to classify these instruments as financial liabilities, but amend their measurement so that changes in their fair value would not be recognised;

(b)   to amend IAS 32 to require separation of all puttable instruments into a put option and a host instrument; or

(c)   to amend IAS 32 to provide a limited scope exception so that financial instruments puttable at fair value would be classified as equity, if specified conditions were met.

Amend the measurement of some puttable financial instruments so that changes in their fair value would not be recognised

BC53　The Board decided against this approach because:

(a)　it is inconsistent with the principle in IAS 32 and IAS 39[*] that only equity instruments are not remeasured after their initial recognition;

(b)　it retains the disadvantage that entities whose instruments are all puttable would have no equity instruments; and

(c)　it introduces a new category of financial liabilities to IAS 39, and thus increases complexity.

Separate all puttable instruments into a put option and a host instrument

BC54　The Board concluded that conducting further research into an approach that splits a puttable share into an equity component and a written put option component (financial liability) would duplicate efforts of the Board's longer-term project on liabilities and equity. Consequently, the Board decided not to proceed with a project at this stage to determine whether a puttable share should be split into an equity component and a written put option component.

Classify as equity instruments puttable instruments that represent a residual interest in the entity

BC55　The Board decided to proceed with proposals to amend IAS 32 to require puttable financial instruments that represent a residual interest in the net assets of the entity to be classified as equity provided that specified conditions are met. The proposals represented a limited scope exception to the definition of a financial liability and a short-term solution, pending the outcome of the longer-term project on liabilities and equity. In June 2006 the Board published an exposure draft proposing that financial instruments puttable at fair value that meet specific criteria should be classified as equity.

BC56　In response to comments received from respondents to that exposure draft, the Board amended the criteria for identifying puttable instruments that represent a residual interest in the entity, to those included in paragraphs 16A and 16B. The Board decided on those conditions for the following reasons:

(a)　to ensure that the puttable instruments, as a class, represent the residual interest in the net assets of the entity;

(b)　to ensure that the proposed amendments are consistent with a limited scope exception to the definition of a financial liability; and

(c)　to reduce structuring opportunities that might arise as a result of the amendments.

BC57　The Board decided that the instrument must entitle the holder to a pro rata share of the net assets on liquidation because the net assets on liquidation represent the ultimate residual interest of the entity.

---

[*]　In November 2009 the requirements on measurement of assets within the scope of IAS 39 were moved from IAS 39 to IFRS 9 *Financial Instruments*.

BC58   The Board decided that the instrument must be in the class of instruments that is subordinate to all other classes of instruments on liquidation in order to represent the residual interest in the entity.

BC59   The Board decided that all instruments in the class that is subordinate to all other classes of instruments must have identical contractual terms and conditions. In order to ensure that the class of instruments as a whole is the residual class, the Board decided that no instrument holder in that class can have preferential terms or conditions in its position as an owner of the entity.

BC60   The Board decided that the puttable instruments should contain no contractual obligation to deliver a financial asset to another entity other than the put. That is because the amendments represent a limited scope exception to the definition of a financial liability and extending that exception to instruments that also contain other contractual obligations is not appropriate. Moreover, the Board concluded that if the puttable instrument contains another contractual obligation, that instrument may not represent the residual interest because the holder of the puttable instrument may have a claim to some of the net assets of the entity in preference to other instruments.

BC61   As well as requiring a direct link between the puttable instrument and the performance of the entity, the Board also decided that there should be no financial instrument or contract with a return that is more residual. The Board decided to require that there must be no other financial instrument or contract that has total cash flows based substantially on the performance of the entity and has the effect of significantly restricting or fixing the return to the puttable instrument holders. This criterion was included to ensure that the holders of the puttable instruments represent the residual interest in the net assets of the entity.

BC62   An instrument holder may enter into transactions with the issuing entity in a role other than that of an owner. The Board concluded that it is inappropriate to consider cash flows and contractual features related to the instrument holder in a non-owner role when evaluating whether a financial instrument has the features set out in paragraph 16A or paragraph 16C. That is because those cash flows and contractual features are separate and distinct from the cash flows and contractual features of the puttable financial instrument.

BC63   The Board also decided that contracts (such as warrants and other derivatives) to be settled by the issue of puttable financial instruments should be precluded from equity classification. That is because the Board noted that the amendments represent a limited scope exception to the definition of a financial liability and extending that exception to such contracts is not appropriate.

Amendment for obligations to deliver to another party a pro rata share of the net assets of the entity only on liquidation

BC64   Issues similar to those raised by constituents relating to classification of puttable financial instruments apply to some financial instruments that create an obligation only on liquidation of the entity.

BC65　In the exposure draft published in June 2006, the Board proposed to exclude from the definition of a financial liability a contractual obligation that entitles the holder to a pro rata share of the net assets of the entity only on liquidation of the entity. The liquidation of the entity may be:

(a)　certain to occur and outside the control of the entity (limited life entities); or

(b)　uncertain to occur but at the option of the holder (for example, some partnership interests).

BC66　Respondents to that exposure draft were generally supportive of the proposed amendment.

BC67　The Board decided that an exception to the definition of a financial liability should be made for instruments that entitle the holder to a pro rata share of the net assets of an entity only on liquidation if particular requirements are met. Many of those requirements, and the reasons for them, are similar to those for puttable financial instruments. The differences between the requirements are as follows:

(a)　there is no requirement that there be no other contractual obligations;

(b)　there is no requirement to consider the expected total cash flows throughout the life of the instrument;

(c)　the only feature that must be identical among the instruments in the class is the obligation for the issuing entity to deliver to the holder a pro rata share of its net assets on liquidation.

The reason for the differences is the timing of settlement of the obligation. The life of the financial instrument is the same as the life of the issuing entity; the extinguishment of the obligation can occur only at liquidation. Therefore, the Board concluded that it was appropriate to focus only on the obligations that exist at liquidation. The instrument must be subordinate to all other classes of instruments and represent the residual interests only at that point in time. However, if the instrument contains other contractual obligations, those obligations may need to be accounted for separately in accordance with the requirements of IAS 32.

Non-controlling interests

BC68　The Board decided that puttable financial instruments or instruments that impose on the entity an obligation to deliver to another party a pro rata share of the net assets of the entity only on liquidation should be classified as equity in the separate financial statements of the issuer if they represent the residual class of instruments (and all the relevant requirements are met). The Board decided that such instruments were not the residual interest in the consolidated financial statements and therefore that non-controlling interests that contain an obligation to transfer a financial asset to another entity should be classified as a financial liability in the consolidated financial statements.

Analysis of costs and benefits

BC69   The Board acknowledged that the amendments made in February 2008 are not consistent with the definition of a liability in the *Framework*, or with the underlying principle of IAS 32, which is based on that definition. Consequently, those amendments added complexity to IAS 32 and introduced the need for detailed rules. However, the Board also noted that IAS 32 contains other exceptions to its principle (and the definition of a liability in the *Framework*) that require instruments to be classified as liabilities that otherwise would be treated as equity. Those exceptions highlight the need for a comprehensive reconsideration of the distinctions between liabilities and equity, which the Board is undertaking in its long-term project.

BC70   In the interim, the Board concluded that classifying as equity the instruments that have all the features and meet the conditions in paragraphs 16A and 16B or paragraphs 16C and 16D would improve the comparability of information provided to the users of financial statements. That is because financial instruments that are largely equivalent to ordinary shares would be consistently classified across different entity structures (eg some partnerships, limited life entities and co-operatives). The specified instruments differ from ordinary shares in one respect; that difference is the obligation to deliver cash (or another financial asset). However, the Board concluded that the other characteristics of the specified instruments are sufficiently similar to ordinary shares for the instruments to be classified as equity. Consequently, the Board concluded that the amendments will result in financial reporting that is more understandable and relevant to the users of financial statements.

BC71   Furthermore, in developing the amendments, the Board considered the costs to entities of obtaining information necessary to determine the required classification. The Board believes that the costs of obtaining any new information would be slight because all of the necessary information should be readily available.

BC72   The Board also acknowledged that one of the costs and risks of introducing exceptions to the definition of a financial liability is the structuring opportunities that may result. The Board concluded that financial structuring opportunities are minimised by the detailed criteria required for equity classification and the related disclosures.

BC73   Consequently, the Board believed that the benefits of the amendments outweigh the costs.

BC74   The Board took the view that, in most cases, entities should be able to apply the amendments retrospectively. The Board noted that IAS 8 *Accounting Policies, Changes in Accounting Estimates and Errors* provides relief when it is impracticable to apply a change in accounting policy retrospectively as a result of a new requirement. Furthermore, the Board took the view that the costs outweighed the benefits of separating a compound financial instrument with an obligation to deliver a pro rata share of the net assets of the entity only on liquidation when the liability component is no longer outstanding on the date of initial application. Hence, there is no requirement on transition to separate such compound instruments.

Dissenting opinions

Dissent of James J Leisenring from the issue of IAS 32 in December 2003

DO1   Mr Leisenring dissents from IAS 32 because, in his view, the conclusions about the accounting for forward purchase contracts and written put options on an issuer's equity instruments that require physical settlement in exchange for cash are inappropriate. IAS 32 requires a forward purchase contract to be recognised as though the future transaction had already occurred. Similarly it requires a written put option to be accounted for as though the option had already been exercised. Both of these contracts result in combining the separate forward contract and the written put option with outstanding shares to create a synthetic liability.

DO2   Recording a liability for the present value of the fixed forward price as a result of a forward contract is inconsistent with the accounting for other forward contracts. Recording a liability for the present value of the strike price of an option results in recording a liability that is inconsistent with the *Framework* as there is no present obligation for the strike price. In both instances the shares considered to be subject to the contracts are outstanding, have the same rights as any other shares and should be accounted for as outstanding. The forward and option contracts meet the definition of a derivative and should be accounted for as derivatives rather than create an exception to the accounting required by IAS 39. Similarly, if the redemption feature is embedded in the equity instrument (for example, a redeemable preference share) rather than being a free-standing derivative contract, the redemption feature should be accounted for as a derivative.

DO3   Mr Leisenring also objects to the conclusion that a purchased put or call option on a fixed number of an issuer's equity instruments is not an asset. The rights created by these contracts meet the definition of an asset and should be accounted for as assets and not as a reduction in equity. These contracts also meet the definition of derivatives that should be accounted for as such consistently with IAS 39.

Dissent of Mary E Barth and Robert P Garnett from the issue of *Puttable Financial Instruments and Obligations Arising on Liquidation* (Amendments to IAS 32 and IAS 1) in February 2008

DO1   Professor Barth and Mr Garnett voted against the publication of *Puttable Financial Instruments and Obligations Arising on Liquidation* (Amendments to IAS 32 and IAS 1 *Presentation of Financial Statements*). The reasons for their dissent are set out below.

DO2   These Board members believe that the decision to permit entities to classify as equity some puttable financial instruments and some financial instruments that entitle the holder to a pro rata share of the net assets of the entity only on liquidation is inconsistent with the *Framework*. The contractual provisions attached to those instruments give the holders the right to put the instruments to the entity and demand cash. The *Framework*'s definition of a liability is that it is a present obligation of the entity arising from a past event, the settlement of which is expected to result in an outflow of resources of the entity. Thus, financial instruments within the scope of the amendments clearly meet the definition of a liability in the *Framework*.

DO3   These Board members do not agree with the Board that an exception to the *Framework* is justified in this situation. First, the Board has an active project on the *Framework*, which will revisit the definition of a liability. Although these Board members agree that standards projects can precede decisions in the *Framework* project, the discussions to date in the *Framework* project do not make it clear that the Board will modify the existing elements definitions in such a way that these instruments would be equity. Second, the amendments would require disclosure of the expected cash outflow on redemption or repurchase of puttable instruments classified as equity. These disclosures are similar to those for financial liabilities; existing standards do not require similar disclosure for equity instruments. The Board's decision to require these disclosures reveals its implicit view these instruments are, in fact, liabilities. Yet, the *Framework* is clear that disclosure is not a substitute for recognition. Third, these Board members see no cost-benefit or practical reasons for making this exception. The amendments require the same or similar information to be obtained and disclosed as would be the case if these obligations were classified as liabilities. Existing standards offer presentation alternatives for entities that have no equity under the *Framework*'s definitions.

DO4   These Board members also do not agree with the Board that there are benefits to issuing these amendments. First, paragraph BC70 in the Basis for Conclusions states that the amendments will result in more relevant and understandable financial reporting. However, as noted above, these Board members do not believe that presenting as equity items that meet the *Framework*'s definition of a liability results in relevant information. Also as noted above, existing standards offer presentation alternatives that result in understandable financial reporting.

DO5   Second, paragraph BC70 states that the amendments would increase comparability by requiring more consistent classification of financial instruments that are largely equivalent to ordinary shares. These Board members believe that the amendments decrease comparability. These instruments are not comparable to ordinary shares because these instruments oblige the entity to transfer its economic resources; ordinary shares do not. Also, puttable instruments and instruments that entitle the holder to a pro rata share of the net assets of the entity only on liquidation will be classified as equity by some entities and as liabilities by other entities, depending on whether the other criteria specified in the amendments are met. Thus, these amendments account similarly for economically different instruments, which decreases comparability.

DO6   Finally, these Board members do not believe that the amendments are based on a clear principle. Rather, they comprise several paragraphs of detailed rules crafted to achieve a desired accounting result. Although the Board attempted to craft these rules to minimise structuring opportunities, the lack of a clear principle leaves open the possibility that economically similar situations will be accounted for differently and economically different situations will be accounted for similarly. Both of these outcomes also result in lack of comparability.

Dissent of James J Leisenring and John T Smith from the issue of *Classification of Rights Issues* in October 2009

DO1   Messrs Leisenring and Smith dissent from the amendment *Classification of Rights Issues* for the reasons set out below.

DO2   Mr Smith agrees with the concept of accounting for a rights issue as equity in specified circumstances and supports both the IFRIC recommendation and staff recommendation in July 2009 that the Board make 'an extremely narrow amendment' to IAS 32 to deal with this issue. However, he dissents because he believes the change is not extremely narrow and will provide a means for an entity to use its equity instruments as a way to engage in speculative foreign currency transactions and structure them as equity transactions, a concern identified by the Board in the Basis for Conclusions on IAS 32.

DO3   In their comment letters on the exposure draft, some respondents expressed concerns that the wording of the amendment was too open-ended and could lead to structuring risks. Mr Smith believes that these concerns are well-founded because there is no limitation on what qualifies as a class of equity. Without some limitation, an entity could, for example, establish a foreign currency trading subsidiary, issue shares to a non-controlling interest and deem the shares to be a class of equity in the consolidated group.

DO4   The staff acknowledged the concerns expressed in comment letters that a new class of equity could be created for the purpose of obtaining a desired accounting treatment. However, the Board decided not to attempt to limit such structuring opportunities. The Board was concerned that a requirement that a pro rata offer of rights must be made to all existing owners (rather than only all existing owners of a particular class) of equity instruments would mean that the amendment would not be applicable to most of the transactions to which the Board intended the amendment to apply.

DO5   Instead of trying to narrow the amendment, the Board simply acknowledged that under the amendment, 'You could set up a new class of shares today and one minute later issue shares to that class and ... speculate in foreign currency without it going through the income statement.' Mr Smith believes the Board should have explored other alternatives. Mr Smith believes that the Board should have sought solutions that could in fact provide a means of narrowing the amendment to limit structuring while accommodating appropriate transactions.

DO6   Mr Smith believes that structuring opportunities could be curtailed significantly if some limitations were placed on the type of class of equity instruments that qualify for the exemption. There are a number of factors or indicators that could have been incorporated into the amendment that would limit the exception. For example, the amendment could have specified that non-controlling interests do not constitute a class. The amendment could have further required that qualification for the exemption is limited to those classes of equity instruments in which (a) ownership in the class is diverse or (b) the class is registered on an exchange and shares are exchanged in the marketplace or (c) shares in that class when issued were offered to the public at large and sold in more than one jurisdiction and there was no agreement to subsequently offer rights to shares of the entity; and the amount of capital provided by the class is substantial relative to the other classes of equity. Clearly, some combination of these and other alternatives could have been used to limit structuring opportunities. Mr Smith believes that a better solution could have been found and without introducing some limits around the type of class of equity instruments that qualify, the Board did not produce an extremely narrow amendment.

DO7 Mr Leisenring agrees that when an entity issues rights to acquire its own equity instruments those rights should be classified as equity. However, he does not accept that the issue must be pro rata to all existing shareholders of a class of non-derivative equity instruments. He does not accept that whether or not the offer is pro rata is relevant to determining if the transaction meets the definition of a liability.

DO8 Paragraph BC4J suggests that the Board limited its conclusion to those transactions issued on a pro rata basis because of concerns about structuring risks. If that is of concern the suggestions contained in Mr Smith's dissent would be much more effective and desirable than introducing a precedent that transactions such as this rights offering must simply be pro rata to be considered a transaction with owners as owners.

DO9 Mr Leisenring would have preferred to conclude that a right granted for a fixed amount of a currency was a 'fixed for fixed' exchange rather than create additional conditions to the determination of a liability.

CONTENTS

IAS 32 *Financial Instruments: Presentation*
Illustrative examples

These examples accompany, but are not part of, IAS 32.

Accounting for contracts on equity instruments of an entity

IE1　The following examples[*] illustrate the application of paragraphs 15–27 and IAS 39 to the accounting for contracts on an entity's own equity instruments (other than the financial instruments specified in paragraphs 16A and 16B or paragraphs 16C and 16D).

Example 1: Forward to buy shares

IE2　This example illustrates the journal entries for forward purchase contracts on an entity's own shares that will be settled (a) net in cash, (b) net in shares or (c) by delivering cash in exchange for shares. It also discusses the effect of settlement options (see (d) below). To simplify the illustration, it is assumed that no dividends are paid on the underlying shares (ie the 'carry return' is zero) so that the present value of the forward price equals the spot price when the fair value of the forward contract is zero. The fair value of the forward has been computed as the difference between the market share price and the present value of the fixed forward price.

Assumptions:

Contract date	1 February 20X2
Maturity date	31 January 20X3
Market price per share on 1 February 20X2	CU100
Market price per share on 31 December 20X2	CU110
Market price per share on 31 January 20X3	CU106
Fixed forward price to be paid on 31 January 20X3	CU104
Present value of forward price on 1 February 20X2	CU100
Number of shares under forward contract	1,000
Fair value of forward on 1 February 20X2	CU0
Fair value of forward on 31 December 20X2	CU6,300
Fair value of forward on 31 January 20X3	CU2,000

---

[*]　In these examples, monetary amounts are denominated in 'currency units (CU)'.

(a) Cash for cash ('net cash settlement')

IE3   In this subsection, the forward purchase contract on the entity's own shares will be settled net in cash, ie there is no receipt or delivery of the entity's own shares upon settlement of the forward contract.

On 1 February 20X2, Entity A enters into a contract with Entity B to receive the fair value of 1,000 of Entity A's own outstanding ordinary shares as of 31 January 20X3 in exchange for a payment of CU104,000 in cash (ie CU104 per share) on 31 January 20X3. The contract will be settled net in cash. Entity A records the following journal entries.

1 February 20X2

The price per share when the contract is agreed on 1 February 20X2 is CU100. The initial fair value of the forward contract on 1 February 20X2 is zero.

No entry is required because the fair value of the derivative is zero and no cash is paid or received.

31 December 20X2

On 31 December 20X2, the market price per share has increased to CU110 and, as a result, the fair value of the forward contract has increased to CU6,300.

Dr	Forward asset	CU6,300	
	Cr Gain		CU6,300

To record the increase in the fair value of the forward contract.

31 January 20X3

On 31 January 20X3, the market price per share has decreased to CU106. The fair value of the forward contract is CU2,000 ([CU106 × 1,000] − CU104,000).

On the same day, the contract is settled net in cash. Entity A has an obligation to deliver CU104,000 to Entity B and Entity B has an obligation to deliver CU106,000 (CU106 × 1,000) to Entity A, so Entity B pays the net amount of CU2,000 to Entity A.

Dr	Loss	CU4,300	
	Cr Forward asset		CU4,300

To record the decrease in the fair value of the forward contract (ie CU4,300 = CU6,300 − CU2,000).

Dr	Cash	CU2,000	
	Cr Forward asset		CU2,000

To record the settlement of the forward contract.

(b) Shares for shares ('net share settlement')

IE4   Assume the same facts as in (a) except that settlement will be made net in shares instead of net in cash. Entity A's journal entries are the same as those shown in (a) above, except for recording the settlement of the forward contract, as follows:

31 January 20X3

The contract is settled net in shares. Entity A has an obligation to deliver CU104,000 (CU104 × 1,000) worth of its shares to Entity B and Entity B has an obligation to deliver CU106,000 (CU106 × 1,000) worth of shares to Entity A. Thus, Entity B delivers a net amount of CU2,000 (CU106,000 – CU104,000) worth of shares to Entity A, ie 18.9 shares (CU2,000/CU106).

Dr Equity	CU2,000	
Cr Forward asset		CU2,000

To record the settlement of the forward contract.

(c) Cash for shares ('gross physical settlement')

IE5   Assume the same facts as in (a) except that settlement will be made by delivering a fixed amount of cash and receiving a fixed number of Entity A's shares. Similarly to (a) and (b) above, the price per share that Entity A will pay in one year is fixed at CU104. Accordingly, Entity A has an obligation to pay CU104,000 in cash to Entity B (CU104 × 1,000) and Entity B has an obligation to deliver 1,000 of Entity A's outstanding shares to Entity A in one year. Entity A records the following journal entries.

1 February 20X2

Dr Equity	CU100,000	
Cr Liability		CU100,000

To record the obligation to deliver CU104,000 in one year at its present value of CU100,000 discounted using an appropriate interest rate (see IAS 39, paragraph AG64).

31 December 20X2

Dr Interest expense	CU3,660	
Cr Liability		CU3,660

To accrue interest in accordance with the effective interest method on the liability for the share redemption amount.

31 January 20X3

Dr Interest expense	CU340	
Cr Liability		CU340

To accrue interest in accordance with the effective interest method on the liability for the share redemption amount.

Entity A delivers CU104,000 in cash to Entity B and Entity B delivers 1,000 of Entity A's shares to Entity A.

Dr Liability	CU104,000	
Cr Cash		CU104,000

To record the settlement of the obligation to redeem Entity A's own shares for cash.

(d) Settlement options

IE6   The existence of settlement options (such as net in cash, net in shares or by an exchange of cash and shares) has the result that the forward repurchase contract is a financial asset or a financial liability. If one of the settlement alternatives is to exchange cash for shares ((c) above), Entity A recognises a liability for the obligation to deliver cash, as illustrated in (c) above. Otherwise, Entity A accounts for the forward contract as a derivative.

Example 2: Forward to sell shares

IE7   This example illustrates the journal entries for forward sale contracts on an entity's own shares that will be settled (a) net in cash, (b) net in shares or (c) by receiving cash in exchange for shares. It also discusses the effect of settlement options (see (d) below). To simplify the illustration, it is assumed that no dividends are paid on the underlying shares (ie the 'carry return' is zero) so that the present value of the forward price equals the spot price when the fair value of the forward contract is zero. The fair value of the forward has been computed as the difference between the market share price and the present value of the fixed forward price.

Assumptions:

Contract date	1 February 20X2
Maturity date	31 January 20X3
Market price per share on 1 February 20X2	CU100
Market price per share on 31 December 20X2	CU110
Market price per share on 31 January 20X3	CU106
Fixed forward price to be paid on 31 January 20X3	CU104
Present value of forward price on 1 February 20X2	CU100
Number of shares under forward contract	1,000
Fair value of forward on 1 February 20X2	CU0
Fair value of forward on 31 December 20X2	(CU6,300)
Fair value of forward on 31 January 20X3	(CU2,000)

(a) Cash for cash ('net cash settlement')

IE8   On 1 February 20X2, Entity A enters into a contract with Entity B to pay the fair value of 1,000 of Entity A's own outstanding ordinary shares as of 31 January 20X3 in exchange for CU104,000 in cash (ie CU104 per share) on 31 January 20X3. The contract will be settled net in cash. Entity A records the following journal entries.

1 February 20X2

No entry is required because the fair value of the derivative is zero and no cash is paid or received.

31 December 20X2

Dr Loss	CU6,300	
Cr Forward liability		CU6,300

To record the decrease in the fair value of the forward contract.

31 January 20X3

Dr Forward liability	CU4,300	
Cr Gain		CU4,300

To record the increase in the fair value of the forward contract (ie CU4,300 = CU6,300 − CU2,000).

The contract is settled net in cash. Entity B has an obligation to deliver CU104,000 to Entity A, and Entity A has an obligation to deliver CU106,000 (CU106 × 1,000) to Entity B. Thus, Entity A pays the net amount of CU2,000 to Entity B.

Dr Forward liability	CU2,000	
Cr Cash		CU2,000

To record the settlement of the forward contract.

(b) Shares for shares ('net share settlement')

IE9 Assume the same facts as in (a) except that settlement will be made net in shares instead of net in cash. Entity A's journal entries are the same as those shown in (a), except:

31 January 20X3

The contract is settled net in shares. Entity A has a right to receive CU104,000 (CU104 × 1,000) worth of its shares and an obligation to deliver CU106,000 (CU106 × 1,000) worth of its shares to Entity B. Thus, Entity A delivers a net amount of CU2,000 (CU106,000 – CU104,000) worth of its shares to Entity B, ie 18.9 shares (CU2,000/CU106).

Dr Forward liability	CU2,000	
Cr Equity		CU2,000

To record the settlement of the forward contract. The issue of the entity's own shares is treated as an equity transaction.

(c) Shares for cash ('gross physical settlement')

IE10 Assume the same facts as in (a), except that settlement will be made by receiving a fixed amount of cash and delivering a fixed number of the entity's own shares. Similarly to (a) and (b) above, the price per share that Entity A will receive in one year is fixed at CU104. Accordingly, Entity A has a right to receive CU104,000 in cash (CU104 × 1,000) and an obligation to deliver 1,000 of its own shares in one year. Entity A records the following journal entries.

1 February 20X2

No entry is made on 1 February. No cash is paid or received because the forward has an initial fair value of zero. A forward contract to deliver a fixed number of Entity A's own shares in exchange for a fixed amount of cash or another financial asset meets the definition of an equity instrument because it cannot be settled otherwise than through the delivery of shares in exchange for cash.

31 December 20X2

No entry is made on 31 December because no cash is paid or received and a contract to deliver a fixed number of Entity A's own shares in exchange for a fixed amount of cash meets the definition of an equity instrument of the entity.

31 January 20X3

On 31 January 20X3, Entity A receives CU104,000 in cash and delivers 1,000 shares.

Dr Cash	CU104,000	
Cr Equity		CU104,000

To record the settlement of the forward contract.

(d) Settlement options

IE11   The existence of settlement options (such as net in cash, net in shares or by an exchange of cash and shares) has the result that the forward contract is a financial asset or a financial liability. It does not meet the definition of an equity instrument because it can be settled otherwise than by Entity A repurchasing a fixed number of its own shares in exchange for paying a fixed amount of cash or another financial asset. Entity A recognises a derivative asset or liability, as illustrated in (a) and (b) above. The accounting entry to be made on settlement depends on how the contract is actually settled.

Example 3: Purchased call option on shares

IE12   This example illustrates the journal entries for a purchased call option right on the entity's own shares that will be settled (a) net in cash, (b) net in shares or (c) by delivering cash in exchange for the entity's own shares. It also discusses the effect of settlement options (see (d) below):

Assumptions:

Contract date	1 February 20X2
Exercise date	31 January 20X3 (European terms, ie it can be exercised only at maturity)
Exercise right holder	Reporting entity (Entity A)
Market price per share on 1 February 20X2	CU100
Market price per share on 31 December 20X2	CU104
Market price per share on 31 January 20X3	CU104
Fixed exercise price to be paid on 31 January 20X3	CU102
Number of shares under option contract	1,000
Fair value of option on 1 February 20X2	CU5,000
Fair value of option on 31 December 20X2	CU3,000
Fair value of option on 31 January 20X3	CU2,000

(a) Cash for cash ('net cash settlement')

IE13   On 1 February 20X2, Entity A enters into a contract with Entity B that gives Entity B the obligation to deliver, and Entity A the right to receive the fair value of 1,000 of Entity A's own ordinary shares as of 31 January 20X3 in exchange for CU102,000 in cash (ie CU102 per share) on 31 January 20X3, if Entity A exercises that right. The contract will be settled net in cash. If Entity A does not exercise its right, no payment will be made. Entity A records the following journal entries.

1 February 20X2

The price per share when the contract is agreed on 1 February 20X2 is CU100. The initial fair value of the option contract on 1 February 20X2 is CU5,000, which Entity A pays to Entity B in cash on that date. On that date, the option has no intrinsic value, only time value, because the exercise price of CU102 exceeds the market price per share of CU100 and it would therefore not be economic for Entity A to exercise the option. In other words, the call option is out of the money.

Dr Call option asset	CU5,000	
Cr Cash		CU5,000

To recognise the purchased call option.

31 December 20X2

On 31 December 20X2, the market price per share has increased to CU104. The fair value of the call option has decreased to CU3,000, of which CU2,000 is intrinsic value ([CU104 − CU102] × 1,000), and CU1,000 is the remaining time value.

Dr Loss	CU2,000	
Cr Call option asset		CU2,000

To record the decrease in the fair value of the call option.

31 January 20X3

On 31 January 20X3, the market price per share is still CU104. The fair value of the call option has decreased to CU2,000, which is all intrinsic value ([CU104 − CU102] × 1,000) because no time value remains.

Dr Loss	CU1,000	
Cr Call option asset		CU1,000

To record the decrease in the fair value of the call option.

On the same day, Entity A exercises the call option and the contract is settled net in cash. Entity B has an obligation to deliver CU104,000 (CU104 × 1,000) to Entity A in exchange for CU102,000 (CU102 × 1,000) from Entity A, so Entity A receives a net amount of CU2,000.

Dr Cash	CU2,000	
Cr Call option asset		CU2,000

To record the settlement of the option contract.

(b) Shares for shares ('net share settlement')

IE14   Assume the same facts as in (a) except that settlement will be made net in shares instead of net in cash. Entity A's journal entries are the same as those shown in (a) except for recording the settlement of the option contract as follows:

31 January 20X3

Entity A exercises the call option and the contract is settled net in shares. Entity B has an obligation to deliver CU104,000 (CU104 × 1,000) worth of Entity A's shares to Entity A in exchange for CU102,000 (CU102 × 1,000) worth of Entity A's shares. Thus, Entity B delivers the net amount of CU2,000 worth of shares to Entity A, ie 19.2 shares (CU2,000/CU104).

Dr Equity	CU2,000	
Cr Call option asset		CU2,000

To record the settlement of the option contract. The settlement is accounted for as a treasury share transaction (ie no gain or loss).

(c) Cash for shares ('gross physical settlement')

IE15   Assume the same facts as in (a) except that settlement will be made by receiving a fixed number of shares and paying a fixed amount of cash, if Entity A exercises the option. Similarly to (a) and (b) above, the exercise price per share is fixed at CU102. Accordingly, Entity A has a right to receive 1,000 of Entity A's own outstanding shares in exchange for CU102,000 (CU102 × 1,000) in cash, if Entity A exercises its option. Entity A records the following journal entries.

1 February 20X2

Dr Equity	CU5,000	
Cr Cash		CU5,000

To record the cash paid in exchange for the right to receive Entity A's own shares in one year for a fixed price. The premium paid is recognised in equity.

31 December 20X2

No entry is made on 31 December because no cash is paid or received and a contract that gives a right to receive a fixed number of Entity A's own shares in exchange for a fixed amount of cash meets the definition of an equity instrument of the entity.

31 January 20X3

Entity A exercises the call option and the contract is settled gross. Entity B has an obligation to deliver 1,000 of Entity A's shares in exchange for CU102,000 in cash.

Dr Equity	CU102,000	
Cr Cash		CU102,000

To record the settlement of the option contract.

(d) Settlement options

IE16   The existence of settlement options (such as net in cash, net in shares or by an exchange of cash and shares) has the result that the call option is a financial asset. It does not meet the definition of an equity instrument because it can be settled otherwise than by Entity A repurchasing a fixed number of its own shares in exchange for paying a fixed amount of cash or another financial asset. Entity A recognises a derivative asset, as illustrated in (a) and (b) above. The accounting entry to be made on settlement depends on how the contract is actually settled.

Example 4: Written call option on shares

IE17   This example illustrates the journal entries for a written call option obligation on the entity's own shares that will be settled (a) net in cash, (b) net in shares or (c) by delivering cash in exchange for shares. It also discusses the effect of settlement options (see (d) below).

Assumptions:

Contract date	1 February 20X2
Exercise date	31 January 20X3 (European terms, ie it can be exercised only at maturity)
Exercise right holder	Counterparty (Entity B)
Market price per share on 1 February 20X2	CU100
Market price per share on 31 December 20X2	CU104
Market price per share on 31 January 20X3	CU104
Fixed exercise price to be paid on 31 January 20X3	CU102
Number of shares under option contract	1,000
Fair value of option on 1 February 20X2	CU5,000
Fair value of option on 31 December 20X2	CU3,000
Fair value of option on 31 January 20X3	CU2,000

(a) Cash for cash ('net cash settlement')

IE18   Assume the same facts as in Example 3(a) above except that Entity A has written a call option on its own shares instead of having purchased a call option on them. Accordingly, on 1 February 20X2 Entity A enters into a contract with Entity B that gives Entity B the right to receive and Entity A the obligation to pay the fair value of 1,000 of Entity A's own ordinary shares as of 31 January 20X3 in exchange for CU102,000 in cash (ie CU102 per share) on 31 January 20X3, if Entity B exercises that right. The contract will be settled net in cash. If Entity B does not exercise its right, no payment will be made. Entity A records the following journal entries.

1 February 20X2

Dr	Cash	CU5,000
	Cr Call option obligation	CU5,000

To recognise the written call option.

31 December 20X2

Dr	Call option obligation	CU2,000
	Cr Gain	CU2,000

To record the decrease in the fair value of the call option.

31 January 20X3

Dr	Call option obligation	CU1,000
	Cr Gain	CU1,000

To record the decrease in the fair value of the option.

On the same day, Entity B exercises the call option and the contract is settled net in cash. Entity A has an obligation to deliver CU104,000 (CU104 × 1,000) to Entity B in exchange for CU102,000 (CU102 × 1,000) from Entity B, so Entity A pays a net amount of CU2,000.

Dr	Call option obligation	CU2,000
	Cr Cash	CU2,000

To record the settlement of the option contract.

(b) Shares for shares ('net share settlement')

IE19 Assume the same facts as in (a) except that settlement will be made net in shares instead of net in cash. Entity A's journal entries are the same as those shown in (a), except for recording the settlement of the option contract, as follows:

31 December 20X3

Entity B exercises the call option and the contract is settled net in shares. Entity A has an obligation to deliver CU104,000 (CU104 × 1,000) worth of Entity A's shares to Entity B in exchange for CU102,000 (CU102 × 1,000) worth of Entity A's shares. Thus, Entity A delivers the net amount of CU2,000 worth of shares to Entity B, ie 19.2 shares (CU2,000/CU104).

Dr	Call option obligation	CU2,000
	Cr Equity	CU2,000

To record the settlement of the option contract. The settlement is accounted for as an equity transaction.

(c) Cash for shares ('gross physical settlement')

IE20 Assume the same facts as in (a) except that settlement will be made by delivering a fixed number of shares and receiving a fixed amount of cash, if Entity B exercises the option. Similarly to (a) and (b) above, the exercise price per share is fixed at CU102. Accordingly, Entity B has a right to receive 1,000 of Entity A's own outstanding shares in exchange for CU102,000 (CU102 × 1,000) in cash, if Entity B exercises its option. Entity A records the following journal entries.

1 February 20X2

Dr Cash	CU5,000	
Cr Equity		CU5,000

To record the cash received in exchange for the obligation to deliver a fixed number of Entity A's own shares in one year for a fixed price. The premium received is recognised in equity. Upon exercise, the call would result in the issue of a fixed number of shares in exchange for a fixed amount of cash.

31 December 20X2

No entry is made on 31 December because no cash is paid or received and a contract to deliver a fixed number of Entity A's own shares in exchange for a fixed amount of cash meets the definition of an equity instrument of the entity.

31 January 20X3

Entity B exercises the call option and the contract is settled gross. Entity A has an obligation to deliver 1,000 shares in exchange for CU102,000 in cash.

Dr Cash	CU102,000	
Cr Equity		CU102,000

To record the settlement of the option contract.

(d) Settlement options

IE21 The existence of settlement options (such as net in cash, net in shares or by an exchange of cash and shares) has the result that the call option is a financial liability. It does not meet the definition of an equity instrument because it can be settled otherwise than by Entity A issuing a fixed number of its own shares in exchange for receiving a fixed amount of cash or another financial asset. Entity A recognises a derivative liability, as illustrated in (a) and (b) above. The accounting entry to be made on settlement depends on how the contract is actually settled.

Example 5: Purchased put option on shares

IE22 This example illustrates the journal entries for a purchased put option on the entity's own shares that will be settled (a) net in cash, (b) net in shares or (c) by delivering cash in exchange for shares. It also discusses the effect of settlement options (see (d) below).

Assumptions:

Contract date	1 February 20X2
Exercise date	31 January 20X3 (European terms, ie it can be exercised only at maturity)
Exercise right holder	Reporting entity (Entity A)
Market price per share on 1 February 20X2	CU100
Market price per share on 31 December 20X2	CU95
Market price per share on 31 January 20X3	CU95
Fixed exercise price to be paid on 31 January 20X3	CU98
Number of shares under option contract	1,000
Fair value of option on 1 February 20X2	CU5,000
Fair value of option on 31 December 20X2	CU4,000
Fair value of option on 31 January 20X3	CU3,000

(a) Cash for cash ('net cash settlement')

IE23 On 1 February 20X2, Entity A enters into a contract with Entity B that gives Entity A the right to sell, and Entity B the obligation to buy the fair value of 1,000 of Entity A's own outstanding ordinary shares as of 31 January 20X3 at a strike price of CU98,000 (ie CU98 per share) on 31 January 20X3, if Entity A exercises that right. The contract will be settled net in cash. If Entity A does not exercise its right, no payment will be made. Entity A records the following journal entries.

1 February 20X2

The price per share when the contract is agreed on 1 February 20X2 is CU100. The initial fair value of the option contract on 1 February 20X2 is CU5,000, which Entity A pays to Entity B in cash on that date. On that date, the option has no intrinsic value, only time value, because the exercise price of CU98 is less than the market price per share of CU100. Therefore it would not be economic for Entity A to exercise the option. In other words, the put option is out of the money.

Dr Put option asset	CU5,000	
Cr Cash		CU5,000

To recognise the purchased put option.

31 December 20X2

On 31 December 20X2 the market price per share has decreased to CU95. The fair value of the put option has decreased to CU4,000, of which CU3,000 is intrinsic value ([CU98 − CU95] × 1,000) and CU1,000 is the remaining time value.

Dr Loss	CU1,000	
Cr Put option asset		CU1,000

To record the decrease in the fair value of the put option.

31 January 20X3

On 31 January 20X3 the market price per share is still CU95. The fair value of the put option has decreased to CU3,000, which is all intrinsic value ([CU98 − CU95] × 1,000) because no time value remains.

Dr Loss	CU1,000	
Cr Put option asset		CU1,000

To record the decrease in the fair value of the option.

On the same day, Entity A exercises the put option and the contract is settled net in cash. Entity B has an obligation to deliver CU98,000 to Entity A and Entity A has an obligation to deliver CU95,000 (CU95 × 1,000) to Entity B, so Entity B pays the net amount of CU3,000 to Entity A.

Dr Cash	CU3,000	
Cr Put option asset		CU3,000

To record the settlement of the option contract.

(b) Shares for shares ('net share settlement')

IE24 Assume the same facts as in (a) except that settlement will be made net in shares instead of net in cash. Entity A's journal entries are the same as shown in (a), except:

31 January 20X3

Entity A exercises the put option and the contract is settled net in shares. In effect, Entity B has an obligation to deliver CU98,000 worth of Entity A's shares to Entity A, and Entity A has an obligation to deliver CU95,000 worth of Entity A's shares (CU95 × 1,000) to Entity B, so Entity B delivers the net amount of CU3,000 worth of shares to Entity A, ie 31.6 shares (CU3,000/CU95).

Dr Equity	CU3,000	
Cr Put option asset		CU3,000

To record the settlement of the option contract.

(c) Cash for shares ('gross physical settlement')

IE25 Assume the same facts as in (a) except that settlement will be made by receiving a fixed amount of cash and delivering a fixed number of Entity A's shares, if Entity A exercises the option. Similarly to (a) and (b) above, the exercise price per share is fixed at CU98. Accordingly, Entity B has an obligation to pay CU98,000 in cash to Entity A (CU98 × 1,000) in exchange for 1,000 of Entity A's outstanding shares, if Entity A exercises its option. Entity A records the following journal entries.

1 February 20X2

Dr Equity	CU5,000	
Cr Cash		CU5,000

To record the cash received in exchange for the right to deliver Entity A's own shares in one year for a fixed price. The premium paid is recognised directly in equity. Upon exercise, it results in the issue of a fixed number of shares in exchange for a fixed price.

31 December 20X2

No entry is made on 31 December because no cash is paid or received and a contract to deliver a fixed number of Entity A's own shares in exchange for a fixed amount of cash meets the definition of an equity instrument of Entity A.

31 January 20X3

Entity A exercises the put option and the contract is settled gross. Entity B has an obligation to deliver CU98,000 in cash to Entity A in exchange for 1,000 shares.

Dr Cash	CU98,000	
Cr Equity		CU98,000

To record the settlement of the option contract.

(d) Settlement options

IE26   The existence of settlement options (such as net in cash, net in shares or by an exchange of cash and shares) has the result that the put option is a financial asset. It does not meet the definition of an equity instrument because it can be settled otherwise than by Entity A issuing a fixed number of its own shares in exchange for receiving a fixed amount of cash or another financial asset. Entity A recognises a derivative asset, as illustrated in (a) and (b) above. The accounting entry to be made on settlement depends on how the contract is actually settled.

Example 6: Written put option on shares

IE27   This example illustrates the journal entries for a written put option on the entity's own shares that will be settled (a) net in cash, (b) net in shares or (c) by delivering cash in exchange for shares. It also discusses the effect of settlement options (see (d) below).

Assumptions:

Contract date	1 February 20X2
Exercise date	31 January 20X3 (European terms, ie it can be exercised only at maturity)
Exercise right holder	Counterparty (Entity B)
Market price per share on 1 February 20X2	CU100
Market price per share on 31 December 20X2	CU95
Market price per share on 31 January 20X3	CU95
Fixed exercise price to be paid on 31 January 20X3	CU98
Present value of exercise price on 1 February 20X2	CU95
Number of shares under option contract	1,000
Fair value of option on 1 February 20X2	CU5,000
Fair value of option on 31 December 20X2	CU4,000
Fair value of option on 31 January 20X3	CU3,000

(a) Cash for cash ('net cash settlement')

IE28   Assume the same facts as in Example 5(a) above, except that Entity A has written a put option on its own shares instead of having purchased a put option on its own shares. Accordingly, on 1 February 20X2, Entity A enters into a contract with Entity B that gives Entity B the right to receive and Entity A the obligation to pay the fair value of 1,000 of Entity A's outstanding ordinary shares as of 31 January 20X3 in exchange for CU98,000 in cash (ie CU98 per share) on 31 January 20X3, if Entity B exercises that right. The contract will be settled net in cash. If Entity B does not exercise its right, no payment will be made. Entity A records the following journal entries.

1 February 20X2

Dr Cash	CU5,000	
Cr Put option liability		CU5,000

To recognise the written put option.

31 December 20X2

Dr Put option liability	CU1,000	
Cr Gain		CU1,000

To record the decrease in the fair value of the put option.

31 January 20X3

Dr Put option liability	CU1,000	
Cr Gain		CU1,000

To record the decrease in the fair value of the put option.

On the same day, Entity B exercises the put option and the contract is settled net in cash. Entity A has an obligation to deliver CU98,000 to Entity B, and Entity B has an obligation to deliver CU95,000 (CU95 × 1,000) to Entity A. Thus, Entity A pays the net amount of CU3,000 to Entity B.

Dr Put option liability	CU3,000	
Cr Cash		CU3,000

To record the settlement of the option contract.

(b) Shares for shares ('net share settlement')

IE29   Assume the same facts as in (a) except that settlement will be made net in shares instead of net in cash. Entity A's journal entries are the same as those in (a), except for the following:

31 January 20X3

Entity B exercises the put option and the contract is settled net in shares. In effect, Entity A has an obligation to deliver CU98,000 worth of shares to Entity B, and Entity B has an obligation to deliver CU95,000 worth of Entity A's shares (CU95 × 1,000) to Entity A. Thus, Entity A delivers the net amount of CU3,000 worth of Entity A's shares to Entity B, ie 31.6 shares (3,000/95).

Dr Put option liability	CU3,000	
Cr Equity		CU3,000

To record the settlement of the option contract. The issue of Entity A's own shares is accounted for as an equity transaction.

(c) Cash for shares ('gross physical settlement')

IE30   Assume the same facts as in (a) except that settlement will be made by delivering a fixed amount of cash and receiving a fixed number of shares, if Entity B exercises the option. Similarly to (a) and (b) above, the exercise price per share is fixed at CU98. Accordingly, Entity A has an obligation to pay CU98,000 in cash to Entity B (CU98 × 1,000) in exchange for 1,000 of Entity A's outstanding shares, if Entity B exercises its option. Entity A records the following journal entries.

1 February 20X2

Dr Cash	CU5,000	
Cr Equity		CU5,000

To recognise the option premium received of CU5,000 in equity.

Dr Equity	CU95,000	
Cr Liability		CU95,000

To recognise the present value of the obligation to deliver CU98,000 in one year, ie CU95,000, as a liability.

31 December 20X2

Dr Interest expense	CU2,750	
Cr Liability		CU2,750

To accrue interest in accordance with the effective interest method on the liability for the share redemption amount.

31 January 20X3

Dr	Interest expense	CU250
	Cr Liability	CU250

To accrue interest in accordance with the effective interest method on the liability for the share redemption amount.

On the same day, Entity B exercises the put option and the contract is settled gross. Entity A has an obligation to deliver CU98,000 in cash to Entity B in exchange for CU95,000 worth of shares (CU95 × 1,000).

Dr	Liability	CU98,000
	Cr Cash	CU98,000

To record the settlement of the option contract.

(d) Settlement options

IE31   The existence of settlement options (such as net in cash, net in shares or by an exchange of cash and shares) has the result that the written put option is a financial liability. If one of the settlement alternatives is to exchange cash for shares ((c) above), Entity A recognises a liability for the obligation to deliver cash, as illustrated in (c) above. Otherwise, Entity A accounts for the put option as a derivative liability.

Entities such as mutual funds and co-operatives whose share capital is not equity as defined in IAS 32

Example 7: Entities with no equity

IE32   The following example illustrates a format of a statement of comprehensive income and statement of finmancial position that may be used by entities such as mutual funds that do not have equity as defined in IAS 32. Other formats are possible.

Statement of comprehensive income for the year ended 31 December 20X1

	20X1	20X0
	CU	CU
Revenue	2,956	1,718
Expenses (classified by nature or function)	(644)	(614)
Profit from operating activities	2,312	1,104
Finance costs		
– other finance costs	(47)	(47)
– distributions to unitholders	(50)	(50)
Change in net assets attributable to unitholders	2,215	1,007

Statement of financial position at 31 December 20X1

	20X1		20X0	
	CU	CU	CU	CU
ASSETS				
Non-current assets				
(classified in accordance with IAS 1)	91,374		78,484	
Total non-current assets		91,374		78,484
Current assets				
(classified in accordance with IAS 1)	1,422		1,769	
Total current assets		1,422		1,769
Total assets		92,796		80,253
LIABILITIES				
Current liabilities				
(classified in accordance with IAS 1)	647		66	
Total current liabilities		(647)		(66)
Non-current liabilities excluding				
net assets attributable to unitholders				
(classified in accordance with IAS 1)	280		136	
		(280)		(136)
Net assets attributable to unitholders		91,869		80,051

Example 8: Entities with some equity

IE33 The following example illustrates a format of a statement of comprehensive income and statement of financial position that may be used by entities whose share capital is not equity as defined in IAS 32 because the entity has an obligation to repay the share capital on demand but does not have all the features or meet the conditions in paragraphs 16A and 16B or paragraphs 16C and 16D. Other formats are possible.

Statement of comprehensive income for the year ended 31 December 20X1

	20X1	20X0
	CU	CU
Revenue	472	498
Expenses (classified by nature or function)	(367)	(396)
Profit from operating activities	105	102
Finance costs		
– other finance costs	(4)	(4)
– distributions to members	(50)	(50)
Change in net assets attributable to members	51	48

Statement of financial position at 31 December 20X1

	20X1		20X0	
	CU	CU	CU	CU
ASSETS				
Non-current assets (classified in accordance with IAS 1)	908		830	
Total non-current assets		908		830
Current assets (classified in accordance with IAS 1)	383		350	
Total current assets		383		350
Total assets		1,291		1,180
LIABILITIES				
Current liabilities (classified in accordance with IAS 1)	372		338	
Share capital repayable on demand	202		161	
Total current liabilities		(574)		(499)
Total assets less current liabilities		717		681
Non-current liabilities (classified in accordance with IAS 1)	187		196	
		(187)		(196)
OTHER COMPONENTS OF EQUITY(a)				
Reserves eg revaluation surplus, retained earnings etc	530		485	
		530		485
		717		681
MEMORANDUM NOTE – Total members' interests				
Share capital repayable on demand		202		161
Reserves		530		485
		732		646

(a) In this example, the entity has no obligation to deliver a share of its reserves to its members.

Accounting for compound financial instruments

Example 9: Separation of a compound financial instrument on initial recognition

IE34   Paragraph 28 describes how the components of a compound financial instrument are separated by the entity on initial recognition. The following example illustrates how such a separation is made.

IE35   An entity issues 2,000 convertible bonds at the start of year 1. The bonds have a three-year term, and are issued at par with a face value of CU1,000 per bond, giving total proceeds of CU2,000,000. Interest is payable annually in arrears at a nominal annual interest rate of 6 per cent. Each bond is convertible at any time up to maturity into 250 ordinary shares. When the bonds are issued, the prevailing market interest rate for similar debt without conversion options is 9 per cent.

IE36   The liability component is measured first, and the difference between the proceeds of the bond issue and the fair value of the liability is assigned to the equity component. The present value of the liability component is calculated using a discount rate of 9 per cent, the market interest rate for similar bonds having no conversion rights, as shown below.

	CU
Present value of the principal – CU2,000,000 payable at the end of three years	1,544,367
Present value of the interest – CU120,000 payable annually in arrears for three years	303,755
Total liability component	1,848,122
Equity component (by deduction)	151,878
Proceeds of the bond issue	2,000,000

Example 10: Separation of a compound financial instrument with multiple embedded derivative features

IE37   The following example illustrates the application of paragraph 31 to the separation of the liability and equity components of a compound financial instrument with multiple embedded derivative features.

IE38   Assume that the proceeds received on the issue of a callable convertible bond are CU60. The value of a similar bond without a call or equity conversion option is CU57. Based on an option pricing model, it is determined that the value to the entity of the embedded call feature in a similar bond without an equity conversion option is CU2. In this case, the value allocated to the liability component under paragraph 31 is CU55 (CU57 – CU2) and the value allocated to the equity component is CU5 (CU60 – CU55).

Example 11: Repurchase of a convertible instrument

IE39   The following example illustrates how an entity accounts for a repurchase of a convertible instrument. For simplicity, at inception, the face amount of the instrument is assumed to be equal to the aggregate carrying amount of its liability and equity components in the financial statements, ie no original issue premium or discount exists. Also, for simplicity, tax considerations have been omitted from the example.

IE40   On 1 January 20X0, Entity A issued a 10 per cent convertible debenture with a face value of CU1,000 maturing on 31 December 20X9. The debenture is convertible into ordinary shares of Entity A at a conversion price of CU25 per share. Interest is payable half-yearly in cash. At the date of issue, Entity A could have issued non-convertible debt with a ten-year term bearing a coupon interest rate of 11 per cent.

IE41   In the financial statements of Entity A the carrying amount of the debenture was allocated on issue as follows:

	CU
Liability component	
Present value of 20 half-yearly interest payments of CU50, discounted at 11%	597
Present value of CU1,000 due in 10 years, discounted at 11%, compounded half-yearly	343
	940
Equity component	
(difference between CU1,000 total proceeds and CU940 allocated above)	60
Total proceeds	1,000

IE42   On 1 January 20X5, the convertible debenture has a fair value of CU1,700.

IE43   Entity A makes a tender offer to the holder of the debenture to repurchase the debenture for CU1,700, which the holder accepts. At the date of repurchase, Entity A could have issued non-convertible debt with a five-year term bearing a coupon interest rate of 8 per cent.

IE44 The repurchase price is allocated as follows:

	Carrying value	Fair value	Difference
Liability component:	CU	CU	CU
Present value of 10 remaining half-yearly interest payments of CU50, discounted at 11% and 8%, respectively	377	405	
Present value of CU1,000 due in 5 years, discounted at 11% and 8%, compounded half-yearly, respectively	585	676	
	962	1,081	(119)
Equity component	60	619[a]	(559)
Total	1,022	1,700	(678)

[a] This amount represents the difference between the fair value amount allocated to the liability component and the repurchase price of CU1,700.

IE45 Entity A recognises the repurchase of the debenture as follows:

Dr Liability component CU962
Dr Debt settlement expense (profit or loss) CU119
    Cr Cash CU1,081

To recognise the repurchase of the liability component.

Dr Equity CU619
    Cr Cash CU619

To recognise the cash paid for the equity component.

IE46 The equity component remains as equity, but may be transferred from one line item within equity to another.

Example 12: Amendment of the terms of a convertible instrument to induce early conversion

IE47 The following example illustrates how an entity accounts for the additional consideration paid when the terms of a convertible instrument are amended to induce early conversion.

IE48 On 1 January 20X0, Entity A issued a 10 per cent convertible debenture with a face value of CU1,000 with the same terms as described in Example 11. On 1 January 20X1, to induce the holder to convert the convertible debenture promptly, Entity A reduces the conversion price to CU20 if the debenture is converted before 1 March 20X1 (ie within 60 days).

IE49   Assume the market price of Entity A's ordinary shares on the date the terms are amended is CU40 per share. The fair value of the incremental consideration paid by Entity A is calculated as follows:

*Number of ordinary shares to be issued to debenture holders under **amended** conversion terms:*

Face amount	CU1,000	
New conversion price	/CU20	per share
Number of ordinary shares to be issued on conversion	50	shares

*Number of ordinary shares to be issued to debenture holders under **original** conversion terms:*

Face amount	CU1,000	
Original conversion price	/CU25	per share
Number of ordinary shares to be issued on conversion	40	shares

Number of incremental ordinary shares issued upon conversion	10	shares

*Value of **incremental** ordinary shares issued upon conversion*

CU40 per share x 10 incremental shares	CU400

IE50   The incremental consideration of CU400 is recognised as a loss in profit or loss.

IASB documents published to accompany

International Accounting Standard 33

Earnings per Share

This version includes amendments resulting from IFRSs issued up to 31 December 2009.

The text of the unaccompanied IAS 33 is contained in Part A of this edition. Its effective date when issued was 1 January 2005. The effective date of the most recent amendments is 1 July 2009. This part presents the following accompanying documents:

Approval by the Board of IAS 33 issued in December 2003

International Accounting Standard 33 *Earnings per Share* (as revised in 2003) was approved for issue by the fourteen members of the International Accounting Standards Board.

Sir David Tweedie — Chairman

Thomas E Jones — Vice-Chairman

Mary E Barth

Hans-Georg Bruns

Anthony T Cope

Robert P Garnett

Gilbert Gélard

James J Leisenring

Warren J McGregor

Patricia L O'Malley

Harry K Schmid

John T Smith

Geoffrey Whittington

Tatsumi Yamada

Basis for Conclusions on
IAS 33 *Earnings per Share*

This Basis for Conclusions accompanies, but is not part of, IAS 33.

Introduction

BC1   This Basis for Conclusions summarises the International Accounting Standards Board's considerations in reaching its conclusions on revising IAS 33 *Earnings Per Share* in 2003. Individual Board members gave greater weight to some factors than to others.

BC2   In July 2001 the Board announced that, as part of its initial agenda of technical projects, it would undertake a project to improve a number of Standards, including IAS 33. The project was undertaken in the light of queries and criticisms raised in relation to the Standards by securities regulators, professional accountants and other interested parties. The objectives of the Improvements project were to reduce or eliminate alternatives, redundancies and conflicts within Standards, to deal with some convergence issues and to make other improvements. In May 2002 the Board published its proposals in an Exposure Draft of *Improvements to International Accounting Standards*, with a comment deadline of 16 September 2002. The Board received over 160 comment letters on the Exposure Draft.

BC3   Because the Board's intention was not to reconsider the fundamental approach to the determination and presentation of earnings per share established by IAS 33, this Basis for Conclusions does not discuss requirements in IAS 33 that the Board has not reconsidered.

Presentation of parent's separate earnings per share

BC4   The Exposure Draft published in May 2002 proposed deleting paragraphs 2 and 3 of the previous version of IAS 33, which stated that when the parent's separate financial statements and consolidated financial statements are presented, earnings per share need be presented only on the basis of consolidated information.

BC5   Some respondents expressed concern that the presentation of two earnings per share figures (one for the parent's separate financial statements and one for the consolidated financial statements) might be misleading.

BC6   The Board noted that disclosing the parent's separate earnings per share amount is useful in limited situations, and therefore decided to retain the option. However, the Board decided that the Standard should prohibit presentation of the parent's separate earnings per share amounts in the consolidated financial statements (either on the face of the financial statements or in the notes).

Contracts that may be settled in ordinary shares or cash

BC7 The Exposure Draft proposed that an entity should include in the calculation of the number of potential ordinary shares in the diluted earnings per share calculation contracts that may be settled in ordinary shares or cash, at the issuer's option, based on a rebuttable presumption that the contracts will be settled in shares. This proposed presumption could be rebutted if the issuer had acted through an established pattern of past practice, published policies, or by having made a sufficiently specific current statement indicating to other parties the manner in which it expected to settle, and, as a result, the issuer had created a valid expectation on the part of those other parties that it would settle in a manner other than by issuing shares.

BC8 The majority of the respondents on the Exposure Draft agreed with the proposed treatment of contracts that may be settled in ordinary shares or cash at the issuer's option. However, the Board decided to withdraw the notion of a rebuttable presumption and to incorporate into the Standard the requirements of SIC-24 *Earnings Per Share—Financial Instruments and Other Contracts that May Be Settled in Shares*. SIC-24 requires financial instruments or other contracts that may result in the issue of ordinary shares of the entity to be considered potential ordinary shares of the entity.

BC9 Although the proposed treatment would have converged with that required by several liaison standard-setters, for example, in US SFAS 128 *Earnings per Share*, the Board concluded that the notion of a rebuttable presumption is inconsistent with the stated objective of diluted earnings per share. The US Financial Accounting Standards Board has agreed to consider this difference as part of the joint short-term convergence project with the IASB.

Calculation of year-to-date diluted earnings per share

BC10 The Exposure Draft proposed the following approach to the year-to-date calculation of diluted earnings per share:

(a) The number of potential ordinary shares is a year-to-date weighted average of the number of potential ordinary shares included in each interim diluted earnings per share calculation, rather than a year-to-date weighted average of the number of potential ordinary shares weighted for the period they were outstanding (ie without regard for the diluted earnings per share information reported during the interim periods).

(b) The number of potential ordinary shares is computed using the average market price during the interim periods, rather than using the average market price during the year-to-date period.

(c) Contingently issuable shares are weighted for the interim periods in which they were included in the computation of diluted earnings per share, rather than being included in the computation of diluted earnings per share (if the conditions are satisfied) from the beginning of the year-to-date reporting period (or from the date of the contingent share agreement, if later).

BC11 The majority of the respondents on the Exposure Draft disagreed with the proposed approach to the year-to-date calculation of diluted earnings per share. The most significant argument against the proposed approach was that the proposed calculation of diluted earnings per share could result in an amount for year-to-date diluted earnings per share that was different for entities that report more frequently, for example, on a quarterly or half-yearly basis, and for entities that report only annually. It was also noted that this problem would be exacerbated for entities with seasonal businesses.

BC12 The Board considered whether to accept that differences in the frequency of interim reporting would result in different earnings per share amounts being reported. However, IAS 34 *Interim Financial Reporting* states 'the frequency of an entity's reporting (annual, half-yearly, or quarterly) should not affect the measurement of its annual results. To achieve that objective, measurements for interim reporting purposes should be made on a year-to-date basis.'

BC13 The Board also considered whether it could mandate the frequency of interim reporting to ensure consistency between all entities preparing financial statements in accordance with IFRSs, ie those that are brought within the scope of IAS 33 by virtue of issuing publicly traded instruments or because they elect to present earnings per share. However, IAS 34 states that, 'This Standard does not mandate which entities should be required to publish interim financial reports, how frequently, or how soon after the end of an interim period.' The frequency of interim reporting is mandated by securities regulators, stock exchanges, governments, and accountancy bodies, and varies by jurisdiction.

BC14 Although the proposed approach for the calculation of year-to-date diluted earnings per share would have converged with US SFAS 128, the Board concluded that the approach was inconsistent with IAS 34 and that it could not mandate the frequency of interim reporting. The US Financial Accounting Standards Board has agreed to consider this difference as part of the joint short-term convergence project with the IASB as well as the issue noted in paragraph BC9.

Other changes

BC15 Implementation questions have arisen since the previous version of IAS 33 was issued, typically concerning the application of the Standard to complex capital structures and arrangements. In response, the Board decided to provide additional application guidance in the Appendix as well as illustrative examples on more complex matters that were not addressed in the previous version of IAS 33. These matters include the effects of contingently issuable shares, potential ordinary shares of subsidiaries, joint ventures or associates, participating equity instruments, written put options, and purchased put and call options.

CONTENTS

IAS 33 *EARNINGS PER SHARE*
ILLUSTRATIVE EXAMPLES

IAS 33 *Earnings per Share*
Illustrative examples

These examples accompany, but are not part of, IAS 33.

Example 1   Increasing rate preference shares

Reference: IAS 33, paragraphs 12 and 15

Entity D issued non-convertible, non-redeemable class A cumulative preference shares of CU100 par value on 1 January 20X1. The class A preference shares are entitled to a cumulative annual dividend of CU7 per share starting in 20X4.

At the time of issue, the market rate dividend yield on the class A preference shares was 7 per cent a year. Thus, Entity D could have expected to receive proceeds of approximately CU100 per class A preference share if the dividend rate of CU7 per share had been in effect at the date of issue.

In consideration of the dividend payment terms, however, the class A preference shares were issued at CU81.63 per share, ie at a discount of CU18.37 per share. The issue price can be calculated by taking the present value of CU100, discounted at 7 per cent over a three-year period.

Because the shares are classified as equity, the original issue discount is amortised to retained earnings using the effective interest method and treated as a preference dividend for earnings per share purposes. To calculate basic earnings per share, the following imputed dividend per class A preference share is deducted to determine the profit or loss attributable to ordinary equity holders of the parent entity:

Year	Carrying amount of class A preference shares 1 January	Imputed(a) dividend	Carrying amount(b) of class A preference shares 31 December	Dividend paid
	CU	CU	CU	CU
20X1	81.63	5.71	87.34	–
20X2	87.34	6.12	93.46	–
20X3	93.46	6.54	100.00	–
Thereafter:	100.00	7.00	107.00	(7.00)

(a) at 7%

(b) This is before dividend payment.

Example 2   Weighted average number of ordinary shares

Reference: IAS 33, paragraphs 19–21

		Shares issued	Treasury(a) shares	Shares outstanding
1 January 20X1	Balance at beginning of year	2,000	300	1,700
31 May 20X1	Issue of new shares for cash	800	–	2,500
1 December 20X1	Purchase of treasury shares for cash	–	250	2,250
31 December 20X1	Balance at year-end	2,800	550	2,250

Calculation of weighted average:

$(1,700 \times \frac{5}{12}) + (2,500 \times \frac{6}{12}) + (2,250 \times \frac{1}{12}) = 2,146$ shares *or*

$(1,700 \times \frac{12}{12}) + (800 \times \frac{7}{12}) - (250 \times \frac{1}{12}) = 2,146$ shares

(a) Treasury shares are equity instruments reacquired and held by the issuing entity itself or by its subsidiaries.

Example 3   Bonus issue

Reference: IAS 33, paragraphs 26, 27(a) and 28

Profit attributable to ordinary equity holders of the parent entity 20X0	CU180
Profit attributable to ordinary equity holders of the parent entity 20X1	CU600
Ordinary shares outstanding until 30 September 20X1	200
Bonus issue 1 October 20X1	2 ordinary shares for each ordinary share outstanding at 30 September 20X1
	$200 \times 2 = 400$

Basic earnings per share 20X1 $\qquad \dfrac{CU600}{(200 + 400)} = CU1.00$

Basic earnings per share 20X0 $\qquad \dfrac{CU180}{(200 + 400)} = CU0.30$

Because the bonus issue was without consideration, it is treated as if it had occurred before the beginning of 20X0, the earliest period presented.

Example 4   Rights issue

Reference: IAS 33, paragraphs 26, 27(b) and A2

	20X0	20X1	20X2
Profit attributable to ordinary equity holders of the parent entity	CU1,100	CU1,500	CU1,800

Shares outstanding before rights issue	500 shares
Rights issue	One new share for each five outstanding shares (100 new shares total)
	Exercise price: CU5.00
	Date of rights issue: 1 January 20X1
	Last date to exercise rights: 1 March 20X1
Market price of one ordinary share immediately before exercise on 1 March 20X1:	CU11.00
Reporting date	31 December

Calculation of theoretical ex-rights value per share

$$\frac{\text{Fair value of all outstanding shares before the exercise of rights + total amount received from exercise of rights}}{\text{Number of shares outstanding before exercise + number of shares issued in the exercise}}$$

$$\frac{(CU11.00 \times 500 \text{ shares}) + (CU5.00 \times 100 \text{ shares})}{500 \text{ shares} + 100 \text{ shares}}$$

Theoretical ex-rights value per share = CU10.00

Calculation of adjustment factor

$$\frac{\text{Fair value per share before exercise of rights}}{\text{Theoretical ex-rights value per share}} \qquad \frac{CU11.00}{CU10.00} = 1.10$$

Calculation of basic earnings per share

		20X0	20X1	20X2
20X0 basic EPS as originally reported:	CU1,100 ÷ 500 shares	CU2.20		
20X0 basic EPS restated for rights issue:	$\dfrac{CU1,100}{(500 \text{ shares} \times 1.1)}$	CU2.00		
20X1 basic EPS including effects of rights issue:	$\dfrac{CU1,500}{(500 \times 1.1 \times \frac{2}{12}) + (600 \times \frac{10}{12})}$		CU2.54	
20X2 basic EPS:	CU1,800 ÷ 600 shares			CU3.00

Example 5   Effects of share options on diluted earnings per share

Reference: IAS 33, paragraphs 45–47

Profit attributable to ordinary equity holders of the parent entity for year 20X1	CU1,200,000
Weighted average number of ordinary shares outstanding during year 20X1	500,000 shares
Average market price of one ordinary share during year 20X1	CU20.00
Weighted average number of shares under option during year 20X1	100,000 shares
Exercise price for shares under option during year 20X1	CU15.00

Calculation of earnings per share

	Earnings	Shares	Per share
Profit attributable to ordinary equity holders of the parent entity for year 20X1	CU1,200,000		
Weighted average shares outstanding during year 20X1		500,000	
Basic earnings per share			CU2.40
Weighted average number of shares under option		100,000	
Weighted average number of shares that would have been issued at average market price: (100,000 × CU15.00) ÷ CU20.00	(a)	(75,000)	
Diluted earnings per share	CU1,200,000	525,000	CU2.29

(a)   Earnings have not increased because the total number of shares has increased only by the number of shares (25,000) deemed to have been issued for no consideration (see paragraph 46(b) of the Standard).

Example 5A Determining the exercise price of employee share options

Weighted average number of unvested share options per employee	1,000
Weighted average amount per employee to be recognised over the remainder of the vesting period for employee services to be rendered as consideration for the share options, determined in accordance with IFRS 2 *Share-based Payment*	CU1,200
Cash exercise price of unvested share options	CU15

Calculation of adjusted exercise price

Fair value of services yet to be rendered per employee:	CU1,200
Fair value of services yet to be rendered per option: (CU1,200 ÷ 1,000)	CU1.20
Total exercise price of share options: (CU15.00 + CU1.20)	CU16.20

Example 6   Convertible bonds[*]

Reference: IAS 33, paragraphs 33, 34, 36 and 49

Profit attributable to ordinary equity holders of the parent entity	CU1,004
Ordinary shares outstanding	1,000
Basic earnings per share	CU1.00
Convertible bonds	100
Each block of 10 bonds is convertible into three ordinary shares	
Interest expense for the current year relating to the liability component of the convertible bonds	CU10
Current and deferred tax relating to that interest expense	CU4

Note: the interest expense includes amortisation of the discount arising on initial recognition of the liability component (see IAS 32 Financial Instruments: Presentation).

Adjusted profit attributable to ordinary equity holders of the parent entity	CU1,004 + CU10 – CU4 = CU1,010
Number of ordinary shares resulting from conversion of bonds	30
Number of ordinary shares used to calculate diluted earnings per share	1,000 + 30 = 1,030
Diluted earnings per share	$\dfrac{CU1,010}{1,030} = CU0.98$

---

[*] This example does not illustrate the classification of the components of convertible financial instruments as liabilities and equity or the classification of related interest and dividends as expenses and equity as required by IAS 32.

Example 7   Contingently issuable shares

Reference: IAS 33, paragraphs 19, 24, 36, 37, 41-43 and 52

Ordinary shares outstanding during 20X1	1,000,000 (there were no options, warrants or convertible instruments outstanding during the period)

An agreement related to a recent business combination provides for the issue of additional ordinary shares based on the following conditions:

	5,000 additional ordinary shares for each new retail site opened during 20X1
	1,000 additional ordinary shares for each CU1,000 of consolidated profit in excess of CU2,000,000 for the year ended 31 December 20X1
Retail sites opened during the year:	one on 1 May 20X1
	one on 1 September 20X1
Consolidated year-to-date profit attributable to ordinary equity holders of the parent entity:	CU1,100,000 as of 31 March 20X1
	CU2,300,000 as of 30 June 20X1
	CU1,900,000 as of 30 September 20X1 (including a CU450,000 loss from a discontinued operation)
	CU2,900,000 as of 31 December 20X1

Basic earnings per share

	First quarter	Second quarter	Third quarter	Fourth quarter	Full year
Numerator (CU)	1,100,000	1,200,000	(400,000)	1,000,000	2,900,000
Denominator:					
Ordinary shares outstanding	1,000,000	1,000,000	1,000,000	1,000,000	1,000,000
Retail site contingency	–	3,333[a]	6,667[b]	10,000	5,000[c]
Earnings contingency[d]	–	–	–	–	–
Total shares	1,000,000	1,003,333	1,006,667	1,010,000	1,005,000
Basic earnings per share (CU)	1.10	1.20	(0.40)	0.99	2.89

(a) 5,000 shares × ⅔

(b) 5,000 shares + (5,000 shares × ⅓)

(c) 5,000 shares × 8/12) + (5,000 shares × 4/12)

(d) The earnings contingency has no effect on basic earnings per share because it is not certain that the condition is satisfied until the end of the contingency period. The effect is negligible for the fourth-quarter and full-year calculations because it is not certain that the condition is met until the last day of the period.

Diluted earnings per share

	First quarter	Second quarter	Third quarter	Fourth quarter	Full year
Numerator (CU)	1,100,000	1,200,000	(400,000)	1,000,000	2,900,000
Denominator:					
Ordinary shares outstanding	1,000,000	1,000,000	1,000,000	1,000,000	1,000,000
Retail site contingency	–	5,000	10,000	10,000	10,000
Earnings contingency	– (a)	300,000 (b)	– (c)	900,000 (d)	900,000 (d)
Total shares	1,000,000	1,305,000	1,010,000	1,910,000	1,910,000
Diluted earnings per share (CU)	1.10	0.92	(0.40) (e)	0.52	1.52

(a) Company A does not have year-to-date profit exceeding CU2,000,000 at 31 March 20X1. The Standard does not permit projecting future earnings levels and including the related contingent shares.

(b) [(CU2,300,000 – CU2,000,000) ÷ 1,000] × 1,000 shares = 300,000 shares.

(c) Year-to-date profit is less than CU2,000,000.

(d) [(CU2,900,000 – CU2,000,000) ÷ 1,000] × 1,000 shares = 900,000 shares.

(e) Because the loss during the third quarter is attributable to a loss from a discontinued operation, the antidilution rules do not apply. The control number (ie profit or loss from continuing operations attributable to the equity holders of the parent entity) is positive. Accordingly, the effect of potential ordinary shares is included in the calculation of diluted earnings per share.

Example 8 Convertible bonds settled in shares or cash at the issuer's option

Reference: IAS 33, paragraphs 31–33, 36, 58 and 59

An entity issues 2,000 convertible bonds at the beginning of Year 1. The bonds have a three-year term, and are issued at par with a face value of CU1,000 per bond, giving total proceeds of CU2,000,000. Interest is payable annually in arrears at a nominal annual interest rate of 6 per cent. Each bond is convertible at any time up to maturity into 250 ordinary shares. The entity has an option to settle the principal amount of the convertible bonds in ordinary shares or in cash.

When the bonds are issued, the prevailing market interest rate for similar debt without a conversion option is 9 per cent. At the issue date, the market price of one ordinary share is CU3. Income tax is ignored.

Profit attributable to ordinary equity holders of the parent entity Year 1	CU1,000,000
Ordinary shares outstanding	1,200,000
Convertible bonds outstanding	2,000
Allocation of proceeds of the bond issue:	
Liability component	CU1,848,122[a]
Equity component	CU151,878
	CU2,000,000

(a) This represents the present value of the principal and interest discounted at 9% – CU2,000,000 payable at the end of three years; CU120,000 payable annually in arrears for three years.

The liability and equity components would be determined in accordance with IAS 32 *Financial Instruments: Presentation*. These amounts are recognised as the initial carrying amounts of the liability and equity components. The amount assigned to the issuer conversion option equity element is an addition to equity and is not adjusted.

Basic earnings per share Year 1:

$$\frac{CU1,000,000}{1,200,000} = CU0.83 \text{ per ordinary share}$$

Diluted earnings per share Year 1:

It is presumed that the issuer will settle the contract by the issue of ordinary shares. The dilutive effect is therefore calculated in accordance with paragraph 59 of the Standard.

$$\frac{CU1,000,000 + CU166,331^{(a)}}{1,200,000 + 500,000^{(b)}} = CU0.69 \text{ per ordinary share}$$

(a) Profit is adjusted for the accretion of CU166,331 (CU1,848,122 × 9%) of the liability because of the passage of time.

(b) 500,000 ordinary shares = 250 ordinary shares × 2,000 convertible bonds

Example 9   Calculation of weighted average number of shares: determining the order in which to include dilutive instruments[*]

Primary reference: IAS 33, paragraph 44

Secondary reference: IAS 33, paragraphs 10, 12, 19, 31–33, 36, 41–47, 49 and 50

Earnings	CU
Profit from continuing operations attributable to the parent entity	16,400,000
Less dividends on preference shares	(6,400,000)
Profit from continuing operations attributable to ordinary equity holders of the parent entity	10,000,000
Loss from discontinued operations attributable to the parent entity	(4,000,000)
Profit attributable to ordinary equity holders of the parent entity	6,000,000
Ordinary shares outstanding	2,000,000
Average market price of one ordinary share during year	CU75.00

Potential ordinary shares

Options	100,000 with exercise price of CU60
Convertible preference shares	800,000 shares with a par value of CU100 entitled to a cumulative dividend of CU8 per share. Each preference share is convertible to two ordinary shares.
5% convertible bonds	Nominal amount CU100,000,000. Each CU1,000 bond is convertible to 20 ordinary shares. There is no amortisation of premium or discount affecting the determination of interest expense.
Tax rate	40%

---

[*]   This example does not illustrate the classification of the components of convertible financial instruments as liabilities and equity or the classification of related interest and dividends as expenses and equity as required by IAS 32.

Increase in earnings attributable to ordinary equity holders on conversion of potential ordinary shares

		Increase in earnings	Increase in number of ordinary shares	Earnings per incremental share
		CU		CU
Options				
Increase in earnings		Nil		
Incremental shares issued for no consideration	100,000 × (CU75 – CU60) ÷ CU75		20,000	Nil
Convertible preference shares				
Increase in profit	CU800,000 × 100 × 0.08	6,400,000		
Incremental shares	2 × 800,000		1,600,000	4.00
5% convertible bonds				
Increase in profit	CU100,000,000 × 0.05 × (1 – 0.40)	3,000,000		
Incremental shares	100,000 × 20		2,000,000	1.50

The order in which to include the dilutive instruments is therefore:

1   Options

2   5% convertible bonds

3   Convertible preference shares

Calculation of diluted earnings per share

	Profit from continuing operations attributable to ordinary equity holders of the parent entity (control number)	Ordinary shares	Per share	
	CU		CU	
As reported	10,000,000	2,000,000	5.00	
Options	–	20,000		
	10,000,000	2,020,000	4.95	Dilutive
5% convertible bonds	3,000,000	2,000,000		
	13,000,000	4,020,000	3.23	Dilutive
Convertible preference shares	6,400,000	1,600,000		
	19,400,000	5,620,000	3.45	Antidilutive

Because diluted earnings per share is increased when taking the convertible preference shares into account (from CU3.23 to CU3.45), the convertible preference shares are antidilutive and are ignored in the calculation of diluted earnings per share. Therefore, diluted earnings per share for profit from continuing operations is CU3.23:

	Basic EPS	Diluted EPS
	CU	CU
Profit from continuing operations attributable to ordinary equity holders of the parent entity	5.00	3.23
Loss from discontinued operations attributable to ordinary equity holders of the parent entity	(2.00)[a]	(0.99)[b]
Profit attributable to ordinary equity holders of the parent entity	3.00[c]	2.24[d]

(a) (CU4,000,000) ÷ 2,000,000 = (CU2.00)

(b) (CU4,000,000) ÷ 4,020,000 = (CU0.99)

(c) CU6,000,000 ÷ 2,000,000 = CU3.00

(d) (CU6,000,000 + CU3,000,000) ÷ 4,020,000 = CU2.24

Example 10   Instruments of a subsidiary: calculation of basic and diluted earnings per share[*]

Reference: IAS 33, paragraphs 40, A11 and A12

Parent:

Profit attributable to ordinary equity holders of the parent entity	CU12,000 (excluding any earnings of, or dividends paid by, the subsidiary)
Ordinary shares outstanding	10,000
Instruments of subsidiary owned by the parent	800 ordinary shares
	30 warrants exercisable to purchase ordinary shares of subsidiary
	300 convertible preference shares

Subsidiary:

Profit	CU5,400
Ordinary shares outstanding	1,000
Warrants	150, exercisable to purchase ordinary shares of the subsidiary
Exercise price	CU10
Average market price of one ordinary share	CU20
Convertible preference shares	400, each convertible into one ordinary share
Dividends on preference shares	CU1 per share

No inter-company eliminations or adjustments were necessary except for dividends.

For the purposes of this illustration, income taxes have been ignored.

---

[*]   This example does not illustrate the classification of the components of convertible financial instruments as liabilities and equity or the classification of related interest and dividends as expenses and equity as required by IAS 32.

Subsidiary's earnings per share

Basic EPS	CU5.00 calculated:	$\dfrac{CU5,400^{(a)} - CU400^{(b)}}{1,000^{(c)}}$

Diluted EPS	CU3.66 calculated:	$\dfrac{CU5,400^{(d)}}{(1,000 + 75^{(e)} + 400^{(f)})}$

(a) Subsidiary's profit attributable to ordinary equity holders.

(b) Dividends paid by subsidiary on convertible preference shares.

(c) Subsidiary's ordinary shares outstanding.

(d) Subsidiary's profit attributable to ordinary equity holders (CU5,000) increased by CU400 preference dividends for the purpose of calculating diluted earnings per share.

(e) Incremental shares from warrants, calculated: $[(CU20 - CU10) \div CU20] \times 150$.

(f) Subsidiary's ordinary shares assumed outstanding from conversion of convertible preference shares, calculated: 400 convertible preference shares × conversion factor of 1.

Consolidated earnings per share

Basic EPS	CU1.63 calculated:	$\dfrac{CU12,000^{(a)} + CU4,300^{(b)}}{10,000^{(c)}}$

Diluted EPS	CU1.61 calculated:	$\dfrac{CU12,000 + CU2,928^{(d)} + CU55^{(e)} + CU1,098^{(f)}}{10,000}$

(a) Parent's profit attributable to ordinary equity holders of the parent entity.

(b) Portion of subsidiary's profit to be included in consolidated basic earnings per share, calculated: $(800 \times CU5.00) + (300 \times CU1.00)$.

(c) Parent's ordinary shares outstanding.

(d) Parent's proportionate interest in subsidiary's earnings attributable to ordinary shares, calculated: $(800 \div 1,000) \times (1,000$ shares × CU3.66 per share).

(e) Parent's proportionate interest in subsidiary's earnings attributable to warrants, calculated: $(30 \div 150) \times (75$ incremental shares × CU3.66 per share).

(f) Parent's proportionate interest in subsidiary's earnings attributable to convertible preference shares, calculated: $(300 \div 400) \times (400$ shares from conversion × CU3.66 per share).

Example 11 Participating equity instruments and two-class ordinary shares[*]

Reference: IAS 33, paragraphs A13 and A14

Profit attributable to equity holders of the parent entity	CU100,000
Ordinary shares outstanding	10,000
Non-convertible preference shares	6,000
Non-cumulative annual dividend on preference shares (before any dividend is paid on ordinary shares)	CU5.50 per share

After ordinary shares have been paid a dividend of CU2.10 per share, the preference shares participate in any additional dividends on a 20:80 ratio with ordinary shares (ie after preference and ordinary shares have been paid dividends of CU5.50 and CU2.10 per share, respectively, preference shares participate in any additional dividends at a rate of one-fourth of the amount paid to ordinary shares on a per-share basis).

Dividends on preference shares paid	CU33,000	(CU5.50 per share)
Dividends on ordinary shares paid	CU21,000	(CU2.10 per share)

Basic earnings per share is calculated as follows:

	CU	CU
Profit attributable to equity holders of the parent entity		100,000
Less dividends paid:		
Preference	33,000	
Ordinary	21,000	
		(54,000)
Undistributed earnings		46,000

Allocation of undistributed earnings:

Allocation per ordinary share = A

Allocation per preference share = B; B = ¼ A

$$(A \times 10,000) + (¼ \times A \times 6,000) = CU46,000$$
$$A = CU46,000 \div (10,000 + 1,500)$$
$$A = CU4.00$$
$$B = ¼ A$$
$$B = CU1.00$$

Basic per share amounts:

	Preference shares	Ordinary shares
Distributed earnings	CU5.50	CU2.10
Undistributed earnings	CU1.00	CU4.00
Totals	CU6.50	CU6.10

---

[*] This example does not illustrate the classification of the components of convertible financial instruments as liabilities and equity or the classification of related interest and dividends as expenses and equity as required by IAS 32.

Example 12 Calculation and presentation of basic and diluted earnings per share (comprehensive example)[*]

This example illustrates the quarterly and annual calculations of basic and diluted earnings per share in the year 20X1 for Company A, which has a complex capital structure. The control number is profit or loss from continuing operations attributable to the parent entity. Other facts assumed are as follows:

Average market price of ordinary shares: The average market prices of ordinary shares for the calendar year 20X1 were as follows:

First quarter	CU49
Second quarter	CU60
Third quarter	CU67
Fourth quarter	CU67

The average market price of ordinary shares from 1 July to 1 September 20X1 was CU65.

Ordinary shares: The number of ordinary shares outstanding at the beginning of 20X1 was 5,000,000. On 1 March 20X1, 200,000 ordinary shares were issued for cash.

Convertible bonds: In the last quarter of 20X0, 5 per cent convertible bonds with a principal amount of CU12,000,000 due in 20 years were sold for cash at CU1,000 (par). Interest is payable twice a year, on 1 November and 1 May. Each CU1,000 bond is convertible into 40 ordinary shares. No bonds were converted in 20X0. The entire issue was converted on 1 April 20X1 because the issue was called by Company A.

Convertible preference shares: In the second quarter of 20X0, 800,000 convertible preference shares were issued for assets in a purchase transaction. The quarterly dividend on each convertible preference share is CU0.05, payable at the end of the quarter for shares outstanding at that date. Each share is convertible into one ordinary share. Holders of 600,000 convertible preference shares converted their preference shares into ordinary shares on 1 June 20X1.

Warrants: Warrants to buy 600,000 ordinary shares at CU55 per share for a period of five years were issued on 1 January 20X1. All outstanding warrants were exercised on 1 September 20X1.

Options: Options to buy 1,500,000 ordinary shares at CU75 per share for a period of 10 years were issued on 1 July 20X1. No options were exercised during 20X1 because the exercise price of the options exceeded the market price of the ordinary shares.

Tax rate: The tax rate was 40 per cent for 20X1.

---

[*] This example does not illustrate the classification of the components of convertible financial instruments as liabilities and equity or the classification of related interest and dividends as expenses and equity as required by IAS 32.

20X1	Profit (loss) from[a] continuing operations attributable to the parent entity	Profit (loss) attributable to the parent entity
	CU	CU
First quarter	5,000,000	5,000,000
Second quarter	6,500,000	6,500,000
Third quarter	1,000,000	(1,000,000)[b]
Fourth quarter	(700,000)	(700,000)
Full year	11,800,000	9,800,000

(a) This is the control number (before adjusting for preference dividends).

(b) Company A had a CU2,000,000 loss (net of tax) from discontinued operations in the third quarter.

First Quarter 20X1

Basic EPS calculation	CU
Profit from continuing operations attributable to the parent entity	5,000,000
Less: preference share dividends	(40,000)[a]
Profit attributable to ordinary equity holders of the parent entity	4,960,000

Dates	*Shares outstanding*	*Fraction of period*	*Weighted-average shares*
1 January–28 February	5,000,000	⅔	3,333,333
Issue of ordinary shares on 1 March	200,000		
1 March–31 March	5,200,000	⅓	1,733,333
Weighted-average shares			5,066,666
Basic EPS			**CU0.98**

continued...

...continued

Diluted EPS calculation

Profit attributable to ordinary equity holders of the parent entity		CU4,960,000
Plus: profit impact of assumed conversions		
Preference share dividends	CU40,000(a)	
Interest on 5% convertible bonds	CU90,000(b)	
Effect of assumed conversions		CU130,000
Profit attributable to ordinary equity holders of the parent entity including assumed conversions		CU5,090,000
Weighted-average shares		5,066,666
Plus: incremental shares from assumed conversions		
Warrants	0(c)	
Convertible preference shares	800,000	
5% convertible bonds	480,000	
Dilutive potential ordinary shares		1,280,000
Adjusted weighted-average shares		6,346,666
Diluted EPS		***CU0.80***

(a) 800,000 shares × CU0.05

(b) (CU12,000,000 × 5%) ÷ 4; less taxes at 40%

(c) The warrants were not assumed to be exercised because they were antidilutive in the period (CU55 [exercise price] > CU49 [average price])

Second Quarter 20X1

Basic EPS calculation			CU
Profit from continuing operations attributable to the parent entity			6,500,000
Less: preference share dividends			(10,000)[(a)]
Profit attributable to ordinary equity holders of the parent entity			6,490,000

Dates	*Shares outstanding*	*Fraction of period*	*Weighted-average shares*
1 April	5,200,000		
Conversion of 5% bonds on 1 April	480,000		
1 April–31 May	5,680,000	⅔	3,786,666
Conversion of preference shares 1 June	600,000		
1 June–30 June	6,280,000	⅓	2,093,333
Weighted-average shares			5,880,000

Basic EPS	***CU1.10***

Diluted EPS calculation

Profit attributable to ordinary equity holders of the parent entity		CU6,490,000
Plus: profit impact of assumed conversions		
Preference share dividends	CU10,000[(a)]	
Effect of assumed conversions		CU10,000
Profit attributable to ordinary equity holders of the parent entity including assumed conversions		CU6,500,000
Weighted-average shares		5,880,000
Plus: incremental shares from assumed conversions		
Warrants	50,000[(b)]	
Convertible preference shares	600,000[(c)]	
Dilutive potential ordinary shares		650,000
Adjusted weighted-average shares		6,530,000

Diluted EPS	***CU1.00***

(a) 200,000 shares × CU0.05

(b) CU55 × 600,000 = CU33,000,000; CU33,000,000 ÷ CU60 = 550,000; 600,000 − 550,000 = 50,000 shares
OR [(CU60 − CU55) ÷ CU60] × 600,000 shares = 50,000 shares

(c) (800,000 shares × ⅔) + (200,000 shares × ⅓)

Third Quarter 20X1

Basic EPS calculation			CU
Profit from continuing operations attributable to the parent entity			1,000,000
Less: preference share dividends			(10,000)
Profit from continuing operations attributable to ordinary equity holders of the parent entity			990,000
Loss from discontinued operations attributable to the parent entity			(2,000,000)
Loss attributable to ordinary equity holders of the parent entity			(1,010,000)

Dates	Shares outstanding	Fraction of period	Weighted-average shares
1 July–31 August	6,280,000	⅔	4,186,666
Exercise of warrants on 1 September	600,000		
1 September–30 September	6,880,000	⅓	2,293,333
Weighted-average shares			6,480,000
Basic EPS			
Profit from continuing operations			**CU0.15**
Loss from discontinued operations			**(CU0.31)**
Loss			**(CU0.16)**

Diluted EPS calculation		
Profit from continuing operations attributable to ordinary equity holders of the parent entity		CU990,000
Plus: profit impact of assumed conversions		
Preference share dividends	CU10,000	
Effect of assumed conversions		CU10,000
Profit from continuing operations attributable to ordinary equity holders of the parent entity including assumed conversions		CU1,000,000
Loss from discontinued operations attributable to the parent entity		(CU2,000,000)
Loss attributable to ordinary equity holders of the parent entity including assumed conversions		(CU1,000,000)
Weighted-average shares		6,480,000
Plus: incremental shares from assumed conversions		
Warrants	61,538[a]	
Convertible preference shares	200,000	
Dilutive potential ordinary shares		261,538
Adjusted weighted-average shares		6,741,538

continued...

© IASCF

....continued

Diluted EPS

Profit from continuing operations	**CU0.15**
Loss from discontinued operations	**(CU0.30)**
Loss	**(CU0.15)**

(a) [(CU65 - CU55) ÷ CU65] × 600,000 = 92,308 shares; 92,308 × ⅔ = 61,538 shares

Note: The incremental shares from assumed conversions are included in calculating the diluted per-share amounts for the loss from discontinued operations and loss even though they are antidilutive. This is because the control number (profit from continuing operations attributable to ordinary equity holders of the parent entity, adjusted for preference dividends) was positive (ie profit, rather than loss).

Fourth Quarter 20X1

Basic EPS calculation	CU
Loss from continuing operations attributable to the parent entity	(700,000)
Add: preference share dividends	(10,000)
Loss attributable to ordinary equity holders of the parent entity	(710,000)

Dates	Shares outstanding	Fraction of period	Weighted-average shares
1 October–31 December	6,880,000	⅓	6,880,000
Weighted-average shares			6,880,000

Basic and diluted EPS

Loss attributable to ordinary equity holders of the parent entity	**(CU0.10)**

Note: The incremental shares from assumed conversions are not included in calculating the diluted per-share amounts because the control number (loss from continuing operations attributable to ordinary equity holders of the parent entity adjusted for preference dividends) was negative (ie a loss, rather than profit).

Full Year 20X1

Basic EPS calculation	CU
Profit from continuing operations attributable to the parent entity	11,800,000
Less: preference share dividends	(70,000)
Profit from continuing operations attributable to ordinary equity holders of the parent entity	11,730,000
Loss from discontinued operations attributable to the parent entity	(2,000,000)
Profit attributable to ordinary equity holders of the parent entity	9,730,000

Dates	Shares outstanding	Fraction of period	Weighted-average shares
1 January–28 February	5,000,000	$^2/_{12}$	833,333
Issue of ordinary shares on 1 March	200,000		
1 March–31 March	5,200,000	$^1/_{12}$	433,333
Conversion of 5% bonds on 1 April	480,000		
1 April–31 May	5,680,000	$^2/_{12}$	946,667
Conversion of preference shares on 1 June	600,000		
1 June–31 August	6,280,000	$^3/_{12}$	1,570,000
Exercise of warrants on 1 September	600,000		
1 September–31 December	6,880,000	$^4/_{12}$	2,293,333
Weighted-average shares			6,076,667

Basic EPS

Profit from continuing operations	*CU1.93*
Loss from discontinued operations	*(CU0.33)*
Profit	*CU1.60*

continued...

...continued

Diluted EPS calculation

Profit from continuing operations attributable to ordinary equity holders of the parent entity		CU11,730,000
Plus: profit impact of assumed conversions		
Preference share dividends	CU70,000	
Interest on 5% convertible bonds	CU90,000(a)	
Effect of assumed conversions		CU160,000
Profit from continuing operations attributable to ordinary equity holders of the parent entity including assumed conversions		CU11,890,000
Loss from discontinued operations attributable to the parent entity		(CU2,000,000)
Profit attributable to ordinary equity holders of the parent entity including assumed conversions		CU9,890,000
Weighted-average shares		6,076,667
Plus: incremental shares from assumed conversions		
Warrants	14,880(b)	
Convertible preference shares	450,000(c)	
5% convertible bonds	120,000(d)	
Dilutive potential ordinary shares		584,880
Adjusted weighted-average shares		6,661,547

Diluted EPS

Profit from continuing operations	*CU1.78*
Loss from discontinued operations	*(CU0.30)*
Profit	*CU1.48*

(a) (CU12,000,000 × 5%) ÷ 4; less taxes at 40%

(b) [(CU57.125* − CU55) ÷ CU57.125] × 600,000 = 22,320 shares; 22,320 × 8/12 = 14,880 shares
     * The average market price from 1 January 20X1 to 1 September 20X1

(c) (800,000 shares × 5/12) + (200,000 shares × 7/12)

(d) 480,000 shares × 3/12

The following illustrates how Company A might present its earnings per share data in its statement of comprehensive income. Note that the amounts per share for the loss from discontinued operations are not required to be presented in the statement of comprehensive income.

	For the year ended 20X1 CU
Earnings per ordinary share	
Profit from continuing operations	1.93
Loss from discontinued operations	(0.33)
Profit	1.60
Diluted earnings per ordinary share	
Profit from continuing operations	1.78
Loss from discontinued operations	(0.30)
Profit	1.48

The following table includes the quarterly and annual earnings per share data for Company A. The purpose of this table is to illustrate that the sum of the four quarters' earnings per share data will not necessarily equal the annual earnings per share data. The Standard does not require disclosure of this information.

	First quarter CU	Second quarter CU	Third quarter CU	Fourth quarter CU	Full year CU
Basic EPS					
Profit (loss) from continuing operations	0.98	1.10	0.15	(0.10)	1.93
Loss from discontinued operations	–	–	(0.31)	–	(0.33)
Profit (loss)	0.98	1.10	(0.16)	(0.10)	1.60
Diluted EPS					
Profit (loss) from continuing operations	0.80	1.00	0.15	(0.10)	1.78
Loss from discontinued operations	–	–	(0.30)	–	(0.30)
Profit (loss)	0.80	1.00	(0.15)	(0.10)	1.48

IASB documents published to accompany

International Accounting Standard 34

Interim Financial Reporting

This version includes amendments resulting from IFRSs issued up to 31 December 2009.

The text of the unaccompanied IAS 34 is contained in Part A of this edition. Its effective date when issued was 1 January 1999. The effective date of the most recent amendment is 1 July 2009. This part presents the following accompanying documents:

Illustrative examples

These illustrative examples accompany, but are not part of, IAS 34.

A Illustration of periods required to be presented

The following examples illustrate application of the principle in paragraph 20.

Entity publishes interim financial reports half-yearly

A1 The entity's financial year ends 31 December (calendar year). The entity will present the following financial statements (condensed or complete) in its half-yearly interim financial report as of 30 June 20X1:

Statement of financial position:

At	30 June 20X1	31 December 20X0

Statement of comprehensive income:

6 months ending	30 June 20X1	30 June 20X0

Statement of cash flows:

6 months ending	30 June 20X1	30 June 20X0

Statement of changes in equity:

6 months ending	30 June 20X1	30 June 20X0

Entity publishes interim financial reports quarterly

A2 The entity's financial year ends 31 December (calendar year). The entity will present the following financial statements (condensed or complete) in its quarterly interim financial report as of 30 June 20X1:

Statement of financial position:

At	30 June 20X1	31 December 20X0

Statement of comprehensive income:

6 months ending	30 June 20X1	30 June 20X0
3 months ending	30 June 20X1	30 June 20X0

Statement of cash flows:

6 months ending	30 June 20X1	30 June 20X0

Statement of changes in equity:

6 months ending	30 June 20X1	30 June 20X0

B   Examples of applying the recognition and measurement principles

The following are examples of applying the general recognition and measurement principles set out in paragraphs 28–39.

Employer payroll taxes and insurance contributions

B1   If employer payroll taxes or contributions to government-sponsored insurance funds are assessed on an annual basis, the employer's related expense is recognised in interim periods using an estimated average annual effective payroll tax or contribution rate, even though a large portion of the payments may be made early in the financial year. A common example is an employer payroll tax or insurance contribution that is imposed up to a certain maximum level of earnings per employee. For higher income employees, the maximum income is reached before the end of the financial year, and the employer makes no further payments through the end of the year.

Major planned periodic maintenance or overhaul

B2   The cost of a planned major periodic maintenance or overhaul or other seasonal expenditure that is expected to occur late in the year is not anticipated for interim reporting purposes unless an event has caused the entity to have a legal or constructive obligation. The mere intention or necessity to incur expenditure related to the future is not sufficient to give rise to an obligation.

Provisions

B3   A provision is recognised when an entity has no realistic alternative but to make a transfer of economic benefits as a result of an event that has created a legal or constructive obligation. The amount of the obligation is adjusted upward or downward, with a corresponding loss or gain recognised in profit or loss, if the entity's best estimate of the amount of the obligation changes.

B4   This Standard requires that an entity apply the same criteria for recognising and measuring a provision at an interim date as it would at the end of its financial year. The existence or non-existence of an obligation to transfer benefits is not a function of the length of the reporting period. It is a question of fact.

Year-end bonuses

B5   The nature of year-end bonuses varies widely. Some are earned simply by continued employment during a time period. Some bonuses are earned based on a monthly, quarterly, or annual measure of operating result. They may be purely discretionary, contractual, or based on years of historical precedent.

B6   A bonus is anticipated for interim reporting purposes if, and only if, (a) the bonus is a legal obligation or past practice would make the bonus a constructive obligation for which the entity has no realistic alternative but to make the payments, and (b) a reliable estimate of the obligation can be made. IAS 19 *Employee Benefits* provides guidance.

Contingent lease payments

B7   Contingent lease payments can be an example of a legal or constructive obligation that is recognised as a liability. If a lease provides for contingent payments based on the lessee achieving a certain level of annual sales, an obligation can arise in the interim periods of the financial year before the required annual level of sales has been achieved, if that required level of sales is expected to be achieved and the entity, therefore, has no realistic alternative but to make the future lease payment.

Intangible assets

B8   An entity will apply the definition and recognition criteria for an intangible asset in the same way in an interim period as in an annual period. Costs incurred before the recognition criteria for an intangible asset are met are recognised as an expense. Costs incurred after the specific point in time at which the criteria are met are recognised as part of the cost of an intangible asset. 'Deferring' costs as assets in an interim statement of financial position in the hope that the recognition criteria will be met later in the financial year is not justified.

Pensions

B9   Pension cost for an interim period is calculated on a year-to-date basis by using the actuarially determined pension cost rate at the end of the prior financial year, adjusted for significant market fluctuations since that time and for significant curtailments, settlements, or other significant one-time events.

Vacations, holidays, and other short-term compensated absences

B10   Accumulating compensated absences are those that are carried forward and can be used in future periods if the current period's entitlement is not used in full. IAS 19 *Employee Benefits* requires that an entity measure the expected cost of and obligation for accumulating compensated absences at the amount the entity expects to pay as a result of the unused entitlement that has accumulated at the end of the reporting period. That principle is also applied at the end of interim financial reporting periods. Conversely, an entity recognises no expense or liability for non-accumulating compensated absences at the end of an interim reporting period, just as it recognises none at the end of an annual reporting period.

Other planned but irregularly occurring costs

B11   An entity's budget may include certain costs expected to be incurred irregularly during the financial year, such as charitable contributions and employee training costs. Those costs generally are discretionary even though they are planned and tend to recur from year to year. Recognising an obligation at the end of an interim financial reporting period for such costs that have not yet been incurred generally is not consistent with the definition of a liability.

       © IASCF

Measuring interim income tax expense

B12   Interim period income tax expense is accrued using the tax rate that would be applicable to expected total annual earnings, that is, the estimated average annual effective income tax rate applied to the pre-tax income of the interim period.

B13   This is consistent with the basic concept set out in paragraph 28 that the same accounting recognition and measurement principles shall be applied in an interim financial report as are applied in annual financial statements. Income taxes are assessed on an annual basis. Interim period income tax expense is calculated by applying to an interim period's pre-tax income the tax rate that would be applicable to expected total annual earnings, that is, the estimated average annual effective income tax rate. That estimated average annual rate would reflect a blend of the progressive tax rate structure expected to be applicable to the full year's earnings including enacted or substantively enacted changes in the income tax rates scheduled to take effect later in the financial year. IAS 12 *Income Taxes* provides guidance on substantively enacted changes in tax rates. The estimated average annual income tax rate would be re-estimated on a year-to-date basis, consistent with paragraph 28 of this Standard. Paragraph 16(d) requires disclosure of a significant change in estimate.

B14   To the extent practicable, a separate estimated average annual effective income tax rate is determined for each taxing jurisdiction and applied individually to the interim period pre-tax income of each jurisdiction. Similarly, if different income tax rates apply to different categories of income (such as capital gains or income earned in particular industries), to the extent practicable a separate rate is applied to each individual category of interim period pre-tax income. While that degree of precision is desirable, it may not be achievable in all cases, and a weighted average of rates across jurisdictions or across categories of income is used if it is a reasonable approximation of the effect of using more specific rates.

B15   To illustrate the application of the foregoing principle, an entity reporting quarterly expects to earn 10,000 pre-tax each quarter and operates in a jurisdiction with a tax rate of 20 per cent on the first 20,000 of annual earnings and 30 per cent on all additional earnings. Actual earnings match expectations. The following table shows the amount of income tax expense that is reported in each quarter:

	1st Quarter	2nd Quarter	3rd Quarter	4th Quarter	Annual
Tax expense	2,500	2,500	2,500	2,500	10,000

10,000 of tax is expected to be payable for the full year on 40,000 of pre-tax income.

B16 As another illustration, an entity reports quarterly, earns 15,000 pre-tax profit in the first quarter but expects to incur losses of 5,000 in each of the three remaining quarters (thus having zero income for the year), and operates in a jurisdiction in which its estimated average annual income tax rate is expected to be 20 per cent. The following table shows the amount of income tax expense that is reported in each quarter:

	1st Quarter	2nd Quarter	3rd Quarter	4th Quarter	Annual
Tax expense	3,000	(1,000)	(1,000)	(1,000)	0

Difference in financial reporting year and tax year

B17 If the financial reporting year and the income tax year differ, income tax expense for the interim periods of that financial reporting year is measured using separate weighted average estimated effective tax rates for each of the income tax years applied to the portion of pre-tax income earned in each of those income tax years.

B18 To illustrate, an entity's financial reporting year ends 30 June and it reports quarterly. Its taxable year ends 31 December. For the financial year that begins 1 July, Year 1 and ends 30 June, Year 2, the entity earns 10,000 pre-tax each quarter. The estimated average annual income tax rate is 30 per cent in Year 1 and 40 per cent in Year 2.

	Quarter ending 30 Sept Year 1	Quarter ending 31 Dec Year 1	Quarter ending 31 Mar Year 2	Quarter ending 30 June Year 2	Year ending 30 June Year 2
Tax expense	3,000	3,000	4,000	4,000	14,000

Tax credits

B19 Some tax jurisdictions give taxpayers credits against the tax payable based on amounts of capital expenditures, exports, research and development expenditures, or other bases. Anticipated tax benefits of this type for the full year are generally reflected in computing the estimated annual effective income tax rate, because those credits are granted and calculated on an annual basis under most tax laws and regulations. On the other hand, tax benefits that relate to a one-time event are recognised in computing income tax expense in that interim period, in the same way that special tax rates applicable to particular categories of income are not blended into a single effective annual tax rate. Moreover, in some jurisdictions tax benefits or credits, including those related to capital expenditures and levels of exports, while reported on the income tax return, are more similar to a government grant and are recognised in the interim period in which they arise.

Tax loss and tax credit carrybacks and carryforwards

B20   The benefits of a tax loss carryback are reflected in the interim period in which the related tax loss occurs. IAS 12 provides that 'the benefit relating to a tax loss that can be carried back to recover current tax of a previous period shall be recognised as an asset'. A corresponding reduction of tax expense or increase of tax income is also recognised.

B21   IAS 12 provides that 'a deferred tax asset shall be recognised for the carryforward of unused tax losses and unused tax credits to the extent that it is probable that future taxable profit will be available against which the unused tax losses and unused tax credits can be utilised'. IAS 12 provides criteria for assessing the probability of taxable profit against which the unused tax losses and credits can be utilised. Those criteria are applied at the end of each interim period and, if they are met, the effect of the tax loss carryforward is reflected in the computation of the estimated average annual effective income tax rate.

B22   To illustrate, an entity that reports quarterly has an operating loss carryforward of 10,000 for income tax purposes at the start of the current financial year for which a deferred tax asset has not been recognised. The entity earns 10,000 in the first quarter of the current year and expects to earn 10,000 in each of the three remaining quarters. Excluding the carryforward, the estimated average annual income tax rate is expected to be 40 per cent. Tax expense is as follows:

	1st Quarter	2nd Quarter	3rd Quarter	4th Quarter	Annual
Tax expense	3,000	3,000	3,000	3,000	12,000

Contractual or anticipated purchase price changes

B23   Volume rebates or discounts and other contractual changes in the prices of raw materials, labour, or other purchased goods and services are anticipated in interim periods, by both the payer and the recipient, if it is probable that they have been earned or will take effect. Thus, contractual rebates and discounts are anticipated but discretionary rebates and discounts are not anticipated because the resulting asset or liability would not satisfy the conditions in the *Framework* that an asset must be a resource controlled by the entity as a result of a past event and that a liability must be a present obligation whose settlement is expected to result in an outflow of resources.

Depreciation and amortisation

B24   Depreciation and amortisation for an interim period is based only on assets owned during that interim period. It does not take into account asset acquisitions or dispositions planned for later in the financial year.

Inventories

B25   Inventories are measured for interim financial reporting by the same principles as at financial year-end. IAS 2 *Inventories* establishes standards for recognising and measuring inventories. Inventories pose particular problems at the end of any financial reporting period because of the need to determine inventory quantities, costs, and net realisable values. Nonetheless, the same measurement principles are applied for interim inventories. To save cost and time, entities often use estimates to measure inventories at interim dates to a greater extent than at the end of annual reporting periods. Following are examples of how to apply the net realisable value test at an interim date and how to treat manufacturing variances at interim dates.

Net realisable value of inventories

B26   The net realisable value of inventories is determined by reference to selling prices and related costs to complete and dispose at interim dates. An entity will reverse a write-down to net realisable value in a subsequent interim period only if it would be appropriate to do so at the end of the financial year.

B27   [Deleted]

Interim period manufacturing cost variances

B28   Price, efficiency, spending, and volume variances of a manufacturing entity are recognised in income at interim reporting dates to the same extent that those variances are recognised in income at financial year-end. Deferral of variances that are expected to be absorbed by year-end is not appropriate because it could result in reporting inventory at the interim date at more or less than its portion of the actual cost of manufacture.

Foreign currency translation gains and losses

B29   Foreign currency translation gains and losses are measured for interim financial reporting by the same principles as at financial year-end.

B30   IAS 21 *The Effects of Changes in Foreign Exchange Rates* specifies how to translate the financial statements for foreign operations into the presentation currency, including guidelines for using average or closing foreign exchange rates and guidelines for recognising the resulting adjustments in profit or loss, or in other comprehensive income. Consistently with IAS 21, the actual average and closing rates for the interim period are used. Entities do not anticipate some future changes in foreign exchange rates in the remainder of the current financial year in translating foreign operations at an interim date.

B31   If IAS 21 requires translation adjustments to be recognised as income or expense in the period in which they arise, that principle is applied during each interim period. Entities do not defer some foreign currency translation adjustments at an interim date if the adjustment is expected to reverse before the end of the financial year.

Interim financial reporting in hyperinflationary economies

B32   Interim financial reports in hyperinflationary economies are prepared by the same principles as at financial year-end.

B33   IAS 29 *Financial Reporting in Hyperinflationary Economies* requires that the financial statements of an entity that reports in the currency of a hyperinflationary economy be stated in terms of the measuring unit current at the end of the reporting period, and the gain or loss on the net monetary position is included in net income. Also, comparative financial data reported for prior periods are restated to the current measuring unit.

B34   Entities follow those same principles at interim dates, thereby presenting all interim data in the measuring unit as of the end of the interim period, with the resulting gain or loss on the net monetary position included in the interim period's net income. Entities do not annualise the recognition of the gain or loss. Nor do they use an estimated annual inflation rate in preparing an interim financial report in a hyperinflationary economy.

Impairment of assets

B35   IAS 36 *Impairment of Assets* requires that an impairment loss be recognised if the recoverable amount has declined below carrying amount.

B36   This Standard requires that an entity apply the same impairment testing, recognition, and reversal criteria at an interim date as it would at the end of its financial year. That does not mean, however, that an entity must necessarily make a detailed impairment calculation at the end of each interim period. Rather, an entity will review for indications of significant impairment since the end of the most recent financial year to determine whether such a calculation is needed.

C Examples of the use of estimates

The following examples illustrate application of the principle in paragraph 41.

C1 **Inventories:** Full stock-taking and valuation procedures may not be required for inventories at interim dates, although it may be done at financial year-end. It may be sufficient to make estimates at interim dates based on sales margins.

C2 **Classifications of current and non-current assets and liabilities:** Entities may do a more thorough investigation for classifying assets and liabilities as current or non-current at annual reporting dates than at interim dates.

C3 **Provisions:** Determination of the appropriate amount of a provision (such as a provision for warranties, environmental costs, and site restoration costs) may be complex and often costly and time-consuming. Entities sometimes engage outside experts to assist in the annual calculations. Making similar estimates at interim dates often entails updating of the prior annual provision rather than the engaging of outside experts to do a new calculation.

C4 **Pensions:** IAS 19 *Employee Benefits* requires that an entity determine the present value of defined benefit obligations and the market value of plan assets at the end of each reporting period and encourages an entity to involve a professionally qualified actuary in measurement of the obligations. For interim reporting purposes, reliable measurement is often obtainable by extrapolation of the latest actuarial valuation.

C5 **Income taxes:** Entities may calculate income tax expense and deferred income tax liability at annual dates by applying the tax rate for each individual jurisdiction to measures of income for each jurisdiction. Paragraph 14 of Appendix B acknowledges that while that degree of precision is desirable at interim reporting dates as well, it may not be achievable in all cases, and a weighted average of rates across jurisdictions or across categories of income is used if it is a reasonable approximation of the effect of using more specific rates.

C6 **Contingencies:** The measurement of contingencies may involve the opinions of legal experts or other advisers. Formal reports from independent experts are sometimes obtained with respect to contingencies. Such opinions about litigation, claims, assessments, and other contingencies and uncertainties may or may not also be needed at interim dates.

C7 **Revaluations and fair value accounting:** IAS 16 *Property, Plant and Equipment* allows an entity to choose as its accounting policy the revaluation model whereby items of property, plant and equipment are revalued to fair value. Similarly, IAS 40 *Investment Property* requires an entity to determine the fair value of investment property. For those measurements, an entity may rely on professionally qualified valuers at annual reporting dates though not at interim reporting dates.

C8 **Intercompany reconciliations:** Some intercompany balances that are reconciled on a detailed level in preparing consolidated financial statements at financial year-end might be reconciled at a less detailed level in preparing consolidated financial statements at an interim date.

C9 **Specialised industries:** Because of complexity, costliness, and time, interim period measurements in specialised industries might be less precise than at financial year-end. An example would be calculation of insurance reserves by insurance companies.

IASB documents published to accompany

International Accounting Standard 36

Impairment of Assets

This version includes amendments resulting from IFRSs issued up to 31 December 2009.

The text of the unaccompanied IAS 36 is contained in Part A of this edition. Its effective date when issued was 31 March 2004. The effective date of the most recent amendments is 1 January 2013. This part presents the following accompanying documents:

Approval by the Board of IAS 36 issued in March 2004

International Accounting Standard 36 *Impairment of Assets* (as revised in 2004) was approved for issue by eleven of the fourteen members of the International Accounting Standards Board. Messrs Cope and Leisenring and Professor Whittington dissented. Their dissenting opinions are set out after the Basis for Conclusions.

Sir David Tweedie	Chairman
Thomas E Jones	Vice-Chairman
Mary E Barth	
Hans-Georg Bruns	
Anthony T Cope	
Robert P Garnett	
Gilbert Gélard	
James J Leisenring	
Warren J McGregor	
Patricia L O'Malley	
Harry K Schmid	
John T Smith	
Geoffrey Whittington	
Tatsumi Yamada	

CONTENTS

---

* In IFRS 5 *Non-current Assets Held for Sale and Discontinued Operations*, issued by the IASB in 2004, the term 'net selling price' was replaced in IAS 36 by 'fair value less costs to sell'.

Basis for Conclusions on
IAS 36 *Impairment of Assets*

The International Accounting Standards Board revised IAS 36 as part of its project on business combinations. It was not the Board's intention to reconsider as part of that project all of the requirements in IAS 36.

The previous version of IAS 36 was accompanied by a Basis for Conclusions summarising the former International Accounting Standards Committee's considerations in reaching some of its conclusions in that Standard. For convenience the Board has incorporated into its own Basis for Conclusions material from the previous Basis for Conclusions that discusses (a) matters the Board did not reconsider and (b) the history of the development of a standard on impairment of assets. That material is contained in paragraphs denoted by numbers with the prefix BCZ. Paragraphs describing the Board's considerations in reaching its own conclusions are numbered with the prefix BC.

In this Basis for Conclusions the terminology has not been amended to reflect the changes made by IAS 1 Presentation of Financial Statements (as revised in 2007).

Introduction

BC1   This Basis for Conclusions summarises the International Accounting Standards Board's considerations in reaching the conclusions in IAS 36 *Impairment of Assets*. Individual Board members gave greater weight to some factors than to others.

BC2   The International Accounting Standards Committee (IASC) issued the previous version of IAS 36 in 1998. It has been revised by the Board as part of its project on business combinations. That project had two phases. The first resulted in the Board issuing simultaneously in 2004 IFRS 3 *Business Combinations* and revised versions of IAS 36 and IAS 38 *Intangible Assets*. The Board's intention in revising IAS 36 as part of the first phase of the project was not to reconsider all of the requirements in IAS 36. The changes to IAS 36 were primarily concerned with the impairment tests for intangible assets with indefinite useful lives (hereafter referred to as 'indefinite-lived intangibles') and goodwill. The second phase of the project on business combinations resulted in the Board issuing simultaneously in 2008 a revised IFRS 3 and an amended version of IAS 27 *Consolidated and Separate Financial Statements*. The Board amended IAS 36 to reflect its decisions on the measurement of a non-controlling interest in an acquiree (see paragraph BC170A). The Board has not deliberated the other requirements in IAS 36. Those other requirements will be considered by the Board as part of a future project on impairment of assets.

BC3   The previous version of IAS 36 was accompanied by a Basis for Conclusions summarising IASC's considerations in reaching some of its conclusions in that Standard. For convenience, the Board has incorporated into this Basis for Conclusions material from the previous Basis for Conclusions that discusses matters the Board did not consider. That material is contained in paragraphs denoted by numbers with the prefix BCZ. The views expressed in paragraphs denoted by numbers with the prefix BCZ are those of IASC.

Scope (paragraph 2)

BCZ4　　IAS 2 *Inventories* requires an enterprise to measure the recoverable amount of inventory at its net realisable value. IASC believed that there was no need to revise this requirement because it was well accepted as an appropriate test for recoverability of inventories. No major difference exists between IAS 2 and the requirements included in IAS 36 (see paragraphs BCZ37–BCZ39).

BCZ5　　IAS 11 *Construction Contracts* and IAS 12 *Income Taxes* already deal with the impairment of assets arising from construction contracts and deferred tax assets respectively. Under both IAS 11 and IAS 12, recoverable amount is, in effect, determined on an undiscounted basis. IASC acknowledged that this was inconsistent with the requirements of IAS 36. However, IASC believed that it was not possible to eliminate that inconsistency without fundamental changes to IAS 11 and IAS 12. IASC had no plans to revise IAS 11 or IAS 12.

BCZ6　　IAS 19 *Employee Benefits* contains an upper limit on the amount at which an enterprise should recognise an asset arising from employee benefits. Therefore, IAS 36 does not deal with such assets. The limit in IAS 19 is determined on a discounted basis that is broadly compatible with the requirements of IAS 36. The limit does not override the deferred recognition of certain actuarial losses and certain past service costs.

BCZ7　　IAS 39 *Financial Instruments: Recognition and Measurement* sets out the requirements for impairment of financial assets.

BCZ8　　IAS 36 is applicable to all assets, unless specifically excluded, regardless of their classification as current or non-current. Before IAS 36 was issued, there was no International Accounting Standard on accounting for the impairment of current assets other than inventories.

Measuring recoverable amount (paragraphs 18–57)

BCZ9　　In determining the principles that should govern the measurement of recoverable amount, IASC considered, as a first step, what an enterprise will do if it discovers that an asset is impaired. IASC concluded that, in such cases, an enterprise will either keep the asset or dispose of it. For example, if an enterprise discovers that the service potential of an asset has decreased:

(a)　the enterprise may decide to sell the asset if the net proceeds from the sale would provide a higher return on investment than continuing use in operations; or

(b)　the enterprise may decide to keep the asset and use it, even if its service potential is lower than originally expected. Some reasons may be that:

　　(i)　　the asset cannot be sold or disposed of immediately;

　　(ii)　 the asset can be sold only at a low price;

　　(iii)　 the asset's service potential can still be recovered but only with additional efforts or expenditure; or

　　(iv)　 the asset could still be profitable although not to the same extent as expected originally.

IASC concluded that the resulting decision from a rational enterprise is, in substance, an investment decision based on estimated net future cash flows expected from the asset.

BCZ10 IASC then considered which of the following four alternatives for determining the recoverable amount of an asset would best reflect this conclusion:

(a) recoverable amount should be the sum of undiscounted future cash flows.

(b) recoverable amount should be the asset's fair value: more specifically, recoverable amount should be derived primarily from the asset's market value. If market value cannot be determined, then recoverable amount should be based on the asset's value in use as a proxy for market value.

(c) recoverable amount should be the asset's value in use.

(d) recoverable amount should be the higher of the asset's net selling price and value in use.*

Each of these alternatives is discussed below.

BCZ11 It should be noted that fair value, net selling price and value in use all reflect a present value calculation (implicit or explicit) of estimated net future cash flows expected from an asset:

(a) fair value reflects the market's expectation of the present value of the future cash flows to be derived from the asset;

(b) net selling price reflects the market's expectation of the present value of the future cash flows to be derived from the asset, less the direct incremental costs to dispose of the asset; and

(c) value in use is the enterprise's estimate of the present value of the future cash flows to be derived from continuing use and disposal of the asset.

These bases all consider the time value of money and the risks that the amount and timing of the actual cash flows to be received from an asset might differ from estimates. Fair value and net selling price may differ from value in use because the market may not use the same assumptions as an individual enterprise.

Recoverable amount based on the sum of undiscounted cash flows

BCZ12 Some argue that recoverable amount should be measured as the sum of undiscounted future cash flows from an asset. They argue that:

(a) historical cost accounting is not concerned with measuring the economic value of assets. Therefore, the time value of money should not be considered in estimating the amount that will be recovered from an asset.

(b) it is premature to use discounting techniques without further research and debates on:

(i) the role of discounting in the financial statements; and

(ii) how assets should be measured generally.

---

* In IFRS 5 *Non-current Assets Held for Sale and Discontinued Operations*, issued by the IASB in 2004, the term 'net selling price' was replaced in IAS 36 by 'fair value less costs to sell'.

If financial statements include assets that are carried on a variety of different bases (historical cost, discounted amounts or other bases), this will be confusing for users.

(c)   identifying an appropriate discount rate will often be difficult and subjective.

(d)   discounting will increase the number of impairment losses recognised. This, coupled with the requirement for reversals of impairment losses, introduces a volatile element into the income statement. It will make it harder for users to understand the performance of an enterprise.

A minority of commentators on E55 *Impairment of Assets* supported this view.

BCZ13   IASC rejected measurement of recoverable amount based on the sum of undiscounted cash flows because:

(a)   the objective of the measurement of recoverable amount is to reflect an investment decision. Money has a time value, even when prices are stable. If future cash flows were not discounted, two assets giving rise to cash flows of the same amount but with different timings would show the same recoverable amount. However, their current market values would be different because all rational economic transactions take account of the time value of money.

(b)   measurements that take into consideration the time value of money are more relevant to investors, other external users of financial statements and management for resource allocation decisions, regardless of the general measurement basis adopted in the financial statements.

(c)   many enterprises were already familiar with the use of discounting techniques, particularly for supporting investment decisions.

(d)   discounting was already required for other areas of financial statements that are based on expectations of future cash flows, such as long-term provisions and employee benefit obligations.

(e)   users are better served if they are aware on a timely basis of assets that will not generate sufficient returns to cover, at least, the time value of money.

Recoverable amount based on fair value

BCZ14   IAS 32 *Financial Instruments: Disclosure and Presentation*[*] and a number of other International Accounting Standards define fair value as:

'... the amount for which an asset could be exchanged, or a liability settled, between knowledgeable, willing parties in an arm's length transaction ...'

BCZ15   International Accounting Standards include the following requirements or guidance for measuring fair value:

(a)   for the purpose of revaluation of an item of property, plant or equipment to its fair value, IAS 16 *Property, Plant and Equipment* indicates that fair value is usually an asset's market value, normally determined by appraisal

---

[*]   In 2005 the IASB amended IAS 32 as *Financial Instruments: Presentation*.

undertaken by professionally qualified valuers and, if no market exists, fair value is based on the asset's depreciated replacement cost.

(b)   for the purpose of revaluation of an intangible asset to its fair value, IASC proposed in E60 *Intangible Assets* that fair value be determined by reference to market values obtained from an active market. E60 proposed a definition of an active market.*

(c)   IASC proposed revisions to IAS 22 (see E61 *Business Combinations*) so that fair value would be determined without consideration of the acquirer's intentions for the future use of an asset.[†]

(d)   IAS 39[§] indicates that if an active market exists, the fair value of a financial instrument is based on a quoted market price. If there is no active market, fair value is determined by using estimation techniques such as market values of similar types of financial instruments, discounted cash flow analysis and option pricing models.

BCZ16   Some argue that the only appropriate measurement for the recoverable amount of an asset is fair value (based on observable market prices or, if no observable market prices exist, estimated considering prices for similar assets and the results of discounted future cash flow calculations). Proponents of fair value argue that:

(a)   the purpose of measuring recoverable amount is to estimate a market value, not an enterprise-specific value. An enterprise's estimate of the present value of future cash flows is subjective and in some cases may be abused. Observable market prices that reflect the judgement of the marketplace are a more reliable measurement of the amounts that will be recovered from an asset. They reduce the use of management's judgement.

(b)   if an asset is expected to generate greater net cash inflows for the enterprise than for other participants, the superior returns are almost always generated by internally generated goodwill stemming from the synergy of the business and its management team. For consistency with IASC's proposals in E60 that internally generated goodwill should not be recognised as an asset, these above-market cash flows should be excluded from assessments of an asset's recoverable amount.

(c)   determining recoverable amount as the higher of net selling price and value in use is tantamount to determining two diverging measures whilst there should be only one measure to estimate recoverable amount.

A minority of commentators on E55 supported measuring recoverable amount at fair value (based on observable market prices or, if no observable market prices exist, estimated considering prices for similar assets and the results of discounted future cash flow calculations).

---

*   IASC approved an International Accounting Standard on intangible assets in 1998.

†   IASC approved revisions to IAS 22 *Business Combinations* in 1998.

§   The IASB's project to revise IAS 32 and IAS 39 in 2003 resulted in the relocation of the requirements on fair value measurement from IAS 32 to IAS 39.

BCZ17 IASC rejected the proposal that an asset's recoverable amount should be determined by reference to its fair value (based on observable market prices or, if no observable market prices exist, estimated considering prices for similar assets and the results of discounted future cash flow calculations). The reasons are the following:

(a) IASC believed that no preference should be given to the market's expectation of the recoverable amount of an asset (basis for fair value when market values are available and for net selling price) over a reasonable estimate performed by the individual enterprise that owns the asset (basis for fair value when market values are not available and for value in use). For example, an enterprise may have information about future cash flows that is superior to the information available in the marketplace. Also, an enterprise may plan to use an asset in a manner different from the market's view of the best use.

(b) market values are a way to estimate fair value but only if they reflect the fact that both parties, the acquirer and the seller, are willing to enter a transaction. If an enterprise can generate greater cash flows by using an asset than by selling it, it would be misleading to base recoverable amount on the market price of the asset because a rational enterprise would not be willing to sell the asset. Therefore, recoverable amount should not refer only to a transaction between two parties (which is unlikely to happen) but should also consider an asset's service potential from its use by the enterprise.

(c) IASC believed that in assessing the recoverable amount of an asset, it is the amount that an enterprise can expect to recover from that asset, including the effect of synergy with other assets, that is relevant.

The following two examples illustrate the proposal (rejected by IASC) that an enterprise should measure an asset's recoverable amount at its fair value (primarily based on observable market values if these values are available).

Example 1

10 years ago, an enterprise bought its headquarters building for 2,000. Since then, the real estate market has collapsed and the building's market value at balance sheet date is estimated to be 1,000. Disposal costs of the building would be negligible. The building's carrying amount at the balance sheet date is 1,500 and its remaining useful life is 30 years. The building meets all the enterprise's expectations and it is likely that these expectations will be met for the foreseeable future. As a consequence, the enterprise has no plans to move from its current headquarters. The value in use of the building cannot be determined because the building does not generate independent cash inflows. Therefore, the enterprise assesses the recoverable amount of the building's cash-generating unit, that is, the enterprise as a whole. That calculation shows that the building's cash-generating unit is not impaired.

continued...

...continued
Example 1

Proponents of fair value (primarily based on observable market values if these values are available) would measure the recoverable amount of the building at its market value (1,000) and, hence, would recognise an impairment loss of 500 (1,500 less 1,000), even though calculations show that the building's cash-generating unit is not impaired.

IASC did not support this approach and believed that the building was not impaired. IASC believed that, in the situation described, the enterprise would not be willing to sell the building for 1,000 and that the assumption of a sale was not relevant.

Example 2

At the end of 20X0, an enterprise purchased a computer for 100 for general use in its operations. The computer is depreciated over 4 years on a straight-line basis. Residual value is estimated to be nil. At the end of 20X2, the carrying amount of the computer is 50. There is an active market for second-hand computers of this type. The market value of the computer is 30. The enterprise does not intend to replace the computer before the end of its useful life. The computer's cash-generating unit is not impaired.

Proponents of fair value (primarily based on observable market values if these values are available) would measure the recoverable amount of the computer at its market value (30) and, therefore, would recognise an impairment loss of 20 (50 less 30) even though the computer's cash-generating unit is not impaired.

IASC did not support this approach and believed that the computer was not impaired as long as:

(a)   the enterprise was not committed to dispose of the computer before the end of its expected useful life; and

(b)   the computer's cash-generating unit was not impaired.

BCZ18   If no deep and liquid market exists for an asset, IASC considered that value in use would be a reasonable estimate of fair value. This is likely to happen for many assets within the scope of IAS 36: observable market prices are unlikely to exist for goodwill, most intangible assets and many items of property, plant and equipment. Therefore, it is likely that the recoverable amount of these assets, determined in accordance with IAS 36, will be similar to the recoverable amount based on the fair value of these assets.

BCZ19   For some assets within the scope of IAS 36, observable market prices exist or consideration of prices for similar assets is possible. In such cases, the asset's net selling price will differ from the asset's fair value only by the direct incremental costs of disposal. IASC acknowledged that recoverable amount as the higher of net selling price and value in use would sometimes differ from fair value primarily based on market prices (even if the disposal costs are negligible). This is because, as explained in paragraph BCZ17(a), the market may not use the same assumptions about future cash flows as an individual enterprise.

BCZ20   IASC believed that IAS 36 included sufficient requirements to prevent an enterprise from using assumptions different from the marketplace that are unjustified. For example, an enterprise is required to determine value in use using:

(a)   cash flow projections based on reasonable and supportable assumptions and giving greater weight to external evidence; and

(b)   a discount rate that reflects current market assessments of the time value of money and the risks specific to the asset.

Recoverable amount based on value in use

BCZ21   Some argue that value in use is the only appropriate measurement for the recoverable amount of an asset because:

(a)   financial statements are prepared under a going concern assumption. Therefore, no consideration should be given to an alternative measurement that reflects a disposal, unless this reflects the enterprise's intentions.

(b)   assets should not be carried at amounts higher than their service potential from use by the enterprise. Unlike value in use, a market value does not necessarily reflect the service potential of an asset.

Few commentators on E55 supported this view.

BCZ22   IASC rejected this proposal because:

(a)   if an asset's net selling price is higher than its value in use, a rational enterprise will dispose of the asset. In this situation, it is logical to base recoverable amount on the asset's net selling price to avoid recognising an impairment loss that is unrelated to economic reality.

(b)   if an asset's net selling price is greater than its value in use, but management decides to keep the asset, the extra loss (the difference between net selling price and value in use) properly falls in later periods because it results from management's decision in these later periods to keep the asset.

Recoverable amount based on the higher of net selling price and value in use[*]

BCZ23   The requirement that recoverable amount should be the higher of net selling price and value in use stems from the decision that measurement of the recoverable amount of an asset should reflect the likely behaviour of a rational management. Furthermore, no preference should be given to the market's expectation of the recoverable amount of an asset (basis for net selling price) over a reasonable estimate performed by the individual enterprise which owns the asset (basis for value in use) or vice versa (see paragraphs BCZ17–BCZ20 and BCZ22). It is uncertain

---

[*]   In IFRS 5 *Non-current Assets Held for Sale and Discontinued Operations*, issued by the IASB in 2004, the term 'net selling price' was replaced in IAS 36 by 'fair value less costs to sell'.

whether the assumptions of the market or the enterprise are more likely to be true. Currently, perfect markets do not exist for many of the assets within the scope of IAS 36 and it is unlikely that predictions of the future will be entirely accurate, regardless of who makes them.

BCZ24 IASC acknowledged that an enterprise would use judgement in determining whether an impairment loss needed to be recognised. For this reason, IAS 36 included some safeguards to limit the risk that an enterprise may make an over-optimistic (pessimistic) estimate of recoverable amount:

(a) IAS 36 requires a formal estimate of recoverable amount whenever there is an indication that:

(i) an asset may be impaired; or

(ii) an impairment loss may no longer exist or may have decreased.

For this purpose, IAS 36 includes a relatively detailed (although not exhaustive) list of indicators that an asset may be impaired (see paragraphs 12 and 111 of IAS 36).

(b) IAS 36 provides guidelines for the basis of management's projections of future cash flows to be used to estimate value in use (see paragraph 33 of IAS 36).

BCZ25 IASC considered the cost of requiring an enterprise to determine both net selling price and value in use, if the amount determined first is below an asset's carrying amount. IASC concluded that the benefits of such a requirement outweigh the costs.

BCZ26 The majority of the commentators on E55 supported IASC's view that recoverable amount should be measured at the higher of net selling price and value in use.

Assets held for disposal

BCZ27 IASC considered whether the recoverable amount of an asset held for disposal should be measured only at the asset's net selling price. When an enterprise expects to dispose of an asset within the near future, the net selling price of the asset is normally close to its value in use. Indeed, the value in use usually consists mostly of the net proceeds to be received for the asset, since future cash flows from continuing use are usually close to nil. Therefore, IASC believed that the definition of recoverable amount as included in IAS 36 is appropriate for assets held for disposal without a need for further requirements or guidance.

Other refinements to the measurement of recoverable amount

Replacement cost as a ceiling

BCZ28 Some argue that the replacement cost of an asset should be adopted as a ceiling for its recoverable amount. They argue that the value of an asset to the business would not exceed the amount that the enterprise would be willing to pay for the asset at the balance sheet date.

BCZ29   IASC believed that replacement cost techniques are not appropriate to measuring the recoverable amount of an asset. This is because replacement cost measures the cost of an asset and not the future economic benefits recoverable from its use and/or disposal.

Appraisal values

BCZ30   In some cases, an enterprise might seek external appraisal of recoverable amount. External appraisal is not a separate technique in its own right. IASC believed that if appraisal values are used, an enterprise should verify that the external appraisal follows the requirements of IAS 36.

Net selling price (paragraphs 25–29)*

BCZ31   IAS 36 defines net selling price as the amount obtainable from the sale of an asset in an arm's length transaction between knowledgeable, willing parties, less the incremental costs directly attributable to the disposal of the asset.

BCZ32   In other words, net selling price reflects the market's expectations of the future cash flows for an asset after the market's consideration of the time value of money and the risks inherent in receiving those cash flows, less the disposal costs.

BCZ33   Some argue that direct incremental costs of disposal should not be deducted from the amount obtainable from the sale of an asset because, unless management has decided to dispose of the asset, the going concern assumption should apply.

BCZ34   IASC believed that it is appropriate to deduct direct incremental costs of disposal in determining net selling price because the purpose of the exercise is to determine the net amount that an enterprise could recover from the sale of an asset at the date of the measurement and to compare it with the alternative of keeping the asset and using it.

BCZ35   IAS 36 indicates that termination benefits (as defined in IAS 19 *Employee Benefits*) and costs associated with reducing or reorganising a business following the disposal of an asset are not direct incremental costs to dispose of the asset. IASC considered these costs as incidental to (rather than a direct consequence of) the disposal of an asset. In addition, this guidance is consistent with the direction of the project on provisions.†

BCZ36   Although the definition of 'net selling price' would be similar to a definition of 'net fair value', IASC decided to use the term 'net selling price' instead of 'net fair value'. IASC believed that the term 'net selling price' better describes the amount that an enterprise should determine and that will be compared with an asset's value in use.

---

*   In IFRS 5 *Non-current Assets Held for Sale and Discontinued Operations*, issued by the IASB in 2004, the term 'net selling price' was replaced in IAS 36 by 'fair value less costs to sell'.

†   IASC approved an International Accounting Standard on provisions, contingent liabilities and contingent assets in 1998.

Net realisable value

BCZ37   IAS 2 *Inventories* defines net realisable value as:

'... the estimated selling price in the ordinary course of business ... less the estimated costs necessary to make the sale ...'

BCZ38   For the purpose of determining recoverable amount, IASC decided not to use the term 'net realisable value' as defined in IAS 2 because:

(a)   IAS 2's definition of net realisable value does not refer explicitly to transactions carried out on an arm's length basis.

(b)   net realisable value refers to an estimated selling price in the ordinary course of business. In certain cases, net selling price will reflect a forced sale, if management is compelled to sell immediately.

(c)   it is important that net selling price uses, as a starting point, a selling price agreed between knowledgeable, willing buyers and sellers. This is not explicitly mentioned in the definition of net realisable value.

BCZ39   In most cases, net selling price and net realisable value will be similar. However, IASC did not believe that it was necessary to change the definition of net realisable value used in IAS 2 because, for inventories, the definition of net realisable value is well understood and seems to work satisfactorily.

Value in use (paragraphs 30–57 and the Appendix)

BCZ40   IAS 36 defines value in use as the present value of the future cash flows expected to be derived from an asset.

Expected value approach

BCZ41   Some argue that, to better reflect uncertainties in timing and amounts inherent in estimated future cash flows, expected future cash flows should be used in determining value in use. An expected value approach considers all expectations about possible future cash flows instead of the single, most likely, future cash flows.

Example

An enterprise estimates that there are two scenarios for future cash flows: a first possibility of future cash flows amounts to 120 with a 40 per cent probability and a second possibility amounts to 80 with a 60 per cent probability.

The most likely future cash flows would be 80 and the expected future cash flows would be 96 (80 × 60% + 120 × 40%).

BCZ42   In most cases, it is likely that budgets/forecasts that are the basis for cash flow projections will reflect a single estimate of future cash flows only. For this reason, IASC decided that an expected value approach should be permitted but not required.

Future cash flows from internally generated goodwill and synergy with other assets

BCZ43   IASC rejected a proposal that estimates of future cash inflows should reflect only future cash inflows relating to the asset that was initially recognised (or the remaining portion of that asset if part of it has already been consumed or sold). The purpose of such a requirement would be to avoid including in an asset's value in use future cash inflows from internally generated goodwill or from synergy with other assets. This would be consistent with IASC's proposal in E60 *Intangible Assets* to prohibit the recognition of internally generated goodwill as an asset.[*]

BCZ44   In many cases, it will not be possible in practice to distinguish future cash inflows from the asset initially recognised from the future cash inflows from internally generated goodwill or a modification of the asset. This is particularly true when businesses are merged or once an asset has been enhanced by subsequent expenditure. IASC concluded that it is more important to focus on whether the carrying amount of an asset will be recovered rather than on whether the recovery stems partly from internally generated goodwill.

BCZ45   The proposal—that future cash inflows should reflect only future cash inflows relating to the asset that was initially recognised—would also conflict with the requirement under IAS 36 that cash flow projections should reflect reasonable and supportable assumptions that represent management's best estimate of the set of economic conditions that will exist over the remaining useful life of the asset (see paragraph 33 of IAS 36). Therefore, the Standard requires that future cash inflows should be estimated for an asset in its current condition, whether or not these future cash inflows are from the asset that was initially recognised or from its subsequent enhancement or modification.

Example

Several years ago, an enterprise purchased a customer list with 10,000 addresses that it recognised as an intangible asset. The enterprise uses this list for direct marketing of its products. Since initial recognition, about 2,000 customer addresses have been deleted from the list and 3,000 new customer addresses added to it. The enterprise is determining the value in use of the customer list.

Under the proposal (rejected by IASC) that an enterprise should reflect only future cash inflows relating to the asset that was initially recognised, the enterprise would consider only those future cash inflows generated by the remaining 8,000 (10,000 less 2,000) customers from the list acquired.

Under IAS 36, an enterprise considers the future cash inflows generated by the customer list in its current condition, ie by all 11,000 customers (8,000 plus 3,000).

---

[*]   IASC approved an International Accounting Standard on intangible assets in 1998.

Value in use estimated in a foreign currency (paragraph 54)

BCZ46　In response to comments from field test participants, paragraph 54 of IAS 36 includes guidance on calculating the value in use of an asset that generates future cash flows in a foreign currency. IAS 36 indicates that value in use in a foreign currency is translated into the reporting currency[*] using the spot exchange rate at the balance sheet date.

BCZ47　If a currency is freely convertible and traded in an active market, the spot rate reflects the market's best estimate of future events that will affect that currency. Therefore, the only available unbiased estimate of a future exchange rate is the current spot rate, adjusted by the difference in expected future rates of general inflation in the two countries to which the currencies belong.

BCZ48　A value in use calculation already deals with the effect of general inflation since it is calculated either by:

(a)　estimating future cash flows in nominal terms (ie including the effect of general inflation and specific price changes) and discounting them at a rate that includes the effects of general inflation; or

(b)　estimating future cash flows in real terms (ie excluding the effect of general inflation but including the effect of specific price changes) and discounting them at a rate that excludes the effect of general inflation.

BCZ49　To use a forward rate to translate value in use expressed in a foreign currency would be inappropriate. This is because a forward rate reflects the market's adjustment for the differential in interest rates. Using such a rate would result in double-counting the time value of money (first in the discount rate and then in the forward rate).

BCZ50　Even if a currency is not freely convertible or is not traded in an active market— with the consequence that it can no longer be assumed that the spot exchange rate reflects the market's best estimate of future events that will affect that currency—IAS 36 indicates that an enterprise uses the spot exchange rate at the balance sheet date to translate value in use estimated in a foreign currency. This is because IASC believed that it is unlikely that an enterprise can make a more reliable estimate of future exchange rates than the current spot exchange rate.

BCZ51　An alternative to estimating the future cash flows in the currency in which they are generated would be to estimate them in another currency as a proxy and discount them at a rate appropriate for this other currency. This solution may be simpler, particularly where cash flows are generated in the currency of a hyperinflationary economy (in such cases, some would prefer using a hard currency as a proxy) or in a currency other than the reporting currency. However, this solution may be misleading if the exchange rate varies for reasons other than changes in the differential between the general inflation rates in the two countries to which the currencies belong. In addition, this solution is

---

[*]　In IAS 21 *The Effects of Changes in Foreign Exchange Rates*, as revised by the IASB in 2003, the term 'reporting currency' was replaced by 'functional currency'.

inconsistent with the approach under IAS 29 *Financial Reporting in Hyperinflationary Economies*, which does not allow, if the reporting currency* is the currency of a hyperinflationary economy, translation into a hard currency as a proxy for restatement in terms of the measuring unit current at the balance sheet date.

Discount rate (paragraphs 55–57 and A15–A21)

BCZ52   The purpose of discounting future cash flows is to reflect the time value of money and the uncertainties attached to those cash flows:

(a)   assets that generate cash flows soon are worth more than those generating the same cash flows later. All rational economic transactions will take account of the time value of money. The cost of not receiving a cash inflow until some date in the future is an opportunity cost that can be measured by considering what income has been lost by not investing that money for the period. The time value of money, before consideration of risk, is given by the rate of return on a risk-free investment, such as government bonds of the same duration.

(b)   the value of the future cash flows is affected by the variability (ie the risks) associated with the cash flows. Therefore, all rational economic transactions will take risk into account.

BCZ53   As a consequence IASC decided:

(a)   to reject a discount rate based on a historical rate—ie the effective rate implicit when an asset was acquired. A subsequent estimate of recoverable amount has to be based on prevailing interest rates because management's decisions about whether to keep the asset are based on prevailing economic conditions. Historical rates do not reflect prevailing economic conditions.

(b)   to reject a discount rate based on a risk-free rate, unless the future cash flows have been adjusted for all the risks specific to the asset.

(c)   to require that the discount rate should be a rate that reflects current market assessments of the time value of money and the risks specific to the asset. This rate is the return that investors would require if they were to choose an investment that would generate cash flows of amounts, timing and risk profile equivalent to those that the enterprise expects to derive from the asset.

BCZ54   In principle, value in use should be an enterprise-specific measure determined in accordance with the enterprise's own view of the best use of that asset. Logically, the discount rate should be based on the enterprise's own assessment both of the time value of money and of the risks specific to the future cash flows from the asset. However, IASC believed that such a rate could not be verified objectively. Therefore, IAS 36 requires that the enterprise should make its own estimate of future cash flows but that the discount rate should reflect, as far as possible, the market's assessment of the time value of money. Similarly, the discount rate should reflect the premium that the market would require from uncertain future cash flows based on the distribution estimated by the enterprise.

---

*   In IAS 21 *The Effects of Changes in Foreign Exchange Rates*, as revised by the IASB in 2003, the term 'reporting currency' was replaced by 'functional currency'.

BCZ55   IASC acknowledged that a current asset-specific market-determined rate would rarely exist for the assets covered by IAS 36. Therefore, an enterprise uses current market-determined rates for other assets (as similar as possible to the asset under review) as a starting point and adjusts these rates to reflect the risks specific to the asset for which the cash flow projections have not been adjusted.

Additional guidance included in the Standard in 2004

Elements reflected in value in use (paragraphs 30–32)

BC56   The Exposure Draft of Proposed Amendments to IAS 36 proposed, and the revised Standard includes, additional guidance to clarify:

(a)   the elements that are reflected in an asset's value in use; and

(b)   that some of those elements (ie expectations about possible variations in the amount or timing of future cash flows, the price for bearing the uncertainty inherent in the asset, and other factors that market participants would reflect in pricing the future cash flows the entity expects to derive from the asset) can be reflected either as adjustments to the future cash flows or as adjustments to the discount rate.

The Board decided to include this additional guidance in the Exposure Draft in response to a number of requests from its constituents for clarification of the requirements in the previous version of IAS 36 on measuring value in use.

BC57   Respondents to the Exposure Draft generally agreed with the proposals. Those that disagreed varied widely in their views, arguing that:

(a)   IAS 36 should be amended to permit entities to measure value in use using methods other than discounting of future cash flows.

(b)   when measuring the value in use of an intangible asset, entities should be required to reflect the price for bearing the uncertainty inherent in the asset as adjustments to the future cash flows.

(c)   it is inconsistent with the definition of value in use to reflect in that measure the other factors that market participants would reflect in pricing the future cash flows the entity expects to derive from the asset—this element refers to market pricing of an asset rather than to the value to the entity of the asset. Other factors should be reflected in value in use only to the extent that they affect the cash flows the entity can achieve from the asset.

BC58   In considering (a) above, the Board observed that the measure of recoverable amount in IAS 36 (ie higher of value in use and fair value less costs to sell) stems from IASC's decision that an asset's recoverable amount should reflect the likely behaviour of a rational management, with no preference given to the market's expectation of the recoverable amount of an asset (ie fair value less costs to sell) over a reasonable estimate performed by the entity that controls the asset (ie value in use) or vice versa (see paragraph BCZ23). In developing the Exposure Draft and revising IAS 36, the Board concluded that it would be inappropriate to modify the measurement basis adopted in the previous version of IAS 36 for determining recoverable amount until the Board considers and resolves the broader question of the appropriate measurement objective(s) in accounting. Moreover, IAS 36 does not preclude the use of other valuation techniques in estimating fair value less costs to sell. For example, paragraph 27 of the Standard states that 'If there is no binding sale agreement or active market for an asset, fair value less costs to sell is based on the best information available to reflect the amount that an entity could obtain, at the balance sheet date, from the disposal of the asset in an arm's length transaction between knowledgeable, willing parties, after deducting the costs of disposal.'

BC59　　In considering (b) above, the Board observed that the previous version of IAS 36 permitted risk adjustments to be reflected either in the cash flows or in the discount rate, without indicating a preference. The Board could see no justification for amending this approach to require risk adjustments for uncertainty to be factored into the cash flows, particularly given the Board's inclination to avoid modifying the requirements in the previous version of IAS 36 for determining recoverable amount until it considers and resolves the broader question of measurement in accounting. Additionally, the Board as part of its consultative process conducted field visits and round-table discussions during the comment period for the Exposure Draft.* Many field visit participants indicated a preference for reflecting such risk adjustments in the discount rate.

BC60　　In considering (c) above, the Board observed that the measure of value in use adopted in IAS 36 is not a pure 'entity-specific' measure. Although the cash flows used as the starting point in the calculation represent entity-specific cash flows (ie they are derived from the most recent financial budgets/forecasts approved by management and represent management's best estimate of the set of economic conditions that will exist over the remaining useful life of the asset), their present value is required to be determined using a discount rate that reflects current market assessments of the time value of money and the risks specific to the asset. Paragraph 56 of the Standard (paragraph 49 of the previous version of IAS 36) clarifies that 'A rate that reflects current market assessments of the time value of money and the risks specific to the asset is the return that investors would require if they were to choose an investment that would generate cash flows of amounts, timing and risk profile equivalent to those that the entity expects to derive from the asset.' In other words, an asset's value in use reflects how the market would price the cash flows that management expects to derive from that asset.

BC61　　Therefore, the Board concluded that:

(a)　it is consistent with the measure of value in use adopted in IAS 36 to include in the list of elements the other factors that market participants would reflect in pricing the future cash flows the entity expects to derive from the asset.

---

*　The field visits were conducted from early December 2002 to early April 2003, and involved IASB members and staff in meetings with 41 companies in Australia, France, Germany, Japan, South Africa, Switzerland and the United Kingdom. IASB members and staff also took part in a series of round-table discussions with auditors, preparers, accounting standard-setters and regulators in Canada and the United States on implementation issues encountered by North American companies during first-time application of US Statements of Financial Accounting Standards 141 *Business Combinations* and 142 *Goodwill and Other Intangible Assets*, and the equivalent Canadian Handbook Sections, which were issued in June 2001.

(b)   all of the elements proposed in the Exposure Draft (and listed
      in paragraph 30 of the revised Standard) should be reflected in the
      calculation of an asset's value in use.

Estimates of future cash flows (paragraphs 33, 34 and 44)

BC62   The Exposure Draft proposed requiring cash flow projections used in measuring
       value in use to be based on reasonable and supportable assumptions that take
       into account both past actual cash flows and management's past ability to
       forecast cash flows accurately.

BC63   Many respondents to the Exposure Draft disagreed with this proposal, arguing
       that:

(a)   the reasons for past cash flow forecasts differing from actual cash flows
      may be irrelevant to the current projections. For example, if there has been
      a major change in management, management's past ability to forecast cash
      flows might not be relevant to the current projections. Additionally, a poor
      record of forecasting cash flows accurately might be the result of factors
      outside of management's control (such as the events of September 11, 2001),
      rather than indicative of management bias.

(b)   it is unclear how, in practice, the assumptions on which the cash flow
      projections are based could take into account past differences between
      management's forecasts and actual cash flows.

(c)   the proposal is inconsistent with the requirement to base cash flow
      projections on the most recent financial budgets/forecasts approved by
      management.

BC64   The Board observed that, as worded, the proposal would have *required* the
       assumptions on which the cash flow forecasts are based to be adjusted for past
       actual cash flows and management's past ability to forecast cash flows accurately.
       The Board agreed with respondents that it is not clear how, in practice, this might
       be achieved, and that in some circumstances past actual cash flows and
       management's past ability to forecast cash flows accurately might not be relevant
       to the development of current forecasts. However, the Board remained of the
       view that in developing the assumptions on which the cash flow forecasts are
       based, management should remain mindful of, and when appropriate make the
       necessary adjustments for, an entity's actual past performance or previous history
       of management consistently overstating or understating cash flow forecasts.

BC65   Therefore, the Board decided not to proceed with the proposal, but instead to
       include in paragraph 34 of the Standard guidance clarifying that management:

(a)   should assess the reasonableness of the assumptions on which its current
      cash flow projections are based by examining the causes of differences
      between past cash flow projections and actual cash flows; and

(b)   should ensure that the assumptions on which its current cash flow
      projections are based are consistent with past actual outcomes, provided
      the effects of subsequent events or circumstances that did not exist when
      those actual cash flows were generated make this appropriate.

BC66   In finalising the Standard the Board also considered two issues identified by respondents to the Exposure Draft and referred to the Board by the International Financial Reporting Interpretations Committee. Both issues related to the application of paragraphs 27(b) and 37 of the previous version of IAS 36 (now paragraphs 33(b) and 44). The Board did not reconsider those paragraphs when developing the Exposure Draft.

BC67   Paragraph 27(b) required the cash flow projections used to measure value in use to be based on the most recent financial budgets/forecasts that have been approved by management. Paragraph 37, however, required the future cash flows to be estimated for the asset [or cash-generating unit] in its current condition and excluded estimated future cash inflows or outflows that are expected to arise from: (a) a future restructuring to which an enterprise is not yet committed; or (b) future capital expenditure that will improve or enhance the asset [or cash-generating unit] in excess of its originally assessed standard of performance.*

BC68   The first issue the Board considered related to the acquisition of a cash-generating unit when:

(a)   the price paid for the unit was based on projections that included a major restructuring expected to result in a substantial increase in the net cash inflows derived from the unit; and

(b)   there is no observable market from which to estimate the unit's fair value less costs to sell.

Respondents expressed concern that if the net cash inflows arising from the restructuring were not reflected in the unit's value in use, comparison of the unit's recoverable amount and carrying amount immediately after the acquisition would result in the recognition of an impairment loss.

BC69   The Board agreed with respondents that, all else being equal, the value in use of a newly acquired unit would, in accordance with IAS 36, be less than the price paid for the unit to the extent that the price includes the net benefits of a future restructuring to which the entity is not yet committed. However, this does not mean that a comparison of the unit's recoverable amount with its carrying amount immediately after the acquisition will result in the recognition of an impairment loss. The Board observed that:

(a)   recoverable amount is measured in accordance with IAS 36 as the higher of value in use and fair value less costs to sell. Fair value less costs to sell is defined in the Standard as 'the amount obtainable from the sale of an asset or cash-generating unit in an arm's length transaction between knowledgeable, willing parties, less the costs of disposal.'

(b)   paragraphs 25–27 of the Standard provide guidance on estimating fair value less costs to sell. In accordance with that guidance, the best evidence of a recently acquired unit's fair value less costs to sell is likely to be the

---

*   The requirement to exclude future capital expenditure that will improve or enhance the asset in excess of its originally assessed standard of performance was amended in 2003 as a consequential amendment arising from the revision of IAS 16 *Property, Plant and Equipment*. Paragraph 44 of IAS 36 now requires estimates of future cash flows to exclude future cash inflows or outflows that are expected to arise from improving or enhancing the asset's performance.

arm's length price the entity paid to acquire the unit, adjusted for disposal costs and for any changes in economic circumstances between the transaction date and the date at which the estimate is made.

(c)   if the unit's fair value less costs to sell were to be otherwise estimated, it would also reflect the market's assessment of the expected net benefits any acquirer would be able to derive from restructuring the unit or from future capital expenditure on the unit.

BC70   Therefore, all else being equal, the unit's recoverable amount would be its fair value less costs to sell, rather than its value in use. As such, the net benefits of the restructuring would be reflected in the unit's recoverable amount, meaning that an impairment loss would arise only to the extent of any material disposal costs.

BC71   The Board acknowledged that treating the newly acquired unit's fair value less costs to sell as its recoverable amount seems inconsistent with the reason underpinning a 'higher of fair value less costs to sell and value in use' recoverable amount measurement objective. Measuring recoverable amount as the higher of fair value less costs to sell and value in use is intended to reflect the economic decisions that are made when an asset becomes impaired: is it better to sell or keep using the asset?

BC72   Nevertheless, the Board concluded that:

(a)   amending IAS 36 to include in value in use calculations the costs and benefits of future restructurings to which the entity is not yet committed would be a significant change to the concept of value in use adopted in the previous version of IAS 36. That concept is 'value in use for the asset in its current condition'.

(b)   the concept of value in use in IAS 36 should not be modified as part of the Business Combinations project, but should be reconsidered only once the Board considers and resolves the broader question of the appropriate measurement objectives in accounting.

BC73   The second issue the Board considered related to what some respondents suggested was a conflict between the requirements in paragraphs 27(b) and 37 of the previous version of IAS 36 (now paragraphs 33(b) and 44). Paragraph 27(b) required value in use to be based on the most recent forecasts approved by management—which would be likely to reflect management's intentions in relation to future restructurings and future capital expenditure—whereas paragraph 37 required value in use to exclude the effects of a future restructuring to which the enterprise is not yet committed and future capital expenditure that will improve or enhance the asset in excess of its originally assessed standard of performance.[*]

---

[*]   The requirement to exclude future capital expenditure that will improve or enhance the asset in excess of its originally assessed standard of performance was amended in 2003 as a consequential amendment arising from the revision of IAS 16 *Property, Plant and Equipment*. Paragraph 44 of IAS 36 now requires estimates of future cash flows to exclude future cash inflows or outflows that are expected to arise from improving or enhancing the asset's performance.

BC74   The Board concluded that it is clear from the Basis for Conclusions on the previous version of IAS 36 that IASC's intention was that value in use should be calculated using estimates of future cash inflows for an asset in its current condition. The Board nevertheless agreed with respondents that the requirement for value in use to be based on the most recent forecasts approved by management could be viewed as inconsistent with paragraph 37 of the previous version of IAS 36 when those forecasts include either future restructurings to which the entity is not yet committed or future cash flows associated with improving or enhancing the asset's performance.

BC75   Therefore, the Board decided to clarify, in what is now paragraph 33(b) of the revised Standard, that cash flow projections should be based on the most recent financial budgets/forecasts that have been approved by management, but should exclude any estimated future cash inflows or outflows expected to arise from future restructurings or from improving or enhancing the asset's performance. The Board also decided to clarify that when a cash-generating unit contains assets with different estimated useful lives (or, similarly, when an asset comprises components with different estimated useful lives), the replacement of assets (components) with shorter lives is considered to be part of the day-to-day servicing of the unit (asset) when estimating the future cash flows associated with the unit (asset).

Using present value techniques to measure value in use (paragraphs A1–A14)

BC76   The Exposure Draft proposed additional application guidance on using present value techniques in measuring value in use. The Board decided to include this additional guidance in the Exposure Draft in response to requests for clarification of the requirements in the previous version of IAS 36 on measuring value in use.

BC77   Respondents to the Exposure Draft were generally supportive of the additional guidance. Those that were not varied in their views, suggesting that:

(a)   limiting the guidance to a brief appendix to IAS 36 is insufficient.

(b)   although the guidance is useful, it detracts from the main purpose of IAS 36, which is to establish accounting principles for impairment testing assets. Therefore, the guidance should be omitted from the Standard.

(c)   entities should be required to use an expected cash flow approach to measure value in use.

(d)   an expected cash flow approach is not consistent with how transactions are priced by management and should be prohibited.

BC78   In considering (a) and (b) above, the Board noted that the respondents that commented on the additional guidance generally agreed that it is useful and sufficient.

BC79   In considering (c) and (d) above, the Board observed that the previous version of IAS 36 did not require value in use to be calculated using an expected cash flow approach, nor did it prohibit such an approach. The Board could see no justification for requiring or prohibiting the use of an expected cash flow approach, particularly given the Board's inclination to avoid modifying the requirements in the previous version of IAS 36 for determining recoverable amount until it considers and resolves the broader measurement issues in accounting. Additionally, in relation to (d), some field visit participants said that they routinely undertake sensitivity and statistical analysis as the basis for using an expected value approach to budgeting/forecasting and strategic decision-making.

BC80 Therefore, the Board decided to include in the revised Standard the application guidance on using present value techniques that was proposed in the Exposure Draft.

Income taxes

Consideration of future tax cash flows

BCZ81 Future income tax cash flows may affect recoverable amount. It is convenient to analyse future tax cash flows into two components:

(a) the future tax cash flows that would result from any difference between the tax base of an asset (the amount attributed to it for tax purposes) and its carrying amount, after recognition of any impairment loss. Such differences are described in IAS 12 *Income Taxes* as 'temporary differences'.

(b) the future tax cash flows that would result if the tax base of the asset were equal to its recoverable amount.

BCZ82 For most assets, an enterprise recognises the tax consequences of temporary differences as a deferred tax liability or deferred tax asset in accordance with IAS 12. Therefore, to avoid double-counting, the future tax consequences of those temporary differences—the first component referred to in paragraph BCZ81—are not considered in determining recoverable amount (see further discussion in paragraphs BCZ86–BCZ89).

BCZ83 The tax base of an asset on initial recognition is normally equal to its cost. Therefore, net selling price* implicitly reflects market participants' assessment of the future tax cash flows that would result if the tax base of the asset were equal to its recoverable amount. Therefore, no adjustment is required to net selling price to reflect the second component referred to in paragraph BCZ81.

BCZ84 In principle, value in use should include the present value of the future tax cash flows that would result if the tax base of the asset were equal to its value in use— the second component referred to in paragraph BCZ81. Nevertheless it may be burdensome to estimate the effect of that component. This is because:

(a) to avoid double-counting, it is necessary to exclude the effect of temporary differences; and

(b) value in use would need to be determined by an iterative and possibly complex computation so that value in use itself reflects a tax base equal to that value in use.

---

* In IFRS 5 *Non-current Assets Held for Sale and Discontinued Operations*, issued by the IASB in 2004, the term 'net selling price' was replaced in IAS 36 by 'fair value less costs to sell'.

For these reasons, IASC decided to require an enterprise to determine value in use by using pre-tax future cash flows and, hence, a pre-tax discount rate.

Determining a pre-tax discount rate

BCZ85   In theory, discounting post-tax cash flows at a post-tax discount rate and discounting pre-tax cash flows at a pre-tax discount rate should give the same result, as long as the pre-tax discount rate is the post-tax discount rate adjusted to reflect the specific amount and timing of the future tax cash flows. The pre-tax discount rate is not always the post-tax discount rate grossed up by a standard rate of tax.

Example

This example illustrates that a post-tax discount rate grossed-up by a standard rate of tax is not always an appropriate pre-tax discount rate.

At the end of 20X0, the carrying amount of an asset is 1,757 and its remaining useful life is 5 years. The tax base in 20X0 is the cost of the asset. The cost is fully deductible at the end of 20X1. The tax rate is 20%. The discount rate for the asset can be determined only on a post-tax basis and is estimated to be 10%. At the end of 20X0, cash flow projections determined on a pre-tax basis are as follows:

	20X1	20X2	20X3	20X4	20X5
(1) Pre-tax cash flows (CF)	800	600	500	200	100

Value in use determined using post-tax cash flows and a post-tax discount rate

End of 20X0		20X1	20X2	20X3	20X4	20X5
(2) Deduction of the cost of the asset	(1,757)	–	–	–	–
(3) Tax CF [((1) – (2)) × 20%]		(191)	120	100	40	20
(4) Post-tax CF [(1) – (3)]		991	480	400	160	80
(5) Post-tax CF discounted at 10%		901	396	301	109	50
Value in use [$\Sigma(5)$] =						1,757

Value in use determined using pre-tax cash flows and a pre-tax discount rate (determined by grossing-up the post-tax discount rate)

Pre-tax discount rate (grossed-up) [10%/(100% – 20%)] 12.5%

End of 20X0	20X1	20X2	20X3	20X4	20X5
(6) Pre-tax CF discounted at 12.5%	711	475	351	125	55
Value in use [$\Sigma(6)$] =					1,717

continued...

> *...continued*
> **Example**
>
> ---
>
> *Determination of the 'real' pre-tax discount rate*
>
> *A pre-tax discount rate can be determined by an iterative computation so that value in use determined using pre-tax cash flows and a pre-tax discount rate equals value in use determined using post-tax cash flows and a post-tax discount rate. In the example, the pre-tax discount rate would be 11.2%.*
>
> | End of 20X0 | 20X1 | 20X2 | 20X3 | 20X4 | 20X5 |
> |---|---|---|---|---|---|
> | *(7) Pre-tax CF discounted at 11.2%* | *718* | *485* | *364* | *131* | *59* |
> | *Value in use [Σ(7)] =* | | | | | *1,757* |
>
> *The 'real' pre-tax discount rate differs from the post-tax discount rate grossed-up by the standard rate of tax depending on the tax rate, the post-tax discount rate, the timing of the future tax cash flows and the useful life of the asset. Note that the tax base of the asset in this example has been set equal to its cost at the end of 20X0. Therefore, there is no deferred tax to consider in the balance sheet.*

Interaction with IAS 12

BCZ86   IAS 36 requires that recoverable amount should be based on present value calculations, whereas under IAS 12 an enterprise determines deferred tax assets and liabilities by comparing the carrying amount of an asset (a present value if the carrying amount is based on recoverable amount) with its tax base (an undiscounted amount).

BCZ87   One way to eliminate this inconsistency would be to measure deferred tax assets and liabilities on a discounted basis. In developing the revised version of IAS 12 (approved in 1996), there was not enough support to require that deferred tax assets and liabilities should be measured on a discounted basis. IASC believed there was still not consensus to support such a change in existing practice. Therefore, IAS 36 requires an enterprise to measure the tax effects of temporary differences using the principles set out in IAS 12.

BCZ88   IAS 12 does not permit an enterprise to recognise certain deferred tax liabilities and assets. In such cases, some believe that the value in use of an asset, or a cash-generating unit, should be adjusted to reflect the tax consequences of recovering its pre-tax value in use. For example, if the tax rate is 25 per cent, an enterprise must receive pre-tax cash flows with a present value of 400 in order to recover a carrying amount of 300.

BCZ89   IASC acknowledged the conceptual merit of such adjustments but concluded that they would add unnecessary complexity. Therefore, IAS 36 neither requires nor permits such adjustments.

Comments by field visit participants and respondents to the December 2002 Exposure Draft

BC90   In revising IAS 36, the Board considered the requirement in the previous version of IAS 36 for:

(a)   income tax receipts and payments to be excluded from the estimates of future cash flows used to measure value in use; and

(b)   the discount rate used to measure value in use to be a pre-tax rate that reflects current market assessments of the time value of money and the risks specific to the asset for which the future cash flow estimates have not been adjusted.

BC91   The Board had not considered these requirements when developing the Exposure Draft. However, some field visit participants and respondents to the Exposure Draft stated that using pre-tax cash flows and pre-tax discount rates would be a significant implementation issue for entities. This is because typically an entity's accounting and strategic decision-making systems are fully integrated and use post-tax cash flows and post-tax discount rates to arrive at present value measures.

BC92   In considering this issue, the Board observed that the definition of value in use in the previous version of IAS 36 and the associated requirements on measuring value in use were not sufficiently precise to give a definitive answer to the question of what tax attribute an entity should reflect in value in use. For example, although IAS 36 specified discounting pre-tax cash flows at a pre-tax discount rate—with the pre-tax discount rate being the post-tax discount rate adjusted to reflect the specific amount and timing of the future tax cash flows—it did not specify *which* tax effects the pre-tax rate should include. Arguments could be mounted for various approaches.

BC93   The Board decided that any decision to amend the requirement in the previous version of IAS 36 for pre-tax cash flows to be discounted at a pre-tax discount rate should be made only after the Board has resolved the issue of what tax attribute should be reflected in value in use. The Board decided that it should not try to resolve this latter issue as part of the Business Combinations project—decisions on the treatment of tax in value in use calculations should be made only as part of its conceptual project on measurement. Therefore, the Board concluded it should not amend as part of the current revision of IAS 36 the requirement to use pre-tax cash flows and pre-tax discount rates when measuring value in use.

BC94   However, the Board observed that, conceptually, discounting post-tax cash flows at a post-tax discount rate and discounting pre-tax cash flows at a pre-tax discount rate should give the same result, as long as the pre-tax discount rate is the post-tax discount rate adjusted to reflect the specific amount and timing of the future tax cash flows. The pre-tax discount rate is generally not the post-tax discount rate grossed up by a standard rate of tax.

Recognition of an impairment loss (paragraphs 58–64)

BCZ95 IAS 36 requires that an impairment loss should be recognised whenever the recoverable amount of an asset is below its carrying amount. IASC considered various criteria for recognising an impairment loss in the financial statements:

(a) recognition if it is considered that the impairment loss is permanent ('permanent criterion');

(b) recognition if it is considered probable that an asset is impaired, ie if it is probable that an enterprise will not recover the carrying amount of the asset ('probability criterion'); and

(c) immediate recognition whenever recoverable amount is below the carrying amount ('economic criterion').

Recognition based on a 'permanent' criterion

BCZ96 Supporters of the 'permanent' criterion argue that:

(a) this criterion avoids the recognition of temporary decreases in the recoverable amount of an asset.

(b) the recognition of an impairment loss refers to future operations; it is contrary to the historical cost system to account for future events. Also, depreciation (amortisation) will reflect these future losses over the expected remaining useful life of the asset.

This view was supported by only a few commentators on E55 *Impairment of Assets*.

BCZ97 IASC decided to reject the 'permanent' criterion because:

(a) it is difficult to identify whether an impairment loss is permanent. There is a risk that, by using this criterion, recognition of an impairment loss may be delayed.

(b) this criterion is at odds with the basic concept that an asset is a resource that will generate future economic benefits. Cost-based accrual accounting cannot reflect events without reference to future expectations. If the events that led to a decrease in recoverable amount have already taken place, the carrying amount should be reduced accordingly.

Recognition based on a 'probability' criterion

BCZ98 Some argue that an impairment loss should be recognised only if it is considered probable that the carrying amount of an asset cannot be fully recovered. Proponents of a 'probability' criterion are divided between:

(a) those who support the use of a recognition trigger based on the sum of the future cash flows (undiscounted and without allocation of interest costs) as a practical approach to implementing the 'probability' criterion; and

(b) those who support reflecting the requirements in IAS 10 (reformatted 1994) *Contingencies and Events Occurring After the Balance Sheet Date.*[*]

---

[*] The requirements relating to contingencies in the 1994 version of IAS 10 were replaced in 1998 with the requirements in IAS 37 *Provisions, Contingent Liabilities and Contingent Assets*.

Sum of undiscounted future cash flows (without interest costs)

BCZ99 Some national standard-setters use the 'probability' criterion as a basis for recognition of an impairment loss and require, as a practical approach to implementing that criterion, that an impairment loss should be recognised only if the sum of the future cash flows from an asset (undiscounted and without allocation of interest costs) is less than the carrying amount of the asset. An impairment loss, when recognised, is measured as the difference between the carrying amount of the asset and its recoverable amount measured at fair value (based on quoted market prices or, if no quoted market prices exist, estimated considering prices for similar assets and the results of valuation techniques, such as the sum of cash flows discounted to their present value, option-pricing models, matrix pricing, option-adjusted spread models and fundamental analysis).

BCZ100 One of the characteristics of this approach is that the bases for recognition and measurement of an impairment loss are different. For example, even if the fair value of an asset is lower than its carrying amount, no impairment loss will be recognised if the sum of undiscounted cash flows (without allocation of interest costs) is greater than the asset's carrying amount. This might occur, especially if an asset has a long useful life.

BCZ101 Those who support using the sum of undiscounted future cash flows (without allocation of interest costs) as a recognition trigger argue that:

(a) using a recognition trigger based on undiscounted amounts is consistent with the historical cost framework.

(b) it avoids recognising temporary impairment losses and creating potentially volatile earnings that may mislead users of financial statements.

(c) net selling price* and value in use are difficult to substantiate—a price for the disposal of an asset or an appropriate discount rate is difficult to estimate.

(d) it is a higher threshold for recognising impairment losses. It should be relatively easy to conclude that the sum of undiscounted future cash flows will equal or exceed the carrying amount of an asset without incurring the cost of allocating projected cash flows to specific future periods.

This view was supported by a minority of commentators on E55 *Impairment of Assets*.

BCZ102 IASC considered the arguments listed above but rejected this approach because:

(a) when it identifies that an asset may be impaired, a rational enterprise will make an investment decision. Therefore, it is relevant to consider the time value of money and the risks specific to an asset in determining whether an asset is impaired. This is particularly true if an asset has a long useful life.

(b) IAS 36 does not require an enterprise to estimate the recoverable amount of each [depreciable] asset every year but only if there is an indication that an asset may be materially impaired. An asset that is depreciated (amortised)

---

* In IFRS 5 *Non-current Assets Held for Sale and Discontinued Operations*, issued by the IASB in 2004, the term 'net selling price' was replaced in IAS 36 by 'fair value less costs to sell'.

in an appropriate manner is unlikely to become materially impaired unless events or changes in circumstances cause a sudden reduction in the estimate of recoverable amount.

(c) probability factors are already encompassed in the determination of value in use, in projecting future cash flows and in requiring that recoverable amount should be the higher of net selling price and value in use.

(d) if there is an unfavourable change in the assumptions used to determine recoverable amount, users are better served if they are informed about this change in assumptions on a timely basis.

Probability criterion based on IAS 10 (reformatted 1994)

BCZ103 IAS 10 required the amount of a contingent loss to be recognised as an expense and a liability if:

(a) it was probable that future events will confirm that, after taking into account any related probable recovery, an asset had been impaired or a liability incurred at the balance sheet date; and

(b) a reasonable estimate of the amount of the resulting loss could be made.

BCZ104 IASC rejected the view that an impairment loss should be recognised based on the requirements in IAS 10 because:

(a) the requirements in IAS 10 were not sufficiently detailed and would have made a 'probability' criterion difficult to apply.

(b) those requirements would have introduced another unnecessary layer of probability. Indeed, as mentioned above, probability factors are already encompassed in estimates of value in use and in requiring that recoverable amount should be the higher of net selling price and value in use.

Recognition based on an 'economic' criterion

BCZ105 IAS 36 relies on an 'economic' criterion for the recognition of an impairment loss—an impairment loss is recognised whenever the recoverable amount of an asset is below its carrying amount. This criterion was already used in many International Accounting Standards before IAS 36, such as IAS 9 *Research and Development Costs*, IAS 22 *Business Combinations*, and IAS 16 *Property, Plant and Equipment*.

BCZ106 IASC considered that an 'economic' criterion is the best criterion to give information which is useful to users in assessing future cash flows to be generated by the enterprise as a whole. In estimating the time value of money and the risks specific to an asset in determining whether the asset is impaired, factors, such as the probability or permanence of the impairment loss, are subsumed in the measurement.

BCZ107 The majority of commentators on E55 supported IASC's view that an impairment loss should be recognised based on an 'economic' criterion.

Revalued assets: recognition in the income statement versus directly in equity

BCZ108 IAS 36 requires that an impairment loss on a revalued asset should be recognised as an expense in the income statement[*] immediately, except that it should be recognised directly in equity[†] to the extent that it reverses a previous revaluation on the same asset.

BCZ109 Some argue that, when there is a clear reduction in the service potential (for example, physical damage) of a revalued asset, the impairment loss should be recognised in the income statement.

BCZ110 Others argue that an impairment loss should always be recognised as an expense in the income statement. The logic of this argument is that an impairment loss arises only where there is a reduction in the estimated future cash flows that form part of the business's operating activities. Indeed, according to IAS 16, whether or not an asset is revalued, the depreciation charge is always recognised in the income statement. Supporters of this view question why the treatment of an impairment loss on a revalued asset should be different to depreciation.

BCZ111 IASC believed that it would be difficult to identify whether an impairment loss is a downward revaluation or a reduction in service potential. Therefore, IASC decided to retain the treatment used in IAS 16 and to treat an impairment loss of a revalued asset as a revaluation decrease (and similarly, a reversal of an impairment loss as a subsequent revaluation increase).

BCZ112 For a revalued asset, the distinction between an 'impairment loss' ('reversal of an impairment loss') and another 'revaluation decrease' ('revaluation increase') is important for disclosure purposes. If an impairment loss that is material to the enterprise as a whole has been recognised or reversed, more information on how this impairment loss is measured is required by IAS 36 than for the recognition of a revaluation in accordance with IAS 16.

Cash-generating units (paragraphs 66–73)

BCZ113 Some support the principle of determining recoverable amount on an individual asset basis only. This view was expressed by a few commentators on E55. They argued that:

(a) it would be difficult to identify cash-generating units at a level other than the business as a whole and, therefore, impairment losses would never be recognised for individual assets; and

(b) it should be possible to recognise an impairment loss, regardless of whether an asset generates cash inflows that are independent from those of other assets or groups of assets. Commentators quoted examples of assets that have become under-utilised or obsolete but that are still in use.

---

[*] IAS 1 *Presentation of Financial Statements* (as revised in 2007) requires an entity to present all income and expense items in one statement of comprehensive income or in two statements (a separate income statement and a statement of comprehensive income).

[†] As a consequence of the revision of IAS 1 (revised 2007) an impairment loss is recognised in other comprehensive income.

BCZ114 IASC acknowledged that identifying the lowest level of independent cash inflows for a group of assets would involve judgement. However, IASC believed that the concept of cash-generating units is a matter of fact: assets work together to generate cash flows.

BCZ115 In response to requests from commentators on E55, IAS 36 includes additional guidance and examples for identifying cash-generating units and for determining the carrying amount of cash-generating units. IAS 36 emphasises that cash-generating units should be identified for the lowest level of aggregation of assets possible.

Internal transfer pricing (paragraph 70)

BC116 The previous version of IAS 36 required that if an active market exists for the output produced by an asset or a group of assets:

(a) that asset or group of assets should be identified as a cash-generating unit, even if some or all of the output is used internally; and

(b) management's best estimate of the future market prices for the output should be used in estimating:

(i) the future cash inflows that relate to the internal use of the output when determining the value in use of this cash-generating unit; and

(ii) the future cash outflows that relate to the internal use of the output when determining the value in use of the entity's other cash-generating units.

BC117 The requirement in (a) above has been carried forward in the revised Standard. However, some respondents to the Exposure Draft asked for additional guidance to clarify the role of internal transfer pricing versus prices in an arm's length transaction when developing cash flow forecasts. The Board decided to address this issue by amending the requirement in (b) above to deal more broadly with cash-generating units whose cash flows are affected by internal transfer pricing, rather than just cash-generating units whose internally consumed output could be sold on an active market.

BC118 Therefore, the Standard clarifies that if the cash inflows generated by *any* asset or cash-generating unit are affected by internal transfer pricing, an entity should use management's best estimate of future prices that could be achieved in arm's length transactions in estimating:

(a) the future cash inflows used to determine the asset's or cash-generating unit's value in use; and

(b) the future cash outflows used to determine the value in use of other assets or cash-generating units affected by the internal transfer pricing.

Testing indefinite-lived intangibles for impairment

BC119 As part of the first phase of its Business Combinations project, the Board concluded that:

(a) an intangible asset should be regarded as having an indefinite useful life when, based on an analysis of all relevant factors (eg legal, regulatory, contractual, competitive and economic), there is no foreseeable limit on the period over which the asset is expected to generate net cash inflows for the entity; and

(b) an indefinite-lived intangible should not be amortised, but should be tested regularly for impairment.

An outline of the Board's deliberations on each of these issues is provided in the Basis for Conclusions on IAS 38 *Intangible Assets*.

BC120 Having reached these conclusions, the Board then considered the form that the impairment test for indefinite-lived intangibles should take. The Board concluded that:

(a) an indefinite-lived intangible should be tested for impairment annually, or more frequently if there is any indication that it may be impaired; and

(b) the recoverable amounts of such assets should be measured, and impairment losses (and reversals of impairment losses) in respect of those assets should be accounted for, in accordance with the requirements in IAS 36 for assets other than goodwill.

Paragraphs BC121–BC126 outline the Board's deliberations in reaching its conclusion about the frequency and timing of impairment testing indefinite-lived intangibles. Paragraphs BC129 and BC130 outline the Board's deliberations in reaching its conclusions about measuring the recoverable amount of such assets and accounting for impairment losses and reversals of impairment losses.

Frequency and timing of impairment testing (paragraphs 9 and 10(a))

BC121 In developing the Exposure Draft, the Board observed that requiring assets to be remeasured when they are impaired is a valuation concept rather than one of cost allocation. This concept, which some have termed 'the recoverable cost concept', focuses on the benefits to be derived from the asset in the future, rather than on the process by which the cost or other carrying amount of the asset should be allocated to particular accounting periods. Therefore, the purpose of an impairment test is to assess whether the carrying amount of an asset will be recovered through use or sale of the asset. Nevertheless, allocating the depreciable amount of an asset with a limited useful life on a systematic basis over that life provides some assurance against the asset's carrying amount exceeding its recoverable amount. The Board acknowledged that non-amortisation of an intangible asset increases the reliance that must be placed on impairment reviews of that asset to ensure that its carrying amount does not exceed its recoverable amount.

BC122 Accordingly, the Exposure Draft proposed that indefinite-lived intangibles should be tested for impairment at the end of each annual reporting period. The Board concluded, however, that testing such assets annually for impairment is not a substitute for management being aware of events occurring or circumstances changing between annual tests that indicate a possible impairment. Therefore, the Exposure Draft also proposed that an entity should be required to test such assets for impairment whenever there is an indication of possible impairment, and not wait until the next annual test.

BC123　The respondents to the Exposure Draft generally supported the proposal to test indefinite-lived intangibles for impairment annually and whenever there is an indication of possible impairment. Those that disagreed argued that requiring an annual impairment test would be excessively burdensome, and recommended requiring an impairment test only when there is an indication that an indefinite-lived intangible might be impaired. After considering these comments the Board:

(a)　reaffirmed its view that non-amortisation of an intangible asset increases the reliance that must be placed on impairment reviews of that asset to ensure that its carrying amount does not exceed its recoverable amount.

(b)　concluded that IAS 36 should require indefinite-lived intangibles to be tested for impairment annually and whenever there is an indication of possible impairment.

BC124　However, as noted in paragraph BC122, the Exposure Draft proposed that the annual impairment tests for indefinite-lived intangibles should be performed at the end of each annual period. Many respondents to the Exposure Draft disagreed that IAS 36 should mandate the timing of the annual impairment tests. They argued that:

(a)　it would be inconsistent with the proposal (now a requirement) that the annual impairment test for a cash-generating unit to which goodwill has been allocated may be performed at any time during an annual period, provided the test is performed at the same time every year. There is no justification for providing less flexibility in the timing of the annual impairment test for indefinite-lived intangibles.

(b)　if the impairment test for an indefinite-lived intangible is linked to the impairment test for goodwill (ie if the indefinite-lived intangible is assessed for impairment at the same cash-generating unit level as goodwill, rather than individually or as part of a smaller cash-generating unit), the requirement to measure its recoverable amount at the end of the annual period could result in the cash-generating unit to which it (and the goodwill) belongs being tested for impairment at least twice each annual period, which is too burdensome. For example, assume a cash-generating unit contains goodwill and an indefinite-lived intangible, and that the indefinite-lived intangible is assessed for impairment at the same cash-generating unit level as goodwill. Assume also that the entity reports quarterly, has a December year-end, and decides to test goodwill for impairment at the end of the third quarter to coincide with the completion of its annual strategic planning/budgeting process. The proposal that the annual impairment test for an indefinite-lived intangible should be performed at the end of each annual period would mean that the entity would be required:

(i)　to calculate at the end of each September the recoverable amount of the cash-generating unit, compare it with its carrying amount, and, if the carrying amount exceeds the recoverable amount, recognise an impairment loss for the unit by reducing the carrying amount of goodwill and allocating any remaining impairment loss to the other assets in the unit, including the indefinite-lived intangible.

(ii) to perform the same steps again each December to test the indefinite-lived intangible for impairment.

(iii) to perform the same steps again at any other time throughout the annual period if there is an indication that the cash-generating unit, the goodwill or the indefinite-lived intangible may be impaired.

BC125 In considering these comments, the Board indicated a preference for requiring entities to perform the recoverable amount calculations for both goodwill and indefinite-lived intangibles at the end of the annual period. However, the Board acknowledged that, as outlined in paragraph BC124(b), impairment tests for indefinite-lived intangibles will sometimes be linked to impairment tests for goodwill, and that many entities would find it difficult to perform all those tests at the end of the annual period.

BC126 Therefore, consistently with the annual impairment test for goodwill, the Standard permits the annual impairment test for an indefinite-lived intangible to be performed at any time during an annual period, provided it is performed at the same time every year.

Carrying forward a recoverable amount calculation (paragraph 24)

BC127 The Standard permits the most recent detailed calculation of the recoverable amount of an indefinite-lived intangible to be carried forward from a preceding period for use in the current period's impairment test, provided all of the criteria in paragraph 24 of the Standard are met.

BC128 Integral to the Board's decision that indefinite-lived intangibles should be tested for impairment annually was the view that many entities should be able to conclude that the recoverable amount of such an asset is greater than its carrying amount without actually recomputing recoverable amount. However, the Board concluded that this would be the case only if the last recoverable amount determination exceeded the carrying amount by a substantial margin, and nothing had happened since then to make the likelihood of an impairment loss other than remote. The Board concluded that, in such circumstances, permitting a detailed calculation of the recoverable amount of an indefinite-lived intangible to be carried forward from the preceding period for use in the current period's impairment test would significantly reduce the costs of applying the impairment test, without compromising its integrity.

Measuring recoverable amount and accounting for impairment losses and reversals of impairment losses

BC129 The Board could see no compelling reason why the measurement basis adopted for determining recoverable amount and the treatment of impairment losses and reversals of impairment losses for one group of identifiable assets should differ from those applying to other identifiable assets. Adopting different methods would impair the usefulness of the information provided to users about an entity's identifiable assets, because both comparability and reliability, which rest on the notion that similar transactions are accounted for in the same way, would be diminished. Therefore, the Board concluded that the recoverable amounts of indefinite-lived intangibles should be measured, and impairment losses and reversals of impairment losses in respect of those assets should be accounted for, consistently with other identifiable assets covered by the Standard.

BC130 The Board expressed some concern over the measurement basis adopted in the previous version of IAS 36 for determining recoverable amount (ie higher of value in use and net selling price) and its treatment of impairment losses and reversals of impairment losses for assets other than goodwill. However, the Board's intention in revising IAS 36 was *not* to reconsider the general approach to impairment testing. Accordingly, the Board decided that it should address concerns over that general approach as part of its future re-examination of IAS 36 in its entirety, rather than as part of its Business Combinations project.

Testing goodwill for impairment (paragraphs 80–99)

BC131 [Deleted]

BC131A The Board concluded that goodwill should not be amortised and instead should be tested for impairment annually, or more frequently if events or changes in circumstances indicate that it might be impaired. IAS 22 *Business Combinations* required acquired goodwill to be amortised on a systematic basis over the best estimate of its useful life. There was a rebuttable presumption that its useful life did not exceed twenty years from initial recognition. If that presumption was rebutted, acquired goodwill was required to be tested for impairment in accordance with the previous version of IAS 36 at least at each financial year-end, even if there was no indication that it was impaired.

BC131B In considering the appropriate accounting for acquired goodwill after its initial recognition, the Board examined the following three approaches:

(a) straight-line amortisation but with an impairment test whenever there is an indication that the goodwill might be impaired;

(b) non-amortisation but with an impairment test annually or more frequently if events or changes in circumstances indicate that the goodwill might be impaired; and

(c) permitting entities a choice between approaches (a) and (b).

BC131C The Board concluded, and the respondents to ED 3 *Business Combinations* that expressed a clear view on this issue generally agreed, that entities should not be allowed a choice between approaches (a) and (b). Permitting such choices impairs the usefulness of the information provided to users of financial statements because both comparability and reliability are diminished.

BC131D The respondents to ED 3 who expressed a clear view on this issue generally supported approach (a). They put forward the following arguments in support of that approach:

(a) acquired goodwill is an asset that is consumed and replaced by internally generated goodwill. Therefore, amortisation ensures that the acquired goodwill is recognised in profit or loss and no internally generated goodwill is recognised as an asset in its place, consistently with the general prohibition in IAS 38 on the recognition of internally generated goodwill.

(b) conceptually, amortisation is a method of allocating the cost of acquired goodwill over the periods it is consumed, and is consistent with the approach taken to other intangible and tangible fixed assets that do not have indefinite useful lives. Indeed, entities are required to determine the useful lives of items of property, plant and equipment, and allocate their depreciable amounts on a systematic basis over those useful lives. There is no conceptual reason for treating acquired goodwill differently.

(c)   the useful life of acquired goodwill cannot be predicted with a satisfactory level of reliability, nor can the pattern in which that goodwill diminishes be known. However, systematic amortisation over an albeit arbitrary period provides an appropriate balance between conceptual soundness and operationality at an acceptable cost: it is the only practical solution to an intractable problem.

BC131E   In considering these comments, the Board agreed that achieving an acceptable level of reliability in the form of representational faithfulness while striking some balance with what is practicable was the primary challenge it faced in deliberating the subsequent accounting for goodwill. The Board observed that the useful life of acquired goodwill and the pattern in which it diminishes generally are not possible to predict, yet its amortisation depends on such predictions. As a result, the amount amortised in any given period can be described as at best an arbitrary estimate of the consumption of acquired goodwill during that period. The Board acknowledged that if goodwill is an asset, in some sense it must be true that goodwill acquired in a business combination is being consumed and replaced by internally generated goodwill, provided that an entity is able to maintain the overall value of goodwill (by, for example, expending resources on advertising and customer service). However, consistently with the view it reached in developing ED 3, the Board remained doubtful about the usefulness of an amortisation charge that reflects the consumption of acquired goodwill, when the internally generated goodwill replacing it is not recognised. Therefore, the Board reaffirmed the conclusion it reached in developing ED 3 that straight-line amortisation of goodwill over an arbitrary period fails to provide useful information. The Board noted that both anecdotal and research evidence supports this view.

BC131F   In considering respondents' comments summarised in paragraph BC131D(b), the Board noted that although the useful lives of both goodwill and tangible fixed assets are directly related to the period over which they are expected to generate net cash inflows for the entity, the expected physical utility to the entity of a tangible fixed asset places an upper limit on the asset's useful life. In other words, unlike goodwill, the useful life of a tangible fixed asset could never extend beyond the asset's expected physical utility to the entity.

BC131G   The Board reaffirmed the view it reached in developing ED 3 that if a rigorous and operational impairment test could be devised, more useful information would be provided to users of an entity's financial statements under an approach in which goodwill is not amortised, but instead tested for impairment annually or more frequently if events or changes in circumstances indicate that the goodwill might be impaired. After considering respondents' comments to the exposure draft of proposed amendments to IAS 36 on the form that such an impairment test should take, the Board concluded that a sufficiently rigorous and operational impairment test could be devised.

BC132　Paragraphs BC133–BC177 outline the Board's deliberations on the form that the impairment test for goodwill should take:

(a)　paragraphs BC137–BC159 discuss the requirements relating to the allocation of goodwill to cash-generating units and the level at which goodwill is tested for impairment.

(b)　paragraphs BC160–BC170 discuss the requirements relating to the recognition and measurement of impairment losses for goodwill, including the frequency of impairment testing.

(c)　paragraphs BC171–BC177 discuss the requirements relating to the timing of goodwill impairment tests.

BC133　As a first step in its deliberations, the Board considered the objective of the goodwill impairment test and the measure of recoverable amount that should be adopted for such a test. The Board observed that recent North American standards use fair value as the basis for impairment testing goodwill, whereas the previous version of IAS 36 and the United Kingdom standard are based on an approach under which recoverable amount is measured as the higher of value in use and net selling price.

BC134　The Board also observed that goodwill acquired in a business combination represents a payment made by an acquirer in anticipation of future economic benefits from assets that are not capable of being individually identified and separately recognised. Goodwill does not generate cash flows independently of other assets or groups of assets and therefore cannot be measured directly. Instead, it is measured as a residual amount, being the excess of the cost of a business combination over the acquirer's interest in the net fair value of the acquiree's identifiable assets, liabilities and contingent liabilities. Moreover, goodwill acquired in a business combination and goodwill generated after that business combination cannot be separately identified, because they contribute jointly to the same cash flows.*

BC135　The Board concluded that because it is not possible to measure separately goodwill generated internally after a business combination and to factor that measure into the impairment test for acquired goodwill, the carrying amount of goodwill will always be shielded from impairment by that internally generated goodwill. Therefore, the Board took the view that the objective of the goodwill impairment test could at best be to ensure that the carrying amount of goodwill is recoverable from future cash flows expected to be generated by both acquired goodwill and goodwill generated internally after the business combination.

BC136　The Board noted that because goodwill is measured as a residual amount, the starting point in any goodwill impairment test would have to be the recoverable amount of the operation or unit to which the goodwill relates, regardless of the measurement basis adopted for determining recoverable amount. The Board decided that until it considers and resolves the broader question of the appropriate measurement objective(s) in accounting, identifying the appropriate measure of recoverable amount for that unit would be problematic. Therefore, although the Board expressed concern over the measurement basis adopted in

---

*　In the second phase of its business combinations project, the Board revised the definition and measurement of goodwill in IFRS 3. See paragraph 32 and Appendix A of IFRS 3 (as revised in 2008).

IAS 36 for determining recoverable amount, it decided that it should not depart from that basis when measuring the recoverable amount of a unit whose carrying amount includes acquired goodwill. The Board noted that this would have the added advantage of allowing the impairment test for goodwill to be integrated with the impairment test in IAS 36 for other assets and cash-generating units that include goodwill.

Allocating goodwill to cash-generating units (paragraphs 80–87)

BC137 The previous version of IAS 36 required goodwill to be tested for impairment as part of impairment testing the cash-generating units to which it relates. It employed a 'bottom-up/top-down' approach under which the goodwill was in effect tested for impairment by allocating its carrying amount to each of the smallest cash-generating units to which a portion of that carrying amount could be allocated on a reasonable and consistent basis.

BC138 Consistently with the previous version of IAS 36, the Exposure Draft proposed that:

(a) goodwill should be tested for impairment as part of impairment testing the cash-generating units to which it relates; and

(b) the carrying amount of goodwill should be allocated to each of the smallest cash-generating units to which a portion of that carrying amount can be allocated on a reasonable and consistent basis.

However, the Exposure Draft proposed additional guidance clarifying that a portion of the carrying amount of goodwill should be regarded as capable of being allocated to a cash-generating unit on a reasonable and consistent basis only when that unit represents the lowest level at which management monitors the return on investment in assets that include the goodwill. That cash-generating unit could not, however, be larger than a segment based on the entity's primary reporting format determined in accordance with IAS 14 *Segment Reporting*.

BC139 In developing this proposal, the Board noted that because acquired goodwill does not generate cash flows independently of other assets or groups of assets, it can be tested for impairment only as part of impairment testing the cash-generating units to which it relates. However, the Board was concerned that in the absence of any guidance on the precise meaning of 'allocated on a reasonable and consistent basis', some might conclude that when a business combination enhances the value of all of the acquirer's pre-existing cash-generating units, any goodwill acquired in that business combination should be tested for impairment only at the level of the entity itself. The Board concluded that this should not be the case. Rather, there should be a link between the level at which goodwill is tested for impairment and the level of internal reporting that reflects the way an entity manages its operations and with which the goodwill naturally would be associated. Therefore, it was important to the Board that goodwill should be tested for impairment at a level at which information about the operations of an entity and the assets that support them is provided for internal reporting purposes.

BC140   In redeliberating this issue, the Board noted that respondents' and field visit participants' comments indicated that the Board's intention relating to the allocation of goodwill had been widely misunderstood, with many concluding that goodwill would need to be allocated to a much lower level than that intended by the Board. For example, some respondents and field visit participants were concerned that the proposal to allocate goodwill to such a low level would force entities to allocate goodwill arbitrarily to cash-generating units, and therefore to develop new or additional reporting systems to perform the test. The Board confirmed that its intention was that there should be a link between the level at which goodwill is tested for impairment and the level of internal reporting that reflects the way an entity manages its operations. Therefore, except for entities that do not monitor goodwill at or below the segment level, the proposals relating to the level of the goodwill impairment test should *not* cause entities to allocate goodwill arbitrarily to cash-generating units. Nor should they create the need for entities to develop new or additional reporting systems.

BC141   The Board observed from its discussions with field visit participants that much of the confusion stemmed from the definition of a 'cash-generating unit', when coupled with the proposal in paragraph 73 of the Exposure Draft for goodwill to be allocated to each 'smallest cash-generating unit to which a portion of the carrying amount of the goodwill can be allocated on a reasonable and consistent basis'. Additionally, field visit participants and respondents were unclear about the reference in paragraph 74 of the Exposure Draft to 'the lowest level at which management monitors the return on investments in assets that include goodwill', the most frequent question being 'what level of management?' (eg board of directors, chief executive officer, or segment management).

BC142   The Board noted that once its intention on this issue was clarified for field visit participants, they all, with the exception of one company that believes goodwill should be tested for impairment at the entity level, supported the level at which the Board believes goodwill should be tested for impairment.

BC143   The Board also noted the comment from a number of respondents and field visit participants that for some organisations, particularly those managed on a matrix basis, the proposal for cash-generating units to which the goodwill is allocated to be no larger than a segment based on the entity's *primary* reporting format could result in an outcome that is inconsistent with the Board's intention, ie that there should be a link between the level at which goodwill is tested for impairment and the level of internal reporting that reflects the way an entity manages its operations. The following example illustrates this point:

> A company managed on a matrix basis is organised primarily on a geographical basis, with product groups providing the secondary basis of segmentation. Goodwill is acquired as part of an acquisition of a product group that is present in several geographical regions, and is then monitored on an ongoing basis for internal reporting purposes as part of the product group/secondary segment. It is feasible that the secondary segment might, depending on the definition of 'larger', be 'larger' than a primary segment.

BC144   Therefore, the Board decided:

    (a)   that the Standard should require each unit or group of units to which goodwill is allocated to represent the lowest level within the entity at which the goodwill is monitored for internal management purposes.

(b) to clarify in the Standard that acquired goodwill should, from the acquisition date, be allocated to each of the acquirer's cash-generating units, or groups of cash-generating units, that are expected to benefit from the combination, irrespective of whether other assets or liabilities of the acquiree are assigned to those units or groups of units.

(c) to replace the proposal for cash-generating units or groups of units to which goodwill is allocated to be no larger than a segment based on the entity's *primary* reporting format, with the requirement that they be no larger than a segment based on either the entity's primary or the entity's secondary reporting format. The Board concluded that this amendment is necessary to ensure that entities managed on a matrix basis are able to test goodwill for impairment at the level of internal reporting that reflects the way they manage their operations.*

BC145 Some respondents to the Exposure Draft raised the following additional concerns on the allocation of goodwill for impairment testing purposes:

(a) mandating that goodwill should be allocated to at least the segment level is inappropriate—it will often result in arbitrary allocations, and entities would need to develop new or additional reporting systems.

(b) for convergence reasons, the level of the goodwill impairment test should be the same as the level in US Financial Accounting Standards Board Statement of Financial Accounting Standards No. 142 *Goodwill and Other Intangible Assets* (SFAS 142) (ie the reporting unit level).

(c) cash-generating units that constitute businesses with similar characteristics should, as is required by SFAS 142, be aggregated and treated as single units, notwithstanding that they may be monitored independently for internal purposes.

BC146 In relation to (a), the Board reaffirmed the conclusion it reached when developing the Exposure Draft that requiring goodwill to be allocated to at least the segment level is necessary to avoid entities erroneously concluding that, when a business combination enhances the value of all of the acquirer's pre-existing cash-generating units, any goodwill acquired in that combination could be tested for impairment only at the level of the entity itself.

BC147 In relation to (b), the Board noted that SFAS 142 requires goodwill to be tested for impairment at a level of reporting referred to as a 'reporting unit'. A reporting unit is an operating segment (as defined in SFAS 131 *Disclosures about Segments of an Enterprise and Related Information*[†]) or one level below an operating segment (referred to as a component). A component of an operating segment is a reporting

---

* In 2006 IAS 14 was replaced by IFRS 8 *Operating Segments*. IFRS 8 does not require disclosure of primary and secondary segment information. See paragraph BC150A.

† The basis for identifying 'operating segments' under SFAS 131 differs from the basis for identifying segments based on the entity's primary reporting format under IFRS 8. SFAS 131 defines an operating segment as a component of an enterprise (a) that engages in business activities from which it may earn revenues and incur expenses, including revenues and expenses relating to transactions with other components of the enterprise; (b) whose operating results are regularly reviewed by the enterprise's chief operating decision maker to make decisions about resources to be allocated to the segment and assess its performance; and (c) for which discrete financial information is available. IAS 14 was replaced by IFRS 8 in 2006. See paragraph BC150A.

unit if the component constitutes a business for which discrete financial information is available and segment management regularly reviews the operating results of that component. However, two or more components of an operating segment must be aggregated and deemed a single reporting unit if the components have similar economic characteristics. An operating segment is deemed to be a reporting unit if all of its components are similar, if none of its components is a reporting unit, or if it comprises only a single component.

BC148   Therefore, unlike IAS 36, SFAS 142 places a limit on how far goodwill can be 'pushed down' for impairment testing (ie one level below an operating segment).

BC149   In deciding not to converge with SFAS 142 on the level of the goodwill impairment test, the Board noted the following findings from the field visits and North American round-table discussions:

(a)   most of the US registrant field visit participants stated that the Board's proposals on the level of the goodwill impairment test would result, in practice, in goodwill being tested for impairment at the same level at which it is tested in accordance with SFAS 142. However, several stated that under the Board's proposals, goodwill would be tested for impairment at a lower level than under SFAS 142. Nevertheless, they believe that the Board's approach provides users and management with more useful information.

(b)   several round-table participants stated that they (or, in the case of audit firm participants, their clients) manage and have available information about their investments in goodwill at a lower level than the level of the SFAS 142 impairment test. They expressed a high level of dissatisfaction at being prevented by SFAS 142 from recognising goodwill impairments that they knew existed at these lower levels, but which 'disappeared' once the lower level units were aggregated with other units containing sufficient 'cushions' to offset the impairment loss.

BC150   In considering suggestion (c) in paragraph BC145, the Board observed that aggregating units that constitute businesses with similar characteristics could result in the disappearance of an impairment loss that management *knows* exists in a cash-generating unit because the units with which it is aggregated contain sufficient cushions to offset the impairment loss. In the Board's view, if, because of the way an entity is managed, information about goodwill impairment losses is available to management at a particular level, that information should also be available to the users of the entity's financial statements.

BC150A In 2006 IFRS 8 replaced IAS 14 and changed the basis for identifying segments. Under IAS 14, two sets of segments were identified—one based on related products and services, and the other on geographical areas. Under IFRS 8, operating segments are identified on the basis of internal reports that are regularly reviewed by the entity's chief operating decision maker in order to allocate resources to the segment and assess its performance. The objective of the change was to improve the disclosure of segment information, not to change the requirements of IAS 36 relating to the allocation of goodwill for impairment testing. The previous wording of the requirement in IAS 36 that each unit or group of units to which goodwill is allocated shall 'not be larger than a segment based on either the entity's primary or the entity's secondary reporting format determined in accordance with IAS 14' has been amended by IFRS 8 to 'not be larger than an operating segment determined in accordance with IFRS 8'. The arguments set out above in support of the original requirement based on segments determined in accordance with IAS 14 support the revised requirements based on segments determined in accordance with the requirements in IFRS 8.

BC150B Entities adopting IFRS 8 must reconsider the allocation of goodwill to cash-generating units because of the definition of operating segment introduced by IFRS 8. That definition affects the determination of the largest unit permitted by paragraph 80 of IAS 36 for testing goodwill for impairment. In 2008 the Board was made aware that divergent views had developed regarding the largest unit permitted by IAS 36 for impairment testing of goodwill. One view was that the unit is the operating segment level as defined in paragraph 5 of IFRS 8 *before* the aggregation permitted by paragraph 12 of IFRS 8. The other view was that the unit is the operating segment level as defined in paragraph 5 of IFRS 8 *after* the aggregation permitted by paragraph 12 of IFRS 8. The Board noted that the lowest level of the entity at which management monitors goodwill as required in paragraph 80(a) is the same as the lowest level of operating segments at which the chief operating decision maker regularly reviews operating results as defined in IFRS 8. The Board also noted that the linkage of the entity's goodwill monitoring level with the entity's internal reporting level is intentional, as described in paragraph BC140. The Board noted that aggregating operating segments for goodwill impairment testing into a unit larger than the level at which goodwill is monitored contradicts the rationale underlying IAS 36, as set out in paragraphs BC145–BC150. In addition, meeting the aggregation criteria of similar economic characteristics permitted in IFRS 8 does not automatically result in groups of cash-generating units that are expected to benefit from the synergies of allocated goodwill. Similarly, the aggregated segments do not necessarily represent business operations that are economically interdependent or work in concert to recover the goodwill being assessed for impairment. Therefore, in *Improvements to IFRSs* issued in April 2009, the Board amended paragraph 80(b) to state that the required unit for goodwill impairment in IAS 36 is not larger than the operating segment level as defined in paragraph 5 of IFRS 8 before the permitted aggregation.

Completing the initial allocation of goodwill (paragraphs 84 and 85)

BC151 If the initial allocation of goodwill acquired in a business combination cannot be completed before the end of the annual period in which the business combination is effected, the Exposure Draft proposed, and the revised Standard requires, that the initial allocation should be completed before the end of the first annual period beginning after the acquisition date. In contrast, ED 3 proposed, and IFRS 3 requires, that if the initial accounting for a business combination can be determined only provisionally by the end of the period in which the combination is effected, the acquirer should:

(a)   account for the combination using those provisional values; and

(b) recognise any adjustments to those provisional values as a result of completing the initial accounting within twelve months of the acquisition date.*

BC152 Some respondents to the Exposure Draft questioned why the period to complete the initial allocation of goodwill should differ from the period to complete the initial accounting for a business combination. The Board's view is that acquirers should be allowed a longer period to complete the goodwill allocation, because that allocation often might not be able to be performed until after the initial accounting for the combination is complete. This is because the cost of the combination or the fair values at the acquisition date of the acquiree's identifiable assets, liabilities or contingent liabilities, and therefore the amount of goodwill acquired in the combination, would not be finalised until the initial accounting for the combination in accordance with IFRS 3 is complete.

Disposal of a portion of a cash-generating unit containing goodwill (paragraph 86)

BC153 The Exposure Draft proposed that when an entity disposes of an operation within a cash-generating unit to which goodwill has been allocated, the goodwill associated with that operation should be:

(a) included in the carrying amount of the operation when determining the gain or loss on disposal; and

(b) measured on the basis of the relative values of the operation disposed of and the portion of the cash-generating unit retained.

BC154 This proposal has been carried forward in the Standard with one modification. The Standard requires the goodwill associated with the operation disposed of to be measured on the basis of the relative values of the operation disposed of and the portion of the cash-generating unit retained, unless the entity can demonstrate that some other method better reflects the goodwill associated with the operation disposed of.

BC155 In developing the Exposure Draft, the Board concluded that the proposed level of the impairment test would mean that goodwill could not be identified or associated with an asset group at a level lower than the cash-generating unit to which the goodwill is allocated, except arbitrarily. However, the Board also concluded that when an operation within that cash-generating unit is being disposed of, it is appropriate to presume that some amount of goodwill is associated with that operation. Thus, an allocation of the goodwill should be required when the part of the cash-generating unit being disposed of constitutes an operation.

---

* In the second phase of its business combinations project, the Board clarified that adjustments to provisional values should be made only to reflect new information obtained about facts and circumstances that existed as of the acquisition date that, if known, would have affected the measurement of the amounts recognised as of that date. Such adjustments should be made within the measurement period, which shall not exceed one year from the acquisition date.

BC156　Some respondents to the Exposure Draft suggested that although in most circumstances goodwill could not be identified or associated with an asset group at a level lower than the cash-generating unit or group of cash-generating units to which it is allocated for impairment testing, there may be some instances when this is not so. For example, assume an acquiree is integrated with one of the acquirer's pre-existing cash-generating units that did not include any goodwill in its carrying amount. Assume also that almost immediately after the business combination the acquirer disposes of a loss-making operation within the cash-generating unit. The Board agreed with respondents that in such circumstances, it might reasonably be concluded that no part of the carrying amount of goodwill has been disposed of, and therefore no part of its carrying amount should be derecognised by being included in the determination of the gain or loss on disposal.

Reorganisation of reporting structure (paragraph 87)

BC157　The Exposure Draft proposed that when an entity reorganises its reporting structure in a way that changes the composition of cash-generating units to which goodwill has been allocated, the goodwill should be reallocated to the units affected using a relative value approach similar to that used when an entity disposes of an operation within a cash-generating unit.

BC158　In developing the Exposure Draft, the Board concluded that a reorganisation that changes the composition of a cash-generating unit to which goodwill has been allocated gives rise to the same allocation problem as disposing of an operation within that unit. Therefore, the same allocation methodology should be used in both cases.

BC159　As a result, and consistently with the Board's decision to modify its proposal on allocating goodwill when an entity disposes of an operation, the revised Standard requires an entity that reorganises its reporting structure in a way that changes the composition of one or more cash-generating units to which goodwill has been allocated:

(a)　to reallocate the goodwill to the units affected; and

(b)　to perform this reallocation using a relative value approach similar to that used when an entity disposes of an operation within a cash-generating unit (group of cash-generating units), unless the entity can demonstrate that some other method better reflects the goodwill associated with the reorganised units (groups of units).

Recognition and measurement of impairment losses (paragraphs 88–99 and 104)

Background to the proposals in the Exposure Draft

BC160　The Exposure Draft proposed a two-step approach for impairment testing goodwill. The first step involved using a screening mechanism for identifying potential goodwill impairments, whereby goodwill allocated to a cash-generating unit would be identified as potentially impaired only when the carrying amount of the unit exceeded its recoverable amount. If an entity identified the goodwill allocated to a cash-generating unit as potentially impaired, an entity would then determine whether the goodwill allocated to the unit was impaired by comparing its recoverable amount, measured as the 'implied value' of the goodwill, with its carrying amount. The implied value of goodwill would be measured as a residual, being the excess of:

(a)   the recoverable amount of the cash-generating unit to which the goodwill has been allocated, over

(b)   the net fair value of the identifiable assets, liabilities and contingent liabilities the entity would recognise if it acquired the cash-generating unit in a business combination on the date of the impairment test (excluding any identifiable asset that was acquired in a business combination but not recognised separately from goodwill at the acquisition date).

BC161   In developing the Exposure Draft, the Board's discussion focused first on how the recoverable amount of goodwill allocated to a cash-generating unit could be separated from the recoverable amount of the unit as a whole, given that goodwill generated internally after a business combination could not be measured separately. The Board concluded that a method similar to the method an acquirer uses to allocate the cost of a business combination to the net assets acquired could be used to measure the recoverable amount of goodwill after its initial recognition. Thus, the Board decided that some measure of the net assets of a cash-generating unit to which goodwill has been allocated should be subtracted from the recoverable amount of that unit to determine a current implied value for the goodwill. The Board concluded that the measure of the net assets of a cash-generating unit described in paragraph BC160(b) would result in the best estimate of the current implied value of the goodwill, given that goodwill generated internally after a business combination could not be measured separately.

BC162   Having decided on the most appropriate measure of the recoverable amount of goodwill, the Board then considered how often an entity should be required to test goodwill for impairment.   Consistently with its conclusions about indefinite-lived intangibles, the Board concluded that non-amortisation of goodwill increases the reliance that must be placed on impairment tests to ensure that the carrying amount of goodwill does not exceed its recoverable amount. Accordingly, the Board decided that goodwill should be tested for impairment annually.   However, the Board also concluded that the annual test is not a substitute for management being aware of events occurring or circumstances changing between annual tests indicating a possible impairment of goodwill. Therefore, the Board decided that an entity should also be required to test goodwill for impairment whenever there is an indication of possible impairment.

BC163   After the Board decided on the frequency of impairment testing, it expressed some concern that the proposed test would not be cost-effective. This concern related primarily to the requirement to determine the fair value of each identifiable asset, liability and contingent liability within a cash-generating unit that would be recognised by the entity if it had acquired the cash-generating unit in a business combination on the date of the impairment test (to estimate the implied value of goodwill).

BC164 Therefore, the Board decided to propose as a first step in the impairment test for goodwill a screening mechanism similar to that in SFAS 142. Under SFAS 142, goodwill is tested for impairment by first comparing the fair value of the reporting unit to which the goodwill has been allocated for impairment testing purposes with the carrying amount of that unit. If the fair value of the unit exceeds its carrying amount, the goodwill is regarded as not impaired. An entity need estimate the implied fair value of goodwill (using an approach consistent with that described in paragraph BC160) only if the fair value of the unit is less than its carrying amount.

The Board's redeliberations

BC165 Many respondents disagreed with the proposal to adopt a two-step approach to impairment testing goodwill. In particular, the second step of the proposed impairment test and the method for measuring any impairment loss for the goodwill caused considerable concern. Respondents provided the following conceptual arguments against the proposed approach:

    (a) by drawing on only some aspects of the SFAS 142 two-step approach, the result is a hybrid between fair values and value in use. More particularly, not measuring goodwill's implied value as the difference between the unit's fair value and the net fair value of the identifiable net assets in the unit, but instead measuring it as the difference between the unit's recoverable amount (ie higher of value in use and fair value less costs to sell) and the net fair value of the identifiable net assets in the unit, results in a measure of goodwill that conceptually is neither fair value nor recoverable amount. This raises questions about the conceptual validity of measuring goodwill impairment losses as the difference between goodwill's implied value and carrying amount.

    (b) it seems inconsistent to consider goodwill separately for impairment testing when other assets within a unit are not considered separately but are instead considered as part of the unit as a whole, particularly given that goodwill, unlike many other assets, cannot generate cash inflows independently of other assets. The previous version of IAS 36 is premised on the notion that if a series of independent cash flows can be generated only by a group of assets operating together, impairment losses should be considered only for that group of assets as a whole—individual assets within the group should not be considered separately.

    (c) concluding that the recoverable amount of goodwill—which cannot generate cash inflows independently of other assets—should be measured separately for measuring impairment losses makes it difficult to understand how the Board could in the future reasonably conclude that such an approach to measuring impairment losses is also not appropriate for other assets. In other words, if it adopts the proposed two-step approach for goodwill, the Board could in effect be committing itself to an 'individual asset/fair value' approach for measuring impairments of all other assets. A decision on this issue should be made only as part of a broad reconsideration of the appropriate measurement objective for impairment testing generally.

(d) if goodwill is considered separately for impairment testing using an implied value calculation when other assets within a unit are considered only as part of the unit as a whole, there will be asymmetry: unrecognised goodwill will shield the carrying value of other assets from impairment, but the unrecognised value of other assets will not shield the carrying amount of goodwill from impairment. This seems unreasonable given that the unrecognised value of those other assets cannot then be recognised. Additionally, the carrying amount of a unit will be less than its recoverable amount whenever an impairment loss for goodwill exceeds the unrecognised value of the other assets in the unit.

BC166 Additionally, respondents, field visit participants and North American round-table participants raised the following concerns about the practicability and costs of applying the proposed two-step approach:

(a) many companies would be required regularly to perform the second step of the impairment test, and therefore would need to determine the fair values of each identifiable asset, liability and contingent liability within the impaired unit(s) that the entity would recognise if it acquired the unit(s) in a business combination on the date of the impairment test. Although determining these fair values would not, for some companies, pose significant practical challenges (because, for example, fair value information for their significant assets is readily available), most would need to engage, on a fairly wide scale and at significant cost, independent valuers for some or all of the unit's assets. This is particularly the case for identifying and measuring the fair values of unrecognised internally generated intangible assets.

(b) determining the fair values of each identifiable asset, liability and contingent liability within an impaired unit is likely to be impracticable for multi-segmented manufacturers that operate multi-product facilities servicing more than one cash-generating unit. For example, assume an entity's primary basis of segmentation is geographical (eg Europe, North America, South America, Asia, Oceania and Africa) and that its secondary basis of segmentation is based on product groups (vaccinations, over-the-counter medicines, prescription medicines and vitamins/dietary supplements). Assume also that:

(i) the lowest level within the entity at which the goodwill is monitored for internal management purposes is one level below primary segment (eg the vitamins business in North America), and that goodwill is therefore tested for impairment at this level;

(ii) the plants and distribution facilities in each geographical region manufacture and distribute for all product groups; and

(iii) to determine the carrying amount of each cash-generating unit containing goodwill, the carrying amount of each plant and distribution facility has been allocated between each product group it services.

---

* In 2006 IAS 14 was replaced by IFRS 8 *Operating Segments* which does not require disclosure of primary and secondary segment information. See paragraph BC150A.

If, for example, the recoverable amount of the North American vitamins unit were less than its carrying amount, measuring the implied value of goodwill in that unit would require a valuation exercise to be undertaken for *all* North American assets so that a portion of each asset's fair value can then be allocated to the North American vitamins unit. These valuations are likely to be extremely costly and virtually impossible to complete within a reasonable time period (field visit participants' estimates ranged from six to twelve months). The degree of impracticability will be even greater for those entities that monitor, and therefore test, goodwill at the segment level.

BC167　In considering the above comments, the Board noted that:

(a)　all of the US registrant field visit participants and North American round-table participants that have had to perform the second step of the SFAS 142 impairment test were compelled to engage, at significant cost, independent valuers.

(b)　the impairment model proposed in the Exposure Draft, although based on the two-step approach in SFAS 142, differed from the SFAS 142 test and would be unlikely to result in convergence for the following reasons:

(i)　the recoverable amount of a unit to which goodwill is allocated in accordance with IAS 36 would be the higher of the unit's value in use and fair value less costs to sell, rather than fair value. Many of the US registrant field visit participants stated that the measure of recoverable amount they would use under IAS 36 would differ from the fair value measure they would be required to use under SFAS 142.

(ii)　the level at which goodwill is tested for impairment in accordance with SFAS 142 will often be higher than the level at which it would be tested under IAS 36. Many of the US registrant field visit participants stated that goodwill would be tested for impairment in accordance with IAS 36 at a lower level than under SFAS 142 because of either: (1) the limit SFAS 142 places on how far goodwill can be 'pushed down' for impairment testing (ie one level below an operating segment); or (2) the requirement in SFAS 142 to aggregate components with similar economic characteristics. Nevertheless, these participants unanimously agreed that the IAS 36 approach provides users and management with more useful information. The Board also noted that many of the North American round-table participants stated that they (or, in the case of audit firm participants, their clients) manage and have available information about their investments in goodwill at a level lower than a reporting unit as defined in SFAS 142. Many of these participants expressed a high level of dissatisfaction at being prevented by SFAS 142 from recognising goodwill impairments that they knew existed at these lower levels, but 'disappeared' once the lower level units were aggregated with other units containing sufficient 'cushions' to offset the impairment loss.

BC168　The Board also noted that, unlike SFAS 142, it had as its starting point an impairment model in IAS 36 that integrates the impairment testing of *all* assets within a cash-generating unit, including goodwill. Unlike US generally accepted accounting principles (GAAP), which use an undiscounted cash flow screening mechanism for impairment testing long-lived assets other than goodwill, IAS 36 requires the recoverable amount of an asset or cash-generating unit to be measured whenever there is an indication of possible impairment. Therefore, if at the time of impairment testing a 'larger' unit to which goodwill has been allocated there is an indication of a possible impairment in an asset or 'smaller' cash-generating unit included in that larger unit, an entity is required to test that asset or smaller unit for impairment first. Consequently, the Board concluded that it would be reasonable in an IAS 36 context to presume that an impairment loss for the larger unit would, after all other assets and smaller units are assessed for impairment, be likely to relate to the goodwill in the unit. Such a presumption would not be reasonable if an entity were following US GAAP.

BC169   The Board considered converging fully with the SFAS 142 approach. However, although supporting convergence, the Board was concerned that the SFAS 142 approach would not provide better information than an approach under which goodwill is tested for impairment at a lower level (thereby removing many of the 'cushions' protecting the goodwill from impairment) but with the amount of any impairment loss for goodwill measured in accordance with the one-step approach in the previous version of IAS 36.

BC170   The Board concluded that the complexity and costs of applying the two-step approach proposed in the Exposure Draft would outweigh the benefits of that approach. Therefore, the Board decided to retain the approach to measuring impairments of goodwill included in the previous version of IAS 36. Thus, the Standard requires any excess of the carrying amount of a cash-generating unit (group of units) to which goodwill has been allocated over its recoverable amount to be recognised first as an impairment loss for goodwill. Any excess remaining after the carrying amount of goodwill has been reduced to zero is then recognised by being allocated to the other assets of the unit pro rata with their carrying amounts.

Changes as a result of 2008 revisions to IFRS 3 (Appendix C)

BC170A As a result of the changes to IFRS 3 (as revised in 2008), the requirements in Appendix C of the Standard and the related illustrative examples have been amended to reflect the two ways of measuring non-controlling interests: at fair value and as a proportion of the identifiable net assets of the acquiree. Appendix C has also been modified to clarify the requirements of the Standard.

Timing of impairment tests (paragraphs 96–99)

BC171   To reduce the costs of applying the test, and consistently with the proposals in the Exposure Draft, the Standard permits the annual impairment test for a cash-generating unit (group of units) to which goodwill has been allocated to be performed at any time during an annual period, provided the test is performed at the same time every year. Different cash-generating units (groups of units) may be tested for impairment at different times. However, if some or all of the goodwill allocated to a unit (group of units) was acquired in a business combination during the current annual period, that unit (group of units) must be tested for impairment before the end of the current annual period.

BC172   The Board observed that acquirers can sometimes 'overpay' for an acquiree, resulting in the amount initially recognised for the business combination and the resulting goodwill exceeding the recoverable amount of the investment. The Board concluded that the users of an entity's financial statements are provided with representationally faithful, and therefore useful, information about a business combination if such an impairment loss is recognised by the acquirer in the annual period in which the business combination occurs.

BC173   The Board was concerned that it might be possible for entities to delay recognising such an impairment loss until the annual period after the business combination if the Standard included only a requirement to impairment test cash-generating units (groups of units) to which goodwill has been allocated on an annual basis at any time during a period. Therefore, the Board decided to include in the Standard the added requirement that if some or all of the goodwill allocated to a unit (group of units) was acquired in a business combination during the current annual period, the unit (group of units) should be tested for impairment before the end of that period.

Sequence of impairment tests (paragraph 97)

BC174   The Standard requires that if the assets (cash-generating units) constituting the cash-generating unit (group of units) to which goodwill has been allocated are tested for impairment at the same time as the unit (group of units) containing the goodwill, those other assets (units) should be tested for impairment before the unit (group of units) containing the goodwill.

BC175   The Board observed that assets or cash-generating units making up a unit or group of units to which goodwill has been allocated might need to be tested for impairment at the same time as the unit or group of units containing the goodwill when there is an indication of a possible impairment of the asset or smaller unit. The Board concluded that to assess whether the unit or group of units containing the goodwill, and therefore whether the goodwill, is impaired, the carrying amount of the unit or group of units containing the goodwill would need first to be adjusted by recognising any impairment losses relating to the assets or smaller units within that unit or group of units.

Carrying forward a recoverable amount calculation (paragraph 99)

BC176   Consistently with the impairment test for indefinite-lived intangibles, the Standard permits the most recent detailed calculation of the recoverable amount of a cash-generating unit (group of units) to which goodwill has been allocated to be carried forward from a preceding period for use in the current period's impairment test, provided all of the criteria in paragraph 99 are met.

BC177   Integral to the Board's decision that goodwill should be tested for impairment annually was the view that many entities should be able to conclude that the recoverable amount of a cash-generating unit (group of units) to which goodwill has been allocated is greater than its carrying amount without actually recomputing recoverable amount. However, again consistently with its conclusions about indefinite-lived intangibles, the Board concluded that this would be the case only if the last recoverable amount determination exceeded the carrying amount of the unit (group of units) by a substantial margin, and nothing had happened since that last determination to make the likelihood of an impairment loss other than remote. The Board concluded that in such circumstances, permitting a detailed calculation of the recoverable amount of a cash-generating unit (group of units) to which goodwill has been allocated to be carried forward from the preceding period for use in the current period's impairment test would significantly reduce the costs of applying the impairment test, without compromising its integrity.

Allocating an impairment loss between the assets of a cash-generating unit (paragraphs 104–107)

BCZ178 IAS 36 includes requirements for the allocation of an impairment loss for a cash-generating unit that differ from the proposals in E55. In particular, E55 proposed that an impairment loss should be allocated:

    (a)   first, to goodwill;

    (b)   secondly, to intangible assets for which no active market exists;

    (c)   thirdly, to assets whose net selling price* is less than their carrying amount; and

    (d)   then, to the other assets of the unit on a pro-rata basis based on the carrying amount of each asset in the unit.

BCZ179 The underlying reasons for making this proposal were that:

    (a)   an impairment loss for a cash-generating unit should be allocated, in priority, to assets with the most subjective values. Goodwill and intangible assets for which there is no active market were considered to be in that category. Intangible assets for which there is no active market were considered to be similar to goodwill (IASC was thinking of brand names, publishing titles etc).

    (b)   if the net selling price of an asset is less than its carrying amount, this was considered a reasonable basis for allocating part of the impairment loss to that asset rather than to other assets.

BCZ180 Many commentators on E55 objected to the proposal on the grounds that:

    (a)   not all intangible assets for which no active market exists are similar to goodwill (for example, licences and franchise rights). They disagreed that the value of intangible assets is always more subjective than the value of tangible assets (for example, specialised plant and equipment).

    (b)   the concept of cash-generating units implies a global approach for the assets of the units and not an asset-by-asset approach.

In response to these comments, IASC decided to withdraw E55's proposal for the allocation of an impairment loss to intangible assets and assets whose net selling price is less than their carrying amount.

---

* In IFRS 5 *Non-current Assets Held for Sale and Discontinued Operations*, issued by the IASB in 2004, the term 'net selling price' was replaced in IAS 36 by 'fair value less costs to sell'.

BCZ181 IASC rejected a proposal that an impairment loss for a cash-generating unit should be allocated first to any obviously impaired asset. IASC believed that if the recoverable amount of an obviously impaired asset can be determined for the individual asset, there is no need to estimate the recoverable amount of the asset's cash-generating unit. If the recoverable amount of an individual asset cannot be determined, it cannot be said that the asset is obviously impaired because an impairment loss for a cash-generating unit relates to all of the assets of that unit.

Reversing impairment losses for assets other than goodwill (paragraphs 110–123)

BCZ182 IAS 36 requires that an impairment loss for an asset other than goodwill should be reversed if, and only if, there has been a change in the estimates used to determine an asset's recoverable amount since the last impairment loss was recognised.

BCZ183 Opponents of reversals of impairment losses argue that:

(a) reversals of impairment losses are contrary to the historical cost accounting system. When the carrying amount is reduced, recoverable amount becomes the new cost basis for an asset. Consequently, reversing an impairment loss is no different from revaluing an asset upward. Indeed, in many cases, recoverable amount is similar to the measurement basis used for the revaluation of an asset. Hence, reversals of impairment losses should be either prohibited or recognised directly in equity as a revaluation.

(b) reversals of impairment losses introduce volatility in reported earnings. Periodic, short-term income measurements should not be affected by unrealised changes in the measurement of a long-lived asset.

(c) the result of reversals of impairment losses would not be useful to users of financial statements since the amount of a reversal under IAS 36 is limited to an amount that does not increase the carrying amount of an asset above its depreciated historical cost. Neither the amount reversed nor the revised carrying amount have any information content.

(d) in many cases, reversals of impairment losses will result in the implicit recognition of internally generated goodwill.

(e) reversals of impairment losses open the door to abuse and income 'smoothing' in practice.

(f) follow-up to verify whether an impairment loss needs to be reversed is costly.

BCZ184 IASC's reasons for requiring reversals of impairment losses were the following:

(a) it is consistent with the *Framework* and the view that future economic benefits that were not previously expected to flow from an asset have been reassessed as probable.

(b) a reversal of an impairment loss is not a revaluation and is consistent with the historical cost accounting system as long as the reversal does not result in the carrying amount of an asset exceeding its original cost less amortisation/depreciation, had the impairment loss not been recognised. Accordingly, the reversal of an impairment loss should be recognised in the income statement and any amount in excess of the depreciated historical cost should be accounted for as a revaluation.

(c) impairment losses are recognised and measured based on estimates. Any change in the measurement of an impairment loss is similar to a change in estimate. IAS 8 *Net Profit or Loss for the Period, Fundamental Errors and Changes in Accounting Policies* requires that a change in accounting estimate should be included in the determination of the net profit or loss in (a) the period of the change, if the change affects the period only, or (b) the period of the change and future periods, if the change affects both.

(d) reversals of impairment losses provide users with a more useful indication of the potential for future benefits of an asset or group of assets.

(e) results of operations will be more fairly stated in the current period and in future periods because depreciation or amortisation will not reflect a previous impairment loss that is no longer relevant. Prohibition of reversals of impairment losses may lead to abuses such as recording a significant loss one year with the resulting lower amortisation/depreciation charge and higher profits in subsequent years.

BCZ185 The majority of commentators on E55 supported IASC's proposals for reversals of impairment losses.

BCZ186 IAS 36 does not permit an enterprise to recognise a reversal of an impairment loss just because of the unwinding of the discount. IASC supported this requirement for practical reasons only. Otherwise, if an impairment loss is recognised and recoverable amount is based on value in use, a reversal of the impairment loss would be recognised in each subsequent year for the unwinding of the discount. This is because, in most cases, the pattern of depreciation of an asset is different from the pattern of value in use. IASC believed that, when there is no change in the assumptions used to estimate recoverable amount, the benefits from recognising the unwinding of the discount each year after an impairment loss has been recognised do not justify the costs involved. However, if a reversal is recognised because assumptions have changed, the discount unwinding effect is included in the amount of the reversal recognised.

Reversing goodwill impairment losses (paragraph 124)

BC187 Consistently with the proposal in the Exposure Draft, the Standard prohibits the recognition of reversals of impairment losses for goodwill. The previous version of IAS 36 required an impairment loss for goodwill recognised in a previous period to be reversed when the impairment loss was caused by a specific external event of an exceptional nature that was not expected to recur, and subsequent external events had occurred that reversed the effect of that event.

---

* IAS 8 *Net Profit or Loss for the Period, Fundamental Errors and Changes in Accounting Policies* was superseded in 2003 by IAS 8 *Accounting Policies, Changes in Accounting Estimates and Errors.*

BC188 Most respondents to the Exposure Draft agreed that reversals of impairment losses for goodwill should be prohibited. Those that disagreed argued that reversals of impairment losses for goodwill should be treated in the same way as reversals of impairment losses for other assets, but limited to circumstances in which the impairment loss was caused by specific events beyond the entity's control.

BC189 In revising IAS 36, the Board noted that IAS 38 *Intangible Assets* prohibits the recognition of internally generated goodwill. Therefore, if reversals of impairment losses for goodwill were permitted, an entity would need to establish the extent to which a subsequent increase in the recoverable amount of goodwill is attributable to the recovery of the acquired goodwill within a cash-generating unit, rather than an increase in the internally generated goodwill within the unit. The Board concluded that this will seldom, if ever, be possible. Because the acquired goodwill and internally generated goodwill contribute jointly to the same cash flows, any subsequent increase in the recoverable amount of the acquired goodwill is indistinguishable from an increase in the internally generated goodwill. Even if the specific external event that caused the recognition of the impairment loss is reversed, it will seldom, if ever, be possible to determine that the effect of that reversal is a corresponding increase in the recoverable amount of the acquired goodwill. Therefore, the Board concluded that reversals of impairment losses for goodwill should be prohibited.

BC190 The Board expressed some concern that prohibiting the recognition of reversals of impairment losses for goodwill so as to avoid recognising internally generated goodwill might be viewed by some as inconsistent with the impairment test for goodwill. This is because the impairment test results in the carrying amount of goodwill being shielded from impairment by internally generated goodwill. This has been described by some as 'backdoor' capitalisation of internally generated goodwill.

BC191 However, the Board was not as concerned about goodwill being shielded from the recognition of impairment losses by internally generated goodwill as it was about the direct recognition of internally generated goodwill that might occur if reversals of impairment losses for goodwill were permitted. As discussed in paragraph BC135, the Board is of the view that it is not possible to devise an impairment test for acquired goodwill that removes the cushion against the recognition of impairment losses provided by goodwill generated internally after a business combination.

Disclosures for cash-generating units containing goodwill or indefinite-lived intangibles (paragraphs 134 and 135)

Background to the proposals in the Exposure Draft

BC192 The Exposure Draft proposed requiring an entity to disclose a range of information about cash-generating units whose carrying amounts included goodwill or indefinite-lived intangibles. That information included:

(a) the carrying amount of goodwill and the carrying amount of indefinite-lived intangibles.

(b)   the basis on which the unit's recoverable amount had been determined (ie value in use or net selling price).

(c)   the amount by which the unit's recoverable amount exceeded its carrying amount.

(d)   the key assumptions and estimates used to measure the unit's recoverable amount and information about the sensitivity of that recoverable amount to changes in the key assumptions and estimates.

BC193   If an entity reports segment information in accordance with IAS 14 *Segment Reporting*, the Exposure Draft proposed that this information should be disclosed in aggregate for each segment based on the entity's primary reporting format. However, the Exposure Draft also proposed that the information would be disclosed separately for a cash-generating unit when:

(a)   the carrying amount of the goodwill or indefinite-lived intangibles allocated to the unit was significant in relation to the total carrying amount of goodwill or indefinite-lived intangibles; or

(b)   the basis for determining the unit's recoverable amount differed from the basis used for the other units within the segment whose carrying amounts include goodwill or indefinite-lived intangibles; or

(c)   the nature of, or value assigned to the key assumptions or growth rate on which management based its determination of the unit's recoverable amount differed significantly from that used for the other units within the segment whose carrying amounts include goodwill or indefinite-lived intangibles.

BC194   In deciding to propose these disclosure requirements in the Exposure Draft, the Board observed that non-amortisation of goodwill and indefinite-lived intangibles increases the reliance that must be placed on impairment tests of those assets to ensure that their carrying amounts do not exceed their recoverable amounts. However, the nature of impairment tests means that the carrying amounts of such assets and the related assertion that those carrying amounts are recoverable will normally be supported only by management's projections. Therefore, the Board decided to examine ways in which the reliability of the impairment tests for goodwill and indefinite-lived intangibles could be improved. As a first step, the Board considered including a subsequent cash flow test in the revised Standard, similar to that included in UK Financial Reporting Standard 11 *Impairment of Fixed Assets and Goodwill* (FRS 11).

Subsequent cash flow test

BC195   FRS 11 requires an entity to perform a subsequent cash flow test to confirm, ex post, the cash flow projections used to measure a unit's value in use when testing goodwill for impairment. Under FRS 11, for five years following each impairment test for goodwill in which recoverable amount has been based on value in use, the actual cash flows achieved must be compared with those forecast. If the actual cash flows are so much less than those forecast that use of the actual cash flows in the value in use calculation could have required recognition of an impairment in previous periods, the original impairment calculations must be re-performed using the actual cash flows, but without revising any other cash flows or assumptions (except those that change as a direct consequence of the occurrence of the actual cash flows, for example where a major cash inflow has been delayed for a year). Any impairment identified must then be recognised in the current period, unless the impairment has reversed and the reversal of the loss satisfies the criteria in FRS 11 regarding reversals of impairment losses for goodwill.

BC196 The Board noted the following arguments in support of including a similar test in the revised Standard:

(a) it would enhance the reliability of the goodwill impairment test by preventing the possibility of entities avoiding the recognition of impairment losses by using over-optimistic cash flow projections in the value in use calculations.

(b) it would provide useful information to users of an entity's financial statements because a record of actual cash flows continually less than forecast cash flows tends to cast doubt on the reliability of current estimates.

BC197 However, the subsequent cash flow test is designed only to prevent entities from avoiding goodwill write-downs. The Board observed that, given current trends in 'big bath' restructuring charges, the greater risk to the quality of financial reporting might be from entities trying to write off goodwill without adequate justification in an attempt to 'manage' the balance sheet. The Board also observed that:

(a) the focus of the test on cash flows ignores other elements in the measurement of value in use. As a result, it does not produce representationally faithful results in a present value measurement system. The Board considered incorporating into the recalculation performed under the test corrections of estimates of other elements in the measurement of value in use. However, the Board concluded that specifying which elements to include would be problematic. Moreover, adding corrections of estimates of those other elements to the test would, in effect, transform the test into a requirement to perform a comprehensive recalculation of value in use for each of the five annual reporting periods following an impairment test.

(b) the amount recognised as an impairment loss under the test is the amount of the impairment that would have been recognised, provided changes in estimates of remaining cash flows and changes in discount and growth rates are ignored. Therefore, it is a hypothetical amount that does not provide decision-useful information—it is neither an estimate of a current amount nor a prediction of ultimate cash flows.

(c) the requirement to perform the test for each of the five annual reporting periods following an impairment test could result in an entity having to maintain as many as five sets of 5-year computations for each cash-generating unit to which goodwill has been allocated. Therefore, the test is likely to be extremely burdensome, particularly if an entity has a large number of such units, without producing understandable or decision-useful information.

BC198   Therefore, the Board decided not to propose a subsequent cash flow test in the Exposure Draft. However, the Board remained committed to finding some way of improving the reliability of the impairment tests for goodwill and indefinite-lived intangibles, and decided to explore improving that reliability through disclosure requirements.

Including disclosure requirements in the revised Standard

BC199   In developing the Exposure Draft, the Board observed that the *Framework* identifies reliability as one of the key qualitative characteristics that information must possess to be useful to users in making economic decisions. To be reliable, information must be free from material error and bias and be able to be depended upon to represent faithfully that which it purports to represent. The *Framework* identifies relevance as another key qualitative characteristic that information must possess to be useful to users in making economic decisions. To be relevant, information must help users to evaluate past, present or future events, or confirm or correct their past evaluations.

BC200   The Board observed that information that assists users in evaluating the reliability of other information included in the financial statements is itself relevant, increasing in relevance as the reliability of that other information decreases. For example, information that assists users in evaluating the reliability of the amount recognised for a provision is relevant because it helps users to evaluate the effect of both a past event (ie the economic consequences of the past event giving rise to the present obligation) and a future event (ie the amount of the expected future outflow of economic benefits required to settle the obligation). Accordingly, IAS 37 *Provisions, Contingent Liabilities and Contingent Assets* requires an entity to disclose, for each class of provision, information about the uncertainties surrounding the amount and timing of expected outflows of economic benefits, and the major assumptions concerning future events that may affect the amount required to settle the obligation and have been reflected in the amount of the provision.

BC201   The Board concluded that because information that assists users in evaluating the reliability of other information is itself relevant, an entity should disclose information that assists users in evaluating the reliability of the estimates used by management to support the carrying amounts of goodwill and indefinite-lived intangibles.

BC202   The Board also concluded that such disclosures would provide users with more useful information for evaluating the reliability of the impairment tests for goodwill and indefinite-lived intangibles than the information that would be provided by a subsequent cash flow test.

BC203   The Board then considered how some balance might be achieved between the objective of providing users with useful information for evaluating the reliability of the estimates used by management to support the carrying amounts of goodwill and indefinite-lived intangibles, and the potential magnitude of those disclosures.

BC204   The Board decided that a reasonable balance might be achieved between the objective of the disclosures and their potential magnitude by requiring:

(a) information to be disclosed on an aggregate basis for each segment based on the entity's primary reporting format that includes in its carrying amount goodwill or indefinite-lived intangibles; but

(b) information for a particular cash-generating unit within that segment to be excluded from the aggregate information and disclosed separately when either:

    (i) the basis (ie net selling price or value in use), methodology or key assumptions used to measure its recoverable amount differ from those used to measure the recoverable amounts of the other units in the segment; or

    (ii) the carrying amount of the goodwill or indefinite-lived intangibles in the unit is significant in relation to the total carrying amount of goodwill or indefinite-lived intangibles.

The Board's redeliberations

BC205 After considering respondents' and field visit participants' comments, the Board confirmed its previous conclusion that information that assists users in evaluating the reliability of other information is itself relevant, increasing in relevance as the reliability of that other information decreases. Therefore, entities should be required to disclose information that assists users in evaluating the reliability of the estimates used by management to support the carrying amounts of goodwill and indefinite-lived intangibles. The Board noted that almost all field visit participants and many respondents expressed explicit support of its conclusion that, because non-amortisation of goodwill and indefinite-lived intangibles increases the reliance that must be placed on impairment tests of those assets, some additional disclosure is necessary to provide users with information for evaluating the reliability of those impairment tests.

BC206 However, it was clear from field visit participants' responses that the proposed disclosures could not be meaningfully aggregated at the segment level to the extent the Board had hoped might be the case. As a result, the proposal to require the information to be disclosed on an aggregate basis for each segment, but with disaggregated disclosures for cash-generating units in the circumstances set out in paragraph BC193 would not result in a reasonable balance between the objective of the disclosures and their potential magnitude.

BC207 The Board was also sympathetic to field visit participants' and respondents' concerns that the proposed disclosures went beyond their intended objective of providing users with relevant information for evaluating the reliability of the impairment tests for goodwill and indefinite-lived intangibles. For example, field visit participants and respondents argued that:

(a) it would be extremely difficult to distil the recoverable amount calculations into concise but meaningful disclosures because those calculations typically are complex and do not normally result in a single point estimate of recoverable amount—a single value for recoverable amount would normally be determined only when the bottom-end of the recoverable amount range is less than a cash-generating unit's carrying amount. These difficulties make it doubtful that the information, particularly the sensitivity analyses, could be produced on a timely basis.

(b) disclosing the proposed information, particularly the values assigned to, and the sensitivity of, each key assumption on which recoverable amount calculations are based, could cause significant commercial harm to an entity. Users of financial statements might, for example, use the quantitative disclosures as the basis for initiating litigation against the entity, its board of directors or management in the highly likely event that those assumptions prove less than accurate. The increased litigation risk would either encourage management to use super-conservative assumptions, thereby resulting in improper asset write-downs, or compel management to engage independent experts to develop all key assumptions and perform the recoverable amount calculations. Additionally, many of the field visit participants expressed concern over the possible impact that disclosing such information might have on their ability to defend themselves in various legal proceedings.

BC208 Therefore, the Board considered the following two interrelated issues:

(a) if the proposed disclosures went beyond their intended objective, what information *should* be disclosed so that users have sufficient information for evaluating the reliability of impairment tests for goodwill and indefinite-lived intangibles?

(b) how should this information be presented so that there is an appropriate balance between providing users with information for evaluating the reliability of the impairment tests, and the potential magnitude of those disclosures?

BC209 As a result of its redeliberations, the Board decided:

(a) not to proceed with the proposal to require information for evaluating the reliability of the impairment tests for goodwill and indefinite-lived intangibles to be disclosed in aggregate for each segment and separately for cash-generating units within a segment in specified circumstances. Instead, the Standard requires this information to be disclosed only for each cash-generating unit (group of units) for which the carrying amount of goodwill or indefinite-lived intangibles allocated to that unit (group of units) is significant in comparison with the entity's total carrying amount of goodwill or indefinite-lived intangibles.

(b) not to proceed with the proposal to require an entity to disclose the amount by which the recoverable amount of a cash-generating unit exceeds its carrying amount. Instead, the Standard requires an entity to disclose this information only if a reasonably possible change in a key assumption on which management has based its determination of the unit's (group of units') recoverable amount would cause the unit's (group of units') carrying amount to exceed its recoverable amount.

(c) not to proceed with the proposal to require an entity to disclose the value assigned to each key assumption on which management based its recoverable amount determination, and the amount by which that value must change, after incorporating any consequential effects of that change on the other variables used to measure recoverable amount, in order for the unit's recoverable amount to be equal to its carrying amount. Instead, the Standard requires an entity to disclose a description of each key assumption on which management has based its recoverable amount determination, management's approach to determining the value(s) assigned to each key assumption, whether those value(s) reflect past experience or, if appropriate, are consistent with external sources of information, and, if not, how and why they differ from past experience or external sources of information. However, if a reasonably possible change in a key assumption would cause the unit's (group of units') carrying amount to exceed its recoverable amount, the entity is also required to disclose the value assigned to the key assumption, and the amount by which that value must change, after incorporating any consequential effects of that change on the other variables used to measure recoverable amount, in order for the unit's (group of units') recoverable amount to be equal to its carrying amount.

(d) to require information about key assumptions to be disclosed also for any key assumption that is relevant to the recoverable amount determination of multiple cash-generating units (groups of units) that individually contain insignificant amounts of goodwill or indefinite-lived intangibles, but contain, in aggregate, significant amounts of goodwill or indefinite-lived intangibles.

Changes as a result of *Improvements to IFRSs* (2008)[*]

BC209A The Board noted that the disclosures that IAS 36 requires when value in use is used to determine recoverable amount differ from those required when fair value less costs to sell is used. These differing requirements appear inconsistent when a similar valuation methodology (discounted cash flows) has been used. Therefore, as part of *Improvements to IFRSs* issued in May 2008, the Board decided to require the same disclosures for fair value less costs to sell and value in use when discounted cash flows are used to estimate recoverable amount.

Transitional provisions (paragraphs 138–140)

BC210 If an entity elects to apply IFRS 3 from any date before the effective dates outlined in IFRS 3, it is also required to apply IAS 36 from that same date. Paragraphs BC181–BC184 of the Basis for Conclusions on IFRS 3 outline the Board's deliberations on this issue.[†]

BC211 Otherwise, IAS 36 is applied:

(a) to goodwill and intangible assets acquired in business combinations for which the agreement date is on or after 31 March 2004; and

(b) to all other assets prospectively from the beginning of the first annual period beginning on or after 31 March 2004.

---

[*] This heading and paragraph BC209A were added by *Improvements to IFRSs* issued in May 2008.

[†] The Board issued a revised IFRS 3 in 2008. This paragraph relates to IFRS 3 as issued in 2004.

BC212 In developing the requirements set out in paragraph BC211, the Board considered whether entities should be required:

(a) to apply retrospectively the revised impairment test for goodwill; and

(b) to apply retrospectively the requirement prohibiting reversals of impairment losses for goodwill and therefore eliminate any reversals recognised before the date the revised Standard was issued.

BC213 The Board concluded that retrospective application of the revised impairment test for goodwill would be problematic for the following reasons:

(a) it was likely to be impossible in many cases because the information needed may not exist or may no longer be obtainable.

(b) it would require the determination of estimates that would have been made at a prior date, and therefore would raise the problem of how the effect of hindsight could be separated from the factors existing at the date of the impairment test.

BC214 The Board also noted that the requirement for goodwill to be tested for impairment annually, irrespective of whether there is any indication that it may be impaired, will ensure that by the end of the first period in which the Standard is effective, all recognised goodwill acquired before its effective date would be tested for impairment.

BC215 In the case of reversals of impairment losses for goodwill, the Board acknowledged that requiring the elimination of reversals recognised before the revised Standard's effective date might seem appropriate, particularly given the Board's reasons for prohibiting reversals of impairment losses for goodwill (see paragraphs BC187–BC191). The Board concluded, however, that the previous amortisation of that goodwill, combined with the requirement for goodwill to be tested for impairment at least annually, ensures that the carrying amount of the goodwill does not exceed its recoverable amount at the end of the reporting period in which the Standard is effective. Therefore, the Board concluded that the Standard should apply on a prospective basis.

Transitional impairment test for goodwill

BC216 Given that one of the objectives of the first phase of the Business Combinations project was to seek international convergence on the accounting for goodwill, the Board considered whether IAS 36 should include a transitional goodwill impairment test similar to that included in SFAS 142. SFAS 142 requires goodwill to be tested for impairment annually, and between annual tests if an event occurs or circumstances change and would be more likely than not to reduce the fair value of a reporting unit below its carrying amount. The transitional provisions in SFAS 142 require the impairment test for goodwill to be applied prospectively. However, a transitional goodwill impairment test must be performed as of the *beginning* of the fiscal year in which SFAS 142 is applied in its entirety. An impairment loss recognised as a result of a transitional test is recognised as the effect of a change in accounting principle, rather than as an impairment loss. In addition to the transitional test, SFAS 142 requires an entity to perform the required annual goodwill impairment test in the year that SFAS 142 is initially applied in its entirety. In other words, the transitional goodwill impairment test may not be regarded as the initial year's annual test unless an entity designates the beginning of its fiscal year as the date for its annual goodwill impairment test.

BC217   The FASB concluded that goodwill that was not regarded as impaired under US GAAP before SFAS 142 was issued could be determined to be impaired if the SFAS 142 impairment test was applied to that goodwill at the date an entity initially applied SFAS 142. This is because, under previous US GAAP, entities typically tested goodwill for impairment using undiscounted estimates of future cash flows. The FASB further concluded that:

(a)   the preponderance of any transitional impairment losses was likely to result from the change in methods and treating those losses as stemming from changes in accounting principles would therefore be more representationally faithful.

(b)   given that a transitional impairment loss should be reported as a change in accounting principle, the transitional goodwill impairment test should ideally apply as of the date SFAS 142 is initially applied.

BC218   The Board observed that under the previous version of IAS 36, goodwill that was amortised over a period exceeding 20 years was required to be tested for impairment at least at each financial year-end. Goodwill that was amortised over a period not exceeding 20 years was required to be tested for impairment at the balance sheet date if there was an indication that it might be impaired. The revised Standard requires goodwill to be tested for impairment annually or more frequently if there is an indication the goodwill might be impaired. It also carries forward from the previous version of IAS 36 (a) the indicators of impairment, (b) the measure of recoverable amount (ie higher of value in use and fair value less costs to sell), and (c) the requirement for an impairment loss for a cash-generating unit to be allocated first to reduce the carrying amount of any goodwill allocated to the unit.

BC219   Therefore, goodwill tested for impairment in accordance with the previous version of the revised Standard immediately before the beginning of the reporting period in which the revised Standard becomes effective (because it was being amortised over a period exceeding 20 years or because there was an indicator of impairment) could not be identified as impaired under IAS 36 at the beginning of the period in which it becomes effective. This is because application of the Standard results in a goodwill impairment loss being identified only if the carrying amount of the cash-generating unit (group of units) to which the goodwill has been allocated exceeds its recoverable amount, and the impairment test in the previous version of IAS 36 ensures that this will not be the case.

BC220   The Board concluded that there would be only one possible situation in which a transitional impairment test might give rise to the recognition of an impairment loss for goodwill. This would be when goodwill being amortised over a period not exceeding 20 years was, immediately before the beginning of the period in which the revised Standard becomes effective, impaired in the absence of any indicator of impairment that ought reasonably to have been considered by the entity. The Board concluded that this is likely to be a rare occurrence.

BC221 The Board observed that any such impairment loss would nonetheless be recognised as a consequence of applying the requirement in IAS 36 to test goodwill for impairment at least annually. Therefore, the only benefit of applying a transitional impairment test would be, in those rare cases, to separate the impairment loss arising before the period in which the revised Standard is effective from any impairment loss arising after the beginning of that period.

BC222 The Board concluded that given the rare circumstances in which this issue would arise, the benefit of applying a transitional goodwill impairment test would be outweighed by the added costs of the test. Therefore, the Board decided that the revised Standard should not require a transitional goodwill impairment test.

Transitional impairment test for indefinite-lived intangibles

BC223 SFAS 142 also requires a transitional impairment test to be applied, as of the beginning of the fiscal year in which that Standard is initially applied, to intangible assets recognised before the effective date of SFAS 142 that are reassessed as having indefinite useful lives. An impairment loss arising from that transitional impairment test is recognised as the effect of a change in accounting principle rather than as an impairment loss. As with goodwill:

(a) intangible assets that cease being amortised upon initial application of SFAS 142 are tested for impairment in accordance with SFAS 142 using a different method from what had previously applied to those assets. Therefore, it is possible that such an intangible asset not previously regarded as impaired might be determined to be impaired under SFAS 142.

(b) the FASB concluded that the preponderance of any transitional impairment losses would be likely to result from the change in impairment testing methods. Treating those losses as stemming from changes in accounting principles is therefore more representationally faithful.

BC224 The Board considered whether IAS 36 should include a transitional impairment test for indefinite-lived intangibles similar to that in SFAS 142.

BC225 The Board observed that the previous version of IAS 38 *Intangible Assets* required an intangible asset being amortised over a period exceeding 20 years to be tested for impairment at least at each financial year-end in accordance with the previous version of IAS 36. An intangible asset being amortised over a period not exceeding 20 years was required, under the previous version of IAS 36, to be tested for impairment at the balance sheet date only if there was an indication the asset might be impaired. The revised Standard requires an indefinite-lived intangible to be tested for impairment at least annually. However, it also requires that the recoverable amount of such an asset should continue to be measured as the higher of the asset's value in use and fair value less costs to sell.

BC226 As with goodwill, the Board concluded that the revised Standard should not require a transitional impairment test for indefinite-lived intangibles because:

(a) the only circumstance in which a transitional impairment test might give rise to the recognition of an impairment loss would be when an indefinite-lived intangible previously being amortised over a period not exceeding 20 years was, immediately before the beginning of the period in which the revised Standard is effective, impaired in the absence of any indicator of impairment that ought reasonably to have been considered by the entity.

(b) any such impairment loss would nonetheless be recognised as a consequence of applying the requirement in the Standard to test such assets for impairment at least annually. Therefore, the only benefit of such a test would be to separate the impairment loss arising before the period in which the revised Standard is effective from any impairment loss arising after the beginning of that period.

(c) given the extremely rare circumstances in which this issue is likely to arise, the benefit of applying a transitional impairment test is outweighed by the added costs of the test.

Early application (paragraph 140)

BC227 The Board noted that the issue of any Standard demonstrates its opinion that application of the Standard will result in more useful information being provided to users about an entity's financial position, performance or cash flows. On that basis, a case exists for permitting, and indeed encouraging, entities to apply IAS 36 before its effective date. However, the Board also considered that permitting a revised Standard to be applied before its effective date potentially diminishes comparability between entities in the period(s) leading up to that effective date, and has the effect of providing entities with an option.

BC228 The Board concluded that the benefit of providing users with more useful information about an entity's financial position, performance and cash flows by permitting early application of IAS 36 outweighs the disadvantages of potentially diminished comparability. Therefore, entities are encouraged to apply the requirements of IAS 36 before its effective date. However, given that the revision of IAS 36 is part of an integrated package, IAS 36 requires IFRS 3 and IAS 38 (as revised in 2004) to be applied at the same time.

Transitional provision for *Improvements to IFRSs* (2009)

BC228A The Board considered the transition provisions and effective date of the amendment to paragraph 80(b). The Board noted that the assessment of goodwill impairment might involve the use of hindsight in determining the fair values of the cash-generating units at the end of a past reporting period. Considering practicability, the Board decided that the effective date should be for annual periods beginning on or after 1 January 2010 although the Board noted that the effective date of IFRS 8 is 1 January 2009. Therefore, the Board decided that an entity should apply the amendment to paragraph 80(b) made by *Improvements to IFRSs* issued in April 2009 prospectively for annual periods beginning on or after 1 January 2010.

Summary of main changes from the Exposure Draft

BC229 The following are the main changes from the Exposure Draft:

(a) the Exposure Draft proposed that an intangible asset with an indefinite useful life should be tested for impairment at the end of each annual period by comparing its carrying amount with its recoverable amount.

The Standard requires such an intangible asset to be tested for impairment annually by comparing its carrying amount with its recoverable amount. The impairment test may be performed at any time during an annual period, provided it is performed at the same time every year, and different intangible assets may be tested for impairment at different times. However, if such an intangible asset was initially recognised during the current annual period, the Standard requires that intangible asset to be tested for impairment before the end of the current annual period.

(b) the Exposure Draft proposed that the cash flow projections used to measure value in use should be based on reasonable and supportable assumptions that take into account both past actual cash flows and management's past ability to forecast cash flows accurately. This proposal has not been included in the Standard. Instead, the Standard includes guidance clarifying that management:

(i) should assess the reasonableness of the assumptions on which its current cash flow projections are based by examining the causes of differences between past cash flow projections and actual cash flows; and

(ii) should ensure that the assumptions on which its current cash flow projections are based are consistent with past actual outcomes, provided the effects of subsequent events or circumstances that did not exist when those actual cash flows were generated make this appropriate.

(c) the Exposure Draft proposed that if an active market exists for the output produced by an asset or a group of assets, that asset or group of assets should be identified as a cash-generating unit, even if some or all of the output is used internally. In such circumstances, management's best estimate of future market prices for the output should be used in estimating the future cash flows used to determine the unit's value in use. The Exposure Draft also proposed that when estimating future cash flows to determine the value in use of cash-generating units using the output, management's best estimate of future market prices for the output should be used. The Standard similarly requires that if an active market exists for the output produced by an asset or a group of assets, that asset or group of assets should be identified as a cash-generating unit, even if some or all of the output is used internally. However, the Standard clarifies that if the cash inflows generated by *any* asset or cash-generating unit are affected by internal transfer pricing, an entity should use management's best estimate of future price(s) that could be achieved in arm's length transactions in estimating:

(i) the future cash inflows used to determine the asset's or cash-generating unit's value in use; and

(ii) the future cash outflows used to determine the value in use of other assets or cash-generating units affected by the internal transfer pricing.

(d)   the Exposure Draft proposed that goodwill acquired in a business combination should be allocated to one or more cash-generating units, with each of those units representing the smallest cash-generating unit to which a portion of the carrying amount of the goodwill could be allocated on a reasonable and consistent basis. The Exposure Draft also proposed that:

    (i)   a portion of the carrying amount of goodwill should be regarded as capable of being allocated to a cash-generating unit on a reasonable and consistent basis only when that unit represents the lowest level at which management monitors the return on investment in assets that include the goodwill.

    (ii)   each cash-generating unit should not be larger than a segment based on the entity's primary reporting format determined in accordance with IAS 14 *Segment Reporting*.

The Standard requires goodwill acquired in a business combination to be allocated to each of the acquirer's cash-generating units, or groups of cash-generating units, that are expected to benefit from the synergies of the combination, irrespective of whether other assets or liabilities of the acquiree are assigned to those units or groups of units. The Standard also requires each unit or group of units to which the goodwill is so allocated: (1) to represent the lowest level within the entity at which the goodwill is monitored for internal management purposes; and (2) to be not larger than a segment based on either the entity's primary or the entity's secondary reporting format determined in accordance with IAS 14.

(e)   the Exposure Draft proposed that when an entity disposes of an operation within a cash-generating unit to which goodwill has been allocated, the goodwill associated with that operation should be:

    (i)   included in the carrying amount of the operation when determining the gain or loss on disposal; and

    (ii)   measured on the basis of the relative values of the operation disposed of and the portion of the cash-generating unit retained.

This proposal has been included in the Standard with one modification. The Standard requires the goodwill associated with the operation disposed of to be measured on the basis of the relative values of the operation disposed of and the portion of the cash-generating unit retained, unless the entity can demonstrate that some other method better reflects the goodwill associated with the operation disposed of.

(f)   the Exposure Draft proposed that when an entity reorganises its reporting structure in a way that changes the composition of cash-generating units to which goodwill has been allocated, the goodwill should be reallocated to the units affected using a relative value approach similar to that used when an entity disposes of an operation within a cash-generating unit. The Standard similarly requires an entity that reorganises its reporting structure in a way that changes the composition of one or more cash-generating units to which goodwill has been allocated to reallocate the goodwill to the units (groups of units) affected. However, the Standard requires this reallocation to be performed using a relative value approach similar to that used when an entity disposes of an operation within a cash-generating unit, unless the entity can demonstrate that some other method better reflects the goodwill associated with the reorganised units (groups of units).

(g) the Exposure Draft proposed a two-step approach for impairment testing goodwill. The first step involved using a screening mechanism for identifying potential goodwill impairments, whereby goodwill allocated to a cash-generating unit would be identified as potentially impaired only when the carrying amount of the unit exceeded its recoverable amount. If an entity identified the goodwill allocated to a cash-generating unit as potentially impaired, an entity would then determine whether the goodwill allocated to the unit was impaired by comparing its recoverable amount, measured as the implied value of the goodwill, with its carrying amount. The implied value of goodwill would be measured as a residual, being the excess of the recoverable amount of the cash-generating unit to which the goodwill has been allocated, over the net fair value of the identifiable assets, liabilities and contingent liabilities the entity would recognise if it acquired the cash-generating unit in a business combination on the date of the impairment test. The Standard requires any excess of the carrying amount of a cash-generating unit (group of units) to which goodwill has been allocated over its recoverable amount to be recognised first as an impairment loss for goodwill. Any excess remaining after the carrying amount of goodwill has been reduced to zero is then recognised by being allocated to the other assets of the unit pro rata with their carrying amounts.

(h) the Exposure Draft proposed requiring an entity to disclose information about cash-generating units whose carrying amounts included goodwill or indefinite-lived intangibles. That information included the carrying amount of goodwill and the carrying amount of indefinite-lived intangibles, the basis on which the unit's recoverable amount had been determined (ie value in use or net selling price), the amount by which the unit's recoverable amount exceeded its carrying amount, the key assumptions and estimates used to measure the unit's recoverable amount and information about the sensitivity of that recoverable amount to changes in the key assumptions and estimates. If an entity reports segment information in accordance with IAS 14, the Exposure Draft proposed that this information should be disclosed in aggregate for each segment based on the entity's primary reporting format. However, the Exposure Draft also proposed that the information would be disclosed separately for a cash-generating unit if specified criteria were met. The Standard:

(i) does not require information for evaluating the reliability of the impairment tests for goodwill and indefinite-lived intangibles to be disclosed in aggregate for each segment and separately for cash-generating units within a segment when specified criteria are met. Instead, the Standard requires this information to be disclosed for each cash-generating unit (group of units) for which the carrying amount of goodwill or indefinite-lived intangibles allocated to that unit (group of units) is significant in comparison with the entity's total carrying amount of goodwill or indefinite-lived intangibles.

(ii) does not require an entity to disclose the amount by which the recoverable amount of a cash-generating unit exceeds its carrying amount. Instead, the Standard requires an entity to disclose this information only if a reasonably possible change in a key assumption on which management has based its determination of the unit's (group of units') recoverable amount would cause the unit's (group of units') carrying amount to exceed its recoverable amount.

(iii) does not require an entity to disclose the value assigned to each key assumption on which management has based its recoverable amount determination, and the amount by which that value must change, after incorporating any consequential effects of that change on the other variables used to measure recoverable amount, in order for the unit's recoverable amount to be equal to its carrying amount. Instead, the Standard requires an entity to disclose a description of each key assumption on which management has based its recoverable amount determination, management's approach to determining the value(s) assigned to each key assumption, whether those value(s) reflect past experience or, if appropriate, are consistent with external sources of information, and, if not, how and why they differ from past experience or external sources of information. However, if a reasonably possible change in a key assumption would cause the unit's (group of units') carrying amount to exceed its recoverable amount, the entity is also required to disclose the value assigned to the key assumption, and the amount by which that value must change, after incorporating any consequential effects of that change on the other variables used to measure recoverable amount, in order for the unit's (group of units') recoverable amount to be equal to its carrying amount.

(iv) requires information about key assumptions to be disclosed for any key assumption that is relevant to the recoverable amount determination of multiple cash-generating units (groups of units) that individually contain insignificant amounts of goodwill or indefinite-lived intangibles, but which contain, in aggregate, significant amounts of goodwill or indefinite-lived intangibles.

History of the development of a standard on impairment of assets

BCZ230 In June 1996, IASC decided to prepare an International Accounting Standard on Impairment of Assets. The reasons for developing a Standard on impairment of assets were:

(a) to combine the requirements for identifying, measuring, recognising and reversing an impairment loss in one Standard to ensure that those requirements are consistent;

(b) the previous requirements and guidance in International Accounting Standards were not detailed enough to ensure that enterprises identified,

> recognised and measured impairment losses in a similar way, eg there was a need to eliminate certain alternatives for measuring an impairment loss, such as the former option not to use discounting; and

(c) IASC decided in March 1996 to explore whether the amortisation period of intangible assets and goodwill could, in certain rare circumstances, exceed 20 years if those assets were subject to detailed and reliable annual impairment tests.

BCZ231 In April 1997, IASC approved Exposure Draft E55 *Impairment of Assets*. IASC received more than 90 comment letters from over 20 countries. IASC also performed a field test of E55's proposals. More than 20 companies from various business sectors and from 10 different countries participated in the field test. About half of the field test participants prepared their financial statements using International Accounting Standards and the other half reported using other Standards. Field test participants completed a detailed questionnaire and most of them were visited by IASC staff to discuss the results of the application of E55's proposals to some of their assets. A brief summary of the comment letters received on E55 and the results of the field test was published in IASC *Insight* in December 1997.

BCZ232 In October 1997, IASC, together with the Accounting Standards Boards in Australia, Canada, New Zealand, the United Kingdom and the United States, published a discussion paper entitled *International Review of Accounting Standards Specifying a Recoverable Amount Test for Long-Lived Assets* (Jim Paul, from the staff of the Australian Accounting Research Foundation, was the principal author). This discussion paper resulted from the discussions of a 'working group' consisting of some Board members and senior staff members from the standard-setting bodies listed above and IASC. The paper:

(a) noted the key features of the working group members' existing or proposed accounting standards that require an impairment test, and compared those standards; and

(b) proposed the views of the working group on the major issues.

BCZ233 In April 1998, after considering the comments received on E55 and the results of the field test, IASC approved IAS 36 *Impairment of Assets*.

Dissenting opinions

Dissent of Anthony T Cope, James J Leisenring and Geoffrey Whittington

DO1   Messrs Cope and Leisenring and Professor Whittington dissent from the issue of IAS 36.

DO2   Messrs Cope and Leisenring and Professor Whittington dissent because they object to the impairment test that the Standard requires for goodwill.

DO3   Messrs Cope and Leisenring agree with the prohibition, in paragraph 54 of IFRS 3 *Business Combinations*, of amortisation of goodwill.* Research and experience have demonstrated that the amortisation of goodwill produces data that is meaningless, and perhaps even misleading. However, if goodwill is not amortised, its special nature mandates that it should be accounted for with caution. The Basis for Conclusions on IAS 36 (paragraph BC131) states that 'if a rigorous and operational impairment test [for goodwill] could be devised, more useful information would be provided to users of an entity's financial statements under an approach in which goodwill is not amortised, but instead tested for impairment annually or more frequently if events or changes in circumstances indicate that the goodwill might be impaired.' Messrs Cope and Leisenring agree with that statement. However, they believe that the impairment test to which a majority of the Board has agreed lacks the rigour to satisfy that condition.

DO4   Messrs Cope and Leisenring share the reservations of some Board members, as noted in paragraph BC130 of the Basis for Conclusions on IAS 36, about an impairment test based on measuring the recoverable amount of an asset, and particularly an asset with an indefinite life, as the higher of fair value less costs to sell or value in use. Messrs Cope and Leisenring are content, however, for the time being to defer consideration of that general measurement issue, pending more research and debate on measurement principles. (They note that the use of fair value would achieve significant convergence with US GAAP.) But a much more rigorous effort must be made to determine the recoverable amount of goodwill, however measured, than the Board's revised impairment test. The 'two-step' method originally proposed by the Board in the Exposure Draft of Proposed Amendments to IAS 36 and IAS 38 was a more useful approach to determining the 'implied value' of goodwill. That test should have been retained.

DO5   Messrs Cope and Leisenring recognise that some constituents raised objections to the complexity and potential cost of the requirements proposed in the Exposure Draft. However, they believe that many commentators misunderstood the level at which the Board intended impairment testing to be undertaken. This was demonstrated during the field-testing of the Exposure Draft. Furthermore, the provisions of paragraph 99 of IAS 36, specifying when impairment testing need not be undertaken, provide generous relief from the necessity of making frequent calculations. They would have preferred to meet those objections by specifying that the goodwill impairment test should be at the level set out in US Financial Accounting Standards Board's Statement of Financial Accounting Standards No. 142 *Goodwill and Other Intangible Assets*.

---

*   The Board issued a revised IFRS 3 in 2008. The amortisation of goodwill is prohibited, but the paragraph reference no longer exists in IFRS 3 (as revised in 2008).

DO6   Professor Whittington believes that there are two aspects of the proposed impairment test that are particularly unsatisfactory. First, the failure to eliminate the shield from impairment provided by the internally generated goodwill of the acquiring entity at acquisition. This is discussed in paragraph DO7. Second, the lack of a subsequent cash flow test. This is discussed in paragraphs DO8–DO10. The inability to eliminate the shield from impairment provided by internally generated goodwill accruing after the acquisition date is also a problem. However, there is no obvious practical way of dealing with this problem within the framework of conventional impairment tests.

DO7   When an acquired business is merged with an acquirer's existing operations, the impairment test in IAS 36 does not take account of the acquirer's pre-existing internally generated goodwill. Thus, the pre-existing internally generated goodwill of the acquirer provides a shield against impairment additional to that provided by subsequent internally generated goodwill. Professor Whittington believes that the impairment test would be more rigorous if it included a requirement similar to that in UK Financial Reporting Standard 11 *Impairment of Fixed Assets and Goodwill*, which recognises, for purposes of impairment testing, the implied value of the acquirer's goodwill existing at the time of acquisition.

DO8   The subsequent cash flow test is discussed in paragraphs BC195–BC198 of the Basis for Conclusions on IAS 36. A subsequent cash flow test substitutes in past impairment tests the cash flows that actually occurred for those that were estimated at the time of the impairment tests, and requires a write-down if the revised estimates would have created an impairment loss for goodwill. It is thus a correction of an estimate. Such a test is incorporated in FRS 11.

DO9   The Board's reasons for rejecting the subsequent cash flow test are given in paragraph BC197(a)–(c). The preamble to paragraph BC197 claims that the subsequent cash flow test is misdirected because excessive write-downs of goodwill may be a problem that should be prevented. However, the subsequent cash flow test requires only realistic write-downs (based on actual outcomes), not excessive ones. If the statement in paragraph BC197 is correct, this may point to another deficiency in the impairment testing process that requires a different remedy.

DO10   Paragraph BC197(a) asserts that 'it does not produce representationally faithful results' because it ignores other elements in the measurement of value in use. As explained above, it merely substitutes the outcome cash flow for the estimate, which should have a clear meaning and provides a safeguard against over-optimism in the estimation of cash flows. If corrections of estimates of other elements, such as variations that have occurred in interest rates, were considered important in this context, they could be incorporated in the calculation. Paragraph BC197(b) seems to raise the same point as paragraph BC197(a), as to the meaning of the impairment loss under the test. Paragraph BC197(c) complains about the excessive burden that a subsequent cash flow test might impose. Professor Whittington notes that the extent of the burden depends, of course, upon the frequency with which the test is applied. He also notes that the extensive disclosure requirements currently associated with the impairment test might be reduced if the subsequent cash flow test were in place.

CONTENTS

IAS 36 *Impairment of Assets*
Illustrative examples

These examples accompany, but are not part of, IAS 36. All the examples assume that the entities concerned have no transactions other than those described. In the examples monetary amounts are denominated in 'currency units (CU)'.

Example 1   Identification of cash-generating units

The purpose of this example is:

    (a)   to indicate how cash-generating units are identified in various situations; and

    (b)   to highlight certain factors that an entity may consider in identifying the cash-generating unit to which an asset belongs.

A - Retail store chain

Background

IE1   Store X belongs to a retail store chain M. X makes all its retail purchases through M's purchasing centre. Pricing, marketing, advertising and human resources policies (except for hiring X's cashiers and sales staff) are decided by M. M also owns five other stores in the same city as X (although in different neighbourhoods) and 20 other stores in other cities. All stores are managed in the same way as X. X and four other stores were purchased five years ago and goodwill was recognised.

        What is the cash-generating unit for X (X's cash-generating unit)?

Analysis

IE2   In identifying X's cash-generating unit, an entity considers whether, for example:

    (a)   internal management reporting is organised to measure performance on a store-by-store basis; and

    (b)   the business is run on a store-by-store profit basis or on a region/city basis.

IE3   All M's stores are in different neighbourhoods and probably have different customer bases. So, although X is managed at a corporate level, X generates cash inflows that are largely independent of those of M's other stores. Therefore, it is likely that X is a cash-generating unit.

IE4   If X's cash-generating unit represents the lowest level within M at which the goodwill is monitored for internal management purposes, M applies to that cash-generating unit the impairment test described in paragraph 90 of IAS 36. If information about the carrying amount of goodwill is not available and monitored for internal management purposes at the level of X's cash-generating unit, M applies to that cash-generating unit the impairment test described in paragraph 88 of IAS 36.

B - Plant for an intermediate step in a production process

Background

IE5   A significant raw material used for plant Y's final production is an intermediate product bought from plant X of the same entity. X's products are sold to Y at a transfer price that passes all margins to X. Eighty per cent of Y's final production is sold to customers outside of the entity. Sixty per cent of X's final production is sold to Y and the remaining 40 per cent is sold to customers outside of the entity.

For each of the following cases, what are the cash-generating units for X and Y?

Case 1: X could sell the products it sells to Y in an active market. Internal transfer prices are higher than market prices.

Case 2: There is no active market for the products X sells to Y.

Analysis

Case 1

IE6   X could sell its products in an active market and, so, generate cash inflows that would be largely independent of the cash inflows from Y. Therefore, it is likely that X is a separate cash-generating unit, although part of its production is used by Y (see paragraph 70 of IAS 36).

IE7   It is likely that Y is also a separate cash-generating unit. Y sells 80 per cent of its products to customers outside of the entity. Therefore, its cash inflows can be regarded as largely independent.

IE8   Internal transfer prices do not reflect market prices for X's output. Therefore, in determining value in use of both X and Y, the entity adjusts financial budgets/forecasts to reflect management's best estimate of future prices that could be achieved in arm's length transactions for those of X's products that are used internally (see paragraph 70 of IAS 36).

Case 2

IE9   It is likely that the recoverable amount of each plant cannot be assessed independently of the recoverable amount of the other plant because:

(a)   the majority of X's production is used internally and could not be sold in an active market. So, cash inflows of X depend on demand for Y's products. Therefore, X cannot be considered to generate cash inflows that are largely independent of those of Y.

(b)   the two plants are managed together.

IE10   As a consequence, it is likely that X and Y together are the smallest group of assets that generates cash inflows that are largely independent.

C - Single product entity

Background

IE11   Entity M produces a single product and owns plants A, B and C. Each plant is located in a different continent. A produces a component that is assembled in either B or C. The combined capacity of B and C is not fully utilised. M's products are sold worldwide from either B or C. For example, B's production can be sold in C's continent if the products can be delivered faster from B than from C. Utilisation levels of B and C depend on the allocation of sales between the two sites.

For each of the following cases, what are the cash-generating units for A, B and C?

Case 1: There is an active market for A's products.

Case 2: There is no active market for A's products.

Analysis

Case 1

IE12   It is likely that A is a separate cash-generating unit because there is an active market for its products (see Example B - Plant for an intermediate step in a production process, Case 1).

IE13   Although there is an active market for the products assembled by B and C, cash inflows for B and C depend on the allocation of production across the two sites. It is unlikely that the future cash inflows for B and C can be determined individually. Therefore, it is likely that B and C together are the smallest identifiable group of assets that generates cash inflows that are largely independent.

IE14   In determining the value in use of A and B plus C, M adjusts financial budgets/ forecasts to reflect its best estimate of future prices that could be achieved in arm's length transactions for A's products (see paragraph 70 of IAS 36).

Case 2

IE15   It is likely that the recoverable amount of each plant cannot be assessed independently because:

(a)   there is no active market for A's products. Therefore, A's cash inflows depend on sales of the final product by B and C.

(b)   although there is an active market for the products assembled by B and C, cash inflows for B and C depend on the allocation of production across the two sites. It is unlikely that the future cash inflows for B and C can be determined individually.

IE16   As a consequence, it is likely that A, B and C together (ie M as a whole) are the smallest identifiable group of assets that generates cash inflows that are largely independent.

D - Magazine titles

Background

IE17   A publisher owns 150 magazine titles of which 70 were purchased and 80 were self-created. The price paid for a purchased magazine title is recognised as an intangible asset. The costs of creating magazine titles and maintaining the existing titles are recognised as an expense when incurred. Cash inflows from direct sales and advertising are identifiable for each magazine title. Titles are managed by customer segments. The level of advertising income for a magazine title depends on the range of titles in the customer segment to which the magazine title relates. Management has a policy to abandon old titles before the end of their economic lives and replace them immediately with new titles for the same customer segment.

What is the cash-generating unit for an individual magazine title?

Analysis

IE18   It is likely that the recoverable amount of an individual magazine title can be assessed. Even though the level of advertising income for a title is influenced, to a certain extent, by the other titles in the customer segment, cash inflows from direct sales and advertising are identifiable for each title. In addition, although titles are managed by customer segments, decisions to abandon titles are made on an individual title basis.

IE19   Therefore, it is likely that individual magazine titles generate cash inflows that are largely independent of each other and that each magazine title is a separate cash-generating unit.

E - Building half-rented to others and half-occupied for own use

Background

IE20   M is a manufacturing company. It owns a headquarters building that used to be fully occupied for internal use. After down-sizing, half of the building is now used internally and half rented to third parties. The lease agreement with the tenant is for five years.

What is the cash-generating unit of the building?

Analysis

IE21   The primary purpose of the building is to serve as a corporate asset, supporting M's manufacturing activities. Therefore, the building as a whole cannot be considered to generate cash inflows that are largely independent of the cash inflows from the entity as a whole. So, it is likely that the cash-generating unit for the building is M as a whole.

IE22   The building is not held as an investment. Therefore, it would not be appropriate to determine the value in use of the building based on projections of future market related rents.

Example 2   Calculation of value in use and recognition of an impairment loss

In this example, tax effects are ignored.

Background and calculation of value in use

IE23   At the end of 20X0, entity T acquires entity M for CU10,000. M has manufacturing plants in three countries.

Schedule 1. Data at the end of 20X0

End of 20X0	Allocation of purchase price CU	Fair value of identifiable assets CU	Goodwill CU[(a)]
Activities in Country A	3,000	2,000	1,000
Activities in Country B	2,000	1,500	500
Activities in Country C	5,000	3,500	1,500
Total	10,000	7,000	3,000

(a) Activities in each country represent the lowest level at which the goodwill is monitored for internal management purposes (determined as the difference between the purchase price of the activities in each country, as specified in the purchase agreement, and the fair value of the identifiable assets).

IE23A   Because goodwill has been allocated to the activities in each country, each of those activities must be tested for impairment annually or more frequently if there is any indication that it may be impaired (see paragraph 90 of IAS 36).

IE24   The recoverable amounts (ie higher of value in use and fair value less costs to sell) of the cash-generating units are determined on the basis of value in use calculations.   At the end of 20X0 and 20X1, the value in use of each cash-generating unit exceeds its carrying amount. Therefore the activities in each country and the goodwill allocated to those activities are regarded as not impaired.

IE25   At the beginning of 20X2, a new government is elected in Country A. It passes legislation significantly restricting exports of T's main product. As a result, and for the foreseeable future, T's production in Country A will be cut by 40 per cent.

IE26   The significant export restriction and the resulting production decrease require T also to estimate the recoverable amount of the Country A operations at the beginning of 20X2.

IE27   T uses straight-line depreciation over a 12-year life for the Country A identifiable assets and anticipates no residual value.

IE28   To determine the value in use for the Country A cash-generating unit (see Schedule 2), T:

(a)   prepares cash flow forecasts derived from the most recent financial budgets/forecasts for the next five years (years 20X2–20X6) approved by management.

(b)   estimates subsequent cash flows (years 20X7–20Y2) based on declining growth rates. The growth rate for 20X7 is estimated to be 3 per cent. This rate is lower than the average long-term growth rate for the market in Country A.

(c)   selects a 15 per cent discount rate, which represents a pre-tax rate that reflects current market assessments of the time value of money and the risks specific to the Country A cash-generating unit.

Recognition and measurement of impairment loss

IE29   The recoverable amount of the Country A cash-generating unit is CU1,360.

IE30   T compares the recoverable amount of the Country A cash-generating unit with its carrying amount (see Schedule 3).

IE31   Because the carrying amount exceeds the recoverable amount by CU1,473, T recognises an impairment loss of CU1,473 immediately in profit or loss. The carrying amount of the goodwill that relates to the Country A operations is reduced to zero before reducing the carrying amount of other identifiable assets within the Country A cash-generating unit (see paragraph 104 of IAS 36).

IE32 Tax effects are accounted for separately in accordance with IAS 12 *Income Taxes* (see Illustrative Example 3A).

Schedule 2. Calculation of the value in use of the Country A cash-generating unit at the beginning of 20X2

Year	Long-term growth rates	Future cash flows	Present value factor at 15% discount rate[3]	Discounted future cash flows
		CU		CU
20X2 (n=1)		230[1]	0.86957	200
20X3		253[1]	0.75614	191
20X4		273[1]	0.65752	180
20X5		290[1]	0.57175	166
20X6		304[1]	0.49718	151
20X7	3%	313[2]	0.43233	135
20X8	(2)%	307[2]	0.37594	115
20X9	(6)%	289[2]	0.32690	94
20Y0	(15)%	245[2]	0.28426	70
20Y1	(25)%	184[2]	0.24719	45
20Y2	(67)%	61[2]	0.21494	13
Value in use				1,360

[1] Based on management's best estimate of net cash flow projections (after the 40% cut).

[2] Based on an extrapolation from preceding year cash flow using declining growth rates.

[3] The present value factor is calculated as $k = 1/(1+a)^n$, where a = discount rate and n = period of discount.

Schedule 3. Calculation and allocation of the impairment loss for the Country A cash-generating unit at the beginning of 20X2

Beginning of 20X2	Goodwill	Identifiable assets	Total
	CU	CU	CU
Historical cost	1,000	2,000	3,000
Accumulated depreciation (20X1)	–	(167)	(167)
Carrying amount	1,000	1,833	2,833
Impairment loss	(1,000)	(473)	(1,473)
Carrying amount after impairment loss	–	1,360	1,360

Example 3   Deferred tax effects

A - Deferred tax effects of the recognition of an impairment loss

Use the data for entity T as presented in Example 2, with supplementary information as provided in this example.

IE33   At the beginning of 20X2, the tax base of the identifiable assets of the Country A cash-generating unit is CU900. Impairment losses are not deductible for tax purposes. The tax rate is 40 per cent.

IE34   The recognition of an impairment loss on the assets of the Country A cash-generating unit reduces the taxable temporary difference related to those assets. The deferred tax liability is reduced accordingly.

Beginning of 20X2	Identifiable assets before impairment loss	Impairment loss	Identifiable assets after impairment loss
	CU	CU	CU
Carrying amount (Example 2)	1,833	(473)	1,360
Tax base	900	–	900
Taxable temporary difference	933	(473)	460
Deferred tax liability at 40%	373	(189)	184

IE35   In accordance with IAS 12 *Income Taxes*, no deferred tax relating to the goodwill was recognised initially. Therefore, the impairment loss relating to the goodwill does not give rise to a deferred tax adjustment.

B - Recognition of an impairment loss creates a deferred tax asset

IE36　An entity has an identifiable asset with a carrying amount of CU1,000. Its recoverable amount is CU650. The tax rate is 30 per cent and the tax base of the asset is CU800. Impairment losses are not deductible for tax purposes. The effect of the impairment loss is as follows:

	Before impairment	Effect of impairment	After impairment
	CU	CU	CU
Carrying amount	1,000	(350)	650
Tax base	800	–	800
Taxable (deductible) temporary difference	200	(350)	(150)
Deferred tax liability (asset) at 30%	60	(105)	(45)

IE37　In accordance with IAS 12, the entity recognises the deferred tax asset to the extent that it is probable that taxable profit will be available against which the deductible temporary difference can be utilised.

Example 4   Reversal of an impairment loss

Use the data for entity T as presented in Example 2, with supplementary information as provided in this example. In this example, tax effects are ignored.

Background

IE38   In 20X3, the government is still in office in Country A, but the business situation is improving. The effects of the export laws on T's production are proving to be less drastic than initially expected by management. As a result, management estimates that production will increase by 30 per cent. This favourable change requires T to re-estimate the recoverable amount of the net assets of the Country A operations (see paragraphs 110 and 111 of IAS 36). The cash-generating unit for the net assets of the Country A operations is still the Country A operations.

IE39   Calculations similar to those in Example 2 show that the recoverable amount of the Country A cash-generating unit is now CU1,910.

Reversal of impairment loss

IE40   T compares the recoverable amount and the net carrying amount of the Country A cash-generating unit.

Schedule 1. Calculation of the carrying amount of the Country A cash-generating unit at the end of 20X3

	Goodwill	Identifiable assets	Total
	CU	CU	CU
Beginning of 20X2 (Example 2)			
Historical cost	1,000	2,000	3,000
Accumulated depreciation	–	(167)	(167)
Impairment loss	(1,000)	(473)	(1,473)
Carrying amount after impairment loss	–	1,360	1,360
End of 20X3			
Additional depreciation (2 years)[(a)]	–	(247)	(247)
Carrying amount	–	1,113	1,113
Recoverable amount			1,910
Excess of recoverable amount over carrying amount			797

(a)   After recognition of the impairment loss at the beginning of 20X2, T revised the depreciation charge for the Country A identifiable assets (from CU166.7 per year to CU123.6 per year), based on the revised carrying amount and remaining useful life (11 years).

IE41   There has been a favourable change in the estimates used to determine the recoverable amount of the Country A net assets since the last impairment loss was recognised. Therefore, in accordance with paragraph 114 of IAS 36, T recognises a reversal of the impairment loss recognised in 20X2.

IE42   In accordance with paragraphs 122 and 123 of IAS 36, T increases the carrying amount of the Country A identifiable assets by CU387 (see Schedule 3), ie up to the lower of recoverable amount (CU1,910) and the identifiable assets' depreciated historical cost (CU1,500) (see Schedule 2). This increase is recognised immediately in profit or loss.

IE43   In accordance with paragraph 124 of IAS 36, the impairment loss on goodwill is not reversed.

Schedule 2. Determination of the depreciated historical cost of the Country A identifiable assets at the end of 20X3

End of 20X3	Identifiable assets
	CU
Historical cost	2,000
Accumulated depreciation (166.7 × 3 years)	(500)
Depreciated historical cost	1,500
Carrying amount (Schedule 1)	1,113
Difference	387

Schedule 3. Carrying amount of the Country A assets at the end of 20X3

End of 20X3	Goodwill	Identifiable assets	Total
	CU	CU	CU
Gross carrying amount	1,000	2,000	3,000
Accumulated amortisation	–	(414)	(414)
Accumulated impairment loss	(1,000)	(473)	(1,473)
Carrying amount	–	1,113	1,113
Reversal of impairment loss	0	387	387
Carrying amount after reversal of impairment loss	–	1,500	1,500

Example 5   Treatment of a future restructuring

In this example, tax effects are ignored.

Background

IE44   At the end of 20X0, entity K tests a plant for impairment. The plant is a cash-generating unit. The plant's assets are carried at depreciated historical cost. The plant has a carrying amount of CU3,000 and a remaining useful life of 10 years.

IE45   The plant's recoverable amount (ie higher of value in use and fair value less costs to sell) is determined on the basis of a value in use calculation. Value in use is calculated using a pre-tax discount rate of 14 per cent.

IE46   Management approved budgets reflect that:

(a)   at the end of 20X3, the plant will be restructured at an estimated cost of CU100. Since K is not yet committed to the restructuring, a provision has not been recognised for the future restructuring costs.

(b)   there will be future benefits from this restructuring in the form of reduced future cash outflows.

IE47   At the end of 20X2, K becomes committed to the restructuring. The costs are still estimated to be CU100 and a provision is recognised accordingly. The plant's estimated future cash flows reflected in the most recent management approved budgets are given in paragraph IE51 and a current discount rate is the same as at the end of 20X0.

IE48   At the end of 20X3, actual restructuring costs of CU100 are incurred and paid. Again, the plant's estimated future cash flows reflected in the most recent management approved budgets and a current discount rate are the same as those estimated at the end of 20X2.

At the end of 20X0

Schedule 1. Calculation of the plant's value in use at the end of 20X0

Year	Future cash flows	Discounted at 14%
	CU	CU
20X1	300	263
20X2	280	215
20X3	420[1]	283
20X4	520[2]	308
20X5	350[2]	182
20X6	420[2]	191
20X7	480[2]	192
20X8	480[2]	168
20X9	460[2]	141
20X10	400[2]	108
Value in use		2,051

[1] Excludes estimated restructuring costs reflected in management budgets.

[2] Excludes estimated benefits expected from the restructuring reflected in management budgets.

IE49   The plant's recoverable amount (ie value in use) is less than its carrying amount. Therefore, K recognises an impairment loss for the plant.

Schedule 2. Calculation of the impairment loss at the end of 20X0

	Plant
	CU
Carrying amount before impairment loss	3,000
Recoverable amount (Schedule 1)	2,051
Impairment loss	(949)
Carrying amount after impairment loss	2,051

At the end of 20X1

IE50   No event occurs that requires the plant's recoverable amount to be re-estimated. Therefore, no calculation of the recoverable amount is required to be performed.

At the end of 20X2

IE51   The entity is now committed to the restructuring. Therefore, in determining the plant's value in use, the benefits expected from the restructuring are considered in forecasting cash flows. This results in an increase in the estimated future cash flows used to determine value in use at the end of 20X0. In accordance with paragraphs 110 and 111 of IAS 36, the recoverable amount of the plant is re-determined at the end of 20X2.

Schedule 3. Calculation of the plant's value in use at the end of 20X2

Year	Future cash flows	Discounted at 14%
	CU	CU
20X3	420[1]	368
20X4	570[2]	439
20X5	380[2]	256
20X6	450[2]	266
20X7	510[2]	265
20X8	510[2]	232
20X9	480[2]	192
20X10	410[2]	144
Value in use		2,162

[1]   Excludes estimated restructuring costs because a liability has already been recognised.

[2]   Includes estimated benefits expected from the restructuring reflected in management budgets.

IE52   The plant's recoverable amount (value in use) is higher than its carrying amount (see Schedule 4). Therefore, K reverses the impairment loss recognised for the plant at the end of 20X0.

Schedule 4. Calculation of the reversal of the impairment loss at the end of 20X2

	Plant
	CU
Carrying amount at the end of 20X0 (Schedule 2)	2,051
End of 20X2	
Depreciation charge (for 20X1 and 20X2–Schedule 5)	(410)
Carrying amount before reversal	1,641
Recoverable amount (Schedule 3)	2,162
Reversal of the impairment loss	521
Carrying amount after reversal	2,162
Carrying amount: depreciated historical cost (Schedule 5)	2,400 (a)

(a) The reversal does not result in the carrying amount of the plant exceeding what its carrying amount would have been at depreciated historical cost. Therefore, the full reversal of the impairment loss is recognised.

At the end of 20X3

IE53   There is a cash outflow of CU100 when the restructuring costs are paid. Even though a cash outflow has taken place, there is no change in the estimated future cash flows used to determine value in use at the end of 20X2. Therefore, the plant's recoverable amount is not calculated at the end of 20X3.

Schedule 5. Summary of the carrying amount of the plant

End of year	Depreciated historical cost	Recoverable amount	Adjusted depreciation charge	Impairment loss	Carrying amount after impairment
	CU	CU	CU	CU	CU
20X0	3,000	2,051	0	(949)	2,051
20X1	2,700	nc	(205)	0	1,846
20X2	2,400	2,162	(205)	521	2,162
20X3	2,100	nc	(270)	0	1,892

nc = not calculated as there is no indication that the impairment loss may have increased/decreased.

Example 6   Treatment of future costs

In this example, tax effects are ignored.

Background

IE54   At the end of 20X0, entity F tests a machine for impairment. The machine is a cash-generating unit. It is carried at depreciated historical cost and its carrying amount is CU150,000. It has an estimated remaining useful life of 10 years.

IE55   The machine's recoverable amount (ie higher of value in use and fair value less costs to sell) is determined on the basis of a value in use calculation. Value in use is calculated using a pre-tax discount rate of 14 per cent.

IE56   Management approved budgets reflect:

(a)   estimated costs necessary to maintain the level of economic benefit expected to arise from the machine in its current condition; and

(b)   that in 20X4, costs of CU25,000 will be incurred to enhance the machine's performance by increasing its productive capacity.

IE57   At the end of 20X4, costs to enhance the machine's performance are incurred. The machine's estimated future cash flows reflected in the most recent management approved budgets are given in paragraph IE60 and a current discount rate is the same as at the end of 20X0.

At the end of 20X0

Schedule 1. Calculation of the machine's value in use at the end of 20X0

Year	Future cash flows	Discounted at 14%
	CU	CU
20X1	22,165[1]	19,443
20X2	21,450[1]	16,505
20X3	20,550[1]	13,871
20X4	24,725[1,2]	14,639
20X5	25,325[1,3]	13,153
20X6	24,825[1,3]	11,310
20X7	24,123[1,3]	9,640
20X8	25,533[1,3]	8,951
20X9	24,234[1,3]	7,452
20X10	22,850[1,3]	6,164
Value in use		121,128

[1] Includes estimated costs necessary to maintain the level of economic benefit expected to arise from the machine in its current condition.

[2] Excludes estimated costs to enhance the machine's performance reflected in management budgets.

[3] Excludes estimated benefits expected from enhancing the machine's performance reflected in management budgets.

IE58 The machine's recoverable amount (value in use) is less than its carrying amount. Therefore, F recognises an impairment loss for the machine.

Schedule 2. Calculation of the impairment loss at the end of 20X0

	Machine
	CU
Carrying amount before impairment loss	150,000
Recoverable amount (Schedule 1)	121,128
Impairment loss	(28,872)
Carrying amount after impairment loss	121,128

Years 20X1–20X3

IE59 No event occurs that requires the machine's recoverable amount to be re-estimated. Therefore, no calculation of recoverable amount is required to be performed.

At the end of 20X4

IE60 The costs to enhance the machine's performance are incurred. Therefore, in determining the machine's value in use, the future benefits expected from enhancing the machine's performance are considered in forecasting cash flows. This results in an increase in the estimated future cash flows used to determine value in use at the end of 20X0. As a consequence, in accordance with paragraphs 110 and 111 of IAS 36, the recoverable amount of the machine is recalculated at the end of 20X4.

Schedule 3. Calculation of the machine's value in use at the end of 20X4

Year	Future cash flows[a]	Discounted at 14%
	CU	CU
20X5	30,321	26,597
20X6	32,750	25,200
20X7	31,721	21,411
20X8	31,950	18,917
20X9	33,100	17,191
20X10	27,999	12,756
Value in use		122,072

(a) Includes estimated benefits expected from enhancing the machine's performance reflected in management budgets.

IE61 The machine's recoverable amount (ie value in use) is higher than the machine's carrying amount and depreciated historical cost (see Schedule 4). Therefore, K reverses the impairment loss recognised for the machine at the end of 20X0 so that the machine is carried at depreciated historical cost.

Schedule 4. Calculation of the reversal of the impairment loss at the end of 20X4

	Machine
	CU
Carrying amount at the end of 20X0 (Schedule 2)	121,128
End of 20X4	
Depreciation charge (20X1 to 20X4 – Schedule 5)	(48,452)
Costs to enhance the asset's performance	25,000
Carrying amount before reversal	97,676
Recoverable amount (Schedule 3)	122,072
Reversal of the impairment loss	17,324
Carrying amount after reversal	115,000
Carrying amount: depreciated historical cost (Schedule 5)	115,000 [a]

(a) The value in use of the machine exceeds what its carrying amount would have been at depreciated historical cost. Therefore, the reversal is limited to an amount that does not result in the carrying amount of the machine exceeding depreciated historical cost.

Schedule 5. Summary of the carrying amount of the machine

Year	Depreciated historical cost	Recoverable amount	Adjusted depreciated charge	Impairment loss	Carrying amount after impairment
	CU	CU	CU	CU	CU
20X0	150,000	121,128	0	(28,872)	121,128
20X1	135,000	nc	(12,113)	0	109,015
20X2	120,000	nc	(12,113)	0	96,902
20X3	105,000	nc	(12,113)	0	84,789
20X4	90,000		(12,113)		
enhancement	25,000		–		
	115,000	122,072	(12,113)	17,324	115,000
20X5	95,833	nc	(19,167)	0	95,833

nc = not calculated as there is no indication that the impairment loss may have increased/decreased.

Example 7 Impairment testing cash-generating units with goodwill and non-controlling interests

Example 7A Non-controlling interests measured initially as a proportionate share of the net identifiable assets

In this example, tax effects are ignored.

Background

IE62   Parent acquires an 80 per cent ownership interest in Subsidiary for CU2,100 on 1 January 20X3. At that date, Subsidiary's net identifiable assets have a fair value of CU1,500. Parent chooses to measure the non-controlling interests as the proportionate interest of Subsidiary's net identifiable assets of CU300 (20% of CU1,500). Goodwill of CU900 is the difference between the aggregate of the consideration transferred and the amount of the non-controlling interests (CU2,100 + CU300) and the net identifiable assets (CU1,500).

IE63   The assets of Subsidiary together are the smallest group of assets that generate cash inflows that are largely independent of the cash inflows from other assets or groups of assets. Therefore Subsidiary is a cash-generating unit. Because other cash-generating units of Parent are expected to benefit from the synergies of the combination, the goodwill of CU500 related to those synergies has been allocated to other cash-generating units within Parent. Because the cash-generating unit comprising Subsidiary includes goodwill within its carrying amount, it must be tested for impairment annually, or more frequently if there is an indication that it may be impaired (see paragraph 90 of IAS 36).

IE64   At the end of 20X3, Parent determines that the recoverable amount of cash-generating unit Subsidiary is CU1,000. The carrying amount of the net assets of Subsidiary, excluding goodwill, is CU1,350.

Testing Subsidiary (cash-generating unit) for impairment

IE65   Goodwill attributable to non-controlling interests is included in Subsidiary's recoverable amount of CU1,000 but has not been recognised in Parent's consolidated financial statements. Therefore, in accordance with paragraph C4 of Appendix C of IAS 36, the carrying amount of Subsidiary is grossed up to include goodwill attributable to the non-controlling interests, before being compared with the recoverable amount of CU1,000. Goodwill attributable to Parent's 80 per cent interest in Subsidiary at the acquisition date is CU400 after allocating CU500 to other cash-generating units within Parent. Therefore, goodwill attributable to the 20 per cent non-controlling interests in Subsidiary at the acquisition date is CU100.

Schedule 1. Testing Subsidiary for impairment at the end of 20X3

End of 20X3	Goodwill of Subsidiary	Net identifiable assets	Total
	CU	CU	CU
Carrying amount	400	1,350	1,750
Unrecognised non-controlling interests	100	–	100
Adjusted carrying amount	500	1,350	1,850
Recoverable amount			1,000
Impairment loss			850

Allocating the impairment loss

IE66   In accordance with paragraph 104 of IAS 36, the impairment loss of CU850 is allocated to the assets in the unit by first reducing the carrying amount of goodwill.

IE67   Therefore, CU500 of the CU850 impairment loss for the unit is allocated to the goodwill. In accordance with paragraph C6 of Appendix C of IAS 36, if the partially-owned subsidiary is itself a cash-generating unit, the goodwill impairment loss is allocated to the controlling and non-controlling interests on the same basis as that on which profit or loss is allocated. In this example, profit or loss is allocated on the basis of relative ownership interests. Because the goodwill is recognised only to the extent of Parent's 80 per cent ownership interest in Subsidiary, Parent recognises only 80 per cent of that goodwill impairment loss (ie CU400).

IE68   The remaining impairment loss of CU350 is recognised by reducing the carrying amounts of Subsidiary's identifiable assets (see Schedule 2).

Schedule 2. Allocation of the impairment loss for Subsidiary at the end of 20X3

End of 20X3	Goodwill	Net identifiable assets	Total
	CU	CU	CU
Carrying amount	400	1,350	1,750
Impairment loss	(400)	(350)	(750)
Carrying amount after impairment loss	–	1,000	1,000

Example 7B   Non-controlling interests measured initially at fair value and the related subsidiary is a stand-alone cash-generating unit

In this example, tax effects are ignored.

Background

IE68A   Parent acquires an 80 per cent ownership interest in Subsidiary for CU2,100 on 1 January 20X3. At that date, Subsidiary's net identifiable assets have a fair value of CU1,500. Parent chooses to measure the non-controlling interests at fair value, which is CU350. Goodwill of CU950 is the difference between the aggregate of the consideration transferred and the amount of the non-controlling interests (CU2,100 + CU350) and the net identifiable assets (CU1,500).

IE68B   The assets of Subsidiary together are the smallest group of assets that generate cash inflows that are largely independent of the cash inflows from other assets or groups of assets. Therefore, Subsidiary is a cash-generating unit. Because other cash-generating units of Parent are expected to benefit from the synergies of the combination, the goodwill of CU500 related to those synergies has been allocated to other cash-generating units within Parent. Because Subsidiary includes goodwill within its carrying amount, it must be tested for impairment annually, or more frequently if there is an indication that it might be impaired (see paragraph 90 of IAS 36).

Testing Subsidiary for impairment

IE68C   At the end of 20X3, Parent determines that the recoverable amount of cash-generating unit Subsidiary is CU1,650. The carrying amount of the net assets of Subsidiary, excluding goodwill, is CU1,350.

Schedule 1. Testing Subsidiary for impairment at the end of 20X3

End of 20X3	Goodwill	Net identifiable assets	Total
	CU	CU	CU
Carrying amount	450	1,350	1,800
Recoverable amount			1,650
Impairment loss			150

Allocating the impairment loss

IE68D   In accordance with paragraph 104 of IAS 36, the impairment loss of CU150 is allocated to the assets in the unit by first reducing the carrying amount of goodwill.

IE68E   Therefore, the full amount of impairment loss of CU150 for the unit is allocated to the goodwill. In accordance with paragraph C6 of Appendix C of IAS 36, if the partially-owned subsidiary is itself a cash-generating unit, the goodwill impairment loss is allocated to the controlling and non-controlling interests on the same basis as that on which profit or loss is allocated.

Example 7C   Non-controlling interests measured initially at fair value and the related subsidiary is part of a larger cash-generating unit

In this example, tax effects are ignored.

Background

IE68F   Suppose that, for the business combination described in paragraph IE68A of Example 7B, the assets of Subsidiary will generate cash inflows together with other assets or groups of assets of Parent. Therefore, rather than Subsidiary being the cash-generating unit for the purposes of impairment testing, Subsidiary becomes part of a larger cash-generating unit, Z. Other cash-generating units of Parent are also expected to benefit from the synergies of the combination. Therefore, goodwill related to those synergies, in the amount of CU500, has been allocated to those other cash-generating units. Z's goodwill related to previous business combinations is CU800.

IE68G   Because Z includes goodwill within its carrying amount, both from Subsidiary and from previous business combinations, it must be tested for impairment annually, or more frequently if there is an indication that it might be impaired (see paragraph 90 of IAS 36).

Testing Subsidiary for impairment

IE68H   At the end of 20X3, Parent determines that the recoverable amount of cash-generating unit Z is CU3,300. The carrying amount of the net assets of Z, excluding goodwill, is CU2,250.

Schedule 3. Testing Z for impairment at the end of 20X3

End of 20X3	Goodwill	Net identifiable assets	Total
	CU	CU	CU
Carrying amount	1,250	2,250	3,500
Recoverable amount			3,300
Impairment loss			200

Allocating the impairment loss

IE68I   In accordance with paragraph 104 of IAS 36, the impairment loss of CU200 is allocated to the assets in the unit by first reducing the carrying amount of goodwill. Therefore, the full amount of impairment loss of CU200 for cash-generating unit Z is allocated to the goodwill. In accordance with paragraph C7 of Appendix C of IAS 36, if the partially-owned Subsidiary forms part of a larger cash-generating unit, the goodwill impairment loss would be allocated first to the parts of the cash-generating unit, Z, and then to the controlling and non-controlling interests of the partially-owned Subsidiary.

IE68J   Parent allocates the impairment loss to the parts of the cash-generating unit on the basis of the relative carrying values of the goodwill of the parts before the impairment. In this example Subsidiary is allocated 36 per cent of the impairment (450/1,250). The impairment loss is then allocated to the controlling and non-controlling interests on the same basis as that on which profit or loss is allocated.

Example 8   Allocation of corporate assets

In this example, tax effects are ignored.

Background

IE69   Entity M has three cash-generating units: A, B and C. The carrying amounts of those units do not include goodwill. There are adverse changes in the technological environment in which M operates. Therefore, M conducts impairment tests of each of its cash-generating units. At the end of 20X0, the carrying amounts of A, B and C are CU100, CU150 and CU200 respectively.

IE70   The operations are conducted from a headquarters. The carrying amount of the headquarters is CU200: a headquarters building of CU150 and a research centre of CU50. The relative carrying amounts of the cash-generating units are a reasonable indication of the proportion of the headquarters building devoted to each cash-generating unit. The carrying amount of the research centre cannot be allocated on a reasonable basis to the individual cash-generating units.

IE71   The remaining estimated useful life of cash-generating unit A is 10 years. The remaining useful lives of B, C and the headquarters are 20 years. The headquarters is depreciated on a straight-line basis.

IE72   The recoverable amount (ie higher of value in use and fair value less costs to sell) of each cash-generating unit is based on its value in use. Value in use is calculated using a pre-tax discount rate of 15 per cent.

Identification of corporate assets

IE73   In accordance with paragraph 102 of IAS 36, M first identifies all the corporate assets that relate to the individual cash-generating units under review. The corporate assets are the headquarters building and the research centre.

IE74   M then decides how to deal with each of the corporate assets:

(a)   the carrying amount of the headquarters building can be allocated on a reasonable and consistent basis to the cash-generating units under review; and

(b)   the carrying amount of the research centre cannot be allocated on a reasonable and consistent basis to the individual cash-generating units under review.

Allocation of corporate assets

IE75   The carrying amount of the headquarters building is allocated to the carrying amount of each individual cash-generating unit. A weighted allocation basis is used because the estimated remaining useful life of A's cash-generating unit is 10 years, whereas the estimated remaining useful lives of B and C's cash-generating units are 20 years.

Schedule 1. Calculation of a weighted allocation of the carrying amount of the headquarters building

End of 20X0	A	B	C	Total
	CU	CU	CU	CU
Carrying amount	100	150	200	450
Useful life	10 years	20 years	20 years	
Weighting based on useful life	1	2	2	
Carrying amount after weighting	100	300	400	800
Pro-rata allocation of the building	12%	38%	50%	100%
	(100/800)	(300/800)	(400/800)	
Allocation of the carrying amount of the building (based on pro-rata above)	19	56	75	150
Carrying amount (after allocation of the building)	119	206	275	600

Determination of recoverable amount and calculation of impairment losses

IE76 Paragraph 102 of IAS 36 requires first that the recoverable amount of each individual cash-generating unit be compared with its carrying amount, including the portion of the carrying amount of the headquarters building allocated to the unit, and any resulting impairment loss recognised. Paragraph 102 of IAS 36 then requires the recoverable amount of M as a whole (ie the smallest group of cash-generating units that includes the research centre) to be compared with its carrying amount, including both the headquarters building and the research centre.

Schedule 2. Calculation of A, B, C and M's value in use at the end of 20X0

Year	A Future cash flows	A Discount at 15%	B Future cash flows	B Discount at 15%	C Future cash flows	C Discount at 15%	M Future cash flows	M Discount at 15%
	CU	CU	CU	CU	CU	CU	CU	CU
1	18	16	9	8	10	9	39	34
2	31	23	16	12	20	15	72	54
3	37	24	24	16	34	22	105	69
4	42	24	29	17	44	25	128	73
5	47	24	32	16	51	25	143	71
6	52	22	33	14	56	24	155	67
7	55	21	34	13	60	22	162	61
8	55	18	35	11	63	21	166	54
9	53	15	35	10	65	18	167	48
10	48	12	35	9	66	16	169	42
11			36	8	66	14	132	28
12			35	7	66	12	131	25
13			35	6	66	11	131	21
14			33	5	65	9	128	18
15			30	4	62	8	122	15
16			26	3	60	6	115	12
17			22	2	57	5	108	10
18			18	1	51	4	97	8
19			14	1	43	3	85	6
20			10	1	35	2	71	4
Value in use		199		164		271		720(a)

(a) It is assumed that the research centre generates additional future cash flows for the entity as a whole. Therefore, the sum of the value in use of each individual cash-generating unit is less than the value in use of the business as a whole. The additional cash flows are not attributable to the headquarters building.

Schedule 3. Impairment testing A, B and C

End of 20X0	A	B	C
	CU	CU	CU
Carrying amount (after allocation of the building) (Schedule 1)	119	206	275
Recoverable amount (Schedule 2)	199	164	271
Impairment loss	0	(42)	(4)

IE77   The next step is to allocate the impairment losses between the assets of the cash-generating units and the headquarters building.

Schedule 4. Allocation of the impairment losses for cash-generating units B and C

Cash-generating unit	B		C	
	CU		CU	
To headquarters building	(12)	$(42 \times {}^{56}\!/_{206})$	(1)	$(4 \times {}^{75}\!/_{275})$
To assets in cash-generating unit	(30)	$(42 \times {}^{150}\!/_{206})$	(3)	$(4 \times {}^{200}\!/_{275})$
	(42)		(4)	

IE78   Because the research centre could not be allocated on a reasonable and consistent basis to A, B and C's cash-generating units, M compares the carrying amount of the smallest group of cash-generating units to which the carrying amount of the research centre can be allocated (ie M as a whole) to its recoverable amount.

Schedule 5. Impairment testing the smallest group of cash-generating units to which the carrying amount of the research centre can be allocated (ie M as a whole)

End of 20X0	A	B	C	Building	Research centre	M
	CU	CU	CU	CU	CU	CU
Carrying amount	100	150	200	150	50	650
Impairment loss arising from the first step of the test	–	(30)	(3)	(13)	–	(46)
Carrying amount after the first step of the test	100	120	197	137	50	604
Recoverable amount (Schedule 2)						720
Impairment loss for the 'larger' cash-generating unit						0

IE79   Therefore, no additional impairment loss results from the application of the impairment test to M as a whole. Only an impairment loss of CU46 is recognised as a result of the application of the first step of the test to A, B and C.

Example 9 Disclosures about cash-generating units with goodwill or intangible assets with indefinite useful lives

The purpose of this example is to illustrate the disclosures required by paragraphs 134 and 135 of IAS 36.

Background

IE80   Entity M is a multinational manufacturing firm that uses geographical segments for reporting segment information. M's three reportable segments are Europe, North America and Asia. Goodwill has been allocated for impairment testing purposes to three individual cash-generating units—two in Europe (units A and B) and one in North America (unit C)—and to one group of cash-generating units (comprising operation XYZ) in Asia. Units A, B and C and operation XYZ each represent the lowest level within M at which the goodwill is monitored for internal management purposes.

IE81   M acquired unit C, a manufacturing operation in North America, in December 20X2. Unlike M's other North American operations, C operates in an industry with high margins and high growth rates, and with the benefit of a 10-year patent on its primary product. The patent was granted to C just before M's acquisition of C. As part of accounting for the acquisition of C, M recognised, in addition to the patent, goodwill of CU3,000 and a brand name of CU1,000. M's management has determined that the brand name has an indefinite useful life. M has no other intangible assets with indefinite useful lives.

IE82   The carrying amounts of goodwill and intangible assets with indefinite useful lives allocated to units A, B and C and to operation XYZ are as follows:

	Goodwill	Intangible assets with indefinite useful lives
	CU	CU
A	350	
B	450	
C	3,000	1,000
XYZ	1,200	
Total	5,000	1,000

IE83   During the year ending 31 December 20X3, M determines that there is no impairment of any of its cash-generating units or group of cash-generating units containing goodwill or intangible assets with indefinite useful lives. The recoverable amounts (ie higher of value in use and fair value less costs to sell)

of those units and group of units are determined on the basis of value in use calculations. M has determined that the recoverable amount calculations are most sensitive to changes in the following assumptions:

Units A and B	Unit C	Operation XYZ
Gross margin during the budget period (budget period is 4 years)	5-year US government bond rate during the budget period (budget period is 5 years)	Gross margin during the budget period (budget period is 5 years)
Raw materials price inflation during the budget period	Raw materials price inflation during the budget period	Japanese yen/US dollar exchange rate during the budget period
Market share during the budget period	Market share during the budget period	Market share during the budget period
Growth rate used to extrapolate cash flows beyond the budget period	Growth rate used to extrapolate cash flows beyond the budget period	Growth rate used to extrapolate cash flows beyond the budget period

IE84 Gross margins during the budget period for A, B and XYZ are estimated by M based on average gross margins achieved in the period immediately before the start of the budget period, increased by 5 per cent per year for anticipated efficiency improvements. A and B produce complementary products and are operated by M to achieve the same gross margins.

IE85 Market shares during the budget period are estimated by M based on average market shares achieved in the period immediately before the start of the budget period, adjusted each year for any anticipated growth or decline in market shares. M anticipates that:

(a) market shares for A and B will differ, but will each grow during the budget period by 3 per cent per year as a result of ongoing improvements in product quality.

(b) C's market share will grow during the budget period by 6 per cent per year as a result of increased advertising expenditure and the benefits from the protection of the 10-year patent on its primary product.

(c) XYZ's market share will remain unchanged during the budget period as a result of the combination of ongoing improvements in product quality and an anticipated increase in competition.

IE86 A and B purchase raw materials from the same European suppliers, whereas C's raw materials are purchased from various North American suppliers. Raw materials price inflation during the budget period is estimated by M to be consistent with forecast consumer price indices published by government agencies in the relevant European and North American countries.

IE87 The 5-year US government bond rate during the budget period is estimated by M to be consistent with the yield on such bonds at the beginning of the budget period. The Japanese yen/US dollar exchange rate is estimated by M to be consistent with the average market forward exchange rate over the budget period.

IE88   M uses steady growth rates to extrapolate beyond the budget period cash flows for A, B, C and XYX. The growth rates for A, B and XYZ are estimated by M to be consistent with publicly available information about the long-term average growth rates for the markets in which A, B and XYZ operate. However, the growth rate for C exceeds the long-term average growth rate for the market in which C operates. M's management is of the opinion that this is reasonable in the light of the protection of the 10-year patent on C's primary product.

IE89   M includes the following disclosure in the notes to its financial statements for the year ending 31 December 20X3.

Impairment Tests for Goodwill and Intangible Assets with Indefinite Lives

Goodwill has been allocated for impairment testing purposes to three individual cash-generating units—two in Europe (units A and B) and one in North America (unit C)—and to one group of cash-generating units (comprising operation XYZ) in Asia. The carrying amount of goodwill allocated to unit C and operation XYZ is significant in comparison with the total carrying amount of goodwill, but the carrying amount of goodwill allocated to each of units A and B is not. Nevertheless, the recoverable amounts of units A and B are based on some of the same key assumptions, and the aggregate carrying amount of goodwill allocated to those units is significant.

Operation XYZ

The recoverable amount of operation XYZ has been determined based on a value in use calculation. That calculation uses cash flow projections based on financial budgets approved by management covering a five-year period, and a discount rate of 8.4 per cent. Cash flows beyond that five-year period have been extrapolated using a steady 6.3 per cent growth rate. This growth rate does not exceed the long-term average growth rate for the market in which XYZ operates. Management believes that any reasonably possible change in the key assumptions on which XYZ's recoverable amount is based would *not* cause XYZ's carrying amount to exceed its recoverable amount.

Unit C

The recoverable amount of unit C has also been determined based on a value in use calculation. That calculation uses cash flow projections based on financial budgets approved by management covering a five-year period, and a discount rate of 9.2 per cent. C's cash flows beyond the five-year period are extrapolated using a steady 12 per cent growth rate. This growth rate exceeds by 4 percentage points the long-term average growth rate for the market in which C operates. However, C benefits from the protection of a 10-year patent on its primary product, granted in December 20X2. Management believes that a 12 per cent growth rate is reasonable in the light of that patent. Management also believes that any reasonably possible change in the key assumptions on which C's recoverable amount is based would *not* cause C's carrying amount to exceed its recoverable amount.

Units A and B

The recoverable amounts of units A and B have been determined on the basis of value in use calculations. Those units produce complementary products, and their recoverable amounts are based on some of the same key assumptions. Both value in use calculations use cash flow projections based on financial budgets approved by management covering a four-year period, and a discount rate of 7.9 per cent. Both sets of cash flows beyond the four-year period are extrapolated using a steady 5 per cent growth rate. This growth rate does not exceed the long-term average growth rate for the market in which A and B operate. Cash flow projections during the budget period for both A and B are also based on the same expected gross margins during the budget period and the same raw materials price inflation during the budget period. Management believes that any reasonably possible change in any of these key assumptions would *not* cause the aggregate carrying amount of A and B to exceed the aggregate recoverable amount of those units.

	Operation XYZ	Unit C	Units A and B (in aggregate)
Carrying amount of goodwill	CU1,200	CU3,000	CU800
Carrying amount of brand name with indefinite useful life	–	CU1,000	–
Key assumptions used in value in use calculations[a]			
• Key assumption	• Budgeted gross margins	• 5-year US government bond rate	• Budgeted gross margins
• Basis for determining value(s) assigned to key assumption	• Average gross margins achieved in period immediately before the budget period, increased for expected efficiency improvements.	• Yield on 5-year US government bonds at the beginning of the budget period.	• Average gross margins achieved in period immediately before the budget period, increased for expected efficiency improvements.
	• Values assigned to key assumption reflect past experience, except for efficiency improvements. Management believes improvements of 5% per year are reasonably achievable.	• Value assigned to key assumption is consistent with external sources of information	• Values assigned to key assumption reflect past experience, except for efficiency improvements. Management believes improvements of 5% per year are reasonably achievable.

continued...

...continued			
• Key assumption	• Japanese yen/ US dollar exchange rate during the budget period	• Raw materials price inflation	• Raw materials price inflation
• Basis for determining value(s) assigned to key assumption	• Average market forward exchange rate over the budget period.	• Forecast consumer price indices during the budget period for North American countries from which raw materials are purchased.	• Forecast consumer price indices during the budget period for European countries from which raw materials are purchased.
	• Value assigned to key assumption is consistent with external sources of information.	• Value assigned to key assumption is consistent with external sources of information.	• Value assigned to key assumption is consistent with external sources of information.
• Key assumption	• Budgeted market share	• Budgeted market share	
• Basis for determining value(s) assigned to key assumption	• Average market share in period immediately before the budget period.	• Average market share in period immediately before the budget period, increased each year for anticipated growth in market share.	
	• Value assigned to key assumption reflects past experience. No change in market share expected as a result of ongoing product quality improvements coupled with anticipated increase in competition.	• Management believes market share growth of 6% per year is reasonably achievable due to increased advertising expenditure, the benefits from the protection of the 10-year patent on C's primary product, and the expected synergies to be achieved from operating C as part of M's North American segment.	

(a) The key assumptions shown in this table for units A and B are only those that are used in the recoverable amount calculations for both units.

IASB documents published to accompany

International Accounting Standard 37

Provisions, Contingent Liabilities and Contingent Assets

This version includes amendments resulting from IFRSs issued up to 31 December 2009.

The text of the unaccompanied IAS 37 is contained in Part A of this edition. Its effective date when issued was 1 July 1999. The effective date of the most recent amendment is 1 July 2009. This part presents the following accompanying documents:

Guidance on implementing IAS 37 *Provisions, Contingent Liabilities and Contingent Assets*

This guidance accompanies, but is not part of, IAS 37.

A Tables – Provisions, contingent liabilities, contingent assets and reimbursements

The purpose of these tables is to summarise the main requirements of the Standard.

Provisions and contingent liabilities

Where, as a result of past events, there may be an outflow of resources embodying future economic benefits in settlement of: (a) a present obligation; or (b) a possible obligation whose existence will be confirmed only by the occurrence or non-occurrence of one or more uncertain future events not wholly within the control of the entity.		
There is a present obligation that probably requires an outflow of resources.	There is a possible obligation or a present obligation that may, but probably will not, require an outflow of resources.	There is a possible obligation or a present obligation where the likelihood of an outflow of resources is remote.
A provision is recognised (paragraph 14).	No provision is recognised (paragraph 27).	No provision is recognised (paragraph 27).
Disclosures are required for the provision (paragraphs 84 and 85).	Disclosures are required for the contingent liability (paragraph 86).	No disclosure is required (paragraph 86).

A contingent liability also arises in the extremely rare case where there is a liability that cannot be recognised because it cannot be measured reliably. Disclosures are required for the contingent liability.

Contingent assets

Where, as a result of past events, there is a possible asset whose existence will be confirmed only by the occurrence or non-occurrence of one or more uncertain future events not wholly within the control of the entity.		
The inflow of economic benefits is virtually certain.	The inflow of economic benefits is probable, but not virtually certain.	The inflow is not probable.
The asset is not contingent (paragraph 33).	No asset is recognised (paragraph 31).	No asset is recognised (paragraph 31).
	Disclosures are required (paragraph 89).	No disclosure is required (paragraph 89).

Reimbursements

Some or all of the expenditure required to settle a provision is expected to be reimbursed by another party.		
The entity has no obligation for the part of the expenditure to be reimbursed by the other party.	The obligation for the amount expected to be reimbursed remains with the entity and it is virtually certain that reimbursement will be received if the entity settles the provision.	The obligation for the amount expected to be reimbursed remains with the entity and the reimbursement is not virtually certain if the entity settles the provision.
The entity has no liability for the amount to be reimbursed (paragraph 57).	The reimbursement is recognised as a separate asset in the statement of financial position and may be offset against the expense in the statement of comprehensive income. The amount recognised for the expected reimbursement does not exceed the liability (paragraphs 53 and 54).	The expected reimbursement is not recognised as an asset (paragraph 53).
No disclosure is required.	The reimbursement is disclosed together with the amount recognised for the reimbursement (paragraph 85(c)).	The expected reimbursement is disclosed (paragraph 85(c)).

B   Decision tree

The purpose of this diagram is to summarise the main recognition requirements of the Standard for provisions and contingent liabilities.

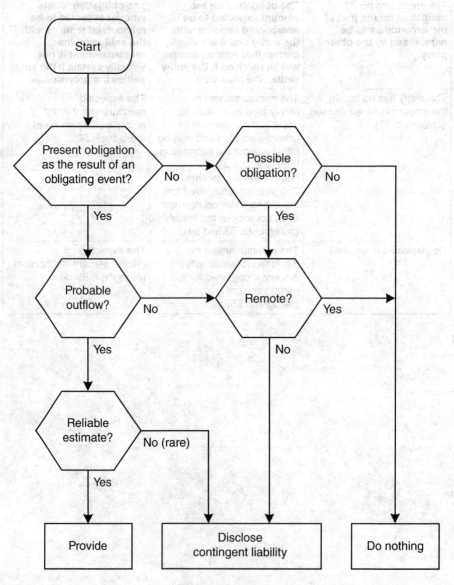

Note: in rare cases, it is not clear whether there is a present obligation. In these cases, a past event is deemed to give rise to a present obligation if, taking account of all available evidence, it is more likely than not that a present obligation exists at the end of the reporting period (paragraph 15 of the Standard).

C   Examples: recognition

All the entities in the examples have 31 December year-ends. In all cases, it is assumed that a reliable estimate can be made of any outflows expected. In some examples the circumstances described may have resulted in impairment of the assets—this aspect is not dealt with in the examples.

The cross-references provided in the examples indicate paragraphs of the Standard that are particularly relevant.

References to 'best estimate' are to the present value amount, where the effect of the time value of money is material.

Example 1 Warranties

A manufacturer gives warranties at the time of sale to purchasers of its product. Under the terms of the contract for sale the manufacturer undertakes to make good, by repair or replacement, manufacturing defects that become apparent within three years from the date of sale. On past experience, it is probable (ie more likely than not) that there will be some claims under the warranties.

Present obligation as a result of a past obligating event – The obligating event is the sale of the product with a warranty, which gives rise to a legal obligation.

An outflow of resources embodying economic benefits in settlement – Probable for the warranties as a whole (see paragraph 24).

Conclusion – A provision is recognised for the best estimate of the costs of making good under the warranty products sold before the end of the reporting period (see paragraphs 14 and 24).

Example 2A Contaminated land – legislation virtually certain to be enacted

An entity in the oil industry causes contamination but cleans up only when required to do so under the laws of the particular country in which it operates. One country in which it operates has had no legislation requiring cleaning up, and the entity has been contaminating land in that country for several years. At 31 December 20X0 it is virtually certain that a draft law requiring a clean-up of land already contaminated will be enacted shortly after the year-end.

Present obligation as a result of a past obligating event – The obligating event is the contamination of the land because of the virtual certainty of legislation requiring cleaning up.

An outflow of resources embodying economic benefits in settlement – Probable.

Conclusion – A provision is recognised for the best estimate of the costs of the clean-up (see paragraphs 14 and 22).

Example 2B Contaminated land and constructive obligation

An entity in the oil industry causes contamination and operates in a country where there is no environmental legislation. However, the entity has a widely published environmental policy in which it undertakes to clean up all contamination that it causes. The entity has a record of honouring this published policy.

Present obligation as a result of a past obligating event – The obligating event is the contamination of the land, which gives rise to a constructive obligation because the conduct of the entity has created a valid expectation on the part of those affected by it that the entity will clean up contamination.

An outflow of resources embodying economic benefits in settlement – Probable.

Conclusion – A provision is recognised for the best estimate of the costs of clean-up (see paragraphs 10 (the definition of a constructive obligation), 14 and 17).

Example 3 Offshore oilfield

An entity operates an offshore oilfield where its licensing agreement requires it to remove the oil rig at the end of production and restore the seabed. Ninety per cent of the eventual costs relate to the removal of the oil rig and restoration of damage caused by building it, and 10 per cent arise through the extraction of oil. At the end of the reporting period, the rig has been constructed but no oil has been extracted.

Present obligation as a result of a past obligating event – The construction of the oil rig creates a legal obligation under the terms of the licence to remove the rig and restore the seabed and is thus an obligating event. At the end of the reporting period, however, there is no obligation to rectify the damage that will be caused by extraction of the oil.

An outflow of resources embodying economic benefits in settlement – Probable.

Conclusion – A provision is recognised for the best estimate of ninety per cent of the eventual costs that relate to the removal of the oil rig and restoration of damage caused by building it (see paragraph 14). These costs are included as part of the cost of the oil rig. The 10 per cent of costs that arise through the extraction of oil are recognised as a liability when the oil is extracted.

Example 4 Refunds policy

A retail store has a policy of refunding purchases by dissatisfied customers, even though it is under no legal obligation to do so. Its policy of making refunds is generally known.

Present obligation as a result of a past obligating event – The obligating event is the sale of the product, which gives rise to a constructive obligation because the conduct of the store has created a valid expectation on the part of its customers that the store will refund purchases.

An outflow of resources embodying economic benefits in settlement – Probable, a proportion of goods are returned for refund (see paragraph 24).

Conclusion – A provision is recognised for the best estimate of the costs of refunds (see paragraphs 10 (the definition of a constructive obligation), 14, 17 and 24).

Example 5A Closure of a division – no implementation before end of the reporting period

On 12 December 20X0 the board of an entity decided to close down a division. Before the end of the reporting period (31 December 20X0) the decision was not communicated to any of those affected and no other steps were taken to implement the decision.

Present obligation as a result of a past obligating event – There has been no obligating event and so there is no obligation.

Conclusion – No provision is recognised (see paragraphs 14 and 72).

Example 5B Closure of a division – communication/implementation before end of the reporting period

On 12 December 20X0, the board of an entity decided to close down a division making a particular product. On 20 December 20X0 a detailed plan for closing down the division was agreed by the board; letters were sent to customers warning them to seek an alternative source of supply and redundancy notices were sent to the staff of the division.

Present obligation as a result of a past obligating event – The obligating event is the communication of the decision to the customers and employees, which gives rise to a constructive obligation from that date, because it creates a valid expectation that the division will be closed.

An outflow of resources embodying economic benefits in settlement – Probable.

Conclusion – A provision is recognised at 31 December 20X0 for the best estimate of the costs of closing the division (see paragraphs 14 and 72).

Example 6 Legal requirement to fit smoke filters

Under new legislation, an entity is required to fit smoke filters to its factories by 30 June 20X1. The entity has not fitted the smoke filters.

(a)   At 31 December 20X0, the end of the reporting period

Present obligation as a result of a past obligating event – There is no obligation because there is no obligating event either for the costs of fitting smoke filters or for fines under the legislation.

Conclusion – No provision is recognised for the cost of fitting the smoke filters (see paragraphs 14 and 17–19).

(b)   At 31 December 20X1, the end of the reporting period

Present obligation as a result of a past obligating event – There is still no obligation for the costs of fitting smoke filters because no obligating event has occurred (the fitting of the filters). However, an obligation might arise to pay fines or penalties under the legislation because the obligating event has occurred (the non-compliant operation of the factory).

An outflow of resources embodying economic benefits in settlement – Assessment of probability of incurring fines and penalties by non-compliant operation depends on the details of the legislation and the stringency of the enforcement regime.

Conclusion – No provision is recognised for the costs of fitting smoke filters. However, a provision is recognised for the best estimate of any fines and penalties that are more likely than not to be imposed (see paragraphs 14 and 17–19).

Example 7 Staff retraining as a result of changes in the income tax system

The government introduces a number of changes to the income tax system. As a result of these changes, an entity in the financial services sector will need to retrain a large proportion of its administrative and sales workforce in order to ensure continued compliance with financial services regulation. At the end of the reporting period, no retraining of staff has taken place.

Present obligation as a result of a past obligating event – There is no obligation because no obligating event (retraining) has taken place.

Conclusion – No provision is recognised (see paragraphs 14 and 17–19).

Example 8 An onerous contract

An entity operates profitably from a factory that it has leased under an operating lease. During December 20X0 the entity relocates its operations to a new factory. The lease on the old factory continues for the next four years, it cannot be cancelled and the factory cannot be re-let to another user.

Present obligation as a result of a past obligating event – The obligating event is the signing of the lease contract, which gives rise to a legal obligation.

An outflow of resources embodying economic benefits in settlement – When the lease becomes onerous, an outflow of resources embodying economic benefits is probable. (Until the lease becomes onerous, the entity accounts for the lease under IAS 17 *Leases*.)

Conclusion – A provision is recognised for the best estimate of the unavoidable lease payments (see paragraphs 5(c), 14 and 66).

Example 9 A single guarantee

On 31 December 20X0, Entity A gives a guarantee of certain borrowings of Entity B, whose financial condition at that time is sound. During 20X1, the financial condition of Entity B deteriorates and at 30 June 20X1 Entity B files for protection from its creditors.

This contract meets the definition of an insurance contract in IFRS 4 *Insurance Contracts*, but is within the scope of IAS 39 *Financial Instruments: Recognition and Measurement*, because it also meets the definition of a financial guarantee contract in IAS 39. If an issuer has previously asserted explicitly that it regards such contracts as insurance contracts and has used accounting applicable to insurance contracts, the issuer may elect to apply either IAS 39 or IFRS 4 to such financial guarantee contracts. IFRS 4 permits the issuer to continue its existing accounting policies for insurance contracts if specified minimum requirements are satisfied. IFRS 4 also permits changes in accounting policies that meet specified criteria. The following is an example of an accounting policy that IFRS 4 permits and that also complies with the requirements in IAS 39 for financial guarantee contracts within the scope of IAS 39.

(a)   At 31 December 20X0

Present obligation as a result of a past obligating event – The obligating event is the giving of the guarantee, which gives rise to a legal obligation.

An outflow of resources embodying economic benefits in settlement – No outflow of benefits is probable at 31 December 20X0.

Conclusion – The guarantee is recognised at fair value.

(b)   At 31 December 20X1

Present obligation as a result of a past obligating event – The obligating event is the giving of the guarantee, which gives rise to a legal obligation.

An outflow of resources embodying economic benefits in settlement – At 31 December 20X1, it is probable that an outflow of resources embodying economic benefits will be required to settle the obligation.

Conclusion – The guarantee is subsequently measured at the higher of (a) the best estimate of the obligation (see paragraphs 14 and 23), and (b) the amount initially recognised less, when appropriate, cumulative amortisation in accordance with IAS 18 *Revenue*.

Example 10 A court case

After a wedding in 20X0, ten people died, possibly as a result of food poisoning from products sold by the entity. Legal proceedings are started seeking damages from the entity but it disputes liability. Up to the date of authorisation of the financial statements for the year to 31 December 20X0 for issue, the entity's lawyers advise that it is probable that the entity will not be found liable. However, when the entity prepares the financial statements for the year to 31 December 20X1, its lawyers advise that, owing to developments in the case, it is probable that the entity will be found liable.

(a)   At 31 December 20X0

Present obligation as a result of a past obligating event – On the basis of the evidence available when the financial statements were approved, there is no obligation as a result of past events.

Conclusion – No provision is recognised (see paragraphs 15 and 16). The matter is disclosed as a contingent liability unless the probability of any outflow is regarded as remote (paragraph 86).

(b)   At 31 December 20X1

Present obligation as a result of a past obligating event – On the basis of the evidence available, there is a present obligation.

An outflow of resources embodying economic benefits in settlement – Probable.

Conclusion – A provision is recognised for the best estimate of the amount to settle the obligation (paragraphs 14–16).

Example 11 Repairs and maintenance

Some assets require, in addition to routine maintenance, substantial expenditure every few years for major refits or refurbishment and the replacement of major components. IAS 16 *Property, Plant and Equipment* gives guidance on allocating expenditure on an asset to its component parts where these components have different useful lives or provide benefits in a different pattern.

Example 11A Refurbishment costs – no legislative requirement

A furnace has a lining that needs to be replaced every five years for technical reasons. At the end of the reporting period, the lining has been in use for three years.

Present obligation as a result of a past obligating event – There is no present obligation.

Conclusion – No provision is recognised (see paragraphs 14 and 17–19).

The cost of replacing the lining is not recognised because, at the end of the reporting period, no obligation to replace the lining exists independently of the company's future actions—even the intention to incur the expenditure depends on the company deciding to continue operating the furnace or to replace the lining. Instead of a provision being recognised, the depreciation of the lining takes account of its consumption, ie it is depreciated over five years. The re-lining costs then incurred are capitalised with the consumption of each new lining shown by depreciation over the subsequent five years.

Example 11B Refurbishment costs – legislative requirement

An airline is required by law to overhaul its aircraft once every three years.

Present obligation as a result of a past obligating event – There is no present obligation.

Conclusion – No provision is recognised (see paragraphs 14 and 17–19).

The costs of overhauling aircraft are not recognised as a provision for the same reasons as the cost of replacing the lining is not recognised as a provision in example 11A. Even a legal requirement to overhaul does not make the costs of overhaul a liability, because no obligation exists to overhaul the aircraft independently of the entity's future actions—the entity could avoid the future expenditure by its future actions, for example by selling the aircraft. Instead of a provision being recognised, the depreciation of the aircraft takes account of the future incidence of maintenance costs, ie an amount equivalent to the expected maintenance costs is depreciated over three years.

D Examples: disclosures

Two examples of the disclosures required by paragraph 85 are provided below.

Example 1 Warranties

A manufacturer gives warranties at the time of sale to purchasers of its three product lines. Under the terms of the warranty, the manufacturer undertakes to repair or replace items that fail to perform satisfactorily for two years from the date of sale. At the end of the reporting period, a provision of 60,000 has been recognised. The provision has not been discounted as the effect of discounting is not material. The following information is disclosed:

A provision of 60,000 has been recognised for expected warranty claims on products sold during the last three financial years. It is expected that the majority of this expenditure will be incurred in the next financial year, and all will be incurred within two years after the reporting period.

Example 2 Decommissioning costs

In 2000, an entity involved in nuclear activities recognises a provision for decommissioning costs of 300 million. The provision is estimated using the assumption that decommissioning will take place in 60–70 years' time. However, there is a possibility that it will not take place until 100–110 years' time, in which case the present value of the costs will be significantly reduced. The following information is disclosed:

A provision of 300 million has been recognised for decommissioning costs. These costs are expected to be incurred between 2060 and 2070; however, there is a possibility that decommissioning will not take place until 2100–2110. If the costs were measured based upon the expectation that they would not be incurred until 2100–2110 the provision would be reduced to 136 million. The provision has been estimated using existing technology, at current prices, and discounted using a real discount rate of 2 per cent.

An example is given below of the disclosures required by paragraph 92 where some of the information required is not given because it can be expected to prejudice seriously the position of the entity.

Example 3 Disclosure exemption

An entity is involved in a dispute with a competitor, who is alleging that the entity has infringed patents and is seeking damages of 100 million. The entity recognises a provision for its best estimate of the obligation, but discloses none of the information required by paragraphs 84 and 85 of the Standard. The following information is disclosed:

Litigation is in process against the company relating to a dispute with a competitor who alleges that the company has infringed patents and is seeking damages of 100 million. The information usually required by IAS 37 Provisions, Contingent Liabilities and Contingent Assets *is not disclosed on the grounds that it can be expected to prejudice seriously the outcome of the litigation. The directors are of the opinion that the claim can be successfully resisted by the company.*

IASB documents published to accompany

International Accounting Standard 38

Intangible Assets

This version includes amendments resulting from IFRSs issued up to 31 December 2009.

The text of the unaccompanied IAS 38 is contained in Part A of this edition. Its effective date when issued was 31 March 2004. The effective date of the most recent amendments is 1 July 2009. This part presents the following accompanying documents:

Approval by the Board of IAS 38 issued in March 2004

International Accounting Standard 38 *Intangible Assets* (as revised in 2004) was approved for issue by thirteen of the fourteen members of the International Accounting Standards Board. Professor Whittington dissented. His dissenting opinion is set out after the Basis for Conclusions.

Sir David Tweedie	Chairman
Thomas E Jones	Vice-Chairman
Mary E Barth	
Hans-Georg Bruns	
Anthony T Cope	
Robert P Garnett	
Gilbert Gélard	
James J Leisenring	
Warren J McGregor	
Patricia L O'Malley	
Harry K Schmid	
John T Smith	
Geoffrey Whittington	
Tatsumi Yamada	

CONTENTS

Basis for Conclusions on
IAS 38 *Intangible Assets*

The International Accounting Standards Board revised IAS 38 as part of its project on business combinations. It was not the Board's intention to reconsider as part of that project all of the requirements in IAS 38.

The previous version of IAS 38 was accompanied by a Basis for Conclusions summarising the former International Accounting Standards Committee's considerations in reaching some of its conclusions in that Standard. For convenience the Board has incorporated into its own Basis for Conclusions material from the previous Basis for Conclusions that discusses (a) matters the Board did not reconsider and (b) the history of the development of a standard on intangible assets. That material is contained in paragraphs denoted by numbers with the prefix BCZ. Paragraphs describing the Board's considerations in reaching its own conclusions are numbered with the prefix BC.

Introduction

BC1   This Basis for Conclusions summarises the International Accounting Standards Board's considerations in reaching the conclusions in IAS 38 *Intangible Assets*. Individual Board members gave greater weight to some factors than to others.

BC2   The International Accounting Standards Committee (IASC) issued the previous version of IAS 38 in 1998. It has been revised by the Board as part of its project on business combinations. That project has two phases. The first has resulted in the Board issuing simultaneously IFRS 3 *Business Combinations* and revised versions of IAS 38 and IAS 36 *Impairment of Assets*. Therefore, the Board's intention in revising IAS 38 as part of the first phase of the project was not to reconsider all of the requirements in IAS 38. The changes to IAS 38 are primarily concerned with:

(a)   the notion of 'identifiability' as it relates to intangible assets;

(b)   the useful life and amortisation of intangible assets; and

(c)   the accounting for in-process research and development projects acquired in business combinations.

BC3   With the exception of research and development projects acquired in business combinations, the Board did not reconsider the requirements in the previous version of IAS 38 on the recognition of internally generated intangible assets. The previous version of IAS 38 was accompanied by a Basis for Conclusions summarising IASC's considerations in reaching some of its conclusions in that Standard. For convenience, the Board has incorporated into this Basis for Conclusions material from the previous Basis for Conclusions that discusses the recognition of internally generated intangible assets (see paragraphs BCZ29– BCZ46) and the history of the development of a standard on intangible assets (see paragraphs BCZ104–BCZ110). The views expressed in paragraphs BCZ29– BCZ46 and BCZ104–BCZ110 are those of IASC.

Definition of an intangible asset (paragraph 8)

BC4 An intangible asset was defined in the previous version of IAS 38 as 'an identifiable non-monetary asset without physical substance held for use in the production or supply of goods or services, for rental to others, or for administrative services'. The definition in the revised Standard eliminates the requirement for the asset to be held for use in the production or supply of goods or services, for rental to others, or for administrative services.

BC5 The Board observed that the essential characteristics of intangible assets are that they:

(a) are resources controlled by the entity from which future economic benefits are expected to flow to the entity;

(b) lack physical substance; and

(c) are identifiable.

The Board concluded that the purpose for which an entity holds an item with these characteristics is not relevant to its classification as an intangible asset, and that all such items should be within the scope of the Standard.

Identifiability (paragraph 12)

BC6 Under the Standard, as under the previous version of IAS 38, a non-monetary asset without physical substance must be identifiable to meet the definition of an intangible asset. The previous version of IAS 38 did not define 'identifiability', but stated that an intangible asset could be distinguished from goodwill if the asset was separable, but that separability was not a necessary condition for identifiability. The revised Standard requires an asset to be treated as meeting the identifiability criterion in the definition of an intangible asset when it is separable, or when it arises from contractual or other legal rights, regardless of whether those rights are transferable or separable from the entity or from other rights and obligations.

Background to the Board's deliberations

BC7 The Board was prompted to consider the issue of 'identifiability' as part of the first phase of its Business Combinations project as a result of changes during 2001 to the requirements in Canadian and United States standards on the separate recognition of intangible assets acquired in business combinations. The Board observed that intangible assets comprise an increasing proportion of the assets of many entities, and that intangible assets acquired in a business combination are often included in the amount recognised as goodwill, despite the requirements in IAS 22 *Business Combinations* and IAS 38 for them to be recognised separately from goodwill. The Board agreed with the conclusion reached by the Canadian and US standard-setters that the usefulness of financial statements would be enhanced if intangible assets acquired in a business combination were distinguished from goodwill. Therefore, the Board concluded that the IFRS arising from the first phase of the Business Combinations project should provide a definitive basis for identifying and recognising intangible assets acquired in a business combination separately from goodwill.

BC8   In revising IAS 38 and developing IFRS 3, the Board affirmed the view in the previous version of IAS 38 that identifiability is the characteristic that conceptually distinguishes other intangible assets from goodwill. The Board concluded that to provide a definitive basis for identifying and recognising intangible assets separately from goodwill, the concept of identifiability needed to be articulated more clearly.

Clarifying identifiability (paragraph 12)

BC9   Consistently with the guidance in the previous version of IAS 38, the Board concluded that an intangible asset can be distinguished from goodwill if it is separable, ie capable of being separated or divided from the entity and sold, transferred, licensed, rented or exchanged. Therefore, in the context of intangible assets, separability signifies identifiability, and intangible assets with that characteristic that are acquired in a business combination should be recognised as assets separately from goodwill.

BC10   However, again consistently with the guidance in the previous version of IAS 38, the Board concluded that separability is not the only indication of identifiability. The Board observed that, in contrast to goodwill, the values of many intangible assets arise from rights conveyed legally by contract or statute. In the case of acquired goodwill, its value arises from the collection of assembled assets that make up an acquired entity or the value created by assembling a collection of assets through a business combination, such as the synergies that are expected to result from combining entities or businesses. The Board also observed that, although many intangible assets are both separable and arise from contractual-legal rights, some contractual-legal rights establish property interests that are not readily separable from the entity as a whole. For example, under the laws of some jurisdictions some licences granted to an entity are not transferable except by sale of the entity as a whole. The Board concluded that the fact that an intangible asset arises from contractual or other legal rights is a characteristic that distinguishes it from goodwill. Therefore, intangible assets with that characteristic that are acquired in a business combination should be recognised as assets separately from goodwill.

Non-contractual customer relationships (paragraph 16)

BC11   The previous version of IAS 38 and the Exposure Draft of Proposed Amendments to IAS 38 stated that 'An entity controls an asset if the entity has the power to obtain the future economic benefits flowing from the underlying resource and also can restrict the access of others to those benefits.' The documents then expanded on this by stating that 'in the absence of legal rights to protect, or other ways to control, the relationships with customers or the loyalty of the customers to the entity, the entity usually has insufficient control over the economic benefits from customer relationships and loyalty to consider that such items meet the definition of intangible assets.'

BC12   However, the Draft Illustrative Examples accompanying ED 3 *Business Combinations* stated that 'If a customer relationship acquired in a business combination does not arise from a contract, the relationship is recognised as an intangible asset separately from goodwill if it meets the separability criterion. Exchange transactions for the same asset or a similar asset provide evidence of separability of a non-contractual customer relationship and might also provide information about exchange prices that should be considered when estimating fair value.' Whilst respondents to the Exposure Draft generally agreed with the Board's conclusions on the definition of identifiability, some were uncertain about the relationship between the separability criterion for establishing whether a non-contractual customer relationship is identifiable, and the control concept for establishing whether the relationship meets the definition of an asset. Additionally, some respondents suggested that non-contractual customer relationships would, under the proposal in the Exposure Draft, be separately recognised if acquired in a business combination, but not if acquired in a separate transaction.

BC13 The Board observed that exchange transactions for the same or similar non-contractual customer relationships provide evidence not only that the item is separable, but also that the entity is able to control the expected future economic benefits flowing from that relationship. Similarly, if an entity separately acquires a non-contractual customer relationship, the existence of an exchange transaction for that relationship provides evidence both that the item is separable, and that the entity is able to control the expected future economic benefits flowing from the relationship. Therefore, the relationship would meet the intangible asset definition and be recognised as such. However, in the absence of exchange transactions for the same or similar non-contractual customer relationships, such relationships acquired in a business combination would not normally meet the definition of an 'intangible asset'—they would not be separable, nor would the entity be able to demonstrate that it controls the expected future economic benefits flowing from that relationship.

BC14 Therefore, the Board decided to clarify in paragraph 16 of IAS 38 that in the absence of legal rights to protect customer relationships, exchange transactions for the same or similar non-contractual customer relationships (other than as part of a business combination) provide evidence that the entity is nonetheless able to control the future economic benefits flowing from the customer relationships. Because such exchange transactions also provide evidence that the customer relationships are separable, those customer relationships meet the definition of an intangible asset.

Criteria for initial recognition

BC15 In accordance with the Standard, as with the previous version of IAS 38, an intangible asset is recognised if, and only if:

(a) it is probable that the expected future economic benefits that are attributable to the asset will flow to the entity; and

(b) the cost of the asset can be measured reliably.

In revising IAS 38 the Board considered the application of these recognition criteria to intangible assets acquired in business combinations. The Board's deliberations on this issue are set out in paragraphs BC16–BC25.

Acquisition as part of a business combination (paragraphs 33–38)

BC16   [Deleted]

BC16A   The Board observed that in a business combination both criteria, the probability criterion and the reliability of measurement criterion, will always be met.

Probability recognition criterion

BC17   In revising IAS 38, the Board observed that the fair value of an intangible asset reflects market expectations about the probability that the future economic benefits associated with the intangible asset will flow to the acquirer. In other words, the effect of probability is reflected in the fair value measurement of an intangible asset. Therefore, the probability recognition criterion is always considered to be satisfied for intangible assets acquired in business combinations.

BC18   The Board observed that this highlights a general inconsistency between the recognition criteria for assets and liabilities in the *Framework* (which states that an item meeting the definition of an element should be recognised only if it is probable that any future economic benefits associated with the item will flow to or from the entity, and the item can be measured reliably) and the fair value measurements required in, for example, a business combination. However, the Board concluded that the role of probability as a criterion for recognition in the *Framework* should be considered more generally as part of a forthcoming Concepts project.

Reliability of measurement recognition criterion

BC19   [Deleted]

BC19A   In developing IFRS 3, the IASB noted that the fair values of identifiable intangible assets acquired in a business combination are normally measurable with sufficient reliability to be recognised separately from goodwill. The effects of uncertainty because of a range of possible outcomes with different probabilities are reflected in measuring the asset's fair value; the existence of such a range does not demonstrate an inability to measure fair value reliably. IAS 38 (as revised in 2004) included a rebuttable presumption that the fair value of an intangible asset with a finite useful life acquired in a business combination can be measured reliably. The Board had concluded that it might not always be possible to measure reliably the fair value of an asset that has an underlying contractual or legal basis. However, IAS 38 (revised 2004) provided that the only circumstances in which it might not be possible to measure reliably the fair value of an intangible asset acquired in a business combination that arises from legal or other contractual rights were if it either:

(a)   is not separable; or

(b)   is separable, but there is no history or evidence of exchange transactions for the same or similar assets, and otherwise estimating fair value would depend on immeasurable variables.

BC19B   In developing the 2005 Business Combinations exposure draft, the Board concluded that separate recognition of intangible assets, on the basis of an estimate of fair value, rather than subsuming them in goodwill, provides better information to the users of financial statements even if a significant degree of judgement is required to estimate fair value. For this reason, the Board decided to propose consequential amendments to IAS 38 to remove the reliability of measurement criterion for intangible assets acquired in a business combination. In redeliberating the proposals in the 2005 Business Combinations exposure draft, the Board affirmed those amendments to IAS 38.

BC19C   When the Board developed IFRS 3 (as revised in 2008), it decided that if an intangible asset acquired in a business combination is separable or arises from contractual or other legal rights, sufficient information exists to measure the fair value of the asset reliably. The Board made related amendments to IAS 38 to reflect that decision. However, the Board identified additional amendments that were needed to reflect clearly its decisions on the accounting for intangible assets acquired in a business combination. Consequently, in *Improvements to IFRSs* issued in April 2009, the Board amended paragraphs 36 and 37 of IAS 38 to clarify the Board's intentions.

BC19D   Additionally, in *Improvements to IFRSs* issued in April 2009, the Board amended paragraphs 40 and 41 of IAS 38 to clarify the description of valuation techniques commonly used to measure intangible assets at fair value when assets are not traded in an active market. The Board also decided that the amendments should be applied prospectively because retrospective application might require some entities to remeasure fair values associated with previous transactions. The Board does not think this is appropriate because the remeasurement might involve the use of hindsight in those circumstances.

BC20– [Deleted]
BC25

Separate acquisition (paragraphs 25 and 26)

BC26   Having decided to include paragraphs 33–38 in IAS 38, the Board also decided that it needed to consider the role of the probability and reliability of measurement recognition criteria for separately acquired intangible assets.

BC27   Consistently with its conclusion about the role of probability in the recognition of intangible assets acquired in business combinations, the Board concluded that the probability recognition criterion is always considered to be satisfied for separately acquired intangible assets. This is because the price an entity pays to acquire separately an intangible asset normally reflects expectations about the probability that the expected future economic benefits associated with the intangible asset will flow to the entity. In other words, the effect of probability is reflected in the cost of the intangible asset.

BC28   The Board also concluded that when an intangible asset is separately acquired in exchange for cash or other monetary assets, sufficient information should exist to measure the cost of that asset reliably. However, this might not be the case when the purchase consideration comprises non-monetary assets. Therefore, the Board decided to carry forward from the previous version of IAS 38 guidance clarifying that the cost of a separately acquired intangible asset can usually be measured reliably, particularly when the purchase consideration is cash or other monetary assets.

Internally generated intangible assets (paragraphs 51–67)

BCZ29   The controversy relating to internally generated intangible assets surrounds whether there should be:

     (a)   a requirement to recognise internally generated intangible assets in the balance sheet whenever certain criteria are met;

     (b)   a requirement to recognise expenditure on all internally generated intangible assets as an expense;

     (c)   a requirement to recognise expenditure on all internally generated intangible assets as an expense, with certain specified exceptions; or

     (d)   an option to choose between the treatments described in (a) and (b) above.

Background on the requirements for internally generated intangible assets

BCZ30   Before IAS 38 was issued in 1998, some internally generated intangible assets (those that arose from development expenditure) were dealt with under IAS 9 *Research and Development Costs*. The development of, and revisions to, IAS 9 had always been controversial.

BCZ31   Proposed and approved requirements for the recognition of an asset arising from development expenditure and other internally generated intangible assets had been the following:

     (a)   in 1978, IASC approved IAS 9 *Accounting for Research and Development Activities*. It required expenditure on research and development to be recognised as an expense when incurred, except that an enterprise had the option to recognise an asset arising from development expenditure whenever certain criteria were met.

     (b)   in 1989, Exposure Draft E32 *Comparability of Financial Statements* proposed retaining IAS 9's option to recognise an asset arising from development expenditure if certain criteria were met and identifying:

         (i)   as a preferred treatment, recognising all expenditure on research and development as an expense when incurred; and

         (ii)   as an allowed alternative treatment, recognising an asset arising from development expenditure whenever certain criteria were met.

     The majority of commentators on E32 did not support maintaining an option or the proposed preferred treatment.

     (c)   in 1991, Exposure Draft E37 *Research and Development Costs* proposed requiring the recognition of an asset arising from development expenditure whenever certain criteria were met. In 1993, IASC approved IAS 9 *Research and Development Costs* based on E37.

     (d)   in 1995, consistently with IAS 9, Exposure Draft E50 *Intangible Assets* proposed requiring internally generated intangible assets—other than those arising from development expenditure, which would still have been covered by IAS 9—to be recognised as assets whenever certain criteria were met.

(e) in 1997, Exposure Draft E60 *Intangible Assets* proposed:

    (i) retaining E50's proposals for the recognition of internally generated intangible assets; but

    (ii) extending the scope of the Standard on intangible assets to deal with all internally generated intangible assets—including those arising from development expenditure.

(f) in 1998, IASC approved:

    (i) IAS 38 *Intangible Assets* based on E60, with a few minor changes; and

    (ii) the withdrawal of IAS 9.

BCZ32 From 1989, the majority view at IASC and from commentators was that there should be only one treatment that would require an internally generated intangible asset—whether arising from development expenditure or other expenditure—to be recognised as an asset whenever certain recognition criteria are met. Several minority views were strongly opposed to this treatment but there was no clear consensus on any other single treatment.

Combination of IAS 9 with the Standard on intangible assets

BCZ33 The reasons for not retaining IAS 9 as a separate Standard were that:

(a) IASC believed that an identifiable asset that results from research and development activities is an intangible asset because knowledge is the primary outcome of these activities. Therefore, IASC supported treating expenditure on research and development activities similarly to expenditure on activities intended to create any other internally generated intangible assets.

(b) some commentators on E50, which proposed to exclude research and development expenditures from its scope,

    (i) argued that it was sometimes difficult to identify whether IAS 9 or the proposed Standard on intangible assets should apply, and

    (ii) perceived differences in accounting treatments between IAS 9 and E50's proposals, whereas this was not IASC's intent.

BCZ34 A large majority of commentators on E60 supported including certain aspects of IAS 9 with the proposed Standard on intangible assets and the withdrawal of IAS 9. A minority of commentators on E60 supported maintaining two separate Standards. This minority supported the view that internally generated intangible assets should be dealt with on a case-by-case basis with separate requirements for different types of internally generated intangible assets. These commentators argued that E60's proposed recognition criteria were too general to be effective in practice for all internally generated intangible assets.

BCZ35 IASC rejected a proposal to develop separate standards (or detailed requirements within one standard) for specific types of internally generated intangible assets because, as explained above, IASC believed that the same recognition criteria should apply to all types of internally generated intangible assets.

Consequences of combining IAS 9 with IAS 38

BCZ36   The requirements in IAS 38 and IAS 9 differ in the following main respects:

(a)   IAS 9 limited the amount of expenditure that could initially be recognised for an asset arising from development expenditure (ie the amount that formed the cost of such an asset) to the amount that was probable of being recovered from the asset. Instead, IAS 38 requires that:

(i)   all expenditure incurred from when the recognition criteria are met until the asset is available for use should be accumulated to form the cost of the asset; and

(ii)   an enterprise should test for impairment, at least annually, an intangible asset that is not yet available for use. If the cost recognised for the asset exceeds its recoverable amount, an enterprise recognises an impairment loss accordingly. This impairment loss should be reversed if the conditions for reversals of impairment losses under IAS 36 *Impairment of Assets* are met.

(b)   IAS 38 permits an intangible asset to be measured after recognition at a revalued amount less subsequent amortisation and subsequent impairment losses. IAS 9 did not permit this treatment. However, it is highly unlikely that an active market (the condition required to revalue intangible assets) will exist for an asset that arises from development expenditure.

(c)   IAS 38 requires consideration of residual values in determining the depreciable amount of an intangible asset. IAS 9 prohibited the consideration of residual values. However, IAS 38 sets criteria that make it highly unlikely that an asset that arises from development expenditure would have a residual value above zero.

BCZ37   IASC believed that, in practice, it would be unlikely that the application of IAS 38 would result in differences from the application of IAS 9.

Recognition of expenditure on all internally generated intangible assets as an expense

BCZ38   Those who favour the recognition of expenditure on all internally generated intangible assets (including development expenditure) as an expense argue that:

(a)   internally generated intangible assets do not meet the *Framework*'s requirements for recognition as an asset because:

(i)   the future economic benefits that arise from internally generated intangible assets cannot be distinguished from future economic benefits that arise from internally generated goodwill; and/or

(ii)   it is impossible to distinguish reliably the expenditure associated with internally generated intangible assets from the expenditure associated with enhancing internally generated goodwill.

(b) comparability of financial statements will not be achieved. This is because the judgement involved in determining whether it is probable that future economic benefits will flow from internally generated intangible assets is too subjective to result in similar accounting under similar circumstances.

(c) it is not possible to assess reliably the amount that can be recovered from an internally generated intangible asset, unless its fair value can be determined by reference to an active market. Therefore, recognising an internally generated intangible asset for which no active market exists at an amount other than zero may mislead investors.

(d) a requirement to recognise internally generated intangible assets at cost if certain criteria are met results in little, if any, decision-useful or predictive information because:

   (i) demonstration of technological feasibility or commercial success in order to meet the recognition criteria will generally not be achieved until substantial expenditure has been recognised as an expense. Therefore, the cost recognised for an internally generated intangible asset will not reflect the total expenditure on that asset.

   (ii) the cost of an internally generated intangible asset may not have any relationship to the value of the asset.

(e) in some countries, users are suspicious about an enterprise that recognises internally generated intangible assets.

(f) the added costs of maintaining the records necessary to justify and support the recognition of internally generated intangible assets do not justify the benefits.

Recognition of internally generated intangible assets

BCZ39 Those who support the mandatory recognition of internally generated intangible assets (including those resulting from development expenditure) whenever certain criteria are met argue that:

(a) recognition of an internally generated intangible asset if it meets the definition of an asset and the recognition criteria is consistent with the *Framework*. An enterprise can, in some instances:

   (i) determine the probability of receiving future economic benefits from an internally generated intangible asset; and

   (ii) distinguish the expenditure on this asset from expenditure on internally generated goodwill.

(b) there has been massive investment in intangible assets in the last two decades. There have been complaints that:

   (i) the non-recognition of investments in intangible assets in the financial statements distorts the measurement of an enterprise's performance and does not allow an accurate assessment of returns on investment in intangible assets; and

        (ii)   if enterprises do not track the returns on investment in intangible assets better, there is a risk of over- or under-investing in important assets. An accounting system that encourages such behaviour will become an increasingly inadequate signal, both for internal control purposes and for external purposes.

    (c)   certain research studies, particularly in the United States, have established a cost-value association for research and development expenditures. The studies establish that capitalisation of research and development expenditure yields value-relevant information to investors.

    (d)   the fact that some uncertainties exist about the value of an asset does not justify a requirement that no cost should be recognised for the asset.

    (e)   it should not matter for recognition purposes whether an asset is purchased externally or developed internally. Particularly, there should be no opportunity for accounting arbitrage depending on whether an enterprise decides to outsource the development of an intangible asset or develop it internally.

IASC's view in approving IAS 38

BCZ40   IASC's view—consistently reflected in previous proposals for intangible assets—was that there should be no difference between the requirements for:

    (a)   intangible assets that are acquired externally; and

    (b)   internally generated intangible assets, whether they arise from development activities or other types of activities.

Therefore, an internally generated intangible asset should be recognised whenever the definition of, and recognition criteria for, an intangible asset are met. This view was also supported by a majority of commentators on E60.

BCZ41   IASC rejected a proposal for an allowed alternative to recognise expenditure on internally generated intangible assets (including development expenditure) as an expense immediately, even if the expenditure results in an asset that meets the recognition criteria. IASC believed that a free choice would undermine the comparability of financial statements and the efforts of IASC to reduce the number of alternative treatments in International Accounting Standards.

Differences in recognition criteria for internally generated intangible assets and purchased intangible assets

BCZ42   IAS 38 includes specific recognition criteria for internally generated intangible assets that expand on the general recognition criteria for intangible assets. It is assumed that these criteria are met implicitly whenever an enterprise acquires an intangible asset. Therefore, IAS 38 requires an enterprise to demonstrate that these criteria are met for internally generated intangible assets only.

Initial recognition at cost

BCZ43 Some commentators on E50 and E60 argued that the proposed recognition criteria in E50 and E60 were too restrictive and that they would prevent the recognition of many intangible assets, particularly internally generated intangible assets. Specifically, they disagreed with the proposals (retained in IAS 38) that:

(a) an intangible asset should not be recognised at an amount other than its cost, even if its fair value can be determined reliably; and

(b) expenditure on an intangible asset that has been recognised as an expense in prior periods should not be reinstated.

They argued that these principles contradict the *Framework* and quoted paragraph 83 of the *Framework*, which specifies that an item that meets the definition of an asset should be recognised if, among other things, its '*cost or value* can be measured with reliability'. These commentators supported recognising an intangible asset—an internally generated intangible asset—at its fair value, if, among other things, its fair value can be measured reliably.

BCZ44 IASC rejected a proposal to allow the initial recognition of an intangible asset at fair value (except if the asset is acquired in a business combination, in exchange for a dissimilar asset* or by way of a government grant) because:

(a) this is consistent with IAS 16 *Property, Plant and Equipment*. IAS 16 prohibits the initial recognition of an item of property, plant or equipment at fair value (except in the specific limited cases as those in IAS 38).

(b) it is difficult to determine the fair value of an intangible asset reliably if no active market exists for the asset. Since active markets with the characteristics set out in IAS 38 are highly unlikely to exist for internally generated intangible assets, IASC did not believe that it was necessary to make an exception to the principles generally applied for the initial recognition and measurement of non-financial assets.

(c) the large majority of commentators on E50 supported the initial recognition of intangible assets at cost and the prohibition of the reinstatement of expenditure on an intangible item that was initially recognised as an expense.

Application of the recognition criteria for internally generated intangible assets

BCZ45 IAS 38 specifically prohibits the recognition as intangible assets of brands, mastheads, publishing titles, customer lists and items similar in substance that are internally generated. IASC believed that internally generated intangible

---

* IAS 16 *Property, Plant and Equipment* (as revised in 2003) requires an entity to measure an item of property, plant and equipment acquired in exchange for a non-monetary asset or assets, or a combination of monetary and non-monetary assets, at fair value unless the exchange transaction lacks commercial substance. Previously, an entity measured such an acquired asset at fair value unless the exchanged assets were similar. The IASB concluded that the same measurement criteria should apply to intangible assets acquired in exchange for a non-monetary asset or assets, or a combination of monetary and non-monetary assets.

items of this kind would rarely, and perhaps never, meet the recognition criteria in IAS 38. However, to avoid any misunderstanding, IASC decided to set out this conclusion in the form of an explicit prohibition.

BCZ46   IAS 38 also clarifies that expenditure on research, training, advertising and start-up activities will not result in the creation of an intangible asset that can be recognised in the financial statements. Whilst some view these requirements and guidance as being too restrictive and arbitrary, they are based on IASC's interpretation of the application of the recognition criteria in IAS 38. They also reflect the fact that it is sometimes difficult to determine whether there is an internally generated intangible asset distinguishable from internally generated goodwill.

2008 Amendments*

BC46A   Paragraph 68 states that expenditure on an internally developed intangible item shall be recognised as an expense when it is incurred. The Board noted that it was unclear to some constituents how this should be interpreted. For example, some believed that an entity should recognise expenditure on advertising and promotional activities as an expense when it received the goods or services that it would use to develop or communicate the advertisement or promotion. Others believed that an entity should recognise an expense when the advertisement or promotion was delivered to its customers or potential customers. Therefore, the Board decided to amend paragraph 69 to clarify the meaning of 'incurred'.

BC46B   The Board noted that advertising and promotional activities enhance or create brands or customer relationships, which in turn generate revenues. Goods or services that are acquired to be used to undertake advertising or promotional activities have no other purpose than to undertake those activities. In other words, the only benefit of those goods or services is to develop or create brands or customer relationships, which in turn generate revenues. Internally generated brands or customer relationships are not recognised as intangible assets.

BC46C   The Board concluded that it would be inconsistent for an entity to recognise an asset in respect of an advertisement that it had not yet published if the economic benefits that might flow to the entity as a result of publishing the advertisement are the same as those that might flow to the entity as a result of the brand or customer relationship that it would enhance or create. Therefore, the Board concluded that an entity should not recognise as an asset goods or services that it had received in respect of its future advertising or promotional activities.

BC46D   In reaching this conclusion the Board noted that, if an entity pays for advertising goods or services in advance and the other party has not yet provided those goods or services, the entity has a different asset. That asset is the right to receive those goods and services. Therefore, the Board decided to retain paragraph 70, which allows an entity to recognise as an asset the right to receive those goods or services. However, the Board did not believe that this paragraph should be used as a justification for recognising an asset beyond the point at which the entity gained a right to access the related goods or received the related services.

---

*   This heading and paragraphs BC46A–BC46I were added by *Improvements to IFRSs* issued in May 2008.

Therefore, the Board decided to amend the paragraph to make clear that a prepayment may be recognised by an entity only until that entity has gained a right to access to the related goods or has received the related services.

BC46E   The Board noted that when the entity has received the related goods or services, it ceases to have the right to receive them. Because the entity no longer has an asset that it can recognise, it recognises an expense. However, the Board was concerned that the timing of delivery of goods should not be the determinant of when an expense should be recognised. The date on which physical delivery is obtained could be altered without affecting the commercial substance of the arrangement with the supplier. Therefore, the Board decided that an entity should recognise an expense for goods when they have been completed by the supplier in accordance with a contract to supply them and the entity could ask for delivery in return for payment—in other words, when the entity had gained a right to access the related goods.

BC46F   A number of commentators on the exposure draft of proposed *Improvements to International Financial Reporting Standards* published in 2007 thought that it was unclear when the Board intended an expense to be recognised. In response to those comments, the Board added paragraph 69A to clarify when entities would gain a right to access goods or receive services.

BC46G   The Board also received a number of comments arguing that mail order catalogues are not a form of advertising and promotion but instead give rise to a distribution network. The Board rejected these arguments, believing that the primary objective of mail order catalogues is to advertise goods to customers. To avoid confusion, the Board decided to include mail order catalogues in the Standard as an example of advertising activities.

BC46H   Some respondents who argued that the cost of mail order catalogues should be capitalised suggested that making an analogy to web site costs in SIC-32 *Intangible Assets—Web Site Costs* would be appropriate. The Board agreed and concluded that its proposed amendments would result in accounting that is almost identical to that resulting from the application of SIC-32. In particular, SIC-32 requires the cost of content (to the extent that it is developed to advertise and promote products and services) to be recognised as an expense as it is incurred. The Board concluded that in the case of a mail order catalogue, the majority of the content is intended to advertise and promote products and services. Therefore, permitting the cost of catalogues to be capitalised while at the same time requiring the cost of developing and uploading web site content used to advertise and promote an entity's products to be recognised as an expense would base the accounting on the nature of the media (paper or electronic) used to deliver the content rather than the nature of the expenditure.

BC46I   The Board also noted that SIC-32 permits expenditure on an internally developed web site to be capitalised only in the 'application and infrastructure development stage'. It requires costs associated with developing the functionality and infrastructure that make a web site operate to be capitalised. In the Board's view, the electronic infrastructure capitalised in accordance with SIC-32 is analogous to the property, plant and equipment infrastructure—for example, a sign—that permits advertising to be displayed to the public not the content that is displayed on that sign.

Subsequent accounting for intangible assets

BC47   The Board initially decided that the scope of the first phase of its Business Combinations project should include a consideration of the subsequent accounting for intangible assets acquired in business combinations. To that end, the Board initially focused its attention on the following three issues:

(a)   whether an intangible asset with a finite useful life and acquired in a business combination should continue to be accounted for after initial recognition in accordance with IAS 38.

(b)   whether, and under what circumstances, an intangible asset acquired in a business combination could be regarded as having an indefinite useful life.

(c)   how an intangible asset with an indefinite useful life (assuming such an asset exists) acquired in a business combination should be accounted for after initial recognition.

BC48   However, during its deliberations of the issues in (b) and (c) of paragraph BC47, the Board decided that any conclusions it reached on those issues would equally apply to recognised intangible assets obtained other than in a business combination. The Board observed that amending the requirements in the previous version of IAS 38 only for intangible assets acquired in business combinations would create inconsistencies in the accounting for intangible assets depending on how they are obtained. Thus, similar items would be accounted for in dissimilar ways. The Board concluded that creating such inconsistencies would impair the usefulness of the information provided to users about an entity's intangible assets, because both comparability and reliability (which rests on the notion of representational faithfulness, ie that similar transactions are accounted for in the same way) would be diminished. Therefore, the Board decided that any amendments to the requirements in the previous version of IAS 38 to address the issues in (b) and (c) of paragraph BC47 should apply to all recognised intangible assets, whether generated internally or acquired separately or as part of a business combination.

BC49   Before beginning its deliberations of the issues identified in paragraph BC47, the Board noted the concern expressed by some that, because of the subjectivity involved in distinguishing goodwill from other intangible assets as at the acquisition date, differences between the subsequent treatment of goodwill and other intangible assets increases the potential for intangible assets to be misclassified at the acquisition date. The Board concluded, however, that adopting the separability and contractual or other legal rights criteria provides a reasonably definitive basis for separately identifying and recognising intangible assets acquired in a business combination. Therefore, the Board decided that its analysis of the accounting for intangible assets after initial recognition should have regard only to the nature of those assets and not to the subsequent treatment of goodwill.

Accounting for intangible assets with finite useful lives acquired in business combinations

BC50 The Board observed that the previous version of IAS 38 required an intangible asset to be measured after initial recognition:

(a) at cost less any accumulated amortisation and any accumulated impairment losses; or

(b) at a revalued amount, being the asset's fair value, determined by reference to an active market, at the date of revaluation less any subsequent accumulated amortisation and any subsequent accumulated impairment losses. Under this approach, revaluations must be made with such regularity that at the balance sheet date the carrying amount of the asset does not differ materially from its fair value.

Whichever of the above methods was used, the previous version of IAS 38 required the depreciable amount of the asset to be amortised on a systematic basis over the best estimate of its useful life.

BC51 The Board observed that underpinning the requirement for all intangible assets to be amortised is the notion that they all have determinable and finite useful lives. Setting aside the question of whether, and under what circumstances, an intangible asset could be regarded as having an indefinite useful life, an important issue for the Board to consider was whether a departure from the above requirements would be warranted for intangible assets acquired in a business combination that have finite useful lives.

BC52 The Board observed that any departure from the above requirements for intangible assets with finite lives acquired in business combinations would create inconsistencies between the accounting for recognised intangible assets based wholly on the means by which they are obtained. In other words, similar items would be accounted for in dissimilar ways. The Board concluded that creating such inconsistencies would impair the usefulness of the information provided to users about an entity's intangible assets, because both comparability and reliability would be diminished.

BC53 Therefore, the Board decided that intangible assets with finite useful lives acquired in business combinations should continue to be accounted for in accordance with the above requirements after initial recognition.

Impairment testing intangible assets with finite useful lives (paragraph 111)

BC54 The previous version of IAS 38 required the recoverable amount of an intangible asset with a finite useful life that is being amortised over a period of more than 20 years, whether or not acquired in a business combination, to be measured at least at each financial year-end.

BC55 The Board observed that the recoverable amount of a long-lived tangible asset needs to be measured only when, in accordance with IAS 36 *Impairment of Assets*, there is an indication that the asset may be impaired. The Board could see no conceptual reason for requiring the recoverable amounts of some identifiable assets being amortised over very long periods to be determined more regularly than for other identifiable assets being amortised or depreciated over similar periods. Therefore, the Board concluded that the recoverable amount of an intangible asset with a finite useful life that is amortised over a period of more than 20 years should be determined only when, in accordance with IAS 36, there is an indication that the asset may be impaired. Consequently, the Board decided to remove the requirement in the previous version of IAS 38 for the recoverable amount of such an intangible asset to be measured at least at each financial year-end.

BC56 The Board also decided that all of the requirements relating to impairment testing intangible assets should be included in IAS 36 rather than in IAS 38. Therefore, the Board relocated to IAS 36 the requirement in the previous version of IAS 38 that an entity should estimate at the end of each annual reporting period the recoverable amount of an intangible asset not yet available for use, irrespective of whether there is any indication that it may be impaired.

Residual value of an intangible asset with a finite useful life (paragraph 100)

BC57 In revising IAS 38, the Board considered whether to retain for intangible assets with finite useful lives the requirement in the previous version of IAS 38 for the residual value of an intangible asset to be assumed to be zero unless:

(a)   there is a commitment by a third party to purchase the asset at the end of its useful life; or

(b)   there is an active market for the asset and:

　　(i)   the asset's residual value can be determined by reference to that market; and

　　(ii)   it is probable that such a market will exist at the end of the asset's useful life.

BC58 The Board observed that the definition in the previous version of IAS 38 (as amended by IAS 16 when revised in 2003) of residual value required it to be estimated as if the asset were already of the age and in the condition expected at the end of the asset's useful life. Therefore, if the useful life of an intangible asset was shorter than its economic life because the entity expected to sell the asset before the end of that economic life, the asset's residual value would not be zero, irrespective of whether the conditions in paragraph BC57(a) or (b) are met.

BC59 Nevertheless, the Board observed that the requirement for the residual value of an intangible asset to be assumed to be zero unless the specified criteria are met was included in the previous version of IAS 38 as a means of preventing entities from circumventing the requirement in that Standard to amortise all intangible assets. Excluding this requirement from the revised Standard for finite-lived intangible assets would similarly provide a means of circumventing the requirement to amortise such intangible assets—by claiming that the residual value of such an asset was equal to or greater than its carrying amount, an entity could avoid amortising the asset, even though its useful life is finite. The Board concluded that it should not, as part of the Business Combinations project, modify the criteria for permitting a finite-lived intangible asset's residual value to be other than zero. However, the Board decided that this issue should be addressed as part of a forthcoming project on intangible assets.

Useful lives of intangible assets (paragraphs 88–96)

BC60   Consistently with the proposals in the Exposure Draft of Proposed Amendments to IAS 38, the Standard requires an intangible asset to be regarded by an entity as having an indefinite useful life when, based on an analysis of all of the relevant factors, there is no foreseeable limit to the period over which the asset is expected to generate net cash inflows for the entity.

BC61   In developing the Exposure Draft and the revised Standard, the Board observed that the useful life of an intangible asset is related to the expected cash inflows that are associated with that asset. The Board observed that, to be representationally faithful, the amortisation period for an intangible asset generally should reflect that useful life and, by extension, the cash flow streams associated with the asset. The Board concluded that it is possible for management to have the intention and the ability to maintain an intangible asset in such a way that there is no foreseeable limit on the period over which that particular asset is expected to generate net cash inflows for the entity. In other words, it is conceivable that an analysis of all the relevant factors (ie legal, regulatory, contractual, competitive, economic and other) could lead to a conclusion that there is no foreseeable limit to the period over which a particular intangible asset is expected to generate net cash inflows for the entity.

BC62   For example, the Board observed that some intangible assets are based on legal rights that are conveyed in perpetuity rather than for finite terms. As such, those assets may have cash flows associated with them that may be expected to continue for many years or even indefinitely. The Board concluded that if the cash flows are expected to continue for a finite period, the useful life of the asset is limited to that finite period. However, if the cash flows are expected to continue indefinitely, the useful life is indefinite.

BC63   The previous version of IAS 38 prescribed a presumptive maximum useful life for intangible assets of 20 years. In developing the Exposure Draft and the revised Standard, the Board concluded that such a presumption is inconsistent with the view that the amortisation period for an intangible asset should, to be representationally faithful, reflect its useful life and, by extension, the cash flow streams associated with the asset. Therefore, the Board decided not to include in the revised Standard a presumptive maximum useful life for intangible assets, even if they have finite useful lives.

BC64   Respondents to the Exposure Draft generally supported the Board's proposal to remove from IAS 38 the presumptive maximum useful life and instead to require useful life to be regarded as indefinite when, based on an analysis of all of the relevant factors, there is no foreseeable limit to the period of time over which the intangible asset is expected to generate net cash inflows for the entity. However, some respondents suggested that an inability to determine clearly the useful life of an asset applies equally to many items of property, plant and equipment. Nonetheless, entities are required to determine the useful lives of those items of property, plant and equipment, and allocate their depreciable amounts on a systematic basis over those useful lives. Those respondents suggested that there is no conceptual reason for treating intangible assets differently.

BC65   In considering these comments, the Board noted the following:

(a)   an intangible asset's useful life would be regarded as indefinite in accordance with IAS 38 only when, based on an analysis of all of the relevant factors, there is no foreseeable limit to the period of time over which the asset is expected to generate net cash inflows for the entity. Difficulties in accurately determining an intangible asset's useful life do not provide a basis for regarding that useful life as indefinite.

(b)   although the useful lives of both intangible and tangible assets are directly related to the period during which they are expected to generate net cash inflows for the entity, the expected physical utility to the entity of a tangible asset places an upper limit on the asset's useful life. In other words, the useful life of a tangible asset could never extend beyond the asset's expected physical utility to the entity.

The Board concluded that tangible assets (other than land) could not be regarded as having indefinite useful lives because there is always a foreseeable limit to the expected physical utility of the asset to the entity.

Useful life constrained by contractual or other legal rights (paragraphs 94–96)

BC66   The Board noted that the useful life of an intangible asset that arises from contractual or other legal rights is constrained by the duration of those rights. The useful life of such an asset cannot extend beyond the duration of those rights, and may be shorter. Accordingly, the Board concluded that in determining the useful life of an intangible asset, consideration should be given to the period that the entity expects to use the intangible asset, which is subject to the expiration of the contractual or other legal rights.

BC67   However, the Board also observed that such rights are often conveyed for limited terms that may be renewed. It therefore considered whether renewals should be assumed in determining the useful life of such an intangible asset. The Board noted that some types of licences are initially issued for finite periods but renewals are routinely granted at little cost, provided that licensees have complied with the applicable rules and regulations. Such licences are traded at prices that reflect more than the remaining term, thereby indicating that renewal at minimal cost is the general expectation. However, renewals are not assured for other types of licences and, even if they are renewed, substantial costs may be incurred to secure their renewal.

BC68   The Board concluded that because the useful lives of some intangible assets depend, in economic terms, on renewal and on the associated costs of renewal, the useful lives assigned to those assets should reflect renewal when there is evidence to support renewal without significant cost.

BC69   Respondents to the Exposure Draft generally supported this conclusion. Those that disagreed suggested that:

(a)   when the renewal period depends on the decision of a third party and not merely on the fulfilment of specified conditions by the entity, it gives rise to a contingent asset because the third-party decision affects not only the cost of renewal but also the probability of obtaining it. Therefore, useful life should reflect renewal only when renewal is not subject to third-party approval.

(b)   such a requirement would be inconsistent with the basis used to measure intangible assets at the date of a business combination, particularly contractual customer relationships. For example, it is not clear whether the fair value of a contractual customer relationship includes an amount that reflects the probability that the contract will be renewed. The possibility of renewal would have a fair value regardless of the costs required to renew. This means the useful life of a contractual customer relationship could be inconsistent with the basis used to determine the fair value of the relationship.

BC70   In relation to (a) above, the Board observed that if renewal by the entity is subject to third-party (eg government) approval, the requirement that there be evidence to support the entity's ability to renew would compel the entity to make an assessment of the likely effect of the third-party approval process on the entity's ability to renew. The Board could see no conceptual basis for narrowing the requirement to situations in which the contractual or legal rights are not subject to the approval of third parties.

BC71   In relation to (b) above, the Board observed the following:

(a)   the requirements relating to renewal periods address circumstances in which *the entity* is able to renew the contractual or other legal rights, notwithstanding that such renewal may, for example, be conditional on the entity satisfying specified conditions, or subject to third-party approval. Paragraph 94 of the Standard states that '... the useful life of the intangible asset shall include the renewal period(s) only if there is evidence to support renewal *by the entity* [emphasis added] without significant cost.' The ability to renew a customer contract normally rests with the customer and not with the entity.

(b)   the respondents seem to regard as a single intangible asset what is, in substance, two intangible assets—one being the customer contract and the other being the related customer relationship. Expected renewals by the customer would affect the fair value of the customer relationship intangible asset, rather than the fair value of the customer contract. Therefore, the useful life of the customer contract would not, under the Standard, extend beyond the term of the contract, nor would the fair value of that customer contract reflect expectations of renewal by the customer. In other words, the useful life of the customer contract would not be inconsistent with the basis used to determine its fair value.

BC72   However, in response to respondents' suggestions, the Board included paragraph 96 in the Standard to provide additional guidance on the circumstances in which an entity should be regarded as being able to renew the contractual or other legal rights without significant cost.

Intangible assets with finite useful lives (paragraph 98)[*]

BC72A   The last sentence of paragraph 98 previously stated, 'There is rarely, if ever, persuasive evidence to support an amortisation method for intangible assets with finite useful lives that results in a lower amount of accumulated amortisation than under the straight-line method.' In practice, this wording was perceived as preventing an entity from using the unit of production method to amortise assets if it resulted in a lower amount of accumulated amortisation than the straight-line method. However, using the straight-line method could be inconsistent with the general requirement of paragraph 38 that the amortisation method should reflect the expected pattern of consumption of the expected future economic benefits embodied in an intangible asset. Consequently, the Board decided to delete the last sentence of paragraph 38.

Accounting for intangible assets with indefinite useful lives (paragraphs 107–110)

BC73   Consistently with the proposals in the Exposure Draft, the Standard prohibits the amortisation of intangible assets with indefinite useful lives. Therefore, such assets are measured after initial recognition at:

(a)   cost less any accumulated impairment losses; or

(b)   a revalued amount, being fair value determined by reference to an active market less any accumulated impairment losses.

Non-amortisation

BC74   In developing the Exposure Draft and the revised Standard, the Board observed that many assets yield benefits to an entity over several periods. Amortisation is the systematic allocation of the cost (or revalued amount) of an asset, less any residual value, to reflect the consumption over time of the future economic benefits embodied in that asset. Thus, if there is no foreseeable limit on the period during which an entity expects to consume the future economic benefits embodied in an asset, amortisation of that asset over, for example, an arbitrarily determined maximum period would not be representationally faithful. Respondents to the Exposure Draft generally supported this conclusion.

BC75   Consequently, the Board decided that intangible assets with indefinite useful lives should not be amortised, but should be subject to regular impairment testing. The Board's deliberations on the form of the impairment test, including the frequency of impairment testing, are included in the Basis for Conclusions on IAS 36. The Board further decided that regular re-examinations should be required of the useful life of an intangible asset that is not being amortised to determine whether circumstances continue to support the assessment that the useful life is indefinite.

---

[*]   This heading and paragraph BC72A were added by *Improvements to IFRSs* issued in May 2008.

Revaluations

BC76 Having decided that intangible assets with indefinite useful lives should not be amortised, the Board considered whether an entity should be permitted to carry such assets at revalued amounts. The Board could see no conceptual justification for precluding some intangible assets from being carried at revalued amounts solely on the basis that there is no foreseeable limit to the period over which an entity expects to consume the future economic benefits embodied in those assets.

BC77 As a result, the Board decided that the Standard should permit intangible assets with indefinite useful lives to be carried at revalued amounts.

Research and development projects acquired in business combinations

BC78 The Board considered the following issues in relation to in-process research and development (IPR&D) projects acquired in a business combination:

(a) whether the proposed criteria for recognising intangible assets acquired in a business combination separately from goodwill should also be applied to IPR&D projects;

(b) the subsequent accounting for IPR&D projects recognised as assets separately from goodwill; and

(c) the treatment of subsequent expenditure on IPR&D projects recognised as assets separately from goodwill.

The Board's deliberations on issue (a), although included in the Basis for Conclusions on IFRS 3, are also, for the sake of completeness, outlined below.

BC79 The Board did not reconsider as part of the first phase of its Business Combinations project the requirements in the previous version of IAS 38 for internally generated intangibles and expenditure on the research or development phase of an internal project. The Board decided that a reconsideration of those requirements is outside the scope of this project.

Initial recognition separately from goodwill

BC80 The Board observed that the criteria in IAS 22 *Business Combinations* and the previous version of IAS 38 for recognising an intangible asset acquired in a business combination separately from goodwill applied to all intangible assets, including IPR&D projects. Therefore, in accordance with those Standards, any intangible item acquired in a business combination was recognised as an asset separately from goodwill when it was identifiable and could be measured reliably, and it was probable that any associated future economic benefits would flow to the acquirer. If these criteria were not satisfied, the expenditure on the cost or value of that item, which was included in the cost of the combination, was part of the amount attributed to goodwill.

BC81 The Board could see no conceptual justification for changing the approach in IAS 22 and the previous version of IAS 38 of using the same criteria for all intangible assets acquired in a business combination when assessing whether those assets should be recognised separately from goodwill. The Board concluded that adopting different criteria would impair the usefulness of the information provided to users about the assets acquired in a combination because both comparability and reliability would be diminished. Therefore, IAS 38 and IFRS 3 require an acquirer to recognise as an asset separately from goodwill any of the acquiree's IPR&D projects that meet the definition of an intangible asset. This will be the case when the IPR&D project meets the definition of an asset and is identifiable, ie is separable or arises from contractual or other legal rights.

BC82 Some respondents to the Exposure Draft of Proposed Amendments to IAS 38 expressed concern that applying the same criteria to all intangible assets acquired in a business combination to assess whether they should be recognised separately from goodwill results in treating some IPR&D projects acquired in business combinations differently from similar projects started internally. The Board acknowledged this point, but concluded that this does not provide a basis for subsuming those acquired intangible assets within goodwill. Rather, it highlights a need to reconsider the conclusion in the Standard that an intangible asset can never exist in respect of an in-process research project and can exist in respect of an in-process development project only once all of the Standard's criteria for deferral have been satisfied. The Board decided that such a reconsideration is outside the scope of its Business Combinations project.

Subsequent accounting for IPR&D projects acquired in a business combination and recognised as intangible assets

BC83 The Board observed that the previous version of IAS 38 required all recognised intangible assets to be accounted for after initial recognition at:

(a) cost less any accumulated amortisation and any accumulated impairment losses; or

(b) revalued amount, being the asset's fair value, determined by reference to an active market, at the date of revaluation less any subsequent accumulated amortisation and any subsequent accumulated impairment losses.

Such assets included: IPR&D projects acquired in a business combination that satisfied the criteria for recognition separately from goodwill; separately acquired IPR&D projects that satisfied the criteria for recognition as an intangible asset; and recognised internally developed intangible assets arising from development or the development phase of an internal project.

BC84 The Board could see no conceptual justification for changing the approach in the previous version of IAS 38 of applying the same requirements to the subsequent accounting for all recognised intangible assets. Therefore, the Board decided that IPR&D projects acquired in a business combination that satisfy the criteria for recognition as an asset separately from goodwill should be accounted for after initial recognition in accordance with the requirements applying to the subsequent accounting for other recognised intangible assets.

Subsequent expenditure on IPR&D projects acquired in a business combination and recognised as intangible assets (paragraphs 42 and 43)

BC85 The Standard requires subsequent expenditure on an IPR&D project acquired separately or in a business combination and recognised as an intangible asset to be:

(a) recognised as an expense when incurred if it is research expenditure;

(b) recognised as an expense when incurred if it is development expenditure that does not satisfy the criteria for recognition as an intangible asset in paragraph 57; and

(c) added to the carrying amount of the acquired IPR&D project if it is development expenditure that satisfies the recognition criteria in paragraph 57.

BC86 In developing this requirement the Board observed that the treatment required under the previous version of IAS 38 of subsequent expenditure on an IPR&D project acquired in a business combination and recognised as an asset separately from goodwill was unclear. Some suggested that the requirements in the previous version of IAS 38 relating to expenditure on research, development, or the research or development phase of an internal project should be applied. However, others argued that those requirements were ostensibly concerned with the initial recognition and measurement of internally generated intangible assets. Instead, the requirements in the previous version of IAS 38 dealing with subsequent expenditure should be applied. Under those requirements, subsequent expenditure on an intangible asset after its purchase or completion would have been recognised as an expense when incurred unless:

(a) it was probable that the expenditure would enable the asset to generate future economic benefits in excess of its originally assessed standard of performance; and

(b) the expenditure could be measured and attributed to the asset reliably.

If these conditions were satisfied, the subsequent expenditure would be added to the carrying amount of the intangible asset.

BC87 The Board observed that this uncertainty also existed for separately acquired IPR&D projects that satisfied the criteria in the previous version of IAS 38 for recognition as intangible assets.

BC88 The Board noted that applying the requirements in the Standard for expenditure on research, development, or the research or development phase of an internal project to subsequent expenditure on IPR&D projects acquired in a business combination and recognised as assets separately from goodwill would result in such subsequent expenditure being treated inconsistently with subsequent expenditure on other recognised intangible assets. However, applying the subsequent expenditure requirements in the previous version of IAS 38 to subsequent expenditure on IPR&D projects acquired in a business combination and recognised as assets separately from goodwill would result in research and development expenditure being accounted for differently depending on whether a project is acquired or started internally.

BC89   The Board concluded that until it has had the opportunity to review the requirements in IAS 38 for expenditure on research, development, or the research or development phase of an internal project, more useful information will be provided to users of an entity's financial statements if all such expenditure is accounted for consistently. This includes subsequent expenditure on a separately acquired IPR&D project that satisfies the Standard's criteria for recognition as an intangible asset.

Transitional provisions (paragraphs 129–132)

BC90   If an entity elects to apply IFRS 3 from any date before the effective dates outlined in IFRS 3, it is also required to apply IAS 38 prospectively from that same date. Otherwise, IAS 38 applies to the accounting for intangible assets acquired in business combinations for which the agreement date is on or after 31 March 2004, and to the accounting for all other intangible assets prospectively from the beginning of the first annual reporting period beginning on or after 31 March 2004. IAS 38 also requires an entity, on initial application, to reassess the useful lives of intangible assets. If, as a result of that reassessment, the entity changes its useful life assessment for an asset, that change is accounted for as a change in an accounting estimate in accordance with IAS 8 *Accounting Policies, Changes in Accounting Estimates and Errors.*

BC91   The Board's deliberations on the transitional issues relating to the initial recognition of intangible assets acquired in business combinations and the impairment testing of intangible assets are addressed in the Basis for Conclusions on IFRS 3 and the Basis for Conclusions on IAS 36, respectively.

BC92   In developing the requirements outlined in paragraph BC90, the Board considered the following three questions:

(a)   should the useful lives of, and the accounting for, intangible assets already recognised at the effective date of the Standard continue to be determined in accordance with the requirements in the previous version of IAS 38 (ie by amortising over a presumptive maximum period of twenty years), or in accordance with the requirements in the revised Standard?

(b)   if the revised Standard is applied to intangible assets already recognised at its effective date, should the effect of a reassessment of an intangible asset's useful life as a result of the initial application of the Standard be recognised retrospectively or prospectively?

(c)   should entities be required to apply the requirements in the Standard for subsequent expenditure on an acquired IPR&D project recognised as an intangible asset retrospectively to expenditure incurred before the effective date of the revised Standard?

BC93   In relation to the first question above, the Board noted its previous conclusion that the most representationally faithful method of accounting for intangible assets is to amortise those with finite useful lives over their useful lives with no limit on the amortisation period, and not to amortise those with indefinite useful lives. Thus, the Board concluded that the reliability and comparability of financial statements would be diminished if the Standard was not applied to intangible assets recognised before its effective date.

BC94   On the second question, the Board observed that a reassessment of an asset's useful life is regarded throughout IFRSs as a change in an accounting estimate, rather than a change in an accounting policy. For example, in accordance with the Standard, as with the previous version of IAS 38, if a new estimate of the expected useful life of an intangible asset is significantly different from previous estimates, the change must be accounted for as a change in accounting estimate in accordance with IAS 8. IAS 8 requires a change in an accounting estimate to be accounted for prospectively by including the effect of the change in profit or loss in:

(a)   the period of the change, if the change in estimate affects that period only; or

(b)   the period of the change and future periods, if the change in estimate affects both.

BC95   Similarly, in accordance with IAS 16 *Property, Plant and Equipment*, if a new estimate of the expected useful life of an item of property, plant and equipment is significantly different from previous estimates, the change must be accounted for prospectively by adjusting the depreciation expense for the current and future periods.

BC96   Therefore, the Board decided that a reassessment of useful life resulting from the initial application of IAS 38, including a reassessment from a finite to an indefinite useful life, should be accounted for as a change in an accounting estimate. Consequently, the effect of such a change should be recognised prospectively.

BC97   The Board considered the view that because the previous version of IAS 38 required intangible assets to be treated as having a finite useful life, a change to an assessment of indefinite useful life for an intangible asset represents a change in an accounting policy, rather than a change in an accounting estimate. The Board concluded that, even if this were the case, the useful life reassessment should nonetheless be accounted for prospectively. This is because retrospective application would require an entity to determine whether, at the end of each reporting period before the effective date of the Standard, the useful life of an intangible asset was indefinite. Such an assessment requires an entity to make estimates that would have been made at a prior date, and therefore raises problems in relation to the role of hindsight, in particular, whether the benefit of hindsight should be included or excluded from those estimates and, if excluded, how the effect of hindsight can be separated from the other factors existing at the date for which the estimates are required.

BC98   On the third question, and as noted in paragraph BC86, it was not clear whether the previous version of IAS 38 required subsequent expenditure on acquired IPR&D projects recognised as intangible assets to be accounted for:

(a)   in accordance with its requirements for expenditure on research, development, or the research or development phase of an internal project; or

(b)   in accordance with its requirements for subsequent expenditure on an intangible asset after its purchase or completion.

The Board concluded that subsequent expenditure on an acquired IPR&D project that was capitalised under (b) above before the effective date of the Standard might not have been capitalised had the Standard applied when the subsequent expenditure was incurred. This is because the Standard requires such expenditure to be capitalised as an intangible asset only when it is development expenditure and all of the criteria for deferral are satisfied. In the Board's view, those criteria represent a higher recognition threshold than (b) above.

BC99 Thus, retrospective application of the revised Standard to subsequent expenditure on acquired IPR&D projects incurred before its effective date could result in previously capitalised expenditure being reversed. Such reversal would be required if the expenditure was research expenditure, or it was development expenditure and one or more of the criteria for deferral were not satisfied at the time the expenditure was incurred. The Board concluded that determining whether, at the time the subsequent expenditure was incurred, the criteria for deferral were satisfied raises the same hindsight issues discussed in paragraph BC97: it would require assessments to be made as of a prior date, and therefore raises problems in relation to how the effect of hindsight can be separated from factors existing at the date of the assessment. In addition, such assessments could, in many cases, be impossible: the information needed may not exist or no longer be obtainable.

BC100 Therefore, the Board decided that the Standard's requirements for subsequent expenditure on acquired IPR&D projects recognised as intangible assets should not be applied retrospectively to expenditure incurred before the revised Standard's effective date. The Board noted that any amounts previously included in the carrying amount of such an asset would, in any event, be subject to the requirements for impairment testing in IAS 36.

Early application (paragraph 132)

BC101 The Board noted that the issue of any Standard reflects its opinion that application of the Standard will result in more useful information being provided to users about an entity's financial position, performance or cash flows. On that basis, a case exists for permitting, and indeed encouraging, entities to apply the revised Standard before its effective date. However, the Board also considered the assertion that permitting a revised Standard to be applied before its effective date potentially diminishes comparability between entities in the period(s) leading up to that effective date, and has the effect of providing entities with an option.

BC102 The Board concluded that the benefit of providing users with more useful information about an entity's financial position and performance by permitting early application of the Standard outweighs the disadvantages of potentially diminished comparability. Therefore, entities are encouraged to apply the requirements of the revised Standard before its effective date, provided they also apply IFRS 3 and IAS 36 (as revised in 2004) at the same time.

Summary of main changes from the Exposure Draft

BC103 The following are the main changes from the Exposure Draft of Proposed Amendments to IAS 38:

(a) The Standard includes additional guidance clarifying the relationship between the separability criterion for establishing whether a non-contractual customer relationship is identifiable, and the control concept for establishing whether the relationship meets the definition of an asset. In particular, the Standard clarifies that in the absence of legal rights to protect customer relationships, exchange transactions for the same or similar non-contractual customer relationships (other than as part of a business combination) provide evidence that the entity is nonetheless able to control the future economic benefits flowing from the customer relationships. Because such exchange transactions also provide evidence that the customer relationships are separable, those customer relationships meet the definition of an intangible asset (see paragraphs BC11–BC14).

(b) The Exposure Draft proposed that, except for an assembled workforce, an intangible asset acquired in a business combination should always be recognised separately from goodwill; there was a presumption that sufficient information would always exist to measure reliably its fair value. The Standard states that the fair value of an intangible asset acquired in a business combination can *normally* be measured with sufficient reliability to qualify for recognition separately from goodwill. If an intangible asset acquired in a business combination has a finite useful life, there is a rebuttable presumption that its fair value can be measured reliably (see paragraphs BC16–BC25).

(c) The Exposure Draft proposed, and the Standard requires, that the useful life of an intangible asset arising from contractual or other legal rights should not exceed the period of those rights. However, if the rights are conveyed for a limited term that can be renewed, the useful life should include the renewal period(s) only if there is evidence to support renewal by the entity without significant cost. Additional guidance has been included in the Standard to clarify the circumstances in which an entity should be regarded as being able to renew the contractual or other legal rights without significant cost (see paragraphs BC66–BC72).

History of the development of a standard on intangible assets

BCZ104 IASC published a Draft Statement of Principles on Intangible Assets in January 1994 and an Exposure Draft E50 *Intangible Assets* in June 1995. Principles in both documents were consistent as far as possible with those in IAS 16 *Property, Plant and Equipment*. The principles were also greatly influenced by the decisions reached in 1993 during the revisions to the treatment of research and development costs and goodwill.

BCZ105 IASC received about 100 comment letters on E50 from over 20 countries. Comment letters on E50 showed that the proposal for the amortisation period for intangible assets—a 20-year ceiling for almost all intangible assets, as required for goodwill in IAS 22 (revised 1993)—raised significant controversy and created serious concerns about the overall acceptability of the proposed standard on intangible assets. IASC considered alternative solutions and concluded in March 1996 that, if an impairment test that is sufficiently robust and reliable could be developed, IASC would propose deleting the 20-year ceiling on the amortisation period for both intangible assets and goodwill.

BCZ106 In August 1997, IASC published proposals for revised treatments for intangible assets and goodwill in Exposure Drafts E60 *Intangible Assets* and E61 *Business Combinations*. This followed the publication of Exposure Draft E55 *Impairment of Assets* in May 1997, which set out detailed proposals for impairment testing.

BCZ107 E60 proposed two major changes to the proposals in E50:

(a)   as explained above, revised proposals for the amortisation of intangible assets; and

(b)   combining the requirements relating to all internally generated intangible assets in one standard. This meant including certain aspects of IAS 9 *Research and Development Costs* in the proposed standard on intangible assets and withdrawing IAS 9.

BCZ108 Among other proposed changes, E61 proposed revisions to IAS 22 to make the requirements for the amortisation of goodwill consistent with those proposed for intangible assets.

BCZ109 IASC received about 100 comment letters on E60 and E61 from over 20 countries. The majority of the commentators supported most of the proposals in E60 and E61, although some proposals still raised significant controversy. The proposals for impairment tests were also supported by most commentators on E55.

BCZ110 After considering the comments received on E55, E60 and E61, IASC approved:

(a)   IAS 36 *Impairment of Assets* (April 1998);

(b)   IAS 38 *Intangible Assets* (July 1998);

(c)   a revised IAS 22 *Business Combinations* (July 1998); and

(d)   withdrawal of IAS 9 *Research and Development Costs* (July 1998).

Dissenting opinions

Dissent of Geoffrey Whittington from IAS 38 issued in March 2004

DO1   Professor Whittington dissents from the issue of this Standard because it does not explicitly require the probability recognition criterion in paragraph 21(a) to be applied to intangible assets acquired in a business combination, notwithstanding that it applies to all other intangible assets.

DO2   The reason given for this (paragraphs 33 and BC17) is that fair value is the required measurement on acquisition of an intangible asset as part of a business combination, and fair value incorporates probability assessments. Professor Whittington does not believe that the *Framework* precludes having a prior recognition test based on probability, even when subsequent recognition is at fair value. Moreover, the application of probability may be different for recognition purposes: for example, it may be the 'more likely than not' criterion used in IAS 37 *Provisions, Contingent Liabilities and Contingent Assets*, rather than the 'expected value' approach used in the measurement of fair value.

DO3   This inconsistency between the recognition criteria in the *Framework* and fair values is acknowledged in paragraph BC18. In Professor Whittington's view, the inconsistency should be resolved before changing the recognition criteria for intangible assets acquired in a business combination.

Dissent of James J Leisenring from amendments issued in May 2008

DO1   Mr Leisenring dissents from the amendments to IAS 38 *Intangible Assets* made by *Improvements to IFRSs* issued in May 2008.

DO2   Mr Leisenring believes that the Board's amendments introduce a logical flaw into IAS 38. Paragraph 68 states that 'expenditure on an intangible item shall be recognised as an expense when it is incurred unless' specific conditions apply. The amendments to paragraph 69 include guidance on the accounting for expenditure on a tangible rather than an intangible item and therefore the amendment to paragraph 69 is inconsistent with paragraph 68.

DO3   Extending the application of IAS 38 to tangible assets used for advertising also raises application concerns. Are signs constructed by a restaurant chain at their location an advertising expense in the period of construction? Would the costs of putting an entity's name on trucks, airplanes and buildings be an advertising expense in the year incurred? The logic of this amendment would suggest an affirmative answer to these questions even though the result of the expenditure benefits several periods.

DO4   Mr Leisenring believes that if an entity acquires goods, including items such as catalogues, film strips or other materials, the entity should determine whether those goods meet the definition of an asset. In his view, IAS 38 is not relevant for determining whether goods acquired by an entity and which may be used for advertising should be recognised as an asset.

DO5   Mr Leisenring agrees that the potential benefit that might result from having advertised should not be recognised as an intangible asset in accordance with IAS 38.

IAS 38 *Intangible Assets*
Illustrative examples

These examples accompany, but are not part of, IAS 38.

Assessing the useful lives of intangible assets

The following guidance provides examples on determining the useful life of an intangible asset in accordance with IAS 38.

Each of the following examples describes an acquired intangible asset, the facts and circumstances surrounding the determination of its useful life, and the subsequent accounting based on that determination.

Example 1 An acquired customer list

A direct-mail marketing company acquires a customer list and expects that it will be able to derive benefit from the information on the list for at least one year, but no more than three years.

The customer list would be amortised over management's best estimate of its useful life, say 18 months. Although the direct-mail marketing company may intend to add customer names and other information to the list in the future, the expected benefits of the acquired customer list relate only to the customers on that list at the date it was acquired. The customer list also would be reviewed for impairment in accordance with IAS 36 *Impairment of Assets* by assessing at the end of each reporting period whether there is any indication that the customer list may be impaired.

Example 2 An acquired patent that expires in 15 years

The product protected by the patented technology is expected to be a source of net cash inflows for at least 15 years. The entity has a commitment from a third party to purchase that patent in five years for 60 per cent of the fair value of the patent at the date it was acquired, and the entity intends to sell the patent in five years.

The patent would be amortised over its five-year useful life to the entity, with a residual value equal to the present value of 60 per cent of the patent's fair value at the date it was acquired. The patent would also be reviewed for impairment in accordance with IAS 36 by assessing at the end of each reporting period whether there is any indication that it may be impaired.

Example 3 An acquired copyright that has a remaining legal life of 50 years

An analysis of consumer habits and market trends provides evidence that the copyrighted material will generate net cash inflows for only 30 more years.

The copyright would be amortised over its 30-year estimated useful life. The copyright also would be reviewed for impairment in accordance with IAS 36 by assessing at the end of each reporting period whether there is any indication that it may be impaired.

Example 4 An acquired broadcasting licence that expires in five years

The broadcasting licence is renewable every 10 years if the entity provides at least an average level of service to its customers and complies with the relevant legislative requirements. The licence may be renewed indefinitely at little cost and has been renewed twice before the most recent acquisition. The acquiring entity intends to renew the licence indefinitely and evidence supports its ability to do so. Historically, there has been no compelling challenge to the licence renewal. The technology used in broadcasting is not expected to be replaced by another technology at any time in the foreseeable future. Therefore, the licence is expected to contribute to the entity's net cash inflows indefinitely.

The broadcasting licence would be treated as having an indefinite useful life because it is expected to contribute to the entity's net cash inflows indefinitely. Therefore, the licence would not be amortised until its useful life is determined to be finite. The licence would be tested for impairment in accordance with IAS 36 annually and whenever there is an indication that it may be impaired.

Example 5 The broadcasting licence in Example 4

The licensing authority subsequently decides that it will no longer renew broadcasting licences, but rather will auction the licences. At the time the licensing authority's decision is made, the entity's broadcasting licence has three years until it expires. The entity expects that the licence will continue to contribute to net cash inflows until the licence expires.

Because the broadcasting licence can no longer be renewed, its useful life is no longer indefinite. Thus, the acquired licence would be amortised over its remaining three-year useful life and immediately tested for impairment in accordance with IAS 36.

Example 6 An acquired airline route authority between two European cities that expires in three years

The route authority may be renewed every five years, and the acquiring entity intends to comply with the applicable rules and regulations surrounding renewal. Route authority renewals are routinely granted at a minimal cost and historically have been renewed when the airline has complied with the applicable rules and regulations. The acquiring entity expects to provide service indefinitely between the two cities from its hub airports and expects that the related supporting infrastructure (airport gates, slots, and terminal facility leases) will remain in place at those airports for as long as it has the route authority. An analysis of demand and cash flows supports those assumptions.

Because the facts and circumstances support the acquiring entity's ability to continue providing air service indefinitely between the two cities, the intangible asset related to the route authority is treated as having an indefinite useful life. Therefore, the route authority would not be amortised until its useful life is determined to be finite. It would be tested for impairment in accordance with IAS 36 annually and whenever there is an indication that it may be impaired.

Example 7 An acquired trademark used to identify and distinguish a leading consumer product that has been a market-share leader for the past eight years

The trademark has a remaining legal life of five years but is renewable every 10 years at little cost. The acquiring entity intends to renew the trademark continuously and evidence supports its ability to do so. An analysis of (1) product life cycle studies, (2) market, competitive and environmental trends, and (3) brand extension opportunities provides evidence that the trademarked product will generate net cash inflows for the acquiring entity for an indefinite period.

The trademark would be treated as having an indefinite useful life because it is expected to contribute to net cash inflows indefinitely. Therefore, the trademark would not be amortised until its useful life is determined to be finite. It would be tested for impairment in accordance with IAS 36 annually and whenever there is an indication that it may be impaired.

Example 8 A trademark acquired 10 years ago that distinguishes a leading consumer product

The trademark was regarded as having an indefinite useful life when it was acquired because the trademarked product was expected to generate net cash inflows indefinitely. However, unexpected competition has recently entered the market and will reduce future sales of the product. Management estimates that net cash inflows generated by the product will be 20 per cent less for the foreseeable future. However, management expects that the product will continue to generate net cash inflows indefinitely at those reduced amounts.

As a result of the projected decrease in future net cash inflows, the entity determines that the estimated recoverable amount of the trademark is less than its carrying amount, and an impairment loss is recognised. Because it is still regarded as having an indefinite useful life, the trademark would continue not to be amortised but would be tested for impairment in accordance with IAS 36 annually and whenever there is an indication that it may be impaired.

Example 9 A trademark for a line of products that was acquired several years ago in a business combination

At the time of the business combination the acquiree had been producing the line of products for 35 years with many new models developed under the trademark. At the acquisition date the acquirer expected to continue producing the line, and an analysis of various economic factors indicated there was no limit to the period the trademark would contribute to net cash inflows. Consequently, the trademark was not amortised by the acquirer. However, management has recently decided that production of the product line will be discontinued over the next four years.

Because the useful life of the acquired trademark is no longer regarded as indefinite, the carrying amount of the trademark would be tested for impairment in accordance with IAS 36 and amortised over its remaining four-year useful life.

IASB documents published to accompany

International Accounting Standard 39

Financial Instruments: Recognition and Measurement

This version includes amendments resulting from IFRSs issued up to 31 December 2009.

The text of the unaccompanied IAS 39 is contained in Part A of this edition. Its effective date when issued was 1 January 2005. The effective date of the most recent amendments is 1 January 2013. This part presents the following accompanying documents:

Approval by the Board of IAS 39 issued in December 2003

International Accounting Standard 39 *Financial Instruments: Recognition and Measurement* (as revised in 2003) was approved for issue by eleven of the fourteen members of the International Accounting Standards Board. Messrs Cope, Leisenring and McGregor dissented. Their dissenting opinions are set out after the Basis for Conclusions.

Sir David Tweedie   Chairman

Thomas E Jones   Vice-Chairman

Mary E Barth

Hans-Georg Bruns

Anthony T Cope

Robert P Garnett

Gilbert Gélard

James J Leisenring

Warren J McGregor

Patricia L O'Malley

Harry K Schmid

John T Smith

Geoffrey Whittington

Tatsumi Yamada

Approval of *Fair Value Hedge Accounting for a Portfolio Hedge of Interest Rate Risk* (Amendments to IAS 39) by the Board issued in March 2004

Fair Value Hedge Accounting for a Portfolio Hedge of Interest Rate Risk (Amendments to IAS 39) was approved for issue by thirteen of the fourteen members of the International Accounting Standards Board. Mr Smith dissented. His dissenting opinion is set out after the Basis for Conclusions.

Sir David Tweedie	Chairman
Thomas E Jones	Vice-Chairman
Mary E Barth	
Hans-Georg Bruns	
Anthony T Cope	
Robert P Garnett	
Gilbert Gélard	
James J Leisenring	
Warren J McGregor	
Patricia L O'Malley	
Harry K Schmid	
John T Smith	
Geoffrey Whittington	
Tatsumi Yamada	

Approval by the Board of *Transition and Initial Recognition of Financial Assets and Financial Liabilities* (Amendments to IAS 39) issued in December 2004

Transition and Initial Recognition of Financial Assets and Financial Liabilities (Amendments to IAS 39) was approved for issue by the fourteen members of the International Accounting Standards Board.

Sir David Tweedie   Chairman

Thomas E Jones   Vice-Chairman

Mary E Barth

Hans-Georg Bruns

Anthony T Cope

Jan Engström

Robert P Garnett

Gilbert Gélard

James J Leisenring

Warren J McGregor

Patricia L O'Malley

John T Smith

Geoffrey Whittington

Tatsumi Yamada

Approval by the Board of *Cash Flow Hedge Accounting of Forecast Intragroup Transactions* (Amendments to IAS 39) issued in April 2005

Cash Flow Hedge Accounting of Forecast Intragroup Transactions (Amendments to IAS 39) was approved for issue by the fourteen members of the International Accounting Standards Board.

Sir David Tweedie   Chairman

Thomas E Jones   Vice-Chairman

Mary E Barth

Hans-Georg Bruns

Anthony T Cope

Jan Engström

Robert P Garnett

Gilbert Gélard

James J Leisenring

Warren J McGregor

Patricia L O'Malley

John T Smith

Geoffrey Whittington

Tatsumi Yamada

Approval by the Board of *The Fair Value Option* (Amendments to IAS 39) issued in June 2005

The Fair Value Option (Amendments to IAS 39) was approved for issue by eleven of the fourteen members of the International Accounting Standards Board. Professor Barth, Mr Garnett and Professor Whittington dissented. Their dissenting opinions are set out after the Basis for Conclusions.

Sir David Tweedie	Chairman
Thomas E Jones	Vice-Chairman
Mary E Barth	
Hans-Georg Bruns	
Anthony T Cope	
Jan Engström	
Robert P Garnett	
Gilbert Gélard	
James J Leisenring	
Warren J McGregor	
Patricia L O'Malley	
John T Smith	
Geoffrey Whittington	
Tatsumi Yamada	

　　　　　　　　　　© IASCF

Approval by the Board of *Financial Guarantee Contracts* (Amendments to IAS 39 and IFRS 4) issued in August 2005

Financial Guarantee Contracts (Amendments to IAS 39 and IFRS 4 *Insurance Contracts*) was approved for issue by the fourteen members of the International Accounting Standards Board.

Sir David Tweedie	Chairman
Thomas E Jones	Vice-Chairman
Mary E Barth	
Hans-Georg Bruns	
Anthony T Cope	
Jan Engström	
Robert P Garnett	
Gilbert Gélard	
James J Leisenring	
Warren J McGregor	
Patricia L O'Malley	
John T Smith	
Geoffrey Whittington	
Tatsumi Yamada	

Approval by the Board of *Eligible Hedged Items* (Amendment to IAS 39) issued in July 2008

Eligible Hedged Items (Amendment to IAS 39) was approved for issue by the thirteen members of the International Accounting Standards Board.

Sir David Tweedie	Chairman
Thomas E Jones	Vice-Chairman
Mary E Barth	
Stephen Cooper	
Philippe Danjou	
Jan Engström	
Robert P Garnett	
Gilbert Gélard	
James J Leisenring	
Warren J McGregor	
John T Smith	
Tatsumi Yamada	
Wei-Guo Zhang	

Approval by the Board of *Reclassification of Financial Assets* (Amendments to IAS 39 and IFRS 7) issued in October 2008

Reclassification of Financial Assets (Amendments to IAS 39 *Financial Instruments: Recognition and Measurement* and IFRS 7 *Financial Instruments: Disclosures*) was approved for issue by eleven of the thirteen members of the International Accounting Standards Board. Messrs Leisenring and Smith dissented. Their dissenting opinions are set out after the Basis for Conclusions.

Sir David Tweedie	Chairman
Thomas E Jones	Vice-Chairman
Mary E Barth	
Stephen Cooper	
Philippe Danjou	
Jan Engström	
Robert P Garnett	
Gilbert Gélard	
James J Leisenring	
Warren J McGregor	
John T Smith	
Tatsumi Yamada	
Wei-Guo Zhang	

Approval by the Board of *Reclassification of Financial Assets—Effective Date and Transition* (Amendments to IAS 39 and IFRS 7) issued in November 2008

Reclassification of Financial Assets—Effective Date and Transition (Amendments to IAS 39 *Financial Instruments: Recognition and Measurement* and IFRS 7 *Financial Instruments: Disclosures*) was approved for issue by the thirteen members of the International Accounting Standards Board.

Sir David Tweedie	Chairman
Thomas E Jones	Vice-Chairman
Mary E Barth	
Stephen Cooper	
Philippe Danjou	
Jan Engström	
Robert P Garnett	
Gilbert Gélard	
James J Leisenring	
Warren J McGregor	
John T Smith	
Tatsumi Yamada	
Wei-Guo Zhang	

Contents

DISSENTING OPINIONS

Basis for Conclusions on
IAS 39 *Financial Instruments: Recognition and Measurement*

This Basis for Conclusions accompanies, but is not part of, IAS 39.

In this Basis for Conclusions the terminology has not been amended to reflect the changes made by IAS 1 Presentation of Financial Statements *(as revised in 2007).*

In November 2009 the Board amended the requirements of IAS 39 relating to classification and measurement of assets within the scope of IAS 39 and relocated them to IFRS 9 Financial Instruments. *Accordingly, the following were deleted: paragraphs BC13 and BC14, the heading above paragraph BC25 and paragraphs BC25–BC29, paragraph BC70, the heading above paragraph BC104A and paragraphs BC104A–BC104E, the headings above paragraphs BC125, BC127 and BC129 and paragraphs BC125–BC130, the heading above paragraph BC221 and that paragraph and the heading above paragraph BC222 and that paragraph.*

BC1   This Basis for Conclusions summarises the International Accounting Standards Board's considerations in reaching the conclusions on revising IAS 39 *Financial Instruments: Recognition and Measurement* in 2003. Individual Board members gave greater weight to some factors than to others.

BC2   In July 2001 the Board announced that, as part of its initial agenda of technical projects, it would undertake a project to improve a number of Standards, including IAS 32 *Financial Instruments: Disclosure and Presentation* and IAS 39 *Financial Instruments: Recognition and Measurement*. The objectives of the Improvements project were to reduce the complexity in the Standards by clarifying and adding guidance, eliminating internal inconsistencies and incorporating into the Standards elements of Standing Interpretations Committee (SIC) Interpretations and IAS 39 implementation guidance. In June 2002 the Board published its proposals in an Exposure Draft of Proposed Amendments to IAS 32 *Financial Instruments: Disclosure and Presentation* and IAS 39 *Financial Instruments: Recognition and Measurement*, with a comment deadline of 14 October 2002. In August 2003 the Board published a further Exposure Draft of Proposed Amendments to IAS 39 on *Fair Value Hedge Accounting for a Portfolio Hedge of Interest Rate Risk*, with a comment deadline of 14 November 2003.

BC3   Because the Board's intention was not to reconsider the fundamental approach to the accounting for financial instruments established by IAS 32 and IAS 39, this Basis for Conclusions does not discuss requirements in IAS 39 that the Board has not reconsidered.

Background

BC4   The original version of IAS 39 became effective for financial statements covering financial years beginning on or after 1 January 2001. It reflected a mixed measurement model in which some financial assets and financial liabilities are measured at fair value and others at cost or amortised cost, depending in part on an entity's intention in holding an instrument.

BC5   The Board recognises that accounting for financial instruments is a difficult and controversial subject. The Board's predecessor body, the International Accounting Standards Committee (IASC) began its work on the issue some 15 years ago, in 1988. During the next eight years it published two Exposure Drafts, culminating in the issue of IAS 32 on disclosure and presentation in 1995. IASC decided that its initial proposals on recognition and measurement should not be progressed to a Standard, in view of:

- the critical response they had attracted;

- evolving practices in financial instruments; and

- the developing thinking by national standard-setters.

BC6   Accordingly, in 1997 IASC published, jointly with the Canadian Accounting Standards Board, a discussion paper that proposed a different approach, namely that all financial assets and financial liabilities should be measured at fair value. The responses to that paper indicated both widespread unease with some of its proposals and that more work needed to be done before a standard requiring a full fair value approach could be contemplated.

BC7   In the meantime, IASC concluded that a standard on the recognition and measurement of financial instruments was needed urgently. It noted that although financial instruments were widely held and used throughout the world, few countries apart from the United States had any recognition and measurement standards for them. In addition, IASC had agreed with the International Organization of Securities Commissions (IOSCO) that it would develop a set of 'core' International Accounting Standards that could be endorsed by IOSCO for the purpose of cross-border capital raising and listing in all global markets. Those core standards included one on the recognition and measurement of financial instruments. Accordingly, IASC developed the version of IAS 39 that was issued in 2000.

BC8   In December 2000 a Financial Instruments Joint Working Group of Standard Setters (JWG), comprising representatives or members of accounting standard-setters and professional organisations from a range of countries, published a Draft Standard and Basis for Conclusions entitled *Financial Instruments and Similar Items*. That Draft Standard proposed far-reaching changes to accounting for financial instruments and similar items, including the measurement of virtually all financial instruments at fair value. In the light of feedback on the JWG's proposals, it is evident that much more work is needed before a comprehensive fair value accounting model could be introduced.

BC9   In July 2001 the Board announced that it would undertake a project to improve the existing requirements on the accounting for financial instruments in IAS 32 and IAS 39. The improvements deal with practice issues identified by audit firms, national standard-setters, regulators and others, and issues identified in the IAS 39 implementation guidance process or by IASB staff.

BC10   In June 2002 the Board published an Exposure Draft of proposed amendments to IAS 32 and IAS 39 for a 116-day comment period. More than 170 comment letters were received.

BC11   Subsequently, the Board took steps to enable constituents to inform it better about the main issues arising out of the comment process, and to enable the Board to explain its views of the issues and its tentative conclusions. These consultations included:

(a)   discussions with the Standards Advisory Council on the main issues raised in the comment process.

(b)   nine round-table discussions with constituents during March 2003 conducted in Brussels and London. Over 100 organisations and individuals took part in those discussions.

(c)   discussions with the Board's liaison standard-setters of the issues raised in the round-table discussions.

(d)   meetings between members of the Board and its staff and various groups of constituents to explore further issues raised in comment letters and at the round-table discussions.

BC11A   Some of the comment letters on the June 2002 Exposure Draft and participants in the round-tables raised a significant issue for which the June 2003 Exposure Draft had not proposed any changes. This was hedge accounting for a portfolio hedge of interest rate risk (sometimes referred to as 'macro hedging') and the related question of the treatment in hedge accounting of deposits with a demand feature (sometimes referred to as 'demand deposits' or 'demandable liabilities'). In particular, some were concerned that it was very difficult to achieve fair value hedge accounting for a macro hedge in accordance with previous versions of IAS 39.

BC11B   In the light of these concerns, the Board decided to explore whether and how IAS 39 might be amended to enable fair value hedge accounting to be used more readily for a portfolio hedge of interest rate risk. This resulted in a further Exposure Draft of Proposed Amendments to IAS 39 that was published in August 2003 and on which more than 120 comment letters were received. The amendments proposed in the Exposure Draft were finalised in March 2004.

BC11C   After those amendments were issued in March 2004 the Board received further comments from constituents calling for further amendments to the Standard. In particular, as a result of continuing discussions with constituents, the Board became aware that some, including prudential supervisors of banks, securities companies and insurers, were concerned that the fair value option might be used inappropriately. These constituents were concerned that:

(a)   entities might apply the fair value option to financial assets or financial liabilities whose fair value is not verifiable. If so, because the valuation of these financial assets and financial liabilities is subjective, entities might determine their fair value in a way that inappropriately affects profit or loss.

(b)   the use of the option might increase, rather than decrease, volatility in profit or loss, for example if an entity applied the option to only one part of a matched position.

(c)   if an entity applied the fair value option to financial liabilities, it might result in an entity recognising gains or losses in profit or loss associated with changes in its own creditworthiness.

In response to those concerns, the Board published in April 2004 an Exposure Draft of proposed restrictions to the fair value option. In March 2005 the Board held a series of round-table meetings to discuss proposals with invited constituents. As a result of this process, the Board issued an amendment to IAS 39 in June 2005 relating to the fair value option.

BC11D   In September 2007, following a request from the International Financial Reporting Interpretations Committee (IFRIC), the Board published *Exposures Qualifying for Hedge Accounting*, an exposure draft of proposed amendments to IAS 39. The Board's objective was to clarify its requirements on exposures qualifying for hedge accounting and to provide additional guidance by specifying eligible risks and portions of cash flows. The Board received 75 responses to the exposure draft. Many respondents raised concerns about the rule-based approach proposed in the exposure draft. Their responses indicated that there was little diversity in practice regarding the designation of hedged items. However, the responses demonstrated that diversity in practice existed, or was likely to occur, in the two situations set out in paragraph BC172C. After considering the responses, the Board decided to focus on those two situations. Rather than specifying eligible risks and portions as proposed in the exposure draft, the Board decided to address those situations by adding application guidance to illustrate how the principles underlying hedge accounting should be applied. The Board subsequently issued *Eligible Hedged Items* (Amendment to IAS 39) in July 2008. The rationale for the amendment is set out in paragraphs BC172B–BC172J.

BC11E   In October 2008 the Board received requests to address differences between the reclassification requirements of IAS 39 and US GAAP (Statements of Financial Accounting Standards No. 115 *Accounting for Certain Investments in Debt and Equity Securities* (SFAS 115) and No. 65 *Accounting for Certain Mortgage Banking Activities* (SFAS 65) issued by the US Financial Accounting Standards Board). In response the Board issued *Reclassification of Financial Assets* (Amendments to IAS 39 and IFRS 7) in October 2008. The amendments to IAS 39 permit non-derivative financial assets held for trading and available-for-sale financial assets to be reclassified in particular situations. The rationale for the amendments is set out in paragraphs BC104A–BC104E.[*]

BC11F   Following the issue of *Reclassification of Financial Assets* (Amendments to IAS 39 and IFRS 7) in October 2008 constituents told the Board that there was uncertainty about the interaction between those amendments and IFRIC 9 regarding the assessment of embedded derivatives. In response the Board issued *Embedded Derivatives* (Amendments to IFRIC 9 and IAS 39) in March 2009. The amendment to IAS 39 clarifies the consequences if the fair value of the embedded derivative that would have to be separated cannot be measured separately.[†]

---

[*]   Superseded by IFRS 9 *Financial Instruments*

[†]   IFRS 9 *Financial Instruments* applies to combined instruments in which a derivative is embedded in a host that is within the scope of IFRS 9. However, the requirements of IAS 39 continue to apply to derivatives embedded in non-financial hosts and financial hosts outside the scope of IFRS 9.

BC12   The Board did not reconsider the fundamental approach to accounting for financial instruments contained in IAS 39.* Some of the complexity in existing requirements is inevitable in a mixed measurement model based in part on management's intentions for holding financial instruments and given the complexity of finance concepts and fair value estimation issues. The amendments reduce some of the complexity by clarifying the Standard, eliminating internal inconsistencies and incorporating additional guidance into the Standard.

BC13–   [Deleted]
BC14

Scope

Loan commitments (paragraphs 2(h) and 4)

BC15   Loan commitments are firm commitments to provide credit under pre-specified terms and conditions. In the IAS 39 implementation guidance process, the question was raised whether a bank's loan commitments are derivatives accounted for at fair value under IAS 39. This question arises because a commitment to make a loan at a specified rate of interest during a fixed period of time meets the definition of a derivative. In effect, it is a written option for the potential borrower to obtain a loan at a specified rate.

BC16   To simplify the accounting for holders and issuers of loan commitments, the Board decided to exclude particular loan commitments from the scope of IAS 39. The effect of the exclusion is that an entity will not recognise and measure changes in fair value of these loan commitments that result from changes in market interest rates or credit spreads. This is consistent with the measurement of the loan that results if the holder of the loan commitment exercises its right to obtain financing, because changes in market interest rates do not affect the measurement of an asset measured at amortised cost (assuming it is not designated in a category other than loans and receivables).†

BC17   However, the Board decided that an entity should be permitted to measure a loan commitment at fair value with changes in fair value recognised in profit or loss on the basis of designation at inception of the loan commitment as a financial liability through profit or loss. This may be appropriate, for example, if the entity manages risk exposures related to loan commitments on a fair value basis.

BC18   The Board further decided that a loan commitment should be excluded from the scope of IAS 39 only if it cannot be settled net. If the value of a loan commitment can be settled net in cash or another financial instrument, including when the entity has a past practice of selling the resulting loan assets shortly after

---

*   In November 2009 the Board amended the requirements of IAS 39 relating to classification and measurement of assets within the scope of IAS 39 and relocated them to IFRS 9 *Financial Instruments*. IFRS 9 applies to all assets within the scope of IAS 39.

†   IFRS 9 *Financial Instruments*, issued in November 2009, eliminated the category of loans and receivables.

origination, it is difficult to justify its exclusion from the requirement in IAS 39 to measure at fair value similar instruments that meet the definition of a derivative.

BC19　Some comments received on the Exposure Draft disagreed with the Board's proposal that an entity that has a past practice of selling the assets resulting from its loan commitments shortly after origination should apply IAS 39 to all of its loan commitments. The Board considered this concern and agreed that the words in the Exposure Draft did not reflect the Board's intention. Thus, the Board clarified that if an entity has a past practice of selling the assets resulting from its loan commitments shortly after origination, it applies IAS 39 only to its loan commitments in the same class.

BC20　Finally, the Board decided that commitments to provide a loan at a below-market interest rate should be initially measured at fair value, and subsequently measured at the higher of (a) the amount that would be recognised under IAS 37 and (b) the amount initially recognised less, where appropriate, cumulative amortisation recognised in accordance with IAS 18 *Revenue*. It noted that without such a requirement, liabilities that result from such commitments might not be recognised in the balance sheet, because in many cases no cash consideration is received.

BC20A　As discussed in paragraphs BC21–BC23E, the Board amended IAS 39 in 2005 to address financial guarantee contracts. In making those amendments, the Board moved the material on loan commitments from the scope section of the Standard to the section on subsequent measurement (paragraph 47(d)). The purpose of this change was to rationalise the presentation of this material without making substantive changes.

Financial guarantee contracts (paragraphs 2(e), 9, 47(c), AG4 and AG4A)

BC21　In finalising IFRS 4 *Insurance Contracts* in early 2004, the Board reached the following conclusions:

(a)　Financial guarantee contracts can have various legal forms, such as that of a guarantee, some types of letter of credit, a credit default contract or an insurance contract. However, although this difference in legal form may in some cases reflect differences in substance, the accounting for these instruments should not depend on their legal form.

(b)　If a financial guarantee contract is not an insurance contract, as defined in IFRS 4, it should be within the scope of IAS 39. This was the case before the Board finalised IFRS 4.

(c)　As required before the Board finalised IFRS 4, if a financial guarantee contract was entered into or retained on transferring to another party financial assets or financial liabilities within the scope of IAS 39, the issuer should apply IAS 39 to that contract even if it is an insurance contract, as defined in IFRS 4.

(d)　Unless (c) applies, the following treatment is appropriate for a financial guarantee contract that meets the definition of an insurance contract:

(i)   At inception, the issuer of a financial guarantee contract has a recognisable liability and should measure it at fair value. If a financial guarantee contract was issued in a stand-alone arm's length transaction to an unrelated party, its fair value at inception is likely to equal the premium received, unless there is evidence to the contrary.

(ii)   Subsequently, the issuer should measure the contract at the higher of the amount determined in accordance with IAS 37 *Provisions, Contingent Liabilities and Contingent Assets* and the amount initially recognised less, when appropriate, cumulative amortisation recognised in accordance with IAS 18 *Revenue*.

BC22   Mindful of the need to develop a 'stable platform' of Standards for 2005, the Board finalised IFRS 4 in early 2004 without specifying the accounting for these contracts and then published an Exposure Draft *Financial Guarantee Contracts and Credit Insurance* in July 2004 to expose for public comment the conclusion set out in paragraph BC21(d). The Board set a comment deadline of 8 October 2004 and received more than 60 comment letters. Before reviewing the comment letters, the Board held a public education session at which it received briefings from representatives of the International Credit Insurance & Surety Association and of the Association of Financial Guaranty Insurers.

BC23   Some respondents to the Exposure Draft of July 2004 argued that there were important economic differences between credit insurance contracts and other forms of contract that met the proposed definition of a financial guarantee contract. However, both in developing the Exposure Draft and in subsequently discussing the comments received, the Board was unable to identify differences that would justify differences in accounting treatment.

BC23A   Some respondents to the Exposure Draft of July 2004 noted that some credit insurance contracts contain features, such as cancellation and renewal rights and profit-sharing features, that the Board will not address until phase II of its project on insurance contracts. They argued that the Exposure Draft did not give enough guidance to enable them to account for these features. The Board concluded it could not address such features in the short term. The Board noted that when credit insurers issue credit insurance contracts, they typically recognise a liability measured as either the premium received or an estimate of the expected losses. However, the Board was concerned that some other issuers of financial guarantee contracts might argue that no recognisable liability existed at inception. To provide a temporary solution that balances these competing concerns, the Board decided the following:

(a)   If the issuer of financial guarantee contracts has previously asserted explicitly that it regards such contracts as insurance contracts and has used accounting applicable to insurance contracts, the issuer may elect to apply either IAS 39 or IFRS 4 to such financial guarantee contracts.

(b)   In all other cases, the issuer of a financial guarantee contract should apply IAS 39.

BC23B   The Board does not regard criteria such as those described in paragraph BC23A(a) as suitable for the long term, because they can lead to different accounting for contracts that have similar economic effects. However, the Board could not find a more compelling approach to resolve its concerns for the short term. Moreover, although the criteria described in paragraph BC23A(a) may appear imprecise, the Board believes that the criteria would provide a clear answer in the vast majority of cases. Paragraph AG4A gives guidance on the application of those criteria.

BC23C   The Board considered convergence with US GAAP. In US GAAP, the requirements for financial guarantee contracts (other than those covered by US standards specific to the insurance sector) are in FASB Interpretation 45 *Guarantor's Accounting and Disclosure Requirements for Guarantees, Including Indirect Guarantees of Indebtedness of Others* (FIN 45). The recognition and measurement requirements of FIN 45 do not apply to guarantees issued between parents and their subsidiaries, between entities under common control, or by a parent or subsidiary on behalf of a subsidiary or the parent. Some respondents to the Exposure Draft of July 2004 asked the Board to provide a similar exemption. They argued that the requirement to recognise these financial guarantee contracts in separate or individual financial statements would cause costs disproportionate to the likely benefits, given that intragroup transactions are eliminated on consolidation. However, to avoid the omission of material liabilities from separate or individual financial statements, the Board did not create such an exemption.

BC23D   The Board issued the amendments for financial guarantee contracts in August 2005. After those amendments, the recognition and measurement requirements for financial guarantee contracts within the scope of IAS 39 are consistent with FIN 45 in some areas, but differ in others:

(a)   Like FIN 45, IAS 39 requires initial recognition at fair value.

(b)   IAS 39 requires systematic amortisation, in accordance with IAS 18, of the liability recognised initially. This is compatible with FIN 45, though FIN 45 contains less prescriptive requirements on subsequent measurement. Both IAS 39 and FIN 45 include a liability adequacy (or loss recognition) test, although the tests differ because of underlying differences in the Standards to which those tests refer (IAS 37 and SFAS 5).

(c)   Like FIN 45, IAS 39 permits a different treatment for financial guarantee contracts issued by insurers.

(d)   Unlike FIN 45, IAS 39 does not contain exemptions for parents, subsidiaries or other entities under common control. However, any differences are reflected only in the separate or individual financial statements of the parent, subsidiaries or common control entities.

BC23E   Some respondents to the Exposure Draft of July 2004 asked for guidance on the treatment of financial guarantee contracts by the holder. However, this was beyond the limited scope of the project.

Contracts to buy or sell a non-financial item (paragraphs 5–7 and AG10)

BC24 Before the amendments, IAS 39 and IAS 32 were not consistent with respect to the circumstances in which a commodity-based contract meets the definition of a financial instrument and is accounted for as a derivative. The Board concluded that the amendments should make them consistent on the basis of the notion that a contract to buy or sell a non-financial item should be accounted for as a derivative when it (i) can be settled net or by exchanging financial instruments and (ii) is not held for the purpose of receipt or delivery of the non-financial item in accordance with the entity's expected purchase, sale or usage requirements (a 'normal' purchase or sale). In addition, the Board concluded that the notion of when a contract can be settled net should include contracts:

(a) where the entity has a practice of settling similar contracts net in cash or another financial instrument or by exchanging financial instruments;

(b) for which the entity has a practice of taking delivery of the underlying and selling it within a short period after delivery for the purpose of generating a profit from short-term fluctuations in price or dealer's margin; and

(c) in which the non-financial item that is the subject of the contract is readily convertible to cash.

Because practices of settling net or taking delivery of the underlying and selling it within a short period after delivery also indicate that the contracts are not 'normal' purchases or sales, such contracts are within the scope of IAS 39 and are accounted for as derivatives. The Board also decided to clarify that a written option that can be settled net in cash or another financial instrument, or by exchanging financial instruments, is within the scope of the Standard and cannot qualify as a 'normal' purchase or sale.

Business combination forward contracts

BC24A The Board was advised that there was diversity in practice regarding the application of the exemption in paragraph 2(g) of IAS 39. Paragraph 2(g) applies to particular contracts associated with a business combination and results in those contracts not being accounted for as derivatives while, for example, necessary regulatory and legal processes are being completed.

BC24B As part of the *Improvements to IFRSs* issued in April 2009, the Board concluded that paragraph 2(g) should be restricted to forward contracts between an acquirer and a selling shareholder to buy or sell an acquiree in a business combination at a future acquisition date and should not apply to option contracts, whether or not currently exercisable, that on exercise will result in control of an entity.

BC24C The Board concluded that the purpose of paragraph 2(g) is to exempt from the provisions of IAS 39 contracts for business combinations that are firmly committed to be completed. Once the business combination is consummated, the entity follows the requirements of IFRS 3. Paragraph 2(g) applies only when completion of the business combination is not dependent on further actions of either party (and only the passage of a normal period of time is required). Option contracts allow one party to control the occurrence or non-occurrence of future events depending on whether the option is exercised.

BC24D   Several respondents to the exposure draft expressed the view that the proposed amendment should also apply to contracts to acquire investments in associates, referring to paragraph 20 of IAS 28. However, the acquisition of an interest in an associate represents the acquisition of a financial instrument. The acquisition of an interest in an associate does not represent an acquisition of a business with subsequent consolidation of the constituent net assets. The Board noted that paragraph 20 of IAS 28 explains only the methodology used to account for investments in associates. This should not be taken to imply that the principles for business combinations and consolidations can be applied by analogy to accounting for investments in associates and joint ventures. The Board concluded that paragraph 2(g) should not be applied by analogy to contracts to acquire investments in associates and similar transactions. This conclusion is consistent with the conclusion the Board reached regarding impairment losses on investments in associates as noted in the *Improvements to IFRSs* issued in May 2008 and stated in paragraph BC27 of the Basis for Conclusions on IAS 28.

BC24E   Some respondents to the exposure draft raised concerns about the proposed transition requirement. The Board noted that determining the fair value of a currently outstanding contract when its inception was before the effective date of this amendment would require the use of hindsight and might not achieve comparability. Accordingly, the Board decided not to require retrospective application. The Board also rejected applying the amendment prospectively only to new contracts entered into after the effective date because that would create a lack of comparability between contracts outstanding as of the effective date and contracts entered into after the effective date. Therefore, the Board concluded that the amendment to paragraph 2(g) should be applied prospectively to all unexpired contracts for annual periods beginning on or after 1 January 2010.

Definitions

BC25–   [Deleted]
BC29

Effective interest rate (paragraphs 9 and AG5–AG8)

BC30   The Board considered whether the effective interest rate for all financial instruments should be calculated on the basis of estimated cash flows (consistently with the original IAS 39) or whether the use of estimated cash flows should be restricted to groups of financial instruments with contractual cash flows being used for individual financial instruments. The Board agreed to reconfirm the position in the original IAS 39 because it achieves consistent application of the effective interest method throughout the Standard.

BC31   The Board noted that future cash flows and the expected life can be reliably estimated for most financial assets and financial liabilities, in particular for a group of similar financial assets or similar financial liabilities. However, the Board acknowledged that in some rare cases it might not be possible to estimate the timing or amount of future cash flows reliably. It therefore decided to require that if it is not possible to estimate reliably the future cash flows or the expected life of a financial instrument, the entity should use contractual cash flows over the full contractual term of the financial instrument.

BC32   The Board also decided to clarify that expected future defaults should not be included in estimates of cash flows because this would be a departure from the incurred loss model for impairment recognition. At the same time, the Board noted that in some cases, for example, when a financial asset is acquired at a deep discount, credit losses have occurred and are reflected in the price. If an entity does not take into account such credit losses in the calculation of the effective interest rate, the entity would recognise a higher interest income than that inherent in the price paid. The Board therefore decided to clarify that such credit losses are included in the estimated cash flows when computing the effective interest rate.

BC33   The revised IAS 39 refers to all fees 'that are an integral part of the effective interest rate'. The Board included this reference to clarify that IAS 39 relates only to those fees that are determined to be an integral part of the effective interest rate in accordance with IAS 18.

BC34   Some commentators noted that it was not always clear how to interpret the requirement in the original IAS 39 that the effective interest rate must be based on discounting cash flows through maturity or the next market-based repricing date. In particular, it was not always clear whether fees, transaction costs and other premiums or discounts included in the calculation of the effective interest rate should be amortised over the period until maturity or the period to the next market-based repricing date.

BC35   For consistency with the estimated cash flows approach, the Board decided to clarify that the effective interest rate is calculated over the expected life of the instrument or, when applicable, a shorter period. A shorter period is used when the variable (eg interest rates) to which the fee, transaction costs, discount or premium relates is repriced to market rates before the expected maturity of the instrument. In such a case, the appropriate amortisation period is the period to the next such repricing date.

BC35A   The Board identified an apparent inconsistency in the guidance in the revised IAS 39. It related to whether the revised or the original effective interest rate of a debt instrument should be applied when remeasuring the instrument's carrying amount on the cessation of fair value hedge accounting. A revised effective interest rate is calculated when fair value hedge accounting ceases. The Board removed this inconsistency as part of *Improvements to IFRSs* issued in May 2008 by clarifying that the remeasurement of an instrument in accordance with paragraph AG8 is based on the revised effective interest rate calculated in accordance with paragraph 92, when applicable, rather than the original effective interest rate.

Accounting for a change in estimates

BC36   The Board considered the accounting for a change in the estimates used in calculating the effective interest rate. The Board agreed that if an entity revises its estimates of payments or receipts, it should adjust the carrying amount of the financial instrument to reflect actual and revised estimated cash flows. The adjustment is recognised as income or expense in profit or loss. The entity recalculates the carrying amount by computing the present value of remaining cash flows at the original effective interest rate of the financial instrument.

The Board noted that this approach has the practical advantage that it does not require recalculation of the effective interest rate, ie the entity simply recognises the remaining cash flows at the original rate. As a result, this approach avoids a possible conflict with the requirement when assessing impairment to discount estimated cash flows using the original effective interest rate.

Embedded derivatives

Embedded foreign currency derivatives (paragraphs 10 and AG33(d))[*]

BC37   A rationale for the embedded derivatives requirements is that an entity should not be able to circumvent the recognition and measurement requirements for derivatives merely by embedding a derivative in a non-derivative financial instrument or other contract, for example, a commodity forward in a debt instrument. To achieve consistency in accounting for such embedded derivatives, all derivatives embedded in financial instruments that are not measured at fair value with gains and losses recognised in profit or loss ought to be accounted for separately as derivatives. However, as a practical expedient IAS 39 provides that an embedded derivative need not be separated if it is regarded as closely related to its host contract. When the embedded derivative bears a close economic relationship to the host contract, such as a cap or a floor on the interest rate on a loan, it is less likely that the derivative was embedded to achieve a desired accounting result.

BC38   The original IAS 39 specified that a foreign currency derivative embedded in a non-financial host contract (such as a supply contract denominated in a foreign currency) was not separated if it required payments denominated in the currency of the primary economic environment in which any substantial party to the contract operates (their functional currencies) or the currency in which the price of the related good or service that is acquired or delivered is routinely denominated in international commerce (such as the US dollar for crude oil transactions). Such foreign currency derivatives are regarded as bearing such a close economic relationship to their host contracts that they do not have to be separated.

BC39   The requirement to separate embedded foreign currency derivatives may be burdensome for entities that operate in economies in which business contracts denominated in a foreign currency are common. For example, entities domiciled in small countries may find it convenient to denominate business contracts with entities from other small countries in an internationally liquid currency (such as the US dollar, euro or yen) rather than the local currency of any of the parties to the transaction. In addition, an entity operating in a hyperinflationary economy may use a price list in a hard currency to protect against inflation, for example, an entity that has a foreign operation in a hyperinflationary economy that denominates local contracts in the functional currency of the parent.

---

[*]   IFRS 9 *Financial Instruments* applies to combined instruments in which a derivative is embedded in a host that is within the scope of IFRS 9. However, the requirements of IAS 39 continue to apply to derivatives embedded in non-financial hosts and financial hosts outside the scope of IFRS 9.

BC40   In revising IAS 39, the Board concluded that an embedded foreign currency derivative may be integral to the contractual arrangements in the cases mentioned in the previous paragraph. It decided that a foreign currency derivative in a contract should not be required to be separated if it is denominated in a currency that is commonly used in business transactions (that are not financial instruments) in the environment in which the transaction takes place. A foreign currency derivative would be viewed as closely related to the host contract if the currency is commonly used in local business transactions, for example, when monetary amounts are viewed by the general population not in terms of the local currency but in terms of a relatively stable foreign currency, and prices may be quoted in that foreign currency (see IAS 29 *Financial Reporting in Hyperinflationary Economies*).

Inability to measure an embedded derivative separately (paragraph 12)[*]

BC40A   As described in paragraph BC11F, the Board also considered another issue related to a reclassification of a hybrid (combined) financial asset out of the fair value through profit or loss category. If the fair value of the embedded derivative that would have to be separated cannot be measured separately, the Board decided to clarify that the hybrid (combined) financial asset in its entirety should remain in the fair value through profit or loss category. The Board noted that the clarification to paragraph 12 would prevent reclassification of a hybrid (combined) financial asset out of that category between financial reporting dates, and hence avoid a requirement to reclassify the hybrid (combined) financial asset back into the fair value through profit or loss category at the end of the financial reporting period. The amendments were issued in March 2009.

Embedded prepayment penalties (paragraph AG30(g))

BC40B   The Board identified an apparent inconsistency in the guidance in IAS 39. The inconsistency related to embedded prepayment options in which the exercise price represented a penalty for early repayment (ie prepayment) of the loan.[†] The inconsistency related to whether these are considered closely related to the loan.

BC40C   The Board decided to remove this inconsistency by amending paragraph AG30(g). The amendment makes an exception to the examples in paragraph AG30(g) of embedded derivatives that are not closely related to the underlying. This exception is in respect of prepayment options, the exercise prices of which compensate the lender for the loss of interest income because the loan was prepaid. This exception is conditional on the exercise price compensating the lender for loss of interest by reducing the economic loss from reinvestment risk.

---

[*]   IFRS 9 *Financial Instruments* applies to combined instruments in which a derivative is embedded in a host that is within the scope of IFRS 9. However, the requirements of IAS 39 continue to apply to derivatives embedded in non-financial hosts and financial hosts outside the scope of IFRS 9.

[†]   IFRS 9 *Financial Instruments* eliminated the requirement to separate embedded derivatives from financial hosts within the scope of IFRS 9. However, this amendment is still relevant to derivatives embedded in host insurance contracts and other host contracts outside the scope of IFRS 9.

Recognition and derecognition*

Derecognition of a financial asset (paragraphs 15–37)

The original IAS 39

BC41 Under the original IAS 39, several concepts governed when a financial asset should be derecognised. It was not always clear when and in what order to apply these concepts. As a result, the derecognition requirements in the original IAS 39 were not applied consistently in practice.

BC42 As an example, the original IAS 39 was unclear about the extent to which risks and rewards of a transferred asset should be considered for the purpose of determining whether derecognition is appropriate and how risks and rewards should be assessed. In some cases (eg transfers with total returns swaps or unconditional written put options), the Standard specifically indicated whether derecognition was appropriate, whereas in others (eg credit guarantees) it was unclear. Also, some questioned whether the assessment should focus on risks and rewards or only risks and how different risks and rewards should be aggregated and weighed.

BC43 To illustrate, assume an entity sells a portfolio of short-term receivables of CU100[†] and provides a guarantee to the buyer for credit losses up to a specified amount (say CU20) that is less than the total amount of the receivables, but higher than the amount of expected losses (say CU5). In this case, should (a) the entire portfolio continue to be recognised, (b) the portion that is guaranteed continue to be recognised or (c) the portfolio be derecognised in full and a guarantee be recognised as a financial liability? The original IAS 39 did not give a clear answer and the IAS 39 Implementation Guidance Committee—a group set up by the Board's predecessor body to resolve interpretative issues raised in practice—was unable to reach an agreement on how IAS 39 should be applied in this case. In developing proposals for improvements to IAS 39, the Board concluded that it was important that IAS 39 should provide clear and consistent guidance on how to account for such a transaction.

Exposure draft

BC44 To resolve the problems, the Exposure Draft proposed an approach to derecognition under which a transferor of a financial asset continues to recognise that asset to the extent the transferor has a continuing involvement in it. Continuing involvement could be established in two ways: (a) a reacquisition provision (such as a call option, put option or repurchase agreement) and (b) a provision to pay or receive compensation based on changes in value of the transferred asset (such as a credit guarantee or net cash settled option).

BC45 The purpose of the approach proposed in the Exposure Draft was to facilitate consistent implementation and application of IAS 39 by eliminating conflicting concepts and establishing an unambiguous, more internally consistent and

---

* In November 2009 the requirements for the recognition of assets within the scope of IAS 39 were relocated in IFRS 9 *Financial Instruments*.

† In this Basis for Conclusions, monetary amounts are denominated in 'currency units (CU)'.

workable approach to derecognition. The main benefits of the proposed approach were that it would greatly clarify IAS 39 and provide transparency on the face of the balance sheet about any continuing involvement in a transferred asset.

Comments received

BC46   Many respondents agreed that there were inconsistencies in the existing derecognition requirements in IAS 39. However, there was limited support for the continuing involvement approach proposed in the Exposure Draft. Respondents expressed conceptual and practical concerns, including:

(a)   any benefits of the proposed changes did not outweigh the burden of adopting a different approach that had its own set of (as yet unidentified and unsolved) problems;

(b)   the proposed approach was a fundamental change from that in the original IAS 39;

(c)   the proposal did not achieve convergence with US GAAP;

(d)   the proposal was untested; and

(e)   the proposal was not consistent with the *Framework*.

BC47   Many respondents expressed the view that the basic approach in the original IAS 39 should be retained in the revised Standard and the inconsistencies removed. The reasons included: (a) the existing IAS 39 was proven to be reasonable in concept and operational in practice and (b) the approach should not be changed until the Board developed an alternative comprehensive approach.

Revisions to IAS 39

BC48   In response to the comments received, the Board decided to revert to the derecognition concepts in the original IAS 39 and to clarify how and in what order the concepts should be applied. In particular, the Board decided that an evaluation of the transfer of risks and rewards should precede an evaluation of the transfer of control for all types of transactions.

BC49   Although the structure and wording of the derecognition requirements have been substantially amended, the Board concluded that the requirements in the revised IAS 39 are not substantially different from those in the original IAS 39. In support of this conclusion, it noted that the application of the requirements in the revised IAS 39 generally results in answers that could have been obtained under the original IAS 39. In addition, although there will be a need to apply judgement to evaluate whether substantially all risks and rewards have been retained, this type of judgement is not new compared with the original IAS 39. However, the revised requirements clarify the application of the concepts in circumstances in which it was previously unclear how IAS 39 should be applied. The Board concluded that it would be inappropriate to revert to the original IAS 39 without such clarifications.

BC50   The Board also decided to include guidance in the Standard that clarifies how to evaluate the concepts of risks and rewards and of control. The Board regards such guidance as important to provide a framework for applying the concepts in IAS 39. Although judgement is still necessary to apply the concepts in practice, the guidance should increase consistency in how the concepts are applied.

BC51 More specifically, the Board decided that the transfer of risks and rewards should be evaluated by comparing the entity's exposure before and after the transfer to the variability in the amounts and timing of the net cash flows of the transferred asset. If the entity's exposure, on a present value basis, has not changed significantly, the entity would conclude that it has retained substantially all risks and rewards. In this case, the Board concluded that the asset should continue to be recognised. This accounting treatment is consistent with the treatment of repurchase transactions and some assets subject to deep in-the-money options under the original IAS 39. It is also consistent with how some interpreted the original IAS 39 when an entity sells a portfolio of short-term receivables but retains all substantive risks through the issue of a guarantee to compensate for all expected credit losses (see the example in paragraph BC43).

BC52 The Board decided that control should be evaluated by looking to whether the transferee has the practical ability to sell the asset. If the transferee can sell the asset (eg because the asset is readily obtainable in the market and the transferee can obtain a replacement asset should it need to return the asset to the transferor), the transferor has not retained control because the transferor does not control the transferee's use of the asset. If the transferee cannot sell the asset (eg because the transferor has a call option and the asset is not readily obtainable in the market, so that the transferee cannot obtain a replacement asset), the transferor has retained control because the transferee is not free to use the asset as its own.

BC53 The original IAS 39 also did not contain guidance on when a part of a financial asset could be considered for derecognition. The Board decided to include such guidance in the Standard to clarify the issue. It decided that an entity should apply the derecognition principles to a part of a financial asset only if that part contains no risks and rewards relating to the part not being considered for derecognition. Accordingly, a part of a financial asset is considered for derecognition only if it comprises:

(a) only specifically identified cash flows from a financial asset (or a group of similar financial assets);

(b) only a fully proportionate (pro rata) share of the cash flows from a financial asset (or a group of similar financial assets); or

(c) only a fully proportionate (pro rata) share of specifically identified cash flows from a financial asset (or a group of similar financial assets).

In all other cases the derecognition principles are applied to the financial asset in its entirety.

Arrangements under which an entity retains the contractual rights to receive the cash flows of a financial asset but assumes a contractual obligation to pay the cash flows to one or more recipients (paragraph 19)

BC54 The original IAS 39 did not provide explicit guidance about the extent to which derecognition is appropriate for contractual arrangements in which an entity retains its contractual right to receive the cash flows from an asset, but assumes a contractual obligation to pay those cash flows to another entity (a 'pass-through arrangement'). Questions were raised in practice about the appropriate accounting treatment and divergent interpretations evolved for more complex structures.

BC55 To illustrate the issue using a simple example, assume the following. Entity A makes a five-year interest-bearing loan (the 'original asset') of CU100 to Entity B. Entity A then enters into an agreement with Entity C in which, in exchange for a cash payment of CU90, Entity A agrees to pass to Entity C 90 per cent of all principal and interest payments collected from Entity B (as, when and if collected). Entity A accepts no obligation to make any payments to Entity C other than 90 per cent of exactly what has been received from Entity B. Entity A provides no guarantee to Entity C about the performance of the loan and has no rights to retain 90 per cent of the cash collected from Entity B nor any obligation to pay cash to Entity C if cash has not been received from Entity B. In the example above, does Entity A have a loan asset of CU100 and a liability of CU90 or does it have an asset of CU10? To make the example more complex, what if Entity A first transfers the loan to a consolidated special purpose entity (SPE), which in turn passes through to investors the cash flows from the asset? Does the accounting treatment change because Entity A first sold the asset to an SPE?

BC56 To address these issues, the Exposure Draft of proposed amendments to IAS 39 included guidance to clarify under which conditions pass-through arrangements can be treated as a transfer of the underlying financial asset. The Board concluded that an entity does not have an asset and a liability, as defined in the *Framework*, when it enters into an arrangement to pass through cash flows from an asset and that arrangement meets specified conditions. In these cases, the entity acts more as an agent of the eventual recipients of the cash flows than as an owner of the asset. Accordingly, to the extent that those conditions are met the arrangement is treated as a transfer and considered for derecognition even though the entity may continue to collect cash flows from the asset. Conversely, to the extent the conditions are not met, the entity acts more as an owner of the asset with the result that the asset should continue to be recognised.

BC57 Respondents to the Exposure Draft were generally supportive of the proposed changes. Some respondents asked for further clarification of the requirements and the interaction with the requirements for consolidation of special purpose entities (in SIC-12 *Consolidation—Special Purpose Entities*). Respondents in the securitisation industry noted that under the proposed guidance many securitisation structures would not qualify for derecognition.

BC58 Considering these and other comments, the Board decided to proceed with its proposals to issue guidance on pass-through arrangements and to clarify that guidance in finalising the revised IAS 39.

BC59 The Board concluded that the following three conditions must be met for treating a contractual arrangement to pass through cash flows from a financial asset as a transfer of that asset:

(a) The entity has no obligation to pay amounts to the eventual recipients unless it collects equivalent amounts from the original asset. However, the entity is allowed to make short-term advances to the eventual recipient so long as it has the right of full recovery of the amount lent plus accrued interest.

(b)   The entity is prohibited by the terms of the transfer contract from selling or pledging the original asset other than as security to the eventual recipients for the obligation to pay them cash flows.

(c)   The entity has an obligation to remit any cash flows it collects on behalf of the eventual recipients without material delay. In addition, during the short settlement period, the entity is not entitled to reinvest such cash flows except for investments in cash or cash equivalents and where any interest earned from such investments is remitted to the eventual recipients.

BC60   These conditions follow from the definitions of assets and liabilities in the *Framework*. Condition (a) indicates that the transferor has no liability (because there is no present obligation to pay cash), and conditions (b) and (c) indicate that the transferor has no asset (because the transferor does not control the future economic benefits associated with the transferred asset).

BC61   The Board decided that the derecognition tests that apply to other transfers of financial assets (ie the tests of transferring substantially all the risks and rewards and control) should also apply to arrangements to pass through cash flows that meet the three conditions but do not involve a fully proportional share of all or specifically identified cash flows. Thus, if the three conditions are met and the entity passes on a fully proportional share, either of all cash flows (as in the example in paragraph BC55) or of specifically identified cash flows (eg 10 per cent of all interest cash flows), the proportion sold is derecognised, provided the entity has transferred substantially all the risks and rewards of ownership. Thus, in the example in paragraph BC55, Entity A would report a loan asset of CU10 and derecognise CU90. Similarly, if an entity enters into an arrangement that meets the three conditions above, but the arrangement is not on a fully proportionate basis, the contractual arrangement would have to meet the general derecognition conditions to qualify for derecognition. This ensures consistency in the application of the derecognition model, whether a transaction is structured as a transfer of the contractual right to receive the cash flows of a financial asset or as an arrangement to pass through cash flows.

BC62   To illustrate a disproportionate arrangement using a simple example, assume the following. Entity A originates a portfolio of five-year interest-bearing loans of CU10,000. Entity A then enters into an agreement with Entity C in which, in exchange for a cash payment of CU9,000, Entity A agrees to pay to Entity C the first CU9,000 (plus interest) of cash collected from the loan portfolio. Entity A retains rights to the last CU1,000 (plus interest), ie it retains a subordinated residual interest. If Entity A collects, say, only CU8,000 of its loans of CU10,000 because some debtors default, Entity A would pass on to Entity C all of the CU8,000 collected and Entity A keeps nothing of the CU8,000 collected. If Entity A collects CU9,500, it passes CU9,000 to Entity C and retains CU500. In this case, if Entity A retains substantially all the risks and rewards of ownership because the subordinated retained interest absorbs all of the likely variability in net cash flows, the loans continue to be recognised in their entirety even if the three pass-through conditions are met.

BC63 The Board recognises that many securitisations may fail to qualify for derecognition either because one or more of the three conditions in paragraph 19 are not met or because the entity has retained substantially all the risks and rewards of ownership.

BC64 Whether a transfer of a financial asset qualifies for derecognition does not differ depending on whether the transfer is direct to investors or through a consolidated SPE or trust that obtains the financial assets and, in turn, transfers a portion of those financial assets to third party investors.

Transfers that do not qualify for derecognition (paragraph 29)

BC65 The original IAS 39 did not provide guidance about how to account for a transfer of a financial asset that does not qualify for derecognition. The amendments include such guidance. To ensure that the accounting reflects the rights and obligations that the transferor has in relation to the transferred asset, there is a need to consider the accounting for the asset as well as the accounting for the associated liability.

BC66 When an entity retains substantially all the risks and rewards of the asset (eg in a repurchase transaction), there are generally no special accounting considerations because the entity retains upside and downside exposure to gains and losses resulting from the transferred asset. Therefore, the asset continues to be recognised in its entirety and the proceeds received are recognised as a liability. Similarly, the entity continues to recognise any income from the asset along with any expense incurred on the associated liability.

Continuing involvement in a transferred asset (paragraphs 30–35)

BC67 The Board decided that if the entity determines that it has neither retained nor transferred substantially all of the risks and rewards of an asset and that it has retained control, the entity should continue to recognise the asset to the extent of its continuing involvement. This is to reflect the transferor's continuing exposure to the risks and rewards of the asset and that this exposure is not related to the entire asset, but is limited in amount. The Board noted that precluding derecognition to the extent of the continuing involvement is useful to users of financial statements in such cases, because it reflects the entity's retained exposure to the risks and rewards of the financial asset better than full derecognition.

BC68 When the entity transfers some significant risks and rewards and retains others and derecognition is precluded because the entity retains control of the transferred asset, the entity no longer retains all the upside and downside exposure to gains and losses resulting from the transferred asset. Therefore, the revised IAS 39 requires the asset and the associated liability to be measured in a way that ensures that any changes in value of the transferred asset that are not attributed to the entity are not recognised by the entity.

BC69 For example, special measurement and income recognition issues arise if derecognition is precluded because the transferor has retained a call option or written a put option and the asset is measured at fair value. In those situations, in the absence of additional guidance, application of the general measurement and income recognition requirements for financial assets and financial liabilities in IAS 39 may result in accounting that does not represent the transferor's rights and obligations related to the transfer.

BC70   [Deleted]

Measurement*

Definitions (paragraph 9)

BC70A   The definition of a financial asset or financial liability at fair value through profit or loss excludes derivatives that are designated and effective hedging instruments. Paragraph 50 of IAS 39 prohibits the reclassification of financial instruments into or out of the fair value through profit or loss category after initial recognition. The Board noted that the prohibition on reclassification in paragraph 50 might be read as preventing a derivative financial instrument that becomes a designated and effective hedging instrument from being excluded from the fair value through profit or loss category in accordance with the definition. Similarly, it might be read as preventing a derivative that ceases to be a designated and effective hedging instrument from being accounted for at fair value through profit or loss.

BC70B   The Board decided that the prohibition on reclassification in paragraph 50 should not prevent a derivative from being accounted for at fair value through profit or loss when it does not qualify for hedge accounting and vice versa. Therefore, in *Improvements to IFRSs* issued in May 2008, the Board amended the definitions in paragraph 9(a) and added paragraph 50A to address this point.

Fair value option (paragraph 9)

BC71   The Board concluded that it could simplify the application of IAS 39 (as revised in 2000) for some entities by permitting the use of fair value measurement for any financial instrument. With one exception (see paragraph 9), this greater use of fair value is optional. The fair value measurement option does not require entities to measure more financial instruments at fair value.

BC72   IAS 39 (as revised in 2000)† did not permit an entity to measure particular categories of financial instruments at fair value with changes in fair value recognised in profit or loss. Examples included:

   (a)   originated loans and receivables, including a debt instrument acquired directly from the issuer, unless they met the conditions for classification as held for trading in paragraph 9.

---

*   The relevant paragraphs relating to measurement of assets within the scope of IAS 39 have been relocated in the Basis for Conclusions on IFRS 9 *Financial Instruments*. The remaining paragraphs still apply to financial liabilities within the scope of IAS 39 and have not been amended.

†   IFRS 9 *Financial Instruments* eliminated the loans and receivables and available-for-sale categories from IAS 39.

(b)　financial assets classified as available for sale, unless as an accounting policy choice gains and losses on all available-for-sale financial assets were recognised in profit or loss or they met the conditions for classification as held for trading in paragraph 9.

(c)　non-derivative financial liabilities, even if the entity had a policy and practice of actively repurchasing such liabilities or they formed part of an arbitrage/customer facilitation strategy or fund trading activities.

BC73　The Board decided in IAS 39 (as revised in 2003) to permit entities to designate irrevocably on initial recognition any financial instruments as ones to be measured at fair value with gains and losses recognised in profit or loss ('fair value through profit or loss'). To impose discipline on this approach, the Board decided that financial instruments should not be reclassified into or out of the category of fair value through profit or loss. In particular, some comments received on the Exposure Draft of proposed amendments to IAS 39 published in June 2002 suggested that entities could use the fair value option to recognise selectively changes in fair value in profit or loss. The Board noted that the requirement to designate irrevocably on initial recognition the financial instruments for which the fair value option is to be applied results in an entity being unable to 'cherry pick' in this way. This is because it will not be known at initial recognition whether the fair value of the instrument will increase or decrease.

BC73A　Following the issue of IAS 39 (as revised in 2003), as a result of continuing discussions with constituents on the fair value option, the Board became aware that some, including prudential supervisors of banks, securities companies and insurers, were concerned that the fair value option might be used inappropriately (as discussed in paragraph BC11C). In response to those concerns, the Board published in April 2004 an Exposure Draft of proposed restrictions to the fair value option contained in IAS 39 (as revised in 2003). After discussing comments received from constituents and a series of public round-table meetings, the Board issued an amendment to IAS 39 in June 2005 permitting entities to designate irrevocably on initial recognition financial instruments that meet one of three conditions (see paragraphs 9(b)(i), 9(b)(ii) and 11A) as ones to be measured at fair value through profit or loss.

BC74　In the amendment to the fair value option, the Board identified three situations in which permitting designation at fair value through profit or loss either results in more relevant information (cases (a) and (b) below) or is justified on the grounds of reducing complexity or increasing measurement reliability (case (c) below). These are:

(a)　when such designation eliminates or significantly reduces a measurement or recognition inconsistency (sometimes referred to as an 'accounting mismatch') that would otherwise arise (paragraphs BC75–BC75B);

(b)　when a group of financial assets, financial liabilities or both is managed and its performance is evaluated on a fair value basis, in accordance with a documented risk management or investment strategy (paragraphs BC76-BC76B); and

(c)　when an instrument contains an embedded derivative that meets particular conditions (paragraphs BC77–BC78).

BC74A The ability for entities to use the fair value option simplifies the application of IAS 39 by mitigating some anomalies that result from the different measurement attributes in the Standard. In particular, for financial instruments designated in this way:

(a) it eliminates the need for hedge accounting for hedges of fair value exposures when there are natural offsets, and thereby eliminates the related burden of designating, tracking and analysing hedge effectiveness.

(b) it eliminates the burden of separating embedded derivatives.

(c) it eliminates problems arising from a mixed measurement model when financial assets are measured at fair value and related financial liabilities are measured at amortised cost. In particular, it eliminates volatility in profit or loss and equity that results when matched positions of financial assets and financial liabilities are not measured consistently.

(d) the option to recognise unrealised gains and losses on available-for-sale financial assets in profit or loss is no longer necessary.

(e) it de-emphasises interpretative issues around what constitutes trading.

Designation as at fair value through profit or loss eliminates or significantly reduces a measurement or recognition inconsistency (paragraph 9(b)(i))

BC75 IAS 39, like comparable standards in some national jurisdictions, imposes a mixed-attribute measurement model. It requires some financial assets and liabilities to be measured at fair value, and others to be measured at amortised cost. It requires some gains and losses to be recognised in profit or loss, and others to be recognised initially as a component of equity.[*] This combination of measurement and recognition requirements can result in inconsistencies, which some refer to as 'accounting mismatches', between the accounting for an asset (or group of assets) and a liability (or group of liabilities). The notion of an accounting mismatch necessarily involves two propositions. First, an entity has particular assets and liabilities that are measured, or on which gains and losses are recognised, inconsistently; second, there is a perceived economic relationship between those assets and liabilities. For example, a liability may be considered to be related to an asset when they share a risk that gives rise to opposite changes in fair value that tend to offset, or when the entity considers that the liability funds the asset.

BC75A Some entities can overcome measurement or recognition inconsistencies by using hedge accounting or, in the case of insurers, shadow accounting. However, the Board recognises that those techniques are complex and do not address all situations. In developing the amendment to the fair value option, the Board considered whether it should impose conditions to limit the situations in which an entity could use the option to eliminate an accounting mismatch. For example, it considered whether entities should be required to demonstrate that particular assets and liabilities are managed together, or that a management

---

[*] As a consequence of the revision of IAS 1 *Presentation of Financial Statements* in 2007 these other gains and losses are recognised in other comprehensive income.

strategy is effective in reducing risk (as is required for hedge accounting to be used), or that hedge accounting or other ways of overcoming the inconsistency are not available.

BC75B The Board concluded that accounting mismatches arise in a wide variety of circumstances. In the Board's view, financial reporting is best served by providing entities with the opportunity to eliminate perceived accounting mismatches whenever that results in more relevant information. Furthermore, the Board concluded that the fair value option may validly be used in place of hedge accounting for hedges of fair value exposures, thereby eliminating the related burden of designating, tracking and analysing hedge effectiveness. Hence, the Board decided not to develop detailed prescriptive guidance about when the fair value option could be applied (such as requiring effectiveness tests similar to those required for hedge accounting) in the amendment on the fair value option. Rather, the Board decided to require disclosures in IAS 32[*] about:

- the criteria an entity uses for designating financial assets and financial liabilities as at fair value through profit or loss

- how the entity satisfies the conditions in this Standard for such designation

- the nature of the assets and liabilities so designated

- the effect on the financial statement of using this designation, namely the carrying amounts and net gains and losses on assets and liabilities so designated, information about the effect of changes in a financial liability's credit quality on changes in its fair value, and information about the credit risk of loans or receivables and any related credit derivatives or similar instruments.

A group of financial assets, financial liabilities or both is managed and its performance is evaluated on a fair value basis, in accordance with a documented risk management or investment strategy (paragraph 9(b)(ii))

BC76 The Standard requires financial instruments to be measured at fair value through profit or loss in only two situations, namely when an instrument is held for trading or when it contains an embedded derivative that the entity is unable to measure separately. However, the Board recognised that some entities manage and evaluate the performance of financial instruments on a fair value basis in other situations. Furthermore, for instruments managed and evaluated in this way, users of financial statements may regard fair value measurement as providing more relevant information. Finally, it is established practice in some industries in some jurisdictions to recognise all financial assets at fair value through profit or loss. (This practice was permitted for many assets in IAS 39 (as revised in 2000) as an accounting policy choice in accordance with which gains and losses on all available-for-sale financial assets were reported in profit or loss.)

---

[*] In August 2005, the IASB relocated all disclosures relating to financial instruments to IFRS 7 *Financial Instruments: Disclosures*.

BC76A   In the amendment to IAS 39 relating to the fair value option issued in June 2005, the Board decided to permit financial instruments managed and evaluated on a fair value basis to be measured at fair value through profit or loss. The Board also decided to introduce two requirements to make this category operational. These requirements are that the financial instruments are managed and evaluated on a fair value basis in accordance with a documented risk management or investment strategy, and that information about the financial instruments is provided internally on that basis to the entity's key management personnel.

BC76B   In looking to an entity's documented risk management or investment strategy, the Board makes no judgement on what an entity's strategy should be. However, the Board noted that users, in making economic decisions, would find useful both a description of the chosen strategy and how designation at fair value through profit or loss is consistent with it. Accordingly, IAS 32[*] requires such disclosures. The Board also noted that the required documentation of the entity's strategy need not be on an item-by-item basis, nor need it be in the level of detail required for hedge accounting. However, it should be sufficient to demonstrate that using the fair value option is consistent with the entity's risk management or investment strategy. In many cases, the entity's existing documentation, as approved by its key management personnel, should be sufficient for this purpose.

The instrument contains an embedded derivative that meets particular conditions (paragraph 11A)

BC77   The Standard requires virtually all derivative financial instruments to be measured at fair value. This requirement extends to derivatives that are *embedded* in an instrument that also includes a non-derivative host contract if the embedded derivative meets the conditions in paragraph 11. Conversely, if the embedded derivative does not meet those conditions, separate accounting with measurement of the embedded derivative at fair value is prohibited. Therefore, to satisfy these requirements, the entity must:

(a)   identify whether the instrument contains one or more embedded derivatives,

(b)   determine whether each embedded derivative is one that must be separated from the host instrument or one for which separation is prohibited, and

(c)   if the embedded derivative is one that must be separated, determine its fair value at initial recognition and subsequently.

BC77A   For some embedded derivatives, like the prepayment option in an ordinary residential mortgage, this process is fairly simple. However, entities with more complex instruments have reported that the search for and analysis of embedded derivatives (steps (a) and (b) in paragraph BC77) significantly increase the cost of complying with the Standard. They report that this cost could be eliminated if they had the option to fair value the combined contract.

---

[*]   In August 2005, the IASB relocated all disclosures relating to financial instruments to IFRS 7 *Financial Instruments: Disclosures*.

BC77B   Other entities report that one of the most common uses of the fair value option is likely to be for structured products that contain several embedded derivatives. Those structured products will typically be hedged with derivatives that offset all (or nearly all) of the risks they contain, whether or not the embedded derivatives that give rise to those risks are separated for accounting purposes. Hence, the simplest way to account for such products is to apply the fair value option so that the combined contract (as well as the derivatives that hedge it) is measured at fair value through profit or loss. Furthermore, for these more complex instruments, the fair value of the combined contract may be significantly easier to measure and hence be more reliable than the fair value of only those embedded derivatives that IAS 39 requires to be separated.

BC78   The Board sought to strike a balance between reducing the costs of complying with the embedded derivatives provisions of this Standard and the need to respond to the concerns expressed regarding possible inappropriate use of the fair value option. The Board determined that allowing the fair value option to be used for *any* instrument with an embedded derivative would make other restrictions on the use of the option ineffective, because many financial instruments include an embedded derivative. In contrast, limiting the use of the fair value option to situations in which the embedded derivative must otherwise be separated would not significantly reduce the costs of compliance and could result in less reliable measures being included in the financial statements. Therefore, the Board decided to specify situations in which an entity cannot justify using the fair value option in place of assessing embedded derivatives—when the embedded derivative does not significantly modify the cash flows that would otherwise be required by the contract or is one for which it is clear with little or no analysis when a similar hybrid instrument is first considered that separation is prohibited.

The role of prudential supervisors

BC78A   The Board considered the circumstances of regulated financial institutions such as banks and insurers in determining the extent to which conditions should be placed on the use of the fair value option. The Board recognised that regulated financial institutions are extensive holders and issuers of financial instruments and so are likely to be among the largest potential users of the fair value option. However, the Board noted that some of the prudential supervisors that oversee these entities expressed concern that the fair value option might be used inappropriately.

BC79   The Board noted that the primary objective of prudential supervisors is to maintain the financial soundness of individual financial institutions and the stability of the financial system as a whole. Prudential supervisors achieve this objective partly by assessing the risk profile of each regulated institution and imposing a risk-based capital requirement.

BC79A   The Board noted that these objectives of prudential supervision differ from the objectives of general purpose financial reporting. The latter is intended to provide information about the financial position, performance and changes in financial position of an entity that is useful to a wide range of users in making economic decisions. However, the Board acknowledged that for the purposes of determining what level of capital an institution should maintain, prudential supervisors may wish to understand the circumstances in which a regulated financial institution has chosen to apply the fair value option and evaluate the rigour of the institution's fair value measurement practices and the robustness of its underlying risk management strategies, policies and practices. Furthermore, the Board agreed that certain disclosures would assist both prudential supervisors in their evaluation of capital requirements and investors in making economic decisions. In particular, the Board decided to require an entity to disclose how it has satisfied the conditions in paragraphs 9(b), 11A and 12 for using the fair value option, including, for instruments within paragraph 9(b)(ii), a narrative description of how designation at fair value through profit or loss is consistent with the entity's documented risk management or investment strategy.

Other matters

BC80   IAS 39 (as revised in 2000) contained an accounting policy choice for the recognition of gains and losses on available-for-sale financial assets—such gains and losses could be recognised either in equity or in profit or loss. The Board concluded that the fair value option removed the need for such an accounting policy choice. An entity can achieve recognition of gains and losses on such assets in profit or loss in appropriate cases by using the fair value option. Accordingly, the Board decided that the choice that was in IAS 39 (as revised in 2000) should be removed and that gains and losses on available-for-sale financial assets should be recognised in equity when IAS 39 was revised in 2003.

BC80A   The fair value option permits (but does not require) entities to measure financial instruments at fair value with changes in fair value recognised in profit or loss. Accordingly, it does not restrict an entity's ability to use other accounting methods (such as amortised cost). Some respondents to the Exposure Draft of proposed amendments to IAS 39 published in June 2002 would have preferred more pervasive changes to expand the use of fair values and limit the choices available to entities, such as the elimination of the held-to-maturity category or the cash flow hedge accounting approach. Although such changes have the potential to make the principles in IAS 39 more coherent and less complex, the Board did not consider such changes as part of the project to improve IAS 39.

BC81   Comments received on the Exposure Draft of proposed amendments to IAS 39 published in June 2002 also questioned the proposal that all items measured at fair value through profit or loss should have the descriptor 'held for trading'. Some comments noted that 'held for trading' is commonly used with a narrower meaning, and it may be confusing for users if instruments designated at fair value through profit or loss are also called 'held for trading'. Therefore, the Board considered using a fifth category of financial instruments—'fair value through profit or loss'—to distinguish those instruments to which the fair value option was applied from those classified as held for trading. The Board rejected this possibility because it believed adding a fifth category of financial instruments would unnecessarily complicate the Standard. Rather, the Board concluded that 'fair value through profit or loss' should be used to describe a category that encompasses financial instruments classified as held for trading and those to which the fair value option is applied.

BC82   In addition, the Board decided to include a requirement for an entity to classify a financial liability as held for trading if it is incurred principally for the purpose of repurchasing it in the near term or it is part of a portfolio of identified financial instruments that are managed together and for which there is evidence of a recent pattern of short-term profit-taking. In these circumstances, the absence of a requirement to measure such financial liabilities at fair value permits cherry-picking of unrealised gains or losses. For example, if an entity wishes to recognise a gain, it can repurchase a fixed rate debt instrument that was issued in an environment where interest rates were lower than in the reporting period and if it wishes to recognise a loss, it can repurchase an issued debt instrument that was issued in an environment in which interest rates were higher than in the reporting period. However, a financial liability is not classified as held for trading merely because it funds assets that are held for trading.

BC83   The Board decided to include in revised IAS 32 * a requirement to disclose the settlement amount repayable at maturity of a liability that is designated as at fair value through profit or loss. This gives users of financial statements information about the amount owed by the entity to its creditors in the event of its liquidation.

BC84   The Board also decided to include in IAS 39 (as revised in 2003) the ability for entities to designate a loan or receivable as available for sale (see paragraph 9). The Board decided that, in the context of the existing mixed measurement model, there are no reasons to limit to any particular type of asset the ability to designate an asset as available for sale.

Application of the fair value option to a component or a proportion (rather than the entirety) of a financial asset or a financial liability

BC85   Some comments received on the Exposure Draft of proposed amendments to IAS 39 published in June 2002 argued that the fair value option should be extended so that it could also be applied to a component of a financial asset or a financial liability (eg changes in fair value attributable to one risk such as changes in a benchmark interest rate). The arguments included (a) concerns regarding inclusion of own credit risk in the measurement of financial liabilities and (b) the prohibition on using non-derivatives as hedging instruments (cash instrument hedging).

BC86   The Board concluded that IAS 39 should not extend the fair value option to components of financial assets or financial liabilities. It was concerned (a) about difficulties in measuring the change in value of the component because of ordering issues and joint effects (ie if the component is affected by more than one risk, it may be difficult to isolate accurately and measure the component); (b) that the amounts recognised in the balance sheet would be neither fair value nor cost; and (c) that a fair value adjustment for a component may move the carrying amount of an instrument away from its fair value. In finalising the 2003 amendments to IAS 39, the Board separately considered the issue of cash instrument hedging (see paragraphs BC144 and BC145).

BC86A   Other comments received on the April 2004 Exposure Draft of proposed restrictions to the fair value option contained in IAS 39 (as revised in 2003) suggested that the fair value option should be extended so that it could be applied to a proportion (ie a percentage) of a financial asset or financial liability. The Board was concerned that such an extension would require prescriptive guidance on how to determine a proportion. For example if an entity were to

---

*   In August 2005, the IASB relocated all disclosures relating to financial instruments to IFRS 7 *Financial Instruments: Disclosures.*

issue a bond totalling CU100 million in the form of 100 certificates each of CU1 million, would a proportion of 10 per cent be identified as 10 per cent of each certificate, CU10 million specified certificates, the first (or last) CU10 million certificates to be redeemed, or on some other basis? The Board was also concerned that the remaining proportion, not being subject to the fair value option, could give rise to incentives for an entity to 'cherry pick' (ie to realise financial assets or financial liabilities selectively so as to achieve a desired accounting result). For these reasons, the Board decided not to allow the fair value option to be applied to a proportion of a single financial asset or financial liability. However, if an entity simultaneously issues two or more identical financial instruments, it is not precluded from designating only some of those instruments as being subject to the fair value option (for example, if doing so achieves a significant reduction in a recognition or measurement inconsistency, as explained in paragraph AG4G). Thus, in the above example, the entity could designate CU10 million specified certificates if to do so would meet one of the three criteria in paragraph BC74.

Credit risk of liabilities

BC87   The Board discussed the issue of including changes in the credit risk of a financial liability in its fair value measurement. It considered responses to the Exposure Draft of proposed amendments to IAS 39 published in June 2002 that expressed concern about the effect of including this component in the fair value measurement and that suggested the fair value option should be restricted to exclude all or some financial liabilities. However, the Board concluded that the fair value option could be applied to any financial liability, and decided not to restrict the option in the Standard (as revised in 2003) because to do so would negate some of the benefits of the fair value option set out in paragraph BC74A.

BC88   The Board considered comments on the Exposure Draft that disagreed with the view that, in applying the fair value option to financial liabilities, an entity should recognise income as a result of deteriorating credit quality (and a loan expense as a result of improving credit quality). Commentators noted that it is not useful to report lower liabilities when an entity is in financial difficulty precisely because its debt levels are too high, and that it would be difficult to explain to users of financial statements the reasons why income would be recognised when a liability's creditworthiness deteriorates. These comments suggested that fair value should exclude the effects of changes in the instrument's credit risk.

BC89   However, the Board noted that because financial statements are prepared on a going concern basis, credit risk affects the value at which liabilities could be repurchased or settled. Accordingly, the fair value of a financial liability reflects the credit risk relating to that liability. Therefore, it decided to include credit risk relating to a financial liability in the fair value measurement of that liability for the following reasons:

(a)   entities realise changes in fair value, including fair value attributable to the liability's credit risk, for example, by renegotiating or repurchasing liabilities or by using derivatives;

(b)   changes in credit risk affect the observed market price of a financial liability and hence its fair value;

(c)   it is difficult from a practical standpoint to exclude changes in credit risk from an observed market price; and

(d)   the fair value of a financial liability (ie the price of that liability in an exchange between a knowledgeable, willing buyer and a knowledgeable, willing seller) on initial recognition reflects its credit risk. The Board believes that it is inappropriate to include credit risk in the initial fair value measurement of financial liabilities, but not subsequently.

BC90   The Board also considered whether the component of the fair value of a financial liability attributable to changes in credit quality should be specifically disclosed, separately presented in the income statement, or separately presented in equity. The Board decided that whilst separately presenting or disclosing such changes might be difficult in practice, disclosure of such information would be useful to users of financial statements and would help alleviate the concerns expressed. Therefore, it decided to include in IAS 32[*] a disclosure to help identify the changes in the fair value of a financial liability that arise from changes in the liability's credit risk. The Board believes this is a reasonable proxy for the change in fair value that is attributable to changes in the liability's credit risk, in particular when such changes are large, and will provide users with information with which to understand the profit or loss effect of such a change in credit risk.

BC91   The Board decided to clarify that this issue relates to the credit risk of the financial liability, rather than the creditworthiness of the entity. The Board noted that this more appropriately describes the objective of what is included in the fair value measurement of financial liabilities.

BC92   The Board also noted that the fair value of liabilities secured by valuable collateral, guaranteed by third parties or ranking ahead of virtually all other liabilities is generally unaffected by changes in the entity's creditworthiness.

Measurement of financial liabilities with a demand feature

BC93   Some comments received on the Exposure Draft requested clarification of how to determine fair value for financial liabilities with a demand feature (eg demand deposits), when the fair value measurement option is applied or the liability is otherwise measured at fair value. In other words, could the fair value be less than the amount payable on demand, discounted from the first date that an amount could be required to be paid (the 'demand amount'), such as the amount of the deposit discounted for the period that the entity expects the deposit to be outstanding? Some commentators believe that the fair value of financial liabilities with a demand feature is less than the demand amount, for reasons that include the consistency of such measurement with how those financial liabilities are treated for risk management purposes.

BC94   The Board agreed that this issue should be clarified in IAS 39. It confirmed that the fair value of a financial liability with a demand feature is not less than the amount payable on demand discounted from the first date that the amount could be required to be paid. This conclusion is the same as in the original IAS 32. The Board noted that in many cases, the market price observed for such financial

---

[*]   In August 2005, the IASB relocated all disclosures relating to financial instruments to IFRS 7 *Financial Instruments: Disclosures*.

liabilities is the price at which they are originated between the customer and the deposit-taker—ie the demand amount. It also noted that recognising a financial liability with a demand feature at less than the demand amount would give rise to an immediate gain on the origination of such a deposit, which the Board believes is inappropriate.

Fair value measurement guidance (paragraphs AG69–AG82)

BC95 The Board decided to include in the revised IAS 39 expanded guidance about how to determine fair values, in particular for financial instruments for which no quoted market price is available (Appendix A paragraphs AG74–AG82). The Board decided that it is desirable to provide clear and reasonably detailed guidance about the objective and use of valuation techniques to achieve reliable and comparable fair value estimates when financial instruments are measured at fair value.

Use of quoted prices in active markets (paragraphs AG71–AG73)

BC96 The Board considered comments received that disagreed with the proposal in the Exposure Draft that a quoted price is the appropriate measure of fair value for an instrument quoted in an active market. Some respondents argued that (a) valuation techniques are more appropriate for measuring fair value than a quoted price in an active market (eg for derivatives) and (b) valuation models are consistent with industry best practice, and are justified because of their acceptance for regulatory capital purposes.

BC97 However, the Board confirmed that a quoted price is the appropriate measure of fair value for an instrument quoted in an active market, notably because (a) in an active market, the quoted price is the best evidence of fair value, given that fair value is defined in terms of a price agreed by a knowledgeable, willing buyer and a knowledgeable, willing seller; (b) it results in consistent measurement across entities; and (c) fair value as defined in the Standard does not depend on entity-specific factors. The Board further clarified that a quoted price includes market-quoted rates as well as prices.

Entities that have access to more than one active market (paragraph AG71)

BC98 The Board considered situations in which entities operate in different markets. An example is a trader that originates a derivative with a corporate in an active corporate retail market and offsets the derivative by taking out a derivative with a dealer in an active dealers' wholesale market. The Board decided to clarify that the objective of fair value measurement is to arrive at the price at which a transaction would occur at the balance sheet date in the same instrument (ie without modification or repackaging) in the most advantageous active market to which an entity has immediate access. Thus, if a dealer enters into a derivative instrument with the corporate, but has immediate access to a more advantageously priced dealers' market, the entity recognises a profit on initial recognition of the derivative instrument. However, the entity adjusts the price observed in the dealer market for any differences in counterparty credit risk between the derivative instrument with the corporate and that with the dealers' market.

Bid-ask spreads in active markets (paragraph AG72)

BC99   The Board confirmed the proposal in the Exposure Draft that the appropriate quoted market price for an asset held or liability to be issued is usually the current bid price and, for an asset to be acquired or liability held, the asking price. It concluded that applying mid-market prices to an individual instrument is not appropriate because it would result in entities recognising up-front gains or losses for the difference between the bid-ask price and the mid-market price.

BC100   The Board discussed whether the bid-ask spread should be applied to the net open position of a portfolio containing offsetting market risk positions, or to each instrument in the portfolio. It noted the concerns raised by constituents that applying the bid-ask spread to the net open position better reflects the fair value of the risk retained in the portfolio. The Board concluded that for offsetting risk positions, entities could use mid-market prices to determine fair value, and hence may apply the bid or asking price to the net open position as appropriate. The Board believes that when an entity has offsetting risk positions, using the mid-market price is appropriate because the entity (a) has locked in its cash flows from the asset and liability and (b) potentially could sell the matched position without incurring the bid-ask spread.

BC101   Comments received on the Exposure Draft revealed that some interpret the term 'bid-ask spread' differently from others and from the Board. Thus, IAS 39 clarifies that the spread represents only transaction costs.

No active market (paragraphs AG74–AG82)

BC102   The Exposure Draft proposed a three-tier fair value measurement hierarchy as follows:

(a)   For instruments traded in active markets, use a quoted price.

(b)   For instruments for which there is not an active market, use a recent market transaction.

(c)   For instruments for which there is neither an active market nor a recent market transaction, use a valuation technique.

BC103   The Board decided to simplify the proposed fair value measurement hierarchy by requiring the fair value of financial instruments for which there is not an active market to be determined on the basis of valuation techniques, including the use of recent market transactions between knowledgeable, willing parties in an arm's length transaction.

BC104   The Board also considered constituents' comments regarding whether an instrument should always be recognised on initial recognition at the transaction price or whether gains or losses may be recognised on initial recognition when an entity uses a valuation technique to estimate fair value. The Board concluded that an entity may recognise a gain or loss at inception only if fair value is evidenced by comparison with other observable current market transactions in the same instrument (ie without modification or repackaging) or is based on a valuation technique incorporating only observable market data. The Board concluded that those conditions were necessary and sufficient to provide reasonable assurance that fair value was other than the transaction price for the purpose of recognising up-front gains or losses. The Board decided that in other cases, the transaction price gave the best evidence of fair value. The Board also noted that its decision achieved convergence with US GAAP.

BC104A–[Deleted]
BC104E

Impairment and uncollectibility of financial assets

Impairment of investments in equity instruments (paragraph 61)[*]

BC105   Under IAS 39, investments in equity instruments that are classified as available for sale and investments in unquoted equity instruments whose fair value cannot be reliably measured are subject to an impairment assessment. The original IAS 39 did not include guidance about impairment indicators that are specific to investments in equity instruments. Questions were raised about when in practice such investments become impaired.

BC106   The Board agreed that for marketable investments in equity instruments any impairment trigger other than a decline in fair value below cost is likely to be arbitrary to some extent. If markets are reasonably efficient, today's market price is the best estimate of the discounted value of the future market price. However, the Board also concluded that it is important to provide guidance to address the questions raised in practice.

BC107   The revised IAS 39 includes impairment triggers that the Board concluded were reasonable in the case of investments in equity instruments (paragraph 61). They apply in addition to those specified in paragraph 59, which focus on the assessment of impairment in debt instruments.

Incurred versus expected losses

BC108   Some respondents to the Exposure Draft were confused about whether the Exposure Draft reflected an 'incurred loss' model or an 'expected loss' model. Others expressed concern about the extent to which 'future losses' could be recognised as impairment losses. They suggested that losses should be recognised only when they are incurred (ie a deterioration in the credit quality of an asset or a group of assets after their initial recognition). Other respondents favoured the use of an expected loss approach. They suggested that expected future losses should be considered in the determination of the impairment loss for a group of assets even if the credit quality of a group of assets has not deteriorated from original expectations.

BC109   In considering these comments, the Board decided that impairment losses should be recognised only if they have been incurred. The Board reasoned that it was inconsistent with an amortised cost model to recognise impairment on the basis of expected future transactions and events. The Board also decided that guidance should be provided about what 'incurred' means when assessing whether

---

[*]   IFRS 9 *Financial Instruments*, issued in November 2009, amended the measurement requirements for investments in equity instruments. However, the section on impairment remains relevant for assets that are measured at amortised cost in accordance with IFRS 9.

impairment exists in a group of financial assets. The Board was concerned that, in the absence of such guidance, there could be a range of interpretations about when a loss is incurred or what events cause a loss to be incurred in a group of assets.

BC110 Therefore, the Board included guidance in IAS 39 that specifies that for a loss to be incurred, an event that provides objective evidence of impairment must have occurred after the initial recognition of the financial asset, and IAS 39 now identifies types of such events. Possible or expected future trends that may lead to a loss in the future (eg an expectation that unemployment will rise or a recession will occur) do not provide objective evidence of impairment. In addition, the loss event must have a reliably measurable effect on the present value of estimated future cash flows and be supported by current observable data.

Assets assessed individually and found not to be impaired (paragraphs 59(f) and 64)

BC111 It was not clear in the original IAS 39 whether loans and receivables[*] and some other financial assets, when reviewed for impairment and determined not to be impaired, could or should subsequently be included in the assessment of impairment for a group of financial assets with similar characteristics.

BC112 The Exposure Draft proposed that a loan asset or other financial asset that is measured at amortised cost and has been individually assessed for impairment and found not to be impaired should be included in a collective assessment of impairment. The Exposure Draft also included proposed guidance about how to evaluate impairment inherent in a group of financial assets.

BC113 The comment letters received on the Exposure Draft indicated considerable support for the proposal to include in a collective evaluation of impairment an individually assessed financial asset that is found not to be impaired.

BC114 The Board noted the following arguments in favour of an additional portfolio assessment for individually assessed assets that are found not to be impaired.

(a) Impairment that cannot be identified with an individual loan may be identifiable on a portfolio basis. The *Framework* states that for a large population of receivables, some degree of non-payment is normally regarded as probable. In that case, an expense representing the expected reduction in economic benefits is recognised (*Framework*, paragraph 85). For example, a lender may have some concerns about identified loans with similar characteristics, but not have sufficient evidence to conclude that an impairment loss has occurred on any of those loans on the basis of an individual assessment. Experience may indicate that some of those loans are impaired even though an individual assessment may not reveal this. The amount of loss in a large population of items can be estimated on the basis of experience and other factors by weighing all possible outcomes by their associated probabilities.

(b) Some time may elapse between an event that affects the ability of a borrower to repay a loan and actual default of the borrower. For example, if

---

[*] IFRS 9 *Financial Instruments*, issued in November 2009, eliminated the category of loans and receivables.

the market forward price for wheat decreases by 10 per cent, experience may indicate that the estimated payments from borrowers that are wheat farmers will decrease by 1 per cent over a one-year period. When the forward price decreases, there may be no objective evidence that any individual wheat farmer will default on an individually significant loan. On a portfolio basis, however, the decrease in the forward price may provide objective evidence that the estimated future cash flows on loans to wheat farmers have decreased by 1 per cent over a one-year period.

(c)   Under IAS 39, impairment of loans is measured on the basis of the present value of estimated future cash flows. Estimations of future cash flows may change because of economic factors affecting a group of loans, such as country and industry factors, even if there is no objective evidence of impairment of an individual loan. For example, if unemployment increases by 10 per cent in a quarter in a particular region, the estimated future cash flows from loans to borrowers in that region for the next quarters may have decreased even though no objective evidence of impairment exists that is based on an individual assessment of loans to borrowers in that region. In that case, objective evidence of impairment exists for the group of financial assets, even though it does not exist for an individual asset. A requirement for objective evidence to exist to recognise and measure impairment in individually significant loans might result in delayed recognition of loan impairment that has already occurred.

(d)   Accepted accounting practice in some countries is to establish a provision to cover impairment losses that, although not specifically identified to individual assets, are known from experience to exist in a loan portfolio as of the balance sheet date.

(e)   If assets that are individually not significant are collectively assessed for impairment and assets that are individually significant are not, assets will not be measured on a consistent basis because impairment losses are more difficult to identify asset by asset.

(f)   What is an individually significant loan that is assessed on its own will differ from one entity to another. Thus, identical exposures will be evaluated on different bases (individually or collectively), depending on their significance to the entity holding them. If a collective evaluation were not to be required, an entity that wishes to minimise its recognised impairment losses could elect to assess all loans individually. Requiring a collective assessment of impairment for all exposures judged not to be impaired individually enhances consistency between entities rather than reduces it.

BC115   Arguments against an additional portfolio assessment for individually assessed loans that are found not to be impaired are as follows.

(a)   It appears illogical to make an impairment provision on a group of loans that have been assessed for impairment on an individual basis and have been found not to be impaired.

(b)   The measurement of impairment should not depend on whether a lender has only one loan or a group of similar loans. If the measurement of impairment is affected by whether the lender has groups of similar loans, identical loans may be measured differently by different lenders. To ensure consistent measurement of identical loans, impairment in individually significant financial assets should be recognised and measured asset by asset.

(c) The *Framework* specifies that financial statements are prepared on the accrual basis of accounting, according to which the effects of transactions and events are recognised when they occur and are recognised in the financial statements in the periods to which they relate. Financial statements should reflect the outcome of events that took place before the balance sheet date and should not reflect events that have not yet occurred. If an impairment loss cannot be attributed to a specifically identified financial asset or a group of financial assets that are not individually significant, it is questionable whether an event has occurred that justifies the recognition of impairment. Even though the risk of loss may have increased, a loss has not yet materialised.

(d) The *Framework*, paragraph 94, requires an expense to be recognised only if it can be measured reliably. The process of estimating impairment in a group of loans that have been individually assessed for impairment but found not to be impaired may involve a significant degree of subjectivity. There may be a wide range of reasonable estimates of impairment. In practice, the establishment of general loan loss provisions is sometimes viewed as more of an art than a science. This portfolio approach should be applied only if it is necessary on practical grounds and not to override an assessment made on an individual loan, which must provide a better determination of whether an allowance is necessary.

(e) IAS 39 requires impairment to be measured on a present value basis using the original effective interest rate. Mechanically, it may not be obvious how to do this for a group of loans with similar characteristics that have different effective interest rates. In addition, measurement of impairment in a group of loans based on the present value of estimated cash flows discounted using the original effective interest rate may result in double-counting of losses that were expected on a portfolio basis when the loans were originated because the lender included compensation for those losses in the contractual interest rate charged. As a result, a portfolio assessment of impairment may result in the recognition of a loss almost as soon as a loan is issued. (This question arises also in measuring impairment on a portfolio basis for loans that are not individually assessed for impairment under IAS 39.)

BC116 The Board was persuaded by the arguments in favour of a portfolio assessment for individually assessed assets that are found not to be impaired and decided to confirm that a loan or other financial asset measured at amortised cost that is individually assessed for impairment and found not to be impaired should be included in a group of similar financial assets that are assessed for impairment on a portfolio basis. This is to reflect that, in the light of the law of large numbers, impairment may be evident in a group of assets, but not yet meet the threshold for recognition when any individual asset in that group is assessed. The Board also confirmed that it is important to provide guidance about how to assess impairment on a portfolio basis to introduce discipline into a portfolio assessment. Such guidance promotes consistency in practice and comparability of information across entities. It should also mitigate concerns that collective assessments of impairment should not be used to conceal changes in asset values or as a cushion for potential future losses.

BC117 Some respondents expressed concerns about some of the detailed guidance proposed in the Exposure Draft, such as the guidance about adjusting the discount rate for expected losses. Many entities indicated that they do not have the data and systems necessary to implement the proposed approach. The Board decided to eliminate some of the detailed application guidance (eg whether to make an adjustment of the discount rate for originally expected losses and an illustration of the application of the guidance).

Assets that are assessed individually and found to be impaired (paragraph 64)

BC118 In making a portfolio assessment of impairment, one issue that arises is whether the collective assessment should include assets that have been individually evaluated and identified as impaired.

BC119 One view is that methods used to estimate impairment losses on a portfolio basis are equally valid whether or not an asset has been specifically identified as impaired. Those who support this view note that the law of large numbers applies equally whether or not an asset has been individually identified as impaired and that a portfolio assessment may enable a more accurate prediction to be made of estimated future cash flows.

BC120 Another view is that there should be no need to complement an individual assessment of impairment for an asset that is specifically identified as impaired by an additional portfolio assessment, because objective evidence of impairment exists on an individual basis and expectations of losses can be incorporated in the measurement of impairment for the individual assets. Double-counting of losses in terms of estimated future cash flows should not be permitted. Moreover, recognition of impairment losses for groups of assets should not be a substitute for the recognition of impairment losses on individual assets.

BC121 The Board decided that assets that are individually assessed for impairment and identified as impaired should be excluded from a portfolio assessment of impairment. Excluding assets that are individually identified as impaired from a portfolio assessment of impairment is consistent with the view that collective evaluation of impairment is an interim step pending the identification of impairment losses on individual assets. A collective evaluation identifies losses that have been incurred on a group basis as of the balance sheet date, but cannot yet be identified with individual assets. As soon as information is available to identify losses on individually impaired assets, those assets are removed from the group that is collectively assessed for impairment.

Grouping of assets that are collectively evaluated for impairment (paragraphs 64 and AG87)

BC122 The Board considered how assets that are collectively assessed for impairment should be grouped for the purpose of assessing impairment on a portfolio basis.

In practice, different methods are conceivable for grouping assets for the purposes of assessing impairment and computing historical and expected loss rates. For example, assets may be grouped on the basis of one or more of the following characteristics: (a) estimated default probabilities or credit risk grades; (b) type (for example, mortgage loans or credit card loans); (c) geographical location; (d) collateral type; (e) counterparty type (for example, consumer, commercial or sovereign); (f) past-due status; and (g) maturity. More sophisticated credit risk models or methodologies for estimating expected future cash flows may combine several factors, for example, a credit risk evaluation or grading process that considers asset type, industry, geographical location, collateral type, past-due status, and other relevant characteristics of the assets being evaluated and associated loss data.

BC123　The Board decided that for the purpose of assessing impairment on a portfolio basis, the method employed for grouping assets should, as a minimum, ensure that individual assets are allocated to groups of assets that share similar credit risk characteristics. It also decided to clarify that when assets that are assessed individually and found not to be impaired are grouped with assets with similar credit risk characteristics that are assessed only on a collective basis, the loss probabilities and other loss statistics differ between the two types of asset with the result that a different amount of impairment may be required.

Estimates of future cash flows in groups (paragraphs AG89–AG92)

BC124　The Board decided that to promote consistency in the estimation of impairment on groups of financial assets that are collectively evaluated for impairment, guidance should be provided about the process for estimating future cash flows in such groups. It identified the following elements as critical to an adequate process:

(a)　Historical loss experience should provide the basis for estimating future cash flows in a group of financial assets that are collectively assessed for impairment.

(b)　Entities that have no loss experience of their own or insufficient experience should use peer group experience for comparable groups of financial assets.

(c)　Historical loss experience should be adjusted, on the basis of observable data, to reflect the effects of current conditions that did not affect the period on which the historical loss experience is based and to remove the effects of conditions in the historical period that do not exist currently.

(d)　Changes in estimates of future cash flows should be directionally consistent with changes in underlying observable data.

(e)　Estimation methods should be adjusted to reduce differences between estimates of future cash flows and actual cash flows.

BC125–　[Deleted]
BC130

Hedging

BC131 The Exposure Draft proposed few changes to the hedge accounting guidance in the original IAS 39. The comments on the Exposure Draft raised several issues in the area of hedge accounting suggesting that the Board should consider these issues in the revised IAS 39. The Board's decisions with regard to these issues are presented in the following paragraphs.

Consideration of the shortcut method in SFAS 133

BC132 SFAS 133 *Accounting for Derivative Instruments and Hedging Activities* issued by the FASB allows an entity to assume no ineffectiveness in a hedge of interest rate risk using an interest rate swap as the hedging instrument, provided specified criteria are met (the 'shortcut method').

BC133 The original IAS 39 and the Exposure Draft precluded the use of the shortcut method. Many comments received on the Exposure Draft argued that IAS 39 should permit use of the shortcut method. The Board considered the issue in developing the Exposure Draft, and discussed it in the round-table discussions that were held in the process of finalising IAS 39.

BC134 The Board noted that, if the shortcut method were permitted, an exception would have to be made to the principle in IAS 39 that ineffectiveness in a hedging relationship is measured and recognised in profit or loss. The Board agreed that no exception to this principle should be made, and therefore concluded that IAS 39 should not permit the shortcut method.

BC135 Additionally, IAS 39 permits the hedging of portions of financial assets and financial liabilities in cases when US GAAP does not. The Board noted that under IAS 39 an entity may hedge a portion of a financial instrument (eg interest rate risk or credit risk), and that if the critical terms of the hedging instrument and the hedged item are the same, the entity would, in many cases, recognise no ineffectiveness.

Hedges of portions of financial assets and financial liabilities (paragraphs 81, 81A, AG99A and AG99B)

BC135A IAS 39 permits a hedged item to be designated as a portion of the cash flows or fair value of a financial asset or financial liability. In finalising the Exposure Draft *Fair Value Hedge Accounting for a Portfolio Hedge of Interest Rate Risk*, the Board received comments that demonstrated that the meaning of a 'portion' was unclear in this context. Accordingly, the Board decided to amend IAS 39 to provide further guidance on what may be designated as a hedged portion, including confirmation that it is not possible to designate a portion that is greater than the total cash flows of the asset or liability.

Expected effectiveness (paragraphs AG105–AG113)

BC136 Qualification for hedge accounting is based on expectations of future effectiveness (prospective) and evaluation of actual effectiveness (retrospective). In the original IAS 39, the prospective test was expressed as 'almost fully offset', whereas the retrospective test was 'within a range of 80–125 per cent'. The Board considered whether to amend IAS 39 to permit the prospective effectiveness to be within the range of 80–125 per cent rather than 'almost fully offset'. The Board noted that an undesirable consequence of such an amendment could be that entities would deliberately underhedge a hedged item in a cash flow hedge so as to reduce recognised ineffectiveness. Therefore, the Board initially decided to retain the guidance in the original IAS 39.

BC136A However, when subsequently finalising the requirements for portfolio hedges of interest rate risk, the Board received representations from constituents that some hedges would fail the 'almost fully offset' test in IAS 39, including some hedges that would qualify for the shortcut method in US GAAP and thus be assumed to be 100 per cent effective. The Board was persuaded that the concern described in the previous paragraph that an entity might deliberately underhedge would be met by an explicit statement that an entity could not deliberately hedge less than 100 per cent of the exposure on an item and designate the hedge as a hedge of 100 per cent of the exposure. Therefore, the Board decided to amend IAS 39:

(a) to remove the words 'almost fully offset' from the prospective effectiveness test, and replace them by a requirement that the hedge is expected to be 'highly effective'. (This amendment is consistent with the wording in US GAAP.)

(b) to include a statement in the Application Guidance in IAS 39 that if an entity hedges less than 100 per cent of the exposure on an item, such as 85 per cent, it shall designate the hedged item as being 85 per cent of the exposure and shall measure ineffectiveness on the basis of the change in the whole of that designated 85 per cent exposure.

BC136B Additionally, comments made in response to the Exposure Draft *Fair Value Hedge Accounting for a Portfolio Hedge of Interest Rate Risk* demonstrated that it was unclear how the prospective effectiveness test was to be applied. The Board noted that the objective of the test was to ensure there was firm evidence to support an expectation of high effectiveness. Therefore, the Board decided to amend the Standard to clarify that an expectation of high effectiveness may be demonstrated in various ways, including a comparison of past changes in the fair value or cash flows of the hedged item that are attributable to the hedged risk with past changes in the fair value or cash flows of the hedging instrument, or by demonstrating a high statistical correlation between the fair value of cash flows of the hedged item and those of the hedging instrument. The Board noted that the entity may choose a hedge ratio of other than one to one in order to improve the effectiveness of the hedge as described in paragraph AG100.

Hedges of portions of non-financial assets and non-financial liabilities for risk other than foreign currency risk (paragraph 82)

BC137 The Board considered comments on the Exposure Draft that suggested that IAS 39 should permit designating as the hedged risk a risk portion of a non-financial item other than foreign currency risk.

BC138 The Board concluded that IAS 39 should not be amended to permit such designation. It noted that in many cases, changes in the cash flows or fair value of a portion of a non-financial hedged item are difficult to isolate and measure. Moreover, the Board noted that permitting portions of non-financial assets and non-financial liabilities to be designated as the hedged item for risk other than foreign currency risk would compromise the principles of identification of the hedged item and effectiveness testing that the Board has confirmed because the portion could be designated so that no ineffectiveness would ever arise.

BC139 The Board confirmed that non-financial items may be hedged in their entirety when the item the entity is hedging is not the standard item underlying contracts traded in the market. In this context, the Board decided to clarify that a hedge ratio of other than one-to-one may maximise expected effectiveness, and to include guidance on how the hedge ratio that maximises expected effectiveness can be determined.

Loan servicing rights

BC140 The Board also considered whether IAS 39 should permit the interest rate risk portion of loan servicing rights to be designated as the hedged item.

BC141 The Board considered the argument that interest rate risk can be separately identified and measured in loan servicing rights, and that changes in market interest rates have a predictable and separately measurable effect on the value of loan servicing rights. The Board also considered the possibility of treating loan servicing rights as financial assets (rather than non-financial assets).

BC142 However, the Board concluded that no exceptions should be permitted for this matter. The Board noted that (a) the interest rate risk and prepayment risk in loan servicing rights are interdependent, and thus inseparable, (b) the fair values of loan servicing rights do not change in a linear fashion as interest rates increase or decrease, and (c) concerns exist about how to isolate and measure the interest rate risk portion of a loan servicing right. Moreover, the Board expressed concern that in jurisdictions in which loan servicing right markets are not developed, the interest rate risk portion may not be measurable.

BC143 The Board also considered whether IAS 39 should be amended to allow, on an elective basis, the inclusion of loan servicing rights in its scope provided that they are measured at fair value with changes in fair value recognised immediately in profit or loss. The Board noted that this would create two exceptions to the general principles in IAS 39. First, it would create a scope exception because IAS 39 applies only to financial assets and financial liabilities; loan servicing rights are non-financial assets. Second, *requiring* an entity to measure loan servicing rights at fair value through profit or loss would create a further exception, because this treatment is optional (except for items that are held for trading). The Board therefore decided not to amend the scope of IAS 39 for loan servicing rights.

Whether to permit hedge accounting using cash instruments

BC144 In finalising the amendments to IAS 39, the Board discussed whether an entity should be permitted to designate a financial asset or financial liability other than a derivative (ie a 'cash instrument') as a hedging instrument in hedges of risks other than foreign currency risk. The original IAS 39 precluded such designation because of the different bases for measuring derivatives and cash instruments. The Exposure Draft did not propose a change to this limitation. However, some commentators suggested a change, noting that entities do not distinguish between derivative and non-derivative financial instruments in their hedging and other risk management activities and that entities may have to use a non-derivative financial instrument to hedge risk if no suitable derivative financial instrument exists.

BC145 The Board acknowledged that some entities use non-derivatives to manage risk. However, it decided to retain the restriction against designating non-derivatives as hedging instruments in hedges of risks other than foreign currency risk. It noted the following arguments in support of this conclusion:

(a) The need for hedge accounting arises in part because derivatives are measured at fair value, whereas the items they hedge may be measured at cost or not recognised at all. Without hedge accounting, an entity might recognise volatility in profit or loss for matched positions. For non-derivative items that are not measured at fair value or for which changes in fair value are not recognised in profit or loss, there is generally no need to adjust the accounting of the hedging instrument or the hedged item to achieve matched recognition of gains and losses in profit or loss.

(b) To allow designation of cash instruments as hedging instruments would diverge from US GAAP: SFAS 133 precludes the designation of non-derivative instruments as hedging instruments except for some foreign currency hedges.

(c) To allow designation of cash instruments as hedging instruments would add complexity to the Standard. More financial instruments would be measured at an amount that represents neither amortised cost nor fair value. Hedge accounting is, and should be, an exception to the normal measurement requirements.

(d) If cash instruments were permitted to be designated as hedging instruments, there would be much less discipline in the accounting model because, in the absence of hedge accounting, a non-derivative may not be selectively measured at fair value. If the entity subsequently decides that it would rather not apply fair value measurement to a cash instrument that had been designated as a hedging instrument, it can breach one of the hedge accounting requirements, conclude that the non-derivative no longer qualifies as a hedging instrument and selectively avoid recognising the changes in fair value of the non-derivative instrument in equity (for a cash flow hedge) or profit or loss (for a fair value hedge).

(e) The most significant use of cash instruments as hedging instruments is to hedge foreign currency exposures, which is permitted under IAS 39.

Whether to treat hedges of forecast transactions as fair value hedges

BC146   The Board considered a suggestion made in some of the comment letters received on the Exposure Draft that a hedge of a forecast transaction should be treated as a fair value hedge, rather than as a cash flow hedge. Some argued that the hedge accounting provisions should be simplified by having only one type of hedge accounting. Some also raised concern about an entity's ability, in some cases, to choose between two hedge accounting methods for the same hedging strategy (ie the choice between designating a forward contract to sell an existing asset as a fair value hedge of the asset or a cash flow hedge of a forecast sale of the asset).

BC147   The Board acknowledged that the hedge accounting provisions would be simplified, and their application more consistent in some situations, if the Standard permitted only one type of hedge accounting. However, the Board concluded that IAS 39 should continue to distinguish between fair value hedge accounting and cash flow hedge accounting. It noted that removing either type of hedge accounting would narrow the range of hedging strategies that could qualify for hedge accounting.

BC148   The Board also noted that treating a hedge of a forecast transaction as a fair value hedge is not appropriate for the following reasons: (a) it would result in the recognition of an asset or liability before the entity has become a party to the contract; (b) amounts would be recognised in the balance sheet that do not meet the definitions of assets and liabilities in the *Framework*; and (c) transactions in which there is no fair value exposure would be treated as if there were a fair value exposure.

Hedges of firm commitments (paragraphs 93 and 94)

BC149   The previous version of IAS 39 required a hedge of a firm commitment to be accounted for as a cash flow hedge. In other words, hedging gains and losses, to the extent that the hedge is effective, were initially recognised in equity and were subsequently 'recycled' to profit or loss in the same period(s) that the hedged firm commitment affected profit or loss (although, when basis adjustment was used, they adjusted the initial carrying amount of an asset or liability recognised in the meantime). Some believe this is appropriate because cash flow hedge accounting for hedges of firm commitments avoids partial recognition of the firm commitment that would otherwise not be recognised. Moreover, some believe it is conceptually incorrect to recognise the hedged fair value exposure of a firm commitment as an asset or liability merely because it has been hedged.

BC150   The Board considered whether hedges of firm commitments should be treated as cash flow hedges or fair value hedges. The Board concluded that hedges of firm commitments should be accounted for as fair value hedges.

BC151   The Board noted that, in concept, a hedge of a firm commitment is a fair value hedge. This is because the fair value of the item being hedged (the firm commitment) changes with changes in the hedged risk.

BC152   The Board was not persuaded by the argument that it is conceptually incorrect to recognise an asset or liability for a firm commitment merely because it has been hedged. It noted that for all fair value hedges, applying hedge accounting has the effect that amounts are recognised as assets or liabilities that would otherwise not be recognised. For example, assume an entity hedges a fixed rate loan asset with a pay-fixed, receive-variable interest rate swap. If there is a loss on the swap, applying fair value hedge accounting requires the offsetting gain on the loan to be recognised, ie the carrying amount of the loan is increased. Thus, applying hedge accounting has the effect of recognising a part of an asset (the increase in the loan's value attributable to interest rate movements) that would otherwise not have been recognised. The only difference in the case of a firm commitment is that, without hedge accounting, none of the commitment is recognised, ie the carrying amount is zero. However, this difference merely reflects that the historical cost of a firm commitment is usually zero. It is not a fundamental difference in concept.

BC153   Furthermore, the Board's decision converges with SFAS 133, and thus eliminates practical problems and eases implementation for entities that report under both standards.

BC154   However, the Board clarified that a hedge of the foreign currency risk of a firm commitment may be treated as either a fair value hedge or a cash flow hedge because foreign currency risk affects both the cash flows and the fair value of the hedged item. Accordingly a foreign currency cash flow hedge of a forecast transaction need not be re-designated as a fair value hedge when the forecast transaction becomes a firm commitment.

Basis adjustments (paragraphs 97–99)

BC155   The question of basis adjustment arises when an entity hedges the future purchase of an asset or the future issue of a liability. One example is that of a US entity that expects to make a future purchase of a German machine that it will pay for in euro. The entity enters into a derivative to hedge against possible future changes in the US dollar/euro exchange rate. Such a hedge is classified as a cash flow hedge under IAS 39, with the effect that gains and losses on the hedging instrument (to the extent that the hedge is effective) are initially recognised in equity.[*] The question the Board considered is what the accounting should be once the future transaction takes place. In its deliberations on this issue, the Board discussed the following approaches:

    (a)   to remove the hedging gain or loss from equity and recognise it as part of the initial carrying amount of the asset or liability (in the example above, the machine). In future periods, the hedging gain or loss is automatically recognised in profit or loss by being included in amounts such as depreciation expense (for a fixed asset), interest income or expense (for a financial asset or financial liability), or cost of sales (for inventories). This treatment is commonly referred to as 'basis adjustment'.

---

[*]   As a consequence of the revision of IAS 1 *Presentation of Financial Statements* in 2007 such gains and losses are recognised in other comprehensive income.

(b) to leave the hedging gain or loss in equity. In future periods, the gain or loss on the hedging instrument is 'recycled' to profit or loss in the same period(s) as the acquired asset or liability affects profit or loss. This recycling requires a separate adjustment and is not automatic.

BC156 It should be noted that both approaches have the same effect on profit or loss and net assets for all periods affected, so long as the hedge is accounted for as a cash flow hedge. The difference relates to balance sheet presentation and, possibly, the line item in the income statement.

BC157 In the Exposure Draft, the Board proposed that the 'basis adjustment' approach for forecast transactions (approach (a)) should be eliminated and replaced by approach (b) above. It further noted that eliminating the basis adjustment approach would enable IAS 39 to converge with SFAS 133.

BC158 Many of the comments received from constituents disagreed with the proposal in the Exposure Draft. Those responses argued that it would unnecessarily complicate the accounting to leave the hedging gain or loss in equity when the hedged forecast transaction occurs. They particularly noted that tracking the effects of cash flow hedges after the asset or liability is acquired would be complicated and would require systems changes. They also pointed out that treating hedges of firm commitments as fair value hedges has the same effect as a basis adjustment when the firm commitment results in the recognition of an asset or liability. For example, for a perfectly effective hedge of the foreign currency risk of a firm commitment to buy a machine, the effect is to recognise the machine initially at its foreign currency price translated at the forward rate in effect at the inception of the hedge rather than the spot rate. Therefore, they questioned whether it is consistent to treat a hedge of a firm commitment as a fair value hedge while precluding basis adjustments for hedges of forecast transactions.

BC159 Others believe that a basis adjustment is difficult to justify in principle for forecast transactions, and also argue that such basis adjustments impair comparability of financial information. In other words, two identical assets that are purchased at the same time and in the same way, except for the fact that one was hedged, should not be recognised at different amounts.

BC160 The Board concluded that IAS 39 should distinguish between hedges of forecast transactions that will result in the recognition of a *financial* asset or a *financial* liability and those that will result in the recognition of a *non-financial* asset or a *non-financial* liability.

Basis adjustments for hedges of forecast transactions that will result in the recognition of a financial asset or a financial liability

BC161 For hedges of forecast transactions that will result in the recognition of a financial asset or a financial liability, the Board concluded that basis adjustments are not appropriate. Its reason was that basis adjustments cause the initial carrying amount of acquired assets (or assumed liabilities) arising from forecast transactions to move away from fair value and hence would override the requirement in IAS 39 to measure a financial instrument initially at its fair value.

BC161A If a hedged forecast transaction results in the recognition of a financial asset or a financial liability, paragraph 97 of IAS 39 required the associated gains or losses on hedging instruments to be reclassified from equity to profit or loss as a reclassification adjustment in the same period or periods during which the hedged item affects profit or loss (such as in the periods that interest income or interest expense is recognised).

BC161B The Board was informed that there was uncertainty about how paragraph 97 should be applied when the designated cash flow exposure being hedged differs from the financial instrument arising from the hedged forecast cash flows.

BC161C The example below illustrates the issue:

> An entity applies the guidance in the answer to Question F.6.2 of the guidance on implementing IAS 39. On 1 January 20X0 the entity designates forecast cash flows for the risk of variability arising from changes in interest rates. Those forecast cash flows arise from the repricing of existing financial instruments and are scheduled for 1 April 20X0. The entity is exposed to variability in cash flows for the three-month period beginning on 1 April 20X0 attributable to changes in interest rate risk that occur from 1 January 20X0 to 31 March 20X0.
>
> The occurrence of the forecast cash flows is deemed to be highly probable and all the other relevant hedge accounting criteria are met.
>
> The financial instrument that results from the hedged forecast cash flows is a five-year interest-bearing instrument.

BC161D Paragraph 97 required the gains or losses on the hedging instrument to be reclassified from equity to profit or loss as a reclassification adjustment in the same period or periods during which the asset acquired or liability assumed affected profit or loss. The financial instrument that was recognised is a five-year instrument that will affect profit or loss for five years. The wording in paragraph 97 suggested that the gains or losses should be reclassified over five years, even though the cash flows designated as the hedged item were hedged for the effects of interest rate changes over only a three-month period.

BC161E The Board believes that the wording of paragraph 97 did not reflect the underlying rationale in hedge accounting, ie that the gains or losses on the hedging instrument should offset the gains or losses on the hedged item, and the offset should be reflected in profit or loss by way of reclassification adjustments.

BC161F The Board believes that in the example set out above the gains or losses should be reclassified over a period of three months beginning on 1 April 20X0, and not over a period of five years beginning on 1 April 20X0.

BC161G Consequently, in *Improvements to IFRSs* issued in April 2009, the Board amended paragraph 97 of IAS 39 to clarify that the gains or losses on the hedged instrument should be reclassified from equity to profit or loss during the period that the hedged forecast cash flows affect profit or loss. The Board also decided that to avoid similar confusion paragraph 100 of IAS 39 should be amended to be consistent with paragraph 97.

Basis adjustments for hedges of forecast transactions that will result in the recognition of a non-financial asset or a non-financial liability

BC162   For hedges of forecast transactions that will result in the recognition of a non-financial asset or a non-financial liability, the Board decided to permit entities a choice of whether to apply basis adjustment.

BC163   The Board considered the argument that changes in the fair value of the hedging instrument are appropriately included in the initial carrying amount of the recognised asset or liability because such changes represent a part of the 'cost' of that asset or liability. Although the Board has not yet considered the broader issue of what costs may be capitalised at initial recognition, the Board believes that its decision to provide an option for basis adjustments in the case of non-financial items will not pre-empt that future discussion. The Board also recognised that financial items and non-financial items are not necessarily measured at the same amount on initial recognition, because financial items are measured at fair value and non-financial items are measured at cost.

BC164   The Board concluded that, on balance, providing entities with a choice in this case was appropriate. The Board took the view that allowing basis adjustments addresses the concern that precluding basis adjustments complicates the accounting for hedges of forecast transactions. In addition, the number of balance sheet line items that could be affected is quite small, generally being only property, plant and equipment, inventory and the cash flow hedge line item in equity. The Board also noted that US GAAP precludes basis adjustments and that applying a basis adjustment is inconsistent with the accounting for hedges of forecast transactions that will result in the recognition of a financial asset or a financial liability. The Board acknowledged the merits of these arguments, and recognised that by permitting a choice in IAS 39, entities could apply the accounting treatment required by US GAAP.

Hedging using internal contracts

BC165   IAS 39 does not preclude entities from using internal contracts as a risk management tool, or as a tracking device in applying hedge accounting for external contracts that hedge external positions. Furthermore, IAS 39 permits hedge accounting to be applied to transactions between entities in the same group in the *separate reporting* of those entities. However, IAS 39 does not permit hedge accounting for transactions between entities in the same group in consolidated financial statements. The reason is the fundamental requirement of consolidation that the accounting effects of internal contracts should be eliminated in consolidated financial statements, including any internally generated gains or losses. Designating internal contracts as hedging instruments could result in non-elimination of internal gains and losses and have other accounting effects. The Exposure Draft did not propose any change in this area.

BC166   To illustrate, assume the banking book division of Bank A enters into an internal interest rate swap with the trading book division of the same bank. The purpose is to hedge the net interest rate risk exposure in the banking book of a group of similar fixed rate loan assets funded by floating rate liabilities. Under the swap, the banking book pays fixed interest payments to the trading book and receives variable interest rate payments in return. The bank wants to designate the internal interest rate swap in the banking book as a hedging instrument in its consolidated financial statements.

BC167   If the internal swap in the banking book is designated as a hedging instrument in a cash flow hedge of the liabilities, and the internal swap in the trading book is classified as held for trading, internal gains and losses on that internal swap would not be eliminated. This is because the gains and losses on the internal swap in the banking book would be recognised in equity[*] to the extent the hedge is effective and the gains and losses on the internal swap in the trading book would be recognised in profit or loss.

BC168   If the internal swap in the banking book is designated as a hedging instrument in a fair value hedge of the loan assets and the internal swap in the trading book is classified as held for trading, the changes in the fair value of the internal swap would offset both in total net assets in the balance sheet and profit or loss. However, without elimination of the internal swap, there would be an adjustment to the carrying amount of the hedged loan asset in the banking book to reflect the change in the fair value attributable to the risk hedged by the internal contract. Moreover, to reflect the effect of the internal swap the bank would in effect recognise the fixed rate loan at a floating interest rate and recognise an offsetting trading gain or loss in the income statement. Hence the internal swap would have accounting effects.

BC169   Some respondents to the Exposure Draft and some participants in the round-tables objected to not being able to obtain hedge accounting in the consolidated financial statements for internal contracts between subsidiaries or between a subsidiary and the parent (as illustrated above). Among other things, they emphasised that the use of internal contracts is a key risk management tool and that the accounting should reflect the way in which risk is managed. Some suggested that IAS 39 should be changed to make it consistent with US GAAP, which allows the designation of internal derivative contracts as hedging instruments in cash flow hedges of forecast foreign currency transactions in specified, limited circumstances.

BC170   In considering these comments, the Board noted that the following principles apply to consolidated financial statements:

(a)   financial statements provide financial information about an entity or group as a whole (as that of a single entity). Financial statements do not provide financial information about an entity as if it were two separate entities.

(b)   a fundamental principle of consolidation is that intragroup balances and intragroup transactions are eliminated in full. Permitting the designation of internal contracts as hedging instruments would require a change to the consolidation principles.

(c)   it is conceptually wrong to permit an entity to recognise internally generated gains and losses or make other accounting adjustments because of internal transactions. No external event has occurred.

---

[*]   As a consequence of the revision of IAS 1 *Presentation of Financial Statements* in 2007 such gains and losses are recognised in other comprehensive income.

(d) an ability to recognise internally generated gains and losses could result in abuse in the absence of requirements about how entities should manage and control the associated risks. It is not the purpose of accounting standards to prescribe how entities should manage and control risks.

(e) permitting the designation of internal contracts as hedging instruments violates the following requirements in IAS 39:

(i) the prohibition against designating as a hedging instrument a non-derivative financial asset or non-derivative financial liability for other than foreign currency risk. To illustrate, if an entity has two offsetting internal contracts and one is the designated hedging instrument in a fair value hedge of a non-derivative asset and the other is the designated hedging instrument in a fair value hedge of a non-derivative liability, from the entity's perspective the effect is to designate a hedging relationship between the asset and the liability (ie a non-derivative asset or non-derivative liability is used as the hedging instrument).

(ii) the prohibition on designating a net position of assets and liabilities as the hedged item. To illustrate, an entity has two internal contracts. One is designated in a fair value hedge of an asset and the other in a fair value hedge of a liability. The two internal contracts do not fully offset, so the entity lays off the net risk exposure by entering into a net external derivative. In that case, the effect from the entity's perspective is to designate a hedging relationship between the net external derivative and a net position of an asset and a liability.

(iii) the option to fair value assets and liabilities does not extend to portions of assets and liabilities.

(f) the Board is considering separately whether to make an amendment to IAS 39 to facilitate fair value hedge accounting for portfolio hedges of interest rate risk. The Board believes that that is a better way to address the concerns raised about symmetry with risk management systems than permitting the designation of internal contracts as hedging instruments.

(g) the Board decided to permit an option to measure any financial asset or financial liability at fair value with changes in fair value recognised in profit or loss. This enables an entity to measure matching asset/liability positions at fair value without a need for hedge accounting.

BC171 The Board reaffirmed that it is a fundamental principle of consolidation that any accounting effect of internal contracts is eliminated on consolidation. The Board decided that no exception to this principle should be made in IAS 39. Consistently with this decision, the Board also decided not to explore an amendment to permit internal derivative contracts to be designated as hedging instruments in hedges of some forecast foreign currency transactions, as is permitted by SFAS 138 *Accounting for Certain Derivative Instruments and Certain Hedging Activities.*

BC172 The Board also decided to clarify that IAS 39 does not preclude hedge accounting for transactions between entities in the same group in individual or separate financial statements of those entities because they are not internal to the entity (ie the individual entity).

BC172A Previously, paragraphs 73 and 80 referred to the need for hedging instruments to involve a party external to the reporting entity. In doing so, they used a segment as an example of a reporting entity. However, IFRS 8 *Operating Segments* requires disclosure of information that is reported to the chief operating decision maker even if this is on a non-IFRS basis. Therefore, the two IFRSs appeared to conflict. In *Improvements to IFRSs* issued in May 2008 and April 2009, the Board removed from paragraphs 73 and 80 references to the designation of hedging instruments at the segment level.

Eligible hedged items in particular situations (paragraphs AG99BA, AG99E, AG99F, AG110A and AG110B)

BC172B The Board amended IAS 39 in July 2008 to clarify the application of the principles that determine whether a hedged risk or portion of cash flows is eligible for designation in particular situations. This followed a request by the IFRIC for guidance.

BC172C The responses to the exposure draft *Exposures Qualifying for Hedge Accounting* demonstrated that diversity in practice existed, or was likely to occur, in two situations:

(a) the designation of a one-sided risk in a hedged item

(b) the designation of inflation as a hedged risk or portion in particular situations.

Designation of a one-sided risk in a hedged item

BC172D The IFRIC received requests for guidance on whether an entity can designate a purchased option in its entirety as the hedging instrument in a cash flow hedge of a highly probable forecast transaction in such a way that all changes in the fair value of the purchased option, including changes in the time value, are regarded as effective and would be recognised in other comprehensive income. The exposure draft proposed to amend IAS 39 to clarify that such a designation was not allowed.

BC172E After considering the responses to the exposure draft, the Board confirmed that the designation set out in paragraph BC172D is not permitted.

BC172F The Board reached that decision by considering the variability of future cash flow outcomes resulting from a price increase of a forecast commodity purchase (a one-sided risk). The Board noted that the forecast transaction contained no separately identifiable risk that affects profit or loss that is equivalent to the time value of a purchased option hedging instrument (with the same principal terms as the designated risk). The Board concluded that the intrinsic value of a purchased option, but not its time value, reflects a one-sided risk in a hedged item. The Board then considered a purchased option designated in its entirety as the hedging instrument. The Board noted that hedge accounting is based on a principle of offsetting changes in fair value or cash flows between the hedging instrument and the hedged item. Because a designated one-sided risk does not contain the time value of a purchased option hedging instrument, the Board noted that there will be no offset between the cash flows relating to the time value of the option premium paid and the designated hedged risk. Therefore, the Board concluded that a purchased option designated in its entirety as the hedging instrument of a one-sided risk will not be perfectly effective.

Designation of inflation in particular situations

BC172G The IFRIC received a request for guidance on whether, for a hedge of a fixed rate financial instrument, an entity can designate inflation as the hedged item. The exposure draft proposed to amend IAS 39 to clarify that such a designation was not allowed.

BC172H After considering the responses to the exposure draft, the Board acknowledged that expectations of future inflation rates can be viewed as an economic component of nominal interest. However, the Board also noted that hedge accounting is an exception to normal accounting principles for the hedged item (fair value hedges) or hedging instrument (cash flow hedges). To ensure a disciplined use of hedge accounting the Board noted that restrictions regarding eligible hedged items are necessary, especially if something other than the entire fair value or cash flow variability of a hedged item is designated.

BC172I The Board noted that paragraph 81 permits an entity to designate as the hedged item something other than the entire fair value change or cash flow variability of a financial instrument. For example, an entity may designate some (but not all) risks of a financial instrument, or some (but not all) cash flows of a financial instrument (a 'portion').

BC172J The Board noted that, to be eligible for hedge accounting, the designated risks and portions must be separately identifiable components of the financial instrument, and changes in the fair value or cash flows of the entire financial instrument arising from changes in the designated risks and portions must be reliably measurable. The Board noted that these principles were important in order for the effectiveness requirements set out in paragraph 88 to be applied in a meaningful way. The Board also noted that deciding whether designated risks and portions are separately identifiable and reliably measurable requires judgement. However, the Board confirmed that unless the inflation portion is a contractually specified portion of cash flows and other cash flows of the financial instrument are not affected by the inflation portion, inflation is not separately identifiable and reliably measurable and is not eligible for designation as a hedged risk or portion of a financial instrument.

Fair value hedge accounting for a portfolio hedge of interest rate risk

Background

BC173 The Exposure Draft of proposed improvements to IAS 39 published in June 2002 did not propose any substantial changes to the requirements for hedge accounting as they applied to a portfolio hedge of interest rate risk. However, some of the comment letters on the Exposure Draft and participants in the round-table discussions raised this issue. In particular, some were concerned that portfolio hedging strategies they regarded as effective hedges would not have qualified for fair value hedge accounting in accordance with previous versions of IAS 39. Rather, they would have either:

(a) not qualified for hedge accounting at all, with the result that reported profit or loss would be volatile; or

(b) qualified only for cash flow hedge accounting, with the result that reported equity would be volatile.

BC174 In the light of these concerns, the Board decided to explore whether and how IAS 39 could be amended to enable fair value hedge accounting to be used more readily for portfolio hedges of interest rate risk. As a result, in August 2003 the Board published a second Exposure Draft, *Fair Value Hedge Accounting for a Portfolio Hedge of Interest Rate Risk*, with a comment deadline of 14 November 2003. More than 120 comment letters were received. The amendments proposed in this second Exposure Draft were finalised in March 2004. Paragraphs BC135A–BC136B and BC175–BC220 summarise the Board's considerations in reaching conclusions on the issues raised.

Scope

BC175 The Board decided to limit any amendments to IAS 39 to applying fair value hedge accounting to a hedge of interest rate risk on a portfolio of items. In making this decision it noted that:

(a) implementation guidance on IAS 39[*] explains how to apply cash flow hedge accounting to a hedge of the interest rate risk on a portfolio of items.

(b) the issues that arise for a portfolio hedge of interest rate risk are different from those that arise for hedges of individual items and for hedges of other risks. In particular, the three issues discussed in paragraph BC176 do not arise in combination for such other hedging arrangements.

The issue: why fair value hedge accounting was difficult to achieve in accordance with previous versions of IAS 39

BC176 The Board identified the following three main reasons why a portfolio hedge of interest rate risk might not have qualified for fair value hedge accounting in accordance with previous versions of IAS 39.

(a) Typically, many of the assets that are included in a portfolio hedge are prepayable, ie the counterparty has a right to repay the item before its contractual repricing date. Such assets contain a prepayment option whose fair value changes as interest rates change. However, the derivative that is used as the hedging instrument typically is not prepayable, ie it does not contain a prepayment option. When interest rates change, the resulting change in the fair value of the hedged item (which is prepayable) differs from the change in fair value of the hedging derivative (which is not prepayable), with the result that the hedge may not meet IAS 39's effectiveness tests.[†] Furthermore, prepayment risk may have the effect that

---

* see Q&A F.6.1 and F.6.2

† see IAS 39, paragraph AG105

the items included in a portfolio hedge fail the requirement[*] that a group of hedged assets or liabilities must be 'similar' and the related requirement[†] that 'the change in fair value attributable to the hedged risk for each individual item in the group shall be expected to be approximately proportional to the overall change in fair value attributable to the hedged risk of the group of items'.

(b) IAS 39[§] prohibits the designation of an overall net position (eg the net of fixed rate assets and fixed rate liabilities) as the hedged item. Rather, it requires individual assets (or liabilities), or groups of similar assets (or similar liabilities), that share the risk exposure equal in amount to the net position to be designated as the hedged item. For example, if an entity has a portfolio of CU100 of assets and CU80 of liabilities, IAS 39 requires that individual assets or a group of similar assets of CU20 are designated as the hedged item. However, for risk management purposes, entities often seek to hedge the net position. This net position changes each period as items are repriced or derecognised and as new items are originated. Hence, the individual items designated as the hedged item also need to be changed each period. This requires de- and redesignation of the individual items that constitute the hedged item, which gives rise to significant systems needs.

(c) Fair value hedge accounting requires the carrying amount of the hedged item to be adjusted for the effect of changes in the hedged risk.[ø] Applied to a portfolio hedge, this could involve changing the carrying amounts of many thousands of individual items. Also, for any items subsequently de-designated from being hedged, the revised carrying amount must be amortised over the item's remaining life.[‡] This, too, gives rise to significant systems needs.

BC177 The Board decided that any change to IAS 39 must be consistent with the principles that underlie IAS 39's requirements on derivatives and hedge accounting. The three principles that are most relevant to a portfolio hedge of interest rate risk are:

(a) derivatives should be measured at fair value;

(b) hedge ineffectiveness should be identified and recognised in profit or loss;[#] and

(c) only items that are assets and liabilities should be recognised as such in the balance sheet. Deferred losses are not assets and deferred gains are not liabilities. However, if an asset or liability is hedged, any change in its fair value that is attributable to the hedged risk should be recognised in the balance sheet.

Prepayment risk

BC178 In considering the issue described in paragraph BC176(a), the Board noted that a prepayable item can be viewed as a combination of a non-prepayable item and a prepayment option. It follows that the fair value of a fixed rate prepayable item changes for two reasons when interest rates move:

(a) the fair value of the contracted cash flows to the contractual repricing date changes (because the rate used to discount them changes); and

(b) the fair value of the prepayment option changes (reflecting, among other things, that the likelihood of prepayment is affected by interest rates).

BC179 The Board also noted that, for risk management purposes, many entities do not consider these two effects separately. Instead they incorporate the effect of prepayments by grouping the hedged portfolio into repricing time periods based on *expected* repayment dates (rather than contractual repayment dates). For example, an entity with a portfolio of 25-year mortgages of CU100 may expect 5 per cent of that portfolio to repay in one year's time, in which case it schedules an amount of CU5 into a 12-month time period. The entity schedules all other items contained in its portfolio in a similar way (ie on the basis of expected repayment dates) and hedges all or part of the resulting overall net position in each repricing time period.

BC180 The Board decided to permit the scheduling that is used for risk management purposes, ie on the basis of expected repayment dates, to be used as a basis for the designation necessary for hedge accounting. As a result, an entity would not be required to compute the effect that a change in interest rates has on the fair value of the prepayment option embedded in a prepayable item. Instead, it could incorporate the effect of a change in interest rates on prepayments by grouping the hedged portfolio into repricing time periods based on expected repayment dates. The Board noted that this approach has significant practical advantages for preparers of financial statements, because it allows them to use the data they use for risk management. The Board also noted that the approach is consistent with paragraph 81 of IAS 39, which permits hedge accounting for a portion of a financial asset or financial liability. However, as discussed further in paragraphs BC193–BC206, the Board also concluded that if the entity changes its estimates of the time periods in which items are expected to repay (eg in the light of recent prepayment experience), ineffectiveness will arise, regardless of whether the revision in estimates results in more or less being scheduled in a particular time period.

BC181 The Board also noted that if the items in the hedged portfolio are subject to different amounts of prepayment risk, they may fail the test in paragraph 78 of being similar and the related requirement in paragraph 83 that the change in fair value attributable to the hedged risk for each individual item in the group is expected to be approximately proportional to the overall change in fair value attributable to the hedged risk of the group of items. The Board decided that, in the context of a portfolio hedge of interest rate risk, these requirements could be inconsistent with the Board's decision, set out in the previous paragraph, on how to incorporate the effects of prepayment risk. Accordingly, the Board decided that they should not apply. Instead, the financial assets or financial liabilities included in a portfolio hedge of interest rate risk need only share the risk being hedged.

Designation of the hedged item and liabilities with a demand feature

BC182 The Board considered two main ways to overcome the issue noted in paragraph BC176(b). These were:

(a) to designate the hedged item as the overall net position that results from a portfolio containing assets and liabilities. For example, if a repricing time period contains CU100 of fixed rate assets and CU90 of fixed rate liabilities, the net position of CU10 would be designated as the hedged item.

(b) to designate the hedged item as a portion of the assets (ie assets of CU10 in the above example), but not to require individual assets to be designated.

BC183 Some of those who commented on the Exposure Draft favoured designation of the overall net position in a portfolio that contains assets and liabilities. In their view, existing asset-liability management (ALM) systems treat the identified assets and liabilities as a natural hedge. Management's decisions about additional hedging focus on the entity's remaining net exposure. They observe that designation based on a portion of either the assets or the liabilities is not consistent with existing ALM systems and would entail additional systems costs.

BC184 In considering questions of designation, the Board was also concerned about questions of measurement. In particular, the Board observed that fair value hedge accounting requires measurement of the change in fair value of the hedged item attributable to the risk being hedged. Designation based on the net position would require the assets and the liabilities in a portfolio each to be measured at fair value (for the risk being hedged) in order to compute the fair value of the net position. Although statistical and other techniques can be used to estimate these fair values, the Board concluded that it is not appropriate to assume that the change in fair value of the hedging instrument is equal to the change in fair value of the net position.

BC185 The Board noted that under the first approach in paragraph BC182 (designating an overall net position), an issue arises if the entity has liabilities that are repayable on demand or after a notice period (referred to below as 'demandable liabilities'). This includes items such as demand deposits and some types of time deposits. The Board was informed that, when managing interest rate risk, many entities that have demandable liabilities include them in a portfolio hedge by scheduling them to the date when they *expect* the total amount of demandable liabilities in the portfolio to be due because of net withdrawals from the accounts in the portfolio. This expected repayment date is typically a period covering several years into the future (eg 0–10 years hence). The Board was also informed that some entities wish to apply fair value hedge accounting based on this scheduling, ie they wish to include demandable liabilities in a fair value portfolio hedge by scheduling them on the basis of their expected repayment dates. The arguments for this view are:

(a) it is consistent with how demandable liabilities are scheduled for risk management purposes. Interest rate risk management involves hedging the interest rate margin resulting from assets and liabilities and not the fair value of all or part of the assets and liabilities included in the hedged portfolio. The interest rate margin of a specific period is subject to variability as soon as the amount of fixed rate assets in that period differs from the amount of fixed rate liabilities in that period.

(b) it is consistent with the treatment of prepayable assets to include demandable liabilities in a portfolio hedge based on expected repayment dates.

(c) as with prepayable assets, expected maturities for demandable liabilities are based on the historical behaviour of customers.

(d) applying the fair value hedge accounting framework to a portfolio that includes demandable liabilities would not entail an immediate gain on origination of such liabilities because all assets and liabilities enter the hedged portfolio at their carrying amounts. Furthermore, IAS 39[*] requires the carrying amount of a financial liability on its initial recognition to be its fair value, which normally equates to the transaction price (ie the amount deposited).

(e) historical analysis shows that a base level of a portfolio of demandable liabilities, such as chequing accounts, is very stable. Whilst a portion of the demandable liabilities varies with interest rates, the remaining portion—the base level—does not. Hence, entities regard this base level as a long-term fixed rate item and include it as such in the scheduling that is used for risk management purposes.

(f) the distinction between 'old' and 'new' money makes little sense at a portfolio level. The portfolio behaves like a long-term item even if individual liabilities do not.

BC186 The Board noted that this issue is related to that of how to measure the fair value of a demandable liability. In particular, it interrelates with the requirement in IAS 39[†] that the fair value of a liability with a demand feature is not less than the amount payable on demand, discounted from the first date that the amount could be required to be paid. This requirement applies to all liabilities with a demand feature, not only to those included in a portfolio hedge.

BC187 The Board also noted that:

(a) although entities, when managing risk, may schedule demandable liabilities based on the expected repayment date of the total balance of a portfolio of accounts, the deposit liabilities included in that balance are unlikely to be outstanding for an extended period (eg several years). Rather, these deposits are usually expected to be withdrawn within a short time (eg a few months or less), although they may be replaced by new deposits. Put another way, the balance of the portfolio is relatively stable only because withdrawals on some accounts (which usually occur relatively quickly) are offset by new deposits into others. Thus, the liability being hedged is actually the forecast replacement of existing deposits by the receipt of new deposits. IAS 39 does not permit a hedge of such a forecast transaction to qualify for fair value hedge accounting. Rather, fair value

---

[*] see IAS 39, paragraph AG76

[†] see IAS 39, paragraph 49

hedge accounting can be applied only to the liability (or asset) or firm commitment that exists today.

(b) a portfolio of demandable liabilities is similar to a portfolio of trade payables. Both comprise individual balances that usually are expected to be paid within a short time (eg a few months or less) and replaced by new balances. Also, for both, there is an amount—the base level—that is expected to be stable and present indefinitely. Hence, if the Board were to permit demandable liabilities to be included in a fair value hedge on the basis of a stable base level created by expected replacements, it should similarly allow a hedge of a portfolio of trade payables to qualify for fair value hedge accounting on this basis.

(c) a portfolio of similar core deposits is not different from an individual deposit, other than that, in the light of the 'law of large numbers', the behaviour of the portfolio is more predictable. There are no diversification effects from aggregating many similar items.

(d) it would be inconsistent with the requirement in IAS 39 that the fair value of a liability with a demand feature is not less than the amount payable on demand, discounted from the first date that the amount could be required to be paid, to schedule such liabilities for hedging purposes using a different date. For example, consider a deposit of CU100 that can be withdrawn on demand without penalty. IAS 39 states that the fair value of such a deposit is CU100. That fair value is unaffected by interest rates and does not change when interest rates move. Accordingly, the demand deposit cannot be included in a fair value hedge of interest rate risk—there is no fair value exposure to hedge.

BC188 For these reasons, the Board concluded that demandable liabilities should not be included in a portfolio hedge on the basis of the expected repayment date of the *total balance of a portfolio* of demandable liabilities, ie including expected rollovers or replacements of existing deposits by new ones. However, as part of its consideration of comments received on the Exposure Draft, the Board also considered whether a demandable liability, such as a demand deposit, could be included in a portfolio hedge based on the expected repayment date of the *existing balance of individual deposits*, ie ignoring any rollovers or replacements of existing deposits by new deposits. The Board noted the following.

(a) For many demandable liabilities, this approach would imply a much earlier expected repayment date than is generally assumed for risk management purposes. In particular, for chequing accounts it would probably imply an expected maturity of a few months or less. However, for other demandable liabilities, such as fixed term deposits that can be withdrawn only by the depositor incurring a significant penalty, it might imply an expected repayment date that is closer to that assumed for risk management.

(b) This approach implies that the *fair value* of the demandable liability should also reflect the expected repayment date of the existing balance, ie that the fair value of a demandable deposit liability is the present value of the amount of the deposit discounted from the expected repayment date. The Board noted that it would be inconsistent to permit fair value hedge accounting to be based on the expected repayment date, but to measure the fair value of the liability on initial recognition on a different basis. The Board also noted that this approach would give rise to a difference on initial recognition between the amount deposited and the fair value recognised in the balance sheet. This, in turn, gives rise to the issue of what the difference represents. Possibilities the Board considered include (i) the value of the depositor's option to withdraw its money before the expected maturity, (ii) prepaid servicing costs or (iii) a gain. The Board did not reach a conclusion on what the difference represents, but agreed that if it were to require such differences to be recognised, this would apply to all demandable liabilities, not only to those included in a portfolio hedge. Such a requirement would represent a significant change from present practice.

(c) If the fair value of a demandable deposit liability at the date of initial recognition is deemed to equal the amount deposited, a fair value portfolio hedge based on an expected repayment date is unlikely to be effective. This is because such deposits typically pay interest at a rate that is significantly lower than that being hedged (eg the deposits may pay interest at zero or at very low rates, whereas the interest rate being hedged may be LIBOR or a similar benchmark rate). Hence, the fair value of the deposit will be significantly less sensitive to interest rate changes than that of the hedging instrument.

(d) The question of how to fair value a demandable liability is closely related to issues being debated by the Board in other projects, including Insurance (phase II), Revenue Recognition, Leases and Measurement. The Board's discussions in these other projects are continuing and it would be premature to reach a conclusion in the context of portfolio hedging without considering the implications for these other projects.

BC189 As a result, the Board decided:

(a) to confirm the requirement in IAS 39[*] that 'the fair value of a financial liability with a demand feature (eg a demand deposit) is not less than the amount payable on demand, discounted from the first date that the amount could be required to be paid', and

(b) consequently, that a demandable liability cannot qualify for fair value hedge accounting for any time period beyond the shortest period in which the counterparty can demand payment.

The Board noted that, depending on the outcome of its discussions in other projects (principally Insurance (phase II), Revenue Recognition, Leases and Measurement), it might reconsider these decisions at some time in the future.

BC190 The Board also noted that what is designated as the hedged item in a portfolio hedge affects the relevance of this issue, at least to some extent. In particular, if the hedged item is designated as a portion *of the assets* in a portfolio, this issue is irrelevant. To illustrate, assume that in a particular repricing time period an entity has CU100 of fixed rate assets and CU80 of what it regards as fixed rate liabilities and the entity wishes to hedge its net exposure of CU20. Also assume that all of the liabilities are demandable liabilities and the time period is later

---

[*] see paragraph 49

than that containing the earliest date on which the items can be repaid. If the hedged item is designated as CU20 of *assets*, then the demandable *liabilities* are not included in the hedged item, but rather are used only to determine how much of the assets the entity wishes to designate as being hedged. In such a case, whether the demandable liabilities can be designated as a hedged item in a fair value hedge is irrelevant. However, if the overall net position were to be designated as the hedged item, because the net position comprises CU100 of assets and CU80 of demandable liabilities, whether the demandable liabilities can be designated as a hedged item in a fair value hedge becomes critical.

BC191　Given the above points, the Board decided that a portion of assets or liabilities (rather than an overall net position) may be designated as the hedged item, to overcome part of the demandable liabilities issue. It also noted that this approach is consistent with IAS 39,[*] whereas designating an overall net position is not. IAS 39[†] prohibits an overall net position from being designated as the hedged item, but permits a similar effect to be achieved by designating an amount of assets (or liabilities) equal to the net position.

BC192　However, the Board also recognised that this method of designation would not fully resolve the demandable liabilities issue. In particular, the issue is still relevant if, in a particular repricing time period, the entity has so many demandable liabilities whose earliest repayment date is before that time period that (a) they comprise nearly all of what the entity regards as its fixed rate liabilities and (b) its fixed rate liabilities (including the demandable liabilities) exceed its fixed rate assets in this repricing time period. In this case, the entity is in a net liability position. Thus, it needs to designate an amount of the *liabilities* as the hedged item. But unless it has sufficient fixed rate liabilities other than those that can be demanded before that time period, this implies designating the demandable liabilities as the hedged item. Consistently with the Board's decision discussed above, such a hedge does not qualify for fair value hedge accounting. (If the liabilities are non-interest bearing, they cannot be designated as the hedged item in a cash flow hedge because their cash flows do not vary with changes in interest rates, ie there is no cash flow exposure to interest rates.[§] However, the hedging relationship may qualify for cash flow hedge accounting if designated as a hedge of associated assets.)

What portion of assets should be designated and the impact on ineffectiveness

BC193　Having decided that a portion of assets (or liabilities) could be designated as the hedged item, the Board considered how to overcome the systems problems noted in paragraph BC176(b) and (c). The Board noted that these problems arise from designating individual assets (or liabilities) as the hedged item. Accordingly, the Board decided that the hedged item could be expressed as an *amount* (of assets or liabilities) rather than as individual assets or liabilities.

---

[*]　see IAS 39, paragraph 84

[†]　see IAS 39, paragraph AG101

[§]　see Guidance on Implementing IAS 39, Question and Answer F.6.3.

BC194 The Board noted that this decision—that the hedged item may be designated as an amount of assets or liabilities rather than as specified items—gives rise to the issue of how the amount designated should be specified. The Board considered comments received on the Exposure Draft that it should not specify any method for designating the hedged item and hence measuring effectiveness. However, the Board concluded that if it provided no guidance, entities might designate in different ways, resulting in little comparability between them. The Board also noted that its objective, when permitting an amount to be designated, was to overcome the systems problems associated with designating individual items whilst achieving a very similar accounting result. Accordingly, it concluded that it should require a method of designation that closely approximates the accounting result that would be achieved by designating individual items.

BC195 Additionally, the Board noted that designation determines how much, if any, ineffectiveness arises if actual repricing dates in a particular repricing time period vary from those estimated or if the estimated repricing dates are revised. Taking the above example of a repricing time period in which there are CU100 of fixed rate assets and the entity designates as the hedged item an amount of CU20 of assets, the Board considered two approaches (a layer approach and a percentage approach) that are summarised below.

Layer approach

BC196 The first of these approaches, illustrated in figure 1, designates the hedged item as a 'layer' (eg (a) the bottom layer, (b) the top layer or (c) a portion of the top layer) of the assets (or liabilities) in a repricing time period. In this approach, the portfolio of CU100 in the above example is considered to comprise a hedged layer of CU20 and an unhedged layer of CU80.

Figure 1: Illustrating the designation of an amount of assets as a layer

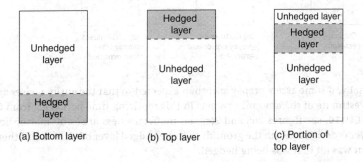

(a) Bottom layer　　　　(b) Top layer　　　　(c) Portion of top layer

BC197 The Board noted that the layer approach does not result in the recognition of ineffectiveness in all cases when the estimated amount of assets (or liabilities) changes. For example, in a bottom layer approach (see figure 2), if some assets prepay earlier than expected so that the entity revises downward its estimate of the amount of assets in the repricing time period (eg from CU100 to CU90), these reductions are assumed to come first from the unhedged top layer (figure 2(b)). Whether any ineffectiveness arises depends on whether the downward revision reaches the hedged layer of CU20. Thus, if the bottom layer is designated as the hedged item, it is unlikely that the hedged (bottom) layer will be reached and that any ineffectiveness will arise. Conversely, if the top layer is designated (see figure 3), any downward revision to the estimated amount in a repricing time period will reduce the hedged (top) layer and ineffectiveness will arise (figure 3(b)).

Figure 2: Illustrating the effect on changes in prepayments in a bottom layer approach

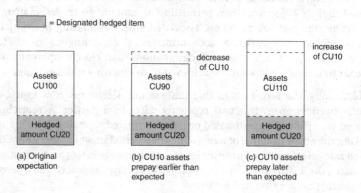

Figure 3: Illustrating the effect on changes in prepayments in a top layer approach

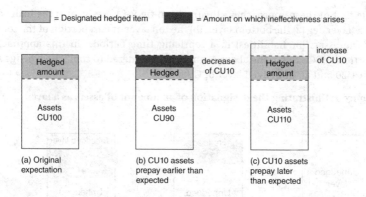

BC198   Finally, if some assets prepay *later* than expected so that the entity revises *upwards* its estimate of the amount of assets in this repricing time period (eg from CU100 to CU110, see figures 2(c) and 3(c)), no ineffectiveness arises no matter how the layer is designated, on the grounds that the hedged layer of CU20 is still there and that was all that was being hedged.

Percentage approach

BC199   The percentage approach, illustrated in figure 4, designates the hedged item as a percentage of the assets (or liabilities) in a repricing time period. In this approach, in the portfolio in the above example, 20 per cent of the assets of CU100 in this repricing time period is designated as the hedged item (figure 4(a)). As a result, if some assets prepay *earlier* than expected so that the entity revises *downwards* its estimate of the amount of assets in this repricing time period (eg from CU100 to CU90, figure 4(b)), ineffectiveness arises on 20 per cent of the decrease (in this case ineffectiveness arises on CU2). Similarly, if some assets prepay *later* than expected so that the entity revises *upwards* its estimate of the amount of assets in this repricing time period (eg from CU100 to CU110, figure 4(c)), ineffectiveness arises on 20 per cent of the increase (in this case ineffectiveness arises on CU2).

Figure 4: Illustrating the designation of an amount of assets as a percentage

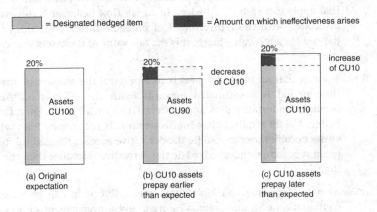

Figure 4: Illustrating the designation of an amount of assets as a percentage

□ = Designated hedged item   ■ = Amount on which ineffectiveness arises

(a) Original expectation — Assets CU100 — 20%

(b) CU10 assets prepay earlier than expected — Assets CU90 — 20% — decrease of CU10

(c) CU10 assets prepay later than expected — Assets CU110 — 20% — increase of CU10

Arguments for and against the layer approach

BC200   The arguments for the layer approach are as follows:

(a)   Designating a bottom layer would be consistent with the answers to Questions F.6.1 and F.6.2 of the Guidance on Implementing IAS 39, which allow, for a cash flow hedge, the 'bottom' portion of reinvestments of collections from assets to be designated as the hedged item.

(b)   The entity is hedging interest rate risk rather than prepayment risk. Any changes to the portfolio because of changes in prepayments do not affect how effective the hedge was in mitigating interest rate risk.

(c)   The approach captures all ineffectiveness on the hedged portion. It merely allows the hedged portion to be defined in such a way that, at least in a bottom layer approach, the first of any potential ineffectiveness relates to the unhedged portion.

(d)   It is correct that no ineffectiveness arises if changes in prepayment estimates cause more assets to be scheduled into that repricing time period. So long as assets equal to the hedged layer remain, there is no ineffectiveness and upward revisions of the amount in a repricing time period do not affect the hedged layer.

(e)   A prepayable item can be viewed as a combination of a non-prepayable item and a prepayment option. The designation of a bottom layer can be viewed as hedging a part of the life of the non-prepayable item, but none of the prepayment option. For example, a 25-year prepayable mortgage can be viewed as a combination of (i) a non-prepayable, fixed term, 25-year mortgage and (ii) a written prepayment option that allows the borrower to repay the mortgage early. If the entity hedges this asset with a 5-year derivative, this is equivalent to hedging the first five years of component (i). If the position is viewed in this way, no ineffectiveness arises when interest rate changes cause the value of the prepayment option to change (unless the option is exercised and the asset prepaid) because the prepayment option was not hedged.

BC201 The arguments against the layer approach are as follows:

(a) The considerations that apply to a fair value hedge are different from those that apply to a cash flow hedge. In a cash flow hedge, it is the cash flows associated with the reinvestment of probable future collections that are hedged. In a fair value hedge it is the fair value of the assets that currently exist.

(b) The fact that no ineffectiveness is recognised if the amount in a repricing time period is re-estimated upwards (with the effect that the entity becomes underhedged) is not in accordance with IAS 39. For a fair value hedge, IAS 39 requires that ineffectiveness is recognised both when the entity becomes overhedged (ie the derivative exceeds the hedged item) and when it becomes underhedged (ie the derivative is smaller than the hedged item).

(c) As noted in paragraph BC200(e), a prepayable item can be viewed as a combination of a non-prepayable item and a prepayment option. When interest rates change, the fair value of both of these components changes.

(d) The objective of applying fair value hedge accounting to a hedged item designated in terms of an amount (rather than as individual assets or liabilities) is to obtain results that closely approximate those that would have been obtained if individual assets or liabilities had been designated as the hedged item. If individual prepayable assets had been designated as the hedged item, the change in both the components noted in (c) above (to the extent they are attributable to the hedged risk) would be recognised in profit or loss, both when interest rates increase and when they decrease. Accordingly, the change in the fair value of the hedged asset would differ from the change in the fair value of the hedging derivative (unless that derivative includes an equivalent prepayment option) and ineffectiveness would be recognised for the difference. It follows that in the simplified approach of designating the hedged item as an amount, ineffectiveness should similarly arise.

(e) All prepayable assets in a repricing time period, and not just a layer of them, contain a prepayment option whose fair value changes with changes in interest rates. Accordingly, when interest rates change, the fair value of the hedged assets (which include a prepayment option whose fair value has changed) will change by an amount different from that of the hedging derivative (which typically does not contain a prepayment option), and ineffectiveness will arise. This effect occurs regardless of whether interest rates increase or decrease—ie regardless of whether re-estimates of prepayments result in the amount in a time period being more or less.

(f) Interest rate risk and prepayment risk are so closely interrelated that it is not appropriate to separate the two components referred to in paragraph BC200(e) and designate only one of them (or a part of one of them) as the hedged item. Often the biggest single cause of changes in prepayment rates is changes in interest rates. This close relationship is the reason why IAS 39[*] prohibits a held-to-maturity asset[†] from being a hedged item with respect to either interest rate risk or prepayment risk. Furthermore, most entities do not separate the two components for risk management purposes. Rather, they incorporate the prepayment option by scheduling amounts based on expected maturities. When entities choose to use risk management practices—based on not separating prepayment and interest rate risk—as the basis for designation for hedge accounting purposes, it is not appropriate to separate the two components referred to in paragraph BC200(e) and designate only one of them (or a part of one of them) as the hedged item.

(g) If interest rates change, the effect on the fair value of a portfolio of prepayable items will be different from the effect on the fair value of a portfolio of otherwise identical but non-prepayable items. However, using a layer approach, this difference would not be recognised—if both portfolios were hedged to the same extent, both would be recognised in the balance sheet at the same amount.

BC202 The Board was persuaded by the arguments in paragraph BC201 and rejected layer approaches. In particular, the Board concluded that the hedged item should be designated in such a way that if the entity changes its estimates of the repricing time periods in which items are expected to repay or mature (eg in the light of recent prepayment experience), ineffectiveness arises. It also concluded that ineffectiveness should arise both when estimated prepayments decrease, resulting in more assets in a particular repricing time period, and when they increase, resulting in fewer.

Arguments for a third approach—measuring directly the change in fair value of the entire hedged item

BC203 The Board also considered comments on the Exposure Draft that:

(a) some entities hedge prepayment risk and interest rate risk separately, by hedging to the expected prepayment date using interest rate swaps, and hedging possible variations in these expected prepayment dates using swaptions.

(b) the embedded derivatives provisions of IAS 39 require some prepayable assets to be separated into a prepayment option and a non-prepayable host contract[§] (unless the entity is unable to measure separately the prepayment option, in which case it treats the entire asset as held for trading[ø]). This seems to conflict with the view in the Exposure Draft that the two risks are too difficult to separate for the purposes of a portfolio hedge.

---

[*]   see IAS 39, paragraph 79

[†]   IFRS 9 *Financial Instruments*, issued in November 2009, eliminated the held-to-maturity category.

[§]   see IAS 39, paragraphs 11 and AG30(g)

[ø]   see IAS 39, paragraph 12

BC204   In considering these arguments, the Board noted that the percentage approach described in paragraph AG126(b) is a proxy for measuring the change in the fair value of the *entire* asset (or liability)—including any embedded prepayment option—that is attributable to changes in interest rates. The Board had developed this proxy in the Exposure Draft because it had been informed that most entities (a) do not separate interest rate risk and prepayment risk for risk management purposes and hence (b) were unable to value the change in the value of the entire asset (including any embedded prepayment option) that is attributable to changes in the hedged interest rates. However, the comments described in paragraph BC203 indicated that in some cases, entities may be able to measure this change in value directly. The Board noted that such a direct method of measurement is conceptually preferable to the proxy described in paragraph AG126(b) and, accordingly, decided to recognise it explicitly. Thus, for example, if an entity that hedges prepayable assets using a combination of interest rate swaps and swaptions is able to measure directly the change in fair value of the entire asset, it could measure effectiveness by comparing the change in the value of the swaps and swaptions with the change in the fair value of the entire asset (including the change in the value of the prepayment option embedded in them) that is attributable to changes in the hedged interest rate. However, the Board also decided to permit the proxy proposed in the Exposure Draft for those entities that are unable to measure directly the change in the fair value of the entire asset.

Consideration of systems requirements

BC205   Finally, the Board was informed that, to be practicable in terms of systems needs, any approach should not require tracking of the amount in a repricing time period for multiple periods. Therefore it decided that ineffectiveness should be calculated by determining the change in the estimated amount in a repricing time period between one date on which effectiveness is measured and the next, as described more fully in paragraphs AG126 and AG127. This requires the entity to track how much of the change in each repricing time period between these two dates is attributable to revisions in estimates and how much is attributable to the origination of new assets (or liabilities). However, once ineffectiveness has been determined as set out above, the entity in essence starts again, ie it establishes the new amount in each repricing time period (including new items that have been originated since it last tested effectiveness), designates a new hedged item, and repeats the procedures to determine ineffectiveness at the next date it tests effectiveness. Thus the tracking is limited to movements between one date when effectiveness is measured and the next. It is not necessary to track for multiple periods. However, the entity will need to keep records relating to each repricing time period (a) to reconcile the amounts for each repricing time period with the total amounts in the two separate line items in the balance sheet (see paragraph AG114(f)), and (b) to ensure that amounts in the two separate line items are derecognised no later than when the repricing time period to which they relate expires.

BC206   The Board also noted that the amount of tracking required by the percentage approach is no more than what would be required by any of the layer approaches. Thus, the Board concluded that none of the approaches was clearly preferable from the standpoint of systems needs.

The carrying amount of the hedged item

BC207   The last issue noted in paragraph BC176 is how to present in the balance sheet the change in fair value of the hedged item. The Board noted the concern of respondents that the hedged item may contain many—even thousands of—individual assets (or liabilities) and that to change the carrying amounts of each of these individual items would be impracticable. The Board considered dealing with this concern by permitting the change in value to be presented in a single line item in the balance sheet. However, the Board noted that this could result in a decrease in the fair value of a financial asset (financial liability) being recognised as a financial liability (financial asset). Furthermore, for some repricing time periods the hedged item may be an asset, whereas for others it may be a liability. The Board concluded that it would be incorrect to present together the changes in fair value for such repricing time periods, because to do so would combine changes in the fair value of assets with changes in the fair value of liabilities.

BC208   Accordingly, the Board decided that two line items should be presented, as follows:

(a)   for those repricing time periods for which the hedged item is an asset, the change in its fair value is presented in a single separate line item within assets; and

(b)   for those repricing time periods for which the hedged item is a liability, the change in its fair value is presented in a single separate line item within liabilities.

BC209   The Board noted that these line items represent changes in the fair value of the hedged item. For this reason, the Board decided that they should be presented next to financial assets or financial liabilities.

Derecognition of amounts included in the separate line items

Derecognition of an asset (or liability) in the hedged portfolio

BC210   The Board discussed how and when amounts recognised in the separate balance sheet line items should be removed from the balance sheet. The Board noted that the objective is to remove such amounts from the balance sheet in the same periods as they would have been removed had individual assets or liabilities (rather than an amount) been designated as the hedged item.

BC211   The Board noted that this objective could be fully met only if the entity schedules individual assets or liabilities into repricing time periods and tracks both for how long the scheduled individual items have been hedged and how much of each item was hedged in each time period. In the absence of such scheduling and tracking, some assumptions would need to be made about these matters and, hence, about how much should be removed from the separate balance sheet line items when an asset (or liability) in the hedged portfolio is derecognised. In addition, some safeguards would be needed to ensure that amounts included in the separate balance sheet line items are removed from the balance sheet over a reasonable period and do not remain in the balance sheet indefinitely. With these points in mind, the Board decided to require that:

(a)   whenever an asset (or liability) in the hedged portfolio is derecognised—whether through earlier than expected prepayment, sale or write-off from impairment—any amount included in the separate balance sheet line item relating to that derecognised asset (or liability) should be removed from the balance sheet and included in the gain or loss on derecognition.

(b)   if an entity cannot determine into which time period(s) a derecognised asset (or liability) was scheduled:

    (i)   it should assume that higher than expected prepayments occur on assets scheduled into the first available time period; and

    (ii)   it should allocate sales and impairments to assets scheduled into all time periods containing the derecognised item on a systematic and rational basis.

(c)   the entity should track how much of the total amount included in the separate line items relates to each repricing time period, and should remove the amount that relates to a particular time period from the balance sheet no later than when that time period expires.

Amortisation

BC212   The Board also noted that if the designated hedged amount for a repricing time period is reduced, IAS 39[*] requires that the separate balance sheet line item described in paragraph 89A relating to that reduction is amortised on the basis of a recalculated effective interest rate. The Board noted that for a portfolio hedge of interest rate risk, amortisation based on a recalculated effective interest rate could be complex to determine and could demand significant additional systems requirements. Consequently, the Board decided that in the case of a portfolio hedge of interest rate risk (and only in such a hedge), the line item balance may be amortised using a straight-line method when a method based on a recalculated effective interest rate is not practicable.

The hedging instrument

BC213   The Board was asked by commentators to clarify whether the hedging instrument may be a portfolio of derivatives containing offsetting risk positions. Commentators noted that previous versions of IAS 39 were unclear on this point.

BC214   The issue arises because the assets and liabilities in each repricing time period change over time as prepayment expectations change, as items are derecognised and as new items are originated. Thus the net position, and the amount the entity wishes to designate as the hedged item, also changes over time. If the hedged item decreases, the hedging instrument needs to be reduced. However, entities do not normally reduce the hedging instrument by disposing of some of the derivatives contained in it. Instead, entities adjust the hedging instrument by entering into new derivatives with an offsetting risk profile.

BC215   The Board decided to permit the hedging instrument to be a portfolio of derivatives containing offsetting risk positions for both individual and portfolio hedges. It noted that all of the derivatives concerned are measured at fair value.

---

[*]   see paragraph 92

© IASCF

It also noted that the two ways of adjusting the hedging instrument described in the previous paragraph can achieve substantially the same effect. Therefore the Board clarified paragraph 77 to this effect.

Hedge effectiveness for a portfolio hedge of interest rate risk

BC216   Some respondents to the Exposure Draft questioned whether IAS 39's effectiveness tests* should apply to a portfolio hedge of interest rate risk. The Board noted that its objective in amending IAS 39 for a portfolio hedge of interest rate risk is to permit fair value hedge accounting to be used more easily, whilst continuing to meet the principles of hedge accounting. One of these principles is that the hedge is highly effective. Thus, the Board concluded that the effectiveness requirements in IAS 39 apply equally to a portfolio hedge of interest rate risk.

BC217   Some respondents to the Exposure Draft sought guidance on how the effectiveness tests are to be applied to a portfolio hedge. In particular, they asked how the prospective effectiveness test is to be applied when an entity periodically 'rebalances' a hedge (ie adjusts the amount of the hedging instrument to reflect changes in the hedged item). The Board decided that if the entity's risk management strategy is to change the amount of the hedging instrument periodically to reflect changes in the hedged position, that strategy affects the determination of the term of the hedge. Thus, the entity needs to demonstrate that the hedge is expected to be highly effective only for the period until the amount of the hedging instrument is next adjusted. The Board noted that this decision does not conflict with the requirement in paragraph 75 that 'a hedging relationship may not be designated for only a portion of the time period during which a hedging instrument remains outstanding'. This is because the entire hedging instrument is designated (and not only some of its cash flows, for example, those to the time when the hedge is next adjusted). However, expected effectiveness is assessed by considering the change in the fair value of the entire hedging instrument only for the period until it is next adjusted.

BC218   A third issue raised in the comment letters was whether, for a portfolio hedge, the retrospective effectiveness test should be assessed for all time buckets in aggregate or individually for each time bucket. The Board decided that entities could use any method to assess retrospective effectiveness, but noted that the chosen method would form part of the documentation of the hedging relationship made at the inception of the hedge in accordance with paragraph 88(a) and hence could not be decided at the time the retrospective effectiveness test is performed.

Transition to fair value hedge accounting for portfolios of interest rate risk

BC219   In finalising the amendments to IAS 39, the Board considered whether to provide additional guidance for entities wishing to apply fair value hedge accounting to a portfolio hedge that had previously been accounted for using cash flow hedge accounting. The Board noted that such entities could apply paragraph 101(d) to revoke the designation of a cash flow hedge and re-designate a new fair value

---

*   see paragraph AG105

hedge using the same hedged item and hedging instrument, and decided to clarify this in the Application Guidance. Additionally, the Board concluded that clarification was not required for first-time adopters because IFRS 1 already contained sufficient guidance.

BC220 The Board also considered whether to permit retrospective designation of a portfolio hedge. The Board noted that this would conflict with the principle in paragraph 88(a) that 'at the inception of the hedge there is formal designation and documentation of the hedging relationship' and accordingly, decided not to permit retrospective designation.

BC221– [Deleted]
BC222

Dissenting opinions

Dissent of Anthony T Cope, James J Leisenring and Warren J McGregor from the issue of IAS 39 in December 2003

DO1   Messrs Cope, Leisenring and McGregor dissent from the issue of this Standard.

DO2   Mr Leisenring dissents because he disagrees with the conclusions concerning derecognition, impairment of certain assets and the adoption of basis adjustment hedge accounting in certain circumstances.

DO3   The Standard requires in paragraphs 30 and 31 that to the extent of an entity's continuing involvement in an asset, a liability should be recognised for the consideration received. Mr Leisenring believes that the result of that accounting is to recognise assets that fail to meet the definition of assets and to record liabilities that fail to meet the definition of liabilities. Furthermore, the Standard fails to recognise forward contracts, puts or call options and guarantees that are created, but instead records a fictitious 'borrowing' as a result of rights and obligations created by those contracts. There are other consequences of the continuing involvement approach that has been adopted. For transferors, it results in very different accounting by two entities when they have identical contractual rights and obligations only because one entity once owned the transferred financial asset. Furthermore, the 'borrowing' that is recognised is not accounted for like other loans, so no interest expense may be recorded. Indeed, implementing the proposed approach requires the specific override of measurement and presentation standards applicable to other similar financial instruments that do not arise from derecognition transactions. For example, derivatives created by derecognition transactions are not accounted for at fair value. For transferees, the approach also requires the override of the recognition and measurement requirements applicable to other similar financial instruments. If an instrument is acquired in a transfer transaction that fails the derecognition criteria, the transferee recognises and measures it differently from an instrument that is acquired from the same counterparty separately.

DO4   Mr Leisenring also disagrees with the requirement in paragraph 64 to include an asset that has been individually judged not to be impaired in a portfolio of similar assets for an additional portfolio assessment of impairment. Once an asset is judged not to be impaired, it is irrelevant whether the entity owns one or more similar assets as those assets have no implications for whether the asset that was individually considered for impairment is or is not impaired. The result of this accounting is that two entities could each own 50 per cent of a single loan. Both entities could conclude the loan is not impaired. However, if one of the two entities happens to have other loans that are similar, it would be allowed to recognise an impairment with respect to the loan where the other entity is not. Accounting for identical exposures differently is unacceptable. Mr Leisenring believes that the arguments in paragraph BC115 are compelling.

DO5   Mr Leisenring also dissents from paragraph 98 which allows but does not require basis adjustment for hedges of forecast transactions that result in the recognition of non-financial assets or liabilities. This accounting results in always adjusting the recorded asset or liability at the date of initial recognition away from its fair value. It also records an asset, if the basis adjustment alternative is selected, at an amount other than its cost as defined in IAS 16 *Property, Plant and Equipment* and further described in paragraph 16 of that Standard. If a derivative were to be considered a part of the cost of acquiring an asset, hedge accounting in these circumstances should not be elective to be consistent with IAS 16. Mr Leisenring also objects to creating this alternative as a result of an improvement project that ostensibly had as an objective the reduction of alternatives. The non-comparability that results from this alternative is both undesirable and unnecessary.

DO6   Mr Leisenring also dissents from the application guidance in paragraph AG71 and in particular the conclusion contained in paragraph BC98. He does not believe that an entity that originates a contract in one market should measure the fair value of the contract by reference to a different market in which the transaction did not take place. If prices change in the transacting market, that price change should be recognised when subsequently measuring the fair value of the contract. However, there are many implications of switching between markets when measuring fair value that the Board has not yet addressed. Mr Leisenring believes a gain or loss should not be recognised based on the fact a transaction could occur in a different market.

DO7   Mr Cope dissents from paragraph 64 and agrees with Mr Leisenring's analysis and conclusions on loan impairment as set out above in paragraph DO4. He finds it counter-intuitive that a loan that has been determined not to be impaired following careful analysis should be subsequently accounted for as if it were impaired when included in a portfolio.

DO8   Mr Cope also dissents from paragraph 98, and, in particular, the Board's decision to allow a free choice over whether basis adjustment is used when accounting for hedges of forecast transactions that result in the recognition of non-financial assets or non-financial liabilities. In his view, of the three courses of action open to the Board— retaining IAS 39's requirement to use basis adjustment, prohibiting basis adjustment as proposed in the June 2002 Exposure Draft, or providing a choice—the Board has selected the worst course. Mr Cope believes that the best approach would have been to prohibit basis adjustment, as proposed in the Exposure Draft, because, in his opinion, basis adjustments result in the recognition of assets and liabilities at inappropriate amounts.

DO9   Mr Cope believes that increasing the number of choices in international standards is bad policy. The Board's decision potentially creates major differences between entities choosing one option and those choosing the other. This lack of comparability will adversely affect users' ability to make sound economic decisions.

DO10   In addition, Mr Cope notes that entities that are US registrants may choose not to adopt basis adjustment in order to avoid a large reconciling difference to US GAAP. Mr Cope believes that increasing differences between IFRS-compliant entities that are US registrants and those that are not is undesirable.

DO11   Mr McGregor dissents from paragraph 98 and agrees with Mr Cope's and Mr Leisenring's analyses and conclusions as set out above in paragraphs DO5 and DO8–DO10.

DO12   Mr McGregor also dissents from this Standard because he disagrees with the conclusions about impairment of certain assets.

DO13   Mr McGregor disagrees with paragraphs 67 and 69, which deal with the impairment of equity investments classified as available for sale. These paragraphs require impairment losses on such assets to be recognised in profit or loss when there is objective evidence that the asset is impaired. Previously recognised impairment losses are not to be reversed through profit and loss when the assets' fair value increases. Mr McGregor notes that the Board's reasoning for prohibiting reversals through profit or loss of previously impaired available-for-sale equity investments, set out in paragraph BC130 of the Basis for Conclusions, is that it '..could not find an acceptable way to distinguish reversals of impairment losses from other increases in fair value'. He agrees with this reasoning but believes that it applies equally to the recognition of impairment losses in the first place. Mr McGregor believes that the significant subjectivity involved in assessing whether a reduction in fair value represents an impairment (and thus should be recognised in profit or loss) or another decrease in value (and should be recognised directly in equity) will at best lead to a lack of comparability within an entity over time and between entities, and at worst provide an opportunity for entities to manage reported profit or loss.

DO14   Mr McGregor believes that all changes in the fair value of assets classified as available for sale should be recognised in profit or loss. However, such a major change to the Standard would need to be subject to the Board's full due process. At this time, to overcome the concerns expressed in paragraph DO13, he believes that for equity investments classified as available for sale, the Standard should require all changes in fair value below cost to be recognised in profit or loss as impairments and reversals of impairments and all changes in value above cost to be recognised in equity. This approach treats all changes in value the same way, no matter what their cause. The problem of how to distinguish an impairment loss from another decline in value (and of deciding whether there is an impairment in the first place) is eliminated because there is no longer any subjectivity involved. In addition, the approach is consistent with IAS 16 *Property, Plant and Equipment* and IAS 38 *Intangible Assets*.

DO15   Mr McGregor disagrees with paragraph 106 of the Standard and with the consequential amendments to paragraph 27[*] of IFRS 1 *First-time Adoption of International Financial Reporting Standards*. Paragraph 106 requires entities to apply the derecognition provisions prospectively to financial assets. Paragraph 27 of IFRS 1 requires first-time adopters to apply the derecognition provisions of IAS 39 (as revised in 2003) prospectively to non-derivative financial assets and financial liabilities. Mr McGregor believes that existing IAS 39 appliers should apply the derecognition provisions retrospectively to financial assets, and that first-time adopters should apply the derecognition provisions of IAS 39 retrospectively to all financial assets and financial liabilities. He is concerned that financial assets may have been derecognised under the original IAS 39 by entities that were subject to

---

[*]   As a result of the revision of IFRS 1 in November 2008, paragraph 27 became paragraph B2.

it, which might not have been derecognised under the revised IAS 39. He is also concerned that non-derivative financial assets and financial liabilities may have been derecognised by first-time adopters under previous GAAP that would not have been derecognised under the revised IAS 39. These amounts may be significant in many cases. Not requiring recognition of such amounts will result in the loss of relevant information and will impair the ability of users of financial statements to make sound economic decisions.

Dissent of John T Smith from the issue in March 2004 of *Fair Value Hedge Accounting for a Portfolio Hedge of Interest Rate Risk* (Amendments to IAS 39)

DO1   Mr Smith dissents from these Amendments to IAS 39 Financial Instruments: Recognition and Measurement—*Fair Value Hedge Accounting for a Portfolio Hedge of Interest Rate Risk*. He agrees with the objective of finding a macro hedging solution that would reduce systems demands without undermining the fundamental accounting principles related to derivative instruments and hedging activities. However, Mr Smith believes that some respondents' support for these Amendments and their willingness to accept IAS 39 is based more on the extent to which the Amendments reduce recognition of ineffectiveness, volatility of profit or loss, and volatility of equity than on whether the Amendments reduce systems demands without undermining the fundamental accounting principles.

DO2   Mr Smith believes some decisions made during the Board's deliberations result in an approach to hedge accounting for a portfolio hedge that does not capture what was originally intended, namely a result that is substantially equivalent to designating an individual asset or liability as the hedged item. He understands some respondents will not accept IAS 39 unless the Board provides still another alternative that will further reduce reported volatility. Mr Smith believes that the Amendments already go beyond their intended objective. In particular, he believes that features of these Amendments can be applied to smooth out ineffectiveness and achieve results substantially equivalent to the other methods of measuring ineffectiveness that the Board considered when developing the Exposure Draft. The Board rejected those methods because they did not require the immediate recognition of all ineffectiveness. He also believes those features could be used to manage earnings.

Dissent of Mary E Barth, Robert P Garnett and Geoffrey Whittington from the issue in June 2005 of *The Fair Value Option* (Amendment to IAS 39)

DO1   Professor Barth, Mr Garnett and Professor Whittington dissent from the amendment to IAS 39 Financial Instruments: Recognition and Measurement—*The Fair Value Option*. Their dissenting opinions are set out below.

DO2   These Board members note that the Board considered the concerns expressed by the prudential supervisors on the fair value option as set out in the December 2003 version of IAS 39 when it finalised IAS 39. At that time the Board concluded that these concerns were outweighed by the benefits, in terms of simplifying the practical application of IAS 39 and providing relevant information to users of financial statements, that result from allowing the fair value option to be used for any financial asset or financial liability. In the view of these Board members, no substantive new arguments have been raised that would cause them to revisit this conclusion. Furthermore, the majority of constituents have clearly expressed a preference for the fair value option as set out in the December 2003 version of IAS 39 over the fair value option as contained in the amendment.

DO3   Those Board members note that the amendment introduces a series of complex rules, including those governing transition which would be entirely unnecessary in the absence of the amendment. There will be consequential costs to preparers of financial statements, in order to obtain, in many circumstances, substantially the same result as the much simpler and more easily understood fair value option that was included in the December 2003 version of IAS 39. They believe that the complex rules will also inevitably lead to differing interpretations of the eligibility criteria for the fair value option contained in the amendment.

DO4   These Board members also note that, for paragraph 9(b)(i), application of the amendment may not mitigate, on an ongoing basis, the anomaly of volatility in profit or loss that results from the different measurement attributes in IAS 39 any more than would the option in the December 2003 version of IAS 39. This is because the fair value designation is required to be continued even if one of the offsetting instruments is derecognised. Furthermore, for paragraphs 9(b)(i), 9(b)(ii) and 11A, the fair value designation continues to apply in subsequent periods, irrespective of whether the initial conditions that permitted the use of the option still hold. Therefore, these Board members question the purpose of and need for requiring the criteria to be met at initial designation.

Dissent of James J Leisenring and John T Smith from the issue in October 2008 of *Reclassification of Financial Assets* (Amendments to IAS 39 and IFRS 7)

DO1   Messrs Leisenring and Smith dissent from *Reclassification of Financial Assets* (Amendments to IAS 39 and IFRS 7). The amendments to IAS 39 are asserted to level the playing field with US GAAP. It accomplishes that with respect to the reclassification of financial instruments to the held-to-maturity category of loans and receivables from other classifications. However, once reclassified, the measurement of impairment and when that measurement is required are quite different and a level playing field in accounting for these instruments is not achieved. Messrs Leisenring and Smith would have been willing to support the alternative approach considered by the Board that would have closely aligned the impairment requirements of US GAAP with IFRSs.

DO2   As described in paragraph BC11E, in October 2008 the Board received requests to address differences between the reclassification requirements of IAS 39 and US GAAP. SFAS 115 permits a security to be reclassified out of the trading category in rare situations. SFAS 65 permits a loan to be reclassified out of the Held for Sale category if the entity has the intention to hold the loan for the foreseeable future or until maturity. IAS 39 permitted no reclassifications for financial assets classified as held for trading. The Board was asked to consider allowing entities applying IFRSs the same ability to reclassify a financial asset out of the held-for-trading category as is permitted by SFAS 115 and SFAS 65.

DO3   Messrs Leisenring and Smith both believe that the current requirements in IFRSs for reclassification are superior to US GAAP and that the accounting for impairments in US GAAP is superior to the requirements of IAS 39.

DO4   Furthermore, Messrs Leisenring and Smith do not believe that amendments to standards should be made without any due process.

IAS 39 *Financial Instruments: Recognition and Measurement*
Illustrative example

This example accompanies, but is not part of, IAS 39.

Facts

IE1   On 1 January 20X1, Entity A identifies a portfolio comprising assets and liabilities whose interest rate risk it wishes to hedge. The liabilities include demandable deposit liabilities that the depositor may withdraw at any time without notice. For risk management purposes, the entity views all of the items in the portfolio as fixed rate items.

IE2   For risk management purposes, Entity A analyses the assets and liabilities in the portfolio into repricing time periods based on expected repricing dates. The entity uses monthly time periods and schedules items for the next five years (ie it has 60 separate monthly time periods).[*] The assets in the portfolio are prepayable assets that Entity A allocates into time periods based on the expected prepayment dates, by allocating a percentage of all of the assets, rather than individual items, into each time period. The portfolio also includes demandable liabilities that the entity expects, on a portfolio basis, to repay between one month and five years and, for risk management purposes, are scheduled into time periods on this basis. On the basis of this analysis, Entity A decides what amount it wishes to hedge in each time period.

IE3   This example deals only with the repricing time period expiring in three months' time, ie the time period maturing on 31 March 20X1 (a similar procedure would be applied for each of the other 59 time periods). Entity A has scheduled assets of CU100 million[†] and liabilities of CU80 million into this time period. All of the liabilities are repayable on demand.

IE4   Entity A decides, for risk management purposes, to hedge the net position of CU20 million and accordingly enters into an interest rate swap[§] on 1 January 20X1 to pay a fixed rate and receive LIBOR, with a notional principal amount of CU20 million and a fixed life of three months.

IE5   This example makes the following simplifying assumptions:

(a)   the coupon on the fixed leg of the swap is equal to the fixed coupon on the asset;

(b)   the coupon on the fixed leg of the swap becomes payable on the same dates as the interest payments on the asset; and

---

[*]   In this example principal cash flows have been scheduled into time periods but the related interest cash flows have been included when calculating the change in the fair value of the hedged item. Other methods of scheduling assets and liabilities are also possible. Also, in this example, monthly repricing time periods have been used. An entity may choose narrower or wider time periods.

[†]   In this example monetary amounts are denominated in 'currency units (CU)'.

[§]   The example uses a swap as the hedging instrument. An entity may use forward rate agreements or other derivatives as hedging instruments.

(c) the interest on the variable leg of the swap is the overnight LIBOR rate. As a result, the entire fair value change of the swap arises from the fixed leg only, because the variable leg is not exposed to changes in fair value due to changes in interest rates.

In cases when these simplifying assumptions do not hold, greater ineffectiveness will arise. (The ineffectiveness arising from (a) could be eliminated by designating as the hedged item a portion of the cash flows on the asset that are equivalent to the fixed leg of the swap.)

IE6 It is also assumed that Entity A tests effectiveness on a monthly basis.

IE7 The fair value of an equivalent non-prepayable asset of CU20 million, ignoring changes in value that are not attributable to interest rate movements, at various times during the period of the hedge is as follows:

	1 Jan 20X1	31 Jan 20X1	1 Feb 20X1	28 Feb 20X1	31 Mar 20X1
Fair value (asset) (CU)	20,000,000	20,047,408	20,047,408	20,023,795	Nil

IE8 The fair value of the swap at various times during the period of the hedge is as follows:

	1 Jan 20X1	31 Jan 20X1	1 Feb 20X1	28 Feb 20X1	31 Mar 20X1
Fair value (liability) (CU)	Nil	(47,408)	(47,408)	(23,795)	Nil

Accounting treatment

IE9 On 1 January 20X1, Entity A designates as the hedged item an amount of CU20 million of assets in the three-month time period. It designates as the hedged risk the change in the value of the hedged item (ie the CU20 million of assets) that is attributable to changes in LIBOR. It also complies with the other designation requirements set out in paragraphs 88(d) and AG119 of the Standard.

IE10 Entity A designates as the hedging instrument the interest rate swap described in paragraph IE4.

End of month 1 (31 January 20X1)

IE11 On 31 January 20X1 (at the end of month 1) when Entity A tests effectiveness, LIBOR has decreased. Based on historical prepayment experience, Entity A estimates that, as a consequence, prepayments will occur faster than previously estimated. As a result it re-estimates the amount of assets scheduled into this time period (excluding new assets originated during the month) as CU96 million.

IE12 The fair value of the designated interest rate swap with a notional principal of CU20 million is (CU47,408)[*] (the swap is a liability).

---

[*] see paragraph IE8.

IE13 Entity A computes the change in the fair value of the hedged item, taking into account the change in estimated prepayments, as follows.

(a) First, it calculates the percentage of the initial estimate of the assets in the time period that was hedged. This is 20 per cent (CU20 million ÷ CU100 million).

(b) Second, it applies this percentage (20 per cent) to its revised estimate of the amount in that time period (CU96 million) to calculate the amount that is the hedged item based on its revised estimate. This is CU19.2 million.

(c) Third, it calculates the change in the fair value of this revised estimate of the hedged item (CU19.2 million) that is attributable to changes in LIBOR. This is CU45,511 (CU47,408* × (CU19.2 million ÷ CU20 million)).

IE14 Entity A makes the following accounting entries relating to this time period:

Dr Cash	CU172,097	
Cr Profit or loss (interest income)[a]		CU172,097

To recognise the interest received on the hedged amount (CU19.2 million).

Dr Profit or loss (interest expense)	CU179,268	
Cr Profit or loss (interest income)		CU179,268
Cr Cash		Nil

To recognise the interest received and paid on the swap designated as the hedging instrument.

Dr Profit or loss (loss)	CU47,408	
Cr Derivative liability		CU47,408

To recognise the change in the fair value of the swap.

Dr Separate line item in the statement of financial position	CU45,511	
Cr Profit or loss (gain)		CU45,511

To recognise the change in the fair value of the hedged amount.

(a) This example does not show how amounts of interest income and interest expense are calculated.

IE15 The net result on profit or loss (excluding interest income and interest expense) is to recognise a loss of (CU1,897). This represents ineffectiveness in the hedging relationship that arises from the change in estimated prepayment dates.

Beginning of month 2

IE16 On 1 February 20X1 Entity A sells a proportion of the assets in the various time periods. Entity A calculates that it has sold 8$\frac{1}{3}$ per cent of the entire portfolio of assets. Because the assets were allocated into time periods by allocating a percentage of the assets (rather than individual assets) into each time period,

---

* ie CU20,047,408 − CU20,000,000. See paragraph IE7.

Entity A determines that it cannot ascertain into which specific time periods the sold assets were scheduled. Hence it uses a systematic and rational basis of allocation. Based on the fact that it sold a representative selection of the assets in the portfolio, Entity A allocates the sale proportionately over all time periods.

IE17   On this basis, Entity A computes that it has sold $8^1/3$ per cent of the assets allocated to the three-month time period, ie CU8 million ($8^1/3$ per cent of CU96 million). The proceeds received are CU8,018,400, equal to the fair value of the assets.[*] On derecognition of the assets, Entity A also removes from the separate line item in the statement of financial position an amount that represents the change in the fair value of the hedged assets that it has now sold. This is $8^1/3$ per cent of the total line item balance of CU45,511, ie CU3,793.

IE18   Entity A makes the following accounting entries to recognise the sale of the asset and the removal of part of the balance in the separate line item in the statement of financial position:

Dr Cash		CU8,018,400
Cr Asset		CU8,000,000
Cr Separate line item in the statement of financial position		CU3,793
Cr Profit or loss (gain)		CU14,607

To recognise the sale of the asset at fair value and to recognise a gain on sale.

Because the change in the amount of the assets is not attributable to a change in the hedged interest rate no ineffectiveness arises.

IE19   Entity A now has CU88 million of assets and CU80 million of liabilities in this time period. Hence the net amount Entity A wants to hedge is now CU8 million and, accordingly, it designates CU8 million as the hedged amount.

IE20   Entity A decides to adjust the hedging instrument by designating only a proportion of the original swap as the hedging instrument. Accordingly, it designates as the hedging instrument CU8 million or 40 per cent of the notional amount of the original swap with a remaining life of two months and a fair value of CU18,963.[†] It also complies with the other designation requirements in paragraphs 88(a) and AG119 of the Standard. The CU12 million of the notional amount of the swap that is no longer designated as the hedging instrument is either classified as held for trading with changes in fair value recognised in profit or loss, or is designated as the hedging instrument in a different hedge.[§]

---

[*]   The amount realised on sale of the asset is the fair value of a prepayable asset, which is less than the fair value of the equivalent non-prepayable asset shown in paragraph IE7.

[†]   CU47,408 × 40 per cent

[§]   The entity could instead enter into an offsetting swap with a notional principal of CU12 million to adjust its position and designate as the hedging instrument all CU20 million of the existing swap and all CU12 million of the new offsetting swap.

IE21   As at 1 February 20X1 and after accounting for the sale of assets, the separate line item in the statement of financial position is CU41,718 (CU45,511 – CU3,793), which represents the cumulative change in fair value of CU17.6[*] million of assets. However, as at 1 February 20X1, Entity A is hedging only CU8 million of assets that have a cumulative change in fair value of CU18,963.[†] The remaining separate line item in the statement of financial position of CU22,755[§] relates to an amount of assets that Entity A still holds but is no longer hedging. Accordingly Entity A amortises this amount over the remaining life of the time period, ie it amortises CU22,755 over two months.

IE22   Entity A determines that it is not practicable to use a method of amortisation based on a recalculated effective yield and hence uses a straight-line method.

End of month 2 (28 February 20X1)

IE23   On 28 February 20X1 when Entity A next tests effectiveness, LIBOR is unchanged. Entity A does not revise its prepayment expectations. The fair value of the designated interest rate swap with a notional principal of CU8 million is (CU9,518)[ø] (the swap is a liability). Also, Entity A calculates the fair value of the CU8 million of the hedged assets as at 28 February 20X1 as CU8,009,518.[‡]

IE24   Entity A makes the following accounting entries relating to the hedge in this time period:

Dr   Cash   CU71,707
        Cr   Profit or loss (interest income)   CU71,707
To recognise the interest received on the hedged amount (CU8 million).

Dr   Profit or loss (interest expense)   CU71,707
        Cr   Profit or loss (interest income)   CU62,115
        Cr   Cash   CU9,592
To recognise the interest received and paid on the portion of the swap designated as the hedging instrument (CU8 million).

Dr   Derivative liability   CU9,445
        Cr   Profit or loss (gain)   CU9,445
To recognise the change in the fair value of the portion of the swap designated as the hedging instrument (CU8 million) (CU9,518 – CU18,963).

Dr   Profit or loss (loss)   CU9,445
        Cr   Separate line item in the statement of financial position   CU9,445
To recognise the change in the fair value of the hedged amount (CU8,009,518 – CU8,018,963).

---

*   CU19.2 million – ($8^1/3\%$ × CU19.2 million)

†   CU41,718 × (CU8 million ÷ CU17.6 million)

§   CU41,718 – CU18,963

ø   CU23,795 [see paragraph IE8] × (CU8 million ÷ CU20 million)

‡   CU20,023,795 [see paragraph IE7] × (CU8 million ÷ CU20 million)

IE25   The net effect on profit or loss (excluding interest income and interest expense) is nil reflecting that the hedge is fully effective.

IE26   Entity A makes the following accounting entry to amortise the line item balance for this time period:

Dr   Profit or loss (loss)   CU11,378
       Cr   Separate line item in the statement of financial position   CU11,378[a]

To recognise the amortisation charge for the period.

(a) CU22,755 ÷ 2

End of month 3

IE27   During the third month there is no further change in the amount of assets or liabilities in the three-month time period. On 31 March 20X1 the assets and the swap mature and all balances are recognised in profit or loss.

IE28   Entity A makes the following accounting entries relating to this time period:

Dr   Cash   CU8,071,707
       Cr   Asset (statement of financial position)   CU8,000,000
       Cr   Profit or loss (interest income)   CU71,707

To recognise the interest and cash received on maturity of the hedged amount (CU8 million).

Dr   Profit or loss (interest expense)   CU71,707
       Cr   Profit or loss (interest income)   CU62,115
       Cr   Cash   CU9,592

To recognise the interest received and paid on the portion of the swap designated as the hedging instrument (CU8 million).

Dr   Derivative liability   CU9,518
       Cr   Profit or loss (gain)   CU9,518

To recognise the expiry of the portion of the swap designated as the hedging instrument (CU8 million).

Dr   Profit or loss (loss)   CU9,518
       Cr   Separate line item in the statement of financial position   CU9,518

To remove the remaining line item balance on expiry of the time period.

IE29   The net effect on profit or loss (excluding interest income and interest expense) is nil reflecting that the hedge is fully effective.

IE30   Entity A makes the following accounting entry to amortise the line item balance for this time period:

Dr   Profit or loss (loss)   CU11,377

    Cr   Separate line item in the statement of financial position   CU11,377[a]

To recognise the amortisation charge for the period.

(a)   CU22,755 ÷ 2

Summary

IE31   The tables below summarise:

(a)   changes in the separate line item in the statement of financial position;

(b)   the fair value of the derivative;

(c)   the profit or loss effect of the hedge for the entire three-month period of the hedge; and

(d)   interest income and interest expense relating to the amount designated as hedged.

Description	1 Jan 20X1	31 Jan 20X1	1 Feb 20X1	28 Feb 20X1	31 Mar 20X1
	CU	CU	CU	CU	CU
Amount of asset hedged		19,200,000	8,000,000	8,000,000	8,000,000

(a) Changes in the separate line item in the statement of financial position

Brought forward:

Balance to be amortised	Nil	Nil	Nil	22,755	11,377
Remaining balance	Nil	Nil	45,511	18,963	9,518
Less: Adjustment on sale of asset	Nil	Nil	(3,793)	Nil	Nil
Adjustment for change in fair value of the hedged asset	Nil	45,511	Nil	(9,445)	(9,518)
Amortisation	Nil	Nil	Nil	(11,378)	(11,377)

Carried forward:

Balance to be amortised	**Nil**	**Nil**	**22,755**	**11,377**	**Nil**
Remaining balance	**Nil**	**45,511**	**18,963**	**9,518**	**Nil**

(b) The fair value of the derivative

	1 Jan 20X1	31 Jan 20X1	1 Feb 20X1	28 Feb 20X1	31 Mar 20X1
CU20,000,000	Nil	47,408	–	–	–
CU12,000,000	Nil	–	28,445	No longer designated as the hedging instrument.	
CU8,000,000	Nil	–	18,963	9,518	Nil
Total	**Nil**	**47,408**	**47,408**	**9,518**	**Nil**

(c) Profit or loss effect of the hedge

	1 Jan 20X1	31 Jan 20X1	1 Feb 20X1	28 Feb 20X1	31 Mar 20X1
Change in line item: asset	Nil	45,511	N/A	(9,445)	(9,518)
Change in derivative fair value	Nil	(47,408)	N/A	9,445	9,518
Net effect	**Nil**	**(1,897)**	**N/A**	**Nil**	**Nil**
Amortisation	**Nil**	**Nil**	**N/A**	**(11,378)**	**(11,377)**

In addition, there is a gain on sale of assets of CU14,607 at 1 February 20X1.

continued...

...continued

(d) Interest income and interest expense relating to the amount designated as hedged

Profit or loss recognised for the amount hedged	1 Jan 20X1	31 Jan 20X1	1 Feb 20X1	28 Feb 20X1	31 Mar 20X1
Interest income					
– on the asset	Nil	172,097	N/A	71,707	71,707
– on the swap	Nil	179,268	N/A	62,115	62,115
Interest expense					
– on the swap	Nil	(179,268)	N/A	(71,707)	(71,707)

CONTENTS

F.5   Cash flow hedges

F.6   Hedges: other issues

SECTION G   OTHER

Guidance on implementing
IAS 39 *Financial Instruments: Recognition and Measurement*

This guidance accompanies, but is not part of, IAS 39.

Section A Scope

A.1 Practice of settling net: forward contract to purchase a commodity

Entity XYZ enters into a fixed price forward contract to purchase one million kilograms of copper in accordance with its expected usage requirements. The contract permits XYZ to take physical delivery of the copper at the end of twelve months or to pay or receive a net settlement in cash, based on the change in fair value of copper. Is the contract accounted for as a derivative?

While such a contract meets the definition of a derivative, it is not necessarily accounted for as a derivative. The contract is a derivative instrument because there is no initial net investment, the contract is based on the price of copper, and it is to be settled at a future date. However, if XYZ intends to settle the contract by taking delivery and has no history for similar contracts of settling net in cash or of taking delivery of the copper and selling it within a short period after delivery for the purpose of generating a profit from short-term fluctuations in price or dealer's margin, the contract is not accounted for as a derivative under IAS 39. Instead, it is accounted for as an executory contract.

A.2 Option to put a non-financial asset

Entity XYZ owns an office building. XYZ enters into a put option with an investor that permits XYZ to put the building to the investor for CU150 million. The current value of the building is CU175* million. The option expires in five years. The option, if exercised, may be settled through physical delivery or net cash, at XYZ's option. How do both XYZ and the investor account for the option?

XYZ's accounting depends on XYZ's intention and past practice for settlement. Although the contract meets the definition of a derivative, XYZ does not account for it as a derivative if XYZ intends to settle the contract by delivering the building if XYZ exercises its option and there is no past practice of settling net (IAS 39.5 and IAS 39.AG10).

The investor, however, cannot conclude that the option was entered into to meet the investor's expected purchase, sale or usage requirements because the investor does not have the ability to require delivery (IAS 39.7). In addition, the option may be settled net in cash. Therefore, the investor has to account for the contract as a derivative. Regardless of past practices, the investor's intention does not affect whether settlement is by delivery or in cash. The investor has written an option, and a written option in which the holder has a choice of physical settlement or net cash settlement can never satisfy the normal delivery requirement for the exemption from IAS 39 because the option writer does not have the ability to require delivery.

However, if the contract were a forward contract rather than an option, and if the contract required physical delivery and the reporting entity had no past practice of settling net in cash or of taking delivery of the building and selling it within a short period after delivery for the purpose of generating a profit from short-term fluctuations in price or dealer's margin, the contract would not be accounted for as a derivative.

---

*   In this guidance, monetary amounts are denominated in 'currency units (CU)'.

Section B Definitions

B.1 Definition of a financial instrument: gold bullion

Is gold bullion a financial instrument (like cash) or is it a commodity?

It is a commodity. Although bullion is highly liquid, there is no contractual right to receive cash or another financial asset inherent in bullion.

B.2 Definition of a derivative: examples of derivatives and underlyings

What are examples of common derivative contracts and the identified underlying?

IAS 39 defines a derivative as follows:

A derivative is a financial instrument or other contract within the scope of this Standard with all three of the following characteristics:

(a)   its value changes in response to the change in a specified interest rate, financial instrument price, commodity price, foreign exchange rate, index of prices or rates, credit rating or credit index, or other variable, provided in the case of a non-financial variable that the variable is not specific to a party to the contract (sometimes called the 'underlying');

(b)   it requires no initial net investment or an initial net investment that is smaller than would be required for other types of contracts that would be expected to have a similar response to changes in market factors; and

(c)   it is settled at a future date.

Type of contract	Main pricing-settlement variable (underlying variable)
Interest rate swap	Interest rates
Currency swap (foreign exchange swap)	Currency rates
Commodity swap	Commodity prices
Equity swap	Equity prices (equity of another entity)
Credit swap	Credit rating, credit index or credit price
Total return swap	Total fair value of the reference asset and interest rates
Purchased or written treasury bond option (call or put)	Interest rates
Purchased or written currency option (call or put)	Currency rates
Purchased or written commodity option (call or put)	Commodity prices
Purchased or written stock option (call or put)	Equity prices (equity of another entity)

continued...

...continued

Type of contract	Main pricing-settlement variable (underlying variable)
Interest rate futures linked to government debt (treasury futures)	Interest rates
Currency futures	Currency rates
Commodity futures	Commodity prices
Interest rate forward linked to government debt (treasury forward)	Interest rates
Currency forward	Currency rates
Commodity forward	Commodity prices
Equity forward	Equity prices (equity of another entity)

The above list provides examples of contracts that normally qualify as derivatives under IAS 39. The list is not exhaustive. Any contract that has an underlying may be a derivative. Moreover, even if an instrument meets the definition of a derivative contract, special provisions of IAS 39 may apply, for example, if it is a weather derivative (see IAS 39.AG1), a contract to buy or sell a non-financial item such as commodity (see IAS 39.5 and IAS 39.AG10) or a contract settled in an entity's own shares (see IAS 32.21–IAS 32.24). Therefore, an entity must evaluate the contract to determine whether the other characteristics of a derivative are present and whether special provisions apply.

B.3 Definition of a derivative: settlement at a future date, interest rate swap with net or gross settlement

For the purpose of determining whether an interest rate swap is a derivative financial instrument under IAS 39, does it make a difference whether the parties pay the interest payments to each other (gross settlement) or settle on a net basis?

No. The definition of a derivative does not depend on gross or net settlement.

To illustrate: Entity ABC enters into an interest rate swap with a counterparty (XYZ) that requires ABC to pay a fixed rate of 8 per cent and receive a variable amount based on three-month LIBOR, reset on a quarterly basis. The fixed and variable amounts are determined based on a CU100 million notional amount. ABC and XYZ do not exchange the notional amount. ABC pays or receives a net cash amount each quarter based on the difference between 8 per cent and three-month LIBOR. Alternatively, settlement may be on a gross basis.

The contract meets the definition of a derivative regardless of whether there is net or gross settlement because its value changes in response to changes in an underlying variable (LIBOR), there is no initial net investment, and settlements occur at future dates.

B.4 Definition of a derivative: prepaid interest rate swap (fixed rate payment obligation prepaid at inception or subsequently)

If a party prepays its obligation under a pay-fixed, receive-variable interest rate swap at inception, is the swap a derivative financial instrument?

Yes.

To illustrate: Entity S enters into a CU100 million notional amount five-year pay-fixed, receive-variable interest rate swap with Counterparty C. The interest rate of the variable part of the swap is reset on a quarterly basis to three-month LIBOR. The interest rate of the fixed part of the swap is 10 per cent per year. Entity S prepays its fixed obligation under the swap of CU50 million (CU100 million × 10 per cent × 5 years) at inception, discounted using market interest rates, while retaining the right to receive interest payments on the CU100 million reset quarterly based on three-month LIBOR over the life of the swap.

The initial net investment in the interest rate swap is significantly less than the notional amount on which the variable payments under the variable leg will be calculated. The contract requires an initial net investment that is smaller than would be required for other types of contracts that would be expected to have a similar response to changes in market factors, such as a variable rate bond. Therefore, the contract fulfils the 'no initial net investment or an initial net investment that is smaller than would be required for other types of contracts that would be expected to have a similar response to changes in market factors' provision of IAS 39. Even though Entity S has no future performance obligation, the ultimate settlement of the contract is at a future date and the value of the contract changes in response to changes in the LIBOR index. Accordingly, the contract is regarded as a derivative contract.

Would the answer change if the fixed rate payment obligation is prepaid subsequent to initial recognition?

If the fixed leg is prepaid during the term, that would be regarded as a termination of the old swap and an origination of a new instrument that is evaluated under IAS 39 and IFRS 9.

B.5 Definition of a derivative: prepaid pay-variable, receive-fixed interest rate swap

If a party prepays its obligation under a pay-variable, receive-fixed interest rate swap at inception of the contract or subsequently, is the swap a derivative financial instrument?

No. A prepaid pay-variable, receive-fixed interest rate swap is not a derivative if it is prepaid at inception and it is no longer a derivative if it is prepaid after inception because it provides a return on the prepaid (invested) amount comparable to the return on a debt instrument with fixed cash flows. The prepaid amount fails the 'no initial net investment or an initial net investment that is smaller than would be required for other types of contracts that would be expected to have a similar response to changes in market factors' criterion of a derivative.

To illustrate: Entity S enters into a CU100 million notional amount five-year pay-variable, receive-fixed interest rate swap with Counterparty C. The variable leg of the swap is reset on a quarterly basis to three-month LIBOR. The fixed interest payments under the swap are calculated as 10 per cent times the swap's notional amount, ie CU10 million per year. Entity S prepays its obligation under the variable leg of the swap at inception at current market rates, while retaining the right to receive fixed interest payments of 10 per cent on CU100 million per year.

The cash inflows under the contract are equivalent to those of a financial instrument with a fixed annuity stream since Entity S knows it will receive CU10 million per year over the life of the swap. Therefore, all else being equal, the initial investment in the contract should equal that of other financial instruments that consist of fixed annuities. Thus, the initial net investment in the pay-variable, receive-fixed interest rate swap is equal to the investment required in a non-derivative contract that has a similar response to changes in market conditions. For this reason, the instrument fails the 'no initial net investment or an initial net investment that is smaller than would be required for other types of contracts that would be expected to have a similar response to changes in market factors' criterion of IAS 39. Therefore, the contract is not accounted for as a derivative under IAS 39 or IFRS 9. By discharging the obligation to pay variable interest rate payments, Entity S in effect provides a loan to Counterparty C.

B.6 Definition of a derivative: offsetting loans

Entity A makes a five-year fixed rate loan to Entity B, while B at the same time makes a five-year variable rate loan for the same amount to A. There are no transfers of principal at inception of the two loans, since A and B have a netting agreement. Is this a derivative under IAS 39?

Yes. This meets the definition of a derivative (that is to say, there is an underlying variable, no initial net investment or an initial net investment that is smaller than would be required for other types of contracts that would be expected to have a similar response to changes in market factors, and future settlement). The contractual effect of the loans is the equivalent of an interest rate swap arrangement with no initial net investment. Non-derivative transactions are aggregated and treated as a derivative when the transactions result, in substance, in a derivative. Indicators of this would include:

- they are entered into at the same time and in contemplation of one another

- they have the same counterparty

- they relate to the same risk

- there is no apparent economic need or substantive business purpose for structuring the transactions separately that could not also have been accomplished in a single transaction.

The same answer would apply if Entity A and Entity B did not have a netting agreement, because the definition of a derivative instrument in IAS 39.9 does not require net settlement.

B.7 Definition of a derivative: option not expected to be exercised

The definition of a derivative in IAS 39.9 requires that the instrument 'is settled at a future date'. Is this criterion met even if an option is expected not to be exercised, for example, because it is out of the money?

Yes. An option is settled upon exercise or at its maturity. Expiry at maturity is a form of settlement even though there is no additional exchange of consideration.

B.8 Definition of a derivative: foreign currency contract based on sales volume

Entity XYZ, whose functional currency is the US dollar, sells products in France denominated in euro. XYZ enters into a contract with an investment bank to convert euro to US dollars at a fixed exchange rate. The contract requires XYZ to remit euro based on its sales volume in France in exchange for US dollars at a fixed exchange rate of 6.00. Is that contract a derivative?

Yes. The contract has two underlying variables (the foreign exchange rate and the volume of sales), no initial net investment or an initial net investment that is smaller than would be required for other types of contracts that would be expected to have a similar response to changes in market factors, and a payment provision. IAS 39 does not exclude from its scope derivatives that are based on sales volume.

B.9 Definition of a derivative: prepaid forward

An entity enters into a forward contract to purchase shares of stock in one year at the forward price. It prepays at inception based on the current price of the shares. Is the forward contract a derivative?

No. The forward contract fails the 'no initial net investment or an initial net investment that is smaller than would be required for other types of contracts that would be expected to have a similar response to changes in market factors' test for a derivative.

To illustrate: Entity XYZ enters into a forward contract to purchase one million T ordinary shares in one year. The current market price of T is CU50 per share; the one-year forward price of T is CU55 per share. XYZ is required to prepay the forward contract at inception with a CU50 million payment. The initial investment in the forward contract of CU50 million is less than the notional amount applied to the underlying, one million shares at the forward price of CU55 per share, ie CU55 million. However, the initial net investment approximates the investment that would be required for other types of contracts that would be expected to have a similar response to changes in market factors because T's shares could be purchased at inception for the same price of CU50. Accordingly, the prepaid forward contract does not meet the initial net investment criterion of a derivative instrument.

B.10 Definition of a derivative: initial net investment

Many derivative instruments, such as futures contracts and exchange traded written options, require margin accounts. Is the margin account part of the initial net investment?

No. The margin account is not part of the initial net investment in a derivative instrument. Margin accounts are a form of collateral for the counterparty or clearing house and may take the form of cash, securities or other specified assets, typically liquid assets. Margin accounts are separate assets that are accounted for separately.

B.11 Definition of held for trading: portfolio with a recent actual pattern of short-term profit-taking

The definition of a financial asset or financial liability held for trading states that 'a financial asset or financial liability is classified as held for trading if it is ... part of a portfolio of identified financial instruments that are managed together and for which there is evidence of a recent actual pattern of short-term profit-taking'. What is a 'portfolio' for the purposes of applying this definition?

Although the term 'portfolio' is not explicitly defined in IAS 39, the context in which it is used suggests that a portfolio is a group of financial assets or financial liabilities that are managed as part of that group (IAS 39.9). If there is evidence of a recent actual pattern of short-term profit-taking on financial instruments included in such a portfolio, those financial instruments qualify as held for trading even though an individual financial instrument may in fact be held for a longer period of time.

B.12–B.23 [Deleted]

B.24 Definition of amortised cost: perpetual debt instruments with fixed or market-based variable rate

Sometimes entities purchase or issue debt instruments that are required to be measured at amortised cost and in respect of which the issuer has no obligation to repay the principal amount. Interest may be paid either at a fixed rate or at a variable rate. Would the difference between the initial amount paid or received and zero ('the maturity amount') be amortised immediately on initial recognition for the purpose of determining amortised cost if the rate of interest is fixed or specified as a market-based variable rate?

No. Since there are no repayments of principal, there is no amortisation of the difference between the initial amount and the maturity amount if the rate of interest is fixed or specified as a market-based variable rate. Because interest payments are fixed or market-based and will be paid in perpetuity, the amortised cost (the present value of the stream of future cash payments discounted at the effective interest rate) equals the principal amount in each period (IAS 39.9).

B.25 Definition of amortised cost: perpetual debt instruments with decreasing interest rate

If the stated rate of interest on a perpetual debt instrument decreases over time, would amortised cost equal the principal amount in each period?

No. From an economic perspective, some or all of the interest payments are repayments of the principal amount. For example, the interest rate may be stated as 16 per cent for the first ten years and as zero per cent in subsequent periods. In that case, the initial amount is amortised to zero over the first ten years using the effective interest method, since a portion of the interest payments represents repayments of the principal amount. The amortised cost is zero after year 10 because the present value of the stream of future cash payments in subsequent periods is zero (there are no further cash payments of either principal or interest in subsequent periods).

B.26 Example of calculating amortised cost: financial asset

How is amortised cost calculated for financial assets measured at amortised cost in accordance with IFRS 9?

Under IAS 39, amortised cost is calculated using the effective interest method. The effective interest rate inherent in a financial instrument is the rate that exactly discounts the estimated cash flows associated with the financial instrument through the expected life of the instrument or, where appropriate, a shorter period to the net carrying amount at initial recognition. The computation includes all fees and points paid or received that are an integral part of the effective interest rate, directly attributable transaction costs and all other premiums or discounts.

The following example illustrates how amortised cost is calculated using the effective interest method. Entity A purchases a debt instrument with five years remaining to maturity for its fair value of CU1,000 (including transaction costs). The instrument has a principal amount of CU1,250 and carries fixed interest of 4.7 per cent that is paid annually (CU1,250 × 4.7 per cent = CU59 per year). The contract also specifies that the borrower has an option to prepay the instrument and that no penalty will be charged for prepayment. At inception, the entity expects the borrower not to prepay.

It can be shown that in order to allocate interest receipts and the initial discount over the term of the debt instrument at a constant rate on the carrying amount, they must be accrued at the rate of 10 per cent annually. The table below provides information about the amortised cost, interest income and cash flows of the debt instrument in each reporting period.

Year	(a) Amortised cost at the beginning of the year	(b = a × 10%) Interest income	(c) Cash flows	(d = a + b − c) Amortised cost at the end of the year
20X0	1,000	100	59	1,041
20X1	1,041	104	59	1,086
20X2	1,086	109	59	1,136
20X3	1,136	113	59	1,190
20X4	1,190	119	1,250 + 59	–

On the first day of 20X2 the entity revises its estimate of cash flows. It now expects that 50 per cent of the principal will be prepaid at the end of 20X2 and the remaining 50 per cent at the end of 20X4. In accordance with IAS 39.AG8, the opening balance of the debt instrument in 20X2 is adjusted. The adjusted amount is calculated by discounting the amount the entity expects to receive in 20X2 and subsequent years using the original effective interest rate (10 per cent). This results in the new opening balance in 20X2 of CU1138. The adjustment of CU52 (CU1,138 – CU1,086) is recorded in profit or loss in 20X2. The table below provides information about the amortised cost, interest income and cash flows as they would be adjusted taking into account the change in estimate.

Year	(a)	(b = a × 10%)	(c)	(d = a + b – c)
	Amortised cost at the beginning of the year	Interest income	Cash flows	Amortised cost at the end of the year
20X0	1,000	100	59	1,041
20X1	1,041	104	59	1,086
20X2	1,086 + 52	114	625 + 59	568
20X3	568	57	30	595
20X4	595	60	625 + 30	–

If the debt instrument becomes impaired, say, at the end of 20X3, the impairment loss is calculated as the difference between the carrying amount (CU595) and the present value of estimated future cash flows discounted at the original effective interest rate (10 per cent).

B.27 Example of calculating amortised cost: debt instruments with stepped interest payments

Sometimes entities purchase or issue debt instruments with a predetermined rate of interest that increases or decreases progressively ('stepped interest') over the term of the debt instrument. If a debt instrument with stepped interest and no embedded derivative is issued at CU1,250 and has a maturity amount of CU1,250, would the amortised cost equal CU1,250 in each reporting period over the term of the debt instrument?

No. Although there is no difference between the initial amount and maturity amount, an entity uses the effective interest method to allocate interest payments over the term of the debt instrument to achieve a constant rate on the carrying amount (IAS 39.9).

The following example illustrates how amortised cost is calculated using the effective interest method for an instrument with a predetermined rate of interest that increases or decreases over the term of the debt instrument ('stepped interest').

On 1 January 2000, Entity A issues a debt instrument for a price of CU1,250. The principal amount is CU1,250 and the debt instrument is repayable on 31 December 2004. The rate of interest is specified in the debt agreement as a percentage of the principal amount as follows: 6.0 per cent in 2000 (CU75), 8.0 per cent in 2001 (CU100), 10.0 per cent in 2002 (CU125), 12.0 per cent in 2003 (CU150), and 16.4 per cent in 2004 (CU205). In this case, the interest rate that exactly discounts the stream of future cash payments through maturity is 10 per cent. Therefore, cash interest payments are reallocated over the term of the debt instrument for the purposes of determining amortised cost in each period. In each period, the amortised cost at the beginning of the period is multiplied by the effective interest rate of 10 per cent and added to the amortised cost. Any cash payments in the period are deducted from the resulting number. Accordingly, the amortised cost in each period is as follows:

Year	(a)	(b = a × 10%)	(c)	(d = a + b – c)
	Amortised cost at the beginning of the year	Interest income	Cash flows	Amortised cost at the end of the year
20X0	1,250	125	75	1,300
20X1	1,300	130	100	1,330
20X2	1,330	133	125	1,338
20X3	1,338	134	150	1,322
20X4	1,322	133	1,250 + 205	–

B.28 Regular way contracts: no established market

Can a contract to purchase a financial asset be a regular way contract if there is no established market for trading such a contract?

Yes. IAS 39.9 refers to terms that require delivery of the asset within the time frame established generally by regulation or convention in the marketplace concerned. Marketplace, as that term is used in IAS 39.9, is not limited to a formal stock exchange or organised over-the-counter market. Rather, it means the environment in which the financial asset is customarily exchanged. An acceptable time frame would be the period reasonably and customarily required for the parties to complete the transaction and prepare and execute closing documents.

For example, a market for private issue financial instruments can be a marketplace.

B.29 Regular way contracts: forward contract

Entity ABC enters into a forward contract to purchase one million of M's ordinary shares in two months for CU10 per share. The contract is with an individual and is not an exchange-traded contract. The contract requires ABC to take physical delivery of the shares and pay the counterparty CU10 million in cash. M's shares trade in an active public market at an average of 100,000 shares a day. Regular way delivery is three days. Is the forward contract regarded as a regular way contract?

No. The contract must be accounted for as a derivative because it is not settled in the way established by regulation or convention in the marketplace concerned.

B.30 Regular way contracts: which customary settlement provisions apply?

If an entity's financial instruments trade in more than one active market, and the settlement provisions differ in the various active markets, which provisions apply in assessing whether a contract to purchase those financial instruments is a regular way contract?

The provisions that apply are those in the market in which the purchase actually takes place.

To illustrate: Entity XYZ purchases one million shares of Entity ABC on a US stock exchange, for example, through a broker. The settlement date of the contract is six business days later. Trades for equity shares on US exchanges customarily settle in three business days. Because the trade settles in six business days, it does not meet the exemption as a regular way trade.

However, if XYZ did the same transaction on a foreign exchange that has a customary settlement period of six business days, the contract would meet the exemption for a regular way trade.

B.31 Regular way contracts: share purchase by call option

Entity A purchases a call option in a public market permitting it to purchase 100 shares of Entity XYZ at any time over the next three months at a price of CU100 per share. If Entity A exercises its option, it has 14 days to settle the transaction according to regulation or convention in the options market. XYZ shares are traded in an active public market that requires three-day settlement. Is the purchase of shares by exercising the option a regular way purchase of shares?

Yes. The settlement of an option is governed by regulation or convention in the marketplace for options and, therefore, upon exercise of the option it is no longer accounted for as a derivative because settlement by delivery of the shares within 14 days is a regular way transaction.

B.32 Recognition and derecognition of financial liabilities using trade date or settlement date accounting

IAS 39 has special rules about recognition and derecognition of financial assets using trade date or settlement date accounting. Do these rules apply to transactions in financial instruments that are classified as financial liabilities, such as transactions in deposit liabilities and trading liabilities?

No. IAS 39 does not contain any specific requirements about trade date accounting and settlement date accounting in the case of transactions in financial instruments that are classified as financial liabilities. Therefore, the general recognition and derecognition requirements in IAS 39.14 and IAS 39.39 apply. IAS 39.14 states that financial liabilities are recognised on the date the entity 'becomes a party to the contractual provisions of the instrument'. Such contracts generally are not recognised unless one of the parties has performed or the contract is a derivative contract not exempted from the scope of IAS 39. IAS 39.39 specifies that financial liabilities are derecognised only when they are extinguished, ie when the obligation specified in the contract is discharged or cancelled or expires.

Section C Embedded derivatives

C.1 Embedded derivatives: separation of host debt instrument

If an embedded non-option derivative is required to be separated from a host debt instrument, how are the terms of the host debt instrument and the embedded derivative identified? For example, would the host debt instrument be a fixed rate instrument, a variable rate instrument or a zero coupon instrument?

The terms of the host debt instrument reflect the stated or implied substantive terms of the hybrid contract. In the absence of implied or stated terms, the entity makes its own judgement of the terms. However, an entity may not identify a component that is not specified or may not establish terms of the host debt instrument in a manner that would result in the separation of an embedded derivative that is not already clearly present in the hybrid contract, that is to say, it cannot create a cash flow that does not exist. For example, if a five-year debt instrument has fixed interest payments of CU40,000 annually and a principal payment at maturity of CU1,000,000 multiplied by the change in an equity price index, it would be inappropriate to identify a floating rate host contract and an embedded equity swap that has an offsetting floating rate leg in lieu of identifying a fixed rate host. In that example, the host contract is a fixed rate debt instrument that pays CU40,000 annually because there are no floating interest rate cash flows in the hybrid contract.

In addition, the terms of an embedded non-option derivative, such as a forward or swap, must be determined so as to result in the embedded derivative having a fair value of zero at the inception of the hybrid contract. If it were permitted to separate embedded non-option derivatives on other terms, a single hybrid contract could be decomposed into an infinite variety of combinations of host debt instruments and embedded derivatives, for example, by separating embedded derivatives with terms that create leverage, asymmetry or some other risk exposure not already present in the hybrid contract. Therefore, it is inappropriate to separate an embedded non-option derivative on terms that result in a fair value other than zero at the inception of the hybrid contract. The determination of the terms of the embedded derivative is based on the conditions existing when the financial instrument was issued.

C.2 Embedded derivatives: separation of embedded option

The response to Question C.1 states that the terms of an embedded non-option derivative should be determined so as to result in the embedded derivative having a fair value of zero at the initial recognition of the hybrid contract. When an embedded option-based derivative is separated, must the terms of the embedded option be determined so as to result in the embedded derivative having either a fair value of zero or an intrinsic value of zero (that is to say, be at the money) at the inception of the hybrid contract?

No. The economic behaviour of a hybrid contract with an option-based embedded derivative depends critically on the strike price (or strike rate) specified for the option feature in the hybrid contract, as discussed below. Therefore, the separation of an option-based embedded derivative (including any embedded put, call, cap, floor, caption, floortion or swaption feature in a hybrid contract) should be based on the stated terms of the option feature documented in the hybrid contract. As a result, the embedded derivative would not necessarily have a fair value or intrinsic value equal to zero at the initial recognition of the hybrid contract.

If an entity were required to identify the terms of an embedded option-based derivative so as to achieve a fair value of the embedded derivative of zero, the strike price (or strike rate) generally would have to be determined so as to result in the option being infinitely out of the money. This would imply a zero probability of the option feature being exercised. However, since the probability of the option feature in a hybrid contract being exercised generally is not zero, it would be inconsistent with the likely economic behaviour of the hybrid contract to assume an initial fair value of zero. Similarly, if an entity were required to identify the terms of an embedded option-based derivative so as to achieve an intrinsic value of zero for the embedded derivative, the strike price (or strike rate) would have to be assumed to equal the price (or rate) of the underlying variable at the initial recognition of the hybrid contract. In this case, the fair value of the option would consist only of time value. However, such an assumption would not be consistent with the likely economic behaviour of the hybrid contract, including the probability of the option feature being exercised, unless the agreed strike price was indeed equal to the price (or rate) of the underlying variable at the initial recognition of the hybrid contract.

The economic nature of an option-based embedded derivative is fundamentally different from a forward-based embedded derivative (including forwards and swaps), because the terms of a forward are such that a payment based on the difference between the price of the underlying and the forward price will occur at a specified date, while the terms of an option are such that a payment based on the difference between the price of the underlying and the strike price of the option may or may not occur depending on the relationship between the agreed strike price and the price of the underlying at a specified date or dates in the future. Adjusting the strike price of an option-based embedded derivative, therefore, alters the nature of the hybrid contract. On the other hand, if the terms of a non-option embedded derivative in a host debt instrument were determined so as to result in a fair value of any amount other than zero at the inception of the hybrid contract, that amount would essentially represent a borrowing or lending. Accordingly, as discussed in the answer to Question C.1, it is not appropriate to separate a non-option embedded derivative in a host debt instrument on terms that result in a fair value other than zero at the initial recognition of the hybrid contract.

C.3 [Deleted]

C.4 Embedded derivatives: equity kicker

In some instances, venture capital entities providing subordinated loans agree that if and when the borrower lists its shares on a stock exchange, the venture capital entity is entitled to receive shares of the borrowing entity free of charge or at a very low price (an 'equity kicker') in addition to interest and repayment of principal. As a result of the equity kicker feature, the interest on the subordinated loan is lower than it would otherwise be. Assuming that the subordinated loan is not measured at fair value with changes in fair value recognised in profit or loss (IAS 39.11(c)), does the equity kicker feature meet the definition of an embedded derivative even though it is contingent upon the future listing of the borrower?

Yes. The economic characteristics and risks of an equity return are not closely related to the economic characteristics and risks of a host debt instrument (IAS 39.11(a)). The equity kicker meets the definition of a derivative because it has a value that changes in response to the change in the price of the shares of the borrower, it requires no initial net investment or an initial net investment that is smaller than would be required for other types of contracts that would be expected to have a similar response to changes in market factors, and it is settled at a future date (IAS 39.11(b) and IAS 39.9(a)). The equity kicker feature meets the definition of a derivative even though the right to receive shares is contingent upon the future listing of the borrower. IAS 39.AG9 states that a derivative could require a payment as a result of some future event that is unrelated to a notional amount. An equity kicker feature is similar to such a derivative except that it does not give a right to a fixed payment, but an option right, if the future event occurs.

C.5 [Deleted]

C.6 Embedded derivatives: synthetic instruments

Entity A issues a five-year floating rate debt instrument. At the same time, it enters into a five-year pay-fixed, receive-variable interest rate swap with Entity B. Entity A regards the combination of the debt instrument and swap as a synthetic fixed rate instrument. Entity A contends that separate accounting for the swap is inappropriate since IAS 39.AG33(a) requires an embedded derivative to be classified together with its host instrument if the derivative is linked to an interest rate that can change the amount of interest that would otherwise be paid or received on the host debt contract. Is the entity's analysis correct?

No. Embedded derivative instruments are terms and conditions that are included in non-derivative host contracts. It is generally inappropriate to treat two or more separate financial instruments as a single combined instrument ('synthetic instrument' accounting) for the purpose of applying IAS 39 or IFRS 9. Each of the financial instruments has its own terms and conditions and each may be transferred or settled separately. Therefore, the debt instrument and the swap are classified separately. The transactions described here differ from the transactions discussed in Question B.6, which had no substance apart from the resulting interest rate swap.

C.7 Embedded derivatives: purchases and sales contracts in foreign currency instruments

A supply contract provides for payment in a currency other than (a) the functional currency of either party to the contract, (b) the currency in which the product is routinely denominated in commercial transactions around the world and (c) the currency that is commonly used in contracts to purchase or sell non-financial items in the economic environment in which the transaction takes place. Is there an embedded derivative that should be separated under IAS 39?

Yes. To illustrate: a Norwegian entity agrees to sell oil to an entity in France. The oil contract is denominated in Swiss francs, although oil contracts are routinely denominated in US dollars in commercial transactions around the world, and Norwegian krone are commonly used in contracts to purchase or sell non-financial items in Norway. Neither entity carries out any significant activities in Swiss francs. In this case, the Norwegian entity regards the supply contract as a host contract with an embedded foreign currency forward to purchase Swiss francs. The French entity regards the supply contact as a host contract with an embedded foreign currency forward to sell Swiss francs. Each entity includes fair value changes on the currency forward in profit or loss unless the reporting entity designates it as a cash flow hedging instrument, if appropriate.

C.8 Embedded foreign currency derivatives: unrelated foreign currency provision

Entity A, which measures items in its financial statements on the basis of the euro (its functional currency), enters into a contract with Entity B, which has the Norwegian krone as its functional currency, to purchase oil in six months for 1,000 US dollars. The host oil contract is not within the scope of IAS 39 because it was entered into and continues to be for the purpose of delivery of a non-financial item in accordance with the entity's expected purchase, sale or usage requirements (IAS 39.5 and IAS 39.AG10). The oil contract includes a leveraged foreign exchange provision that states that the parties, in addition to the provision of, and payment for, oil will exchange an amount equal to the fluctuation in the exchange rate of the US dollar and Norwegian krone applied to a notional amount of 100,000 US dollars. Under IAS 39.11, is that embedded derivative (the leveraged foreign exchange provision) regarded as closely related to the host oil contract?

No, that leveraged foreign exchange provision is separated from the host oil contract because it is not closely related to the host oil contract (IAS 39.AG33(d)).

The payment provision under the host oil contract of 1,000 US dollars can be viewed as a foreign currency derivative because the US dollar is neither Entity A's nor Entity B's functional currency. This foreign currency derivative would not be separated because it follows from IAS 39.AG33(d) that a crude oil contract that requires payment in US dollars is not regarded as a host contract with a foreign currency derivative.

The leveraged foreign exchange provision that states that the parties will exchange an amount equal to the fluctuation in the exchange rate of the US dollar and Norwegian krone applied to a notional amount of 100,000 US dollars is in addition to the required payment for the oil transaction. It is unrelated to the host oil contract and therefore separated from the host oil contract and accounted for as an embedded derivative under IAS 39.11.

C.9 Embedded foreign currency derivatives: currency of international commerce

IAS 39.AG33(d) refers to the currency in which the price of the related goods or services is routinely denominated in commercial transactions around the world. Could it be a currency that is used for a certain product or service in commercial transactions within the local area of one of the substantial parties to the contract?

No. The currency in which the price of the related goods or services is routinely denominated in commercial transactions around the world is only a currency that is used for similar transactions all around the world, not just in one local area. For example, if cross-border transactions in natural gas in North America are routinely denominated in US dollars and such transactions are routinely denominated in euro in Europe, neither the US dollar nor the euro is a currency in which the goods or services are routinely denominated in commercial transactions around the world.

C.10 Embedded derivatives: holder permitted, but not required, to settle without recovering substantially all of its recognised investment

If the terms of a combined contract permit, but do not require, the holder to settle the combined contract in a manner that causes it not to recover substantially all of its recognised investment and the issuer does not have such a right (for example, a puttable debt instrument), does the contract satisfy the condition in IAS 39.AG33(a) that the holder would not recover substantially all of its recognised investment?

No. The condition that 'the holder would not recover substantially all of its recognised investment' is not satisfied if the terms of the combined contract permit, but do not require, the investor to settle the combined contract in a manner that causes it not to recover substantially all of its recognised investment and the issuer has no such right. Accordingly, an interest-bearing host contract with an embedded interest rate derivative with such terms is regarded as closely related to the host contract. The condition that 'the holder would not recover substantially all of its recognised investment' applies to situations in which the holder can be forced to accept settlement at an amount that causes the holder not to recover substantially all of its recognised investment.

C.11 [Deleted]

Section D Recognition and derecognition

D.1 Initial recognition

D.1.1 Recognition: cash collateral

Entity B transfers cash to Entity A as collateral for another transaction with Entity A (for example, a securities borrowing transaction). The cash is not legally segregated from Entity A's assets. Should Entity A recognise the cash collateral it has received as an asset?

Yes. The ultimate realisation of a financial asset is its conversion into cash and, therefore, no further transformation is required before the economic benefits of the cash transferred by Entity B can be realised by Entity A. Therefore, Entity A recognises the cash as an asset and a payable to Entity B while Entity B derecognises the cash and recognises a receivable from Entity A.

D.2 Regular way purchase or sale of a financial asset

D.2.1 Trade date vs settlement date: amounts to be recorded for a purchase

How are the trade date and settlement date accounting principles in the Standard applied to a purchase of a financial asset?

The following example illustrates the application of the trade date and settlement date accounting principles in the Standard for a purchase of a financial asset. On 29 December 20X1, an entity commits itself to purchase a financial asset for CU1,000, which is its fair value on commitment (trade) date. Transaction costs are immaterial. On 31 December 20X1 (financial year-end) and on 4 January 20X2 (settlement date) the fair value of the asset is CU1,002 and CU1,003, respectively. The amounts to be recorded for the asset will depend on how it is classified and whether trade date or settlement date accounting is used, as shown in the two tables below.

Settlement date accounting			
Balances	Financial assets measured at amortised cost	Financial assets measured at fair value with changes presented in other comprehensive income	Financial assets measured at fair value through profit or loss
29 December 20X1			
Financial asset	–	–	–
Financial liability	–	–	–
31 December 20X1			
Receivable	–	2	2
Financial asset	–	–	–
Financial liability	–	–	–
Other comprehensive income (fair value adjustment)	–	(2)	–
Retained earnings (through profit or loss)	–	–	(2)
4 January 20X2			
Receivable	–	–	–
Financial asset	1,000	1,003	1,003
Financial liability	–	–	–
Other comprehensive income (fair value adjustment)	–	(3)	–
Retained earnings (through profit or loss)	–	–	(3)

Trade date accounting			
Balances	Financial assets measured at amortised cost	Financial assets measured at fair value with changes presented in other comprehensive income	Financial assets measured at fair value through profit or loss
29 December 20X1			
Financial asset	1,000	1,000	1,000
Financial liability	(1,000)	(1,000)	(1,000)
31 December 20X1			
Receivable	–	–	–
Financial asset	1,000	1,002	1,002
Financial liability	(1,000)	(1,000)	(1,000)
Other comprehensive income (fair value adjustment)	–	(2)	–
Retained earnings (through profit or loss)	–	–	(2)
4 January 20X2			
Receivable	–	–	–
Financial asset	1,000	1,003	1,003
Financial liability	–	–	–
Other comprehensive income (fair value adjustment)	–	(3)	–
Retained earnings (through profit or loss)	–	–	(3)

D.2.2 Trade date vs settlement date: amounts to be recorded for a sale

How are the trade date and settlement date accounting principles in the Standard applied to a sale of a financial asset?

The following example illustrates the application of the trade date and settlement date accounting principles in the Standard for a sale of a financial asset. On 29 December 20X2 (trade date) an entity enters into a contract to sell a financial asset for its current fair value of CU1,010. The asset was acquired one year earlier for CU1,000 and its amortised cost is CU1,000. On 31 December 20X2 (financial year-end), the fair value of the asset is CU1,012. On 4 January 20X3 (settlement date), the fair value is CU1,013. The amounts to be recorded will depend on how the asset is classified and whether trade date or settlement date accounting is used as shown in the two tables below (any interest that might have accrued on the asset is disregarded).

A change in the fair value of a financial asset that is sold on a regular way basis is not recorded in the financial statements between trade date and settlement date even if the entity applies settlement date accounting because the seller's right to changes in the fair value ceases on the trade date.

Settlement date accounting		
Balances	Financial assets measured at amortised cost	Financial assets measured at fair value through profit or loss
29 December 20X2		
Receivable	–	–
Financial asset	1,000	1,010
Other comprehensive income (fair value adjustment)	–	–
Retained earnings (through profit or loss)	–	10
31 December 20X2		
Receivable	–	–
Financial asset	1,000	1,000
Other comprehensive income (fair value adjustment)	–	–
Retained earnings (through profit or loss)	–	10
4 January 20X3		
Other comprehensive income (fair value adjustment)	–	–
Retained earnings (through profit or loss)	10	10

Trade date accounting		
Balances	Financial assets measured at amortised cost	Financial assets measured at fair value through profit or loss
29 December 20X2		
Receivable	1,010	1,010
Financial asset	–	–
Other comprehensive income (fair value adjustment)	–	–
Retained earnings (through profit or loss)	10	10
31 December 20X2		
Receivable	1,010	1,010
Financial asset	–	–
Other comprehensive income (fair value adjustment)	–	–
Retained earnings (through profit or loss)	10	10
4 January 20X3		
Other comprehensive income (fair value adjustment)	–	–
Retained earnings (through profit or loss)	10	10

D.2.3 Settlement date accounting: exchange of non-cash financial assets

If an entity recognises sales of financial assets using settlement date accounting, would a change in the fair value of a financial asset to be received in exchange for the non-cash financial asset that is sold be recognised in accordance with IAS 39.57?

It depends. Any change in the fair value of the financial asset to be received would be accounted for under IAS 39.57 if the entity applies settlement date accounting for that category of financial assets. However, if the entity classifies the financial asset to be received in a category for which it applies trade date accounting, the asset to be received is recognised on the trade date as described in IAS 39.AG55. In that case, the entity recognises a liability of an amount equal to the carrying amount of the financial asset to be delivered on settlement date.

To illustrate: on 29 December 20X2 (trade date) Entity A enters into a contract to sell Note Receivable A, which is measured at amortised cost, in exchange for Bond B, which meets the definition of held for trading and is measured at fair value. Both assets have a fair value of CU1,010 on 29 December, while the amortised cost of Note Receivable A is CU1,000. Entity A uses settlement date accounting for financial assets measured at amortised cost and trade date accounting for assets that meet the definition of held for trading. On 31 December 20X2 (financial year-end), the fair value of Note Receivable A is

CU1,012 and the fair value of Bond B is CU1,009. On 4 January 20X3, the fair value of Note Receivable A is CU1,013 and the fair value of Bond B is CU1,007. The following entries are made:

29 December 20X2

Dr Bond B	CU1,010	
Cr Payable		CU1,010

31 December 20X2

Dr Trading loss	CU1	
Cr Bond B		CU1

4 January 20X3

Dr Payable	CU1,010	
Dr Trading loss	CU2	
Cr Note Receivable A		CU1,000
Cr Bond B		CU2
Cr Realisation gain		CU10

Section E Measurement

E.1 Initial measurement of financial assets and financial liabilities

E.1.1 Initial measurement: transaction costs

Transaction costs should be included in the initial measurement of financial assets and financial liabilities other than those at fair value through profit or loss. How should this requirement be applied in practice?

For financial assets not measured at fair value through profit or loss, transaction costs are added to the fair value at initial recognition. For financial liabilities, transaction costs are deducted from the fair value at initial recognition.

For financial instruments that are measured at amortised cost, transaction costs are subsequently included in the calculation of amortised cost using the effective interest method and, in effect, amortised through profit or loss over the life of the instrument.

Transaction costs expected to be incurred on transfer or disposal of a financial instrument are not included in the measurement of the financial instrument.

E.2 Fair value measurement considerations

E.2.1 Fair value measurement considerations for investment funds

IAS 39.AG72 states that the current bid price is usually the appropriate price to be used in measuring the fair value of an asset held. The rules applicable to some investment funds require net asset values to be reported to investors on the basis of mid-market prices. In these circumstances, would it be appropriate for an investment fund to measure its assets on the basis of mid-market prices?

No. The existence of regulations that require a different measurement for specific purposes does not justify a departure from the general requirement in IAS 39.AG72 to use the current bid price in the absence of a matching liability position. In its financial statements, an investment fund measures its assets at current bid prices. In reporting its net asset value to investors, an investment fund may wish to provide a reconciliation between the fair values recognised in its statement of financial position and the prices used for the net asset value calculation.

E.2.2 Fair value measurement: large holding

Entity A holds 15 per cent of the share capital in Entity B. The shares are publicly traded in an active market. The currently quoted price is CU100. Daily trading volume is 0.1 per cent of outstanding shares. Because Entity A believes that the fair value of the Entity B shares it owns, if sold as a block, is greater than the quoted market price, Entity A obtains several independent estimates of the price it would obtain if it sells its holding. These estimates indicate that Entity A would be able to obtain a price of CU105, ie a 5 per cent premium above the quoted price. Which figure should Entity A use for measuring its holding at fair value?

Under IAS 39.AG71, a published price quotation in an active market is the best estimate of fair value. Therefore, Entity A uses the published price quotation (CU100). Entity A cannot depart from the quoted market price solely because independent estimates indicate that Entity A would obtain a higher (or lower) price by selling the holding as a block.

E.3 Gains and losses

E.3.1–E.3.2 [Deleted]

E.3.3 IFRS 9, IAS 39 and IAS 21 Exchange differences arising on translation of foreign entities: other comprehensive income or profit or loss?

IAS 21.32 and IAS 21.48 states that all exchange differences resulting from translating the financial statements of a foreign operation should be recognised in other comprehensive income until disposal of the net investment. This would include exchange differences arising from financial instruments carried at fair value, which would include financial assets measured at fair value through profit or loss in accordance with IFRS 9 *Financial Instruments*.

If the foreign operation is a subsidiary whose financial statements are consolidated with those of its parent, in the consolidated financial statements how are IFRS 9 and IAS 21.39 applied?

IFRS 9 applies in the accounting for financial instruments in the financial statements of a foreign operation and IAS 21 applies in translating the financial statements of a foreign operation for incorporation in the financial statements of the reporting entity.

To illustrate: Entity A is domiciled in Country X and its functional currency and presentation currency are the local currency of Country X (LCX). A has a foreign subsidiary (Entity B) in Country Y whose functional currency is the local currency of Country Y (LCY). B is the owner of a debt instrument, which meets the definition of held for trading and is therefore measured at fair value.

In B's financial statements for year 20X0, the fair value and carrying amount of the debt instrument is LCY100 in the local currency of Country Y. In A's consolidated financial statements, the asset is translated into the local currency of Country X at the spot exchange rate applicable at the end of the reporting period (2.00). Thus, the carrying amount is LCX200 (= LCY100 × 2.00) in the consolidated financial statements.

At the end of year 20X1, the fair value of the debt instrument has increased to LCY110 in the local currency of Country Y. B recognises the trading asset at LCY110 in its statement of financial position and recognises a fair value gain of LCY10 in its profit or loss. During the year, the spot exchange rate has increased from 2.00 to 3.00 resulting in an increase in the fair value of the instrument from LCX200 to LCX330 (= LCY110 × 3.00) in the currency of Country X. Therefore, Entity A recognises the trading asset at LCX330 in its consolidated financial statements.

Entity A translates the statement of comprehensive income of B 'at the exchange rates at the dates of the transactions' (IAS 21.39(b)). Since the fair value gain has accrued through the year, A uses the average rate as a practical approximation ([3.00 + 2.00] / 2 = 2.50, in accordance with IAS 21.22). Therefore, while the fair value of the trading asset has increased by LCX130 (= LCX330 – LCX200), Entity A recognises only LCX25 (= LCY10 × 2.5) of this increase in consolidated profit or loss to comply with IAS 21.39(b). The resulting exchange difference, ie the remaining increase in the fair value of the debt instrument (LCX130 – LCX25 = LCX105), is accumulated in equity until the disposal of the net investment in the foreign operation in accordance with IAS 21.48.

E.3.4 IFRS 9, IAS 39 and IAS 21 Interaction between IFRS 9, IAS 39 and IAS 21

IFRS 9 and IAS 39 include requirements about the measurement of financial assets and financial liabilities and the recognition of gains and losses on remeasurement in profit or loss. IAS 21 includes rules about the reporting of foreign currency items and the recognition of exchange differences in profit or loss. In what order are IAS 21, IFRS 9 and IAS 39 applied?

Statement of financial position

Generally, the measurement of a financial asset or financial liability at fair value, cost or amortised cost is first determined in the foreign currency in which the item is denominated in accordance with IFRS 9 and IAS 39. Then, the foreign currency amount is translated into the functional currency using the closing rate or a historical rate in accordance with IAS 21 (IAS 39.AG83). For example, if a monetary financial asset (such as a debt instrument) is measured at amortised cost in accordance with IFRS 9, amortised cost is calculated in the currency of denomination of that financial asset. Then, the foreign currency amount is recognised using the closing rate in the entity's financial statements (IAS 21.23). That applies regardless of whether a monetary item is measured at cost, amortised cost or fair value in the foreign currency (IAS 21.24). A non-monetary financial asset (such as an investment in an equity instrument) is translated using the closing rate if it is measured at fair value in the foreign currency (IAS 21.23(c)).

As an exception, if the financial asset or financial liability is designated as a hedged item in a fair value hedge of the exposure to changes in foreign currency rates under IAS 39, the hedged item is remeasured for changes in foreign currency rates even if it would otherwise have been recognised using a historical rate under IAS 21 (IAS 39.89), ie the foreign currency amount is recognised using the closing rate. This exception applies to non-monetary items that are carried in terms of historical cost in the foreign currency and are hedged against exposure to foreign currency rates (IAS 21.23(b)).

Profit or loss

The recognition of a change in the carrying amount of a financial asset or financial liability in profit or loss depends on a number of factors, including whether it is an exchange difference or other change in carrying amount, whether it arises on a monetary item (for example, most debt instruments) or non-monetary item (such as most equity investments), whether the associated asset or liability is designated as a cash flow hedge of an exposure to changes in foreign currency rates, and whether it results from translating the financial statements of a foreign operation. The issue of recognising changes in the carrying amount of a financial asset or financial liability held by a foreign operation is addressed in a separate question (see Question E.3.3).

Any exchange difference arising on recognising a *monetary item* at a rate different from that at which it was initially recognised during the period, or recognised in previous financial statements, is recognised in profit or loss or in other comprehensive income in accordance with IAS 21 (IAS 39.AG83, IAS 21.28 and IAS 21.32), unless the monetary item is designated as a cash flow hedge of a highly probable forecast transaction in foreign currency, in which case the requirements for recognition of gains and losses on cash flow hedges in IAS 39 apply (IAS 39.95). Differences arising from recognising a monetary item at a foreign currency amount different from that at which it was previously recognised are accounted for in a similar manner, since all changes in the carrying amount relating to foreign currency movements should be treated consistently. All other changes in the statement of financial position measurement of a monetary item are recognised in profit or loss or in other comprehensive income in accordance with IFRS 9 or IAS 39.

Any changes in the carrying amount of a *non-monetary item* are recognised in profit or loss or in other comprehensive income in accordance with IFRS 9 or IAS 39 (IAS 39.AG83). If the non-monetary item is designated as a cash flow hedge of an unrecognised firm commitment or a highly probable forecast transaction in foreign currency, the requirements for recognition of gains and losses on cash flow hedges in IAS 39 apply (IAS 39.95).

When some portion of the change in carrying amount is recognised in other comprehensive income and some portion is recognised in profit or loss, an entity cannot offset those two components for the purposes of determining gains or losses that should be recognised in profit or loss or in other comprehensive income.

E.4 Impairment and uncollectibility of financial assets

E.4.1 Objective evidence of impairment

Does IAS 39 require that an entity be able to identify a single, distinct past causative event to conclude that it is probable that an impairment loss on a financial asset has been incurred?

No. IAS 39.59 states 'It may not be possible to identify a single, discrete event that caused the impairment. Rather the combined effect of several events may have caused the impairment.' Also, IAS 39.60 states that 'a downgrade of an entity's credit rating is not, of itself, evidence of impairment, although it may be evidence of impairment when considered with other available information'. Other factors that an entity considers in determining whether it has objective evidence that an impairment loss has been incurred include information about the debtors' or issuers' liquidity, solvency and business and financial risk exposures, levels of and trends in delinquencies for similar financial assets, national and local economic trends and conditions, and the fair value of collateral and guarantees. These and other factors may, either individually or taken together, provide sufficient objective evidence that an impairment loss has been incurred in a financial asset or group of financial assets.

E.4.2 Impairment: future losses

Does IAS 39 permit the recognition of an impairment loss through the establishment of an allowance for future losses when a loan is given? For example, if Entity A lends CU1,000 to Customer B, can it recognise an immediate impairment loss of CU10 if Entity A, based on historical experience, expects that 1 per cent of the principal amount of loans given will not be collected?

No. Paragraph 5.1 of IFRS 9 requires a financial asset to be initially measured at fair value. For a loan asset, the fair value is the amount of cash lent adjusted for any fees and costs (unless a portion of the amount lent is compensation for other stated or implied rights or privileges). In addition, paragraph 5.2.2 of IFRS 9 requires an entity to apply the impairment requirements in IAS 39. IAS 39.58 requires that an impairment loss is recognised only if there is objective evidence of impairment as a result of a past event that occurred after initial recognition. Accordingly, it is inconsistent with paragraph 5.1 of IFRS 9 and IAS 39.58 to reduce the carrying amount of a loan asset on initial recognition through the recognition of an immediate impairment loss.

E.4.3 Assessment of impairment: principal and interest

Because of Customer B's financial difficulties, Entity A is concerned that Customer B will not be able to make all principal and interest payments due on a loan in a timely manner. It negotiates a restructuring of the loan. Entity A expects that Customer B will be able to meet its obligations under the restructured terms. Would Entity A recognise an impairment loss if the restructured terms are as reflected in any of the following cases?

(a)   Customer B will pay the full principal amount of the original loan five years after the original due date, but none of the interest due under the original terms.

(b)   Customer B will pay the full principal amount of the original loan on the original due date, but none of the interest due under the original terms.

(c)   Customer B will pay the full principal amount of the original loan on the original due date with interest only at a lower interest rate than the interest rate inherent in the original loan.

(d)   Customer B will pay the full principal amount of the original loan five years after the original due date and all interest accrued during the original loan term, but no interest for the extended term.

(e)   Customer B will pay the full principal amount of the original loan five years after the original due date and all interest, including interest for both the original term of the loan and the extended term.

IAS 39.58 indicates that an impairment loss has been incurred if there is objective evidence of impairment. The amount of the impairment loss for a loan measured at amortised cost is the difference between the carrying amount of the loan and the present value of future principal and interest payments discounted at the loan's original effective interest rate. In cases (a)–(d) above, the present value of the future principal and interest payments discounted at the loan's original effective interest rate will be lower than the carrying amount of the loan. Therefore, an impairment loss is recognised in those cases.

In case (e), even though the timing of payments has changed, the lender will receive interest on interest, and the present value of the future principal and interest payments discounted at the loan's original effective interest rate will equal the carrying amount of the loan. Therefore, there is no impairment loss. However, this fact pattern is unlikely given Customer B's financial difficulties.

E.4.4 Assessment of impairment: fair value hedge

A loan with fixed interest rate payments is hedged against the exposure to interest rate risk by a receive-variable, pay-fixed interest rate swap. The hedge relationship qualifies for fair value hedge accounting and is reported as a fair value hedge. Thus, the carrying amount of the loan includes an adjustment for fair value changes attributable to movements in interest rates. Should an assessment of impairment in the loan take into account the fair value adjustment for interest rate risk?

Yes. The loan's original effective interest rate before the hedge becomes irrelevant once the carrying amount of the loan is adjusted for any changes in its fair value attributable to interest rate movements. Therefore, the original effective interest rate and amortised cost of the loan are adjusted to take into account recognised fair value changes. The adjusted effective interest rate is calculated using the adjusted carrying amount of the loan.

An impairment loss on the hedged loan is calculated as the difference between its carrying amount after adjustment for fair value changes attributable to the risk being hedged and the estimated future cash flows of the loan discounted at the adjusted effective interest rate. When a loan is included in a portfolio hedge of interest rate risk, the entity should allocate the change in the fair value of the hedged portfolio to the loans (or groups of similar loans) being assessed for impairment on a systematic and rational basis.

E.4.5 Impairment: provision matrix

A financial institution calculates impairment in the unsecured portion of financial assets measured at amortised cost on the basis of a provision matrix that specifies fixed provision rates for the number of days a financial asset has been classified as non-performing (zero per cent if less than 90 days, 20 per cent if 90–180 days, 50 per cent if 181–365 days and 100 per cent if more than 365 days). Can the results be considered to be appropriate for the purpose of calculating the impairment loss on the financial assets measured at amortised cost under IAS 39.63?

Not necessarily. IAS 39.63 requires impairment or bad debt losses to be calculated as the difference between the asset's carrying amount and the present value of estimated future cash flows discounted at the financial instrument's original effective interest rate.

E.4.6 Impairment: excess losses

Does IAS 39 permit an entity to recognise impairment or bad debt losses in excess of impairment losses that are determined on the basis of objective evidence about impairment in identified individual financial assets or identified groups of similar financial assets?

No. IAS 39 does not permit an entity to recognise impairment or bad debt losses in addition to those that can be attributed to individually identified financial assets or identified groups of financial assets with similar credit risk characteristics (IAS 39.64) on the basis of objective evidence about the existence of impairment in those assets (IAS 39.58). Amounts that an entity might want to set aside for additional possible impairment in financial assets, such as reserves that cannot be supported by objective evidence about impairment, are not recognised as impairment or bad debt losses under IAS 39. However, if an entity determines that no objective evidence of impairment exists for an individually assessed financial asset, whether significant or not, it includes the asset in a group of financial assets with similar credit risk characteristics (IAS 39.64).

E.4.7 Recognition of impairment on a portfolio basis

IAS 39.63 requires that impairment be recognised for financial assets carried at amortised cost. IAS 39.64 states that impairment may be measured and recognised individually or on a portfolio basis for a group of similar financial assets. If one asset in the group is impaired but the fair value of another asset in the group is above its amortised cost, does IAS 39 allow non-recognition of the impairment of the first asset?

No. If an entity knows that an individual financial asset carried at amortised cost is impaired, IAS 39.63 requires that the impairment of that asset should be recognised.

It states: 'the amount of the loss is measured as the difference between *the asset's* carrying amount and the present value of estimated future cash flows (excluding future credit losses that have not been incurred) discounted at the financial asset's original effective interest rate' (emphasis added). Measurement of impairment on a portfolio basis under IAS 39.64 may be applied to groups of small balance items and to financial assets that are individually assessed and found not to be impaired when there is indication of impairment in a group of similar assets and impairment cannot be identified with an individual asset in that group.

E.4.8 Impairment: recognition of collateral

If an impaired financial asset is secured by collateral that does not meet the recognition criteria for assets in other Standards, is the collateral recognised as an asset separate from the impaired financial asset?

No. The measurement of the impaired financial asset reflects the fair value of the collateral. The collateral is not recognised as an asset separate from the impaired financial asset unless it meets the recognition criteria for an asset in another Standard.

E.4.9–E.4.10 [Deleted]

Section F Hedging

F.1 Hedging instruments

F.1.1 [Deleted]

F.1.2 Hedging with a non-derivative financial asset or liability

Entity J's functional currency is the Japanese yen. It has issued a fixed rate debt instrument with semi-annual interest payments that matures in two years with principal due at maturity of 5 million US dollars. It has also entered into a fixed price sales commitment for 5 million US dollars that matures in two years and is not accounted for as a derivative because it meets the exemption for normal sales in paragraph 5. Can Entity J designate its US dollar liability as a fair value hedge of the entire fair value exposure of its fixed price sales commitment and qualify for hedge accounting?

No. IAS 39.72 permits a non-derivative asset or liability to be used as a hedging instrument only for a hedge of a foreign currency risk.

Alternatively, can Entity J designate its US dollar liability as a cash flow hedge of the foreign currency exposure associated with the future receipt of US dollars on the fixed price sales commitment?

Yes. IAS 39 permits the designation of a non-derivative asset or liability as a hedging instrument in either a cash flow hedge or a fair value hedge of the exposure to changes in foreign exchange rates of a firm commitment (IAS 39.87). Any gain or loss on the non-derivative hedging instrument that is recognised in other comprehensive income during the period preceding the future sale is reclassified from equity to profit or loss as a reclassification adjustment when the sale takes place (IAS 39.95).

Alternatively, can Entity J designate the sales commitment as the hedging instrument instead of the hedged item?

No. Only a derivative instrument or a non-derivative financial asset or liability can be designated as a hedging instrument in a hedge of a foreign currency risk. A firm commitment cannot be designated as a hedging instrument. However, if the foreign currency component of the sales commitment is required to be separated as an embedded derivative under IAS 39.11 and IAS 39.AG33(d), it could be designated as a hedging instrument in a hedge of the exposure to changes in the fair value of the maturity amount of the debt attributable to foreign currency risk.

F.1.3 Hedge accounting: use of written options in combined hedging instruments

Issue (a) – Does IAS 39.AG94 preclude the use of an interest rate collar or other derivative instrument that combines a written option component and a purchased option component as a hedging instrument?

It depends. An interest rate collar or other derivative instrument that includes a written option cannot be designated as a hedging instrument if it is a net written option, because IAS 39.AG94 precludes the use of a written option as a hedging instrument unless it is designated as an offset to a purchased option. An interest rate collar or other derivative instrument that includes a written option may be designated as a hedging instrument, however, if the combination is a net purchased option or zero cost collar.

Issue (b) – What factors indicate that an interest rate collar or other derivative instrument that combines a written option component and a purchased option component is not a net written option?

The following factors taken together suggest that an interest rate collar or other derivative instrument that includes a written option is not a net written option.

(a)   No net premium is received either at inception or over the life of the combination of options. The distinguishing feature of a written option is the receipt of a premium to compensate the writer for the risk incurred.

(b)   Except for the strike prices, the critical terms and conditions of the written option component and the purchased option component are the same (including underlying variable or variables, currency denomination and maturity date). Also, the notional amount of the written option component is not greater than the notional amount of the purchased option component.

F.1.4 Internal hedges

Some entities use internal derivative contracts (internal hedges) to transfer risk exposures between different companies within a group or divisions within a single legal entity. Does IAS 39.73 prohibit hedge accounting in such cases?

Yes, if the derivative contracts are internal to the entity being reported on. IAS 39 does not specify how an entity should manage its risk. However, it states that internal hedging transactions do not qualify for hedge accounting. This applies both (a) in consolidated financial statements for intragroup hedging transactions, and (b) in the individual or separate financial statements of a legal entity for hedging transactions between divisions in the entity. The principles of preparing consolidated financial statements in IAS 27.24 require that 'intragroup balances, transactions, income and expenses shall be eliminated in full'.

On the other hand, an intragroup hedging transaction may be designated as a hedge in the individual or separate financial statements of a group entity, if the intragroup transaction is an external transaction from the perspective of the group entity. In addition, if the internal contract is offset with an external party the external contract may be regarded as the hedging instrument and the hedging relationship may qualify for hedge accounting.

The following summarises the application of IAS 39 to internal hedging transactions.

•   IAS 39 does not preclude an entity from using internal derivative contracts for risk management purposes and it does not preclude internal derivatives from being accumulated at the treasury level or some other central location so that risk can be managed on an entity-wide basis or at some higher level than the separate legal entity or division.

•   Internal derivative contracts between two separate entities within a consolidated group can qualify for hedge accounting by those entities in their individual or separate financial statements, even though the internal contracts are not offset by derivative contracts with a party external to the consolidated group.

•   Internal derivative contracts between two separate divisions within the same legal entity can qualify for hedge accounting in the individual or separate financial statements of that legal entity only if those contracts are offset by derivative contracts with a party external to the legal entity.

- Internal derivative contracts between separate divisions within the same legal entity and between separate entities within the consolidated group can qualify for hedge accounting in the consolidated financial statements only if the internal contracts are offset by derivative contracts with a party external to the consolidated group.

- If the internal derivative contracts are not offset by derivative contracts with external parties, the use of hedge accounting by group entities and divisions using internal contracts must be reversed on consolidation.

To illustrate: the banking division of Entity A enters into an internal interest rate swap with the trading division of the same entity. The purpose is to hedge the interest rate risk exposure of a loan (or group of similar loans) in the loan portfolio. Under the swap, the banking division pays fixed interest payments to the trading division and receives variable interest rate payments in return.

If a hedging instrument is not acquired from an external party, IAS 39 does not allow hedge accounting treatment for the hedging transaction undertaken by the banking and trading divisions. IAS 39.73 indicates that only derivatives that involve a party external to the entity can be designated as hedging instruments and, further, that any gains or losses on intragroup or intra-entity transactions should be eliminated on consolidation. Therefore, transactions between different divisions within Entity A do not qualify for hedge accounting treatment in the financial statements of Entity A. Similarly, transactions between different entities within a group do not qualify for hedge accounting treatment in consolidated financial statements.

However, if in addition to the internal swap in the above example the trading division enters into an interest rate swap or other contract with an external party that offsets the exposure hedged in the internal swap, hedge accounting is permitted under IAS 39. For the purposes of IAS 39, the hedged item is the loan (or group of similar loans) in the banking division and the hedging instrument is the external interest rate swap or other contract.

The trading division may aggregate several internal swaps or portions of them that are not offsetting each other and enter into a single third party derivative contract that offsets the aggregate exposure. Under IAS 39, such external hedging transactions may qualify for hedge accounting treatment provided that the hedged items in the banking division are identified and the other conditions for hedge accounting are met.

F.1.5 Offsetting internal derivative contracts used to manage interest rate risk

If a central treasury function enters into internal derivative contracts with subsidiaries and various divisions within the consolidated group to manage interest rate risk on a centralised basis, can those contracts qualify for hedge accounting in the consolidated financial statements if, before laying off the risk, the internal contracts are first netted against each other and only the net exposure is offset in the marketplace with external derivative contracts?

No. An internal contract designated at the subsidiary level or by a division as a hedge results in the recognition of changes in the fair value of the item being hedged in profit or loss (a fair value hedge) or in the recognition of the changes in the fair value of the internal derivative in other comprehensive income (a cash flow hedge). There is no basis for changing the measurement attribute of the item being hedged in a fair value hedge unless the exposure is offset with an external derivative. There is also no basis for recognising the gain or loss on the internal derivative in other comprehensive income for one entity and recognising it in profit or loss by the other entity unless it is offset with an external derivative. In cases where two or more internal derivatives are used to manage interest rate risk on assets or liabilities at the subsidiary or division level and those internal derivatives are offset at the treasury level, the effect of designating the internal derivatives as hedging instruments is that the hedged non-derivative exposures at the subsidiary or division levels would be used to offset each other on consolidation. Accordingly, since IAS 39.72 does not permit designating non-derivatives as hedging instruments, except for foreign currency exposures, the results of hedge accounting from the use of internal derivatives at the subsidiary or division level that are not laid off with external parties must be reversed on consolidation.

It should be noted, however, that there will be no effect on profit or loss and other comprehensive income of reversing the effect of hedge accounting in consolidation for internal derivatives that offset each other at the consolidation level if they are used in the same type of hedging relationship at the subsidiary or division level and, in the case of cash flow hedges, where the hedged items affect profit or loss in the same period. Just as the internal derivatives offset at the treasury level, their use as fair value hedges by two separate entities or divisions within the consolidated group will also result in the offset of the fair value amounts recognised in profit or loss, and their use as cash flow hedges by two separate entities or divisions within the consolidated group will also result in the fair value amounts being offset against each other in other comprehensive income. However, there may be an effect on individual line items in both the consolidated statement of comprehensive income and the consolidated statement of financial position, for example when internal derivatives that hedge assets (or liabilities) in a fair value hedge are offset by internal derivatives that are used as a fair value hedge of other assets (or liabilities) that are recognised in a different line item in the statement of financial position or statement of comprehensive income. In addition, to the extent that one of the internal contracts is used as a cash flow hedge and the other is used in a fair value hedge, gains and losses recognised would not offset since the gain (or loss) on the internal derivative used as a fair value hedge would be recognised in profit or loss and the corresponding loss (or gain) on the internal derivative used as a cash flow hedge would be recognised in other comprehensive income.

Question F.1.4 describes the application of IAS 39 to internal hedging transactions.

F.1.6 Offsetting internal derivative contracts used to manage foreign currency risk

If a central treasury function enters into internal derivative contracts with subsidiaries and various divisions within the consolidated group to manage foreign currency risk on a centralised basis, can those contracts be used as a basis for identifying external transactions that qualify for hedge accounting in the consolidated financial statements if, before laying off the risk, the internal contracts are first netted against each other and only the net exposure is offset by entering into a derivative contract with an external party?

It depends. IAS 27 *Consolidated and Separate Financial Statements* requires all internal transactions to be eliminated in consolidated financial statements. As stated in IAS 39.73, internal hedging transactions do not qualify for hedge accounting in the consolidated financial statements of the group. Therefore, if an entity wishes to achieve hedge accounting in the consolidated financial statements, it must designate a hedging relationship between a qualifying external hedging instrument and a qualifying hedged item.

As discussed in Question F.1.5, the accounting effect of two or more internal derivatives that are used to manage interest rate risk at the subsidiary or division level and are offset at the treasury level is that the hedged non-derivative exposures at those levels would be used to offset each other on consolidation. There is no effect on profit of loss or other comprehensive income if (a) the internal derivatives are used in the same type of hedge relationship (ie fair value or cash flow hedges) and (b), in the case of cash flow hedges, any derivative gains and losses that are initially recognised in other comprehensive income are reclassified from equity to profit or loss in the same period(s). When these two conditions are met, the gains and losses on the internal derivatives that are recognised in profit or loss or in other comprehensive income will offset on consolidation resulting in the same profit or loss and other comprehensive income as if the derivatives had been eliminated. However, there may be an effect on individual line items, in both the consolidated statement of comprehensive income and the consolidated statement of financial position, that would need to be eliminated. In addition, there is an effect on profit or loss and other comprehensive income if some of the offsetting internal derivatives are used in cash flow hedges, while others are used in fair value hedges. There is also an effect on profit or loss and other comprehensive income for offsetting internal derivatives that are used in cash flow hedges if the derivative gains and losses that are initially recognised in other comprehensive income are reclassified from equity to profit or loss in different periods (because the hedged items affect profit or loss in different periods).

As regards foreign currency risk, provided that the internal derivatives represent the transfer of foreign currency risk on underlying non-derivative financial assets or liabilities, hedge accounting can be applied because IAS 39.72 permits a non-derivative financial asset or liability to be designated as a hedging instrument for hedge accounting purposes for a hedge of a foreign currency risk. Accordingly, in this case the internal derivative contracts can be used as a basis for identifying external transactions that qualify for hedge accounting in the consolidated financial statements even if they are offset against each other. However, for consolidated financial statements, it is necessary to designate the hedging relationship so that it involves only external transactions.

Furthermore, the entity cannot apply hedge accounting to the extent that two or more offsetting internal derivatives represent the transfer of foreign currency risk on underlying forecast transactions or unrecognised firm commitments. This is because an unrecognised firm commitment or forecast transaction does not qualify as a hedging instrument under IAS 39. Accordingly, in this case the internal derivatives cannot be used as a basis for identifying external transactions that qualify for hedge accounting in the consolidated financial statements. As a result, any cumulative net gain or loss on an internal derivative that has been included in the initial carrying amount of an asset or liability (basis adjustment) or recognised in other comprehensive income would have to be reversed on consolidation if it cannot be demonstrated that the offsetting internal derivative represented the transfer of a foreign currency risk on a financial asset or liability to an external hedging instrument.

F.1.7 Internal derivatives: examples of applying Question F.1.6

In each case, FC = foreign currency, LC = local currency (which is the entity's functional currency), and TC = treasury centre.

Case 1 Offset of fair value hedges

Subsidiary A has trade receivables of FC100, due in 60 days, which it hedges using a forward contract with TC. Subsidiary B has payables of FC50, also due in 60 days, which it hedges using a forward contact with TC.

TC nets the two internal derivatives and enters into a net external forward contract to pay FC50 and receive LC in 60 days.

At the end of month 1, FC weakens against LC. A incurs a foreign exchange loss of LC10 on its receivables, offset by a gain of LC10 on its forward contract with TC. B makes a foreign exchange gain of LC5 on its payables offset by a loss of LC5 on its forward contract with TC. TC makes a loss of LC10 on its internal forward contract with A, a gain of LC5 on its internal forward contract with B, and a gain of LC5 on its external forward contract.

At the end of month 1, the following entries are made in the individual or separate financial statements of A, B and TC. Entries reflecting intragroup transactions or events are shown in italics.

A's entries

Dr	Foreign exchange loss	LC10	
	Cr Receivables		LC10
Dr	*Internal contract TC*	*LC10*	
	Cr Internal gain TC		*LC10*

B's entries

Dr	Payables	LC5	
	Cr Foreign exchange gain		LC5
Dr	*Internal loss TC*	*LC5*	
	Cr Internal contract TC		*LC5*

TC's entries

Dr	*Internal loss A*	*LC10*	
	Cr Internal contract A		*LC10*
Dr	*Internal contract B*	*LC5*	
	Cr Internal gain B		*LC5*
Dr	External forward contract	LC5	
	Cr Foreign exchange gain		LC5

Both A and B could apply hedge accounting in their individual financial statements provided all conditions in IAS 39 are met. However, in this case, no hedge accounting is required because gains and losses on the internal derivatives and the offsetting losses and gains on the hedged receivables and payables are recognised immediately in profit or loss of A and B without hedge accounting.

In the consolidated financial statements, the internal derivative transactions are eliminated. In economic terms, the payable in B hedges FC50 of the receivables in A. The external forward contract in TC hedges the remaining FC50 of the receivable in A. Hedge accounting is not necessary in the consolidated financial statements because monetary items are measured at spot foreign exchange rates under IAS 21 irrespective of whether hedge accounting is applied.

The net balances before and after elimination of the accounting entries relating to the internal derivatives are the same, as set out below. Accordingly, there is no need to make any further accounting entries to meet the requirements of IAS 39.

	Debit	Credit
Receivables	–	LC10
Payables	LC5	–
External forward contract	LC5	–
Gains and losses	–	–
Internal contracts	–	–

Case 2 Offset of cash flow hedges

To extend the example, A also has highly probable future revenues of FC200 on which it expects to receive cash in 90 days. B has highly probable future expenses of FC500 (advertising cost), also to be paid for in 90 days. A and B enter into separate forward contracts with TC to hedge these exposures and TC enters into an external forward contract to receive FC300 in 90 days.

As before, FC weakens at the end of month 1. A incurs a 'loss' of LC20 on its anticipated revenues because the LC value of these revenues decreases. This is offset by a 'gain' of LC20 on its forward contract with TC.

B incurs a 'gain' of LC50 on its anticipated advertising cost because the LC value of the expense decreases. This is offset by a 'loss' of LC50 on its transaction with TC.

TC incurs a 'gain' of LC50 on its internal transaction with B, a 'loss' of LC20 on its internal transaction with A and a loss of LC30 on its external forward contract.

A and B complete the necessary documentation, the hedges are effective, and both A and B qualify for hedge accounting in their individual financial statements. A recognises the gain of LC20 on its internal derivative transaction in other comprehensive income and B recognises the loss of LC50 in other comprehensive income. TC does not claim hedge accounting, but measures both its internal and external derivative positions at fair value, which net to zero.

At the end of month 1, the following entries are made in the individual or separate financial statements of A, B and TC. Entries reflecting intragroup transactions or events are shown in italics.

A's entries

Dr	Internal contract TC	LC20	
	Cr Other comprehensive income		LC20

B's entries

Dr	Other comprehensive income	LC50	
	Cr Internal contract TC		LC50

TC's entries

Dr	Internal loss A	LC20	
	Cr Internal contract A		LC20
Dr	Internal contract B	LC50	
	Cr Internal gain B		LC50
Dr	Foreign exchange loss	LC30	
	Cr External forward contract		LC30

For the consolidated financial statements, TC's external forward contract on FC300 is designated, at the beginning of month 1, as a hedging instrument of the first FC300 of B's highly probable future expenses. IAS 39 requires that in the consolidated financial statements at the end of month 1, the accounting effects of the internal derivative transactions must be eliminated.

However, the net balances before and after elimination of the accounting entries relating to the internal derivatives are the same, as set out below. Accordingly, there is no need to make any further accounting entries in order for the requirements of IAS 39 to be met.

	Debit	Credit
External forward contract	–	LC30
Other comprehensive income	LC30	–
Gains and losses	–	–
Internal contracts	–	–

Case 3 Offset of fair value and cash flow hedges

Assume that the exposures and the internal derivative transactions are the same as in cases 1 and 2. However, instead of entering into two external derivatives to hedge separately the fair value and cash flow exposures, TC enters into a single net external derivative to receive FC250 in exchange for LC in 90 days.

TC has four internal derivatives, two maturing in 60 days and two maturing in 90 days. These are offset by a net external derivative maturing in 90 days. The interest rate differential between FC and LC is minimal, and therefore the ineffectiveness resulting from the mismatch in maturities is expected to have a minimal effect on profit or loss in TC.

As in cases 1 and 2, A and B apply hedge accounting for their cash flow hedges and TC measures its derivatives at fair value. A recognises a gain of LC20 on its internal derivative transaction in other comprehensive income and B recognises a loss of LC50 on its internal derivative transaction in other comprehensive income.

At the end of month 1, the following entries are made in the individual or separate financial statements of A, B and TC. Entries reflecting intragroup transactions or events are shown in italics.

A's entries

Dr Foreign exchange loss	LC10	
Cr Receivables		LC10
Dr Internal contract TC	*LC10*	
Cr Internal gain TC		*LC10*
Dr Internal contract TC	*LC20*	
Cr Other comprehensive income		*LC20*

B's entries

Dr Payables	LC5	
Cr Foreign exchange gain		LC5
Dr Internal loss TC	*LC5*	
Cr Internal contract TC		*LC5*
Dr Other comprehensive income	*LC50*	
Cr Internal contract TC		*LC50*

TC's entries

Dr Internal loss A	*LC10*	
Cr Internal contract A		*LC10*
Dr Internal loss A	*LC20*	
Cr Internal contract A		*LC20*
Dr Internal contract B	*LC5*	
Cr Internal gain B		*LC5*
Dr Internal contract B	*LC50*	
Cr Internal gain B		*LC50*
Dr Foreign exchange loss	LC25	
Cr External forward contract		LC25

TOTAL (for the internal derivatives)	A	B	Total
	LC	LC	TC
Profit or loss (fair value hedges)	10	(5)	5
Other comprehensive income (cash flow hedges)	20	(50)	(30)
Total	30	(55)	(25)

Combining these amounts with the external transactions (ie those not marked in italics above) produces the total net balances before elimination of the internal derivatives as follows:

	Debit	Credit
Receivables	–	LC10
Payables	LC5	–
Forward contract	–	LC25
Other comprehensive income	LC30	–
Gains and losses	–	–
Internal contracts	–	–

For the consolidated financial statements, the following designations are made at the beginning of month 1:

- the payable of FC50 in B is designated as a hedge of the first FC50 of the highly probable future revenues in A. Therefore, at the end of month 1, the following entries are made in the consolidated financial statements: Dr Payable LC5; Cr Other comprehensive income LC5;

- the receivable of FC100 in A is designated as a hedge of the first FC100 of the highly probable future expenses in B. Therefore, at the end of month 1, the following entries are made in the consolidated financial statements: Dr Other comprehensive income LC10; Cr Receivable LC10; and

- the external forward contract on FC250 in TC is designated as a hedge of the next FC250 of highly probable future expenses in B. Therefore, at the end of month 1, the following entries are made in the consolidated financial statements: Dr Other comprehensive income LC25; Cr External forward contract LC25.

In the consolidated financial statements at the end of month 1, IAS 39 requires the accounting effects of the internal derivative transactions to be eliminated.

However, the total net balances before and after elimination of the accounting entries relating to the internal derivatives are the same, as set out below. Accordingly, there is no need to make any further accounting entries to meet the requirements of IAS 39.

	Debit	Credit
Receivables	–	LC10
Payables	LC5	–
Forward contract	–	LC25
Other comprehensive income	LC30	–
Gains and losses	–	–
Internal contracts	–	–

Case 4 Offset of fair value and cash flow hedges with adjustment to carrying amount of inventory

Assume similar transactions as in case 3, except that the anticipated cash outflow of FC500 in B relates to the purchase of inventory that is delivered after 60 days. Assume also that the entity has a policy of basis-adjusting hedged forecast non-financial items. At the end of month 2, there are no further changes in exchange rates or fair values. At that date, the inventory is delivered and the loss of LC50 on B's internal derivative, recognised in other comprehensive income in month 1, is adjusted against the carrying amount of inventory in B. The gain of LC20 on A's internal derivative is recognised in other comprehensive income as before.

In the consolidated financial statements, there is now a mismatch compared with the result that would have been achieved by unwinding and redesignating the hedges. The external derivative (FC250) and a proportion of the receivable (FC50) offset FC300 of the anticipated inventory purchase. There is a natural hedge between the remaining FC200 of anticipated cash outflow in B and the anticipated cash inflow of FC200 in A. This relationship does not qualify for hedge accounting under IAS 39 and this time there is only a partial offset between gains and losses on the internal derivatives that hedge these amounts.

At the end of months 1 and 2, the following entries are made in the individual or separate financial statements of A, B and TC. Entries reflecting intragroup transactions or events are shown in italics.

A's entries (all at the end of month 1)

Dr Foreign exchange loss	LC10	
Cr Receivables		LC10
Dr Internal contract TC	*LC10*	
Cr Internal gain TC		*LC10*
Dr Internal contract TC	*LC20*	
Cr Other comprehensive income		*LC20*

B's entries

At the end of month 1:

Dr Payables	LC5	
Cr Foreign exchange gain		LC5
Dr Internal loss TC	*LC5*	
Cr Internal contract TC		*LC5*
Dr Other comprehensive income	*LC50*	
Cr Internal contract TC		*LC50*

At the end of month 2:

Dr Inventory	LC50	
Cr Other comprehensive income		LC50

TC's entries (all at the end of month 1)

Dr Internal loss A	*LC10*	
Cr Internal contract A		*LC10*

continued...

...continued

Dr	Internal loss A	*LC20*
	Cr Internal contract A	*LC20*
Dr	Internal contract B	*LC5*
	Cr Internal gain B	*LC5*
Dr	Internal contract B	*LC50*
	Cr Internal gain B	*LC50*
Dr	Foreign exchange loss	LC25
	Cr Forward	LC25

TOTAL (for the internal derivatives)	A	B	Total
	LC	LC	TC
Profit or loss (fair value hedges)	10	(5)	5
Other comprehensive income (cash flow hedges)	20	–	20
Basis adjustment (inventory)	–	(50)	(50)
Total	30	(55)	(25)

Combining these amounts with the external transactions (ie those not marked in italics above) produces the total net balances before elimination of the internal derivatives as follows:

	Debit	Credit
Receivables	–	LC10
Payables	LC5	–
Forward contract	–	LC25
Other comprehensive income	–	LC20
Basis adjustment (inventory)	LC50	–
Gains and losses	–	–
Internal contracts	–	–

For the consolidated financial statements, the following designations are made at the beginning of month 1:

- the payable of FC50 in B is designated as a hedge of the first FC50 of the highly probable future revenues in A. Therefore, at the end of month 1, the following entry is made in the consolidated financial statements: Dr Payables LC5; Cr Other comprehensive income LC5.

- the receivable of FC100 in A is designated as a hedge of the first FC100 of the highly probable future expenses in B. Therefore, at the end of month 1, the following entries are made in the consolidated financial statements: Dr Other comprehensive income LC10; Cr Receivable LC10; and at the end of month 2, Dr Inventory LC10; Cr Other comprehensive income LC10.

- the external forward contract on FC250 in TC is designated as a hedge of the next FC250 of highly probable future expenses in B. Therefore, at the end of month 1, the following entry is made in the consolidated financial statements: Dr Other comprehensive income LC25; Cr External forward contract LC25; and at the end of month 2, Dr Inventory LC25; Cr Other comprehensive income LC25.

The total net balances after elimination of the accounting entries relating to the internal derivatives are as follows:

	Debit	Credit
Receivables	–	LC10
Payables	LC5	–
Forward contract	–	LC25
Other comprehensive income	–	LC5
Basis adjustment (inventory)	LC35	–
Gains and losses	–	–
Internal contracts	–	–

These total net balances are different from those that would be recognised if the internal derivatives were not eliminated, and it is these net balances that IAS 39 requires to be included in the consolidated financial statements. The accounting entries required to adjust the total net balances before elimination of the internal derivatives are as follows:

(a) to reclassify LC15 of the loss on B's internal derivative that is included in inventory to reflect that FC150 of the forecast purchase of inventory is not hedged by an external instrument (neither the external forward contract of FC250 in TC nor the external payable of FC100 in A); and

(b) to reclassify the gain of LC15 on A's internal derivative to reflect that the forecast revenues of FC150 to which it relates is not hedged by an external instrument.

The net effect of these two adjustments is as follows:

Dr Other comprehensive income		LC15
Cr Inventory		LC15

F.1.8 Combination of written and purchased options

In most cases, IAS 39.AG94 prohibits the use of written options as hedging instruments. If a combination of a written option and purchased option (such as an interest rate collar) is transacted as a single instrument with one counterparty, can an entity split the derivative instrument into its written option component and purchased option component and designate the purchased option component as a hedging instrument?

No. IAS 39.74 specifies that a hedging relationship is designated by an entity for a hedging instrument in its entirety. The only exceptions permitted are splitting the time value and intrinsic value of an option and splitting the interest element and spot price on a forward. Question F.1.3 addresses the issue of whether and when a combination of options is considered as a written option.

F.1.9 Delta-neutral hedging strategy

Does IAS 39 permit an entity to apply hedge accounting for a 'delta-neutral' hedging strategy and other dynamic hedging strategies under which the quantity of the hedging instrument is constantly adjusted in order to maintain a desired hedge ratio, for example, to achieve a delta-neutral position insensitive to changes in the fair value of the hedged item?

Yes. IAS 39.74 states that 'a dynamic hedging strategy that assesses both the intrinsic value and time value of an option contract can qualify for hedge accounting'. For example, a portfolio insurance strategy that seeks to ensure that the fair value of the hedged item does not drop below a certain level, while allowing the fair value to increase, may qualify for hedge accounting.

To qualify for hedge accounting, the entity must document how it will monitor and update the hedge and measure hedge effectiveness, be able to track properly all terminations and redesignations of the hedging instrument, and demonstrate that all other criteria for hedge accounting in IAS 39.88 are met. Also, it must be able to demonstrate an expectation that the hedge will be highly effective for a specified short period of time during which the hedge is not expected to be adjusted.

F.1.10 [Deleted]

F.1.11 Hedging instrument: proportion of the cash flows of a cash instrument

In the case of foreign exchange risk, a non-derivative financial asset or non-derivative financial liability can potentially qualify as a hedging instrument. Can an entity treat the cash flows for specified periods during which a financial asset or financial liability that is designated as a hedging instrument remains outstanding as a proportion of the hedging instrument under IAS 39.75, and exclude the other cash flows from the designated hedging relationship?

No. IAS 39.75 indicates that a hedging relationship may not be designated for only a portion of the time period in which the hedging instrument is outstanding. For example, the cash flows during the first three years of a ten-year borrowing denominated in a foreign currency cannot qualify as a hedging instrument in a cash flow hedge of the first three years of revenue in the same foreign currency. On the other hand, a non-derivative financial asset or financial liability denominated in a foreign currency may potentially qualify as a hedging instrument in a hedge of the foreign currency risk associated with a hedged item that has a remaining time period until maturity that is equal to or longer than the remaining maturity of the hedging instrument (see Question F.2.17).

F.1.12 Hedges of more than one type of risk

Issue (a) – Normally a hedging relationship is designated between an entire hedging instrument and a hedged item so that there is a single measure of fair value for the hedging instrument. Does this preclude designating a single financial instrument simultaneously as a hedging instrument in both a cash flow hedge and a fair value hedge?

No. For example, entities commonly use a combined interest rate and currency swap to convert a variable rate position in a foreign currency to a fixed rate position in the functional currency. IAS 39.76 allows the swap to be designated separately as a fair value hedge of the currency risk and a cash flow hedge of the interest rate risk provided the conditions in IAS 39.76 are met.

Issue (b) – If a single financial instrument is a hedging instrument in two different hedges, is special disclosure required?

IFRS 7.22 requires disclosures separately for designated fair value hedges, cash flow hedges and hedges of a net investment in a foreign operation. The instrument in question would be reported in the IFRS 7.22 disclosures separately for each type of hedge.

F.1.13 Hedging instrument: dual foreign currency forward exchange contract

Entity A's functional currency is the Japanese yen. Entity A has a five-year floating rate US dollar liability and a ten-year fixed rate pound sterling-denominated note receivable. The principal amounts of the asset and liability when converted into the Japanese yen are the same. Entity A enters into a single foreign currency forward contract to hedge its foreign currency exposure on both instruments under which it receives US dollars and pays pounds sterling at the end of five years. If Entity A designates the forward exchange contract as a hedging instrument in a cash flow hedge against the foreign currency exposure on the principal repayments of both instruments, can it qualify for hedge accounting?

Yes. IAS 39.76 permits designating a single hedging instrument as a hedge of multiple types of risk if three conditions are met. In this example, the derivative hedging instrument satisfies all of these conditions, as follows.

(a)   The risks hedged can be identified clearly. The risks are the exposures to changes in the exchange rates between US dollars and yen, and yen and pounds, respectively.

(b)   The effectiveness of the hedge can be demonstrated. For the pound sterling loan, the effectiveness is measured as the degree of offset between the fair value of the principal repayment in pounds sterling and the fair value of the pound sterling payment on the forward exchange contract. For the US dollar liability, the effectiveness is measured as the degree of offset between the fair value of the principal repayment in US dollars and the US dollar receipt on the forward exchange contract. Even though the receivable has a ten-year life and the forward protects it for only the first five years, hedge accounting is permitted for only a portion of the exposure as described in Question F.2.17.

(c)   It is possible to ensure that there is specific designation of the hedging instrument and different risk positions. The hedged exposures are identified as the principal amounts of the liability and the note receivable in their respective currency of denomination.

F.1.14 Concurrent offsetting swaps and use of one as a hedging instrument

Entity A enters into an interest rate swap and designates it as a hedge of the fair value exposure associated with fixed rate debt. The fair value hedge meets the hedge accounting criteria of IAS 39. Entity A simultaneously enters into a second interest rate swap with the same swap counterparty that has terms that fully offset the first interest rate swap. Is Entity A required to view the two swaps as one unit and therefore precluded from applying fair value hedge accounting to the first swap?

It depends. IAS 39 is transaction-based. If the second swap was not entered into in contemplation of the first swap or there is a substantive business purpose for structuring the transactions separately, then the swaps are not viewed as one unit.

For example, some entities have a policy that requires a centralised dealer or treasury subsidiary to enter into third-party derivative contracts on behalf of other subsidiaries within the organisation to hedge the subsidiaries' interest rate risk exposures. The dealer or treasury subsidiary also enters into internal derivative transactions with those subsidiaries in order to track those hedges operationally within the organisation. Because the dealer or treasury subsidiary also enters into derivative contracts as part of its trading operations, or because it may wish to rebalance the risk of its overall portfolio, it may enter into a derivative contract with the same third party during the same business day that has substantially the same terms as a contract entered into as a hedging instrument on behalf of another subsidiary. In this case, there is a valid business purpose for entering into each contract.

Judgement is applied to determine whether there is a substantive business purpose for structuring the transactions separately. For example, if the sole purpose is to obtain fair value accounting treatment for the debt, there is no substantive business purpose.

F.2 Hedged items

F.2.1 Whether a derivative can be designated as a hedged item

Does IAS 39 permit designating a derivative instrument (whether a stand-alone or separately recognised embedded derivative) as a hedged item either individually or as part of a hedged group in a fair value or cash flow hedge, for example, by designating a pay-variable, receive-fixed Forward Rate Agreement (FRA) as a cash flow hedge of a pay-fixed, receive-variable FRA?

No. Derivative instruments always meet the definition of held for trading and are measured at fair value with gains and losses recognised in profit or loss unless they are designated and effective hedging instruments (IAS 39.9 and IFRS 9 paragraphs 4.1-4.5, 5.4.1 and 5.4.3). As an exception, IAS 39.AG94 permits the designation of a purchased option as the hedged item in a fair value hedge.

F.2.2 Cash flow hedge: anticipated issue of fixed rate debt

Is hedge accounting allowed for a hedge of an anticipated issue of fixed rate debt?

Yes. This would be a cash flow hedge of a highly probable forecast transaction that will affect profit or loss (IAS 39.86) provided that the conditions in IAS 39.88 are met.

To illustrate: Entity R periodically issues new bonds to refinance maturing bonds, provide working capital and for various other purposes. When Entity R decides it will be issuing bonds, it may hedge the risk of changes in the long-term interest rate from the date it decides to issue the bonds to the date the bonds are issued. If long-term interest rates go up, the bond will be issued either at a higher rate or with a higher discount or smaller premium than was originally expected. The higher rate being paid or decrease in proceeds is normally offset by the gain on the hedge. If long-term interest rates go down, the bond will be issued either at a lower rate or with a higher premium or a smaller discount than was originally expected. The lower rate being paid or increase in proceeds is normally offset by the loss on the hedge.

For example, in August 2000 Entity R decided it would issue CU200 million seven-year bonds in January 2001. Entity R performed historical correlation studies and determined that a seven-year treasury bond adequately correlates to the bonds Entity R expected to issue, assuming a hedge ratio of 0.93 futures contracts to one debt unit. Therefore, Entity R hedged the anticipated issue of the bonds by selling (shorting) CU186 million worth of futures on seven-year treasury bonds. From August 2000 to January 2001 interest rates increased. The short futures positions were closed in January 2001, the date the bonds were issued, and resulted in a CU1.2 million gain that will offset the increased interest payments on the bonds and, therefore, will affect profit or loss over the life of the bonds. The hedge qualifies as a cash flow hedge of the interest rate risk on the forecast issue of debt.

F.2.3 Hedge accounting: core deposit intangibles

Is hedge accounting treatment permitted for a hedge of the fair value exposure of core deposit intangibles?

It depends on whether the core deposit intangible is generated internally or acquired (eg as part of a business combination).

Internally generated core deposit intangibles are not recognised as intangible assets under IAS 38. Because they are not recognised, they cannot be designated as a hedged item.

If a core deposit intangible is acquired together with a related portfolio of deposits, the core deposit intangible is required to be recognised separately as an intangible asset (or as part of the related acquired portfolio of deposits) if it meets the recognition criteria in paragraph 21 of IAS 38 *Intangible Assets*. A recognised core deposit intangible asset could be designated as a hedged item, but only if it meets the conditions in paragraph 88, including the requirement in paragraph 88(d) that the effectiveness of the hedge can be measured reliably. Because it is often difficult to measure reliably the fair value of a core deposit intangible asset other than on initial recognition, it is unlikely that the requirement in paragraph 88(d) will be met.

F.2.4 Hedge accounting: hedging of future foreign currency revenue streams

Is hedge accounting permitted for a currency borrowing that hedges an expected but not contractual revenue stream in foreign currency?

Yes, if the revenues are highly probable. Under IAS 39.86(b) a hedge of an anticipated sale may qualify as a cash flow hedge. For example, an airline entity may use sophisticated models based on experience and economic data to project its revenues in various currencies. If it can demonstrate that forecast revenues for a period of time into the future in a particular currency are 'highly probable', as required by IAS 39.88, it may designate a currency borrowing as a cash flow hedge of the future revenue stream. The portion of the gain or loss on the borrowing that is determined to be an effective hedge is recognised in other comprehensive income until the revenues occur.

It is unlikely that an entity can reliably predict 100 per cent of revenues for a future year. On the other hand, it is possible that a portion of predicted revenues, normally those expected in the short term, will meet the 'highly probable' criterion.

F.2.5 Cash flow hedges: 'all in one' hedge

If a derivative instrument is expected to be settled gross by delivery of the underlying asset in exchange for the payment of a fixed price, can the derivative instrument be designated as the hedging instrument in a cash flow hedge of that gross settlement assuming the other cash flow hedge accounting criteria are met?

Yes. A derivative instrument that will be settled gross can be designated as the hedging instrument in a cash flow hedge of the variability of the consideration to be paid or received in the future transaction that will occur on gross settlement of the derivative contract itself because there would be an exposure to variability in the purchase or sale price without the derivative. This applies to all fixed price contracts that are accounted for as derivatives under IAS 39 and IFRS 9.

For example, if an entity enters into a fixed price contract to sell a commodity and that contract is accounted for as a derivative under IAS 39 and IFRS 9 (for example, because the entity has a practice of settling such contracts net in cash or of taking delivery of the underlying and selling it within a short period after delivery for the purpose of generating a profit from short-term fluctuations in price or dealer's margin), the entity may designate the fixed price contract as a cash flow hedge of the variability of the consideration to be received on the sale of the asset (a future transaction) even though the fixed price contract is the contract under which the asset will be sold. Also, if an entity enters into a forward contract to purchase a debt instrument that will be settled by delivery, but the forward contract is a derivative because its term exceeds the regular way delivery period in the marketplace, the entity may designate the forward as a cash flow hedge of the variability of the consideration to be paid to acquire the debt instrument (a future transaction), even though the derivative is the contract under which the debt instrument will be acquired.

F.2.6 Hedge relationships: entity-wide risk

An entity has a fixed rate asset and a fixed rate liability, each having the same principal amount. Under the terms of the instruments, interest payments on the asset and liability occur in the same period and the net cash flow is always positive because the interest rate on the asset exceeds the interest rate on the liability. The entity enters into an interest rate swap to receive a floating interest rate and pay a fixed interest rate on a notional amount equal to the principal of the asset and designates the interest rate swap as a fair value hedge of the fixed rate asset. Does the hedging relationship qualify for hedge accounting even though the effect of the interest rate swap on an entity-wide basis is to create an exposure to interest rate changes that did not previously exist?

Yes. IAS 39 does not require risk reduction on an entity-wide basis as a condition for hedge accounting. Exposure is assessed on a transaction basis and, in this instance, the asset being hedged has a fair value exposure to interest rate increases that is offset by the interest rate swap.

F.2.7 Cash flow hedge: forecast transaction related to an entity's equity

Can a forecast transaction in the entity's own equity instruments or forecast dividend payments to shareholders be designated as a hedged item in a cash flow hedge?

No. To qualify as a hedged item, the forecast transaction must expose the entity to a particular risk that can affect profit or loss (IAS 39.86). The classification of financial instruments as liabilities or equity generally provides the basis for determining whether transactions or other payments relating to such instruments are recognised in profit or loss (IAS 32). For example, distributions to holders of an equity instrument are debited by the issuer directly to equity (IAS 32.35). Therefore, such distributions cannot be designated as a hedged item. However, a declared dividend that has not yet been paid and is recognised as a financial liability may qualify as a hedged item, for example, for foreign currency risk if it is denominated in a foreign currency.

F.2.8 Hedge accounting: risk of a transaction not occurring

Does IAS 39 permit an entity to apply hedge accounting to a hedge of the risk that a transaction will not occur, for example, if that would result in less revenue to the entity than expected?

No. The risk that a transaction will not occur is an overall business risk that is not eligible as a hedged item. Hedge accounting is permitted only for risks associated with recognised assets and liabilities, firm commitments, highly probable forecast transactions and net investments in foreign operations (IAS 39.86).

F.2.9–F.2.11 [Deleted]

F.2.12 Hedge accounting: prepayable financial asset

If the issuer has the right to prepay a financial asset, can the investor designate the cash flows after the prepayment date as part of the hedged item?

Cash flows after the prepayment date may be designated as the hedged item to the extent it can be demonstrated that they are 'highly probable' (IAS 39.88). For example, cash flows after the prepayment date may qualify as highly probable if they result from a group or pool of similar assets (for example, mortgage loans) for which prepayments can be estimated with a high degree of accuracy or if the prepayment option is significantly out of the money. In addition, the cash flows after the prepayment date may be designated as the hedged item if a comparable option exists in the hedging instrument.

F.2.13 Fair value hedge: risk that could affect profit or loss

Is fair value hedge accounting permitted for exposure to interest rate risk in fixed rate loans that are measured at amortised cost?

Yes. Under IFRS 9, some fixed rate loans are measured at amortised cost. Banking institutions in many countries hold the bulk of their fixed rate loans to collect their contractual cash flows. Thus, changes in the fair value of such fixed rate loans that are due to changes in market interest rates will not affect profit or loss. IAS 39.86 specifies that a fair value hedge is a hedge of the exposure to changes in fair value that is attributable to a particular risk and that can affect profit or loss. Therefore, IAS 39.86 may appear to preclude fair value hedge accounting for fixed rate loans. However, the entity could sell them and the change in fair values would affect profit or loss. Thus, fair value hedge accounting is permitted for fixed rate loans.

F.2.14 Intragroup and intra-entity hedging transactions

An Australian entity, whose functional currency is the Australian dollar, has forecast purchases in Japanese yen that are highly probable. The Australian entity is wholly owned by a Swiss entity, which prepares consolidated financial statements (which include the Australian subsidiary) in Swiss francs. The Swiss parent entity enters into a forward contract to hedge the change in yen relative to the Australian dollar. Can that hedge qualify for hedge accounting in the consolidated financial statements, or must the Australian subsidiary that has the foreign currency exposure be a party to the hedging transaction?

The hedge can qualify for hedge accounting provided the other hedge accounting criteria in IAS 39 are met. Since the Australian entity did not hedge the foreign currency exchange risk associated with the forecast purchases in yen, the effects of exchange rate changes between the Australian dollar and the yen will affect the Australian entity's profit or loss and, therefore, would also affect consolidated profit or loss. IAS 39 does not require that the operating unit that is exposed to the risk being hedged be a party to the hedging instrument.

F.2.15 Internal contracts: single offsetting external derivative

An entity uses what it describes as internal derivative contracts to document the transfer of responsibility for interest rate risk exposures from individual divisions to a central treasury function. The central treasury function aggregates the internal derivative contracts and enters into a single external derivative contract that offsets the internal derivative contracts on a net basis. For example, if the central treasury function has entered into three internal receive-fixed, pay-variable interest rate swaps that lay off the exposure to variable interest cash flows on variable rate liabilities in other divisions and one internal receive-variable, pay-fixed interest rate swap that lays off the exposure to variable interest cash flows on variable rate assets in another division, it would enter into an interest rate swap with an external counterparty that exactly offsets the four internal swaps. Assuming that the hedge accounting criteria are met, in the entity's financial statements would the single offsetting external derivative qualify as a hedging instrument in a hedge of a part of the underlying items on a gross basis?

Yes, but only to the extent the external derivative is designated as an offset of cash inflows or cash outflows on a gross basis. IAS 39.84 indicates that a hedge of an overall net position does not qualify for hedge accounting. However, it does permit designating a part of the underlying items as the hedged position on a gross basis. Therefore, even though the purpose of entering into the external derivative was to offset internal derivative contracts on a net basis, hedge accounting is permitted if the hedging relationship is defined and documented as a hedge of a part of the underlying cash inflows or cash outflows on a gross basis. An entity follows the approach outlined in IAS 39.84 and IAS 39.AG101 to designate part of the underlying cash flows as the hedged position.

F.2.16 Internal contracts: external derivative contracts that are settled net

Issue (a) – An entity uses internal derivative contracts to transfer interest rate risk exposures from individual divisions to a central treasury function. For each internal derivative contract, the central treasury function enters into a derivative contract with a single external counterparty that offsets the internal derivative contract. For example, if the central treasury function has entered into a receive-5 per cent-fixed, pay-LIBOR interest rate swap with another division that has entered into the internal contract with central treasury to hedge the exposure to variability in interest cash flows on a pay-LIBOR borrowing, central treasury would enter into a pay-5 per cent-fixed, receive-LIBOR interest rate swap on the same principal terms with the external counterparty. Although each of the external derivative contracts is formally documented as a separate contract, only the net of the payments on all of the external derivative contracts is settled since there is a netting agreement with the external counterparty. Assuming that the other hedge accounting criteria are met, can the individual external derivative contracts, such as the pay-5 per cent-fixed, receive-LIBOR interest rate swap above, be designated as hedging instruments of underlying gross exposures, such as the exposure to changes in variable interest payments on the pay-LIBOR borrowing above, even though the external derivatives are settled on a net basis?

Generally, yes. External derivative contracts that are legally separate contracts and serve a valid business purpose, such as laying off risk exposures on a gross basis, qualify as hedging instruments even if those external contracts are settled on a net basis with the same external counterparty, provided the hedge accounting criteria in IAS 39 are met. See also Question F.1.14.

Issue (b) – Treasury observes that by entering into the external offsetting contracts and including them in the centralised portfolio, it is no longer able to evaluate the exposures on a net basis. Treasury wishes to manage the portfolio of offsetting external derivatives separately from other exposures of the entity. Therefore, it enters into an additional, single derivative to offset the risk of the portfolio. Can the individual external derivative contracts in the portfolio still be designated as hedging instruments of underlying gross exposures even though a single external derivative is used to offset fully the market exposure created by entering into the external contracts?

Generally, yes. The purpose of structuring the external derivative contracts in this manner is consistent with the entity's risk management objectives and strategies. As indicated above, external derivative contracts that are legally separate contracts and serve a valid business purpose qualify as hedging instruments. Moreover, the answer to Question F.1.14 specifies that hedge accounting is not precluded simply because the entity has entered into a swap that mirrors exactly the terms of another swap with the same counterparty if there is a substantive business purpose for structuring the transactions separately.

F.2.17 Partial term hedging

IAS 39.75 indicates that a hedging relationship may not be designated for only a portion of the time period during which a hedging instrument remains outstanding. Is it permitted to designate a derivative as hedging only a portion of the time period to maturity of a hedged item?

Yes. A financial instrument may be a hedged item for only a portion of its cash flows or fair value, if effectiveness can be measured and the other hedge accounting criteria are met.

To illustrate: Entity A acquires a 10 per cent fixed rate government bond with a remaining term to maturity of ten years. Entity A classifies the bond as measured at amortised cost. To hedge itself against fair value exposure on the bond associated with the present value of the interest rate payments until year 5, Entity A acquires a five-year pay-fixed, receive-floating swap. The swap may be designated as hedging the fair value exposure of the interest rate payments on the government bond until year 5 and the change in value of the principal payment due at maturity to the extent affected by changes in the yield curve relating to the five years of the swap.

F.2.18 Hedging instrument: cross-currency interest rate swap

Entity A's functional currency is the Japanese yen. Entity A has a five-year floating rate US dollar liability and a 10-year fixed rate pound sterling-denominated note receivable. Entity A wishes to hedge the foreign currency exposure on its asset and liability and the fair value interest rate exposure on the receivable and enters into a matching cross-currency interest rate swap to receive floating rate US dollars and pay fixed rate pounds sterling and to exchange the dollars for the pounds at the end of five years. Can Entity A designate the swap as a hedging instrument in a fair value hedge against both foreign currency risk and interest rate risk, although both the pound sterling and US dollar are foreign currencies to Entity A?

Yes. IAS 39.81 permits hedge accounting for components of risk, if effectiveness can be measured. Also, IAS 39.76 permits designating a single hedging instrument as a hedge of more than one type of risk if the risks can be identified clearly, effectiveness can be demonstrated, and specific designation of the hedging instrument and different risk positions can be ensured. Therefore, the swap may be designated as a hedging instrument in a fair value hedge of the pound sterling receivable against exposure to changes in its fair value associated with changes in UK interest rates for the initial partial term of five years and the exchange rate between pounds and US dollars. The swap is measured at fair value with changes in fair value recognised in profit or loss. The carrying amount of the receivable is adjusted for changes in its fair value caused by changes in UK interest rates for the first five-year portion of the yield curve. The receivable and payable are remeasured using spot exchange rates under IAS 21 and the changes to their carrying amounts recognised in profit or loss.

F.2.19–F.2.20 [Deleted]

F.2.21 Hedge accounting: netting of assets and liabilities

May an entity group financial assets together with financial liabilities for the purpose of determining the net cash flow exposure to be hedged for hedge accounting purposes?

An entity's hedging strategy and risk management practices may assess cash flow risk on a net basis but IAS 39.84 does not permit designating a net cash flow exposure as a hedged item for hedge accounting purposes. IAS 39.AG101 provides an example of how a bank might assess its risk on a net basis (with similar assets and liabilities grouped together) and then qualify for hedge accounting by hedging on a gross basis.

F.3 Hedge accounting

F.3.1 Cash flow hedge: fixed interest rate cash flows

An entity issues a fixed rate debt instrument and enters into a receive-fixed, pay-variable interest rate swap to offset the exposure to interest rate risk associated with the debt instrument. Can the entity designate the swap as a cash flow hedge of the future interest cash outflows associated with the debt instrument?

No. IAS 39.86(b) states that a cash flow hedge is 'a hedge of the exposure to variability in cash flows'. In this case, the issued debt instrument does not give rise to any exposure to variability in cash flows since the interest payments are fixed. The entity may designate the swap as a fair value hedge of the debt instrument, but it cannot designate the swap as a cash flow hedge of the future cash outflows of the debt instrument.

F.3.2 Cash flow hedge: reinvestment of fixed interest rate cash flows

An entity manages interest rate risk on a net basis. On 1 January 2001, it forecasts aggregate cash inflows of CU100 on fixed rate assets and aggregate cash outflows of CU90 on fixed rate liabilities in the first quarter of 2002. For risk management purposes it uses a receive-variable, pay-fixed Forward Rate Agreement (FRA) to hedge the forecast net cash inflow of CU10. The entity designates as the hedged item the first CU10 of cash inflows on fixed rate assets in the first quarter of 2002. Can it designate the receive-variable, pay-fixed FRA as a cash flow hedge of the exposure to variability to cash flows in the first quarter of 2002 associated with the fixed rate assets?

No. The FRA does not qualify as a cash flow hedge of the cash flow relating to the fixed rate assets because they do not have a cash flow exposure. The entity could, however, designate the FRA as a hedge of the fair value exposure that exists before the cash flows are remitted.

In some cases, the entity could also hedge the interest rate exposure associated with the forecast reinvestment of the interest and principal it receives on fixed rate assets (see Question F.6.2). However, in this example, the FRA does not qualify for cash flow hedge accounting because it increases rather than reduces the variability of interest cash flows resulting from the reinvestment of interest cash flows (for example, if market rates increase, there will be a cash inflow on the FRA and an increase in the expected interest cash inflows resulting from the reinvestment of interest cash inflows on fixed rate assets). However, potentially it could qualify as a cash flow hedge of a portion of the refinancing of cash outflows on a gross basis.

F.3.3 Foreign currency hedge

Entity A has a foreign currency liability payable in six months' time and it wishes to hedge the amount payable on settlement against foreign currency fluctuations. To that end, it takes out a forward contract to buy the foreign currency in six months' time. Should the hedge be treated as:

(a)   a fair value hedge of the foreign currency liability with gains and losses on revaluing the liability and the forward contract at the year-end both recognised in profit or loss; or

(b)   a cash flow hedge of the amount to be settled in the future with gains and losses on revaluing the forward contract recognised in other comprehensive income?

IAS 39 does not preclude either of these two methods. If the hedge is treated as a fair value hedge, the gain or loss on the fair value remeasurement of the hedging instrument and the gain or loss on the fair value remeasurement of the hedged item for the hedged risk are recognised immediately in profit or loss. If the hedge is treated as a cash flow hedge with the gain or loss on remeasuring the forward contract recognised in other comprehensive income, that amount is recognised in profit or loss in the same period or periods during which the hedged item (the liability) affects profit or loss, ie when the liability is remeasured for changes in foreign exchange rates. Therefore, if the hedge is effective, the gain or loss on the derivative is released to profit or loss in the same periods during which the liability is remeasured, not when the payment occurs. See Question F.3.4.

F.3.4 Foreign currency cash flow hedge

An entity exports a product at a price denominated in a foreign currency. At the date of the sale, the entity obtains a receivable for the sale price payable in 90 days and takes out a 90-day forward exchange contract in the same currency as the receivable to hedge its foreign currency exposure.

Under IAS 21, the sale is recorded at the spot rate at the date of sale, and the receivable is restated during the 90-day period for changes in exchange rates with the difference being taken to profit or loss (IAS 21.23 and IAS 21.28).

If the foreign exchange contract is designated as a hedging instrument, does the entity have a choice whether to designate the foreign exchange contract as a fair value hedge of the foreign currency exposure of the receivable or as a cash flow hedge of the collection of the receivable?

Yes. If the entity designates the foreign exchange contract as a fair value hedge, the gain or loss from remeasuring the forward exchange contract at fair value is recognised immediately in profit or loss and the gain or loss on remeasuring the receivable is also recognised in profit or loss.

If the entity designates the foreign exchange contract as a cash flow hedge of the foreign currency risk associated with the collection of the receivable, the portion of the gain or loss that is determined to be an effective hedge is recognised in other comprehensive income, and the ineffective portion in profit or loss (IAS 39.95). The amount recognised in other comprehensive income is reclassified from equity to profit or loss as a reclassification adjustment in the same period or periods during which changes in the measurement of the receivable affect profit or loss (IAS 39.100).

F.3.5 Fair value hedge: variable rate debt instrument

Does IAS 39 permit an entity to designate a portion of the risk exposure of a variable rate debt instrument as a hedged item in a fair value hedge?

Yes. A variable rate debt instrument may have an exposure to changes in its fair value due to credit risk. It may also have an exposure to changes in its fair value relating to movements in the market interest rate in the periods between which the variable interest rate on the debt instrument is reset. For example, if the debt instrument provides for annual interest payments reset to the market rate each year, a portion of the debt instrument has an exposure to changes in fair value during the year.

F.3.6 Fair value hedge: inventory

IAS 39.86(a) states that a fair value hedge is 'a hedge of the exposure to changes in fair value of a recognised asset or liability ... that is attributable to a particular risk and could affect profit or loss'. Can an entity designate inventories, such as copper inventory, as the hedged item in a fair value hedge of the exposure to changes in the price of the inventories, such as the copper price, although inventories are measured at the lower of cost and net realisable value under IAS 2 *Inventories*?

Yes. The inventories may be hedged for changes in fair value due to changes in the copper price because the change in fair value of inventories will affect profit or loss when the inventories are sold or their carrying amount is written down. The adjusted carrying amount becomes the cost basis for the purpose of applying the lower of cost and net realisable value test under IAS 2. The hedging instrument used in a fair value hedge of inventories may alternatively qualify as a cash flow hedge of the future sale of the inventory.

F.3.7 Hedge accounting: forecast transaction

For cash flow hedges, a forecast transaction that is subject to a hedge must be 'highly probable'. How should the term 'highly probable' be interpreted?

The term 'highly probable' indicates a much greater likelihood of happening than the term 'more likely than not'. An assessment of the likelihood that a forecast transaction will take place is not based solely on management's intentions because intentions are not verifiable. A transaction's probability should be supported by observable facts and the attendant circumstances.

In assessing the likelihood that a transaction will occur, an entity should consider the following circumstances:

(a) the frequency of similar past transactions;

(b) the financial and operational ability of the entity to carry out the transaction;

(c) substantial commitments of resources to a particular activity (for example, a manufacturing facility that can be used in the short run only to process a particular type of commodity);

(d) the extent of loss or disruption of operations that could result if the transaction does not occur;

(e)   the likelihood that transactions with substantially different characteristics might be used to achieve the same business purpose (for example, an entity that intends to raise cash may have several ways of doing so, ranging from a short-term bank loan to an offering of ordinary shares); and

(f)   the entity's business plan.

The length of time until a forecast transaction is projected to occur is also a factor in determining probability. Other factors being equal, the more distant a forecast transaction is, the less likely it is that the transaction would be regarded as highly probable and the stronger the evidence that would be needed to support an assertion that it is highly probable.

For example, a transaction forecast to occur in five years may be less likely to occur than a transaction forecast to occur in one year. However, forecast interest payments for the next 20 years on variable rate debt would typically be highly probable if supported by an existing contractual obligation.

In addition, other factors being equal, the greater the physical quantity or future value of a forecast transaction in proportion to the entity's transactions of the same nature, the less likely it is that the transaction would be regarded as highly probable and the stronger the evidence that would be required to support an assertion that it is highly probable. For example, less evidence generally would be needed to support forecast sales of 100,000 units in the next month than 950,000 units in that month when recent sales have averaged 950,000 units per month for the past three months.

A history of having designated hedges of forecast transactions and then determining that the forecast transactions are no longer expected to occur would call into question both an entity's ability to predict forecast transactions accurately and the propriety of using hedge accounting in the future for similar forecast transactions.

F.3.8 Retrospective designation of hedges

Does IAS 39 permit an entity to designate hedge relationships retrospectively?

No. Designation of hedge relationships takes effect prospectively from the date all hedge accounting criteria in IAS 39.88 are met. In particular, hedge accounting can be applied only from the date the entity has completed the necessary documentation of the hedge relationship, including identification of the hedging instrument, the related hedged item or transaction, the nature of the risk being hedged, and how the entity will assess hedge effectiveness.

F.3.9 Hedge accounting: designation at the inception of the hedge

Does IAS 39 permit an entity to designate and formally document a derivative contract as a hedging instrument after entering into the derivative contract?

Yes, prospectively. For hedge accounting purposes, IAS 39 requires a hedging instrument to be designated and formally documented as such from the inception of the hedge relationship (IAS 39.88); in other words, a hedge relationship cannot be designated retrospectively. Also, it precludes designating a hedging relationship for only a portion of the time period during which the hedging instrument remains outstanding (IAS 39.75). However, it does not require the hedging instrument to be acquired at the inception of the hedge relationship.

F.3.10 Hedge accounting: identification of hedged forecast transaction

Can a forecast transaction be identified as the purchase or sale of the last 15,000 units of a product in a specified period or as a percentage of purchases or sales during a specified period?

No. The hedged forecast transaction must be identified and documented with sufficient specificity so that when the transaction occurs, it is clear whether the transaction is or is not the hedged transaction. Therefore, a forecast transaction may be identified as the sale of the first 15,000 units of a specific product during a specified three-month period, but it could not be identified as the last 15,000 units of that product sold during a three-month period because the last 15,000 units cannot be identified when they are sold. For the same reason, a forecast transaction cannot be specified solely as a percentage of sales or purchases during a period.

F.3.11 Cash flow hedge: documentation of timing of forecast transaction

For a hedge of a forecast transaction, should the documentation of the hedge relationship that is established at inception of the hedge identify the date when, or time period in which, the forecast transaction is expected to occur?

Yes. To qualify for hedge accounting, the hedge must relate to a specific identified and designated risk (IAS 39.AG110) and it must be possible to measure its effectiveness reliably (IAS 39.88(d)). Also, the hedged forecast transaction must be highly probable (IAS 39.88(c)). To meet these criteria, an entity is not required to predict and document the exact date a forecast transaction is expected to occur. However, it is required to identify and document the time period during which the forecast transaction is expected to occur within a reasonably specific and generally narrow range of time from a most probable date, as a basis for assessing hedge effectiveness. To determine that the hedge will be highly effective in accordance with IAS 39.88(d), it is necessary to ensure that changes in the fair value of the expected cash flows are offset by changes in the fair value of the hedging instrument and this test may be met only if the timing of the cash flows occur within close proximity to each other. If the forecast transaction is no longer expected to occur, hedge accounting is discontinued in accordance with IAS 39.101(c).

F.4 Hedge effectiveness

F.4.1 Hedging on an after-tax basis

Hedging is often done on an after-tax basis. Is hedge effectiveness assessed after taxes?

IAS 39 permits, but does not require, assessment of hedge effectiveness on an after-tax basis. If the hedge is undertaken on an after-tax basis, it is so designated at inception as part of the formal documentation of the hedging relationship and strategy.

F.4.2 Hedge effectiveness: assessment on cumulative basis

IAS 39.88(b) requires that the hedge is expected to be highly effective. Should expected hedge effectiveness be assessed separately for each period or cumulatively over the life of the hedging relationship?

Expected hedge effectiveness may be assessed on a cumulative basis if the hedge is so designated, and that condition is incorporated into the appropriate hedging documentation. Therefore, even if a hedge is not expected to be highly effective in a particular period, hedge accounting is not precluded if effectiveness is expected to remain sufficiently high over the life of the hedging relationship. However, any ineffectiveness is required to be recognised in profit or loss as it occurs.

To illustrate: an entity designates a LIBOR-based interest rate swap as a hedge of a borrowing whose interest rate is a UK base rate plus a margin. The UK base rate changes, perhaps, once each quarter or less, in increments of 25–50 basis points, while LIBOR changes daily. Over a period of 1–2 years, the hedge is expected to be almost perfect. However, there will be quarters when the UK base rate does not change at all, while LIBOR has changed significantly. This would not necessarily preclude hedge accounting.

F.4.3 Hedge effectiveness: counterparty credit risk

Must an entity consider the likelihood of default by the counterparty to the hedging instrument in assessing hedge effectiveness?

Yes. An entity cannot ignore whether it will be able to collect all amounts due under the contractual provisions of the hedging instrument. When assessing hedge effectiveness, both at the inception of the hedge and on an ongoing basis, the entity considers the risk that the counterparty to the hedging instrument will default by failing to make any contractual payments to the entity. For a cash flow hedge, if it becomes probable that a counterparty will default, an entity would be unable to conclude that the hedging relationship is expected to be highly effective in achieving offsetting cash flows. As a result, hedge accounting would be discontinued. For a fair value hedge, if there is a change in the counterparty's creditworthiness, the fair value of the hedging instrument will change, which affects the assessment of whether the hedge relationship is effective and whether it qualifies for continued hedge accounting.

F.4.4 Hedge effectiveness: effectiveness tests

How should hedge effectiveness be measured for the purposes of initially qualifying for hedge accounting and for continued qualification?

IAS 39 does not provide specific guidance about how effectiveness tests are performed. IAS 39.AG105 specifies that a hedge is normally regarded as highly effective only if (a) at inception and in subsequent periods, the hedge is expected to be highly effective in achieving offsetting changes in fair value or cash flows attributable to the hedged risk during the period for which the hedge is designated, and (b) the actual results are within a range of 80–125 per cent. IAS 39.AG105 also states that the expectation in (a) can be demonstrated in various ways.

The appropriateness of a given method of assessing hedge effectiveness will depend on the nature of the risk being hedged and the type of hedging instrument used. The method of assessing effectiveness must be reasonable and consistent with other similar hedges unless different methods are explicitly justified. An entity is required to document at the inception of the hedge how effectiveness will be assessed and then to apply that effectiveness test on a consistent basis for the duration of the hedge.

Several mathematical techniques can be used to measure hedge effectiveness, including ratio analysis, ie a comparison of hedging gains and losses with the corresponding gains and losses on the hedged item at a point in time, and statistical measurement techniques such as regression analysis. If regression analysis is used, the entity's documented policies for assessing effectiveness must specify how the results of the regression will be assessed.

F.4.5 Hedge effectiveness: less than 100 per cent offset

If a cash flow hedge is regarded as highly effective because the actual risk offset is within the allowed 80–125 per cent range of deviation from full offset, is the gain or loss on the ineffective portion of the hedge recognised in other comprehensive income?

No. IAS 39.95(a) indicates that only the effective portion is recognised in other comprehensive income. IAS 39.95(b) requires the ineffective portion to be recognised in profit or loss.

F.4.7 Assuming perfect hedge effectiveness

If the principal terms of the hedging instrument and of the entire hedged asset or liability or hedged forecast transaction are the same, can an entity assume perfect hedge effectiveness without further effectiveness testing?

No. IAS 39.88(e) requires an entity to assess hedges on an ongoing basis for hedge effectiveness. It cannot assume hedge effectiveness even if the principal terms of the hedging instrument and the hedged item are the same, since hedge ineffectiveness may arise because of other attributes such as the liquidity of the instruments or their credit risk (IAS 39.AG109). It may, however, designate only certain risks in an overall exposure as being hedged and thereby improve the effectiveness of the hedging relationship. For example, for a fair value hedge of a debt instrument, if the derivative hedging instrument has a credit risk that is equivalent to the AA-rate, it may designate only the risk related to AA-rated interest rate movements as being hedged, in which case changes in credit spreads generally will not affect the effectiveness of the hedge.

F.5 Cash flow hedges

F.5.1 Hedge accounting: non-derivative monetary asset or non-derivative monetary liability used as a hedging instrument

If an entity designates a non-derivative monetary asset as a foreign currency cash flow hedge of the repayment of the principal of a non-derivative monetary liability, would the exchange differences on the hedged item be recognised in profit or loss (IAS 21.28) and the exchange differences on the hedging instrument be recognised in other comprehensive income until the repayment of the liability (IAS 39.95)?

No. Exchange differences on the monetary asset and the monetary liability are both recognised in profit or loss in the period in which they arise (IAS 21.28).

IAS 39.AG83 specifies that if there is a hedge relationship between a non-derivative monetary asset and a non-derivative monetary liability, changes in fair values of those financial instruments are recognised in profit or loss.

F.5.2 Cash flow hedges: performance of hedging instrument (1)

Entity A has a floating rate liability of CU1,000 with five years remaining to maturity. It enters into a five-year pay-fixed, receive-floating interest rate swap in the same currency and with the same principal terms as the liability to hedge the exposure to variable cash flow payments on the floating rate liability attributable to interest rate risk. At inception, the fair value of the swap is zero. Subsequently, there is an increase of CU49 in the fair value of the swap. This increase consists of a change of CU50 resulting from an increase in market interest rates and a change of minus CU1 resulting from an increase in the credit risk of the swap counterparty. There is no change in the fair value of the floating rate liability, but the fair value (present value) of the future cash flows needed to offset the exposure to variable interest cash flows on the liability increases by CU50. Assuming that Entity A determines that the hedge is still highly effective, is there ineffectiveness that should be recognised in profit or loss?

No. A hedge of interest rate risk is not fully effective if part of the change in the fair value of the derivative is attributable to the counterparty's credit risk (IAS 39.AG109). However, because Entity A determines that the hedge relationship is still highly effective, it recognises the effective portion of the change in fair value of the swap, ie the net change in fair value of CU49, in other comprehensive income. There is no debit to profit or loss for the change in fair value of the swap attributable to the deterioration in the credit quality of the swap counterparty, because the cumulative change in the present value of the future cash flows needed to offset the exposure to variable interest cash flows on the hedged item, ie CU50, exceeds the cumulative change in value of the hedging instrument, ie CU49.

Dr Swap		CU49
Cr Other comprehensive income		CU49

If Entity A concludes that the hedge is no longer highly effective, it discontinues hedge accounting prospectively as from the date the hedge ceased to be highly effective in accordance with IAS 39.101.

Would the answer change if the fair value of the swap instead increases to CU51 of which CU50 results from the increase in market interest rates and CU1 from a decrease in the credit risk of the swap counterparty?

Yes. In this case, there is a credit to profit or loss of CU1 for the change in fair value of the swap attributable to the improvement in the credit quality of the swap counterparty. This is because the cumulative change in the value of the hedging instrument, ie CU51, exceeds the cumulative change in the present value of the future cash flows needed to offset the exposure to variable interest cash flows on the hedged item, ie CU50. The difference of CU1 represents the excess ineffectiveness attributable to the derivative hedging instrument, the swap, and is recognised in profit or loss.

Dr Swap		CU51
Cr Other comprehensive income		CU50
Cr Profit or loss		CU1

F.5.3 Cash flow hedges: performance of hedging instrument (2)

On 30 September 20X1, Entity A hedges the anticipated sale of 24 tonnes of pulp on 1 March 20X2 by entering into a short forward contract on 24 tonnes of pulp. The contract requires net settlement in cash determined as the difference between the future spot price of pulp on a specified commodity exchange and CU1,000. Entity A expects to sell the pulp in a different, local market. Entity A determines that the forward contract is an effective hedge of the anticipated sale and that the other conditions for hedge accounting are met. It assesses hedge effectiveness by comparing the entire change in the fair value of the forward contract with the change in the fair value of the expected cash inflows. On 31 December, the spot price of pulp has increased both in the local market and on the exchange. The increase in the local market exceeds the increase on the exchange. As a result, the present value of the expected cash inflow from the sale on the local market is CU1,100. The fair value of Entity A's forward contract is negative CU80. Assuming that Entity A determines that the hedge is still highly effective, is there ineffectiveness that should be recognised in profit or loss?

No. In a cash flow hedge, ineffectiveness is not recognised in the financial statements when the cumulative change in the fair value of the hedged cash flows exceeds the cumulative change in the value of the hedging instrument. In this case, the cumulative change in the fair value of the forward contract is CU80, while the fair value of the cumulative change in expected future cash flows on the hedged item is CU100. Since the fair value of the cumulative change in expected future cash flows on the hedged item from the inception of the hedge exceeds the cumulative change in fair value of the hedging instrument (in absolute amounts), no portion of the gain or loss on the hedging instrument is recognised in profit or loss (IAS 39.95(b)). Because Entity A determines that the hedge relationship is still highly effective, it recognises the entire change in fair value of the forward contract (CU80) in other comprehensive income.

Dr Other comprehensive income		CU80
Cr Forward		CU80

If Entity A concludes that the hedge is no longer highly effective, it discontinues hedge accounting prospectively as from the date the hedge ceases to be highly effective in accordance with IAS 39.101.

F.5.4 Cash flow hedges: forecast transaction occurs before the specified period

An entity designates a derivative as a hedging instrument in a cash flow hedge of a forecast transaction, such as a forecast sale of a commodity. The hedging relationship meets all the hedge accounting conditions, including the requirement to identify and document the period in which the transaction is expected to occur within a reasonably specific and narrow range of time (see Question F.2.17). If, in a subsequent period, the forecast transaction is expected to occur in an earlier period than originally anticipated, can the entity conclude that this transaction is the same as the one that was designated as being hedged?

Yes. The change in timing of the forecast transaction does not affect the validity of the designation. However, it may affect the assessment of the effectiveness of the hedging relationship. Also, the hedging instrument would need to be designated as a hedging instrument for the whole remaining period of its existence in order for it to continue to qualify as a hedging instrument (see IAS 39.75 and Question F.2.17).

F.5.5 Cash flow hedges: measuring effectiveness for a hedge of a forecast transaction in a debt instrument

A forecast investment in an interest-earning asset or forecast issue of an interest-bearing liability creates a cash flow exposure to interest rate changes because the related interest payments will be based on the market rate that exists when the forecast transaction occurs. The objective of a cash flow hedge of the exposure to interest rate changes is to offset the effects of future changes in interest rates so as to obtain a single fixed rate, usually the rate that existed at the inception of the hedge that corresponds with the term and timing of the forecast transaction. During the period of the hedge, it is not possible to determine what the market interest rate for the forecast transaction will be at the time the hedge is terminated or when the forecast transaction occurs. In this case, how is the effectiveness of the hedge assessed and measured?

During this period, effectiveness can be measured on the basis of changes in interest rates between the designation date and the interim effectiveness measurement date. The interest rates used to make this measurement are the interest rates that correspond with the term and occurrence of the forecast transaction that existed at the inception of the hedge and that exist at the measurement date as evidenced by the term structure of interest rates.

Generally it will not be sufficient simply to compare cash flows of the hedged item with cash flows generated by the derivative hedging instrument as they are paid or received, since such an approach ignores the entity's expectations of whether the cash flows will offset in subsequent periods and whether there will be any resulting ineffectiveness.

The discussion that follows illustrates the mechanics of establishing a cash flow hedge and measuring its effectiveness. For the purpose of the illustrations, assume that an entity expects to issue a CU100,000 one-year debt instrument in three months. The instrument will pay interest quarterly with principal due at maturity. The entity is exposed to interest rate increases and establishes a hedge of the interest cash flows of the debt by entering into a forward starting interest rate swap. The swap has a term of one year and will start in three months to correspond with the terms of the forecast debt issue. The entity will pay a fixed rate and receive a variable rate, and the entity designates the risk being hedged as the LIBOR-based interest component in the forecast issue of the debt.

Yield curve

The yield curve provides the foundation for computing future cash flows and the fair value of such cash flows both at the inception of, and during, the hedging relationship. It is based on current market yields on applicable reference bonds that are traded in the marketplace. Market yields are converted to spot interest rates ('spot rates' or 'zero coupon rates') by eliminating the effect of coupon payments on the market yield. Spot rates are used to discount future cash flows, such as principal and interest rate payments, to arrive at their fair value. Spot rates also are used to compute forward interest rates that are used to compute variable and estimated future cash flows. The relationship between spot rates and one-period forward rates is shown by the following formula:

Spot-forward relationship

$$F = \frac{(1 + SR_t)^t - 1}{(1 + SR_{t-1})^{t-1}}$$

where   F = forward rate (%)

SR = spot rate (%)

t = period in time (eg 1, 2, 3, 4, 5)

Also, for the purpose of this illustration, assume that the following quarterly-period term structure of interest rates using quarterly compounding exists at the inception of the hedge.

Yield curve at inception – (beginning of period 1)					
Forward periods	*1*	*2*	*3*	*4*	*5*
Spot rates	3.75%	4.50%	5.50%	6.00%	6.25%
Forward rates	3.75%	5.25%	7.51%	7.50%	7.25%

The one-period forward rates are computed on the basis of spot rates for the applicable maturities. For example, the current forward rate for Period 2 calculated using the formula above is equal to $[1.0450^2/1.0375] - 1 = 5.25$ per cent. The current one-period forward rate for Period 2 is different from the current spot rate for Period 2, since the spot rate is an interest rate from the beginning of Period 1 (spot) to the end of Period 2, while the forward rate is an interest rate from the beginning of Period 2 to the end of Period 2.

Hedged item

In this example, the entity expects to issue a CU100,000 one-year debt instrument in three months with quarterly interest payments. The entity is exposed to interest rate increases and would like to eliminate the effect on cash flows of interest rate changes that may happen before the forecast transaction takes place. If that risk is eliminated, the entity would obtain an interest rate on its debt issue that is equal to the one-year forward coupon rate currently available in the marketplace in three months. That forward coupon rate, which is different from the forward (spot) rate, is 6.86 per cent, computed from the term structure of interest rates shown above. It is the market rate of interest that exists at the inception of the hedge, given the terms of the forecast debt instrument. It results in the fair value of the debt being equal to par at its issue.

At the inception of the hedging relationship, the expected cash flows of the debt instrument can be calculated on the basis of the existing term structure of interest rates. For this purpose, it is assumed that interest rates do not change and that the debt would be issued at 6.86 per cent at the beginning of Period 2. In this case, the cash flows and fair value of the debt instrument would be as follows at the beginning of Period 2.

Issue of fixed rate debt					
Beginning of period 2 - No rate changes (spot based on forward rates)					
	Total				
Original forward periods		1	2	3	4	5
Remaining periods			1	2	3	4
Spot rates			5.25%	6.38%	6.75%	6.88%
Forward rates			5.25%	7.51%	7.50%	7.25%
	CU		*CU*	*CU*	*CU*	*CU*
Cash flows:						
Fixed interest @ 6.86%			1,716	1,716	1,716	1,716
Principal						100,000
Fair value:						
Interest	6,592		1,694	1,663	1,632	1,603
Principal	93,408					93,408 [a]
Total	100,000					

(a) CU100,000/(1 + [0.0688/4]) ^{4}

Since it is assumed that interest rates do not change, the fair value of the interest and principal amounts equals the par amount of the forecast transaction. The fair value amounts are computed on the basis of the spot rates that exist at the inception of the hedge for the applicable periods in which the cash flows would occur had the debt been issued at the date of the forecast transaction. They reflect the effect of discounting those cash flows on the basis of the periods that will remain after the debt instrument is issued. For example, the spot rate of 6.38 per cent is used to discount the interest cash flow that is expected to be paid in Period 3, but it is discounted for only two periods because it will occur two periods after the forecast transaction.

The forward interest rates are the same as shown previously, since it is assumed that interest rates do not change. The spot rates are different but they have not actually changed. They represent the spot rates one period forward and are based on the applicable forward rates.

Hedging instrument

The objective of the hedge is to obtain an overall interest rate on the forecast transaction and the hedging instrument that is equal to 6.86 per cent, which is the market rate at the inception of the hedge for the period from Period 2 to Period 5. This objective is accomplished by entering into a forward starting interest rate swap that has a fixed rate of 6.86 per cent. Based on the term structure of interest rates that exist at the inception of the hedge, the interest rate swap will have such a rate. At the inception of the hedge, the fair value of the fixed rate payments on the interest rate swap will equal the fair value of the variable rate payments, resulting in the interest rate swap having a fair value of zero. The expected cash flows of the interest rate swap and the related fair value amounts are shown as follows.

Interest rate swap						
	Total					
Original forward periods		1	2	3	4	5
Remaining periods			1	2	3	4
	CU		*CU*	*CU*	*CU*	*CU*
Cash flows:						
Fixed interest @6.86%			1,716	1,716	1,716	1,716
Forecast variable interest			1,313	1,877	1,876	1,813
Forecast based on forward rate			5.25%	7.51%	7.50%	7.25%
Net interest			(403)	161	160	97
Fair value:						
Discount rate (spot)			5.25%	6.38%	6.75%	6.88%
Fixed interest	6,592		1,694	1,663	1,632	1,603
Forecast variable interest	6,592		1,296	1,819	1,784	1,693
Fair value of interest rate swap	0		(398)	156	152	90

At the inception of the hedge, the fixed rate on the forward swap is equal to the fixed rate the entity would receive if it could issue the debt in three months under terms that exist today.

Measuring hedge effectiveness

If interest rates change during the period the hedge is outstanding, the effectiveness of the hedge can be measured in various ways.

Assume that interest rates change as follows immediately before the debt is issued at the beginning of Period 2.

Yield curve - Rates increase 200 basis points				
Forward periods 1	2	3	4	5
Remaining periods	1	2	3	4
Spot rates	5.75%	6.50%	7.50%	8.00%
Forward rates	5.75%	7.25%	9.51%	9.50%

Under the new interest rate environment, the fair value of the pay-fixed at 6.86 per cent, receive-variable interest rate swap that was designated as the hedging instrument would be as follows.

Fair value of interest rate swap						
	Total					
Original forward periods		1	2	3	4	5
Remaining periods			1	2	3	4
	CU	CU	CU	CU	CU	CU
Cash flows:						
Fixed interest @6.86%			1,716	1,716	1,716	1,716
Forecast variable interest			1,438	1,813	2,377	2,376
Forecast based on new forward rate			5.25%	7.25%	9.51%	9.50%
Net interest			(279)	97	661	660
Fair value:						
New discount rate (spot)			5.75%	6.50%	7.50%	8.00%
Fixed interest	6,562		1,692	1,662	1,623	1,585
Forecast variable interest	7,615		1,417	1,755	2,248	2,195
Fair value of net interest	1,053		(275)	93	625	610

In order to compute the effectiveness of the hedge, it is necessary to measure the change in the present value of the cash flows or the value of the hedged forecast transaction. There are at least two methods of accomplishing this measurement.

Method A Compute change in fair value of debt						
	Total					
Original forward periods		1	2	3	4	5
Remaining periods			1	2	3	4
	CU		CU	CU	CU	CU
Cash flows:						
Fixed interest @6.86%			1,716	1,716	1,716	1,716
Principal						100,000
Fair value:						
New discount rate (spot)			5.75%	6.50%	7.50%	8.00%
Interest	6,562		1,692	1,662	1,623	1,585
Principal	92,385					92,385 [a]
Total	98,947					
Fair value at inception	100,000					
Fair value difference	(1,053)					

(a) $CU100,000/(1 + [0.08/4])^4$

Under Method A, a computation is made of the fair value in the new interest rate environment of debt that carries interest that is equal to the coupon interest rate that existed at the inception of the hedging relationship (6.86 per cent). This fair value is compared with the expected fair value as of the beginning of Period 2 that was calculated on the basis of the term structure of interest rates that existed at the inception of the hedging relationship, as illustrated above, to determine the change in the fair value. Note that the difference between the change in the fair value of the swap and the change in the expected fair value of the debt exactly offset in this example, since the terms of the swap and the forecast transaction match each other.

Method B Compute change in fair value of cash flows					
Total					
Original forward periods	1	2	3	4	5
Remaining periods		1	2	3	4
Market rate at inception		6.86%	6.86%	6.86%	6.86%
Current forward rate		5.75%	7.25%	9.51%	9.50%
Rate difference		1.11%	(0.39%)	(2.64%)	(2.64%)
Cash flow difference (principal × rate)		CU279	(CU97)	(CU661)	(CU660)
Discount rate (spot)		5.75%	6.50%	7.50%	8.00%
Fair value of difference	(CU1,053)	CU275	(CU93)	(CU625)	(CU610)

Under Method B, the present value of the change in cash flows is computed on the basis of the difference between the forward interest rates for the applicable periods at the effectiveness measurement date and the interest rate that would have been obtained if the debt had been issued at the market rate that existed at the inception of the hedge. The market rate that existed at the inception of the hedge is the one-year forward coupon rate in three months. The present value of the change in cash flows is computed on the basis of the current spot rates that exist at the effectiveness measurement date for the applicable periods in which the cash flows are expected to occur. This method also could be referred to as the 'theoretical swap' method (or 'hypothetical derivative' method) because the comparison is between the hedged fixed rate on the debt and the current variable rate, which is the same as comparing cash flows on the fixed and variable rate legs of an interest rate swap.

As before, the difference between the change in the fair value of the swap and the change in the present value of the cash flows exactly offset in this example, since the terms match.

Other considerations

There is an additional computation that should be performed to compute ineffectiveness before the expected date of the forecast transaction that has not been considered for the purpose of this illustration. The fair value difference has been determined in each of the illustrations as of the expected date of the forecast transaction immediately before the forecast transaction, ie at the beginning of Period 2. If the assessment of hedge effectiveness is done before the forecast transaction occurs, the difference should be discounted to the current date to arrive at the actual amount of ineffectiveness. For example, if the measurement date were one month after the hedging relationship was established and the forecast transaction is now expected to occur in two months, the amount would have to be discounted for the remaining two months before the forecast transaction is expected to occur to arrive at the actual fair value. This step would not be necessary in the examples provided above because there was no ineffectiveness. Therefore, additional discounting of the amounts, which net to zero, would not have changed the result.

Under Method B, ineffectiveness is computed on the basis of the difference between the forward coupon interest rates for the applicable periods at the effectiveness measurement date and the interest rate that would have been obtained if the debt had been issued at the market rate that existed at the inception of the hedge. Computing the change in cash flows based on the difference between the forward interest rates that existed at the inception of the hedge and the forward rates that exist at the effectiveness measurement date is inappropriate if the objective of the hedge is to establish a single fixed rate for a series of forecast interest payments. This objective is met by hedging the exposures with an interest rate swap as illustrated in the above example. The fixed interest rate on the swap is a blended interest rate composed of the forward rates over the life of the swap. Unless the yield curve is flat, the comparison between the forward interest rate exposures over the life of the swap and the fixed rate on the swap will produce different cash flows whose fair values are equal only at the inception of the hedging relationship. This difference is shown in the table below.

	Total				
Original forward periods	1	2	3	4	5
Remaining periods		1	2	3	4
Forward rate at inception		5.25%	7.51%	7.50%	7.25%
Current forward rate		5.75%	7.25%	9.51%	9.50%
Rate difference		(0.50%)	0.26%	(2.00%)	(2.25%)
Cash flow difference (principal × rate)		(CU125)	CU64	(CU501)	(CU563)
Discount rate (spot)		5.75%	6.50%	7.50%	8.00%
Fair value of difference	(CU1,055)	(CU123)	CU62	(CU474)	(CU520)
Fair value of interest rate swap	CU1,053				
Ineffectiveness	(CU2)				

If the objective of the hedge is to obtain the forward rates that existed at the inception of the hedge, the interest rate swap is ineffective because the swap has a single blended fixed coupon rate that does not offset a series of different forward interest rates. However, if the objective of the hedge is to obtain the forward coupon rate that existed at the inception of the hedge, the swap is effective, and the comparison based on differences in forward interest rates suggests ineffectiveness when none may exist. Computing ineffectiveness based on the difference between the forward interest rates that existed at the inception of the hedge and the forward rates that exist at the effectiveness measurement date would be an appropriate measurement of ineffectiveness if the hedging objective is to lock in those forward interest rates. In that case, the appropriate hedging instrument would be a series of forward contracts each of which matures on a repricing date that corresponds with the date of the forecast transactions.

It also should be noted that it would be inappropriate to compare only the variable cash flows on the interest rate swap with the interest cash flows in the debt that would be generated by the forward interest rates. That methodology has the effect of measuring ineffectiveness only on a portion of the derivative, and IAS 39 does not permit the bifurcation of a derivative for the purposes of assessing effectiveness in this situation (IAS 39.74). It is recognised, however, that if the fixed interest rate on the interest rate swap is equal to the fixed rate that would have been obtained on the debt at inception, there will be no ineffectiveness assuming that there are no differences in terms and no change in credit risk or it is not designated in the hedging relationship.

F.5.6 Cash flow hedges: firm commitment to purchase inventory in a foreign currency

Entity A has the Local Currency (LC) as its functional currency and presentation currency. On 30 June 20X1, it enters into a forward exchange contract to receive Foreign Currency (FC) 100,000 and deliver LC109,600 on 30 June 20X2 at an initial cost and fair value of zero. It designates the forward exchange contract as a hedging instrument in a cash flow hedge of a firm commitment to purchase a certain quantity of paper on 31 March 20X2 and the resulting payable of FC100,000, which is to be paid on 30 June 20X2. All hedge accounting conditions in IAS 39 are met.

As indicated in the table below, on 30 June 20X1, the spot exchange rate is LC1.072 to FC1, while the twelve-month forward exchange rate is LC1.096 to FC1. On 31 December 20X1, the spot exchange rate is LC1.080 to FC1, while the six-month forward exchange rate is LC1.092 to FC1. On 31 March 20X2, the spot exchange rate is LC1.074 to FC1, while the three-month forward rate is LC1.076 to FC1. On 30 June 20X2, the spot exchange rate is LC1.072 to FC1. The applicable yield curve in the local currency is flat at 6 per cent per year throughout the period. The fair value of the forward exchange contract is negative LC388 on 31 December 20X1 $\{([1.092 \times 100,000] - 109,600)/1.06^{(6/12)}\}$, negative LC1.971 on 31 March 20X2 $\{([1.076 \times 100,000] - 109,600)/1.06^{(3/12)})\}$, and negative LC2,400 on 30 June 20X2 $\{1.072 \times 100,000 - 109,600\}$.

Date	Spot rate	Forward rate to 30 June 20X2	Fair value of forward contract
30 June 20X1	1.072	1.096	–
31 December 20X1	1.080	1.092	(388)
31 March 20X2	1.074	1.076	(1,971)
30 June 20X2	1.072	–	(2,400)

Issue (a) – What is the accounting for these transactions if the hedging relationship is designated as being for changes in the fair value of the forward exchange contract and the entity's accounting policy is to apply basis adjustment to non-financial assets that result from hedged forecast transactions?

The accounting entries are as follows.

30 June 20X1

Dr Forward	LC0	
Cr Cash		LC0

To record the forward exchange contract at its initial amount of zero (IAS 39.43). The hedge is expected to be fully effective because the critical terms of the forward exchange contract and the purchase contract and the assessment of hedge effectiveness are based on the forward price (IAS 39.AG108).

31 December 20X1

Dr	Other comprehensive income	LC388
	Cr Forward liability	LC388

To record the change in the fair value of the forward exchange contract between 30 June 20X1 and 31 December 20X1, ie LC388 – 0 = LC388, in other comprehensive income (IAS 39.95). The hedge is fully effective because the loss on the forward exchange contract (LC388) exactly offsets the change in cash flows associated with the purchase contract based on the forward price $[(LC388) = \{([1.092 \times 100,000] - 109,600)/1.06^{(6/12)}\} - \{([1.096 \times 100,000] - 109,600)/1.06\}]$.

31 March 20X2

Dr	Other comprehensive income	LC1,583
	Cr Forward liability	LC1,583

To record the change in the fair value of the forward exchange contract between 1 January 20X2 and 31 March 20X2 (ie LC1,971 – LC388 = LC1,583) in other comprehensive income (IAS 39.95). The hedge is fully effective because the loss on the forward exchange contract (LC1,583) exactly offsets the change in cash flows associated with the purchase contract based on the forward price $[(LC1,583) = \{([1.076 \times 100,000] - 109,600)/1.06^{(3/12)}\} - \{([1.092 \times 100,000] - 109,600)/1.06^{(6/12)}\}]$.

Dr	Paper (purchase price)	LC107,400
Dr	Paper (hedging loss)	LC1,971
	Cr Other comprehensive income	LC1,971
	Cr Payable	LC107,400

To recognise the purchase of the paper at the spot rate (1.074 × FC100,000) and remove the cumulative loss on the forward exchange contract that has been recognised in other comprehensive income (LC1,971) and include it in the initial measurement of the purchased paper. Accordingly, the initial measurement of the purchased paper is LC109,371 consisting of a purchase consideration of LC107,400 and a hedging loss of LC1,971.

30 June 20X2

Dr	Payable	LC107,400
	Cr Cash	LC107,200
	Cr Profit or loss	LC200

To record the settlement of the payable at the spot rate (FC100,000 × 1.072 = 107,200) and the associated exchange gain of LC200 (LC107,400 − LC107,200).

Dr Profit or loss		LC429
Cr Forward liability		LC429

To record the loss on the forward exchange contract between 1 April 20X2 and 30 June 20X2 (ie LC2,400 − LC1,971 = LC429) in profit or loss. The hedge is regarded as fully effective because the loss on the forward exchange contract (LC429) exactly offsets the change in the fair value of the payable based on the forward price (LC429 = ([1.072 × 100,000] − 109,600 − {([1.076 × 100,000] − 109,600)/1.06$^{(3/12)}$})).

Dr Forward liability		LC2,400
Cr Cash		LC2,400

To record the net settlement of the forward exchange contract.

Issue (b) − What is the accounting for these transactions if the hedging relationship instead is designated as being for changes in the spot element of the forward exchange contract and the interest element is excluded from the designated hedging relationship (IAS 39.74)?

The accounting entries are as follows.

30 June 20X1

Dr Forward		LC0
Cr Cash		LC0

To record the forward exchange contract at its initial amount of zero (IAS 39.43). The hedge is expected to be fully effective because the critical terms of the forward exchange contract and the purchase contract are the same and the change in the premium or discount on the forward contract is excluded from the assessment of effectiveness (IAS 39.AG108).

31 December 20X1

Dr Profit or loss (interest element)		LC1,165
Cr Other comprehensive income (spot element)		LC777
Cr Forward liability		LC388

To record the change in the fair value of the forward exchange contract between 30 June 20X1 and 31 December 20X1, ie LC388 − 0 = LC388. The change in the present value of spot settlement of the forward exchange contract is a gain of LC777 ({([1.080 × 100,000] − 107,200)/1.06$^{(6/12)}$} − {([1.072 × 100,000] − 107,200)/1.06}), which is recognised in other comprehensive income (IAS 39.95(a)). The change in the interest element of the forward exchange contract (the residual change in fair value) is a loss of LC1,165 (388 + 777), which is recognised in profit or loss (IAS 39.74 and IAS 39.55). The hedge is fully effective because the gain in the spot element of the forward contract (LC777) exactly offsets the change in the purchase price at spot rates (LC777 = {([1.080 × 100,000] − 107,200)/1.06$^{(6/12)}$} − {([1.072 × 100,000] − 107,200)/1.06}).

31 March 20X2

Dr	Other comprehensive income (spot element)	LC580
Dr	Profit or loss (interest element)	LC1,003
	Cr Forward liability	LC1,583

To record the change in the fair value of the forward exchange contract between 1 January 20X2 and 31 March 20X2, ie LC1,971 – LC388 = LC1,583. The change in the present value of the spot settlement of the forward exchange contract is a loss of LC580 ({{[1.074 × 100,000] – 107,200}/1.06$^{(3/12)}$} – {([1.080 × 100,000] – 107,200)/1.06$^{(6/12)}$}), which is recognised in other comprehensive income (IAS 39.95(a)). The change in the interest element of the forward exchange contract (the residual change in fair value) is a loss of LC1,003 (LC1,583 – LC580), which is recognised in profit or loss (IAS 39.74 and IAS 39.55). The hedge is fully effective because the loss in the spot element of the forward contract (LC580) exactly offsets the change in the purchase price at spot rates [(580) = {([1.074 × 100,000] – 107,200)/1.06$^{(3/12)}$} – {([1.080 × 100,000] – 107,200) /1.06$^{(6/12)}$}].

Dr	Paper (purchase price)	LC107,400
Dr	Other comprehensive income	LC197
	Cr Paper (hedging gain)	LC197
	Cr Payable	LC107,400

To recognise the purchase of the paper at the spot rate (= 1.074 × FC100,000) and remove the cumulative gain on the spot element of the forward exchange contract that has been recognised in other comprehensive income (LC777 – LC580 = LC197) and include it in the initial measurement of the purchased paper. Accordingly, the initial measurement of the purchased paper is LC107,203, consisting of a purchase consideration of LC107,400 and a hedging gain of LC197.

30 June 20X2

Dr	Payable	LC107,400
	Cr Cash	LC107,200
	Cr Profit or loss	LC200

To record the settlement of the payable at the spot rate (FC100,000 × 1.072 = LC107,200) and the associated exchange gain of LC200 (– [1.072 – 1.074] × FC100,000).

Dr	Profit or loss (spot element)	LC197
Dr	Profit or loss (interest element)	LC232
	Cr Forward liability	LC429

To record the change in the fair value of the forward exchange contract between 1 April 20X2 and 30 June 20X2 (ie LC2,400 – LC1,971 = LC429). The change in the present value of the spot settlement of the forward exchange contract is a loss of LC197 ([1.072 × 100,000] – 107,200 – {([1.074 × 100,000] – 107,200)/1.06$^{(3/12)}$}), which is recognised in profit or loss. The change in the interest element of the forward exchange contract (the residual change in fair value) is a loss of LC232 (LC429 – LC197), which is recognised in profit or loss. The hedge is fully effective because the loss in the spot element of the forward contract (LC197) exactly offsets the change in the present value of the spot settlement of the payable $[(LC197) = \{[1.072 \times 100{,}000] - 107{,}200 - \{([1.074 \times 100{,}000] - 107{,}200)/1.06^{(3/12)}\}]$.

Dr Forward liability	LC2,400
Cr Cash	LC2,400

To record the net settlement of the forward exchange contract.

The following table provides an overview of the components of the change in fair value of the hedging instrument over the term of the hedging relationship. It illustrates that the way in which a hedging relationship is designated affects the subsequent accounting for that hedging relationship, including the assessment of hedge effectiveness and the recognition of gains and losses.

Period ending	Change in spot settlement	Fair value of change in spot settlement	Change in forward settlement	Fair value of change in forward settlement	Fair value of change in interest element
	LC	LC	LC	LC	LC
June 20X1	–	–	–	–	–
December 20X1	800	777	(400)	(388)	(1,165)
March 20X2	(600)	(580)	(1,600)	(1,583)	(1,003)
June 20X2	(200)	(197)	(400)	(429)	(232)
Total	–	–	(2,400)	(2,400)	(2,400)

F.6   Hedges: other issues

F.6.1   Hedge accounting: management of interest rate risk in financial institutions

Banks and other financial institutions often manage their exposure to interest rate risk on a net basis for all or parts of their activities. They have systems to accumulate critical information throughout the entity about their financial assets, financial liabilities and forward commitments, including loan commitments. This information is used to estimate and aggregate cash flows and to schedule such estimated cash flows into the applicable future periods in which they are expected to be paid or received. The systems generate estimates of cash flows based on the contractual terms of the instruments and other factors, including estimates of prepayments and defaults. For risk management purposes, many financial institutions use derivative contracts to offset some or all exposure to interest rate risk on a net basis.

If a financial institution manages interest rate risk on a net basis, can its activities potentially qualify for hedge accounting under IAS 39?

Yes. However, to qualify for hedge accounting the derivative hedging instrument that hedges the net position for risk management purposes must be designated for accounting purposes as a hedge of a gross position related to assets, liabilities, forecast cash inflows or forecast cash outflows giving rise to the net exposure (IAS 39.84, IAS 39.AG101 and IAS 39.AG111). It is not possible to designate a net position as a hedged item under IAS 39 because of the inability to associate hedging gains and losses with a specific item being hedged and, correspondingly, to determine objectively the period in which such gains and losses should be recognised in profit or loss.

Hedging a net exposure to interest rate risk can often be defined and documented to meet the qualifying criteria for hedge accounting in IAS 39.88 if the objective of the activity is to offset a specific, identified and designated risk exposure that ultimately affects the entity's profit or loss (IAS 39.AG110) and the entity designates and documents its interest rate risk exposure on a gross basis. Also, to qualify for hedge accounting the information systems must capture sufficient information about the amount and timing of cash flows and the effectiveness of the risk management activities in accomplishing their objective.

The factors an entity must consider for hedge accounting purposes if it manages interest rate risk on a net basis are discussed in Question F.6.2.

F.6.2 Hedge accounting considerations when interest rate risk is managed on a net basis

If an entity manages its exposure to interest rate risk on a net basis, what are the issues the entity should consider in defining and documenting its interest rate risk management activities to qualify for hedge accounting and in establishing and accounting for the hedge relationship?

Issues (a)–(l) below deal with the main issues. First, Issues (a) and (b) discuss the designation of derivatives used in interest rate risk management activities as fair value hedges or cash flow hedges. As noted there, hedge accounting criteria and accounting consequences differ between fair value hedges and cash flow hedges. Since it may be easier to achieve hedge accounting treatment if derivatives used in interest rate risk management activities are designated as cash flow hedging instruments, Issues (c)–(l) expand on various aspects of the accounting for cash flow hedges. Issues (c)–(f) consider the application of the hedge accounting criteria for cash flow hedges in IAS 39, and Issues (g) and (h) discuss the required accounting treatment. Finally, Issues (i)–(l) elaborate on other specific issues relating to the accounting for cash flow hedges.

Issue (a) – Can a derivative that is used to manage interest rate risk on a net basis be designated under IAS 39 as a hedging instrument in a fair value hedge or a cash flow hedge of a gross exposure?

Both types of designation are possible under IAS 39. An entity may designate the derivative used in interest rate risk management activities either as a fair value hedge of assets, liabilities and firm commitments or as a cash flow hedge of forecast transactions, such as the anticipated reinvestment of cash inflows, the anticipated refinancing or rollover of a financial liability, and the cash flow consequences of the resetting of interest rates for an asset or a liability.

In economic terms, it does not matter whether the derivative instrument is regarded as a fair value hedge or as a cash flow hedge. Under either perspective of the exposure, the derivative has the same economic effect of reducing the net exposure. For example, a receive-fixed, pay-variable interest rate swap can be considered to be a cash flow hedge of a variable rate asset or a fair value hedge of a fixed rate liability. Under either perspective, the fair value or cash flows of the interest rate swap offset the exposure to interest rate changes. However, accounting consequences differ depending on whether the derivative is designated as a fair value hedge or a cash flow hedge, as discussed in Issue (b).

To illustrate: a bank has the following assets and liabilities with a maturity of two years.

	Variable interest	Fixed interest
	CU	CU
Assets	60	100
Liabilities	(100)	(60)
Net	(40)	40

The bank takes out a two-year swap with a notional principal of CU40 to receive a variable interest rate and pay a fixed interest rate to hedge the net exposure. As discussed above, this may be regarded and designated either as a fair value hedge of CU40 of the fixed rate assets or as a cash flow hedge of CU40 of the variable rate liabilities.

Issue (b) – What are the critical considerations in deciding whether a derivative that is used to manage interest rate risk on a net basis should be designated as a hedging instrument in a fair value hedge or a cash flow hedge of a gross exposure?

Critical considerations include the assessment of hedge effectiveness in the presence of prepayment risk and the ability of the information systems to attribute fair value or cash flow changes of hedging instruments to fair value or cash flow changes, respectively, of hedged items, as discussed below.

For accounting purposes, the designation of a derivative as hedging a fair value exposure or a cash flow exposure is important because both the qualification requirements for hedge accounting and the recognition of hedging gains and losses for these categories are different. It is often easier to demonstrate high effectiveness for a cash flow hedge than for a fair value hedge.

Effects of prepayments

Prepayment risk inherent in many financial instruments affects the fair value of an instrument and the timing of its cash flows and impacts on the effectiveness test for fair value hedges and the highly probable test for cash flow hedges, respectively.

Effectiveness is often more difficult to achieve for fair value hedges than for cash flow hedges when the instrument being hedged is subject to prepayment risk. For a fair value hedge to qualify for hedge accounting, the changes in the fair value of the derivative hedging instrument must be expected to be highly effective in offsetting the changes in the fair value of the hedged item (IAS 39.88(b)). This test may be difficult to meet if, for example, the derivative hedging instrument is a forward contract having a fixed term and the financial assets being hedged are subject to prepayment by the borrower. Also, it may be difficult to conclude that, for a portfolio of fixed rate assets that are subject to prepayment, the changes in the fair value for each individual item in the group will be expected to be approximately proportional to the overall changes in fair value attributable to the hedged risk of the group. Even if the risk being hedged is a benchmark interest rate, to be able to conclude that fair value changes will be proportional for each item in the portfolio, it may be necessary to disaggregate the asset portfolio into categories based on term, coupon, credit, type of loan and other characteristics.

In economic terms, a forward derivative instrument could be used to hedge assets that are subject to prepayment but it would be effective only for small movements in interest rates. A reasonable estimate of prepayments can be made for a given interest rate environment and the derivative position can be adjusted as the interest rate environment changes. If an entity's risk management strategy is to adjust the amount of the hedging instrument periodically to reflect changes in the hedged position, the entity needs to demonstrate that the hedge is expected to be highly effective only for the period until the amount of the hedging instrument is next adjusted. However, for that period, the expectation of effectiveness has to be based on existing fair value exposures and the potential for interest rate movements without consideration of future adjustments to those positions. Furthermore, the fair value exposure attributable to prepayment risk can generally be hedged with options.

For a cash flow hedge to qualify for hedge accounting, the forecast cash flows, including the reinvestment of cash inflows or the refinancing of cash outflows, must be highly probable (IAS 39.88(c)) and the hedge expected to be highly effective in achieving offsetting changes in the cash flows of the hedged item and hedging instrument (IAS 39.88(b)). Prepayments affect the timing of cash flows and, therefore, the probability of occurrence of the forecast transaction. If the hedge is established for risk management purposes on a net basis, an entity may have sufficient levels of highly probable cash flows on a gross basis to support the designation for accounting purposes of forecast transactions associated with a portion of the gross cash flows as the hedged item. In this case, the portion of the gross cash flows designated as being hedged may be chosen to be equal to the amount of net cash flows being hedged for risk management purposes.

Systems considerations

The accounting for fair value hedges differs from that for cash flow hedges. It is usually easier to use existing information systems to manage and track cash flow hedges than it is for fair value hedges.

Under fair value hedge accounting, the assets or liabilities that are designated as being hedged are remeasured for those changes in fair values during the hedge period that are attributable to the risk being hedged. Such changes adjust the carrying amount of the hedged items and, for interest sensitive assets and liabilities, may result in an adjustment of the effective interest rate of the hedged item (IAS 39.89). As a consequence of fair value hedging activities, the changes in fair value have to be allocated to the assets or liabilities being hedged in order for the entity to be able to recompute their effective interest rate, determine the subsequent amortisation of the fair value adjustment to profit or loss, and determine the amount that should be reclassified from equity to profit or loss when assets are sold or liabilities extinguished (IAS 39.89 and IAS 39.92). To comply with the requirements for fair value hedge accounting, it will generally be necessary to establish a system to track the changes in the fair value attributable to the hedged risk, associate those changes with individual hedged items, recompute the effective interest rate of the hedged items, and amortise the changes to profit or loss over the life of the respective hedged item.

Under cash flow hedge accounting, the cash flows relating to the forecast transactions that are designated as being hedged reflect changes in interest rates. The adjustment for changes in the fair value of a hedging derivative instrument is initially recognised in other comprehensive income (IAS 39.95). To comply with the requirements for cash flow hedge accounting, it is necessary to determine when the cumulative gains and losses recognised in other comprehensive income from changes in the fair value of a hedging instrument should be reclassified to profit or loss (IAS 39.100 and IAS 39.101). For cash flow hedges, it is not necessary to create a separate system to make this determination. The system used to determine the extent of the net exposure provides the basis for scheduling the changes in the cash flows of the derivative and the recognition of such changes in profit or loss.

The timing of the recognition in profit or loss can be predetermined when the hedge is associated with the exposure to changes in cash flows. The forecast transactions that are being hedged can be associated with a specific principal amount in specific future periods composed of variable rate assets and cash inflows being reinvested or variable rate liabilities and cash outflows being refinanced, each of which creates a cash flow exposure to changes in interest rates. The specific principal amounts in specific future periods are equal to the notional amount of the derivative hedging instruments and are hedged only for the period that corresponds to the repricing or maturity of the derivative hedging instruments so that the cash flow changes resulting from changes in interest rates are matched with the derivative hedging instrument. IAS 39.100 specifies that the amounts recognised in other comprehensive income should be reclassified from equity to profit or loss in the same period or periods during which the hedged item affects profit or loss.

Issue (c) – If a hedging relationship is designated as a cash flow hedge relating to changes in cash flows resulting from interest rate changes, what would be included in the documentation required by IAS 39.88(a)?

The following would be included in the documentation.

The hedging relationship - The maturity schedule of cash flows used for risk management purposes to determine exposures to cash flow mismatches on a net basis would provide part of the documentation of the hedging relationship.

The entity's risk management objective and strategy for undertaking the hedge - The entity's overall risk management objective and strategy for hedging exposures to interest rate risk would provide part of the documentation of the hedging objective and strategy.

The type of hedge - The hedge is documented as a cash flow hedge.

The hedged item - The hedged item is documented as a group of forecast transactions (interest cash flows) that are expected to occur with a high degree of probability in specified future periods, for example, scheduled on a monthly basis. The hedged item may include interest cash flows resulting from the reinvestment of cash inflows, including the resetting of interest rates on assets, or from the refinancing of cash outflows, including the resetting of interest rates on liabilities and rollovers of financial liabilities. As discussed in Issue (e), the forecast transactions meet the probability test if there are sufficient levels of highly probable cash flows in the specified future periods to encompass the amounts designated as being hedged on a gross basis.

The hedged risk - The risk designated as being hedged is documented as a portion of the overall exposure to changes in a specified market interest rate, often the risk-free interest rate or an interbank offered rate, common to all items in the group. To help ensure that the hedge effectiveness test is met at inception of the hedge and subsequently, the designated hedged portion of the interest rate risk could be documented as being based on the same yield curve as the derivative hedging instrument.

The hedging instrument - Each derivative hedging instrument is documented as a hedge of specified amounts in specified future time periods corresponding with the forecast transactions occurring in the specified future time periods designated as being hedged.

The method of assessing effectiveness - The effectiveness test is documented as being measured by comparing the changes in the cash flows of the derivatives allocated to the applicable periods in which they are designated as a hedge to the changes in the cash flows of the forecast transactions being hedged. Measurement of the cash flow changes is based on the applicable yield curves of the derivatives and hedged items.

Issue (d) – If the hedging relationship is designated as a cash flow hedge, how does an entity satisfy the requirement for an expectation of high effectiveness in achieving offsetting changes in IAS 39.88(b)?

An entity may demonstrate an expectation of high effectiveness by preparing an analysis demonstrating high historical and expected future correlation between the interest rate risk designated as being hedged and the interest rate risk of the hedging instrument. Existing documentation of the hedge ratio used in establishing the derivative contracts may also serve to demonstrate an expectation of effectiveness.

Issue (e) – If the hedging relationship is designated as a cash flow hedge, how does an entity demonstrate a high probability of the forecast transactions occurring as required by IAS 39.88(c)?

An entity may do this by preparing a cash flow maturity schedule showing that there exist sufficient aggregate gross levels of expected cash flows, including the effects of the resetting of interest rates for assets or liabilities, to establish that the forecast transactions that are designated as being hedged are highly probable to occur. Such a schedule should be supported by management's stated intentions and past practice of reinvesting cash inflows and refinancing cash outflows.

For example, an entity may forecast aggregate gross cash inflows of CU100 and aggregate gross cash outflows of CU90 in a particular time period in the near future. In this case, it may wish to designate the forecast reinvestment of gross cash inflows of CU10 as the hedged item in the future time period. If more than CU10 of the forecast cash inflows are contractually specified and have low credit risk, the entity has strong evidence to support an assertion that gross cash inflows of CU10 are highly probable to occur and to support the designation of the forecast reinvestment of those cash flows as being hedged for a particular portion of the reinvestment period. A high probability of the forecast transactions occurring may also be demonstrated under other circumstances.

Issue (f) – If the hedging relationship is designated as a cash flow hedge, how does an entity assess and measure effectiveness under IAS 39.88(d) and IAS 39.88(e)?

Effectiveness is required to be measured at a minimum at the time an entity prepares its annual or interim financial reports. However, an entity may wish to measure it more frequently on a specified periodic basis, at the end of each month or other applicable reporting period. It is also measured whenever derivative positions designated as hedging instruments are changed or hedges are terminated to ensure that the recognition in profit or loss of the changes in the fair value amounts on assets and liabilities and the recognition of changes in the fair value of derivative instruments designated as cash flow hedges are appropriate.

Changes in the cash flows of the derivative are computed and allocated to the applicable periods in which the derivative is designated as a hedge and are compared with computations of changes in the cash flows of the forecast transactions. Computations are based on yield curves applicable to the hedged items and the derivative hedging instruments and applicable interest rates for the specified periods being hedged.

The schedule used to determine effectiveness could be maintained and used as the basis for determining the period in which the hedging gains and losses recognised initially in other comprehensive income are reclassified from equity to profit or loss.

Issue (g) – If the hedging relationship is designated as a cash flow hedge, how does an entity account for the hedge?

The hedge is accounted for as a cash flow hedge in accordance with the provisions in IAS 39.95–IAS 39.100, as follows:

(i)   the portion of gains and losses on hedging derivatives determined to result from effective hedges is recognised in other comprehensive income whenever effectiveness is measured; and

(ii)   the ineffective portion of gains and losses resulting from hedging derivatives is recognised in profit or loss.

IAS 39.100 specifies that the amounts recognised in other comprehensive income should be reclassified from equity to profit or loss in the same period or periods during which the hedged item affects profit or loss. Accordingly, when the forecast transactions occur, the amounts previously recognised in other comprehensive income are reclassified from equity to profit or loss. For example, if an interest rate swap is designated as a hedging instrument of a series of forecast cash flows, the changes in the cash flows of the swap are reclassified from equity to profit or loss in the periods when the forecast cash flows and the cash flows of the swap offset each other.

Issue (h) – If the hedging relationship is designated as a cash flow hedge, what is the treatment of any net cumulative gains and losses recognised in other comprehensive income if the hedging instrument is terminated prematurely, the hedge accounting criteria are no longer met, or the hedged forecast transactions are no longer expected to take place?

If the hedging instrument is terminated prematurely or the hedge no longer meets the criteria for qualification for hedge accounting, for example, the forecast transactions are no longer highly probable, the net cumulative gain or loss recognised in other comprehensive income remains in equity until the forecast transaction occurs (IAS 39.101(a) and IAS 39.101(b)). If the hedged forecast transactions are no longer expected to occur, the net cumulative gain or loss is reclassified from equity to profit or loss (IAS 39.101(c)).

Issue (i) – IAS 39.75 states that a hedging relationship may not be designated for only a portion of the time period in which a hedging instrument is outstanding. If the hedging relationship is designated as a cash flow hedge, and the hedge subsequently fails the test for being highly effective, does IAS 39.75 preclude redesignating the hedging instrument?

No. IAS 39.75 indicates that a derivative instrument may not be designated as a hedging instrument for only a portion of its remaining period to maturity. IAS 39.75 does not refer to the derivative instrument's original period to maturity. If there is a hedge effectiveness failure, the ineffective portion of the gain or loss on the derivative instrument is recognised immediately in profit or loss (IAS 39.95(b)) and hedge accounting based on the previous designation of the hedge relationship cannot be continued (IAS 39.101). In this case, the derivative instrument may be redesignated prospectively as a hedging instrument in a new hedging relationship provided this hedging relationship satisfies the necessary conditions. The derivative instrument must be redesignated as a hedge for the entire time period it remains outstanding.

Issue (j) – For cash flow hedges, if a derivative is used to manage a net exposure to interest rate risk and the derivative is designated as a cash flow hedge of forecast interest cash flows or portions of them on a gross basis, does the occurrence of the hedged forecast transaction give rise to an asset or liability that will result in a portion of the hedging gains and losses that were recognised in other comprehensive income remaining in equity?

No. In the hedging relationship described in Issue (c) above, the hedged item is a group of forecast transactions consisting of interest cash flows in specified future periods. The hedged forecast transactions do not result in the recognition of assets or liabilities and the effect of interest rate changes that are designated as being hedged is recognised in profit or loss in the period in which the forecast transactions occur. Although this is not relevant for the types of hedges described here, if instead the derivative is designated as a hedge of a forecast purchase of a financial asset or issue of a financial liability, the associated gains or losses that were recognised in other comprehensive income are reclassified from equity to profit or loss in the same period or periods during which the hedged forecast cash flows affect profit or loss (such as in the periods that interest expenses are recognised). However, if an entity expects at any time that all or a portion of a net loss recognised in other comprehensive income will not be recovered in one or more future periods, it shall reclassify immediately from equity to profit or loss the amount that is not expected to be recovered.

Issue (k) – In the answer to Issue (c) above it was indicated that the designated hedged item is a portion of a cash flow exposure. Does IAS 39 permit a portion of a cash flow exposure to be designated as a hedged item?

Yes. IAS 39 does not specifically address a hedge of a portion of a cash flow exposure for a forecast transaction. However, IAS 39.81 specifies that a financial asset or liability may be a hedged item with respect to the risks associated with only a portion of its cash flows or fair value, if effectiveness can be measured. The ability to hedge a portion of a cash flow exposure resulting from the resetting of interest rates for assets and liabilities suggests that a portion of a cash flow exposure resulting from the forecast reinvestment of cash inflows or the refinancing or rollover of financial liabilities can also be hedged. The basis for qualification as a hedged item of a portion of an exposure is the ability to measure effectiveness. This is further supported by IAS 39.82, which specifies that a non-financial asset or liability can be hedged only in its entirety or for foreign currency risk but not for a portion of other risks because of the difficulty of isolating and measuring the appropriate portion of the cash flows or fair value changes attributable to a specific risk. Accordingly, assuming effectiveness can be measured, a portion of a cash flow exposure of forecast transactions associated with, for example, the resetting of interest rates for a variable rate asset or liability can be designated as a hedged item.

Issue (l) – In the answer to Issue (c) above it was indicated that the hedged item is documented as a group of forecast transactions. Since these transactions will have different terms when they occur, including credit exposures, maturities and option features, how can an entity satisfy the tests in IAS 39.78 and IAS 39.83 requiring the hedged group to have similar risk characteristics?

IAS 39.78 provides for hedging a group of assets, liabilities, firm commitments or forecast transactions with similar risk characteristics. IAS 39.83 provides additional guidance and specifies that portfolio hedging is permitted if two conditions are met, namely: the individual items in the portfolio share the same risk for which they are designated, and the change in the fair value attributable to the hedged risk for each individual item in the group will be expected to be approximately proportional to the overall change in fair value.

When an entity associates a derivative hedging instrument with a gross exposure, the hedged item typically is a group of forecast transactions. For hedges of cash flow exposures relating to a group of forecast transactions, the overall exposure of the forecast transactions and the assets or liabilities that are repriced may have very different risks. The exposure from forecast transactions may differ depending on the terms that are expected as they relate to credit exposures, maturities, options and other features. Although the overall risk exposures may be different for the individual items in the group, a specific risk inherent in each of the items in the group can be designated as being hedged.

The items in the portfolio do not necessarily have to have the same overall exposure to risk, provided they share the same risk for which they are designated as being hedged. A common risk typically shared by a portfolio of financial instruments is exposure to changes in the risk-free or benchmark interest rate or to changes in a specified rate that has a credit exposure equal to the highest credit-rated instrument in the portfolio (ie the instrument with the lowest credit risk). If the instruments that are grouped into a portfolio have different credit exposures, they may be hedged as a group for a portion of the exposure. The risk they have in common that is designated as being hedged is the exposure to interest rate changes from the highest credit rated instrument in the portfolio. This ensures that the change in fair value attributable to the hedged risk for each individual item in the group is expected to be approximately proportional to the overall change in fair value attributable to the hedged risk of the group. It is likely there will be some ineffectiveness if the hedging instrument has a credit quality that is inferior to the credit quality of the highest credit-rated instrument being hedged, since a hedging relationship is designated for a hedging instrument in its entirety (IAS 39.74). For example, if a portfolio of assets consists of assets rated A, BB and B, and the current market interest rates for these assets are LIBOR+20 basis points, LIBOR+40 basis points and LIBOR+60 basis points, respectively, an entity may use a swap that pays fixed interest rate and for which variable interest payments based on LIBOR are made to hedge the exposure to variable interest rates. If LIBOR is designated as the risk being hedged, credit spreads above LIBOR on the hedged items are excluded from the designated hedge relationship and the assessment of hedge effectiveness.

F.6.3 Illustrative example of applying the approach in Question F.6.2

The purpose of this example is to illustrate the process of establishing, monitoring and adjusting hedge positions and of qualifying for cash flow hedge accounting in applying the approach to hedge accounting described in Question F.6.2 when a financial institution manages its interest rate risk on an entity-wide basis. To this end, this example identifies a methodology that allows for the use of hedge accounting and takes advantage of existing risk management systems so as to avoid unnecessary changes to it and to avoid unnecessary bookkeeping and tracking.

The approach illustrated here reflects only one of a number of risk management processes that could be employed and could qualify for hedge accounting. Its use is not intended to suggest that other alternatives could not or should not be used. The approach being illustrated could also be applied in other circumstances (such as for cash flow hedges of commercial entities), for example, hedging the rollover of commercial paper financing.

Identifying, assessing and reducing cash flow exposures

The discussion and illustrations that follow focus on the risk management activities of a financial institution that manages its interest rate risk by analysing expected cash flows in a particular currency on an entity-wide basis. The cash flow analysis forms the basis for identifying the interest rate risk of the entity, entering into hedging transactions to manage the risk, assessing the effectiveness of risk management activities, and qualifying for and applying cash flow hedge accounting.

The illustrations that follow assume that an entity, a financial institution, had the following expected future net cash flows and hedging positions outstanding in a specific currency, consisting of interest rate swaps, at the beginning of Period X0. The cash flows shown are expected to occur at the end of the period and, therefore, create a cash flow interest exposure in the following period as a result of the reinvestment or repricing of the cash inflows or the refinancing or repricing of the cash outflows.

The illustrations assume that the entity has an ongoing interest rate risk management programme. Schedule I shows the expected cash flows and hedging positions that existed at the beginning of Period X0. It is included here to provide a starting point in the analysis. It provides a basis for considering existing hedges in connection with the evaluation that occurs at the beginning of Period X1.

Schedule I End of period: expected cash flows and hedging positions							
Quarterly period	X0	X1	X2	X3	X4	X5	...n
(units)	CU	CU	CU	CU	CU	CU	CU
Expected net cash flows		1,100	1,500	1,200	1,400	1,500	x,xxx
Outstanding interest rate swaps:							
Receive-fixed, pay-variable (notional amounts)	2,000	2,000	2,000	1,200	1,200	1,200	x,xxx
Pay-fixed, receive-variable (notional amounts)	(1,000)	(1,000)	(1,000)	(500)	(500)	(500)	x,xxx
Net exposure after outstanding swaps		100	500	500	700	800	x.xxx

The schedule depicts five quarterly periods. The actual analysis would extend over a period of many years, represented by the notation '...n'. A financial institution that manages its interest rate risk on an entity-wide basis re-evaluates its cash flow exposures periodically. The frequency of the evaluation depends on the entity's risk management policy.

For the purposes of this illustration, the entity is re-evaluating its cash flow exposures at the end of Period X0. The first step in the process is the generation of forecast net cash flow exposures from existing interest-earning assets and interest-bearing liabilities, including the rollover of short-term assets and short-term liabilities. Schedule II below illustrates the forecast of net cash flow exposures. A common technique for assessing exposure to interest rates for risk management purposes is an interest rate sensitivity gap analysis showing the gap between interest rate-sensitive assets and interest rate-sensitive liabilities over different time intervals. Such an analysis could be used as a starting point for identifying cash flow exposures to interest rate risk for hedge accounting purposes.

Schedule II Forecast net cash flow and repricing exposures							
Quarterly period	Notes	X1	X2	X3	X4	X5	...n
(units)		CU	CU	CU	CU	CU	CU
CASH INFLOW AND REPRICING EXPOSURES - from assets							
Principal and interest payments:							
Long-term fixed rate	(1)	2,400	3,000	3,000	1,000	1,200	x,xxx
Short-term (roll over)	(1)(2)	1,575	1,579	1,582	1,586	1,591	x,xxx
Variable rate – principal payments	(1)	2,000	1,000	–	500	500	x,xxx
Variable rate – estimated interest	(2)	125	110	105	114	118	x,xxx
Total expected cash inflows		6,100	5,689	4,687	3,200	3,409	x,xxx
Variable rate asset balances	(3)	8,000	7,000	7,000	6,500	6,000	x,xxx
Cash inflows and repricings	(4)	**14,100**	**12,689**	**11,687**	**9,700**	**9,409**	**x,xxx**
CASH OUTFLOW AND REPRICING EXPOSURES - from liabilities							
Principal and interest payments:							
Long-term fixed rate	(1)	2,100	400	500	500	301	x,xxx
Short-term (roll over)	(1)(2)	735	737	738	740	742	x,xxx
Variable rate – principal payments	(1)	–	–	2,000	–	1,000	x,xxx
Variable rate – estimated interest	(2)	100	110	120	98	109	x,xxx
Total expected cash outflows		2,935	1,247	3,358	1,338	2,152	x,xxx
Variable rate liability balances	(3)	8,000	8,000	6,000	6,000	5,000	x,xxx
Cash outflows and repricings	(4)	**10,935**	**9,247**	**9,358**	**7,338**	**7,152**	**x,xxx**
NET EXPOSURES	(5)	3,165	3,442	2,329	2,362	2,257	x,xxx

1   The cash flows are estimated using contractual terms and assumptions based on management's intentions and market factors. It is assumed that short-term assets and liabilities will continue to be rolled over in succeeding periods. Assumptions about prepayments and defaults and the withdrawal of deposits are based on market and historical data. It is assumed that principal and interest inflows and outflows will be reinvested and refinanced, respectively, at the end of each period at the then current market interest rates and share the benchmark interest rate risk to which they are exposed.

2   Forward interest rates obtained from Schedule VI are used to forecast interest payments on variable rate financial instruments and expected rollovers of short-term assets and liabilities. All forecast cash flows are associated with the specific time periods (3 months, 6 months, 9 months and 12 months) in which they are expected to occur. For completeness, the interest cash flows resulting from reinvestments, refinancings and repricings are included in the schedule and shown gross even though only the net margin may actually be reinvested. Some entities may choose to disregard the forecast interest cash flows for risk management purposes because they may be used to absorb operating costs and any remaining amounts would not be significant enough to affect risk management decisions.

3   The cash flow forecast is adjusted to include the variable rate asset and liability balances in each period in which such variable rate asset and liability balances are repriced. The principal amounts of these assets and liabilities are not actually being paid and, therefore, do not generate a cash flow. However, since interest is computed on the principal amounts for each period based on the then current market interest rate, such principal amounts expose the entity to the same interest rate risk as if they were cash flows being reinvested or refinanced.

4   The forecast cash flow and repricing exposures that are identified in each period represent the principal amounts of cash inflows that will be reinvested or repriced and cash outflows that will be refinanced or repriced at the market interest rates that are in effect when those forecast transactions occur.

5   The net cash flow and repricing exposure is the difference between the cash inflow and repricing exposures from assets and the cash outflow and repricing exposures from liabilities. In the illustration, the entity is exposed to interest rate declines because the exposure from assets exceeds the exposure from liabilities and the excess (ie the net amount) will be reinvested or repriced at the current market rate and there is no offsetting refinancing or repricing of outflows.

Note that some banks regard some portion of their non-interest bearing demand deposits as economically equivalent to long-term debt. However, these deposits do not create a cash flow exposure to interest rates and would therefore be excluded from this analysis for accounting purposes.

Schedule II *Forecast net cash flow and repricing exposures* provides no more than a starting point for assessing cash flow exposure to interest rates and for adjusting hedging positions. The complete analysis includes outstanding hedging positions and is shown in Schedule III *Analysis of expected net exposures and hedging positions*. It compares the forecast net cash flow exposures for each period (developed in Schedule II) with existing hedging positions (obtained from Schedule I), and provides a basis for considering whether adjustment of the hedging relationship should be made.

Schedule III	Analysis of expected net exposures and hedging positions					
Quarterly period	X1	X2	X3	X4	X5	...n
(units)	CU	CU	CU	CU	CU	CU
Net cash flow and repricing exposures (Schedule II)	3,165	3,442	2,329	2,362	2,257	x,xxx
Pre-existing swaps outstanding:						
Receive-fixed, pay-variable (notional amounts)	2,000	2,000	1,200	1,200	1,200	x,xxx
Pay-fixed, receive-variable (notional amounts)	(1,000)	(1,000)	(500)	(500)	(500)	x,xxx
Net exposure after pre-existing swaps	2,165	2,442	1,629	1,662	1,557	x,xxx
Transactions to adjust outstanding hedging positions:						
Receive-fixed, pay variable swap 1 (notional amount, 10-years)	2,000	2,000	2,000	2,000	2,000	x,xxx
Pay-fixed, receive-variable swap 2 (notional amount, 3-years)			(1,000)	(1,000)	(1,000)	x,xxx
Swaps ...X						x,xxx
Unhedged cash flow and repricing exposure	165	442	629	662	557	x,xxx

The notional amounts of the interest rate swaps that are outstanding at the analysis date are included in each of the periods in which the interest rate swaps are outstanding to illustrate the impact of the outstanding interest rate swaps on the identified cash flow exposures. The notional amounts of the outstanding interest rate swaps are included in each period because interest is computed on the notional amounts each period, and the variable rate components of the outstanding swaps are repriced to the current market rate quarterly. The notional amounts create an exposure to interest rates that in part is similar to the principal balances of variable rate assets and variable rate liabilities.

The exposure that remains after considering the existing positions is then evaluated to determine the extent to which adjustments of existing hedging positions are necessary. The bottom portion of Schedule III shows the beginning of Period X1 using interest rate swap transactions to reduce the net exposures further to within the tolerance levels established under the entity's risk management policy.

Note that in the illustration, the cash flow exposure is not entirely eliminated. Many financial institutions do not fully eliminate risk but rather reduce it to within some tolerable limit.

Various types of derivative instruments could be used to manage the cash flow exposure to interest rate risk identified in the schedule of forecast net cash flows (Schedule II). However, for the purpose of the illustration, it is assumed that interest rate swaps are used for all hedging activities. It is also assumed that in periods in which interest rate swaps should be reduced, rather than terminating some of the outstanding interest rate swap positions, a new swap with the opposite return characteristics is added to the portfolio.

In the illustration in Schedule III above, swap 1, a receive-fixed, pay-variable swap, is used to reduce the net exposure in Periods X1 and X2. Since it is a 10-year swap, it also reduces exposures identified in other future periods not shown. However, it has the effect of creating an over-hedged position in Periods X3-X5. Swap 2, a forward starting pay-fixed, receive-variable interest rate swap, is used to reduce the notional amount of the outstanding receive-fixed, pay-variable interest rate swaps in Periods X3-X5 and thereby reduce the over-hedged positions.

It also is noted that in many situations, no adjustment or only a single adjustment of the outstanding hedging position is necessary to bring the exposure to within an acceptable limit. However, when the entity's risk management policy specifies a very low tolerance of risk a greater number of adjustments to the hedging positions over the forecast period would be needed to further reduce any remaining risk.

To the extent that some of the interest rate swaps fully offset other interest rate swaps that have been entered into for hedging purposes, it is not necessary to include them in a designated hedging relationship for hedge accounting purposes. These offsetting positions can be combined, de-designated as hedging instruments, if necessary, and reclassified for accounting purposes from the hedging portfolio to the trading portfolio. This procedure limits the extent to which the gross swaps must continue to be designated and tracked in a hedging relationship for accounting purposes. For the purposes of this illustration it is assumed that CU500 of the pay-fixed, receive-variable interest rate swaps fully offset CU500 of the receive-fixed, pay-variable interest rate swaps at the beginning of Period X1 and for Periods X1-X5, and are de-designated as hedging instruments and reclassified to the trading account.

After reflecting these offsetting positions, the remaining gross interest rate swap positions from Schedule III are shown in Schedule IV as follows.

Schedule IV Interest rate swaps designated as hedges						
Quarterly period	X1	X2	X3	X4	X5	...n
(units)	CU	CU	CU	CU	CU	CU
Receive-fixed, pay-variable (notional amounts)	3,500	3,500	2,700	2,700	2,700	x,xxx
Pay-fixed, receive-variable (notional amounts)	(500)	(500)	(1,000)	(1,000)	(1,000)	x,xxx
Net outstanding swaps positions	3,000	3,000	1,700	1,700	1,700	x,xxx

For the purposes of the illustrations, it is assumed that swap 2, entered into at the beginning of Period X1, only partially offsets another swap being accounted for as a hedge and therefore continues to be designated as a hedging instrument.

Hedge accounting considerations

Illustrating the designation of the hedging relationship

The discussion and illustrations thus far have focused primarily on economic and risk management considerations relating to the identification of risk in future periods and the adjustment of that risk using interest rate swaps. These activities form the basis for designating a hedging relationship for accounting purposes.

The examples in IAS 39 focus primarily on hedging relationships involving a single hedged item and a single hedging instrument, but there is little discussion and guidance on portfolio hedging relationships for cash flow hedges when risk is being managed centrally. In this illustration, the general principles are applied to hedging relationships involving a component of risk in a portfolio having multiple risks from multiple transactions or positions.

Although designation is necessary to achieve hedge accounting, the way in which the designation is described also affects the extent to which the hedging relationship is judged to be effective for accounting purposes and the extent to which the entity's existing system for managing risk will be required to be modified to track hedging activities for accounting purposes. Accordingly, an entity may wish to designate the hedging relationship in a manner that avoids unnecessary systems changes by taking advantage of the information already generated by the risk management system and avoids unnecessary bookkeeping and tracking. In designating hedging relationships, the entity may also consider the extent to which ineffectiveness is expected to be recognised for accounting purposes under alternative designations.

The designation of the hedging relationship needs to specify various matters. These are illustrated and discussed here from the perspective of the hedge of the interest rate risk associated with the cash inflows, but the guidance can also be applied to the hedge of the risk associated with the cash outflows. It is fairly obvious that only a portion of the gross exposures relating to the cash inflows is being hedged by the interest rate swaps. Schedule V *The general hedging relationship* illustrates the designation of the portion of the gross reinvestment risk exposures identified in Schedule II as being hedged by the interest rate swaps.

Schedule V The general hedging relationship						
Quarterly period	X1	X2	X3	X4	X5	...n
(units)	CU	CU	CU	CU	CU	CU
Cash inflow repricing exposure (Schedule II)	14,100	12,689	11,687	9,700	9,409	x,xxx
Receive-fixed, pay-variable swaps (Schedule IV)	3,500	3,500	2,700	2,700	2,700	x,xxx
Hedged exposure percentage	24.8%	27.6%	23.1%	27.8%	28.7%	xx.x%

The hedged exposure percentage is computed as the ratio of the notional amount of the receive-fixed, pay-variable swaps that are outstanding divided by the gross exposure. Note that in Schedule V there are sufficient levels of forecast reinvestments in each period to offset more than the notional amount of the receive-fixed, pay-variable swaps and satisfy the accounting requirement that the forecast transaction is highly probable.

It is not as obvious, however, how the interest rate swaps are specifically related to the cash flow interest risks designated as being hedged and how the interest rate swaps are effective in reducing that risk. The more specific designation is illustrated in Schedule VI *The specific hedging relationship* below. It provides a meaningful way of depicting the more complicated narrative designation of the hedge by focusing on the hedging objective to eliminate the cash flow variability associated with future changes in interest rates and to obtain an interest rate equal to the fixed rate inherent in the term structure of interest rates that exists at the commencement of the hedge.

The expected interest from the reinvestment of the cash inflows and repricings of the assets is computed by multiplying the gross amounts exposed by the forward rate for the period. For example, the gross exposure for Period X2 of CU14,100 is multiplied by the forward rate for Periods X2–X5 of 5.50 per cent, 6.00 per cent, 6.50 per cent and 7.25 per cent, respectively, to compute the expected interest for those quarterly periods based on the current term structure of interest rates. The hedged expected interest is computed by multiplying the expected interest for the applicable three-month period by the hedged exposure percentage.

Schedule VI The specific hedging relationship								
			Term structure of interest rates					
Quarterly period			*X1*	*X2*	*X3*	*X4*	*X5*	*...n*
Spot rates			5.00%	5.25%	5.50%	5.75%	6.05%	x.xx%
Forward rates[a]			5.00%	5.50%	6.00%	6.50%	7.25%	x.xx%
Cash flow exposures and expected interest amounts								
Repricing period	Time to forecast transaction	Gross amounts exposed			Expected interest			
			CU	CU	CU	CU	CU	CU
2	3 months	14,100	→	194	212	229	256	
3	6 months	12,689			190	206	230	xxx
4	9 months	11,687				190	212	xxx
5	12 months	9,700					176	xxx
6	15 months	9,409						xxx
Hedged percentage (Schedule V) in the previous period				24.8%	27.6%	23.1%	27.8%	xx.x%
Hedged expected interest				48	52	44	49	xx

(a) The forward interest rates are computed from the spot interest rates and rounded for the purposes of the presentation. Computations that are based on the forward interest rates are made based on the actual computed forward rate and then rounded for the purposes of the presentation.

It does not matter whether the gross amount exposed is reinvested in long-term fixed rate debt or variable rate debt, or in short-term debt that is rolled over in each subsequent period. The exposure to changes in the forward interest rate is the same. For example, if the CU14,100 is reinvested at a fixed rate at the beginning of Period X2 for six months, it will be reinvested at 5.75 per cent. The expected interest is based on the forward interest rates for Period X2 of 5.50 per cent and for Period X3 of 6.00 per cent, equal to a blended rate of 5.75 per cent $(1.055 \times 1.060)^{0.5}$, which is the Period X2 spot rate for the next six months.

However, only the expected interest from the reinvestment of the cash inflows or repricing of the gross amount for the first three-month period after the forecast transaction occurs is designated as being hedged. The expected interest being hedged is represented by the shaded cells. The exposure for the subsequent periods is not hedged. In the example, the portion of the interest rate exposure being hedged is the forward rate of 5.50 per cent for Period X2. In order to assess hedge effectiveness and compute actual hedge ineffectiveness on an ongoing basis, the entity may use the information on hedged interest cash inflows in Schedule VI and compare it with updated estimates of expected interest cash inflows (for example, in a table that looks like Schedule II). As long as expected interest cash inflows exceed hedged interest cash inflows, the entity may compare the cumulative change in the fair value of the hedged cash inflows with the cumulative change in the fair value of the hedging instrument to compute actual hedge effectiveness. If there are insufficient expected interest cash inflows, there will be ineffectiveness. It is measured by comparing the cumulative change in the fair value of the expected interest cash flows to the extent they are less than the hedged cash flows with the cumulative change in the fair value of the hedging instrument.

Describing the designation of the hedging relationship

As mentioned previously, there are various matters that should be specified in the designation of the hedging relationship that complicate the description of the designation but are necessary to limit ineffectiveness to be recognised for accounting purposes and to avoid unnecessary systems changes and bookkeeping. The example that follows describes the designation more fully and identifies additional aspects of the designation not apparent from the previous illustrations.

Example designation

Hedging objective

The hedging objective is to eliminate the risk of interest rate fluctuations over the hedging period, which is the life of the interest rate swap, and in effect obtain a fixed interest rate during this period that is equal to the fixed interest rate on the interest rate swap.

Type of hedge

Cash flow hedge.

Hedging instrument

The receive-fixed, pay-variable swaps are designated as the hedging instrument. They hedge the cash flow exposure to interest rate risk.

Each repricing of the swap hedges a three-month portion of the interest cash inflows that results from:

- the forecast reinvestment or repricing of the principal amounts shown in Schedule V.

- unrelated investments or repricings that occur after the repricing dates on the swap over its life and involve different borrowers or lenders.

continued...

...continued

Example designation

The hedged item—General

The hedged item is a portion of the gross interest cash inflows that will result from the reinvestment or repricing of the cash flows identified in Schedule V and are expected to occur within the periods shown on such schedule. The portion of the interest cash inflow that is being hedged has three components:

- the principal component giving rise to the interest cash inflow and the period in which it occurs,

- the interest rate component, and

- the time component or period covered by the hedge.

The hedged item—The principal component

The portion of the interest cash inflows being hedged is the amount that results from the first portion of the principal amounts being invested or repriced in each period:

- that is equal to the sum of the notional amounts of the received-fixed, pay-variable interest rate swaps that are designated as hedging instruments and outstanding in the period of the reinvestment or repricing, and

- that corresponds to the first principal amounts of cash flow exposures that are invested or repriced at or after the repricing dates of the interest rate swaps.

The hedged item—The interest rate component

The portion of the interest rate change that is being hedged is the change in both of the following:

- the credit component of the interest rate being paid on the principal amount invested or repriced that is equal to the credit risk inherent in the interest rate swap. It is that portion of the interest rate on the investment that is equal to the interest index of the interest rate swap, such as LIBOR, and

- the yield curve component of the interest rate that is equal to the repricing period on the interest rate swap designated as the hedging instrument.

The hedged item—The hedged period

The period of the exposure to interest rate changes on the portion of the cash flow exposures being hedged is:

- the period from the designation date to the repricing date of the interest rate swap that occurs within the quarterly period in which, but not before, the forecast transactions occur, and

- its effects for the period after the forecast transactions occur equal to the repricing interval of the interest rate swap.

It is important to recognise that the swaps are not hedging the cash flow risk for a single investment over its entire life. The swaps are designated as hedging the cash flow risk from different principal investments and repricings that are made in each repricing period of the swaps over their entire term. The swaps hedge only the interest accruals that occur in the first period following the reinvestment. They are hedging the cash flow impact resulting from a change in interest rates that occurs up to the repricing of the swap. The exposure to changes in rates for the period from the repricing of the swap to the date of the hedged reinvestment of cash inflows or repricing of variable rate assets is not hedged. When the swap is repriced, the interest rate on the swap is fixed until the next repricing date and the accrual of the net swap settlements is determined. Any changes in interest rates after that date that affect the amount of the interest cash inflow are no longer hedged for accounting purposes.

Designation objectives

Systems considerations

Many of the tracking and bookkeeping requirements are eliminated by designating each repricing of an interest rate swap as hedging the cash flow risk from forecast reinvestments of cash inflows and repricings of variable rate assets for only a portion of the lives of the related assets. Much tracking and bookkeeping would be necessary if the swaps were instead designated as hedging the cash flow risk from forecast principal investments and repricings of variable rate assets over the entire lives of these assets.

This type of designation avoids keeping track of gains and losses recognised in other comprehensive income after the forecast transactions occur (IAS 39.97 and IAS 39.98) because the portion of the cash flow risk being hedged is that portion that will be reclassified from equity to profit or loss in the period immediately following the forecast transactions that corresponds with the periodic net cash settlements on the swap. If the hedge were to cover the entire life of the assets being acquired, it would be necessary to associate a specific interest rate swap with the asset being acquired. If a forecast transaction is the acquisition of a fixed rate instrument, the fair value of the swap that hedged that transaction would be reclassified from equity to profit or loss to adjust the interest income on the asset when the interest income is recognised. The swap would then have to be terminated or redesignated in another hedging relationship. If a forecast transaction is the acquisition of a variable rate asset, the swap would continue in the hedging relationship but it would have to be tracked back to the asset acquired so that any fair value amounts on the swap recognised in other comprehensive income could be reclassified from equity to profit or loss upon the subsequent sale of the asset.

It also avoids the necessity of associating with variable rate assets any portion of the fair value of the swaps that is recognised in other comprehensive income. Accordingly, there is no portion of the fair value of the swap that is recognised in other comprehensive income that should be reclassified from equity to profit or loss when a forecast transaction occurs or upon the sale of a variable rate asset.

This type of designation also permits flexibility in deciding how to reinvest cash flows when they occur. Since the hedged risk relates only to a single period that corresponds with the repricing period of the interest rate swap designated as the hedging instrument, it is not necessary to determine at the designation date whether the cash flows will be reinvested in fixed rate or variable rate assets or to specify at the date of designation the life of the asset to be acquired.

Effectiveness considerations

Ineffectiveness is greatly reduced by designating a specific portion of the cash flow exposure as being hedged.

- Ineffectiveness due to credit differences between the interest rate swap and hedged forecast cash flow is eliminated by designating the cash flow risk being hedged as the risk attributable to changes in the interest rates that correspond with the rates inherent in the swap, such as the AA rate curve. This type of designation prevents changes resulting from changes in credit spreads from being considered as ineffectiveness.

- Ineffectiveness due to duration differences between the interest rate swap and hedged forecast cash flow is eliminated by designating the interest rate risk being hedged as the risk relating to changes in the portion of the yield curve that corresponds with the period in which the variable rate leg of the interest rate swap is repriced.

- Ineffectiveness due to interest rate changes that occur between the repricing date of the interest rate swap and the date of the forecast transactions is eliminated by simply not hedging that period of time. The period from the repricing of the swap and the occurrence of the forecast transactions in the period immediately following the repricing of the swap is left unhedged. Therefore, the difference in dates does not result in ineffectiveness.

Accounting considerations

The ability to qualify for hedge accounting using the methodology described here is founded on provisions in IAS 39 and on interpretations of its requirements. Some of those are described in the answer to Question F.6.2 *Hedge accounting considerations when interest rate risk is managed on a net basis*. Some additional and supporting provisions and interpretations are identified below.

Hedging a portion of the risk exposure

The ability to identify and hedge only a portion of the cash flow risk exposure resulting from the reinvestment of cash flows or repricing of variable rate instruments is found in IAS 39.81 as interpreted in the answers to Questions F.6.2 Issue (k) and F.2.17 *Partial term hedging*.

Hedging multiple risks with a single instrument

The ability to designate a single interest rate swap as a hedge of the cash flow exposure to interest rates resulting from various reinvestments of cash inflows or repricings of variable rate assets that occur over the life of the swap is founded on IAS 39.76 as interpreted in the answer to Question F.1.12 *Hedges of more than one type of risk*.

Hedging similar risks in a portfolio

The ability to specify the forecast transaction being hedged as a portion of the cash flow exposure to interest rates for a portion of the duration of the investment that gives rise to the interest payment without specifying at the designation date the expected life of the instrument and whether it pays a fixed or variable rate is founded on the answer to

Question F.6.2 Issue (l), which specifies that the items in the portfolio do not necessarily have to have the same overall exposure to risk, providing they share the same risk for which they are designated as being hedged.

Hedge terminations

The ability to de-designate the forecast transaction (the cash flow exposure on an investment or repricing that will occur after the repricing date of the swap) as being hedged is provided for in IAS 39.101 dealing with hedge terminations. While a portion of the forecast transaction is no longer being hedged, the interest rate swap is not de-designated, and it continues to be a hedging instrument for the remaining transactions in the series that have not occurred. For example, assume that an interest rate swap having a remaining life of one year has been designated as hedging a series of three quarterly reinvestments of cash flows. The next forecast cash flow reinvestment occurs in three months. When the interest rate swap is repriced in three months at the then current variable rate, the fixed rate and the variable rate on the interest rate swap become known and no longer provide hedge protection for the next three months. If the next forecast transaction does not occur until three months and ten days, the ten-day period that remains after the repricing of the interest rate swap is not hedged.

F.6.4 Hedge accounting: premium or discount on forward exchange contract

A forward exchange contract is designated as a hedging instrument, for example, in a hedge of a net investment in a foreign operation. Is it permitted to amortise the discount or premium on the forward exchange contract to profit or loss over the term of the contract?

No. The premium or discount on a forward exchange contract may not be amortised to profit or loss under IAS 39 or IFRS 9. Derivatives are always measured at fair value in the statement of financial position. The gain or loss resulting from a change in the fair value of the forward exchange contract is always recognised in profit or loss unless the forward exchange contract is designated and effective as a hedging instrument in a cash flow hedge or in a hedge of a net investment in a foreign operation, in which case the effective portion of the gain or loss is recognised in other comprehensive income. In that case, the amounts recognised in other comprehensive income are reclassified from equity to profit or loss when the hedged future cash flows occur or on the disposal of the net investment, as appropriate. Under IAS 39.74(b), the interest element (time value) of the fair value of a forward may be excluded from the designated hedge relationship. In that case, changes in the interest element portion of the fair value of the forward exchange contract are recognised in profit or loss.

F.6.5 IAS 39 and IAS 21 Fair value hedge of asset measured at cost

If the future sale of a ship carried at historical cost is hedged against the exposure to currency risk by foreign currency borrowing, does IAS 39 require the ship to be remeasured for changes in the exchange rate even though the basis of measurement for the asset is historical cost?

No. In a fair value hedge, the hedged item is remeasured. However, a foreign currency borrowing cannot be classified as a fair value hedge of a ship since a ship does not contain any separately measurable foreign currency risk. If the hedge accounting conditions in IAS 39.88 are met, the foreign currency borrowing may be classified as a cash flow hedge of an anticipated sale in that foreign currency. In a cash flow hedge, the hedged item is not remeasured.

To illustrate: a shipping entity in Denmark has a US subsidiary that has the same functional currency (the Danish krone). The shipping entity measures its ships at historical cost less depreciation in the consolidated financial statements. In accordance with IAS 21.23(b), the ships are recognised in Danish krone using the historical exchange rate. To hedge, fully or partly, the potential currency risk on the ships at disposal in US dollars, the shipping entity normally finances its purchases of ships with loans denominated in US dollars.

In this case, a US dollar borrowing (or a portion of it) may be designated as a cash flow hedge of the anticipated sale of the ship financed by the borrowing provided the sale is highly probable, for example, because it is expected to occur in the immediate future, and the amount of the sales proceeds designated as being hedged is equal to the amount of the foreign currency borrowing designated as the hedging instrument. The gains and losses on the currency borrowing that are determined to constitute an effective hedge of the anticipated sale are recognised in other comprehensive income in accordance with IAS 39.95(a).

Section G Other

G.1 Disclosure of changes in fair value

IAS 39 and IFRS 9 require remeasurement of financial assets and financial liabilities measured at fair value. Unless a financial asset or a financial liability is designated as a cash flow hedging instrument, fair value changes for financial assets and financial liabilities at fair value through profit or loss are recognised in profit or loss, and fair value changes for financial assets designated at fair value through other comprehensive income are recognised in other comprehensive income. What disclosures are required regarding the amounts of the fair value changes during a reporting period?

IFRS 7.20 requires items of income, expense and gains and losses to be disclosed. This disclosure requirement encompasses items of income, expense and gains and losses that arise on remeasurement to fair value. Therefore, an entity provides disclosures of fair value changes, distinguishing between changes that are recognised in profit or loss and changes that are recognised in other comprehensive income. Further breakdown is provided of changes that relate to:

(a)   financial assets or financial liabilities at fair value through profit or loss, showing separately those fair value changes on financial assets or financial liabilities (i) designated as such upon initial recognition and (ii) mandatorily classified as such in accordance with IFRS 9; and

(b)   hedging instruments.

In addition, IFRS 7.20A requires an entity to disclose the amount of gain or loss recognised in other comprehensive income for financial assets measured at fair value through other comprehensive income, including any amount transferred within equity.

IFRS 7 neither requires nor prohibits disclosure of components of the change in fair value by the way items are classified for internal purposes. For example, an entity may choose to disclose separately the change in fair value of those derivatives that meet the definition of held for trading in IAS 39, but the entity classifies as part of risk management activities outside the trading portfolio.

In addition, IFRS 7.8 requires disclosure of the carrying amounts of financial assets or financial liabilities at fair value through profit or loss, showing separately: (i) those designated as such upon initial recognition and (ii) those mandatorily classified as such in accordance with IAS 39 and IFRS 9.

G.2 IAS 39 and IAS 7 Hedge accounting: statements of cash flows

How should cash flows arising from hedging instruments be classified in statements of cash flows?

Cash flows arising from hedging instruments are classified as operating, investing or financing activities, on the basis of the classification of the cash flows arising from the hedged item. While the terminology in IAS 7 has not been updated to reflect IAS 39, the classification of cash flows arising from hedging instruments in the statement of cash flows should be consistent with the classification of these instruments as hedging instruments under IAS 39.

IASB documents published to accompany

International Accounting Standard 40

Investment Property

This version includes amendments resulting from IFRSs issued up to 31 December 2009.

The text of the unaccompanied IAS 40 is contained in Part A of this edition. Its effective date when issued was 1 January 2005. The latest amendments refer to IFRS 9 *Financial Instruments*, which has an effective date of 1 January 2013. This part presents the following accompanying documents:

Approval by the Board of IAS 40 issued in December 2003

International Accounting Standard 40 *Investment Property* (as revised in 2003) was approved for issue by the fourteen members of the International Accounting Standards Board.

Sir David Tweedie	Chairman
Thomas E Jones	Vice-Chairman
Mary E Barth	
Hans-Georg Bruns	
Anthony T Cope	
Robert P Garnett	
Gilbert Gélard	
James J Leisenring	
Warren J McGregor	
Patricia L O'Malley	
Harry K Schmid	
John T Smith	
Geoffrey Whittington	
Tatsumi Yamada	

Basis for Conclusions on
IAS 40 *Investment Property*

This Basis for Conclusions accompanies, but is not part of, IAS 40.

Introduction

BC1   This Basis for Conclusions summarises the International Accounting Standards Board's considerations in reaching its conclusions on revising IAS 40 *Investment Property* in 2003. Individual Board members gave greater weight to some factors than to others.

BC2   In July 2001 the Board announced that, as part of its initial agenda of technical projects, it would undertake a project to improve a number of Standards, including IAS 40. The project was undertaken in the light of queries and criticisms raised in relation to the Standards by securities regulators, professional accountants and other interested parties. The objectives of the Improvements project were to reduce or eliminate alternatives, redundancies and conflicts within Standards, to deal with some convergence issues and to make other improvements. In May 2002 the Board published its proposals in an Exposure Draft of *Improvements to International Accounting Standards*, with a comment deadline of 16 September 2002. The Board received over 160 comment letters on the Exposure Draft.

BC3   Because the Board's intention was not to reconsider the fundamental approach to the accounting for investment property established by IAS 40, this Basis for Conclusions does not discuss requirements in IAS 40 that the Board has not reconsidered. The IASC Basis for Conclusions on IAS 40 (2000) follows this Basis.

Scope

Property interests held under an operating lease

BC4   Paragraph 14 of IAS 17 *Leases* requires a lease of land with an indefinite economic life to be classified as an operating lease, unless title is expected to pass to the lessee by the end of the lease term. Without the provisions of IAS 40 as amended, this operating lease classification would prevent a lessee from classifying its interest in the leased asset as an investment property in accordance with IAS 40. As a result, the lessee could not remeasure its interest in the leased asset to fair value and recognise any change in fair value in profit or loss. However, in some countries, interests in property (including land) are commonly—or exclusively—held under long-term operating leases. The effect of some of these leases differs little from buying a property outright. As a result, some contended that such leases should be accounted for as finance leases or investment property, or as both.

BC5   The Board discussed possible solutions to this issue. In particular, it considered deleting paragraph 14 of IAS 17, so that a long-term lease of land would be classified as a finance lease (and hence could qualify as an investment property) when the conditions for finance lease classification in paragraphs 4–13 of

IAS 17 are met. However, the Board noted that this would not resolve all cases encountered in practice. Some leasehold interests held for investment would remain classified as operating leases (eg leases with significant contingent rents), and hence could not be investment property in accordance with IAS 40.

BC6 In the light of this, the Board decided to state separately in paragraph 6 (rather than amend IAS 40's definition of investment property) that a lessee's interest in property that arises under an operating lease could qualify as investment property. The Board decided to limit this amendment to entities that use the fair value model in IAS 40, because the objective of the amendment is to permit use of the fair value model for similar property interests held under finance and operating leases. Put another way, a lessee that uses the cost model for a property would not be permitted to recognise operating leases as assets. The Board also decided to make the change optional, ie a lessee that has an interest in property under an operating lease is allowed, but not required, to classify that property interest as investment property (provided the rest of the definition of investment property is met). The Board confirmed that this classification alternative is available on a property-by-property basis.

BC7 When a lessee's interest in property held under an operating lease is accounted for as an investment property, the Board decided that the initial carrying amounts of that interest and the related liability are to be accounted for as if the lease were a finance lease. This decision places such leases in the same position as investment properties held under finance leases in accordance with the previous version of IAS 40.

BC8 In doing so, the Board acknowledged that this results in different measurement bases for the lease asset and the lease liability. This is also true for owned investment properties and debt that finances them. However, in accordance with IAS 39 *Financial Instruments: Recognition and Measurement,*[*] as revised in 2003, an entity can elect to measure such debt at fair value, but lease liabilities cannot be remeasured in accordance with IAS 17.

BC9 The Board considered changing the scope of IAS 39,[*] but concluded that this would lead to a fundamental review of lease accounting, especially in relation to contingent rentals. The Board decided that this was beyond the limited revisions to IAS 40 to facilitate application of the fair value model to some operating leases classified as investment properties. The Board did, however, indicate that it wished to revisit this issue in a later project on lease accounting. The Board also noted that this was the view of the Board of the former IASC as expressed in its Basis for Conclusions, in paragraphs B25 and B26.[†]

BC10 Finally, the Board noted that the methodology described in paragraphs 40 and 50(d) of IAS 40, whereby a fair valuation of the property that takes all lease obligations into account is adjusted by adding back any liability that is recognised

---

[*] In November 2009 the Board amended the requirements of IAS 39 relating to classification and measurement of assets within the scope of IAS 39 and relocated them to IFRS 9 *Financial Instruments.* IFRS 9 applies to all assets within the scope of IAS 39.

[†] These paragraphs in the IASC Basis are no longer relevant and have been deleted.

for these obligations, would, in practice, enable entities to ensure that net assets in respect of the leased interest are not affected by the use of different measurement bases.*

The choice between the cost model and the fair value model

BC11   The Board also discussed whether to remove the choice in IAS 40 of accounting for investment property using a fair value model or a cost model.

BC12   The Board noted that IASC had included a choice for two main reasons. The first was to give preparers and users time to gain experience with using a fair value model. The second was to allow time for countries with less-developed property markets and valuation professions to mature. The Board decided that more time is needed for these events to take place (IAS 40 became mandatory only for periods beginning on or after 1 January 2001). The Board also noted that requiring the fair value model would not converge with the treatment required by most of its liaison standard-setters. For these reasons, the Board decided not to eliminate the choice as part of the Improvements project, but rather to keep the matter under review with a view to reconsidering the option to use the cost model at a later date.

BC13   The Board did not reconsider IAS 40 in relation to the accounting by lessors. The definition of investment property requires that such a property is held by the owner or a lessee under a finance lease. As indicated above, the Board agreed to allow a lessee under an operating lease, in specified circumstances, also to be a 'holder'. However, a lessor that has provided a property to a lessee under a finance lease cannot be a 'holder'. Such a lessor has a lease receivable, not an investment property.

BC14   The Board did not change the requirements for a lessor that leases property under an operating lease that is classified and accounted for by the lessee as investment property. The Board acknowledged that this would mean that two parties could both account as if they 'hold' interests in the property. This could occur at various levels of lessees who become lessors in a manner consistent with the definition of an investment property and the election provided for operating leases. Lessees who use the property in the production or supply of goods or services or for administrative purposes would not be able to classify that property as an investment property.

Scope

Investment property under construction

BC15   In response to requests for guidance, the Board revisited the exclusion of investment property under construction from the scope of IAS 40. The Board noted that investment property being redeveloped remained in the scope of the

---

*   Subsequently, the Board concluded that the drafting of paragraph 50(d) was misleading because it implied that the fair value of an investment property asset held under a lease was equal to the net fair value plus the carrying amount of any recognised lease liability. Therefore, in *Improvements to IFRSs* issued in May 2008 the Board amended paragraph 50(d) to clarify the intended meaning.

Standard and that the exclusion of investment property under construction gave rise to a perceived inconsistency. In addition, the Board concluded that with increasing experience with the use of fair value measures since the Standard was issued, entities were more able to measure reliably the fair value of investment property under construction. Therefore, in the exposure draft of proposed *Improvements to International Financial Reporting Standards* published in 2007 the Board proposed amending the scope of the Standard to include investment property under construction.

BC16 Many respondents supported the Board's proposal. However, many expressed concern that including in IAS 40 investment property under construction might result in fewer entities measuring investment property at fair value. This was because the fair value model in the Standard requires an entity to establish whether fair value can be determined reliably when a property first becomes an investment property. If not, the property is accounted for using the cost model until it is disposed of. In some situations, the fair value of investment property under construction cannot be measured reliably but the fair value of the completed investment property can. In these cases, including in the Standard investment property under construction would have required the properties to be accounted for using the cost model even after construction had been completed.

BC17 Therefore, the Board concluded that, in addition to including investment property under construction within the scope of the Standard, it would also amend the Standard to allow investment property under construction to be measured at cost if fair value cannot be measured reliably until such time as the fair value becomes reliably measurable or construction is completed (whichever comes earlier).

CONTENTS

Basis for Conclusions on
IAS 40 (2000) *Investment Property*

This Basis for Conclusions accompanies, but is not part of, IAS 40. It was issued by the Board of the former International Accounting Standards Committee (IASC) in 2000. Apart from the deletion of paragraphs B10–B20, B25 and B26, this Basis has not been revised by the IASB—those paragraphs are no longer relevant and have been deleted to avoid the risk that they might be read out of context. However, cross-references to paragraphs in IAS 40 as issued in 2000 have been marked to show the corresponding paragraphs in IAS 40 as revised by the IASB in 2003 (superseded references are struck through and new references are underlined). Paragraphs are treated as corresponding if they broadly address the same matter even though the guidance may differ. In addition, the text has been annotated where references to material in other standards are no longer valid, following the revision of those standards. Reference should be made to the IASB's Basis for Conclusions on the amendments made in 2003.

Background

B1   The IASC Board (the "Board") approved IAS 25 *Accounting for Investments* in 1986. In 1994, the Board approved a reformatted version of IAS 25 presented in the revised format adopted for International Accounting Standards from 1991. Certain terminology was also changed at that time to bring it into line with then current IASC practice. No substantive changes were made to the original approved text.

B2   IAS 25 was one of the standards that the Board identified for possible revision in E32 *Comparability of Financial Statements*. Following comments on the proposals in E32, the Board decided to defer consideration of IAS 25, pending further work on Financial Instruments. In 1998, the Board approved IAS 38 *Intangible Assets* and IAS 39 *Financial Instruments: Recognition and Measurement*, leaving IAS 25 to cover investments in real estate, commodities and tangible assets such as vintage cars and other collectors' items.

B3   In July 1999, the Board approved E64 *Investment Property*, with a comment deadline of 31 October 1999. The Board received 121 comment letters on E64. Comment letters came from various international organisations, as well as from 28 individual countries. The Board approved IAS 40 *Investment Property* in March 2000. Paragraph B67 below summarises the changes that the Board made to E64 in finalising IAS 40.

B4   IAS 40 permits entities to choose between a fair value model and a cost model. As explained in paragraphs B47–B48 below, the Board believes that it is impracticable, at this stage, to require a fair value model for all investment property. At the same time, the Board believes that it is desirable to permit a fair value model. This evolutionary step forward will allow preparers and users to gain greater experience working with a fair value model and will allow time for certain property markets to achieve greater maturity.

Need for a Separate Standard

B5   Some commentators argued that investment property should fall within the scope of IAS 16 *Property, Plant and Equipment*, and that there is no reason to have a separate standard on investment property. They believe that:

(a) it is not possible to distinguish investment property rigorously from owner-occupied property covered by IAS 16 and without reference to management intent. Thus, a distinction between investment property and owner-occupied property will lead to a free choice of different accounting treatments in some cases; and

(b) the fair value accounting model proposed in E64 is not appropriate, on the grounds that fair value is not relevant and, in some cases, not reliable in the case of investment property. The accounting treatments in IAS 16 are appropriate not only for owner-occupied property, but also for investment property.

B6 Having reviewed the comment letters, the Board still believes that the characteristics of investment property differ sufficiently from the characteristics of owner-occupied property that there is a need for a separate Standard on investment property. In particular, the Board believes that information about the fair value of investment property, and about changes in its fair value, is highly relevant to users of financial statements. The Board believes that it is important to permit a fair value model for investment property, so that entities can report fair value information prominently. The Board tried to maintain consistency with IAS 16, except for differences dictated by the choice of a different accounting model.

Scope

Investment Property Entities

B7 Some commentators argued that the Standard should cover only investment property held by entities that specialise in owning such property (and, perhaps, also other investments) and not cover investment property held by other entities. The Board rejected this view because the Board could find no conceptual and practical way to distinguish rigorously any class of entities for which the fair value model would be less or more appropriate.

Investment Property Reportable Segments

B8 Some commentators suggested that the Board should limit the scope of the Standard to entities that have a reportable segment whose main activity is investment property. These commentators argued that an approach linked to reportable segments would require an entity to adopt the fair value model when the entity considers investment property activities to be an important element of its financial performance and would allow an entity to adopt IAS 16 in other cases.

B9 An approach linked to reportable segments would lead to lack of comparability between investment property held in investment property segments and investment property held in other segments. For this reason, the Board rejected such an approach.

B10–B20 [Deleted]

Property Occupied by Another Entity in the Same Group

B21　In some cases, an entity owns property that is leased to, and occupied by, another entity in the same group. The property does not qualify as investment property in consolidated financial statements that include both entities, because the property is owner-occupied from the perspective of the group as a whole. However, from the perspective of the individual entity that owns it, the property is investment property if it meets the definition set out in the Standard.

B22　Some commentators believe that the definition of investment property should exclude properties that are occupied by another entity in the same group. Alternatively, they suggest that the Standard should not require investment property accounting in individual financial statements for properties that do not qualify as investment property in consolidated financial statements. They believe that:

(a)　it could be argued (at least in some such cases) that the property does not meet the definition of investment property from the perspective of a subsidiary whose property is occupied by another entity in the same group—the subsidiary's motive for holding the property is to comply with a directive from its parent and not necessarily to earn rentals or to benefit from capital appreciation. Indeed, the intragroup lease may not be priced on an arm's length basis;

(b)　this requirement would lead to additional valuation costs that would not be justified by the limited benefits to users. For groups with subsidiaries that are required to prepare individual financial statements, the cost could be extensive as entities may create a separate subsidiary to hold each property;

(c)　some users may be confused if the same property is classified as investment property in the individual financial statements of a subsidiary and as owner-occupied property in the consolidated financial statements of the parent; and

(d)　there is a precedent for a similar exemption (relating to disclosure, rather than measurement) in paragraph 4(c) of IAS 24 *Related Party Disclosures*, which does not require disclosures in a wholly-owned subsidiary's financial statements if its parent is incorporated in the same country and provides consolidated financial statements in that country.*

B23　Some commentators believe that the definition of investment property should exclude property occupied by any related party. They argue that related parties often do not pay rent on an arm's length basis, that it is often difficult to establish whether the rent is consistent with pricing on an arm's length basis and that rental rates may be subject to arbitrary change. They suggest that fair values are less relevant where property is subject to leases that are not priced on an arm's length basis.

---

*　IAS 24 *Related Party Disclosures* as revised by the IASB in 2003 no longer provides the exemption mentioned in paragraph B22(d).

B24   The Board could find no justification for treating property leased to another entity in the same group (or to another related party) differently from property leased to other parties. Therefore, the Board decided that an entity should use the same accounting treatment, regardless of the identity of the lessee.

B25–B26 [Deleted]

Government Grants

B27   IAS 20 *Accounting for Government Grants and Disclosure of Government Assistance* permits two methods of presenting grants relating to assets—either setting up a grant as deferred income and amortising the income over the useful life of the asset or deducting the grant in arriving at the carrying amount of the asset. Some believe that both of those methods reflect a historical cost model and are inconsistent with the fair value model set out in this Standard. Indeed, Exposure Draft E65 *Agriculture*, which proposes a fair value model for biological assets, addresses certain aspects of government grants, as these are a significant factor in accounting for agriculture in some countries.

B28   Some commentators urged IASC to change the accounting treatment of government grants related to investment property. However, most commentators agreed that IASC should not deal with this aspect of government grants now. The Board decided not to revise this aspect of IAS 20 in the project on Investment Property.

B29   Some commentators suggested that IASC should begin a wider review of IAS 20 as a matter of urgency. In early 2000, the G4+1 group of standard setters published a Discussion Paper *Accounting by Recipients for Non-Reciprocal Transfers, Excluding Contributions by Owners: Their Definition, Recognition and Measurement*. The Board's work plan does not currently include a project on the accounting for government grants or other forms of non-reciprocal transfer.

Definition of Investment Property

B30   The definition of investment property excludes:

(a)   owner-occupied property—covered by IAS 16 *Property, Plant and Equipment*. Under IAS 16, such property is carried at either depreciated cost or revalued amount less subsequent depreciation. In addition, such property is subject to an impairment test; and

(b)   property held for sale in the ordinary course of business—covered by IAS 2 *Inventories*. IAS 2 requires an entity to carry such property at the lower of cost and net realisable value.

B31   These exclusions are consistent with the existing definitions of property, plant and equipment in IAS 16 and inventories in IAS 2. This ensures that all property is covered by one, and only one, of the three Standards.

B32   Some commentators suggested that property held for sale in the ordinary course of business should be treated as investment property rather than as inventories (covered by IAS 2). They argued that:

(a) it is difficult to distinguish property held for sale in the ordinary course of business from property held for capital appreciation; and

(b) it is illogical to require a fair value model for land and buildings held for long-term capital appreciation (investment property) when a cost model is still used for land and buildings held for short-term sale in the ordinary course of business (inventories).

B33 The Board rejected this suggestion because:

(a) if fair value accounting is used for property held for sale in the ordinary course of business, this would raise wider questions about inventory accounting that go beyond the scope of this project; and

(b) it is arguably more important to use fair value accounting for property that may have been acquired over a long period and held for several years (investment property) than for property that was acquired over a shorter period and held for a relatively short time (inventories). With the passage of time, cost-based measurements become increasingly irrelevant. Also, an aggregation of costs incurred over a long period is of questionable relevance.

B34 Some commentators suggested requiring (or at least permitting) entities, particularly financial institutions such as insurance companies, to use the fair value model for their owner-occupied property. They argued that some financial institutions regard their owner-occupied property as an integral part of their investment portfolio and treat it for management purposes in the same way as property leased to others. In the case of insurance companies, the property may be held to back policyholder liabilities. The Board believes that property used for similar purposes should be subject to the same accounting treatment. Accordingly, the Board concluded that no class of entities should use the fair value model for their owner-occupied property.

B35 Some commentators suggested that the definition of investment property should exclude property held for rentals, but not for capital appreciation. In their view, a fair value model may be appropriate for dealing activities, but is inappropriate where an entity has historically held rental property for many years and has no intention of selling it in the foreseeable future. They consider that holding property for long-term rental is a service activity and the assets used in that activity should be treated in the same way as assets used to support other service activities. In their view, holding an investment in property in such cases is similar to holding "held-to-maturity investments", which are measured at amortised cost under IAS 39.[*]

B36 In the Board's view, the fair value model provides useful information about property held for rental, even if there is no immediate intention to sell the property. The economic performance of a property can be regarded as being made up of both rental income earned during the period (net of expenses) and changes in the value of future net rental income. The fair value of an investment property can be regarded as a market-based representation of the value of the future net rental income, regardless of whether the entity is likely to sell the property in the

---

[*] IFRS 9 *Financial Instruments*, issued in November 2009, eliminated the held-to-maturity category.

© IASCF

near future. Also, the Standard notes that fair value is determined without deducting costs of disposal—in other words, the use of the fair value model is not intended as a representation that a sale could, or should, be made in the near future.

B37　The classification of hotels and similar property was controversial throughout the project and commentators on E64 had mixed views on this subject. Some see hotels essentially as investments, while others see them essentially as operating properties. Some requested a detailed rule to specify whether hotels (and, perhaps, other categories of property, such as restaurants, bars and nursing homes) should be classified as investment property or as owner-occupied property.

B38　The Board concluded that it is preferable to distinguish investment property from owner-occupied property on the basis of general principles, rather than have arbitrary rules for specific classes of property. Also, it would inevitably be difficult to establish rigorous definitions of specific classes of property to be covered by such rules. Paragraphs 9–11 11–13 of the Standard discuss cases such as hotels in the context of the general principles that apply when an entity provides ancillary services.

B39　Some commentators requested quantitative guidance (such as a percentage) to clarify whether an "insignificant portion" is owner-occupied (paragraph 8 10) and whether ancillary services are "significant" (paragraphs 9–11 11–13 of the Standard). As for similar cases in other Standards, the Board concluded that quantitative guidance would create arbitrary distinctions.

Subsequent Expenditure

B40　Some believe that there is no need to capitalise subsequent expenditure in a fair value model and that all subsequent expenditure should be recognised as an expense. However, others believe—and the Board agreed—that the failure to capitalise subsequent expenditure would lead to a distortion of the reported components of financial performance. Therefore, the Standard requires that an entity should determine whether subsequent expenditure should be capitalised using a test similar to the test used for owner-occupied property in IAS 16.

B41　Some commentators suggested that the test for capitalising subsequent expenditure should not refer to the originally assessed standard of performance. They felt that it is impractical and irrelevant to judge against the originally assessed standard of performance, which may relate to many years in the past. Instead, they suggested that subsequent expenditure should be capitalised if it enhances the previously assessed standard of performance—for example, if it increases the current market value of the property or is intended to maintain its competitiveness in the market. The Board saw some merit in this suggestion.

B42　Nevertheless, the Board believes that a reference to the previously assessed standard of performance would require substantial additional guidance, might not change the way the Standard is applied in practice and might cause confusion. The Board also concluded that it was important to retain the existing reference to the originally assessed standard of performance[*] to be consistent with IAS 16 and IAS 38.

Subsequent Measurement

Accounting Model

B43   Under IAS 25, an entity was permitted to choose from among a variety of accounting treatments for investment property (depreciated cost under the benchmark treatment in IAS 16 *Property, Plant and Equipment*, revaluation with depreciation under the allowed alternative treatment in IAS 16, cost less impairment under IAS 25 or revaluation under IAS 25).[†]

B44   E64 proposed that all investment property should be measured at fair value. Supporters of the fair value model believe that fair values give users of financial statements more useful information than other measures, such as depreciated cost. In their view, rental income and changes in fair value are inextricably linked as integral components of the financial performance of an investment property and measurement at fair value is necessary if that financial performance is to be reported in a meaningful way.

B45   Supporters of the fair value model also note that an investment property generates cash flows largely independently of the other assets held by an entity. In their view, the generation of independent cash flows through rental or capital appreciation distinguishes investment property from owner-occupied property. The production or supply of goods or services (or the use of property for administrative purposes) generates cash flows that are attributable not merely to property, but also to other assets used in the production or supply process. Proponents of the fair value model for investment property argue that this distinction makes a fair value model more appropriate for investment property than for owner-occupied property.

B46   Those who oppose measurement of investment property at fair value argue that:

(a)   there is often no active market for investment property (unlike for many financial instruments). Real estate transactions are not frequent and not homogeneous. Each investment property is unique and each sale is subject to significant negotiations. As a result, fair value measurement will not enhance comparability because fair values are not determinable on a reliable basis, especially in countries where the valuation profession is less well established. A depreciated cost measurement provides a more consistent, less volatile, and less subjective measurement;

---

[*]   IAS 16 *Property, Plant and Equipment* as revised by the IASB in 2003 requires all subsequent costs to be covered by its general recognition principle and eliminated the requirement to reference the originally assessed standard of performance. IAS 40 was amended as a consequence of the change to IAS 16.

[†]   IAS 16 *Property, Plant and Equipment* as revised by the IASB in 2003 eliminated all references to 'benchmark' treatment and 'allowed alternative' treatments. They are replaced with cost model and revaluation model.

(b)   IAS 39 does not require fair value measurement for all financial assets, even some that are realised more easily than investment property. It would be premature to consider extending the fair value model until the Joint Working Group on financial instruments has completed its work;

(c)   a cost basis is used for "shorter term" assets (such as inventories) for which fair value is, arguably, more relevant than for "held for investment" assets; and

(d)   measurement at fair value is too costly in relation to the benefits to users.

B47   This is the first time that the Board has proposed requiring a fair value accounting model for non-financial assets. The comment letters on E64 showed that although many support this step, many others still have significant conceptual and practical reservations about extending a fair value model to non-financial assets, particularly (but not exclusively) for entities whose main activity is not to hold property for capital appreciation. Also, some entities feel that certain property markets are not yet sufficiently mature for a fair value model to work satisfactorily. Furthermore, some believe that it is impossible to create a rigorous definition of investment property and that this makes it impracticable to require a fair value model at present.

B48   For those reasons, the Board believes that it is impracticable, at this stage, to require a fair value model for investment property. At the same time, the Board believes that it is desirable to permit a fair value model. This evolutionary step forward will allow preparers and users to gain greater experience working with a fair value model and will allow time for certain property markets to achieve greater maturity.

B49   IAS 40 permits entities to choose between a fair value model and a cost model. An entity should apply the model chosen to all its investment property. [This choice is not available to a lessee accounting for an investment property under an operating lease as if it were a finance lease—refer to the IASB's Basis for Conclusions on the amendments made in 2003.] The fair value model is the model proposed in E64: investment property should be measured at fair value and changes in fair value should be recognised in the income statement. The cost model is the benchmark treatment[*] in IAS 16 *Property, Plant and Equipment*: investment property should be measured at depreciated cost (less any accumulated impairment losses). An entity that chooses the cost model should disclose the fair value of its investment property.

B50   Under IAS 8 *Net Profit or Loss for the Period, Fundamental Errors and Changes in Accounting Policies*,[†] a change in accounting policies from one model to the other model should be made only if the change will result in a more appropriate presentation of events or transactions.[§] The Board concluded that this is highly unlikely to be the case for a change from the fair value model to the cost model and paragraph 25 31 of the Standard reflects this conclusion.

---

[*]   IAS 16 *Property, Plant and Equipment* as revised by the IASB in 2003 eliminated all references to 'benchmark' treatment and 'allowed alternative' treatments.

[†]   revised by the IASB in 2003 as IAS 8 *Accounting Policies, Changes in Accounting Estimates and Errors*

[§]   The IASB conformed the terminology used in paragraph 31 to the terminology used in IAS 8 by *Improvements to IFRSs* issued in May 2008.

B51   The Board believes that it is undesirable to permit three different accounting treatments for investment property. Accordingly, if an entity does not adopt the fair value model, the Standard requires the entity to use the benchmark treatment in IAS 16 and does not permit the use of the allowed alternative treatment. However, an entity may still use the allowed alternative for other properties covered by IAS 16.[*]

Guidance on Fair Value

B52   The valuation profession will have an important role in implementing the Standard. Accordingly, in developing its guidance on the fair value of investment property, the Board considered not only similar guidance in other IASC literature, but also International Valuation Standards (IVS) issued by the International Valuation Standards Committee (IVSC). The Board understands that IVSC intends to review, and perhaps revise, its Standards in the near future.

B53   The Board believes that IASC's concept of fair value is similar to the IVSC concept of market value. IVSC defines market value as "the estimated amount for which an asset should exchange on the date of valuation between a willing buyer and a willing seller in an arm's length transaction after proper marketing wherein the parties had each acted knowledgeably, prudently and without compulsion." The Board believes that the guidance in paragraphs 29-30 36, 37 and 32-38 39-44 of the Standard is, in substance (and largely in wording as well), identical with guidance in IVS 1.

B54   Paragraphs 31 38 and 39-46 45-52 have no direct counterpart in the IVSC literature.   The Board developed much of this material in response to commentators on E64, who asked for more detailed guidance on determining the fair value of investment property.   In developing this material, the Board considered guidance on fair value in other IASC Standards and Exposure Drafts, particularly those on financial instruments (IAS 32 and IAS 39), intangible assets (IAS 38) and agriculture (E65).

Independent Valuation

B55   Some commentators believe that fair values should be determined on the basis of an independent valuation, to enhance the reliability of the fair values reported. Others believe, on cost-benefit grounds, that IASC should not require (and perhaps not even encourage) an independent valuation. They believe that it is for preparers to decide, in consultation with auditors, whether an entity has sufficient internal resources to determine reliable fair values. Some also believe that independent valuers with appropriate expertise are not available in some markets.

B56   The Board concluded that an independent valuation is not always necessary. Therefore, as proposed in E64, the Standard encourages, but does not require, an entity to determine the fair value of all investment property on the basis of a valuation by an independent valuer who holds a recognised and relevant

---

[*]   IAS 16 *Property, Plant and Equipment* as revised by the IASB in 2003 eliminated all references to 'benchmark' treatment and 'allowed alternative' treatments.

professional qualification and who has recent experience in the location and category of the investment property being valued. This approach is consistent with the approach to actuarial valuations in IAS 19 *Employee Benefits* (see IAS 19, paragraph 57).

Inability to Measure Fair Value Reliably

B57   E64 included a rebuttable presumption that an entity will be able to determine reliably the fair value of property held to earn rentals or for capital appreciation. E64 also proposed a reliability exception: IAS 16 should be applied if evidence indicates clearly, when an entity acquires or constructs a property, that fair value will not be determinable reliably on a continuing basis.

B58   Some commentators opposed various aspects of this proposal, on one or more of the following grounds:

(a)   the rebuttable presumption underestimates the difficulties of determining fair value reliably. This will often be impossible, particularly where markets are thin or where there is not a well-established valuation profession;

(b)   the accounting model under IAS 16 includes an impairment test under IAS 36. However, it is illogical to rely on an impairment test when fair value cannot be determined using cash flow projections, because an impairment test under IAS 36 is also difficult in such cases;

(c)   where fair value cannot be determined reliably, this fact does not justify charging depreciation. Instead, the property in question should be measured at cost less impairment losses; and

(d)   to avoid the danger of manipulation, all efforts should be made to determine fair values, even in a relatively inactive market. Even without an active market, a range of projected cash flows is available. If there are problems in determining fair value, an entity should measure the property at the best estimate of fair value and disclose limitations on the reliability of the estimate. If it is completely impossible to determine fair value, fair value should be deemed to be zero.

B59   The Board concluded that the rebuttable presumption and the reliability exception should be retained, but decided to implement them in a different way. In E64, they were implemented by excluding a property from the definition of investment property if the rebuttable presumption was overcome. Some commentators felt that it was confusing to include such a reliability exception in a definition. Accordingly, the Board moved the reliability exception from the definition to the section on subsequent measurement (paragraphs 47–49 53–55).

B60   Under E64, an entity should not stop using the fair value model if comparable market transactions become less frequent or market prices become less readily available. Some commentators disagreed with this proposal. They argued that there may be cases when reliable estimates are no longer available and that it would be misleading to continue fair value accounting in such cases. The Board decided that it is important to keep the E64 approach, because otherwise entities might use a reliability exception as an excuse to discontinue fair value accounting in a falling market.

B61   In cases where the reliability exception applies, E64 proposed that an entity should continue to apply IAS 16 until disposal of the property. Some commentators proposed that an entity should start applying the fair value model once the fair value becomes measurable reliably. The Board rejected this proposal because it would inevitably be a subjective decision to determine when fair value has become measurable reliably and this subjectivity could lead to inconsistent application.

B62   E64 proposed no specific disclosure where the reliability exception applies. Some commentators felt that disclosure would be important in such cases. The Board agreed and decided to include disclosures consistent with paragraph 170(b) of IAS 39[*] (see paragraphs 68 and 69(e) 78 and 79(e) of IAS 40). Paragraph 170(b) of IAS 39 requires disclosures for financial assets whose fair value cannot be reliably measured.

Gains and Losses on Remeasurement to Fair Value

B63   Some commentators argued that there should be either a requirement or an option to recognise changes in the fair value of investment property in equity, on the grounds that:

(a)   the market for property is not liquid enough and market values are uncertain and variable. Investment property is not as liquid as financial instruments and IAS 39 allows an option for available-for-sale investments;[†]

(b)   until performance reporting issues are resolved more generally, it is premature to require recognition of fair value changes in the income statement;

(c)   recognition of unrealised gains and losses in the income statement increases volatility and does not enhance transparency, because revaluation changes will blur the assessment of an entity's operating performance. It may also cause a presumption that the unrealised gains are available for distribution as dividends;

(d)   recognition in equity is more consistent with the historical cost and modified historical cost conventions that are a basis for much of today's accounting. For example, it is consistent with IASC's treatment of revaluations of property, plant and equipment under IAS 16 and with the option available for certain financial instruments under IAS 39;

(e)   for properties financed by debt, changes in the fair value of the properties resulting from interest rate changes should not be recognised in the income statement, since the corresponding changes in the fair value of the debt are not recognised under IAS 39;

(f)   under paragraphs 92 and 93 of the *Framework*, income should be recognised only when it can be measured with sufficient certainty. For example, IAS 11 *Construction Contracts* requires certain conditions before an entity can

---

*   In August 2005, the IASB relocated all disclosures relating to financial instruments to IFRS 7 *Financial Instruments: Disclosures*.

†   IFRS 9 *Financial Instruments*, issued in November 2009, eliminated the category of available-for-sale financial assets.

use the percentage-of-completion method. These conditions are not normally met for investment property; and

(g) results from operations should be distinguished from changes in values. For example, under IAS 21, unrealised exchange differences on a foreign entity* are recognised in equity.

B64 Some commentators suggested that increases should be recognised in equity and decreases should be recognised in profit or loss. This is similar to the revaluation model that forms the allowed alternative treatment[†] in IAS 16 (except for the lack of depreciation).

B65 As proposed in E64, the Board concluded that, in a fair value model, changes in the fair value of investment property should be recognised in the income statement as part of profit or loss for the period. The arguments for this approach include the following:

(a) the conceptual case for the fair value model is built largely on the view that this provides the most relevant and transparent view of the financial performance of investment property. Given this, it would be inconsistent to permit or require recognition in equity;

(b) recognition of fair value changes in equity would create a mismatch because net rental income would be recognised in the income statement, whereas the related consumption of the service potential (recognised as depreciation under IAS 16) would be recognised in equity. Similarly, maintenance expenditure would be recognised as an expense while related increases in fair value would be recognised in equity;

(c) using this approach, there is no need to resolve some difficult and controversial issues that would arise if changes in the fair value of investment property were recognised in equity. These issues include the following:

(i) should fair value changes previously recognised in equity be transferred ("recycled") to profit or loss on disposal of investment property; and

(ii) should fair value changes previously recognised in equity be transferred ("recycled") to profit or loss when investment property is impaired? If so, how should such impairment be identified and measured; and

(d) given the difficulty in defining investment property rigorously, entities will sometimes have the option of applying the investment property standard or either of the two treatments in IAS 16. It would be undesirable to include two choices in the investment property standard, as this would give entities a choice (at least occasionally) between four different treatments.

---

* In IAS 21 *The Effects of Changes in Foreign Exchange Rates*, as revised by the IASB in 2003, the term 'foreign entity' was replaced by 'foreign operation'.

† IAS 16 *Property, Plant and Equipment* as revised by the IASB in 2003 eliminated all references to 'benchmark' treatment and 'allowed alternative' treatments.

Transfers

B66 When an owner-occupied property carried under the benchmark treatment under IAS 16 becomes an investment property, the measurement basis for the property changes from depreciated cost to fair value. The Board concluded that the effect of this change in measurement basis should be treated as a revaluation under IAS 16 at the date of change in use. The result is that:

(a) the income statement excludes cumulative net increases in fair value that arose before the property became investment property. The portion of this change that arose before the beginning of the current period does not represent financial performance of the current period; and

(b) this treatment creates comparability between entities that had previously revalued the property under the allowed alternative treatment in IAS 16 and those entities that had previously used the IAS 16 benchmark treatment.*

Summary of Changes to E64

B67 The most important change between E64 and the final Standard was the introduction of the cost model as an alternative to the fair value model. The other main changes are listed below.

(a) The guidance on determining fair value was expanded, to clarify the following:

(i) the fair value of investment property is not reduced by transaction costs that may be incurred on sale or other disposal (paragraph 30 37 of the Standard). This is consistent with the measurement of financial assets under paragraph 69 of IAS 39.† E64 was silent on the treatment of such costs;

(ii) measurement is based on valuation at the balance sheet date (paragraph 31 38);

(iii) the best evidence of fair value is normally given by current prices on an active market for similar property in the same location and condition and subject to similar lease and other contracts (paragraph 39 45). In the absence of such evidence, fair value reflects information from a variety of sources and an entity needs to investigate reasons for any differences between the information from different sources (paragraphs 40–41 46 and 47);

(iv) market value differs from value in use as defined in IAS 36 *Impairment of Assets* (paragraph 43 49);

(v) there is a need to avoid double counting of investment property and separately recognised assets and liabilities. Integral equipment (such

---

* IAS 16 *Property, Plant and Equipment* as revised by the IASB in 2003 eliminated all references to 'benchmark' treatment and 'allowed alternative' treatments.

† Paragraph 69 was replaced by paragraph 46 when the IASB revised IAS 39 in 2003. In 2009 paragraph 46 of IAS 39 was replaced by paragraph 5.2.1 of IFRS 9 *Financial Instruments*.

as elevators or air-conditioning) is generally included in the investment property, rather than recognised separately (paragraph 44 50);

(vi) the fair value of investment property does not reflect future capital expenditure that will improve or enhance the asset and does not reflect the related future benefits from this future expenditure (paragraph 45 51);

(vii) an entity uses IAS 37 to account for any provisions associated with investment property (paragraph 46 52); and

(viii) in the exceptional cases when fair value cannot be determined reliably, measurement is under the IAS 16 benchmark treatment[*] only (in such cases, revaluation under IAS 16 would also not be reliable) and residual value is assumed to be zero (given that fair value cannot be determined reliably) (paragraphs 47–48 53 and 54).

(b) In relation to the scope of the Standard and the definition of investment property:

(i) paragraph 3 4 now clarifies that the Standard does not apply to forests and similar regenerative natural resources and to mineral rights, the exploration for and extraction of minerals, oil, natural gas and similar non-regenerative resources. This wording is consistent with a similar scope exclusion in IAS 16 *Property, Plant and Equipment*. The Board did not wish to prejudge its decision on the treatment of such items in the current projects on Agriculture and the Extractive Industries;

(ii) land held for a currently undetermined future use is a further example of investment property (paragraph 6(b) 8(b)), on the grounds that a subsequent decision to use such land as inventory or for development as owner-occupied property would be an investment decision;

(iii) new examples of items that are not investment property are: property held for future use as owner-occupied property, property held for future development and subsequent use as owner-occupied property, property occupied by employees (whether or not the employees pay rent at market rates) and owner-occupied property awaiting disposal (paragraph 7(e) 9(c));

(iv) property that is being constructed or developed for future use as investment property is now covered by IAS 16 and measured at cost, less impairment losses, if any (paragraph 7(d) 9(d)). E64 proposed that investment property under construction should be measured at fair value; and

(v) the reference to reliable measurement of fair value (and the related requirements in paragraphs 14–15 of E64) was moved from the

---

* IAS 16 *Property, Plant and Equipment* as revised by the IASB in 2003 eliminated all references to 'benchmark' treatment and 'allowed alternative' treatments.

definition of investment property into the section on subsequent measurement (paragraphs 47–49 53–55).

(c) New paragraph 20 23 deals with start up costs, initial operating losses and abnormal wastage (based on paragraphs 17 and 18 of IAS 16[*]). The Board considered adding guidance on the treatment of incidental revenue earned during the construction of investment property. However, the Board concluded that this raised an issue in the context of IAS 16 and decided that it was beyond the scope of this project to deal with this.

(d) There is an explicit requirement on determining gains or losses on disposal (paragraph 62 69). This is consistent with IAS 16, paragraph 56.[†] There are also new cross-references to:

(i) IAS 17 *Leases* and IAS 18 *Revenue*, as guidance for determining the date of disposal (paragraph 61 67); and

(ii) IAS 37 *Provisions, Contingent Liabilities and Contingent Assets*, for liabilities retained after disposal (paragraph 64 71).

(e) The Standard states explicitly that an entity should transfer an investment property to inventories when the entity begins to develop the property for subsequent sale in the ordinary course of business (paragraphs 51(b) and 52 57(b) and 58). E64 proposed that all transfers from investment properties to inventories should be prohibited. The Standard also deals more explicitly than E64 with certain other aspects of transfers.

(f) New disclosure requirements include:

(i) extension of the required disclosure on methods and significant assumptions, which are now to include disclosure of whether fair value was supported by market evidence, or whether the estimate is based on other data (which the entity should disclose) because of the nature of the property and the lack of comparable market data (paragraph 66(b) 75(d));

(ii) disclosures of rental income and direct operating expenses (paragraph 66(d) 75(f)); and

(iii) disclosures in the exceptional cases when fair value is not reliably determinable (paragraphs 68 and 69(e) 78 and 79(e)).

(g) E64 proposed a requirement to disclose the carrying amount of unlet or vacant investment property. Some commentators argued that this disclosure was impracticable, particularly for property that is partly vacant. Some also felt that this is a matter for disclosure in a financial review by management, rather than in the financial statements. The Board deleted this disclosure requirement. It should be noted that some indication of vacancy levels may be available from the required disclosure of rental income and from the IAS 17 requirement to disclose cash flows from

---

[*] In IAS 16 *Property, Plant and Equipment* as revised by the IASB in 2003, paragraphs 17 and 18 were replaced by paragraphs 19–22.

[†] In IAS 16 *Property, Plant and Equipment* as revised by the IASB in 2003, paragraph 56 was replaced by paragraphs 68 and 71.

© IASCF

non-cancellable operating leases (split into less than one year, one to five years and more than five years).

(h) E64 included no specific transitional provisions, which means that IAS 8 would apply. There is a risk that restatement of prior periods might allow entities to manipulate their reported profit or loss for the period by selective use of hindsight in determining fair values in prior periods. Accordingly, the Board decided to prohibit restatement in the fair value model, except where an entity has already publicly disclosed fair values for prior periods (paragraph ~~70~~ 80).

IASB documents published to accompany

International Accounting Standard 41

Agriculture

This version includes amendments resulting from IFRSs issued up to 31 December 2009.

The text of the unaccompanied IAS 41 is contained in Part A of this edition. Its effective date when issued was 1 January 2003. The effective date of the latest amendments is 1 January 2013. This part presents the following accompanying documents:

Basis for Conclusions on
IAS 41 *Agriculture*

This Basis for Conclusions accompanies, but is not part of, IAS 41.

Introduction

BC1   This Basis for Conclusions summarises the International Accounting Standards Board's considerations in reaching its conclusions on amending IAS 41 *Agriculture* by *Improvements to IFRSs* in May 2008. Individual Board members gave greater weight to some factors than to others.

BC2   Because the Board's intention was not to reconsider the fundamental approach to the accounting for agriculture established by IAS 41, this Basis for Conclusions does not discuss requirements in IAS 41 that the Board has not reconsidered. The IASC Basis for Conclusions on IAS 41 follows this Basis.

Scope

Costs to sell (paragraph 5)

BC3   Before the *Improvements to IFRSs* issued in May 2008, IAS 41 used the term 'point-of-sale costs'. This term was not used elsewhere in IFRSs. The term 'costs to sell' is used in IFRS 5 *Non-current Assets Held for Sale and Discontinued Operations* and IAS 36 *Impairment of Assets*. The Board decided that 'point-of-sale costs' and 'costs to sell' meant the same thing in the context of IAS 41. The word 'incremental' in the definition of 'costs to sell' excludes costs that are included in the fair value measurement of a biological asset, such as transport costs. It includes costs that are necessary for a sale to occur but that would not otherwise arise, such as commissions to brokers and dealers, levies by regulatory agencies and commodity exchanges, and transfer taxes and duties. Both terms relate to transaction costs arising at the point of sale.

BC4   Therefore, the Board decided to replace the terms 'point-of-sale costs' and 'estimated point-of-sale costs' with 'costs to sell' to make IAS 41 consistent with IFRS 5 and IAS 36.

Recognition and measurement

Discount rate (paragraph 20)

BC5   As part of the annual improvements project begun in 2007, the Board reconsidered whether it is appropriate to require a pre-tax discount rate in paragraph 20 when measuring fair value. The Board noted that a fair value measurement should take into account the attributes, including tax attributes, that a market participant would consider when pricing an asset or liability.

BC6   The Board noted that a willing buyer would factor into the amount that it would be willing to pay the seller to acquire an asset (or would receive to assume a liability) all incremental cash flows that would benefit that buyer. Those incremental cash flows would be reduced by expected income tax payments using appropriate tax rates (ie the tax rate of a market participant buyer). Accordingly, fair value takes into account future income taxes that a market participant purchasing the asset (or assuming the liability) would be expected to pay (or to receive), without regard to an entity's specific tax situation.

BC7   Therefore, the Board decided to keep the requirement to use a current market-based discount rate but in *Improvements to IFRSs* issued in May 2008 removed the reference to a pre-tax discount rate in paragraph 20.

Additional biological transformation (paragraph 21)

BC8   Sometimes the fair value of an asset in its current location and condition is estimated using discounted cash flows. Paragraph 21 could be read to exclude from such calculations increases in cash flows arising from 'additional biological transformation'. Diversity in practice had developed from different interpretations of this requirement. The Board decided that not including these cash flows resulted in a carrying amount that is not representative of the asset's fair value. The Board noted that an entity should consider the risks associated with cash flows from 'additional biological transformation' in determining the expected cash flows, the discount rate, or some combination of the two. Therefore, the Board decided to amend IAS 41 to remove the prohibition on an entity taking into account the cash flows resulting from 'additional biological transformation' when estimating the fair value of a biological asset.

BC9   In its exposure draft of proposed *Improvements to International Financial Reporting Standards* published in 2007, the Board proposed changing the definition of biological transformation to include harvest. This was because the Board wished to make clear that harvest altered the condition of a biological asset. Some commentators objected to this change on the basis that harvest is a human activity rather than a biological transformation. The Board agreed with this argument and decided not to include the harvest in the definition of biological transformation. Instead, the Board amended the Standard to refer to biological transformation or harvest when applicable to make clear that harvest changes the condition of an asset.

BC10   Because applying the changes discussed in paragraphs BC8 and BC9 retrospectively might require some entities to remeasure the fair value of biological assets at a past date, the Board decided that these amendments should be applied prospectively.

Contents

Basis for IASC's Conclusions on
IAS 41 *Agriculture*

This Basis for Conclusions accompanies, but is not part of, IAS 41. It was prepared by the IASC Staff in 2000 but was not approved by the IASC Board. It summarises the Board's reasons for:

(a)   initiating and proposing an International Accounting Standard on agriculture; and

(b)   accepting or rejecting certain alternative views.

Individual Board members gave greater weight to some factors than to others.

This Basis has not been revised by the IASB and the terminology has not been amended to reflect the changes made by Improvements to IFRSs *issued in May 2008.*

Background

B1   In 1994, the IASC Board (the 'Board') decided to develop an International Accounting Standard on agriculture and appointed a Steering Committee to help define the issues and develop possible solutions. In 1996, the Steering Committee published a Draft Statement of Principles ('DSOP') setting out the issues, alternatives, and the Steering Committee's proposals for resolving the issues and inviting public comment. In response, 42 comment letters were received. The Steering Committee reviewed the comments, revised certain of its recommendations, and submitted them to the Board.

B2   In July 1999, the Board approved Exposure Draft E65 *Agriculture* with a comment deadline of 31 January 2000. The Board received 62 comment letters on E65. They came from various international organisations, as well as from 28 individual countries. In April 2000, the IASC Staff sent a questionnaire to entities that undertake agricultural activity in an attempt to determine the reliability of the fair value measurement proposed in E65 and received 20 responses from 11 countries. In December 2000, after considering the comments on E65 and responses to the questionnaire, the Board approved IAS 41 *Agriculture* (the Standard). Paragraph B82 below summarises the changes that the Board made to E65 in finalising the Standard.

The need for an International Accounting Standard on agriculture

B3   A main objective of the IASC is to develop International Accounting Standards that are relevant in the general purpose financial statements of all businesses. While most International Accounting Standards apply to entities in all activities, some International Accounting Standards, for example IAS 30 *Disclosures in the Financial Statements of Banks and Similar Financial Institutions*[*] and IAS 40 *Investment Property*, deal with issues that arise in particular activities. IASC has also undertaken industry-specific projects on insurance and extractive industries.

---

[*]   In August 2005, IFRS 7 *Financial Instruments: Disclosures* superseded IAS 30.

B4   Diversity in accounting for agricultural activity has occurred because:

(a)   prior to the development of the Standard, assets related to agricultural activity and changes in those assets were excluded from the scope of International Accounting Standards:

(i)   IAS 2 *Inventories* excluded 'producers' inventories of livestock, agricultural and forest products... to the extent that they are measured at net realisable value in accordance with well established practices in certain industries';

(ii)   IAS 16 *Property, Plant and Equipment* did not apply to 'forests and similar regenerative natural resources';

(iii)   IAS 18 *Revenue* did not deal with revenue arising from 'natural increases in herds, and agricultural and forest products'; and

(iv)   IAS 40 *Investment Property* did not apply to 'forests and similar regenerative natural resources';

(b)   accounting guidelines for agricultural activity developed by national standard setters have, in general, been piecemeal, developed to resolve a specific issue related to a form of agricultural activity of significance to that country; and

(c)   the nature of agricultural activity creates uncertainty or conflicts when applying traditional accounting models, particularly because the critical events associated with biological transformation (growth, degeneration, production, and procreation) that alter the substance of biological assets are difficult to deal with in an accounting model based on historical cost and realisation.

B5   Most business organisations involved in agricultural activity are small, independent, cash and tax focused, family-operated business units, often perceived as not being required to produce general purpose financial statements. Some believe that because of this an International Accounting Standard on agriculture would not have widespread application. However, even small agricultural entities seek outside capital and subsidies, particularly from banks or government agencies, and these capital providers increasingly request financial statements. Moreover, an international trend towards deregulation, an increasing number of cross-border listings and more investment have resulted in increasing scale, scope, and commercialism of agricultural activity. This has created a greater need for financial statements based on sound and generally accepted accounting principles. For the above reasons, in 1994 the Board added to its agenda a project on agriculture.

B6   The DSOP specifically asked for views on the feasibility of developing a comprehensive International Accounting Standard on agriculture. Some commentators felt that the diversity of agricultural activity prevents the development of a single International Accounting Standard on accounting for all agricultural activities. Others said that different principles should attach to agricultural activity with short and long production cycles. Some cited the need to develop International Accounting Standards that are simple to apply and broad in application. Commentators on the DSOP also noted that agriculture is a significant industry in many countries, particularly in developing and newly industrialised countries. In many such countries it is the most important industry.

B7   After considering the comments on the DSOP, the Board reaffirmed its conclusion that an International Accounting Standard is needed. The Board believes that the principles set forth in the Standard have wide application and provide a clear set of principles.

Scope

B8   The Standard prescribes, among other things, the accounting treatment for biological assets and for the initial measurement of agricultural produce harvested from an entity's biological assets at the point of harvest. However, the Standard does not deal with the processing of agricultural produce after harvest, since the Board did not consider it appropriate to undertake a partial revision of IAS 2 *Inventories* which deals with the accounting treatment for inventories under the historical cost system.* The processing after harvest is accounted for under IAS 2 or another applicable International Accounting Standard (for example, if an entity harvests logs† and decides to use them for constructing its own building, IAS 16 *Property, Plant and Equipment* is applied in accounting for the logs).

B9   Some may think of such processing as agricultural activity, particularly if it is done by the same entity that developed the agricultural produce (for example, the processing of grapes into wine by a vintner who has grown the grapes). While such processing may be a logical and natural extension of agricultural activity, and the events taking place may bear some similarity to biological transformation, such processing is not included within the definition of agricultural activity in the Standard.

B10   In particular, the Board considered whether to include circumstances where there is a long ageing or maturation process after harvest (for example, for wine production from grapes and cheese production from milk) in the scope of the Standard. Those who believe that the Standard should cover such processing argue that:

      (a)   such a long ageing or maturation process is similar to biological transformation and fundamental to assessing the performance of an entity; and

      (b)   many agricultural entities are vertically integrated and involved in, for example, producing both grapes and wine.

---

*   The term 'historical cost system' is no longer applicable owing to revisions made to IAS 2 in December 2003.

†   As the result of an amendment by the IASB, contained in *Improvements to IFRSs* issued in May 2008, 'logs' is an example of produce that has been processed rather than an example of unprocessed produce.

B11   The Board decided not to include such circumstances in the scope of the Standard because of concerns about difficulties in differentiating them from other manufacturing processes (such as conversion of raw materials into marketable inventories as defined in IAS 2). The Board concluded that the requirements in IAS 2 or another applicable International Accounting Standard would be suited to accounting for such processes.

B12   The Board also considered whether to deal with contracts for the sale of a biological asset or agricultural produce and government grants related to agricultural activity in the Standard.   These issues are discussed below (see paragraphs B47–54 and B63–73).

Measurement

Biological assets

Fair value versus cost

B13   The Standard requires an entity to use a fair value approach in measuring its biological assets related to agricultural activity as proposed in the DSOP and E65, except for cases where the fair value cannot be measured reliably on initial recognition.

B14   Those who support fair value measurement argue that the effects of changes brought about by biological transformation are best reflected by reference to the fair value changes in biological assets. They believe that fair value changes in biological assets have a direct relationship to changes in expectations of future economic benefits to the entity.

B15   Those who support fair value measurement also note that the transactions entered into to effect biological transformation often have only a weak relationship with the biological transformation itself and, thus, a more distant relationship to expected future economic benefits. For example, patterns of growth in a plantation forest directly affect expectations of future economic benefits but differ markedly, in timing, from patterns of cost incurrence. No income might be reported until first harvest and sale (perhaps 30 years) in a plantation forestry entity using a transaction-based, historical cost accounting model. On the other hand, income is measured and reported throughout the period until initial harvest if an accounting model is used that recognises and measures biological growth using current fair values.

B16   Further, those who support fair value measurement cite reasons for concluding that fair value has greater relevance, reliability, comparability, and understandability as a measurement of future economic benefits expected from biological assets than historical cost, including:

(a)   many biological assets are traded in active markets with observable market prices. Active markets for these assets provide a reliable measure of market expectations of future economic benefits. The presence of such markets significantly increases the reliability of market value as an indicator of fair value;

(b)   measures of the cost of biological assets are sometimes less reliable than measures of fair value because joint products and joint costs can create situations in which the relationship between inputs and outputs is ill-defined, leading to complex and arbitrary allocations of cost between the different outcomes of biological transformation. Such allocations become even more arbitrary if biological assets generate additional biological assets (offspring) and the additional biological assets are also used in the entity's own agricultural activity;

(c)   relatively long and continuous production cycles, with volatility in both the production and market environment, mean that the accounting period often does not depict a full cycle. Therefore, period-end measurement (as opposed to time of transaction) assumes greater significance in deriving a measure of current period financial performance or position. The less significant current year harvest is in relation to total biological transformation, the greater the significance of period-end measures of asset change (growth and degeneration). In relatively high turnover, short production cycle, highly controlled agricultural systems (for example, broiler chicken or mushroom production) in which the majority of biological transformation and harvesting occurs within a year, the relationship between cost and future economic benefits appears more stable. This apparent stability does not alter the relationship between current market value and future economic benefits, but it makes the difference in measurement method less significant; and

(d)   different sources of replacement animals and plants (home-grown or purchased) give rise to different costs in a historical cost approach. Similar assets should give rise to similar expectations with regard to future benefits. Considerably enhanced comparability and understandability result when similar assets are measured and reported using the same basis.

B17   Those who oppose measuring biological assets at fair value believe there is superior reliability in cost measurement because historical cost is the result of arm's length transactions, and therefore provides evidence of an open-market value at that point in time, and is independently verifiable. More importantly, they believe fair value is sometimes not reliably measurable and that users of financial statements may be misled by presentation of numbers that are indicated as being fair value but are based on subjective and unverifiable assumptions. Information regarding fair value can be provided other than in a single number in the financial statements. They believe the scope of the Standard is too broad. They also argue that:

(a)   market prices are often volatile and cyclical and not appropriate as a basis of measurement;

(b)   it may be onerous to require fair valuation at each balance sheet date, especially if interim reports are required;

(c)   the historical cost convention is well established and commonly used. The use of any other basis should be accompanied by a change in the IASC *Framework for the Preparation and Presentation of Financial Statements* (the '*Framework*'). For consistency with other International Accounting

Standards and other activities, biological assets should be measured at their cost;

(d)   cost measurement provides more objective and consistent measurement;

(e)   active markets may not exist for some biological assets in some countries. In such cases, fair value cannot be measured reliably, especially during the period of growth in the case of a biological asset that has a long growth period (for example, trees in a plantation forest);

(f)   fair value measurement results in recognition of unrealised gains and losses and contradicts principles in International Accounting Standards on recognition of revenue; and

(g)   market prices at a balance sheet date may not bear a close relationship to the prices at which assets will be sold, and many biological assets are not held for sale.

B18   The *Framework* is neutral with respect to the choice of measurement basis, identifying that a number of different bases are employed to different degrees and in varying combinations, though noting that historical cost is most commonly adopted. The alternatives specifically identified are historical cost, current cost, realisable value, and present value. Precedents for fair value measurement exist in other International Accounting Standards.

B19   The Board concluded that the Standard should require a fair value model for biological assets related to agricultural activity because of the unique nature and characteristics of agricultural activity. However, the Board also concluded that, in some cases, fair value cannot be measured reliably. Some respondents to the questionnaire, as well as some commentators on E65, expressed significant concern about the reliability of fair value measurement for some biological assets, arguing that:

(a)   active markets do not exist for some biological assets, in particular for those with a long growth period;

(b)   present value of expected net cash flows is often an unreliable measure of fair value due to the need for, and use of, subjective assumptions (for example, about weather); and

(c)   fair value cannot be measured reliably prior to harvest.

Some commentators on E65 suggested that the Standard should include a reliability exception for cases where no active market exists.

B20   The Board decided there was a need to include a reliability exception for cases where market-determined prices or values are not available and alternative estimates of fair value are determined to be clearly unreliable. In those cases, biological assets should be measured at their cost less any accumulated depreciation and any accumulated impairment losses. In determining cost, accumulated depreciation and accumulated impairment losses, an entity considers IAS 2 *Inventories*, IAS 16 *Property, Plant and Equipment* and IAS 36 *Impairment of Assets*.

B21   The Board rejected a benchmark treatment of fair value and an allowed alternative treatment of historical cost because of the greater comparability and understandability achieved by a mandatory fair value approach in the presence of active markets. The Board is also uncomfortable with options in International Accounting Standards.

Treatment of point-of-sale costs

B22   The Standard requires that a biological asset should be measured at its fair value less estimated point-of-sale costs. Point-of-sale costs include commissions to brokers and dealers, levies by regulatory agencies and commodity exchanges, and transfer taxes and duties. Point-of-sale costs exclude transport and other costs necessary to get assets to a market. Such transport and other costs are deducted in determining fair value (that is, fair value is a market price less transport and other costs necessary to get an asset to a market).

B23   E65 proposed that pre-sale disposal costs that will be incurred to place an asset on the market (such as transport costs) should be deducted in determining fair value, if a biological asset will be sold in an active market in another location. However, E65 did not specify the treatment of point-of-sale costs. Some commentators suggested that the Standard should clarify the treatment of point-of-sale costs, as well as pre-sale disposal costs.

B24   Some argue that point-of-sale costs should not be deducted in a fair value model. They argue that fair value less estimated point-of-sale costs would be a biased estimate of markets' estimate of future cash flows, because point-of-sale costs would in effect be recognised as an expense twice if the acquirer pays point-of-sale costs on acquisition; once related to the initial acquisition of biological assets and once related to the immediate measurement at fair value less estimated point-of-sale costs. This would occur even when point-of-sale costs would not be incurred until a future period or would not be paid at all for a bearer biological asset that will not be sold.

B25   On the other hand, some believe that point-of-sale costs should be deducted in a fair value model. They believe that the carrying amount of an asset should represent the economic benefits that are expected to flow from the asset. They argue that fair value less estimated point-of-sale costs would represent the markets' estimate of the economic benefits that are expected to flow to the entity from that asset at the balance sheet date. They also argue that failure to deduct estimated point-of-sale costs could result in a loss being deferred until a sale occurs.

B26   The Board concluded that fair value less estimated point-of-sale costs is a more relevant measurement of biological assets, acknowledging that, in particular, failure to deduct estimated point-of-sale costs could result in a loss being deferred.

Hierarchy in fair value measurement

B27   The Standard requires that, if an active market exists for a biological asset, the quoted price in that market is the appropriate basis for determining the fair value of that asset. If an active market does not exist, an entity uses market-determined prices or values (such as the most recent market transaction price) when available.

However, in some circumstances, market-determined prices or values may not be available for a biological asset in its present condition. In these circumstances, the Standard indicates that an entity uses the present value of expected net cash flows* from the asset.

B28   E65 proposed that, if an active market exists for a biological asset, an entity should use the market price in the active market. If an active market does not exist, E65 proposed that an entity should consider other measurement bases such as the price of the most recent transaction for the same type of asset, sector benchmarks, and present value of expected net cash flows. E65 did not set a hierarchy in cases where no active market exists; that is, E65 did not indicate which basis is preferable to the other bases.

B29   The Board considered setting an explicit hierarchy in cases where no active market exists. Some believe that using market-determined prices or values; for example, the most recent market transaction price, would always be preferable to present value of expected net cash flows. On the other hand, some believe that market-determined prices or values would not necessarily be preferable to present value of expected net cash flows, especially when an entity uses market prices for similar assets with adjustment to reflect differences.

B30   The Board concluded that a detailed hierarchy would not provide sufficient flexibility to appropriately deal with all the circumstances that may arise and decided not to set a detailed hierarchy in cases where no active market exists. However, the Board decided to indicate that an entity uses all available market-determined prices or values since otherwise there is a possibility that entities may opt to use present value of expected net cash flows from the asset even when useful market-determined prices or values are available. Of the 20 companies that responded to the questionnaire, six companies used present value of expected net cash flows as a basis of fair value measurement and, in addition, two companies indicated that it was impossible to measure their biological assets reliably since the present value of expected net cash flows would not be reliable (as they would need to use present value as a basis).

B31   When an entity has access to different markets, the Standard indicates that the entity uses the most relevant one. For example, if an entity has access to two active markets, it uses the price existing in the market expected to be used. Some believe that the most advantageous price in the accessible markets should be used. The Standard reflects the view that the most relevant measurement results from using the market expected to be used.

Frequency of fair value measurement

B32   Some argue that less frequent measurement of fair value should be permitted because of concerns about burdens on entities. The Board rejected this approach because of the:

(a)   continuous nature of biological transformation;

---

* Paragraph 20 of the previous version of IAS 41 required entities to use a pre-tax discount rate when measuring fair value. The IASB decided to maintain the requirement to use a current market-based discount rate but removed the reference to a pre-tax discount rate by *Improvements to IFRSs* issued in May 2008.

(b) lack of direct relationships between financial transactions and the outcomes of biological transformation; and

(c) general availability of reliable measures of fair value at reasonable cost.

Independent valuation

B33 A significant number of commentators on the DSOP indicated that, if present value of expected net cash flows is used to determine fair value, an external independent valuation should be required. The Board rejected this proposal since it believes that external independent valuations are not commonly used for certain agricultural activity and it would be burdensome to require an external independent valuation. The Board believes that it is for entities to decide how to determine fair value reliably, including the extent to which independent valuers need to be involved.

Inability to measure fair value reliably

B34 As noted previously, the Board decided to include a reliability exception in the Standard for cases where fair value cannot be measured reliably on initial recognition. The Standard indicates a presumption that fair value can be measured reliably for a biological asset. However, that presumption can be rebutted only on initial recognition for a biological asset for which market-determined prices or values are not available and for which alternative estimates of fair value are determined to be clearly unreliable. In such a case, that biological asset should be measured at its cost less any accumulated depreciation and any accumulated impairment losses. Once the fair value of such a biological asset becomes reliably measurable, the Standard requires that an entity should start measuring the biological asset at its fair value less estimated point-of-sale costs.

B35 Some believe that, if an entity was previously using the reliability exception, the entity should not be allowed to start fair value measurement (that is, an entity should continue to use a cost basis). They argue that it could be a subjective decision to determine when fair value has become reliably measurable and that this subjectivity could lead to inconsistent application and, potentially, abuse. The Board noted, however, that in agricultural activity, it is likely that fair value becomes measurable more reliably as biological transformation occurs and that fair value measurement is preferable to cost in those cases. Thus, the Board decided to require fair value measurement once fair value becomes reliably measurable.

B36 If an entity has previously measured a biological asset at its fair value less estimated point-of-sale costs, the Standard requires that the entity should continue to measure the biological asset at its fair value less estimated point-of-sale costs until disposal. Some argue that reliable estimates may cease to be available. The Board believed that this would rarely, if ever, occur. Accordingly, the Board decided to prohibit entities from changing their measurement basis from fair value to cost, because otherwise an entity might use a reliability exception as an excuse to discontinue fair value accounting in a falling market.

B37   If an entity uses the reliability exception, the Standard requires additional disclosures. The additional disclosures include information on biological assets held at the end of the period such as a description of the assets and an explanation of why fair value cannot be measured reliably. The additional disclosures also include the gain or loss recognised for the period on disposal of biological assets measured at cost less any accumulated depreciation and any accumulated impairment losses, even though those biological assets are not held at the end of the period.

Gains and losses

B38   The Standard requires that a gain or loss arising on initial recognition of a biological asset and from a change in fair value less estimated point-of-sale costs of a biological asset should be included in net profit or loss[*] for the period in which it arises. Those who support this treatment argue that biological transformation is a significant event that should be included in net profit or loss because:

(a)   the event is fundamental to understanding an entity's performance; and

(b)   this is consistent with the accrual basis of accounting.

B39   Some commentators on the DSOP and E65 argued that fair value changes should be included directly in equity, through the statement of changes in equity, until realised, arguing that:

(a)   the effects of biological transformation cannot be measured reliably and, therefore, should not be reported as income;

(b)   fair value changes should only be included in net profit or loss when the earnings process is complete;

(c)   recognition of unrealised gains and losses in net profit or loss increases volatility of earnings;

(d)   the results of biological transformation may never be realised, particularly given the risks to which biological assets are exposed; and

(e)   it is premature to require recognition of fair value changes in net profit or loss, until performance reporting issues are resolved.

B40   The Board rejected requiring changes in fair value to be included directly in equity since it is difficult to find any conceptual basis for reporting any portion of the changes in fair value of biological assets related to agricultural activity directly in equity. No distinction is made in the *Framework* between recognition in the balance sheet and recognition in the income statement.

---

[*]   IAS 1 *Presentation of Financial Statements* (revised in 2003) replaced the term 'net profit or loss' with 'profit or loss'.

Agricultural produce

B41 The Standard requires that agricultural produce harvested from an entity's biological assets should be measured at its fair value less estimated point-of-sale costs at the point of harvest. Such measurement is the cost at that date when applying IAS 2 *Inventories* or another applicable International Accounting Standard.

B42 The Board noted that the same basis of measurement should generally be applied to agricultural produce on initial recognition and to the biological asset from which it is harvested. Because the fair value of a biological asset takes into account the condition of the agricultural produce that will be harvested from the biological asset, it would be illogical to measure the agricultural produce at cost when the biological asset is measured at fair value. For example, the fair value of a sheep with half fleece will differ from the fair value of a similar sheep with full fleece. It would be inconsistent and distort reporting of current period performance if, upon shearing, the shorn fleece is measured at its cost when the fair value of the sheep is reduced by the fair value of the fleece.

B43 As noted previously, certain biological assets are measured at their cost less any accumulated depreciation and any accumulated impairment losses, if the reliability exception is applied. Some argue that a reliability exception should exist for measurement of agricultural produce. The Board rejected this view because many of the arguments for a reliability exception do not apply to agricultural produce. For example, markets more often exist for agricultural produce than for biological assets. The Board also noted that it is generally not practicable to reliably determine the cost of agricultural produce harvested from biological assets.

B44 With regard to measurement after harvest, some argue that agricultural produce should be measured at its fair value both at the point of harvest and at each balance sheet date until sold, consumed, or otherwise disposed of. They argue that this approach would ensure that all agricultural produce of a similar type is measured similarly irrespective of date of harvest, thus enhancing comparability and consistency.

B45 The Board concluded that fair value less estimated point-of-sale costs at the point of harvest should be the cost when applying IAS 2 or another applicable International Accounting Standard, since this is consistent with the historical cost accounting model applied to manufacturing processes in general and other types of inventory.

B46 In reaching the above conclusion, the Board noted that entities undertaking agricultural activity sometimes purchase agricultural produce for resale, and other entities often engage in processing purchased agricultural produce into consumable products. If agricultural produce would be measured at its fair value after harvest, a desire for consistency would suggest revaluing purchased inventories as well, and such a treatment would be inconsistent with IAS 2. The Board did not consider it appropriate to undertake a partial revision of IAS 2.

Sales contracts

B47   Entities often enter into contracts to sell at a future date their biological assets or agricultural produce. The Standard indicates that contract prices are not necessarily relevant in determining fair value and that the fair value of a biological asset or agricultural produce is not adjusted because of the existence of a contract.

B48   E65 did not propose how to account for a contract for the sale of a biological asset or agricultural produce. Some commentators suggested prescribing the treatment of sales contracts since such sales contracts are common in certain agricultural activity. Some commentators also pointed out that certain sales contracts are not within the scope of IAS 39 *Financial Instruments: Recognition and Measurement** and that no other International Accounting Standards deal with those contracts.

B49   Some argue that contract prices should be used in measuring the related biological assets when an entity expects to settle the contract by delivery and believe this would result in the most relevant carrying amount for the biological asset. Others argue that contract prices are not necessarily relevant in measuring the biological assets at fair value since fair value reflects the current market in which a willing buyer and seller would enter into a transaction.

B50   The Board concluded that contract prices should not be used in measuring related biological assets, because contract prices do not necessarily reflect the current market in which a willing buyer and seller would enter into a transaction and therefore do not necessarily represent the fair value of assets. The Board wished to maintain a consistent approach to the measurement of assets. The Board instead considered whether it might require that sales contracts be measured at fair value. It is logical to measure a sales contract at fair value to the extent that a related biological asset is also measured at fair value.

B51   However, the Board noted that to achieve symmetry between the measurement of a biological asset and a related sales contract the Standard would have to carefully restrict the sales contracts to be measured at fair value. An entity may enter into a contract to sell agricultural produce to be harvested from the entity's biological assets. The Board concluded that it would not be appropriate to require fair value measurement for a contract to sell agricultural produce that does not yet exist (for example, milk to be harvested from a cow), since no related asset has yet been recognised or measured at fair value and to do so would be beyond the scope of the project on agriculture.

B52   Thus, the Board considered restricting the sales contracts to be measured at fair value to those for the sale of an entity's existing biological assets and agricultural produce. However, the Board noted that it is difficult to differentiate existing agricultural produce from agricultural produce that does not exist. For example:

    (a)   if an entity enters into a contract to sell fully-grown wheat at a future date and has half-grown wheat at a balance sheet date, it seems clear that the

---

*   In November 2009 the IASB amended some of the requirements of IAS 39 and relocated them to IFRS 9 *Financial Instruments*. IFRS 9 applies to all assets within the scope of IAS 39.

                © IASCF

wheat to be delivered under the contract does not yet exist at the balance sheet date; but

(b)   on the other hand, if an entity enters into a contract to sell mature cattle at a future date and has mature cattle at a balance sheet date, it could be argued that the cattle exist in the form in which they will be sold at the balance sheet date. However, it could also be argued that the cattle do not yet exist in the form in which they will be sold at the balance sheet date since further biological transformation will occur between the balance sheet date and the date of delivery.

B53   The Board also noted that the Standard would have to require an entity to stop fair value measurement for sales contracts once agricultural produce to be sold under the contract is harvested from an entity's biological assets, since accounting for agricultural produce is not dealt with in the Standard except for initial measurement and IAS 2 *Inventories* or another applicable International Accounting Standard applies after harvest. It would be illogical to continue fair value measurement when the agricultural produce is measured at historical cost. The Board noted that it would be anomalous to require an entity to start measuring a contract at fair value once the related asset exists and to stop doing that at a later date.

B54   The Board concluded that no solution is practicable without a complete review of the accounting for commodity contracts that are not within the scope of IAS 39.* Because of the above difficulties, the Board concluded that the Standard should not deal with the measurement of sales contracts that are not within the scope of IAS 39. Instead, the Board decided to include an observation that those sales contracts may be onerous contracts under IAS 37 *Provisions, Contingent Liabilities and Contingent Assets*.

Land related to agricultural activity

B55   The Standard does not establish any new principles for land related to agricultural activity. Rather, an entity follows IAS 16 *Property, Plant and Equipment* or IAS 40 *Investment Property* depending on which standard is appropriate in the circumstances. IAS 16 requires land to be measured either at its cost less any accumulated impairment losses, or at a revalued amount. IAS 40 requires land that is investment property to be measured at its fair value, or cost less any accumulated impairment losses.

B56   Some argue that land attached to biological assets related to agricultural activity should also be measured at its fair value. They argue that fair value measurement of land results in consistency of measurement with the fair value measurement of biological assets. They also argue that it is sometimes difficult to measure the fair value of such biological assets separately from the land since an active market often exists for the combined assets (that is, land and biological assets; for example, trees in a plantation forest).

---

*   In November 2009 the IASB amended some of the requirements of IAS 39 and relocated them to IFRS 9 *Financial Instruments*. IFRS 9 applies to all assets within the scope of IAS 39.

B57   The Board rejected this approach, primarily because requiring the fair value measurement of land related to agricultural activity would be inconsistent with IAS 16.

Intangible assets

B58   The Standard does not establish any new principles for intangible assets related to agricultural activity. Rather, an entity follows IAS 38 *Intangible Assets*. IAS 38 requires an intangible asset, after initial recognition, to be measured at its cost less any accumulated amortisation and impairment losses, or at a revalued amount.

B59   E65 proposed that an entity should be encouraged to follow the revaluation alternative in IAS 38 for intangible assets related to agricultural activity, to enhance consistency of measurement with the fair value measurement of biological assets. Some commentators on E65 disagreed with having the encouragement. They argued that a unique treatment for intangible assets related to agricultural activity is not warranted.

B60   The Board did not include the encouragement in E65 in the Standard. The Board concluded that IAS 38 should be applied to intangible assets related to agricultural activity, as it is to intangible assets related to other activities.

Subsequent expenditure

B61   The Standard does not explicitly prescribe how to account for subsequent expenditure related to biological assets. E65 proposed that costs of producing and harvesting biological assets should be charged to expense when incurred and that costs that increase the number of units of biological assets owned or controlled by the entity should be added to the carrying amount of the asset.

B62   Some believe that there is no need to capitalise subsequent expenditure in a fair value model and that all subsequent expenditure should be recognised as an expense. Some also argue that it would sometimes be difficult to prescribe which costs should be recognised as expenses and which costs should be capitalised; for example, in the case of vet fees paid for delivering a calf. The Board decided not to explicitly prescribe the accounting for subsequent expenditure related to biological assets in the Standard, because it believes to do so is unnecessary with a fair value measurement approach.

Government grants

B63   The Standard requires that an unconditional government grant related to a biological asset measured at its fair value less estimated point-of-sale costs should be recognised as income when, and only when, the government grant becomes receivable. If a government grant is conditional, including where a government grant requires an entity not to engage in specified agricultural activity, an entity should recognise the government grant as income when, and only when, the conditions attaching to the government grant are met.

B64 The Standard requires a different treatment from IAS 20 *Accounting for Government Grants and Disclosure of Government Assistance* in the circumstances described above. IAS 20 is to be applied only to government grants related to biological assets measured at cost less any accumulated depreciation and any accumulated impairment losses.

B65 IAS 20 requires that government grants should not be recognised until there is reasonable assurance that:

(a) the entity will comply with the conditions attaching to them; and

(b) the grants will be received.

IAS 20 also requires that government grants should be recognised as income over the periods necessary to match them with the related costs that they are intended to compensate, on a systematic basis. In relation to the presentation of government grants related to assets, IAS 20 permits two methods—setting up a government grant as deferred income or deducting the government grant from the carrying amount of the asset.

B66 The latter method of presentation—deducting a government grant from the carrying amount of the related asset—is inconsistent with a fair value model in which an asset is measured and presented at its fair value. Using the deduction from carrying value approach, an entity would first deduct the government grant from the carrying amount of the related asset and then measure that asset at its fair value. In effect, an entity would recognise a government grant as income immediately, even for a conditional government grant. This conflicts with the requirement in IAS 20 that government grants should not be recognised until there is reasonable assurance that the entity will comply with the conditions attaching to them.

B67 Because of the above, the Board concluded that there was a need to deal with government grants related to biological assets measured at their fair value. Some argued that IASC should begin a wider review of IAS 20 rather than provide special rules in individual International Accounting Standards. The Board acknowledged that this might be a more appropriate approach, but concluded that such a review would be beyond the scope of the project on agriculture. Instead, the Board decided to deal with government grants in the Standard, since the Board noted that government grants related to agricultural activity are common in some countries.

B68 E65 proposed that, if an entity receives a government grant in respect of a biological asset that is measured at its fair value and the grant is unconditional, the entity should recognise the grant as income when the government grant becomes receivable. E65 also proposed that, if a government grant is conditional, the entity should recognise it as income when there is reasonable assurance that the conditions are met.

B69 The Board noted that, if a government grant is conditional, an entity is likely to have costs and ongoing obligations associated with satisfying the conditions attaching to the government grant. It may be possible that the inflow of economic benefits is much less than the amount of the government grant. Given that possibility, the Board acknowledged that the criterion for recognising income from a conditional government grant in E65, when there is reasonable assurance that the conditions are met, may give rise to income recognition that is inconsistent with the *Framework*. The *Framework* indicates that income is recognised in the income statement when an increase in future economic benefits related to an increase in an asset or a decrease in a liability has arisen that can be measured reliably. The Board also noted that it would inevitably be a subjective decision as to when there is reasonable assurance that the conditions are met and that this subjectivity could lead to inconsistent income recognition.

B70 The Board considered two alternative approaches:

(a) an entity should recognise a conditional government grant as income when it is probable that the entity will meet the conditions attaching to the government grant; and

(b) an entity should recognise a conditional government grant as income when the entity meets the conditions attaching to the government grant.

B71 Proponents of approach (a) argue that this approach is generally consistent with the revenue recognition requirements in IAS 18 *Revenue*. IAS 18 requires that revenue should be recognised, among other things, when it is probable that the economic benefits associated with the transaction will flow to the entity.

B72 Proponents of approach (b) believe that, until the conditions attaching to the government grant are met, a liability should be recognised under the *Framework* rather than income since an entity has a present obligation to satisfy the conditions arising from past events. They also argue that income recognition under approach (a) would still be subjective and inconsistent with the recognition criteria indicated in the *Framework*.

B73 The Board concluded that approach (b) is more appropriate. The Board also decided that a government grant that requires an entity not to engage in specified agricultural activity should also be accounted for in the same way as a conditional government grant related to a biological asset measured at its fair value less estimated point-of-sale costs.

Disclosure

Separate disclosure of physical and price changes

B74 The Standard encourages, but does not require, separate disclosure of the effects of the factors resulting in changes to the carrying amount of biological assets, physical change and price change, when there is a production cycle of more than one year. Physical change is attributable to changes in the assets themselves while price change is attributable to changes in unit fair values.

B75 Some argue that the separate disclosure should be required since it is useful in appraising current period performance and future prospects in relation to production from, and maintenance and renewal of, biological assets. Others argue that it may be impracticable to separate these elements and the two components cannot be separated reliably.

B76 The Board concluded that the separate disclosure should not be required because of practicability concerns. However, the Board decided to encourage the separate disclosure, given that such disclosure may be useful and practically determinable in some circumstances. The separate disclosure is not encouraged when the production cycle is less than one year (for example, when raising broiler chickens or growing cereal crops) since that information is less useful in that circumstance.

B77 Some argue that physical changes should be included in net profit or loss and that price changes should be included directly in equity, through the statement of changes in equity. The Board rejected this approach because both components are indicative of management's performance.

Disaggregation of the gain or loss

B78 The Standard requires that an entity should disclose the aggregate gain or loss arising during the current period on initial recognition of biological assets and agricultural produce and from the change in fair value less estimated point-of-sale costs of biological assets. The Standard does not require or encourage disaggregating the gain or loss, except that the Standard encourages separate disclosure of physical changes and price changes as discussed above.

B79 The Board considered requiring, or encouraging, disclosure of the gain or loss on a disaggregated basis; for example, requiring separate disclosure of the gain or loss related to biological assets and the gain or loss related to agricultural produce. Those who supported disaggregating the gain or loss believe that such information is useful in appraising current period performance in relation to biological transformation. Others argued that disaggregation would be impracticable and require a subjective procedure.

Other disclosures

B80 E65 proposed disclosing the:

(a) extent to which the carrying amount of biological assets reflects a valuation by an external independent valuer, or if there has been no valuation by an external independent valuer, that fact;

(b) activities that are unsustainable with an estimated date of cessation of the activities;

(c) aggregate carrying amount of an entity's agricultural land and the basis (cost or revalued amount) on which the carrying amount was determined under IAS 16 *Property, Plant and Equipment*; and

(d) carrying amount of agricultural produce either on the face of the balance sheet or in the notes.

B81 The Board did not include the above disclosures in the Standard. The Board noted that requiring item (a) above would not be appropriate since external independent valuations are not commonly used for assets related to agricultural activity, unlike for certain other assets such as investment property. The Board also noted that item (b) is not required in other International Accounting Standards and a unique disclosure requirement is not warranted for agricultural activity. Items (c) and (d) would be outside the scope of the Standard and covered by other International Accounting Standards (IAS 16 or IAS 2 *Inventories*).

Summary of changes to E65

B82   The Standard made the following principal changes to the proposals in E65:

(a)   The Standard includes a reliability exception for biological assets on initial recognition. If the exception is applied, the biological asset should be measured at its cost less any accumulated depreciation and any accumulated impairment losses (paragraph 30 of the Standard). As a consequence, the Standard includes disclosure requirements consistent with paragraph 170(b) of IAS 39 *Financial Instruments: Recognition and Measurement** and paragraph 68 of IAS 40 *Investment Property*† (paragraphs 54(a)–(c) and 55 of the Standard), and consistent with paragraphs 60(b)–(d) and 60(e)(v)–(vii) of IAS 16 *Property, Plant and Equipment*§ (paragraphs 54(d)–(f) and 55).

(b)   If the reliability exception is applied but fair value subsequently becomes reliably measurable and, therefore, an entity has started measuring the biological assets at their fair value less estimated point-of-sale costs, the Standard requires the entity to disclose a description of the biological assets, an explanation of why fair value has become reliably measurable, and the effect of the change (paragraph 56).

(c)   E65 did not specify how to account for point-of-sale costs (such as commissions to brokers). The Standard requires that biological assets and agricultural produce should be measured at their fair value less estimated point-of-sale costs (paragraphs 12–13).

(d)   E65 included net realisable value as one of the measurement bases in cases where no active market exists. Net realisable value was deleted from the bases since it is not a market-determined value.

(e)   The Standard indicates that market-determined prices or values are used when available. The Standard also indicates that, in some circumstances, market-determined prices or values may not be available for an asset in its present condition. In these circumstances, an entity uses the present value of expected net cash flows (paragraphs 18–20).

(f)   Guidance on the performance of present value calculations was added (paragraphs 21–23).

(g)   E65 did not specify how to account for contracts for the sale of a biological asset or agricultural produce. The Standard indicates that the fair value of

---

*   Paragraph 170(b) of IAS 39 was replaced by paragraph 90 of IAS 32 *Financial Instruments: Disclosure and Presentation* when the IASB revised those standards in 2003. In 2005, the IASB relocated all disclosures relating to financial instruments to IFRS 7 *Financial Instruments: Disclosures*.

†   Paragraph 68 of IAS 40 was replaced by paragraph 78 when the IASB revised IAS 40 in 2003.

§   Paragraph 60 of IAS 16 was replaced by paragraph 73 when IAS 16 was revised in 2003.

a biological asset or agricultural produce is not adjusted because of the existence of a sales contract (paragraph 16).

(h) E65 did not explicitly indicate that a gain or loss may arise on initial recognition of agricultural produce. The Standard clarifies that a gain or loss may arise on initial recognition of agricultural produce; for example, as a result of harvesting and that such a gain or loss should be included in net profit or loss* for the period in which it arises (paragraphs 28–29).

(i) E65 proposed that costs of producing and harvesting biological assets should be charged to expense when incurred, and that costs that increase the number of units of biological assets owned or controlled by the entity should be added to the carrying amount of the asset. The Standard does not explicitly prescribe how to account for subsequent expenditure related to biological assets.

(j) E65 proposed that an entity should recognise a conditional government grant as income when there is reasonable assurance that the conditions are met. The Standard requires that a conditional government grant related to a biological asset measured at its fair value less estimated point-of-sale costs, including where a government grant requires an entity not to engage in specified agricultural activity, should be recognised as income when, and only when, the conditions attaching to the government grant are met. The Standard also indicates that IAS 20 *Accounting for Government Grants and Disclosure of Government Assistance* is applied to a government grant related to a biological asset measured at its cost less any accumulated depreciation and any accumulated impairment losses (paragraphs 34–35 and 37).

(k) E65 provided the following encouragements specific to agricultural activity with regard to alternative treatments allowed in other International Accounting Standards, to achieve consistency with the accounting treatment of activities covered by E65:

   (i) analysing expenses by nature, as set out in IAS 1 *Presentation of Financial Statements*; and

   (ii) revaluing certain intangible assets used in agricultural activity if an active market exists, as set out in IAS 38 *Intangible Assets*.

   The Board did not include these encouragements in the Standard. The Board noted that IAS 1 and IAS 38 apply to entities that undertake agricultural activity, as well as to those in other activities.

(l) New disclosure requirements include disclosing the:

   (i) basis for making distinctions between consumable and bearer biological assets or between mature and immature biological assets, when an entity provides a quantified description of each group of biological assets (paragraph 43);

---

* IAS 1 *Presentation of Financial Statements* (revised in 2003) replaced the term 'net profit or loss' with 'profit or loss'.

      (ii)   methods and significant assumptions applied in determining the fair value of each group of agricultural produce at the point of harvest (paragraph 47);

      (iii) fair value less estimated point-of-sale costs of agricultural produce harvested during the period, determined at the point of harvest (paragraph 48);

      (iv) increases resulting from business combinations in the reconciliation of the carrying amount of biological assets (paragraph 50(e)); and

      (v)   significant decreases expected in the level of government grants related to agricultural activity covered by the Standard (paragraph 57(c)).

(m)   E65 proposed disclosing the:

      (i)   extent to which the carrying amount of biological assets reflects a valuation by an external independent valuer or, if there has been no valuation by an external independent valuer, that fact;

      (ii)   activities that are unsustainable with an estimated date of cessation of the activities;

      (iii) aggregate carrying amount of an entity's agricultural land and the basis (cost or revalued amount) on which the carrying amount was determined under IAS 16; and

      (iv) carrying amount of agricultural produce either on the face of the balance sheet or in the notes.

The Standard does not include the above disclosures.

(n)   The amendment to IAS 17 *Leases* now clarifies that IAS 17 should not be applied to the measurement by:

      (i)   lessees of biological assets held under finance leases; and

      (ii)   lessors of biological assets leased out under operating leases.

Biological assets held under finance leases and those leased out under operating leases are measured under the Standard rather than IAS 17. A lease of a biological asset is classified as a finance lease or operating lease under IAS 17. If a lease is classified as a finance lease, the lessee recognises the leased biological asset under IAS 17 and thereafter measures and presents it under the Standard. In that case, the lessee makes disclosures both under the Standard and IAS 17. A lessor of a biological asset under an operating lease measures and presents the biological asset under the Standard, and makes disclosures both under the Standard and IAS 17.

Illustrative examples

These examples, which were prepared by the IASC staff but were not approved by the IASC Board, accompany, but are not part of, IAS 41. They have been updated to take account of the changes made by IAS 1 Presentation of Financial Statements *(as revised in 2007) and* Improvements to IFRSs *issued in 2008.*

A1   Example 1 illustrates how the disclosure requirements of this Standard might be put into practice for a dairy farming entity. This Standard encourages the separation of the change in fair value less costs to sell of an entity's biological assets into physical change and price change. That separation is reflected in Example 1. Example 2 illustrates how to separate physical change and price change.

A2   The financial statements in Example 1 do not conform to all of the disclosure and presentation requirements of other Standards. Other approaches to presentation and disclosure may also be appropriate.

Example 1 XYZ Dairy Ltd

Statement of financial position

XYZ Dairy Ltd Statement of financial position	Notes	31 December 20X1	31 December 20X0
ASSETS			
Non-current assets			
Dairy livestock – immature[a]		52,060	47,730
Dairy livestock – mature[a]		372,990	411,840
Subtotal – biological assets	3	425,050	459,570
Property, plant and equipment		1,462,650	1,409,800
Total non-current assets		**1,887,700**	**1,869,370**
Current assets			
Inventories		82,950	70,650
Trade and other receivables		88,000	65,000
Cash		10,000	10,000
Total current assets		**180,950**	**145,650**
Total assets		**2,068,650**	**2,015,020**
EQUITY AND LIABILITIES			
Equity			
Issued capital		1,000,000	1,000,000
Retained earnings		902,828	865,000
Total equity		**1,902,828**	**1,865,000**
Current liabilities			
Trade and other payables		165,822	150,020
Total current liabilities		**165,822**	**150,020**
Total equity and liabilities		**2,068,650**	**2,015,020**

[a] An entity is encouraged, but not required, to provide a quantified description of each group of
 biological assets, distinguishing between consumable and bearer biological assets or between
 mature and immature biological assets, as appropriate. An entity discloses the basis for making
 any such distinctions.

Statement of comprehensive income*

XYZ Dairy Ltd Statement of comprehensive income	Notes	Year ended 31 December 20X1
Fair value of milk produced		518,240
Gains arising from changes in fair value less costs to sell of dairy livestock	3	39,930
		558,170
Inventories used		(137,523)
Staff costs		(127,283)
Depreciation expense		(15,250)
Other operating expenses		(197,092)
		(477,148)
Profit from operations		**81,022**
Income tax expense		(43,194)
Profit/comprehensive income for the year		**37,828**

---

* This statement of comprehensive income presents an analysis of expenses using a classification based on the nature of expenses. IAS 1 *Presentation of Financial Statements* requires that an entity present, either in the statement of comprehensive income or in the notes, an analysis of expenses using a classification based on either the nature of expenses or their function within the entity. IAS 1 encourages presentation of an analysis of expenses in the statement of comprehensive income.

Statement of changes in equity

XYZ Dairy Ltd
Statement of changes in equity
Year ended 31 December 20X1

	Share capital	Retained earnings	Total
Balance at 1 January 20X1	1,000,000	865,000	1,865,000
Profit/comprehensive income for the year		37,828	37,828
Balance at 31 December 20X1	1,000,000	902,828	1,902,828

Statement of cash flows*

XYZ Dairy Ltd Statement of cash flows	Notes	Year ended 31 December 20X1
Cash flows from operating activities		
Cash receipts from sales of milk		498,027
Cash receipts from sales of livestock		97,913
Cash paid for supplies and to employees		(460,831)
Cash paid for purchases of livestock		(23,815)
		111,294
Income taxes paid		(43,194)
Net cash from operating activities		68,100
Cash flows from investing activities		
Purchase of property, plant and equipment		(68,100)
Net cash used in investing activities		(68,100)
Net increase in cash		0
Cash at beginning of the year		10,000
Cash at end of the year		10,000

---

* This statement of cash flows reports cash flows from operating activities using the direct method. IAS 7 *Statement of Cash Flows* requires that an entity report cash flows from operating activities using either the direct method or the indirect method. IAS 7 encourages use of the direct method.

Notes

1 **Operations and principal activities**

XYZ Dairy Ltd ('the Company') is engaged in milk production for supply to various customers. At 31 December 20X1, the Company held 419 cows able to produce milk (mature assets) and 137 heifers being raised to produce milk in the future (immature assets). The Company produced 157,584kg of milk with a fair value less costs to sell of 518,240 (that is determined at the time of milking) in the year ended 31 December 20X1.

2 **Accounting policies**

Livestock and milk

Livestock are measured at their fair value less costs to sell. The fair value of livestock is determined based on market prices of livestock of similar age, breed, and genetic merit. Milk is initially measured at its fair value less costs to sell at the time of milking. The fair value of milk is determined based on market prices in the local area.

3 **Biological assets**

Reconciliation of carrying amounts of dairy livestock	20X1
Carrying amount at 1 January 20X1	459,570
Increases due to purchases	26,250
Gain arising from changes in fair value less costs to sell attributable to physical changes*	15,350
Gain arising from changes in fair value less costs to sell attributable to price changes*	24,580
Decreases due to sales	(100,700)
Carrying amount at 31 December 20X1	425,050

4 **Financial risk management strategies**

The Company is exposed to financial risks arising from changes in milk prices. The Company does not anticipate that milk prices will decline significantly in the foreseeable future and, therefore, has not entered into derivative or other contracts to manage the risk of a decline in milk prices. The Company reviews its outlook for milk prices regularly in considering the need for active financial risk management.

---

* Separating the increase in fair value less costs to sell between the portion attributable to physical changes and the portion attributable to price changes is encouraged but not required by this Standard.

Example 2 Physical change and price change

The following example illustrates how to separate physical change and price change. Separating the change in fair value less costs to sell between the portion attributable to physical changes and the portion attributable to price changes is encouraged but not required by this Standard.

A herd of 10 2 year old animals was held at 1 January 20X1. One animal aged 2.5 years was purchased on 1 July 20X1 for 108, and one animal was born on 1 July 20X1. No animals were sold or disposed of during the period. Per-unit fair values less costs to sell were as follows:

2 year old animal at 1 January 20X1	100
Newborn animal at 1 July 20X1	70
2.5 year old animal at 1 July 20X1	108
Newborn animal at 31 December 20X1	72
0.5 year old animal at 31 December 20X1	80
2 year old animal at 31 December 20X1	105
2.5 year old animal at 31 December 20X1	111
3 year old animal at 31 December 20X1	120

Fair value less costs to sell of herd at 1 January 20X1 (10 × 100)		1,000
Purchase on 1 July 20X1 (1 × 108)		108
Increase in fair value less costs to sell due to price change:		
10 × (105 − 100)	50	
1 × (111 − 108)	3	
1 × (72 − 70)	2	55
Increase in fair value less costs to sell due to physical change:		
10 × (120 − 105)	150	
1 × (120 − 111)	9	
1 × (80 − 72)	8	
1 × 70	70	237
Fair value less costs to sell of herd at 31 December 20X1		
11 × 120	1,320	
1 × 80	80	1,400

Documents published to accompany

IFRIC Interpretation 1

Changes in Existing Decommissioning, Restoration and Similar Liabilities

This version includes amendments resulting from IFRSs issued up to 31 December 2009.

The text of the unaccompanied IFRIC 1 is contained in Part A of this edition. Its effective date when issued was 1 September 2004. The effective date of the amendments is 1 January 2009. This part presents the following accompanying documents:

IFRIC Interpretation 1
Illustrative examples

These examples accompany, but are not part of, IFRIC 1.

Common facts

IE1   An entity has a nuclear power plant and a related decommissioning liability. The nuclear power plant started operating on 1 January 2000. The plant has a useful life of 40 years. Its initial cost was CU120,000 *; this included an amount for decommissioning costs of CU10,000, which represented CU70,400 in estimated cash flows payable in 40 years discounted at a risk-adjusted rate of 5 per cent. The entity's financial year ends on 31 December.

Example 1: Cost model

IE2   On 31 December 2009, the plant is 10 years old. Accumulated depreciation is CU30,000 (CU120,000 × $^{10}/_{40}$ years). Because of the unwinding of discount (5 per cent) over the 10 years, the decommissioning liability has grown from CU10,000 to CU16,300.

IE3   On 31 December 2009, the discount rate has not changed. However, the entity estimates that, as a result of technological advances, the net present value of the decommissioning liability has decreased by CU8,000. Accordingly, the entity adjusts the decommissioning liability from CU16,300 to CU8,300. On this date, the entity makes the following journal entry to reflect the change:

		CU	CU
Dr	decommissioning liability	8,000	
	Cr cost of asset		8,000

IE4   Following this adjustment, the carrying amount of the asset is CU82,000 (CU120,000 − CU8,000 − CU30,000), which will be depreciated over the remaining 30 years of the asset's life giving a depreciation expense for the next year of CU2,733 (CU82,000 ÷ 30). The next year's finance cost for the unwinding of the discount will be CU415 (CU8,300 × 5 per cent).

IE5   If the change in the liability had resulted from a change in the discount rate, instead of a change in the estimated cash flows, the accounting for the change would have been the same but the next year's finance cost would have reflected the new discount rate.

Example 2: Revaluation model

IE6   The entity adopts the revaluation model in IAS 16 whereby the plant is revalued with sufficient regularity that the carrying amount does not differ materially from fair value. The entity's policy is to eliminate accumulated depreciation at the revaluation date against the gross carrying amount of the asset.

---

*   In these examples, monetary amounts are denominated in 'currency units (CU)'.

IE7   When accounting for revalued assets to which decommissioning liabilities attach, it is important to understand the basis of the valuation obtained. For example:

(a)   if an asset is valued on a discounted cash flow basis, some valuers may value the asset without deducting any allowance for decommissioning costs (a 'gross' valuation), whereas others may value the asset after deducting an allowance for decommissioning costs (a 'net' valuation), because an entity acquiring the asset will generally also assume the decommissioning obligation. For financial reporting purposes, the decommissioning obligation is recognised as a separate liability, and is not deducted from the asset. Accordingly, if the asset is valued on a net basis, it is necessary to adjust the valuation obtained by adding back the allowance for the liability, so that the liability is not counted twice.*

(b)   if an asset is valued on a depreciated replacement cost basis, the valuation obtained may not include an amount for the decommissioning component of the asset. If it does not, an appropriate amount will need to be added to the valuation to reflect the depreciated replacement cost of that component.

IE8   Assume that a market-based discounted cash flow valuation of CU115,000 is obtained at 31 December 2002. It includes an allowance of CU11,600 for decommissioning costs, which represents no change to the original estimate, after the unwinding of three years' discount. The amounts included in the statement of financial position at 31 December 2002 are therefore:

	CU
Asset at valuation (1)	126,600
Accumulated depreciation	nil
Decommissioning liability	(11,600)
Net assets	115,000
Retained earnings (2)	(10,600)
Revaluation surplus (3)	15,600

Notes:

(1)   Valuation obtained of CU115,000 plus decommissioning costs of CU11,600, allowed for in the valuation but recognised as a separate liability = CU126,600.

(2)   Three years' depreciation on original cost CU120,000 × $3/40$ = CU9,000 plus cumulative discount on CU10,000 at 5 per cent compound = CU1,600; total CU10,600.

(3)   Revalued amount CU126,600 less previous net book value of CU111,000 (cost CU120,000 less accumulated depreciation CU9,000).

---

*   For examples of this principle, see IAS 36 *Impairment of Assets* and IAS 40 *Investment Property*.

IE9   The depreciation expense for 2003 is therefore CU3,420 (CU126,600 × ¹⁄₃₇) and the discount expense for 2003 is CU600 (5 per cent of CU11,600). On 31 December 2003, the decommissioning liability (before any adjustment) is CU12,200 and the discount rate has not changed. However, on that date, the entity estimates that, as a result of technological advances, the present value of the decommissioning liability has decreased by CU5,000. Accordingly, the entity adjusts the decommissioning liability from CU12,200 to CU7,200.

IE10   The whole of this adjustment is taken to revaluation surplus, because it does not exceed the carrying amount that would have been recognised had the asset been carried under the cost model. If it had done, the excess would have been taken to profit or loss in accordance with paragraph 6(b). The entity makes the following journal entry to reflect the change:

		CU	CU
Dr	decommissioning liability	5,000	
	Cr revaluation surplus		5,000

IE11   The entity decides that a full valuation of the asset is needed at 31 December 2003, in order to ensure that the carrying amount does not differ materially from fair value. Suppose that the asset is now valued at CU107,000, which is net of an allowance of CU7,200 for the reduced decommissioning obligation that should be recognised as a separate liability. The valuation of the asset for financial reporting purposes, before deducting this allowance, is therefore CU114,200. The following additional journal entry is needed:

		CU	CU
Dr	accumulated depreciation (1)	3,420	
	Cr asset at valuation		3,420
Dr	revaluation surplus (2)	8,980	
	Cr asset at valuation (3)		8,980

Notes:

(1)   Eliminating accumulated depreciation of CU3,420 in accordance with the entity's accounting policy.

(2)   The debit is to revaluation surplus because the deficit arising on the revaluation does not exceed the credit balance existing in the revaluation surplus in respect of the asset.

(3)   Previous valuation (before allowance for decommissioning costs) CU126,600, less cumulative depreciation CU3,420, less new valuation (before allowance for decommissioning costs) CU114,200.

IE12   Following this valuation, the amounts included in the statement of financial position are:

	CU
Asset at valuation	114,200
Accumulated depreciation	nil
Decommissioning liability	(7,200)
Net assets	107,000
Retained earnings (1)	(14,620)
Revaluation surplus (2)	11,620

Notes:

(1)   CU10,600 at 31 December 2002 plus 2003's depreciation expense of CU3,420 and discount expense of CU600 = CU14,620.

(2)   CU15,600 at 31 December 2002, plus CU5,000 arising on the decrease in the liability, less CU8,980 deficit on revaluation = CU11,620.

Example 3: Transition

IE13   The following example illustrates retrospective application of the Interpretation for preparers that already apply IFRSs. Retrospective application is required by IAS 8 *Accounting Policies, Changes in Accounting Estimates and Errors*, where practicable, and is the benchmark treatment in the previous version of IAS 8. The example assumes that the entity:

(a)   adopted IAS 37 on 1 July 1999;

(b)   adopts the Interpretation on 1 January 2005; and

(c)   before the adoption of the Interpretation, recognised changes in estimated cash flows to settle decommissioning liabilities as income or expense.

IE14   On 31 December 2000, because of the unwinding of the discount (5 per cent) for one year, the decommissioning liability has grown from CU10,000 to CU10,500. In addition, based on recent facts, the entity estimates that the present value of the decommissioning liability has increased by CU1,500 and accordingly adjusts it from CU10,500 to CU12,000. In accordance with its then policy, the increase in the liability is recognised in profit or loss.

IE15   On 1 January 2005, the entity makes the following journal entry to reflect the adoption of the Interpretation:

	CU	CU
Dr cost of asset	1,500	
Cr accumulated depreciation		154
Cr opening retained earnings		1,346

IE16   The cost of the asset is adjusted to what it would have been if the increase in the estimated amount of decommissioning costs at 31 December 2000 had been capitalised on that date. This additional cost would have been depreciated over 39 years. Hence, accumulated depreciation on that amount at 31 December 2004 would be CU154 (CU1,500 × $^{4}/_{39}$ years).

IE17   Because, before adopting the Interpretation on 1 January 2005, the entity recognised changes in the decommissioning liability in profit or loss, the net adjustment of CU1,346 is recognised as a credit to opening retained earnings. This credit is not required to be disclosed in the financial statements, because of the restatement described below.

IE18   IAS 8 requires the comparative financial statements to be restated and the adjustment to opening retained earnings at the start of the comparative period to be disclosed. The equivalent journal entries at 1 January 2004 are shown below. In addition, depreciation expense for the year ended 31 December 2004 is increased by CU39 from the amount previously reported:

	CU	CU
Dr cost of asset	1,500	
Cr accumulated depreciation		115
Cr opening retained earnings		1,385

Basis for Conclusions on
IFRIC Interpretation 1 *Changes in Existing Decommissioning, Restoration and Similar Liabilities*

This Basis for Conclusions accompanies, but is not part of, IFRIC 1.

The original text has been marked up to reflect the revision of IAS 1 Presentation of Financial Statements *in 2007: new text is underlined and deleted text is struck through.*

Introduction

BC1   This Basis for Conclusions summarises the IFRIC's considerations in reaching its consensus. Individual IFRIC members gave greater weight to some factors than to others.

Background

BC2   IAS 16 *Property, Plant and Equipment* requires the cost of an item of property, plant and equipment to include the initial estimate of the costs of dismantling and removing an asset and restoring the site on which it is located, the obligation for which an entity incurs either when the item is acquired or as a consequence of having used the item during a particular period for purposes other than to produce inventories during that period.

BC3   IAS 37 *Provisions, Contingent Liabilities and Contingent Assets* requires that the measurement of the liability, both initially and subsequently, should be the estimated expenditure required to settle the present obligation at the ~~balance sheet date~~ end of the reporting period and should reflect a current market-based discount rate. It requires provisions to be reviewed at ~~each balance sheet date~~ the end of each reporting period and adjusted to reflect the current best estimate. Hence, when the effect of a change in estimated outflows of resources embodying economic benefits and/or the discount rate is material, that change should be recognised.

BC4   The IFRIC was asked to address how to account for changes in decommissioning, restoration and similar liabilities. The issue is whether changes in the liability should be recognised in current period profit or loss, or added to (or deducted from) the cost of the related asset. IAS 16 contains requirements for the initial capitalisation of decommissioning costs and IAS 37 contains requirements for measuring the resulting liability; neither specifically addresses accounting for the effect of changes in the liability. The IFRIC was informed that differing views exist, resulting in a risk of divergent practices developing.

BC5   Accordingly, the IFRIC decided to develop guidance on accounting for the changes. In so doing, the IFRIC recognised that the estimation of the liability is inherently subjective, since its settlement may be very far in the future and estimating (a) the timing and amount of the outflow of resources embodying economic benefits (eg cash flows) required to settle the obligation and (b) the discount rate often involves the exercise of considerable judgement. Hence, it is likely that revisions to the initial estimate will be made.

Scope

BC6   The scope of the Interpretation addresses the accounting for changes in estimates of existing liabilities to dismantle, remove and restore items of property, plant and equipment that fall within the scope of IAS 16 and are recognised as a provision under IAS 37. The Interpretation does not apply to changes in estimated liabilities in respect of costs that fall within the scope of other IFRSs, for example, inventory or production costs that fall within the scope of IAS 2 *Inventories*. The IFRIC noted that decommissioning obligations associated with the extraction of minerals are a cost either of the property, plant and equipment used to extract them, in which case they are within the scope of IAS 16 and the Interpretation, or of the inventory produced, which should be accounted for under IAS 2.

Basis for Consensus

BC7   The IFRIC reached a consensus that changes in an existing decommissioning, restoration or similar liability that result from changes in the estimated timing or amount of the outflow of resources embodying economic benefits required to settle the obligation, or a change in the discount rate, should be added to or deducted from the cost of the related asset and depreciated prospectively over its useful life.

BC8   In developing its consensus, the IFRIC also considered the following three alternative approaches for accounting for changes in the outflow of resources embodying economic benefits and changes in the discount rate:

   (a)   capitalising only the effect of a change in the outflow of resources embodying economic benefits that relate to future periods, and recognising in current period profit or loss all of the effect of a change in the discount rate.

   (b)   recognising in current period profit or loss the effect of all changes in both the outflow of resources embodying economic benefits and the discount rate.

   (c)   treating changes in an estimated decommissioning, restoration and similar liability as revisions to the initial liability and the cost of the asset. Under this approach, amounts relating to the depreciation of the asset that would have been recognised to date would be reflected in current period profit or loss and amounts relating to future depreciation would be capitalised.

BC9   The IFRIC rejected alternative (a), because this approach does not treat changes in the outflow of resources embodying economic benefits and in the discount rate in the same way, which the IFRIC agreed is important, given that matters such as inflation can affect both the outflow of economic benefits and the discount rate.

BC10   In considering alternative (b), the IFRIC observed that recognising all of the change in the discount rate in current period profit or loss correctly treats a change in the discount rate as an event of the present period. However, the IFRIC decided against alternative (b) because recognising changes in the estimated outflow of resources embodying economic benefits in current period profit or loss would be inconsistent with the initial capitalisation of decommissioning costs under IAS 16.

BC11   Alternative (c) was the approach proposed in draft Interpretation D2 *Changes in Decommissioning, Restoration and Similar Liabilities*, published on 4 September 2003. In making that proposal, the IFRIC regarded the asset, from the time the liability for decommissioning is first incurred until the end of the asset's useful life, as the unit of account to which decommissioning costs relate. It therefore took the view that revisions to the estimates of those costs, whether through revisions to estimated outflows of resources embodying economic benefits or revisions to the discount rate, ought to be accounted for in the same manner as the initial estimated cost. The IFRIC still sees merit in this proposal, but concluded on balance that, under current standards, full prospective capitalisation should be required for the reasons set out in paragraphs BC12–BC18.

IAS 8 and a change in accounting estimate

BC12   IAS 8 *Accounting Policies, Changes in Accounting Estimates and Errors* requires an entity to recognise a change in an accounting estimate prospectively by including it in profit or loss in the period of the change, if the change affects that period only, or the period of the change and future periods, if the change affects both. To the extent that a change in an accounting estimate gives rise to changes in assets or liabilities, or relates to an item of equity, it is required to be recognised by adjusting the asset, liability or equity item in the period of change.

BC13   Although the IFRIC took the view that the partly retrospective treatment proposed in D2 is consistent with these requirements of IAS 8, most responses to the draft Interpretation suggested that IAS 8 would usually be interpreted as requiring a fully prospective treatment. The IFRIC agreed that IAS 8 would support a fully prospective treatment also, and this is what the Interpretation requires.

IAS 16 and changes in accounting estimates for property, plant and equipment

BC14   Many responses to the draft Interpretation argued that the proposal in D2 was inconsistent with IAS 16, which requires other kinds of change in estimate for property, plant and equipment to be dealt with prospectively. For example, as IAS 8 also acknowledges, a change in the estimated useful life of, or the expected pattern of consumption of the future economic benefits embodied in, a depreciable asset affects depreciation expense for the current period and for each future period during the asset's remaining useful life. In both cases, the effect of the change relating to the current period is recognised in profit or loss in the current period. The effect, if any, on future periods is recognised in profit or loss in those future periods.

BC15   Some responses to the draft Interpretation noted that a change in the estimate of a residual value is accounted for prospectively and does not require a catch-up adjustment. They observed that liabilities relating to decommissioning costs can be regarded as negative residual values, and suggested that the Interpretation should not introduce inconsistent treatment for similar events. Anomalies could result if two aspects of the same change are dealt with differently—for example, if the useful life of an asset was extended and the present value of the decommissioning liability reduced as a result.

BC16   The IFRIC agreed that it had not made a sufficient case for treating changes in estimates of decommissioning and similar liabilities differently from other changes in estimates for property, plant and equipment. The IFRIC understood that there was no likelihood of the treatment of other changes in estimate for such assets being revisited in the near future.

BC17   The IFRIC also noted that the anomalies that could result from its original proposal, if other changes in estimate were dealt with prospectively, were more serious than it had understood previously, and that a fully prospective treatment would be easier to apply consistently.

BC18   The IFRIC had been concerned that a fully prospective treatment could result in either unrealistically large assets or negative assets, particularly if there are large changes in estimates toward the end of an asset's life. The IFRIC noted that the first concern could be dealt with if the assets were reviewed for impairment in accordance with IAS 36 *Impairment of Assets*, and that a zero asset floor could be applied to ensure that an asset did not become negative if cost estimates reduced significantly towards the end of its life. The credit would first be applied to write the carrying amount of the asset down to nil and then any residual credit adjustment would be recognised in profit or loss. These safeguards are included in the final consensus.

Comparison with US GAAP

BC19   In reaching its consensus, the IFRIC considered the US GAAP approach in Statement of Financial Accounting Standards No. 143, *Accounting for Asset Retirement Obligations* (SFAS 143). Under that standard, changes in estimated cash flows are capitalised as part of the cost of the asset and depreciated prospectively, but the decommissioning obligation is not required to be revised to reflect the effect of a change in the current market-assessed discount rate.

BC20   The treatment of changes in estimated cash flows required by this Interpretation is consistent with US GAAP, which the proposal in D2 was not. However, the IFRIC agreed that because IAS 37 requires a decommissioning obligation to reflect the effect of a change in the current market-based discount rate (see paragraph BC3), it was not possible to disregard changes in the discount rate. Furthermore, SFAS 143 did not treat changes in cash flows and discount rates in the same way, which the IFRIC had agreed was important.

The interaction of the Interpretation and initial recognition under IAS 16

BC21　In developing the Interpretation, the IFRIC considered the improvements that have been made to IAS 16 by the Board and agreed that it would explain the interaction of the two.

BC22　IAS 16 (as revised in 2003) clarifies that the initial measurement of the cost of an item of property, plant and equipment should include the cost of dismantling and removing the item and restoring the site on which it is located, if this obligation is incurred either when the item is acquired or as a consequence of having used the item during a particular period for purposes other than to produce inventories during that period. This is because the Board concluded that whether the obligation is incurred upon acquisition of the item or as a consequence of using it, the underlying nature of the cost and its association with the asset are the same.

BC23　However, in considering the improvements to IAS 16, the Board did not address how an entity would account for (a) changes in the amount of the initial estimate of a recognised obligation, (b) the effects of accretion of, or changes in interest rates on, a recognised obligation or (c) the cost of obligations that did not exist when the entity acquired the item, such as an obligation triggered by a change in a law enacted after the asset is acquired. The Interpretation addresses issues (a) and (b).

The interaction of the Interpretation and the choice of measurement model under IAS 16

BC24　IAS 16 allows an entity to choose either the cost model or the revaluation model for measuring its property, plant and equipment, on a class-by-class basis. The IFRIC's view is that the measurement model that an entity chooses under IAS 16 would not be affected by the Interpretation.

BC25　Several responses to the draft Interpretation sought clarification of how it should be applied to revalued assets. The IFRIC noted that:

(a)　if the entity chooses the revaluation model, IAS 16 requires the valuation to be kept sufficiently up to date that the carrying amount does not differ materially from that which would be determined using fair value at the balance sheet date.* This Interpretation requires a change in a recognised decommissioning, restoration or similar liability generally to be added to or deducted from the cost of the asset. However, a change in the liability does not, of itself, affect the *valuation* of the asset for financial reporting purposes, because (to ensure that it is not counted twice) the separately recognised liability is excluded from its valuation.

(b)　rather than changing the valuation of the asset, a change in the liability affects the difference between what would have been reported for the asset under the cost model, under this Interpretation, and its valuation. In other

---

*　IAS 1 *Presentation of Financial Statements* (revised 2007) replaced the term 'balance sheet date' with 'end of the reporting period'.

words, it changes the revaluation surplus or deficit that has previously been recognised for the asset. For example, if the liability increases by CU20, which under the cost model would have been added to the cost of the asset, the revaluation surplus reduces (or the revaluation deficit increases) by CU20. Under the revaluation model set out in IAS 16, cumulative revaluation surpluses for an asset are accounted for in equity,* and cumulative revaluation deficits are accounted for in profit or loss. The IFRIC decided that changes in the liability relating to a revalued asset should be accounted for in the same way as other changes in revaluation surpluses and deficits under IAS 16.

(c) although a change in the liability does not directly affect the value of the asset for financial reporting purposes, many events that change the value of the liability may also affect the value of the asset, by either a greater or lesser amount. The IFRIC therefore decided that, for revalued assets, a change in a decommissioning liability indicates that a revaluation may be required. Any such revaluation should be taken into account in determining the amount taken to profit or loss under (b) above. If a revaluation is done, IAS 16 requires all assets of the same class to be revalued.

(d) the depreciated cost of an asset (less any impairment) should not be negative, regardless of the valuation model, and the revaluation surplus on an asset should not exceed its value. The IFRIC therefore decided that, if the reduction in a liability exceeds the carrying amount that would have been recognised had the asset been carried under the cost model, the excess reduction should always be taken to profit or loss. For example, if the depreciated cost of an unimpaired asset is CU25, and its revalued amount is CU100, there is a revaluation surplus of CU75. If the decommissioning liability associated with the asset is reduced by CU30, the depreciated cost of the asset should be reduced to nil, the revaluation surplus should be increased to CU100 (which equals the value of the asset), and the remaining CU5 of the reduction in the liability should be taken to profit or loss.

The unwinding of the discount

BC26 The IFRIC considered whether the unwinding of the discount is a borrowing cost for the purposes of IAS 23 *Borrowing Costs*. This question arises because if the unwinding of the discount rate were deemed a borrowing cost for the purposes of IAS 23, in certain circumstances this amount might be capitalised under the allowed alternative treatment of capitalisation.† The IFRIC noted that IAS 23 addresses funds borrowed specifically for the purpose of obtaining a particular

---

* As a consequence of the revision of IAS 1 *Presentation of Financial Statements* in 2007 the increase is recognised in other comprehensive income and accumulated in equity under the heading of revaluation surplus.

† In March 2007, IAS 23 was revised to require the previously allowed alternative treatment of capitalisation. Capitalisation of borrowing costs for a qualifying asset becomes the only accounting treatment. That revision does not affect the reasoning set out in this Basis for Conclusions.

asset. It agreed that a decommissioning liability does not fall within this description since it does not reflect funds (ie cash) borrowed. Hence, the IFRIC concluded that the unwinding of the discount is not a borrowing cost as defined in IAS 23.

BC27   The IFRIC agreed that the unwinding of the discount as referred to in paragraph 60 of IAS 37 should be reported in profit or loss in the period it occurs.

Disclosures

BC28   The IFRIC considered whether the Interpretation should include disclosure guidance and agreed that it was largely unnecessary because IAS 16 and IAS 37 contain relevant guidance, for example:

(a)   IAS 16 explains that IAS 8 requires the disclosure of the nature and effect of changes in accounting estimates that have an effect in the current period or are expected to have a material effect in subsequent periods, and that such disclosure may arise from changes in the estimated costs of dismantling, removing or restoring items of property, plant and equipment.

(b)   IAS 37 requires the disclosure of:

(i)   a reconciliation of the movements in the carrying amount of the provision for the period.

(ii)   the increase during the period in the discounted amount arising from the passage of time and the effect of any change in the discount rate.

(iii)   a brief description of the nature of the obligation and the expected timing of any resulting outflows of economic benefits.

(iv)   an indication of the uncertainties about the amount or timing of those outflows, and where necessary the disclosure of the major assumptions made concerning future events (eg future interest rates, future changes in salaries, and future changes in prices).

BC29   However, in respect of assets measured using the revaluation model, the IFRIC noted that changes in the liability would often be taken to the revaluation surplus. These changes reflect an event of significance to users, and the IFRIC agreed that they should be given prominence by being separately disclosed and described as such in the statement of changes in equity.*

Transition

BC30   The IFRIC agreed that preparers that already apply IFRSs should apply the Interpretation in the manner required by IAS 8, which is usually retrospectively. The IFRIC could not justify another application method, especially when IAS 37 requires retrospective application.

---

*   As a consequence of the revision of IAS 1 *Presentation of Financial Statements* in 2007 such changes are presented in the statement of comprehensive income.

BC31   The IFRIC noted that, in order to apply the Interpretation retrospectively, it is necessary to determine both the timing and amount of any changes that would have been required by the Interpretation. However, IAS 8 specifies that:

(a)   if retrospective application is not practicable for all periods presented, the new accounting policy shall be applied retrospectively from the earliest practicable date; and

(b)   if it is impracticable to determine the cumulative effect of applying the new accounting policy at the start of the current period, the policy shall be applied prospectively from the earliest date practicable.

BC32   The IFRIC noted that IAS 8 defines a requirement as impracticable when an entity cannot apply it after making every reasonable effort to do so, and gives guidance on when this is so.

BC33   However, the provisions of IAS 8 on practicability do not apply to IFRS 1 *First-time Adoption of International Financial Reporting Standards*. Retrospective application of this Interpretation at the date of transition to IFRSs, which is the treatment required by IFRS 1 in the absence of any exemptions, would require first-time adopters to construct a historical record of all such adjustments that would have been made in the past. In many cases this will not be practicable. The IFRIC agreed that, as an alternative to retrospective application, an entity should be permitted to include in the depreciated cost of the asset at the date of transition an amount calculated by discounting the liability at that date back to, and depreciating it from, when it was first incurred. This Interpretation amends IFRS 1 accordingly.

Document published to accompany

IFRIC Interpretation 2

Members' Shares in Co-operative Entities and Similar Instruments

This version includes amendments resulting from IFRSs issued up to 31 December 2009.

The text of the unaccompanied IFRIC 2 is contained in Part A of this edition. Its effective date when issued was 1 September 2004. The effective date of the amendments is 1 January 2009. This part presents the following accompanying document:

page

BASIS FOR CONCLUSIONS
B1492

Basis for Conclusions on
IFRIC Interpretation 2 *Members' Shares in Co-operative Entities and Similar Instruments*

This Basis for Conclusions accompanies, but is not part of, IFRIC 2.

Introduction

BC1 This Basis for Conclusions summarises the IFRIC's considerations in reaching its consensus. Individual IFRIC members gave greater weight to some factors than to others.

Background

BC2 In September 2001, the Standing Interpretations Committee instituted by the former International Accounting Standards Committee (IASC) published Draft Interpretation SIC D-34 *Financial Instruments - Instruments or Rights Redeemable by the Holder*. The Draft Interpretation stated: 'The issuer of a Puttable Instrument should classify the entire instrument as a liability.'

BC3 In 2001 the International Accounting Standards Board (IASB) began operations in succession to IASC. The IASB's initial agenda included a project to make limited amendments to the financial instruments standards issued by IASC. The IASB decided to incorporate the consensus from Draft Interpretation D-34 as part of those amendments. In June 2002 the IASB published an exposure draft of amendments to IAS 32 *Financial Instruments: Disclosure and Presentation* that incorporated the proposed consensus from Draft Interpretation D-34.

BC4 In their responses to the Exposure Draft and in their participation in public round-table discussions held in March 2003, representatives of co-operative banks raised questions about the application of the principles in IAS 32 to members' shares. This was followed by a series of meetings between IASB members and staff and representatives of the European Association of Co-operative Banks. After considering questions raised by the bank group, the IASB concluded that the principles articulated in IAS 32 should not be modified, but that there were questions about the application of those principles to co-operative entities that should be considered by the IFRIC.

BC5 In considering the application of IAS 32 to co-operative entities, the IFRIC recognised that a variety of entities operate as co-operatives and these entities have a variety of capital structures. The IFRIC decided that its proposed Interpretation should address some features that exist in a number of co-operatives. However, the IFRIC noted that its conclusions and the examples in the Interpretation are not limited to the specific characteristics of members' shares in European co-operative banks.

Basis for consensus

BC6   Paragraph 15 of IAS 32 states:

> The issuer of a financial instrument shall classify the instrument, or its component parts, on initial recognition as a financial liability, a financial asset or an equity instrument in accordance with the *substance of the contractual arrangement* and the definitions of a financial liability, a financial asset and an equity instrument. [Emphasis added]

BC7   In many jurisdictions, local law or regulations state that members' shares are equity of the entity. However, paragraph 17 of IAS 32 states:

> With the exception of the circumstances described in paragraphs 16A and 16B or paragraphs 16C and 16D, a critical feature in differentiating a financial liability from an equity instrument is *the existence of a contractual obligation of one party to the financial instrument (the issuer) either to deliver cash or another financial asset to the other party (the holder) or to exchange financial assets or financial liabilities with the holder under conditions that are potentially unfavourable to the issuer.* Although the holder of an equity instrument may be entitled to receive a pro rata share of any dividends or other distributions of equity, the issuer does not have a contractual obligation to make such distributions because it cannot be required to deliver cash or another financial asset to another party. [Emphasis added]

BC8   Paragraphs cited in the examples in the Appendix and in the paragraphs above show that, under IAS 32, the terms of the contractual agreement govern the classification of a financial instrument as a financial liability or equity. If the terms of an instrument create an unconditional obligation to transfer cash or another financial asset, circumstances that might restrict an entity's ability to make the transfer when due do not alter the classification as a financial liability. If the terms of the instrument give the entity an unconditional right to avoid delivering cash or another financial asset, the instrument is classified as equity. This is true even if other factors make it likely that the entity will continue to distribute dividends or make or other payments. In view of those principles, the IFRIC decided to focus on circumstances that would indicate that the entity has the unconditional right to avoid making payments to a member who has requested that his or her shares be redeemed.

BC9   The IFRIC identified two situations in which a co-operative entity has an unconditional right to avoid the transfer of cash or another financial asset. The IFRIC acknowledges that there may be other situations that may raise questions about the application of IAS 32 to members' shares. However, it understands that the two situations are often present in the contractual and other conditions surrounding members' shares and that interpretation of those two situations would eliminate many of the questions that may arise in practice.

BC10   The IFRIC also noted that an entity assesses whether it has an unconditional right to avoid the transfer of cash or another financial asset on the basis of local laws, regulations and its governing charter in effect at the date of classification. This is because it is local laws, regulations and the governing charter in effect at the classification date, together with the terms contained in the instrument's documentation that constitute the terms and conditions of the instrument at that date. Accordingly, an entity does not take into account expected future amendments to local law, regulation or its governing charter.

The right to refuse redemption (paragraph 7)

BC11   An entity may have the unconditional right to refuse redemption of a member's shares. If such a right exists, the entity does not have the obligation to transfer cash or another financial asset that IAS 32 identifies as a critical characteristic of a financial liability.

BC12   The IFRIC considered whether the entity's history of making redemptions should be considered in deciding whether the entity's right to refuse requests is, in fact, unconditional. The IFRIC observed that a history of making redemptions may create a reasonable expectation that all future requests will be honoured. However, holders of many equity instruments have a reasonable expectation that an entity will continue a past practice of making payments. For example, an entity may have made dividend payments on preference shares for decades. Failure to make those payments would expose the entity to significant economic costs, including damage to the value of its ordinary shares. Nevertheless, as outlined in IAS 32 paragraph AG26 (cited in paragraph A3), a holder's expectations about dividends do not cause a preferred share to be classified as a financial liability.

Prohibitions against redemption (paragraphs 8 and 9)

BC13   An entity may be prohibited by law or its governing charter from redeeming members' shares if doing so would cause the number of members' shares, or the amount of paid-in capital from members' shares, to fall below a specified level. While each individual share might be puttable, a portion of the total shares outstanding is not.

BC14   The IFRIC concluded that conditions limiting an entity's ability to redeem members' shares must be evaluated sequentially. Unconditional prohibitions like those noted in paragraph 8 of the consensus prevent the entity from *incurring a liability* for redemption of all or some of the members' shares, regardless of whether it would otherwise be able to satisfy that financial liability. This contrasts with conditional prohibitions that prevent payments being made only if specified conditions—such as liquidity constraints—are met. Unconditional prohibitions prevent a liability from coming into existence, whereas the conditional prohibitions may only defer the payment of a liability already incurred. Following this analysis, an unconditional prohibition affects classification when an instrument subject to the prohibition is issued or when the prohibition is enacted or added to the entity's governing charter. In contrast, conditional restrictions such as those described in paragraphs 19 and AG25 of IAS 32 do not result in equity classification.

BC15   The IFRIC discussed whether the requirements in IAS 32 can be applied to the classification of members' shares as a whole subject to a partial redemption prohibition. IAS 32 refers to 'a financial instrument', 'a financial liability' and 'an equity instrument'. It does not refer to groups or portfolios of instruments. In view of this the IFRIC considered whether it could apply the requirements in IAS 32 to the classification of members' shares subject to partial redemption prohibitions. The application of IAS 32 to a prohibition against redeeming some portion of members' shares (eg 500,000 shares of an entity with 1,000,000 shares outstanding) is unclear.

BC16   The IFRIC noted that classifying a group of members' shares using the individual instrument approach could lead to misapplication of the principle of 'substance of the contract' in IAS 32. The IFRIC also noted that paragraph 23 of IAS 32 requires an entity that has entered into an agreement to purchase its own equity instruments to recognise a financial liability for the present value of the redemption amount (eg for the present value of the forward repurchase price, option exercise price or other redemption amount) even though the shares subject to the repurchase agreement are not individually identified. Accordingly, the IFRIC decided that for purposes of classification there are instances when IAS 32 does not require the individual instrument approach.

BC17   In many situations, looking at either individual instruments or all of the instruments governed by a particular contract would result in the same classification as financial liability or equity under IAS 32. Thus, if an entity is prohibited from redeeming any of its members' shares, the shares are not puttable and are equity. On the other hand, if there is no prohibition on redemption and no other conditions apply, members' shares are puttable and the shares are financial liabilities. However, in the case of partial prohibitions against redemption, the classification of members' shares governed by the same charter will differ, depending on whether such a classification is based on individual members' shares or the group of members' shares as a whole. For example, consider an entity with a partial prohibition that prevents it from redeeming 99 per cent of the highest number of members' shares ever outstanding. The classification based on individual shares considers each share to be potentially puttable and therefore a financial liability. This is different from the classification based on all of the members' shares. While each member's share may be redeemable individually, 99 per cent of the highest number of shares ever outstanding is not redeemable in any circumstances other than liquidation of the entity and therefore is equity.

Measurement on initial recognition (paragraph 10)

BC18   The IFRIC noted that when the financial liability for the redemption of members' shares that are redeemable on demand is initially recognised, the financial liability is measured at fair value in accordance with paragraph 49 of IAS 39 *Financial Instruments: Recognition and Measurement*. Paragraph 49 states: 'The fair value of a financial liability with a demand feature (eg a demand deposit) is not less than the amount payable on demand, discounted from the first date that the amount could be required to be paid'. Accordingly, the IFRIC decided that the fair value of the financial liability for redemption of members' shares redeemable on demand is the maximum amount payable under the redemption provisions of its governing charter or applicable law. The IFRIC also considered situations in which the number of members' shares or the amount of paid-in capital subject to prohibition against redemption may change. The IFRIC concluded that a change in the level of a prohibition against redemption should lead to a transfer between financial liabilities and equity.

Subsequent measurement

BC19   Some respondents requested additional guidance on subsequent measurement of the liability for redemption of members' shares. The IFRIC noted that the focus of this Interpretation was on clarifying the classification of financial instruments rather than their subsequent measurement. Also, the IASB has on its agenda a project to address the accounting for financial instruments (including members' shares) that are redeemable at a pro rata share of the fair value of the residual interest in the entity issuing the financial instrument. The IASB will consider certain measurement issues in this project. The IFRIC was also informed that the majority of members' shares in co-operative entities are not redeemable at a pro rata share of the fair value of the residual interest in the co-operative entity thereby obviating the more complex measurement issues. In view of the above, the IFRIC decided not to provide additional guidance on measurement in the Interpretation.

Presentation

BC20   The IFRIC noted that entities whose members' shares are not equity could use the presentation formats included in paragraphs IE32 and IE33 of the Illustrative Examples with IAS 32.

Alternatives considered

BC21   The IFRIC considered suggestions that:

(a)   members' shares should be classified as equity until a member has requested redemption. That member's share would then be classified as a financial liability and this treatment would be consistent with local laws. Some commentators believe this is a more straightforward approach to classification.

(b)   the classification of members' shares should incorporate the probability that members will request redemption. Those who suggest this view observe that experience shows this probability to be small, usually within 1–5 per cent, for some types of co-operative. They see no basis for classifying 100 per cent of the members' shares as liabilities on the basis of the behaviour of 1 per cent.

BC22   The IFRIC did not accept those views. Under IAS 32, the classification of an instrument as financial liability or equity is based on the 'substance of the contractual arrangement and the definitions of a financial liability, a financial asset and an equity instrument.' In paragraph BC7 of the Basis for Conclusions on IAS 32, the IASB observed:

> Although the legal form of such financial instruments often includes a right to the residual interest in the assets of an entity available to holders of such instruments, the inclusion of an option for the holder to put the instrument back to the entity for cash or another financial asset means that the instrument meets the definition of a financial liability. The classification as a financial liability is independent of considerations such as when the right is exercisable, how the amount payable or receivable upon exercise of the right is determined, and whether the puttable instrument has a fixed maturity.

BC23   The IFRIC also observed that an approach similar to that in paragraph BC21(a) is advocated in the Dissenting Opinion of one Board member on IAS 32. As the IASB did not adopt that approach its adoption here would require an amendment to IAS 32.

Transition and effective date (paragraph 14)

BC24   The IFRIC considered whether its Interpretation should have the same transition and effective date as IAS 32, or whether a later effective date should apply with an exemption from IAS 32 for members' shares in the interim. Some co-operatives may wish to amend their governing charter in order to continue their existing practice under national accounting requirements of classifying members' shares as equity. Such amendments usually require a general meeting of members and holding a meeting may not be possible before the effective date of IAS 32.

BC25   After considering a number of alternatives, the IFRIC decided against any exemption from the transition requirements and effective date in IAS 32. In reaching this conclusion, the IFRIC noted that it was requested to provide guidance on the application of IAS 32 when it is first adopted by co-operative entities, ie from 1 January 2005. Also, the vast majority of those who commented on the draft Interpretation did not object to the proposed effective date of 1 January 2005. Finally, the IFRIC observed that classifying members' shares as financial liabilities before the date that the terms of these shares are amended will affect only 2005 financial statements, as first-time adopters are not required to apply IAS 32 to earlier periods. As a result, any effect of the Interpretation on first-time adopters is expected to be limited. Furthermore, the IFRIC noted that regulators are familiar with the accounting issues involved. A co-operative entity may be required to present members' shares as a liability until the governing charter is amended. The IFRIC understands that such amendments, if adopted, could be in place by mid-2005. Accordingly, the IFRIC decided that the effective date for the Interpretation would be annual periods beginning on or after 1 January 2005.

Documents published to accompany

IFRIC Interpretation 4

Determining whether an Arrangement contains a Lease

This version includes amendments resulting from IFRSs issued up to 31 December 2009.

The text of the unaccompanied IFRIC 4 is contained in Part A of this edition. Its effective date when issued was 1 January 2006. The effective date of the most recent amendments is 1 January 2013. This part presents the following accompanying documents:

IFRIC Interpretation 4
Illustrative examples

These examples accompany, but are not part of, IFRIC 4.

Example of an arrangement that contains a lease

Facts

IE1   A production company (the purchaser) enters into an arrangement with a third party (the supplier) to supply a minimum quantity of gas needed in its production process for a specified period of time. The supplier designs and builds a facility adjacent to the purchaser's plant to produce the needed gas and maintains ownership and control over all significant aspects of operating the facility. The agreement provides for the following:

- The facility is explicitly identified in the arrangement, and the supplier has the contractual right to supply gas from other sources. However, supplying gas from other sources is not economically feasible or practicable.

- The supplier has the right to provide gas to other customers and to remove and replace the facility's equipment and modify or expand the facility to enable the supplier to do so. However, at inception of the arrangement, the supplier has no plans to modify or expand the facility. The facility is designed to meet only the purchaser's needs.

- The supplier is responsible for repairs, maintenance, and capital expenditures.

- The supplier must stand ready to deliver a minimum quantity of gas each month.

- Each month, the purchaser will pay a fixed capacity charge and a variable charge based on actual production taken. The purchaser must pay the fixed capacity charge irrespective of whether it takes any of the facility's production. The variable charge includes the facility's actual energy costs, which amount to about 90 per cent of the facility's total variable costs. The supplier is subject to increased costs resulting from the facility's inefficient operations.

- If the facility does not produce the stated minimum quantity, the supplier must return all or a portion of the fixed capacity charge.

Assessment

IE2   The arrangement contains a lease within the scope of IAS 17 *Leases*. An asset (the facility) is explicitly identified in the arrangement and fulfilment of the arrangement is dependent on the facility. Although the supplier has the right to supply gas from other sources, its ability to do so is not substantive. The purchaser has obtained the right to use the facility because, on the facts presented—in particular, that the facility is designed to meet only the purchaser's needs and the supplier has no plans to expand or modify the facility—it is remote that one or more parties other than the purchaser will take more than an insignificant amount of the facility's output and the price the purchaser will pay is neither contractually fixed per unit of output nor equal to the current market price per unit of output as of the time of delivery of the output.

Example of an arrangement that does not contain a lease

Facts

IE3   A manufacturing company (the purchaser) enters into an arrangement with a third party (the supplier) to supply a specific component part of its manufactured product for a specified period of time. The supplier designs and constructs a plant adjacent to the purchaser's factory to produce the component part. The designed capacity of the plant exceeds the purchaser's current needs, and the supplier maintains ownership and control over all significant aspects of operating the plant. The arrangement provides for the following:

- The supplier's plant is explicitly identified in the arrangement, but the supplier has the right to fulfil the arrangement by shipping the component parts from another plant owned by the supplier. However, to do so for any extended period of time would be uneconomic.

- The supplier is responsible for repairs, maintenance, and capital expenditures of the plant.

- The supplier must stand ready to deliver a minimum quantity. The purchaser is required to pay a fixed price per unit for the actual quantity taken. Even if the purchaser's needs are such that they do not need the stated minimum quantity, they still pay only for the actual quantity taken.

- The supplier has the right to sell the component parts to other customers and has a history of doing so (by selling in the replacement parts market), so it is expected that parties other than the purchaser will take more than an insignificant amount of the component parts produced at the supplier's plant.

Assessment

IE4   The arrangement does not contain a lease within the scope of IAS 17. An asset (the plant) is explicitly identified in the arrangement and fulfilment of the arrangement is dependent on the facility. Although the supplier has the right to supply component parts from other sources, the supplier would not have the ability to do so because it would be uneconomic. However, the purchaser has not obtained the right to use the plant because the purchaser does not have the ability or right to operate or direct others to operate the plant or control physical access to the plant, and the likelihood that parties other than the purchaser will take more than an insignificant amount of the component parts produced at the plant is more than remote, on the basis of the facts presented. In addition, the price that the purchaser pays is fixed per unit of output taken.

Basis for Conclusions on
IFRIC Interpretation 4 *Determining whether an Arrangement contains a Lease*

This Basis for Conclusions accompanies, but is not part of, IFRIC 4.

Introduction

BC1   This Basis for Conclusions summarises the IFRIC's considerations in reaching its consensus. Individual IFRIC members gave greater weight to some factors than to others.

Background (paragraphs 1–3)

BC2   The IFRIC noted that arrangements have developed in recent years that do not take the legal form of a lease but convey rights to use items for agreed periods of time in return for a payment or series of payments. Examples of such arrangements are set out in paragraph 1 of the Interpretation. The IFRIC observed that these arrangements share many features of a lease because a lease is defined in paragraph 4 of IAS 17 *Leases* as 'an agreement whereby the lessor conveys to the lessee in return for a payment or series of payments *the right to use an asset* for an agreed period of time' (emphasis added). The IFRIC noted that all arrangements meeting the definition of a lease should be accounted for in accordance with IAS 17 (subject to the scope of that Standard) regardless of whether they take the legal form of a lease. In other words, just as the Standing Interpretations Committee concluded in SIC-27 *Evaluating the Substance of Transactions Involving the Legal Form of a Lease* that an arrangement that is described as a lease is not necessarily accounted for as a lease, the IFRIC concluded that an arrangement can be within the scope of IAS 17 even if it is not described as a lease. The IFRIC therefore decided that it should issue guidance to assist in determining whether an arrangement is, or contains, a lease.

BC3   The IFRIC published Draft Interpretation D3 *Determining whether an Arrangement contains a Lease* for public comment in January 2004 and received 51 comment letters in response to its proposals. In addition, in order to understand better the practical issues that would have arisen on implementing the proposed Interpretation, IASB staff met a number of preparer constituents.

BC4   There was broad support for the IFRIC issuing an Interpretation on this topic (even among those respondents who disagreed with the criteria in D3 for determining whether a lease exists). However, some respondents to D3 questioned whether the proposals were a legitimate *interpretation* of IAS 17. In particular, some suggested that the proposals anticipated the Board's current research project on leasing.

BC5   In considering these comments, the IFRIC concluded that they primarily arose from its observation in the Basis for Conclusions on D3 that 'the lease asset under IAS 17 is the right to use [and] that this asset should not be confused with the underlying item [in the arrangement]' (eg an item of property, plant or equipment). As a result, the IFRIC understood that some respondents were concerned that D3 was requiring (or permitting) purchasers (lessees) to recognise an intangible asset for the right of use, even for leases classified as operating leases.

BC6　During redeliberation, the IFRIC affirmed its view that conceptually IAS 17 regards the asset as the right of use (although it acknowledged that in a finance lease, a lessee recognises an asset and accounts for that asset as if it were within the scope of IAS 16 *Property, Plant and Equipment* or IAS 38 *Intangible Assets*). However, the IFRIC decided to emphasise that the objective of the Interpretation is only to identify whether an arrangement contains a lease, not to change the requirements of IAS 17. Accordingly, having identified a lease, an entity accounts for that lease in accordance with IAS 17. This includes following the requirements of paragraphs 7–19 of IAS 17 to determine whether the lease should be classified as an operating lease or as a finance lease. This means, for example, that if a purchaser satisfies the criteria in the Interpretation, it (a) recognises an asset only if substantially all the risks and rewards incidental to ownership are transferred and (b) treats the recognised asset as a leased item, rather than an intangible asset for the right to use that item.

BC7　The IFRIC reconsidered its use of the term 'item' in D3 (as in right to use an item). The IFRIC noted that it had used 'item' rather than 'asset' to refer to the underlying asset in the arrangement (eg an item of property, plant or equipment) in order to emphasise that the asset that is the subject of the Interpretation is the right of use and not the underlying item or asset. However, given that many found the use of the term confusing, the IFRIC decided in finalising the Interpretation to revert to the phrase in IAS 17 'right to use an asset'.

Multiple-element arrangements

BC8　The IFRIC observed that many of the arrangements that fall within the scope of the Interpretation are likely to involve services as well as a right to use an asset. In other words, the arrangement is what is sometimes referred to as a multiple-element arrangement. The IFRIC concluded that IAS 17 allows for separate recognition of a lease that is embedded or contained within a multiple-element arrangement because IAS 17 states (paragraph 3) that it applies to 'agreements that transfer the right to use assets even though substantial services by the lessor may be called for in connection with the operation or maintenance of such assets.' In addition, the definition of minimum lease payments in paragraph 4 of IAS 17 clarifies that such payments exclude costs for services. The Interpretation therefore addresses whether a multiple-element arrangement contains a lease and not just whether an *entire* arrangement is a lease.

Portions of an asset (paragraph 3)

BC9　The Interpretation (like D3) does not address what constitutes the underlying asset in the arrangement. In other words, it does not address when a portion of a larger asset can be the subject of a lease.

BC10   Some respondents to D3 suggested that this omission pointed to a flaw in the proposals. They were troubled by the potential inconsistency between the accounting for a take-or-pay arrangement for substantially all of the output from a specific asset (which could have contained a lease) and one for a smaller portion of the output (which would not have been required to be treated as containing a lease). Other respondents argued that D3 would have allowed undue flexibility and that the IFRIC should either explicitly rule out portions or provide additional guidance to clarify which portions should be recognised (for example, those that are physically distinguishable).

BC11   From an early stage in this project, the IFRIC decided that it should not address the issue of portions and should focus on the main question, ie what constitutes a lease. The IFRIC noted that the subject of portions was important in itself and had much wider applicability than the Interpretation. The IFRIC affirmed this view during its redeliberations and therefore rejected the suggestion that it also should address portions in the Interpretation. The IFRIC also concluded that it would be inappropriate to specify that the Interpretation should not be applied to an arrangement that contains a right to use a portion of an asset (whether that portion be a physically distinguishable portion of an asset, or defined by reference to the output of the asset or the time the asset is made available) because this would conflict with IAS 17. The IFRIC agreed that the phrase 'right to use an asset' does not preclude the asset being a portion of a larger asset.

BC12   However, in the light of comments from respondents, the IFRIC decided to clarify that the Interpretation should be applied to arrangements in which the underlying asset would represent the unit of account in either IAS 16 or IAS 38.

Scope (paragraph 4)

BC13   The objective of the Interpretation is to determine whether an arrangement contains a lease that falls within the scope of IAS 17. The lease is then accounted for in accordance with that Standard. Because the Interpretation should not be read as overriding any of the requirements of IAS 17, the IFRIC decided that it should clarify that if an arrangement is found to be, or contains, a lease or licensing agreement that is excluded from the scope of IAS 17, an entity need not apply IAS 17 to that lease or licensing agreement.

BC14   The IFRIC considered whether the scope of the Interpretation might overlap with IAS 39 *Financial Instruments: Recognition and Measurement.*[*] In particular it noted the view that an arrangement for output might meet the definition of a derivative under IAS 39 but also be determined to contain a lease under this Interpretation. The IFRIC concluded that there should not be an overlap because an arrangement for output that is a derivative would not meet the criteria in paragraphs 6–9 of the Interpretation. In particular, the IFRIC noted that such an arrangement would be for a product with a quoted market price available in an active market and would therefore be unlikely to depend upon the use of a specifically identified asset.

---

[*]   In November 2009 the Board amended some of the requirements of IAS 39 and relocated them to IFRS 9 *Financial Instruments*. IFRS 9 applies to all assets within the scope of IAS 39.

BC14A   The IFRIC considered whether the scope of the Interpretation might overlap with IFRIC 12, which was developed from draft Interpretations D12–D14. In particular it noted the views expressed by some respondents to the proposals that the contractual terms of some public-to-private service concession arrangements would be regarded as leases under IFRIC 4 and would also be regarded as meeting the scope criterion of D12–D14. The IFRIC did not regard the choice between accounting treatments as appropriate because it could lead to different accounting treatments for contracts that have similar economic effects. The IFRIC therefore amended IFRIC 4 to specify that if a public-to-private service concession arrangement met the scope requirements of IFRIC 12 it would not be within the scope of IFRIC 4.

Consensus (paragraphs 6–15)

Criteria for determining whether an arrangement contains a lease (paragraphs 6–9)

BC15   In D3 the IFRIC proposed that three criteria would all need to be satisfied for an arrangement to be, or contain, a lease:

(a)   The arrangement depends upon a specific item or items (the item). The item need not be explicitly identified by the contractual provisions of the arrangement. Rather it may be implicitly identified because it is not economically feasible or practical for the supplier to fulfil the arrangement by providing use of alternative items.

(b)   The arrangement conveys a right to use the item for a specific period of time such that the purchaser is able to exclude others from using the item.

(c)   Payments under the arrangement are made for the time that the item is made available for use rather than for actual use of the item.

BC16   D3 also proposed that arrangements in which there is only a remote possibility that parties other than the purchaser will take more than an insignificant amount of the output produced by an item would meet the second of the criteria above.

BC17   In its Basis for Conclusions on D3, the IFRIC drew attention to the similarities between its Interpretation and Issue No. 01-8 *Determining Whether an Arrangement Contains a Lease* published by the US Emerging Issues Task Force (EITF) in May 2003. The IFRIC concluded that '[a]lthough the wording of Issue 01-8 and the draft Interpretation differ, ... a similar assessment of whether an arrangement contains a lease is likely under both interpretations.'

BC18   Some respondents disagreed with the IFRIC's conclusion and suggested that the differences between the two interpretations were, in fact, significant. The IFRIC, however, maintained its original conclusion. In particular, it noted that both it and the EITF had concluded that a right of use can be conveyed in arrangements in which purchasers have rights to acquire the output that will be produced by an asset, regardless of any right or ability physically to operate or control access to that asset. Accordingly, many take-or-pay (and similar contracts) would have been similarly assessed under the two interpretations.

BC19　Nonetheless, the IFRIC agreed that some arrangements would be regarded as leases under Issue 01-8 but not under D3. The IFRIC concluded that there were two main reasons for this. First, the effect of the third criterion in D3 ('payments under the arrangement are made for the time that the item is made available for use rather than for actual use of the item') was that a purchaser would always be required to assume some pricing risk in an arrangement for there to be a lease. This is not the case under Issue 01-8. Secondly, the second criterion in D3 ('the arrangement conveys a right to use the item ... such that the purchaser is able to exclude others from using the item') suggested that a right of use is conveyed in an arrangement for the output from an asset only when the purchaser is taking *substantially all* of the output from a specific asset. Under Issue 01-8, a right of use is also conveyed if the purchaser controls or operates the underlying specific asset while taking more than a *minor amount* of the output from an asset.

BC20　The IFRIC noted that the definition of a lease in IAS 17 is similar to its definition in the US standard SFAS 13 *Accounting for Leases*. Given this, the IFRIC concluded that there was no compelling reason for different assessments of whether an arrangement contains a lease under IFRSs and US GAAP. Furthermore, the IFRIC was sympathetic to the practical difficulties highlighted by some respondents that would arise in cases when an agreement would need to be assessed against two similar, but different, sets of criteria. Therefore, the IFRIC decided that it should seek to eliminate the differences between the approach in D3 and Issue 01-8 for determining whether an arrangement contains a lease. The IFRIC concluded that the most effective way of achieving this objective would be to modify its criteria to conform them more fully to the approach in Issue 01-8.

BC21　The IFRIC decided that as far as possible it should adopt the actual words from Issue 01-8, subject to differences between IAS 17 and SFAS 13. It concluded that differences in wording would not promote convergence and would be likely to cause confusion. Therefore, paragraphs 7–9 are virtually identical to Issue 01-8, except that:

(a)　the Interpretation uses the term 'asset' rather than 'property, plant or equipment' as in Issue 01-8. The IFRIC noted that IAS 17 covers a broader range of leases than SFAS 13 and that there was no reason for restricting this Interpretation only to items of property, plant or equipment.

(b)　the phrase 'more than a minor amount of the output' in Issue 01-8 has been expressed as 'more than an insignificant amount of the output'. This is because the latter is the more customary form of words under IFRSs and is therefore consistent with other Standards. In this context, however, the IFRIC intends 'minor' and 'insignificant' to have the same meaning.

BC22　Apart from small modifications to the wording of the first criterion in D3, the effect of converging fully with the criteria in Issue 01-8 for determining whether an arrangement contains a lease is that the second and third criteria in D3 are replaced by one criterion, requiring the arrangement to convey to the purchaser the right to control the use of the underlying asset.

BC23　Although the requirements for determining whether an arrangement contains a lease are the same under IFRSs and US GAAP, the IFRIC emphasises that any lease identified by the Interpretation may be accounted for differently under IFRSs and US GAAP because of differences between their respective leasing standards.

　　　　　　　　　　© IASCF

Fulfilment of the arrangement is dependent on the use of a specific asset (paragraphs 7 and 8)

BC24 The IFRIC agreed that a specific asset needs to be identified in the arrangement for there to be a lease. The IFRIC concluded that this follows from the definition of a lease, which refers to a 'right to use *an* asset' (emphasis added). The IFRIC also observed that dependence on a specifically identified asset is a feature that distinguishes a lease from other arrangements that also convey rights to use assets but are not leases (eg some service arrangements).

BC25 However, the IFRIC concluded that the identification of the asset in the arrangement need not be explicit. Rather, the facts and circumstances could implicitly identify an asset because it would not be economically feasible or practical for the supplier to perform its obligation by providing the use of alternative assets. Examples of when an asset may be implicitly identified are when the supplier owns only one suitable asset; the asset used to fulfil the contract needs to be at a particular location or specialised to the purchaser's needs; and the supplier is a special purpose entity formed for a limited purpose.

BC26 Some respondents to D3 noted that the effect of this first criterion is that the *purchaser's* accounting could depend on how the *supplier* chooses to fulfil the arrangement. They noted that the purchaser might have no control over this because (in form) the purchaser has contracted for output. Some respondents were also troubled by the lack of comparability, because similar arrangements for the output of an asset could be accounted for differently according to whether they depend on the use of a specific asset.

BC27 In response to the first of these comments, the IFRIC noted that how an entity chooses to obtain a product normally determines the accounting treatment; for example, an entity requiring power may choose to lease a power plant or connect to the grid and the two options would result in different accounting. Although in the respondents' example the choice is the supplier's (rather than the purchaser's), the IFRIC concluded that the critical matter is the end position of the entity (ie is there a lease?) not how it got to that position (ie whether it chose that outcome or it was imposed).

BC28 In response to the second comment, the IFRIC observed that it is important to consider the combined effect of the criteria in the Interpretation rather than considering the criteria individually. On reconsidering the proposals in D3 and the requirements of Issue 01-8, the IFRIC concluded that in the context of current IFRSs, in which executory contracts are generally not accounted for, the Interpretation identifies contracts (or an element therein) that for a purchaser warrant recognition (if the definition of a finance lease is satisfied). The IFRIC concluded that identifying and accounting for the lease element would represent an improvement to existing accounting practice.

Arrangement conveys a right to use the asset (paragraph 9)

BC29 Following Issue 01-8, the Interpretation specifies that a right of use can be conveyed if any of three criteria is satisfied.

BC30   The first two criteria consider the purchaser's ability to control physically the use of the underlying asset, either through operations or access, while obtaining or controlling more than an insignificant amount of the output of the asset. For example, a purchaser's ability to operate the asset may be evidenced by its ability to hire, fire or replace the operator of the asset or its ability to specify significant operating policies and procedures in the arrangement (as opposed to a right to monitor the supplier's activities) with the supplier having no ability to change such policies and procedures.

BC31   In D3 the IFRIC explained that it did not regard the ability of a purchaser to operate physically the underlying asset as determinative of whether a right of use has been conveyed. The IFRIC noted that asset managers 'operate' assets, but this does not necessarily convey a right of use. However, the IFRIC noted that under Issue 01-8, in addition to the ability to operate the asset, the purchaser has to be taking more than a minor amount of the output. The IFRIC agreed that in such cases the arrangement would convey a right of use.

BC32   The IFRIC agreed with the EITF that a right of use has been conveyed in arrangements in which the purchaser has the ability to control physically the use of the underlying asset through access (while obtaining or controlling more than a minor amount of the output of the asset). The IFRIC noted that in such arrangements the purchaser would have the ability to restrict the access of others to economic benefits of the underlying asset.

BC33   The third criterion for determining whether a right of use has been conveyed considers whether the purchaser is taking all or substantially all of the output or other utility of the underlying asset.

BC34   As noted above, D3 similarly specified that a right of use could be conveyed in arrangements in which there is only a remote possibility that other parties could take more than an insignificant amount of the output of an asset. Among the respondents who disagreed with the proposals in D3, it was this criterion that was considered most troublesome. They disagreed that, in certain specified circumstances, a purchaser's right to acquire the output from an asset could be equated with a right of use that asset. Among the arguments put to the IFRIC were:

(a)   A right of use requires the purchaser to have the ability to control the way in which the underlying asset is used during the term of the arrangement: for example, the right for the purchaser's employees to assist or supervise the operation of the asset.

(b)   In addition to the right to the output, the purchaser needs to have control over the delivery profile of the output; in other words it also needs the ability to determine when the output flows, otherwise it is simply consuming the output of the underlying asset rather than using the asset in its business.

(c)   In most supply arrangements, the purchaser would not have access to the plant in the event of default by the supplier but would receive damages. The absence of this right points to there not being a lease. If the arrangement did contain a lease, the purchaser would have the ability to receive the output from the plant in the arrangement by replacing the original supplier with another service provider.

(d) D3 dismisses 'risks and rewards incidental to ownership' of the asset in determining whether an arrangement contains a lease. Therefore, arrangements in which the supplier retains significantly all of the risks and rewards of operation and ownership of the asset could be deemed to contain leases. However, in such arrangements the supplier's cash flows may have significantly more potential for variability than a 'true' lessor and the supplier may demand a return significantly above the market rate for a lessor.

BC35 In its redeliberations, the IFRIC reaffirmed its view that a purchaser that is taking substantially all of the output from an asset has the ability to restrict the access of others to the output from that asset. The purchaser therefore has a right of use because it controls access to the economic benefits to be derived from the asset. The IFRIC therefore did not agree that the absence of the ability to control physically the way in which the underlying asset is used precludes the existence of a right of use (although, as noted above, such an ability may indicate that a right of use has been conveyed).

BC36 With respect to the other points, the IFRIC noted the following:

(a) A purchaser that is taking substantially all of the output from an asset in cases when it is remote that others will be taking more than an insignificant amount of the output does in effect determine when the output flows.

(b) In most straightforward leases, any lessee that terminates the lease because of default by the lessor would no longer have access to the asset. Furthermore, in many leases that contain both a right of use and a service element, the related service contract does not operate independently (eg the lessee cannot terminate the service element alone). Indeed, the IFRIC noted that the purchaser's entitlement to damages in the event of default by the supplier indicates that a right of use was originally conveyed, and that the supplier is compensating the purchaser for withdrawing that right.

(c) Risks and rewards are in general relevant for determining lease classification rather than whether an arrangement is a lease. The IFRIC noted that in many straightforward short-term operating leases, substantially all the risks and rewards are retained by the lessor. Even if it were desirable to specify that a certain level of risks and rewards needed to be transferred for there to be a lease, the IFRIC was doubtful that such a criterion could be made operable. Nonetheless, an arrangement that conveys the right to use an asset will also convey certain risks and rewards incidental to ownership. Therefore, the transfer of risks and rewards of ownership may indicate that the arrangement conveys the right to use an asset. For example, if an arrangement's pricing provides for a fixed capacity charge designed to recover the supplier's capital investment in the underlying asset, the pricing may be persuasive evidence that it is remote that parties other than the purchaser will take more than an insignificant amount of the output or other utility that will be produced or generated by the asset, and the criterion in paragraph 9(c) is satisfied.

BC37 In adopting the approach from Issue 01-8, the IFRIC has specified that an arrangement for all or substantially all of the output from a specific asset does not convey the right to use the asset if the price that the purchaser will pay is contractually fixed per unit of output or equal to the current market price per unit of output as of the time of delivery of the output. This is because in such cases the purchaser is paying for a product or service rather than paying for the right to use the asset. In D3, the IFRIC proposed making a similar distinction by the combination of the second and third criteria (see paragraph BC15(b) and (c) above).

BC38 The IFRIC noted that its Interpretation could result in take-or-pay arrangements, in which purchasers are committed to purchase substantially all of the output from specific assets, being determined to contain leases. This is because in such arrangements the purchaser makes payments for the time that the underlying asset is made available for use rather than on the basis of actual use or output (resulting in the arrangement's pricing being neither fixed per unit of output nor equal to the current market price per unit of output). In many take-or-pay arrangements, the purchaser is contractually committed to pay the supplier regardless of whether the purchaser uses the underlying asset or obtains the output from that asset. Payments are therefore made for the right to use that asset. The IFRIC agreed that the overall effect of such a take-or-pay arrangement is similar to that of a lease plus contracts for related services and supplies (such as contracts for the operation of the asset and the purchase of inputs).

BC39 The IFRIC observed that if an arrangement contains a lease, and the lease is an operating lease, applying the Interpretation is likely to result in the same assets, liabilities and expenses being recognised as if no lease had been identified. However, the IFRIC noted that IAS 17 requires lessors and lessees to recognise operating lease payments on a straight-line basis over the lease term (unless another systematic basis is more representative of the time pattern of the benefit derived from the leased asset), and thus adjustments to the recognition profile of the payments for the lease element might be required in some instances. Also, the IFRIC noted that the Interpretation would often result in additional disclosure, because IAS 17 requires the lessor and lessee to disclose the future minimum lease payments. The IFRIC observed that, for a purchaser, the arrangements discussed in the Interpretation typically represent significant future commitments, and yet these commitments are not specifically required to be disclosed in the financial statements by Standards other than IAS 17. The IFRIC concluded that bringing such arrangements within the scope of IAS 17 would provide users of financial statements with relevant information that is useful for assessing the purchaser's solvency, liquidity and adaptability. The IFRIC acknowledged that the disclosed information might relate only to the lease element of the arrangement; however, it agreed that it would be beyond the scope of this Interpretation to address disclosure of executory contracts more generally.

Assessing or reassessing whether an arrangement contains a lease (paragraphs 10 and 11)

BC40   In D3 the IFRIC proposed that the assessment of whether an arrangement contains a lease should be made at the inception of the arrangement on the basis of the facts and circumstances existing at that time and that, consistently with IAS 17, an arrangement should be reassessed only if there was a change in the terms of the arrangement. Hence, under D3, a supplier that subsequently obtained additional assets with which it could fulfil the arrangement, would not have reassessed the arrangement.

BC41   Some respondents disagreed with this conclusion and argued that the analogy with the requirements for reclassifying a lease in IAS 17 was not relevant because the objective of the Interpretation is to determine whether an arrangement is within the scope of IAS 17. They noted that since this depends on factors such as whether the arrangement depends on a specific asset, it was logical that reassessment should be required if those factors change.

BC42   The IFRIC was persuaded by this argument and concluded that it outweighed the concerns that it had expressed in D3 about it being unduly burdensome to require purchasers to reassess arrangements. The IFRIC also noted that its proposal in D3 was different from Issue 01-8. Given that it had modified its approach to determining whether a lease exists to converge with Issue 01-8, the IFRIC decided that it should also specify the same treatment as Issue 01-8 for reassessments.

BC43   The IFRIC noted that the requirements in paragraphs 10 and 11 relate only to determining when the arrangement should be reassessed and that they do not alter the requirements of IAS 17. Hence if an arrangement that contains a lease is required to be reassessed and found still to contain a lease, the lease is reclassified as a finance lease or operating lease only if so required by paragraph 13 of IAS 17.

Separating payments for the lease from other payments (paragraphs 12–15)

BC44   D3 proposed, and the Interpretation requires, payments in an arrangement containing both a lease and other elements (eg services) to be separated into those for the lease and those for other elements on the basis of their relative fair values. The IFRIC concluded that fair value is the most relevant and faithful representation of the underlying economics of the transaction.

BC45   The IFRIC noted that this requirement could be more onerous for purchasers than for suppliers, particularly when a purchaser has no access to the supplier's pricing information. The IFRIC therefore agreed that it should provide some guidance to assist purchasers in separating the lease from other elements in the arrangement. Nonetheless, the IFRIC acknowledged that in rare cases it might be impracticable for the purchaser to separate the payments reliably. The IFRIC noted that if this was the case and the lease was a finance lease, then the requirements of IAS 17 would ensure that the purchaser would not capitalise an amount greater than the fair value of the asset (since paragraph 20 of IAS 17 requires a lessee to recognise a finance lease asset at the fair value of the leased property or, if lower, the present value of the minimum lease payments). Accordingly, the IFRIC decided to specify that in such cases the purchaser should recognise the fair value of the underlying asset as the leased asset. If the lease is an operating lease and it is impracticable to separate the payments reliably, the IFRIC agreed, as a practical accommodation, that the purchaser should disclose all the payments under the arrangement when disclosing the minimum lease payments, and state that these also include payment for other elements in the arrangement.

BC46 Some respondents to D3 noted that if a purchaser with an operating lease does not separate the payments, the usefulness of the disclosures required by IAS 17 would be reduced. The IFRIC agreed that the minimum lease payments are often used by users of financial statements to estimate the value of assets held under operating leases and therefore concluded that lease payments that also include payments for other elements should be disclosed separately.

Transition (paragraph 17)

BC47 D3 proposed, and the Interpretation requires, retrospective application. Some respondents proposed that the Interpretation should be applied only to new arrangements starting after its effective date. Two main arguments were put forward in support of this view:

(a) convergence with Issue 01-8 (which applies to arrangements starting or modified after the beginning of an entity's next reporting period beginning after 28 May 2003); and

(b) to ease transition, particularly in the case of longer arrangements that started some years ago and where it might be difficult to make the assessments required by D3 retrospectively.

BC48 The IFRIC noted that EITF Abstracts are usually applied prospectively. In contrast, IFRSs (including Interpretations) are applied retrospectively following the principle articulated in IAS 8 *Accounting Policies, Changes in Accounting Estimates and Errors*. The IFRIC could see no compelling argument for departing from this principle. The IFRIC also noted that unless it were to specify exactly the same effective date as Issue 01-8 (which was before D3 was published), reconciling items with US GAAP would still arise.

BC49 In addition, the IFRIC decided that the continuation of some arrangements for many years emphasised the need for retrospective application. Without retrospective application, an entity could be accounting for similar arrangements differently for many years with a consequent loss of comparability.

BC50 However, the IFRIC was sympathetic to the practical difficulties raised by full retrospective application, in particular the difficulty of going back potentially many years and determining whether the criteria would have been satisfied at that time. Although IAS 8 provides relief from fully retrospective application in cases where such treatment would be impracticable, the IFRIC decided that it should provide transitional relief for existing preparers of IFRSs in the Interpretation itself. The IFRIC emphasises that this relief does not alter the transition requirements of IAS 17 and therefore if an arrangement is determined to contain a lease an entity applies IAS 17 from the inception of the arrangement.

Document published to accompany

IFRIC Interpretation 5

Rights to Interests arising from Decommissioning, Restoration and Environmental Rehabilitation Funds

This version includes amendments resulting from IFRSs issued up to 31 December 2009.

The text of the unaccompanied IFRIC 5 is contained in Part A of this edition. Its effective date is 1 January 2006. This part presents the following accompanying document:

	page
BASIS FOR CONCLUSIONS	**B1514**

Basis for Conclusions on
IFRIC Interpretation 5 *Rights to Interests arising from Decommissioning, Restoration and Environmental Rehabilitation Funds*

This Basis for Conclusions accompanies, but is not part of, IFRIC 5.

The original text has been marked up to reflect the revision of IAS 1 Presentation of Financial Statements *in 2007: new text is underlined and deleted text is struck through.*

Introduction

BC1   This Basis for Conclusions summarises the IFRIC's considerations in reaching its consensus. Individual IFRIC members gave greater weight to some factors than to others.

Background (paragraphs 1–3)

BC2   The IFRIC was informed that an increasing number of entities with decommissioning obligations are contributing to a separate fund established to help fund those obligations. The IFRIC was also informed that questions have arisen in practice over the accounting treatment of interests in such funds and that there is a risk that divergent practices may develop. The IFRIC therefore concluded that it should provide guidance to assist in answering the questions in paragraph 6, in particular on the accounting for the asset of the right to receive reimbursement from a fund. On the issue of whether the fund should be consolidated or equity accounted, the IFRIC concluded that the normal requirements of IAS 27 *Consolidated and Separate Financial Statements*, SIC-12 *Consolidation—Special Purpose Entities*, IAS 28 *Investments in Associates* or IAS 31 *Interests in Joint Ventures* apply and that there is no need for interpretative guidance. The IFRIC published its proposed Interpretation on 15 January 2004 as D4 *Decommissioning, Restoration and Environmental Rehabilitation Funds*.

BC3   Paragraphs 1–3 describe ways in which entities might arrange to fund their decommissioning obligations. Those that are within the scope of the Interpretation are specified in paragraphs 4–6.

Scope (paragraphs 4 and 5)

BC4   D4 did not precisely define the scope because the IFRIC believed that the large variety of schemes in operation would make any definition inappropriate. However, some respondents to D4 disagreed and commented that the absence of any definition made it unclear when the Interpretation should be applied. As a result, the IFRIC has specified the scope by identifying the features that make an arrangement a decommissioning fund. It has also described the different types of fund and the features that may (or may not) be present.

BC5   The IFRIC considered whether it should issue a wider Interpretation that addresses similar forms of reimbursement, or whether it should prohibit the application of the Interpretation to other situations by analogy. The IFRIC rejected any widening of the scope, deciding instead to concentrate on the matter referred to it. The IFRIC also decided that there was no reason to prohibit the application of the Interpretation to other situations by analogy and thus the hierarchy of criteria in paragraphs 7–12 of IAS 8 *Accounting Policies, Changes in Accounting Estimates and Errors* would apply, resulting in similar accounting for reimbursements under arrangements that are not decommissioning funds, but have similar features.

BC6 The IFRIC considered comments from respondents that a contributor may have an interest in the fund that extends beyond its right to reimbursement. In response, the IFRIC added clarification that a residual interest in a fund, such as a contractual right to distributions once all the decommissioning has been completed or on winding up the fund, may be an equity instrument within the scope of IAS 39 *Financial Instruments: Recognition and Measurement.**

Basis for consensus

Accounting for an interest in a fund (paragraphs 7–9)

BC7 The IFRIC concluded that the contributor should recognise a liability unless the contributor is not liable to pay decommissioning costs even if the fund fails to pay. This is because the contributor remains liable for the decommissioning costs. Additionally, IAS 37 *Provisions, Contingent Liabilities and Contingent Assets* provides that:

(a) when an entity remains liable for expenditure, a provision should be recognised even where reimbursement is available; and

(b) if the reimbursement is virtually certain to be received when the obligation is settled, then it should be treated as a separate asset.

BC8 In concluding that the contributor should recognise separately its liability to pay decommissioning costs and its interest in the fund, the IFRIC also noted the following:

(a) There is no legally enforceable right to set off the rights under the decommissioning fund against the decommissioning liabilities. Also, given that the main objective is reimbursement, it is likely that settlement will not be net or simultaneous. Accordingly, treating these rights and liabilities as analogous to financial assets and financial liabilities would not result in offset because the offset criteria in IAS 32 *Financial Instruments: Disclosure and Presentation*† are not met.

(b) Treating the decommissioning obligation as analogous to a financial liability would not result in derecognition through extinguishment. If the fund does not assume the obligation for decommissioning, the criteria in IAS 39 for derecognition of financial liabilities through extinguishment are

---

* In November 2009 the Board amended the requirements of IAS 39 relating to classification and measurement of assets within the scope of IAS 39 and relocated them to IFRS 9 *Financial Instruments*. IFRS 9 applies to all assets within the scope of IAS 39.

† In August 2005, IAS 32 was amended as IAS 32 *Financial Instruments: Presentation*.

not met. At best, the fund acts like an in-substance defeasance that does not qualify for derecognition of the liability.

(c)   It would not be appropriate to treat decommissioning funds as analogous to pension funds, which are presented net of the related liability. This is because, in allowing a net presentation for pension plans in IAS 19 *Employee Benefits*, the International Accounting Standards Board's predecessor organisation, IASC, stated that it believed the situation is 'unique to employee benefit plans and [it did] not intend to permit this net presentation for other liabilities if the conditions in IAS 32 and IAS 39 are not met' (IAS 19, Basis for Conclusions paragraph BC68I).

BC9   As to the accounting for the contributor's interest in the fund, the IFRIC noted that some interests in funds would be within the scope of IAS 27, IAS 28, IAS 31 or SIC-12. As noted in paragraph BC2, the IFRIC concluded that, in such cases, the normal requirements of those Standards would apply and there is no need for interpretative guidance.

BC10   Otherwise, the IFRIC concluded that the contributor has an asset for its right to receive amounts from the fund.

The right to receive reimbursement from a fund and amendment to the scope of IAS 39

BC11   The IFRIC noted that under existing IFRSs, there are two forms of rights to reimbursement that would be accounted for differently:

(a)   A contractual right to receive reimbursement in the form of cash. This meets the definition of a financial asset and is within the scope of IAS 39.[*] Such a financial asset would be classified as an available-for-sale financial asset (unless accounted for using the fair value option) because it does not meet the definitions of a financial asset held for trading, a held-to-maturity investment or a loan or receivable.[†]

(b)   A right to reimbursement other than a contractual right to receive cash. This does not meet the definition of a financial asset and is within the scope of IAS 37.

BC12   The IFRIC concluded that both these forms of reimbursement have economically identical effects. Therefore accounting for both forms in the same way would provide relevant and reliable information to a user of the financial statements. However, the IFRIC noted that this did not appear possible under existing IFRSs

---

[*]   IFRS 9 *Financial Instruments*, issued in November 2009, eliminated the category of available-for-sale financial assets.

[†]   An interest in a decommissioning fund would not meet the definition of held for trading because it is not acquired or incurred principally for the purpose of selling or repurchasing it in the near term, nor of a held-to-maturity investment because it does not have fixed or determinable maturity. In addition, an interest in a fund is excluded from the definition of loans and receivables in IAS 39 since it is 'an interest acquired in a pool of assets that are not loans and receivables'.

because some such rights are within the scope of IAS 39,[*] and others are not. Therefore, it asked the Board to amend the scope of IAS 39 to exclude rights to reimbursement for expenditure required to settle:

(a)   a provision that has been recognised in accordance with IAS 37; and

(b)   obligations that had been originally recognised as provisions in accordance with IAS 37, but are no longer provisions because their timing or amount is no longer uncertain. An example of such a liability is one that was originally recognised as a provision because of uncertainty about the timing of the cash outflow, but subsequently becomes another type of liability because the timing is now certain.

BC13   This amendment was approved by the Board and is set out in the Appendix of IFRIC 5.[†] As a result, all such rights to reimbursement are within the scope of IAS 37.

BC14   The IFRIC noted that paragraph 53 of IAS 37 specifies the accounting for rights to receive reimbursement. It requires this right to reimbursement to be separately recognised when it is virtually certain that reimbursement will be received if the contributor settles the obligation. The IFRIC also noted that this paragraph prohibits the recognition of an asset in excess of the recognised liability. For example, rights to receive reimbursement to meet decommissioning liabilities that have yet to be recognised as a provision are not recognised. Accordingly, the IFRIC concluded that when the right to reimbursement is virtually certain to be received if the contributor settles its decommissioning obligation, it should be measured at the lower of the amount of the decommissioning obligation recognised and the reimbursement right.

BC15   The IFRIC discussed whether the reimbursement right should be measured at:

(a)   the contributor's share of the fair value of the net assets of the fund attributable to contributors, taking into account any inability to access any surplus of the assets of the fund over eligible decommissioning costs (with any obligation to make good potential defaults of other contributors being treated separately as a contingent liability); or

(b)   the fair value of the reimbursement right (which would normally be lower than (a) because of the risks involved, such as the possibility that the contributor may be required to make good defaults of other contributors).

BC16   The IFRIC noted that the right to reimbursement relates to a decommissioning obligation for which a provision would be recognised and measured in accordance with IAS 37. Paragraph 36 of IAS 37 requires such provisions to be measured at 'the best estimate of the expenditure required to settle the present obligation at the ~~balance sheet date~~ end of the reporting period'. The IFRIC noted that the amount in paragraph BC15(a)— ie the contributor's share of the fair value of the net assets of the fund attributable to contributors, taking into account any inability to access any surplus of the assets of the fund over eligible

---

[*]   In November 2009 the Board amended the requirements of IAS 39 relating to classification and measurement of assets within the scope of IAS 39 and relocated them to IFRS 9 *Financial Instruments*. IFRS 9 applies to all assets within the scope of IAS 39.

[†]   The amendment has been incorporated into the text of IAS 39 as published in this volume.

decommissioning costs—is the best estimate of the amount available to the contributor to reimburse it for expenditure it had incurred to pay for decommissioning. Thus, the amount of the asset recognised would be consistent with the amount of the liability recognised.

BC17   In contrast, the IFRIC noted that the amount in paragraph BC15(b)—ie the fair value of the reimbursement right—would take into account the factors such as liquidity that the IFRIC believed to be difficult to measure reliably. Furthermore, this amount would be lower than that in paragraph BC15(a) because it reflects the possibility that the contributor may be required to make potential additional contributions in the event of default by other contributors. The IFRIC noted that its decision that the obligation to make potential additional contributions should be treated as a contingent liability in accordance with IAS 37 (see paragraphs BC22–BC25) would result in double-counting of the risk of the additional contribution being required if the measure in paragraph BC15(b) were to be used.

BC18   Consequently, the IFRIC concluded that the approach in paragraph BC15(a) would provide the most useful information to users.

The asset cap

BC19   Many respondents to D4 expressed concern about the 'asset cap' that is imposed by the requirement in paragraph 9. This asset cap limits the amount recognised as a reimbursement asset to the amount of the decommissioning obligation recognised. These respondents argued that rights to benefit in excess of this amount give rise to an additional asset, separate from the reimbursement asset. Such an additional asset may arise in a number of ways, for example:

(a)   the contributor has the right to benefit from a repayment of any surplus in the fund that exists once all the decommissioning has been completed or on winding up the fund.

(b)   the contributor has the right to benefit from reduced contributions to the fund or increased benefits from the fund (eg by adding new sites to the fund for no additional contributions) in the future.

(c)   the contributor expects to obtain benefit from past contributions in the future, based on the current and planned level of activity. However, because contributions are made before the decommissioning obligation is incurred, IAS 37 prevents recognition of an asset in excess of the obligation.

BC20   The IFRIC concluded that a right to benefit from a repayment of any surplus in the fund that exists once all the decommissioning has been completed or on winding up the fund may be an equity instrument within the scope of IAS 39,[*] in which case IAS 39 would apply. However, the IFRIC agreed that an asset should not be recognised for other rights to receive reimbursement from the fund. Although the IFRIC had sympathy with the concerns expressed by constituents that there may be circumstances in which it would seem appropriate to recognise an asset in excess of the reimbursement right, it concluded that it would be inconsistent

---

[*]   In November 2009 the Board amended the requirements of IAS 39 relating to classification and measurement of assets within the scope of IAS 39 and relocated them to IFRS 9 *Financial Instruments*. IFRS 9 applies to all assets within the scope of IAS 39.

with paragraph 53 of IAS 37 (which requires that 'the amount recognised for the reimbursement should not exceed the amount of the provision') to recognise this asset. The IFRIC also noted that the circumstances in which this additional asset exists are likely to be limited, and apply only when a contributor has restricted access to a surplus of fund assets that does not give it control, joint control or significant influence over a fund. The IFRIC expects that most such assets would not meet the recognition criteria in the *Framework* because they are highly uncertain and cannot be measured reliably.

BC21   The IFRIC also considered arguments that there should not be a difference between the treatment of a surplus when a fund is accounted for as a subsidiary, joint venture or associate, and when it is not. However, the IFRIC noted that, under IFRSs, restrictions on assets in subsidiaries, joint ventures or associates do not affect recognition of those assets. Hence it concluded that the difference in treatment between funds accounted for as subsidiaries, joint ventures or associates and those accounted for as a reimbursement right is inherent in IFRSs. The IFRIC also concluded that this is appropriate because, in the former case, the contributor exercises a degree of control not present in the latter case.

Obligations to make additional contributions (paragraph 10)

BC22   In some cases, a contributor has an obligation to make potential additional contributions, for example, in the event of the bankruptcy of another contributor.

BC23   The IFRIC noted that by 'joining' the fund, a contributor may assume the position of guarantor of the contributions of the other contributors, and hence become jointly and severally liable for the obligations of other contributors. Such an obligation is a present obligation of the contributor, but the outflow of resources associated with it may not be probable. The IFRIC noted a parallel with the example in paragraph 29 of IAS 37, which states that 'where an entity is jointly and severally liable for an obligation, the part of the obligation that is expected to be met by other parties is treated as a contingent liability.' Accordingly, the IFRIC concluded that a liability would be recognised by the contributor only if it is probable that it will make additional contributions. The IFRIC noted that such a contingent liability may arise both when the contributor's interest in the fund is accounted for as a reimbursement right and when it is accounted for in accordance with IAS 27, IAS 28, IAS 31 or SIC-12.

BC24   The IFRIC considered the argument that an obligation to make good potential shortfalls of other contributors is a financial instrument (ie a financial guarantee) as defined in IAS 32 and hence should be accounted for in accordance with IAS 39.[*] The grounds for this point of view are that the contributor has an obligation to deliver cash to the fund, and the fund has a right to receive cash from the contributor if a shortfall in contributions arises. However, the IFRIC noted that:

(a)   a contractual obligation to make good shortfalls of other contributors is a financial guarantee. Financial guarantee contracts that provide for

---

[*] In November 2009 the Board amended the requirements of IAS 39 relating to classification and measurement of assets within the scope of IAS 39 and relocated them to IFRS 9 *Financial Instruments*. IFRS 9 applies to all assets within the scope of IAS 39.

payments to be made if the debtor fails to make payment when due are excluded from the scope of IAS 39.

(b) when the obligation is not contractual, but rather arises as a result of regulation, it is not a financial liability as defined in IAS 32 nor is it within the scope of IAS 39.

BC25 Therefore, the IFRIC concluded that an obligation to make additional contributions in the event of specified circumstances should be treated as a contingent liability in accordance with IAS 37.

Disclosure (paragraphs 11–13)

BC26 The IFRIC noted that the contributor may not be able to access the assets of the fund (including cash or cash equivalents) for many years (eg until it undertakes the decommissioning), if ever. Therefore, the IFRIC concluded that the nature of the contributor's interest and the restriction on access should be disclosed. The IFRIC also concluded that this disclosure is equally relevant when a contributor's interest in a fund is accounted for by consolidation, proportional consolidation or using the equity method because the contributor's ability to access the underlying assets may be similarly restricted.

Effective date and transition (paragraphs 14 and 15)

BC27 D4 proposed that the Interpretation should be effective for annual periods beginning on a date set at three months after the Interpretation was finalised. The IFRIC considered the view of some respondents that the Interpretation should apply from 1 January 2005 (an earlier date) on the grounds that this is the date from which many entities will adopt IFRSs, and hence adopting the Interpretation at that time would promote comparability between periods. However, the IFRIC noted its general practice is to allow at least three months between finalising an Interpretation and its application, to enable entities to obtain the Interpretation and implement any necessary systems changes. In addition, the IFRIC considered the Board's concern that the amendment to IAS 39 issued as part of the Interpretation would change the 'stable platform' of Standards that are in force for entities that will apply IFRSs for the first time in 2005. Therefore, the IFRIC decided to require that the Interpretation should be applied for annual periods beginning on or after 1 January 2006, with earlier application encouraged.

BC28 The IFRIC observed that the implementation of the Interpretation is not expected to be problematic. Therefore, the IFRIC concluded that IAS 8 should apply. Respondents to D4 did not disagree with this conclusion.

Document published to accompany

IFRIC Interpretation 6

Liabilities arising from Participating in a Specific Market—Waste Electrical and Electronic Equipment

The text of the unaccompanied IFRIC 6 is contained in Part A of this edition. Its effective date is 1 December 2005. This part presents the following accompanying document:

Basis for Conclusions on
IFRIC Interpretation 6 *Liabilities arising from Participating in a Specific Market—Waste Electrical and Electronic Equipment*

This Basis for Conclusions accompanies, but is not part of, IFRIC 6.

BC1   This Basis for Conclusions summarises the IFRIC's considerations in reaching its consensus. Individual IFRIC members gave greater weight to some factors than to others.

BC2   The IFRIC was informed that the European Union's Directive on Waste Electrical and Electronic Equipment (WE&EE) had given rise to questions about when a liability for the decommissioning of WE&EE for certain goods should be recognised. The IFRIC therefore decided to develop an Interpretation that would provide guidance regarding what constitutes an obligating event in the circumstances created by the Directive.

BC3   The IFRIC's proposals were set out in Draft Interpretation D10 *Liabilities arising from Participating in a Specific Market—Waste Electrical and Electronic Equipment*, which was published in November 2004. The IFRIC received 22 comment letters on the proposals.

BC4   The Directive indicates that it is participation in the market during the measurement period that triggers the obligation to meet the costs of waste management.

BC5   For example, an entity selling electrical equipment in 20X4 has a market share of 4 per cent for that calendar year. It subsequently discontinues operations and is thus no longer in the market when the waste management costs for its products are allocated to those entities with market share in 20X7. With a market share of 0 per cent in 20X7, the entity's obligation is zero. However, if another entity enters the market for electronic products in 20X7 and achieves a market share of 3 per cent in that period, then that entity's obligation for the costs of waste management from earlier periods will be 3 per cent of the total costs of waste management allocated to 20X7, even though the entity was not in the market in those earlier periods and has not produced any of the products for which waste management costs are allocated to 20X7.

BC6   The IFRIC concluded that the effect of the cost attribution model specified in the Directive is that the making of sales during the measurement period is the 'past event' that requires recognition of a provision under IAS 37 *Provisions, Contingent Liabilities and Contingent Assets* over the measurement period. Aggregate sales for the period determine the entity's obligation for a proportion of the costs of waste management allocated to that period. The measurement period is independent of the period when the cost allocation is notified to market participants. The timing of the obligating event may also be independent of the particular period in which the activities to perform the waste management are undertaken and the related costs incurred. Incurring costs in the performance of the waste management activities is a separate matter from incurring the obligation to share in the ultimate cost of those activities.

BC7   Some constituents asked the IFRIC to consider the effect of the following possible national legislation: the waste management costs for which a producer is responsible because of its participation in the market during a specified period (for example 20X6) are not based on the market share of the producer during that period but on the producer's participation in the market during a previous period (for example 20X5). The IFRIC noted that this affects only the measurement of the liability and that the obligating event is still participation in the market during 20X6.

BC8   The IFRIC considered whether its conclusion is undermined by the principle that the entity will continue to operate as a going concern. If the entity will continue to operate in the future, it treats the costs of doing so as future costs. For these future costs, paragraph 18 of IAS 37 emphasises that 'Financial statements deal with the financial position of an entity at the end of its reporting period and not its possible position in the future. Therefore, no provision is recognised for costs that need to be incurred to operate in the future.'

BC9   The IFRIC considered an argument that manufacturing or selling products for use in private households constitutes a past event that gives rise to a constructive obligation. Allocating waste management costs on the basis of market share would then be a matter of measurement rather than recognition. Supporters of this argument emphasise the definition of a constructive obligation in paragraph 10 of IAS 37 and point out that in determining whether past actions of an entity give rise to an obligation it is necessary to consider whether a change in practice is a realistic alternative. These respondents believed that when it would be necessary for an entity to take some unrealistic action in order to avoid the obligation then a constructive obligation exists and should be accounted for.

BC10   The IFRIC rejected this argument, concluding that a stated intention to participate in a market during a future measurement period does not create a constructive obligation for future waste management costs. In accordance with paragraph 19 of IAS 37, a provision can be recognised only in respect of an obligation that arises independently of the entity's future actions. For historical household equipment the obligation is created only by the future actions of the entity. If an entity has no market share in a measurement period, it has no obligation for the waste management costs relating to the products of that type which it had previously manufactured or sold and which otherwise would have created an obligation in that measurement period. This differentiates waste management costs, for example, from warranties (see Example 1 in Appendix C to IAS 37), which represent a legal obligation even if the entity exits the market. Consequently, no obligation exists for the future waste management costs until the entity participates in the market during the measurement period.

Documents published to accompany

IFRIC Interpretation 7

Applying the Restatement Approach under IAS 29 *Financial Reporting in Hyperinflationary Economies*

This version includes amendments resulting from IFRSs issued up to 31 December 2009.

The text of the unaccompanied IFRIC 7 is contained in Part A of this edition. Its effective date when issued was 1 March 2006. The effective date of the amendments is 1 January 2009. This part presents the following accompanying documents:

IFRIC Interpretation 7
Illustrative example

This example accompanies, but is not part of, IFRIC 7.

IE1   This example illustrates the restatement of deferred tax items when an entity restates for the effects of inflation under IAS 29 *Financial Reporting in Hyperinflationary Economies*. As the example is intended only to illustrate the mechanics of the restatement approach in IAS 29 for deferred tax items, it does not illustrate an entity's complete IFRS financial statements.

Facts

IE2   An entity's IFRS statement of financial position at 31 December 20X4 (before restatement) is as follows:

Note	Statement of financial position	20X4[(a)]	20X3
		CU million	CU million
	ASSETS		
1	Property, plant and equipment	300	400
	Other assets	XXX	XXX
	Total assets	XXX	XXX
	EQUITY AND LIABILITIES		
	Total equity	XXX	XXX
	Liabilities		
2	Deferred tax liability	30	20
	Other liabilities	XXX	XXX
	Total liabilities	XXX	XXX
	Total equity and liabilities	XXX	XXX

continued...

> *...continued*
>
> **Notes**
>
> 1 *Property, plant and equipment*
>
> All items of property, plant and equipment were acquired in December 20X2. Property, plant and equipment are depreciated over their useful life, which is five years.
>
> 2 *Deferred tax liability*
>
> The deferred tax liability at 31 December 20X4 of CU30 million is measured as the taxable temporary difference between the carrying amount of property, plant and equipment of 300 and their tax base of 200. The applicable tax rate is 30 per cent. Similarly, the deferred tax liability at 31 December 20X3 of CU20 million is measured as the taxable temporary difference between the carrying amount of property, plant and equipment of CU400 and their tax base of CU333.
>
> (a) In this example, monetary amounts are denominated in 'currency units (CU)'.

IE3   Assume that the entity identifies the existence of hyperinflation in, for example, April 20X4 and therefore applies IAS 29 from the beginning of 20X4. The entity restates its financial statements on the basis of the following general price indices and conversion factors:

	General price indices	Conversion factors at 31 Dec 20X4
December 20X2[a]	95	2.347
December 20X3	135	1.652
December 20X4	223	1.000

(a) For example, the conversion factor for December 20X2 is 2.347=223/95.

Restatement

IE4   The restatement of the entity's 20X4 financial statements is based on the following requirements:

- Property, plant and equipment are restated by applying the change in a general price index from the date of acquisition to the end of the reporting period to their historical cost and accumulated depreciation.

- Deferred taxes should be accounted for in accordance with IAS 12 *Income Taxes.*

- Comparative figures for property, plant and equipment for the previous reporting period are presented in terms of the measuring unit current at the end of the reporting period.

- Comparative deferred tax figures should be measured in accordance with paragraph 4 of the Interpretation.

IE5   Therefore the entity restates its statement of financial position at 31 December 20X4 as follows:

Note	Statement of financial position (restated)	20X4	20X3
		CU million	CU million
	ASSETS		
1	Property, plant and equipment	704	939
	Other assets	XXX	XXX
	Total assets	XXX	XXX
	EQUITY AND LIABILITIES		
	Total equity	XXX	XXX
	Liabilities		
2	Deferred tax liability	151	117
	Other liabilities	XXX	XXX
	Total liabilities	XXX	XXX
	Total equity and liabilities	XXX	XXX

continued...

...*continued*

Notes

1 *Property, plant and equipment*

All items of property, plant and equipment were purchased in December 20X2 and depreciated over a five-year period. The cost of property, plant and equipment is restated to reflect the change in the general price level since acquisition, ie the conversion factor is 2.347 (223/95).

	Historical CU million	Restated CU million
Cost of property, plant and equipment	500	1,174
Depreciation 20X3	(100)	(235)
Carrying amount 31 December 20X3	400	939
Depreciation 20X4	(100)	(235)
Carrying amount 31 December 20X4	300	704

2 *Deferred tax liability*

The nominal deferred tax liability at 31 December 20X4 of CU30 million is measured as the taxable temporary difference between the carrying amount of property, plant and equipment of CU300 and their tax base of CU200. Similarly, the deferred tax liability at 31 December 20X3 of CU20 million is measured as the taxable temporary difference between the carrying amount of property, plant and equipment of CU400 and their tax base of CU333. The applicable tax rate is 30 per cent.

In its restated financial statements, at the end of the reporting period the entity remeasures deferred tax items in accordance with the general provisions in IAS 12, ie on the basis of its restated financial statements. However, because deferred tax items are a function of carrying amounts of assets or liabilities and their tax bases, an entity cannot restate its comparative deferred tax items by applying a general price index. Instead, in the reporting period in which an entity applies the restatement approach under IAS 29, it (a) remeasures its comparative deferred tax items in accordance with IAS 12 after it has restated the nominal carrying amounts of its non-monetary items at the date of the opening statement of financial position of the current reporting period by applying the measuring unit at that date, and (b) restates the remeasured deferred tax items for the change in the measuring unit from the date of the opening statement of financial position of the current period up to the end of the reporting period.

continued...

...continued

In the example, the restated deferred tax liability is calculated as follows:

	CU million
At the end of the reporting period:	
Restated carrying amount of property, plant and equipment (see note 1)	704
Tax base	(200)
Temporary difference	504
@ 30 per cent tax rate = Restated deferred tax liability 31 December 20X4	151
Comparative deferred tax figures:	
Restated carrying amount of property, plant and equipment [either 400 × 1.421 (conversion factor 1.421 = 135/95), or 939/1.652 (conversion factor 1.652 = 223/135)]	568
Tax base	(333)
Temporary difference	235
@ 30 per cent tax rate = Restated deferred tax liability 31 December 20X3 at the general price level at the end of 20X3	71
Restated deferred tax liability 31 December 20X3 at the general price level at the end of 20X4 (conversion factor 1.652 = 223/135)	117

IE6 In this example, the restated deferred tax liability is increased by CU34 to CU151 from 31 December 20X3 to 31 December 20X4. That increase, which is included in profit or loss in 20X4, reflects (a) the effect of a change in the taxable temporary difference of property, plant and equipment, and (b) a loss of purchasing power on the tax base of property, plant and equipment. The two components can be analysed as follows:

	CU million
Effect on deferred tax liability because of a decrease in the taxable temporary difference of property, plant and equipment (-CU235 + CU133) × 30%	31
Loss on tax base because of inflation in 20X4 (CU333 × 1.652 – CU333) × 30%	(65)
Net increase of deferred tax liability	(34)
Debit to profit or loss in 20X4	34

The loss on tax base is a monetary loss. Paragraph 28 of IAS 29 explains this as follows:

> The gain or loss on the net monetary position is included in net income. The adjustment to those assets and liabilities linked by agreement to changes in prices made in accordance with paragraph 13 is offset against the gain or loss on net monetary position. Other income and expense items, such as interest income and expense, and foreign exchange differences related to invested or borrowed funds, are also associated with the net monetary position. Although such items are separately disclosed, it may be helpful if they are presented together with the gain or loss on net monetary position in the statement of comprehensive income.

Basis for Conclusions on
IFRIC Interpretation 7 *Applying the Restatement Approach under IAS 29* Financial Reporting in Hyperinflationary Economies

This Basis for Conclusions accompanies, but is not part of, IFRIC 7.

In this Basis for Conclusions the terminology has not been amended to reflect the changes made by IAS 1 Presentation of Financial Statements (as revised in 2007).

Introduction

BC1   This Basis for Conclusions summarises the IFRIC's considerations in reaching its consensus. Individual IFRIC members gave greater weight to some factors than to others.

Background

BC2   The IFRIC was asked for guidance on how an entity should restate its financial statements when it starts to apply IAS 29 *Financial Reporting in Hyperinflationary Economies*. There was uncertainty whether the opening balance sheet at the beginning of the reporting period should be restated to reflect changes in prices before that date.

BC3   In addition, there was uncertainty about the measurement of comparative deferred tax items in the opening balance sheet. IAS 29 states that at the balance sheet date deferred tax items of the restated financial statements should be measured in accordance with IAS 12 *Income Taxes*. However, it was not clear how an entity should account for the corresponding deferred tax figures.

BC4   In response, the IFRIC developed and published Draft Interpretation D5 *Applying IAS 29* Financial Reporting in Hyperinflationary Economies *for the First Time* for public comment in March 2004. It received 30 letters in response to the proposals.

Basis for consensus

The restatement approach

BC5   In developing D5, the IFRIC observed that the purpose of restating financial statements in hyperinflationary economies in accordance with IAS 29 is to reflect the effect on an entity of changes in general purchasing power. Paragraph 2 of IAS 29 states:

> In a hyperinflationary economy, reporting of operating results and financial position in the local currency without restatement is not useful. Money loses purchasing power at such a rate that comparison of amounts from transactions and other events that have occurred at different times, even within the same accounting period, is misleading.

This purpose applies to the financial statements of the first reporting period in which an entity identifies the existence of hyperinflation in the economy of its functional currency as well as to subsequent reporting periods (if the criteria for a hyperinflationary economy are still met).

BC6   The IFRIC considered the meaning of paragraph 4 of IAS 29, which states:

> ... this Standard applies to the financial statements of any entity from the beginning of the reporting period in which it identifies the existence of hyperinflation in the country in whose currency it reports.

The IFRIC noted that some may interpret this provision as restricting the restatement of an entity's opening balance sheet in the reporting period in which it identifies the existence of hyperinflation. Consequently, the opening balance sheet should be restated to reflect the change in a general price index for the reporting period only and not for changes in a general price index before the beginning of the reporting period, even though some balance sheet items may have been acquired or assumed before that date. However, the IFRIC also noted that paragraph 34 of IAS 29 requires:

> *Corresponding figures for the previous reporting period*, whether they were based on a historical cost approach or a current cost approach, are restated by applying a general price index so that the comparative financial statements are *presented in terms of the measuring unit current at the end of the reporting period*. Information that is disclosed in respect of earlier periods is also expressed in terms of the measuring unit current at the end of the reporting period ... [emphasis added]

BC7   The IFRIC considered a possible inconsistency between the restriction in paragraph 4 of IAS 29 and the requirement in paragraph 34. The IFRIC noted that paragraph 4 is a scope paragraph, which identifies when an entity has to comply with the Standard. The paragraph clarifies that an entity applies the requirements of the Standard to its financial statements from the beginning of the reporting period to the balance sheet date and not only from the date when it identifies the existence of hyperinflation. However, paragraph 4 does not deal with the restatement and presentation of the financial statements (either at the balance sheet date or in relation to the comparative figures). Hence, paragraph 4 of IAS 29 does not exclude from the restatement of an entity's opening balance sheet changes in the general price level before the beginning of the reporting period in which the entity identifies the existence of hyperinflation.

BC8   The IFRIC concluded that, in the context of the purpose of the Standard, the restatement of the financial statements for the reporting period in which an entity identifies the existence of hyperinflation should be consistent with the restatement approach applied in subsequent reporting periods.

BC9   Some respondents to D5 expressed concerns about whether the restatement approach in IAS 29 was always practicable for preparers and whether it provided decision-useful information to users. Though the IFRIC understood those concerns, the IFRIC observed that such concerns reflected broader aspects related to the accounting for hyperinflation in general, rather than how an entity has to apply the current Standard.

BC10   Nevertheless, the IFRIC considered how an entity should apply the Standard if, for example, detailed records of the acquisition dates of items of property, plant and equipment are not available. The IFRIC noted that, in those circumstances, paragraph 16 of IAS 29 states:

> ... In these rare circumstances, it may be necessary, in the first period of application of this Standard, to use an independent professional assessment of the value of the items as the basis for their restatement.

The IFRIC also noted that a similar exemption exists when a general price index may not be available. Paragraph 17 of IAS 29 states:

> ... In these circumstances, it may be necessary to use an estimate based, for example, on the movements in the exchange rate between the functional currency and a relatively stable foreign currency.

BC11 The IFRIC observed that, in developing IFRS 1 *First-time Adoption of International Financial Reporting Standards*, the International Accounting Standards Board discussed whether IFRS 1 should exempt first-time adopters of IFRSs from the effects of restatement in their first IFRS financial statements. Paragraph BC67 of IFRS 1 states:

> Some argued that the cost of restating financial statements for the effects of hyperinflation in periods before the date of transition to IFRSs would exceed the benefits, particularly if the currency is no longer hyperinflationary. However, the Board concluded that such restatement should be required, because hyperinflation can make unadjusted financial statements meaningless or misleading.

BC12 However, the IFRIC also observed that first-time adopters of IFRSs could use, for example, the fair value at transition date as deemed cost for property, plant and equipment, and, in some instances, also for investment property and intangible assets. Hence, if a first-time adopter that would otherwise have to apply IAS 29 at its transition to IFRSs applies the fair value measurement exemption of IFRS 1, it would apply IAS 29 to periods only after the date for which the fair value was determined. Such remeasurements would therefore reduce the need for a first-time adopter to restate its financial statements.

BC13 The IFRIC noted that the exemptions from the general restatement approach for preparers that already apply IFRSs, as stated in paragraph BC10 above, apply only in specific circumstances, whereas a first-time adopter may always elect to use the fair value remeasurement exemption for property, plant and equipment in IFRS 1. Nevertheless, the IFRIC concluded that the application of the exemptions in the Standards is clear and, therefore, extending the exemptions in IAS 29 to permit preparers that already apply IFRSs to elect fair value remeasurement of property, plant and equipment when applying the restatement approach under IAS 29 would require amendments of the Standard itself, rather than an Interpretation.

BC14 Respondents to D5 also argued that the procedures, as proposed to be clarified, are inconsistent with the accounting for a change in functional currency under IAS 21 *The Effect of Changes in Foreign Exchange Rates*, which in their view is comparable to moving into a state of hyperinflation. Moreover, they noted that retrospective application is also inconsistent with the US GAAP approach, which accounts for a change in hyperinflation status prospectively.

BC15 In relation to the reference to a change in functional currency, the IFRIC observed that the existence of hyperinflation may (but not necessarily should) initiate such a change. The IFRIC noted that a change in functional currency is a change in the currency that is normally used to determine the pricing of an entity's transactions. As clarified in paragraph BC5 above, the purpose of restatement for the effects of hyperinflation is to reflect the effect of changes in purchasing power in the economy of an entity's functional currency. Therefore, the IFRIC did not believe that the application of accounting for hyperinflation should be based on the accounting for the change in an entity's functional currency.

BC16　The IFRIC also observed that respondents' reference to prospective application under US GAAP reflects requirements only for investments in foreign entities in hyperinflationary economies. In this case, paragraph 11 of SFAS 52 *Foreign Currency Translation* states:

> The financial statements of a foreign entity in a highly inflationary economy shall *be remeasured as if the functional currency were the reporting currency*. Accordingly, the financial statements of those entities shall be remeasured into the reporting currency according to the requirements of paragraph 10 ... [emphasis added]

Therefore, under US GAAP a foreign entity's financial statements are remeasured into its investor's functional currency. The IFRIC noted that this approach is different from the restate/translate approach under IFRSs. US GAAP provides different guidance for reporting entities operating with a hyperinflationary functional currency. APB Statement No. 3 *Financial Statements Restated for General Price-Level Changes* is also based on a restatement approach, and would require retrospective application, as under IAS 29. The IFRIC observed that for the purpose of presenting comparative amounts in a different presentation currency under IFRSs paragraphs 42(b) and 43 of IAS 21 apply. In such instances, an entity will have relief from the required restatement of comparatives under IAS 29. Paragraph BC22 of IAS 21 explains the reasoning for this specific exemption as follows:

> ... If exchange rates fully reflect differing price levels between the two economies to which they relate, the SIC-30 approach will result in the same amounts for the comparatives as were reported as current year amounts in the prior year financial statements. Furthermore, the Board noted that in the prior year, the relevant amounts had been already expressed in the non-hyperinflationary presentation currency, and there was no reason to change them.

BC17　D5 proposed that applying the restatement approach under IAS 29 should be regarded as a change in circumstances, rather than a change in accounting policy. Some respondents to D5 believed this was inconsistent. This is because IAS 8 *Accounting Policies, Changes in Accounting Estimates and Errors*, paragraph 16, states that a change in circumstances is not a change in accounting policy and an entity would not apply IAS 29 retrospectively. However, the IFRIC observed that IAS 29 contains specific requirements on this point, as noted in paragraphs BC5–BC16 above. The IFRIC concluded that the opening balance sheet for the reporting period in which an entity identifies the existence of hyperinflation ought to be restated as if the entity had always applied the restatement approach under IAS 29. The IFRIC reconfirmed its view that this treatment is similar to the retrospective application of a change in accounting policy described in IAS 8.

Deferred tax items

BC18　The IFRIC was asked for guidance on the accounting for deferred tax items when an entity restates its financial statements according to IAS 29. In particular, the IFRIC was asked for guidance on measuring deferred tax items in the opening balance sheet for the reporting period in which an entity identifies the existence of hyperinflation.

BC19　The IFRIC observed that paragraph 32 of IAS 29 states:

> The restatement of financial statements in accordance with this Standard may give rise to differences between the carrying amount of individual assets and liabilities in the balance sheet and their tax bases. These differences are accounted for in accordance with IAS 12 *Income Taxes*.

Therefore, at the closing balance sheet date of the reporting period an entity remeasures its deferred tax items on the basis of the restated financial statements, rather than by applying the general restatement provisions for monetary items or non-monetary items. However, the IFRIC noted that it was not clear how an entity should account for its comparative deferred tax items.

BC20　In developing D5, the IFRIC considered the following options:

(a)　restatement of deferred tax items as monetary items;

(b)　restatement of deferred tax items as non-monetary items; or

(c)　remeasurement of deferred tax items as if the economy of the entity's functional currency had always been hyperinflationary.

BC21　D5 proposed clarifying that deferred tax items are neither clearly monetary nor non-monetary in nature. This was because deferred tax items are determined by the assets' (and liabilities') relative carrying amounts and tax bases. However, some respondents to D5 objected to that view, for various reasons. Some argued that deferred tax items, by nature, are received or paid in a fixed or determinable number of units of currency, and so should be considered as monetary items in accordance with paragraph 8 of IAS 21. Others noted that general practice is to classify deferred taxes as non-monetary items.

BC22　When considering respondents' comments the IFRIC confirmed that its conclusion in paragraph BC17 above should also apply to deferred tax items. In other words, the deferred tax items in the opening balance sheet for the reporting period in which an entity identifies the existence of hyperinflation should be calculated as if the environment had always been hyperinflationary, ie option (c) in paragraph BC20. Although the IFRIC acknowledged that deferred tax items may meet the definition of monetary items it noted that the purposes of option (c) would not be achieved if opening deferred tax items were restated in the same manner as applied generally for monetary items.

BC23　The IFRIC observed that some respondents to D5 suggested that deferred tax items in the opening balance sheet should be remeasured after restating the opening balance sheet with the measurement unit current at the closing balance sheet date of the reporting period. In the IFRIC's view, that proposal would (in case of a deferred tax liability) overstate the deferred tax item recognised in the opening balance sheet and, accordingly, understate the costs recognised in the reporting period. This is because the loss on the tax base caused by the inflation in the reporting period would be recognised directly in opening equity. The IFRIC illustrated this by the following example:

> At the end of Year 1, a non-monetary asset is restated at the measurement unit current at that date. Its restated amount is CU1,000* and its tax base is CU500. If the tax rate is 30 per cent, the entity would remeasure a deferred tax liability of CU150. In Year 2 inflation is 100 per cent. Assuming that nothing has changed the entity would, in its restated financial statements, recognise an asset of CU2,000 (both at the closing balance sheet date of the reporting period and in the comparative figures). At the closing balance sheet date, the deferred tax liability is remeasured at CU450 ((CU2,000 − CU500) × 0.3). However, if the comparative deferred tax liability is remeasured after restating the asset by the measuring unit current at the closing balance sheet date of the reporting period, the entity should recognise an opening deferred tax liability of CU450, and there would be no impact on profit or loss (CU450 − CU450). On the other hand, if the comparatives are stated as proposed in D5, the restated opening deferred tax liability would be CU300 ((CU1,000 − CU500) × 0.3) × 100% + CU150). Accordingly, the entity should recognise a loss of CU150 (CU450 − CU300), which is the loss of purchasing power on the tax base in the reporting period.

BC24   The IFRIC observed that paragraph 18 of Appendix A to IAS 12 explains:[†]

> Non-monetary assets are restated in terms of the measuring unit current at the balance sheet date (see IAS 29 *Financial Reporting in Hyperinflationary Economies*) and no equivalent adjustment is made for tax purposes. *(notes: (1) the deferred tax is charged in the income statement;[§] and (2) if, in addition to the restatement, the non-monetary assets are also revalued, the deferred tax relating to the revaluation is charged to equity [ø]and the deferred tax relating to the restatement is charged in the income statement.)*

BC25   Consequently, the IFRIC confirmed its conclusion that restatement of comparative deferred tax items would require an entity, first, to remeasure its deferred tax items on the basis of the financial statements of the previous reporting period, which have been restated by applying a general price index reflecting the price level at the end of that period. Secondly, the entity should restate those calculated deferred tax items by the change in the general price level for the reporting period.

---

*   In this example monetary amounts are denominated in 'currency units (CU)'.

†   Paragraph 18 has been amended as a consequence of the changes made by IAS 1 *Presentation of Financial Statements* (as revised in 2007).

§   IAS 1 (revised 2007) requires an entity to present all income and expense items in one statement of comprehensive income or in two statements (a separate income statement and a statement of comprehensive income).

ø   Under IAS 1 (revised 2007), such effect is recognised in other comprehensive income.

Documents published to accompany

IFRIC Interpretation 9

Reassessment of Embedded Derivatives

This version includes amendments resulting from IFRSs issued up to 31 December 2009.

The text of the unaccompanied IFRIC 9 is contained in Part A of this edition. Its effective date when issued was 1 June 2006. The effective date of the most recent amendment is 1 July 2009. This part presents the following accompanying documents.

Approval by the Board of *Embedded Derivatives* (Amendments to IFRIC 9 and IAS 39) issued in March 2009

Embedded Derivatives (Amendments to IFRIC 9 and IAS 39) was approved for issue by the fourteen members of the International Accounting Standards Board.

Sir David Tweedie	Chairman
Thomas E Jones	Vice-Chairman
Mary E Barth	
Stephen Cooper	
Philippe Danjou	
Jan Engström	
Robert P Garnett	
Gilbert Gélard	
Prabhakar Kalavacherla	
James J Leisenring	
Warren J McGregor	
John T Smith	
Tatsumi Yamada	
Wei-Guo Zhang	

Basis for Conclusions on
IFRIC Interpretation 9 *Reassessment of Embedded Derivatives*

This Basis for Conclusions accompanies, but is not part of, IFRIC 9.

Introduction

BC1   This Basis for Conclusions summarises the IFRIC's considerations in reaching its consensus. Individual IFRIC members gave greater weight to some factors than to others.

BC2   As explained below, the IFRIC was informed that uncertainty existed over certain aspects of the requirements of IAS 39 *Financial Instruments: Recognition and Measurement*[*] relating to the reassessment of embedded derivatives. The IFRIC published proposals on the subject in March 2005 as D15 *Reassessment of Embedded Derivatives* and developed IFRIC 9 after considering the thirty comment letters received.

BC3   IAS 39 requires an entity, when it first becomes a party to a contract, to assess whether any embedded derivative contained in the contract needs to be separated from the host contract and accounted for as a derivative under the Standard. However, the issue arises whether IAS 39 requires an entity to continue to carry out this assessment after it first becomes a party to a contract, and if so, with what frequency. The Standard is silent on this issue and the IFRIC was informed that as a result there was a risk of divergence in practice.

BC4   The question is relevant, for example, when the terms of the embedded derivative do not change but market conditions change and the market was the principal factor in determining whether the host contract and embedded derivative are closely related. Instances when this might arise are given in paragraph AG33(d) of IAS 39. Paragraph AG33(d) states that an embedded foreign currency derivative is closely related to the host contract provided it is not leveraged, does not contain an option feature, and requires payments denominated in one of the following currencies:

(a)   the functional currency of any substantial party to that contract;

(b)   the currency in which the price of the related good or service that is acquired or delivered is routinely denominated in commercial transactions around the world (such as the US dollar for crude oil transactions); or

(c)   a currency that is commonly used in contracts to purchase or sell non-financial items in the economic environment in which the transaction takes place (eg a relatively stable and liquid currency that is commonly used in local business transactions or external trade).

---

[*]   IFRS 9 *Financial Instruments*, issued in November 2009, amended the requirements in IAS 39 to identify and separately account for derivatives embedded in a financial host within the scope of IFRS 9. The requirements in IAS 39 continue to apply for derivatives embedded in non-financial hosts and financial hosts outside the scope of IFRS 9.

BC5   Any of the currencies specified in (a)–(c) above may change. Assume that when an entity first became a party to a contract, it assessed the contract as containing an embedded derivative that was closely related (because it was in one of the three categories in paragraph BC4) and hence not accounted for separately. Assume that subsequently market conditions change and that if the entity were to reassess the contract under the changed circumstances it would conclude that the embedded derivative is not closely related and therefore requires separate accounting. (The converse could also arise.) The issue is whether the entity should make such a reassessment.

BC5A   In 2009 the International Accounting Standards Board observed that the changes to the definition of a business combination in the revisions to IFRS 3 *Business Combinations* (as revised in 2008) caused the accounting for the formation of a joint venture by the venturer to be within the scope of IFRIC 9. Similarly, the Board noted that common control transactions might raise the same issue depending on which level of the group reporting entity is assessing the combination.

BC5B   The Board observed that during the development of the revised IFRS 3, it did not discuss whether it intended IFRIC 9 to apply to those types of transactions. The Board did not intend to change existing practice by including such transactions within the scope of IFRIC 9. Accordingly, in *Improvements to IFRSs* issued in April 2009, the Board amended paragraph 5 of IFRIC 9 to clarify that IFRIC 9 does not apply to embedded derivatives in contracts acquired in a combination between entities or businesses under common control or the formation of a joint venture.

BC5C   Some respondents to the exposure draft *Post-implementation Revisions to IFRIC Interpretations* published in January 2009 expressed the view that investments in associates should also be excluded from the scope of IFRIC 9. Respondents noted that paragraphs 20–23 of IAS 28 *Investments in Associates* state that the concepts underlying the procedures used in accounting for the acquisition of a subsidiary are also adopted in accounting for the acquisition of an investment in an associate.

BC5D   In its redeliberations, the Board confirmed its previous decision that no scope exemption in IFRIC 9 was needed for investments in associates. However, in response to the comments received, the Board noted that reassessment of embedded derivatives in contracts held by an associate is not required by IFRIC 9 in any event. The investment in the associate is the asset the investor controls and recognises, not the underlying assets and liabilities of the associate.

Reassessment of embedded derivatives

BC6   The IFRIC noted that the rationale for the requirement in IAS 39 to separate embedded derivatives is that an entity should not be able to circumvent the recognition and measurement requirements for derivatives merely by embedding a derivative in a non-derivative financial instrument or other contract (for example, by embedding a commodity forward in a debt instrument). Changes in external circumstances (such as those set out in paragraph BC5) are not ways to circumvent the Standard. The IFRIC therefore concluded that reassessment was not appropriate for such changes.

BC7　The IFRIC noted that as a practical expedient IAS 39 does not require the separation of embedded derivatives that are closely related. Many financial instruments contain embedded derivatives. Separating all of these embedded derivatives would be burdensome for entities. The IFRIC noted that requiring entities to reassess embedded derivatives in all hybrid instruments could be onerous because frequent monitoring would be required. Market conditions and other factors affecting embedded derivatives would have to be monitored continuously to ensure timely identification of a change in circumstances and amendment of the accounting treatment accordingly. For example, if the functional currency of the counterparty changes during the reporting period so that the contract is no longer denominated in a currency of one of the parties to the contract, then a reassessment of the hybrid instrument would be required at the date of change to ensure the correct accounting treatment in future.

BC8　The IFRIC also recognised that although IAS 39 is silent on the issue of reassessment it gives relevant guidance when it states that for the types of contracts covered by paragraph AG33(b) the assessment of whether an embedded derivative is closely related is required only at inception. Paragraph AG33(b) states:

> An embedded floor or cap on the interest rate on a debt contract or insurance contract is closely related to the host contract, provided the cap is at or above the market rate of interest and the floor is at or below the market rate of interest *when the contract is issued*, and the cap or floor is not leveraged in relation to the host contract. Similarly, provisions included in a contract to purchase or sell an asset (eg a commodity) that establish a cap and a floor on the price to be paid or received for the asset are closely related to the host contract if both the cap and floor were out of the money *at inception* and are not leveraged. [Emphasis added]

BC9　The IFRIC also considered the implications of requiring subsequent reassessment. For example, assume that an entity, when it first becomes a party to a contract, separately recognises a host asset and an embedded derivative liability. If the entity were required to reassess whether the embedded derivative was to be accounted for separately and if the entity concluded some time after becoming a party to the contract that the derivative was no longer required to be separated, then questions of recognition and measurement would arise. In the above circumstances, the IFRIC identified the following possibilities:

(a)　the entity could remove the derivative from its balance sheet and recognise in profit or loss a corresponding gain or loss. This would lead to recognition of a gain or loss even though there had been no transaction and no change in the value of the total contract or its components.

(b)　the entity could leave the derivative as a separate item in the balance sheet. The issue would then arise as to when the item was to be removed from the balance sheet. Should it be amortised (and, if so, how would the amortisation affect the effective interest rate of the asset), or should it be derecognised only when the asset is derecognised?

(c)　the entity could combine the derivative (which is recognised at fair value) with the asset (which is recognised at amortised cost). This would alter both the carrying amount of the asset and its effective interest rate even though there had been no change in the economics of the whole contract. In some cases, it could also result in a negative effective interest rate.

The IFRIC noted that, under its view that subsequent reassessment is appropriate only when there has been a change in the terms of the contract that significantly modifies the cash flows that otherwise would be required by the contract, the above issues do not arise.

BC10   The IFRIC noted that IAS 39 requires an entity to assess whether an embedded derivative needs to be separated from the host contract and accounted for as a derivative when it first becomes a party to a contract. Consequently, if an entity purchases a contract that contains an embedded derivative it assesses whether the embedded derivative needs to be separated and accounted for as a derivative on the basis of conditions at that date.

BC11   The IFRIC considered an alternative approach of making reassessment optional. It decided against this approach because it would reduce comparability of financial information. Also, the IFRIC noted that this approach would be inconsistent with the embedded derivative requirements in IAS 39 that either require or prohibit separation but do not give an option. Accordingly, the IFRIC concluded that reassessment should not be optional.

BC11A   Following the issue of *Reclassification of Financial Assets* (Amendments to IAS 39 and IFRS 7) in October 2008 constituents told the International Accounting Standards Board that there was uncertainty about the interaction between those amendments and IFRIC 9 regarding the assessment of embedded derivatives. Some of those taking part in the public round-table meetings held by the Board and the US Financial Accounting Standards Board in November and December 2008 in response to the global financial crisis also raised that issue. They asked the Board to consider further amendments to IFRSs to prevent any practice developing whereby, following reclassification of a financial asset, embedded derivatives that should be separately accounted for are not.

BC11B   In accordance with paragraph 7 of IFRIC 9, assessment of the separation of an embedded derivative after an entity first became a party to the contract is prohibited unless there is a change in the terms of the contract that significantly modifies the cash flows that otherwise would be required under the contract. Constituents told the Board that some might interpret IFRIC 9 as prohibiting the separation of an embedded derivative on the reclassification of a hybrid (combined) financial asset out of the fair value through profit or loss category unless there is a concurrent change in its contractual terms.

BC11C   The Board noted that when IFRIC 9 was issued, reclassifications out of the fair value through profit or loss category were prohibited and hence IFRIC 9 did not consider the possibility of such reclassifications.

BC11D   The Board was clear that it did not intend the requirements to separate particular embedded derivatives from hybrid (combined) financial instruments to be circumvented as a result of the amendments to IAS 39 issued in October 2008. Therefore, the Board decided to clarify IFRIC 9 by amending paragraph 7.

BC11E   The Board believes that unless assessment and separation of embedded derivatives is done when reclassifying hybrid (combined) financial assets out of the fair value through profit or loss category, structuring opportunities are created that the embedded derivative accounting requirements in IAS 39 were intended to prevent. This is because, by initially classifying a hybrid (combined) financial instrument as at fair value through profit or loss and later reclassifying it into another category, an entity can circumvent requirements for separation of an embedded derivative. The Board also noted that the only appropriate accounting for derivative instruments is to be included in the fair value through profit or loss category.

BC11F   The Board decided also to clarify that an assessment on reclassification should be made on the basis of the circumstances that existed when the entity first became a party to the contract, or, if later, the date of a change in the terms of the contract that significantly modified the cash flows that otherwise would be required under the contract. This date is consistent with one of the stated purposes of embedded derivative accounting (ie preventing circumvention of the recognition and measurement requirements for derivatives) and provides some degree of comparability. Furthermore, because the terms of the embedded features in the hybrid (combined) financial instrument have not changed, the Board did not see a reason for arriving at an answer on separation different from what would have been the case at initial recognition of the hybrid (combined) contract (or a later date of a change in the terms of the contract). In addition, the Board clarified that paragraph 11(c) of IAS 39 should not be applied in assessing whether an embedded derivative requires separation. The Board noted that before reclassification the hybrid (combined) financial instrument is necessarily classified at fair value through profit or loss so that for the purpose of the assessment on reclassification this criterion is not relevant but would, if applied for assessments made in accordance with paragraph 7A of the Interpretation, always result in no embedded derivative being separated.

First-time adopters of IFRSs

BC12   In the Implementation Guidance with IFRS 1 *First-time Adoption of International Financial Reporting Standards*, paragraph IG55 states:

> When IAS 39 requires an entity to separate an embedded derivative from a host contract, the initial carrying amounts of the components at the date when the instrument first satisfies the recognition criteria in IAS 39 reflect circumstances at that date (IAS 39 paragraph 11). If the entity cannot determine the initial carrying amounts of the embedded derivative and host contract reliably, it treats the entire combined contract as a financial instrument held for trading (IAS 39 paragraph 12). This results in fair value measurement (except when the entity cannot determine a reliable fair value, see IAS 39 paragraph 46(c)), with changes in fair value recognised in profit or loss.

BC13   This guidance reflects the principle in IFRS 1 that a first-time adopter should apply IFRSs as if they had been in place from initial recognition. This is consistent with the general principle used in IFRSs of full retrospective application of Standards. The IFRIC noted that the date of initial recognition referred to in paragraph IG55 is the date when the entity first became a party to the contract and not the date of first-time adoption of IFRSs. Accordingly, the IFRIC concluded that IFRS 1 requires an entity to assess whether an embedded derivative is required to be separated from the host contract and accounted for as a derivative on the basis of conditions at the date when the entity first became a party to the contract and not those at the date of first-time adoption.

Document published to accompany

IFRIC Interpretation 10

Interim Financial Reporting and Impairment

This version includes amendments resulting from IFRSs issued up to 31 December 2009.

The text of the unaccompanied IFRIC 10 is contained in Part A of this edition. Its effective date when issued was 1 November 2006. The effective date of the most recent amendments is 1 January 2013. This part presents the following accompanying document:

page

BASIS FOR CONCLUSIONS   **B1548**

Basis for Conclusions on
IFRIC Interpretation 10 *Interim Financial Reporting and Impairment*

This Basis for Conclusions accompanies, but is not part of, IFRIC 10.

BC1   This Basis for Conclusions summarises the IFRIC's considerations in reaching its consensus. Individual IFRIC members gave greater weight to some factors than to others.

BC2   IAS 34 requires an entity to apply the same accounting policies in its interim financial statements as it applies in its annual financial statements. For annual financial statements, IAS 36 prohibits an entity from reversing an impairment loss on goodwill that it recognised in a prior annual period. Similarly, IAS 39[*] prohibits an entity from reversing in a subsequent annual period an impairment loss on an investment in an equity instrument or in a financial asset carried at cost. These requirements might suggest that an entity should not reverse in a subsequent interim period an impairment loss on goodwill or an investment in an equity instrument or in a financial asset carried at cost that it had recognised in a prior interim period. Such impairment losses would not be reversed even if no loss, or a smaller loss, would have been recognised had the impairment been assessed only at the end of the subsequent interim period.

BC3   However, IAS 34 requires year-to-date measures in interim financial statements. This requirement might suggest that an entity should reverse in a subsequent interim period an impairment loss it recognised in a prior interim period. Such impairment losses would be reversed if no loss, or a smaller loss, would have been recognised had the impairment been assessed only at the end of the subsequent interim period.

BC4   The IFRIC released Draft Interpretation D18 *Interim Financial Reporting and Impairment* for public comment in January 2006. It received more than 50 letters in response.

BC5   The IFRIC noted that many of the respondents believed that in attempting to address contradictions between standards, D18 was beyond the scope of the IFRIC. Some believed that the issue addressed could be better resolved by amending IAS 34. Before finalising its views, the IFRIC asked the International Accounting Standards Board to consider this point. The Board, however, did not wish to amend IAS 34 and asked the IFRIC to continue with its Interpretation.

BC6   Respondents to D18 were divided on whether the proposed Interpretation should prohibit the reversal of impairment losses on goodwill or investments in equity instruments or in financial assets carried at cost that had been recognised in interim periods. The IFRIC considered these responses but

---

[*]   In November 2009 the IASB amended the requirements of IAS 39 relating to classification and measurement of assets within the scope of IAS 39 and relocated them to IFRS 9 *Financial Instruments*. Consequently, no financial assets are carried at cost.

© IASCF

maintained its view that such losses should not be reversed in subsequent financial statements. The IFRIC observed that the wide divergence of views evident from respondents' letters underlined the need for additional guidance and it therefore decided to issue the Interpretation with few changes from D18.

BC7　The IFRIC considered the example of Entity A and Entity B, which each hold the same equity investment with the same acquisition cost. Entity A prepares quarterly interim financial statements and Entity B prepares half-yearly financial statements. The entities have the same year-end. The IFRIC noted that if there was a significant decline in the fair value of the equity instrument below its cost in the first quarter, Entity A would recognise an impairment loss in its first quarter interim financial statements. However, if the fair value of the equity instrument subsequently recovered, so that by the half-year date there had not been a significant decline in fair value below cost, Entity B would not recognise an impairment loss in its half-yearly financial statements if it tested for impairment only at its half-yearly reporting dates. Therefore, unless Entity A reversed the impairment loss that had been recognised in an earlier interim period, the frequency of reporting would affect the measurement of its annual results when compared with Entity B's approach. The IFRIC also noted that the recognition of an impairment loss could similarly be affected by the timing of the financial year-ends of the two entities.

BC8　The IFRIC noted paragraph B36 of Appendix B accompanying IAS 34, which provides examples of applying the general recognition and measurement principles of that standard and states that IAS 34 requires an entity to apply the same impairment testing, recognition, and reversal criteria at an interim date as it would at the end of its financial year.

BC9　The IFRIC concluded that the prohibitions on reversals of recognised impairment losses on goodwill in IAS 36 and on investments in equity instruments and in financial assets carried at cost in IAS 39[*] should take precedence over the more general statement in IAS 34 regarding the frequency of an entity's reporting not affecting the measurement of its annual results.

BC10　Furthermore, the IFRIC concluded that the rationale for the non-reversal of impairment losses relating to goodwill and investments in equity instruments, as set out in paragraph BC189 of IAS 36 and paragraph BC130 of IAS 39, applies at both interim and annual reporting dates.

BC11　The IFRIC considered a concern that this conclusion could be extended to other areas of potential conflict between IAS 34 and other standards. The IFRIC has not studied those areas and therefore has not identified any general principles that might apply both to the Interpretation and to other areas of potential conflict. The IFRIC therefore added a prohibition against extending the consensus by analogy to other areas of potential conflict between IAS 34 and other standards.

---

[*]　In November 2009 the IASB amended the requirements of IAS 39 relating to classification and measurement of assets within the scope of IAS 39 and relocated them to IFRS 9 *Financial Instruments*. Consequently, no financial assets are carried at cost.

BC12 D18 proposed fully retrospective application. A number of comment letters stated that this could be read as being more onerous than the first-time adoption requirements of IAS 36. The IFRIC revised the wording of the transition requirements to make clear that the Interpretation should not be applied to periods before an entity's adoption of IAS 36 in the case of goodwill impairments and IAS 39 in the case of impairments of investments in equity instruments or in financial assets carried at cost.

Documents published to accompany

IFRIC Interpretation 12

Service Concession Arrangements

This version includes amendments resulting from IFRSs issued up to 31 December 2009.

The text of the unaccompanied IFRIC 12 is contained in Part A of this edition. Its effective date when issued was 1 January 2008. The effective date of the latest amendments is 1 January 2013. This part presents the following accompanying documents:

Information note 1

Accounting framework for public-to-private service arrangements

This note accompanies, but is not part of, IFRIC 12.

The diagram below summarises the accounting for service arrangements established by IFRIC 12.

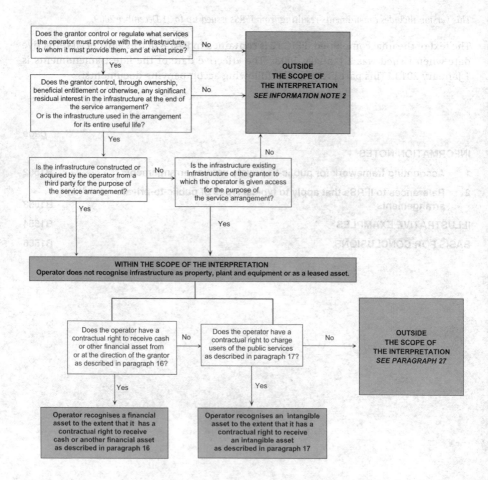

© IASCF

Information note 2

References to IFRSs that apply to typical types of public-to-private arrangements

This note accompanies, but is not part of, IFRIC 12.

The table sets out the typical types of arrangements for private sector participation in the provision of public sector services and provides references to IFRSs that apply to those arrangements. The list of arrangements types is not exhaustive. The purpose of the table is to highlight the continuum of arrangements. It is not the IFRIC's intention to convey the impression that bright lines exist between the accounting requirements for public-to-private arrangements.

Category	Lessee	Service provider			Owner	
Typical arrangement types	Lease (eg Operator leases assets from grantor)	Service and/or maintenance contract (specific tasks eg debt collection)	Rehabilitate-operate-transfer	Build-operate-transfer	Build-own-operate	100% Divestment/ Privatisation/ Corporation
Asset ownership	Grantor				Operator	
Capital investment	Grantor		Operator			
Demand risk	Shared	Grantor	Operator and/or Grantor		Operator	
Typical duration	8–20 years	1–5 years	25–30 years			Indefinite (or may be limited by licence)
Residual interest	Grantor				Operator	
Relevant IFRSs	IAS 17	IAS 18	IFRIC 12		IAS 16	

Illustrative examples

These examples accompany, but are not part of, IFRIC 12.

Example 1: The grantor gives the operator a financial asset

Arrangement terms

IE1 The terms of the arrangement require an operator to construct a road—completing construction within two years—and maintain and operate the road to a specified standard for eight years (ie years 3–10). The terms of the arrangement also require the operator to resurface the road at the end of year 8—the resurfacing activity is revenue-generating. At the end of year 10, the arrangement will end. The operator estimates that the costs it will incur to fulfil its obligations will be:

Table 1.1 *Contract costs*

	Year	CU[(a)]
Construction services	1	500
	2	500
Operation services (per year)	3–10	10
Road resurfacing	8	100

(a) in this example, monetary amounts are denominated in 'currency units (CU)'.

IE2 The terms of the arrangement require the grantor to pay the operator 200 currency units (CU200) per year in years 3–10 for making the road available to the public.

IE3 For the purpose of this illustration, it is assumed that all cash flows take place at the end of the year.

Contract revenue

IE4 The operator recognises contract revenue and costs in accordance with IAS 11 *Construction Contracts* and IAS 18 *Revenue*. The costs of each activity—construction, operation and resurfacing—are recognised as expenses by reference to the stage of completion of that activity. Contract revenue—the fair value of the amount due from the grantor for the activity undertaken—is recognised at the same time. Under the terms of the arrangement the operator is obliged to resurface the road at the end of year 8. In year 8 the operator will be reimbursed by the grantor for resurfacing the road. The obligation to resurface the road is measured at zero in the statement of financial position and the revenue and expense are not recognised in profit or loss until the resurfacing work is performed.

IE5　The total consideration (CU200 in each of years 3–8) reflects the fair values for each of the services, which are:

Table 1.2 *Fair values of the consideration received or receivable*

	Fair value		
Construction services	Forecast cost	+	5%
Operation services	"	" +	20%
Road resurfacing	"	" +	10%
Effective interest rate	6.18% per year		

IE6　In year 1, for example, construction costs of CU500, construction revenue of CU525 (cost plus 5 per cent), and hence construction profit of CU25 are recognised in profit or loss.

Financial asset

IE7　IFRS 9 *Financial Instruments* may require the entity to measure the amounts due from the grantor at amortised cost, unless the entity designates those amounts as measured at fair value through profit or loss. If the receivable is measured at amortised cost in accordance with IFRS 9, it is measured initially at fair value and subsequently at amortised cost, ie the amount initially recognised plus the cumulative interest on that amount calculated using the effective interest method minus repayments.

IE8　If the cash flows and fair values remain the same as those forecast, the effective interest rate is 6.18 per cent per year and the receivable recognised at the end of years 1–3 will be:

Table 1.3 *Measurement of receivable*

	CU
Amount due for construction in year 1	525
Receivable at end of year 1[(a)]	**525**
Effective interest in year 2 on receivable at the end of year 1 (6.18% × CU525)	32
Amount due for construction in year 2	525
Receivable at end of year 2	**1,082**
Effective interest in year 3 on receivable at the end of year 2 (6.18% × CU1,082)	67
Amount due for operation in year 3 (CU10 × (1 + 20%))	12
Cash receipts in year 3	(200)
Receivable at end of year 3	**961**

(a)　No effective interest arises in year 1 because the cash flows are assumed to take place at the end of the year.

Overview of cash flows, statement of comprehensive income and statement of financial position

IE9 For the purpose of this illustration, it is assumed that the operator finances the arrangement wholly with debt and retained profits. It pays interest at 6.7 per cent per year on outstanding debt. If the cash flows and fair values remain the same as those forecast, the operator's cash flows, statement of comprehensive income and statement of financial position over the duration of the arrangement will be:

Table 1.4 Cash flows *(currency units)*

Year	1	2	3	4	5	6	7	8	9	10	Total
Receipts	-	-	200	200	200	200	200	200	200	200	1,600
Contract costs[a]	(500)	(500)	(10)	(10)	(10)	(10)	(10)	(110)	(10)	(10)	(1,180)
Borrowing costs[b]	-	(34)	(69)	(61)	(53)	(43)	(33)	(23)	(19)	(7)	(342)
Net inflow/ (outflow)	(500)	(534)	121	129	137	147	157	67	171	183	78

(a) Table 1.1
(b) Debt at start of year (table 1.6) × 6.7%

Table 1.5 Statement of comprehensive income *(currency units)*

Year	1	2	3	4	5	6	7	8	9	10	Total
Revenue	525	525	12	12	12	12	12	122	12	12	1,256
Contract costs	(500)	(500)	(10)	(10)	(10)	(10)	(10)	(110)	(10)	(10)	(1,180)
Finance income[a]	-	32	67	59	51	43	34	25	22	11	344
Borrowing costs[b]	-	(34)	(69)	(61)	(53)	(43)	(33)	(23)	(19)	(7)	(342)
Net profit	25	23	-	-	-	2	3	14	5	6	78

(a) Amount due from grantor at start of year (table 1.6) × 6.18%
(b) Cash/(debt) (table 1.6) × 6.7%

Table 1.6 Statement of financial position *(currency units)*

End of year	1	2	3	4	5	6	7	8	9	10
Amount due from grantor[a]	525	1,082	961	832	695	550	396	343	177	-
Cash/(debt)[b]	(500)	(1,034)	(913)	(784)	(647)	(500)	(343)	(276)	(105)	78
Net assets	25	48	48	48	48	50	53	67	72	78

(a) Amount due from grantor at start of year, plus revenue and finance income earned in year (table 1.5), less receipts in year (table 1.4)
(b) Debt at start of year plus net cash flow in year (table 1.4)

IE10   This example deals with only one of many possible types of arrangements. Its purpose is to illustrate the accounting treatment for some features that are commonly found in practice. To make the illustration as clear as possible, it has been assumed that the arrangement period is only ten years and that the operator's annual receipts are constant over that period. In practice, arrangement periods may be much longer and annual revenues may increase with time. In such circumstances, the changes in net profit from year to year could be greater.

Example 2: The grantor gives the operator an intangible asset (a licence to charge users)

Arrangement terms

IE11   The terms of a service arrangement require an operator to construct a road—completing construction within two years—and maintain and operate the road to a specified standard for eight years (ie years 3–10). The terms of the arrangement also require the operator to resurface the road when the original surface has deteriorated below a specified condition. The operator estimates that it will have to undertake the resurfacing at the end of the year 8. At the end of year 10, the service arrangement will end. The operator estimates that the costs it will incur to fulfil its obligations will be:

Table 2.1 Contract costs

	Year	CU[(a)]
Construction services	1	500
	2	500
Operation services (per year)	3–10	10
Road resurfacing	8	100

(a) in this example, monetary amounts are denominated in 'currency units (CU)'.

IE12   The terms of the arrangement allow the operator to collect tolls from drivers using the road. The operator forecasts that vehicle numbers will remain constant over the duration of the contract and that it will receive tolls of 200 currency units (CU200) in each of years 3–10.

IE13   For the purpose of this illustration, it is assumed that all cash flows take place at the end of the year.

Intangible asset

IE14   The operator provides construction services to the grantor in exchange for an intangible asset, ie a right to collect tolls from road users in years 3–10. In accordance with IAS 38 *Intangible Assets*, the operator recognises the intangible asset at cost, ie the fair value of consideration transferred to acquire the asset, which is the fair value of the consideration received or receivable for the construction services delivered.

IE15   During the construction phase of the arrangement the operator's asset (representing its accumulating right to be paid for providing construction services) is classified as an intangible asset (licence to charge users of the infrastructure). The operator estimates the fair value of its consideration received to be equal to the forecast construction costs plus 5 per cent margin. It is also assumed that, in accordance with IAS 23 *Borrowing Costs*, the operator capitalises the borrowing costs, estimated at 6.7 per cent, during the construction phase of the arrangement:

Table 2.2 *Initial measurement of intangible asset*

	CU
Construction services in year 1 (CU500 × (1 + 5%))	525
Capitalisation of borrowing costs (table 2.4)	34
Construction services in year 2 (CU500 × (1 + 5%))	525
Intangible asset at end of year 2	1,084

IE16   In accordance with IAS 38, the intangible asset is amortised over the period in which it is expected to be available for use by the operator, ie years 3–10. The depreciable amount of the intangible asset (CU1,084) is allocated using a straight-line method. The annual amortisation charge is therefore CU1,084 divided by 8 years, ie CU135 per year.

Construction costs and revenue

IE17   The operator recognises the revenue and costs in accordance with IAS 11 *Construction Contracts*, ie by reference to the stage of completion of the construction. It measures contract revenue at the fair value of the consideration received or receivable. Thus in each of years 1 and 2 it recognises in its profit or loss construction costs of CU500, construction revenue of CU525 (cost plus 5 per cent) and, hence, construction profit of CU25.

Toll revenue

IE18   The road users pay for the public services at the same time as they receive them, ie when they use the road. The operator therefore recognises toll revenue when it collects the tolls.

Resurfacing obligations

IE19   The operator's resurfacing obligation arises as a consequence of use of the road during the operating phase. It is recognised and measured in accordance with IAS 37 *Provisions, Contingent Liabilities and Contingent Assets*, ie at the best estimate of the expenditure required to settle the present obligation at the end of the reporting period.

IE20 For the purpose of this illustration, it is assumed that the terms of the operator's contractual obligation are such that the best estimate of the expenditure required to settle the obligation at any date is proportional to the number of vehicles that have used the road by that date and increases by CU17 (discounted to a current value) each year. The operator discounts the provision to its present value in accordance with IAS 37. The charge recognised each period in profit or loss is:

Table 2.3 *Resurfacing obligation* (currency units)

Year	3	4	5	6	7	8	Total
Obligation arising in year (CU17 discounted at 6%)	12	13	14	15	16	17	87
Increase in earlier years' provision arising from passage of time	0	1	1	2	4	5	13
Total expense recognised in profit or loss	12	14	15	17	20	22	100

Overview of cash flows, statement of comprehensive income and statement of financial position

IE21 For the purposes of this illustration, it is assumed that the operator finances the arrangement wholly with debt and retained profits. It pays interest at 6.7 per cent per year on outstanding debt. If the cash flows and fair values remain the same as those forecast, the operator's cash flows, statement of comprehensive income and statement of financial position over the duration of the arrangement will be:

Table 2.4 *Cash flows* (currency units)

Year	1	2	3	4	5	6	7	8	9	10	Total
Receipts	-	-	200	200	200	200	200	200	200	200	1,600
Contract costs[a]	(500)	(500)	(10)	(10)	(10)	(10)	(10)	(110)	(10)	(10)	(1,180)
Borrowing costs[b]	-	(34)	(69)	(61)	(53)	(43)	(33)	(23)	(19)	(7)	(342)
Net inflow/ (outflow)	(500)	(534)	121	129	137	147	157	67	171	183	78

(a) Table 2.1
(b) Debt at start of year (table 2.6) × 6.7%

Table 2.5 *Statement of comprehensive income* (currency units)

Year	1	2	3	4	5	6	7	8	9	10	Total
Revenue	525	525	200	200	200	200	200	200	200	200	2,650
Amortisation	-	-	(135)	(135)	(136)	(136)	(136)	(136)	(135)	(135)	(1,084)
Resurfacing expense	-	-	(12)	(14)	(15)	(17)	(20)	(22)	-	-	(100)
Other contract costs	(500)	(500)	(10)	(10)	(10)	(10)	(10)	(10)	(10)	(10)	(1,080)
Borrowing costs[a][b]	-	-	(69)	(61)	(53)	(43)	(33)	(23)	(19)	(7)	(308)
Net profit	25	25	(26)	(20)	(14)	(6)	1	9	36	48	78

(a) Borrowing costs are capitalised during the construction phase.

(b) Table 2.4

Table 2.6 *Statement of financial position* (currency units)

End of year	1	2	3	4	5	6	7	8	9	10
Intangible asset	525	1,084	949	814	678	542	406	270	135	-
Cash/(debt)[a]	(500)	(1,034)	(913)	(784)	(647)	(500)	(343)	(276)	(105)	78
Resurfacing obligation	-	-	(12)	(26)	(41)	(58)	(78)	-	-	-
Net assets	25	50	24	4	(10)	(16)	(15)	(6)	30	78

(a) Debt at start of year plus net cash flow in year (table 2.4)

IE22   This example deals with only one of many possible types of arrangements. Its purpose is to illustrate the accounting treatment for some features that are commonly found in practice. To make the illustration as clear as possible, it has been assumed that the arrangement period is only ten years and that the operator's annual receipts are constant over that period. In practice, arrangement periods may be much longer and annual revenues may increase with time. In such circumstances, the changes in net profit from year to year could be greater.

Example 3: The grantor gives the operator a financial asset and an intangible asset

Arrangement terms

IE23   The terms of a service arrangement require an operator to construct a road—completing construction within two years—and to operate the road and maintain it to a specified standard for eight years (ie years 3–10). The terms of the arrangement also require the operator to resurface the road when the original surface has deteriorated below a specified condition. The operator estimates that it will have to undertake the resurfacing at the end of year 8. At the end of year 10, the arrangement will end. The operator estimates that the costs it will incur to fulfil its obligations will be:

Table 3.1 *Contract costs*

	Year	CU[a]
Construction services	1	500
	2	500
Operation services (per year)	3–10	10
Road resurfacing	8	100

(a)   in this example, monetary amounts are denominated in 'currency units (CU)'.

IE24   The operator estimates the consideration in respect of construction services to be cost plus 5 per cent.

IE25   The terms of the arrangement allow the operator to collect tolls from drivers using the road.   In addition, the grantor guarantees the operator a minimum amount of CU700 and interest at a specified rate of 6.18 per cent to reflect the timing of cash receipts.   The operator forecasts that vehicle numbers will remain constant over the duration of the contract and that it will receive tolls of CU200 in each of years 3–10.

IE26   For the purpose of this illustration, it is assumed that all cash flows take place at the end of the year.

Dividing the arrangement

IE27   The contractual right to receive cash from the grantor for the services and the right to charge users for the public services should be regarded as two separate assets under IFRSs.   Therefore in this arrangement it is necessary to divide the operator's consideration into two components—a financial asset component based on the guaranteed amount and an intangible asset for the remainder.

Table 3.2 *Dividing the operator's consideration*

Year	Total	Financial asset	Intangible asset
Construction services in year 1 (CU500 × (1 + 5%))	525	350	175
Construction services in year 2 (CU500 × (1 + 5%))	525	350	175
Total construction services	1,050	700	350
	100%	67%[a]	33%
Finance income, at specified rate of 6.18% on receivable (see table 3.3)	22	22	-
Borrowing costs capitalised (interest paid in years 1 and 2 × 33%) (see table 3.7)	11	-	11
Total fair value of the operator's consideration	1,083	722	361

(a)   Amount guaranteed by the grantor as a proportion of the construction services

Financial asset

IE28   IFRS 9 *Financial Instruments* may require the entity to measure the amount due from or at the direction of the grantor in exchange for the construction services at amortised cost. If the receivable is measured at amortised cost in accordance with IFRS 9, it is measured initially at fair value and subsequently at amortised cost, ie the amount initially recognised plus the cumulative interest on that amount minus repayments.

IE29   On this basis the receivable recognised at the end of years 2 and 3 will be:

Table 3.3 *Measurement of receivable*

	CU
Construction services in year 1 allocated to the financial asset	350
Receivable at end of year 1	350
Construction services in year 2 allocated to the financial asset	350
Interest in year 2 on receivable at end of year 1 (6.18% × CU350)	22
Receivable at end of year 2	722
Interest in year 3 on receivable at end of year 2 (6.18% × CU722)	45
Cash receipts in year 3 (see table 3.5)	(117)
Receivable at end of year 3	650

Intangible asset

IE30   In accordance with IAS 38 *Intangible Assets*, the operator recognises the intangible asset at cost, ie the fair value of the consideration received or receivable.

IE31   During the construction phase of the arrangement the operator's asset (representing its accumulating right to be paid for providing construction services) is classified as a right to receive a licence to charge users of the infrastructure. The operator estimates the fair value of its consideration received or receivable as equal to the forecast construction costs plus 5 per cent. It is also assumed that, in accordance with IAS 23 *Borrowing Costs*, the operator capitalises the borrowing costs, estimated at 6.7 per cent, during the construction phase:

Table 3.4 *Initial measurement of intangible asset*

	CU
Construction services in year 1 (CU500 × (1 + 5%) × 33%)	175
Borrowing costs (interest paid in years 1 and 2 × 33%) (see table 3.7)	11
Construction services in year 2 (CU500 × (1 + 5%) × 33%)	175
Intangible asset at the end of year 2	361

IE32　In accordance with IAS 38, the intangible asset is amortised over the period in which it is expected to be available for use by the operator, ie years 3–10. The depreciable amount of the intangible asset (CU361 including borrowing costs) is allocated using a straight-line method. The annual amortisation charge is therefore CU361 divided by 8 years, ie CU45 per year.

Contract revenue and costs

IE33　The operator provides construction services to the grantor in exchange for a financial asset and an intangible asset. Under both the financial asset model and intangible asset model, the operator recognises contract revenue and costs in accordance with IAS 11 *Construction Contracts*, ie by reference to the stage of completion of the construction. It measures contract revenue at the fair value of the consideration receivable. Thus in each of years 1 and 2 it recognises in profit or loss construction costs of CU500 and construction revenue of CU525 (cost plus 5 per cent).

Toll revenue

IE34　The road users pay for the public services at the same time as they receive them, ie when they use the road. Under the terms of this arrangement the cash flows are allocated to the financial asset and intangible asset in proportion, so the operator allocates the receipts from tolls between repayment of the financial asset and revenue earned from the intangible asset:

Table 3.5 *Allocation of toll receipts*

Year	CU
Guaranteed receipt from grantor	700
Finance income (see table 3.8)	237
Total	937
Cash allocated to realisation of the financial asset per year (CU937/8 years)	117
Receipts attributable to intangible asset (CU200 × 8 years – CU937)	663
Annual receipt from intangible asset (CU663/8 years)	83

Resurfacing obligations

IE35　The operator's resurfacing obligation arises as a consequence of use of the road during the operation phase. It is recognised and measured in accordance with IAS 37 *Provisions, Contingent Liabilities and Contingent Assets*, ie at the best estimate of the expenditure required to settle the present obligation at the end of the reporting period.

IE36　For the purpose of this illustration, it is assumed that the terms of the operator's contractual obligation are such that the best estimate of the expenditure required to settle the obligation at any date is proportional to the number of vehicles that have used the road by that date and increases by CU17 each year. The operator discounts the provision to its present value in accordance with IAS 37. The charge recognised each period in profit or loss is:

Table 3.6 Resurfacing obligation (currency units)

Year	3	4	5	6	7	8	Total
Obligation arising in year (CU17 discounted at 6%)	12	13	14	15	16	17	87
Increase in earlier years' provision arising from passage of time	0	1	1	2	4	5	13
Total expense recognised in profit or loss	12	14	15	17	20	22	100

Overview of cash flows, statement of comprehensive income and statement of financial position

IE37   For the purposes of this illustration, it is assumed that the operator finances the arrangement wholly with debt and retained profits. It pays interest at 6.7 per cent per year on outstanding debt. If the cash flows and fair values remain the same as those forecast, the operator's cash flows, statement of comprehensive income and statement of financial position over the duration of the arrangement will be:

Table 3.7 Cash flows (currency units)

Year	1	2	3	4	5	6	7	8	9	10	Total
Receipts	–	–	200	200	200	200	200	200	200	200	1,600
Contract costs[(a)]	(500)	(500)	(10)	(10)	(10)	(10)	(10)	(110)	(10)	(10)	(1,180)
Borrowing costs[(b)]	–	(34)	(69)	(61)	(53)	(43)	(33)	(23)	(19)	(7)	(342)
Net inflow/ (outflow)	(500)	(534)	121	129	137	147	157	67	171	183	78

(a) Table 3.1

(b) Debt at start of year (table 3.9) × 6.7%

© IASCF

Table 3.8 Statement of comprehensive income (currency units)

Year	1	2	3	4	5	6	7	8	9	10	Total
Revenue on construction	525	525	-	-	-	-	-	-	-	-	1,050
Revenue from intangible asset	-	-	83	83	83	83	83	83	83	83	663
Finance income[a]	-	22	45	40	35	30	25	19	13	7	237
Amortisation	-	-	(45)	(45)	(45)	(45)	(45)	(45)	(45)	(46)	(361)
Resurfacing expense	-	-	(12)	(14)	(15)	(17)	(20)	(22)	-	-	(100)
Construction costs	(500)	(500)									(1,000)
Other contract costs[b]			(10)	(10)	(10)	(10)	(10)	(10)	(10)	(10)	(80)
Borrowing costs (table 3.7)[c]	-	(23)	(69)	(61)	(53)	(43)	(33)	(23)	(19)	(7)	(331)
Net profit	25	24	(8)	(7)	(5)	(2)	0	2	22	27	78

(a) Interest on receivable

(b) Table 3.1

(c) In year 2, borrowing costs are stated net of amount capitalised in the intangible (see table 3.4).

Table 3.9 Statement of financial position (currency units)

End of year	1	2	3	4	5	6	7	8	9	10
Receivable	350	722	650	573	491	404	312	214	110	-
Intangible asset	175	361	316	271	226	181	136	91	46	-
Cash/(debt)[a]	(500)	(1,034)	(913)	(784)	(647)	(500)	(343)	(276)	(105)	78
Resurfacing obligation	-	-	(12)	(26)	(41)	(58)	(78)	-	-	-
Net assets	25	49	41	34	29	27	27	29	51	78

(a) Debt at start of year plus net cash flow in year (table 3.7)

IE38　This example deals with only one of many possible types of arrangements. Its purpose is to illustrate the accounting treatment for some features that are commonly found in practice. To make the illustration as clear as possible, it has been assumed that the arrangement period is only ten years and that the operator's annual receipts are constant over that period. In practice, arrangement periods may be much longer and annual revenues may increase with time. In such circumstances, the changes in net profit from year to year could be greater.

Basis for Conclusions on
IFRIC Interpretation 12 *Service Concession Arrangements*

This Basis for Conclusions accompanies, but is not part of, IFRIC 12.

Introduction

BC1   This Basis for Conclusions summarises the IFRIC's considerations in reaching its consensus. Individual IFRIC members gave greater weight to some factors than to others.

Background (paragraphs 1–3)

BC2   SIC-29 *Service Concession Arrangements: Disclosures* (formerly *Disclosure—Service Concession Arrangements*) contains disclosure requirements in respect of public-to-private service arrangements, but does not specify how they should be accounted for.

BC3   There was widespread concern about the lack of such guidance. In particular, operators wished to know how to account for infrastructure that they either constructed or acquired for the purpose of a public-to-private service concession arrangement, or were given access to for the purpose of providing the public service. They also wanted to know how to account for other rights and obligations arising from these types of arrangements.

BC4   In response to this concern, the International Accounting Standards Board asked a working group comprising representatives of the standard-setters of Australia, France, Spain and the United Kingdom (four of the countries that had expressed such concern) to carry out initial research on the subject. The working group recommended that the IFRIC should seek to clarify how certain aspects of existing accounting standards were to be applied.

BC5   In March 2005 the IFRIC published for public comment three draft Interpretations: D12 *Service Concession Arrangements—Determining the Accounting Model*, D13 *Service Concession Arrangements—The Financial Asset Model* and D14 *Service Concession Arrangements—The Intangible Asset Model*. In response to the proposals 77 comment letters were received. In addition, in order to understand better the practical issues that would have arisen on implementing the proposed Interpretations, IASB staff met various interested parties, including preparers, auditors and regulators.

BC6   Most respondents to D12–D14 supported the IFRIC's proposal to develop an Interpretation. However, nearly all respondents expressed concern with fundamental aspects of the proposals, some urging that the project be passed to the Board to develop a comprehensive standard.

BC7   In its redeliberation of the proposals the IFRIC acknowledged that the project was a large undertaking but concluded that it should continue its work because, given the limited scope of the project, it was by then better placed than the Board to deal with the issues in a timely way.

Terminology

BC8   SIC-29 used the terms 'Concession Provider' and 'Concession Operator' to describe, respectively, the grantor and operator of the service arrangement. Some commentators, and some members of the IFRIC, found these terms confusingly similar. The IFRIC decided to adopt the terms 'grantor' and 'operator', and amended SIC-29 accordingly.

Scope (paragraphs 4–9)

BC9   The IFRIC observed that public-to-private service arrangements take a variety of forms. The continued involvement of both grantor and operator over the term of the arrangement, accompanied by heavy upfront investment, raises questions over what assets and liabilities should be recognised by the operator.

BC10   The working group recommended that the scope of the IFRIC's project should be restricted to public-to-private service concession arrangements.

BC11   In developing the proposals the IFRIC decided to address only arrangements in which the grantor (a) controlled or regulated the services provided by the operator, and (b) controlled any significant residual interest in the infrastructure at the end of the term of the arrangement. It also decided to specify the accounting treatment only for infrastructure that the operator constructed or acquired from a third party, or to which it was given access by the grantor, for the purpose of the arrangement. The IFRIC concluded that these conditions were likely to be met in most of the public-to-private arrangements for which guidance had been sought.

BC12   Commentators on the draft Interpretations argued that the proposals ignored many arrangements that were found in practice, in particular, when the infrastructure was leased to the operator or, conversely, when it was held as the property, plant and equipment of the operator before the start of the service arrangement.

BC13   In considering these comments, the IFRIC decided that the scope of the project should not be expanded because it already included the arrangements most in need of interpretative guidance and expansion would have significantly delayed the Interpretation. The scope of the project was considered at length during the initial stage, as indicated above. The IFRIC confirmed its view that the proposed Interpretation should address the issues set out in paragraph 10. Nonetheless, during its redeliberation the IFRIC considered the range of typical arrangements for private sector participation in the provision of public services, including some that were outside the scope of the proposed Interpretation. The IFRIC decided that the Interpretation could provide references to relevant standards that apply to arrangements outside the scope of the Interpretation without giving guidance on their application. If experience showed that such guidance was needed, a separate project could be undertaken at a later date. Information Note 2 contains a table of references to relevant standards for the types of arrangements considered by the IFRIC.

Private-to-private arrangements

BC14 Some respondents to the draft Interpretations suggested that the scope of the proposed Interpretation should be extended to include private-to-private service arrangements. The IFRIC noted that addressing the accounting for such arrangements was not the primary purpose of the project because the IFRIC had been asked to provide guidance for public-to-private arrangements that meet the requirements set out in paragraph 5 and have the characteristics described in paragraph 3. The IFRIC noted that application by analogy would be appropriate under the hierarchy set out in paragraphs 7–12 of IAS 8 *Accounting Policies, Changes in Accounting Estimates and Errors.*

Grantor accounting

BC15 The Interpretation does not specify the accounting by grantors, because the IFRIC's objective and priority were to establish guidance for operators. Some commentators asked the IFRIC to establish guidance for the accounting by grantors. The IFRIC discussed these comments but reaffirmed its view. It noted that in many cases the grantor is a government body, and that IFRSs are not designed to apply to not-for-profit activities in the private sector, public sector or government, though entities with such activities may find them appropriate (see *Preface to IFRSs* paragraph 9).

Existing assets of the operator

BC16 The Interpretation does not specify the treatment of existing assets of the operator because the IFRIC decided that it was unnecessary to address the derecognition requirements of existing standards.

BC17 Some respondents asked the IFRIC to provide guidance on the accounting for existing assets of the operator, stating that the scope exclusion would create uncertainty about the treatment of these assets.

BC18 In its redeliberations the IFRIC noted that one objective of the Interpretation is to address whether the operator should recognise as its property, plant and equipment the infrastructure it constructs or to which it is given access. The accounting issue to be addressed for existing assets of the operator is one of derecognition, which is already addressed in IFRSs (IAS 16 *Property, Plant and Equipment*). In the light of the comments received from respondents, the IFRIC decided to clarify that certain public-to-private service arrangements may convey to the grantor a right to use existing assets of the operator, in which case the operator would apply the derecognition requirements of IFRSs to determine whether it should derecognise its existing assets.

The significant residual interest criterion

BC19 Paragraph 5(b) of D12 proposed that for a service arrangement to be within its scope the residual interest in the infrastructure handed over to the grantor at the end of the arrangement must be significant. Respondents argued, and the IFRIC agreed, that the significant residual interest criterion would limit the usefulness of the guidance because a service arrangement for the entire physical life of the infrastructure would be excluded from the scope of the guidance. That result was not the IFRIC's intention. In its redeliberation of the proposals, the IFRIC decided that it would not retain the proposal that the residual interest in the infrastructure handed over to the grantor at the end of the arrangement must be significant. As a consequence, 'whole of life' infrastructure (ie where the infrastructure is used in a public-to-private service arrangement for the entirety of its useful life) is within the scope of the Interpretation.

Treatment of the operator's rights over the infrastructure (paragraph 11)

BC20   The IFRIC considered the nature of the rights conveyed to the operator in a service concession arrangement. It first examined whether the infrastructure used to provide public services could be classified as property, plant and equipment of the operator under IAS 16. It started from the principle that infrastructure used to provide public services should be recognised as property, plant and equipment of the party that controls its use. This principle determines which party should recognise the property, plant and equipment as its own. The reference to control stems from the *Framework*:

(a)   an asset is defined by the *Framework* as 'a resource controlled by the entity as a result of past events and from which future economic benefits are expected to flow to the entity.'

(b)   the *Framework* notes that many assets are associated with legal rights, including the right of ownership. It goes on to clarify that the right of ownership is not essential.

(c)   rights are often unbundled. For example, they may be divided proportionately (undivided interests in land) or by specified cash flows (principal and interest on a bond) or over time (a lease).

BC21   The IFRIC concluded that treatment of infrastructure that the operator constructs or acquires or to which the grantor gives the operator access for the purpose of the service arrangement should be determined by whether it is controlled by the grantor in the manner described in paragraph 5. If it is so controlled (as will be the case for all arrangements within the scope of the Interpretation), then, regardless of which party has legal title to it during the arrangement, the infrastructure should not be recognised as property, plant and equipment of the operator because the operator does not control the use of the public service infrastructure.

BC22   In reaching this conclusion the IFRIC observed that it is control of the right to use an asset that determines recognition under IAS 16 and the creation of a lease under IAS 17 *Leases*. IAS 16 defines property, plant and equipment as tangible items that 'are held for use in the production or supply of goods or services, for rental to others or for administrative purposes ...'. It requires items within this definition to be recognised as property, plant and equipment unless another standard requires or permits a different approach. As an example of a different approach, it highlights the requirement in IAS 17 for recognition of leased property, plant and equipment to be evaluated on the basis of the transfer of risks and rewards. That standard defines a lease as 'an agreement whereby the lessor conveys to the lessee in return for a series of payments the right to use an asset' and it sets out the requirements for classification of leases. IFRIC 4 *Determining whether an Arrangement contains a Lease* interprets the meaning of right to use an asset as 'the arrangement conveys the right to control the use of the underlying asset.'

BC23   Accordingly, it is only if an arrangement conveys the right to control the use of the underlying asset that reference is made to IAS 17 to determine how such a lease should be classified. A lease is classified as a finance lease if it transfers substantially all the risks and rewards incidental to ownership. A lease is classified as an operating lease if it does not transfer substantially all the risks and rewards incidental to ownership.

BC24   The IFRIC considered whether arrangements within the scope of IFRIC 12 convey 'the right to control the use of the underlying asset' (the public service infrastructure) to the operator. The IFRIC decided that, if an arrangement met the conditions in paragraph 5, the operator would not have the right to control the use of the underlying asset and should therefore not recognise the infrastructure as a leased asset.

BC25   In arrangements within the scope of the Interpretation the operator acts as a service provider. The operator constructs or upgrades infrastructure used to provide a public service. Under the terms of the contract the operator has access to operate the infrastructure to provide the public service on the grantor's behalf. The asset recognised by the operator is the consideration it receives in exchange for its services, not the public service infrastructure that it constructs or upgrades.

BC26   Respondents to the draft Interpretations disagreed that recognition should be determined solely on the basis of control of use without any assessment of the extent to which the operator or the grantor bears the risks and rewards of ownership. They questioned how the proposed approach could be reconciled to IAS 17, in which the leased asset is recognised by the party that bears substantially all the risks and rewards incidental to ownership.

BC27   During its redeliberation the IFRIC affirmed its decision that if an arrangement met the control conditions in paragraph 5 of the Interpretation the operator would not have the right to control the use of the underlying asset (public service infrastructure) and should therefore not recognise the infrastructure as its property, plant and equipment under IAS 16 or the creation of a lease under IAS 17. The contractual service arrangement between the grantor and operator would not convey the right to use the infrastructure to the operator. The IFRIC concluded that this treatment is also consistent with IAS 18 *Revenue* because, for arrangements within the scope of the Interpretation, the second condition of paragraph 14 of IAS 18 is not satisfied. The grantor retains continuing managerial involvement to the degree usually associated with ownership and control over the infrastructure as described in paragraph 5.

BC28   In service concession arrangements rights are usually conveyed for a limited period, which is similar to a lease. However, for arrangements within the scope of the Interpretation, the operator's right is different from that of a lessee: the grantor retains control over the use to which the infrastructure is put, by controlling or regulating what services the operator must provide, to whom it must provide them, and at what price, as described in paragraph 5(a). The grantor also retains control over any significant residual interest in the infrastructure throughout the period of the arrangement. Unlike a lessee, the operator does not have a right of use of the underlying asset: rather it has access to operate the infrastructure to provide the public service on behalf of the grantor in accordance with the terms specified in the contract.

BC29   The IFRIC considered whether the scope of the Interpretation might overlap with IFRIC 4. In particular, it noted the views expressed by some respondents that the contractual terms of certain service arrangements would be regarded as leases under IFRIC 4 and would also be regarded as meeting the scope criterion set out in paragraph 5 of IFRIC 12. The IFRIC did not regard the choice between accounting treatments as appropriate because it could lead to different accounting treatments for contracts that have similar economic effects. In the light of comments received the IFRIC amended the scope of IFRIC 4 to specify that if a service arrangement met the scope requirements of IFRIC 12 it would not be within the scope of IFRIC 4.

Recognition and measurement of arrangement consideration (paragraphs 12 and 13)

BC30   The accounting requirements for construction and service contracts are addressed in IAS 11 *Construction Contracts* and IAS 18. They require revenue to be recognised by reference to the stage of completion of the contract activity. IAS 18 states the general principle that revenue is measured at the fair value of the consideration received or receivable. However, the IFRIC observed that the fair value of the construction services delivered may in practice be the most appropriate method of establishing the fair value of the consideration received or receivable for the construction services. This will be the case in service concession arrangements, because the consideration attributable to the construction activity often has to be apportioned from a total sum receivable on the contract as a whole and, if it consists of an intangible asset, may also be subject to uncertainty in measurement.

BC31   The IFRIC noted that IAS 18 requires its recognition criteria to be applied separately to identifiable components of a single transaction in order to reflect the substance of the transaction. For example, when the selling price of a product includes an identifiable amount for subsequent servicing, that amount is deferred and is recognised as revenue over the period during which the service is performed. The IFRIC concluded that this requirement was relevant to service arrangements within the scope of the Interpretation. Arrangements within the scope of the Interpretation involve an operator providing more than one service, ie construction or upgrade services, and operation services. Although the contract for each service is generally negotiated as a single contract, its terms call for separate phases or elements because each separate phase or element has its own distinct skills, requirements and risks. The IFRIC noted that, in these circumstances, IAS 18 paragraphs 4 and 13 require the contract to be separated into two separate phases or elements, a construction element within the scope of IAS 11 and an operations element within the scope of IAS 18. Thus the operator might report different profit margins on each phase or element. The IFRIC noted that the amount for each service would be identifiable because such services were often provided as a single service. The IFRIC also noted that the combining and segmenting criteria of IAS 11 applied only to the construction element of the arrangement.

BC32   In some circumstances, the grantor makes a non-cash payment for the construction services, ie it gives the operator an intangible asset (a right to charge users of the public service) in exchange for the operator providing construction services. The operator then uses the intangible asset to generate further revenues from users of the public service.

BC33   Paragraph 12 of IAS 18 states:

> When goods are sold or services are rendered in exchange for dissimilar goods or services, the exchange is regarded as a transaction which generates revenue. The revenue is measured at the fair value of the goods or services received, adjusted by the amount of any cash or cash equivalents transferred. When the fair value of the goods or services received cannot be measured reliably, the revenue is measured at the fair value of the goods or services given up, adjusted by the amount of any cash or cash equivalents transferred.

BC34   The IFRIC noted that total revenue does not equal total cash inflows. The reason for this outcome is that, when the operator receives an intangible asset in exchange for its construction services, there are two sets of inflows and outflows rather than one. In the first set, the construction services are exchanged for the intangible asset in a barter transaction with the grantor. In the second set, the intangible asset received from the grantor is used up to generate cash flows from users of the public service. This result is not unique to service arrangements within the scope of the Interpretation. Any situation in which an entity provides goods or services in exchange for another dissimilar asset that is subsequently used to generate cash revenues would lead to a similar result.

BC35   Some IFRIC members were uncomfortable with such a result, and would have preferred a method of accounting under which total revenues were limited to the cash inflows. However, they accepted that it is consistent with the treatment accorded to a barter transaction, ie an exchange of dissimilar goods or services.

Consideration given by the grantor to the operator (paragraphs 14–19)

BC36   The IFRIC observed that the contractual rights that the operator receives in exchange for providing construction services can take a variety of forms. They are not necessarily rights to receive cash or other financial assets.

BC37   The draft Interpretations proposed that the nature of the operator's asset depended on who had the primary responsibility to pay the operator for the services. The operator should recognise a financial asset when the grantor had the primary responsibility to pay the operator for the services. The operator should recognise an intangible asset in all other cases.

BC38   Respondents to the draft Interpretations argued that determining which accounting model to apply by looking at who has the primary responsibility to pay the operator for the services, irrespective of who bears demand risk (ie ability and willingness of users to pay for the service), would result in an accounting treatment that did not reflect the economic substance of the arrangement. Respondents were concerned that the proposal would require operators with essentially identical cash flow streams to adopt different accounting models. This would impair users' understanding of entities involved in providing public-to-private service concession arrangements. Several gave the example of a shadow toll road and a toll road, where the economics (demand risk) of the arrangements would be similar, pointing out that under the proposals the two arrangements would be accounted for differently. In the light of comments received on the proposals, the IFRIC decided to clarify (see paragraphs 15–19) the extent to which an operator should recognise a financial asset and an intangible asset.

BC39   Responses to the draft Interpretations provided only limited information about the impact of the proposals. To obtain additional information, IASB staff arranged for discussions with preparers, auditors and regulators. The consensus of those consulted was that the identity of the payee has no effect on the risks to the operator's cash flow stream. The operator typically relies on the terms of the service arrangement contract to determine the risks to its cash flow stream. The operator's cash flows may be guaranteed by the grantor, in which case the grantor bears demand risk, or the operator's cash flows may be conditional on usage levels, in which case the operator bears demand risk.

BC40   The IFRIC noted that the operator's cash flows are guaranteed when (a) the grantor agrees to pay the operator specified or determinable amounts whether or not the public service is used (sometimes known as take-or-pay arrangements) or (b) the grantor grants a right to the operator to charge users of the public service and the grantor guarantees the operator's cash flows by way of a shortfall guarantee described in paragraph 16. The operator's cash flows are conditional on usage when it has no such guarantee but must obtain its revenue either directly from users of the public service or from the grantor in proportion to public usage of the service (road tolls or shadow tolls for example).

A financial asset (operator's cash flows are guaranteed by the grantor)

BC41   Paragraph 11 of IAS 32 *Financial Instruments: Presentation* defines a financial asset to include 'a contractual right to receive cash or another financial asset from another entity'. Paragraph 13 of that standard clarifies that 'contractual' refers to 'an agreement between two or more parties that has clear economic consequences that the parties have little, if any, discretion to avoid, usually because the agreement is enforceable by law.'

BC42   The IFRIC decided that a financial asset should be recognised to the extent that the operator has an unconditional present right to receive cash from or at the direction of the grantor for the construction services; and the grantor has little, if any, discretion to avoid payment, usually because the agreement is enforceable by law. The operator has a contractual right to receive cash for the construction services if the grantor contractually guarantees the operator's cash flows, in the manner described in paragraph 16. The IFRIC noted that the operator has an unconditional right to receive cash to the extent that the grantor bears the risk (demand risk) that the cash flows generated by the users of the public service will not be sufficient to recover the operator's investment.

BC43   The IFRIC noted that:

(a)   an agreement to pay for the shortfall, if any, between amounts received from users of the service and specified or determinable amounts does not meet the definition of a financial guarantee in paragraph 9 of IAS 39 *Financial Instruments: Recognition and Measurement* because the operator has an unconditional contractual right to receive cash from the grantor. Furthermore, the amendments made to IAS 39 in August 2005 by *Financial Guarantee Contracts* do not address the treatment of financial guarantee contracts by the holder. The objective of the amendments was to ensure that issuers of financial guarantee contracts recognise a liability for the obligations the guarantor has undertaken in issuing that guarantee.

(b)   users or the grantor may pay the contractual amount receivable directly to the operator. The method of payment is a matter of form only. In both cases the operator has a present, unconditional, contractual right to receive the specified or determinable cash flows from or at the direction of the grantor. The nature of the operator's asset is not altered solely because the contractual amount receivable may be paid directly by users of the public service. The IFRIC observed that accounting for these contractual cash flows in accordance with IASs 32 and 39 faithfully reflects the economics of the arrangements, which is to provide finance to the grantor for the construction of the infrastructure.

Operator's cash flows are contingent on the operator meeting specified quality or efficiency requirements

BC44   The IFRIC concluded that the definition of a financial asset is met even if the contractual right to receive cash is contingent on the operator meeting specified quality or efficiency requirements or targets. Before the grantor is required to pay the operator for its construction services, the operator may have to ensure that the infrastructure is capable of generating the public services specified by the grantor or that the infrastructure is up to or exceeds operating standards or efficiency targets specified by the grantor to ensure a specified level of service and capacity can be delivered. In this respect the operator's position is the same as that of any other entity in which payment for goods or services is contingent on subsequent performance of the goods or service sold.

BC45   Therefore IFRIC 12 treats the consideration given by the grantor to the operator as giving rise to a financial asset irrespective of whether the contractual amounts receivable are contingent on the operator meeting levels of performance or efficiency targets.

An intangible asset (operator's cash flows are conditional on usage)

BC46   IAS 38 *Intangible Assets* defines an intangible asset as 'an identifiable non-monetary asset without physical substance'. It mentions licences as examples of intangible assets. It describes an asset as being identifiable when it arises from contractual rights.

BC47 The IFRIC concluded that the right of an operator to charge users of the public service meets the definition of an intangible asset, and therefore should be accounted for in accordance with IAS 38. In these circumstances the operator's revenue is conditional on usage and it bears the risk (demand risk) that the cash flows generated by users of the public service will not be sufficient to recover its investment.

BC48 In the absence of contractual arrangements designed to ensure that the operator receives a minimum amount (see paragraphs BC53 and BC54), the operator has no contractual right to receive cash even if receipt of the cash is highly probable. Rather, the operator has an opportunity to charge those who use the public service in the future. The operator bears the demand risk and hence its commercial return is contingent on users using the public service. The operator's asset is a licence, which would be classified as an intangible asset within the scope of IAS 38. And, as clarified in paragraph AG10 of the application guidance in IAS 32:

> Physical assets (such as inventories, property, plant and equipment), leased assets and intangible assets (such as patents and trademarks) are not financial assets. Control of such physical and intangible assets creates an opportunity to generate an inflow of cash or another financial asset, but it does not give rise to a present right to receive cash or another financial asset.

BC49 The IFRIC considered whether a right to charge users unsupported by any shortfall guarantee from the grantor could be regarded as an indirect right to receive cash arising from the contract with the grantor. It concluded that although the operator's asset might have characteristics that are similar to those of a financial asset, it would not meet the definition of a financial asset in IAS 32: the operator would not at the balance sheet date have a contractual right to receive cash from another entity. That other entity (ie the user) would still have the ability to avoid any obligation. The grantor would be passing to the operator an opportunity to charge users in future, not a present right to receive cash.

Contractual arrangements that eliminate substantially all variability in the operator's return

BC50 The IFRIC considered whether agreements incorporating contractual arrangements designed to eliminate substantially all variability in the operator's return would meet the definition of a financial asset, for example:

(a) the price charged by the operator would be varied by regulation designed to ensure that the operator received a substantially fixed return; or

(b) the operator would be permitted to collect revenues from users or the grantor until it achieved a specified return on its investment, at which point the arrangement would come to an end.

BC51 The IFRIC noted that, as a result of such contractual arrangements, the operator's return would be low risk. Only if usage were extremely low would the contractual mechanisms fail to give the operator the specified return. The likelihood of usage being that low could be remote. Commercially, the operator's return would be regarded as fixed, giving its asset many of the characteristics of a financial asset.

BC52   However, the IFRIC concluded that the fact that the operator's asset was low risk did not influence its classification. IAS 32 does not define financial assets by reference to the amount of risk in the return—it defines them solely by reference to the existence or absence of an unconditional contractual right to receive cash. There are other examples of licences that offer the holders of the rights predictable, low risk returns, but such licences are not regarded as giving the holder a contractual right to cash. And there are other industries in which price regulation is designed to provide the operators with substantially fixed returns—but the rights of operators in these other industries are not classified as financial assets as a result. The operator's asset is a variable term licence, which would be classified as an intangible asset within the scope of IAS 38.

A financial asset and an intangible asset

BC53   The IFRIC concluded that if the operator is paid for its construction services partly by a financial asset and partly by an intangible asset it is necessary to account separately for each component of the operator's consideration. The IFRIC included the requirement to account separately for each component (sometimes known as a bifurcated arrangement) of the operator's consideration in response to a concern raised on the draft Interpretations. The concern was that, in some arrangements, both parties to the contract share the risk (demand risk) that the cash flows generated by users of the public service will not be sufficient to recover the operator's investment. In order to achieve the desired sharing of risk, the parties often agree to arrangements under which the grantor pays the operator for its services partly by a financial asset and partly by granting a right to charge users of the public service (an intangible asset). The IFRIC concluded that in these circumstances it would be necessary to divide the operator's consideration into a financial asset component for any guaranteed amount of cash or other financial asset and an intangible asset for the remainder.

BC54   The IFRIC concluded that the nature of consideration given by the grantor to the operator is determined by reference to the contract terms and when it exists, relevant contract law. The IFRIC noted public-to-private service agreements are rarely if ever the same; technical requirements vary by sector and country. Furthermore, the terms of the contractual agreement may also depend on the specific features of the overall legal framework of the particular country. Public-to-private service contract laws, where they exist, may contain terms that do not have to be repeated in individual contracts.

Contractual obligations to restore the infrastructure to a specified level of serviceability (paragraph 21)

BC55   The IFRIC noted that IAS 37 *Provisions, Contingent Liabilities and Contingent Assets* prohibits an entity from providing for the replacement of parts of its own property, plant and equipment. IAS 16 requires such costs to be recognised in the carrying amount of an item of property, plant and equipment if the recognition criteria in paragraph 7 are met. Each part of an item of property, plant and equipment with a cost that is significant in relation to the total cost of the item is depreciated separately. The IFRIC concluded that this prohibition would not apply to arrangements within the scope of the Interpretation because the operator does not recognise the infrastructure as its own property, plant and equipment. The operator has an unavoidable obligation that it owes to a third party, the grantor, in respect of the infrastructure. The operator should recognise its obligations in accordance with IAS 37.

BC56 The IFRIC considered whether the Interpretation should contain guidance on the timing of recognition of the obligations. It noted that the precise terms and circumstances of the obligations would vary from contract to contract. It concluded that the requirements and guidance in IAS 37 were sufficiently clear to enable an operator to identify the period(s) in which different obligations should be recognised.

Borrowing costs (paragraph 22)

BC57 IAS 23 *Borrowing Costs* permits borrowing costs to be capitalised as part of the cost of a qualifying asset to the extent that they are directly attributable to its acquisition, construction or production until the asset is ready for its intended use or sale. That Standard defines a qualifying asset as 'an asset that necessarily takes a substantial period of time to get ready for its intended use or sale'.

BC58 For arrangements within the scope of the Interpretation, the IFRIC decided that an intangible asset (ie the grantor gives the operator a right to charge users of the public service in return for construction services) meets the definition of a qualifying asset of the operator because generally the licence would not be ready for use until the infrastructure was constructed or upgraded. A financial asset (ie the grantor gives the operator a contractual right to receive cash or other financial asset in return for construction services) does not meet the definition of a qualifying asset of the operator. The IFRIC observed that interest is generally accreted on the carrying value of financial assets.

BC59 The IFRIC noted that financing arrangements may result in an operator obtaining borrowed funds and incurring associated borrowing costs before some or all of the funds are used for expenditure relating to construction or operation services. In such circumstances the funds are often temporarily invested. Any investment income earned on such funds is recognised in accordance with IAS 39,[*] unless the operator adopts the allowed alternative treatment, in which case investment income earned during the construction phase of the arrangement is accounted for in accordance with paragraph 16 of IAS 23.[†]

---

[*] In November 2009 the IASB amended the requirements of IAS 39 relating to classification and measurement of assets within the scope of IAS 39 and relocated them to IFRS 9 *Financial Instruments*. IFRS 9 applies to all assets within the scope of IAS 39.

[†] In March 2007, IAS 23 was revised to require the previously allowed alternative treatment of capitalisation. Therefore, an entity is required to capitalise borrowing costs as part of the cost of a qualifying asset to the extent that they are directly attributable to its acquisition, construction or production until the asset is ready for its intended use or sale. That revision does not affect the reasoning set out in this Basis for Conclusions.

Financial asset (paragraphs 23–25)[*]

BC60 Paragraph 9 of IAS 39 identifies and defines four categories of financial asset: (i) those held at fair value through profit or loss; (ii) held-to-maturity investments; (iii) loans and receivables; and (iv) available-for-sale financial assets.

BC61 Paragraph 24 of IFRIC 12 assumes that public-to-private service arrangement financial assets will not be categorised as held-to-maturity investments. Paragraph 9 of IAS 39 states that a financial asset may not be classified as a held-to-maturity investment if it meets the definition of a loan or receivable. An asset that meets the definition of a held-to-maturity investment will meet the definition of a loan or receivable unless:

(a) it is quoted in an active market; or

(b) the holder may not recover substantially all of its initial investment, other than because of credit deterioration.

It is not envisaged that a public-to-private service arrangement financial asset will be quoted in an active market. Hence the circumstances of (a) will not arise. In the circumstances of (b), the asset must be classified as available for sale (if not designated upon initial recognition as at fair value through profit or loss).

BC62 The IFRIC considered whether the contract would include an embedded derivative if the amount to be received by the operator could vary with the quality of subsequent services to be provided by the operator or performance or efficiency targets to be achieved by the operator. The IFRIC concluded that it would not, because the definition of a derivative in IAS 39 requires, among other things, that the variable is not specific to a party to the contract. The consequence is that the contract's provision for variations in payments does not meet the definition of a derivative and, accordingly, the requirements of IAS 39 in relation to embedded derivatives do not apply. The IFRIC observed that if the amount to be received by the operator is conditional on the infrastructure meeting quality or performance or efficiency targets as described in paragraph BC44, this would not prevent the amount from being classified as a financial asset. The IFRIC also concluded that during the construction phase of the arrangement the operator's asset (representing its accumulating right to be paid for providing construction services) should be classified as a financial asset when it represents cash or another financial asset due from or at the direction of the grantor.

Intangible asset (paragraph 26)

BC63 The Interpretation requires the operator to account for its intangible asset in accordance with IAS 38. Among other requirements, IAS 38 requires an intangible asset with a finite useful economic life to be amortised over that life. Paragraph 97 states that 'the amortisation method used shall reflect the pattern in which the asset's future economic benefits are expected to be consumed by the entity.'

---

[*] IFRS 9 *Financial Instruments*, issued in November 2009, amended the requirements in IAS 39 for the classification of assets within the scope of IAS 39. This Basis for Conclusions has not been updated for changes in requirements since IFRIC 12 was issued.

BC64   The IFRIC considered whether it would be appropriate for intangible assets under paragraph 26 to be amortised using an 'interest' method of amortisation, ie one that takes account of the time value of money in addition to the consumption of the intangible asset, treating the asset more like a monetary than a non-monetary asset. However, the IFRIC concluded that there was nothing unique about these intangible assets that would justify use of a method of depreciation different from that used for other intangible assets. The IFRIC noted that paragraph 98 of IAS 38 provides for a number of amortisation methods for intangible assets with finite useful lives. These methods include the straight-line method, the diminishing balance method and the unit of production method. The method used is selected on the basis of the expected pattern of consumption of the expected future economic benefits embodied in the asset and is applied consistently from period to period, unless there is a change in the expected pattern of consumption of those future economic benefits.

BC65   The IFRIC noted that interest methods of amortisation are not permitted under IAS 38. Therefore, IFRIC 12 does not provide exceptions to permit use of interest methods of amortisation.

BC66   The IFRIC considered when the operator should first recognise the intangible asset. The IFRIC concluded that the intangible asset (the licence) received in exchange for construction services should be recognised in accordance with general principles applicable to contracts for the exchange of assets or services.

BC67   The IFRIC noted that it is current practice not to recognise executory contracts to the extent that they are unperformed by both parties (unless the contract is onerous). IAS 37 describes executory contracts as 'contracts under which neither party has performed any of its obligations or both parties have partially performed their obligations to an equal extent'. Paragraph 91 of the *Framework* states:

> In practice, obligations under contracts that are equally proportionately unperformed (for example, liabilities for inventory ordered but not yet received) are generally not recognised as liabilities in the financial statements.

BC68   Therefore, the IFRIC concluded that contracts within the scope of the Interpretation should not be recognised to the extent that they are executory. The IFRIC noted that service concession arrangements within the scope of the Interpretation are generally executory when the contracts are signed. The IFRIC also concluded that during the construction phase of the arrangement the operator's asset (representing its accumulating right to be paid for providing construction services) should be classified as an intangible asset to the extent that it represents a right to receive a right (licence) to charge users of the public service (an intangible asset).

Items provided to the operator by the grantor (paragraph 27)

BC69   For service arrangements within the scope of the Interpretation, pre-existing infrastructure items made available to the operator by the grantor for the purpose of the service arrangement are not recognised as property, plant and equipment of the operator.

BC70 However, different considerations apply to other assets provided to the operator by the grantor if the operator can keep or deal with the assets as it wishes. Such assets become assets of the operator and so should be accounted for in accordance with general recognition and measurement principles, as should the obligations undertaken in exchange for them.

BC71 The IFRIC considered whether such assets would represent government grants, as defined in paragraph 3 of IAS 20 *Accounting for Government Grants and Disclosure of Government Assistance*:

> Government grants are assistance by government in the form of transfers of resources to an entity in return for past or future compliance with certain conditions relating to the operating activities of the entity. They exclude those forms of government assistance which cannot reasonably have a value placed upon them and transactions with government which cannot be distinguished from the normal trading transactions of the entity.

The IFRIC concluded that if such assets were part of the overall consideration payable by the grantor on an arms' length basis for the operator's services, they would not constitute 'assistance'. Therefore, they would not meet the definition of government grants in IAS 20 and that standard would not apply.

Transition (paragraphs 29 and 30)

BC72 IAS 8 *Accounting Policies, Changes in Accounting Estimates and Errors* states that an entity shall account for a change in accounting policy resulting from initial application of an Interpretation in accordance with any specific transitional provisions in that Interpretation. In the absence of any specific transitional provisions, the general requirements of IAS 8 apply. The general requirement in IAS 8 is that the changes should be accounted for retrospectively, except to the extent that retrospective application would be impracticable.

BC73 The IFRIC noted that there are two aspects to retrospective determination: reclassification and remeasurement. The IFRIC took the view that it will usually be practicable to determine retrospectively the appropriate classification of all amounts previously included in an operator's balance sheet, but that retrospective remeasurement of service arrangement assets might not always be practicable.

BC74 The IFRIC noted that, when retrospective restatement is not practicable, IAS 8 requires prospective application from the earliest practicable date, which could be the start of the current period. Under prospective application, the operator could be applying different accounting models to similar transactions, which the IFRIC decided would be inappropriate. The IFRIC regarded it as important that the correct accounting model should be consistently applied.

BC75 The Interpretation reflects these conclusions.

Amendments to IFRS 1

BC76 The amendments to IFRS 1 *First-time Adoption of International Financial Reporting Standards* are necessary to ensure that the transitional arrangements are available to both existing users and first-time adopters of IFRSs. The IFRIC believes that the requirements will ensure that the balance sheet will exclude any items that would not qualify for recognition as assets and liabilities under IFRSs.

Summary of changes from the draft Interpretations

BC77   The main changes from the IFRIC's proposals are as follows:

(a)   The proposals were published in three separate draft Interpretations, D12 *Service Concession Arrangements—Determining the Accounting Model*, D13 *Service Concession Arrangements—The Financial Asset Model* and D14 *Service Concession Arrangements—The Intangible Asset Model*. In finalising IFRIC 12, the IFRIC combined the three draft Interpretations.

(b)   By contrast with IFRIC 12 the draft Interpretations did not explain the reasons for the scope limitations and the reasons for the control approach adopted by the IFRIC in paragraph 5. The IFRIC added Information Note 2 to IFRIC 12 to provide references to standards that apply to arrangements outside the scope of the Interpretation.

(c)   The scope of the proposals did not include 'whole of life infrastructure' (ie infrastructure used in a public-to-private service arrangement for its entire useful life). IFRIC 12 includes 'whole of life infrastructure' within its scope.

(d)   Under the approach proposed, an entity determined the appropriate accounting model by reference to whether the grantor or the user had primary responsibility to pay the operator for the services provided. IFRIC 12 requires an entity to recognise a financial asset to the extent that the operator has an unconditional contractual right to receive cash from or at the direction of the grantor.   The operator should recognise an intangible asset to the extent that it receives a right to charge users of the public service.

(e)   By contrast with IFRIC 12, the draft Interpretations implied that the nature of asset recognised (a financial asset or an intangible asset) by the operator as consideration for providing construction services determined the accounting for the operation phase of the arrangement.

(f)   Under the approach proposed in the draft Interpretations, an entity could capitalise borrowing costs under the allowed alternative treatment in IAS 23. IFRIC 12 requires borrowing costs to be recognised as an expense in the period in which they are incurred unless the operator has a contractual right to receive an intangible asset (a right to charge users of the public service), in which case borrowing costs attributable to the arrangement may be capitalised in accordance with the allowed alternative treatment under IAS 23.[*]

(g)   In finalising IFRIC 12, the IFRIC decided to amend IFRIC 4.

---

[*]   In March 2007, IAS 23 was revised to require the previously allowed alternative treatment of capitalisation. Therefore, an entity is required to capitalise borrowing costs as part of the cost of a qualifying asset to the extent that they are directly attributable to its acquisition, construction or production until the asset is ready for its intended use or sale. That revision does not affect the reasoning set out in this Basis for Conclusions.

Documents published to accompany

IFRIC Interpretation 13

Customer Loyalty Programmes

The text of the unaccompanied IFRIC 13 is contained in Part A of this edition. Its effective date is 1 July 2008. This part presents the following accompanying documents:

Illustrative examples

These examples accompany, but are not part of, IFRIC 13.

Example 1—Awards supplied by the entity

IE1   A grocery retailer operates a customer loyalty programme. It grants programme members loyalty points when they spend a specified amount on groceries. Programme members can redeem the points for further groceries. The points have no expiry date. In one period, the entity grants 100 points. Management expects 80 of these points to be redeemed. Management estimates the fair value of each loyalty point to be one currency unit (CU1), and defers revenue of CU100.

Year 1

IE2   At the end of the first year, 40 of the points have been redeemed in exchange for groceries, ie half of those expected to be redeemed. The entity recognises revenue of (40 points/80* points) × CU100 = CU50.

Year 2

IE3   In the second year, management revises its expectations. It now expects 90 points to be redeemed altogether.

IE4   During the second year, 41 points are redeemed, bringing the total number redeemed to $40^{\dagger}$ + 41 = 81 points. The cumulative revenue that the entity recognises is (81 points/$90^{\S}$ points) × CU100 = CU90. The entity has recognised revenue of CU50 in the first year, so it recognises CU40 in the second year.

Year 3

IE5   In the third year, a further nine points are redeemed, taking the total number of points redeemed to 81 + 9 = 90. Management continues to expect that only 90 points will ever be redeemed, ie that no more points will be redeemed after the third year. So the cumulative revenue to date is (90 points/$90^{\emptyset}$ points) × CU100 = CU100. The entity has already recognised CU90 of revenue (CU50 in the first year and CU40 in the second year). So it recognises the remaining CU10 in the third year. All of the revenue initially deferred has now been recognised.

---

*   total number of points expected to be redeemed

†   number of points redeemed in year 1

§   revised estimate of total number of points expected to be redeemed

ø   total number of points still expected to be redeemed.

       © IASCF

Example 2—Awards supplied by a third party

IE6   A retailer of electrical goods participates in a customer loyalty programme operated by an airline. It grants programme members one air travel point with each CU1 they spend on electrical goods. Programme members can redeem the points for air travel with the airline, subject to availability. The retailer pays the airline CU0.009 for each point.

IE7   In one period, the retailer sells electrical goods for consideration totalling CU1 million. It grants 1 million points.

Allocation of consideration to travel points

IE8   The retailer estimates that the fair value of a point is CU0.01. It allocates to the points 1 million × CU0.01 = CU10,000 of the consideration it has received from the sales of its electrical goods.

Revenue recognition

IE9   Having granted the points, the retailer has fulfilled its obligations to the customer. The airline is obliged to supply the awards and entitled to receive consideration for doing so. Therefore the retailer recognises revenue from the points when it sells the electrical goods.

Revenue measurement

IE10   If the retailer has collected the consideration allocated to the points on its own account, it measures its revenue as the gross CU10,000 allocated to them. It separately recognises the CU9,000 paid or payable to the airline as an expense. If the retailer has collected the consideration on behalf of the airline, ie as an agent for the airline, it measures its revenue as the net amount it retains on its own account. This amount of revenue is the difference between the CU10,000 consideration allocated to the points and the CU9,000 passed on to the airline.

Basis for Conclusions on
IFRIC Interpretation 13 *Customer Loyalty Programmes*

This Basis for Conclusions accompanies, but is not part of, IFRIC 13.

BC1 This Basis for Conclusions summarises the IFRIC's considerations in reaching its consensus. Individual IFRIC members gave greater weight to some factors than to others.

Scope

BC2 Customer loyalty programmes are widespread, being used by businesses as diverse as supermarkets, airlines, telecommunications operators, hotels and credit card providers. IFRSs lack specific guidance on how entities should account for the awards offered to customers in these programmes. As a result, practices have diverged.

BC3 The main area of diversity concerns award credits that entities grant to their customers as part of a sales transaction, and that the customers can redeem in the future for free or discounted goods or services. The Interpretation applies to such award credits.

BC4 In some sales transactions, the entity receives consideration from an intermediate party, rather than directly from the customer to whom it grants the award credits. For example, credit card providers may provide services and grant award credits to credit card holders but receive consideration for doing so from vendors accepting payment by credit card. Such transactions are within the scope of the Interpretation and the wording of the consensus has been drafted to accommodate them.

Issues

BC5 Different views have emerged about how the entity granting award credits should recognise and measure its obligation to provide free or discounted goods or services if and when customers redeem award credits.

BC6 One view is that the obligation should be recognised as an expense at the time of the initial sale and be measured by reference to the amount required to settle it, in accordance with IAS 37 *Provisions, Contingent Liabilities and Contingent Assets*. In support of this view, it is argued that:

(a) customer loyalty programmes are marketing tools designed to enhance sales volumes. Therefore the costs of the programmes are marketing expenses.

(b) the value of awards is often insignificant compared with the value of the purchases required to earn them. The obligation to exchange award credits for awards is not a significant element of the sales transaction. Thus, when the initial sale is made, the entity has met the conditions set out in IAS 18 *Revenue* for recognising revenue from that sale. Paragraph 16 of IAS 18 indicates that a selling entity can recognise revenue before it has completed all of the acts required of it under the contract, providing it does not retain the significant risks and rewards of ownership of the goods sold. Paragraph 19 requires expenses relating to the sale, including those for costs still to be incurred, to be recognised at the same time as the revenue.

BC7 A second view is that some of the consideration received in respect of the initial sale should be allocated to the award credits and recognised as a liability until the entity fulfils its obligations to deliver awards to customers. The liability would be measured by reference to the value of the award credits to the customer (not their cost to the entity) and recognised as an allocation of revenue (not an expense). In support of this view, it is argued that:

(a) award credits granted to a customer as a result of a sales transaction are an element of the transaction itself, ie the market exchange of economic benefits between the entity and the customer. They represent rights granted to the customer, for which the customer is implicitly paying. They can be distinguished from marketing expenses because they are granted to the customer as part of the sales transaction. Marketing expenses, in contrast, are incurred independently of the sales transactions they are designed to secure.

(b) award credits are separately identifiable from the other goods or services sold as part of the initial sale. Paragraph 13 of IAS 18 states that:

> The recognition criteria in this Standard are usually applied separately to each transaction. However, in certain circumstances, it is necessary to apply the recognition criteria to the separately identifiable components of a single transaction in order to reflect the substance of the transaction. For example, when the selling price of a product includes an identifiable amount for subsequent servicing, that amount is deferred and recognised as revenue over the period during which the service is performed.

Because loyalty awards are not delivered to the customer at the same time as the other goods or services, it is necessary to divide the initial sale into components and apply the recognition criteria separately to each component in order to reflect the substance of the transaction.

BC8 A third view is that the accounting should depend on the nature of the customer loyalty programme. The criteria for determining which accounting treatment should be adopted could refer to the relative value or nature of the awards, or the method of supplying them. Award credits would be regarded as marketing expenses if, say, their value were insignificant and/or they were redeemable for goods or services not supplied by the entity in the course of its ordinary activities. In contrast, award credits would be regarded as a separate component of the initial sales transaction if their value were significant and/or they were redeemable for goods or services supplied by the entity in the course of its ordinary activities.

Consensus

Attributing revenue to award credits

BC9   The consensus reflects the second view, described in paragraph BC7. In reaching its consensus, the IFRIC noted that:

(a)   the first and second views apply different paragraphs of IAS 18. The first view (paragraph BC6) applies paragraph 19 to recognise the cost of the awards at the time of the initial sale. The second view applies paragraph 13 to identify the award credits as a separate component of the initial sale. The issue is to identify which of the two paragraphs should be applied. IAS 18 does not give explicit guidance. However, the aim of IAS 18 is to recognise revenue when, and to the extent that, goods or services have been delivered to a customer. In the IFRIC's view, paragraph 13 applies if a single transaction requires two or more separate goods or services to be delivered at different times; it ensures that revenue for each item is recognised only when that item is delivered. In contrast, paragraph 19 applies only if the entity has to incur further costs directly related to items already delivered, eg to meet warranty claims. In the IFRIC's view, loyalty awards are not costs that directly relate to the goods and services already delivered—rather, they are separate goods or services delivered at a later date.

(b)   the third view, described in paragraph BC8, would be difficult to justify conceptually. It can be argued that the substance of the incentives is the same, whatever their form or value. A dividing line could lead to inconsistencies and accounting arbitrage. Particular difficulties could arise if a programme offered customers a choice of awards, only some of which would be supplied by the entity in the course of its ordinary activities.

BC10   The IFRIC considered an objection that the costs of applying the approach set out in the consensus view in paragraph BC7 would exceed the benefits. Those raising the objection argued that:

- the approach is more complicated to apply than a cost accrual approach;

- it produces information that is less reliable, and no more relevant; and

- the additional costs are not merited because the amounts involved are often relatively insignificant.

BC11   The IFRIC acknowledged that entities might have to incur costs to change systems and procedures to comply with the Interpretation. However, it did not agree that the ongoing costs would exceed the benefits. It noted that most of the variables that have to be estimated to measure the revenue attributable to award credits (such as redemption rates, timing of redemption etc) also need to be estimated to measure the future cost of fulfilling the obligation. In the IFRIC's view, benefits to users will arise from customer loyalty award obligations being measured on the same basis as other separately identifiable performance obligations to customers.

Allocation method

BC12   IAS 18 requires revenue to be measured at the fair value of the consideration received or receivable. Hence the amount of revenue attributed to award credits should be the fair value of the consideration received for them. The IFRIC noted that this amount is often not directly observable because the award credits are granted as part of a larger sale. In such circumstances, it must be estimated by allocating the total consideration between the award credits and other goods or services sold, using an appropriate allocation method.

BC13   IAS 18 does not prescribe an allocation method for multiple-component sales. However, its overall objective is to determine the amount the customer is paying for each component, which can be estimated by drawing on the entity's experience of transactions with similar customers. Hence, the Interpretation requires the consideration allocated to award credits to be measured by reference to their fair value.

BC14   The Interpretation does not specify whether the amount allocated to the award credits should be:

(a)   equal to their fair value (irrespective of the fair values of the other components); or

(b)   a proportion of the total consideration based on the fair value of the award credits relative to the fair values of the other components of the sale.

The IFRIC noted that IAS 18 does not specify which of these methods should be applied, or in what circumstances. The IFRIC decided that the Interpretation should not be more prescriptive than IAS 18. The selection of one or other method is therefore left to management's judgement.

Revenue recognition—awards supplied by the entity

BC15   The consideration allocated to award credits represents the amount that the entity has received for accepting an obligation to supply awards if customers redeem the credits. This amount reflects both the value of the awards and the entity's expectations regarding the proportion of credits that will be redeemed, ie the risk of a claim being made. The entity has received the consideration for accepting the risk, whether or not a claim is actually made. Hence, the Interpretation requires revenue to be recognised as the risk expires, ie based on the number of award credits that have been redeemed relative to the total number expected to be redeemed.

BC16   After granting award credits, the entity may revise its expectations about the proportion that will be redeemed. The change in expectations does not affect the consideration that the entity has received for supplying awards: this consideration (the revenue) was fixed at the time of the initial sale. Hence the change in expectations does not affect the measurement of the original obligation. Instead, it affects the amount of revenue recognised in respect of award credits that are redeemed in the period. The change in expectations is thus accounted for as a change in estimate in the period of change and future periods, in accordance with paragraph 36 of IAS 8 *Accounting Policies, Changes in Accounting Estimates and Errors*.

BC17   A change in expectations regarding redemption rates may also affect the costs the entity expects to incur to supply awards. If estimated redemption rates increase to the extent that the unavoidable costs of supplying awards are expected to exceed the consideration received and receivable for them, the entity has onerous contracts. The Interpretation therefore highlights the requirement of IAS 37 to recognise a liability for the excess.

Revenue recognition—awards supplied by a third party

BC18   Some customer loyalty programmes offer customers awards in the form of goods and services supplied by a third party. For example, a grocery retailer may offer customers an option to redeem award credits for air travel points or a voucher for free goods from an electrical retailer. The IFRIC noted that, depending on the terms of the arrangement, the reporting entity (the grocery retailer in this example) may retain few, if any, obligations in respect of the supply of the awards. In such circumstances, the customer is still receiving the benefits of—and implicitly paying the entity consideration for—the rights to awards. Hence, consideration should be allocated to the award credits.

BC19   However, the entity may in substance be collecting the consideration on behalf of the third party, ie as an agent for the third party. If so, paragraph 8 of IAS 18 would need to be taken into consideration. This paragraph states that:

> Revenue includes only the gross inflows of economic benefits received and receivable by the entity on its own account. ... in an agency relationship, the gross inflows of economic benefits include amounts collected on behalf of the principal and which do not result in increases in equity for the entity. The amounts collected on behalf of the principal are not revenue. Instead, revenue is the amount of commission.

BC20   Depending on the terms of the agreement between the entity, award credit holders and the third party, the gross consideration attributable to the award credits might not represent revenue for the entity. Rather, the entity's revenue might be only the net amount it retains on its own account, ie the difference between the consideration allocated to the award credits and the amount paid or payable by the entity to the third party for supplying the awards.

BC21   The IFRIC noted that, if the entity is acting as an agent for a third party, its revenue arises from rendering agency services to that third party, not from supplying awards to the award credit holders. The entity should therefore recognise revenue in accordance with paragraph 20 of IAS 18. As the outcome of the transaction can be estimated reliably (the consideration has been received and the amount payable to the third party agreed), revenue is recognised in the periods in which the entity renders its agency services, ie when the third party becomes obliged to supply the awards and entitled to receive consideration for doing so.

Changes from draft Interpretation D20

BC22   A draft of the Interpretation—D20 *Customer Loyalty Programmes*—was published for comment in September 2006. The most significant changes made in the light of comments received relate to:

(a)   *allocation of consideration to award credits.* D20 proposed that consideration should be allocated between award credits and other components of the sale by reference to their relative fair values. The IFRIC accepted suggestions that another allocation method—whereby the award credits are allocated an amount equal to their fair value—could also be consistent with IAS 18, and would be simpler to apply. So, as explained in paragraph BC14, the consensus has been revised to avoid precluding this latter method.

(b)   *awards supplied by a third party.* The consensus in D20 did not refer to the possibility that an entity may have collected consideration on behalf of the third party, and hence that its revenue may need to be measured net of amounts passed on to the third party. However, as some commentators pointed out, awards are often supplied by third parties and so this possibility will often need to be considered for transactions within the scope of the Interpretation. The requirements of IAS 18 in this respect have therefore been added to paragraph 8 of the consensus and are explained in paragraphs BC19–BC21.

(c)   *customer relationship intangible assets.* Customer loyalty programmes may create or enhance customer relationship intangible assets. The consensus in D20 had pointed out that such assets should be recognised only if the recognition criteria in IAS 38 *Intangible Assets* had been met. The IFRIC accepted that this comment appeared to suggest that there would be circumstances in which intangible assets were recognised, whereas the requirements of IAS 38 were such that recognition was very unlikely. It also decided that the comment was peripheral to the issues being addressed in the Interpretation. It deleted the comment from the consensus.

(d)   *guidance on measuring the fair value of award credits.* Paragraph AG2 explains that the fair value of award credits may be measured by reference to the fair value of the awards for which they could be redeemed, reduced to take into account various factors. The list of factors in D20 had referred to the time value of money. However, the IFRIC accepted suggestions that the effect of the time value of money will often not be material—especially if awards are specified in non-monetary terms—and that it should not therefore be highlighted as a factor that will routinely need to be measured.

(e)   *location of application guidance.* Two paragraphs of the consensus in D20 comprised guidance on how to apply the paragraphs that preceded them. They have been moved to an appendix, and supplemented by additional explanation that had been located in the Basis for Conclusions in D20.

(f)   *illustrative examples.* These have been added to help readers understand how to apply the revenue recognition requirements, especially in relation to forfeited award credits and changes in estimates of forfeiture rates.

Documents published to accompany

IFRIC Interpretation 14

IAS 19—The Limit on a Defined Benefit Asset, Minimum Funding Requirements and their Interaction

The text of the unaccompanied IFRIC 14 is contained in Part A of this edition. Its effective date when issued was 1 January 2008. The effective date of the most recent amendments is 1 January 2011. This part presents the following accompanying documents:

Approval by the Board of *Prepayments of a Minimum Funding Requirement* issued in November 2009

Prepayments of a Minimum Funding Requirement (Amendments to IFRIC 14) was approved for issue by the fifteen members of the International Accounting Standards Board.

Sir David Tweedie	Chairman

Stephen Cooper

Philippe Danjou

Jan Engström

Patrick Finnegan

Robert P Garnett

Gilbert Gélard

Amaro Luiz de Oliveira Gomes

Prabhakar Kalavacherla

James J Leisenring

Patricia McConnell

Warren J McGregor

John T Smith

Tatsumi Yamada

Wei-Guo Zhang

Illustrative examples

These examples accompany, but are not part of, IFRIC 14.

Example 1—Effect of the minimum funding requirement when there is an IAS 19 surplus and the minimum funding contributions payable are fully refundable to the entity

IE1   An entity has a funding level on the minimum funding requirement basis (which is measured on a different basis from that required under IAS 19) of 82 per cent in Plan A. Under the minimum funding requirements, the entity is required to increase the funding level to 95 per cent immediately. As a result, the entity has a statutory obligation at the end of the reporting period to contribute 200 to Plan A immediately. The plan rules permit a full refund of any surplus to the entity at the end of the life of the plan. The year-end valuations for Plan A are set out below.

Market value of assets	1,200
Present value of defined benefit obligation under IAS 19	(1,100)
Surplus	100
Defined benefit asset (before consideration of the minimum funding requirement)[(a)]	100

(a) For simplicity, it is assumed that there are no unrecognised amounts.

Application of requirements

IE2   Paragraph 24 of IFRIC 14 requires the entity to recognise a liability to the extent that the contributions payable are not fully available. Payment of the contributions of 200 will increase the IAS 19 surplus from 100 to 300. Under the rules of the plan this amount will be fully refundable to the entity with no associated costs. Therefore, no liability is recognised for the obligation to pay the contributions.

Example 2—Effect of a minimum funding requirement when there is an IAS 19 deficit and the minimum funding contributions payable would not be fully available

IE3   An entity has a funding level on the minimum funding requirement basis (which is measured on a different basis from that required under IAS 19) of 77 per cent in Plan B. Under the minimum funding requirements, the entity is required to increase the funding level to 100 per cent immediately. As a result, the entity has a statutory obligation at the end of the reporting period to pay additional contributions of 300 to Plan B. The plan rules permit a maximum refund of 60 per cent of the IAS 19 surplus to the entity and the entity is not permitted to reduce its contributions below a specified level which happens to equal the IAS 19 service cost. The year-end valuations for Plan B are set out below.

Market value of assets	1,000
Present value of defined benefit obligation under IAS 19	(1,100)
Deficit	(100)
Defined benefit (liability) (before consideration of the minimum funding requirement)[(a)]	(100)

(a) For simplicity, it is assumed that there are no unrecognised amounts.

Application of requirements

IE4   The payment of 300 would change the IAS 19 deficit of 100 to a surplus of 200. Of this 200, 60 per cent (120) is refundable.

IE5   Therefore, of the contributions of 300, 100 eliminates the IAS 19 deficit and 120 (60 per cent of 200) is available as an economic benefit. The remaining 80 (40 per cent of 200) of the contributions paid is not available to the entity.

IE6   Paragraph 24 of IFRIC 14 requires the entity to recognise a liability to the extent that the additional contributions payable are not available to it.

IE7   Therefore, the entity increases the defined benefit liability by 80. As required by paragraph 26 of IFRIC 14, 80 is recognised immediately in accordance with the entity's adopted policy for recognising the effect of the limit in paragraph 58 and the entity recognises a net liability of 180 in the statement of financial position. No other liability is recognised in respect of the statutory obligation to pay contributions of 300.

Summary

Market value of assets	1,000
Present value of defined benefit obligation under IAS 19	(1,100)
Deficit	(100)
Defined benefit liability (before consideration of the minimum funding requirement)[(a)]	(100)
Adjustment in respect of minimum funding requirement	(80)
Net liability recognised in the statement of financial position	(180)

(a) For simplicity, it is assumed that there are no unrecognised amounts.

IE8   When the contributions of 300 are paid, the net asset recognised in the statement of financial position will be 120.

Example 3—Effect of a minimum funding requirement when the contributions payable would not be fully available and the effect on the economic benefit available as a future contribution reduction

IE9   An entity has a funding level on the minimum funding basis (which it measures on a different basis from that required by IAS 19) of 95 per cent in Plan C. The minimum funding requirements require the entity to pay contributions to increase the funding level to 100 per cent over the next three years. The contributions are required to make good the deficit on the minimum funding basis (shortfall) and to cover future service.

IE10   Plan C also has an IAS 19 surplus at the end of the reporting period of 50, which cannot be refunded to the entity under any circumstances. There are no unrecognised amounts.

IE11   The nominal amounts of contributions required to satisfy the minimum funding requirements in respect of the shortfall and the future service for the next three years are set out below.

Year	Total contributions for minimum funding requirement	Contributions required to make good the shortfall	Contributions required to cover future service
1	135	120	15
2	125	112	13
3	115	104	11

Application of requirements

IE12   The entity's present obligation in respect of services already received includes the contributions required to make good the shortfall but does not include the contributions required to cover future service.

IE13   The present value of the entity's obligation, assuming a discount rate of 6 per cent per year, is approximately 300, calculated as follows:

$[120/(1.06) + 112/(1.06)^2 + 104/(1.06)^3]$.

IE14   When these contributions are paid into the plan, the present value of the IAS 19 surplus (ie the fair value of assets less the present value of the defined benefit obligation) would, other things being equal, increase from 50 to 350 (300 + 50).

IE15   However, the surplus is not refundable although an asset may be available as a future contribution reduction.

IE16   In accordance with paragraph 20 of IFRIC 14, the economic benefit available as a reduction in future contributions is the sum of:

(a) any amount that reduces future minimum funding requirement contributions for future service because the entity made a prepayment (ie paid the amount before being required to do so); and

(b) the estimated future service cost in each period in accordance with paragraphs 16 and 17, less the estimated minimum funding requirement contributions that would be required for future service in those periods if there were no prepayment as described in (a).

IE17 In this example there is no prepayment as described in paragraph 20(a). The amounts available as a reduction in future contributions when applying paragraph 20(b) are set out below.

Year	IAS 19 service cost	Minimum contributions required to cover future service	Amount available as contribution reduction
1	13	15	(2)
2	13	13	0
3	13	11	2
4+	13	9	4

IE18 Assuming a discount rate of 6 per cent, the present value of the economic benefit available as a future contribution reduction is therefore equal to:

$$(2)/(1.06) + 0/(1.06)^2 + 2/(1.06)^3 + 4/(1.06)^4 \dots = 56.$$

Thus in accordance with paragraph 58(b) of IAS 19, the present value of the economic benefit available from future contribution reductions is limited to 56.

IE19 Paragraph 24 of IFRIC 14 requires the entity to recognise a liability to the extent that the additional contributions payable will not be fully available. Therefore, the entity reduces the defined benefit asset by 294 (50 + 300 − 56).

IE20 As required by paragraph 26 of IFRIC 14, the 294 is recognised immediately in accordance with the entity's adopted policy for recognising the effect of the limit in paragraph 58 and the entity recognises a net liability of 244 in the statement of financial position. No other liability is recognised in respect of the obligation to make contributions to fund the minimum funding shortfall.

Summary

Surplus	50
Defined benefit asset (before consideration of the minimum funding requirement)	50
Adjustment in respect of minimum funding requirement	(294)
Net liability recognised in the statement of financial position[a]	(244)

(a) For simplicity, it is assumed that there are no unrecognised amounts.

IE21 When the contributions of 300 are paid into the plan, the net asset recognised in the statement of financial position will become 56 (300 − 244).

Example 4—Effect of a prepayment when a minimum funding requirement exceeds the expected future service charge

IE22 An entity is required to fund Plan D so that no deficit arises on the minimum funding basis. The entity is required to pay minimum funding requirement contributions to cover the service cost in each period determined on the minimum funding basis.

IE23 Plan D has an IAS 19 surplus of 35 at the beginning of 20X1. There are no cumulative unrecognised net actuarial losses and past service costs. This example assumes that the discount rate and expected return on assets are 0 per cent, and that the plan cannot refund the surplus to the entity under any circumstances but can use the surplus for reductions of future contributions.

IE24 The minimum contributions required to cover future service are 15 for each of the next five years. The expected IAS 19 service cost is 10 in each year.

IE25 The entity makes a prepayment of 30 at the beginning of 20X1 in respect of years 20X1 and 20X2, increasing its surplus at the beginning of 20X1 to 65. That prepayment reduces the future contributions it expects to make in the following two years, as follows:

Year	IAS 19 service cost	Minimum funding requirement contribution before prepayment	Minimum funding requirement contribution after prepayment
20X1	10	15	0
20X2	10	15	0
20X3	10	15	15
20X4	10	15	15
20X5	10	15	15
Total	50	75	45

Application of requirements

IE26　In accordance with paragraphs 20 and 22 of IFRIC 14, at the beginning of 20X1, the economic benefit available as a reduction in future contributions is the sum of:

(a)　30, being the prepayment of the minimum funding requirement contributions; and

(b)　nil. The estimated minimum funding requirement contributions required for future service would be 75 if there was no prepayment. Those contributions exceed the estimated future service cost (50); therefore the entity cannot use any part of the surplus of 35 noted in paragraph IE23 (see paragraph 22).

IE27　Assuming a discount rate of 0 per cent, the present value of the economic benefit available as a reduction in future contributions is equal to 30. Thus in accordance with paragraph 58 of IAS 19 the entity recognises an asset of 30 (because this is lower than the IAS 19 surplus of 65).

Basis for Conclusions on
IFRIC Interpretation 14 *IAS 19—The Limit on a Defined Benefit Asset, Minimum Funding Requirements and their Interaction*

This Basis for Conclusions accompanies, but is not part of, IFRIC 14.

The original text has been marked up to reflect the revision of IAS 1 Presentation of Financial Statements *in 2007: new text is underlined and deleted text is struck through.*

BC1   This Basis for Conclusions summarises the IFRIC's considerations in reaching its consensus. Individual IFRIC members gave greater weight to some factors than to others.

BC2   The IFRIC noted that practice varies significantly with regard to the treatment of the effect of a minimum funding requirement on the limit placed by paragraph 58 of IAS 19 *Employee Benefits* on the amount of a defined benefit asset. The IFRIC therefore decided to include this issue on its agenda. In considering the issue, the IFRIC also became aware of the need for general guidance on determining the limit on the measurement of the defined benefit asset, and for guidance on when that limit makes a minimum funding requirement onerous.

BC3   The IFRIC published D19 *IAS 19—The Asset Ceiling: Availability of Economic Benefits and Minimum Funding Requirements* in August 2006. In response, the IFRIC received 48 comment letters.

BC3A In November 2009 the International Accounting Standards Board amended IFRIC 14 to remove an unintended consequence arising from the treatment of prepayments in some circumstances when there is a minimum funding requirement (see paragraphs BC30A–BC30D).

Definition of a minimum funding requirement

BC4   D19 referred to statutory or contractual minimum funding requirements. Respondents to D19 asked for further guidance on what constituted a minimum funding requirement. The IFRIC decided to clarify that for the purpose of the Interpretation a minimum funding requirement is any requirement for the entity to make contributions to *fund* a post-employment or other long-term defined benefit plan.

Interaction between IAS 19 and minimum funding requirements

BC5   Funding requirements would not normally affect the accounting for a plan under IAS 19. However, paragraph 58 of IAS 19 limits the amount of the defined benefit asset to the available economic benefit plus unrecognised amounts. The interaction of a minimum funding requirement and this limit has two possible effects:

(a)   the minimum funding requirement may restrict the economic benefits available as a reduction in future contributions, and

(b) the limit may make the minimum funding requirement onerous because contributions payable under the requirement in respect of services already received may not be available once they have been paid, either as a refund or as a reduction in future contributions.

BC6 These effects raised general questions about the availability of economic benefits in the form of a refund or a reduction in future contributions.

Availability of the economic benefit

BC7 One view of 'available' would limit the economic benefit to the amount that is realisable immediately at the end of the reporting period balance sheet date.

BC8 The IFRIC disagreed with this view. The *Framework* defines an asset as a resource 'from which future economic benefits are expected to flow to the entity.' Therefore, it is not necessary for the economic benefit to be realisable immediately. Indeed, a reduction in future contributions cannot be realisable immediately.

BC9 The IFRIC concluded that a refund or reduction in future contributions is available if it could be realisable at some point during the life of the plan or when the plan liability is settled. Respondents to D19 were largely supportive of this conclusion.

BC10 In the responses to D19, some argued that an entity may expect to use the surplus to give improved benefits. Others noted that future actuarial losses might reduce or eliminate the surplus. In either case there would be no refund or reduction in future contributions. The IFRIC noted that the existence of an asset at the end of the reporting period balance sheet date depends on whether the entity has the right to obtain a refund or reduction in future contributions. The existence of the asset at that date is not affected by possible future changes to the amount of the surplus. If future events occur that change the amount of the surplus, their effects are recognised when they occur. Accordingly, if the entity decides to improve benefits, or future losses in the plan reduce the surplus, the consequences are recognised when the decision is made or the losses occur. The IFRIC noted that such events of future periods do not affect the existence or measurement of the asset at the end of the reporting period balance sheet date.

The asset available as a refund of a surplus

BC11 The IFRIC noted that a refund of a surplus could potentially be obtained in three ways:

(a) during the life of the plan, without assuming that the plan liabilities have to be settled in order to get the refund (eg in some jurisdictions, the entity may have a right to a refund during the life of the plan, irrespective of whether the plan liabilities are settled); or

(b) assuming the gradual settlement of the plan liabilities over time until all members have left the plan; or

(c) assuming the full settlement of the plan liabilities in a single event (ie as a plan wind-up).

BC12   The IFRIC concluded that all three ways should be considered in determining whether an economic benefit was available to the entity. Some respondents to D19 raised the question of when an entity controls an asset that arises from the availability of a refund, in particular if a refund would be available only if a third party (for example the plan trustees) gave its approval. The IFRIC concluded that an entity controlled the asset only if the entity has an unconditional right to the refund. If that right depends on actions by a third party, the entity does not have an unconditional right.

BC13   If the plan liability is settled by an immediate wind-up, the costs associated with the wind-up may be significant. One reason for this may be that the cost of annuities available on the market is expected to be significantly higher than that implied by the IAS 19 basis. Other costs include the legal and other professional fees expected to be incurred during the winding-up process. Accordingly, a plan with an apparent surplus may not be able to recover any of that surplus on wind-up.

BC14   The IFRIC noted that the available surplus should be measured at the amount that the entity could receive from the plan. The IFRIC decided that in determining the amount of the refund available on wind-up of the plan, the amount of the costs associated with the settlement and refund should be deducted if paid by the plan.

BC15   The IFRIC noted that the costs of settling the plan liability would be dependent on the facts and circumstances of the plan and it decided not to issue any specific guidance in this respect.

BC16   The IFRIC also noted that the present value of the defined benefit obligation and the fair value of assets are both measured on a present value basis and therefore take into account the timing of the future cash flows. The IFRIC concluded that no further adjustment for the time value of money needs to be made when measuring the amount of a refund determined as the full amount or a proportion of the surplus that is realisable at a future date.

The asset available in the form of a future contribution reduction

BC17   The IFRIC decided that the amount of the contribution reduction available to the entity should be measured with reference to the amount that the entity would have been required to pay had there been no surplus. The IFRIC concluded that is represented by the cost to the entity of accruing benefits in the plan, in other words by the future IAS 19 service cost. Respondents to D19 broadly supported this conclusion.

BC18   When the issue of the availability of reductions in future contributions was first raised with the IFRIC, some expressed the view that an entity should recognise an asset only to the extent that there was a formal agreement between the trustees and the entity specifying contributions payable lower than the IAS 19 service cost. The IFRIC disagreed, concluding instead that an entity is entitled to assume that, in general, it will not be required to make contributions to a plan in order to maintain a surplus and hence that it will be able to reduce contributions if the plan has a surplus. (The effects of a minimum funding requirement on this assumption are discussed below.)

BC19   The IFRIC considered the assumptions that underlie the calculation of the future service cost. In respect of the discount rate, IAS 19 requires the measurement of the present value of the future contribution reduction to be based on the same discount rate as that used to determine the present value of the defined benefit obligation.

BC20   The IFRIC considered whether the term over which the contribution reduction should be calculated should be restricted to the expected future working lifetime of the active membership. The IFRIC disagreed with that view. The IFRIC noted that the entity could derive economic benefit from a reduction in contributions beyond that period. The IFRIC also noted that increasing the term of the calculation has a decreasing effect on the incremental changes to the asset because the reductions in contributions are discounted to a present value. Thus, for plans with a large surplus and no possibility of receiving a refund, the available asset will be limited even if the term of the calculation extends beyond the expected future working lifetime of the active membership to the expected life of the plan. This is consistent with paragraph 77 of the Basis for Conclusions on IAS 19, which states that 'the limit [on the measurement of the defined benefit asset] is likely to come into play *only* where ... the plan is very mature and has a very large surplus that is more than large enough to eliminate *all* future contributions and cannot be returned to the entity' (emphasis added). If the contribution reduction were determined by considering only the term of the expected future working lifetime of the active membership, the limit on the measurement of the defined benefit asset would come into play much more frequently.

BC21   Most respondents to D19 were supportive of this view. However, some argued that the term should be the shorter of the expected life of the plan and the expected life of the entity. The IFRIC agreed that the entity could not derive economic benefits from a reduction in contributions beyond its own expected life and has amended the Interpretation accordingly.

BC22   Next, the IFRIC considered what assumptions should be made about a future workforce. D19 proposed that the assumptions for the demographic profile of the future workforce should be consistent with the assumptions underlying the calculation of the present value of the defined benefit obligation at the end of the reporting period balance sheet date. Some respondents noted that the calculation of service costs for future periods requires assumptions that are not required for the calculation of the defined benefit obligation. In particular, the assumptions underlying the present value of the defined benefit obligation calculation do not include an explicit assumption for new entrants.

BC23   The IFRIC agreed that this is the case. The IFRIC noted that assumptions are needed in respect of the size of the future workforce and future benefits provided by the plan. The IFRIC decided that the future service cost should be based on the situation that exists at the end of the reporting period balance sheet date determined in accordance with IAS 19. Therefore, increases in the size of the workforce or the benefits provided by the plan should not be anticipated. Decreases in the size of the workforce or the benefits should be included in the assumptions for the future service cost at the same time as they are treated as curtailments in accordance with IAS 19.

The effect of a minimum funding requirement on the economic benefit available as a refund

BC24   The IFRIC considered whether a minimum funding requirement to make contributions to a plan in force at the end of the reporting period ~~balance sheet date~~ would restrict the extent to which a refund of surplus is available. The IFRIC noted that there is an implicit assumption in IAS 19 that the specified assumptions represent the best estimate of the eventual outcome of the plan in economic terms, while a requirement to make additional contributions is often a prudent approach designed to build in a risk margin for adverse circumstances. Moreover, when there are no members left in the plan, the minimum funding requirement would have no effect. This would leave the IAS 19 surplus available. To the extent that the entity has a right to this eventual surplus, the IAS 19 surplus would be available to the entity, regardless of the minimum funding restrictions in force at the end of the reporting period ~~balance sheet date~~. The IFRIC therefore concluded that the existence of a minimum funding requirement may affect the timing of a refund but does not affect whether it is ultimately available to the entity.

The effect of a minimum funding requirement on the economic benefit available as a reduction in future contributions

BC25   The entity's minimum funding requirements at a given date can be analysed into the contributions that are required to cover (a) an existing shortfall for past service on the minimum funding basis and (b) future service.

BC26   Contributions required to cover an existing shortfall may give rise to a liability, as discussed in paragraphs BC31–BC37 below. But they do not affect the availability of a reduction in future contributions for future service.

BC27   In contrast, future contribution requirements in respect of future service do not generate an additional liability at the end of the reporting period ~~balance sheet date~~ because they do not relate to past services received by the entity. However, they may reduce the extent to which the entity can benefit from a reduction in future contributions. Therefore, the IFRIC decided that the available asset from a contribution reduction should be calculated as the present value of the IAS 19 future service cost less the minimum funding contribution requirement in respect of future service in each year.

BC28   If the minimum funding contribution requirement is consistently greater than the IAS 19 future service cost, that calculation may be thought to imply that a liability exists. However, as noted above, an entity has no liability at the end of the reporting period ~~balance sheet date~~ in respect of minimum funding requirements that relate to future service. The economic benefit available from a reduction in future contributions can be nil, but it can never be a negative amount.

BC29   The respondents to D19 were largely supportive of these conclusions.

BC30   The IFRIC noted that future changes to regulations on minimum funding requirements might affect the available surplus. However, the IFRIC decided that, just as the future service cost was determined on the basis of the situation existing at the end of the reporting period ~~balance sheet date~~, so should the effect of a minimum funding requirement. The IFRIC concluded that when determining the amount of an asset that might be available as a reduction in future contributions, an entity should not consider whether the minimum funding requirement might change in the future. The respondents to D19 were largely supportive of these conclusions.

Prepayments of a minimum funding requirement

BC30A   If an entity has prepaid future minimum funding requirement contributions and that prepayment will reduce future contributions, the prepayment generates economic benefits for the entity. However, to the extent that the future minimum funding requirement contributions exceeded future service costs, the original version of IFRIC 14 did not permit entities to consider those economic benefits in measuring a defined benefit asset. After issuing IFRIC 14, the Board reviewed the treatment of such prepayments. The Board concluded that such a prepayment provides an economic benefit to the entity by relieving the entity of an obligation to pay future minimum funding requirement contributions that exceed future service cost. Therefore, considering those economic benefits in measuring a defined benefit asset would convey more useful information to users of financial statements. In May 2009 the Board published that conclusion in an exposure draft *Prepayments of a Minimum Funding Requirement*. After considering the responses to that exposure draft, the Board amended IFRIC 14 by issuing *Prepayments of a Minimum Funding Requirement* in November 2009.

BC30B   Some respondents noted that the amendments increase the effect of funding considerations on the measurement of a defined benefit asset and liability and questioned whether funding considerations should ever affect the measurement. However, the Board noted that the sole purpose of the amendments was to eliminate an unintended consequence in IFRIC 14. Thus, the Board did not re-debate the fundamental conclusion of IFRIC 14 that funding is relevant to the measurement when an entity cannot recover the additional cost of a minimum funding requirement in excess of the IAS 19 service cost.

BC30C   Many respondents noted that the proposals made the assessment of the economic benefit available from a prepayment different from the assessment for a surplus arising from actuarial gains. Most agreed that a prepayment created an asset, but questioned why the Board did not extend the underlying principle to other surpluses that could be used to reduce future payments of minimum funding requirement contributions.

BC30D   The Board did not extend the scope of the amendments to surpluses arising from actuarial gains because such an approach would need further thought and the Board did not want to delay the amendments for prepayments. However, the Board may consider the matter further in a future comprehensive review of pension cost accounting.

Onerous minimum funding requirements

BC31 Minimum funding requirements for contributions to cover an existing minimum funding shortfall create an obligation for the entity at the end of the reporting period ~~balance sheet date~~ because they relate to past service. Nonetheless, usually minimum funding requirements do not affect the measurement of the defined benefit asset or liability under IAS 19. This is because the contributions, once paid, become plan assets and the additional net liability for the funding requirement is nil. However, the IFRIC noted that the limit on the measurement of the defined benefit asset in paragraph 58 of IAS 19 may make the funding obligation onerous, as follows.

BC32 If an entity is obliged to make contributions and some or all of those contributions will not subsequently be available as an economic benefit, it follows that when the contributions are made the entity will not be able to recognise an asset to that extent. However, the resulting loss to the entity does not arise on the payment of the contributions but earlier, at the point at which the obligation to pay arises.

BC33 Therefore, the IFRIC concluded that when an entity has an obligation under a minimum funding requirement to make additional contributions to a plan in respect of services already received, the entity should reduce the ~~balance sheet~~ asset or increase the liability recognised in the statement of financial position to the extent that the minimum funding contributions payable to the plan will not be available to the entity either as a refund or a reduction in future contributions.

BC34 Respondents to D19 broadly supported this conclusion. But some questioned whether the draft Interpretation extended the application of paragraph 58 of IAS 19 too far. They argued that it should apply only when an entity has a defined benefit asset. In particular, it should not be used to classify a funding requirement as onerous, thereby creating an additional liability to be recognised beyond that arising from the other requirements of IAS 19. Others agreed that such a liability existed, but questioned whether it fell within the scope of IAS 19 rather than IAS 37 *Provisions, Contingent Liabilities and Contingent Assets*.

BC35 The IFRIC did not agree that the Interpretation extends the application of paragraph 58 of IAS 19. Rather, it applies the principles in IAS 37 relating to onerous contracts in the context of the requirements of IAS 19, including paragraph 58. On the question whether the liability falls within the scope of IAS 19 or IAS 37, the IFRIC noted that employee benefits are excluded from the scope of IAS 37. The IFRIC therefore confirmed that the interaction of a minimum funding requirement and the limit on the measurement of the defined benefit asset could result in a decrease in a defined benefit asset or an increase in a defined benefit liability.

BC36 The IFRIC also discussed whether the liability in respect of the minimum funding requirement and the effect of any subsequent remeasurement should be recognised immediately in profit or loss or whether they should be eligible for the options for deferred recognition or recognition outside profit or loss that IAS 19 specifies for actuarial gains and losses. The IFRIC noted that the liability in respect of any minimum funding requirements arises only because of the limit on the measurement of the ~~balance sheet~~ asset recognised in the statement of financial position under paragraph 58 of IAS 19. Furthermore, all consequences of paragraph 58 should be treated consistently.

BC37 Therefore, the IFRIC concluded that any liability in respect of a minimum funding requirement and the effect of any subsequent remeasurement should be recognised immediately in accordance with paragraph 61(g) or 93C of IAS 19. This is consistent with the recognition of other adjustments to the net ~~balance sheet~~ asset or liability recognised in the statement of financial position under paragraph 58 of IAS 19. The respondents to D19 broadly agreed with this requirement.

Transitional provisions

BC38 In D19, the IFRIC proposed that the draft Interpretation should be applied retrospectively. The draft Interpretation required immediate recognition of all adjustments relating to the minimum funding requirements. The IFRIC therefore argued that retrospective application would be straightforward.

BC39 Respondents to D19 noted that paragraph 58A of IAS 19 causes the limit on the defined benefit asset to affect the deferred recognition of actuarial gains and losses. Retrospective application of the Interpretation could change the amount of that limit for previous periods, thereby also changing the deferred recognition of actuarial gains and losses. Calculating these revised amounts retrospectively over the life of the plan would be costly and of little benefit to users of financial statements.

BC40 The IFRIC agreed with this view. The IFRIC therefore amended the transitional provisions so that IFRIC 14 is to be applied only from the beginning of the first period presented in the financial statements for annual periods beginning on or after the effective date.

Summary of changes from D19

BC41 The Interpretation has been altered in the following significant respects since it was exposed for comment as D19:

(a) The issue of when an entity controls an asset arising from the availability of a refund has been clarified (paragraphs BC10 and BC12).

(b) Requirements relating to the assumptions underlying the measurement of a reduction in future contributions have been clarified (paragraphs BC22 and BC23).

(c) The transitional requirements have been changed from retrospective application to application from the beginning of the first period presented in the first financial statements to which the Interpretation applies (paragraphs BC38–BC40).

(d) In November 2009 the Board amended IFRIC 14 to require entities to recognise as an economic benefit any prepayment of minimum funding requirement contributions. At the same time, the Board removed references to 'present value' from paragraphs 16, 17, 20 and 22 and 'the surplus in the plan' from paragraph 16 because these references duplicated references in paragraph 58 of IAS 19. The Board also amended the term 'future accrual of benefits' to 'future service' for consistency with the rest of IAS 19.

Documents published to accompany

IFRIC Interpretation 15

Agreements for the Construction of Real Estate

The text of the unaccompanied IFRIC 15 is contained in Part A of this edition. Its effective date is 1 January 2009. This part presents the following accompanying documents:

Information note

Analysis of a single agreement for the construction of real estate

This note accompanies, but is not part of, IFRIC 15.

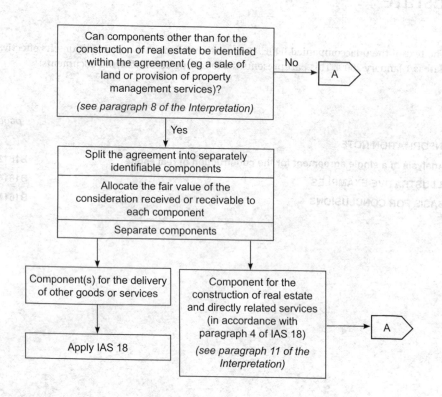

continued...

...continued

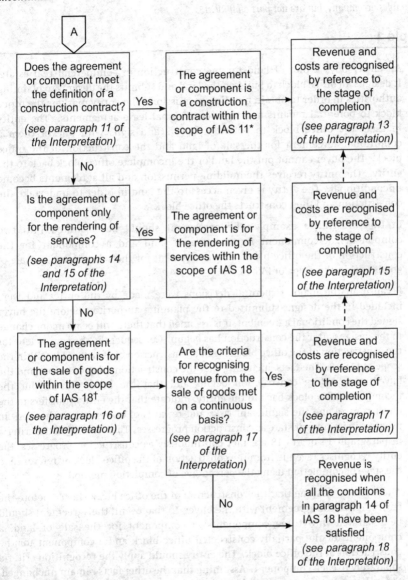

* The construction contract may need to be segmented in accordance with paragraph 8 of IAS 11
† Directly related services may need to be separated in accordance with paragraph 13 of IAS 18

Illustrative examples

These examples accompany, but are not part of, IFRIC 15.

Example 1

IE1 An entity buys a plot of land for the construction of commercial real estate. It designs an office block to build on the land and submits the designs to planning authorities in order to obtain building permission. The entity markets the office block to potential tenants and signs conditional lease agreements. The entity markets the office block to potential buyers and signs with one of them a conditional agreement for the sale of land and the construction of the office block. The buyer cannot put the land or the incomplete office block back to the entity. The entity receives the building permission and all agreements become unconditional. The entity is given access to the land in order to undertake the construction and then constructs the office block.

IE2 In this illustrative example, the agreement should be separated into two components: a component for the sale of land and a component for the construction of the office block. The component for the sale of land is a sale of goods within the scope of IAS 18.

IE3 Because all the major structural decisions were made by the entity and were included in the designs submitted to the planning authorities before the buyer signed the conditional agreement, it is assumed that there will be no major change in the designs after the construction has begun. Consequently, the component for the construction of the office block is not a construction contract and is within the scope of IAS 18. The facts, including that the construction takes place on land the buyer owns before construction begins and that the buyer cannot put the incomplete office block back to the entity, indicate that the entity transfers to the buyer control and the significant risks and rewards of ownership of the work in progress in its current state as construction progresses. Therefore, if all the criteria in paragraph 14 of IAS 18 are met continuously as construction progresses, the entity recognises revenue from the construction of the office block by reference to the stage of completion using the percentage of completion method.

IE4 Alternatively, assume that the construction of the office block started before the entity signed the agreement with the buyer. In that event, the agreement should be separated into three components: a component for the sale of land, a component for the partially constructed office block and a component for the construction of the office block. The entity should apply the recognition criteria separately to each component. Assuming that the other facts remain unchanged, the entity recognises revenue from the component for the construction of the office block by reference to the stage of completion using the percentage of completion method as explained in paragraph IE3.

IE5 In this example, the sale of land is determined to be a separately identifiable component from the component for the construction of real estate. However, depending on facts and circumstances, the entity may conclude that such a component is not separately identifiable. For example, in some jurisdictions, a condominium is legally defined as the absolute ownership of a unit based on a legal description of the airspace the unit actually occupies, plus an undivided interest in the ownership of the common elements (that includes the land and actual building itself, all the driveways, parking, lifts, outside hallways, recreation and landscaped areas) that are owned jointly with the other condominium unit owners. In this case, the undivided interest in the ownership of the common elements does not give the buyer control and the significant risks and rewards of the land itself. Indeed, the right to the unit itself and the interest in the common elements are not separable.

Example 2

IE6   An entity is developing residential real estate and starts marketing individual units (apartments) while construction is still in progress. Buyers enter into a binding sale agreement that gives them the right to acquire a specified unit when it is ready for occupation. They pay a deposit that is refundable only if the entity fails to deliver the completed unit in accordance with the contracted terms. Buyers are also required to make progress payments between the time of the initial agreement and contractual completion. The balance of the purchase price is paid only on contractual completion, when buyers obtain possession of their unit. Buyers are able to specify only minor variations to the basic design but they cannot specify or alter major structural elements of the design of their unit. In the jurisdiction, no rights to the underlying real estate asset transfer to the buyer other than through the agreement. Consequently, the construction takes place regardless of whether sale agreements exist.

IE7   In this illustrative example, the terms of the agreement and all the surrounding facts and circumstances indicate that the agreement is not a construction contract. The agreement is a forward contract that gives the buyer an asset in the form of a right to acquire, use and sell the completed real estate at a later date and an obligation to pay the purchase price in accordance with its terms. Although the buyer might be able to transfer its interest in the forward contract to another party, the entity retains control and the significant risks and rewards of ownership of the work in progress in its current state until the completed real estate is transferred. Therefore, revenue should be recognised only when all the criteria in paragraph 14 of IAS 18 are met (at completion in this example).

IE8   Alternatively, assume that, in the jurisdiction, the law requires the entity to transfer immediately to the buyer ownership of the real estate in its current state of completion and that any additional construction becomes the property of the buyer as construction progresses. The entity would need to consider all the terms of the agreement to determine whether this change in the timing of the transfer of ownership means that the entity transfers to the buyer control and the significant risks and rewards of ownership of the work in progress in its current state as construction progresses. For example, the fact that if the agreement is terminated before construction is complete, the buyer retains the work in progress and the entity has the right to be paid for the work performed, might indicate that control is transferred along with ownership. If it does, and if all the criteria in paragraph 14 of IAS 18 are met continuously as construction progresses, the entity recognises revenue by reference to the stage of completion using the percentage of completion method taking into account the stage of completion of the whole building and the agreements signed with individual buyers.

Example 3

IE9 Determining whether the entity will retain neither continuing managerial involvement to the degree usually associated with ownership nor effective control over the constructed real estate to an extent that would preclude recognition of some or all of the consideration as revenue depends on the terms of the agreement and all the surrounding facts and circumstances. Such a determination requires judgement. The Interpretation assumes the entity has reached the conclusion that it is appropriate to recognise revenue from the agreement and discusses how to determine the appropriate pattern of revenue recognition.

IE10 Agreements for the construction of real estate may include such a degree of continuing managerial involvement by the entity undertaking the construction that control and the significant risks and rewards of ownership are not transferred even when construction is complete and the buyer obtains possession. Examples are agreements in which the entity guarantees occupancy of the property for a specified period, or guarantees a return on the buyer's investment for a specified period. In such circumstances, recognition of revenue may be delayed or precluded altogether.

IE11 Agreements for the construction of real estate may give the buyer a right to take over the work in progress (albeit with a penalty) during construction, eg to engage a different entity to complete the construction. This fact, along with others, may indicate that the entity transfers to the buyer control of the work in progress in its current state as construction progresses. The entity that undertakes the construction of real estate will have access to the land and the work in progress in order to perform its contractual obligation to deliver to the buyer completed real estate. If control of the work in process is transferred continuously, that access does not necessarily imply that the entity undertaking the construction retains continuing managerial involvement with the real estate to the degree usually associated with ownership to an extent that would preclude recognition of some or all of the consideration as revenue. The entity may have control over the activities related to the performance of its contractual obligation but not over the real estate itself.

Basis for Conclusions on
IFRIC Interpretation 15 *Agreements for the Construction of Real Estate*

This Basis for Conclusions accompanies, but is not part of, IFRIC 15.

Introduction

BC1 This Basis for Conclusions summarises the IFRIC's considerations in reaching its consensus. Individual IFRIC members gave greater weight to some factors than to others.

BC2 The IFRIC released draft Interpretation D21 *Real Estate Sales* for public comment in July 2007 and received 51 comment letters in response.

Scope

BC3 Agreements for the construction of real estate are widespread and may relate to residential, commercial or industrial developments. Construction often spans more than one accounting period, may take place on land the buyer owns or leases before construction begins and agreements may require progress payments.

BC4 The main area of divergence in practice concerns the identification of the applicable accounting standard for agreements for the construction of real estate. In some jurisdictions, the prevailing practice is to apply IAS 11 *Construction Contracts* and to recognise revenue as construction progresses. In others, it is to apply the requirements for the sale of goods in IAS 18 *Revenue* and to recognise revenue only when the completed real estate is delivered to the buyer.

BC5 The IFRIC considered whether the scope of the Interpretation should be confined to agreements for the construction of real estate. It concluded in D21 that the scope should be limited to the request received to clarify the requirements of IAS 18 with respect to 'real estate sales' because that was the area identified as having the most diversity in practice. In redeliberating the issue, the IFRIC took the view that the notion of 'real estate sales' in D21 might create confusion and clarified that this Interpretation applies to 'agreements for the construction of real estate'. The primary issue of whether an agreement is within the scope of IAS 11 or IAS 18 arises only when agreements include construction activities. Such agreements may or may not meet the definition of a construction contract. The IFRIC also clarified that the Interpretation might affect entities that undertake the construction of real estate, directly or through subcontractors.

BC6 The IFRIC noted that respondents to D21 were concerned about the implications of the IFRIC's conclusions for agreements that required manufacture of goods to a customer's specifications in industries other than real estate. The IFRIC reconsidered the scope of the Interpretation after it had redeliberated its conclusions with respect to agreements for the construction of real estate. It concluded that the scope of the Interpretation should remain confined to agreements for the construction of real estate. The IFRIC noted that it might be applied by analogy to industries other than real estate in accordance with IAS 8 *Accounting Policies, Changes in Accounting Estimates and Errors.*

Issue

BC7   The issue is when should revenue from the construction of real estate be recognised? In International Financial Reporting Standards (IFRSs), two standards deal with accounting for revenue: IAS 18 and IAS 11. Because many agreements involve the construction or manufacture of an asset to meet customer's specifications, the IFRIC was asked to clarify how to determine whether an agreement for the construction of real estate is a construction contract within the scope of IAS 11.

Consensus

BC8   The nature and extent of the entity's continuing managerial involvement with the item sold may affect the accounting for the transaction. It may be accounted for as a sale, or as a financing, leasing or some other profit-sharing arrangement. Because the issue addressed in this Interpretation is a revenue recognition issue, the Interpretation assumes that the entity has previously analysed the agreement for the construction of real estate and any related agreements and concluded that it will retain neither continuing managerial involvement to the degree usually associated with ownership nor effective control over the constructed real estate to an extent that would preclude recognition of some or all of the consideration as revenue. This assumption, that the entity would recognise revenue at some point and the issue was one of timing, was implicit in D21 but was not clearly stated. In response to comments received, the IFRIC clarified that an entity must have concluded that the arrangement will result in the recognition of revenue to be within the scope of the Interpretation.

BC9   Some respondents to D21 asked the IFRIC to provide guidance on agreements with multiple components so the Interpretation would cover the more complex transactions that often occur in practice.

BC10   In its redeliberations, the IFRIC noted that, in addition to the construction of real estate, an agreement may include the delivery of other goods or services (eg a sale of land or provision of property management services). In accordance with paragraph 13 of IAS 18, such an agreement may need to be split into separately identifiable components, including one for the construction of real estate. Because IAS 18 is the standard that sets out requirements for revenue recognition in general, the IFRIC decided to consider the issue in the context of IAS 18, ie an entity should first determine whether an agreement that includes the construction of real estate also includes other components that do not need further analysis in this Interpretation.

BC11   The IFRIC noted that IFRIC 12 *Service Concession Arrangements* and IFRIC 13 *Customer Loyalty Programmes* already provide guidance on determining whether a single agreement should be divided into components and, if so, how to allocate the fair value of the total consideration received or receivable for the agreement to each component (see paragraph 13 of IFRIC 12 and paragraphs 5–7 of IFRIC 13). Therefore, the IFRIC concluded that this Interpretation should include only a reminder in paragraph 8 that such identification and allocation are required.

BC12 Regarding the issue of whether and when there is a separately identifiable component for the sale of land, the IFRIC concluded from the existing guidance that the identification of a component for the sale of land should be undertaken when first analysing any potential components. Depending on facts and circumstances, the entity may or may not conclude that such a component is separately identifiable from the component for the construction of real estate.

BC13 The IFRIC noted that respondents were uncertain whether an entity applying D21 would follow the guidance on combining and segmenting contracts in IAS 18 or that in IAS 11. The approach adopted in the Interpretation makes it clear that the specific criteria for contract segmentation in IAS 11 are applied only after the entity has concluded that the agreement is within the scope of that standard.

Determining whether the agreement is within the scope of IAS 11 or IAS 18

BC14 One view is that IAS 11 applies to all agreements for the construction of real estate. In support of this view, it is argued that:

(a) these agreements are in substance construction contracts. The typical features of a construction contract—land development, structural engineering, architectural design and construction—are all present.

(b) IAS 11 requires a percentage of completion method of revenue recognition for construction contracts. Revenue is recognised progressively as work is performed. Because many real estate development projects span more than one accounting period, the rationale for this method—that it 'provides useful information on the extent of contract activity and performance during a period' (IAS 11 paragraph 25)—applies to real estate development as much as it does to other construction contracts. If revenue is recognised only when the IAS 18 conditions for recognising revenue from the sale of goods are met, the financial statements do not reflect the entity's economic value generation in the period and are susceptible to manipulation.

(c) US Statement of Financial Accounting Standards No. 66 *Accounting for Sales of Real Estate* requires a percentage of completion method for recognising profit from sales of units in condominium projects or time-sharing interests (provided specified criteria are met). Thus US generally accepted accounting principles (GAAP) acknowledge that such real estate sales have the same economic substance as construction-type contracts. IFRSs can and should be interpreted in the same way to avoid unnecessary differences.

BC15 A second view is that IAS 11 applies only when the agreement meets the definition of a construction contract. When the agreement does not meet the definition of a construction contract, the agreement is within the scope of IAS 18.

BC16 The consensus reflects the second view. In reaching this consensus, the IFRIC noted that:

(a) the facts that the construction spans more than one accounting period and requires progress payments are not relevant features to consider when determining the applicable standard and the timing of revenue recognition.

(b)   determining whether an agreement for the construction of real estate is within the scope of IAS 11 or IAS 18 depends on the terms of the agreement and all the surrounding facts and circumstances. Such a determination requires judgement with respect to each agreement. It is not an accounting policy choice.

(c)   IAS 11 lacks specific guidance on the definition of a construction contract and further application guidance is needed to help identify construction contracts.

(d)   differences exist between the requirements in IFRSs and US GAAP for revenue recognition in general and for construction contracts in particular. They cannot be eliminated by interpretation. They are being addressed in a general project on revenue recognition conducted jointly by the IASB and the US Financial Accounting Standards Board.

BC17   The IFRIC noted that when IAS 11 applies, for accounting purposes, the construction contract also includes contracts for the rendering of services that are directly related to the construction of the real estate in accordance with paragraph 4 of IAS 18 and paragraph 5(a) of IAS 11.

BC18   In D21 the IFRIC concluded that an agreement for the construction of real estate would be within the scope of IAS 11 in two circumstances—if the agreement met the definition of a construction contract and/or if control and the significant risks and rewards of ownership of the work in progress in its current state transferred to the buyer continuously as construction progresses. Many respondents pointed out that IAS 11 does not require 'continuous transfer' for the use of the percentage of completion method, only that the contract be a 'construction contract'. The IFRIC clarified in the consensus that IAS 11 applies only when the agreement meets the definition of a construction contract and carried forward into the Interpretation the guidance in paragraphs 9(a), 10(a) and BC5(a) of D21.

BC19   In addition, many respondents asked the IFRIC to provide guidance to distinguish between construction contracts that meet the definition included in D21 and other agreements for the manufacture of goods to a customer's specifications. The IFRIC concluded that the most important distinguishing feature is whether the customer is actually specifying the main elements of the structural design. In situations involving the manufacture of goods to a customer's specifications, the customer generally does not have the ability to specify or alter the basic design of the product. Rather, the customer is simply choosing elements from a range of options specified by the seller or specifying only minor variations to the basic design. The IFRIC decided to include guidance to this effect in the Interpretation to help clarify the application of the definition of a construction contract.

Accounting for revenue from the construction of real estate

BC20   When the agreement is within the scope of IAS 11 and its outcome can be estimated reliably, the entity should recognise revenue by reference to the stage of completion in accordance with IAS 11.

BC21　When the agreement does not meet the definition of a construction contract, the agreement is within the scope of IAS 18. The IFRIC identified the following types of agreements for the construction of real estate that are within the scope of IAS 18 and that are distinguishable in substance:

(a)　agreements for the rendering of services only;

(b)　two types of agreements for the sale of goods:

(i)　agreements in which the entity transfers to the buyer control and the significant risks and rewards of ownership of the work in progress in its current state as construction progresses;

(ii)　agreements in which the entity transfers to the buyer control and the significant risks and rewards of ownership of the real estate in its entirety at a single time (eg at completion, upon or after delivery).

BC22　The IFRIC noted that a customer may decide to act in essence as its own general contractor and enter into agreements with individual suppliers for specific goods and services. When the entity is responsible only for assembling materials supplied by others (ie it has no inventory risk for the construction materials), the agreement is an agreement for the rendering of services. The IFRIC noted that, if the criteria in paragraph 20 are met, IAS 18 requires revenue to be recognised by reference to the stage of completion using the percentage of completion method. IAS 18 then refers to IAS 11 and states that the requirements of IAS 11 are generally applicable to the recognition of revenue and the associated expenses for such a transaction.

BC23　The IFRIC also noted that construction activities often require an entity that undertakes the construction of real estate, directly or through subcontractors, to provide services together with construction materials. However, the entity delivers to the buyer a real estate asset, either completed or in its current stage of completion. Therefore, the IFRIC concluded that the criteria in paragraph 14 of IAS 18 for recognition of revenue from the sale of goods should apply to such agreements.

BC24　As noted in paragraph BC18, the IFRIC agreed with respondents to D21 that IAS 11 does not require the entity to transfer to the buyer control and the significant risks and rewards of ownership of the work in process in its current state as construction progresses ('continuous transfer') in order to use the percentage of completion method, only that the contract be a 'construction contract'. In its redeliberations, the IFRIC noted that the criterion it included in paragraph 9(b) of D21 was actually one of the criteria in IAS 18 for recognition of revenue from the sale of goods. Although these agreements may not meet the definition of construction contracts, the IFRIC concluded that they may result in the entity meeting all of the criteria for recognising revenue from the sale of goods in IAS 18 (including the transfer of control and the significant risks and rewards of ownership) continuously as construction progresses, as opposed to at a single time (eg at completion, upon or after delivery).

BC25　The IFRIC concluded that if all these criteria are met continuously, an entity should recognise revenue on the same basis (by reference to the stage of completion). Like paragraph 21 of IAS 18 for the rendering of services, the Interpretation refers entities to IAS 11 for guidance on applying the percentage of completion method.

The IFRIC observed that this conclusion was consistent with the basis for using the percentage of completion method in Statement of Position No. 81-1 *Accounting for Performance of Construction-Type and Certain Production-Type Contracts* issued by the American Institute of Certified Public Accountants, which states:

> ... the business activity taking place supports the concept that in an economic sense performance is, in effect, a continuous sale (transfer of ownership rights) that occurs as the work progresses ...

BC26   The IFRIC noted that agreements with 'continuous transfer' might not be encountered frequently. However, the IFRIC decided that the Interpretation should address the accounting for such agreements because some respondents to D21 identified agreements with these characteristics.

BC27   The IFRIC also identified agreements for the construction of real estate in which the entity transfers to the buyer control and the significant risks and rewards of ownership of the real estate in its entirety at a single time (eg at completion, upon or after delivery). The IFRIC reaffirmed its conclusion in D21 that these agreements are sales of goods within the scope of IAS 18. Such agreements give the buyer only an asset in the form of a right to acquire, use and sell the completed real estate at a later date. The IFRIC concluded that revenue from such agreements should be recognised only when all the criteria in paragraph 14 of IAS 18 are satisfied.

BC28   The IFRIC noted that this conclusion is consistent with revenue recognition requirements for significant contracts for the delivery of multiple units of goods manufactured to the customer's specifications over more than one accounting period, such as subway cars. In such circumstances, the entity recognises revenue as individual units (or groups of units) are delivered. However, in contrast to the contracts described in paragraph BC24, control and the significant risks and rewards of ownership of the work in process in its current state do not transfer to the buyer as construction/manufacture progresses. This transfer takes place only on delivery of the completed units. In this case, the entity would apply the requirements of paragraph 14 of IAS 18 at that time; use of the percentage of completion method would not be appropriate.

BC29   In some circumstances, an entity has to perform further work on real estate already delivered to the buyer. The IFRIC noted that IFRIC 13 *Customer Loyalty Programmes* already provides guidance on how to apply paragraphs 13 and 19 of IAS 18. Paragraph BC9 of IFRIC 13 states that:

> ... IAS 18 does not give explicit guidance. However, the aim of IAS 18 is to recognise revenue when, and to the extent that, goods or services have been delivered to a customer. In the IFRIC's view, paragraph 13 applies if a single transaction requires two or more separate goods or services to be delivered at different times; it ensures that revenue for each item is recognised only when that item is delivered. In contrast, paragraph 19 applies only if the entity has to incur further costs directly related to items already delivered, eg to meet warranty claims. In the IFRIC's view, loyalty awards are not costs that directly relate to the goods and services already delivered— rather, they are separate goods or services delivered at a later date ...

BC30   The IFRIC concluded that the Interpretation should provide similar guidance.

Disclosures

BC31   The IFRIC noted that IAS 1 *Presentation of Financial Statements* (as revised in 2007) requires an entity to provide disclosures about its significant accounting policies (paragraph 117), judgements management has made in applying those policies (paragraph 122) and major sources of estimation uncertainty.

BC32   For greater certainty, the IFRIC concluded that, for agreements with 'continuous transfer', the Interpretation should require specific disclosures similar to those of paragraphs 39 and 40 of IAS 11 to satisfy the general requirements of IAS 1.

BC33   The IFRIC noted that this conclusion was generally consistent with D21 because D21 included such agreements in the scope of IAS 11 and therefore implicitly required the full disclosures of that standard.

Changes from draft Interpretation D21

BC34   Most respondents to D21 supported the IFRIC's conclusion that it should develop an interpretation on this issue. However, nearly all respondents expressed concern with some aspects of the proposals or the possible application by analogy to industries other than real estate.

BC35   The most significant changes made from D21 in the light of comments received relate to:

(a)   *scope.* D21 referred to 'real estate sales'. The IFRIC clarified that the Interpretation applies to agreements for the construction of real estate.

(b)   *applicable standard.* D21 listed typical features, including 'continuous transfer', to help determine whether an agreement for the construction of real estate is within the scope of IAS 11 or IAS 18. The IFRIC concluded that only agreements that meet the definition of a construction contract are within the scope of IAS 11 and carried forward into the Interpretation the guidance in paragraphs 9(a), 10(a) and BC5(a) of D21 on when a contract satisfies that definition.

(c)   *continuous transfer.* Many respondents believed that the indicator of 'continuous transfer' (the entity transfers to the buyer control and the significant risks and rewards of ownership of the work in progress in its current state as construction progresses) set out in paragraph 9(b) of D21 was relevant, although not specifically included in IAS 11. The IFRIC took the view that when the criteria for recognising revenue from the sale of goods set out in paragraph 14 of IAS 18 are met continuously, it is appropriate to recognise revenue as the criteria are met. The IFRIC carried forward the criterion set out in paragraph 9(b) of D21 and concluded that the percentage of completion method appropriately recognises revenue in such circumstances. However, the IFRIC did not carry forward the features set out in paragraph 9(b)(i)–(iii) of D21 on the basis that the criterion was sufficiently clear. Overall, the Interpretation and D21 provide similar revenue recognition conclusions for agreements with 'continuous transfer' but for different reasons.

(d)   *multiple components.* Some respondents to D21 asked the IFRIC to address the issue of a single agreement with multiple components in order to cover the more complex transactions that often occur in practice. The requirements of IAS 18 in this respect have been included in the consensus and the issue is also addressed in an illustrative example.

(e)   *disclosures.* D21 did not specify disclosures because agreements with 'continuous transfer' were included in the scope of IAS 11 and its disclosure requirements would have automatically applied. Paragraphs 20 and 21 of the Interpretation have been added to require specific disclosures for such agreements that now fall within the scope of IAS 18.

(f)   *flow chart and illustrative examples.* The IFRIC decided that a flow chart and illustrative examples should accompany, but not be part of, the Interpretation to help entities apply the Interpretation.

Documents published to accompany

IFRIC Interpretation 16

Hedges of a Net Investment in a Foreign Operation

This version includes amendments resulting from IFRSs issued up to 31 December 2009.

The text of the unaccompanied IFRIC 16 is contained in Part A of this edition. Its effective date when issued was 1 October 2008. The effective date of the amendments is 1 July 2009. This part presents the following accompanying documents:

Illustrative example

This example accompanies, but is not part of, IFRIC 16.

Disposal of a foreign operation (paragraphs 16 and 17)

IE1   This example illustrates the application of paragraphs 16 and 17 in connection with the reclassification adjustment on the disposal of a foreign operation.

Background

IE2   This example assumes the group structure set out in the application guidance and that Parent used a USD borrowing in Subsidiary A to hedge the EUR/USD risk of the net investment in Subsidiary C in Parent's consolidated financial statements. Parent uses the step-by-step method of consolidation. Assume the hedge was fully effective and the full USD/EUR accumulated change in the value of the hedging instrument before disposal of Subsidiary C is ε24 million (gain). This is matched exactly by the fall in value of the net investment in Subsidiary C, when measured against the functional currency of Parent (euro).

IE3   If the direct method of consolidation is used, the fall in the value of Parent's net investment in Subsidiary C of ε24 million would be reflected totally in the foreign currency translation reserve relating to Subsidiary C in Parent's consolidated financial statements. However, because Parent uses the step-by-step method, this fall in the net investment value in Subsidiary C of ε24 million would be reflected both in Subsidiary B's foreign currency translation reserve relating to Subsidiary C and in Parent's foreign currency translation reserve relating to Subsidiary B.

IE4   The aggregate amount recognised in the foreign currency translation reserve in respect of Subsidiaries B and C is not affected by the consolidation method. Assume that using the direct method of consolidation, the foreign currency translation reserves for Subsidiaries B and C in Parent's consolidated financial statements are ε62 million gain and ε24 million loss respectively; using the step-by-step method of consolidation those amounts are ε49 million gain and ε11 million loss respectively.

Reclassification

IE5   When the investment in Subsidiary C is disposed of, IAS 39 requires the full ε24 million gain on the hedging instrument to be reclassified to profit or loss. Using the step-by-step method, the amount to be reclassified to profit or loss in respect of the net investment in Subsidiary C would be only ε11 million loss. Parent could adjust the foreign currency translation reserves of both Subsidiaries B and C by ε13 million in order to match the amounts reclassified in respect of the hedging instrument and the net investment as would have been the case if the direct method of consolidation had been used, if that was its accounting policy. An entity that had not hedged its net investment could make the same reclassification.

© IASCF

Basis for Conclusions on
IFRIC Interpretation 16 *Hedges of a Net Investment in a Foreign Operation*

This Basis for Conclusions accompanies, but is not part of, IFRIC 16.

Introduction

BC1   This Basis for Conclusions summarises the IFRIC's considerations in reaching its consensus. Individual IFRIC members gave greater weight to some factors than to others.

Background

BC2   The IFRIC was asked for guidance on accounting for the hedge of a net investment in a foreign operation in the consolidated financial statements. Interested parties had different views of the risks eligible for hedge accounting purposes. One issue is whether the risk arises from the foreign currency exposure to the functional currencies of the foreign operation and the parent entity, or whether it arises from the foreign currency exposure to the functional currency of the foreign operation and the presentation currency of the parent entity's consolidated financial statements.

BC3   Concern was also raised about which entity within a group could hold a hedging instrument in a hedge of a net investment in a foreign operation and in particular whether the parent entity holding the net investment in a foreign operation must also hold the hedging instrument.

BC4   Accordingly, the IFRIC decided to develop guidance on the accounting for a hedge of the foreign currency risk arising from a net investment in a foreign operation.

BC5   The IFRIC published draft Interpretation D22 *Hedges of a Net Investment in a Foreign Operation* for public comment in July 2007 and received 45 comment letters in response to its proposals.

Consensus

Hedged risk and hedged item

Functional currency versus presentation currency (paragraph 10)

BC6   The IFRIC received a submission suggesting that the method of consolidation can affect the determination of the hedged risk in a hedge of a net investment in a foreign operation. The submission noted that consolidation can be completed by either the direct method or the step-by-step method. In the direct method of consolidation, each entity within a group is consolidated directly into the ultimate parent entity's presentation currency when preparing the consolidated financial statements. In the step-by-step method, each intermediate parent entity prepares consolidated financial statements, which are then consolidated into its parent entity until the ultimate parent entity has prepared consolidated financial statements.

BC7   The submission stated that if the direct method was required, the risk that qualifies for hedge accounting in a hedge of a net investment in a foreign operation would arise only from exposure between the functional currency of the foreign operation and the presentation currency of the group. This is because each foreign operation is translated only once into the presentation currency. In contrast, the submission stated that if the step-by-step method was required, the hedged risk that qualifies for hedge accounting is the risk between the functional currencies of the foreign operation and the immediate parent entity into which the entity was consolidated. This is because each foreign operation is consolidated directly into its immediate parent entity.

BC8   In response to this, the IFRIC noted that IAS 21 *The Effects of Changes in Foreign Exchange Rates* does not specify a method of consolidation for foreign operations. Furthermore, paragraph BC18 of the Basis for Conclusions on IAS 21 states that the method of translating financial statements will result in the same amounts in the presentation currency regardless of whether the direct method or the step-by-step method is used. The IFRIC therefore concluded that the consolidation mechanism should not determine what risk qualifies for hedge accounting in the hedge of a net investment in a foreign operation.

BC9   However, the IFRIC noted that its conclusion would not resolve the divergence of views on the foreign currency risk that may be designated as a hedge relationship in the hedge of a net investment in a foreign operation. The IFRIC therefore decided that an Interpretation was needed.

BC10   The IFRIC considered whether the risk that qualifies for hedge accounting in a hedge of a net investment in a foreign operation arises from the exposure to the functional currency of the foreign operation in relation to the presentation currency of the group or the functional currency of the parent entity, or both.

BC11   The answer to this question is important when the presentation currency of the group is different from an intermediate or ultimate parent entity's functional currency. If the presentation currency of the group and the functional currency of the parent entity are the same, the exchange rate being hedged would be identified as that between the parent entity's functional currency and the foreign operation's functional currency. No further translation adjustment would be required to prepare the consolidated financial statements. However, when the functional currency of the parent entity is different from the presentation currency of the group, a translation adjustment will be included in other comprehensive income to present the consolidated financial statements in a different presentation currency. The issue, therefore, is how to determine which foreign currency risk may be designated as the hedged risk in accordance with IAS 39 *Financial Instruments: Recognition and Measurement* in the hedge of a net investment in a foreign operation.

BC12   The IFRIC noted the following arguments for permitting hedge accounting for a hedge of the presentation currency:

(a)   If the presentation currency of the group is different from the ultimate parent entity's functional currency, a difference arises on translation that is recognised in other comprehensive income. It is argued that a reason for allowing hedge accounting for a net investment in a foreign operation is to remove from the financial statements the fluctuations resulting from the translation to a presentation currency. If an entity is not allowed to use hedge accounting for the exposure to the presentation currency of the group when it is different from the functional currency of the parent entity, there is likely to be an amount included in other comprehensive income that cannot be offset by hedge accounting.

(b)   IAS 21 requires an entity to reclassify from equity to profit or loss as a reclassification adjustment any foreign currency translation gains and losses included in other comprehensive income on disposal of a foreign operation. An amount in other comprehensive income arising from a different presentation currency is therefore included in the amount reclassified to profit or loss on disposal. The entity should be able to include the amount in a hedging relationship if at some stage it is recognised along with other reclassified translation amounts.

BC13   The IFRIC noted the following arguments for allowing an entity to designate hedging relationships solely on the basis of differences between functional currencies:

(a)   The functional currency of an entity is determined on the basis of the primary economic environment in which that entity operates (ie the environment in which it generates and expends cash). However, the presentation currency is an elective currency that can be changed at any time. To present amounts in a presentation currency is merely a numerical convention necessary for the preparation of financial statements that include a foreign operation. The presentation currency will have no economic effect on the parent entity. Indeed, a parent entity may choose to present financial statements in more than one presentation currency, but can have only one functional currency.

(b)   IAS 39 requires a hedging relationship to be effective in offsetting changes in fair values or cash flows attributable to the hedged risk. A net investment in a foreign operation gives rise to an exposure to changes in exchange rate risk for a parent entity. An economic exchange rate risk arises only from an exposure between two or more functional currencies, not from a presentation currency.

BC14   When comparing the arguments in paragraphs BC12 and BC13, the IFRIC concluded that the presentation currency does not create an exposure to which an entity may apply hedge accounting. The functional currency is determined on the basis of the primary economic environment in which the entity operates. Accordingly, functional currencies create an economic exposure to changes in cash flows or fair values; a presentation currency never will. No commentators on the draft Interpretation disagreed with the IFRIC's conclusion.

Eligible risk (paragraph 12)

BC15   The IFRIC considered which entity's (or entities') functional currency may be used as a reference point for the hedged risk in a net investment hedge. Does the risk arise from the functional currency of:

(a)   the immediate parent entity that holds directly the foreign operation;

(b)   the ultimate parent entity that is preparing its financial statements; or

(c)   the immediate, an intermediate or the ultimate parent entity, depending on what risk that entity decides to hedge, as designated at the inception of the hedge?

BC16   The IFRIC concluded that the risk from the exposure to a different functional currency arises for any parent entity whose functional currency is different from that of the identified foreign operation. The immediate parent entity is exposed to changes in the exchange rate of its directly held foreign operation's functional currency. However, indirectly every entity up the chain of entities to the ultimate parent entity is also exposed to changes in the exchange rate of the foreign operation's functional currency.

BC17   Permitting only the ultimate parent entity to hedge its net investments would ignore the exposures arising on net investments in other parts of the entity. Conversely, permitting only the immediate parent entity to undertake a net investment hedge would imply that an indirect investment does not create a foreign currency exposure for that indirect parent entity.

BC18   The IFRIC concluded that a group must identify which risk (ie the functional currency of which parent entity and of which net investment in a foreign operation) is being hedged. The specified parent entity, the hedged risk and hedging instrument should all be designated and documented at the inception of the hedge relationship. As a result of comments received on the draft Interpretation, the IFRIC decided to emphasise that this documentation should also include the entity's strategy in undertaking the hedge as required by IAS 39.

Amount of hedged item that may be hedged (paragraphs 11 and 13)

BC19   In the draft Interpretation the IFRIC noted that, in financial statements that include a foreign operation, an entity cannot hedge the same risk more than once. This comment was intended to remind entities that IAS 39 does not permit multiple hedges of the same risk. Some respondents asked the IFRIC to clarify the situations in which the IFRIC considered that the same risk was being hedged more than once. In particular, the IFRIC was asked whether the same risk could be hedged by different entities within a group as long as the amount of risk being hedged was not duplicated.

BC20   In its redeliberations, the IFRIC decided to clarify that the carrying amount of the net assets of a foreign operation that may be hedged in the consolidated financial statements of a parent depends on whether any lower level parent of the foreign operation has hedged all or part of the net assets of that foreign operation and that accounting has been maintained in the parent's consolidated financial statements. An intermediate parent entity can hedge some or all of the risk of its net investment in a foreign operation in its own consolidated financial statements. However, such hedges will not qualify for hedge accounting at the ultimate parent entity level if the ultimate parent entity has also hedged the same risk. Alternatively, if the risk has not been hedged by the ultimate parent entity or another intermediate parent entity, the hedge relationship that qualified in the immediate parent entity's consolidated financial statements will also qualify in the ultimate parent entity's consolidated financial statements.

BC21 In its redeliberations, the IFRIC also decided to add guidance to the Interpretation to illustrate the importance of careful designation of the amount of the risk being hedged by each entity in the group.

Hedging instrument

Location of the hedging instrument (paragraph 14) and assessment of hedge effectiveness (paragraph 15)

BC22 The IFRIC discussed where in a group structure a hedging instrument may be held in a hedge of a net investment in a foreign operation. Guidance on the hedge of a net investment in a foreign operation was originally included in IAS 21. This guidance was moved to IAS 39 to ensure that the hedge accounting guidance included in paragraph 88 of IAS 39 would also apply to the hedges of net investments in foreign operations.

BC23 The IFRIC concluded that any entity within the group, other than the foreign operation being hedged, may hold the hedging instrument, as long as the hedging instrument is effective in offsetting the risk arising from the exposure to the functional currency of the foreign operation and the functional currency of the specified parent entity. The functional currency of the entity holding the instrument is irrelevant in determining effectiveness.

BC24 ~~The IFRIC concluded that the foreign operation being hedged could not hold the hedging instrument because that instrument would be part of, and denominated in the same currency as, the net investment it was intended to hedge. In this circumstance, hedge accounting is unnecessary. The foreign exchange differences between the parent's functional currency and both the hedging instrument and the functional currency of the net investment will automatically be included in the group's foreign currency translation reserve as part of the consolidation process. The balance of the discussion in this Basis for Conclusions does not repeat this restriction.~~[*]

BC24A Paragraph 14 of IFRIC 16 originally stated that the hedging instrument could not be held by the foreign operation whose net investment was being hedged. The restriction was included in draft Interpretation D22 (from which IFRIC 16 was developed) and attracted little comment from respondents. As originally explained in paragraph BC24, the IFRIC concluded, as part of its redeliberations, that the restriction was appropriate because the foreign exchange differences between the parent's functional currency and both the hedging instrument and the functional currency of the net investment would automatically be included in the group's foreign currency translation reserve as part of the consolidation process.

---

[*] Paragraph BC24 was deleted and paragraphs BC24A–BC24D and paragraph BC40A added as a consequence of *Improvements to IFRSs* issued in April 2009.

BC24B   After IFRIC 16 was issued, it was brought to the attention of the International Accounting Standards Board that this conclusion was not correct. Without hedge accounting, part of the foreign exchange difference arising from the hedging instrument would be included in consolidated profit or loss. Therefore, in *Improvements to IFRSs* issued in April 2009, the Board amended paragraph 14 of IFRIC 16 to remove the restriction on the entity that can hold hedging instruments and deleted paragraph BC24.

BC24C   Some respondents to the exposure draft *Post-implementation Revisions to IFRIC Interpretations* (ED/2009/1) agreed that a parent entity should be able to use a derivative held by the foreign operation being hedged as a hedge of the net investment in that foreign operation. However, those respondents recommended that the amendment should apply only to derivative instruments held by the foreign operation being hedged. They asserted that a non-derivative financial instrument would be an effective hedge of the net investment only if it were issued by the foreign operation in its own functional currency and this would have no foreign currency impact on the profit or loss of the consolidated group. Consequently, they thought that the rationale described in paragraph BC24B to support the amendment did not apply to non-derivative instruments.

BC24D   In its redeliberations, the Board confirmed its previous decision that the amendment should not be restricted to derivative instruments. The Board noted that paragraphs AG13–AG15 of IFRIC 16 illustrate that a non-derivative instrument held by the foreign operation does not need to be considered to be part of the parent's net investment. As a result, even if it is denominated in the foreign operation's functional currency a non-derivative instrument could still affect the profit or loss of the consolidated group. Consequently, although it could be argued that the amendment was not required to permit non-derivative instruments to be designated as hedges, the Board decided that the proposal should not be changed.

BC25   The IFRIC also concluded that to apply the conclusion in paragraph BC23 when determining the effectiveness of a hedging instrument in the hedge of a net investment, an entity computes the gain or loss on the hedging instrument by reference to the functional currency of the parent entity against whose functional currency the hedged risk is measured, in accordance with the hedge documentation. This is the same regardless of the type of hedging instrument used. This ensures that the effectiveness of the instrument is determined on the basis of changes in fair value or cash flows of the hedging instrument, compared with the changes in the net investment as documented. Thus, any effectiveness test is not dependent on the functional currency of the entity holding the instrument. In other words, the fact that some of the change in the hedging instrument is recognised in profit or loss by one entity within the group and some is recognised in other comprehensive income by another does not affect the assessment of hedge effectiveness.

BC26   In the draft Interpretation the IFRIC noted Question F.2.14 in the guidance on implementing IAS 39, on the location of the hedging instrument, and considered whether that guidance could be applied by analogy to a net investment hedge. The answer to Question F.2.14 concludes:

> IAS 39 does not require that the operating unit that is exposed to the risk being hedged be a party to the hedging instrument.

This was the only basis for the IFRIC's conclusion regarding which entity could hold the hedging instrument provided in the draft Interpretation. Some respondents argued that the Interpretation should not refer to implementation guidance as the sole basis for an important conclusion.

BC27 In its redeliberations, the IFRIC considered both the International Accounting Standards Board's amendment to IAS 21 in 2005 and the objective of hedging a net investment described in IAS 39 in addition to the guidance on implementing IAS 39.

BC28 In 2005 the Board was asked to clarify which entity is the reporting entity in IAS 21 and therefore what instruments could be considered part of a reporting entity's net investment in a foreign operation. In particular, constituents questioned whether a monetary item must be transacted between the foreign operation and the reporting entity to be considered part of the net investment in accordance with IAS 21 paragraph 15, or whether it could be transacted between the foreign operation and any member of the consolidated group.

BC29 In response the Board added IAS 21 paragraph 15A to clarify that 'The entity that has a monetary item receivable from or payable to a foreign operation described in paragraph 15 may be any subsidiary of the group.' The Board explained its reasons for the amendment in paragraph BC25D of the Basis for Conclusions:

> The Board concluded that the accounting treatment in the consolidated financial statements should not be dependent on the currency in which the monetary item is denominated, nor on which entity within the group conducts the transaction with the foreign operation.

In other words, the Board concluded that the relevant reporting entity is the group rather than the individual entity and that the net investment must be viewed from the perspective of the group. It follows, therefore, that the group's net investment in any foreign operation, and its foreign currency exposure, can be determined only at the relevant parent entity level. The IFRIC similarly concluded that the fact that the net investment is held through an intermediate entity does not affect the economic risk.

BC30 Consistently with the Board's conclusion with respect to monetary items that are part of *the net investment*, the IFRIC concluded that monetary items (or derivatives) that are *hedging instruments* in a hedge of a net investment may be held by any entity within the group and the functional currency of the entity holding the monetary items can be different from those of either the parent or the foreign operation. The IFRIC, like the Board, agreed with constituents who noted that a hedging item denominated in a currency that is not the functional currency of the entity holding it does not expose the group to a greater foreign currency exchange difference than arises when the instrument is denominated in that functional currency.

BC31 The IFRIC noted that its conclusions that the hedging instrument can be held by any entity in the group and that the foreign currency is determined at the relevant parent entity level have implications for the designation of hedged risks. As illustrated in paragraph AG5 of the application guidance, these conclusions make it possible for an entity to designate a hedged risk that is not apparent in the currencies of the hedged item or the foreign operation. This possibility is unique to hedges of net investments. Consequently, the IFRIC specified that the conclusions in the Interpretation should not be applied by analogy to other types of hedge accounting.

BC32   The IFRIC also noted that the objective of hedge accounting as set out in IAS 39 is to achieve offsetting changes in the values of the *hedging instrument* and of the *net investment* attributable to the hedged risk. Changes in foreign currency rates affect the value of the entire *net investment* in a foreign operation, not only the portion IAS 21 requires to be recognised in profit or loss in the absence of hedge accounting but also the portion recognised in other comprehensive income in the parent's consolidated financial statements. As noted in paragraph BC25, it is the total change in the hedging instrument as result of a change in the foreign currency rate with respect to the parent entity against whose functional currency the hedged risk is measured that is relevant, not the component of comprehensive income in which it is recognised.

Reclassification from other comprehensive income to profit or loss (paragraphs 16 and 17)

BC33   In response to requests from some respondents for clarification, the IFRIC discussed what amounts from the parent entity's foreign currency translation reserve in respect of both the hedging instrument and the foreign operation should be recognised in profit or loss in the parent entity's consolidated financial statements when the parent disposes of a foreign operation that was hedged. The IFRIC noted that the amounts to be reclassified from equity to profit or loss as reclassification adjustments on the disposition are:

(a)   the cumulative amount of gain or loss on a hedging instrument determined to be an effective hedge that has been reflected in other comprehensive income (IAS 39 paragraph 102), and

(b)   the cumulative amount reflected in the foreign currency translation reserve in respect of that foreign operation (IAS 21 paragraph 48).

BC34   The IFRIC noted that when an entity hedges a net investment in a foreign operation, IAS 39 requires it to identify the cumulative amount included in the group's foreign currency translation reserve as a result of applying hedge accounting, ie the amount determined to be an effective hedge. Therefore, the IFRIC concluded that when a foreign operation that was hedged is disposed of, the amount reclassified to profit or loss from the foreign currency translation reserve in respect of the hedging instrument in the consolidated financial statements of the parent should be the amount that IAS 39 requires to be identified.

Effect of consolidation method

BC35   Some respondents to the draft Interpretation argued that the method of consolidation creates a difference in the amounts included in the ultimate parent entity's foreign currency translation reserve for individual foreign operations that are held through intermediate parents. These respondents noted that this difference may become evident only when the ultimate parent entity disposes of a second tier subsidiary (ie an indirect subsidiary).

BC36   The difference becomes apparent in the determination of the amount of the foreign currency translation reserve that is subsequently reclassified to profit or loss. An ultimate parent entity using the direct method of consolidation would reclassify the cumulative foreign currency translation reserve that arose between its functional currency and that of the foreign operation. An ultimate parent entity using the step-by-step method of consolidation might reclassify the cumulative foreign currency translation reserve reflected in the financial statements of the intermediate parent, ie the amount that arose between the functional currency of the foreign operation and that of the intermediate parent, translated into the functional currency of the ultimate parent.

BC37 In its redeliberations, the IFRIC noted that the use of the step-by-step method of consolidation does create such a difference for an *individual* foreign operation although the aggregate net amount of foreign currency translation reserve for all the foreign operations is the same under either method of consolidation. At the same time, the IFRIC noted that the method of consolidation *should not* create such a difference for an individual foreign operation, on the basis of its conclusion that the economic risk is determined in relation to the ultimate parent's functional currency.

BC38 The IFRIC noted that the amount of foreign currency translation reserve for an individual foreign operation determined by the direct method of consolidation reflects the economic risk between the functional currency of the foreign operation and that of the ultimate parent (if the parent's functional and presentation currencies are the same). However, the IFRIC noted that IAS 21 does not require an entity to use this method or to make adjustments to produce the same result. The IFRIC also noted that a parent entity is not precluded from determining the amount of the foreign currency translation reserve in respect of a foreign operation it has disposed of as if the direct method of consolidation had been used in order to reclassify the appropriate amount to profit or loss. However, it also noted that making such an adjustment on the disposal of a foreign operation is an accounting policy choice and should be followed consistently for the disposal of all net investments.

BC39 The IFRIC noted that this issue arises when the net investment disposed of was not hedged and therefore is not strictly within the scope of the Interpretation. However, because it was a topic of considerable confusion and debate, the IFRIC decided to include a brief example illustrating its conclusions.

Transition (paragraph 19)

BC40 In response to respondents' comments, the IFRIC clarified the Interpretation's transitional requirements. The IFRIC decided that entities should apply the conclusions in this Interpretation to existing hedging relationships on adoption and cease hedge accounting for those that no longer qualify. However, previous hedge accounting is not affected. This is similar to the transition requirements in IFRS 1 *First-time Adoption of International Financial Reporting Standards* paragraph 30,[*] for relationships accounted for as hedges under previous GAAP.

---

[*] Paragraph B6 in the revised version of IFRS 1 issued in November 2008.

Effective date of amended paragraph 14

BC40A The Board amended paragraph 14 in April 2009. In ED/2009/01 the Board proposed that the amendment should be effective for annual periods beginning on or after 1 October 2008, at the same time as IFRIC 16. Respondents to the exposure draft were concerned that permitting application before the amendment was issued might imply that an entity could designate hedge relationships retrospectively, contrary to the requirements of IAS 39. Consequently, the Board decided that an entity should apply the amendment to paragraph 14 made in April 2009 for annual periods beginning on or after 1 July 2009. The Board also decided to permit early application but noted that early application is possible only if the designation, documentation and effectiveness requirements of paragraph 88 of IAS 39 and of IFRIC 16 are satisfied at the application date.

Summary of main changes from the draft Interpretation

BC41 The main changes from the IFRIC's proposals are as follows:

    (a) Paragraph 11 clarifies that the carrying amount of the net assets of a foreign operation that may be hedged in the consolidated financial statements of a parent depends on whether any lower level parent of the foreign operation has hedged all or part of the net assets of that foreign operation and that accounting has been maintained in the parent's consolidated financial statements.

    (b) Paragraph 15 clarifies that the assessment of effectiveness is not affected by whether the hedging instrument is a derivative or a non-derivative instrument or by the method of consolidation.

    (c) Paragraphs 16 and 17 and the illustrative example clarify what amounts should be reclassified from equity to profit or loss as reclassification adjustments on disposal of the foreign operation.

    (d) Paragraph 19 clarifies transitional requirements.

    (e) The appendix of application guidance was added to the Interpretation. Illustrative examples accompanying the draft Interpretation were removed.

    (f) The Basis for Conclusions was changed to set out more clearly the reasons for the IFRIC's conclusions.

Documents published to accompany

IFRIC Interpretation 17

Distributions of Non-cash Assets to Owners

The text of the unaccompanied IFRIC 17 is contained in Part A of this edition. Its effective date is 1 July 2009. This part presents the following accompanying documents:

Illustrative examples

These examples accompany, but are not part of, IFRIC 17.

Scope of the Interpretation (paragraphs 3–8)

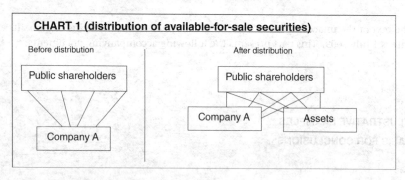

CHART 1 (distribution of available-for-sale securities)

Before distribution — Public shareholders — Company A

After distribution — Public shareholders — Company A — Assets

IE1   Assume Company A is owned by public shareholders. No single shareholder controls Company A and no group of shareholders is bound by a contractual agreement to act together to control Company A jointly. Company A distributes certain assets (eg available-for-sale securities) pro rata to the shareholders. This transaction is within the scope of the Interpretation.

IE2   However, if one of the shareholders (or a group bound by a contractual agreement to act together) controls Company A both before and after the transaction, the entire transaction (including the distributions to the non-controlling shareholders) is not within the scope of the Interpretation. This is because in a pro rata distribution to all owners of the same class of equity instruments, the controlling shareholder (or group of shareholders) will continue to control the non-cash assets after the distribution.

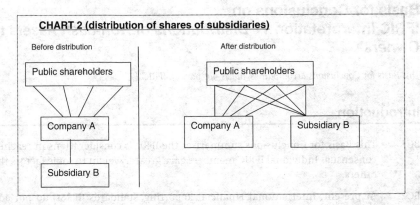

CHART 2 (distribution of shares of subsidiaries)

Before distribution

Public shareholders

Company A

Subsidiary B

After distribution

Public shareholders

Company A

Subsidiary B

IE3　Assume Company A is owned by public shareholders. No single shareholder controls Company A and no group of shareholders is bound by a contractual agreement to act together to control Company A jointly. Company A owns all of the shares of Subsidiary B. Company A distributes all of the shares of Subsidiary B pro rata to its shareholders, thereby losing control of Subsidiary B. This transaction is within the scope of the Interpretation.

IE4　However, if Company A distributes to its shareholders shares of Subsidiary B representing only a non-controlling interest in Subsidiary B and retains control of Subsidiary B, the transaction is not within the scope of the Interpretation. Company A accounts for the distribution in accordance with IAS 27 *Consolidated and Separate Financial Statements* (as amended in 2008). Company A controls Company B both before and after the transaction.

Basis for Conclusions on
IFRIC Interpretation 17 *Distributions of Non-cash Assets to Owners*

This Basis for Conclusions accompanies, but is not part of, IFRIC 17.

Introduction

BC1   This Basis for Conclusions summarises the IFRIC's considerations in reaching its consensus. Individual IFRIC members gave greater weight to some factors than to others.

BC2   At present, International Financial Reporting Standards (IFRSs) do not address how an entity should measure distributions to owners acting in their capacity as owners (commonly referred to as dividends). The IFRIC was told that there was significant diversity in practice in how entities measured distributions of non-cash assets.

BC3   The IFRIC published draft Interpretation D23 *Distributions of Non-cash Assets to Owners* for public comment in January 2008 and received 56 comment letters in response to its proposals.

Scope (paragraphs 3–8)

Should the Interpretation address all transactions between an entity and its owners?

BC4   The IFRIC noted that an asset distribution by an entity to its owners is an example of a transaction between an entity and its owners. Transactions between an entity and its owners can generally be categorised into the following three types:

(a)   exchange transactions between an entity and its owners.

(b)   non-reciprocal transfers of assets by owners of an entity to the entity. Such transfers are commonly referred to as contributions from owners.

(c)   non-reciprocal transfers of assets by an entity to its owners. Such transfers are commonly referred to as distributions to owners.

BC5   The IFRIC concluded that the Interpretation should not address exchange transactions between an entity and its owners because that would probably result in addressing all related party transactions. In the IFRIC's view, such a scope was too broad for an Interpretation. Instead, the IFRIC concluded that the Interpretation should focus on distributions of assets by an entity to its owners acting in their capacity as owners.

BC6   In addition, the IFRIC decided that the Interpretation should not address distributions in which owners of the same class of equity instrument are not all treated equally. This is because, in the IFRIC's view, such distributions might imply that at least some of the owners receiving the distributions indeed gave up something to the entity and/or other owners. In other words, such distributions might be more in the nature of exchange transactions.

Should the Interpretation address all types of asset distributions?

BC7   The IFRIC was told that there was significant diversity in the measurement of the following types of non-reciprocal distributions of assets by an entity to its owners acting in their capacity as owners:

    (a)   distributions of non-cash assets (eg items of property, plant and equipment, businesses as defined in IFRS 3, ownership interests in another entity or disposal groups as defined in IFRS 5 *Non-current Assets Held for Sale and Discontinued Operations*) to its owners; and

    (b)   distributions that give owners a choice of receiving either non-cash assets or a cash alternative.

BC8   The IFRIC noted that all distributions have the same purpose, ie to distribute assets to an entity's owners. It therefore concluded that the Interpretation should address the measurement of all types of asset distributions with one exception set out in paragraph 5 of the Interpretation.

A scope exclusion: a distribution of an asset that is ultimately controlled by the same party or parties before and after the distribution

BC9   In the Interpretation, the IFRIC considered whether it should address how an entity should measure a distribution of an asset (eg an ownership interest in a subsidiary) that is ultimately controlled by the same party or parties before and after the distribution. In many instances, such a distribution is for the purpose of group restructuring (eg separating two different businesses into two different subgroups). After the distribution, the asset is still controlled by the same party or parties.

BC10   In addition, the IFRIC noted that dealing with the accounting for a distribution of an asset within a group would require consideration of how a transfer of any asset within a group should be accounted for in the separate or individual financial statements of group entities.

BC11   For the reasons described in paragraphs BC9 and BC10, the IFRIC concluded that the Interpretation should not deal with a distribution of an asset that is ultimately controlled by the same party or parties before and after the distribution.

BC12   In response to comments received on the draft Interpretation, the IFRIC redeliberated whether the scope of the Interpretation should be expanded to include a distribution of an asset that is ultimately controlled by the same party or parties before and after the distribution. The IFRIC decided not to expand the scope of the Interpretation in the light of the Board's decision to add a project to its agenda to address common control transactions.

BC13   The IFRIC noted that many commentators believed that most distributions of assets to an entity's owners would be excluded from the scope of the Interpretation by paragraph 5. The IFRIC did not agree with this conclusion. It noted that in paragraph B2 of IFRS 3 *Business Combinations* (as revised in 2008), the Board concluded that a group of individuals would be regarded as controlling an entity only when, as a result of contractual arrangements, they collectively have the power to govern its financial and operating policies so as to obtain benefits from its activities. In addition, in *Cost of an Investment in a Subsidiary, Jointly Controlled Entity or Associate* in May 2008, the Board clarified in the amendments to IAS 27 *Consolidated and Separate Financial Statements* that the distribution of equity interests in a new parent to shareholders in exchange for their interests in the existing parent was not a common control transaction.

BC14 Consequently, the IFRIC decided that the Interpretation should clarify that unless there is a contractual arrangement among shareholders to control the entity making the distribution, transactions in which the shares or the businesses of group entities are distributed to shareholders outside the group (commonly referred to as a spin-off, split-off or demerger) are not transactions between entities or businesses under common control. Therefore they are within the scope of the Interpretation.

BC15 Some commentators on D23 were concerned about situations in which an entity distributes some but not all of its ownership interests in a subsidiary and retains control. They believed that the proposed accounting for the distribution of ownership interests representing a non-controlling interest in accordance with D23 was inconsistent with the requirements of IAS 27 (as amended in 2008). That IFRS requires changes in a parent's ownership interest in a subsidiary that do not result in a loss of control to be accounted for as equity transactions. The IFRIC had not intended the Interpretation to apply to such transactions so did not believe it conflicted with the requirements of IAS 27. As a result of the concerns expressed, the IFRIC amended the Interpretation to make this clear.

BC16 Some commentators on D23 were also concerned about situations in which a subsidiary with a non-controlling interest distributes assets to both the parent and the non-controlling interests. They questioned why only the distribution to the controlling entity is excluded from the scope of the Interpretation. The IFRIC noted that when the parent controls the subsidiary before and after the transaction, the entire transaction (including the distribution to the non-controlling interest) is not within the scope of the Interpretation and is accounted for in accordance with IAS 27.

BC17 Distributions to owners may involve significant portions of an entity's operations. In such circumstances, sometimes referred to as split-off, some commentators on D23 were concerned that it would be difficult to determine which of the surviving entities had made the distribution. They thought that it might be possible for each surviving entity to recognise the distribution of the other. The IFRIC agreed with commentators that identifying the distributing entity might require judgement in some circumstances. However, the IFRIC concluded that the distribution could be recognised in only one entity's financial statements.

When to recognise a dividend payable (paragraph 10) and amendment to IAS 10

BC18 D23 did not address when an entity should recognise a liability for a dividend payable and some respondents asked the IFRIC to clarify this issue. The IFRIC noted that in IAS 10 *Events after the Reporting Period* paragraph 13 states that 'If dividends are declared (ie the dividends are appropriately authorised and no longer at the discretion of the entity) after the reporting period but before the financial statements are authorised for issue, the dividends are not recognised as a liability at the end of the reporting period because no obligation exists at that time.'

BC19   Some commentators stated that in many jurisdictions a commonly held view is that the entity has discretion until the shareholders approve the dividend. Therefore, constituents holding this view believe a conflict exists between 'declared' and the explanatory phrase in the brackets in IAS 10 paragraph 13. This is especially true when the sentence is interpreted as 'declared by *management but before the shareholders' approval*'. The IFRIC concluded that the point at which a dividend is appropriately authorised and no longer at the discretion of the entity will vary by jurisdiction.

BC20   Therefore, as a consequence of this Interpretation the IFRIC decided to recommend that the Board amend IAS 10 to remove the perceived conflict in paragraph 13. The IFRIC also noted that the principle on when to recognise a dividend was in the wrong place within the IASB's authoritative documents. The Board agreed with the IFRIC's conclusions and amended IAS 10 as part of its approval of the Interpretation. The Board confirmed that this Interpretation had not changed the principle on when to recognise a dividend payable; however, the principle was moved from IAS 10 into the Interpretation and clarified but without changing the principle.

How should an entity measure a dividend payable? (paragraphs 11–13)

BC21   IFRSs do not provide guidance on how an entity should measure distributions to owners. However, the IFRIC noted that a number of IFRSs address how a liability should be measured. Although IFRSs do not specifically address how an entity should measure a dividend payable, the IFRIC decided that it could identify potentially relevant IFRSs and apply their principles to determine the appropriate measurement basis.

Which IFRSs are relevant to the measurement of a dividend payable?

BC22   The IFRIC considered all IFRSs that prescribe the accounting for a liability. Of those, the IFRIC concluded that IAS 37 *Provisions, Contingent Assets and Contingent Liabilities* and IAS 39 *Financial Instruments: Recognition and Measurement* [*] were the most likely to be relevant. The IFRIC concluded that other IFRSs were not applicable because most of them addressed only liabilities arising from exchange transactions and some of them were clearly not relevant (eg IAS 12 *Income Taxes*). As mentioned above, the Interpretation addresses only non-reciprocal distributions of assets by an entity to its owners.

---

[*]   In November 2009 the IASB amended the requirements of IAS 39 relating to classification and measurement of assets within the scope of IAS 39 and relocated them to IFRS 9 *Financial Instruments*. IFRS 9 applies to all assets within the scope of IAS 39.

BC23 Given that all types of distributions have the purpose of distributing assets to owners, the IFRIC decided that all dividends payable should be measured the same way, regardless of the types of assets to be distributed. This also ensures that all dividends payable are measured consistently.

BC24 Some believed that IAS 39 was the appropriate IFRS to be used to measure dividends payable. They believed that, once an entity declared a distribution to its owners, it had a contractual obligation to distribute the assets to its owners. However, IAS 39 would not cover dividends payable if they were considered to be non-contractual obligations. In addition, IAS 39 covers some but not all obligations that require an entity to deliver non-cash assets to another entity. It does not cover a liability to distribute non-financial assets to owners. The IFRIC therefore concluded that it was not appropriate to conclude that all dividends payable should be within the scope of IAS 39.

BC25 The IFRIC then considered IAS 37, which is generally applied in practice to determine the accounting for liabilities other than those arising from executory contracts and those addressed by other IFRSs. IAS 37 requires an entity to measure a liability on the basis of the best estimate of the expenditure required to settle the present obligation at the end of the reporting period. Consequently, in D23 the IFRIC decided that it was appropriate to apply the principles in IAS 37 to all dividends payable (regardless of the types of assets to be distributed). The IFRIC decided that to apply IAS 37 to measure a liability for an obligation to distribute non-cash assets to owners, an entity should consider the fair value of the assets to be distributed. The fair value of the assets to be distributed is clearly relevant no matter which approach in IAS 37 is taken to determine the best estimate of the expenditure required to settle the liability.

BC26 However, in response to comments received on D23, the IFRIC reconsidered whether the Interpretation should specify that all dividends payable should be measured in accordance with IAS 37. The IFRIC noted that many respondents were concerned that D23 might imply that the measurement attribute in IAS 37 should always be interpreted to be fair value. This was not the intention of D23 as that question is part of the Board's project to amend IAS 37. In addition, many respondents were not certain whether measuring the dividend payable 'by reference to' the fair value of the assets to be distributed required measurement at their fair value or at some other amount.

BC27 Therefore, the IFRIC decided to modify the proposal in D23 to require the dividend payable to be measured at the fair value of the assets to be distributed, without linking to any individual standard its conclusion that fair value is the most relevant measurement attribute. The IFRIC also noted that if the assets being distributed constituted a business, its fair value could be different from the simple sum of the fair value of the component assets and liabilities (ie it includes the value of goodwill or the identified intangible assets).

Should any exception be made to the principle of measuring a dividend payable at the fair value of the assets to be distributed?

BC28   Some are concerned that the fair value of the assets to be distributed might not be reliably measurable in all cases. They believe that exceptions should be made in the following circumstances:

   (a)   An entity distributes an ownership interest of another entity that is not traded in an active market and the fair value of the ownership interest cannot be measured reliably. The IFRIC noted that IAS 39 does not permit investments in equity instruments that do not have a quoted market price in an active market and whose fair value cannot be measured reliably to be measured at fair value.*

   (b)   An entity distributes an intangible asset that is not traded in an active market and therefore would not be permitted to be carried at a revalued amount in accordance with IAS 38 *Intangible Assets*.

BC29   The IFRIC noted that in accordance with IAS 39 paragraphs AG80 and AG81,† the fair value of equity instruments that do not have a quoted price in an active market is reliably measurable if:

   (a)   the variability in the range of reasonable fair value estimates is not significant for that instrument, or

   (b)   the probabilities of the various estimates within the range can be reasonably assessed and used in estimating fair value.

BC30   The IFRIC noted that, when the management of an entity recommends a distribution of a non-cash asset to its owners, one or both of the conditions for determining a reliable measure of the fair value of equity instruments that do not have a quoted price in an active market is likely to be satisfied. Management would be expected to know the fair value of the asset because management has to ensure that all owners of the entity are informed of the value of the distribution. For this reason, it would be difficult to argue that the fair value of the assets to be distributed cannot be determined reliably.

BC31   In addition, the IFRIC recognised that in some cases the fair value of an asset must be estimated. As mentioned in paragraph 86 of the *Framework for the Preparation and Presentation of Financial Statements*, the use of reasonable estimates is an essential part of the preparation of financial statements and does not undermine their reliability.

---

*   IFRS 9 *Financial Instruments*, issued in November 2009, requires all investments in equity instruments to be measured at fair value.

†   IFRS 9 *Financial Instruments*, issued in November 2009, amended paragraphs AG80 and AG81 of IAS 39 so that they apply only to derivatives on unquoted equity instruments.

BC32   The IFRIC noted that a reason why IAS 38 and IAS 39[*] require some assets to be measured using a historical cost basis is cost-benefit considerations. The cost of determining the fair value of an asset not traded in an active market at the end of each reporting period could outweigh the benefits. However, because an entity would be required to determine the fair value of the assets to be distributed only once at the time of distribution, the IFRIC concluded that the benefit (ie informing users of the financial statements of the value of the assets distributed) outweighs the cost of determining the fair value of the assets.

BC33   Furthermore, the IFRIC noted that dividend income, regardless of whether it is in the form of cash or non-cash assets, is within the scope of IAS 18 *Revenue* and is required to be measured at the fair value of the consideration received. Although the Interpretation does not address the accounting by the recipient of the non-cash distribution, the IFRIC concluded that the Interpretation did not impose a more onerous requirement on the entity that makes the distribution than IFRSs have already imposed on the recipient of the distribution.

BC34   For the reasons described in paragraphs BC28–BC33, the IFRIC concluded that no exceptions should be made to the requirement that the fair value of the asset to be distributed should be used in measuring a dividend payable.

Whether an entity should remeasure the dividend payable (paragraph 13)

BC35   The IFRIC noted that paragraph 59 of IAS 37 requires an entity to review the carrying amount of a liability at the end of each reporting period and to adjust the carrying amount to reflect the current best estimate of the liability. Other IFRSs such as IAS 19 *Employee Benefits* similarly require liabilities that are based on estimates to be adjusted each reporting period. The IFRIC therefore decided that the entity should review and adjust the carrying amount of the dividend payable to reflect its current best estimate of the fair value of the assets to be distributed at the end of each reporting period and at the date of settlement.

BC36   The IFRIC concluded that, because any adjustments to the best estimate of the dividend payable reflect changes in the estimated value of the distribution, they should be recognised as adjustments to the amount of the distribution. In accordance with IAS 1 *Presentation of Financial Statements* (as revised in 2007), distributions to owners are required to be recognised directly in the statement of changes in equity. Similarly, adjustments to the amount of the distribution are also recognised directly in the statement of changes in equity.

BC37   Some commentators argued that the changes in the estimated value of the distribution should be recognised in profit or loss because changes in liabilities meet the definition of income or expenses in the *Framework*. However, the IFRIC decided that the gain or loss on the assets to be distributed should be recognised in profit or loss when the dividend payable is settled. This is consistent with other IFRSs (IAS 16, IAS 38, IAS 39) that require an entity to recognise in profit or loss any gain or loss arising from derecognition of an asset. The IFRIC concluded that the changes in the dividend payable before settlement related to changes in the estimate of the distribution and should be accounted for in equity (ie adjustments to the amount of the distribution) until settlement of the dividend payable.

---

[*]   IFRS 9 *Financial Instruments*, issued in November 2009, eliminated the requirement in IAS 39 for some assets to be measured using a historical cost basis.

When the entity settles the dividend payable, how should it account for any difference between the carrying amount of the assets distributed and the carrying amount of the dividend payable? (paragraph 14)

BC38   When an entity distributes the assets to its owners, it derecognises both the assets distributed and the dividend payable.

BC39   The IFRIC noted that, at the time of settlement, the carrying amount of the assets distributed would not normally be greater than the carrying amount of the dividend payable because of the recognition of impairment losses required by other applicable standards. For example, paragraph 59 of IAS 36 *Impairment of Assets* requires an entity to recognise an impairment loss in profit or loss when the recoverable amount of an asset is less than its carrying amount. The recoverable amount of an asset is the higher of its fair value less costs to sell and its value in use in accordance with paragraph 6 of IAS 36. When an entity has an obligation to distribute the asset to its owners in the near future, it would not seem appropriate to measure an impairment loss using the asset's value in use. Furthermore, IFRS 5 requires an entity to measure an asset held for sale at the lower of its carrying amount and its fair value less costs to sell. Consequently, the IFRIC concluded that when an entity derecognises the dividend payable and the asset distributed, any difference will always be a credit balance (referred to below as the credit balance).

BC40   In determining how the credit balance should be accounted for, the IFRIC first considered whether it should be recognised as an owner change in equity.

BC41   The IFRIC acknowledged that an asset distribution was a transaction between an entity and its owners. The IFRIC also observed that distributions to owners are recognised as owner changes in equity in accordance with IAS 1 (as revised in 2007). However, the IFRIC noted that the credit balance did not arise from the distribution transaction. Rather, it represented the cumulative unrecognised gain associated with the asset. It reflects the performance of the entity during the period the asset was held until it was distributed.

BC42   Some might argue that, since an asset distribution does not result in the owners of an entity losing the future economic benefits of the asset, the credit balance should be recognised directly in equity. This view would be based upon the proprietary perspective in which the reporting entity does not have substance of its own separate from that of its owners. However, the IFRIC noted that the *Framework* requires an entity to consider the effect of a transaction from the perspective of the entity for which the financial statements are prepared. Under the entity perspective, the reporting entity has substance of its own, separate from that of its owners. In addition, when there is more than one class of equity instruments, the argument that all owners of an entity have effectively the same interest in the asset would not be valid.

BC43   For the reasons described in paragraphs BC41 and BC42, the IFRIC concluded that the credit balance should not be recognised as an owner change in equity.

BC44   The IFRIC noted that, as explained in the Basis for Conclusions on IAS 1, the Board explicitly prohibited any income or expenses (ie non-owner changes in equity) from being recognised directly in the statement of changes in equity. Any such income or expenses must be recognised as items of comprehensive income first.

BC45   The statement of comprehensive income in accordance with IAS 1 includes two components: items of profit or loss, and items of other comprehensive income. The IFRIC therefore discussed whether the credit balance should be recognised in profit or loss or in other comprehensive income.

BC46   IAS 1 does not provide criteria for when an item should be recognised in profit or loss. However, paragraph 88 of IAS 1 states: 'An entity shall recognise all items of income and expense in a period in profit or loss unless an IFRS requires or permits otherwise.'

BC47   The IFRIC considered the circumstances in which IFRSs require items of income and expense to be recognised as items of other comprehensive income, mainly as follows:

     (a)   some actuarial gains or losses arising from remeasuring defined benefit liabilities provided that specific criteria set out in IAS 19 are met.

     (b)   a revaluation surplus arising from revaluation of an item of property, plant and equipment in accordance with IAS 16 or revaluation of an intangible asset in accordance with IAS 38.

     (c)   an exchange difference arising from the translation of the results and financial positions of an entity from its functional currency into a presentation currency in accordance with IAS 21 *The Effects of Changes in Foreign Exchange Rates*.

     (d)   an exchange difference arising from the translation of the results and financial position of a foreign operation into a presentation currency of a reporting entity for consolidation purposes in accordance with IAS 21.

     (e)   a change in the fair value of an available-for-sale[*] investment in accordance with IAS 39.

     (f)   a change in the fair value of a hedging instrument qualifying for cash flow hedge accounting in accordance with IAS 39.

BC48   The IFRIC concluded that the requirement in IAS 1 prevents any of these items from being applied by analogy to the credit balance. In addition, the IFRIC noted that, with the exception of the items described in paragraph BC47(a)–(c), the applicable IFRSs require the items of income and expenses listed in paragraph BC47 to be reclassified to profit or loss when the related assets or liabilities are derecognised. Those items of income and expenses are recognised as items of other comprehensive income when incurred, deferred in equity until the related assets are disposed of (or the related liabilities are settled), and reclassified to profit or loss at that time.

---

[*]   IFRS 9 *Financial Instruments*, issued in November 2009, eliminated the category of available-for-sale financial assets.

BC49 The IFRIC noted that, when the dividend payable is settled, the asset distributed is also derecognised. Therefore, given the existing requirements in IFRSs, even if the credit balance were recognised as an item of other comprehensive income, it would have to be reclassified to profit or loss immediately. As a result, the credit balance would appear three times in the statement of comprehensive income—once recognised as an item of other comprehensive income, once reclassified out of other comprehensive income to profit or loss and once recognised as an item of profit or loss as a result of the reclassification. The IFRIC concluded that such a presentation does not faithfully reflect what has occurred. In addition, users of financial statements were likely to be confused by such a presentation.

BC50 Moreover, when an entity distributes its assets to its owners, it loses the future economic benefit associated with the assets distributed and derecognises those assets. Such a consequence is, in general, similar to that of a disposal of an asset. IFRSs (eg IAS 16, IAS 38, IAS 39 and IFRS 5) require an entity to recognise in profit or loss any gain or loss arising from the derecognition of an asset. IFRSs also require such a gain or loss to be recognised when the asset is derecognised. As mentioned in paragraph BC42, the *Framework* requires an entity to consider the effect of a transaction from the perspective of an entity for which the financial statements are prepared. For these reasons, the IFRIC concluded that the credit balance and gains or losses on derecognition of an asset should be accounted for in the same way.

BC51 Furthermore, paragraph 92 of the *Framework* states: 'Income is recognised in the income statement when an increase in future economic benefits related to an increase in an asset or *a decrease of a liability* has arisen that can be measured reliably' (emphasis added). At the time of the settlement of a dividend payable, there is clearly a decrease in a liability. Therefore, the credit balance should be recognised in profit or loss in accordance with paragraph 92 of the *Framework*. Some might argue that the entity does not receive any additional economic benefits when it distributes the assets to its owners. As mentioned in paragraph BC41, the credit balance does not represent any additional economic benefits to the entity. Instead, it represents the unrecognised economic benefits that the entity obtained while it held the assets.

BC52 The IFRIC also noted that paragraph 55 of the *Framework* states: 'The future economic benefits embodied in an asset may flow to the entity in a number of ways. For example, an asset may be: (a) used singly or in combination with other assets in the production of goods or services to be sold by the entity; (b) exchanged for other assets; (c) used to settle a liability; or (d) *distributed to the owners of the entity* [emphasis added].'

BC53 In the light of these requirements, in D23 the IFRIC concluded that the credit balance should be recognised in profit or loss. This treatment would give rise to the same accounting results regardless of whether an entity distributes non-cash assets to its owners, or sells the non-cash assets first and distributes the cash received to its owners. Most commentators on D23 supported the IFRIC's conclusion and its basis.

BC54   Some IFRIC members believed that it would be more appropriate to treat the distribution as a single transaction with owners and therefore recognise the credit balance directly in equity. This alternative view was included in D23 and comments were specifically invited. However, this view was not supported by commentators. To be recognised directly in equity, the credit balance must be considered an owner change in equity in accordance with IAS 1. The IFRIC decided that the credit balance does not arise from the distribution transaction. Rather, it represents the increase in value of the assets. The increase in the value of the asset does not meet the definition of an owner change in equity in accordance with IAS 1. Rather, it meets the definition of income and should be recognised in profit and loss.

BC55   The IFRIC recognised respondents' concerns about the potential 'accounting mismatch' in equity resulting from measuring the assets to be distributed at carrying amount and measuring the dividend payable at fair value. Consequently, the IFRIC considered whether it should recommend that the Board amend IFRS 5 to require the assets to be distributed to be measured at fair value.

BC56   In general, IFRSs permit remeasurement of assets only as the result of a transaction or an impairment. The exceptions are situations in which the IFRSs prescribe current measures on an ongoing basis as in IASs 39 and 41 *Agriculture*, or permit them as accounting policy choices as in IASs 16, 38 and 40 *Investment Property*. As a result of its redeliberations, the IFRIC concluded that there was no support in IFRSs for requiring a remeasurement of the assets because of a decision to distribute them. The IFRIC noted that the mismatch concerned arises only with respect to assets that are not carried at fair value already. The IFRIC also noted that the accounting mismatch is the inevitable consequence of IFRSs using different measurement attributes at different times with different triggers for the remeasurement of different assets and liabilities.

BC57   If a business is to be distributed, the fair value means the fair value of the business to be distributed. Therefore, it includes goodwill and intangible assets. However, internally generated goodwill is not permitted to be recognised as an asset (paragraph 48 of IAS 38). Internally generated brands, mastheads, publishing titles, customer lists and items similar in substance are not permitted to be recognised as intangible assets (paragraph 63 of IAS 38). In accordance with IAS 38, the carrying amounts of internally generated intangible assets are generally restricted to the sum of expenditure incurred by an entity. Consequently, a requirement to remeasure an asset that is a business would contradict the relevant requirements in IAS 38.

BC58   Furthermore, in addition to the lack of consistency with other IFRSs, changing IFRS 5 this way (ie to require an asset held for distribution to owners to be remeasured at fair value) would create internal inconsistency within IFRS 5. There would be no reasonable rationale to explain why IFRS 5 could require assets that are to be sold to be carried at the lower of fair value less costs to sell and carrying value but assets to be distributed to owners to be carried at fair value. The IFRIC also noted that this 'mismatch' would arise only in the normally short period between when the dividend payable is recognised and when it is settled. The length of this period would often be within the control of management. Therefore, the IFRIC decided not to recommend that the Board amend IFRS 5 to require assets that are to be distributed to be measured at fair value.

Amendment to IFRS 5

BC59   IFRS 5 requires an entity to classify a non-current asset (or disposal group) as held for sale if its carrying amount will be recovered principally through a sale transaction rather than through continuing use. IFRS 5 also sets out presentation and disclosure requirements for a discontinued operation.

BC60   When an entity has an obligation to distribute assets to its owners, the carrying amount of the assets will no longer be recovered principally through continuing use. The IFRIC decided that the information required by IFRS 5 is important to users of financial statements regardless of the form of a transaction. Therefore, the IFRIC concluded that the requirements in IFRS 5 applicable to non-current assets (or disposal groups) classified as held for sale and to discontinued operations should also be applied to assets (or disposal groups) held for distribution to owners.

BC61   However, the IFRIC concluded that requiring an entity to apply IFRS 5 to non-current assets (disposal groups) held for distribution to owners would require amendments to IFRS 5. This is because, in the IFRIC's view, IFRS 5 at present applies only to non-current assets (disposal groups) held for sale.

BC62   The Board discussed the IFRIC's proposal at its meeting in December 2007. The Board agreed with the IFRIC's conclusion that IFRS 5 should be amended to apply to non-current assets held for distribution to owners as well as to assets held for sale. However, the Board noted that IFRS 5 requires an entity to classify a non-current asset as held for sale when the sale is highly probable and the entity is *committed* to a plan to sell (emphasis added). Consequently, the Board directed the IFRIC to invite comments on the following questions:

(a)   Should an entity apply IFRS 5 when it is committed to make a distribution or when it has an obligation to distribute the assets concerned?

(b)   Is there a difference between those dates?

(c)   If respondents believe that there is a difference between the dates and that an entity should apply IFRS 5 at the commitment date, what is the difference? What indicators should be included in IFRS 5 to help an entity to determine that date?

BC63   On the basis of the comments received, the IFRIC noted that, in many jurisdictions, shareholders' approval is required to make a distribution. Therefore, in such jurisdictions there could be a difference between the commitment date (ie the date when management is committed to the dividend) and the obligation date (ie the date when the dividend is approved by the shareholders). On the other hand, some commentators think that, when a distribution requires shareholders' approval, the entity cannot be committed until that approval is obtained: in that case, there would be no difference between two dates.

BC64   The IFRIC concluded that IFRS 5 should be applied at the commitment date at which time the assets must be available for immediate distribution in their present condition and the distribution must be *highly probable*. For the distribution to be highly probable, it should meet essentially the same conditions required for assets held for sale. Further, the IFRIC concluded that the probability of shareholders' approval (if required in the jurisdiction) should be considered as part of the assessment of whether the distribution is highly probable. The IFRIC noted that shareholder approval is also required for the sale of assets in some jurisdictions and concluded that similar consideration of the probability of such approval should be required for assets held for sale.

BC65 The Board agreed with the IFRIC's conclusions and amended IFRS 5 as part of its approval of the Interpretation.

Summary of main changes from the draft Interpretation

BC66 The main changes from the IFRIC's proposals in D23 are as follows:

(a) Paragraphs 3–8 were modified to clarify the scope of the Interpretation.

(b) Paragraph 10 clarifies when to recognise a dividend payable.

(c) Paragraphs 11–13 were modified to require the dividend payable to be measured at the fair value of the assets to be distributed without linking the IFRIC's conclusion that fair value is the most relevant measurement attribute to any individual standard.

(d) Illustrative examples were expanded to set out clearly the scope of the Interpretation.

(e) The Interpretation includes the amendments to IFRS 5 and IAS 10.

(f) The Basis for Conclusions was changed to set out more clearly the reasons for the IFRIC's conclusions.

Documents published to accompany

IFRIC Interpretation 18

Transfers of Assets from Customers

The text of the unaccompanied IFRIC 18 is contained in Part A of this edition. Its effective date is 1 July 2009. This part presents the following accompanying documents:

Illustrative examples

These examples accompany, but are not part of, IFRIC 18.

Example 1

IE1   A real estate company is building a residential development in an area that is not connected to the electricity network. In order to have access to the electricity network, the real estate company is required to construct an electricity substation that is then transferred to the network company responsible for the transmission of electricity. It is assumed in this example that the network company concludes that the transferred substation meets the definition of an asset. The network company then uses the substation to connect each house of the residential development to its electricity network. In this case, it is the homeowners that will eventually use the network to access the supply of electricity, although they did not initially transfer the substation. By regulation, the network company has an obligation to provide ongoing access to the network to all users of the network at the same price, regardless of whether they transferred an asset. Therefore, users of the network that transfer an asset to the network company pay the same price for the use of the network as those that do not. Users of the network can choose to purchase their electricity from distributors other than the network company but must use the company's network to access the supply of electricity.

IE2   Alternatively, the network company could have constructed the substation and received a transfer of an amount of cash from the real estate company that had to be used only for the construction of the substation. The amount of cash transferred would not necessarily equal the entire cost of the substation. It is assumed that the substation remains an asset of the network company.

IE3   In this example, the Interpretation applies to the network company that receives the electricity substation from the real estate company. The network company recognises the substation as an item of property, plant and equipment and measures its cost on initial recognition at its fair value (or at its construction cost in the circumstances described in paragraph IE2) in accordance with IAS 16 *Property, Plant and Equipment*. The fact that users of the network that transfer an asset to the network company pay the same price for the use of the electricity network as those that do not indicates that the obligation to provide ongoing access to the network is not a separately identifiable service of the transaction. Rather, connecting the house to the network is the only service to be delivered in exchange for the substation. Therefore, the network company should recognise revenue from the exchange transaction at the fair value of the substation (or at the amount of the cash received from the real estate company in the circumstances described in paragraph IE2) when the houses are connected to the network in accordance with in paragraph 20 of IAS 18 *Revenue*.

Example 2

IE4   A house builder constructs a house on a redeveloped site in a major city. As part of constructing the house, the house builder installs a pipe from the house to the water main in front of the house. Because the pipe is on the house's land, the owner of the house can restrict access to the pipe. The owner is also responsible for the maintenance of the pipe. In this example, the facts indicate that the definition of an asset is not met for the water company.

IE5   Alternatively, a house builder constructs multiple houses and installs a pipe on the commonly owned or public land to connect the houses to the water main. The house builder transfers ownership of the pipe to the water company that will be responsible for its maintenance. In this example, the facts indicate that the water company controls the pipe and should recognise it.

Example 3

IE6   An entity enters into an agreement with a customer involving the outsourcing of the customer's information technology (IT) functions. As part of the agreement, the customer transfers ownership of its existing IT equipment to the entity. Initially, the entity must use the equipment to provide the service required by the outsourcing agreement. The entity is responsible for maintaining the equipment and for replacing it when the entity decides to do so. The useful life of the equipment is estimated to be three years. The outsourcing agreement requires service to be provided for ten years for a fixed price that is lower than the price the entity would have charged if the IT equipment had not been transferred.

IE7   In this example, the facts indicate that the IT equipment is an asset of the entity. Therefore, the entity should recognise the equipment and measure its cost on initial recognition at its fair value in accordance with paragraph 24 of IAS 16. The fact that the price charged for the service to be provided under the outsourcing agreement is lower than the price the entity would charge without the transfer of the IT equipment indicates that this service is a separately identifiable service included in the agreement. The facts also indicate that it is the only service to be provided in exchange for the transfer of the IT equipment. Therefore, the entity should recognise revenue arising from the exchange transaction when the service is performed, ie over the ten-year term of the outsourcing agreement.

IE8   Alternatively, assume that after the first three years, the price the entity charges under the outsourcing agreement increases to reflect the fact that it will then be replacing the equipment the customer transferred.

IE9   In this case, the reduced price for the services provided under the outsourcing agreement reflects the useful life of the transferred equipment. For this reason, the entity should recognise revenue from the exchange transaction over the first three years of the agreement.

Basis for Conclusions on
IFRIC Interpretation 18 *Transfers of Assets from Customers*

This Basis for Conclusions accompanies, but is not part of, IFRIC 18.

Introduction

BC1   This Basis for Conclusions summarises the IFRIC's considerations in reaching its consensus. Individual IFRIC members gave greater weight to some factors than to others.

BC2   The IFRIC released draft Interpretation D24 *Customer Contributions* for public comment in January 2008 and received 59 comment letters in response.

Background

BC3   The IFRIC received a request to issue guidance on the accounting for transfers of items of property, plant and equipment by entities that receive such transfers from their customers. Divergence had arisen in practice with some entities recognising the transferred item at fair value and others recognising it at a cost of nil. Among those that recognised the item at fair value, some recognised the resulting credit as revenue immediately, while others recognised it over some longer service period. The IFRIC decided to develop an Interpretation in response to that divergence in practice.

Scope

BC4   This Interpretation applies to the accounting for transfers of items of property, plant and equipment by entities that receive such transfers from their customers. In developing the Interpretation, the IFRIC decided that it would not address how the customers should account for the transfers because the main issue is how the entity receiving the asset should recognise revenue.

BC5   Some respondents questioned whether transfers of assets other than those within the scope of this Interpretation, ie transfers of intangible assets from customers, would lead to the same answer. In its redeliberations, the IFRIC decided not to expand the scope to assets other than those already considered in D24 but did not prohibit application by analogy in accordance with IAS 8 *Accounting Policies, Changes in Accounting Estimates and Errors*.

BC6   In its redeliberations, the IFRIC clarified in paragraph 3 that, for convenience, this Interpretation refers to the entity transferring the item of property, plant and equipment as the customer even though that entity may not be the entity that will eventually have ongoing access to the supply of goods or services and will be the recipient of those goods or services. The IFRIC also added an example to illustrate such a situation.

BC7   Some respondents commented that, in practice, customers often transfer cash instead of transferring an item of property, plant and equipment. The IFRIC reaffirmed its view that transfers of cash should be within the scope of the Interpretation (see also paragraph BC24).

BC8   Many respondents were concerned that D24 could create unintended overlaps with existing IFRSs such as IFRIC 12 *Service Concession Arrangements* and IAS 20 *Accounting for Government Grants and Disclosure of Government Assistance*. In its redeliberations, the IFRIC noted that in a public-to-private service concession arrangement within the scope of IFRIC 12 the grantor controls the infrastructure, not the operator. Therefore, the IFRIC concluded that this Interpretation does not apply to agreements in which the transfer is an item of infrastructure used in a service concession arrangement that is within the scope of IFRIC 12. The IFRIC also clarified that IAS 20 does not apply because transfers of assets from customers do not meet the definition of a government grant in accordance with paragraph 3 of IAS 20.

BC9   Some respondents to D24 questioned the application by analogy to situations other than utility entities providing connection and access to their networks (eg electricity, gas, water or telecommunication networks). In its redeliberations, the IFRIC noted that this Interpretation might also be relevant to industries other than utilities. The IFRIC also clarified the background section of the Interpretation adding an example of an information technology outsourcing agreement.

Issues

BC10   When an entity receives an item of property, plant and equipment from a customer, it should assess whether the transferred item meets the definition of an asset.

BC11   If the entity concludes that the transferred item of property, plant and equipment meets the definition of an asset, it should recognise the transferred item in accordance with paragraph 7 of IAS 16. In that case, the next issues are at what amount it should be recognised on initial recognition and how to account for the resulting credit.

BC12   The last issue the IFRIC considered is how the entity should account for the receipt of cash instead of a transfer of an item of property, plant and equipment.

Consensus

Is the definition of an asset met?

BC13   In its redeliberations, the IFRIC discussed the different steps that D24 required an entity to follow to determine whether an asset should be recognised, including the consideration of IFRIC 4 *Determining whether an Arrangement contains a Lease* and IAS 17 *Leases*. The IFRIC decided to simplify the proposals by focusing on who controls the asset. The Interpretation provides guidance based on the definition of an asset set out in paragraph 49(a) of the *Framework* and the additional guidance in paragraphs 55 and 57 of the *Framework*.

How should the transferred item of property, plant and equipment be measured on initial recognition?

BC14 The IFRIC concluded that, in a normal trading transaction, the item of property, plant and equipment is received in exchange for something, ie the provision of services such as connection to a network, provision of ongoing access to a supply of goods or services, or both.

BC15 The IFRIC noted that both paragraph 24 of IAS 16 *Property, Plant and Equipment* and paragraph 12 of IAS 18 *Revenue* lead to the same measurement attribute for such exchange transactions, ie the item received should be measured at fair value on initial recognition. Therefore, if the entity concludes that the definition of an asset is met, it should recognise the transferred asset as an item of property, plant and equipment in accordance with paragraph 7 of IAS 16 and measure it on initial recognition at its fair value in accordance with paragraph 24 of that Standard. The IFRIC also noted that respondents to D24 generally agreed with that conclusion.

How should the credit be accounted for?

BC16 The following discussion assumes that the entity receiving an item of property, plant and equipment from a customer has concluded that the transferred item should be recognised and measured at its fair value on initial recognition. It also assumes that the services to be provided in exchange for the transferred item are part of the ordinary activities of the entity.

Identifying the separately identifiable services

BC17 D24 identified only one service to be delivered in exchange for the transferred item of property, plant and equipment: the provision of ongoing access to a supply of goods or services. Many respondents, including utility entities, questioned whether an entity receiving an asset from a customer always has an obligation to provide ongoing access to a supply of goods or services as a result of the transfer. For example, some respondents argued that when a utility company is required by law or regulation to provide access to a supply of a commodity to all customers at the same price it may have no further obligation once the service connection has been made. They also argued that an obligation to provide ongoing services to the customer who transferred the asset may exist only if the customer obtains in exchange some exclusive right of access to a supply of goods or services, eg a reduced price. Overall, these respondents asked the IFRIC to reconsider the revenue recognition issue on the basis of an IAS 18 approach.

BC18 In its redeliberations, the IFRIC noted that an entity may agree to deliver one or two services in exchange for the transferred item of property, plant and equipment, such as connecting the customer to a network, providing the customer with ongoing access to a supply of goods or services, or both. The IFRIC concluded that identifying the separately identifiable services of a single agreement depends on facts and circumstances and that judgement is required. The IFRIC also acknowledged that a practical weakness of IAS 18 is that it gives insufficient guidance on agreements that deliver more than one good or service to the customer. Therefore, the IFRIC decided to develop guidance based on paragraph 13 of IAS 18 to help identify the services to be delivered in exchange for the transferred asset. This decision resulted in including the indicators in paragraphs 15–17 of the Interpretation and the examples illustrating their application.

Revenue recognition

BC19   In accordance with paragraph 13 of IAS 18, the IFRIC decided that the Interpretation should require that when more than one service is identified the fair value of the total consideration received or receivable for the agreement should be allocated to each service and that the recognition criteria of IAS 18 should be applied to each service. The IFRIC noted that IFRIC 12 *Service Concession Arrangements* and IFRIC 13 *Customer Loyalty Programmes* provide guidance on how to allocate the fair value of the total consideration received or receivable for the agreement to each component (see paragraph 13 of IFRIC 12 and paragraphs 5–7 of IFRIC 13). Therefore, the IFRIC concluded that this Interpretation should include only a reminder in paragraph 19 that such allocation is required if more than one service is identified.

BC20   If a separately identifiable ongoing service is part of the agreement, the entity must identify the period over which revenue should be recognised. Paragraph 20 of D24 stated that 'although the period over which an entity has an obligation to provide access to a supply of goods or services using a contributed asset may be shorter than the useful economic life of the asset, it cannot be longer.' Some respondents asked the IFRIC to clarify whether that period may be determined by the terms of the agreement and why that period cannot be longer than the economic life of the contributed asset.

BC21   The IFRIC clarified that the period over which revenue should be recognised for the ongoing service is generally determined by the terms of the agreement with the customer. If the arrangement does not specify a period, the IFRIC reaffirmed its view that the revenue should be recognised over a period no longer than the useful life of the transferred asset used to provide the ongoing service. This is because the entity can only use the transferred asset to provide ongoing access to a supply of goods or services during its useful life. Any obligation that exists after the asset is replaced does not arise from the original transfer but from the terms of the entity's operating licence or other regulation.

BC22   Almost all respondents disagreed with paragraph BC22 of D24 that the time value of money should be taken into account when measuring revenue. The IFRIC agreed with respondents and noted that paragraph 11 of IAS 18 requires taking the time value of money into account only when payments are deferred.

How should the entity account for a transfer of cash from its customer?

BC23   Respondents were generally supportive of the IFRIC's proposals related to transfers of cash. However, some respondents asked the IFRIC to clarify the circumstances in which a cash transfer would be within the scope of the Interpretation.

BC24   In its redeliberations, the IFRIC discussed the accounting for agreements in which an entity receives a transfer of cash from a customer instead of an item of property, plant and equipment. The IFRIC reaffirmed its view in D24: when that amount of cash must be used only to construct or acquire an item of property, plant and equipment and the entity must then use the item of property, plant and equipment to deliver goods or services to the customer, the economic effect of the transfer of cash is similar to that of a transfer of an item of property, plant and equipment.

Transition

BC25   The IFRIC noted that applying the change in accounting policy retrospectively would require entities to establish a carrying amount for assets that had been transferred in the past. That carrying amount would be based on historical fair values. Those fair values may not be based on an observable price or observable inputs. Therefore, the IFRIC concluded that retrospective application may be impracticable and that the Interpretation should require prospective application to transfers received after its effective date. However, the IFRIC also concluded that earlier application should be permitted provided the valuations and other information needed to apply the Interpretation to past transfers were obtained at the time those transfers occurred.

Changes from draft Interpretation D24

BC26   The most significant changes made from D24 in the light of comments received relate to:

(a)   *Recognition of transferred assets.* As stated in paragraph BC13, the IFRIC decided to simplify the requirements. It addressed the issue of which entity controls the asset by giving guidance based on the definition of an asset set out in the *Framework*.

(b)   *Revenue recognition.* The IFRIC decided that an entity receiving an item of property, plant and equipment from a customer may not always have an obligation to provide ongoing access to a supply of goods or services as a result of the transfer. Therefore, the IFRIC also decided to develop guidance based on paragraph 13 of IAS 18 to help identify the separately identifiable services to be delivered in exchange for the transferred asset.

(c)   *Title of the Interpretation.* The IFRIC noted that in some jurisdictions, the term 'contribution' has the implication of a donation rather than an exchange transaction. In addition, the IFRIC noted that this term might be difficult to translate into some languages. For that reason, the IFRIC decided to use the term 'transfer' and redrafted the Interpretation accordingly.

(d)   *Illustrative examples.* The IFRIC decided that illustrative examples should accompany, but not be part of, the Interpretation to help entities apply the Interpretation.

Document published to accompany

IFRIC Interpretation 19

Extinguishing Financial Liabilities with Equity Instruments

The text of the unaccompanied IFRIC 19 is contained in Part A of this edition. Its effective date is 1 July 2010. This part presents the following accompanying document:

page

BASIS FOR CONCLUSIONS   **B1662**

Basis for Conclusions on
IFRIC Interpretation 19 *Extinguishing Financial Liabilities with Equity Instruments*

This Basis for Conclusions accompanies, but is not part of, IFRIC 19.

Introduction

BC1   This Basis for Conclusions summarises the IFRIC's considerations in reaching its consensus. Individual IFRIC members gave greater weight to some factors than to others.

BC2   The IFRIC received a request for guidance on the application of IAS 39 *Financial Instruments: Recognition and Measurement* and IAS 32 *Financial Instruments: Presentation* when an entity issues its own equity instruments to extinguish all or part of a financial liability. The question is how the entity should recognise the equity instruments issued.

BC3   The IFRIC noted that lenders manage loans to entities in financial difficulty in a variety of ways including one or more of the following:

(a)   selling the loans in the market to other investors/lenders;

(b)   renegotiating the terms of the loan (eg extension of the maturity date or lower interest payments); or

(c)   accepting the creditor's equity instruments in full or partial settlement of the liability (sometimes referred to as a 'debt for equity swap').

BC4   The IFRIC was informed that there was diversity in practice in how entities measure the equity instruments issued in full or partial settlement of a financial liability following renegotiation of the terms of the liability. Some recognise the equity instruments at the carrying amount of the financial liability and do not recognise any gain or loss in profit or loss. Others recognise the equity instruments at the fair value of either the liability extinguished or the equity instruments issued and recognise a difference between that amount and the carrying amount of the financial liability in profit or loss.

BC5   In August 2009 the IFRIC published draft Interpretation D25 *Extinguishing Financial Liabilities with Equity Instruments* for public comment. It received 33 comment letters in response to the proposals.

Scope

BC6   The IFRIC concluded that its Interpretation should address only the accounting by an entity when the terms of a financial liability are renegotiated and result in the entity issuing equity instruments to a creditor of the entity to extinguish part or all of the liability. It does not address the accounting by the creditor because other IFRSs already set out the relevant requirements.

BC7   The IFRIC considered whether to provide guidance on transactions in which the creditor is also a direct or indirect shareholder and is acting in its capacity as an existing direct or indirect shareholder. The IFRIC concluded that the Interpretation should not address such transactions. It noted that determining whether the issue of equity instruments to extinguish a financial liability in such situations is considered a transaction with an owner in its capacity as an owner would be a matter of judgement depending on the facts and circumstances.

BC8   In its redeliberations, the IFRIC clarified that transactions when the creditor and the entity are controlled by the same party or parties before and after the transaction are outside the scope of the Interpretation when the substance of the transaction includes an equity distribution by, or contribution to, the entity. The IFRIC acknowledged that the allocation of consideration between the extinguishment of all or part of a financial liability and the equity distribution or contribution components may not always be reliably measured.

BC9   Some respondents questioned whether the Interpretation should be applied to transactions when the extinguishment of the financial liability by issuing equity shares is in accordance with the original terms of the liability. In its redeliberations the IFRIC decided that these transactions should be excluded from the scope of the Interpretation, noting that IAS 32 includes specific guidance on those financial instruments.

Are an entity's equity instruments 'consideration paid'?

BC10   The IFRIC noted that IFRSs do not contain specific guidance on the measurement of an entity's equity instruments issued to extinguish all or part of a financial liability. Paragraph 41 of IAS 39 requires an entity to recognise in profit or loss the difference between the carrying amount of the financial liability extinguished and the consideration paid. That paragraph describes 'consideration paid' as including non-cash assets transferred, or liabilities assumed, and does not specifically mention equity instruments issued. Consequently, some are of the view that equity instruments are not 'consideration paid'.

BC11   Holders of this view believe that, because IFRSs are generally silent on how to measure equity instruments on initial recognition (see paragraph BC15), a variety of practices has developed. One such practice is to recognise the equity instruments issued at the carrying amount of the financial liability extinguished.

BC12   However, the IFRIC observed that both IFRS 2 *Share-based Payment* and IFRS 3 *Business Combinations* make it clear that equity instruments are used as consideration to acquire goods and services as well as to obtain control of businesses.

BC13   The IFRIC also observed that the issue of equity instruments to extinguish a financial liability could be analysed as consisting of two transactions—first, the issue of new equity instruments to the creditor for cash and second, the creditor accepting payment of that amount of cash to extinguish the financial liability.

BC14   As a result of its analysis, the IFRIC concluded that the equity instruments issued to extinguish a financial liability are 'consideration paid' in accordance with paragraph 41 of IAS 39.

How should the equity instruments be measured?

BC15   The IFRIC observed that although IFRSs do not contain a general principle for the initial recognition and measurement of equity instruments, guidance on specific transactions exists, including:

(a)   *initial recognition of compound instruments* (IAS 32). The amount allocated to the equity component is the residual after deducting the fair value of the financial liability component from the fair value of the entire compound instrument.

(b)   *cost of equity transactions and own equity instruments ('treasury shares') acquired and reissued or cancelled* (IAS 32). No gain or loss is recognised in profit or loss on the purchase, sale, issue or cancellation of an entity's own equity instruments. These are transactions with an entity's owners in their capacity as owners.

(c)   *equity instruments issued in share-based payment transactions* (IFRS 2). For equity-settled share-based payment transactions, the entity measures the goods or services received, and the corresponding increase in equity, directly, at the fair value of the goods or services received, unless that fair value cannot be estimated reliably. If the entity cannot estimate reliably the fair value of the goods or services received (eg transactions with employees), the entity measures their value, and the corresponding increase in equity, indirectly, by reference to the fair value of the equity instruments granted.

(d)   *consideration transferred in business combinations* (IFRS 3).   The total consideration transferred in a business combination is measured at fair value. It includes the acquisition-date fair values of any equity interests issued by the acquirer.

BC16   The IFRIC noted that the general principle of IFRSs is that equity is a residual and should be measured initially by reference to changes in assets and liabilities (the *Framework* and IFRS 2). IFRS 2 is clear that when goods or services are received in return for the issue of equity instruments, the increase in equity is measured directly at the fair value of the goods or services received.

BC17   The IFRIC decided that the same principles should apply when equity instruments are issued to extinguish financial liabilities. However, the IFRIC was concerned that entities might encounter practical difficulties in measuring the fair value of both the equity instruments issued and the financial liability, particularly when the entity is in financial difficulty. Therefore, the IFRIC decided in D25 that equity instruments issued to extinguish a financial liability should be measured initially at the fair value of the equity instruments issued or the fair value of the liability extinguished, whichever is more reliably determinable.

BC18   However, in response to comments received on D25, the IFRIC reconsidered whether the entity should initially measure equity instruments issued to a creditor to extinguish all or part of a financial liability at the fair value of the equity instruments issued or the fair value of the liability extinguished. The IFRIC noted that many respondents proposed that a preferred measurement basis should be determined to avoid an 'accounting choice' developing in practice, acknowledging that both measurement approaches would need to be used to identify which was more reliably determinable.

BC19　Therefore the IFRIC decided to modify the proposal in D25 and identify a preferred measurement basis. In identifying this preferred measurement basis, the IFRIC noted that many respondents considered that the principles in IFRS 2 and the *Framework* referred to in paragraph BC16 support a measurement based on the fair value of the liability extinguished.

BC20　However, some respondents argued that the fair value of the equity issued should be the proposed measurement basis. They pointed out that this approach would be consistent with the consensus that the issue of an entity's equity instruments is consideration paid in accordance with paragraph 41 of IAS 39. They also argued that the fair value of the equity issued best reflects the total amount of consideration paid in the transaction, which may include a premium that the creditor requires to renegotiate the terms of the financial liability.

BC21　The IFRIC considered that the fair value of the equity issued should be the proposed measurement basis for the reasons described in paragraph BC20. Consequently the IFRIC concluded that an entity should initially measure equity instruments issued to a creditor to extinguish all or part of a financial liability at the fair value of the equity instruments issued, unless that fair value cannot be reliably measured. If the fair value of the equity instruments issued cannot be reliably measured then these equity instruments should initially be measured to reflect the fair value of the liability extinguished.

BC22　In redeliberations, the IFRIC noted that these transactions often take place in situations when the terms of the financial liability are breached and the liability becomes repayable on demand. The IFRIC agreed with comments received that paragraph 49 of IAS 39 is not applied in measuring the fair value of all or part of a financial liability extinguished in these situations. This is because the extinguishment transaction suggests that the demand feature is no longer substantive.

BC23　In response to comments, the IFRIC also clarified that the equity instruments issued should be recognised initially and measured at the date the financial liability (or part of that liability) is extinguished. This is consistent with paragraphs BC341 and BC342 of the Basis for Conclusions on IFRS 3, which discuss the views on whether equity instruments issued as consideration in a business combination should be measured at fair value at the agreement date or acquisition date, concluding that measurement should be at the acquisition date.

How should a difference between the carrying amount of the financial liability and the consideration paid be accounted for?

BC24　In accordance with paragraph 41 of IAS 39, the entity should recognise a gain or loss in profit or loss for any difference between the carrying amount of the financial liability extinguished and the consideration paid. This requirement is consistent with the *Framework*'s discussion of income:

  (a)　Income is increases in economic benefits during the accounting period in the form of inflows or enhancements of assets or *decreases of liabilities that result in increases in equity*, other than those relating to contributions from equity participants. (paragraph 70(a)) (emphasis added)

(b) Gains represent other items that meet the definition of income and may, or may not, arise in the course of the ordinary activities of an entity. Gains represent increases in economic benefits ... (paragraph 75)

(c) Income may also result from the settlement of liabilities. For example, an entity may provide goods and services to a lender in settlement of an obligation to repay an outstanding loan. (paragraph 77)

Full extinguishment

BC25   The IFRIC noted that, as discussed in paragraph BC13, a transaction in which an entity issues equity instruments to extinguish a liability can be analysed as first, the issue of new equity instruments to the creditor for cash and second, the creditor accepting payment of that amount of cash to extinguish the financial liability. Consistently with paragraph BC24, when the creditor accepts cash to extinguish the liability, the entity should recognise a gain or loss in profit or loss.

BC26   Similarly, the IFRIC noted that, in accordance with IAS 32, when an entity amends the terms of a convertible instrument to induce early conversion, the entity recognises in profit or loss the fair value of any additional consideration paid to the holder. Thus, the IFRIC concluded that when an entity settles an instrument by issuing its own equity instruments and that settlement is not in accordance with the original terms of the financial liability, the entity should recognise a gain or loss in profit or loss.

BC27   As a result of its conclusions, the IFRIC decided that the entity should recognise a gain or loss in profit or loss. This gain or loss is equal to the difference between the carrying amount of the financial liability and the fair value of the equity instruments issued, or fair value of the liability extinguished if the fair value of the equity instruments issued cannot be reliably measured.

Partial extinguishment

BC28   The IFRIC also observed that the restructuring of a financial liability can involve both the partial settlement of the liability by the issue of equity instruments to the creditor and the modification of the terms of the liability that remains outstanding. Therefore, the IFRIC decided that the Interpretation should also apply to partial extinguishments. In the case of a partial extinguishment, the discussion in paragraphs BC25–BC27 applies to the part of the liability extinguished.

BC29   Many respondents requested clarification of the guidance on partial extinguishment included in D25. During its redeliberations, the IFRIC acknowledged that the issue of an entity's equity shares may reflect consideration paid for both the extinguishment of part of a financial liability and the modification of the terms of the part of the liability that remains outstanding.

BC30   The IFRIC decided that to reflect this, an entity should allocate the consideration paid between the part of the liability extinguished and the part of the liability that remains outstanding. The entity would consider this allocation in determining the profit or loss to be recognised on the part of the liability extinguished and in its assessment of whether the terms of the remaining liability have been substantially modified.

BC31   The IFRIC concluded that providing additional guidance on determining whether the terms of the part of the financial liability that remains outstanding has been substantially modified in accordance with paragraph 40 of IAS 39 was outside the scope of the Interpretation.

Presentation

BC32   The IFRIC decided that an entity should disclose the gain or loss on the extinguishment of the financial liability by the issue of equity instruments as a separate line item in profit or loss or in the notes. This requirement is consistent with the *Framework* and the requirements in other IFRSs, for example:

(a)   When gains are recognised in the income statement, they are usually displayed separately because knowledge of them is useful for the purpose of making economic decisions. (paragraph 76 of the *Framework*)

(b)   An entity shall present additional line items, headings and subtotals in the statement of comprehensive income and the separate income statement (if presented), when such presentation is relevant to an understanding of the entity's financial performance. (paragraph 85 of IAS 1 *Presentation of Financial Statements*)

(c)   An entity shall disclose net gains or net losses on financial liabilities either in the statement of comprehensive income or in the notes. (paragraph 20 of IFRS 7 *Financial Instruments: Disclosures*)

Transition

BC33   The IFRIC decided that the Interpretation should be applied retrospectively even though it acknowledged that determining fair values retrospectively may be problematic. The IFRIC noted that IAS 8 *Accounting Policies, Changes in Accounting Estimates and Errors* provides guidance on circumstances in which retrospective application might be impracticable. The IFRIC concluded that it was preferable to require entities that could apply the Interpretation retrospectively to do so, rather than requiring all entities to apply it prospectively to future transactions. However, to simplify transition, the IFRIC also concluded that it should require retrospective application only from the beginning of the earliest comparative period presented because application to earlier periods would result only in a reclassification of amounts within equity.

Summary of main changes from the draft Interpretation

BC34   The main changes from the IFRIC's proposals in D25 are as follows:

(a)   Paragraph 3 was added because the IFRIC identified specific transactions that are outside of the scope of the Interpretation.

(b)   Paragraph 6 was modified to state that measurement should be based on the fair value of the equity instruments issued, unless that fair value cannot be reliably measured.

(c)   Paragraph 7 was added to reflect the modification to paragraph 6. It also clarifies the intention of the IFRIC that in measuring the fair value of a financial liability extinguished that includes a demand feature (eg a demand deposit), paragraph 49 of IAS 39 is not applied.

(d) Paragraph 8 was added, and paragraph 10 was modified, to clarify how the Interpretation should be applied when only part of the financial liability is extinguished by the issue of equity instruments.

(e) Paragraph 9 was modified to state when the equity instruments issued should be initially measured.

Material published to accompany

SIC Interpretation 7

Introduction of the Euro

This version includes amendments resulting from IFRSs issued up to 31 December 2009.

The text of the unaccompanied Interpretation is contained in Part A of this edition. Its effective date when issued was 1 June 1998. The effective date of the most recent amendment is 1 July 2009. This part presents the following accompanying material:

Basis for Conclusions on
SIC Interpretation 7 *Introduction of the Euro*

This Basis for Conclusions accompanies, but is not part of, SIC-7.

[The original text has been marked up to reflect the revision of IAS 21 in 2003 and IAS 1 in 2007 and the amendment of IAS 27 in 2008: new text is underlined and deleted text is struck through.]

5   IAS 21.23~~11~~(a) requires that foreign currency monetary items (as defined by IAS 21.8~~07~~) be reported using the closing rate at ~~each balance sheet date~~ the end of each reporting period. According to IAS 21.28~~15~~, exchange differences arising from the translation of monetary items generally should be recognised as income or as expenses in the period in which they arise. The effective start of the EMU after the reporting period ~~balance sheet date~~ does not change the application of these requirements at the end of the reporting period ~~balance sheet date~~; in accordance with IAS 10.10~~28~~* it is not relevant whether or not the closing rate can fluctuate after the ~~balance sheet date~~ reporting period.

6   IAS 21.5~~14~~ states that the Standard does not apply to ~~deal with~~ hedge accounting~~, except in restricted circumstances~~. Therefore, this Interpretation does not address how foreign currency hedges should be accounted for. IAS 8.4~~2~~ would allow such a change in accounting policy only if the change would result in a more appropriate presentation of events or transactions.[†] The effective start of EMU, of itself, does not justify a change to an entity's established accounting policy related to ~~anticipatory~~ hedges of forecast transactions because the changeover does not affect the economic rationale of such hedges. Therefore, the changeover should not alter the accounting policy where gains and losses on financial instruments used as ~~anticipatory~~ hedges of forecast transactions are ~~currently deferred~~ initially recognised in ~~equity~~ other comprehensive income and matched with the related income or expense in a future period.

7   IAS 21.48~~37~~ requires the cumulative amount of exchange differences relating to the translation of the financial statements of a foreign operation ~~entity which~~ that have been ~~deferred in equity~~ recognised in other comprehensive income and accumulated in a separate component of equity in accordance with IAS 21.~~17, 19 or 30~~32 or 39(c) to be ~~recognised as income or expenses~~ reclassified from equity to profit or loss in the same period in which the gain or loss on disposal or partial disposal of the foreign operation ~~entity~~ is recognised. The fact that the cumulative amount of exchange differences will be fixed under EMU does not justify immediate recognition as income or expenses ~~since~~ because the wording and the rationale of IAS 21.48~~37~~ clearly preclude such a treatment.

8   ~~Under the Allowed Alternative Treatment of IAS 21.21, exchange differences resulting from severe devaluations of currencies are included in the carrying amount of the related assets in certain limited circumstances. Those circumstances do not apply to the currencies participating in the changeover since the event of severe devaluation is incompatible with the required stability of participating currencies.~~

---

*   ~~IAS 10 (revised in 1999), paragraph 20, contains similar requirements.~~

†   The accounting for hedges is now covered under IAS 39 *Financial Instruments: Recognition and Measurement*. As SIC-7 was issued before IAS 39, the previous version of this Interpretation could refer only to the entity's own accounting policies on the matter.

Material published to accompany

SIC Interpretation 10

Government Assistance—No Specific Relation to Operating Activities

This version includes amendments resulting from IFRSs issued up to 31 December 2009.

The text of the unaccompanied Interpretation is contained in Part A of this edition. Its effective date when issued was 1 August 1998. The effective date of the most recent amendment is 1 January 2009. This part presents the following accompanying material:

page

BASIS FOR CONCLUSIONS **B1672**

Basis for Conclusions on
SIC Interpretation 10 *Government Assistance—No Specific Relation to Operating Activities*

This Basis for Conclusions accompanies, but is not part of, SIC-10.

4   IAS 20.03 defines government grants as assistance by the government in the form of transfers of resources to an entity in return for past or future compliance with certain conditions relating to the operating activities of the entity. The general requirement to operate in certain regions or industry sectors in order to qualify for the government assistance constitutes such a condition in accordance with IAS 20.03. Therefore, such assistance falls within the definition of government grants and the requirements of IAS 20 apply, in particular paragraphs 12 and 20, which deal with the timing of recognition as income.

Material published to accompany

SIC Interpretation 12

Consolidation—Special Purpose Entities

This version includes amendments resulting from IFRSs issued up to 31 December 2009.

The text of the unaccompanied Interpretation is contained in Part A of this edition. Its effective date when issued was 1 June 1999. The effective date of the most recent amendment is 1 January 2005. This part presents the following accompanying material:

Basis for Conclusions on
SIC Interpretation 12 *Consolidation—Special Purpose Entities*

This Basis for Conclusions accompanies, but is not part of, SIC-12.

[The original text has been marked up to reflect the revision of IASs 1, 8 and 27 in 2003: new text is underlined and deleted text is struck through. Paragraphs 15A–15E were added by IFRIC Amendment to SIC-12 issued on 11 November 2004.]

12   IAS 27.12~~11~~ states that 'a ~~parent which issues~~ Consolidated financial statements shall include ~~should consolidate~~ all subsidiaries of the parent'. IAS 27.04~~06~~ defines a parent as 'an entity that has one or more subsidiaries', a subsidiary as 'an entity, including an unincorporated entity such as a partnership, that is controlled by another entity (known as the parent)', and control as 'the power to govern the financial and operating policies of an entity so as to obtain benefits from its activities.' Paragraph 35 of the *Framework* and IAS 8.10(b)(ii) ~~1.20(b)(ii) (revised 1997)~~ require that transactions and other events are accounted for in accordance with their substance and economic reality, and not merely their legal form.

13   Control over another entity requires having the ability to direct or dominate its decision-making, regardless of whether this power is actually exercised. Under the definitions of IAS 27.04~~06~~, the ability to govern decision-making alone, however, is not sufficient to establish control. The ability to govern decision-making must be accompanied by the objective of obtaining benefits from the entity's activities.

14   SPEs frequently operate in a predetermined way so that no entity has explicit decision-making authority over the SPE's ongoing activities after its formation (ie they operate on 'autopilot'). Virtually all rights, obligations, and aspects of activities that could be controlled are predefined and limited by contractual provisions specified or scheduled at inception. In these circumstances, control may exist for the sponsoring party or others with a beneficial interest, even though it may be particularly difficult to assess, because virtually all activities are predetermined. However, the predetermination of the activities of the SPE through an 'autopilot' mechanism often provides evidence that the ability to control has been exercised by the party making the predetermination for its own benefit at the formation of the SPE and is being perpetuated.

~~15   IAS 27.13(b) indicates that a subsidiary should be excluded from consolidation when it 'operates under severe long-term restrictions which significantly impair its ability to transfer funds to the parent.' Predetermination of the activities of an SPE by an enterprise (the sponsor or other party with a beneficial interest) is often a demonstration of control over ongoing activities as determined by that enterprise and would not represent the type of restrictions referred to in IAS 27.13(b).~~

15A   In 2004, the IFRIC amended the scope of SIC-12. That Amendment is effective for annual periods beginning on or after 1 January 2005, unless an entity applied IFRS 2 for an earlier period, in which case the Amendment is effective for that earlier period. Before that Amendment, SIC-12 excluded from its scope equity compensation plans and post-employment benefit plans. Paragraphs 15B–15E summarise the IFRIC's considerations in reaching its consensus to amend the scope of SIC-12. Individual IFRIC members gave greater weight to some factors than to others.

15B   The IFRIC was asked by the IASB to consider whether the scope exclusion in SIC-12 for equity compensation plans should be removed when IFRS 2 becomes effective. Equity compensation plans were excluded from the scope of SIC-12 because they were within the scope of IAS 19 and that Standard did not specify recognition and measurement requirements for equity compensation benefits. However, once IFRS 2 became effective, IAS 19 would no longer apply to equity compensation plans. IFRS 2 specifies recognition and measurement requirements for equity compensation benefits.

15C   Also, IFRS 2 amended IAS 32, to state that paragraphs 33 and 34, which relate to the treatment of treasury shares, should be applied to treasury shares purchased, sold, issued or cancelled in connection with employee share option plans, employee share purchase plans, and all other share-based payment arrangements. However, in some cases, those shares might be held by an employee benefit trust (or similar entity) set up by the entity for the purposes of its share-based payment arrangements. Removing the scope exclusion in SIC-12 would require an entity that controls such a trust to consolidate the trust and, in so doing, to apply the requirements of IAS 32 to treasury shares held by the trust.

15D   The IFRIC therefore concluded that, to ensure consistency with IFRS 2 and IAS 32, the scope of SIC-12 should be amended by removing the exclusion of equity compensation plans.

15E   At the same time, the IFRIC discussed the scope exclusion in SIC-12 for post-employment benefit plans. The IFRIC noted that, although SIC-12 did not exclude other long-term employee benefit plans from its scope, IAS 19 nevertheless requires those plans to be accounted for in a manner similar to the accounting for post-employment benefit plans. The IFRIC therefore concluded that, to ensure consistency with IAS 19, the scope exclusion in SIC-12 should also apply to other long-term employee benefit plans.

Guidance on implementing SIC-12

This guidance accompanies, but is not part of, SIC-12.

Indicators of control over an SPE

The examples in paragraph 10 of this Interpretation are intended to indicate types of circumstances that should be considered in evaluating a particular arrangement in light of the substance-over-form principle. The guidance provided in the Interpretation and below is not intended to be used as 'a comprehensive checklist' of conditions that must be met cumulatively in order to require consolidation of an SPE.

(a)   *Activities*

The activities of the SPE, in substance, are being conducted on behalf of the reporting entity, which directly or indirectly created the SPE according to its specific business needs.

Examples are:

* the SPE is principally engaged in providing a source of long-term capital to an entity or funding to support an entity's ongoing major or central operations; or

* the SPE provides a supply of goods or services that is consistent with an entity's ongoing major or central operations which, without the existence of the SPE, would have to be provided by the entity itself.

Economic dependence of an entity on the reporting entity (such as relations of suppliers to a significant customer) does not, by itself, lead to control.

(b)   *Decision-making*

The reporting entity, in substance, has the decision-making powers to control or to obtain control of the SPE or its assets, including certain decision-making powers coming into existence after the formation of the SPE. Such decision-making powers may have been delegated by establishing an 'autopilot' mechanism.

Examples are:

* power to unilaterally dissolve an SPE;

* power to change the SPE's charter or bylaws; or

* power to veto proposed changes of the SPE's charter or bylaws.

(c)   *Benefits*

The reporting entity, in substance, has rights to obtain a majority of the benefits of the SPE's activities through a statute, contract, agreement, or trust deed, or any other scheme, arrangement or device. Such rights to benefits in the SPE may be indicators of control when they are specified in favour of an entity that is engaged in transactions with an SPE and that entity stands to gain those benefits from the financial performance of the SPE.

Examples are:

- rights to a majority of any economic benefits distributed by an entity in the form of future net cash flows, earnings, net assets, or other economic benefits; or

- rights to majority residual interests in scheduled residual distributions or in a liquidation of the SPE.

(d)   *Risks*

An indication of control may be obtained by evaluating the risks of each party engaging in transactions with an SPE. Frequently, the reporting entity guarantees a return or credit protection directly or indirectly through the SPE to outside investors who provide substantially all of the capital to the SPE. As a result of the guarantee, the entity retains residual or ownership risks and the investors are, in substance, only lenders because their exposure to gains and losses is limited.

Examples are:

- the capital providers do not have a significant interest in the underlying net assets of the SPE;

- the capital providers do not have rights to the future economic benefits of the SPE;

- the capital providers are not substantively exposed to the inherent risks of the underlying net assets or operations of the SPE; or

- in substance, the capital providers receive mainly consideration equivalent to a lender's return through a debt or equity interest.

Material published to accompany

SIC Interpretation 13

Jointly Controlled Entities—
Non-monetary Contributions by Venturers

This version includes amendments resulting from IFRSs issued up to 31 December 2009.

The text of the unaccompanied Interpretation is contained in Part A of this edition. Its effective date when issued was 1 January 1999. The effective date of the most recent amendment is 1 January 2009. This part presents the following accompanying material:

page

BASIS FOR CONCLUSIONS **B1680**

Basis for Conclusions on
SIC Interpretation 13 *Jointly Controlled Entities—Non-monetary Contributions by Venturers*

This Basis for Conclusions accompanies, but is not part of, SIC-13.

[The original text has been marked up to reflect the revision of IAS 16 and IAS 31 in 2003; new text is underlined and deleted text is struck through.]

8   IAS 31.~~48~~39 requires that, while the assets are retained in the joint venture, the venturer should recognise only that portion of the gain or loss which is attributable to the interests of the other venturers. Additional losses are recognised if required by IAS 31.~~48~~39.

9   IAS 31.~~48~~39 refers to the transfer of the 'significant risks and rewards of ownership' as a condition for recognition of gains or losses resulting from transactions between venturers and joint ventures. IAS 18.16(a) to (d) contain examples of situations where the risks and rewards of ownership are typically not transferred. This guidance also applies by analogy to the recognition of gains or losses resulting from contributions of non-monetary assets to JCEs. Since the venturer participates in joint control of the JCE, it retains some 'continuing managerial involvement' in the asset transferred. However, this does not generally preclude the recognition of gains or losses since joint control does not constitute control to the degree usually associated with ownership (IAS 18.14(b)).

10   Paragraph 92 of the *Framework* states: 'income is recognised in the income statement when an increase in future economic benefits related to an increase in an asset or a decrease of a liability has arisen that can be measured reliably'. IAS 18.14(c) requires, among other conditions, that revenue from the sale of goods should be recognised when 'the amount of revenue can be measured reliably'. The requirement for reliable measurement also applies to the recognition of gains or losses resulting from a contribution of non-monetary assets to a JCE.

11   IAS 18.12 explains that 'when goods and services are exchanged or swapped for goods or services which are of similar nature and value, the exchange is not regarded as a transaction which generates revenue'. ~~IAS 16.22 says that 'an item of property, plant and equipment may be acquired in exchange for a similar asset that has a similar use in the same line of business and which has a similar fair value. An item of property, plant and equipment may also be sold in exchange for an equity interest in a similar asset. In both cases, since the earnings process is incomplete, no gain or loss is recognised on the transaction'.~~ The same rationale applies to a contribution of non-monetary assets since a contribution to a JCE is, in substance, an exchange of assets with the other venturers at the level of the JCE.

---

*   IAS 16 *Property, Plant and Equipment* as revised by the IASB in 2003 requires an entity to measure an item of property, plant and equipment acquired in exchange for a non-monetary asset or assets, or a combination of monetary and non-monetary assets, at fair value unless the exchange transaction lacks commercial substance. Previously, an entity measured such an acquired asset at fair value unless the exchanged assets were similar.

12   To the extent that the venturer also receives cash or non-monetary assets dissimilar to the assets contributed in addition to equity interests in the JCE, the realisation of which is not dependent on the future cash flows of the JCE, the earnings process is complete. Accordingly, the appropriate portion of the gain on the non-monetary contribution is recognised in profit or loss for the period.

13   It is not appropriate to present unrealised gains or losses on non-monetary assets contributed to JCEs as deferred items since such items do not meet the recognition criteria for assets or liabilities as defined in the *Framework* (paragraphs 53 to 64 and paragraphs 89 to 91).

Material published to accompany

SIC Interpretation 15

Operating Leases—Incentives

This version includes amendments resulting from IFRSs issued up to 31 December 2009.

The text of the unaccompanied Interpretation is contained in Part A of this edition. Its effective date when issued was 1 January 1999. The effective date of the most recent amendment is 1 January 2009. This part presents the following accompanying material:

Basis for Conclusions on
SIC Interpretation 15 *Operating Leases—Incentives*

This Basis for Conclusions accompanies, but is not part of, SIC-15.

[The original text has been marked up to reflect the revision of IASs 8 and 17 in 2003 and of IAS 1 in 2007: new text is underlined and deleted text is struck through.]

7   Paragraph 35 of the *Framework* explains that if information is to represent faithfully the transactions and events that it purports to represent, it is necessary that transactions and events are accounted for and presented in accordance with their substance and economic reality and not merely their legal form. IAS 1.20(b)(ii) 8.10(b)(ii) also requires the application of accounting policies which reflect economic substance.

8   Paragraph 22 of the *Framework* and IAS 1.2527 require the preparation of financial statements under the accrual basis of accounting. IAS 17.3325 and IAS 17.5042 specify the basis on which lessees and lessors respectively should recognise amounts payable or receivable under operating leases.

9   The underlying substance of operating lease arrangements is that the lessor and lessee exchange the use of an asset for a specified period for the consideration of a net amount of money. The accounting periods in which this net amount is recognised by either the lessor or the lessee is not affected by the form of the agreement or the timing of payments. Payments made by a lessor to or on behalf of a lessee, or allowances in rental cost made by a lessor, as incentives for the agreement of a new or renewed lease are an inseparable part of the net amount receivable or payable under the operating lease.

10   Costs incurred by the lessor as incentives for the agreement of new or renewed operating leases are not considered to be part of those initial costs which may be recognised as an expense in the income statements in the period in which they are incurred are added to the carrying amount of the leased asset and recognised as an expense over the lease term on the same basis as the lease income in accordance with under IAS 17.5244. Initial costs, such as direct costs for administration, advertising and consulting or legal fees, are incurred by a lessor to arrange a contract, whereas incentives in an operating lease are, in substance, related to the consideration for the use of the leased asset.

11   Costs incurred by the lessee on its own behalf are accounted for using the applicable recognition requirements. For example, relocation costs are recognised as an expense in profit or loss the income statement in the period in which they are incurred. The accounting for such costs does not depend on whether or not they are effectively reimbursed through an incentive arrangement as they are not related to the consideration for the use of the leased asset.

Illustrative examples

These examples accompany, but are not part of, SIC-15.

Example application of SIC-15

Example 1

An entity agrees to enter into a new lease arrangement with a new lessor. The lessor agrees to pay the lessee's relocation costs as an incentive to the lessee for entering into the new lease. The lessee's moving costs are 1,000. The new lease has a term of 10 years, at a fixed rate of 2,000 per year.

The accounting is:

The lessee recognises relocation costs of 1,000 as an expense in Year 1. Net consideration of 19,000 consists of 2,000 for each of the 10 years in the lease term, less a 1,000 incentive for relocation costs. Both the lessor and lessee would recognise the net rental consideration of 19,000 over the 10 year lease term using a single amortisation method in accordance with paragraphs 4 and 5 of this Interpretation.

Example 2

An entity agrees to enter into a new lease arrangement with a new lessor. The lessor agrees to a rent-free period for the first three years as incentive to the lessee for entering into the new lease. The new lease has a term of 20 years, at a fixed rate of 5,000 per year for years 4 through 20.

The accounting is:

Net consideration of 85,000 consists of 5,000 for each of 17 years in the lease term. Both the lessor and lessee would recognise the net consideration of 85,000 over the 20 year lease term using a single amortisation method in accordance with paragraphs 4 and 5 of this Interpretation.

Material published to accompany

SIC Interpretation 25

Income Taxes—Changes in the Tax Status of an Entity or its Shareholders

This version includes amendments resulting from IFRSs issued up to 31 December 2009.

The text of the unaccompanied Interpretation is contained in Part A of this edition. Its effective date when issued was 15 July 2000. The effective date of the most recent amendment is 1 January 2009. This part presents the following accompanying material:

page

BASIS FOR CONCLUSIONS   **B1690**

Basis for Conclusions on
SIC Interpretation 25 *Income Taxes—Changes in the Tax Status of an Entity or its Shareholders*

This Basis for Conclusions accompanies, but is not part of, SIC-25.

[The original text has been marked up to reflect the amendment to IAS 12 in 2003, and the revision of IAS 38 Intangible Assets *in 2004 and IAS 1* Presentation of Financial Statements *in 2007: new text is underlined and deleted text is struck through.]*

5   IAS 12.58 requires current and deferred tax to be included in the net profit or loss for the period, except to the extent the tax arises from a transaction or event that is recognised outside profit or loss either in other comprehensive income or directly in equity, in the same or a different period, (or arises from a business combination that is an acquisition). IAS 12.61A requires that current and deferred tax to be recognised outside profit or loss charged or credited directly to equity if the tax relates to items that are recognised credited or charged, in the same or a different period, outside profit or loss directly to equity.

5A   IAS 12.62 identifies examples of circumstances in which a transaction or event is recognised in other comprehensive income as permitted or required by another IFRS. All of these circumstances result in changes in the recognised amount of equity through recognition in other comprehensive income.

6   IAS 12.62A identifies examples of circumstances in which a transaction or event is recognised directly in equity as is permitted or required by another IFRS International Financial Reporting Standard. All of these circumstances result in changes in the recognised amount of equity through recognition of a credit or charge directly to equity.

7   IAS 12.65 explains that where the tax base of a revalued asset changes, any tax consequence is recognised in other comprehensive income directly in equity only to the extent that a related accounting revaluation was or is expected to be recognised in other comprehensive income directly in equity (revaluation surplus).

8   Because tax consequences recognised outside profit or loss, whether in other comprehensive income or directly in equity, must relate to a transaction or event recognised outside profit or loss directly in equity in the same or a different period, the cumulative amount of tax charged or credited directly to equity recognised outside profit or loss can be expected to be the same amount that would have been recognised outside profit or loss charged or credited directly to equity if the new tax status had applied previously. IAS 12.63(b) acknowledges that determining the tax consequences of a change in the tax rate or other tax rules that affects a deferred tax asset or liability and relates to an item previously recognised outside profit or loss charged or credited to equity may prove to be difficult. Because of this, IAS 12.63 suggests that an allocation may be necessary.

          © IASCF

Material published to accompany

SIC Interpretation 27

Evaluating the Substance of Transactions Involving the Legal Form of a Lease

This version includes amendments resulting from IFRSs issued up to 31 December 2009.

The text of the unaccompanied Interpretation is contained in Part A of this edition. Its effective date when issued was 31 December 2001. The effective date of the most recent amendment is 1 January 2009. This part presents the following accompanying material:

Basis for Conclusions on
SIC Interpretation 27 *Evaluating the Substance of Transactions Involving the Legal Form of a Lease*

This Basis for Conclusions accompanies, but is not part of, SIC-27.

[The original text has been marked up to reflect the revision of IAS 39 in 2003 and subsequently the issue of IFRS 4: new text is underlined and deleted text is struck through]

12   Paragraph 9 of IAS 11 *Construction Contracts* requires a group of contracts to be treated as a single contract when the group of contracts is negotiated as a single package, the contracts are so closely interrelated that they are, in effect, part of a single project with an overall profit margin, and the contracts are performed concurrently or in a continuous sequence. In such a situation, a series of transactions that involve the legal form of a lease are linked and accounted for as one transaction, because the overall economic effect cannot be understood without reference to the series of transactions as a whole.

13   An agreement is accounted for as a lease in accordance with IAS 17 when it conveys to the lessee in return for a payment or series of payments the right to use an asset for an agreed period of time. For information to represent faithfully the transactions it purports to represent, paragraph 35 of the *Framework* indicates that it is necessary that transactions are accounted for and presented in accordance with their substance and economic reality, not merely their legal form.

14   When an Entity does not control the assets that will be used to satisfy the lease payment obligations, and is not obligated to pay the lease payments, it does not recognise the assets and lease payment obligations, because the definitions of an asset and a liability have not been met. This is different from the circumstance when an Entity controls the assets, is obligated to pay the lease payments, and then later transfers assets to a third party (including a trust). In that circumstance, the transfer of assets (sometimes called an 'in-substance' defeasance) does not by itself relieve the Entity of its primary obligation, in the absence of legal release. A financial asset and a financial liability, or a portion of either, are derecognised only when the requirements of ~~IAS 39.35–65~~ paragraphs 15–37, 39–42, AG36–AG52 and AG57–AG63 of IAS 39 are met.

15   ~~In addition to addressing the general requirements for recognition of a provision, IAS 37 IAS 39~~ IFRS 4 provides guidance for recognising and measuring financial guarantees and similar instruments that provide for payments to be made if the debtor fails to make payments when due, if that contract transfers significant insurance risk to the issuer. ~~IAS 37 also provides guidance when disclosure of a contingent liability is required.~~ Financial guarantee contracts that provide for payments to be made in response to changes in relation to a variable (sometimes referred to as an 'underlying') are subject to IAS 39.

16   IAS 18 addresses the accounting treatment of revenue. Paragraph 75 of the *Framework* indicates that gains are no different in nature from revenue. Therefore, the requirements of IAS 18 apply by analogy or otherwise. Example 14(c) in the illustrative examples accompanying IAS 18 states that a fee earned on the execution of a significant act, which is much more significant than any other act, is recognised as income when the significant act has been completed. The example also indicates that it is necessary to distinguish between fees earned on completion of a significant act and fees related to future performance or risks retained.

Guidance on implementing SIC-27

This guidance accompanies, but is not part of, SIC-27.

A Linked transactions

A1　The Interpretation requires consideration of whether a series of transactions that involve the legal form of a lease are linked to determine whether the transactions are accounted for as one transaction.

A2　Extreme examples of transactions that are viewed as a whole and accounted for as single transactions, include:

(a)　An Entity leases an asset to an Investor (the headlease) and leases the same asset back for a shorter period of time (the sublease). At the end of the sublease period, the Entity has the right to buy back the rights of the Investor under a purchase option. If the Entity does not exercise its purchase option, the Investor has options available to it under each of which the Investor receives a minimum return on its investment in the headlease—the Investor may put the underlying asset back to the Entity, or require the Entity to provide a return on the Investor's investment in the headlease.

The predominant purpose of the arrangement is to achieve a tax advantage for the Investor, which is shared with the Entity in the form of a fee, and not to convey the right to use an asset. The Investor pays the fee and prepays the lease payment obligations under the headlease. The agreement requires the amount prepaid to be invested in risk-free assets and, as a requirement of finalising the execution of the legally binding arrangement, placed into a separate investment account held by a Trustee outside of the control of the Entity. The fee is retained by the Entity.

Over the term of the sublease, the sublease payment obligations are satisfied with funds of an equal amount withdrawn from the separate investment account. The Entity guarantees the sublease payment obligations, and will be required to satisfy the guarantee should the separate investment account have insufficient funds. The Entity, but not the Investor, has the right to terminate the sublease early under certain circumstances (eg a change in local or international tax law causes the Investor to lose part or all of the tax benefits, or the Entity decides to dispose of (eg replace, sell or deplete) the underlying asset) and upon payment of a termination value to the Investor. If the Entity chooses early termination, then it would pay the termination value from funds withdrawn from the separate investment account, and if the amount remaining in the separate investment account is insufficient, the difference would be paid by the Entity. The underlying asset is a specialised asset that the Entity requires to conduct its business.

(b)　An entity leases an asset to another entity for its entire economic life and leases the same asset back under the same terms and conditions as the original lease. The two entities have a legally enforceable right to set off the amounts owing to one another, and an intention to settle these amounts on a net basis.

(c) An entity (Entity A) leases an asset to another entity (Entity B), and obtains a non-recourse loan from a financier (by using the lease rentals and the asset as collateral). Entity A sells the asset subject to the lease and the loan to a trustee, and leases the same asset back. Entity A also concurrently agrees to repurchase the asset at the end of the lease for an amount equal to the sale price. The financier legally releases Entity A from the primary responsibility for the loan, and Entity A guarantees repayment of the non-recourse loan if Entity B defaults on the payments under the original lease. Entity B's credit rating is assessed as AAA and the amounts of the payments under each of the leases are equal. Entity A has a legally enforceable right to set off the amounts owing under each of the leases, and an intention to settle the rights and obligations under the leases on a net basis.

(d) An entity (Entity A) legally sells an asset to another entity (Entity B) and leases the same asset back. Entity B is obligated to put the asset back to Entity A at the end of the lease period at an amount that has the overall practical effect, when also considering the lease payments to be received, of providing Entity B with a yield of LIBOR plus 2 per cent per year on the purchase price.

B   The substance of an arrangement

B1   The Interpretation requires consideration of the substance of an arrangement to determine whether it includes the conveyance of the right to use an asset for an agreed period of time.

B2   In each of the examples described in Part A of this guidance, the arrangement does not, in substance, involve a lease under IAS 17 for the following reasons:

(a)   in the example described in paragraph A2(a), the arrangement is designed predominantly to generate tax benefits that are shared between the two entities. Even though the periods of the headlease and sublease are different, the options available to each of the entities at the end of the sublease period are structured such that the Investor assumes only an insignificant amount of asset risk during the headlease period. The substance of the arrangement is that the Entity receives a fee for executing the agreements, and retains the risks and rewards incident to ownership of the underlying asset.

(b)   in the example described in paragraph A2(b), the terms and conditions and period of each of the leases are the same. Therefore, the risks and rewards incident to ownership of the underlying asset are the same as before the arrangement. Further, the amounts owing are offset against one another, and so there is no retained credit risk. The substance of the arrangement is that no transaction has occurred.

(c)   in the example described in paragraph A2(c), Entity A retains the risks and rewards incident to ownership of the underlying asset, and the risk of payment under the guarantee is only remote (due to the AAA credit rating). The substance of the arrangement is that Entity A borrows cash, secured by the underlying asset.

(d)   in the example described in paragraph A2(d), Entity A's risks and rewards incident to owning the underlying asset do not substantively change. The substance of the arrangement is that Entity A borrows cash, secured by the underlying asset and repayable in instalments over the lease period and in a final lump sum at the end of the lease period. The terms of the option preclude recognition of a sale. Normally, in a sale and leaseback transaction, the risks and rewards incident to owning the underlying asset sold are retained by the seller only during the period of the lease.

Material published to accompany

SIC Interpretation 29

Service Concession Arrangements: Disclosures

This version includes amendments resulting from IFRSs issued up to 31 December 2009.

The text of the unaccompanied Interpretation is contained in Part A of this edition. Its effective date when issued was 31 December 2001. The effective date of the most recent amendment is 1 January 2009. This part presents the following accompanying material:

page

BASIS FOR CONCLUSIONS **B1698**

Basis for Conclusions on
SIC Interpretation 29 *Service Concession Arrangements: Disclosures*

This Basis for Conclusions accompanies, but is not part of, SIC-29.

[The original text of paragraphs 8 and 9 has been marked up to reflect the revision of IAS 1 in 2003 and 2007 and the issue of IFRIC 12 in 2006: new text is underlined and deleted text is struck through]

8   Paragraph 15 of the *Framework* states that the economic decisions taken by users of financial statements require an evaluation of the ability of the entity to generate cash and cash equivalents and of the timing and certainty of their generation. Paragraph 21 of the *Framework* states that financial statements also contain notes and supplementary schedules and other information. For example, they may contain additional information that is relevant to the needs of users about the items in the statement of financial position balance sheet and statement of comprehensive income statement. They may also include disclosures about the risks and uncertainties affecting the entity and any resources and obligations not recognised in the statement of financial position balance sheet.

9   A service concession arrangement often has provisions or significant features that warrant disclosure of information necessary to assist in assessing the amount, timing and certainty of future cash flows, and the nature and extent of the various rights and obligations involved. The rights and obligations associated with the services to be provided usually involve a high level of public involvement (eg to provide electricity to a city). Other obligations could include significant acts such as building an infrastructure asset (eg power plant) and delivering that asset to the Concession Provider grantor at the end of the concession period.

    The text of paragraph 10 has been marked up to reflect the revision of IAS 1 in 2007. Previous amendments to the paragraph, reflecting the revision of IAS 1 in 2003, have been incorporated into the text to avoid confusion with the new amendments in 2007.

10   IAS 1.112(c)103(c) requires an entity's notes to provide additional information that is not presented elsewhere in the financial statements on the face of the balance sheet, income statement, statement of changes in equity or cash flow statement, but is relevant to an understanding of any of them. The definition of notes in IAS 1.7 11 indicates that notes provide narrative descriptions or disaggregations of items disclosed in the statement of financial position balance sheet, statement of comprehensive income, separate income statement (if presented), statement of changes in equity and statement of cash flows statement, as well as information about items that do not qualify for recognition in those statements.

Material published to accompany

SIC Interpretation 31

Revenue—Barter Transactions Involving Advertising Services

This version includes amendments resulting from IFRSs issued up to 31 December 2009.

The text of the unaccompanied Interpretation is contained in Part A of this edition. Its effective date when issued was 31 December 2001. The effective date of the most recent amendment is 1 January 2005. This part presents the following accompanying material:

page

BASIS FOR CONCLUSIONS   **B1700**

Basis for Conclusions on
SIC Interpretation 31 *Revenue—Barter Transactions Involving Advertising Services*

This Basis for Conclusions accompanies, but is not part of, SIC-31.

6   IAS 18.9 requires revenue to be measured at the fair value of the consideration received or receivable. When the fair value of the services received cannot be measured reliably, the revenue is measured at the fair value of the services provided, adjusted by the amount of any cash or cash equivalents transferred. IAS 18.26 states that when the outcome of a transaction involving the rendering of services cannot be estimated reliably (eg the amount of revenue cannot be measured reliably), revenue should be recognised only to the extent of the expenses recognised that are recoverable. As explained in IAS 18.27, this means that revenue is recognised only to the extent of costs incurred that are expected to be recoverable and, as the outcome of the transactions cannot be estimated reliably, no profit is recognised.

7   Paragraph 31 of the *Framework* states that information has the quality of reliability when it is free from material error and bias and is representationally faithful. Measuring revenue at the fair value of advertising services received from the Customer in a barter transaction is impracticable, because reliable information not available to the Seller is required to support the measurement. Consequently, revenue from a barter transaction involving advertising services is measured at the fair value of the advertising services provided by the Seller to the Customer.

8   IAS 18.7 defines fair value as the amount for which an asset could be exchanged, or a liability settled, between knowledgeable, willing parties in an arm's length transaction. A published price of a service does not constitute reliable evidence of its fair value, unless the price is supported by transactions with knowledgeable and willing parties in an arm's length transaction. For transactions to provide a relevant and reliable basis for support, the services involved are similar, there are many transactions, valuable consideration that can be reliably measured is exchanged, and independent third parties are involved. Consequently, the fair value of advertising services provided in a barter transaction is reliably measurable only when it is supportable by reference to non-barter transactions that have these characteristics.

9   However, a swap of cheques, for example, for equal or substantially equal amounts between the same entities that provide and receive advertising services does not provide reliable evidence of fair value. An exchange of advertising services that also includes only partial cash payment provides reliable evidence of the fair value of the transaction to the extent of the cash component (except when partial cash payments of equal or substantially equal amounts are swapped), but does not provide reliable evidence of the fair value of the entire transaction.

10   Reliable measurement of the fair value of a service also depends on a number of other factors, including the industry, the number of market participants, the nature of the services, and the number of market transactions. In the case of barter transactions involving advertising, the fair value of advertising services is reliably measurable when independent non-barter transactions involving similar advertising provide reliable evidence to substantiate the fair value of the barter exchange.

Material published to accompany

SIC Interpretation 32

Intangible Assets—Web Site Costs

This version includes amendments resulting from IFRSs issued up to 31 December 2009.

The text of the unaccompanied Interpretation is contained in Part A of this edition. Its effective date when issued was 25 March 2002. The effective date of the most recent amendment is 1 January 2009. This part presents the following accompanying material:

Basis for Conclusions on
SIC Interpretation 32 *Intangible Assets—Web Site Costs*

This Basis for Conclusions accompanies, but is not part of, SIC-32.

[The original text has been marked up to reflect the revision of IAS 16 in 2003 and the subsequent issue of IFRS 3: new text is underlined and deleted text is struck through]

11   An intangible asset is defined in IAS 38.87 as an identifiable non-monetary asset without physical substance held for use in the production or supply of goods or services, for rental to others, or for administrative purposes. IAS 38.98 provides computer software as a common example of an intangible asset. By analogy, a web site is another example of an intangible asset.

12   IAS 38.68.56 requires expenditure on an intangible item to be recognised as an expense when incurred unless it forms part of the cost of an intangible asset that meets the recognition criteria in IAS 38.18–.67.55. IAS 38.69.57 requires expenditure on start-up activities to be recognised as an expense when incurred. An entity developing its own web site for internal or external access is not undertaking a start-up activity to the extent that an internally generated intangible asset is created. The requirements and guidance in IAS 38.52–.67.40.55, in addition to the general requirements described in IAS 38.21.19 for recognition and initial measurement of an intangible asset, apply to expenditure incurred on the development of an entity's own web site. As described in IAS 38.65–.67.53–.55, the cost of a web site recognised as an internally generated intangible asset comprises all expenditure that can be directly attributed, or allocated on a reasonable and consistent basis, and is necessary to creating, producing and preparing the asset for it to be capable of operating in the manner intended by management its intended use.

13   IAS 38.54.42 requires expenditure on research (or on the research phase of an internal project) to be recognised as an expense when incurred. The examples provided in IAS 38.56.44 are similar to the activities undertaken in the Planning stage of a web site's development. Consequently, expenditure incurred in the Planning stage of a web site's development is recognised as an expense when incurred.

14   IAS 38.57.45 requires an intangible asset arising from the development phase of an internal project to be recognised only if an entity can demonstrate fulfilment of the six criteria specified. One of the criteria is to demonstrate how a web site will generate probable future economic benefits (IAS 38.57.45(d)). IAS 38.60.48 indicates that this criterion is met by assessing the economic benefits to be received from the web site and using the principles in IAS 36 *Impairment of Assets*, which considers the present value of estimated future cash flows from continuing use of the web site. Future economic benefits flowing from an intangible asset, as stated in IAS 38.17, may include revenue from the sale of products or services, cost savings, or other benefits resulting from the use of the asset by the entity. Therefore, future economic benefits from a web site may be assessed when the web site is capable of generating revenues. A web site developed solely or primarily for advertising and promoting an entity's own products and services is

not recognised as an intangible asset, because the entity cannot demonstrate the future economic benefits that will flow. Consequently, all expenditure on developing a web site solely or primarily for promoting and advertising an entity's own products and services is recognised as an expense when incurred.

15   Under IAS 38.21~~19~~, an intangible asset is recognised if, and only if, it meets specified criteria. IAS 38.65~~53~~ indicates that the cost of an internally generated intangible asset is the sum of expenditure incurred from the date when the intangible asset first meets the specified recognition criteria. When an entity acquires or creates content for purposes other than to advertise and promote an entity's own products and services, it may be possible to identify an intangible asset (eg a licence or a copyright) separate from a web site. However, a separate asset is not recognised when expenditure is directly attributed, ~~or allocated on a reasonable and consistent basis,~~ to creating, producing, and preparing the web site for <u>it to be capable of operating in the manner intended by management</u> ~~its intended use~~ —the expenditure is included in the cost of developing the web site.

16   IAS 38.65~~57~~(c) requires expenditure on advertising and promotional activities to be recognised as an expense when incurred. Expenditure incurred on developing content that advertises and promotes an entity's own products and services (eg digital photographs of products) is an advertising and promotional activity, and consequently recognised as an expense when incurred ~~in accordance with IAS 38.57(c).~~

17   ~~Once development of a web site is complete, an enterprise begins the activities described in the Operating stage. Subsequent expenditure to enhance or maintain an enterprise's own web site is recognised as an expense when incurred unless it meets the recognition criteria in IAS 38.60. IAS 38.61 explains that if the expenditure is required to maintain the asset at its originally assessed standard of performance, then the expenditure is recognised as an expense when incurred.*~~ <u>Once development of a web site is complete, an entity begins the activities described in the Operating stage. Subsequent expenditure to enhance or maintain an entity's own web site is recognised as an expense when incurred unless it meets the recognition criteria in IAS 38.18. IAS 38.20 explains that most subsequent expenditures are likely to maintain the future economic benefits embodied in an existing intangible asset rather than meet the definition of an intangible asset and the recognition criteria set out in IAS 38. In addition, it is often difficult to attribute subsequent expenditure directly to a particular intangible asset rather than to the business as a whole. Therefore, only rarely will subsequent expenditure—expenditure incurred after the initial recognition of a purchased intangible asset or after completion of an internally generated intangible asset—be recognised in the carrying amount of an asset.</u>[†]

---

*   ~~IAS 16 *Property, Plant and Equipment* as revised by the IASB in 2003 requires all subsequent costs to be covered by its general recognition principle and eliminated the requirement to reference the originally assessed standard of performance. IAS 38 was amended as a consequence of the change to IAS 16 and the paragraphs specifically referred to were eliminated. This paragraph has been struck through to avoid any confusion.~~

†   <u>The new text was added by IFRS 3 *Business Combinations* in 2004.</u>

18   An intangible asset is measured after initial recognition by applying the requirements of IAS 38.~~72–~~.87~~63–.78~~. The <u>revaluation model</u> ~~Allowed Alternative Treatment~~ in IAS 38.~~75~~64 is applied only when the fair value of an intangible asset can be determined by reference to an active market. However, as an active market is unlikely to exist for web sites, the <u>cost model</u> ~~Benchmark Treatment~~ applies. Additionally, ~~since IAS 38.84 states that an intangible asset always has a finite useful life, a web site that is recognised as an asset is amortised over the best estimate of its useful life under IAS 38.79.~~ ~~As~~ <u>as</u> indicated in IAS 38.~~92~~81, many intangible assets are susceptible to technological obsolescence, and given the history of rapid changes in technology, the useful life of web sites will be short.

Illustrative example

This example accompanies, but is not part of, SIC-32. Its purpose is to illustrate examples of expenditure that occur during each of the stages described in paragraphs 2 and 3 of SIC-32 and illustrate application of SIC-32 to assist in clarifying its meaning. It is not intended to be a comprehensive checklist of expenditure that might be incurred.

Example application of SIC-32

Stage/nature of expenditure	Accounting treatment
Planning	
• undertaking feasibility studies	Recognise as an expense when incurred in accordance with IAS 38.54
• defining hardware and software specifications	
• evaluating alternative products and suppliers	
• selecting preferences	
Application and infrastructure development	
• purchasing or developing hardware	Apply the requirements of IAS 16
• obtaining a domain name	Recognise as an expense when incurred, unless the expenditure can be directly attributed to preparing the web site to operate in the manner intended by management, and the web site meets the recognition criteria in IAS 38.21 and IAS 38.57[(a)]
• developing operating software (eg operating system and server software)	
• developing code for the application	
• installing developed applications on the web server	
• stress testing	
Graphical design development	
• designing the appearance (eg layout and colour) of web pages	Recognise as an expense when incurred, unless the expenditure can be directly attributed to preparing the web site to operate in the manner intended by management, and the web site meets the recognition criteria in IAS 38.21 and IAS 38.57[(a)]

continued...

...*continued* **Stage/nature of expenditure**	**Accounting treatment**
Content development	
• creating, purchasing, preparing (eg creating links and identifying tags), and uploading information, either textual or graphical in nature, on the web site before the completion of the web site's development. Examples of content include information about an entity, products or services offered for sale, and topics that subscribers access	Recognise as an expense when incurred in accordance with IAS 38.69(c) to the extent that content is developed to advertise and promote an entity's own products and services (eg digital photographs of products). Otherwise, recognise as an expense when incurred, unless the expenditure can be directly attributed to preparing the web site to operate in the manner intended by management, and the web site meets the recognition criteria in IAS 38.21 and IAS 38.57[a]
Operating	
• updating graphics and revising content • adding new functions, features and content • registering the web site with search engines • backing up data • reviewing security access • analysing usage of the web site	Assess whether it meets the definition of an intangible asset and the recognition criteria set out in IAS 38.18, in which case the expenditure is recognised in the carrying amount of the web site asset
Other	
• selling, administrative and other general overhead expenditure unless it can be directly attributed to preparing the web site for use to operate in the manner intended by management • clearly identified inefficiencies and initial operating losses incurred before the web site achieves planned performance [eg false start testing] • training employees to operate the web site	Recognise as an expense when incurred in accordance with IAS 38.65–.70
[a] All expenditure on developing a web site solely or primarily for promoting and advertising an entity's own products and services is recognised as an expense when incurred in accordance with IAS 38.68.	

Approval by the Board of *Improvements to IFRSs* issued in May 2008

In May 2008 the International Accounting Standards Board issued *Improvements to IFRSs*. The document contained miscellaneous amendments to International Financial Reporting Standards (IFRSs) and the related Bases for Conclusions and guidance made in the Board's first annual improvements project.

The annual improvements project provides a vehicle for making non-urgent but necessary amendments to IFRSs. The amendments have been incorporated into the text of the IFRSs set out in this edition.

Improvements to IFRSs was approved for issue by the thirteen members of the International Accounting Standards Board, except that:

• Mr Yamada dissented from one of the amendments to IAS 28 *Investments in Associates*.

• Mr Leisenring dissented from one of the amendments to IAS 38 *Intangible Assets*.

The dissenting opinions of those Board members are set out after the Basis for Conclusions on the IFRSs affected.

Sir David Tweedie	Chairman
Thomas E Jones	Vice-Chairman
Mary E Barth	
Stephen Cooper	
Philippe Danjou	
Jan Engström	
Robert P Garnett	
Gilbert Gélard	
James J Leisenring	
Warren J McGregor	
John T Smith	
Tatsumi Yamada	
Wei-Guo Zhang	

Approval by the Board of *Improvements to IFRSs* issued in April 2009

In April 2009 the International Accounting Standards Board issued *Improvements to IFRSs*. The document contained miscellaneous amendments to International Financial Reporting Standards (IFRSs) and the related Bases for Conclusions and guidance made in the Board's second annual improvements project.

The annual improvements project provides a vehicle for making non-urgent but necessary amendments to IFRSs. The amendments have been incorporated into the text of the IFRSs set out in this edition.

Improvements to IFRSs was approved for issue by the fourteen members of the International Accounting Standards Board, except that:

• Mr Cooper dissented from the amendment to IFRS 8 *Operating Segments*.

• Mr Leisenring dissented from the amendment to IAS 17 *Leases*.

The dissenting opinions of those Board members are set out after the Basis for Conclusions on the IFRSs affected.

Sir David Tweedie	Chairman
Thomas E Jones	Vice-Chairman
Mary E Barth	
Stephen Cooper	
Philippe Danjou	
Jan Engström	
Robert P Garnett	
Gilbert Gélard	
Prabhakar Kalavacherla	
James J Leisenring	
Warren J McGregor	
John T Smith	
Tatsumi Yamada	
Wei-Guo Zhang	

Framework for the Preparation and Presentation of Financial Statements

The IASB Framework was approved by the IASC Board in April 1989 for publication in July 1989, and adopted by the IASB in April 2001.

Contents

© IASCF

> *The* Framework *has not been amended to reflect the changes made by IAS 1* **Presentation of** **Financial Statements** *(as revised in 2007).*

Preface

Financial statements are prepared and presented for external users by many entities around the world. Although such financial statements may appear similar from country to country, there are differences which have probably been caused by a variety of social, economic and legal circumstances and by different countries having in mind the needs of different users of financial statements when setting national requirements.

These different circumstances have led to the use of a variety of definitions of the elements of financial statements; that is, for example, assets, liabilities, equity, income and expenses. They have also resulted in the use of different criteria for the recognition of items in the financial statements and in a preference for different bases of measurement. The scope of the financial statements and the disclosures made in them have also been affected.

The International Accounting Standards Committee (IASC) is committed to narrowing these differences by seeking to harmonise regulations, accounting standards and procedures relating to the preparation and presentation of financial statements. It believes that further harmonisation can best be pursued by focusing on financial statements that are prepared for the purpose of providing information that is useful in making economic decisions.

The Board of IASC believes that financial statements prepared for this purpose meet the common needs of most users. This is because nearly all users are making economic decisions, for example, to:

(a) decide when to buy, hold or sell an equity investment;

(b) assess the stewardship or accountability of management;

(c) assess the ability of the entity to pay and provide other benefits to its employees;

(d) assess the security for amounts lent to the entity;

(e) determine taxation policies;

(f) determine distributable profits and dividends;

(g) prepare and use national income statistics; or

(h) regulate the activities of entities.

The Board recognises, however, that governments, in particular, may specify different or additional requirements for their own purposes. These requirements should not, however, affect financial statements published for the benefit of other users unless they also meet the needs of those other users.

Financial statements are most commonly prepared in accordance with an accounting model based on recoverable historical cost and the nominal financial capital maintenance concept. Other models and concepts may be more appropriate in order to meet the objective of providing information that is useful for making economic decisions although there is presently no consensus for change. This *Framework* has been developed so that it is applicable to a range of accounting models and concepts of capital and capital maintenance.

Introduction

Purpose and status

1   This *Framework* sets out the concepts that underlie the preparation and presentation of financial statements for external users. The purpose of the *Framework* is to:

    (a)   assist the Board of IASC in the development of future International Accounting Standards and in its review of existing International Accounting Standards;

    (b)   assist the Board of IASC in promoting harmonisation of regulations, accounting standards and procedures relating to the presentation of financial statements by providing a basis for reducing the number of alternative accounting treatments permitted by International Accounting Standards;

    (c)   assist national standard-setting bodies in developing national standards;

    (d)   assist preparers of financial statements in applying International Accounting Standards and in dealing with topics that have yet to form the subject of an International Accounting Standard;

    (e)   assist auditors in forming an opinion as to whether financial statements conform with International Accounting Standards;

    (f)   assist users of financial statements in interpreting the information contained in financial statements prepared in conformity with International Accounting Standards; and

    (g)   provide those who are interested in the work of IASC with information about its approach to the formulation of International Accounting Standards.

2   This *Framework* is not an International Accounting Standard and hence does not define standards for any particular measurement or disclosure issue. Nothing in this *Framework* overrides any specific International Accounting Standard.

3   The Board of IASC recognises that in a limited number of cases there may be a conflict between the *Framework* and an International Accounting Standard. In those cases where there is a conflict, the requirements of the International Accounting Standard prevail over those of the *Framework*. As, however, the Board of IASC will be guided by the *Framework* in the development of future Standards and in its review of existing Standards, the number of cases of conflict between the *Framework* and International Accounting Standards will diminish through time.

4   The *Framework* will be revised from time to time on the basis of the Board's experience of working with it.

Scope

5   The *Framework* deals with:

    (a)   the objective of financial statements;

(b)   the qualitative characteristics that determine the usefulness of information in financial statements;

(c)   the definition, recognition and measurement of the elements from which financial statements are constructed; and

(d)   concepts of capital and capital maintenance.

6   The *Framework* is concerned with general purpose financial statements (hereafter referred to as 'financial statements') including consolidated financial statements. Such financial statements are prepared and presented at least annually and are directed toward the common information needs of a wide range of users. Some of these users may require, and have the power to obtain, information in addition to that contained in the financial statements. Many users, however, have to rely on the financial statements as their major source of financial information and such financial statements should, therefore, be prepared and presented with their needs in view. Special purpose financial reports, for example, prospectuses and computations prepared for taxation purposes, are outside the scope of this *Framework*. Nevertheless, the *Framework* may be applied in the preparation of such special purpose reports where their requirements permit.

7   Financial statements form part of the process of financial reporting. A complete set of financial statements normally includes a balance sheet, an income statement, a statement of changes in financial position (which may be presented in a variety of ways, for example, as a statement of cash flows or a statement of funds flow), and those notes and other statements and explanatory material that are an integral part of the financial statements. They may also include supplementary schedules and information based on or derived from, and expected to be read with, such statements. Such schedules and supplementary information may deal, for example, with financial information about industrial and geographical segments and disclosures about the effects of changing prices. Financial statements do not, however, include such items as reports by directors, statements by the chairman, discussion and analysis by management and similar items that may be included in a financial or annual report.

8   The *Framework* applies to the financial statements of all commercial, industrial and business reporting entities, whether in the public or the private sectors. A reporting entity is an entity for which there are users who rely on the financial statements as their major source of financial information about the entity.

Users and their information needs

9   The users of financial statements include present and potential investors, employees, lenders, suppliers and other trade creditors, customers, governments and their agencies and the public. They use financial statements in order to satisfy some of their different needs for information. These needs include the following:

(a)   *Investors*. The providers of risk capital and their advisers are concerned with the risk inherent in, and return provided by, their investments. They need information to help them determine whether they should buy, hold or sell. Shareholders are also interested in information which enables them to assess the ability of the entity to pay dividends.

(b) *Employees*. Employees and their representative groups are interested in information about the stability and profitability of their employers. They are also interested in information which enables them to assess the ability of the entity to provide remuneration, retirement benefits and employment opportunities.

(c) *Lenders*. Lenders are interested in information that enables them to determine whether their loans, and the interest attaching to them, will be paid when due.

(d) *Suppliers and other trade creditors*. Suppliers and other creditors are interested in information that enables them to determine whether amounts owing to them will be paid when due. Trade creditors are likely to be interested in an entity over a shorter period than lenders unless they are dependent upon the continuation of the entity as a major customer.

(e) *Customers*. Customers have an interest in information about the continuance of an entity, especially when they have a long-term involvement with, or are dependent on, the entity.

(f) *Governments and their agencies*. Governments and their agencies are interested in the allocation of resources and, therefore, the activities of entities. They also require information in order to regulate the activities of entities, determine taxation policies and as the basis for national income and similar statistics.

(g) *Public*. Entities affect members of the public in a variety of ways. For example, entities may make a substantial contribution to the local economy in many ways including the number of people they employ and their patronage of local suppliers. Financial statements may assist the public by providing information about the trends and recent developments in the prosperity of the entity and the range of its activities.

10 While all of the information needs of these users cannot be met by financial statements, there are needs which are common to all users. As investors are providers of risk capital to the entity, the provision of financial statements that meet their needs will also meet most of the needs of other users that financial statements can satisfy.

11 The management of an entity has the primary responsibility for the preparation and presentation of the financial statements of the entity. Management is also interested in the information contained in the financial statements even though it has access to additional management and financial information that helps it carry out its planning, decision-making and control responsibilities. Management has the ability to determine the form and content of such additional information in order to meet its own needs. The reporting of such information, however, is beyond the scope of this *Framework*. Nevertheless, published financial statements are based on the information used by management about the financial position, performance and changes in financial position of the entity.

The objective of financial statements

12   The objective of financial statements is to provide information about the financial position, performance and changes in financial position of an entity that is useful to a wide range of users in making economic decisions.

13   Financial statements prepared for this purpose meet the common needs of most users. However, financial statements do not provide all the information that users may need to make economic decisions since they largely portray the financial effects of past events and do not necessarily provide non-financial information.

14   Financial statements also show the results of the stewardship of management, or the accountability of management for the resources entrusted to it. Those users who wish to assess the stewardship or accountability of management do so in order that they may make economic decisions; these decisions may include, for example, whether to hold or sell their investment in the entity or whether to reappoint or replace the management.

Financial position, performance and changes in financial position

15   The economic decisions that are taken by users of financial statements require an evaluation of the ability of an entity to generate cash and cash equivalents and of the timing and certainty of their generation. This ability ultimately determines, for example, the capacity of an entity to pay its employees and suppliers, meet interest payments, repay loans and make distributions to its owners. Users are better able to evaluate this ability to generate cash and cash equivalents if they are provided with information that focuses on the financial position, performance and changes in financial position of an entity.

16   The financial position of an entity is affected by the economic resources it controls, its financial structure, its liquidity and solvency, and its capacity to adapt to changes in the environment in which it operates. Information about the economic resources controlled by the entity and its capacity in the past to modify these resources is useful in predicting the ability of the entity to generate cash and cash equivalents in the future. Information about financial structure is useful in predicting future borrowing needs and how future profits and cash flows will be distributed among those with an interest in the entity; it is also useful in predicting how successful the entity is likely to be in raising further finance. Information about liquidity and solvency is useful in predicting the ability of the entity to meet its financial commitments as they fall due. Liquidity refers to the availability of cash in the near future after taking account of financial commitments over this period. Solvency refers to the availability of cash over the longer term to meet financial commitments as they fall due.

17   Information about the performance of an entity, in particular its profitability, is required in order to assess potential changes in the economic resources that it is likely to control in the future. Information about variability of performance is important in this respect. Information about performance is useful in predicting the capacity of the entity to generate cash flows from its existing resource base. It is also useful in forming judgements about the effectiveness with which the entity might employ additional resources.

18   Information concerning changes in the financial position of an entity is useful in order to assess its investing, financing and operating activities during the reporting period. This information is useful in providing the user with a basis to assess the ability of the entity to generate cash and cash equivalents and the needs of the entity to utilise those cash flows. In constructing a statement of changes in financial position, funds can be defined in various ways, such as all financial resources, working capital, liquid assets or cash. No attempt is made in this *Framework* to specify a definition of funds.

19   Information about financial position is primarily provided in a balance sheet. Information about performance is primarily provided in an income statement. Information about changes in financial position is provided in the financial statements by means of a separate statement.

20   The component parts of the financial statements interrelate because they reflect different aspects of the same transactions or other events. Although each statement provides information that is different from the others, none is likely to serve only a single purpose or provide all the information necessary for particular needs of users. For example, an income statement provides an incomplete picture of performance unless it is used in conjunction with the balance sheet and the statement of changes in financial position.

Notes and supplementary schedules

21   The financial statements also contain notes and supplementary schedules and other information. For example, they may contain additional information that is relevant to the needs of users about the items in the balance sheet and income statement. They may include disclosures about the risks and uncertainties affecting the entity and any resources and obligations not recognised in the balance sheet (such as mineral reserves). Information about geographical and industry segments and the effect on the entity of changing prices may also be provided in the form of supplementary information.

Underlying assumptions

Accrual basis

22   In order to meet their objectives, financial statements are prepared on the accrual basis of accounting. Under this basis, the effects of transactions and other events are recognised when they occur (and not as cash or its equivalent is received or paid) and they are recorded in the accounting records and reported in the financial statements of the periods to which they relate. Financial statements prepared on the accrual basis inform users not only of past transactions involving the payment and receipt of cash but also of obligations to pay cash in the future and of resources that represent cash to be received in the future. Hence, they provide the type of information about past transactions and other events that is most useful to users in making economic decisions.

Going concern

23 The financial statements are normally prepared on the assumption that an entity is a going concern and will continue in operation for the foreseeable future. Hence, it is assumed that the entity has neither the intention nor the need to liquidate or curtail materially the scale of its operations; if such an intention or need exists, the financial statements may have to be prepared on a different basis and, if so, the basis used is disclosed.

Qualitative characteristics of financial statements

24 Qualitative characteristics are the attributes that make the information provided in financial statements useful to users. The four principal qualitative characteristics are understandability, relevance, reliability and comparability.

Understandability

25 An essential quality of the information provided in financial statements is that it is readily understandable by users. For this purpose, users are assumed to have a reasonable knowledge of business and economic activities and accounting and a willingness to study the information with reasonable diligence. However, information about complex matters that should be included in the financial statements because of its relevance to the economic decision-making needs of users should not be excluded merely on the grounds that it may be too difficult for certain users to understand.

Relevance

26 To be useful, information must be relevant to the decision-making needs of users. Information has the quality of relevance when it influences the economic decisions of users by helping them evaluate past, present or future events or confirming, or correcting, their past evaluations.

27 The predictive and confirmatory roles of information are interrelated. For example, information about the current level and structure of asset holdings has value to users when they endeavour to predict the ability of the entity to take advantage of opportunities and its ability to react to adverse situations. The same information plays a confirmatory role in respect of past predictions about, for example, the way in which the entity would be structured or the outcome of planned operations.

28 Information about financial position and past performance is frequently used as the basis for predicting future financial position and performance and other matters in which users are directly interested, such as dividend and wage payments, security price movements and the ability of the entity to meet its commitments as they fall due. To have predictive value, information need not be in the form of an explicit forecast. The ability to make predictions from financial statements is enhanced, however, by the manner in which information on past transactions and events is displayed. For example, the predictive value of the income statement is enhanced if unusual, abnormal and infrequent items of income or expense are separately disclosed.

Materiality

29   The relevance of information is affected by its nature and materiality. In some cases, the nature of information alone is sufficient to determine its relevance. For example, the reporting of a new segment may affect the assessment of the risks and opportunities facing the entity irrespective of the materiality of the results achieved by the new segment in the reporting period. In other cases, both the nature and materiality are important, for example, the amounts of inventories held in each of the main categories that are appropriate to the business.

30   Information is material if its omission or misstatement could influence the economic decisions of users taken on the basis of the financial statements. Materiality depends on the size of the item or error judged in the particular circumstances of its omission or misstatement. Thus, materiality provides a threshold or cut-off point rather than being a primary qualitative characteristic which information must have if it is to be useful.

Reliability

31   To be useful, information must also be reliable. Information has the quality of reliability when it is free from material error and bias and can be depended upon by users to represent faithfully that which it either purports to represent or could reasonably be expected to represent.

32   Information may be relevant but so unreliable in nature or representation that its recognition may be potentially misleading. For example, if the validity and amount of a claim for damages under a legal action are disputed, it may be inappropriate for the entity to recognise the full amount of the claim in the balance sheet, although it may be appropriate to disclose the amount and circumstances of the claim.

Faithful representation

33   To be reliable, information must represent faithfully the transactions and other events it either purports to represent or could reasonably be expected to represent. Thus, for example, a balance sheet should represent faithfully the transactions and other events that result in assets, liabilities and equity of the entity at the reporting date which meet the recognition criteria.

34   Most financial information is subject to some risk of being less than a faithful representation of that which it purports to portray. This is not due to bias, but rather to inherent difficulties either in identifying the transactions and other events to be measured or in devising and applying measurement and presentation techniques that can convey messages that correspond with those transactions and events. In certain cases, the measurement of the financial effects of items could be so uncertain that entities generally would not recognise them in the financial statements; for example, although most entities generate goodwill internally over time, it is usually difficult to identify or measure that goodwill reliably. In other cases, however, it may be relevant to recognise items and to disclose the risk of error surrounding their recognition and measurement.

Substance over form

35   If information is to represent faithfully the transactions and other events that it purports to represent, it is necessary that they are accounted for and presented in accordance with their substance and economic reality and not merely their legal form. The substance of transactions or other events is not always consistent with that which is apparent from their legal or contrived form. For example, an entity may dispose of an asset to another party in such a way that the documentation purports to pass legal ownership to that party; nevertheless, agreements may exist that ensure that the entity continues to enjoy the future economic benefits embodied in the asset. In such circumstances, the reporting of a sale would not represent faithfully the transaction entered into (if indeed there was a transaction).

Neutrality

36   To be reliable, the information contained in financial statements must be neutral, that is, free from bias. Financial statements are not neutral if, by the selection or presentation of information, they influence the making of a decision or judgement in order to achieve a predetermined result or outcome.

Prudence

37   The preparers of financial statements do, however, have to contend with the uncertainties that inevitably surround many events and circumstances, such as the collectability of doubtful receivables, the probable useful life of plant and equipment and the number of warranty claims that may occur. Such uncertainties are recognised by the disclosure of their nature and extent and by the exercise of prudence in the preparation of the financial statements. Prudence is the inclusion of a degree of caution in the exercise of the judgements needed in making the estimates required under conditions of uncertainty, such that assets or income are not overstated and liabilities or expenses are not understated. However, the exercise of prudence does not allow, for example, the creation of hidden reserves or excessive provisions, the deliberate understatement of assets or income, or the deliberate overstatement of liabilities or expenses, because the financial statements would not be neutral and, therefore, not have the quality of reliability.

Completeness

38   To be reliable, the information in financial statements must be complete within the bounds of materiality and cost. An omission can cause information to be false or misleading and thus unreliable and deficient in terms of its relevance.

Comparability

39   Users must be able to compare the financial statements of an entity through time in order to identify trends in its financial position and performance. Users must also be able to compare the financial statements of different entities in order to evaluate their relative financial position, performance and changes in financial

position. Hence, the measurement and display of the financial effect of like transactions and other events must be carried out in a consistent way throughout an entity and over time for that entity and in a consistent way for different entities.

40 An important implication of the qualitative characteristic of comparability is that users be informed of the accounting policies employed in the preparation of the financial statements, any changes in those policies and the effects of such changes. Users need to be able to identify differences between the accounting policies for like transactions and other events used by the same entity from period to period and by different entities. Compliance with International Accounting Standards, including the disclosure of the accounting policies used by the entity, helps to achieve comparability.

41 The need for comparability should not be confused with mere uniformity and should not be allowed to become an impediment to the introduction of improved accounting standards. It is not appropriate for an entity to continue accounting in the same manner for a transaction or other event if the policy adopted is not in keeping with the qualitative characteristics of relevance and reliability. It is also inappropriate for an entity to leave its accounting policies unchanged when more relevant and reliable alternatives exist.

42 Because users wish to compare the financial position, performance and changes in financial position of an entity over time, it is important that the financial statements show corresponding information for the preceding periods.

Constraints on relevant and reliable information

Timeliness

43 If there is undue delay in the reporting of information it may lose its relevance. Management may need to balance the relative merits of timely reporting and the provision of reliable information. To provide information on a timely basis it may often be necessary to report before all aspects of a transaction or other event are known, thus impairing reliability. Conversely, if reporting is delayed until all aspects are known, the information may be highly reliable but of little use to users who have had to make decisions in the interim. In achieving a balance between relevance and reliability, the overriding consideration is how best to satisfy the economic decision-making needs of users.

Balance between benefit and cost

44 The balance between benefit and cost is a pervasive constraint rather than a qualitative characteristic. The benefits derived from information should exceed the cost of providing it. The evaluation of benefits and costs is, however, substantially a judgemental process. Furthermore, the costs do not necessarily fall on those users who enjoy the benefits. Benefits may also be enjoyed by users other than those for whom the information is prepared; for example, the provision of further information to lenders may reduce the borrowing costs of an entity. For these reasons, it is difficult to apply a cost-benefit test in any particular case. Nevertheless, standard-setters in particular, as well as the preparers and users of financial statements, should be aware of this constraint.

Balance between qualitative characteristics

45   In practice a balancing, or trade-off, between qualitative characteristics is often necessary. Generally the aim is to achieve an appropriate balance among the characteristics in order to meet the objective of financial statements. The relative importance of the characteristics in different cases is a matter of professional judgement.

True and fair view/fair presentation

46   Financial statements are frequently described as showing a true and fair view of, or as presenting fairly, the financial position, performance and changes in financial position of an entity. Although this *Framework* does not deal directly with such concepts, the application of the principal qualitative characteristics and of appropriate accounting standards normally results in financial statements that convey what is generally understood as a true and fair view of, or as presenting fairly such information.

The elements of financial statements

47   Financial statements portray the financial effects of transactions and other events by grouping them into broad classes according to their economic characteristics. These broad classes are termed the elements of financial statements. The elements directly related to the measurement of financial position in the balance sheet are assets, liabilities and equity. The elements directly related to the measurement of performance in the income statement are income and expenses. The statement of changes in financial position usually reflects income statement elements and changes in balance sheet elements; accordingly, this *Framework* identifies no elements that are unique to this statement.

48   The presentation of these elements in the balance sheet and the income statement involves a process of sub-classification. For example, assets and liabilities may be classified by their nature or function in the business of the entity in order to display information in the manner most useful to users for purposes of making economic decisions.

Financial position

49   The elements directly related to the measurement of financial position are assets, liabilities and equity. These are defined as follows:

    (a)   An asset is a resource controlled by the entity as a result of past events and from which future economic benefits are expected to flow to the entity.

    (b)   A liability is a present obligation of the entity arising from past events, the settlement of which is expected to result in an outflow from the entity of resources embodying economic benefits.

    (c)   Equity is the residual interest in the assets of the entity after deducting all its liabilities.

50   The definitions of an asset and a liability identify their essential features but do not attempt to specify the criteria that need to be met before they are recognised in the balance sheet. Thus, the definitions embrace items that are not recognised as assets or liabilities in the balance sheet because they do not satisfy the criteria for recognition discussed in paragraphs 82 to 98. In particular, the expectation that future economic benefits will flow to or from an entity must be sufficiently certain to meet the probability criterion in paragraph 83 before an asset or liability is recognised.

51   In assessing whether an item meets the definition of an asset, liability or equity, attention needs to be given to its underlying substance and economic reality and not merely its legal form. Thus, for example, in the case of finance leases, the substance and economic reality are that the lessee acquires the economic benefits of the use of the leased asset for the major part of its useful life in return for entering into an obligation to pay for that right an amount approximating to the fair value of the asset and the related finance charge. Hence, the finance lease gives rise to items that satisfy the definition of an asset and a liability and are recognised as such in the lessee's balance sheet.

52   Balance sheets drawn up in accordance with current International Accounting Standards may include items that do not satisfy the definitions of an asset or liability and are not shown as part of equity. The definitions set out in paragraph 49 will, however, underlie future reviews of existing International Accounting Standards and the formulation of further Standards.

Assets

53   The future economic benefit embodied in an asset is the potential to contribute, directly or indirectly, to the flow of cash and cash equivalents to the entity. The potential may be a productive one that is part of the operating activities of the entity. It may also take the form of convertibility into cash or cash equivalents or a capability to reduce cash outflows, such as when an alternative manufacturing process lowers the costs of production.

54   An entity usually employs its assets to produce goods or services capable of satisfying the wants or needs of customers; because these goods or services can satisfy these wants or needs, customers are prepared to pay for them and hence contribute to the cash flow of the entity. Cash itself renders a service to the entity because of its command over other resources.

55   The future economic benefits embodied in an asset may flow to the entity in a number of ways. For example, an asset may be:

(a)   used singly or in combination with other assets in the production of goods or services to be sold by the entity;

(b)   exchanged for other assets;

(c)   used to settle a liability; or

(d)   distributed to the owners of the entity.

56   Many assets, for example, property, plant and equipment, have a physical form. However, physical form is not essential to the existence of an asset; hence patents and copyrights, for example, are assets if future economic benefits are expected to flow from them to the entity and if they are controlled by the entity.

57   Many assets, for example, receivables and property, are associated with legal rights, including the right of ownership. In determining the existence of an asset, the right of ownership is not essential; thus, for example, property held on a lease is an asset if the entity controls the benefits which are expected to flow from the property. Although the capacity of an entity to control benefits is usually the result of legal rights, an item may nonetheless satisfy the definition of an asset even when there is no legal control. For example, know-how obtained from a development activity may meet the definition of an asset when, by keeping that know-how secret, an entity controls the benefits that are expected to flow from it.

58   The assets of an entity result from past transactions or other past events. Entities normally obtain assets by purchasing or producing them, but other transactions or events may generate assets; examples include property received by an entity from government as part of a programme to encourage economic growth in an area and the discovery of mineral deposits. Transactions or events expected to occur in the future do not in themselves give rise to assets; hence, for example, an intention to purchase inventory does not, of itself, meet the definition of an asset.

59   There is a close association between incurring expenditure and generating assets but the two do not necessarily coincide. Hence, when an entity incurs expenditure, this may provide evidence that future economic benefits were sought but is not conclusive proof that an item satisfying the definition of an asset has been obtained. Similarly the absence of a related expenditure does not preclude an item from satisfying the definition of an asset and thus becoming a candidate for recognition in the balance sheet; for example, items that have been donated to the entity may satisfy the definition of an asset.

Liabilities

60   An essential characteristic of a liability is that the entity has a present obligation. An obligation is a duty or responsibility to act or perform in a certain way. Obligations may be legally enforceable as a consequence of a binding contract or statutory requirement. This is normally the case, for example, with amounts payable for goods and services received. Obligations also arise, however, from normal business practice, custom and a desire to maintain good business relations or act in an equitable manner. If, for example, an entity decides as a matter of policy to rectify faults in its products even when these become apparent after the warranty period has expired, the amounts that are expected to be expended in respect of goods already sold are liabilities.

61   A distinction needs to be drawn between a present obligation and a future commitment. A decision by the management of an entity to acquire assets in the future does not, of itself, give rise to a present obligation. An obligation normally arises only when the asset is delivered or the entity enters into an irrevocable agreement to acquire the asset. In the latter case, the irrevocable nature of the

agreement means that the economic consequences of failing to honour the obligation, for example, because of the existence of a substantial penalty, leave the entity with little, if any, discretion to avoid the outflow of resources to another party.

62 The settlement of a present obligation usually involves the entity giving up resources embodying economic benefits in order to satisfy the claim of the other party. Settlement of a present obligation may occur in a number of ways, for example, by:

(a) payment of cash;

(b) transfer of other assets;

(c) provision of services;

(d) replacement of that obligation with another obligation; or

(e) conversion of the obligation to equity.

An obligation may also be extinguished by other means, such as a creditor waiving or forfeiting its rights.

63 Liabilities result from past transactions or other past events. Thus, for example, the acquisition of goods and the use of services give rise to trade payables (unless paid for in advance or on delivery) and the receipt of a bank loan results in an obligation to repay the loan. An entity may also recognise future rebates based on annual purchases by customers as liabilities; in this case, the sale of the goods in the past is the transaction that gives rise to the liability.

64 Some liabilities can be measured only by using a substantial degree of estimation. Some entities describe these liabilities as provisions. In some countries, such provisions are not regarded as liabilities because the concept of a liability is defined narrowly so as to include only amounts that can be established without the need to make estimates. The definition of a liability in paragraph 49 follows a broader approach. Thus, when a provision involves a present obligation and satisfies the rest of the definition, it is a liability even if the amount has to be estimated. Examples include provisions for payments to be made under existing warranties and provisions to cover pension obligations.

Equity

65 Although equity is defined in paragraph 49 as a residual, it may be sub-classified in the balance sheet. For example, in a corporate entity, funds contributed by shareholders, retained earnings, reserves representing appropriations of retained earnings and reserves representing capital maintenance adjustments may be shown separately. Such classifications can be relevant to the decision-making needs of the users of financial statements when they indicate legal or other restrictions on the ability of the entity to distribute or otherwise apply its equity. They may also reflect the fact that parties with ownership interests in an entity have differing rights in relation to the receipt of dividends or the repayment of contributed equity.

66   The creation of reserves is sometimes required by statute or other law in order to give the entity and its creditors an added measure of protection from the effects of losses. Other reserves may be established if national tax law grants exemptions from, or reductions in, taxation liabilities when transfers to such reserves are made. The existence and size of these legal, statutory and tax reserves is information that can be relevant to the decision-making needs of users. Transfers to such reserves are appropriations of retained earnings rather than expenses.

67   The amount at which equity is shown in the balance sheet is dependent on the measurement of assets and liabilities. Normally, the aggregate amount of equity only by coincidence corresponds with the aggregate market value of the shares of the entity or the sum that could be raised by disposing of either the net assets on a piecemeal basis or the entity as a whole on a going concern basis.

68   Commercial, industrial and business activities are often undertaken by means of entities such as sole proprietorships, partnerships and trusts and various types of government business undertakings. The legal and regulatory framework for such entities is often different from that applying to corporate entities. For example, there may be few, if any, restrictions on the distribution to owners or other beneficiaries of amounts included in equity. Nevertheless, the definition of equity and the other aspects of this *Framework* that deal with equity are appropriate for such entities.

Performance

69   Profit is frequently used as a measure of performance or as the basis for other measures, such as return on investment or earnings per share. The elements directly related to the measurement of profit are income and expenses. The recognition and measurement of income and expenses, and hence profit, depends in part on the concepts of capital and capital maintenance used by the entity in preparing its financial statements. These concepts are discussed in paragraphs 102 to 110.

70   The elements of income and expenses are defined as follows:

   (a)   Income is increases in economic benefits during the accounting period in the form of inflows or enhancements of assets or decreases of liabilities that result in increases in equity, other than those relating to contributions from equity participants.

   (b)   Expenses are decreases in economic benefits during the accounting period in the form of outflows or depletions of assets or incurrences of liabilities that result in decreases in equity, other than those relating to distributions to equity participants.

71   The definitions of income and expenses identify their essential features but do not attempt to specify the criteria that would need to be met before they are recognised in the income statement. Criteria for the recognition of income and expenses are discussed in paragraphs 82 to 98.

72   Income and expenses may be presented in the income statement in different ways so as to provide information that is relevant for economic decision-making. For example, it is common practice to distinguish between those items of income and expenses that arise in the course of the ordinary activities of the entity and

those that do not. This distinction is made on the basis that the source of an item is relevant in evaluating the ability of the entity to generate cash and cash equivalents in the future; for example, incidental activities such as the disposal of a long-term investment are unlikely to recur on a regular basis. When distinguishing between items in this way consideration needs to be given to the nature of the entity and its operations. Items that arise from the ordinary activities of one entity may be unusual in respect of another.

73 Distinguishing between items of income and expense and combining them in different ways also permits several measures of entity performance to be displayed. These have differing degrees of inclusiveness. For example, the income statement could display gross margin, profit or loss from ordinary activities before taxation, profit or loss from ordinary activities after taxation, and profit or loss.

Income

74 The definition of income encompasses both revenue and gains. Revenue arises in the course of the ordinary activities of an entity and is referred to by a variety of different names including sales, fees, interest, dividends, royalties and rent.

75 Gains represent other items that meet the definition of income and may, or may not, arise in the course of the ordinary activities of an entity. Gains represent increases in economic benefits and as such are no different in nature from revenue. Hence, they are not regarded as constituting a separate element in this *Framework*.

76 Gains include, for example, those arising on the disposal of non-current assets. The definition of income also includes unrealised gains; for example, those arising on the revaluation of marketable securities and those resulting from increases in the carrying amount of long-term assets. When gains are recognised in the income statement, they are usually displayed separately because knowledge of them is useful for the purpose of making economic decisions. Gains are often reported net of related expenses.

77 Various kinds of assets may be received or enhanced by income; examples include cash, receivables and goods and services received in exchange for goods and services supplied. Income may also result from the settlement of liabilities. For example, an entity may provide goods and services to a lender in settlement of an obligation to repay an outstanding loan.

Expenses

78 The definition of expenses encompasses losses as well as those expenses that arise in the course of the ordinary activities of the entity. Expenses that arise in the course of the ordinary activities of the entity include, for example, cost of sales, wages and depreciation. They usually take the form of an outflow or depletion of assets such as cash and cash equivalents, inventory, property, plant and equipment.

79 Losses represent other items that meet the definition of expenses and may, or may not, arise in the course of the ordinary activities of the entity. Losses represent decreases in economic benefits and as such they are no different in nature from other expenses. Hence, they are not regarded as a separate element in this *Framework*.

80   Losses include, for example, those resulting from disasters such as fire and flood, as well as those arising on the disposal of non-current assets. The definition of expenses also includes unrealised losses, for example, those arising from the effects of increases in the rate of exchange for a foreign currency in respect of the borrowings of an entity in that currency. When losses are recognised in the income statement, they are usually displayed separately because knowledge of them is useful for the purpose of making economic decisions. Losses are often reported net of related income.

Capital maintenance adjustments

81   The revaluation or restatement of assets and liabilities gives rise to increases or decreases in equity. While these increases or decreases meet the definition of income and expenses, they are not included in the income statement under certain concepts of capital maintenance. Instead these items are included in equity as capital maintenance adjustments or revaluation reserves. These concepts of capital maintenance are discussed in paragraphs 102 to 110 of this *Framework*.

Recognition of the elements of financial statements

82   Recognition is the process of incorporating in the balance sheet or income statement an item that meets the definition of an element and satisfies the criteria for recognition set out in paragraph 83. It involves the depiction of the item in words and by a monetary amount and the inclusion of that amount in the balance sheet or income statement totals. Items that satisfy the recognition criteria should be recognised in the balance sheet or income statement. The failure to recognise such items is not rectified by disclosure of the accounting policies used nor by notes or explanatory material.

83   An item that meets the definition of an element should be recognised if:

(a)   it is probable that any future economic benefit associated with the item will flow to or from the entity; and

(b)   the item has a cost or value that can be measured with reliability.

84   In assessing whether an item meets these criteria and therefore qualifies for recognition in the financial statements, regard needs to be given to the materiality considerations discussed in paragraphs 29 and 30. The interrelationship between the elements means that an item that meets the definition and recognition criteria for a particular element, for example, an asset, automatically requires the recognition of another element, for example, income or a liability.

The probability of future economic benefit

85   The concept of probability is used in the recognition criteria to refer to the degree of uncertainty that the future economic benefits associated with the item will flow to or from the entity. The concept is in keeping with the uncertainty that characterises the environment in which an entity operates. Assessments of the degree of uncertainty attaching to the flow of future economic benefits are made on the basis of the evidence available when the financial statements are prepared.

For example, when it is probable that a receivable owed to an entity will be paid, it is then justifiable, in the absence of any evidence to the contrary, to recognise the receivable as an asset. For a large population of receivables, however, some degree of non-payment is normally considered probable; hence an expense representing the expected reduction in economic benefits is recognised.

Reliability of measurement

86   The second criterion for the recognition of an item is that it possesses a cost or value that can be measured with reliability as discussed in paragraphs 31 to 38 of this *Framework*. In many cases, cost or value must be estimated; the use of reasonable estimates is an essential part of the preparation of financial statements and does not undermine their reliability. When, however, a reasonable estimate cannot be made the item is not recognised in the balance sheet or income statement. For example, the expected proceeds from a lawsuit may meet the definitions of both an asset and income as well as the probability criterion for recognition; however, if it is not possible for the claim to be measured reliably, it should not be recognised as an asset or as income; the existence of the claim, however, would be disclosed in the notes, explanatory material or supplementary schedules.

87   An item that, at a particular point in time, fails to meet the recognition criteria in paragraph 83 may qualify for recognition at a later date as a result of subsequent circumstances or events.

88   An item that possesses the essential characteristics of an element but fails to meet the criteria for recognition may nonetheless warrant disclosure in the notes, explanatory material or in supplementary schedules. This is appropriate when knowledge of the item is considered to be relevant to the evaluation of the financial position, performance and changes in financial position of an entity by the users of financial statements.

Recognition of assets

89   An asset is recognised in the balance sheet when it is probable that the future economic benefits will flow to the entity and the asset has a cost or value that can be measured reliably.

90   An asset is not recognised in the balance sheet when expenditure has been incurred for which it is considered improbable that economic benefits will flow to the entity beyond the current accounting period. Instead such a transaction results in the recognition of an expense in the income statement. This treatment does not imply either that the intention of management in incurring expenditure was other than to generate future economic benefits for the entity or that management was misguided. The only implication is that the degree of certainty that economic benefits will flow to the entity beyond the current accounting period is insufficient to warrant the recognition of an asset.

Recognition of liabilities

91   A liability is recognised in the balance sheet when it is probable that an outflow of resources embodying economic benefits will result from the settlement of a present obligation and the amount at which the settlement will take place can be

measured reliably. In practice, obligations under contracts that are equally proportionately unperformed (for example, liabilities for inventory ordered but not yet received) are generally not recognised as liabilities in the financial statements. However, such obligations may meet the definition of liabilities and, provided the recognition criteria are met in the particular circumstances, may qualify for recognition. In such circumstances, recognition of liabilities entails recognition of related assets or expenses.

Recognition of income

92   Income is recognised in the income statement when an increase in future economic benefits related to an increase in an asset or a decrease of a liability has arisen that can be measured reliably. This means, in effect, that recognition of income occurs simultaneously with the recognition of increases in assets or decreases in liabilities (for example, the net increase in assets arising on a sale of goods or services or the decrease in liabilities arising from the waiver of a debt payable).

93   The procedures normally adopted in practice for recognising income, for example, the requirement that revenue should be earned, are applications of the recognition criteria in this *Framework*. Such procedures are generally directed at restricting the recognition as income to those items that can be measured reliably and have a sufficient degree of certainty.

Recognition of expenses

94   Expenses are recognised in the income statement when a decrease in future economic benefits related to a decrease in an asset or an increase of a liability has arisen that can be measured reliably. This means, in effect, that recognition of expenses occurs simultaneously with the recognition of an increase in liabilities or a decrease in assets (for example, the accrual of employee entitlements or the depreciation of equipment).

95   Expenses are recognised in the income statement on the basis of a direct association between the costs incurred and the earning of specific items of income. This process, commonly referred to as the matching of costs with revenues, involves the simultaneous or combined recognition of revenues and expenses that result directly and jointly from the same transactions or other events; for example, the various components of expense making up the cost of goods sold are recognised at the same time as the income derived from the sale of the goods. However, the application of the matching concept under this *Framework* does not allow the recognition of items in the balance sheet which do not meet the definition of assets or liabilities.

96   When economic benefits are expected to arise over several accounting periods and the association with income can only be broadly or indirectly determined, expenses are recognised in the income statement on the basis of systematic and rational allocation procedures. This is often necessary in recognising the expenses associated with the using up of assets such as property, plant, equipment, goodwill, patents and trademarks; in such cases the expense is referred to as depreciation or amortisation. These allocation procedures are intended to recognise expenses in the accounting periods in which the economic benefits associated with these items are consumed or expire.

97　　An expense is recognised immediately in the income statement when an expenditure produces no future economic benefits or when, and to the extent that, future economic benefits do not qualify, or cease to qualify, for recognition in the balance sheet as an asset.

98　　An expense is also recognised in the income statement in those cases when a liability is incurred without the recognition of an asset, as when a liability under a product warranty arises.

Measurement of the elements of financial statements

99　　Measurement is the process of determining the monetary amounts at which the elements of the financial statements are to be recognised and carried in the balance sheet and income statement. This involves the selection of the particular basis of measurement.

100　　A number of different measurement bases are employed to different degrees and in varying combinations in financial statements. They include the following:

(a) *Historical cost.* Assets are recorded at the amount of cash or cash equivalents paid or the fair value of the consideration given to acquire them at the time of their acquisition. Liabilities are recorded at the amount of proceeds received in exchange for the obligation, or in some circumstances (for example, income taxes), at the amounts of cash or cash equivalents expected to be paid to satisfy the liability in the normal course of business.

(b) *Current cost.* Assets are carried at the amount of cash or cash equivalents that would have to be paid if the same or an equivalent asset was acquired currently. Liabilities are carried at the undiscounted amount of cash or cash equivalents that would be required to settle the obligation currently.

(c) *Realisable (settlement) value.* Assets are carried at the amount of cash or cash equivalents that could currently be obtained by selling the asset in an orderly disposal. Liabilities are carried at their settlement values; that is, the undiscounted amounts of cash or cash equivalents expected to be paid to satisfy the liabilities in the normal course of business.

(d) *Present value.* Assets are carried at the present discounted value of the future net cash inflows that the item is expected to generate in the normal course of business. Liabilities are carried at the present discounted value of the future net cash outflows that are expected to be required to settle the liabilities in the normal course of business.

101　　The measurement basis most commonly adopted by entities in preparing their financial statements is historical cost. This is usually combined with other measurement bases. For example, inventories are usually carried at the lower of cost and net realisable value, marketable securities may be carried at market value and pension liabilities are carried at their present value. Furthermore, some entities use the current cost basis as a response to the inability of the historical cost accounting model to deal with the effects of changing prices of non-monetary assets.

Concepts of capital and capital maintenance

Concepts of capital

102 A financial concept of capital is adopted by most entities in preparing their financial statements. Under a financial concept of capital, such as invested money or invested purchasing power, capital is synonymous with the net assets or equity of the entity. Under a physical concept of capital, such as operating capability, capital is regarded as the productive capacity of the entity based on, for example, units of output per day.

103 The selection of the appropriate concept of capital by an entity should be based on the needs of the users of its financial statements. Thus, a financial concept of capital should be adopted if the users of financial statements are primarily concerned with the maintenance of nominal invested capital or the purchasing power of invested capital. If, however, the main concern of users is with the operating capability of the entity, a physical concept of capital should be used. The concept chosen indicates the goal to be attained in determining profit, even though there may be some measurement difficulties in making the concept operational.

Concepts of capital maintenance and the determination of profit

104 The concepts of capital in paragraph 102 give rise to the following concepts of capital maintenance:

(a) *Financial capital maintenance.* Under this concept a profit is earned only if the financial (or money) amount of the net assets at the end of the period exceeds the financial (or money) amount of net assets at the beginning of the period, after excluding any distributions to, and contributions from, owners during the period. Financial capital maintenance can be measured in either nominal monetary units or units of constant purchasing power.

(b) *Physical capital maintenance.* Under this concept a profit is earned only if the physical productive capacity (or operating capability) of the entity (or the resources or funds needed to achieve that capacity) at the end of the period exceeds the physical productive capacity at the beginning of the period, after excluding any distributions to, and contributions from, owners during the period.

105 The concept of capital maintenance is concerned with how an entity defines the capital that it seeks to maintain. It provides the linkage between the concepts of capital and the concepts of profit because it provides the point of reference by which profit is measured; it is a prerequisite for distinguishing between an entity's return on capital and its return of capital; only inflows of assets in excess of amounts needed to maintain capital may be regarded as profit and therefore as a return on capital. Hence, profit is the residual amount that remains after expenses (including capital maintenance adjustments, where appropriate) have been deducted from income. If expenses exceed income the residual amount is a loss.

106　　The physical capital maintenance concept requires the adoption of the current cost basis of measurement. The financial capital maintenance concept, however, does not require the use of a particular basis of measurement. Selection of the basis under this concept is dependent on the type of financial capital that the entity is seeking to maintain.

107　　The principal difference between the two concepts of capital maintenance is the treatment of the effects of changes in the prices of assets and liabilities of the entity. In general terms, an entity has maintained its capital if it has as much capital at the end of the period as it had at the beginning of the period. Any amount over and above that required to maintain the capital at the beginning of the period is profit.

108　　Under the concept of financial capital maintenance where capital is defined in terms of nominal monetary units, profit represents the increase in nominal money capital over the period. Thus, increases in the prices of assets held over the period, conventionally referred to as holding gains, are, conceptually, profits. They may not be recognised as such, however, until the assets are disposed of in an exchange transaction. When the concept of financial capital maintenance is defined in terms of constant purchasing power units, profit represents the increase in invested purchasing power over the period. Thus, only that part of the increase in the prices of assets that exceeds the increase in the general level of prices is regarded as profit. The rest of the increase is treated as a capital maintenance adjustment and, hence, as part of equity.

109　　Under the concept of physical capital maintenance when capital is defined in terms of the physical productive capacity, profit represents the increase in that capital over the period. All price changes affecting the assets and liabilities of the entity are viewed as changes in the measurement of the physical productive capacity of the entity; hence, they are treated as capital maintenance adjustments that are part of equity and not as profit.

110　　The selection of the measurement bases and concept of capital maintenance will determine the accounting model used in the preparation of the financial statements. Different accounting models exhibit different degrees of relevance and reliability and, as in other areas, management must seek a balance between relevance and reliability. This *Framework* is applicable to a range of accounting models and provides guidance on preparing and presenting the financial statements constructed under the chosen model. At the present time, it is not the intention of the Board of IASC to prescribe a particular model other than in exceptional circumstances, such as for those entities reporting in the currency of a hyperinflationary economy. This intention will, however, be reviewed in the light of world developments.

IASC Foundation Constitution

Preface

This Constitution was approved in its original form by the Board of the former International Accounting Standards Committee (IASC) in March 2000 and by the members of IASC at a meeting in Edinburgh on 24 May 2000.

At its meeting in December 1999, the IASC Board had appointed a Nominating Committee to select the first Trustees. Those Trustees were nominated on 22 May 2000 and took office on 24 May 2000 as a result of the approval of the Constitution. In execution of their duties under the Constitution, the Trustees formed the International Accounting Standards Committee Foundation on 6 February 2001. As a consequence of a resolution by the Trustees, Part C of the revised Constitution approved on 24 May 2000 ceased to have effect and was deleted.

Reflecting the Trustees' decision to create the International Financial Reporting Interpretations Committee, and following public consultation, the Constitution was revised on 5 March 2002. Subsequently the Trustees amended the Constitution, with effect from 8 July 2002, to reflect other changes that had taken place since the formation of the IASC Foundation.

The Constitution requires the Trustees to review the Constitution every five years. The Trustees initiated the first review in November 2003 and following extensive consultation completed the review in June 2005. The changes were adopted and approved by the Trustees on 21 June 2005 and came into effect on 1 July 2005. Further amendments were adopted and approved by the Trustees on 31 October 2007 for immediate effect.

The Trustees formally initiated their second five-yearly review of the organisation's constitutional arrangements in February 2008. This version reflects changes adopted after the first part of that review, which focused on public accountability and the composition and size of the International Accounting Standards Board. The Trustees approved the changes on 15 January 2009 for effect on 1 February 2009.

IASC Foundation Constitution

(approved by the Members of IASC at a meeting in Edinburgh, Scotland on 24 May 2000 and revised by the IASC Foundation Trustees on 5 March and 8 July 2002, 21 June 2005, 31 October 2007 and 15 January 2009)

> This Constitution consists of Part A and Part B. Part A deals with the organisation's name and objectives, and the membership and appointment of Trustees. Part B sets out the provisions that came into effect when the Trustees formed the International Accounting Standards Committee Foundation on 6 February 2001, following a Trustees' Resolution.

Part A

Name and objectives

1   The name of the organisation shall be the International Accounting Standards Committee Foundation (abbreviated as 'IASC Foundation'). The International Accounting Standards Board (abbreviated as 'IASB'), whose structure and functions are laid out in Sections 24–38, shall be the standard-setting body of the IASC Foundation.

2   The objectives of the IASC Foundation are:

    (a)   to develop, in the public interest, a single set of high quality, understandable and enforceable global accounting standards that require high quality, transparent and comparable information in financial statements and other financial reporting to help participants in the world's capital markets and other users make economic decisions;

    (b)   to promote the use and rigorous application of those standards;

    (c)   in fulfilling the objectives associated with (a) and (b), to take account of, as appropriate, the special needs of small and medium-sized entities and emerging economies; and

    (d)   to bring about convergence of national accounting standards and International Accounting Standards and International Financial Reporting Standards to high quality solutions.

Governance of the IASC Foundation

3   The governance of the IASC Foundation shall rest with the Trustees and such other governing organs as may be appointed by the Trustees in accordance with the provisions of this Constitution. The Trustees shall use their best endeavours to ensure that the requirements of this Constitution are observed; however, they are empowered to make minor variations in the interest of feasibility of operation if such variations are agreed by 75 per cent of all the Trustees.

Trustees

4   The Trustees shall comprise twenty-two individuals.

5   The Monitoring Board (described further in Sections 18–23) shall be responsible for the approval of all Trustee appointments and reappointments. In approving such selection, the Monitoring Board shall be bound by the criteria set out in Sections 6 and 7. The Trustees and the Monitoring Board shall agree a nomination process that will entitle the Monitoring Board to recommend candidates and provide other input. In administering the nomination process and putting forward nominations to the Monitoring Board for approval, the Trustees shall consult international organisations as set out in Section 7.

6   All Trustees shall be required to show a firm commitment to the IASC Foundation and the IASB as a high quality global standard-setter, to be financially knowledgeable, and to have an ability to meet the time commitment. Each Trustee shall have an understanding of, and be sensitive to, the challenges associated with the adoption and application of high quality global accounting standards developed for use in the world's capital markets and by other users. The mix of Trustees shall broadly reflect the world's capital markets and diversity of geographical and professional backgrounds. The Trustees shall be required to commit themselves formally to acting in the public interest in all matters. In order to ensure a broad international basis, there shall be:

   (a)   six Trustees appointed from the Asia/Oceania region;

   (b)   six Trustees appointed from Europe;

   (c)   six Trustees appointed from North America; and

   (d)   four Trustees appointed from any area, subject to establishing overall geographical balance.

7   The Trustees shall comprise individuals that as a group provide an appropriate balance of professional backgrounds, including auditors, preparers, users, academics, and other officials serving the public interest. Normally, two of the Trustees shall be senior partners of prominent international accounting firms. To achieve such a balance, Trustees should be selected after consultation with national and international organisations of auditors (including the International Federation of Accountants), preparers, users and academics. The Trustees shall establish procedures for inviting suggestions for appointments from these relevant organisations and for allowing individuals to put forward their own names, including advertising vacant positions.

8   Trustees shall normally be appointed for a term of three years, renewable once: in order to provide continuity, some of the initial Trustees will serve staggered terms so as to retire after four or five years.

9   Subject to the voting requirements in Section 14, the Trustees may terminate the appointment of an individual as a Trustee on grounds of poor performance, misbehaviour or incapacity.

10   The Chairman of the Trustees shall be appointed by the Trustees from among their own number, subject to the approval of the Monitoring Board. With the agreement of the Trustees, regardless of prior service as a Trustee, the appointee may serve as the Chairman for a term of three years, renewable once, from the date of appointment as Chairman.

11   The Trustees shall meet at least twice each year and shall be remunerated by the IASC Foundation with an annual fee and a per-meeting fee, commensurate with the responsibilities assumed, such fees to be determined by the Trustees. Expenses of travel on IASC Foundation business shall be met by the IASC Foundation.

12   In addition to the powers and duties set out in Section 13, the Trustees may make such operational commitments and other arrangements as they deem necessary to achieve the organisation's objectives, including, but without limitation, leasing premises and agreeing contracts of employment with IASB members.

13   The Trustees shall:

(a)   assume responsibility for establishing and maintaining appropriate financing arrangements;

(b)   establish or amend operating procedures for the Trustees;

(c)   determine the legal entity under which the IASC Foundation shall operate, provided always that such legal entity shall be a Foundation or other body corporate conferring limited liability on its members and that the legal documents establishing such legal entity shall incorporate provisions to achieve the same requirements as the provisions contained in this Constitution;

(d)   review in due course the location of the IASC Foundation, both as regards its legal base and its operating location;

(e)   investigate the possibility of seeking charitable or similar status for the IASC Foundation in those countries where such status would assist fundraising;

(f)   open their meetings to the public but may, at their discretion, hold certain discussions (normally only about selection, appointment and other personnel issues, and funding) in private; and

(g)   publish an annual report on the IASC Foundation's activities, including audited financial statements and priorities for the coming year.

14   There shall be a quorum for meetings of the Trustees if 60 per cent of the Trustees are present in person or by telecommunications: Trustees shall not be represented by alternates. Each Trustee shall have one vote, and a simple majority of those voting shall be required to take decisions on matters other than termination of the appointment of a Trustee, amendments to the Constitution, or minor variations made in the interest of feasibility of operations, in which cases a 75 per cent majority of all Trustees shall be required; voting by proxy shall not be permitted on any issue. In the event of a tied vote, the Chairman shall have an additional casting vote.

     © IASCF

Part B

Trustees

15 In addition to the duties set out in Part A, the Trustees shall:

   (a) appoint the members of the IASB and establish their contracts of service and performance criteria;

   (b) appoint the members of the International Financial Reporting Interpretations Committee and the Standards Advisory Council;

   (c) review annually the strategy of the IASC Foundation and the IASB and its effectiveness, including consideration, but not determination, of the IASB's agenda;

   (d) approve annually the budget of the IASC Foundation and determine the basis for funding;

   (e) review broad strategic issues affecting accounting standards, promote the IASC Foundation and its work and promote the objective of rigorous application of International Accounting Standards and International Financial Reporting Standards, provided that the Trustees shall be excluded from involvement in technical matters relating to accounting standards;

   (f) establish and amend operating procedures, consultative arrangements and due process for the IASB, the International Financial Reporting Interpretations Committee and the Standards Advisory Council;

   (g) review compliance with the operating procedures, consultative arrangements and due process as described in (f);

   (h) approve amendments to this Constitution after following a due process, including consultation with the Standards Advisory Council and publication of an exposure draft for public comment and subject to the voting requirements given in Section 14;

   (i) exercise all powers of the IASC Foundation except for those expressly reserved to the IASB, the International Financial Reporting Interpretations Committee and the Standards Advisory Council; and

   (j) foster and review the development of educational programmes and materials that are consistent with the IASC Foundation's objectives.

16 The Trustees may terminate the appointment of a member of the IASB, the International Financial Reporting Interpretations Committee or the Standards Advisory Council, on grounds of poor performance, misbehaviour, incapacity or other failure to comply with contractual requirements, and the Trustees shall develop procedures for such termination.

17 The accountability of the Trustees shall be ensured *inter alia* through:

   (a) a commitment made by each Trustee to act in the public interest;

   (b) their commitment to report to and engage with the Monitoring Board according to the terms described in Sections 18–23.

(c) their undertaking a review of the entire structure of the IASC Foundation and its effectiveness, such review to include consideration of changing the geographical distribution of Trustees in response to changing global economic conditions, and publishing the proposals of that review for public comment, the review commencing three years after the coming into force of this Constitution, with the objective of implementing any agreed changes five years after the coming into force of this Constitution (6 February 2006, five years after the date of the incorporation of the IASC Foundation); and

(d) their undertaking a similar review subsequently every five years.

The Monitoring Board

18   A Monitoring Board will provide a formal link between the Trustees and public authorities. This relationship seeks to replicate, on an international basis, the link between accounting standard-setters and those public authorities that have generally overseen accounting standard-setters. A Memorandum of Understanding will be agreed between the Monitoring Board and the Trustees describing the interaction of the Monitoring Board with the Trustees. This Memorandum of Understanding will be made available to the public.

19   The responsibilities of the Monitoring Board shall be:

(a) to participate in the process for appointing Trustees and to approve the appointment of Trustees according to the guidelines in Sections 5–8.

(b) to review and provide advice to the Trustees on their fulfilment of the responsibilities set out in Sections 13 and 15. The Trustees shall make an annual written report to the Monitoring Board.

(c) to meet the Trustees or a subgroup of the Trustees at least once annually, and more frequently as appropriate. The Monitoring Board shall have the authority to request meetings with the Trustees or separately with the Chairman of the Trustees (with the Chairman of the IASB as appropriate) about any area of work of either the Trustees or the IASB. These meetings may include discussion of, and any IASC Foundation or IASB proposed resolution of, issues that the Monitoring Board has referred for timely consideration by the IASC Foundation or the IASB.

20   The Monitoring Board shall develop a charter that sets out its organisational, operating and decision-making procedures. The charter shall be made public.

21   Initially, the Monitoring Board shall comprise:

(a) the responsible member of the European Commission,

(b) the chair of the IOSCO Emerging Markets Committee,

(c) the chair of the IOSCO Technical Committee (or vice chair or designated securities commission chair in cases where either the chairman of an EU securities regulator, commissioner of the Japan Financial Services Agency or chairman of the US Securities and Exchange Commission is the chair of the IOSCO Technical Committee),

© IASCF

(d)   the commissioner of the Japan Financial Services Agency,

(e)   the chairman of the US Securities and Exchange Commission, and

(f)   as an observer, the chairman of the Basel Committee on Banking Supervision.

22   The Monitoring Board shall reconsider its composition from time to time relative to its objectives.

23   The Monitoring Board shall reach decisions to approve the appointment of Trustees and establish any common positions by consensus.

IASB

24   The IASB shall comprise fourteen members, increasing to sixteen members at a date no later than 1 July 2012. The members of the IASB are appointed by the Trustees under Section 15(a). Up to three members may be part-time members (the expression 'part-time' meaning that the members concerned commit most of their time in paid employment to the IASC Foundation) and shall meet appropriate guidelines of independence established by the Trustees. The remaining members shall be full-time members (the expression 'full-time' meaning that the members concerned commit all of their time in paid employment to the IASC Foundation). The work of the IASB shall not be invalidated by its failure at any time to have a full complement of members, although the Trustees shall use their best endeavours to achieve a full complement.

25   The main qualifications for membership of the IASB shall be professional competence and practical experience. The Trustees shall select members of the IASB, consistently with the Criteria for IASB Members set out in the Annex to the Constitution, so that it will comprise a group of people representing, within that group, the best available combination of technical expertise and diversity of international business and market experience in order to contribute to the development of high quality, global accounting standards. The members of the IASB shall be required to commit themselves formally to acting in the public interest in all matters. No individual shall be both a Trustee and an IASB member at the same time.

26   In a manner consistent with the Criteria for IASB Members as set out in the Annex to the Constitution and in order to ensure a broad international basis, there shall normally be, by 1 July 2012:

(a)   four members from the Asia/Oceania region;

(b)   four members from Europe;

(c)   four members from North America;

(d)   one member from Africa;

(e)   one member from South America; and

(f)   two members appointed from any area, subject to maintaining overall geographical balance.

The work of the IASB shall not be invalidated by its failure at any time to have a full complement of members according to the above geographical allocation, although the Trustees shall use their best endeavours to achieve the geographical allocation.

27   The Trustees shall select IASB members so that the IASB as a group provides an appropriate mix of recent practical experience among auditors, preparers, users and academics.

28   The IASB will, in consultation with the Trustees, be expected to establish and maintain liaison with national standard-setters and other official bodies concerned with standard-setting in order to promote the convergence of national accounting standards and International Accounting Standards and International Financial Reporting Standards.

29   Each full-time and part-time member of the IASB shall agree contractually to act in the public interest and to have regard to the IASB *Framework* (as amended from time to time) in deciding on and revising standards.

30   The Trustees shall appoint one of the full-time members as Chairman of the IASB, who shall also be the Chief Executive of the IASC Foundation. One of the full-time members of the IASB shall also be designated by the Trustees as Vice-Chairman, whose role shall be to chair meetings of the IASB in the absence of the Chairman in unusual circumstances (such as illness). The appointment of the Chairman and the designation as Vice-Chairman shall be for such term as the Trustees decide. The title of Vice-Chairman would not imply that the individual concerned is the Chairman-elect.

31   Members of the IASB shall be appointed for a term of up to five years, renewable once. The Trustees shall develop rules and procedures to ensure that the IASB is, and is seen to be, independent, and, in particular, on appointment, full-time members of the IASB shall sever all employment relationships with current employers and shall not hold any position giving rise to economic incentives which might call into question their independence of judgement in setting accounting standards. Secondments and any rights to return to an employer would therefore not be permitted. Part-time members of the IASB would not be expected to sever all other employment arrangements.

32   The terms of appointment of members of the IASB shall be staggered so that not all members retire at once. To accomplish this, the Trustees shall consider initial terms of three years for some members, four years for others and a full five years for the remaining initial members.

33   Full-time and part-time members of the IASB shall be remunerated at rates commensurate with the respective responsibilities assumed: such rates shall be determined by the Trustees. Expenses of travel on IASB business shall be met by the IASC Foundation.

34   The IASB shall meet at such times and locations as it determines: meetings of the IASB shall be open to the public, but certain discussions (normally only about selection, appointment and other personnel issues) may be held in private at the discretion of the IASB.

35 Each member of the IASB shall have one vote. On both technical and other matters, proxy voting shall not be permitted nor shall members of the IASB be entitled to appoint alternates to attend meetings. In the event of a tied vote, on a decision that is to be made by a simple majority of the members of the IASB present at a meeting in person or by telecommunications, the Chairman shall have an additional casting vote.

36 The publication of an exposure draft, or an International Financial Reporting Standard (including an International Accounting Standard or an Interpretation of the International Financial Reporting Interpretations Committee) shall require approval by nine members of the IASB, if there are fewer than 16 members, or by ten members if there are 16 members. Other decisions of the IASB, including the publication of a discussion paper, shall require a simple majority of the members of the IASB present at a meeting that is attended by at least 60 per cent of the members of the IASB, in person or by telecommunications.

37 The IASB shall:

(a) have complete responsibility for all IASB technical matters including the preparation and issuing of International Accounting Standards, International Financial Reporting Standards and exposure drafts, each of which shall include any dissenting opinions, and final approval of Interpretations by the International Financial Reporting Interpretations Committee;

(b) publish an exposure draft on all projects and normally publish a discussion document for public comment on major projects;

(c) have full discretion in developing and pursuing the technical agenda of the IASB and over project assignments on technical matters: in organising the conduct of its work, the IASB may outsource detailed research or other work to national standard-setters or other organisations;

(d) (i) establish procedures for reviewing comments made within a reasonable period on documents published for comment,

(ii) normally form working groups or other types of specialist advisory groups to give advice on major projects,

(iii) consult the Standards Advisory Council on major projects, agenda decisions and work priorities, and

(iv) normally issue bases for conclusions with International Accounting Standards, International Financial Reporting Standards, and exposure drafts;

(e) consider holding public hearings to discuss proposed standards, although there is no requirement to hold public hearings for every project;

(f) consider undertaking field tests (both in developed countries and in emerging markets) to ensure that proposed standards are practical and workable in all environments, although there is no requirement to undertake field tests for every project; and

(g) give reasons if it does not follow any of the non-mandatory procedures set out in (b), (d)(ii), d(iv), (e) and (f).

38   The authoritative text of any exposure draft or International Accounting Standard or International Financial Reporting Standard or draft or final Interpretation shall be that published by the IASB in the English language. The IASB may publish authorised translations or give authority to others to publish translations of the authoritative text of exposure drafts and International Accounting Standards and International Financial Reporting Standards and draft and final Interpretations.

International Financial Reporting Interpretations Committee

39   The International Financial Reporting Interpretations Committee shall comprise fourteen voting members, appointed by the Trustees under Section 15(b) for renewable terms of three years. The Trustees shall select members of the Committee so that it comprises a group of people representing, within that group, the best available combination of technical expertise and diversity of international business and market experience in the practical application of International Financial Reporting Standards (IFRSs) and analysis of financial statements prepared in accordance with IFRSs. Expenses of travel on Committee business shall be met by the IASC Foundation.

40   The Trustees shall appoint a member of the IASB, the Director of Technical Activities or another senior member of the IASB staff, or another appropriately qualified individual, to chair the Committee. The Chair has the right to speak to the technical issues being considered but not to vote. The Trustees, as they deem necessary, shall appoint as non-voting observers representatives of regulatory organisations, who shall have the right to attend and speak at meetings.

41   The Committee shall meet as and when required and ten voting members present in person or by telecommunications shall constitute a quorum: one or two IASB members shall be designated by the IASB and shall attend meetings as non-voting observers; other members of the IASB may attend and speak at the meetings. On exceptional occasions, members of the Committee may be allowed to send non-voting alternates, at the discretion of the Chair of the Committee. Members wishing to nominate an alternate should seek the consent of the Chair in advance of the meeting concerned. Meetings of the Committee shall be open to the public, but certain discussions (normally only about selection, appointment and other personnel issues) may be held in private at the Committee's discretion.

42   Each member of the Committee shall have one vote. Members vote in accordance with their own independent views, not as representatives voting according to the views of any firm, organisation or constituency with which they may be associated. Proxy voting shall not be permitted. Approval of draft or final Interpretations shall require that not more than four voting members vote against the draft or final Interpretation.

43   The Committee shall:

    (a)   interpret the application of International Accounting Standards (IASs) and International Financial Reporting Standards (IFRSs) and provide timely guidance on financial reporting issues not specifically addressed in IASs and IFRSs, in the context of the IASB *Framework*, and undertake other tasks at the request of the IASB;

(b)   in carrying out its work under (a) above, have regard to the IASB's objective of working actively with national standard-setters to bring about convergence of national accounting standards and IASs and IFRSs to high quality solutions;

(c)   publish after clearance by the IASB draft Interpretations for public comment and consider comments made within a reasonable period before finalising an Interpretation; and

(d)   report to the IASB and obtain the approval of nine of its members for final Interpretations.

Standards Advisory Council

44   The Standards Advisory Council, whose members shall be appointed by the Trustees under Section 15(b), provides a forum for participation by organisations and individuals, with an interest in international financial reporting, having diverse geographical and functional backgrounds, with the objective of:

(a)   giving advice to the IASB on agenda decisions and priorities in the IASB's work,

(b)   informing the IASB of the views of the organisations and individuals on the Council on major standard-setting projects and

(c)   giving other advice to the IASB or the Trustees.

45   The Council shall comprise thirty or more members, having a diversity of geographical and professional backgrounds, appointed for renewable terms of three years. The Chairman of the Council shall be appointed by the Trustees, and shall not be a member of the IASB or a member of its staff. The Trustees shall invite the Chairman of the Council to attend and participate in the Trustees' meetings, as appropriate.

46   The Council shall normally meet at least three times a year. Meetings shall be open to the public. The Council shall be consulted by the IASB in advance of IASB decisions on major projects and by the Trustees in advance of any proposed changes to this Constitution.

Chief Executive and staff

47   As provided under Section 24, the Chairman of the IASB shall also be the Chief Executive of the IASC Foundation, and shall be subject to supervision by the Trustees.

48   The Chief Executive shall be responsible for the staffing of the IASB, which shall include a Director of Technical Activities appointed by the Chief Executive in consultation with the Trustees: the Director of Technical Activities, while not a member of the IASB, shall be entitled to participate in the debate but not to vote at meetings of the IASB and the International Financial Reporting Interpretations Committee.

49   A Director of Operations and a Commercial Director shall also be appointed by the Chief Executive in consultation with the Trustees. They shall have responsibility for publications and copyright, communications, administration, and finance under the supervision of the Chief Executive and for fundraising under the supervision of the Trustees.

Administration

50   The administrative office of the IASC Foundation shall be located in such location as may be determined by the Trustees in accordance with Section 13(d).

51   The IASC Foundation shall be a legal entity as determined by the Trustees and shall be governed by this Constitution and by any laws which apply to such legal entity, including, if appropriate, laws applicable because of the location of its registered office.

52   The IASC Foundation shall be bound by the signature(s) of such person or persons as may be duly authorised by the Trustees.

© IASCF

ANNEX

International Accounting Standards Committee Foundation
Criteria for IASB Members

The following would represent criteria for IASB membership:

1   **Demonstrated Technical Competency and Knowledge of Financial Accounting and Reporting**. All members of the IASB, regardless of whether they are from the accounting profession, preparers, users, or academics, should have demonstrated a high level of knowledge and technical competency in financial accounting and reporting. The credibility of the IASB and its individual members and the effectiveness and efficiency of the organisation will be enhanced with members who have such knowledge and skills.

2   **Ability to Analyse**. IASB members should have demonstrated the ability to analyse issues and consider the implications of that analysis for the decision-making process.

3   **Communication Skills**. Effective oral and written communication skills are necessary. These skills include the ability to communicate effectively in private meetings with IASB members, in public meetings, and in written materials such as accounting standards, speeches, articles, memos and correspondence with constituents. Communication skills also include the ability to listen to and consider the views of others. While a working knowledge of English is necessary, there should not be discrimination in selection against those for whom English is not their first language.

4   **Judicious Decision-making**. IASB members should be capable of considering varied viewpoints, weighing the evidence presented in an impartial fashion, and reaching well-reasoned and supportable decisions in a timely fashion.

5   **Awareness of the Financial Reporting Environment**. High quality financial reporting will be affected by the financial, business and economic environment. IASB members should have an understanding of the global economic environment in which the IASB operates. This global awareness should include awareness of business and financial reporting issues that are relevant to, and affect the quality of, transparent financial reporting and disclosure in the various capital markets worldwide, including those using International Financial Reporting Standards.

6   **Ability to Work in a Collegial Atmosphere**. Members should be able to show respect, tact and consideration for one another's and constituents' views. Members must be able to work with one another in reaching consensus views based on the IASB's objective of developing high quality and transparent financial reporting. Members must be able to put the objective of the IASB above individual philosophies and interests.

7   **Integrity, Objectivity and Discipline**. The credibility of members should be demonstrated through their integrity and objectivity. This includes intellectual integrity as well as integrity in dealing with fellow IASB members and constituents. Members should demonstrate an ability to be objective in reaching decisions. Members also should demonstrate an ability to show rigorous discipline and carry a demanding workload.

8   **Commitment to the IASC Foundation's Mission and Public Interest**. Members should be committed to achieving the objective of the IASC Foundation of establishing international accounting and financial reporting standards that are of high quality, comparable, and transparent. A candidate for the IASB also should be committed to serving the public interest through a private standard-setting process.

International Accounting Standards Committee Foundation

Due Process Handbook for the International Accounting Standards Board (IASB)

Approved by the Trustees March 2006. Amended version approved by the Trustees October 2008

CONTENTS

APPENDIX I

The IASB's due process: extracts from the Constitution *not reproduced here*

APPENDIX II

Due process: extract from the *Preface to International Financial Reporting Standards* *not reproduced here*

APPENDIX III

Standards Advisory Council: Terms of reference and operating procedures

APPENDIX IV

The Trustees' oversight role—extract from the Constitution *not reproduced here*

HANDBOOK OF CONSULTATIVE ARRANGEMENTS
International Accounting Standards Board

I   Introduction

1   This Handbook describes the consultative arrangements of the International Accounting Standards Board (IASB). It is based on the existing framework of the due process laid out in the Constitution of the International Accounting Standards Committee (IASC) Foundation and the *Preface to International Financial Reporting Standards* (IFRSs) issued by the IASB. It reflects the public consultation conducted by the IASB in 2004 and 2005 and enhancements made to the due process since then.

2   The Trustees of the IASC Foundation have a committee—the Trustees' Due Process Oversight Committee—which has the task of regularly reviewing and, if necessary, amending the procedures of due process in the light of experience and comments from the IASB and constituents. The Committee reviews proposed procedures for the IASB's due process on new projects and the composition of working groups and ensures that their membership reflects a diversity of views and expertise.

3   The Trustees approved this amended Handbook on 9 October 2008.

II   Summary

4   The IASB is the standard-setting body of the IASC Foundation. The foremost objective of the organisation is to develop, in the public interest, a single set of high quality, understandable and enforceable global accounting standards.

5   The IASB is an independent group of experts with an appropriate mix of recent practical experience of standard-setting, or of the user, accounting, academic or preparer communities. Members of the IASB are selected and considered for reappointment through an open and rigorous process, which includes advertising vacancies and consulting relevant organisations. The Trustees' Nominating Committee makes recommendations to the full Trustees on candidates to serve on the IASB, and reviews annually the performance of IASB members.

6   In accordance with the IASC Foundation's Constitution, the IASB has full discretion in developing and pursuing its technical agenda and in organising the conduct of its work. In order to gain a wide range of views from interested parties throughout all stages of a project's development, the Trustees and the IASB have established consultative procedures to govern the standard-setting process. The framework for, and the minimum requirements of, the IASB's 'due process' are set out in the Constitution (see Appendix I) and the IASB's *Preface to International Financial Reporting Standards* (see Appendix II).

7   The IASB uses many steps in its consultation process to gain a better understanding of different accounting alternatives and the potential impact of proposals on affected parties. In the light of its consultation, the IASB considers its position, and decides whether to modify its approach to standard-setting issues.

8   In establishing its consultative arrangements, the IASB originally drew upon and expanded the practices of national standard-setters and other regulatory bodies. The IASB sought to enhance its procedures in 2004 and proposed a series of steps to improve transparency. Those steps, after public consultation, were incorporated into practice. This Handbook describes the procedures that were established and have been subsequently enhanced.

9   The procedures described in this Handbook address the following requirements:

- transparency and accessibility

- extensive consultation and responsiveness

- accountability.

Transparency and accessibility

10   The IASB considers adding topics to its agenda after consultations with constituents and on the basis of research conducted by or in conjunction with IASB staff. Potential agenda items are discussed in IASB meetings. Those meetings, as well as meetings of the Standards Advisory Council (the SAC), the International Financial Reporting Interpretations Committee (the IFRIC) and the IASB's working groups, are open to the public for observation. IASB meetings are also broadcast and archived on the IASB's website.

11   Comment letters from interested organisations, IASB meeting observer notes and IASB decisions are posted on the IASB's website. Discussion papers and exposure drafts are also posted on the website and published for public comment (see paragraph 111).

Extensive consultation and responsiveness

12   The IASB solicits views and suggestions through its consultations with a wide range of interested parties and a formal process of inviting public comment on discussion papers and exposure drafts. Organisations that the IASB consults include, among others, the SAC, standard-setting organisations and various regulatory bodies. The IASB may also arrange public hearings and field visits and set up working groups to promote discussions.

13   IASB members hold a large number of meetings with groups of preparers, users, academics and others to test proposals and to understand concerns raised by affected parties. Additionally, IASB members and senior staff appear at many public events to exchange views with constituents.

14   The IASB listens to, evaluates and, where the IASB considers it appropriate, adopts suggestions received during the consultations. It also debates different views on technical matters in public IASB meetings, conferences and seminars. In response to public comments, the IASB considers alternatives to its proposals.

15   Comments received from interested parties as part of the consultation process are summarised, analysed and considered by the staff, who make recommendations for the IASB to consider in its public meetings. Using its website, project summaries and feedback statements, the IASB informs the public of its position on major points raised in the comment letters received.

Accountability

16   Adopting the 'comply or explain' approach that is used by various regulatory bodies, the IASB explains its reasons if it decides to omit any non-mandatory step of its consultative process as described in the Constitution (see paragraphs 112–114 below).

17   In addition, the Trustees review and ensure compliance with the IASB's procedures and mandate, consider the IASB's agenda, and conduct annual reviews of the IASB's performance (see paragraphs 115 and 116).

III   The six stages of standard-setting

18   The IASB's standard-setting process comprises six stages, with the Trustees having the opportunity to ensure compliance at various points throughout the process.

Stage 1: Setting the agenda

19   The IASB, by developing high quality accounting standards, seeks to address a demand for better quality information that is of value to all users of financial statements. Users include present and potential investors, employees, lenders, suppliers and other trade creditors, customers, governments and their agencies and the public. Better quality information will also be of value to preparers of financial statements.

20   Although not all of the information needs of these users can be met by financial statements, there are common needs for all users. As investors are providers of risk capital to the entity, the provision of financial statements that meet their needs will also meet most of the needs of other users. The IASB therefore evaluates the merits of adding a potential item to its agenda mainly by reference to the needs of investors.

21   When deciding whether a proposed agenda item will address users' needs the IASB considers:

(a)   the relevance to users of the information and the reliability of information that could be provided

(b)   existing guidance available

(c)   the possibility of increasing convergence

(d)   the quality of the IFRS to be developed

(e)   resource constraints.

For further discussion see paragraphs 54–60.

22   To help the IASB in considering its future agenda, its staff are asked to identify, review and raise issues that might warrant the IASB's attention. New issues may also arise from a change in the IASB's conceptual framework. In addition, the IASB raises and discusses potential agenda items in the light of comments from other standard-setters and other interested parties, the SAC and the IFRIC, and staff research and other recommendations.

23   The IASB receives requests to interpret, review or amend IFRSs. The staff consider all such requests, summarise major or common issues raised, and present them to the IASB from time to time as candidates for when the IASB is next considering its agenda (see paragraphs 62 and 63).

24   The IASB's discussion of potential projects and its decisions to adopt new projects take place in public IASB meetings. Before reaching such decisions the IASB consults the SAC and accounting standard-setting bodies on proposed agenda items and setting priorities. In making decisions regarding its agenda priorities, the IASB also considers factors related to its convergence initiatives with accounting standard-setters. The IASB's approval to add agenda items, as well as its decisions on their priority, is by a simple majority vote at an IASB meeting.

25   When the IASB considers potential agenda items, it may decide that some issues require additional research before it can take a decision on whether to add the item to its active agenda. Such issues may be addressed as research projects on the IASB's research agenda. A research project normally requires extensive background information that other standard-setters or similar organisations with sufficient expertise, time and staff resources could provide.

26   Research projects are normally carried out by other standard-setters under the supervision of, and in collaboration with, the IASB. In the light of the result of the research project (normally a discussion paper, see paragraph 32), the IASB may decide, in its public meetings, to move an issue from the research project to its active agenda.

Stage 2: Project planning

27   When adding an item to its active agenda, the IASB also decides whether to conduct the project alone, or jointly with another standard-setter. Similar due process is followed under both approaches.

28   After considering the nature of the issues and the level of interest among constituents, the IASB may establish a working group (see paragraphs 92–95) at this stage.

29   The directors of the technical staff select a project team for the project, and the project manager draws up a project plan under the supervision of those directors (see paragraphs 64–68). The project team may also include members of staff from other accounting standard-setters, as deemed appropriate by the IASB.

Stage 3: Development and publication of a discussion paper

30   Although a discussion paper is not a mandatory step in its due process, the IASB normally publishes a discussion paper as its first publication on any major new topic as a vehicle to explain the issue and solicit early comment from constituents. If the IASB decides to omit this step, it will state its reasons.

31   Typically, a discussion paper includes a comprehensive overview of the issue, possible approaches in addressing the issue, the preliminary views of its authors or the IASB, and an invitation to comment. This approach may differ if another accounting standard-setter develops the research paper.

32   Discussion papers may result either from a research project being conducted by another accounting standard-setter or as the first stage of an active agenda project carried out by the IASB. In the first case, the discussion paper is drafted by another accounting standard-setter and published by the IASB. Issues related to the discussion paper are discussed in IASB meetings, and publication of such a paper requires a simple majority vote by the IASB. If the discussion paper includes the preliminary views of other authors, the IASB reviews the draft discussion paper to ensure that its analysis is an appropriate basis on which to invite public comments.

33   For discussion papers on agenda items that are under the IASB's direction, or include the IASB's preliminary views, the IASB develops the paper or its views on the basis of analysis drawn from staff research and recommendations, as well as suggestions made by the SAC (see paragraphs 88–91), working groups and accounting standard-setters and presentations from invited parties. All discussions of technical issues related to the draft paper take place in public sessions according to the procedures described in paragraphs 69–75.

34   When the draft is completed and the IASB has approved it for publication (see paragraphs 76–83), the discussion paper is published to invite public comment.

35   The IASB normally allows a period of 120 days for comment on a discussion paper, but may allow a longer period on major projects (which are those projects involving pervasive or difficult conceptual or practical issues).

36   After the comment period has ended the project team analyses and summarises the comment letters for the IASB's consideration. Comment letters are posted on the website. In addition, a summary of the comments is posted on the website as a part of IASB meeting observer notes.

37   If the IASB decides to explore the issues further, it may seek additional comment and suggestions by conducting field visits, or by arranging public hearings and round-table meetings (see paragraphs 96–108).

Stage 4: Development and publication of an exposure draft

38   Publication of an exposure draft is a mandatory step in due process. Irrespective of whether the IASB has published a discussion paper, an exposure draft is the IASB's main vehicle for consulting the public. Unlike a discussion paper, an exposure draft sets out a specific proposal in the form of a proposed IFRS (or amendment to an IFRS).

39   The development of an exposure draft begins with the IASB considering issues on the basis of staff research and recommendations, as well as comments received on any discussion paper, and suggestions made by the SAC, working groups and accounting standard-setters and arising from public education sessions.

40   After resolving issues at its meetings, the IASB instructs the staff to draft the exposure draft. When the draft has been completed, and the IASB has balloted on it (see paragraphs 76–83), the IASB publishes it for public comment.

41   An exposure draft contains an invitation to comment on a draft IFRS, or draft amendment to an IFRS, that proposes requirements on recognition, measurement and disclosures. The draft may also include mandatory application guidance and implementation guidance, and will be accompanied by a basis for conclusions on the proposals and the alternative views of dissenting IASB members (if any).

42   The IASB normally allows a period of 120 days for comment on an exposure draft as clarified in paragraph 100 below.

43   The project team collects, summarises and analyses the comments received for the IASB's deliberation. A summary of the comments is posted on the website as a part of IASB meeting observer notes.

44   After the comment period ends, the IASB reviews the comment letters received and the results of other consultations. As a means of exploring the issues further, and soliciting further comments and suggestions, the IASB may conduct field visits, or arrange public hearings and round-table meetings. The IASB is required to consult the SAC and maintains contact with various groups of constituents.

Stage 5: Development and publication of an IFRS

45   The development of an IFRS is carried out during IASB meetings, when the IASB considers the comments received on the exposure draft. Changes from the exposure draft are posted on the website.

46   After resolving issues arising from the exposure draft, the IASB considers whether it should expose its revised proposals for public comment, for example by publishing a second exposure draft.

47   In considering the need for re-exposure, the IASB

● identifies substantial issues that emerged during the comment period on the exposure draft that it had not previously considered

● assesses the evidence that it has considered

● evaluates whether it has sufficiently understood the issues and actively sought the views of constituents

● considers whether the various viewpoints were aired in the exposure draft and adequately discussed and reviewed in the basis for conclusions on the exposure draft.

48   The IASB's decision on whether to publish its revised proposals for another round of comment is made in an IASB meeting. If the IASB decides that re-exposure is necessary, the due process to be followed is the same as for the first exposure draft (see Stage 4 at paragraph 40).

49   As it moves towards completing a new IFRS or major amendment to an IFRS, the IASB prepares a project summary and feedback statement. These:

● give direct feedback to those who submitted comments on the exposure draft

● identify the most significant matters raised in the comment process and

- explain how the IASB responded to those matters.

50   At the same time, the IASB prepares an analysis of the likely effects of the forthcoming IFRS or major amendment. The IASB has undertaken to provide such information to jurisdictions that adopt IFRSs. The IASB is committed to imparting information and sharing knowledge on the likely costs of implementing a new requirement and the ongoing associated costs. The IASB also documents what it learned during the development of the IFRS about the likely costs of implementing a new requirement and the subsequent ongoing costs, and the likely effect of an IFRS on the quality of the information that entities will provide to users. The analysis will therefore attempt to assess the likely effects of the new IFRS on:

- the financial statements of those applying IFRSs

- the possible compliance costs for preparers

- the costs of analysis for users (including the costs of extracting data, identifying how the data have been measured and adjusting data for the purposes of including them in, for example, a valuation model)

- the comparability of financial information between reporting periods for an individual entity and between different entities in a particular reporting period and

- the quality of the financial information and its usefulness in assessing the future cash flows of an entity.

51   When the IASB is satisfied that it has reached a conclusion on the issues arising from the exposure draft, it instructs the staff to draft the IFRS. A pre-ballot draft is usually subject to external review, normally by the IFRIC. Shortly before the IASB ballots the standard, a near-final draft is posted on its limited access website for paying subscribers. Finally, after the due process is completed, all outstanding issues are resolved, and the IASB members have balloted in favour of publication, the IFRS is issued, followed by publication of any project summary and feedback statement and any effect analysis. See paragraphs 76–83 for details on balloting and drafting.

Stage 6: Procedures after an IFRS is issued

52   After an IFRS is issued, IASB members and staff hold regular meetings with interested parties, including other standard-setting bodies, to help understand unanticipated issues related to the practical implementation and potential impact of its provisions. The IASC Foundation also fosters educational activities to ensure consistency in the application of IFRSs.

53   The IASB carries out a post-implementation review of each new IFRS or major amendment. This is normally carried out two years after the new requirements have become mandatory and been implemented. Such reviews are normally limited to important issues identified as contentious during the development of the pronouncement and consideration of any unexpected costs or implementation problems encountered. A review may also be prompted by:

- changes in the financial reporting environment and regulatory requirements

- comments made by the SAC, the IFRIC, standard-setters and constituents about the quality of the IFRS.

The review may lead to items being added to the IASB's agenda. The IASB may also continue informal consultations throughout the implementation of the IFRS or amendment.

IV How the due process is applied

Setting the agenda

54 As mentioned above, the development of a single set of global standards relevant to users' needs is the foremost objective of the IASB. When developing IFRSs to achieve this objective, the IASB evaluates the merits of adding a potential item to its agenda primarily on the basis of the needs of users of financial statements. As investors are providers of risk capital to the entity, the provision of financial statements that meet their needs will also meet most of the needs of other users.

55 The IASB considers the following factors when adding agenda items:

(a) the relevance to users of the information involved and the reliability of information that could be provided

(b) existing guidance available

(c) the possibility of increasing convergence

(d) the quality of the IFRSs to be developed

(e) resource constraints.

The relevance to users of the information involved and the reliability of information that could be provided

56 The IASB considers whether the project would address the needs of users across different jurisdictions, taking into account the following factors:

- changes in the financial reporting and regulatory environment—whether the issue is internationally relevant, and has emerged as a result of changes in the financial reporting environment and regulatory requirements across jurisdictions.

- pervasiveness—whether the issue is one that (a) affects more than a few entities and more than a few jurisdictions, (b) gives rise to problems that are frequent and material and (c) will persist if not resolved.

- urgency—whether requests have been received from constituents, with reasonable justifications, that the IASB should address the issue as a matter of priority.

- consequences—whether the absence of an IFRS might cause users to make suboptimal decisions.

Existing guidance available

57   After assessing the significance of an issue, the IASB considers whether the project will address an area on which existing guidance is insufficient. The following aspects are taken into account:

- no guidance exists.

- there is diversity in national standards, which results in a lack of comparability in financial reporting.

- there is diversity in practice, or IFRSs are difficult to apply because

  - they are unclear or unnecessarily complex,

  - the cost of complying outweighs benefits to users, or

  - the IFRSs are out of date and the information they generate no longer appropriately reflects economic conditions or results.

The possibility of increasing convergence

58   As specified in the Constitution, the IASB is tasked with bringing about the convergence of national and international accounting standards to high quality solutions. Therefore, in parallel with the review of existing guidance on an issue, the IASB considers whether undertaking a project would increase the possibility of achieving the convergence of the accounting standards in different jurisdictions.

The quality of the IFRSs to be developed

59   After evaluating the existing IFRSs including the prospects of further convergence, the IASB considers the qualitative aspects of the IFRSs that are proposed to be developed. The following factors are taken into account:

- availability of alternative solutions—whether when an issue is addressed, there are alternative solutions to improve *relevance, faithful representation, application of fundamental qualitative characteristics, comparability, verifiability, timeliness and understandability* in financial reporting, and it is likely that sufficient IASB support and approval will be attainable for IFRSs developed.

- cost/benefit considerations—whether it is likely that the expected benefits to users of the improved financial reporting will exceed the costs of implementation.

- feasibility—whether it is feasible to develop a technically sound solution within a reasonable time period without awaiting completion of other projects.

Resource constraints

60   The IASB then considers whether there are sufficient resources to undertake a project in its agenda. The following factors are taken into account:

- availability of expertise outside the IASB—whether there is expertise available at the national level that the IASB can employ to address the issue; or certain accounting standard-setters have already committed resources to the project or have undertaken research to address the issue.

- amount of additional research required—whether there is sufficient research about the topic to form a basis for beginning the project, although more may be needed.

- availability of resources—whether there are adequate resources and expertise available to the IASB and its staff to complete the project and undertake the necessary due process activities.

Other considerations

61 As mentioned in paragraph 24, before approving the addition of an item to its agenda item and deciding on the priority of agenda items, the IASB consults the SAC and standard-setters.

62 As mentioned in paragraph 23, the IASB may also discuss potential agenda items in the light of requests received. The following requests are considered:

- requests to clarify IFRSs

- requests to resolve conflicts between IFRSs

- requests for guidance on issues for which no relevant IFRS has been established.

63 Before the IASB's discussion, the staff, under the supervision of the directors, review the requests and recommend whether any issues should be added to the IASB's agenda. On the basis of the five factors described in paragraph 55, the IASB decides whether any specific issues are to be added to its agenda. Such evaluations are carried out regularly.

Project planning

64 Project plans are prepared by the staff under the supervision of the directors. The plans provide an overview of the proposed timetable, staffing, the documents that are expected to be produced and the due process to be followed.

65 In planning a project, the staff divide a project into manageable components. Each component is assigned a target date of completion. The documents to be produced for each component include drafts (or sections of drafts) of the proposed publication (discussion paper, exposure draft or IFRS).

66 A project team may include a senior project manager, one or more project managers, a practice fellow or a research associate, IASB members and staff. A project team may also include members of staff from other accounting standard-setters, as deemed appropriate by the IASB. Project teams may, where appropriate, seek advice from IASB members on specific topics during their research. Individual IASB members may also seek information from staff and project teams.

67   In developing staff recommendations, to preserve the quality of staff proposals, project teams are expected not to seek to favour the views of individual IASB members, and individual IASB members are required not to try to influence unduly or improperly projects teams' conclusions outside of the IASB's public meetings.

68   The duties of project managers include:

- proposing the due process and a timetable for the IASB's consideration
- preparing IASB meeting materials, including observer notes
- developing staff recommendations
- presenting the different views of constituents and facilitating debates during IASB meetings
- preparing materials for meetings and assisting with communications with working groups and constituents
- preparing updates for the IASB's website to enable the public to follow the progress of the project
- co-ordinating the due process throughout the life of the project.

IASB meetings

69   The IASB's discussions of technical issues take place during public IASB meetings. The IASB normally meets once every month (except August) for a period of three to five days. Additional meetings may be convened at the Chairman's request.

70   In accordance with the Constitution, meetings of the IASB are open to the public. Individuals may attend meetings as observers, or, for a nominal fee to help cover the cost of transmission, view or listen to the meetings through an Internet broadcast. Past meetings are archived on the website.

71   Before IASB meetings, the staff prepare IASB papers and observer notes for review and approval by the directors. IASB papers are distributed to the IASB members on or before the second Wednesday before the IASB meeting date. Meeting agendas and observer notes are normally posted on the website five days before the IASB meeting day. Observer notes normally include the following:

- background to the issues to be considered by the IASB
- all illustrations and examples given to the IASB
- all PowerPoint presentations and spreadsheets used at IASB meetings
- staff recommendations.

72   The numbering of paragraphs in observer notes matches the numbers used in IASB papers. Staff analysis may be omitted from the observer notes to allow staff to express their views freely.

73   During the week when the IASB meets, the staff may from time to time conduct open educational and informational sessions. Individuals or organisations with interests or expertise in a particular project may be invited to provide background briefings to the IASB and to respond to questions.

74   During its meetings, the IASB also discusses comments and suggestions arising from research by the staff, and from consultations with the IFRIC, the SAC, working groups and other interested parties from public hearings, field visits, education sessions and comment letters.

75   Soon after the meeting, the staff summarise the IASB's decisions, and a decision summary—IASB *Update*—is published. This publication, together with a webcast recording of the IASB meeting, is available from the website. When project plans (including consultative arrangements) have been discussed in the meeting, the staff update and revise those plans to reflect the IASB's decisions.

Balloting and drafting

76   The voting requirements for the IASB's publications are as follows:

Simple majority of members in favour	Nine votes in favour
• Agenda and topic decisions	• Exposure drafts (including revised proposals, and proposed amendments of existing standards and the conceptual framework)
• Discussion paper	
• Other discussion documents (such as those prepared by other standard-setters)	
	• IFRSs
• Administrative decisions	• Interpretations of IFRSs

77   Before instructing the staff to start drafting a document to be voted upon, the Chairman of the IASB polls IASB members during an IASB meeting to gauge the level of support on a particular issue. If there is sufficient support, the IASB instructs the staff to prepare a pre-ballot draft of the document (discussion paper, exposure draft or IFRS). IASB members review the pre-ballot draft individually, and further pre-ballot drafts may be required if new issues ('sweep issues') arise during IASB members' review.

78   If the document being drafted is an IFRS, the pre-ballot draft is sent to selected parties (normally the IFRIC) for a 'fatal flaw' review. After considering the results of this review, together with IASB members' comments, the staff prepare a ballot draft. To enhance the transparency of the drafting process, the IASB posts on the website changes from the exposure draft. In addition, at about the same time a near-final draft is posted on the IASB's limited-access website for paying subscribers.

79   The ballot draft of a discussion paper, exposure draft or IFRS is ready for balloting after all outstanding issues are cleared and the IASB agrees to proceed with balloting.

80   A balloting package includes the following:

    •   a balloting form

    •   a memorandum summarising major changes from the pre-ballot draft

- the ballot draft, in two versions:

    - the text, marked up to show changes from the previous pre-ballot draft

    - the 'clean' text.

81   Balloting takes place outside meetings. The staff circulate the balloting package to IASB members individually. After reviewing the balloting package, IASB members complete the ballot form to record whether they assent to, or dissent from, publication of the ballot draft. IASB members may suggest late editorial improvements to the text; depending on the number of such changes, the staff report to the IASB after the ballot or prepare and circulate to the IASB a post-ballot draft showing the final changes.

82   The IASB publishes its pronouncements and consultative documents by posting them on its limited-access website for paying subscribers. Discussion papers, exposure drafts and draft Interpretations are freely available on the IASB's website. With the exception of IFRIC documents, IASB publications are normally also published in hard copy.

83   IASB members who propose to dissent from publication of an exposure draft or IFRS make their intentions known during the poll at the IASB meeting. Dissenting opinions are prepared by the IASB member concerned in collaboration with the staff. In exposure drafts, dissenting opinions are presented as alternative views. Dissenting opinions and alternative views are incorporated in the pre-ballot and ballot drafts for the other IASB members to see before balloting.

Liaison activities

84   Liaison activities take place throughout the due process cycle. Their purpose is to promote co-operation and communication between the IASB and parties interested in standard-setting. Liaison is conducted at many levels within the IASB's structure and operations.

85   Close co-ordination between the IASB's due process and the due process of other accounting standard-setters is important to the success of the IASB. At its inception, the IASB established formal liaison relationships with standard-setters in Australia and New Zealand, Canada, France, Germany, Japan, the United Kingdom and the United States. The Technical Expert Group of the European Financial Reporting Advisory Group (EFRAG) was given the same rights as those bodies formally designated as liaison standard-setters. Since then, the concept of liaison with accounting standard-setters has been broadened. Members of the IASB are assigned to liaison not only with formerly designated liaison standard-setters and EFRAG, but also with other accounting standard-setters throughout the world.

86   While the extent and depth of liaison with accounting standard-setters required depends on the organisation involved, the IASB determines particular liaison responsibilities in consultation with the Trustees. The IASB meets the chairmen of other accounting standard-setters and regularly organises regional and global meetings with standard-setters.

87   Liaison activities extend beyond interaction with accounting standard-setters. The IASB interacts with a wide range of interested parties throughout a project which can include practical business analysis. IASB members and senior staff of the IASB and the IASC Foundation also regularly hold educational sessions, attend meetings and conferences of interested parties, invite interested organisations to voice their views, and announce major events of the organisation on the website.

Consultation with the SAC

88   The SAC provides broad strategic advice on the IASB's operations. In accordance with the Constitution and the SAC Charter (at Appendix III), the IASB consults the SAC on its technical agenda, project priorities, project issues related to application and implementation of IFRSs, and possible benefits and costs of particular proposals. The SAC also serves as a sounding board for the IASB, and can be used to gather views that supplement the normal consultative process.

89   The SAC normally meets three times a year for a period of two days. The directors of the technical staff and those IASB members and staff who are responsible for items on the SAC meeting agenda are normally required to attend the meetings.

90   IASB staff normally provide an update for the SAC, and invite questions and comments from SAC members. Depending on the issue, the chairman of the meeting may call for a formal poll to demonstrate to the IASB the extent of support within the SAC for a particular point of view. If the IASB ultimately takes a position on a particular issue that differs from a polled expression of the SAC, the IASB gives the SAC its reasons for coming to a different position.

91   In addition to receiving advice from the SAC, the IASB also considers comments from SAC subcommittees.

Working groups

92   Working groups give the IASB access to additional practical experience and expertise. The IASB normally establishes working groups for its major projects. If the IASB decides to omit this step, it will state its reasons.

93   Working groups are set up during the project planning stage. Before setting up a working group, the IASB advertises for nominations and applications. The composition of a working group reflects the diversity and breadth of interest involved in a particular area. The Trustees' Due Process Oversight Committee reviews the proposed composition of each group to ensure that there is a satisfactory balance of perspectives. Meetings of working groups are attended by some IASB members and technical staff.

94   In consultation with the Trustees and the members of working groups, the IASB sets working groups a clear mandate and objectives, and the groups are not asked to develop formal recommendations. Once work starts, the IASB consults the groups on important decisions, and provides regular updates on the progress of the project.

95   Meetings of working groups are announced in advance, open to the public, and chaired by an IASB member. Comments from group members are included in the materials for discussion in IASB meetings.

Comment letters

96   Comment letters play a vital role in the IASB's formal deliberative process. To give the public timely access to the comment letters sent to the IASB, the staff regularly post the letters on the website.

97   The IASB members review comment letters that are received within the comment period. The staff normally provide a summary and analysis of the comments received. Summaries of comments are posted on the website as part of IASB meeting observer notes.

98   To be responsive to views received in comment letters, the IASB posts on the website a summary of its position on the major points raised in the letters, once they have been considered. In addition the IASB responds to the main issues raised in comment letters.

Comment period

99   The following documents are published by the IASB to solicit public comments:

(a)   discussion papers

(b)   exposure drafts of IFRSs and amendments to IFRSs

(c)   draft IFRIC Interpretations and draft amendments to Interpretations.

100   The IASB normally allows a period of 120 days for comment on its consultation documents. For exposure drafts, if the matter is exceptionally urgent, the document is short, and the IASB believes that there is likely to be a broad consensus on the topic, the IASB may consider a comment period of no less than 30 days. For major projects, the IASB will normally allow a period of more than 120 days for comments. The comment period on draft IFRIC Interpretations is usually 60 days, but may be less in urgent cases.

Field visits and field tests

101   The IASB often uses field visits to gain a better understanding of industry practices and how proposed standards could affect them. Conducted at a later stage of a project's development, they enable the IASB to assess the cost of possible changes in practice.

102   Although field visits are not described in the Constitution or the *Preface to International Financial Reporting Standards*, the IASB often uses them. Field visits are usually made after the publication of a discussion paper or exposure draft. However, sometimes they take place earlier. The focus of such visits is principally on transaction-specific issues. Participants in the field visits normally include companies or other parties affected by the proposals, and are identified by the IASB in consultation with working groups.

103   Field tests normally require collaboration with interested companies that are willing to be involved in testing the proposed IFRS, sometimes over an extended period. During field tests, the IASB staff work closely with participating companies in data collection, preparation of financial reports using the proposed IFRS, and evaluation of the results of the tests.

104   The IASB recognises the high costs of field tests, for financial resources and staff arrangements required from the IASB and the participating entities, and the possibility that the tests will delay the timely introduction of IFRSs. As the costs may exceed any benefits, the IASB expects to conduct field tests in rare circumstances. If the IASB decides to omit this step, it will state its reasons.

Public hearings (including round-table meetings)

105   In addition to inviting comment letters to solicit views and suggestions, the IASB often considers holding public meetings with interested organisations to listen to and exchange views on specific topics. Such public meetings can be convened as public hearings, public round tables or other formats. Notice is given to the public in advance of those meetings.

106   Public hearings are regarded as most usefully held after the comment period, when the IASB has reviewed the views raised by constituents. Participating entities are required to provide written submissions in advance of the hearing. During the hearings, participants make brief presentations, and question and answer sessions follow.

107   As an alternative to public hearings, the IASB may arrange public round-table meetings to discuss issues with interested parties. The format of such meetings is similar to that of an SAC meeting, in that the IASB raises previously circulated questions and invites participants to give their comments and views.

108   Throughout the due process, and in particular during the comment period, constituents may propose public meetings to explain their concerns about the IASB's proposals or existing IFRSs. In response to such requests, the IASB may assign individual IASB members and staff to attend such meetings. The staff summarise the information received at the different meetings for the IASB's consideration.

Impact analysis

109   The IASB gains insight on the impact of IFRSs through its consultations, both in consultative publications (discussion papers and exposure drafts) and communications with interested parties (liaison activities, meetings etc). The IASB's views on impact analysis questions are reflected explicitly in the basis for conclusions published with each exposure draft and IFRS. The IASB weighs impact analysis considerations as a part of its deliberation when considering and drafting its analysis of likely effects. However, it is rarely possible to make a formal quantitative assessment of the impact of IFRSs.

110   In forming its judgement on the evaluation of impact analysis, the IASB considers

- the costs incurred by preparers of financial statements

- the costs incurred by users of financial statements when information is not available

- the comparative advantage that preparers have in developing information, when compared with the costs that users would incur to develop surrogate information

- the benefit of better economic decision-making as a result of improved financial reporting.

Information on the organisation's website

111   Publications and information related to the IASB's due process that are freely available on the organisation's website are as follows:

- meeting schedules of the Trustees, the IASB, the SAC, the Working Groups, the IFRIC, public hearings and other public meetings
- comment letters and written submissions
- exposure drafts of IFRSs and amendments
- draft Interpretations and draft amendments to Interpretations
- discussion papers
- project summaries and feedback statements
- effect analyses
- IASB *Update* and IFRIC *Update*
- project updates
- comparisons of exposure drafts and current proposals of the IASB following IASB redeliberations
- post-implementation reviews
- press releases
- other relevant information.

'Comply or explain' approach

112   The following due process steps are mandatory:

- developing and pursuing the IASB's technical agenda
- preparing and issuing IFRSs and publishing exposure drafts, each of which is to include any dissenting opinions
- establishing procedures for reviewing comments made within a reasonable period on documents published for comment
- consulting the SAC on major projects, agenda decisions and work priorities
- publishing bases for conclusions with IFRSs and exposure drafts.

113   Other steps specified in the Constitution are not mandatory. They include:

- publishing a discussion document (eg a discussion paper)
- establishing working groups or other types of specialist advisory groups
- holding public hearings

- undertaking field tests (both in developed countries and in emerging markets).

114 If the IASB decides not to undertake those non-mandatory steps defined by the Constitution, it will, as required by the Constitution, state its reasons. Explanations are normally made at IASB meetings, and are published in the decision summaries and in the basis for conclusions with the exposure draft or IFRS in question.

Trustees' oversight role

115 As mentioned in paragraph 17, the Trustees of the IASC Foundation oversee the IASB's operations. The Trustees' Due Process Oversight Committee reviews the composition of working groups and ensures that their membership reflects a diversity of views and expertise. The Committee also reviews proposed procedures for the IASB's due process on new projects.

116 Other oversight duties of the Trustees in relation to the IASB's due process include

- reviewing annually the IASB's strategy and its effectiveness

- considering, but not determining, the IASB's agenda

- reviewing the IASB's compliance with its due process

- establishing and amending the IASB's operating procedures, consultative arrangements and due process

- engaging the chairman of the SAC to participate in the Trustees' meetings.

Appendix IV sets out the relevant Constitution sections regarding the Trustees' oversight role.

117 Questions about adherence to the procedures described in this Handbook should be addressed to the IASC Foundation's Director of Operations.

Appendix I
The IASB's due process: extracts from the Constitution

This appendix, which contains Sections 28, 30 and 31 of the Constitution, is not reproduced here.

Appendix II

Due process:
extract from the *Preface to International Financial Reporting Standards*

This appendix, which contains paragraph 18 of the Preface, *is not reproduced here.*

Appendix III

Standards Advisory Council
Terms of reference and operating procedures

I Objectives and scope of activities

1   The primary objective of the Standards Advisory Council of the International Accounting Standards Board (SAC) is to provide a forum where the International Accounting Standards Board (IASB) consults individuals, and representatives of organisations affected by its work, that are committed to the development of high quality International Financial Reporting Standards (IFRSs). As part of that consultative process the SAC gives advice to the IASB on a range of issues which includes, but is not limited to, the following:

   • input on the IASB's agenda;

   • input on the IASB's project timetable (work programme) including project priorities, and consultation on any changes in agenda and priorities; and

   • advice on projects, with particular emphasis on practical application and implementation issues, including matters relating to existing standards that may warrant consideration by the International Financial Reporting Interpretations Committee.

   In view of the importance of the IASB's agenda and priorities, once these have been determined by the IASB, changes thereto are expected to be the subject of consultation with the SAC.

When considered appropriate by the members of the SAC, or on the request of the Trustees of the International Accounting Standards Committee Foundation (the 'Trustees'), the SAC also provides input to the Trustees on matters relating to the activities of the SAC or the IASB and any other relevant issues.

2   A secondary objective of the SAC is to support the IASB in the promotion and adoption of IFRSs throughout the world. This may include the publishing of articles supportive of IFRSs and addressing public meetings on the same subject. Any such views expressed are personal, and should not create the impression that they are the opinions of the SAC. (This objective does not preclude SAC members from participating in genuine and objective critiques of the work of the IASB to assist better understanding and transparency of issues and solutions.)

II   Composition and membership

3   The SAC is composed of individuals, or representatives of organisations, interested in the development of high quality IFRSs. The membership provides for a broad geographical spread and a range of functional backgrounds that include members drawn from user groups, preparers, financial analysts, academics, auditors, regulators and professional accounting bodies. In addition, certain international organisations may be granted permanent seats on the SAC by the Trustees. Official observer status may also be granted by the Trustees to other bodies and organisations that are influential in the global financial community.

4   A panel of the Trustees considers nominations and, where applicable, their origins and/or the organisations that may be represented, to determine whether nominee associations and individuals are suitable for membership and to ensure a broad geographical spread and a range of functional backgrounds.

5   Members are appointed for an initial term of three years and, depending upon the need to maintain a proper balance and for continuity, may be asked to remain for a further period of up to three years. A maximum period of service of six years is permitted.

6   In the interests of retaining an active and engaged membership, individuals who do not attend in person three consecutive meetings will be asked to stand down from the SAC.

7   The Trustees appoint members to the SAC in an individual or representative capacity, and at SAC meetings members are expected to express their individual views unless it is expressly stated that they are the opinions of the organisations they represent. No sourcing record is made of organisational or individual views in the SAC minutes. In adopting this convention the SAC is mindful that discussion at a SAC meeting may often be free-ranging and an individual's contribution might be unduly hampered if reference had to be made back to an organisation before a view was expressed at the meeting. SAC members are free to table written materials for circulation, prior to the meeting, should they wish.

III   Chairman

8   The Chairman of the SAC is appointed by the Trustees from nominations submitted by the SAC. The term of office of the Chairman is three years renewable for up to three years, subject to a maximum of six years.

9   The Chairman provides leadership to the SAC in ensuring that the IASB receives timely and effective input that contributes to the development of high quality IFRSs enjoying broad acceptance. To achieve this goal, the Chairman actively monitors the progress of the IASB's work programme, projects and priorities and works closely with the Chairman of the IASB and senior staff to identify, on a timely basis, matters on which the SAC's advice should be sought. Specifically, the duties of the Chairman include, but are not limited to, the following:

- working with the senior staff of the IASB and IASC Foundation to ensure the preparation of timely and appropriate materials to facilitate the conduct of the SAC meetings;

- conducting meetings of the SAC;

- reviewing the draft minutes of SAC meetings before distribution to members;

- appointing the Agenda Committee of the SAC;

- acting as the liaison between the SAC and the IASB and the Trustees;

- keeping abreast of developments within the IASB and informing members of the SAC of these matters, if considered necessary, between meetings;

- assisting the Trustees in the identification of new members of the SAC;

- briefing new members of the SAC on its operations and their role and responsibilities;

- assisting the Chairman of the IASB in promoting the adoption of IFRSs throughout the world; and

- at the request of the Trustees, attending and participating in the Trustees' meetings.

IV   Operating procedures

10   In order to ensure that the SAC operates efficiently and effectively the following operating procedures are adopted.

Meeting details

11   Generally, the SAC meets three times per year for a period of two days, but additional meetings may be convened at the request of the Chairman.

12   The Chairman of the IASB, the IASB's Director of Technical Activities and those IASB members and staff who are responsible for items on the agenda are required to attend SAC meetings. IASB members are generally required to attend the meetings so that they can hear at first hand the views of the SAC.

13 Secretarial support for the meetings, as well as the recording of the minutes, is the responsibility of a designated member of the IASB secretariat.

14 The meetings of the SAC are open to the public except for administrative items, which are dealt with in closed session.

Meeting agenda and papers

15 The Agenda Committee, appointed by the Chairman from amongst the members, is responsible for preparing the agenda for each meeting in consultation with the IASB secretariat. All SAC members are encouraged to submit to the Agenda Committee items for consideration for inclusion in the agenda in advance of the meeting date and in accordance with the timing determined by the Chairman.

16 Written materials supporting SAC agenda items are provided before each meeting. A briefing paper highlighting those issues on which specific guidance is sought from the SAC is usually prepared for each technical item on the agenda. The extent of the supporting documentation is dependent on the complexity of the issues involved and the need for SAC members to be adequately briefed. The following should be the norms for distribution of material to SAC members by the Secretariat:

- minutes of each meeting are distributed to SAC members within thirty days following each SAC (or subcommittee of SAC) meeting;

- the agenda for each SAC meeting, including a brief description of each agenda item, is distributed to SAC members at least thirty days before each SAC meeting; and

- all detailed agenda papers are distributed to SAC members at least ten days before each SAC meeting.

Conduct of meetings

17 The conduct of technical topics is generally prefaced by an introduction of the topic by the relevant IASB member or staff, and may include papers prepared and/or delivered by SAC members. The extent of these briefings is dependent on the complexity of the topic. At the meeting members are invited to comment on the questions raised by the IASB or any other related matters. Depending upon the issue, the Chair may call for a formal poll to demonstrate to the IASB the extent of support within the SAC for a particular point of view. If the IASB ultimately takes a position on a particular issue that differs from a polled expression of the SAC, feedback is given at the next meeting of the SAC on the reasons for the IASB's decision.

Subcommittees

18 In order to improve the quality of comment submitted to the IASB on a specialised topic, the Chairman may call for the establishment of a subcommittee of knowledgeable SAC members to provide expert comment. This subcommittee reports to the SAC, which in turn presents its views to the IASB.

V Travel and accommodation costs

19 Members of the SAC or the organisations they represent meet their own travel and accommodation costs.

VI Approval and changes

20 The Trustees have approved the terms of reference and operating procedures and any changes thereto require their concurrence.

Appendix IV

The Trustees' oversight role—extract from the Constitution

This appendix, which contains Section 15 of the Constitution, is not reproduced here.

International Accounting Standards Committee Foundation

Due Process Handbook
for the International Financial Reporting
Interpretations Committee (IFRIC)

Approved by the Trustees January 2007

CONTENTS

APPENDIX A
The IFRIC's due process – extracts from the Constitution

APPENDIX B
Template for submission of a potential agenda item request to the IFRIC

DUE PROCESS HANDBOOK
International Financial Reporting Interpretations Committee

Introduction

1   The International Financial Reporting Interpretations Committee (IFRIC) assists the International Accounting Standards Board (IASB) in improving financial reporting through timely identification, discussion and resolution of financial reporting issues within the framework of International Financial Reporting Standards (IFRSs). The IFRIC was established in March 2002 by the Trustees of the International Accounting Standards Committee (IASC) Foundation, when it replaced the previous interpretations committee, the Standing Interpretations Committee.

2   This Handbook was published in draft for public comment in May 2006. It is based on the existing framework of the due process laid out in the Constitution of the IASC Foundation (see Appendix A) and the *Preface to International Financial Reporting Interpretations* issued by the IASB. It reflects the public consultation conducted in 2005 and 2006, and supersedes the *Preface to International Financial Reporting Interpretations*.

3   The Trustees of the IASC Foundation have set up a committee—the Trustees' Procedures Committee—with the task of regularly reviewing and, if necessary, amending the procedures of due process in the light of experience and comments from the IFRIC, the IASB and constituents.

4   The Trustees have approved this Handbook following public consultation and public debate by the IFRIC, the IASB and the Trustees.

Responsibilities of the IFRIC and scope of its work

5   In the context of its requirements for due process, the IFRIC reviews newly identified financial reporting issues not specifically addressed in IFRSs or issues where unsatisfactory or conflicting interpretations have developed, or seem likely to develop in the absence of authoritative guidance, with a view to reaching a consensus on the appropriate treatment.

6   In providing interpretative guidance, the IFRIC applies a principle-based approach founded on the *Framework for the Preparation and Presentation of Financial Statements*. The IFRIC considers the principles established in relevant IFRSs to develop its interpretative guidance and to determine that the proposed guidance does not conflict with IFRSs. It follows that, in providing interpretative guidance, the IFRIC is not seeking to create an extensive rule-oriented environment. Nor does it act as an urgent issues group.

7   The IFRIC does not reach a consensus that changes or conflicts with IFRSs or the *Framework*. If the IFRIC concludes that the requirements of an IFRS differ from the *Framework*, it obtains direction from the IASB before providing guidance. In reaching a consensus, the IFRIC also has due regard for the need for international convergence.

8   The IFRIC informs the IASB of any existing or emerging issues that it perceives as indicative of inadequacies in IFRSs or the *Framework*. If the IFRIC believes that an IFRS or the *Framework* should be modified or an additional IFRS should be developed, it refers such conclusions to the IASB for its consideration.

9   When the IFRIC reaches a consensus on an issue, it develops an Interpretation (or an Amendment to an Interpretation) to make that consensus publicly available to interested parties on a timely basis and requests the IASB to approve it for issue. IFRIC Interpretations are developed in accordance with a due process of consultation and debate including making draft Interpretations available for public comment.

Membership

10   The IFRIC has twelve voting members appointed by the Trustees. The members are selected for their ability to maintain an awareness of current issues as they arise and the technical ability to resolve them. They would normally include accountants in industry and public practice and users of financial statements, with a reasonably broad geographical representation. The lack of a full complement of members does not restrict the IFRIC's ability to meet. The membership shall not include more than one person from the same entity.

11   Members of the IFRIC are appointed for fixed renewable terms of three years. The Trustees recognise that continuity of membership is important to the IFRIC's work, and therefore expect to appoint some members for more than one term.

12   The IFRIC is chaired by a member of the IASB, the Director of Technical Activities or another senior member of the IASB staff, or another appropriately qualified individual. The Chairman of the IFRIC is appointed by the Trustees. The Chairman has the right to speak on the technical issues being considered but not to vote.

13   The IFRIC also includes appointed observers (currently from the International Organization of Securities Commissions and the European Commission) and liaison members of the IASB. Appointed observers and liaison IASB members have the right to attend and speak at IFRIC meetings but not to vote. Similarly, members of the IASB other than those specifically designated for liaison with the IFRIC may attend IFRIC meetings, with the right to speak but not to vote.

14   IFRIC members and appointed observers are expected to attend all meetings. Membership is personal; members vote in accordance with their own independent views, not as representatives voting according to the views of the firm, organisation or constituency with which they are associated. If an IFRIC member or appointed observer is unable to attend a meeting, he or she may designate an alternate who will attend in his or her stead. The alternate is nominated in advance in consultation with, and with the agreement of, the Chairman and should be fully briefed by the member in advance of the meeting. Alternates have the right to speak but are not included in determining whether quorum requirements are satisfied and do not have the right to vote.

15   A member's continued membership will be reconsidered by the Trustees if the member is absent from two successive meetings of the IFRIC or is absent from three meetings of the IFRIC held during a period of one year. The member's appointment will be terminated unless reasonable grounds for the absence and an assurance of future attendance are provided.

16   The quorum and voting requirements are detailed in paragraphs 28 and 29.

Due process

17   The IFRIC due process comprises seven stages.

Stage 1: Identification of issues

18   The primary responsibility for identifying issues to be considered by the IFRIC is that of its members and appointed observers. Preparers, auditors and others with an interest in financial reporting are encouraged to refer issues to the IFRIC when they believe that divergent practices have emerged regarding the accounting for particular transactions or circumstances or when there is doubt about the appropriate accounting treatment and it is important that a standard treatment is established.

19   An issue may be put forward by any individual or organisation. A template for submission is available on the IASB Website (see Appendix B). A submission can be made either by email to ifric@iasb.org or by post to the IASB address for the attention of the IFRIC Co-ordinator. A submission should contain both a detailed description of the issue (including a description of alternative solutions referring to the relevant IASB pronouncements) and an evaluation of the issue using the criteria for agenda items set out in paragraph 24.

20   The source of a suggested agenda item is not revealed to the IFRIC or to others.

21   A consensus of the IFRIC has general applicability. The IFRIC does not resolve issues that are specific to the circumstances of a particular entity.

22   The IASB staff assess the issue and prepare an analysis concerning the scope of the issue and whether it meets the agenda criteria. The staff may seek input from members of the IASB and the IFRIC and other knowledgeable parties in undertaking this work.

Stage 2: Setting the agenda

23   The IFRIC decides after debate in a public meeting whether to add an issue to its agenda.

24   The IFRIC assesses proposed agenda items against the following criteria. An issue does not have to satisfy all the criteria to qualify for the agenda.

(a)   The issue is widespread and has practical relevance.

(b)   The issue indicates that there are significantly divergent interpretations (either emerging or already existing in practice). The IFRIC will not add an item to its agenda if IFRSs are clear, with the result that divergent interpretations are not expected in practice.

(c) Financial reporting would be improved through elimination of the diverse reporting methods.

(d) The issue can be resolved efficiently within the confines of existing IFRSs and the *Framework*, and the demands of the interpretation process. The issue should be sufficiently narrow in scope to be capable of interpretation, but not so narrow that it is not cost-effective for the IFRIC and its constituents to undertake the due process associated with an Interpretation.

(e) It is probable that the IFRIC will be able to reach a consensus on the issue on a timely basis.

(f) If the issue relates to a current or planned IASB project, there is a pressing need to provide guidance sooner than would be expected from the IASB's activities. The IFRIC will not add an item to its agenda if an IASB project is expected to resolve the issue in a shorter period than the IFRIC requires to complete its due process.

25 A consultative period applies to issues that are not added to the agenda. The draft reason for not adding an item to the agenda is published in *IFRIC Update* and electronically on the IASB Website with a comment period of not less than 30 days. The comments received are placed on the public record, unless confidentiality is specifically requested by the commentator (supported by good reason such as commercial confidence), and form part of the deliberation that takes place at the next available IFRIC meeting. At that meeting the IFRIC decides whether to add the issue to its agenda.

26 A simple majority of IFRIC members present at the meeting can agree to add any issue to the IFRIC agenda. The reasons for not adding an item to the IFRIC agenda are posted on the IASB Website as a historical record of decisions taken. That record is not updated as standards are amended and does not form part of IFRSs.

27 To ensure that the IFRIC considers only issues on which timely guidance can be provided, over the course of a project the IFRIC reassesses from time to time whether the issues can be appropriately addressed within the mandate. If an issue has been considered at three meetings and there is still no consensus in prospect for either a draft or final Interpretation, the IFRIC considers whether it should be removed from the agenda. The IFRIC may extend consideration of the issue for an additional period, normally not more than one or two meetings. If the IFRIC has concluded that it will not be able to reach a consensus, it will discontinue work on the issue, inform the IASB and publish the fact that work has been discontinued. The IFRIC may recommend that the matter be taken up by the IASB.

Stage 3: IFRIC meetings and voting

28 The IFRIC meets in public and follows procedures similar to the IASB's general policy for its Board meetings. At such meetings the IFRIC debates both matters that are on its agenda and items proposed to be added to its agenda. IFRIC members and appointed observers are expected to attend meetings in person.

However, meetings may be held using teleconference or any other communication facilities that permit simultaneous communication among all members and appointed observers and allow public observers to hear all participants.

29   Nine voting members of the IFRIC present in person or by telecommunications constitute a quorum.

30   Each IFRIC voting member has one vote. Members vote in accordance with their own independent views, not as representatives voting according to the views of any firm, organisation or constituency with which they may be associated. Proxy voting is not permitted.

31   The Chairman may invite others to attend meetings of the IFRIC as advisers when specialised input is required. A member or an appointed observer may also, with the prior consent of the Chairman, bring to a meeting an adviser who has specialised knowledge of a topic to be discussed. Such invited advisers will have the right to speak.

32   The IFRIC may conduct business electronically or by mail between meetings, for example to confirm drafting of a proposed draft or final Interpretation or for the IASB staff to obtain information on a proposed topic so that it can be developed appropriately for public discussion. All technical decisions, however, are made in meetings that are open for public observation.

Stage 4: Development of a draft Interpretation

33   The IFRIC reaches its conclusions on the basis of information contained in Issue Summaries that are prepared under the supervision of IASB staff. An Issue Summary describes the issue to be discussed and provides the information necessary for IFRIC members to gain an understanding of the issue and make decisions about it. An Issue Summary is developed for the IFRIC's consideration after a thorough review of the authoritative accounting literature and possible alternatives, including consultation where appropriate with national standard-setters. An Issue Summary may include:

(a)   a brief description of the transaction or event.

(b)   the specific issues or questions to be considered by the IFRIC.

(c)   the relevant concepts from the *Framework*.

(d)   a description of potential appropriate alternative treatments based on those concepts, with the arguments in favour and against each alternative.

(e)   a list of the relevant IASB pronouncements as well as those of national standard-setters, identifying any inconsistency between the alternative treatments, the relevant concepts, and the standards.

(f)   recommendations on the appropriate accounting treatment.

34   A draft Interpretation is developed on which the IFRIC votes. Voting takes place at a public meeting. A consensus is achieved when no more than three members have voted against the proposal.

35   An Interpretation includes:

(a)   a summary of the accounting issues identified;

(b)   the consensus reached on the appropriate accounting;

(c)   references to relevant IFRSs, parts of the *Framework* and other pronouncements that have been drawn upon to support the consensus; and

(d)   the effective date and transitional provisions.

The reasons for the consensus are set out in the Basis for Conclusions.

Stage 5: The IASB's role in the release of a draft Interpretation

36   IASB members have access to all IFRIC agenda papers. They are expected to comment on technical matters as the issues are being considered, particularly if they have concerns about alternatives the IFRIC is considering.

37   IASB members are informed when the IFRIC reaches a consensus on a draft Interpretation. The draft Interpretation is released for public comment unless four or more IASB members object within a week of being informed of its completion.

38   If a draft Interpretation is not released because of IASB members' objections, the issue will be considered at the next IASB meeting. On the basis of discussion at the meeting, the IASB will decide whether the draft Interpretation should be published or whether the matter should be referred back to the IFRIC, added to its own agenda or not be the subject of any further action.

Stage 6: Comment period and deliberation

39   Draft Interpretations are made available for public comment for not less than 60 days. All comments received during the comment period are considered by the IFRIC before an Interpretation is finalised. Comment letters are made publicly available unless confidentiality is requested by the commentator (supported by good reason such as commercial confidence). A staff summary and analysis of the comment letters are provided to the IFRIC.

40   If the proposed Interpretation is changed significantly, the IFRIC will consider whether it should be re-exposed. Re-exposure is not required automatically and will depend on the significance of the changes contemplated, whether they were raised in the Basis for Conclusions on the draft Interpretation or in questions posed by the IFRIC, their significance for practice and what might be learned by the IFRIC from re-exposure.

41   The IFRIC votes to confirm the consensus set out in the final Interpretation. A consensus is achieved when no more than three members have voted against the proposal.

Stage 7: The IASB's role in an Interpretation

42   When the IFRIC has reached a consensus on an Interpretation, the Interpretation is put to the IASB for ratification, in a public meeting, before being issued. Approval by the IASB requires at least nine IASB members to be in favour. The IASB votes on the Interpretation as submitted by the IFRIC. If an Interpretation is not approved by the IASB, the IASB provides the IFRIC with an analysis of the objections and concerns of those voting against the Interpretation. On the basis of this analysis, the IASB will decide whether the matter should be referred back to the IFRIC, added to its own agenda or not be the subject of any further action.

43   Approved Interpretations are issued by the IASB.

Authority of IFRIC Interpretations

44   IFRIC Interpretations set out the consensus that entities are required to apply if their financial statements are described as being prepared in accordance with IFRSs. The authoritative text of a draft Interpretation or an Interpretation is that published by the IASB in the English language.

45   IFRIC Interpretations usually apply to periods beginning on or after a specified effective date (usually three months from the date of issue). However, the IFRIC may choose to vary that approach. Transitional provisions that apply on initial application of an IFRIC consensus are specified in the Interpretation. In keeping with IFRSs, the presumption is that IFRIC Interpretations will be applied retrospectively in accordance with IAS 8 *Accounting Policies, Changes in Accounting Estimates and Errors*. The IFRIC also considers the effect of the transitional provisions on first-time adopters of IFRSs, including the interaction of the transitional provisions with those of IFRS 1 *First-time Adoption of International Financial Reporting Standards*.

46   An IFRIC Interpretation is withdrawn when an IFRS or other authoritative document issued by the IASB that overrides or confirms a previously issued IFRIC consensus becomes effective. The IFRIC Interpretations that would be affected by an authoritative IASB document are identified in the exposure draft of that document. The IASB informs the IFRIC when an exposure draft proposes the withdrawal of an IFRIC Interpretation.

Communication

47   IFRIC members and appointed observers are encouraged to discuss, in general terms, technical issues being considered by the IFRIC with associates who have an interest and expertise in such matters. Informal consultation of this kind offers members the opportunity to bring a variety of views to bear on the decisions to be made. The IFRIC agenda papers and drafts of proposed Interpretations are not to be distributed to other parties without the consent of the Chairman.

48   Information about the deliberations of the IFRIC is made available to the public. The IFRIC meeting agenda is posted on the IASB Website in advance of each meeting. Observer notes are prepared before the IFRIC meeting to allow public observers to follow the debate and discussion during the meeting. About two weeks after the IFRIC meeting the IASB staff post *IFRIC Update* on the IASB Website,

summarising the IFRIC's decisions and recent developments. Shortly afterwards *IFRIC Update* is published in hard copy. The IFRIC publishes on the IASB Website details of items on its agenda, and a record of its decisions in respect of items not taken on to the agenda.

49   The IFRIC regularly reports to the IASB on matters relating to its procedures, progress with its agenda and other administrative matters. In addition, the IFRIC reviews its mandate and operating procedures at least every five years. The results of this review are communicated to the IASB for consideration and, after consultation with the Standards Advisory Council, the IASB may make recommendations to the Trustees for change.

Relationship with national standard-setters and national interpretative groups

50   The IASB staff maintain liaison with national standard-setters (NSSs) and national interpretative groups (NIGs) to identify interpretative issues that the IFRIC might need to consider. IFRIC members and appointed observers are encouraged to identify issues that may indicate emerging divergence in the interpretation of IFRSs.

51   NSSs and NIGs are encouraged to refer interpretative issues to the IFRIC for its consideration. The IFRIC, however, will not give assurance that a local interpretation is either consistent or inconsistent with IFRSs.

Appendix A

The IFRIC's due process: extracts from the Constitution

This appendix, which contains extracts from Sections 15, 16, 30–36 and 41 of the Constitution, is not reproduced here.

Appendix B

Template for submission of a potential agenda item request to the IFRIC

Any individual or organisation may put forward suggestions of potential agenda items for consideration by the IFRIC. Anyone doing so is asked to submit a brief proposal, which will be presented to the IFRIC without identifying the submitter. The proposal should include the following:

1   **The issue.** A description of the issue including, where relevant, any aspects that should be addressed separately.

2   **Current practice.** A brief description of current or emerging accounting practices, outlining the major alternatives, and referring to the relevant IASB pronouncements.

3   **Reasons for the IFRIC to address the issue.** The issue should be evaluated using the following criteria:

    (a)   Is the issue widespread and practical?

    (b)   Does the issue involve significantly divergent interpretations (either emerging or already existing in practice)?

    (c)   Would financial reporting be improved through elimination of the diversity?

    (d)   Is the issue sufficiently narrow in scope to be capable of interpretation within the confines of IFRSs and the *Framework for the Preparation and Presentation of Financial Statements*, but not so narrow that it is inefficient to apply the interpretation process?

    (e)   If the issue relates to a current or planned IASB project, is there a pressing need for guidance sooner than would be expected from the IASB project? (The IFRIC will not add an item to its agenda if an IASB project is expected to resolve the issue in a shorter period than the IFRIC would require to complete its due process.)

A template is set out below (see next page).

Please submit the completed template by either email to ifric@iasb.org or post to:

IFRIC Co-ordinator
International Accounting Standards Board
First Floor
30 Cannon Street
London EC4M 6XH
United Kingdom

IFRIC POTENTIAL AGENDA ITEM REQUEST

The issue:

Current practice:

Reasons for the IFRIC to address the issue:

Submitted by
Name:
Organisation:
Address:
Telephone:
Email:

Glossary of Terms

This glossary is extracted from the International Financial Reporting Standards (IFRSs) including International Accounting Standards (IASs) issued by the IASB as at 31 December 2009. References are by Standard and paragraph number.

The glossary also includes extracts from the *Framework for the Preparation and Presentation of Financial Statements*. References to the *Framework* are preceded by F.

References set out below in (brackets) indicate minor variations in wording.

accounting policies	The specific principles, bases, conventions, rules and practices applied by an entity in preparing and presenting financial statements.	IAS 8.5
accounting profit	Profit or loss for a period before deducting tax expense.	IAS 12.5
accrual basis of accounting	The effects of transactions and other events are recognised when they occur (and not as cash or its equivalent is received or paid) and they are recorded in the accounting records and reported in the financial statements of the periods to which they relate.	F.22
accumulating compensated absences	Compensated absences that are carried forward and can be used in future periods if the current period's entitlement is not used in full.	IAS 19.13
acquiree	The business or businesses that the acquirer obtains control of in a business combination.	IFRS 3.A
acquirer	The entity that obtains control of the acquiree.	IFRS 3.A
acquisition date	The date on which the acquirer obtains control of the acquiree.	IFRS 3.A
active market	A market in which all the following conditions exist: (a) the items traded within the market are homogeneous; (b) willing buyers and sellers can normally be found at any time; and (c) prices are available to the public.	IAS 36.6, (IAS 38.8), IAS 41.8
active market	A financial instrument is regarded as quoted in an active market if quoted prices are readily and regularly available from an exchange, dealer, broker, industry group, pricing service or regulatory agency, and those prices represent actual and regularly occurring market transactions on an arm's length basis.	IAS 39.AG71

actuarial assumptions	An entity's unbiased and mutually compatible best estimates of the demographic and financial variables that will determine the ultimate cost of providing post-employment benefits.	IAS 19.72–73
actuarial gains and losses	(a) Experience adjustments (the effects of differences between the previous actuarial assumptions and what has actually occurred); and (b) the effects of changes in actuarial assumptions.	IAS 19.7
actuarial present value of promised retirement benefits	The present value of the expected payments by a retirement benefit plan to existing and past employees, attributable to the service already rendered.	IAS 26.8
adjusting events after the reporting period	See 'events after the reporting period'	
agricultural activity	The management by an entity of the biological transformation and harvest of biological assets for sale or for conversion into agricultural produce or into additional biological assets.	IAS 41.5
agricultural produce	The harvested product of the entity's biological assets.	IAS 41.5
amortisation (depreciation)*	The systematic allocation of the depreciable amount of an asset over its useful life.	IAS 36.6, IAS 38.8
amortised cost of a financial asset or financial liability	The amount at which the financial asset or financial liability is measured at initial recognition minus principal repayments, plus or minus the cumulative amortisation using the effective interest method of any difference between that initial amount and the maturity amount, and minus any reduction (directly or through the use of an allowance account) for impairment or uncollectibility.	IAS 39.9
antidilution	An increase in earnings per share or a reduction in loss per share resulting from the assumption that convertible instruments are converted, that options or warrants are exercised, or that ordinary shares are issued upon the satisfaction of specified conditions.	IAS 33.5
asset	A resource: (a) controlled by an entity as a result of past events; and (b) from which future economic benefits are expected to flow to the entity.	IAS 38.8, (F.49(a))

---

* In the case of an intangible asset, the term 'amortisation' is generally used instead of 'depreciation'. The two terms have the same meaning.

assets held by a long-term employee benefit fund	Assets (other than non-transferable financial instruments issued by the reporting entity) that:	IAS 19.7

(a) are held by an entity (a fund) that is legally separate from the reporting entity and exists solely to pay or fund employee benefits; and

(b) are available to be used only to pay or fund employee benefits, are not available to the reporting entity's own creditors (even in bankruptcy), and cannot be returned to the reporting entity, unless either:

    (i) the remaining assets of the fund are sufficient to meet all the related employee benefit obligations of the plan or the reporting entity; or

    (ii) the assets are returned to the reporting entity to reimburse it for employee benefits already paid.

associate	An entity, including an unincorporated entity such as a partnership, over which the investor has significant influence and that is neither a subsidiary nor an interest in a joint venture.	IAS 28.2
basic earnings per share	Profit or loss attributable to ordinary equity holders of the parent entity (the numerator) divided by the weighted average number of ordinary shares outstanding during the period (the denominator).	IAS 33.10
biological asset	A living animal or plant.	IAS 41.5
biological transformation	The processes of growth, degeneration, production, and procreation that cause qualitative or quantitative changes in a biological asset.	IAS 41.5
borrowing costs	Interest and other costs that an entity incurs in connection with the borrowing of funds.	IAS 23.5
business	An integrated set of activities and assets that is capable of being conducted and managed for the purpose of providing a return in the form of dividends, lower costs or other economic benefits directly to investors or other owners, members or participants.	IFRS 3.A
business combination	A transaction or other event in which an acquirer obtains control of one or more businesses. Transactions sometimes referred to as 'true mergers' or 'mergers of equals' are also business combinations as that term is used in IFRS 3.	IFRS 3.A

capital	Under a financial concept of capital, such as invested money or invested purchasing power, the net assets or equity of the entity. The financial concept of capital is adopted by most entities.	F.102
	Under a physical concept of capital, such as operating capability, the productive capacity of the entity based on, for example, units of output per day.	
capitalisation	Recognising a cost as part of the cost of an asset.	IAS 23.9
carrying amount	The amount at which an asset is recognised after deducting any accumulated depreciation (amortisation) and accumulated impairment losses thereon.	IAS 16.6, IAS 36.6, IAS 38.8
carrying amount	The amount at which an asset is recognised in the statement of financial position.	IAS 40.5, IAS 41.8
cash	Cash on hand and demand deposits.	IAS 7.6
cash equivalents	Short-term, highly liquid investments that are readily convertible to known amounts of cash and which are subject to an insignificant risk of changes in value.	IAS 7.6
cash flows	Inflows and outflows of cash and cash equivalents.	IAS 7.6
cash-generating unit	The smallest identifiable group of assets that generates cash inflows that are largely independent of the cash inflows from other assets or groups of assets.	IAS 36.6, IFRS 5.A
cash-settled share-based payment transaction	A share-based payment transaction in which the entity acquires goods or services by incurring a liability to transfer cash or other assets to the supplier of those goods or services for amounts that are based on the price (or value) of equity instruments (including shares or share options) of the entity or another group entity.	IFRS 2.A
cedant	The policyholder under a reinsurance contract.	IFRS 4.A
change in accounting estimate	An adjustment of the carrying amount of an asset or a liability, or the amount of the periodic consumption of an asset, that results from the assessment of the present status of, and expected future benefits and obligations associated with, assets and liabilities. Changes in accounting estimates result from new information or new developments and, accordingly, are not corrections of errors.	IAS 8.5
class of assets	A grouping of assets of a similar nature and use in an entity's operations.	IAS 16.37, IAS 36.127, IAS 38.119

class of financial instruments	Grouping of financial instruments that is appropriate to the nature of the information disclosed and that takes into account the characteristics of those financial instruments.	IFRS 7.6
close members of the family of a person	Those family members who may be expected to influence, or be influenced by, that person in their dealings with the entity and include:	IAS 24.9

    (a) that person's children and spouse or domestic partner;

    (b) children of that person's spouse or domestic partner

    (c) dependants of that person or that person's spouse or domestic partner.

closing rate	The spot exchange rate at the end of the reporting period.	IAS 21.8
commencement of the lease term	The date from which the lessee is entitled to exercise its right to use the leased asset. It is the date of initial recognition of the lease (ie the recognition of the assets, liabilities, income or expenses resulting from the lease, as appropriate).	IAS 17.4

compensation	Includes all employee benefits (as defined in IAS 19) including employee benefits to which IFRS 2 applies. Employee benefits are all forms of consideration paid, payable or provided by the entity, or on behalf of the entity, in exchange for services rendered to the entity. It also includes such consideration paid on behalf of a parent of the entity in respect of the entity. Compensation includes:	IAS 24.9

(a) short-term employee benefits, such as wages, salaries and social security contributions, paid annual leave and paid sick leave, profit-sharing and bonuses (if payable within twelve months of the end of the period) and non-monetary benefits (such as medical care, housing, cars and free or subsidised goods or services) for current employees;

(b) post-employment benefits such as pensions, other retirement benefits, post-employment life insurance and post-employment medical care;

(c) other long-term employee benefits, including long-service leave or sabbatical leave, jubilee or other long-service benefits, long-term disability benefits and, if they are not payable wholly within twelve months after the end of the period, profit-sharing, bonuses and deferred compensation;

(d) termination benefits; and

(e) share-based payment.

component of an entity	Operations and cash flows that can be clearly distinguished, operationally and for financial reporting purposes, from the rest of the entity.	IFRS 5.A
compound financial instrument	A financial instrument that, from the issuer's perspective, contains both a liability and an equity element.	IAS 32.28–29
consolidated financial statements	The financial statements of a group presented as those of a single economic entity.	IAS 27.4, IAS 28.2
construction contract	A contract specifically negotiated for the construction of an asset or a combination of assets that are closely interrelated or interdependent in terms of their design, technology and function or their ultimate purpose or use.	IAS 11.3

constructive obligation	An obligation that derives from an entity's actions where:	IAS 37.10
	(a) by an established pattern of past practice, published policies or a sufficiently specific current statement, the entity has indicated to other parties that it will accept certain responsibilities; and	
	(b) as a result, the entity has created a valid expectation on the part of those other parties that it will discharge those responsibilities.	
contingent asset	A possible asset that arises from past events and whose existence will be confirmed only by the occurrence or non-occurrence of one or more uncertain future events not wholly within the control of the entity.	IAS 37.10
contingent consideration	Usually, an obligation of the acquirer to transfer additional assets or equity interests to the former owners of an acquiree as part of the exchange for control of the acquiree if specified future events occur or conditions are met. However, contingent consideration also may give the acquirer the right to the return of previously transferred consideration if specified conditions are met.	IFRS 3.A
contingent liability	(a) A possible obligation that arises from past events and whose existence will be confirmed only by the occurrence or non-occurrence of one or more uncertain future events not wholly within the control of the entity; or	IAS 37.10
	(b) a present obligation that arises from past events but is not recognised because:	
	(i) it is not probable that an outflow of resources embodying economic benefits will be required to settle the obligation; or	
	(ii) the amount of the obligation cannot be measured with sufficient reliability.	
contingent rent	That portion of the lease payments that is not fixed in amount but is based on the future amount of a factor that changes other than with the passage of time (eg percentage of future sales, amount of future use, future price indices, future market rates of interest).	IAS 17.4
contingent share agreement	An agreement to issue shares that is dependent on the satisfaction of specified conditions.	IAS 33.5

contingently issuable ordinary shares	Ordinary shares issuable for little or no cash or other consideration upon the satisfaction of specified conditions in a contingent share agreement.	IAS 33.5
contract	An agreement between two or more parties that has clear economic consequences that the parties have little, if any, discretion to avoid, usually because the agreement is enforceable at law. Contracts may take a variety of forms and need not be in writing.	IAS 32.13
control (of an entity)	The power to govern the financial and operating policies of an entity so as to obtain benefits from its activities.	IAS 24.9, IAS 27.4, IAS 28.2, (IAS 31.3), IFRS 3.A
corporate assets	Assets other than goodwill that contribute to the future cash flows of both the cash-generating unit under review and other cash-generating units.	IAS 36.6
'corridor'	A range around an entity's best estimate of post-employment benefit obligations.	IAS 19.95
cost	The amount of cash or cash equivalents paid or the fair value of the other consideration given to acquire an asset at the time of its acquisition or construction, or, when applicable, the amount attributed to that asset when initially recognised in accordance with the specific requirements of other IFRSs, eg IFRS 2.	IAS 16.6, IAS 38.8, IAS 40.5
cost of inventories	All costs of purchase, costs of conversion and other costs incurred in bringing the inventories to their present location and condition.	IAS 2.10
cost of purchase	All of the purchase price, import duties and other taxes (other than those subsequently recoverable by the entity from the taxing authorities), and transport, handling and other costs directly attributable to the acquisition of the item. Trade discounts, rebates and other similar items are deducted in determining the costs of purchase.	IAS 2.11
cost plus contract	A construction contract in which the contractor is reimbursed for allowable or otherwise defined costs, plus a percentage of these costs or a fixed fee.	IAS 11.3
costs of conversion	Costs directly related to the units of production, such as direct labour together with a systematic allocation of fixed and variable production overheads that are incurred in converting materials into finished goods.	IAS 2.12

costs of disposal	Incremental costs directly attributable to the disposal of an asset, excluding finance costs and income tax expense.	IAS 36.6
costs to sell	The incremental costs directly attributable to the disposal of an asset (or disposal group), excluding finance costs and income tax expense.	IFRS 5.A (IAS 41.5)
credit risk	The risk that one party to a financial instrument will cause a financial loss for the other party by failing to discharge an obligation.	IFRS 7.A
currency risk	The risk that the fair value or future cash flows of a financial instrument will fluctuate because of changes in foreign exchange rates.	IFRS 7.A

current asset An entity shall classify an asset as current when: IAS 1.66, (IFRS 5.A)

(a) it expects to realise the asset or intends to sell or consume it in its normal operating cycle;

(b) it holds the asset primarily for the purpose of trading;

(c) it expects to realise the asset within twelve months after the reporting period

(d) the asset is cash or a cash equivalent (as defined in IAS 7) unless the asset is restricted from being exchanged or used to settle a liability for at least twelve months after the reporting period.

An entity shall classify all other assets as non-current.

current cost The amount of cash or cash equivalents that would have to be paid if the same or an equivalent asset was acquired currently. F.100(b)

The undiscounted amount of cash or cash equivalents that would be required to settle an obligation currently.

current liability An entity shall classify a liability as current when: IAS 1.69

(a) it expects to settle the liability in its normal operating cycle;

(b) it holds the liability primarily for the purpose of trading;

(c) the liability is due to be settled within twelve months after the reporting period; or

(d) the entity does not have an unconditional right to defer settlement of the liability for at least twelve months after the reporting period.

An entity shall classify all other liabilities as non-current.

current service cost	The increase in the present value of the defined benefit obligation resulting from employee service in the current period.	IAS 19.7
current tax	The amount of income taxes payable (recoverable) in respect of the taxable profit (tax loss) for a period.	IAS 12.5
curtailment (of a defined benefit plan)	A curtailment occurs when an entity either:	IAS 19.111
	(a) is demonstrably committed to make a significant reduction in the number of employees covered by a plan; or	
	(b) amends the terms of a defined benefit plan so that a significant element of future service by current employees will no longer qualify for benefits, or will qualify only for reduced benefits.	
date of transition to IFRSs	The beginning of the earliest period for which an entity presents full comparative information under IFRSs in its first IFRS financial statements.	IFRS 1.A
deductible temporary differences	Temporary differences between the carrying amount of an asset or liability in the balance sheet and its tax base that will result in amounts that are deductible in determining taxable profit (tax loss) of future periods when the carrying amount of the asset or liability is recovered or settled.	IAS 12.5
deemed cost	An amount used as a surrogate for cost or depreciated cost at a given date. Subsequent depreciation or amortisation assumes that the entity had initially recognised the asset or liability at the given date and that its cost was equal to the deemed cost.	IFRS 1.A
deferred tax assets	The amounts of income taxes recoverable in future periods in respect of:	IAS 12.5
	(a) deductible temporary differences;	
	(b) the carryforward of unused tax losses; and	
	(c) the carryforward of unused tax credits.	
deferred tax liabilities	The amounts of income taxes payable in future periods in respect of taxable temporary differences.	IAS 12.5

defined benefit liability	The net total of the following amounts:	IAS 19.54
	(a) the present value of the defined benefit obligation at the end of the reporting period;	
	(b) plus any actuarial gains (less any actuarial losses) not recognised;	
	(c) minus any past service cost not yet recognised;	
	(d) minus the fair value at the end of the reporting period of plan assets (if any) out of which the obligations are to be settled directly.	
defined benefit obligation (present value of)	The present value, without deducting any plan assets, of expected future payments required to settle the obligation resulting from employee service in the current and prior periods.	IAS 19.7
defined benefit plans	Post-employment benefit plans other than defined contribution plans.	IAS 19.7
defined benefit plans	Retirement benefit plans under which amounts to be paid as retirement benefits are determined by reference to a formula usually based on employees' earnings and/or years of service.	IAS 26.8
defined contribution plans	Post-employment benefit plans under which an entity pays fixed contributions into a separate entity (a fund) and will have no legal or constructive obligation to pay further contributions if the fund does not hold sufficient assets to pay all employee benefits relating to employee service in the current and prior periods.	IAS 19.7
defined contribution plans	Retirement benefit plans under which amounts to be paid as retirement benefits are determined by contributions to a fund together with investment earnings thereon.	IAS 26.8
demonstrably committed	An entity is demonstrably committed to pay termination benefits when, and only when, an entity has a detailed formal plan for the termination and is without realistic possibility of withdrawal. The detailed plan shall include, as a minimum:	IAS 19.134
	(a) the location, function, and approximate number of employees whose services are to be terminated;	
	(b) the termination benefits for each job classification or function; and	
	(c) the time at which the plan will be implemented. Implementation shall begin as soon as possible and the period of time to complete implementation shall be such that material changes to the plan are not likely.	

deposit component	A contractual component that is not accounted for as a derivative under IAS 39 and would be within the scope of IAS 39 if it were a separate instrument.	IFRS 4.A
depreciable amount	The cost of an asset, or other amount substituted for cost (in the financial statements), less its residual value.	IAS 16.6, (IAS 36.6, IAS 38.8)
depreciation (amortisation)*	The systematic allocation of the depreciable amount of an asset over its useful life.	IAS 16.6, IAS 36.6
derecognition (of a financial instrument)	The removal of a previously recognised financial asset or financial liability from an entity's statement of financial position.	IAS 39.9
derivative	A financial instrument or other contract within the scope of IAS 39 (see paragraphs 2–7) with all three of the following characteristics:	IAS 39.9

(a) its value changes in response to the change in a specified interest rate, financial instrument price, commodity price, foreign exchange rate, index of prices or rates, credit rating or credit index, or other variable, provided in the case of a non-financial variable that the variable is not specific to a party to the contract (sometimes called the 'underlying');

(b) it requires no initial net investment or an initial net investment that is smaller than would be required for other types of contracts that would be expected to have a similar response to changes in market factors; and

(c) it is settled at a future date.

---

* In the case of an intangible asset, the term 'amortisation' is generally used instead of 'depreciation'. The two terms have the same meaning.

derivative financial instruments	Financial instruments such as financial options, futures and forwards, interest rate swaps and currency swaps, which create rights and obligations that have the effect of transferring between the parties to the instrument one or more of the financial risks inherent in an underlying primary financial instrument. On inception, derivative financial instruments give one party a contractual right to exchange financial assets or financial liabilities with another party under conditions that are potentially favourable, or a contractual obligation to exchange financial assets or financial liabilities with another party under conditions that are potentially unfavourable. However, they generally do not result in a transfer of the underlying primary financial instrument on inception of the contract, nor does such a transfer necessarily take place on maturity of the contract. Some instruments embody both a right and an obligation to make an exchange. Because the terms of the exchange are determined on inception of the derivative instrument, as prices in financial markets change those terms may become either favourable or unfavourable.	IAS 32. AG15–AG16
development	The application of research findings or other knowledge to a plan or design for the production of new or substantially improved materials, devices, products, processes, systems or services before the start of commercial production or use.	IAS 38.8
diluted earnings per share	Profit or loss attributable to ordinary equity holders of the parent entity (the numerator), divided by the weighted average number of ordinary shares outstanding during the period (the denominator), both adjusted for the effects of all dilutive potential ordinary shares.	IAS 33.31
dilution	A reduction in earnings per share or an increase in loss per share resulting from the assumption that convertible instruments are converted, that options or warrants are exercised, or that ordinary shares are issued upon the satisfaction of specified conditions.	IAS 33.5
dilutive potential ordinary shares	Potential ordinary shares whose conversion to ordinary shares would decrease earnings per share or increase loss per share from continuing operations.	IAS 33.41
direct insurance contract	An insurance contract that is not a reinsurance contract.	IFRS 4.A

direct method of reporting cash flows from operating activities	A method whereby major classes of gross cash receipts and gross cash payments are disclosed.	IAS 7.18(a)

discontinued operation

A component of an entity that either has been disposed of or is classified as held for sale and:

(a) represents a separate major line of business or geographical area of operations,

(b) is part of a single co-ordinated plan to dispose of a separate major line of business or geographical area of operations or

(c) is a subsidiary acquired exclusively with a view to resale.

IFRS 5.A

discretionary participation feature

A contractual right to receive, as a supplement to guaranteed benefits, additional benefits:

(a) that are likely to be a significant portion of the total contractual benefits;

(b) whose amount or timing is contractually at the discretion of the issuer; and

(c) that are contractually based on:

(i) the performance of a specified pool of contracts or a specified type of contract;

(ii) realised and/or unrealised investment returns on a specified pool of assets held by the issuer; or

(iii) the profit or loss of the company, fund or other entity that issues the contract.

IFRS 4.A

disposal group

A group of assets to be disposed of, by sale or otherwise, together as a group in a single transaction, and liabilities directly associated with those assets that will be transferred in the transaction. The group includes goodwill acquired in a business combination if the group is a cash-generating unit to which goodwill has been allocated in accordance with the requirements of paragraphs 80–87 of IAS 36 or if it is an operation within such a cash-generating unit.

IFRS 5.A

dividends

Distributions of profits to holders of equity investments in proportion to their holdings of a particular class of capital.

IAS 18.5

economic life	Either:	IAS 17.4
	(a) the period over which an asset is expected to be economically usable by one or more users; or	
	(b) the number of production or similar units expected to be obtained from the asset by one or more users.	
effective interest method	A method of calculating the amortised cost of a financial asset or a financial liability (or group of financial assets or financial liabilities) and of allocating the interest income or interest expense over the relevant period.	IAS 39.9
effective interest rate	The rate that exactly discounts estimated future cash payments or receipts through the expected life of the financial instrument or, when appropriate, a shorter period to the net carrying amount of the financial asset or financial liability. When calculating the effective interest rate, an entity shall estimate cash flows considering all contractual terms of the financial instrument (for example, prepayment, call and similar options) but shall not consider future credit losses. The calculation includes all fees and points paid or received between parties to the contract that are an integral part of the effective interest rate (see IAS 18), transaction costs, and all other premiums or discounts. There is a presumption that the cash flows and the expected life of a group of similar financial instruments can be estimated reliably. However, in those rare cases when it is not possible to estimate reliably the cash flows or the expected life of a financial instrument (or group of financial instruments), the entity shall use the contractual cash flows over the full contractual term of the financial instrument (or group of financial instruments).	IAS 39.9

embedded derivative	A component of a hybrid (combined) contract that also includes a non-derivative host contract—with the effect that some of the cash flows of the combined contract vary in a way similar to a stand-alone derivative. An embedded derivative causes some or all of the cash flows that otherwise would be required by the contract to be modified according to a specified interest rate, financial instrument price, commodity price, foreign exchange rate, index of prices or rates, credit rating or credit index, or other variable, provided in the case of a non-financial variable that the variable is not specific to a party to the contract. A derivative that is attached to a financial instrument but is contractually transferable independently of that instrument, or has a different counterparty from that instrument, is not an embedded derivative, but a separate financial instrument.	IAS 39.10
employee benefits	All forms of consideration given by an entity in exchange for service rendered by employees.	IAS 19.7
employees and others providing similar services	Individuals who render personal services to the entity and either (a) the individuals are regarded as employees for legal or tax purposes, (b) the individuals work for the entity under its direction in the same way as individuals who are regarded as employees for legal or tax purposes, or (c) the services rendered are similar to those rendered by employees. For example, the term encompasses all management personnel, ie those persons having authority and responsibility for planning, directing and controlling the activities of the entity, including non-executive directors.	IFRS 2.A
entity-specific value	The present value of the cash flows an entity expects to arise from the continuing use of an asset and from its disposal at the end of its useful life or expects to incur when settling a liability.	IAS 16.6, IAS 38.8
equity	The residual interest in the assets of the entity after deducting all its liabilities.	F.49(c)
equity instrument	A contract that evidences a residual interest in the assets of an entity after deducting all of its liabilities.	IAS 32.11, IFRS 2.A
equity instrument granted	The right (conditional or unconditional) to an equity instrument of the entity conferred by the entity on another party, under a share-based payment arrangement.	IFRS 2.A
equity interests	In IFRS 3 is used broadly to mean ownership interests of investor-owned entities and owner, member or participant interests of mutual entities.	IFRS 3.A

equity method	A method of accounting whereby the investment is initially recognised at cost and adjusted thereafter for the post-acquisition change in the investor's share of net assets of the investee. The profit or loss of the investor includes the investor's share of the profit or loss of the investee.	IAS 28.2
equity-settled share-based payment transaction	A share-based payment transaction in which the entity (a) receives goods or services as consideration for its own equity instruments (including shares or share options), or (b) receives goods or services but has no obligation to settle the transaction with the supplier.	IFRS 2.A
events after the reporting period	Those events, favourable and unfavourable, that occur between the end of the reporting period and the date when the financial statements are authorised for issue. Two types of events can be identified: (a) those that provide evidence of conditions that existed at the end of the reporting period (adjusting events after the reporting period); and (b) those that are indicative of conditions that arose after the reporting period (non-adjusting events after the reporting period).	IAS 10.3
exchange difference	The difference resulting from translating a given number of units of one currency into another currency at different exchange rates.	IAS 21.8
exchange rate	The ratio of exchange for two currencies.	IAS 21.8
expenses	Decreases in economic benefits during the accounting period in the form of outflows or depletions of assets or incurrences of liabilities that result in decreases in equity, other than those relating to distributions to equity participants.	F.70(b)
experience adjustments	The effects of differences between previous actuarial assumptions and what has actually occurred.	IAS 19.7
exploration and evaluation assets	Exploration and evaluation expenditures recognised as assets in accordance with the entity's accounting policy.	IFRS 6.A
exploration and evaluation expenditures	Expenditures incurred by an entity in connection with the exploration for and evaluation of mineral resources before the technical feasibility and commercial viability of extracting a mineral resource are demonstrable.	IFRS 6.A

exploration for and evaluation of mineral resources	The search for mineral resources, including minerals, oil, natural gas and similar non-regenerative resources after the entity has obtained legal rights to explore in a specific area, as well as the determination of the technical feasibility and commercial viability of extracting the mineral resource.	IFRS 6.A
fair value	The amount for which an asset could be exchanged, or a liability settled, between knowledgeable, willing parties in an arm's length transaction.	IAS 2.6, (IAS 16.6), IAS 17.4, IAS 18.7, (IAS 19.7), (IAS 20.3), IAS 21.8, IAS 32.11, (IAS 38.8), IAS 39.9, (IAS 40.5), IAS 41.8, IFRS 1.A, IFRS 3.A, IFRS 4.A, IFRS 5.A
fair value	The amount for which an asset could be exchanged, a liability settled, or an equity instrument granted could be exchanged, between knowledgeable, willing parties in an arm's length transaction.	IFRS 2.A
fair value less costs to sell	The amount obtainable from the sale of an asset or cash-generating unit in an arm's length transaction between knowledgeable, willing parties, less the costs of disposal.	IAS 36.6
FIFO (first-in, first-out)	The assumption that the items of inventory that were purchased or produced first are sold first, and consequently the items remaining in inventory at the end of the period are those most recently purchased or produced.	IAS 2.27
finance lease	A lease that transfers substantially all the risks and rewards incidental to ownership of an asset. Title may or may not eventually be transferred.	IAS 17.4

financial asset   Any asset that is: IAS 32.11

(a) cash;

(b) an equity instrument of another entity;

(c) a contractual right:

   (i) to receive cash or another financial asset from another entity; or

   (ii) to exchange financial assets or financial liabilities with another entity under conditions that are potentially favourable to the entity; or

(d) a contract that will or may be settled in the entity's own equity instruments and is:

   (i) a non-derivative for which the entity is or may be obliged to receive a variable number of the entity's own equity instruments; or

   (ii) a derivative that will or may be settled other than by the exchange of a fixed amount of cash or another financial asset for a fixed number of the entity's own equity instruments. For this purpose the entity's own equity instruments do not include puttable financial instruments classified as equity instruments in accordance with paragraphs 16A and 16B of IAS 32, instruments that impose on the entity an obligation to deliver to another party a pro rata share of the net assets of the entity only on liquidation and are classified as equity instruments in accordance with paragraphs 16C and 16D of IAS 32, or instruments that are themselves contracts for the future receipt or delivery of the entity's own equity instruments.

financial asset or financial liability held for trading	A financial asset or financial liability that:	IAS 39.9

(a) is acquired or incurred principally for the purpose of selling or repurchasing it in the near term;

(b) on initial recognition is part of a portfolio of identified financial instruments that are managed together and for which there is evidence of a recent actual pattern of short-term profit-taking; or

(c) is a derivative (except for a derivative that is a financial guarantee contract or a designated and effective hedging instrument).

financial guarantee contract	A contract that requires the issuer to make specified payments to reimburse the holder for a loss it incurs because a specified debtor fails to make payment when due in accordance with the original or modified terms of a debt instrument.	IAS 39.9, IFRS 4.A
financial instrument	Any contract that gives rise to a financial asset of one entity and a financial liability or equity instrument of another entity.	IAS 32.11

financial liability	Any liability that is:	IAS 32.11

(a) a contractual obligation:

  (i) to deliver cash or another financial asset to another entity; or

  (ii) to exchange financial assets or financial liabilities with another entity under conditions that are potentially unfavourable to the entity; or

(b) a contract that will or may be settled in the entity's own equity instruments and is:

  (i) a non-derivative for which the entity is or may be obliged to deliver a variable number of the entity's own equity instruments; or

  (ii) a derivative that will or may be settled other than by the exchange of a fixed amount of cash or another financial asset for a fixed number of the entity's own equity instruments. For this purpose, rights, options or warrants to acquire a fixed number of the entity's own equity instruments for a fixed amount of any currency are equity instruments if the entity offers the rights, options or warrants pro rata to all of its existing owners of the same class of its own non-derivative equity instruments. Also, for these purposes the entity's own equity instruments do not include puttable financial instruments that are classified as equity instruments in accordance with paragraphs 16A and 16B of IAS 32, instruments that impose on the entity an obligation to deliver to another party a pro rata share of the net assets of the entity only on liquidation and are classified as equity instruments in accordance with paragraphs 16C and 16D of IAS 32, or instruments that are contracts for the future receipt or delivery of the entity's own equity instruments.

As an exception, an instrument that meets the definition of a financial liability is classified as an equity instrument if it has all the features and meets the conditions in paragraphs 16A and 16B or paragraphs 16C and 16D of IAS 32.

financial liability at fair value through profit or loss	A financial liability that meets either of the following conditions.	IAS 39.9
	(a) It meets the definition of held for trading.	
	(b) Upon initial recognition it is designated by the entity as at fair value through profit or loss. An entity may use this designation only when permitted by IAS 39 paragraph 11A (embedded derivatives) or when doing so results in more relevant information, because either	
	(i) it eliminates or significantly reduces a measurement or recognition inconsistency (sometimes referred to as 'an accounting mismatch') that would otherwise arise from measuring assets or liabilities or recognising the gains and losses on them on different bases; or	
	(ii) a group of financial liabilities or financial assets and financial liabilities is managed and its performance is evaluated on a fair value basis, in accordance with a documented risk management or investment strategy, and information about the group is provided internally on that basis to the entity's key management personnel (as defined in IAS 24).	
financial position	The relationship of the assets, liabilities and equity of an entity, as reported in the balance sheet [statement of financial position].	F.47, IAS 1.54
financial risk	The risk of a possible future change in one or more of a specified interest rate, financial instrument price, commodity price, foreign exchange rate, index of prices or rates, credit rating or credit index or other variable, provided in the case of a non-financial variable that the variable is not specific to a party to the contract.	IFRS 4.A

financial statements	A complete set of financial statements comprises: (a) a statement of financial position as at the end of the period; (b) a statement of comprehensive income for the period; (c) a statement of changes in equity for the period; (d) a statement of cash flows for the period; (e) notes, comprising a summary of significant accounting policies and other explanatory information; and (f) a statement of financial position as at the beginning of the earliest comparative period when an entity applies an accounting policy retrospectively or makes a retrospective restatement of items in its financial statements, or when it reclassifies items in its financial statements.	IAS 1.10, (F.7)
financing activities	Activities that result in changes in the size and composition of the contributed equity and borrowings of the entity.	IAS 7.6
firm commitment	A binding agreement for the exchange of a specified quantity of resources at a specified price on a specified future date or dates.	IAS 39.9
firm purchase commitment	An agreement with an unrelated party, binding on both parties and usually legally enforceable, that (a) specifies all significant terms, including the price and timing of the transactions, and (b) includes a disincentive for non-performance that is sufficiently large to make performance highly probable.	IFRS 5.A
first IFRS financial statements	The first annual financial statements in which an entity adopts International Financial Reporting Standards (IFRSs), by an explicit and unreserved statement of compliance with IFRSs.	IFRS 1.A
first IFRS reporting period	The latest reporting period covered by an entity's first IFRS financial statements.	IFRS 1.A
first-time adopter	An entity that presents its first IFRS financial statements.	IFRS 1.A
fixed price contract	A construction contract in which the contractor agrees to a fixed contract price, or a fixed rate per unit of output, which in some cases is subject to cost escalation clauses.	IAS 11.3

fixed production overheads	Those indirect costs of production that remain relatively constant regardless of the volume of production, such as depreciation and maintenance of factory buildings and equipment, and the cost of factory management and administration.	IAS 2.12
forecast transaction	An uncommitted but anticipated future transaction.	IAS 39.9
foreign currency	A currency other than the functional currency of the entity.	IAS 21.8
foreign currency transaction	A transaction that is denominated in or requires settlement in a foreign currency.	IAS 21.20
foreign operation	An entity that is a subsidiary, associate, joint venture or branch of the reporting entity, the activities of which are based or conducted in a country or currency other than those of the reporting entity.	IAS 21.8
forgivable loans	Loans which the lender undertakes to waive repayment of under certain prescribed conditions.	IAS 20.3
functional currency	The currency of the primary economic environment in which the entity operates.	IAS 21.8
funding (of post-employment benefits)	Contributions by an entity, and sometimes its employees, into an entity, or fund, that is legally separate from the reporting entity and from which the employee benefits are paid.	IAS 19.49
funding (of retirement benefits)	The transfer of assets to an entity (the fund) separate from the employer's entity to meet future obligations for the payment of retirement benefits.	IAS 26.8
future economic benefit	The potential to contribute, directly or indirectly, to the flow of cash and cash equivalents to the entity. The potential may be a productive one that is part of the operating activities of the entity. It may also take the form of convertibility into cash or cash equivalents or a capability to reduce cash outflows, such as when an alternative manufacturing process lowers the costs of production.	F.53
gains	Increases in economic benefits and as such no different in nature from revenue.	F.75
general purpose financial statements	Financial statements that are intended to meet the needs of users who are not in a position to require an entity to prepare reports tailored to their particular information needs.	IAS 1.7, F.6
going concern	The financial statements are prepared on a going concern basis unless management either intends to liquidate the entity or to cease trading, or has no realistic alternative but to do so.	IAS 1.25, (F.23)

goodwill	An asset representing the future economic benefits arising from other assets acquired in a business combination that are not individually identified and separately recognised.	IFRS 3.A
government	Government, government agencies and similar bodies whether local, national or international.	IAS 20.3 IAS 24.9
government assistance	Action by government designed to provide an economic benefit specific to an entity or range of entities qualifying under certain criteria.	IAS 20.3
government grants	Assistance by government in the form of transfers of resources to an entity in return for past or future compliance with certain conditions relating to the operating activities of the entity. They exclude those forms of government assistance which cannot reasonably have a value placed upon them and transactions with government which cannot be distinguished from the normal trading transactions of the entity.	IAS 20.3
government-related entity	An entity that is controlled, jointly controlled or significantly influenced by a government.	IAS 24.9
grant date	The date at which the entity and another party (including an employee) agree to a share-based payment arrangement, being when the entity and the counterparty have a shared understanding of the terms and conditions of the arrangement. At grant date the entity confers on the counterparty the right to cash, other assets, or equity instruments of the entity, provided the specified vesting conditions, if any, are met. If that agreement is subject to an approval process (for example, by shareholders), grant date is the date when that approval is obtained.	IFRS 2.A
grants related to assets	Government grants whose primary condition is that an entity qualifying for them should purchase, construct or otherwise acquire long-term assets. Subsidiary conditions may also be attached restricting the type or location of the assets or the periods during which they are to be acquired or held.	IAS 20.3
grants related to income	Government grants other than those related to assets.	IAS 20.3
gross investment in the lease	The aggregate of: (a) the minimum lease payments receivable by the lessor under a finance lease, and (b) any unguaranteed residual value accruing to the lessor.	IAS 17.4

group	A parent and all its subsidiaries.	IAS 21.8, IAS 27.4
group administration (employee benefit) plans	An aggregation of single employer plans combined to allow participating employers to pool their assets for investment purposes and reduce investment management and administration costs, but the claims of different employers are segregated for the sole benefit of their own employees.	IAS 19.33
group of biological assets	An aggregation of similar living animals or plants.	IAS 41.5
guaranteed benefits	Payments or other benefits to which a particular policyholder or investor has an unconditional right that is not subject to the contractual discretion of the issuer.	IFRS 4.A
guaranteed element	An obligation to pay guaranteed benefits, included in a contract that contains a discretionary participation feature.	IFRS 4.A
guaranteed residual value	(a) For a lessee, that part of the residual value that is guaranteed by the lessee or by a party related to the lessee (the amount of the guarantee being the maximum amount that could, in any event, become payable); and	IAS 17.4
	(b) for a lessor, that part of the residual value that is guaranteed by the lessee or by a third party unrelated to the lessor that is financially capable of discharging the obligations under the guarantee.	
harvest	The detachment of produce from a biological asset or the cessation of a biological asset's life processes.	IAS 41.5
hedge effectiveness	The degree to which changes in the fair value or cash flows of the hedged item that are attributable to a hedged risk are offset by changes in the fair value or cash flows of the hedging instrument (see IAS 39 paragraphs AG105–AG113).	IAS 39.9
hedged item	An asset, liability, firm commitment, highly probable forecast transaction or net investment in a foreign operation that (a) exposes the entity to risk of changes in fair value or future cash flows and (b) is designated as being hedged (IAS 39 paragraphs 78–84 and AG98–AG101 elaborate on the definition of hedged items).	IAS 39.9

hedging instrument	A designated derivative or (for a hedge of the risk of changes in foreign currency exchange rates only) a designated non-derivative financial asset or non-derivative financial liability whose fair value or cash flows are expected to offset changes in the fair value or cash flows of a designated hedged item (IAS 39 paragraphs 72–77 and AG94–AG97 elaborate on the definition of a hedging instrument).	IAS 39.9
held for trading	See 'financial asset or financial liability held for trading.	IAS 39.9
highly probable	Significantly more likely than probable.	IFRS 5.A
hire purchase contract	The definition of a lease includes contracts for the hire of an asset that contain a provision giving the hirer an option to acquire title to the asset upon the fulfilment of agreed conditions. These contracts are sometimes known as hire purchase contracts.	IAS 17.6
historical cost	A measurement basis according to which assets are recorded at the amount of cash or cash equivalents paid or the fair value of the consideration given to acquire them at the time of their acquisition. Liabilities are recorded at the amount of proceeds received in exchange for the obligation, or in some circumstances (for example, income taxes), at the amounts of cash or cash equivalents expected to be paid to satisfy the liability in the normal course of business.	F.100(a)

hyperinflation	Loss of purchasing power of money at such a rate that comparison of amounts from transactions and other events that have occurred at different times, even within the same accounting period, is misleading.	IAS 29.2–3

Hyperinflation is indicated by characteristics of the economic environment of a country which include, but are not limited to, the following:

(a) the general population prefers to keep its wealth in non-monetary assets or in a relatively stable foreign currency. Amounts of local currency held are immediately invested to maintain purchasing power.

(b) the general population regards monetary amounts not in terms of the local currency but in terms of a relatively stable foreign currency. Prices may be quoted in that currency.

(c) sales and purchases on credit take place at prices that compensate for the expected loss of purchasing power during the credit period, even if the period is short.

(d) interest rates, wages and prices are linked to a price index.

(e) the cumulative inflation rate over three years is approaching, or exceeds, 100%.

identifiable	An asset is identifiable if it either:	IFRS 3.A

(a) is separable, ie capable of being separated or divided from the entity and sold, transferred, licensed, rented or exchanged, either individually or together with a related contract, identifiable asset or liability, regardless of whether the entity intends to do so; or

(a) arises from contractual or other legal rights, regardless of whether those rights are transferable or separable from the entity or from other rights and obligations.

impairment loss	The amount by which the carrying amount of an asset exceeds its recoverable amount.	IAS 16.6, (IAS 36.6), IAS 38.8
impracticable	Applying a requirement is impracticable when the entity cannot apply it after making every reasonable effort to do so.	IAS 1.7, (IAS 8.5)

imputed rate of interest	The more clearly determinable of either:	IAS 18.11
	(a) the prevailing rate for a similar instrument of an issuer with a similar credit rating; or	
	(b) a rate of interest that discounts the nominal amount of the instrument to the current cash sales price of the goods or services.	
inception of a lease	The earlier of the date of the lease agreement and the date of commitment by the parties to the principal provisions of the lease.	IAS 17.4
income	Increases in economic benefits during the accounting period in the form of inflows or enhancements of assets or decreases of liabilities that result in increases in equity, other than those relating to contributions from equity participants.	F.70(a)
incremental borrowing rate of interest (lessee's)	The rate of interest the lessee would have to pay on a similar lease or, if that is not determinable, the rate that, at the inception of the lease, the lessee would incur to borrow over a similar term, and with a similar security, the funds necessary to purchase the asset.	IAS 17.4
indirect method of reporting cash flows from operating activities	A method whereby profit or loss is adjusted for the effects of transactions of a non-cash nature, any deferrals or accruals of past or future operating cash receipts or payments, and items of income or expense associated with investing or financing cash flows.	IAS 7.18(b)
initial direct costs	Incremental costs that are directly attributable to negotiating and arranging a lease, except for such costs incurred by manufacturer or dealer lessors.	IAS 17.4
insurance asset	An insurer's net contractual rights under an insurance contract.	IFRS 4.A
insurance contract	A contract under which one party (the insurer) accepts significant insurance risk from another party (the policyholder) by agreeing to compensate the policyholder if a specified uncertain future event (the insured event) adversely affects the policyholder. (See IFRS 4 Appendix B for guidance on this definition.)	IFRS 4.A
insurance liability	An insurer's net contractual obligations under an insurance contract.	IFRS 4.A
insurance risk	Risk, other than financial risk, transferred from the holder of a contract to the issuer.	IFRS 4.A

insured event	An uncertain future event that is covered by an insurance contract and creates insurance risk.	IFRS 4.A
insurer	The party that has an obligation under an insurance contract to compensate a policyholder if an insured event occurs.	IFRS 4.A
intangible asset	An identifiable non-monetary asset without physical substance.	IAS 38.8, IFRS 3.A
interest cost (for an employee benefit plan)	The increase during a period in the present value of a defined benefit obligation which arises because the benefits are one period closer to settlement.	IAS 19.7
interest rate implicit in the lease	The discount rate that, at the inception of the lease, causes the aggregate present value of (a) the minimum lease payments and (b) the unguaranteed residual value to be equal to the sum of (i) the fair value of the leased asset and (ii) any initial direct costs of the lessor.	IAS 17.4
interest rate risk	The risk that the fair value or future cash flows of a financial instrument will fluctuate because of changes in market interest rates.	IFRS 7.A
interim financial report	A financial report containing either a complete set of financial statements (as described in IAS 1) or a set of condensed financial statements (as described in IAS 34) for an interim period.	IAS 34.4
interim period	A financial reporting period shorter than a full financial year.	IAS 34.4
International Financial Reporting Standards (IFRSs)	Standards and Interpretations adopted by the International Accounting Standards Board (IASB). They comprise: (a) International Financial Reporting Standards; (b) International Accounting Standards; and (c) Interpretations developed by the International Financial Reporting Interpretations Committee (IFRIC) or the former Standing Interpretations Committee (SIC).	IAS 1.7, IAS 8.5, IFRS 1.A
intrinsic value	The difference between the fair value of the shares to which the counterparty has the (conditional or unconditional) right to subscribe or which it has the right to receive, and the price (if any) the counterparty is (or will be) required to pay for those shares. For example, a share option with an exercise price of CU15,* on a share with a fair value of CU20, has an intrinsic value of CU5.	IFRS 2.A

---

* Monetary items are denominated in 'currency units (CU)'.

inventories	Assets:	IAS 2.6,
	(a) held for sale in the ordinary course of business;	IAS 2.8
	(b) in the process of production for such sale; or	
	(c) in the form of materials or supplies to be consumed in the production process or in the rendering of services.	
	Inventories encompass goods purchased and held for resale including, for example, merchandise purchased by a retailer and held for resale, or land and other property held for resale. Inventories also encompass finished goods produced, or work in progress being produced, by the entity and include materials and supplies awaiting use in the production process. In the case of a service provider, inventories include the costs of the service, as described in IAS 2 paragraph 19, for which the entity has not yet recognised the related revenue (see IAS 18).	
investing activities	The acquisition and disposal of long-term assets and other investments not included in cash equivalents.	IAS 7.6
investment property	Property (land or a building—or part of a building—or both) held (by the owner or by the lessee under a finance lease) to earn rentals or for capital appreciation or both, rather than for:	IAS 40.5
	(a) use in the production or supply of goods or services or for administrative purposes; or	
	(b) sale in the ordinary course of business.	
investor in a joint venture	A party to a joint venture that does not have joint control over that joint venture.	IAS 31.3
joint control	The contractually agreed sharing of control over an economic activity.	IAS 24.9
joint control	The contractually agreed sharing of control over an economic activity; it exists only when the strategic financial and operating decisions relating to the activity require the unanimous consent of the parties sharing control (the venturers).	IAS 28.2, IAS 31.3
joint venture	A contractual arrangement whereby two or more parties undertake an economic activity that is subject to joint control.	IAS 31.3, IFRS 3.A

jointly controlled entity	A joint venture that involves the establishment of a corporation, partnership or other entity in which each venturer has an interest. The entity operates in the same way as other entities, except that a contractual arrangement between the venturers establishes joint control over the economic activity of the entity.	IAS 31.24
key management personnel	Those persons having authority and responsibility for planning, directing and controlling the activities of the entity, directly or indirectly, including any director (whether executive or otherwise) of that entity.	IAS 24.9
lease	An agreement whereby the lessor conveys to the lessee in return for a payment or series of payments the right to use an asset for an agreed period of time.	IAS 17.4
lease term	The non-cancellable period for which the lessee has contracted to lease the asset together with any further terms for which the lessee has the option to continue to lease the asset, with or without further payment, when at the inception of the lease it is reasonably certain that the lessee will exercise the option.	IAS 17.4
legal obligation	An obligation that derives from: (a) a contract (through its explicit or implicit terms); (b) legislation; or (c) other operation of law.	IAS 37.10
lessee's incremental borrowing rate of interest	The rate of interest the lessee would have to pay on a similar lease or, if that is not determinable, the rate that, at the inception of the lease, the lessee would incur to borrow over a similar term, and with a similar security, the funds necessary to purchase the asset.	IAS 17.4
liability	A present obligation of the entity arising from past events, the settlement of which is expected to result in an outflow from the entity of resources embodying economic benefits.	IAS 37.10, F.49(b)
liability adequacy test	An assessment of whether the carrying amount of an insurance liability needs to be increased (or the carrying amount of related deferred acquisition costs or related intangible assets decreased), based on a review of future cash flows.	IFRS 4.A
liquidity	The availability of cash in the near future after taking account of financial commitments over this period.	F.16

liquidity risk	The risk that an entity will encounter difficulty in meeting obligations associated with financial liabilities that are settled by delivering cash or another financial asset.	IFRS 7.A
loans payable	Financial liabilities other than short-term trade payables on normal credit terms.	IFRS 7.A
losses	Decreases in economic benefits and as such no different in nature from other expenses.	F.79
market condition	A condition upon which the exercise price, vesting or exercisability of an equity instrument depends that is related to the market price of the entity's equity instruments, such as attaining a specified share price or a specified amount of intrinsic value of a share option, or achieving a specified target that is based on the market price of the entity's equity instruments relative to an index of market prices of equity instruments of other entities.	IFRS 2.A
market risk	The risk that the fair value or future cash flows of a financial instrument will fluctuate because of changes in market prices. Market risk comprises three types of risk: currency risk, interest rate risk and other price risk.	IFRS 7.A
master netting arrangement	An arrangement providing for an entity that undertakes a number of financial instrument transactions with a single counterparty to make a single net settlement of all financial instruments covered by the agreement in the event of default on, or termination of, any one contract.	IAS 32.50
matching of costs with revenues	A process in which expenses are recognised in the income statement [statement of comprehensive income] on the basis of a direct association between the costs incurred and the earning of specific items of income. This process involves the simultaneous or combined recognition of revenues and expenses that result directly and jointly from the same transactions or other events. However, the application of the matching concept does not allow the recognition of items in the balance sheet [statement of financial position] which do not meet the definition of assets or liabilities.	F.95

material	Omissions or misstatements of items are material if they could, individually or collectively, influence the economic decisions that users make on the basis of the financial statements. Materiality depends on the size and nature of the omission or misstatement judged in the surrounding circumstances. The size or nature of the item, or a combination of both, could be the determining factor.	IAS 1.7, IAS 8.5
materiality	Information is material if its omission or misstatement could influence the economic decisions of users taken on the basis of the financial statements.	F.30
measurement	The process of determining the monetary amounts at which the elements of the financial statements are to be recognised and carried in the balance sheet [statement of financial position] and income statement [statement of comprehensive income].	F.99
measurement date	The date at which the fair value of the equity instruments granted is measured for the purposes of IFRS 2. For transactions with employees and others providing similar services, the measurement date is grant date. For transactions with parties other than employees (and those providing similar services), the measurement date is the date the entity obtains the goods or the counterparty renders service.	IFRS 2.A
minimum lease payments	The payments over the lease term that the lessee is or can be required to make, excluding contingent rent, costs for services and taxes to be paid by and reimbursed to the lessor, together with:	IAS 17.4
	(a) for a lessee, any amounts guaranteed by the lessee or by a party related to the lessee; or	
	(b) for a lessor, any residual value guaranteed to the lessor by:	
	(i) the lessee;	
	(ii) a party related to the lessee; or	
	(iii) a third party unrelated to the lessor that is financially capable of discharging the obligations under the guarantee.	
minority interest	See 'non-controlling interest'	
monetary assets	Money held and assets to be received in fixed or determinable amounts of money.	IAS 38.8
monetary items	Units of currency held and assets and liabilities to be received or paid in a fixed or determinable number of units of currency.	IAS 21.8

monetary items	Money held and items to be received or paid in money.	IAS 29.12
multi-employer (benefit) plans	Defined contribution plans (other than state plans) or defined benefit plans (other than state plans) that:	IAS 19.7
	(a) pool the assets contributed by various entities that are not under common control; and	
	(b) use those assets to provide benefits to employees of more than one entity, on the basis that contribution and benefit levels are determined without regard to the identity of the entity that employs the employees concerned.	
mutual entity	An entity, other than an investor-owned entity, that provides dividends, lower costs or other economic benefits directly to its owners, members or participants. For example, a mutual insurance company, a credit union and a co-operative entity are all mutual entities.	IFRS 3.A
net assets available for benefits	The assets of a plan less liabilities other than the actuarial present value of promised retirement benefits.	IAS 26.8
net investment in a foreign operation	The amount of the reporting entity's interest in the net assets of that operation.	IAS 21.8
net investment in the lease	The gross investment in the lease discounted at the interest rate implicit in the lease.	IAS 17.4
net realisable value	The estimated selling price in the ordinary course of business less the estimated costs of completion and the estimated costs necessary to make the sale.	IAS 2.6–7
	Net realisable value refers to the net amount that an entity expects to realise from the sale of inventory in the ordinary course of business. Fair value reflects the amount for which the same inventory could be exchanged between knowledgeable and willing buyers and sellers in the marketplace. The former is an entity-specific value; the latter is not. Net realisable value for inventories may not equal fair value less costs to sell.	
neutrality	Freedom from bias of the information contained in financial statements.	F.36
non-adjusting events after the reporting period	See 'events after the reporting period'	

non-cancellable lease	A lease that is cancellable only: (a) upon the occurrence of some remote contingency; (b) with the permission of the lessor; (c) if the lessee enters into a new lease for the same or an equivalent asset with the same lessor; or (d) upon payment by the lessee of such an additional amount that, at inception of the lease, continuation of the lease is reasonably certain.	IAS 17.4
non-controlling interest	The equity in a subsidiary not attributable, directly or indirectly, to a parent.	IAS 27.4, IFRS 3.A
non-current asset	An asset that does not meet the definition of a current asset.	IFRS 5.A
normal capacity of production facilities	The production expected to be achieved on average over a number of periods or seasons under normal circumstances, taking into account the loss of capacity resulting from planned maintenance.	IAS 2.13
notes	Notes contain information in addition to that presented in the statement of financial position, statement of comprehensive income, separate income statement (if presented), statement of changes in equity and statement of cash flows. Notes provide narrative descriptions or disaggregations of items presented in those statements and information about items that do not qualify for recognition in those statements.	IAS 1.7
obligating event	An event that creates a legal or constructive obligation that results in an entity having no realistic alternative to settling that obligation.	IAS 37.10
obligation	A duty or responsibility to act or perform in a certain way. Obligations may be legally enforceable as a consequence of a binding contract or statutory requirement. Obligations also arise, however, from normal business practice, custom and a desire to maintain good business relations or act in an equitable manner.	F.60
offsetting	See 'set-off, legal right of'	
onerous contract	A contract in which the unavoidable costs of meeting the obligations under the contract exceed the economic benefits expected to be received under it.	IAS 37.10
opening IFRS statement of financial position	An entity's statement of financial position at the date of transition to IFRSs.	IFRS 1.A

operating activities	The principal revenue-producing activities of an entity and other activities that are not investing or financing activities.	IAS 7.6, IAS 14.8
operating cycle	The time between the acquisition of assets for processing and their realisation in cash or cash equivalents.	IAS 1.68
operating lease	A lease other than a finance lease.	IAS 17.4
operating segment	An operating segment is a component of an entity:	IFRS 8.A

(a) that engages in business activities from which it may earn revenues and incur expenses (including revenues and expenses relating to transactions with other components of the same entity),

(b) whose operating results are regularly reviewed by the entity's chief operating decision maker to make decisions about resources to be allocated to the segment and assess its performance, and

(c) for which discrete financial information is available.

options, warrants and their equivalents	Financial instruments that give the holder the right to purchase ordinary shares.	IAS 33.5
ordinary equity holders	Holders of ordinary shares.	IAS 33.5–9
ordinary share	An equity instrument that is subordinate to all other classes of equity instruments.	IAS 33.5
originated loans and receivables	See 'loans and receivables'	
other comprehensive income	Items of income and expense (including reclassification adjustments) that are not recognised in profit or loss as required or permitted by other IFRSs.	IAS 1.7
other long-term employee benefits	Employee benefits (other than post-employment benefits and termination benefits) that are not due to be settled within twelve months after the end of the period in which the employees render the related service.	IAS 19.7
other price risk	The risk that the fair value or future cash flows of a financial instrument will fluctuate because of changes in market prices (other than those arising from interest rate risk or currency risk), whether those changes are caused by factors specific to the individual financial instrument or its issuer, or factors affecting all similar financial instruments traded in the market.	IFRS 7.A

owner-occupied property	Property held (by the owner or by the lessee under a finance lease) for use in the production or supply of goods or services or for administrative purposes.	IAS 40.5
owners	Holders of instruments classified as equity.	IAS 1.7
owners	In IFRS 3 owners is used broadly to include holders of equity interests of investor-owned entities and owners or members of, or participants in, mutual entities.	IFRS 3.A
parent	An entity that has one or more subsidiaries.	IAS 27.4, IFRS 3.A
participants	The members of a retirement benefit plan and others who are entitled to benefits under the plan.	IAS 26.8
past due	A financial asset is past due when a counterparty has failed to make a payment when contractually due.	IFRS 7.A
past service cost	The change in the present value of the defined benefit obligation for employee service in prior periods, resulting in the current period from the introduction of, or changes to, post-employment benefits or other long-term employee benefits. Past service cost may be either positive (when benefits are introduced or changed so that the present value of the defined benefit obligation increases) or negative (when existing benefits are changed so that the present value of the defined benefit obligation decreases).	IAS 19.7
percentage of completion method	The recognition of revenue and expenses by reference to the stage of completion of a contract. Under this method contract revenue is matched with the contract costs incurred in reaching the stage of completion, resulting in the reporting of revenue, expenses and profit which can be attributed to the proportion of work completed.	IAS 11.25
performance	The relationship of the income and expenses of an entity, as reported in the income statement [statement of comprehensive income].	F.47
plan assets (of an employee benefit plan)	(a) Assets held by a long-term employee benefit fund; and (b) qualifying insurance policies.	IAS 19.7
policyholder	A party that has a right to compensation under an insurance contract if an insured event occurs.	IFRS 4.A
post-employment benefits	Employee benefits (other than termination benefits) which are payable after the completion of employment.	IAS 19.7

post-employment benefit plans	Formal or informal arrangements under which an entity provides post-employment benefits for one or more employees.	IAS 19.7
potential ordinary share	A financial instrument or other contract that may entitle its holder to ordinary shares.	IAS 33.5
presentation currency	The currency in which the financial statements are presented.	IAS 21.8
present value	A current estimate of the present discounted value of the future net cash flows in the normal course of business.	F.100(d)
present value of a defined benefit obligation	See 'defined benefit obligation (present value of)'	IAS 19.7
previous GAAP	The basis of accounting that a first-time adopter used immediately before adopting IFRSs.	IFRS 1.A
primary financial instruments	Financial instruments, such as receivables, payables and equity securities, that are not derivative financial instruments.	IAS 32.AG15
prior period errors	Omissions from, and misstatements in, the entity's financial statements for one or more prior periods arising from a failure to use, or misuse of, reliable information that: (a) was available when financial statements for those periods were authorised for issue; and (b) could reasonably be expected to have been obtained and taken into account in the preparation and presentation of those financial statements. Such errors include the effects of mathematical mistakes, mistakes in applying accounting policies, oversights or misinterpretations of facts, and fraud.	IAS 8.5
probable	More likely than not.	IFRS 5.A, (IAS 37.23)
profit	The residual amount that remains after expenses (including capital maintenance adjustments, where appropriate) have been deducted from income. Any amount over and above that required to maintain the capital at the beginning of the period is profit.	F.105, F.107
profit or loss	The total of income less expenses, excluding the components of other comprehensive income.	IAS 1.7

projected unit credit method	An actuarial valuation method that sees each period of service as giving rise to an additional unit of benefit entitlement and measures each unit separately to build up the final obligation (sometimes known as the accrued benefit method pro-rated on service or as the benefit/years of service method).	IAS 19.64–66
property, plant and equipment	Tangible items that:	IAS 16.6
	(a) are held for use in the production or supply of goods or services, for rental to others, or for administrative purposes; and	
	(b) are expected to be used during more than one period.	
proportionate consolidation	A method of accounting and reporting whereby a venturer's share of each of the assets, liabilities, income and expenses of a jointly controlled entity is combined line by line with similar items in the venturer's financial statements or reported as separate line items in the venturer's financial statements.	IAS 31.3
prospective application	Prospective application of a change in accounting policy and of recognising the effect of a change in an accounting estimate, respectively, are:	IAS 8.5
	(a) applying the new accounting policy to transactions, other events and conditions occurring after the date as at which the policy is changed; and	
	(b) recognising the effect of the change in the accounting estimate in the current and future periods affected by the change.	
provision	A liability of uncertain timing or amount.	IAS 37.10
prudence	The inclusion of a degree of caution in the exercise of the judgements needed in making the estimates required under conditions of uncertainty, such that assets or income are not overstated and liabilities or expenses are not understated.	F.37
put options (on ordinary shares)	Contracts that give the holder the right to sell ordinary shares at a specified price for a given period.	IAS 33.5

puttable instrument	A financial instrument that gives the holder the right to put the instrument back to the issuer for cash or another financial asset or is automatically put back to the issuer on the occurrence of an uncertain future event or the death or retirement of the instrument holder.	IAS 32.11
qualifying asset	An asset that necessarily takes a substantial period of time to get ready for its intended use or sale.	IAS 23.5
qualifying insurance policy	An insurance policy issued by an insurer that is not a related party (as defined in IAS 24) of the reporting entity, if the proceeds of the policy:	IAS 19.7

(a) can be used only to pay or fund employee benefits under a defined benefit plan;

(b) are not available to the reporting entity's own creditors (even in bankruptcy) and cannot be paid to the reporting entity, unless either:

    (i) the proceeds represent surplus assets that are not needed for the policy to meet all the related employee benefit obligations; or

    (ii) the proceeds are returned to the reporting entity to reimburse it for employee benefits already paid.

realisable value	The amount of cash or cash equivalents that could currently be obtained by selling an asset in an orderly disposal.	F.100(c)
reclassification adjustments	Amounts reclassified to profit or loss in the current period that were recognised in other comprehensive income in the current or previous periods.	IAS 1.7
reclassification date	The first day of the first reporting period following the change in business model that results in an entity reclassifying financial assets.	IFRS 9.A
recognition	The process of incorporating in the balance sheet [statement of financial position] or income statement [statement of comprehensive income] an item that meets the definition of an element and satisfies the following criteria for recognition:	F.82–83

(a) it is probable that any future economic benefit associated with the item will flow to or from the entity; and

(b) the item has a cost or value that can be measured with reliability.

recoverable amount	The higher of an asset's (or cash-generating unit's) fair value less costs to sell and its value in use.	IAS 16.6, IAS 36.6, IFRS 5.A

regular way purchase or sale	A purchase or sale of a financial asset under a contract whose terms require delivery of the asset within the time frame established generally by regulation or convention in the marketplace concerned.	IAS 39.9
reinsurance assets	A cedant's net contractual rights under a reinsurance contract.	IFRS 4.A
reinsurance contract	An insurance contract issued by one insurer (the reinsurer) to compensate another insurer (the cedant) for losses on one or more contracts issued by the cedant.	IFRS 4.A
reinsurer	The party that has an obligation under a reinsurance contract to compensate a cedant if an insured event occurs.	IFRS 4.A

related party A person or entity that is related to the entity that is   IAS 24.9
preparing its financial statements (in IAS 24 referred
to as the 'reporting entity').

(a) A person or a close member of that person's
family is related to a reporting entity if that
person:

(i) has control or joint control over the
reporting entity;

(ii) has significant influence over the
reporting entity; or

(iii) is a member of the key management
personnel of the reporting entity or of a
parent of the reporting entity.

(b) An entity is related to a reporting entity if any
of the following conditions applies:

(i) The entity and the reporting entity are
members of the same group (which
means that each parent, subsidiary and
fellow subsidiary is related to the others).

(ii) One entity is an associate or joint
venture of the other entity (or an
associate or joint venture of a member of
a group of which the other entity is a
member).

(iii) Both entities are joint ventures of the
same third party.

(iv) One entity is a joint venture of a third
entity and the other entity is an associate
of the third entity.

(v) The entity is a post-employment benefit
plan for the benefit of employees of
either the reporting entity or an entity
related to the reporting entity. If the
reporting entity is itself such a plan, the
sponsoring employers are also related to
the reporting entity.

(vi) The entity is controlled or jointly
controlled by a person identified in (a).

(vii) A person identified in (a)(i) has
significant influence over the entity or is
a member of the key management
personnel of the entity (or of a parent of
the entity).

related party transaction	A transfer of resources, services or obligations between a reporting entity and a related party, regardless of whether a price is charged.	IAS 24.9
relevance	Information has the quality of relevance when it influences the economic decisions of users by helping them evaluate past, present or future events or confirming, or correcting, their past evaluations.	F.26
reliability	Information has the quality of reliability when it is free from material error and bias and can be depended upon by users to represent faithfully that which it either purports to represent or could reasonably be expected to represent.	F.31
reload feature	A feature that provides for an automatic grant of additional share options whenever the option holder exercises previously granted options using the entity's shares, rather than cash, to satisfy the exercise price.	IFRS 2.A
reload option	A new share option granted when a share is used to satisfy the exercise price of a previous share option.	IFRS 2.A
reportable segment	An operating segment for which IFRS 8 requires information to be disclosed.	IFRS 8.11
reporting entity	An entity for which there are users who rely on the financial statements as their major source of financial information about the entity.	F.8
research	Original and planned investigation undertaken with the prospect of gaining new scientific or technical knowledge and understanding.	IAS 38.8
residual value (of an asset)	The estimated amount that an entity would currently obtain from disposal of an asset, after deducting the estimated costs of disposal, if the asset were already of the age and in the condition expected at the end of its useful life.	IAS 16.6, (IAS 38.8)
restructuring	A programme that is planned and controlled by management, and materially changes either: (a) the scope of a business undertaken by an entity; or (b) the manner in which that business is conducted.	IAS 37.10
retirement benefit plans	Arrangements whereby an entity provides benefits for its employees on or after termination of service (either in the form of an annual income or as a lump sum) when such benefits, or the employer's contributions towards them, can be determined or estimated in advance of retirement from the provisions of a document or from the entity's practices. (See also 'post-employment benefit plans'.)	IAS 26.8

retrospective application	Applying a new accounting policy to transactions, other events and conditions as if that policy had always been applied.	IAS 8.5
retrospective restatement	Correcting the recognition, measurement and disclosure of amounts of elements of financial statements as if a prior period error had never occurred.	IAS 8.5
return on plan assets (of an employee benefit plan)	Interest, dividends and other revenue derived from the plan assets, together with realised and unrealised gains or losses on the plan assets, less any costs of administering the plan (other than those included in the actuarial assumptions used to measure the defined benefit obligation) and less any tax payable by the plan itself.	IAS 19.7
revaluation	Restatement of assets and liabilities.	F.81
revalued amount of an asset	The fair value of an asset at the date of a revaluation less any subsequent accumulated depreciation and subsequent accumulated impairment losses.	IAS 16.31
revenue	The gross inflow of economic benefits during the period arising in the course of the ordinary activities of an entity when those inflows result in increases in equity, other than increases relating to contributions from equity participants.	IAS 18.7
reverse acquisition	An acquisition where the acquirer is the entity whose equity interests have been acquired and the issuing entity is the acquiree. This might be the case when, for example, a private entity arranges to have itself 'acquired' by a smaller public entity as a means of obtaining a stock exchange listing.	IFRS 3.21
rewards associated with a leased asset	Rewards may be represented by the expectation of profitable operation over the asset's economic life and of gain from appreciation in value or realisation of a residual value.	IAS 17.7
risks associated with a leased asset	Risks include possibilities of losses from idle capacity or technological obsolescence and of variations in return because of changing economic conditions.	IAS 17.7
sale and leaseback transaction	The sale of an asset and the leasing back of the same asset. The lease payment and the sale price are usually interdependent because they are negotiated as a package.	IAS 17.58

separate financial statements	Those presented by a parent, an investor in an associate or a venturer in a jointly controlled entity, in which the investments are accounted for on the basis of the direct equity interest rather than on the basis of the reported results and net assets of the investees.	IAS 27.4, IAS 28.2, IAS 31.3
set-off, legal right of	A debtor's legal right, by contract or otherwise, to settle or otherwise eliminate all or a portion of an amount due to a creditor by applying against that amount an amount due from the creditor.	IAS 32.45
settlement (of employee benefit obligations)	A transaction that eliminates all further legal or constructive obligation for part or all of the benefits provided under a defined benefit plan, for example, when a lump-sum cash payment is made to, or on behalf of, plan participants in exchange for their rights to receive specified post-employment benefits.	IAS 19.112
settlement date	The date that a financial asset is delivered to or by an entity.	IAS 39.AG56
settlement value	The undiscounted amounts of cash or cash equivalents expected to be paid to satisfy the liabilities in the normal course of business.	F.100(c)
share-based payment arrangement	An agreement between the entity (or another group[*] entity or any shareholder of the group entity) and another party (including an employee) that entitles the other party to receive	IFRS 2.A

(a)   cash or other assets of the entity for amounts that are based on the price (or value) of equity instruments (including shares or share options) of the entity or another group entity, or

(b)   equity instruments (including shares or share options) of the entity or another group entity,

provided the specified vesting conditions, if any, are met.

---

[*]   A 'group' is defined in paragraph 4 of IAS 27 *Consolidated and Separate Financial Statements* as 'a parent and its subsidiaries' from the perspective of the reporting entity's ultimate parent.

share-based payment transaction	A transaction in which the entity	IFRS 2.A
	(a) receives goods or services from the supplier of those goods or services (including an employee) in a share-based payment arrangement, or	
	(b) incurs an obligation to settle the transaction with the supplier in a share-based payment arrangement when another group entity receives those goods or services.	
share option	A contract that gives the holder the right, but not the obligation, to subscribe to the entity's shares at a fixed or determinable price for a specific period of time.	IFRS 2.A
short seller	An entity that sells financial assets that it has borrowed and does not yet own.	IAS 39.AG15
short-term employee benefits	Employee benefits (other than termination benefits) that are due to be settled within twelve months after the end of the period in which the employees render the related service.	IAS 19.7
significant influence	The power to participate in the financial and operating policy decisions of an entity, but not control over those policies. Significant influence may be gained by share ownership, statute or agreement.	IAS 24.9, (IAS 28.2), (IAS 31.3)
solvency	The availability of cash over the longer term to meet financial commitments as they fall due.	F.16
spot exchange rate	The exchange rate for immediate delivery.	IAS 21.8
state (employee benefit) plan	Employee benefit plans established by legislation to cover all entities (or all entities in a particular category, for example a specific industry) and operated by national or local government or by another body (for example an autonomous agency created specifically for this purpose) which is not subject to control or influence by the reporting entity.	IAS 19.37
subsidiary	An entity, including an unincorporated entity such as a partnership, that is controlled by another entity (known as the parent).	IFRS 3.A, IAS 27.4, IAS 28.2
substance over form	The principle that transactions and other events are accounted for and presented in accordance with their substance and economic reality and not merely their legal form.	F.35, (IAS 8.7–10)

tax base of an asset or liability	The amount attributed to that asset or liability for tax purposes.	IAS 12.5
tax expense (tax income)	The aggregate amount included in the determination of profit or loss for the period in respect of current tax and deferred tax. Tax expense (tax income) comprises current tax expense (current tax income) and deferred tax expense (deferred tax income).	IAS 12.5, IAS 12.6
taxable profit (tax loss)	The profit (loss) for a period, determined in accordance with the rules established by the taxation authorities, upon which income taxes are payable (recoverable).	IAS 12.5
taxable temporary differences	Temporary differences that will result in taxable amounts in determining taxable profit (tax loss) of future periods when the carrying amount of the asset or liability is recovered or settled.	IAS 12.5
temporary differences	Differences between the carrying amount of an asset or liability in the statement of financial position and its tax base. Temporary differences may be either: (a) taxable temporary differences; or (b) deductible temporary differences.	IAS 12.5
termination benefits	Employee benefits payable as a result of either: (a) an entity's decision to terminate an employee's employment before the normal retirement date; or (b) an employee's decision to accept voluntary redundancy in exchange for those benefits.	IAS 19.7
total comprehensive income	The change in equity during a period resulting from transactions and other events, other than those changes resulting from transactions with owners in their capacity as owners.	IAS 1.7
trade date	The date that an entity commits itself to purchase or sell an asset.	IAS 39.AG55
transaction costs (financial instruments)	Incremental costs that are directly attributable to the acquisition, issue or disposal of a financial asset or financial liability (see IAS 39 paragraph AG13). An incremental cost is one that would not have been incurred if the entity had not acquired, issued or disposed of the financial instrument.	IAS 39.9

transitional liability (defined benefit plans)	For an entity on first adopting IAS 19:	IAS 19.154
	(a) the present value of the obligation at the date of adoption;	
	(b) minus the fair value, at the date of adoption, of plan assets (if any) out of which the obligations are to be settled directly;	
	(c) minus any past service cost that shall be recognised in later periods.	
treasury shares	An entity's own equity instruments, held by the entity or other members of the consolidated group.	IAS 32.33
unbundle	Account for the components of a contract as if they were separate contracts.	IFRS 4.A
understandability	Information provided in financial statements has the quality of understandability when it is comprehensible to users who have a reasonable knowledge of business and economic activities and accounting and a willingness to study the information with reasonable diligence.	F.25
unearned finance income	The difference between:	IAS 17.4
	(a) the gross investment in the lease, and	
	(b) the net investment in the lease.	
unguaranteed residual value	That portion of the residual value of the leased asset, the realisation of which by the lessor is not assured or is guaranteed solely by a party related to the lessor.	IAS 17.4
useful life	The estimated remaining period, from the commencement of the lease term, without limitation by the lease term, over which the economic benefits embodied in the asset are expected to be consumed by the entity.	IAS 17.4
useful life	Either:	IAS 16.6, IAS 36.6, IAS 38.8
	(a) the period over which an asset is expected to be available for use by an entity; or	
	(b) the number of production or similar units expected to be obtained from the asset by the entity.	
value in use	The present value of estimated future cash flows expected to arise from the continuing use of an asset and from its disposal at the end of its useful life.	IFRS 5.A
value in use	The present value of the future cash flows expected to be derived from an asset or cash-generating unit.	IAS 36.6

variable production overheads	Those indirect costs of production that vary directly, or nearly directly, with the volume of production, such as indirect materials and indirect labour.	IAS 2.12
venturer	A party to a joint venture that has joint control over that joint venture.	IAS 31.3
vest	To become an entitlement. Under a share-based payment arrangement, a counterparty's right to receive cash, other assets or equity instruments of the entity vests when the counterparty's entitlement is no longer conditional on the satisfaction of any vesting conditions.	IFRS 2.A
vested benefits	Benefits, the rights to which, under the conditions of a retirement benefit plan, are not conditional on continued employment.	IAS 26.8
vested employee benefits	Employee benefits that are not conditional on future employment.	IAS 19.7
vesting conditions	The conditions that determine whether the entity receives the services that entitle the counterparty to receive cash, other assets or equity instruments of the entity, under a share-based payment arrangement. Vesting conditions are either service conditions or performance conditions. Service conditions require the counterparty to complete a specified period of service. Performance conditions require the counterparty to complete a specified period of service and specified performance targets to be met (such as a specified increase in the entity's profit over a specified period of time). A performance condition might include a market condition.	IFRS 2.A
vesting period	The period during which all the specified vesting conditions of a share-based payment arrangement are to be satisfied.	IFRS 2.A
warrant	A financial instrument that gives the holder the right to purchase ordinary shares.	IAS 33.5
weighted average cost formula	Under this formula, the cost of each item is determined from the weighted average of the cost of similar items at the beginning of a period and the cost of similar items purchased or produced during the period. The average may be calculated on a periodic basis, or as each additional shipment is received, depending upon the circumstances of the entity.	IAS 2.27

© IASCF

weighted average number of ordinary shares outstanding during the period	The number of ordinary shares outstanding at the beginning of the period, adjusted by the number of ordinary shares bought back or issued during the period multiplied by a time-weighting factor.	IAS 33.20

Index

The index to this volume is a comprehensive index. It references not only all International Financial Reporting Standards—IFRSs, IASs and Interpretations—but also all related documentation including Bases for Conclusions, Implementation Guidance, Application Guidance, Appendices and Illustrative Examples. In addition, it includes references to the IASC Foundation Constitution, the IASB *Framework*, the *Preface to IFRSs* and the Due Process Handbooks for the IASB and the IFRIC.

References to IFRSs, IASs, Interpretations and supporting documentation are by Standard number and paragraph number. This method provides an absolute reference rather than a relative one. The index uses prefix notations to identify the document to which paragraphs and subparagraphs belong. These prefix notations are as follows:

Section	Prefix	Examples	Reference
International Financial Reporting Standards (IFRSs) 1–9	IF	IF1.1—47A	IFRS 1, paragraphs 1 to 47A
		IF3.3A(c)	IFRS 3, paragraph 3A subparagraph (c)
International Accounting Standards (IASs) 1–41	no prefix	12.26(a)	IAS 12, paragraph 26 subparagraph (a)
		37.10	IAS 37, paragraph 10
Basis for Conclusions on IFRSs	BC	IF2.BC19–22	Basis for Conclusions on IFRS 2, paragraphs BC19 to BC22
		IF4.BC61(d)	Basis for Conclusions on IFRS 4, paragraph BC61 subparagraph (d)
Basis for Conclusions on IASs	B, BC or BCZ	24.BC8–14	Basis for Conclusions on IAS 24, paragraphs BC8 to BC14
		36.BCZ108–112	Basis for Conclusions on IAS 36, paragraphs BCZ108 to BCZ112
Implementation Guidance on IFRSs and IASs	IG	39.IG Q&A E.4.2	Implementation Guidance on IAS 39 Q&A E.4.2,
		IF4.IG6–10	Implementation Guidance on IFRS 4, paragraphs IG6 to IG10
Illustrative Examples on IFRSs and IASs	IE	33.IE1	IAS 33, Illustrative Example 1
Application Guidance	AG	32.AG25–26	Application Guidance on IAS 32, paragraphs AG25 to AG26
		39.Appendix A AG84–93	IAS 39.Appendix A: Application Guidance on IAS 39, paragraphs AG84 to AG93
Appendices to IFRSs and IASs	Appendix	IF1 Appendices A–C	IFRS 1, Appendices A to C
		36.Appendix A4	IAS 36,.Appendix A, paragraph A4

Other prefixes are: IASC Foundation Constitution–**CN**; Preface to International Financial Reporting Standards–**IFRS Preface**; Due Process Handbook for the IASB–**DPH**; IFRIC Interpretation–**IFRIC**; SIC Interpretation–**SIC**; Due Process Handbook for the IFRIC–**IDPH**; IASB *Framework*–**F**.

© IASCF

© IASCF

© IASCF

© IASCF

NOTES

NOTES

NOTES

NOTES

NOTES

NOTES

NOTES

NOTES

NOTES

NOTES

NOTES

NOTES

NOTES

NOTES

NOTES

NOTES

NOTES

NOTES

NOTES

NOTES

Printed in UK by CPI William Clowes Beccles NR34 7TL